INTERNATIONAL ENCYCLOPEDIA OF DANCE

INTERNATIONAL ENCYCLOPEDIA OF

DANCE

A project of Dance Perspectives Foundation, Inc.

FOUNDING EDITOR

Selma Jeanne Cohen

AREA EDITORS

George Dorris Nancy Goldner Beate Gordon
Nancy Reynolds David Vaughan
Suzanne Youngerman

CONSULTANTS

Thomas F. Kelly Horst Koegler Richard Ralph
Elizabeth Souritz

VOLUME 6

OXFORD UNIVERSITY PRESS
New York   2004   Oxford

OXFORD
UNIVERSITY PRESS

Oxford   New York

Auckland   Bangkok   Buenos Aires   Cape Town   Chennai
Dar es Salaam   Delhi   Hong Kong   Istanbul   Karachi   Kolkata
Kuala Lumpur   Madrid   Melbourne   Mexico City   Mumbai   Nairobi
São Paulo   Shanghai   Taipei   Tokyo   Toronto

First published by Oxford University Press, Inc., 1998
198 Madison Avenue, New York, New York 10016
www.oup.com

First issued as an Oxford University Press paperback, 2004

This work was initiated with funds granted by the
National Endowment for the Humanities,
a federal agency

Library of Congress Cataloging-in-Publication Data
International encyclopedia of dance : a project of Dance
Perspectives Foundation, Inc. / founding editor, Selma Jeanne Cohen;
area editors, George Dorris et al.; consultants, Thomas F. Kelly et al.
p. cm.
Includes bibliographical references and index.
1. Dance—Encyclopedias. 2. Ballet—Encyclopedias. I. Cohen,
Selma Jeanne, 1920-. II. Dance Perspectives Foundation.
GV1585.1586 1998 97-36562 792.6'2'03—dc21 CIP

ISBN 0-19-517369-4 (set)
ISBN 0-19-517590-5 (vol. 6)

Printing (last digit): 9 8 7 6 5 4 3 2 1

Printed in the United States of America
on acid-free paper

STRATE, GRANT (born 7 December 1927 in Cardston, Alberta), Canadian dancer, choreographer, and educator. Strate had just embarked on a law career when, with only rudimentary dance training, he was invited by Celia Franca to join the newly established National Ballet of Canada in 1951. Continuing his training with Franca and with Betty Oliphant, ballet mistress of the company, he was promoted to soloist rank in 1953 and soon achieved public notice as a talented character dancer. He also displayed a marked gift for administration, which enabled him to assist Franca in her responsibilities as artistic director of the company.

Strate's primary interest and primary talent, however, lay neither in performing nor in administration but in choreography. Appointed resident choreographer for the National Ballet in 1958, he served the company in that capacity for eleven years, until 1969. During his tenure he created numerous original works, some of them overtly modernistic. Among the most successful were three works set to the music of Canadian composer Harry Somers: *The*

Fisherman and His Soul (1956), *Ballad* (1958), and, best known of all, *The House of Atreus* (1964). Other works that entered the National Ballet repertory included *The Willow* (1957), to music by Arthur Foote; *Antic Spring* (1960), to music by Jacques Ibert; *Triptych* (1965), to music by Mozart; *Pulcinella* (1966), to the Stravinsky score; *Studies in White* (1967), to music by Telemann; *The Arena* (1968), to music by Benjamin Britten; and *Phases* (1969), to music by Eric Satie. He also created or restaged ballets for the Studio Ballet of Antwerp, the Royal Swedish Ballet, and several Canadian modern dance companies and solo dancers, often employing Canadian composers and designers.

In 1970 Strate left the National Ballet of Canada to become founding chairman of the Dance Department at York University, Toronto, where he remained as professor until his appointment in 1978 as director of the Centre for the Arts at Simon Fraser University, Burnaby, British Columbia. During his years at York, he also played a crucial role, as founding chairman and board member of the

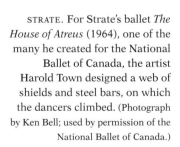

STRATE. For Strate's ballet *The House of Atreus* (1964), one of the many he created for the National Ballet of Canada, the artist Harold Town designed a web of shields and steel bars, on which the dancers climbed. (Photograph by Ken Bell; used by permission of the National Ballet of Canada.)

Dance in Canada Association from 1973 to 1978, in establishing the organization as a national service agency for the dance community. Since his retirement from his university post in 1993, Strate has remained active as an adviser to several Canadian dance companies and cultural organizations, as a guest teacher, and as an organizer of choreographic seminars. His influence on the development of the recent generation of Canadian dancers and choreographers has been profound. He was appointed to the Order of Canada in 1995 and was the recipient of the Governor General's Performing Arts Award in 1996.

BIBLIOGRAPHY
Bell, Ken, and Celia Franca. *The National Ballet of Canada: A Celebration.* Toronto, 1978.
Crabb, Michael. "Prime Mover Number One: Grant Strate and Dance in Canada." *Dance in Canada,* no. 38 (Winter 1983–1984): 15–19.
Neufeld, James. *Power to Rise: The Story of the National Ballet of Canada.* Toronto, 1996.

MICHAEL CRABB

STRAUSS FAMILY, a Viennese family of bandleaders and composers who flourished during the nineteenth century and whose name became synonymous with the popular Viennese waltz. Notable members include the father, Johann Strauss the elder, and his children, Johann Strauss the younger, Josef Strauss, and Eduard Strauss.

Johann Strauss the elder (Johann Baptist Strauss [I]; born 14 March 1804 in Vienna, died 25 September 1849 in Vienna), conductor and composer. Johann Strauss began his career as a violist in dance ensembles playing in the inns and public dance halls of Vienna. In the 1820s he and Joseph Lanner (1801–1843), who both led their ensembles on the violin, became established as the foremost dance bandleaders in Vienna when the waltz became a popular craze. They built orchestras of twenty to thirty string and wind instrumentalists—sometimes even more for special functions such as the Habsburg court balls of the 1830s and 1840s. Their compositions included not only waltzes but also galops and later quadrilles and polkas; it was the waltz, however, that spread their fame. Strauss was more ebullient in both temperament and musical style than Lanner and built on the popularity of his compositions, even taking his orchestra abroad. He performed at concerts and balls throughout Britain in 1838, Queen Victoria's coronation year, and returned there in 1849 just a few weeks before his death.

In the early nineteenth century the waltz dance program typically consisted of an ad hoc sequence of short, simple melodies. Under Lanner and Strauss, the classical waltz form became established as a set sequence of perhaps five two-part waltz sections (making ten waltz melodies in all), preceded by a short introduction and ended by a coda that recapitulated the main theme. When the introductory section became a mood-setting passage and the whole program was given a picturesque title, each waltz composition acquired an individual identity.

These traditions, established by Lanner and Strauss and practiced by others such as the Bohemian Joseph Labitzky (1802–1881) in Carlsbad and the Hungarian Joseph Gungl (1809–1889) in Berlin, were developed further by Johann Strauss's three sons. The eldest, **Johann Strauss the younger** (Johann Baptist Strauss [II], also known as the Waltz King; born 25 October 1825 in Vienna, died 3 June 1899 in Vienna), composer and conductor, is the most famous of the three sons. **Josef Strauss** (born 20 August 1827 in Vienna, died 22 July 1870 in Vienna), engineer, conductor, and composer. Josef is considered by connoisseurs of the family's music to have had the more profound talent. His introverted nature is reflected in harmonically adventurous introductions and a great emotional range in his waltz melodies. Considered to be less inspired was the youngest son, **Eduard Strauss** (born 15 March 1835 in Vienna, died 28 December 1916 in Vienna), conductor and composer.

Johann the younger and Josef produced dance music that is exceptional in transcending the constraints of dance rhythms. To the polka's regular beat they added a unique range of picturesque invention, often discreetly using special effects to give each piece individuality. No other practitioners could match their melodic invention or their abilities to tug at the heart with yearning waltz themes and to string together melodies varied in shape and mood—alternately bold, reflective, teasing, or caressing, each melody reestablishing the listener's attention with its originality. The introduction of each waltz became a miniature tone poem, giving the whole composition an elegant orchestral context that was as worthy of the concert hall as of the dance hall. It has been Johann's waltzes that have most readily captured the popular imagination. His music gained a place in the orchestral repertory unlike that of any other composer with origins in the dance hall.

Particularly celebrated are the younger Johann's waltz classics of the 1860s: "Accelerations" (1860), "Morning Papers" (1864), "By the Beautiful Blue Danube" (1867), "Artist's Life" (1867), "Tales from the Vienna Woods" (1868), and "Wine, Woman, and Song" (1869). His most famous polkas include the "Anna Polka" (1852), "Chit-Chat Polka" (1858), "In Thunder and Lightning" (1868), and the "Pizzicato Polka" (1869), which was composed with Josef.

After 1870, Johann the younger concentrated on composing operettas, establishing the distinctively Viennese operetta style built around the waltz. Other waltz composers became prominent, such as the Frenchman Émile Waldteufel (1837–1915) and the Viennese Carl Michael Ziehrer (1843–1922), but Strauss still matched them with the occasional outstanding waltz, such as "Vienna Blood" (1873), "Voices of Spring" (1883), devised as a coloratura soprano showpiece, and the majestic "Emperor Waltz" (1889). In addition, he successfully arranged waltzes on themes from his operettas, such as "1001 Nights" from *Indigo* (1871) and "Roses from the South" from *The Queen's Lace Handkerchief* (1880).

In all, the younger Johann composed some 180 waltzes, 130 polkas, 30 quick polkas or galops, 30 polka mazurkas, 80 quadrilles, and 50 marches. Besides his 15 operettas, he composed one opera, *Ritter Pázmán* (best known for its ballet music), and one full-length ballet, *Cinderella*. In the years since his death, many stage works have been created using his melodies, including the ballet scores for Léonide Massine's *Le Beau Danube* and David Lichine's *Graduation Ball*. Publication of a complete edition of the younger Johann Strauss's works in full score was begun under the imprint of Doblinger and Universal Edition of Vienna, but it has made limited progress.

[*For related discussion, see* Music for Dance, *article on* Western Music, 1800–1900.]

BIBLIOGRAPHY

Carner, Mosco. *The Waltz.* New York, 1948.

Carner, Mosco, and Max Schönherr. "Strauss." In *The New Grove Dictionary of Music and Musicians.* London, 1980.

Decsey, Ernst. *Johann Strauss.* Stuttgart, 1922.

Eisenberg, L. *Johann Strauss: Ein Lebensbild.* Leipzig, 1894.

Jacob, Heinrich E. *Johann Strauss und das Neunzehnte Jahrhundert.* Amsterdam, 1937.

Kemp, Peter. *The Strauss Family: Portrait of a Musical Dynasty.* Tunbridge Wells, Kent, 1985.

Lamb, Andrew. "Waltz." In *The New Grove Dictionary of Music and Musicians.* London, 1980.

Mailer, Franz. *Joseph Strauss: Genie wider Willen.* Vienna, 1977.

Mailer, Franz, ed. *Johann Strauss (Sohn): Leben und Werk in Briefen und Dokumenten.* Tutzing, 1983–.

Pastene, Jerome. *Three-Quarter Time: The Life and Music of the Strauss Family of Vienna.* New York, 1951.

Prawy, Marcel. *Johann Strauss: Weltgeschichte im Waltzertakt.* Vienna, 1975.

Schönherr, Max, and Karl Reinöhl. *Johann Strauss Vater: Ein Werkverzeichnis.* London, 1954.

Schönherr, Max. "Ästhetik des Walzers." *Österreichische Musikzeitschrift* 31 (February 1976): 57–120.

Wechsberg, Joseph. *The Waltz Emperors: The Life and Times and Music of the Strauss Family.* London, 1973.

ANDREW LAMB

STRAVINSKY, IGOR (Igor' Fedorovich Stravinskii; born 5 [17] June 1882 in Oranienbaum, Russia, died 6 April 1971 in New York City), composer. Stravinsky was one of the most important composers of the twentieth century and its most significant composer of ballet music. Stravinsky's father was a leading bass singer at the Maryinsky Theater in Saint Petersburg. The third of four children, the young Igor was frequently exposed to music and theater in the city and to folk music during summers spent at relatives' country estates. He began piano lessons at the age of nine and later received private instruction in harmony and counterpoint. Although his family insisted that he read law at the university, his attention to these studies was desultory. Long before his graduation in 1906, his interest in musical composition had led him to seek the advice of Nikolai Rimsky-Korsakov, whose son Vladimir was a fellow student; his private lessons in composition with Rimsky-Korsakov continued from 1902 until the master's death in 1908. In January 1906 Stravinsky married his first cousin, Katerina Nossenko; they had four children.

Early Career. Although some of Stravinsky's works from these years, including a dirge on his teacher's death, are lost, a piano sonata (1904) and a symphony (1907) composed under Rimsky-Korsakov's tutelage document Stravinsky's absorption of the Russian cosmopolitan, or Western, style, epitomized by Petr Ilich Tchaikovsky and Aleksandr Glazunov and the antithesis of the folkloric style of which Rimsky-Korsakov was a leading proponent. Two orchestral scores, the *Scherzo Fantastique* and *Feu d'Artifice*, both completed in 1908, also show the influence of the modern French school, exemplified by Paul Dukas and Claude Debussy. Performed at a concert in Saint Petersburg on 6 February 1909, these two works attracted the attention of Serge Diaghilev, who commissioned some orchestrations from Stravinsky for his 1909 Paris season. Diaghilev also turned to Stravinsky to compose *The Firebird*, a Michel Fokine ballet intended for the 1910 Ballets Russes season in Paris, when Anatoly Lyadov required too much time to do so.

Russian and Western influences are constructively juxtaposed in *The Firebird* (1910), a brilliantly colorful and pictorial score based on folkloric material; as in Rimsky-Korsakov's opera *Le Coq d'Or*, chromatic writing for the supernatural creatures is contrasted with modal-diatonic music for the human figures. Its success launched Stravinsky's international career, centered in Paris, where he soon became a figure in the musical world and a friend of Debussy and Maurice Ravel. Two further ballets for Diaghilev followed, also on Russian subjects. An opera, *Le Rossignol*, based on a Hans Christian Andersen tale, begun before *The Firebird*, was not completed until 1914; in 1917 Stravinsky arranged from it a symphonic poem, *Le Chant du Rossignol*, which was staged by Diaghilev in 1920, with sets by Henri Matisse and choreography by Léonide Massine.

Stravinsky's *Petrouchka* (1911), described as a "burlesque," is a tale of a puppet hero, set in the milieu of the Saint Petersburg Shrovetide fair. Devised in collaboration with the designer Alexandre Benois, it was also choreographed by Fokine. As in *The Firebird*, Stravinsky drew on folk and popular material, this time in an increasingly dissonant and rhythmically irregular context; a *concertante* piano soloist represents Petrouchka in the orchestra, and the material of the central scenes, based on the superimposed chords of C major and F-sharp major, was in fact first conceived as a concert piece for piano and orchestra. The out-of-doors scenes vividly evoke the milieu and the sounds of the street fair.

Le Sacre du Printemps (1913), enacting a ritual of human sacrifice, was developed in collaboration with Nikolai Roerich (who also designed it) and choreographed by Vaslav Nijinsky. In this score Stravinsky elevated to a constructive principle the metrical irregularities prominent in the preceding works: rhythm in *Le Sacre* is no longer a matter of subdividing a regular pulse but of cumulating groups of beats in ever-changing numbers. Equally revolutionary (and profoundly antithetical to traditional Western modes of symphonic development) are the formal techniques of montage: sequential crosscutting between, and simultaneous layering of, musical materials. These had been employed representationally in the fair scenes of *Petrouchka* but were now used structurally in their own right. They continued to be a basic stylistic feature of Stravinsky's music throughout his life. The speeds of the montaged materials are always carefully coordinated, and Stravinsky assigns such metrical relationships a role often as significant as that of tonal relationships in earlier music.

Research by Lawrence Morton and Richard Taruskin has demonstrated the importance of Russian folk music as a source for the melodic material of *Le Sacre*, despite Stravinsky's subsequent emphatic denials of such origins; from the standpoint of his later aesthetic preoccupations, he preferred to regard it as concert music without ethnological purport. The work's harmony centers on the superimposed chords of E-flat major and F-flat major, which make up the famous "chugging" sonority in the "Dance of the Adolescents"; although highly dissonant, these harmonies are essentially static in nature and function. Pieter van den Toorn has demonstrated Stravinsky's extensive reliance throughout his career on the octatonic scale, a pattern of alternating half and whole steps. Although *Le Sacre* is a work of explicit primitivism, its monumental orchestration marks it as still very much a part of the post-Wagnerian European high culture that Stravinsky, and many others, were soon to reject violently. Its premiere on 29 May 1913 in Paris was the occasion of one of the most famous theatrical demonstrations of modern times, inspired equally by the brutalism of the music and the unconventionality of Nijinsky's choreography.

Cut off from Russia and the revenues from his German publishers and his Russian estate by the beginning of World War I, Stravinsky settled in neutral Switzerland. Working from various collections of Russian folk poetry, some of which he had hastily retrieved on a brief trip home in July 1914, he composed a number of small works, mostly vocal, developing musical ideas related to the language of *Le Sacre* but in a less violent expressive framework. By this time Stravinsky's internalization of his native musical folklore was as complete as Béla Bartók's. Inspired by traditional Russian theatrical genres, he turned from the grandiose scale of Diaghilev, whose operations had in any case been curtailed by the war, to novel and economical combinations of music, dance, speech, and pantomime. Thus began a series of theater works—continuing through *Perséphone* in 1934—that, because they call for singers, actors, or special instrumentations, fall outside, or between, the resources of most institutional repertory companies.

Le Renard (1916) is a "burlesque in song and dance," with a text assembled by Stravinsky from Russian folk material. *The Soldier's Tale* (1918), a collaboration with the Swiss writer C. F. Ramuz, after a Russian folk transmutation of the Faust legend, is "to be read, played, and danced" as a traveling theater piece, in the tradition of the oral folk theater of Russian soldiers and convicts. At this time Stravinsky became fascinated by the cimbalom, a Hungarian stringed instrument played with mallets, which he used in *Le Renard* and in the instrumental piece *Rag-time* (1918). Like many European composers at the end of the war, Stravinsky was interested in American jazz although at this point Stravinsky knew only printed music, not performed and improvised jazz.

However, the principal project of these years was *Les Noces*, intended for the Ballets Russes. Although he began the work in 1914 and substantially completed the score by 1917, Stravinsky experimented with several novel orchestrations. It was not until 1923 that he completed the final version, in which vocal soloists and chorus are accompanied by the "black and white" ensemble of four pianos and percussion. Stravinsky had wanted the instruments on stage with the dancers, but this was not achieved in Bronislava Nijinska's original production. The stylized, ritualistic character of *Les Noces* and *Le Renard* is underlined by the vocal layout, as the solo singers have no specific identities in the action.

Exile in France. With the success of the Bolshevik Revolution in Russia, the exile of Stravinsky and of Diaghilev became permanent. The impresario turned primarily to France and to French composers and, following the lead of Jean Cocteau, espoused a more conservative, "objective" aesthetic in preference to his prewar avant-gardism. In the aftermath of the war, this explicitly involved rejection of any traces of Wagnerianism and of the German Romantic sensibility. Stravinsky followed in this path, but the composer, cut off not only from his Russian roots but from a Russian audience, also faced the problem of a language for vocal music. His only subsequent major work in Russian would be the opera *Mavra* (1922)—dedicated, significantly, to the great cosmopolitan Westernizers of Russian culture, Aleksandr Pushkin, Mikhail Glinka, and Tchaikovsky. Although he took up residence in France in 1920, Stravinsky's next major vocal works would be in Latin: *Oedipus Rex* (1927) and the Symphony of Psalms (1930).

With the abandonment of the Russian language, Stravinsky also stopped drawing on the Russian folk material that had stimulated much of his music for more than a decade. As early as the dance episodes of *The Soldier's Tale*, stylistic parody of Western materials had begun to play a role in his music. The decisive experience for his reorientation came with *Pulcinella* (1920), a "ballet with song" for Diaghilev based on eighteenth-century pieces (attributed to Giambattista Pergolesi, but now known to be the work of other composers), with sets by Pablo Picasso and choreography by Massine. Diaghilev presumably expected something along the lines of *Les Femmes de Bonne Humeur*, Vincenzo Tommasini's slick modern orchestrations of Domenico Scarlatti keyboard sonatas, but *Pulcinella* turned out to be something quite different: "art about art," in which by subtle adjustments the eighteenth-century surface was made to embrace Stravinskian asymmetry and nondirectional harmony. The ostensibly eighteenth-century orchestration, incorporating the Baroque contrast of small and larger ensembles, nonetheless yielded a characteristic sonority. Stravinsky even found ways to elicit percussive sounds without percussion instruments. *Pulcinella* showed Stravinsky a direction in which he could move away from Russia without becoming entirely rootless, and it inaugurated his so-called neoclassical period, which would last about twenty-five years.

The Symphonies of Wind Instruments (1920), dedicated to the memory of Debussy, and especially the Octet (1923) confirmed the new direction. In part because of financial pressures, Stravinsky began in 1924 to be active as a touring pianist and composed several works for his own use: Concerto for Piano and Winds (1924), Piano Sonata (1924), Serenade in A (1925), Capriccio for Piano and Orchestra (1929), and the Concerto for Two Solo Pianos (1935). He had also begun to conduct his own music. After a period during which he made piano-roll recordings of most of his music, Stravinsky in 1925 turned his attention to the phonograph, regularly recording his own performances of his new works and rerecording his older ones to new technical standards. Even if they failed in their professed purpose of fixing his interpretation as an inviolate standard—and indeed they differ significantly among themselves and are variously flawed in detail and execution—Stravinsky's recordings played an important role in propagating his music.

Although Stravinsky's works of the neoclassical period have their definable stimuli in earlier music, they always are wholly Stravinskian; each work establishes its own world of harmonic and rhythmic tensions, its own characteristic sonority. What to early listeners often seemed willful defacement of classical styles has with time established a stylistic identity of its own.

Although no further dance works for the Ballets Russes followed *Les Noces*, the opera-oratorio *Oedipus Rex* (1927) was composed to celebrate Diaghilev's twentieth anniversary as an impresario. However, relations with Diaghilev became strained by Stravinsky's acceptance of patronage from other quarters. *Apollon Musagète* (1928) was commissioned by the American Elizabeth Sprague Coolidge and first performed at the Library of Congress with choreography by Adolph Bolm; six weeks later George Balanchine made his classic version for Diaghilev. The allegorical ballet *Le Baiser de la Fée* (1928), based on music by Tchaikovsky, thereby affirming Stravinsky's new preference for the cosmopolitan rather than the nationalistic tradition of Russian music, was written for Ida Rubinstein. After Diaghilev's death in 1929, Rubinstein also commissioned the melodrama *Perséphone* (1934), with a text by André Gide, in which she recited as well as danced. Completed the year he became a French citizen, this was Stravinsky's only setting of French words since a pair of Verlaine songs in 1910.

In the early 1930s Stravinsky and American violinist Samuel Dushkin undertook a series of concert tours, for which new works were specially made: the Violin Concerto in D (1931), the Duo Concertante for Violin and Piano (1932), and a variety of transcriptions of earlier works. Perhaps as a result of such tours, additional commissions came from the United States. Lincoln Kirstein and Edward Warburg commissioned *Jeu de Cartes*, a "ballet in three deals" (1936) for Balanchine's American Ballet; Mr. and Mrs. Robert Woods Bliss, the Concerto in E-flat for Chamber Orchestra (*Dumbarton Oaks*, 1938); and the Chicago Symphony, the Symphony in C (1940).

Immigration to the United States. In March 1939 Stravinsky's wife died of tuberculosis; their eldest child had died the year before, and the composer himself suffered with tuberculosis at this time. In September 1939, with the onset of war in Europe, he moved to the United States, where he had been invited to deliver the Charles Eliot Norton lectures at Harvard University. His lectures, published under the title *Poetics of Music* (1947), were actually written by the French critic Alexis Roland-Manuel; earlier his *Autobiography* (1936) had been ghosted by Diaghilev's associate Walter Nouvel. On 9 March 1940 Stravinsky married Vera de Bosset, regularizing a long-standing liaison. The Stravinskys, who would become naturalized American citizens in 1945, settled in Beverly Hills, California, which remained their home until the fall of 1969.

During World War II, commissions were hard to come by. Besides continuing his conducting and playing activities, Stravinsky worked for some improbable patrons: the *Circus Polka*, "for a young elephant" (1942), was written for Ringling Brothers and Barnum & Bailey circus; the bandleaders Paul Whiteman and Woody Herman commissioned, respectively, *Scherzo à la Russe* (1944) and *Ebony Concerto* (1945); the Broadway producer Billy Rose ordered *Scènes de Ballet* for the revue *The Seven Lively Arts* (1944). Ostensibly a concert work, *Danses Concertantes* (1942), commissioned by the conductor Werner Janssen, has the structure of a ballet score and was choreographed by Balanchine in 1944. In 1945 Stravinsky completed a major orchestral work, the Symphony in Three Movements.

After the war, a new publishing arrangement with the firm of Boosey and Hawkes placed the composer on a sounder financial basis. Because Russia and the United States had not been adherents of the Berne copyright convention, Stravinsky's earlier works were in the public domain in the United States; Stravinsky now sought to reestablish control over them by preparing revised editions. The most radical alteration among the theater scores was the rescoring of *Petrouchka* for a smaller orchestra, and many errors in this and other scores were corrected.

Stravinsky's major ballet of this period was *Orpheus* (1947), commissioned by Kirstein for Balanchine and Ballet Society. The following years were devoted principally to the composition of the three-act opera *The Rake's Progress* (1951), with a libretto by W. H. Auden and Chester Kallman suggested by William Hogarth's famous series of paintings. Stravinsky's only full-evening theater work and an homage to the eighteenth-century number opera (made up of separate arias and ensembles rather than through-composed in the Wagnerian manner), it culminated Stravinsky's neoclassical period.

In the early 1950s, encouraged by Robert Craft, a young musician who had joined his household in 1948 as a secretary and assistant, Stravinsky interested himself in the music and compositional technique of Arnold Schoenberg and his disciples, Alban Berg and Anton Webern. At first in songs and chamber works, Stravinsky began cautious experiments with aspects of Schoenberg's twelve-tone method. These discoveries were gradually absorbed into his style during the composition of the ballet *Agon*, begun in 1953 but not completed until 1957. For this plotless work, another Kirstein commission for Balanchine's company, now the New York City Ballet, Stravinsky was stimulated by the French court dances described in François de Lauze's *Apologie de la Danse* and by music examples in the writings of French mathematician Marin Mersenne.

Craft, a man of wide interests in literature and philosophy as well as music, vastly stimulated the Stravinskys' intellectual life, introducing them to new music, new books,

and new friends; by forcing them to speak English, he brought them into closer contact with American culture. Craft also functioned as Stravinsky's assistant conductor, rehearsing orchestras for concerts and recordings; as the composer grew older and his new music became more difficult to conduct, Craft also acted as co-conductor. Beginning in 1959, he collaborated with Stravinsky on a series of books that take the form of conversations. The exact nature of the collaboration, especially during Stravinsky's final years, has been a subject of some controversy.

Agon was Stravinsky's final ballet score, although *The Flood* (1962), composed for CBS television, also included dance episodes choreographed by Balanchine and has been performed theatrically. In his later years, Stravinsky composed a number of religious vocal pieces: *Canticum Sacrum* (1955), *Threni* (1958), *A Sermon, a Narrative, and a Prayer* (1961), *Abraham and Isaac* (1963), and *Requiem Canticles* (1966). These continued a strain in his work dating back to the mid-1920s, when he had rejoined the Russian Orthodox Church, and also manifest in the Symphony of Psalms and the Mass, completed in 1948. Another preoccupation of the 1950s and 1960s was writing memorial pieces for, among others, Dylan Thomas, Raoul Dufy, John F. Kennedy, and T. S. Eliot. He also composed two substantial orchestral works: *Movements* (1959), for piano and orchestra, and *Variations* (1964), which was dedicated to the memory of Aldous Huxley. With their dense and often contrapuntal textures, angular melodies, and somber colors, the works of Stravinsky's seventies and eighties have not yet found a wide audience.

In 1962, at the invitation of the Soviet government in honor of his eightieth birthday, Stravinsky made a much-publicized return to Russia—his first trip there in forty-eight years. After this journey, Stravinsky's public appearances and the range of his compositional activity were gradually curtailed by ill health. His last completed work was a setting for voice and piano of Edward Lear's "The Owl and the Pussycat," one of his wife's favorite poems (1966); subsequently, he made instrumentations of two songs by Hugo Wolf and worked at scoring some pieces from Johann Sebastian Bach's *Well-Tempered Clavier*. In the fall of 1969 the Stravinskys moved to New York and remained there until the composer's death, some fourteen months short of his ninetieth birthday.

Contributions. Thanks to what Jeremy Noble has described as Stravinsky's "ability to express physical gestures and movements (and the psychological states that prompt them) in purely musical terms—a gift in which he has had no rival since Wagner," and to the inexhaustible fertility of his rhythmic invention, his music has consistently commanded the interest of choreographers. Few (if any) of his scores, whatever their initial purpose, have failed to find their way into theatrical use. The weight of his major works and their central concerns—rituals of purification and regeneration *(Le Sacre du Printemps, Les Noces, Oedipus Rex, Perséphone, The Rake's Progress)* and myths of artistic creation *(Apollon Musagète, Orpheus)*—have ensured their prominence in twentieth-century theatrical experience.

Stravinsky's connection with Diaghilev fixed a lifelong relationship to ballet and accustomed Stravinsky to a culture of novelty and avant-gardism and to the uses of publicity. His unpredictable stylistic transformations, variously stimulated by geography, patronage, and economic circumstances, were major events in the artistic world. If his early scores remained the most popular with the general public, the neoclassical style was long the most influential with composers, in both France and the United States, through the example of the music itself and through the teaching of Nadia Boulanger, the formidable French pedagogue and Stravinsky disciple. In the 1950s Stravinsky's conversion to serialism lent enormous prestige to the worldwide movement to use such techniques. At his death, he was widely recognized as the last representative of a long tradition of great composers of international stature.

[*See also* Agon; Apollo; Firebird, The; Noces, Les; Petrouchka; *and* Sacre du Printemps, Le.]

BIBLIOGRAPHY

Balanchine, George. "The Dance Elements in Stravinsky's Music." *Ballet Review* 10 (Summer 1982): 14–18.

Boucourechliev, André. *Stravinsky.* Translated by Martin Cooper. New York, 1987.

Garafola, Lynn. *Diaghilev's Ballets Russes.* New York, 1989.

Harris, Dale. "Balanchine: Working with Stravinsky." *Ballet Review* 10 (Summer 1982): 19–24.

Karlinsky, Simon. "Stravinsky and Russian Pre-Literate Theater." *Nineteenth-Century Music* 6 (Spring 1983): 232–240.

Kirstein, Lincoln. "Working with Stravinsky." In Kirstein's *By With To and From.* New York, 1991.

Lederman, Minna, ed. *Stravinsky in the Theatre.* New York, 1949.

Pasler, Jann C. "Debussy, Stravinsky, and the Ballets Russes." Ph.D. diss., University of Chicago, 1981.

Schouvaloff, Alexander, and Victor Borovsky. *Stravinsky on Stage.* London, 1982.

Stravinsky, Igor. *Stravinsky: Autobiography.* New York, 1936.

Stravinsky, Igor. *Poetics of Music.* Translated by Arthur Knodel and Ingolf Dahl. New York, 1947.

Stravinsky, Igor, and Robert Craft. *Conversations with Igor Stravinsky.* Garden City, N.Y., 1959.

Stravinsky, Igor, and Robert Craft. *Memories and Commentaries.* Berkeley, 1960.

Stravinsky, Igor, and Robert Craft. *Expositions and Developments.* Garden City, N.Y., 1962.

Stravinsky, Igor, and Robert Craft. *Dialogues and a Diary.* Garden City, N.Y., 1963.

Stravinsky, Igor, and Robert Craft. *Themes and Episodes.* New York, 1966.

Stravinsky, Igor, and Robert Craft. *Retrospectives and Conclusions.* New York, 1969.

Stravinsky, Igor. *Selected Correspondence.* 3 vols. Translated and edited by Robert Craft. New York, 1982–1985.

Stravinsky, Vera, and Robert Craft. *Stravinsky in Pictures and Documents.* New York, 1978.

Taruskin, Richard. *Stravinsky and the Russian Traditions: A Biography of the Works through Mavra.* 2 vols. Berkeley, 1996.

Toorn, Pieter C. van den. *The Music of Igor Stravinsky.* New Haven, 1983.

White, Eric W. *Stravinsky: The Composer and His Works.* 2d ed. Berkeley, 1979.

White, Eric W., and Jeremy Noble. "Stravinsky, Igor." In *The New Grove Dictionary of Music and Musicians.* London, 1980.

DAVID HAMILTON

STRIPTEASE. *See* Fan Dancing.

STRUCHKOVA, RAISA (Raisa Stepanovna Struchkova; born 5 October 1925 in Moscow), Russian dancer and teacher. Struchkova graduated from the Moscow School of Choreography in 1944. Her teacher and coach was Elisaveta Gerdt, who brought the classicism of the Saint Petersburg school to Moscow. From 1944 to 1978 Struchkova was the leading ballerina of the Bolshoi Ballet. After leaving the stage she continued to coach the

STRUCHKOVA. With Yuri Zhdanov as Albrecht in act 1 of *Giselle,* c.1955. Struchkova's interpretation was marked by a sweetness and simplicity that set her apart from other famous performers of the role at the Bolshoi Theater. (Photograph by Fritz Peyer; from a private collection.)

company, and in 1968 she began teaching also at the Lunacharsky Institute of Theatrical Art. In 1981, she became editor in chief of *Sovietskii balet* (Soviet Ballet) magazine.

A classical ballerina in the grand style and a talented actress, Struchkova was famous for the musicality of her dance in a broad range of roles, including lyrical, dramatic, and comic characters. She danced more than thirty roles in the classical and modern repertory, creating, among others, Leili in *Leili and Medzhnun* (1964), choreographed by Kasyan Goleizovsky, and the Maid of Honor in *Lieutenant Kijé* (1963), by Aleksandr Lapauri and Olga Tarasova, set to music by Sergei Prokofiev. She starred in the ballet feature films *The Crystal Shoe (Cinderella), Lieutenant Kijé,* and *I Am Your Name* (music by Francis Poulenc, choreography by Lapauri and Tarasova to poetry of Paul Éluard). She danced in a broad concert repertory and performed with her partner and husband Lapauri in *Moszkowski Waltz* and Reinhold Glière's *Étude* with great success, demonstrating a nearly acrobatic virtuosity.

STRUCHKOVA. With Aleksandr Lapauri in their most celebrated concert number, sometimes billed as *Moszkowski Waltz* and sometimes simply as *Waltz,* c.1960. Choreographed by Vasily Vainonen to a rousing waltz by Moritz Moszkowski, it is arguably the most exciting number ever performed on a ballet stage. Dancing with joyous abandon, Struchkova was the embodiment of reckless happiness. As she gleefully soared through the air, with complete trust in her partner and complete disregard of danger, audiences were invariably thrilled. (Photograph reprinted from a Bolshoi Ballet souvenir program, 1962.)

Struchkova's distinctive talents lay particularly in the improvisational playfulness of her dancing. Her dancing was fresh and original; in the established roles she found her own interpretations rather than copying others' performances. It is customary to consider Struchkova a fundamentally lyrical dancer. However, she was fascinating as the temperamental Kitri in Rostislav Zakharov's version of *Don Quixote,* as the clambering Bacchante in Leonid Lavrovsky's *Walpurgis Night,* and as the sparkling title character in Vasily Vainonen's *Mirandolina,* based on motifs from the plays of Carlo Goldoni. The contemporary comedy-satire *Lieutenant Kijé* revealed still another facet of her talent as an actress. Marina Semenova wrote of her, "I do not recall Struchkova ever making a mistake in dancing her role or feigning sincerity on the stage. This is perhaps what matters most in Struchkova as an actress; her genuine sincerity. This is the essence of her art." Struchkova's guest performances in more than thirty-five countries evoked the admiration of her audiences. The fame of the Bolshoi Ballet in the West was for many years associated with her name as a prime representative of Soviet ballet theater, with its traditions of realism, psychological penetration, and philosophical profundity.

Struchkova won First Prize at the World Festival of Youth and Students in Prague (1947), Budapest (1949), and Berlin (1951). She was named People's Artist of the USSR in 1959 and professor of the chair of choreography at the Lunacharsky Institute of Theatrical Art in 1978. She has served as a member of the jury of ballet competitions at home and abroad.

BIBLIOGRAPHY

Dolgopolov, Mikhail. "Raisa Struchkova." *The Dancing Times* (September 1949): 689–690.

Fradkin, Herman. *Raisa Struchkova* (in English). Moscow, 1956.

Greskovic, Robert. "The Bolshoi: The Picture Changes." *Ballet Review* 4.5 (1973): 35–49.

Moore, Lillian. "The Bolshoi Ballet Arrives on Film." *Dance Magazine* (January 1958): 36–43.

Poesio, Giannandrea. "Raissa Struchkova." *The Dancing Times* (July 1993): 971–972.

Semenova, Marina. "V osobom mire baleta." *Ogonek* 42 (1975).

Sinclair, Janet. "Raissa Struchkova: An Appreciation." *Ballet Today* (November 1963): 14–15.

Sluzhenie iskusstvu. Moscow, 1979. Booklet of the Moscow Bolshoi on the thirty-fifth anniversary of the stage activities of Struchkova.

Zakharov, Rostislav. "V ee tantsakh—sama zhizn." *Sovetskaia Kul'tura* (27 April 1973).

GALINA V. BELYAYEVA-CHELOMBITKO
Translated from Russian

STUTTGART BALLET, formerly known as the Ballet of the Württemberg State Theater (Ballett der Württembergischen Staatstheater Stuttgart). Until 1759 the

Stuttgart court opera ballet was a company like many others in Germany: patronized by petty princes and largely directed by French ballet masters. In that year, Duke Karl Eugen of Württemberg, an absolutist ruler but a lavish patron of the arts, appointed the young French choreographer Jean-Georges Noverre as his court ballet master. For the next seven years Stuttgart became the capital of the burgeoning fashion for *ballets d'action*, with Noverre creating a large number of works, often in collaboration with Niccolò Jommelli, the internationally famous Stuttgart court *Kapellmeister*.

Thus, at the nearby Ludwigsburg court theater, many historic works had their premieres, including *Renaud et Armide* (c.1760), *Admète et Alceste* (1761), *Médée et Jason* (1763), *Der Sieg des Neptun* (The Triumph of Neptune; 1763), *Hypernestra* (also known as *Les Danaïdes*, 1764), and *Der Raub der Proserpina* (The Abduction of Persephone; 1766). These works were performed by a company that listed seven male and seven female solo dancers and forty-four other dancers, evenly divided by sex; they were augmented occasionally by guest stars such as Gaëtan Vestris, Maximilien Gardel, Jean Dauberval, Anna Friedrike Heinel, and Nicolas Sauveur.

The duke's extravagance, however, created ever-mounting debt problems, and one of the court's first economic remedies was the drastic reduction of the ballet company, which led Noverre to leave for Vienna in 1767. Ballet in Stuttgart returned to its former inconspicuous state although a ballet school attached to the court theater lasted from 1771 until 1794. Stuttgart regained some of its former splendor when Filippo Taglioni was engaged as court ballet master at the end of 1824; he stayed through March 1828. Taglioni replaced Noverre's heroic approach with Romantic idylls in productions featuring his ballerina daughter Marie, partnered principally by Anton Stuhlmüller. This brief association saw the premier of *Jocko, the Brazilian Ape* (1826), which soon left Stuttgart for the international circuit.

After the Taglionis, Stuttgart returned to its ballet provincialism. The next date of historic significance was not until 1922, with the first performance of Oskar Schlemmer's *Triadic Ballet*. This, however, had no lasting consequences for the repertory of the company, which favored such classics as *The Fairy Doll*. Even after World War II there was no marked change in the role of ballet when the Stuttgart State Opera resumed operation.

Not until the 1958 arrival of Nicholas Beriozoff did the company, now known as the Ballet of the Württemberg State Theater, assume a stronger identity. Beriozoff insisted on strengthening the company's classical base, concentrating on a repertory of classics from the nineteenth century as well as from his own years with the Ballets Russes and on improving the teaching standards at the at-

STUTTGART BALLET. Marcia Haydée and Richard Cragun in John Cranko's comic masterpiece *The Taming of the Shrew*, created for the company in 1969. (Photograph from the Dance Collection, New York Public Library for the Performing Arts.)

tached opera ballet school. He also collaborated with the local Noverre Society, established in 1958 to further the cause of ballet and to assist young dancers and aspiring choreographers through the awarding of scholarhips and creation of a platform on which they might demonstrate their gifts. Beriozoff was succeeded in 1961 by John Cranko, and under the latter's guidance, which lasted until his death in 1973, the Stuttgart Ballet acquired its present international reputation.

Drawing from his experiences with the British Sadler's Wells Ballet and the Royal Ballet, and collaborating with Anne Woolliams and Peter Wright, Cranko built a company that soon drew international attention. Basing its repertory on highly individual productions of the classics and on British revivals, the Stuttgart Ballet was especially strong in such full-length works as Cranko's *Romeo and Juliet*, *Onegin*, and *The Taming of the Shrew*. These were supplemented by a few Balanchine imports and occasional contributions from Kenneth MacMillan, who created *Las Hermanas*, *Das Lied von der Erde*, and, after Cranko's death, *Requiem* and *My Brother, My Sisters*. Em-

STUTTGART BALLET. Using music by Aleksandr Scriabin, Cranko created *Poème de l'Extase* for guest artist Margot Fonteyn in 1970. She is seen here with Richard Cragun (left) and Egon Madsen (center). (Photograph from the Dance Collection, New York Public Library for the Performing Arts.)

phasizing the dramatic potential of ballet, Cranko carefully nurtured the dancers to express his ideas. Early on he found his ideal ballerina in Marcia Haydée, whom he surrounded with an ensemble of individualistic artists such as Ray Barra, Richard Cragun, Birgit Keil, Egon Madsen, and Heinz Clauss.

One of Cranko's special concerns was the school's consolidation, which included the addition of a boarding wing. He also was active as a lecturer at the matinees of

STUTTGART BALLET. Heinz Spoerli's *Sackgasse* (Dead End), set to music by Igor Stravinsky, was created for the company in 1982, with leading roles for Birgit Keil and Vladimir Klos. Keil is pictured here with Christopher Boatwright in a later performance. (Photograph © by Hannes Kilian; used by permission.)

the Noverre Society, which increasingly developed into a forum for the promotion of new choreographers such as Ashley Killar, Gray Veredon, John Neumeier, and Jiří Kylián. Thus Cranko created new ballet awareness not only in Stuttgart but also in other German cities (both Berlin and Munich tried to lure him away); this appreciation increased when the company returned from its first successful tours abroad. The company and city were shocked when Cranko died suddenly in 1973.

After a leaderless season, Glen Tetley was appointed as Cranko's successor from 1974 to 1976, but he never truly took control of the company, which survived because of its solid Cranko repertory. In 1976 Marcia Haydée became artistic director of the company, maintaining its by now rather obsolete Cranko orientation but infusing new blood by encouraging younger dancer-choreographers such as Patrice Montagnon, William Forsythe, and Uwe Scholz. This honest effort, however, was slow to pay dividends. Haydée was more successful in inviting John Neumeier to create *The Lady of the Camellias* and *A Streetcar Named Desire* for the company and relied mostly on works by Hans van Manen and Maurice Béjart.

Although most of the company's present dancers never worked with Cranko, the company's international status in the 1980s rested largely on his repertory, performed by such Cranko stalwarts as Keil, Cragun, Susanne Hanke, and Haydée herself. Until Haydée's resignation in the summer of 1996, the repertory consisted mainly of works by Cranko, van Manen, Neumeier, and Béjart, along with Haydée's highly successful production of *The Sleeping Beauty*. There were also contributions from such young choreographers as Nacho Duato, Renato Zanella, Stefan Thoss, and Roberto de Oliveira. For the 1996/97 season,

STUTTGART BALLET. Maurice Béjart mounted his production of *Die Zauberflöte* (The Magic Flute) for the company in 1994. The dancers in this beautifully geometric grouping are Benito Marcelino (in arabesque), Tamas Detrich, and Marion Jäger. The striking scenic design was made by Béjart. (Photograph © by Gundel Kilian; used by permission.)

Reid Anderson was appointed artistic director, with a three-year contract.

[*See also the entries on Noverre, Cranko, and other principal figures mentioned herein.*]

BIBLIOGRAPHY

Ballett Annual. Stuttgart, 1978–. Published by the John Cranko Gesellschaft und Württembergische Staatstheater Stuttgart.
Kilian, Gundel. *Stuttgarter Ballett.* New ed. Weingarten, 1991.
Koegler, Horst. *Stuttgart Ballet.* London, 1978.
Schmidt, Jochen. "The Guardians of Cranko's Legacy." *Ballett International* 9 (October 1986): 18–23.

HORST KOEGLER

SUBLIGNY, MARIE-THÉRÈSE (Marie-Thérèse Perdou [Perdoult] de Subligny; born July 1666 in Paris, death date unknown), French dancer. According to the *Dictionnaire critique de biographie et d'histoire* (Paris, 1878): "On 18 July 1666, was baptized Marie-Thérèse, daughter of Adrien-Thomas Pardoult [*sic*], *escuyer*, Sieur de Subligny, and dlle. Claude Bourgoin, the mother, living at rue de Richelieu. The godfather: Martin Ducas [Lucas], *conseiller aumonier* of the King; the godmother: Dame Elisabeth de Villaret (Villares), mother of the Sieur de Subligny." Her paternal grandparents were Adrien Perdou and Elisabeth de Villars; her maternal grandparents were Jean Bourgoin, seigneur d'Ailly, one of the king's secretaries, and Claude de Saucort. Marie-Thérèse Subligny belonged to a somewhat noble lineage, or at least to one with pretensions to some nobility. At the time of her parents' marriage, on 5 September 1667, she was already "thirteen months old or about" and her "legalization" had to be completed. Her father was a writer and a journalist, author of *Fausse Clélie* (1677) and of *Muze Dauphine*, a gazette written in verse, in imitation of the renowned *Muze historique* (1650) by Jean Loret.

Almost nothing personal is known about this famous dancer, whose career can be traced through ballet programs only. She appeared in the last court ballets given by Louis XIV. In *Ballet de Flore* (January 1689), she danced with Mesdemoiselles de La Fontaine, Lesueur, and Durieux. At the Paris Opera, her name is first seen in the cast of *Cadmus et Hermione* (1690) and appeared regularly in all the ballets until her retirement in 1705. Many of Subligny's dances have survived, thanks to the Feuillet notation system. Her famous partnership with Claude Ballon brought them an invitation to perform in England in 1699, where they scored a popular success. In 1703, the *London Stage* was still advertising a "new dance by the Devonshire girl [Mrs. Campion] in imitation of Mademoiselle Subligny." Her name made its last appearance on Opera programs in 1705, for the ballets *Roland*, *La Fêtes Vénitiennes*, and *Le Triomphe de l'Amour.*

Two racy anecdotes found in a police report indicate that Marie-Thérèse de Subligny was still living in 1735. She was said to be sharing an apartment in rue Saint Honoré with a woman friend named Madeleine Bailleul, without servants (Archives Nationales y. 10.750).

BIBLIOGRAPHY

Hilton, Wendy. *Dance of Court and Theatre: The French Noble Style, 1690–1725.* Princeton, 1981.
Lajarte, Théodore de. *Bibliothèque musicale du Théâtre de l'Opéra* (1878). 2 vols. Geneva, 1969.
Maurepas, Jean. *Recueil de chansons.* N.p., 1696. Manuscript located in Paris, Bibliothèque Nationale, fr.12644.
Migel, Parmenia. *The Ballerinas: From the Court of Louis XIV to Pavlova.* New York, 1972.
Parfaict, François, and Claude Parfaict. *Histoire manuscrite de l'Académie Royale de Musique.* Paris, n.d. Manuscript located in Paris, Bibliothèque Nationale, fr.12355.
Winter, Marian Hannah. *The Pre-Romantic Ballet.* London, 1974.

RÉGINE ASTIER

SUB-SAHARAN AFRICA. [*To survey the diverse dance traditions found in sub-Saharan Africa, this entry comprises three articles:*

An Overview

Popular Dance

Dance Research and Publication

The first article presents the importance of dance in African societies, the variety of dance styles, and the evolution of theatrical styles based on traditional dances; the second explores recreational forms of social dancing; the third focuses on dance scholarship and writing. For related discussion, see Central and East Africa; Southern Africa; *and* West Africa. *For more general discussion, see* Aesthetics, *article on* African Aesthetics; Costume in African Traditions; Mask and Makeup; Music for Dance, *article on* African Music; *and* Ritual Dance.]

An Overview

In indigenous sub-Saharan African societies, dance serves diverse functions as an integral part of communal life, in which people share language, religious belief, and social organization. Although functionally similar, the dances of Africa's diverse cultures display radically different styles.

Social Function. Within an indigenous traditional society, a dance usually has a principal overt function and several related subsidiary associations that may be conscious expressions or implicit reflections of the society's organization and its people's traditional values. This multiplicity of intentions is exemplified in the dance performed in the Yoruba town of Ijio, Nigeria, by the Efe masquerader at the Gelede ceremonies. A dramatic midnight appearance of this key figure is designed at a ritual level to appease the Great Earth Mother and the women on whom she bestows mystic powers. The Efe masquerade enters the market dancing to the Bembe drum rhythms with an aggressive display of stamping feet and rapid turns that awe the spectators. The Ososo drums take over as he moves around the square, pausing to sing and dance in honor of the ritual and political leaders present. He thus reaffirms the social hierarchy within the community. As night wears on, the Efe dancer relaxes into informal songs and dances. Using mimetic gestures, he ridicules improper behavior by selected individuals over the past year, thus exercising social control while entertaining his audience.

In sub-Saharan African cultures, dance is used as an expression of social organization. It differentiates and defines the roles of individuals and groups. Members related by status, age, sex, or work express their identity and cohesion in dances appropriate to the occasion, which emphasize the qualities proper to the performers. In the hierarchical society of the Yoruba, dance is used as a validation of leadership. A ruler is expected to state his

authority in formal dances, and failure to meet the required standard may be a serious threat to his prestige. His wives and lesser chiefs also have dances through which they express their dignity and status. In Ghana, the Asantehene, ruler of the Akan, dances the *kete* in his palace, with gestures conveying that "apart from the Gods and the Earth, there is no one greater than the Asantehene." Other chiefs honor their leader in dance, each with his own formalized gestures that express his allegiance and position.

For priests and priestesses, dance is a statement of their spiritual leadership. When they are possessed by the powers they serve, their gestures give mimetic expression to the nature of the deity or spirit. Initiates have their own styles of dance in which they act as supporting choruses for the ritual leaders. For example, Yoruba priests in Benin who serve Shango, the god of thunder, express his wrath in the lightning speed of their arm gestures and the "thunderous" roll of their shoulders in the highly formalized rhythms of their *lanku* dance. At the same time, women praise-singers dance in honor of the god by forming a circle and raising their headdresses when they mention his name. In Zimbabwe, the Mhondora spirit mediums connect the Shona people with the guardian spirits of the dead. They move into a state of trance as they sing and perform a characteristic dance of rhythmic foot patterns to the music of the *mbira* (a hand piano).

Masquerade dancers are a feature of religious societies in most African cultures. Four main types, with different roles, can be identified: those who embody deities or spirits; those who embody the ancestral spirits returning to guide their descendants; those who placate the spirits; and those who perform principally as entertainers.

In Mali, the animal-spirit masqueraders of the Bambara carry stylized carvings of bush animals and dance in imitation of their movements to ensure fertility in their community. *Bedu* masquerade dancers of the Nafana in Côte d'Ivoire make their night appearance wearing abstract animal masks that are the central feature of their purification rites. The heavier the mask, the less freedom for dance: *Epa* masqueraders of the Ekiti Yoruba wear complex head masks, whose weight allows them to perform only stately processional dances. Costume can also facilitate dance: the voluminous cloth costumes of the ancestral *ikhien-ani-mhin* masquerades of the Ishan permit leaping turns that demand virtuosic skill.

Secular masqueraders who perform as entertainers have emerged from the ritual societies. The Egúngún entertainers of the Nigerian Yoruba appear at the Egúngún festival but may also be invited to perform for a fee and travel abroad to earn money, although they are bound to offer sacrifice to their ancestors before performing. The company usually starts its performance with simple acrobatic dances and then displays its magic powers by changing into a series of costumes and masks that represent gods, heroes, and animals or that satirically impersonate politicians, wrongdoers, and strangers, such as visiting Europeans.

In societies that stress stratification by age people born around the same date belong to an age set and move together through several life stages with prescribed roles and rites of passage. The qualities proper to a particular phase of life are expressed in its dances. For example, certain dances are intended to keep young men physically fit and teach them the discipline necessary for warfare. The dances of young Zulu and Ndebele (Matabele) men in southern Africa, as well as the *takai* dance of the male aristocrats of the Barabra in western Africa recall the victories of past warriors. Among the Owo Yoruba, male adolescents perform the lively *ajabure* with ceremonial swords, while the stately *totorigi* dance is for older men and women. The transition from one life stage to the next may be marked by ritual ceremonies, as in initiation rites for adolescents, when dances stress sexual fertility and customary behavior between the sexes. In the *otufo* initiation rites for girls among the Ga of Accra in Ghana, dance is part of preparation for womanhood and enables them to display their charms to suitors. The *sikyi* dance of the Akan allows formalized flirtation between the sexes. The mixed-sex dances of the Ika people in Nigeria are openly erotic, and this is unusual; in most traditional sub-Saharan African dances, men and women do not perform the same style of dance or dance in direct relation to each other. This is becoming more frequent, however, in areas where the original context of the dance has been disrupted by external influences. As a rule, idealized male and female qualities are expressed in the movements of each gender's dances. Even if both join a circle or share a dance rhythm, their movement patterns are usually quite distinct. The erotic is expressed with humor.

Men of an age set often work together and celebrate a successful project with beer-drinking and vigorous dances that express their occupational skills. For example, Nupe fishermen are renowned for their net-throwing, which they have formalized in dance patterns; young Irigwe men at agricultural festivals on the Jos Plateau in Nigeria leap to encourage symbolically the growth of crops.

Professional organizations or guilds of experts such as blacksmiths, hunters, and woodcarvers also have their own expressive dances in sub-Saharan Africa. Hunters may reenact their exploits or mime the movements of animals as a ritual means of controlling both wild beasts and their own fears. The *abofour* dance of the Akan is a mime dance staged after the killing of a dangerous animal. It placates the spirit of the beast and informs the community of the manner in which it was killed.

In many cultures, established dance groups are invited to perform as part of the celebration of important social occasions, such as marriages and funerals, as well as to entertain visitors at the bidding of the elders. Dance is a particularly important part of the funeral service, where it may be performed during or after burial ceremonies or at a later anniversary celebration honoring the dead. Some dances are specifically designed for the occasion; in the *igogo* dance of the Owo Yoruba, young men use stamping movements to pack the earth of the grave into place. Others are social dances that can be performed on various occasions, including honoring the dead and comforting the bereaved.

Dance clubs have become popular in Africa's urban centers. They allow people of the same culture to perpetuate their heritage in a multicultural environment. People of both sexes and various ages meet to perfect their skill in traditional dances, which are tailored for performance in

SUB-SAHARAN AFRICA: An Overview. Among the Baga people of Guinea, the dance of the female mask Sörsörne is performed by a male dancer. The expandable costume is seen here extended to its full height; the carved mask at top is characterized by curved horns and prominent breasts. (Photograph © 1987 by Frederick Lamp; used by permission.)

a new setting. Dance teams are formed, and as their reputations grow, they are invited to perform on social occasions.

Dance is also important as an educational medium. Repetitive dance patterns teach children physical control and stress traditional behavior patterns and standards of conduct. Children may form their own dance and masquerade groups, as among the Kalabari of Nigeria; they may join adults at the end of a dance line, as in the dances of the Gungawa (Reshe) in Borgu Division, Nigeria; or they may simply have a space allocated to them in a performing area at the time of a festival.

Ritual dance is used as therapy in many cultures, particularly in West Africa. Cults commonly known as *bori* (or *ajun* among the Jukun) have female elders who treat women with mental disturbances, by exorcising the evil spirits thought to be responsible, in ceremonies that initiate the sufferers into the cult. During a three-month preparation period in a house shrine, a patient is taught songs and dances that play a therapeutic role. The period culminates in a ceremony in which the initiate publicly joins the members of the society to perform the *ajun-kpa* dance.

Throughout Africa, dance is the most popular form of recreation. In towns, members of different age groups meet informally on occasions when men and women may dance together. In villages, informal dancing may take place in the evenings, but relations between the sexes are more tightly overseen and controlled.

Dancing Style. The variety of sub-Saharan African dancing styles arises in part from the physical contexts of cultures. Differing musical styles are interrelated with

dance, as well. A third factor determining style is the history of a society and its external relations.

Influence of environment and material culture. Africa has extensive areas of both open savanna and dense forest, tropical and subtropical; and the continent displays extremes of barren desert and moist temperate lands. The physical environment has influenced the way in which people conceive space and time, two of the cultural constructs on which they have patterned their movements; so undoubtedly the environment has affected their styles of dance.

The Lopawa farmers of Nigeria live on the solid earth of the savanna, surrounded by open spaces extending to the far horizon. When dancing, they place their feet firmly on the sun-baked earth as they follow their team leader through the clearly defined circular pattern; with upright carriage they perform simple foot patterns to a steady tempo. This is a basic style of dance for many of the savanna farmers. The various cultures have, however, devised a wide variety of movements on the basic pattern.

The Ijo-speaking people live in the mangrove swamps of the Niger Delta, where their villages are regularly flooded. Canoes provide their transport and fishing their livelihood; the women's dances reflect this. They use light, precise foot beats, moving their weight rapidly from heel to toe and side to side in a variety of rhythmic patterns as they lean forward from the hips, with their arms extended to the sides as though balancing in an unsteady canoe or wading. Similarly, the Nembe women of mime paddling as they dance. These are common patterns of dance in riverine cultures.

Like many of Africa's desert peoples, the Kanuri of the

SUB-SAHARAN AFRICA: An Overview. The Wè (or Guéré) people live in the southwestern region of the Côte d'Ivoire. At a village festival at Zilebli, Canton Bo, this woman danced as an *oudhué*-spirit, wearing a warrior's headdress and brandishing hair whisks. Behind her are two supporting women dancers and an audience of appreciative villagers. (Photograph © 1985 by Monni Adams; used by permission.)

desert fringes conserve their energy by performing stately, measured dances with economical movements, extending their gestures into manipulation of their flowing robes. In contrast, the dances of forest-dwellers, such as the southern Yoruba, are freer and faster. Their foot patterns and sequences of body movements are performed in time to drums. The leading drummer may unexpectedly change the tempo and rhythm of the dance. Such alterations and their movement patterns suggest movement through forest undergrowth and alert reactions to the unexpected.

Environmental conditions are basic to a society's subsistence patterns. The movements used in such work, in turn, contribute to styles of dance. The knee-bend accompanying the farmer's swing of his machete can be recognized in the heightened elaboration of a dance gesture. Architecture, furniture, and dress are other cultural elements that influence posture, gesture, and the use of energy. For example, the Kambari of Nigeria must bend forward to enter the low doors of their houses, and their dance posture reflects this. The Nigerian Nupe, like most other Africans, sit on low stools or on the floor with their legs crossed or extended. Their flexible knees and strong leg tendons allow them to perform continuous deep knee-bends in their dance movements. Igbo boys in Nigeria wear short dance skirts that allow them a variety of rapid dance patterns with minimal expenditure of energy (in contrast to dancers in flowing robes, who use their energy in gestures away from the body center).

These basic influences in the development of African dance styles have been obscured by historical events—such as migrations—for example, the movement of Bantu-speaking peoples to the east and south, of Kwa speakers down the western coast, or of many populations along trade routes. For centuries, intertribal wars, and more recently religious persecution by Muslims and Christians, have also displaced people.

The boundaries that were established by colonial regimes to demarcate modern states often cut through traditional territories of homogeneous peoples, while bringing together entirely disparate cultures in a single new state. In some areas, neighbors now share a basic style of dance; in others, they perform in radically different styles. Thus, groups in widely separated locations in East, West, Central, and southern Africa may have dance styles that share features not present in the dance of their immediate neighbors. Nigeria, the largest nation in sub-Saharan Africa, has more than four hundred distinct ethnic groups, with elements of the dance styles that exist in most of sub-Saharan Africa. Yet dances in some regions may differ markedly in detail, and a few—such as the high-kicking dance of Zulu men and the leaping dances of the East African Masai—are not present in Nigeria.

Rhythmic patterns. African dances are based on a wide variety of rhythmic arrangements, many of which give the

SUB-SAHARAN AFRICA: An Overview. Women of the royal court of Dahomey (present-day Benin) dancing in homage to the family of King Justin Hao, at Abomey in the late 1950s. The black-and-white dresses and elaborate hair styles were mandatory for court dress. Each hair style, sculpted with the aid of oil and wire, could take an entire day to create. This undulating dance around the court was the beginning of a fetishistic ritual. (Photograph by Dominique Darbois; reprinted from *African Dance*, Prague, 1962, p. 26.)

dances their names. The most elementary is the continuous repetition of a simple rhythmic pattern throughout a dance. The Kambari of Nigeria use this technique in their *maranji* dance. A team of men moves in a circle around two drummers playing a two-beat rhythm on large *kagbandari* (snare drums). The dancers progress by sliding one foot forward while the other stamps out the rhythmic beat, which is emphasized by iron leg rattles. Each forward-inclined dancer turns slowly on his own axis. The dance continues for hours. At the end of the circle, standing upright, women dancers sing and step to the beats of the same rhythm.

By contrast, Urhobo women in Nigeria dance with strong contractions of the torso, thrusting their arms back and forth to a repetitive drum rhythm. As the dance progresses, the tempo accelerates to encourage ecstatic individuals to emerge from the group and dance in a state of trancelike possession.

The *ikhien-ani-mhin* masqueraders of the Ishan (Esan) are improvisational soloists. Each starts his acrobatic

SUB-SAHARAN AFRICA: An Overview. This festive group of Ijo people in Nigeria left their homes and went out on a highway to welcome home a local man who had just received a university degree. Their celebratory dance of greeting incorporated movements from traditional dances of the region. (Photograph © 1990 by Judith Gleason; used by permission.)

dance to the rhythms of the Okpodu drummers. They in turn conform to his rhythm as he begins to accelerate his movements. These include leaping turns in which the dancer begins in an upright position and then abruptly leans over at an angle. The turn speeds increase, reaching a climax in which the dancer's body revolves parallel to the ground while he maintains his rotation by touching the earth, in passing, with a foot or a hand. The dance displays amazing skill—the drummer and dancer are one in a repetitive, steadily mounting crescendo of rhythm.

Many cultures have team dances involving the repetition of a rhythmic phrase at a steady tempo. For example, in the *lwele le dag chun* dance of Birom girls in northern Nigeria, the girls take four running steps along a circle line, ending in a half turn with their feet spread. They then bend forward and mime the cutting of the vegetable *accha* using three arm-beats and ending in a half turn to the starting position.

The Afo men of Nassarrawa, Nigeria, perform the *goro goro*, a ritual dance to awaken their oracle in which a simple rhythmic phrase is extended during the performance. The dance begins with eleven men in a circle, each carrying a large metal *kokpo* gong on a handle of buffalo horn. Seven times they run, stopping to stamp in the center. The seventh time, they strike their gongs three times. This new pattern is repeated; then they add three kicks to the gong; this elongated pattern is also repeated. The tempo increases until the rhythm and movement phase ends with the dancers swinging the gongs around their bodies and striking them vigorously.

Many savanna farmers dance in teams and play instruments simultaneously to establish the rhythm. The Nga in Shiwer village blow fourteen large buffalo horns as they perform the repetitive step pattern of the *rumada* dance, in which they move along a circle or in and out of its center. Neighboring Chip men, playing flutes of four different pitches that blend to form a rhythmic melody, perform a dance in which they run lightly; at the end of each phrase, the dancers turn to the center and execute a series of light hopping movements. The close-knit relationship between music and dance limits innovation in choreography.

The Igbo of eastern Nigeria dance to a range of sophisticated rhythms. A dance performed by a boys' team with an adult leader, the *ubi-ogazu* (guinea fowl), is a version of the popular *etilogwu* dance and a good example of the most elaborate style of team dancing. The lead dancer plays an *oga* (flute) to set the rhythm, supported by an *igba* (drum), an *ududu* (pot drum), two *igedegwa* (xylophones), and an *ekwe* (bamboo gong). The dance consists of thirteen variations, each with a distinct rhythm and pattern of movement. Each variation is danced for five minutes, while the rhythm repeats with a rising tempo. The beat is light and rapid, and the boys dance in unison, with rhythmic precision, moving from one variation to the next with strong attack.

In contrast to the precision and teamwork required for the *ubi-ogazu*, the *apala* dance of the Yoruba allows a solo dancer to move freely among his fellow dancers in a pattern of his own devising. He relates directly to the rhythm of the leading drum and chooses his own sequence of movements within the recognized style of the dance. He competes with fellow dancers in interpretation of the rhythm and swift response to changes or unexpected nuances within it. The dancers are accompanied by an ensemble of Bata drummers. At a certain point in the dance, the leading drummer joins an outstanding dancer in a rhythmic exchange, urging him to yet greater feats of invention. These may include a variety of subtle foot patterns leading into turns, kicks, or small neat jumps accompanied by flourishes with a horse tail and a range of restrained and expansive dance movements.

Tradition and creativity. An Igbo dance performance presents a series of rehearsed dances of calculated variety, developed in rehearsal by the leader, who introduces new themes and creates movements to interpret them. Months of practice are required before a dance group is permitted by the elders to perform on a public occasion. The Yoruba dancer, by contrast, learns his skill as a child and uses his creativity to interpret the drum rhythm. African dance tradition is not static but a vital expression of immediate experience, skillfully ordered and formalized into various styles by generations of master dancers. The hierarchical Yoruba allow their dancers great personal freedom of in-terpretation and invention, albeit based on years of disciplined training. The more democratic Igbos place emphasis on team discipline under the strict control of a leader, who is responsible for innovations. The Igbo tradition has grown out of a horizontal social structure organized by age group, while the status-conscious Yoruba are highly competitive individualists in dance as well as in every other aspect of their lives.

Common Elements. Throughout sub-Saharan Africa, dance has common and basic formal features. Rhythm is the central element from which the dance form emerges. This rhythm is provided by musicians playing percussion instruments or by singers. Dancers may wear rattles that emphasize rhythms as they move. Normally the musicians lead the dancers, but in some cultures the dancer takes the initiative in establishing a dialogue of rhythmic exchange. The musicians initiate the performance by playing the basic pulse of the rhythm; the dancer warms up by shifting his weight from one part of the body to another—feet, knees, hips, or shoulders—until the rhythm is established by the musicians accenting and eliminating pulses to form the required pattern.

SUB-SAHARAN AFRICA: An Overview. The mating dance of young Sara people from Maro, in southwestern Chad. The groups of girls (in the foreground) and boys (at right, in the background) clap accompaniment as couples pair up, face off, and perform stamping dances to display their temperament and physical beauty. (Photograph © 1994 by Michel Huet / Hoa-Qui; used by permission.)

To dance rhythmically, the dancer uses relaxed knees as springs to transfer weight from one foot or one hip to the other. The back is held straight, with the center of control in the lower spine; the head is lightly poised. The shoulders are relaxed and move independently of the torso.

The dancer's weight is usually directed toward the ground. The performer does not resist gravity but rather emphasizes the body's weight in response to the rhythmic beats of the dance. The Earth Mother, a key figure in many African religions, controls the fertility of the earth and of people. Guardian ancestral spirits live within her domain, and dancers celebrate this deep-rooted relationship.

African dancers employ three characteristic dance postures. The first is an upright position with the back straight, typically used in the dance of chiefs, expressing their authority. The second posture requires a forward inclination from the hips, which directs the dancer's attention and gestures toward the earth. This posture may be maintained throughout a dance, as the Kambari do, or the dancer may move from the upright to the inclined position, as in the Yoruba *apala* dance. In the third posture, the dancer inclines the back parallel to the ground, bearing the body weight on the balls of the feet. Many riverine people use this posture in their dances, either throughout the performance or in alternation with the inclined and upright postures.

The fact that dancers are weighted toward the earth does not necessarily mean that they are heavy-footed. In some cultures, the dancers use the full foot to stamp out the rhythms; in others, they leap while performing light foot movements. Whatever the style of movement, however, the weight is pulled toward the earth, and leaps accent the return to the earth.

SUB-SAHARAN AFRICA: An Overview. This historic photograph, taken sometime between 1909 and 1915 near Rungu, in the Belgian Congo, shows an entire village of Bangba people engaged in a circle dance. An American explorer, a member of the expeditionary team, can be seen standing in the background, wearing a white shirt and a pith helmet. (Photograph by Herbert Lang; from the Department of Library Services, American Museum of Natural History, New York [no. 224585]; used by permission.)

Formal Elements: A Basis for Analysis. Any analysis of African dance must emphasize the time element of rhythm, which is experienced in the performance of rhythmic dance patterns and which forms an inseparable bond between dancers and musicians, as well as between a dance leader and the members of his team. A dancer is evaluated according to ability to follow the percussive musical rhythm—"to play the drums with one's feet" or with whatever part of the body that articulates the rhythm. This rhythmic skill underlies the abilities to hold the correct posture with the essential straight back and to use the means of progression and the gestures required by the dance style at the correct tempo. The dancer allows the rhythm to move through the body in accordance with the norms of the tradition.

Each dance has a characteristic movement pattern by which it is immediately identified. Some dance styles are exemplified by foot patterns, others by contraction of the torso, strong shoulder beats, or rapid vibrations or twists of the buttocks. The duration of a movement may be limited or unlimited, depending on how much physical exertion the dance requires and its context.

In addition to patterns of bodily movements, dances are characterized by the patterns of progression traced on the ground or floor surface—either formal or free-flowing, or a combination of these. Among the formal patterns used by teams are circles or circling lines, in which dancers usually move counterclockwise. Some linear patterns suggest the influence of drill routines from the West, but they are in fact traditional in the dances of warriors. Free-flowing patterns allow the members of a group to dance freely among themselves. A loosely organized linear or half-circle formation allows a soloist to emerge and interpret the music personally, rather than through a leader.

Spatial movements grow out of the rhythm; the dancer moves through rather than to each position, creating sculptural rather than geometric shapes. Precision is rhythmic rather than spatial, in contrast to dances traditional to most Western cultures. This characteristic does not imply simplicity; in fact, body rhythms are percussive and far more complex than those in most Western dance forms. A dancer may sustain two or three distinct rhythms simultaneously with different body parts.

The arts of Africa are united in performance. From childhood, specialist musicians, singers, dancers, sculptors, and costume-makers have learned family skills. The dance masquerader, in elaborate costume carrying a carved mask, embodies all the arts of Africa.

From Tradition to Theater. Dance in Africa may be divided into three interrelated categories—traditional, neotraditional, and theatrical. In African societies, the year revolves around a series of festivals at which traditional arts may be seen in the contexts for which they were created, performed by leading artists in a form of village the-ater. Five main types of festival are distinguished by their functions: (1) ritual festivals in honor of the guardian spirits, such as the Kpledzo festival of the Ga; (2) festivals in honor of ancestors, such as the Ade festival of the Akan; (3) those that reinvest a divinely appointed king with power, such as the royal festivals of the Bini; (4) those that commemorate historical events, such as the Dumba festival in Ghana, at which Muslims celebrate the birth of the prophet Muḥammad; (5) and those that mark the annual work cycle, such as the Kundum festival of the Nzema and Ahanta. Placatory sacrificial rites at a shrine are followed by processions of key figures through the town or village, featuring music and dance and culminating in the market square, where the theme of the festival is stated in artistic terms.

In a village community, the spectators at a ceremony or social celebration are familiar with the style and intention of the dance. They are present to participate in artistic reaffirmation of the customs and values that sustain their communal life. A close-knit relationship is established between the performers and the audience who surround them, creating their dance space and supporting them by clapping or singing if the occasion allows. Audiences also assess the performances and decide whether innovations accord with tradition. Only highly skilled dancers are selected by the elders to perform at important public events. Master dancers hold a position of prestige which they must work to maintain, because spectators are fiercely critical of errors or mishaps. For example, a stilt dancer who falls is ordered out of the area in disgrace by the organizer, who may discipline audience and performers alike.

Within the various traditions, gradual changes in dance styles usually occur under the guidance of dance leaders. But when a sudden or major cultural change—such as invasion, religious conversion, or the introduction of universal primary education—occurs in a country or community, the pattern of life alters radically, as are attitudes toward dance. Conversion to Christianity banned or minimized dances in the past; now Muslims too often forbid converts to attend traditional festivals or perform their dances. Today some Christian churches attempt to Africanize their liturgies with music and dance, bringing familiar styles into new contexts, so gestures and tempos have to be rethought.

The introduction of long-term formal education to Africa since World War II has meant that many children had no time to learn traditional dancing skills. Ghana's Ministry of Education introduced dance and music into the school syllabus in the 1960s. This has affected dance styles in the towns and villages to which the pupils return. Dances in schools are performed in a different environment and with different intentions than those that are part of a village tradition. When the two coincide, the

SUB-SAHARAN AFRICA: An Overview. Men of the Tutsi tribe in Rwanda performing the dance of the *intore*, the warrior elite of the kingdom. Wearing their typical headdresses with long raffia manes and richly bedecked with bead necklaces and leopard skins, the *intore* perform a vigorous, leaping dance while brandishing bows and spears. Accompaniment is provided by horn players and by the jangling of bells strapped to the dancers' ankles. (Photograph © 1994 by Michel Huet / Hoa-Qui; used by permission.)

dance styles are affected by changes in organization, duration, and dress; the resulting performances successfully met a new need, so the altered dance styles became accepted.

Modern transport has affected dance styles by bringing together people from diverse cultures, at times with spectacular results. The introduction of modern media, such as transistor radios played in villages, has led the young to turn to new styles of dance, with emphasis on entertainment and recreation. When a master dancer dies nowadays, he may have no replacement; however, the changing pattern of village life stimulates creative individuals to build new dance patterns that reflect modern interests. More radical changes occur as dancers move to urban centers where westernized lifestyles, films, and television are common.

A major catalyst for change has been governmental organization of civic arts festivals to promote traditional arts. Cultural officials, with varying knowledge of the arts, hold village competitions, selecting the best dancers to compete in a series of elimination events from town to national levels.

When a traditional dance is taken out of its village context and performed for a diverse audience unfamiliar with its original intention or style, the dance may be regarded as pure entertainment, and the motivation and intention of the performers may change as well. The performers may restructure traditional dances to emphasize spectacular elements in attempts to please the audience or gain prizes, fees, or prestige. Cultural officials often rearrange performances on the basis of audience reaction, limiting duration and encouraging a concentration of spectacular movements from several dances into a single performance. Costumes may be changed to suit occasions or to express national sentiments. Movement patterns may be altered to suit modern stages or to please important donors. When traditional dance forms are thus disrupted, a neotraditional style emerges.

The highly organized teams of the Igbo, however, perform in a number of contexts within their village tradition. Their discipline and rehearsal technique allow them to make the transition to a modern stage with spectacular results, especially if the master dancers are allowed to alter the dance patterns in creative response to the stimulation of fresh venues and foreign audiences. Nonetheless, with continuous repetition for purely commercial motives even such lively dances as the *etilogwu* or the Zulu war dance can become hackneyed and faded.

Neotraditional dance styles may imitate the externals of traditional styles yet lose the vital motivation that gives the dance meaning for performer and audience. Master dancers may become or give way to theatrical choreographers who can create works for the contemporary theater that are meaningful specifically in performance terms, not merely compromised versions of traditional dances. At the University of Ife in Nigeria, at the Mudra Centre in Dakar, Senegal, and in Guinea, contemporary training for African dance theater has been established. The technique taught at Ife has been based purely on dance patterns drawn from a wide range of African traditions; the Mudra Centre, established in 1977, has imported theatrical techniques from the West.

Dance drama has become a popular form in African theaters, but the most common role for theatrical dance is in conjunction with other performing arts in theater productions, preserving the essence of the traditional interrelation of artists in different performance media. The first professional theaters in West Africa were companies created by actor-managers, most of whom had been schoolteachers experienced in dramatizing Bible stories in Christian churches. They set up traveling companies that performed in native languages, utilizing full ranges of theater arts to reach both urban and rural audiences. Programs, readily adaptable, could be toured to halls, open spaces, or theaters.

The Yoruba opera companies are examples of this popular form of theater in Nigeria. Each company works under the artistic direction of the actor-manager, who plays leading parts. In productions based on musical ensembles, the performers move fluidly from the use of words in song, poetry, and dialogue to the use of movement in mime and dance. Dialogue is initially improvised and finally scripted. The dance, music, poetry, and costumes are

SUB-SAHARAN AFRICA: An Overview. The *ngodo*, the elaborate orchestral dance of the Chopi people of Mozambique, is an ancient tradition, having been documented by Portuguese explorers in the sixteenth century. The orchestra is composed of xylophones made in five pitches (treble, alto, tenor, bass, and double bass), seen here in the foreground. In front of the seated xylophone players stand four rattle players. The dancers have just made their entrance into the performing area and have turned to face the orchestra. A complete dance may have as many as nine to fifteen sections and take up to an hour to perform. The complexities of the dance, the poetry of the lyrics, and the beauty of the music place the Chopi *ngodo* in a class by itself among the performing arts of sub-Saharan Africa. (Photograph by Merlyn Severn; reprinted by permission from Hugh Tracey, *African Dances of the Witwatersrand Gold Mines*, Johannesburg, 1952, p. 131.)

drawn from Yoruba traditions and used creatively in a dramatic setting.

The themes in the works of the leading companies' dramatists indicate their range of material. Duro Lapido based his work on Yoruba mythology. Actor and mime Kola Ogunmola created domestic comedies focused on his brilliant use of mime, while Herbert Ogunde staged social narratives and political satires, using music and dance influenced by the British concert-hall performances in vogue when he began his career in Lagos in the 1930s. Ladipo died in 1973, hailed in Nigeria as a leading theatrical innovator for his use of African traditions as a basis of contemporary theater.

In Ghana, since the 1920s the popular Bob Cole worked, through improvisation, to produce theatrical comedies that combined music and dance with dialogue. These are known in Africa as the Trios, and their influence as indigenous theater is apparent in the works of contemporary choreographic directors.

In many African states, government ministries have set up national dance schools that feed dance companies promoted to tour in Africa and abroad. Some companies, such as the National Ballet of Senegal, are neotraditional rather than theatrical and offer sophisticated adaptations

SUB-SAHARAN AFRICA: An Overview. A troupe of Zulu youths performing a gumboot dance at the Robinson Deep Mine dance arena, near Johannesburg. To the accompaniment of a guitar, the dancers perform in unison, slapping their boots and stamping their feet to create elaborate rhythmic patterns. The percussive effects achieved with heavy rubber Wellington boots are not unlike those in tap dancing. The dome-shaped straw hut is typically Zulu. (Photograph by Merlyn Severn; reprinted by permission from Hugh Tracey, *African Dances of the Witwatersrand Gold Mines*, Johannesburg, 1952, p. 52.)

of traditional dance styles in fast-moving productions. Others, such as Les Ballets Africains, use these traditions to create contemporary African styles. [*See* Ballets Africains, Les; *and* National Ballet of Senegal.] National theater companies may be static, promoting conservative works, or inventive, aiming to appeal to all strata of society. For example, the National Theatre of Kenya was established in the 1960s under the directorship of Ngugi Wa'Thiongo, who was later banished to his village. There, he set up a cooperative theater in which villagers worked together, using the full range of performing arts in productions that spoke of their lives and problems. At the other extreme are the musical extravaganzas on stereotyped African themes that were sponsored by South Africa's government to support its former doctrine of *apartheid*, such as the stage musical *Ipo-Tombi*, presented in London and New York. An effective response was the refreshing simplicity and artistic excellence of the musical *Poppie Nongena*, in which a small cast of black South Africans based their performance on song and used dance as an integral part of the drama.

Contemporary theater in Africa is at its most successful when a creative director works with talented artists who have not lost the strength and vigor of the traditional arts. Other twentieth-century phenomena are the growth of popular dance forms, such as highlife and juju, and the counterinfluence of African-American and Caribbean music and dance on new African styles and genres.

BIBLIOGRAPHY

Åkesson, Birgit. *Källvattnets mask: Om dans i Afrika.* Stockholm, 1983.
Briginshaw, Valerie A. "African Dance Bibliography." *Africana Journal* 10.1 (1979).
Hanna, Judith Lynne. "African Dance Research: Past, Present, and Future." *Africana Journal* 11.1–2 (1980): 33–51.
Harper, Peggy. "Dance in a Changing Society." *African Arts* 1 (Fall 1967): 10–13, 76–80.
Harper, Peggy. "Dance in Nigeria." In *Dance in Africa, Asia, and the Pacific*, edited by Judy Van Zile. New York, 1976.
Harper, Peggy. "The Arts of Theatre and Ritual." *Theoria of Theory* 2.3 (1977).
Harper, Peggy. "Dance." In *The Cambridge Encyclopedia of Africa*. Cambridge, 1981.
Huet, Michel. *The Dance, Art, and Ritual of Africa.* New York, 1978.
Huet, Michel, and Claude Savary. *Africa Dances.* London, 1995.
Kubik, Gerhard. *Maskentraditionen im bantu-sprachigen Afrika.* Munich, 1993.
Nketia, J. H. Kwabena. *The Music of Africa.* New York, 1974.
Opoku, Albert M. "The Presentation of Traditional Music and Dance in the Theatre." *World of Music* 18.4 (1976): 58–67.
Schaeffner, André. *Le sistre et le hochet: Musique, théâtre et danse dans les sociétés africaines.* Paris, 1990.
Thompson, Robert Farris. *African Art in Motion: Icon and Act.* 2d ed. Los Angeles, 1979.
Thompson-Drewal, Margaret, and Glorianne Jackson, comps. *Sources on African and African-Related Dance.* New York, 1974.
Tiérou, Alphonse. *Dooplé: The Eternal Law of African Dance.* Translated by Deirdre McMahon. Chur, 1992.

PEGGY HARPER

Popular Dance

In the context of sub-Saharan Africa, the term *popular dance* refers to purely recreational forms of social dancing that developed in the growing urban centers of the colonial period (sixteenth to twentieth centuries). These dances rapidly diffused into the countryside, where they have thrived as irrepressibly as in urban settings. During the twentieth century, large towns have served as centers of invention and dissemination for popular dance. In rural areas, precolonial or traditional recreational dances and older styles of popular dance still flourish. Rural areas not only provide a constant source of enrichment for urban dance culture but also are continually reinvigorated by new influences from the cities.

African popular music and dance emerged from the confrontation and confluence of indigenous and foreign cultures around 1900. Their development and performance represent a creative response to the demands of a challenging and rapidly changing environment. African popular dances exemplify the process of syncretism, in which stylistic elements drawn from two or more cultures in contact not only blend but also cross-fertilize in response to new social needs. The actual forms these dances take depend on the social experiences, cognitive cultural models, and expressive resources of their creators.

Widely distributed throughout English-speaking West Africa is highlife, a popular dance style and an example of syncretism. The term *highlife* seems first to have attained popularity during the 1920s, although the creative origins of the dance may go back another century to the beginning of a significant British presence in Ghana (the former Gold Coast). The British employed Africans throughout the lower levels of their colonial administration. To succeed within the system, Africans had to learn the cultural forms of their employers. This they did in the mission churches and schools, the colonial service, and the enterprises of the colonial economy. Adopting European forms of social dancing was a creative and enjoyable aspect of acceding to cultural imperialism.

Both the British expatriates and the African colonial elite needed dance music, so before recordings became available African musicians were trained on Western in-

SUB-SAHARAN AFRICA: Popular Dance. The famous New Year's Carnival in Cape Town, South Africa, draws visitors from far and near. These youngsters, wearing matching outfits and carrying yellow parasols, are typical of the numerous groups organized to go dancing in the streets of the city. (Photograph by Doug Pithey; used by permission of the Cape Newspaper Picture Service.)

struments in the mission schools and in the military bands of the West African Frontier Force. Soon these musicians came together in dance bands to play for the social events of the colonial elite, both white and black. Obliged to perform while fellow Africans in formal dress disported themselves in the manner of the British, these musicians named this music "highlife," a satirical reference to the social ambitions of their patrons. Specifically, the term denoted indigenous African melodies that were orchestrated for dance bands, as well as to European hymns and march tunes that were transformed into dance music by the influence of African intonations, harmonies, and rhythms. West Indian, Latin American, and African-American music entered the mix via Europe and the dance craze of the 1920s.

As a dance, highlife displayed the same complex syncretism as the music, using a relatively uncomplicated set of steps. Unlike traditional African dances, highlife was performed by couples in the European fashion; rather than holding onto each other, however, partners moved individually, smoothly orchestrating simultaneous movements of head, shoulders, hips, and feet in a graceful alternating two-step, to the multiple accents of an easy calypso-like rhythm.

During the same period, another form of highlife was also developing out of a different colonial experience. African artisans from the Gold Goast, who had been sent to work in the coastal towns of Sierra Leone, Nigeria, and Cameroon, learned and brought back new dances and musical influences. In such ports as Sekondi-Takoradi (in Ghana), they met Liberian, West Indian, and African-American sailors, who were introducing the guitar into West African urban folk music. Soon a tradition of guitar band or "palm wine" highlife developed among the new urban African working class. Among its most famous innovators was Yao Amponsah, after whom the most common highlife rhythm is named. Amponsah claimed to have learned guitar in the 1920s from a Liberian Kru sailor at Takoradi.

Unlike dance-band highlife, guitar-band highlife emphasized lengthy narrative songs of social commentary and satire that were similar to the traditional ballads of the Akan-speaking peoples of Ghana. They were performed to the accompaniment of guitar and traditional percussion instruments, often for casual listeners and dancers at the palm wine bars found throughout Ghana's urban working-class neighborhoods. In the countryside, and in precolonial towns such as the Ashanti capital, Kumasi, guitar highlife was strongly influenced by traditional dances such as *adowa*, which led to the emergence of new virtuosic styles of solo dancing—traditional highlife and highlife *adowa*.

Following Ghanaian independence in 1957, dance-band and guitar-band highlife gradually converged, becoming part of the emerging cultural nationalism of postcolonial Africa. Well before this, highlife had spread to Nigeria and other West African countries, and bands from several countries toured throughout the region. In Congo (formerly Zaïre), a popular guitar-band style—based on Afro-Latin rhythms and Mediterranean, African, and West Indian melodies—emerged and spread throughout East and Francophone Africa. Called "Congo Beat," it is still sub-Saharan Africa's most widely played and popular style of music and dance. In Nigeria, *juju* music has become the most popular form; its exponents perform regularly in Britain and the United States as well as in West Africa. In southern Africa, the blending of African dance with African-American soul and jazz has produced the energetic jive style.

At nightclubs and social gatherings throughout sub-Saharan Africa today, styles of homegrown popular dance flourish side by side with the latest imported recordings and African-American dances. Together, all these factors nourish the continuing vitality of African dance and provide a means of cultural expression, representation, and reorientation.

BIBLIOGRAPHY
African Urban Notes 5.4 (1970).
African Urban Studies 6 (Winter 1979–1980).
Coplan, David. "Go to My Town, Cape Coast! The Social History of Ghanaian Highlife." In *Eight Urban Musical Cultures: Tradition and Change*, edited by Bruno Nettl. Urbana, Ill., 1978.
Coplan, David. *In Township Tonight! South Africa's Black City Music and Theatre*. Johannesburg, 1985.
Roberts, John Storm. *Black Music of Two Worlds*. New York, 1972.

RECORDINGS.   King Sunny Ade and His African Beats, *Juju Music* (Mango Records, MLPS 9712). African Brothers Dance Band, *African Brothers Dance Band (International)* (Afribros, PAB 110). Eric Agyeman, *Highlife Safari* (Apogee Records, BEBLOP 013). Dollar Brand, *Mannenburg—Is Where It's Happening* (The Sun, SRK 786134). Franco et le T.P. O.K. Jazz, *Disque d'or et maracas d'or 1982*, vol. 6 (Disco Stock Makossa, DM 5004). Fela Ransome Kuti and the Africa 70, *Shakara* (Editions Makossa International, EM 23.05). Tabu Ley et l'Afrisa International, *Rochereau*, vol. 6 (Star Musique, SMP 6006). Prince Nico Mbarga & Rocafil Jazz, *Sweet Mother* (Rounder Records, 5007). Ebenezer Obey, *Chief Commander Ebenezer Obey and His International Brothers* (Decca [West Africa], WAP 38). Oboade, *Kpanlogo Party with Oboade* (Lyrichord, LLST7251). Soul Brothers, *Dumela* (Masterpiece, LMS 528). *Sound d'Afrique* (Mango Records, MLPS 9697).

DAVID COPLAN

Dance Research and Publication

Few Western scholars who have done sustained field-work in Africa have had specific training in observing, describing, documenting, and analyzing dance. Among the few who have such training are Odette Blum, Margaret Thompson-Drewal, Judith Lynne Hanna, and Peggy Harper. Blum (1973) characterized certain dance styles in four Ghanaian cultures. Margaret Thompson-Drewal, Hanna, and Harper studied dance primarily in Nigeria. Hanna's

1963 fieldwork among the Ubakala Igbo (1976, 1977a, 1977b, 1979) considered the functions of dance as a communicative system. Harper worked with filmmaker Francis Speed and used effort-shape theory to establish a relationship between dance styles and work movements (1968a, 1968b, 1969, 1970a, 1970b, 1972). Margaret Thompson-Drewal, both alone (1975, 1978, 1984) and with Henry John Drewal (1987) investigated indigenous concepts of performance, their bases in philosophies, and the ways in which dance articulates those philosophies and concepts. A semiological approach is of particular interest to Céline Baduel-Mathon (1969).

Since 1970, much of the available information on African dance has come from the writings of anthropologists, art historians, and musicologists; dance performance, however, is only incidental to their primary interests. The art historian Robert Farris Thompson, for example, wrote *African Art in Motion* (1974; 2d ed., 1979). Two of Thompson's former students, Frederick Lamp (1978) and Judith Bettelheim (1976), also explored dance. Lamp studied with Irmgard Bartenieff in preparation for fieldwork among the Temne people of Sierra Leone, and Bettelheim concentrated on documenting African influences in Caribbean performance genres.

Perhaps the best contributions of art historians to dance scholarship come from their studies of masked performances, a genre that combines their interests in costumes and sculpted masks with the context of dance. Works by Jean Borgatti (1976, 1979), Henry John Drewal (1977, 1979), Wilson Perkins Foss (1973), and René Bravmann (1977) are of particular note.

Ethnomusicologists—including Paul Berliner (1975–1976), John Blacking (1977), Gerhard Kubik (1977), and J. H. Kwabena Nketia (1974, pp. 206–230)—and the art historians Thompson (1966) and Borgatti have also been interested in dance styles and performances. Films, too, provide rich glimpses of African dance styles; see Margaret Thompson-Drewal and Glorianne Jackson (1974), also Ruth M. Stone (1982).

Anthropological information on African dance has often come as a byproduct of research on ritual, especially its functional and symbolic dimensions. Anthropologists who have concentrated specifically on dance include Jacques Binet (1972), James W. Fernandez (1975–1976), T. O. Ranger (1975), and Victor Turner (1968). Their work reveals how dance functions as a part of social processes, but not how dancers actually perform or how such performance relates to those social processes or to a culture's total symbolic system. Exceptions are found in works by Walter H. Sangree (1976) and by Judith Lynne Hanna. Hanna's studies consider formal and stylistic elements of Ubakala Igbo dance plays within a functionalist interpretation.

Possession trance is one important area of research that has been explored by both anthropologists and ethnomusicologists (see Walker 1972; Zaretsky and Shambaugh, 1978). The literature on possession in Africa, however, concentrates on neurological and psycho-physiological explanations of trance. Dance scholars can provide fresh insights into this phenomenon by examining it as performance—because trance in Africa is frequently expressed in dance that varies greatly even within cultures (as among the Yoruba) and requires a certain level of technical mastery. Dance scholars can analyze and compare the formal aspects of possession trance, the training of performers, and their movement styles and techniques.

The issue of gender should also be an important consideration in dance research in Africa. Earlier scholars tended either to accept men's and women's dances as cultural givens or to explain them in terms of corresponding social roles, without accounting for dance roles and categories as cultural constructions. Questions arise, then, about how gender concepts shape dance, and vice versa.

Poststructuralist trends in anthropology suggest new directions in African dance research. A view has developed that holds traditional African dance to be unfixed, fluid, always emerging through interpretive processes, and thus simultaneously created anew and re-presented at each performance.

BIBLIOGRAPHY

Baduel-Mathon, Céline. "Pour une semiologie du geste en Afrique occidentale." *Semiotica* 1 (1969).

Berliner, Paul. "Music and Spirit Possession at a Shona Bira." *African Music Society Journal* 5 (1975–1976).

Bettelheim, Judith. "The Jonkonnu Festival: Its Relation to Caribbean and African Masquerades." *Jamaica Journal* 10 (1976).

Binet, Jacques. *Sociétés de danse chez les Fang du Gabon*. Paris, 1972.

Blacking, John. "An Introduction to Venda Traditional Dances." *Dance Studies* 2 (1977): 34–56.

Blum, Odette. "Dance in Ghana." *Dance Perspectives*, no. 56 (Winter 1973).

Borgatti, Jean. "The Festival as Art Event: Form and Iconography." Ph.D.diss., University of California, Los Angeles, 1976.

Borgatti, Jean. *From the Hands of Lawrence Ajanaku*. Los Angeles, 1979.

Bravmann, René A. "Gyinna-Gyinna: Making the Djinn Manifest." *African Arts* 10 (April 1977).

Drewal, Henry John. "Art and the Perception of Women in Yoruba Culture." *Cahiers d'études africaines* 17 (1977).

Drewal, Henry John. "Pageantry and Power in Yoruba Costuming." In *The Fabrics of Culture*, edited by Justine M. Cordwell and Ronald A. Schwarz. The Hague, 1979.

Fernandez, James W. "Dance Exchange in Western Equatorial Africa." *Dance Research Journal* 8 (Fall–Winter 1975–1976): 1–7.

Foss, Wilson Perkins. "Festival of Ohwóru at Evwreni." *African Arts* 6 (1973).

Hanna, Judith Lynne. "The Anthropology of Dance Ritual: Nigeria's Ubakala Nkwa di Iche Iche." Ph.D.diss., Columbia University, 1976.

Hanna, Judith Lynne. "Ubakala Dance Movement: Aesthetics, Sex, and Other Sociocultural Patterns." *African Studies Papers* (1977).

Hanna, Judith Lynne. "Dance and Social Structure: The Ubakala of Nigeria." *Journal of Communication* 29 (Autumn 1979): 184–191.

Harper, Peggy. *The Irigwe Dancers of Miango Village on the Jos Plateau.* Studies in Nigerian Dance, no. 2. Ibadan, 1968a.

Harper, Peggy. *Tiv Women: The Icough Dance.* Studies in Nigerian Dance, no. 1. Ibadan, 1968b.

Harper, Peggy. "Dance in Nigeria." *Ethnomusicology* 13.2 (1969): 280–295.

Harper, Peggy. "Icough: A Tiv Dance." *African Notes* 6 (1970a).

Harper, Peggy. "The Role of Dance in the Gelede Ceremonies of the Village of Ijio." *Odu,* n.s. 4 (1970b).

Harper, Peggy. "The Kambari People and Their Dances." *Odu,* n.s. 7 (April 1972).

Kubik, Gerhard. "Patterns of Body Movement in the Music of Boys' Initiation in South-East Angola." In *The Anthropology of the Body,* edited by John Blacking. London, 1977.

Lamp, Frederick. "Frogs into Princes: The Temne Rabai Initiation." *African Arts* 11 (January 1978).

Nketia, J. H. Kwabena. *The Music of Africa.* New York, 1974.

Ranger, T. O. *Dance and Society in Eastern Africa, 1890–1970: The Beni Ngoma.* London, 1975.

Sangree, Walter H. "Dancers as Emissaries in Irigwe, Nigeria." *Dance Research Journal* 8 (Spring-Summer 1976): 31–35.

Stone, Ruth M. "Twenty-Five Years of Selected Films in Ethnomusicology: Africa." *Ethnomusicology* 26 (1982).

Thompson, Robert Farris. "An Aesthetic of the Cool: West African Dance." *African Forum* 2.2 (1966): 85–102.

Thompson, Robert Farris. *African Art in Motion: Icon and Act.* 2d ed. Los Angeles, 1979.

Thompson-Drewal, Margaret, and Glorianne Jackson, comps. *Sources on African and African-Related Dance.* New York, 1974.

Thompson-Drewal, Margaret. "Symbols of Possession: A Study of Movement and Regalia in an Anago-Yoruba Ceremony." *Dance Research Journal* 7 (Spring–Summer 1975): 15–24.

Thompson-Drewal, Margaret, and Henry John Drewal. "More Powerful Than Each Other: An Egbado Classification of Egungun." *African Arts* 11 (Spring 1978).

Thompson-Drewal, Margaret. "Appendix B (Dance)." In *From the Hands of Lawrence Ajanaku,* by Jean Borgatti. Los Angeles, 1979.

Thompson-Drewal, Margaret, and Henry John Drewal. "Composing Time and Space in Yoruba Art." In *The Relationship of the Verbal and Visual Arts among the Yoruba,* edited by Rowland Abiodun. 1987.

Thompson-Drewal, Margaret. "Dancing for Ogun in Yorubaland and in Brazil." In *Africa's Ogun: Old World and New,* edited by Sandra T. Barnes. Bloomington, 1989.

Turner, Victor. *The Drums of Affliction: A Study of Religious Processes among the Ndembu of Zambia.* Oxford, 1968.

Walker, Sheila S. *Ceremonial Spirit Possession in Africa and Afro-America.* Leiden, 1972.

Zaretsky, Irving I., and Cynthia Shambaugh. *Spirit Possession and Spirit Mediumship in Africa and Afro-America: An Annotated Bibliography.* New York, 1978.

MARGARET THOMPSON-DREWAL

SUDAN. *See* Nuba Dance; *and* Zār. *For discussion of Sudanese influence on Egyptian traditional dance, see* Egypt, *article on* Traditional Dance.

SUFI DANCE. *See* Dance and Islam. *See also* Turkey.

SUITE FOR FIVE. Original title: *Suite for Five in Space and Time.* Choreography: Merce Cunningham. Music: *Music for Piano 8–84,* John Cage. Costumes: Robert Rauschenberg. First performance: 18 May 1956, University of Notre Dame, South Bend, Indiana, Merce Cunningham Dance Company. Dancers: Merce Cunningham, Carolyn Brown, Viola Farber, Marianne Preger, Remy Charlip.

Suite for Five is an expanded version of Merce Cunningham's 1953 *Solo Suite in Space and Time.* To the original five solos, Cunningham added a trio (for Farber, Preger, and Charlip), a duet (for Cunningham and Brown), and a quintet. In the first performance the order was solo ("At Random"), trio ("Transition"), solo ("Stillness"), duet ("Extended Moment"), solo ("Repetition"), solo ("Excursion"), quintet ("Meetings"), solo ("For the Air"). Subsequently the solos "Repetition" and "For the Air" were omitted. In 1958, for a duet version titled *Suite for Two,* Cunningham choreographed "A Meander," a solo for Carolyn Brown. It was interpolated between the opening solo and the trio in the group version and this became the definitive *Suite for Five.* From 1953 until 1973 the solo, duet, and quintet versions were in the Cunningham company repertory, seen throughout the United States, Europe, and Asia.

Cunningham and Cage used chance operation in the choreography and music composition. A detailed explanation of Cage's process may be found in his *Silence.* Cunningham used Cage's process to determine the space, spatial relationships, and durations of phrases. Each dance has a designated time length. "This was one of the first dances where meter was completely abandoned," according to Cunningham, "and [the] dancers had to rely on [their] own dance timing to guard the length of any phrase, and the timing of a complete dance" (*A John Cage Reader,* p. 111). The following note appeared in the program: "The events and sounds of this dance revolve around a quiet center, which, though silent and unmoving, is the source from which it happens." *Suite for Five* is a seminal work that explores movement in time and space, and one might describe it as Cunningham's earliest choreographic realization of the hypothesis that time and space cannot be defined independently of motion.

BIBLIOGRAPHY
Cunningham, Merce. *Changes: Notes on Choreography.* Edited by Frances Starr. New York, 1968.
Cage, John. *Silence.* Middletown, Connecticut, 1961.
A John Cage Reader. New York, 1982.

CAROLYN BROWN

SULAWESI. *See* Indonesia, *article on* Dance Traditions of the Outlying Islands.

SUMATRA. *See* Indonesia, *article on* Sumatran Dance Traditions.

SUMMERSPACE. Full title: *Summerspace—A Lyric Dance.* Choreography: Merce Cunningham. Music: *Xion,* Morton Feldman. Scenery and costumes: Robert Rauschenberg. First performance: 17 August 1958, Connecticut College, New London, Connecticut, Merce Cunningham Dance Company. Dancers: Merce Cunningham, Carolyn Brown, Viola Farber, Cynthia Stone, Marilyn Wood, Remy Charlip.

Summerspace is the second in a series of dances by Merce Cunningham named for the four seasons. *Springweather and People* (1955), *Rune* (originally *Autumn Rune*; 1959), and *Winterbranch* (1964) complete the cycle. *Time* Magazine (29 February 1960) described *Summerspace* as "an impressionistic work evoking the shimmering heat of summer, the play of light and shade . . . danced before a pointillistic back drop. . . . The dancers wore similarly dappled costumes which permitted them to disappear into and emerge from the scenery as if they were passing through a wall."

"With *Summerspace* (the summer part of the title came after the dance was finished, but the notion of space was always present), the principal momentum was a concern for steps that carry one through space, and not only into it," wrote Cunningham in 1968. "Like the passage of birds, stopping for moments on the ground and then going on, or automobiles more relentlessly throbbing along turnpikes and under and over cloverleaves. This led to the idea of using kinds of movement that would be continuous, and would carry the dancer into the playing area, and out of it." In his notes, Cunningham explains his use of chance procedures applied to a gamut of movement to determine such things as direction, speed, shape of the space, number of dancers involved in a particular action, and so on.

Summerspace is one of the best known of Cunningham's dances for two reasons: its unusual and striking pointillist decor by Robert Rauschenberg and the fact that it is one of the few works Cunningham choreographed for his own company that has been performed by other companies, namely the New York City Ballet, the Cullberg Ballet, the Boston Ballet, and the Théâtre du Silence in La Rochelle, France. In both the New York City Ballet and the Boston Ballet productions the womens' roles were danced in pointe shoes.

The first performance of *Summerspace* at Connecticut College in 1958 was virtually ignored by the dance press. On the Cunningham company's 1964 six-month world tour, *Summerspace* was seen by audiences in London, Paris, Brussels, Venice, New Delhi, and Tokyo, among other cities, and received considerable press coverage. But in 1965, when the company gave two performances at the New York State Theater the dance once again received little attention from American critics. However, the same work on the same stage performed by the New York City Ballet only one year later was greeted with reviews in six New York City daily newspapers and much preperformance publicity, and yet many agreed with Walter Terry that it was Cunningham's dancers rather than Balanchine's who communicated a sense of alertness, of responsiveness to stillness as well as to sound.

BIBLIOGRAPHY

Cunningham, Merce. "*Summerspace* Story." *Dance Magazine* (June 1966): 52–54.
Cunningham, Merce. *Changes: Notes on Choreography.* Edited by Frances Starr. New York, 1968.
Reynold, Nance, and Susan Reimer-Torn. *Dance Classics.* Pennington, N.J., 1991.
Terry, Walter. Review. *New York Herald Tribune* (15 April 1966).

CAROLYN BROWN

SUNDA. *See* Indonesia, *article on* Sundanese Dance Traditions.

SUSANA (Susana Janssen-Audeoud; born 10 October 1916 in Köniz, Switzerland), performer, teacher, and choreographer of Spanish dance. Although dance was not cultivated in her childhood home, Susana Janssen-Audeoud expressed herself even as a little girl in dances of her own invention. She danced in response to an inner need and without any urging from her parents. Later, when she began formal studies of classical and modern dance, she discovered Spanish dancing and recognized it as her true métier. Because Spanish dancing sought a connection with the earth as intensely as it sought passion and an opening upward, it corresponded closely to her own nature, and it became the medium through which she developed as an artist.

Despite her Swiss birth, Susana became an embodiment of Spanish dance. Juan Estampio and Cojo de Sevilla had the most decisive artistic impact upon her during her formative years. Beginning in 1948, she spent twenty years touring with José Udaeta as the dance team of Susana y José. They toured the world with a repertory that included theatricalized folk dances and their own creations in the spirit of Spanish dance.

In 1970, Susana became intensively involved in dance education and was soon a much sought-after teacher of Spanish dance, giving courses of instruction at the National Ballet School of Canada, in Toronto; at Mudra, Maurice Béjart's name for the École de Danse et d'Interpretation Artistique, in Brussels; and at the international summer Academy of Dance in Cologne. As vivacious and intuitive a teacher as a performer, Susana developed a precisely structured course of instruction based on a variety of forms of Spanish dance in a sequence of exercises comparable to those taught in a classical ballet class.

In developing this material, Susana became increasingly aware of the rich and genuine vocabulary of movement that Spanish dance offered, and she began to wonder if it could be used in developing theatrical works, as was the classical vocabulary. In addition to bringing explicitly Spanish dances to the stage, Susana used Spanish material in independent choreographic figurations of dance themes. Toward these ends, she was greatly helped by her collaboration with the composer Antonio Robledo, who willingly included the rhythmic and melodic material of flamenco in his ballet scores, which closely followed her own creative ideas. The results of their collaboration were a merging of music and choreography virtually unseen since the days of Serge Diaghilev.

Two notable works from their repertory are *Ronda de Toros* (1977) and *Los Siete Puñales* (1981), Susana's version of Federico García Lorca's *Blood Wedding*. In *Los Siete Puñales* (The Seven Daggers), the story is told in pantomime enriched by Spanish dance, and the situation and characters are expressed through elements of Spanish dance used in innovative ways. This choreographic approach was particularly successful in the depiction of the seducer Leonardo and in the duel, where dramatic tension is expressed chiefly by the *zapateado* heelwork of the onlookers.

In 1985, Susana and Robledo formed their own small company, which they called Flamencos en Route. In the following five years the two artists created for it their two masterpieces, *Soledad* and *A Juan*. In both these works, Spanish folklore is transformed into a language of high art, combining the power and energy of dance with the expressive sensibility of music.

BIBLIOGRAPHY
Merz, Richard. "En Route: Susana." *Ballet-Info* 4 (June 1981): 15–18.
Merz, Richard. "What Is a Dance Event?" *Ballett International* 11 (March 1988): 10–15.
Pastori, Jean-Pierre. *Dance and Ballet in Switzerland.* Translated by Jacqueline Gartmann. 2d ed., rev. and enl. Zurich, 1989.
Zacharias, Gerhard. *Susana y José.* Vienna, 1970.

RICHARD MERZ
Translated from German

SVETLOV, VALERIAN (Valerian Iakovlevich Ivchenko; born 1860 in Saint Petersburg, died 1934 in Paris), Russian critic, writer, and editor. Svetlov was an associate of Serge Diaghilev, a founding member of the Association for the Organization of the Russian Seasons Abroad, and an ardent champion of Michel Fokine's innovations in choreography. He was a prolific writer both in Russia and in France following his 1917 emigration there. Svetlov was the third husband of the dancer Vera Trefilova.

Editor of the popular literary journal *Niva*, Svetlov also wrote numerous full-length works as well as articles that appeared in such periodicals as *Peterburgskaia gazeta, Birzhevye vedomosti, Slovo, Le temps russe, Vozrozhdenie, Dancing Times, Archives internationales de la danse,* and *American Dancer*. He contributed extensive accounts of Diaghilev's Paris seasons to the Russian press and always enthusiastically supported Fokine's work. In 1910, for instance, Svetlov summarized the season by noting that "Diaghilev not only organized this mighty and serious artistic enterprise but served as its inspiration, breathing new life into an art that had frozen in a state of senility. He provided a broad arena for Fokine's outstanding talents." Svetlov's accounts of Diaghilev productions were not always full of praise, however. In 1912 Svetlov wrote two lengthy articles about *L'Après-midi d'un Faune* in which he argued that although Léon Bakst's decor was "beautiful and striking in its use of color, creating a Bacchanalia of all possible spots, like a multicolored, attractive rug," it was completely out of keeping with the ballet's bas-relief theme. In Svetlov's view, the ballet's illustrious creators had simply made a *faux pas*, and he predicted that the *Faune* failure would simply go unnoticed.

In addition to being Fokine's chief supporter among the critics, Svetlov collaborated with Fokine on the production of *Eros* in 1915. His story "The Fiesole Angel" provided the scenario for the ballet.

Svetlov is perhaps best remembered for his 1911 book *Sovremennyi balet*, published the following year in French as *Le ballet contemporain*. Among the first expositions of the new ballet and its influence on western Europe, the book also served as a compilation and summary of Svetlov's own views about the new ballet. The book includes a chapter on the Petipa legacy, Svetlov's accounts of the first Russian season in Paris, a discussion of French critical reaction to the Diaghilev enterprise, and an article on Isadora Duncan. Duncan, Svetlov wrote, "arrived in the dead of winter, nude, like an ancient goddess, and transported us back to that faraway land of blue skies and golden sunshine where the plastic arts were born."

[*For related discussion, see the entries on Koni, Levinson, Volynsky, and Zotov.*]

BIBLIOGRAPHY
Karsavina, Tamara. *Theatre Street.* Rev. and enl. ed. London, 1948.
Scholl, Tim. "From Apollon to Apollo." *Ballet Review* 21 (Winter 1993): 82–96.
Svetlov, Valerian. *Terpsikhora: Stati, ocherki, zamietki.* St. Petersburg, 1906.
Svetlov, Valerian. *Sovremennyi balet.* St. Petersburg, 1911.
Svetlov, Valerian. *Le ballet contemporain.* St. Petersburg, 1912.
Svetlov, Valerian. *Anna Pavlova.* Translated by A. Grey. Paris, 1922.
Svetlov, Valerian. *Thamar Karsavina.* London, 1922.
Svetlov, Valerian. *Bakst.* New York, 1927.
Svetlov, Valerian. "The Diaghileff Ballet in Paris." *The Dancing Times* (December 1929): 263–274; (January 1930): 460–463; (February 1930): 569–574.

SUSAN COOK SUMMER

SWAINE, ALEXANDER VON (Alexander Freiherr von Swaine; born 28 December 1905 in Munich), German dancer and teacher. Swaine was one of the most versatile and technically brilliant dancers of his time. The peaks of his artistic career in Europe were in the 1930s and the 1950s. The most striking feature of his dance style was his ability to fascinate with his expressive power in both classical and modern dance.

From 1924 to 1928 Swaine studied classical dance in Berlin with Evgenia Eduardova, a veteran of Pavlova's company. At the same time he worked with Max Reinhardt in Berlin and Salzburg, appearing as Puck in *A Midsummer Night's Dream*. In 1928 he went on tour with his own dance evening; its program bore the strong imprint of interpretive dance, but its classical background was also recognizable. In 1932 he continued his studies with Margaret Craske in London. In 1933 he was hired as a solo dancer with the Berlin City Opera, but in 1935 he left this position and joined the Berlin State Opera as soloist.

Swaine quickly made a name for himself as a dancer of tremendous dramatic power. His tension-filled characterizations, reinforced by mime and physical endowments as well as dance technique, fitted him for both classical roles and for interpretive dance on the concert stage. Numerous tours, some of them with Darja Collin and Rosalia Chladek, won him high esteem in other countries. During World War II, he lived and taught in Java and India. In 1947, after being interned by the British, he returned to Germany.

With the Hungarian dancer Lisa Czobel, whose repertory similarly included both classical and modern dance, Swaine appeared in joint programs for almost twenty years thereafter, making numerous tours throughout Europe and overseas. In 1960 Swaine was hired as a teacher of classical and modern dance at the School of Fine Arts in Mexico City. In 1965 he appeared in a final dance evening with Czobel. Thereafter he concentrated on teaching, an activity that also led to guest assignments outside Mexico, including some in the United States.

BIBLIOGRAPHY

Ballett in Berlin, 1945–1978. Berlin, 1978.
Haskell, Arnold L. "The Art of Alexander von Swaine." *The Dancing Times* (January 1938): 508–509.
Huwe, Gisela, ed. *Der Deutsche Oper Berlin.* Berlin, 1984.
Peters, Kurt. "Alexander von Swaine." *Das Tanzarchiv* 28 (December 1980): 717–720.
Regitz, Hartmut, ed. *Tanz in Deutschland: Ballett seit 1945.* Berlin, 1984.

HEDWIG MÜLLER
Translated from German

SWAN, THE. *See* Dying Swan, The.

SWAN LAKE. [*This entry comprises of two articles on ballets choreographed to the score for "Swan Lake," written by Petr Ilich Tchaikovsky: the first describes the original Russian production choreographed by Wentzel Reisinger, the later version choreographed by Marius Petipa and Lev Ivanov, and subsequent productions by other choreographers in Russia; the second is a survey of productions outside Russia.*]

Productions in Russia

There is no extant draft of the original score of *Swan Lake*, and neither the librettist nor his sources are identified on the announcements or programs of the premiere. The plot was in essence similar to the one that is familiar today, telling of the maiden-turned-swan and the prince who swears he loves her but is tricked by an evil magician into betraying her. Asked by the directorate of the Bolshoi Theater to compose a ballet, Tchaikovsky requested a chivalrous theme. Given only six months to create the four-act score (in the end it took two years), he evidently planned to use material from his unfinished opera *Ondine* and needed a similar theme. (A comparison of the finished scores shows that the final duet of *Ondine* is identical to the second-act adagio of *Swan Lake*.)

Tchaikovsky began working on the score late in May 1875. He had previously used dance music in his operas, instrumental works, and even symphonies, making them more accessible to the public by introducing elements of popular music. In composing *Swan Lake* he pursued no reformist objectives, but his penchant for innovation was nevertheless at work. He did not use the method of sustained symphonic development that he would later apply in *The Sleeping Beauty* and *The Nutcracker*, but even here the music served the dance as more than an elementary rhythmic pattern by conveying its own dramatic message and complex characterizations. The integrity of the score was ensured not only by the leitmotifs that occurred throughout but also by the tonal interdependence of the episodes, which constituted an intricate system of layered associations based on the thematic material.

Original Production. Russian title: *Lebedinoe Ozero*. Ballet in four acts. Choreography: Julius (Wentzel) Reisinger. Music: Petr Ilich Tchaikovsky. Libretto: Vladimir Begichev and Vasily Geltser. Scenery: Karl Valz, Ivan Shanguine, and Karl Gropius. First performance: 20 February [4 March] 1877, Bolshoi Theater, Moscow. Principals: Polina Karpakova (Odette), Arnold Gillert (Siegfried).

In writing his score, Tchaikovsky had acted as a ballet dramatist, laying down new principles of organization that, in turn, required innovative choreographic thinking. The ballet dramaturgy of the day failed to realize this and consequently the first production of *Swan Lake* did not

SWAN LAKE: Productions in Russia. Anyone naming the great Swan Queens in Russian ballet history could not fail to mention Maya Plisetskaya. She first danced the dual role of Odette-Odile in 1947, and after the retirement of Galina Ulanova in 1962 she became the undisputed owner of the role at the Bolshoi Theater. She is pictured here in act 2, with Nikolai Fadeyechev as Siegfried and members of the female ensemble as the enchanted swan-maidens. (Photograph from the Dance Collection, New York Public Library for the Performing Arts.)

succeed. The critics found Reisinger's dances weak and gymnastic; the swan scenes were monotonous and poor in fantasy. The choreographer had failed to penetrate the complex world of Tchaikovsky's musical-psychological drama and seemingly had no feeling for its inherent lyricism. For the fourth performance on 25 April 1877 Anna Sobeshchanskaya replaced Polina Karpakova in the role of Odette, performing a new pas de deux she had commissioned from Marius Petipa.

Further alterations followed. On 13 January 1880 Joseph Hansen choreographed a new *Swan Lake* with Evdokia Kalmykova as Odette and Alfred Bekefi as Siegfried. Before it was dropped from the repertory in 1883 the ballet had been given forty-one performances. In 1888 the second act, choreographed by Augustin Berger, was shown at a concert given in honor of Tchaikovsky in Prague. In response the composer wrote in a letter to his family that he had experienced a moment of blissful happiness.

In 1894 the same act, this time choreographed by Lev Ivanov, was shown in a program at the Maryinsky Theater in Saint Petersburg commemorating Tchaikovsky, who had died the year before. After this successful showing, the decision was made to restage the entire ballet.

Petipa-Ivanov Version. Fantastic ballet in three acts and four scenes. Choreography: Marius Petipa and Lev Ivanov. Music: Petr Ilich Tchaikovsky. Libretto: Vladimir Begichev and Vasily Geltser. Scenery by Colonel Andreyev, Mikhail Bocharov, and Heinrich Levogt. Costumes by Evgeny Ponomaryov. First performance: 15 [27] January 1895, Maryinsky Theater, Saint Petersburg. Principals: Pierina Legnani (Odette-Odile), Pavel Gerdt (Prince Siegfried). Supporting cast: Sergei Bulgakov (Von Rothbart, the Evil Genie), Giuseppina Cecchetti (A Sovereign Princess, Siegfried's Mother), Aleksandr Oblakov (Benno).

For the new version of *Swan Lake*, Tchaikovsky's brother, Modest, considerably revised the original score and edited the libretto newly written by Vladimir Begichev and Vasily Geltser. Many details were altered that clarified the action and made Prince Siegfried more serious and sympathetic. The score was reworked to accommodate the revised libretto: some of the composer's piano pieces were added and some numbers were deleted or altered, while others were repositioned. Riccardo Drigo prepared a new orchestration. The first and third scenes were choreographed by Petipa; the second and fourth by Ivanov, who also staged the Hungarian and Venetian dances in the third scene.

In this version the psychological drama that Tchaikovsky had conceived gave way to magic and fairy tale. Petipa misunderstood the musical logic of the first act, regarding it as an insignificant prelude to the main events, rather than the portrait of Siegfried that Tchaikovsky had intended. (It was no accident that in later productions of the ballet it was the first scene that was most often revised.) Petipa staged the third scene (act 2) after the stereotypical model of a "ball *divertissement*," creating the impressive pas de deux for the black swan, Odile, and Siegfried as a *pas d'action* that echoed the adagio for Siegfried and the white swan, Odette, in the second scene of act 1. Nevertheless, the production owed its success to Ivanov, whose profound understanding of the music enabled him to devise scenes of intense lyricism, in which the geometry of lines was often sharpened by the asymmetric positions of the corps de ballet and all the movement configurations reflected the image of captive, enchanted beauty. Despite the mixture of styles, the ballet was a success.

Subsequent Productions. Following the success of the Petipa-Ivanov version, numerous choreographers mounted productions of *Swan Lake* at various theaters in Russia. Notable among them are those of Aleksandr Gorsky, Agrippina Vaganova, Fedor Lopukhov, Vladimir Burmeister, and Yuri Grigorovich.

Gorsky production. In 1901 Aleksandr Gorsky introduced the Petipa-Ivanov version to the Moscow stage, but with a number of changes. In the first and third scenes he sought to intensify the dramatic elements and to clarify the psychological motivation. Later revivals of Gorsky's staging tended to present the tale as a straightforward conflict between good and evil, the good Prince Siegfried opposed to the evil sorcerer Rothbart.

Vaganova production. Attempts to depart from the Petipa-Ivanov version were also undertaken in Leningrad. In 1933 Agrippina Vaganova—collaborating with the artist Vladimir Dmitriev, who also wrote the new libretto, and the musicologist Boris Asafiev—offered her own interpretation. This staging was of fundamental significance and influenced all later Soviet productions. Previously deleted musical pieces were restored, while the mystical and fantastic elements of the plot were intensified. The action was transferred from the Middle Ages to the Romantic period of the early nineteenth century. The lake scenes emerged as if in the imagination of Siegfried, danced elegiacally by Konstantin Sergeyev. The roles of the Swan (Odette) and Odile (reimagined as the daughter of a ruined landlord rather than an evil magician) were now danced by different ballerinas, Galina Ulanova and Olga Jordan, respectively. Vaganova replaced the pantomime episodes with danced scenes that have been retained in contemporary stagings. She also accentuated the imitative movements of the swan corps de ballet.

Lopukhov and Burmeister productions. Fedor Lopukhov gave *Swan Lake* a more classical appearance in Leningrad in 1945. He restored the plot of the Petipa-Ivanov version but strengthened the role of Siegfried. His interpretation was the starting point for Vladimir Burmeister, who produced the ballet for the Stanislavsky and Nemirovich-Danchenko Musical Theater in Moscow in 1956. Burmeister used the original sequence of musical numbers but provided crudely literal explanations for the actions.

Grigorovich production. In 1969 Yuri Grigorovich produced the ballet at the Bolshoi Theater in Moscow, making extensive revisions in all but the second act. Adhering to the original conception of the plot, he avoided modernization. The first act was an extended exposition that contrasted the worlds of Siegfried and Rothbart. The latter, now with more dancing than mime, became Siegfried's alter ego, a symbol of the dark, subconscious forces dormant in the human soul. This opposition also reflected the conflict between the white and black swans. In his final version Grigorovich preserved the happy ending that became common in Russian productions.

Swan Lake's role of Odette-Odile has been an important vehicle for many ballerinas over time, including Tamara Karsavina, Olga Spessivtseva, Marina Semenova, Maya Plisetskaya, and Natalia Bessmertnova. The ballet has been staged in all the republics of the former Soviet Union.

[*See also the entries on the principal figures mentioned herein.*]

BIBLIOGRAPHY

Beaumont, Cyril W. *Complete Book of Ballets*. Rev. ed. London, 1951.
Brown, David. "Tchaikovsky's Ballets: Swan Lake." *Dance Now* 2 (Spring 1993): 26–34.
Demidov, Alexander P. *Lebedinoe Ozero*. Moscow, 1985.
Grigorovich, Yuri, and Alexander Demidov. *The Official Bolshoi Ballet Book of Swan Lake*. Translated by Yuri S. Shirokov. Neptune, N.J., 1986.
Krasovskaya, Vera. *Russkii baletnyi teatr vtoroi poloviny deviatnadtsatogo veka*. Leningrad, 1963.
Macaulay, Alastair. "Why a Swan?" *Dance Ink* 3 (Summer 1992): 16–20.
Ross, Janice, ed. *Why a Swan?* San Francisco, 1989.
Slonimsky, Yuri. *P. I. Chaikovskii i baletnyi teatr ego vremeni*. Moscow, 1956.
Souritz, Elizabeth. *Soviet Choreographers in the 1920s*. Translated by Lynn Visson. Durham, N.C., 1990.
Vanslov, Victor V. *Balety Grigorovicha i problemy khoreografii*. 2d ed. Moscow, 1971.
Wiley, Roland John. *Tchaikovsky's Ballets: "Swan Lake," "Sleeping Beauty," "Nutcracker."* Oxford, 1985.
Wiley, Roland John. *The Life and Ballets of Lev Ivanov*. Oxford, 1997.

ALEXANDER P. DEMIDOV
Translated from Russian

Productions outside Russia

There is a succession of phases in the history of the ballet *Swan Lake* in the West: exports of the scenario, nearly always with the original score by Petr Ilich Tchaikovsky;

tours of the 1895 Saint Petersburg production by companies of Russian dancers; re-creations of the 1895 Saint Petersburg production by companies in the West; and revisions of the ballet and its score according to the many choreographers' experimentations with its characterizations and themes. These phases are continuous for more than one hundred years, beginning within several years of the ballet's 1877 premiere in Moscow.

The 1877 choreography by Julius Reisinger for the Bolshoi was revised by Joseph Hansen in 1880 and 1882. Soon afterward, Hansen left Russia and became ballet master at the Alhambra Theatre in London where he mounted a ballet called *The Swans*, to music by Georges Jacobi, the Alhambra's music director. Although a December 1884 announcement in London's *Daily Telegraph* referred to an 1813 Christmas pantomime produced at Covent Garden as its antecedent, the action of the one-act ballet at the Alhambra resembled the Bolshoi version: a Swan Queen falls in love with Roland, leader of the hunters; it takes place in a forest where the swans transform themselves into "pretty feminine shapes"; at the end, the Swan Queen and Roland are united in a boat drawn by the swans across the water.

The first production set to Tchaikovsky's music outside Russia was mounted at the Prague National Theater on 21 February 1888, during a visit by the composer. The ballet master August Berger, who also took the role of the Prince, choreographed act 2 for the second of two concerts in which Tchaikovsky conducted some of his own works. Adolph Cech conducted for the ballet performances, and Giulietta Paltrinieri-Bergrova appeared as the Swan Queen. Eight performances were given of Berger's version.

Despite these early versions of *Swan Lake*, only the transmission of the choreography by Marius Petipa and Lev Ivanov for the Maryinsky Theater production in Saint Petersburg has inspired subsequent generations. The Petipa-Ivanov *Swan Lake*, which remained in the Saint Petersburg repertory, became one of the most renowned artistic exports from Russia. In 1908, Anna Pavlova and Adolph Bolm, who led the first tour of wholly trained Russian dancers to the West, presented the middle two acts of *Swan Lake* in Scandinavia and Germany. In 1909, the czar's dancers visited a wider circuit of European cities, including Vienna. Pavlova, with Nicholas Legat as partner, danced *Swan Lake's* leading role in a three-act version. The ballet was seen in London on 16 May 1910 in a production at the London Hippodrome starring Olga Preobrajenska and a group of twenty performers; it was in New York at the Metropolitan Opera House on 20 December 1911 in a production staged by Mikhail Mordkin for fourteen solo dancers and a corps de ballet—Ekaterina Geltser appeared as the Swan Queen, with Mordkin as the Prince.

Although an early production of *Swan Lake* was choreographed in 1907 by Archille Viscusi in Prague, the version for Diaghilev's Ballets Russes, which premiered in London on 30 November 1911, is generally considered the first major production outside Russia.

Accounts by Diaghilev inner-circle members Serge Grigoriev and Alexandre Benois suggest that Diaghilev included *Swan Lake* in the repertory to entice Matilda Kshessinska, *prima ballerina assoluta* of the Maryinsky company, into appearing with the troupe. Diaghilev shortened *Swan Lake* to two acts and three scenes, because, in Grigoriev's words, "he considered some of the choreography dull and repetitive" (Grigoriev, 1953, p. 59). The first scene of the Saint Petersburg original was deleted. The second scene and second act were retained with revisions. The last act was shortened into a brief scene by the lake and amended without a break to the ballroom act. The choreography was attributed to Petipa, except for the waltz and the dance of the Prince in the second scene, by Michel Fokine. A new role, the Fiancée of the Prince, was created. Tchaikovsky's score was shortened and amended with the "Dance of the Sugarplum Fairy" from *The Nutcracker* added for the Prince and an interpretation of music by Andrei Kadlets for Kshessinska's solo. Vaslav Nijinsky and Kshessinska led the cast on opening night, with Enrico Cecchetti as Master of Ceremonies, Bronislava Nijinska and Ludmilla Schollar as the leading Swan Maidens, and Adolph Bolm and Sofia Fedorova in the ballroom *divertissements* in the "Spanish Dance." Mischa Elman played the violin solos at the opening.

Some changes in the libretto were made for the performances at Monte Carlo in 1912, but the two-act *Swan Lake* remained in Diaghilev's Ballets Russes repertory from 1911 to 1914 and was revived after World War I, from 1923 to 1926. For the last four years of the company's existence, a one-act version was performed, starring Alexandra Danilova and Olga Spessivtseva. George Balanchine made minor alterations in the one-act version while he was ballet master, deleting part of the Swan Queen's mime and rearranging ensemble movements for a corps de ballet decreased in size.

After Diaghilev's death and the dispersal of the Ballets Russes in 1929, one-act reductions of *Swan Lake* were presented at the Chicago Civic Opera House in 1930 with choreography by Laurent Novikoff, by Colonel W. de Basil's Ballets Russes in 1934, and by the Ballet Russe de Monte Carlo in 1938.

One of the Russian ballet émigrés to the West had more than just memories of *Swan Lake's* complete production as it was performed in Saint Petersburg before the Russian Revolution. Nicholas Sergeyev, former dancer and regisseur for the Maryinsky Theater, had used the Stepanov system of notation to record the classic repertory; he had brought his notebooks, scores, and memorabilia out of Russia in 1918. In London, Ninette de Valois, director of the Sadler's Wells Ballet, hired Sergeyev to stage the full-length *Swan Lake* for her company in 1934. Alicia Markova and Anton Dolin had already mounted act 2 for her in 1932, based on their memories of the Diaghilev production.

Sergeyev's notebooks contained directions for twenty-three dances from the original, with steps and floor plans. The notations were a compendium of the various changes that had been made in the production from 1895 to the end of the Imperial period. The only omission in Sergeyev's production for Sadler's Wells was the Venetian Dance in act 3. The Sadler's Wells premiere took place on 20 November 1934, with Alicia Markova and Robert Helpmann leading the cast.

Margot Fonteyn danced her first *Swan Lake* for Sadler's Wells as Odette, with Ruth French as Odile, on 16 December 1935. Fonteyn danced the dual role for the first time on 15 November 1938. The production was redressed with new sets and costumes by Leslie Hurry on 7 September 1943, and it was first performed in the United States on 10 October 1949. Additions by Frederick Ashton were made in 1952—the *valse pas de six* in act 2 and the pas de deux Neapolitan tarantella made on the unused "Venetian Dance." In 1963, Ashton added a prologue that was dropped in 1967; a new pas de six; a pas de quatre in act 2, later moved to act 3; a "Spanish Dance" for act 3; and a new choreography for the last act. In the 1973/74 season, after forty years of revisions to Sergeyev's production, his setting of the original Petipa-Ivanov version was restored.

Sergeyev also produced the complete work for Mona Inglesby's International Ballet, with decor and costumes by Hugh Stevenson, which premiered 18 March 1947, at the Adelphi Theatre in London, with Nana Gollner and Paul Petroff. It was virtually identical to the 1934 Sadler's Wells version but included the "Venetian Dance." After Sergeyev's death, in an appreciation written by Inglesby, she remembered that Sergeyev's mission was to "preserve the spirit

SWAN LAKE: Productions outside Russia. In 1963, Robert Helpmann staged a new production of the Petipa-Ivanov classic for Britain's Royal Ballet, with additional choreography by Frederick Ashton and designs by Carl Toms. Pictured here in act 2 are Georgina Parkinson as Odette and Anthony Dowell as Siegfried, c.1968. (Photograph by Houston Rogers; used by permission of the Board of Trustees of the Theatre Museum, London.)

SWAN LAKE: Productions outside Russia. In London in 1996, Matthew Bourne created an all-male version of *Swan Lake* for his company, Adventures in Motion Pictures, to critical acclaim. Adam Cooper is pictured here in the starring role, as the Swan. (Photograph © by Andrew Cockrill; used by permission.)

and atmosphere of the original rendering" of the ballets (Inglesby, 1951, p. 655).

The first full-length American production of *Swan Lake* was produced by the San Francisco Ballet within two years of the company's founding. Artistic director William Christensen provided the choreography "after Petipa and Ivanov," with the help of the large colony of Russian émigrés living in the city. Jacqueline Martin danced Odette, Janet Reed danced Odile, and Lew Christensen appeared as Prince Siegfried at the ballet's premiere at the War Memorial Opera House on 25 September 1940. The company included the production in its 1941/42 winter tour of the Midwest and Pacific Northwest.

By the 1940s, the story and music of *Swan Lake* were widely recognized in the United States as the paradigm for ballet. Balanchine had choreographed a capsule version for the 1940 Twentieth Century–Fox film *I Was an Adventuress*, with Vera Zorina as the Swan Queen and Lew Christensen as the Prince. Balanchine was seen in the film as the orchestra leader conducting the ballet. Catherine Littlefield produced a *Swan Lake* on ice skates for the extravaganza called *It Happens on Ice* at the Center Theater in New York on 10 October 1940. A *Swan Lake* in East Indian idiom was choreographed and performed by the American ethnic dancer La Meri on 20 February 1944.

In 1951, Balanchine choreographed a shortened *Swan Lake*, the first traditional ballet to enter the New York City Ballet repertory. The thirty-five-minute work was a composite of acts 2 and 4 of Ivanov's portions of the ballet. Balanchine kept only the central adagio, the Swan Queen's variation and coda, and the pas de quatre of the

cygnets. Balanchine's new choreography of the group passages and his elimination of all mime passages resulted in a greatly enlarged role for the corps de ballet. Balanchine cast twenty-four women as swans and eight men as hunters; Maria Tallchief was Swan Queen and André Eglevsky was the Prince at the New York premiere at the City Center of Music and Drama on 20 November 1951. The scenery and costumes had been designed by Cecil Beaton. Balanchine's version has remained in the repertory since then, but he continued to tinker with the choreography. New productions were mounted by the New York City Ballet in 1964 (scenery and costumes by Rouben Ter-Arutunian) and in 1986 (designed by Alain Vaes); in the 1986 production, the swans were clad in black, except for the Swan Queen.

The British dancer David Blair went to Atlanta, Georgia, in 1965 to stage a full-length production of *Swan Lake* and star as Prince Siegfried for the Municipal Theater. A company of fifty-eight dancers was recruited from companies in New York and Chicago and from regional ballet companies in Georgia, Florida, Alabama, North Carolina, Virginia, and Tennessee. As a member of Sadler's Wells Ballet (and the Royal Ballet), Blair was able to restage the traditional Petipa-Ivanov choreography, assisted by his wife Maryon Lane. Lupe Serrano of American Ballet Theatre danced the Swan Queen at the premiere. Blair also mounted the first full-length *Swan Lake* for American Ballet Theatre. It premiered on 16 February 1967 at the Civic Opera House, Chicago, and was similar to the Sadler's Wells production. Nadia Nerina and Royes Fernandez danced the leading roles in Chicago, while Toni Lander and Bruce Marks danced the leads at the New York premiere on 9 May 1967. Lucia Chase, director of the company, appeared as the Queen Mother. In 1981, American Ballet Theatre mounted a new production, staged by Mikhail Baryshnikov.

Inspiration for revisionist thinking on *Swan Lake* came partially from Soviet ballet master Vladimir Burmeister's staging of the work for the ballet company of Moscow's Stanislavsky and Nemirovich-Danchenko Musical Theater. Burmeister used Tchaikovsky's autograph score and added a prologue to the main "swan theme" for the production, which the Russian company brought to the Paris Opera in 1956. He made the Prince a character in his own right, not merely a partner for the Swan Queen. Erik Bruhn claims to have been influenced by his memories of the 1956 visit, and Rudolf Nureyev danced in the Burmeister version choreographed at the Paris Opera in 1960. The Soviet choreographer also staged act 2 for the London Festival Ballet in 1961 and a version for the same company in 1965, co-choreographed by Vaslav Orlikovsky.

John Cranko, Nureyev, and Bruhn created full-length versions of *Swan Lake* that focused on the Prince as the major character. Cranko's Siegfried, in his version for the

Stuttgart Ballet (premiere 14 November 1963), was a tragic hero, doomed to death in the waves that flooded the stage in act 4. Prince Siegfried, as choreographed and performed by Nureyev for the Vienna State Opera Ballet with Margot Fonteyn as the Swan Queen (premiere 15 October 1964), was a suffering hero, described by the critic Clive Barnes as "manic-depressive"; he not only failed to win Odette but was killed by Von Rothbart. In Bruhn's Freudian version for the National Ballet of Canada (premiere 27 March 1967 at O'Keefe Centre, Toronto), the magician Von Rothbart opposes Prince Siegfried and is changed to a Black Queen, the alter ego of the Prince's mother. At the end of the ballet, Siegfried is killed by the corps of swan maidens.

Two more recent productions of *Swan Lake* have framed the ballet as a dream. John Neumeier's production for the Hamburg Ballet (1976) made Prince Ludwig of Bavaria the protagonist who recalls his past obsession with *Swan Lake*. His identification with Siegfried accounts for the recollections that follow. Nureyev's 1986 production for the Paris Opera revised the scenario so that the Prince's tutor and Von Rothbart were combined into one character (danced by Nureyev). Siegfried, asleep on a throne, sees the action as a dream, which then follows the standard scenario. At the end, when Siegfried is dying of despair over the loss of his idealized love, the image returns of the hero with his dream.

In March 1987, Anthony Dowell staged a "new" production of *Swan Lake* for the Royal Ballet. Dowell enlisted a team of collaborators that included Professor Roland John Wiley, an expert on the Stepanov notations that Sergeyev had used to mount the 1934 Vic-Wells production. The notations are now housed in the Harvard Theater Collection. Dowell's intention was to strip away the accretions of the many revivals of *Swan Lake* so as to restore the Petipa choreography. The critical reviews were mixed. The settings were designed by Yolanda Sonnabend, who set the court scenes in Imperial Russia. Cynthia Harvey and Jonathan Cape were the first-cast leads, with Deanne Bergsma as Siegfried's mother and Derek Rencher as Rothbart.

The Boston Ballet produced an American-Soviet *Swan Lake* during May 1990. The company imported Konstantin Sergeyev and his wife, the former ballerina Natalia Dudinskaya, from Leningrad to teach Sergeyev's version of the traditional ballet to the Boston dancers. John Conklin designed the sets. Anna-Marie Holmes assisted in the staging, and Bruce Marks brought in Soviet dancers to partner members of the Boston Ballet in the leads. The first-cast leads were Nina Ananiashvili partnered by Fernando Bujones, with Daniel Meja as the Jester, a Soviet interpolation, and Simon Dow as Von Rothbart. Other guest Soviet dancers were Tatiana Terekhova and Konstantin Zaklinsky of the Kirov Ballet. The production was highly praised for its flowing performance, with Sergeyev omitting much of the mime. The production was revived in 1992 and 1994.

Perhaps Professor Wiley is correct in calling *Swan Lake* a "work in progress," since there seems to be no end to variations on the theme.

BIBLIOGRAPHY

Barnes, Clive. "Swan Lake" (parts 1–2). *Dance and Dancers* (December 1963–January 1964).

Beaumont, Cyril W. *The Ballet Called Swan Lake.* London, 1952.

Briginshaw, Valerie A. "Analysis of Variation in Choreography and Performance: *Swan Lake* Act II Pas de Deux." In *Dance Analysis: Theory and Practice*, by Janet Adshead et al. London, 1988.

Cook, Michael. *Swan Lake: The Making of a Ballet.* Sydney, 1978.

Dorris, George. "Once More to the Lake." *Ballet Review* 6.4 (1977–1978): 99–108.

Grigoriev, S. L. *The Diaghilev Ballet 1909–1929.* Translated and edited by Vera Bowen. London, 1953.

Guest, Ivor. "Swan Lake." *About the House* 1 (December 1963): 24–28.

Hellman, Eric. "The *Swan* That Got Away." *Ballet Review* 20 (Fall 1992): 47–53.

Kirstein, Lincoln. *Movement and Metaphor: Four Centuries of Ballet.* New York, 1970.

Maynard, Olga. "*Swan Lake:* USA, USSR." *Dance Magazine* (May 1990): 39–43.

Pudełek, Janina. "*Swan Lake* in Warsaw, 1900." *Dance Chronicle* 13 (Winter 1990–1991): 359–367.

Ross, Janice. "High Tide on *Swan Lake*." *Dance Magazine* (August 1988): 36–41.

Ross, Janice, and Stephan Cobbett Steinberg, comps. *Why a Swan? Essays, Interviews, and Conversations on "Swan Lake."* San Francisco, 1989.

Wiley, Roland John. "The Revival of *Swan Lake*." *The Dancing Times* (March 1987): 492.

ARCHIVE. The Sergeyev Collection, consisting of choreographic notations and memorabilia, is housed at the Harvard Theatre Collection, Pusey Library, Cambridge, Massachusetts.

IRIS M. FANGER

SWEDEN. [*To survey the dance traditions of Sweden, this entry comprises seven articles:*

Traditional Dance
Theatrical Dance before 1771
Theatrical Dance, 1771–1900
Theatrical Dance since 1900
Court Theaters
Dance Education
Dance Research and Publication

For further discussion of theatrical dance, see the entries on individual companies, choreographers, and dancers.]

Traditional Dance

Swedish culture, including dance and dance music, is in many ways similar to that of the neighboring countries. In western Sweden, along the border with Norway, much of the dance and music is very like the Norwegian. In the eastern counties of Sweden, indigenous Swedish characteristics are more pronounced than those shared with neighboring countries. In the far north of Sweden live Finnish-speaking and Saami (Lapp) minorities; in the southernmost region, Scania, it is possible to see cultural similarities with Denmark and Germany.

Traditional dances and dancing, usually called folk dance or old-time dance, have a rather low status and profile in contemporary Swedish culture and the education system. There is no obligatory folk dance taught in schools, and at the National College of Dance (Danshögskolan) the folk dance department is new and small compared with those for other dance genres. When dance is spoken of in official cultural and political discussion, it is above all ballet and modern dance that are meant, never folk dance or ballroom dance.

For most Swedes, folk dances are those done in folk dance clubs. There are associations for folk costume and for dance performances at Midsummer's Eve. Today there is little if any interaction between folk dance and court, social, or popular dances. Folk dance is restricted to dance clubs.

Interactions between folk dance and stage genres are also rare today. Choreographers have occasionally incorporated folkloric images into ballets, and in a few cases they have actually used folk dance movement motifs. Ivo Cramér used folk dance movements in some of his dance creations. The Swedish Folk Dance Ensemble (Svensk Folkdansensamble), a semiprofessional group that existed between 1976 and 1994, performed a dance drama based on August Strindberg's *Kronbruden*. Theatrical productions have also used folk dance as a basic movement repertory; an example is Västanå Teater's version of Selma Lagerlöf's *Gösta Berlings Saga*.

The majority of Swedish folk dances used today were documented, reconstructed, or composed between the end of the nineteenth century and the first half of the twentieth. Older sources are rare and difficult to interpret in isolation. The Swedish bishop Olaus Magnus, who immigrated to Rome during the Reformation, wrote in 1555 in his *Historia de gentibus septentrionalibus* (History of Nordic People), our oldest source, about the Sword Dance *(svärdsdans)* and the Bow Dance *(bågdans)*, but they are not really described, just mentioned. From the mid-eighteenth century there are some dance descriptions made by Carl von Linné (Linnaeus), the famous Swedish botanist, who traveled extensively in Sweden and wrote on many topics other than botany. He mentions, for example, the Weaving Dance *(väva vadmal)* and the longdance from Mora *(Mora långdans)*.

It was in the twentieth century, however, that the greater part of Swedish folk dances were first documented, mainly by members of the Swedish folk dance movement, such as Gustav Karlsson, Johan Larsson, Ingvar Norman, Göran Karlholm, and Börje Wallin. In the 1970s and 1980s Henry Sjöberg, who played a vital role in establishing the Archive for Folk Dance, was an important inspiration for many young researchers, teachers, and performers of folk dance.

In the academic field, the most important folk dance researchers have been Tobias Norlind, Ernst Klein, and Mats Rehnberg. As early as the 1920s Klein used film for dance documentation, a technique that unfortunately was not continued. Not until around 1970 were film and video once again used regularly in field documentation, in the work of Henry Sjöberg. All dance descriptions have been made with words rather than with any notation system.

The collection of dances during the nineteenth and twentieth centuries was carried out in the name of nationalism, but it reflected more a spirit of provincialism and local patriotism. At the end of the nineteenth century, Artur Hazelius founded the Nordic Museum (Nordiska Museet), the national museum for folk culture, and Skansen, an outdoor museum with buildings brought from throughout Sweden. At Skansen, folk dance and music performances are held in summer.

Although sources are scarce, it is still possible to construct a fairly valid Swedish dance history. In addition to the dances mentioned by Olaus Magnus and Linné, sources from the Middle Ages mention circle dances, line dances, and chain dances of the branle and farandole type, danced both to ballad singing and to instrumental accompaniment. During the seventeenth century couple dances appeared, often referred to as *polska*, which appear under many local names, such as *springlek, bleking, slängpolska, trinning,* or *hamburska*.

Group dances, often called *engelska* ("English"), became common during the eighteenth century, along with the quadrille *(kadrilj)* and minuet *(menuett)*. During the second half of the nineteenth century, first the waltz *(vals)* and then the polka, schottische, and mazurka became the most popular social dances. Today these couple dances from the nineteenth century are collectively termed *gammaldanser* ("old-time dances"). The *hambo*, the best-known Swedish folk dance, is probably a local variation of the mazurka danced to *polska* music; it became very popular throughout Sweden around 1900.

After about 1910 American dances such as the two-step, one-step, and fox trot became popular among young Swedes. Older dances such as the waltz, polka and schottische, as well as folk dances such as the *engelska* and quadrille, gradually disappeared from general social use and became limited to clubs of enthusiasts.

Swedish folk dances are nearly always couple dances or group dances based on couples. There are a few gender-specific dances, such as the *björndans* ("bear dance"), and a few solo dances, such as the *halling*, for men, and the *sjuskevilappen* ("messy fool") for women.

There is no evidence for ritual dance in Swedish culture since the Middle Ages. Swedish dancing has been and is still a social event for amusement. There are, however, some competition dances in which it is possible to show dance and balance skill, such as the "Dansa på Strå" (Dance on a Straw) and "Skinnkompass" (from French, *cinque pas*).

The basic repertory of folk dance clubs in the twentieth century is made up not of rural dances but of dances choreographed for stage use during the Romantic era. For example, the ballet master at the Royal Opera, Anders Selinder, composed and stylized folk dances for *Värmlän-ningarna* (People of Varmland) in 1846. Among these "Selinder dances" are "Fryksdalspolska", "Vingåkers-dans", "Skrälåt", and "Daldans", dances that still are an important part of the folk dance club repertory.

When the first Swedish folk dance club, Philochoros, started in 1880, it was the Selinder dances and dances stylized by club members that largely formed its repertory. In 1920 several folk dance clubs formed a national organization, which a year later took the name Svenska Ungdomsringen för Bygdekultur (Swedish Youth Clubs for Country Culture). As the name indicates, there was a great interest in all forms of folk art and folk culture, including dance.

The repertory of the folk dance organizations continued to be the dances of Selinder and Philochoros, augmented with rediscovered, reconstructed, and newly choreographed dances, such as "Västgötapolska" and "Fjäll-näspolska". Many of these new compositions were of the quadrille type, as were the dances of Selinder and Philochoros.

In Sweden, dancers and musicians do not interact much during the dancing; the music merely provides the meter and rhythm. Dance music may be in even measure, 2/4 and 4/4 (schottische, polka, quadrille, and *engelska*), or in uneven measure, 3/4 (*polska*, waltz, mazurka, *hambo*). Throughout the nineteenth and twentieth centuries, the most important instruments for making dance music were the fiddle and accordion (*fiol, dragspel*). From the Middle Ages onward, and in a few places today, dance music was played on the key harp, bagpipe, clarinet, and drum (*nyckelharpa, säckpipa, klar-inett,* and *trumma*).

Today folk dance is performed nearly exclusively at festivals and in dance clubs. There are approximately four hundred clubs with about thirty thousand members in the largest organization, Svenska Ungdomsringen för Bygdekultur. A smaller number of clubs are grouped in other nationwide organizations; for example, old-time dancers have their own national network, and revival groups from the 1970s form Riksföreingen för Folkmusik och Dans (Swedish Folk Music and Folk Dance Association).

It is possible to join clubs and to dance just for fun. A common goal, however, is to prepare programs for performance at festivals or on tours abroad. At Midsummer's Eve nearly all clubs give performances around the maypole. The public usually does not participate in these performances, but after the display there is communal song and dancing in which everyone, especially children, takes part.

The summer Rättvik Folklore Festival is the most important folk dance festival in Sweden. There are also a number of smaller local festivals and *spelmansstämmor* (dance musicians' gatherings), with dancing throughout the country. Also in the summer is the Hälsingehambon, the world championship in *hambo* dancing, in which about fifteen hundred couples compete for titles.

In Swedish schools, folk dance, if it is taught at all, is an optional subject. If dance is on the curriculum, it is usually a part of athletics—or occasionally of music or other aesthetic or cultural subjects.

There are a few professional Swedish folk dance teachers educated at the National College of Dance (Dans-högskolan), but there is no professional dance ensemble or theater group that has folk dance as basic repertory. Education in practical folk dancing is offered at the National College of Dance and at some *folkhögskolor* (schools for continuing education). Folk dance as a theoretical subject is offered, together with folk song, only in a five-week course at the Department of Ethnology of Gothenburg University. Sometimes folk dance is included in basic anthropology and ethnology courses, and it is possible to choose folk dance as a subject of individual interest at higher levels in these fields.

[*For related discussion, see* European Traditional Dance.]

BIBLIOGRAPHY

Dąbrowska, Grażyna, et al. *International Monograph on Folk Dance,* vol. 2, *Poland, Portugal, Sweden.* Budapest, 1987.
Klein, Ernst. *Om folkdans.* Stockholm, 1978.
Norlind, Tobias. *Studier i svensk folklore.* Lund, 1911.
Norlind, Tobias. *Dansens historia med särskild hänsyn till dansen i Sverige.* Stockholm, 1941.
Olaus Magnus. *Historia om de nordiska folken* (1555). Edited by John Granlund. Stockholm, 1976.
Rehnberg, Mats. *Klackarna i taket: Om halling och jössehäradspolska.* Stockholm, 1966.
Salvén, Erik. *Dances of Sweden.* Translated by Veronica Wright. London, 1949.
Sjöberg, Henry, and Anita Etzler. *Folklig dans.* 3 vols. Stockholm, 1970–1976.
Svenska folkdanser. 2 vols. 5th ed. Stockholm, 1964–1971.

ARCHIVES. Arkivet för Folklig Dans, Dansmuseet, Stockholm, which holds the largest public collection of videotapes and films on Swedish folk dances. Danshögskolan, Stockholm. Department of Ethnology, Gothenburg University. Riksföreingen för Folkmusik och Dans. Svenska Ungdomsringen för Bygdekultur, Stockholm.

MATS NILSSON

Theatrical Dance before 1771

The art of ballet reached Sweden in 1637, when the Swedish Royal Council imported Antoine de Beaulieu to polish the nobility's courtly behavior. In less than a year, the courtiers were so accomplished in dance that Beaulieu produced the first court ballet in Sweden on 28 January 1638. The *Ballet des Plaisirs de la Vie des Enfans sans Soucy* (Pleasures of Carefree Childhood) was a typical French *ballet à entrées*, with thirteen *entrées* (or *divertissements*) and a grand ballet for twelve nobles in a style that was simultaneously burlesque and pompous.

In 1645, Beaulieu mounted his fourth ballet, *Le Monde Reiovi* (Rejoicing Worlds), which introduced Italian stage machinery, three settings (Heaven, the Sea, and Earth), twenty-four *entrées*, and fifty roles. The entertainment's style had become distinguished and heroic. In 1646, the dance master Monsieur Daniel presented *L'Amour Constant*, which offered a legitimate plot about Ulysses and Penelope; all previous presentations had been little more than pleas for Queen Christina to marry.

In 1649, Christina expressed her own ideas about marriage in *Den Fångne Cupido* (Cupid Out of His Humor), which had a text by the Parisian poet Hélie Poirier; Christina herself danced as Diana in her conquest of Cupid. This was the first ballet to be published in three languages—French, German, and Swedish (in a more elaborate translation by George Stiernhielm)—and to include both women and men. It was revived by Mary Skeaping for the court theater in 1956.

Soon after, *La Naissance de la Paix* (The Birth of Peace) was presented to the court. This ballet is remarkable not only because it was written by the mathematician and philosopher René Descartes but also because it showed the inglorious side of warfare. What had been burlesque in earlier ballets now became a sinister *danse macabre* of mutilated soldiers and peasants. Christina danced this time as Pallas, the goddess of temperance who arranges for peace—just as Christina herself had mediated peace at Westphalia in 1648. Several entertainments were presented in 1650, with and without dance; the culmination was the New Year's Day 1651 presentation of the ballet *Parnassus Triumphans* by George Stiernhielm. The performance included more than one hundred ten roles for sixty-eight participants, all male except for the lone woman who played Aurora; there were thirty *entrées* in different settings, and magnificent stage machinery by Antonio Brunati.

These three ballets—*Den Fångne Cupido*, *La Naissance de la Paix*, and *Parnassus Triumphans*—constituted a high point in form and ideas and were judged the equal of contemporary French works. Beaulieu was then succeeded by his assistant, Des Aunez (also written Desaunai and de Sonnes), and Stiernhielm retired to the country.

Urban Chevreau's *Les Liberalités des Dieux* (The Bounties of the Gods; 1652) was written for twenty-two couples and had only fifteen *entrées*. One concerned three Swedish ghosts, evidence of a growing interest in native folklore. Christina made a last appearance in the 1653 ballet *Gudarnas Högtid* (The Feast of the Gods), a *bergerette* or pastoral. All Christina's guests appeared as gods, she was the shepherdess Amaranta, and her courtiers were shepherds and shepherdesses. At the conclusion she presented jewels from her dress to guests she chose to honor; thus was inaugurated the Swedish Order of Amarant.

After Christina's abdication in 1654, few occasions arose for true court ballets. Still, for the 1654 wedding of Charles X Gustav, Christina's successor, Chevreau arranged *Ballet de la Félicité* in three parts. His subjects included the five senses, happiness, and the gifts of nature and the noble soul. In 1669 the Swedish poet Erik Lindesköld wrote *Den stora genius* (The Great Genius), which was performed by sixty noble couples in twenty *entrées* and a grand ballet. The young Charles XI appeared as a Turk in a rather solemn allegory of evil and good genius. In 1689, the last true Baroque court ballet, *Lycko-Priis* (The Price of Happiness), was danced; however, it used as much speech and singing as it did dance, and of the seventy-one roles, only eighteen were solely danced.

In 1699, a troupe of professional French dancers under a Monsieur Rosidor was invited to Sweden. It introduced in 1701 the new French comedy and Italian *commedia dell'arte* in the farcical *Ballet Mêlé de Chants Héroïques*. The music by Andreas Düben is the earliest preserved example of this type of ballet. The company soon left Sweden, however, because it could not find a regular audience.

During the first half of the eighteenth century, comedies were danced and played primarily by enthusiastic court amateurs. Such was the case with *Feste Royal* (1706), whose four intermezzi were sandwiched between three comedies in the Medici style of the fifteenth century.

In the 1720s a new royal dance master, Jean-Baptiste Landé, introduced the court to the new French style with such dances as the *rigaudon*, *loure*, *gigue*, and *menuet*. Professional dancers returned to Sweden in 1753 with a royal invitation to another French company. The twelve Italian and French dancers were led by Louis Frossard.

In 1758 Frossard left for Paris and Vienna, and Louis Gallodier took his place. The following year an Italian opera company under Francesco Uttini arrived for a ten-year stay to perform complete operas with ballet in the Paris style. In addition, the 1750s saw operas by Charles-Simon Favart and Jean-Jacques Rousseau, with choreography by Gallodier.

BIBLIOGRAPHY
Gustafsson, Lars. "Amor et Mars vaincu." In *Queen Christina of Sweden: Documents and Studies*. Analecta Reginensia, 1. Stockholm, 1966.

Skeaping, Mary. "Ballet under the Three Crowns." *Dance Perspectives*, no. 32 (1967).

MAGNUS BLOMKVIST

Theatrical Dance, 1771–1900

The pre-Romantic style in the Swedish theater is associated with King Gustav III. He looked upon theater not only as a courtly entertainment (among others), but as a vehicle for his political ambition. He wished to be an absolute ruler, looked to as a father by the people, and to lead a national cultural revival. The theater was to help to cultivate the Swedish language and, above all, in dramatic form, to give a picture of Sweden's glorious history. As a child, the theater had been Gustav's favorite occupation. His fantasy had fed on the repertory of the French troupe imported by his mother, Queen Lovisa Ulrika, sister of Frederick II of Prussia. Gustav was to be a skilled actor, a playwright, and a stage director. When he came to the throne in 1771 he dismissed his mother's French company to build up a national Swedish theater. The lack of skilled Swedish actors and playwrights compelled him to concentrate his ingenuity and economic resources on creating a Swedish opera.

Count Ehrenswärd, who was to be the first director of the Royal Opera, wrote,

> An opera which consists of pleasing and catchy music, a properly trained ballet, attractive costumes, and beautiful, well-painted scenery is so captivating that ear, eye, and all the other senses are satisfied at the same time. In this way one gets accustomed to the language, whose harshness is minimized by absorption in the music.

The old Tennis Court Theater in Stockholm was restored and equipped with new stage machinery. There were some first-class singers and musicians in Stockholm, as well as the conductor and composer Francesco Antonio Uttini, who had been part of the Italian opera company in Lovisa Ulrika's day. The dancers from the dismissed French company were also still in Stockholm and became the nucleus of the opera-ballet.

Gustav III's efforts were brought to fruition in the 1780s: plays and operas were given at the new (1782) opera house in Stockholm. The company even performed for the court at theaters in palaces outside Stockholm—at Ulriksdal and Gripsholm and in the Drottningholm Theater (that had been built in 1766), which was still in its original state, its scenery and stage machinery untouched. In 1781 a new French acting company, under the leadership of Boutet de Monvel, was imported. In 1787 the king at last initiated his much longed-for national dramatic theater company. The repertory consisted of original compositions based mostly on French prototypes and foreign operas translated into Swedish. Christoph Willbald

Gluck's opera *Orfeo ed Euridice* was presented even before its Paris premiere. Most Gustavian operas were influenced by Gluck, both their music (by the German composers Joseph Martin Kraus, Johann Gottlieb Naumann, and Johann Christian Friedrich Haeffner) and libretti (by the Swedish poets Kellgren and Adlerbeth among others). More original were the historical-romantic operas with the king's own text. His greatest success was *Gustav Wasa* (1786).

Gustav III even added music and dance to plays, the first attempt being *Birger Jarl* (1774). With these and many other works, the king succeeded in bringing Swedish history to life and arousing enthusiasm for some of his royal predecessors. The people were portrayed as true-hearted peasants, loyal to the king. A certain amount of realism was reflected in costumes, dance, and music—an early instance of genuine folklore in the theater. The choreography was integrated in the dramatic plot, following the ideas of Jean-Georges Noverre.

The most important figure in establishing Gustav III's opera-ballet was Louis Gallodier, who arrived in Sweden in 1758 to join Lovisa Ulrika's French troupe and was to become the first ballet master of the Swedish Royal Opera (1773–1795). Gallodier obtained dancers for the new compagny—Louis Frossand and his wife Ninon Bubois, and Le Clerc, and Madame Soligny from the dismissed French company. Others were imported from France, most of them trained by Jean Dauberval: Didelot the elder, Madame Du Tillet from the Royal Theater in Copenhagen, Giovanna Bassi, Antoine Bournonville, Julie Bournonville-Alix, and Jean Marcadet, who was also a gifted choreographer. The dancers were generously paid—better paid than the singers and actors. The Swedish dancers in the company first had to be trained. At the start, there were only about thirty dancers, but by the 1780s there were about seventy-two. Unfortunately, Sweden lost two of its dancers who became outstanding choreographers—Charles-Louis Didelot and Antoine Bournonville (who, in 1792, settled in Copenhagen). Despite Noverre's influence on ballet in Sweden, the king did not take Noverre into his service, even though Noverre, in 1791, had requested the post of ballet master to the Swedish court. Political disturbances at the time had left Gustav III with no energy for or interest in the theater. In March 1792, he was assassinated at a masked ball in the opera house. A glorious period came to an end, and the Swedish ballet was left out of the mainstream of dance for more than a century.

The history of the Romantic ballet in Sweden is the story of decline. The theater was no longer sufficiently supported by the court and the government, either economically or artistically. The directors of the Royal Theater had to consider the audience's taste and the repertory had to have box-office appeal. For ballet, this meant giving *divertissements* and ballet-pantomimes in the comic and sentimental genres, most of them remnants of the Gustavian era, which endured into the 1830s. Although ballet had declined to a mere entertainment in Sweden, technical skills, it seems, were kept to a tolerable level by members of the old Gustavian company.

After the death of Gustav III, Marcadet left Sweden. Gallodier remained ballet master until his death in 1803. From 1795 onward, he was assisted by Federico Nadi Terrade, then newly arrived from Italy. Terrade was responsible for most of the dances in the operas. Meanwhile, the young Louis Joseph Deland, sent by Gustav III to be a student of Pierre Gardel's in Paris from 1783 to 1788, returned to Stockholm and followed the French style, so that the repertory was dominated by such Parisian pantomime ballets as *Le Jugement de Pâris* (1793) and *La Dansomanie* (1800). The decade that bridged the centuries witnessed the most intense dance activity yet seen in Stockholm, with nine new ballets a year and several new choreographies for the favorite operas, which sometimes included up to thirty-five separate numbers.

All this activity was silenced in 1806 when war with Russia and shortage of funds caused the young king, Gustav IV Adolph, to close the opera house and dismiss the entire ballet company. The French tradition endured because of Sophie Daguin, who had been trained by Didelot in Paris. She was a dancer at the Stockholm Royal Theater in 1815, and from 1830 to 1856 she trained students at the ballet school.

More important to Swedish ballet was the first native-born ballet master, Ander Selinder. He entered the ballet school of the Royal Theater as a boy and was nominated premier danseur in 1829 and ballet master in 1833. After his retirement from the Royal Theater in 1856, he started a company with talented children that gave ballet and vaudeville performances at various boulevard theaters until 1871. He composed about eighteen ballets for the Royal Theater company, most of them *divertissements* and small pantomine ballets. In addition, he arranged the dances for the Romantic operas of Giacomo Meyerbeer and Vincento Bellini.

Of importance to Swedish dance history are the folk dances Selinder arranged for some Swedish Romantic plays from the middle of the 1840s onward. As dramatic texts these plays are weak but, in performance, together with the dances, songs, music, costumes, and scenery, they evoked Swedish peasant life. They were genuinely Romantic in spirit, unlike the picturesque peasantry of the Gustavian era, and the dances were authentic folk dances arranged for the stage. One of these plays, *Värmlänningarna* (1846), remains popular. Selinder also continued to arrange folk dances for his children's company.

The most talented dancer of the period was Christian Johansson. Born in Stockholm in 1817, he entered the Royal Theater's ballet school in 1829. In the 1830s he was sent to August Bournonville in Copenhagen for advanced studies. He returned to Stockholm in 1837 and was nominated premier danseur. Selinder did not make use of Johansson's talent, and in 1840 Johansson went to Saint Petersburg, where he became one of the founders of the Russian school of dancing. He only returned to Sweden once, in 1841, when he partnered Marie Taglioni in her guest performances in Stockholm. [*See the entry on Johansson.*] Her repertory contained the pas de deux and ballet from act 3 of *Robert of Normandie*, scenes from *La Sylphide*, *Le Lac des Fées*, and *L'Élève de L'Amour*, and some *divertissements*. Her success was enormous—spectators became almost hysterical. It may not be without significance that she was part Swedish. Her father, Filippo Taglioni, had worked at the Royal Opera in 1803 and 1804, where he met and married Sofia Karsten, the daughter of the great Swedish singer C. C. Karsten. In 1818 Filippo returned to Stockholm for three months as ballet master. In 1843 Paul Taglioni visited to mount *La Sylphide*, with Marie in the title role. [*See the entry on the Taglioni family.*]

The visits of August Bournonville had a more lasting influence. He came from Copenhagen with some of his dancers in 1839 for a brief guest performance. In 1847 he paid another visit, as choreographer, and mounted his ballets *The Toreador*, *Faust*, and *Bellman* with great success. In 1857 he returned once more to stage *Festival in Albano*, *The Dancing School*, and *The Wedding Festival in Hardanger*. This time the criticism was somewhat sour: dance was no longer regarded as fitting for the Royal Theater. His most important and lasting influence on the Swedish theater was as superintendent and stage director, from 1861 to 1864, at the Royal Theater. He was responsible for opera and drama but not for ballet. According to him, at that time the quality of the dance and choreography had hit bottom.

BIBLIOGRAPHY

Beijer, Agne. *Drottningholms slottsteater på Lovisa Ulrikas och Gustaf III:s tid.* Stockholm, 1981.

Bournonville, August. *My Theatre Life* (1848–1978). 3 vols. Translated and edited by Patricia McAndrew. Middletown, Conn., 1979.

Dahlgren, F. A. *Förteckning öfver svenska skådespel uppförda på Stockholms teatrar, 1737–1863.* Stockholm, 1866.

Dahms, Sibylle. "The 'Ballet d'Action' in Theory and Practice." In *Proceedings of the Stockholm Symposium on Opera and Dance in the Gustavian Era, 1711–1809.* Stockholm, 1986.

Koegler, Horst. "From the Early Days of Ballet." *Ballett International* 9 (October 1986): 24–27.

Koegler, Horst. "The Swedes and Their Theatre King." *Dance Chronicle* 10.2 (1987): 223–229.

Mattson, Inger, ed. *Gustavian Opera: An Interdisciplinary Reader in Swedish Opera, Dance, and Theatre, 1771–1809.* Translated by Paul B. Austin. Stockholm, 1991.

Proceedings of the Stockholm Symposium on Opera and Dance in the Gustavian Era, 1771–1809. Stockholm, 1986.

Skeaping, Mary. "Ballet under the Three Crowns." *Dance Perspectives*, no. 32 (1967).

Stribolt, Barbro, ed. *The Drottningholm Theatre Museum*. Drottningholm, 1984.

Strömbeck, K. G., et al. *Kungliga Teatern i Stockholm repertoar 1773–1973*. Stockholm, 1974.

Winter, Marian Hannah. *The Pre-Romantic Ballet*. London, 1974.

KIRSTEN GRAM HOLMSTROM

Theatrical Dance since 1900

At the beginning of the twentieth century two guest performances made the Stockholm public aware of new trends in dance: Isadora Duncan danced in 1906 and made a lasting impression; Anna Pavlova arrived in 1908 with her ensemble and performed ballets from the repertory of the Maryinsky Theater. It was Pavlova's first venture abroad, and her overwhelming reception in Stockholm encouraged her to start an international career. Duncan and Pavlova paved the way for a dance revival.

Michel Fokine had fallen out with Serge Diaghilev in 1912, so was free from the Ballets Russes. The Royal Theater in Stockholm approached him, and Fokine accepted a position as guest choreographer. He spent working periods in Stockholm in 1913 and 1914 and staged five of the ballets with which the Diaghilev Ballets Russes had recently conquered Paris. He and his wife, Vera Fokina, danced the main roles and then turned them over to Swedish dancers. *Cléopâtre*, *Les Sylphides*, *Le Spectre de la Rose*, *Carnaval*, and *Schéhérazade* offered new and exciting possibilities. Fokine also discovered and encouraged young talent.

Fokine brought the painter Boris Anisfeld to Stockholm from Saint Petersburg. He painted decor based on sketches by Léon Bakst and created a romantic setting for *Les Sylphides*, which has been used for this ballet's frequent revivals. The Royal Theater has also preserved Anisfeld's decor for *Schéhérazade*, based on Bakst. Its colorful splendor was used by Ulf Gadd for his 1993 version of *Schéhérazade*.

Fokine and his ballets were enthusiastically received. Newspapers and literary magazines were filled with articles about the "new" ballet. Fokine influenced not only dance in Sweden but also art, design, and theater. There were negotiations with Fokine to take over the leadership of the Royal Swedish Ballet, but World War I intervened and he returned to Paris. After the Russian Revolution Fokine lived in Denmark. Swedish dancers journeyed there to study with him, and some of them—Jean Börlin, Jenny Hasselquist, and Carina Ari—joined Les Ballets Suédois in Paris in 1920. Sven Tropp, Lisa Steier, and others returned to Stockholm and assumed responsibility for the company, not an easy task since Les Ballets Suédois had robbed the ensemble of one third of its dancers. Lisa Steier introduced her own choreographies

SWEDEN: Theatrical Dance since 1900. Elsa-Marianne von Rosen and Julius Mengarelli, as the original Julie and Jean in *Miss Julie* (1950), Birgit Cullberg's ballet based on the 1888 play by August Strindberg. (Photograph © by Enar Merkel Rydberg; used by permission.)

for Igor Stravinsky's *The Firebird* and *Pulcinella* at the Royal Theater in 1927. She died young, a short time later.

In Sweden during the 1930s and 1940s ballet was again overshadowed by opera. Very few ballets were staged to Swedish music and with Swedish themes. The repertory reflected to some extent the legacy of Diaghilev's Ballets Russes; attempts were made to stage classics or parts of them, and new works of varied value were introduced. The economic depression was felt, and World War II broke out, limiting cultural exchange.

Renaissance of the Royal Swedish Ballet. The postwar ballet renaissance in Europe and the United States also reached Sweden, through visits by excellent ballet companies. The Royal Theater decided to encourage its own ballet. Antony Tudor came as ballet director for the 1949/50 season, followed by Mary Skeaping in 1953; she remained with the company until 1962. In these very fruitful years, she gave it a classical repertory. Between the wars the ballet world had been hostile to modern dancers, but now the Royal Swedish Ballet was ready to

SWEDEN: Theatrical Dance since 1900. Antony Tudor created his *Ekon av Trumpeter* (Echoing of Trumpets), for the Royal Swedish Ballet in 1963. In this scene, Gerd Andersson reaches for the body of her executed lover and is restrained by Mario Mengarelli, as the leading Nazi soldier. Sets and costumes were designed by Birger Bergling. (Photograph © by Enar Merkel Rydberg; used by permission.)

try new dance styles and invited three Swedish choreographers to work with the dancers. Birgit Cullberg, Birgit Åkesson, and Ivo Cramér created dance dramas in different styles. The influence of Kurt Jooss was felt in Cullberg's dramatic ballets. Åkesson belonged to the avant-garde and collaborated with contemporary composers and painters, often using texts by the poet Erik Lindegren. Cramér took his themes from folklore and history. Tudor returned on several occasions, staged his old ballets, and created a new one, *Echoing of Trumpets* (1963). George Balanchine's beautiful, musical ballets were much admired when performed on tour by New York City Ballet. He generously shared the best of his productions, and the Royal Swedish Ballet was happy to get five of them. During this decade the company toured Europe and China.

In the 1950s Mary Skeaping began to revive ballets from Swedish dance history for the Drottningholm Court Theater. Her dancers learned early steps and techniques and mastered old styles. Ivo Cramér joined her as co-choreographer, and Regina Beck-Friis became her assistant and successor. The Royal Swedish Ballet was now able to perform dance from four centuries.

During its formative years the company could rely on soloists with distinctive personalities and dramatic talent. Important roles were performed by Ellen Rasch, Teddy Rhodin, Bjørn Holmgren, Elsa-Marianne von Rosen, Julius Mengarelli, and Gunnel Lindgren; they were supplemented in time by Mariane Orlando, Gerd Andersson, Caj Selling, Verner Klavsen, Kari Sylwan, Conny Borg, Mario Mengarelli, and Berit Sköld.

In 1962 Yuri Grigorovich staged *The Stone Flower* for the Swedes, their first exposure to the virtuoso Soviet style. He had just been named ballet master of the Bolshoi Theater in Moscow, and this was his first assignment outside the Soviet Union. More guests arrived from the USSR, some to dance and Nathalie Conus to stage a new version of *Swan Lake*. The Canadian Brian Macdonald led the ballet between 1964 and 1967 and was house choreographer, stimulating the public with a spring ballet festival. He was succeeded in 1967 by Erik Bruhn, who strengthened the modern repertory with some masterpieces.

Jerome Robbins staged his version of *Les Noces,* and Kenneth MacMillan his *Romeo and Juliet;* both ballets have been carefully preserved in the repertory. An important period in the history of modern dance was illuminated when José Limón visited Stockholm in 1970 and introduced *There Is a Time, The Exiles,* and *Missa Brevis;* in 1972 he brought *The Moor's Pavane.* A younger generation of American choreographers was represented by Glen

Tetley with *Ricercare* and *Embrace Tiger and Return to Mountain,* and by Eliot Feld with *At Midnight* and *The Consort.*

New dancers came to the fore: Kerstin Lidström, Annette av Paul, Jonas Kåge, Maria Lang, Ulf Gadd, Nils-Åke Häggbom, Istvan Kisch, and Jens Graff. Marianne Orlando remained *prima ballerina* throughout her stage career.

The Royal Swedish Ballet had for many years been oriented toward the Anglo-Saxon dance world. It was a special occasion when Frederick Ashton came in 1972 to stage *La Fille Mal Gardée* with Kerstin Lidström as Lise, Imre Dózsa as Colas, and Istvan Kisch as Mother Simone.

When Ivo Cramér became ballet director in 1975, he found that it was high time to explore continental Europe. From Stuttgart he acquired John Cranko's *Onegin* and *The Taming of the Shrew,* both giving ballerina Astrid Strüwer roles that suited her temperament and virtuosity. Cramér also contacted Jiří Kylián, whose first assignment outside the Netherlands Dance Theater was at Stockholm in 1977 with *Blue Skin.* Since then four of Kylián's works have been staged at the Royal Theater; his *Intimate Letters* was staged for Swedish television.

In 1980 Gunilla Roempke assumed the post of ballet director, and the company began to make room for more Swedish choreography. Birgit Cullberg had returned in 1976 to do a ballet on a large scale. She used Allan Pettersson's Seventh Symphony to make her choreographic

SWEDEN: Theatrical Dance since 1900. *(above)* Scene from the Royal Swedish Ballet's 1969 production of Kenneth MacMillan's *Romeo and Juliet,* with Annette av Paul and Nils-Åke Häggbom as the young lovers. *(right)* Kerstin Lidström and Imre Dózsa in Frederick Ashton's *La Fille Mal Gardée,* first staged for the Royal Swedish Ballet in 1972. (Photograph above © by Enar Merkel Rydberg; used by permission. Photograph at right from the Dance Collection, New York Public Library for the Performing Arts.)

Report on the condition of the world and the gap between rich and poor. Her son Niklas Ek, former soloist with Maurice Béjart's Ballet du XXe Siècle and the Cullberg Ballet, danced the leading role and then joined the Royal Swedish Ballet as a principal dancer. Roempke invited three young choreographers to work with the company: Ulf Gadd presented *Orpheus;* Mats Ek created *Cain and Abel;* and the modern dancer Per Jonsson was introduced to the public in 1984 with his first work, *Shaft.* Jonsson, a farmer's son from the north, was recognized as an unusual talent with his own approach to movement and form. A welcome addition to the repertory of classics and large-scale dance dramas was Kenneth MacMillan's *Manon* in 1980. *The Sleeping Beauty,* staged by Beryl Grey, was an appreciated classic. Principal dancers during the 1980s were Anneli Alkhanko, Per-Arthur Segerström, Johanna Björnson, Madeleine Onne, Weit Carlson, Pär Isbert, Hans Nilsson, and Mats Wegmann.

After a short spell with Egon Madsen as ballet director, Nils-Åke Häggbom, a former principal dancer, took over

SWEDEN: Theatrical Dance since 1900. Mats Ek staged his *Vårof-fer* (Rite of Spring) in Japanese style for the Cullberg Ballet. The dancers seen here are Ana Laguna and Yvan Auzely. (Photograph by Lesley Leslie-Spinks; from the Dance Collection, New York Public Library for the Performing Arts.)

in 1987. The first new ballet he offered the public was by Ulf Gadd, who based his dance drama on the novel *Gösta Berling's Saga* by the Nobel Prize winner Selma Lagerlöf. Next season brought an old classic, Petipa's *La Bayadère,* staged by Natalia Makarova; it was succeeded by Frederick Ashton's *Cinderella.* Häggbom then approached John Neumeier in Hamburg, regarded as the last master of the type of European dance drama that had for decades dominated theaters in Russia, England, Germany, and Scandinavia. Neumeier staged his masterpieces *A Midsummer Night's Dream* in 1990 and his *Peer Gynt* in 1992.

Häggbom also made room for other contemporary choreographers. Maurice Béjart was represented by *Lieder eines Fahrenden Gesellen* and *Le Sacre du Printemps;* Nils Christe by *Before Nightfall;* and, in 1993, Ulysses Dove with his remarkable *Dancing on the Front Porch of Heaven.* Glen Tetley's *The Tempest* was also added to the repertory in 1993.

Regular workshops were fruitful. Several dancers were asked to do choreography for operas, as well as short ballets. Most active among them was the principal dancer Pär Isbert, who created television ballets and works for the theater. During the 1995 Christmas season he presented a new version of *The Nutcracker,* inspiried by pictures in popular Swedish children's books by Elsa Beskow.

The Swedish Ballet School produced many male dancers of quality. In the 1990s the company had such leading male dancers as Göran Svalberg, Jan-Erik Wikström and Anders Nordström. There was also Maria Lindqvist, a talented ballerina.

Since the foundation of the Royal Theater in 1773, outstanding singers have been given the title of court singer. In 1990 King Charles XVI Gustav decided to honor dance, and the first court dancers named were Anneli Alhanko and Per-Arthur Segerström, followed by Johanna Björnson, Madeleine Onne, and Hans Nilsson.

The Royal Swedish Ballet with its ensemble of seventy-five dancers often went abroad on tour during the 1980s and 1990s. The company danced in Spain, England, Finland, Norway, Japan, and Brazil.

Other Companies. There are other dance companies in Sweden besides the Royal Swedish Ballet. In Göteborg, Ballet at Teatern (Great Theater) flourished under Conny Borg and Elsa-Marianne von Rosen, but especially since Ulf Gadd became ballet director in 1979. Gadd gave his ensemble a distinctive profile in a series of strong dance dramas. He retired in 1988 and spent seven years in Bali studying and dancing, but he was recalled in 1995 to replace Robert North and became director of the ballet, now resident in the new opera house.

Malmö had a ballet attached to the Stadsteatern; its directors included Teddy Rhodin, Conny Borg, Elsa-Marianne von Rosen, and Jonas Kåge. Here full-length classics were favored. Because of a reorganization of the theater

SWEDEN: Theatrical Dance since 1900. Per Jonsson, one of Sweden's foremost modern dance choreographers, staged his *Mellan Två Trädgårdar* (Between Two Gardens), for the Cullberg Ballet in 1985. (Photograph by Lesley Leslie-Spinks; courtesy of Anna Greta Ståhle.)

in 1994, the ballet was moved to the university town of Lund to work independently.

The umbrella organization Riksteatern administered two touring companies: the Cullberg Ballet, founded in 1967, and the Cramér Ballet, active from 1968 to 1986. In 1971 a small company was formed at the regional theater Östgötateatern. This company has specialized in contemporary works by young choreographers. Since the early 1970s independent companies of dancers of modern, ethnic, or historical styles have been active in Sweden; their organization Danscentrum gives support.

Modern dance has a long tradition in Sweden, and interest in new dance styles is growing fast. Some of the modern groups became internationally known: L'Étoile du Nord, Wind Witches, and the Pyramides, whose choreographers were Susanne Valentin, Eva Lundqvist, and Margaretha Åsberg, respectively. Lundqvist and Åsberg opened the first theaters devoted to modern dance in Stockholm, Glashuset and Moderna Dansteatern. An experimental avant-garde group called Rubicon was founded in Göteborg in 1978 by Gun Lund, Eva Ingemarsson, and Gunilla Witt; in 1987 Rubicon moved into a theater of its own. In the 1990s young modern choreographers such as Per Jonsson and Jens Östberg came to the fore, attracted many followers, and founded their own groups.

[*For further discussion, see the entries on Åkesson, Ari, Åsberg, Beck-Friis, Behle, Cramér, Cullberg, Ek, Gadd, Johansson, Orlando, Rosen, and Skeaping.*]

BIBLIOGRAPHY

Baer, Nancy Van Norman, ed. *Paris Modern: The Swedish Ballet, 1920–1925*. San Francisco, 1995. Exhibition catalog.

Beijer, Agne. *Drottningholms slottsteater på Lovisa Ulrikas och Gustaf III:s tid*. Stockholm, 1981.

Dahlgren, F. A. *Förteckning öfver svenska skådespel uppförda på Stockholms teatrar, 1737–1863*. Stockholm, 1866.

Engdahi, Horace. *Swedish Ballet and Dance: A Critic's View*. Translated by Paul Kessel and Erika Svedberg. Stockholm, 1992.

Gustafsson, Lars. "Amor et Mars vaincu." In *Queen Christina of Sweden: Documents and Studies*. Analecta Reginensia, I. Stockholm, 1966.

Hood, Robin [Idestam-Almqvist, Bengt]. *Svensk balett*. Malmö, 1951.

Palmqvist, Bertil. *Malmöbaletten*. Malmö, 1985.

Riwkin-Brick, Anna. *Svensk danskonst på scen och i skola*. Stockholm, 1932.

Rootzén, Kajsa. *Den svenska baletten*. Stockholm, 1945.

Sjögren, Margareta. *Biljett till balett*. Stockholm, 1957.

Sjögren, Margareta. *Skandinavisk balett*. Stockholm, 1988.

Skeaping, Mary. "Ballet under the Three Crowns." *Dance Perspectives*, no. 32 (1967).

Skeaping, Mary, and Anna Greta Ståhle. *Balett på Stockholmsoperan*. Stockholm, 1979.

Strömbeck, K. G., et al. *Kungliga Teatern i Stockholm repertoar 1773–1973*. Stockholm, 1974.

Winter, Marian Hannah. *The Pre-Romantic Ballet*. London, 1974.

ANNA GRETA STAHLE

Court Theaters

The royal palace of Drottningholm, three miles (ten kilometers) west of Stockholm, is best known now for its theater, where seventeenth- and eighteenth-century ballets and opera are staged in authentic surroundings. The palace was built from 1661 to 1681 but gained its final form in 1750. In 1756 Carl Fredrik Adelcrantz designed and constructed a theater at the palace, to replace an ear-

SWEDEN: Court Theaters. In 1956, Mary Skeaping staged *Cupid Out of His Humor* in the style of the seventeenth-century court ballets, for the Drottningholm Court Theater. In this scene, the four continents (Istvan Kisch, Per Arthur Segerström, Verner Klavsen, and Nils-Åke Häggbom) pay their respects to the god of love (Nisse Winqvist, center). (Photograph © by Enar Merkel Rydberg; used by permission.)

lier theater. Although it caught fire during a performance in 1762 and was destroyed, Queen Lovisa Ulrika immediately ordered Adelcrantz to have a new theater built on the same site; it opened in 1766 and is still in use.

If outwardly rather modest in appearance, the theater possesses one of the world's most beautiful eighteenth-century interiors. The stage is a reflection of the auditorium, which was decorated by Adrien Masreliez; it is almost sixty feet (nineteen meters) in depth, with a proscenium almost thirty feet (nine meters) wide and about twenty-one feet (seven meters) high. Ingenious stage machinery, constructed by Donato Stopani, permits as many as four rapid changes of scene.

After King Gustav III received the palace in 1777 from his mother, Lovisa Ulrika, most of Sweden's important theatrical productions were staged at Drottningholm until the new royal opera house in Stockholm opened in 1782. After the king was assassinated in 1792, however, Drottningholm was considered old-fashioned; with the advance of more realistic staging, the theater was closed.

In 1921 the historian Agne Beijer rediscovered the theater. He realized that it constituted a treasure, with its thirty complete sets from the end of the eighteenth century and its still functional stage machinery. After careful restoration the theatre was opened to the public in 1922. A demonstration of all the stage effects was given, and members of the Ballet School performed minuets arranged by Lisa Steier.

No general performances were scheduled until 1935, however—merely the occasional show for a visiting congress or society. These entertainments often included dances by members of the Ballet School, and Valborg Franchi, director of the school from 1924 through 1949, was principally responsible for arranging them. She introduced dances from Uttini's *Thetis och Pelée*, along with minuets by Mozart and Haydn. In 1935 plans were laid for more ambitious performances, and three short ballad-operas, by Höpken, Kraus, and Bellman, were presented that fall. They included dances choreographed by Franchi and continued to be given during the 1940s.

On the twentieth anniversary of the theater's resurrection, 1941/42, the Royal Swedish Ballet appeared at Drottningholm in a mixed program of dances arranged by George Gé. These were criticized as being too far from eighteenth-century style to be suited to that stage, as were the dances by Sven Tropp that were introduced into Mozart's opera *Bastien und Bastienne*, written in 1768 when he was only twelve.

In 1947, Cissi Olsson-Åhrberg, a former *prima ballerina*, first choreographed at Drottningholm. She returned in 1949 with an evening of dances from the Baroque era to the Romantic era, after studying the work of the eighteenth-century theorist Gennaro Magri in Paris (where she also acquired an old version of *Giselle* from Alexandre Volinine, once Pavlova's partner). The program included highlights from André Campra's *L'Europe Galante* of 1697; they suited the theater perfectly and remained in the repertory for three years.

In 1951 the Royal Swedish Opera agreed to stage performances at Drottningholm each summer, which allowed it to present complete operas. When Mary Skeaping became director of the Royal Swedish Ballet in 1953, she realized what opportunities the Drottningholm theater offered for research into seventeenth- and eighteenth-century ballet, which the company developed under her guidance.

Skeaping's first production, *Den Fångne Cupido* (Cupid Out of His Humor), in 1956, was in the style of seventeenth-century court ballet, to music by Henry Purcell. It was followed in 1957 by Christoph Willibald Gluck's *Orfeo ed Euridice* (1762), with all the dances included. This enjoyed such success that an entire cycle of Gluck operas was produced in the 1960s—*Iphigénie en Tauride* in 1960, *Alcestes* in 1962, and *Iphigénie en Aulide* in 1963—all three had been in the original repertory at Drottningholm.

In 1964 Skeaping staged *Atis och Camilla*, a ballet based on an eighteenth-century poem by the Swedish poet Gustav Philip Creutz, set to music by Johan Helmich Roman. The choreography was her own, but the steps derived from authentic eighteenth-century sources. In 1966, she

staged a reconstruction of Filippo Taglioni's *Le Retour du Printemps* (The Return of Spring), which evoked a pre-Romantic sensibility; in 1968 her staging of act 2 of *Giselle* revived the true Romantic-era's style.

That same year Skeaping's assistant, Regina Beck-Friis, showed the same accuracy of style in the dances she arranged for operas by Scarlatti and Grétry. In 1969, the company staged George Frideric Handel's *Il Pastor Fido* (1712), with a large portion of the dances by Skeaping, and it introduced to Sweden Vincenzo Galeotti's *Amors og Balletmesterens Luner* (The Whims of Cupid and the Ballet Master), given in the 1786 version from Copenhagen, revived by Elsa-Marianne von Rosen. *Orfeo ed Euridice* was restaged in 1971, this time with choreography by Beck-Friis on the pattern of a 1774 production. She revived with splendid success such Baroque period French *opéra-ballets* as Lully's *Le Carnaval* in 1975 and Rameau's *Platée* in 1978.

Skeaping joined Ivo Cramér in 1971 in a fruitful collaboration that led to re-creations of Antoine Bournonville's eighteenth-century ballet *Fiskarena* (The Fishermen), to the original music by Joseph Martin Kraus, and in 1976 a presentation of Pierre Gardel's *La Dansomanie* (1800).

SWEDEN: Court Theaters. Pierre Gardel's *La Dansomanie*, first performed at Stockholm's Royal Opera in 1804, was revived by Ivo Cramér, with assistance from Mary Skeaping, for the Drottningholm Court Theater in 1976. (Photograph © by Enar Merkel Rydberg; used by permission.)

Cramér subsequently did further research on ballets of the Gustavian period. He restaged *La Mort d'Arlequin* (1796), originally by Terrade, and *Arlequin, Magicien par Amour* (1793), originally by Marcadet; both of them fully exploit the fabulous stage machinery of the Drottningholm theater.

In 1985 Beck-Friis created a new version of Gasparo Angiolini's *Don Juan* of 1761, to the original music by Gluck, using the technique of Gennaro Magri according to Mary Skeaping's translation of his *Trattato teorico-prattica di ballo* (1779). This successful ballet stimulated a new interest in Angiolini, his predecessor Franz Hilverding, and their style of *ballet d'action*.

The Stockholm vicinity is blessed with two more eighteenth-century theaters, the Ulriksdal Court Theater and the Gripsholm Court Theater. The Ulriksdal Court Theater, originally built as a riding school, was transformed by Carl Fredrik Adelcrantz to a small theater in 1753 for Queen Lovisa Ulrika. During her reign and that of her son Gustav III, it was used exclusively for the court's amusement, with a repertory mostly of French plays, *opéra-comique*, and *divertissements*. In the nineteenth century it was damaged and turned into a royal hunting lodge; later, like Drottningholm, it was forgotten.

In 1976 it was decided to reconstruct the theater, and the next year a *divertissement* was given in the theater, still decorated with hunting motifs. During the 1980s all the audience area was restored, but the stage was newly built. Under the artistic direction of Kjerstin Dellert the theater, now called Confidencen, grew more and more authentic in style, with a repertory of ballets and musical theater of the eighteenth century and later epochs, choreographed by Beck-Friis and Cramér.

The Gripsholm Court Theater was originally designed in 1772 by Carl Fredrik Adelcrantz in the upper floor of one of the towers of the medieval castle, after a suggestion of Gustave III himself. It was a very small theater, for the frequent dramatic activities of the royal court during the winters of 1775 to 1779. In 1782 the young architect Eric Palmstedt was asked to build a new, larger theater in the same tower, which resulted in a real architectual jewel of the neoclassical style. The audience area is rounded like the tower, while the small stage, equipped with full stage machinery, extends into the queen's wing and is raised to the same level as the tower.

Like the other court theaters the Gripsholm was forgotten in the nineteenth century but restored to functional order in the twentieth by Agne Beijer. Now it is primarily a museum; from time to time *divertissements*, plays, and concerts are given for small audiences in connection with the visits of dignitaries.

BIBLIOGRAPHY

Beijer, Agne. *Drottningholms slottsteater på Lovisa Ulrikas och Gustaf III:s tid.* Stockholm, 1981.

MAGNUS BLOMKVIST

Dance Education

The Royal Swedish Ballet School was founded in 1773, together with the Royal Opera, by King Gustav III. After an unbroken tradition of 210 years the school moved out of the Royal Opera House in 1983 to become the Swedish Ballet School, a communal and state-supported school integrated into the communal school of Högalid in Stockholm. From 1983 to 1992 the school expanded greatly and now has about two hundred fifty pupils in a basic school of six grades and a high school of three year-levels. The school belongs to the largest and best known in Europe and has a reputation for producing fine male dancers. In the basic school classical ballet, modern dance, jazz, and character dance are taught, as well as pas de deux and repertory. In the high school two alternative programs exist, one with a focus on traditional classical ballet and repertory, and the other (since 1989) for modern dance, jazz, and creativity.

Aside from the Swedish Ballet School in Stockholm, similar professional schools have been integrated into school systems in the towns of Göteborg and Malmö (1992 and 1993), where the pupils also complete their ordinary schoolwork. The high school attached to the Swedish Ballet School in Stockholm is available after entrance examination to students from throughout Sweden, and offers a high school diploma.

The Choreographic Institute of the Royal Academy of Music, now University College of Dance, was founded in 1963. An independent college under the Department of Education, the college offers four full-time courses: two, dance education and choreography (three years), lead to the equivalent of a bachelor of fine arts degree; two others, folk dance and further education for dancers in modern and contemporary dance (two years), lead to a university diploma. The college also organizes single-subject courses on a regular basis in historical dance and dance therapy. The college aims to educate students for careers in dance and to provide an environment for research and artistic experimentation.

In recent years several communities in Sweden have started to include dance education in the preschools and elementary schools. The upper secondary school curriculum has added a program for practical and artistic subjects, with a special option in dance and theater.

Private dance schools flourished in Sweden earlier in the twentieth century, but few survive today. Their courses in dance for adults and children have been integrated into ten organizations that promote adult education. The largest and most popular of these is Balettakademien, a part of Folkuniversitetet, the extramural department of Stockholm University, which has eleven thousand pupils in dance, thirty-six hundred of them in Stockholm. Of these students, seventy of age sixteen to twenty-one attend a full-time professional school. Balettakademien arranges annual summer courses in ballet, modern dance, and jazz dance. Internationally famous teachers from Europe and the United States are invited to Stockholm for stints of five weeks.

BIBLIOGRAPHY

Cullberg, Birgit, and Lilian Karina Vasarhelyi. *Balettskolan.* Vastaras, 1960.

Cullberg, Birgit. "Why Study Ballet?" *Dance Magazine* (May 1961): 27–28.

Feinberg, Gunilla. *Lär dig dansa: 200 års danslåroböcker.* Malmö, 1989.

Hood, Robin [Idestam-Almqvist, Bengt]. *Svensk balett/The Ballet in Sweden.* Malmö, 1951.

Palmqvist, Bertil. *Malmöbaletten.* Malmö, 1985.

Riwkin-Brick, Anna. *Svensk danskonst på scen och i skola.* Stockholm, 1932.

LULLI SVEDIN

Dance Research and Publication

The study of Swedish folk dance began during the late 1800s and early 1900s and was a consequence of romantic nationalism and a general interest in folklore during that period. Ernst Klein, curator of the Nordiska Museet in Stockholm, was a pioneer in this field; Mats Rehnberg pursued the study of folk dance in the next generation. The Dance Museum (Dansmuseet) in Stockholm opened a special section for folk dance, with Henry Sjöberg as curator. Sjöberg established an archive of all existing literature on folk and social dancing in Sweden, both collecting original books and obtaining photocopies of material in other libraries. Contributors to the Dance Museum's folk dance section have studied and preserved folk dances by embarking on expeditions to the countryside, where traditions still live, and filming authentic folk dances. Contributors to Svenska Visarkivet, the archive for Swedish songs and ballads, have undertaken similar expeditions; however, they emphasize the musical aspect of song dance.

The first ballet criticism published in Sweden was written by Johan Henrik Kellgren, a major poet and writer representative of the Enlightenment. When King Gustav III founded the Swedish Academy in 1786, Kellgren was chosen to be one of the first thirteen members. He was a regular contributor to the *Stockholmsposten* from its inception in 1778. One of his first articles is a review of an opera performance, Uttini's *Aline, Queen of Golconda.* He gave the newly-engaged dancer Jean Marcadet credit for a joyful shepherd's dance but adds that the ballets need more vitality and that most of the time there are only poses to look at. He wrote, "All theatrical dance should be an imitation of human actions and passions. The steps are only the mechanism, but the pantomime the very soul."

In subsequent articles Kellgren championed Jean-Georges Noverre's ideas of the new *ballet d'action.* He kept Noverre's *Lettres sur la danse* in his private library; not surprisingly, two of Noverre's letters were translated and published in the *Stockholmsposten* in 1781. Since the *Stockholmsposten* exerted a strong influence on intellectual and artistic circles in Stockholm, Kellgren's pressure was effective. In 1782 the Royal Theater engaged Noverre's pupil Antoine Bournonville as *premier danseur* and choreographer; consequently, the repertory of *ballets d'action* grew and the dancing improved.

Kellgren was familiar with the writings of C. J. Dorat and used his "Notions sur la danse ancienne et moderne" (an addition in prose to his cycle of poems *La déclamation théâtrale: La danse*) to publish in the *Stockholmsposten* in 1779 the first dance history written in Swedish. The piece is not a strict translation of Dorat; rather, Kellgren enlarged and commented on it in his own elegant, witty style. In 1782 he wrote a short piece in the *Stockholmsposten* that provided the French recipe for saving boring, wooden operas: lengthen the ballets and shorten the skirts.

Ballet criticism in the modern sense, written by dance experts, is a recent phenomenon in Sweden, beginning in the 1940s. Before that time, during the early decades of the twentieth century, music critics and authorities on arts and crafts covered dance events in daily newspapers and literary magazines.

A special category of writers to emerge was the first generation of newspaperwomen, all of them suffragettes, who gave modern dance their support. Isadora Duncan's guest appearance in Stockholm in 1906 had a great impact on the young generation. When the Swede Anna Behle, a pupil of Duncan and Émile Jaques-Dalcroze, returned from abroad and started to perform and teach, the press filled many columns with articles about the new dance and the ideals behind it.

One music critic, Kajsa Rootzén of the conservative *Svenska dagbladet,* explored the history of dance more thoroughly than her contemporaries. In 1945 she wrote the first history of Swedish ballet, *Den svenska baletten,* covering the development of the Royal Swedish Ballet from 1773 until her own time.

In the 1940s new dance critics appeared in the daily newspapers. Bengt Idestam-Almquist was a supporter of pure classical ballet and author of *Svensk balett* (1951). Bengt Häger wrote criticism and the book *Balett klassisk og fri* (Ballet Classical and Modern, first published in Denmark in 1945) and *Les Ballets Suédois* (1989); he became active as curator of the Dance Museum at its foundation in 1953. Anna Greta Ståhle, critic and editor of the entertainment pages of the *Dagens nyheter,* was later a lecturer at Stockholm University and the State Dance College. Margareta Sjögren succeeded Rootzén and wrote *Biljett till balett* (1957), which included chapters about Swedish dancers and choreographers in the 1950s; she published

Skandinavisk balett in 1988. Madeleine Katz, who wrote for the *Expressen*, was a former dancer writing about dance and literature, especially psychology. Erik Näslund, author of monographs on Birgit Cullberg and Carina Ari, editor of the magazine *Dans* from 1973 to 1981, and dance critic of the *Svenska dagbladet*, became director of the Dansmuseet in Stockholm. Other writers on dance include Gunilla Jensen, a playwright working for Swedish television, and Brit Svedbert from Göteborg, an artist and writer who has published and exhibited her drawings of dancers. Horace Engdahl is critic of the *Dagens nyheter* and contributor to the cultural section of articles on literature and philosophy; his knowledge and support of modern dance has been of great value. Engdal is the author of *Swedish Ballet and Dance* (1992).

With five ballet companies and a growing number of modern dance groups, more coverage is needed. New writers in the 1990s are Bodil Persson, Anna Ångström, and Margareta Sörenson. *Dans tidningen*, a magazine devoted to dance, has been published regularly since 1991. Photographers have contributed to preserving dance history by their records of performances. Important photographic pioneers in Sweden were Beata Bergström and Enar Merkel Rydberg, later followed by Leslie Leslie-Spinks and Tomas Gidén.

Research in Swedish archives, conducted by Mary Skeaping and continued by Ivo Cramér and Regina Beck-Friis, resulted in the reconstruction of ballets depicting the period of Gustav III. Another specialist is Gunilla Roempke. Her research led to an exhibition of Gustavian ballet at the Dansmuseet and to a book about the lives of some Gustavian ballerinas. Magnus Blomkvist produced the articles "Public Entertainment in Stockholm 1773–1806" and "Ballet Music at the Royal Academy of Music 1773–1806" in 1972 and 1973. A symposium held in Stockholm in 1987 centered on theatrical dance and opera at the Drottningholm Court Theater.

Dance has also entered the curricula of Swedish universities. Since 1988 it has been possible to study the history and aesthetics of dance at Stockholm University. Students have prepared papers on specific dance subjects, for example, "Fokine in Sweden." Others have written about Birgit Cullberg, Ivo Cramér, Birgit Åkesson, and Ronny Johansson. In the early 1990s several doctoral dissertations were completed. Lena Hammergren wrote "Form och mening i Dansen" (Form and Meaning in Dance); and Cecilia Olsson wrote "Dansföreställningar" (Dance Performances), centering on George Balanchine and Antony Tudor. In the field of ethnic dance Owe Ronström studied the dances of Yugoslav immigrants and their evolution. In 1995 Erik Näslund presented "Birgit Cullberg's Fröken Julie, en svensk Balettklassiker" (Birgit Cullberg's *Miss Julia*, a Swedish Ballet Classic).

The State Dance College has encouraged research and university studies. Several teachers have prepared papers on children's dances for the university's departments of pedagogy and psychology; Erna Grönlund of the State Dance College presented a 1994 dissertation, "Barns känslor bearbetade i dans: Dansterapi för barn med tidiga störningar" (Dance Therapy as a Treatment for Children with Early Emotional Disturbances). Peter Rajka, also at the State Dance College, is experimenting with a new form of dance notation.

Anna Greta Ståhle

SWEIGARD, LULU. *See* Body Therapies, *overview article.*

SWING DANCE. *See* Lindy Hop.

SWISS MILKMAID, THE. Originally titled *Das Schweizer Milchmädchen;* also known as *Nathalie, ou La Laitière Suisse.* Ballet in two acts. Choreography: Filippo Taglioni. Music: Adalbert Gyrowetz. Scenery: Janitz, Gail, and Pran. Costumes: Philipp Stubenrauch. First performance: 8 October 1821, Kärntnertor Theater, Vienna. Principals: Johanna Bretel (Henriette), Théodore Rozier (Nathalie), Therese Heberle (Nannette), Filippo Taglioni (Alexis).

Inspired by Gaetano Gioja's ballet *I Minatori Valacchi,* which had its premiere on 9 February 1814, Filippo Taglioni used French-speaking Switzerland as the scene of the story for *The Swiss Milkmaid.* Alexis, an army officer, is in love with Henriette and has her abducted to the castle. In a series of pantomime scenes, the peasant girl expresses her amazement at her lordly surroundings while standing in front of a statue of Alexis. Unknown to her, Alexis has substituted himself for the statue at a moment when she was not looking. Enraptured with Henriette, Alexis falls at her feet and declares his love. After she recovers from the shock of her discovery, she agrees to marry him. Other principal characters include Henriette's father and two sisters, and the lord of the castle.

The ballet was a sensation in Europe. It offered the principal dancer an opportunity to show off her qualities as a mime—qualities that Fanny Elssler possessed to a greater degree than any other ballerina of the Romantic era. Antoine Titus produced the ballet for the Berlin debut of the Elssler sisters on 8 October 1830. On 4 February 1831, Elssler danced the role for the first time in Vienna. The dancers added two pas de deux, which she danced partnered by her sisters.

On 25 September 1823, Titus (who had worked in Vienna in 1822) produced the ballet at the Théâtre de la

Porte-Saint-Martin in Paris. In 1832, Filippo Taglioni did the ballet under the title *Nathalie, ou La Laitière Suisse*, with additional music by Michele Carafa, and with his daughter Marie in the title role. For this Paris version of the ballet, Taglioni changed both the characters' names and the story. Although Marie Taglioni was successful in this role, which she also danced in a London production at the King's Theatre, the role nevertheless remained linked with the name of her rival Elssler.

In August 1840 Elssler danced the ballet for the first time in New York, where it had been performed the previous year in a production by Paul Taglioni, who also produced his father's ballet in 1841 in Copenhagen. Elssler danced the milkmaid for the last time on 16 December 1849, at the Bolshoi Theater in Saint Petersburg, where Titus had already produced the ballet in 1832. This version, by Marius Petipa jointly with Jules Perrot, was Petipa's first work for Saint Petersburg. The ballet now went under the title *Lida, oder Das Schweizer Milchmädchen*.

In 1980 Pierre Lacotte created a reconstruction of the ballet for the Classical Ballet of Moscow, with Ekaterina Maximova in the title role.

[*See also the entries on the principal figures mentioned herein.*]

BIBLIOGRAPHY

Beaumont, Cyril W. *Complete Book of Ballets.* London, 1937.
Guest, Ivor. *The Romantic Ballet in England.* London, 1972.
Guest, Ivor. *The Romantic Ballet in Paris.* 2d rev. ed. London, 1980.

ARCHIVE. Riki Raab Archives, Vienna.

GUNHILD OBERZAUCHER-SCHÜLLER
Translated from German

SWITZERLAND.

To reflect the current state of dance in Switzerland, any survey must take account not only of the historical mainstream of dance in municipal theaters and opera houses, including the "ballet boom" following World War II, but also of the "dance explosion," a phenomenon of extratheatrical dance activity, that has occurred in the later decades of the twentieth century.

Early History. Although the eighteenth-century Swiss elite followed the French example and on occasion staged dance spectacles, it was not until the nineteenth century, when municipal theaters were founded for opera and drama, that the theatrical arts were established in Switzerland on an ongoing basis. During the first decades of the century, many artists employed in theaters were amateurs. It is known, for instance, that many well-trained but nonprofessional musicians played in theater orchestras. Very little, however, is known about stage dance at the time. While it might be assumed that amateur dancers were as common as amateur musicians, the parallel could be misleading, for, although high-caliber musical instruction was common among the Swiss middle class, dance instruction beyond the level of social dance was comparatively rare.

Throughout the nineteenth century and well into the twentieth, most stage dancing took the form of operatic interludes. Some independent performances were staged, but they remained peripheral to the overall concerns of theater artists and audiences. One notable exception was *The Fairy Doll*, Joseph Hassreiter's perennially popular pantomime ballet, which enjoyed a number of performances in various Swiss theaters around the turn of the century. More typical were the statistics associated with the Zurich municipal theater: during its first fifty years (1891–1941), productions on its stage included only twenty-five ballets, most of which were performed a mere five or six times.

In the first half of the twentieth century, German modern dance, called *Ausdruckstanz* ("expressive dance"), had a far greater impact in Switzerland that did classical ballet. Émile Jaques-Dalcroze, whose theories of eurhythmics formed the basis of much of early modern dance, began his teaching career in 1892 at the Conservatoire de Musique in Geneva. In 1910 he left to work at Hellerau in Germany, but from 1915 until his death in 1950 he continued his work in Geneva at the institute that still bears his name. In the years surrounding World War I, Rudolf Laban and Mary Wigman, the originators of German modern dance, worked in Ascona, an artists' colony on the shore of Lake Maggiore in the Swiss Alps, near the Italian

SWITZERLAND. In Basel in 1978, Heinz Spoerli created what is perhaps the quintessential Swiss ballet. Based on Swiss folklore, it is entitled *Chäs* (Cheese). Seen here are Martin Schläpfer (kicking his heel over his head) and members of the ensemble in a typically frolicsome moment. The ballet was set to music by André Bauer and Edi Baer and was danced in front of a backdrop created by Hannes Meyer. The costumes, in bright yellow and red, relieved by black and white, were designed by Anuschka Meyer-Riehl. (Photograph © by Gundel Kilian; used by permission.)

border. Their circle of dancers included Sophie Täuber, who performed at the Dada Gallery in Zurich. The intensive experimental work of these German artists laid the groundwork for later developments throughout central Europe.

After World War I, modern dance reached a larger public. Charlotte Bara, a German dancer who took Berlin by storm in the 1920s, settled near Ascona and in 1927–1928 opened her Teatro San Materno. Designed specifically for dance, it was considered to be the first truly modern theater in Switzerland. There, Bara presented not only her own productions but also those of other modernists on tour, including Valeska Gert, Rosalia Chladek, and Trudi Schoop. Schoop, a Swiss-born dancer who had studied in Germany and who had opened a school in Zurich in 1926, trained a company that toured at home and abroad from 1930 to 1947. During the same period, the frequent tours of Clothilde and Alexander Sakharoff popularized modern dance for a broad theatergoing public.

From 1939 to 1957, Mara Jovanovits, a dancer trained by Gret Palucca, directed the dance ensemble at the small theater in Sankt Gallen (Saint Gall). In the isolation of the war years, Jovanovits's choreographic style became increasingly classical. In this way her work showed a natural evolution away from *Ausdruckstanz* and anticipated the postwar turn toward ballet. Unlike the state theaters in Germany, where the performing arts were brought to a virtual standstill during World War II, Swiss theaters continued to function more or less normally, yet after the war Swiss artists and audiences, like those in Germany, found ballet far more compelling than modern dance. To postwar audiences in both Switzerland and Germany, ballet was considered a novelty, whereas, ironically, "modern" dance was considered old-fashioned.

The Ballet Boom. The postwar ballet boom centered on the six government-subsidized ballet ensembles at theaters in Basel, Bern, Geneva, Lucerne, Saint Gall, and Zurich. The status of these companies has depended largely on the support, or lack thereof, offered by the general director of the theater and by the strength of personality projected by the resident choreographer or ballet master. Not surprisingly, each of the six companies has experienced high and low points.

Basel. In the late 1950s and early 1960s Vaslav Orlikovsky guided the Basel Ballet to renown as a "Swiss ballet miracle" comparable to John Cranko's "Stuttgart ballet miracle." In 1973, Heinz Spoerli began a long and distinguished tenure that brought the company to a second peak of international fame. In 1991, when Spoerli left for Düsseldorf, he was replaced by Youri Vámos, and in 1996 the Basel Ballet was disbanded and replaced by a *Tanztheater* directed by Joachim Schlömer. [*See* Basel Ballet.]

Geneva. Regular ballet performances in Geneva began only in the early 1960s, following the opening of the rebuilt Grand Théâtre. The first directors of the Geneva Ballet were Janine Charrat (1962–1964) and Serge Golovine (1964–1969), who presented a conventional repertory. The arrival of Alfonso Catà in 1969 signaled a major change. Catà, a Cuban-American who had danced with the New York City Ballet, persuaded George Balanchine to become an artistic adviser to the company and to help build a repertory featuring his ballets. Patricia Neary continued this policy during her tenure as director of the company from 1973 to 1978. She was succeeded by Peter van Dyk (1978–1980) and Oscar Araiz (1980–1988), who replaced the neoclassical repertory with his own scenic works. From 1988 to 1996 the Geneva Ballet was directed by Gradimir Pankov. At the center of his repertory were works by Jiří Kylián, Ohad Naharin, and Christopher Bruce.

Zurich. Nicholas Beriozoff built a strong ballet audience in Zurich during the 1960s, but in the 1970s the company was plagued by frequent changes in artistic directorship. In the early 1980s, Patricia Neary built up a broad-based repertory, starting with the works by Balanchine that she had mounted earlier at the Grand Théâtre de Genève and then proving the versatility and strength of the Zurich company with performances of works ranging from such Romantic classics as *Giselle*, as staged by Heinz Spoerli, to the violently contemporary *Love Songs* by William Forsythe. In 1985, Neary was replaced as head of the Zurich Ballet by Uwe Scholz, who had the company concentrate on his own choreography. In 1991 Scholz was succeeded by Bernd Roger Biernert, who held the directorship for five confused years before being replaced, in 1996, by Spoerli, who was persuaded to return to Switzerland from Germany. [*See* Zurich Ballet.]

Lucerne. As ballet master at the municipal theater in Lucerne, the Swiss dancer and choreographer Riccardo Duse built a versatile and imaginative repertory in the early 1970s. Taking over from Duse in 1976, Dieter Ammann creatively guided the ballet company in the late 1970s and the 1980s. Then, in 1990, the Lucerne company created a small sensation by obtaining star dancer Ben van Cauwenberg as director and former Kirov ballerina Galina Panova as soloist and ballet mistress. Their tenure was relatively brief, and they were followed in 1992 by the young choreographer and director Thorsten Kreissig, whose free and easy works met with huge success, arous-

ing the spirited approval of Lucerne audiences. In 1996, Kreissig was replaced by Richard Wherlock, who introduced instead of ballet the currently fashionable style of *Tanztheater.*

Bern and Saint Gall. The relatively small cities of Bern and Saint Gall have not been widely known as centers of theatrical dance. Riccardo Duse worked at the municipal theater in Bern in the early 1980s, and in 1991 the French dancer François Klaus took over the ballet company there. His story ballets, such as *Peer Gynt*, were highly successful. Since 1994, the company has been directed by Martin Schläpfer, formerly a soloist with Spoerli's Basel Ballet, who has given it a level of quality and a range of style almost unprecedented for such a small company performing on such a small stage. With even more restricted means, Marianne Fuchs has since 1990 built for the small company in Saint Gall an interesting repertory, including works by such well-known choreographers as Tom Schilling. Considering that the company directors in Bern and Saint Gall, like their colleague in Lucerne, work with troupes of fewer than twenty members and are frequently called upon to stage dances in operas and operettas, their achievements are especially impressive.

Lausanne. In addition to the six cities that support municipal ballet companies, Lausanne, at the eastern end of Lake Geneva, has played a prominent part in the dance history of Switzerland. Thanks to the Festival de Lausanne, the city's Théâtre Beaulieu has been the principal Swiss venue for ballet and modern dance companies from abroad. In 1973, the Prix de Lausanne was established by a group of culturally minded industrialists to provide a

SWITZERLAND. Thorsten Kreissig's *Dornröschen—Die Schlafende Schönheit* was presented at the Municipal Theater in Lucerne in 1993. Audiences expecting to see a production of *The Sleeping Beauty* were, however, in for a surprise. Although set to the familiar Tchaikovsky score, the ballet told a completely different story. Critics admitted that it was entertaining but complained about misuse of a classic musical score. (Photograph by Peter Schnetz; reprinted from *World Ballet and Dance, 1993–1994,* Oxford, 1994, p. 136).

scholarship to a talented teenage ballet dancer who has not yet begun a professional career. It is awarded each year by a international jury of about ten prominent teachers and choreographers to the winner of a four-day competition.

In 1987, the noted French choreographer and company director Maurice Béjart disbanded his famed Ballet du XXᵉ Siècle in Brussels, relocated to Lausanne, and founded a new company, which he named the Ballet Béjart Lausanne. In 1992, following the model of his Brussels school, Mudra, he founded in Lausanne the École-Atelier Rudra Béjart Lausanne. He has continued to be a prolific choreographer and a master of theatrical spectacle.

The Dance Explosion. Since the 1960s, Switzerland has been the site of explosive growth in all types of dance. It is difficult to determine whether the increased esteem for theater dance has encouraged and facilitated the extratheatrical activities or whether the extratheatrical activities have themselves attracted larger audiences for performances of theater dance. Perhaps the influence is reciprocal.

Opera houses and municipal theaters often sponsor studio demonstrations and experimental workshop performances in addition to ballet evenings. The number of professional dancers working outside the subsidized theater has increased exponentially, while small, nonsubsidized groups have proliferated, although many have been short-lived. It is impossible to assess or even survey all of the performances taking place on small stages and in improvised theaters throughout the country.

It is clear, however, that these performances exhibit a wide range of styles and types of musical accompaniment. Although scores by Swiss composers written specifically for dance constitute only a small fraction of the repertory, a quiet explosion has occurred even in this domain. Since 1900, more than one hundred composers have written more than two hundred and fifty scores specifically for dance. Still, composers of music for dance receive little direct support or official encouragement.

In contrast, the needs of other dance professionals and related institutions are well supported. The Migros training scholarship, for example, and the Prix de Lausanne both aim to encourage talented young dancers. The Schweizerischer Dachverband, a kind of umbrella organization, coordinates activities in a wide range of areas, while local associations have focused their support on specific institutions. Several different organizations look after the interests of teachers. In 1996, there were more than five hundred ballet schools in Switzerland, of which more than fifty provided professional training.

Perhaps most surprising is the widespread participation in extratheatrical dance. In dance studios all over the country, amateurs study ballet, modern dance, and jazz.

Even small towns boast popular discothèques and dance clubs, and American fads such as break dancing and hip-hop are imported immediately. In recent years, residents of Zurich have even cultivated a Carnival tradition, taking Basel's famous Fasnacht as their model. For three consecutive nights every year, a dense crowd dances in the squares of the Old City, stamping their feet and whirling about to the rhythms of traditional tunes as well as modern music. In just a few decades, attitudes toward dance have changed decisively in Switzerland, enabling it to become an integral part of theatrical and extratheatrical life.

[*See also the entries on the principal figures mentioned herein.*]

BIBLIOGRAPHY

Baumann, Dorothea, ed. *Théâtre musical: L'oeuvre de compositeurs suisses du vingtième siècle.* Bonstetten, 1983.

Buffat, Serge. *Oscar Araiz: Carnets de danse, Genève 1980–1988.* Lausanne, 1988.

Cunha, Antonio. "Le Béjart Ballet de Lausanne et les enjeux de la politique culturelle." In *La danse, art du XXe siècle.* Lausanne, 1990.

Flury, Phillip, and Peter Kaufmann. *Heinz Spoerli: Ballett-Fazination.* 2d ed. Zurich, 1996.

Levieux, Francette. *Prix de Lausanne: Un tremplin pour les jeunes danseurs de talents.* Lausanne, 1989.

Merz, Richard. "Von zweitrangiger Bedeutung zu unerwarteter Popularität: Ballett in der Schweiz." In *Tanz in Deutschland: Ballett seit 1945,* edited by Hartmut Regitz. Berlin, 1984.

Muriset, Yvan, and Jean-Pierre Pastori. *Béjart, le tournant.* New ed. Lausanne, 1988.

Pastori, Jean-Pierre. "The Emancipation of Dance in the Municipal Theatres." *Ballett International* 10 (June 1987): 12–18.

Pastori, Jean-Pierre. *Dance and Ballet in Switzerland.* Translated by Jacqueline Gartmann. 2d ed., rev. and enl. Zurich, 1989.

Pastori, Jean-Pierre. *De Diaghilev à Béjart: Lausanne danse, 1915–1993.* Lausanne, 1993.

Schouvaloff, Alexander. *Set and Costume Designs for Ballet and Theatre.* London, 1987.

Vollmer, Horst. "Direktorenkarussell." *Tanz und Gymnastik* 51.3 (1995): 42–46.

Weber, Conrad G. *Brauchtum in der Schweiz.* Zurich, 1985.

RICHARD MERZ
Translated from German

SWORD DANCE. The linked, closed-circle, hilt-and-point sword dance is known throughout Europe but is especially concentrated in the Germanic countries and in the northeast of England. The dance has considerable regional variety, but the core choreographic principle is to weave a number of figures without releasing the swords, culminating in the tying and display of a polygonal braid of the swords. Dancers hold the hilt of their swords in their right hand and the point of their neighbor's in their left hand, to form a closed circle. In England there are two types of sword dance—the long-sword and the rapper, the latter an outgrowth of the former.

The sword dance proper, especially in the long-sword

traditions, is only part of a much larger seasonal ceremonial. The performance begins with the captain of the team singing a "calling-on" song, the signal that allows him to clear a space for the dance and to introduce the dancers one by one. Each of the dancers is mythologized as a hero or a villain, and the song concludes with an exhortation to dance. The closed, hilt-and-point circle is formed and a few figures are danced. One of the performers is (mock) slain, then a play, recited in doggerel, is enacted, ending in the appearance of a quack doctor who through general horseplay resurrects the dead man. The dancers complete their stock of figures and finish by tying a lock.

Traditionally, the sword dance is performed at Christmastime. Each team takes its performance on a tour of important points around the village or group of neighboring villages. The overt function of the dance is to entertain and to earn some pocket money by passing the hat. Implicitly, though, the dance serves to maintain and strengthen social solidarity by providing a locally recognizable and significant aesthetic focus to general festival activity.

The long-sword dance is performed in and around Yorkshire by six or eight men wearing quasi-military or uniform costumes decked with rosettes and ribbons; each man carries a dancing sword, a thirty- to forty-inch (about one meter) lath of steel with a fixed, wooden handle. The stepping is a rhythmic, slightly dotted, running step using any 4/4, 2/2, or 6/8 tune that can be played at a moderate pace. The basic figure from which the others start is a wide, closed ring circling clockwise. Each of the figures is performed with all possible combinations of dancers; for example, if the first dancer raises his sword and the rest file under it ("single under"), then the second through the sixth (or eighth) dancers will do likewise in turn. Other figures include "over your own sword" (each dancer hops over his sword in turn), "over your neighbor's sword," and "single over" (the dancers file over a sword held as a hurdle). The overall aesthetic effect is of a hypnotic, mathematical certainty.

The rapper dance almost certainly developed out of the long-sword tradition in the eighteenth century, although it did not reach its present form until the early part of the twentieth century. It is performed almost exclusively by coal miners from Northumbria. There are five central dancers dressed in white shirts decorated with rosettes, dark open-knee breeches, and white stockings. They are accompanied by two characters, Tommy and Bessy, who serve as clowns, occasionally joining in the main dance. One of the characters sings the calling-on song. Plays are no longer performed, although two are known from the mid-nineteenth century. The dance is performed to double jigs played very fast, with the dancers alternating a running step with a 6/8 shuffle-tap step. Each dancer carries a rapper, a twenty-eight-inch (about 0.75 meter) lath of flexible spring steel, with a swivel handle at one end and a fixed one at the other. The characteristics of this strange implement (of unknown origin or function outside the dance) make the dance unique. In the long-sword dance the lock is the final figure because strength and precision timing are required to tie it and because it is virtually impossible to untie it without breaking the circle. With the flexible rappers, however, the lock, called a *nut*, can be easily tied and untied by turning the circle inside out without the dancers releasing the rappers. This has made the aesthetic of the rapper dance a display of the different ways that the nut can be tied.

The speed of the rapper dance does not allow for the wide circles and generous motions of the long-sword dance. The set is always tightly packed, and all movement is carried out shoulder to shoulder. The characteristic rapper figure is two counterrotating circles with various possibilities for crossing from one circle to the opposite, tangling the rappers in a seemingly hopeless mess. At the end of the dance Tommy and Bessy may enter the set, making the counterrotating circles and the resultant jumble of rappers even more amazing and the final nut more complex.

Early folklorists speculated that the sword dance, with its death-and-resurrection motif, is a remnant of a pre-Christian ritual cycle designed to propitiate the forces of nature in midwinter and to ensure the return of the sun. Apart from imputing to early Europeans a naïveté that contemporary anthropology has shown to be unwarranted, the historical evidence for such a theory does not exist. The earliest reference to the sword dance in Europe is in Nuremberg in 1350, and the earliest in England is 1638. Because the great majority of sword dances are native to areas with old mining sites, there has been theoretical speculation that the earliest dancers were members of a sacral brotherhood of metal workers that performed essential rituals during the annual cycle. The more mundane explanation is that it was easiest to have special swords for dancing made at mining sites, which were also centers for metal working. There is as yet no sound theory of the origin and evolution of hilt-and-point sword dancing in Europe.

[*See also* Great Britain, *article on* English Traditional Dance; Jig; Matachins; *and* Morris Dance.]

BIBLIOGRAPHY

Alford, Violet. *Sword Dance and Drama.* London, 1962.

Cawte, E. C. "A History of the Rapper Dance." *Folk Music Journal* 4.2 (1981): 79–116.

Corrsin, Stephen D. *Sword Dancing: A History.* Enfield Lock, 1996.

Sharp, Cecil J. *The Sword Dances of Northern England.* 3 vols. London, 1912–1913. 2d ed. London, 1951.

JOHN FORREST

SYDNEY DANCE COMPANY. Acclaimed for its large and varied repertory of contemporary and theatrically innovative works, Sydney Dance Company has mostly Australian choreographers. From the beginning of their association with the company, current artistic director Graeme Murphy and his assistant artistic director Janet Vernon have aimed to develop a repertory that is relevant to contemporary Australians, with a style that reflects contemporary Australian society.

The company was called the Dance Company (NSW) when Murphy took over its direction at the end of 1976. The Dance Company (NSW) had been founded by Suzanne Musitz in 1965 as a dance-in-education group, but it developed as a full-fledged performing company that was led first by Musitz and then in 1975 and 1976 by Jaap Flier. Murphy changed its name to Sydney Dance Company in 1979, hoping to give the company a stronger image and a recognizable sense of place. The company

SYDNEY DANCE COMPANY. Carl Morrow and Victoria Taylor in *Daphnis and Chloe*, choreographed by the company's longtime director Graeme Murphy to the score by Maurice Ravel. (Photograph by Branco Gaica; used by permission.)

survived financial difficulties that had it on the brink of receivership in 1983, and is now the only major dance company, classical or modern, whose permanent base is in Sydney. It is often regarded as one of Sydney's cultural icons, although its frequent national and overseas tours have ensured that it is now widely known outside the city that gave it birth.

The company's repertory consists largely of works choreographed by Murphy. They range from full-length works, his first being *Poppy* (1978) inspired by the life and art of French author Jean Cocteau, to shorter one-act pieces. They are sometimes clearly narrative-based, although Murphy frequently manipulates or reworks a given narrative. Thus *After Venice* (1984) was based on the Thomas Mann novella *Death in Venice*, but it focused on the character of Tadzio and presented a psychological exploration of his relations with the other characters in the novella. Some works have Australian themes, such as *Rumours* (1978/79), *Homelands* (1982), *Wilderness* (1982) and *Nearly Beloved* (1986), although in recent years Murphy has rarely chosen an overtly Australian subject. At other times Murphy's works for Sydney Dance Company are strongly nonnarrative. *Kraanerg* (1988) and *Piano Sonata* (1992), for example, were influenced in their choreographic structure by the music Murphy chose, a score by Iannis Xenakis for *Kraanerg* and a sonata by Carl Vine for *Piano Sonata*. The works are often also multimedia creations, making use of film, slide projections, and complex stage machinery and lighting.

Murphy has always seen Sydney Dance Company as a vehicle for the showing of work by Australian visual artists and composers and the company has a strong history of commissioning music and design. In recent years the company has worked with live performance ensembles who appear on stage and who have become an intrinsic part of the dance work, as in *Synergy with Synergy* (1992) made with the Australian percussion group Synergy. *Free Radicals* (1996) took this process one step further when both the music, by four percussionists, and the choreography were created side by side in the rehearsal process.

The repertory of Sydney Dance Company includes works by choreographers other than Murphy, such as Louis Falco, Ralph Lemon, Ohad Naharin, and Douglas Wright; the several Australians include Paul Mercurio, Gideon Obarzanek, Stephen Page, Garth Welch, and Kim Walker. Many company dancers have contributed to the repertory over the years, often in workshop seasons, and the company has also nurtured some dancers who have gone on to start their own or direct other companies, including Mercurio (Australian Choreographic Ensemble), Obarzanek (Chunky Move), and Page (Bangarra Dance Theatre).

In the mid-1990s, Sydney Dance Company took on an

entrepreneurial role in order, Murphy says, to expand the choices available to Australian dance audiences. The company has brought a number of French and American companies to Australia often to perform as part of a Sydney Dance Company season. Companies that have come to Australia under this arrangement include those led by Maguy Marin and Angelin Preljocaj as well as Momix and the Parsons Dance Company.

Sydney Dance Company dancers all have a strong classical training, although not all have the perfectly proportioned classical body. Although it does not promote a hierarchical system of star dancers, certain dancers have come to be closely identified with the company, especially Janet Vernon, who, as well as assisting Murphy with artistic direction, has danced with it since 1976. Vernon and Murphy had a notable dancing partnership in early Sydney Dance Company seasons and Vernon's performance skills as a dancer and actor are strongly individualistic. She is also often described as Murphy's muse, and Murphy has created many of the leading roles in his works on her, including those in some of his most recent works like *The Protecting Veil* (1994) and *Fornicon* (1995).

The company's first international opportunity came in 1980 when it visited Italy. In 1981 it went to New York where its novelty, originality, and sheer theatrical quality received favorable notice. *New York Times* critic Clive Barnes wrote:

> Murphy is the kind of choreographer you will want to tell your grandchildren about. The man is a major find—and so is his company.

In the same year recitals were given at the Spoleto Festival in Charleston, South Carolina, and in Washington, D.C. In 1985, it returned to New York and soon became the first contemporary dance company to perform in China. In 1988, after a long tour to Europe, the company shared a program with the Australian Ballet at the Royal Opera House in London. Since then Sydney Dance Company has continued to tour internationally, visiting the United States, Europe, China, and South America.

[*See also* Australia, *article on* Modern Dance; *and the entry on* Murphy.]

BIBLIOGRAPHY
Pask, Edward H. *Ballet in Australia: The Second Act, 1940–1980*. Melbourne, 1982.
Sydney Dance Company: Repertoire and Touring History. Sydney, 1995.
Ulzen, Karen van. "'Kraanerg' and the Rest." *Dance Australia*, no. 39 (December 1988–January 1989): 18–20.

INTERVIEWS. Graeme Murphy, by Hazel de Berg (April 1981), National Library of Australia, Canberra (de B 1222/3). Graeme Murphy, by Shirley McKechnie (May 1990), National Library of Australia, Canberra (TRC 2680). Graeme Murphy, by Michelle Potter (August 1996), National Library of Australia, Canberra (TRC 3478).

MICHELLE POTTER

SYLPHIDE, LA. Ballet in two acts. Choreography: Filippo Taglioni. Music: Jean Schneitzhoeffer. Libretto: Adolphe Nourrit. Scenery: Pierre Ciceri. Costumes: Eugène Lami. First performance: 12 March 1832, Académie Royale de Musique, Paris. Principals: Marie Taglioni (The Sylphide), Joseph Mazilier (James), Lise Noblet (Effie).

Although *La Sylphide* has earned the title of the first Romantic ballet, none of the components for which it is famed (pointe work, the white muslin ballet skirt, gas lighting, and the use of supernatural beings as characters) was literally new in ballet in 1832. *La Sylphide*, however, united these components and made them serve a powerful and evocative Romantic theme, that of a mortal torn between two realms—the material and the spiritual. The Sylphide of the title, personified as a beautiful young woman dressed in white, symbolized a transcendental world that a mortal may perceive and aspire to, yet never attain. The popularity of this ballet led to a host of imitations centering on white-clad supernatural heroines (hence the term *ballet blanc*); few of these ballets, however, could match the poetry of *La Sylphide*.

LA SYLPHIDE. A lithograph of Marie Taglioni in the title role of *La Sylphide*. This famous image was first published as a plate in *Les danseuses de l'Opéra*, issued in Paris in 1865. (Dance Collection, New York Public Library for the Performing Arts.)

The mysterious and unreal world represented in act 2 of *La Sylphide* was foreshadowed by Jean Coralli's sylphides ballet in a melodramatic version of *Faust* (1828) and the "Ballet of the Nuns" in Giacomo Meyerbeer's opera *Robert le Diable* (1831). The "Ballet of the Nuns," the direct predecessor of *La Sylphide*, was choreographed by Filippo Taglioni for his daughter Marie, who, dressed in a white habit, led the ensemble of seductive ghosts. The ballet was set in a medieval cloister spectrally illuminated by gas lighting. During the opera's rehearsals, the tenor Adolphe Nourrit, who sang the role of Robert, wrote a ballet libretto loosely based on Charles Nodier's story *Trilby, ou Le Lutin d'Argaïl* (1822), a tale of a male sprite who falls in love with the wife of a Scottish fisherman. Marie and Filippo Taglioni approved of the libretto but reversed the male and female roles—thus *La Sylphide* was born.

Set in Scotland, the ballet opens on the wedding day of James Reuben, who is discovered asleep in an armchair, watched over by the Sylphide. Waking him with a kiss, she vanishes up the chimney. As James and his kinsfolk prepare for the wedding, the Sylphide appears again and again, distracting him from his fiancée Effie. Madge, a hideous witch whom James tries to eject from the house, reads Effie's palm and tells her that it is Gurn, James's rival, and not James, who truly loves her. The wedding festivities begin, but as James is about to place his ring on Effie's finger, the Sylphide snatches it away and flies from the house, with James in hot pursuit.

In the forest, Madge and her coven cast spells around a cauldron. James enters in search of the Sylphide, who eludes all his efforts to retain her. In desperation he accepts Madge's aid: an enchanted scarf that will compel the Sylphide to remain beside him. He wraps it around the Sylphide; her wings fall off; she sinks to the ground, dying. As her sister sylphs bear her aloft, James sees in the distance the bridal procession of Effie and Gurn.

Taglioni's dancing, polished by her father, reached a zenith of perfection in the role of the Sylphide. Abjuring the mannerisms and technical displays of the *danse noble*, she danced in a more natural style, rising to her pointes not as an acrobatic stunt but as a means of depicting the Sylphide's insubstantiality. Her lightness and fluidity of movement were enhanced by her gauzy white skirts, which became the uniform of the ballet, the Romantic tutu. [*See* Tutu.]

Taglioni's success in *La Sylphide* not only ensured her personal fame but also paved the way for the nineteenth-century reign of the ballerina. Paradoxically, many writers view James, not the Sylphide, as the focal point of the story. Although the ballet is superficially a love story, the characters are most significant as symbols. James represents the Romantic artist, restless, discontent with the world as it is, and filled with inchoate longings. The Sylphide is a symbol of his longings given feminine form, like

LA SYLPHIDE. Ghislaine Thesmar in the title role in Pierre Lacotte's "reconstitution" of Taglioni's *La Sylphide*, broadcast on French television in April 1971. (Photograph by Colette Masson; used by permission of Agence Enguerand/Iliade, Paris.)

Liberty in Eugène Delacroix's painting *The 28th July* (1830).

The ballet soon became an international sensation. Taglioni danced it in London and Berlin in the year of its premiere; in 1837 she danced it in Russia, where Antoine Titus had already staged it in 1835. Madame Celeste danced an excerpt of it in New York in 1835, but it was not until 1839 that a complete and authentic version was presented in the United States by Paul and Amalia Taglioni. Upon Marie Taglioni's return to Paris in 1840, she added a pas de trois for James, Effie, and the Sylphide, using choreography that she had danced first in Vienna in 1839 (Guest, 1980) and probably in her father's ballet *L'Ombre* in Saint Petersburg later that year. The Paris Opera last revived it in 1858 for the ill-fated Emma Livry.

Filippo Taglioni's choreography survived longer in Russia but was revised in 1892 by Marius Petipa. In 1946 Victor Gsovsky, Boris Kochno, and Roland Petit attempted to reconstruct Taglioni's work, on the basis of contemporary prints and writings, for the Ballets des Champs-Élysées; a similar attempt was made by Richard Adama for the Bremen Ballet in 1965. Pierre Lacotte's "reconstitution," filmed in 1971 and presented at the Paris Opera in 1972, is the best-known reconstruction of Taglioni's choreography. In addition to the materials used previously, he also consulted Filippo's annotated musical scores, sketches, performance notes, and class notebooks.

Most revivals have been based on the version choreographed by August Bournonville in Copenhagen in 1836 to a new score by Herman Løvenskjold. Lucile Grahn danced the Sylphide, while James was danced by Bournonville himself. His version is noted for a stronger sense of drama than Taglioni's, a greater emphasis on male dancing, and a heightened contrast between the folk dances in act 1 and the more academic choreography for the sylphides. It has formed the basis of revivals by Harald Lander, Elsa-Marianne von Rosen, Erik Bruhn, Hans Brenaa, Peter Schaufuss, Peter Martins, and others.

The use of pointe work has caused controversy in many revivals. Following Bournonville's lead, pointe work is often limited to the sylphides, thus preserving the distinction between mortals and supernaturals. Lacotte, however, contends that Taglioni placed the Scottish girls on pointe and also gave the ballerina more demanding pointe

work than was previously thought possible for the period. In Adama's version, only the Sylphide dances on pointe.

Over the years both versions of the ballet have been subjected to cuts and additions. James, Gurn, and Effie are often given new solos; some revivals also add a pas de deux for James and Effie. Lacotte added to act 1 a pas de deux comparable to the peasant pas de deux in *Giselle;* Schaufuss added a pas de huit for the wedding guests. Lander and Schaufuss elaborated the witches' scene, strengthening Madge's motive of revenge. In act 2, the dances of the Sylphide, James, and the ensemble of sylphides have frequently been revised.

[*Many of the figures herein are the subjects of independent entries.*]

BIBLIOGRAPHY

Aschengreen, Erik. "The Beautiful Danger: Facets of the Romantic Ballet." Translated by Patricia McAndrew. *Dance Perspectives,* no. 58 (Summer 1974).

Beaumont, Cyril W. "La Sylphide." In Beaumont's *Complete Book of Ballets.* London, 1937.

Bournonville, August. "La Sylphide." Translated by Patricia McAndrew in *Dance as a Theatre Art,* edited by Selma Jeanne Cohen. New York, 1974.

Guest, Ivor. *The Ballet of the Second Empire.* London, 1974.

Guest, Ivor. *The Romantic Ballet in Paris.* 2d rev. ed. London, 1980.

Hallar, Marianne, and Alette Scavenius, eds. *Bournonvilleana.* Translated by Gaye Kynoch. Copenhagen, 1992.

Lacotte, Pierre. "Looking for *La Sylphide.*" *Dance and Dancers* (October 1982): 14–16.

Levinson, André. *Marie Taglioni* (1929). Translated by Cyril W. Beaumont. London, 1977.

Macaulay, Alastair. "The Author of *La Sylphide,* Adolphe Nourrit." *The Dancing Times* (November 1989): 140–143.

Maynard, Olga. "The Ballet of La Sylphide." In Maynard's *The Ballet Companion.* Philadelphia, 1957.

Moore, Lillian. "*La Sylphide:* Epitome of the Romantic Ballet." *Dance Magazine* (March 1965): 42–47.

Sowell, Debra Hickenlooper. "'Virtue (almost) Triumphant' Revisited: Of Sylphs and Silfidi." *Dance Chronicle* 18.2 (1995): 293–301.

SUSAN AU

LA SYLPHIDE. August Bournonville's version of *La Sylphide* has rarely been absent from the repertory of the Royal Danish Ballet since he mounted it in 1836. Firmly in the tradition of the great Danish interpreters of the roles of James Reuben and the Sylphide are Erik Bruhn and Margrethe Schanne, pictured here in 1952. (Photograph © by Rigmor Mydstkov; used by permission.)

SYLPHIDES, LES.

[*To document the origins and development of Michel Fokine's seminal ballet, this entry comprises two articles. The first gives details of the versions presented in Saint Petersburg in 1907–1909; the second discusses the historic production by Diaghilev's Ballets Russes in Paris in June 1909.*]

Russian Origins

The ballet that was to become widely known as Michel Fokine's masterpiece, *Les Sylphides,* took shape gradually, as Fokine reworked it and reshaped it over the course of some two years. The first version, entitled *Chopiniana,* was presented to the public on 10 February 1907, at a charity performance at the Maryinsky Theater, Saint Petersburg, for the Society for the Prevention of Cruelty to Children. It consisted of five scenes set to a suite of piano pieces by Frédéric Chopin orchestrated by Aleksandr Glazunov: a polonaise, a nocturne, a mazurka, a waltz, and a tarantella. The scenery and costumes were selected from the wardrobes and costume rooms of the Imperial Theaters, with the exception of the ballerina's costume for the waltz, which was designed especially for the occasion by Léon Bakst.

The opening Polonaise in A Major (op. 40, no. 1) was staged as "a ballroom in Warsaw" and was danced by a group of couples in colorful Polish costumes. Then, to the music of the Nocturne in F Major (op. 15, no. 1), the second scene depicted Chopin (Aleksei Bulgakov), in his music room in Majorca. In his feverish dreams, the ominous shadows of monks were superseded by the radiant vision of his muse, danced by A. P. Urakova. The third scene, set to the Mazurka in C-sharp Minor (op. 50, no. 3), was staged as "A Peasant Wedding in a Polish Village," where, at the height of the ceremonies, the young bride (Julia Sedova) threw her engagement ring to the elderly bridegroom and eloped with her lover. Then came the Waltz in C-sharp Minor (op. 64, no. 2), and the scene called "Moonlight Vision," a pas de deux for a sylphide and a youth, danced by Anna Pavlova and Mikhail Obukov in a Romantic style reminiscent of Marie Taglioni and Jules Perrot. The final scene was "A Square in Naples," where the lively Tarantella in A-flat Major (op. 43) was performed by a group of dancers led by Vera Fokina and Aleksandr Shiriaev. Fokine later wrote that each scene of *Chopiniana* was designed to illustrate the diversity of the paths open to ballet.

For the February charity performance the following year, 1908, Fokine was obliged to mount a work on short notice, owing to the last-minute cancelation of plans for a series of *divertissements*. He had been working on a new ballet based on the Romantic motifs of the *Chopiniana* waltz and set to an expanded score orchestrated by Maurice Keller. As neither the ballet nor the orchestrations were yet complete, he decided to present excerpts from this work danced to piano accompaniment. Thus at the charity performance at the Maryinsky Theater on 16 February 1908 a work entitled *Danses sur la Musique de Chopin* featured a solo mazurka by Anna Pavlova, the *Chopiniana* waltz danced by Pavlova and Fokine himself, and a nocturne and a waltz performed by twenty members of the female corps de ballet wearing long white dresses copied from the one designed by Bakst for Pavlova the previous year.

Only a few weeks later, Keller's orchestrations were completed, and Fokin's new ballet was given at a benefit performance at the Maryinsky on 8 March 1908 under the title *Rêverie Romantique: Ballet sur la Musique de Chopin.* It included a nocturne, a waltz, a mazurka, a second

waltz, a prelude, a second mazurka, and a concluding *grande valse brillante,* and it was danced by Anna Pavlova, Olga Preobrajenska, Tamara Karsavina, Vaslav Nijinsky, and a corps de ballet of sixteen women. The female soloists and the corps de ballet all wore long white tutus. Nijinsky, only recently graduated from the Imperial Theater School but already recognized as a phenomenal dancer, wore a costume designed for him by Bakst for his appearances with Matilda Kshessinska in a pas de deux called *Nocturnes:* a black velvet tunic over a filmy white shirt, a blond wig, and white tights. Fokine had choreographed a mazurka solo for Nijinsky only the day before the performance, and he continued to make changes in the groupings with the corps de ballet even during the intermission on the day of performance. When the curtain rose, the scene was revealed as a moonlit glade, with the dancers posed before an improvised backdrop, a section of the forest panorama designed for *The Sleeping Beauty.*

Only three weeks later, on 6 April 1908, this version of the work was again performed at the Maryinsky Theater, this time by ballet students in Fokine's class at the Imperial Theater School. The choreography remained essentially the same as in the March performance, but the title of the work was once again changed: at the student performance the work was billed as *Grand Pas sur la Musique de Chopin.*

At the February charity performance the following year, which took place on 19 February 1909, the work was once again entitled *Chopiniana* and was once again danced by artists of the Imperial Ballet: Pavlova, Preobrajenska, Karsavina, and Nijinsky. At this performance, for which a polonaise was played as an overture, the corps de ballet included Nijinsky's younger sister, Bronislava, who later vividly recalled the performance in her memoirs (Nijinska, 1981, pp. 251–252). Thereafter, the ballet became a part of the permanent repertory of the Maryinsky Theater.

As performed in Saint Petersburg today, *Chopiniana* is danced by three female soloists, a male soloist, and a corps de ballet of sixteen. It opens with the Polonaise in A Major (op. 40, no. 1), played as the overture. Then comes the Nocturne in A-flat Major (op. 32, no. 2), performed by the corps de ballet, two female soloists, and the lone male dancer. This is followed by the Waltz in G-flat Major (op. 70, no. 1), performed by three female soloists; the Mazurka in C Major (op. 33, no. 3), danced by the male soloist; the Mazurka in D Major (op. 33, no. 2), performed by the first female soloists; the Prelude in A Major (op. 28, no. 7), performed by the second female soloist; the Waltz in C-sharp Minor (op. 64, no. 2), danced by the first female soloist and the male soloist; and the final Grand Waltz in E-flat Major (op. 18, no. 1), for the entire ensemble.

The final version of *Chopiniana* has the sylphides and the youth dancing against the backdrop of a poetic, bosky landscape. By combining the image of the ethereal sylphide created by Marie Taglioni with the music of Chopin, Fokine sought to resurrect the concept of Romantic ballet. The various miniatures that comprise *Chopiniana* exhibit the utmost subtleties of choreographic art, as Fokine used a new, freer vocabulary of movement to suggest the Romantic moods of languor, anticipation, sorrow, and joy that characterize the dances of the three principal sylphides and the young man. Abandoning the episodic and narrative elements of Romantic ballet, he was able to suggest, purely through dance, the inner world of his characters' imagination, a world of poetic fantasy and dreams. In the final version of his *Grand Pas*, Fokine created the first plotless ballet of the twentieth century.

BIBLIOGRAPHY

Dobrovolskaya, Galina N. "*Chopiniana* M. Fokina i puti zarubezhnogo baleta." In *Zapiski o teatre*, edited by L. A. Levbarg. Leningrad, 1968.
Fokine, Michel. *Memoirs of a Ballet Master*. Translated by Vitale Fokine. Edited by Anatole Chujoy. London, 1961.
Horwitz, Dawn Lille. *Michel Fokine*. Boston, 1985.
Karsavina, Tamara. *Theatre Street*. Rev. and enl. ed. London, 1948.
Krasovskaya, Vera. *Russkii baletnyi teatr nachala dvadtatogo veka*. 2 vols. Leningrad, 1971–1972.
Krasovskaya, Vera. *Nijinsky*. Translated by John E. Bowlt. New York, 1979.
Lazzarini, John, and Roberta Lazzarini. *Pavlova: Repertoire of a Legend*. New York, 1980.
Nijinska, Bronislava. *Early Memoirs*. Translated and edited by Irina Nijinska and Jean Rawlinson. New York, 1981.

GALINA N. DOBROVOLSKAYA
Translated from Russian

LES SYLPHIDES: Diaghilev Production. The poster designed by Valentin Serov for Diaghilev's first season in Paris featured a drawing of Anna Pavlova in *Les Sylphides*. (Photograph from the Dance Collection, New York Public Library for the Performing Arts.)

Diaghilev Production

Title: *Les Sylphides*. Ballet in one act. Choreography: Michel Fokine. Music: Frédéric Chopin, orchestrated by Aleksandr Glazunov, Igor Stravinsky, Nikolai Tcherepnin, and Anatol Liadov. Scenery and costumes: Alexandre Benois. First performance: 2 June 1909, Théâtre du Châtelet, Paris, Ballets Russes de Serge Diaghilev. Principals: Anna Pavlova, Tamara Karsavina, Alexandra Baldina, Vaslav Nijinsky.

Les Sylphides, Fokine's one-act abstract ballet to music by Chopin, may be the most widely and consistently performed ballet of this century, surviving as a popular example of Fokine's contributions to the development of modern ballet choreography. The ballet originated in two distinct versions presented in Saint Petersburg in 1907 and 1908, but it took its final form only when Fokine staged it for Serge Diaghilev's Saison Russe in Paris in June 1909. Several minor but significant changes were made from the second version Fokine had staged in Russia: the title was changed, at Diaghilev's suggestion, from *Chopiniana* to *Les Sylphides;* new scenery and costumes were designed by Alexandre Benois; the Prelude in A Ma-

jor (op. 28, no. 7) replaced the Polonaise in A Major (op. 40, no. 1) as the overture; and Stravinsky (in his first commission for Diaghilev) reorchestrated the Nocturne in A-flat Major (op. 32, no. 2) and the Grand Waltz in E-flat Major (op. 18, no. 1). Fokine's choreography, however, remained essentially the same as in his second Russian version.

Although the ballet's Western premiere attracted little attention in the press, the work has since accumulated abundant critical literature. Through repeated performances, Diaghilev established *Les Sylphides* as a signature piece in his company's repertory. For the European public nurtured on Ballets Russes productions between 1909 and 1929, *Les Sylphides* epitomized the essence of ballet: purity of line, expressiveness, and soft, flowing movements executed by clusters of women dressed in long white skirts.

The Prelude overture sets a quiet, contemplative mood. The curtain rises on a moonlit glade near an ancient ruin. The opening tableau shows three ballerinas surrounding the *danseur*, one on each arm, another reclined at his feet, while the corps pose symmetrically around them. In the

Nocturne, the corps undulate their arms, echoing the music's pulse while the soloists dance the melody, weaving in and among the corps's ever-shifting patterns. The Waltz soloist marks the music's joyous rhythms with each *enchaînement,* ending suddenly with her back to the audience. The Mazurka soloist soars diagonally across stage doing *grands jetés,* while the corps trace her flight with softly waving arms. Sustained jumps and balances characterize the male variation, where the movements match the curved line of melody. The Prelude soloist sweeps noiselessly about the stage, pauses, and seems to listen to a distant call. In the pas de deux, the ballerina appears descending from her partner's arms, the dance marked by evanescent poses and swift, fluttering movements that correspond to the contrasting moods of the melody. The final Grand Waltz is the livliest section: the whole cast sprints about before calmly reforming the opening tableau.

The structure and technique of *Les Sylphides* identify Fokine's choreographic innovations. These include the expansion of flowing port de bras and an extended use of *épaulement,* the liberation of the ensemble from the hierarchial groupings employed in nineteenth-century ballets, and the emphasis on the more subtle qualities of controlled balances, the seemingly effortless flow of the dancers' movements, and their ability to create and sustain a mood. In contrast to Petipa ballets, there is no announcement of solos, no virtuoso steps to show off the dancer's prowess, and each variation ends differently. *Les Sylphides* employs an arabesque motif that unifies the choreography. The corps move in silence in between each section to give added continuity to the string of dances and allowing no breaks for applause. The ballet includes turning the back to the audience as a direct reference to Romantic ballets such as *Giselle.* The work's abstract nature introduces the idea of introspection to twentieth-century ballet. In his *Memoirs,* Fokine tells how he implored his dancers not to project their movements toward the audience but to dance for themselves.

Les Sylphides is the twentieth century's first successful abstract ballet and remains a classic in international repertory. Fokine staged the work for the Royal Swedish Ballet in 1913, the Royal Danish Ballet in 1925, René Blum's Ballet Russe de Monte Carlo in 1936; Ballet Russe de Monte Carlo (Massine) in 1939; and Ballet Theatre (later American Ballet Theatre) in 1940. Other companies received the ballet from ballerinas who worked directly under Fokine, and a surprising consistency in steps and performance style has been maintained in the West. Karsavina staged the work for Marie Rambert's Dancers (later Ballet Rambert) in 1930, and the Royal Ballet's staging is by Alicia Markova, originally set for the Vic-Wells Ballet in 1932. A slightly different version is danced in Russia as *Chopiniana,* where the Polonaise in

A Major (op. 40, no. 1) is still played as the overture and an alternate male variation is performed to the Mazurka in C Major (op. 33, no. 3). The production as a whole is faster paced and more extroverted than its Western counterpart.

An experiment in separating *Les Sylphides* from its Romantic trappings was given by the New York City Ballet in 1972. Alexandra Danilova restaged the work and dressed the dancers in plain practice clothes. This performance showed the purity and strength of the choreography but raised questions concerning the importance of scenery and costumes in the work. The ballet in this form had only a brief existence.

BIBLIOGRAPHY

Balanchine, George, and Francis Mason. *One Hundred and One Stories of the Great Ballets.* New York, 1989.
Benois, Alexandre. *Reminiscences of the Russian Ballet.* Translated by Mary Britnieva. London, 1941.
Fokine, Michel. *Memoirs of a Ballet Master.* Translated by Vitale Fokine. Edited by Anatole Chujoy. London, 1961.
Garafola, Lynn. *Diaghilev's Ballets Russes.* New York, 1989.
Goodwin, Noël. "Fokine and Chopin." *Dance and Dancers* (November 1991): 15–17.
Gregory, John. *Les Sylphides—Chopiniana.* Croesor, Wales, 1989.
Horwitz, Dawn Lille. *Michel Fokine.* Boston, 1985.
Lomax, Sondra. "Fokine's Manifesto and *Les Sylphides.*" In *New Directions in Dance,* edited by Diana Theodores Taplin. Toronto, 1979.
Maynard, Olga. *"Les Sylphides." Dance Magazine* (December 1971): 44–63.
Vaughan, David. "Fokine in the Contemporary Repertory." *Ballet Review* 7.2–3 (1978–1979): 19–27.

INTERVIEWS: Alexandra Danilova and Nathalie Krassovska, by Sondra Lomax.

Sᴏɴᴅʀᴀ Lᴏᴍᴀx

SYLVIA. Full French title: *Sylvia, ou La Nymphe de Diane.* Ballet in three acts and four scenes. Choreography: Louis Mérante. Music: Léo Delibes. Libretto: Jules Barbier and Baron de Reinach, based on the pastoral play *Aminta* by Torquato Tasso. Scenery and costumes: Jules Cheret, August Rubé, Philippe Chaperon, and Eugène Lacoste. First performance: 14 June 1876, Théâtre de l'Opéra, Paris. Principals: Rita Sangalli (Sylvia), Louis Mérante (Aminta), Louise Marquet (Diana), Marie Sanlaville (Eros), and Francesco Magri (Orion).

Synopsis. The nymph Sylvia and her companions discover the sleeping shepherd Aminta while they are slaking their thirst at a stream. The shepherd falls in love with Sylvia. She feels that the love of a mere mortal is unworthy of a nymph, and she aims an arrow at a statue of Eros, god of love, erected near the site. The arrow wounds Aminta, who is trying to protect the god. The statue comes to life and shoots an arrow of his own, wounding Sylvia in turn. Disturbed, she remains alone while her companions go off. Orion, the Dark Hunter, who has desired Sylvia for a long time, arrives at that moment, surprises her, and carries her off. Meanwhile, an old witch has been taking care of Aminta, who is able to set out in pursuit of the nymph, thanks to instructions given him by Eros.

In the second act, Sylvia is a prisoner in Orion's cave. She gets Orion drunk, then tries unsuccessfully to flee. She prays to Eros to come to her assistance. The grotto disappears, and the discouraged shepherd is seen sitting on a rock. In the third act, thanks to the efforts of Eros, Sylvia is restored to Aminta. But Orion comes looking for her. In despair, the lovers beg the protection of Diana. Orion is then killed by the goddess, who remains unbending when the young couple try to obtain her forgiveness. Diana softens, however, when Eros pleads for them, in-voking the memory of Diana and Endymion. She pardons them, and there is general rejoicing.

History. In 1876 the Théâtre de l'Opéra was relatively new, and Olivier Halanzier, the director, was eager to mount new productions. The authors of the book for *Sylvia* contacted Léo Delibes, who prepared an outline of the score in collaboration with the choreographer and the star dancer. Some pieces were written several times, as for *Coppélia*, which is why the score follows the scenic action so closely. The best-known sections include the *valse lente* in the first act; the grotto scene, in which violincellos and bassoons evoke the passion of the hunter; the brilliant bacchanal at the beginning of the third act; the famous pizzicato, to which the veiled Sylvia reveals her identity to Aminta; the *pas* of the slaves, in which the drum punctuates the melody of the woodwinds; Sylvia's waltz variation; and the somber passage expressing Diana's anger. The score of *Sylvia* is one of the most homogeneous and complete in the repertory. Petr Ilich Tchaikovsky was fond of saying that if he had known the music of *Sylvia*, he

SYLVIA. Frederick Ashton mounted his version of *Sylvia* for the Sadler's Wells Ballet in 1952, with Margot Fonteyn in the title role and Michael Somes as Aminta. Robin and Christopher Ironside designed the elaborate scenery and costumes. (Photograph from the Dance Collection, New York Public Library for the Performing Arts.)

would never have dared to compose *Swan Lake* (Mannoni, 1982, p. 112). Delibes used it as the source for a very graceful orchestral suite. [*See the entry on Delibes.*]

Sylvia remained in the repertory of the Paris Opera until 1893. Although less gifted than his predecessor Arthur Saint-Léon, Louis Mérante was nevertheless a competent partner for Rita Sangalli, and as a soloist he was fully able to perform variations of a high degree of virtuosity. Rosita Mauri succeeded Sangalli in 1892, but her physique was not very suitable for the character. A fire destroyed the sets in 1894, and the ballet disappeared from the repertory for more than twenty years. It was restaged in 1919 under Léo Staats, with Carlotta Zambelli as Sylvia, Albert Aveline as Aminta, and Staats himself in the expanded role of Orion. Zambelli was an ideal Sylvia, and her name remains permanently connected with the role, which she danced until 1929. A new and shorter version was created in 1941 by Serge Lifar and was danced by Suzanne Lorcia, Solange Schwarz, and Lycette Darsonval.

In 1946, Albert Aveline, a teacher at the Paris Opera Ballet School, restaged the ballet following Mérante's original choreography. He sought Zambelli's help in refreshing his memory of the version they had danced in 1919. Zambelli herself passed on the pizzicato variation to her students. At the premiere in November 1946, Lycette Darsonval again danced the title role and again showed the brilliant pointe work for which she was famous. More than thirty years later, in November 1979, with the help of Violette Verdy, then dance director of the Opera, Darsonval reconstructed Aveline's staging and mounted *Sylvia* with sets and costumes by Bernard Daydé and with Noëlla Pointois, Jean-Yves Lormeau, and Cyril Atanassoff in the principal roles. [*See the entry on Darsonval.*]

Outside France, *Sylvia* has been mounted by numerous choreographers. It was produced in Vienna in 1877 and in Berlin in 1884. In 1886, Giorgio Saracco mounted it at the Teatro alla Scala in Milan, with Carlotta Brianza in the title role. In Saint Petersburg the production mounted by Lev Ivanov in 1901 at the Maryinsky Theater was notable not only for the performance of Olga Preobrajenska as Sylvia but for the dispute that led to Serge Diaghilev's resignation from the theater staff. In London an abridged version was presented in 1911 at the Empire Theatre with choreography by Fred Farren and with Lydia Kyasht in the principal role.

In the United States, George Balanchine, who was very fond of the music, created his *Sylvia: Pas de Deux* for the New York City Ballet in 1950, using the *valse lente* from act 1 and the pas de deux from act 3. In costumes designed by Barbara Karinska, the original performers were Maria Tallchief and Nicholas Magallanes. This showpiece was frequently televised and was later staged, sometimes with the choreography credited to André Eglevsky, for numerous companies in the United States and Canada.

In England, Frederick Ashton staged a complete version of *Sylvia* for the Sadler's Wells Ballet in September 1952, with sets and costumes by Robin and Christopher Ironside. The original cast featured Margot Fonteyn as Sylvia, Michael Somes as Aminta, John Hart as Orion, and Alexander Grant as Eros. The noted historian and critic Cyril Beaumont disliked this production but acknowledged that Fonteyn's performance of "the well-known Polka Pizzicato, concluding with a series of accelerated *coupés jetés posés sur la pointe* travelled on a straight line, is theatrically effective" (Beaumont, 1954, p. 36).

In later years *Sylvia* continued to be mounted by various choreographers around the globe. László Seregi's version, originally staged at the Budapest Opera in 1972, was mounted for the Zurich Ballet in 1976. Lycette Darsonval's version was mounted for the National Ballet of China in Beijing in 1980, and Balanchine's pas de deux was staged for the Matsuyama Ballet in Tokyo in 1981.

BIBLIOGRAPHY

Balanchine, George, with Francis Mason. *Balanchine's Complete Stories of the Great Ballets.* Rev. and enl. ed. Garden City, N.Y., 1977.
Beaumont, Cyril W. *Complete Book of Ballets.* Rev. ed. London, 1951.
Beaumont, Cyril W. *Ballets of Today: Being a Second Supplement to the Complete Book of Ballets.* London, 1954.
Guest, Ivor. "*Sylvia*, from Mérante to Ashton." *Ballet Annual* 8 (1954): 67–72.
Macdonald, Nesta. "Hijacked." *Dance and Dancers* (January–February 1992): 19–22.
Mannoni, Gérard. *Grands ballets de l'Opéra de Paris.* Paris, 1982.
Vaughan, David. *Frederick Ashton and His Ballets.* London, 1977.

MONIQUE BABSKY
Translated from French

SYMPHONIC BALLET. *See the entry on Léonide Massine.*

SYMPHONIC VARIATIONS. Ballet in one act. Choreography: Frederick Ashton. Music: César Franck, Symphonic Variations for Piano and Orchestra (1885). Scenery and costumes: Sophie Fedorovitch. First performance: 24 April 1946, Royal Opera House, Covent Garden, London, Sadler's Wells Ballet. Principals: Margot Fonteyn, Pamela May, Moira Shearer, Michael Somes, Brian Shaw, Henry Danton.

Ashton's original scheme for *Symphonic Variations* included a blend of spiritual ideas—divine love, a mystical marriage, and the cycle of the seasons. As he began the choreography, however, he became anxious to eliminate all traces of such material. In reaction against the literary or symbolic content of much British choreography of the day, he wished to demonstrate that "the subject of ballet is dancing." For him, therefore, *Symphonic Variations* became a testament, emphasizing dance values, formal organization, harmonious coordination, and musicality.

The six dancers never leave the stage, although some or all of them often stand on its borders. The ground patterns complement the linear geometries of Sophie Fedorovitch's backdrop. The six dancers begin spaced about the perimeters of the stage, with one foot crossed over the other and resting on *pointe tendue*. This stance and some *ports de bras* in the opening dance for the women become choreographic motifs. Further elaborations build up in a sequence of quartets, duets, sextets, and solos. The ballet's musicality also moves from ritualistic simplicity to subtle counterpoint.

To its early audiences, sequences involving the three women and leading danseur evoked memories of *Les Sylphides* and *Apollo;* the critic A. V. Coton considered *Symphonic Variations* to be, after those two, the century's third masterpiece of plotless ballet. Its refinement of English style was emphasized by the casting of three ballerinas of the utmost accomplishment; all three danced Aurora in *The Sleeping Beauty* at that time. The avoidance of hierarchy, the concern with stage geometries, and the incorporation of both academic ballet and simple movements such as running, were typical Ashton characteristics.

Symphonic Variations was also a test of stamina and stylistic purity that made new demands, especially on the male dancers. The original cast was greatly admired, particularly Margot Fonteyn for her radiance and tranquility within the harmonious ensemble. The ballet was widely considered the Royal Ballet's signature work for many years.

BIBLIOGRAPHY

Ashton, Frederick. "A Conversation with Clement Crisp." In *Dance as a Theatre Art,* edited by Selma Jeanne Cohen. New York, 1974.

Buckle, Richard. Interview with Ashton. *Ballet* 4.5 (1947).

Fonteyn, Margot. *Margot Fonteyn: Autobiography.* London, 1975.

Rigby, Cormac. "A Ballet of Perfect Englishness." *Dance Now* 1 (Winter 1992–1993): 22–27.

Vaughan, David. *Frederick Ashton and His Ballets.* London, 1977.

ALASTAIR MACAULAY

SYMPHONY IN C. Original title: *Le Palais de Cristal.* Ballet in four movements. Choreography: George Balanchine. Music: Georges Bizet; Symphony no. 1 in C Major. Scenery and costumes: Léonor Fini. First performance: 28 July 1947, Théâtre National de l'Opéra, Paris Opera Ballet. Principals: Lycette Darsonval, Alexandre Kalioujny; Tamara Toumanova, Roger Ritz; Micheline Bardin, Michel Renault; Madeleine Lafon, Max Bozzoni. Restaged as *Symphony in C:* 22 March 1948, City Center of Music and Drama, New York, Ballet Society. Lighting: Jean Rosenthal. Principals: Maria Tallchief, Nicholas Magallanes; Tanaquil Le Clercq, Francisco Moncion; Beatrice Tompkins, Herbert Bliss; Elise Reiman, John Taras.

The original title of Balanchine's opulent ballet to Bizet's first symphony, *Le Palais de Cristal,* was singularly apt, for this work is indeed a palatial construction, exhibiting a crystalline purity of design and an unashamedly ornate ballet vocabulary. Mounted on the Paris Opera Ballet, it paid tribute to the grandeur of the Opera's heritage while forging ahead by fully exploiting the resources of classical technique. Léonor Fini's scenery included a staircase, balconies, galleries, and gargoyles, creating the kind of elaborate setting to which Parisian audiences had been long accustomed. Somewhat unexpected, however, were Fini's costumes for the women, which were not classical tutus but flowing dresses in jewel tones of red, brown, green, and yellow. The cast was huge, consisting of the eight principals, two demi-soloist couples in each movement, and a corps de ballet of six women in each movement, for a total of forty-eight. Lycette Darsonval danced the sparkling first movement, and Tamara Toumanova, a woman of almost unearthly beauty, performed the pivotal adagio in the second movement.

When Balanchine transferred the work to Ballet Society, his own company in New York, he staged a streamlined version, dispensing with the elaborate setting and using fewer dancers, who doubled in the corps from movement to movement. At the premiere of this production, in March 1948, the featured ballerinas in the first and second movements were Maria Tallchief and Tanaquil Le Clercq. On 11 October 1948, *Symphony in C,* as the work was then called, was performed on the first program of the New York City Ballet, along with *Concerto Barocco* and *Orpheus,* at New York's City Center of Music and Drama. A new production was mounted in 1950 with spectacular women's costumes designed by Barbara Karinska: shimmering tutus of ivory satin and tulle, accented by headpieces of jewels and flowers. By 1971 the growth of the company had allowed expansion of the cast to a total of fifty-two.

Symphony in C is as elegant and as grandly proportioned as its score, written when its prodigiously talented composer was only seventeen years old, in 1855. The first two movements are designed to present the talents of two quite different ballerinas, the first commanding, the second ethereal and expansive. The demanding "Scottish" folk dance in the third movement calls for parallel unison dancing by the principal couple. All cast members join forces in the fourth movement, a recapitulative climactic finale. The corps de ballet forms a three-sided frame around the soloists and demi-soloists, whose unison dancing builds to a powerful crescendo of movement, as the music rises in key and as row upon row of dancers enters into the joyous conclusion of the work.

Over the years, *Symphony in C* has wielded a strong influence on dancers and has been a significant work in the history of New York City Ballet. Jerome Robbins, for instance, was so impressed by a performance of it in 1949 that he asked to join the company. Other dancers found in it roles perfectly suited to their particular talents. Patricia McBride and Merrill Ashley both gave memorable bravura performances in the dizzying sequences of the first movement; Edward Villella, John Clifford, Ethan Stiefel, and Peter Boal have been outstanding among many male dancers who have bounded happily through the exuberant third movement.

It is, however, in the renowned adagio of the second movement that a number of ballerinas made an indelible impression, among them Allegra Kent, Mimi Paul, and Suzanne Farrell, who danced it in her first performance upon returning to the company in 1975 after a five-year absence, and again, as a memorial to Balanchine, on the day of his death, 30 April 1983. Others who have shone in the role include the Danish dancer Mona Vangsaae, who was partnered by Erik Bruhn in the 1953 production in Copenhagen; the French ballerina Sylvie Guillem, who danced in a revival of *Le Palais de Cristal* by the Paris Opera Ballet in 1986; and the Georgian dancer Nina Ananiashvili, who appeared as a guest artist with New York City Ballet in 1988.

Symphony in C remains a part of the permanent repertory of New York City Ballet. It has also been mounted for La Scala Ballet, the Royal Swedish Ballet, the Dutch National Ballet, the Hamburg Ballet, the German Opera Ballet (Berlin), the Rome Opera Ballet, the Stuttgart Ballet, the Hungarian State Opera Ballet, the Zurich Ballet, the Royal Ballet (London), and numerous regional companies in the United States.

BIBLIOGRAPHY

Balanchine, George, with Francis Mason. *Balanchine's Complete Stories of the Great Ballets.* Rev. and enl. ed. Garden City, N.Y., 1977.

Barnes, Clive. "Balanchine: Mercilessly Inquisitive." *New York Times* (23 November 1975).

Barnes, Clive. "The Danish Festival." *Dance and Dancers* 5 (July 1954): 13–15.

Barzel, Ann, et al. "A Symposium." *Ballet Annual* 7 (1953): 63–75.

Choreography by George Balanchine: A Catalogue of Works. New York, 1984.

Kaplan, Larry. "Corps Choreography by Balanchine." *Ballet Review* 15 (Winter 1988): 64–75.

Kirstein, Lincoln. *Thirty Years: The New York City Ballet.* New York, 1978.

Reynolds, Nancy. *Repertory in Review: Forty Years of the New York City Ballet.* New York, 1977.

Scholl, Tim. *From Petipa to Balanchine: Classical Revival and the Modernization of Ballet.* New York, 1994.

Terry, Walter. Review. *New York Herald Tribune* (23 March 1948).

NOTATED SCORES. *Symphony in C,* Benesh notation documented by Jürg Lanzrein (1973). *Symphony in C,* Labanotation documented by Ann Hutchinson Guest (1948), held in the Dance Notation Bureau.

FILM. *Lincoln Center Day* (1963) presents the second and fourth movements of the ballet, available in the Dance Collection, New York Public Library for the Performing Arts.

REBA ANN ADLER

SZEGED CONTEMPORARY BALLET. The youngest of the four full-time companies of Hungary, the Szeged Contemporary Ballet adopted its present name in 1993. Its history goes back to 1946, however, when Károly Zsedényi, solo dancer of the Budapest Opera, staged *Schéhérazade;* the following year he staged *Coppélia* and Gyula Harangozó's *Scene in the Inn.* Full-evening ballets could also be staged since many of the dancers came from the Kolozsvár (today Cluj) Opera. The company functioned under ballet director György Lőrinc until 1949, when he staged Belá Bartók's *The Miraculous Mandarin.*

In 1958, classically trained dancers formed the company of the Szeged National Theater with compositions by guest choreographers in styles that deviated somewhat from the academic. Zoltán Imre started his dancing and creative career with his 1966 *Metamorphosis,* to music by Endre Szervánszky, and his 1968 *Combat of Forms,* to music by Johann Sebastian Bach. For economic reasons, the staff slowly departed and Imre left the country.

In 1986, after the reconstruction of the theater, writer and manager Roland Bokor re-launched the company with dancers trained in a variety of styles; he then called Imre back from abroad to supervise the repertory. Imre conveyed his knowledge of such contemporary techniques as Martha Graham's and José Limón's to his dancers and, in 1987, organized a "Night of Hungarian Choreographers Working Abroad." He staged György Vámos's *Rhapsody,* to music by Sergei Rachmaninov; Ferenc Barbay's *Firebird—A Pas de Deux,* to music by Igor Stravinsky and Tomita; Zoltán Imre's *Woman's Love— Woman's Fate,* to music by Robert Schumann; and Imre's *The Demon,* to music by Robert Wittinger. The multifaceted stylistic training of the dancers even made them suitable for performing dances in musicals such as Eva Reinthaller's *Jesus Christ Superstar* and Gyula Harangozó's *Polovtsian Dances* from *Prince Igor* in 1988. Their first important tour was to the Babylon Festival, and their repertory was enlarged with Saad Munir Bashir's piece *Ishtar,* to his own music. László Seregi taught them Leonard Bernstein's musical *On the Town,* and there were two premieres—György Krámer's *The Wind Is Rising,* to music by István Márta, and Imre's ballet to Giovanni Pergolesi's *Stabat Mater.*

Imre staged his *Infernal Games* in memory of Jean Cocteau to a montage of Claudio Monteverdi and Aleksandr Scriabin, the hit of the season in December 1989, which gave young Tamás Juronics the chance of scoring a great success as the principal (he is now head of the company). At the end of the same season, the chamber theater gave its stage to a triple bill with Matthew Hawkins' *The Fruits of Labour,* the music consisting of Scottish folk songs; Imre's *The Medium,* an Alban Berg and Arnold Schoenberg montage; and Krámer's *Exodus,* to music by

W. Kylar. This essentially constituted a second stage for ballet.

In 1990 Imre created the Szeged Studio Ballet, which functioned until 1993 and produced contemporary ballets like Tamás Juronics's 1990 *Dances Born from Need,* set to folk music and 1991's *The Reminiscences of a Hardly Used Clothes Line,* to a musical montage. Both hits were incorporated in the repertory of the big theatre. The other premieres of the 1990/91 season included Katalin Lőrinc's *Tatyana and the Others,* to music by Tchaikovsky, and Jorma Uotinen's *Beyond Dreams,* to a musical montage. Open to foreign influences and exposed to the creative impetus of Juronics, the Studio Ballet closed its 1992/93 season with ballets, including Imre's *Dream about Kafka,* to music by Alban Berg; Yvette Bozsik's *Expectation,* to music by Erik Satie; Juronics's *Our Cell,* to music by Maurice Jarre; Bertrand d'At's *The Night,* to a modern montage; and Roberto Galvan's *Concerto for Piano, Accordion and Orchestra,* to music by Astor Piazzola.

The company started the 1993/94 season under the name of Szeged Contemporary Ballet, headed by Tamás Juronics but under the dominating choreographic personality of Roberto Galvan. Their first night in November 1993 included Juronics's *Croquis,* to music by Arvo Pärt and Galvan's *Requiem,* to music by Mozart. Since then, mainly foreign guest artists have choreographed for the company.

BIBLIOGRAPHY

Dienes, Gedeon. "Balett vidéken 1945 és 1985 között." In *A szinpadi tánc története Magyarországon,* edited by Gedeon Dienes and L. Fuchs, Budapest.

Körtvélyes, Géza. "Korszerű tendenciák a magyar táncműsészetben 1957 ésö 1977 köztt. In *Tánctudányi tanulmányck 1978–1979,* edited by Gedeon Dienes and E. Pesovár. Budapest, 1979.

Kővágó, Zsuzsa. "Szegedi Balett 1987–1993." In *Fordulatok. Hungarian Theatres 1994.* Jászberény, 1994.

Lőrinc, Katalin. "Szegedi Kortárs Balett 1993–1995." In *Magyar táncművészet 1990 és 1995 között.* Budapest, 1996.

Vitáni, Iván. "Uj törekvések a magyar balettművészetben." In *Tánctudományi tanulmányok 1969–1970,* edited by Gedeon Dienes and L. Maácz. Budapest, 1970.

ZSUZSA KŐVÁGÓ

T

TAGLIONI FAMILY, family of Italian dancers, choreographers, and ballet masters of the late eighteenth and nineteenth centuries. One of the great dancing dynasties, their lives were closely intertwined with those of other leading dancers and choreographers of the day. Most of the family were well traveled, though the men eventually settled down to establish their own spheres of influence: Carlo and Salvatore in Italy (the later particularly in Naples), Filippo in Warsaw, and Paul in Berlin. All the men choreographed original ballets, as did at least one of the women, the elder Marie. The most notable members were Carlo Taglioni; his children Filippo, Salvatore, Giuseppa, and Louise; Filippo's children Marie and Paul; Salvatore's daughter Louise; and Paul's daughter Marie.

Carlo Taglioni (born c.1750 in Turin), dancer and choreographer. Little is known about the early life of Carlo Taglioni. He began to dance, usually in the grotesque genre, in various Italian cities during the 1770s. In 1774 and 1775 he appeared in his native Turin in dances arranged by Innocenzo Gambuzzi for the operas *Merope* and *Alcina e Ruggiero;* he also danced in Gambuzzi's works in Milan in 1778. He performed in the serious or noble genre in Venice in 1782, where he danced in the ballets of Gaspero Angiolini. He worked in Rome in 1785–1786, at the same time as Salvatore Viganò.

Although Carlo Taglioni may have started to choreograph in the 1770s, his early works have fallen into obscurity. He created *Il Villano Rincivilito, ossia Il Barone Molletta di Rocca Antica,* a comic ballet, in Florence in 1790, following it with *Li Due Sindaci, ossia La Vendemmia* (The Two Mayors, or The Grape Harvest) in Lucca during the same year. In Venice, where he worked as a choreographer from 1796 to 1798, he mounted *La Scuola Olandese, ossia L'Amante in Statua* (The Dutch School, or The Statue of the Lover), *La Sposa Rapita* (The Abducted Bride), *La Recluta con Ingano* (The Deceived Recruit), and other ballets.

Carlo Taglioni made several trips to Paris to recruit French dancers for Italian companies. There he choreographed ballets for the Gaîté and Porte-Saint-Martin theaters in the early 1800s. According to Lillian Moore (1938), he had Bonapartist connections: he taught dancing to Joachim Murat's corps of pages in Naples, then went to Paris at the request of Lucien Bonaparte "to infuse new life into the ballet of the Italian opera."

Carlo Taglioni married Maria Petracchi, who may have danced under her married name, Maria Taglioni, thus becoming the first bearer of an exalted name in dance history. Of their five children, two sons (Filippo and Salvatore) and both daughters (Giuseppa and Louise) became dancers.

Giuseppa Taglioni (born c.1780 in Turin), dancer and choreographer. Beyond the fact that she made her debut at the Teatro La Fenice in Venice in 1797 and probably toured with her father and brothers in Italy, little is known about Giuseppa. A renowned beauty, she retired early to marry the Venetian count Antonio Contarini.

Louise Taglioni (also known as Luisa or Luigia; born c.1785), dancer. The first of two dancers of that name, she studied with Jean-François Coulon in Paris and is said to have made her debut at the Opera with her brother Filippo in 1799 in the opera *La Caravane.* Her roles at the Opera included Terpsichore in *Psyché* and Eucharis in *Télémaque,* both choreographed by Pierre Gardel; she also danced a featured role in Louis-Jacques Milon's *Les Noces de Gamache* (1801). In 1827, when her niece Marie made her Opera debut, the journal *Le réunion* published a letter that affectionately recalled Louise as "fresh, affable, and as light as a sylphide" (quoted by Guest, 1980).

Louise Taglioni resigned from the Opera in 1806 when her brother Salvatore's exorbitant contractual demands (which had included a promotion and raise in salary for Louise) were turned down by the administration. She accompanied him to Lyon, where she met and married Count Aimé Dubourg and consequently retired from the stage.

Salvatore Taglioni (born 1789 in Palermo, died 1868 in Naples), dancer, choreographer, and teacher. Carlo's son Salvatore also studied with Coulon in Paris, where he made his Opera debut in 1806. Vaillat (1942) stated that he was of medium height and very well made, and would have been handsome if not for a turned-up nose and chin. He was not engaged by the Opera because of his inflated demands, which included three months' vacation and the right to dance what he chose and to choreograph his own steps. He and Louise went to Lyon, where he married the dancer Adélaïde Perrault (or Perraud), who appeared in his ballets.

TAGLIONI FAMILY. Louise Taglioni the younger (1823–1893), depicted in a *divertissement* from Halévy's opera *Le Juif Errant* (1852). Arthur Saint-Léon choreographed it for her to a *grande valse brillante* by Friedrich Burgmüller. (Courtesy of Madison U. Sowell and Debra H. Sowell, Brigham Young University, Provo, Utah.)

A prolific choreographer, Salvatore Taglioni did most of his work in Naples, with some at the Teatro alla Scala in Milan and in Turin. In 1812 he and Louis Henry founded the school of ballet at the Teatro San Carlo in Naples at the order of Joachim Murat, then king of Naples. Salvatore taught the *classe de perfectionnement*, a position he held for most of his life. As his first choreographic assignment, Salvatore restaged Jean Dauberval's *La Fille Mal Gardée* in Naples. Many of his early works were in the fashionable mythological or historical mode. *La Conquista di Malacca, ossia I Portoghesi nell'Indie* (The Conquest of Malacca, or The Portuguese in the Indies; 1819), *Castore e Polluce* (1820), *Sesostri* (1823), and *Tippoo-Saeb* (1823).

In 1826 Fanny and Thérèse Elssler danced in Salvatore's ballets in Naples. Fanny played Briseis in his mythological ballet *L'Ira di Achille* (The Wrath of Achilles) and also appeared in *Alcibiade*. Both sisters performed in *Acbar Gran Mogul*, which Salvatore completed after the death of its original choreographer, Gaetano Gioja.

In 1832 Salvatore choreographed one of his best-known ballets, *Romanow*. This historical ballet was noted for its use of horses on stage, particularly in a scene where a young Russian girl on horseback jumped from a bridge.

The Neapolitan ballerina Fanny Cerrito probably studied with Salvatore and gained performing experience in his works of the 1830s, among them the Chinese ballet *L'Ombra di Tsi-Ven, ossia La Costanza Premiata* (The Shade of Tsi-Ven, or Loyalty Rewarded). She and Carlotta Grisi respectively played the roles of Iris and Amor in Salvatore's *Amore e Psiche*. Jules Perrot, soon to become Grisi's mentor and lover, partnered Amalia Brugnoli in Salvatore's *Il Ritorno di Ulisse* in 1836; Grisi was also a member of the cast.

Salvatore's ballet *Faust* (1838) earned acclaim in Naples ten years before Perrot's treatment of the same theme at La Scala. Brugnoli returned to dance in his fantasy-ballet *Nadan, o L'Orgoglio Punito* (Nadan, or Pride Punished, 1839), in which Salvatore's daughter Louise also appeared. The historical ballet *Marco Visconti* and the romantic *La Foresta d'Hermanstadt* (both 1841), were also admired. Gustave Carey, a member of another famous dancing dynasty, choreographed sequences in both ballets. One of Perrot's earliest choreographic efforts, a pas de deux for himself and Grisi, was inserted into Salvatore's *Il Rajah de Benares* (1841).

In the first volume of *My Theatre Life*, published in 1848, August Bournonville called Salvatore Taglioni "the finest living ballet composer in Italy." He singled out for praise *Romanow*, *Ettore Fieramosca*, and *Marco Visconti*.

In 1854 Salvatore choreographed *Hulda*, with a libretto by his son-in-law Alexandre Fuchs and a pas de deux by Louis Mérante, a future ballet master at the Paris Opera. He continued his association with Carey, who collaborated with him on restagings of Giovanni Casati's *Shakespeare* (1855) and Perrot's *La Filleule des Fées*, which they retitled *Isaura* (1856).

Salvatore continued to choreograph until the early 1860s. Among his last ballets were *Rita* and *Il Figlio dello Shak*, both produced in Naples.

Louise Taglioni (born 13 March 1823 in Naples, died April 1893 in Cufrofiano [Lecce]), dancer and choreographer. Salvatore's daughter Louise became the second Louise Taglioni to dance at the Paris Opera. She probably began her career in Naples, where she danced in her father's ballet *Nadan, o L'Orgoglio Punito* in 1839. In 1841 she danced with Bournonville in two excerpts from his ballets, the *grand pas de deux* from *Waldemar* and the *bolero* from *The Toreador*.

By 1846 Louise the younger had traveled north to London, where she appeared in Perrot's ballets at Her Majesty's Theatre. Reviews of her London debut as Venus in the *pas de modèles* of *Catarina* noted her "grace, distinction and modesty of manner" and her "poetry of motion" (quoted by Guest, 1984). She danced in the pas de neuf in *Lalla Rookh* and played one of the three Graces in *Le Jugement de Pâris*, in which her renowned cousin, the elder Marie, took a leading role. Louise also played Gian-nina, the hero's mortal sweetheart, in a revival of Perrot's *Ondine*, and took the leading female role in Perrot's *Un Bal sous Louis XIV*, with Lucile Grahn, *en travesti*, as her cavalier.

Louise Taglioni the younger was engaged by the Paris Opera in 1848, making her debut in a solo in Auguste Mabille's *Nisida;* however, she returned to London for guest engagements at Covent Garden every year between 1849 and 1851. Among the roles she created at the Opera were the benevolent Pink Fairy in Perrot's *La Filleule des Fées;* Louiselle, who ultimately relinquishes her fiancé to the eponymous heroine of Arthur Saint-Léon's *Stella* (1850); one of the Graces in Joseph Mazilier's *Aelia et Mysis* (1853); and the bride Marietta in Cerrito's *Gemma* (1854). With Nadezdha Bogdanova, she led Saint-Léon's *divertissement Les Abeilles* in Fromenthal Halévy's opera *Le Juif Errant* (1852), and she played Effie when Saint-Léon revived *La Sylphide* in 1852. Around 1850 she married Alexandre Fuchs, also a dancer at the Opera, and she occasionally danced under the name Taglioni-Fuchs.

In 1855 the younger Louise appeared at the National Theater in New York City, performing Irish and Scottish character dances, including a solo to "Comin' through the Rye." After leaving the Paris Opera with her husband in 1857, she became the director of a school of theatrical dancing in Naples. She retired from this position after her husband's death.

Filippo Taglioni (also known as Philippe; born 5 November 1777 in Milan, died 11 September 1871 in Como), dancer and choreographer. Filippo was Carlo's eldest son and, after his own daughter Marie, the best-known member of the clan. He may have appeared on stage as early as 1783, playing a cupid; by the mid-1790s he was playing female roles *en travesti* in various Italian cities. In 1799 he went to Paris to study with Coulon, and he is said to have made his Opera debut with his sister Louise in the opera *La Caravane*. According to Léandre Vaillat (1942), however, his debut came about by chance, much as Marie Camargo's had in an earlier day: he went on at the last minute to replace an indisposed *premier danseur*. During his engagement at the Opera he danced in Milon's *Les Noces de Gamache* and in Gardel's *La Dansomanie* and *Le Retour de Zéphire*. Despite his popularity, however, he left the Opera in 1802 to assume the position of *premier danseur* and ballet master in Stockholm.

This decision had historic consequences for ballet, for in Stockholm Filippo Taglioni met and married Edwige Sofia Karsten, the daughter of a Swedish opera singer. The couple moved to Vienna when their daughter Marie was barely a year old, and Filippo first tried his hand at choreography there, restaging Gardel's *La Dansomanie*.

Although Filippo's family accompanied him to Kassel, where he served as *premier danseur* and ballet master under King Jerome of Westphalia, he left them behind when he went to Italy in 1816, and they subsequently settled in Paris. During the late 1810s Filippo worked in Munich, Stockholm, Copenhagen, Hamburg, and Berlin, as well as in various Italian cities. Bournonville saw him dance during this period and praised his virtuosity. By 1819 Filippo had established himself in Vienna, where he assumed the post of ballet master at the Hoftheater (Court Theater) after the departure of Jean-Louis Aumer in 1821. That year he choreographed *Das Schweizer Milchmädchen* (The Swiss Milkmaid), a ballet that he revived repeatedly under several different names in the 1830s.

Filippo's family joined him in Vienna in 1821, and he began to prepare Marie for her debut. Filippo's wife had misled him as to the extent of Marie's progress under Coulon in Paris, and when Marie arrived in Vienna Filippo discovered that she was far from ready to dance on stage. He immediately set her to work for six hours a day, concentrating on different aspects of ballet technique. In later life Marie attributed her success to her father's rigorous teaching. The style he instilled in her emphasized elevation, effortlessness, fluidity, and suppleness. In addition, he demanded of his daughter a modest and well-bred demeanor that Louis Véron, the director of the Paris Opera, later contrasted favorably with the coquettish behavior encouraged by the teaching of Auguste Vestris.

By June 1822 Filippo deemed Marie ready to dance in public and choreographed the ballet in which she made her debut, *La Réception d'une Jeune Nymphe à la Cour de Terpsichore*. He appeared in it himself in a pas de trois with her and Therese Heberle.

From that time until 1843 Filippo's fortunes were symbiotically linked with those of Marie. He had refined her technique and shaped her unique style. He traveled throughout Europe with her, advised her, negotiated her contracts, and used his insight as father and teacher to create ballets that would best display her special gifts.

Despite his preoccupation with his daughter, Filippo had other concerns. His own career as a dancer continued until the late 1820s or early 1830s. He sometimes danced with Marie: in Louis Henry's *Les Amazones*, which they performed in Vienna in 1823, she took him captive and dragged him off by his hair, to the great delight of the audience. Both of them were engaged as dancers in Stuttgart from 1824 to 1828, in a company that included Louise Pierson, Anton Stuhlmüller, Angelica Saint-Romain, and Filippo's son Paul. In 1831 father and daughter danced a minuet and gavotte at the King's Theatre in London.

Filippo also had to create works for other ballerinas. Fanny Elssler was a junior member of the Viennese company and danced in Filippo's *Lodoïska* in 1823. Amalia Brugnoli and Elise Vaque-Moulin, early exponents of the pointe technique, appeared as guest artists in Vienna. According to Winter (1974), iconographic evidence suggests that many of the female dancers in Filippo's Stuttgart company danced on pointe. Despite his use of this innovation, Winter continues, his choreography preserved an equality between male and female dancing.

Filippo took his family to Paris in 1824 in an attempt to obtain an engagement for Marie at the Opera, but he was unsuccessful. Although some sources state that Marie danced at the Théâtre de la Porte-Saint-Martin at this time, no evidence of this has been found (Guest, 1980). Filippo had to content himself with an engagement in Stuttgart, where in 1826 he choreographed the very popular *Danina, oder Jocko der Brasilianische Affe* (Danina, or Jocko the Brazilian Ape), inspired by Charles Mazurier's success in the similarly titled *Jocko, ou Le Singe du Brésil* at the Porte-Saint-Martin in 1825.

A personal friend of Filippo, Baron Laflèche, smoothed the way for a second attempt on the Opera in 1827. Filippo choreographed the dance, inserted into the ballet *Le Sicilien*, in which Marie first appeared before the Parisian public. She was awarded a contract, and Filippo was able

TAGLIONI FAMILY. Marie Taglioni's performance in *La Sylphide* (1832) is legendary for its ascendency on both the physical and spiritual planes. In this mezzotint, after an 1834 painting by Gabriel Lépaulle, Taglioni is pictured as the weightless Sylphide, gently resting beside the sleeping James. (Courtesy of Madison U. Sowell and Debra H. Sowell, Brigham Young University, Provo, Utah.)

to insist on the condition that she would dance only in his choreography.

After a final season in Stuttgart, Filippo's family moved to Paris in the spring of 1828 to take up Marie's new engagement. In 1830 Filippo choreographed her first great role, Zoloë in Daniel Auber's opera *Le Dieu et la Bayadère*. Marie had to mime as well as dance, and Filippo created an affecting dance of supplication before the god Brahmā. His *pas de shalls*, a formula much used by himself and others, proved to be surprisingly effective, particularly in the moment when the scarves of the dancing girls were arranged to make Marie resemble a Botticellian Venus standing on her scallop shell.

Filippo's and Marie's next triumph was the "Ballet of the Nuns" in Giacomo Meyerbeer's opera *Robert le Diable* (1831). Aided by the ghostly ambience of gas-lighting (introduced at the Opera less than a decade before), and by the opera's tale of supernatural beings and sensational events, Filippo wove a dance that blended fear and seduction. The dead nuns, led by Marie as their abbess Helena, rose from their tombs to abandon themselves to unholy revels in their ruined cloister.

This performance made such an impression on Adolphe Nourrit, the tenor who sang the role of Robert, that he conceived a ballet scenario for Marie. Filippo was the natural choice to choreograph this new ballet, *La Sylphide* (1832). In it he took Marie's greatest gifts—elevation, ease, and pointe work—and presented them within an otherworldly framework suggested by the "Ballet of the Nuns." For the first time, pointe work was justified as a means of poetic expression, and Filippo's choreography ensured that his daughter made the most of the opportunity. [See Sylphide, La.]

La Sylphide was the high point of Filippo's career; none of his other ballets would achieve its lasting fame. He continued, however, to choreograph new vehicles for Marie. *Nathalie*, presented at the Opera in November 1832, was a revival of *Das Schweizer Milchmädchen*, which Filippo had resurrected earlier that year as *Divertissement Suisse* in Berlin and *La Ressemblance* in London. Its simple story involved a farmer's daughter who is abducted by a lord and who expresses her love for him before his statue without noticing that the real lord has taken its place. All ends happily when he offers her honorable marriage.

Filippo's much-lauded dances in the ballroom scene of Auber's opera *Gustave* (1833) did not include Marie. He created amusing dances for ingeniously costumed couples, and an intoxicating galop for one hundred and twenty-two performers ended the scene. Louis Henry, however, accused Filippo of plagiarizing it from a ballet Henry had produced in Milan in 1830.

Henry's accusations followed Filippo to his next ballet, *La Révolte au Sérail* (1833), allegedly taken from Henry's *Les Amazones*, which Filippo and Marie had danced in Vienna. As Zulma in her father's ballet, Marie incited a harem to revolt against its master and led the women in military drills. One of the highlights was a pas de deux for her and the high-leaping Perrot.

Filippo's last ballet for the Opera, *La Fille du Danube* (1836), was considered a rehash of his earlier successes. Its complicated fairy-tale plot revolved around Fleur-des-Champs (Marie) and her lover Rudolph (Joseph Mazilier), who successfully identifies her among the water sprites of the Danube. The critics agreed that Marie's performance alone saved the ballet.

Filippo left the Opera in 1837 to accompany Marie to Saint Petersburg, where they played five seasons between 1837 and 1842. Some of the new ballets he choreographed for her there were subsequently restaged in the West. In *Miranda*, loosely based on Shakespeare's *The Tempest*, the daughter of the Good Genius wins the love of a shipwrecked Spaniard. *La Gitana*, the story of a girl abducted as a child by Gypsies, gave Marie the opportunity to perform the type of balleticized Spanish dances that had made Fanny Elssler's name. *L'Ombre* was a ghost story about a murdered girl who is ultimately reunited with her lover in death. Filippo's Russian works also included the pirate tale *L'Écumeur de Mer; Le Lac des Fées*, which was suggested by Tsar Nicholas I; and *Herta, la Reine des Elfrides*. In *Aglaë, ou L'Élève d'Amour*, which bore the same title as a ballet Filippo had first presented in Munich in the 1820s, Marie took a dancing lesson with Cupid, awakening the love of a youth and a faun.

The Russian seasons were interspersed with engagements in London and Milan. In 1843, however, Filippo and Marie apparently parted company. Filippo went to Warsaw, where he became the ballet master and director of the ballet company and school. He was also named a member of the directorate of government theaters in Warsaw. According to Janina Pudełek, he staged nine new ballets before his retirement in 1853, among them *Indian Morning, A Day at the Carnival in Venice, The Isle of the Amazons, The Lame Little Devil*, and *A Panorama of Naples*.

Filippo spent his final years in a villa on Lake Como. During a visit to Paris in 1860 he watched a rehearsal of Marie's ballet *Le Papillon*, which he criticized for not being in time, though he conceded that the dances were "well arranged and very pretty" (quoted by Guest, 1953–1955).

Marie Taglioni (born 23 April 1804 in Stockholm, died 22 April 1884 in Marseille), dancer and choreographer. Even though Marie may not have satisfied her father as a choreographer, she was matchless as a dancer. During her lifetime she became the standard by which other ballerinas were measured, and her name is still invoked today as an exemplar of the art.

Her 1822 debut in *La Réception d'une Jeune Nymphe à la*

TAGLIONI FAMILY. Marie Taglioni dancing the mazurka from Filippo Taglioni's *La Gitana* (1838). (Courtesy of Madison U. Sowell and Debra H. Sowell, Brigham Young University, Provo, Utah.)

Cour de Terpsichore, which took the form of a dancing lesson given by Terpsichore and her nymphs, required Marie to display her proficiency in all styles of dance—noble, *demi-caractère*, and comic. Fanny Elssler, who was destined to become her greatest rival, may have been among the corps at Marie's debut; she is listed as a Bacchante in the ballet's second performance.

In Vienna, Marie had the opportunity to observe the pointe technique of Brugnoli and Vaque-Moulin, and it is recorded that she rather waspishly remarked on the efforts Brugnoli made with her arms in order to stay on pointe. She probably learned to dance on pointe at this stage of her career, but the technique still held an odor of the circus; not until Filippo's *La Sylphide* would it be transformed into poetry.

During the 1820s Marie performed in Vienna, Munich, and Stuttgart in ballets by her father and other choreographers. She played Venus in Armand Vestris's *Psyché* and the eponymous heroine in her father's popular *Danina, oder Jocko der Brasilianische Affe*. For Filippo's *Aglaë, ou L'Élève d'Amour*, her mother made her a costume that was a prototype of her Sylphide tutu, white and diaphanous, with a ribbon girdle and a wreath of flowers in her hair.

Although her father failed in his first attempt in 1824 to get her an engagement at the Paris Opera, Marie was granted permission in 1827 to make the six debut performances required before a contract could be negotiated. She first appeared on 23 July in a pas de deux with her brother. It contained a considerable amount of pointe work, which was not entirely new to Paris, having been introduced in the 1810s by Geneviève Gosselin; however, combined with Marie's other qualities—lightness, fluidity, ease, and modesty—it made an indelible impression. She was hailed as the progenitor of a new style; her example inspired the other dancers to "taglionize," and the Opera awarded her a three-year contract.

Despite the public favor she had won at her debut, Marie was not always given principal roles during her first years at the Opera. Also, by the terms of her contract she was limited to her father's choreography. She pleased the audience, however, in dances such as "La Naïade" in Aumer's *Sleeping Beauty* and the "Tyrolienne" in Gioacchino Rossini's opera *Guillaume Tell*, both of which she performed throughout her career. In 1830 she danced in a revival of Charles-Louis Didelot's *Flore et Zéphire* in London and repeated her triumph in Paris the following year, with Perrot "the aerial" as her partner.

Marie's performance as Zoloë in *Le Dieu et la Bayadère* sealed her position as a leading ballerina of the Opera. Although she was considered disappointing in the mimed portions of the role, her father's choreography highlighted her special gifts as a dancer, presenting her as ethereal rather than sensual. The Opera awarded her a six-year contract, from 1831 to 1837. Between seasons she danced in London and Berlin, often in revivals of Parisian triumphs.

The crucial year of 1831 brought Marie the role of the ghostly yet enticing abbess Helena in *Robert le Diable*, which in turn led to the creation of *La Sylphide* (1832). Although this ballet is generally associated today with the use of the pointe technique, and Marie's name has come down in history as the dancer who gave artistic legitimacy to toe-dancing, Marie never regarded pointe work as an end in itself. It was simply part of an arsenal that included her supernal lightness and elasticity in steps of elevation (a quality that led critics to speak of her *ballonné* style); the ease and fluidity of her arm movements, which showed none of the strain for which she had criticized Brugnoli; and the effortlessness that characterized her dancing as a whole, earning her the sobriquet "Marie full of grace." These qualities made Marie's Sylphide the prototype of the ethereal, otherworldly heroines who began to take over the Opera in the 1830s, their pale and diaphanous costumes providing the name of a new genre, the "white ballet."

The fact that Marie's performances often salvaged her father's undistinguished choreography, such as that of *La Révolte au Sérail* and *La Fille du Danube,* did not go unnoticed by the critics. Charles de Boigne remarked, "All Father Taglioni's ballets are alike: a complete absence of ideas, second-hand stuff, always the same. . . . But the ballerina is there to rescue the choreographer, the daughter to rescue the father" (quoted by Guest, 1980). This working relationship continued when Marie left the Opera in 1837 on the expiration of her contract and went to dance in Saint Petersburg. There Filippo choreographed for her the ballet that enabled her to meet Elssler on her own ground, *La Gitana* (1838).

The rivalry between Marie and Elssler, who was six years younger, had developed gradually. Prior to Elssler's debut at the Opera in 1834, the two had shared stages in Vienna and London. By 1836, however, Elssler had perfected a style that many viewers considered antithetical to Marie's. Théophile Gautier's often-quoted comparison of the two as the "pagan" dancer (Elssler) and the "Christian" (Marie) succinctly describes the difference in their stage personalities, just as the opposition of the terms *taqueté* (Elssler) and *ballonné* (Marie) contrasts their technical styles: one exploited brilliant but earthbound steps, while the other emphasized lightness and elevation. The Opera's director, Véron, considered the rivalry good for business and encouraged the factionalism of the "Taglionists" and the "Elsslerists."

Marie, however, was no stranger to Elssler's specialty, character dancing, as her repeated performances of the "Tyrolienne" indicate. *La Gitana* gave her a mazurka and a Spanish dance in the style of Elssler's signature dance, the *cachucha*. She impressed her own qualities on the Spanish dance, which one observer described as "a succession of flying movements expressive of alarm" (quoted by Beaumont, 1937). *La Gitana* was a great success and long remained in her repertory.

Marie traveled widely in the late 1830s and the 1840s, appearing in Britain, Italy, Austria, Poland, France, Belgium, and her native Sweden. In 1841 she danced for the first time at La Scala, where she became embroiled in a rivalry with Fanny Cerrito in 1843. In the final years of her career she enjoyed a second spring of adulation at Her Majesty's Theatre in London, where she appeared in Perrot's *Pas de Quatre* (1845) and *Le Jugement de Pâris* (1846). She was undeniably the cynosure of these star-studded *divertissements*, and the other ballerinas (Grisi, Cerrito, and Grahn) unquestioningly deferred to her. Her performances in Perrot's one-act version of *La Sylphide* inspired the famous series of lithographs by Alfred Chalon, *La Sylphide: Souvenir d'adieu de Marie Taglioni* (1845). She gave her farewell performance in London on 21 August 1847, dancing in *Le Jugement de Pâris*.

Although her performing career had ended, Marie returned to the world of dance in 1858, soon after the debut of Emma Livry in *La Sylphide*. Livry, who reincarnated

Marie's own qualities as a dancer, became her protégée, and in 1860 Marie choreographed for her *Le Papillon,* a fairy tale of a girl who is magically transformed into a butterfly. Despite its complicated plot, the ballet was well received, and Marie had begun to rehearse a second work for Livry, *Zara,* when Livry's costume caught fire during a rehearsal, burning her severely. After her death some months later, a few attempts were made to produce *Zara* with other ballerinas, but this ballet was never realized.

In the meantime Marie had been appointed as *inspectrice de la danse* at the Opera and later as *professeur de la classe de perfectionnement.* These positions allowed her to institute certain reforms at the Opera, including a system of examinations (she sat on the first jury) for promotions within the ranks of the corps de ballet.

During the 1860s Marie lost her fortune (according to some sources, through Filippo's speculations). In 1870 she opened a school of ballroom dancing and deportment in London, where, as a former pupil recalled, she paid particular attention to graceful movements of the arms, curtsying, and the pointing of the toes. In 1880 she retired to Marseille to live with her son Georges. She was survived by him and by her daughter Eugénie-Marie-Edwige.

Paul Taglioni (born 12 January 1800 in Vienna, died 6 January 1884 in Berlin), dancer and choreographer. Paul studied dancing with his father Filippo and with Coulon, making his debut in Stuttgart in 1824 or 1825. He was engaged as a soloist in Vienna from 1826 to 1829, although in 1827 he partnered his sister Marie in her debut appearances at the Paris Opera. In 1829 he married the German ballerina Amalia Galster (c.1808–1881), who became his regular partner.

Although Paul danced in Paris and London in the early 1830s, by 1835 he had settled in Berlin, which became his home base. Some of his earliest ballets were choreographed there, among them *Amors Triumph* and *Der Arme Fischer* (both 1835), as well as his first major work, *Undine* (1836), which was based on Friedrich de La Motte-Fouqué's romance about a water nymph who falls in love with a knight.

Paul and Amalia accepted an engagement in the United States in 1839, appearing in New York, Baltimore, Philadelphia, Boston, and Providence. They made their American debut in New York's Park Theater on 22 May in the first full-length version of *La Sylphide* presented in the United States; their repertory also included *Undine* and Filippo's *Nathalie* and *Le Dieu et la Bayadère.* They were very well received; Paul's virtuosity was particularly admired, for good male dancers were rare in the United States at the time.

The *Spirit of the Times* (New York) described Paul as "Italian in appearance, wondrously well formed—limbs clean and sinewy like those of a race-horse, with a face which reminds you of the pictures of his famous sister,

particularly about the mouth" (quoted by Moore, 1942). The same journal later commented upon "his remarkable activity, and his muscular power," though it faulted him for lack of grace.

In 1841 Paul was asked to replace August Bournonville temporarily in Copenhagen, an engagement that ended in disaster when his restaging of *Nathalie* was hissed at its second performance, causing him to break his contract and leave. He remained on friendly terms, however, with Bournonville, who used Paul's choreography for the final *seguidillas* in his ballet *La Ventana* (1853).

In 1844 and 1845 Paul and Amalia made guest appearances in Warsaw, where Filippo was ballet master. According to Pudełek, Paul's ballets *Les Plaisirs de l'Hiver* and *La Prima Ballerina, ou L'Embuscade* were first produced here in 1845 rather than in London in 1849, as was formerly believed. The ice-skating scene of *Les Plaisirs de l'Hiver* anticipated Frederick Ashton's twentieth-century *Les Patineurs.* *La Prima Ballerina* was purportedly based on an actual experience of Marie's, in which bandits stopped her carriage on a deserted road but let her go free after she danced for them.

Paul served as ballet master at Her Majesty's Theatre in London from 1847 to 1851, sharing the post with Perrot in his first two years. He restaged *Undine* (retitled *Coralia* to avoid confusion with Perrot's *Ondine*), as well several new ballets. In the rather sugary *Théa, ou La Fée aux Fleurs,* the heroine (Carolina Rosati) wins her prince's love only after she has been transformed into a rosebush. *Electra,* which was famous for its use of electric lighting on stage, featured Grisi as a star that comes to earth. As the protean heroine of *Les Métamorphoses* (later restaged in Berlin as *Santanella*), Grisi played both male and female roles, among them a coquette and the cavalier who woos her. Paul himself danced the male leads in many of his ballets. His choreography tended to emphasize dancing at the expense of dramatic action, but this evidently accorded with contemporary taste; the *Times* praised *Théa* as "so much better than those long pieces of action in which the public is worn out with processions and nondancing magnificence. It is, in fact, one blaze of brilliant dancing from the beginning to the end" (quoted by Beaumont, 1937).

Beginning in the 1850s Paul worked as ballet master in Naples and Vienna as well as London and Berlin. He also began to stage ballets at La Scala during the 1860s. His most popular and frequently revived ballet, *Flick und Flocks Abenteuer* (Berlin, 1858), depicted the magical adventures of two friends who visit the kingdom of the gnomes and the undersea palace of Amphitrite. Arthur Saint-Léon, who saw the ballet some years after its premiere, criticized it as "a sort of faery with every known trick—out of date rococo groups, no delicacy, not a witty idea—and, if only one could forget it, the cocking-the-snook dance." He conceded, however, that "there is much precision in the general dances" (Guest, 1981).

Paul's penchant for extravagant fantasies enlivened with much dancing and elaborate scenery evidently persisted into the next decade, when Bournonville noted these characteristics in *Fantasca* (Berlin, 1869). "I admire his skill in choreographic arrangement, which, regardless of dramatic worth or poetic inspiration, must enrapture the avid spectator," confessed the Danish choreographer. Although the full range of Paul's works has yet to be studied, he appears to have been a skillful purveyor of the type of spectacular ballets favored in the late nineteenth century. He remained active as a choreographer in Berlin until 1883, a year before his death.

Marie Taglioni (born 27 October 1830 in Berlin, died 27 April 1891 in Neu-Aigen, near Vienna), dancer. Paul's daughter Marie was called "the second," "the younger," or "Marie Paul" in order to distinguish her from her illustrious aunt. She made her debut in 1847 at Her Majesty's Theatre in London, where her father was ballet master. In a review of her solo *pas de la rosière* in Paul's *Coralia*, the *Times* described her as "light, agile, graceful, and, at the

TAGLIONI FAMILY. Marie Taglioni the younger (1830–1891) in the title role of *Saltanella*. This lithograph, by Louis Veit after a photograph, was printed in Eduard Bloch's *Album der Bühnen-Costüme*, Berlin, 1859. (Courtesy of Madison U. Sowell and Debra H. Sowell, Brigham Young University, Provo, Utah.)

same time, possessed of remarkable power of muscle" (quoted by Beaumont, 1937). She also created the role of the Flower Fairy in her father's *Théa*. Her strength, also an attribute of Paul, was again noted the following year when she played Hertha in Paul's *Fiorita*.

During the same year Marie also created the role of Winter in Perrot's *Les Quatre Saisons*, dancing alongside Cerrito, Grisi, and Rosati. She played one of the rival goddesses, with Cerrito and Rosati, in a revival of Perrot's *Le Jugement de Pâris*. Marie also assumed the title role of *Théa* in Berlin that year. After seeing her in this role, her aunt Marie wrote, "I find her charming, very suited to the stage: she has much aplomb and ease, and sufficient elevation; she is graceful in pantomime. She will bring honor to the name of Taglioni" (quoted by Vaillat, 1942).

Along with her father, Marie returned repeatedly to Her Majesty's Theatre. In the role of Edda in Paul's *Electra* (1849), she danced the pas de deux "Le Lutte" with Grisi, in which the two vied for the love of Ehrick, played by Paul. She also appeared that year as Myrtha in *Giselle*. In 1850 she danced in Paul's ballets *Les Grâces* and *Les Métamorphoses;* she later took the title role in the latter ballet when it was restaged in Berlin as *Santanella*. She danced her aunt's famous role of the Sylphide in London in 1851.

In 1851 Marie also paid a visit to Warsaw, where her grandfather Filippo was ballet master, and danced before the court and at the Wielki Theater. She spent the years 1853 to 1856 in Vienna, then joined her father at the Berlin Court Opera from 1856 to 1866, with a few guest appearances in London, dancing in Paul's ballets *Flick und Flocks Abenteur*, *Des Malers Traumbild*, and *Sardanapal*. She retired from the stage in 1866 after her marriage to Prince Josef von Windisch-Graetz.

[*See also entries on the principal figures mentioned herein.*]

BIBLIOGRAPHY

Beaumont, Cyril W. *Complete Book of Ballets.* Rev. ed. London, 1951.

Binney, Edward, 3rd. *Longing for the Ideal: Images of Marie Taglioni in the Romantic Ballet.* Cambridge, Mass., 1984.

Bournonville, August. *My Theatre Life* (1848–1878). Translated by Patricia McAndrew. Middletown, Conn., 1979.

Cavalletti, Lavinia. "Salvatore Taglioni re di Napoli." *La Danza Italiana* 8–9 (Winter 1990): 109–134.

Celi, Claudia, and Andrea Toschi. "Alla ricerca dell'anello mancante: 'Flik e Flok' e l'Unità d'Italia." *Chorégraphie* 1 (Autumn 1993): 58–72.

Chazin-Bennahum, Judith. *Dance in the Shadow of the Guillotine.* Carbondale, Ill., 1988.

Guest, Ivor. *Fanny Elssler.* London, 1970.

Guest, Ivor. *The Romantic Ballet in England.* London, 1972.

Guest, Ivor. *The Ballet of the Second Empire.* London, 1974.

Guest, Ivor. *Fanny Cerrito.* 2d rev. ed. London, 1974.

Guest, Ivor. *The Romantic Ballet in Paris.* 2d rev. ed. London, 1980.

Guest, Ivor. *Jules Perrot.* London, 1984.

Guest, Ivor. "L'Italia e il balletto romantico." *La Danza Italiana* 8–9 (Winter 1990): 7–25.

Heiberg, Johanne L. "Memories of Taglioni and Elssler." Translated by Patricia McAndrew. *Dance Chronicle* 4.1 (1981): 14–18.

Hill, Lorna. *La Sylphide: The Life of Marie Taglioni.* London, 1967.

Lecomte, Nathalie. "Marie Taglioni alla Scala." *La Danza Italiana* 8–9 (Winter 1990): 47–71.

Levinson, André. *Marie Taglioni* (1929). Translated by Cyril W. Beaumont. London, 1977.

Lifar, Serge. *A History of Russian Ballet.* Translated by Arnold L. Haskell. New York, 1954.

Migel, Parmenia. *The Ballerinas: From the Court of Louis XIV to Pavlova.* New York, 1972.

Moore, Lillian. *Artists of the Dance.* New York, 1938.

Moore, Lillian. "A Dancer's Odyssey: Paul and Amelie Taglioni" (1942). In Moore's *Echoes of American Ballet.* Brooklyn, 1976.

Pudełek, Janina. "The Warsaw Ballet under the Directorships of Maurice Pion and Filippo Taglioni, 1832–1853." *Dance Chronicle* 11.2 (1988): 219–273.

Roslavleva, Natalia. *Era of the Russian Ballet* (1966). New York, 1979.

Saint-Léon, Arthur. *Letters from a Ballet Master: The Correspondence of Arthur Saint-Léon.* Edited by Ivor Guest. New York, 1981.

Sasportes, José. "La danza, 1737–1900." In *Il Teatro di San Carlo,* edited by Bruno Cagli and Agostino Ziino. Naples, 1987.

Tani, Gino. "Taglioni." In *Enciclopedia dello spettacolo.* Rome, 1954–.

Testa, Alberto. "Duecentocinquanta anni di balletto al Teatro oli San Carlo." In *Il Teatro di San Carlo 1737–1987.* 2 vols., Naples (1987): 333–344.

Testa, Alberto. "Taglioni." In *Storia della Danzae del Balletto.* Rome, 1994.

Vaillat, Léandre. *La Taglioni, ou, La vie d'une danseuse.* Paris, 1942.

Véron, Louis Désiré. "Behind the Scenes at the Opéra in Marie Taglioni's Day." Translated by Cyril W. Beaumont. *The Dancing Times* (January 1924): 403–407.

Wiley, Roland John, trans. and ed. *A Century of Russian Ballet: Documents and Accounts, 1810–1910.* Oxford, 1990. Includes Filippo Taglioni's libretto of *La Fille du Danube* and an account of the Taglionis in Russia.

Wiley, Roland John. "Images of *La Sylphide:* Two Accounts by a Contemporary Witness of Marie Taglioni's Appearances in St. Petersburg." *Dance Research* 13 (Summer 1995): 21–32.

Winter, Marian Hannah. *The Pre-Romantic Ballet.* London, 1974.

Woodcock, Sarah C. "Margaret Rolfe's Memoirs of Marie Taglioni" (parts 1–2). *Dance Research* 7 (Spring 1989): 3–19; 7 (Autumn 1989): 55–69.

ARCHIVE. Dance Collection, New York Public Library for the Performing Arts, in particular the files of unpublished research notes by Lillian Moore and the Walter Toscanini collection of research materials in dance.

ALBERTO TESTA
Translated from Italian

TAHITI. The largest and most populous of the Society Islands, Tahiti is the capital and administrative center for French Polynesia, an overseas territory of France comprising five culturally differentiated island groups in the southern Pacific Ocean. Because Tahiti is also the best-known island in the Society chain and enjoys a central position in the economic, political, and cultural life of the archipelago, the term *Tahitian* generally designates the language, people, and culture shared throughout the nine islands of that archipelago. In its larger sense, it may also refer to French Polynesia as a whole.

TAHITI. Female dancers posing for a photograph, c.1910. (Photograph from the Department of Library Services, American Museum of Natural History, New York [no. 33110]; used by permission.)

History. Early European visitors to Tahiti (the first was the English navigator Samuel Wallis in 1767) described a society in which dance was a favorite source of entertainment, beauty, and excitement. It was moreover an integral part of daily life, included in such varied activities as community projects and celebrations, certain rites of passage, war, politics, and religion. Europeans wrote about the elegant and beautiful motions of the hands and fingers, of a rapid circular hip movement employed by the women, of dances that incorporated various "lascivious postures," and of the fact that facial distortion was highly admired by the Tahitians. They noted that most dances were accompanied by the drum (*pahu*) and the nose flute (*vivo*), and that costuming varied widely, from nudity to elaborate costumes made of prized bark cloth.

Western influence and the missionaries' suppression of native dance—forbidden by law as early as the 1820s—have left a dance culture that today is considerably different from the original. In 1928 the Tahitian chronicler Teuira Henry lamented that "the ancient dancers would not recognize the modern form." Most contemporary Tahitians, however, do not focus on the past, but view their dance as part of a vibrant artistic life woven from many threads of change. The years since the 1950s have brought a proliferation of both amateur and professional dance groups, an increased respect for traditional dance in the eyes of modern Tahitians, and substantial government support of dance groups and folklore research. Influences from other Polynesian islands have also left their mark on the performing arts as Tahitians turned to neighboring cultures for ideas to fuel their creativity and desire for innovative material. In the 1990s, choreographers have added movements and techniques to the basic core of Tahitian dance, ushering in a new era of artistic transformation and prompting new definitions of traditional dance.

Dance in Contemporary Tahiti. The popular Western partner dances are the norm for social dancing at parties, celebrations, and evenings in night spots. Western classical dance is not widely known and is represented by only one ballet school in the capital, Papeete. Traditional Tahitian dance, however, can be viewed regularly in tourist hotels and at school, church, tourist-related, and official events throughout the year. The Heiva dance competitions in summer are considered the highlight of the dance year.

TAHITI. Men dancing in Papeete, c.1925. The vigorous knee-flapping, caught mid-motion here, is a characteristic feature of many Tahitian men's dances. (Photograph by R. H. Beck; from the Department of Library Services, American Museum of Natural History, New York [no. 122415]; used by permission.)

A notable feature of Tahitian dance in the 1990s is the emergence and growth of dance schools, a development representing a conspicuous change in the way Tahitians transmit dance knowledge. Whereas earlier generations learned dance through observation and repetition in informal group rehearsals, young dancers in the 1990s prefer to enroll in classes at the government-sponsored Conservatoire Artistique Territorial or at private dance schools established by Tahiti's well-known dancers. Such classes stress the acquisition and perfection of technique, thereby encouraging both increased virtuosity in dance and the codification of dance technique and vocabulary.

Tahitian dance is a group activity (competition groups in 1995 and 1996 had as many as 120 dancers; hotel performances may have only ten), choreographed and directed by a group leader and accompanied by a minimum of five musicians. Costumes may feature the simple *pareu*, the wraparound cloth, or finely worked natural materials (such as the inner bark of the purau tree, dried or fresh leaves, shells, seeds, and flowers) made into dance skirts with elaborately decorated belts, headdresses or head garlands, breast coverings, and neck ornaments.

Most dances call for gender-specific movements, revolving hip movements for women (*fa'arapu*) and a vigorous opening and closing of the knees for men (*pa'oti*). These movements, properly known as *'ori tahiti* (Tahitian dance), are also popularly referred to as the *tāmūrē*. The following are genres of Tahitian dance found today.

Once a men's dance, the *'ōte'a* today is performed by all-male, all-female, or mixed groups. The best known of all Tahitian dances, it is marked by a fast pace, the strong rhythmic drive of accompanying drums (slit drums and membranophones), the use of *'ori tahiti* movements, and predominantly abstract arm gestures. The dancers stand in columns facing the front of the performing area and use changing configurations to provide choreographic variety or to express the overall theme of the dance.

The *pā'ō'ā* is said by many Tahitians to have originated in the work of making bark cloth. Today it is a dance in which a group leader joins the drummers in the middle of a full or partial circle formed by a seated, mixed group. As the group members slap their thighs in rhythm with the basic pulse, one or two dancers rise and improvise a dance based on *'ori tahiti* movements. Accounts from the turn of the twentieth century describe the *pā'ō'ā* as having a solo female dancer; today the dance may be performed by a male-female couple.

The *hivinau* ("heave, now!") takes its name from the shouts of sailors lifting anchor on the nineteenth-century schooners that traveled between the islands. Used as a social mixer in the early years of the twentieth century, the *hivinau* now occurs within the context of presentational dance. It is performed in a double concentric circle formation (one circle male, one female) enclosing the group leader and the drummers. The men and women move in opposite directions using a stylized walking step, then stop momentarily to share a brief *'ori tahiti* dance with the person opposite.

The *'aparima* is a storytelling dance in which the gestures of the arms and hands play an important role. Two basic types of *'aparima* are found. Both may be performed by a mixed or same-sex group. The *'aparima vāvā* (mute *'aparima*) is a mimed dance accompanied by a drumming ensemble. Its gestures represent activities of daily life (fishing, canoe-paddling, or making coconut milk). It is performed in a seated or kneeling position.

The *'aparima hīmene* ("sung" *'aparima*) tells a story by means of a song text and accompanying hand and arm gestures. Gestures are predominantly symbolic or mimetic in nature and relate to the text of the song, highlighting important words or amplifying underlying meanings in the text. Choreographers also employ ornamental, nontext-related gestures to provide visual interest and fill the visual space between highlighted words.

'Aparima hīmene dances are accompanied by stringed instruments (guitars and locally made ukuleles) and bass drum; they may be performed seated, kneeling, or standing. In the 1980s standing dances began to exhibit increasing variety in foot and lower torso movements. Whereas the older *'aparima* used a simple sideways step (similar to the Hawaiian *kāholo*) or were performed in

place with dancers marking the basic pulse of the music by tapping one heel or foot, dances in the 1990s incorporate level changes, locomotion, and a wide assortment of foot and hip movements (including many from Hawaiian hula).

Tahitian dance in the mid-1990s is clearly an art form molded by a global culture, interweaving elements from other artistic traditions with local motifs and yet remaining a recognizable symbol of Tahitian cultural identity for both islanders and visitors. As the dance becomes more virtuosic and institutionalized, increasingly complex and sophisticated performances will become the norm in urban areas, even as rural communities continue to feature amateur dance based on older models and older definitions of what it means to be Tahitian—both styles contributing to the richness and viability of Tahitian dance culture.

[*See also* Oceanic Dance Traditions *and* Polynesia.]

BIBLIOGRAPHY

Henry, Teuira. *Ancient Tahiti*. Bishop Museum Bulletin, no. 48. Honolulu, 1928.
Moulin, Jane Freeman. *The Dance of Tahiti*. Papeete, Tahiti, 1979.
Oliver, Douglas L. *Ancient Tahitian Society*. Honolulu, 1974.

JANE FREEMAN MOULIN

TAIWAN. An island in the western Pacific Ocean, Taiwan (formerly called Formosa) lies between the East and the South China seas, some ninety miles (145 kilometers) from the coast of the Chinese mainland. Taiwan and thirteen small islands of the Taiwan group constitute 12,847 square miles (35,860 square kilometers); since 1949, when the People's Republic of China (PRC) was established, the government of the Republic of China (ROC) and millions of Chinese moved to Taiwan, with their capital at Taipei. Some twenty million people now live on Taiwan, including the pre-Chinese indigenous peoples, collectively called Kaoshan. The Chinese began arriving in the seventeenth century; before 1945 they were rice farmers and fisherfolk from Fujian and Guangdong provinces, speaking Cantonese, Hakka, or Min dialects (they are known as Taiwanese). From 1945 to 1950, some three million anti-Communist Chinese from every province arrived, many from Shanghai. Today, both Taiwanese and Chinese constitute 98.5 percent of the population and speak Mandarin Chinese (the official dialect of both the ROC and PRC governments).

Dance in Taiwan has a long and rich cultural legacy. Some traditional dance genres include Kaoshan indigenous dance, the ancient Confucian ritual dance (*yayue*) of the Han people of China, the banquet music and dance (*yanyue*) dating from the Tang dynasty (618–906), as well as other types of Kaoshan, Taiwanese, and Chinese folk dance. Dancers stage numerous performances as part of traditional ritual ceremonies, appearing in theaters and even in the streets of Taiwan. In the 1940s, Western ballet and modern dance came to Taiwan.

Indigenous Dance. There are nine aboriginal peoples in Taiwan—the Ami, Atayal, Bunun, Paiwan, Puyuma, Rukai, Saisiyat, Tsou, and Yami. Their religious beliefs are based on ancestor worship and animism, a polytheism of nature gods and spirits. The Yami experience an intense awe of the dead, and many believe in and practice shamanism. [*See* Shamanism.] The indigenous dance of all the peoples of Taiwan is intimately related to traditional religious beliefs; the dances and songs are an intrinsic part of ceremonies, which include the worship of the ancestors and the souls of the dead. Song and dance also accompany rituals that celebrate sexual maturity and marriage, the harvesting of food, and the hunt—they express respect and gratitude to the ancestors and reenactment of heroic deeds and historic events. Less formally, singing and dancing also provide them with a source of pleasure and amusement in their daily lives.

Aboriginal dance is not accompanied by musical instruments. After the lead singer provides the first line, the dancers join in, singing and dancing. The rhythms are usually 4/4, 2/4, 6/4, 8/4, and 3/4. Some steps can be used with a variety of songs. Songs are sung spontaneously to welcome guests or for simple pleasure and amusement, and some degree of improvisation often occurs. Such dancing is often joyful and relaxing.

Aboriginal dance formations include the closed circle, the open semicircle, the spiral, and the lateral row. A variety of steps include walking, running, stamping, pointing, hopping, jumping, and zig-zaging in circular patterns, both clockwise and counterclockwise. Another step, the gallop, is found in the Paiwan people's hunting dance. Aboriginal dance does not place much emphasis on arm movements; most often, dancers join hands and move their arms up and down to the rhythm of the dance. They employ a movement with their hands swung back and forth and from left to right; occasionally they simply clap their hands. They use their torsos to sway from side to side, often bending forward in a deep bow, to mime the waves of the ocean. One very famous dance performed by Yami women is called the Hair Dance. Women with long, loose tresses line up side by side and take hands, kicking rhythmically, bending forward and back, and tossing their hair in the air, again, as if communing with the ocean.

Traditional aboriginal costumes are very colorful, and each people has its own distinctive ones. Costumes and accessories may include pants for men, blouses, skirts, leggings, headpieces, garlands, necklaces, bells, and bags of betel nuts. Yami men often wear simple T-pants for casual dancing but don embroidered shirts and silver hats for formal rituals. Paiwanese noblemen dance in blouses embroidered in patterns of poisonous snakes. Tsou male dancers engage in singing and dancing to honor their ancestors and the nature deities, but there is a taboo against women and children taking part or appearing at the altar.

Traditional Chinese Dance. Confucian ritual dance (*yayue*) is the oldest traditional dance of the Han people of

TAIWAN. Performers of the Formosa Aboriginal Dance Troupe of Taiwan in a dance of the Tsou people from the village of Tufuya. (Photograph © 1993 by Linda Vartoogian; used by permission.)

China. This dance was an important part of the scholarly curriculum in ancient China, and its performance was obligatory in rituals. After 1911, the Republic of China was founded, and many of China's traditions underwent changes; with the overthrow of the emperor and traditional absolutism, the rituals for sacrifices to heaven and earth, the mountains, the rivers, and the ancestors were generally abandoned. Thus, Confucian ritual music and dance lost its high status in Chinese society. Today, only four kinds of ancient Confucian dances are performed in Taiwan. (1) The ancient Yi Dance has been performed over the centuries in rituals of ancestor worship. Five variations, with a description and figures, are recorded in historical documents. The Yi Dance is performed annually in the Temple of Confucius on 28 September, his birthday. The reconstruction used has been taken from figure drawings and illustrations dating from the Qing dynasty (1644–1912). (2) The World Completely Reformed is a civil dance. (3) Majesty Invests the Four Seas, a martial dance, were composed by Ye Fang in December of 1089. Their movements/meaning were recorded at the time, and both pieces were performed during the Emperor's court gatherings and rituals. (In 1984, Liu Feng-Shueh reconstructed and staged them; both are now recorded in Labanotation.) (4) Dance of the People, choreographed by Chu Tsai-yü (1536–c.1610), served as an educational dance for children and is imbued with a strong moral sense.

Some characteristics of Confucian ritual dance may now be discussed. Dance formations as well as the number of dancers are strictly limited. Rituals devoted to ancestor worship, sacrifices to heaven and earth, and those in honor of the grain harvest were often hosted by the emperor. On such an occasion the dance consisted of sixty-four dancers—eight dancers arranged in eight rows. If the host and high priest were feudal lords, the required number of dancers was reduced to thirty-six—six dancers in six rows (sometimes a row had eight dancers, making forty-eight dancers in all). If the host and high priest were merely high ranking officers, the number of dancers would be sixteen, with four dancers in four rows (or eight dancers in four rows, making thirty-two dancers in all). If the host and high priest were but common civilians, then there would be two dancers in two rows (or eight dancers in two rows, sixteen in all). The significance of such arrangements was based on numerical symbolism and a striving for harmony and social order as expressed in music, dance, and rituals.

The patterns of movement in Confucian ritual dance were not intended to explore the expressive aspect of dance, since the beauty of the dance lies in its spirit. The purpose of life was to arrive at moral fulfillment and to attain the ideal sphere in which humans become an integral part of nature. These and other related ideas are ex-

TAIWAN. *Chun Ying Chuan* (Oriole's Chirping) is a Tang-dynasty court dance. Upon hearing orioles singing one morning, Emperor Tang Gaozong (650–683) ordered his court musician Bai Mingda to compose the music and dance. Preserved by the Japanese court, the dance also symbolizes ancient Chinese women's beauty and spirituality. Liu Feng-Shueh staged the reconstruction pictured here with dancers Liu Jen-ying, Chao Huey-ren, Chen Chuen-mey, Shih Show-tseng, Cheng Guey-mei, Cheng Ten-shiang, and Lin Shou-shiang. (Photograph courtesy of the Neo-Classical Dance Company, Taiwan.)

pressed in Confucian ritual dance. Many movements are thematic; for example, in The World Completely Reformed, saluting, declining, and modesty are types of comportment that follow strict rules of social etiquette. In the Dance of the People, eight traditional Confucian moral virtues are revealed—loyalty, filial piety, love, benevolence, righteousness, wisdom, propriety, and faithfulness—through eight different movements. In Majesty Invests the Four Seas, the dance extols the achievements of the imperial army. In general, Confucian ritual dances are performed for the sake of increasing one's self-discipline and devotion to others.

Singing and music accompany the dance. Three of the dances—the Yi Dance, The World Completely Reformed, and Majesty Invests the Four Seas—have three song parts, with eight lines in each part, four words in each line. Each word corresponds to one note and one movement. During the first wine offering of the rituals, the first part is performed. The second part is performed during the middle wine offering, and the third part during the final wine offering. The costumes for these three Confucian ritual dances consisted of the ceremonial dress of the period. At performances of the civil dance, the dancer typically holds a flute in his left hand and a feather in his right hand. The dancer in the martial dance bears a shield in his left hand and a pike in his right hand. The dancer in the Dance of the People does not have anything in his hands; he waves his sleeves in a token of respect.

Banquet music and dance. This dance genre, called *yanyue*, was performed during major court ceremonies and national banquets of the Tang dynasty (618–906). According to Tang-era records, more than three hundred of such dances were performed at the court. Most came from India, Iran, and the northwestern part of China, while others were created by the Han people. The musical scores for most of them are no longer extant, but some fragments exist. Of these, "The Scores of Dunhuang" has been examined by the scholar Peng Song and has been recorded in Labanotation. Liu Feng-Shueh initiated

TAIWAN. A scene from the Cloud Gate Dance Theater's production of *Nine Songs*, chorographed by Lin Hwai-min. Pictured here are Lee Ching-chun as the Shaman and Deng Kei-fu as the Sun God in a 1993 performance at the National Theater, Taipei. (Photograph © 1993 by Deng Yu-lin; used by permission.)

TAIWAN. Liu Feng-Shueh's *The Seance* (1974), a modern dance work inspired by a poem from *Chu Tsu,* incorporates elements of witchcraft, folk dance practices from northern China and Taiwan, and narrative exploring the self-searching process of the artist. The dancer seen here is Shih Kun-cheng. (Photograph by Li Ming-hsun; courtesy of the Neo-Classical Dance Company, Taiwan.)

his study of Tang banquet dance in 1957 and in 1983 completed his reconstruction of a major work, entitled "The Emperor Destroys the Formations." This dance, martial in nature, was originally created in 634 and was brought to Japan in 701. Liu Feng-Shueh reconstructed the work based on a Japanese description, then recorded it in Labanotation (the music has been reproduced by L. E. R. Picken of Cambridge University). The dance includes a prelude and a broaching; it is twenty-five minutes long. Four dancers form a square, and their steps range from walking and stamping to pointing and sliding. Arm gestures include forward and sideward motions, swaying sideways, hitting, and cutting. Body movements include turns, forward tilts, and diagonal forward and backward tilts, accompanied by the fanning out of wide sleeves. The movements represent a typical Chinese martial manner and attitude. The color of the costumes is primarily red; costumes include blouses, pants, short skirts, long tails, belts, headpieces, and boots. Although "The Emperor Destroys the Formations" is a martial dance, the four dancers are not armed for the performance.

Theatrical Dance. Since the 1940s, ballet has become increasingly popular in Taiwan. Many children began studying ballet in private studios after regular school hours. Since the 1960s, ballet has become a required course in college dance departments. In the 1970s, small semiprofessional ballet troupes began making their appearance. Occasionally they have attempted creative works characterized and inspired by local events, but the general public prefers to attend the classical grand ballets, such as *Swan Lake*.

In Taiwan, modern dance started to develop along with ballet in the 1940s. For fifty years, however, these two dance genres have gone in different directions. Early local development was based on the theory and approaches to modern dance of Rudolf Laban and Mary Wigman. Thereafter, the approaches of Doris Humphrey, Martha Graham, and Jośe Limón were widely adopted by dance professionals in Taiwan. In the 1990s, because of the enlightened government policy, national support for dance groups has increased substantially. Moreover, with the cross-fertilization between Eastern and Western schools, the world of dance has begun flourishing. Dance education has become innovative and creative, with an emphasis placed on individual talent and development. A growing number of excellent dancers exist and their skill has earned them a glowing reputation.

Since the 1980s, numerous theaters have been built in Taiwan with the support of both local and national governments. This has resulted in more opportunities and sites for Taiwan's wide range of modern dance groups and choreographers, rich in personal expression and creativity. The most well-known dance companies in Taiwan are the Cloud Gate Dance Theater, the Henry Yu Dance Company, and the Neo-Classic Dance Company.

[*See also* China.]

BIBLIOGRAPHY

Ch'ên Yang. *Yüeh Shu* (1101). Reprinted, Kuang Chou, 1987.

Chu Ts'ai-yü. *Lü-Lü Ching-i* (1596). Reprinted by Shang-wu Yin-shu-kuan, Taipei, 1967.

Li Chih-tso. *P'an Kung Li yüeh shu* (1615). Reprinted by Wei-wên t'u-shu ch'u-pan-shê, Taipei, 1970.

Liu Feng-Shueh. "A Documented Historical and Analytical Study of Chinese Ritual and Ceremonial Dance from the Second Millennium BC to the Thirteenth Century." Ph.D. diss., Laban Centre for Movement and Dance at the University of London, Goldsmiths' College, 1986.

Picken, L. E. R. *Music from the T'ang Court.* 2 vols. Oxford, 1981. Reprinted, Cambridge, 1985.

Sung Shih (1345). In *Ssŭ-pu t'sung-k'an.* 128 vols. Reprinted, Shang-wu Yin-shu-kuan, Shanghai, 1936.

LIU FENG-SHUEH

TAJIKISTAN. Inhabited by Persians from the sixth century BCE onward, Tajikistan in Central Asia was subject throughout its history to a series of invasions by its neighbors—China on the east, Afghanistan on the south, Uzbekistan and Kyrgyzstan on the west and north—and by Arabs who in the seventh and eighth centuries converted the nation to Islam. Part of Tajikistan belonged to the emirate of Bukhara, under despotic Uzbek rule, until Russian suzerainty was imposed in the late nineteenth century; then Tajikistan was incorporated into Russian Turkistan. In 1924 Tajikistan became a Soviet autonomous republic within the Uzbek domain and in 1929 a constituent republic of the USSR. Tajikistan achieved independence in 1991 with the Soviet Union's dissolution.

After becoming a dominated region—by Islamic law, by tsarist repression, and later by Soviet conformism—cultural development in Tajikistan was circumscribed. The lives of women, in particular, were severely restricted: hidden from strangers under the *yashmak*, women were allowed to sing and dance only in the half of the home reserved for them; exception was made for harem dancers in wealthier households, who had been introduced by foreign conquerors. Despite the successive invasions of the country, Tajiki dance did manage to survive, so some traditions are known, but much was irretrievably lost.

Not until 1935 was the Tajiki musical theater founded. Teachers from Russia introduced regular classes in acting and classical dance. The first national musical, staged in 1939, was *Lola* (Tulip), choreographed by A. Islamova and Gafur Balamat-zade to music by Sergei Balasanian and S. Urbach. Conforming to Socialist Realism, it shows neighboring farmers who, having completed their plan of spring work, assemble for a traditional tulip festival. A competition of skill among singers, dancers, and jesters takes place on a lawn in front of a teahouse; modern social and round dances are also represented. The production thus combined contemporary motifs with traditional folk dance.

In 1940 the musical theater in the capital, Stalinabad (now Dushanbe), became an opera and ballet theater named after S. Aini, who had campaigned for progress in Tajikistan. The first national ballet, *The Two Roses*, was produced in 1941, choreographed by Kasyan Goleizovsky to music by Aleksandr Lensky. Set in the early years of Soviet Tajikistan, the story tells of two young girls who are so good and so beautiful that people call them roses. One is betrothed to an honorable man, but the other's fiancé is unwittingly involved with the *basmachis*, a group of counterrevolutionaries. Upon seeing them rob a rich landowner and try to run off with the two girls, the youth realizes the identity of his associates. Both fiancés help the border guards to unarm the gang and save the two roses. The opposing sides are characterized by differing musical and choreographic themes: "Rakcikamchin," a dance with whips, communicates the anger of the *bas-machis;* the dances "Panj-gul" (Five Roses) and "Merzon" (Trembling) are the basis of the women's movement, and "Striking Eagles" the men's. The genre scenes include a bazaar, a holiday concluding with a dance on stilts, a dance with clay pots, and a performance of traveling comedians and mummers.

Balamat-zade was chief choreographer of the company in the 1940s and staged a number of ballet classics. He also created new works, including *Leili and Medzhnun* (1947, reproduced by Goleizovsky in 1964 for the Bolshoi Ballet) to music by Balasanian, which was based on an oriental legend; *Dilbar* (1954) was set to music by Lensky, an early Tajik attempt to express a modern theme in classical dance. In 1965 Balamat-zade founded the Lola Tajik Dance Company to stage works based on oriental folk dance; the company has toured abroad.

In the 1950s and 1960s a number of young Tajik ballet dancers graduated from the Vaganova Ballet School in Leningrad and returned to Dushanbe to join their native ballet company. Among them was Malika Sabirova, who created a number of important roles. Her former partner, Muzafar Burkhanov, directed the company in the 1980s. Carefully maintaining continuity with the past, the company preserves Tajiki traditions and adapts them to meet modern sensibilities.

[*See also the entry on Goleizovsky.*]

BIBLIOGRAPHY
Azimova, A. *Tantsevalnoe iskusstvo Tadzhikistana.* Stalinabad, 1957.
Nurdzhanov, N. K. *Tadzhikskii narodnyi teatr.* Moscow, 1956.

YURI P. TYURIN
Translated from Russian

TAKARAZUKA (Takarazuka Girls' Opera) is a Japanese all-female company that presents musical shows. Founded in 1914 by Kobayashi Ichizo, the troupe was one of the attractions at his amusement park at Takarazuka, a suburb between Osaka and Kobe. Kobayashi owned not only the park but also the connecting Hankyu Railway; his intention in forming Takarazuka was to increase attendance at the park and use of the railway.

At first the company presented only Japanese dance, but in the early 1930s, the repertory was strongly influenced by Parisian revues. Through Takarazuka, many French *chansons* of that period became popular in Japan. Modified versions of European operettas and *kabuki* dance dramas were also staged.

The stars of the company, especially those playing male roles, attracted many female admirers, ranging from junior high school girls to rich housewives. Popular stars received showers of expensive gifts. During World War II, this "Takarazuka fever" caused concern to the government, which tried to restrain it, with only partial success.

After the war, Takarazuka flourished again, now under the influence of the Broadway musical. Its repertory, both Western and Japanese, became more varied and opulent, and Broadway directors and *kabuki* actors were often invited to supervise productions.

The stars of the company always retire at an early age, because the girls' youth is one of the troupe's main attractions and because company policy forbids Takarazuka actresses to marry. Some former Takarazuka stars, such as Koshiji Fubuki, have gone on to careers as popular singers; others, like Awashima Chikage and Otowa Nobuko, have become successful movie actresses.

Takarazuka has an affiliated school that gives the girls a two-year education in Western and Japanese music, ballet, modern and jazz dance, and traditional Japanese dance and acting. The girls range in age from fifteen to eighteen, and the school accepts forty to fifty girls annually, chosen from about ten times that many applicants.

The Takarazuka company toured Europe in 1938, 1965, and 1975, the United States in 1939, 1959, and 1992, and Southeast Asia in 1973, always with great success.

BIBLIOGRAPHY
Doraisamy, Cyril. "That's Entertainment, Japanese Style." *Dance Australia* (June–July 1995): 54–57.
Hirai, Takane. "External Influences in the Transformation of Japanese Dance." In *Culture Embodied*, edited by Michael Moerman et al. Senri Ethnological Studies, no. 27. Osaka, 1990.
Japan Centre, International Theatre Institute. *Theatre in Japan 1994.* Tokyo, 1995.
Newman, Barbara. "Takarazuka." *The Dancing Times* (September 1994): 1195–1197.
Ortolani, Benito. *The Japanese Theatre: From Shamanistic Ritual to Contemporary Pluralism.* Rev. ed. Princeton, 1995.
Shoemaker, Barbara. "The Takarazuka Dance Theatre." *Dance Magazine* (September 1959): 40–43.
Tobias, Tobi. "Wishful Thinking." *New York Magazine* (30 November 1992).
Wechsler, Bert. "Takarazuka." *Attitude* 9 (Winter 1993): 27–28.

USUI KENJI

TALE OF THE STONE FLOWER, THE. *See* Stone Flower, The.

TALLCHIEF, MARIA (Elizabeth Marie Tall Chief; born 24 January 1925 in Fairfax, Oklahoma), American ballet dancer, teacher, and company director. Although Maria Tallchief spent several seasons with the Ballet Russe de Monte Carlo, where she was a protégée of Bronislava Nijinska, and pursued an international career for twenty-five years, she will be best remembered for her association with George Balanchine during the New York City Ballet's early years of greatness, when she was the young company's first true star. She lacked the long-limbed proportions favored by Balanchine, but she personified another kind of Balanchine ideal: she moved with blazing speed, energy, unmannered brilliance—what the critics called "brio." At the height of her career, critic Walter Terry wrote that she could "spin across the stage faster and more accurately than any ballerina I [have] ever seen [and] flash through allegro passages with such authority that one [has] the feeling a partner [is] not necessary."

Daughter of an Osage Indian father and a Scotch-Irish mother, Tallchief trained in Hollywood with Ernest Belcher (father of Marge Champion) and Nijinska, joining the Ballet Russe de Monte Carlo as a teenager in 1942. (Nijinska was then in residence as guest choreographer.) At the age of eighteen, Tallchief appeared in Nijinska's *Chopin Concerto,* a performance that caused *New York Times* critic John Martin to refer to her as possible "ballerina material," with a "lovely simplicity of style and ease which certainly look hard to spoil." A year later she met Balanchine, who cast her as Alexandra Danilova's understudy in "Anitra's Dance" from *Song of Norway* and changed her life. With Ballet Russe, she performed solos in Balanchine's *Danses Concertantes, Ballet Imperial, Mozartiana,* and *Raymonda* and leading roles of the Coquette in *The Night Shadow* and the Fairy in *Le Baiser de la Feé* as well as roles in numerous other ballets in the repertory (including all the old chestnuts, such as *Schéhérazade* and *Gaîté Parisienne*).

At this time, in 1945, dance critic Edwin Denby noted her "thrilling power of momentum." In 1947, she became the first American since Augusta Maywood a century before to dance at the Paris Opera, where Balanchine staged *Serenade, Le Baiser de la Feé,* and *Apollo.* With Balanchine's tiny group called Ballet Society (1946–1948), Tallchief performed as ballerina in *Symphony in C, Symphonie Concertante,* and, perhaps most important, as Eurydice in *Orpheus,* the work that led to the formation of the New York City Ballet.

It was Balanchine's *Firebird* (1949) that established the reputation of the new company—and of its ballerina Maria Tallchief. Lillian Moore wrote that Tallchief danced the Firebird "like a flame." Walter Terry found her feats "breathtaking. In off-center spins, in sudden lifts, [her movements] seem to defy gravity, and in their alert, graceful, and sharp explorations of space, they define the characteristics of a magical, air-borne creature." It was at this time that she was referred to (not entirely accurately) as the first "homegrown" ballerina—an American of international stature who had neither trained in Europe nor made her reputation there.

For the next seven years or so, Tallchief was Balanchine's first dancer, creating roles in all of his virtuoso pieces, including *Sylvia: Pas de Deux* (1950), *Swan Lake* (1951), *The Nutcracker* (1954), *Pas de Dix* (1955), and *Allegro Brillante* (1956), among many others. Her frequent partner was André Eglevsky. Of *Pas de Dix,* Doris Hering wrote (in a comment typical of the time)—that "there was something almost crystalline in the way she moved through space—turning, tossing her head, arching her back . . . [with] a tantalizing combination of fire and detachment." Commenting on the art and philosophy of Balanchine, to whom she was married (1946–1950), and who was her greatest artistic influence, Tallchief said, "It's a way of timing, of attacking, of not holding back, of giving every ounce of your energy. You're never comfortable. To be comfortable and careful—that's not dancing."

Nevertheless, Tallchief's ethereal rendering of the Sylph in *Scotch Symphony* (1952) revealed that not everything about her art was hard brilliance. Dancing a version of *The Dying Swan* as Anna Pavlova in the Hollywood movie *The Million Dollar Mermaid* (1952), she displayed remarkable softness and a particularly graceful *port de bras.* These qualities were also notable in her portrayal of Ellida in Birgit Cullberg's *Lady from the Sea,* which she danced with American Ballet Theatre in the early 1960s.

TALLCHIEF. In 1950, Tallchief and André Eglevsky danced together for the first time, in Balanchine's *Sylvia: Pas de Deux,* a virtuoso showpiece. They subsequently performed it on stages all over the world. (Photograph from the archives at Jacob's Pillow, Becket, Massachusetts. Choreography by George Balanchine © The George Balanchine Trust.)

By the end of the 1950s, Tallchief's important years with Balanchine were over, although she remained with his company intermittently until 1965. Throughout her career, she made numerous television appearances and frequently danced as a guest artist with various companies, performing dramatic roles as well as virtuoso classics. With American Ballet Theatre (1960–1962), for example, her repertory included the title role in Cullberg's *Miss Julie* and Caroline in Antony Tudor's *Jardin aux Lilas* as well as Harald Lander's *Études* and the Black Swan pas de deux. At this time she renewed a partnership with Erik Bruhn. During a season with Ballet Russe de Monte Carlo (1954/55), she was reportedly the world's most highly paid ballerina. She appeared as well with Ruth Page's Chicago Opera Ballet, the Chicago Lyric Opera, the San Francisco Ballet, and the Royal Danish Ballet. One of her last roles was that of Cinderella in Peter van Dyk's production for the Hamburg State Opera in 1966. She retired from the stage soon thereafter.

In 1974, Tallchief established the Ballet School of the Lyric Opera in Chicago, and by 1980 she was able to form an independent school (affiliated with Balanchine's School of American Ballet in New York) and to found a company. The Chicago City Ballet, with Tallchief as artistic director, Paul Mejia as resident choreographer, and Suzanne Farrell and Balanchine as artistic advisers, produced its first season in June 1981. One of its principal successes was Mejia's version of *Cinderella* with Farrell, dancing as guest artist, in the title role. Although she was a fine teacher, Tallchief found herself unsuited to the role of artistic director. She severed her association with the company in 1987.

Over the years, many awards and honors have been bestowed upon Tallchief. Among the earliest was an achievement award presented by the Women's National Press Club in 1953, the same year in which she was elected an honorary princess of the Osage tribe. This was followed by a *Dance Magazine* Award in 1960 and the Capezio Award in 1965. In 1996 she was inducted into the National Women's Hall of Fame and was a recipient of a Kennedy Center Honor, awarded in recognition of a lifetime contribution to the nation's culture.

[*See also* New York City Ballet *and the entry on Balanchine.*]

BIBLIOGRAPHY

Anderson, Jack. *The One and Only: The Ballet Russe de Monte Carlo.* New York, 1981.

Cargill, Mary. "Talking with Maria Tallchief." *Dance View* 13 (Autumn 1995): 3–5.

Chujoy, Anatole. *The New York City Ballet.* New York, 1953.

Gruen, John. "Tallchief and the Chicago City Ballet." *Dance Magazine* (December 1984): HC24–HC27. Interview with Tallchief.

Hardy, Camille. "Chicago's Soaring City Ballet." *Dance Magazine* (April 1982): 70–76.

Hardy, Camille. "Tallchief on Balanchine: Passing on the Magic." *American Arts* (May 1984).

Livingston, Lili Cockerille. *American Indian Ballerinas.* Norman, Okla., 1997.

Maynard, Olga. *Bird of Fire: The Story of Maria Tallchief.* New York: 1961.

Reynolds, Nancy. *Repertory in Review: Forty Years of the New York City Ballet.* New York, 1977.

Tallchief, Maria, with Larry Kaplan. *Maria Tallchief: America's Prima Ballerina.* New York, 1997.

Taper, Bernard. *Balanchine: A Biography.* New rev. ed. Berkeley, 1996.

Tracy, Robert, and Sharon DeLano. *Balanchine's Ballerinas: Conversations with the Muses.* New York: 1983.

ARCHIVES.   The Dance Collection of the New York Public Library for the Performing Arts has extensive holdings of still photographs of Tallchief and of materials pertinent to her performing career. The Barzel Collection, Newberry Library, Chicago, contains the archives of the Chicago City Ballet.

FILMS AND VIDEOTAPES.   The Dance Collection of the New York Public Library for the Performing Arts has a large collection of videotapes showing, in whole or in part, Tallchief's performances in *The Firebird, Harlequinade Pas de Deux, Pas de Dix, Scotch Symphony, Symphony in C* (first movement), *Allegro Brillante, Don Quixote* (pas de deux), *Flower Festival in Genzano* (pas de deux), *The Nutcracker,* and *Sylvia: Pas de Deux,* among others. Anne Belle's *Dancing for Mr. B: Six Balanchine Ballerinas* (Seahorse Films, 1996), which contains a lengthy segment on Tallchief, is available commercially from Nonesuch/WarnerVision Entertainment. The George Balanchine Foundation Interpreters Archive, distributed to dance reference collections, includes several tapes of Tallchief coaching her important Balanchine roles.

NANCY REYNOLDS

TAMASHA. The popular musical theater of Maharashtra state, west-central India, tamasha is a kind of musical comedy with many racy songs and dances. The themes vary; they may deal with chiefs and kings, quarrels over land, domestic tales of henpecked husbands, historical romances, or stories from mythology.

Although today most of the performers in tamasha come from the lower-caste Mahar, Manj, and Kolhati communities, in the past a number of high-caste brahmans were celebrated as lyricists and composers of tamasha songs. Some of these brahman composers even formed their own tamasha troupes, although this usually resulted in their being ostracized by their families.

The history of tamasha (spelled *tamāśa* in Indian languages, *tamasha* in English) begins in the late seventeenth or early eighteenth century. It flourished for the next hundred years or so, but the takeover of the Maratha state by the British in the early nineteenth century put an end to court patronage of tamasha. Over the years, its popularity has waxed and waned. Today there are at least eight hundred established troupes, performing on tour in the countryside as well as in the cities. The troupes employ an estimated forty thousand actors, dancers, and musicians who make their living in this regional folk theater.

BIBLIOGRAPHY

Abrams, Tevia. "Tamasha: People's Theatre of Maharashtra State, India." Ph.D. diss., Michigan State University, 1974.

Gargi, Balwant. *Folk Theater of India.* Seattle, 1966.

Sawant, K. R. *Tamasha: A Unique Folk Theatre of Maharashtra.* Bombay, 1983.

Tendulkar, Vijay, and Kumud Mehta. "Dadu Indurikar." *Quarterly Journal of the National Centre for the Performing Arts* 2 (December 1973): 21–40.

CLIFFORD REIS JONES

BIBLIOGRAPHY

Blades, James. "Tambourin. II (de Provence)." In *The New Grove Dictionary of Music and Musicians.* London, 1980.

Little, Meredith Ellis. "Tambourin. I." In *The New Grove Dictionary of Music and Musicians.* London, 1980.

Little, Meredith Ellis, and Carol G. Marsh. *La Danse Noble: An Inventory of Dances and Sources.* Williamstown, Mass., 1992.

Quantz, Johann Joachim. *On Playing the Flute* (1752). Translated by Edward R. Reilly. London, 1966.

Seefrid, Gisela. *Die Airs de danse in den Bühnenwerken von Jean-Philippe Rameau.* Wiesbaden, 1969.

REBECCA HARRIS-WARRICK

TAMBOURIN. A lively duple-meter dance of Provençal origin, the *tambourin* was frequently used on the French stage during the eighteenth century. The *tambourin* was traditionally accompanied by a single musician playing pipe and tabor, or in French, the *galoubet* and *tambourin*, the large, double-headed drum that gave the dance its name. In orchestral settings of the dance, the drumbeats are imitated by the rhythmic repetition of a single bass note, thus providing a static but accented harmonic foundation over which the lively melody moves. The time signature of the *tambourin* is usually 2/4, and it was always described in the eighteenth century as quick and gay. Johann Joachim Quantz wrote in 1752 that the *tambourin* is to be played a little faster than the *bourrée* and *rigaudon*, thus making it one of the fastest of the French dances.

The *tambourin* made its first appearance on the French stage in Marin Marais's opera *Alcione* (1706). It reached the height of its success in the ballets and operas of Jean-Philippe Rameau, written for the Paris Opera between 1733 and 1760, in which the *tambourin* was one of the most frequently occurring dance types. Most of Rameau's *tambourins* come in pairs, one in a major key followed by one in a minor key, with a subsequent repetition of the first *tambourin*. Some of the *tambourins* were danced by Provençal characters, as in the first *entrée* ("Le Turc Généreux") in *Les Indes Galantes*, but most have no discernible connection with the regional origins of the dance. Rameau frequently used a pair of *tambourins* to end an act, which suggests that such *tambourins* were group dances. The scant stage indications in the scores and livrets, however, reveal little about the size or character of the performing forces for the dances and nothing at all about the choreography.

The only *tambourin* in Feuillet notation is a couple dance by Guillaume-Louis Pecour that appeared in the *Recüeil de danses pour l'année 1719*, one of a series of social-dance collections. It is a typical French couple dance with symmetrical figures based on the social dance step vocabulary and probably has a limited relationship with the stage *tambourins* of the following decades.

TAMIRIS, HELEN (Helen Becker; born 23 April 1903 in New York City, died 4 August 1966 in New York City), American dancer, choreographer, teacher, and theater director. During the late 1920s through the 1930s, Tamiris participated in the origin and development of the concert dance form of modern dance in the United States. Then, through the 1940s and 1950s, she solidified its place in the musical theater of New York's Broadway.

Trained in Italian ballet technique at the Metropolitan Opera, Russian ballet technique at Michel Fokine's studio, and natural dancing at an Isadora Duncan studio, Tamiris became a member of the corps of the Metropolitan Opera Ballet, a leading soloist in the Bracale Opera Company in a tour of South America, a specialty dancer in nightclubs and revues and in the stage shows of movie houses, and a featured dancer in the 1924–1925 Music Box Revue. Taking the name of "Ruthless Queen" Tamiris, and rejecting mimed stories, theatricality, and technical tricks, she turned to concert works by presenting a solo recital on 9 October 1927 at the Little Theater in New York (within a year of Martha Graham), with Louis Horst at the piano. "Dancing is simply movement with a personal conception of rhythm," she declared in a program note.

Tamiris created twenty-seven solo dances in two years and presented them in seven concerts—four in New York and three in Europe (Paris, Berlin, and the Salzburg Festival of 1938): a reflection of urban life in *Dance of the City* (1929) with siren accompaniment; the aura of Ernest Hemingway in *Impressions of the Bull Ring* (1927) with its flashing colors; a foreshadowing of concert jazz dance in *1927* (1927) to Gershwin rhythms; a summary of the 1920s "Champion of . . ." in *Prize Fight Studies* (1928) with its opening swagger performed to the beating of piano strings; a glimpse of Freud in *Subconscious* (1927), which included nudity; and a statement on sex in *Twentieth Century Bacchante* (1928), with its frank voluptuousness. Tamiris attacked affected Madonna interpretations in *Hypocrisy* (1928); she performed *The Queen Walks in the Garden* (1927) in silence; the spirit

TAMIRIS. A studio portrait of Tamiris in costume for one of her dances set to Negro spirituals. (Photograph from the Dance Collection, New York Public Library for the Performing Arts.)

of the Negro spiritual became her métier in *Nobody Knows de Trouble I See* (1928), *Swing Low, Sweet Chariot* (1929), and *Joshua Fit de Battle ob Jericho* (1928); and she sounded the call of the next decade in *Revolutionary March* (1929), using three kettle drums resounding alone and a flaglike costume: these were the awakenings of the social Tamiris. She was known as the "Harlem savage" who viewed life as conflict and said so verbally, physically, and artistically.

Tamiris was a leader in the development of the Dance Repertory Theatre of 1930 and 1931, during which the emerging modern dancers—Martha Graham, Doris Humphrey, and Charles Weidman (Agnes de Mille appeared in 1931)—banded together for financial reasons to give a series of their individual works at a common time in a common theater with a single staff. All did group works, Tamiris continuing to base hers on life as conflict. Accompaniment grew out of movement: in *Triangle Dance* (1930), instruments were carried; *Gris-Gris Ceremonial* (1932) used gourd rattles; and elbows beating on drums characterized *Mourning Ceremonial* (1931).

By 1934 Tamiris and Her Group was one of those forging the concert art called modern dance in *Walt Whitman Suite* (1934), a statement of yearning and being; *Toward the Light* (1934), a proccupation with freedom and existence; *Composition for Group* (1932), a sarcastic deriding of effeminacy and decadence; *Cycle of Unrest* (1935), a writhing manifesto of conflict and optimism; *Harvest 1935* (1935), a revolting denunciation of war; and *Momentum* (1936), a dramatic encounter between "haves" and "have-nots." The addition of *Crucifixion* (1931), *Git on Board, Lil Chillen* (1932), and *Go Down, Moses* (1932) completed what became her signature work, a suite of solos based on Negro spirituals, which, while expressing her sympathy for the oppressed human being, also reflected her own uninhibited nature and extemporaneous air and her love of the free flow of life, the impromptu, and the unpremeditated.

The concert dance *Mass Study* (1935) and the theater dances in the play *Gold Eagle Guy* (1934) were two results of Tamiris's affiliation with Group Theater, which developed into a reciprocal arrangement whereby she taught movement classes to its actors and the theater gave acting classes to her dancers. Lee Strasberg's adaptation of the Konstantin Stanislavsky method helped affirm and clarify Tamiris's approach to theatrical performance, direction, and choreography. It confirmed her search for specific human motivations for movement rather than reaching for abstract artistic applications.

Tamiris developed no characteristic technique that she could hand down to her followers. For her, no one way of moving could be true for everyone and for every moment. Instead she brought out the personal and existential style of each of her students, as she did for herself. Her own style became as immediate as her life itself—vital, warm, lusty, and powerful. She had sought and found movement, essentially primitive, that had the torso as its center, the face and limbs as the fringes of outflow. This movement grew out of her lusty affirmation of immediate life, a childlike wonder about its possibilities, and an innate respect for its endemic form. Thus Tamiris's style was found in her dance's dynamic actualities—the physicality of its movement, the forcefulness of its moment, and the clarity of its form.

John Martin described her impact in a review in the *New York Times:*

> What a really thrilling dancer she is when she breaks free from the moorings of sobriety and lets what a European critic once called 'the magnificent lust of motion' take possession of her! . . . there is a vitality, a warmth about her that relates her movements inevitably to human living. . . . What we need from her is more and more of that affirmation upon which she has laid so much stress; and we need it not only because it is part and parcel of her art but also, since she is interested in 'social content' in her dancing, because there is probably nothing anywhere to be found in the way of content that is more strongly social.   (15 November 1936)

By contrast, critical reaction to Tamiris's choreography during the 1930s was limited and insular. Neither esoteric enough to be accepted by reviewers for the Louis Horst journal, *Dance Observer*, nor sufficiently submerged in social protest to be acceptable to the *Daily Worker*, her works adhered to no exterior law. Whether making solo dances for herself in the 1920s, ensemble work for Tamiris and Her Group or mass dances for the Federal Theater in the 1930s, or chorus dances for Broadway musical theater after World War II, she worked from the premise that the here and now determined her art. Because of her ephemeral approach, Tamiris left no technique *per se* and few dances. A molder of the art form of modern dance as much as Martha Graham, Charles Weidman, Doris Humphrey, or Hanya Holm, she was left out of the Bennington Group, a fact that has caused parochial historians to discount her contribution to the development of that art form.

Tamiris was the one who was driven to use the new form to shape the consciousness of people, not merely to make artistic statements for a narrow coterie. Thus for much of the 1930s she served as the catalyst for dancers in the Works Progress Administration (WPA) Federal Art Project. It was she who had the sense of mission required for advancing the welfare of dancers as individuals and the expansion of modern dance as art. Groups she supported included the Concert Dancers' League (fighting sabbath laws), the Dancers' Emergency Association (providing financial support), and the New Dance League (advocating social action), and she formulated and chaired the American Dance Association, which was successful in setting up the Federal Dance Project. In 1936 the project sponsored Tamiris's *Salut au Monde*, five episodes depicting race struggle, and in 1937 the double bill of Weidman's *Candide* and Tamiris's *How Long, Brethren?*. With the last, Tamiris achieved "status." Based on seven Negro protest songs and sung by a Negro chorus, its choreography was awarded *Dance Magazine's* first award for outstanding group choreography.

Financial cuts and infighting gradually hamstrung the project by 1939 but not before Tamiris had produced *Trojan Incident* (1938), a short play about the subjugation of Troy (set off by dancers and onstage singers), and *Adelante* (1939), a seventy-five minute, all-dance work on Loyalist Spain, subsequently recognized by Margaret Lloyd as the first of the big modern ballets.

From 1939 to 1944, Tamiris (who now added the name of Helen to her single name) found herself without a company (hers had disappeared into the Federal Dance Project; the other modern dancers had kept theirs distinct) and with a politically suspect reputation. Unions came in, ballet flourished, the war spurred the economy. After her work in the Federal Theatre Project, which drew masses of people to modern dance, Tamiris turned to Broadway as the best place to draw similar crowds to this new art. Between 1943 and 1957 she choreographed modern dances in eighteen musical comedies, six of which had long runs. Rather than using chorus lines or technical displays to advance the script or to enhance the music, Tamiris integrated dance into such theater pieces as *Up in Central Park* (1945) with its Currier and Ives "Skating Ballet"; *Annie Get Your Gun* (1946), with Daniel Nagrin in its

TAMIRIS. *How Long, Brethren?* (1937), with Helen Tamiris and Her Group. Produced by the Federal Dance Project as part of a double bill with Charles Weidman's *Candide*, Tamiris's suite of dances to Negro songs of protest had a long, successful run on Broadway. Although the work dealt with the plight of African Americans, it was originally performed by an all-white cast of women. In the early 1990s, the African-American choreographer Dianne McIntyre reconstructed this work for several U.S. student groups. (Photograph from the Dance Collection, New York Public Library for the Performing Arts.)

"Wild Horse Ceremonial Dance"; and *Inside U.S.A.* (1948), with Valerie Bettis in "Tiger Lily" and "Haunted House." *By the Beautiful Sea* (1954) had an underwater ballet, and *Plain and Fancy* starred Nagrin in the poignant "By Lantern Light." Instinctively, Tamiris integrated dance action with acting, speech, song, and stage pictorialism. All elements were equally fused for the whole that was musical theater in the 1940s and 1950s.

Tamiris's choreography for *Touch and Go* (1949) won the Antoinette Perry ("Tony") Award for the best choreography of the season. *Up in Central Park* had a national tour in 1946–1947 and then toured Europe after World War II; in 1948 it became a motion picture (Universal International) and included her dances. The string of Broadway performances of *Annie Get Your Gun*—1,147— was extended in 1947 to a London production as well as a U.S. tour in 1947–1948. The 1954 production *Fanny* also had a long run on Broadway and a U.S. tour in 1956–1957. Other musicals choreographed by Tamiris included *Stovepipe Hat* (1944); a new production of *Show Boat* (1946) with white and black member choruses; *Park Avenue* (1946); *The Great Campaign* (1947), which was staged by the Experimental Theater; *Great to Be Alive* (1950); *Bless You All* (1950); *Flahooley* (1951); *Carnival in Flanders* (1953); and, for Utah's centennial, *The Promised Valley* (1947).

Although she did not always have a studio, Tamiris continually taught not only dance but also body movement for actors and directors, including stage movement for directors at the American Dance Festival in Connecticut (1960), the Perry-Mansfield School of Theater and Dance in Colorado (1956–1958), the Tamiris-Nagrin Dance Workshop, which was based in New York and had summers in Maine (1957–1964), and C. W. Post College, on Long Island (summer 1962, 1963). Tamiris had returned to concert modern dance in 1957. The Tamiris-Nagrin Dance Company, formed with her husband, Daniel Nagrin (married 1946, separated 1964), who was co-director and leading dancer, performed intermittently between 1960 and 1964.

[*See also* Federal Dance Project *and the entries on the principal figures mentioned herein.*]

BIBLIOGRAPHY

Lloyd, Margaret. *The Borzoi Book of Modern Dance.* New York, 1949.
Markoff, Luba. "Dance in the Political Arena: The Federal Dance Project and Helen Tamiris." Master's thesis, San Jose State University, 1992.
McDonagh, Don, ed. *The Complete Guide to Modern Dance.* New York, 1976.
Nagrin, Daniel. "Helen Tamiris and the Dance Historians." In *Proceedings of the Twelfth Annual Conference, Society of Dance History Scholars, Arizona State University, 17–19 February 1989,* compiled by Christena L. Schlundt. Riverside, Calif., 1989.
Prickett, Stacey. "'The People': Issues of Identity within the Revolutionary Dance." *Studies in Dance History* 5 (Spring 1994): 14–22.
Schlundt, Christena L. "Tamiris: A Chronicle of Her Dance Career, 1927–1955." New York, 1972. Reprinted in *Studies in Dance History* 1 (Fall–Winter 1989): 65–154.
Sorell, Walter, ed. *The Dance Has Many Faces.* New York, 1951.
Tamiris, Helen. "Tamiris in Her Own Voice: Draft of an Autobiography." Edited by Daniel Nagrin. *Studies in Dance History* 1 (Fall–Winter 1989): 1–64.
Tish, Pauline. "Remembering Helen Tamiris." *Dance Chronicle* 17.3 (1994): 327–360.

FILM AND VIDEOTAPE. *Helen Tamiris in Her Negro Spirituals* (1959). "Trailblazers of Modern Dance" (1977).

Christena L. Schlundt

TANAKA MIN (born 10 March 1945 in Hachioji-shi, Tokyo Prefecture, Japan), *butō* performer and choreographer. While at Tokyo Kyoiku University, which he had entered as a basketball player, Tanaka became a dancer. He studied ballet and modern dance, beginning his career as a professional modern dancer in 1966. Among his early works were *Dance-State Series* (1975), *Drive Series* (1977), and *Hyper-Dance* (1977).

In 1978, Tanaka created the Body Weather Laboratory, a sequenced series of exercises that he and others who have learned the technique teach in workshops. In 1981, he founded the Maijuku company in Tokyo, and in 1985 he established the Body Weather Farm in Yamanashi, a rural area several hours' drive from Tokyo. Tanaka has sought inspiration for his choreography in farming and communal life: he operates Body Weather as an organic farm; he established an annual festival, the Art Camp Hakushu, at the farm in 1988; and, every summer, he holds Body Weather Laboratory workshops there.

Tanaka first turned to *butō* in 1984, collaborating with Hijikata Tatsumi on the piece *Ren-ai Butō-ha* (Love *Butō*). Tanaka's later works have included two commissioned by the Paris Opéra-Comique: *Peut-on Danser une Paysage?* (Can We Dance a Landscape?, 1989), in collaboration with Dutch visual artist Karel Appel, and *Le Sacre du Printemps* (The Rite of Spring, 1990), in collaboration with sculptor Richard Serra; it has also commissioned *Tree* (1990). Tanaka has performed numerous times in the United States.

BIBLIOGRAPHY

Durland, Steven. "Weekend in the Country." *High Performance* (Summer 1990): 46–49.
"Min Tanaka at Bennington College." *Contact Quarterly* 19 (Summer-Fall 1994): 35–40.
Rouland, Katy. "Entretiens avec Min Tanaka." *Empreintes*, no. 6 (February 1984): 34–41.
Schmidt, Jochen. "The Individual as Microcosm." *Ballett International* 12 (November 1989): 18–21.
Stein, Bonnie Sue. "Min Tanaka: Farmer/Dancer or Dancer/Farmer." *Drama Review* 30 (Summer 1986): 142–151.
Tanaka Min. *Bodyprint.* Tokyo, 1981.

Hasegawa Roku
Translated from Japanese

TANGO. A complex popular genre in South America, tango involves dance, music, poetry, song, gesture, and narrative as well as philosophy and ethical values. During the late nineteenth century it was a vehicle that accelerated social integration in the Río de la Plata region of South America, weaving aesthetic and other cultural features from African, American, and European peoples. *Gauchos, criollos* (Creoles), European immigrants, and African Argentines participated in the formation of the genre.

Origins and Development of the Tango. The word *tango* is of Bantu origin (from central and southern Africa), meaning "drums" or "a social gathering with dances." Since the late 1700s, "tango" has referred to many different forms of dance and music (in chronological order): *tango de negros, tango americano* or *habanera, tango andaluz* or *tango español, tango criollo, tango rioplatense,* and *tango argentino.* The candombes, tambos, and tangos danced by Africans and African Argentines at the end of the eighteenth and the beginning of the nineteenth centuries were prohibited for "Christianizing" reasons by the viceroy and by the *cabildo* (town council). All these dances had no physical contact. The tango, as a dance of embrace, was born between 1860 and 1890 in the cities of Buenos Aires, Argentina, and Montevideo, Uruguay.

During this period when the tango crystallized as urban dance in the region of the Río de la Plata, Argentina was undergoing profound changes in the makeup of its population. In 1778 African Argentines constituted 29.7 percent of the population of Buenos Aires; by 1887 that percentage had declined to 1.8 percent, as African Argentines were displaced by European immigrants. Between 1821 and 1932 Argentina was second only to the United States among nations receiving immigrants (Canada was third). These immigrants came from all over Europe as well as from Lebanon and Syria, with the largest number coming from Italy and the second largest from Spain. In 1879, General Julio A. Roca's settlement program, the Conquest of the Desert, which attained land for cattle and agriculture, also contributed to the transformation of the Argentine population—it decimated a majority of the Araucanians, a native people. In 1880, the port city of Buenos Aires was named the federal capital of the Argentine Republic— *la Gran Aldea* would soon be a metropolis.

Until the middle of the nineteenth century, the European dances of the Río de la Plata region were the minuet, gavotte, contredance, and quadrille. From the 1840s until the end of the century, the waltz, polka, mazurka, and schottische were popular. In the 1830s African-Argentine dances and songs had begun to be imitated on stage. Between 1856 and 1865 the *compañías españolas de zarzuelas* performed *bailes de negros* and sang *tangos americanos* or Cuban *habaneras.* Minstrel shows, such as Christy's Minstrels (1869) from the United States, also imitated

TANGO. By 1920, from *barrio* to elegant cafe, the tango was danced at every level of Argentine society. On 6 September 1936 people danced it in the streets to celebrate the four hundreth anniversary of the founding of Buenos Aires. (Photograph from the Archivo General de la Nación, Buenos Aires.)

African dances and songs when they performed in Buenos Aires. At the same time, in their quest for social mobility, African Argentines began to imitate Europeans and incorporated the mazurka, the polka, and the waltz into their dances. The dance halls *(academias de baile)* provided the meeting place for the *candombe, habanera,* polka, mazurka, *milonga* (a form of improvised song to which choreography was added about 1860, it was first called the *habanera con cortes y quebradas* and later *baile con corte*), and the tango. The African-Argentine dances provided the movement and cadence of the tango and inspired the curves that form the tango poses. The figure called *ocho* ("eight") in the tango comes from the *candombe,* which is composed of a succession of eights drawn on the floor. The *ocho* is the base for all movements in the tango, as all other steps pass through it. The typical male dancers in the *academias de baile, compadres (gauchos* of the Argentine pampas who moved to the city but maintained their traditional attire and independent attitude), and *compadritos* (young men from the outskirts of Buenos Aires who imitated the attitudes of the *compadres*) mimicked and mocked the leg movements of the African Argentines.

Musical accompaniment to the *milonga tango* was played in 2/4 time on violin, guitar, and flute, with the harp sometimes replacing the guitar. Later the mandolin, the clarinet, the piano, and sometimes the accordion were added; at the turn of the century the *bandoneón* (large button accordion) was incorporated. In the 1910s the double bass, the violoncello, and the viola joined what had become a small orchestra. The tango, until then strongly influenced by the *habanera* and the *milonga*, began to assimilate Italian influences, as evidenced by the

TANGO. A popular aspect of feature films from the 1930s and 1940s, the tango was danced in RKO's *Flying Down to Rio* (1933) and Fox's *Down Argentine Way* (1940). In this photogaph, tango dancer and actor Elías Alippi holds an unidentified partner in the Argentine film *Así Es la Vida* (1939). (Photograph courtesy of María Susana Azzi.)

changing pathos of the music as well as the remarkable number of Italian surnames among the musicians.

The tango was danced in urban neighborhoods and in the *arrabales* ("suburbs"). It was primarily a dance of the brothels but also was danced on *patios* of the *conventillos* ("tenements"), where Italian, Spanish, Polish, and other immigrants shared crowded living quarters. Until this point, the tango was considered to be a marginal, immoral, and indecent dance and as such was rejected by the *porteño*—the Buenos Aires high society. Nevertheless, the *niños bien* (sons of well-to-do families) frequented the brothels, where they danced and often fought with the *compadritos*.

In 1907 the tango made its way to Paris and from there spread to other European capitals as well as to New York City. In the aristocratic ballrooms, the tango became "decent" and stylized, leaving aside the *cortes y quebradas* (suggestive contorsions followed by a pause). Upon its return to Buenos Aires, the upper class took up this new, "clean" tango. The middle class of Buenos Aires also modified the tango in the dance halls of the Italian and Spanish associations, where they danced the *tango liscio* or *liso*. The dance no longer had complicated leg movements, but the dancers retained the stamp of elegance and the walk, and they executed the rhythm and tempo with exactitude. This smooth *tango de salón* replaced the tango *canyengue* and the *tango orillero* (both styles full of exaggerated steps and adornments), which could not be accommodated in crowded dance halls. In exhibitions, where there was more space, dancers continued to use more complicated movements, performing what was then called the *tango fantasía*. In the 1920s, the tango was as popular in the heart of the city as it was in the *barrios* ("neighborhoods"), although the styles remained distinct. In the city center, the dance was stylized; in the *barrios*, dancers continued to adorn it with curves. When the great internal migration of the 1940s brought thousands of people from the Argentine provinces to the capital city of Buenos Aires, the tango underwent another transformation. In the 1950s, 1960s, and 1970s, however, the popularity of the tango declined significantly.

The Dance. The tango is a dance of embrace, meaning that the woman dances in the man's arms (the embrace is borrowed from the waltz). Although the man is the engine that generates the movement—he leads—the work of the dance is shared equally by the man and the woman. Always moving counterclockwise, the man walks the tango, indicating the figures and the poses by gently pressing his right hand against the woman's back. With an attitude that is creative and active rather than passive or submissive, the woman intuits the movements her partner desires. She plays and adorns with her feet and must know how to turn and twirl. If the male dancer does not walk the tango, he does not dance it. If he only makes figures, he cannot pause, which is when the woman plays. If the man's role is more difficult because he leads, the woman must be a good solo dancer, to capture the moment in movement but bridle it when tempering is needed. The man proposes, and the woman offers counterproposals. The posture, the embrace, and the ability to place one's foot "just so" defines the good dancer. When danced slowly, simply, and elegantly, "the tango," as Jorge Luis Borges has written, "is a way of walking."

The tango is a dance with a non-rigid structure that developed through trial and error; it is continually transformed through improvisation and is passed on from generation to generation. Improvisation has come to lie in the order of the steps and figures and not in the conceptualization of the dance itself, as the movements have become substantially standardized. For example, the tango can open with a figure *ocho* forward or backward. Some tangos inspire the dancers to adorn it, others to just walk it; there are sad and joyful tangos. The dancer or choreographer creates the structures from which to improvise the steps and figures: *ocho, boleo, sentada, quebrada*. Dancing slowly is very difficult because the dancer has to feel the motion, cadence, and pauses; the movement is not continuous. The woman feels the man mark the movement according to what he feels; he transmits messages, she receives and interprets them. When danced smoothly, the tango is poetic. The good dancer has the capacity to arouse emotions in his or her partner and in an audience. Among the principal male dancers of the tango have been Casimiro Aín ("El Vasco"), José Ovidio Bianquet ("El Cachafaz"), Carlos Alberto Estévez ("Petróleo"), Ramón Ribera ("Fino"), Juan Carlos Copes, Jorge Orcaizaguirre ("Virulazo"), Pepito Avellaneda (José Domingo Monteleone), Antonio Todaro, and Miguel Angel Zotto. The principal female dancers have been Edith Peggy, Olga San Juan, Carmencita Calderón, María Nieves, Elvira Santamaría, and Milena Plebs.

The tango is different when it is danced in a dance hall than when it is performed onstage. In a dance hall (*milonga*) the man dances with a variety of partners and the woman dances with various men; there is no choreography, only improvisation. The dancers' intuitions must be keen. Each dancer marks and feels the tango distinctly. The woman adapts her body to what her partner tells her with his marks. The man guides, the woman accompanies. The woman can adorn this dance with wantonness, sentimentality, or other emotions—or, she can follow closely what the man feels. The *milonguero* is an artist produced by "authentic" conditions in the *milongas*. Onstage, professional tango partners do a gymnastic and acrobatic dance. The movements are choreographed, not improvised, richly adorned, and exaggerated—otherwise it becomes visually dull. Onstage stylization derives from the tango developed in Paris. Partners dance upright, and the poses are distinct. It is a technical and structured tango that does not transmit the popular sentiment, the cadence, the pause, or the adagio of the music; the manner of walking one sees in the *milongas* is not conveyed. Audiences like the display, the drama, the passion, the dips.

Music, Arts, and Literature. The rhythm of tango music reflects its Andalusian and its African roots, while the melody is Italian. Tango music has evolved dramatically since it was first played by small bands at the beginning of the twentieth century: from trios, quartets, sextets, and full orchestras to the avant-garde and the innovative musician Astor Piazzolla. When the *bandoneón* was incorporated, the joy of the tango music became solemn; the *bandoneón* produces a serious sound, and the tango has become a serious matter. "The tango is a sad thought that can be danced," Enrique Santos Discépolo, one of the most talented tango poets, has said. It has become impossible to separate the concept of the tango from the timbre of the *bandoneón*; the sound of this instrument has generated a cultural memory. The repertory of instrumental

TANGO. Premiered in Paris in 1983, *Tango Argentino* became a worldwide hit. "La Cumparsita," a turn-of-the-century tango danced by María and Carlos Rivarola, was an audience favorite. (Photograph © 1985 by Linda Vartoogian; used by permission.)

TANGO. One of the most dramatic and popular tango shows ever produced, *Tango Argentino* soon made its way to Broadway. In this 1985 photograph, Noanim Timoyko and Nélida Rodríguez perform a tango during one of the show's visits to New York City. (Photograph © 1985 by Jack Vartoogian; used by permission.)

and sung tango is vast, yet two of the great tango figures take center stage in Argentina's cultural memory. Carlos Gardel (1890–1935) developed a style of tango singing that brought him enduring renown as its greatest vocal interpreter—he embodied the tango-song; Astor Piazzolla (1921–1992), whose music synthesized tango, jazz, and classical music, revolutionized the way of playing the *bandoneón*.

Tango Argentino, the Broadway hit created by Claudio Segovia and Héctor Orezzoli, opened for six days at the Festival d'Automne, Paris, in 1983. In 1993 it completed a ten-year run of fifty-seven cities in the United States, Europe, Japan, and Latin America. Dancers in the original cast were Juan Carlos Copes and María Nieves, Virulazo and Elvira, Gloria and Eduardo, Nélida and Nelson, Mayoral and Elsa María, María del Carmen and Carlos Rivarola, and "Los Dinzel" (Gloria and Rodolfo). The show's great success resulted in a demand for additional professors of dance; the opening of Argentine tango schools in Argentina, Europe, Japan, and the United States; and the creation of other similar shows, such as *Tango × 2*. The

rebirth of tango dance in Argentina has been directly related to the worldwide success of *Tango Argentino*.

The tango permeates the life and culture of the Argentine people (primarily the people in the Río de la Plata region), as one hears in frequent references to tango lyrics in daily life as well as in the works of many of the great twentieth-century Argentine writers, such as Roberto Arlt, Adolfo Bioy Casares, Jorge Luis Borges, Julio Cortázar, Ricardo Güiraldes, Leopoldo Lugones, Eduardo Mallea, Leopoldo Marechal, Ezequiel Martínez Estrada, and Ernesto Sábato. For Argentines, the tango continues to be both a central cultural reference and a strong source of cultural cohesion.

[*See also* Nieves and Copes *and* Plebs and Zotto. *For discussion in a broader context, see* Social Dance, *article on* Twentieth-Century Social Dance to 1960.]

BIBLIOGRAPHY

Andrews, George Reid. *The Afro-Argentines of Buenos Aires, 1800–1900*. Madison, Wis., 1980.

Azzi, María Susana. *Antropología del tango: Los protagonistas*. Buenos Aires, 1991.

Azzi, María Susana. "Multicultural Tango: The Impact and the Contribution of the Italian Immigration to the Tango in Argentina." *International Journal of Musicology* 5 (1996).

Azzi, María Susana. "The Golden Age and After: 1920s–1990s." In *¡Tango!*, by Simon Collier et al. London, 1995: 114–160.

Azzi, María Susana. "Tango Argentino." In *The Universe of Music: A World History*, vol. 11, *Latin America and the Caribbean*, edited by Malena Kuss. Washington, D.C. (forthcoming).

Borges, Jorge Luis. *Evaristo Carriego: A Book about Old-Time Buenos Aires*. Translated by Norman Thomas di Giovanni. New York, 1984.

Castro, Donald S. *The Argentine Tango as Social History, 1880–1955*. Lewiston, N.Y., 1991.

Collier, Simon. *The Life, Music, and Times of Carlos Gardel*. Pittsburgh, 1986.

Collier, Simon. "The Tango Is Born, 1880s–1920." In *¡Tango!*, by Simon Collier et al. London, 1995: 18–64.

Copes, Juan Carlos. *Let's Dance: Bailemos tango*. Buenos Aires, 1984.

Ferrer, Horacio. *El libro del tango*. Buenos Aires, 1980.

Gesualdo, Vicente. *Historia de la música en la Argentina*. Buenos Aires, 1961.

Hanna, Gabriela. *Así bailaban el tango*. Berlin, 1993.

La historia del tango. 19 vols. Buenos Aires, 1976–1987.

Jakubs, Deborah L. "From Baudy House to Cabaret: The Evolution of the Tango as an Expression of Argentine Popular Culture." *Journal of Popular Culture* 18 (Summer 1984): 133–145.

Novati, Jorge, et al. *Antología del tango rioplatense*. Vol. 1. Buenos Aires, 1980.

Savigliano, Marta. *Tango and the Political Economy of Passion*. Boulder, Colo., 1995.

Taylor, Julie M. "Tango: Theme of Class and Nation." *Ethnomusicology* 20.2 (1977): 273–291.

Tienken, Arthur A. "Carlos Gardel: Fifty Years Later." *Studies in Latin American Popular Culture* 7 (1988): 309–314.

Vass, Winifred Kellersberger. *The Bantu-Speaking Heritage of the United States*. Los Angeles, 1979.

Zlotchew, Clark M. "Tango, *Lunfardo*, and the Popular Culture of Buenos Aires." *Studies in Latin American Popular Culture* 8 (1989): 271–285.

MARÍA SUSANA AZZI
Translated from Spanish

TANKARD, MERYL (born 8 September 1955 in Darwin), Australian dancer and choreographer. Since 1989, when she was appointed artistic director of a permanent company, Tankard has emerged as one of Australia's most innovative choreographers of dance theater. She began her professional dance career with the Australian Ballet, which she joined in 1975 after graduating from the Australian Ballet School. She spent three years as a dancer with the company. During that time she choreographed her first piece, *Birds behind Bars,* for a special program presented by the Australian Ballet in 1977 as a tribute to retiring artistic director Dame Peggy van Praagh.

While on a study tour in Europe in 1978, Tankard's career moved in a major new direction when she encountered the work of the German choreographer Pina Bausch. Tankard joined Bausch's Tanztheater Wuppertal in 1978 and until 1984 performed as a soloist with the company, taking major roles in many of Bausch's works, including *Le Sacre du Printemps* and *Bluebeard.* While in Wuppertal she also co-wrote and performed in an experimental film, *Sydney on the Wupper,* which won a gold award at the Berlin Film Festival in 1983.

Tankard returned to Australia in 1984 to choreograph *Echo Point* and to freelance as a choreographer, performer, and director. Between 1984 and 1988 she also frequently returned to Bausch's company, touring with it as guest artist throughout Europe and in Canada and the United States. From 1989 to 1992 she was director of the Canberra-based Meryl Tankard Company. In 1993 she became director of the Australian Dance Theatre in Adelaide, which she renamed the Meryl Tankard Australian Dance Theatre.

Tankard's choreography builds on her experiences with Bausch. Some of her works stand in a direct line of descent from specific pieces in the Bausch repertory. Tankard's *Two Feet,* with its stress on the compulsive behavior often associated with performers and performances, recalls Bausch's *Bandoneon,* while the flooding of the stage with water in the final moments of *Two Feet* is reminiscent of Bausch's *Arien.* Like Bausch, Tankard also works from an emotional rather than a technical base. Bausch has remarked that she is not interested so much in how people move as what moves them, which could equally apply to Tankard.

Tankard builds her choreography from real experiences, often ones that develop during the rehearsal period. Her work is strongly image-based, with a new vocabulary emerging for each piece. In 1993 she made *Furioso* in which her dancers, attached to ropes and harnesses, were airborne for large sections of the piece. Since then, her choreography has continued to explore parts of the stage space not normally used in dance. She usually uses a collage of music taken from a variety of sources—although a number of her pieces, including *Songs with Mara* and *Banshee*—have involved collaboration with live musicians who have a distinct performing role in the works. An important influence on her work has been that of her associate artist, photographer, and scenic designer, Régis Lansac. Lansac's use of slide projections, exemplified by his work for *Nuti,* in which images are projected onto moving bodies, is often an intrinsic part of a Tankard production. Tankard's other credits include work for film and television and the choreography for two productions by the Australian Opera, *Death in Venice* (1989), *Orphée et Euridyce* (1993), and *The Deep End* (1996), a commissioned one-act work for the Australian Ballet.

BIBLIOGRAPHY

Halligan, Marion. "The Meryl Tankard Company." *Fremantle Arts Review* 5 (June 1990): 17–19.
Kiernander, Adrian. "Meryl Tankard's Australian Dance Theatre." *Theatre Forum,* no. 6 (Winter/Spring 1995): 5–11.
Nugent, Ann. "Meryl Tankard: An Impression." *Writings on Dance,* no. 5 (Autumn 1990): 52–62.
Potter, Michelle. *A Passion for Dance.* Canberra, 1997.
Potter, Michelle et al. "Meryl Tankard: The Canberra Record 1989–1992." *Brolga,* no. 3 (December 1995): 49–52.

INTERVIEW. Meryl Tankard, by Shirley McKechnie (July 1990), National Library of Australia, Canberra (TRC 2602). Meryl Tankard, by Michelle Potter (July 1996), National Library of Australia, Canberra (TRC 3477).

MICHELLE POTTER

TANZANIA. *See* Central and East Africa.

TAP DANCE. An American art form that fuses West African and British Isles dance traditions, tap dance slowly evolved between the mid-1600s and early 1800s from two sets of parent forms: British Isles soft-shoe and hard-shoe step dances, such as the jig, reel, and various clog dances, and a variety of secular and religious African step dances labeled *juba* and *ringshout* dances. In general, as tap's African elements became more formal and diluted, its European elements became more fluid and rhythmic. When African rhythms and performance styles fused with European techniques of footwork, the American tap hybrid was born.

What distinguishes tap from all other forms of dance based on percussive footwork is its unique jazz rhythms and syncopations. The rhythms, for example, of traditional clog dancing, classic flamenco *estampe,* or North Indian *kathak* sound very different from tap rhythms, yet all these dance styles share common techniques of footwork. Because their accent patterns, syncopations, and rhythm patterns differentiate one dance style from another, the polyrhythmic, multimetric African percussive sensibility is considered to have exerted the most profound influence on the development of tap.

Examples of tap's double heritage suggest ways in which African and European dance might have blended. Because it was done on the bare earth in bare feet, much African dance favored gliding, dragging, shuffling, and stamping footwork, with the body held in a gently crouched position. Tap's assimilation of these features is clear in its use of slides, drags, shuffles, and chugs and in its relaxed body attitude. Conversely, in step dances such as the jig and in clog dances the body was held erect; usually performed in hard-soled shoes or clogs on wooden floors, these dances favored the articulated and highly codified heel-and-toe actions that would provide the technical amplification for tap's percussive development. It is important to note that the old-style (*sean-nós* in Irish) step dances in England and Ireland were very different from later exhibition and competition forms. The old close-to-the-floor style of solo step dancing (and the step-dance vocabulary that occurs in the social form called set dances) was the main British Isles influence on the development of tap from 1600 to 1800. Theatricalized versions of step dances, such as the hornpipe and jig, only made their way to the United States (and began to influence the evolution of tap) with itinerant exhibition dancers after 1800. African dance, like African music, is polyrhythmic and multimetric, pushed forward by a propulsive tempo that accents the *offbeat* (the basis of jazz), a rhythmic signature whose imprint is seen in the performance of American social dance and heard in the percussions of tap. In African animal dances, details of the animal's behavior are realistically imitated in the whole body; these dances have enriched tap's vocabulary with such steps and gestures as pecking, shimmies, and snake hips. The term *buck-and-wing* described an early tap combination of shuffles and wings (in a "wing" the tapper jumps in the air while simultaneously executing a three-beat shuffle with the toes of one foot; excellent tappers can execute a five- or six-beat shuffle before landing), whereas *buck dancer* was an early term used to describe a solo male tap dancer, presumably because the rapid shuffling of the feet resembled pawing, prancing hooves.

TAP DANCE. A ninenteenth-century print by Matt Morgan of the flat-footed African-American step dancing that was a precursor to modern tap. Here, wooden planks supported by barrels serve as a resonant platform. Musicians are pictured playing banjo, fiddle, and tambourine, the typical accompaniment for this type of dance. (Collection of Sally R. Sommer and William G. Sommer.)

TAP DANCE. This postcard, captioned "Waiting for the Sunday Boat," shows a buck dancer "heel-and-toeing," c.1900. (Collection of Sally R. Sommer and William G. Sommer.)

Whites and blacks undoubtedly watched each other dance because between the seventeenth and nineteenth centuries blacks adapted the figures and partner relationships of European dances for their own use. Blacks adopted the form of men and women dancing together, following the figures of reels and quadrilles, but retained their African steps and rhythms. After 1825, with the rise of minstrelsy, the borrowing was reversed: white minstrelmen frankly copied African and African-American dance and musical styles and used them as their stage material, and after 1890 black social dances were rapidly assimilated into mainstream white culture—a trend that has dominated American social dancing in the twentieth century. [See United States of America, *articles on African-American dance traditions.*]

As the number of slaves in the colonies increased, so did the number of rules governing their behavior. One law in particular, first passed in 1739 in the Carolinas and soon legislated by the other colonies, directly affected the development of tap. As a result of a slave uprising known as the Cato Conspiracy or the Stono Insurrection, white slave masters, convinced (wrongly) that the sound of drums echoing throughout the countryside had called the slaves to revolt, made it illegal and punishable for slaves to play drums or congregate. In place of the forbidden drums, the slaves had to rely on tambourines, bones, banjos, fiddles, and "patting"—also known as "hamboning"—whereby the body is slapped as if it were a drum set. It was the feet, however, that became one of the most important of the slaves' percussive instruments, and this development was noted in contemporary accounts throughout the 1700s. Increasingly there were references to the popularity of "patting juba" and descriptions of feet slapping the floors at slave "frolics," beating against the ground like hail pounding on rooftops.

House slaves observed their masters dancing (or taking lessons from itinerant dancing masters) and may have seen some of the fine Irish step dancers who toured the South as entertainers. By the late 1700s and early 1800s, jig dancing contests were held between competing plantations, with owners placing bets on their favorite slave dancers. A couple of large planks were placed across supporting sawhorses or barrels to serve as a dancing platform and the winner was the dancer who executed the most complex footwork and daring turns without losing rhythm or balance. Similar contests took place on the docks and levees of the great rivers, and in urban centers jigging contests were held on market days, with the planks laid down on cobblestones in the city square.

By this time the term *jig* was beginning to be loosely applied to all African-American step dances, indicating, perhaps, that black and white styles looked similar and were blending together. It was with the rise of the minstrel show in the late 1820s, however, that tap quickly developed into a codified stage dance. White minstrelmen (usually Irish) blackened their faces with burnt cork and created stage performances based on their interpretations of plantation slaves and their music and dance forms—competing among themselves to see who had the most "authentic" material. Between 1840 and 1890 minstrel shows were the most popular form of American entertainment. Featuring a variety of songs, jokes, dancing, and music in a loose format, minstrel shows could have as few as four performers or as many as 150; at the peak of the shows' popularity, more than sixty companies crisscrossed the United States, and many regularly toured Europe. At best,

TAP DANCE. A portrait of Bill ("Bojangles") Robinson, who developed a light, crisp style by tapping up on his toes and departing from the flat-footed buck-and-wing tradition. (Photograph by James J. Kriegsmann; from the collection of Frankie Manning and Cynthia R. Millman.)

these minstrelmen could offer only pale copies of the African-American originals; at worst, they presented degrading racial stereotypes and caricatures. Nevertheless, the long-term popularity of the minstrel show testifies to the increasing influence of and interest in black culture in the United States, even in these whited-out formulas.

Before 1865 (and the end of the Civil War), black and white performers rarely were permitted to appear on stage together. One notable exception was Master Juba (William Henry Lane), an important figure in the history of tap dance. Born free in about 1825, Lane became a well-known dancer in the Five Points area of New York City when he was a teenager. A skilled Irish-jig and clog dancer, Lane was famous for his skillful and precise imitations of the best-known minstrel dancers of his day. Furthermore, he created his own rhythmically complex and virtuosic form of dance and was declared the champion dancer of his time, winning that title in the many minstrel dance competitions fiercely promoted by the various minstrel companies. Four of the best companies vied for his services, and they all gave him featured billing above his white colleagues. When Lane traveled to London with

Pell's Ethiopian Serenaders in 1848, enthralled English critics—discerning judges of the traditional jigs and clogs—hailed Lane's dancing as unique both in its new rhythms and in his method of beating time with his feet. Clearly Lane had forged a style of dance that was neither African nor European but something in between. Grafting African-American rhythms onto the exacting techniques of the hard-shoe step dances and clogs, Lane set the standard for excellence. Although he died young (in about 1852), he was so respected that for years after his death minstrelmen would advertise their skills by announcing that they danced in the style of the late Master Juba. (*Juba* was an honorary name given to many fine minstrel dancers, but *late* referred specifically to Lane.) [*See the entry on Juba.*]

If Lane imitated white dance styles, white minstrelmen did the reverse. Skilled step and clog dancers hastened the development of tap every time they performed their imitations and interpretations of plantation dancing. Whether their intentions were parodic or purely derogatory, they internalized African-American rhythms and performance styles, thereby unintentionally contributing to the tap hybrid.

After the Civil War many black or mixed minstrel companies were founded—ironically, African Americans had to perform in blackface—and freshness and a new vitality were brought to the dance by performers in touch with their own culture. By the late 1890s the tap vocabulary included syncopated *stop times*, using silence to punctuate the rhythms; *sand dancing*, using the gritty abrasive sound of feet scraping on sand as the source of percussion; the *essence*, a rapid pigeon-toeing motion that made the dancer appear to slip across the stage as if on rollers; the *soft-shoe*, a graceful dance usually performed to a languid 4/4 tempo, originally done in soft-soled shoes and later with taps (later still, the soft-shoe became an elegant tap dance and style of performance); the *waltz clog*, a basic clog step done to an easy 3/4 tempo; and the *time step*, the most basic combination in tap, which uses syncopated accents in a 4/4 tempo.

Between 1890 and 1915 all sorts of steps and phrases from vernacular social dances—such as the cakewalk strut, rubber-legging, and the camel walk—were incorporated into tap. The body had softened and relaxed from the erect position of the clog dancer, the knees were slightly bent, and the shoulders and arms were used for witty and whimsical gestures. The term *tap* came into popular use very late; it may have been first used in public advertising by Ziegfeld Follies' dance director Ned Wayburn in 1902. Previously the dance had been called buck-and-wing, buck dancing, or flat-footed dancing (because of the shuffles, drags, and slides that differed from traditional clog steps); it also went by the older names step, clog, and jig dancing. Metal plates attached to the bot-toms of heel and toe did not come into common use until after 1910. Before then, a typical shoe had leather uppers and wooden soles split at the ball of the foot or soles with wooden pieces set into toe and heel. A variation was shoes with hobnails or pennies pounded into toe and heel (an old Irish practice that continued into the twentieth century); yet another shoe had soles made from several layers of leather covered at toe and heel with tiny nails sanded smooth.

With the rise of vaudeville and of traveling black road shows and Broadway revues and musicals, numerous performance opportunities opened up for tap as its haphazard but vigorous growth continued. [*See* Vaudeville.] Still, racism was insidious, and black and white performers essentially danced on different theatrical circuits for different audiences. In white vaudeville, several large syndicates (such as E. F. Albee and B. F. Keith's) linked hundreds of theaters together under a single artistic management. The Theater Owners' Booking Association (TOBA) was the single black syndicate; at its peak in the 1920s, TOBA controlled more than two hundred vaudeville theaters. The tap dance chorus line became entrenched on the larger stages of white, mainstream Broadway theaters where big-budget productions enjoyed long runs. Unrestrained by touring costs that limited the size of vaudeville shows, Broadway producers could hire professional dance directors and large chorus lines. Yet the quality of tap technique and choreography deteriorated. The reason is clear: the more dancers in a line, the simpler the rhythms tend to become, because complicated combinations are blurred by the multiplication of feet. The cycle of mediocrity continued as studios were established (often by the dance directors) to train the dancers with technique sufficient only to perform the simple routines and techniques necessary for chorus work.

Unlike other dance genres, tap has never been characterized by great teaching institutions where choreographers and dancers could go to learn the large and varied vocabulary that has evolved through the years. In the world of black tap dance in particular, traditions and techniques have almost always been learned through an informal process of observation and imitation followed by apprenticeship. In earlier decades, performance skills were sharpened in informal tap competitions or "tap-offs"; the winner was the dancer with the most daring improvisations and inventive step combinations. There was—and still is—an emphasis on developing individual styles. A tacit rule of this system is: you can copy my steps but not exactly, which bespeaks an attitude opposed to the practice of the well-drilled classroom.

Vaudeville, rather than Broadway, became the nursery for great tap-dancing talent. Indeed, the artistry of tap is perhaps best refined in the individual performer or in the small team of three to eight members, whose virtuosic rhythms can be clearly heard. The practice of playing before many different types of audiences enabled vaudeville performers to perfect their work, which kept the quality of their tap dancing extraordinarily high. The variety format was typical of all popular entertainment forms—on Broadway, in revues, and in vaudeville. In order to satisfy the public's taste and to define personal styles, performers drew on their imaginations to come up continually with something new. Gradually tap became roughly divisible into categories of performance styles. Good performers often merged different styles, and the lines that divide one classification from another are blurred at best.

Eccentric tap relied on idiosyncratic body movements: the body was almost as loose as a wet mop, unable to remain upright while the feet tapped out chattering rhythms below. This style was perfected by Ray Bolger and the lesser known but superb "Rubberneck" Holmes, a favorite performer on the TOBA circuit. *Comedy* tap always involved two or more dancers and often employed eccentric moves. The team of Bert Williams and George Walker personified this style: Williams's legs seemed to be

TAP DANCE. John W. Bubbles and Ford Lee ("Buck") Washington began collaborating in Louisville, Kentucky, in the 1910s, forming the famous singing-and-dancing act Buck and Bubbles. They are pictured here at the Zanzibar nightclub in 1943: Buck plays the piano as Bubbles dances. (Photograph from the collection of Sally R. Sommer and William G. Sommer.)

made of rubber, and as he did a slow and lazy hip grind he seemed on the verge of tripping over his rapidly shuffling feet. Walker, elegant in dress and manner, was a "class act" tapper and cakewalker who acted as a foil to Williams. *Flash* tap refers to spectacular tricks incorporated into tap phrases; done well, these touches add spice and visual interest.

Perhaps the best-known and most respected tap performers who used elements of flash techniques in their routines were the extremely elegant tap dance team known as the Nicholas Brothers (Harold and Fayard Nicholas). They would leap from platforms or stairs (one platform they used is said to have been more than ten feet high), land in full splits, bounce up, and continue with their tap phrases. [*See the entry on the Nicholas brothers.*] There were also acrobatic teams who extended flash tap by combining acrobatic maneuvers with their regular routines. The most elegant of these teams was the versatile Berry Brothers (Ananias, James, and Warren), who used many different stylistic elements in their dancing, including spectacular acrobatic work. [*See the entry on the Berry brothers.*] The art of acrobatic tap is to time each feat precisely and accurately so that the rhythms of the dance are

TAP DANCE. *Ruby Keeler and Paul Draper in the Hollywood film* Colleen *(Warner Brothers, 1936). Keeler was an early tap star of the movies. Draper, who combined intricate footwork with smooth body movements, is noted for performing tap dance to classical music. (Photograph from the collection of Rusty E. Frank.)*

not disturbed. *Class acts,* as the term suggests, were debonair in manner, sophisticated in dress, and charming, elegant, and casual in dancing style. Fred Astaire personified this tap style on film, and the equally remarkable Charles ("Honi") Coles epitomized it on the stage.

The years 1920 to 1935 constituted the heyday of the Harlem Renaissance, the nightclub, black Broadway, and vaudeville, and throughout these years tap was the most popular of all the stage dances. The best known of all the tap dancers was Bill ("Bojangales") Robinson, who performed in each of these arenas as well as on film. Admired for his neat, clean footwork and for his style of dancing up on his toes with minimal heel taps, Robinson created dances that were brilliantly shaded with tonal nuance and dynamic shifts, using easily heard and economical rhythmic lines. Robinson's buoyant performances and style of phrasing set new standards in the evolution of tap; the typical patterning of the eight-bar phrase was three two-bar phrases followed by a two-bar contrasting phrase (known as the *break*). Considered to be the classic structure of tap, this pattern is still fundamental to the genre. Robinson always performed in split, wooden-soled shoes, preferring their mellow sound to the clatter of metallic plates. The stair dance may not have originated with Robinson, but he brought it to such a level of excellence that it has become synonymous with his name—perhaps the most famous example being the routine he performed with Shirley Temple in the 1935 movie *The Little Colonel.* [*See the entry on Robinson.*]

A younger man, John W. Bubbles (John ["Bubber"] Sublett), was known as the father of *rhythm* tap because he perfected this unique style and, like Robinson before him, influenced future generations of tappers. By bringing down his heels, Bubbles brought tap down from the toes; slapping his heels against the floor like a drummer hitting the bass drum, Bubbles added a new range of syncopated accents to his rhythmical lines. His rhythms were contemporary with—and in some cases preceded—the complex syncopations that developed in jazz music during the late 1920s and early 1930s and that would evolve further in bebop. Bubbles freed tap from the classic eight bar phrase ending in a two-bar break by "running" the bars, hooking together longer nonrepetitive phrases and lacing them across as many as sixteen bars. This style has continued to predominate in tap performances. [*See the entry on Bubbles.*]

A favorite offstage haunt for Bubbles and others of his generation was the Hoofers' Club, located on 131st Street in Harlem; it was really nothing more than a small back room that the sympathetic owner of a pool hall set aside for tap dancers. Open twenty-four hours a day, the club became the gathering place for tap dancers, the tap summit where famous improvisational contests were held. The best challenged the best, and because the aspiring dancers learned from the experts through observation and imitation, the Hoofers' Club earned its reputation as the best unofficial tap school in the country. The improvisational spirit comes from tap's African heritage and did much to foster its technical development, particularly among African-American tap dancers. When the Hoofers' Club closed in the late 1930s, something vital was lost, yet by then the tradition of the tap challenge had become part of tap's technique and performance, and it has remained one of the most important ingredients in the modern tap vocabulary.

With the rise of film and the demise of vaudeville during the 1930s, performers had to compete for audiences in a shrinking market. As a result, tap routines got trickier, filled with flash and increasingly dangerous acrobatics that kept audiences gasping. Writing in the *New Yorker*, prescient critic Robert Benchley discerned the trend:

> Up until three or four years ago I was the Peer of Tap-Dance-Enjoyers. . . . It didn't seem as if I could get enough tap-dancing. But I did. More than enough. With every revue and musical comedy offering a complicated tap routine every seven minutes throughout the program, and each dancer vying with the rest to upset the easy rhythm of the original dance form, tap-dancing lost its tang.

In the early 1930s, with the importation to Hollywood of Broadway dance directors, such as Sammy Lee, Seymour Felix, and especially Busby Berkeley, the tap dancing chorus line was taken to its surrealistic limit. Once again, as in the huge Broadway chorus lines, the artistry of tap was not enhanced by the chorus line numbers. The increasing mobility of the camera, as well as the ability of the editors to juxtapose and layer images in the cutting room, decreased, even further, the necessity for any tap technique. One of the notable exceptions to this declining excellence were the Russell Market Girls, a well-drilled and highly skilled tap-dancing chorus line. The quality of tap choreography inevitably suffered. However, Hollywood also preserved some of the finest tap dancing in the solo performances of Hal Leroy, Ann Miller, Buddy Ebsen, Ray Bolger, Eleanor Powell, Donald O'Connor, Vera-Ellen, Ginger Rogers and, above all, in the tap dance performances of Gene Kelly and the brilliant Fred Astaire. Astaire and Kelly epitomized the range of American tap styles. Kelly was athletic and smooth. The roles he usually played in film—reflected in his tap style as well—were unpretentious, everyday, working-class characters. In contrast, Astaire, whose tap style was elegant, classy and graceful, usually played debonair, charming characters who were themselves professional dancers. Astaire is certainly America's most famous tap dancer. Indeed, were it not for the continuing popularity of the Astaire films, the art of tap dancing probably would have been completely forgotten by the American public from the mid-1950s to

TAP DANCE. Fred Astaire in *Three Little Words* (MGM, 1950). (Photograph courtesy of the Kobal Collection, London.)

the mid-1970s, when tap all but disappeared from public view.

Broadway tastes shifted in the 1940s, when a new kind of dance, derived from ballet, modern-dance, and jazz-dance vocabularies, was introduced to audiences in *Pal Joey* and *Oklahoma!* Vaudeville was dead, and tap dancers had few places to perform. They traveled with the big bands as speciality acts and continued to appear in prologues, live entertainments that preceded the showing of films. Over the next twenty years tap gradually went into decline, kept alive only by a few remaining clubs and the reruns of Astaire's superb films.

The tap revival began slowly. The first flare was set off at the 1962 Newport Jazz Festival by jazz and tap historian Marshall Stearns when he brought eight of the older black tap percussionists back to the stage. Although the audience and the critics were dazzled, they believed that this was tap's swan song. In the 8 July edition of the *Boston Herald*, critic George Frazier praised the tappers, noting how "their Shim Sham sanctified the sunlight, so that if you had never seen this before, you could hardly believe that creativeness could seem so casual. Then for more than an hour these men—this dying breed—made a lithe litany." Fortunately, everyone was mistaken: these performances heralded a rebirth. In 1968 a series of concerts called *Tap Happenings* lit up the stage of the Dixie Hotel in Manhattan. Standing in the traditional semicircle, legendary figures of the African-American jazz-tap world each stepped out to take a solo riff. The success of this show reawakened the world of dance to the jazz-tap heritage it had almost let slip away. Suddenly the tap masters were teaching and performing once more.

The revival of *No, No, Nanette* with Ruby Keeler brought tap back to Broadway in 1971, followed by *The Wiz* (1975) and *Bubblin' Brown Sugar* (1976). Then, in quick succession, came *Sugar Babies* (1979), *42nd Street* (1980), *Sophisticated Ladies* (1981), *The Tap Dance Kid* (1982), and *My One and Only* (1983). Also during this pe-

TAP DANCE. Jimmy Slyde, a master of rhythm tap, in performance, c.1984. (Photograph from the collection of Sally R. Sommer and William G. Sommer.)

riod, tap dance was brought to dance concertgoers, thereby gaining new audiences and critical acclaim from a hitherto unexposed section of the dance world. Throughout its history, tap had been treated as entertainment, but now it was being considered as art, and a new generation of dancers began to study tap and to form small tap dance companies that performed in modern-dance concert halls.

Jazz appealed to the minimalist aesthetic of the 1970s that revered improvisation and advocated an unstressed, pedestrian style of movement. The dexterous footwork of tap can be viewed as a flamboyant celebration of the walk. In tap, dancer and musician are the same, exemplified by the simple elegance of "tacet" tapping, with the sounds of taps as the only music.

Conspicuously, during the 1970s, the younger tap dancers actively sought out older African-American tap masters to teach them the jazz-tap or rhythm-tap style, strongly identified with John Bubbles, that flourished most markedly in the black tap and jazz communities. The traditional system of informal apprenticeship, with the tap competition or challenge as an essential evolutionary force, was maintained and refined. Instead of learning just an exacting tap vocabulary and unchangeable routine, the dancers were now taught to think of themselves as percussive instrumentalists with an improvisational sensibility. Although set routines are frequently used in jazz tap, the tapper does not necessarily need to adhere to the precise choreography. The routine may merely provide a structure within which the dancer creates improvisational rhythmic riffs—in the same way the jazz musician improvises with the well-known tune.

During the next fifteen years, extraordinary tap masters passed on the craft of jazz tap. Important mentors in New York were Charles ("Cookie") Cook, Charles ("Honi") Coles, Marion Coles, Chuck Green, Harriet Browne, Burt ("Gip") Gibson, Lon Chaney, Ralph Brown, Howard ("Sandman") Sims, Buster Brown; in Los Angeles, Eddie Brown, John Bubbles, and Jack Johnson; in Boston, Stanley Green, Leon Collins, Jimmy Slyde; in Florida, Steve Condos; in Chicago, Jimmy Payne.

From the mid-1970s through the mid-1980s, tap choreography was taken forward by a generation of dancers who were most often white, female, and trained in modern dance techniques. Although they learned jazz tap technique from the older Black tap masters, they choreographed by fusing traditional jazz-tap material with a modern-dance aesthetic, a fusion which shaped tap's concert presentation during the 1980s. Notable among these companies are Brenda Bufalino and the American Tap Dance Orchestra; Lynn Dally's Jazz Tap Ensemble; Heather Cornell's Manhattan Tap; and Linda Sohl-Donnell's Rhapsody in Taps.

In the 1980s and 1990s national tap festivals and conferences began to be held, initiated with By Word of Foot, organized by Jane Goldberg in 1981. These gatherings of venerated tap teachers, performers, and historians helped strengthen the community by offering opportunities for study, performances, and tap exchanges among tappers from all over the country. Concurrently, Europe slowly began rediscovering tap and appreciating its expatriot and younger tap dancers.

At the end of the 1980s, inspired by the Broadway success of *Black and Blue* (1989), and especially inspired by tap dancer Gregory Hines, who starred in *Sophisticated Ladies* (1983) and in *Jelly's Last Jam* (1991), along with Savion Glover, as well as in the Hollywood films *White Nights* (1985) and *Tap* (1989), many young African-American male dancers were attracted to tap.

The unquestioned leader of this youthful avant-garde was the brilliant Savion Glover. Profoundly influenced by the harsh vibrancy of 1990s hip-hop music with its heavy bass beats, political rap poetry, and fierce, inner-city sensibility, Glover's hip-hop–funk tap caused a major stylistic revolution within the field. Most importantly, it brought tap in line with the newest musical developments. Sometimes called "power tapping," the style is distinguished by dense, hard-hitting rhythms. The body hunkers over, the arms are used pragmatically to maintain balance, the knees are deeply bent, and the feet seem to attack and pound the floor. Little attempt is made to please the audience with smiles or eye contact and the dancer's focus remains inward as he searches to "find the groove." "Finding the groove" happens when the tapper plays with his rhythms until he creates a baseline beat, a rhythmic cadence around which he can weave his varied riffs. When the groove is good, it causes an almost trancelike state. The style—masculine, heavy, and fast—defines the George Wolfe–Savion Glover collaborative dance drama, *Bring in 'da Noise, Bring in 'da Funk: A Hip Hop Discourse on the Staying Power of the Beat,* which opened on Broadway in the fall of 1996.

At the end of the twentieth century, tap continues to maintain a varied cultural tradition that is intergenerational, multiracial, and interdisciplinary, maintaining a high level of choreographic inventions. Tap has taken its place on concert as well as musical stages, in film, and in television. Its choreographic expressions range from traditional jazz tap to tap dance "orchestras" and experimental fusions of new music with tap performance. With the passing of the elder tap masters, the next generation of tap dancers has taken up the responsibility of keeping the legacy alive. In many respects tap seems new because it was virtually lost for two decades. Although tap is still a small part of the dance world, it continues to undergo vigorous change and growth; and because it has yet to discover its full potential, or reach its limitations, tap re-

TAP DANCE. The leader of a new generation of rhythm tappers, Savion Glover, in a 1991 performance. (Photograph © 1991 by Jack Vartoogian; used by permission.)

mains one of the more vital elements in the American dance world.

[*For related discussion, see also* United States of America, *article on* Musical Theater; *and the entries on Astaire, Baby Laurence, Bates, Berkeley, Bolger, Coles, Draper, Four Step Brothers, Green, Hines, Kelly, Miller, O'Connor, Powell, Sims, Temple, and the Whitman sisters.*]

BIBLIOGRAPHY

Balliett, Whitney. *Such Sweet Thunder.* Indianapolis, 1966.
Benchley, Robert. *The New Yorker* (16 May 1931).
Emery, Lynne Fauley. *Black Dance from 1619 to Today.* 2d rev. ed. Princeton, 1988.
Frank, Rusty E. *Tap! The Greatest Tap Dance Stars and Their Stories, 1900–1955.* Rev. ed. New York, 1994.
Frazier, George. *Boston Herald* (8 July 1962).
Gilbert, Douglas. *American Vaudeville: Its Life and Times.* New York, 1940.
Lahr, John. "King Tap." *New Yorker* (30 October 1995).
Murray, Albert. *The Omni-Americans: Some Alternatives to the Folklore of White Supremacy.* New York, 1983.

Nathan, Hans. *Dan Emmett and the Rise of Early Negro Minstrelsy.* Norman, Okla., 1962.

Sommer, Sally R. "Feet, Talk to Me!" *Dance Magazine* (September 1988): 56–60.

Southern, Eileen. *The Music of Black Americans.* New York, 1971.

Stearns, Marshall, and Jean Stearns. *Jazz Dance.* Rev. ed. New York, 1994.

Toll, Robert C. *Blacking Up: The Minstrel Show in Nineteenth-Century America.* New York, 1974.

Winter, Marian Hannah. "Juba and American Minstrelsy." In *Chronicles of the American Dance: From the Shakers to Martha Graham,* edited by Paul Magriel. New York, 1948.

FILM AND VIDEOTAPE. *History of American Tap,* series of documentaries on Louis DaPron, Nanette Fabray, Fred Kelly, Hal Leroy, Fayard Nicholas, and Jack Williams, held in the Dance Collection of the New York Public Library for the Performing Arts. Chris Bould and Bruce Goldstein. *The Nicholas Brothers* (EMI Records, 1992). George T. Nerenberg, *No Maps on My Taps* (1979). Christian Blackwood, *Tap Dancin'* (1980). Jolyon Wimhurst, *Masters of Tap* (1983). *About Tap* (Direct Cinema Ltd., 1985). *Tap* (Orion Pictures, 1989). "Tap," *Dance in America* (WNET-TV, New York, 1989). Robert Kuperberg, *Dance Crazy in Hollywood* (1990), a documentary on Hollywood choreographer Hermes Pan. Gerald Fox, *Opening Shot: Savion Glover* (1993).

ARCHIVES. Dance Collection, New York Public Library for the Performing Arts, Tap Dance clippings file. Schomburg Center for Research in Black Culture, New York Public Library. George T. Nerenberg Productions, New York.

SALLY R. SOMMER

TARANTELLA. Although the tarantella is firmly entrenched in the Western mind as an expression of the gaiety and vivacity of southern Italy, there is no set structure for the dance. The figures of the tarantella, which are made up of light hopping steps executed in 3/8 or 6/8 time, often in accelerating tempo, may be executed in any order the dancers please. In addition, there are regional differences in the number, sex, and demeanor of the dancers and in the musical instruments used to accompany the dance.

The tarantella has roots in ancient history; it is said to derive its name from the city of Tarentum (modern-day Taranto), formerly a Greek settlement on the southern coast of Italy. Historians have identified representations of the dance in ancient Greek vase paintings and on the wall paintings at Pompeii. Elba Farabegoli Gurzau (1981) notes, however, that the name *tarantella* came into use only within the last four or five centuries, and that the dance was formerly known as the *lucia,* *sfessania,* or *villanella,* among other names. She further observes that it became fused with the *fandango* and acquired the use of castanets when Spain dominated southern Italy in the late fifteenth century.

According to a widespread legend, the dance acquired its name because it was used as a cure for the poisonous bite of the tarantula spider. Gurzau reports that this etymological point was debated at the Venice Congress and Folk Festival in 1949, and the participants concluded that the legend was based on the similarity of the two words rather than actuality. In apparent contradiction to this conclusion is the fact that the tarantella is performed as a kind of exorcism by the practitioners of Tarantism, an Italian possession cult comparable to the *zār* cult of Ethiopia or Vodun in Haiti. Ernesto de Martino, whose *La terra del rimorso* (1961) is considered the principal monograph on Tarantism, has discovered, however, that the cult's association with the bite of the tarantula is more symbolic than real because its members, the majority of whom are women, tend to be concentrated in particular families, and their attacks usually occur annually around the time of the feast of Saint Paul.

W. G. Raffé's dictionary (1964), which contains three separate entries for the tarantella, identifies the dance with the *treguenda,* or *danza alla strega,* a witches' ritual in which an invisible web was woven to entrap unwary travelers, and the *danza dell'arco,* a mimed love story performed by pilgrims to Mount Virgine near Naples. The latter, he notes, is "not merely a technically executed folk-dance."

Gurzau (1981) records several regional variations of the tarantella as well as some modern-day arrangements created by folk dance groups. In Apulia (region on the southeastern coast of Italy, on the Adriatic Sea and Gulf of Taranto), the tarantella is usually danced by a man and a woman, with other dancers in a circle around them; when either partner tires, he or she is replaced from the circle. The women preserve a shy demeanor as they dance, keeping their heads bent and their eyes on the ground. Musical accompaniment is provided by the accordion, castanets, and tambourines. In Sicily, where the tarantella is often performed during wedding festivities, rhythmic clapping accompanies the dance instead of castanets or tambourines. The women of Campania (the region that includes Naples and Sorrento) dance with their heads up and a sense of self-pride. Two women may dance together as a third plays the tambourine; they may also make patterns with a long ribbon or sash. Bagpipes, tambourines, castanets, clapping, and finger-snapping accompany the dance.

Stylized tarantellas have been used to add a touch of local color to the ballet stage. An early example is the tarantella created for Fanny Elssler in Jean Coralli's ballet *La Tarentule* (1836), the plot of which centers around real and feigned bites of the tarantula. In making this dance, Coralli cannily exploited Elssler's previous success in character dances such as the *cachucha.* Inspired by his visit to Italy in 1841, August Bournonville's *Napoli* (1842) contained a tarantella that, as the master proudly notes, "was unanimously declared to be the finest composition of its kind" (1979). A comparison of his choreography

TARANTELLA. A nineteenth-century engraving showing a couple dancing the tarantella to the accompaniment of tambourines and a mandolin. Reflecting Spanish influence, the man dances with castanets. (Courtesy of Madison U. Sowell and Debra H. Sowell, Brigham Young University, Provo, Utah.)

with Gurzau's descriptions suggests that he may have conflated different regional variations of the dance.

Dolls dressed in Italian peasant costume performed a tarantella in Léonide Massine's *La Boutique Fantasque* (1919). George Balanchine's lively *Tarantella* (1964) was created as a display piece for two virtuosic dancers, Patricia McBride and Edward Villella. The choreographer modestly denied any claim of authenticity, stating, "[It] is 'Neapolitan' if you like and *'demi-caractère.'* The costumes are inspired by Italy, anyhow, and there are tambourines" (1977).

[*For related discussion, see* Character Dancing.]

BIBLIOGRAPHY

Balanchine, George, with Francis Mason. *Balanchine's Complete Stories of the Great Ballets.* Rev. and enl. ed. Garden City, N.Y., 1977.

Bournonville, August. *My Theatre Life* (1848–1878). Translated by Patricia McAndrew. Middletown, Conn., 1979.

de Martino, Ernesto. *La terra del rimorso.* Milan, 1961.

Gurzau, Elba Farabegoli. *Folk Dances, Costumes, and Customs of Italy.* 2d ed. Philadelphia, 1981.

Pillosu, Clotilde. "Deux danses de possession italiennes: La 'Tarentelle' des Pouilles et la danse de l''Argia' en Sardaigne." *Recherche en Danse,* no. 1 (June 1982): 133–138.

Raffé, W. G., ed. *Dictionary of the Dance.* New York, 1964.

Reynolds, Nancy. "Balanchine: An Introduction to the Ballets." *Dance Notation Journal* 6 (Winter–Spring 1988–1989): 15–74.

SUSAN AU

TARASOV, NIKOLAI (Nikolai Ivanovich Tarasov; born 6 [19] December 1902 in Moscow, died 8 February 1975 in Moscow), dancer and teacher. Tarasov developed an interest in ballet at an early age, influenced by his father, Ivan Tarasov, a dancer of note with the Bolshoi Ballet. In 1920 Nikolai graduated from the Moscow Ballet School, where he had studied under Nikolai Domashov and Nikolai Legat. Tarasov almost immediately became a principal dancer at the Bolshoi Theater, where he danced the male leads in ballets such as *Swan Lake, Giselle, La Bayadère, La Esmeralda, Coppélia, Raymonda, The Nutcracker, Don Quixote, The Red Poppy,* and *La Fille Mal Gardée.* He was partnered by some of the foremost ballerinas of the day, including Ekaterina Geltser, Viktorina Kriger, Marina Semenova, Liubov Bank, Margarita Kandaurova, and Nina Podgoretskaya. In her memoirs Viktorina Kriger recalled, "Tarasov was a superb dancer in the strict academic style. He never tried to dance for effect, for the sake of achieving quick success." Tarasov's precise, clean line and his unaffected manner sprang from a harmonious blend of technical brilliance and an intelligent, refined approach to the art.

Between 1923 and 1960 Tarasov taught at the Moscow Ballet School, from 1942 to 1946 holding the dual post of artistic director and managing director, and again in 1953 and 1954 serving as artistic director. A handsome man of noble stature, in class by his very presence Tarasov created a stimulating atmosphere conducive to the pursuit of artistic excellence. A paragon of punctuality and discipline, he felt he had a right to expect his students to measure up to his standards. Tarasov groomed his students to a high level of professionalism, putting them through a finely graded sequence of exercises and getting them to polish each element. He emphasized the barre exercises, seeing them as the foundation for mastery of the most complicated elements of classical technique, and loaded each combination with carefully selected movements that built in complexity. As a result Tarasov's students had an impressive range of sophisticated technique. Among the male dancers Tarasov trained were Yuri Zhdanov, Aleksandr Lapauri, Mikhail Lavrovsky, Maris Liepa, and Yaroslav Sekh. From 1923 to 1936 Tarasov had conducted the class for soloists of the Bolshoi Ballet; some of the best-known dancers, including Aleksei Yermolayev, Mikhail Gabovich, and Asaf Messerer, flourished under his competent guidance.

When the Lunacharsky Theater Technicum created a choreography department in 1947, Tarasov was appointed to teach the method and composition of classical dance. In 1958 he organized a choreographic training unit there, and in 1962 he received a professorship. Tarasov trained a great many ballet teachers, *répétiteurs*, and choreographers who went out to teach classical dance throughout the communist bloc. The wealth of experience he gained in teaching, coupled with that of his predecessors, enabled him to evolve his own philosophy and teaching method, both of which he described in detail in *Ballet Technique for the Male Dancer;* first published in 1971, the book won a national prize in 1975.

BIBLIOGRAPHY

Kholfina, Serafima. *Vospominania masterov moskovskogo baleta.* Moscow, 1990.

Puttke, Martin. "The Straight Line Is Godless." *Ballett International* 1 (January 1995): 26–31.

Struchkova, Raisa. "Nash liubimyi professor." *Sovetskii balet,* no. 1 (1983).

Tarasov, Nikolai. *Klassicheskii tanets, shkola muzhskogo ispolnitel'stva.* Moscow, 1971. Translated by Elizabeth Kraft as *Ballet Technique for the Male Dancer* (Garden City, N. Y., 1985).

RAISA S. STRUCHKOVA
Translated from Russian

TAVERNER, SONIA (born 18 May 1936 in Byfleet, Surrey), English-born Canadian ballet dancer. At age twelve Sonia Taverner began her dance studies in the weekly ballet classes of a local teacher, and at age sixteen she enrolled at the Elmhurst Ballet School, which offered a curriculum of academic courses combined with a program in the fine arts. Obviously talented, she was the 1954 winner of the Dame Adeline Genée silver medal for the most promising student. She also won a scholarship to the Senior School of the Sadler's Wells Ballet, where she continued her training and found her most inspiring instructor in Winifred Edwards, who had been a member of Anna Pavlova's company.

Taverner joined the corps of the Sadler's Wells Ballet early in 1955 and danced with the company, which was dubbed the Royal Ballet in 1956, for the next year and a half. Apprehensive about her chances for rising through the ranks of such a large organization, she was happy to join her family in relocating to a new home in Winnipeg, Canada. She was soon accepted into the Royal Winnipeg Ballet, where she was promoted to one of three leading female dancers for the season 1957/58. Among her first roles were leads in two early works by Brian Macdonald, *Aimez-vous Bach?* and *Pas d'Action*, which she created. Other works in which she danced leading roles were *Chinese Nightingale* by Heino Heiden, *Concerto* and *Romance* by Gweneth Lloyd, *Pas de Dix* by George Balanchine, and numerous pas de deux from the classical ballet repertory, in which her frequent partner was Fredric Strobel.

Aspiring to dance in full-length productions of the classics and attracted by the varied repertory of Les Grands Ballets Canadiens, Taverner moved in 1965 to Montreal and joined the company headed by Ludmilla Chiriaeff and Fernand Nault. In the classical repertory she shone in such works as *Giselle, The Nutcracker,* and *La Fille Mal Gardée.* She also found congenial roles in Nault's *Pas Rompu, Divertissement Glazounov,* and *Cérémonie;* in Balanchine's *Theme and Variations* and *Allegro Brillante;* and in Norman Walker's *Trionfo di Afrodite.* In classical and neoclassical works, she was often partnered by Richard Beaty, whose elegant style and looks provided a perfect foil for her own regal bearing and dark beauty.

After six years with Les Grands Ballets Canadiens, Taverner joined the Pennsylvania Ballet as principal dancer for the 1971/72 season and enjoyed the same success with American audiences as she had with those in Canada. She

TAVERNER. With Richard Beaty as her partner, Taverner danced a leading role in Fernand Nault's *Carmina Burana* during the Expo 67 season of Les Grands Ballets Canadiens. (Photograph © 1966 by Jack Mitchell; used by permission.)

gave notable performances in Balanchine's *Symphony in C* and *Raymonda Variations* and as the Innocent Girl in John Butler's *Villon*. Returning to Canada, she appeared with the newly formed Festival Ballet of Ottawa, dancing in Brydon Paige's *Songs for a Dark Voice,* and once again with Les Grands Ballets Canadiens. In February 1974 she gave a highly praised series of performances of *Giselle,* partnered by Vincent Warren.

Later that year Taverner relocated to western Canada and in 1975 was invited to head the ballet program at Grant MacEwan Community College in Edmonton, Alberta. For the next five years she taught classes, staged performances, and appeared as occasional guest artist with the Alberta Ballet and Les Grands Ballets Canadiens. Since 1980 she has taught at her own school near Edmonton.

BIBLIOGRAPHY
Goodman, Saul. "Sonia Taverner." *Dance Magazine* (October 1967): 58.
Maynard, Olga. "Idea, Image, and Purpose: Ballet in Canada Today." *Dance Magazine* (April 1971): 32–65.

CLAUDE CONYERS

TAYLOR, PAUL (Paul Bellville Taylor; born 29 July 1930 in Edgewood, Pennsylvania), American dancer and choreographer. During the first decade of Paul Taylor's dance career, he worked with several of America's most influential teachers and choreographers. Even his first steps in dance indicated his early eclecticism: Taylor's debut as a performer was in 1950 at Syracuse University—where he was studying painting, funded in part by a swimming scholarship—and his first choreography, *Hobo Ballet,* was created for students in the university's Dance department. Taylor has likened his training and competing with the Syracuse swim team to the commitment required in his early dance career. After moving to New York City in 1952, he trained for a year at the Juilliard School and also took classes with Margaret Craske and Antony Tudor at the Metropolitan Opera Ballet School; he performed in works by Doris Humphrey (1952), Merce Cunningham (1953–1954), Charles Weidman (1954), Martha Graham (1955–1962), and George Balanchine (1959); he worked in commercial theater and television; and from 1954 on, he created further performing opportunities for himself through his own choreography. Importantly, it was through these varied experiences that Taylor evolved his own pluralist aesthetic.

He was an extremely versatile performer. His tall, athletic physique created a striking presence on stage and he was particularly acclaimed in performances with the Martha Graham Dance Company; he created roles in *Clytemnestra* (1958), *Acrobats of God* and *Alcestis* (both 1960), *Visionary Recital* and *One More Gaudy Night* (both 1961), and *Phaedra* (1962). It was through this association that Taylor worked with George Balanchine on *Episodes,* the 1959 co-production which brought together Graham's company and the New York City Ballet.

During Taylor's formative years as a choreographer, he also collaborated with painter Robert Rauschenberg. In order to finance their early careers, both worked as window dressers (alongside another aspiring artist, Jasper Johns) at Tiffany's, the famous New York jewelers. After their first collaboration on *Jack and the Beanstalk* (1954) Rauschenberg designed all eleven works choreographed by Taylor during the 1950s, including *Three Epitaphs* (1956) and *Seven New Dances* (1957). Just as Rauschenberg's paintings challenged the lofty conventions of the abstract expressionists, Taylor's early choreography was seen as a rejection of mainstream American ballet and modern dance, and particularly of the highly codified styles developed by Balanchine and Graham.

Jack and the Beanstalk was the opening work in a Dance Associates program entitled A Theater for New Dance, Music, and Design. (Dance Associates was set up by choreographer James Waring to present shared programs of new, experimental work.) Previously, Taylor and Rauschenberg had worked separately at Black Mountain

TAYLOR. Linda Hodes and Taylor in *Insects and Heroes* (1961). (Photograph by William Schipp; from the Dance Collection, New York Public Library for the Performing Arts.)

College in North Carolina where some of the earliest postmodern explorations occurred. It was there that John Cage developed and disseminated many of his ideas on chance, indeterminacy, and silence, the latter resulting in his 1952 work *4′33″*, created in response to a series of Rauschenberg's "white" paintings.

4′33″ was the inspiration for Taylor's *Duet*, part of his *Seven New Dances* concert. In the same way as Cage had experimented with music, ambient sound, and silence, Taylor was attempting to discover an individual vocabulary through a detailed study of stylized and pedestrian movement, and of stillness, in each of his seven dances. (He has described these studies as his "ABC" of dance postures, gestures, and steps.) While *Three Epitaphs*, his oldest surviving work, is now regarded as a Taylor classic, *Seven New Dances* is remembered for its single, controversial performance. The work that caused the greatest furor was *Duet*, Taylor's stage interpretation of Cage's score—four minutes and thirty-three seconds of silence and stillness. Relatively few people had attended the concert but Louis Horst's nonreview in *Dance Observer*—a blank column, identifying only the date and place of performance—was largely responsible for Taylor's first taste of fame (at a time when the choreographer had neither

the administrative nor the financial resources to orchestrate his own publicity campaign) and, thus, he became the *enfant terrible* of the New York dance scene.

Critics and audiences were unable to reconcile Taylor's popularity as a performer in works by Graham and Balanchine with the seemingly nondance content of his choreography. His early works explored many of the ideas and practices of the American postmodernists but, even at his most experimental, Taylor never fully embraced their notion of performance—most particularly, their emphasis on process and their rejection of established theater venues. Nevertheless, he created ten further works following *Seven New Dances* and made two successful European tours with his own group of dancers (in 1960 and 1962) before establishing himself as a choreographer in New York. The turning point was *Aureole*, not least because audiences could applaud its seamless, skimming combinations of steps, set to music by Handel in five clearly structured sections. Moreover, the second movement featured Taylor in the work's main solo, an extended adagio in which his upper body virtually swims through space during an unbroken series of slow, controlled promenades and *penchées*, thereby highlighting his strong technique and lyricism. *Aureole* has become an enduring repertory favourite and, through its many restagings for other companies, it is one of Taylor's most performed works. Also, it was the success of this work that convinced him to leave Graham's company in order to work full time with his own group of dancers.

Today, the appeal of *Aureole* tends to overshadow other significant works created by Taylor during the same period, especially *Insects and Heroes* and *Junction* (both 1961), *Piece Period* (1962), and *Scudorama* (1963). It was undoubtedly this series of works that led critics to identify an alternating dark/light sequence in Taylor's choreography—he wanted *Scudorama* to be "as dark as *Aureole* is sunny"—and while the numerous works created since the 1960s cannot be confined to only two categories, the most telling and consistent aspect of Taylor's dancemaking is that he has resisted being pigeonholed by repeatedly doing the unexpected. (That the lyrical and plotless *Aureole*, danced to Baroque music, was created for the 1962 American Dance Festival was itself risqué because, at that time, the festival was predominantly a platform for America's more expressionist modern dance choreographers.)

Junction was Taylor's first choreography to Baroque music. Indeed, his aim in working with two of J. S. Bach's cello suites was to develop his musicality and, from 1961 on, a closer dance-music relationship can be detected in his work. (*Junction* was also the first work designed by Taylor's long-term associate, painter Alex Katz.) Musically, *Aureole* was an extension rather than a new direction for Taylor and he made further strides with *Piece Period*. The latter was a direct response to both the national and period styles of seven pieces of music by Beethoven, Haydn, Scarlatti, Vivaldi, and other pre-twentieth century composers, and it was this work that initiated Taylor's collaboration with designer John Rawlings. Subsequently, Rawlings designed such seminal Taylor works as *From Sea to Shining Sea* (1965), *Esplanade* (1975), and *Le Sacre du Printemps (The Rehearsal)* in 1980. (The latter was their last collaboration because Rawlings died later the same year.)

Scudorama, in its final form, was performed to a commissioned score by Clarence Jackson as part of Taylor's first Broadway season in December 1963. (The premiere, in August at the 1963 American Dance Festival, was performed without accompaniment because Jackson's score arrived too late. Also, although Katz's costumes were ready in time, his set for *Scudorama* was added later.) During rehearsals, Taylor worked with Igor Stravinsky's *Le Sacre du Printemps*. The aggression and dissonance of *Scudorama* stem largely from its original accompaniment and, typically, when Taylor returned to the two-piano version for his *Le Sacre du Printemps (The Rehearsal)* in 1980, he sought a completely different interpretation of Stravinsky's music. (Taylor's *Le Sacre*, set in a dance studio and Chinatown, is a double narrative in which the Chosen Maiden is, respectively, a dancer who submits herself to the daily ritual of rehearsals and a distraught mother whose baby has been kidnapped by gangsters.)

While *Piece Period* revealed Taylor's witty side, *Scudorama* was his first representation of evil and social disinte-

gration. Whereas Graham chose allegory and ancient myths in order to critique human weakness, the most joyless and macabre of Taylor's dances are contemporary morality tales. Some could even be deemed futuristic, especially *Big Bertha* (1971) and *Last Look* (1986) where the abuse and destruction faced by present-day stereotypes are cautionary signs for tomorrow's world. Similarly, Taylor's treatment of history borders on the postmodern in its use of pastiche and irony: for example, in *From Sea to Shining Sea*, *Orbs* (1966) and the evening-length epic *American Genesis* (1974), his characterization of historical figures and natural phenomena—ranging from several biblical characters, the Statue of Liberty, and a Thanksgiving turkey to the planets, sun, and moons of the solar system—is irreverent and funny. The exception in Taylor's Americana series is *Speaking in Tongues* (1988), which some writers have compared to Graham's *Appalachian Spring* (1944). In both works, a religious protagonist controls the lives of a small-town community, but where Graham's work extols the simplicity and order of America's pioneer past, Taylor's is an indictment of such late twentieth-century ills as hypocrisy, evangelism, and violence. His Man of the Cloth is closer in kind to his Followers than to some divine power and is as prone as they are to temptation and prejudice.

Humor, doom, and ritual are recurrent themes in Taylor's choreography. However, particular ideas are most often suggested rather than described. Sometimes, Taylor identifies specific characters and provides clues such as

TAYLOR. The original cast of *Aureole* (1962), included (left to right) Sharon Kinney, Renee Kimball, Dan Wagoner, and Liz Walton. A series of clearly structured dances set to orchestral music by Handel, *Aureole* is one of Taylor's most popular works. It has been staged for many other companies, including the Royal Danish Ballet (1968) and the Paris Opera Ballet (1974). (Photograph © 1962 by Jack Mitchell; used by permission.)

subtitles in his program but he encourages an open interpretation of his dances. He believes that movement in itself is expressive and this is borne out by his ongoing interest in nonnarrative choreography. Possibly the most extreme example of this is the two-part *Polaris*, created in 1976 to a commissioned score by Donald York. Choreographically the second part is an identical repeat of the first but, by using two different casts and by responding to the contrasting dynamics of the music in the two sections, Taylor's aim was to highlight how individual dancers imbue movement with distinct nuances through their different physiques and personalities. In *Esplanade*, too, he shows how the same movement can appear very different by simply changing a dancer's stage position or facing, and how even the simplest, pedestrian actions are transformed into dance when set on a proscenium stage. Together with other devices, such as truncating or extending a gesture, altering its timing or directing it toward another dancer, Taylor captures the inherent dramatic potential of "pure" movement.

Throughout his career, Taylor has emphasized the theatrical possibilities of formalist choreography first explored in *Junction* and *Aureole*. Together, they can be seen as the prototype for *Airs* (1978), *Arden Court* (1981), *Mercuric Tidings* (1982), *Equinox* (1983), and *Brandenburgs* (1988), and it is no coincidence that these plotless works have all been choreographed to some of the finest pre–twentieth century music. By working closely with the orchestration and dynamics of his accompaniment, Taylor has developed a highly sophisticated sense of phrasing and sectioning. Other works, too, are essentially plotless. Only the dancers' costumes and certain associations—as suggested by Spinoza's "Man is a social animal" in the program for *Cloven Kingdom* (1976); by subtitles for *Musical Offering* (1986): "a requiem for gentle primitives," and *Syzygy* (1987): "the nearly straight line configuration of three or more celestial bodies in a gravitational system"; or by Taylor's structuring of six male-female duets in the romantic *Roses* (1985) and his dramatic use of a soloist/ensemble division in both *Spindrift* (1993) and *Moonbine* (1994)—make it possible for these works to be read as quasi narratives. There is no delineation of characters or situations; all of these works are a direct response to their musical accompaniment.

Several of Taylor's plotless works have been restaged by classical ballet companies around the world. After *Aureole* and *Company B* (1991), the most frequently performed works are *Airs*, *Arden Court*, *Cloven Kingdom*, *Esplanade*, and *Three Epitaphs*. While this has created international exposure for his choreography, it has popularized only part of Taylor's diverse style. (Conversely, only a few of his narrative works—specifically, *Big Bertha*, *Le Sacre du Printemps*, and *Speaking in Tongues*—have been restaged for other companies.) Such exposure has also highlighted certain aspects of Taylor's movement vocabulary more than others. Although some movements and step combinations do recur, both within and across works, his choreography incorporates an infinite number of pedestrian actions and postures, and a wide range of codified movements. Taylor has developed a technique—contrary to his

TAYLOR. *Esplanade* (1975), set to music by J. S. Bach, was Taylor's first major work created after his retirement from performing in 1974. It is generally considered his signature work. The pedestrian event of a girl running to catch a bus served as a starting image for the dance. Here, Lila York jumps over each of her fellow company members in series. (Photograph © 1977 by Jack Vartoogian; used by permission.)

earlier disclaimers. It is not a system of training, as are the techniques evolved by Graham, Cunningham, and other choreographers, but it comprises a clearly devised sequence of exercises and terminology. With elements such as "chugs," "paddle turns," and distinct C-arms, V-arms, and wrap-arms, Taylor's terminology is not so poetic as Graham's, nor as pragmatic as Cunningham's, yet it conveys both the type and quality of movement required. Also, it reveals Taylor's unpretentious attitude to his work.

The same is true of his views on dancers. Consistently, he has selected an unusual mix of personalities and physiques, with Taylor's female dancers often being both the shortest and tallest members of his company. He prefers to be inspired by their individual differences, rather than work with a homogenous group. A sense of unity stems from two common characteristics: Taylor's dancers manifest the same unmannered and athletic abilities as he did as a dancer; and they all share his fearless attitude to movement—not only when performing high-speed, high-risk traveling steps (in *Esplanade* and *Mercuric Tidings*, especially) but also in their commitment to other forms of abandoned movement, such as the disturbingly grotesque in *Dust* (1977), *Nightshade* (1979), and *Last Look*, and the extremely zany in *Aphrodisiamania* (1977), *Minikin Fair* (1989), and *Offenbach Overtures* (1995). Taylor describes this special quality as "zunch." In a letter to his dancers in 1975, he defined it as the "oomph that sets the exciting dancer apart from the adequate one"; "a kind of St. Elmo's fire that radiates all round the dancer, the defined space and the audience."

In 1974 Taylor collapsed during the New York premiere of *American Genesis*, his first full-evening work. (Taylor's 1974 New York season also marked the twentieth anniversary of his professional debut as a dancer-choreographer in *Jack and the Beanstalk*.) Initially, he anticipated only a short break from performing—with his roles "on loan" to other dancers—but within months, he decided to retire permanently. Thus, Taylor's letter was written at a crucial time in his career, in the year he retired from performing and immediately before the creation of *Esplanade*. Just as *Aureole* had launched his own full-time company and repertory, *Esplanade* confirmed that both of these could be successful without him at center stage. Also, after his retirement, Taylor began to tour less with his company and this enabled him to devote more time to the prerehearsal preparations for his next choreography. Listening to a wider selection of music was a significant part of this process, as can be seen in subsequent works by Taylor's more ambitious use of twentieth-century scores by Claude Debussy (*Images*), Francis Poulenc (*Dust*), Darius Milhaud (*House of Cards*), Edgard Varèse (. . . *Byzantium*), György Ligeti (*Counterswarm*), and Charles Ives (*Danbury Mix*); and his commissioning of contemporary composers Gerald Busby (for *Runes* later in 1975), Jan Radzynski

TAYLOR. Carolyn Adams and Christopher Gillis in a duet from *Airs* (1978), set to music by Handel. (Photograph © 1979 by Jack Vartoogian; used by permission.)

(*Profiles*), and Donald York (*Polaris; Diggity; Lost, Found and Lost; Snow White; Last Look;* and *Syzygy*).

Most importantly, Taylor's experience of choreographing *Esplanade* and then *Runes* "from outside" led to a new working relationship with his dancers and to a new phase of creativity. During the next decade, he developed a company of very talented dancers, several of whom he also encouraged as choreographers, while simultaneously choreographing some of his best works: *Esplanade* and *Runes* were followed by *Cloven Kingdom* and *Polaris* in 1976, *Images* and *Dust* in 1977, *Airs* and *Diggity* in 1978; and, during the early 1980s, by *Le Sacre du Printemps (The Rehearsal)*, *Arden Court*, *Mercuric Tidings*, *Sunset* (1983), and *Last Look*.

The culmination of this stream of creativity was *Musical Offering*, choreographed in 1986 to one of J. S. Bach's last compositions. In its scale, complex musicality, and structure, *Musical Offering* was a high point in Taylor's career but it was also a watershed. Soon afterward, many of the dancers who had featured prominently as soloists in this work retired from performing or left to form their own companies. (Sadly, some have also died from AIDS-related illnesses.) Since 1986, Taylor's company has been transformed through a complete turnover of dancers; however, his curiosity about movement—the dance potential of particular ideas and personalities—remains undimmed. This is borne out by the creation of, on average, two works per year and, most notably, by *Speaking in Tongues, Company B,* and *Spindrift*. Like *Musical Offering*, all three recent works explore the physical possibilities and the inherent

TAYLOR. Three dancers in *Sunset* (1983): Kate Johnson, Jeff Wadlington, and Christopher Gillis. (Photograph © 1989 by Jack Vartoogian; used by permission.)

dramatic connotations of solo and group choreography: in *Musical Offering*, the female protagonist summons and controls the ritualized activities of the ensemble; in *Speaking in Tongues*, as well as Taylor's *Man of the Cloth*, other dancers emerge successively as archetypes, for example, A Mismatched Couple, A Party Girl, The Odd Man Out. In *Spindrift*, the leading male dancer often stands alone from the group, separated by distance (and possibly by a life/death divide), while *Company B*, taking its title from the Andrews Sisters' rendition of the song "Boogie Woogie Bugle-Boy" and the seventh section solo, illuminates various types of relationships (for example, the romantic contrasts between the male-female couple in "Pennsylvania Polka" and in "There Will Never Be Another You," and the soloist/group inversions of "Oh Johnny, Oh Johnny, Oh!" and "Rum and Coca-Cola."). As each song concludes, the slow-motion falling of the male dancers echoes Taylor's linking theme, namely the large-scale loss caused by war and its impact on loved ones.

Company B is one of Taylor's landmark dances. In this work, he began to feature several of his newest dancers as soloists—a policy that has proved highly successful in discovering and developing new talent. Today, these dancers have become Taylor's latest muses and, in working with him so closely, they have also assimilated the technical and performance styles of earlier choreography (as the revivals of *Junction* and *Private Domain* in 1992 and *Musical Offering* in 1995 confirmed). *Company B* was the first of a series of works set to popular songs, followed by *Field of Grass* (1993) and *Funny Papers* (1994). Furthermore *Company B*, which was made possible by a grant awarded to the Kennedy Center in Washington, D.C., brought Taylor considerable public acclaim. Six companies were se-

lected to present new choreography there and, as part of the project, the Houston Ballet chose Taylor to create his first work for them. (Subsequently, the Houston Ballet has also performed *Sunset*.) *Company B* was the first premiere to result from the project, a high-profile event attended by then President George Bush and his wife, Barbara.

Most telling, however, was the genesis of *Company B*. Although commissioned and premiered by the Houston Ballet, Taylor created the choreography on his own company in New York. Taylor prefers to tease out movement ideas on dancers he knows well and, even though several of his works are performed by other companies, he has seldom assumed the role of guest choreographer. (None of the works created by Taylor for other companies have survived in repertory. Also, following his abortive attempt to choreograph *Airs* for American Ballet Theatre in 1978, he began anew with his own dancers. The Taylor company version was subsequently taken into American Ballet Theatre's repertory.)

Two other landmark dances of recent years are *Danbury Mix* and *Of Bright & Blue Birds & the Gala Sun*. The former was first performed during the 1988 American Music Festival, to a selection of music by Charles Ives. (The title makes reference to the composer's home in Danbury, Connecticut.) Choreographically, *Danbury Mix* resembles two of Taylor's former collages, *From Sea to Shining Sea* and *American Genesis*. Americana themes and characters have been borrowed from these earlier commentaries and, created in the same year as *Speaking in Tongues*, *Danbury Mix* presents a satirical, but equally probing, critique of American cultural mores.

Morality underpins much of Taylor's choreography. In *Of Bright & Blue Birds & the Gala Sun* (1990), his second full-evening work, journey, spiritual struggle, exorcism, and prodigal return are developed sequentially. As with *American Genesis*, narrative and scenic progression are of epic proportions and, like the hour-long *Orbs*, *Of Bright & Blue Birds* alludes to the scale and order of the solar system (with Heaven and Hell inspiring the strongest "planetary" activity). *American Genesis* had incorporated two recent dances (*So Long Eden* and *Noah's Minstrels*); similarly, *Of Bright & Blue Birds* evolved from *Syzygy*. It was first performed as part of the Taylor company's thirty-fifth anniversary season at City Center, New York and, as with *Syzygy*, it involved two of Taylor's longtime associates, music director and composer Donald York and lighting designer Jennifer Tipton. (Santo Loquasto, who has designed almost all of Taylor's work since 1988, created the costumes and sets.)

Now in his mid-sixties, Taylor is acutely aware of his place in America's ever-evolving dance tradition. Increasingly, he has involved himself in the retrieval of lost choreography: in 1986, he re-created his 1959 solo in *Episodes* for the New York City Ballet dancer Peter Frame; in 1992, he revived *Epic*, one of his early postmodernist experiments from the 1957 concert, *Seven New Dances*. Also in 1992, the National Endowment for the Arts awarded a challenge grant of $850,000 to help Taylor's company launch its Repertory Preservation Project. The aim of the five-year project is to document approximately thirty dances (on film, in written form, and in Labanotation) and this will involve the revival of lost works, such as other sections from the *Seven New Dances* program. A side outcome of the project has been the setting-up of a junior company, Taylor 2, which recruits its dancers from the Paul Taylor Dance School. Each year, this smaller group learns at least one of the works included in the project and, thus, these young dancers will not only preserve Taylor's choreography in performance but will also benefit from learning a series of major works at a crucial stage in their career.

The Paul Taylor Dance Company moved into improved premises in a building adjacent to their longtime home on Broadway in 1987 and here, as part of the Repertory Preservation Project, the company is establishing an archive. This is certainly timely because Taylor has been saving press cuttings, programs, and other important materials since the early 1950s. Moreover, though his work has been consistently well documented, by dance critics and by Taylor himself, access to information has been restricted. (Until the publication of Taylor's autobiography, *Private Domain*, in 1987, few comprehensive sources on his career were widely available, except as single-chapter accounts in dance texts, such as Mazo's *Prime Movers*.)

Taylor's sense of history is evident in several dances created during the last decade—. . . *Byzantium* (1984), *Kith and Kin* (1987), *Company B*, and *Field of Grass* are his most overt period pieces—and the historical importance of his work has been formally recognized through the Repertory Preservation Project. As he acknowledges on a videotape to promote the project, "My attitude is that I've been handed down so many wonderful things from the generations that came before me, it's a duty to keep doing that for others."

Undoubtedly, that duty, together with the many important works that constitute Taylor's legacy, will secure him a prominent place in America's dance history.

[*See also* Esplanade; Musical Offering; Spindrift; *and* Three Epitaphs.]

BIBLIOGRAPHY

Adams, Carolyn. "The Paul Taylor Mystique." *Dance Theatre Journal* 1 (Spring 1983): 7–9.

Anderson, Jack. "Taylor's Domain." *Dance Chronicle* 11.1 (1988): 130–132.

Coe, Robert. *Dance in America*. New York, 1985.

Croce, Arlene. *Sight Lines*. New York, 1987.

Dalva, Nancy. "Paul Taylor: A Very Appealing Genius." *Dance Magazine* (October 1991): 38–43.

Jacobson, Daniel. "Private Domains in Public Spaces." *Ballet Review* 17 (Spring 1989): 67–75.

Jowitt, Deborah. "A Fishy Conversation with an Obliging Giant." *Village Voice* (23 April 1979). Reprinted in *The Dance in Mind*. (Boston, 1985): 45–50.

Kane, Angela. "A Catalogue of Works Choreographed by Paul Taylor." *Dance Research* no. 2 (Winter 1996): 3–7.

Lobenthal, Joel. "Christopher Gillis: Dancing for Paul Taylor." *Ballet Review* 13 (Summer 1985): 10–22.

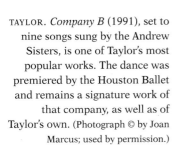

TAYLOR. *Company B* (1991), set to nine songs sung by the Andrew Sisters, is one of Taylor's most popular works. The dance was premiered by the Houston Ballet and remains a signature work of that company, as well as of Taylor's own. (Photograph © by Joan Marcus; used by permission.)

Lobenthal, Joel. "Victoria Uris: Dancing for Paul Taylor." *Ballet Review* 15 (Spring 1987): 26–37.

Mazo, Joseph. "Nikolais, Ailey, Taylor—Three Specialists." In *Prime Movers: The Makers of Modern Dance in America*. Princeton, 1977.

Reiter, Susan. "In Orbit." *Ballet News* 6 (April 1985): 16–19.

Reiter, Susan. "Baroque and Beyond with Paul Taylor." *Ballet Review* 14 (Fall 1986): 65–71.

Rosen, Lillie. "A Few Insights into Paul Taylor and One of His Finest, Longest Staying Dancers, Elie Chaib." *Attitude* 9 (Winter 1993): 6–15.

Sorens, Ina. "Taylor Reconstructs Balanchine." *Ballet Review* 14 (Summer 1986): 54–65.

Taylor, Paul. *Private Domain*. New York, 1987.

Tobias, Tobi. "A Conversation with Paul Taylor and George Tacit." *Dance Magazine* (April 1985): 54–60.

ANGELA KANE

TCHAIKOVSKY, PETR ILICH (Petr Il'ich Chaikovskii; born 7 May 1840 in Kamsko-Votkinok, Russia, died 6 November 1893 in Saint Petersburg), Russian composer whose three full-length ballets—*Swan Lake* (1877), *The Sleeping Beauty* (1890), and *The Nutcracker* (1892)—remain masterworks of the classical repertory. Tchaikovsky, the second son of a mining engineer, showed an interest in music at an early age. He started piano lessons when he was four and quickly showed exceptional skill. At the age of ten, he entered the School of Jurisprudence at Saint Petersburg and the same year was taken by his mother to see Mikhail Glinka's opera *A Life for the Tsar*, which made a deep and lasting impression on him. He spent nine years at the school, and his mother's death when he was fourteen was a shock that caused deep-rooted psychological disturbances. He sought emotional release by turning even more to music, adding singing lessons to piano studies and starting to compose.

He began work in 1859 as a clerk in the Ministry of Justice, giving up thoughts of a musical career for lack of financial support. Still, he involved himself socially in Saint Petersburg musical circles and took technique classes at the new conservatory there. During a tour to western Europe in 1861, he acted as interpreter for a friend of his father's and was greatly impressed by Germany, Belgium, Britain, and France. On his return, he joined the composition class taught by the conservatory's director, Anton Rubinstein, who in 1863 encouraged him to resign his job and concentrate on music study. Although this involved financial hardship, because his only income was from the private teaching of piano and theory, he managed to continue studies for two years, including flute and organ as well as composition. In 1864, he composed an overture on Aleksandr Ostrovsky's play *Groza* (The Storm), his first work of substance; a suite entitled *Characteristic Dances* then brought the first public performance of his music, in 1865, at an open-air concert conducted by the younger Johann Strauss, "The Waltz King."

Early Career. Tchaikovsky graduated in 1866, gaining a diploma and silver medal. He moved to Moscow as a teacher of harmony at the conservatory headed by Anton Rubinstein's brother Nikolai, with whom he lodged. He soon found the household distracting and the teaching duties irksome, but the experience brought him a new circle of influential acquaintances and the beginnings of a reputation.

The composition of Tchaikovsky's First Symphony ("Winter Daydreams"; 1866), at the insistence of Nikolai Rubenstein, was a long and difficult labor. Tchaikovsky's instinct was always much stronger for theater music than for symphonic discourse, and when his symphony was completed, in 1867, he turned to *Voyevoda* (Dream on the Volga), the first of his ten completed operas. Based on another Ostrovsky drama, it had no great success at its Moscow premiere in 1869; but a suite of "Hay Maidens Dances" from act 2 had made a favorable impression in concert performances beforehand, both in Moscow and Saint Petersburg. The dances, derived from his earlier *Characteristic Dances*, were published separately as a suite for piano duet. In David Brown's 1978 biography of Tchaikovsky, he writes of the "ravishingly chaste diatonicism" of the opening dance and declares that if the rest of the opera's invention had been as fine, it would have been a masterpiece. Tchaikovsky soon destroyed the *Voyevoda* score, although fragments were used in his 1877 ballet *Swan Lake*—the prelude to the opera's act 3 and a passage from that act are used in the entr'act before the ballet's act 4 and in the reunion of Prince Siegfried and Odette, respectively.

Tchaikovsky also destroyed his second opera, *Ondine* (1869), the romantic fairy tale of a water nymph, after it was turned down for production. Once again, fragments were salvaged for other purposes, the most notable being the final love duet from act 3. With its vocal themes transcribed for solo violin and cello, it achieved lasting fame as the White Swan pas de deux for Odette and Siegfried in *Swan Lake*, act 2 (no. 13e), which Lev Ivanov would one day choreograph.

From 1870 to 1872, Tchaikovsky wrote another opera, *The Oprichnik* (The Life Guardsman). Letters from this period mention a project for a four-act ballet, *Cinderella*, but nothing else survives to indicate its origins or whether any music was written. His letters and papers make no further reference to it.

The Oprichnik incorporates a round dance *(khorovod)* as the finale to act 1 and a suite of wedding dances in act 4, all based on themes from Russian folk songs. Five of these had been arranged by Tchaikovsky for piano duet in his *Fifty Russian Folksongs*, published in 1869. His next opera was *Vakula the Smith*, composed in 1874, and it incorporates earthy peasant humor and folk-tale fantasy. It features the Ukrainian *gopak*, danced in a variety of ways—as a Russian dance and as a Cossack dance in the ballroom scene of act 3, which itself begins with a *grande polonaise*.

Swan Lake. In the spring of 1875, Tchaikovsky was approached by the directorate of Russia's Imperial Theaters to compose the four-act ballet *Swan Lake* for production at Moscow's Bolshoi Theater. Tchaikovsky had attended ballets, but he was unimpressed by their prevailing musical standard. In a letter written later in 1875 to composer Nikolai Rimsky-Korsakov, Tchaikovsky wrote, "I accepted the work, partly because I want the money, but also because I have long had the wish to try my hand at this kind of music." The fee paid was eight hundred rubles, not a pittance but by no means generous.

A few years before this commission—probably in 1871—Tchaikovsky had himself staged another "Swan Lake," this one a domestic family entertainment. During one of several summer visits Tchaikovsky made to his married sister, Aleksandra (Sasha) Davydova, at her country home at Kamenka, near Kiev, Tchaikovsky contrived a dance pantomime based on the tale of the Swan Princess. He performed it for the entertainment of Sasha's children, and the event was long remembered in the family, with the story being passed on to Sasha's youngest son, Yuri (born in 1876). In a recollection published in 1962, he recounted what had happened:

> The staging of the ballet was done entirely by Pyotr Ilyich. He invented the steps and the pirouettes, and danced them himself to show the performers what he required of them. At such moments Uncle Pyotr, red in the face, wet with perspiration as he sang the tune, presented a pretty amusing sight. Yet in the children's eyes he was so perfect in the art of choreography that for many years the memories of this remained with them down to the finest details. (Davydov, 1962)

Davydov insisted that he recognized one tune in the mature ballet as having come from the earlier entertainment. This is thought to be the oboe tune in the finale to act 1 (no. 9), although no score for the entertainment has survived.

Tchaikovsky began work on *Swan Lake* in the summer of 1875. He sketched two acts by the end of September, scoring as he went along and, pressing himself, finished the ballet on 22 April 1876 at Glebovo, the country estate near Moscow belonging to his friend Konstantin Shilovsky. Earlier that month, a run-through of act 1 was held in the Bolshoi Theater school, the music played by a single *répétiteur* violinist, as was the custom for ballet rehearsals. He told his brother Modest that he thought it a rather ridiculous way to go about it, but that what was heard had been greatly admired.

How Tchaikovsky went about the composition of *Swan Lake* is uncertain. He must have had a scenario to determine the outline and some content for each act, as represented by the titles and descriptive cues in the score, but who was responsible for this remains unknown. Most sources suggest a collaboration among theater director Vladimir Begichev, dancer Vasily Geltser, ballet master and choreographer Julius (Wentzel) Reisinger, and the composer himself, who no doubt had his own ideas after devising the Davydov entertainment. What Tchaikovsky did not have was much experience of the way ballets were created and produced in the theater, how the music was expected to relate to the choreographer's intentions, or the leading dancers' prerogatives. As a result, *Swan Lake* is musically, in effect, a four-part tone poem, the narrative and mime scenes interspersed with set dances. It was composed with a degree of musical imagination that disconcerted both the orchestra and the dancers at first, introducing as it did a strong and organic element.

Swan Lake's score has a carefully organized and close-knit structure of key sequences and harmonic relationships around a central key (both major and minor) of B, the unison note on which the ballet ends. Within this scheme, Tchaikovsky reserved mainly flat keys for the forces of evil and bewitchment and sharp keys for the *divertissements*. Except for some recall of particular themes for reminiscence, the music is not concerned with symphonic devices and achieves continuity by repetition, as for example the "Dance of the Swans" in act 2 (no. 13) as a rondo, begun and linked by a waltz theme.

Roland Wiley's study of Tchaikovsky's ballets (1985) has much detail concerning the origins of *Swan Lake* and its composition. He explores the ballet's key relationships as a diagramed "circle of fifths," each with particular associations as to character and/or situation. In his study, David Brown drew particular attention to the range and variety of Tchaikovsky's abundant invention, especially in waltz rhythm, and "his ability to order different waltz themes to make a larger entity." Quoting opening bars from seven waltzes that occur in the ballet, Brown noted:

> The accompaniment is always of the simplest, always explicitly triple time, yet the themes themselves show endless rhythmic variety, partly through details of phrasing prescribed by Tchaikovsky, mainly by fertilizing the basic triple meter with duple-time inflexions. (Brown, 1978)

Other dance forms in *Swan Lake* include the czardas, bolero, tarantella, and mazurka among the national dances of act 3, to which Tchaikovsky added the "Russian Dance" for the benefit of Pelagia Karpakova, the first Odette-Odile. Her successor at the fifth performance, Anna Sobeshchanskaya, had gone to Saint Petersburg to obtain an extra pas de deux from the choreographer Marius Petipa, because Reisinger could not make it showy enough; it was choreographed to music by Léon Minkus, but Tchaikovsky found this unacceptable and wrote his own music to suit the choreography. The "Additional Pas de Deux," like the "Russian Dance," is published as an appendix to the full score in the complete Tchaikovsky edition. Only one version survived as Tchaikovsky's orchestration, however, the *Swan Lake* music having otherwise been replaced bit by bit until in the twentieth century a two-violin *répétiteur* score was found, bound into a score of the ballet *Le Corsaire*. The Tchaikovsky score was then re-orchestrated by Vissarion Shebalin for a Bolshoi Ballet production in 1953.

Tchaikovsky's refusal to accept another composer's music for his *Swan Lake* makes it unlikely that there was even one alien interpolation at the ballet's first performance. Nikolai Kashkin (1896), who did the first piano arrangement of the full score, wrote that with later performances "nearly one-third of the music of *Swan Lake* was replaced by extracts from other ballets which were, to say the least, mediocre." Most of these were probably occasioned by the change of choreographer, to Joseph Hansen, for the 1880 Moscow production. The ballet then continued in repertory until 1883, after which it was not seen again during Tchaikovsky's lifetime. Tchaikovsky seems not to have concerned himself with the Hansen production. By then Tchaikovsky had endured the trauma of his disastrous marriage and consequent mental breakdown, had resigned his conservatory post, and had found himself the beneficiary of unsolicited but welcome financial support from a wealthy widow, Nadezhda von Meck. Her assistance, however, was accompanied by the delicate stipulation—rigidly kept—that they never meet. [*See* Swan Lake.]

The Sleeping Beauty. Twelve years elapsed between *Swan Lake* and Tchaikovsky's next involvement with dance. Between European conducting tours in 1888 and 1889, he received a letter from the director of Russia's Imperial Theaters, Ivan Vsevolozhsky, proposing *The Sleeping Beauty* as a subject for ballet and inviting him to compose its music. Vsevolozhsky, appointed in 1881, was a man of taste and discernment, and a great admirer of Tchaikovsky's music. He helped to bring about the 1884 double production of the composer's opera *Mazeppa* at Moscow and Saint Petersburg only a few days apart, an unusual occurrence. In 1886, he abolished the post of staff ballet composer (then held by Minkus) in the interests of raising the standard of ballet music and sought to interest Tchaikovsky, who, however, had turned down the suggested subjects, *Ondine* and *Salammbô*.

The Sleeping Beauty (1889) was much more to Tchaikovsky's taste. Vsevolozhsky had sketched the scenario (he was also a playwright), and the composer was delighted. Evidence from Galina von Meck, granddaughter of Tchaikovsky's patroness, indicates that the subject had already been treated as another family entertainment at Kamenka years before; Tchaikovsky again retained some of its music for the mature ballet (Warrack, 1979).

To avoid any conflict of form and content between music and dance, as had been a factor in *Swan Lake*, Vsevolozhsky arranged for Petipa to be involved with the composer from the outset, and thus a collaborator in the fullest sense. Petipa wrote a detailed plan for each act, a working draft describing the narrative and the dances, with suggestions for the length and character of the music desired. Tchaikovsky noted progress in his diary, showing no evidence that he found Petipa's requirements irksome, as some historians have supposed; rather, the music would seem to indicate that the method was more a help than a hindrance.

Without slavishly following Petipa, Tchaikovsky worked close to the ideas, modifying them when he thought the musical interest was justified. In his four-part score (prologue and three acts), the discipline of the key relationships that was basic to *Swan Lake* was changed to a musical structure built from the contrast of narrative and dance character. Thematic references were confined to the Lilac Fairy and to Carabosse, as symbols of good and evil, presented clearly in the introduction and skillfully worked together at crucial dramatic moments. The role of Princess Aurora was associated not with a theme but with the waltz rhythm, which presented some of Tchaikovsky's most fertile invention, both for solo and ensemble purposes. His other formal dances are the act 2 minuet, gavotte, and so-called farandole (as named in the score, which is musically a mazurka); a polonaise, saraband, and mazurka are in act 3. The Sapphire Fairy variation (no. 23c) early in act 3 is in the unusual 5/4 meter that Tchaikovsky later employed in his Symphony no. 6 ("Pathétique") for the celebrated "limping waltz" movement (*allegro con grazia*) and in his "Valse à Cinqtemps" for piano (op. 72, no. 16). In *The Sleeping Beauty*, his only quotation from elsewhere is the old French song "Vive Henri Quatre," for the ballet's apotheosis (no. 31), which brings about the odd effect of a happy ending in a minor key. [*See* Sleeping Beauty, The]

The Nutcracker. Following the shock of von Meck's withdrawal of financial support, Tchaikovsky was asked for a one-act opera and a two-act ballet to be performed as a double bill at the Maryinsky Theater. The opera became *Iolanta* (1891), derived at three removes from a Hans Christian Andersen tale; the ballet was *The Nutcracker* (1892), adapted from one of the tales of E. T. A. Hoffmann.

Tchaikovsky began with the ballet and sketched act 1 before leaving for Paris on his way to the United States for his only visit in May of 1891. He conducting concerts in New York, Baltimore, and Philadelphia. He continued to compose while traveling and, having complained in a letter about "the absolute impossibility of depicting the Sugarplum Fairy in music," found the answer to his problem in Paris on discovering Auguste Mustel's newly invented keyboard instrument, the celeste, with distinctively bell-like tones. His anxiety to keep the celeste from rival composers so that he could be the first to use it perhaps led him to take the unusual step of performing a concert suite of music from *The Nutcracker*, including the Sugarplum Fairy's dance, some nine months before the ballet's production. The suite comprised "Overture," "March," "Waltz of the Flowers," and five character dances from act 2; almost every number was encored.

Tchaikovsky had considered using toy instruments as an element in the music, after the manner of Leopold Mozart's *Toy Symphony* (then attributed to Haydn), but decided to achieve his effects through his orchestration, such as leaving out all low-register instruments from the overture. The remaining fifteen numbers, in two acts as prescribed and again composed to a Petipa plan, include folk song themes from Germany ("Grossvatertanz," no. 5), France ("La Mère Gigogne," no. 12g), and Georgia ("Arabian Dance," no. 12b); otherwise the music is Tchaikovsky's invention. He looked on the suite with childlike imagination and with the intention of being charming rather than dramatic, avoiding the most sinister aspects of Hoffmann's tale. An optional wordless vocalise of children's voices is written into the "Waltz of the Snowflakes" (no. 9). An English dance in the form of a jig was originally composed among the act 2 character dances, but it seems to have been dropped before the first performance; it was not included in the published score, surviving only in a piano version, from which it was orchestrated for inclusion in later productions of the ballet. For various reasons, more visual than musical, the ballet, choreographed by Lev Ivanov, was only a partial success at its premiere performances. [*See* Nutcracker, The.]

The Final Years. Tchaikovsky made one more journey to England, conducting a Philharmonic Society concert (shared with Camille Saint-Saëns) in London and his tone poem *Francesca da Rimini* (1876) in Cambridge as part of a concert marking the university's conferral on him of an honorary doctorate in musical. Back in Russia, he conducted the premiere of his Symphony no. 6 in Saint Petersburg at the end of October 1893. Nine days later, he died; the cause of death given was cholera. It has been claimed that he actually died from arsenic poisoning, an act of suicide carried out in the threat of scandal about a homosexual relationship with a prominent nobleman (Orlova, 1979). Whether his alleged suicide was committed at the instigation of a "kangaroo court" or "court of honor" of his friends and associates has also been suggested but also remains unproven.

Contributions. What can be accepted is that the character of Tchaikovsky's music, theatrical and symphonic, was to a great extent formed by his acknowledged homosexuality, sternly repressed as it was by the laws and social conventions of his time. His music became a means of expressing thoughts and feelings that could not otherwise have found an outlet. A century later, his listeners are vastly the richer for the musicality, wealth, and candor of his emotions, put into forms that are universally accessible and as universally cherished.

The close relationship that exists between much of Tchaikovsky's ballet music and his concert music has led almost every choreographer of note in the twentieth century to make use of his concert music. Some of Tchaikovsky's concert pieces have suggested narrative themes, such as *Hamlet*, choreographed by both Serge Lifar and Robert Helpmann; *Romeo and Juliet*, by Lifar; *Manfred*, by Rudolf Nureyev; *Francesca da Rimini*, by both Michel Fokine and David Lichine; *Onegin*, by John Cranko (to the nonoperatic pieces); and *Anastasia*, by Kenneth MacMillan (to Symphonies 1 and 3). Music utilized for plotless ballets includes "Serenade for Strings," set by both Fokine and George Balanchine; Piano Concerto no. 1, by Bronislava Nijinska; Piano Concertos 2 and 3, by Balanchine; Symphony no. 1, by both Vladimir Burmeister and Peter Martins; Symphony no. 3, by Balanchine; Symphony no. 5, by Léonide Massine; and Symphony no. 6, by Serge Lifar, by Maurice Béjart, and by George Balanchine. In 1981, George Balanchine and the New York City Ballet staged a Tchaikovsky Festival for ten days at the New York State Theater. Twelve premieres were among the twenty-four ballets presented, and Balanchine then declared, "If it were not for Tchaikovsky, there wouldn't be any dancing."

BIBLIOGRAPHY

Acocella, Joan. "The Mystery, Magic, and the Majesty of Tchaikovsky and the Ballet." *Dance Magazine* (June 1981): 53–56.
Brown, David. *Tchaikovsky: The Early Years, 1840–1874*. London, 1978.
Brown, David. *Tchaikovsky: The Crisis Years, 1874–1878*. London, 1983.
Davydov, I. L. *Zapiski o P. I. Chaikovskom*. Moscow, 1962.
Kashkin, Nikolai. *Vospominaniia o P. I. Chaikovskom*. Moscow, 1896.
Kendall, Alan. *Tchaikovsky: A Biography*. London, 1988.
New York City Ballet program (June 1981).
Orlova, Alexandra. "Tchaikovsky: The Last Chapter." *Music and Letters* 1 (1979).
Tchaikovsky, Petr Ilich. *To My Best Friend: Correspondence between Tchaikovsky and Nadezhda von Meck, 1876–1878*. Translated by Galina von Meck. Oxford, 1993.
Warrack, John. *Tchaikovsky Ballet Music*. London, 1979.
Wiley, Roland John. *Tchaikovsky's Ballets*. Oxford, 1985.

NOËL GOODWIN

TCHAIKOVSKY PIANO CONCERTO NO. 2. *See* Ballet Imperial.

TCHELITCHEV, PAVEL (Pavel Fedorovich Chelishchev; born 21 September 1898 in Moscow, died 31 July 1957 in Frascati, Italy), Russian-American painter, illustrator, and stage designer. The painter Pavel Tchelitchev brought many innovative ideas to his stage designs, introducing new uses of stage lighting and the first use of film projections in a ballet. He preferred to approach the stage as a sculptor rather than as a painter. His sets were not merely painted backdrops; they incorporated elements that became integrated with the action: for example, gauzes to diffuse the shapes made by dancers or ropes manipulated by dancers to create geometric forms in space.

Born into an aristocratic and wealthy Russian family, Tchelitchev was exposed to the fine arts at an early age. At one time he wished to become a ballet dancer, an ambition his father firmly discouraged. In 1918, the aftermath of the Russian Revolution forced his family to flee to Kiev, Ukraine, where he began formal art lessons. Two of his teachers, Alexandra Exter and Isaac Rabinovitch, fostered his interest in stage design. He was commissioned in 1919 to design an operetta, *The Geisha,* which was never produced.

In 1920 Tchelitchev left Ukraine for Turkey, where he designed ballets for Victor Zimine's Istanbul-based company. After moving to Berlin in 1921, he worked for the cabaret theater group Der Blaue Vogel and for the Russian Romantic Theater, for which he designed ballets choreographed by Boris Romanov. In 1923 Serge Diaghilev saw Romanov's *Bojarenhochzeit (*The Wedding Feast of the Boyar*)* and invited Tchelitchev to work for the Ballets Russes. At this time Tchelitchev was strongly influenced by constructivism (a style that combined geometric abstraction and the use of modern industrial materials) and Russian folk art; the latter dominated his designs for Rimsky-Korsakov's opera *Le Coq d'Or,* commissioned by the Berlin State Opera in 1923.

Tchelitchev's move to Paris in July 1923 was marked by a stylistic shift toward naturalism. His painting *Basket of Strawberries,* exhibited at the Salon d'Automne of 1925, won him the notice of art collector Gertrude Stein. He was briefly associated with the neo-Romantic group of painters (among them Eugene Berman and Christian Bérard) and shared in their exhibition in 1926. His first experiments with multiple images (best known through his painting *Hide-and-Seek,* c.1940) began at this time.

His long-awaited collaboration with Diaghilev was realized in 1928 with Léonide Massine's ballet *Ode.* He was deeply involved in this project and even made extensive changes in Nicholas Nabokov's scenario. With his technical assistant, Pierre Charbonnier, an expert in neon lighting, he introduced many novel effects, including the placement of lights behind onstage screens, the use of mannequins suspended from ropes to create false perspectives, and the projection of time-lapse films. The ballet's success won him his first one-man show, at the Claridge Gallery in London in July 1928.

In 1933 he collaborated for the first time with George Balanchine, on the ballet *L'Errante,* where he experimented with transparent fabrics and mobile lights. He helped Lincoln Kirstein persuade Balanchine to emigrate

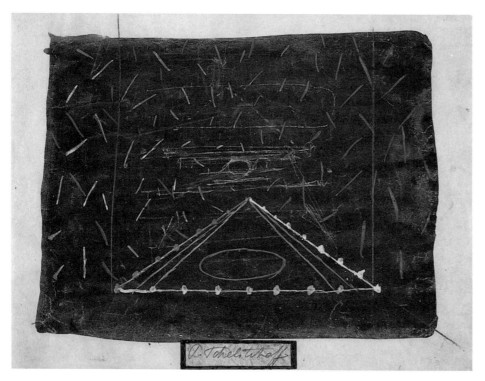

TCHELITCHEV. A design for Léonide Massine's *Ode* (1928), Tchelitchev's first project for Diaghilev's company. Interestingly, this gouache shows the triangular configuration of the stage space but omits the hanging mannequins considered a visual hallmark of the work. (Photograph from the Dance Collection, New York Public Library for the Performing Arts.)

to America; Tchelitchev himself first visited in 1934 and subsequently became a U.S. citizen. In 1936 he collaborated with Balanchine on the conception and design of Gluck's opera *Orfeo ed Euridice* for the Metropolitan Opera. Kirstein (1978) later described this controversial production as "a fusion of the Great Western traditions of myth which joined the mourning for Eurydice with Saint Veronica's Veil, and hell seen as a concentration camp." Tchelitchev also designed Balanchine's *Magic* (1936), *Balustrade* (1941), *Pas de Trois for Piano and Two Dancers, Apollon Musagète*, and *Concierto de Mozart* (all 1942; the latter two for the Teatro Colón, Buenos Aires). In *Apollon* he applied his experiments with multiple images to the ballet, using a single set that was transformed by lighting into a landscape of human faces. He had previously used similar transformations in Jean Giraudoux's play *Ondine*, produced in Paris in 1939.

Tchelitchev continued to advise Kirstein and Balanchine long after he gave up stage design in 1942. His scenario and sketches for the unrealized ballet *Cave of Sleep* (1941) were intended for them. He also designed Ruth Page's *Variations on Euclid* (1933) and Massine's *Saint Francis*, also known as *Nobilissima Visione* (1938).

[*See also* Scenic Design.]

BIBLIOGRAPHY. The most comprehensive analysis of Tchelitchev's stage designs is offered by Donald Windham, "The Stage and Ballet Designs of Pavel Tchelitchew," *Dance Index* 3 (January–February 1944): 4–32. Lincoln Kirstein, *Thirty Years: The New York City Ballet* (New York, 1978), gives many fascinating details about Tchelitchev's interaction with Balanchine and Kirstein. See as well Kirstein's most recent volume, *Tchelitchev* (Santa Fe, 1994). An extensive bibliography is provided in the exhibition catalog, *Pavel Tchelitchew: An Exhibition in the Gallery of Modern Art, 20 March through 19 April 1964* (New York, 1964), which also includes an excellent biographical essay by Kirstein and a chronology by Parker Tyler.

SUSAN AU

TCHERINA, LUDMILA (Monika [Monique] Avenirovna Tchmerzina; born 10 October 1924 in Paris), French ballet dancer, actress, painter, sculptor, and writer. Daughter of a Georgian father and a French mother, Monique Tchmerzina began her ballet training in the Paris studio of the great Russian dancer Olga Preobrajenska in 1931, when she was six. In 1933, at eight, she became a pupil of the Italian dancer Blanche d'Alessandri, who had been trained by Enrico Cecchetti. On holidays in Nice she took class with Ivan Clustine (who taught her Anna Pavlova's famous solo *The Dying Swan*), and she later studied with Julie Sedova and Gustave Ricaux, among others.

Perhaps because her family was poor, Tchmerzina became a performer for hire while still a child. Exhibiting unusual maturity, possessing formidable technical command, and already showing evidence of the stunning beauty she would eventually become, she led the life of a child prodigy, appearing at galas and salons in Paris and tea parties at the Nice Casino. At the age of twelve she met Michel Tverskoi, who had been a stage director in Moscow, and he began coaching her in the dramatic repertory. Her first important recitals as a dancer were in Paris, at the Maison de la Chimie in 1938 and at the École Normale de Musique in 1939.

The outbreak of World War II found Tchmerzina and her mother in Nice, where she met Marcel Sablon, then the manager of the Ballets de Monte-Carlo, who signed her as ballerina of the company. She was sixteen years old. In 1942 she met Serge Lifar, who gave her her big chance by choosing her to dance with him in his new ballet, *Romeo and Juliet*. She made her Paris debut in this ballet, set to Tchaikovsky's music, on 16 June 1942 at the Salle Pleyel. Lifar also chose the name by which she was to be known. At the Marseille Opera, where she danced in *Giselle, Swan Lake*, and several operas *(Manon Lescaut, Aida, Faust)*, Tcherina met the dancer Édmond Audran, whom she married.

In 1945 Tcherina joined Roland Petit's Ballets des Champs-Élysées for its first season, dancing in *Les Forains* and pas de deux from *The Sleeping Beauty* and *Swan Lake*. She and her young husband put on dance concerts of their own from 1946 to 1951. In 1946 Audran choreographed *Madame La Lune* for her, to his own musical score, and *Le Loup et l'Agneau*, to music of Alessandro Scarlatti. That same year she created one of her favorite roles, the Young Bonaparte, in Lifar's *À la Memoire d'un Héros* for the Nouveaux Ballets de Monte-Carlo, where she and Audran were among the leading dancers.

At this time, Tcherina began a film career, appearing first in *Les Rendezvous*, directed by Christian Jacques, and then in two films directed by Michael Powell: *The Red Shoes* (1948) and *The Tales of Hoffmann* (1951), in which she co-starred with Moira Shearer, Robert Helpmann, and Léonide Massine. *The Tales of Hoffmann* would make her internationally famous and would bring her an Academy Award (an "Oscar") in 1952. Just when her career was in the ascendant, the tragic death of her young husband in an automobile accident in 1951 caused her to halt, as she was almost overwhelmed by grief.

She resumed performing as an international guest artist in 1954, when she appeared in *Giselle* at the Teatro alla Scala in Milan. In 1957 she appeared as a dancer and an actress in the title role of Lifar's production of *Le Martyre de Saint-Sébastien* at the Paris Opera, and in 1958 she founded her own company, which toured France, Britain, and Italy. The Ballets de Ludmila-Tcherina appeared in Paris in 1959 at the Théâtre Sarah-Bernhardt in a season of new productions that included Milko Šparemblek's *Les Amants de Teruel* and Paul Goubé's *Feu de Poudre*. The former work, which was called a *"ballet total"* at the time, was made into a full-length film and commercially distrib-

TCHERINA. In the film *The Lovers of Teruel* (1962), Tcherina appeared with the famous Spanish dancer Antonio, here pictured in a flying leap. Choreography was by Léonide Massine, set to music by Michel Theodorakis. Sets and costumes were designed by Evor Beddoes. (Photograph by Michael Powell Productions.)

uted in Anglophone countries as *The Lovers of Teruel*. In 1959 Tcherina went to Russia to dance in *Swan Lake* with both the Kirov Ballet in Saint Petersburg and the Bolshoi Ballet in Moscow.

During the 1960s, Tcherina was often to be seen in Italy. In 1960 she became a producer and principal dancer at the Teatro San Carlo in Naples; in 1961 she created the principal role in Maurice Béjart's *Gala*, presented by his Ballet du XXᵉ Siècle at the Teatro La Fenice in Venice; and in 1967 she created a principal part in Ugo dell'Ara's historic revival of Luigi Manzotti's *Excelsior* at the Teatro Communale in Florence. That same year she appeared at the Metropolitan Opera in New York as principal dancer in Joseph Lazzini's production of *The Miraculous Mandarin* (1967), which was also filmed and televised. During the 1970s, she made numerous appearances on television and in films, and in 1972 she appeared in Palermo in the title role of Daniel Auber's opera *La Muette de Portici*.

As a dancer, Tcherina excelled in dramatic roles in ballets such as Lifar's *Le Martyre de Saint-Sébastien* and Goubé's *L'Atlantide* (both 1957); as an actress, she was admired as much for her exceptional beauty and strong presence as for her dramatic ability. She also established a reputation as a painter and sculptor, with several exhibitions of her work in Paris, Seville, and Strasbourg, and she is known as the author of two novels about the world of ballet, *L'amour au miroir* (1983) and *La femme à l'envers* (1986). She was named Officier des Arts et Lettres in 1979 and Officier de la Légion d'Honneur in 1980.

BIBLIOGRAPHY
Garaudy, Roger. *Ludmila Tcherina: Érotisme et mystique*. Paris, 1975.
Hirsch, Nicole. *Ludmila Tcherina*. Paris, 1958.
Lido, Irène, and Serge Lido. *Ludmila Tcherina: Tragédienne de la danse*. Paris, 1967.

MONIQUE BABSKY
Translated from French

TCHERNICHEVA, LUBOV (Liubov' Pavlovna Chernyshova; born 17 September 1890 in Saint Petersburg, died 1 March 1976 in Richmond, Surrey), Russian ballet dancer and teacher. A student of Michel Fokine at the Imperial Theater School in Saint Petersburg, Lubov Chernyshova entered the Maryinsky corps de ballet after her graduation in 1908. The following year she married Serge Grigoriev, who served as *régisseur* for the Ballets Russes de Serge Diaghilev during its spring and summer Saisons Russes in France. In 1911, she participated in Diaghilev's Paris season (with her surname spelled in the French fashion) and eventually became one the Ballets Russes' most popular dancers.

A woman of striking beauty with lovely hand and arm movements, Tchernicheva was a postwar favorite in the title roles of *Cléopâtre* and *Thamar* and as Chiarina in *Le Carnaval*, Zobeide in *Schéhérazade*, and Costanza in *Les Femmes de Bonne Humeur*. As Costanza, her solo of gently drifting *bourrées* on pointe was remembered by Lydia Sokolova as "truly exquisite" (Sokolova, 1960). Along with such *demi-caractère* parts as the Nursemaid in *Petrouchka*, the Tsarevna in *The Firebird*, the Principal Nymph in *L'Après-midi d'un Faune*, the Miller's Wife in *Le Tricorne*, and the Chanson Dansée in *Les Biches*, her repertory included classical solos in *Les Sylphides*, *The Sleeping Princess*, and *Apollon Musagète*.

In 1926, Tchernicheva succeeded Nikolai Legat and assumed the duties of ballet mistress for Diaghilev's Ballets Russes, a position she held until the company was disbanded upon Diaghilev's death in 1929. In 1932, Tchernicheva became ballet mistress for Colonel Wassily de Basil's Ballets Russes de Monte Carlo, where her coaching and teaching were highly esteemed. She remained in this position until 1952, throughout the life of the various companies managed by Colonel de Basil.

In 1935, Tchernicheva came out of premature retirement to dance her old roles in *Schéhérazade*, *Le Tricorne*, and *Thamar* (1936), earning critical praise for her powerful sense of theater and miming. In 1937, she created the title role in David Lichine's *Francesca da Rimini*. After the demise of the de Basil company, she settled in England, where she taught at the Sadler's Wells School and, with her husband, staged revivals of *The Firebird* (1954), *Les Sylphides* (1955), *Petrouchka* (1957), and the Polovtsian Dances from *Prince Igor* (1965) for Britain's Royal Ballet. In 1957, she made a last stage appearance as Juliet's mother in John Cranko's *Romeo and Juliet*.

BIBLIOGRAPHY

Anthony, Gordon. "Lubov Tchernicheva." *The Dancing Times* (February 1976): 248–249.

Beaumont, Cyril W. *Bookseller at the Ballet: Memoirs, 1891 to 1929*. London, 1975.

Garafola, Lynn. *Diaghilev's Ballets Russes*. New York and Oxford, 1989.

García-Márquez, Vicente. *The Ballets Russes: Colonel de Basil's Ballets Russes de Monte Carlo, 1932–1952*. New York, 1990.

Grigoriev, Serge. *The Diaghilev Ballet, 1909–1929*. Translated and edited by Vera Bowen. London, 1953.

Sokolova, Lydia. *Dancing for Diaghilev*. Edited by Richard Buckle. London, 1960.

Sorley Walker, Kathrine. *De Basil's Ballets Russes*. New York, 1983.

LYNN GARAFOLA

TEATRO ALLA SCALA. *See* Scala Ballet.

TEATRODANZA CONTEMPORANEA DI ROMA

(Contemporary Dance Theater of Rome) is a modern dance company founded by Elsa Piperno in 1972 and directed by Piperno and the Italian-American dancer Joseph Fontano. The company and its school have been responsible in large measure for the diffusion of modern dance in Italy. This has been a difficult process in a country and a city where dance has traditionally been an elite enthusiasm, overwhelmed by the popular taste for opera and closed to the new forms of dance expression coming from the United States.

With determination and obstinacy, Piperno (a former pupil of the National Academy of Dance in Rome) went to London in 1967 to become a student of Robert Cohan, himself a disciple of Martha Graham, and later a dancer with his London Contemporary Dance Theatre. Upon her return to Italy in 1971, Piperno began a series of lecture performances designed to demonstrate and spread the teaching of the Cohan-Graham technique. She and Fontano, a student of Paul Sanasardo, constituted the nucleus of the Teatrodanza Contemporanea di Roma. The group and its school soon became the most important point of reference for modern dance in Italy. The doors of the Rome school opened to modern American artists of all stamps for seminars, lectures, and demonstrations.

The company's repertory was enriched by Piperno's choreographies, including *Stripsmania* (1980), set to selections from Luciano Berio's *Sequenza IV*, sung by Cathy Berberian; *Autofocus* (1981), to music by Brian Eno, J. S. Bach, and Nina Hagen; and *Aquile e Aquiloni* (1981), to music by J. M. Jarre, Genesis, A. Coppola, and P. Schiavoni. Also in the repertory are works by Fontano, including *Duetto in Nero* (1977), to the music of Jean Guillou; *On the Radio* (1980), set to pop and rock music by various composers; and *Sala B* (1982), to music by Eugenio Bennato and Toni Esposito. In the 1980s Teatrodanza Contemporanea has produced a number of modern dance teachers and dancers of great quality, who in Rome and other Italian cities continue to promote and popularize dance, as Elsa Piperno had done in the early 1970s.

BIBLIOGRAPHY

Bentivoglio, Leonetta. *La danza contemporanea*. Milan, 1985.

Doglio, Vittoria, and Elisa Vaccarino. *L'Italia in ballo*. Rome, 1993.

VITTORIA OTTOLENGHI
Translated from Italian

TECHNICAL MANUALS. [*To discuss the importance of published materials as aids in the understanding of technical requirements of early court and theatrical dance and ballet, this entry comprises three articles:*

Publications, 1445–1725
Publications, 1765–1859
Publications since 1887

For related discussion, see Medieval Dance; Renaissance Dance Technique; *and* Ballet Technique, History of.]

Publications, 1445–1725

A technical manual instructs the reader in the technique of dancing. In nearly all instances the technical portion of a manual contains sections on style, gesture, manners, the proper handling of accessories (swords, hats, fans, cloaks, gloves, kerchiefs, and so on) and on musical performance practice, meter, rhythm, and instrumentation. With few exceptions the technical manuals from the early Renaissance to the middle of the seventeenth century contain choreographic descriptions of dances, with or without musical accompaniment, in addition to their theoretical-technical introductions.

The first technical manual was the treatise of Domenico da Piacenza (c.1445), which was followed by Antonio Cornazano's manual (1455 and 1465) and Guglielmo Ebreo's treatises (1463 and undated exemplars). All three authors conceived of dance as an activity involving body, mind, and emotion. For this reason and because the treatises were addressed to persons who had already mastered the fundamentals of dancing, the technical information is embedded in a general discourse on dance, memory, space, and dance composition. A systematization of the steps is given by Domenico; all three fifteenth-century dancing masters dealt with the time values of the steps in relation to one another, with the combination of steps and ornamental motions into larger units (tempi), and with the interchangeability of the tempi in the various dance meters.

Compiled late in the fifteenth century but reflecting an earlier manner of dancing are the French Burgundian *bassedanse* sources, the Brussels manuscript, and Michel Toulouze's *L'art et instruction de bien dancer* (c.1488). The manual of Englishman Robert Coplande (1521) stands in the same tradition as does the so-called Moderne treatise (c.1540). In the theoretical introductions of all of these, the portions dealing with actual technique are often no more than a few sentences, but they are essential for understanding the dances themselves.

The dominant teaching method used in the technical manuals of the fifteenth century is direct didaxis: the teaching dialogue, a discussion between the master and his disciple. The device was first used by Guglielmo Ebreo in some of his treatises and was later used by Thoinot Arbeau and Fabritio Caroso.

Only two dance instruction books appeared during the century that separated the fifteenth-century treatises from the next group of major technical manuals, which begins with Caroso's *Il ballarino* of 1581. One was the *bassedanse*-related Moderne treatise; the other was Antonius de Arena's *Leges dansandi*, written in the macaronic Latin verse then fashionable in the literary circles of Avignon. Arena describes the steps one by one (the first viable reverence description for men and women comes from Arena) and gives extensive attention to manners. University students in the early sixteenth century obviously needed careful instruction in the social graces that a courtier acquired gradually as part of his education in his elevated social environment. Although the main focus of Arena's *Leges dansandi* is still the *bassedanse*, the dance types *branle*, *pavane*, and *tourdion* are mentioned for the first time.

Precise technical information is supplied by Fabritio Caroso and Cesare Negri, whose manuals appeared in the years 1581 to 1630. Large segments of their treatises describe steps in minute detail, each step in its own chapter *(regola)*. Many chapters contain the authors' laments about dancers' bad habits and mistakes, making it possible to distinguish the proper version of a given step from an unsatisfactory one. Composite steps, like *galliard* and *canario* sequences, and step-units modeled after the meters of classical Greek verse (Caroso, *Della nobiltà di dame*) are all included in the *regole;* so too are chapters on men's and ladies' ballroom etiquette, as well as on sitting, walking, and greeting an equal or a superior. Negri's treatise *Le gratie d'amore* (1602) is especially rich in technical

information, and it is Negri who gives the clearest images of the demanding theatrical dance technique of the Renaissance as it must have been employed in operas by Giulio Caccini and Claudio Monteverdi, in court ballets, *intermedi*, and other dance spectacles of the period.

Less technical manuals than technical reference books are Lutio Compasso's *Ballo della gagliarda* (1560), Prospero Luti di Sulmona's *Opera bellissima . . . di gagliarda* (1589), and Livio Lupi da Caravaggio's *Libro di gagliarda, tordiglione, passo è mezzo canario è passeggi* (1600, 1607). All three authors give almost no descriptions of steps or full choreographies, instead giving hundreds of step combinations to be used in the composition of new *galliards*, *tourdions*, *passo e mezzo*s, and *canaries* and in *passeggi*, the connecting passages between the figures of Renaissance dances that are performed hand-in-hand. Many of the step names mentioned are not described by Caroso and Negri.

The English *Treatise of Daunces* (1581) describes dances of the contemporary repertory and names the steps with which to do them, but it is not strictly speaking a technical manual.

The only technical manual from France in the late sixteenth century is Thoinot Arbeau's *Orchésographie* (1589, 1596). Arbeau, in a way, reaches back to the method used in the early Renaissance: his technical dance information is embedded in a teaching dialogue between himself and his student, Capriol, interwoven with remarks about style, manners, occasional excursions into history, and recurring statements about the benefits to be obtained from faultless mastery of the art of dancing. Arbeau's opening section—which deals with military movement and its music, with drum rhythms, signal tunes, and melodies for the fife *(arigot)*—is unique. In addition to the text Arbeau provides a series of pictures of dancers executing the most prevalent steps, a simple but effective teaching device that helps the reader now, as then, to understand the essential components of the French dance technique of the Renaissance.

In the first half of the seventeenth century, technical manuals were published in France and in Spain. François de Lauze's *Apologie de la danse* (1623) is, according to the full title, "the perfect method to teach [dancing] as much to the gentlemen as to the ladies." More than in any previous manual, emphasis is placed here on exercises, for the "assured grace and dignity" required for the flawless execution of the courante, branle, gavotte, and gaillard could only be acquired with diligent practice. The turnout from the hip is stressed again and again; attention is given to the glance and to facial expression; *révérence* steps for men and women in various social settings are dealt with extensively; the five positions, although not yet called by name, are clearly described, as are [bends] and rises that constitute the *mouvement* of the Baroque technique—all this makes de Lauze's *Apologie* the first technical manual of the Baroque era.

The same trend, although less pronounced, is evident in Esquivel de Navarro's *Discvrsos sobre el arte del dancado*. This manual also gives step descriptions and exercise sequences, but, as in de Lauze's manual, dance descriptions are kept to a minimum, and there is no music. Juan Antonio Jaque, in his *Libro de danzar* (c.1680), includes the descriptions of six fashionable social dances, together with instructions for steps and figures.

During the remainder of the seventeenth century, no further technical manuals were produced. The English country dance collections by John Playford (from 1651), Thomas Bray (1699 and later editions), and others exerted their influence on French ballroom practices, namely, André Lorin's *Livre de contredance présenté au Roy* (manuscript, c.1685) and his *Livre de la contredance du Roy* (1688). All contain some advice regarding the execution of steps; their main concern, however, is the transmission of choreographies, occasionally enhanced by elegant drawings of dancing couples (Lorin), not the teaching of dance.

The decade of the 1680s in France saw the eruption of an enormous concern with the creation of a viable dance notation. Lorin, Jean Favier, Pierre Beauchamps, and Sieur De La Haise each developed his own system (for details, see Harris-Warrick and Marsh, 1994, pp. 82ff.), but neither Lorin's nor Favier's notations (the latter summarized in the article "Chorégraphie" in volume 3 of Denis Diderot and Jean Le Rond d'Alembert's *Encyclopédie* of 1753) assumed the format of a technical manual. Beauchamps's efforts, in contrast, formed the background, albeit unacknowledged, to Raoul-Auger Feuillet's didactic masterpiece, the *Chorégraphie, ou L'art de décrire la dance* of 1700.

In Feuillet's *Chorégraphie*, which, as the title page states, is intended for the self-instruction of amateurs "in every kind of dance" as well as for the use of dancing masters, he takes his reader step by step through all the elements of his notational system. He deals with the dancing space, with the positioning of dancers in that space, and with floor patterns. He describes the five positions, the "good" ones as well as the *fausses*, with the toes turned in. He describes and notates a variety of ornamental leg gestures, explains the use of the arms, discusses *"la batterie des castagnettes,"* with practice sequences, and provides tables of hundreds of steps—*coupés, pas de bourrée*, pirouettes, cabrioles, and so on—in every direction. A relatively brief chapter is devoted to the correlation of the steps with the most common musical meters; practice phrases are included there also.

At the end of his treatise, Feuillet added a collection of fifteen notated *entrées de ballet* of his own composition, some of considerable difficulty, as a challenge to masters

of the dance and to advanced students (see preface to *Chorégraphie*). This was followed by a separate collection of nine ballroom dances by Guillaume-Louis Pecour (see Witherell, 1983).

Not long after its first printing, *Chorégraphie* was translated into English in 1706 both by P. Siris and by John Weaver (whose later edition, with three additional dances, appeared in the early 1720s). Gottfried Taubert included a German translation in his *Rechtschaffener Tantz-Meister* of 1717.

The importance and viability of this dance notation was recognized immediately, as witnessed by the numerous dances that were published singly or in small groups each November, for the beginning of the "season" (see Annual Collections), and by the larger collections of choreographies for use in the ballroom and/or in the theater, such as the ones by Gaudrau (c.1712–1715) and Anthony L'Abbé, the last published by F. Le Rousseau (c.1725; see Marsh, 1991; Little and Marsh, 1992). None of these is a teaching manual, strictly speaking; rather, each represents the repertory that dance enthusiasts in Europe could learn to master through diligent study of the instruction books and in their dancing schools.

The line of manuals devoted to the teaching of Beauchamps-Feuillet notation, not infrequently with modifications (as, for example, the detailed treatment of arms, hands, and fingers in Malpied, c.1780), continued through the entire eighteenth century. It included works by authors from Germany, England, Italy, Spain, and Portugal, all attesting to the far-reaching influence of the French style of dancing during the Baroque era (for individual listings and commentaries, see Schwartz-Schlundt, 1987).

In addition, a large group of instruction manuals describe in words the technique and style of the *danse noble* as well as, with increasing frequency, the *danse haute* of the theatre, nearly always in combination with directives for proper etiquette, descriptions of festivities of all kinds, excursions into history, and the like.

To this group belong Pierre Rameau's *Le Maître à danser* (1725; translated as *The Dancing Master* by John Essex, 1728), the textbook *par excellence* for early eighteenth-century social dancing; Louis Bonin's *Die Neueste Art zur Galanten und Theatralischen Tanzkunst* (1711); Gottfried Taubert's *Tantz-Meister* (1717); Kellom Tomlinson's *The Art of Dancing Explained* (1724/1735); Giambatista Dufort's *Trattato del Ballo Nobile* (1728); and, later in the century, Gennaro Magri's *Trattato* (1779) and Malpied's *Traîté* (c.1780).

Not quite satisfied with the purely verbal explanations of the dance technique of his time as he gave them in *Le maître à danser*, Rameau also published in 1725 his *Abbrégé de la nouvelle méthode dans l'art d'écrire ou de traçer toutes sortes de danses de ville*, a notation book intended as an aide-mémoire for persons who may have interrupted their dance studies but also useful for dancing masters. Tables of steps were given in a manner similar to that of Feuillet, but in each case Rameau juxtaposed the "ancienne Chorégraphie avec la nouvelle" (p. 85 ff), and he accompanied the notations with verbal descriptions of each step. Twelve dances by Pecour in "the new corrected and augmented" notation form part 2 of *Abbrégé*.

In many of these publications, the explanatory text was enhanced by engravings, showing persons in the execution of individual steps (Rameau) or step-sequences (Tomlinson), depicting arm and wrist motions (Rameau), arm and leg positions (Behr), dancing couples (Tomlinson, Rameau, Bickham, Dubois, Guillaume), an entire grand ball presided over by the king (Rameau), and so on. A particularly lovely set of illuminations can be found in Pablo Minguet e Yrol's *Arte de danzar à la francesa* (1758/1768). Practically all the manuals mentioned contain one or more sample dances in notation.

Volumes are also devoted to one dance type only, such as George Bickham (1738) and G. M. de Chavanne (1767) on the minuet; or Simon Guillaume (1769) and Dubois (late eighteenth century) on the allemande.

The minuet, which has enjoyed a lasting popularity since the 1660s, and demanded the utmost in control and elegance from those who dance it, normally one solo couple (see Hilton, 1981, p. 191ff. for details), occupies large sections of the more general instruction books as well (Tomlinson, Malpied, Magny, and others).

The technique of stage dancing, serious as well as grotesque, was given full attention in the writings of John Weaver (see Ralph, 1985) and Louis Bonin (1711), in book 2 of Taubert's *Tantz-Meister,* in Noverre's *Lettres* (1760), in Gaspero Angiolini's extensive forewords to his ballets *Don Juan* (1760) and *Semiramis* (1765; for both, see Brown, 1991 and Brainard, 1996) and in Gennaro Magri's *Trattato* (1779). The instruction manuals for actors cited in Dene Barnett's important study on gesture on the eighteenth-century tragic stage (1987) provide us with the material needed to fill in the gaps that the dance treatises left open.

Theater dances for all kinds of personages are depicted in Gregorio Lambranzi's *Neue und Curieuse Theatrialische Tantz-Schul* (Nürnberg, 1716). On the title page, next to a portrait of the author, is a scroll with one figure of a *loure* for a couple in Feuillet notation; no other example of that notation appears in the 101 engravings that make up the two parts of the book. Printed at the top of each page is the tune for each dance; below that is the image of a stage with a few flats and the dancing figures; at the bottom is a decorative medallion that frames the names of the steps the performers are to execute, with directives for the action, some very brief, some extensive enough to amount to small scenarios.

As Lambranzi explains in his foreword to part 1, his

aim is not to describe in detail the choreography of these dances or any particular *pas,* still less to depict all their possible variations. . . . I shall portrait a principal character in appropriate costume, the style of his dance and the manner of its execution. . . . However, it is not my intention to restrict anyone to my method, but to leave each dancer free to adapt it as he pleases.   (Beaumont edition, p. 15)

Lambranzi's opus is a treasure-trove of information on the dancing style and technique of Italian *commedia dell'arte* characters, on that of various professions and trades, on highly acrobatic buffoonery, and on the dancing of persons of elegance who move in the manner of Spain, of Rome, and, of course, of France.

National and regional dances are taught in a number of technical manuals from Spain by Juan Antonio Jaque (c.1680; see Subirá, 1950 and Gingell, 1991), Pablo Minguet and Minguet E Yrol (1750s), Felipe Rejo de Flores (1793); German, Polish, Hungarian and "a multitude of English dances" (eine Unzahl Englischer Tänze) appear in C. J. Feldtenstein's *Erweiterung der Kunst nach der Chorographie* [sic] *zu tanzen* (1772; 1775; 1776).

Parallel to the manuals that teach the technique and style of noble and theatrical dancing were publications devoted to the increasingly popular, more relaxed *contredanses,* country dances, quadrilles, and cotillons, some in verbal descriptions such as the Playford series and the Caledonian dances from Scotland, others in simplified Feuillet notation in which mainly the dancers' path is given and steps are written in only at crucial moments. Feuillet's own *Recüeil de contredances* (1706) is followed by similar collections by Jacques Dezais (1712), John Essex (1710), Ernest August Jayme (1717), Pablo Minguet e Yrol (1758), and De La Cuisse (1762), all the way to Gennaro Magri (1779) and beyond. Choreographies for *contredanses* are also included in many of the other instruction books, usually at the end, after the more formal dances have been presented (see Schwartz-Schlundt, 1987; also Guilcher, 1969).

Finally, a large number of publications have main objectives that are the aesthetics, and often the history, of the performing arts—of dance, music, and theater. These provide us with innumerable, valuable details concerning topics that are treated elsewhere in more or less cursory fashion, and they throw light on some of the heated discussions that occupied the minds of theorists and practitioners of the dance in the seventeenth and the eighteenth centuries. These include the manufacturing and wearing of masks, the execution of gestures in various dramatic situations, the relationship of music and dance, the composition of ballets, the education and training of dancers, the role of the grotesque versus that of the serious dancer on the Baroque stage, and so on.

There are far too many authors to mention them all by name (see Schwartz-Schlundt, 1987; Harris-Warrick and Marsh, 1994; among others). The list, of necessity, includes Marin Mersenne, Claude-François Ménestrier, Louis Bonin, Louis de Cahusac, Michel de Pure, John Weaver, Gaspero Angiolini, Jean-Georges Noverre, Giovanni Andrea Gallini, and Gennaro Magri; and, on the musical side, Michael Praetorius, Johann Mattheson, Thomas Mace, George Muffat, and Jean-Philippe Rameau. Important information is also transmitted in the Diderot-d'Alembert *Encyclopédie* and in the many dictionaries on music and dance subjects published during the Baroque period.

BIBLIOGRAPHY

Barnett, Dene, with Jeanette Massy-Westropp. *The Art of Gesture: The Practices and Principles of 18th Century Acting.* Heidelberg, 1987.

Beaumont, Cyril W., ed., and Derra de Moroda. *Gregorio Lambranzi: New and Curious School of Theatrical Dancing.* New York, 1966.

Brainard, Ingrid. "Die Choreographie der Hoftänze in Burgund, Frankreich und Italien im 15. Jahrhundert." Ph.D. diss., University of Göttingen, 1956.

Brainard, Ingrid. "Bassedanse, Bassadanza, and Ballo in the Fifteenth Century." In *Dance History Research: Perspectives from Related Arts and Disciplines,* edited by Joann W. Kealiinohomoku. New York, 1970.

Brainard, Ingrid. *The Art of Courtly Dancing in the Early Renaissance.* West Newton, Mass., 1981.

Brainard, Ingrid. "Der Höfische Tanz: Darstellende Kunst und Höfische Repräsentation." In *Europäische Hofkultur im 16. und 17. Jahrhundert,* edited by August Buck et al. Hamburg, 1981.

Brainard, Ingrid. "The Speaking Body: Gaspero Angiolini's *Rhétorique Muette* and the *Ballet d'Action* in the Eighteenth Century." In *Critica Musica: Essays in Honor of Paul Brainard.* Amsterdam, 1996.

Brown, Bruce Alan. *Gluck and the French Theatre in Vienna.* Oxford, 1991.

Chadima, Helen Gower. "The Use of Castanets in Baroque Dance." In *Proceedings of the Sixth Annual Conference, Society of Dance History Scholars, the Ohio State University, 11–13 February 1983,* edited by Christena L. Schlundt, pp. 84–94. Riverside, Calif., 1983.

Crane, Frederick. *Materials for the Study of the Fifteenth-Century Basse Danse.* Brooklyn, 1968.

Francalanci, Andrea. "The *Copia di Mº Giorgio del Guido di ballare basse danze e balletti* as Found in the New York Public Library." *Basler Jahrbuch für Historische Musikpraxis* 14 (1990): 87–179. Italian text only.

Gallo, F. Alberto. "Il 'ballare lombardo,' circa 1435–1475." *Studi musicali* 8 (1979): 61–84.

Gerbes, Angelika. "Gottfried Taubert on Social and Theatrical Dance of the Early Eighteenth Century." Ph.D. diss., Ohio State University, 1972.

Gingell, Jane. "Spanish Dance in the Golden Age: The Dance Text of Juan Antonio Jaque." In *Dance in Hispanic Cultures: Proceedings of the Fourteenth Annual Conference, Society of Dance History Scholars, New World School of the Arts, Miami, Florida, 8–10 February 1991,* compiled by Christena L. Schlundt. Riverside, Calif., 1991.

Goff, Moira. "Edmund Pemberton, Dancing-Master and Publisher." *Dance Research* 9.1 (1993): 52–81.

Goff, Moira, and Jennifer Thorp. "Dance Notations Published in England c.1700–1740 and Related Manuscript Material." *Dance Research* 9.2 (1993): 32–50.

Goff, Moira. "'The Art of Dancing Demonstrated by Characters and Figures': French and English Sources for Court and Theatre Dance, 1700–1750." In *The British Library Journal* 21.2 (1995): 202–231.

Goff, Moira. "George Bickham Junior and the Art of Dancing." In *Factotum* 34 (1993): 14–18.

Guilcher, Jean Michel. *La contredanse et les renouvellements de la danse française.* Paris, 1969.

Guthrie, John, and Marino Zorzi. "Rules of Dancing: Antonius Arena." *Dance Research* 4 (Autumn 1986): 3–53. Original text with English translation.

Harris-Warrick, Rebecca, and Carol G. Marsh. *Musical Theatre at the Court of Louis XIV: Le Mariage de la Grosse Cathos.* Cambridge, 1994.

Helwig, Christine, and Marshall Barron. *Thomas Bray's Country Dances, 1699.* New Haven, 1988.

Hilton, Wendy. *Dance of Court and Theatre: The French Noble Style, 1690–1725.* Princeton, 1981.

Hudson, Richard. *The Allemande, the Balletto, and the Tanz.* 2 vols. Cambridge, 1986.

Inglehearn, Madeleine, and Peggy Forsyth. *The Book on the Art of Dancing: Antonio Cornazano.* London, 1981. English translation only.

Jones, Pamela. "The Relation between Music and Dance in Cesare Negri's 'Le gratie d'amore' (1602)." 2 vols. Ph.D. diss., University of London, 1988.

Keller, Kate Van Winkle, and Genevieve Shimer. *The Playford Ball.* 2d ed. Northampton, Mass., 1994.

Kendall, Yvonne. "*Le gratie d'amore* (1602) by Cesare Negri: Translation and Commentary." Ph.D. diss., Stanford University, 1985. Original Italian text in facsimile with English translation.

Little, Meredith Ellis, and Carol G. Marsh. *La Danse Noble: An Inventory of Dances and Sources.* Williamstown, 1992.

Marrocco, W. Thomas. *Inventory of Fifteenth-Century Bassedanze, Balli, and Balletti in Italian Dance Manuals.* New York, 1981.

Marsh, Carol. "French Court Dance in England, 1706–1740: A Study of the Sources." Ph.D. diss., City University of New York, 1985.

Marsh, Carol G., and John M. Ward, eds. *Anthony L'Abbé, A New Collection of Dances.* Facsimile. Music for London Entertainment, 1660–1800, series D, vol. 2. Boston 1991.

Mather, Betty Bang, with Dean M. Karns. *Dance Rhythms of the French Baroque: A Handbook for Performance.* Bloomington, 1987.

Ralph, Richard. *The Life and Works of John Weaver.* New York, 1985.

Rebman, Elizabth Huttig. "Chorégraphie: An Annotated Bibliography of Eighteenth Century Printed Instruction Books." M.A. thesis, Stanford University, 1981.

Sasportes, José. *História de dança em Portugal.* Lisbon, 1970.

Schwartz, Judith L., and Christena L. Schlundt. *French Court Dance and Dance Music: A Guide to Primary Source Writings, 1643–1789.* Stuyvesant, N.Y., 1987.

Smith, A. William, trans. and ed. *Fifteenth-Century Dance and Music: The Complete Transcribed Italian Treatises and Collections in the Tradition of Domenico da Piacenza.* 2 vols. Stuyvesant, N.Y., 1995.

Sparti, Barbara. *Guglielmo Ebreo of Pesaro: On the Practice or Art of Dancing.* Oxford, 1993. Original Italian text with English translation.

Sparti, Barbara. *Ballo della Gagliarda: Lutio Compasso.* Freiburg, 1995. Italian text only.

Subirá, José. "Juan Antonio Jaque: Libro de Danzar de Baltazar de Rojas Pantoia." *Anuario musical* 5 (1950): 190–198.

Sutton, Julia. "Reconstruction of Sixteenth-Century Dance." In *Dance History Research: Perspectives from Related Arts and Disciplines,* edited by Joann W. Kealiinohomoku. New York, 1970.

Sutton, Julia. "Arbeau, Thoinot," "Caroso, Fabritio," and "Negri, Cesare." In *The New Grove Dictionary of Music and Musicians.* London, 1980.

Sutton, Julia. *Fabritio Caroso: Nobiltà di Dame (1600).* Music transcribed and edited by F. Marian Walker. Oxford, 1986. English translation only.

Taubert, Karl Heinz. *Höfische Tänze: Ihre Geschichte und Choreographie.* Mainz, 1968.

Tomlinson, Kellom. *A Work Book by Kellom Tomlinson: Commonplace Book of an Eighteenth-Century English Dancing Master (c.1708–1722).* Edited by Jennifer Shennan. Stuyvesant, N.Y., 1992.

Wilson, D. R. *Domenico of Piacenza (Paris, Bibliothèque Nationale, MS ital. 972).* Corr. ed. Cambridge, 1995. Italian text only.

Witherell, Anne L. *Louis Pécour's 1700 Recüeil de dances.* Ann Arbor, Mich., 1983.

INGRID BRAINARD

Publications, 1765–1859

The period from 1765 to 1859 marks a transition from the dance of the Baroque court and theater to the Romantic ballet; thus, the technical manuals of the time reflect both the old style and the new. Books devoted to theatrical dance technique, rare in previous periods, appear with more frequency, if mostly in numerous editions and translations of a few works, often still containing chapters on social, or "private," dancing. In the absence of any extant ballet repertory from the period preserving a semblance of its original choreography (with the possible exception of Vincenzo Galeotti's *The Whims of Cupid and the Ballet Master,* 1786), the value of the following technical manuals, with their insights into the changes that were occurring, is considerable.

The most important manual treating theatrical dance technique and execution in the latter part of the eighteenth century is Gennaro Magri's *Trattato teorico-prattico di ballo* (Naples, 1779). Magri discusses steps familiar from earlier in the century, usually giving French terms and their Italian equivalents, but his extensive list includes many later steps and exercises that reappear in the manuals of the next century. He often suggests which movements are appropriate for the various types of dancer—the serious, the *demi-caractère,* and the comic. Of particular interest is his information about the steps and style of the *grotteschi,* an impressive account of the skill and dexterity their art demanded. In contrast, the treatises by Claude Marc Magny (1765) and Malpied (c.1789) closely follow Raoul-Auger Feuillet's early text, *Chorégraphie* (1700). Although some additional steps are included, the predominant emphasis is on older forms, with special attention given to the minuet. The technical descriptions in Charles Compan's *Dictionnaire de danse* (1787) also reflect the style of the early eighteenth century. The *Encyclopédie méthodique* (1786), acknowledging its debt to the *traité* of Pierre Rameau as well as to the work of Louis de Cahusac and Jean-Georges Noverre, includes, among its technical material, an extensive discussion of arm movements.

The first important text devoted exclusively to theatrical dancing in the nineteenth century was written in 1820 by Carlo Blasis, *Traité élémentaire théorique et pratique de l'art de la danse.* The young author explains and illustrates many of the requisites still observed in ballet technique today, including complete turnout of the legs. His outline of "the lesson" provides some description of the "elementary exercises" to be "performed with the hand resting upon something firm," and a listing, but not an explanation, of the exercises to be practiced in center floor.

Although Blasis's is the first nineteenth-century account of the ballet lesson, his preface indicates that his instructions emanate "from the schools of leading masters who have contributed immensely to the progress and beauty of modern dancing." Indeed, an almost identical format of elementary exercises had been described earlier by J. H. Gourdoux-Daux (1817). His *Principes et notions élémentaires sur l'art de la danse,* published in 1811, had been preceded by a private printing in 1804. It clearly demonstrates the continuity between social and theatrical dancing.

In *Notes upon Dancing, Historical and Practical,* Blasis (1847) recalls the various translations of his *Traité* into Italian, Danish, Spanish, English, and French. His *The Code of Terpsichore,* written in England, was prepared for a printing in 1828, but because of the publisher's financial straits only a few copies were bound. The book finally appeared in 1830, with a French edition, *Manueal complete de la danse,* published that same year. The chapters on technique are virtually identical with those in the *Traité,* with the addition of a section on the "New Method of Instruction" and different engravings. [*See the entry on Blasis.*]

For this period, social dance publications continue to be helpful in explaining the step vocabulary found both on the stage and in the ballroom. Examples include *Elements of the Art of Dancing* by Alexander Strathy (1822) and *A Short Essay on the French Danse de Société* by Charles Mason (1827). The most extensive description of steps of the period appears in Giacoma Costa's *Saggio analitico-pratico intorno all'arte della danza per uso di civile conversazione* (1831). Although written as a text for social dancing, Costa's manual contains highly complex steps and some charming combinations (*ligazione*). Costa is easier to decipher than Magri, and his illustrations resemble those of Blasis.

E. A. Théleur's *Letters on Dancing* (1831) tried to accommodate the changing technical style with new nomenclature for the positions of the feet and arms. Although his efforts failed to be adopted, his technical descriptions, along with his two easily deciphered notation systems, his explanations of proper execution, and his illustrations (including the first depiction in a technical manual of a dancer on full pointe) give the clearest account of early nineteenth-century technique. His description of the dance lesson closely resembles Blasis's, but Théleur's account is more explicit. Included in the manual is the duet "Gavotte de Vestris," notated in both of Théleur's systems.

Although never published, the four handwritten notebooks by Léon Michel (who preferred to be known as Michel St. Léon) include numerous exercises, *enchaînements*, and *entrées* (and their music) for one to three dancers, composed or compiled during his tenure as dancing master at the court of Würtemberg. St. Léon also includes some solo and pas de deux selections from the Paris Opera ballet repertory by Pierre Gardel, Jean-Pierre Aumer, and Albert (François Decombe). These notebooks, together with works by August Bournonville, particularly his manuscript, *Méthode de Vestris* (c.1826) and his later published works on dance theory and notation, *Études chorégraphiques* (1855, 1861), provide important insights into the teaching methods developed by Jean-François Coulon and most especially by Auguste Vestris at the Paris Opera's School of Dance.

For a more complete understanding of the actual performance of ballet technique in the early nineteenth century, later texts must be consulted. Two especially pertinent ones are Arthur Saint-Léon's *La sténochorégraphie* (1852) and Giovanni Léopold Adice's *Théorie de la gymnastique de la danse théâtrale* (1859). Saint-Léon both describes and notates in his own system classroom combinations mentioned earlier by both Blasis and Théleur, as well as *enchaînements* from the collection of his father, Léon Michel. His notation is correlated with music for the *enchaînements* as well as for a pas de six from his ballet *La Vivandière*.

One section of Adice's book is devoted to the explication of Blasis's classes, which Adice extols over lessons of his own day. In the chapter on Blasis's *barre* work, Adice enumerates the repetitions of each exercise—altogether some 648 gymnastic movements. Substantial portions of this section are translated in *Dance as a Theatre Art*, edited in 1974 by Selma Jeanne Cohen. Some of the material from Adice, Blasis, Saint-Léon, and Théleur, is correlated and reconstructed in Sandra Noll Hammond's *Ballet: Beyond the Basics* (1982).

BIBLIOGRAPHY

Adice, G. Léopold. *Théorie de la gymnastique de la danse théâtrale.* Paris, 1859. Excerpts translated by Leonore Loft in *Dance as a Theatre Art*, edited by Selma Jeanne Cohen (New York, 1974).

Blasis, Carlo. *An Elementary Treatise upon the Theory and Practice of the Art of Dancing* (1820). Translated by Mary Stewart Evans. New York, 1944.

Blasis, Carlo. *The Code of Terpsichore: A Practical and Historical Treatise on the Ballet, Dancing, and Pantomime.* London, 1828.

Blasis, Carlo. *The Art of Dancing Comprising Its Theory and Practice, and a History of Its Rise and Progress, from the Earliest Times.*
Translated by R. Barton. London, 1831. Second edition of *The Code of Terpsichore* (above).

Blasis, Carlo. *Notes upon Dancing, Historical and Practical.* Translated by R. Barton. London, 1847.

Bournonville, August. *Méthode de Vestris.* Undated manuscript located in Copenhagen, Royal Library, NKS 3285 4°.

Bournonville, August. *Etudes Chorégraphiques.* Copenhagen, 1855 and 1861.

Compan, Charles. *Dictionnaire de danse.* Paris, 1787.

Costa, Giacomo. *Saggio analitico-pratico intorno all'arte della danza per uso di civile conversazione.* Turin, 1831.

Encyclopédie méthodique: Arts académiques, équitation, escrime, danse, et art de nager. Paris, 1786.

Feuillet, Raoul-Auger. *Chorégraphie, ou L'art de décrire la dance, par caractères, figures et signes démonstratifs, avec lesquels on apprend facilement de soy-même toutes sortes de dances.* Paris, 1700. Translated by John Weaver as *Orchesography, or, The Art of Dancing* (London, 1706).

Flindt, Vivi, and Knud Arne Jürgensen. *Bournonville Ballet Technique.* London, 1992.

Gallini, Giovanni. *Critical Observations on the Art of Dancing, to Which Is Added a Collection of Cotillons or French Dances.* London, c.1770.

Gourdoux-Daux, J. H. *Principes et notions élémentaires sur l'art de la danse.* 2d ed. Paris, 1811. Translated by Victor Guillou as *Elements and Principles of the Art of Dancing* (Philadelphia, 1817).

Hammond, Sandra Noll. *Ballet: Beyond the Basics.* Palo Alto, Calif., 1982.

Jürgensen, Knud Arne and Ann Hutchinson Guest. *The Bournonville Heritage, A Choreographic Record 1829–1875.* London, 1990.

Magny, Claude Marc. *Principes de chorégraphie, suivis d'un traité de la cadence.* Paris, 1765.

Magri, Gennaro. *Trattato teorico-prattico di ballo.* Naples, 1779. Translated by Mary Skeaping as *Theoretical and Practical Treatise on Dancing* (London, 1988).

Malpied. *Traité sur l'art de la danse.* Paris, c.1785. 2d ed., rev. and enl. Paris, c.1789.

Mason, Charles. *A Short Essay on the French Danse de Société.* London, 1827.

Noverre, Jean-Georges. *Lettres sur la danse et sur les ballets.* Stuttgart and Lyon, 1760. Translated by Cyril W. Beaumont as *Letters on Dancing and Ballets* (London, 1930).

Saint-Léon, Arthur. *La sténochorégraphie.* Paris, 1852.

St. Léon, Michel. *Exercices de 1829, cahier d'exercices pour LL. AA. Royalles les Princesses de Würtemburg 1830, 2me cahier exercices de 1830.* Untitled volume containing Exercises de 1833, 1834, and 1836. Manuscripts located in Paris, Bibliothèque de l'Opéra, Res. 1137 and 1140.

Strathy, Alexander. *Elements of the Art of Dancing.* Edinburgh, 1822.

Théleur, E. A. *Letters on Dancing, Reducing This Elegant and Healthful Exercise to Easy Scientific Principles.* London, 1831.

Warner, MaryJane. "Gavottes and Bouquets: A Comparative Study of Changes in Dance Style between 1700 and 1850." Ph.D. diss., Ohio State University, 1974.

Winter, Marian Hannah. *The Pre-Romantic Ballet.* London, 1974.

Sandra Noll Hammond

Publications since 1887

From the late nineteenth century until World War I, ballet manuals were not widespread; however, books on natural movement and social and folk dancing became increasingly popular. Natural movement or physical culture manuals described various approaches to movement intended to create total body coordination. Social dance manuals described dances and discussed steps, styles, etiquette, and even the cost of holding social evenings. Recording folk dances was an aspect of the developing interest in heritage preservation.

In 1887 Friedrich Zorn published *Grammar of the Art of Dancing*. The industrious author is responsible for the last manual in the "old" style, in which a single author explained all aspects of dancing—history, technique, theatrical and social dance, and his own notation system. Subsequent technical manuals discussed fewer topics in more depth. In 1890 Berthe Bernay produced *La danse au théâtre*, a general educational reader. Probably around this time, Eugène Giraudet published his *Traité de la danse* (5th ed., 1891), collecting his many lectures on dance. Although mainly a description of social dances, it includes a section on theatrical dance, obviously inspired by Carlo Blasis.

Dictionnaire de la danse (1895) was written by G. Desrat to update the 1787 Compan book. It included a compendious bibliography of books written on dance.

Perhaps because of World War I, and because the presentation of Serge Diaghilev's Ballets Russes demanded a new evaluation of ballet technique, the decade 1910–1920 was sparse in manuals. In 1913, teacher Édouard Espinosa had his *Technical Dictionary of Dancing* published by the *Dancing Times* in London. His discussions of technique and ballet principles helped stimulate the English dance world to organize, leading to the formation of what is now the Royal Academy of Dancing (RAD). The popular *First Steps in Ballet* (1934), followed by *Intermediate Steps in Ballet* (1947) and *Advanced Steps in Ballet* (1950), by Ruth French and Felix Demery, updated Espinosa's discussion of technique and his terminology.

The teaching methods of Enrico Cecchetti, ballet master of the Ballets Russes, were published in 1922 as *A Manual of The Theory and Practice of Classical Theatrical Dancing (Méthode Cecchetti)* (1922), the most important technical manual of the time. The balletomane and publisher Cyril Beaumont, aided by the former Diaghilev dancer Stanislas Idzikowski, deciphered and analyzed Cecchetti's Italian-Russian mixture of ballet technique under the master's close guidance. This is a more detailed study than the 1894 *Manuel des exercices de danse théâtrale* (Saint Petersburg), handwritten by Cecchetti and including exercises notated in Arthur Saint-Léon's Sténochorégraphie. The 1922 book was complete in its discussion, from *barre* to *adage*. The *allegro* section was supplemented by *The Theory and Practice of Allegro in Classical Ballet (Cecchetti Method)* by Beaumont and Margaret Craske (1930), and *The Theory and Practice of Advanced Allegro in Classical Ballet (Cecchetti Method)* by Craske and Friderica de Moroda, (1956). The last book

lists Cecchetti's *enchaînements* of center pirouettes as well as his daily combinations. Cecchetti's and Espinosa's books helped to establish a new foundation for ballet technique in England.

During the same period in New York, the Russian-trained teacher Louis H. Chalif wrote a series of three technical manuals: *The Chalif Text Book of Dancing, Book I* (1914), *Book II* (1915), and *Book III, Greek Dancing* (1920). Written from an experienced and successful teacher's point of view, the texts are spirited and straightforward. A practice exercise accompanies each step, which is then described both technically and aesthetically. Although the terminology may be outdated, his philosophies remain valid. In 1923 Luigi Albertieri published *The Art of Terpsichore*, a book inspired by Cecchetti's but with its many helpful line drawings and commentary not so dry.

Although a spate of technical manuals was published between 1930 and 1934, it was not until 1934 that the next definitive work appeared. In Basic Principles *of Classic Ballet* (1934), outstanding Russian teacher Agrippina Vaganova reevaluated ballet technique from an anatomical perspective. This manual has become the basis for Russian teaching methods and helped to create a new Russian style. The pre-Soviet style of Nikolai Legat was not published until *Ballet Education* (1947) was written by his wife, the former dancer Nadine Nikolaeva Legat; it was later discussed by André Eglevsky and John Gregory in *Heritage of a Ballet Master: Nicholas Legat* (1977) and updated with Gregory's *The Legat Saga: An Anecdotal Study of the Life and Times of Nicolai Legat* (1995).

Until the end of World War II the publication of ballet manuals was limited. In 1943 Kay Ambrose's *Ballet-Lover's Pocket-Book, Technique without Tears* included a section on ballet technique written in popular style. Its wide success was matched in 1951 by *Ballet For Beginners* by Nancy Draper and Margaret F. Atkinson.

In the 1950s detailed ballet studies were made from various perspectives. The anatomist Celia Sparger discussed technique in *Anatomy and Ballet* (1949). Joan Lawson continued this anatomical approach in *Teaching of Classical Ballet* (1973) and *Teaching Young Dancers* (1975). Former Ballets Russes members who turned to teaching published works explaining the principles of technique that guided them through their careers. In *Lifar on Classical Ballet* (1951), Serge Lifar explained, through text and line drawings, the subtleties of technique and style that separated great from good dancers. Tamara Karsavina, in *Ballet Technique* (1956) and *Classical Ballet: The Flow of Movement* (1962) offered practical solutions to specific movement problems. Historically valuable is Olga Spessivtseva's *Technique for the Ballet Artiste* (1967).

The most important technical manual published in the 1950s was *The Classical Ballet: Basic Technique and Termi-*

nology (1952), written by Muriel Stuart with Lincoln Kirstein and associated with George Balanchine's School of American Ballet. Although the emphasis is on Russian methods (the author was trained by Pavlova), Cecchetti material is also included. Highlighting clean, detailed line drawings are near-mathematical analyses of a vast catalog of ballet movements.

Asaf Messerer in *Classes in Classical Ballet*, originally published in Moscow in 1967, and Nikolai I. Tarasov in *Ballet Technique for the Male Dancer*, published in Moscow in 1971, chose to elucidate specific areas of Vaganova's training methods. It was becoming clear, however, that there was a need for new discussion of Russian technique. This came in the exhaustive *School of Classical Dance* (1978) by Vera Kostrovitskaya and Alexei Pisarev, which provides hundreds of step combinations as well as a detailed eight-year syllabus.

There are also technical manuals written from a historical perspective. Documenting the Bournonville method of training are two books, Erik Bruhn and Lillian Moore's *Bournonville and Ballet Technique* (1961) and Kirsten Ralov's *The Bournonville School* (1979). The Ralov manual is a set of four books, one for classwork music and three describing technique—one in words, one in Benesh notation, and one in Labanotation. As well, *Bournonville Ballet Technique: Fifty Enchaînements*, selected and reconstructed by Vivi Flindt and Knud Arne Jürgensen (1996) is presented in both book and video formats.

More and more, movement notation systems, especially Benesh and Labanotation, are being included in technical manuals, augmenting, or sometimes replacing verbal descriptions. Two good examples of other new directions in the explanation of technique are Merrill Ashley's *Dancing for Balanchine* (1984) with its hundreds of rapid-sequence photographs demonstrating subtleties of the Balanchine style, and *The Video Dictionary of Classical Ballet* (1983) a four-videotape set produced in association with the Metropolitan Opera Guild. In the latter, the former Royal Ballet principal dancer Georgina Parkinson elucidates the classical technique as superbly demonstrated by Merrill Ashley and Kevin McKenzie.

There is a plethora of new video studies, analyzing every aspect of ballet for all ages. David Howard's tapes *Ballet Class for Beginners* (1986); *Intermediate and Advanced* (1986); and *Take a Master Class with David Howard* (1991) are popular, as is *Pointe by Pointe* (1990) by Barbara Fewster OBE.

[*See also the entries on the principal figures mentioned herein.*]

BIBLIOGRAPHY

Albertieri, Luigi. *The Art of Terpsichore.* New York, 1923.
Ambrose, Kay. *The Ballet-Lover's Pocket-Book: Technique without Tears.* 2d ed. New York, 1945.
Ashley, Merrill. *Dancing for Balanchine.* New York, 1984.
Beaumont, Cyril W., and Stanislas Idzikowski. *A Manual of the Theory and Practice of Classical Theatrical Dancing.* London, 1922.
Bernay, Berthe. *La danse au théâtre.* Paris, 1890.
Bruhn, Erik, and Lillian Moore. *Bournonville and Ballet Technique.* London, 1961.
Cecchetti, Enrico. *Manuel des exercices de danse théâtrale.* St. Petersburg, 1894.
Chalif, Louis H. *The Chalif Text Book of Dancing.* 5 vols. New York, 1914–1924.
Craske, Margaret, and Cyril W. Beaumont. *The Theory and Practice of Allegro in Classical Ballet (Cecchetti Method).* London, 1930.
Craske, Margaret, and Friderica Derra de Moroda. *The Theory and Practice of Advanced Allegro in Classical Ballet (Cecchetti Method).* London, 1956.
Desrat, G. *Dictionnaire de la danse.* Paris, 1895.
Draper, Nancy, and Margaret F. Atkinson. *Ballet for Beginners.* New York, 1951.
Eglevsky, André, and John Gregory. *Heritage of a Ballet Master: Nicholas Legat.* New York, 1977.
Espinosa, Édouard. *Technical Dictionary of Dancing.* London, 1913.
French, Ruth, and Felix Demery. *First Steps in Ballet.* Rev. ed. London, 1938.
French, Ruth, and Felix Demery. *Intermediate Steps in Ballet.* London, 1947.
French, Ruth, and Felix Demery. *Advanced Steps in Ballet.* London, 1950.
Giraudet, Eugène. *Traité de la danse.* 2 vols. Paris, 1890–1900.
Gregory, John. *The Legat Saga: An Anecdotal Study of the Life and Times of Nicolai Legat.* New York, 1995.
Karsavina, Tamara. *Ballet Technique.* London, 1956.
Karsavina, Tamara. *Classical Ballet: The Flow of Movement.* London, 1962.
Kostrovitskaya, Vera, and Alexei Pisarev. *School of Classical Dance.* Translated by John Barker. Moscow, 1978.
Lawson, Joan. *The Teaching of Classical Ballet.* London, 1973.
Lawson, Joan. *Teaching Young Dancers.* New York, 1975.
Legat, Nadine Nikolaeva. *Ballet Education.* London, 1947.
Lifar, Serge. *Lifar on Classical Ballet.* Translated by D. M. Dinwiddie. London, 1951.
Messerer, Asaf. *Classes in Classical Ballet.* Translated by Oleg Briansky. Garden City, N. Y., 1975.
Parkinson, Georgina. *The Video Dictionary of Classical Ballet.* 1983.
Ralov, Kirsten, ed. *The Bournonville School.* 4 vols. New York, 1979.
Sparger, Celia. *Anatomy and Ballet.* London, 1949.
Spessivtseva, Olga. *Technique for the Ballet Artiste.* London, 1967.
Stuart, Muriel, et al. *The Classic Ballet.* New York, 1952.
Tarasov, Nikolai. *Ballet Technique for the Male Dancer.* Translated by Elizabeth Kraft. Garden City, N.Y., 1985.
Vaganova, Agrippina. *Basic Principles of Classical Ballet: Russian Ballet Technique* (1934). Translated by Anatole Chujoy. Edited by Peggy van Praagh. 2d ed. London, 1953.
Zorn, Friedrich Albert. *Grammar of the Art of Dancing* (1887). Translated by Benjamin P. Coates. Boston, 1905.

VIDEOTAPES. Ashley, Merrill, and Suki Schorer. *The Balanchine Essays: Arabesque* (1995); *Bournonville Ballet Technique. Fifty Enchaînements* (Dance Horizons, 1992), performed by principals of the Royal Danish Ballet; *Bujones in Class* (Kulthur, 1986), featuring Fernando Bujones; Dickinson, Patricia. *Basic Principles of Pointe* (Dance Horizons, 1994) and *Pointe to Pointe* (Dance Horizons, 1994); Mahler, Roni. *How to: Improve your Ballet Technique* (1991), *How to: Improve your Pirouettes* (1993), and *How to: Improve your Pointe Technique* (1994).

KENNETHA R. MCARTHUR

TELEVISION. [*This entry comprises articles surveying the history of dance on television in three areas of the Western world where coverage has been especially rich: Canada, Europe, and the United States.*]

Dance on Television in Canada

Television came to Canada with the opening of CBFT in Montreal on Saturday, 6 September 1952. Ballet made its appearance the next evening with the beginning of a Sunday series from French television featuring Janine Charrat and her Ballets de France. On the following day, Monday, 8 September 1952, CBLT in Toronto began broadcasting. These two stations, CBFT and CBLT, thus became the flagships of the publicly owned television network called, in the country's two official languages, Société Radio-Canada (SRC) and the Canadian Broadcasting Corporation (CBC). Each organization maintains its own stations and affiliates, broadcasts in its own language, and is responsible for its own programming. Although SRC/CBC is funded by the federal government, the network also generates revenue from commercial advertising.

Variety programming, a staple of early television, was instrumental in developing a roster of versatile choreographers able to work in any style, be it classical, contemporary, or musical comedy. Alan and Blanche Lund, Don Gillies, Gladys Forrester, and Willy Blok Hanson created dance segments for the CBC. Hanson's *Maria Chapdelaine*—based on the novel by French-Canadian au-

thor Louis Hémon, set to a commissioned score by Calvin Jackson, and directed by Norman Campbell—was the first complete modern dance work shown on Canadian television when it aired on 12 December 1952 on the CBC. In Montreal, Ludmilla Chiriaeff and, later, Brian Macdonald, choreographed for SRC variety shows. Program directors at both the CBC and the SRC early on mastered the craft of capturing dance effectively on camera. In fact, the dance programs of Campbell (CBC) and Pierre Morin (SRC) would be acclaimed for their innovative camera work and imaginative special effects and would earn them many awards for excellence.

In those heady, early days of television, network executives such as Gabriel Charpentier, head of the SRC's Organisation et Direction Artistique (Télévision), and Franz Kraemer, CBC's executive producer of features, mandated that the performing arts be given prime-time exposure. What is interesting is the difference in emphasis. Charpentier, a well-known composer, focused on concert music, opera, and dance in the SRC's *L'Heure du Concert*, which premiered on 14 January 1954. In the CBC's *Scope*, which first aired on 19 December 1954, Kraemer showcased a potpourri of drama, music, dance, and documentary. In the former show, dance was featured once or twice a month; in the latter, dance averaged two programs a season.

The remarkable *L'Heure du Concert* was unique to North American television. Each week producers such as Pierre Mercure (another well-known composer), Noël Gauvin, Françoys Bernier, and Pierre Morin would set

TELEVISION: Dance on Television in Canada. In the 1950s, one of the most popular programs on Montreal's French-language public television service was *L'Heure du Concert*. Regular performers on this weekly program were a group of dancers formed by Ludmilla Chiriaeff. She is pictured here with Roger Rochon (left), Brydon Paige (right), and members of the ensemble in Eric Hyrst's *Variations sur un Thème de Haydn* (1955). (Photograph by Henri Paul; from the archives of Les Grands Ballets Canadiens, courtesy of Ludmilla Chiriaeff.)

opera, concert music, or dance within an artistic presentation. As well as showcasing original Canadian ballets by Chiriaeff, Macdonald, Fernand Nault, and Eric Hyrst and presenting original Canadian modern dance works by Françoise Sullivan, Jeanne Renaud, and Françoise Riopelle, *L'Heure du Concert* featured works by choreographers and their companies from the United States and Europe. Indeed, the list of choreographers whose works appeared on *L'Heure du Concert* reads like an international Who's Who, including George Balanchine, Jerome Robbins, Murray Louis, Alwin Nikolais, Janine Charrat, and Roland Petit. The SRC archives are a rich repository of notable performances captured on film and videotape, including, for example, the only extant footage of the New York City Ballet's Tanaquil Le Clercq and Jacques d'Amboise performing Robbins's *Afternoon of a Faun,* recorded on 6 October 1955.

Among the Canadians, Ludmilla Chiriaeff was remarkably creative, participating in some three hundred programs broadcast on the SRC. She gradually withdrew from choreographing for variety programs to concentrate on creating ballets for *L'Heure du Concert* and on building up a group of classically trained dancers. Her version of *Les Noces,* set to Igor Stravinsky's familiar score, was presented for the first time in Canada on the broadcast of 8 March 1956. The following autumn, Les Ballets Chiriaeff scored a triumph when it presented this work during the Montreal Festival season, a success that led the mayor of Montreal to suggest the formation of a permanent ballet company for the city. When Les Grands Ballets Canadiens

gave its first performance in April 1958, dance historians noted the astonishing fact that a television network had given birth to a ballet company. [*See* Grands Ballets Canadiens, Les; *and the entry on Chiriaeff.*]

In September 1966, *L'Heure du Concert* was replaced with the weekly *Les Beaux Dimanches,* but the high quality and frequency of dance programming remained. Performances by Canadian and international ballet and contemporary companies were often featured. The first full-length ballet to be broadcast in color on either the English or the French network was Brian Macdonald's *Rose Latulippe.* Choreographed to an original score by Harry Freedman, it was performed on 7 May 1967 by the Royal Winnipeg Ballet under the direction of Pierre Morin. Other Morin highlights include the world television premiere of Maurice Béjart's Le Ballet du XXᵉ Siècle performing *Messe pour le Tempes Présent* (1972). Morin ended his distinguished career in 1992 with the Emmy-nominated film of *Na Floresta,* choreographed by Nacho Duato and performed by Les Grands Ballets Canadiens.

The National Ballet of Canada made its first appearance on CBC's *Scope* in a performance of act 2 of *The Nutcracker* on Sunday, 26 December 1954. *Scope* (1954–1955) was followed by arts programs variously called *Folio* (1955–1959), *Festival* (1960–1969), *Musicamera* (1973–1978), and *Spectrum* (1979–1980). The first of Campbell's three productions of *Swan Lake* featuring the National Ballet made its live debut on *Folio* on 12 December 1956, starring Lois Smith and David Adams. This production

TELEVISION: Dance on Television in Canada. In a studio of Société Radio-Canada, Ludmilla Chiriaeff strikes a pose for the television camera during the same performance pictured opposite. During the 1950s, before widespread use of videotape, dancers performed on "live television," hampered by limited performance space and unyielding concrete floors. (Photograph by Henri Paul; from the archives of Les Grands Ballets Canadiens, courtesy of Ludmilla Chiriaeff.)

was the first full-length televised ballet by a Canadian company and the first North American television presentation of the beloved Russian classic. (Taped versions would follow in 1961 and 1967, the latter of which was the Erik Bruhn production.) Campbell's first non-studio production was the National Ballet's *Sleeping Beauty*, choreographed by Rudolf Nureyev; this Emmy-winning program was captured with six cameras at Toronto's O'Keefe Centre in 1972.

Producer Harvey Hart, who was primarily interested in modern dance, was responsible for the appearances on *Folio* of American companies such as those of José Limón, Pearl Lang, Donald McKayle, and Katherine Dunham as well as for commissioning original works from Canadian choreographers such as Gladys Forrester. Vancouver's Anna Wyman Dance Theatre was given national exposure via regional director Keith Christie's *Anna in Graz* (1974) and *Klee Wyck: A Ballet for Emily* (1975). Dance documentaries also played an important part in CBC programming, including the profile of Mikhail Baryshnikov by famed filmmaker Harry Rasky made shortly after the Russian dancer defected from the Soviet Union in Toronto in the summer of 1974.

By the 1980s, the CBC was losing viewers to the more popular, lowbrow programs available on American television and two competing private Canadian networks. The ratings game forced CBC to relegate arts programming to Sunday afternoon or the occasional prime-time special. This decade saw Norman Campbell capture on camera an average of one ballet production a year, mostly from the repertory of the National Ballet of Canada, although performances by the Royal Winnipeg Ballet and Les Grands Ballets Canadiens were also featured. Contemporary dance was given exposure in *Canadance* (1985), showcasing Montreal's La La La Human Steps, the Winnipeg Contemporary Dancers, Vancouver's Judith Marcuse Repertory Company, and Toronto's National Ballet in the work of Constantin Patsalas—with each segment produced by different regional teams.

As funding began to decline in the 1980s, CBC/SRC joined with other broadcasters or production companies as co-producers or pre-buy licensees. In 1985, the SRC co-produced a two-part series featuring the New York City Ballet to do homage to Balanchine directed by Morin with WNET/Thirteen (New York) and the BBC. From 1986 to 1991, the last six Campbell ballet productions that aired on CBC were the National Ballet in John Cranko's *Onegin*, Ronald Hynd's *The Merry Widow*, and Glen Tetley's *La Ronde* and *Alice*; the Royal Winnipeg Ballet in Jacques LeMay's *The Big Top*; and the documentary *Karen Kain: Prima Ballerina*. All were co-produced by Toronto's Primedia with the CBC and/or RM Arts of Britain. Ottawa's enterprising Sound Ventures co-produced with CBC/SRC an English and French version of Frank Augustyn's *The Tin Soldier / Le Soldat du Plomb*, featuring the Ottawa Ballet, which aired in 1992.

In the last decade of the century, there is only one prime-time show on CBC devoted to the arts. The magazine format *Adrienne Clarkson Presents* has featured profiles on such Canadian choreographers as Montreal's Gilles Maheu of Carbon Quatorze, Toronto's Baroque-period Opera Atelier, and Vancouver's John Alleyne of Ballet British Columbia. In-house programming has moved away from capturing extant works to focus on artists or special events. Vancouver-based Tony Papa has produced a documentary on ballet superstar Vladimir Malakhov, formerly of the National Ballet, while *A Salute to "Dancers for Life,"* produced by former National Ballet ballerina Veronica Tennant, recreated a studio version of an annual Toronto AIDS benefit presented by dance artists and companies from across Canada.

While facing stiff competition from the private French-language TVA network and dubbed American programs, SRC has not been dragged to quite the level of the common denominator as has the CBC. As the century turns, *Les Beaux Dimanches* is still a going concern despite cutbacks. SRC remains committed to dance, airing approximately seven or eight programs a season, but the majority of these are acquisitions. The focus is on dance that is out of the ordinary or that represents a new current, such as a program of highlights featuring international companies and artists appearing at Montreal's biennial Festival International de Nouvelle Danse. A limited number of in-house programs is being realized by a new generation of gifted directors such as Bernard Picard, who has filmed Jean-Pierre Perreault's *Joe*, and Jocelyn Barnabé, who has presented *Infante C'est Destroy* with Édouard Lock and his La La La Human Steps.

Cable television has widened the horizons of dance on television. Provincial educational broadcasters—Radio-Québec (1968), TVOntario (1970) and its French wing TFO (1987), ACCESS in Alberta (1973), and Knowledge Network (KNOW) in British Columbia (1980)—have shown dance, either produced, co-produced, or acquired, on a continuing basis. It is of interest to note that the French educational networks follow SRC in scheduling such programs dedicated to the performing arts as TFO's *Dimanches Classiques* and Radio-Québec's *Samedi C* and *Hors-Circuit*.

The educational networks have also functioned as producers and co-producers. Radio-Québec's archive includes profiles on dancers Marie Chouinard and Margie Gillis; a profile on Martine Époque, one of the founders of the seminal Montreal modern dance company Le Groupe Nouvelle Aire; and the documentary *Les Vingt-cinq Ans des Grands Ballets*. KNOW has produced *Point of Depar-*

ture, a six-part series that demonstrates imaginative use of the camera with dance.

TFO is working with producer Mark Hammond to bring together three directors and three choreographers to produce original dance film as a pilot for a new series. With various partners, TVO co-produced the six-part series *The Dancemakers* (1988), directed by Moze Mossanen, which profiles contemporary choreographers David Earle, Christopher House, Danny Grossman, Constantin Patsalas, James Kudelka, and Ginette Laurin. It was also responsible for independent filmmaker Anthony Azzopardi's *Making Ballet,* which documents the creation of James Kudelka's *The Actress* (1994), starring Karen Kain and the National Ballet of Canada. TVO is currently planning to commit funds that once purchased Euro-dance productions to filming small-scale Canadian dance works.

Two other cable networks feature dance programming. Vision, which first went on the air in 1988, is mandated to schedule television shows motivated by spiritual or humanitarian concerns. A wide range of acquisitions includes *Shumka: Return of the Whirlwind,* focusing on the Edmonton-based Shumka dancers and documenting their emotional 1990 tour of the Ukraine, the company's ancestral homeland. Vision has also co-produced such documentaries as *Making of a Dancer: Stephane Léonard,* profiling a Montrealer who attended the Vaganova Ballet School in Saint Petersburg, and *Moment of Light: The Dance of Evelyn Hart.* Francophones across Canada have access to TV5, which features programming from the best of French-language television around the world. This network is noted for its magazine shows, particularly *au current reportage* of rehearsals in progress and interviews with choreographers and dancers in the Francophone world.

The two most famous production companies in Canada are Toronto's Rhombus Media, headed by Niv Fichman, Barbara Willis Sweete, and Larry Weinstein, and Montreal's Ciné Qua Non, run by Bernar Hébert. Each company has won numerous awards and has attracted co-producers from around the world. Both companies produce work for television of innovative brilliance and have demonstrated that creating dance film is an art in its own right. Hébert productions include *Déluge* (1995), with choreography by Ginette Laurin, and *Le Petit Musée de Vélasquez,* based on Édouard Lock's *Infante C'est Destroy* (1994). Willis Sweete, who has become the dance specialist of Rhombus Media, has produced Purcell's *Dido and Aeneas* (1995), a "danced opera" with choreography by Mark Morris, and *The Sorceress* (1993), starring Kiri Te Kanawa, with arias interpolated from Handel's "magic operas" and choreography by Toronto's Opera Atelier, which specializes in works of the Baroque era.

With the publicly funded networks in a financial squeeze, the great hope of dance on television in Canada lies with Bravo!, the specialty arts cable network that began broadcasting on 1 January 1995. An earlier television service offering arts programming on a pay-per-view basis, C Channel, lasted only six months in 1983 because of a lack of subscribers. Bravo! is not pay-per-view television and is readily available on extended cable service. The name is licensed from its U.S. counterpart, but the Canadian Bravo! is an independent entity. In its brief lifetime, C Channel did present a wide range of dance programming, including Canadian premieres of works by Alvin Ailey, George Balanchine, and John Neumeier. Original C Channel productions included Brian Macdonald's *Newcomers,* created for the National Ballet, which uses the music of four Canadian composers to depict nineteenth-century immigration, and *I Am a Hotel,* a dance drama set to music by Leonard Cohen and featuring choreography by Ann Ditchburn.

Bravo! presents the arts in themes, and one day a week is devoted to dance, where the programming runs the gamut from conventionally staged ballet to experimental dance film. The backbone of programming is made up of international acquisitions and works from the Rhombus, Primedia, and National Film Board of Canada catalogs. (The catalog of the National Film Board lists over fifty dance films.) Bravo! creates new dance films by underwriting short video productions from its Bravo!Fact foundation or by supporting projects through development grants or pre-buy license fees. Original series, in conjunction with Sound Ventures of Ottawa, include the thirteen-part *Foot Notes: The Classics of Ballet with Frank Augustyn,* hosted by a former star of the National Ballet of Canada. Within its second year of operation, Bravo! was involved with the production of eighteen new Canadian dance films from experienced directors like Sweete, Fichman, and Hébert to a new generation of filmmakers from Winnipeg, Halifax, Regina, Vancouver, and Whitehorse in the Yukon.

One cannot leave a discussion of dance on television in Canada without mention of the rise of Canadian dance film. The annual Moving Pictures Festival of Dance on Film and Video, the first in North America to be dedicated to the art form, began in Toronto in 1992 and has become an important national and international showcase. The Media and Visual Arts Department of the Banff Centre for the Arts in Alberta is co-producer for approximately ten dance films a year, and the annual Banff Film and Video Festival is one of the most important in the world. Workshops on dance and the camera given by the Banff Centre (1992), Vancouver's Dance Centre (1994), and Toronto's Dance Umbrella (1996) invited choreographers to receive hands-on training from Sweete, Hébert, and Bob Lockyer, the BBC producer who is largely responsible for the growth of dance film in Britain. These workshops are already bearing fruit. In 1996 Lee Eisler, a workshop trainee and Vancouver choreographer, was given money to make a Bravo!Fact based on her previous output.

[See also Canada, *articles on theatrical dance.*]

BIBLIOGRAPHY

Canadian Broadcasting Corporation. *CBC Times* 4.1 (July 1951–July 1952); 22.27 (July 1969–December 1969). Toronto, 1948–1970.

Carpenter, Bernadette. *SPOTLIGHT newsletters 1951–1959.* Toronto, 1995.

McClelland & Stewart, Inc. *The Canadian Encyclopedia Plus* (CD-ROM). Toronto, 1996.

Officer, Jill, ed. *The Encyclopedia of Theatre Dance in Canada* (electronic). Toronto, 1989.

Tembeck, Iro. *Dancing in Montreal: Seeds of a Choreographic History.* Studies in Dance History, vol. 5.2. Madison, Wis., 1994.

PAULA CITRON

Dance on Television in Europe

The world's first high-definition television transmissions were started by the British Broadcasting Corporation (BBC) on 2 November 1936. They continued until the outbreak of World War II in 1939. Between November 1936 and September 1939 Ballet Rambert, Ballets Russes, and the Vic-Wells Ballet made regular telecasts. As early as 1926, dance first appeared on television. In 1928, the BBC authorized experimental regularly scheduled broadcasts,

TELEVISION: Dance on Television in Europe. Margot Fonteyn and Michael Somes in the BBC Television broadcast of the Royal Ballet production of *The Sleeping Beauty,* in 1955. (Photograph from the Dance Collection, New York Public Library for the Performing Arts.)

after tests that had begun in 1925. On 15 March 1933 Dame Adeline Genée gave her farewell performance for John Logie Baird, one of the inventors and pioneers of early television. The audiences for these early telecasts were very small—limited to those who had purchased television sets (receivers) or who built home receivers—those who could receive the signal transmitted from the Alexandra Palace on a hill in North London. After World War II, the BBC resumed television transmissions on 7 June 1946, and on 21 June, it broadcast Antony Tudor's ballet *Gala Performance.*

Regularly scheduled telecasts began in the USSR (1931), France (1934), and Germany (1935). In 1936 the Olympic Games were telecast from Berlin. After World War II, general European programming began. Where dance was already established, as in Denmark, it found a place in the schedules of this new form of public entertainment. Until the 1950s all shows were broadcast live, however, the arrival of kinescope (the recording of the electronic pictures on 35-millimeter black-and-white film) made it possible to record performances and start an archive. The first complete dance performance in the BBC Film and Video Library is a performance of *Les Sylphides* with a cast that included Alicia Markova. The arrival of videotape recording in the 1960s and its subsequent development changed the nature of dance on television.

For dance on television the relationship between the program's director and the choreographer or company is most important. In the United Kingdom, Margaret Dale, a former dancer with Sadler's Wells Ballet, did pioneer work transferring works from the Royal Ballet repertory to television. These programs were made in television studios and included Frederick Ashton's *La Fille Mal Gardée* (1962) and Dame Ninette de Valois's *Checkmate* (1963). Later Colin Nears developed a close working relationship with Ballet Rambert and its choreographer Christopher Bruce, winning the Prix Italia in 1982 with *Cruel Garden,* a ballet based on the works of Spanish poet Federico García Lorca as choreographed by Bruce and directed by Lindsay Kemp. The Prix Italia has done much to promote television dance; it is an annual competition established in 1948 at the instigation of RAI (Radiotelevision Italia) to stimulate radio's music, drama, and documentary, and is open to broadcasters throughout the world. With the inclusion of television in 1957, dance played an important part in this competition. Bob Lockyer, working with Robert Cohan and the London Contemporary Dance Theatre, transferred to television many of Cohan's dances. In Denmark, Thomas Grimm has had a similar relationship with the Royal Danish Ballet, winning the RAI Prize with Glen Tetley's *The Firebird* at the Prix Italia in 1982.

In the United Kingdom, dance programs (not including dance acts or light entertainment routines) fall into three main types: documentaries, performances, and created works. Documentaries are either portraits of stars, such as *Markova,* a portrait of Alicia Markova produced by Keith Cheetham (BBC, 1980), and *All the Superlatives,* a portrait of Anthony Dowell by Colin Nears (BBC, 1976); films about companies, such as Margaret Dale's history of the Ballet Rambert, *Rambert at Fifty* (BBC, 1976); or programs like *MacMillan's "Mayerling,"* a documentary that included the historical background to the ballet. This program, made for London Weekend Television by Derek Bailey, won the Prix Italia in 1978.

Dance performances are either recorded as outside broadcasts, taking the television cameras and equipment into the theater and recording the program, often at a public performance, or taking the production into a television studio. For the great nineteenth-century ballets that demand theatrical effect, a television recording from the theater usually produces the best result. For the modern works and the shorter classical works the best results are obtained by taking the dance into the studio and remaking the ballet for television. However, this takes time. Rehearsal in the studio is important because dance is the hardest of the performance arts to televise, requiring an understanding between dancer, choreographer, cameraman, and director—unlike music recitals or opera where stand-ins for rehearsals are typical.

Dance made specially for television has been rare. An early example was Antony Tudor's *Fugue for Four Cameras,* which he created on 2 March 1937 as a solo for Maude Lloyd. In it she was first seen dancing in the center screen; then, as the second theme was introduced in the music, her movement took her to one side, and she was joined by a replica of herself, and so on, until she was dancing in quadruplicate.

When the Swedish choreographer Birgit Cullberg was asked to transfer her ballet *Miss Julie* to television, and wanting to retain control of the ballet in this new medium, she devised the idea of a single fixed camera; she changed the choreography to fit into the camera's unchanging field of view. With the advent of color television and the use of chroma key, Cullberg again broke new ground with *Red Wine in Green Glasses* (1971), a pas de deux where the performers danced inside the paintings of, among others, Jean-Antoine Watteau, Jean Honoré Fragonard, and Jan and Pieter Bruegel.

In Denmark, Flemming Flindt's ballet *The Lesson* (1963), an adaptation of the Ionesco play, was made for television before being remade for the stage. In the following years Flindt worked on many television ballets, including *The Young Man Must Marry* (1968) and *Felix Luna* (1973). In the United Kingdom, the BBC has not commissioned many dance works in recent years, but in 1970 Alwin Nikolais made *The Relay,* one of the most exciting and successful creative uses of dance and television.

TELEVISION: Dance on Television in Europe. Ross Parkes, Lynn Kothera, and members of the Glen Tetley Dance Company in a performance of Tetley's popular ballet *Mythical Hunters,* broadcast on West German television in 1969. (Photograph from the Dance Collection, New York Public Library for the Performing Arts.)

In the late 1970s increasing production costs caused broadcast and production companies to look for partners to share costs. In many cases this led to only the "safe" works being televised and recorded, often using the same international dance stars. Since the arrival of lightweight video equipment it has now been possible for smaller independent program makers and the dance companies themselves to make videos of exciting dance works or make dance for the camera. This work is then sold to major distributors and broadcasters.

Because of this, in 1988 IMZ (International Music Center, based in Vienna) in association with CID-UNESO, set up the Grand Prix International Vidéo Danse. It was held first at Nîmes and is now in Sète in the south of France.

In 1990, IMZ broke away and founded Dance Screen. The first was held at the Alte Oper Frankfurt and since then six other festivals have been held around Europe. The published catalogs show a move away from large-scale productions made by national broadcasters to smaller projects made by independent production compa-

TELEVISION: Dance on Television in Europe. Birgit Keil found one of her best roles as Mathilde Wesendonk in Heinz Spoerli's *Traume*, first performed on Swiss television in October 1979. Set to Richard Wagner's "Wesendonk Lieder," this ballet was later staged in both Basel and Stuttgart. (Photograph by Schweizer Fernsehen DRS, Zurich; courtesy of Heinz Spoerli.)

BIBLIOGRAPHY

Cullberg, Birgit. "Television Ballet." In *The Dance Has Many Faces*, edited by Walter Sorell. 2d ed. New York, 1966.

Dale, Margaret. "Ballet and BBC-TV." *The Dancing Times* (March 1963): 332–334.

Davis, Janet Rowson. "Ballet on British Television, 1933–1939." *Dance Chronicle* 5.3 (1983): 245–304.

Davis, Janet Rowson. "Ballet on British Television, 1932–1935: A Supplement." *Dance Chronicle* 7.3 (1984–1985): 294–325.

Davis, Janet Rowson. "Ballet on British Television: Christian Simpson, Producer, 1949–1959—Divine or Diabolic?" *Dance Chronicle* 19.1 (1996): 17–92.

IMZ *Dance Screen Catalogues* (1990–). Vienna.

Jordon, Stephany, and Dave Allen, eds. *Parrallell Lines*. London, 1993.

Penman, Robert, comp. *A Catalogue of Ballet and Contemporary Dance in the BBC Television, Film, and Videotape Library, 1937–1984*. London, 1987.

BOB LOCKYER

nies with the help of a mix of funders. In 1992 the Arts Council of England and BBC Television set a trend when it transmitted *Dance House*—a series of twelve short dance films made collaboratively by various choreographers and directors. This was followed by *Dance for the Camera*, and to date twenty-eight short dance film/videos have been commissioned. This example has been followed in many other countries including Spain, the Netherlands (Four TokenS), and Australia (Macrodance).

Choreographers' and directors' interest in film and video as a tool to make dance works has also led to a growing number of master classes and workshops to be held around the world. Many of these have been run by Elliot Caplan from the Cunningham Foundation or Bob Lockyer. Nearly all the major dance festivals worldwide include video dance showcases. Sadly, major changes in public broadcasting, film production, and television distribution are putting these exciting projects in jeopardy just as this new art form begins its emergence.

Dance on Television in the United States

Dance, in one form or another, has been part of North American television since the 1930s. Dancers began appearing regularly on experimental television broadcasts in 1931. The medium's limitations at this stage were formidable, and it would take decades before many of its problems were satisfactorily overcome. Studio size was restricted; screen clarity was minimal; and directors and technicians often butchered the choreography by a combination of poor framing and graceless camera movement.

Nevertheless, the future for dance broadcasts was heralded with enthusiasm—the manager of the National Broadcasting Corporation (NBC) in 1939 proclaimed that television would do for dance what radio had done for speech. When commercial transmission began in 1941, dance programs were scheduled frequently. The Columbia Broadcasting System (CBS) offered several dance shows featuring the work of Erick Hawkins, Agnes de Mille, Katherine Dunham, Ruth Page, and Eugene Loring. In 1946 Pauline Koner and her partner Kitty Doner began a successful weekly program that was one of the first to experiment with television choreography. Dances were specially staged for the camera, and special effects, such as superimpositions, were selectively employed.

Television's enormous postwar expansion was accompanied by an increase in dance programming. The networks, not quite locked into their lowest common-denominator orientation, experimented with occasional offerings of ballet. Alicia Markova and Anton Dolin appeared on *NBC Concert Hall* in 1948. In 1949 the Ford Motor Company sponsored a weekly series of half-hour programs on CBS under the title *Through the Crystal Ball*, each of which consisted of an original ballet choreographed for television. Before being abruptly suspended, the series opened with *Robinson Crusoe*, choreographed by Michael Kidd and Talley Beatty, and went on to present a *Cinderella* by George Balanchine, to music of Tchaikovsky, *Ali Baba* by Helen Tamiris, *The Wild West* by Todd Bolender, *Alice in Wonderland* by Pauline Koner, *Fiesta* by Anna Sokolow, and *Casey at the Bat* by Paul Godkin. American Ballet Theatre was seen in a full-length presentation of *Giselle* (featuring Nora Kaye and Igor Youskevitch) in 1950.

The chief forum for television dance in the 1950s was the popular variety programs. Most shows had their own five- or six-member dance company and a resident choreographer responsible for staging several new dances each week. Cramped for space and forced to deal with a frenzied rehearsal schedule and the pressures of live performing, choreographers such as James Starbuck on *Your Show of Shows*, Tony Charmoli on *Your Hit Parade*, and Peter Gennaro on *The Perry Como Show* perfected a lighthearted, casual dance style that suited the medium's small-scale visual demands.

Beginning in the mid-1950s, the commercial networks started to restrict ballet to one of three different formats. The most popular was a five- or six-minute number in variety shows seeking an occasional dose of high culture. Programs such as *The Bell Telephone Hour*, *The Voice of Firestone*, and even *The Ed Sullivan Show* frequently featured *The Nutcracker* and *Swan Lake* pas de deux danced by such performers as Margot Fonteyn and Michael

Somes, André Eglevsky and Melissa Hayden, and Edward Villella and Patricia McBride.

Once or twice a year the networks also offered special events designed to boost their cultural prestige. In 1955 NBC imported the Royal Ballet from London to present *The Sleeping Beauty* adapted by Frederick Ashton, which surprised everyone by attracting an audience of thirty million viewers. Two years later the Royal Ballet was brought back to perform Ashton's *Cinderella* in a version that used many electronic effects. Perhaps the most famous, or notorious, dance presentation of the period was CBS's 1962 broadcast of Igor Stravinsky and George Balanchine's *The Flood*, which was widely attacked for its twenty minutes of undistinguished abstract choreography and forty minutes of pretentious lecture material and rehearsal footage that surrounded it.

However, other than these scattered prime-time appearances, serious dance, like most cultural programming, was increasingly pushed to Sunday morning and afternoon time slots, where ratings were not as important. The most notable, semi-regular forum during the 1950s was *Omnibus*, an arts magazine supported by funds from the

TELEVISION: Dance on Television in the United States. Peter Gennaro was the choreographer and featured dancer on *The Perry Como Show* for several years. Seen here in his number set to "South Rampart Street Parade," he displays his characteristic charm. (Photograph © by Jack Mitchell; used by permission.)

TELEVISION: Dance on Television
in the United States. In the 1950s
the June Taylor Dancers were a
regular feature of *The Jackie
Gleason Show*, opening the
program with precision tap
routines, like the "bellhop"
number seen here. (Photograph
by Herb Flatow; from the archives of
the Museum of Television and Radio,
New York.)

Ford Foundation. Among its many dance programs were a 1953 version of *Billy the Kid* narrated by Eugene Loring, two lively shows on the history of ballet and choreography written and presented by Agnes de Mille, and a lecture-demonstration by Gene Kelly proving that male dancers are just as skilled (and manly) as male athletes. CBS's Sunday morning schedule was a rare haven for new dance. Its religious programs, such as *Lamp unto My Feet*, offered many commissions for original choreography based on biblical themes, and its innovative culture series, *Camera Three*, provided one of the few places on television hospitable to modern dance.

The formation of National Educational Television (NET) in the mid-1950s offered an alternative to choreographers unable or unwilling to work within restricted commercial demands. Martha Graham, who first appeared on television in an experimental NBC broadcast in 1939, was seen on several NET programs beginning in 1957. In the mid-1960s NET launched a pioneering series, *USA: Dance*, produced by Jac Venza, that demonstrated the expressive possibilities of videotaped dance performances. Among the program's highlights were a striking rendition of Anna Sokolow's *Rooms* and a collection of Balanchine pas de deux danced by the New York City Ballet, with occasional commentary by Balanchine, Arthur Mitchell, and Jacques d'Amboise.

Nevertheless, many choreographers were still reluctant to let their work be seen on television because of the medium's technological limitations and economic pressures. The small screen size made it difficult to see more than four or five dancers on stage at any one time. Further, the often gimmicky camera work directors employed to promote visual interest, the lack of adequate rehearsal time, and the inherent distortions of television's two-dimensional space posed serious obstacles. These problems were compounded by the fact that most television ballet and dance consisted of performances of existing repertory, rather than attempts to choreograph works specifically for the medium. Although calls have been raised since the 1940s for original dance created expressly for the camera, this has remained an infrequently fulfilled dream on broadcast television because of budgetary restrictions and a programming philosophy that favors the known and the safe over the new and the experimental.

A turning point, at least for the reproduction of repertory dance on television, occurred in 1976 when the Public Broadcasting Service (PBS, the successor to NET) initiated *Dance in America* as a showcase for the best dance companies in the country. Each program offered a bit of company choreographic philosophy, a little history, some documentary footage, and unusually intelligent television translations of repertory pieces. Producers Emile Ardolino and Merrill Brockway worked closely with each choreographer to reshape his or her work for the best possible television presentation. This often meant changing the lines and movements of individual dances to accommodate screen size and camera perspective, and the results, aided by sensitive direction, were frequently impressive.

Not the least of the achievements of *Dance in America* has been the diversity of its focus. The series not only lured mainstream choreographers who had remained skeptical of television's abilities, such as Jerome Robbins, Graham, and Balanchine, but it also examined companies that had rarely, if ever, received national exposure, including Paul Taylor, Pilobolus, the Pennsylvania Ballet, the Dance Theatre of Harlem, and Feld Ballet. Programs have also been devoted to the life and work of Katherine Dunham, a survey of avant-garde dancing in New York, a special rechoreographed-for-video sampler by Merce Cunningham, and works by Balanchine and Graham reconceived for television by their creators.

Dance in America was not the only innovative PBS program that looked at dance. Thanks to new low-light cameras, series such as *Live from Lincoln Center* and *In Performance at Wolf Trap* could telecast live events without

disturbing the audience in the theater. The network also aired a few programs exploring video dance. WGBH in Boston produced several dance programs that used video technology as a direct choreographic tool, and Twyla Tharp's *Making Television Dance* was the result of her experiments with the equipment and facilities of WNET in New York. *Alive from Off Center*, from KTCA in Minneapolis, and *New Television*, from WGBH in Boston, have both served as showcases for experimental dance videos.

There is little doubt that the creation of PBS in 1967 freed the commercial networks from a sense of responsibility toward cultural programming. The number of shows featuring dance on CBS, NBC, and ABC (American Broadcasting Corporation) since the late 1960s has been minimal. Other than a few broadcasts of *The Nutcracker* at Christmas time, and a well-meaning but ill-fated experiment by NBC, *Live from Studio 8H*, dance has been left to fend for itself on PBS and a few upscale cable networks.

TELEVISION: Dance on Television in the United States. George Balanchine as Herr Drosselmeyer, with children and members of the New York City Ballet, in the CBS-TV production of *The Nutcracker*, broadcast Christmas Day, 1958. (Photograph from the Dance Collection, New York Public Library for the Performing Arts. Choreography by George Balanchine © The George Balanchine Trust.)

TELEVISION: Dance on Television in the United States. A camera-man filming members of the Paul Taylor Dance Company in *Company B*, one of three of Taylor's dances on a program entitled "Wrecker's Ball," presented as part of the *Dance in America* series. (Photograph © 1996 by Johan Elbers; used by permission.)

Over the last decade, even these environments have provided less and less of a welcome. Though they began in the 1980s with some original dance programming, cable networks like Bravo! and the Arts and Entertainment network now rely on a very limited menu of imported dance fare. More troubling is the diminished state of the once trailblazing PBS. Continuing budgetary cutbacks have led to a severe reduction of its dance commitment. At a time when American choreographers are being celebrated throughout the world, *Dance in America*'s presentations are increasingly foreign co-productions, with only a few original domestic programs.

Dance has never been a staple on American television, but it has often been approached with freshness and so-phistication. U.S. producers and directors discovered innovative methods to translate the sweep of choreography to the limitations of the small screen. Their contributions have played an important role in changing the face of dance on television.

[*For related discussion, see* American Bandstand.]

BIBLIOGRAPHY

Balanchine, George, and Bernard Taper. "Television and Ballet." In *The Eighth Art*, edited by Robert L. Shayon. New York, 1962.

Barzel, Ann. "Looking at TV." *Dance Magazine* (March 1953–December 1969). Monthly column on television dance, renamed "Reviewing the Tube" when Norma McLain Stoop became critic in December 1971 and changed to "Dancevision" under John Gruen in September 1980.

Bettis, Valerie, et al. "Dance on Television." In *Television: The Creative Experience*, edited by A. William Bluem and Roger Manvell. New York, 1967.

Bohen, Tullia. "Making Television Dance." *Ballet News* 1 (May 1980): 26–29.

Dance Theatre Journal (Summer 1988). Dance and television issue.

Feigay, Paul. "The Dance of 'Omnibus.'" *Dance Magazine* (March 1955): 23–27.

Grossman, Peter Z. "Video and Dance." *Videography* 2 (September 1977): 16–19.

Grossman, Peter Z. "Talking with Merce Cunningham about Video." *Dance Scope* 13 (Winter-Spring 1979): 56–68.

Koner, Pauline, and Kitty Doner. "Technological Progress and the Dance in Television." In *The Dance Has Many Faces*, edited by Walter Sorell. New York, 1951.

Lorber, Richard. "'Dance in America' on TV in America." *Dance Scope* 10 (Spring–Summer 1976): 19–28.

Lorber, Richard. "Experiments in Videodance." *Dance Scope* 12 (Fall–Winter 1977–1978): 7–16.

Mueller, John. "Twyla Tharp and the Wide-Angle Lens." *Dance Magazine* (September 1977): 99.

Mueller, John. "Martha Graham, Then and Now." *Dance Magazine* (December 1977): 107.

Mueller, John. "The Close-Up, the Dissolve, and Martha Graham." *Dance Magazine* (January 1978): 94–95.

Neal, Nelson D. "Early Television Dance." *Dance Scope* 13 (Winter–Spring 1979): 51–55.

Rose, Brian. *Television and the Performing Arts*. Westport, Conn., 1986.

Rose, Brian. *Televising the Performing Arts: Interviews with Merrill Brockway, Kirk Browning, and Roger Englander*. Westport, Conn., 1992.

Simpson, Herbert. "American Dance on Television: The Changing Picture." *Dance Magazine* (January 1977): 41–45.

Simpson, Herbert. "WNET TV's Dance in America." *Dance Magazine* (January 1977): 45–50.

Vaughan, David. "TV." *Ballet News* (May 1979–). Monthly column examining dance on television.

Venza, Jac. "Educational TV Loves Dance." *Dance Magazine* (September 1965): 43.

VIDEOTAPES.   The following is a selected list of videotapes available for screening in the Dance Collection of the New York Public Library for the Performing Arts: Eugene Loring, "Billy the Kid," *Omnibus* (CBS, 8 November 1953). "Appalachian Spring" (National Educational Television, 1959). Alvin Ailey, "Revelations," *Lamp Unto My Feet* (CBS, 3 March 1962). George Balanchine, "Noah and the Flood" (CBS, 14 June 1962). "Four Pioneers," featuring a re-creation of Doris Humphrey's *Pasacaglia, USA: Dance* (National Educational Television, 1965). "New York City Ballet," featuring four Balanchine pas de deux (National Education Television, 1966). Twyla Tharp, "Bix Pieces," *Camera Three* (CBS, 7 October 1973). "Merce Cunningham: A Video Event," *Camera Three* (CBS, 27 October and 3 November 1974). *Dance in America* (WNET-TV, New York, 1976–). The following are available from the Museum of Television and Radio, New York and Los Angeles: Agnes de Mille, "The Art of Choreography," *Omnibus* (CBS, 30 December 1956). Frederick Ashton, "Cinderella," *Producer's Showcase* (NBC, 29 April 1957). Gene Kelly, "Dancing: A Man's Game," *Omnibus* (ABC, 21 December 1958).

BRIAN ROSE

TEMPLE, SHIRLEY (Shirley Jane Temple; born 23 April 1928 in Santa Monica, California), child tap dancer, singer, and actress. Shirley's trademarks were dimples, bright eyes, and curly golden hair, and she had a film musical named for each. Throughout her childhood, her fame was colossal.

When barely three years old, Shirley became a student at the Ethel Meglin Dance Studio and simultaneously a "Famous Meglin Kiddie." There she was discovered for Educational Films, for a new series of 1932 and 1933 one-reel comedies called *Baby Burlesks*. Temple soon astounded the film industry with her featured spot in *Stand Up and Cheer* (1934) for Fox with James Dunn. She performed with him again in *Baby Take a Bow* (1934).

From 1934 to 1940, Temple made twenty-four films; of those, fifteen included musical sequences in which she tap danced. When not performing alone, she was accompanied by first-rate veteran tap talent and vaudevillians. She has said:

> I didn't really have any dancing teachers, per se, at the time I was working on these films. My dancing "teachers" were just the ones I was working with . . . Bill [Robinson], or Buddy [Ebsen], or George [Murphy].   (Frank, 1994)

TEMPLE. With the eccentric tapper Buddy Ebsen, Temple is pictured here in the number "At the Codfish Ball," from the film *Captain January* (Fox, 1936). (Photograph from the collection of Rusty E. Frank.)

Temple was first paired with Bill ("Bojangles") Robinson in *The Little Colonel* (1935). The combination proved so winning, they were featured together in three more films: *The Littlest Rebel* (1935), *Rebecca of Sunnybrook Farm* (1938), and *Just around the Corner* (1938). Not only did she and Robinson become great friends, they were the first interracial couple in films. Explained Temple:

> Everyone I danced with was wonderful to work with . . . Buddy and George were certainly two of the finest ones. But Bill Robinson was my favorite. He was the easiest teacher I had, because we could do it by holding hands. I learned most of it by listening to the sounds of the taps.   (Frank, 1994)

She danced with Ebsen in *Captain January* (1936) and with Alice Faye and Jack Haley in *Poor Little Rich Girl* (1936). She danced with Murphy in *Little Miss Broadway* (1938), with Arthur Treacher in *The Little Princess* (1939), and with Charlotte Greenwood and Jack Oakie in *Young People* (1940).

Temple's movies were magic at the box office—she was the top box-office attraction from 1935 to 1938. At the beginning of her success, the *Motion Picture Herald* listed her as number eight of the top ten money-making stars for 1934. One year later, she skyrocketed in popularity to become the number one box-office star and held that position through 1938, ranking above Clark Gable, Fred Astaire and Ginger Rogers, Joan Crawford, Gary Cooper, and Spencer Tracy. Temple's intelligent but unaffected personality and her uncanny abilities charmed audiences and critics alike. Temple continued making films until 1949 but her adolescent and adult films did not feature her dancing.

[*See also* Tap Dance.]

BIBLIOGRAPHY
Black, Shirley Temple. *Child Star.* New York, 1988.
Frank, Rusty E. *Tap! The Greatest Tap Dance Stars and Their Stories, 1900–1955.* Rev. ed. New York, 1994.
Stearns, Marshall, and Jean Stearns. *Jazz Dance: The Story of American Vernacular Dance.* Rev. ed. New York, 1994.
Thomas, Tony. *That's Dancing.* New York, 1984.

RUSTY E. FRANK

TENNANT, VERONICA (born 15 January 1947 in London), British-Canadian ballet dancer. As one of a new generation of Canadian dancers to emerge during the 1960s, Veronica Tennant demonstrated that it had become possible to have a distinguished and fulfilling international career without having to abandon her adopted homeland.

Tennant began her training at the Cone-Ripman School in London. When her family moved to Toronto in 1955, she continued her studies and joined the newly created National Ballet School of Canada, from which she was graduated in 1963. An injury delayed her entry into the National Ballet of Canada until 1965. Hired as a principal dancer, Tennant quickly established herself as a dancer-actress of extraordinary intensity and individuality in the role of Juliet in John Cranko's *Romeo and Juliet.* She soon built a repertory that included the leading roles in almost all the National Ballet's full-length classics, proving herself as adept in roles in the Petipa repertory—Aurora, Odette-Odile, and the Sugarplum Fairy—as in the Romantic roles of Giselle and La Sylphide.

As the leading ballerina of the company, Tennant starred in several award-winning CBC-TV ballet presentations, including *Romeo and Juliet* (Prix René-Barthélemy, Monte Carlo, 1965), Celia Franca's *Cinderella* (Emmy award, 1968) and Rudolf Nureyev's *The Sleeping Beauty* (Emmy award, 1972). She was the first to dance with Mikhail Baryshnikov after his defection from the Soviet Union, as his partner in a CBC-TV production of Erik Bruhn's *La Sylphide,* broadcast 26 July 1974, the day before Baryshnikov's American stage debut.

A knee operation in December 1976 kept Tennant from the stage for fourteen months, but she returned with deepened maturity and a newly refined musicality that was particularly apparent in such roles as Lise in Frederick Ashton's *La Fille Mal Gardée* and Titania in his *The*

TENNANT. An action photograph of Tennant in the title role of Celia Franca's *Cinderella,* in 1968. A broadcast of this production by CBC-TV helped make Tennant a household name throughout Canada. (Photograph by Ken Bell; used by permission of the National Ballet of Canada.)

Dream. Always a strong supporter of choreographers emerging from the ranks of the National Ballet, Tennant created numerous roles in works by James Kudelka, Constantin Patsalas, and David Allan. Among her most notable later roles were Tatiana in John Cranko's *Onegin*—acquired by artistic director Alexander Grant in 1985 as a particularly suitable vehicle for Tennant's dramatic talent—and Hanna in Ronald Hynd's *The Merry Widow,* which she danced in 1986.

Although she was most often partnered by Raymond Smith, Tennant danced with all the National Ballet's principal men and with numerous international guest stars, among them Anthony Dowell, Rudolf Nureyev, Fernando Bujones, Iván Nagy, Edward Villella, Peter Schaufuss, and Jean-Charles Gil. Her compatibility with dancers of such varied styles and dispositions is indicative of her own mastery of the stylistic spectrum of the National Ballet's repertory. She was as much at home playing the light-hearted heroines of *Coppélia, Napoli,* and *Don Quixote* as she was portraying an enchanted princess in *Swan Lake* or *The Sleeping Beauty.* Having announced her retirement in 1988, she recreated the role of Juliet for her final performance with the National Ballet of Canada on 12 February 1989.

Tennant is the author of two children's books, *On Stage, Please* (1977), a novel, and *The Nutcracker* (1985). She was the subject of a CBC-TV documentary, *Veronica Tennant: A Dancer of Distinction* (1983), and she became a frequent host and interviewer of radio and television arts programs. She is now an arts producer for CBC Television. The first dancer to be invested with the Order of Canada, in 1975, and the recipient of the Toronto Arts Award for the Performing Arts, she holds several honorary doctorates from Canadian universities.

BIBLIOGRAPHY

Howard, Sebastian. "Veronica Tennant: A Dancer of Distinction." *Dance in Canada* (Autumn 1989).
Kelly, Deirdre. "Dancing on the Town." *Performing Arts in Canada* (Summer 1992).
Maynard, Olga. "Veronica Tennant, a Canadian Ballerina." *Dance Magazine* (May 1972): 40–44.
Neufeld, James. *Power to Rise: The Story of the National Ballet of Canada.* Toronto, 1996.
Odom, Selma Landen. "Spotlight on Veronica Tennant." *Dance Magazine* (March 1977): 68-70.

MICHAEL CRABB

TERABUST, ELISABETTA (Elisabetta Magli; born 5 August 1946 in Varese, Lombardy), Italian ballet dancer and company director. Raised and educated in Rome, Elisabetta Terabust received her dance training at the ballet school of the Teatro dell'Opera under the direction of Attilia Radice, one of the last pupils of Enrico Cecchetti. Upon her graduation in 1962, Terabust was immediately engaged for the corps de ballet of the theater. She caught the public's attention when she first performed as a soloist, particularly in the role of Myrtha in *Giselle,* in which she was pallid, sublime, and merciless, with an excellent technique evidenced in her jumps and turns. She also triumphed in the spirited role of a Silver Sole in *Roi des Gourmets* by Jean Babilée, presented at the Teatro dell'Opera in 1964.

Terabust first danced the title role in *Giselle* at the Opera in 1965, partnered by Gianni Notari; she subsequently danced this role with several other illustrious partners, including Paolo Bortoluzzi, Peter Schaufuss, and Rudolf Nureyev. Small, slender, and graceful, with large black eyes, she was sought by Erik Bruhn in 1967 as a partner in *Flower Festival in Genzano,* for which she was taught the basics of the Danish technique and many aspects of the role of Giselle.

Dissatisfied with the scarce scheduling of dance in the lyrical seasons of the Rome Opera, Terabust followed the example of Carla Fracci and left her country. She first went to France, where she was the star (1974–1977) of the Ballet National de Marseille under the direction of Roland Petit. She appeared in revivals of his *Carmen* and *Nôtre-Dame de Paris,* as well as the new *Schiaccianoci.*

Terabust then became a star with London Festival Ballet in 1977. Here she refined the quality of her technique, which in her long association with Peter Schaufuss, her favorite partner, reached the highest level in both the classical tradition of Italy, France, and Russia and in the Bournonville tradition of Denmark. She appeared in revivals of Schaufuss's *La Sylphide,* with the London Festival Ballet (1978) and of *Napoli* with the National Ballet of Canada (1981). In 1982, Kenneth MacMillan created *Verdi Variations* for Terabust and Schaufuss; Glen Tetley created the role of Pimpenella in *Pulcinella* for her in 1984.

Within the framework of London Festival Ballet, where she danced the full classical and modern classical repertory, Terabust began to address herself to innovative contemporary productions—for example, the revival of Glen Tetley's *Sphinx* (1979), which was one of her best interpretations. This modern direction, although still within pure academic foundations, was confirmed and broadened in the early 1980s, when she was a guest start with Aterballetto in Reggio nell'Emilia. With this young and dynamic Italian company, Terabus danced many of the creations of Amedeo Amodio, notably *Psiche a Manhattan* (1984), and of William Forsythe, including *Artifact 2* (1984).

During the 1980s Terabust appeared as a guest artist with the National Ballet of Canada, with the Rome Opera Ballet, and with the ballet companies of the Teatro Comunale di Firenze, the Arena of Verona, the Teatro San Carlo in Naples, and the Teatro alla Scala in Milan. In 1990, she returned to Rome to direct the Rome Opera Ballet and its associated school. She effected great improvements in a short time, but she failed to win the support of the public or the officials of the Opera. She resigned her post in 1993 to go to Milan as artistic director of La Scala Ballet.

BIBLIOGRAPHY

Agostini, Alfio. "Elisabetta, Giuletta et Figlio prodigo." *Balletto oggi* (February 1987).

Doglio, Vittoria, and Elisa Vaccarino. *L'Italia in ballo.* Rome, 1993.

Fitzgerald, Brendan. "Rome's Prima Ballerina Finds Stardom in Paris." *New York Times* (27 February 1977).

Ottolenghi, Vittoria. "Elisabetta, la nostra stella." *Balletto oggi* 2 (March–May 1981).

Ottolenghi, Vittoria. "1983: L'anno di E.T." *Musica viva* 2 (February 1983).

Ottolenghi, Vittoria. "Elisabetta Terabust e Roland Petit." *Balletto oggi* (March 1992):12–13.

"London Festival Ballet: The Biographies." In *Ballet in London Year Book 1988/89.* London, 1988.

"Terabust, Elisabetta." In *Enciclopedia dello spettacolo.* Rome, 1954–.

Testa, Alberto, et al. *Il balletto nel novecento.* Turin, 1983.

Testa, Alberto. "Elisabetta Terabust." *Danza & danza* (November 1991).

VITTORIA OTTOLENGHI
Translated from Italian

TER-ARUTUNIAN, ROUBEN (born 24 July 1920 in Tiflis, died 17 October 1992 in New York City), Armenian-American stage designer. An extremely prolific and eclectic designer, Rouben Ter-Arutunian worked in every aspect of theater, from opera to television, from Shakespeare to Broadway musicals. He had his greatest effect, however, as premier designer for the New York City Ballet, in a long series of collaborations with George Balanchine.

Educated in Berlin, Vienna, and Paris, Ter-Arutunian worked in the theaters of these cities before emigrating to the United States in 1951. His German experience served him in his first work with Balanchine, the honky-tonk expressionism of the revival of *The Seven Deadly Sins* (1958). He went on to work in a spare, abstract idiom with choreographers such as Martha Graham, Paul Taylor, and Glen Tetley, but it is his grandly traditional redesign of Balanchine's *The Nutcracker* for the New York State Theater (1964) that has endured. The first act is a masterpiece of domestic poetry, a perfect unity of choreography and design; the setting is vividly detailed, faithful to what Balanchine called "a bourgeois Biedermeier home," yet more atmospheric than realistic, suffused with a nostalgic warmth which gives way before one's eye to the vast blue-white realm of the Snowflakes.

Never classifiable in style, Ter-Arutunian's designs for Balanchine range from the toy theater of *Harlequinade* (1965), adapted from opera scenery, to the comic grotesquerie of the stage-consuming cape in *Variations pour une Porte et un Soupir* (1974). His diversified scenery for *Vienna Waltzes* (1977), combined with Barbara Karinska's costumes, provided the most successful stage designs for the New York City Ballet since *The Nutcracker.* Once again there is theatrical magic in onstage transformation: as the dappled trees of the first scene rise into the flies, their dangling roots become decorative hangings of a *fin-de-siècle* salon. The last scene's glittering, mirrored ballroom doubles the full-company surge of dancers in Balanchine's great finale.

[*See also* Scenic Design.]

BIBLIOGRAPHY

Baker, Rob. "Designing Articulate Space." *Soho Weekly News* (18 May 1978).

Current Biography (June 1963). Includes an extensive list of works through the early 1960s.

Ter-Arutunian, Rouben. "In Search of Design." *Dance Perspectives,* no. 28 (Winter 1966).

Ter-Arutunian, Rouben. "Elegant Minimal Settings." *Theatre Crafts* (October 1971). Interview.

ARCHIVE.   Dance Collection, New York Public Library for the Performing Arts.

CLAUDIA ROTH PIERPONT

TERPSICHORE, one of the Muses (or Moisai) of Greek mythology, has come to be known as the patroness of dance. In the earliest extant account of the Muses in Greek mythology, Hesiod describes them as the nine daughters of Zeus and Mnemosyne (Memory), who danced and sang atop Mount Helicon (*Theogony* 1–100). In poets' stories they were credited as the sources of inspiration: the epic, lyric, and dramatic authors called upon a Muse but did not invoke her by a specific name. Hesiod in his *Theogony* cited their names as Calliope, Clio, Erato, Euterpe, Melpomene, Polyhymnia (or Polymnia), Terpsichore, Thalia, and Urania. Later, less celebrated versions (for example, Diodorus Siculus) accounted for only three or four Muses, often with different names and different parentage.

Designating a fixed domain of patronage to each Muse was not a preoccupation until Roman times. Diodorus Siculus, writing in the first century BCE, attempted to assign different functions to each Muse by analyzing the supposed etymological components of her name (4.7). For example, he maintained that Terpsichore's name derived from the way she delighted *(terpein)* her followers with good things that came from education, and Polyhymnia's from the acclaim she brought to writers through her great *(pollē)* praises *(hymnēsis).*

In the same way, Plutarch in the first to second century CE treats the name Terpsichore as a compound of the words for enjoyment *(terpsis)* and seeing *(horan)*—thus, she is the Muse governing the visual delights ("Quaestiones convivales" 9.14). Ausonius's fourth-century poem on the Muses arbitrarily names Erato as patroness of the dance and Terpsichore as governess of emotions (*Appendix* 3). Only the latest classical references link Terpsichore with the dance and confirm Polyhymnia as mistress of the Roman pantomime (*Greek Anthology* 5.504–505). Western writers on dance have since appropriated Terpsichore for their discipline and use the word "terpsichorean" to indicate an association with dance.

In addition to the Muses, the ancient Greeks perceived the three Graces (Charitēs) as another divine dancing chorus, and they are represented frequently in epic and lyric poetry. While the Muses are led in dance by Apollo, the Graces have Pan as their leader in literature and art. As William Mullen has noted, Pindar seems to distinguish between the Muses and the Graces when invoking them in his lyric poetry (*Olympian Odes* 14).

[*See also* Greece, *article on* Dance in Ancient Greece.]

BIBLIOGRAPHY

Mullen, William. *Choreia: Pindar and Dance.* Princeton, 1982.

LIBBY SMIGEL

TESHIGAWARA SABURŌ (born 15 September 1953 in Sendagaya, Tokyo Prefecture, Japan), Japanese modern dancer and choreographer. After studying sculpture at an art institute, Teshigawara studied ballet with Saiga Toshiko. He began to give solo dance concerts in 1981, and in 1985 he founded the Teshigawara Saburō and Karas Dance Company. It performed its inaugural dance, *The Pale Boy,* as part of the Tokyo Scene Dance Series of 1986. Following this successful performance, his work *The Point of the Wind* was nominated for the international choreography competition in Bagnolet, France, in 1986 and won the silver prize. That same year, Teshigawara performed in France, at Éspace Quiron in Paris and at the Festival d'Aix in Aix-en-Provence.

Returning to Japan, Teshigawara presented new works including *The Arm of the Blue Sky* (1987), *The Moon Is Quicksilver* (1987), and *A Thought in the Night* (1988). More recent works include *Dah-Dah-Sko-Dah-Dah* (1991), *Bones in Pages* (1991), and *Noiject,* which premiered in 1992 and was also performed at the Brooklyn Academy of Music's Next Wave Festival in 1994 and at the Festival d'Avignon. *Noiject,* whose name is a coinage in English combining "noise" and "object," is considered one of Teshigawara's masterpieces; its score—noise blasted at excruciatingly high volume—contributes to a mood of crisis that is often present in Teshigawara's work.

Teshigawara has also directed a film, *Keshioko* (1993), and written a book, *Hone to Kuki* (Bone and Air), published in 1994.

BIBLIOGRAPHY

Boxberger, Edith. "A Change of Paradigms in Dance." *Ballett International/Tanz Aktuell* 2 (February 1994): 28–32.

Boxberger, Edith. "Expeditions into the Essence of Time." *Ballett International/Tanz Aktuell* 8 (August-September 1994): 64–69.

Durland, Steven. "Making the Air Dance." *High Performance* (Summer 1990): 38–43.

Hughes, David. "Ishi-No-Hana (Stone Garden)." *Dance Theatre Journal* 7 (February 1990): 16.

Hunt, Marilyn. "Saburo Teshigawara." *Dance Magazine* (April 1991): 50–53.

Hunt, Marilyn. "A Terrible Beauty Attenuated." *Dance Theatre Journal* 9 (Spring 1992): 28–29.

Kennedy, Gilles. "Escaping from the Swans." *Ballett International* 13 (January 1990): 111–115.

Nugent, Ann. "Through a Wide-Angled Lens." *Dance Now* 2 (Winter 1993–1994): 22–27.

Slater, Lizzie. "Rising Post-Butoh Dance Artist Saburo Teshigawara." *Dance Theatre Journal* 7 (Winter 1989): 7.

Svane, Christina. "The Pro Series." *Contact Quarterly* 18.2 (1993): 15–20.

Tsuki wa suigin: Teshigawara Saburō no buyō. Tokyo, 1988.

HASEGAWA ROKU
Translated from Japanese

TETLEY, GLEN (Glenford Andrew Tetley, Jr.; born 3 February 1926 in Cleveland, Ohio), American choreographer. In Europe, where his choreographic career has been centered, Tetley is rightly regarded as one of the pivotal figures in the emergence of a vigorous contemporary ballet idiom. His idiosyncratic, highly personalized vocabulary evolved from his eclectic background as an American performer with both ballet and modern companies, as well as on Broadway.

After pre-medical studies at Franklin and Marshall College, Tetley moved to New York and began studying modern dance with Hanya Holm and Martha Graham, later adding classes in classical technique from Margaret Craske and Antony Tudor at the Metropolitan Opera Ballet School. He received a bachelor of science degree from New York University in 1948 and became a teacher at Holm's School of Contemporary Dance. He appeared in Holm's Broadway productions of *Kiss Me Kate* (1948) and *Juno* (1959), among others, and danced in the premiere of Gian-Carlo Menotti's *Amahl and the Night Visitors* (NBC Television, 1951), choreographed by John Butler. Tetley's performance career also included seasons with the New York City Opera Ballet (1952–1954) and John Butler's American Dance Theatre (1951–1955). He was one of the original members of the Joffrey Ballet (1956–1957) and appeared with Martha Graham from 1957 to 1959, creating roles in *Clytemnestra* and *Embattled Garden.* He also danced with American Ballet Theatre (1959–1961) and with Jerome Robbins's Ballets: USA (1961–1962).

Tetley formed his own chamber company in 1962, for which he created *Pierrot Lunaire,* his first major work. Set to Arnold Schoenberg's 1912 song cycle, this often ribald, occasionally wistful series of vignettes used *commedia* archetypes. Tetley already showed a flair for the theatrical and a tendency to mix ballet and contemporary idioms without strict allegiance to the conventions of either. Originally danced by Tetley, Linda Hodes, and Robert Powell, this work has become a repertory staple for many European ballet companies. In 1969, following a government-sponsored tour of Europe, the company was officially disbanded.

Concurrent with the formation of his own troupe, Tetley accepted an appointment with the Netherlands Dance Theater. A guest choreographer, he also danced with the company (1962–1965), and in 1969 he became codirector with Hans van Manen. His major Netherlands contributions include *The Anatomy Lesson* (1964), inspired by the Rembrandt painting; *Mythical Hunters*, originally created in 1965 for Batsheva Dance Company; *Arena* (1968), a sextet for men; and *Embrace Tiger and Return to Mountain*, inspired by *taijiquan* and first staged for Ballet Rambert in 1968.

Begun in 1967 at the invitation of Norman Morrice, Tetley's ongoing association with Ballet Rambert has often been cited as one of the major contributing factors in Rambert's development of a new contemporary performance style. Tetley has staged ten ballets for Rambert, notably *Embrace Tiger, Ziggurat* (1967), *The Tempest* (1979)—his only full-length ballet to date—and *Murderer Hope of Women* (1983). The last was inspired by Oskar Kokoschka's brief expressionist pageant of 1909; it includes almost the entire Kokoschka text, interspersed throughout the dancing and chanted by the performers. The work was created

with the support of the 1983 Tennent Caledonian Award for premiere at the Edinburgh Festival.

The Tempest (original score by Arne Nordheim) was also created through a commission, this one given to Tetley by the Schwetzingen Festival in Germany. Awarded during his tenure as artistic director of the Stuttgart Ballet (1974–1976), it was not realized until 1979 with Ballet Rambert. Tetley's replacement of John Cranko as head of the Stuttgart company led to the creation of *Voluntaries* (a memorial to Cranko), (1973), *Greening* (1975), and *Daphnis and Chloe* (1975).

After 1976 he worked extensively as a freelance choreographer. During the late 1970s several of his works, including *Rite of Spring* (originally staged for Munich State Opera, 1973) were taken into the repertory of American Ballet Theatre, for which he also created *Sphinx* (1977) for Martine van Hamel, and *Contredances* (1979) for Natalia Makarova and Anthony Dowell. Tetley's association with the Royal Ballet began with *Field Figures* (1970) and *Laborintus* (1972); the choreographer can be seen rehearsing the former in the Rudolf Nureyev film *I Am a Dancer*. Other stagings and creations for the Royal Ballet include *Dances of Albion–Dark Night: Glad Day*, for which he received the Queen Elizabeth II Coronation Award in 1981. Several of his Royal Danish Ballet productions, including *The Firebird* (1981), have been filmed for television. Tetley was artistic associate of the National Ballet of Canada from 1987 through 1989, choreographing several

TETLEY. In 1973, Tetley created his version of Stravinsky's ballet *The Rite of Spring* for the Bavarian State Opera Ballet in Munich. In 1976, he mounted it for the Stuttgart Ballet and cast Richard Cragun in the pivotal role of The Sacrifice, here seen tossed overhead by members of the male ensemble. Minimal scenery and costumes were designed by Nadine Baylis. (Photograph © 1976 by Leslie E. Spatt; used by permission.)

works for the company including *Alice* (1986), *La Ronde* (1987), and *Tagore* (1989). He has created or staged works for nearly every major ballet company in the Western world.

Tetley's work is characterized by fervid intensity, sinuous nonstop propulsion, and voluptuous physicality. A stance of epic grandeur (not unlike Graham's) can be found in his approach to ballet. He rarely creates abstract ballets, but rather utilizes movement as a means to convey his meditations on themes from myth, music, theater, and literature. Tetley's tendency toward abstruse intellectualism, coupled with the openly sexual impetus of his movement vocabulary, has sometimes been derided by American critics who find his stylistically distinct work overly mannered; in Europe, however where he is regarded as one of the major innovators of the century, his critical and popular reputation is of the highest order.

BIBLIOGRAPHY

Brinson, Peter, and Clement Crisp. *The Pan Book of Ballet and Dance.* Rev. ed. London, 1981.

Christofis, Lee. "Glen Tetley: Fusing Classical and Modern." *Dance Australia*, no. 57 (1991–1992): 33–36.

Crabb, Michael F. "Tetley Makes La Ronde Go 'Round." *Dance Magazine* (July 1988): 36–40.

Rogosin, Elinor. *The Dance Makers: Conversations with American Choreographers.* New York, 1980.

Williams, Peter. "Prospero's Island: Glen Tetley Talks to Peter Williams." *Dance and Dancers* (May 1979): 20–21.

ALLEN ROBERTSON

TEYYAM. The term *Teyyam* denotes both a Hindu festival and the deity propitiated in it. Teyyam festivals are held in both private and community Hindu shrines throughout the northern part of Kerala state and in contiguous parts of South Kanara and Coorg in southwestern India.

The festival is organized around the invocation of village ancestors, local heroes, and Puranic deities, who are worshipped with the whole spectrum of performing arts—drumming, singing, processions, feasting, and entertainment. The central performance progresses through a series of stages in which the low-caste dancer is transformed into a deity. Each stage has its own particular text, costume, ritual objects, and interactions among participants. In the first stage, the dancer calls down the spirit of the deity. In the second, the history and origin of the deity are recited. Wearing elaborate costume and makeup, the performer becomes possessed and dances in the third stage. Finally, he calls members of the community in order of their ritual and social importance and blesses them. Individual or communal problems can be brought up before the deity, who sometimes takes the role of mediator.

Until the 1960s and before the government redistributed land in the area, Teyyam performances could be seen as expressive of the local hierarchy. Elaborate rituals of deference, asymmetrical reciprocity, and ritual inversion sanctified the power and authority of the high-caste landowner, while allowing for the controlled aggression of the lower caste (in the person of the dancer) toward a rigid power structure. With the end of the old feudal order in 1972, however, and the concomitant freeing up of the social structure and reallocation of wealth from landowners to tenants, Teyyam performances have begun to assert different messages. They are now saying less about caste hierarchy and interdependence and more about caste mobility and independence.

BIBLIOGRAPHY

Kurup, K. K. N. *The Cult of Teyyam and Hero Worship in Kerala.* Calcutta, 1973.

WAYNE ASHLEY

THAILAND. A constitutional monarchy, the Kingdom of Thailand was formerly known as Siam. Thais are ethnically related to the Shan of Myanmar (Burma) and the Lao of Laos. Thai state religion is Theravāda Buddhism. The Thais moved south to this area from China in the thirteenth century, establishing kingdoms at Sukhothai in 1238 and Ayudhayā in about 1350. Portuguese traders in the 1500s marked the beginning of Siam's relations with the West. Although threatened by French and British colonization, Thailand retained its independence through the centuries.

Dance Genres. The major genres of Thai dance are *rambam phün muang* (folk dance), *nātasin* (classical dance), and *lakhǫn ram* (dance drama). Although at times these Thai arts have suffered from a lack of appreciation and understanding among some political authorities, they have been revived by traditionalists, and Thai classical and folk dance as well as dance drama remain living arts.

In both the folk and the classical style Thai dancers hold their bodies straight from the neck to the hips and move up and down, with knees bending and extending to the rhythm of the music. The arms and hands are kept in curves *(wong)* at various levels—high, medium, or low—and the legs are bent with knees opening outward to make an angle *(liem)*. The grace and beauty of the dancer depend on how well the *wong* and *liem* are kept in relationship and proportion to the whole body. The *wong* and *liem* of male dancers and characters are wide and open, while those of the female are narrow and closed.

For Thai dance, the symbolic hand gestures (*mudrā*s) of dance from India are simplified to a few basic gestures, such as the *čhip*, in which the thumb and index finger are pinched together; in other gestures all the fingers are held away from the thumb. The foot movements are slower in Thai dancing than in Indian dancing, with the toes mostly flexed upward or kept flat at an angle with the legs, never pointed as in Indian dance and Western ballet. Head and neck movements are slight, while the shoulders remain horizontal, resulting in their being at different angles to the moving body. The body moves in diagonal lines to the left and the right; it is rarely twisted in curves—one exception is the *nōrā chātri*, a southern dance drama. These rules apply to most Thai dance, with some variations.

Folk Dance. Each of the four regions of Thailand has its own folk dances, usually associated with agricultural and social activities such as rice planting, harvest festivals, and religious celebrations. The styles of these regional dances are unique to their localities and societies.

Northern folk dance, called *fōn*, is slow and graceful, with simple hand, arm, and leg movements to the musical accompaniment of the *khōng* (gong), *klōng* (drum), *pi* (oboe), and *chāp* (cymbals). Northeastern dance, called *soeng*, is faster in steps and tempo. Hand and leg movements remain simple, with the addition of sensual hip-shaking and swaying. The major instruments accompanying these dances are *khaen* (pipe flute), *klōng*, and *khōng*.

The folk dances of the central region, such as *ram srinuan* and *ram prop kai*, are more refined. Around the time of World War II, *ram wong* was created by Premier Phibulsongkhram's government to counteract the popularity of Western ballroom dancing. *Ram wong* is now a national folk dance.

Southern dances are closer in origin to Indian and Sri Lankan (Ceylonese) dance, as reflected in their fast rhythms and swift hand and leg movements. The southern style of dancing is called *ram sat*. The *ram sat chātri*'s movements are sensual, imitating the natural movements of mating birds and animals. The dance is accompanied by *pi*, *klōng tuk* (a pair of drums), *mong* (gong), *ching* (small cymbals), *thap* or *thōn* (a pair of one-faced drums), and *krae* (bamboo-stick castanets). Dancers of both the north and south usually wear long, curved bronze fingernails.

Classical Dance. *Nātasin* developed from the basic movements of Thai folk dances, later incorporating the elaborate hand gestures and arm and leg movements of the Indian *bharata nāṭyam* transmitted either directly or through the ancient Mons and Khmers. Although influenced by Indian dance, Thai *nātasin* maintains its own national characteristics.

The development of *nātasin* can be traced to the Sukhōthai period of the thirteenth and fourteenth centuries. The terms *rabam* (choreographed dances for specific functions or occasions), *ram* (dancing with emphasis on hand movements), and *ten* (dancing with emphasis on leg and foot movements) are first mentioned in a stone inscription from the reign of King Rāmkhamhaeng the Great (1279–1300). *Ten* probably refers to *khōn* (masked dance drama) and *nang* (shadow-puppet dance drama), because these two arts use foot movements in a martial style. However, it was probably not until the Ayudhayā

period (1351–1767) that Thai classical dance and dance drama fully developed the forms and styles that continue to the present.

The long reign of King Boromakōt of Ayudhayā (1732–1758), a time of peace and prosperity, was also a golden age of Thai classical dancing and the dance drama of the royal court. The dance teachers and members of the royal family, who were responsible for the training of Ayudhayā court dancers, carried on the tradition through the Thonburi period (1767–1782) and the Ratanakōsin period (1782 to the present) after the fall of the ancient capital in 1767 in a war with the Burmese. Then, a large number of Thai court dancers were taken to the Burmese royal court; they settled in Yodia (Ayudhayā) village and taught Thai *nātasin* to the Burmese.

Dance Drama and Masked Dance Drama. Dance theater developed in the Ayudhayā period in the forms of *lakhǭn* (dance drama) and *khōn* (masked dance drama). One of the oldest forms of *lakhǭn* is the *nōrā chātri* of the south, which incorporates movements from Thai *nātasin*, Indian *bharata nāṭyam*, and the indigenous naturalistic style of southern dance. Other subgenres of dance theater are *lakhǭn nōk* (folk dance drama, originally performed by male dancers, and later by a mixed ensemble) and *lakhǭn nai* (female dance drama of the royal court). In

THAILAND. An early twentieth-century portrait of two *khōn* dancers of the royal court. (Photograph from a private collection.)

to survive through the era of westernization and into the present.

All the kings from King Tāksin, the sole monarch of the Thonburi period, to the present king, Bhūmiphol Adulayadēj, contributed in one way or another to classical dance and dance drama. In preserving the classical tradition, many talented artists and dramatists introduced new dimensions and directions to the content, style, form, expression, and stage presentation of Thai dance. The royal court maintained its role as the center of Thai classical dance and dance drama and set the royal style as the national model for public troupes and theaters.

King Rama II (1809–1824) was responsible for most of the royal choreographies and dramatic texts for *khōn* and *lakhōn* that are preserved by the royal and national dance troupes today. Teachers of the National Academy of Dance and the National Theater come from a long line of artists of the royal courts of Ayudhayā, Thonburi, and Ratanakosin that has continued without interruption despite wars and political crises.

Dance Education. After the revolution of 1932, the government's Department of Fine Arts, under the Ministry of Education, took over the function of training dancers and producing dance and dance drama. Thai *nātasin*, *khōn*, *lakhōn*, music, and art are now taught by modern methods along with academic subjects from the elementary to the college level. The natural, lifelong method of teaching used by traditional artists was changed to a system with a rigid curriculum for each academic year, dur-

THAILAND. Performers of *Manōhrā*, a dance drama depicting the romance between a mythical bird-maiden and a human prince, are called *nōrā* dancers and are traditionally all male. Golden headdresses and long golden fingernails are characteristic items of their costumes. (Photograph from the archives of The Asia Society, New York.)

the nineteenth century many new styles were developed from these traditional dances—for example, *lakhōn dŭkdamban* (from *lakhōn nai* and *lakhōn nōk*), *lakhōn phanthāng* (from *lakhōn nōk*), *lakhōn rōng* (Thai operetta), and *liké* (folk dance drama). *Liké*, because of its popular themes, wit, and humor, is the only form that survives as a people's art; the others are performed by the National Theater as classical dance drama.

The first Western-style theater building with a proscenium stage, called the Prince Theater, was constructed in the nineteenth century by Čhao Phrayā Mahin. Tickets were sold for the first time in the history of Thai theater. Other troupes followed suit and theater houses proliferated. Modern painted architectural sets with three-dimensional perspectives were introduced by Prince Narisaranuwadhiwong (1863–1947). Dance drama from this period onward was divided into acts and scenes, following Western tradition, a change from the traditional, free performance that was presented continuously for three to seven days and nights. The modernization and expansion of classical dance and dance drama in the reigns of King Chulalongkorn (1868–1910) and King Vajiravudh (1910–1925) enabled this centuries-old cultural heritage

THAILAND. *Khōn* perfomance at the National Theater, Bangkok. A masked dance drama, *khōn* enacts stories from the *Rāmakian*, the Thai version of the *Rāmāyaṇa*. Here, Phra Ram (Rāma), Phra Lak (Lakṣmaṇa), and the monkey army progress to the battlefield. (Photograph © Jukka Miettinen; used by permission.)

ing which students take academic courses in the morning and dance, music, and art in the afternoon. Both teachers and students participate in the National Theatre productions for the public. A graduate of the National Academy and College of Dance receives either a certificate of dance or a bachelor's degree in education with a specialization in *nātasin*. Thailand's Ministry of Education now prescribes Thai classical dance and music as compulsory courses in elementary and secondary schools. The National Academy of Dance has branches in the four major regions of Thailand to teach or to advise local schools, and the academy's traveling dance troupes perform in the country's provinces and abroad in Asia, Southeast Asia, Europe, and the United States.

Many universities and colleges offer elective courses in Thai classical dance and dance drama or extracurricular dramatic activities. During the 1990s, two leading universities, Chulalongkorn and Thammasat, began to offer bachelor degrees in Thai and Western dance. The Thammasat Faculty of Fine and Applied Arts emphasizes research, choreography, notation, theory, and methodology for the teaching of Thai classical, modern, and contemporary dance.

Students of Thai classical dance start their training at the age of eight to ten, learning the basic dance movements, called *phlēng chā* (series of slow movements) and *phlēng reo* (series of fast movements). They repeat the sounds of the *taphōn* (one-faced drum), which provides the rhythm for the dance while they do their daily exercise routine, chanting "čha-čhong-čha, thing-čhong-thing" for the *phlēng chā* and "tup-thing-thing" for the *phlēng reo*. Then they proceed to learn the basic patterns of dance for each character, called *mae bot* (mother chapter).

The next phase for students of classical dance drama is to learn the *ram nā phāt* (dances for specific actions and occasions in a play or ceremony). The most basic *nā phāt* (dance tunes and patterns for these actions) are *smoe*, used for walking and going from one place to another in a slow or moderate tempo, and *choet*, used for fast entrances or exits or other rapid actions, such as fighting. More elaborate *nā phāt* are for special kinds of actions, such as *tra nimit* for supernatural actions, *kuk phāt* for very violent and forceful actions, and *rua* to presage magical or supernatural actions. Each type of *nā phāt* is again divided into subtypes for specific purposes, occasions, and characters. All *nā phāt* are revered as sacred and must be performed with great respect, concentration, and care—as if the dancer were in a magical or religious trance.

THAILAND. Students who specialize in the portrayal of noble male characters practice at the College of Dramatic Arts, Bangkok. (Photograph © by Jukka Miettinen; used by permission.)

Certain *nā phāt* are considered very powerful, to the extent that they could cause accidents or even death to dancers who perform them improperly. An example is the "Dance of Phra Phirāp," performed in the dancers' invocation and initiation ceremony. Phra Phirāp is a god of dance, a destructive, monstrous form of the Hindu god Śiva (Shiva), the creator and destroyer, whose dance gives both life and death to the universe. Phirāp is also the name of a demon guardian of Śiva's garden in the *Rāmakian,* the Thai version of India's *Rāmāyana* epic.

To perform well in dance drama, performers have to learn the language of gestures, *phāsā thā.* The narratives and dialogues in classical dance and dance drama of all forms are interpreted with gestures by the dancer, either word by word or phrase by phrase. The expression of emotions is also mimed with elaborate hand movements. These gestures are more fixed in the classical dance forms than in the folk and modern forms. The gestures have even influenced the daily language and expression of Thai people.

Each dancer has to practice *ti-bot,* the interpretation of scripts and characters. Dancers and actors who succeed in interpreting well are said to "smash the script and character to pieces." Although strict patterns of movement and gesture must be observed as an artistic skill, dancers can still explore their individual talents and ingenuity as creative artists.

Present trends include experimentation with adapting Thai classical dance to contemporary music, thus giving modern interpretations to classical dance drama. Examples are Professor Mattani Rutnin's *Busaba-Unakan* (1994) and *Rama-Sida* (1996), his modern version of the *Rāmakien;* Parichart Jungwiwattanaporn's *Phimphilalai* (1995), based on *Khun Chang Kun Phaen;* and *Savitri* (1996), performed under the title of *Love and Death* by a British-educated contemporary dancer, Nuchawadee Bamrungtrakul, and graduates of Chulalongkorn University.

[*See also* Khōn; Lakhōn; *and* Manōhrā.]

BIBLIOGRAPHY

Maha Vajiravudh. "Notes on the Siamese Theatre." *Journal of the Siam Society* 55.1 (1967): 1–30.

Miettinen, Jukka O. *Classical Dance and Theatre in South-East Asia.* New York, 1992.

Rutnin, Mattani, Mojdara ed. *The Siamese Theatre.* Bangkok, 1975.

Rutnin, Mattani Mojdara. *Dance, Drama, and Theatre in Thailand.* Tokyo, 1993.

Rutnin, Mattani Mojara. "Phatthanākān Khǫng Lakhǫn Thai Smai Mai." In *Arayatham Thai.* Bangkok, 1997.

Morton, David. "Thailand." In *The New Grove Dictionary of Music and Musicians.* London, 1980.

Virulrak, Surapone. "Theatre in Thailand Today." *Asian Theatre Journal* 7 (Spring 1990): 95–104.

Yupho, Dhanit. *Classical Siamese Theatre.* Bangkok, 1952.

MATTANI MOJDARA RUTNIN

THARP, TWYLA (born 1 July 1941 in Portland, Indiana), American dancer and choreographer. Best known as a modern dance choreographer, Twyla Tharp has also worked in ballet, film, theater, television, and even sports. In all these venues her choreography is characterized by wit, inventiveness, complexity, and physical rigor. The glamor and daring of her movement style, as well as her frequent use of American popular music from rags to rock, have made her dances appealing to a wide audience; at the same time, they are works of scrupulous logic, demanding extraordinary technique.

Born to a Quaker family of farmers and entrepreneurs, Tharp was the oldest of four children. When she was eight the family moved to southern California, eventually settling in San Bernardino. Her parents ran several businesses in the area, including—most important for Tharp—a drive-in movie theater. She began helping out at the drive-in as a child and continued through high school, absorbing the Hollywood movies of the 1950s.

Tharp's mother, who had studied to be a concert pianist, started her on a variety of music and dance lessons. Tharp had been introduced to ear training and piano by her mother while in Indiana, where she also studied "Hawaiian tap" in a neighbor's garage. In California she continued piano lessons with a professional teacher, studied ballet with one of Anna Pavlova's former company members, Beatrice Collenette, and later undertook violin, viola, drums, tap, and baton. Her daily practice schedule was formidable, but she developed habits of discipline and concentration that still influence her work in the studio.

After graduating from Pacific High School, Tharp entered Pomona College, planning to become a psychiatrist. The summer following her freshman year, however, she took classes at the Los Angeles studios of Lester Horton, Eugene Loring, and John Butler. She spent one more semester at Pomona before committing herself to dance and moving to New York, where she entered Barnard College. While majoring in art history at Barnard she studied at numerous schools of modern dance, including those of Martha Graham, Merce Cunningham, Alwin Nikolais, and Erick Hawkins; she also studied jazz with Luigi and ballet with Igor Schwezoff and Richard Thomas.

By the time Tharp graduated from Barnard in 1963 she was already a member of the Paul Taylor Dance Company. Although she spent less than two years with Taylor and had only small parts, her dancing won considerable praise; nonetheless, she was too independent and ambitious to be content working for someone else. On leaving the company she choreographed her first work, *Tank Dive,* which premiered on 29 April 1965 at Hunter College. It lasted only a few minutes and made up the entire program: highlights included Tharp in a diver's pose wearing outsized flippers, and Tharp holding a *relevé* in second position while Petula Clark's "Downtown" was played.

Tharp's work over the next five years came in the wake of the Judson Dance Theater but was only partially associated with the postmodern sensibility that reigned at the time. These early pieces were performed dispassionately to silence, metronomes, or spoken counts. They were structured so precisely and rigorously that Tharp could, and often did, diagram the dance on paper, using numbers, colors, and geometrical figures.

Like many others in this era, Tharp preferred non-proscenium spaces, staging events in gymnasiums, museums, and parks. *Medley* (1969), commissioned by the American Dance Festival, had six company members and about thirty students working in squadrons on a huge parade ground. *Dancing in the Streets of London and Paris, Continued in Stockholm and Sometimes Madrid* (1969), the biggest and most elaborate work of these years, took place simultaneously in different areas of the Hartford

THARP. Mikhail Baryshnikov and Marianna Tcherkassky in *Push Comes to Shove* (1976). (Photograph © by Herbert Migdoll; used by permission.)

THARP. Richard Colton and Tharp in her *Baker's Dozen* (1979), an upbeat dance for twelve performers that is filled with flowing movement. (Photograph © 1979 by Jack Vartoogian; used by permission.)

Atheneum in Hartford, Connecticut; closed-circuit television augmented the performance, and there were opportunities for audience participation.

Unlike many postmodernists, Tharp still believed in classical technique and in dance movement as distinct from pedestrian activity. From the beginning she worked with distinguished dancers, including Sara Rudner, Rose Marie Wright, and Kenneth Rinker; some of the most notable dancers she worked with later included Shelley Washington, Richard Colton, Tom Rawe, Jennifer Way, John Carrafa, Christine Uchida, and William Whitener.

By 1969 critics saw in Tharp's work a mixture of ballet, athletics, and knockabout play, with a style described by Deborah Jowitt in the *Village Voice* as "acquiring a strong classical technique and then learning to fling it around without ever really losing control." Arlene Croce—discussing *Group Activities* (1969), performed at the Brooklyn Academy of Music with the audience seated on two sides of the stage and the dancers working in the space between—noted "the near-collisions, the sudden crowding or circling in a gang (in a jumping phrase), the as-sudden dispersals," and said it looked "brilliantly irrational."

During this period Tharp was working to develop movement as intrinsically logical as music, with a structure based on retrograde, inversion, reversal, and other manipulations of the phrase. The culmination of this work, and of all Tharp's Judson-era dances, was *The Fugue* (1970), a trio performed in boots on a miked stage and displaying the unadorned architecture of a series of intricately related phrases.

With her next dance Tharp turned a corner. She kept the mathematical surety of musical structure but let the music itself be heard; she also freed her sense of humor and her affection for American popular culture, both historic and contemporary. *Eight Jelly Rolls* (1971), choreographed to the music of Jelly Roll Morton, was called by critic John Rockwell "an astounding masterpiece which pays tribute to jazz dance and a whole era and stratum of American life without ever slipping away from Tharp's own style." Later Tharp used the music of Bix Beiderbecke, Scott Joplin, Fats Waller, and Willie ("The Lion") Smith, as well as Chuck Berry and Paul Simon; in addition, she has choreographed to Bach, Mozart, Haydn, and Brahms.

As Tharp's style took shape in the 1970s, it came to be identified with risky, intricate partnering, sudden leaps and lifts, offhanded virtuoso displays, and a relentless urge to keep moving. Sometimes frantic, often funny, the movement seems spontaneous (audience members at lecture-demonstrations used to ask if the dances were improvised) because the counts and the phrasing are invisible. Yet the effect is harmonious, as if rules of classical propriety were operating covertly.

With *Deuce Coupe* (1973) Tharp became the first modern dance choreographer of her generation to cross over to ballet. Commissioned by the Joffrey Ballet and choreographed to songs of the Beach Boys, *Deuce Coupe* was performed by Joffrey and Tharp dancers together. Tharp also choreographed *As Time Goes By* (1973) for the Joffrey. Her works for American Ballet Theatre include *Push Comes to Shove* (1976), a witty and vigorous reassessment of balletic behavior set to rags and Haydn; *The Little Ballet* (1984) to music by Aleksandr Glazunov; *Sinatra Suite* (1984); and *Bach Partita* (1984). All but the last were made for Mikhail Baryshnikov, whose work with Tharp has been deeply illuminating for both artists. In collaboration with Jerome Robbins she created *Brahms/Handel* (1984) for New York City Ballet.

In 1986 Tharp altered the format of her company to include several classically trained ballet dancers so that she could choreograph ballet as well as modern styles for her own dancers. Her best-known work from this period was *In the Upper Room* (1986), to a score by Philip Glass. In 1988 she disbanded her company, despite its critical and popular success, because she felt that the burdens of administration and fundraising were making it impossible

THARP. A personal characteristic of Tharp's choreography is her willingness to draw on movement from all sources. *Fait Accompli* (1983), pictured here with Tharp at center, features movement derived from boxing. Lighting designer Jennifer Tipton created brightly lit haze, evoking the feel of a sports arena. The designs for *Fait Accompli* evolved into the most famous Tharp-Tipton collaboration, *In the Upper Room* (1986). (Photograph © 1984 by Beatriz Schiller; used by permission.)

for her to work creatively. She joined American Ballet Theatre as an associate artistic director, and several of her dancers followed her. After Baryshnikov left the company in 1989, Tharp's formal association with it ended. She went on to create works for the Boston Ballet, the Paris Opera Ballet, and the Royal Ballet, as well as choreographing for American Ballet Theatre; and she has toured widely with pickup companies of ballet and modern dancers. In 1990 she granted permission to Chicago's Hubbard Street Dance Company to perform several of her early works.

Long attracted to the idea of presenting a full-evening theater piece, Tharp created *When We Were Very Young* (1980) with playwright Thomas Babe, to a score by John Simon. The piece was based on the A. A. Milne poem "Disobedience," and the company portrayed a chaotic family, with Tharp as the crazed, courageous mother. A bigger, more complex theater piece followed a year later—*The Catherine Wheel*, with music by David Byrne. Densely symbolic but rich with dancing and theatricality, the piece has another tormented family, this time struggling with apoca-

THARP. *In the Upper Room* (1986) is perhaps Tharp's most popular work. In her autobiography, Tharp says that it is her only dance that consistently receives a standing ovation. A craftily constructed dance, set to a driving score by Philip Glass, *In the Upper Room* features a mixed cast of ballet and modern dancers. In this scene, Christine Uchida (left) and Shelley Washington (right), whose roles were inspired by black-and-white china bulldogs, guard the stage. (Photograph © 1987 by Jack Vartoogian; used by permission.)

lypse both inside and out. Turning to more traditional theater, Tharp directed and choreographed a Broadway production of *Singin' in the Rain* (1985), employing members of her company in the chorus. The show received poor reviews but ran successfully for nearly a year.

Early in her career Tharp became interested in the possibilities for video in creating, sustaining, and conveying dance. During her pregnancy (1970–1971), she videotaped herself doing the same movement every day; elements of these phrases appeared in her 1979 dance *Baker's Dozen.* Her first major television project was the award-winning "Making Television Dance" (1977), a co-production with WNET, in which she applied various video techniques to movement as well as providing an introduction to her company at work. Since then she has directed several video productions of her work, including a restaging of *The Catherine Wheel* (1983). For "Baryshnikov by Tharp" (1985), a public television production of three of her ballets for Baryshnikov, Tharp and co-director Don Mischer won two Emmy awards and a Directors' Guild of America award.

Tharp's fascination with film dates back to her childhood, and she has choreographed the dances for three films directed by Milos Forman—*Hair* (1979), *Ragtime* (1980), and *Amadeus* (1984); for the last she also staged the opera sequences. She also supplied some choreography for the film *White Nights* (1985), starring Baryshnikov and Gregory Hines.

Tharp has undertaken two special projects in the sports world. *After All* (1976) was choreographed for Olympic gold medal–winning figure skater John Curry, and "Dance Is a Man's Sport, Too" (1980), made for ABC's *Omnibus,* featured Peter Martins and football player Lynn Swann.

Tharp's numerous honors include the Brandeis University Creative Citation in Dance (1972), the Dance Magazine Award (1981), the Barnard College Medal of Distinction (1982), the New York City Mayor's Award of Honor for Arts and Culture (1984), the Columbia University Medal of Excellence (1986), and the Samuel H. Scripps American Dance Festival Award (1990).

BIBLIOGRAPHY

Acocella, Joan. "Balancing Act." *Dance Magazine* (October 1990): 54–59.

Albert, Steven. "Utopia Lost—and Found? A Look at Tharp's Way." *Ballet Review* 14 (Spring 1986): 17–35.

Croce, Arlene. "Twyla Tharp's Red Hot Peppers." *Ballet Review* 4.1 (1971): 33–40.

Foster, Susan Leigh. *Reading Dancing: Bodies and Subjects in Contemporary American Dance.* Berkeley, 1986.

Jowitt, Deborah. "Far-Out Ladies." *The Village Voice* (13 February 1969).

Jowitt, Deborah. "Twyla Tharp's New Kick." *New York Times Magazine* (4 January 1976).

Macaulay, Alastair. "Let's Twist Again." *New Yorker* (17 February 1992).

Nugent, Ann. "*Till* and Twyla: A Myth and a Legend." *Dance Now* 3 (Spring 1994): 10–17.

Reynolds, Nancy, and Susan Reimer-Torn. "Push Comes to Shove." In *Dance Classics.* Pennington, N.J., 1991.

Rockwell, John. "Tharp Troupe in L.A. Debut." *Los Angeles Times* (11 April 1972).

Rogosin, Elinor. *The Dance Makers: Conversations with American Choreographers.* New York, 1980.

Shapiro, Laura. "Something in the Way She Moves." *Rolling Stone* (2 June 1977).

Tharp, Twyla. *Push Comes to Shove: An Autobiography.* New York, 1992.

LAURA SHAPIRO

THEATERS FOR DANCE. In Western cultures, dance has been performed in every kind of space, indoors and out. With few exceptions, theatrical dance is performed in borrowed spaces because it does not have sufficient mass appeal to support a permanent home. Companies and choreographers who have home theaters, however, may shape their works for a particular stage, demonstrating that the dance space itself is an important determinant of style. For touring companies, the conditions of presentation are always changing; the same work can vary greatly in different spaces or even when viewed from different places in the same theater. The style of a work arises from what the dancer does with the body, how it relates to space, and how the audience sees the body in space. These factors are inextricably connected to the place of performance.

The general characteristics of the performing space for Western theatrical dance have evolved over the centuries. At the same time the relationship between audience and dancers also evolved.

Classical Antiquity. The space for choral performance in ancient Greek theaters is well known. One example, the theater at Epidauros (c.350 BCE), reflects the order and harmony of the classical style. It has a circular orchestra about sixty-seven feet (about 20 meters) in diameter set well into a *cavea* (amphitheater) accommodating fourteen thousand in fifty-five rows of stone seats. Privileged members of the audience sat in the lower seats with an excellent view of the dithyrambic and dramatic choruses, while the lowest class, the slaves, viewed the performance from a great distance.

In a theater where the orchestra was more than half surrounded by an audience seated in a graded construction, movement would have been seen from many points of view. We have limited knowledge of ancient choreographic method; sculptural (three-dimensional) movement by individuals or massed groups, gestural movement, rank-and-file figures, and circular figures were probably all used, but it is not known how these movements were connected in space or time.

Eventually the orchestra was reduced to a semicircle, and the *cavea* no longer "engulfed" the dance space. Audience and player were thus separated; seats of honor were moved to higher rows for a better perspective on the raised stage. The chorus exited when not performing, and its importance in the play was gradually reduced. The action was increasingly confined to the stage, where any danced movement would have taken a different form than it had in the orchestra. The long, narrow stage with a frontal aspect may have called for a more upright, two-dimensional use of the body, probably limited in range of motion and force.

The Romans made pervasive structural contributions to theater-building. They connected and enclosed the stage and auditorium, developed sophisticated audience circulation systems, and made the theater a free-standing edifice.

Inside the theater, the orchestra was walled off from the spectators. The movement emphasis shifted to the personal expressiveness of the solo performer instead of groups in formations. The rise of the pantomimist can thus be understood in a spatial context: this popular performer mimed on a shallow stage against a background of an elaborate *scaenae frons* (a wall with architectural embellishments) several stories high. Individual virtuosity could be accommodated in the limited space.

In the Middle Ages, before architecturally specific spaces began to be built, performances were held in basilicas, marketplaces, ceremonial halls, and other multipurpose sites. Performers and audience were often mobile, creating an individualized viewing perspective in which the movement was multivalent in style and meaning.

Renaissance Italy. The revival of classical theater-building in Renaissance Italy in the late fifteenth century was intended for the presentation of plays, but the scenic and architectural activity that ensued influenced all types of formal spectacle. There were two spaces available for theatrical dancing: the open space, or pit, in front of the stage; or the raised stage also occupied by painted, illusionistic perspective scenery, machines, and traps.

THEATERS FOR DANCE. The Theater of the Sanctuary of Apollo (fourth century BCE) at Delphi, Greece, a prototype for theaters in the Western world. (Photograph from a private collection.)

THEATERS FOR DANCE. This engraving in *Orbis sensualium pictus* (translated into English in 1658) shows a seventeenth-century raised stage surrounded by painted scenery. The audience gathered in front of the stage to view the performance. (Reprinted from Allardyce Nicolle, *Stuart Masques and the Renaissance Stage*, New York, 1938.)

Illustrations of court entertainments show steps or ramps connecting stage to pit, leading to an earlier assumption that steps were used. However, Nagler's descriptions of the Medici entertainments (1539–1637) indicate that steps were often painted on the front of the raised stage (the trap room), and stairs were actually built only if the choreography required it. The open space was not always available for dancing, because the patron and his entourage could be seated there on their own platform. In this case, the dancing was confined to about a twenty-foot (6-meter) depth of the raised stage. A famous Callot etching of the Uffizi in Florence in 1617 shows the use of the pit for a ballet, but this does not suggest an unvarying practice. In *Le Nozze degli Dei* (The Marriage of the Gods; 1637), the final scene used the entire stage to show a "celestial ballet" in layers of vertical space created by four levels of cloud machines. [*See* Nozze degli Dei, Le.]

Patrician families of Venice began producing opera not just for amusement of the private patron but also for a wider audience that paid to attend. To cover costs and return a profit, the maximum number of paying customers had to be accommodated; to this end, the pit filled with benches and multiple tiers of boxes replaced the galleries and graduated constructions derived from the classical *cavea*. The musicians were placed between audience and stage, further reducing access to the pit. The first theater so designed was the Teatro San Cassiano (1637); by 1699, Venice had sixteen such theaters.

France in the Baroque Era. Theater for profit had important implications for the expressive and technical use of the body. In France, it forced a transition between about 1615 and 1650 from the figured dance tradition of

the *ballet à entrée* to the step tradition of the *danse d'école*.

The French were using ceremonial halls, tennis courts, or parks as theaters, temporarily arranged for each event. All of the interiors were in the *teatro da sala* tradition of rectangular rooms with one or two tiers of permanent galleries. The Palais du Louvre had five areas suitable for theatrical presentation, but none of them were used exclusively for that purpose. At Versailles most performances were held in a park theater, although in the late seventeenth century, plans were drafted for a *salle des ballets*. The spaces in regular use were the Grande Salle du Louvre, the Salle du Petit Bourbon, and the Palais Royal (home of the opera from 1673).

The Petit Bourbon was a huge room in the Hotel de Bourbon (now the site of the colonnade of the Louvre). Here *Le Balet Comique de la Royne* (1581) was produced, as were balls and other spectacles. Patin's well-known etching of the opening scene from the *Balet Comique* is drastically out of scale. Other illustrations of the Petit Bourbon suggest more plausible proportions and volume for this space. For example, a 1615 etching shows a room 221 by 48 feet (70 by 15 meters) with ground-level seating, an apse, and a vaulted ceiling that accommodated the machines omitted from the Patin etching. The king sat in the apsidal east end opposite Circe's garden, which rested on a sloped platform one foot (0.3 meter) high in front. A true raised stage with traps and machines underneath was not introduced in French court entertainments for another thirty-three years. Until then the settings were one with the dance space in the central area.

In 1596 Tomaso Francini, an Italian architect and engineer, came to France, where he created scenes and machines for several court ballets. Among the ballets was the *Triomphe de Minerve* (1615) produced in the Petit Bourbon, which used a six-foot-high (2-meter-high) raised stage or trap room with ramps to the floor on either side so that characters entering through the scene could descend to the floor for dancing. The raised stage effectively separated the decor from the audience, but the dancers still used the pit until the 1640s. When Giacomo Torelli was hired in 1645 to convert the Petit Bourbon fully to the Italianate style, his production of *La Finta Pazza* set a precedent for confining action to the stage. Performers were now on display in a new sense in the raised, picture-frame stage, which came to be regarded as a place distinct from the theatrical and social settings of the court. While amateurs retreated from such situations, professional dancers developed their art to be seen in Torelli's venue.

Illustrations of subsequent French court productions show a raised stage without ramps or steps into the pit. The orchestra pit begins to appear in its present position early in the eighteenth century. At the back of the pit was an amphitheater of ten or more rows of graded construction. The unfurnished front section was a pit for standing spectators in the public theaters, but at court it was reserved for the king. The Petit Bourbon was torn down in the 1660s to make way for an addition to the Louvre.

A magnificent but bizarre theater, Gaspare Vigarani's Salle des Machines (or Théâtre des Tuileries), was built for production of lavish machine plays (those using elaborate special effects). The stage of the new theater was the largest in Europe at 132-feet (40-meters) deep and had one machine that could hold as many as three hundred people. The theater had severe acoustic problems and fell into disuse, leaving only one theater in Paris—the Palais Royal—suitable for fully mounted productions of opera and opéra-ballet.

Paris Opera. Built during Cardinal Richelieu's residence (c.1640), the Palais Royal was the Paris Opera's first permanent home. It had a raised stage with flat wings, a proscenium arch, and steps into the pit. The painting *Le Soir* shows the theater with Richelieu and Louis XIII at a performance. Remodeled by Torelli in 1646 for Mazarin's Italian opera productions, it reverted to use for the more popular *ballet à entrée*. This space was home to many distinguished artists and their collaborators, notably Molière and Lully. A late plan of this theater (1745) shows a narrowing of the horseshoe toward the back of the house, possibly an attempt to improve sightlines.

From the late seventeenth century until the late eighteenth, choreography at the opera revolved around displays of steps in formal, stiff costumes including wigs, masks, armor, panniers, and heeled shoes. Changing subject matter included heroic pantomime and exotic and folk themes. These added variety to the *danse d'école*, but until dresses became soft at the end of the eighteenth century, the use of the body in the picture-frame stage could not have changed a great deal.

While the architect Pierre-Louis Moreau-Desproux built a new theater on the ruins of the old, the Opera was housed at the Théâtre des Tuileries (1764–1770). The new theater, still called the Palais Royal, measured 180 by 92 feet (about 57 by 30 meters). Formed on a truncated oval, it lost the look of a remodeled ceremonial hall. The house measured 48 by 46 feet (about 15 by 14 meters), with four tiers of boxes; the stage was 36 by 56 feet (about 11 by 17 meters). It lasted eleven years (1770–1781). Compared to other theater plans in the opera-house tradition, Moreau's was a compromise. His wider and shallower

THEATERS FOR DANCE. A vertical section of an eighteenth-century theater in Stuttgart shows two tiers of boxes, for viewing, and the orchestra, which is separated from the audience by a barrier. This is one of the theaters used by Jean-Georges Noverre during the time he served as *maître de ballet* to the court of the duke of Württemberg. (Reprinted from Jean-Georges Noverre, *Letters on Dancing and Ballet*, translated by Cyril W. Beaumont, London, 1951, p. 94.)

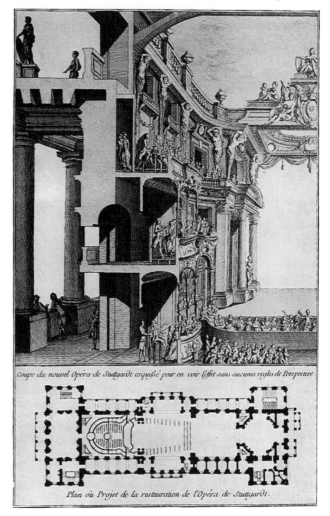

Coupe du nouvel Opéra de Stuttgardt esquissé pour en voir l'effet sans aucunes regles de Perspective.

Plan où Projet de la restauration de l'Opéra de Stuttgardt.

THEATERS FOR DANCE. Architect François Debret created a home for the Paris Opera by dismantling and reconstructing the Théâtre des Arts in the 1820s. This lithograph, made c.1850 by Jean-Baptiste Arnout, shows an 1831 performance of the "Ballet of the Nuns" in Meyerbeer's opera *Robert le Diable*. The theater burned in 1873. (Photograph from the Dance Collection, New York Public Library for the Performing Arts)

stage house and auditorium brought spectator and performer closer together. The stage itself had more functional space because new angled perspectives claimed less depth.

Jean-Georges Noverre's ill-fated years (1776–1779) as ballet master of the Paris Opera were spent in this theater. His *ballet d'action* repertory had been developed on well-equipped provincial and foreign stages. The ballets required a set with props to establish locale and situation, but open space was also needed for the danced parts. Such an arrangement was perfectly compatible with the opera, with which ballet always shared the evening. At Stuttgart (1760–1766) Noverre had had virtually everything he needed under the patronage of the duke of Wurtemberg, including a theater with a deep stage for the "new style of ballet." As in Moreau's theater, elaborate three-dimensional Italian vistas gave way to a more

painted environment in which there was functional space available for the dance.

Again between homes after the new Palais Royal burned in 1781, the Opera was situated uncomfortably in the Porte Saint-Martin until 1793. A new theater had just opened, built by Marguerite Brunet Montansier for her own company, which included Charles Didelot. It had been designed to order by Victor Louis expressly for plays, operas, and dance on a grand scale. Louis's theater at Bordeaux (1772), where *La Fille Mal Gardée* premiered, was already famous for its grand staircase and circular plan. He had solved the problem of supporting a massive domed ceiling by a complex system of vaulting and semi-domes that rested on giant columns encircling the audience. This technical masterpiece was widely imitated by subsequent architects and was used in the Montansier theater, which became the Opera's home in 1794 when the revolutionary government removed Montansier and her company. The building was renamed the Théâtre des Arts and alterations were made to the pit. In 1820, after the duc de Berry was assassinated there, the building was ordered demolished. Instead, the architect François Debret dismantled and reconstructed much of it in another part of Paris, creating a magnificent home for the Romantic ballet. Debret's theater also became a test house for gas lighting, already used in street lighting. All this brought the Opera back to artistic dominance during the years 1821–1850. This building was to have been a temporary house (though it lasted until it burned in 1873), and in 1860 plans were made for a new theater. Charles Garnier's theater building in the Place de l'Opéra, much in debt to Victor Louis, opened in 1875 after years of delays. Garnier's opera house remains one of the best-equipped and most admired in all of Europe.

England and the United States. The home of ballet and opera in England was London's Italian Opera House, built in 1705 in the Haymarket. The house was called the King's or Her Majesty's, according to the gender of the monarch, throughout its existence. It was a fashionable

house requiring formal dress even for the pit. After it burned, a new theater opened in 1791 with a 37-foot (12-meter) proscenium opening and a deep, rather old-fashioned forestage which thrust the performers well past those seated in the stage boxes.

The English forestage was a desirable feature of the King's because of the building's poor acoustics and because it provided space for the danced sections of the *ballet d'action*. The stage boxes, which became popular in opera houses after Louis Véron introduced them in Paris in 1830, were a negative feature of the theater. Named after the new public transit vehicles, these "omnibus boxes" held large parties of subscribers who often became rowdy. The house could hold 2,500 people in five closely spaced tiers with a huge gallery. The pit was raked and filled with benches, leaving a wide center aisle known as "Fop's Alley."

In the United States, foreign dance artists first appeared in English-style theaters. Philadelphia's Chestnut Street Theatre, New York's Park Theatre, and Charleston's City Theatre were the major houses from the 1790s through

THEATERS FOR DANCE. Built in 1778 and renovated in 1838, the Teatro alla Scala in Milan is, like most Italian theaters, primarily an opera house, although dance performances are regularly presented. This photograph was shot at a performance of *Swan Lake* during the 1963/64 season. (Photograph from the Dance Collection, New York Public Library for the Performing Arts.)

the mid-1800s. Fanny Elssler appeared at all these theaters, beginning with her debut at the Park in 1840.

Russia. From the late eighteenth century, dance activity in Russia was housed in permanent public theaters in the opera-house tradition. Today the Bolshoi Theater in Moscow and the Maryinsky in Saint Petersburg are notable for their enormous stages and large companies of 180 to 250 dancers, which have developed an expansive style of dancing to fill and command the dance space.

In 1860 the Maryinsky Theater was built by Alberto Cavos with a capacity of more than 1,760 and a stage 97 feet wide and 72 feet deep (31 by 23 meters). The pit is nearly flat; the auditorium is bell-shaped, with five tiers of boxes and a gallery in the topmost tier offering the lowest-priced seats. In the center there is a royal box rising three tiers from the floor.

In the Bolshoi Theater of Saint Petersburg (1783–1889), the works of Charles Didelot were produced during the years 1801–1811 and 1816–1833. When Didelot first went to Russia, the Bolshoi was the only theater with the flight machinery and understage space needed for production of his Anacreontic ballets. In the new theater Marius Petipa created *The Sleeping Beauty* (1890) and, with Ivanov, *The Nutcracker* (1892) and *Swan Lake* (1895). The theater has had four name changes since the 1917 revolution; long known as the S. M. Kirov State Theater of Opera and Ballet, it reverted to the name Maryinsky Theater in 1992.

The name *Bolshoi* ("great") identifies both the theater and its company. The present building in Moscow (two have burned on its site) was built in 1865, seats two thousand, and has a stage 85 feet (28 meters) wide and 77 feet (25 meters) deep. Its predecessor, the smaller Petrovsky Theater (1780–1805), was intimate by comparison, seating eight hundred in three tiers of boxes and a gallery. The pit had benches and armchairs for special guests and

could be raised to stage level for use as a ballroom, a common feature in opera-house design.

When Serge Diaghilev took his Ballets Russes to Paris in 1909, he transformed the Théâtre du Châtelet, which by Russian standards was primitively equipped. Elaborate hatches, traps, and fountains were installed for Mikhail Fokine's *Le Pavillon d'Armide*. The whole stage floor was then relaid and the interior of the auditorium redecorated for the premiere. Diaghilev took complete charge of productions, especially the lighting, seeking to provide the right environment for each ballet. The huge painted canvases used as backdrops provided the dance with space, color, and atmosphere in a manner previously unseen in the West.

Evolution of European Theater Design. By the mid-eighteenth century there were permanent theaters in the Italian opera-house style all over Europe; however, they were judged not by the appropriateness of their function but by the opulence of their interiors. Theatergoing was primarily a social activity, and elegant interiors and grand staircases were places for meeting and gathering, for reinforcing class distinctions, and for displaying fashion and wealth. The idea of the theater thus became definitively linked with the box-tier system.

In practice, however, the box-tier has never provided an adequate auditorium for viewing a performance. In any horseshoe-shaped house with a picture-frame stage, 25 to 40 percent of the audience have an impeded view of the stage. Architectural theorists and theater designers have since 1771 criticized this system as inappropriate for illusion theater, while others have justified its continued use on socioeconomic grounds. Recent study shows that the box-tier system was a structural development in which two performance types of the Renaissance were combined—the "motion theater" of outdoor tournaments and entries, and the picture-frame "illusion theater" for simu-

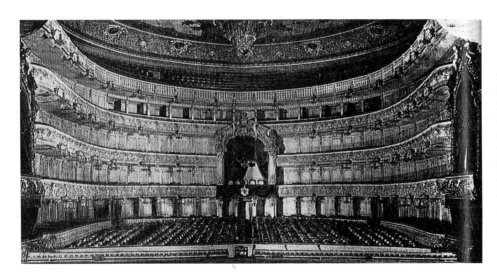

THEATERS FOR DANCE. This view from the stage of Saint Petersburg's Maryinsky Theater, built in 1869, shows the large royal box (located in the center), which rises through three tiers from the floor. (Photograph reprinted from Matilda Kshessinska, *Dancing in Petersburg*, translated by Arnold Haskell, London, 1960, p. 25.)

lation of reality. While the two types coexisted, their physical spaces were joined by ramps. By about 1650, the three-dimensional, corporeal motion theater had been entirely replaced by the simulated reality of illusion theater. The action moved to the stage and the ramps were removed, but box-tier seating did not change for more than two hundred years.

Theatrical dance developed in service of the illusion theater. The use of the body on the picture-frame stage may be seen as a series of transitions centering on costume. Body movement was inhibited by the stiff dresses in vogue from 1650 to 1750, but dance acquired a fuller use of expressive gesture by the late 1700s. The extension of the limbs, flights, and pointe and partner work developed with the softening of dress in the early nineteenth century. The Romantic tutu completed the costume repertory as ballet crystallized on the picture-frame stage. Ballet remained the pervasive style until the twentieth century, when modern dance and its experiments looked ahead to an exploration of the absolute values of the stage space.

The problem of sightline distortion was finally addressed by the composer Richard Wagner in the context of total musical-dramatic theater. Opening in 1876 in Bayreuth, Wagner's Festspielhaus was the most revolutionary theater in four centuries; it featured "continental seating," a fan-shaped pit with all seats facing the stage. The rows were spaced well apart to allow transverse access to side aisles. The orchestra, unseen by the audience, performed in a deep pit within an open acoustic shell. As a result of these innovations, the audience had an unimpeded view of the stage with no visual distractions caused by the shape of the auditorium.

Two other improvements influenced auditorium design. One, the dish-shaped pit with seating alternated so that patrons were never seated one exactly behind the other, was an innovation by the French architects Gabriel Davioud and J. D. Bourdais in 1875. The second involved a major change in engineering and materials. The use of iron in place of wood made possible deep balconies supported with bracketlike structures. G. H. Holloway designed such a cantilevered system in 1891 for what is now London's Palace Theatre. Balconies could be extended out over the pit, increasing auditorium capacity, yet all the seats faced the stage and provided a full view. With these changes the alternative shapes of the auditorium in the bipartite theater were established.

A coincident impetus in expressionist architecture was the People's Theater movement in Europe, especially Germany, from the 1890s to the 1920s. Repudiating the theater as elitist, directors such as Max Reinhardt provided large auditoriums, inexpensive seats, and thrust or arena stages to break down barriers between art and the people. The movement generated architectural experiments and

alternative spaces intended to move and involve the viewer spiritually.

For the movement artist, there was an increasing acceptance of the whole body and a willingness to experiment both within and apart from tradition. There was a growing awareness of the stage as an environment, and concern that it be appropriate for the art form presented.

Twentieth-Century Innovations. The American dancer Isadora Duncan disliked opera houses, preferring to dance in the open-air space of the Greek theater. To achieve a neutral background for her performances, she toured with her own blue-grey draperies; to protect her bare feet, she laid groundcloths on the distressed opera-house stages.

Loie Fuller had her own theater built for the Paris Exposition of 1900. The theater was designed in Art Nouveau style by Henri Sauvage for her *Danses Lumineuses*. Fuller's unique lighting, costuming, and staging methods could be effective only under strictly controlled conditions, necessitating a custom-made theater. Perhaps no dance artist before her had achieved such precise fulfillment of production and artistic requirements.

Adolphe Appia, in collaboration with Émile Jaques-Dalcroze and other designers, created a theater for Dalcroze's lecture demonstrations at Hellerau in 1910, in a large hall with six hundred seats in continental arrangement. There was no proscenium arch and no sunken pit, and the walls were covered with transparent canvas which masked light sources, resulting in an ambient space with a one-room effect. The stage was arranged in levels of varying heights, its space further defined by light to create a three-dimensional environment for human movement.

The architect Norman Bel Geddes envisioned a theater that Rudolf Laban later recognized as an ideal space for his "plastic forms" (works that could be seen from all sides). Bel Geddes designed his "intimate" Theatre 14 in 1922 and submitted it for the Chicago World's Fair of 1933 and 1934. This was a theater-in-the-round with concentric circles of steep raked seating; all viewers were about the same distance from the stage. Laban wrote:

> Of all the arts dance suffers most from the inability of the audience to see properly. In most halls . . . the dancers' legs are hidden up to the knees by the heads of people sitting in front. The subtlety of gesture gets lost as the distance from the stage increases while those sitting in front, see details of mime too clearly and at the same time do not have full view of the whole dance area.   (Laban, 1975, p. 162)

Based on his own architectural background and his theoretical study of space, Laban planned several performance environments, none of which was ever built. He recognized the need for a variety of dance spaces for different uses: theaters for stage dance; open-air pavilions ("dance temples") for choric dance by lay performers; and to fend

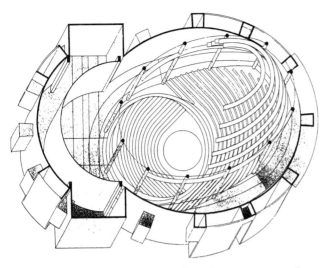

THEATERS FOR DANCE. A view into the auditorium, as seen from above, for the Total Theater (1926) of Bauhaus founder Walter Gropius. By rotating the big stage platform, the small proscenium stage is moved to the center of the theater. Scenery can be projected on screens that are placed between the twelve main columns. (Reprinted from Gropius, 1961, p. 13.)

off the weather for mass performances, a vault-like Kilometrehouse in the spirit of Buckminster Fuller's geodesic domes.

The Total Theater (1926) of Bauhaus founder Walter Gropius was a multiform design in response to the post-World War I demand for new performance spaces. The theater's mechanized stage and seating areas made it possible to alter the relationship of viewing and playing areas even during a production.

Oskar Schlemmer, a colleague of Gropius, sought a three-dimensional use of the body through a nonnarrative, nondecorative approach to movement. He experimented with studies in line, color, form, and space in an effort to eliminate all but absolute values. Schlemmer's work is better understood in the context of Rudolf Laban's polyhedral analysis of the kinesphere, known as *choreutics*. Out of the same "man in space" concept, Schlemmer sought ideas to generate movement and Laban created a tool for analysis, observation, and communication about movement.

The expressionist viewpoint which encouraged dance artists to work from the "inside out" also let them eschew the traditional theater both as content and as space. In the 1930s in New York City, modern dancers often performed on concert hall stages. Enclosed on three sides by a dark velour drape, the space presented a "strident bareness" in keeping with the artistic focus on the movement rather than on the decoration. This "symbolical stage," according to George Beiswanger (1939, p. 221) "lasted only until the dancer had become conscious of the fact that move-

ment was doing something to the space . . . articulating it in terms of direction and level, radiation and bounds, channels and focal spots, points of energy flow and places of climax." Hanya Holm, by virtue of her German training, was perhaps the most articulate and intellectual in her recognition of the use of space. In 1938 the designer Arch Lauterer created a stage for Holm's work *Trend*, "geometrically parsed," functional, and clean as a movement environment. The amorphous folds of the draperies were replaced by flat panels angled like fins at the sides for entrances and exits. The use of low upstage platforms and a downstage open dance space was reminiscent of Adolphe Appia's spatial sensibilities.

About 1928 Doris Humphrey began using a collection of boxes and platforms designed by Erika Klein. These could be arranged in a multitude of ways to create representational, symbolic, or practical definitions of the stage space. For Martha Graham, Isamu Noguchi's sculp-

THEATERS FOR DANCE. Using the Piazzo San Marco in Venice as an alternative theater, the Merce Cunningham Dance Company performed *Event*, a program consisting of sections of pre-existing works spliced together, on 14 September 1972. (Photograph © by James Klosty; used by permission.)

THEATERS FOR DANCE. *(top)* Loft spaces have historically served as performance venues for modern and postmodern dance. In *Spiral* (1974), Trisha Brown utilized support pillars, an architectural feature of many lofts, by having her dancers, suspended in harnesses, wind their way around them. *(bottom)* Brown has designed works for other unconventional settings, including *Raft Piece* (1989) in the Hudson River at Battery Park City, New York. (Top photograph © 1974 by Babette Mangolte; used by permission. Bottom photograph © 1989 by Johan Elbers; used by permission.)

tural sets served "to wed the total void of theatre to form an action" and were symbolic participants in the work. Other artists, such as Jean Rosenthal, explored the effects of color and body definition through the use of light.

From 1930 to 1960, modern choreographers generally maintained the convention of frontal viewing and sought theaters that could provide at least an approximation of the proscenium space. Beginning with more experimental activity in the 1960s, there was a move away from design values and frontal viewing to street theater, loft concerts, and even rooftop performances. Merce Cunningham led a trend in the use of alternate spaces which was exploited by the choreographers of the Judson Dance Theater. The lighting designer Jennifer Tipton (1970) commented that such choreographers "are concerned with the spaces they're in, not stages but gyms, forests, lawns. They do not make it look always the same." Cunningham was among the most flexible in this respect, accepting that old dances in new places were in fact new dances.

Lacking mass appeal, modern dance in the twentieth century held little interest for theater owners primarily concerned with profit. The audience had to be built over three-quarters of a century, an effort bolstered by the fitness movement which became popular in the United States in the mid-1970s.

During that period dance artists and architects continued planning, adapting, and dreaming about ideal performance conditions. These were first provided by colleges and universities where dance was a part of the curriculum. In 1952 Marcel Breuer designed for Sarah Lawrence College a five-hundred-seat multipurpose theater with a steeply raked auditorium and a low stage to improve audience perspective.

Theaters in the opera-house style continue to be used and built in the service of tradition and public expectations. The New York State Theater at Lincoln Center (1964) is a throwback to the nineteenth-century neo-Baroque auditorium. At the same time, it is the only theater in a major North American city that provides a permanent home for its dance company, the New York City Ballet.

There is sparse but significant evidence of substantial architectural change for dance. Two renovated New York theaters provide intimate seating and excellent sightlines—the Joyce Theater (1981; a former movie house) and The Space at the City Center for Music and Dance (1982). Premiere Dance Theatre, opened in Toronto in 1983, was expressly designed for choreographic performance. These efforts indicate a new public and corporate willingness to support dance as an art form by providing permanent space for its performance.

[*See also the entries on the principal figures mentioned herein.*]

BIBLIOGRAPHY

Armstrong, Leslie, and Roger Morgan. *Space for Dance: An Architectural Design Guide.* New York, 1984.
Arnott, James F., et al., eds. *Theatre Space/Des Raum des Theaters.* Munich, 1977. See articles by Baldry, Zielske, Izenour.
Beiswanger, George. "The Stage for the Modern Dance." *Theatre Arts Monthly* 23 (March 1939).
Campbell, Larry G. "Finding a Home for Dance." *Dance Scope* 7.1 (1972–1973): 19–28.
Coeyman, Barbara. "Theatres for Opera and Ballet during the Reigns of Louis XIV and Louis XV." *Early Music* 18 (February 1990): 22–37.
Craig, Gordon. "Some Old Theatre Plans." *The Mask* 13.4 (1927).
Evans, Mary Stewart. "London Homes of the Romantic Ballet." *The Dancing Times* (March 1966): 294–297.
Foster, Susan Leigh. *Reading Dancing.* Berkeley, 1986.
Geddes, Norman Bel. *Horizons.* Boston, 1932.
Gropius, Walter, ed. *The Theater of the Bauhaus.* Translated by Arthur S. Wensinger. Middletown, Conn., 1961.
Hedstrom, Cynthia, and Judy Padow. "Space and Support." *Dance Scope* 14.4 (1980): 8–17.
Izenour, George. *Theatre Design.* New York, 1977.
Laban, Rudolf von. *A Life for Dance: Reminiscences.* Translated and edited by Lisa Ullmann. New York, 1975.
Lauterer, Arch. "Stage Design in Our Time." *Impulse* (1959): 56–58.
Lawler, Lillian B. *The Dance of the Ancient Greek Theatre.* Iowa City, 1964.
Lawrenson, T. E. *The French Stage in the XVIIth Century.* 2d ed. New York, 1986.
Leclerc, Hélène. *Les origines italiennes de l'architecture théâtrale moderne.* Paris, 1946.
Lloyd, Margaret. *The Borzoi Book of Modern Dance.* New York, 1949.
Lynham, Deryck. *The Chevalier Noverre: Father of Modern Ballet.* London, 1950.
MacClintock, Carol, and Lander MacClintock, trans. *Balet Comique de la Royne, 1581.* N.p., 1971. English translation and modern transcription of the music.
McGowan, Margaret M. *L'art du ballet de cour en France, 1581–1643.* Paris, 1963.
Nagler, A. M. *Theatre Festivals of the Medici, 1539–1637.* New Haven, 1964.
Nicoll, Allardyce. *The Development of the Theatre.* 5th ed., rev. New York, 1967.
Patté, Pierre. *Essai sur l'architecture théâtrale.* Paris, 1782.
Pehnt, Wolfgang. *Expressionist Architecture.* New York, 1973.
Prunières, Henry. *Le ballet de cour en France avant Benserade et Lully.* Paris, 1914.
Rice, Paul F. *The Performing Arts at Fontainebleau from Louis XIV to Louis XVI.* Ann Arbor, 1989.
Sachs, Edwin O. *Modern Opera Houses and Theatres.* New York, 1896.
Silin, Charles I. *Benserade and His Ballets de Cour.* Baltimore, 1940.
Silverman, Maxwell. *Contemporary Theatre Architecture.* New York, 1965.
Southern, Richard. *The Seven Ages of the Theatre.* New York, 1961.
Swift, Mary Grace. *A Loftier Flight: The Life and Accomplishments of Charles Louis Didelot.* Middletown, Conn., 1974.
Tipton, Jennifer. "Innovation in Lighting Design." *Theatre Design and Technology* 22 (October 1970).
Troili, Giulio, et al. *The Italian Baroque Stage.* Translated and edited by Dunbar H. Ogden. Berkeley, 1978.
Worsthorne, Simon T. *Venetian Opera in the Seventeenth Century.* Oxford, 1954.

DIANNE L. WOODRUFF

THERAPY. *See* Dance and Movement Therapy.

THREE-CORNERED HAT, THE. *See* Tricorne, Le.

THREE EPITAPHS. Choreography: Paul Taylor. Music: early New Orleans jazz music as recorded by the Laneville-Johnson Union Brass Band. Costumes: Robert Rauschenberg. First performance: 27 March 1956, Master Institute of United Artists, New York City, Dance Associates. Dancers: Paul Taylor, Carol Rubenstein, Therese Cura, Doris Thurston.

Paul Taylor's *Three Epitaphs* was first performed at a Dance Associates concert, as part of a shared program of new choreography. It is his oldest surviving work: a telling example both of his early choreography and of enduring Taylor-style traits. *Three Epitaphs* was created primarily as a performance vehicle for Taylor himself and three women, and like much of his early choreography, it was regarded initially as yet another of his avant-garde experiments. In this work, however, Taylor began to explore body stance, stillness, and postural changes, and to juxtapose large and small gestures—choreographic ideas that he would pursue more fully in *Seven New Dances* the following year. Moreover, it was in *Three Epitaphs* that he introduced signature traits such as the contracted, concave torso with its correspondingly weighted, parallel legs and relaxed wrists. Described by Taylor's dancers as "the Slump," it recurs in many subsequent works, most notably in *Cloven Kingdom* (1976). In *Three Epitaphs*, the Slump is often seen in profile. As the dancers recover from it by first lifting then twisting at the waist, the upper body turns *en face*, thereby presaging another aspect of Taylor's style: his use of two-dimensional movement, as seen in *Images* (1977), *Profiles* (1979), *Le Sacre du Printemps (The Rehearsal),* (1980) and *Moonbine* (1994).

Similarly, although the music for *Three Epitaphs* seemed typical of Taylor's eclectic and unconventional choices during the 1950s, it also reveals a great deal about his ability to find meaning and an appropriate movement vocabulary from particular sound stimuli. And, as with later works such as *Scudorama* (1963) and *Field of Grass* (1993), *Three Epitaphs* evolved in rehearsals through a radical change of accompaniment. Taylor started choreographing the work to music by Debussy but then switched to early jazz music, a form played at weddings and funerals in the southern United States. This slurred, syncopated music, with its contrastingly funny and dirgelike tone, influenced a dynamic change in Taylor's choreography (and most probably contributed to the "Epitaphs" of his title).

The title also reflects the A-B-A structure of the final, five-minute version of *Three Epitaphs*. (A first reworking was *Four Epitaphs* in May 1956 and further revisions were made to the work, under its original title, during the late 1950s and early 1960s. Taylor's last reworking of *Three Epitaphs* included the addition of a second male dancer.) The first and third sections feature the full ensemble, all clad identically in dark, hooded leotards and tights designed by Robert Rauschenberg. The dancers are costumed from head to foot, their faces covered completely, with only small mirrors to suggest eyes and to distinguish the palms of their hands. Taylor and Rauschenberg collaborated many times during the 1950s, one of their shared aims being to challenge the modernist aesthetic of the New York mainstream. The choreography and costumes for *Three Epitaphs* certainly challenged established notions of body design, image, and projection. Even some of Taylor's dancers became disillusioned with such pre-

Judson, postmodern ideas, thus prompting several cast changes during the work's early days.

Despite the anonymity of Rauschenberg's costumes, Taylor's powerful, triangular physique was unmistakable in *Three Epitaphs*. Through differentiating individual dancers by height, he not only distinguished himself as the leader of an otherwise indiscernible group; he also provided the work with many of its humorous moments. (Since Taylor retired from performing in 1974, his role has been danced by one of his tallest male dancers.) *Three Epitaphs* begins and ends with the most marked tall/small contrast: the "leader" is positioned downstage left, towering over the slouched contour of the group's smallest dancer, the runt of the litter who spends much of the work following two steps behind. Taylor's opening phrase—a series of arm gestures and shifts of weight *sur place*—is a synthesis of the work's main vocabulary and, as other dancers enter upstage left and start to echo many of his movements, the follow-the-leader theme of the work is further established. (Follow the leader is also a recurring structural device in Taylor's choreography.)

Taylor's role was most strongly differentiated in the short solo that forms the central section of *Three Epitaphs*. Performed without accompaniment, it is essentially a mime section in which, on reentering the stage, the dancer adopts a confident, upright stance—the most vertical of the entire work—before realizing that he has misjudged his stage position. Slightly unsettled, he steps into the center-stage spotlight and, after resuming his previous stance, rolling his shoulders alternately and raising one arm, he starts to groom himself as if reacting to the reflection in his mirrored palm. It seems to be a prelude to more complex dance movement until unexpectedly, he shrugs his shoulders and walks offstage. Only then do we realize that this brief, twenty-second sequence *was* the second epitaph.

Throughout his career, Taylor has continued to do the unexpected. In 1991, having established *Three Epitaphs* as a repertory classic, he attempted to rekindle some of its early, experimental appeal. One of his two premieres that year was *Fact and Fancy*. It begins with a complete performance of *Three Epitaphs*, followed by six new sections for Taylor's now much enlarged company of eighteen dancers. As the last drones of *Three Epitaphs* come to an end, the stage is transformed into a rehearsal studio. The backdrop and side flats disappear; towels, newspapers and furniture litter the floor; the dancers engage in various nondance activities—all accompanied by reggae music.

In its pluralist, pedestrian style, *Fact & Fancy* recalls Taylor's early postmodernist work. Aptly subtitled *3 Epitaphs & All*, it is a return to some of the ideas that he explored as a young choreographer during the 1950s, especially the distinctions between dance process and

performance; between natural and stylized movement; the contrasting effects of metric, nonmetric, and unaccompanied choreography. Such fundamental ideas not only inspired *Three Epitaphs* but launched Taylor on his long, prolific career.

BIBLIOGRAPHY

Guthman, Louise. "Dance Associates." *Dance Observer* (May 1956): 73–74.

Jowitt, Deborah. "A Fishy Conversation with an Obliging Giant." *Village Voice* (23 April 1979). Reprinted in *The Dance in Mind.* (Boston, 1985): 45–50.

Manchester, P. W. "Dances by Paul Taylor and James Waring." *Dance News* (June 1956): 8.

Mazo, Joseph. "Nikolais, Ailey, Taylor—Three Specialists." In *Prime Movers: The Makers of Modern Dance in America.* Princeton, 1977. 231–270.

MacDonagh, Don. *The Complete Guide to Modern Dance.* New York, 1976: 313–325.

Taylor, Paul. *Private Domain.* New York, 1987: 75, 99.

ANGELA KANE

TIBET. A high plateau surrounded by mountain ranges including the Himalayas, Tibet is today an autonomous region of the People's Republic of China. It has some two million people in 475,000 square miles (1.2 million square kilometers) and is bordered by India, Bhutan, and Nepal to the south, Kashmir to the west, Myanmar (formerly Burma) to the southeast, and China to the north and northeast. The Tibetans are mainly pastoral people, raising yaks and other livestock and growing barley and vegetable crops. A Tibetan kingdom was flourishing by the seventh century CE. It came under the control of China in the seventeenth century and remained so until the overthrow of the emperor in 1911. Tibet was then independent until 1950, when the newly established People's Republic of China invaded and instituted repressive measures against Tibetan Buddhism, which is called Lamaism.

Ritual Dance. Ritual has played a major role in Tibetan life since ancient times. Scholars have limited knowledge about the indigenous pre-Buddhist religion known as the "religion of men," but its successor has been well documented—the shamanistic Bon religion, which is still practiced. Elaborate Bon rituals include dance. For example, when a Tibetan king was crowned, accompanied by a Bon priest of the royal household, he performed a dance to generate the supernatural power vested in the ruler and to maintain the cosmic and social order. Oral tradition relates that Bon priests, carrying drums, performed ritual dances on ceremonial occasions. Some say that these are the predecessors of the Buddhist Black Hat Dance. Other Bon ritual dances were performed by lay men and women (not of the priesthood), and some dances with animal costumes may have come from as far away as Persia.

Buddhism, which first came to Tibet from India in the seventh century, was not firmly established until the eighth century, when Padmasambhava, the great tantric master, was invited from India to subdue the forces that opposed the new religion. He introduced Vajrayāna Buddhism, which is based on a body of esoteric texts (*tantra*s) that include ritual practices using *mudrā*s (ritual gestures), *mantra*s (symbolic incantations), visualizations of the deity, and *maṇḍala*s (sacred squared circles). Padmasambhava demonstrated the efficacy of these practices in eliminating the obstacles which threatened to halt the construction of the first Buddhist monastery in Tibet. Dance was not considered contrary to religion but rather an integral part of its worship: Padmasambhava rose into the sky, where he performed a threatening dance that dispelled the opposition, and the shadow he cast on the ground marked the boundaries of Bsam-yas monastery.

The oral tradition and the texts agree that the first known Buddhist dance in Tibet was performed during the time of Padmasambhava. However, other forms of masked dance and musical and theatrical events have appeared in documents covering the royal dynastic period from the seventh to the ninth centuries. Tibetans claim the lineage of the masked monastic dances can be traced back through a succession of deities to Padmasambhava, while scholars maintain that these dances are based on early Buddhist texts translated and taught in Tibet during the time of Padmasambhava.

Some ritual dances are also performed by the lay community; however, of those performed by the religious order, the monastic dances attributed to Padmasambhava have become known to the world through the photographs and writings of Western explorers.

Ritual dance in Tibet most probably developed from Indian ritual dance and theater and Bon dance. Indian dances are known to have been performed in front of statues of the Buddha portraying different gestures that may, themselves, have been inspiration for the dance. Masked dances rooted in Indian Tantrism, such as the Buddhist *cham*, spread from India to Tibet, China, Korea, and Japan, where they were adapted within the several cultural environments.

Dances in the Tibetan Buddhist style are performed by Tibetans and among the indigenous Buddhist peoples of the Himalayas in the areas of Ladakh, Sikkim, Bhutan, and in the Buddhist areas of Nepal; there are scattered Tibetan refugee settlements throughout these areas and in India.

In Tibet, mime dance, drama, and folk opera were developed and presented as a skillful means of transmitting Tibetan history and customs in what was predominantly an illiterate society. Ritual dances symbolically presenting esoteric teachings, through gesture and dance, varied in date of presentation, content, and style of presentation among the four Tibetan Buddhist sects, from area to area, and from monastery to monastery. These dances, representing the earliest type of Tibetan theatrical presentation, are similar to medieval European Christian mystery plays; however, they have no plot or story, but the dances and characters (well-known Tibetan deities) are symbolic. The performance is an extension of the Buddhist liturgy, which consists of creating the pure realm *(mandala)* of the deity.

Tibetan dance rituals have all been composed by great teachers who recorded the dances of celestial figures they had seen in dreams or during meditations. Although the music and movements have been precisely recorded in texts, the secret information, such as the meaning of the ritual and the proper interpretation of the movement, is orally transmitted—this, to ensure that only those chosen to perform a dance will be able to execute it perfectly, for the entire ritual must be performed without error to be efficacious.

Tibetan dance rituals are presented with the objective of attaining special goals; for example, to eradicate negative forces and engender positive circumstances—long life, wealth, or inner transformation. All forms of Tibetan ritual dance are considered the vehicles of instantaneous enlightenment, since any spectator might spontaneously comprehend the otherwise secret meaning of the ritual. The dances are aural and visual offerings to a deity, enticing him or her to attend the dance and bless all present. As the dancers offer the beautiful movements of their bodies, their melodic speech (*mantras* or song), and the devotional thought of their minds, these are ritually transformed into the *mandala*s of the body, speech, and mind of the deity.

The *mandala*, a sacred squared circle, is an important symbol in Vajrayāna Buddhism. It can represent the temporal world, with the sacred mountain at its center, or, in its purified form, the Buddha realm, with the palace in which the deity resides at the center. Practitioners engage in the *mandala* through ritual practices that reveal to them that the deity is a reflection of one's own mind. Tibetan ritual dance is mandalic in form. The dancers whirl in a pattern that circles the deity, who is at the center of the dance ground, until they become united as the deity-and-his-retinue in their pure land.

The first part of any Tibetan Buddhist ritual is the creation of the *mandala;* this sacred space is specially created by purifying and protecting it from hostile outside forces through exorcism, ritual offerings, incantations, and ritual gestures made to pacify the local spirits. Ritual dancers move in a clockwise manner, creating a boundary around the sacred space, protecting it from harmful influence, and thereby allowing the ritual of transformation to take place. The *mandala* space is sanctified by the circling of the dancers, who empower both themselves and the space they enclose by revolving around the center—in the same direction as they perceive the planets revolving around the sun.

Monastic Dance. There are two main types of Tibetan monastic dance: *gar* and *cham*. The highest meditative ritual dance, *gar,* is the more complex and esoteric of the two and is performed privately for the initiates within the monastery. The movement is focused in the hands, which execute a series of stylized ritual gestures in an increasing tempo. This type of dance is generally performed by an individual or by a small group of dancers.

Cham is a large public ceremony of many dancers performing one or more dances, and most of the movement is executed with the feet. The performance lasts from sunset to sundown during a period of one to seven days. Originally the *chams* were performed secretly for the initiates within the monastery. Now, rehearsals may be private, but the lay community is welcomed into the monastery for the performance.

Different *cham*s are performed at different ceremonial occasions throughout the year. Their subjects range from the lives of the saints to the expulsion of negative influences. For example, a *cham* to ward off evil is the highlight of the lunar New Year celebration. Dancers in a variety of costumes and masks enact the different sections of the liturgy. In some dances, the performers wear heavy brocade gowns and oversized wooden or *papier-mâché* masks that personify sublimely peaceful or fiercely compassionate or wrathful deities. For example, the skeleton costume for the Lords of the Cemeteries—a dance common to all four sects of Tibetan Buddhism—consists of a skull-shaped mask and pajamas with bones painted on them. The Black Hat Dance, which is performed without masks but with elaborate headresses, is also common to many *cham*s. [*See* Black Hat Dance.]

In the New Year *cham*, dancers make offerings to the deities and local spirits and eventually the ceremony culminates with the exorcistic stabbing of a dough effigy of a demon (representing the ego) into which all harmful forces have been conjured. When the figure is dismembered by a ritual dagger, misconception and negativity are annihilated and dispelled for the next year. Thus, the communal psyche is restored to balance; peace, health, happiness, and prosperity are ushered in.

Performance takes place in the courtyard of a monastery. The temple serves as a dressing room for the dancers. First the musicians and monks file into the courtyard to begin the ceremony with music and chanting. Led by the music master, an orchestra of horns, drums, cymbals, and conch shells accompanies the dancers as they circle the courtyard in a series of stamps, steps, and hops. These movements, which have names such as "half-thunderbolt," are to be performed smoothly and gracefully by a dancer who should have a gentle demeanor. The dancers have been chosen for their interest, dancing skill, and degree of meditative realization. They have prepared for their performance by meditating on the

TIBET. Itinerant performers of Tibetan folk opera. The masks worn by two of the group may be guises of divinities. (Photograph by S. Singh; from the Dance Collection, New York Public Library for the Performing Arts.)

deity they are to portray and by spiritually identifying with the deity. Through meditation they must come to understand and be able to demonstrate in dance the principles of detachment, clarity, and emptiness. As they dance, they must execute the correct movements, sing or recite *mantra*s, and focus their thoughts on the deity. They study with a dance master, who is in charge of the technical details of the performance. He accompanies the dancers in rehearsal with cymbals to help them count the beat.

Some performances of *cham*s contain dramatic comic interludes sandwiched between ritual dance sequences. The actors, who are often chosen from the lay community, portray through mime such stock characters as the stupid servant; some even mock the deities of the *cham* itself. The audiences of lay persons particularly enjoy performances that serve to attract attention and hold interest.

Ritual dances are not only performed by monks and nuns but also by devoted members of the lay community who are not confined by monastic restrictions; so, in costume, the lay population of men and women perform together. In one such dance, called "Ling-dro-dechen-rolmo," the dancers perform movements similar to folk dance and accompany themselves with a song of praise and devotion to the deity. Another *cham*, one of an exorcistic nature, is performed as an offering to increase the lifespan of a great teacher. The performers, young women or monks, portray celestial female messengers *(dakinis)* who have gathered to escort the teacher to the Buddha realms, symbolic of his death. They conclude the dance by accepting an effigy as a substitute for the teacher's person.

The number of Tibetan ritual dance performances has diminished since the Chinese occupation in 1959 (after an anti-Chinese uprising was put down). Some monasteries

that have been modestly resettled in India have continued to carry on the dance tradition despite a lack of costumes and financial resources. Dance performances may often be shortened; sections may be omitted with the death of a dance master, or the loss of a text, or because many monks now must work as farmers. However, the long tradition of ritual dance—which includes various forms of *cham, gar,* and *dro* (the dance of lay people)—continues to develop through the new dreams and meditational visions of Tibetan teachers.

Folk Opera. There are two types of Tibetan dance drama: *cham*s and *ache lhamo*, Tibetan folk opera (a choral dance drama). Named after sister goddesses, *ache lhamo* was created in the late fourteenth century by the great mystic, deified saint, and god of drama, Than-tog-gyal-po. To this day all performances of it are dedicated to him and offerings are made to him during each performance at an altar erected in the center of the performance area.

In the past, the performances were presented both as popular entertainment in central Tibet and as an offering to please the spirits of the soil, to secure the well-being of the community, and to ensure a plentiful harvest. In Tibet, troupes of *lhamo* performers wandered from village to village. The actors were usually peasant farmers or small shopkeepers who closed up shop once or twice a year to present their day-long performances. Gradually, some of these companies developed into professional troupes that performed for profit in monasteries and private homes.

The plots of the operas range from national history to Buddhist themes. Buddhism, which pervades Tibetan thought, has been integrated into the plays. Often their themes are about the life and former lives of the Buddha and other religious figures, and the moral message they convey is the triumph of good over evil. The deified characters wear masks, whereas the Tibetan and Chinese characters do not. The main plot is interspersed with satirical skits and parody. A dance precedes each opera and is performed between sets of operatic singing. The dramatic structure seems to have originated in India, while the style of song, makeup, and gesture are similar to those of regional Chinese opera.

The script is based on literary texts. From these are extracted the dialogues for the actors and the descriptive materials for the narrators. The more traditional troupes closely follow the original text, while others use it as a basis for improvisation. The dramatic portion of the opera is presented in a series of tableaux, in which one or two actors sing and the chorus echoes the last phrase of each line or stanza. A narrator presents the background of the story and describes each main character in an extremely rapid recitation.

For a change of scene or a new character, the actors dance into new positions on the stage. They move in a

clockwise direction toward the back of the altar, for the action is performed in the round. Each character in the play has his or her own costume, mask, and characteristic musical theme to which he or she enters; the characters' movement styles reveal their personalities. The performers dance on stage in single file. A chorus of "hunters"—distinguished by large flat masks with stylized eyes and mouth, a triangular nose, moustache, and beard—enters, executing a leaping-and-turning dance accompanied by drums and cymbals. Often two groups of male dancers compete by leaping around the performance area. A group of young women, who compose the main part of the chorus, perform restrained flowing movements to music; they represent the sister goddesses for whom *ache lhamo* is named.

Folk Dance. In Tibet, the people danced whenever an occasion arose: to celebrate the harvest, the lunar New Year, gatherings of friends and relatives, and receptions for important personages. The dance genre they performed, *dro*, had no choreographers or oral or written directives and was thus flexible, vital, and strongly influenced by regional variation.

The folk dance styles and costumes varied from place to place. Western and central Tibetan dances emphasized

TIBET. A troupe from Lhasa dancing the ritual overture that traditionally begins a Tibetan opera performance. (Photograph from the archives of The Asia Society, New York.)

complex footwork in rhythmic patterns, while the phrases of eastern Tibetan folk dance were longer and slower, and the movements were more simple and flowing. Since folk songs have been said to travel from west to east in Tibet, it is assumed that the dances they accompany have followed the same route.

Tibetan folk dancers are most often accompanied by a capella singing or by the music of one or a few instruments. On occasion, however, the dancers remain silent as an ensemble or an orchestra of flutes and/or strings plays; the instruments are most often the long-necked, plucked lute that sounds like a banjo, and the transverse and vertical flutes. The songs that accompany folk dances are drawn from daily activities such as traveling, herding, churning butter, and winnowing or from such universal topics as love and thanksgiving.

As they perform the vigorous stamps and turns that distinguish *dro* movement style, the dancers make either circular or linear floor patterns that often cross, intermesh, or unravel.

[*See also* Costume in Asian Traditions.]

BIBLIOGRAPHY

Aris, Michael. "Sacred Dances of Bhutan." *Natural History* 89 (March 1980): 28–37.

Fantin, Mario. *Mani Rimdu, Nepal.* Singapore, 1976.

Hoetzlein, Nanci A. "Sacred Dances of Tibet's Gelugpa Sect." In *Hong Kong International Dance Conference.* Hong Kong, 1990.

Jerstad, Luther. *Mani Rimdu.* Calcutta, 1969.

Lerner, Lin. "Lingdro Dechen Rolmo: A Tibetan Ritual Dance in Mandalic Form." In *A Spectrum of World Dance*, edited by Lynn Ager Wallen and Joan Acocella. New York, 1987.

Nebesky-Wojkowitz, René de. *Oracles and Demons of Tibet.* The Hague, 1956.

Pearlman, Ellen. "Tibet: At the Crossroads of the Global Village." *Ear Magazine* 15 (October 1990): 16–23.

Samuel, Geoffrey. "Songs of Lhasa." *Ethnomusicology* 20 (September 1976): 407–449.

Snellgrove, David L., and Hugh E. Richardson. *A Cultural History of Tibet.* New York, 1968.

Snyder, Jeanette. "A Preliminary Study of the Lha Mo." *Asian Music* 10.2 (1979): 23–62.

Tethong, Rakra. "Conversations on Tibetan Musical Traditions." *Asian Music* 10.2 (1979): 5–22.

LIN LERNER

TIGUA DANCE. At Ysleta del Sur pueblo near El Paso, Texas, live about six hundred Tigua, descended from Isleta people, who were relocated there by the Spanish in the late seventeenth century. Tigua ceremonial culture features many dances, both masked and unmasked, largely associated with agriculture and the *kachina* (*katsina*) dance culture of the peoples of the southwestern pueblos. Masked dances are performed by young men known as "grandfathers" (*awelos*, from Spanish *abuelos*); in Ysleta del Sur these characters strongly resemble *kachinas* in that they descend from nearby mountains to lead dancers and impose social sanctions. Other than the grandfathers, the dancers are unmasked; unmasked clown society members participate as ceremonial police.

The dancers of Ysleta del Sur traditionally performed for major Roman Catholic festivals. Today, the ceremony of the feast day of Saint Anthony, 13 June, is the most regularly performed of their rituals. Surrounding the ceremonial drum, a chorus of male singers provides the music. Both the drum and the songs are said to have been brought by the original inhabitants of the pueblo. Other instruments include rattles worn by male dancers and a shotgun fired at the conclusion of each song.

Both men and women take part in the dances, sometimes jointly, as in their round dances and the Greeting, Hovina (Charging of the Drum), and Figura dances; or in paired duets, as in the Evergreen Dance. Dancing is always performed by the group, never by individuals. The dance movements for women are usually limited to the lower arms and legs, with straight, stiff torsos. Men's movements are also limited to the lower arms and legs, but the torsos are slightly hunched. The arms move from the elbows, causing the forearms to raise and lower. The legs alternately lift from one side to another. This stepping movement is subdued for women but almost a prance when performed by men.

The Tigua of Ysleta del Sur are no longer an agrarian people and, as a result, the meanings of their ceremonies have changed. The dances are now prayers and affirmations of Tigua identity. The participants have individual reasons for dancing: to acknowledge answered prayers, to pray for strength to overcome a problem, or to answer the call of the drum; but the format of the prayer—through dance—has not changed. Taking part in the ceremony reminds the individual of his or her Tigua past, ancestors, duties, and uniqueness in the world.

[*See also* Matachins, *article on* Matachines Dances in the Southwest United States; *and* Native American Dance.]

BIBLIOGRAPHY

Diamond, Tom. *The Tigua Indians of El Paso.* New York, 1966.

Griffith, James Seavey. "Kachinas and Masking." In *Handbook of North American Indians*, vol. 10, *Southwest*, pp. 764–777. Washington, D.C., 1983.

CARLOS LOZANO

TIKHOMIROV, VASILY (Vasilii Dmitrievich Tikhomirov; born 17 [29] March 1876 in Moscow, died 20 June 1956 in Moscow), Russian dancer and teacher. Tikhomirov studied from 1886 to 1891 at the Moscow Imperial Theater School under Ivan Yrmolov, and from 1892 to 1893 at the Saint Petersburg Imperial Theater School, where his teachers were Pavel Gerdt, Platon Karsavin, and Aleksandr Shiriaev. Beginning in 1893 he was the leading dancer of the Bolshoi Theater ballet company, performing mainly roles in the classical repertory. He was an ardent champion of preserving intact ballets of the classical heritage and objected to innovations introduced by the chief choreographer Aleksandr Gorsky. In Gorsky's original ballets he danced less often and not always in principal roles, for example, Narr-Avas in *Salammbô* in 1910. A classical dancer of the strictly academic school, Tikhomirov demonstrated a strong and refined technique, an elegant but virile manner of execution, and a somewhat static image. A skillful partner, he danced often with his wife, Ekaterina Geltser, beginning in 1898. At a mature age he created several noble characters: Conrad in *Le Corsaire* in 1912; Phoebus in *Esmeralda* in 1926.

Tikhomirov held a number of administrative posts at the Bolshoi: assistant *régisseur* of the ballet (1908), *régisseur* of the ballet (1909), assistant choreographer (1913), and chief ballet master of the company (1925–1930). He staunchly pursued his own line, struggling to preserve ballet in its traditional forms, and opposed in particular Kasyan Goleizovsky's experiments of the 1920s. He revived a number of productions: Kingdom of the Shades from *La Bayadère* in 1923, *The Sleeping Beauty* in 1924, and the second act of *La Sylphide* in 1925. In 1926 he revived *Esmeralda*, with music completed by Reinhold Glière, and reinforced the social message of the ballet.

In 1927 Tikhomirov collaborated in the staging of *The Red Poppy*, to music by Glière. He was responsible for the second act, "The Dream of Tao-Hoa," which he developed as a choreographic and mime *tour de force* for Geltser. He himself was one of the interpreters of the Captain. His dances drew a negative press; they were judged archaic and in bad taste. Nevertheless, Tikhomirov had a point when he sought to prove the right of classical dance to exist as extended ensembles and complex choreographic forms at a time when choreography of this kind was being renounced, but his example demonstrated that replication alone was lifeless.

Tikhomirov had started teaching in 1896 and brought to the Moscow ballet the style knowledge that he had gained during his training at Saint Petersburg. He taught until the 1930s and was director of the school from 1917 to 1931. All dancers of the Bolshoi, male and female, studied in his class or at the theater at various times. The strong and elegant style of dance demonstrated by Mikhail Mordkin, Laurent Novikoff, Viktor Smoltsov, and others was largely developed at lessons directed by Tikhomirov. He also regularly coached Geltser.

BIBLIOGRAPHY
Abolimov, P. F., ed. *Vasilii Dmitrievich Tikhomirov*. Moscow, 1971.
Guest, Ivor. *Ballet in Leicester Square*. London, 1992.
Krasovskaya, Vera. *Russkii baletnyi teatr nachala dvadtsatogo veka*, vol. 2, *Tantsovshchiki*. Leningrad, 1972.
Roslavleva, Natalia. "Moscow Assoluta." *Dance and Dancers* (April 1963): 23–25.
Smakov, Gennady. *The Great Russian Dancers*. New York, 1984.
Souritz, Elizabeth. *Soviet Choreographers in the 1920s*. Translated by Lynn Visson. Durham, N.C., 1990.
Swift, Mary Grace. *The Art of the Dance in the U.S.S.R.* Notre Dame, 1968.

ELIZABETH SOURITZ

TILLER, JOHN. *See* Precision Dancing.

TIMOFEYEVA, NINA (Nina Vladimirovna Timofeeva; born 11 June 1935 in Leningrad), dancer. Timofeyeva graduated in 1953 from the Leningrad Choreographic Institute, where she studied under Natalia Kamkova. In 1952, when she was still a student, she made her debut at the Kirov Theater as Masha in Vasily Vainonen's version of *The Nutcracker*. In 1953 she joined the Kirov company, and in 1954 danced Odette-Odile in *Swan Lake*. In 1966 Timofeyeva moved to the Bolshoi Ballet and became a leading soloist of the company. A virtuoso in command of all the subtleties of technique, she was considered too bold in the early years of her career. Eventually she learned to blend her academic precision with emotional truth and was well received in classical roles. But it was as an exponent of Soviet choreography that she made her name. She created the roles of the Girl in Leonid Lavrovsky's *Night City* (1961, set to Béla Bartók's *The Miraculous Mandarin*), the title role in Oleg Vinogradov's *Asel* (1967), Aegina in Yuri Grigorovich's *Spartacus* (1968), and Lady Macbeth in Vladimir Vasiliev's *Macbeth* (1980). Her talent as a tragedian was revealed with great force in one of her best roles, Mekhmene-Banu in Grigorovich's *Legend of Love*. Timofeyeva created a total of fifty roles in the classical and modern repertory. She also has fifteen films to her credit, among them *Fedra and the Twilight Nights* (1971), after Dostoyevsky, *Raymonda* (1974), and *The Three Cards* (1983), after Aleksandr Pushkin's *Queen of Spades*.

Timofeyeva was named People's Artist of the USSR in 1969 and was chosen a deputy of the Supreme Soviet of the USSR. In 1980 she graduated from the Choreography Department of the Lunacharsky Theater Technicum in Moscow, where she studied under Rostislav Zakharov. She retired in 1988 but has frequently returned to the Bolshoi as a coach.

BIBLIOGRAPHY
Demidov, Alexander P. *The Russian Ballet: Past and Present*. Translated by Guy Daniels. Garden City, N.Y., 1977.
Grigorovich, Yuri. "Edva li ne samaya sovremennaya." *Teatralnaia zhizn*, no. 13 (1969).
Lvov-Anokhin, Boris. "Nina Timofeyeva of the Bolshoi Ballet." *Ballet Today* (July 1960): 14–15.
Timofeyeva, Nina. *Mir baleta*. Moscow, 1993.

YURI P. TYURIN
Translated from Russian

TINIKLING. A performance by members of the Philippine Dance Company of New York. (Photograph courtesy of Reynaldo Gamboa Alejandro.)

TINIKLING.

Among the many mimetic bird dances of the Philippines, the most famous is the *tinikling*, named after the *tikling* bird, which has long legs and a long neck. This dance, which originated on the island of Leyte, has two versions—the regular *tinikling*, danced between two bamboo poles, and one danced between two long pestles, called *tinikling ha bayo*. This dance is usually performed by a couple to the accompaniment of singers and guitar players.

The *tinikling* imitates the movements of the *tikling* birds as they walk and prance in the forest and ricefields. Some say the movements imitate the hopping and jumping of these birds as they try to escape bamboo traps hidden in the grass.

In the old days the *tinikling* was usually accompanied by a song with a slow 3/4 beat. Bamboo poles are struck together in time to the music while the dancers perform between the poles. In the 1950s the beat was accelerated, and the dance was stylized for the stage, an innovation by the dance scholar Leonor Orosa Goquingco.

The *tinikling* was once part of a curing ceremony, much like the rites observed by the Spanish, who colonized the Philippines in the 1500s. In Sitio Tubig-ginoo in Kawayan, Leyte, a curing ceremony was witnessed by Father Richard Arens of the Society of the Divine Word in 1950. In the second part of this ceremony, called *pana-ad*, women with red kerchiefs on their heads danced around the fire, and the men danced a kind of *tinikling*. The source of *tinikling* may therefore have been a pre-Hispanic ritual dance.

[*See also* Philippines.]

BIBLIOGRAPHY

Alejandro, Reynaldo Gamboa. *Philippine Dance: Mainstream and Crosscurrents.* Quezon City, 1978.

Arens, Richard. "Folk Practices and Beliefs of Leyte and Samar." *Leyte Samar Studies* 5 (1971): 107–121.

Baty, Gregoria. "Tinikling in Labanotation: A Search for Transcribing a Non-Western Dance." In *Hong Kong International Dance Conference.* Hong Kong, 1990.

Enriquez, Marge. "Orosa-Goquingco, Leonor Luna." In *Encyclopedia of Philippine Art.* Manila, 1994.

Joaquin, Nick. *La Orosa: The Dance-Drama That Is Leonor Goquingco.* Manila, 1994.

Reyes Tolentino, Francisca. *Philippine National Dances.* New York, 1946.

REYNALDO GAMBOA ALEJANDRO

TIV DANCE.

The Tiv are an energetic and fiercely egalitarian people, about four million of whom live mostly in the valley of the Benue River in central eastern Nigeria. They work at fishing or as farmers on the open savanna land, living in small rural communities, each based on an extended polygamous family.

Their social organization features age sets, through which men close in age help one another in work and dance together in teams. The wives of men married within the same three-year period also dance together; unmarried girls from the husbands' compounds may join these teams.

Dance plays a central role at marriage and funeral ceremonies and is a popular form of entertainment at the lavish feasts held by elders to gain prestige and entertain visitors. The same styles of dance may be used for a variety of occasions. At village markets, held every five days, men and women perform in their separate teams for hours, encircled by dense crowds of enthusiastic spectators. Gifts of money are lavished on skilled performers, who hold a position of prestige because their dance has the power to dispel witchcraft and "mend the earth."

A dance song, "The Sun Is a Man, the Moon Is a Woman," voices the contrast between men's and women's dance. Men express their strength in a variety of dance styles. In the *ingough*, they circle around four drummers in a dance divided into a number of sections, each with its own rhythm, initiated by the master drummer and accompanied by a gong. The leader starts each rhythm with a walk, accelerating into a loping run that ends in a different movement pattern for each section. The first is a stamping pattern; the second is based on leaps ending with a turn; and in subsequent patterns the dancers take a stance that allows for repetitive contractions in the torso and shoulders. This is a familiar style in Tiv men's dance, but the *ingough* ends each section with the dancers abruptly adopting a grotesque posture with abdomens distended and faces distorted, creating a comic dramatic effect—to distance disease-causing painful deformities by satirizing them. The dancers wear amulets and charms, and each carries a small animal skin stuffed with protective medicine to negate the power of wizards who cause disease. Solo dances, such as the *ibiamegh*, are performed by a male elder who carries two long spears as he performs the strong, sustained body rhythms and arm gestures from a static position.

The *ajo* dance combines two styles. The master drummer plays a snare drum *(kunkun)* at the center of a circle of men squatting on low stools; their costume is characterized by two decorative crossed sticks tied to the upper back with leather thongs hanging down over the shoulders. They sing and drum as a chorus, beating tension drums *(ajo)*, as two men move center to dance with powerful shoulder thrusts, causing the thongs to whirl. Two *ajo* players join them as partners in an intense rhythmic exchange between drummer and dancer, which mounts as the dancers compete in a spectacular performance revealing the Tiv talent for invention, often based on skillful adaptation of their neighbors' arts. On an important occasion, the *ajo* circle is surrounded by an outer circle of men dancing a simple foot pattern to the *kunkun*.

During the dry season when work lightens, the leaders of the women's *icough* teams compose new songs referring to recent events, each with a distinctive rhythm. The Tiv are perfectionists and spend months practicing the new dance for performance. The dance is not entirely innovative, but rather continues the *icough* style, with variations of gesture, movement patterns, and tempo that follow the rhythm of the drums *(agbande)* or flute *(agya)*.

The outstanding feature of *icough* is the sustained, controlled flow of the movement through the body and limbs as the dancer passes through the basic positions of the dance. In the stance, the weight is placed on the whole foot, the knees are flexed, and the upper body moves from an upright position to a slight or deep forward inclination, according to the dance pattern. A gentle contraction-release of the shoulders extends into the body, creating a wavelike motion as the weight is used positively in pressing and wringing or released in light floating and gliding gestures.

Many teams include a section in which the women kneel on the ground throughout the dance. In a standing posture, the performers may remain stationary, either facing the drummers or along the line of the circle. In some sequences they progress slowly, using an elementary step

pattern; in others, each dancer turns to face a partner with whom she exchanges position once or twice during the sequences.

The dancers on the circle perform the contrasting patterns of the dance sections in rhythmic unison. The leader, however, dances as a soloist within the circle, moving around to supervise their movement with an upright posture. Meanwhile, an elderly "mother of the dance" encourages the performers with ululation from outside the circle. (These *icough* styles were recorded between 1963 and 1965.)

In 1966 the Tiv tradition of expressing important events in dance was evident in the *gburka*, a soldiers' dance popular during the Nigerian civil war. The leader was dressed in a uniform and the women carried small wooden guns. A male "commander" joined the circle to shout drill commands to start the dance, to which the dancers responded with comic stiffened gestures. On the command "Fire!" the drums took over as the women held the guns forward with a series of abrupt gestures, after which the rhythm developed into a recognizable *icough* style.

In 1976, a spectacular *suwa* dance was created in the Gboko district for competition at FESTAC 77 in Lagos. Their song related to fishing activities; the team leader danced within the circle carrying a small replica of a fishing net. The best dancer on the circle led twenty women in unison, using rhythmic patterns from a stationary position. In place of a rattle, each woman carried a minute calabash in one hand. The "dance mother" moved around the outside gesturing with a hoe to encourage her dancers. The rhythms were far more complex than usual, and the tempo accelerated and declined twice within each rhythmic section. The sections were also longer, allowing the dance patterns to elaborate. The movements demanded great physical virtuosity, resulting in the development of a style that could be described as theatrical. The dance theme was based on a fishing experience: when the women found the river flowing too swiftly to catch fish, they built a dam with hand tools, emptied out the water with calabashes, and caught the stranded fish in their nets. The stylization of working movements is a conscious source of dance postures, movements, and gestures in Tiv women's dance.

By 1983, the *icough* dance in the Gboko district had lost much of its flow, subtlety, and invention. A more upright posture using walks and runs alternated with rhythmic patterns in a stationary position—reminiscent of the men's dances, as marked differences eroded between male and female dancing under urban influences.

Dance clubs have been popular in Tiv towns since the 1950s. There, young people perform simple adaptations of traditional dances, as recreation, to highlife beats played on a combination of Tiv, Hausa, and Western instruments. In the 1960s, cabaret dance by solo virtuoso dancers was performed with great skill in improvisation in a style called *swange*. Their influence may still be seen in the popular styles at present-day clubs.

[*See also* West Africa.]

BIBLIOGRAPHY

Harper, Peggy. "Dance in Nigeria." *Ethnomusicology* 13.2 (1969): 280–295.

Harper, Peggy. "Icough: A Tiv Dance." *African Notes* 6 (1970).

Harper, Peggy. *Dance: The Living Cultures of Nigeria*. N.p., 1975.

Keil, Charles. *Tiv Song*. Chicago, 1979.

Kerr, Julie A. "Tiv Dance Aesthetics." In *Congress on Research in Dance: Progress and Possibilities*. New York, 1987.

PEGGY HARPER

TODD, MABEL ELSWORTH. *See* Body Therapies, *overview article.*

TOMASSON, HELGI (born 8 October 1942 in Reykjavik, Iceland), dancer, choreographer, and company director. A dancer who would be noted for the clarity, refinement, and musicality of his dancing, Tomasson began training at age ten in Iceland. In 1958 he began performing with the Tivoli Pantomime Theater in Copenhagen. With the support of Jerome Robbins, he studied for several months at the School of American Ballet, and with the encouragement of Erik Bruhn he was invited to join the Robert Joffrey Theatre Ballet in 1962. He danced successfully there in a wide-ranging repertory

TOMASSON. Jerome Robbins created *A Beethoven Pas de Deux* for Tomasson and Gelsey Kirkland in 1973. It was later retitled *Four Bagatelles*. (Photograph from the Dance Collection, New York Public Library for the Performing Arts.)

until 1964, when he joined the newly formed Harkness Ballet. In 1969 he won the silver medal (to Mikhail Baryshnikov's gold) at the International Ballet Competition in Moscow.

In 1970 Tomasson joined the New York City Ballet as a principal dancer; he flourished there until his retirement as a performer in 1985. Considered to be one of the finest male dancers of his generation, he acquired a large and varied repertory and was known as an exemplar of style in works by both George Balanchine and Robbins. Balanchine created numerous roles for him, including an unusual solo in *Divertimento from "Le Baiser de la Fée"* (1972) and the *demi-caractère* role of Franz in his new staging of *Coppélia* (1974). Robbins also created parts for him in numerous works, including the pure dance *The Goldberg Variations* and the dance drama *Dybbuk Variations*. Tomasson performed the role of Albrecht in *Giselle* with American Ballet Theatre in 1977 and a few years later with the Royal Danish Ballet.

Although relatively short for a dancer (five feet, seven inches), Tomasson was a handsome young man with good proportions. He became an excellent partner, working with Violette Verdy, Melissa Hayden, Gelsey Kirkland, and especially Patricia McBride.

Tomasson began his choreographic career with a work for the School of American Ballet Workshop performance in 1982. His second work, *Ballet d'Isoline* (1983), was later taken into the repertory of the New York City Ballet. His choreography, like his dancing, is noted for its formal refinement and musicality. He has been especially successful in creating roles for men.

In 1985 Tomasson was invited to become the artistic director of the San Francisco Ballet. He is credited with raising the technical standards of the company and providing it with a cohesive look. He developed a balanced repertory, including works by such masters as Marius Petipa, Balanchine, and Frederick Ashton, as well as such innovators as William Forsythe, James Kudelka, and Mark Morris. He has continued to choreograph many works of his own for the company. His *Handel—A Celebration* (1989) was particularly successful. He has also staged notable productions of *Swan Lake* (1988), *The Sleeping Beauty* (1990, later added to the repertory of the Royal Danish Ballet), and *Romeo and Juliet* (1994). In 1995 he sponsored UNited We Dance, a festival in honor of the fiftieth anniversary of the signing of the United Nations Charter that featured premiers by thirteen international companies.

His awards include Iceland's Knight of the Order of the Falcon (1974; he was its youngest recipient) and Commander of the Order of the Falcon (1990) as well as the 1992 *Dance Magazine* Award. He has been married since 1965 to former Harkness dancer Marlene Rizzo and has two sons.

BIBLIOGRAPHY
Current Biography. New York, 1982.
Gruen, John. "Interview with Helgi Tomasson." In Gruen's *The Private World of Ballet.* New York, 1975.
Hellman, Eric. "Tomasson's Coming of Age." *Ballet Review* 19 (Spring 1991): 85–87.
Kisselgoff, Anna. *Helgi Tomasson.* Brooklyn, 1975.
Mason, Francis, ed. *I Remember Balanchine.* New York, 1991.
Ross, Janice. "San Francisco Ballet: Helgi's Domain." *Dance Magazine* (September 1991): 38–45.
Tomasson, Helgi, et al. "The Male Image." *Dance Perspectives* (Winter 1969).

KATY MATHESON

also became known outside Poland through his company's regular tours and frequent appearances in various festivals. The Wrocław Mime Theater won the Critics Prize at the Parisian Festival of the Theater of Nations in 1962 and the Gold Star at the Festival International de Danse in Paris in 1970.

BIBLIOGRAPHY
Hausbrandt, Andrej. *Tomaszewski-pantomima.* Warsaw, 1974.
Neuer, Adam, ed. *Polish Opera and Ballet of the Twentieth Century: Operas, Ballets, Pantomimes, Miscellaneous Works.* Translated by Jerzy Zawadzki. Kraków, 1986.

PAWEŁ CHYNOWSKI

TOMASZEWSKI, HENRYK (born 20 November 1925 in Poznań), Polish dancer, mime, choreographer, teacher, and company director. Tomaszewski studied dance with Feliks Parnell and acting with Iwo Gall. After performing as a soloist of the Wrocław Opera Ballet from 1949 to 1955, he established a mime studio, converted in 1958 into the Wrocław Mime Theater.

As a dancer, Tomaszewski always preferred dramatic, mimic, and character roles. He was expressive, full of invention, and talented in improvisation. He created many leading roles in his own dance dramas, shaping the style of interpretation in Polish mime theater. Early in his career as a choreographer for his mime company, he created short, strict mime in the style of Marcel Marceau. Later he developed an original type of narrative theater of movement based on his own scenarios, utilizing mime, modern dance, ballet, and acrobatics. The music in Tomaszewski's works fulfills an illustrative, ornamental function.

Among Tomaszewski's more important works are *A Harlequin's Masks* (1959), *The Sorcerer's Apprentice* (1960), *The Peculiar Closet* (1961), *Entrance to the Labyrinth* (1963), *The Minotaur* (1964), *The Rocking Horse* (1965), *The Garden of Love* and *The Dress* (both 1966), *Gilgamesh* and *Bagage* (both 1968), *Faust's Departure* (1970), *A November Night's Dream* (1971), *The Menagerie of Empress Philissa* (1972), *I Am Coming Tomorrow* (1974), *Fantastic Scenes from the Legend of Pan Twardowski* (1976), *The Dispute* (1978), *Hamlet—Irony and Mourning* (1979), *King Arthur's Knights* (1981), and *The Prodigal Son* (1983).

Tomaszewski also occasionally choreographed ballets for Polish opera companies or for foreign ballet companies. For the Dutch National Ballet, he created *The Bull* (1965), to music by Augustyn Bloch; *Labyrinth*, performed in silence, *Pit and Bolster*, to music by Charles Mingus, and *The Dream*, to music by Bloch (all 1969); and *Before Five Passed* (1972), set to music by Juliusz Luciuk. For the Royal Danish Ballet, he set *Bagage* (1969) to music by Giovanni Pergolesi.

Many films of Tomaszewski's dance dramas were broadcast in Poland and other European countries. His work

TOMLINSON, KELLOM (also known as Kenelm, Mr. Kellom; born c.1690, died after 1753), English dancing master and choreographer. Tomlinson is best known as the author of *The Art of Dancing* (1735). He was apprenticed to Thomas Caverley at his ladies' dancing and boarding school on Bedford Street in London in April 1707, where he remained until 1714. His instructor in theatrical dancing at that time was René Cherrier. Tomlinson also knew Anthony L'Abbé and was a contemporary at Caverley's with John Shaw, the theatrical dancer.

Tomlinson set himself up as a genteel dancing master at his lodgings on the corner of King's Gate Street, Holborn, and immediately began to notate and publish his own annual dance, following the examples of Mister Isaac, L'Abbé, P[eter?] Siris, and others. A series of six dances, for the years 1715 to 1720, was issued in a collected edition in 1721 as *Six Dances Composed by Mr. Kellom Tomlinson*, including "The Passepied Round O" (1715); "The Shepherdess" (1716); "The Submission" (1717), which was performed by Marie and Francis Sallé at Lincoln's Inn Fields theater as "Mr. Kellom's New Dance"; "The Prince Eugene" (1718); "The Address: A New Rigadoon" (1719); and "The Gavot" (1720). In 1721 he also published his "Passacaille Diana," dedicated to L'Abbé. These dances were for the "use and improvement" of his students and "for the further Encouragement of dancing." His most successful pupil was John Topham, who first appeared on the stage as "Mr. Kellom's scholar" and later danced in John Weaver's *Orpheus and Eurydice* (1718).

Tomlinson moved into his own house on Southampton Street, Holborn, in 1717 or 1718 after marrying Mary Alston (25 July 1717), and in 1719 they moved to Devonshire Street, near Queen's Square, Holborn. Although this suggests increasing prosperity, Tomlinson's failure to obtain enough subscribers led to a crucial delay in the publication of his major work *The Art of Dancing*. He finished the book in 1724 and advertised it as ready for press in October 1726, but it was not actually published until 1735.

The expense of Tomlinson's work (which accounted for

the long delay) was due to the cost of the fine plates by Gerard Vandergucht, George Bickhan, George Vertue, and others. The novel idea of the treatise, for which Tomlinson was eager to take credit, was to make the notation of dances more useful to the amateur and student: the manner of performance was described in words and dancers performing the steps were depicted graphically in addition to the steps being notated. The work is clearly set out and written in accordance with the principles and rules that Tomlinson had garnered from observing the outstanding masters of genteel dancing, including Caverley and others. Thirty named dances by English and French dancing masters published since 1700 are referred to in the text. The work was reissued as a second edition in 1744 and was one of the most finely produced of all dance books, subscribed to by the greatest in the British world of dance; it has continuing importance and interest for students of dance technique and bibliography.

Tomlinson disclaimed all knowledge of Pierre Rameau's *Le maître à danser* (1725) and maintained that John Essex's translation, *The Dancing-Master: or, The Art of Dancing Explained* (1728), which had a larger format than the original and sold at half the proposed cost of Tomlinson's book, was designed to destroy his market. A workbook apparently compiled by Tomlinson between 1708 and 1721 has come to light in New Zealand that contains six previously unknown dances by Tomlinson. Three of those dances were performed in London in a 1716 production of *The Island Princess* and used again, with two additional dances, in 1721. The collection also contains a solo *sarabande* for a man, performed in 1716, and a hitherto unknown version of Caverley's "Slow Minuet," which differs in several respects from Pemberton's engraved version.

BIBLIOGRAPHY
Brinson, Peter, ed. *The Ballet in Britain.* London, 1962.
Marsh, Carol. "French Court Dance in England, 1706–1740: A Study of the Sources." Ph.D. diss., City University of New York, 1985.
Petre, Robert. "Six New Dances by Kellom Tomlinson: A Recently Discovered Manuscript." *Early Music* 18 (August 1990): 381–390.
Scott, Edward. "Notes on the Minuet as Represented by Kellom Tomlinson." *Dancing Times* (December 1922): 243–245.
Shennan, Jennifer. "Discovery of New Kellom Tomlinson Manuscript." *Dance Research Journal* 22 (Spring 1990): 58–61.
Tomlinson, Kellom. *A Work Book by Kellom Tomlinson: Commonplace Book of an Eighteenth-Century English Dancing Master* (c.1708–1722). Edited by Jennifer Shennan. Stuyvesant, N.Y., 1992.
RICHARD RALPH and JENNIFER THORP

TONGA. The Kingdom of Tonga, in Polynesia, is in the southern Pacific Ocean, southwest of Samoa; it is an independent member nation of the British Commonwealth, composed of some 150 islands with about 100,000 people. Its parliamentary political system is headed by a king who traces his ancestry back to the Polynesian gods who are

TONGA. Men from Lapaha performing the *m'etu'upaki* at the centenary celebration of the Tongan constitution, at Nuku'alofa, 1975. (Photograph © 1976 by Adrienne L. Kaeppler; used by permission.)

said to have created and peopled the islands. Dance is a functional part of the present sociopolitical system, which combines traditional social stratification with a system of appointed nobles.

No notable occasion, from national celebration to informal get-together, is complete without the performance of some kind of dancing. The most important dances performed on formal occasions can be characterized as metaphorical danced speeches. These include *lakalaka*, usually a standing dance ideally performed by all the men and women of a village, and *mā'ulu'ulu*, a sitting dance performed by many individuals of one or both sexes from a school, church, village, or other corporate group. In these dances the basic text is structured along the lines of a formal speech in a series of concepts and references to past and present events, places, and people. Movements allude to selected words of the poetry or to underlying concepts to which the poetry alludes. Thus, Tongan dance creates a double abstraction; while movements are in themselves abstract, they also allude to multiple words, meanings, and concepts.

The aesthetic concept of *heliaki* (to say one thing but mean another) is found both in the melodically and rhythmically rendered poetry and in the movements that allude to it. Another aesthetic element, *fakateki* (side head tilt), expresses a state of inner exhilaration called *māfana*. In *lakalaka*, leg movements are primarily a series of sidesteps executed nearly in place, while in *mā'ulu'ulu* and other seated dances no leg movements are made except for a rhythmic pulse kept with one foot. Thus the most important movements are those of the hands and arms, which form a series of movement motifs—movements interpreting a selected word or concept, beautiful movements that ornament or complete certain phrases, and motifs that divide stanzas or sections of poetry.

Movement motifs are based on flexible wrists and the rotation of the lower arms, in conjunction with various finger movements and positions and palm facings, which occur in a limited number of arm positions. These motifs are known by the general term *haka*, and a number of the motifs also have specific names. For example, *milolua* is a movement that derives from the wringing of *kava (Piper methysticum)*, plant material used to make a ceremonial drink. Arm movements for women are soft and graceful, and foot and leg movements are small, in keeping with the stricture of always keeping the thighs parallel and close together, even while seated. Men's movements are larger and more virile, delivered with stiffer wrists; the steps are wider and the legs more separated, and there is more body movement, including moving to one knee, striking the ground with feet or hands, and even rolling on the ground.

TONGA. Men and women from Kanokupolu performing a *lakalaka* at the centenary celebration of the Tongan constitution, at Nuku'alofa, 1975. (Photograph © 1976 by Adrienne L. Kaeppler; used by permission.)

Older dances that are still performed but no longer created include *me'etu'upaki*, a men's standing dance in which dance paddles are manipulated; and a women's dance, *fa'ahiula*, which includes a seated section called *'otuhaka* and a standing section called *ula*. The *ula* has been largely replaced by *tau'olunga*, an acculturated dance that combines Tongan and Samoan movements with Tongan poetry rendered in a form based on European melodic contours and played on stringed instruments.

[*For general discussion, see* Oceanic Dance Traditions *and* Polynesia. *See also* Music for Dance, *article on* Oceanic Music.]

BIBLIOGRAPHY

Kaeppler, Adrienne L. "Tongan Dance: A Study in Cultural Change." *Ethnomusicology* 14.2 (1970): 266–277.

Kaeppler, Adrienne L. "Aesthetics of Tongan Dance." *Ethnomusicology* 15.2 (1971): 175–185.

Kaeppler, Adrienne L. "Method and Theory in Analyzing Dance Structure, with an Analysis of Tongan Dance." *Ethnomusicology* 16.2 (1972): 173–217.

Kaeppler, Adrienne L. "Melody, Drone, and Decoration: Underlying Structures and Surface Manifestations in Tongan Art and Society." In *Art in Society: Studies in Styles, Cultures, and Aesthetics,* edited by Michael Greenhalgh and Vincent Megaw. London, 1978.

Kaeppler, Adrienne L. "Structured Movement Systems in Tonga." In *Society and the Dance: The Social Anthropology of Process and Performance,* edited by Paul Spencer. Cambridge, 1985.

Kaeppler, Adrienne L. *Poetry in Motion: Studies in Tongan Dance.* Nuku'alofa, Tonga, 1993.

ADRIENNE L. KAEPPLER

TOPÉNG. *See* Indonesia, *article on* Balinese Mask Theater.

TORDION (also Eng., *turgion;* Fr., *tourdion;* It., *tordiglione, dordigilone*), a lively triple-meter sixteenth-century dance type of unknown origins, similar to the galliard. French and Italian sources first mention the tordion in 1499, in *La grant danse macabre* (see Heartz, 1949–1979, p. 590) and in a letter to Isabella d'Este, which refers to a drummer playing a *dordoglione* in an *intermedio* (Pirrotta and Povoledo, 1982, p. 50). An early English reference appears in Thomas Elyot's guide to a prince's education, the *Boke Named the Gouvernour* (1531): "We have nowe, base daunsis, bargenettes, pavions, turgions, and roundes." There is no choreography, however, before 1581. The dance seems to have died out in Italy and France shortly after 1600, although references to it continue in Spain.

In musical collections of the early sixteenth century, the tordion was often an after-dance to the *bassedanse* (e.g., Pierre Attaingnant, *18 basses dances*, 1530), but the only contemporary choreographic reference, in Antonius de Arena's treatise *A suos compagnones studiantes* (1528), merely gives comical hints of sprightly "passages" in macaronic verse.

Choreographic details appear much later in Fabritio Caroso (1581, 1600), Thoinot Arbeau (1588), Cesare Negri (1602, 1604), and Livio Lupi (1600, 1607). Whatever the tordion was originally, it and the galliard are, by this time, recognized as related, if not actually identical. Arbeau equates the dances musically and choreographically but distinguishes between them also by saying that the tordion follows the *retour* of the *bassedanse*. He states further that it differs from the galliard because it is "danced close to the ground to a light, lively beat and the galliard is danced higher off the ground to a slower, stronger beat." He also supplies two simple variations.

The far more complex Italian choreographies blur even these small distinctions. Caroso's (two) and Negri's (one) *tordiglione* have passages and variations couched entirely in galliard terms; because all three dances have the same short music, whose six-beat units may be read as needed in triple (3/2) or duple (6/4), the Italian *tordiglione* may simply be a galliard to a specific tune or chord scheme. Caroso, however, has *tordiglione* variations (for the lady) in galliard movements of *balletto* suites to other music, such as "Nido d'Amore" (Caroso, 1600, p. 290). He says, in fact, that the *tordiglione* is a galliard (Caroso, 1600, p. 320). Nevertheless, Lupi's long lists of *tordiglione* variations (100 in 1600 and 140 for the gentleman and 30 for the lady in 1607) are kept separate from his even longer lists of galliard passages and variations. Thus, differences were apparently perceived by some that are not now evident but that more study and statistical analyses may yet reveal.

The mystery of the dance is further deepened by John Florio's definition of the *tordiglione* as "a kind of dance in Spaine" (Florio, 1598, 1600); yet Spanish references to this dance are from the seventeenth century only (Esses, 1992).

[*For related discussion, see* Galliard.]

BIBLIOGRAPHY: SOURCES

Arbeau, Thoinot. *Orchesographie et traicte en forme de dialogve, par leqvel tovtes personnes pevvent facilement apprendre & practiquer l'honneste exercice des dances.* Langres, 1588, 1589. Facsimile reprint, Langres, 1988. Reprinted with expanded title as *Orchesographie, metode, et teorie en forme de discovrs et tablatvre povr apprendre a dancer, battre le Tambour en toute sorte & diuersité de batteries, Iouët du fifre & arigot, tirer des armes & escrimer, auec autres honnestes exercices fort conuenables à la Ieunesse.* Langres, 1596. Facsimile reprint, Geneva, 1972.

Arbeau, Thoinot. *Orchesography.* 1589. Translated into English by Mary Stewart Evans. New York, 1948. Reprint with corrections, a new introduction, and notes by Julia Sutton, and representative steps and dances in Labanotation by Mireille Backer. New York, 1967.

Arena, Antonius. *Ad suos compagnones studiantes.* Lyon, 1528. Translated by John Guthrie and Marino Zorzi in "*Rules of Dancing* by Antonius Arena." *Dance Research* 4 (1986): 3–53.

Caroso, Fabritio. *Il ballarino* (1581). Facsimile reprint, New York, 1967.

Caroso, Fabritio. *Nobiltà di dame.* Venice, 1600, 1605. Facsimile reprint, Bologna, 1970. Reissued with order of illustrations changed as *Raccolta di varij balli.* Rome, 1630. Translated into English with eight introductory chapters by Julia Sutton, the music transcribed by F. Marian Walker. Oxford, 1986. Reprint with step manual in Labanotation by Rachelle Palnick Tsachor and Julia Sutton, New York, 1995.

Florio, John. *A World of Wordes.* London, 1598. Facsimile reprint, Hildesheim, 1972. 2d ed., *Queen Anna's New World of Words.* London, 1611. Facsimile reprint of 1611 ed., Menston, England, 1973.

Lupi, Livio. *Libro di gagliarda, tordiglione, passo e mezzo, canari e passeggi.* Palermo, 1600. Rev. ed., Palermo, 1607.

Negri, Cesare. *Le gratie d'amore.* Milan, 1602. Reissued as *Nuove invenzione di balli.* Milan, 1604. Translated into Spanish by Don Balthasar Carlos for Señor Condé, Duke of Sanlucar, 1630. Manuscript located in Madrid, Biblioteca Nacional, MS 14085. Facsimile reprint of 1602, New York and Bologna, 1969. Literal translation into English and musical transcription by Yvonne Kendall. D.M.A. diss., Stanford University, 1985.

BIBLIOGRAPHY: OTHER STUDIES

Brooks, Lynn Matluck. *The Dances of the Processions of Seville in Spain's Golden Age.* Kassel, 1988.

Esses, Maurice. *Dance and Instrumental Diferencias in Spain during the Seventeenth and Early Eighteenth Centuries.* Stuyvesant, N.Y., 1992.

Heartz, Daniel. "Sources and Forms of the French Instrumental Dance in the Sixteenth Century." Ph.D. diss., Harvard University, 1957.

Heartz, Daniel. *Preludes, Chansons, and Dances for Lute Published by Pierre Attaingnant, Paris, 1529–1530.* Neuilly-sur-Seine, 1964.

Heartz, Daniel. *Keyboard Dances from the Earlier Sixteenth Century.* American Institute of Musicology, Corpus of Early Keyboard Music, 8. Dallas, 1965.

Heartz, Daniel. "Tourdion." In *Die Musik in Geschichte und Gegenwart.* 1st ed., vol. 13, 1966. Kassel, 1949–1979. Recast in *The New Grove Dictionary of Music and Musicians.* London, 1980.

Pirrotta, Nino, and Elena Povoledo. *Music and Theatre from Poliziano to Monteverdi.* Translated by Karen Eals. Cambridge, 1982.

Tani, Gino. "Tourdion." In *Enciclopedio dello spettacolo.* 9 vols. Rome, 1954–1968.

JULIA SUTTON
with David Hahn

TORNEO. *See* Barriera, Torneo, and Battaglia.

TORVILL AND DEAN. Jayne Torvill (born 7 October 1957 in Nottingham) and Christopher Dean (Christopher Colin Dean, born 27 July 1958 in Nottingham), English ice dancers and choreographers. Torvill and Dean revolutionized ice dancing, bringing it closer to art while indirectly casting doubt upon its viability as a sport. During their amateur career, which culminated with a gold medal at the 1984 Olympic Games, the couple amassed more perfect scores than any other competitors in skating history and transformed the sport through Dean's choreography, its imitation by others, and the rules changes aimed at reducing its influence. As professionals, Torvill and Dean's skating remained at the highest standard. In 1994 they returned to the Olympics under new eligibility rules, and their technically challenging and charismatic performance to "Let's Face the Music and Dance" was awarded a bronze medal for third place. The decision of the judges was highly controversial, and the suspicion that Torvill and Dean had been unfairly penalized renewed speculation that the highly subjective sport might be eliminated from Olympic competition.

Both Jayne Torvill and Christopher Dean started skating at about age ten, and both quickly achieved recognition in amateur competitions: Dean won a British junior dance championship (1974) with Sandra Elson, whereas Torvill won the British senior pairs championship (1971) with Michael Hutchinson. When both were left by their partners, they formed a dance team in 1975. In 1980, they were able to leave their jobs (Torvill was an insurance clerk, Dean, a policeman) to train full-time on a grant from the Nottingham City Council. They won four consecutive world championships, starting in 1981.

Their 1982 programs set new standards of artistry for the sport. "Summertime," a required Blues number, conveyed a feeling of passionate desolation, and its intriguing air of intimacy became a hallmark of the Torvill and Dean mystique (genuine, but also carefully cultivated). The desire of audiences to see them as a couple remained undisturbed by their subsequent marriages to others. The popularity of their free dance based on the failed Broadway musical *Mack and Mabel* stimulated revivals of the show. The 1983 free dance "Barnum" tightly integrated mime and dance, and was polished with the assistance of the show's London star, Michael Crawford. Their amateur competitive career climaxed at the Sarajevo Olympics in 1984. Their required Paso Doble strikingly depicted a bullfighter (Dean) and his cape (Torvill), but it was the free dance to Ravel's *Boléro* that captured a perfect score for artistic impression as well as the world's attention, becoming not just a sporting event but part of a collective cultural consciousness. As professionals, Torvill and Dean mounted their own ice shows and made several television specials. The most lavish of these was *Fire and Ice* (1986), which featured choreography by Graeme Murphy and, uniquely, Dean dancing without skates.

Christopher Dean's choreography contains several identifiable traits: carriage is straight-bodied and open; skaters frequently skate between or underneath each other's feet; and besides the traditional holds derived from ballroom or folk dancing, he employs three distinctive types—"behind-the-back," "leg," and "neck" holds. In the first, one partner holds the other with one or both arms behind the back; in the other two, one partner is held and guided by the leg (now illegal in amateur competition) or the neck (sometimes the cheek), often with the supported

TORVILL AND DEAN. Noted for elegance and precision, Torvill and Dean also excelled in dramatic numbers. "Missing" (1987), inspired by news stories of the fate of political dissidents in South America, was skated to "Dolencias," a song composed and performed by the popular South American music group Incantation. (Photograph courtesy of Torvill and Dean.)

partner stretched at an angle to the ice. The partners are equal in choreographic interest, and the woman frequently supports or guides the man. Overall, Dean's choreography gives a sense of continuously evolving movement that tends to relate literally to music. A striking exception is "Oscar Tango" (1990), with the sound largely provided by the skaters' blades.

Other significant choreography includes "Encounter" (1984), a highly detailed dance based on the simple motif of a bent knee; "Tribute to Fred and Ginger" (1987), a modernist's analytical interpretation of the Astaire-Rogers style; "Tribute to John Lennon" (1990), an exploration of action and reaction with overt physical aggression influenced by Édouard Lock; "Hat Trick" (1990), an intricate, amusing competition for a shiny red hat; "Iceworks" (1991), a choreography for video, incorporating skate sounds into the original music; and "Missing" (1987), a controversial piece that, despite Dean's refutation, draws on the theme, music, and choreographic motifs of Christopher Bruce's "Ghost Dances" (1981). Considered

as "Dean after Bruce," however, "Missing" is a masterly synthesis of the multicharacter one-act ballet into a brief duet. A revised version was performed in 1990 by the French-Canadian team of Paul Duchesnay and his sister Isabelle, to whom Dean was briefly married. The Duchesnays won the world championships in 1991 with a hastily choreographed "sequel," after judges and audiences resoundingly rejected the abstract "Mirror Image," which highlighted the siblings' physical similarity. Other notable choreography created by Dean for the Duchesnays includes two 1988 programs, a comic tango and "Tribal [Savage] Rites," skating's equivalent to *Le Sacre du Printemps*. Dean has also choreographed for other dance and pairs teams and has received a commission to create works for the English National Ballet.

TORVILL AND DEAN. The famous couple in "Rumba," an original dance performed to "History of Love" by Carlos Almaran. This number was part of their 1994 program at the British championships, where they won the gold medal; at the European championships, where they won the gold medal; and at the Winter Olympic Games in Lillehammer, Norway, where, to the dismay of millions of television viewers, they were denied the gold medal and were awarded the bronze instead. (Photograph courtesy of Torvill and Dean.)

BIBLIOGRAPHY

Copley-Graves, Lynn. *Figure Skating History: The Evolution of Dance on Ice.* Columbus, Ohio, 1992.

Hennessey, John. *Torvill and Dean.* London, 1983.

Hilton, Christopher. *Torvill and Dean: The Full Story.* London, 1994.

Torvill, Jayne, and Christopher Dean. *Facing the Music.* London and New York, 1995.

VIDEOTAPES. *Path to Perfection* (1984). *Fire and Ice* (1986). *Torvill and Dean and the Russian All-Stars* (1990). *The Best of Torvill and Dean* (1994), which includes *Path to Perfection, Fire and Ice,* and the 1994 British National Championships.

ROBYNN J. STILWELL

TOTENTANZ. *See* Dance of Death.

TOULOUSE-LAUTREC, HENRI DE (Henri-Marie-Raymond de Toulouse-Lautrec-Monfa; born 24 November 1864 in Albi, France, died 9 September 1901 in Malrome, France), French painter. The name Toulouse-Lautrec evokes one of the most memorable and crucial eras in the history of both art and dance. The artist's celebrated images of Parisian life during the city's Belle Époque captured the excitement and, at times, despair of a modern France emerging. Toulouse-Lautrec's art had its own modernity. In 1891 he was asked to design a poster for the highly contemporary nightclub Moulin Rouge. The poster, with its bold color, sensuous line, and distorted space, revolutionized poster design and not only succeeded in advertising the dance hall but also brought immortality to the dancer it pictured, La Goulue (Louise Weber). Toulouse-Lautrec's reputation was secured; from then on, despite repeated critical attacks for his unconventional painting style and indecorous subject matter, he was in great demand. His posters, paintings, and prints of leading dance halls and their stars ensured the widespread popularity of both the artist and his work throughout Paris and abroad.

Born into one of the oldest noble families in France, Toulouse-Lautrec enjoyed a childhood typical of his class. However, as an adolescent he broke his legs in two successive accidents only months apart. His legs ceased to grow, leaving him permanently deformed. Deprived of the sport and hunt he loved so well, he turned instead to art, and what was once a leisure activity became a serious pursuit.

At the urging of fellow students at the school of Fernand Cormon, Toulouse-Lautrec settled in the bohemian Montmartre section of Paris in 1884. He had received some formal academic training but now looked more toward the innovative approaches of contemporary illustrators, Édouard Manet and the impressionists, Japanese art, and the painter he most admired, Edgar Degas. Subscribing to the modern theories of such writers as the French symbolist poet Charles Baudelaire, who insisted that truth and beauty could exist only in an art based on direct experience, Toulouse-Lautrec immersed himself in the night life of Paris and portrayed its most celebrated as well as its most downtrodden residents and places.

With a sardonic wit and the sharp eye of a journalist, he pinpointed the salient aspects of character, movement, and ambience in each subject. More than a mere observer, Toulouse-Lautrec identified personally with the entertainers, prostitutes, and clowns he portrayed. They, too, were considered misfits and "could stand as equivalent to the derided, unrecognized artist" (Thompson, 1977).

Among his most memorable subjects, however, are images of dancers and the dance. Like Degas, Toulouse-Lautrec studied ballerinas but preferred the wild contortions of *quadrille* dancers such as La Goulue and her partner Valentin le Désossé. Sketching horses as a child had developed his lightning skill at capturing movement, and he would spend hours sketching in his favorite dance halls or cabarets. Among the sights that caught his attention were the spectacular theatrics of Loie Fuller's skirt dance. Her innovative lighting effects and undulating drapery are rendered with an economy of means in his famous lithograph *Miss Loie Fuller* (1893). He also went numerous times to see operetta star Marcelle Lender dance the bolero in Chilpéric: "I came only to see [her] back! Look at it, you will hardly ever see anything so wonderful again" (Sorell, 1953). Yet Toulouse-Lautrec was concerned with more than mere movement, stage effects, or physiognomy. His artistic greatness rested on his ability to express the character and soul of his subject, be it person or place. Jane Avril's face reveals the hardships of her early life, whether she is depicted dancing, entering the Moulin Rouge, or sitting in attendance at the Divan Japonais.

The art and life of Toulouse-Lautrec are inextricably linked. Unfortunately, the same lifestyle that produced such an original, poignant body of work eventually destroyed the artist. He continued to work after suffering a nervous breakdown in 1899 but died two years later from the effects of alcohol abuse.

[*See also* Prints and Drawings. *For related discussion, see* Artists and Dance.]

BIBLIOGRAPHY.   The basic text for the study of Toulouse-Lautrec is the comprehensive catalog in six volumes of all his work, M. G. Dortu, *Toulouse-Lautrec et son oeuvre* (New York, 1971). A useful, annotated list of characters and places that recur in Toulouse-Lautrec's work appears in *The Complete Paintings of Toulouse-Lautrec,* introduced by Denys Sutton (rev. ed., New York, 1987). Other sources include the following.

Adhémar, Jean. *Toulouse-Lautrec: His Complete Lithographs and Drypoints.* New York, 1965.

Amaya, Mario. "The Dance in Art, 1: 1850–1925" and "The Dance in Art, 3: The Little Genius of Montmartre." *Dance and Dancers* 11 (December 1960): 18–23+; 12 (April 1961): 18–21+.

Goldschmidt, Lucien, and Herbert Schimmel, eds. *Unpublished Correspondence of Henri de Toulouse-Lautrec*. London, 1969.

Murray, G. B. "The Theme of the Naturalist Quadrille in the Art of Toulouse-Lautrec: Its Origins, Meaning, Evolution, and Relationship to Later Realism." *Arts Magazine* 55 (December 1980).

Sorell, Walter. "The Dancers of Toulouse Lautrec." *Dance Magazine* (March 1953): 26–29.

Stuckey, Charles F. *Toulouse-Lautrec: Paintings*. Chicago, 1979. Exhibition catalogue.

Thompson, Richard. *Toulouse-Lautrec*. London, 1977.

ELLEN BREITMAN

TOUMANOVA, TAMARA (Tamara Vladimirovna Tumanova; born 2 March 1919 in Tyumen, Siberia, died 29 May 1996 in Santa Monica, California), Russian-American ballerina. Toumanova was born near Shanghai in a boxcar of a train in which her parents were leaving Russia after the Revolution. In China, where the family stayed for a few years, she received her first lessons in ballet when she was barely more than a toddler. After the family moved to Paris, she renewed her ballet training with Olga Preobrajenska in 1924, when she was five years old. The following year she was chosen by Anna Pavlova to dance in a benefit performance at the Trocadéro, and by the time she was ten, in 1929, she had developed such a formidable technique and charismatic presence that she was cast in a leading role in *L'Éventail de Jeanne*, a ballet with a cast of children, at the Paris Opera. André Levinson, a leading critic of the time, declared that the extraordinary virtuosity of this "prodigious child" was not only astounding but also somewhat frightening.

In 1931 Toumanova was invited to join the Ballets Russes de Monte Carlo by George Balanchine, ballet master of the company being formed under the direction of René Blum and Colonel Wassily de Basil. When the company made its debut in the spring of 1932, Toumanova, at age thirteen, was one of its three "baby ballerinas" (along with Irina Baronova, thirteen, and Tatiana Riabouchinska, fifteen). She created roles in four works by Balanchine—*Cotillon*, *La Concurrence*, *Le Bourgeois Gentilhomme*, and *Suite de Danse*—and in Léonide Massine's *Jeux d'Enfants*. When Balanchine left the company at the end of 1932 to form Les Ballets 1933, Toumanova went with him as leading dancer, appearing in Paris and London and creating principal roles in his *Mozartiana* and *Les Songes*. She returned to the Ballets Russes de Monte Carlo in October 1933, during its first London season at the Alhambra, and created roles in the first and fourth movements of Massine's *Choreartium*.

For the next several years Toumanova remained with the de Basil company, which from 1934 to 1937 was billed as the Ballets Russes de Colonel W. de Basil, dancing leading roles in the repertory and creating roles in several important new ballets, among them, Massine's *Le Bal* (1935) and *Symphonie Fantastique* (1936). In 1938 she joined the

TOUMANOVA. A studio portrait, posed *sur les pointes*, reveals Toumanova's fabled beauty. (Photograph by Maurice Seymour; used by permission.)

new Ballet Russe de Monte Carlo, headed by Massine as artistic director and Sergei Denham as managing director. During this company's famous London season in June 1938 she appeared for the first time in the title role of *Giselle*, for which she was to be acclaimed throughout her career. The following year, 1939, found her in New York in a supporting role in the Broadway musical *Stars in Your Eyes*, directed by Joshua Logan and starring Ethel Merman and Jimmy Durante.

At the end of 1939, as war threatened to engulf Europe, Toumanova rejoined the de Basil company, by then called Original Ballet Russe, and appeared with it on tour in Australia, the United States, and Canada. Her affinity for Balanchine's choreography and his appreciation of her as a performer were notable in the dances he created for her in the third and fourth movements of his *Balustrade* (1941), set to Igor Stravinsky's Concerto in D for violin and orchestra. When her contract with de Basil expired in March 1941, she left his company to rejoin Denham's Ballet Russe de Monte Carlo, where she remained as ballerina until the end of the 1942 season.

Thereafter, Toumanova became internationally famous as a guest artist with numerous ballet companies in North and South America and in Europe. Among others, she danced with Ballet Theatre (1944–1945), in New York; with the San Francisco Ballet (1948); with the Paris Opera Ballet (1947, 1950, 1959); with Le Grand Ballet du Marquis de Cuevas (1949); with La Scala Ballet (1951, 1952, 1956), in Milan; and with London's Festival Ballet (1952, 1954–1955). In 1947, at the Paris Opera, she created the spectacular adagio role of the ballerina in the second movement of Balanchine's *Le Palais de Cristal* (later called *Symphony in C*). From 1959 onward she made frequent appearances in concert performances, often with her partner Vladimir Oukhtomsky. Acclaimed for her beauty and her acting skills as well as her dancing, Toumanova also appeared in numerous films: *Days of Glory* (1944, the producer of which, Casey Robinson, she married that year), *Tonight We Sing* (1953), *Deep in My Heart* (1954), *Invitation to the Dance* (directed by Gene Kelly; 1956), *Torn Curtain* (1966), and *The Private Life of Sherlock Holmes* (1970) as well as *Spanish Fiesta* (1941), the film of Massine's *Capriccio Espagnol*.

Toumanova's beauty and virtuosity as a ballerina were coupled with great versatility. Although her popular image was as a tragic or romantic dancer in the grand manner, she danced comedy roles with great success. Among her finest creations were the Girl in Balanchine's *Cotillon* (1932), the Beloved in Massine's *Symphonie Fantastique* (1936), and Potiphar's Wife in Margarete Wallmann's production of *Legend of Joseph* (1951), at La Scala in Milan. One of her greatest triumphs was the title role of *Phèdre*, staged at the Paris Opera in 1950 by Serge Lifar and Jean Cocteau to a score by Georges Auric. In addition to her Giselle, Toumanova was widely recognized as one of the foremost interpreters of Odette-Odile in *Swan Lake* and of the Miller's Wife in Massine's *Le Tricorne*.

BIBLIOGRAPHY

Anastos, Peter. "A Conversation with Tamara Toumanova." *Ballet Review* 11 (Winter 1984): 33–57.

Anderson, Jack. *The One and Only: The Ballet Russe de Monte Carlo.* New York, 1981.

Finch, Tamara. "The First Baby Ballerinas." *The Dancing Times* (August 1985): 952–954.

García-Márquez, Vicente. *The Ballets Russes: Colonel de Basil's Ballets Russes de Monte Carlo, 1932–1952.* New York, 1990.

García-Márquez, Vicente. *Massine: A Biography.* New York, 1995.

Healy, Katherine. "The Baby Ballerina on Trial." *Dance Now* 2 (Summer 1993): 19–27.

"An Informal Interview with Tamara Toumanova" (parts 1–2). *Dance Digest* (March–April 1957).

Lesser, Wendy. "Tamara Toumanova: Portrait of a Ballerina." *Dance Ink* (Fall 1994): 4–5.

Mason, Francis. "Tamara Toumanova (1916–1996)." *Ballet Review* 24.3 (Fall 1996): 35–62.

Sorley Walker, Kathrine. *De Basil's Ballets Russes.* New York, 1983.

Swisher, Viola Helgi. "Tamara Toumanova." *Dance Magazine* (September 1970): 46–63.

Tracy, Robert, and Sharon Delano. *Balanchine's Ballerinas: Conversations with the Muses.* New York, 1983.

KATHRINE SORLEY WALKER

TOURS EN L'AIR. *See* Ballet Technique, *article on* Turning Movements.

TOVIL. In Sri Lanka, one of the most dramatic forms of dance occurs in exorcist healing rituals variously called *tovil, thovil, toile, yakuma, yakun-natima,* and *yakun-natanava.* The *tovil* is part of the folk tradition of Sinhala-speaking Buddhists, and though not officially a part of Buddhism has been greatly influenced by it.

Techniques of *tovil* singing and dancing are handed down from teacher to pupil and from father to son (women do not perform); these traditions are said to be two thousand years old. Influences that are also identifiable come from South India, Malaysia, and Europe (the Portuguese established colonies on the island of Ceylon [now Sri Lanka] in 1505).

The *tovil* is performed by exorcists, combatting diseases believed to be caused by demons and ghosts. A temporary arena symbolizing the forest, a favorite haunting place for demons, is prepared on level ground near the patient's house, with a canopy, shrines, and trays for spirit offerings decorated with leaves, strips of banana stem, and coconut fronds. A pallet for the patient is set at one end of the arena. Relatives and friends gather around to offer their sympathies to the patient and to enjoy the performance, which runs from dusk to dawn.

The senior exorcist is usually accompanied by several younger men, who do most of the singing and dancing, and by one or two drummers. The dancers wear costumes and facial makeup; they frequently hold tufts of young coconut leaves or burning torches soaked in coconut oil. Smoke and the smell of incense fill the air.

The dancing begins slowly and grows progressively more energetic, sometimes led by the beat of the drums and sometimes in counterpoint to it. Singing, the chanting of spells and charms, and presentations to gods and demons are interlaced with vigorous dancing and loud drumming. The atmosphere is informal, with people coming and going, visiting and sleeping, eating and playing cards; yet excitement and tension build as the ceremony progresses to a dramatic conclusion. The patient may become possessed by a demon and dance to the rhythm of the drums. The patient must be settled, the gods appeased, and the demons conjured, all before sunrise, if a cure is to be achieved. The conclusion to the ceremony is a series of comic masked dances designed to depict and to placate a particularly nasty set of disease-causing demons.

TOVIL. The exorcist-dancer Samapala, performing the *pandam paliya* (torch ritual). (Photograph from the archives of The Asia Society, New York.)

Obeyesekere, Gananath. "The Ritual Drama of the Sanni Demons: Collective Representations of Disease in Ceylon." *Comparative Studies in Society and History* 11.2 (1969): 174–216.
Pertold, Otaker. *Ceremonial Dances of the Sinhalese* (1930). Colombo, 1973.
Seneviratna, Anuradha. *Traditional Dance of Sri Lanka*. Colombo, 1984.

FILM. Yvonne Hannemann, *The Work of Gomis* (Oakland, Calif.: Serious Business Co.).

ARCHIVES. The following museums contain major collections of Sri Lankan dance masks: American Museum of Natural History, New York; Canadian Museum of Civilization, Hull, Quebec; Chicago Field Museum; Ethnographic Museum, Stockholm; Hamburgisches Museum für Volkerkunde, Hamburg; Horniman Museum, London; Museum für Volkerkunde, Berlin; Museum für Volkerkunde, Leipzig; Museum of Anthropology, Vancouver, B.C.; Museum of Mankind, London; National Museum, Colombo; Science Museum, London; Smithsonian Institution, Washington, D.C.; Ubersee Museum, Bremen.

M. M. AMES

The *tovil* drum, the principal musical instrument, is cylindrical, about one foot in diameter and three feet long; it is fitted with leather and strung together with hide, which can be tightened or loosened to vary the sound. A reed flute, bells, and jingles tied to the arms and ankles complete the dancer's equipment.

The *tovil* is a multipurpose performance: a socially integrative and entertaining public gathering of friends and relatives, a ritual dramatization of illness, a cathartic and therapeutic encounter for the patient, and a theological discourse. As monstrous as the demons may appear, they can be combated and subjugated if the proper procedures are followed, and so, by analogy, can other misfortunes of daily life.

Tovil is today thought to be a dying art, gradually being replaced by Buddhist pietism, Western medicine, and faith-healing cults. The drums can still be heard occasionally in rural areas, however, and—as one of the ironies of the modern world—*tovil* may be undergoing a modest revival as a form of tourist entertainment in urban areas.

[*For articles on other dance traditions in Sri Lanka, see also* Kandyan Dance; Kandy Perahera; Kohomba Kan Kariya; *and* Ves Dance. *For related discussion, see* Costume in Asian Traditions *and* Mask and Makeup, *article on* Asian Traditions.]

BIBLIOGRAPHY
Ames, M. M. "Tovil: Exorcism by White Magic." *Natural History* 87.1 (1978): 42–49.
Ames, M. M. "Tovil: The Ritual Chanting, Dance, and Drumming of Exorcism in Sri Lanka." *International Journal of Asian Studies* 2.2 (1982).
Gunawardana, A. J. *Theatre in Sri Lanka*. Colombo, 1976.
Loviconi, Alain. *Masques et exorcismes de Ceylan*. Paris, 1981.

TRADITIONAL DANCE. *See* European Traditional Dance; Folk Dance History. *See also* Methodologies in the Study of Dance, *article on* Ethnography; *and the folk and traditional dance articles within individual country entries.*

TRANCE DANCE. An altered (or alternate) state of consciousness (ASC) is frequently associated with dance, particularly in the context of religious rituals. The result is often called *trance dance*. Gregory Bateson (1975) writes, "The use of dance as an entry into ecstasy and an ego-alien world is ancient and perhaps worldwide." Adrienne Kaeppler (1978) describes the aesthetic experience connected with dance as "a heightened state of experience [that] may be related to trance." "Ecstasy" and "trance" as used here refer to forms of ASC.

An ASC is characterized as a deviation from the ordinary states in any or all aspects of mental functioning; it may involve changes in sensations and perceptions, including perceptions of time and space, or modifications of thought processes, memory, and awareness of self and others. Arnold Ludwig (1966) notes changes in meaning or significance, a sense of the ineffable, feelings of rejuvenation, and hypersuggestibility.

ASCs have been classified by different criteria, such as the manner of induction, the sociocultural context, or the categories used in native explanatory systems. Ludwig, who groups ASCs by the means used to produce them, distinguishes between states induced by altered levels of either internal or external stimuli and those induced by somatopsychological factors. The latter include drugs, physical disease (such as fever), and mental illness (such as hallucinatory or delusional states of psychosis).

The states treated here, even those that may be considered pathological in nature, are culturally interpreted, patterned, and controlled. They may be grouped by sociocultural context as either sacred or profane. In the sacred sense, trance dances are most frequently found in connection with either worship or curing; in secular contexts, they are usually forms of entertainment. Sacred ritual, however, often evolves into entertainment, and often the line between the two cannot be clearly drawn.

When ASC is linked to dance, it is usually also related to music. Gilbert Rouget (1985) established a music-based classification. More restricted than Ludwig's, it deals primarily with intentionally produced states. Rouget distinguishes between two states, ecstasy and trance. Ecstasy is characterized by immobility, silence, solitude, sensory deprivation, absence of seizures, heightened memory, and hallucination. Ecstatic states result from various types of meditation and are experienced by mystics in certain religions. Ecstasy thus defined is not included in this discussion.

In contrast to ecstasy, Rouget defines trance as typically involving movement, noise, sensory overstimulation, seizures, amnesia, and the absence of hallucination. Possession trance and shamanistic trance are the two principal subtypes, and each relates distinctively with the invisible world. In possession trance, spirits are believed to visit humans, acting through the bodies of possession trancers. In shamanistic trance, the shaman leaves the body to encounter various spiritual forces or beings. Because the shaman typically brings back messages from these spirit journeys, the absence of hallucination and memory is a questionable criterion for this classification. Rouget also finds a difference between the use of music in the two trance forms: the shaman is his own musician, usually singing and drumming, whereas the music for possession trance is provided by others.

Rouget's classification largely parallels one by Bourguignon (1973) based on native categories. She distinguishes between those states interpreted by participants as due to possession by spirits and those not so interpreted. Rouget's "ecstasy" and "shamanistic trance" belong to this second category, as do many nonintentional states, whether they are religious or secular. Bourguignon's classification depends not on features visible to or measurable by an observer, but on the explanation of the states by the cultural group in which they occur.

Possession trance in this classification is not simply an impersonation of other beings by a human actor but rather is a behavior that is culturally defined as being caused by the actual presence of these beings in the actor. Such a trance, which is frequently followed by amnesia, may include activities uncharacteristic of the individual: transsexual behaviors, eating foods considered repulsive, or performing spectacular feats. Such activities provide evidence to trancers of the presence of other beings in their own bodies. As such, possession trance is quite distinct experientially and cognitively from other forms of impersonation, such as conscious imitation or impersonation in a theatrical performance or a masking ritual. A mask may simply hide the identity of the actor or serve as an aid to imitation; if a spirit is believed to be present, it is generally thought to reside in the mask, not in the impersonator's body as in possession trance. Masked actors may experience an ASC, but this phenomenon has not been thoroughly investigated.

An ASC may be voluntary or involuntary. The demonic possessions recorded in the European and Euro-American Christian and Jewish traditions are typically, in their first manifestations, involuntary. Attempts at exorcism generally involve inducing an ASC (calling the spirits to be expelled). Such possessions—which are negative, undesired states, whether spontaneous or voluntary—do not involve music or dance. Apparent exceptions are the dancing manias of the late Middle Ages in Germany and the Low Countries and twentieth-century tarantism of southern Italy. In these cases, the sound of music was said to cause uncontrollable dancing, but music and dance were also used to cure the possessed.

Possession trance rituals occur in all parts of the world, all periods of history, and societies of various degrees of complexity and modernization. They are widespread in Africa—examples include Hausa *bori; zār* in Ethiopia, Somalia, Sudan, and Egypt; and *orisha* rituals among the Yoruba of Nigeria, among many others. African rituals were brought to the Americas with the slave trade and now appear in newer forms such as Santería in Cuba and Florida, Vodun *(vodoun)* in Haiti and New York, Shango in Trinidad and in a great variety of Afro-Brazilian religions, such as Candomblé, Macumba, Umbanda, Xângo, and others. Throughout Southeast Asia, possession trance is present in Bali, Malaysia, Thailand, Myanmar (formerly Burma), Vietnam, Cambodia and Laos, as well as in Sri Lanka. Such practices are known from European antiquity—for example, in the Dionysian cults of Greece. They also occur in movements of radical religious innovation, such as the eighteenth-century Shakers in England and America, and in nativistic movements, such as the Ghost Dance of the Plains Indians in the late nineteenth century. [*See* Ghost Dance.] Nonpossession trance is characteristic of Native American societies. It is often linked to hunting and gathering societies, while possession trance is typical of agricultural and pastoral groups.

Shamanism is or was widespread in northern Europe and Asia and among the native peoples of the Americas, Australia, and New Guinea. In Korea and Nepal, for example, some ritual practices combine features of both shamanistic and possession trance. Nepalese shamans experience possession trance early in their spiritual development; after additional levels of initiation, they engage in spirit voyages as part of their healing rituals.

Dance and ASCs typically occur in the larger context of rituals that may include sacrifice, feasting, curing, divining, praying, preaching, dramatic performances, spectacular acts (including proofs of invulnerability), acrobatics, and sleight-of-hand. They thus constitute a narrow range of activities within a larger field.

The relationship between dance and ASC is complex and variable. Adrienne Kaeppler (1978) notes that "trance and other altered states of consciousness are often associated with structured movement systems, yet they usually are not dance." She asks whether dance is created only when the participants themselves consider the movements to belong to a stylized category that corresponds to the Western concept of dance. Judith Lynne Hanna (1979) introduces a related problem by describing dance as involving the "manipulation of ordinary motor activities within an aesthetic domain." Although some structured movements occur frequently in conjunction with ASCs, they may not be defined by the participating group as dance or as occurring in an aesthetic domain.

Jeannette Henney (1973) has described possession trance in a fundamentalist Christian church on the Caribbean island of Saint Vincent, in which worshipers seek to experience the presence of the Holy Spirit during certain rituals. At the incipient stage of possession trance, individuals exhibit random behavior, such as bending at the waist or flexing the knees. At the second stage, each person repeats his or her own action pattern in unison with the movement and breathing of others. Although Henney writes that "people move as if in a dance line," depicts a "choral dance aspect of the possession trance phenomenon," and elsewhere refers to the patterns of movement as "aesthetically pleasing," neither she nor the participants appear to consider possession trance behavior as a form of dance. Nonetheless, it incorporates both ASC and a structured movement system.

Central to the experience reported by these Saint Vincent possession trancers is the sense of "being shaken," which starts as a "trembling within." The tremor is visible to the observer. Trembling as a feature of ASCs, at significant stages or throughout the experience, has been reported in many parts of the world.

Describing the ceremonial dances of the Kwakiutl of British Columbia, Franz Boas (1972) notes the "quivering of hands as well as the entire body." He remarks that "all these vibrations require a definite ecstatic quality in order to be executed." The participants recognize that the vibrations result involuntarily from a certain level of excitement that is recognized and named as an aspect of the dances.

Among the Kwakiutl, quivering is a patterned part of the dance. Elsewhere it is a sign that an ASC has been achieved, but it is not part of any choreography. Quivering can be seen vividly in a film by Jean Rouch, *Les maîtres fous*, which records possession trance rituals of the Haouka cult in Accra, Ghana. Here the only element resembling dance consists of a group of participants walking around in a circle to the sound of a violin. Those about to go into trance drop out of the circle. When the ASC begins, the camera clearly shows a series of small tremors, beginning in the feet and fingers of a seated individual, rising through the legs and arms to the trunk and the head. The tremor is typical and expected, but neither rhythmical nor a dance pattern. It does modify the behavior of the possession trancers while the ASC lasts: ordinary motor behavior, such as walking, becomes extraordinary, modified by the tremor and by a certain staccato quality that reveals a substantial effort to maintain control.

Tremor may also be used as an intentional means to induce trance. Bateson describes how little girls in Bali are put into trance in order to dance as if possessed by *dedari* ("angels"). Puppets, representing the angels, are made to dance by involuntary twitching (clonus) in the arms of the two men who support them suspended on a string between two bamboo poles. Grasping one of the poles, a girl is shaken violently by the twitching of the men's arms. With the pole, she beats out a few bars of the song being sung, falls back in a trance, is dressed for her role, and then dances in trance. She has been entered by the spirit of the angels, the state being induced through the pole by a form of contagion. An illustration (Bateson, 1975, plate 18) shows several Balinese girls being put into trance simultaneously. Here, shaking, brought about externally and mechanically, is preliminary to the trance. Child possession trancers are rare in any society. The Balinese girls dance with great balance and grace, often standing on the shoulders of men.

As they relate to ASCs, shaking and tremors may also occur outside the context of dance, as in the seated drumming of Nepali shamans. Larry Peters (1981) describes how his own conscious shaking developed into an automatic process, so that "after a few moments my whole body began to shake and I bounced all over the room."

Another frequent and characteristic motor pattern associated with ASCs is motion of the head. Eric Dodds (1951) notes that maenads, ancient Greek possession trancers, are often depicted in Greek art with tossed-back heads and hair swinging loose. Similar trance behavior is observed in ritual states in many parts of the world (for example, in Balinese *keris* dancers) as well as in nineteenth-century French clinical observations of hysterics.

Three types of relations between dance and ASC can be distinguished—dance as an expression of an ASC, as a means of producing an ASC, and as a means of controlling an ASC. Such distinctions are useful for ordering available information, although some categories inevitably overlap.

Dance as expression of an ASC occurs in two subforms, spontaneous trance dancing and intentionally induced ASC. In the first, the ASC is accompanied by extraordinary motion patterns such as whirling, hopping, jumping, trembling, twitching, staccato motions, convulsive movements, crawling, head-tossing, and grimacing. The interpretation of such behavior depends on the cultural context. Does it appear to be uncontrolled? Does it deviate significantly from behavior patterns deemed appropriate for the occasion? Are uncontrolled deviations interpreted as spirit interventions? Do they occur in the presence of music? If so, they may be considered dance of either human or supernatural origin. Spirit entities reveal themselves by the dancer's behavior, which mimes spirit characteristics.

The actions of Saint Vincent possession trancers include singing and clapping, and the extraordinary motion patterns are said to be caused by the presence of the Holy Spirit in the participants. In medieval dancing manias and southern Italian Tarantism, dance is the irresistible response to music. Included in Tarantism, as Michell and André Martin (1975) observe, was imitation of the behavior of the tarantula, whose bite was believed to cause the condition. [*See* Tarantella.]

In an example of an ASC resulting from intentional induction, Balinese girl-trancers express ASCs as complex acrobatic dancing after an initial seizure revealed by a fall. Bourguignon (1965) describes the hopping and whirling that result from the hypnotic induction of a Haitian possession trancer. Barbara Wright (1980) notes that in the *main petri* healing rituals of Kelantan, Malaysia, the onset of possession trance is signaled by dancing. At different points in the rituals the male healer or the female patient dance in trance.

In many possession trance rituals, the behavior of the dancers reveals the characteristics and identity of the individual spirit entities who are impersonated. In Greece, especially Macedonia, firewalking is practiced annually in honor of Saint Constantine and Saint Helen by dancers in trance who believe they are under the saints' control and protection. Firewalking occurs in many parts of the world and in different systems of belief. Like other spectacular trance activities, such as balancing on blades or stabbing oneself without experiencing harm, it involves both skill and fearlessness. [*See* Anastenárides.]

Michael Lambeck (1981) describes a possession trance ritual in the Comoro Islands. Those who are possessed dance in the fashion characteristic of a particular group of spirits, yet each adds personal touches as well:

They moved in short steps or hops, a kind of light bounce, as if they were not touching the ground. Each dancer faced in one direction, moving two or three steps to the right, then rotating the upper part of the body, went two or three steps to the left, rotated again and turned to the right, so that the eventual path was a series of zigzags.   (Lambeck, 1981)

This ritual focuses on healing, but at the end of a long night of dance, sacrifice, and personal consultation, it ends in lively entertainment.

Dance may be used formally to train dancers to enter an ASC, as is done by the Mevlevi dervishes of Konya, Turkey, who induce an ASC by means of a vigorous whirling dance. Esther Pressel (1974) observed special training sessions for novices in the Umbanda cult of São Paulo, Brazil. Among the dance-related techniques used are several leading to disturbances of balance and a loosening of contact with the environment, by spinning or rocking on the heels, followed by head- and chest-jerking movements that signal possession. Dancers also learn the special characteristics of each class of spirits, such as the stooped postures of old black spirits *(prêtos velhos)*, or the upright, virile carriage of Indians *(caboclos)*.

In ceremonial settings, induction of possession trance by a spinning dance is usually accompanied by polyrhythmic drumming, singing, and handclapping. Besides affecting balance and contact with the environment, vigorous dancing may also cause hyperventilation and euphoria.

Self-torture to induce visionary trance is rare in dance, with the important exception of the Sun Dance of the Great Plains, in which male supplicants for power sometimes danced while attached to a central pole by thongs passed through the skin of the breast or back until the skin broke. Attempts have recently been made to revive this practice, which was prohibited by the U.S. government at the beginning of the twentieth century.

The imposition of rhythm and structure on involuntary movement exercises an important control function, so that individual erratic behavior becomes structured and responsive to external cues. This control may be achieved through collective behavior, as in Saint Vincent, or through the use of music and ritualization, as in Tarantism.

Trance dance in some cultures is used as therapy. In the Brazilian Umbanda cult, possession trancers are mediums who deal with the afflictions of others. Many, however, join the cult to mitigate their own problems, and one of the symptoms of undeveloped mediumship is a spontaneous, uncontrolled ASC. Learning trance dancing in a controlled ritual environment offers a way to transform an involuntary state into a controlled, voluntary one. David Akstein (1974), a Brazilian psychiatrist influenced by Umbanda, reports on a method called terpsychore-trance therapy, which applies trance dance techniques to secular psychotherapy.

Trance dance also functions as entertainment in both traditional and modern contexts. Most possession trance rituals, in which diverse characters are acted out, are likely to include amusing or trickster personages. For observers, possession trance rituals often serve as entertainment. In Java and Bali, performances by folk trancers who act out various animal-spirit roles are popular. Balinese traditional kris trance rituals are now sometimes performed for tourists, as are staged ceremonies of Haitain Vodun. Firewalking is frequently performed for entertainment and, in the United States, as a sport as well as a spiritual exercise in the context of New Age religions, as described by Danforth.

An ASC may occur in the context of secular dancing, such as rock dancing, with loud and rhythmic music and large crowds in prolonged contact, to which young people come with high anticipation. In such cases, dance appears to be secondary to other factors in inducing the ASC.

[*For further discussion of related issues, see* Brazil, *article on* Ritual and Popular Dance; Shamanism; Vodun; *and* Zār.]

BIBLIOGRAPHY

Akstein, David. "Psychosocial Perspectives on the Application of Terpsychoretrancetherapy." *Psychopathologie Africaine* 10 (1974).

Bateson, Gregory. "Some Components of Socialization for Trance." *Ethos* 3 (Summer 1975).

Boas, Franz. "Dance and Music in the Life of the Northwest Coast Indians of North America (Kwakiutl)." In *The Function of Dance in Human Society*, edited by Franziska Boas. 2d ed. Brooklyn, 1972.

Bourguignon, Erika. "The Self, the Behavioral Environment, and the Theory of Spirit Possession." In *Context and Meaning in Cultural Anthropology*, edited by Melford E. Spiro. New York, 1965.

Bourguignon, Erika. Introduction to *Religion, Altered States of Consciousness, and Social Change*, edited by Erika Bourguignon. Columbus, Ohio, 1973.

de Martino, Ernesto. *La terra del rimorso*. Milan, 1961.

Dodds, E. R. *The Greeks and the Irrational*. Berkeley, 1951.

Hanna, Judith Lynne. *To Dance Is Human*. Austin, 1979.

Hecker, J. F. C. *The Dancing Mania of the Middle Ages* (1837). Translated by B. G. Babington. New York, 1970.

Henney, Jeannette H. "The Shakers of St. Vincent: A Stable Religion." In *Religion, Altered States of Consciousness, and Social Change*, edited by Erika Bourguignon. Columbus, Ohio, 1973.

Kaeppler, Adrienne L. "Dance in Anthropological Perspective." *Annual Review of Anthropology* 7 (1978).

Lambeck, Michael. *Human Spirits: A Cultural Account of Trance in Mayotte*. Cambridge, 1981.

Ludwig, Arnold M. "Altered States of Consciousness." *Archives of General Psychiatry* 15 (1966).

Martin, Michelle, and André Martin. *Les noires vallées du repentir*. Paris, 1975.

Peters, Larry. *Ecstasy and Healing in Nepal*. Malibu, 1981.

Pressel, Esther. "Umbanda Trance and Possession in São Paulo, Brazil." In *Trance, Healing, and Hallucination*, by Felicitas D. Goodman et al. New York, 1974.

Rouget, Gilbert. *Music and Trance*. Chicago, 1985.

Wright, Barbara S. "Dance Is the Cure: The Arts as Metaphor for Healing in Kelantanese Malay Spirit Exorcisms." *Dance Research Journal* 12 (Spring-Summer 1980): 3–10.

FILMS.   Maya Deren, *Divine Horsemen: The Living Gods of Haiti* (1947–1952). Gregory Bateson and Margaret Mead, *Trance and Dance in Bali* (1951). Jean Rouch, *Les maîtres fous* (1954). John K. Marshall, *N/um T'chai* (1957). Peter Adair, *The Holy Ghost People* (1967). P. C. Haramis and K. Kakouri, *The Anastenaria* (1969). Karen Kramer, *The Jolo Serpent Handlers* (n.d.). Karen Kramer, *To Serve the Gods* (n.d.). *Sucking Doctor* (n.d.).

ERIKA BOURGUIGNON

TRAVESTY originally signified a male playing a female role *(en travesti)*. This Western tradition of female impersonation originated in ancient Greece, where women were excluded from the stage and male actors and the chorus made use of masks and female costumes to portray women. The early Christian church perpetuated and dogmatized the prohibition of women onstage while, despite antitheatrical polemics, incorporating dramatic forms in its liturgy—mimetic processions, morality plays, and the like. Priests used music, dance, mime, costume, masks, and eventually elaborate scenic effects to vivify biblical history and to celebrate feast days within the cathedral.

Women played no part in the services or offices of the church, so the acting was done by clerics and choir boys; when such presentations were expanded to take place in the open air, away from church ritual, religious content and custom ensured the continuation of an all-male tradition. Yet records show that women occasionally took part. In doing so they were caught in a stigmatic double bind: considered unworthy of the somewhat priestly function of impersonating biblical characters, at the same time they were considered in jeopardy by association with the so-called unchaste and immodest practices of the theater. Because the idea was repugnant (running counter to anything that ordinary Christian folk felt about women) and because actors had no social standing outside the arena in which they played, women who joined them were regarded as disreputable. Until the late seventeenth century in Europe, it seemed quite natural and acceptable for men to play female parts.

In Shakespeare's time (1564–1616), boys were trained in the techniques of female impersonation. In Renaissance court spectacles, masks permitted young men to convincingly portray women in danced *entrées* and tableaux. In these private entertainments, women performed alongside men as well as with men *en travesti*, avoiding only the comic or grotesque roles that were generally taken by professional male performers. Men danced female roles without the embarrassment of any sexual ambiguity or social stigma as a matter of theatrical convention that was disassociated from private conduct.

The English Puritans of the seventeenth century became responsible for the demise of boy actors *en travesti* and the gradual substitution of women playing female roles throughout most of Europe. They based their attack on the theater, and on female impersonation in particular, on the Bible: "The woman shall not wear that which pertaineth unto a man, neither shall a man put on a woman's garment; for all that do so are abomination unto the Lord thy God" (*Deut.* 22.5). English theaters were closed and all public playgoing and acting banned between 1642 and 1660, the period of the Commonwealth. This brief period of prohibition seems to have been sufficient to interrupt the tradition of female impersonation. After it for the first time actresses came into vogue—even playing boys' parts on occasion and to some degree avoiding the brunt of antitheatrical stigma. By the end of the seventeenth century, men *en travesti* ceased to perform on the refined, serious level that derived from the Elizabethan period and began to burlesque female characters. Very soon the unprecedented popularity of female ballet dancers (Marie Sallé, Marie Camargo, Marie-Madeleine Guimard, among them) further diminished the demand for men *en travesti*. The prohibition against actresses persisted in Italy, however, and male travesty remained a matter of papal preference there until the close of the eighteenth century.

The biblical proscription against cross-dressing was applied with full force to women and interpreted to mean that pants were an absolute masculine prerogative not to be imitated by women, even concealed under skirts as underclothing. The separation of a woman's legs by any form of clothing was thought to be obscene and unholy, and underdrawers were not accepted as a respectable and conventional necessity until the middle of the nineteenth century. However, from the beginning of the eighteenth century, dancers and acrobats wore precautionary drawers *(caleçon de précaution)* while performing. These were a feature of European theatrical life that contributed to the association between sexual depravity and performers in the public's imagination.

The slightly perverse eroticism of this concealed transvestism—especially stimulating because it was revealed only now and then—was the basis on which actresses and female dancers began to impersonate men on the stage toward the end of the eighteenth century. Wearing "false disguise" with no pretense at concealing their real sexual identity, they exploited the salacious attitude that men held toward women in any form of male garb. Their costumes were androgynous adaptations of historical male fashions, designed to emphasize female proportions and, in particular, to show the forbidden upper leg to advantage in tights.

For about thirty years (1780–1810), male and female dancers impersonating one another performed together, sharing the stage with dancers not *en travesti*. Gradually, however, through this same period female dancers began to develop the use of pointe work, and by the 1830s the Romantic period found its fullest expression in the *ballet*

TRAVESTY. Janet Hiligsberg *en travesti* in the ballet *Le Jaloux Puni*, which premiered 1 June 1793 at the King's Theatre, London. This engraving is by Jean Condé after H. de Janvry. (Courtesy of Madison U. Sowell and Debra H. Sowell, Brigham Young University, Provo, Utah.)

blanc—legions of white-clad sylphs floated in nocturnal light. Except for a few male dancers of extraordinary talent, women dominated the Romantic ballet; male dancers were relegated to the role of *porteur*, whose function was to make the ballerina appear weightless and effortless in her performance. Since supported adagio and lifts were such an essential factor in the choreographic illusion of weightlessness, male dancers, though somewhat ignored by audiences, remained essential to the *ballet blanc* and women *en travesti* appeared in numbers only after *ballet blanc* began to go out of fashion.

In the meantime, actresses *en travesti* were by no means a novelty. In the 1817 London production of *Giovanni in London*, the actress-singer Madame Vestris played in doublet and hose, sporting a plumed hat and brandishing a riding crop with such success that she continued in similar roles for twenty years.

About 1860, when the public began to tire of the ballet, choreographers experimented freely with novelty, such as *danseuses de travesti*. Because two women could not execute the lifts that were possible with a male partner, pas de deux *en travesti* required a more even distribution of choreographic display. Ballet masters concentrated on the acrobatic possibilities of sustained pointe work, such as multiple pirouettes, extended balances, and hops on toe, new steps of tour de force that could be done in unison to display the rather full-blown charms of both dancers. Female ballet costumes became somewhat abbreviated and frankly erotic, and the style favored for travesty was a loosely adapted version of the already anachronistic *style troubadour* worn by male actors. This was a fanciful combination of medieval and Renaissance fashions—a tunic or a doublet and hose, padded, puffed, or slashed, with a plume-decorated beret. In adapting this costume to women, personal attraction played a more important part in the choice of design than did historical accuracy. Instead of any effort to simulate masculine proportions, waists were corseted, hips were padded, and everything possible was done to enhance the curvilinear proportions of the female anatomy.

The ballet spectacles that followed the Romantic period—those produced by Luigi Manzotti in Italy, those of

TRAVESTY. In this scene from a Royal Ballet production of *La Fille Mal Gardée*, Merle Park appears as Lise with Stanley Holden, *en travesti*, as Lise's mother, the Widow Simone. David Blair observes from the loft. (Photograph by Houston Rogers; used by permission of the Board of Trustees of the Theatre Museum, London.)

the Paris Opera and London's Alhambra and Empire theaters, and *The Black Crook*, which toured the United States—all featured legions of *danseuses de travesti* in every conceivable adaptation of male dress. Because male ballet dancers were at the time practically unemployable, their training was neglected, and the antitheatrical prejudice against them became more firmly fixed in Western culture than at any previous time.

Fortunately, the ballet in Russia had taken its own course; the tradition of strong male dancing survived there, to be reintroduced throughout Europe and America in the early twentieth century by Michel Fokine, Vaslav Nijinsky, and Serge Diaghilev. After seeing Diaghilev's Ballets Russes, audiences were never again willing to accept the substitution of women in men's roles.

Travesty survived into the twentieth century as a comedic tradition in vaudeville, in music halls, in the principal boys and dame comedians of English pantomime, and in the female impersonators of drag shows. (The term *drag* originated in the 1800s, derived from the dragging trains of women's dresses.)

In contemporary ballet, travesty roles for women are rare, with the exception of those roles that call for a temporary disguise that is not intended to deceive the audience as to the performer's true identity. Freudian self-consciousness about sexuality seems to have diminished the possibility of suspended disbelief when it comes to travesty, male or female. Cross-dressing (transvestism) is now considered a more serious psychological aberration than in the past, and any form of sexual ambiguity on the stage is apt to provoke distaste, uneasy laughter, or lecherous sneers. The exception is male travesty, providing that it offers a comic or grotesque impersonation far enough removed from reality and broad enough in its techniques or portrayal.

Male travesty roles still have an important place in ballet repertories. In *La Fille Mal Gardée*, the part of the heroine's mother, a comic peasant farmer, is often taken by a man. The great Italian ballet master Enrico Cecchetti danced this role and originated that of the wicked fairy Carabosse in *The Sleeping Beauty*. In the Kingdom of Sweets scene in *The Nutcracker*, Mother Ginger, a towering figure played by a man in a massive farthingale, enters and releases a horde of small children from beneath her skirts. The Headmistress in David Lichine's *Graduation Ball* is an absurdly flirtatious spinster, always danced by a man, whose pratfalls and broadly burlesqued choreographic gaffs leave no doubt as to his real identity. In 1948 Frederick Ashton choreographed *Cinderella* to the music of Prokofiev for the Sadler's Wells Ballet, casting himself and Robert Helpmann as the Stepsisters. The hilariously subtle characterizations of these two expert mimes contributed substantially to the success of the ballet.

In 1974 Les Ballets Trockadero, a company of male

TRAVESTY. Olga Tchikaboumskaya of Les Ballets Trockadero de Monte Carlo, a company of male dancers who perform classical ballets *en travesti*, in Peter Anastos's parodic work *Yes, Virginia, Another Piano Ballet*. (Photograph © 1977 by Jack Vartoogian; used by permission.)

dancers *en travesti* performing abbreviated, comedic versions of the classics, attracted attention in New York City; within a few seasons it was successful internationally with both critics and dance audiences. Most of the dancers in the company were poorly equipped for the arduous ballerina roles on pointe that they danced, and few of them had physical characteristics that would make it possible to pass for women onstage should they have wished to. Their subtle comic mime and attention to balletic nuance achieved something unique in the history of travesty—sometimes they conveyed the essential artistry and beauty of the balletic tradition while sending it up as broad comedy in performances that were both poignant and hilarious.

BIBLIOGRAPHY
Baker, Roger. *Drag: A History of Female Impersonation on the Stage.* London, 1968.
Baker, Roger. *Drag: A History of Female Impersonation in the Performing Arts.* London and New York, 1994.

MALCOLM McCORMICK

TREFILOVA, VERA (Vera Aleksandrovna Trefilova; born 29 September [8 October] 1875, died 11 July 1943 in Paris), Russian ballet dancer and teacher. Destined to become one of the great Maryinsky ballerinas of the first decade of the twentieth century, Vera Trefilova graduated from the Imperial Theater School in Saint Petersburg in 1894 and joined the corps de ballet at the Maryinsky Theater. She enjoyed her first success in the title role of *Graziella* in 1900, and after her promotion to soloist in 1901 she received important parts in *Le Corsaire, The Naïad and the Fisherman, Bluebeard, The Tulip of Haarlem*, and *Coppélia*. Classes with Enrico Cecchetti, Rosita Mauri, and Caterina Beretta strengthened her technique. Following triumphs in the roles of Aurora in *The Sleeping Beauty* (1904), Kitri in *Don Quixote* (1906), and Odette-Odile in *Swan Lake* (1906), she was promoted to the rank of ballerina. In 1910, Trefilova retired prematurely, perhaps driven away by the jealousy of Matilda Kshessinska, who would brook no rival, or perhaps dissatisfied by the innovations then being introduced by Michel Fokine and others. She returned to the stage of the Mikhailovsky Theater in 1915 as a dramatic actress.

Having emigrated after the Russian Revolution, Trefilova danced Aurora in Serge Diaghilev's production of *The Sleeping Princess* at London's Alhambra Theatre (1921/22) and Odette-Odile in his shortened version of *Swan Lake*, presented in Monte Carlo in 1924. Of her performance in *Aurora's Wedding* at the Paris Opera (1922), André Levinson wrote, "Her technique is absolute . . . the total expression of a harmonious being. In the adagio, the play of curves and verticals is of unequaled purity; her *développé* is like an opening flower. She is a . . . dancing Stradivarius." Settling in Paris, she served as ballet mistress of the Théâtre du Châtelet and opened a studio where she taught such well-known dancers as Nina Vyroubova and Marina Svetlova. She married the ballet critic Valerian Svetlov, her third husband, in emigration.

BIBLIOGRAPHY
Haskell, Arnold L. *Vera Trefilova: A Study in Classicism.* London, 1928.
Ivchenko [Svetlov], Valerian. "The Recent Creations of Vera Trefilova." *The Dancing Times* (December 1928): 343–345; (January 1929): 517–522.
Krasovskaya, Vera. *Russkii baletnyi teatr nachala dvadtatogo veka*, vol. 2, *Tantsovshchiki.* Leningrad, 1972.
Levinson, André. *La danse au théâtre.* Paris, 1924.
Smakov, Gennady. *The Great Russian Dancers.* New York, 1984.

LYNN GARAFOLA

TREND. Choreography: Hanya Holm. Music: Wallingford Riegger. Scenery: Arch Lauterer. First performance: 1937, Vermont State Armory, Bennington, Hanya Holm Company. Principals: Eve Gentry, Louise Kloepper, Bernice van Gelder, Lucretia Wilson, Elizabeth Waters.

Trend, the signature work of Hanya Holm, was choreographed and first performed during the Bennington Summer School in 1937. A fifty-five-minute epic of heroic proportions, *Trend* used a large all-female group (because male dancers were not available) juxtaposed against a series of solos depicting a society being destroyed by false values. The multilevel, double stage set of ramps, steps, and platforms by Arch Lauterer was hailed by John Martin of the *New York Times* as "the first truly modern stage setting that the dance has seen."

Trend is divided into six major sections: "Mask Motions," "Episodes," "Cataclysms," "The Gates Are Desolate," "Resurgence," and "Assurance." The "Episodes" section was further subdivided into solo themes: "The Effete" (Louise Kloepper), "Lucre Lunacy" (Bernice van Gelder), "From Heaven Ltd." (Lucretia Wilson), "Lest We Remember" (Elizabeth Waters), and "He the Great" (Eve Gentry). According to John Martin, "The sections are independent though related, treated more as if they were several acts in a drama, steadily carrying forward the central theme to its resolution. . . . There is a superb organization of material and a masterly instinct for balancing the values of group movement."

Company member Eve Gentry recalls one section:

An endless line of tall women in long dresses, shoulder to shoulder, moved with their backs to the audience. They slowly inched sidewards, subtly, almost imperceptibly, shifting weight from one foot to another, a curtain of movement. The whole atmosphere was permeated with a tense excitement and vibration. It grew in volume; it became a wave of people breathing together.

The original score for *Trend* was by Wallingford Riegger; the "Resurgence" section added "Ionization" by Edgard Varèse, and the music for "Assurance" was Varèse's "Octandre." The score makes much use of percussion instruments, a Holm trademark.

When *Trend* was transported from Bennington to the Mecca Auditorium (now City Center) in New York in December 1937, Holm closed off the orchestra seats so people could only sit in the mezzanine and balconies and look down on the full architectural design. The work has never been remounted owing to its cost and to Holm's desire to rechoreograph sections for men as well as women. It was never recorded and is documented only in photographs.

BIBLIOGRAPHY

Martin, John. Review. *New York Times* (2 January 1938).
Sorell, Walter. *Hanya Holm: The Biography of an Artist.* Middletown, Conn., 1969.
Tobias, Tobi. "Hanya Holm: A Young Octogenarian." *Dance News* (March 1979): 1.

INTERVIEWS.   Eve Gentry, Louise Kloepper, and Bernice van Gelder (Peterson), by Theresa Bowers, Oral History Research Office, Columbia University.

VIDEOTAPE.   Marilyn Cristofori, "Hanya: Portrait of a Dance Pioneer" (1984), Dance Collection, New York Public Library for the Performing Arts.

NANCY MASON HAUSER

TRICORNE, LE. Ballet in one act. Choreography: Léonide Massine. Music: Manuel de Falla. Libretto: Martinez Sierra. Scenery and costumes: Pablo Picasso. First performance: 22 July 1919, Alhambra Theatre, London, Ballets Russes de Serge Diaghilev. Principals: Léonide Massine (The Miller), Tamara Karsavina (The Miller's Wife), Leon Woizikowski (The Corregidor), Stanislas Idzikowski (The Dandy).

Le Tricorne (The Three-Cornered Hat) is a signature piece of Léonide Massine's career. The ballet was born from the collaboration of Massine, Pablo Picasso, and Manuel de Falla under the direct supervision of Serge Diaghilev.

While the Ballets Russes was immobilized in Spain during World War I, Diaghilev began sowing the seeds for a Spanish ballet. Massine was enraptured by Spanish flamenco dance and began intensive training in that style, while Diaghilev engaged the talents of Falla to compose an authentic Spanish score. As Falla integrated basic forms of Spanish music, Massine translated ethnic dance onto the ballet stage. The artistic exchange began in 1917, but progress on the ballet was halted until 1919. When the work resumed, Diaghilev employed Picasso to design the sets and costumes.

The ballet, set in a small, eighteenth-century Spanish village, centers around the flirtations between the Miller, his Wife, and the Corregidor, who wears a three-cornered hat emblematic of his position and social class. Picasso effectively captured the essence of the Spanish temperament in the drop cloth; black borders denoting Spanish dignity enclosed bold colors reflecting the gaiety of the people. The costumes were based on authentic eighteenth-century styles.

The dancing was lively, to an underlying *jota* rhythm. Massine's understanding of the use of groups on the stage and the coordination of their movements as a congruent whole was very evident. The crowds were necessary within the story to create atmosphere, but there was always a logical reason for the group to exit when a solo was to be performed. The Miller's Wife had a brilliant *fandango* solo heavily laced with traditional Spanish steps yet in keeping with the theatrical setting. The pas de deux between the Miller and his Wife was also a kind of *fandango*, but it had more classical steps in its teasing, flirtatious content. Finally, the Miller's solo was an explosive, fiery *farruca*. With rapid staccato footwork, great jumps, and *tours en l'air*, this solo, like the *fandango*, integrated authentic Spanish, classical, and theatrical dance.

Massine was highly acclaimed for the rhythmic nature and musicality of the choreography in *Le Tricorne*. The *demi-caractère* quality of the work created a new subgenre in ballet.

[*See also the entry on Massine.*]

BIBLIOGRAPHY

Balanchine, George, with Francis Mason. *Balanchine's Complete Stories of the Great Ballets*. Rev. and enl. ed. Garden City, N.Y., 1977.

Fusillo, Lisa A. "Léonide Massine: Choreographic Genius with a Collaborative Spirit." Ph.D. diss., Texas Woman's University, 1982.

García-Márquez, Vicente. *Massine: A Biography*. New York, 1995.

Massine, Léonide. *My Life in Ballet*. New York, 1968.

LISA A. FUSILLO

TRIPUDIUM (plural, *tripudiī*) is a Latin term important to the history of Christian liturgical dance, related to the intransitive verb *tripudiō, tripudiāre*, with an occasional variant, *tripodium*, found in written sources from c.200 BCE to 1600 CE.

Etymology and Usage. No single term adequately translates *tripudium;* in various contexts *tripudium* may mean (1) "dance," generally (and at times metaphorically, as in "dancing for joy"); (2) "rejoicing" or "jubilation" (du Cange); or (3) an auspicious omen in Roman augury rites, which overlaps in usage with the first two meanings from at least 100 to 15 BCE but is obsolete after c.400 to 600 CE. This favorable omen is also seen as *tripudium solistimum*, for example in Livy's reference to a rite in which "the sacred chickens ate so greedily that the grain dropped [Foster et al. has "danced"] on the ground."

Despite the word's syllabic composition (see below), no primary texts positively support the widely held notion of *tripudium* as a "three-step dance," or *Dreischritt* (Pauly, Sachs); or as having "return" or "recovery" motifs in its step formulation (Sachs, Adams); nor is there adequate justification for generalizing the rebounding movement qualities suggested both by the augury ritual and some other instances of the term to all interpretations of it (Backman); these are all contextual rather than connotational associations. Especially to be resisted is the attempt to define a reconstructible "*tripudium* step" with "three steps forward, one step back . . . done over thousands of years" (Adams), a description championed in the mid- to late 1900s as part of a larger effort to insinuate modern liturgical dance into contemporary Christian worship as the recovery of a lost traditional practice rather than as the revelatory *novum*, with historical precedents and precursors, which it more likely is (La Rue, 1995, 1996).

Classical writers, including Livy, Cicero, and Seneca used *tripudium* infrequently; however, both Livy and Cicero used the word in all three of its meanings throughout their oeuvre. It appears twice in the instructions to the *Arval Brethren Hymn* (see below), once in the Latin Vulgate Bible (*Esther* 8.32), and in the retrospective etymologiara of the fifth to seventh centuries by Festus and Isidore of Seville (Migne). Later it occurs in the lyrics to Christian hymns such as "Tripudians Martyr," a tenth-century hymn to Saint Martial of Limoges (Dreves), "Stella Splendens," from the thirteenth-century Spanish *Llibre Vermell* (Brainard), and others; in the title of Guglielmo Ebreo's 1463 treatise, *De practica seu arte tripudii*, and, most problematically for recent writers, in a series of references to the "hopping saints" or *springenden Heiligen* of Echternach, which Backman connects with a processional folk dance observed in the town around 1940.

Tripudium's derivations as well as its meanings are uncertain. It may have come from the Greek τρίποδον (tripodon), "to trot" (Pauly), or from τρίποδίος (tripodios), "a poetic line of three metrical feet." Cicero's derivation from *terripavium*, "to strike the ground" (*De divinatione*, 2.34.72), is considered contrived. Some scholars associate specific dance movements such as "three-step," "hop-dance," "line-" or "circle-dance," and "religious dance" with *tripudium*. While no primary source positively defines the word thus, the segments *tri-, tres-* ("three") and *-pud, -pes, -pedis* ("foot" or "feet" or, possibly, "steps") and the possible derivation from *tripodios* appear to many writers to suggest a step with a pattern of three footfalls, or three beats, or both. Evidence from the *Carmen Fratrem Arvale* (Arval Brethren Hymn), a cryptic inscription from Rome dated to 218 CE that appears to provide instructions for a danced hymn whose refrains repeat three times (Ernout), taken together with the *tripodios* definition, might support this view, but the hymn's meter does not allow us to make assumptions about any movement that may have accompanied it, as Sachs implies. It should also be noted that this cluster of references alluding to the Salii of the late Roman republic (in Livy and Seneca) and to the Arval Brethren deserves attention. Both involved a sacred priesthood of twelve members dedicated to the cult of Mars, whose ceremonies are described as including a processional *tripudium;* it is slightly possible that the Fratres Arvales represent a revival of an earlier priesthood, perhaps undertaken as an act of piety in the turbulent days of the late empire.

Leaping or hopping steps associated with *tripudium* might explain the augur's use of the term to describe bouncing grain (in the third definition above); they would also be consistent with such Indo-European roots as *trep-*, "trepidation," and *trem-*, "to tremble"; this etymology for *tripudium* would moreover contradict the syllabic division of the word often used to suggest "triple steps." The *tripodon* derivation seems more likely in this case; even Cicero's intent in providing an etymology through *terripavium* becomes plausible. An eleventh-century reference to the procession of Saint Willibrod also uses the term, as

Backman demonstrates, although his irregular treatment of *tripudium* throughout his work is probably one cause of confusion among contemporary liturgical writers on the subject.

The range of formal shapes and movement patterns associated with *tripudium* varies widely as well. Some *tripudia* are clearly processionals, either linear or in phalangeal array (close ranks); however, "line dance" is conjectural. Translating *tripudium* as "circle dance" is probably also too specific. In the qualified phrase *tripudium rotundum*, which appears in the rubrics of the fourteenth-century hymn "Stella Splendens," if *tripudium* means "circle dance," then *rotundum* is superfluous (or perhaps pleonastic). But cases where *tripudium* is best rendered simply "dance" (Ebreo's title, *De practica seu arte tripudii*, for one) make a translation with fewer formal movement implications more useful.

Many but not all *tripudia* have religious associations. These include Roman "armed or victory dances" (Livy, 21.42.3; 23.26.9; Aeppli; Brainard), "funeral dances" (Livy, 25.17.5), the honorific dances of an elect priesthood like the Salii, and the cosmic dance of Roman mythological figures, glorified Christian saints, and angels delighting in the joys of Creation, as related in *De nuptiis* (Miller) and "Tripudians Martyr." *Tripudii* in these contexts are spiritually or emotionally expressive dances, often but not exclusively of a communal nature. There are also no grounds for accepting Chailley's effort to locate celebrative dances called *tripudii* in any specific part of the pagan calendrical or Christian liturgical year, especially as opposed to those called *caroles*, which are known to have occurred throughout the year.

It is important to remember that *tripudium* may not always mean "dance," but may mean "rejoice," especially in religious sources, where figurative or symbolic language often occurs: a "dance of joy," for example, may be a metaphoric image for joy and not an actual dance at all. In the hymn cited above, for example, *tripudians* may as easily mean "rejoicing" as "dancing" martyr; and its presence in the lyrics in no way proves the hymn was ever danced, as Backman claims.

No one meaning can be imposed on every source in which *tripudium* occurs. Throughout its currency, the uses of *tripudium* range with the uses of dance itself; this alone favors a general over a specific meaning for the term. It seems wisest to leave the question open to further research and to urge a contextually sensitive, conservative approach to the sources themselves.

Historiography. As a historiographic case, the study of *tripudium* is also instructive. As Lawler notes, confusion about early terms takes a particular turn where an ephemeral, nonartifactual medium such as dance leaves only a few enigmatic clues behind. Paucity of information pressures the analyst to wrest as much meaning as possible from a given source; a scarcity of correctives leaves the field open to a variety of interpretations.

The clearest example of this attends the contemporary introduction of liturgical dance noted above. Danced exposition of the tenets of Christianity, regularly approved and encouraged by an ecclesial hierarchy responsible for planning services of worship, has appeared sporadically in the past (though the written record is probably biased in favor of upper-class ecclesiastical references during much of the period of *tripudium*'s usage, since most lettered historians were in the employ of the church, the courts, or both). Nor can liturgical dance be said to occupy a central place in the life of most congregations today.

Proponents of an epiphanic event like danced worship, which interrupts but does not rupture the fabric of traditional Christianity, have introduced it as a restoration, rather than a revelation, of a vital practice of faith to a church historically suspicious of enthusiastic liturgical innovation. This must be considered in terms of the philosophical and theological beliefs that prevailed during the period in question. Creedally, the church holds that the human spirit is incarnate—not incarcerate—in the human body. Yet the church has only rarely and ineffectually attempted to dispel the strong current of Gnostic antimaterialistic dualism riding along on the underbelly of popular theology. [*See* Christianity and Dance.]

In addition, the references to such a supposed tradition are both geographically and chronologically disparate, and the original compendium of these references (Fiske-Taylor, as cited or reprinted in Adams, and in Apostopoulos-Cappadona) requires intensive review. These sources—anecdotal references, hymn lyrics, misunderstood visual sources (the dancing angels in Fra Angelico's *Last Judgment*, for example, are probably heavenly courtiers, not exponents of liturgical practice), misinterpreted florilegaic articles on dance from late nineteenth-century liturgical dictionaries, and disconnected local dance and processional practices scattered about western Europe from the tenth to the eighteenth century—each require better analysis on their own terms before they can be described as fitting into the historical sequence of repeated events that the term *tradition* usually implies (the liturgical term *traditio* actually represents a much broader concept). As a dynamic ethical icon, modeling an active response to faith and a valuation of the physical body as a fit vessel for praise, danced prayer functions well within the range of self-understood Christian creedal affirmations emphasizing a holistic cosmology and anthropology.

Moreover, there is no need to overdetermine words such as *tripudium* or to overinterpret sources referring to religious dance simply to assuage the fears of those who are wary of the new. Developing a functional theology of applications for liturgical dance (Rock, 1978, 1988; La Rue 1995, 1996), educating congregations and dancers alike to the many ways beyond a fundamental gestural literalism in which dance can communicate meaning, and attending to areas of resonance within the broader understanding of *traditio* offers a more balanced approach. Careful attention to the quality of danced worship as well as to its proper function—of forwarding the intentions of the gathered assembly through prayerful submission to both the craft and the expressive potential of the work—is less disruptive to the fabric of dance history in general and the understanding of terms like *tripudium* in particular, is more respectful of the richer historical situation, and may best establish the place of liturgical dance.

BIBLIOGRAPHY

Adams, Doug. *Congregational Dancing in Christian Worship.* North Aurora, Ill., 1980.

Aeppli, Fritz. *Die wichtigsten Ausdrücke für das Tanzen in den romanischen Sprachen.* Halle, 1925.

Apostoulos-Capadona, Diane, and Doug Adams, eds. *Dance as Religious Studies.* San Francisco, 1992.

Backman, Eugène Louis. *Religious Dances in the Christian Church and in Popular Medicine.* Translated by E. Classen. London, 1952.

Brainard, Ingrid. "Dance: Middle Ages and Early Renaissance." In *The New Grove Dictionary of Music and Musicians.* London, 1980.

Chailley, Jacques. "La danse réligieuse au Moyen Âge." In *Arts libéraux et philosophie au Moyen Âge: Actes du quatrième congrès international de philosophie médiévale.* Montreal, 1969.

Cicero. *De divinatione.* Translated by William Armistead Falconer. Cambridge, Mass., 1979.

Dreves, Guido Maria, and Clemens Blume, eds. *Analecta Hymnica Medii Aevi.* Vol. 49, no. 372. Leipzig, 1922.

Du Cange, Charles Du Fresne. *Glossarium mediae et infimae latinitatis.* Paris, 1937.

Ernout, Alfred. *Recueil de textes latins archaïques.* Paris, 1973. See entry 146.

Fiske-Taylor, Margaret. *A Time to Dance.* North Aurora, Ill., 1976.

La Rue, Donna. "Tripudium: Its Uses and Meanings from 200 BCE to 1600 CE, or, More Than Just Another Pretty Word Study." *ARTS Journal* (September 1995).

La Rue, Donna. "Both a Performance and a Prayer: Towards an Aesthetic and Theology of Liturgical Dance." Unpublished seminar paper, January, 1996.

Lawler, Lillian. *The Dance in Ancient Greece.* Seattle, 1967.

Livy. *Ab urbe condita.* Translated by B. O. Foster et al. Cambridge, Mass., 1970.

Miller, James. *Measures of Wisdom: The Cosmic Dance in Classical and Christian Antiquity.* Buffalo, 1986.

Migne, J.-P. *Patrologiae cursus, series Latina.* "De Ecclesiasticus Officis Lib. I." Vol. 83, col. 775.

Pauly, August Friedrich von. *Real-Encyclopädie der klassischen Altertumswissenschaft.* Stuttgart, 1894.

Rock, Judith. *Theology in the Shape of Dance.* Austin, Tex., 1978.

Rock, Judith, and Norman Mealey. *Performer as Priest and Prophet.* San Francisco, 1988.

Sachs, Curt. *World History of the Dance.* Translated by Bessie Schönberg. New York, 1957.

Seneca. *Epistolae morales.* Translated by Richard M. Gummere. Cambridge, Mass., 1979.

DONNA LA RUE

TUDOR, ANTONY (William John Cook; born 4 April 1909 in London, died 19 April 1987 in New York City), British choreographer. Tudor created a new dance genre, the psychological ballet, in which the characters' inner states were externalized through movement. Though Tudor himself asserted that "principles from other choreographers did not actively or consciously affect my works," he carried to its ultimate conclusion Michel Fokine's "second principle," that dance movement and gesture should be expressive of the characters' thoughts and feelings. It is probable that he was also influenced by Sigmund Freud and Konstantin Stanislavsky.

As a child Tudor was captivated by dancers he saw in music halls and Christmas pantomimes, but he did not study dance seriously until he was about twenty. At that time he was working as a clerk in London's Smithfield meat market. After a few classes at adult education institutions, he presented himself to Marie Rambert, who took him on as a pupil.

In spite of his late start, Tudor quickly became proficient enough to pass the Cecchetti examination in 1929 and that of the Imperial Society of Teachers of Dancing a year later. He danced in the performances by Rambert's dancers at the Lyric Theater, Hammersmith, and at the Ballet Club, and at the beginning of the Ballet Club's second season he choreographed his first ballet, *Cross-Garter'd*, to music by Girolamo Frescobaldi (1583–1643), based on an episode from Shakespeare's *Twelfth Night*. Tudor himself danced the role of Malvolio.

Like Frederick Ashton, Tudor learned two important lessons in ballet making from working on the tiny stage of what came to be called the Mercury Theater: how to achieve his effects with the utmost economy of means and how to build the structure of a ballet on the basis of the chosen musical score. Tudor's approach was quite different from Ashton's; he was intellectual, whereas Ashton was intuitive. Ashton used a basically classic vocabulary with some jazz and Latin American elements, while Tudor incorporated natural movement and colloquial gesture, eventually finding his way to what is now recognized as a modern dance idiom. He briefly studied central European dance and saw performances by Mary Wigman, Harald Kreutzberg, and Les Ballets Jooss; at Rambert's studio he met Agnes de Mille and worked with her.

Tudor's second ballet, *Lysistrata, or The Strike of Wives* (March 1932), was also based on a literary source, Aristophanes' comedy. For this Tudor selected piano pieces by Sergei Prokofiev, which Rambert considered unsuitable, as did the composer when he saw the ballet. But again Tudor successfully conveyed the comedy of character through movement, and the ballet remained in the repertory of the Ballet Rambert until 1940.

Male dancers were in demand in the early days of British ballet. In January 1932 Tudor began dancing with

TUDOR. *The Descent of Hebe*, set to Ernest Bloch's Concerto Grosso no. 1 in B Minor, was created for the Ballet Club in 1935. In a 1940 performance by Ballet Rambert, Leo Kersley and Lisa Serova appeared in the roles of Mercury and Night, originally danced by Hugh Laing and Maude Lloyd. (Photograph by Cyril Arapoff; from the Dance Collection, New York Public Library for the Performing Arts.)

the Vic-Wells Ballet and also appeared in the Camargo Society's performances. He choreographed a ballet for the society, *Adam and Eve* (December 1932), to the music by Constant Lambert that Serge Diaghilev had used for Bronislava Nijinska's *Romeo and Juliet*. At Sadler's Wells Tudor was allowed to choreograph the ballet in *Faust* (1933), but its artistic director Ninette de Valois refused to let him choreograph for the ballet company proper, advising him to join the Ballets Russes du Colonel W. de Basil for a year or two to learn his craft by working with such esteemed choreographers as Michel Fokine and Léonide Massine. Tudor declined to take this advice, and it was not until Ashton succeeded de Valois as director more than thirty years later that Tudor was invited to choreograph for the company, which by then had become the Royal Ballet.

Tudor's next two ballets at the Ballet Club, although unsuccessful, were important because they marked the beginning of two important artistic and personal associations. In *Pavane pour une Infante Défunte* (1933), he worked for the first time with designer Hugh Stevenson, and in *Atalanta of the East* (May 1933), Hugh Laing danced for the first time.

It was in his next ballet that Tudor's genius began to manifest itself. This was *The Planets* (October 1934), to three movements from the orchestral suite of that name by Gustav Holst. Both the designs and the concept were by Stevenson, and each scene showed the influence of the

planet on mortals born under it: Venus on a pair of lovers; Mars on a young man (Laing) whose conflict was as much within himself as with an external enemy; Neptune on a mystic who "longs to unit herself with the infinite." This last role was created by Kyra Nijinsky, Vaslav Nijinsky's daughter. The movement ranged from the lyricism of "Venus" through the pounding, percussive modern idiom of "Mars" to the austere, reductive tranquility of "Neptune."

Although Tudor was often emotionally remote and at times cruel in his comments, he began to collect around himself a group of dancers who were in all of his ballets and were deeply devoted to him: Laing, Maude Lloyd, and Peggy van Praagh. When Tudor found a flat with a studio large enough to rehearse in, the group worked long hours away from Rambert's watchful and jealous eye.

Tudor started dancing too late to become a virtuoso and probably had no ambitions in that direction, but he was an authoritative performer of character roles in his own and other choreographers' ballets and was also an excellent teacher. A trained musician, he chose unusual, often difficult scores for his ballets. His approach to the music was not analytical: he knew it thoroughly and choreographed in long phrases that went "through" the music. An exception to this practice was the final section of his next ballet, *The Descent of Hebe* (April 1935), to Ernest Bloch's Concerto Grosso no. 1, a choreographic fugue that exactly mirrored the musical one.

Rambert paid her choreographers one British pound per minute for a staged ballet, with no royalties, so Tudor augmented his income by choreographing elsewhere. In the summer of 1935 he arranged the ballets for Thomas Beecham's opera season at Covent Garden, and he also began to work in the commercial theater and in the earliest British Broadcasting Corporation (BBC) television transmissions. He did pioneering work in the new medium, such as the *Fugue for Four Cameras* with Maude Lloyd in 1937.

In January 1936 Tudor produced his first unquestionable masterpiece, *Jardin aux Lilas*, to music by Ernest Chausson (*Poème* for violin and orchestra). Again Stevenson not only designed the ballet but had much to do with its final form. The action devised by Stevenson and Tudor can be summarized in the descriptions of the four main characters: Caroline, the bride-to-be (Lloyd); Her Lover (Laing); The Man She Must Marry (Tudor); and An Episode in His Past (van Praagh). The various emotions flowing among these four people were expressed in dance movement and in small, subtle gestures. Supported adagio was used not for acrobatic effects but to heighten the drama of a moment—Caroline's lover steps in from the wings to stop her at the end of a solitary pirouette; the Other Woman throws herself headlong into the bridegroom's arms. The most audacious stroke occurs at the point of crisis, coinciding with the highest climax in the music. All the characters who have been seeking and avoiding each other in the moonlit garden, snatching moments together or being torn apart, suddenly coalesce in a frozen group, from which Caroline alone detaches herself, moving slowly in a circle as though in a trance, overcome by a despair she cannot outwardly express. As Lloyd has said, "she walks out of time." It was Tudor's boldest use so far of stasis as a positive choreographic element.

Tudor's last ballet for Rambert was *Dark Elegies* (February 1937), to Gustav Mahler's *Kindertotenlieder*. The choice of music was a daring one for the time. Tudor did not make the mistake of pantomiming the words: the ballet is an abstraction of grief, of mourning, and of eventual resignation. Nor did he attempt a slavish visualization of the music; more than ever the movement parted company with the music and went its own way, coming together with it at certain key points. The ballet's lineage may be traced back both to Nijinsky's *Le Sacre du Printemps* and to Nijinska's *Les Noces*. Like those works, it depicts a community confronted with a momentous event, in this case, the death of its children. The community enacts a ritual in which individuals emerge from the group only to be absorbed back again. Although the women were on pointe, the vocabulary is not that of the classic dance. The feet are usually in parallel, and the thrust of the movement is downward into the floor. Much of the movement was developed from folk dance or everyday gesture; for all intents and purposes, *Dark Elegies* is a modern dance work.

By this time Tudor was ready to strike out on his own, in part because Rambert was a difficult person to work with. In the summer of 1937, he and Agnes de Mille joined forces in a company called Dance Theatre, which gave a short season at the Playhouse in Oxford and then promptly folded. He took with him some of his favorite dancers (not including Lloyd), and some of his most important ballets, and he made one new one—*Gallant Assembly*, which the painter Lawrence Gowing described as "an inconsequent and pleasantly disreputable Rococo frolic."

During the following season Tudor worked in television to accumulate funds for a more permanent company of his own. As a curtain raiser to a production of Nikolai Gogol's play *Marriage*, Tudor choreographed the bitterly sardonic *The Judgment of Paris*, set in a sleazy French bordello, to a suite from Kurt Weill's *Dreigroschenoper;* de Mille was the voluptuous, vacuous Venus.

In December 1938 Tudor's new company, the London Ballet, opened after months of rehearsal in the new four-hundred-seat theater at Toynbee Hall, an adult education institution where Tudor had been lecturing on dance history. This time Lloyd was with him, as were Laing, van Praagh, and some new dancers. In addition to *Hebe, Jardin aux Lilas, Elegies,* and *The Planets* (with a new fourth scene, "Mercury"), the repertory included *Gallant Assembly* and *The Judgment of Paris* as well as two new ballets—*Soirée Musicale*, to music by Gioacchino Rossini as augmented by Benjamin Britten, a charming *divertisse-*

TUDOR. The four principal dancers in the original cast of *Jardin aux Lilas* (1936): Maude Lloyd (second from left) as Caroline, Hugh Laing as Her Lover, Antony Tudor as The Man She Must Marry, and Peggy van Praagh as An Episode in His Past. Scenery and costumes were designed by Hugh Stevenson. (Photograph from the Dance Collection, New York Public Library for the Performing Arts.)

TUDOR. *Dark Elegies*, set to Gustav Mahler's *Kindertotenlieder*, was first performed by Ballet Rambert at the Duchess Theatre in London in 1937. After immigrating to the United States, Tudor staged it for Ballet Theatre in 1940 and appeared with Nora Kaye in "Second Song." (Photograph by Carl Van Vechten; used by permission.)

ment, and *Gala Performance*, to music of Sergei Prokofiev. *Gala*, about the rivalry of three ballerinas from Moscow, Milan, and Paris, provided a witty commentary on the different styles of classic ballet that they exemplified.

The company's first season ran through April 1939, with weekly performances, and in the spring Tudor again choreographed the opera ballets at Covent Garden for his company (Margot Fonteyn was guest artist in *Aída*). He was already preparing new works for the following season, among them a ballet to Arnold Schoenberg's *Verklärte Nacht* (Transfigured Night), but the London Ballet did not present another season under his direction. Soon after the outbreak of war in Europe in the fall of 1939, Tudor, Laing, and Andrée Howard, another of Rambert's choreographers, sailed for New York to join the newly formed Ballet Theatre. Lloyd and van Praagh kept the London company going for a season or two; it was then reabsorbed into the Ballet Rambert.

Tudor immediately set to work rehearsing three of the most successful ballets he had made in London, *Jardin aux Lilas* (its title usually given in English as *Lilac Gar-*

den), *The Judgment of Paris,* and *Dark Elegies,* all of which were given during the first two weeks of Ballet Theatre's inaugural season in January 1940 at the Center Theater. On opening night, 11 January 1940, Tudor danced a leading role in Eugene Loring's *The Great American Goof.*

The first new ballet that Tudor choreographed in the United States was a minor work, *Goya Pastoral,* given at the College of the City of New York's Lewisohn Stadium that summer. The work's primary *raison d'être* was to make use of some beautiful scenery and costumes that Nicholas de Molas had designed for an unsuccessful ballet, *Goyescas,* by José Fernandez, which had been on the same program with *Jardin Aux Lilas.* Tudor's ballet survived into the following season, when it too was called *Goyescas.*

No new ballet by Tudor was presented during Ballet Theatre's second season. *Gala Performance* was revived in February 1941. His first truly "American" ballet was made at the invitation of Lincoln Kirstein, for the American Ballet Caravan's goodwill tour of South America in the summer of 1941. *Time Table,* another minor work, set in a railroad station during World War I and danced to Aaron Copland's *Music for the Theatre.* It was shown at an open dress rehearsal in New York before the company left and was briefly revived in 1949 during the first season of New York City Ballet.

In the meantime Tudor had resumed work on his ballet to *Verklärte Nacht,* which finally reached the stage as *Pillar of Fire,* first performed at the Metropolitan Opera House on 8 April 1942 after being in rehearsal for more than a year. It immediately established Tudor as a choreographer of the first rank and Nora Kaye as the greatest dramatic ballerina of her time. Kaye had danced a small role and later that of Caroline in *Jardin aux Lilas* and the role of the Russian Ballerina in *Gala Performance.* Critic Walter Terry had described *Jardin* as "almost a psychological ballet"; *Pillar* went further, a danced case history of Hagar, whose repressed emotions and desires are made clear to the audience in her smallest gestures. Critical reception to Tudor's earlier ballets had been only moderately enthusiastic, but in the light of this new, great work, they were reassessed. Critic John Martin proclaimed Tudor to be "the most important figure in the contemporary ballet."

Certainly it was Tudor's ballets that gave artistic stature to Ballet Theatre, even after Sol Hurok took over management of the company in the 1941/42 season and, advertising it as "the greatest in Russian Ballet," started to bring in new and old ballets by Fokine, Massine, George Balanchine, Nijinska, and David Lichine and the ballerinas Alicia Markova and Irina Baronova. Tudor often performed in his own ballets, but both he and Laing had leading roles in Massine's *Aleko* (1942), and Tudor sometimes played the king in Fokine's burlesque, *Bluebeard.*

Tudor was never a prolific choreographer, and his next ballet, *Romeo and Juliet*, was still incomplete at its scheduled premiere, 6 April 1943; the finished ballet was not given until four nights later. It was danced not to Prokofiev's famous score, then unknown in the West, but to a selection of orchestral pieces by Frederick Delius, which proved to be surprisingly apt for Tudor's approach, described by dance critic Edwin Denby as "a meditation on the play." Originally, the ballet was to be designed by Salvador Dali, but Tudor rejected his sketches and insisted that the commission be given to Eugene Berman. The result was one of the most beautiful scenic investitures in modern ballet. Laing was a natural choice for the impetuous, passionate Romeo, but Tudor's casting of Juliet was much less obvious: Markova danced the role in a red wig; it was one of her greatest roles outside the classic repertory. Kaye later took it over, with Tudor himself as Tybalt.

Tudor's *Dim Lustre* (October 1943) was a ballet on the Proustian theme of "mixing memory and desire." The action takes place at a ball where the scent of a woman's perfume and the sight of a man's white tie trigger memories of previous loves in the minds of a couple (Laing and Kaye). Some of the episodes were amusing, and Tudor devised some brilliant dance passages to the *Burlesca* of Richard Strauss, but the stagecraft of the transitions from present to remembered action was surprisingly clumsy.

Tudor revived *Dim Lustre* for New York City Ballet in 1964, but its 1985 revival by American Ballet Theatre was unsuccessful.

The intervals between Tudor's new ballets became longer. After *Dim Lustre* a year and a half passed before the appearance of *Undertow* (April 1945), Tudor's only work to a commissioned score, by William Schuman. The theme, a kind of Freudian analysis in dance terms, was suggested by playwright John van Druten. The protagonist, a young man (Laing), is driven to commit what Martin called "a sordid sex murder" as a consequence of a traumatic experience in childhood. The ballet is full of sensational incidents, beginning with as realistic a depiction of birth as is possible on the ballet stage and going on to scenes involving prostitutes, drunken bawds, the gang rape of a vicious little girl (danced by Alicia Alonso), and the seduction of the transgressor by the temptress who became his victim. To convey universal significance, the characters had names from Greek mythology. Again Kaye was not in the original cast but later took over the role of the seductress Medusa, first danced by Nana Gollner, who was previously known for such roles as Odette-Odile in *Swan Lake*.

Three years elapsed between *Undertow* and Tudor's next ballet, although in 1945 he choreographed several musical comedies (so-called serious choreographers were in demand on Broadway after de Mille's success with *Okla-*

TUDOR. The principal dancers in the original cast of *Pillar of Fire*, created for Ballet Theatre in 1942: Annabelle Lyon as The Youngest Sister, Antony Tudor as The Friend, Lucia Chase as The Eldest Sister, Nora Kaye as Hagar, and Hugh Laing as The Young Man from the House Opposite. Scenery and costumes were designed by Jo Mielziner. (Photograph from the Dance Collection, New York Public Library for the Performing Arts.)

homa!). In the summer of 1946 Ballet Theatre visited London for the first time, and Tudor's major American works *Pillar of Fire, Romeo and Juliet,* and *Undertow* were seen at Covent Garden. In the following season Lucia Chase and Oliver Smith, who had taken over the direction of Ballet Theatre in 1945, named Tudor its artistic administrator.

As early as the late 1930s, Tudor had considered making a ballet to Gustav Mahler's symphony *Das Lied von der Erde,* and he finally succeeded in 1948 with *Shadow of the Wind.* Although the piece had its adherents, the combination of Chinese poetry in Mahler's setting with a largely ballet dance idiom was criticized by others. It did not survive beyond the season of its creation.

After restaging *Time Table* for New York City Ballet, Tudor spent most of the 1948/49 season in Stockholm, where he revived *Jardin aux Lilas* and *Gala Performance* for the Royal Swedish Ballet. He returned briefly to Ballet Theatre the following year and, in May 1950, produced a slight piece, *Nimbus,* to music by Louis Gruenberg, in which Kaye portrayed a Working Girl and Laing her "Dream Beau."

In the 1950/51 season Laing and Diana Adams, who had married, left Ballet Theatre to join New York City Ballet; they were followed a few months later by Kaye and Tudor. Tudor's first work for New York City Ballet was *The Lady of the Camellias,* presented in February 1951 to a selection of music by Giuseppe Verdi (but none from *La Traviata*). Its main *raison d'être,* other than as a vehicle for Adams and Laing, was to make use of scenery and costumes designed by Cecil Beaton for an earlier *Camille* ballet by John Taras for Original Ballet Russe. Tudor, who appeared under a pseudonym in the role of Armand's father, later described his task as that of "a short order cook." Given the circumstances, except for the lovers' pastoral duet, the result was mediocre.

Tudor's attempt to provide a vehicle for Kaye was not much better. In *La Gloire* (February 1952), Kaye portrayed a Sarah Bernhardt-like actress both onstage (as Lucretia, Phaedra, and Hamlet) and off (with her lovers). The work was in three scenes, and the music consisted of three

TUDOR. *Gala Performance,* made for the London Ballet in 1938, was restaged and revised for Ballet Theatre in 1941. A spoof of mannerisms of rival *prima ballerinas* from Russia, Italy, and France, it remained a repertory staple for many years. In a 1946 performance, the three ballerinas were portrayed by Nora Kaye (kneeling, at left of center), as La Reine de la Danse (from Moscow); Alicia Alonso (center), as La Déesse de la Danse (from Milan); and Norma Vance (bowing, at right of center) as La Fille de Terpsichore (from Paris). They are flanked by Tudor (at left) and Hugh Laing (at right) as their cavaliers. (Photograph from the Dance Collection, New York Public Library for the Performing Arts.)

Beethoven overtures, which tended to overwhelm the dance action.

Tudor's most successful work for New York City Ballet was a 1951 revival of *Jardin aux Lilas* (restaged as *Lilac Garden*), with Kaye, Laing, and Tudor in their familiar roles and with Tanaquil Le Clercq as the Other Woman. The elaborate decor by Horace Armistead was later used for several other ballets in the repertory. Kaye and Laing did not stay long with New York City Ballet, but Adams remained and became one of Balanchine's favorite ballerinas. Tudor also severed his connection with the company.

For the next few years Tudor devoted himself chiefly to teaching. He was an extraordinary teacher who challenged his students intellectually as well as physically. He had been spending summers at Jacob's Pillow in Massachusetts since the late 1940s; in 1950 he had become director of the Metropolitan Opera Ballet School; and he joined the faculty of the Juilliard dance department when it opened in 1951. Starting in 1973 he was a frequent guest instructor at the University of California, Irvine. He also served as administrative director of the Metropolitan Opera Ballet but refrained from choreographing any of the operas himself (although he had choreographed three during the 1949/50 season). Most of his choreographic work in this period consisted of small pieces for his students.

Tudor was also teaching in Philadelphia and in 1954 put on a program of ballets there, including revivals of *Les Sylphides* and Nijinsky's *L'Après-midi d'un Faune* and a new ballet, *Offenbach in the Underworld,* to the arrangement of Offenbach tunes originally used by Massine for his *Gaîté Parisienne.* This ballet subsequently went into the repertories of the Komaki Ballet, Tokyo (where Kaye was a guest artist later in 1954), of the National Ballet of Canada (1955), of Ballet Theatre when Kaye and Laing returned (1956), and of the Joffrey Ballet (1975). The piece is a hybrid: a Tudor treatment of a Massine subject, with a rowdy can-can and a characteristic passage where the various denizens of the "Bar du Can-can" wonder if they have paired off with the right partners.

Others of Tudor's ballets were revived over the years in many places, but new ballets were few: in Buenos Aires, a version of Strauss's *Die Josephslegende* (Teatro Colón, 1958); for ballet evenings at the Metropolitan Opera, *Hail and Farewell* (1959), also to music of Strauss, including his *Four Last Songs,* with Kaye as guest artist, and *Concerning Oracles,* to music of Jacques Ibert (1966); for the Royal Swedish Ballet, where Tudor returned as guest choreographer and artistic adviser from 1961 to 1963, *Ekon av Trumpeter* (1963), to music of Bohuslav Martinů. Of these, only the last was of consequence, and under the name *Echoing of Trumpets* it was taken into the repertories of American Ballet Theatre in 1967 and London Festival Ballet in 1973. Some considered this ballet, based on

TUDOR. *Dim Lustre* (1943), set to Richard Strauss's Burlesque in D Minor for Piano and Orchestra, was a ballet about love and illusion, about old, fragile passions vaguely recalled and glimpsed through the scrim of memory. Tudor staged it for the New York City Ballet in 1964, with Patricia McBride as The Lady with Him and Edward Villella as The Gentleman with Her. Costumes were designed by Beni Montresor. (Photograph by Fred Fehl; used by permission.)

the massacre of the Czech village of Lidice by the Nazis in World War II, a great dramatic work; others thought it synthetic and exploitative.

When Frederick Ashton became director of the Royal Ballet in 1963, he wanted to correct the injustice of the company's neglect of Tudor, the other great contemporary British choreographer. Tudor finally went to London in 1966 to create a new ballet, *Shadowplay,* which had its premiere in January 1967. The libretto was suggested by Rudyard Kipling's *The Jungle Book,* as was the music by Charles Koechlin. Tudor cast Anthony Dowell as the Boy who undergoes an initiation at the hands of a Terrestrial (Derek Rencher) and a Celestial (Merle Park). The ballet itself is unsatisfactory, but under Tudor's coaching Dowell gained considerable artistic maturity, making the role his own in a way that Mikhail Baryshnikov failed to do in a subsequent revival by American Ballet Theatre.

Tudor's association with the Royal Ballet continued the following year; in November 1968 the main company revived *Jardin aux Lilas* at Covent Garden (even with Svetlana Beriosova as Caroline it was unsuccessful), and the touring section presented a new ballet, *Knight Errant,* to music of Richard Strauss, with a libretto drawn from Pierre Choderlos de Laclos's *Les liaisons dangéreuses.*

Again Tudor made a central role that brought out the talent of a young male star, in this case David Wall, who played the Philandering Hero (though not at the first performance, when he was out with an injury. Neither of these ballets remained for long in the respective repertories; in 1980 the Royal Ballet revived *Dark Elegies*, with no greater success.

In the summer of 1969 Tudor was invited by the Australian Ballet to revive *Pillar of Fire* and to make a new piece, *The Divine Horsemen*, with music by Werner Egk, based on the book by Maya Deren. Both were designed by Hugh Laing, who had designed the original costumes for *The Judgment of Paris* and in 1970 designed *Gala Performance* for the Royal Danish Ballet.

Tudor often made small pieces for his students. Among these, *Little Improvisations*, to music by Robert Schumann, given at Jacob's Pillow in 1953 and at Juilliard in 1960, and *Fandango*, to music by Antonio Soler, given at the Metropolitan Opera Ballet Studio in 1963, have gone into the repertories of several companies. In 1971 Tudor received a choreographic grant from the National Endowment for the Arts, in fulfillment of which he made three short, originally untitled, ballets for his Juilliard students.

TUDOR. Created in 1967 for the Royal Ballet, *Shadowplay* was revived in 1975 for American Ballet Theatre. Mikhail Baryshnikov is pictured here in the principal role of The Boy with Matted Hair; behind him stands Danilo Radojevich as the dominating figure of The Terrestrial. Set to music by Charles Koechlin, the scenario is an allegory of life based loosely on Rudyard Kipling's *The Jungle Book*. (Photograph © 1976 by Linda Vartoogian; used by permission.)

Later called *Sunflowers*, to music of Leoš Janáček; *Cereus*, to music by Geoffrey Guy; and *Continuo*, to music by Johann Pachelbel, these were made available to virtually any company that wanted to do them.

In 1974 Tudor was appointed associate director of American Ballet Theatre, and in the company's 1975 summer season at the New York State Theater two of his ballets were added to the repertory, *Shadowplay* and the new *The Leaves Are Fading*, a lyrical, even rhapsodic work about young love. The story depicted in the ballet seems to take place in the memory of a woman who passes across the stage at the work's beginning and end. Like many people, Tudor was apparently captivated by the fullness and fearlessness of Gelsey Kirkland's dancing at that stage of her career, for he cast her both as The Celestial in *Shadowplay* and as the woman in the leading couple in *Leaves*. The new ballet suffered from an excessive evenness of texture, induced perhaps by the music, a selection of Antonín Dvořák's lesser string pieces.

The Tiller in the Fields (December 1978), also to Dvořák (movements from two symphonies and an overture), was a kind of sequel. Again the leading role was danced by Kirkland and seemed to be built around her offbeat personality as much as her gifts as a dancer. She played the Gypsy Girl who is seduced by (or who seduces) the Peasant Lad, and she appears at the end with padding to simulate pregnancy. The theme recalls Janáček's song cycle *Diary of One Who Vanished*. Unlike its predecessor, which has returned to the American Ballet Theatre repertory from time to time (and was revived by the Royal Danish Ballet in 1984), *The Tiller in the Fields* was soon dropped. It was Tudor's last ballet, though he continued to be listed as choreographer emeritus by American Ballet Theatre.

In February 1985 the Paris Opera Ballet presented an evening in homage to Tudor, whose works were hardly known in France. The program consisted of *Shadowplay*, *Jardin aux Lilas*, *Continuo*, and *Dark Elegies*. Tudor was not in attendance.

Any study of Tudor's career must ask why his creativity faded after producing a handful of masterpieces in his first fifteen years as a choreographer? Was this a deliberate abdication on his part—a withdrawal from the spotlight? Always reclusive, Tudor was for years a resident of the First Zen Institute in New York, and he seems to have been convinced that he had nothing more to express. Lack of movement invention was not his problem, but too often in his later ballets the subject matter was not made manifest through the dancing itself. As Denby wrote of *Undertow*, "one keeps watching the movement all through for the intellectual meaning its pantomime conveys more than for its physical impetus as dancing." Even in his most productive period Tudor was never prolific in the way that his contemporaries, Ashton and Balanchine,

TUDOR. Gelsey Kirkland, Tudor's last muse, with Iván Nagy in a 1980 performance of *The Leaves Are Fading*, created for her in 1975 to music by Antonín Dvořák. Costumes were designed by Patricia Zipprodt. (Photograph © 1980 by Max Waldman; used by permission.)

BIBLIOGRAPHY

Chazin-Bennahum, Judith. *The Ballets of Antony Tudor: Studies in Psyche and Satire.* New York, 1995.

Cohen, Selma Jeanne. "Antony Tudor: The Years in America and After." *Dance Perspectives*, no. 18 (1963).

Coton, A. V. *Writings on Dance, 1938–1968.* Edited by Kathrine Sorley Walker and Lilian Haddakin. London, 1975.

Heppenstall, Rayner. *Apology for Dancing.* London, 1936.

Jordan, Stephanie. "Antony Tudor: His Use of Music and Movement." *Eddy*, no. 8 (Spring–Summer 1976): 18–23.

Lloyd, Maude. "Some Recollections of the English Ballet." *Dance Research* 3 (Autumn 1984): 39–52.

Percival, John. "Antony Tudor: The Years in England." *Dance Perspectives*, no. 17 (1963).

Perlmutter, Donna. *Shadowplay/The Life of Antony Tudor.* New York, 1991.

Van Praagh, Peggy. "Working with Antony Tudor." *Dance Research* 2 (Summer 1984): 56–67.

Vaughan, David. "Antony Tudor's Early Ballets." In *The Myriad Faces of Dance: Proceedings of the Eighth Annual Conference, Society of Dance History Scholars, University of New Mexico, 15–17 February 1985*, compiled by Christena L. Schlundt. Riverside, Calif., 1985.

DAVID VAUGHAN

were, and it may be that a failure to exercise the craft of choreography in the end caused a stoppage of his creativity.

Nevertheless, any choreographer will be ultimately judged on only a few works. It is tragic that Tudor's *The Planets, The Descent of Hebe*, and above all *Romeo and Juliet*—the finest of all ballets on that overworked subject—have been lost. Tudor's reputation must rest on the few ballets that survive: judged by such works as *Jardin aux Lilas, Dark Elegies*, and *Pillar of Fire*, Tudor's status as one of the greatest choreographers of the twentieth century beyond dispute.

In 1986 Tudor received the Capezio Dance Award and New York City's Handel Medallion, and he was a recipient of the Kennedy Center Honors. At the Capezio award ceremony, Mikhail Baryshnikov, then artistic director of American Ballet Theatre, said, "We do Tudor's ballets because we must. Tudor is our conscience." Until a day or two before his death Tudor was rehearsing a new cast for *Pillar of Fire* with American Ballet Theatre.

[*See also* Dark Elegies; Jardin aux Lilas; *and* Pillar of Fire.]

TULSA BALLET THEATRE. Since its inception in 1956, the thirty-member Tulsa Ballet Theatre, based in one of the major cities of Oklahoma, has been characterized by fine, classical training and a conservative approach to repertory selection. Its founding directors, Roman Jasinski and Moscelyne Larkin, married in 1943 when they were dancers with Colonel de Basil's Original Ballet Russe. They later joined Sergei Denham's Ballet Russe de Monte Carlo. Outstanding works from the repertories of these companies have gained a home with the Tulsa Ballet Theatre.

The company has also revived ballets that otherwise might never have been seen again. In 1978 David Lichine's version of *The Prodigal Son*, originally danced by Jasinski, was revived for his son, Roman L. Jasinski. Serge Lifar's *Icare* was also revived. In 1982 the "Hand of Fate" pas de deux from George Balanchine's *Cotillon* received avid critical attention when the company took it to New York. The same was true in 1987, when Balanchine's *Mozart Violin Concerto* was revived. In 1990 Michel Fokine's *Paganini* was also returned to the stage.

Until his death in 1991, Jasinski was the company's principal choreographer. Although he preferred to create abstract works, such as *Tribute, Convolutions*, and *Zingara*, one of his most successful productions was *The Bamboo Princess*, a dramatic ballet created in 1983 in collaboration with Sahomi Tachibana. Jasinski's early training was at the Warsaw Opera Ballet School, whereas Larkin's training began in Tulsa at the school of her mother, Eva Matlagova, and later continued in New York. From the outset the couple's Tulsa school was characterized by their mutually high standards.

Unlike most other regional companies in the United States, Tulsa Ballet Theatre does not have a substantial nucleus of Balanchine ballets, nor does it foster new or experimental choreographers from outside the company or from within its ranks. Its specially commissioned works have included *Cinderella* and *Romeo and Juliet*, staged by Alun Jones, director of the Louisville Ballet. It also has acquired such repertory staples as Eugene Loring's *Billy the Kid*, Lew Christensen's *Con Amore*, the Ruth Page–Bentley Stone *Frankie and Johnny*, Agnes de Mille's *Rodeo*, and Léonide Massine's *Gaîté Parisienne*. Of more recent vintage are Peter Anastos's *Yes, Virginia, Another Piano Ballet* and Lisa de Ribere's *Casey at the Bat*.

Because of its somewhat popular approach to repertory, Tulsa Ballet Theatre's finances have remained unusually stable. In 1992, it was able to dedicate a handsome new home structured from a former public school building.

In 1991, after his father's death and a relatively brief career with the Cincinnati Ballet and American Ballet Theatre, Roman L. Jasinski became artistic director, and his mother functioned actively as artistic director emerita. Jasinski's tenure was turbulent. He resigned in 1994, as did the company's longtime general manager Connie Cronley. In 1995, Marcello Angelini, a dancer with the Cincinnati Ballet, became Tulsa Ballet Theatre's new artistic director.

BIBLIOGRAPHY
Anderson, Jack. *The One and Only: The Ballet Russe de Monte Carlo.* New York, 1981.
Anderson, Jack. Obituary: Roman Jasinski. *New York Times* (17 April 1991).
Garafola, Lynn. "Fokine's *Paganini* Resurrected." *Ballet Review* 14 (Spring 1986): 69–71.
Livingston, Lili Cockerille. "Tulsa Ballet Theatre's Ballet Russe Renaissance." *Dance Magazine* (February 1988): 54–63.
Livingston, Lili Cockerille. "Jasinski Leaves Tulsa Ballet Theatre." *Dance Magazine* (February 1995): 28–34.
Souvenir Program. Tulsa Ballet Theatre, 1992.

INTERVIEW.   Roman Jasinski, by Doris Hering (July 1976), Dance Collection, Oral History Tapes, New York Public Library for the Performing Arts.

DORIS HERING

TUNE, TOMMY (Thomas James Tune; born 28 February 1939 in Witchita Falls, Texas), American director, choreographer, and dancer. As a youngster, Tune studied ballet and produced theatrical entertainments in his family's garage in Witchita Falls. By the time he reached his full height—six feet, six inches—in high school, he had grown too tall for a classical dance career and instead set his sights on the theater. He took courses at Lon Morris Junior College, earned a Bachelor of Fine Arts degree in dramatic arts from the University of Texas at Austin in 1962, and pursued graduate studies the following year at the University of Houston.

New York City seemed a better venue than Houston for pursuing stardom, and Tune got a job on his first day in town with a U.S. touring production of the Broadway musical *Irma La Douce*. His New York debut was on 16 February 1965, when he appeared as a chorus dancer in *Baker Street* at the Broadway Theater. During the following year he appeared in *A Joyful Noise*, with dances by Michael Bennett, and was given a solo in the 1967 *How Now Dow Jones?*

Tune choreographed a tour of *The Canterbury Tales*, then moved to Hollywood in 1969 to play Ambrose Kemper in the film *Hello, Dolly!*, remaining in California as a television series regular on *Dean Martin Presents the Golddiggers*. He was cast in the 1971 film version of *The Boyfriend*, starring the willowy former model Twiggy. While shooting the movie in London, lean and lanky Tune recognized Twiggy as his perfect dancing partner, although the two did not appear together onstage until the 1983 production of *My One and Only*.

Back in New York, he was cast as David in Bennett's production of *Seesaw*, which opened on 18 March 1973 at the Uris Theater and subsequently moved to the Mark Hellinger. Troubled with money problems, *Seesaw* was still a significant critical success, completing a respectable Broadway run and national tour. For it, Tune won his first Tony Award as Best Supporting or Featured Actor in a Musical.

Tune's first New York directing assignment came in 1976, for Eve Merriman's satirical *The Club* at Circle in the Square. His colorful sex-role charades gave a light touch to sometimes dark material, which became a hallmark of his work. The following year he directed *Sunset* at the Studio Arena in Buffalo and began a collaboration on what would become his first blockbuster, *The Best Little Whorehouse in Texas*.

With co-director Peter Masterson and co-choreographer Thomie Walsh, Tune was able to capitalize on his Texas heritage. Among many colorful numbers, the dance he devised for football players, cheerleaders, and stuffed dummies is probably the most memorable. The popular success of *The Best Little Whorehouse in Texas* at the Entermedia caused the production to be moved to Broadway's Forty-sixth Street Theater. For it, he won a 1978 Tony as Best Director of a Musical.

Again collaborating with Walsh, Tune was recognized during the following season for direction and choreography for *A Day in Hollywood/A Night in the Ukraine*, notable for its inventive "ankle stage." For this production he won two 1980 Tonys, as Best Director of a Musical and as Best Choreographer, and he received the 1979/80 Drama Desk awards for Best Choreography and Best Staging of a Musical.

Caryl Churchill's nonmusical *Cloud 9* (1981) was Tune's next success. Produced off-Broadway at the Theatre de Lys, the play was given a strongly visual interpretation by Tune, who again used gender-changing role modeling as a technique for revealing both text and subtext. In the spring, he directed and choreographed *Nine*, adapted from Fellini's film *8½*. *Nine* won five Tonys, including for Tune Best Musical and Best Director of a Musical; he also accepted Drama Desk awards as Best Director of a Musical *(Nine)* and Best Director of a Play *(Cloud 9)*. With a 1982 Obie as Best Director for *Cloud 9* as well, Tune's was a distinctive triple-crown Broadway achievement.

The sweetness of Tune's onstage persona was best expressed in the role of Captain Billy Buck Chandler in *My One and Only* (1983), in which he starred, directed and co-choreographed with Walsh. At last paired with Twiggy, Tune evoked the romance of an earlier era in top hat and tails, dancing to the silky tunes of George Gershwin from *Funny Face*, with a new book by Timothy Mayer. An effervescent sense of theatrical wonder and joy permeated *My One and Only*, presenting theatergoers with a perfect prescription for elegant escape. Tune and Walsh shared Tony and Drama Desk Awards for Choreography, and Tune received a 1983 Tony for Best Actor in a Musical. In that same year he directed the initial, problematic version of *Steppin' Out*. He was presented the *Dance Magazine* Award for 1984, and Twiggy attended the ceremony to take photographs from the first row of the audience.

With co-choreographer Marge Champion, Tune directed another edition of *Steppin' Out* in 1987 that received neither critical nor popular endorsement. He soon turned his creative sights from frothier confections to darker flirtations with the lavish and compelling *Grand Hotel* (1989). Set in the gilded decadence of 1920s Berlin, *Grand Hotel* presented some of Tune's most vivid couple dances (partly inspired by the triumphant 1985 New York appearance of *Tango Argentino*). The titilating presentation of feminine charms was a highlight of *The Will Rogers Follies*, which opened at the Palace Theater on 1 May 1991; the production won six Tony awards and Tune was honored as Best Choreographer.

The film *That's Dancing* (1984) and the television special "Irving Berlin's 100th Birthday Salute" (CBS, 1988) gave Tune opportunities that have continued with other television experiments. Besides the creativity of his tap and softshoe compositions, Tune is credited with breaking up and opening out the narrow range of body types that had become associated with chorus lines. His own height made him especially sensitive to size, and his productions have focused on dancers of many shapes and lengths, rather than on a single profile. He is noted principally for his innovative choreography and musical staging, for stylish comedy, and for adapting material from other media for the theater.

TUNE. *My One and Only* (1983) featured Tune and Twiggy singing and dancing to a selection of show tunes by George Gershwin. With Tune not only co-starring but co-choreographing, the dancing vied with Gershwin's beloved melodies as the highlight of the show. (Photograph by Kenn Duncan; used by permission of Virginia Duncan Shearer.)

BIBLIOGRAPHY
Bordman, Gerald. *American Musical Theatre: A Chronicle.* 2d ed. New York and Oxford, 1992.

ARCHIVES. Dance Collection and Theater Collection, New York Public Library for the Performing Arts.

CAMILLE HARDY

TUNISIA. Once part of Phoenician Carthage, Tunisia was conquered by Rome in the second century BCE and by the Muslims spreading Islam in the seventh century CE. The Ottoman Empire ruled from the sixteenth century until the *beys* (governors) gained their independence and founded a center for corsairing in the eighteenth and nineteenth centuries. France established a protectorate in 1881; it was the site of fierce battles during World War II, and Tunisia became independent in 1956.

A small North African country with a fairly homogeneous population, Tunisia has extensive contact and interchange among its various regions, which accounts, at least in part, for the similarity of its traditional dance styles. In general, many dances typical of North Africa are also found in Tunisia. Rifle and sword dances, once common throughout the country, can still be seen in isolated areas, such as the southern oasis town of Nefta. The exorcistic rites of the sub-Saharan brotherhoods, called *stambeli* in Tunisia, consist primarily of singing. Their dance is a simple procession in which they accompany themselves with the typical *chakchakas* (forged iron percussion instruments).

On the islands of Djerba and Kerkenna, male musicians dressed in nineteenth-century costumes dance while playing the *tbal* (large two-headed drum) and the *mizwid* (bagpipe) or the *darabukka* (clay goblet drum) and the *zikra* (folk oboe). Their dancing includes complex pelvic rotations, graceful walking, and smoothly executed squat turns. In the southern coastal area, around Medenine, male dancers dressed in flowing robes dance with canes and handkerchiefs to a drum made from a shallow bowl covered with a skin. The dance consists primarily of simple walking and running steps.

In Tunisia, as in North Africa generally, numerous ecstatic brotherhoods are attached to the shrines of local saints. They hold special commemorative gatherings during which they sing, speak in tongues, mortify the flesh, or dance. One of the brotherhoods of Sidi Alī in Nefta is an example of the latter. Their meeting takes place in a courtyard. The members dance in a loose line, facing a row of musicians playing *bendirs* (circular frame drums). The dancers throw their torsos violently, but rhythmically, up and down. Their heads move reciprocally, producing a slight undulating quality. This motion is similar to a movement common in Moroccan Berber dances but is more extreme. As the dance progresses, the drummers shift into different rhythmic patterns, producing a gradual acceleration and growing excitement. The dancers repeat the same movement over and over until some fall to the ground unconscious. The dancing may go on all night.

In the small towns of Tunisia, song and dance play an especially important role. They occur at every wedding and at most large celebrations, as well as at home. Often, after the family dinner is over, someone may sing a popular song or two. If the mood is festive enough, dancing will begin. All present—men, women, and children—are urged to participate.

Traditional social dancing is an improvisational form performed as a solo or duo. Tunisian dancing does not differ appreciably whether performed by a male or a female (as is true generally in North African dance). The movements of the torso are so integral a part of the folk culture that country people use them unself-consciously. Although performing this style of dance in public is frowned upon, almost anyone can enjoy dancing among friends and family.

Tunisians dance to the music of the *darabukka* and the *mizwid* and, especially at large outdoor celebrations, the *tbal* and the *zikra*. The most usual dance rhythms are 6/8 and 12/16. The dance style is characterized by light, glid-

TUNISIA. The Ali Suissi ensemble from the island of Kerkenna, in a 1977 performance at the Dar Shaab in Sfax. In North Africa, it is not uncommon for dancers to play musical instruments while dancing. (Photograph by Aisha Ali; from the collection of Mardi Rollow.)

TUNISIA. Nabila, a professional dancer, demonstrates the Tunisian women's style at a performance at the Dar Shaab in Sfax, 1977. (Photograph by Aisha Ali; from the collection of Mardi Rollow.)

ing steps and vigorous horizontal hip movements, which are accentuated by the fullness of the traditional dress, called *melia* or *palla*, and the flying ends of the yarn belts commonly worn. The rural women have excellent carriage; the vigor of their hip movements does not interfere with the gliding character of their steps.

A Tunisian woman dances with her arms held slightly forward and to the sides, with fingertips up and palms away from the body. Her arms are relaxed, although she sometimes accentuates the sharp movements of her hips with strong reciprocal arm motions.

Occasionally, a woman will dance with scarves, moving them from side to side and up and down, in a manner complementary to the hip accents. Professional dancers sometimes add sharp shimmies to the usual repertory of movements. They may sit and perform a number of simple mimetic movements, such as preparing a meal of couscous, combing the hair, and applying makeup. Balancing a water jar on the head is a popular embellishment.

Tunisia has a national folk-dance company, the National Ensemble of Popular Arts, based in Tunis, that presents highly choreographed versions of folk styles. Although company members have been recruited from all over Tunisia, they do not necessarily perform dances from their own regions. Fortunately, there are still places, such as Djerba, Medenine, and Nefta, where the local inhabitants perform their dances much as they may have done for centuries.

[*See also* North Africa.]

BIBLIOGRAPHY
Rollow, Mardi. "Traditional Dance in Tunisia." *Arabesque* 5 (May–June 1979): 10–15.

RECORDING. *Music of the Shikhat and Dance Music of Tunisia* (Disques Maghrébins 5001).

VIDEOTAPE. *Dances of North Africa: Vol. 1, Morocco and Tunisia* (Araf, 1995).

AISHA ALI, MARDI ROLLOW, and LEONA WOOD

TURCZYNOWICZ, ROMAN (born 14 March 1813 in Radom, Poland, died 21 May 1882 in Warsaw), Polish dancer, choreographer, and ballet director. Turczynowicz trained at the ballet school attached to Warsaw's Wielki Theater, where he performed as a principal dancer from 1825 to 1843. Although he preferred character roles, he also played classical roles, such as James in *La Sylphide*, Alidor in *Fee und Ritter*, and Alvar in *Hertha's Sacrifice*.

In 1843 Turczynowicz began choreographing with the support of Filippo Taglioni, the newly engaged director of the Warsaw Ballet. Three years later he made his choreographic debut with *Peasant Feast near Kielce*. His interest in Romantic and national themes continued throughout his career. As second company choreographer he staged his own versions of *Le Diable à Quatre* (1847), *Giselle* (1848), *Catarina, ou La Fille de Bandit* (1850), and *Esmeralda* (1851). His stagings maintained a balance between mime and pure dance and between male and female dancing.

From 1853 to 1866 Turczynowicz served as director of the school and company. Although the Russian authorities forbade ballets on national themes, he set stage versions of national dances in almost every ballet in the repertory, crowning the whole series with *mazur, polonez,* and Highlanders' dances for Stanisław Miniuszko's opera *Halka* in 1858, which remained in the repertory until 1917. He also emphasized character dancing in the curriculum of the school.

Turczynowicz's wife, Konstancja (1818–1880), was a principal dancer from 1832 to 1853 at the Wielki Theater, excelling in both character and classical roles. She taught Marie Taglioni the *mazur*. In 1842 she appeared with her husband in a program of Polish national dances at the Paris Opera. From 1832 to 1853 she taught at the ballet school affiliated with the Wielki Theater.

BIBLIOGRAPHY

Chynowski, Paweł, and Janina Pudełek. *Almanach baletu warszawskiego, 1785–1985/Le ballet de Varsovie, 1785–1985.* Warsaw, 1987.

Pudełek, Janina. *Warszawski balet romantyczny, 1802–1866.* Warsaw, 1968.

Pudełek, Janina. *Two Hundred Years of Polish Ballet, 1785–1985.* Warsaw, 1985.

JANINA PUDEŁEK

TURKEY. The Turks, descendants of nomadic peoples of Central Asia, had been living on the Anatolian Plateau for centuries before they began an agressive advance into neighboring eastern Europe, the Levant, northern Africa, and western Asia to create an empire—the Ottoman Empire—which lasted from the fourteenth to the twentieth century. The Turks had practiced shamanism, then Buddhism and Manichaeism, but with their conquest of Constantinople in 1453, then capital of the Byzantine Empire, they accepted Islam. The city was renamed Istanbul and it became the capital of both their empire and the Islamic caliphate. With the demise of the empire after World War I, the Republic of Turkey, with its new capital at Ankara, was founded as a secular, Western-style country.

Traditional Dance. Because many cultures have lived in and crossed Anatolia, the dances of Anatolian Turkey possess a rich heritage of movement and gesture. Even with this heterogeneous heritage, Turkish folklore never lost the flexibility to add new components. Turkish folk dances are therefore a blend of the cultural traditions of several folk cultures.

After the Anatolian tradition, the two most important influences on Turkish dance come from Asia, including one directly from the shamanistic rituals of the Ural-Altaic region [*see* Shamanism], from which the Turkish peoples originated, and one indirectly from other Asian cultures, such as the Chinese. The dances of Turkestan (a region between the Caspian Sea and the Gobi Desert), which were brought west to Turkey, were probably introduced to China as well, where dances from Central Asia had been enjoyed in antiquity. Contemporary Anatolian folk dances bear myriad signs of shamanistic influences. The most important of these is dancing to the accompaniment of the drum in which the Anatolian drum *(davul)* is the primary instrument. Also widespread in both urban and rural Turkey is animal mimicry—simulated by gesture or by masks and other disguises, just as shamans donned animal skins. Some of these dances are relics of ancient Anatolia, but others reflect a synthesis of Anatolian and Central Asian cultures.

The third major influence on Turkish dance is that of Islam. Because Islam is fundamentally antagonistic to dance, its influence has been largely negative. (There is a ban against women dancing with men, for example.) Positive aspects, however, have been acquired from increased

TURKEY. A member of the Mevlevi order of Sufis, performing the whirling dance characteristic of the order, founded in the thirteenth century by the poet-philosopher Jalāl al-Dīn Rūmī. Through their revolving dance, the dervishes (the word refers to a person on the threshold of enlightenment) strive to detach themselves from earth and become spiritually united with a nonpersonified God. (Collection of Metin And.)

contact with other Islamic traditions—mainly the Arab and Persian. Islamic puritanism did not greatly affect Turkish peasants, who retained both their ethnic unity and their dancing. Despite Islamic bans, in many of the peasant dances, men and women do dance together, especially among the heterodox (non-Sunni Islamic) tribes. The fourth influence was caused by the expansion of the Turkish empire, with ensuing cultural exchanges among its varied peoples.

The fifth has been the influences of Western civilization. From the Republic of Turkey's modern and secular beginnings under Kemal Atatürk in the 1920s, westernization has set Turkey apart from the other Muslim nations. Modern improvements in communications and other factors have been lessening the practice and purity of folk dancing, yet more than a thousand traditional Turkish dances remain. The heterodox Turkish tribes living across Anatolia, some still seminomadic, have preserved a form of traditional Turkish culture.

The Turkish word *oyun*, for "dance," covers a wide field of concepts that have little to do with dance; Turkish *raks* (from Arabic *raqṣ*) means both "dancing" and "a form of dance." In 1975 the State Folk Dance Company was formed to present Turkey's rich heritage of dance at home and abroad.

Ecstatic and Sacred Dance. Despite Islamic bans, the Sufi concept of music and dancing as part of religious experience gained acceptance in Turkey; various Muslim religious orders of dervishes practice Sufi mysticism. The central Asian shamanistic influence may still be felt most strongly in the quasi-religious dances of these orders, especially the Bektaşi and Kalendar dervishes, who had a powerful influence among nomadic heterodox tribes and people of the Alevi sect, an Anatolian offshoot of Shiism. In Sufism, *sema* (Ar., *samāᶜ*) is the practice of listening to music, singing, and chanting to attain a state of religious ecstasy; *zikr* (Ar., *dhikr*), the repeated recital of short invocations to Allah with movements to vocal or instrumental accompaniment, helps to free physical effort from conscious thought. The complex ceremonial dances of the dervish orders usually begin with a slow movement that increases in speed. The Mevlevi (Mawlawīyah) order (the "whirling dervishes") was founded by the poet and mystic Jalāl al-Dīn Rūmī (known in Turkish as Mevlana Celaleddin Rumi) in the thirteenth-century city of Konya, then the capital of the Seljuk Turks. The dancers are first blessed by their leader. Then, with arms crossed on their breasts, heads bent, and feet close together, they turn very slowly, resting on each heel in turn. As the speed of their spinning increases, their long white skirts flare outward. Sometimes the right hand is raised, palm upward, and the left lowered, palm downward, symbolizing the belief that the influence of heaven is handed down to the world. The whirling symbolizes the celestial motions—the earth turning on its axis as it revolves around the sun. As the dervishes spin, they circle the hall (termed "the hall of celestial sound").

The quasi-religious dances of the Alevi (see above) parallel these. Some of these people are still seminomadic and hold indoor parties at which there is male-female dancing. These carefully guarded dances are performed in secrecy from fear of the Sunni bans. As the Alevi do not intermarry with other sects, their cultural unity has preserved their dances. Despite the sacred air of these mixed-sex dances, they usually have a social nature. Two to sixteen dancers take part. Sometimes a master of ceremonies invites both men and women, who sit on opposite sides of the room, to dance. They face each other, extend their arms forward, cross them on their chests, and dance without ever touching each other. When a dancer is tired, a man goes to a man, and a woman to a

TURKEY. Unlike most devout Muslims, members of the Alevi sect, an offshoot of Shiism, enjoy male-female dancing on social occasions. These dancers are from one of the seminomadic groups of Alevi who live in rural Turkey. Characteristically, they do not touch each other while dancing. (Photograph from the collection of Metin And.)

woman, inviting the person to replace him or her with a kiss on the knees, called *niyaz*.

Professional Dancing. Some Turkish dancing is primarily designed to entertain spectators; it is performed by professional boy and girl dancers, buffoons, grotesque dancers, and dancers in theatrical performances. Like most Asian theater, traditional Turkish theater fuses dance, music, acrobatics, song, and story. Turkish shadow puppet theater seems to have borrowed movements and costumes from the Ottoman jesters and grotesque dancers who entertained long before the shadow theater. Also, throughout rural Anatolia countless unsophisticated dramas are enacted, accompanied by singing, dancing, and mime; some use masks and animal mimicry—probably a legacy of ancient shamanistic and religious rites.

TURKEY. Often performing acrobatic and virtuosic dances, buffoon characters were popular acts in Ottoman processions. This eighteenth-century buffoon carries an implement used to strike the small drum worn at his waist. (Collection of Metin And.)

Dancing by buffoons, wandering dervishes, and boys dressed as females was an important part of Ottoman spectacular processions, both in cities and villages. Comic dancers, *curcunabaz*, were members of the same companies as boy dancers, acrobats, and tumblers; their grotesque costumes and postures contrasted with the boys' artistic eroticism. The buffoons sometimes wore masks and sometimes imitated animals. The dancers displayed their virtuosity: the *kasebaz* danced and twirled *majolica* plates on their fingers, while other dancers performed acrobatics and contortions, and still others danced on stilts.

Boy and girl dancers, hired for exhibition dancing, are still an established institution throughout the Middle East. In Ottoman Turkey the word *çengi*, which referred both to the boys and the girls, was basically synonymous with the French terms *comédiant(e)* and *joueur de farce*. A "company" of these boys or girls was a *kol*, their "leader" was the *kolbşı*.

The dancing boys called *köçek* cultivated a feminine appearance; they often grew their hair long and dressed like girls, dancing with languid movements and suggestive gestures, and marking time with clappers or by finger snapping. They danced rapidly, with somersaults, wrestling, and mimicry; in the dance *tavşan raksı*, they sprang lightly and moved the muscles of their faces like rabbits *(tavşan)*. Their popularity among the urban population caused trouble, so *köçek* performances were banned by the sultan in 1857. Nevertheless, in Anatolian villages both amateur and professional *köçek* still perform at weddings and other parties, some wearing wide, multicolored skirts. When these boys are older, they often become drummers for younger *köçek*.

The *çengi* dancing girls were very popular. Holding a silk scarf, they performed sensuous contortions and pantomimes of physical love—alternatively acting coy or alluring. The *kolbaşı* was an older woman, and a *kol* usually included twelve dancing girls and four musicians playing a fiddle, a double drum called a *nekkare*, and two tambourines. In addition to dancing for male audiences, they danced in women's public bathhouses and in the women's quarters in the houses of the wealthy. The *çengi* girls often dressed as boys or men and were believed to arouse lesbian desires among women in their audience. First

TURKEY. A nineteenth-century print of a dancing girl with finger cymbals. (Collection of Metin And.)

they sang, saluted the audience, and marched around in rhythm. Then, with finger cymbals clicking, they quivered and gyrated their bodies in sensuous undulations. In the third part of their performance, in the *tavşan rakşı*, they wore trousers and whirled and jumped. The final part of the performance was more a pantomime with singing. A favorite role was the *kalyoncu* (galley sailor), in which the principal dancer mimed a braggart captain challenging his rivals.

Although the dancing girls were not banned in 1857, as the boys were, their popularity has waned. Today, their dancing is merely the corrupt belly dancing [*see* Danse du Ventre] of nightclubs; in Anatolian villages, however, female *çengi* still perform occasionally.

Nonprofessional Dancing. As a reflection of the pure joy of dancing, and not for the admiration of spectators, dancing by nonprofessionals serves to reinforce social solidarity. Such dances include all folk dancing and those dances with magico-religious purposes whose origins are lost in antiquity. The dances easily disappear in urban surroundings but have survived in great variety in the Turkish countryside. Turkish folk dances are regional, but among some common elements of basic movement the most widespread is crouching or kneeling, possibly a central Asian influence. Other characteristic movements are lifting one knee to a half-bent position; the sole of the foot remains parallel to the ground while the other leg supports the weight of the body. One arm is extended above the shoulder while the other points downward. Heavy foot stamping is also typical. In many dances, for both men and women, either every dancer holds a handkerchief in the right hand or the leader of the line holds it. There are line, ring, couple, and solo dances, some danced only by men, some only by women, and some by both—although the sexes rarely touch. The accompaniment may be instrumental or vocal.

In eastern Anatolia, the word for "group dances" is *bar*. In central Anatolia the most popular dances are *kaşık oyunu*, in which each dancer uses a pair of wooden spoons like castanets, and *halay*, in which the dancers hold one another's hands or shoulders in a line, from which the leader may break away to perform a solo. In the north of Turkey and on the Black Sea coast the typical dance is the *horon;* in southwest Anatolia, it is the *teke;* and in western Turkey and on the Aegean coast, it is the *zeybek*. One of the best-known Turkish dances can be performed by one dancer or by several, in a special solemn, heroic style; in Turkish Thrace, the word for this dance is *karşılama* (a solo) or *sirto* (usually a chain dance). Considerable regional overlapping exists, however, so one word may be used to describe different dances in the different regions.

Turkish dances may be themeless or mimetic. The latter can be categorized in five groups, by the subject imitated:

TURKEY. Women from the Black Sea area performing a line dance. (Photograph from the collection of Metin And.)

the actions of animals; the daily routine of village life or seasonal work; the personification of nature; combat, with or without weapons; and courtship. In the first group of dances the performer is disguised as an animal or uses stylized movements to suggest the animal. Both may be vestiges of ancient rites. The trembling movements in the *horon* are thought to symbolize the local *hamsi* ("anchovies")—the dance being a vestige of a fertility or an abundance rite. There are many variants of an eagle dance, *kartal halayı*, that depict the hopping, sidling advance of the bird toward its prey, while the arms of the dancers mimic wings. In a *kartal halayı* from Tokat, a hat placed in the circle symbolizes the prey; near the end of the dance one dancer attacks this and grasps it with his teeth.

A typical mimetic dance of everyday life is the *köy halayı* from the Sivas area, in which the dancers mime various village tasks and conclude with a lively dance called *hoplatma*, a kind of thanksgiving. In *esnaf* ("craftsman"), a mimicking song and dance from Kastamonu performed by women and children, the gestures reflect movements used in various trades—there are countless dances of this type.

Of dances personifying nature, a graceful chain dance for women is "Ben Bir Kavak" (I Am a Poplar Tree). In it, the dancers glide sideways, gently swaying their bodies and arms. A typical combat dance is the *hançer barı* from Erzerum, in which two dancers, each holding a dagger in both hands, depict movements of attack and defense. In Giresun on the Black Sea, a rifle dance, *çandırlı tüfek oyunu*, is danced before the bride's house when the crowd comes to take her to her groom's village. There are many sword and shield dances, for couples and for lines facing each other. In a popular Anatolian dance, *sinsin*, dancers form a ring around a bonfire and each in turn stands in the center. In turn, the dancer in the center hits another

TURKEY. Combat dancers that utilize rifles or swords are popular, as seen in this photograph of men from eastern Anatolia. (Photograph from the collection of Metin And.)

on the back, to signal his turn in the center. The encircling dancers increase their speed, with each in turn leaping over the fire.

In courtship dances, the man seldom touches his partner—and sometimes a man dressed as a woman dances the female part. In many dances from eastern Turkey the man follows the woman closely, with open arms (like barriers encircling her), while the woman makes expressive movements with her hands and wrists.

Theatrical Dance. Before 1947 in Turkey, classical ballet was known from a few performances by visiting companies. In that year, Dame Ninette de Valois was invited by the Turkish government to visit the country and study the feasibility of setting up a ballet school within the existing State Conservatory of Music and Drama. The school officially opened in Istanbul in 1948, but in 1950 it moved to the Ankara State Conservatory. Its first professional performance as a full company took place in 1960, when Robert Harrold mounted Manuel de Falla's *El Amor Brujo* with all Turkish dancers. The company is now known as the Ankara State Ballet; in 1970, a second company was founded, the Istanbul State Ballet.

In the 1965/66 season, the first large-scale ballet was set to music by a Turkish composer, Ferit Tüzün. The production, *Çeşmebaşı* (At the Fountain) was choreographed for the company by de Valois using elements of Turkish folk dance. The 1967/68 season presented *Sinfonietta*, choreographed by de Valois to music by Nevit Kodalı. The work combines classical ballet with Turkish folk dance steps in a lighthearted romantic intrigue. *Hançerli Hanım* (The Lady with the Dagger), choreographed by Richard Glas-

stone to music by Bülent Tarcan, was also performed. In it, a legend of love, jealousy, and murder in seventeenth-century Istanbul is reenacted in a dream sequence. These ballets paved the way for an indigenous Turkish ballet style. The company now has its own choreographers, who work with both Turkish and non-Turkish material. At the same time, the company is constantly enlarging its repertory of the great classical ballets.

In 1968, for the first time, the company performed a ballet by a native choreographer, Sait Sökmen. His ballet *Çark* (The Wheel), an abstract work, visually follows the musical line and structure of Maurice Ravel's String Quartet in F. In 1973, Oytun Turfanda choreographed *Pembe Kadın* (A Woman Called Rosy), set to music by Necil Kazim Akses and based on Hidayet Sayın's drama depicting the ignorance and hopelessness of Turkish peasant women. Turfanda has also choreographed *Yoz Döngü* (Vicious Circle), an exciting abstract ballet set to Turkish folk melodies; *Güzelleme;* and the three-act *Hürrem Sultan,* the story of the second wife of the emperor Süleyman the Magnificent. The individual style of Duygu Aykal, another choreographer, combines classical technique with free modern dance forms. *Çoğul* (Plurality), set to music by Cengiz Tanc, concerns the metamorphosis of a miniature world. Her second ballet, *Oluşum* (Evolution) to music by Ilhan Uzmanbaş, resembles *Çoğul* in style, since both deal with people as symbols of time and events and their struggles with the elements of life. Later ballets by Aykal are *Bulutlar Nereye Gidiyor* (Where Do the Clouds Go?) and *Insan-Insan* (Human, Human).

Geyvan Yılmas McMillan, a Turkish modern dance

choreographer, has created four one-act ballets: *Baharda Duet* (Spring Duet), *Anadolu Gecesi* (Anatolian Night), *Mavı Düşler* (Blue Dreams), and *Delta*. Other additions to the Ankara company's repertory are *Köçekce*, choreographed by Oya Aruoba to a dance rhapsody composed by Ulvi Cemal Erkin in 1943; *Ebru*, the stormy love affair and dethroning of Sultan Selim III, by Altan Tekin to music by Kodalı; and *Saray Eğlenceleri* (Istanbul Palace Amusements) by Aruoba to music by Evinç Sunal.

BIBLIOGRAPHY

And, Metin. "Dances of Anatolian Turkey." *Dance Perspectives*, no. 3 (Summer 1959).

And, Metin. *A Pictorial History of Turkish Dancing.* Ankara, 1976.

And, Metin. "Opera and Ballet in Modern Turkey." In *The Transformation of Turkish Culture: The Atatürk Legacy,* edited by Günsel Renda and C. Max Kortepeter. Princeton, 1986.

And, Metin. "Les rituals et les danses extatiques mystiques de la Confrérie des Bektachis et des Alevis d'Anatolie." In *Transe, Chamanisme, Possession: De la fête à l'extase; Actes des deuxièmes rencontres internationales sur la fête et la communication, Nice Acropolis, 24–28 avril 1985.* Nice, 1986.

Arabesque. New York, 1975–.

Berger, Morroe. "A Curious and Wonderful Gymnastic: The Arab Danse du Ventre." *Dance Perspectives*, 10 (Spring 1961): 4–41.

Faruqi, Lois Lamya' al-. "Dances of the Muslim Peoples." *Dance Scope* 11.1 (1976–1977): 43–51.

Faruqi, Lois Lamya' al-. "Dance as an Expression of Islamic Culture." *Dance Research Journal* 10.2 (1978): 6–13.

Halman, Talat Sait, and Metin And. *Mevlana Celaleddin Rumi and the Whirling Dervishes.* Istanbul, 1983.

Haq, Sirajul. "Samāʿ and Raqṣ of the Darwishes." *Islamic Culture* 18.2 (1944): 111–130.

James, D. W. "Some Turkish Folk Dances." *The Dancing Times* (October 1946): 14–15.

Masʿūdī, Abū al-Ḥasan ʿAlī al-. *Les prairies d'or (Murūj al-dhahab wa maʿādin al-jawhar).* Vol. 8. Translated by C. A. C. Barbier de Meynard. Paris, 1874.

Molé, Marijan. "La danse extatique en Islam." In *Les danses sacrées,* edited by Jean Cazeneuve. Paris, 1963.

Rezvani, Madjid K. *Le théâtre et la danse en Iran.* Paris, 1962.

Saygun, Ahmed Adnun. "Des danses d'Anatolie et de leur caractère rituel." *Journal of the International Folk Music Council* 2 (1950): 10–14.

Shiloah, Amnon. "Réflexions sur la danse artistique musulmane au moyen âge." *Cahiers de Civilisation Médiévale* 6 (October–November 1962): 463–474.

Tabbārah, Shafīq. *Al-raqṣ fī lubnān.* Beirut, 1957.

Yönetken, Halil. "Turkish Folk Dances." *Rosin the Bow* 4.7 (1952).

METIN AND

TURKMENISTAN.

Sharing a long northern and eastern border with Uzbekistan and a corner of Kazakhstan, with Afghanistan and Iran on the south and the Caspian Sea on the west, Turkmenistan, in Central Asia, is largely covered by a desert, the Kara Kum. Long occupied by fiercely independent horse-riding tribes, it became a province of ancient Persia, then passed successively to Arab, Mongol, and Uzbek Khiva khanate rule to become a Turkic-speaking Muslim nation. It became part of Rus-sian Turkistan in the late 1800s, and a constituent republic of the USSR in 1925. With the dissolution of the USSR in 1991, Turkmenistan became an independent state.

Turkmenistan has no documented history of dance prior to the early twentieth century. The feudal system, tribal strife, oppression by the khanate, predatory raids by foreigners, and restrictive national and religious customs precluded a focus on dance.

In 1936 a group of Turkmen children was sent to the Leningrad Choreographic Institute, and two years later the first Turkmenian ballet school and workshop was established in the capital, Ashkhabad, with the assistance of Russian teachers. In 1939 the workshop's choreographer, Leonid Yakobson, created the first Turkmenian piece, *Ak-Eshekli.* Further work was carried out by Nikolai Kholfin at the Ashkhabad Opera and Ballet Theater, which opened in 1941; the first full evening of ballet took place that year. Also in 1941 the Turkmenian folk dance company was established under the leadership of Ivan Boiko. The first dances he staged were based on traditional folk art motifs: carpet weaving, carving, games, and rituals. The company gave its first concert in 1942.

The first ballet on a national theme was Kholfin's *Aldar Kose* (1942) to music by Klimenty Korchmarev. It tells the story of the folk hero of Turkmenistan, who is the protector of the poor; thanks to his courage he conquers the khan. For the idolized hero Kholfin created stylized Turkmenian folk dances and incorporated innovative narrative passages, familiar folk games, and imitations of work movements. A later version by Kosha Japarov enriched the movement vocabulary of the ballet, which deepened and consolidated its message. Still a favorite, the production is considered a landmark in the history of Turkmenian ballet.

In the 1980s the dancers Gulbakhar Musaeva and Akhmed Pursianov enjoyed special popularity, creating roles in both the national and classical repertories. During the early 1990s, there was practically no ballet activity.

BIBLIOGRAPHY

Ataev, S. A. *Tantsuet Turkmenistan.* Ashkhabad, 1965.

Uralskaya, Valeria. "Sozdanie traditsii." *Sovetskii balet,* no. 5 (1982).

N. P. RADKINA
Translated from Russian

TURNER, HAROLD

(born 2 December 1909 in Manchester, died 2 July 1962 in London), British dancer, teacher, and ballet master. Turner began his training at sixteen with Alfred Haines and made his debut with the Haines English Ballet; encouraged by Léonide Massine, he studied next with Marie Rambert in London. In 1930 Tamara Karsavina joined Rambert's company as a guest artist and chose Turner to partner her in *Le Spectre de la Rose* and *Les Sylphides.* During the next several years, after dancing his first dazzling Bluebird and a Harlequin of overflowing gaiety to Karsavina's Columbine in *Le Carnaval,* Turner emerged as the first male virtuoso produced by British training.

Previously a guest artist, he joined the Vic-Wells Ballet as a principal in 1935, creating both the elegant Dancing Master and the crazed Gentleman with a Rope in *The Rake's Progress.* He followed these in 1937 with his two most important creations: the impudent Blue Skater in Frederick Ashton's *Les Patineurs* and the grim, zealous Red Knight in Ninette de Valois's *Checkmate.* He stamped all his roles with classical virtuosity and personal magnetism.

Turner left the company during the 1940s to perform and choreograph for the Arts Theatre Ballet and International Ballet and complete his military service; he returned in 1945, danced his first Rake, and then became the first British dancer to portray the Miller in *Le Tricorne,* succeeding Massine in 1947. He chose this vigorous *demi-caractère* role for his farewell performance in 1950.

Upon retiring, Turner became the ballet master of the Covent Garden Opera Ballet, an honored teacher at the Sadler's Wells School, and an occasional guest artist with the Sadler's Wells Ballet. Enlisted to appear as the old Marquis di Luca in the 1962 revival of Massine's *The Good-Humored Ladies,* he died on the way to his dressing room after a rehearsal.

BIBLIOGRAPHY

Anthony, Gordon. "Harold Turner." In Anthony's *A Camera at the Ballet: Pioneer Dancers of the Royal Ballet.* Newton Abbot, 1975.
Turner, Harold. "Ballet in Opera." *The Dancing Times* (April 1958): 315–316.
Vaughan, David. *Frederick Ashton and His Ballets.* London, 1977.

BARBARA NEWMAN

TURNOUT. [*This entry comprises two articles. The first examines physical turnout of the dancer's legs and the second surveys the history and aesthetics of the practice.*]

Physical Mechanics

In dancers' parlance, "turnout" refers to a position of the legs that is effected by lateral rotation of the hip joints.

Anatomically, the form of the hip joint is analogous to a ball and socket. This form provides the greatest mobility of all the body's joints, in all three dimensions: forward and backward, side to side, and rotationally outward and inward. Many athletic activities, and dance in particular, exploit the mobility of the ball and socket joints; even walking requires the rhythmic motions of these joints for smooth striding over changing terrains.

Lateral rotation is measured in degrees of the arc through which the toes pass as the ball of the hip swivels

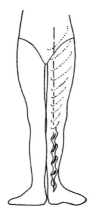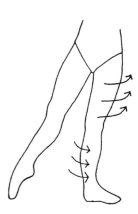

TURNOUT: Physical Mechanics. Turnout comes from the rotation of the femur (thigh bone) in the hip socket and is an active movement rather than a static placement of the leg. (Drawing by Naomi Rosenblatt; reprinted by permission from Valerie Grieg, *Inside Ballet Technique,* Pennington, N.J., 1994, p. 53.)

in the socket of the pelvis. Zero degrees is indicated where the toes are oriented straight forward. This basic anatomical position is referred to as "parallel." From parallel, each leg is normally capable of lateral rotation of between 15 and 50 degrees.

The parallel position provides a convenient but inexact standard. The numerous bones and many joints of the leg all affect the alignment and movement of the limb. Genetic variations from one individual to another are manifold, so the range of "normal" bone alignment and joint configuration is necessarily broad.

It is normal for the foot to be oriented 15 to 30 degrees laterally from the anterior orientation of the knee. The knee may also be oriented between five degrees medial or inward rotation to 15 degrees lateral rotation within the normal genetic range. Therefore, an absolute parallel alignment of the foot and knee with the anterior or forward aspect of the hip is a rare anatomical configuration. Furthermore, the science of arthrometry (joint measurement) has identified nine independent genetic factors at the hip alone that delimit the motions of the entire leg.

Positions in dance techniques, although absolute in the manuals, are actually different for each body, in much the same way that anatomical parallel is different from person to person. Turnout in ballet and most modern dance techniques is, optimally, 50 degrees for beginning students and 90 degrees for advanced students. Considering that 50 degrees of rotation is the maximum normal range, anything approaching optimal turnout must be achieved by compensating elsewhere, often by hyperextending the lower back or rolling inward on the arches of the feet.

Turnout training emphasizes use of the twelve small muscles deep within the pelvis that are the prime movers for lateral rotation of the hips. Because these muscles are neither visible beneath the skin nor clearly and independently sensed by feedback mechanisms, the dancer has no direct image of their sizes, insertions, or feeling of their force of contraction. Therefore the dancer must learn to judge proper placement from external appearances and from hands-on instruction.

Increases of from 5 to 10 degrees in turnout are not unusual as a result of careful training of adults. Greater increases almost invariably impose stresses on the weakest joints of the leg, on the ligaments, tendons, and cartilages. Turnout in children can be increased by as much as 30 degrees, but this should be done slowly and with great care. The individual's structure might not be genetically designed to operate efficiently in that altered configuration, and the consequences of forcing the turnout can be severe and irreversible.

BIBLIOGRAPHY

"A Guide to the Impairment of the Extremities and Back." *Journal of the American Medical Association* (15 February 1958): 82–83.

Moore, Margaret L. "Clinical Assessment of Joint Motion." In *Therapeutic Exercise*, vol. 6.1, edited by John V. Basmajian. 5th ed. Baltimore, 1990.

Napier, John. "The Antiquity of Human Walking." *Scientific American* 216 (April 1967): 56–66.

Steindler, Arthur. *Kinesiology.* Springfield, Ill., 1955.

Stuart, Muriel, et al. *The Classic Ballet.* New York, 1952. See pages 26–27.

Wilson, John M. "Kinesiology for Dance." *Arts* 2.2 (1981): 8–14.

JOHN M. WILSON

History and Aesthetics

Turnout is the rotation outward, or *en dehors,* of the legs from the hip joints. For contemporary classical ballet, ideal turnout allows the feet to form a straight line, or a 180-degree angle, when the heels are placed together in first position. To be fully turned outward was deemed the "first essential for the legs" by Carlo Blasis in 1820. However, the desirability of performing social and theatrical dances with turned-out legs can be documented for the two hundred years preceding Blasis, for aesthetic as well as utilitarian reasons.

François de Lauze, writing in 1623, advised that steps be made with "the toes well outward" so that movements "free from all timidity, proceed from the hip." Even though a lady's feet might not show beneath her long gown, they should be turned outward, for it was much more graceful to dance in that manner, according to de Lauze.

Earlier indications of turnout appeared in the 1589 publication of *Orchesography* by Thoinot Arbeau, who suggested that the degree of the angle of the feet be left to the discretion of the dancer. However, he believed that the "natural rotation of the leg will not permit it to exceed a

right angle." Furthermore, a gentleman's toes should not be "too positively turned out," for that gave a "feminine appearance." However, as Ingrid Brainard (1983) notes, fifteenth-century Burgundian gentlemen posed, stepped, and danced with feet turned outward as a matter of expediency when wearing shoes with fashionably long points. Italians of the same period, in more modest footwear, are pictured with their legs and feet in parallel positions. Indeed, any degree of turnout was discouraged by Italian dancing masters of the sixteenth and early seventeenth centuries. Fabritio Caroso, for instance, cautioned that, whether dancing or not, it was a most ugly sight to "point one foot south and the other north," as if the feet were misshapen by nature (Caroso, 1600).

Despite such objections, turnout of the legs was incorporated in the codification of the five positions of the feet by the end of the seventeenth century. As depicted in Feuillet's *Chorégraphie* (1700), the angle of turnout in first position was about ninety degrees and remained no more than an obtuse angle throughout most of the century.

In the mid-eighteenth century, Jean-Georges Noverre, an advocate of a return to more "natural" movement and gesture, nevertheless believed that "in order to dance well . . . nothing is so important as the turning outward of the thigh" (Noverre, 1760). Elegance and grace made it imperative "to reverse the order of things and force the limbs, by means of exercise" into a "totally different position from that which is natural to them." Condemning the use of the *tourne-hanche,* or hip-turner machine, Noverre advocated regular practice of *ronds de jambe* and *grands battements tendus,* "working from the hip" in order to become well turned outward.

By the nineteenth century, it was so essential to be turned out that Blasis advised aspiring dancers be given careful physical examinations before being allowed to "embark upon a career which demands certain natural endowments," such as the capacity for extreme turnout (Blasis, 1820).

In the twentieth century, complete 180-degree turnout continues to be espoused for both aesthetic and practical purposes. According to Edward Villella (1992), "Turnout initiates movement; turnout extends movement." Thus, he believes that turnout "isn't a position. It's the constant rotation of the body outward from the center." For André Levinson (1925) a completely turned out fifth position is the very "spirit of classic dancing."

Rebellion against the strictures of classic dancing led early twentieth-century choreographers to abandon turnout as they sought new, freer approaches to dance movement. By the 1950s, however, turnout of the legs had been incorporated into most modern-dance techniques, again justified by both aesthetic and practical considerations.

[*See also* Ballet Technique, *article on* Feet Positions.]

BIBLIOGRAPHY

Arbeau, Thoinot. *Orchesography* (1589). Translated by Mary Stewart Evans. New York, 1948. Reprinted with introduction, corrections, and notes by Julia Sutton, New York, 1967.

Beaumont, Cyril W., and Stanislas Idzikowski. *A Manual of the Theory and Practice of Classical Theatrical Dancing (Méthode Cecchetti).* London, 1922. New York, 1975.

Blasis, Carlo. *An Elementary Treatise upon the Theory and Practice of the Art of Dancing* (1820). Translated by Mary Stewart Evans. New York, 1944.

Brainard, Ingrid. "Modes, Manners, Movement: The Interaction of Dance and Dress from the Late Middle Ages to the Renaissance." In *Proceedings of the Sixth Annual Conference, Society of Dance History Scholars, Ohio State University, 11–13 February 1983,* compiled by Christena L. Schlundt. Milwaukee, 1983.

Caroso, Fabritio. *Nobiltà di dame* (1600). Translated and edited by Julia Sutton. Oxford, 1986.

Feuillet, Raoul-Auger. *Chorégraphie, ou L'art de décrire la dance, par caractères, figures et signes démonstratifs, avec lesquels on apprend facilement de soy-même toutes sortes de dances.* Paris, 1700. Translated by John Weaver as *Orchesography, or, The Art of Dancing* (London, 1706).

Lauze, François de. *Apologie de la danse, 1623: A Treatise of Instruction in Dancing and Deportment.* Translated by Joan Wildeblood. London, 1952.

Levinson, André. "The Spirit of the Classic Dance" (1925). In *Dance as a Theatre Art,* edited by Selma Jeanne Cohen. New York, 1974.

Noverre, Jean-Georges. *Lettres sur la danse et sur les ballets.* Stuttgart and Lyon, 1760. Translated by Cyril W. Beaumont as *Letters on Dancing and Ballets* (London, 1930).

Rameau, Pierre. *Le maître à danser.* Paris, 1725. Translated by Cyril W. Beamont as *The Dancing Master* (London, 1931).

Villella, Edward. *Prodigal Son.* New York, 1992.

SANDRA NOLL HAMMOND

TURNS. *For discussion of turning movements in ballet, see* Ballet Technique, *article on* Turning Movements.

TUTU. Claude Bessy, a *première danseuse étoile* at the Paris Opera (1956–1971), in a typically French tutu, somewhat shorter and puffier than the platelike tutus usually worn in such Russian classics as *Swan Lake* and *The Sleeping Beauty.* Note that the bodice, made in several sections and heavily boned, is perfectly fitted to the dancer's torso. (Photograph by Studio Liseg, Paris; from the Dance Collection, New York Public Library for the Performing Arts.)

TUTU. A woman's ballet costume, a tutu consists of a closefitting bodice and a bouffant skirt made of many layers of tarlatan, muslin, tulle, gauze, silk, nylon, or other thin, lightweight fabrics. The word, which is said to derive from French children's slang for the human buttocks, is sometimes used to indicate the skirt only. The length of the skirt varies; it is often called a "classical" tutu if it is knee-length or shorter and a "Romantic" tutu if it reaches to the midcalf or ankle. Although the tutu, along with toe shoes, has come to symbolize ballet to the popular mind, it did not make its appearance until the nineteenth century and is no longer considered compulsory by today's choreographers and costume designers, having been superseded to some extent by softer, more free-flowing skirts of chiffon, nylon, or other fabrics.

The Romantic tutu, so called because of its association with the Romantic period in ballet, developed first. It originated in the late 1820s, probably evolving gradually out of the costumes of the time. The basic silhouette of the Romantic tutu appears in a costume designed by Hippolyte Lecomte for Pauline Montessu to wear in *La Somnambule* (1827). Marie Taglioni wore a similar costume as the Naiad in Jean Aumer's *La Belle au Bois Dormant* (1829) and as Flora in a revival of Charles-Louis Didelot's *Flore et Zéphire* (1831). The origin of the tutu is sometimes traced to the costume worn by Taglioni in the title role of *La Sylphide* (1832), and its invention is sometimes credited to Eugène Lami, the costume designer of the ballet. However, no actual design for the Sylphide was found among Lami's sketches for the ballet. Ivor Guest (1981) believes that the Sylphide costume "differed little from the basic costume that a ballerina would have worn in class," and that it was distinguished from its predecessors mainly by its simplicity and white color.

The tutu proved to be the perfect costume for the supernatural creatures that dominated the Romantic ballet, for its floating skirts lent them a weightless quality and its white color symbolized their pure, ethereal nature. It could also be adapted for the use of more earthly beings by altering the cut and color of the bodice and skirt and by adding details and accessories that suggested national or period costumes. The shape of the skirt was influenced by contemporary women's fashions such as the crinoline; it became shorter and more bouffant, and when the bustle came into vogue in the 1870s, the tutu showed a corresponding fullness in back. The Italian ballerinas of the mid-1870s shortened their skirts to several inches above the knee in order to display their virtuosic technique. Necklines were lowered as the dancers strove to emphasize their sexual attractiveness.

By the late nineteenth century the tutu had become the ballerina's uniform. Although the corps de ballet and supernumeraries might be dressed in costumes closely approximating the authentic, the ranking ballerina wore a tutu regardless of the ballet's period or setting. The Egyptian princess in Marius Petipa's *La Fille de Pharaon* (1862) wore a tutu with an overskirt bearing "Egyptian" decorations. When Michel Fokine began to call for reforms in ballet, he protested against this practice.

In the twentieth century the so-called classical tutu achieved its platelike form, standing out stiffly from the hips. The French critic André Levinson remarked upon the contrast between the immobile skirt and the active movement performed in it.

The use of the tutu in contemporary ballet is often dictated by the mood or style the choreographer wishes to convey. Lyrical works often use the drifting, flowing Romantic tutu; an example is George Balanchine's *Serenade* (1935), which was originally costumed in brief tunics. A ballet that emphasizes academic formalism may use the more revealing classical tutu, as does Harald Lander's *Études* (1948). The tutu may also evoke a specific historical period. Fokine used the Romantic tutu in *Les Sylphides* (1909), his tribute to Taglioni's era. Balanchine's *Ballet Imperial* (1941), intended as a tribute to the late nineteenth-century classicism of Petipa and the Imperial Russian Ballet, was costumed in classical tutus. When he stripped the ballet of its imperial associations in 1973, retitling it *Tchaikovsky Piano Concerto No. 2*, the tutus were replaced by soft chiffon skirts.

[*For related discussions, see* Costume in Western Traditions *and* Designing for Dance.]

BIBLIOGRAPHY

Chaffee, George. "Three or Four Graces: A Centenary Salvo." *Dance Index* 3 (September–November 1944): 136–211.
Guest, Ivor. "Costume and the Nineteenth-Century Dancer." In *Designing for the Dancer*, by Roy Strong et al. London, 1981.
Kahane, Martine, and Delphine Pinasa. *Le tutu guide*. Paris, 1997.
Lawson, Joan, and Peter Revitt. *Dressing for the Ballet*. London, 1958.

SUSAN AU

TWO PIGEONS, THE. Original title: *Les Deux Pigeons*. Ballet in two acts. Choreography: Frederick Ashton. Music: André Messager, arranged by John Lanchbery. Libretto: Frederick Ashton, after La Fontaine. Scenery and costumes: Jacques Dupont. First performance: 14 February 1962, Royal Opera House, Covent Garden, London, Royal Ballet Touring Company. Principals: Christopher Gable (The Young Man), Lynn Seymour (The Young Girl), Elizabeth Anderton (A Gypsy Girl), Richard Farley (Her Lover).

Ashton's ballet was not the first to be mounted to Messager's score, which had been commissioned for an 1886 production at the Paris Opera. Choreographed by Louis Mérante, starring Mérante and Rosita Mauri, and with a libretto by Mérante and Henry Régnier, *Les Deux Pigeons* was an elaborate three-act ballet based on a fable by La Fontaine. Pepino, longing for a life of adventure, leaves his fiancée, Gourouli, to join a band of Gypsies. But Gourouli disguises herself as a Gypsy and wins him back. A one-act version was staged by Albert Aveline for Carlotta Zambelli at the Paris Opera in 1919.

For his version, Frederick Ashton also drew upon La Fontaine's fable, but his treatment was allegorical, set in

THE TWO PIGEONS. Lynn Seymour and Christopher Gable in the final pas de deux, in which the young lovers are reconciled. (Photograph © by Zoë Dominic; used by permission.)

late nineteenth-century bohemian Paris. In his studio, a young painter tires of the young woman who is both his model and his mistress. When a group of Gypsies enters, he is at once attracted to an alluring Gypsy girl and eventually leaves the studio in pursuit of her. In act 2, scene 1 (the Gypsy camp), the Gypsy girl encourages the rivalry of the artist and her own lover. Eventually the Gypsies manhandle the artist and throw him from the encampment. He returns to his studio to find his old lover alone. Their pas de deux of reconciliation, reaching heights of passion and intimacy, ends the ballet.

Ashton uses the classical ballet vocabulary, with entirely different inflections for the tender, intimate "pigeons," his protagonists—who use pigeonlike movements at many points—and the bold, sensual Gypsies. Comedy and pathos are combined and contrasted. The narrative theme of a man learning the nature of love from his experiences with more than one woman, treated several times by this choreographer, is developed with particular poetic precision in this work.

Jacques Dupont, in his only collaboration with Ashton, produced very successful designs, including a studio with a broad view of Parisian rooftops and Degas-style dresses for the heroine and her friends. The two leading roles were choreographed for Lynn Seymour and Donald Britton; at the first performances, however, the injured Britton was replaced by Christopher Gable. As a result, the original concept of an older man irritated with his youthful girlfriend was replaced by the story of an immature man's experience.

Retitled *The Two Pigeons* when Ashton staged it for the main company of the Royal Ballet in October 1962, the ballet quickly became popular and was frequently performed in London and in other cities of Great Britain. It has been mounted for CAPAB Ballet (1968), the Australian Ballet (1975), the National Ballet of Canada (1978), the Houston Ballet (1983), Les Ballets de Monte Carlo (1987), and the ballet company of the Teatro Regio in Turin (1992).

BIBLIOGRAPHY
Macaulay, Alastair. "Performing Pigeons." *Ballet Review* 8.1 (1980): 85–95.
Macaulay, Alastair. "Taking Flight." *Ballet News* 4 (May 1983): 33–35.
Vaughan, David. *Frederick Ashton and His Ballets*. London, 1977.

VIDEOTAPE. "A Real Choreographer," BBC-TV (1979).

ALASTAIR MACAULAY

U

UBAKALA DANCE. One of about two hundred formerly politically autonomous Igbo groups in Nigeria, the Ubakala are a patrilineal, egalitarian, achievement-oriented agricultural people. Reincarnation and ancestor honor are key tenets in their traditional polytheistic religion, which persists to some degree even among Christian converts. The most important Ubakala dance form is the dance play *nkwa*, which encompasses all phases of Ubakala life.

Although Ubakala groups transmit dance plays from one generation to the next, innovation through individual or group creation and borrowing from others are common. Social, psychological, or ecological factors catalyze the performance of a dance play. A village market, family birth or death, or festival celebration makes participation in a dance play as a performer or spectator virtually obligatory. The dry season or a moonlit night provides an opportunity for the pleasure of a *nkwa*. Motivations and desired rewards for participating in a dance play include fear of being shamed for not meeting expectations; enjoyment, social approval, prestige, or money received for a praiseworthy performance; promotion of positive social relations; the desire to introduce novelty; and the opportunity to present publicly a grievance, mediate conflict, or keep informed of current events. Furthermore, once a performance is successfully underway, it commands attention.

The Ubakala dance plays both reflect what is and suggest what might be. They send messages through rich symbolism—about values (fertility, egalitarianism, innovation, respect, and reciprocity), beliefs, and norms—which is clarified and dramatized. Movement, song texts, costume, music, and action (who does what, when, where, why, and how) clarify social relationships and their transitions. The *nkwa* delineates the roles of child, wife, mother, husband, father, grandparent, and ancestor, and promotes interdependency within and between families.

Young people of both sexes have relatively similar dance movements. Elderly men and women have their own patterns. However, when the age of both sexes is close and the biological and social sex role differentiation is greatest, there is strong contrast in the dance-movement patterns between women as life-creating and nurturing and men as life-taking warriors, actually or symbolically. Men's directional changes are more angular, their body shapes more varied and complex. Men dance in a circle extrusively, stepping in and out, leaping up and down, and moving on the ball of the foot; in contrast, women use the circle intrusively, have a more homogeneous spatial level, and move predominantly on the whole foot. Rapid speed and varied spatial use connote destruction, while more deliberate movements and limited spatial use connote construction. The warrior's killing thrust is swift; he ventures abroad. A woman's gestation-and-suckling period (about two and three-quarters years) somewhat restricts her mobility.

Because women and youths are excluded from formal ritual and political decision-making organizations, the dance play offers these groups an accepted means of demanding redress of grievances. The so-called Women's War of 1929, which was sparked by what Ubakala women believed to be unfair taxation, illustrates the *nkwa*'s potential for social drama and change. When the women's complaints expressed through the *nkwa* went unresolved, they went on a rampage, inciting riots, releasing prisoners, and attacking European trading stores. These actions moved the British to alter their colonial administration of eastern Nigeria.

[*See also* Sub-Saharan Africa *and* West Africa.]

BIBLIOGRAPHY

Hanna, Judith Lynne. *To Dance Is Human: A Theory of Nonverbal Communication* (1979). Chicago, 1987.

Hanna, Judith Lynne. "African Dance Frame by Frame: Revelation of Sex Roles through Distinctive Feature Analysis and Comments on Field Research, Film, and Notation." *Journal of Black Studies* 19 (June 1989): 422–441.

JUDITH LYNNE HANNA

UGANDA. *See* Central and East Africa. *See also* Pokot Dance.

UKRAINE. [*To survey dance in Ukraine, this entry comprises two articles: the first article discusses traditional dance; the second traces the history of ballet.*]

Traditional Dance

One of the largest countries of Europe, Ukraine occupies 233,000 square miles (600,000 square kilometers) and has a population of some fifty-two million. It borders on Poland, Belarus, Russia, the Slovak Republic, Hungary, Romania, and Moldova; the Black Sea and the Sea of Azov are to the south. The complex history of Ukraine involves numerous changes in political sovereignty and territorial definition since Neolithic pastoralists first settled in the Dnipro and Dnister valleys. Most of Ukraine was ruled by Scythia from the eighth to the first century BCE. Scythians, Sarmatians, Goths, Huns, Avars, Khazars, and other groups lived in these territories over the centuries. The leaders of Kyivan Rus' (Kievan Rus or Kievan Russia; c.900–1240) adopted Eastern Christianity and ruled a large and powerful state. The Mongols of the Golden Horde conquered Ukrainian territory in the thirteenth century, and Poland-Lithuania ruled from the fourteenth to the seventeenth century. A Cossack state was established in the mid-seventeenth century, but most of Ukraine came under the control of the Russian and Austro-Hungarian empires by the late eighteenth century. During World War I, Ukraine was the battleground of the Eastern Front. The collapse of tsarist Russia resulted in an independent Ukrainian National Republic until 1922, when Ukraine became part of the new Soviet Union. After World War II, Ukraine remained within the Soviet bloc after treaties enlarged it and gave it a seat in the United Nations. Since 1991, Ukraine has been independent.

The majority of Ukrainian territory consists of fertile steppes drained by major rivers that empty into the Black Sea and the Sea of Azov. The Carpathian mountain range crosses a small area in the southwest and the Polissian lowlands (Prypiat Marshes) lie in the northwest. Agriculture has provided good subsistence for several mellennia.

Ukraine was industrialized in the second half of the nineteenth century. This and other factors contributed to the retention of a relatively integrated and archaic peasant culture longer than in some other areas of Europe. The rich folk tradition has led to a strong emphasis on folklore and ethnography in the development of Ukrainian national consciousness.

Some 27 percent of the population of Ukraine constitute minority ethnic groups, including Russians, Jews, Belorusians, Romanians, and others. Some 14.5 million people of Ukrainian origin live outside the borders of Ukraine, either because the political boundaries do not now correspond with historical ethnolinguistic patterns or as a result of immigration since the 1880s to European Russia, Siberia, the United States, Canada, South America, western Europe, and other destinations.

Ritual and Participatory Dance. In Ukrainian territory the beginnings of human habitation are known through archaeological evidence. Speculation on dance types, functions, and contexts in the prehistoric and pre-Christian times is based on extrapolations from comparative studies and the remnants of old rituals. Since the acceptance of Christianity in 988, churchmen fighting paganism have noted that ritual ceremonies involved dance. Frescoes help shed some light on dance as part of the performances of *skomorokhy,* palace entertainers in the time of Kyivan Rus'.

UKRAINE: Traditional Dance. A nineteenth-century woodcut showing two villagers from west-central Ukraine dancing outdoors after an engagement ceremony. The dancer on the left is performing a *prisiadka,* a step typical of Ukrainian and Russian folk dances done by men. (Photograph reprinted from I. Belichko and A. V'iunyk, *Ukrains'ke narodne vesillia,* Kiev, 1969, fig. 12.)

UKRAINE: Traditional Dance. A bride, Svitlana Rusnak, dancing *rus'ka* with her brother Iurii (center) and their friends at the commencement of her wedding ceremonies in the village of Toporivtsi, Bukovina, in August 1995. (Photograph by Andriy Nahachewsky; from the Ukrainian Folklore Archives, University of Alberta.)

The oldest Ukrainian dances are characterized by circle, chain, and line formations, now preserved primarily in lyrical ritual dance-songs *(vesnianky, haivky, khorovody)* and in children's games. Dances during midwinter ritual visitations *(plias, malanka* mumming) and for wedding processionals are also seen as remnants of the ancient culture. In western Ukraine, old circular dance forms *(kolomyika, hutsulka)* continue to be common. Dances with a virtuosic improvisatory focus *(hopak, kozachok),* most characteristic of central and eastern Ukraine, seem to constitute a slightly newer style of dance connected with the Cossack baroque. The whirling couple dances (many polka derivatives, the waltz), quadrille-forms *(kateryna, lintsei)* and new improvisatory dance styles (rock-and-roll) are common in all parts of Ukraine. This basic historical pattern correlates with the rest of Europe.

Geographic boundaries did not limit the spread of dance in Ukraine; shifting political boundaries often allowed direct contact with western Europe, Russia, the Caucasus, and Asia Minor. Common dance elements can therefore be observed with neighbors in all directions. Cosmopolitan aspects of elite dance culture were sometimes adopted by the lower classes—for example by servants in the palaces of their landlords. Contact of all kinds has increased since the 1700s through experiences at marketplaces, factories, and military service in distant lands. The spread of dance styles from the peasantry to members of the elite occurred mostly in the second half of the 1800s, inspired by the growing romantic nationalism of the time; this occurred again but somewhat differently in the time of Soviet socialist realism. Peasant dances were sometimes adapted for the ballroom but more often, they were portrayed onstage. The Soviet policy of raising the culture of the masses to so-called higher forms supported the development of stage dance.

Ritual dances continue to have their place during rites of passage. The elaborate wedding ritual involves dance, as do christenings, farewell parties for emigration and military conscription, and even funerals in some areas. Nowadays, dance events for adolescents and dance traditions associated with holidays of the calendar cycle remain numerous. *Haivky* were performed across western Ukraine on the traditional three days of Easter; in central and eastern Ukraine, similar dance-songs were performed, generally, throughout the spring season. Minor dance traditions are related to Pentecost, Kupalo (the Feast of Saint John the Baptist near midsummer), harvest, Christmas, New Year's, and before Lent in the spring and Advent in the fall. At some ritual occasions, the actual dances performed are the same as those danced during social events.

A great diversity of dance forms have been documented in Ukraine. Couple dances predominate in a variety of forms (polka, *hutsulka,* waltz). Some dances are structurally simple to allow a fair amount of improvisation. In western Ukraine, many couple dances are performed in a large circle. Some circular dances survive from older tra-

UKRAINE: Traditional Dance. Four members of the Ukrainian Dance Company perform acrobatic leaps in a Cossack dance, a *zaporozhtsi.* (Photograph from the Dance Collection, New York Public Library for the Performing Arts.)

ditions (*holubka, metelytsia,* some *hutsulka* variants), but others are newly popular forms (*sim-sorok,* often rock-and-roll). Dances for men only *(arkan, kozak,)* are less common, as are trio dances *(ocheret, verkhovyna),* and thematic forms (*shevchyky* [shoemakers], *holiar* [barber]).

Traditionally, social dancers were held on village commons or in homes on Sunday afternoons and on other holy days, except during lenten periods. In the Soviet era, the organization of social events was taken over by local branches of the Communist youth organization or other official institutions. Dances took place in "palaces of culture," in schools, and in other facilities with large rooms. Although the Soviet authorities tried to limit access to rock-and-roll, Western genres of music and dance, including rock, jazz, disco, break dancing, rap, and heavy metal, have became extremely popular—attendance at this type of dance event was usually limited to adolescents and young adults.

Wedding dances involve a much greater age range. Rural weddings typically take place in a large tent constructed near the host's house; urban weddings often take place in rented restaurants. Most ritual and participatory dance forms in Ukraine are learned informally, by observation and participation. Adolescents and unmarried adults dance most often, but married people and even seniors participate at weddings and other family-based events. In Ukrainian diaspora communities, remnants of participatory dance forms that were popular prior to emigration may be seen in Canada, Brazil, the United States, and other countries. Of particular note is a virtuosic *kolomyika* form that evolved in North America in the 1960s.

Musical traditions are very rich and vary according to region, time, and rural/urban customs. Traditional musical groups typically involved three or four performers. Violins and, more recently, accordions, carry the melody line, while flutes, hammer dulcimers, double basses, drums, tambourines, small cymbals, and other instruments are also played. Clarinets, saxophones, banjos, guitars, electronic keyboards, and many other instruments have become popular since the 1960s. Musical groups remain most desirable for weddings and other traditional dance occasions, though recorded music is less expensive and has been used on occasion. Discotheques play recorded popular music for evenings of dancing.

Folk Dance Onstage. The first Ukrainian dance performed onstage was most probably during the 1819 premiere of Ivan Kotliarevsky's play *Natalka Poltavka.* Theater was important to the growth of the Ukrainian national (independence) movement in the late 1800s and early 1900s. Comedies and melodramas with village settings were popular, and they established the tradition of presenting peasant customs, dress, song, and dance onstage. Staged folk dances evolved into a variety of formats, including folkloric-ethnographic tableaux, dramas, variety concerts, and cabarets.

After the establishment of the Soviet Union, policy required that nationalistic elements in all forms of Ukrainian dance be severely downplayed, although the great local popularity of dance and its potential for international public relations continued to be exploited. For example, the State Folk Dance Ensemble of the Ukrainian S.S.R. was formed in Kyiv (Kiev) in 1937 under the direction of Mykola Bolotov and Pavlo (Pavel) Virsky. The movement to establish this professional ensemble was based on 1930s developments in local ballet and the success of the Ukrainian performers at the 1936 International Festival of Folk Dance in London. It was also related to general developments in Soviet art dance at that time. After World War II, professional folk-stage ensembles were founded in almost all of the twenty-five provinces in Ukraine; thousands of amateur ensembles were organized through the Ministry of Culture, the Ministry of Education, and the Workers' Unions. The Ukrainian State Dance Ensemble (later named for long-time director Pavlo Virsky) has become well known. Since the 1950s, many of Virsky's choreographies have become classics, inspiring imitative compositions both in Ukraine and abroad. [*See the entry on Virsky.*] Other key choreographers include Klara Balog, Lidia Cherneshova, Iaroslav Chuperchuk, Leonid Kalinin, Anatolii (Anatole) Kryvokhyzha, Darii (Dare) Lastivka, Volodymyr Nerodenko, Mykola Vantukh, and Kim Vasylenko. By 1983, the organized amateur dance movement in Ukraine involved an estimated 425,000 participants; folk-stage dance (as it is called) was more popular than the classical ballet, ballroom, and historical dance whose ranks were also included within this number. Thousands of trained professional choreographers, rehersal directors, administrators, educators, accompanists, and wardrobe managers were employed in the industry. Dance attracted many as a form of healthy exercise, a chance for socializing, and particularly as an opportunity to travel, sometimes even abroad. With the dissolution of the Soviet Union, the cultural industries have experienced a sharp decline in funding, resulting in instability and disenchantment. If opportunities for travel have increased for some, many dance collectives have become smaller or disbanded completely.

With a few notable exceptions, the early leaders of the Ukrainian folk-stage dance movement approached this activity from the perspective of ballet professionals. The Soviet tradition of folk-stage dance (*narodno-stsenichnyi tanets'*) evolved as a semi-autonomous genre related to character dance (*kharakternyi tanets'*), which itself had always been a part of ballet. The choreographers and dancers were not so much concerned with reproducing village forms but instead placed their emphasis on creating theatrical art. The extended visual line of ballet, its postures, movements, and terminology all strongly influenced the style of folk-stage movement, as did ballet's strong frontal orientation to the proscenium, its concern with monumentality, massiveness, compositional density, and technical virtuosity. High energy and color were prized, with great variety developing from the diversity of the cultures represented and the range of repertory within each. By the late 1980s and early 1990s, a rethinking of aesthetics occurred in some quarters, resulting in a slightly greater appreciation of intimacy over bravado, plus a striving for greater connection with earlier village forms and with the rising national consciousness of an independent Ukraine.

In diaspora communities, Ukrainian stage dance is extremely popular, a visible symbol of Ukrainian ethnicity owing to the efforts of Vasile (Vasily) Avramenko as early as the 1920s and the several generations of enthusiasts that followed. In the diaspora, choreographers and audiences generally declare a concern for heritage retention and fidelity to village prototypes. This stated concern for authenticity is often not reflected in the dances, however,

which since the 1960s have been increasingly influenced by the appeal of technically virtuosic Soviet-style folk-stage dance.

In Soviet Ukraine, ballroom dance and the related *estrada* were popular for theatrical, participation, and competition purposes.

Institutional Structures and Research. As in other European countries, the major impetus for studying traditional dance in Ukraine was nineteenth-century Romanticism—the links to ones rural past—and the associated growth of a national consciousness, and independence movement. Song texts and music connected with peasant dance were collected, arranged, and published increasingly by the end of the 1800s. Oskar Kolberg and Volodymyr Shukhevych contributed early descriptions of such dances. This movement also gave rise to both the study of participatory dance traditions and the stage dance movement. The first book on traditional dance was published in 1919 by V. Verkovynets'. Hundreds of Soviet publications later dealt with the theatrical presentation of Ukrainian dance, and they include descriptions of repertory as well as methodological advice for leaders of dance collectives. Roman Harasymchuk (Harasymczuk) and Andrii (Andre) Humeniuk, both with ethnomusicological training, are the most important researchers of participatory dance. Harasymchuk's work remains largely unpublished, however. Some field notes and films of ritual and participatory dancing are found in archives, but these remain scattered and unsystematized, while a great deal remains in private collections. English publications on Ukrainian dance are few at this time.

Except for Harasymchuk and Humeniuk's work at Ukraine's Institute of Art Studies, Folklore, and Ethnography, and for incidental archival support, almost all institutional involvement in dance in Ukraine is connected with stage presentation and the training of performing artists. The department of dance at the Institute of Culture grants postsecondary diplomas, and dozens of pedagogical institutes and specialized high schools prepare professional dancers for work in schools as well as for amateur and professional ensembles. Research on staged dance activity has been conducted in the offices of the Ministry of Culture, the Ministry of Education, and the Workers' Unions for the republic and for provincial and local levels, since folk-stage dance had been financed by these organizations during the Soviet period. The most important authors on methodology are Iroida Antypova, Luidmila Bondarenko, and Kim Vasylenko.

BIBLIOGRAPHY

Avramenko, Vasile. *Ukrains'ki natsional'ni tanky, muzyka i strii.* Winnipeg, 1947.
Borymska, Henrietta. *Samotsvity ukrains'koho tantsiu.* Kiev, 1974.
Harasymczuk, Roman. *Tance Huculskie.* Prace Etnograficzne, vol. 5. Lvov, 1939.

Hnatiuk, Volodymyr. *Haivky.* In *Materiialy do ukrains'koi etnolohii.* Vol. 12. Lvov (Lemberg), 1909.

Humeniuk, Andrii. *Narodne khoreohrafichne mystetstvo Ukrainy.* Kiev, 1963.

Humeniuk, Andrii. *Ukrains'ki narodni tantsi.* 2d exp. ed. Kiev, 1968.

Klymasz, Robert B., ed. *The Ukrainian Folk Dance: A Symposium.* Toronto, 1961.

Nahachewsky, Andriy. "The Kolomyika: Change and Diversity in Canadian Ukrainian Folk Dance." Ph.D.diss., University of Alberta, 1991.

Nahachewsky, Andriy. *Bibliography of Ukrainian Dance: Materials Available in Canada.* Edmonton, 1993.

Shatulsky, Myron. *The Ukrainian Folk Dance.* Toronto, 1986.

Verkhovynets' [Kostiv], Vasyl'. *Teoria ukrains'koho narodnoho tanka.* 5th rev. ed. Kiev, 1990.

Zaitsev, Ievhen. *Osnovy narodno-stsenichnoho tantsiu.* 2 vols. Kiev, 1975–1976.

Zerebecky, Bohdan. *Ukrainian Dance Curriculum and Teacher's Guide.* Ukrainian Dance Resource Booklets, Series 3. Saskatoon, 1988.

ANDRIY NAHACHEWSKY

Theatrical Dance

Ukrainian dances were first seen on the professional stage in 1780 in Kharkov, at the Gorodsky (City) Theater, where a ballet company led by P. I. Ivanitsky, a dancer from Saint Petersburg, performed *divertissements* based on folk song motifs. In 1819 I. P. Kotliarevsky's drama *Natalka Poltavka*, including many round dances, the Kasachok tap dance, and comic dances, was staged at the City Theater of Poltava. A few years later, in 1823, a number of national dances by an unknown choreographer were included in a production of the opera *A Ukrainian Maiden, or The Magic Castle*, staged at the opening of the City Theater in Kiev.

Thereafter, throughout the 1820s and 1830s, Ukrainian dances and ballets were often performed in the cities of Kharkov, Kiev, and Odessa by touring theatrical companies led by I. F. Stein and L. I. Mlotkovsky. After 1840, Russian and Polish ballet companies began to make fairly frequent tours in Ukraine, and during the 1860s ballets from the standard repertory (e.g., *Esmeralda, Giselle,* and *Catarina, ou La Fille du Bandit*) were seen on the stage of the Italian Opera House in Kiev. A permanent Russian Opera House was opened in Kiev in 1867, but the resident ballet company was too small to mount major dance works. In 1893, however, the ballet company was expanded and, under the direction of various Polish choreographers, gave regular performances for the next twenty-five years. Works bearing such titles as *The Ukrainian Ballet, A Holiday at the Seaside, Harvesting in the Ukraine,* and *Festival of Hungarian Gypsies* typically included Ukrainian folk dances. More modern works were introduced in 1915, when Bronislava Nijinska and her husband, Aleksandr Kochetovsky, spent two years in Kiev staging ballets from the repertory of Diaghilev's Ballets Russes.

The development of Ukrainian theatrical dance was associated with the activities of the Ukrainian classical theater in the late nineteenth century, especially with the musical dramas and operas produced by M. L. Kropivnitsky and M. P. Staritsky. In 1899 Kropivnitsky successfully collaborated with the Polish dancer and choreographer Foma Nijinsky, who produced dances for Nikolai Arkas's opera *Katerina*. This work, which is among the earliest Ukrainian operas, was based on a poem by Taras Shevchenko, generally considered the father of Ukrainian

UKRAINE: Theatrical Dance. Members of the Virsky Academic Dance Company of Ukraine in a scene from the last act of *The Sleeping Beauty,* performed in Kiev in December 1938. (Photograph by B. Kosiuk; from the Dance Collection, New York Public Library for the Performing Arts.)

UKRAINE: Theatrical Dance. Members of the Donetsk Ballet in *Paquita*. (Photograph © 1989 by Jack Vartoogian; used by permission.)

national literature. Productions of Shevchenko's plays also often included folk dances.

In the early twentieth century, the Ukrainian permanent theater in Kiev staged not only dramas and comedies but also many national operas and operettas with dances created by the choreographer and folklorist V. N. Verkhovinets. In 1919 the first Ukrainian opera and ballet theater, called the Ukrainian Musical Drama, was opened in Kiev, where ballets were staged by Mikhail Mordkin and others. In 1924, in Kharkov, the first production of the Ukrainian heroic opera *Taras Bulba*, composed in 1890 by Mykola Lysenko, was a significant event. It included dance scenes staged by the choreographers R. I. Balanotti, M. A. Sobol, and V. N. Verkhovinets. The following year, 1925, the first national opera and ballet theater was opened in Kharkov, and the dance company, led by Balanotti, Sobol, and Verkhovinets, soon built up a repertory of both classical and national choreography.

In 1926 the theaters of Kharkov, Kiev, and Odessa formed an association under the guidance of artistic director I. M. Lapitsky. The Kharkov company, led by Mikhail P. Moiseyev, was the first in Ukraine to stage the Soviet ballet *The Red Poppy* (1927). Other companies soon followed with versions of their own. In 1931 Vasily Litvinenko, collaborating with Verkhovinets, staged in Kharkov the heroic ballet *Pan Kanevsky* to music by M. I. Velikovsky. This was the first Ukrainian ballet to integrate the language and forms of classical dance and Ukrainian folk dance, the traditions of ballet and the national musical drama theater. Theatrical folk dance was further de-

veloped in operas such as Boris Liatoshinsky's *The Golden Hoop* (1929), in which the dances were staged by Pavel Virsky, Verkhovinets, and Sobol. The latter two were invited to Kiev in 1934, and Virsky was appointed head of the ballet company of the opera house there in 1936. The following year, with N. A. Bolotov, Virsky founded the Ukrainian State Folk Dance Company, for which he tapped the roots of Ukrainian folkore in choreographed works such as *Zaporazhe Cossacks, Polzunets,* and *Why Is the Willow Tree Weeping?* After his death in 1979 Miroslav Vantukh was appointed artistic director of the company; he maintains the Virsky repertory and adds new works of his own in the same style.

In 1940 the ballet *Lilea* was presented in Kiev with choreography by G. A. Berezova and Sobol. The score by Konstantin Dankevich was based on motifs in Shevchenko's poems, and the story of the ballet is dramatic. A landlord separates a loving peasant couple, Lilea and Stephan. She becomes a dancer in the serf theater; he goes to the Cossack War and, after losing his sight in a battle, becomes a musician. Some time later, rebels burst into the home of the landowner, where guests are being entertained by his dancers. Stephan is with the rebels, but Lilea perishes in the skirmish. The rebels raise her corpse overhead and carry her as a symbol of undying love and freedom.

Lilea is important because of the way in which folk elements form the dramatic base of the choreography, defining the distinctiveness of the work as a whole. The search for a modern, national choreographic language was continued in the heroic ballet *Svetlana,* staged in Kharkov by Pavel Yorkin in 1941.

Meanwhile, works from the classical repertory were also staged in various Ukrainian cities. In 1940 the Franko Opera and Ballet Theater was opened in Lvov. In 1943 in Kharkov the composer and conductor Grigory Veriovka formed a choral and dance group to celebrate pan-Ukrainian indigenous culture. Called Veriovka Ukrainian National Dance Company, now under the direction of Anatoly Avdevsky, the dance portion of the company comprises young, ballet-trained dancers. Touring the United States in 1996, the company presented theatricalized folk dances, such as the "Gopak," "Taras Bulba," and dances of the Carpathian region, as well as folk-based scenes staged by the chief choreographer, Aleksei Gomon (who had worked with Virsky's company), and works by other choreographers—Anatoly Shekera's "The Fern Is Blooming" and Yaroslav Chuperchuk's "Turtle-Dove."

During the years of World War II, the ballet companies of Kiev and Kharkov worked in Irkutsk, while the groups of Odessa and Dnepropetrovsk went to Krasnoiarsk. After the war, a number of large-scale ballets based on Ukrainian literary sources were staged—for example, *The Forest Song* (1946), *Marusya Boguslavka* (1951), *Rostislava* (1955), *The Shadows of Forgotten Ancestors* (1960), and *Oksana* (1964)—and more works from the classical repertory— *Romeo and Juliet, Cinderella, The Stone Flower, Spartacus,* and, of course, *Swan Lake, The Sleeping Beauty,* and *Raymonda*—were produced by Russian ballet masters. In the 1960s and 1970s principles of symphonism enriched the choreography of the national ballets, with new works being created by Vakhtang Vronsky, Virsky, and Anatoly Shekera. Shekera's *The Stone Ruler* (1972), based on the drama by Lesya Ukrainka, was important in this development. At the same time, the process of gathering and analyzing national folklore continued, as it does today.

Since the 1960s Ukrainian companies have made frequent tours abroad. They have won numerous awards, and in 1964 the company of the Shevchenko Opera and Ballet Theater in Kiev won first prize at the International Dance Festival in Paris. There are now six opera and ballet theaters in Ukraine, and the Kharkov, Odessa, and Lvov theaters have associated ballet schools. The State Ballet School, established in Kiev in 1934, trains dancers for both ballet and folk dance companies, and the Department of Theatrical Arts at the M. F. Rylsky Institute of Art Research, Folklore, and Ethnography, with branches in Kiev and Lvov, has long been the center for the study of the history of theatrical dance in Ukraine.

[*See also the entry on Virsky.*]

BIBLIOGRAPHY

Schreyer-Tkachenko, A., ed. *Istoriya ukrainskoy muzyki.* Moscow, 1981.

Stanishevsky, Yuri. *Ukrainsky radyansky balet.* Kiev, 1963.

Stanishevsky, Yuri. *Ukrainsky radyansky muzychny teatr, 1917–1967.* Kiev, 1970.

Stanishevsky, Yuri. *Baletnyi teatr Sovetskoi Ukrainy, 1925–1985.* Kiev, 1986.

Warrack, John, and Ewan West. *The Oxford Dictionary of Opera.* Oxford and New York, 1992.

ARCHIVES. The Ukrainian State Museum of Theatrical, Musical, and Cinematographic Art and the Karpenko-Kary State Theatrical Institute, both in Kiev, contain extensive holdings of books and archival materials.

YURI A. STANISHEVSKY
Translated from Russian

ULANOVA, GALINA (Galina Sergeevna Ulanova; born 8 January 1910 in Saint Petersburg), Russian ballet dancer. Ulanova was born into a family of dancers. Her father, Sergei Nikolaevich Ulanov, was a dancer and ballet master; her mother, Maria Fedorovna Romanova, was a dancer and her daughter's first teacher at the Petrograd (Leningrad) Choreographic Institute. In the advanced class Ulanova's teacher was Agrippina Vaganova. From the beginning Ulanova was a hard worker at the ballet barre, and her talents were soon recognized. For her graduation performance in 1928 she danced the waltz and mazurka from Michel Fokine's *Chopiniana.* In her first season as a member of the Kirov Ballet, she danced Princess Florine in *The Sleeping Beauty;* in her second season, she danced Odette-Odile in *Swan Lake* and Aurora in *The Sleeping Beauty.* At the beginning of World War II she was evacuated with the company to Tashkent and then to Perm. In 1944 she was transferred to the Bolshoi Ballet, where she was *prima ballerina* until she retired in 1962; thereafter she served as the company's ballet mistress and coach.

Ulanova danced leading roles in many ballets of the standard repertory. After *Swan Lake* and *The Sleeping Beauty,* she danced *Giselle* in 1932 and *The Nutcracker* in 1934. She became best known, however, for her creation of roles in new ballets, especially Maria in Rostislav Zakharov's *The Fountain of Bakhchisarai* (1934) and Juliet in Leonid Lavrovsky's *Romeo and Juliet* (1940). She was also instrumental in the shaping of new versions of Soviet ballets, including Zakharov's *Cinderella* (1945), and Lavrovsky's *The Red Poppy* (1949) and his *The Tale of the Stone Flower* (1954). Notable among her concert numbers was her rendition of Fokine's *The Dying Swan.*

Ulanova was widely praised for her musicality. She described dance as the movement of music, that which makes music visible (Kahn, 1962, p. 31). She seemed to respond to the subtlest nuances of music not only in the precise rhythm of her dancing but also in the play of her arms and hands, and even her glances, pauses, and the inclination of her head. Her dramatic ability was equally notable. Each movement, each fleeting glance, was an im-

ULANOVA. Thanks to the 1954 Soviet film of Leonid Lavrovsky's production of *Romeo and Juliet,* Ulanova can still be seen in one of her greatest roles. This still photograph, taken from the film, shows her as Juliet with Yuri Zhdanov as Romeo. (Photograph from the Dance Collection, New York Public Library for the Performing Arts.)

portant link, defining the meaning of the sequence to follow. In the words of Konstantin Stanislavsky, she strove to express the life of the human soul. Seeking inspiration in the works of Aleksandr Pushkin and Shakespeare, she created profound tragic images, conveying through dance the most complex dramatic conflicts.

With Ulanova, the almost imperceptible moment of suspended animation was neither an interruption of the dance nor an ending; rather, it seemed as if the moment were gradually fading, melting, and dissolving into the air. This unique art in her plastique of *ritardando* or fading away created a *pianissimo* effect of great expressiveness. Ulanova avoided abrupt stops; her dance flowed freely, reflecting the movements of the spirit. Her virtuosity, not flamboyant, gave priority to the living, vibrating flexibility of line. Without sharp accents or staccato rhythms she embodied the most delicate, tremulous images of femininity, weightlessness, and softness. Truly Russian, her art combined the poetic lucidity of Pushkin with the modesty and laconic manner of Chekhov—a perfect match for the music of Tchaikovsky.

Ulanova wrote that she loved the role of Maria in *The Fountain of Bakhchisarai* because it expressed Pushkin's poetry so well. She felt at once that the character of the captured princess had to be individualized, but her concept of the character developed over the years. At first, she felt, her portrayal of Maria was one of all-pervading grief. The portrait later changed, becoming more intricate and brighter, with hints of joy and youth in the first act. The

character of Juliet developed from the music, although Ulanova found Prokofiev's music difficult, often abrupt, and bewildering with its frequent changes of rhythm. Nevertheless, she soon found in the score a harmony of thought and action. For her, Juliet appeared as a character of strong will, ready to fight and die for happiness, like the contemporary "heroine of the people" ready to die for a patriotic cause. This made the centuries-old tragedy seem new. This kind of concern also attracted her to the character of Tao-Hoa in *The Red Poppy,* a role requiring both lyricism and valor.

A traditionalist, Ulanova excelled in dance drama, appearing uninterested in abstract works or in the modern experiments that were prevalent in the Soviet Union in her time. An isolated venture into the latter was the role of Komsomolka in Vasily Vainonen, Leonid Yakobson, and Vladimir Chesnakov's *The Golden Age* (1930). She told Albert Kahn (1962): "For me, the value of my work lies in the conviction that the language of the ballet can convey to people great and vital truths about life, about the beauty in life and in the human heart."

ULANOVA. The British film *The Bolshoi Ballet,* released by the Rank Organisation in 1957, contains a complete performance of *Giselle,* with Ulanova in the title role. (Photograph from the Dance Collection, New York Public Library for the Performing Arts.)

In the 1950s Ulanova's art won her worldwide recognition in places as far-flung as Egypt and China. She first danced in western Europe at the Maggio Musicale Fiorentino in 1951. This was followed by performances with the Bolshoi Ballet in Berlin (1954), London (1956), Japan (1957), Paris (1958), and the United States and Canada (1959, 1962). In a London review Richard Buckle wrote of her Giselle that she "painted all the shyness, doubts and delicate hesitations of first love and at times she conveyed rapture. . . . There was a delicious exhilaration in her *petits battements,* and her *pas ballonnés* were like a draft of mountain air." In New York the *New York Times* critic John Martin described her Juliet as one of the greatest, spoken or unspoken. Seeing her when she was nearly fifty years old, he claimed that her youthfulness in the role transcended in artistic values the youthfulness of nature.

After retiring from the stage Ulanova dedicated herself to directing and teaching. Among her students who became major figures in Soviet ballet are Nina Timofeyeva, Ekaterina Maximova, Vladimir Vasiliev, Ludmila Semenyaka, Malika Sabirova, and Nina Semizorova. In her role as mentor Ulanova has said that she wanted to develop the imagination of the young dancers, to help them to think creatively. "The artist creates the role; the teacher molds the personality of the artist into one capable of creating an artistic image," she wrote (1959). Maximova has testified to Ulanova's emphasis in coaching on the development of the character of the role, a task requiring not only physical effort, for perfect technical control, but emotional and intellectual work.

As chairman of the Bolshoi Ballet Council, Ulanova participated in the programming of performances and casting and was involved in the general supervision of the company's affairs. She was also chairman of the examining board of the Bolshoi school, and she frequently served as both the chairperson and a member of the jury of the international ballet competitions held in Moscow and Varna. She received numerous honors in the USSR and internationally: Honored Artist of the USSR (1939), National Artist of the USSR (1940), states prizes (1941, 1946, 1947, 1950), People's Artist of the USSR (1951), the Biotti Prize in Italy (1959), honorary memberships in the Academy of Arts of the German Democratic Republic (1959) and the American Academy of Science and Art (1960), and Hero of Socialist Labor (1974, 1980).

In 1981 in Paris, UNESCO sponsored a gala in honor of Ulanova for which Vasiliev created *Tribute to Ulanova.* In 1984 in Stockholm and in Leningrad sculptures of her were installed.

BIBLIOGRAPHY

Bogdanov-Berezovskii, V. M. *Ulanova and the Development of the Soviet Ballet.* Translated by Stephen Garry and Joan Lawson. London, 1952.

Brinson, Peter, ed. *Ulanova, Moiseyev, and Zakharov on Soviet Ballet.* Translated by E. Fox and D. Fry. London, 1954.

Clarke, Mary. *Six Great Dancers.* London, 1957.

Golubov, Vladimir. *Tanets Galiny Ulanovoi.* Leningrad, 1948.

Gould, Susan. "Talking with Galina Ulanova." *Dance Scope* 14 (September 1980): 8–15.

Ilupina, Anna. *Ballerina: The Life and Work of Galina Ulanova.* Philadelphia, 1965.

Kahn, Albert E. *Days with Ulanova.* New York, 1962.

Potapov, Vladimir. "Galina Ulanova." In *The Soviet Ballet,* by Yuri Slonimsky et al. New York, 1947.

Lvov-Anokhin, Boris. *Galina Ulanova* (in English). 2d ed. Moscow, 1984.

Smakov, Gennady. *The Great Russian Dancers.* New York, 1984.

Swift, Mary Grace. *The Art of the Dance in the U.S.S.R.* Notre Dame, 1968.

Ulanova, Galina. *The Making of a Ballerina.* Translated by S. Rosenberg. Moscow, 1959.

BORIS A. LVOV-ANOKHIN
Translated from Russian

ULRICH, JOCHEN (born 3 August 1944 in Osterode), German dancer, choreographer, and company director. Having studied at the Cologne Institute of Theater Dance from 1964 to 1967, Jochen Ulrich became a member of the Cologne State Opera Ballet in 1967. A talented dancer, he was soon cast in soloist roles. He was also quickly given the opportunity to try his hand at choreography, which allowed him to experiment with modern forms of dance movement. With the support of some of his colleagues in the company, Ulrich managed over the next few years to transform the opera ballet company into a contemporary dance company. Although still attached to the Cologne opera house, the company was modeled on such experimental troupes as the Netherlands Dance Theater and Ballet Rambert. The daily classes for the dancers came to be less strictly based on the classical ballet vocabulary and increasingly influenced by the modern technique of Martha Graham.

In 1971 the company was officially renamed the Tanz-Forum der Oper der Stat Köln (Dance Forum of the Cologne State Opera). Ulrich functioned as first among equals in a tripartite directorship shared with Helmut Baumann—later replaced by Jürg Burth—and Gray Veredon. Since the 1978/79 season, Ulrich has been the sole director and chief choreographer of the Cologne Dance Forum, which he has developed into one of the foremost modern-oriented German dance companies, frequently collaborating with such international choreographers as Glen Tetley, Hans van Manen, and Christopher Bruce. Under his aegis, the company has performed in many countries. In 1995, the Cologne Dance Forum became an independent company, with a guaranteed number of performances at the Cologne opera house but otherwise detached from it.

Ulrich has created a large repertory of works for the

Cologne Dance Forum and has served as guest choreographer for the Wiesbaden, Munich, and Vienna State Opera ballet companies. His ballets—many of them full-length productions—shun all classical academic material. They are rather lean and somewhat strenuous, coolly sensual, lissome, and elastic. When Ulrich has occasionally dealt with topical subjects, he has always sided strongly with the socially underprivileged and economically deprived. His musical taste is catholic, and he has worked with very different kinds of music by various composers.

Notable among Ulrich's earlier works are *Lewis C.* (1970; music by Ivo Malec), *Waltz Dreams* (1977; music by Kurt Schwertsik), *The Miraculous Mandarin* (1980; music by Béla Bartók), *American Landscapes* (1983; music by George Gershwin and Charles Ives), *Lyric Suite* (1984; music by Alban Berg), and *Der Wanderer* (1984; music by Wilhelm Killmayer and Franz Schubert). His works from more recent years include *Neue und Curieuse Theatralische Tanz-Schul* (1988; music by Mauricio Kagel), *Lulu* (1990; music by Nino Rota), *Graf Dracula* (1991; music by Samuelina Tahija), *Yerma* (1992; music by Salvador Pueyo), *Carmen* (1993; music by Egberto Gismondi), *Peer Gynt* (1994; music by Jean Sibelius and Henryk Gorecki), *Goya* (1995; music by Bo Spaenc), and *Get Up Early* (1996; music by Joachim Kühn).

BIBLIOGRAPHY

Nevill, Timothy, trans. *Ballet and Dance in the Federal Republic of Germany.* Bonn, 1988.
Weigelt, Gert. *Tanz-Forum Köln.* Cologne, 1986.

HORST KOEGLER

UMEWAKA MAKIO (born 11 February 1941 in Tokyo), *nō* actor of the Kanze school, fourteenth headmaster of the Kichinojō branch of the Umewaka family, leader of the Umewaka Kennōkai troupe. Makio is the great-grandson of Umewaka Minoru I (1828–1909), who with Hōshō Kurō (1837–1917) and Sakurama Bamba (1835–1917) preserved *nō* at the beginning of the Meiji era and who taught *nō* to Ernest Fenollosa (1853–1908), the first foreigner to study it as a performing art. Makio is also the elder son of Umewaka Manzaburō II (1908–1991), who in 1956 was designated Bearer of an Important Intangible Cultural Asset by the Japanese government and whose dream was to spread *nō* around the world. (It was Manzaburō who in 1979 accepted the first non-Japanese, Stephen Comee, to train as a professional *nō* actor.)

The earliest known reference to the Umewaka family appears in a diary kept by Emperor Go-Komatsu (ruled 1392–1412) in the entry for 9 March 1416. Descended from the medieval Tamba *sarugaku* troupe, the Umewaka family also claims descent from Prince Regent Shōtoku (572–621) through Tachibana no Moroe (684–757), famous as one of the compilers of the *Man'yōshū* (Anthology of Ten Thousand Leaves for Ten Thousand Ages). The family, which had been established as the *tsure* (accompanying actor) branch of the Kanze school in 1868 by warlord Toyotomi Hideyoshi (1536–1598), broke away from the Kanze school when its headmaster fled with the defeated shogun; it remained in Tokyo, where it struggled to preserve *nō* and its traditions. In 1921 the Umewaka family, supported by the Kanze school's Tetsunojō branch, declared itself an independent school, but it again rejoined the Kanze school in 1954.

Makio debuted on the *nō* stage at the age of three, performed his first *shite* (main actor) role at seven, and at fourteen gave his first performance with a mask (indicating that a youth is now a full-fledged *nō* actor) in the play *Okina*. He participated in the official *nō* tours to Europe six times (1967–1975); led a cultural tour that performed in the United States, Canada, and Mexico (1978); performed at the University of British Columbia (1984); gave

UMEWAKA MAKIO. As the beautiful Spirit of the Wisteria *(fuji)*, Umewaka is shown dancing with joy after having attained buddhahood, in the *nō* drama *Fuji*. (Photograph by Morita Toshiro; used by permission.)

lecture-demonstrations at the Vancouver Museum (1985); and led the official Japanese delegation to perform *nō* at Canada's World's Fair in Vancouver in 1986. Makio also participated in Belgium's Europalia '89–Japan, led his troupe on a tour through France (1990), and performed and gave lecture-demonstrations throughout the United Kingdom as part of Japan Festival '91. He was dispatched by the Japan Foundation to perform *nō* for the first time in Moscow (1991). Since 1992, he has toured Hong Kong, Italy, Germany, and other countries, while remaining active in Japan, not only performing in theaters all over the country but also participating in an overwhelming number of popular torch-lit *nō* performances each year.

Makio's art is especially characterized by the flowing, balletic grace of his "dance of the angel" *(tennyo-no-mai)* and the shimmering yet dark elegance of his women, as well as by the intense power of his evil spirits (as in *Aoi no Ue* and *Dōjōji*). The fluidity of his movement adds depth and dimension to his dancing. His chanting is sung in a lyrical yet powerful manner, and the intensity of his acting draws the audience deep within its vortex. He both studied the works of Zeami and often performed with the great Kanze Hisao. At present, he is recognized as one of Japan's leading *nō* actors and often performs with Hisao's younger brother, Kanze Tetsunojō VIII.

Among the numerous awards he has received is the Prix d'Honneur of the Osaka Cultural Prize (1988); he was designated Bearer of an Important Intangible Cultural Asset by the Japanese government in 1991.

[*See also* Kanze School *and* Nō.]

BIBLIOGRAPHY

Keene, Donald. *Nō: The Classical Theatre of Japan*. New York, 1966.
Kodansha Encyclopedia of Japan. Tokyo, 1983. See the entries "Kanze School," "Nō," and "Zeami."
Komparu Kunio. *The Noh Theater: Principles and Perspectives*. Translated by Jane Corddry and Stephen Comee. New York, 1983.
Nishino Haruo and Hata Hisashi, eds. *Nō, kyōgen jiten* (Dictionary of Noh and Kyogen). 2d ed. Tokyo, 1988.
Shirasu Masako. *Umewaka Minoru kikigaki*. Tokyo, 1951.
Umewaka Kennōkai, ed. *Nō: Umewaka Kennōkai*. Tokyo, 1990.
Umewaka Manzaburō. *Manzaburō geidan*. Osaka, 1946.

STEPHEN COMEE

UNDINE. *See* Ondine.

UNITED STATES OF AMERICA. [*To survey the dance traditions of the United States of America, this entry comprises nine articles:*

> An Overview
> African-American Dance Traditions
> African-American Social Dance
> Regional Dance Companies

> Musical Theater
> Ballet Education
> Social, Folk, and Modern Dance Education
> Dance Research and Publication
> Contemporary Criticism

The introductory article views dance in the context of recurring cultural contacts and assimilation; the second and third explore the syncretism of African and European forms in theatrical and social dance traditions; the fourth focuses on the development of regional dance companies; the fifth discusses the development of American musical theater and attendant forms of theatrical dancing; the sixth and seventh articles consider the diversity of dance education; the concluding articles examine dance scholarship and writing. For a discussion of dance traditions of indigenous peoples, see Native American Dance.]

An Overview

Dance in the United States is a culturally diverse and complex phenomenon. Woven into its development are all the strands of American cultural history: patterns of immigration, settlement, and cultural contact; shifts of geographical boundaries; developments in transportation and communication; growth of industry, economy, and business life; diverse religious and philosophical attitudes; and varied expressions in social life and amusements. What we call dance in the United States is bound by two central problems that must be examined in order to understand historically patterned expressive movement experience: human physiognomy, both in terms of developing medical knowledge and the general assimilation of that knowledge by populations, and cultural perceptions and attitudes toward the human body.

More particularly, the history of dance in the United States is a story of recurring cultural contacts and assimilation through the most direct channel available to people, their bodies. It is also the story of the creation and rationalization of forms of amusement and theatrical performances by people who saw these innovations as broadly and democratically contributing to the concept of a national character and the growth of the nation.

The study of dance in the United States begins with the dances of Native Americans. The written record on dance commences with the first sustained European contact with the native peoples of the North American continent. Not until the United States developed a national identity, however, were dominant political and social groups able to reach a tacit consensus and communicate an "American" style of dance. Prior to the early decades of the nineteenth century, descriptions of dance were shared by and associated among people sharing similar ethnic background and social class. Nevertheless, while there was not yet a wholly American dance in 1800, unique experiences in the nation's development were molding the culture of the new nation and creating the basis for its dance.

The Colonial Period. From 1492 to 1660 early European colonial ventures in Virginia, Georgia, South Carolina, Massachusetts, and Connecticut, as well as those in what is now Mexico and California, served commercial purposes for their mother countries and provided political and religious asylum for many settlers. Diverse immigrants, brought together in the common necessity to survive, included military men, aristocrats, traders, adventurers, prisoners, slaves, and indentured servants, predominantly from England, France, and Spain but also from Holland, Sweden, and Africa. Residents of these first settlements maintained their indigenous dance traditions and behavioral expressions, but they sometimes responded to their frontier isolation and spare, marginal living conditions with keen observation and adaptations. Native American dancing and ceremonies, as well as the dancing and ceremonies of foreign neighbors, inspired some early cross-cultural exchanges. Noteworthy examples come from accounts of fur trappers and traders who associated with both Native American tribes and the predominantly white, Anglo-Saxon world.

Immigrants, however, often reacted to the wilderness and the freedom of the American frontier—as they would a century later in the wilderness of crowded urban environments—by projecting notions of proper and improper behavior on the bodily expression and dancing of others in order to fortify and separate their own community values. Historian Michael Zuckerman has drawn the portrait of Thomas Morton, a trader who, after erecting a Maypole at Merry Mount, Massachusetts, in 1626, fell to "frisking," reviving the early, roisterous English holidays. Zuckerman showed that the merriment, which included dancing, was emblematic of the clash of consciousness between Elizabethan traditions and Puritanism.

Relatively few sources of later seventeenth- and early eighteenth-century settlements mention dance. Those rare observations are by predominantly Anglo-Saxon and upper-class writers. Prominent among these are the sermons of New England Puritans (for example, Reverend Increase Mather [1639–1723] and later his son Cotton Mather [1663–1728]); diaries and letters of middle-colony and southern plantation owners; observations by European and colonial travelers; and court records dealing with infractions of community laws regarding public gatherings. Historical methods, such as demographics, that attempt to define the activities of "invisible" (middle-, lower-class, and illiterate populations) have not yet been applied to dance in the United States. Consequently what emerges as dance in these early years of the colonial period is a view biased by the thin historical record created by literate, Anglo-Saxon, upper-class witnesses.

European theatrical performers who came to the colonies in the late seventeenth and early eighteenth centuries encountered widely separated, culturally diverse, and generally sparse populations with few of the refinements common in Europe. Yet, like European cities, the Atlantic seaboard communities were multicultural, had many of the same religious and political strictures, and provided a range of audiences comparable to those in Europe. Early theatrical dancers were itinerants who performed on the tight and slack ropes, enacted comic sketches, and exhibited their virtuoso physical skills and feats in solo dances—such as hornpipes, *galliards*, jigs—and acrobatics. They often joined acting companies as actors. Historical records in southern colonies show instances in which these itinerant performers entertained at plantation parties. For the most part, early itinerant theatrical performers have not been systematically investigated and remain anonymous.

Fashion and taste in Europe influenced both theatrical trends and social amusements in the United States. Formal occasions for performances of such court dances as the *pavane, allemande, corrante, sarabande, galliard, passepied*, and *menuet* were, at first, infrequent, and musicians and dancers competent to perform them were scarce. After the mid-eighteenth century, gains in population, growing local economies encouraging varied occupations especially within towns, and rising standards of living gradually supported hierarchical social strata and styles of living closer to those of Europe. A white, Anglo-Saxon society whose wealth, power, and status arose from trade and political influence with European powers dominated the colonies. At the higher end of the social scale more leisure time was available for dances of society. People of the middle class who wished to make an impression on more powerful individuals and obtain the attention of their peers emulated the manners, dance fashions, and tastes of the colonial aristocracy.

Among religious liberals (particularly in the middle and southern colonies), a kind of consumer class for "the art of dancing" began to form. The growth of dancing as an amusement, social accomplishment, symbol of gentility, and occasion for meeting favorable marriage partners is evidenced by the growing number of references about teachers of dancing in newspapers, diaries, and letters. Among the names are George Brownell, Peter Pelham, and Charles and Mrs. Stagg. Occasions vary from military tributes and encampment celebrations to birthnight balls and festivities for visiting dignitaries. The increasing number of music and dancing masters attests to the growth of general interest in court dances of the eighteenth century, such as the *menuet, rigaudon*, and *gavotte*, which required professional instruction. Dance publications from Europe, such as John Playford's *The English Dancing Master* (1651–1726), and, after 1720, sheet music and other notes for informal French dances were available to purchasers. The availability of published guides and music led to country dance versions performed with little or no knowledge of formal steps by an untutored general public. Books found in estate inventories of the period reveal the close connection between European and American dance tastes and fashions. For example, the inventory of Virginian Charles Stagg's estate made after his death in 1735 contained two dance instruction books: one by John Weaver, *Orchesography* (1706), and the other by John Essex, *For the Further Improvement of Dancing* (1710). Both these volumes are translations of Raoul-Auger Feuillet, and both are entitled in the inventory as *The Art of Dancing*.

Throughout the early eighteenth century slow transatlantic travel (and consequently, slow communication) resulted in a time warp for fashions and styles from one side of the Atlantic to the other. Coupled with the colonists' adherence to traditions (first- and second-generation American customs), this situation sometimes caused theatrical and social dance fashions and tastes to become curiously combined and layered. For example, as late as 1770 a "banqueting house" reminiscent of sixteenth-century entertainments was erected in Virginia for "good Neighborhood" and fit to entertain annually the subscribers and their wives, sweethearts, and friends. At the same time, a colonial governor might have been receiving his order for a suit tailored in the latest English fashion or a list of the dances performed at the yearly Birthnight Ball of the English court just a few weeks or months before. Meanwhile, outbreaks of Maypole dancing in various colonies shocked those members of the population who viewed such dancing as primitive and ritualistic.

Other socioeconomic and ethnic communities had their own dance expressions. For example, sailors danced their competitive jigs and hornpipes (official exercises aboard ship), and African slaves performed tribal animal-imitation dances and ritual dances for special occasions such as marriages and harvest. Although the dances of such subcultural groups have not been thoroughly investigated, scholars assume that they were important to their performers in maintaining social solidarity in an alien environment and that they may have influenced individuals outside the group. These early, overlapping patterns of diversity of physical movement created the foundation for an emerging American consciousness—attitudes and responsiveness—to all types of dance and tolerance or aversion to the physical expressions and behaviors entailed therein.

Theatrical dance shared an early and parallel development with the beginnings of theater in the United States. European theatrical dance traditions presented in the United States range from the early touring of itinerant performers whose various dancing skills did not necessarily include classical training to highly trained, professional classical dancers such as Londoner Henry Holt

(1738), "Monsieur Denoier" (Philip Desnoyer, 1751), Pietro Sode (1774), and Louis Roussel (1783). It was not uncommon to have a rope dancer on the same program with a ballet performance. The colonial period in the United States witnessed the introduction of dancers in groups (later called "ballet companies") associated both with early acting companies and with the construction of permanent theaters.

Tradition has it that theater in the United States dates from 1716, when William Livingston established the first playhouse in Williamsburg, Virginia. However, evidence exists of earlier banqueting halls with social entertainments that featured the talents of paid performers and gentlemen amateurs. Later, urban musical societies and clubs, like the Philadelphia Dancing Assemblies (founded in 1748) and the Saint Cecilia Society of Charleston, South Carolina (1762), sanctioned private and exclusive social and theatrical performances of music and dance. The musical concert coupled with a dancing party continued well into the nineteenth century as a refined and respectable evening entertainment in which professional musicians and amateur dancers (both men and women) might have appeared. During these entertainments, dancing masters would often exhibit the most skilled of their young pupils.

The American Revolutionary era, from 1760 through 1789, had its effect on dancing in society and in the theater. In October 1774 the First Continental Congress passed a resolution that strongly recommended the closing of all public places of amusement. In this time of political unrest, public theatrical performances and dancing were considered not only unrefined but likely to be emotionally and politically inflammatory. As a result, Loyalists in the dancing profession returned to England. Some antitheatrical laws remained in effect until 1789. Similarly, court dances, such as *menuets* and *gavottes*, carried a controversial message. They were reminders of hierarchical power relationships at a time when American's democratic republic was being tested. French quadrilles and cotillions and English country dances and reels were less exclusive and more neutral forms to which "as many as will" could be added. These dances symbolized the democratic ideals of the new nation. After the Revolutionary War, British dancers returned and French expatriates began to seek refuge in America.

Prior to 1815, four major theater companies with affiliated dancers presented dance events periodically. The American Company (1783) formed the basis of a permanent theater in New York City. Beginning in 1796 a Frenchman named Jean-Baptiste Francisqui, previously a member of Alexandre Placide's Charleston, South Carolina, company, became its ballet master. The Chestnut Street Theatre (1794–1815) in Philadelphia, managed by Thomas Wignell and Alexander Reinagle, retained William Francis as ballet master. The Federal Street Theatre (1793) in Boston also presented ballet. French expatriate Alexandre Placide (c.1750–1812), manager of the City Theatre (1795) in Charleston from 1798 to 1812, danced in all these theaters and was perhaps the single most influential theatrical dance figure of the post-Revolutionary period in America.

From these four theatrical centers emanated four major touring circuits before 1815: Charleston north to Richmond; Philadelphia south to Baltimore, Annapolis, and Washington, D.C.; New York City and environs; and Boston, including New England. Performances were given usually three times a week, and typical programs are described in a monograph (originally published 1960; reprinted 1976) that dance historian Lillian Moore titled *New York City's First Ballet Season.* The John Street Theatre opened on a night in January 1792 with projected programs that included a play, a ballet or pantomime, interludes of dancing or acrobatics, and sometimes a farce. Ballets and pantomimes like *The Bird Catcher; The Two Philosophers, or The Merry Girl;* and *Harlequin Protected by Cupid, or The Enchanted Nosegay* mixed with interlude dances, such as "Menuet de la Cour," "a Gavotte," "an Allemande," "a Sabottiere Dance," and "a Hornpipe."

It is useful to note that both dancers and teachers from the mid-eighteenth century are conventionally distinguished in newspapers as professional dancers touring from Europe, or immigrants, or native-born. This information is a clue to the historian regarding the establishment of beginnings of "an American dance," that is, one rising from a native-born population and not imported from Europe.

Early touring dancers, such as the popular Madame Anna Gardie and the immigrant dancer and choreographer William Francis, are familiar because of extant comments made by their contemporaries. Many other dancers, like Mr. and Mrs. Aivre, Monsieur Lege, and Mr. and Mrs. Oscar Byrne, remain more obscure. The first American-born theatrical dancer is generally considered to be John Durang (1768–1822). [*See the entry on Durang.*] His son Charles Durang (1794–1870) performed with Placide's company and at New York City's Bowery Theatre. Actor, ballet and social dancing master, stage manager, author and early critic, Charles Durang wrote several guides to the dances of society that reveal his familiarity with the principles of continental ballet technique of Jean-Georges Noverre and Carlo Blasis. The many names of and references to dances and dancers in newspapers and letters after 1800 attest that theatrical dance had appreciative and large audiences and that the business of teaching society to dance was a widely acceptable occupation in early America.

Prominent choreography by native-born Americans, unlike dramatic works, appears to have been sparse. At least four choreographers of this period were well known,

UNITED STATES OF AMERICA: An Overview. A watercolor self-portrait of John Durang (1768–1822), considered the first American-born theatrical dancer, performing a hornpipe. (Courtesy of the Historical Society of York County, Pennsylvania.)

Placide, Francisqui, Byrne, and Francis. European ballets were restaged in the United States. Moore credited *La Fôret Noire* as "the first serious ballet to be given in this country" (Magriel, 1948). Patriotic pantomimes with ballets—"a medley of plot, singing, and dancing, adorned with elaborate scenery and costumes, and using complicated mechanical devices to produce spectacular effect"—like *American Independence, or The 4th of July 1776* (1794) by French choreographer Jean-Baptiste Val—were a genre with symbols of liberty and national meaning that appealed to American audiences (Cohen, 1976). Pantomimes like *Harlequin Panattaha, or Genii of the Algonquins,* presented in 1810 at the Park Theatre in New York City, and dances like the Indian Dance in the opera *Tammany* (1794)—the first opera ballet in America—helped audiences assimilate their own unique American experiences.

A major issue in the study of dance of the early nineteenth century in the United States is the change of performance technique and style from the classical presentation of the body and steps formulated in French court dancing beginning in the mid-seventeenth century to the Romantic ideal of the early nineteenth century developed in the theater schools of Europe. Another issue is the fact that the *danse d'école,* or ballet, and the dancing of the society were inextricably meshed throughout the late eighteenth and the early nineteenth century. The last dancing master in the United States to teach French court dancing to both performers and society died in the 1840s. Curiously, in the mid-nineteenth century, both in Europe and the United States, a revival of French court dancing mixed with the Romantic ballet as the latter began to wane.

Theatrical ballet stars and society personalities were models for performance, and they popularized the dances with which they were identified. Examples taken from sheet music popular in the early part of the nineteenth century include "Commodore Perry's March," by P. L. Duport (Baltimore, 1813); "Miss M. A. Cowper's Favorite Waltz," by Frederich L. Abel (Philadelphia, 1819); the "Elssler Quadrilles, Selected from her Favorite Dance," composed by C. T. Geslain (New York, 1840); the "Ravel Polka Quadrilles," composed by M. Keller (c.1847); and "The Cally Waltz," by Allen Dodworth, named in honor of his wife in the 1840s.

Dancing masters often taught both members of society and aspirants to the stage. Often teaching both theatrical and social dancing contributed to the mixing of conventions, techniques, and forms. Elite clientele demanded the newest and most respected social dances, and they had the leisure time to learn some technique. Complications and competition in the teaching profession resulted when dance exponents had sparse training and experience. Exotic, foreign-sounding names often disguised their lack of experience. Dance instruction was competitive both in quality and in the variety of prices established for the diverse customers who might decide that knowledge in dance, as well as access to proper social customs and individuals associated with dancing circles, was worth the price.

The Nineteenth Century. Tremendous national growth marked the years from 1789 to 1865. In 1803 the Louisiana Purchase doubled the size of the United States. With the later annexation of territories as states, such as California in 1850, the young country extended west to the Pacific and south to Mexico. Significant to the development of dancing in the United States were the cultures that these new annexations officially brought into the country: Native American; Spanish and, later, Mexican-owned parts of the Southwest and California; and French interests in New Orleans, Florida, and the Northwest. Russian contact occurred in northern California and the Pacific Northwest. Although not annexed territory, the French and English colonies of Canada also influenced the northeastern region of the United States. Settlements in these borderlands were characterized by specific cultural tastes and dancing customs, and therefore became distinctive regions of cultural contact that have continued to be influential. In contrast to these borderlands and to isolated cultural pockets like the Appalachian Mountains, seaport cities and junctions along major transportation and trade routes were more cosmopolitan. Also in this period, certain preferences—stemming from the dominant political, religious, and social values of the old colonial gentry and the *nouveaux riches* of the rapidly growing northeastern postindustrial society—controlled and shaped the development of dance in the United States.

One such trend during this early period was widespread religious evangelism, which had been unevenly fanned by the flames of revivalism since the mid-eighteenth century. Perhaps as a result of social conservatism and its recoil from sensuality rekindled by the Second Great Awakening, which began in New England in the 1790s and spread with the westward expansion of settlements in the early decades of the nineteenth century, from about 1820 to 1835 some dancing masters found themselves no longer as essential to the old colonial gentry and to the relatively small urban elite. Performance of quadrilles, cotillions, and country dances—the hallmarks of the new republic—had become repetitious, even stagnant; the waltz had not become the mania in America that it was in Europe. The polka had yet to burst upon the popular stage. Conservative Americans disapproved of the potential immorality presented by closed couple dances and of what a closed couple symbolized as a loss of control over previously dominant community values.

UNITED STATES OF AMERICA: An Overview. A watercolor painted c.1830 depicting members of the Moravian community of York, Pennsylvania, dancing to a small instrumental ensemble and mixed chorus. (Courtesy of the Historical Society of York County, Pennsylvania.)

By 1835 both of America's leading evangelists, Lyman Beecher and Charles G. Finney, had abandoned their urban outposts to take up academic chairs in colleges in the West. Thereafter second-rate men and reform crusades diluted revivalism, yet they brought the Christian gospel to broader and more dispersed audiences. In this less intense and more receptive social environment teachers of dance found another opportunity to expand their profession. Just as Beecher and Finney changed their focus to become lecturers—moving from conducting revivals (inspiration) to delivering advice on how to conduct revivals (methodology)—dancing masters moved to conduct "proper" dancing parties and to teach "correct techniques" for achieving what they collectively agreed was "morality in motion." To complement this more conservative social milieu, dancing masters advocated physical education and such related social reforms as functional dress and outward displays of social grace and gentility as a national standard of etiquette. By the 1850s, when new social dances such as the mazurka, *redowa,* and five-, three-, and two-step waltzes were becoming familiar to more people, a wider populace accepted the dancing master as a social arbiter between the potentially volatile expressions of the human body and its practiced control.

Early social reform and educational crusades encouraged American intellectual and cultural institutions to support dance in education by using the argument of the benefits of physical education. They also made later serious study of dance possible. Self-education systems—the Lyceum movement (1826–1861), the Transcendentalist philosophy of "self-culture," and the beginnings of free public education—focused the nation on the significance of physical training and supported the consideration of exercise programs, gymnastics, and dancing as means to physical improvement. The rhetoric of physical education for a healthier body and a healthier nation persuaded the general population to accept dancing as a legitimate cultural amusement and theatrical art form. The moral and healthful virtues of gymnastic movements thus carried over into social dancing.

The vocabulary of simple rhythmic steps used in physical exercise and gymnastic programs such as Catharine Beecher's 1837 calisthenic exercises, Dio Lewis's New Gymnastics, and Adolph Spiess's revival of the folk roundel paralleled the move of social dance from classical ballet terminology and theatrical standards of execution. Dancing masters were believed to be necessary to teach deportment and refinement of steps and for chaperoning couple dancing, but mass audiences on their own increasingly could find refuge and a easy level of competency in the simple stepping patterns of standardized social dances.

Social movements against slavery, nativism, anti-Catholicism, and the struggle for women's rights also had their effects on the formation of an American dance. These and other issues and reforms tacitly called attention to deviancy in appearance and behavior from an implied national norm. The appearance and expressive display of the human body had long been a means to assess the inner morality of people. Such focus on the human body and its movements supported interest in social and cultural stereotypes, for example, the simple morality involved in the contrasts between thrift and idleness, temperance and intemperance. These moral directives appeared in novels and popular prints and were put into movement on the stage in character delineations and satires. Blatant ill manners, some uncontrolled body gestures, certain crooked postures, excessive display of emotions and "humors," and overly sloppy, gaudy, or inappropriate dress and conduct expressed bad character. Exaggerated self-control of emotions, severely plain and simple dress, which the wearer's "good nature" was supposed to ornament, and proper conduct (often perceived as tight and formal) expressed good character.

Physical expressions of moral lessons were also acted out in real life by assigning body movements certain cultural meaning. Restrictions of movement (such as that between the rib cage and pelvis, thus presenting the torso as a single unit) and the rigid prescription of gender roles (for example, stereotypical ways that men physically displayed strength and independence and that women exhibited dependency) affected how dancing was perceived and to be performed. Clothing proper to the occasion of dancing supported preferred body movement patterns.

Led by the steamboat, canal systems, toll roads, and railroads, new means of transportation and communication instigated a great social and economic expansion in antebellum America. In the first decade of the nineteenth century this expansion opened the West for settlement and encouraged new theatrical touring circuits as well as created new employment possibilities for dance instructors. Itinerant dancing masters, traditionally respected for their offerings of "gentility" and "polite education," brought cosmopolitan culture to remote geographic areas. They plied their trade in the expanding frontier areas of the Ohio Valley, the Mississippi River, the Old Northwest, and California to bring the socially useful, external displays of virtue and grace, or "manners," to the new social leaders of these rough-hewn communities. Middle- and upper-class social circles in well-established smaller towns retained respectable and long-tenured dancing teachers who taught what their clientele needed, and wanted, to participate in "polite society." At the same time, powerful oral and participatory instruction introduced traditional dances to the young of immigrant and ethnic communities and, as a consequence, initiated them to their native customs of social interaction and preferred patterns of deportment. Traditional culture and new-forming society had to mediate between behavioral options; for many the dance floor was a sanctioned space for trying on new and different movement fashions.

Growth of industry and commerce, of occupations, and of the labor force assisted by influxes of new immigrants (notably from Ireland and Germany) supported larger towns and dense population areas that, in turn, created new customers for a growing form of respectable amusement, the social dance party. Those of the middle classes who wished to capture respectability felt that socially controlled dancing parties (or balls) ensured properly conducted courtships and marriages and, in turn, the continuance of the positive socializing influence of the family. All this was to lead spirally to the proper conduct and refinement of the community, city, and nation. The more people understood the beneficial aspects of social dance—its gentle form of physical exercise and its containment of undesirable behaviors in aesthetic form—the more they would understand the rationale and beauty of theatrical

dance. There were also larger audiences for theatrical dance, particularly the morally didactic and "family entertainment" of companies such as the Ravels. [*See the entry on the Ravel family.*]

Some Europeans and dissenters against centralized power continued to regard the United States as an asylum and a place for utopian experimentation. Thus religious communal societies and various religious and social utopian models—as widely diverse as the religious sect called Shakers (founded c.1777) and Pullman, Illinois, a community planned for laborers (founded in 1880 on the outskirts of Chicago by railroad magnate George Pullman)—condoned expressive physical activities, some of which included dance. These communities were artificial environments whose social and religious rationales supported dancing and other physical activities. [*See Shaker Dance.*]

At mid-nineteenth century, the fear of urban violence erupting uncontrolled from groups of dislocated and dissatisfied peoples began to threaten traditional authority and power. Nativism and fear of social contamination encouraged society's upper strata to use organized, private dancing classes and complicated dance forms, such as the

UNITED STATES OF AMERICA: An Overview. Couples dancing at "The Great Russian Ball," held at the Academy of Music, New York, on 5 November 1863. (Reprinted from *Harper's Weekly,* November 1963; courtesy of Elizabeth Aldrich.)

German cotillion, as a social defense. Knowledge of an elaborate dance was a password as well as certification of social acceptance. The upper classes believed that pure dance forms and polite manners would cement class loyalty and keep the impure elements of society from contaminating "the right people." Dances from the eighteenth century, such as *menuets* and *gavottes,* which were reminiscent of a seemingly more virtuous and simple time, were thought to promote the gentility and refinements necessary to a moral and polite society.

Also at mid-century, burgeoning population—particularly in the cities—created favorable conditions for more and larger theaters and for more theatrical touring. Itinerant musical and dancing masters continued to follow the same routes as did itinerant theatrical and ballet companies. New roads, more efficient modes of water transportation, and the new railroad lines supported two major theatrical touring routes: the Ohio River Valley circuit established by Samuel Drake (1769–1854) and the Mississippi Valley circuit controlled by James H. Caldwell (1793–1863) from 1825 to 1835 and after 1835 by Noah Ludlow (1795–1886) and his partner, Solomon Smith (1801–1869).

The social and cultural climate of the United States—embroiled in such issues as public education, temperance, peace, rights for women, abolition, criminal reform, workers' rights, and domesticity, and preoccupied with social purity and law and order—did not view the theatrical arts, especially dancing, as a cultural or social imperative in national progress. As a consequence, Americans did not support the training of American theatrical dancers. Because the U.S. government did not support national academies devoted to the theater arts as in Europe, and because there were widely divergent ideas on the legitimacy and morality of dancing, foreign dancers continued to dominate the American stage well into the twentieth century. A sampling of these foreign classical dancers—initially and largely English and French, later Italian, and finally Russian—includes some of the century's most brilliant stars: Edmund H. Conway (1824–?), Claude and Madame Labasse (1822–1831), Fanny Achille (1827–?), Charles and Maria Ronzi Vestris (1828–1829), the Ravel family (1823–1868), Paul and Amalia Galster Taglioni (1839), Madame Augusta (1836–1839), Fanny Elssler (1840–1842), the Montplaisir Ballet (1847–1856), Domenico Ronzani and the Ronzani Ballet (1857–1868), Madame Celeste (1827–1866), whom Charles Durang, in his *The Philadelphia Stage* (1854), described as "probably the most successful female star ever to appear on the American boards," Giuseppina Morlacchi (1866–?), Anna Pavlova (1910–1916), and Serge Diaghilev's Ballets Russes (1916).

The nineteenth century was distinguished by a few prominent native-born dancers: Mary Ann Lee, whom

UNITED STATES OF AMERICA: An Overview. The Italian dancer Giuseppina Morlacchi, one of a number of European ballet stars to tour the United States, made her New York debut on 23 October 1867. This portrait shows her in costume for the can-can she created several months later during a stay in Boston. (Photograph by L. R. Burnham; from the Hotlibzelle Theatre Arts Library, University of Texas at Austin.)

Moore credited with being "the first American dancer to attain nation-wide fame as an exponent of the classical ballet" (Moore, 1948), Julia Turnbull (1822–1887), and Augusta Maywood (1835–1876?), America's first internationally famous *prima ballerina.* The life of George Washington Smith (1825–1899) exemplifies the versatility expected of an American dancer. He danced in *grand ballet,* opera, and the circus, working for both P. T. Barnum and Edwin Booth. Smith did entr'actes, clowned, and partnered almost every great ballerina who visited the United States from 1840 to the end of the century. He also choreographed, taught social dancing, and trained dancers for the theater. [*See the entries on Lee, Maywood, and George Washington Smith.*]

In popular theatrical dance, William Henry Lane (c.1825–1852), an African American known as Master

Juba, took the uniquely American theatrical dance art of African Americans to Europe. The emergence of black musicians, dancers, and actors on the American stage in the late 1830s marked the historical beginnings of one of the most original contributions of the United States to dance, an aspect of the jazz idiom that historians Marshall and Jean Stearns have termed "American vernacular dance." [*See the entry on Juba.*]

UNITED STATES OF AMERICA: An Overview. William Henry Lane, known as Master Juba, is an important figure in the development of American dance. As a skilled Irish jig and clog dancer, as well as a virtuosic minstrel dance competitor, Lane fused African-American rhythms with the techniques of hard-shoe step dancing. He traveled to London with Pell's Ethiopian Serenaders in 1848, where he was hailed by critics. This print shows him performing a jig at Vauxhall Gardens, London. (Reprinted from *Illustrated London News*, 5 August 1848.)

Those Americans in the middle and upper social strata continued to be more attracted to European tastes and fashions than to their own creative potential until after the Civil War. Spectacle productions with dance and acrobatics, like those of the Ravels, and the Romantic ballets, such as *Giselle* (1841), *La Esmeralda* (1844), and *Le Corsaire* (1856), were more prominent in the theater.

The Civil War had a positive effect on one particular aspect of dancing: revivals of dances from the eighteenth century—symbolic of the nation's genesis and union—achieved their greatest impetus during the campaign, beginning in the 1850s, to purchase and preserve George Washington's home, Mount Vernon, as a symbol of national unity. In the wake of this movement, eighteenth-century dances, again fashionable, spread to a popular audience. The American Centennial Celebration in 1876 further continued support of this early preservation movement of "old-fashioned" (eighteenth-century) dances. This new interest in history, as expressed by attention to a national folklore, to the English Arts and Crafts Movement in the United States, and to the need for models of a national standard of etiquette and manners, sustained this dance revival to the turn of the century.

The Civil War also marked the culminating point of the American brass band movement. Brass bands and the concomitant establishment of town bands and professional organizations of musicians contributed to the general spread of popular musical arts in America. These orchestras and bands provided music for both social and theatrical dance. New York musician and society dancing master Allen Dodworth and his family represented the popularity of all types of music and dance during this period. The beginnings of a professionalized American musical community drew dance and music more closely together and created conditions necessary for dance innovations.

The period from 1865 to 1900 marks the rise of "modern America." Characterized by the establishment and consolidation of business and social hierarchies and the stabilization of social, economic, and political relationships, the nation knit farming, ranching, and industry and brought the New South, the mining frontiers, the expansion of the railroad West, and agriculture to new power an influence. The period marks the advent of great cities and associated problems aggravated by increasing numbers of immigrants, including massive influxes of peoples from middle and eastern Europe. The U.S. political policy of economic isolationism ended, and this brought the country in closer diplomatic and commercial contact with foreign cultures, particularly those in East Asia.

Like benign rulers, the new wealthy industrialists of the 1870s and 1880s focused a portion of their influence on what they considered to be their moral responsibility and duty to the nation. Their idea of *noblesse oblige* motivated cultural philanthropy. Beautiful public structures, such as libraries, and cultural arts programs and events including dance and dance-related arts were to transform cities and regenerate the spiritual lives of their inhabitants.

The "modern America" period also introduced a new focus on child nurturing. This new attention developed largely through the work of theologian Horace Bushnell and in education through the model of the German kindergarten. Childhood education brought new regard to the importance of children's play, games, and dances. Accompanying this interest in children was a generalized fear that industrialization and modernity were ending a cultural age of innocence: old traditions were dying and needed to be saved. One response to this fear was an emphasis on physical regeneration as implied by the support of adult physical education and sports, which included new programs of exercise and spectator events.

The configuration of cultural interests in this period encouraged new attitudes toward the function of dance in American life. Four key trends in this transformation were the movement to professionalize teachers of dancing; the development of physical education in public schools and in community recreation programs that included forms of dance; the widespread popularity of systems of physical expression; and a new appreciation of history and culture consciousness in broad segments of the population, which led to the revival and popularity of dances from the past and from other cultures. These trends resulted in new attitudes toward all kinds of dancing and catalyzed the attention and concern of a mass, popular audience toward dance. The perception that dance was not only morally but socially useful began the process through which dance education and dance arts gained credibility and became more popular after the middle of the twentieth century.

Dancing masters, like architects, doctors, and lawyers, did not have any nationwide guild structures in the early decades of the nineteenth century. Two emerging phenomena, the dance teaching family and the professional and national organization of dancing masters, pointed to the professionalization of dancing masters at midcentury. Just as small "dynasties" of theatrical and stage dancing families like the Booths and the Ravels began to appear on the American theatrical scene, urban social dancing families (like the Durangs, the Dodworths, the Bourniques, the Ferreros, and the Carusis) became involved in teaching social dance. These family "businesses" had respectability and, unlike theatrical families, geographical stability.

Three professional organizations formed in the last quarter of the nineteenth century represent the first formal and broadly inclusive attempts to organize, standardize, and professionalize dance teaching and teachers in the United States. In Europe such organization had begun much earlier with government-established and tightly controlled theaters and academies. The American Society of Professors of Dancing was founded on 19 January 1879 and incorporated 20 October 1883. The American National Association of Masters of Dancing, United States and Canada, was founded in Boston on 15 June 1883. The Western Association Normal School, Masters of Dancing was started in Saint Louis in June 1894. Membership in all three groups reflected a broad geographical membership—for example, from Toronto; Louisville, Kentucky; and Oakland, California. Some members made regular trips to New York City and regularly corresponded in order to learn new dances, exchange ideas about dance, and keep up on musical and dance trends. By 1896 all three societies were flourishing. *The Director* (December 1987–November 1898), believed to be the first magazine devoted to dances published in America, gave a subtle sense of the relationship between these groups that begs further inquiry when it reported a bit too positively that "although the societies are distinct and working upon somewhat different principles, they should be in harmony and in friendly relation with each other. We have no reason to doubt that such a relation does exist, and we trust that it may continue."

Dancing masters such as E. B. Reilley and Judson Sause pointedly related their art to healthful exercise, physical culture, and gymnastics in order to stress its moral necessity to society. Like other dogma, gospel, rituals, and literature from the fields of business, medicine, and the publications industry that claimed to make Americans more successful, wealthy, and better persons, dancing manuals and the American Society of Professors of Dancing professed to accomplish similar transformations.

Dancing masters also capitalized on dance literature to influence their audiences. Dance, like other literature, was made possible at a reasonable cost because of mid-nineteenth-century inventions and improvements in printing presses that boosted production capabilities. Among the diverse books and pamphlets whose numbers steadily increased after the Civil War was a genre of technical manuals on a wide range of how-to subjects, from horseshoeing to beekeeping. How-to dance literature superficially mirrored the scientific, technical approach of these publications and made dance available to a large reading audience. Whether or not Charles Durang's *Terpsichore* (1847), Thomas Hillgrove's *Scholar's Companion and Ball-Room Guide* (1858), Elias Howe's *American Dancing Master* (1862), and Edward Ferrero's *Art of Dancing* (1859), as well as hundreds of anonymously written dance manuals, were read and used, they had the effect of standardizing and systematizing specific dances, like waltzes and quadrilles, and stimulating interest in popular American social and theatrical dance forms. The American body as well as character was being shaped through a common set of instructions.

Publications on dance burgeoned particularly after 1870, when new federal copyright laws permitted dance teachers to better protect their writings and notations (both written and shorthand methods) of their dances. Grassroots-oriented programs such as the ongoing Chautauqua movement, which began in 1874 as a Sunday school assembly in upstate New York and later became a forum for education, religion, arts, and public issues, were among the many educational projects that depended upon a variety of publications for lectures and correspondence courses. The Chautauqua School of Physical Education was founded in 1886 and directed until 1904 by William G. Anderson. Among his course offerings to the twelve to fifteen hundred physical education teachers who came to Chautauqua from all regions of the United States was an "Americanized Delsarte" system of expression. Continuing earlier self-culture attitudes and Lyceum programs from the first half of the century, Chautauqua also brought the subject of the moral and healthful benefits of dance to widely dispersed audiences across the country. It supported ideas about and provided a forum for the integration of dance into education as a vital aspect of American life.

Systems of physical expression contributed to the changing attitudes of Americans toward the morality of the human body and, by extension, of dance. The term *expression* in the nineteenth century included "physical culture, pantomime, dramatics . . . interpersonal communication, [and] . . . professional training for public speaking" (Ruyter, 1979). Expression was taught by instructors of elocution who emphasized the role of posture and gesture in effectively communicating with others in a variety of settings, from legal courts to public balls. As the Lyceum movement and later the Chautauqua movement provided more opportunities for both men and women to persuade and to teach their peers, the subject of expression became appropriate for all ranks of people.

The most popular of these expression systems used in the United States was the Delsarte system, developed by François Delsarte (1822–1871). As a professor of music, Delsarte developed a system of rhythmic exercises that combined singing, declamation, gymnastics, and dancing. Key to its broad acceptance in the United States was the Reverend William R. Alger, a Boston Unitarian clergyman, who, in his lectures, advocated the system's appeal to morality. He saw Delsartism as a religious culture that would redeem the earth. Delsartism brought broad segments of the population into contact with physical culture and dance, and it sanctioned dancelike activities in respectable homes, places of business, and educational institutions. [*See* Delsarte System of Expression.]

Marches and formations of the "musical drill" were another contribution to the creation of an American dance style. From approximately 1865 to 1885 drills evolved in civilian life in conjunction with English and American fraternal militias. Musical drills, more or less artistically arranged exercises set to music, not infrequently included dance steps and relied for effect on spatial patterns and, like chorales, upon large numbers of persons. German cotillions that were "staged" for several hundred participants often used drill formations and spatial emblems. The musical drill appeared simultaneously in several aspects of American culture: military training for the Spanish-American War; physical education in public schools and on public playgrounds; historical pageantry; stage dancing; social dancing; and rituals involving sororal and fraternal organizations. Wherever large crowds had to be managed with some degree of order, the musical marching drill was effective because it could be either called by simple "left" and "right" directions or comprehended easily by simple diagrams.

As dances incorporated physical exercise and gymnastic elements, physical educators began to use dance in their programs. In 1887 the director of the Boston Turnverein, a Mr. Eberhard, taught a new genre called "Fancy Steps" at the Harvard Summer School of Physical Education. Also in 1887, Dr. W. G. Anderson began a new genre called "gymnastic dancing." As head of the Brooklyn Normal School of Gymnastics, he believed that dancing could be used to arouse greater interest in gymnastics, and so he introduced jigs, reels, and clogs (an umbrella term he used for any ethnic dance) into the school's exercise program in order to develop the ear as well as the grace of his students (many of whom were the sons and daughters of immigrants). Anderson's and Eberhard's approaches were ways in which the new muscular morality was made to fit into the performance of American social dances.

After 1890 Elizabeth Burchenal and Dr. C. Ward Crampton, both of New York City and leaders in the new folk dance movement, began to collect and preserve European folk dances. Once considered a resource for the steps of gymnastic dancing, folk dances and their steps now became a separate and legitimate area of study. In 1918 Burchenal published the first modern book of traditional American dances, *Twenty Eight Contra Dances, Largely from the New England States.* Dr. Luther Gulick, a medical doctor as well as a leader in the profession of physical training, published *The Healthful Art of Dancing* (1910), through which he united, with new authority, the ideas of healthful exercise, folk dance, and public morality. Other university-educated instructors, such as M. B. Gilbert (Harvard Summer School of Physical Education) and O. L. Herbert (physical director of the Providence YMCA), further united social dancing with physical exercise and the concepts of folk dancing.

The Twentieth Century. By 1901, continuing demands for political, economic, and social change had ushered in the Progressive Era, a period of massive collective efforts to correct inequities caused by corruption in big business and by increasing waves of immigration. President Theodore Roosevelt led the attack against immorality in American society by calling for physical fitness and exercise. Progressive educational theory—espoused by philosopher Herbert Spencer, psychologist and educator G. Stanley Hall, philosopher William James, philosopher and educator John Dewey, and psychoanalyst Sigmund Freud—developed previous arguments for the rationalization of dance through art and physical education programs as a necessary means to healthy personal development.

UNITED STATES OF AMERICA: An Overview. Classical Greek sculpture and philosophy inspired many American dancers, choreographers, and dance educators in the late nineteenth and early twentieth centuries. Greek ideals of sport and education were part of the Progressive Era philosophy that brought dance into college and university settings. Pictured here are students at Barnard College's annual Greek dance competition in 1927. (Photograph by White Studios, New York; from the collection of Sally R. Sommer and William G. Sommer.)

Reactions against old definitions of the arts and social life, which characterized the period up to World War I, heightened contrasts and created concepts of "high" and "low" culture as well as of tradition and modernism. In the arts, the era has been defined as the "American Renaissance." Guided by the Pre-Raphaelites, who extolled the sixteenth century as a golden age of integrity in workmanship, American architects, city planners, mural painters, and dramatists tapped the ideals of Renaissance Europe to enrich what they felt were thin artistic currents in the United States.

In the area of dance, inspiration came from bygone eras in which the spirit as well as the body was honored. Elizabethan England bestowed the idea of wholesome pastimes and reinforced Anglo-American identity and traditions—especially in folk dance, and English folk dance in particular. Ancient Greece projected compelling images of serenity, the preciousness of youth before its decay, and the promise of light—inspiration—in contrast to the public image of American corruption. The Orient bequeathed mystery, eccentricity, and a kind of antimasque—

"unimaginable antiquity, inhuman beauty, boundless distance" (Said, 1978)—to the Anglo-European experience.

The ideals of the Progressive Era forged the concept of a "modern dance" in two areas: aesthetics and the theater, and education. Through programs in colleges and universities, a uniquely American vision of dance emerged. Gertrude Colby of Teacher's College, Columbia University, and Margaret H'Doubler of the University of Wisconsin took the theories of the new philosophers, educators, and artists and brought those ideas to fruition in dance curricula. [*See the entry on H'Doubler.*] The discipline heralded dance as a nurturing and spontaneous activity and as preparation for democracy by "strengthening body, cultivating love of beauty, stimulating imagination, challenging the intellect and social capabilities, and prompting individualization and self-expression" (Ruyter, 1979). The growth of dance in education continued to nourish a new professional modern dance by providing teaching and performing opportunities as well as informed audiences for new directions in dance as art.

Beginning in 1915 and extending through 1930, the rise in theater ticket prices, competition from spectator sports, and the appearance of films caused the popularity of big Broadway theaters to decline. As a consequence, there was little support for theatrical dancing scenes associated with expressive and elaborate productions and realistic spectacles, which had been used to provide touches of mood and verisimilitude to such shows as Augustin Daly's *Frou-Frou* (1870) and *The Taming of the Shrew* (1892) and David Belasco's *The Heart of Maryland* (1895) and *A Girl of the Golden West* (1905). Prior to this period, theatrical dancing had moved from the Romantic ballets of the 1840s and 1850s to the spectacle feats and chorus-line patterns of *The Black Crook* (1866) to the technically faultless, but emotionally arid, skill of the Italian ballerinas of 1860–1880, Marie Bonfanti, Giuseppina Morlacchi, and Rita Sangalli. Various kinds of popular dancing—like the chorus line and revue—gradually began to dominate the turn of the century. [*See* Black Crook, The; *and the entries on Bonfanti, Morlacchi, and Sangalli.*]

New popular entertainment genres—vaudeville, burlesque, and carnival and tent shows—that used precision, tap, and ethnic dances, ballet, and specialty acts and dances (acrobatics, adagio, exhibition ballroom, and striptease) absorbed hopeful theatrical dancers. The chorus line and precision dancing, a major choreographic attraction, dominated musical comedies and revues (particularly those mounted by Florenz Ziegfeld [1869–1932] as the *Ziegfeld Follies*). Theater audiences who had been exposed to dance through physical education and military training had an immediate appreciation for staged choreographic figures of columns and lines. Later, New York City's new Radio City Music Hall (1932), with its chorus line of thirty-six precision dancers, would carry this dance genre into present times. [*See* Radio City Music Hall *and the entry on Ziegfeld.*]

At the same time, a variety of public programs continued to expose mass audiences to new visions of dance in relation to American social reform, national unity, morality, and health. These public programs included the Playground Association of America (later the Playground and Recreation Association of America) founded in 1906; the American Pageant Association, officially founded in 1913; and more strongly developed German *Turnverein* and gymnastic exercise programs, begun in earnest after 1850. Further refinements in the training and certification of dancing teachers legitimized theatrical as well as social and folk forms of dancing and earned the broad support of participants as well as political and social audiences. Proponents of these public performances were firmly united in their social interests in public art, physical education, recreation, medicine, and ceremonies supporting nationalism. Traditional dances were supported by wealthy industrialists and cultural philanthropists such as Henry Ford and John D. Rockefeller. Ford became keenly interested in early American and international dances and music as a means to "Americanize" factory workers. His sense of duty to a seemingly nonexistent American dance catalyzed the attention of the nation through publicity in magazine and newspaper articles and, later, radio and Edison cylinders. Dances made up of simple lines and emblems and featuring large groups of performers created a positive and orderly image that could assuage the fears that American manufacturers had of managing dissimilar populations, riots, and disruptive union activities.

In the first decade of the twentieth century, just as Henry Ford had streamlined production techniques with the assembly line, standardized and published versions of teaching "methods" and dances—whether the mechanized chorus line or square dancing—spread to broader audiences across the country. Dance teachers as different as theatrical chorine trainer and choreographer Ned Wayburn and society dancing masters T. George Dodworth of New York and Alvar Bournique of Chicago turned away from the earlier dance "academies" toward modern dance "schools"—literally factories—run on business principles. At a different level of society, taxi dance halls wherein one could buy a dance and syndicated dance studios made their appearance.

In the first quarter of the century social dancing expressed two directions of American society: Traditional dancing masters, their businesses built on the needs of the social elites—clients preoccupied with the display of wealth, style, and fashion—moved to find novel attractions to counteract the staleness of old society dances and to keep their consumers conspicuous and stylish. Audiences at the new places of entertainment—first hotel ballrooms, then, in the 1920s, nightclubs—began to move to new, expressive dance rhythms originating in the various ethnic communities of the city and from countries such as Cuba and Central and South America, with whom the United States was, for the first time, exploring diplomatic relations, policies, and markets. Black American and American Creole communities were the source of the cakewalk. The syncopated rhythms of the one-step (its variants including the Turkey Trot and Bunny Hug), the Argentine tango, and the fox trot contrasted sharply with the smoothness of society dance. Dancing teams, especially that of Irene and Vernon Castle, promoted these new dances internationally in hotel ballrooms, nightclubs, and vaudeville houses. [*See the entry on Irene and Vernon Castle.*]

One of America's first independent artists in dance—Isadora Duncan—exemplified the spirit of a new form of American dance. Duncan's revolution can be best understood against the American compulsion to systematize and standardize expressive bodily movement. An aversion to "schools," systems, and artifices and an underlying anxiety about the loss of cultural innocence, symbolized by the expressive freedom of a child, motivated a few socially conscious and liberal thinkers of Duncan's era. In an age when most people turned to revivals of the past for guidance, Duncan, and later Ruth St. Denis, found more than old form: they found their own unique inspirations to create new dances. Duncan equated natural and freely expressive body movements in dance with hope for modern humanity. Her art was a reaction to the hegemony of the French academy, with its rules of proportion, composition, suitable subjects, and other matters that together legitimized "the academy" approach to general education and traditional art. Reactions against the status quo were not yet widespread. It was too early for Duncan to find support for her modern art in the United States, so she turned to Europe. [*See the entries on Duncan and St. Denis.*]

On 13 February 1913 a select group of progressive painters organized the Armory Show in New York City as a means of combating the doldrums of the artistic spirit in the United States. Called "pathological" by the *New York Times*, the show included for the first time in the United States the work of European postimpressionists and futurists. In an era when "the academy" had a corner on respectability in all arts, including dance, this exhibition focused the attention of the art world on the tension between traditionalism and modernism. The influence of both reached the art of dance through aesthetic principles of abstraction and expressionism. Both guided the tastes of new audiences in appreciating form and content in abstract representations of the body and its emotions. What was novel was that modern intellectual currents supported self-expression that promised both creative and psychological well-being.

The earlier appearance of Russian dancers Anna Pavlova and Mikhail Mordkin at the Metropolitan Opera House in New York in 1910 had exposed American audiences to the expressive, new vitality in classical ballet; but when Serge Diaghilev's Ballets Russes came to the United States in 1916, the company's modernism "rocked a widespread minority of interested people all over America to their imaginative foundation" (Kirstein, 1967). Russian dancers who stayed in America, like Michel Fokine and Léonide Massine, revitalized ballet teaching with Russian technique but were not able to capture the electric modernism of Diaghilev's repertory. It would be seventeen more years before Russian George Balanchine, influenced by American culture, would infuse vital new choreography into classical ballet in the United States. In 1916 insufficient organization and management of opera houses, inadequately trained dancers, and the need for permanent dance companies—all necessary to support ballet's theatrical illusion—were still underdeveloped. [*See the entries on Balanchine, Fokine, Massine, Mordkin, and Pavlova.*]

An accretion of dance types, both traditional and modern, meshed into a new wave of theatrical dance. Around 1912, and in emulation of the independent theaters of Europe, several so-called little theaters and art schools became established in the United States. Significant to the dance world was the momentum of the movement, as it supported the creative inclinations of individual dance artists upon whom modernism was having an effect. Exemplary was the Neighborhood Playhouse, established by Irene and Alice Lewisohn in 1915 in New York City as an adjunct to the Henry Street Settlement. Originally designed not as a social experiment but to serve the needs and creative interests of residents of the area, the Neighborhood Playhouse evolved out of festivals for children of the settlement. Individual dance artists also started their own little theaters and schools. In 1914 Nellie Cornish established the Cornish School in Seattle, and in 1915 the Ruth St. Denis School of Dancing and Its Related Arts opened in Los Angeles as Denishawn. [*See* Denishawn.]

In 1912 Jesse L. Lasky, Samuel Goldwyn, and Cecil B. De Mille headed west to make the film *The Squaw Man*. Early American cinema included the first recording of dance in the United States. Theatrical dancing depicted in Hollywood films provided mass audiences with images—albeit stereotypic—of dance in the lives of Americans. These first films included Broadway musical comedies and revues adapted for the silver screen as well as scenes set in nightclubs and frontier towns. A major resource for dance historians, early films have provided the history of other forms of dance, often inadvertently caught in newsreels, home movies, and early documentaries. [*See* Film musicals, *article on* Hollywood Film Musicals.]

After World War I—a point that conventionally marks the end of American cultural naïveté and of the massive

UNITED STATES OF AMERICA: An Overview. Students at the Denishawn school in Los Angeles, c.1920. This canopied, open-air studio provided the perfect environment for the Denishawn curriculum, which included at various times courses in dramatic gesture, assorted "Oriental" dance techniques (Indian, Arabian, Siamese, et al.), ballet, "Greek" dancing, music visualization, piano, the French language, and craft-work. (Photograph from the archives at Jacob's Pillow, Becket, Massachusetts.)

immigration from eastern Europe that began in the 1880s—new emphasis was put on an "American-styled" dance. By performing American and European folk dances in their mass-participant, outdoor spectacles and civic pageants, both the American Pageant Association and the community theater movement had served to define these dances to a general public. Both agencies renewed audience and producers' interests in programs that acknowledged cultural roots of the United States and those of recent arrivals. These civic programs aroused interest in and directed research of historical American dress, dances, and folklore.

A kind of forced self-consciousness caused by being relegated to overcrowded urban and northern ghettos, such as New York City's Harlem, contributed to the emergence of a new black American assertiveness and intellectualism. Black Americans uncovered their own historical and cultural motifs and incorporated them into new forms of artistic expression. For white intellectuals, Harlem was an opportunity to discover and experience the exotic in an otherwise staid, conformist, and mechanistic world. The Harlem Renaissance of the late 1910s and the 1920s brought to popularity social dances of ragtime and early jazz, like the Black Bottom, the Shimmy, and the Charleston. The Cotton Club, a Harlem night spot, is notable for having introduced black performers such as Ethel Waters, Cab Calloway, Maude Russell, and Bill Robinson. Gramophone recordings and national radio broadcasts brought the new dance sounds to popular attention.

By 1928 the juncture of the development of modern aesthetic theories and the support of the intellectual community; the emergence of "new schools" (some of which supported dance performances); the extraordinary appearance of expressionism in dance in Diaghilev's Ballets Russes; and the awareness brought to "an American dance" by civic festivals and film created a receptive environment for independent and nonconformist young dancers to experiment with modernism in dance. Four such individuals are exemplary: Doris Humphrey and Charles Weidman, Martha Graham (with composer and music director Louis Horst), and Helen Tamiris. All choreographed, performed, and taught in a network of "new schools" and, on occasion, in the Neighborhood School of the Theater. All anchored, in their individual ways, their choreographic ideas in the expression of American culture. For example, the titles of Graham's early works—*Immigrant, Revolt, Four Insecurities,* and *Heretic*—evoke both the social consciousness and the psychological issues that were current in the late 1920s and early 1930s. Similarly, Graham's pieces of the 1930s—*Primitive Mysteries* and *Ceremonials,* followed by *Frontier*

and *American Document,* demonstrate the influence of American themes. [*See the entries on Graham, Horst, Humphrey, and Weidman.*]

The invention of synchronous sound for motion pictures in 1927 and the Great Depression that followed the stock market crash of October 1929 were serious blows to Broadway theaters. In the 1930s, as part of President Franklin Roosevelt's New Deal to American artists, the Federal Dance Project (1935–1939), subsidized by the Works Progress Administration (WPA), attempted to cut unemployment drastically in the theatrical dance field. Although administered in various cities, the Federal Dance Project was most active in Chicago and New York. Also in the early 1930s, numerous groups in New York City, including the Red Dancers and the New Dance Group, joined to form the Workers' Dance League. Dedicated to making dance a weapon in the class struggle and a means of social protest, the league produced dances of revolution. As the decade went on, however, its themes shifted to issues of war, fascism, and censorship. [*See* New Dance Group.]

The accomplishments of the Federal Dance Project reflected the variety of directions that theatrical dancing took after the turn of the century. There was a children's festival, entitled Folk Dances of All Nations, choreographed by Lillian Mehlman, and there were perfor-

UNITED STATES OF AMERICA: An Overview. Maude Russell and Her Ebony Steppers, who were a featured act at several Harlem clubs in the 1920s. (Photograph from the Dance Collection, New York Public Library for the Performing Arts.)

UNITED STATES OF AMERICA: An Overview. A former Denishawn dancer, Martha Graham was one of the most influential, and long-lived, modern dance pioneers. She swirls here in *Letter to the World* (1940), a work inspired by the life and poetry of Emily Dickinson, which premiered at the Bennington Festival in Vermont. (Photograph © by Barbara Morgan; used by permission of the Barbara Morgan Archives, Hastings-on-Hudson, New York.)

of dancing began to appear in the 1930s: Lincoln Kirstein's *Dance: A Short History of Classical Theatrical Dancing* (1935) was closely followed by the English translation of the musicologist Curt Sachs's pioneering study *World History of the Dance* (1937). Sachs's book had been published in Germany just before he took up residence in New York City as professor of music at the Graduate School of Liberal Arts, New York University, and as music consultant to the New York Public Library.

The WPA had identified and made legitimate, if only briefly, federal responsibility for the nation's arts. The 1930s also witnessed renewed attempts to establish American professional dance companies and schools for classical ballet training. The founding of the School of American Ballet in 1933 and of the American Ballet in 1934 by Lincoln Kirstein and Edward M. Warburg with George Balanchine (whom they had invited to the United States to direct and organize the company) reflected a growing

mances by the new modern dancers Humphrey, Weidman, Tamiris, and Katherine Dunham. The project brought together the diverse forms of theatrical dance that had developed over the previous fifty years and presented many of them side by side on the same stage. For instance, tap and chorus line routines were mixed with classical ballet in a Chicago revue called *O Say, Can You See?* Current social and political issues were expressed in movement, for example, Tamiris's *How Long Brethren?* (1937). Most importantly, in many cities the records of the region's performing arts were brought together in research studies for the first time, and the WPA led to the development of some of the first modern chronologies of early American dance, music, and theater history. [*See* Federal Dance Project; *and the entry on* Tamiris.]

The swing-band era of Benny Goodman, Glenn Miller, and others introduced social dances such as the boogie-woogie and jitterbug. These dances, free and improvised, further marked the move away form the close embrace of couple dancing. New sounds of maracas, claves, and Cuban drums popularized Latin American dances like the rumba, samba, and *maxixe*.

Dance increasingly became a more serious subject in colleges and universities as well as in the scheme of national cultural life. The first modern studies of the history

UNITED STATES OF AMERICA: An Overview. Katherine Dunham was director of the Negro Unit of the Federal Dance Project in Chicago for a period in the late 1930s. During her tenure there, she presented her ballet *L'Ag'ya* under the FDP's auspices. She appears here, at center, with three male dancers of her company, in this work inspired by her research in Martinique. (Photograph from the Dance Collection, New York Public Library for the Performing Arts.)

interest in American ballet. In 1946 Balanchine and Kirstein also organized Ballet Society, a membership organization for the encouragement of lyric theater; in 1948 it was renamed New York City Ballet. Three brothers, who epitomized the development of dance in America—Willam, Lew, and Harold Christensen—established ballet schools in the far western United States. [*See* American Ballet; New York City Ballet; *and the entries on the Christensen brothers and Kirstein.*]

To some, ballet remained controversial until the 1950s. Essentially an assertion of high culture in a country whose population and potential audiences responded to popular entertainments and pastimes, ballet was not a standard aspect of university and college dance programs until the 1960s. Connoisseurship of classical dance, the result of exposure and education, grew steadily as a consequence of early dance tours like those of Ballet Caravan and that company's exploration of American subjects in choreography. Ballet Caravan's innovative repertory included *Pocahontas* (1936) by Lew Christensen, with music by Elliott Carter; *Yankee Clipper* (1937) by Eugene Loring, with music by Paul Bowles; *Filling Station* (1937) by Lew Christensen, with music by Virgil Thomson; and *Billy the Kid* (1938) by Eugene Loring, with music by Aaron Copland. [*See* Ballet Caravan.]

Also in the 1930s, American square dancing began as a nationwide recreational dance movement, having received impetus from the back-to-the-land movement prior to the stock market crash of 1929 and from the emergence of middle-class vacationers and auto tourists. Vacationing created a demand for "country customs" and brought local performers to the attention of travelers on holiday. Out of this trend arose a number of dance enthusiasts from all ranks who began "collecting" early dances on the model provided by English musicologist Cecil Sharp, who had founded the English Folk Dance Society of America in 1915, simultaneously in New York, Boston, Chicago, and Pittsburgh. In 1932 the English group became the English Dance and Song Society; later the United States branch became the Country Song and Dance Society of America.

Several books published after 1930 attest to the vitality of the country dance movement: Beth Tolman and Ralph Page's *The Country Dance Book* (1937), Lloyd Shaw's *Cowboy Dances* (1939), Grace L. Ryan's *Dance of Our Pioneers,* and Lucile K. Czarnowski's *Dances of Early California Days* (1950). These enthusiasts responded to the belief that they were preserving the dances of older members of their communities. They sponsored traditional dances at new-fashioned dude ranches and ski resorts, and they joined together to make a tacit folk community whose

UNITED STATES OF AMERICA: An Overview. Agnes de Mille's *Rodeo* is a paragon of balletic Americana. Premiered by the Ballet Russe de Monte Carlo in 1942, it was restaged for Ballet Theatre in 1950 in the production seen here, with the original designs by Oliver Smith (scenery) and Kermit Love (costumes). (Photograph from the archives of American Ballet Theatre.)

networks have since grown steadily, some of whose members have emerged as professional performers.

Summer festivals and dance camps for all varieties of dance put young dancers together with mature performing artists and subject specialists. Beginning with summer pageants, Charlotte Perry and Portia Mansfield's summer dance camp in Steamboat Springs, Colorado (1914), Cecil Sharp's camps in Eliot, Maine, and Amherst Agricultural College, Massachusetts (1915), and later, the modern dance sessions at Bennington College in Vermont (1934–1946) and Mills College in California (1934), these intensive periods of study drew dancers and increased slowly in number and geographical location until their peak in the mid-1970s.

Against the background of these developments up to World War II, the Broadway musical *Oklahoma!* (1943), choreographed by Agnes de Mille, appeared as a milestone in American theatrical dance. In de Mille's choreography, elements of the growing traditional dance move-

ment were united with classical ballet steps in a popular musical theater production on an American theme. The production brought many diverse aspects of American dance together, and the result was a dance form that attracted a large and popular audience. [*See the entry on de Mille.*]

American theatrical dance continued to attract large audiences after World War II, when ethnic, folk, and social genres began to support intellectual, social, and aesthetic diversity. Developments in national cultural life again guided the dance's multifarious directions. Foreign policy debates, the escalating Cold War between the USSR and the United States, loyalty checks and other ramifications of McCarthyism, economic and political reconstructions abroad, and the post–New Deal economy combined to create an aura of insecurity at home and abroad.

The population of the United States in 1952 was double that of 1900. Only 10 percent depended upon farming for their livelihood. Beginning in the 1950s, white collar workers outnumbered manual laborers, and manufacturers and suppliers in all professions increased markedly. Social progress began to be made in the fields of civil rights, health, and welfare. After 1950 dancing as an art form—enhanced by government support to arts and phys-

UNITED STATES OF AMERICA: An Overview. A scene from Yvonne Rainer's *Carriage Discreteness*, from *Nine Evenings: Theater and Engineering* (1966), a series of performances in which avant-garde artists collaborated with engineers from Bell Telephone Laboratories at the Sixty-ninth Regiment Armory, New York. (Photograph © 1966 by Peter Moore; used by permission.)

UNITED STATES OF AMERICA: An Overview. Trisha Brown devised the movement for *Locus* (1975) by assigning letters to points on an imaginary cube surrounding her body and then "spelling" out an autobiographical text through actions directed at these points. From left to right, Brown, Elizabeth Garren, Mona Sulzman, and Judith Ragir appear in different phases of this articulation. *Locus* was pivotal in the development of Brown's efficient, yet fluid, style of movement, which has been influential among dancers and choreographers throughout the world. (Photograph © by Babette Mangolte; used by permission.)

ical education programs in colleges and universities; growing national economic security; an increase in the number of educated viewers; television exposure; and finally the establishment of the national endowments—entered a period of growth that exploded by the mid-1970s.

Classical ballet companies began to develop all over the world and by the 1960s had become international symbols of national or civic prestige. The successful visit of Great Britain's Sadler's Wells Ballet (renamed the Royal Ballet in 1956) from Covent Garden to New York City in 1949 marked the beginning of regular international cultural exchanges of dance companies. Impresario Sol Hurok (1888–1974) was a major figure in these exchanges. In the 1950s he arranged for visits by the Bolshoi Ballet, the Kirov Ballet, the Moiseyev Dance Company, and the Azumi Kabuki troupe as well as tours by American artists such as Martha Graham to Europe and East Asia.

Beginning in 1956, with the first regional ballet festival in Atlanta, Georgia, the regional ballet movement began to provide one solution to the problem of training young dancers for ballet companies, nationally and abroad. Consisting of nonprofessional companies attached to schools, the activity complemented the earlier civic theater movement. It brought support to its members, served the communities with which it was affiliated, and was one answer to the need for developing young talent for professional careers. After the formation of the Regional Ballet Festival Association (later the National Association for Regional Ballet), the design spread to the Northeast (1959), Southwest (1963), Pacific Western (1966) and Middle States (1972) regions.

Against the canvas of expanding professional dance organization and touring companies, the off-Broadway movement, whose performances took place in out-of-the-way theaters and improvised auditoriums in order to cut production costs, supported new waves of young modern dancers who pursued the path of individual expression established by Graham, Humphrey, Tamiris, and Hanya Holm. Dancers such as Merce Cunningham, Alwin Nikolais, and Paul Taylor began to steer choreography and performance technique away from its expressionist focus. Cunningham created a style of dancing that embodied flexibility, multiplicity change, and idiosyncrasy. Other modern dancers, like Anna Halprin, explored the cacophony of modern life and found new ways to create sense from its diverse elements with happenings, wherein any raw material—simultaneous phenomena, sounds, or objects—could become part of the dance event. [*See the entries on Cunningham, Halprin, Holm, Nikolais, and Taylor.*]

A simplified version of the jitterbug, the jive, and "smooch" dancing to quiet music characterized post–World War II social dancing. Soon, however, rock-and-roll (popularized by Bill Haley and the Comets in 1955) became the rage, and dances like the Twist (popularized by Chubby Checker in the early 1960s) and the Shake became the popular "fast" dances. All could be danced in groups without partners. Electric guitars and organs, along with rhythm and sometimes brass instruments, created a new dance sound that entertained widespread audiences through records played at home, at school proms, on jukeboxes, and on the radio. [*See* Social Dance, *article on* Social Dance since 1960.]

From 1961 through 1968, the presidencies of John F. Kennedy and Lyndon Johnson, the population of the United States increased by twenty-four million—with 60 percent living in metropolitan areas, 5 percent on farms. In a phantasmagorical scene induced by national and international events, the country witnessed domestic wars on poverty and racism convergent with U.S. involvement in Vietnam. A confrontation on a national scale over the potential end of the world's natural resources coincided with and exacerbated the media images and felt consequences of environmental destruction and the sacrifice of lives in war as a means to peace. By 1970 American society appeared to have stalled: within ten years it had confronted the paradox of being both the best and the worst of nations. Dancing reflected the times in terms of choreographic themes and artistic approaches as well as through its growth boosted by federal programs for the arts and humanities. In 1966 the U.S. Congress initiated governmental support of the nation's arts with passage of the National Foundation on the Arts and Humanities Act. Touring and funding for dance projects began in 1966, and in the early 1970s the National Endowment for the Arts (NEA) Dance Program became a special umbrella for dance as a performing art.

The increasing diversity of dance styles and genres after 1960 was met by a conscious joining of styles and the disassembling of dance movements—directions in dance that have served to create expressive new dimensions in the arts. Examples can be drawn from divergent levels of society and training. Inspired by choreographer Cunningham, artists Allan Kaprow, Robert Rauschenberg, and Jasper Johns, and composer John Cage, postmodern dancers such as Steve Paxton, Yvonne Rainer, Trisha Brown, and David Gordon explored invention and change as a means of disengaging from ideas of tradition, personal expression, craftsmanship, and composition. Their dances not only evaluate space, time, and weight; but they also play with perception, arbitrary assemblages, fragmentation, and juxtaposition; movement is demystified and allowed to be ordinary, mundane. [*See the entries on Trisha Brown, Cage, Gordon, Johns, Paxton, Rainer, and Rauschenberg.*]

UNITED STATES OF AMERICA: An Overview. Catherine Turocy's New York Baroque Dance Company and James Richman's Concert Royal revived Rameau's 1745 *opéra-ballet Le Temple de la Gloire* in 1991. Here, Venus (dancer Patricia Beaman) and Mars (dancer Todd Putman) crown the Roman emperor Trajan (tenor Frederick Urrey) with a laurel wreath in an allegory of ideal kingship; Glory (soprano Christine Brandes) observes from the clouds above. (Photograph © 1991 by Jack Vartoogian; used by permission.)

UNITED STATES OF AMERICA: An Overview. Zydeco is a Cajun couple dance performed to lively two-step music. Pictured here are dancers doing the Nouveau Zydeco at the Twelfth Annual Original Southwest Louisiana Zydeco Music Festival in Plaisance, Louisiana, in 1994. (Photograph © 1994 by Jack Vartoogian; used by permission.)

American dance after the 1960s reflected the work of choreographers like Glen Tetley, who, trained in both classical and modern styles, brought the rational and cool steps, position, and attitudes of ballet together with the free and independently expressive use of space, time, and rhythm in modern dance. [*See the entry on Tetley.*] In a similar vein, but from another dance community, break dancing—a movement art that used wrists, shoulders, and heads more than feet in a stunning array of twists, kicks, and spins—superseded "dancing" on roller skates as the urban dance art of the 1980s. Most break dancers were black or Hispanic male teenagers who gathered on the streets or in discos to display their talents. Frequently accompanied by a "rapper," a nondancer who gave a "soliloquy in rhyme about the hard knocks, crime, and life in the ghetto" (Sandler, 1984), the dancing incorporated movements similar to gymnastics, wrestling, and martial arts. [*See* Break Dancing.]

In the 1960s and early 1970s, social dances like the Frug, the Hustle, and salsa moved into discotheques. A revival of rock-and-roll and renewed interest in country-western music rejuvenated dances from the 1950s as well as country swing, the Texas Two-Step, Cotton-Eyed Joe, and clogging. Late 1950s and early 1960s Latin dances such as the cha-cha and the bossa nova infused more formal ballroom practices, and a revival of "tea dancing" in urban hotels renewed interest in the fox trot, waltz, and other ballroom dances.

Professional associations founded since the 1960s express contemporary and burgeoning diversity of dance interests, from dance history to movement therapy to aerobics. These groups reflect developments in physical education, ethnic and traditional dancing, dance criticism, dance therapy, cheerleading, dance music, dance revivalism, games, and play. Dance revivalism, the impulse to preserve dances from the past—a phenomenon in American dance history as far back as the eighteenth century—has become almost a science, involving a combination of sensitivity to theatrical and social history with procedures of analysis, scholarship, and expressive movement reconstruction. As a result, an ironic situation has developed: American scholars in historical dance have played an important role in bringing forth reconstructed early court-dance choreographies to European audiences. The Baroque Dance Ensemble under the direction of Shirley Wynne was the first such American company in Europe at Spoleto, Italy, in the summer of 1979. Two of her company members, Catherine Turocy and Ann Jacoby, co-founders of the New York Baroque Dance Company, presented the premiere performance in Europe of Jean-Philippe Rameau's opera *Les Bordéades* in Aix-en-Provence, France, in the summer of 1982.

As the turn of the twenty-first century approaches, dance art in the United States is like any other medium and cultural commodity that must keep pace in both the intellectual marketplace and the supermarket of consumerism. Performers, musicians, choreographers, choreographies, and audiences are globally accessible and performers interchangeable within a vast array of professional movement styles. A good theatrical dance experience, like most American cars, may have performers, director, and expressive and technical components from multiple international communities. Like postmodern choreographer and dancer Mark Morris, American dance artists have played an increasingly significant role in the development of dance arts in Europe. In 1984, the American Dance Festival in Durham, North Carolina, produced its first International Modern Dance Festival and its first International Choreographers Workshop, which led to the formation of the International Choreographers Commissioning Program in 1987. The year 1993 saw the first International Dance Critics Conference. Activities were not limited to the United States; by 1994, twenty-four foreign countries had offered classes and workshops led by American Dance Festival faculty. [*See* American Dance Festival; *and the entry on Morris.*]

In 1985, New York's Dance Theater Workshop founded The Suitcase Fund: A Project of Ideas and Means in Cross-Cultural Artist Relations. The Fund was organized to assist independent professional artists and their progressive producers in overcoming the economic and political barriers that deny artists access to other cultures. In addition, the fund now also helps producers and writers travel to major meetings and festivals in order to build ongoing relationships with their peers. By 1995 both the American Dance Festival and Dance Theater Workshop were sponsoring cooperative activities with Africa, Asia, Europe, and Latin America.

U.S. dance magazines and scholarly publications regularly cover international dance in Denmark, France, the Netherlands, and some Asian countries. There are now international ballet seminars. A child studying dance in

UNITED STATES OF AMERICA: An Overview. Mark Morris set his *Pièces en Concert* to selections from François Couperin's work of the same title. Pictured here, in the 1986 premiere performance at the Brooklyn Academy of Music, are Susan Hadley, Morris, and Rob Besserer. (Photographs © 1986 by Jack Vartoogian; used by permission.)

UNITED STATES OF AMERICA: An Overview. The Pacific Northwest Ballet, directed by Kent Stowell and Francia Russell, is one of the most successful dance companies in the United States. In Stowell's production of *Cinderella* (1994), Ross Yearsley as the Prince partnered Louise Nadeau in the title role. (Photograph courtesy of Pacific Northwest Ballet.)

Omaha, Nebraska, can aspire to join a dance company in almost any part of the globe. Likewise, complementing fine televised programming of all types of dance—accessible to countless audiences worldwide—the World Wide Web and internet permit audience, performer, and choreographer to exchange information instantly and to see bodies move across their computer screens. In such a frantic and fragmented world, meaning in expressive body gestures and dance language is one of "references," a postmodern trend that lets us view body movement from our theater seats much as we view scenery from a fast-moving car. The embodied performance—not self-conscious—is the *rara avis,* and yet it is sought out by ethnologists and sociologists and can, when captured, become, in an Erving Goffman manner, a kind of theater experience in itself. As Adam Gopnik remarked in the *New Yorker,* "Post-modernist art is, above all, post-audience art."

The broad acceptance of American dance, its diverse manifestations and definitions, expresses a uniquely American cultural consciousness. Dance historians examine past webs of ideas, and the pathways that dancers have been asked by their society and culture to travel. Dance anthropologists and musicologists challenge the public to see the movement performance of others within the performers' own cultural systems. Sociologists urge spectators to find structured relationships in vernacular dancing events. Folklorists and psychologists show how dance events and interpersonal behaviors create vital circuits of communication between participants and how

the values and attitudes related to dance postures and gestures are encoded in culture and society so that they are saved, used, and perpetuated. Dance therapists call attention to how body-movement patterns and preferences impede or assist growth, development, and perception. The history of dance in the United States is thus best understood from a broad, interdisciplinary base of inquiry that seeks to define and explain dance expressions in the tangled variety of cultural situations that are the American experience.

BIBLIOGRAPHY.   Primary sources available for the study of dance in the United States are virtually without limit. The ephemeral and all-encompassing activity of dance makes it necessary to consider a broad variety of sources in order to understand what diverse groups of Americans have thought about their bodies and those of others, and what principles have helped to shape people's expressive postures and gestures as well as forms in dance. Standard documents for the investigation of dancing include diaries and journals, letters, newspapers, magazines, and books. Graphics such as paintings, magazine and newspaper illustrations, and photographs—though laden with artistic conventions and limited by the medium as well as by the artist—reveal cultural ideas about dancing and the body. Film is one of the most immediate, but least available, records of dance. Oral histories can provide information to the folklorist as well as to the historian in dance. Less obvious sources are municipal, state, and federal records, ship passenger lists, and legal records.

Abrahams, Roger D. "Moving in America." *Prospects* 3 (1977): 63–82.
"American Dancing." *Dance Magazine* (July 1976): 44–78.
Andrews, Edward D. *The Gift to Be Simple: Songs, Dances, and Rituals of the American Shakers.* New York, 1940.
Aschenbrenner, Joyce. *Katherine Dunham: Reflections on the Social and Political Contexts of Afro-American Dance.* CORD Dance Research Annual, 12. New York, 1981.
Banes, Sally. *Terpsichore in Sneakers: Post-Modern Dance.* Boston, 1980.
Barker[-Warner], Barbara. *Ballet or Ballyhoo: The American Careers of Maria Bonfanti, Rita Sangalli, and Giuseppina Morlacchi.* New York, 1984.
Barzel, Ann. "European Dance Teachers in the United States." *Dance Index* 3 (April–June 1944): 56–100.
Benson, Norman A. "The Itinerant Dancing and Music Masters of Eighteenth-Century America." Ph.D. diss., University of Minnesota, 1963.
Blaustein, Richard J. "Traditional Music and Social Change: The Old Time Fiddler's Association Movement in the United States." Master's thesis, Indiana University, 1975.
Brockett, Oscar G. *History of the Theatre.* 7th ed. Boston, 1995.
Brooks, Lynn Matluck. "The Philadelphia Dancing Assembly in the Eighteenth Century." *Dance Research Journal* 21 (Spring 1989): 1–6.
Brown, Richard D. *Modernization: The Transformation of American Life, 1600–1865.* New York, 1976.
Cohen, Selma Jeanne. "The Fourth of July, or, The Independence of American Dance." *Dance Magazine* (July 1976): 49–53.
Dance Research Journal (Spring 1983). Special issue entitled "Popular Dance in Black America."
Delamater, Jerome. *Dance in the Hollywood Musical.* Ann Arbor, Mich., 1981.
de Mille, Agnes. *Dance to the Piper.* Boston, 1952.
Emery, Lynne Fauley. *Black Dance from 1619 to Today.* Rev. ed. Princeton, 1988.

Garafola, Lynn, ed. *Of, By, and For the People: Dancing on the Left in the 1930s*. Madison, Wis., 1994.

Glassberg, David. "Restoring a 'Forgotten Childhood': American Play and the Progressive Era's Elizabethan Past." *American Quarterly* 32 (Fall 1980): 351–368.

Handlin, Oscar. *The Uprooted: The Epic Story of the Great Migrations That Made the American People*. 2d enl. ed. Boston, 1973.

Harris, Neil. *The Artist in American Society: The Formative Years, 1790–1860*. Chicago, 1966.

Haskins, James. *The Cotton Club: A Pictorial and Social History of the Most Famous Symbol of the Jazz Era*. New York, 1977.

Haskins, James. *Black Dance in America: A History through Its People*. New York, 1990.

Hazzard-Gordon, Katrina. *Jookin': The Rise of Social Dance Formations in African-American Culture*. Philadelphia, 1990.

Howe, Daniel Walker, ed. *Victorian America*. Philadelphia, 1976.

Humphrey, Doris. *Doris Humphrey, an Artist First: An Autobiography*. Edited by Selma Jeanne Cohen. Middletown, Conn., 1977.

Kirstein, Lincoln. *Ballet, Bias, and Belief: Three Pamphlets Collected and Other Dance Writings*. New York, 1983.

Lally, Kathleen A. "A History of the Federal Dance Theatre of the Works Progress Administration, 1935–1939." Master's thesis, Texas Women's University, 1978.

Lehman, Rhea H. "Virtue and Virtuosity: America's Vision of the Romantic Ballet, 1827–1840." Ph.D. diss., University of Wisconsin, Madison, 1986.

Lynes, Russell. *The Tastemakers*. New York, 1954.

Magriel, Paul, ed. *Chronicles of the American Dance: From the Shakers to Martha Graham*. New York, 1948.

Marks, Joseph E. III. *America Learns to Dance: A Historical Study of Dance Education in America before 1900*. New York, 1957.

Marks, Joseph E. III. *The Mathers on Dancing*. Brooklyn, 1975.

Martin, Carol. *Dance Marathons: Performing American Culture of the 1920s and 1930s*. Jackson, Miss., 1994.

Martin, John. *The Modern Dance*. New York, 1933.

Matlaw, Myron, ed. *American Popular Entertainment: Program and Papers of the Conference on the History of American Popular Entertainment*. Westport, Conn., 1979.

McDermott, Douglas. "The Development of Theatre on the American Frontier, 1750–1890." *Theatre Survey* 19 (May 1978): 63–78.

Moore, Lillian. "Moreau de Saint-Méry and 'Danse.'" *Dance Index* 5 (October 1946): 232–260.

Moore, Lillian. "Some Early American Dancers." *Dancing Times* (August 1950): 668–671.

Moore, Lillian. "The Duport Mystery." *Dance Perspectives*, no. 7 (1960).

Moore, Lillian. "New York's First Ballet Season, 1792." *Bulletin of the New York Public Library* (September 1960).

Moore, Lillian. *Echoes of American Ballet: A Collection of Seventeen Articles Written and Selected by Lillian Moore*. Edited by Ivor Guest. Brooklyn, 1976.

Moulton, Robert D. "Choreography in Musical Comedy and Revue on the New York Stage from 1925 through 1950." Master's thesis, University of Minnesota, 1957.

Nye, Russell Blaine. *The Cultural Life of the New Nation, 1776–1830*. New York, 1963.

Nye, Russell Blaine. *The Unembarrassed Muse: The Popular Arts in America*. New York, 1970.

Nye, Russell Blaine. *Society and Culture in America, 1830–1860*. New York, 1974.

Oliver, George B. "Changing Pattern of Spectacle on the New York Stage, 1850–1890." Ph.D. diss., Pennsylvania State University, 1956.

Prevots, Naima. "American Pageantry and American Modern Dance." In *Proceedings of the Sixth Annual Conference, Society of Dance History Scholars, the Ohio State University, 11–13 February 1983*, compiled by Christena L. Schlundt. Milwaukee, 1983.

Richman, Marjorie L., and Gertrude R. Schmiedler. "Changes in a Folk Dance Accompanying Cultural Change." *Journal of Social Psychology* 42 (1955): 333–336.

Ruyter, Nancy Lee Chalfa. *Reformers and Visionaries: The Americanization of the Art of Dance*. New York, 1979.

Said, Edward W. *Orientalism*. New York, 1978.

Sandler, Ken. "Breakdancing! Spinning into the Big Time." *Washington Post* (January 1984).

Schneider, Gretchen. "Dance as an Expressive Response to Frontier Life in the Mining Camps of California, 1848–1855." Master's thesis, University of California, Los Angeles, 1968.

Schneider, Gretchen. "Pigeon Wings and Polkas: The Dance of the California Miners." *Dance Perspectives*, no. 39 (1969): 1–57.

Schneider, Gretchen. "Using Nineteenth-Century American Social Dance Manuals." *Dance Research Journal* 14.1–2 (1981–1982): 39–42.

Seeger, Mike. *Talking Feet: Buck, Flatfoot, and Tap: Solo Southern Dance of the Appalachian, Piedmont, and Blue Ridge Mountain Regions*. Berkeley, 1992.

Shelton, Suzanne. *Divine Dancer: A Biography of Ruth St. Denis*. Garden City, N.Y., 1981.

Stearns, Marshall, and Jean Stearns. *Jazz Dance*. New York, 1968.

Theeman, Margaret. "Rhythms of Community: The Sociology of Expressive Body Movement." Ph.D. diss., Harvard University, 1973.

Thompson, Robert Farris. *African Art in Motion: Icon and Act*. 2d ed. Los Angeles, 1979.

Van Cleef, Joy. "Rural Felicity: Social Dance in Eighteenth-Century Connecticut." *Dance Perspectives*, no. 65 (Spring 1976): 3–45.

Van Cleef, Joy, and Kate Van Winkle Keller. "Selected American Country Dances and Their English Sources." In *Music in Colonial Massachusetts, 1630–1820*, vol. 1, *Music in Public Places*. Boston, 1980.

Van Dyke, Jan. *Modern Dance in a Postmodern World: An Analysis of Federal Arts Funding and Its Impact on the Field of Modern Dance*. Reston, Va., 1992.

Winter, Marian Hannah. "American Theatrical Dancing from 1750 to 1800." *Musical Quarterly* 24 (January 1938): 58–73.

Wynne, Shirley S. "From Ballet to Ballroom: Dance in the Revolutionary Era." *Dance Scope* 10 (Fall–Winter 1975–1976): 65–73.

Zuckerman, Michael. "Pilgrims in the Wilderness: Community, Modernity, and the Maypole at Merry Mount." *New England Quarterly* 50 (June 1977): 255–277.

RECORDINGS. *Nineteenth-Century American Ballroom Music* (Nonesuch, 1975). *Come and Trip It: Instrumental Dance Music, 1780s–1920s* (New York, 1978).

VIDEOTAPES. Catherine Turocy, *The Art of Dancing: An Introduction to Baroque Dance* (New York, 1979). Mike Seeger, *Talking Feet: Buck, Flatfoot, and Tap* (El Cerrito, Calif., 1987).

GRETCHEN SCHNEIDER

African-American Dance Traditions

African-American dance, a syncretism of African and European dance, evolved in the United States out of plantation and frontier life and came to the popular stage through minstrelsy. Its path and pattern of development delineate the tenor of American racial segregation and discrimination. The progression from minstrelsy to the concert stage—from mid-nineteenth century to the present—parallels the availability to African Americans of additional performance environments in successive eras of American history.

The earliest outlets were tent shows, road shows, and the minstrel stage, followed by white burlesque houses—the lowest rung on the white show business ladder. (Nineteenth-century burlesque was a variety entertainment genre. Striptease developed in the twentieth century.) Next came segregated theaters on African-American vaudeville circuits (1900–1940s). A few black Americans performed in white vaudeville and on Broadway during the first few decades of the twentieth century, but only occasionally were they so engaged. Community-based college and repertory theater productions of African-American concert dance (beginning in the 1920s) preceded the earliest professional concert recitals (1930s).

Additional performance outlets stimulated experimentation, innovation, and the creation of new dance genres, but the root connection with African and plantation forms remained. Refined and developed, the earliest African-American form, plantation dance, was the basis for minstrel dance. With the advent of drinking houses and dance halls in southern and frontier labor communities during Reconstruction, new dances—social dances—evolved. African Americans on Broadway and in vaudeville created a generous variety of theatrical and social dances in the 1920s and 1930s. Drawing upon its rich legacy of a past rooted in vernacular and popular stage traditions, African-American concert dance comprises a wide variety of styles and approaches and represents a healthy interchange between theatrical and vernacular, African and European, forms.

Minstrelsy. The most popular genre of American entertainment during the mid-nineteenth century, minstrelsy was the first professional performance outlet for African Americans, and the training ground for early vaudevillians. It carried African-American vernacular forms into American popular culture, preserved plantation dances, and laid the groundwork for the creation of new dances. It also sanctioned the use of white forms (jig, clogging, ballads, arias) by black Americans and offered them employment and the opportunity to develop theatrical talent. On the other hand, minstrelsy established and perpetuated the negative character stereotypes that have haunted African Americans and continued to circumscribe their social and theatrical achievements into the present. This overriding characteristic of the genre looms large enough to neutralize its positive contributions.

William Henry Lane, known as Master Juba (c.1825–c.1852), was one of the few African Americans in antebellum minstrelsy. Blending jigs and clogging with African-based rhythm and syncopation, he created a new dance style and came to be considered the father of tap dance. [See the entry on Juba.]

African Americans did not gain general access to the minstrel stage until after the Civil War. Setting a precedent that continued into vaudeville, minstrel performers were multitalented. They danced, sang, and played one or more musical instruments and were comedians as well as masters of ceremonies, managers, and directors.

Plantation dances that were preserved and developed in minstrelsy include the Virginia Essence, the cakewalk, the buck-and-wing, Pattin' Juba, and the walk-around. The Virginia Essence was a refined shuffle in which the performer's feet moved so smoothly as to appear not to move at all. Billy Kersands was famous for his development and performance of this dance, which is the precursor of the vaudeville soft-shoe as well as the first African-American dance to gain popularity on the American stage. The plantation buck dance, another variation on shuffle steps (which form a fundamental component in African-American vernacular dance), was combined with hopping—or wing—steps and became the minstrel buck-and-wing, a major early form of tap dance. Pattin' Juba developed out of a West African ceremonial dance called Giouba. Plantation owners outlawed the use of drums, so ingenious slaves substituted interrelated systems of syncopated foot patting, vocal punctuation, and the patting or clapping of various parts of the body. This dance, known as Pattin' Juba, was transposed to the minstrel stage as a specialty number involving the rhythmical patting of chest, hips, and thighs. Remnants exist in children's handclapping games and in the hambone routine that is performed to the folk rhyme of the same name.

The cakewalk, a plantation challenge dance, with a cake as the prize, was a paradigm of African-American continuity with African forms and syncretism with European forms. It contained elements of competition and improvisation basic to African dance. The characteristic strutting steps originally parodied the plantation owners, whom slaves observed dancing European forms at social functions. Forerunner of the strut and the jazz walk familiar to musical comedy and jazz dance, it was used for the finale in African-American minstrelsy. By the 1890s it became the first social fad dance to gain popularity in both black and white circles, with cakewalk contests a common occurrence.

The cakewalk finale was performed as a walk-around, the secular equivalent of the plantation ring shout, which replicated the structure of traditional West African dance: onlookers stood or moved in a circle around a soloist or couple who improvised in the center, then joined the circle to be replaced by someone else. It continued into early vaudeville and was replaced by the Shim-Sham finale of the swing era of the 1930s and 1940s. [See Cakewalk.]

Of the many outstanding African-American minstrels, mention must be made of Sam Lucas, Tom Fletcher, and Billy Kersands. Others who began their careers as min-

UNITED STATES OF AMERICA: African-American Dance Traditions. A parade of cakewalk dancers depicted in a photo-montage by H. M. Pettit, after a film made by Thomas Edison, c.1896. The cakewalk, which began as a competitive plantation dance, became a popular feature of many theatrical entertainments. (Collection of Sally R. Sommer and William G. Sommer.)

strels include James Bland, W. C. Handy, Gussie L. Davis, Ernest Hogan, George Walker, Bert Williams, and Dewey ("Pigmeat") Markham. After leaving minstrelsy, Williams and Markham continued to perform in burnt-cork makeup as vaudevillians.

Greatly reduced in scope and concept and overshadowed by new theatrical genres, minstrelsy declined in national popularity but survived through the 1960s as road-show fare in the rural South.

Vaudeville and Social Dance. Dance formed the matrix of African-American performance in minstrelsy, musical comedy, and vaudeville. Stars such as Ethel Waters, Ralph Cooper, Lena Horne, and Dorothy Dandridge all began as dancers. In turn, concert dancers such as Katherine Dunham and Lavinia Williams-Yarborough spent part of their career on the popular stage. [*See the entries on Dunham and Williams-Yarborough.*]

Minstrelsy declined as the all-male format was challenged externally by the rising interest in female performers, the film industry, and the cabaret and internally by repetitiveness and lack of innovation. By 1890 African-

American minstrel shows had added women, forerunners of the chorus line, and ushered in the "coon show" era, exemplified by productions such as *The Creole Show* (1890); *The Octoroons* (1895); *Oriental America* (1896), the first African-American show to run on Broadway; and *Black Patti's Troubadours* (1897), which subsequently toured for eighteen seasons as a road show. *A Trip to Coontown* and *Clorindy, or The Origin of the Cakewalk* (both 1898) were the first African-American shows to make a complete break with the minstrel format. These productions laid the groundwork for the contributions of George Walker and Bert Williams, multitalented African-American performers, producers, and directors who created a series of operettas (1897–1907) and popularized the cakewalk.

During this period African-American song and dance became trendsetters for white American popular culture. Through popular entertainment outlets of the 1900s and 1920s white audiences learned such plantation-derived dances as the cakewalk, the Turkey Trot, the Grizzly Bear, the Black Bottom, Ballin' the Jack, the Charleston, the Shimmy, and the Mooche. African-American songwriters such as Perry Bradford ("The Bullfrog Hop," 1912; "The Original Black Bottom Dance," 1919), Chris Smith ("Ballin' the Jack," 1913), and Sheldon Brooks ("Walkin' the Dog," 1917) wrote dance instruction songs that were sold in sheet form.

African Americans performed in road shows, medicine

shows, carnivals, and circuses throughout the South and the Midwest, either in the segregated units of white companies or as part of independent African-American outfits, such as the *Whitman Sisters' Roadshow* (1910s–1930s), Salem Tutt Whitney's *Silas Green from New Orleans* show (1904–1940s), and Irvin C. Miller's *Brownskin Models* (1920s–1950s).

By 1920 African-American theaters that had been built in the South and the Midwest early in the twentieth century were organized into the Theater Owners' Booking Association (TOBA), which booked complete shows and independent acts through the 1930s. Ethel Waters, Bessie Smith, Willie Bryant, Bill Robinson, Eddie Rector, and the Berry Brothers were but a few of the many performers who began their career on "TOBY-Time." Its demise was owed, in part, to the expanding influence of white managers and to the growth of the film industry (double features meant the end of the movie-with-variety-show format). [*See the entries on the Berry Brothers and Robinson.*]

After George Walker retired from the stage in 1907, Bert Williams joined the *Ziegfeld Follies.* African-American shows disappeared from Broadway (until 1921, with the opening of *Shuffle Along*) and survived in African-American repertory theaters across the nation. In Harlem, the Lincoln, Crescent, Alhambra, and Lafayette theaters, which originally produced farces, serious dramas, and variety shows, by the 1920s had become vaudeville houses. The Lafayette Theater's 1913 production of *Darktown Follies* featured Eddie Rector, whose tapping was characterized by light-footed grace and elegance—instead of a shuffling stereotype—and who was the predecessor of the swing-era "class act." This *Follies* also featured Toots Davis, whose acrobatic tapping foreshadowed the swing-era "flash act," and it introduced an African-American dance hall favorite, the Texas Tommy, forerunner of the Lindy Hop. It was one of the last shows to feature a cakewalk finale. The show's final act was bought by Florenz Ziegfeld and used for his *Follies* in 1913, with no credit given to J. Leubrie Hill, who was director, writer, and producer of the original, or to cast members (such as dancer Cora La Redd) who taught the new routines to Ziegfeld's white, downtown dancers.

The co-opting of African-American choreography and music by the white world began in white minstrelsy and continued in vaudeville and on Broadway. Choreographer Buddy Bradley created routines for stars such as Adele Astaire and Clifton Webb but was given no credit. [*See the entry on Bradley.*] James Reese Europe's Memphis Students Band was the first "big band" and in 1912 was the first to play jazz music in a concert setting, although the Paul Whiteman 1921 concert generally is cited as the first such instance. African Americans also initiated the "dancing conductor," later epitomized by musicians such as

Cab Calloway. It was Europe and Ford Dabney's band that played for Irene and Vernon Castle, created the fox trot for them, and initiated the custom of African-American musicians playing at white social dance events. This trend was reversed by the mid-1930s. The white world turned away from African-American bands after white bands, led by Benny Goodman and others, had mastered the sound that had once been the exclusive domain of bands led by the likes of Fletcher Henderson, Duke Ellington, and Jimmie Lunceford. African-American nightclubs fell into decline as whites took their business to white clubs.

The 1920s and 1930s was a period of dense cultural interchange between blacks and whites. African-American choreographers opened dance studios and created routines for white performers. White composers, including Harold Arlen, Jimmy McHugh, and Dorothy Fields, contributed music to the New York Cotton Club revues; Cotton Clubs and Plantation Clubs in cities across the United States offered exclusively African-American entertainment for exclusively white audiences. White choreographers such as Jean De Meaux and composers such as Armand Lamet devised routines and musical arrangements for the white ballroom repertory (waltzes, tangos, and so forth) of African-American dance teams, such as Norton and Margot. Whites wrote black Broadway shows; and black arrangers, such as James Mundy, Billy Strayhorn, Benny Carter, Will Vodery, and Don Redman—to name only a few—were behind the swing music of many white big bands.

Big band music and ballrooms evolved out of a need for sound to accompany and space to accommodate the various social dance crazes that began at the turn of the century and peaked in the 1920s and 1930s. Americans of both races danced in Harlem ballrooms such as the Savoy, Alhambra, and Renaissance.

A healthy interchange took place between the ballroom and nightclub dance floor and the vaudeville and Broadway stage. Updated, theatricalized versions of age-old African and plantation steps were introduced to whites by African-American performers who used them as the basis for their routines. White audiences took these steps back to their ballrooms. Broadway shows such as *Runnin' Wild* (1923), which introduced an old African-American dance, the Charleston, and *Dixie to Broadway* (1924), which introduced another vintage African-derived dance, the Black Bottom, served the same function. The African American performing to white audiences was the means of dissemination from black world to white. As choreographer Buddy Bradley later recalled:

> We thought nothing of the fact that everybody in and out of colored show business seemed to know a million old jive steps. . . . We all knew those movements as kids . . . they were a part of our life that we took for granted—and it was some time be-

UNITED STATES OF AMERICA: African-American Dance Traditions. Choreographer Buddy Bradley taught African-American dance steps to many of the white stars of musical theater. He is seen here, c.1927, demonstrating Ballin' the Jack (left), the Baltimore Jazz (center), and the Breakdown (right). (Photographs by Nasib; collection of Sally R. Sommer and William G. Sommer.)

fore I realized that they were pretty new to Broadway and that most white people couldn't begin to do any of them.

(Quoted in Stearns, 1994, p. 165)

Fad dances such as Truckin', the Susie Q, the Shorty-George, Peckin', and the Scronch originated as Cotton Club production numbers and subsequently caught on as ballroom dances. By the time they reached white circles, they had been simplified and toned down—and replaced by new fad dances created in African-American circles. [*For discussion of social dances see* Big Apple, Lindy Hop, *and the entry on Frankie Manning.*]

The influence of African-American "dance directors" on Broadway changed the nature of American musical comedy dance and introduced the precision chorus line to Broadway. These "directors" included Bradley, Clarence Robinson, Leonard Harper, Elida Webb, Charlie Davis, Herbie Harper, Charlie White, Addison Carey, Leonard Reed, Sammy Dyer, and Frank Montgomery. By the 1930s, however, black Broadway's heyday was over, killed by the Great Depression and by white lyricists and composers who produced their own versions of materials originally generated by the likes of Sissle and Blake, Miller and Lyles. As in minstrelsy, the churning out of formula shows led to self-induced obsolescence. [*See the article on* Musical Theater, *below.*]

Vaudeville dance acts manifested a staggering variety of genres, including tap, eccentric, comedy, acrobatic, exotic, social (fad dances), and ballroom. As with pure acrobatics, ballroom was a small category, epitomized by the team of Norton and Margot, who dared to break the stereotype of speed, rhythm, or exoticism and who danced in the style and repertory of white teams such as Veloz and Yolanda.

As big bands declined, so did the dances they accompanied. In the late 1940s, after a major depression and two world wars—crises spanning three decades through which Americans sang, danced, and reveled in spite of themselves—the American temperament experienced a major shift from an outgoing to an introspective national personality. This shift was marked by such diverse cultural trends as widespread ownership of the automobile; television viewing; small-group, bebop music; mass migration to the suburbs (a reversal of urban migration patterns of the preceding half-century); xenophobia elicited and revealed by McCarthyism; and increased use of psychoanalysis.

African-American dance lost its national footing in the 1950s. It receded from white scrutiny and survived on the so-called Chitlin' Circuit comprising neighborhood bars in the various Harlems throughout the nation. Resurgent national attention to African-American vernacular forms was occasioned by the animal dance craze of the 1960s (the Monkey, the Pony, the Philly Dog, and other spinoffs of the Twist), the Hustle of the 1970s, and disco dancing in the 1970s and 1980s. [*See* Social Dance, *article on* Social Dance since 1963.]

Vaudeville dance and the vaudeville stage no longer exist. The concert dance arena, including modern dance, ballet, and staged versions of African-based ceremonial dance, is the contemporary frontier for African-American dance.

Theatrical Dance. In 1932, reviewing an African-American recital, critic John Martin termed concert dance "the white man's art" (quoted in Emery, 1972, p. 314). This subjective value judgment aptly reflects the prevailing biases to which African Americans were subjected when they entered the concert dance arena. It was an updated version of the point of view that had obtained in minstrelsy, on Broadway, and in vaudeville: African Americans fit certain stereotypes and nothing more. As late as the 1960s Martin and Ernestine Stodelle asserted that the African American was culturally and anatomically unfit for ballet (Emery, 1972, pp. 282, 287). This myth, which has persisted in the world of classical ballet, conceals the fundamental problem, the root racism that pervades American culture and society. Despite the fact that African-American dance types have influenced every type of white dance, the black dancer has not been considered fit to dance "the white man's art."

> The success of a dancer depends on whether he has lived up to the audience's expectations. If the dancer is black, the audience frequently has a preconceived notion of the type of dance he should be performing.   (Emery, 1972)

In 1931 Hemsley Winfield and his New Negro Art Dancers gave a concert dance recital in New York City. The program reflected Denishawn, African, and African-American themes. Company member Edna Guy was one of the first to dance to Negro spirituals in the genre that became known as the dance spiritual.

Winfield was preceded (in the 1920s) by Charles H. Williams's Hampton Institute Creative Dance Group. Through contact with African exchange students, they staged reconstructions of traditional African dances, thereby setting a precedent that was followed by Asadata Dafora in the 1930s. Williams's group reconstructed traditional African-American dances, such as the Juba and the cakewalk; they also established the prototype for African-American, college-based concert dance groups, such as those established at Spelman, Howard, Fisk, and Tuskegee. In 1934 Dafora produced *Kykunkor,* the first professional concert version of traditional African dance and the forerunner of the stage genre embraced by African national dance companies and African-American groups, such as those of Michael Olatunji, Nana Dinizulu, Chuck Davis, and Charles Moore, to name but a few.

Eugene Von Grona's American Negro Ballet premiered in 1937, performing modern ballets (barefoot, on *demi-pointe*) to the music of Bach, Ellington, and Gershwin. The same year, Katherine Dunham presented her first New York concert, a shared bill at the Ninety-second Street Young Men's and Young Women's Hebrew Association (YM-YWHA). A trained anthropologist, Dunham based her productions on original field material, and her unique combination of ballet, modern, and traditional Caribbean dance became famous as the Dunham technique. The Dunham School of Dance in New York City

UNITED STATES OF AMERICA: African-American Dance Traditions. Hemsley Winfield (on the floor) with members of his New Negro Art Theater Dance Group in *Life and Death.* From 1931, when he founded his company, to 1934, the year of his premature death, Winfield presented concert works that probed issues of black aesthetics. (Photograph from the Dance Collection, New York Public Library for the Performing Arts.)

(1940–1955) and the company's Broadway and film appearances had a pervasive influence on American dance, black and white. Often the style was appropriated, with no credit given to Dunham. Just as J. Leubrie Hill and Buddy Bradley had taught white Broadway dancers, Dunham dancers taught in Hollywood and New York City and saw their technique reappear in all-white films and routines. [*See the entry on Dunham.*] Talley Beatty, Lavinia Williams-Yarborough, Vanoye Aikens, Carmencita Romero, Tommy Gomez, Lucille Ellis, Syvilla Fort, Lenwood Morris, Claude Marchant, Hope Clarke, and Jean-Léon Destiné are among Dunham's legatees.

In 1943, Pearl Primus, also a trained anthropologist, debuted at the Ninety-second Street YM-YWCA with a program including staged West African dances as well as protest dances highlighting the plight of black Americans. Although African-American dancers have since explored many styles and themes, unsolved problems of racism have compelled many to reaffirm connections with Africa and New World African cultures while protesting the oppression of blacks.

White critics have often concluded that black artists only deal adeptly with recognizably "black" material, which is interpreted as making a social statement in itself. Donald McKayle's *Rainbow 'Round My Shoulder* (1959), a testament to the suffering of Southern chain gangs, fits this critical framework; yet his *Games* (1951) and *District Storyville* (1962), based on African-American folklore, are political works only in that showing a previously underrepresented social reality on stage is a necessarily political act.

Many black choreographers since Primus have made dances without particular social content or African-derived movement, such as Eleo Pomare's dance drama *Las Desenamorados* (1967), based on Federico García Lorca's play *The House of Bernarda Alba*. Gus Solomons, Jr., is known for abstract essays in a style related to that of Merce Cunningham, with whom he performed. By contrast, Garth Fagan, celebrated for his lyrical athleticism, mines diverse sources of motion and music from the African diaspora in such pieces as *From Before* (1978), which abstracts and isolates African movements and regroups them in a minimalist framework. Postmodern dancers such as Blondell Cummings and Bebe Miller approach movement conceptually, with a basis in improvisation. Even in *The Hendrix Project* (1992), celebrating Jimi Hendrix, an iconic black musician, Miller's vocabulary owes little to black dance forms. Ralph Lemon, known for his expansive, release-oriented idiom, has examined such varied themes as the *commedia dell'arte* and the myth of Persephone; he exemplifies the freedom many black choreographers of his generation feel from an obligation to focus on political content.

Other choreographers stress political commitments perhaps even fiercer than Primus's. Rod Rodgers's *Box* (1971)

is a non-narrative social commentary inspired by the jailing of black militant George Jackson. Bill T. Jones's *Still/Here* (1994) concerns heroism, mortality, and survival among sufferers of AIDS and cancer; while his sprawling *Last Supper at Uncle Tom's Cabin/The Promised Land* (1990) mines diverse sources of myth, as well as his family history (his mother appears in the work) to confront racial stereotypes. Like Jones, Ron Brown examines homophobia and sexism as often as racism and invokes both his family and racial heritage in such dances as *Combat Review/Witches' Response* (1992–1993). Yet both choreographers are also preoccupied with movement invention and problems of formal structure. The range of approaches represented by Louis Johnson, Dianne McIntyre, Fred Benjamin, Arthur Hall, and Donald Byrd is similarly diverse.

Given that white companies tend to exclude black dancers, African-American companies would be justified in employing only blacks. Ironically, the only major integrated American dance company is the (African-American) Alvin Ailey American Dance Theater, truly American and truly representative of the multicultural ideal.

UNITED STATES OF AMERICA: African-American Dance Traditions. Eugene Von Grona, founder of the American Negro Ballet, 1938. (Photograph by Carl Van Vechten; used by permission.)

UNITED STATES OF AMERICA: African-American Dance Traditions. (*left*) Maxine Sherman and Donna Wood (right) of the Alvin Ailey American Dance Theater in a 1980 performance of George Faison's *Suite Otis*. (*below*) Ralph Lemon in his solo *Joy* (1990). (*above*) A scene from Bill T. Jones's *Havoc* (1992) with Seán Curran (left) and Odile Reine-Adelaide. (Photographs left and above © 1980 and 1992 by Jack Vartoogian; photograph below © 1993 by Beatriz Schiller; all used by permission.)

At the end of the century ballet was still a no-man's land for the African-American dancer. Neither Arthur Mitchell's entry into New York City Ballet in 1956 nor the creation of his company, the Dance Theatre of Harlem in 1969, paved the way for meaningful black entry into white ballet despite the professional talent of, among others, Ronald Perry, Kevin Pugh, Virginia Johnson, Mel Tomlinson, and Christopher Boatwright as well as their illustrious predecessors Billy Wilson, Sylvester Campbell, Delores Brown, Raven Wilkerson, Paul Russell, Keith Lee, Christian Holder, and John Jones.

Dance is a measure of society. The history of African-American dance is a measure of the history of American racial oppression. The survival and proliferation of African-American dance is thus a testament to its substantive strength and indestructibility.

[*See also* Alvin Ailey American Dance Theater; Dance Theatre of Harlem; Tap Dance; Vaudeville; *and the entries on Beatty, Dafora, Fagan, Bill T. Jones, McKayle, Mitchell, Primus, and Zollar.*]

BIBLIOGRAPHY

Aschenbrenner, Joyce. *Katherine Dunham: Reflections on the Social and Political Contexts of Afro-American Dance.* CORD Dance Research Annual, 12. New York, 1981.

Dixon-Stowell, Brenda. "Dancing in the Dark: The Life and Times of Margot Webb in Aframerican Vaudeville of the Swing Era." 2 vols. Ph.D. diss., New York University, 1981.

Dixon Gottschild, Brenda. *Digging the Africanist Presence in American Performance: Dance and Other Contexts.* Westport, Conn. 1996.

Emery, Lynne Fauley. *Black Dance in the United States from 1619 to 1970.* Palo Alto, Calif., 1972. Rev. ed. Princeton, 1988.

Malone, Jacqui. *Steppin' on the Blues: The Visible Rhythms of African American Dance.* Urbana and Chicago, 1996.

Sampson, Henry T. *Blacks in Blackface: A Source Book on Early Black Musical Shows.* Metuchen, N.J., 1980.

Stearns, Marshall, and Jean Stearns. *Jazz Dance* (1968). New York, 1994.

Toll, Robert C. *Blacking Up: The Minstrel Show in Nineteenth-Century America.* New York, 1974.

ARCHIVES. Dance Collection, New York Public Library for the Performing Arts. Katherine Dunham Collection, Morris Library, Southern Illinois University, Carbondale. Hatch-Billops Collection, New York. Joseph Nash Collection, New York. Schomburg Center for Research in Black Culture, New York Public Library.

BRENDA DIXON GOTTSCHILD

African-American Social Dance

In the sub-Saharan African population groups from which slaves were taken, dance was integrated with daily life. Ceremonial dance expressed philosophical ideas, community attitudes, and individual identities. The brutality of the slave experience, regardless of where it was, transformed Africans' cultural lives and dance. This experience of slavery varied somewhat from place to place, country to country, or colony to colony. For the most part, slaves from several African societies lived and worked together, often in all-male units. On plantations, males and females worked both in the master's house and on the land. This article describes the situation in the colonies that became the United States, and emphasizes the evolution from plantation dances to contemporary social dances. Slavery existed in the British colonies of the 1600s and lasted legally in the United States until 1 January 1863.

New African-American dances emerged and varied according to context and with the work rhythms of the tasks performed. On the plantation, the slaves' social activities were restricted, but they took every opportunity to create new alternatives. Slaves used dancing to perform a variety of functions: education, resistance, community sanction, and the establishment of social norms. Dances were held in the woods or in other isolated locations when the slave owners were least vigilant. Although most masters permitted dancing on Saturdays, Sundays, and holidays such as Christmas, Thanksgiving, and the Fourth of July, they also encouraged dancing to increase their own profits, for example, dances were held to stimulate the shucking of corn. Of all the types of plantation dances, corn-shucking dances were the slaves' favorite. Held after work, shuckings involved teams of slaves from two or more plantations. The corn was divided, and each team competed to finish first. During and after the work, dancing contributed to an atmosphere of frolic and release.

Urban slave dances were more heterogeneous than plantation dances. Held on the edge of a town, these dances could attract two hundred to seven hundred slaves, both agricultural and urban. Like the smaller secret dances, the larger urban gatherings provided rare opportunities to plan and stage acts of resistance. Dance was the natural camouflage most frequently chosen to stage acts of self-determination, such as setting a fire, running away, or organizing a rebellion. These dances often took place near major cities, such as Charleston, South Carolina, and Mobile, Alabama, but the most famous occurred at Congo Square in New Orleans. Even after the Emancipation of 1863 and until about 1890, blacks gathered until sunset on Sundays, drumming and dancing the calenda, the bamboula, and the chica-congo.

Emancipation, including the breakup of both rural and

UNITED STATES OF AMERICA: African-American Social Dance. A characteristic depiction of early African-American step dancing. The dancer plays castanet-like bones, to the accompaniment of banjo and fiddle. The "get-down" position of his body and the angular arrangment of his limbs show a strong African influence, whereas the position of his arms overhead, framing the body, reveal the influence of European folk dancing. (Engraving c.1888 by G. W. Breeneman; collection of Sally R. Sommer and William G. Sommer.)

urban slave quarters and the reorganization of black labor under the sharecropping system, contributed to the transformation of the nature of African-American dance. During the period following Emancipation, African-American dance experienced accelerated cross-fertilization, reworking, and fine-tuning. The primary institutional context for most social dance was called the jook, a poorly constructed shelter used for dancing, drinking, and social activity. At the jooks, older plantation dances such as the Buzzard Lope, Snake Hips, the Breakdown, the Juba, and the Buck Dance could combine with new, urbanized forms. From the jooks came great American dance crazes: the Black Bottom, the Charleston, and the Twist, as well as the Turkey Trot and the Big Apple.

Between the end of Reconstruction—the reorganizing of the states that had seceded and reestablishing them in the Union (1867–1877)—and the beginning of World War I in 1914, African-American social dance became better known among the general public. Dance experienced a new level of development as Southern black migration to urban areas and then a rapidly changing war economy influenced black Americans—who created new music and new fashions while experiencing new economic and cultural demands. The dances from the plantations and the jooks were rapidly redefined in the cities. New social institutions provided African-American dance with additional variations on an already richly varied tradition. Urban dance halls, membership clubs, and honky-tonks provided places in which dances could relinquish some of their rural characteristics, such as flatfootedness, and acquire a more urbane polish. The institutional complex formed by the jooks, honky-tonks, dance halls, and membership clubs enabled African Americans to experience an ever-widening variety of sociocultural options; these were directly reflected in the proliferation of and variations on African-American dance.

After World War I, when some social and cultural choices for blacks increased, social dance became more sophisticated. Cabarets and "rent parties" (gatherings to contribute to a friend's monthly rent, when needed) provided new situations for social interaction. Although dancing had been unrefined and intimate, public expectation influenced cabaret dancing, frequently rendering it self-conscious, theatrical, and performance-oriented. During the Great Depression of the 1930s and as World War II approached, black migration to the industrial North intensified. The jook-house tradition also went north and cross-fertilized the dances developing among northern urban blacks.

Among the characteristics of African-American social dance are competition, dancing apart (couples do not touch), improvisation, call and response, mimicry, and derision. These elements can be observed in the competitive high kicking of the cakewalk, the apart dancing of the Black Bottom and the Charleston, and the improvisational Lindy Hop breakaway. The Susie Q, Truckin', the Shorty-George, and the Slop are all dances that have been used in a competitive, improvisational manner. Along

UNITED STATES OF AMERICA: African-American Social Dance. Whitey's Lindy Hoppers, a group of Savoy Ballroom dancers organized by Herby ("Whitey") White, performed their synchronized Lindy routines in nightclubs, theaters, revues, and films. The three couples pictured here are (left to right) Norma Walker and Frankie Manning, Lucille Middleton and Jerome Williams, and Billy Williams and Mildred Cruse. (Photograph from the collection of Frankie Manning.)

UNITED STATES OF AMERICA: African-American Social Dance. Robert Taylor demonstrates three characteristic break dancing moves: the Turtle (left), Back Spin (center), and Downrocking (right). (Photographs by Michael Ginsburg; courtesy of Sally R. Sommer and William G. Sommer.)

with dances from the plantations, these formed the core vocabulary of African-American social dance. Nevertheless, negative influences limited the structural development and content of African-American social dance.

Although a good amount of American social dance has resulted from African-American culture, for nearly a century after Emancipation, blacks were barred (in the segregated South) from public social activity with whites. In the first half of the twentieth century, however, in New York, Chicago, Saint Louis, New Orleans, and other cities with large African-American populations, jazz flourished and nightclubs and theaters were patronized by whites as well as blacks; here, on phonograph records, and in Hollywood films, African-American music and dance entered the American mainstream. Not until the 1960s, however, were the final vestiges of legal segregation at all public facilities in the United States removed by act of Congress. And in that decade African-American dance rediscovered and reestablished some of its original characteristics. Dancing apart characterized many of the popular dances of the decade: the Twist, Boogaloo, African Twist, Sophisticated Sissy, Philly Dog, Horse, Chicken, Watusi, Shing-a-ling, Monkey, Swim, Waddle, Mashed Potato, and Four Corners. This period of intense social change renewed and strengthened black identification with African-American social dance traditions.

In the 1970s, a trend toward intense competition culminated in the development of break dancing. "Breaking," a predominantly male activity, demonstrates through the characteristic use of competition, mimicry, and derision an acrobatic, theatricalized, and highly self-conscious cultural response. Breaking has also altered the traditional male-female partnering relationship; dancers compete to outdance one another in a fashion reminiscent of the corn-shucking dances and the dance contests engaged in at rent parties.

Many contemporary African-American dances may be recycled versions of older ones. A good example is Pop Locking, a variation on the old plantation dance Snake Hips. Done in the Georgia Sea Islands prior to emancipation, Snake Hips was popularized in the 1920s by performer Earl ("Snake Hips") Tucker. In the 1950s, it reappeared in the urban Midwest as Poppin' the Hips. The Jerk of the 1960s appropriated part of its technique and vocabulary. Its snapping and joint-locking technique was utilized in the Robot of the 1970s, and its fluidity was redefined in the break dancing of the 1980s.

[*See also* Cakewalk *and* Lindy Hop. *For general discussion, see* Social Dance, *article on* Twentieth-Century Social Dance to 1960.]

BIBLIOGRAPHY

Begho, Felix D. "Black Dance Continuum: Reflections on the Heritage Connection between African Dance and Afro-American Jazz Dance." Ph.D. diss., New York University, 1985.

Emery, Lynne Fauley. *Black Dance from 1619 to Today.* 2d rev. ed. Princeton, 1988.

Hanna, Judith Lynne. "Moving Message: Identity and Desire in Popular Music and Social Dance." In *Popular Music and Communication,* edited by James Lull. 2d ed. Newbury Park, Calif., 1992.

Hanna, Judith Lynne. "What Is Black Dance? Report on 'Choreographing the Future: Dance, Politics, and the African Diaspora.'" *Dance Teacher Now* 16 (October 1994): 69–72.

Hazzard-Gordon, Katrina. *Jookin': The Rise of Social Dance Formations in African-American Culture.* Philadelphia, 1990.

Perpener, John O. "African-American Dance and Sociological Positivism during the 1930s." *Studies in Dance History* 5 (Spring 1994): 23–30.

Stearns, Marshall, and Jean Stearns. *Jazz Dance.* Rev. ed. New York, 1994.

Szwed, John F., and Morton Marks. "The Afro-American Transformation of European Set Dances and Dance Suites." *Dance Research Journal* 20 (Summer 1988): 29–36.

KATRINA HAZZARD-DONALD

Regional Dance Companies

Decentralized or regional dance takes place outside New York City. The companies discussed herein have additional identifying characteristics. They are resident in their communities, which means that the core of their performing takes place in the home city, usually with a subscription series as the basis of their earned income. Outside their home communities they tend to perform under regional consortia, such as the Southern Arts Federation, either as part of tour plans initiated by their state arts agencies or as the guests of local sponsors. Regional ballet companies usually identify with the home city or state by using geographically related titles, whereas modern dance companies tend to use the names of their directors, although some, such as the Dayton Contemporary Dance Company and Philadanco (Philadelphia Dance Company), prefer geographical nomenclature.

Despite a heartening increase in the quantity and quality of televised dance, millions of Americans would see little live dance were it not for regional companies. The high costs of widespread touring have curtailed the itineraries of major New York companies. More and more, regional companies are filling this gap. The touring of regional companies, though, even in the case of a well-traveled ensemble like the Bella Lewitzky Company, is rarely national. The closest to national in exposure are the Boston Ballet, the Houston Ballet, the Pacific Northwest Ballet, and the San Francisco Ballet.

Despite the economic hazards, more young people than ever before are looking to dance as a career. New York City cannot accommodate them all. Regional companies not only provide needed employment, they also help to identify dance artists not as nomads but as respected members of their communities. The companies help provide sociological identity for the American dancer.

Twentieth-century America has fostered a unique group of dance pioneers. They were and are the founders of regional dance companies. As individuals they have shared certain traits: they were receptive to all forms of dance; they had taste; and they were dedicated teachers who not only imparted technique but knew how to shape artists. All had boundless energy and strength of character. Most important, they related effectively to their communities and their trustees. The leaders were Dorothy Alexander (Atlanta), Josephine and Hermene Schwarz (Dayton), and Willam Christensen (Salt Lake City). All were determined to make dance happen in their communities at a time when there were no precedents.

The Atlanta Ballet, founded in 1929, is the oldest ballet company in the United States. The Dayton Ballet came along in 1937. Christensen organized the San Francisco Ballet in 1934. In 1951 his brothers Lew and Harold took over the company and school while Willam moved to their native Salt Lake City and formed what is now Ballet West. Other distinctive companies, such as the Littlefield Ballet and the Pavley-Oukrainsky Ballet, also emerged during the 1930s but did not survive.

World War II meant an inevitable hiatus in the formation of dance companies. It was not until the 1950s that a crop of new pioneering directors emerged. Among them were Thomas Armour (Miami Ballet, 1951), Barbara and Deane Crockett (Sacramento Ballet, 1954), Jan Collum (Balletacoma, 1955), Lisa Gardiner and Mary Day (Washington Ballet, 1956), Moscelyne Larkin and Roman Jasinski (Tulsa Ballet Theatre, 1956), and E. Virginia Williams (Boston Ballet, 1958). From the 1960s one might add Jeraldyne Blunden (Dayton Contemporary Dance Company), Madeline Culpo (Berkshire Ballet), Lila Zali (Ballet Pacifica), Loyce Houlton (Minnesota Dance Theatre), Audrée Estey (American Repertory Ballet), Leona Norman (Marin Ballet), and Barbara Weisberger (Pennsylvania Ballet). Younger artistic directors, while sharing many traits with their predecessors, have had the benefit of role models and service organizations.

In the Southwest, a once-strong Ballet Russe influence was stimulated by the extensive touring in that area of the Ballet Russe de Monte Carlo. The Houston Ballet, for example, did not begin under a pioneering director. Instead, the company was initiated by a board of trustees that first selected Tatiana Semenova and then Nina Popova as artistic director. Both had Ballet Russe credentials. The company's artistic identity did not take shape, however, until the advent of artistic director Ben Stevenson, whose background is British. The Dallas Ballet began with a sequence of guest artistic directors, all of Ballet Russe origin. These included Marina Svetlova, Nathalie Krassovska, Mia Slavenska, Alexandra Danilova, and eventually George Skibine. Not long after Skibine's death in 1981, the company was dissolved. In 1993 the Fort Worth Ballet was renamed Fort Worth–Dallas Ballet. Under Moscelyne Larkin and Roman Jasinski, Tulsa Ballet Theatre conscientiously revived pillars of the Ballet Russe repertory, such as Léonide Massine's *Gaîté Parisienne* and *Le Beau Danube*, David Lichine's *Prodigal Son*, and Michel Fokine's *Schéhérazade*. With Jasinski's death in 1991, the company's focus began to shift.

Since the mid-1980s, the strongest influence on American regional companies has been that of George Balanchine. His death expanded that influence because the Balanchine Trust under Barbara Horgan has made his ballets readily available. Furthermore, former Balanchine dancers are directing companies all across the United States. The earliest seeds of the Balanchine influence were sown with the celebrated Ford Foundation Program. This included the establishment in 1960 of regional scholarships for promising young dancers to study in New York at the School of American Ballet. The following year introduced the first of a series of free teachers' seminars conducted by Balanchine. In 1963 the foundation distributed $7,756,000 to seven ballet companies: New York City Ballet, San Francisco Ballet, Boston Ballet, Pennsylvania Ballet, Houston Ballet, National Ballet, and Ballet West.

In addition to underscoring Balanchine's contribution to American dance, the plan also encouraged the entire dance world to pay more attention to the need for fiscal stability. Until that time, most companies had been rather haphazardly funded or had depended upon a single benefactor. Now these same organizations began to augment their boards of trustees and to engage experienced executive directors. For better or for worse, dance began to assume the characteristics of the corporate world.

UNITED STATES OF AMERICA: Regional Dance Companies. Members of the Atlanta Civic Ballet Junior Group in *The Princess's Magic Mirror* (1954), choreographed by Merrilee Smith and Marie Ellen Roberts to music from Josef Bayer's *Rouge et Noir*. By 1954, its twenty-fifth year, the Atlanta Civic Ballet had developed three distinct sections of its repertory: adult programs, children's programs, and lecture-demonstrations. This three-act ballet was based on the children's story "The Plain Little Princess" by Phyllis McGinley. (Photograph by Ben Damon; reprinted from a souvenir program, courtesy of Claude Conyers.)

The earliest Balanchine dancers to head regional companies were Fred Danieli (Garden State Ballet), Robert Barnett (who, in 1963, succeeded Dorothy Alexander in Atlanta), and Robert Lindgren (North Carolina Dance Theatre). In the mid-1990s the ranks were led by Todd Bolender (State Ballet of Missouri), Daniel Duell (Chicago City Ballet), Paul Mejia (Fort Worth–Dallas Ballet), Bryan Pitts and Laura Flagg (Ballet Oklahoma), Francia Russell and Kent Stowell (Pacific Northwest Ballet), Helgi Tomasson (San Francisco Ballet), Edward Villella (Miami Ballet), and Patricia Wilde (Pittsburgh Ballet Theatre).

While the Balanchine repertory exercised its influence, it was *The Nutcracker* that continued to be performed by more ballet companies than any other work, and audiences for *The Nutcracker* proved to be double that for any other program. Also in demand were *Romeo and Juliet* and *Cinderella*.

In modern dance, Martha Graham stands equal to Balanchine as a twentieth-century influence. But because she did not allow her works to be set on any American company other than her own, her influence has not become choreographic. There is, however, a strong stylistic impact because so many directors and choreographers of modern companies have studied with Graham or her disciples.

It is easy to trace choreographic trends filtering down from the top, and to credit regional companies with pro-

ducing at least three generations of impressive American dancers, but what has been the imprint of these regional companies on American choreography? One of the most distinctive voices was that of Loyce Houlton. Her works abounded in surreal, free-associative imagery enhanced by sophisticated theatrical effects. Among the most prolific of the company directors are Heinz Poll, Dennis Nahat, and Helgi Tomasson. All three work in the classical mold, Poll with great vigor and energy; Nahat in a flowing, musically aware style; and Tomasson with elegance and structural finesse. Other company directors who create a substantial portion of each season's repertory are Martin Fredmann (Colorado Ballet), Ronn Guidi (Oakland Ballet), Alun Jones (Louisville Ballet), Lambros Lambrou (Ballet Austin), Paul Mejia (Fort Worth–Dallas Ballet), David Nixon (BalletMet), Kirk Peterson (Hartford Ballet), Kent Stowell (Pacific Northwest Ballet), and Septime Webre (American Repertory Ballet).

Most modern companies, such as Garth Fagan Dance and the Margaret Jenkins Dance Company, are centered around the creative output of a single choreographer. Others, like Dance Kaleidoscope, Oberlin Dance Collective, and the Hubbard Street Dance Company, rely upon several. Some of the freelance and resident choreographers, now deceased, who initially developed their skills on regional companies were Choo San Goh, Patricia Olalde, Tom Pazik, Stuart Sebastian, and Norbert Vesak. Heading the later generation are Peter Anastos, Jill Eathorne Bahr, Val Caniparolli, Lisa de Ribere, Bill Evans, Jon Rodriguez, Bess Saylor, Lynne Taylor-Corbett, and Bruce Wells.

Making quality choreography available to regional companies was one of the principal concerns of the National Association for Regional Ballet. The evolution of this service organization for decentralized companies began in 1955. Anatole Chujoy, then publisher of *Dance News*, had previously attended regional ballet festivals in Canada. He suggested to Dorothy Alexander that she initiate a similar project in Atlanta. In April 1956, with the Atlanta Ballet as host, Alexander invited the companies she knew in the Southeast for a weekend of performing, classes, and social activities. The impact of the event was so strong that it provided the impetus for Alexi Ramov (Scranton Ballet), with Barbara Weisberger (Wilkes-Barre Ballet Guild), to host the first Northeast Festival in 1959. The Southwest followed in 1963, with Barbara and David Carson (Austin Civic Ballet) as hosts. In 1966 the Sacramento Civic Ballet, under Deane and Barbara Crockett, brought the Pacific region into the fold. In 1972 the Mid-States began in Kansas City under Tom Steinhoff (Kansas City Civic Ballet).

With continuity apparent, it was deemed wise to consolidate the regions under a national office with a professional staff. Funding from the National Endowment for the Arts stimulated this move in 1972. Doris Hering, who

had just completed three terms as the association's president, became its first executive director, with Dorothy Alexander as founder-consultant and Barbara Crockett as president. While some of the members' choreographic needs were already being addressed, the national office widened their scope. For example, the Craft of Choreography Conferences had begun in 1960. Under the guidance of Josephine Schwarz, the directors in the Northeast region had come together in the summer to work intensively at their craft. Gradually the project was expanded to the other regions, and it began to attract not only the directors but the young choreographers rising through their companies, plus a nucleus of freelance choreographers.

The National Endowment for the Arts, several state arts agencies, and the Monticello College Foundation were instrumental in the development of the conferences and in the allocation of scholarships to dancers and emerging choreographers. Among the artists who have served as creative directors of the conferences are Salvatore Aiello, Martha Hill, Saeko Ichinohe, Elizabeth Keen, Phyllis Lamhut, Bella Lewitzky, Dennis Nahat, Lynne Taylor-Corbett, Glen Tetley, and Norman Walker.

To help meet the constantly growing repertory needs of its member companies, the national association evolved additional programs. The National Choreography Plan, formed with the aid of the Andrew W. Mellon Foundation, offered an index of the strongest works performed at festivals since the beginning. Forty-three companies received ballets of their choice, with the national office subsidizing the choreographers' fees and expenses.

While these and several other related projects were designed to strengthen the companies artistically, another evolving need began to be addressed. Initially the role of the artistic director had been that of pioneer and leader. During the early 1970s the identity began to change from leader to employee of the board of trustees, with the executive director often exceeding the artistic director in institutional prestige. To help correct this imbalance and to redefine and strengthen the role of the artistic director, the National Association for Regional Ballet, with the aid of the Andrew W. Mellon Foundation and the L. J. and Mary C. Skaggs Foundation, initiated the Artistic Directors Seminar in 1985.

In 1987 the office and services of the National Association for Regional Ballet were for the most part discontinued. The organization, retitled Regional Dance America, returned to functioning as it had initially, with the festivals as the primary focus. But it had already made its impact. Whereas there had been virtually no professional dance companies outside New York City in the early 1960s, by the 1990s there were approximately fifty fully professional companies, plus another two hundred that were engaged in serving their communities on substantial technical and creative levels. Decentralization had indeed proven to be a major force in twentieth-century American dance.

[*See also* Atlanta Ballet; Boston Ballet; Cleveland–San Jose Ballet; Dayton Ballet; Dayton Contemporary Dance Company; Houston Ballet; Ohio Ballet; Pacific Northwest Ballet; Pennsylvania Ballet; Pittsburgh Ballet Theatre; San Francisco Ballet; Tulsa Ballet Theatre; *and* Washington Ballet.]

ARCHIVES.   Records of the National Association for Regional Ballet (NARB) reside in the Dance Collection of the New York Public Library for the Performing Arts, Lincoln Center. They include festival souvenir programs for the five regions—Mid-States (1972–1987), Northeast (1959–1987), Pacific (1966–1987), Southeast (1956–1987), and Southwest (1963–1987)—as well as company souvenir programs (1956–1987), NARB brochures, NARB Choreography Conference brochures (1972–1987), National Choreography Plan (1976–1987), rosters of member companies (1972–1987), Twenty-fifth Anniversary Press Kit (1981), national board of directors fiscal information and minutes of semi-annual meetings, pictures of festivals and choreography conferences, records of Artistic Directors Seminar (1986).

Records of Regional Dance America, also held in the Dance Collection, New York Public Library for the Performing Arts, Lincoln Center, consist of festival souvenir programs for the five regions (1988–1996). Other archival materials are held in the homes of various officers; locales change as the officers change.

DORIS HERING

Musical Theater

Two productions in the middle of the nineteenth century laid the foundation from which the American musical comedy, and its attendant forms of theatrical dancing, evolved. When *The Black Crook* opened at Niblo's Garden on 12 September 1866, spectators witnessed a lush extravaganza designed by W. T. Voegtlin, the acrobatic contortions of the Majilitons, and classically trained Italian *danseuses* Marie Bonfanti and Rita Sangalli along with a corps of Amazons, girls with shields and helmets whose drills used simple steps to execute complicated patterns. All of this splendor was unified by a complex, slightly moralizing plot. *The Black Crook* was so popular that it could be seen in revivals until 1929, when the young Agnes de Mille appeared in the Bonfanti role. [*See* Black Crook, The.]

With the opening of *Ixion* at Wood's Museum on 28 September 1868, Lydia Thompson and Her British Blondes showed New Yorkers that ladies in fleshings, as the pink tights were called, could provide innocently titillating entertainment. The battalion of chorines, or "ballet girls," who subsequently trooped across American stages needed good legs rather than technique to retain a spot in the limelight. The taste for foreign extravaganza and Victorian burlesque established the practice of alternating precision drills by large female choruses with variations by legitimate ballerinas.

The season of 1879 brought two additional shows to New York that greatly influenced the next phase of development. *The Brook* (12 May 1879) incorporated a flimsy plot device to string together vaudeville turns, thus providing the seeds for both the revue format and the much later book musical. Gilbert and Sullivan's *H.M.S. Pinafore* introduced operetta to an audience with whom it remained fashionable, particularly in Viennese editions, until 1930, when realistic techniques of the legitimate theater and the new "talking" motion pictures made the romantic fantasies of operetta seem naïve.

The operetta was a nineteenth-century phenomenon that had multinational roots in the Italian *opera buffa*, the German *Singspiel*, and the British ballad opera. Among its illustrious antecedents was Adam de la Halle's play *Le Jeu de Robin et de Marion*, into which the author inserted songs during the 1283 presentation for the French court at Naples. Dancing was an integral part of a later French variant—*comédie-ballet*—of which the best example is Molière's *Le Bourgeois Gentilhomme*, first performed for Louis XIV on 14 October 1670, with a score by Jean-Baptiste Lully and steps by the royal ballet master Pierre Beauchamp. John Gay's *The Beggar's Opera*, produced in London at Lincoln's Inn Fields in 1728, added provocative, low-life characters such as Peachum and Macheath to the milieu, and Mozart's *Le Nozze di Figaro* (1786) centered all actions on the peasant hero of Pierre-Augustin Caron de Beaumarchais's comedy.

Hundreds of operettas were composed between 1855 and 1930. The earliest center was Paris, where some elements from the boulevard theaters, vaudeville, and the magical transformations of Romantic ballet fused into a new form. Composer Adolphe Adam and playwright Eugene Scribe (both well known to French balletomanes) contributed to several of the earliest productions. The real

UNITED STATES OF AMERICA: Musical Theater. Members of the female ensemble of *The Black Crook* chorus as they appeared at Niblo's Garden, New York, in 1866. (Photograph from the Dance Collection, New York Public Library for the Performing Arts.)

master was Jacques Offenbach (1819–1880), whose *La Vie Parisienne* (1866) owed as much to the waltzes, polkas, and formal quadrilles of the public balls as it did to the risqué can-can of café society. Offenbach's *Tales of Hoffmann* has been the basis for theater, film, and ballet productions.

The waltz transformed the operetta in Vienna into a distinctive world standard. *Die Fledermaus*, by Johann Strauss the younger, had its premiere in April 1874 and remains a classic of the genre. *Fledermaus* has the requisite satire, romance, and mistaken identities that later joined with exotic locales to become hallmarks of operetta. This popular entertainment brought complex variants of social dances out of the grand salons and into the theaters. While the swirling patterns of ländlers, polkas, and waltzes were common on Continental stages, the real impact of couple dances—particularly the waltz—did not peak in the United States for another thirty years, until Franz Lehár's *The Merry Widow*.

British productions by William Gilbert and Arthur Sullivan offered other links to operetta practices in Paris and to the emerging concert stage. In 1871 John D'Auban staged the first Gilbert and Sullivan collaboration. D'Auban was a British dancer who had been employed at Paris's Théâtre de la Porte-Saint-Martin; in the cities of Saint Petersburg, Saint-Quentin, and Brussels; and in sixteen English theaters, including the Alhambra, the Gaiety, and Drury Lane. It was D'Auban who experimented with his sister on a dance that featured the manipulation of her long skirt in a sketch titled "'Ain't She Very Shy." He later coached Kate Vaughan, who became the leading British skirt dancer. Following its London premiere on 25 May 1878, *H.M.S. Pinafore* opened on 25 November at the Boston Museum. Its popularity with American audiences was so great that by March 1879 eight separate companies were performing *Pinafore* in New York alone.

During the last decade of the nineteenth century, several events occurred in the United States that caused the walking and marching of chorines to be superseded by buck-and-wing, jig, cakewalk, high kicks, skirt dancing, and other artful innovations. Spanish dancer Carmencita made her American debut in August 1889 and a year later gained a rival in the fiery Carolina Otéro. Carmencita and Otéro introduced the sensuous and expressive potential of the solo female form to a wide spectrum of dazzled viewers. The Chicagoan Loie Fuller was the first of the extraordinary trio of artists (including Ruth St. Denis and Isadora Duncan) to perform an experimental dance in the commercial theater. Fuller (1861–1928) was an actress-singer-dancer who created a sensation with her *Serpentine Dance*, seen originally in the play *The Quack M.D.* (1 October 1891). The magical impression of her solo was effected by colored light projections onto yards of silk that she manipulated around her body while she dipped and turned. On 24 February 1892, as featured dancer, she joined the cast of Charles Hoyt's smash hit *A Trip to Chinatown*, the show that set the record for the longest Broadway run of the nineteenth century. By the time Fuller left the production the following spring to go to Europe, her dance discovery had gained acceptance and inspired a host of imitators. [*See the entry on Fuller.*]

Julian Mitchell (c.1854–1926), who staged most of Hoyt's innovative musical farce-comedies, was the earliest example of the successful Broadway director-choreographer and was one of the period's most sought-after dance arrangers. He helped to create vehicles for Loie Fuller, Maud Allan, Mademoiselle Dazie, and scores of other luminaries, and he staged the American debuts of Anna Held and Adeline Genée. As burlesque, spectacles, and operettas grew to number as many as one hundred and fifty in their choruses, Mitchell had to deal simultaneously with an entirely different theatrical dimension. Between 1895 and 1904, the golden years of Weber and Fields's memorable partnership at the Music Hall, Mitchell staged several successful productions there despite the tiny stage, which could accommodate fewer than a dozen members of the music hall's adulated Beauty Chorus. Mitchell and another colleague, Gus Sohlke, compensated for the small scale by incorporating more complicated steps and combinations into the dances. Mitchell's Broadway blockbusters—among them Victor Herbert's *The Idol's Eye* (25 October 1897) and *The Fortune Teller* (26 September 1898) along with the director's hits of the 1903/04 season *The Wizard of Oz* and *Babes in Toyland*—made him the highest-paid person in the business. Because of this reputation, the young Florenz Ziegfeld hired him as general director for all of his productions. Among other Ziegfeld assignments, Mitchell conceived and staged the first seven editions of the annual *Follies*, which began in 1907.

The extravaganza began to lose favor at the end of the century, although one of the last and most acclaimed of these productions, George Lederer's *The Man in the Moon* (24 April 1899), introduced a new trend setter. Not the little-known Ruth St. Denis, who appeared in the chorus, but the Pony Ballet—eight petite dynamos from the John Tiller School in England—caused the excitement. The crisp precision routines of the Tiller Girls became a mainstay of theatrical dancing. Welcomed in New York intermittently until after World War II, they were the model for the American Rockettes.

The influence of realism and the fascination with settings that sported verisimilitude led to the use of narrative as a device for unifying music, drama, and dance in musicals. Economic as well as aesthetic factors reduced the size of the female chorus, which in turn raised the level of skill that was demanded. The appeal of variety was maintained in the more sophisticated revue, in which recherché themes, often centering on the battle of the sexes, served as a framework for specialty numbers. The prototype for the American revue, a genre that amused audiences for the next fifty years, was *The Passing Show* (12 May 1894). Produced by George Lederer and Sydney Rosenfeld, the production mingled French nuances with elements from English music halls and Yankee vaudeville houses.

The late nineteenth-century obsession with hygiene, coupled with the connection that had been made between dance and healthful exercise, helped to alter earlier biases against dancing and expand the number of teaching studios. A wave of gifted immigrants, products of the great European academies, arrived to teach classes and to arrange dances for the stage. They included Marie Bonfanti, Mamert Bibberyan, Léon Espinosa, Luigi Albertieri, and Louis Chalif along with the revered native George Washington Smith, who in 1881 had partnered Fanny Elssler on her legendary American tour as well as opened his studio in Philadelphia.

New Dimensions and Inspirations. The technical level of theatrical dancing was not high at the turn of the century, but by then the commercial stage offered a variety of styles that were vigorous, highly expressive, and appealing to an audience just beginning to develop its tastes.

Besides the smaller (though by no means small) group-

ings, a new dimension was added to the female chorus in 1900. Again inspiration came from a British import: *Floradora* (12 November) boasted a sextet of tall, willowy redheads who established the statuesque charms of the "show girl," known above all else for her visual allure. The distinction of the "broiler," a girl of action, a vivacious category of chorine noted for actual dancing skills plus a winsome figure, developed that same season.

The musical adventure stories of Reginald De Koven, operettas by Victor Herbert and Franz Lehár, as well as George M. Cohan's distinctive shows enlivened Broadway during the first decade of the twentieth century. A production with far-reaching influences, Ziegfeld's *A Parisian Model* (27 November 1906) touted glamour on a lavish scale. A superficial plot provided the structure for what was, in fact, a revue. The ultimate showman was a trend setter. In addition to dozens of the most beautiful girls—who danced on roller skates with delectable Anna Held—Ziegfeld inserted a ballroom number. Held performed the *maxixe* with Gertrude Hoffman in travesty. Hoffman, a talented dancer and choreographer, was the first in a distinguished group of art dancers whom Ziegfeld presented in his revues and musicals. Some of these include Mademoiselle Dazie, Bessie Clayton, Adeline Genée (the only genuine ballerina most Americans had seen), and, in 1927, Ruth St. Denis and Ted Shawn. Julian Mitchell's staging of *A Parisian Model* inspired the choreographer's greatest brainchild: in the following year Ziegfeld premiered his unmatched series with the *Follies of 1907*.

The other smash of that season—affecting everything from fashions to bonbons—was Lehár's *The Merry Widow* (21 October 1907). Overnight the popularity of Viennese operetta soared. Everyone waltzed. The number of male

UNITED STATES OF AMERICA: Musical Theater. George M. Cohan as the title character in *Little Johnny Jones* (1904). The first of Cohan's shows with a theme of American patriotism, *Little Johnny Jones* featured two unforgettable numbers: Cohan's flag-waving song and dance to "The Yankee Doodle Boy" (or "I'm a Yankee Doodle Dandy") and a spectacular "transformation scene" set to "Give My Regards to Broadway." (Photograph from the Museum of the City of New York; used by permission.)

dancers slowly increased along with the demand for couples in ballroom displays. The *apache*, the tango, the fox trot, the *maxixe*, the polka, and other dance inventions blossomed. Nearly all were demonstrated by Irene and Vernon Castle, who personified the crest of ballroom fervor from their marriage in 1911 until Vernon's death in 1918.

The Metropolitan Opera Ballet School opened in 1909 under the direction of Malvina Cavallazzi to offer first-rate, professional training. Instruction was free, though graduates were expected to remain for three years, with pay, in the opera's corps de ballet. Some did; many others defected to higher-paying Broadway ventures. One of the decade's most sensational dances was produced at the Met. Biancha Froelich's "Dance of the Seven Veils," an erotic solo that was widely parodied in the commercial theater, caused such a furor that Richard Strauss's *Salomé* was taken out of the Metropolitan repertory until 1934. Audiences also got their first glimpse of Russian classicism at the Met. Anna Pavlova, partnered by Mikhail Mordkin, made her American debut there on 28 February 1910. During the next season, Gertrude Hoffman presented a Russian ballet ensemble headed by Theodore Koslov and Maria Baldina. Spectators' standards for technical execution rose considerably.

The second decade of the twentieth century was the last period in which the American musical theater depended to any appreciable extent on foreign imports. Significant elements emerged that became characteristics of the lyric stage after World War I. As operettas flourished and the book musical made some appreciable progress, revues gained ascendancy. Actors' Equity was founded in 1912, and some of the vagaries of the profession began to be addressed. Low pay was not as burning an issue as the policy of no rehearsal pay. Under the common practice, it was possible to rehearse for months without a salary. If the show closed after a single night, no recompense other than for one performance was required. In its earliest days Equity began efforts to improve standards of safety for dancers as well as negotiations with producers to provide rehearsal shoes, among other compensations. Attaining these ends took decades.

One of the true masterworks of the musical stage opened in 1910. Victor Herbert's *Naughty Marietta* (7 November) was commissioned by Oscar Hammerstein I for his Manhattan Opera Company. Herbert (1859–1924), the leading composer of the New York theater, was the only U.S.-based musician to gain an international reputation for his operettas. Among his many achievements, Herbert wrote cohesive scores to support plots that centered, eventually, on romance rather than on the antics of comics. *Naughty Marietta* was a transitional production that pointed the way toward a more integral relationship between libretto and accompanying music. Pauline Ver-

hoeven, a Belgian classicist, staged the dances. She had made her New York debut in 1904 at the Metropolitan Opera House. Verhoeven subsequently became ballet mistress to Hammerstein's ensemble and eventually directed the Metropolitan Opera Ballet School. With *Naughty Marietta* she set an important precedent: it was the first time that a choreographer and dancers associated, primarily, with a ballet troupe were used in a commercial production. Theatergoers saw the Danish ballerina Adeline Genée, once again, in *The Bachelor Belles*, which had its premiere on the same evening as Herbert's triumph.

In the next year *The Pink Lady* (13 March) was praised for the fact that its songs developed logically out of dramatic situations. As staged by Julian Mitchell, this Ziegfeld show capitalized on the passionate craze for ballroom dances. Eccentric routines were featured in his contribution to *Follies of 1911*, which introduced New Yorkers to the dancing Dolly Sisters. An updated revival of Charles Hoyt's *A Trip to Chinatown*, retitled *A Winsome Widow* (11 April 1912), gave Mitchell and Ziegfeld another success. Mitchell, who had collaborated with Hoyt on the original, staged a dance on ice for the new production, and the graceful skaters astonished the crowds. Equipment was installed in the theater to freeze the one-inch-thick sheet of ice for this number.

The Shubert organization (run by brothers Sam, Lee, and J. J.) offered the greatest Broadway competition to Ziegfeld's enterprises. To ensure summer business at their major house, the Winter Garden, and to take advantage of the innovations of the *Follies*, the Shuberts inaugurated *The Passing Show of 1912*. It, too, was a revue but remained closer than the *Follies* to the format established by Weber and Fields at the Music Hall. The first edition offered "The Ballet of 1830," originally mounted in London, as its first act. In the *Follies of 1913*, Ziegfeld introduced the dancing soubrette Ann Pennington. The Shuberts countered in *The Passing Show of 1914* by presenting the Broadway debut of Marilyn Miller, who became one of the most beloved dancing stars.

"The Dance Craze," as the demand for ballroom shenanigans was termed, was abetted on 3 February 1913 by the premiere of *The Sunshine Girl*. An English import with American performers, the production starred Julia Sanderson and featured Irene and Vernon Castle as well as the venerable Joseph Cawthorn. The plot revolved around a soap factory and the stipulation that its heir not become engaged or marry for a period of time. Castle, as the young lord "Bingo," impersonated the new owner of the establishment. He performed a tango with Sanderson and a Turkey Trot with his wife, establishing, in the words of critic Charles Darnton, "a new reputation for himself as a dancer." Presidents Roosevelt, Taft, and Wilson were portrayed in ballet skirts in a comic number called "Who's the Boss?"

A hit show by twenty-six-year-old Irving Berlin, *Watch Your Step* (8 December 1914), ensured the ambitious musician's tenure on Broadway. The syncopation of ragtime and a complete score based on native rhythms and melodies were Berlin's chief aims. The presence of the Castles at the head of the cast and the centerpiece number "The Syncopated Walk" were evidence of the production's dance emphasis. In "I'm a Dancing Teacher Now," Vernon Castle parodied the burgeoning number of dance studios that had been established to meet the national demand for private lessons, and Irene Castle led the troops in "Show Us How to Do the Fox Trot."

The *Follies of 1914* was a turning point for Ziegfeld. A quarrel with Mitchell caused a rift in their relationship that lasted until 1924, and comic Leon Errol staged most of the numbers for this edition. With an arrangement of "The Star Spangled Banner" in its first-act finale, the *Follies of 1914* presaged the patriotism and preoccupation with the military that characterized the World War I era. Typical of many hits of the period, the highlight of *Hip-Hip Hooray* (30 September 1915) was music by "the March King," John Philip Sousa. Entrepreneur and choreographer Ned Wayburn left the Shuberts to join the Ziegfeld team in 1915. Along with Viennese set designer Joseph Urban, Wayburn helped to take Ziegfeld's revues into the realm of legend. [*See the entry on Wayburn.*]

Scores by Rudolf Friml and Sigmund Romberg strengthened Broadway's operetta holdings. Some of the most influential music in the teens was written by Jerome Kern (1885–1946) for *Nobody Home* (20 April 1915), the first of the Princess Theater shows that launched the intimate musical. These productions were stripped of the huge number of chorus members, the preoccupation with lavish spectacle, and many of the other aspects that had linked the American musical stage with native and European extravaganzas. Located on West Thirty-ninth Street in Manhattan, the Princess had only 292 seats and a diminutive stage to match. There Kern, teamed with wordsmith Guy Bolton, helped to create in *Nobody Home* the theatrical prototype that integrated both songs and jokes into the dramatic action. The practice was unheard of at the time either in British music halls or on American stages, and Kern worked on both sides of the Atlantic.

What was trimmed in quantity was made up for in quality. The sets and costumes for *Nobody Home* were beautifully executed on a small scale that prized elegance and charm. Like many of Mitchell's choreographic innovations that were the result of the tiny dimensions of Weber and Fields's Music Hall, the staging for *Nobody Home* emphasized inventiveness rather than large audiences. The popularity of *Nobody Home* was exceeded by its successor, *Very Good Eddie.* P. G. Wodehouse, the British critic for *Vanity Fair*, joined Bolton and Kern to compose additional shows for the Princess, among which were *Oh, Boy!* and

UNITED STATES OF AMERICA: Musical Theater. Irene and Vernon Castle in the Broadway musical *Watch Your Step* (1914), with book by Charles Dillingham and music by Irving Berlin. (Photograph from the Dance Collection, New York Public Library for the Performing Arts.)

Oh, Lady! Lady!! The rehearsal pianist for the latter was the youthful George Gershwin. Produced by Bessie Marbury and Ray Comstock, the Princess musicals foreshadowed the first great masterpiece of the American lyric theater: Ziegfeld's *Show Boat* (27 December 1927), composed by Kern, was both landmark and harbinger of the book musical that evolved into the exquisitely integrated productions of the 1940s.

Some of the greatest composers for the musical stage were already working on Broadway in the teens. Besides Kern and Berlin, two younger musicians began making their mark, Gershwin and Cole Porter. Oscar Hammerstein II was at the beginning of his extraordinary career as a lyricist. Visually, audiences at the Metropolitan Opera House were taken by storm by the 1916 appearance of the Ballets Russes de Serge Diaghilev. Vaslav Nijinsky gave a considerable boost to the image of the *danseur* and excited the growing interest in ballet.

The number of revues—wonderful vehicles for soloists, stars, and chorus dancers—began to escalate. Kern composed the majority of songs for the *Follies of 1916*. George M. Cohan got in on the act with *The Cohan Revue of 1916* (9 February). Florence O'Denishawn, a product of the Denishawn school founded by Ruth St. Denis and Ted Shawn in California, appeared in *Kitchy-Koo of 1918* and in its sequel the following year. O'Denishawn reaffirmed the link for dancers between the concert stage and the commercial theater. Former hoofer George White (born Weitz) instituted a revue notable, above all, for its dancing sequences. The *Scandals of 1919* was the maiden production of the annual series to which White later gave his name. Tapping, shimmying, and acrobatic feats delighted viewers and provided more competition for Ziegfeld. *Greenwich Village Nights*, renamed *Greenwich Village Follies* (15 July 1919), added to the revue's development.

Two book musicals in 1919 advanced that evolving genre. Victor Herbert's *The Velvet Lady* (3 February) was not one of his finest scores, but Julian Mitchell's direction turned it into a dancing phenomenon, especially for Georgia O'Ramsey. *Irene* (18 November) was a significant benchmark because its plot dealt with realistic characters who took believable actions that provided logical situations and motivations for songs as well as dances. Meanwhile, the Actors' Equity strike of 1919 resulted in bitter recriminations as performers attempted to improve their salaries and working conditions.

The Innovative Twenties. The 1920s ushered in the jazz age, which was more idiosyncratically American than any previous era. World War I had solidified a national identity that firmly recognized the United States as a lead-

ing world power. Syncopated rhythms, art deco visuals, and an explosion of dance styles set a racy pulse. The revue reached its zenith, a level that has never been equaled. In spite of scores of imitators, Ziegfeld's *Follies* reigned supreme. Nearly fifty new musicals were produced in the 1920/21 season alone, most of them revues. Some emphasized music; a few showcased dance, comedy, or even nudity. The Shuberts' *Passing Show*, White's *Scandals*, and Ziegfeld's *Follies* plus his *Midnight Frolics* continued to dominate the scene, but there were some notable additions—and incidents.

The 22 September 1921 premiere of *The Music Box Revue* was a spectacular christening for the Music Box Theater. For the *Greenwich Village Follies of 1923* (20 September), Martha Graham danced in a Spanish fiesta number and in "The Garden of Kama," an exotic replication from her Denishawn days. Earl Carroll's *Vanities* (5 July 1923) appeared with the 1923 production. *The Grand Street Follies* were so successful as a private event that the series went public with *The Grand Street Follies of 1924* on 20 May. The Shuberts flirted with nudity in *Artists and Models of 1924* (15 October). *The Garrick Gaieties* (17 May 1925) affirmed the songwriting abilities of young Richard Rodgers. One of the best and most remarkable revues, *Blackbirds of 1928*, featured the footwork of Bill ("Bojangles") Robinson. Jazz and the black performer were acclaimed, respected, and legitimized on the Great White Way. By 1929 Broadway was so saturated that *Ned Wayburn's Gambols* ran for only thirty-one nights.

The *Charlot Revue of 1926* received some unusually negative press coverage. The roster for this British import was headed by Gertrude Lawrence, Beatrice Lillie, and Jack Buchanan, who also staged some of the dances and several of the Noël Coward songs. A letter from "a Wrathful Playgoer" to the management of the Selwyn Theater complained about the lackluster entertainment and uninspired cast. Journalist Alexander Woollcott gave Miss Lawrence space in his column so that she could reply

UNITED STATES OF AMERICA: Musical Theater. Chorus girls in *Shuffle Along* (1921). Josephine Baker stands sixth from the right. This show was the first all-black "smash hit" on Broadway, thanks mainly to the danceable tunes of Eubie Blake. (Photograph from the archives of Noble Sissle and Eubie Blake; reprinted from Robert Kimball and William Bolcom, *Reminiscing with Sissle and Blake*, New York, 1973, p. 128.)

UNITED STATES OF AMERICA: Musical Theater. An English precision dance group founded by John Tiller in 1901, the Tiller Girls were a popular attraction at the *Zigfield Follies* in 1922, 1924, and 1925. (Photograph by White Studio, New York; from the Dance Collection, New York Public Library for the Performing Arts.)

publicly to her detractors. The lady confessed to exhaustion, due to her intensive effort to make a good impression on New Yorkers.

Magnificent music seemed to be everywhere. Three operettas, *The Student Prince, The Vagabond King,* and *The Desert Song,* exemplified the genre's last glorious blaze before losing favor to more realistic lyric theater pieces and to films. Both Rudolf Friml (1879–1972) and Sigmund Romberg (1887–1951) were Europeans who had trained as classical musicians in Prague and Vienna, respectively, before immigrating to the United States. The two also contributed significantly in the transition from operetta to musical comedy that took place in the 1920s. Romberg's *Student Prince* (2 December 1924) retained the aura of unrequited love in a Ruritanian setting, but his *Desert Song* (30 November 1926), with its contemporary French North Africa locale, moved closer to the realm of musical drama. In *The Vagabond King* (20 September 1925), Friml dealt with issues surrounding political upheaval, an indication that serious ideas were being tested on the lyric stage. With *Rose-Marie* (2 September 1924), he struck a balance between Old World romance and contemporary accents, captivating spectators and setting a box office record that remained unbroken for nearly twenty years. Melody and beat propelled the dancers in David Bennett's *Rose-Marie,* its choreography including the Charleston, the Black Bottom, and the Lindy Hop plus adagio, toe-tapping, and Tiller Girl precision routines. The "Totem Tom-Tom" production number in act 1 presented one hundred dancers in formations that are associated with a later era of Hollywood musicals.

The book musical coalesced in the 1920s and proved to be the American musical theater's vehicle of the future. *Irene* and George M. Cohan's *Mary* (18 October 1920) piqued the taste for heroine-centered sagas. Ziegfeld's *Sally* (21 October 1920) was a runaway favorite, with Marilyn Miller as star, Jerome Kern as composer with additional ballet music by Victor Herbert, and Joseph Urban as designer. Miller's performance in the "Butterfly Ballet" was so enchanting that the entire number was interpolated into a subsequent edition of the *Follies*. Miller triumphed again in *Sunny* (22 September 1925), produced by Charles Dillingham and directed by Julian Mitchell not long before his death. *Sunny* was the first Kern-Hammerstein collaboration and was staged by Mitchell in conjunction with David Bennett, Alexis Kosloff, and John Tiller. The altering relationship between book and music did not affect Ziegfeld's production methods. For one of Miller's numbers in Romberg and Gershwin's *Rosalie* (10 January 1928), he surrounded his star with fifty beauties adorned in "simple peasant costumes of satin and chiffon."

The 2 February 1927 premiere of *Rio Rita* opened the exquisite, egg-shaped Ziegfeld Theater. For all the future-shock elegance of the auditorium and settings, *Rio Rita* was something of a dated, swashbuckling operetta, with one exception: Albertina Rasch fashioned a stunning ballet for the Albertina Rasch Girls, who wore black-and-white costumes by Joseph Urban. Many of the other sequences were staged by Sammy Lee, who had succeeded Ned Wayburn as Ziegfeld's dance director in 1923. [*See the entry on Rasch.*]

In a decade brimming with hits, some unusual talents and new themes emerged. Fred Astaire, who gave up

UNITED STATES OF AMERICA: Musical Theater. Marilyn Miller in the title role of *Rosalie* (1928), with music by Sigmund Romberg and George Gershwin. As a princess from the Ruritanian country of Romanza who falls in love with a West Point cadet, Miller danced in several elaborate numbers staged by Seymour Felix. (Photograph from the Billy Rose Theater Collection, New York Public Library for the Performing Arts.)

vaudeville and between 1917 and 1932 appeared in ten Broadway shows with his sister Adele, began choreographing and performing his own solos in George and Ira Gershwin's *Lady, Be Good!* (1 December 1924). The Astaires displayed their enormous charms in *Funny Face* (22 November 1927) and took three of their New York successes to London during the 1920s. Tap dancing was eulogized by adorable flappers in the frothy, amusing *No, No, Nanette* (16 September 1925). At the opposite end of the spectrum *Show Boat*, with dances by Sammy Lee, examined tough social issues such as racism and divorce. Based on Edna Ferber's novel, the book by Oscar Hammerstein II and Jerome Kern's score set a precedent for revealing the interplay of serious emotions on the musical stage. The same season introduced Vincent Youman's talent in *Hit the Deck!* (25 April 1927). Staged by Seymour Felix, the show featured an eccentric, "knee-twisting" ballet performed by Madeline Cameron. *The Three Muske-*

teers (13 March 1928) allowed Ziegfeld and Urban to dabble with historical settings, and it provided the occasion for Rasch to insert a *ballet de cour* in act 2 of Friml's score. In *Whoopee* (4 December 1928), Ziegfeld explored the Wild West, Urban reinvented the Grand Canyon, and Eddie Cantor pranced his way to stardom.

Two shows were outstanding for the work of their choreographers rather than for breathtaking box office records. *The Street Singer* (17 September 1929), a Shubert venture that borrowed heavily from the Folies-Bergère, was co-produced by Busby Berkeley, who created a touching "Green Room Ballet" for Queenie Smith. Best remembered as a singer, Smith actually began her career as a soloist with the Metropolitan Opera Ballet. Ziegfeld's *The Show Girl* (2 July 1929) allowed Rasch to cap the decade in which she had begun choreographing so successfully. With a Gershwin score and Ruby Keeler in the lead, Rasch had glorious material to work with. Her coup was a ballet to Gershwin's *An American in Paris* that featured Harriet Hoctor.

Rasch, known as the "Czarina of Broadway," was a classically trained Viennese dancer who had appeared in major opera houses, in vaudeville, and as the entr'acte entertainment on a South American tour with Sarah Bernhardt. A brilliant teacher and choreographer, she created dances for the Hippodrome for fifty of her dancers and sent out groups of "Albertina Rasch Girls" numbered to suit the scale of specific stages. She helped, also, to convince Sol Hurok to bring the German expressionist Mary Wigman to the United States for a tour in 1930. Both she and Berkeley became major influences in film choreography during the 1930s.

The invention of the talkies collided with the stock market crash of October 1929, and the bright lights dimmed on Broadway.

Experimentation and a Seriousness of Purpose. The Great Depression had a profound effect on the American theater, contributing to one of the most creative periods in its history. Whereas the 1920s had witnessed the culmination of innovations begun at the turn of the century, the 1930s marked radical changes in the nation's social, economic, and political fabric that were reflected in the highly experimental nature of the era's theatrical achievements. Productions that confronted pressing social and labor issues were mounted simultaneously with those that offered purely escapist fare. The seriousness of purpose and rich quantity of talent caused this decade to uncover ideas that were refined for many years afterward.

A Gershwin score was teamed with a book by George S. Kaufman for *Strike Up the Band* (14 January 1930), a musical that dealt with war, international politics, and big business. Jazz syncopations were exchanged for "swing" melodies. A few of the pit musicians for the production

UNITED STATES OF AMERICA: Musical Theater. *(above)* The Albertina Rasch Dancers and soloist Harriet Hoctor (right) in Rasch's ballet set to Gershwin's *An American in Paris,* in Ziegfeld's production of *Show Girl* (1929). *(below)* In *The Band Wagon* (1931), Rasch choreographed an inventive number to "Dancing in the Dark" for Tilly Losch, in the role of a glamorous ballerina, and Fred Astaire, as a stagedoor beggar who dances with her in a dream. They performed the number on a raked stage with a mirrored floor. (Photographs from the Billy Rose Theater Collection, New York Public Library for the Performing Arts.)

were Benny Goodman, Gene Krupa, Glenn Miller, and Jimmy Dorsey. George Hale arranged the dances for this show, which set a new tone for Broadway.

The golden days of the revue were over, although the genre was still in evidence. In *The Band Wagon* (3 June 1931), Tilly Losch danced on a raked, mirrored floor in a set that incorporated revolving stages. Albertina Rasch choreographed, and the Astaires appeared together for the last time, as Adele Astaire was about to exchange her stage career for marriage. The last *Follies* that Ziegfeld supervised personally was in 1931. After his death in 1932, editions were produced sporadically—usually staged by Robert Alton—but these never equaled the standard set by Ziegfeld himself. Another revue, *Hellzapoppin* (22 September 1938), established a box office record and featured a precedent-setting use of film footage in its opening production number. [*See the entry on Ziegfeld.*]

Of Thee I Sing (26 December 1931) was the first musical to win a Pulitzer Prize. Collaborators George and Ira Gershwin, George S. Kaufman, and Morrie Ryskind were floored, as was George Hale, their choreographer.

Broadway began losing many of its finest talents to more lucrative film ventures in Hollywood, a situation

that enhanced the abundance of movie musicals that were produced over the next two decades. Typical of this exodus are the examples of Fred Astaire and Albertina Rasch. Astaire's last stage musical was *Gay Divorce* (29 November 1932) with Claire Luce. Appearing for the first time in a book show with a woman who was not his sister, Astaire began, in *Gay Divorce*, to explore the deft, romantic comedy that became the framework for all his films: sophistication rather than sentiment is the touchstone, and the most important love scenes are the danced duets. *The Great Waltz* (22 September 1934) was an operetta produced, like earlier behemoths, on an extravagant scale. The lives of the Johann Strausses—father and son—served as plot and motive for using the Waltz King's superb music. On stage, the show incorporated two hundred performers, several sweeping numbers by Rasch, and $250,000 worth of sets and costumes. In the 1938 Metro-Goldwyn-Mayer (MGM) movie, Rasch was able to mount her dance sequences on an even more lavish scale.

The days of great producers in the Ziegfeld mold were over. Yet an interesting roster of producing organizations emerged. The Works Progress Administration (WPA) Federal Theatre and Dance Projects supported new composers, such as Eubie Blake in *Swing It* (22 July 1937) and Lehman Engel in *A Hero Is Born* (1 October 1937). Under Federal auspice, *The Swing Mikado* (1 March 1939) was produced in Chicago, inspiring Michael Todd's *The Hot Mikado* (23 March 1939) in New York City with Bill Robinson. The Group Theater produced Paul Green's *Johnny Johnson* (19 November 1936). The Mercury Theater and the Theater Guild joined the action. Plays with music and dance were mounted, such as the 1933 productions *Run, Little Chillun* and *School for Husbands* for which Doris Humphrey created the dances. The Ladies Garment Workers Union renamed the Princess Theater the Labor Stage and on 27 November 1937 opened the politically activist *Pins and Needles*, which included some dances by Katherine Dunham.

Many figures from the concert field came to work on Broadway. José Limón staged the Dance of the Seven Mannequins in *Roberta* (18 November 1933), which featured Bob Hope and Fay Templeton and used only twenty-eight chorus girls. George Balanchine made history with "Slaughter on Tenth Avenue" for *On Your Toes* (11 April 1936), introducing Ray Bolger and proving that dance could be integrated with the dramatic plot. Balanchine asked to be billed as "choreographer" for the show, the first listing of the term in a Broadway program.

The Russian genius began his forrays into the commercial theater in London, where he created dances for

UNITED STATES OF AMERICA: Musical Theater. Two jazz versions of Gilbert and Sullivan's comic opera *The Mikado*, with all-black casts, opened on Broadway in March 1939. *The Hot Mikado*, produced by impresario Mike Todd, starred Bill Robinson, who strutted through his role wearing a gold suit, gold shoes, and a gold hat and carrying a gold cane. He is pictured here with an unidentified player and the "three little maids from school": Gwendolyn Reyde, Frances Broch, and Rosetta Le Noire. After its Broadway run, the show moved to the grounds of the World's Fair in Flushing, Queens. (Photograph from the Museum of the City of New York.)

UNITED STATES OF AMERICA: Musical Theater. The "Pernambuco" number from *Where's Charley?* (1948), choreographed by George Balanchine. Ray Bolger as a *caballero* is seen at center wooing Allyn Ann McLerie. (Photograph by Eileen Darby, Graphic House, Inc.; used by permission.)

Charles B. Cochran's *Revue* (1930 and 1931) and for Sir Oswald Stoll's *Variety Show* (1931). In the United States Balanchine staged or made dances for five movies and nearly twenty musicals, casting leading ballet performers and bringing up the standards of choreography to a par with those for musical composition. For *Babes in Arms* (14 April 1937) he made Broadway's first dream ballet: "Peter's Journey" in act 2 took the hero to Hollywood, Europe, and Africa and ultimately returned him to reality. Balanchine's association with black dancers began with the tap dancing Nicholas Brothers in *Babes in Arms*. He later worked with Katherine Dunham in the stage and movie versions of *Cabin in the Sky* (1940) and the film *Star Spangled Rhythm* (1942). During his association with *House of Flowers* (30 December 1954)—the cast of which starred Pearl Bailey and Diahann Carroll and included Arthur Mitchell and Alvin Ailey—Balanchine designed the staging and was instrumental in Geoffrey Holder's arrangement of the Banda Dance. Besides using ballerinas Tamara Geva and Vera Zorina on Broadway, Balanchine cast Alexandra Danilova and Frederic Franklin, along with an entire ensemble from Ballet Russe de Monte Carlo, in *Song of Norway* (21 August 1944). He choreographed for Ray Bolger in *On Your Toes*, *Where's Charley?*, and *Keep Off the Grass*, in which José Limón and

Jerome Robbins also appeared. Young chorus dancers in *Great Lady* included Robbins and, in *The Lady Comes Across*, the youthful Gower Champion. Among Balanchine's greatest musical theater successes were *I Married an Angel* (11 May 1938), *The Boys from Syracuse* (23 November 1938), and *The Merry Widow* (4 August 1943). [*See the entry on Balanchine.*]

Development of Theatrical Choreography. Serious theatrical choreography began to develop almost simultaneously with the demise of a leading American composer, the death of George Gershwin in Hollywood in 1937. Initially inspired by Jerome Kern's songs, Gershwin had entered the musical theater at a time when most of its scores were trite, old fashioned, or cliché-ridden. He fused jazz syncopations, big symphonic arrangements, and an often-haunting lyricism into distinctive scores, many of which are equally at home in a concert hall or in a Broadway orchestra pit. The last Gershwin shows coincided with the first of Cole Porter's long string of hits, beginning with *Anything Goes* (21 November 1934), for which Robert Alton arranged numbers for the chorus and leading lady Ethel Merman. Another Porter show, *DuBarry Was a Lady* (6 December 1939), introduced the novice dancer Betty Grable.

The book musical clearly defined itself as a distinguished art form during the 1940s, when all production elements were organically integrated and the form reached the sort of apex attained by the revue in the 1920s. There were several strong forerunners to the new importance of librettos created by serious writers.

UNITED STATES OF AMERICA:
Musical Theater. Agnes de Mille's
landmark choreography for
Oklahoma! (1943) fused ballet
and modern dance idioms to
create a new-style Americana
musical. The original cast
members seen here include, at
left, Katherine Sergava as Laurey
and Bambi Linn as Child. Marc
Platt as Curley heads the cowboys
on the right. (Photograph by
Vandamm Studio, New York.)

Maxwell Anderson had joined Kurt Weill to create *Knickerbocker Holiday* (19 October 1938), and Gertrude Stein had collaborated with Virgil Thomson on *Four Saints in Three Acts* (20 February 1934), "an opera to be sung," as Stein described it. The positive national image following World War II contributed to the blossoming of theatrical expressiveness. The first major-league American ballet troupes—now known as New York City Ballet and American Ballet Theatre—came into being in the forties and evinced strong classical training and technique. Modern dancers added their singular gifts as both choreographers and performers.

Three productions opened new 1940s directions. *Cabin in the Sky* (25 October 1940), with Ethel Waters and Katherine Dunham as stars and Balanchine as choreographer, took a close look at black lifestyles. Robert Alton's dances for Gene Kelly in *Pal Joey* (25 December 1940), along with the show's script and score, brought three-dimensional characters to life in a situation that engendered cynicism rather than idealized love. Like numerous other musicals in this period, both became popular movies. For *Lady in the Dark* (23 January 1941), Albertina Rasch used dance to explore the psychological ramifications of dreams. The most famous dream ballet ever created was staged two years later by Agnes de Mille.

De Mille's choreography for *Oklahoma!* (31 March 1943) elaborated character as well as plot, used idiomatic American gestures and folk forms, and firmly allied Broadway with professionals from ballet and concert stages. In the celebrated sequence "Laurey Makes Up Her Mind," de Mille cast dancers in roles that paralleled the principal characters and had them demonstrate the interior struggle Laurey experienced in choosing her beau. Directed by Rouben Mamoulian, *Oklahoma!* transformed Alfred Drake, Celeste Holm, and Joan Roberts into leading stage personalities. The original cast for the dream ballet comprised Katherine Sergava as Laurey, Bambi Linn as Child, George Church as Jud, and Marc Platt as Curley. The two men were subsequently replaced by Vladimir Kostenko and Erick Hawkins. Other *Oklahoma!* dancers who were part of the relatively recent practice of incorporating serious dance artists in commercial ventures included Diana Adams, John Butler, Marian Horosko, Joan McCracken, and later, Gemze de Lappe and Mavis Ray. [*See the entry on de Mille.*]

This pattern continued and expanded in *One Touch of Venus* (7 October 1943), Cheryl Crawford's production that combined the experimental approach of the Group Theater with the proven attraction of de Mille's choreography. Elia Kazan directed the show—his first musical—that had a book by S. J. Perelman with Ogden Nash and a score by Kurt Weill. Mary Martin starred as Venus, and Sono Osato was featured as *première danseuse*. Kermit Love designed the dance costumes. De Mille staged, among other numbers, the ballets "Forty-five Minutes for Lunch," "Foolish Heart," and "Venus in Ozone Heights." Some of the dancers were Diana Adams, Ann Hutchinson, Pearl Lang, Duncan Noble, Welland Lathrop, and, briefly, Merce Cunningham, who appeared in the cast for a week in Boston.

At thirty-four, de Mille had impressive credentials. She had already completed a Charles Cochran revue in London for Gertrude Lawrence; dances for the 1936 film version of *Romeo and Juliet* with Norma Shearer and Leslie Howard; *Drums Beat in Hackensack* for Les Ballets Jooss; *Three Virgins and a Devil* for Ballet Theatre; and *Rodeo* for Ballet Russe de Monte Carlo. Her "Civil War Ballet" in *Bloomer Girl* (5 October 1944) had less to do with the plot than with touching national consciousness with regard to grief for husbands and sons who were fighting overseas and in its plea for racial tolerance. With the ballet-pantomime to the overture of *Carousel* (19 April 1945), de Mille set a poetic dimension for the entire production. Teamed with Frederick Lowe and Alan Jay Lerner for *Brigadoon* (13 March 1947), she again extended the range of feeling and mood that could be sustained by dance in the musical theater, especially with the chasing of Harry Beaton and the mourning ritual for his death.

With Sono Osato and Nancy Walker as winsome principals, *On the Town* (28 December 1944) was the first Broadway show to evolve from a ballet, Jerome Robbins's *Fancy Free*. It also was the debut of what became a spectacular theatrical partnership between Robbins and Leonard Bernstein. Next, Robbins choreographed the ballet *Interplay*—for himself, Janet Reed, John Kriza, and

UNITED STATES OF AMERICA: Musical Theater. The final tableau of the "Mack Sennett Ballet" from *High Button Shoes* (1947), choreographed by Jerome Robbins. (Photograph reprinted from a souvenir program.)

Michael Kidd, among others—for Billy Rose's *Concert Varieties* (1 June 1945), which had an exceedingly short run. He scored another hit with his hilarious "Mack Sennett Ballet" in *High Button Shoes* (9 October 1947), which had music by Jule Styne. In *Look, Ma, I'm Dancin'* (29 January 1948) Robbins spoofed the ballet world with a cast featuring Nancy Walker and Harold Lang. [*See the entry on Robbins.*]

Another influx of dancemakers came to Broadway from the concert circuit. Helen Tamiris evoked pure magic in her Currier and Ives "Skating Ballet" for *Up in Central Park* (27 January 1945); she enlivened the Wild West with *Annie Get Your Gun* (16 May 1946), Irving Berlin's tailor-made score for Ethel Merman; and she staged dances for a revival of *Show Boat* in the same season. Michael Kidd also demonstrated a flair for blending ballet with theatrical dance forms. One of his earliest achievements was *Finian's Rainbow* (10 January 1947), an unusual mixture of serious issues and escapism; Kidd created an entire

role for the speechless character Sharon out of dance and mime passages. Some of his best work was done in the film *Seven Brides for Seven Brothers* (1954), which utilized company members from both Ballet Theatre and the New York City Ballet. *Kiss Me, Kate* (30 December 1948), widely considered to be one of the most perfect musicals, matched the gifts of Shakespeare with those of Cole Porter and Hanya Holm, who used preclassic dance forms (pavane and tarantella) to lend a Renaissance dimension to her choreography.

Concert soloists also made an impact on the commercial theater. Katherine Dunham appeared in several revues and in *Carib Song* (27 September 1945). Pearl Primus led the cast for *Caribbean Carnival* (5 December 1947), an artistic and aesthetic breakthrough even though it was not well received at the box office, an indication that audiences were not yet comfortable with the exuberance of African and Latino exoticism. Modern dancer Valerie Bettis stunned spectators in the revue *Inside U.S.A.* (30 April 1948).

The American Society of Composers, Authors and Publishers (ASCAP), the composers' union, called a strike during the 1948 season. Despite complaints against it, ASCAP had been instrumental in bringing about an important artistic change, beginning in the 1930s. Until then, it was common to have several composers contribute to a production, a situation that stemmed both from the revue format and from the custom in nineteenth-century opera houses of having several staff musicians write part of the music for a ballet. Even a major accomplishment such as Ziegfeld's *Rosalie* incorporated melodies by Sigmund

UNITED STATES OF AMERICA: Musical Theater. The pavane from Cole Porter's *Kiss Me, Kate* (1948), choreographed by Hanya Holm. Decor and costumes were designed by Lemuel Ayres. (Photograph by Eileen Darby, Graphic House, Inc.; used by permission.)

Romberg and George Gershwin, and Jerome Kern's *Show Boat* included Charles K. Harris's period song "After the Ball." The move to have an entire score written by one composer was a crucial step in unifying musical productions. ASCAP's efforts at one-show-one-composer were abetted by the strong personalities and musical gifts of Kern and Gershwin. Kern's work at the Princess Theater and Gershwin's score for *Strike Up the Band* provided favorable evidence in support of change. Kern's *The Cat and the Fiddle* (15 October 1931) and Gershwin's *Of Thee I Sing* (26 December 1931) helped to establish this practice, which was standard procedure by the late 1940s.

Rodgers and Hammerstein finished the decade with their Pulitzer Prize–winner *South Pacific* (7 April 1949). Anderson and Weill collaborated for the last time before Weill's death with their poignant *Lost in the Stars* (30 October 1949). Carol Channing began her long love affair with theatergoers in *Gentlemen Prefer Blondes* (8 December 1949), with steps made to measure by de Mille.

Emergence of the Director-Choreographer. The concept of the single director-choreographer—another attempt at production unity—began in the 1950s and became increasingly prominent in subsequent decades. Writing in *And Promenade Home*, de Mille attributed this, primarily, to a choreographer's need to have control over his or her work without interference from a director or producer. Both Julian Mitchell and Gus Sohlke had functioned in this solo capacity at the turn of the century. The advantage of a single creative vision is, normally, a tightly integrated production. During the 1950s, Jerome Robbins and Michael Kidd took over directorial and choreographic responsibilities, often producing their own shows as well.

A harsher realism entered the theater in the 1950s and slowly supplanted the apple-pie values and traditional American idioms that had been so well served in the 1940s. The "beat generation" grooved to rock-and-roll. The scope of the lyric stage widened to encompass ethnic variety as well as streetwise figures and tactics. When exotic locales were featured, they usually provided background for the encounters of three-dimensional characters. Choreographers were able to add a kinetic veracity in the process of role development. The time span between *Oklahoma!* (1943) and *Fiddler on the Roof* (1964) is the richest period in American musical theater. A growing emphasis on human values and an onstage synthesis of the performing and visual arts produced a body of work that has yet to be matched in substance or number.

The modest appeal of the immodest *Michael Todd's Peep Show* (28 June 1950) revealed the by-then limited draw of revues. That same year witnessed the premiere of one of the masterpiece musicals, *Guys and Dolls* (24 November 1950), with a book by Abe Burrows, score by Frank Loesser, and dances by Michael Kidd, whose crap game for Sky Masterson and his friends to "Luck Be a Lady

Tonight" is a pinnacle of choreography for males on the musical stage, rarely equaled except for Kidd's ensembles in the film *Seven Brides for Seven Brothers,* Fred Astaire's movie dances, and some of Robbins's work. For *The King and I* (29 March 1951), Robbins used poses from Siamese classical dance to fashion "The Small House of Uncle Thomas," a complete miniature ballet that could stand alone as a concert piece. Although de Mille's dance hall girls in *Paint Your Wagon* (12 November 1951) were fully realized characters, the Old West had lost the power to rivet popular imaginations. Two foreign-flavored offerings sparked the 1953 season. Kidd racked up another winner in *Can-Can* (7 May), starring Lilo and Gwen Verdon and brandishing a fine Cole Porter score. *Kismet* (3 December), with its seductive themes borrowed subtly from Aleksandr Borodin, was enhanced by Jack Cole's choreography. A former Denishawn member, Cole was a pioneer of jazz dancing. He trained Verdon and Carol Haney as well as many other dancers, coached Marilyn Monroe, and collaborated on several movies. [*See the entry on Cole.*]

The Pajama Game (13 May 1954), Richard Adler's first hit with Jerry Ross, employed two directors, George Abbott and Jerome Robbins. Bob Fosse staged the dances, and his "Steam Heat" brought instant recognition for himself and Carol Haney, his leading dancer. Fosse brought his tight-bodied jazz to Broadway again almost immediately with *Damn Yankees* (5 May 1955), a baseball spoof with Gwen Verdon as the sexy vamp Lola. David Merrick began to develop a reputation as a producer that was reminiscent of the 1920s' theater tycoons and of Ziegfeld. His *Peter Pan* (20 October 1954), conceived and staged by Robbins with Mary Martin as the eternal youth, became an all-time classic.

Robbins's greatest musical theater achievement to date was accomplished with Leonard Bernstein on *West Side Story* (26 September 1957). Created with Peter Gennaro, the dances and fights proved that gesture could convey the full range of emotion from tenderness to violence, providing spectators with an Aristotelian catharsis along the way. Its foundation based in Shakespeare's *Romeo and Juliet, West Side Story* transposed the noble houses of Capulet and Montague—as well as their transgressions—to the warring street gangs of Sharks and Jets. As drama critic Walter Terry observed in the *New York Herald,* "The great wonder of *West Side Story* is that realistic action flows into dancing and out of it again without a hitch or break, just as speech swells or snarls its way into poetry and song." Throughout the production, music and dance heightened adolescent interactions, vividly articulating feelings that the young are unable to express. Male dancers gained a new macho dimension in the public eye. These were not street toughs but kids from the corps de ballet, notably, in the film, Russ Tamblyn and Eliot Feld. Both the stage and film versions of *West Side Story* continue to fill theaters around the world because of its timeless power as a metaphor of youth and death. The show also brought a new lyricist to Broadway, Stephen Sondheim.

Other interesting and off-beat attractions included *House of Flowers,* with a book by Truman Capote; the dancerly spy thriller, *Silk Stockings* (24 February 1955), with choreography by Eugene Loring, which was appropriate as the Cold War commenced; and *Flower Drum Song* (1 December 1958), one of several attempts to reinvoke the lucrative Oriental splendors of *The King and I.*

My Fair Lady (15 March 1956), one of the great box office colossuses, was a musical theater jewel in its original production. Again, the principal librettist was a man of letters: George Bernard Shaw's *Pygmalion* was adapted by Lerner and Lowe into a witty, sophisticated tryst for Rex Harrison and Julie Andrews. Hanya Holm, a wizard with period movement, exceeded her own standards with the bustling Covent Garden sequences, the understated "Ascot Gavotte," and the ripsnorting "Get Me to the Church on Time."

With *Gypsy* (21 May 1959), Robbins staged the last of the big, traditional musical comedies. The wonderful burlesque-hall tale of Mama Rose and her fetching daughter Gypsy Rose Lee had a score by Jule Styne and lyrics by Stephen Sondheim. The great-hearted *Fiorello!* (23 November 1959), with dances by Peter Gennaro, marked the end of an era. The decade's finale, *The Sound of Music* (16 November 1959), immortalized the Trapp family in a production that placed top value on music rather than dance.

Radical Concepts and New Energy. The 1960s brought on a severe crisis in American confidence and a splintering of national identity that was disorienting on nearly all levels. The early optimism that began with the Kennedy administration was gradually eaten away by the emotional and financial costs of the war in Vietnam. Civil rights, political assassinations, street violence, campus rebellions, women's liberation, and flower children further fragmented traditional alliances. Acid rock and psychedelic imaginings expressed a free-falling loss of innocence that characterized the decade. The stage, as a result, produced an eclectic assortment of odd bed fellows: the avant-garde flourished next to the traditional. A great deal of experimentation took place with radical concepts and energy coming from communal performance groups, postmodern artists, and pop culture.

Escalating costs that continued to push ticket prices up caused cast numbers to shrink in most productions. Appropriately, the music that holds the record for the longest off-Broadway run helped to christen the decade. *The Fantasticks* (3 May 1960), Tom Jones and Harvey Schmidt's romance for seven players, echoed the simplicity of a parable and became a touchstone for the sixties' generation. Stock production numbers were hardly the point

with such a tiny cast, yet this entire show was conceived in dance terms, and one of the seven characters is a white-faced mime. Like the functional, unpretentious props that were taken out of an onstage trunk as needed, the choreography wove simple steps and movement into lyrical sequences that bound together the dramatic action. The Boy (Matt) and The Girl (Luisa) had a fanciful turn of swirling embraces in "Soon It's Gonna Rain," the two fathers executed a soft-shoe routine in "They Did It 'Cause We Said No," and the first act ended with "The Rape Ballet." The initial production investment was $16,500. *The Fantasticks* was still running in 1997, demonstrating the antitraditional stance and creative vitality that still permeates off- and off-off-Broadway venues.

One of the liveliest of these was the Judson Poets' Theatre, housed in the Judson Church at 55 Washington Square South. Under the stewardship of its associate minister, Al Carmines, an insouciant musician and composer, the arts program at the church added the Judson Dance Theater to its aegis in 1962. New programs of dance, theater, and musical theater were given every month or so. *What Happened* (October 1963), which typified the Judson participatory democracy, won the annual Obie award for best production of a musical. The Gertrude Stein script was directed by Lawrence Kornfeld and had a score that was composed and performed by Carmines. Three male singers and five female dancers—Joan Baker, Lucinda Childs, Aileen Pasloff, Yvonne Rainer, and Arlene Rothlein—performed postmodern games and tasks. Five separate sections were sorted out by Jerry Tallmer in the *New York Post:* skipping rope and chases; counting sweet cadence; wedding and slicing; hop-scotch and crossings; and falling down and photographs. The James Waring Dance Company appeared in *Poet's Vaudeville* on the same bill. By scrutinizing the essence of movement and dissecting all styles of dance, these artists pushed out the boundaries of the art form.

The success of Judson's *In Circles* (13 October 1967) caused the production to be moved from the church to the Cherry Lane Theater and, ultimately, to Grammercy Arts. Stein's syllabic collisions that made up the script of *In Circles* were again staged by Kornfeld and accompanied by a Carmines score. The singing-dancing company included Rothlein, Theo Barnes, Elaine Summers, and David Vaughan, who performed an overture out of the phrase "Poppa knowes that Momma blows her noses." Carmines's whimsical *Promenade* (4 June 1969) opened the Promendade Theater and helped to propel some of the experimentation uptown. The pattern of moving popular experimental productions into commercial houses, inaugurated in the 1960s, was refined over the next decade into a standard operating procedure by Joseph Papp's Shakespeare Festival.

On the mainstream musical front, Gower Champion

joined the front ranks of Broadway creators with *Bye Bye Birdie* (14 April 1960), which he choreographed and directed. *Birdie* dealt with the generation gap, motorcycles, television, and Shriners. Dick Van Dyke and Chita Rivera starred.

At the opposite extreme were the presentations of idealized worlds. *Camelot* (3 December 1960) brought Holm back into the theater to create May dances and medieval games for a cast headed by Richard Burton, Julie Andrews, and Robert Goulet. Based on *The Rainmaker, 110 in the Shade* (24 October 1963) was de Mille's last Broadway original. Jones and Schmidt retained their delicacy in libretto and score. With "Everything Wonderful Happens at Night," de Mille conjured up a spell of ice cream socials and fragile first love—quaint, but too tame and too distant to fire audience imaginations. Jack Cole left Hollywood temporarily to stage *Man of La Mancha* (22 November 1965). This musical tale of Don Quixote is one of the most chivalrous of love stories. Canadian Onna White fashioned period steps to contemporary melodies both for *Half a Sixpence* (25 April 1965), which introduced British teen idol Tommy Steele to Americans, and for *1776* (16 March 1969), which presented the nation's founding fathers in a historic gambol. *George M!* (10 April 1968) brought director-choreographer Joe Layton out of his television studio and back into the limelight. Layton combined patriotism, zippy theatrics, and tap dancing in his brash and sassy view of vaudeville.

Reversing the former stage-to-screen route, a number of sixties' musicals were adaptations from films. *Sweet Charity* (29 January 1966), based on Federico Fellini's *Le Notti di Cabiria* (Nights of Cabiria), was one of the most successful of these and brought a great deal of acclaim to choreographer-director Bob Fosse. Neil Simon Americanized the script into a saga of Charity (Gwen Verdon) and her more worldly cohorts (Helen Gallagher and Thelma Oliver) at the Fan-Dango Ballroom. For "Hey, Big Spender" Fosse lined up his tough corps of hostesses along a railing just over the orchestra pit and gave them the twitchy, grinding posturings that became his choreographic signature. The Cy Coleman score with Dorothy Fields lyrics provided springing-off points for everything from a hippie spiritual, "The Rhythm of Life," to a show-stopping soft-shoe for Charity, "If They Could See Me Now." Among other achievements, *Sweet Charity* refurbished the Palace Theater, reclaiming the famed pinnacle of vaudeville as a legitimate Broadway house.

The blockbusters of the 1960s were nearly all built around a single star. In these productions, Broadway capitalized on the early phase of the dance boom that trained high-caliber performers and inspired a massive following of fans who adored watching them. The 1964 season alone produced three of the biggest shows. Champion directed and choreographed the first. *Hello, Dolly!* (16 January 1964) brought Carol Channing back to her adoring fans and, in a later all-black cast, did the same for Pearl Bailey. The script, adapted from Thornton Wilder's *The Matchmaker,* was accompanied by a Jerry Herman score. In the irrepressible "Waiters' Gallop," Champion had his male dancers leaping back and forth across the orchestra pit from the stage to a ramp in the front rows of the auditorium. *Funny Girl* (26 March 1964), choreographed by Carol Haney, was a star vehicle for Barbra Streisand based on a period telling of the life of comedienne Fanny

UNITED STATES OF AMERICA: Musical Theater. The "Big Spender" number from a 1986 revival of *Sweet Charity* (1966), directed and choreographed by Bob Fosse. (Photograph by Alan Pappé, Lee Gross Inc.; from the Billy Rose Theater Collection, New York Public Library for the Performing Arts.)

Brice. The third and most sensationally popular of the three was *Fiddler on the Roof* (22 September 1964). Directed and staged by Robbins as a lyrical paean to the Jewish family, the cast was headed by Zero Mostel. Another later production in this category was *Mame* (24 May 1966), in which Angela Lansbury played everybody's favorite auntie. Onna White's dances included a death-defying fox hunt and smoothie, 1920s ballroom routines.

Musicals that heralded the future were those that dealt acerbically with the perils of urban life. These were the "now" shows that focused on fast-paced banter, rhythms, and steps. *How to Succeed in Business without Really Trying* (14 October 1961) was staged by Bob Fosse with Hugh Lambert. *Subways Are for Sleeping* (27 December 1961) was choreographed by Michael Kidd. *Promises, Promises* (1 December 1968) introduced another candidate for the top echelon of director-choreographers in Michael Bennett and a composer new to Broadway in Burt Bacharach. Satire and nostalgia were served by *You're a Good Man, Charlie Brown* (7 March 1967) and *Dames at Sea* (20 December 1968). No two choreographers could have been less alike. Patricia Birch, a former Graham dancer, set the rompish movement for the "Peanuts" gang of Charles M. Schulz's comic strip. Neal Kenyan directed and staged the delicious period tap routines for Bernadette Peters and her cronies in *Dames at Sea*.

German decadence with Bertolt Brecht–Kurt Weill overtones set the atmosphere for *Cabaret* (20 November 1966). Ron Field choreographed absinthe-etched numbers, and Joel Grey hosted the proceedings with chilly precision. Grey, an example of the triple-threat singing-dancing actor, gained prominence during the 1960s with spectators who developed a taste for virtuosity. The "Age of Aquarius" arrived with Tom O'Horgan's *Hair* (29 April 1968), the archetypal communal love orgy. To diminish barriers between art and life and to decry the need for technique, the cast invited the audience onstage to participate in the finale.

Rock and Revivals. Economic constrictions became an even greater factor during the 1970s. Inflation spiraled, and the energy crisis affected nearly every aspect of social and professional life. For most of the decade, four patterns could be identified. Rock music and country-western music became increasingly popular in various manifestations. Several outstanding black musicals were mounted. The single director-choreographer retained favor as a cost-effective method of evolving an integrated show. Original scripts and scores were fewer, with producers relying on the revival of proven bonanzas as the way to make profits on their investments.

Gaudy, irreverent *Jesus Christ Superstar* (12 October 1971) not only epitomized the fervency of rock fans, it also heralded the growing preoccupation with technology over human talent in musical theater. The *Superstar* con-

cept started as a two-volume record album of this cultish dramatization of the last seven days of Christ. Andrew Lloyd Webber's music and Tim Rice's lyrics depicted long-haired Jesus, played by Jeff Fenolt, as a poet-prophet whose awesome howls riveted his followers. Staged by Tom O'Horgan, the over-amplified production made it necessary for practically the entire cast to carry hand-held microphones with long, sinewy gray chords. Machines and hallucinatory imagery were the keys to O'Horgan's movement. Ben Vereen as Judas made an entrance on the wings of a gigantic butterfly. At one point the stage floor itself rose in three sections to become a vertical field for crawling and wiggling. Smaller, more trenchant rock productions were *Grease* (14 February 1972) and *Godspell*, the latter an experimental show developed in 1971 at Café La Mama out of a retelling of the gospel according to Matthew. Its success transported it first to the Cherry Lane Theater and then uptown, where it ran until 1977.

The influx of musicals starring black performers began with the near failure of *Ain't Supposed to Die a Natural Death* (20 October 1963). An advertising campaign conducted in black neighborhoods to boost attendance succeeded in attracting a significant new audience to the theater district. Black patrons grew in number with *Purlie* (15 March 1970), a less controversial production with choreography by Cleavon Little. Veteran dance man Donald McKayle did the musical numbers for *Raisin* (18 October 1973), the lyrical version of Lorraine Hansberry's *A Raisin in the Sun*, which had originated at the Arena Stage in Washington, D.C., to open as a successful Broadway show in 1959. A wonderful extravaganza, *The Wiz* (5 January 1975), directed by Geoffrey Holder with dances by George Faison, was a funky retelling of Frank Baum's *The Wonderful Wizard of Oz*. Stephanie Mills, as Dorothy, led the cast in everything from boogie-woogie and tap routines to the latest disco dance fads. Among the shows that capitalized on earlier black dance and music traditions were *Bubblin' Brown Sugar* (2 March 1976), choreographed by Vernon Washington with tap sequences by Bill Robinson; the Fats Waller tribute *Ain't Misbehavin'* (9 May 1978), staged by Arthur Faria; and *Eubie!* (20 September 1978), with dances by Billy Wilson.

Risks were taken with a number of shows. Bob Fosse chose an unlikely hero for *Pippin* (23 October 1972) in the historically curious figure of Charlemagne's young son. The *Pippin* innovation that was to have the greatest consequence was the use of television advertising to sell a musical to the public, a factor that increased ticket sales but also drove up production costs considerably. Another Fosse brainchild was *Dancin'* (27 March 1978), a plotless production led by Ann Reinking in which sixteen performers capitalized on America's absorption with dance. [*See the entry on Fosse.*]

Dancin' had been inspired by the record-breaking bo-

UNITED STATES OF AMERICA: Musical Theater. The original cast of
A Chorus Line (1975). Donna McKechnie is the eighth from right.
(Photograph © by Herbert Migdoll; used by permission.)

nanza of the 1970s, Michael Bennett's *A Chorus Line,* originally produced under the auspices of Joseph Papp's
Shakespeare Festival. The script was based on improvised
material from biographical sketches of dancers—gypsies
whose dreams of stardom began, and sometimes ended,
by making it into a Broadway chorus lineup. On 29 September 1983 *A Chorus Line* completed its 3,389th performance, establishing it as the longest-running legitimate
musical on the American stage. (It would later be over-
taken by *Cats* in the summer of 1997.) At the June 1984
ceremonies in the Gershwin Theater, Bennett received a
special Tony award and was treated to an unusual acco-
lade. The finale from *A Chorus Line* was presented as the
evening's climax, with 332 performers who had appeared
in various editions of the show. [*See the entry on Bennett.*]

Bennett had additional successes, some, financial, others, artistic. *Company* (26 April 1970) used a Sondheim
score to reveal the perils and lonely victories of the urban
swinging singles' scene. The "Tick-Tock Dance" commented wryly on the so-called sexual revolution. *Follies* (4
April 1971), another collaboration with Sondheim, was a
ghostly and beautiful invocation of the Ziegfeld productions as "remembered" by former stars, dancing acts, and
the exquisite show girls who drifted through the Winter
Garden Theater like mythic godesses. The realization of
his short-lived *Ballroom* in 1979 cost Bennett $2 million of
his own money. Although it was a box office disaster, *Ballroom* was critically acclaimed for its sensitive treatment
of middle-aged romance and for its dancers. Most of this

lively corps—all of whom were well past forty—had been
young gypsies in the halcyon days of *Oklahoma!* and
South Pacific. Youth, they proved, was but one aspect of
theatrical magic.

At least one other venturesome production was a big-
scale experiment. *Pacific Overtures* (11 January 1976), a
lavish, sophisticated amalgam of Japanese and American
elements, featured choreography by Patricia Birch, who
had also contributed to the surprising popularity of the
1974 Leonard Bernstein hit, *Candide.* Eighteen years earlier the show had flopped badly, but the peripatetic staging, which took the cast around and through the audience, and Birch's loosely structured dances, added to the
compelling music, gave the newer production its bitter-
sweet appeal.

Less daring revivals of, among others, *Oklahoma!, Peter
Pan,* and *Kismet* (the last disguised as *Timbuktu*), were
gauged to make profits out of nostalgia. Notable among
these was the 1971 revival of *No, No, Nanette,* for which
Busby Berkeley, the legendary mogul of 1930s' movie musicals, came out of retirement to supervise production
numbers. Choreographer Larry Fuller received praise for
both *Sweeney Todd* (1 March 1977) and Andrew Lloyd
Webber's *Evita* (25 September 1979), though neither was
a dance-oriented show. Staging for the musical numbers
in *Annie* (21 April 1977) was created by Peter Gennaro,
whose major work at the time was done with the Rockettes at Radio City Music Hall.

Two of the freshest talents on Broadway were Tommy
Tune and his sometimes choreographic collaborator
Thommie Walsh. *The Best Little Whorehouse in Texas* (19
June 1978), the first popular country and western musi-
cal, started its run at the Entermedia Theater and then

moved to Broadway. The musical showcased two of Tune's funniest dances. One took place in a men's locker room. The other, a parody of football cheerleaders, mixed pneumatic, life-sized puppets with dancers who personified vacuously charming bubbleheads. Tune's lanky ease as a performer was matched by his facility for producing colorful and inventive staging. Two small, madcap productions—*A Day in Hollywood, A Night in the Ukraine* (1 May 1980), created with Walsh, and *Cloud 9* (18 May 1981)—won Tune a considerable following. The production of *Nine* (9 May 1982), directed by Tune and choreographed by Walsh, won five Tony awards. As the star with Twiggy, the British model with whom he had appeared in Ken Russell's film version of *The Boy Friend*, Tune had a resounding success in the updated period musical *My One and Only* (1 May 1983). This production, adapted with Walsh, included songs from Gershwin's 1927 *Funny Face*.

Commerce over Creativity. Recalling Broadway of the Roaring Twenties reveals a sharp contrast with that of the 1980s. Whereas in 1920 there had been premieres of fifty new musicals, the 1982/83 theatrical lineup reflected the worst financial slump in a decade. The fewest premieres in Broadway history were staged the following season. There were only fifteen musicals; four were revivals, and only five of the remainder ran for more than one hundred performances. In a hotly debated 1985 decision, no Tony was awarded for musical theater choreography because no entry in the 1984/85 season was deemed worthy of recognition.

Musical production costs had escalated astronomically because of the rising price of materials, the high wages demanded by union designers and stagehands, and the expense of advertising. Producers appealed to the spectator's visual sense, made keener by film and video spectacles, with hundreds of thousands of dollars worth of scenery, costumes, and special effects. Choreographers had learned how film techniques of montage and cross cuts could be used effectively on stage. The integrated book musical coexisted with less linear narratives that used flashbacks, simultaneous sequences, and fast-forwards at a relentless pace that simulated urban lifestyles.

The average ticket price for a musical had reached $28, and choice seats were $47.50. The financial situation placed strict limits on experimentation and put live Broadway performances out of the reach of thousands of theatergoers. Ironically, this occurred at a time when New York was heralded as the world capital of dance in terms of both creative and performance capabilities. If life in the 1980s was more expensive, it also was more stressful because of new anxieties over the federal budget deficit and random acts of violence by international terrorists. The American Dream seemed to be giving way at the seams. This tension, along with an obsessive drive to succeed,

was evident in the theater. Interest in creating productions of high quality was less evident than the commercial urge to latch onto a Broadway jackpot.

Michael Bennett's *Amadeus* (17 December 1980), a stunning stage production on the life of Mozart, subsequently enjoyed a truly cinematic transposition to the screen. Dances for the movie were created by Twyla Tharp and performed by her company with a sly, tongue-in-cheek nod to eighteenth-century technique and practices. With *Dreamgirls* (20 December 1981), Bennett captured the scheming competition in the Motown capital of the rock empire. His synthesis of black styles with rock and musical theater dance was accomplished in a glittering array of scenic spectacle and special effects.

Another shrewd and glamorous idea was the jazz musical *Sophisticated Ladies* (1 March 1981). Conceived by Donald McKayle, the show had difficulty reaching its premiere and was unable to sustain a satisfying run. Many talented artists were involved. Michael Smuin, then artistic director of the San Francisco Ballet, collaborated with McKayle on direction and choreography; Henry Le Tang staged the tap numbers. Cast members included Hinton Battle, Mercedes Ellington, Gregory Hines, and Judith Jamison, a principal member of the Alvin Ailey American Dance Theater.

The standout seller of the early 1980s was *Cats* (7 October 1982), a bold adaptation of T. S. Eliot's *Old Possum's Book of Practical Cats*, with a score by Andrew Lloyd Webber. Gillian Lynne's choreography had the feline dancers slinking into every cranny of the Winter Garden Theater—even the balcony rail. Her emphasis was on acrobatics and sex appeal, a high-voltage combination that thrilled viewers but resulted in a high incidence of turnovers in the dance corps because of injuries.

An accent on acrobatics and slapstick was Joe Layton's concept for *Barnum* (30 April 1980), built around the British comedian and dancer Jim Dale. Travesty was the gimmick in *La Cage aux Folles* (21 August 1983), with its chorus line of male dancers in show-girl attire. Hinton Battle personally triumphed in *The Tap Dance Kid* (21 December 1983), which featured choreography by Danny Daniels. Graciela Daniele staged dances in the short-lived *The Rink* (9 February 1984), for which Chita Rivera won a Tony.

There were gratifying attempts to reignite a partnership between the commercial and concert stages. The revival of *On Your Toes* (1 May 1983), with musical numbers by Donald Saddler, called on the talents of both the New York City Ballet and American Ballet Theatre. Balanchine's choreography was reconstructed with additional ballet sequences by Peter Martins, by then a ballet master in chief of City Ballet. Ballet Theatre principal George De La Pena appeared in the Ray Bolger part, and Russian *prima ballerina* Natalia Makarova starred. The legendary

"Slaughter on Tenth Avenue" was introduced to a new generation and reentered the New York City Ballet repertory. Two years later Martins choreographed the second, all-dancing act of *Song and Dance* (18 September 1985), with Bernadette Peters and Christopher d'Amboise in the leading roles.

A pair of stage musicals that originated as films reflected a growing demand for novel material that nonetheless had a record of strong audience appeal to protect backers' interests. *Forty-second Street,* adapted from the Berkeley film starring Ruby Keeler, opened in Washington at the Kennedy Center to an unfavorable response. Producer David Merrick and director-choreographer Gower Champion doctored the whole considerably, adding dances and cutting some of the expository material. In one of the more macabre incidents in musical comedy history, Merrick announced Champion's death from the stage following the New York premiere on 25 August 1980. The show was a hit.

Singin' in the Rain (2 July 1985), directed and choreographed by Twyla Tharp, was the most costly production in Broadway history. Its $5-million tab seemed particularly exorbitant when compared to the Ziegfeld spectacles, none of which exceeded $300,000. Based on the all-time favorite movie musical from 1952 starring Gene Kelly, Donald O'Connor, and Debbie Reynolds, the stage version—with Don Correia, Peter Slutsker, and Mary D'Arcy—reconstructed most of the original choreography by Kelly and Stanley Donen. Tharp's skill at making dances for the concert stage, screen, and television was evident only in the second act, which opened with a zany parade of live Hollywood toys that skittered around the stage to several tunes, including "Wedding of the Painted Doll." Later, a wacky interpolation in the movie-within-the-show, *The Dancing Cavalier,* mixed roller skates with the "movie's" period French costumes; and in the finale the full cast cavorted to the title song in bright yellow slickers.

This was Tharp's first directorial assignment. Some of the high points and some of the inherent difficulties stemmed from the problematic relationship between screen and stage. The rushes of *The Dancing Cavalier,* designed and shot by Gordon Willis, were delightfully satiric. The overall production was staged in a style consistent with the pageant approach of musical theater in the mid-1950s, which obliterated the cinematic qualities of the script and many of the musical numbers. *Singin' in the Rain* drew crowds to the 1,992-seat Gershwin Theater largely on the basis of its technology: the famous soft-shoe number in the rain was danced in the most spectacular man-made shower ever produced on stage.

Noncommercial dancing that also mesmerized theatergoers included 1985 appearances by Grand Kabuki of Japan at the Metropolitan Opera House and *Tango Ar-* *gentino* at City Center. Under the direction of Claudio Segovia and Hector Orezzoli, the Argentinian dancers and musicians were such a success in initial New York performances that the ensemble opened at the Mark Hellinger Theater on 9 October 1985 for a six-month run and subsequent national tour.

Bob Fosse's short-lived *Big Deal* (10 April 8–June 1986) won him the 1986 Tony award for Best Choreography, which he shared with his associate Christopher Chadman, and a revival of Fosse's *Sweet Charity* on 27 April at the Minskoff brought additional accolades. The 1986/87 season was notable for the success of *Me and My Girl* (10 August 1986) at the Marquis Theater, with dances by Gillian Gregory, and the failure of *Steppin' Out* (1 January-15 March 1987), a choreographic collaboration by Tommy Tune and Marge Champion. *Starlight Express* (15 March 1987) brought the avant garde focus at the time on stamina and risk to the Great White Way. Arlene Phillips staged the entire production on roller skates, with far more brutal routines than those done three years earlier by Graciela Daniele for *The Rink.*

Modern dance choreographer Lar Lubovitch added hops, skips and gentle jumps to the grownup fairy tales by Stephen Sondheim (music and lyrics) and James Lapine (book and direction) for *Into the Woods* (5 November 1987) at the Martin Beck Theater, with a stunning cast headed by Bernadette Peters as the wicked and very funny witch. The traditional stories of archetypal heroines like Cinderella and Rapunzel were assigned contemporary outcomes, with adultery and random death given equal time to the quiet heroism of peons and mankind's courage to carry on against the emptiness of the unknown. Partly influenced by the October 1987 plunge of the New York Stock Exchange, some of the most admired musicals for the next two years were preoccupied with less-than-gleeful subject matter. Especially distinguished for choreography were Tommy Tune's *Grand Hotel* (12 November 1989) and *City of Angels* (12 December 1989), with musical staging by Walter Painter.

Almost as a talisman, *Singin' in the Rain* seemed to signal the opening of an obsessive Broadway emphasis on revivals, encompassing everything from *Oklahoma!* to Michael Bennett's quite recent *Dreamgirls.* With some significant exceptions between 1984 and 1994, productions from bygone eras seemed to alternate most frequently with new works by Andrew Lloyd Webber, whose scores leave little space outside the emotional pyrotechnics for dancing. Gillian Lynne's staging for *Phantom of the Opera* (26 January 1988) flirted with figures from nineteenth-century Parisian stages and ballrooms, and *Sunset Boulevard,* which reached New York in 1994 by way of London and Los Angeles, was a harmonized version of the movie. The February 1997 announcement by director Harold Prince that Lloyd Webber's *Whistle in the Wind* was "not ready" to open on Broadway as scheduled seemed to herald the end of the British tunester's influence on American audiences.

During the last two decades of the twentieth century, some of the most innovative dance influences in musical theater came from multicultural productions that focused on ethnic styles. *Flamenco Puro* (19 October 1986) was the second offering by Argentinian producers Segovia and Orezzoli, switching in this instance from tango to dazzling flamenco forms. *Oba Oba* (29 March 1987), a Brazilian extravaganza with choreography by Roberto Abrahao, brought Carnival themes and rhythmns to Broadway. *Sarafina!* (28 January 1988) was a presentation from South Africa with dances by Ndaba Mhlongo. *Black and Blue* (26 January 1989), an African-American revue, embellished the stardom of Savion Glover and sported staging and routines by Cholly Atkins, Henry Le Tang, Frankie Manning and Fayard Nicholas of the legendary Nicholas Brothers. Choreographed and directed by Graciela

UNITED STATES OF AMERICA: Musical Theater. Pierre Dulaine as the Gigolo and Yvonne Marceau as the Countess in *Grand Hotel* (1989), directed and choreographed by Tommy Tune. (Photograph by Martha Swope © Time Inc.; used by permission.)

Daniele, *Once on This Island* (18 October 1990) was a Caribbean tale told exclusively through music and dance. Glover was again the headliner for *Jelly's Last Jam* (26 April 1992), with choreography by Hope Clarke and Gregory Hines, and for *Bring in 'da Noise, Bring in 'da Funk*, which moved from the Public Theater—where the production originated—to Broadway in April 1996. *Tommy* and *Grease* in revivals and *Stomp* were principal theatrical interests for rock music lovers.

Other sources beyond Broadway also contributed to dance vitality in the 1990s. American Ballet Theatre acquired Lar Lubovich's *Ballet of the Red Shoes* from the ill-fated musical that closed after a handful of performances in December 1993 and added the piece to the company's spring 1994 season at the Metropolitan Opera House. In that year City Center began Encores!, concert productions of musicals from previous eras that might have limited audience appeal, yet represent significant milestones in the evolution of the American form. *Fiorello!*, featuring a high-stepping number by Christopher Chadman for Donna McKechnie, launched the series. The 1996 Encores! presentation of *Chicago* with Bob Fosse's original choreography, restaged by Ann Reinking, gained such a following that moves to the Richard Rodgers Theater and on to the Shubert Theater were necessary to accommodate crowds that had been missing in the original run in 1975. San Diego's Old Globe Theater brought a delightful revival of *Damn Yankees* to the Marquis Theater in 1994, with dances by Rob Marshall (who staged some of the numbers for *Kiss of the Spider Woman*, the 1993 Tony award for Best Musical), but without the distinguished Fosse choreography. A beautiful 1994 version of Rodgers and Hammerstein's *Carousel* at Lincoln Center's Vivian Beaumont Theater also appeared with some dances by Sir Kenneth MacMillan, yet minus the glorious work of Agnes de Mille. In a day of widespread notation, recording devices and living resources, it seems appropriate to treat a production's choreography with the same respect given to the score and book. While updating may be critical in some instances, in others—especially with regard to work by giants like de Mille and Fosse—re-exposure of the original choreography could prove enlightening to contemporary spectators.

For more than fifty years, Jerome Robbins has been an exalted creative presence in American musicals on stage and screen. His *Jerome Robbins' Broadway*, which opened at the Imperial Theater on 26 February 1989, featured a collection of his finest Broadway choreography mounted under his own supervision. From that production, *West Side Story Suite* entered the repertory of the New York City Ballet. Subsequent editions of his choreography were also seen in revivals that included *Fiddler on the Roof* (1990), *Gypsy* (1991), *Peter Pan* (1991), and *The King and I* (1995).

UNITED STATES OF AMERICA: Musical Theater. Savion Glover as Young Jelly and Gregory Hines as Jelly Roll Morton in the number "The Whole World's Waitin' to Sing Your Song" from the musical *Jelly's Last Jam* (1993). (Photograph by Martha Swope © Time, Inc.; used by permission.)

With a facility that may some day match Robbins's, Susan Stroman gained experience making dances in regional theater, on television, and for such New York City Opera enterprises as the 1991 production of *A Little Night Music*. She choreographed *Crazy for You* (a retake on George Gershwin's *Girl Crazy* that was the recipient of the 1992 Tony award for Best Musical), was also represented on Broadway by Jerome Kern's *Show Boat,* and has won Tony, Drama Desk, and Outer Circle recognition. Stroman made the dances for *Steel Pier* (24 April 1997), which centered on a 1933 dance marathon in Atlantic City. With a background similar to Stroman's, Lynne Taylor-Corbett choreographed *Titanic* (23 April 1997).

The New Forty-Second Street, a ten-year urban renewal project undertaken by the City of New York, implies a lively and changing profile for musical theater in Times Square. Following an $11.5 million renovation, the New Victory Theater opened on 11 December 1995 with a mandate to commission and to produce entertainment for children and families. On 29 April 1996, *Rent*—acclaimed as the most creative musical of the 1990s—opened one block away on Forty-first Street at the Nederlander Theater. In April 1997, Disney reopened Florenz Ziegfeld's fabled New Amsterdam Theater with *The Lion King* in a production for the stage by Julie Taymor, whose *Juan Darién* won critical praise during a short holiday run in 1996 at the Vivian Beaumont Theater. Another milestone in this undertaking, the Ford Center for the Performing Arts opened with a production of *Ragtime* on 26 December 1997. While a low point for dance on Broadway may have occurred when Stephen Sondheim's *Passion,* winner of the 1994 Tony for Best Musical, had no dancing at all, the direction for the twenty-first century points to increased collaboration among dance artists in commercial, film, and concert performance venues.

[*See also* Film Musicals, *article on* Hollywood Film Musicals; Tap Dance; Vaudeville; *and the entries on* Astaire, Berkeley, Bernstein, Dunham, Hines, Holm, Kidd, McKayle, Martins, Primus, Tharp, *and* Tune.]

BIBLIOGRAPHY

Block, Geoffrey. *Enchanted Evenings: The Broadway Musical from "Show Boat" to Sondheim.* New York, 1997.

Bordman, Gerald. *American Musical Theatre: A Chronicle.* New York, 1978.

Gänzl, Kurt. *The Encyclopedia of Musical Theatre.* 2 vols. New York, 1994.

Hardy, Camille. "Bessie Clayton: An American Genée." *Dance Chronicle* 2.4 (1978–1979): 251–278.

Hardy, Camille. "The American Debut of Adeline Genée." In *New Directions in Dance,* edited by Diana Theodores Taplin. Toronto, 1979.

Hardy, Camille. "Ballet Girls and Broilers." *Ballet Review* 1.1 (1980): 96–127.

Hardy, Camille. "Art Dancing on Broadway: Loie Fuller in *A Trip to Chinatown.*" In *Musical Theatre in America,* edited by Glenn Loney. Westport, Conn., 1984.

Kirstein, Lincoln, et al. *Choreography by George Balanchine: A Catalogue of Works.* New York, 1983.

Smith, Cecil, and Glenn Litton. *Musical Comedy in America.* 2d ed. New York, 1981.

Traubner, Richard. *Operetta: A Theatrical History.* Garden City, N.Y., 1983.

ARCHIVES. Dance Collection and Theater Collection, New York Public Library for the Performing Arts.

CAMILLE HARDY

Ballet Education

The teaching of classical ballet in the United States began around 1830. Before then, retired dancers occasionally took pupils, most often the children of theatrical families, to train in their own sitting rooms, and professional performers and ballet masters trained apprentices on dimly lit, off-duty theater stages. In 1837, Paul H. Hazard, a retired dancer trained at the Paris Opera, established a ballet school in Philadelphia. Augusta Maywood and Mary Ann Lee were among his first pupils. French-trained ballet dancers Jules Martin and Eugénie Lecomte (his sister) also opened a school in Philadelphia. Charles Durang, son of America's first native dancer, John Durang, added ballet to the ballroom dancing he and his wife taught in Philadelphia. Pauline Desjardins, a member of Fanny Elssler's company, remained after the 1841 tour to teach in New York. All through the 1840s, European ballet dancers toured America. Most of them took themselves and their dollars back across the Atlantic, but a few remained to teach French, fencing, and dance.

In 1852, Léon Espinosa, then twenty-seven years old and finished with his studies at the Paris Opera, was the ballet master for a troupe that danced a varied repertory for an entire season in the Varieties Theatre in Saint Louis, Missouri. Espinosa enlarged his company, teaching the Americans he recruited with a notice that read, "Young ladies wanted to dance in *La Bayadère*." Giuseppina Morlacchi, trained at the Teatro alla Scala in Milan, came to New York in 1867 to dance in *The Devil's Auction,* and subsequently headed her own company. In the 1880s she taught in Lowell, Massachusetts. These teachers were all trained in the methods and traditions of the Paris Opera and Milan's La Scala with its roots in the codified technique of Carlo Blasis. Their students, however, were not motivated by anything beyond the elementary dance training needed for a career in the music halls. J. F. Cardella, who reported in an interview that he had studied with Blasis, was ballet master of the Theatre Comique in Saint Louis in 1879, where he directed and taught the locally recruited corps de ballet. He gave three-hour classes but deplored the lack of technique and noted that there was no "sideboard practice." Indeed, *barre* work was a rarity in American dance schools until the twentieth century.

A demand for female dancers developed when versions of *The Black Crook,* a musical extravaganza, proliferated and toured. Because badly trained female dancers were employed, the public gained an inaccurate idea of ballet. The original *Black Crook* ballerina, La Scala–trained Marie Bonfanti, opened a school in New York in 1897, where she taught until 1916. In the wake of *The Black Crook,* extravaganzas were popular and toured the country in the last decades of the nineteenth century. In 1876, Elizabeth Menzeli was the dance star of *Ali Baba.* She retired to teach in New York and New Jersey (and, much later, in Cleveland). The Bonfanti and Menzeli schools had stability, and ballet was taught in a manner consistent with academy traditions. To judge from pictures of the classes and the caliber of the students, their activities could honestly be regarded as classical ballet.

The political upheavals in Europe in the 1870s sent many immigrants to the United States. Among these were dance masters who brought with them the new educational idea of "aesthetic gymnastics." The new Americans established dancing academies in many cities, especially in the Midwest. They featured ballroom dancing and included drills and "fancy dancing," the latter being neither ballroom nor folk but a free form that had elements of ballet and *demi-caractère.* The clientele of these academies was middle class, and the dance masters were respected members of the community, socially notches above the theatrical "maestros" who were never part of the mainstream.

In 1879, the American Society of Professors of Dancing was formed, followed in 1883 by the American National Association of Dancing Masters (later Dancing Masters of America). At their annual conventions, ballroom dance trends were a major concern, but, aware of changing demands, the organizations also engaged experts to teach dances suitable for fancy dancing. Eventually, the need for instruction of technique was recognized, and the only technique known was that of classical ballet. Therefore, the organizations hired noted ballet masters such as Stefano Mascagno to teach the dance masters during the convention. For many years, Mascagno was "convention principal" of the Dancing Masters of America.

At these conventions some of the dancing masters acquired the fundamentals of ballet technique to bring back to their pupils in such cities as Omaha, Kansas City, Cincinnati, and Portland. Friedrich Albert Zorn's *The Grammar of the Art of Dancing* (1887) was the authoritative reference for terminology and technique. By 1930, members in the dance masters' organizations numbered in the hundreds and, although the classical ballet taught in their schools was limited and quite elementary, the associations invited fine teachers to serve on the convention faculties. Such artists as Michel Fokine, Adolph Bolm,

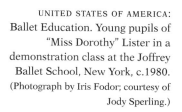

UNITED STATES OF AMERICA: Ballet Education. Young pupils of "Miss Dorothy" Lister in a demonstration class at the Joffrey Ballet School, New York, c.1980. (Photograph by Iris Fodor; courtesy of Jody Sperling.)

Muriel Stuart, and Catherine Littlefield planted seeds that later bore fruit.

New theories of child psychology and new ideas about physical education for girls developed at the turn of the century. Dance was recommended for both the naturally active child and for girls, who now attended high schools and colleges in greater numbers. "Normal" courses for teachers offered a dilute form of ballet with simple steps and positions; *jeté, arabesque,* and *pirouette* were taught with no *barre* work and nary a thought of placement. The subject matter was "material," that is, these were simple dances with no concern for technique. However, with the normal courses, dance attained a measure of respect in the educational world.

Inevitably, individual interest and ambition were aroused. Some pupils sought more exact training. They went to the professional dancing academies, where astute ballroom teachers included classical ballet in their offerings. The teachers of ballet classes were too often poorly prepared. Conditions were aggravated by cement-hard toe shoes. Toe dancing of an excruciatingly bad type discredited classical ballet.

However, a distinctly new type of American dance instructor developed: young women trained as physical education teachers who became deeply interested in dance, studied more, and gained honest perceptions of the art. They became excellent teachers, left the gymnasiums, and opened their own dance studios. Edna McRae of Chicago is a notable example.

To train dancers for opera ballets, the Metropolitan Opera Ballet in New York started a school in 1909, directed first by Malvina Cavallazzi, who taught ballet of a decent level. The Chicago and San Francisco operas had no official schools until the 1920s. However, when Andreas Pavley and Serge Oukrainsky became the ballet masters of the Chicago Grand Opera Company in 1916, they conducted their own school, which trained dancers

for the opera ballet. As they expanded, many American teachers studied with them, especially in their summer quarters in South Haven, Michigan. The South Haven location was one of the first vacation-site dance schools, initiating a fashion for dance camps.

Classical training in the United States received its greatest impetus from Russian ballet. First came Anna Pavlova, whose dancing struck sparks wherever she appeared. The 1917 Russian Revolution led several noted ballet dancers to settle eventually in the United States, conduct classes in established schools, and found their own schools. These included Fokine, Bolm, Theodore Koslov, Mikhail Mordkin, and Bronislava Nijinska. They focused attention on classical ballet as an art.

From 1910 to 1930, opportunities for careers in dance attracted many students to dance schools. Vaudeville, which presented theatrical acts of many kinds, was America's most popular entertainment. The existence of several hundred vaudeville theaters in the land created a demand for performers, and ballet dancers, both excellent and mediocre, worked regularly. Another prime source of employment was the "stage show" or "prologue" presented between film screenings in dozens of magnificent new "cinema palaces." Many theaters hired ballet groups for year-round work, while others brought in touring units or shows that included ballet groups.

In the fall of 1933, Colonel W. de Basil's Ballets Russes de Monte Carlo appeared in New York and then toured the country. It toured annually, soon followed by the Littlefield Ballet, Lincoln Kirstein's Ballet Caravan, Ballet Theatre, and Serge Denham's Ballet Russe de Monte Carlo. These touring companies had a profound effect on the teaching of classical ballet. Inspired students came to ballet schools with ambitions to dance in companies. Though male students did not exactly flock to classes, the number studying classical ballet increased. More attention was paid to strengthening and purifying technique, particularly in the matter of turnout, line, and footwork. Virtuosity was encouraged. The practice costume changed. Gone were the tunics, tutus, bloomers, and rompers. Tights and leotards became the rule.

Of special significance was the founding of the School of American Ballet in 1934 under the direction of Lincoln Kirstein and George Balanchine with a faculty that included George Balanchine, Pierre Vladimiroff, and then Muriel Stuart, Anatole Oboukhoff, and Dorothie Littlefield, among others. The prime function of the school is the training of dancers for the New York City Ballet in the style developed by Balanchine. In the decades since its founding the faculty has been increased, especially with retired New York City Ballet dancers. The prestige of the school, the quality of the teachers, and the standards of technique affected the teaching of ballet, especially with new summer courses for dance teachers. At the School of American Ballet, more attention was paid to placement and turnout. Footwork was fastidious. Speed and suppleness were cultivated. Line became more elegant. Variations from classical repertory and supported adagio were taught, influencing scores of schools to do the same. There was a new selectivity of students: the petite feminine female was superseded by the sleek, long-limbed young woman with high extensions.

The School of American Ballet trains dancers in the Balanchine-approved style of dancing that company's repertory. Other companies have developed similar schools. Many ballets including the Joffrey, San Francisco, Boston, Houston, Pittsburgh, Tulsa, Colorado, and Milwaukee train students to perform in their companies.

Because of the expanding interest and respect for classical dance, ballet has been invited into U.S. colleges. An academic interest has legitimated the history of ballet and the philosophy of its styles. More surprising is the acceptance of ballet as a physical movement science to be taught by a knowledgeable faculty.

Ballet teachers in colleges often are retired dancers whose prestigious performing, directing, or choreographing careers are accepted as experience in lieu of the academic degrees required of most university faculty members. Notable among them have been Willam Christensen (University of Utah), George Verdak and William Glen (Butler University), Lawrence Rhodes (New York University), Elisabeth Carroll (Skidmore College), Jean-Pierre Bonnefous (Indiana University), Igor Youskevitch and Leon Danielian (University of Texas at Austin), George Zoritch (University of Arizona), Nicholas Petroff and Kenneth Johnson (Point Park College), and Carol Walker (succeeding Royes Fernandez at the State University of New York at Purchase).

Many performing artists have recently settled down as teachers. Their broad experiences, including dancing in ballets by several imaginative choreographers, are re-flected in an eclectic style of ballet that recognizes many new elements. Increasingly lithe and freer torsos are emphasized, and some teachers cultivate greater virtuosity—multiple pirouettes, high extensions, and great jumps.

The faculty of the School of the Arts at the University of North Carolina, Chapel Hill, originally directed by Robert Lindgren, exemplifies many of these trends. Although they did not emphasize virtuosity, an appreciation of a wide range of ballet influences was taught by Bentley Stone and Walter Camryn, who conducted a school in Chicago for forty years and whose many students, now teachers, are carrying on these precepts. One of Camryn's innovative courses was American Character Dance, in which the gait and style of folk dances of several regions was taught. Among the teachers with original and eclectic styles have been Benjamin Harkarvy, Maggie Black, Carmelita Maracci, and Loyce Houlton. Eclecticism is common, but some do teach distinctive methods and styles. From England's Royal Ballet have come Margaret Craske in New York, Stanley Holden in California, Christine DuBoulay and Richard Ellis in Chicago, and several, such as Ben Stevenson in Houston, who conduct schools in connection with companies. The Bournonville style is not the sole one in any school as yet, but guests such as Kirsten Ralov and Kirsten Simone have introduced the style in several schools. The former Soviet style of Russian ballet, as distinct from the Imperial Ballet style of the first wave of Russians, was taught by Valentina Pereyaslavec and Alexander Mintz; with freedom to travel after the breakup of the Soviet Union in 1991, many Soviet-trained teachers came to the United States.

Modern dance has been finding ballet amenable and has in turn influenced classical ballet. Some of its elements were in the plastique exercises once presented by Muriel Stuart at the School of American Ballet. Many ballet schools now have special classes of modern dance. But more noteworthy is the fact that modern dance has influenced the range of classical ballet. Some teachers introduce subtle modifications into the execution of standard steps, and they also invent movements based on ballet technique that employ a more lithe torso and expressive arms.

The study of classical ballet has emerged from the sitting rooms and twilight theater stages of colonial times to large, airy studios with special floors and competent faculties. Hundreds of dedicated students perform their *pliés*, *battements tendus*, and so on—and not exactly in the same old ways.

BIBLIOGRAPHY.   Ann Barzel, "European Dance Teachers in the United States," *Dance Index* 3 (April–June 1944): 56–100, is the only systematic history of classical training in America. But various articles and particularly the advertisements in dance teacher periodicals reveal a great deal about the teaching of ballet in America from the turn of the century. Some of these are *The Two Step* (Buffalo, N.Y., 1890s); *The Ballroom* (Kansas City,

Mo., 1896–1897); *The Dancing Master* (St. Joseph, Mo., 1900–1901); *Terpsichorean* (Chicago, c.1918–1920s); *The Dancing Master* (Chicago, 1920s); *Dance Lovers* (New York, 1920s); *The Dance* (New York, 1929–1931); *The American Dancer* (Calif. and New York, 1930s); and *Dance Magazine* (New York, 1940s–). The Newberry Library, Chicago, contains an extensive archive of such periodicals, as well as other dance memorabilia.

ANN BARZEL

Social, Folk, and Modern Dance Education

In the United States, dance training exists in general education, recreational, and professional contexts. Dance in general education has been important since colonial times with each era focusing on what would best reflect the predominant ideals of the day. Recreational dance has been enjoyed by people of all classes also from colonial times and may or may not involve formal training. The preparation of professional dancers for the stage, while introduced on a limited basis early in the nation's history, has proliferated in the twentieth century.

Ballroom dance, for example, was important to the colonial aristocracy and to succeeding social elites as well as those who aspired to them. Folk and popular dances were adapted to educational purposes in the wake of nineteenth-century democratization. Modern and creative dance came to the fore with middle-class progressive education of the twentieth century. Related, but not always parallel to general education curriculums, private teachers and specialized institutions have offered a range of techniques, including social dances; theatrical dance forms; and, to a lesser extent, dances from the international arena. Recreation departments and some religious organizations similarly have covered the gamut of dance genres but with emphasis on social and folk dance.

The development of dance education has been cumulative. By the 1980s all kinds of dance were being offered in the various settings. Popularity makes some genres more available at certain times than others, but in major urban areas classes in all types of dance are offered.

Social Dance. The colonists brought their social dances with them from the Old World, and by the late seventeenth century American society was sufficiently developed to support formal training in the art. Despite sporadic attacks by moralists, the urban and rural gentry followed European tradition and included dance in their children's education. Dance was justified in terms of educational functions: it fostered good carriage and gentle manners, instilled a sense of form in life, and prepared one to be an acceptable member of society.

Proper dance skill and behavior were taught by English, French, and American dance masters in pupils' homes, in taverns or other rented rooms, and in schools, colleges, and military academies. Basing his instruction on European theory and practice, the master taught his students the minuet, cotillon, rigaudon, hornpipe, and country dances, and he also served as master of ceremonies at balls. Colonial diaries, letters, wills, financial records, and newspapers contain numerous references to dance masters and dance occasions as well as some mentions of dance treatises.

Throughout the nineteenth century, social dancing continued to be a popular activity for all classes of Americans in every region. As the new nation grew, so did the number of dance teachers and schools to serve those who could afford such training: the wealthy, of course, and the growing middle class. Despite some opposition, social dancing was still promoted for training in grace and manners—and for its value as exercise. It continued to be offered in private schools and academies, but for many leaders in the burgeoning field of public education, it was frivolous, had an elitist orientation, and was suspected of posing a risk to public health and morals. When dance finally entered nineteenth-century public education, it was in the context of physical education; social aspects of the dance experience were minimized.

By the end of the nineteenth century, dance teaching was an established profession with organizations and a growing body of literature. With the founding in 1879 of the American Society of Professors of Dancing and of other national organizations, dance teachers gained a means of accreditation, a forum for the exchange of ideas and dances, and the strength of numbers to promote policies and standards. The publication of numerous articles and books by dance teachers also contributed to the respectability of the profession and to the level of knowledge and theory within it.

Important leaders in nineteenth-century dance education included Melvin Ballou Gilbert, Allen Dodworth, A. E. Bournique, and Carl Marweg. Gilbert (1847–1910) taught for forty years in New England, wrote books, and founded and edited *The Director* (1897–1898), one of the earliest known dance magazines in the United States. Gilbert was typical of his profession in that he taught not only ballroom dance but also related subjects, such as etiquette, stage and exhibition dancing, teaching methods, and what he called "aesthetic calisthenics."

Interest in social dance continued in the twentieth century, and the rapid succession of new dance fashions usually ensured the stability of social dance teaching as a profession. Also since many of the popular dances of the twentieth century were first danced on stage or screen in forms too difficult for the public, the professional teacher has profited from adapting such dances for general use. A temporary decline was suffered from the 1950s to the 1970s, however, when dance styles became improvisatory.

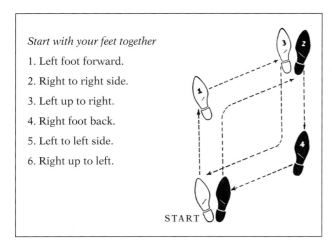

Start with your feet together

1. Left foot forward.
2. Right to right side.
3. Left up to right.
4. Right foot back.
5. Left to left side.
6. Right up to left.

START

UNITED STATES OF AMERICA: Social, Folk, and Modern Dance Education. Drawings of footprints were a signature part of Arthur Murray's instructional method, allowing students to learn dances on their own. The diagram here shows the box step of the rumba. (Reprinted from Arthur Murray, *How to Become a Good Dancer*, New York, 1947, p. 140.)

The twentieth-century social dance teacher taught in many contexts: secondary schools, in higher education, and for recreation departments, churches, and community centers. By far the most important setting has been the private studio or dance studio chain (such as those associated with Fred Astaire and Arthur Murray). In contrast to earlier times—when social graces were perceived as the concomitants of social dance skill—twentieth-century ballroom dance schools emphasized attractiveness to the opposite sex in their advertising.

In the late twentieth century, mature adults sought instruction in what were by then thought of as "classical" ballroom dances, such as the waltz, fox trot, and tango. Young people, in contrast, usually only wanted to learn what was new and popular. After nearly two decades of individual improvisation in the rock-and-roll era, young people in the late 1970s were drawn to dances that once again involved skill and coordination with a partner. Both disco dancing and country and western dances required instruction and practice. At the same time, young people developed a new interest in traditional ballroom dances and in certain "fad" dances of the past, such as swing, Lindy Hop, mambo, and cha-cha. As a consequence of both developments, the ballroom dance teacher regained importance in the social dance scene. [*For related discussion, see* Social Dance, *articles on nineteenth- and twentieth-century social dance.*]

From Gymnastics to Folk Dance. Physical education began to develop in the 1820s in tandem with public education, and it featured heavy gymnastics training for robust men and lighter programs for women, children, and sedentary men. The latter systems, as exemplified by Catharine Beecher's calisthenics and Dio Lewis's "New Gymnastics," were accompanied by music, but their creators disclaimed any relation to dancing. After 1865 heavy gymnastics for men began to include exercises that were based on folk dance steps. This "gymnastic dance" was eventually introduced into physical education training schools, and from there it made its way into the public school curriculum. Modern counterparts to such conditioning exercise set to music are jazzercise and aerobic dance.

From the 1880s onward, educators sought to adapt known dance material to educational goals. In these early years there was apparently no interest in presenting authentic folk or popular dances as cultural artifacts or artistic entities. Rather, selected patterns were extrapolated for their presumed effectiveness in physical training and conditioning. In 1887, for example, William G. Anderson introduced at his Brooklyn Normal School of Gymnastics a dance course incorporating step patterns he had learned from his study of Irish, Dutch, and southern black folk dances. In the same year, Dudley A. Sargent engaged Christian Eberhard of the Boston Turnverein to teach gymnastics dance at the Harvard School of Physical Education. Then, in 1894, Sargent introduced Gilbert's "aesthetic calisthenics" (later called "aesthetic dancing"), which was an adaptation of ballet, social, and folk dance steps and was widely used in women's physical education courses until approximately 1915.

After 1900 folk dance continued to be important in the curriculum. Specialists began to collect and notate actual dances from various nationalities. The material came to be valued educationally not only for its contribution to physical conditioning but also for the understanding it provided of different cultures and past eras. Early leaders of the folk dance movement, such as Elizabeth Burchenal, Mary Wood Hinman, and Louis Chalif, conducted research, published collections of dances, trained teachers, and were active in professional organizations.

Folk dance instruction takes place in various settings. In elementary education it is often tied in with multicultural studies and the production of festivals. The majority of U.S. colleges and universities have folk dance courses or clubs where dances are regularly taught. Churches or fraternal organizations with a national orientation—such as Greek, Armenian, or Russian—and synagogues often provide training to strengthen cultural identity, and the traditional dances usually are enjoyed by those of all ages at both religious and secular festivities. In addition a nationwide network of recreational folk dance clubs and organizations sponsors dance events and courses, publishes magazines, directories, and dance descriptions, and sets standards of teaching and authenticity. Teachers of folk dance include nonspecialists, such as elementary school teachers; international or area folk dance specialists who constantly increase their own repertory by attending special courses both in the United States and abroad; and native dancers who have inherited a folk dance tradition and teach solely from their own heritage.

Folk dance as it has been described herein is a social activity for the participants, not a display for observers. Character dance (balletic versions of folk dance patterns) was a part of ballet from its beginning, and dances with various national motifs were featured in popular stage entertainments. Only in the twentieth century were folk or ethnic dance ensembles established. Training for participation in an ensemble is specialized, rigorous, and performance-oriented and usually is conducted or at least supervised by the ensemble director. Although some of these ensembles are professional, most are amateur and connected with a university, church, recreation center, or national community group. A prominent example is the Duquesne University Tamburitzans, which is made up of young dancers and musicians who receive university scholarships in exchange for their participation.

Modern and Creative Dance. By the early twentieth century, dance was generating much interest among educators. In 1905 it was chosen as a theme for the American Physical Education Association's New York convention, which featured folk and popular dances and Gilbert's aesthetic dance. The cause of dance was taken up also by such figures as G. Stanley Hall, leading Darwinian educator and psychologist, who widened the perspective on dance by emphasizing that its benefits were not necessarily limited to the physical but could be psychological, intellectual, moral, and emotional as well.

With the progressive education movement that reached full development in the twentieth century came an emphasis on self-direction, self-expression, and creativity in the educational process. Seeking a more creative approach to dance, physical educators sought ideas from American Delsartism, Dalcroze eurhythmics, the dancing of Isadora Duncan, and the productions of Denishawn. They developed a kind of dance that was educational but included theatrical performance, emphasized expression but also included technique, and offered creative opportunities but also developed discipline.

The first influential figure in the new educational dance was Gertrude Colby of Teachers College, Columbia University. Active from 1913 to 1931, Colby trained hundreds of teachers in a nontechnical approach to movement expression that she called "natural dance." The most important center for the continuing development of what was new and progressive in educational dance was the University of Wisconsin at Madison. In 1917 Margaret H'Doubler began to work on an approach to educational dance based on scientific physical principles, a problem-solving instructional method, and a belief in the value of individual creativity. It was soon offered in a physical education course and then in a teacher-training program. Finally, in 1927, Wisconsin established the first dance major to be offered in an institution of higher education.

An important aspect of the Wisconsin program was Orchesis, a club first organized in 1918 to present performances in the new idiom. The result of learning and creativity was the finished dance piece—an art product. The Orchesis idea stimulated much interest among students in the new dance and spread to other institutions. Dance courses and Orchesis groups began to appear in colleges and universities throughout the country from the early 1920s on.

Since that time dance departments and major programs have proliferated in colleges and universities. The main offering has continued to be some form of modern dance, although the curriculum often includes other dance techniques, theory and history courses, notation, and related subjects. Some of the historically influential dance departments have been at Bennington College (Bennington, Vermont), Ohio State University (Columbus), Mills College (Oakland, California), Sarah Lawrence (Bronxville, New York), the University of California at Los Angeles, and, in the conservatory setting, at the Juilliard School in New York City.

Summer schools of dance have been particularly important in promoting modern dance along with other theatrical dance forms. The Bennington School of Dance (1934–1939), for example, offered instruction and new works by the great modern dance innovators such as Martha Graham and Doris Humphrey. Also important have been the American Dance Festival (first at Connecticut College), the Perry-Mansfield School, Jacob's Pillow, and the summer program at Colorado College under the direction of Hanya Holm. Countless teachers as well as performers have been trained in these programs. The consequent effect on dance education has been enormous, as the aesthetic principles, artistic standards, technical systems, and choreographic approaches of the professional dance world have been disseminated to educational institutions throughout the United States. [*See* American Dance Festival; Bennington School of the Dance; *and* Jacob's Pillow.]

From the beginning there has been a close collaboration between modern dance departments in higher education and professional modern dance artists. The professionals have depended on the universities for teaching stints and performance engagements, and the educators have valued the stimulus from the professional world—even though at times they have questioned how closely educational dance should emulate the professional. That question has receded, however, as professional training in the arts has gradually made a place for itself in the academic setting. As a result, dance departments have moved from physical education into the fine arts and have begun to train to professional standards and for professional careers.

Modern dance in higher education has been a nation-wide phenomenon. The important and influential departments are scattered throughout the country, and there is a network of communication through organizations, publications, conferences, touring groups, visiting teachers, and changing personnel. The educational dance world has variety, optimism, dynamic growth, and artistic validity that makes it a significant element in the United States cultural scene.

Modern dance has been offered in other educational settings but to a lesser degree. Private studios offering modern dance can hardly exist outside of urban areas, such as New York or Boston. Modern dance, however, is often a part of high school physical education programs, some of which include the Orchesis type of public presentation. There are also a few professional performing arts high schools, the High School of Performing Arts in New York City, for example, where modern dance is featured. Creative children's dance, an offshoot of modern dance, is sometimes offered in primary schools, in recreation programs, or by private dance teachers.

At the end of the twentieth century, except among those communities whose religion forbids dancing, almost every American was in contact with some facet of dance education. In its many manifestations, training in dance has become a ubiquitous part of American culture.

[*See also* Delsarte System of Expression.]

BIBLIOGRAPHY

Casey, Betty. *International Folk Dancing U.S.A.* Garden City, N.Y., 1981.

Dancemagazine College Guide 1996–1997: A Directory to Dance in North American Colleges and Universities. New York, 1996.

Kraus, Richard, Sarah Chapman Hilsendagger, and Brenda Dixon. *History of the Dance in Art and Education.* 3d ed. Englewood Cliffs, N.J., 1991.

Marks, Joseph E., III. *America Learns to Dance: A Historical Study of Dance Education in America before 1900.* New York, 1957.

O'Brien, Dorothy Adella. "Theoretical Foundations of Dance in American Higher Education, 1885–1932." Ph.D. diss., University of Southern California, 1966.

Rogers, Frederick R., ed. *Dance: A Basic Educational Technique.* New York, 1941.

Ruyter, Nancy Lee Chalfa. *Reformers and Visionaries: The Americanization of the Art of Dance.* New York, 1979.

NANCY LEE CHALFA RUYTER

Dance Research and Publication

As in most other countries, dance scholars in the United States began with enthusiasm and learned their skills along the way. As late as the 1930s, American universities offered no courses in dance history, and those libraries that possessed a few serious books on dance shelved them next to treatises on other "physical" activities, such as basketball and swimming, where casual researchers would hardly be likely to discover them.

But in 1928, Lillian Moore, then a young dancer with the Metropolitan Opera Ballet, found her way to the New York Public Library and between rehearsals began investigating her professional heritage. After old newspapers and magazines yielded their treasurers to her, she traveled to find descendants of legendary performers and sought out long-forgotten names and dates on long-neglected gravestones. Although she did not live to complete her comprehensive history of American dance, her individual studies in Americana remain invaluable, as do her essays on styles of ballet technique. [*See the entry on Moore.*]

Also in the 1920s, a young graduate of Harvard had discovered the ballet. Lincoln Kirstein involved himself in many forms of art as producer, director, and writer but still found time to publish America's first major book of dance history in 1935. From the beginning he favored classical ballet—its discipline, clarity, and purity. In later books he continued his proselytizing as he developed his early themes with fervor and erudite brilliance. [*See the entry on Kirstein.*]

Countering Kirstein's preference for ballet, John Martin promoted the new modern dance, not only in the pages of the *New York Times* but also in books, such as *The Modern Dance* (1933), that allowed him to probe more deeply into the nature of this expressive style and into the kinesthetic experience of its audience. Martin was the first American to formulate a theory of dance based on its communicative powers and, as such, deserves more attention than he has received from aestheticians. From 1934 to 1937 Martin taught a course in dance history at the Bennington School of the Dance in Vermont. [*See the entry on Martin.*]

Paul Magriel's pioneering effort in documenting American dance, *A Bibliography of Dancing*, was published in 1936, but few serious dance books appeared in the 1930s and 1940s. The field was not ready for them.

The dance audience was growing, however, and in time the fan books began to appear—ballet stories, elementary technique manuals, picture books, and biographies full of adulation but often lacking accurate, factual information. *Dance Magazine* (then titled *The American Dancer*), the oldest and long the most popular dance publication, began in 1927 under the aegis of Ruth Eleanor Howard. At first focused on the needs of the teacher and later of the performer, the periodical soon sought to serve the dance audience as well by offering reviews. *Dance News*, started in 1942 by Anatole Chujoy, who was later joined by P. W. Manchester, favored an elitist, ballet-oriented readership; although concerts in other dance forms were reviewed, they were not featured. For future historians these early publications would provide significant insights into America's attitude toward theatrical dance in the early decades of the twentieth century. A beginning had been made.

As the dance audience grew in size, it became more heterogeneous. New members of that audience—teachers and scholars working in such fields as art, music, and theater history—were disappointed to find so little academic discipline applied to their new area of interest. Unable to find the books they wanted, they set out to write their own. Musicologists explored the dances of the Middle Ages and the Renaissance. Some mavericks appeared: a professor of ancient Greek, Lillian Lawler, produced the authoritative study of Grecian dance, *The Dance in Ancient Greece* (1954); a nun, Sister Mary Grace Swift, wrote the authoritative biography of Charles-Louis Didelot, *A Loftier Flight* (1973).

The group of dancers interested in dance history grew as well and, in time, they had more opportunities to pursue their interests. By the mid-1990s more than one hundred American colleges and universities offered at least a one-year survey course in dance history, and many had graduate courses. The University of Chicago pioneered graduate study with three summer seminars from 1974 to 1976. York University in Toronto, Canada, was the first to offer a continuing graduate program, initiated in 1971 by Grant Strate. Christena Schlundt established a master's degree curriculum at the University of California, Riverside, in 1981; a Ph.D. program was launched there in 1993. New York University also began to offer degrees in dance through its departments of education and performance studies.

Although extensive interest in dance scholarship is of recent origin, enterprising individuals have been sponsoring serious periodicals for some time. In 1934 Louis Horst founded the *Dance Observer,* a monthly magazine devoted primarily to modern dance. The magazine survived until Horst's death in 1964. Although it consisted largely of reviews, some theoretical and analytical articles appeared as well; a notable contribution was "Symbolism and the Dance" by mythologist Joseph Campbell. From 1942 to 1948 Lincoln Kirstein, assisted for some years by Marian Eames, edited *Dance Index,* which presented the results of important historical research and original theorizing, most of it devoted to classical ballet. In its seven years of publication, only a single issue—the last in the entire series of monthly monographs—was devoted to non-Western dance: Colin McPhee's "Dance in Bali."

Dance Perspectives (1959–1976) also published monographs. Founded by A. J. Pischl and edited by Selma Jeanne Cohen, the quarterly journal covered a wider range than had *Dance Index* and devoted one issue each year to a form of ethnic dance. It also produced several symposium-like issues, such as those on music for dance, dance films, and dance aesthetics. *Ballet Review* (1965–), edited first by Arlene Croce and later by Francis Mason, has specialized in well-written, often provocative, articles dealing with contemporary issues and performances.

Dance Research Journal has been published by the Congress on Research in Dance since 1974. Its early issues, co-edited by Lois Andreasen and Elizabeth Burtner, concentrated on educational and ethnological subjects. In the 1980s the scope widened to cover theatrical dance. Since its founding in 1977, *Dance Chronicle,* which is focused on Western theatrical dance, with forays into music and scene design, has been co-edited by Jack Anderson and George Dorris. Although *Ballet News* (1979–1986) was devoted largely to reviews, editor Karl Reuling managed to produce some special issues dealing with historical context, as in the issue devoted to the August Bournonville centennial.

As interest in dance developed, more periodicals were produced. Among them was *Studies in Dance History,* a biannual series of monographs, initiated in 1990 by the Society of Dance History Scholars and first edited by Barbara Palfy. Most of the issues have been devoted to in-depth research of areas of Western theatrical dance. Two provocative journals dealing with the contemporary dance scene are *Dance Ink,* edited by Lise Friedman from 1990 to 1996, and *Dance View,* edited by Alexandra Tomalonis since 1992.

American dance historians have made their primary contributions in the area of fact-finding. The methodologies that were initially applied to dance research evolved from other disciplines. The first model came from anthropologists who incorporated analyses of dances into their investigations of ethnic groups. A prominent example was Ruth Benedict's *Patterns of Culture* (1934). What followed were studies that concentrated on the role of dance in particular societies. The acknowledged American pioneer in this field was Gertrude Prokosch Kurath, who, beginning in the 1940s, published numerous works on Native Americans.

Most of those who followed concentrated on particular ethnic areas, seeking through direct observation, as well as through the study of documents and artifacts, to determine the original purposes and structures of the dances of a society and then to pursue their history and development. This field grew with increasing vigor in the 1980s; both dancers and anthropologists were attracted to the tasks of refining research techniques and extending the areas of exploration.

Less formal in their methodology, many folk dance researchers have based their studies on seeing and performing the recreational dances of many lands. Fascinated by discoveries of cross-cultural themes, they have also sought the specific movement flavor of individual cultures and countries. Mary Ann Herman wrote extensively on pervasive patterns and their national variations.

Growing numbers of scholars are concerned with dances of the past. Using notated records (when they exist), technical manuals, costume designs, and written commentaries, these researchers have sought out contemporary clues not only to steps but also to performance styles. In addition to writing about their discoveries, they perform them: for example, Ingrid Brainard's group does European court and urban dances of the fifteenth to eighteenth centuries, and Catherine Turocy leads the New York Baroque Dance Company.

In 1973 Dance Perspectives Foundation established the de la Torre Bueno Prize, honoring the late J. R. de la Torre Bueno, who founded the dance book program at Wesleyan University Press. The prize is awarded annually for what is judged the best work of dance scholarship published in the preceding year. Other university presses have also become increasingly interested in the subject. Important books from the past have been reprinted by Dance Horizons, whereas the Princeton Book Company has published both historical treatises and technical guides for young readers.

In the 1990s an important move was made toward interdisciplinary approaches to dance scholarship. Viewed within the contexts of culture or gender studies, dance takes on new kinds of significance. [*See, for example,* Methodologies in the Study of Dance, *article on* New Areas of Inquiry.] It has also gained respect in academia, where scholars in other disciplines have discovered that dance can provide them with sources of fresh insights relevant to their own fields. Journals published by the American Society for Aesthetics, the Society for Ethnomusicology, and the American Society for Theatre Research frequently publish articles on dance. In 1996 the Society of Dance History Scholars became the first dance organization to be admitted to membership in the American Council of Learned Societies.

The comprehensive history of American dance that Lillian Moore had been planning has yet to be written. Now, however, that history may take a number of forms, each viewing its subject from a different perspective, within a different context, and reaching an audience larger than earlier writers would ever have imagined.

[*For repositories and locations of major collections, see* Libraries and Museums.]

SELMA JEANNE COHEN

Contemporary Criticism

American dance criticism developed in tandem with the emergence of dance as a performing art, to be considered as refined and richly varied as were music and drama. Few indications remain of how professional writers viewed staged dance in the 1790s, fifty years after the first recorded performance of ballet in America. Ballet was a very popular entertainment, however, with French ballet dancers performing on theatrical circuits from Boston to New Orleans. Their activities can be charted in brief newspaper items on performers, upcoming performances, duels, and deaths; in the letters to the editor from critical readers; and in the detailed advertisements that appeared in the newspapers of the nine major touring cities. Actual reviews tended to be "vague and pretty and not at all definite," as dance historian Lillian Moore observed of American dance reviewing in the mid-nineteenth century. "Madam Gardie . . . gave us a delight altogether new," *New York Magazine* reported in a review of a 1794 performance by Anna Gardie, the first ballet star to appear in the United States. "Her face, figure, and action were . . . prepossessing beyond any example on our stage." Boston critics observed that Gardie had "a certain something in her action and expression, which ravishes the senses," and they delighted in the ballerina's power "to melt, to fascinate, and astonish." Perhaps these were, after all, critical enough responses to dance performed generally for simple amusement and entertainment.

Gardie's murder in 1794 was reported in every newspaper in cities along the circuit, and ballet would not receive quite such widespread publicity until the mid-nineteenth century, when the European soloist Fanny Elssler swept through the United States on a wave of adulation. Although the level of ballet dancing had declined at the beginning of the nineteenth century, new European touring companies soon arrived, most notably those of Eugénie Lecomte and Paul and Amalia Taglioni, whose popularity among Americans was enhanced by the news that they were related to the great soloist Marie Taglioni. If the Taglionis noted with disgust the low quality of corps dancers they were forced to enlist on their American tour, so did the writers of the time. Nevertheless, the 1830s were a time of renewed popularity for ballet in America. "Why cannot the ballet be attached permanently to our theaters?" an anonymous critic wrote plaintively in 1839, in the *Spirit of the Times;* it was one of several popular theater journals then published in New York City, each with regular commentary on dance in America and abroad. Reviews from the 1830s show an increased awareness of "the scientific quality and brilliant execution" of ballet, as a reviewer of the ballet *La Fille Mal Gardeé* put it in 1838, in Philadelphia's *Public Ledger,* casually using such technical terms as pas de deux and pirouette.

Americans were thus ready to see—and write about—Elssler when she arrived in 1840. No dancer of her caliber had yet performed in the United States, and she was greeted with incessant, gossipy publicity of a kind not repeated in the nation until the arrival of Anna Pavlova in 1910. Some American writers pressed the "peerless Fanny" to their readers' hearts through breathless exclamations, but others described her dancing with the sense of occasion and poetics that existed in English and French dance writing of the time. The critic of New York's *Evening Post,* for example, compared Elssler to Taglioni in vivid but telling prose. Critics became sufficiently confident and well versed in the art of ballet to suggest, in reviews in New York publications, that a visiting foreign star limit himself to comic rather than Romantic-hero roles and to write about improvements in the technique of various young American dancers or to compare them favorably with foreign visitors

The long success of *The Black Crook* (1866)—an American extravaganza that was performed continuously into the early twentieth century—and its vaudevillian successors helped revive the American puritanical spirit that had objected to stage dancing a century before. At the same time, the style of much mid-nineteenth-century dance writing cheapened, wavering among the empty praise of earlier years, pompous declamations, and what read like perfumed parodies of Théophile Gautier. With a few exceptions, writing on dance would not take itself seriously in America until the late 1920s, when it began to become the specialized (if poorly remunerated) profession it would be by the end of the century.

Early in the twentieth century, foreign ballet flourished in the United States, when highly popular tours by Anna Pavlova and the Ballets Russes de Serge Diaghilev drew sensational, innocently idolatrous, and even serious coverage from U.S. newspapers and journals. The Metropolitan Opera Company, founded in 1883, offered a continuous dance presence throughout the early years of the twentieth century. Isadora Duncan and Ruth St. Denis also performed in America during the century's first decade, and their innovative work initiated the stirrings of a new American dance that would require new scrutiny and new sympathy from the music, drama, feature, and sports writers who commonly served as dance reviewers. An iconoclastic modern dance pioneer named Martha Graham gave her first solo recital in New York City in 1926, and ballet created and performed by Americans began to come into its own in the 1930s.

There were music and drama critics who wrote perceptively and intelligently about dance, among them H. T. Parker of the *Boston Evening Transcript* (1904–1934), Carl Van Vechten of the *New York Times* (1906–1907 and 1910–1913), Alfred Frankenthaler of the *San Francisco Chronicle*, and Cecil Smith of both the *Chicago Daily Tribune* and *Theatre Arts Monthly*. Claudia Cassidy, who succeeded Smith at the *Tribune* in 1942, brought notoriety to dance in Chicago through her acid but very popular reviews.

Van Vechten, the nation's first acknowledged critic of dance, wrote about dance events of the early twentieth century with sophisticated enthusiasm, knowledge, and a poetically evocative style, and he thereby played an important part in the creation of public taste. Mary F. Watkins of the *New York Herald Tribune* (1927–1934) became the nation's first full-time dance critic employed

on a daily newspaper, switching from music to dance a few weeks before the hiring of John Martin at the *New York Times* in 1927. Martin, whose tenure at the *Times* did not end until 1962, established dance criticism as a profession. That seal was set in 1976, when dance critic Alan Kriegsman, who had been at the *Washington Post* since 1966, was awarded the Pulitzer Prize for criticism.

Watkins brought a distanced eye and a tart, polished writing style to dance criticism. Martin saw himself as an educator, helping in particular to explain the unfamiliar art of modern dance to early audiences and encouraging young dance revolutionaries to form their own choreographic styles. His successor, Allen Hughes, who was at the *Times* only until 1965, brought a similarly open mind to the early experimentation of postmodernism. For many years dance critics perceived their primary responsibility as one of education and advocacy, a position exemplified in the work of Margaret Lloyd of the *Christian Science Monitor* (1936–1960).

Walter Terry—critic for the *Boston Herald* (1936–1939), the *New York Herald Tribune* (1939–1942 and 1945–1967), the *World Journal Tribune* (1967–1968), and the *Saturday Review/World* (1968–1982)—was dance's popularizer. Like Martin and most of the critics who followed him, Terry had had some training in dance. Also like Martin, he wrote prolifically on dance in reviews, features, and books and lectured extensively throughout the United States. Terry's genial style, which made him an exceptionally popular public figure both in the United States and abroad, was characterized by a high level of enthusiasm that occasionally masked the abundance of firsthand knowledge he brought to his work. Clive Barnes, also a popularizer, wrote for the *New York Times* from 1965 to 1977, then joined the *New York Post*. Reversing the traditional process, Barnes became the *Times*'s drama critic in 1967, bringing a consequent celebrity as well as a witty style to his reviewing. He was succeeded as dance critic by Anna Kisselgoff, who had been at the *Times* since 1968. Her reviews were distinguished by their sense of the historical context of a given dance event.

Although generally plainspoken and optimistic, American dance criticism has had its idiosyncratic stylists, most notably B. H. Haggin of the *Hudson Review* (1958–1972) and Jill Johnston, who covered postmodernist dance for the *Village Voice* in the 1960s. It has had its essayists, too. Arlene Croce, who joined the *New Yorker* in 1974, stood out for her rigorous, meditative writing that addressed both the event and the field itself from the viewpoint of an informed observer. George Beiswanger of *Theatre Arts Monthly* (1939–1944) and the *Atlanta Journal* (1967–1972) offered journalistic analyses that were particularly thoughtful. Equally thoughtful was the work of Nancy Goldner, whose analytical reviews and features for a number of nondance publications in the 1970s and 1980s revealed both an extrinsic and an intrinsic knowledge of dance.

Edwin Denby of *Modern Music* (1936–1942) and the *New York Herald Tribune* (1942–1945) was, along with Martin and Terry, a dean of American dance criticism. Dancer, choreographer, and poet, Denby was the influential founder of the intrinsic school of criticism. He brought to reviewing a vivid sense of how it feels to move through space, the ability to describe that, and the objective analysis of ballet in technical, stylistic, and psychological terms. More explicitly a critic with a highly developed sense of kinetic empathy was Deborah Jowitt of the *Village Voice*, who, beginning in 1967, brought to reviewing the perceptions of a former dancer and choreographer.

Jowitt and Marcia B. Siegel have been influential in training dance reviewers—first in private, informal classes that the two taught in the late 1960s and later through seminars conducted at the various critics' conferences that flourished briefly across the nation during the "dance boom" years of the 1970s. The most established of these seminars, the Critics Conference of the American Dance Festival, grew out of a dance festival course taught by Selma Jeanne Cohen in 1967. Still held each summer, the conference first convened in 1970 under the aegis of the Dance Program of the National Endowment for the Arts.

Dance of new and greater variety was touring nationally in the 1970s, under the auspices of the endowment's Dance Touring Program; regional dance companies, particularly ballet, then flourished and became important alternatives to performing in the nation's urban dance capitals. The conference worked to train regional critics to respond with sophistication to this proliferation of dance, some of it new and unfamiliar. By the 1980s, dance criticism had become a highly specialized profession. Critics shared a body of knowledge that was once unimaginable and they had begun to meet yearly at conferences conducted in New York City by the Dance Critics Association, a national group formed in 1974. Increasingly, dance criticism became part of university dance curricula.

Landmarks in U.S. dance publishing had been John Martin's *The Modern Dance* (1933) and *The Dance Encyclopedia* (1949). Dance books proliferated in the 1980s and were regularly reviewed in the national and dance media; opportunities for the study of dance history became available at the Dance Collection of the New York Public Library and other archives. Numerous specialty publications—the oldest and most popular is *Dance Magazine*, which dates from 1926—offer reviews, news, and historical features. Critics of major newspapers across the country were regularly expected to contribute interviews and essays to them on the dance. More and more, dance was preserved on film, most popularly in the Public Broadcasting Service (PBS) series *Dance in America*, which brought dance to vast national audiences beginning in 1975.

During this heyday of dance writing, the movement was away from the traditional, judgmental role of the critic and toward the attempt to report objectively on movement in dance, emphasizing choreography over performance and description over overt analysis. By the end of the 1980s, dance criticism had become more institutionalized and dance critics generally brought more specialized cultural perspectives to the field than did the music and drama writers of previous decades. Jobs for dance critics continued to be scarce in America, and writers outside the nation's biggest cities often found themselves having to adopt, once again, the roles of advocates and educators, which had been so much a part of the earlier dance criticism.

Once again, dance writing had thrived with the prospering fortunes of American dance; yet by the early 1990s, the scene had begun to change drastically, both for dance and dance writing. Increased cutbacks in government funding for dance were followed by the cutbacks and revamping of private aid, especially for programs that advocated crossover dance—dance that blurred the distinctions between classical ballet and modern dance. Most major American dance institutions struggled to survive. Newspapers did, too, as electronic media (television and interactive computers) became the media of choice. With general staff cutbacks and retirements, the number of jobs for dancers and dance writers decreased. By the late 1990s, the *New York Times* was the only national newspaper still to have full-time staff critics whose sole job was to write about dance.

Dance publishing in the 1990s, both of books and general dance periodicals, also decreased. University critical writing courses, like the dance departments, were being phased out. The scarcity of places to publish thinned the ranks of the new generation of dance writers. At the same time, however, new (but unpaid) possibilities emerged on the Internet for dance writing, from the simple publicizing of dance events to reviews and features. By the late 1990s, even small dance institutions had their own websites, and information about dance could be shared within minutes with readers throughout the world.

Writing for Dance Online was still unpaid by 1997, two years after the start of this pioneering major dance website. Nevertheless, the new electronic media promise new ways of looking at and studying dance; the potential also exists for the development of a new generation of dance writers whose shorter reviews, relatively informal personal styles, and international readership should bring profound changes to the field of dance criticism.

JENNIFER DUNNING

UNIVERSITY OF CAPE TOWN BALLET. *See* CAPAB Ballet.

URUGUAY. The Republic of Uruguay was a Spanish colony in South America until independence in the early 1800s; it has about 72,000 square miles (187,000 square kilometers) located on the Rio de la Plata between Brazil to the northeast and Argentina to the southwest. Its population, some 3.1 million, mainly Roman Catholics, is about 90 percent of European descent. There has been no indigenous population since the late nineteenth century, when mass European immigration began (to serve the grazing and meat-packing industries). The Europeans are mainly Spanish and Italian but also German, eastern European, and British. The other 10 percent of the population are of African descent, mulattos (mixed European and African), and *mestizos* (mixed European and Native American). The capital city of Montevideo is the major cultural center, where more than half the people live.

Folk Dance. In 1943 the eminent musicologist Lauro Ayestaran began collecting Uruguayan folk dances and classifying them in four major categories. The four thousand field recordings he made, now in the Museo Histórico Nacional in Montevideo, reveal that the music of the old European dances has been preserved in Uruguayan folk tradition. Ayestaran's wife, Flor de María Rodriguez de Ayestaran, was able to reconstruct twenty dances by using various archival sources. In 1973 she founded the Ballet Folklórico del Uruguay, which has made Uruguayan folk dances better known both within the country and abroad and has won her many prizes. In 1977 she established the Ballet Flor de Ceibo, which is sponsored by both Uruguay's Ministry of Culture and the Argentine embassy in Uruguay; it also performs in Argentina. In all nineteen of the departments (provinces) of Uruguay there are "nativist societies" working to preserve the "native" colonial culture. All have folk dance groups specializing in dances of the Rio de la Plata region.

In 1975 the Ministry of Education and Culture established the National Dance School in Montevideo, with two sections: ballet, under the direction of Margaret Graham, and folklore, under the direction of Flor de María Rodríguez de Ayestaran. The school trains dancers and dance teachers from the nation's secondary schools. Unfortunately, no dance is taught at the university level, even as an extracurricular subject.

Uruguay has an African minority that dances the *candombe*, the country's only "living" folk dance. This African-Uruguayan dance originated in Montevideo and is the only one of its kind in the Rio de la Plata region. *Candombe* characters still dance in the streets and in nightclubs in the city. During Carnival there is a parade called Llamadas ("calls") in which descendants of African slaves dance while drums beat continuously. The *candombe*'s standard characters are La Mama Vieja (The Old Mother), El Escobero (The Broom Man), El Gramillero (A kind of witch doctor), La Dama Joven (The Young Woman), and the Vedette, a glamorous female character who entered the repertory in the 1940s because of the popularity of Josephine Baker, the beautiful African-American entertainer who performed in Paris nightclubs.

Other ethnic communities also have dance groups in Uruguay. Dances from the different regions of Spain are represented by the groups of Rosario Penalver, Lydia Revilla, Spikerman Reyno, Pepe Montoya, and other ensembles. There are Italian, Tyrolese, Scottish, Yugoslavian (the Balkan states), and Jewish folk dance groups; particularly noteworthy is the Lithuanian ensemble Azuolinas, under the direction of J. A. Stanevicius, which has performed successfully in the United States and Canada. The Indio-American Folklore Association collects Native American folk dances from all of Latin America.

SODRE Ballet. Uruguay has a state ballet that operates under the auspices of the state radio system, SODRE (Servicio Oficial de Difusión Radio Eléctrica). The radio system was established in 1929, its ballet in 1935. The SODRE Ballet was first led by the Uruguyan Alberto Pouyanne, then by numerous directors of international repute, including Gala Shabelska, Tamara Grigorieva, Vaslav Veltchek, Roger Fenonjois, Alexander Sakharoff, and Clotilde Sakharoff. The Pole Yurek Shabelevsky directed the SODRE Ballet from 1954 to 1957, and from 1965 to 1980 it was under the direction of the Argentine Eduardo Ramírez. In 1980 the *prima ballerina* Margaret Graham assumed directorship; then, following a short interval in which the Argentine Amalia Lozano was in charge, the Uruguayan José Brum was appointed director in 1982.

The SODRE Ballet has had no home since a fire destroyed its theater in 1973. As a result, it is unable to have long seasons and is generally scheduled to take advantage of available dates at other state theaters, which are, however, unsuitable for dance performances. The SODRE Ballet also performs outdoors during summer seasons and tours the country. Its international repertory includes *Giselle, Les Sylphides,* act 2 of *Swan Lake,* the pas de deux from *Le Corsaire* and *Don Quixote, Aurora's Wedding, Boléro, Capriccio Espagnol, La Fille Mal Gardée, The Firebird, The Duel,* and *Graduation Ball.* These works alternate with choreographies by Amalia Lozano, Tito Barbon, Margaret Graham, Adriana Coll, and Eduardo Ramírez, and the Uruguayans Elsa Vallarino, Domingo Vera, and Alejandro Godoy. Worthy of mention is the Uruguayan choreographer Violeta López Lomba, whose *Contemporary Suite* was first performed in 1959, to music by Héctor Tosar. Although not performed again and ceasing to be part of the usual repertory, this piece is significant as a relevant work by the pioneer of Uruguayan contemporary dance, who died in 1968.

Vilen Galstian came to the SODRE Ballet from the Soviet Union in 1986 and 1987 to stage productions of *Don Quixote, Giselle,* and *Gayané.* In 1986 Alberto Alonso came from Cuba to choreograph the new ballet *Delmira Agustini,* based on Uruguayan themes; and Uruguayan choreographer Domingo Vera went to Cuba to stage his *Retrato* (Portrait), based on songs of Edith Piaf.

In 1988 the Cuban teacher Lydia Díaz became director of the SODRE Ballet. During her tenure the company staged several works by the Cuban Gustavo Herrera, one of which, *Candomballet,* used both academic dance and African folk dance. During this time also, Romanian choreographer Gheorghe Caciuleanu produced three important ballets, *The Four Seasons* (1988) to music by Vivaldi, *Symphonie Fantastique* (1989) to music by Berlioz, and *Mozartissimo* (1991) to music by Mozart.

Since 1994, the SODRE Ballet has been directed by the Cuban teacher Olga Madan Vera. She has presented a new version of *Les Sylphides,* based on choreography by Alicia Alonso, and a series of renowned pas de deux. Uruguayan choreographer Domingo Vera presented *Canto Hondo a España* in 1992 and *Gloria* in 1995 (to music by Vivaldi), both with the SODRE Ballet. SODRE House is being rebuilt; this began in 1995, to be completed about 1999. Until completion, the ballet continues to work out of its provisional home.

Independent Groups. Violeta López Lomba, student of Alexander and Clothilde Sakharoff, was one of the first people in Uruguayan dance to come into contact with North American contemporary dance. During that period, the 1950s, independent groups devoted to new dance genres began to appear.

The first of these, DALICA (Danza Libre de Cámara, or Free Chamber Dance), directed by the dancer, choreographer, and painter Elsa Vallarino, was founded in 1957. Since then it has performed in uninterrupted seasons throughout the country. It has its own dance school. Vallarino has made many trips to the United States, Brazil, Costa Rica, and other countries. Some of her students are now part of the SODRE Ballet or have formed their own small dance groups abroad. Her dance often uses themes from popular music, and on several occasions she has presented choreographies with Uruguayan musicians playing on stage.

The Ballet de Cámara de Montevideo (Montevideo Chamber Ballet) has been directed since its founding in 1958 by Hebe Rosa. At first the group danced in a neoclassical style, but Rosa, influenced by German dance technique and by José Limón, turned to expressionist choreography, although her dance school still includes ballet in its curriculum.

The Taller Mouret (Mouret Workshop) gave its first performance in 1966 under the direction of Iris Mouret, formerly with the Ballet de Cámara. It maintains the expressionist tendency of the latter both in its performances and in its dance school.

The Teatro Danza Company (Dance Theater Company) was founded in 1968. Its first performance was *Danza, Luz, Sonidos* (Dance, Light, Sound), under the direction of Julia Gade and her husband, José Claudio. An experimental group, it incorporates all branches of theater and is producing video performances. The style of Teatro Danza is personal, achieving an integration of balance, sound, and silences in purely regional abstract works. It has performed throughout Uruguay and in Argentina. Since 1974 the artist Fernando Álvarez Cozzi has been a third creative member of the group and has contributed films, slides, and video recordings. In 1978 the group opened a contemporary dance school to promote its experimental work.

Grupo Moebius was formed in 1974 under the direction of Cristina Martínez. It performs contemporary and experimental dance and also operates a school. Grupo Gestus is an expressionistic group created by the former SODRE ballerina María Minetti. Its first performance took place in 1980.

Group Concertante de Balle (Ballet Concert Group) is the only academic dance group independent of the state. Under the direction of former SODRE Ballet director Eduardo Ramírez, it has its own repertory, which is performed by pupils of its own school together with SODRE's star dancers.

On 1 March 1985 Julio María Sanguinetti was elected president of Uruguay, ending almost twelve years of military dictatorship. The new political situation stimulated developments in the arts, and independent dance prospered with the return of artists who had left Uruguay during the period of the dictatorship. Choreographers Ema Häberli and Numen Vilariño have created the Center of Contemporary Art in Montevideo. Teresa Trujillo, the modern dance teacher, has returned from Europe. Florence Varela, influenced by both American and German modern dance, founded the Contradanza Group. Dancers from several schools joined together to form the Babinka Group. Babinka and Contradanza merged in 1991, and work under the name Contradanza. Uruguayan dancer and choreographer Graciela Figueroa (who danced for Twyla Tharp in 1969) has returned to Uruguay; she directs her own Dance Group in Montevideo after spending many years traveling, dancing, and teaching in Chile, Brazil, and Europe (mainly Spain). Teresa Trujillo is teaching Eutony, a body technique based on the studies of Gerda Alexander (1908–1994).

Since December 1985, Ana Rosa Rodríguez Cravanzola has conducted a weekly program on SODRE television;

called "El Mundo de la Danza" (Dance World); it includes dance news, interviews with artists, and filmed dance.

BIBLIOGRAPHY

Assunção, Fernando O. *Evolución de los bailes populares tradicionales en el Río de la Plata*. Buenos Aires, 1978.

Carvalho Neto, Paulo de. "The Candombe: A Dramatic Dance from Afro-Uruguayan Folklore." *Ethnomusicology* 6 (September 1962): 164–174.

"Entretien avec Lolita Parent." *La Danse* (March 1957): 29–30.

Figari, Pedro, and Fernando Guibert. *Tango y candombe en el Río de la Plata, 1861–1979*. Río de la Plata, 1979.

Gilbert, Isabel. "Teresa Trujillo, bailarina y coreógrafa." *Cuba en el Ballet* 3 (May 1972): 36–39.

Gimelfarb, Norberto. "Le tour du monde en quatre-vingts tours de piste." In *La danse: Art du XXe siècle*. Lausanne, 1990.

Lauro Ayestaran, Flor de Maria R. de Ayestaran. *Las musicas infantiles en el Uruguay* (includes coreografia). Montevideo, 1995.

Legido, Juan Carlos. *La orilla oriental del tango: Historia del tango uruguayo*. Montevideo, 1994.

Omara, Grania. "Panorama del ballet en el Uruguay." *Ballet* (Lima) 2.3 (1953): 10–11.

Rodríguez de Ayestarán, Flor de María. "Methodology in the Reconstruction of Extinct Folk Dances." *Dance Studies* 8 (1984): 67–74.

Rodríguez de Ayestarán, Flor de María. *La danza popular en el Uruguay*. Montevideo, 1994.

Sclavo, Jorge. *Los tangos del Cuque*. Montevideo, 1990.

El tango uruguayo. Montevideo, 1994.

CLAUDIO SANGUINETTI GAMBARO
Translated from Spanish

USTINOVA, TATIANA (Tat'iana Alekseevna Ustinova; born 19 December 1908 in Tver [formerly Kalinin], Russia), choreographer and teacher. Ustinova graduated from the Moscow ballet school in 1931. From 1931 to 1938 she was a choreographer and dancer at the Moscow Theater of Young Audiences. From 1938 onward she was chief choreographer for the Piatnitsky State Academic Russian Folk Choir.

Ustinova created more than one hundred original dance scenes and various dances during her long career, using elements of Russian folk dances as a primary means of expression. She studied original folk dances for many years, beginning with her first ethnographic expeditions to the villages of her native Kalinin region. She gradually expanded her expeditions to include other areas of the Soviet Union. Ustinova's intimate knowledge of the folk material, coupled with her mastery of all its nuances, have lent a sense of authenticity to her stage compositions. Ustinova's dances are all original works, which she choreographs explicitly for the stage and according to her personal vision of the world. Ustinova founded the school of academic-style Russian folk dance.

"Northern Round Dances," staged by Ustinova in 1954, portrayed the Russian North, with its serenely flowing rivers and vast expanses. The majestic and tranquil movements of the region's women, wrapped in large embroidered shawls, the fluid transitions between dance numbers, and the rhythms of the North were all depicted on the stage. An entirely different rhythm carried the spectator away in the rollicking *chastushka* dance "Timonya" (1947). The gaiety that erupts from the circle of dancers creates a festive atmosphere characteristic of the southern regions of Russia. In Kursk and Belgorod it is precisely in this way that people celebrated—openly and sincerely, alternating the vivacious *chastushka* with the diversified rhythmic and improvised round dance. Ustinova's dances, united in a single program, conveyed the diversity of Russia.

"Siberian Polka" (1957) and "The Golden Chain" (1959) were built on elements characteristic of Siberian dances. "The Ural Shestera" is a quadrille characteristic of that region. The Kalinin (1938) and Yaroslavl (1950) quadrilles are lyrical and ornate, and capture the essence of the central regions of European Russia. "Voronezh Round Dance" (1944), "The Smolensk Goose Dance" (1945), "Moscow Round Dances" (1952), "Vologda Naparochka" (1963), "The Bryansk Igrishcha" (1978), "Kaluga Perebory" (1980), and many other dances incorporate characteristics of the folk cultures of the cities and villages of Russia.

Ustinova also had a keen sense of the present. Consequently, among her creations there are a number of compositions that in form are close to ballet, although these numbers are usually performed in variety shows by ensemble groups. Such dances include "The Star Round Dance" (1961), "Bloom" and "Springtime Land" (1963), "The Red Carnation" (1976), "Greetings, Volga!" (1978), "A Tale of the Russian Land" (1978), and "Zimushka" (1980). In her productions Ustinova also made use of the imagery of Russian folk poetry: "Willow Tree," a personification of woman, mother, the motherland; "White Swans," beautiful maidens; "Evil Kites," an enemy force; "Fearless Falcons," brave youths. *A Tale of the Russian Land* had three scenes: peace, war, and again peace. This structure was at once characteristic of the folk dance tradition and profoundly contemporary, expressing ordinary people's eternal yearning for peace and evoking memories of the dead. The poetic image of the Russian woman, the chastity of her dance, represented a special theme in Ustinova's work, which found expression in the woman's role in the dance "And I Walk in the Meadow" (once performed by Ustinova herself), "Ivushka," *A Tale of the Russian Land*, "Carnations," and others.

Ustinova wrote many books on dance. The major ones include *Russkie tantsy* (Russian Dances), 1950; *Berech krasotu russkogo tantsa* (To Preserve the Beauty of Russian Dance), 1959; *Zvezdnie khorovody* (The Star Round Dance), 1964; and *Russkii narodnyi tanets* (Russian Folk Dance), 1976. Ustinova has also written numerous articles in journals, anthologies, and newspapers. She has been a prominent public figure and the founder of folk dance studios, and created a curriculum for Russian dance that is taught at dance schools and institutes of higher education. Ensembles that perform her dances have enjoyed success. Ustinova is People's Artist of the USSR (1961), Laureate of the State Prize (1949, 1952), and winner of the Glinka Prize (1971).

BIBLIOGRAPHY

Klimov, A. A. Article in *Sovetskii Balet*, no. 6 (1983).
Uralskaya, Valeria. *Poiski i resheniia: Tanets v russkom khore.* Moscow, 1973.
Ustinova, Tatiana. *Russkie tantsy.* Moscow, 1955.
Ustinova, Tatiana. *Berech krasoty russkogo tantsa.* Moscow, 1959.

VALERIA I. URALSKAYA
Translated from Russian

UTHOFF, ERNST (born 28 December 1904 in Duisburg, Germany, died 19 February 1993), dancer, teacher, director, and choreographer. As a youth, Uthoff was initially interested in acting. His parents did not object as long as he also acquired a "serious profession." Hence, Uthoff served a two-year apprenticeship with an import-export firm and then joined the Bank of Dresden. At the same time he studied with Rudolf Laban. After obtaining a scholarship to study with Kurt Jooss, Uthoff devoted himself to dancing full-time.

UTHOFF. Oscar Escauríaza and Hans Züllig of the Ballet Nacional Chileno in Uthoff's late-1950s ballet *Wunder auf der Alameda*, based on *Die Puppenfee*. (Photograph by Bob Borwicz.)

In 1932, when Les Ballets Jooss won the Archives Internationales de la Danse choreographic competition with *The Green Table*, Uthoff danced the role of the Standard Bearer; he also created other roles, such as the Libertine in *Big City*. The company, supportive of its Jewish members, emigrated from Nazi Germany to England in the mid-1930s. On one of its tours (1940), it performed in Chile; a year later, when the company returned to England, Uthoff—with Lola Botka, whom he had married in 1938, and another dancer, Rudolf Pescht—settled in Santiago to found the University of Chile's dance school.

The success of Uthoff's version of *Coppélia* (1945) established the budding dance school on the local scene. It became the Ballet Nacional Chileno and, until his retirement in 1965, Uthoff's career was linked with it. As director and chief choreographer, he formed a compact company of approximately thirty dancers, trained in the Kurt Jooss–Sigurd Leeder technique. At first, several of Uthoff's ballets (*Drosselbart, Petrouchka, The Prodigal Son*) were on themes already choreographed by Jooss; later, however, he struck out on his own with works such as *Alotria*, a humorous circus ballet, and his greatest success, a ballet to Carl Orff's oratorio *Carmina Burana* (1937, 1960).

Uthoff's work, which in its later phase incorporated elements of classical technique, is best described as dance theater, defined by a clear and logical development of character and story line. A meticulous worker, he spent months on the preparation and rehearsal of each of his ballets, constantly demanding that the dancers not only perform the steps but interpret their roles, giving each instant its precise meaning. During the late 1950s and early 1960s, Uthoff and the Ballet Nacional Chileno undertook several very successful Latin American tours. In 1964, the company also performed at Lincoln Center in New York City. Uthoff retired in 1967 and, in 1984, belatedly received Chile's National Art Award.

BIBLIOGRAPHY

Cánepa Guzmán, Mario. *El Teatro Municipal en sus 125 años de sufrimientos y esplendor.* Santiago, 1985.
Ehrmann, Hans. "A Descendant of the Jooss Ballet Thrives in Chile." *Dance Magazine* (April 1957): 30–33.
Ewart, Germán. "Ernesto Uthoff." *El Mercurio* (24 September 1961).

HANS EHRMANN

UZBEKISTAN. The dance traditions of present-day Uzbekistan have been enriched by numerous cultures over the centuries because of the country's central location on the Silk Road, the ancient trade routes that linked China with the Mediterranean. Formerly known as Bactria, Transoxiana, Maveranaher, and Turkestan, the area was inhabited at least fifty-five thousand years ago. The ancient tribes that lived in Central Asia left petroglyphs, bas-reliefs, clay sculptures, and other artifacts depicting dancers and musicians. Later peoples continued to portray dancing figures in wood and clay sculptures, wall paintings, ornaments, and drawings on serving vessels of precious metal. Pictures dating from the first centuries CE show religious, mythological, and secular subjects in which dancing figures play an important part. From the fourth to eighth centuries CE the professional dancers of Samarkand, Bukhara, and Tashkent were so well known that they were in demand at the court of the Chinese emperor. The Arab invasion of Central Asia in the seventh century and the adoption of Islam promoted sexual segregation and the practice of veiling. Women danced for each other in the *ich kari,* or women's quarters. Public performances of dance were the domain of the *batcha,* or dancing boy, who dressed in women's clothing, wore makeup, and mimicked female behavior. A notable exception to this practice were the female court dancers depicted in miniature paintings produced from the Middle Ages until the nineteenth century.

The surviving dance heritage of the Uzbek people includes both folk and professional traditions. Folk dances fall into two general categories: dances performed at a specific time and linked to specific occasions, and dances performed at any time for entertainment. The first group consists of ritual dances performed at festivals associated with the seasons and reflecting humans' relationship with nature. Especially popular are the songs and dances devoted to the pre-Islamic festival Navruz (Nawrūz), which takes place on the spring equinox. In addition to an all-night ritual of stirring a large caldron to make *sumelek,* a special dish made from seven grains, festivities also include the *suskhotin,* a dance asking for rain, and the *mazhnun tal,* a dance by girls with fluffy willow buds woven into their braided hair. Other folk dances depict daily chores, seasonal work, or important events. Some dances relate to ceremonies such as weddings and funerals. Vestiges of Central Asian shamanism can be linked to the incantational dances of healers and fortunetellers, which were still common at the beginning of the twentieth century. Also still performed is the *zikr, (dhikr),* a Sufi ritual in which dancers travel in a circle with repetitive movements, accompanied by chanting and percussion, and sometimes reaching a trance state.

Entertainment dances include the *koshuk* and *kairakufari,* each distinctive to a particular area, which feature the playing of *kairok,* castanets made from smooth, flat river stones or metal. The *lapar* is a duet to sung couplets; the *yalla* is a solo dance accompanied by song. *Gul ufari* (jocular rhythms) or *khaivonlar ufari* (animal rhythms) are sometimes obvious imitations of animals, birds, or fish; at other times they are sophisticated dances representing stylized images of wild or domesticated animals.

"Tanovar", a classical dance from the Ferghana Valley, exists in at least twelve different variations. It expresses the hopes and longings of women and is somewhat melancholy in nature. Another classical dance, "Munadzhat", reflects the sentiment of an eponymous poem by Alisher Navoi, a prayerful lament entreating God for succor.

Uzbek dance is characterized by intricate arm and hand movements, a variety of spins and turns, backbends, shoulder isolations, and animated facial expressions. Portions of the dance are often performed kneeling on the floor. Footwork is relatively simple; high leaps and pelvic isolations are absent. Dancing is done mostly by women and girls. Musical accompaniment takes many forms, ranging from purely rhythmic patterns and melodies of narrow tonal range perfomed by a single percussion instrument or two-stringed instruments, to classical *maqom* (complex compositions of many parts), or even music performed by a large orchestra of folk instruments with singers.

The professional dance tradition falls into three categories. The first includes *raqş, oyin,* and *ufari,* technically sophisticated dances performed by virtuosos who may improvise on the basic patterns. The second group is *gul ufari,* a humorous, imitative form developed by dancers of the Uzbek theater of Maskharaboz. The third category consists of dances performed by traditional circus artists that include various acrobatic stunts.

Three regional styles of Uzbek dance, each with clearly defined styles and systems of training, developed in the separate political entities that existed in Turkestan prior to its incorporation into the Soviet Union. The Khanate of Kokand in the Ferghana Valley, the Khanate of Khiva in the Khorezm region, and the Emirate of Bukhara produced the Ferghana, Khorezm, and Bukharan styles, respectively. The most lyrical of the three schools, Ferghana dance, is characterized by intricate wrist circles and undulations of the hands and arms, with pliant bending of the spine and a shy yet playful demeanor. Khorezm dances often feature trembling of the hands and torso, side-to-side movements of the head, and comic elements. The most popular Khorezm dance, the *lazgi,* was originally a healing dance, traditionally performed with the dancer standing on a large platter. Dances from Bukhara feature a proud carriage and the juxtaposition of soft, undulating movements with crisp, staccato ones. The Bukharan style is the most acrobatic of the three, requiring fast spins, sudden drops to the floor, and deep backbends. In all three schools, dancers sometimes wear wrist bells to add a percussive element to their movements. Traditionally, both folk and professional Uzbek dance were solos, group dances being virtually nonexistent.

Although Russia conquered Turkestan in the mid-nineteenth century, local traditions went largely undisturbed until 1924, when the region was incorporated into

UZBEKISTAN. Dressed in traditional Uzbek costume, Mukarram Turgunbaeva (left) and Tamara Khanum (right) in a photograph from the 1920s perform a dance from the Ferghana Valley. (Photograph by K. Romeev; courtesy of Laurel Victoria Gray.)

the Soviet Union. The Bolshevik campaign to eliminate the custom of veiling soon led to public performances of dance by women. Born in Margillan in 1906, Tamara Khanum (*khanum,* an honorific meaning "madame" or "lady," was her sobriquet) was one of the first women to defy tradition and perform unveiled, often courting death at the hands of fundamentalists. In 1924 she performed Uzbek dance at the World Exposition in Paris, the first time in modern history that Central Asian dance had been seen in the West. One of Tamara Khanum's colleagues, a young dancer named Nurkhon, was murdered by her own brother for dishonoring the family by dancing in public. Nurkhon later became the subject of a musical drama by Kamil Yashin. [*See the entry on Khanum.*]

The Uzbek Ethnographic Company was established in 1926 to create concerts staged by masters of traditional dance. Ten years later the first Uzbek folk song and dance ensemble was formed; in 1956 another collective, Shodlik (Joy), was established. In 1958 an ethnographic song and dance company was created in Khorezm. The most celebrated of all Uzbek dance ensembles, Bakhor (Spring), was founded in 1957. Under the artistic direction of Mukarram Turgunbaeva, Bakhor developed a repertory of group and solo dances based on Uzbek traditions but employing Western techniques of staging and choreography. Bakhor has toured throughout the world and at its zenith consisted of forty-five young dancers who performed with an orchestra of native musicians. Nearly one hundred amateur companies exist, some of which perform dances reflecting local themes and genres.

The first contemporary dance studios were founded between 1927 and 1932. Isadora Duncan performed in Tashkent and Samarkand in 1924; one of her adopted daughters later taught special classes at the Tashkent Choreographic Institute. In 1947 the Tashkent ballet school was founded, with departments for both classical

and folk dance. Since 1970 folk dance choreographers have been trained at the Tashkent Institute of Culture under teachers from Leningrad and Moscow as well as Tashkent. The first Uzbek musical theater was established in 1929. The pantomime *Pakhta* (Cotton) was staged there in 1933, with choreography by Konstantin Bek, Usta Kamilov, and Turgunbaeva. Five years later the theater staged *Shakhuda,* a ballet on the theme of the struggle against the Basmachi bandits, with choreography by Kamilov, Turgunbaeva, and Aleksandr Tomsky. In both cases, the dances were based on folk idioms with classical elements introduced. In 1939 the State Academic Bolshoi Theater of Opera and Ballet (Uzbek Opera and Ballet Theater), named for Alisher Navoi, opened in Tashkent. Two of Uzbekistan's first native ballerinas were Galiya Izmailova and Bernara Karyeva, who performed traditional Uzbek dance as well as classical ballet.

In addition to ballets from the classical repertory, Uzbek choreographers have created their own works, developing new forms through a synthesis of classical and traditional dance. *Amulet of Love, Poem of Two Hearts,* and *Tomiris* are examples. One of the most popular is *Guliandom* (1940) by Vera Gubstkaya, Ilya Arbatov, and Tamara Khanum. On the basis of folk melodies collected by

UZBEKISTAN. Galiya Izmailova in a dance from the Khorezm region. (Photograph by K. Romeev; courtesy of Laurel Victoria Gray.)

Gavkhar Rakhimova, the composer Evgeny Brusilovsky created the score, introducing quotations from folk themes. The choreographers created the character of the hero by combining classical ballet with traditional Uzbek dance elements. Leading contemporary choreographers of classical and traditional dance are Galiya Izmailova, Ibraghim Yusupov, Kadir Muminov, Viktoria Akilova, Yulduz Ismatova, Damira Sagirova, Akbar Muminov, Sonmas Burkhanov, Takhir Dusmetov, and Inna Gorlina.

Uzbekistan declared its independence on 31 August 1991 and annually celebrates this event with festivities in which dance plays a central role. Each year members of Tashkent's professional dance ensembles participate in a mass dance, with specially created music and choreography. The ancient celebration of the spring holiday, Navruz, has also enjoyed a renaissance in the post-Soviet era, with numerous concerts featuring dance and a competition between professional dance companies for the best new festival program. Economic reforms have forced many companies to reduce their size and some professional dancers and musicians to seek employment outside the arts. Small, privately sponsored dance groups have sprung up to entertain tourists, foreign business people, and nightclub audiences. Traditional Uzbek dance has become more commercial in nature, abandoning many of the older dances in favor of lively numbers performed to ethno-pop-style music. Access to foreign materials has resulted in traditional-style costuming being replaced by sequined gowns and rhinestone tiaras. Arabic and Turkish-style dances and more revealing costumes have also become popular at concerts. Some professional companies and numerous amateur ensembles, however, endeavor to preserve Uzbek dance traditions. Dance remains central to Uzbek life; no wedding is complete without it, and televised dance performances enjoy great popularity, giving leading dancers celebrity status.

Expanded contact with the outside world, especially in the 1980s, encouraged Western dance forms to flourish in Uzbekistan, including ballroom dance and American break dancing, aerobics, and hip-hop. Cultural exchange, notably through the sister-city relationship between Tashkent and Seattle, resulted in an increased interest in Uzbek dance abroad, with non-Uzbeks in the United States and Europe studying and performing traditional dances. In 1985 the Uzbek Dance and Culture Society was founded in the United States to preserve and promote Central Asian culture; today it has members in the United States, Europe, Canada, and Australia.

BIBLIOGRAPHY

Allworth, Edward. *The Modern Uzbeks.* Stanford, Calif., 1990.
Avaz, Sotim, and O. Madrakhimov. *Madrakhim sherozii.* Tashkent, 1991.
Avdeeva, Lubov. *Tamara Khanum.* Tashkent, 1959.
Avdeeva, Lubov. *Tantseval'noe iskusstvo Uzbekistana.* Tashkent, 1960.
Avdeeva, Lubov. *Balet Uzbekistana.* Tashkent, 1973.
Avdeeva, Lubov. *Tanets Bernary Karyevoi.* Tashkent, 1973.
Avdeeva, Lubov. *Galiia Izmailova.* Tashkent, 1975.
Avdeeva, Lubov. *Tanets Mukarram Turgunbayevoi.* Tashkent, 1989.
Cohen, Selma Jeanne. "Report from Tashkent: East Meets West in Central Asia." *Dance Magazine* (July 1990): 45–48.
Gray, Laurel Victoria. "A Living Legacy: Women's Dances in Uzbekistan." *Arabesque* (January–February 1983): 6–7.
Gray, Laurel Victoria. "Tamara Khanum: Uzbekistan's Heroine of Dance." *Arabesque* (January–February 1985): 14–15.
Gray, Laurel Victoria. "Uzbek Women Dance through Time." *Middle Eastern Dancer* (April 1985): 17–20.
Gray, Laurel Victoria. "Uzbek Women's Dances, Past and Present." *Viltis* 43 (March–April 1985): 7–9.
Gray, Laurel Victoria. "Dancing Boys." *Arabesque* (May–June 1986): 8–11.
Gray, Laurel Victoria. "Americans Dance in Uzbekistan." *Dance Magazine* (September 1988): 10.
Gray, Laurel Victoria. "Poesie und Anmut des Herzens." Part 1: "Ferghana." Part 2: "Bukhara." Part 3: "Khorezm." *TanzOriental* (1994).
Gray, Laurel Victoria. "Uzbeks Adapt to Independence." *Dance Magazine* (August 1994): 22–23.
Gray, Laurel Victoria. "The Splendor of Uzbek Dance, Part 1: Khorezm." *Habibi* (Spring 1995): 12, 27.
Gray, Laurel Victoria. "The Splendor of Uzbek Dance, Part 2: Ferghana." *Habibi* (Summer 1995): 14, 31.
Karimova, Roziia. *Ferganskii tanets.* Tashkent, 1973.
Karimova, Roziia. *Khorezmskii tanet.* Tashkent, 1975.
Karimova, Roziia. *Bukharskii tanets.* Tashkent, 1977.
Karimova, Roziia. *Tantsy ansamblia Bakhor.* Tashkent, 1979.
Karimova, Roziia. *Tanovar.* Tashkent, 1993.
Lakov, Nikolai A., and Vera P. Sokolovskaia. *Kostiumy k tantsam narodov SSSR.* Moscow, 1964.
Khamrayeva, Gul'sum R. "Obshche Zakony Stsenicheskoi Khoreografii i Natsional'nyi Obraz Tantsa." Ph.D. diss., Khamza Institute of Art Studies, Tashkent, 1986.
Pulatova, Ogulkhon M. *Istoki Formirovaniya i Dal'neishego Razvitiya Terminologii Tantseval'nogo Iskusstva Uzbekskogo Yazyka.* Tashkent, 1992.
Shirokaia, O. I. *Al'bom Tamara Khanum.* Tashkent, 1972.
Swift, Mary Grace. *The Art of the Dance in the U.S.S.R.* Notre Dame, 1968.
Tkachenko, Tamara. *Narodnyi tanets.* 2d ed. Moscow, 1967.

VIDEOTAPES. "An Introduction to Uzbek Dance" (Uzbek Dance Society, 1986). "In Concert: The Bakhor Ensemble" (Uzbek Dance Society, 1989). "The Mukhimi Theatre Presents: Nurkhon" (Uzbek Dance Society, 1989).

ARCHIVE. Museum of Tamara Khanum, Tashkent.

LAUREL VICTORIA GRAY
With material provided by Lubov Avdeeva

VAGANOVA, AGRIPPINA (Agrippina Iakovlevna Vaganova; born 14 [26] June 1879 in Saint Petersburg, died 5 February 1951 in Leningrad), dancer, choreographer, and teacher. Vaganova studied at Saint Petersburg's theater school under Aleksandr Obladov, Lev Ivanov, Ekaterina Vazem, Christian Johansson, and Pavel Gerdt, and later under Olga Preobrajenska and Nikolai Legat. Upon graduation in 1897 she joined the corps de ballet of the Maryinsky Theater, where, despite her superlative technique, she made slow progress in her stage career (*coryphée* from 1903, soloist from 1906, *prima ballerina* from 1915). Vaganova danced leading roles in Marius Petipa's versions of Arthur Saint-Léon's *The Little Humpbacked Horse* and Jean Coralli and Jules Perrot's *Giselle;* Petipa's own *Les Caprices du Papillon* and *Le Talisman;* Petipa and Lev Ivanov's *Swan Lake* and *Le Réveil de Flore* as well as their version of Jean Dauberval's *La Fille Mal Gardée;* Aleksandr Gorsky's *Don Quixote;* Saint-Léon's *La Source,* restaged by Achille Coppini; Nikolai Legat's revival of Petipa's *Les Saisons;* and Michel Fokine's *Le Carnaval* and *Chopiniana.* Legat also staged for her in 1910 "The Whisper of Flowers," to Franz von Blon's eponymous waltz.

Critics invariably emphasized Vaganova's energetic style. Describing her as the "queen of variations," Valerian Svetlov pointed out in her dancing its chiseled precision, attention to detail, and ease of execution. Vaganova's achievements, such as the role of Odette-Odile in *Swan Lake* in 1913, came at the end of her stage career. She retired from the stage in 1916 and devoted herself to teaching.

One of Vaganova's first works in choreography was the miniature *The Visions of a Poet* (1927), to music by Arseny Gladkovsky, at the theater of the Leningrad ballet school. Vaganova revived Fokine's *Chopiniana* at the same theater in 1931; it was later staged at the Leningrad Opera and Ballet Theater. As the art director of the ballet company of the Opera and Ballet Theater from 1931 to 1937, Vaganova gave every encouragement to the company's interest in the modern repertory and revived two classic ballets: *Swan Lake* in 1933 and *La Esmeralda* in 1935. In these productions Vaganova sought to achieve the integrity of choreographic drama, to sharpen the dramatic conflict (social conflict in *La Esmeralda*) by enhancing the role played by mass scenes and consistent psychological

motivation of the action. The scene of the first meeting between Siegfried and Odette, which she staged anew, was included in subsequent versions of the ballet; in act 2, the "swan act," Vaganova carefully preserved Ivanov's choreographic text.

Vaganova began teaching at the School of Russian Ballet run by Akim Volynsky in Petrograd. From 1921 to 1951 she taught at the Petrograd ballet school; she was named professor in 1946. In 1957 the school was renamed after Vaganova. From 1934 to 1941 she also taught in the ballet teachers' department of that school, and from 1943 to 1944 she taught at the Bolshoi Theater in Moscow. From 1946 to 1951 she was the chair of choreography at the Leningrad Conservatory.

As a teacher, Vaganova contributed to the survival of classical ballet in the complex conditions of the emergence of a new culture in the country. The efficient and well-planned system of instruction in classical dance that she had established became the foundation of Soviet ballet art and training. This system was based on both the traditions of pure academic dance that Vaganova had adopted from her teachers and the selection of the finest achievements of the past, with a critical revision of what had been introduced into Russian ballet by representatives of various European schools in the late nineteenth century. Vaganova rejected the outward decorative effects and mannerisms that were characteristic of the French school of the late nineteenth century as well as the self-centered technique of the Italian school, with its exaggerated, angular dance style. She summed up and imaginatively used in her teaching the experience of the distinctive Russian school of dance and choreography that had taken shape at the turn of the century. At the same time she took into account the innovations of the Russian choreographers who had succeeded Petipa. Following Johansson, Vaganova interpreted virtuosity not as an aim in itself but as a means of artistic expression, subordinated to the general conception of a role and the choreography of the ballet as a whole.

Vaganova attached great significance to the strict carriage of the body and to its core of stability, the spine. This theoretical prerequisite played an important part in her pedagogical practice. For Vaganova, movement necessarily began from the body, for this gave support and artistic freedom to dance. At the beginning stage of training she also gave considerable attention to *épaulement*—the skill to hold the head and shoulders freely, not straining the muscles of the neck—as the first sign of future artistry. The correctly placed body, leading to perfect aplomb, was the foundation for steps of elevation, including turns and complicated jumps in allegro. In Vaganova's pedagogical system, steely aplomb was connected to correctly placed hands and the natural beauty of their movements, and to unconstrained *port de bras* and its organic connection with the control of the head. The hands, in Vaganova's opinion, should not only complete the contour of the visual image but also actively help the movement in jumps and turns. Vaganova's method enables ballet dancers to use the time-tested technique of academic style to adapt freely to the sophisticated tasks set in modern choreography. It has indirectly influenced the development of male dance by the universality of its main principles.

Vaganova described her system in her book *Fundamentals of the Classic Dance*, published in Russian in Leningrad, 1934, which has been translated into many languages. She greatly influenced the pedagogical principles of the Soviet and world school of classical ballet. Most of Vaganova's pupils were not only outstanding dancers but also teachers who imaginatively used her experience in their own work. Vaganova was awarded the title of People's Artist of the Russian Federation in 1934 and the State Prize of the USSR in 1946.

BIBLIOGRAPHY

Bogdanov-Berezovskii, V. M. *A. Ia. Vaganova.* Moscow, 1950.
Gregory, John. *The Legat Saga.* 2d ed. London, 1993.
Greskovic, Robert. "Ballet, Barre, and Center, on the Bookshelf." *Ballet Review* 6.2 (1977–1978): 1–56.
Iuzhina, Kamila. "Agrippina Vaganova and the Art of Teaching." *Dance Magazine* (November 1979): 36.
Kendall, Elizabeth B. "In Search of the Classichiski." *Dance Connection* 11.4 (1993–1994): 13–16, 53–54.
Krasovskaya, Vera. *Agrippina Iakovlevna Vaganova.* Leningrad, 1989.
Kremshevskaia, G. D. *Agrippina Iakovlevna Vaganova.* Leningrad, 1981.
Vaganova, Agrippina. *Stati, vospominaniia, dokumenty.* Leningrad, 1958.
Vaganova, Agrippina. *Basic Principles of Classical Ballet: Russian Ballet Technique* (1934). Translated by Anatole Chujoy. Edited by Peggy van Praagh. 2d ed. London, 1953; reprint New York, 1969.
Volkov, Nikolai D. "Agrippina Vaganova." In *The Soviet Ballet*, by Yuri Slonimsky et al. New York, 1947.

VALERY A. KULAKOV
Translated from Russian

VAINONEN, VASILY (Vasilii Ivanovich Vainonen; born 8 [21] February 1901 in Saint Petersburg, died 23 March 1964 in Moscow), dancer, choreographer, and librettist. Vainonen graduated from the Petrograd ballet school, where he studied under Vladimir Ponomarev, in 1919. From then until 1933 he danced with the Petrograd/Leningrad Opera and Ballet Theater, mainly in character roles. He started to work as a choreographer in the early 1920s and during the ensuing decade staged a few dances, including *Nocturnes* (1923), to Chopin; the Russian sailors' dance "Yablochko" (Little Apple; 1927); *Moszkowski Waltz* (1930); and *The Musical Snuffbox* (1932), to music by Anatol Liadov. These works evidenced his fascination with Isadora Duncan's art and also that of Michel Fokine. In addition to his work in ballet, Vainonen staged dances in operas. He was choreographer at the Leningrad Opera and Ballet Theater from 1930 to 1938 and at Moscow's Bolshoi Theater from 1946 to 1950 and 1954 to 1958.

Vainonen's first significant choreographic work was *The Golden Age*, to Dmitri Shostakovich's score, which he created with Vladimir Chesnakov and Leonid Yakobson at the Leningrad Opera and Ballet Theater in 1930. The production was largely experimental, with parody and the grotesque prevailing. Vainonen relied on his experience in variety dance and made an attempt to enrich the dance vocabulary with that of related arts: cinematography and propaganda posters. Vainonen's 1932 premiere of *The Flames of Paris*, to Boris Asafiev's score, at the Leningrad Opera and Ballet Theater was a milestone event in the history of Soviet ballet. (A new version was presented in 1936 and 1950; restaged at Moscow's Bolshoi Theater 1933, 1947, 1960, and at the National Opera House in Budapest in 1950.) Turning to the historical theme of the French Revolution, Vainonen made the people the protagonist; in his development of mass dance scenes the influence of gala performances of the early post-Revolutionary years could be noted. In his choreography, with its action dance and quest for a new plastique language containing elements of folk dance as well as virtuosic leaps and spins, he pursued the aim of presenting the image of a new hero: vigorous, rebellious, and determined to act. That was of major significance for the advancement of Soviet ballet, and largely anticipated the heroic style of Vakhtang Chabukiani's productions. [*See* Flames of Paris, The, *and* Golden Age, The.]

In later years Vainonen turned to modern themes in *Partisan Days* (1936, revised 1937) and *Militsa* (1947), both to scores by Asafiev and presented at Leningrad's Opera and Ballet Theater; *The Coast of Happiness* (1952), to music by Antonio Spadavecchia, in Novosibirsk; and Aram Khachaturian's *Gayané* in 1957 at Moscow's Bolshoi Theater. Using classical dance enriched with elements of comedy and drama, Vainonen choreographed *Mirandolina* (1949), to music by Sergei Vasilenko and a libretto based on Carlo Goldoni's play *La Locandiera*, for the Bolshoi Theater in Moscow.

Vainonen also produced original versions of the classics, such as *The Nutcracker* in 1934 for the Leningrad Opera and Ballet Theater, and Riccardo Drigo's *Har-*

lequinade in 1945 for the Belarussian Opera and Ballet Theater. For *The Nutcracker* Vainonen revised Marius Petipa's libretto, eliminated the naive doll-like character of the ballet, enriched the psychological motivations of the protagonists, and presented a new choreographic interpretation of Tchaikovsky's score. Other Petipa ballets that Vainonen restaged were *Raymonda* in 1938, with a new libretto by himself and Yuri Slonimsky, for the Kirov Opera and Ballet Theater, and *The Sleeping Beauty* in 1952 for the Novosibirsk Opera and Ballet Theater. He collaborated on the libretto for Aleksandr Radunsky's new version of *The Little Humpbacked Horse* in 1960. An article, "Notes on the Language of Choreography," was published in the September 1940 issue of the journal *Teatr*. Vainonen was awarded Merited Artist of the Russian Federation in 1939 and the State Prize of the USSR in 1947 and 1949.

BIBLIOGRAPHY
Armashevskaia, Klaudiia, and Nikita Vainonen. *Baletmeister Vainonen.* Moscow, 1971.
Roslavleva, Natalia. *Era of the Russian Ballet* (1966). New York, 1979.
Swift, Mary Grace. *The Art of the Dance in the U.S.S.R.* Notre Dame, 1968.

VALERY A. KULAKOV
Translated from Russian

VAIN PRECAUTIONS. *See* Fille Mal Gardée, La.

VALBERKH, IVAN (Ivan Lessogorov; Ivan Ivanovich Val'berkh; born 3 [14] July 1766 in Moscow; died 14 [26] July 1819 in Saint Petersburg), dancer, choreographer, teacher, and man of letters. Valberkh graduated from the Saint Petersburg Theater School in 1786 and was immediately appointed a soloist with its ballet troupe. Studying under Gaspero Angiolini and Giuseppe Canziani, he developed a taste for pantomime and mastered its technique. Charles Le Picq, the famous French dancing master, exercised a great influence on the young Valberkh. An inquisitive and thoughtful dancer, Valberkh took a creative approach to whatever he was learning by executing the dance in his own new way.

With his polished technique and attractive stage presence, Valberkh quickly made his mark as *premier danseur*, with a special gift for dramatic roles. He is best remembered for his brilliant Jason in *Médée et Jason*, choreographed by Le Picq after Jean-Georges Noverre; Alexis in *Le Déserteur*, choreographed by himself after Jean Dauberval; Romeo in his own *Romeo and Juliet;* and Ivan in *Russians in Germany, or The Effects of Love for the Motherland*, mounted by himself and Auguste Poireau. Press reviews praised him as a first-class dancer whose pantomime and dance technique were faultless.

An adherent of eighteenth-century theatrical aesthetics,

Valberkh shared Noverre's views on the *ballet d'action*. In his compositions Valberkh freely alternated dances with dramatized mime scenes. He was fully aware of literary and artistic trends of the day and was open to them, but he rejected both the rationalism of Noverre's ballets and the limitations of mythological themes. He was the first in Russia to present on the ballet stage the heroes of Shakespeare and Jean-Pierre Bernardin de Saint-Pierre. The content of his ballet *The New Sterne* (1801) was drawn from Laurence Sterne's novel *A Sentimental Journey*. Valberkh kept a close watch on the repertory and stage practices of the dramatic theater of the period; as a result, melodrama had profound influence on the style of his productions.

Valberkh produced thirty-six original ballets, revived ten ballets staged by other choreographers, and composed and arranged dances and mime scenes for forty-two grand operas. His ballets varied widely in genre and theme, including mythological subjects (*Orpheus and Eurydice*, 1808) and fairy tales (*Raoul Barbe-Bleue*, 1807). But Valberkh was proudest of his "moral" ballets, products of the sentimental trend in choreography. In these he departed from mythological themes and titanic images, instead drawing empathetic inspiration from the experiences of ordinary people. He praised virtue, repentance, and the triumph of justice, and often resorted to melodramatic effects. Moralizing and edifying principles dominated his productions, as even the titles indicate, from his debut as a choreographer on 8 February 1795 with *A Happy Repentance*, a pantomime-ballet, through *Blanca, or A Marriage of Revenge* (1803), *The Count Castelli, or The Criminal Brother* (1804), *Clara, or Return to Virtue* (1806), *Romeo and Juliet* (1809), *An American Heroine, or Treachery Punished* (1814), and *Henry IV, or Virtue Rewarded* (1816). All were marked by sentimentality and the praise of virtue.

Valberkh's *The New Werther* (1799) had a libretto based on a true story of two lovers who committed suicide in a cemetery in Moscow. The wealthy parents of the young woman opposed the marriage because the young man was only a poor infantry officer. The idiom of the dances was subordinated to the theme, especially in the duets, and the dancers performed in contemporary dress. Valberkh's quest to link ballet with the arts of his epoch was crowned by the great success of *A New Heroine, or The Cossack Woman* (1811). The libretto was based on another true story, that of Nadezhda Durova, a girl who disguised herself as an army officer and took part in the difficult battles waged by the Russians against Napoleon's encroaching army. The ballet had a long run at theaters in Moscow and Saint Petersburg. During the 1812 war, Valberkh initiated a new genre—a folk *divertissement* as an organic blend of dances, songs, and music. The war inspired him to produce *Russians in Germany, or The Effects of Love for the Motherland* (1813) and several other patriotic ballets.

From 1794 to the day he died, Valberkh taught at the Imperial Theater School. Evgenia Kolosova, Arina Tukmanova, Agrafina Makhayeva, Constance Pletin, Isaac Ablets, and Adam Glushkovsky were among his pupils. An active dancer, choreographer, and teacher, Valberkh also found time to pursue the career of a man of letters. He knew several languages, translated twenty-seven plays staged by Russian theaters, and left informative memoirs of early nineteenth-century French ballet, in which he presented his philosophy of art. In dancing he valued, above all, harmony and the ability to express ideas; he opposed those who saw these qualities only as a way to display a dancer's technical brilliance.

BIBLIOGRAPHY

Bakhrushin, Yuri. *Istoriia russkogo baleta*. 3d ed. Moscow, 1977.
Roslavleva, Natalia. *Era of the Russian Ballet* (1966). New York, 1979.
Sorley Walker, Kathrine. "Ballet in Imperial Russia." *Dance Gazette* (October 1982): 38–40.
Swift, Mary Grace. *A Loftier Flight: The Life and Accomplishments of Charles Louis Didelot*. Middletown, Conn., 1974.
Valberkh, Ivan. *Iz arkhiva baletmeistera*. Moscow, 1948.
Winter, Marian Hannah. *The Pre-Romantic Ballet*. London, 1974.

NIKOLAI I. ELYASH
Translated from Russian

VALLI (Alarmel Valli; born 14 September 1956 in Madras), Indian dancer. Trained in the Pandanallur technique of classical *bharata nāṭyam* by the guru Chokkalingam Pillai, Valli began her studies at the age of seven. Later she expanded her repertory with her master's son, Subbaraya Pillai. She studied *abhinaya* (expressive dance) with Kalanidhi Narayanan. Like many of her contemporaries, she also studied Oḍissi dance, but she decided to concentrate solely on *bharata nāṭyam*.

Valli's dancing is marked by a sparkling quality. To the typically forceful movement style of Pandanallur dance, she brings a refreshing approach which adds grace without stripping the style of its grandeur. Her style is not a forceful one, either in the movements of the arms or in the execution of *adavu*s, the dance units that build up the architectonic structure of *bharata nāṭyam*. Rather, her signature lies in softening the movements gracefully while preserving the essential vigor. Her steps uncoil and flow, revealing beauty in the dance's unfolding. Her *utplavan*s (jumps) are light and her landings perfect, drawing exquisite, lingering curves. Her dancing is playful; her eyes do not move as prescribed in the classical treatises but rather enhance the movements and give a joyous touch to the presentation. Nonetheless, both her repertory and performance adhere to tradition. Studying music has developed in her the keen musicality essential to a *bharata nāṭyam* dancer.

Valli has also choreographed several *bharata nāṭyam* works that recast traditional sequences to create beautiful movement patterns. She has participated in many national and international festivals and conferences, winning critical acclaim. She has explored the combination of *bharata nāṭyam* and Oḍissi dance with Oḍissi exponent Madhavi Mughal, but she is best known as a soloist.

Valli lives in Madras, where she trains young dancers at her academy. Her performances were filmed by Prakash Jha in a series produced for the Festival of India. Her honors include the Nritya Choodamani award from Shri Krishna Gana Sabha, Madras, and the Kalaimamani award from the Tamil Nadu State Sangeet Natak Akademi, as well as many other honors from various arts organizations.

BIBLIOGRAPHY

Kliger, George, ed. *Bharata Nāṭyam in Cultural Perspective*. Manohar, 1993.
Kothari, Sunil, ed. *Bharata Natyam: Indian Classical Dance Art*. Bombay, 1979.
Meisner, Nadine. "Festival of India." *Dance and Dancers* (June 1982): 31–32.

SUNIL KOTHARI

VAN PRAAGH, PEGGY (born 1 September 1910 in London, died 15 January 1990 in Melbourne, Australia), British dancer, teacher, and ballet director. Van Praagh studied with Aimée Phipps, Margaret Craske, Lydia Sokolova, Vera Volkova, Tamara Karsavina, Gertrud Bodenwieser, and Agnes de Mille. She made her debut at the Coliseum Theatre in London on 16 September 1929 in a company formed by Anton Dolin, and in 1932 she passed her advanced Cecchetti examination. Subsequently she danced in Camargo Society performances and then as a soloist with the Ballet Club/Ballet Rambert (1933–1938), working particularly with Frederick Ashton and Antony Tudor. She also danced in many musicals, in opera ballets at Covent Garden, and in some of the earliest television transmissions. In 1938 she joined Tudor's London Ballet, where she created roles in his *Jardin aux Lilas* (1936), *Dark Elegies* (1937), *Soirée Musicale* and *Gala Performance* (both 1938), and *The Planets* (extended version, 1939).

At the beginning of World War II, van Praagh took over the Craske studio in London and became joint director with Maude Lloyd of the London Ballet, revived initially for lunchtime performances during the blitz. When the company was absorbed into Ballet Rambert in 1941, she joined Sadler's Wells as teacher and principal dancer, later making a particular impression in *demi-caractère* and virtuoso roles such as one of the Blue Girls in Ashton's *Les Patineurs* and Swanilda in *Coppélia*.

Van Praagh was appointed ballet mistress of the newly established Sadler's Wells Theatre Ballet in 1946 and was assistant director to Ninette de Valois from 1951 to 1955. In that position she nurtured the early choreographic works of John Cranko and Kenneth MacMillan and the early careers of many dancers who became leaders of the Royal Ballet. She also pioneered many outreach programs to popularize and explain classical ballet through lectures and lecture-demonstrations.

After she left Sadler's Wells in 1955 to freelance, van Praagh staged ballets by Ashton, de Valois, and Tudor in Canada, West Germany, Sweden, Norway, the United States, and France. She also produced many ballets for BBC Television between 1949 and 1958 and directed the Edinburgh International Ballet in 1958.

In 1960 she went to Australia as guest teacher for the Borovansky Ballet, for which she staged *Coppélia* and *Les Rendezvous*. She was appointed artistic director of the Australian Ballet for 1963–1974 and 1978–1979. As such she is considered the principal influence in the development of classical ballet in Australia, where she fostered dancers, teachers, and choreographers and continued her outreach work on television as well as in personal lectures and demonstrations.

An examiner and London committee member of the Cecchetti Society since 1937, she was considered one of its leading teachers and achieved an international reputation as an exponent of the Cecchetti method of training. She received many honors, including the Queen Elizabeth II Coronation Award, Royal Academy of Dancing (of which she was vice president), 1965; Commander of the Order of the British Empire (CBE), 1966; Dame Commander of the Order of the British Empire (DBE), 1970; honorary doctor of letters, University of New South Wales, Armidale, 1974; Distinguished Artist Award of Australian Art Circle, 1975; honorary doctor of laws, Melbourne University, 1981.

[*See also* Australia, *article on* Ballet.]

BIBLIOGRAPHY

Brinson, Peter. "Married to the Ballet." *Brolga*, no. 3 (December 1995): 24–48.

Pelly, Noël. "A Tribute to Dame Peggy." *Dance Australia* (April–May 1990): 31–34.

Sexton, Christopher. *Peggy van Praagh: A Life of Dance.* South Melbourne, 1985.

Sorley Walker, Kathrine. "A Sort of Dedication." *The Dancing Times* (December 1974): 128–130.

van Praagh, Peggy. *How I Became a Ballet Dancer.* New York, 1954.

van Praagh, Peggy, and Peter Brinson. *The Choreographic Art.* London, 1963.

van Praagh, Peggy. *Ballet in Australia.* Melbourne, 1965.

van Praagh, Peggy. "Working with Antony Tudor." *Dance Research* 2 (Summer 1984): 56–67.

Woodcock, Sarah C. *The Sadler's Wells Royal Ballet.* London, 1991.

PETER BRINSON

VANUATU. *See* Melanesia.

VASILIEV, VLADIMIR (Vladimir Viktorovich Vasil'ev; born 18 April 1940 in Moscow), Russian dancer, choreographer, and teacher. Vasiliev graduated from the Moscow Ballet School, Mikhail Gabovich's class, in 1958 and became a leading soloist of the Bolshoi Ballet. His ballet teachers and coaches were Aleksei Yermolayev, Asaf Messerer, and Galina Ulanova. He graduated from Rostislav Zakharov's course in choreography at the Lunacharsky Theater Technicum in 1981.

Vasiliev's talent combined consummate technique with highly artistic and original acting. He made a brilliant debut in the 1959 Bolshoi staging of Yuri Grigorovich's *The Stone Flower*, portraying the leading role of Danila, a Russian folk artist. Vasiliev's Ivanushka in Aleksandr Radunsky's *The Little Humpbacked Horse* and Petrouchka in Michel Fokine's eponymous ballet, revived by Konstantin Boyarsky for the Bolshoi, were distinctive for their rich national coloring. Another of his remarkable roles was Medzhnun, which was created for him by Kasyan Goleizovsky in *Leili and Medzhnun* (1964). In this ballet Vasiliev mastered a style of choreography unusual for its variety in nuances, just as he later did in Maurice Béjart's productions of *Romeo and Juliet* and *Petrouchka*. Able to immerse himself in his roles and evince each character

VASILIEV. Cast in the title role of Leonid Lavrovsky's *Paganini* in 1962, the youthful Vasiliev relished the opportunity to display his exceptional elevation and virtuosity. (Photograph reprinted from a Bolshoi Ballet souvenir program, 1962.)

VASILIEV. In 1968, Vasililev created the title role of Yuri Grig- orovich's *Spartacus*. This photograph, taken during a perfor- mance, captured a dramatic moment when Spartacus's wife Phrygia (Ekaterina Maximova) throws herself at the knees of her husband to make an impassioned plea. (Photograph from the Dance Collection, New York Public Library for the Performing Arts.)

through movement, Vasiliev gave an innovative interpre- tation to the roles of Romeo in Leonid Lavrovsky's *Romeo and Juliet* and the Prince in Zakharov's *Cinderella*. His vir- tuosity was seen in the traditional role of Basil in Marius Petipa's *Don Quixote*. He brought to Albrecht in *Giselle* and Désiré in *The Sleeping Beauty* the spirit of classicism and poetry in motion. Vasiliev became the exemplary in- terpreter of Grigorovich's ballets, creating the principal roles in *Spartacus, The Nutcracker, Ivan the Terrible,* and *The Angara*.

Vasiliev's dancing influenced the contemporary artistic criteria of ballet. Fedor Lopukhov passed on to Vasiliev from Vakhtang Chabukiani the title "god of the dance." Yermolayev said that with each role Vasiliev adopted a new persona and especially commended his "soft" and "hard" *pliés*, which allowed him a limitless range of move- ment and of roles. Lopukhov (1974) commented with pro- fessional delight on Vasiliev's technique: "His *double tours* to left and right, *entrechats*, simple and *double cabrioles*,

and *double ronds de jambe* are of an amazingly noble pat- tern. He performs, for example, the following unique combination in the pas de deux coda from *Don Quixote:* after making two *jetés en tournant* from the right leg, he makes a *tour en l'air en attitude* and during the turn per- forms an ordinary *rond de jambe*. This combination is re- peated several times *en manège*, and the audience feels en- raptured by the soaring dancer whose feet touch the floor almost imperceptibly."

Vasiliev displayed his mature skill as a choreographer in productions staged at the Bolshoi. Remaining loyal to classical dance and realistic art, he regarded form as the flesh and blood of an idea and sought to polish realistic images into symbols of significance. In his full-length story ballets *Icarus* (1971) and *Macbeth* (1980) he relied on sophisticated technique, which he performed. The flight of Icarus, for example, is an unusual combination: from a swift, springy *chassé* he soared in a high *saut de basque en dedans* on the right leg and, at the moment of turning at the acme of the jump, changed the position of his legs in midair to execute a *grand rond de jambe* with his left leg, then landed in a broad fourth position; this was performed twice. In his plotless ballet *These Charm- ing Sounds* (1978) Vasiliev revealed his search for a wider range of classical dance technique. His work as choreog- rapher and dancer in his ballet film *Aniuta* (1982, ex- panded for the stage in 1986), based on Anton Chekhov's *Anna Round the Neck,* and his one-act productions *I Want to Dance* (later called *Suite Nostalgique*), created in honor of Ulanova, and *Fragments of a Biography*, set to music by Russian and Argentine composers, were acclaimed; *Correo Musical Argentino* magazine wrote that he "created a truly Argentinian elegy by the wonderful singing of his dance. There is no archaeological reconstruction, no eth- nic documentality. Vasiliev has offered us a bunch of Ar- gentinian flowers chosen by an artist in spirit and a uni- versal man in art. His perfect dance, the dignity and integrity of his art, is evidence that he is the greatest dancer of our day."

During the 1980s, while retaining his position at the Bolshoi, Vasiliev was often invited as a guest choreogra- pher to companies outside and inside the Soviet Union— Berlin, Budapest, Naples, Riga, Cheliabinsk, Kasian—as well as performing as a guest artist, usually with his wife, the ballerina Ekaterina Maximova. By the end of the 1980s his disaffection with the Bolshoi had become patent, so that he and Maximova were no longer wel- comed. In 1990 Vasiliev joined the board of the Kremlin Ballet, reviving for the new company his *Macbeth* and cre- ating his version of *Cinderella* (1991), in which he and Maximova danced. Always a champion of the Russian, as opposed to Soviet, style of dancing, Vasiliev formed a small company of dancers, drawn from the Bolshoi and Kirov companies and representing diverse republics, and toured the United States in 1991 in a program of excerpts from his ballets complemented by classical pas de deux. Vasiliev's nomadic existence came to an end when in 1995 Grigorovich was made to step down as director of the Bolshoi Ballet. Vasiliev was named joint director with Vladimir Kokonin of the Bolshoi Theater, overseeing the opera, ballet, and theater companies. His immediate aims are to stabilize the theater's finances, to open the Bolshoi Ballet repertory to foreign choreographers' and new young choreographers' works, to associate the school more directly with the company, and to foster international exchange.

BIBLIOGRAPHY

Avaliani, Noi, and Leonid Zhdanov, comps. *Bolshoi's Young Dancers.* Translated by Natalie Ward. Moscow, 1975.

Belinskii, A. A. "Odin takoi tsantsovschik." *Sovetskii balet*, no. 6 (1983).

Ben-Itzak, Paul. "Vladimir Vasiliev: Hauling the Bolshoi into the Twentieth Century." *Dance Magazine* 70.2 (February 1996): 74–77.

Demidov, Alexander P. *The Russian Ballet: Past and Present.* Translated by Guy Daniels. Garden City, N.Y., 1977.

Garafola, Lynn. "Vladimir Vasiliev." *Dance Magazine* (November 1990): 50–53.

Ignatov, Victor. "Entretien: Vladimir Vassiliev au Bolchoi." *Danser* (June 1995): 34–35.

Kisselgoff, Anna. *Vladimir Vasiliev.* Brooklyn, 1975.

Lazzarini, Roberta. *Maximova & Vasiliev at the Bolshoi.* London, 1995.

Lidova, Irène. "Volodia, il gigante buono." *Ballettoggi* (July–August 1988): 15–18.

Lopukhov, Fedor. "Vladimir Vasiliev." In *Muzyka i khoreografiia sovremennogo baleta.* Leningrad, 1974.

Lvov-Anokhin, Boris. "Vladimir Vasiliev." In Lvov-Anokhin's *Mastera Bolshogo Baleta.* Moscow, 1976.

Ottolenghi, Vittoria. "Vladimir Vassiliev: Autoritratto in due parole." *Ballettoggi* (July–August 1988): 12–14.

Smakov, Gennady. *The Great Russian Dancers.* New York, 1984.

Willis, Margaret E. "Vasiliev through the Viewfinder." *Dance Magazine* (January 1988): 48–51.

GALINA V. BELYAYEVA-CHELOMBITKO
Translated from Russian

VAUDEVILLE. [*This entry is limited to discussion of vaudeville in the United States. For related discussion of European traditions, see* Music Hall.]

Variegated performances of song, dance, comedy, and tumbling had held the American stage since colonial times, but not until the period following the Civil War were they commonly called variety shows. Usually presented within the precincts of a barroom, honky tonk, or concert saloon, these entertainments had to amuse a rowdy and impatient crowd of male boozers. There was no place for the finer points of dance. Ballerinas, imported from Britain or Europe for extravaganzas such as *The Black Crook* and burlesques such as *Ixion*, danced in variety theaters in the off-season or when the taste for such shows faded, but these former *coryphées* merely had to display their stockinetted legs in a few energetic steps. Tony Pastor's more ambitious Opera House boasted its regular corps de ballet of ten "soloists" under the direction of a Monsieur Szollosy.

VAUDEVILLE. The Four Cohans were one of the best-known family acts to tour the vaudeville circuits. George M. Cohan is pictured here with his sister Josephine, his father Jerry J., and his mother Helen. (Photograph from the Museum of the City of New York; used by permission.)

VAUDEVILLE. The specialty act of Earl ("Snake Hips") Tucker exploited his unique, seemingly boneless way of moving. As his nickname suggests, he popularized the Snake Hips—in origin a plantation dance—and was also noted for his undulating Belly Roll. One of the foremost African-American entertainers of his day, Tucker was a regular at Harlem clubs, including the Cotton Club and Connie's Inn. (Photograph from a private collection.)

Most variety dancing was more athletic than aesthetic. Clogging contests, popularized by the phenomenal John Queen, were judged on time, style, and execution. Introduced in 1876 by Jimmy Bradley, sand jig dancing, a style tripped on the balls of the feet in 4/4 time like a schottische, was appraised from beneath the stage in order to gauge the accuracy of cadence. Kitty O'Neill was the first female sand jigger; the Barlow Brothers and the Girard Brothers, the first double acts to perform it. The Majiltons launched "legmania," a frenetic display of high kicks, splits, and three-hand reels played in grotesque wigs and tights; they were widely imitated by, among others, the Daly Brothers, the first act to kick at inanimate objects, such as hats and cigar boxes. In 1877 the Poole Brothers combined legmania and clogging, thereby creating the first acrobatic clog dance.

Throughout the 1870s, variety dancing stressed gimmickry and vigor over technique. Prime novelties were the Egg Dance, a series of pirouettes, dips, and hops carried out among two dozen raw eggs; the Spade Dance, in which the blade served as a kind of pogo stick on which the dancer hopped through an obstacle course; and the Transformation Dance (especially popular with male impersonators), in which costumes were yanked off the performer from the wings by means of strings, enabling her to perform, in succession, a military drill, an Irish jig, and a skipping rope dance, each time clad in appropriate garb. Charlie Dimond started the vogue for soft-shoe, accompanying himself on a harp slung over his shoulder. According to Joe Laurie, Jr. (1953), the Turkey Trot was introduced by Johnny Lorenze in 1886, the same year the first "break" was danced on a piano, by Guy Hawley. In 1888 buck-and-wing dancing was initiated, by Lew Randall; roughhouse dancing, by Charles Guyer and Nellie O'Neill; and double one-legged song and dance, by Harper and Stencil. Dancers working the big time during this period made at most $70 a week in tandem and performed under less than ideal conditions. The brother-sister team of Johnny and Bertha Gleason, wooden-shoe dancers, traveled with their own pianist to ensure accurate music cues and were the first dance team to use a mat of hardwood slats to correct the lack of resilience in the double stage flooring of most theaters. Amateurs had to rehearse for auditions and contests in empty grain cars that had hard, smooth floors.

The opening of Tony Pastor's Fourteenth Street Theatre in 1881 signaled the use of "vaudeville" to imply a higher grade of entertainment, one that was clean and refined. As managers wooed family audiences by promising high-toned amusements, they screened variety dancing for any salacious or sensual overtones. Bubble dances with or without fans and doves, striptease, and *danses du ventre* were strictly relegated to burlesque. Censors were quick to jib at any suggestion of licentiousness in dance. The Cubanola Glide, a cakewalk, was, complained the *American Magazine* in 1909, "a dance so suggestive and so reeking of implied indecency that it is an insult to any respectable woman who happens to hear it." Later, hints of passion in *apache* dances would be attacked by local moralists as overtly sensual, even bestial.

Conversely, children's troupes were thought to guarantee wholesomeness. The Hengler Sisters; Harry Delf "The Kid Romeo"; Elseeta, "The American Dancing Girl"; Eva and Harry Puck; and Rae Dooley had successful careers as juvenile dancers until the "Geary society" (American Society for the Prevention of Cruelty to Children) cracked down on full-time employment of minors.

African-American dance was never presented in the early days of white vaudeville because at first such dances were interpreted by white performers in blackface. Cakewalks came to vaudeville by way of the minstrel show. Johnson and Dean were the earliest black dance team to feature the cakewalk in variety, but it was Irish Dan Burke who spiced the cake with high kicks. The shuffle and sway was first danced by the white George Primrose. The finest black performers were eventually able to break in but initially only in the unpopular number two spot on the bill: Phina and Her Picks (short for *pickaninnies*), George Cooper, and Bill ("Bojangles") Robinson, who developed the stair dance (initiated by Al Leach in 1899) into a full-fledged art form. Exclusively black vaudeville helped to cultivate the talents of Ulysses ("Slow Kid") Thompson, with his legmanic tap dance, the high kicks and leaps of Peg Leg Bates, and the Duo Éclatant of Ollie Burgoyne and Usher Watts. Buck and Bubbles began as ushers at B. F. Keith's in Louisville, Kentucky, before becoming the first black team to perform there (although under burnt cork masks). Long after white vaudeville had entered its decline, the Apollo Theater in Harlem provided a showcase for Snake Hips Tucker and the Berry Brothers, with their combination of acrobatics, soft-shoe, and strut. [*See the entries on the Berry Brothers, Peg Leg Bates, and Robinson.*]

Vaudeville audiences, even in the gilded palaces managed by Keith, E. F. Albee, and F. F. Proctor, remained indifferent to dance as an art but responded enthusiastically to successive waves of novelties. Spanish dance became a rage in 1890, when Carmencita did a *cachucha*, a Santiago waltz, and a *fandango* with castanets at Koster & Bial's in New York City. She was widely imitated, burlesqued, and, six years after her death, impersonated by an imposter in a "farewell" performance at Hammerstein's theater. Her chief rival was Carolina Otéro, known in Paris as La Belle Otéro. The skirt dances and graceful glides of England's Kate Seymour and Kate Vaughan were Americanized at about this time by Amelia Glover and Bessie McCoy. The replacement of gas by electric lighting enabled the experiments of Loie Fuller in manipulating translucent gauze in colored light, and in her wake followed a spate of serpentines, fire dances, and butterfly dances. A certain Papinta embellished her serpentines with mirrors and a glass trapdoor through which she fell in 1895. [*See* Skirt Dance *and the entry on Fuller.*]

In 1894 a performer called Ayesha conveyed to vaudeville a laundered hootchy-kootchy from its birthplace, the World's Columbian Exposition in Chicago. The number was then headlined at Hammerstein's by one "Rajah," formerly of Huber's Museum on the Bowery, where she had danced with a chair in her teeth. Hammerstein's later featured Djemille Fatimah in Algerian dances. Hawaiian dancing arrived in 1908 with Toots Paka's company, and by 1916 Doraldina was packaging an act comprising the hula, a harem dance, and similar exotica.

Bare feet were given a veneer of scriptural authority in 1908 with the Salome that Gertrude Hoffman (Kitty Hayes) copied from Maud Allan (who was prevented by a booking war from dancing it in the United States). Once again the pattern of imitation, exaggeration (Eva Tanguay omitted the veils), and derision (Fanny Brice as a Yiddish Salome) continued for years, eventuating in the Salome of La Belle Marie (Marie Gillian), a "Terpsichorean Dream" that verged on striptease. The Salome craze ushered in a series of symbolic storytelling dances, obvious allegories readily comprehended, such as Joseph Herbert and Lillian Goldsmith's *Dance of the Siren* and Alice Eis and Bert French in *Rouge et Noir* (1912), a gambling scenario. More cryptic and hence less popular were Valeska Surratt's *Black Crepe and Diamonds* and the Orientalia of Ruth St. Denis, who loathed performing for vaudeville audiences.

By 1915 ragtime dominated, with shoulder shaking, finger snapping, wriggling, the fox trot, the Turkey Trot, and the one-step. A leading exponent was Joe Smith of the Avon Comedy Four, a specialist in step dances and the buck-and-wing. Later Bee Palmer and Gilda Gray would perform a toned-down Shimmy. During World War I dance halls lost appeal, as young men vanished from the

VAUDEVILLE. A nightclub performer whose heyday was in the 1910s, Gilda Gray became famous as the inventor of the Shimmy. She is seen here in a 1940 portrait. (Photograph by Carl Van Vechten; used by permission.)

floors and paid partners were scorned as shirkers. Social dancing found a haven in vaudeville, where in the 1920s the Charleston, the Black Bottom, or the Toodle-oo would be exhibited, albeit in expurgated versions.

Before World War I, Maurice Mauvet and Florence Walton were among the earliest teams to demonstrate genteel with ballroom techniques to middle-class audiences. Their well-tailored demeanor contrasted sharply with that of Irene and Vernon Castle, with their "languid energy, drooping strenuousness [and] whimsical seriousness" (Caffin, 1914, p. 103). In her autobiography, however, Irene Castle claimed that she and Vernon "only went into vaudeville when we were hard up." On the Orpheum circuit, Ivy and Douglas Crane were billed as "The Vernon and Irene Castle of the West." Jack Clifford and Evelyn Nesbit exploited her involvement in the sensational Harry Thaw murder trial by creating a "modest and proper" act that played the Keith circuit from 1913 to 1917. Between film engagements, Mae Murray and Clifton Webb toured in *Society Dances*, disseminating throughout the provinces such urban fads as a "Valse d'Arlequin," a "Brazilian Maxixe," a "Cinquante-Cinquante Tango," and a "Barcarole Waltz." Other popular teams included Mr. and Mrs. Carter De Haven, the "Beau Ideals"; the French Mitty and Tillo; the English Ted Trevor and Diane Harris; the suave and syncopated Tony and Renée De Marco; and Fred and Adele Astaire. The Astaire siblings played vaudeville as early as 1908 (Hudson Theater, New York City) in an act written by Ned Wayburn; their steps ranged from toe to the more popular hard-shoe, but they displeased the vari-

VAUDEVILLE. Edna Covey developed a comedic act that showed her special skills as a ballet-dancing contortionist. She was a featured performer in several editions of the *Ziegfeld Follies* in the 1920s. (Photograph from the Dance Collection, New York Public Library for the Performing Arts.)

VAUDEVILLE. Acts featuring Oriental or exotic themes were a staple of variety shows. This alluring, barefoot dancer was billed as Mademoiselle Armen Ohanian, "The Dancer of Shamahka." An advertisement in *The Morning Telegraph* announced her appearance at the Aeolian Hall, New York, in April 1924. (Photograph from the Dance Collection, New York Public Library for the Performing Arts.)

ety public: Fred seemed too effeminate. This was a frequent charge leveled at male exhibition dancers, who often were stigmatized as "lounge lizards" and "gigolos."

The ballet school tradition was perpetuated by La Petite Adelaide (Mary Dickey) in her dollie act and by Mademoiselle Dazie (Daisy Peterkin), originally known as Le Domino Rouge, expert at the *eschoppe*, or rock step. To keep from seeming stilted or mechanical, vaudeville toe dancing had to be a sprightly form of acrobatics. Mazie King was the first to jump off a table several feet in the air and come down on pointe, whereas Titenia would trip up and down stairs on her toes. Bessie Clayton, described by Caroline Caffin (1914) as a "sportive, laughing elfin creature" in a Pierrot costume, performed eccentric toe steps in unblocked shoes. Even Sally Rand, later notorious for her fans, toe danced at the Palace in New York City, waving ostrich plumes to Debussy's *Clair de Lune*.

The influence of Diaghilev's Ballets Russes was to be diffused throughout vaudeville. Gertrude Hoffman presented picturesque Russian dance dramas, and a number of authentic émigrés, such as Anna Pavlova and defectors from the Ballets Russes as well as Americans with Slavic sobriquets offered cut-rate renditions of Russian ballets to one-horse towns across the nation. Shura Rulowa's Ballet Russe, for example, toured the Pantages, Orpheum, Loew, and Keith theater circuits from 1922 to 1926, showering the fruits of enlightenment upon flocks of corn-fed ballerinas. Mockery ensued, often on the same bill. Sammy Krevoff did an infant travesty of Michel Fokine's *Le Spectre de la Rose*, and Fanny Brice dealt the *coup de grâce* to *The Dying Swan*.

The old standbys of acrobatic and comic dancing maintained a tenuous hold. Even the Albertina Rasch Dancers with its pastel, pompadour ambience had to feature a contortionist, for refinement was commercial only if it was enlivened by physical exertion. Legmania was revital-

VAUDEVILLE. The sight of two identically clad dancers moving in perfect synchrony has always held an appeal for the American public. *(left)* Inez Courtney and Gertrude McDonald holding a pose from their "Broadway Whirl" number, c.1921. *(right)* The young Verlon and Berlon Griffin are seen here in a mirror-image "Egyptian" pose, c.1923. The Griffin Twins were headliners on B. F. Keith's vaudeville circuit. (Photograph at right by Progress Studio, New York; both from the Dance Collection, New York Public Library for the Performing Arts.)

ized by Evelyn Law and Charlotte Greenwood; wooden-shoe acts, by Pat Rooney and Marion Bent; and the Texas Tommies flung one another around with frank good humor. There were dancers who imitated animals (Arthur Borani and Annie Nevaro, Rita Le Roy), scarecrow dancers (Montgomery and Stone; Macmahon, Diamond, and Clemence), and performers who specialized in drunken falls down staircases (Leon Errol, Willie Solar). When adagio dancing came into favor it was teeming with acrobats: Percy Oakes spun his partner Pamela Latour over his head, threw her on his back, and then whirled over the stage. The craze for the *apache* dance, launched by Giovanni Molasso, was capitalized on by French and Eis in their *Vampire Dance* (1909). [*See* Apache Dance.] Even in the late 1920s Janette Hackett stunned audiences with her "bad girl" act melding stunt work with tendentious allegory: upon finding her partner (Cesar Romero) to be Death, the fast-living siren rushes up a flight of stairs, clutches a heavy drape, and, swathed in it, rolls back down to the bottom.

The hoofer (a term coined about 1890 by the minstrel Billy Emerson but not heard commonly until the 1920s) did not necessarily specialize. Almost every comic could "shuffle off to Buffalo" to get offstage, and virtually every singer could fill in between verses with a sketchy soft-shoe. Some celebrities, such as the Dolly Sisters, could

barely move in time to the music, but their looks and charm were adequate recompense. It was a comedian, Joe Frisco, who originated the bent-knee jazz dance accompanied by cigar and derby. By 1923, the peak revenue year of vaudeville, usually three or four dance acts, the best earning upward of $250 a week, were on a "class" bill and scheduled in a strong spot directly after intermission. The dancers' technical expertise improved over the decades as audiences became more adept at distinguishing finesse from flat feet.

But vaudeville's yearning for sophistication and refinement proved to be its undoing. Large ensembles, tasteful costumes, and elaborate sets began to cut into profits: expenses of the Albertina Rasch Dancers totaled $2,500 a week. In 1921 the critic Marsden Hartley wrote how he regretted that

> now we get little more in the field of acrobatics beyond a varied buck and wing; everything seems tuxedoed for drawingroom purposes. *(Adventures in the Arts*, p. 156)

Audiences began to drift away, first to the automobile, now a viable commodity, which emptied theaters on weekends; then to the radio, which had the audacity to broadcast unseen tap dancers; and, most definitively, to the movies, where the lavish theatrics of a Busby Berkeley spectacular could be amplified by the live musical numbers, or "prologs," that preceded the films. The Palace Theater in New York stopped playing two-a-day vaudeville in 1932, and after an interim of mixed live and filmed entertainment, converted exclusively to movies in 1934.

As a result of this waning, many who had started as dancers metamorphosed into actors, the most conspicuous examples being George Raft, the hottest of Charlestoneers; James Cagney; and Buddy Ebsen, a popular adagio dancer. Adagio teams moved to the nightclubs, which had proliferated with Prohibition (1920–1933), and beat out the clean-cut varsity acts that had predominated there; ballet dancers found a berth in revue, a form intended for smaller, more elite audiences; and eccentric dancers received featured spots in musical comedy. A recrudescence of sorts occurred in the early 1940s, when the Palace revived vaudeville for a wartime public; and again during the 1950s on television, when it relied heavily on variety programming. Then, such troupers as the June Taylor Dancers and Mata & Hari garnered a vast new public for time-honored precision dancing and for spoofs of outdated styles. As Bernard Sobel (1961) has written, "Vaudeville is dead, but vaudevillians live on."

[*See also* Fan Dance; Tap Dance; United States of America, *articles on African-American dance traditions*.]

BIBLIOGRAPHY

Caffin, Caroline. *Vaudeville*. New York, 1914.
Castle, Irene. *Castles in the Air*. Garden City, N.Y., 1958.
Cooper, H. E. "Variety, Vaudeville, and Virtue: From the Naughty Nineties to Respectability." *Dance Magazine* (December 1926): 31–32.
Donahue, Jack. *Letters of a Hoofer to His Ma*. New York, 1931.
Fletcher, Tom. *One Hundred Years of the Negro in Show Business*. New York, 1954.
Laurie, Joe, Jr. *Vaudeville*. New York, 1953.
Martin, John. "Variety Revival Finds New Blood in an Old Medium." *New York Times* (10 May 1942).
Sampson, Henry T. *Blacks in Blackface: A Source Book on Early Black Musical Shows*. Metuchen, N.J., 1980.
Slide, Anthony. *The Vaudevillians: A Dictionary of Vaudeville Performers*. Westport, Conn., 1981.
Smith, Bill. *The Vaudevillians*. New York, 1976.
Sobel, Bernard. *A Pictorial History of Vaudeville*. New York, 1961.
Stearns, Marshall, and Jean Stearns. *Jazz Dance* (1968). New York, 1994.
Stein, Charles W., ed. *American Vaudeville as Seen by Its Contemporaries*. New York, 1984.
Terry, Walter. "Variety Dancers." *Dance Magazine* (July 1942): 12–13.
Terry, Walter. "Vaudeville Dance." *New York Tribune* (16 May 1942).
White, Stanley. "The Art and Agony of Toe-Dancing." *Royal Magazine* (June 1902).

FILMS. The following films may be found at the New York Public Library for the Performing Arts, unless otherwise noted. *Amy Muller* (Edison, 1896), featuring legmania, George Eastman House, Rochester, N.Y. *Annabella* (Edison, 1897). *Fougère* (American Mutoscope and Bioscope Co., 1902), with the ragtime cakewalk. *A "Tough" Dance* (American Mutoscope and Bioscope Co., 1902), with Kid Foly and Sailor Lil performing an *apache* dance. *Ameta* (American Mutoscope and Bioscope Co., 1903). *Franchonetti Sisters* (American Mutoscope and Bioscope Co., 1903). Edwin S. Porter, *Uncle Tom's Cabin* (Edison, 1903), with the time step, breaks, and street cakewalk. *She Would Be an Actress* (Lubin, 1907). *Tillie's Punctured Romance* (Sennett, 1914), featuring exhibition ballroom dancing and a parody by Marie Dressler and Charlie Chaplin, Museum of Modern Art, New York. Michael Curtiz, *Yankee Doodle Dandy* (Warner Brothers, 1942), featuring reconstructed and modernized vaudeville dance routines performed by veteran vaudevillians James Cagney and Walter Huston. *Dance Program* (George Amberg, c.1945), with clips of the Sisters Daineff, Loie Fuller, Alla Nazimova, and the Charlestons.

VIDEOTAPE. *The History of Jazz Dancing* (KQED-TV, San Francisco, 1970), Dance Collection, New York Public Library for the Performing Arts.

LAURENCE SENELICK

VEDANTAM SATYAM (Vedantam Satyanarayan Sarma; born 15 August 1934, Kuchipudi, Andhra Pradesh), Indian dancer. Vedantam Satyam is renowned for his enactment of female roles in traditional Kuchipudi dance drama. Trained from early childhood by his elder brother Prahlad Sarma and other teachers, he soon attracted the attention of connoisseurs with his exceptional expressive talent. His portrayals of Satyabhama in *Bhama Kalapam* and of Usha in *Usha Parinayam* have been universally hailed as the finest. He imparts an uncanny authority and assurance to his female roles and commands style, empathy, and erudition. His total identification with his roles draws crowds again and again. Many wonder how his masculine mind can comprehend and elicit the intensity of expression and ethos so intimately associated with women; however, the questions become irrelevant when one witnesses his compelling and communicative female portrayals that bring forth the essence of a *nāyikā* (heroine in a Sanskrit drama) with remarkable ease and abandon. Indeed, he belongs to the class of legendary dancers such as the Oḍissi guru Kelucharan Mahapatra and the late Balasaraswati and Mylapore Gauri Amma. Even when the physical form is no more than that of a young maiden, Vedantam Satyam's metamorphosis and evocation of female roles continue to surprise audiences.

Regarded as the foremost Kuchipudi dancer of recent times, Vedantam Satyam also served as principal of the Kuchipudi Art Academy and as a lead actor in the Venkataram Natya Mandali company of traditional male performers. In recognition of his rare gifts, he was made a fellow of the Central Sangeet Natak Akademi at the young age of twenty-six and received the academy's major aware. The government of India bestowed the Padamshri award on him; he also received the prestigious Kalidasa Sanman award for his services to Kuchipudi. Married and the father of two daughters and a son, Vedantam Satyam lives in Kuchipudi village, from which he travels to perform throughout India and abroad.

BIBLIOGRAPHY
Jonnalagadda, Anuradha. *Kuchipudi Who is Who.* Hyderabad, India, 1993.
Ragini Devi. *Dance Dialects of India.* 2d rev. ed. Delhi, 1990.
SUNIL KOTHARI

VEIGL, EVA MARIA. *See* Violette, Eva Maria.

VEMPATI CHINNA SATYAM (born 28 October 1929 in Kuchipudi, Andhra Pradesh), Indian dancer, choreographer, and teacher. Born into a traditional family of Kuchipudi performers, Vempati Chinna Satyam was trained by the legendary Vedantam Lakshminarayan Sastri, Tadepalli Pariya Satyam, and others from early childhood. Like other traditional male dancers, he began by performing female roles and later took male roles.

In the late 1950s Vempati moved to Madras to choreograph for films. In 1965 he established the Kuchipudi Art Academy, where he trained many young female dancers, an innovation in a dance drama genre which until then had been the preserve of men. His disciple Shobha Naidu interpreted his solo dances remarkably, establishing him as a brilliant choreographer.

Soon Vempati began choreographing dance dramas on mythological themes, working with a team of musicians to build up a large repertory of both solo and group works. His solo numbers featured lilting music, an arresting dance style, rapid footwork, and undulating vertical movements. What had begun as a folk genre three decades before, with loose, ill-defined movements, acquired sophistication in his hands. He applied the principles of classical Indian dance manuals to Kuchipudi technique, raising it to the level of such classical genres as *bharata nāṭyam, kathakaḷi,* and *kathak.* His dance dramas, especially *Krishna Parijata, Padmavati Srinivasa Kalyanam, Hara Vilasa, Ramayana,* and *Chandalika,* are a precious legacy.

The many dancers who studied with Vempati have transformed Kuchipudi dance; notable are Shashikala, Bala, Padma Menon, Kamala Reddy, and the late Kamadeva. His son Vempati Ravi Shankar is also a noted dancer and teaches with his father at their academy in Madras. Among Vempati's honors are the Central Sangeet Natak Akademi award, the Kalidasa Sanman, and many awards from art institutions in Andhra Pradesh.

BIBLIOGRAPHY
Misra, Susheela. *Some Dancers of India.* New Delhi, 1992.
Ramachandran, Anandhi. "Interview: Vempati Chinna Satyam." *Sruti* (Madras), no. 13 (November 1984): 32–34.
Satyanajayana, Andavilli, and Premaraju Surya Rao. *Dr. Vempati—Maestro with a Mission.* Vijaywordan, 1993.
SUNIL KOTHARI

VENDA DANCE. Most of the traditional dances of the Venda, a Bantu people, were developed in an enclave within the Transvaal, South Africa, that was declared an independent republic in 1979. This is a lush, mountainous region directly south of Zimbabwe, between the South African town of Louis Trichardt and Kruger National Park. Its 1987 population of approximately six hundred thousand included minorities speaking Tsonga and Northern Sotho (Pedi). Several hundred thousand Venda live in the Republic of South Africa, especially in Soweto, where some fine performances of men's dances can be seen because of the many dance teams that rehearse and perform regularly.

The teams are organized in much the same way as those in the rural areas but with the difference that the dancing is the focus of social activity, rather than a part of rituals and social events organized by rulers and healers. Team members contribute regularly to the general expenses and particularly to the cost of beer. Each team has a manager and an assistant manager, a musical director and his assistant, and a dance director and his assistant, who are responsible for demonstrating the steps. This system of organization existed in Venda before the arrival of Europeans, as did indigenous terms for the officers, their functions, the accompanying musical instruments, and the music played on them.

Two types of dance are performed, and teams generally specialize in one or the other; both are circle dances. The dancers move counterclockwise around the drums, and each dancer blows a single pitch on a stopped pipe so that the whole ensemble produces sequences of melody that are filled out with chords. The *givha*, *visa*, and related dances are played on pipes tuned to a pentatonic scale, while the pipes of the *tshikona* are heptatonic. Traditionally, the two sets of pipes are made from different types of reed and tuned to different pitches, so that pentatonic melodies cannot be played on heptatonic pipes; this distinction is observed even when the pipes are made from pieces of tubing or hose.

The *tshikona* is the most sacred and important of the Venda dances and was originally performed by adult men and women on state and ritual occasions. The *givha* and *visa* are comparatively new versions of ancient play dances for young people. Various tunes are used for the *visa*, *mutshaini*, *givha*, and *tshikanganga*, but many dance steps are common to all of them. There is only one *tshikona* melody but many different steps, some representational and others abstract and named after their inventor, or after a ruler whom the choreographer wanted to honor. The representational steps portray baboons, the gathering of peanuts, sowing seeds, and other horticultural activities related to the first-fruits rites at which *tshikona* is performed.

Dzhombo (children's dances) and *tshigombela* (a recreational dance for adolescent and preadolescent girls) are classified as games *(mitambo)* and are similar in form to the *givha* and *visa*. In contrast, the *domba* premarital initiation dance, the female puberty rites *vhusha* and *ndayo* (which resembled physical-training exercises), the *ngoma dza midzimu* dances of spirit possession, the dances of the *sungwi* girls' initiation, and the *tshikona* are all classified as sacred, serious acts *(dzingoma)*.

There are contrasts within many events between communal dancing in a circle or spiral (expressed by the lexical root -*mona*)—which is also referred to by the general word meaning "to dance" (-*tshina*)—and improvised solo exhibition dancing (-*gaya*). In *tshigombela*, girls dance *gaya* in groups of two, three, or four and always rehearse their coordinated step routines. In dances of spirit possession, which are performed by cult members and are centered on medicine, healing, and ancestral spirits, *tshina* and *gaya* are condensed into sequences of steps danced by individuals who come out in turn into the arena. Each one alternately spins around for sixteen beats and dances toward three drummers for another sixteen beats. In the important dancing to *malende* beer-drinking songs, however, the style is that of solo *gaya*, but it is always called *tshina*.

The basic posture in Venda dances for both men and women is relaxed, with feet parallel and a slight tilt forward from the hips. Dancers never try to fight against gravity, except when men and youths leap high in *malende* or *gaya*. The legs and arms are not fully extended, although girls and women often flex the foot when lifting it so that the sole is nearly parallel to the ground. The men's style contrasts with that of women; it is light and opposed to the ground, while the women's is sharp and earthbound, with the feet kicking the ground. Men move outward, perform bigger movements, and use all available space; women use the more limited space underneath themselves, using the front-back plane without extending their limbs.

In traditional Venda society, everyone dances during childhood and youth, and most men and women dance *tshikona* or *malende*, or both, whenever they can. Dancing is an integral part of both informal and formal education. It can also help people achieve the transcendent states necessary for direct experience of the "real world" of the spirit.

[*See also* South Africa, *article on* Indigenous Dance; *and* Southern Africa.]

BIBLIOGRAPHY

Blacking, John. "An Introduction to Venda Traditional Dances." *Dance Studies* 2 (1977): 34–56. Contains photographs and Benesh notation of dances by Dora Frankel.

Blacking, John. "Songs and Dances of the Venda People." In *Music and Dance*, edited by David Tunley. Nedlands, W.A., 1982.

Blacking, John. "The Context of Venda Possession Music: Reflections on the Effectiveness of Symbols." *Yearbook of the International Council for Traditional Music* 17 (1985).

Grau, Andrée. "Some Problems in the Analysis of Dance Style, with Special Reference to the Venda of South Africa." Master's thesis, Queen's University of Belfast, 1979.

Stayt, Hugh A. *The Bavenda.* Oxford, 1931.

JOHN BLACKING

VENEZUELA. During the precolonial era, dance in Venezuela was associated with religious ceremonies. In the early years of independence and throughout the nineteenth century, dances were performed for entertainment, among them zarzuelas, *sainetes*, and musical comedies. Ballet was not then a part of the national culture.

The visit of Anna Pavlova and her ballet company in 1917 marked the first time Venezuelans saw ballet in their own country. In 1930 Gally de Mamay, a former member of Diaghilev's Ballets Russes, arrived in Caracas. She taught private classes for the city's privileged youth, usually using large rooms in their own homes.

From 1864 to 1935 Venezuela had been ruled by a military dictatorship. During a brief democratic spell, Nena Coronil, who had studied with de Mamay, founded the National School of Ballet in 1948. There were scholarships for selected students, with each of the nation's twenty states contributing financial support. By 1953 the school had one hundred pupils. The faculty consisted of

William Lundy, an American, the Russians Irina Yovanovitch and Lila Nikolska, and Miro Anton, a Czech.

In 1953, Henry Danton from England's Sadler's Wells Ballet headed the school, and Coronil established the Ballet Nena Coronil. This was the nation's first professional company, but its repertory was limited by the elementary level of the dancers. Progress was also impeded by the lack of a sense of organization and risk, typical of the country at that time. In addition, Coronil and Danton relied on the standard European ballet heritage rather than attempting to create an image more appropriate to the regional culture. In 1954, Coronil staged fragments of the classics—*Swan Lake, Giselle,* and *The Sleeping Beauty.* Nevertheless, Coronil's efforts were important: they familiarized the Venezuelan audience with the art of ballet; they also formed a generation of Venezuelan dancers, among them Graciela Henríquez, Julián Pérez, Belén Lobo, Vicente Nebrada, Maruja Leiva, Margot Contreras, and Irma Contreras.

Meanwhile, Grishka Holguín, a student of Waldeen and Guillermina Bravo, arrived in Caracas from Mexico. He and Conchita Crededio founded the Venezuelan School of Contemporary Dance, which functioned from 1948 to 1959. Among Holguín's best choreographic works were *Mampulorio* (1956), *Hiroshima* (1957), and *Medea* (1957). His student Sonia Sanoja established her own group in 1963, but her idiosyncratic style hindered the formation of a lasting company.

Another attempt at founding a company supported by a school was made in 1957 by Irma Contreras. The National Ballet of Venezuela began with members of the newly disbanded Coronil company and was associated with the Interamerican Academy of Ballet. In addition to staging classics and fragments, Contreras sought to create new works; however, the dancers, not yet fully attuned to the classical tradition, were not ready for this move, nor was the public. The company disbanded in 1968. The Interamerican Academy of Ballet and the National Ballet had, however, achieved one exceptional result: they produced Zhandra Rodríguez. After six years at the school, Rodríguez began dancing major roles with the company at the age of fourteen. She then studied at the School of American Ballet in New York and danced with American Ballet Theatre before returning to Venezuela in 1975.

Irma Contreras resigned from the National Ballet in 1968. Her place was taken by Elías Pérez Borjas, who had been the company's *régisseur* since its founding. Seeking to establish a national identity, Pérez Borjas introduced the company to modern dance. As the Ballet del INCIBA (Instituto Nacional de Cultura y Bellas Artes), the group was a success despite the desertion of many of the original dancers. Pérez Borjas became an important presence on the cultural scene. He brought to Venezuela a new way of viewing dance and of organizing a company.

VENEZUELA. Zhandra Rodríguez was Venezuela's leading ballerina from the 1960s to the 1980s. Partnered by Zane Wilson, she appeared in Vicente Nebrada's neoclassical *Nuestros Valses* in a 1977 performance with the Ballet Internacional de Caracas. (Photograph by Miguel Gracia, courtesy of Belén Lobo.)

In 1968 the Ballet del INCIBA staged the debut of the choreographer Graciela Henríque. With her first work, *Tres,* she established her position in the vanguard of Venezuelan dance and achieved her desire, to reveal through movement the personality of a human being—dancer, woman, or worker. Another of her works, *Mujeres,* was more polemical.

A new policy of subsidizing arts groups was announced by the National Institute of Culture and Fine Arts in 1974 but was not immediately put into practice. As a consequence, unemployed dancers looked for new ways to continue their professions, and a new kind of organization, the independent group, emerged. Among them were the Taller de Danza Contemporánea, founded by José Ledezma; Macrodanza, directed by Norah Parissi; and Contradanza, directed by Hercilia López. These remain active and are now supported by the state.

The 1970s were marked by the reshaping of concepts of modern dance, influenced by the work of Martha Graham, Merce Cunningham, and Alwin Nikolais. Drama, gesture, and daily actions were incorporated. The sisters Adriana and Luz Urdaneta, who had graduated from The

Place in London, formed the group Danzahoy in 1980. The Urdanetas' search for a Latin American style was embodied in such successful Venezuelan works as Henríquez's *Oraciones* (1982), Carlos Orta's *Un Modo de Andar por la Vida* (1980), and the collective creations *Selva* (1981), *Momentos Hostiles* (1987), *40 Grades de la Sombra* (1988), and *Ventana* (1990).

Two companies had important impacts on dance in Venezuela. Both the Ballet Internacional de Caracas, founded in 1975, and the Ballet Fundación Teresa Carreño, founded in 1980, enjoy substantial financial support. The Ballet Internacional had Zhandra Rodríguez as principal ballerina and Vicente Nebrada, who had been with New York's Harkness Ballet, as artistic director and resident choreographer. Essential to Nebrada's work was a corps of strong, athletic dancers, most of whom he recruited from the defunct Harkness group. Only a few Venezuelan dancers were able to work in the new company. The Americans Alvin Ailey and Margo Sappington were invited to stage their works for the BIC, as was the Canadian Brian Macdonald. The company toured Europe, performed at the Spoleto Festival in Italy, and danced in New York. Disunity undermined the company, however, as Rodríguez came into conflict with Nebrada.

In 1983, the Ballet Nuevo Mundo (Ballet of the New World) emerged from the BIC with Rodríguez and Dale Talley as artistic directors and principal dancers. The company gathered many of the BIC dancers and reserved the rights to certain of its choreographic works. While the Ballet Internacional de Caracas oriented itself in the direction of the Harkness Ballet and American Ballet Theatre, the Ballet of the New World commissioned occasional works from new choreographers and from Carlos Orta. In 1987 the Ballet of the New World toured Europe and Asia.

The Teatro Teresa Carreño opened in 1983, providing a cultural and theatrical complex comparable to New York's Lincoln Center, with technologically sophisticated scenographic devices. It became the home of La Fundación Ballet Teresa Carreño, founded by the Argentinian teacher Rodolfo Rodríguez. With the intention of staging the classical repertory, Rodríguez invited such foreign stars as Rudolf Nureyev, Ekaterina Maximova, and Fernando Bujones to interpret principal roles, letting the Venezuelans dance in the corps. This procedure was in contrast to that of the Ballet of the New World, where only Venezuelan dancers performed.

With Pérez Borjas in charge at the Teresa Carreño, Nebrada returned to choreography with great success in his 1984 version of *The Firebird*, which featured elaborate scenery and a brilliant company. Nebrada clearly revealed the neoclassical direction of the company by staging his choreographies such as *Géminis*, *Percussion for Six Men*, *Nuestros Valses*, *Doble Corchea*, *George Sand*, and, later, versions of *Romeo and Juliet*, *Coppélia*, *Don Quixote*, *Swan Lake*, and *Cinderella*. The Teresa Carreño Foundation successfully blended dancers from different companies and schools, including the Metropolitan Ballet, directed by Keyla Ermecheo; the Ballet Nina Novak, directed by Nina

VENEZUELA. Dancers of the Ballet Nacional de Caracas Teresa Carreño (originally the Ballet Fundación Teresa Carreño) in a 1986 performance of Vicente Nebrada's *Doble Corchea*, set to music by Benjamin Britten. (Photograph by Miguel Gracia, courtesy of Belén Lobo.)

VENEZUELA. Members of the Danzahoy group perform Adriana Urdaneta's *Huespedes* (1994), to music by Aquíles Báez. (Photograph by Ana María Yánez, courtesy of Adriana Urdaneta.)

Novak; Ballet Arte, directed by Lidija Franklin; Conjunto Coreográfico (Choreographic Alliance) of the state of Carabobo, directed by Nina Nikaronova; and the Ballet School of Taormina Guevara, directed by Taormina Guevara until her death. In 1986 Danzahoy became the resident company of the Teatro Teresa Carreño.

Additional small groups were formed. Danza Teatro, directed by Abelardo Gameche, formerly with the Taller de Danza Contemporánea, was oriented toward experiments with postmodern tendencies. While also dancing with the José Limón company in the United States, Orta established a group of his own, Choreoarte, planning to develop choreography based on folklore.

La Fundación Ballet Teresa Carreño, called Ballet Nacional de Caracas Teresa Carreño since 1984, participated in the United We Dance festival held in 1995 in San Francisco, California. In the area of modern dance, Venezuela's encouragement for young choreographers has seen notable development as a result of the Festival de Jóvenes Coreógraphos. At this time in Venezuela there are six active classical dance companies and thirteen active modern dance companies, all subsidized by the Consejo Nacional de la Cultura.

BIBLIOGRAPHY
Alvarenga, Teresa. *Zhandra Rodríguez y el Ballet de Caracas*. Caracas, 1980.
Barrios, Maria Eugenia. *Por amor a la danza*. Caracas, 1985.
Danzaluz. *Directorio latinoamericano*. Maracaibo, 1991.
Danzaluz. *Cuadernos de danza (Terminología de danza académica y contemporánea)*. Maracaibo, 1991.
Fernandez Palazzi, Federico. *Las dos caras de la danza*. Caracas, 1990.
Ferrari, Marisol. *Danzaluz: Veinticinco aniversario*. Maracaibo, 1994.
Guerra, Ramiro. *Apreciación de la danza*. Maracaibo, 1990.
Leon, Carlos Augusto. *Vivencia de la danza*. Caracas, 1974.
Lobo, Belén. "La danza en Venezuela: De Gally de Mamay a Vicente Nebreda." *Enciclopedia conocer a Venezuela*, 1986.
Lobo, Belén. *Pasión de la danza*. (Revista M. 93) Caracas, 1990.
Lobo, Belén. "La danza clásica y contemporánea en Venezuela." *Enciclopedia temática de Venezuela*. Caracas, 1993.
Lobo, Belén. *Nebreda/Nebrada*. Caracas, 1996.
Monasterios, Ruben. *B.I.C. Imágen de un ballet perdido*. Caracas, 1981.
Monasterios, Ruben. *Cuerpos en el espacio*. Caracas, 1986.
Perez Borjas, Elias. *La danza en Venezuela*. Caracas, 1966.
Sanoja, Sonia, *Duraciones visuales*. Caracas, 1963.
Sanoja, Sonia. *A través de la danza*. Caracas, 1971.
Sanoja, Sonia. *Bajo el signo de la danza, 1992*. Caracas, 1992.
Sassone, Helena, and Roland Streuli. *La danza en Venezuela*. Caracas, 1989.
Stahl, Steffy. *El amanecer de la danza en Venezuela*. Caracas, 1992.
Viana, Luis. *La metáfora de la violencia*. Caracas, 1994.
Womutt, Andreina. *Movimiento perpetuo*. Caracas, 1991.

BELÉN LOBO

VERCHININA, NINA (Nina Verchinina de Beausacq; born 1912 in Moscow, died 16 December 1995 in Rio de Janiero, Brazil), dancer. By the first half of the twentieth century many ballet companies were touring Brazil, and some of the dancers stayed to open schools and found companies. Until the arrival of the Russian dancer Nina Verchinina in 1954, Brazil's exposure to theatrical dance was almost exclusively to classical ballet. After arriving in the country as an independent choreographer, Verchinina became a pioneer, introducing the basic principles of modern dance.

Nina Verchinina had a noble background. Born in Moscow and raised in Shanghai, she held the title of countess of Beausacq. As a child she began taking dance lessons with two of the most prominent Russian instructors of the time, Olga Preobajenska, master of the classical technique, and Bronislava Nijinska, one of the first to introduce modern dance worldwide. After absorbing Nijinska's teachings, Verchinina went to Germany to study with Rudolf Laban.

Verchinina began her professional career in 1929 as a member of Ida Rubinstein's dance company. At that time, the company had Nijinska as a choreographer and Igor Stravinsky and Maurice Ravel as contributing composers. Verchinina soon became a soloist for the Ballets Russes de Monte Carlo, and when the company split, Verchinina stayed with Colonel Wassily de Basil's group, then called the Original Ballets Russes. She danced intermittently for the company from 1933 to 1937, 1939 to 1941, and 1946 to 1947.

During her years with the Ballets Russes, Verchinina was known for her idiosyncratic style, juxtaposing classical pointe technique with dramatic gesture and modern angular steps. Because of these characteristics, she was often referred to as "Mary Wigman on pointe."

VERCHININA. As one of the picnickers in the third movement, "In the Country," of Léonide Massine's *Symphonie Fantasque* (1936). (Photograph from the Dance Collection, New York Public Library for the Performing Arts.)

Beginning in 1937, while dancing with the Original Ballet Russe, Verchinina began experimenting with choreography. She worked initially as invited choreographer for the San Francisco Ballet in the 1937/38 season, and later at the Ballet Opera of Havana, from 1942 to 1945.

In 1949, while established in Madrid, Spain, Verchinina founded her own dance group. Works such as *The Quest* and *Valsa Triste*, created then, are now part of the repertory of many companies worldwide.

During the 1950s Verchinina built an independent career in South America. In 1950 she went to Argentina and worked in Buenos Aires, La Plata, and Mendoza. Four years later, she settled in Brazil. In 1954 and 1955, Verchinina was based at the Rio de Janeiro City Theater as invited choreographer. There she was responsible for the *mise-en-scène* of *Narciso* and *Rhapsody in Blue*. From 1957 to 1960, Verchinina began creating dances for the same company, based on the work of Brazilian composers. The results included *Tahina Can*, to music by Heitor Villa-Lobos, and *Zuimaaluti*, to music by Claudio Santoro.

In the 1960s, Nina Verchinina stopped choreographing and dedicated her time exclusively to teaching dance. Her style, combining a strong classical background with modernist movement and an expressionist repertory of gestures, was carried into her teaching. It has been of incomparable value to the development of theatrical dance in Brazil.

BIBLIOGRAPHY

Faro, Antonio José. *Pequena história da dança*. Rio de Janeiro, 1986.
Faro, Antonio José. *A dança no Brasil e seus constructores*. Rio de Janeiro, 1988.
Portinari, Maribel. *História da dança*. Rio de Janeiro, 1989.
Sucena, Eduardo. *A dança teatral no Brasil*. Rio de Janeiro, 1988.

KATIA CANTON

VERDON, GWEN (Gwyneth Evelyn Verdon; born 13 January 1925 in Culver City, California), American dancer, singer, actress, choreographer, and dance educator. Because she was "knock-kneed," Verdon began to study dance with her mother, Gertrude, a Denishawn dancer, while very young. She continued with the Cecchetti, method taught by Ernest Belcher and Aida Broadbent and explored Spanish dance with Eduardo Cansino (Rita Hayworth's father). Chosen "Miss California" at the age of fourteen, she danced with Broadbent's ballet corps in Los Angeles Civic Light Opera productions of *Rosalinda* and *The Three Musketeers* (1947) and even formed a comedy ballroom team, Verdon and Del Velle.

After a brief marriage at the age of sixteen, motherhood, and a three-year interlude from dance, she returned to study ballet with Carmelita Maracci and East Indian dance with La Meri. She joined Jack Cole's landmark dance company in nightclubs and on stage in *Bonanza Bound* (out of town, 1947) and *Alive and Kicking* (Broadway, 1950). With her strong technique and immaculate isolation, she became one of the leading exponents of Cole's inventive jazz style, first assisting him on *Magdalena* (Broadway, 1948).

Under contract to Twentieth Century–Fox, Verdon and Cole, who was the dance director, explored erotic honesty in onscreen dance, often causing havoc with the censors. In 1951 she blistered the screen as a slave girl in *David and Bathsheba*, was featured with Betty Grable in *Meet Me after the Show*, and led the ensemble of *On the Riviera*. After choreographing and dancing in *Dreamboat*, she was back illuminating Cole's work in *The "I Don't Care" Girl* and *The Merry Widow* (1952). In 1953, she had an acting role and again danced with Grable in *The Farmer Takes a Wife* and performed a steamy Voodoo-ceremony dance (which she choreographed) in *Mississippi Gambler*.

At the invitation of choreographer Michael Kidd, she auditioned for the role of Claudine in *Can-Can* (1953). On opening night on Broadway, she created a sensation, and she subsequently won her first Tony award for her performance. Hollywood lost its best dancer, although she did briefly rejoin Cole for *Gentlemen Marry Brunettes* (1955). Cast next as the temptress Lola in *Damn Yankees* (1955), Verdon collaborated with another film expatriate, choreographer Bob Fosse. With her impudent explosion of flame-red hair, uniquely lovable squeaky voice, and innocent farm-girl face, Verdon, planted firmly on her well-controlled and well-proportioned body, became the definitive dancing-singing star of American musicals.

With Verdon as his inspiration and muse, Fosse continued to experiment and define his style. Together they created a succession of hit shows, with Verdon as their star, as the Broadway musical moved into its choreographer-as-director era: *New Girl in Town* (1957), *Redhead* (1959), *Sweet Charity* (1966), and, finally, *Chicago* (1975). Verdon and Fosse had married in 1960 and had a daughter together in 1963. Although they subsequently divorced, Verdon continued to assist Fosse on the film version of *Sweet Charity* (1969, for which she coached Shirley MacLaine), staged the second company of *Chicago*, and served as dance mistress on *Dancin'* (Broadway, 1978).

In addition to multiple Tony, Donaldson, Grammy, and *Dance Magazine* awards for her stage performances, Verdon also has the distinction of being the quintessential interpreter of the work of two of the twentieth century's most innovative stage and film choreographers. One of her stage roles, in *Damn Yankees* (1958), was captured on film: the crispness and clarity of her technique and her unique vulnerability and sense of humor and style are riveting.

VERDON. The sultry "Whatever Lola Wants," choreographed by Bob Fosse, was one of the hit numbers of *Damn Yankees* (1955). Verdon is pictured here as Lola, a 172-year-old witch sent by Satan to seduce an uncooperative baseball player (Stephen Douglass). Her provocative striptease was an extraordinary mix of East Indian hand gestures, flamenco-like footwork, French burlesque, and purely American jazz dance. (Photograph by Photofest, New York; used by permission.)

BIBLIOGRAPHY

"1961 Award Winner Profile." *Dance Magazine* (March 1962).

Grubb, Kevin Boyd. *Razzle Dazzle: The Life and Work of Bob Fosse.* New York, 1989.

Mordden, Ethan. *Broadway Babies.* New York, 1983.

Who's Who in Entertainment, 1992–1993. Wilmette, Ill., 1993.

LARRY BILLMAN

VERDY, VIOLETTE (Nelly Armande Guillerm; born 1 December 1933 in Pont l'Abbé), French dancer and teacher. Verdy began ballet lessons at the age of eight. Following studies with Carlotta Zambelli and Rousanne Sarkissian, she made her professional debut in 1945 in Roland Petit's *Le Poète*, soon afterward becoming a member of his Ballets des Champs-Élysées. For three years she

VERDY. Her vivacity and extraordinary musicality made Verdy an audience favorite wherever she appeared. She is pictured here in an exuberant *saut de chat* in George Balanchine's *Donizetti Variations*, in 1960. (Photograph by Fred Fehl; used by permission. Choreography by George Balanchine © The George Balanchine Trust.)

danced cameo roles until chosen by film director Ludwig Berger to star in his 1950 release *Ballerina*. It was at this time that she adopted the stage name of Verdy.

Although *Ballerina* was generally considered an insignificant film, Verdy's sincere acting and pure technique led to numerous guest appearances at festivals and galas and to contracts with the reorganized Ballets des Champs-Élysées, the Ballet de Marigny, and the Ballets de Paris de Roland Petit. While with the latter group she created the embattled heroine in Petit's *Le Loup* (1953), a portrayal that marked her artistic coming-of-age. After the Ballets de Paris disbanded, Verdy toured the United States with the London Festival Ballet. Injury temporarily interrupted her career, but by 1957 she was appearing with the Ballet Rambert in her first full-length *Coppélia* and *Giselle*.

An amateur film made during Verdy's Festival Ballet tour and shown to Nora Kaye led, in 1957, to an invitation for Verdy to join American Ballet Theatre. Thereafter, with brief exceptions, the focus of her career shifted to the United States. Her ability to adapt herself to the tastes of the American public in such works as *Gala Performance*, *Offenbach in the Underworld*, and *Theme and Variations* was summed up by a reviewer for *Dance News* (November 1957): "Violette Verdy has acclimatized herself to the company and is part of the repertory with no ado. Her unmannered style is the secret of the ease with which she fits

into British, French, and American Ballet." Beside dancing the standard repertory, Verdy also created the title role in the American Ballet Theatre production of Birgit Cullberg's *Miss Julie* (1958).

With the temporary disbanding of American Ballet Theatre in autumn 1958, Verdy became the only company member invited to join the New York City Ballet. Although her physique and training set her apart from the majority of the New York City Ballet dancers, her musicality and intelligence enabled her to blend harmoniously into George Balanchine's choreographic conceptions. For close to two decades she brought vitality and incisive musical understanding to her interpretations of *Symphony in C, Divertimento No. 15,* Polyhymnia in *Apollo, Stars and Stripes, Scotch Symphony,* and *Allegro Brillante.* Her longtime partner Edward Villella commented on her "extraordinary, complete musical understanding, almost like Balanchine's. The remarkable thing . . . is that a French dancer coming here to another style and another repertoire has pointed up Balanchine's intentions . . . more than any of his other dancers."

In addition to her roles in the standard repertory, Verdy had Balanchine parts crafted for her in *A Midsummer Night's Dream, Episodes, Liebeslieder Walzer, Jewels, La Source,* and *Sonatine.* Throughout the same period she also created roles by other choreographers, including that of Creusa in the American premiere of Cullberg's *Medea* and a solo (op. 25, no. 4) in Jerome Robbins's *Dances at a Gathering,* beside making guest appearances dancing the classics with such companies as England's Royal Ballet, the Paris Opera Ballet, and the Boston Ballet. Her portrayal of Giselle was hailed as one of the finest of her generation, while her partnership with Villella approached the legendary. She also served as a roving talent scout for the School of American Ballet's scholarship program.

Verdy's last years with Balanchine were punctuated by recurrent injuries and by a growing distance between herself and the choreographer, largely because of her independent thinking. In 1977 she left the New York City Ballet to become the first female director of dance at the Paris Opera. For three years she attempted, against some opposition, to bring flexibility into the Opera's rigid hierarchical system, as well as to promote youthful dancers and choreographers. She was also instrumental in obtaining the ballet company's first musical director. When a change of administration necessitated her departure in 1980, Verdy returned to the United States, where she became artistic co-director, later full director, of the Boston Ballet, a position in which she served until 1984. She then rejoined the New York City Ballet, where she is a teaching associate. Known for her broad-ranging skills in the field, Verdy also receives frequent invitations to teach, choreograph, and lecture at other institutions, including England's Royal Ballet, the Paris Opera Ballet school, and Ballet West. She is also active in regional ballet. She has written a book for children, *Of Swans, Sugar Plums, and Satin Slippers,* which was published in 1991.

BIBLIOGRAPHY

Dekle, Nicole. "Summer Secret." *Dance Magazine* (February 1994): 88–93.

Garis, Robert. "The Balanchine Enterprise." *Ballet Review* 21 (Spring 1993): 24–44.

Haggin, B. H. *Ballet Chronicle.* New York, 1970.

Huckenpahler, Victoria. *Ballerina: A Biography of Violette Verdy.* New York, 1978.

Marks, Marcia. "Violette—'Because She Is So Modest.'" *Dance Magazine* (February 1972): 47–62.

Mason, Francis. "The Paris Opéra: A Conversation with Violette Verdy." *Ballet Review* 14 (Fall 1986): 23–30.

Verdy, Violette. *Giselle: A Role for a Lifetime.* New York, 1977.

Verdy, Violette. "Violette Verdy on the Bolshoi." *Ballet Review* 15 (Summer 1987): 15–38.

Whitney, Mary. "Homecoming." *Ballet News* 2 (September 1980): 18–21.

VICTORIA HUCKENPAHLER

VES DANCE. The Sri Lankan ritual dance drama called Kohomba Kankariya, dating to the fifth century BCE, is the spiritual home of the *ves* dancer. The *ves* regalia *(suseta abarana)* is that of a priest-king. No fewer than sixty-four items make up this costume, which is believed to belong to the deity Kohomba and is regarded as a replica of costume of the royal magician Male Rajjuruwo, who was supernaturally lured to the island of Sri Lanka to heal King Panduvasdeva of an incurable malady.

The impressive headgear is a crown of several parts: a silver tiara *(sikha-bandanaya)*; a forehead plate fringed with silver *bo*-leaves *(netti malaya)*; and seven silver spokes rising like rays above the dancer's head. Intricate silver ear plates *(thodupath)* adorn his ears; ornamental plates *(urabahu)* of silver or brass cover his shoulders. He wears three sets of broad silver armlets *(bandi wallalu)*, six on each arm, and necklaces of colored beads *(kara-patiya)*. His bare chest is covered with strings of beads, held together with clasps of carved ivory ornamented with silver. He wears elongated silver wrist plates about two inches (five centimeters) wide.

The clothing of the dancer is called *hangalaya*. From waist to ankle he wears a white cloth *(ududaya)* intricately pleated, about three and a half yards (three meters) in length. Over this he puts another cloth, the *devalla*, which is twenty yards (twenty meters) long, heavily pleated, and extends to the knees. Around the waist he wears yet another cloth *(yoth pota)* of fine material folded to a width of two inches (five centimeters) and flounced at the end to form layers of frills *(neriya)*. A strong string forty-two feet (fourteen meters) long, the *hangal lanuwa*, is wrapped around the dancer's waist to secure the layers of pleated fabric, and a silver belt with a decorated clasp is worn over the cloth. From the center of this belt down to the knees is a drape of bright red velvet decorated with heavy silver bosses *(inahedaya)*, fashioned into nineteen tasseled corners to simulate an elephant's trunk. Around the calves are several sets of brass jingles *(rasu pati)*, and on the feet are anklets *(silambu)* rounded and filled with bells, anchored to the second toe of each foot.

After several years of apprenticeship under a revered *mulyakdessa*, the *ves* dancer *(yakdessa)* is crowned with his silver headgear at an auspicious time with much ceremony; traditionally, this initiation occurs at a Kohomba Kankariya ceremony. The *ves* dancers and drummers display their talents in competitive performances at the Kohomba Kankariya. [*See* Kohomba Kankariya.]

Ves dance has a highly developed classical technique with many variations and synchronizations of mood and rhythm. Its elements include invocatory chants, perfect synchronization of hand and foot movements, and vigorous embellishments. The dancer has to be equally proficient in dancing, drumming, and singing before his initiation.

VES DANCE. Wearing an elaborate traditional costume, the *ves* dancer Surasena demonstrates a characteristic jumping movement. (Photograph from the archives of The Asia Society, New York.)

Ves dancers from traditional families, such as the Nittawela, Thiththapajjala, Rangama, and Amunugama families of the Kandy district, were given lands and settled in certain villages by the Kandyan kings. These masters have passed down their art form in its purity from father to son for perhaps two millennia. The Beravaya community of shamans today preserves the highly evolved art of Kandyan dance. [*See* Kandyan Dance.] In recent times they have provided a grand finale to any public performance of Kandyan dancing, welcomed state guests, and participated in the famous annual street pageant, the Kandy Perahera, held in August.

[*For articles on other dance traditions in Sri Lanka see* Kandy Perahera *and* Touil. *See also* Costume in Asian Traditions *and* Mask and Makeup, *article on* Asian Traditions.]

BIBLIOGRAPHY

Amunugana, Sarath. *Notes on Sinhala Culture.* Colombo, 1980.
Bowers, Faubion. *Theatre in the East: A Survey of Asian Dance and Drama.* New York, 1956.
de Zoete, Beryl. *Dance and Magic Drama in Ceylon.* London, 1957.
Disanayaka, Mudiyanse. *Udarata santikarma saha gami natya sampradaya.* Colombo, 1990.
Gunasinghe, Siri. *Masks of Ceylon.* Colombo, 1962.
Kotelawala, Sicille P. C. *The Classical Dance of Sri Lanka.* New York, 1974.
Makulloluwa, W. B. *Dances of Sri Lanka.* Colombo, 1976.
Nevill, Hugh. "Sinhalese Folklore." *Journal of the Royal Asiatic Society, Ceylon Branch* 14 (1971): 58–90.
Pertold, Otaker. *Ceremonial Dances of the Sinhalese* (1930). Colombo, 1973.
Raghavan, M. D. *Dances of the Sinhalese.* Colombo, 1968.
Sarachchandra, Ediriweera R. *The Folk Drama of Ceylon.* 2d ed. Colombo, 1966.
Sedaraman, J. I. *Nrtya ratnakaraya.* Colombo, 1992.
Sedaraman, J. I., et al. *Udarata natum kalava.* Colombo, 1992.
Seneviratna, Anuradha. *Traditional Dance of Sri Lanka.* Colombo, 1984.

SICILLE P. C. KOTELAWALA

VESTRIS FAMILY, Italian-French family of dancers, of Florentine origin, originally surnamed Vestri. Because of difficulties arising from business irregularities, the Vestri family was forced to leave northern Italy in the late 1730s. The head of the family, Tommaso Maria Ippolito Vestri, and his wife, Beatrice Bruscagli, took refuge in Naples, along with their seven children, Giovanni Battista, Teresa, Gaetano, Angiolo, Maddalena, Francesco, and Violante. Schooled in music and dancing, the older children soon began to appear on stage in Naples and Palermo. After a time, the family left Naples and pursued theatrical work in Bologna, Venice, Genoa, and Vienna. Then the family split, to look for work elsewhere. The mother, Teresa, and Gaetano went to Dresden, and the father and the other children went to Milan. In Dresden, Teresa and Gaetano were hired for the opera, but by the late 1740s both had settled in Paris, where they were joined by Angiolo and Giovanni Battista. Under the French spelling of *Vestris*, the family name was to become famous throughout Europe, thanks chiefly to the genius of Gaetano and his son Auguste.

Jean-Baptiste Vestris (Giovanni Battista Vestri; born 1725 in Florence, died 1801 in Paris). The eldest of the children, Jean-Baptiste retired from the stage in 1753 to maintain the home of his famous brother Gaetano, known as Gaëtan, and later to devote time to the education of his nephew and godchild Auguste. Possessing a good nature and an even temperament, Jean-Baptiste managed the affairs of the family with exceptional skill, always maintaining harmonious relations with the often impetuous and scheming personalities typical of the theatrical world in eighteenth-century Paris.

Thérèse Vestris (Maria Teresa Francesca Vestri; born 1726 in Florence, died 18 January 1808 in Paris). After the family left Italy, Teresa performed for a time in Vienna, but, when her love affair with Prince Esterházy aroused the displeasure of the empress Maria Theresa, she found it prudent to leave the city. She went first to Dresden, then spent eighteen months in Florence, and finally settled in Paris in 1746. She used her social connections to obtain positions for her brothers Gaetano and Angiolo with the Paris Opera, where she herself made her debut on 17 March 1751 in *Le Carnaval du Parnasse.* She also performed in court spectacles. Like her brothers, she reinforced her position at the Opera with backstage intrigues, aimed particularly at her rival Mademoiselle Puvigné, whom she desired to supplant, frequently complaining to the director of the Opera that Puvigné was unfairly favored by the ballet master. After creating a number of incidents, Thérèse and her brothers left the Opera in December 1754 and went to Berlin.

One year later they were back in Paris, appearing in *Roland,* an opera by Robert Quinault and Jean-Baptiste Lully. "The Italian Beauty," as Thérèse was called, often danced as the partner of her famous brother Gaëtan. She performed in Bernard's *opéra-ballet Les Emprises de l'Amour* (In the Grip of Love) and in Lully's *Armide,* and she scored triumphs in Lully's *Alceste* and *Amadis.* Jean-Marie Clément referred to "signorina Teresina" as

the most pleasant ballerina. What legs! — a joy to look at! She has an admirably slender waist, her head is held high and is well positioned. Her eyes, teeth, and lips are charmingly expressive. Her smile is so gracious, there is something so tender, something so voluptuous in all her movements, a graciousness so smooth that it permeates your fantasy: I think of it constantly. (Clément, 1754)

Other reviewers similarly praised her grace and loveliness. Until 1766 she ruled the Opera stage with a seductiveness that won her many admirers.

Gaëtan Vestris (Gaetano Apolline Baldassare Vestri; born 18 April 1729 in Florence, died 23 September 1808 in Paris). After his engagement at the Dresden Opera, Gaëtan went to Paris, where he studied dance with Louis Dupré and was admitted to the ranks of dancers at the Opera. He made his debut in 1749 as a sailor in the comic ballet *Le Carnaval et la Folie*. As few dancers of the day could equal him, he was immediately welcomed and enjoyed great success. In 1750 he appeared in no fewer than six major productions of opera and ballet—Royer's *Almasis*, Campra's *Les Fêtes Vénitiennes* and *Tancrède*, Rebel and Francoeur's *Ismène*, Brassac's *Léandre et Héro*, and Collasse's *Thétis et Pélée*—and was highly acclaimed in them all. Appointed *premier danseur* in 1751, he performed chiefly in works by Lully (e.g., *Alceste*, *Prosperine*, and *Armide*) and Rameau (e.g., *Les Indes Galantes*, *Castor et Pollux*, *Platée*, and *Dardanus*). He also danced in court spectacles with his sister Thérèse and his brother Angiolo. Clément wrote that "the *premier danseur* after Dupré, and of his type, now dancing at the Opera is a young Florentine named Vestris. He is quite tall and long-legged, and nobly built, and he cuts a dashing figure in the theater" (Clément, 1754).

Gaëtan was dismissed from the Opera in 1754 after an awkward incident involving his fellow dancer Jean-Barthélémy Lany. During a rehearsal, a quarrel broke out between Mademoiselle Puvigné and Thérèse Vestris. Lany sided with Puvigné and Gaëtan with his sister. In the heat of the moment, Gaëtan challenged Lany to a duel. Things were smoothed out and the duel did not take place, but some days later, on a report from guards posted at the Opera, Gaëtan was confined to the prison of Fort l'Évêque, where he lived in high style. On his release he accepted an engagement in Berlin. His exile from the Opera was, however, brief. In December 1755 he rejoined the company and appeared with his sister Thérèse in Lully's *tragédie-lyrique Roland*.

By the mid-1750s Gaëtan's public life was becoming increasingly important, and his name was often mentioned in the newspapers. *Le Mercure* of 31 May 1757 praised his performances in Bernard's *opéra-ballet Les Emprises de l'Amour* and in Lully's *Alceste* and *Amadis*. In *Les Indes Galantes* he was greatly admired in the role of Borée for "the brilliance of his steps, the precision of his positions, and the picturesque genius of his dancing." He was called *l'homme à la belle jambe* ("the man with the beautiful legs") and, after Dupré, *le dieu de la danse* ("the god of dance"). In her memoirs (1835–1837) the painter Élisabeth Vigée-Lebrun noted that "he was a very handsome man and perfect in *la danse noble*. I can hardly describe the grace with which he took his hat off and put it back on, and the bow that preceded the minuet."

With each success, Gaëtan's sense of self-importance and his demands for preference increased in proportion to his triumphs, and his romantic affairs supplied much material for the scandal sheets. His numerous liaisons included affairs with Marie Allard, the mother of his son Auguste (born 1760), and Anna Heinel, who also bore him a son, Adolphe (born 1791), and whom he married in 1792, when he was sixty-three.

Between 1760 and 1766 Gaëtan Vestris often danced at the Hoftheater in Stuttgart under the direction of Jean-Georges Noverre. There he created roles in a number of Noverre's ballets, including Admète in *Admète et Alceste* (1761), Hercules in *La Mort d'Hercule* (1762), Jason in *Médée et Jason* (1763), and Orpheus in *Orpheus und Eurydice* (1763), among others. In France he continued to make frequent appearances at the Opera and at the court theater at Fontainebleau. In 1767, he mounted a version of *Médée et Jason*, with choreography "after Noverre," in Vienna, and in Paris, dancing with Marie-Madeleine Guimard, he had a great success in what Gaston Capon (1908) called the "pantomime très voluptueuse" in the ballet *Dardanus*.

Having been assistant ballet master at the Paris Opera since 1761, Gaëtan succeeded Jean-Barthélémy Lany as ballet master in 1770. He lost little time in mounting yet another version of *Médée et Jason*, which by then had become a favorite work. He choreographed a mediocre ballet, *Endymion*, in 1772 and danced in it in March 1773, along with Mademoiselle Guimard and his son Auguste, who by then was a boy of thirteen. In 1775, dancing the role of Jason with Guimard or his sister Thérèse as Medée, he gave still another version of Noverre's *Médée et Jason*. In 1776 he turned over the post of ballet master to Noverre. After a triumphal tour of England with Auguste in 1781, he retired in 1782 but reappeared in 1800 to dance a minuet in Maximilien Gardel's *Ninette à la Cour*.

Gaëtan Vestris began his career as a burlesque dancer, but he adopted to perfection the serious style that had been the glory of his teacher, the great Louis Dupré. A noble reserve lent harmony to his steps, and Noverre said that "while he does the pirouette much better than his son, he is sparing of it; he leaves the audience wanting more." But he was also able to humanize his art by adopting the reforms recommended by such innovators as Gardel and Noverre. Like Gardel, he abandoned the use of masks, and, following Noverre's principles, he "combined with extremely noble and easy execution the rare merit of moving and involving the spectators and speaking to their passions."

Well aware of his talent and popularity, Vestris once declared, "There are only three great men in Europe: the king of Prussia, Monsieur de Voltaire, and me." Despite his vanity and egoism, he nevertheless served the cause of dance with passion, contributed to its growth, and paved the way for his son Auguste, who can justly be considered the first modern dancer.

VESTRIS FAMILY. Auguste Vestris depicted at a gleeful moment during his first visit to London, in 1780–1781. This etching was made from a sketch by Nathaniel Dance that is now in the Fitzwilliam Museum, Cambridge. (Reprinted from Cecil J. Sharp and A. P. Opie, *The Dance: An Historical Survey of Dancing in Europe*, London, 1924.)

Angiolo Vestris (Angiolo Maria Gasparo Vestri; born 1730 in Florence, died 10 June 1809 in Paris). A handsome, blue-eyed blond, Angiolo played the flute in the Concerts de la Reine in Paris, studied dance with Louis Dupré, and joined the Opera as a soloist in 1753. He remained with the Opera until 1757, with an interruption in 1754. Fearing that his brother Gaëtan's fame would overshadow his own, he continued his career in various European theaters before being hired in 1761 for the Stuttgart Opera as *premier danseur*, under the direction of Noverre. There he spent six years and married the comic actress Françoise Rose Gourgaud, a sister of the celebrated mezzo-soprano Louise Dugazon. In 1767 he returned to Paris, where he became an actor, first with the Comédie Italienne and then with the Comédie Française.

Auguste Vestris Marie-Jean-Augustin Vestris; born 27 March 1760 in Paris, died 5 December 1842 in Paris). The son of Gaëtan Vestris and Marie Allard (whence his nickname, Vestr'Allard), Auguste studied dance with his father and showed exceptional gifts at a very early age. As a prodigy of twelve, he appeared on stage at the Paris Opera on 18 September 1772 during the performance of a pastorale called *La Cinquantaine*. Presented by his father in court dress, a sword at his side, the young boy immediately won the hearts of the audience. *Le Mercure* declared

that he combined "brilliance of execution, personal grace, the finesse of art, beauty of bearing, intelligence, and all the advantages of a felicitous nature and a consummate talent." Baron Grimm, a prominent reviewer, noted that Auguste "danced with the same precision, the same aplomb, and almost the same strength as the great [Gaëtan] Vestris" (Grimm, 1812).

Having been applauded at court on 14 November 1772 and admitted to the Opera as a pupil, Auguste danced the role of Eros beside his father and Marie-Madeleine Guimard in *Endymion* in March 1773. Hired for the Opera in 1775, he became a solo dancer in 1776 and performed in *Les Petits Rien, Alceste*, and *Les Caprices de Galathée* of Noverre. He was named *premier danseur* in 1778 and *premier sujet de la danse* in 1780. He then took a six-month leave of absence and toured England with his father. At the King's Theatre in London he triumphed in

VESTRIS FAMILY. Auguste Vestris as the lead dancer in *Les Amans Surpris* (1780), which was first performed at the King's Theatre, London, during Vestris's tour of England. This contemporary lithograph, by J. Thorthwaite after James Roberts, was published in Bell's *British Theatre* (London, 1781). (Courtesy of Madison U. Sowell and Debra H. Sowell, Brigham Young University, Provo, Utah.)

Noverre's *Les Caprices de Galathée* and *Médée et Jason* and in Maximilien Gardel's *Ninette à la Cour* and *Mirza et Lindor*, all of which he had performed at the Paris Opera with Guimard, with whom he had a brief love affair. In addition, Auguste shown in such Gardel ballets as *La Chercheuse d'Esprit* (1778), *La Rosière* (1784), *Le Premier Navigateur, ou Le Pouvoir de l'Amour* (1785), and *Le Coq au Village* (1787). After the French Revolution in 1789, he returned to England and performed at the King's Theatre, where Noverre was directing the ballet.

A man of many love affairs, Auguste married a young Opera dancer, Anne-Catherine Augier (1777–1809), who had made her debut in 1795 under the name of Mademoiselle Aimée, but marriage did not prevent him from continuing his many amorous liaisons. Among others, he had a notable affair with Marie-Adrienne Chameroy (1779–1802), a pupil of Gardel, a charming dancer, and a rival of Auguste's famous partner Guimard. Chameroy accompanied him on one of his tours of the provinces—he repeatedly scored triumphs in Lyon, Montepellier, and Bordeaux—and they enjoyed particular success in Pierre Gardel's ballet *Psyché* (1790). After Pierre Gardel succeeded his brother Maximilien as ballet master of the Opera in 1786, he made a number of ballets that included roles worthy of Auguste's special abilities, among them *Télémaque dans l'Île de Calypso* (1790), *La Dansomanie* (1800), *Achille à Scyros* (1804), and *Paul et Virginie* (1806).

By 1803 Auguste had a rival: the twenty-two-year-old Louis-Antoine Duport, who gradually won the public adulation that Vestris had earlier enjoyed. Their rivalry was a juicy subject for the gossip sheets. Although Vestris was no longer able to astonish spectators as he had in his youth, he was still capable of moving them in such ballets as Pierre Gardel's *L'Enfant Prodigue*, which he created in 1812 and which he danced for his farewell performance on 27 September 1816. Almost twenty years later, at the age of sixty-five, he made his last appearance on the Opera stage, dancing a courtly minuet with Marie Taglioni during a gala performance on 8 August 1835.

The heir to his father's majesty and his mother's sprightliness, noble and charming, full of imagination, Auguste Vestris did not fit into any of the customary classifications. Noverre valued his gifts as a dancer and his knowledge as a performer, stating that "his debut in the serious dance was a triumph; this young dancer was distinguished by the rare qualities of aplomb, daring, sureness, brilliance, beautiful formation of steps, and a sensitive and delicate ear." Speaking of a *pas de pâtres* (shepherds' dance) created by Lany for Vestris and Mademoiselle Théodore, Noverre noted that

> our young Proteus [Auguste] grasped this new genre, so completely opposed to the one taught him by his father, with as much taste as intelligence, and was extremely successful in it. I

used him in *Le Bergère Héroïque*, a fine, delicate, and characteristic work, in which he demonstrated the naive graces and all the expressiveness that could be desired.   (Noverre, 1760)

Regarded as a prodigy and proclaimed the greatest dancer in Europe, Vestris aroused enthusiasm whenever he appeared.

A dancer of great virtuosity as well as artistry, Vestris inspired numerous imitators. Although he was, ultimately, inimitable, his example set a high standard for male dancers of his day. Particularly noteworthy were his cabrioles, his *entrechats* (Serge Lifar [1950] said he could perform the *entrechat douze*), and his pirouettes, although with these he was, according to Noverre, "too generous,"

VESTRIS FAMILY. A much publicized rivalry existed between Auguste Vestris and the younger star of the Paris Opera, Louis-Antoine Duport. In this engraving, Duport is pictured triumphant, as he extends his leg—in perfect *écarté* position—over the fallen body of Vestris. (Engraved frontispiece from Joseph Berchoux's *La danse, ou Les dieux de l'Opéra*, Paris, 1806; courtesy of Madison U. Sowell and Debra H. Sowell, Brigham Young University, Provo, Utah.)

performing them with extraordinary speed if not perfect balance when he stopped. His exceptional elevation was also particularly admired. In her memoirs Madame Vigée-Lebrun (1835–1837) noted that "he was the most amazing dancer to be seen, such was his grace and lightness at one and the same moment. . . . He rose toward the sky in such a prodigious manner that he was believed to have wings."

Vestris was also a choreographer and a teacher. His few choreographies, several *divertissements* and a ballet called *The Nymphs of Diana* (1781), were all presented at the King's Theatre in London and, in sum, added nothing to his glory. As one of the most famous teachers of his day, however, Vestris was able to transmit his art to a significant number of dancers worthy of his lessons, including Charles-Louis Didelot, August Bournonville, and Jules Perrot. But it was as a dancer that Auguste Vestris was indeed supreme. He revealed to audiences that the miraculous emanates from the dance itself, from man transfigured by the conquest of his art. Therein resided his characteristic genius, originality, and modernity.

Armand Vestris (Armand-Auguste Vestris; born 1795 in Paris, died 17 May 1825 in Vienna). Son of Auguste Vestris and Anne-Catherine Augier, Armand Vestris studied dance with his grandfather, Gaëtan. In 1800, at the age of four, he was presented to the Paris Opera audience by his grandfather, still elegant despite his seventy-one years, and his father, then at the height of his glory. Armand followed the family tradition by training as a professional dancer, but in later life he spent little time in Paris. After touring in Italy and Portugal, he went to England in 1809 and stayed for some years in London. There, on 28 June 1813 he married the comic actress Lucia Elizabetta Bartolozzi (1797–1856), who as Madame Vestris became a well-known figure on the London stage. Vestris himself served as choreographer at the King's Theatre from 1813 to 1816, where he successfully mounted several ballets. These included *Le Calife Voleur, Mars et l'Amour*, which was performed by Auguste Vestris, and *Gonzalve de Cordoue*, his most important work. A handsome dancer, Armand Vestris was pleasant to watch, but he did not have the genius of his famous predecessors. He deserted his wife in 1820, left England, and spent the last years of his life in Italy and Vienna.

BIBLIOGRAPHY
Beaumont, Cyril W. "Gaetano and Auguste Vestris in English Caricature." *Ballet* 5 (March 1948): 19–29.
Berchoux, Joseph de. *La danse: Les dieux de l'Opéra.* Paris, 1806.
Campardon, Émile. *L'Académie Royale de Musique du XVIIIe siècle.* 2 vols. Paris, 1884.
Capon, Gaston. *Les Vestris: Le dieu de la danse et sa famille.* Paris, 1908.
Chapman, John V. "Auguste Vestris and the Expansion of Technique." *Dance Research Journal* 19 (Summer 1987): 11–18.
Clément, Pierre. *Les cinq années littéraires.* 2 vols. The Hague, 1754.
Fenner, Theodore. "Ballet in Early Nineteenth-Century London as Seen by Leigh Hunt and Henry Robertson." *Dance Chronicle* 1.2 (1978): 75–95.
Grimm, Friedrich Melchior von. *Correspondance littéraire philosophique et critique.* 17 vols. Paris, 1812–1814.
Guest, Ivor. *The Romantic Ballet in England.* London, 1972.
Guest, Ivor. *The Romantic Ballet in Paris.* 2d rev. ed. London, 1980.
Guest, Ivor. *Jules Perrot: Master of the Romantic Ballet.* London, 1984.
Hammond, Sandra Noll. "The 'Gavotte de Vestris': A Dance of Three Centuries." In *Proceedings of the Seventh Annual Conference, Society of Dance History Scholars, Goucher College, Towson, Maryland, 17–19 February 1984,* compiled by Christena L. Schlundt. Riverside, Calif., 1984.
Lifar, Serge. *Auguste Vestris, le dieu de la danse.* Paris, 1950.
Migel, Parmenia. *The Ballerinas: From the Court of Louis XIV to Pavlova.* New York, 1972.
Moore, Lillian, "Gaetan Vestris and the Vestris Family." In Moore's *Artists of the Dance.* New York, 1938.
Noverre, Jean-Georges. *Lettres sur la danse et sur les ballets.* Stuttgart and Lyon, 1760. Translated by Cyril W. Beaumont as *Letters on Dancing and Ballets* (London, 1930).
Price, Curtis A., et al. *Italian Opera in Late Eighteenth-Century London,* vol. 1, *The King's Theatre, Haymarket, 1778–1791.* London, 1995.
Swift, Mary Grace. *A Loftier Flight: The Life and Accomplishments of Charles Louis Didelot.* Middletown, Conn., 1974.
Vigée-Lebrun, Élisabeth. *Memoirs of Madame Vigée Lebrun (1835–1837).* Translated by Lytton Strachey. London, 1903.
Winter, Marian Hannah. *The Pre-Romantic Ballet.* London, 1974.

JEANNINE DORVANE
Translated from French

VIENNESE KINDERBALLET. Children's theater, in which children play the roles of adults, has a long history. Organized by impresarios with a good business sense, or by choreographers, children's ballet (German, *Kinderballett*) touched feelings in adults that perhaps combined sentimentality and perversity. Vienna appears to have been particularly fruitful soil for this genre: the two most famous children's ballet groups were the Friedrich Horschelt Kinderballett, which performed in the Theater an der Wien, and Josefine Weiss's Danseuses Viennoises.

In the late eighteenth century Vienna had a children's ballet that was artistically quite sophisticated, using choreographers of the stature of Franz Hilverding and Jean-Georges Noverre. To ensure a regular supply of dancers, in 1771 Noverre founded a dance school from which he recruited dancers for his company. The children, who included Antoine and Théodore Bournonville, danced in regular court productions as well as in children's ballets.

When Friedrich Horschelt, who as a child had danced in the Theater an der Wien, returned to work for the theater in 1813, he found that a number of children were dancing there as well as in the court opera house, the Kärntnertor Theater. In 1814 Horschelt became deputy ballet master and in 1816 full ballet master for the Theater an der Wien, which was then under the same management as the Kärntnertor Theater.

On 14 November 1816 Horschelt presented the first production of the children's ballet in a pantomime, *Die Kleine Diebin*, to music by Joseph Kinsky. After the great success of this ballet, a team was formed to adapt existing ballets for children's performances. The two best-known such adaptations were Louis-Antoine Duport's *Aschenbrödel* (Cinderella), performed by as many as 174 children, and *Der Blöde Ritter* (The Bashful Knight), with new music.

In 1815 there were twenty dancers in the children's ensemble. The stars of the troupe were Therese Heberle, Angioletta Mayer, the Schröder sisters Wilhelmine, Betty, and Auguste, Michael Johann Laroche, and Anton Stuhlmüller. Heberle later made a career in Italy; Stuhlmüller became a well-known dancer in central Europe and a partner of Fanny Elssler.

In 1818 this extremely popular and profitable undertaking received its first setback. The Inspectorate of the Vienna Police conducted an investigation and found that the children were in danger of "corruption of morals." Although the investigation was quickly forgotten, Empress Caroline Augusta herself issued a prohibition against the children's ballet, claiming that the children's morals were seriously threatened by "epicures." Count Ferdinand Pálffy, then director of the theater, tried to postpone the decision, arguing that the productions of the children's ballet occupied such an important place in the repertory that it was out of the question to drop them.

Furthermore, he argued, if they were all dismissed immediately, thirty or forty families would be left destitute. An investigation of the domestic conditions of the children in 1820 revealed that the children's ballet had fifty-two members, thirty-seven girls and fifteen boys; the youngest child was eight, the oldest nineteen, and most were between twelve and fifteen. Only thirteen children could return to proper households if dismissed. Most of the others supported their families with their earnings. It was also rumored that a few were supported by "highly placed people," including Count Pálffy.

These findings did nothing to prevent the dissolution of the children's ballet. Horschelt accepted a post as ballet master in Munich in 1822. Apparently the management of the Kärntnertor Theater did not feel that the imperial prohibition applied to it, for by 1824 there were fifty-one child dancers in the theater's employ; however, only dancers who had reached the age of fifteen were allowed to remain in the company.

Children's ballet in Vienna was not revived until 1841, when the dancer Josefine Maudry Weiss accepted the post of a ballet mistress of the Theater in der Josephstadt. She had herself danced at the Kärntnertor Theater and held the post of ballet mistress in the 1830s. As she had already worked with children in Hamburg, she immediately be-

VIENNESE KINDERBALLET. This lithographed music cover, published in the 1840s, shows children of the Danseuses Viennoises in *The Harvest Fête*, performed to music by Max Maretzek at Her Majesty's Theatre, London. (Courtesy of Madison U. Sowell and Debra H. Sowell, Brigham Young University, Provo, Utah.)

gan creating children's dances for the Theater in der Josefstadt. Unlike Horschelt, who created full-length ballets for his children, Weiss limited herself to the composition of short character and national dances, for which she was well known. She inserted them into fairy-tale extravaganzas, musical plays, and other ballets. The music for these dances was written by composers such as Johann Strauss the elder or Joseph Lanner, but chiefly by Anton Emil Titl, conductor at the theater.

In June 1842 Weiss signed contracts with the parents of twenty-eight children, committing the children to a five-year ballet training program. She saw to the physical well-being of the children and guaranteed the parents a payment for each performance. Late in 1844, she took thirty-six female dancers on tour along with her twelve-year-old son Franz, who had been a dancer at the Theater in der Josefstadt since 1843. During the next eight years, the children astonished audiences with the incredible precision of their performances. They toured Austria, Germany, and northern Italy. As the Danseuses Viennoises, the troupe visited Paris (1845, 1846, and 1850), London (1845, 1846, and 1849), and the United States, Canada, and Cuba (1846 and 1847). On tour Weiss had to contend with changes of corrupting the children's morals and problems with immigration authorities.

In December 1852, Weiss unexpectedly died. The director of the Theater in der Josefstadt temporarily became the children's guardian, but the troupe was dissolved later that month. A few Viennese children obtained posts with the Kärntnertor Theater, but most of them—including French, English, and even American children—returned to their parents.

[*See also the entry on the Horschelt family.*]

BIBLIOGRAPHY

Dieke, Gertraude. *Die Blütezeit des Kindertheaters: Ein Beitrag zur Theatergeschichte des 18. und beginnenden 19. Jahrhunderts.* Emsdetten, 1934.

Feigl, Susanne, and Christian Lunzer. "Der Fall Alois Fürst Kaunitz-Rietberg." In *Das Mädchenballett des Fürsten Kaunitz.* Vienna, 1988.

Seyfried, Ferdinand von. *Rückschau in das Theaterleben Wiens seit den letzten fünfzig Jahren.* Vienna, 1864.

GUNHILD OBERZAUCHER-SCHÜLLER
Translated from German

VIENNESE WALTZ.   *See* Ballroom Dance Competition *and* Waltz.

VIETNAM. Situated on the east coast of the Indochinese Peninsula, the Socialist Republic of Vietnam was formed in 1976, uniting the northern and southern regions after some twenty years. This Southeast Asian region had been colonized by France in the nineteenth century and was divided into three administrative regions (empires) at that time: Tonkin in the north, Annam in the center, and Cochin China in the south. The three were formed into French Indochina between 1859 and 1887. During World War II, Japan invaded and occupied the country. In 1945, Vietnam was made an independent nation, but French attempts at regaining authority led to the French Indochina War (1946–1954). A Geneva Conference in 1954 divided the country along the seventeenth parallel, with communist rule in North Vietnam and a noncommunist regime in South Vietnam. Efforts by North Vietnam to reunify led to the Vietnam War (1957–1975). Today, some seventy million people live in about 130,000 square miles (330,000 square kilometers), bordered by China in the north, Laos in the west, and Cambodia in the southwest. The South China Sea lies to the east. About nine million tribal peoples live in the northern and central highlands, and about two million Chinese descendants of precolonial families continue to live in the country. Mahāyāna Buddhism, Confucianism, and Daoism are the prevailing religions.

The region had a neolithic rice-growing society in the Red (Hong) River Delta before it became a province of China from 221 BCE to 939 CE, and again in the fifteenth century. The Vietnamese expanded their own territory gradually, taking the southern portion in the late fifteenth century and incorporating the Mekong Delta from Cambodia in the seventeenth and eighteenth centuries. Beginning in the sixteenth century, however, European traders and clerics had begun their commerce with Southeast Asia.

Traditional dance in Vietnam reflects the various elements that have contributed to the nation's culture—indigenous, Chinese, and Buddhist. Four categories of traditional dance may be distinguished: folk dance, religious dance, court dance, and dance in the traditional music theaters.

Folk Dance. Throughout Vietnam, folk dances are performed by nonprofessional dancers in everyday dress, using simple gestures and few stage properties. The musical accompaniment is from songs sung by the dancers in unison, or from a few drums or clappers. Some of the dances concern the peasants' work in the fields, such as the *mua chay cay* ("dance of the plough") done at Phu Tho in northern Vietnam, or work on the rivers, such as the *mua ba trao* ("rowing dance") done at Knanh Hoà, Huê, and Binh Dinh in central Vietnam. Others are related to folk games, such as the *mua du tiên* ("dance of the fairy swing") or the *mua co nguoi* ("dance of the human chess pieces") in northern Vietnam; to seasonal feasts, such as the *mua lân* ("dance of the unicorn") on New Year's Day in southern Vietnam; to folk customs or beliefs with a ritual character, such as the *mua cau ngu* ("dance in honor of the whale"), performed by fishermen, *mua dua linh* ("funeral dance), *mua dèn* ("dance of the oil lamp"), *mua dâng ruou* ("dance to offer rice wine"), and *mua dao vo* or *mua câu mua* ("dance to implore the rain") in Thanh Hoa in northern Vietnam.

Religious Dance. These dances are performed by dancers who are possessed by spirits or gods and by monks or members of a religious community. In the *mua phu thuy* ("sorcerer's dance"), a sorcerer dances with incense (joss) sticks, a small bell, or a small drum to cure a disease or to chase away evil spirits. *Mua bong* and *mua châu van* are shamanistic dances of southern and northern Vietnam, respectively, performed by a female medium (shaman). In northern Vietnam the shaman performs different dances depending on which deity possesses her: the *mua kiêm* ("sword dance") for the First, Second, Third, and Fourth High Dignitaries; the *mua môi* ("torch dance") for the First Mother in the Sky; the *mua cheo do* ("boat girl dance") for the Mother of Water; the *mua quat* ("fan dance") for the Fourth Ambassador to the Sky; the *mua cung* ("arch dance") and the *mua hèo* ("stick dance") for the Third, Seventh, and Tenth Princes; the *mua thanh long* *dao* ("blue dragon's saber dance") for the Fifth Dragon King; and the *mua lân* ("unicorn dance").

Another religious dance, the mua luc cung ("six offerings dance") is performed by priests in Buddhist temples or by young girls twelve or thirteen years of age. The six offerings are incense, flowers, candles, tea, fruit, and rice cakes.

Court Dance. Certain dances were performed at various ceremonies at the courts of the ancient Vietnamese emperors. The "Bat Dât" dance originated in China and was performed by 128 court dancers—sixty-four for the civilian segment *(van vu)* and sixty-four for the military *(vo vu)*. Other court dances are "Tam Tinh Chuc Tho" (Three Stars Present Wishes for Longevity), "Mua Tu Linh" (Four Fabulous Animals—the dragon, unicorn, phoenix, and tortoise), and "Mua Hoa Dang" (Flowery Lantern Dance). "Nu Tuong Xuat Quan" (Female Warriors' Dance) is performed by female dancers.

Dance in Music Theater. There are two kinds of music theaters in which dances are performed in Vietnam: *hat cheo*, the folk-music theater of the north, and *hat tuông* or *hat bôi*, the classical-music theater of central and southern Vietnam.

Folk and religious dances are disappearing from Vietnam today. Court dances are being restored for study purposes, however, and theatrical dances are still being performed.

BIBLIOGRAPHY

Cuisinier, Jeanne. *Danse sacrée en Indochine et en Indonésie.* Paris, 1957.

Do Bang Doàn and Do Trong Huê. *Nhung dai le ya yu khuc cua yua chua Viet Nam.* Saigon, 1967.

Ky yeu hoi nghi mua dan toc Viet Nam. Hanoi, 1979.

Lâm To Loc. *Nghe thuat mua dan toc Viet.* Hanoi, 1979.

TRÂN VAN KHÊ

VIGANÒ, SALVATORE (born 25 March 1769 in Naples, died 10 August 1821 in Milan), Italian ballet dancer, choreographer, and composer. Salvatore Viganò was a son of Onorato Viganò, a skillful choreographer, and Maria Ester Viganò (née Boccherini), a talented dancer and mime who was a sister of the composer Luigi Boccherini. Initiated into the art of dance by his parents, Viganò also became an avid student of history, the pictorial arts, and literature, gaining knowledge and insights that would win him the esteem of the major cultural figures of the times. The study of music also occupied an important place in his artistic training, and he became a good violinist and an accomplished composer. (It is likely that his uncle, the celebrated Boccherini, contributed to his development.) When he was just seventeen years old, Viganò presented an *opera buffa* in Rome. Thereafter, he frequently composed or adapted the music for his father's ballets as well as his own.

Viganò's dancing debut took place in 1783, when he was fourteen years old. He appeared with his father's company at the Teatro Argentina in Rome in a female role, because women were still forbidden to appear in the theaters of the Papal States. Salvatore performed in his father's company until 1788, then went to Madrid, where he took part in the festivities surrounding the coronation of Charles IV and where he performed until 1789. This was his chance to study Spanish dance and also to meet Jean Dauberval, a follower of Jean-Georges Noverre. Under Dauberval's guidance, Viganò danced in Bordeaux and London, improving his technique and delving deeper into Noverre's concepts of the *ballet d'action*. In Madrid, Viganò had met and then married Maria Medina, a Spanish dancer, whom he subsequently partnered in many successful productions until they separated at the end of the century.

The influence of Dauberval's teachings marked Viganò's first works. In Italy once again, Viganò's presented *Raul, Signore de Crechi*, a ballet based on the plot of an *opéra comique* by Jacques-Marie Monvel and Nicolas Dalayrac but set to his own music. This, the first of Viganò's works shown alongside his father's works, was mounted in 1791 at the Teatro San Samuele in Venice and was followed in 1792 by his revival of Dauberval's *La Fille Mal Gardée*, staged at the Teatro La Fenice.

Shortly afterward, in 1793, the Viganòs moved to Vienna, where his fame became such that it even influenced the style of the times: "There was no hairdo, footwear, or new *contredanse* that was not 'in the manner of Viganò,'" reports Henry Prunières (1921); even the young Ludwig van Beethoven composed a "minuet in the manner of Viganò." Still under the influence of Dauberval, and having assimilated from his father the tradition of grotesque dancing and pantomime, Viganò presented in 1794 his comic ballet *La Fiera di Barcellona* in Vienna, incurring for it the censure of Cornelius von Ayrenhoff, an advocate of Antonio Muzzarelli. During his career, Viganò composed in the comic genre with no less care than in the serious, demonstrating his knowledge and appreciation of comedy in the traditions of dance theater. The characters in his *Mazilli und Orisko*, staged at the Hoftheater in Vienna in 1800, are, for example, directly linked to the figures of sixteenth-century *commedia dell'arte*.

Among other works produced while Viganò was in Vienna, *Richard Löwenherz, König von England* (Richard Lionheart, King of England), to music by Joseph Weigl, stands out. Inspired by Michel-Jean Sedaine and André-Ernest-Modeste Grétry's *opéra comique*, it was first performed at the Kärntnertor Theater in 1795. It evidenced moments of remarkable intensity, a skillful interplay of groups, and use of the leitmotif as a function of dramatic structure. Viganò further developed these devices in subsequent works.

Between 1795 and 1798, Viganò and his wife frequently

toured central Europe, going to Prague, Dresden, Berlin, and Hamburg. In 1798 and 1799 Viganò staged some of his ballets at the Teatro La Fenice in Venice, and in 1799, separated from Medina, he returned to Vienna, where he remained until 1803. His first major work after his return to the Austrian capital was *Die Geschöpfe des Prometheus* (The Creatures of Prometheus; 1801), set to the score by Ludwig van Beethoven. This work, an exaltation of music and dance, was inspired by the heroic myth of Prometheus and was turned into a grand allegory that dramatized universal themes. [*See the entry on Beethoven.*] Some years later, it became the point of departure for Viganò's *Prometeo*, a major work staged at the Teatro alla Scala in Milan in 1813.

Viganò's work in Vienna makes it clear that he was already developing his own poetics, which were destined to surpass those of the *ballet d'action* and even the *divertissement*. His ballet *Die Spanier auf der Insel Christina* (The Spaniards of Christina Island) was performed in 1802 and *I Giuochi Istmici* in 1803. Both were set to music by Weigl. Also in 1802 appeared *Die Zauberschwestern im Beneventer Walde*, set to music by Franz Xaver Süssmayr. (Viganò staged a revised version of this ballet, *Il Noce di Benevento* [The Walnut Tree of Benevento], at La Scala in 1812. Carlo Ritorni, Viganò's biographer, gives a detailed account of this production, asserting that it was received in Milan by some as "an outstanding, pleasantly eccentric, work" and by others as a "hodgepodge of diabolical and grotesque inventions" [Ritorni, 1838]. Stendhal, however, compared Viganò's ballet to Shakespeare's *The Tempest* and to the last act of *The Merry Wives of Windsor.*)

Viganò's debut in Milan took place at the Teatro Carcao with *Marzio Coriolano*, to music composed by Weigl, in 1804. In this work Viganò sacrificed pure dance in favor of dramatic coherence. During the years that followed, some of Viganò's productions were performed in Venice, Milan, Rome, Padua, Bologna, and Turin. He composed *Gli Strelizzi* for the Teatro La Fenice in Venice in 1809. The subject was the Strelitz conspiracy, which occurred in Russia during the reign of Peter the Great, and was portrayed by Viganò with strong emotional energy. Mass movements alternated with pas de deux, among which was that of the Tsar (Viganò) and Elisabetta (Amalia Muzzarelli). The historian Prunières (1921) saw in this ballet "gestures, subordinated to the imperious need of the rhythm," the path that later led to Vaslav Nijinsky's research and to the theories of Émile Jaques-Dalcroze.

After 1811, Viganò worked almost exclusively for the Teatro alla Scala. In Milan, with its lively cultural milieu, he found fertile soil for the creation, with the assistance of a select group of dancer-actors, of a new form of danced drama, which Ritorni (1838) defined as *coreodramma*. This was because of Viganò's way of composing ballets, utilizing solutions adopted by the contemporaneous mu-

sical theater. Thus his drama was neither "quiet, mimed tragedy . . . nor dumb acting, but mute singing."

The most illustrious writers of his time lauded what was one of Viganò's masterpieces, *Prometeo*, performed in 1813—not a revival but a completely new version of *Die Geschöpfe des Prometheus*. The remake used some numbers from Beethoven's score as well as pieces of music by Joseph Weigl, Franz Joseph Haydn, and Viganò himself. Among the scenes at which audiences most marveled was the opening one, which set a powerful image for the ensuing action.

The first scene of act 1 takes place on a desolate heath. Men drag themselves around in a brutish state while Prometheus, surrounded by Virtue, the Arts, and the Muses, contemplates the moment with commiseration, wondering how to awaken their reason. Act 2 shows, with a marvelous use of machinery, the fall of the Titan from Minerva's chariot after the theft of the celestial fire. In act 3, the sparks from the fallen torch give birth to innumerable Cupids, symbolizing the spread of reason among human beings. The men then rescue Prometheus and will be led by him to the Temple of Virtues. Act 4, set in Vulcan's furnace, shows the gods' reaction to Prometheus's theft of fire. In act 5, again in the Temple of Virtues, the Muses, Sciences, Arts, and Graces are about to educate the humans when Cupid, with an arrow, excites love between a man and a woman. The idyll is broken by the appearance of the Cyclopes, who carry Prometheus underground with them. The final act, closer to the traditional myth, shows the men sympathizing with Prometheus, now the bound and tortured Titan. They ask Hercules to free him. In an apotheosis, Prometheus is crowned with immortality by an appeased Jupiter.

The ballet was a resounding success and was repeated in the autumn season. Ritorni (1838) wrote, "I consider myself lucky to have seen, with my own eyes, the *Prometeo*, of which people have a false idea: that it is a spectacle of machines. . . . To the contrary . . . it was a moral spectacle, that is to say a sublime and surprising expression of poetic ideas and dramatic situations."

Several years later, in 1817, Viganò produced another masterpiece, *Mirra, o sia La Vendetta di Venere*. According to the critics, *Mirra* was greater than the tragedy by Count Vittorio Alfieri that had inspired it. Viganò was able to render in the mute language of gestures the torment of the heroine, Mirra, who is secretly in love with her father. The obvious difficulties inherent in the scabrous subject held the risk of being accentuated by the pantomime; Viganò, however was able to sublimate the action to the dancing and obtain a cathartic effect. The internal drama of Mirra was interpreted by Antonia Pallerini, Viganò's favorite artist.

Among Viganò's other outstanding works was the triad *Otello* (Othello), *Dedalo* (Daedalus), and *La Vestale* (The Vestal Virgin) of 1818, all with scenery by Alessandro Sanquirico. In *Otello*, Viganò concentrated the action on the core of the drama. In *La Vestale,* Pallerini created one of her most celebrated characterizations, as Viganò had provided her with yet another role that transcended the division between pantomime and dance. These three works were followed by *I Titani* (The Titans), staged in 1819. Set at the dawn of humanity, this work, the fruition of Viganò's long career, was richly invested with imagination and fantasy, merging classical myths and biblical themes. Although somewhat uneven, it contained moments of rare beauty. After *I Titani,* Viganò composed *Alessandro nelle Indie,* a ballet showing a mature and articulated use of music for dramatic purpose, as well as *Le Sabine in Roma* and *Giovanna d'Arco,* all mounted in 1820.

A painstaking, tireless artist, Viganò died the following year, while he was trying to finish his *Didone.* "A new art died with this great man," said Stendhal (1826). Nonetheless, Viganò left a rich heritage of research and innovations. He was to become the emblem of the choreodramatic genre, his work a lasting touchstone. An imaginative librettist and a poetic visionary, he based his dance dramas on a skillful play of contrast, on the combination of differing elements into a coherent whole. His choreodramatic pieces were animated in successive scenes, always changing for the eyes of the audience. In a process that blended the actions of separated scenic planes, he combined the Baroque legacy of the "marvelous" with the requirements of dramatic verisimilitude that was being pursued by the new theater of his time.

BIBLIOGRAPHY

Ayrenhoff, Cornelius von. *Über die teatralischen Tänze und die Balletmeister Noverre, Muzzarelli und Viganò.* Vienna, 1794. Reprinted in Ayrenhoff's *Sämmtliche Werke,* vol. 5 (Vienna, 1814).

Brinson, Peter. *Background to European Ballet: A Notebook from Its Archives.* Leiden, 1966.

Celi, Claudia. "Il balletto in Italia: Il Ottocento." In *Musica in scena: Storia dello spettacolo musicale,* edited by Alberto Basso, vol. 5, pp. 89–138. Turin, 1995.

Celi, Claudia. "Verso il 'canto muto': Dal danzatore pittore al danzator musico." In *Proceedings of the Conference "Naturale e artificiale nel teatro veneziano del secondo Settecento," Venezia, 10–11 November 1995.* Venice, 1997.

Cohen, Selma Jeanne, ed. *Dance as a Theater Art.* New York, 1974. Reprint, Princeton, 1992.

Guest, Ivor. "L'Italia e il balletto romantico." *La danza italiana* 8–9 (Winter 1990): 7–25.

Ferrari, Donatella. "I libretti comici di Salvatore Viganò." *La danza italiana* 7 (Spring 1989): 79–97.

Girardi, Maria. "I balli di Onorato Viganò a Venezia." *La danza italiana* 5–6 (Autumn 1987): 89–119.

Hadamowsky, Franz. *Die Wiener Hoftheater (Staatstheater),* vol. 1, *1776–1810.* Vienna, 1966.

Kirstein, Lincoln. *Dance: A Short History of Classical Theatrical Dancing.* New York, 1935.

Krasovskaya, Vera. "Ballet Changes, Shakespeare Endures." *Ballet Review* 19 (Summer 1991): 71–80.

Levinson, André. *Meister des balletts.* Potsdam, 1923.

Milloss, Aurelio. "La lezione di Salvatore Viganò." *La danza italiana* 1 (Autumn 1984): 7–19.

Monaldi, Gino. *Le regine della danza nel secolo XIX.* Turin, 1910.

Moore, Lillian. "Salvatore Viganò." In Moore's *Artists of the Dance.* New York, 1938.

Mori, Elisabetta. *Libretti di melodrammi e balli del secolo XVIII.* Florence, 1984.

Mori, Elisabetta. "Dove gli eroi vanno a morir ballando, ovvero la danza a Roma nel Settecento." *La danza italiana* 4 (Spring 1986): 27–47.

Prunières, Henry. "Salvatore Viganò." *La revue musicale* (December 1921): 71–94.

Raimondi, Ezio, ed. *Il sogno del coreodramma: Salvatore Viganò, poeta muto.* Reggio Emilia, 1984.

Ritorni, Carlo. *Commentarii della vita e delle opere coreodrammatiche di Salvatore Viganò e della coreografia e de' corepei.* Milan, 1838.

Rossi, Luigi. *Il ballo alla Scala, 1778–1970.* Milan, 1972.

Saint-Léon, Arthur. *Portraits et biographies des plus célèbres maîtres de ballets et chorégraphes anciens et nouveaux de l'école française et italienne.* Paris, 1852.

Stendhal (Marie-Henri Beyle). *Rome, Naples et Florence.* Paris, 1826.

Terzian, Elizabeth. "Salvatore Viganò: His Ballets at the Teatro La Scala (1811–1821), the Attitudes of His Contemporaries." In *Proceedings of the Tenth Annual Conference, Society of Dance History Scholars, University of California, Irvine, 13–15 February 1987,* compiled by Christena L. Schlundt. Riverside, Calif., 1987.

Winter, Marian Hannah. *The Pre-Romantic Ballet.* London, 1974.

Zambon, Rita. "Sulle traccie dell'immortale Astigiano." *Chorégraphie* 2 (Autumn 1993): 73–84.

CLAUDIA CELI
Translated from Italian

VILLELLA, EDWARD (born 1 October 1936 in Bayside, New York), American ballet dancer, teacher, and company director. Referring to the "dazzling antics" of Edward Villella, Lincoln Kirstein once described him as "born to be both Arlecchino and Pulcinella" (Kirstein, 1973, p. 244). A strong, athletic little boy with a scrappy nature and a cocky attitude, Villella began his dance studies with a local teacher in Bayside, Queens, a suburban neighborhood of New York City. When he was ten, he was awarded a scholarship to the School of American Ballet, where he continued his studies until 1952, when he was sixteen. Then, in what Kirstein further describes as "more than five long and unprofitable years in the Merchant Marine Academy," the young dancer's progress was halted. With his return to the School of American Ballet in 1956, he began to make up for lost time.

Villella joined the New York City Ballet in 1957, on his twenty-first birthday, and soon made his solo debut in Jerome Robbins's *Afternoon of a Faun,* partnering Allegra Kent. In 1958, his natural and remarkable elevation won him the jumping roles of Robert Barnett, such as Candy Cane in *The Nutcracker,* the third movement in *Symphony in C,* and the Thunderer in *Stars and Stripes.* In 1959 George Balanchine cast Villella in the title role of *The Prodigal Son,* which he performed with enormous success, putting his personal stamp on the role to such an extent that his interpretation established a new, definitive

VILLELLA. In *Harlequinade* (1965), George Balanchine made the roles of Harlequin and Columbine especially for Villella and Patricia McBride. Of all the roles they danced together, none suited them better than the sweethearts of the *commedia dell'arte*. (Photograph by Fred Fehl; used by permission. Choreography by George Balanchine © The George Balanchine Trust.)

model. The following year, 1960, he danced the first role that Balanchine created expressly for him, the Prince of Lorraine in *The Figure in the Carpet*.

New, major roles followed, nearly one a year for the next decade, in works created by Balanchine or Jerome Robbins: *Electronics* (1961), *A Midsummer Night's Dream* (1962), *Bugaku* (1963), *Tarantella* (1964), *Harlequinade* (1965), *Brahms-Schoenberg Quartet* (1966), *Jewels* (1967), *Dances at a Gathering* (1969), *Suite No. 3* (1970), and *Watermill, Symphony in Three Movements*, and *Pulcinella* (all 1972). In these and other works in the repertory Villella often danced opposite Patricia McBride, Allegra Kent, or Violette Verdy. With McBride he formed a special partnership and gave unforgettable performances in *Tarantella*, the *Rubies* section of *Jewels*, and *Tchaikovsky Pas de Deux*, to name only three of the many works they danced together. In *Harlequinade*, McBride was the quintessential Columbine (Colombina) to his definitive Harlequin (Arlecchino), perpetrator of the dazzling antics that so charmed Kirstein, along with everyone else who saw them. During these peak years, Villella also made numerous television appearances, including *A Man Who Dances*, a 1968 NBC film with himself as the subject.

In 1962, Villella appeared in the musical *Brigadoon*, in the dancing role of Harry Beaton, at the City Center of Music and Drama in New York. His success was such that he was invited to perform the role in several subsequent revivals of the show. In 1966, he created his first ballet, *Narkissos*, but soon realized that choreography was not his forte. He was, essentially, a performer. Throughout the late 1960s, he not only performed regularly in numerous roles with the New York City Ballet, but he often made guest appearances with other companies, frequently dancing in such nineteenth-century classics as *Giselle* and *La Sylphide*.

By the early 1970s, Villella was beginning to feel the full effects of his late return to dance, of an early injury, and of dancing on concrete surfaces in television studios. In 1973, at the age of only thirty-six, he began the struggle of dancing a physically demanding repertory despite persistent pain in his back and hip. For the Ravel Festival in 1975, Balanchine used him only sparingly in a work set to Ravel's *Shéhérazade*, and in subsequent years he was forced to relinquish a number of his more exuberant roles. He made his last appearances as a member of the New York City Ballet in Robbins's monumentally static *Watermill* in 1979, performing an essentially mime role. Eleven years later, in June 1990, he reprised his role as the principal figure in this mesmerizing work in an official farewell performance. He was fifty-three years old, but the power and nobility of his portrayal were undiminished.

Seeing Villella as the perfect embodiment of both Arlecchino and Pulcinella, as Lincoln Kirstein did, is certainly justifiable, but such a view falls far short of giving a full picture of his artistry. To understand the breadth of his range one must also consider him as the protagonist of *Watermill*, as the Prodigal Son, and as Apollo, which he first performed in 1964 and in which he won great acclaim. In comic roles, he was the epitome of merriment; in dramatic roles, he could be profoundly moving. Perhaps, of all his roles, his part in the third movement of *Brahms-Schoenberg Quartet* best examplifies his style: elegant yet impetuous, powerful yet delicate, straightforward yet sly, romantic yet classical.

After leaving the New York City Ballet, Villella did not immediately stop dancing. Although physically unable to perform a full-scale repertory with a ballet company, he continued to give lecture-demonstrations with ballet students and to teach master classes. In 1980 he became artistic director of the Eglevsky Ballet, on Long Island, New York, a post he held for the next four years, and in 1981 he served for a year as visiting artist at the U.S. Military Academy at West Point, New York. He also served during this period as artistic adviser to Ballet Oklahoma and the New Jersey Ballet, and he worked both as a consultant and as a producer-director for the *Dance in America* series on public television. In 1986, Villella founded the Miami City Ballet, which today he continues to develop and direct. In addition to commissioning new ballets for his dancers, he has restaged a good number of Balanchine works, including *The Prodigal Son, Apollo, Bugaku, The Nutcracker,* and *Jewels.*

Villella's accomplishments have been officially recognized by a *Dance Magazine* Award (1965); an Emmy award (1976), from the Academy of Television Arts and Sciences; the Capezio Award (1989); the National Medal of Arts (1997); and a Kennedy Center Honor for lifetime achievement (1997).

BIBLIOGRAPHY

Barnes, Clive. "Edward Villella." *Dance Magazine* (November 1989).

Bland, Alexander, and John Percival. *Men Dancing: Performers and Performances.* New York, 1984.

Croce, Arlene. "Edward Villella: A Man and His Roles." In *Edward Villella: American Dancer.* West Point, N.Y., 1982. The catalog of an exhibition of photographs, sponsored by the Cadet Fine Arts Forum, 2–28 May 1982, Class of 1929 Gallery, Eisenhower Hall, U.S. Military Academy.

Croce, Arlene. "Slower Is Faster." *The New Yorker* (21 November 1988, 28 November 1988).

Kirsten, Lincoln. *The New York City Ballet.* New York, 1973. With photographs by Martha Swope and George Platt Lynes.

Terry, Walter. *Great Male Dancers of the Ballet.* New York, 1978.

Villella, Edward. "The Male Image." *Dance Perspectives,* no. 40 (Winter 1969).

Villella, Edward, with Larry Kaplan. *Prodigal Son: Dancing for Balanchine in a World of Pain and Magic.* New York, 1992.

ROBERT GRESKOVIC

VILZAK, ANATOLE (Anatolii Iosifovich Vil'tzak; born 29 August 1896 in Vilnius, Lithuania), Russian-American ballet dancer and teacher. Vitzak studied under Michel Fokine at the Imperial Theater School in Saint Petersburg, entering the corps de ballet of the Maryinsky Theater upon his graduation in 1915. He soon came to the attention of Matilda Kshessinska, and with her backing he stepped into leading classical roles, becoming a soloist in 1917.

In 1921, Vilzak left Russia and, with his wife Ludmilla Schollar, joined the Ballets Russes de Serge Diaghilev, dancing the role of Prince Charming in Diaghilev's production of *The Sleeping Princess* at London's Alhambra Theatre (1921/22). Between 1922 and 1925, he became the company's leading male classicist, performing principal roles in *Aurora's Wedding, Les Sylphides, Schéhérazade, Le Carnaval,* and *Les Biches.* Dismissed from the company for supporting a threatened strike in 1925, he appeared in Fokine's *Frolicking Gods* at the London Hippodrome and danced in a number of the choreographer's ballets at the Teatro Colón in Buenos Aires. In 1928, he became Ida Rubinstein's premier danseur, creating the leading male roles in Bronislava Nijinska's *Le Baiser de la Fée, Boléro, La Bien-Aimée,* and *La Valse.*

A matinee idol among the *danseurs nobles* of his generation, Vilzak appeared with Ida Rubinstein's troupe (1931, 1934), the State Opera House in Riga, Latvia (1932), Ni-jinska's Théâtre de Danse (1932–1934), and the Levitov-Dandré Russian Ballet (1934–1935). For René Blum's Ballet Russe de Monte Carlo, he danced the title role in Fokine's *Don Juan* (1936) as well as the leading role in Fokine's version of the *Polovtsian Dances* from *Prince Igor.* From 1935 to 1937, Vilzak appeared with Balanchine's American Ballet at New York's Metropolitan Opera, creating roles in many *divertissements.*

Retiring from the stage, Vilzak became one of the most prominent Russian teachers in the United States, serving on the faculties of the School of American Ballet, the Ballet Russe de Monte Carlo School, the Ballet Theatre School, and the Washington School of Ballet, in addition to conducting his own school in New York with his wife. From 1966 until 1996, when he was one hundred years old, he taught at the San Francisco Ballet School. His *Vilzak Variations after Petipa* for the San Francisco Ballet was premiered in 1982.

BIBLIOGRAPHY

Denny, Carol H. "Viva Vilzak: On His Toes at Eighty-Six." *San Francisco Sunday Examiner and Chronicle* (31 January 1982).

Heymont, George. "A Real Charmer." *Ballet News* 4 (February 1983): 14–18.

Karsavina, Tamara. "Vilzak, Dolin, Malcolm Sargent and Others." *Dancing Times* (May 1968).

Moore, Lillian. "Diaghileff Teachers in America: A Study in Constructive Guidance." *Ballet Annual* 10 (1956): 75–77.

Newman, Barbara. *Striking a Balance: Dancers Talk about Dancing.* Boston, 1982.

Ross, Janice. "Vilzak Variations." *Dance Magazine* (July 1988).

LYNN GARAFOLA

VINOGRADOV, OLEG (Oleg Mikhailovich Vinogradov; born 1 August 1937 in Leningrad), Russian choreographer. Upon graduation in 1958 from the Leningrad Choreographic Institute, where he studied with Aleksandr Pushkin, Vinogradov joined the Novosibirsk Opera and Ballet Theater as a dancer and later assistant choreographer until 1965. From 1968 to 1972 he was choreographer at the Kirov Opera and Ballet Theater in Leningrad, from 1973 to 1977 he held the same post at Leningrad's Maly Opera and Ballet Theater, and since 1977 he has been artistic director and chief choreographer of the Kirov Ballet.

Vinogradov produced Prokofiev's *Cinderella* (Novosibirsk, 1964; Odessa, 1970; Dresden, 1973; Leningrad's Maly Theater, 1977; Budapest, 1983) and *Romeo and Juliet* (Novosibirsk, 1965; Sofia, 1971; Erevan, 1972; new version at the Maly Theater, 1976), and Vladimir Vlasov's *Asel* (for the Bolshoi Ballet, Moscow, 1967). For the Kirov Theater he produced Murad Kazhlayev's *The Mountain Girl* (1968; new versions 1973 and 1984), Prokofiev's *Aleksandr Nevsky* (1969), Arif Melikov's *Two* (1969), Benjamin Britten's *The Prince of the Pagodas* (1972), Tikhon Khrennikov's *The Hussar's Ballad* (1979; with Dmitri Briantzev, new version for the Bolshoi Ballet, 1980), *The Fairy of the Rond Mountains* to Grieg (1980), *The Inspector-General* to

Tchaikovsky (1980), and *Testaments of the Past* (1971), to a pastiche score, for the bicentennial of the Kirov Theater. For the Maly Theater he produced *La Fille Mal Gardée* (1971; Odessa and Saratov, 1973; Berlin's Komische Opera, 1974; Frunze and Riga, 1976; Minsk, 1979; Tallinn, 1980), *Coppélia* (1973), Boris Tishchenko's *Yaroslavna* (1974), and *A Pedagogical Poem* (with Leonid Lebedev to Lebedev's music, 1977). On his return to the Kirov he produced Aleksei Machavariani's *The Knight in Tigerskin* (1985), *Battleship Potemkin* to Tchaikovsky (1986), his own version of *Petrouchka* (1990), which the company presented in Paris, and Samuel Barber's *Adagio* (1991), among others. Vinogradov has been the librettist and designer of many of his own productions.

Vinogradov has clearly tended toward large-scale compositions, in which the corps de ballet is assigned a considerable role and characterization is imaginative and inventive. At the same time his ballets have been quite varied. Besides classical ballets (*The Prince of the Pagodas* and *The Fairy of the Rond Mountains* as well as the standard repertory) he has done experimental productions (*Yaroslavna, A Pedagogical Poem, The Inspector-General*) that have stretched the boundaries of modern choreography, as well as ballets that are tragic (*Romeo and Juliet*), comic (*La Fille Mal Gardée*), and even satirical (*The Inspector-General*). He has believed that the struggles of everyday life can be resolved in ballet, as reflected in *Asel, A Pedagogical Poem,* and *The Mountain Girl.* The latter is especially interesting for its skillful use of the rich folk dance idiom of Daghestan, as is *The Knight in Tigerskin* for its incorporation of Georgian and Indian dances.

The plots of most of Vinogradov's ballets were not previously choreographed, but even with traditional subjects the choreographer's point of view has been manifested. For example, his *Cinderella* is not simply a story of virtue rewarded but of the confrontation between two outlooks on life, the philistine and the artistic. In *Romeo and Juliet,* which is addressed to young audiences, the accent is on the protagonists' travails and the constancy with which they are surmounted, set in a timeless context. Vinogradov's translation into dance of the classic comedy *The Inspector-General,* a text which had seemed inseparable from the caustic and pictorial language of Nikolai Gogol, was daring yet preserved something greater than words: the spirit of Gogol's satire, his famous "laughter through tears."

Vinogradov's choreography and Tishchenko's music for *Yaroslavna* were new in Soviet ballet, in their spirit of bold experimentation, use of modern theater techniques, and rich content. The creators viewed *The Lay of Igor's Campaign* (against the Polovtsians), the remarkable twelfth-century epic on which the ballet is based, through the eyes of modern artists and called on the spectator to reflect on the lessons of history. The dance movement, costumes, and design were pervaded with themes and symbols characteristic of ancient Russian art. Vinogradov has formulated his credo as follows: "In my opinion, a spectator coming to the ballet to admire only the beauty of the dancing deprives himself of what matters most. Modern ballet can and must stir not only emotions, but also thoughts."

As artistic director and chief choreographer of the Kirov Ballet, Vinogradov has also devoted attention and effort to preserving and restoring the classical repertory, especially the Petipa corpus, with emphasis on the intrinsic style of each ballet. Thus he has restored *The Sleeping Beauty* and *Le Corsaire* and set a *divertissement* from *Paquita* for the Paris Opera Ballet. At the same time he was the first Soviet director to bring ballets by Western choreographers into a Russian company's repertory. He is credited by many historians with having raised the Kirov Ballet from a state of decline in the early 1970s to its original eminence. In 1995 Vinogradov was replaced at the Kirov by Valery Gergiev. In 1990 Vinogradov opened a school in Washington, D.C., the Universal Ballet Academy, of which he remains director. Since 1991 he has also been head of the Saint Petersburg Chamber Ballet. Among his awards are the title People's Artist of the USSR (1983), the Petipa Prize in Paris (1979), the Order of Friendship of Nations (1984), and the Nijinsky Prize (1991).

BIBLIOGRAPHY
Alovert, Nina. "An Interview with Oleg Vinogradov." *Dance Magazine* (July 1989): 42–44.
Gregory, John. "Vinogradov's Testament." *The Dancing Times* (August 1982): 822–823.
Ilicheva, Marina A. *Oleg Vinogradov.* Hamburg, 1994.
Krasovskaya, Vera. "V seredine veka, 1950–1960." In *Sovetskii baletnyi teatr, 1917–1967,* edited by Vera Krasovskaya. Moscow, 1976.
Roslavleva, Natalia. "The Cause of Controversy: Oleg Vinogradov." *Dance and Dancers* (November 1967): 24–26.
Universal Ballet Academy. *Oleg Vinogradov: Portrait of a Contemporary Classicist.* Washington, D.C., 1990.

ARSEN B. DEGEN
Translated from Russian

VIOLETTE, EVA MARIA (Eva Maria Veigl [Weig(e)l or Faig(e)l]; born 29 February 1724 in Vienna, died 16 October 1822 in London), Austrian dancer. The daughter of Johann Veigl, valet of the Viennese Count von Paar, Eva Maria obtained ballet lessons at an early age from the prominent Austrian dancing master and choreographer Franz Hilverding. From about 1734 to 1745 she was attached to the ballet companies of the two leading Viennese theaters, the Kärntnertor Theater and the Burgtheater, both of which were under the management of the ballet master Joseph Sellier, perhaps another of her teachers. During this time she changed her name to Violette (*Veigl* is the Viennese dialect word for the German *Veilchen,* "violet").

Early in 1746, Eva Maria Violette and her younger

brother Ferdinand, a dancer who also took the name Violette, accepted an invitation to the London Theatre in the Haymarket. Charles Burney, in his *General History of Music*, erroneously states that Violette's London debut was on 7 January 1746 in the dances between the acts of Christoph Willibald Gluck's opera *La Caduta de' Giganti*. According to some contemporary reports and documents, Violette's arrival in London cannot be dated before the end of February 1746. Burney's comment on "the new dances by Auretti and the charming Violetta, afterward Mrs. Garrick" may well correspond to Violette's real London debut in Gluck's second London opera, *Artamene*, on 4 March 1746.

From that time onward she was extremely successful, both on the London stage and in London society. Her very close connection with the powerful Burlington family, which had taken the young dancer under their wing soon after her arrival in London, gave way to rumors that she might have been Lord Burlington's illegitimate daughter. Violette's contemporaries had little that was specific to say of her style of dancing. In *The Letters of Horace Walpole* she is said to be "the first and most admired dancer in the world" (1903, vol. 2, p. 230). Steedman (1979) quotes others as calling her "exquisite" and one who "inimitably" expresses the role of her character. Her marriage to the great English actor and playwright David Garrick on 22 June 1749, which created a sensation, ended Violette's stage career. The happy marriage ended only when Garrick died in 1779. Eva Maria, who never returned to her home country, outlived her husband by forty-three years and was buried next to him in London in Westminster Abbey.

BIBLIOGRAPHY

Burney, Charles. *A General History of Music*. 4 vols. 2d ed. London, 1789.

Derra de Moroda, Friderica. "The Dancer in Westminster Abbey: Eva Maria Garrick." *The Dancing Times* (June 1967): 476–477.

Garrick, David. *The Letters*. Edited by David M. Little and George M. Karl. London, 1963.

Parsons, Clement. *Garrick and His Circle*. London, 1906.

Steedman, W. "The Early Years of Mrs. Garrick." *Theatre Research International* 4 (February 1979).

Walpole, Horace. *The Letters of Horace Walpole*. London, 1903.

SIBYLLE DAHMS

VIRSALADZE, SIMON (Soliko Bagratovich Virsaladze; born 13 [26] January 1909 in Tbilisi, died 9 February 1989 in Tbilisi), Russian scenery and costume designer. Virsaladze trained at the Tbilisi (1926) and Leningrad (1928–1931) academies of art, and from 1932 to 1936 he was chief designer of the Paliashvili Theater in Tbilisi, where he designed operas as well as ballets. The most distinctive were *Heart of the Hills* (1936) and over twenty years later *Othello* (1957), both choreographed by Vakhtang Chabukiani. At the Kirov Theater in Leningrad he created the decor for the restaging of Chabukiani's *Heart of the Hills* (1938) and his new *Laurencia* (1939). After becoming chief designer there in 1945 he designed Fedor Lopukhov's *Spring Tale* (1947); Konstantin Sergeyev's *Raymonda* (1950), *Swan Lake* (1950), and *The Sleeping Beauty* (1951); and Vasily Vainonen's *The Nutcracker* (1954). In the same period Virsaladze also provided scenery for ballets at Leningrad's Maly Theater, and he later designed decor for theaters in Baku, Novosibirsk, and abroad. Between 1930 and 1950 the art of Virsaladze, along with that of other outstanding artists (Fedor Fedorovsky, Vladimir Dmitriev, Petr Williams, and Vadim Ryndin), largely defined the main principle of ballet design: realism coupled with a creative interpretation of the dramaturgy and characters.

From 1957 until his death Virsaladze worked in ballet exclusively with the choreographer Yuri Grigorovich, at the Kirov until 1962, and at the Bolshoi Theater in Moscow thereafter. His art was inseparably linked with the new principles Grigorovich introduced into ballet. The Grigorovich ballets designed by Virsaladze—*The Stone Flower* (1957), *Legend of Love* (1961), *The Sleeping Beauty* (1963 and 1973), *The Nutcracker* (1966), *Spartacus* (1968), *Swan Lake* (1969), *Ivan the Terrible* (1975), *The Angara* (1976), *Romeo and Juliet* (1979), *The Golden Age* (1982), and *Raymonda* (1984)—largely determined the development of Soviet choreography.

Virsaladze was thoroughly familiar with the requirements of dance design. Leaving the center of the stage free for the choreography, he usually found an expression for the ballet as a whole, which might also appear in specific scenes as the action unfolded. In *The Stone Flower*, for example, the repository of fairy tales in *The Malachite Casket* on which the ballet is based incorporates pictures of every act. Virsaladze's costumes were invariably integral to the character as well as convenient for dancing. He never oversimplified a costume or converted it into a uniform or an abstract sketch. His costumes reflected the traits of the character or had historical and social appropriateness; at the same time the color and cut revealed and emphasized the plastique. They were also related to the scenery in color, thus creating "symphonic paintings" that were integral with the music and dance. Virsaladze was a People's Artist of the USSR and a Fellow of the Soviet Academy of Art. He won the Lenin Prize in 1970 and the State Prize of the USSR in 1949, 1951, and 1977.

BIBLIOGRAPHY

Berezkin, Viktor. "Khudozhnik v sovetskom balete." In *Sovetskii baletnyi teatr, 1917–1967*, edited by Vera Krasovskaya. Moscow, 1976.

Karp, Poel M. "Simon Virsaladze." In *Leningradskie khudozhniki teatra*, edited by E. A. Davydova. Leningrad, 1971.

Obituary. *Dance Magazine* (June 1989): 28–29.

Vanslov, Victor V. *Simon Virsaladze* (in Russian). Moscow, 1969.

VICTOR V. VANSLOV
Translated from Russian

VIRSKY, PAVEL (Pavlo Vir'skyi, known in Russian as Pavel Pavlovich Virskii; born 12 [25] February 1905 in Odessa, Ukraine, died 5 June 1975 in Kiev), dancer and choreographer. Virsky graduated in 1926 from the dance department of the Odessa School of Music and Drama, where he studied under Vladimir Presnyakov, and in 1928 from a theater school in Moscow, where his teachers were Asaf Messerer and Kasyan Goleizovsky. Between 1923 and 1926 Virsky was a ballet dancer, but his interest soon turned to choreography. From 1928 to 1933 he served as chief choreographer of the Odessa Opera and Ballet Theater and 1933 of the Kharkov Opera Theater. In 1935 he worked in the same capacity in Dniepropetrovsk and in 1936 in Kiev.

In 1932, with Nikolai Bolotov, Virsky produced the heroic ballet *La Carmagnole* for the Moscow Art Theater Ballet, then under the directorship of Viktorina Kriger. While relying on the classical tradition, Virsky boldly introduced into his ballet productions the advancements of the contemporary dramatic stage, the latest achievements of folk dance choreography, and modern plastique in an effort to achieve clear-cut dramatic development and to create vivid characters and ensemble dances with full-blooded emotional and substantive content. Some of his best ballet productions created in collaboration with Bolotov are noted for vivid and original dance imagery. They include *The Red Poppy* (1928), *The Little Humpbacked Horse* and *La Esmeralda* (1929), *Swan Lake* (1932), and *Le Corsaire* (1933) in Odessa; *La Esmeralda* (1933) and *Raymonda* (1934) in Kharkov; and the comic ballet *The Burgess from Tuscany* (1935) in Dniepropetrovsk and 1936 in Kiev).

In 1937 Virsky founded a Ukrainian dance ensemble for which he labored to collect, systematize, and realize on the stage the rich heritage of Ukrainian folk dance. He also staged a series of narrative dance numbers and the ballet *Bondarivna* (Kiev, 1938) based on the folk dance idiom with elements of classical dance. In the 1920s and 1930s Virsky also produced dances for Soviet, Ukrainian, and contemporary operas, of which the most significant were the large-scale scenes in Mykola Lysenko's *Taras Bulba*, Semen Gulak-Artemovsky's *The Zaporozhe Cossack beyond the Danube*, and Boris Liatoshinksy's *The Golden Ring* and *Shchors*. Between 1939 and 1943 Virsky was chief choreographer of the song-and-dance ensemble of the Kiev military district, and from 1943 to 1955 he served in the same capacity with the Anatoly Aleksandrov ensemble of the Soviet Army, staging numerous military dances and choreographed scenes.

From 1955 to 1975 Virsky was the artistic director of the State Academic Dance Ensemble of the Ukraine. The ensemble has borne his name since 1975. During this period Virsky displayed every facet of his talent as choreographer. A connoisseur of Ukrainian folk dance, he skillfully theatricalized it by using a combination of dramatic techniques, modern ballet, and pantomime. The large-scale works he staged—*The Zaporozhe Cossacks, We Remember, Why Is the Willow Weeping?*, and *The Guelder Rose*—are noted for a wide range of themes, genres, and styles. He also devised delightfully vivid dance miniatures, such as "Chumak Joys," "Podolyanka," "Polzunets," "Kozachek," and "The Dolls," which revealed new expressive dimensions in Ukrainian dance, reflecting various facets of the distinctive national character, artistic traditions, and folk dance heritage. In 1960 Virsky produced a modern Ukrainian heroic ballet, *Black Gold*, at the Kiev Opera and Ballet Theater, and in 1967 he created the ballet *October Legend*. In 1962, on Virsky's initiative, the ensemble opened a folk dance studio, which has since produced many first-class performances.

For his distinguished services Virsky was honored in 1960 with the title People's Artist of the USSR. He was also awarded state prizes of the USSR in 1950 and 1970 and the Shevchenko State Prize of the Ukrainian SSR.

BIBLIOGRAPHY
Lawson, Joan. "The Ukrainians Return to London." *The Dancing Times* (November 1961): 83.
Stanishevsky, Yuri. *Pavlo Pavlovych Virskyi*. Kiev, 1962.
Stanishevsky, Yuri. *The Ukrainian Ballet, 1786–1986*. Kiev, 1986.
Zürner, Inge. Obituary. *Dance News* (September 1975): 6–7.

YURI A. STANISHEVSKY
Translated from Russian

VLADIMIROFF, PIERRE (Petr Nikolaevich Nikolaev [Vladimirov]; born 1 [13] February? 1893 in Saint Petersburg, died 26 November 1970 in New York), Russian dancer and teacher. Vladimiroff was the prototype of the imperial Russian dancers who found a second career in the West after the Bolshevik Revolution. As the successor to Vaslav Nijinsky at the Maryinsky Theater, he was the favorite partner of the leading Saint Petersburg ballerinas and the object of legendary outbursts of balletomania. He danced in Serge Diaghilev's and Anna Pavlova's companies before settling in the United States, where he taught at the School of American Ballet in New York from its founding until his retirement in 1967.

Vladimiroff trained with Sergei Legat, Samuil Andreonov, and Mikhail Obukhov in the Imperial Theater School. In 1911 he graduated into the Maryinsky company and became *premier danseur* in 1915. In the Fokine repertory he danced *Le Carnaval, Chopiniana, Le Pavillon d'Armide*, and *Le Spectre de la Rose*, and he created the title role of *Eros*. Urged by Michel Fokine, he also performed the classics: *Giselle* with Olga Spessivtseva, *Swan Lake* with Lubov Egorova, and *Paquita, Raymonda, Le Corsaire*, and *The Talisman*.

During leaves of absence in 1912 and 1914, Vladimiroff

danced for Diaghilev, who attempted to recruit him as Nijinsky's permanent replacement, but he refused at the request of his partner, Matilda Kshessinska. Last appearing at the Maryinsky in 1918, he fled the Soviets with his wife, the dancer Felia Doubrovska, in 1920. He danced for Diaghilev as Prince Désiré in *The Sleeping Princess* and with Tamara Karsavina in European and American concerts. In the United States he toured with Adolph Bolm's Ballet Intime and Mikhail Mordkin's Russian Ballet. He was Pavlova's last partner and was said to have been her favorite. Touring with her company from 1928 to 1931 he danced *Dionysus, Chopiniana, Grand Pas Hongrois, The Fairy Doll,* and *Autumn Leaves.*

Vladimiroff returned to the United States in 1933 with a troupe organized by Serge Lifar. In 1934 George Balanchine engaged him for the School of American Ballet, where he taught for thirty-three years. Vladimiroff had been a favorite dancer of Balanchine's at the Maryinsky

VLADIMIROFF. With Anna Pavlova in *Chopiniana*, photographed during a South American tour in 1928. (Photograph by Nicholas Yarovoff; from the Dance Collection, New York Public Library for the Performing Arts.)

and transmitted to American dancers the pure classicism of the Russian tradition.

BIBLIOGRAPHY

Barzel, Ann. "European Dance Teachers in the United States." *Dance Index* 3 (April–June 1944): 56–100.

Borisoglebsky, Mikhail. *Proshloe baletnogo otdeleniia Peterburgskogo teatral'nogo uchilishcha, nyne Leningradskogo gosudarstvennogo khoreograficheskogo uchilishcha: Materialy po istorii russkogo baleta.* Vol. 2. Leningrad, 1939.

Como, William, and Richard Philp. "Pavlova." *Dance Magazine* (January 1976): 43–74.

Doubrovska, Felia. "Pierre Vladimiroff: A Memoir, as Told to Marian Horosko." *Dance Magazine* (February 1971): 43–45.

Krasovskaya, Vera. *Russkii baletnyi teatr nachala dvadtsatogo veka,* vol. 2, *Tantsovshchiki.* Leningrad, 1972.

Relkin, Abbie. "In Pavlova's Shadow." *Ballet News* 2 (January 1981): 26–29.

Smakov, Gennady. *The Great Russian Dancers.* New York, 1984.

SUZANNE CARBONNEAU

VODUN. The dance culture of Haiti is inseparable from the pervasive Africa-based folk religion of the nation, Vodun. Misunderstood and labeled "Voodoo" by outsiders, this tradition is not mere witchcraft based on superstition but a highly structured system fulfilling social and psychological needs. Slaves brought to the Spanish and French colonies on the island of Hispaniola from various regions of sub-Saharan Africa experienced terrible dislocation and nostalgia as well as physical suffering. They were deprived of the family and community in which elders provided security, linking them together. Their land and family spirits were far away. To reconstruct an emotional African background was essential for psychological survival in their new milieu, but that could not be done without the unity possible only through traditional religion.

This religion has survived despite the efforts of slave-owners to suppress it and the desire of some Haitian governments to eradicate it. Today, Vodun constitutes vivid testimony to the African presence in Haiti.

Vodun is an amalgam of the religious practices of several African cultures, including Yoruba, Fon, Congo, Igbo, Bamana, Adja, Akan, Asante, Wolof, Mandinka, Hausa, Mahi, and Ewe. Its greatest influence came from the Fon people of Benin (formerly Dahomey), from whom most Haitians are descended. Vodun is one of the best-preserved Africa-based religions systems in the Americas. Although it has much in common with other New World Africa-based religions—Santería or Lucumi of Cuba; Candomblé, Macumba, and Batuque of Brazil; Kumina of Jamaica; Shango and Nago of Trinidad and Tobago—it differs in some respects. The others are derived to a large extent from the Yoruba (with the exception of Kumina of Jamaica, which is influenced mostly by the religious systems of the Akan and Asante [Ashanti] peoples of Ghana).

VODUN. A man, his face puckered in the throes of possession, dances during a Vodun ceremony in 1960. (Photograph by Pierre Verger; used by permission.)

The word *vodun* means "spirit" in the Fongbe language of Benin. Vodun involves rites of birth, initiation, marriage, death, and burial in conjunction with the worship of its pantheon. (Contrary to popular belief, Vodun is not malevolent but harmless and benevolent in character.) As a religious system, Vodun uses ritual songs and dances that are accompanied by a sacred drum and other musical instruments. A clear picture of this religion is given by Harold Courlander:

> Vodun is clearly more than ritual of the cult temple. It is an integrated system of concepts concerning human behavior, the relation of mankind to those who have lived before, and to the natural and supernatural forces of the universe. It relates the living to the dead and those not yet born. It explains unpredictable principles. In short, it is a true religion which attempts to tie the unknown to the known and thus create order where chaos existed before. (Courlander, 1960, p. 9)

Many students of Vodun conceive of it as geocentric and anthropocentric, unlike Christianity, which is theocentric. The Vodun practitioner is not interested in heaven but believes that humans must do good deeds on earth to join the world of the spirits, where they may be able to help the living. This basic concept is shared by most African religious systems.

The Vodun temple, called a *hounfor*, consists of three sections. In the peristyle (courtyard), where public ceremonies are held, there is a center post, called *poteau mi-tan*, down which spirits descend during ceremonies. The *jevo* is a special sanctuary for confining devotees during initiation and for curing serious illness. The *bagui*, commonly called *kay-miste* or *kay loa* ("house of the spirits"), is a sanctuary room that contains one or more altars *(pe)* on which are arranged a large number of ritual objects. The *hounfor* serves not only as a place of worship but also as a shelter for the homeless; nonmembers are welcome as long as there is enough space.

The *houngan* (Vodun priest) and the *mambo* (Vodun priestess) are the spiritual leaders who officiate at all ceremonies. They are helped by members of the congregation, called *hounsis;* there are two categories, *hounsis bossales* and *hounsis kanzo*, the former noninitiated and the latter initiated. Some of the initiated *hounsis* hold special positions in the congregation's hierarchy. The *laplace*, chief assistant to the *houngan*, ordinarily acts as a master of ceremonies, often carrying a sword or a machete while leading processions within the *hounfor*. The *houngenikon*, a special assistant, leads the choir and assists the *houngan* during sacrifices, taking the *houngan's* place when necessary, especially when the *houngan* is possessed. (Both assistants are final steps before becoming a *houngan*.)

Not every Vodun practitioner belongs to a particular congregation. Some go to a *hounfor* often, but others seek help from a *houngan* or a *mambo* only when faced with a crisis. The *houngan* functions in the community not only as a spiritual leader but also as a medicine person, counselor or social worker, judge, political leader, and policymaker. Not everyone can become a Vodun priest or priestess; one must either inherit knowledge from parents or relatives or be chosen by a spirit—mainly from among the family spirits.

Ritual Objects. A good Vodun priest knows about all the aspects of the Vodun rituals, including the meaning and significance of the ritual and its sacred objects. The drums are the most sacred and the most common musical instrument in African religions. In Vodun their use is specific to certain ceremonies. For example, a Rada drum is not to be used in a Petro ceremony.

The *assoto* drum, the most sacred drum in Vodun, is seven feet (two meters) high. There is a special ceremony held in its honor every year, or every two or three years, depending on the locality. Rada drums are a set of three. The largest, three to four feet (one meter) high, is called *maman;* the middle sized is *segond*, and the smallest is *bula* or *bébé*. They are made of wood, with stretched cowhide skins affixed to the body with wooden pegs. The Rada drums are used during ceremonies honoring the Rada spirits. Petro drums are a set of two. The larger is called *maman* or *gro baka*, and the smaller *pitit* or *ti baka*. They have stretched goatskin attached to the wooden body with sisal strings. The Petro drums are used during ceremonies in honor of the Petro gods.

There are also drums for lesser groups of deities, such as Congo drums or *juba* drums, but these drums are seldom used because some of these spirits belong to the Rada group. The drums also have their own spirit, called Hunto.

The *asson,* another important ritual object, is a pear-shaped gourd rattle covered with multicolored beads that represent the colors of the Vodun deities. It is used by the priest and priestess to help summon the spirits.

The *gavi* is a ritual clay pot into which spirits are drawn down by the priest or priestess. It is also used to house the spirit *mait-tête* ("master of the head") of a deceased devotee. The priest takes the spirit off the corpse's head in a ceremony called *dessounin* and puts it in the *govi*. It also functions as *pot de tête* ("head pot"), holding hair strands and nail parings of the initiated (personal matter that can be used for either good or bad magic).

The *zin,* used during initiation and funeral rites in a ceremony called *boule zin* (pot burning), is usually made of clay but sometimes of iron. The *plate marassa* (twin's dishes and pitchers) are also of clay, but sometimes of wood. They are used to hold offerings of food and drink for the spirits of twins. The *cruche* or *criche* is a clay pitcher that holds water for libations during ceremonies and sometimes fulfills the function of *pot de tête.*

Vodun Pantheon. The Vodun religion has a large pantheon of deities called *loa* (a Congo word meaning "spirit"). Most of them are syncretized with Roman Catholic saints, owing to the pressure on the slaves by their masters who wanted them converted. Early Vodun practitioners first used Catholic elements as camouflage; later they became integral to the religion. Syncretism in Vodun is not limited to saints/*loa*s; it plays an important role in the liturgy, with most Vodun ceremonies begun with Catholic prayers.

The Vodun pantheon has two main categories. Rada deities consist mostly of African entities, whereas Petro deities comprise mostly local or Creole deities. The deities are intermediaries between humans and God, whom Vodun practitioners call Grand Mait' (Great Master).

Rituals and ceremonies in honor of the spirits are an integral part of Vodun. These are called *service loa:* the two most common are the Mange Marassa (food for the twin spirits) and the Mange Yams (eating yams)—a thanksgiving ceremony. There are also ceremonies honoring a *loa*'s day, which often coincides with the celebration of the corresponding Catholic saint; for example, Saint Patrick's day is also Damballah's, and Saint James's day is also Oggun's. Depending on the preference of the spirit, goats, roosters, pigs, pigeons, or occasionally a cow may be offered as sacrifice during a ceremony.

Ceremonies. At the beginning of every ceremony the priest draws symbols on the ground of the *hounfor* with corn flour, especially around the *poteau mitan.* These symbols, called *veves,* are emblems of the deities; they help attract the spirits. Legba, the oldest deity of the pantheon, is the first to be honored in any ceremony.

Songs, rhythmic drumbeats, and especially dance are also attractive forces to the spirits during the ceremony. Each deity has a specific rhythm and dance to attract him or her. The *yanvalou* rhythm and dance, for example, attract Agwe, the spirit of the sea, and Damballah, the snake spirit of fertility; *nago* rhythm and dance attract Oggun, the spirit of war and iron. In the former dance, the devotee mimes the undulating movements of a snake and the waves of the sea by moving gracefully forward and backward. In the second dance, however, the participant's movements recall those of a slave trying to break the chains or a warrior attempting to crush an enemy. In both cases there is a correlation between the character of the deity and his favorite dance.

Vodun is a family religion, and the hereditary element is used to acquire help from a spirit. Each person may inherit a spirit from his mother's or father's side—sometimes from both. In order to benefit fully from the protection of a particular spirit, the protégé must establish a forceful rela-

VODUN. A man dancing in a *hounfor* (temple) during a Vodun ritual. (Photograph by Pierre Verger; used by permission.)

tionship between himself and this spirit protector through initiation. The complex initiation rite, called *kanzo*, lasts twenty-one days and is the first step toward becoming a priest.

Possession by a spirit is one of the main features of Vodun. The gods communicate with devotees either by entering their bodies or in dreams. Possession occurs when the *loa* moves into the individual's head. The person becomes the "horse" of the god, his mouthpiece. The actions and words of the possessed are those of the spirit by whom the devotee is mounted. Possession is not regarded as evil; for the worshipper it is a blessing, because it enables him to carry out difficult tasks such as curing disease or protecting the life of one in great danger. During initiation, a neophyte may be possessed by his spirit two or more times, a good sign, showing communication between the protégé and the protector.

[*See also* Haiti.]

BIBLIOGRAPHY

Bastide, Roger. *African Civilisations in the New World.* Translated from the French by Peter Green, with a foreward by Geoffrey Parrinder. New York, 1971.

Bascom, William R. "The Focus of Cuban Santería." *South Western Journal of Anthropology* 6.1 (1950).

Bastien, Remy, and Harold Courlander. *Religion and Politics in Haiti; Two Essays.* Washington, D.C., 1966.

Cabrea, Lydia. *El Monte.* Miami, 1971.

Courlander, Harold. *The Drum and the Hoe: Life and Lore of the Haitian People.* Berkeley, 1960.

Deren, Maya. *Divine Horsemen: The Living Gods of Haiti.* New York, 1953.

Franck, Harry A. *Roaming through the West Indies.* New York, 1920.

Frank, Henry. "African Religion in the Caribbean: Santería and Voodoo." *Carib* 2.1 (1982).

Gonzalez-Wippler, Migene. *Santería: African Magic in Latin America.* New York, 1973.

Gonzalez-Wippler, Migene. *The Santería Experience.* New Jersey, 1982.

Gonzalez-Wippler, Migene. *Rituals and Spells of Santería.* New York, 1984.

Herskovits, Melville J. *Life in a Haitian Valley.* New York, 1937, reprinted 1964.

Hurbon, Laennec. *Dieu dans le Vaudou Haïtien.* Paris, 1972.

Jahn, Janheiz. *Muntu, the New African Culture.* New York, 1961.

Maximilien, Louis. *Le Voudou Haïtien: Rite Radas-Canzo.* Port-au-Prince, 1945.

Métraux, Alfred. *Vaudou in Haitien.* Translated from the French by Hugo Charteris. New York, 1958.

Murphy, Joseph M. *Santeria, an African Religion in America.* New York, 1988.

Moreau de Saint-Mery, M. L. E. *A Topographical and Political Description of the Spanish Part of Saint-Domingo, Containing General Observations on the Climate, Population, and Productions; on the Character and Manners of the Inhabitants.* Translated from the French by William Cobbett, Philadelphia, 1796.

Planson, Claude. *Voodoo, Un Initié Parle.* Paris, 1974.

Rigaud, Milo. *La Tradition Voudoo et le Voudoo Haïtien: Son Temple, Ses Mysteres, Sa Magie.* Paris, 1953.

HENRY FRANK

VOLININE, ALEXANDRE (Aleksandr Emel'ianovich Volinin; born 4 [16] September 1882 in Moscow, died 3 July 1955 in Paris), Russian-French ballet dancer and teacher. Born to a family of engineers, Volinine received his dance training from Vasily Tikhomirov and Aleksandr Gorsky at the Imperial Theater School in Moscow. Entering the Bolshoi Ballet as a soloist in 1901, he quickly established himself as one of the company's leading classical dancers, admired for his beautiful, flowing line and adagio. In 1904, he replaced Tikhomirov in *The Goldfish*, which led to his promotion to principal dancer. In subsequent years, he added the major classical ballets to his repertory: *Raymonda, La Fille du Pharaon, La Fille Mal Gardée, Coppélia, The Sleeping Beauty,* and *Swan Lake.*

In 1910, Volinine left Russia to dance in Serge Diaghilev's Saison Russe in Paris partnering Ekaterina Geltser in *Les Orientales* and also appearing in *Les Sylphides, Le Carnaval,* and *Schéhérazade.* With Lydia Lopokova, her sister Evgenia, and her brother Fedor Lopukhov, he left Europe on a tour of the United States, subsequently performing in Gertrude Hoffmann's Saisons Russes (1911) and Mikhail Mordkin's All-Star Imperial Russian Ballet (1911–1912). He partnered Adeline Genée on her American and Australian tours (1912–1913) as well as during her farewell season at the London Coliseum (1914).

Later in 1914 Anna Pavlova invited Volinine to join her company, initiating a partnership that lasted with few interruptions until 1926. During these years, Volinine appeared as Pavlova's *danseur noble* in *Giselle, The Sleeping Beauty, The Awakening of Flora, Raymonda, The Fairy Doll,* and *The Magic Flute,* also performing various solo *divertissements.* For P. J. S. Richardson, editor of *The Dancing Times,* he was "the finest male dancer of [his] generation. He has a magnificent presence, and is always manly. His 'Bow and Arrow' dance shows a poise and elevation coupled with a purity of line and perfection of pose that make most *premiers danseurs* seem very small beer indeed." In 1926, Volinine opened a school in Paris where he taught such well-known dancers as Jean Babilée, Zizi Jeanmaire, George Skibine, Janine Charrat, and André Eglevsky. In 1946, he staged *Giselle* for the Royal Danish Ballet.

BIBLIOGRAPHY

Cross, Julia Vincent. "A Volinine Vignette." *Dance Magazine* (February 1957): 42–43.

Krasovskaya, Vera. *Russkii baletnyi teatr nachala dvadtatogo veka,* vol. 2, *Tantsovshchiki.* Leningrad, 1972.

Lazzarini, John, and Roberta Lazzarini. *Pavlova: Repertoire of a Legend.* New York, 1980.

Michaut, Pierre. "Parisian studios de danse." *Ballet Annual* 4 (1950): 124–129.

Money, Keith. *Anna Pavlova: Her Life and Art.* New York, 1982.

Volinine, Alexandre. "My Dance of Life" (parts 1–4). *Dance Magazine* (January–April 1930).

"Volinine at Work." *The Dancing Times* (January 1929): 548–551.

LYNN GARAFOLA

VOLKOVA, VERA (born 7 June 1904 in Saint Petersburg, died 5 May 1975 in Copenhagen), Russian ballet teacher. Volkova was born into the Russian aristrocracy and had her formal education in the Smolny Institute for Young Girls in Saint Petersburg. She started dancing at the age of fourteen. Stimulated by the influential critic Akim Volynsky, she became a pupil at his private school, the Russian School of Choreography. Agrippina Vaganova was a teacher there, and Volkova was a member of the group of pupils on which Vaganova tested her theories. Also among Volkova's teachers was Maria Romanova, the mother of Galina Ulanova.

Volkova danced with the Kirov Ballet, but her performing career was brief. She had intended to go to the West and join Serge Diaghilev's Ballets Russes, but when Diaghilev died in 1929, she defected while on tour with a group of colleagues in Vladivostok. She then settled in Shanghai, where she met the English architect and painter Hugh Finch Williams. They moved to Hong Kong, where they married in 1932, and she established her own school. Among her earliest pupils there was the young Margot Fonteyn, who also studied with Volkova later in England.

In 1937, Volkova moved to London and established an academy on West Street, which for years was attended by the most important English dancers of the period. From 1943 to 1950 she also taught for the Sadler's Wells Ballet. Volkova had great influence on the generation that shaped English ballet after World War II. She was the first and most important exponent of Vaganova's method of training in the West.

In the late 1940s, Volkova went to the Teatro alla Scala in Milan; not satisfied with conditions there, she allowed the head of the Royal Danish Ballet, Harald Lander, to persuade her to join his company in Copenhagen. Volkova organized the training at the Royal Ballet School, combining the Vaganova system with the traditional Danish Bournonville method. She was of decisive importance in setting the technical and spiritual standard that led the company to international fame during the following decade. Among her pupils in Copenhagen was Stanley Williams; in his later position as a teacher she was of great inspiration. Volkova also profoundly influenced such Danish soloists as Kirsten Simone, Erik Bruhn, Henning Kronstam, Peter Martins, Peter Schaufuss, Adam Lüders, and Lis Jeppesen. The American-born choreographer John Neumeier, head of the Hamburg Ballet, also said that his conversations with Volkova in Copenhagen were decisive in his decision to start choreographing. From 1950 to 1957 Volkova watched the Royal Danish Ballet from her seat in the stalls at almost every performance, in order to prepare for her teaching the next day.

From 1958 until 1970 Volkova also taught at Kurt Jooss's Folkwang Schule in Essen, Germany. She was a guest teacher in the United States on several occasions, most often with the Harkness Ballet. In 1956 she was named a Knight of the Order of Dannebrog.

BIBLIOGRAPHY

Aschengreen, Erik. "Hommage à Vera Volkova." *Saisons de la danse,* no. 75 (June 1975): 28.

Hering, Doris. "America Meets Vera Volkova." *Dance Magazine* (September 1959): 36–38.

Kragh-Jacobsen, Svend. "Interview with Vera Volkova." *Ballet Review* 5.4 (1975–1976).

Volkova, Vera. "Agrippina Vaganova." *Ballet Annual* 7 (1953): 44.

EBBE MØRK

VOLTA (Fr., *volte*) is a word used in Italian and French technical terminology for dancing, fencing, and horsemanship (three closely associated "manly arts," many of whose traditions and terms have descended from the Renaissance). *Volta* ("turn") appears in dance terminology as early as the first Italian manuals of the fifteenth century. It is still a standard term in the Italian dance vocabulary, frequently used with modifiers to indicate the degree of turn—for example, *mezza volta* ("half turn") or *volta tonda* ("full turn").

Volta also means "time," in the sense of frequency; its usage in dance is customary, as in *una volta* ("once") and *due volte* ("twice"). In this sense it also appears regularly in Italian Renaissance dance terminology, as in the instruction, in Cesare Negri's dance manual of 1602, *si levarà il salto intorno due volte alla sinistra* ("jump and turn around twice to the left").

The term *volta*, when it means "the turn" (Eng., *the lavolta*; Fr., *la volte*; Prov., *la volto*), seems to have been used generically by a few Renaissance writers for any turning couple dance in any meter; Rinaldo Corso (1555), for example, used the term in this broad sense, saying, "Begin the ball with a *passo e mezzo* [a duple-meter dance related both to the pavan and the galliard], which is a pleasing *volta* halfway between moderate and lively. At the end join together and do the *volta* that is now in fashion." Clearly, in this case the term refers simply to the large group of rapid turning dances that are documented from the Middle Ages to the present in iconography and literature throughout Europe and Scandinavia. The dances are distinguished by the partners, who face and hold one another firmly in embrace position—coordinating their steps to produce the centrifugal force for a full turn or pivot, with or without a lift (e.g., Swedish *polsks*, German *Zwiefacher*, Viennese and French waltzes).

References to the *volta* as a specific dance appear in print and in musical and iconographic sources on courtly life between about 1550 and 1650. Despite the dance's apparent popularity throughout western Europe, Thoinot Arbeau's *Orchésographie* (1588) is the only major dance manual to describe it in detail and correlate it with music. Arbeau says it is a triple-meter couple dance, a variant of the immensely popular galliard. Its distinguishing feature is a leap-turn by the lady, during which the man pivots on one foot while assisting his partner to leap. With one hand he grasps the bottom of her busk (a long rigid piece of thin metal or bone inserted or sewn into the corselet and extending from the breastbone to the crotch) and with the other he presses her back at the waist. At the same time, he turns her around with his other (lifted) knee just under her buttocks. The lady contributes to the lift by jumping strongly off one foot while she simultaneously presses one arm or hand forcefully down on her partner's shoulder using her other arm to keep her skirts from flying too high. She remains absolutely erect during the lift, with her legs straight down but not together. She is set down at the end of each turn. With a preparation, the whole pattern takes six beats and is to be repeated or else done to the other side *ad libitum*.

Arbeau gives two different rhythms for the changes of weight (one verbal and another in tabulation) and two different paths to alternate (one moving forward with a simple galliard variant, the other with the lift-turn). In the turning version, the preparation consists of two kicks, and the assisted lift and turn take the place of the *saut majeur* and *posture* of the last three or four beats of Arbeau's basic galliard pattern. These instructions are briefly confirmed by John Ramsey in about 1606 (Manuscripts of the Inns of Court, Douce 280).

There are numerous musical examples of the sixteenth- and seventeenth-century *volta* from France, England, Italy, and Germany. Like the galliard, it is in 6/2 or 3/2 time, and frequently the second half of its six-beat pattern contains the dotted rhythm of that dance: ♩♩♩♩ ♩·♩♩|. Unlike the galliard, however, the music for the *volta* never became increasingly complex polyphonically and rhythmically (and, hence, slower) as it aged, but remained a plain tune or a tune with simple harmonies. Its slow har-

monic rhythm of only one or two chords to a bar continued to indicate a brisk tempo. As the dance itself retained its focus on the preparation and lift, which was its constant and tempo-controlling feature, so did a number of *volta* melodies also emphasize the leap to the fourth beat of every six. (See Example 1.)

No *volta* instructions appear in Italian large or small dance manuals, although Negri gives a related dance, "La Nizzarda" (The Girl from Nice), a fast and energetic turning dance in embrace position with small jumps and other hopping steps. Some scholars claim that it is the same as the *volta* (Donington, 1980). Negri's rather ambiguous description of "La Nizzarda," however, with its low hopping turns and embrace position, shows only a familial relationship to Arbeau's *volte*. However, a later description by Federico Zuccari in his travel memoirs (1608) describes a *nizzarda* with high lifts and turns that seems closer to Arbeau's choreography. The precise relationship between *volta* and *nizzarda*, both of which may be of Provençal origin, seems still to be in question.

The *volta's* lusty and erotic nature caused it to figure frequently in moral, salacious, or humorous texts that appeared during its greatest popularity at European courts (c.1550–1650). The suggestive embrace position and the spin and lift of the dance provided ample fodder for commentary: for example, Abbé Pierre de Bourdeilles de Brantôme (*Les vies des dames galantes*, c.1570), says of it, "The *volta*, as it swirls the dress up, always shows something delightful to the eye, and as I have seen, has caused many to lose their heads and to be utterly transported"; Guillaume Bouchet (*Les Serées*, 1597) says, "The *volta* [and] the *courante*, . . . which magicians have brought from Italy to France, besides their rude and bold movements, have the misfortune of causing an infinite number of murders and miscarriages, killing and destroying all who are yet unborn"; and the diary of "R. Z." (c.1600) in the Biblioteca di Modena says that the lift involves a tight pivot and is dangerous because if the dancers "are not fast [enough], they may both fall; nor must they allow them-

VOLTA. Example 1. A *volta* from William Byrd's *Fitzwilliam Virginal Book* (c.1612–1619). Note the melodic leap to the fourth beat in three of the four bars.

selves to get dizzy." Even Arbeau, despite his carefully detailed and practical instructions, seems to feel it his churchman's duty to warn his student, Capriol:

> After having spun round for as many cadences as you wish, return the damsel to her place, when, however brave a face she shows, she will feel her brain reeling and her head full of dizzy whirlings; and you yourself will perhaps be no better off. I leave it to you to judge whether it is a becoming thing for a young girl to take long strides and separations of the legs, and whether in this *lavolta* both honour and health are not involved and at stake.   (Arbeau, 1588, pp. 119–121)

Shakespeare, in *Henry V* (act 3, scene 5), is much more approving:

> They [the English] bid us, "to the English dancing-schools,
> And teach lavoltas high and swift corantos—
> Saying, our grace is only in our heels,
> And that we are most lofty runaways.

Early records reveal two assumptions about the *volta*'s origins, one Italian, the other Provençal. Certainly the earliest known references to it are in Italian, or speak of it as Italian: in 1556 Carlois, the secretary of Vielleville, says it has been brought to France from Italy and popularized by Catherine de Médicis and Henri III (Tani, 1954); Bouchet says it is Italian; Arbeau, however, says it is Provençal. In fact, it has been reported in Provence from the sixteenth century to the present day. Whatever its origins, for nearly a century the *volta* at court represented those vigorous and earthy pleasures not yet defeated by Puritanism's proprieties.

The name *volta* (Ger., *wältzen*, "to roll" or "to revolve") was given by the French in the nineteenth century to perhaps the most popular couple dance in the world, the nineteenth-century waltz. At the height of its popularity, the French were delighted to discover that they had an ancient dance of the same name and claimed the *volta* as the French ancestor of the waltz (Desrat, 1895). The claim seems highly unlikely, for the sixteenth-century *volta*, along with the elongated busk it required, had died out by the middle of the seventeenth century; furthermore, the waltz was never characterized by a high lift. Many turning couple dances, with and without lifts, however, had remained important in Scandinavian and German-speaking countries, even in "polite" society (among them the *Weller*, the *Deutscher*, the *Drehtanz*, and the *Ländler*). The *volta* and the waltz may have shared a common ancestor and been equally dizzying, intimate, and sensuous, but they were as different from one another in affect as exuberant lustiness is from ecstatic lyricism.

BIBLIOGRAPHY: SOURCES

Arbeau, Thoinot. *Orchesographie et traicte en forme de dialogve, par leqvel tovtes personnes pevvent facilement apprendre & practiquer l'honneste exercice des dances.* Langres, 1588, 1589. Facsimile reprint, Langres, 1988. Reprinted with expanded title as *Orcheso-graphie, metode, et teorie en forme de discovrs et tablatvre povr apprendre a dancer, battre le Tambour en toute sorte & diuersité de batteries, Iouët du fifre & arigot, tirer des armes & escrimer, auec autres honnestes exercices for conuenables à la Ieunesse.* Langres, 1596. Facsimile reprint, Geneva, 1972.

Arbeau, Thoinot. *Orchesography.* 1589. Translated into English by Mary Stewart Evans. New York, 1948. Reprint with corrections, a new introduction, and notes by Julia Sutton, and representative steps and dances in Labanotation by Mireille Backer. New York, 1967.

Corso, Rinaldo. *Dialogo del ballo.* Venice, 1559. Facsimile reprint, Bologna, 1969.

Manuscript of the Inns of Court. Located in Bodleian Library, Bodleian, Douce 280, ff.66av-66bv (202v-203v).

Negri, Cesare. *Le gratie d'amore.* Milan, 1602. Reissued as *Nuove invenzione di balli.* Milan, 1604. Translated into Spanish by Don Balthasar Carlos for Señor Condé, Duke of Sanlucar, 1630. Manuscript located in Madrid, Biblioteca Nacional, MS 14085. Facsimile reprint of 1602, New York and Bologna, 1969. Literal translation into English and musical transcription by Yvonne Kendall. D.M.A. diss., Stanford University, 1985.

BIBLIOGRAPHY: OTHER STUDIES

Bragaglia, Anton Giulio. *Danze popolari italiane.* Rome, 1950.

Desrat, G. *Dictionnaire de la danse.* Paris, 1895.

Donington, Robert. "Volta." In *The New Grove Dictionary of Music and Musicians.* London, 1980.

Heartz, Daniel. "Volte." In *Die Musik in Geschichte und Gegenwart.* 1st ed., vol. 14, 1968. Kassel, 1949–1979.

Palisca, Claude V. "The Beginnings of Baroque Music: Its Roots in Sixteenth-Century Theory and Polemics." Ph.D. diss., Harvard University, 1953.

Palisca, Claude V. *Humanism in Italian Renaissance Musical Thought.* New Haven, 1985.

Sachs, Curt. *World History of the Dance.* Translated by Bessie Schönberg. New York, 1937.

Tani, Gino. "Nizzarda" and "Volta." In *Enciclopedio dello spettacolo.* 9 vols. Rome, 1954–1968.

Tennevin, Nicolette, and Marie Texier. *Dances of France II: Provence and Alsace.* Vol. 2. Translated by Violet Alford. London, 1951.

Wilson, D. R. "Dancing in the Inns of Court." *Historical Dance* 2.5 (1986–1987): 3–16.

JULIA SUTTON
with Patricia Weeks Rader

VOLYNSKY, AKIM (Akim L'vovich Flekser; born 11 April 1865 in Zhitomir, Russia, died 6 July 1926 in Leningrad), Russian literary and ballet critic and art historian. Volynsky venerated the classical tradition and sought to elevate ballet to a status equal to that of the other arts. He wrote extensively on literature, aesthetics, and art, including a monumental study of Leonardo da Vinci for which he was proclaimed an honorary citizen of Milan.

Volynsky's sharply worded polemics in support of the classical tradition appeared in a number of leading periodicals, including *Birzhevye vedomosti*, *Zhizn' iskusstva*, and *Severnyi vestnik*. Among his many targets over the years was Boris Romanov, whom he forcefully upbraided, describing his works as "expressive bordering on grotesque" and "barbarically breaking the rules" of classical dance. He later criticized Michel Fokine as well as George Balanchine and his Molodoy Balet (Young Ballet) on similar grounds.

In 1921 Volynsky founded the School of Russian Ballet in Petrograd. Many teachers from the Maryinsky Theater Ballet School, including Nikolai Legat and Agrippina Vaganova, taught there. On the basis of his lectures at the school, Volynsky wrote *Kniga likovanii: Azbuka klassicheskogo tantsa* (The Book of Exultation: A Primer in the Classical Dance), published in 1926. This work attempts a formulation of his philosophy of ballet and aesthetics. It includes an examination of ballet in contrast to the other arts and in terms of metaphysics. Additionally the work outlines a basic, suggested ballet school program, including aspects of theory and aesthetics. Volynsky's other major book on dance was *Problemy russkogo baleta* (Problems of the Russian Ballet), published in 1923.

From 1920 to 1922 Volynsky engaged in a fierce debate on the pages of *Zhizn' iskusstva* concerning performances by the Maryinsky Theater and ballet training at its ballet school. He particularly assailed Leonid Leontev, whom he blamed for much of the decline of the Petrograd ballet. Volynsky advocated radical reforms in the school's teaching methodology and changes in the troupe's leadership in order to breathe new life into the company. His attack included an open letter to Anatoly Lunacharsky, the commissar for enlightenment.

Volynsky was likewise embroiled in administrative disputes following Fokine's departure from the Maryinsky Theater. Volynsky wrote a series of articles in 1922–1923 asserting that Nikolai Legat was the only ballet master capable of leading the troupe. He and Legat were united in their belief that Fokine and his experimental diversions had been leading ballet away from its true path of development.

Volynsky's importance rests on his articulate, unflagging defense of classical dance theory and forms. In the words of Fedor Lopukhov, Volynsky was the "first who attempted an explanation of the meaning of each movement in dance . . . and who revealed the wonderful essence of the choreographic art."

[*For similar discussion, see the entries on Koni, Levinson, Svetlov, and Zotov.*]

BIBLIOGRAPHY

Souritz, Elizabeth. *Soviet Choreographers in the 1920s.* Translated by Lynn Visson. Durham, N.C., 1990.
Leontev, L. V. "V zashchitu padaiushchego Gosudarstvennogo baleta." *Zhizn' iskusstva* (26–27 June 1920).
Volynsky, Akim. "Baletmeisterskii vopros (B. G. Romanov)." *Birzhevye vedomosti* (20 February 1915).
Volynsky, Akim. "Reforma Gosudarstvennogo baleta: Otkrytoe pis'mo narkomu prosveshcheniia A. V. Lunacharskomu." *Zhizn' iskusstva* (29–31 May 1920).
Volynsky, Akim. *Leonardo da Vinchi.* St. Petersburg, 1922.
Volynsky, Akim. "Gde byt' russkomu baletu?" *Zhizn' iskusstva* (11 December 1923).
Volynsky, Akim. "Khoreograficheskie arabeski." *Zhizn' iskusstva* (17 April 1923).
Volynsky, Akim. *Problemy russkogo baleta.* Petrograd, 1923.
Volynsky, Akim. *Kniga likovanii: Azbuka klassicheskogo tantsa.* Leningrad, 1926. Translated by Seymour Barofsky as "The Book of Exultation," *Dance Scope* (Spring 1971).

SUSAN COOK SUMMER

VOODOO. *See* Vudun.

VYROUBOVA, NINA (Nina Goursoff; born 4 June 1921 in Crimea), Russian-French dancer and teacher. Vyroubova was a naturally gifted dancer and an heir to the imperial Russian style. In 1924, with her grandmother and widowed mother, she immigrated to Paris, where they lived the difficult life of penniless émigrés. Vyroubova dreamed of dancing from the time she saw Anna Pavlova in *The Fairy Doll* and *The Dying Swan* in 1931 at the Théâtre des Champs-Elysées.

Her career took shape quickly. She began by studying with Olga Preobrajenska; later teachers included the Russian dancers Vera Trefilova and Lubov Egorova. Discovered by Elvira Roné, a pupil and longtime assistant of Preobrajenska, Vyroubova was performing at sixteen as Swanilda in *Coppélia* at the ballet festival in Caen; her partner was Aubrey Hitchins, formerly of Pavlova's company. In 1940 she danced with the Ballets Polonais and the Ballets Russes de Paris; in 1945 she was one of the young dancers who participated in the Dance Fridays at the Théâtre Sarah-Bernhardt (another was Roland Petit, Vyroubova's partner in *Giselle*). In the first production of Petit's *Les Forains* (1945), she created the role of the Sleeping Beauty, also dancing it at the Ballets des Champs-Élysées, which she joined in 1946. In December 1946 she danced the title role in *La Sylphide*, perhaps the peak of her career.

In fall 1949, Vyroubova made her debut as a *première danseuse étoile* at the Paris Opera in the *Divertissement d'Aurore*. Director Serge Lifar called on her to replace Yvette Chauviré; in 1950, Vyroubova triumphed in *Giselle* in Monte Carlo and performed in works of the repertory ranging from *Swan Lake* to George Balanchine's *Le Palais de Cristal*. Edwin Denby (1950) spoke of her as "the brightest hope in Europe for another great ballerina five years from now," adding:

[She has a] delicious figure, limpid style, sweet absorption. . . . She has the sweetest Russian-style virtues. A long foot, quick thigh, delicate bust, small head far from the shoulder. The step has edge, the arms are a classicist's dream, the carriage of the head has distinction, the face makes sense. She is unusually accurate and musical.

In 1956 Vyroubova left the Opera, appearing as a leading dancer with Le Grand Ballet du Marquis de Cuevas from 1957 to 1962. There she performed the great Romantic roles and established a partnership with Serge Golovine. She had roles created for her by Ana Ricarda (in the 1957 *La Chanson de l'Éternelle Tristesse*) and by Lifar (the 1957 *L'Amour et Son Destin*). She created an unforgettable portrayal of the Sleepwalker in Balanchine's *La Sonnambula* and performed the title role of *The Sleeping Beauty* with Rudolf Nureyev as her partner. From 1962 to 1966 she performed as a guest artist throughout the world in such widely dissimilar roles as the ethereal Taglioni in Anton Dolin's *Pas de Quatre* and the fatally seductive Bellastriga in Peter van Dyk's *Abraxas*.

Since 1986 Vyroubova has taught privately in Paris and at the Conservatory of Troyes. Reflecting her personality, her technique combines vivacity and legato, lightness and passion, ease of movement and the slow flowering of the adagio.

In 1957 Vyroubova was awarded the Prix Pavlova for her interpretation of Giselle and the Petipa Prize for her teaching. In 1980 she received the Italian prize Una Vita per la Danza. She is a Chevalier de l'Ordre National du Mérite.

BIBLIOGRAPHY

Denby, Edwin. *Dance Writings*. Edited by Robert Cornfield and William MacKay. New York, 1986.
Dorvane, Jeannine. "Hommage à Nina Vyroubova." *Saisons de la danse*, no. 128 (November 1980): 24–29.
Laurent, Jean. *Nina Vyroubova et ses visages*. Paris, 1958.
Perrin, Olivier. "The Art of Ballet: Interviews." *Opera, Ballet, Music-Hall*, no. 1 (1952): 33–52.
Swinson, Cyril, ed. *Dancers and Critics*. London, 1950.
Zürner, Inge. "Nina Vyroubova." *Ballet Today* (January–February 1964): 14–16.

FILMS. Dominique Delouche, *Le spectre de la danse* (1960) and *L'adage* (1965).

JEANNINE DORVANE
Translated from French

VYROUBOVA. As La Dame in Serge Lifar's *Dramma per Musica*, at the Paris Opera in 1950. (Photograph by Roger-Violett © Lipnitzki-Viollet; used by permission.)

Vyroubova became particularly associated with Lifar's work, dancing in *Suite en Blanc*, *Romeo and Juliet*, *Dramma per Musica*, and *La Mort du Cygne*, as well as in *Phèdre*, in which she succeeded Tamara Toumanova. Lifar also made roles for Vyroubova in *Blanche-Neige* (Snow White; 1951), *Fourberies* (1952), *The Firebird* (1954), and *Les Noces Fantastiques* (1955).

W

WALDEEN (Waldeen Falkenstein; born 1 February 1913 in Dallas, Texas), Mexican dancer, choreographer, ballet director, and teacher. Waldeen received classical ballet lessons from Theodore Koslov and Vera Fredowa. At thirteen she made her debut as a soloist with the Koslov Ballet Company and at the Los Angeles Opera. At fifteen she studied modern dance with Benjamin Zemach—an exponent of the school of Rudolf Laban and

WALDEEN. Guillermina Bravo and Ricardo Silva in Waldeen's *En la Boda* (1954), set to music by Blas Galindo, with costume designs by Carlos Mérida. (Photograph reprinted from *Artes de Mexico*, August 1955.)

Mary Wigman—the director of the Russian Habimah Theater. She also took intensive courses from Harald Kreuzberg at his school in Bern, Switzerland. She joined Michio Ito's dance company on a three-year tour of the United States, Canada, Japan, and Mexico, visiting the last in 1934. In 1939 Waldeen returned to Mexico, where the government commissioned her to form a modern dance company, the Ballet de Bellas Artes.

Waldeen was a pioneer of the Mexican modern dance movement of the 1940s and 1950s. During this period she directed a group of young dancers who produced works stressing nationalistic and Mexican approaches to history and art. In 1940, she presented the ballet *La Coronela* (The Lady Colonel) to Silvestre Revueltas's music; in 1942 she presented the mass ballet *Siembra* (Sowing Time), danced by five thousand people. Her choreography (including *Suite de Danzas, Cinco Danzas en Ritmo Búlgaro, Aleggretto,* and *Elena la Traicionera*) provides aesthetic models for many modern Mexican choreographers, incorporating and reflecting the Mexican spirit on the stage. Waldeen was the teacher of Mexico's first generation of modern dancers.

Strongly influenced by Mexican nationalistic painting and music, Waldeen successfully used the themes and images of Mexico's peoples and cultures. From 1940 to 1942, she took her Ballet de Bellas Artes, as well as her later group, the Waldeen Ensemble, on tours through the United States. In 1946 she went back to New York, where she joined the Choreographers Workshop and the New School for Social Research. In 1948 she returned to Mexico, where she successively directed the Modern Ballet Company, the Bellas Artes Ballet Company, and the Waldeen Ballet Company. In 1962 she traveled to Cuba, where she directed a modern dance school and produced several ballets.

Waldeen returned to Mexico in 1966 to resume her work in choreography and teaching. She also served in an advisory capacity to various government organizations, as well as at her own academy. She now lives in Cuernavaca, Mexico, where she directs a choreography workshop.

[*See also* Mexico, *article on* Theatrical Dance.]

BIBLIOGRAPHY

Dallal, Alberto. *La danza contra la muerte.* 3d ed. Mexico City, 1993.
Dallal, Alberto. *La danza en México.* 3 vols. 2d ed. Mexico City, 1995.

Razetti, Ricardo. *"La coronela": Ballet del Teatro de las Artes.* Mexico City, 1940.
Waldeen. *La danza: Imagen de creación continua.* Mexico City, 1982.

ALBERTO DALLAL

WALKAROUND TIME. Choreography: Merce Cunningham. Music: David Behrman; ". . . for nearly an hour . . . ." Scenery supervised by Jasper Johns; based on Marcel Duchamp's unfinished work *The Large Glass* (1913–1923). Costumes (uncredited): Jasper Johns. First performance: 10 March 1968, Upton Auditorium, State University College at Buffalo, New York, Merce Cunningham Dance Company. Dancers: Merce Cunningham, Carolyn Brown, Barbara Lloyd, Sandra Neels, Valda Setterfield, Meg Harper, Albert Reid, Gus Solomons, Jr., Jeff Slayton.

Walkaround Time is essentially an *hommage à Marcel Duchamp.* In having such a central focus, it differs from most Cunningham collaborations in which artist, composer, and choreographer create relatively independently, their efforts coming together only in performance. Duchamp's interest in pure chance ("a way of going against logical reality") made him a role model or hero figure for John Cage and Cunningham. Like Duchamp's work, Cunningham's choreography is enigmatic. It is laced with references to Duchamp the man, to his work, and specifically to his work *The Large Glass,* or *The Bride Stripped Bare by Her Bachelors, Even.* The dance is divided into two sections by an unchoreographed entr'acte which, according to Cunningham, is "straight out of *Relâche,*" a Dadaist ballet in which Duchamp performed. In the entr'acte the dancers may walk around on and off stage, practice steps, rest, talk with musicians and stage hands, or do anything they choose. This improvisatory section is in sharp contrast to parts 1 and 2, which are characterized by clearly articulated, precisely timed, exacting movement, ranging from basic unadorned classroom material (Duchamp's "readymades") to technical, highly demanding material (Duchamp's "mechanical apparatus"). The title of Behrman's music refers to an earlier Duchamp painting, *To Be Looked at with One Eye, Close to, for Almost an Hour.* The set, which *New York Times* critic Clive Barnes called "the finest decor American dance has ever known," consists of seven vinyl boxes of varying shapes and sizes onto which Jasper Johns transcribed images from *The Large Glass.* The audience looks through the dance to see the painting and through the painting to see the dance, each absorbing the other into its world.

> *"Walkaround Time* is, purely and simply, a masterwork. . . . The entire choreographic aesthetic . . . at once austere, whimsical, transparent and meticulous, is like that of *The Large Glass.*" (John Mueller, *Dance Magazine,* June 1977)

Walkaround Time also exists as a forty-eight minute, 16mm color film performed by the Merce Cunningham Dance Company, with cinematography by Charles Atlas, filmed at the Brooklyn Academy of Music in 1969 and the Théâtre de la Ville, Paris, in 1972.

BIBLIOGRAPHY
Cunningham, Merce. *Changes: Notes on Choreography.* Edited by Frances Starr. New York, 1968.
Cunningham, Merce, in conversation with Jacqueline Lesschaeve. *The Dancer and the Dance.* New York, 1985.
Mazo, Joseph H. *Prime Movers: The Makers of Modern Dance in America.* New York, 1977.
Tomkins, Calvin. *Duchamp.* New York, 1996.

CAROLYN BROWN

WALKOWITZ, ABRAHAM (born 1878 in Tyumen, Siberia, died 27 January 1965 in New York), creator of drawings and watercolors of Isadora Duncan. Walkowitz gained recognition in the dance world for his numerous drawings and watercolors of Isadora Duncan. In his lifetime he made thousands of sketches of the dancer ("more than I have hairs on my head"), which allegedly inspired her to remark, "Walkowitz, you have written my biography in lines without words."

Walkowitz was born in Tyumen, a small city in Siberia. After his father's death, the family immigrated to New York in the late 1880s and settled on the Lower East Side. The young artist enrolled in the National Academy of Design at the age of sixteen and subsequently saved enough money for European travel and two years of study at the Académie Julien in Paris.

Isadora Duncan and Walkowitz were introduced at the studio of the sculptor Auguste Rodin in 1906; the following day Walkowitz saw her perform in a private salon. He saw her dance again in Paris and during Duncan's American tours in 1908 and 1909. "She was an inspiration . . . a Muse," said Walkowitz in an interview in 1958. "She didn't dance according to rules. She created. Her body was music."

Walkowitz's studies of Duncan explore seemingly endless variations of her dance figure. The drawings were done from remembered impressions and sought to convey the visual equivalent of his personal experience. With expressive draftsmanship and fluid lines he summarized the essence of Duncan's form and movement.

Themes other than dance also figured in Walkowitz's art, particularly Manhattan street life and architecture. His early works dating from 1913 and 1914 reveal an interest in and understanding of the rhythm, tensions, and dynamics that were just then beginning to absorb progressive American artists. This same understanding underlies his interpretation of Duncan's art.

The artist's first one-man exhibition in New York in 1908 was followed by several shows between 1912 and

1917 at Alfred Stieglitz's famed "291" gallery. In 1913 he participated in the celebrated Armory Show, and in his lifetime he was accorded retrospectives by the Brooklyn Museum (1939) and the Jewish Museum (1949). Failing eyesight, which began in his fifties, prevented Walkowitz from pursuing his profession in later life. A prodigious body of early work, however, indissolubly links him to the dance and choreography of Isadora Duncan.

BIBLIOGRAPHY

Walkowitz, Abraham. *Isadora Duncan in Her Dances*. Girard, Kansas, 1945.
Werner, Alfred. "Abraham Walker Rediscovered." *American Artist* 43 (August 1979): 54–59.

NANCY VAN NORMAN BAER

WALL, DAVID (born 15 March 1946 in London), British dancer and teacher. A *premier danseur* with a noble manner and a flowing classical technique, Wall was completely trained at the Royal Ballet School, which he entered at the age of ten. Graduating into the Royal Ballet Touring Company in 1963, he informed his dancing with such authority and intelligence that he was promoted to soloist in 1965 and to principal—then the youngest in the history of the Royal Ballet—in 1966.

Wall's meteoric progress seemed inevitable. He won his first solo, in *Napoli*, within months of joining the company, and he followed it swiftly with sharply contrasted debuts as the Young Man in *The Two Pigeons* and as Her Cousin in *The Invitation*. Guided by the company teacher Erling Sunde and company director John Field, he danced the leading male roles in *Giselle, Swan Lake, La Fille Mal Gardée,* and *The Rake's Progress* in 1965, often partnering Doreen Wells. He moved on confidently to *The Dream* and *Coppélia* in 1966 and *The Sleeping Beauty* in 1967. By then he was the mainstay of the company and an experienced and gracious partner.

When the Touring Company disbanded in 1970, Wall transferred to the Royal Ballet at Covent Garden and continued to stretch himself technically and emotionally with debuts as Romeo in *Romeo and Juliet* and Solor in *La Bayadère*. A pure and natural classicist in *Symphonic Variations, Song of the Earth,* and *Agon,* he played the role of Petruchio in *The Taming of the Shrew* with robust delight. His compelling gifts as a dramatic actor, which he first tested as the Rake and developed further as Mercutio and the Prodigal Son, blazed into full maturity with his creation of Lescaut in *Manon* (1974) and the tortured Crown Prince Rudolf in *Mayerling* (1978).

Wall was the company's principal *danseur* through the 1970s. In 1978 he won the *Evening Standard* Award for "the most outstanding achievement in dance in 1977" and was awarded a CBE (Commander of the Order of the British Empire) in 1985. He retired from dancing in 1984 and joined the Royal Academy of Dancing as associate director the same year; he became director in 1986 and retained that position until 1991.

BIBLIOGRAPHY

Maynard, Olga. "David Wall: England Made Him." *Dance Magazine* (August 1974): 53–59.
Newman, Barbara. *Striking a Balance: Dancers Talk about Dancing.* New York, 1982.
Percival, John. "A Whole Dancer." *Dance and Dancers* (August 1984): 24–29.
Woodcock, Sarah C. *The Sadler's Wells Royal Ballet.* London, 1991.

BARBARA NEWMAN

WALLMANN, MARGARETE (also known as Margarita Wallmann; born 22 July 1904 in Vienna, died 2 May 1992 in Monte Carlo), Austrian dancer and choreographer. Wallmann attended the ballet school of the Berlin State Opera and studied with Evgenia Eduardova, Olga Preobrajenska, and Matilda Kshessinska and, starting in 1920, with Heinrich Kröller at the Munich State Opera Ballet school. In 1923 she began studying with Mary Wigman in Dresden; she took over the Wigman school in Berlin in 1929.

In 1930 in Munich, Wallmann and her Tänzer-Kollectiv ensemble performed with Ted Shawn the movement drama *Orpheus Dionysos* to music by Gluck. In the summer of 1931 Wallmann and her troupe were guest performers at the Salzburg Festival, where, as an exponent of contemporary expressionist dance, she staged the premiere of *The Last Judgment* to music by Handel. Thanks to this success, Wallmann was a regular guest at the Salzburg Festival until 1937, where she made her debut as an opera producer in 1933 with Gluck's *Orpheus and Eurydice*. From 1934 to 1938 she was also the leading house choreographer at the Vienna State Opera. Since she was Jewish, she left Vienna after the annexation of Austria by Nazi Germany in 1938.

Wallmann turned away from modern dance and arranged sumptuously staged spectacles to pleasant music with Austrian themes in *divertissement* form, such as *Austrian Farmer's Wedding,* to music by Franz Salmhofer; this had its premiere 6 October 1934 at the Vienna State Opera. In addition, she created dance scenes for Hollywood films, notably *Anna Karenina* (1935). From 1938 to 1948, at the Teatro Colón in Buenos Aires, she presented *Josephslegende* and *Don Juan* as well as ballets with South American themes. After 1949 she choreographed for Teatro alla Scala in Milan and again for the Salzburg Festival before returning to opera production. She was associated with the Metropolitan Opera in New York from 1964 to 1977 and presented numerous productions, with varying degrees of success, in Milan, Rome, Vienna, Paris, Chicago, Naples, Palermo, and elsewhere. Wherever she worked, Wallmann was recognized for her theatricality, her knowledge of stage effects, and her characteristic block use of groups of performers.

BIBLIOGRAPHY

Amort, Andrea. "Die Geschichte des Balletts der Wiener Staatsoper, 1918–1942." Ph.D. diss., University of Vienna, 1981.

Amort, Andrea. "Die Tänze oder Verfewden." *Ballett International/Tanz Aktuell* 8–9 (1995): 64.

Amort, Andrea. "Margarete Wallmann." *Pipers Enzyklopiëdie des Musiktheaters, Oper, Operette, Musical, Ballett.* Vol. 6. Zurich, 1996.

Basaldua, Emilio. "Hector Basaldua and the Colón Theater." *Journal of Decorative and Propaganda Arts* 18 (1992): 32–53.

Shawn, Ted. "Germany's Newest Genius," *Dance Magazine* (August 1930).

"Margarete Wallmann: Zum Tode der Choreographin und Regisseurin." *Tanzdrama*, no. 19 (1992): 8–11.

Wallmann, Margarethe. *Les balcons du ciel.* Paris, 1976.

ANDREA AMORT
Translated from German

WALTER, ERICH (born 30 December 1927 in Fürth, near Nuremberg, died 23 November 1983 in Herdacke), German ballet dancer, choreographer, and company director. Having been trained in ballet by Olympia Alperova in Nuremberg, Erich Walter joined the opera ballet there in 1946. He was with the Göttingen Opera Ballet from 1950 to 1951 and the Wiesbaden Opera Ballet from 1951 to 1953. He was ballet master and choreographer in Wuppertal from 1953 to 1964 and then ballet director and chief choreographer of the Deutsche Oper am Rhine (German Opera on the Rhine), Düsseldorf-Duisburg, from 1964 onward, with numerous guest engagements in Germany (West Berlin, Munich) and abroad (Vienna State Opera, Teatro alla Scala, Zurich Opera). The first classically trained German choreographer to emerge after World War II, Walter became known for his musically am-

WALTER. A scene from Georg Reinhart's production of Hans Werner Henze's *Boulevard Solitude*, first mounted at the Hanover Opera in 1952. Uniting ballet and lyric drama, realism and surrealism, nineteenth-century conventions and modern cinematic illusion, the seven scenes of this evening-length work derived meaning as much from Walter's choreography as from Henze's music, Grete Weil's libretto, or Reinhart's production values. (Photograph by Saurin-Sorani; reprinted from Horst Koegler, *Ballett International*, Berlin, 1960, fig. 142.)

bitious, perfectly integrated ballet productions, which were a product of his close collaboration with the designer Henrich Wendel.

In the course of Walter's long, consistent, and distinguished career there were certain mainstays: the classics (*Giselle, Swan Lake,* and *The Sleeping Beauty,* on all of which he collaborated with Ruzena Mazalová from Prague, an authority on traditional choreography); the Prokofiev full-length ballets *(Romeo and Juliet, Cinderella,* and *The Stone Flower);* and full-length productions based upon musical selections from an individual composer (Monteverdi's *Orfeo,* in a fully choreographed version; *Fantasies,* dealing with episodes from the life of Tchaikovsky; and *Kalevala,* with music by Sibelius). These were, however, far outnumbered by his one-act ballets, choreographed to concert music ranging from Albinoni and Vivaldi to contemporary composers such as Wolfgang Fortner, Hans Werner Henze, and Aribert Reimann. Walter's special sympathies were reserved for Berlioz, Debussy, Janáček, Stravinsky, and Bartók. Among his best ballets must be counted "Dance around the Golden Calf" (1968) in the Düsseldorf production of Schoenberg's opera *Moses und Aron* and his version of Stravinsky's *Le Sacre du Printemps* (1970).

Walter was born in the same year as Maurice Béjart, John Cranko, and Yuri Grigorovich. His ballets may lack the strongly individual flavor of those of his eminent contemporaries, but his choreographies are imprinted with his impeccable musical taste and demands, in which he was obviously schooled by George Balanchine. He was a lyricist rather than a dramatist and always favored a beautiful line and decorous group arrangement rather than striving for originality through distorted movements. At the peak of his career Walter was Germany's most classically minded choreographer.

BIBLIOGRAPHY
Barfuss, Grischa, et al. *Ein Ballett in Deutschland.* Düsseldorf, 1971.
Koegler, Horst. "Ballettgeschichte an der Rheinoper." In *Die Deutsche Oper am Rhein 1964–1980,* pp. 10–11. Düsseldorf, 1986.
Kügler, Ilka, et al. *Poet des Tanzes: Der Choreograph Erich Walter.* Düsseldorf, 1993.

HORST KOEGLER

WALTZ. The word *waltz* is derived from German *wälzen,* meaning "to turn," "to revolve," or "to wander." This European couple dance in triple measure reached its zenith in the nineteenth century, in the capitals of Europe and the Americas. It captivated all strata of society with its heady, romantic rotations, a contrast to the precise protocol of the earlier minuet and the confining geometry of the cotillon and the contradance. Initially, however, genteel society was rather shocked by the intimacy implied by the waltz's embracing position.

Much has been preserved of the nineteenth-century waltz, but its origins are unclear. The waltz cannot be attributed to the inspiration of a specific dancing master or associated with any notable event. Dance historians have traced general similarities to the *volta,* a sixteenth-century court dance done by couples turning and striding to triple measure. The *Weller,* a German peasant turning dance, was mentioned in 1525 by the Nüremberg Meistersinger Has. A dance in which a couple turned together, face to face with hands placed on each other's shoulder or waist is depicted in engravings of the late Renaissance; it is identified as Alpine peasant dancing.

In regard to the music, a seventeenth-century lute manuscript preserved in an Austrian monastery at Kremsmuenster contains melodies that closely resemble the musical form later identified as *Walzer;* they are entitled "Laenderli" and "Steyerische," words associated with Austrian peasant dances in which couples pursue and capture each other, entwine arms in a series of courtship postures, and finally revolve together in unison.

Joseph Schmelzer (1623–1680), *Kapellmeister* to the court of Vienna from 1665, composed music for a "Ballet d'Amoretti e Trattore" performed in the opera *Le Disgrazie d'Amore,* in the form of a *Ländler.* In 1679 Schmelzer's music for the opera *Baldrucca,* performed at the Viennese court of Leopold I, included music to which Schwabian peasants danced in triple time to an aria with clear waltz characteristics.

An obstacle confronting dance historians researching the early waltz is the various applications of words meaning "German" (such as *Allemande* and *Deutscher*) in seventeenth- and eighteenth-century dance description. *Allemande,* for example, originally denoted a processional court dance of the late Renaissance, bearing little resemblance to the waltz. In mid-eighteenth-century France the same word was applied to a different court dance in which partners turned one another with interlaced arms, with steps possibly derived from the *Ländler.* In Austria, *Ländler* were Alpine peasant dances from the Landl district, while *Deutscher* encompassed all Germanic dances. Finally, *walzen, drehen,* and *spinneren* were verbs of general usage describing various motions of turning not necessarily related to dancing.

Around 1750 numerous comedies staged in Vienna were interspersed with musical pieces called *walzer.* In 1760, "waltzende Taenze" were publicly cited there as licentious.

Although dance historians are reluctant to draw connections between minuet and waltz, it is true that Viennese composers of the eighteenth century included rustic *Ländler*-like trios as a contrast to the grand style of the minuet, both in their symphonic minuet arrangements and in music intended solely for dancing. A sonatina by Franz Joseph Haydn, written in 1776, included a "mouvement de valse"—perhaps the first waltz specifically scored for piano. In 1784 an "air pour valser" appeared in André-Ernest-Modeste Grétry's ballet *Colinette à la Coeur,* presented by the Opéra Comique of Paris. In 1786 the comic opera *Una Cosa Rara* by the Spanish composer Vicente Martín y Soler (1754–1806) had its first performance in Vienna; the sensation it created was due less to the music than to the simple peasant turning dance incorporated in it.

The music associated with turning dance of this period, variously labeled *Walzer, Ländler, Allemande,* or *Deutsche,* was usually in the form of two eight-measure phrases in triple measure, repeated as AA/BB. Each beat of the bar was accented more or less evenly, although there are early examples of typical waltz characteristics—anticipation of the first beat, elongation of the second beat, and rubato. Occasionally several *Walzer* were strung together, forming a rudimentary suite.

In 1787, Mozart's opera *Don Giovanni* presented a minuet, *contredanse,* and waltz ingeniously combined. Mozart also wrote numerous "Deutsche Tanze" and *Ländler* intended for social dancing. Beethoven composed twelve *Deutscher* for the Redoutensaal balls in 1795.

Johann Nepomuk Hummel (1778–1837), Mozart's best-known pupil, is credited with introducing dance music to the concert salon in 1808. Joining six somewhat programmatic waltzes with trios to a coda, he expanded the waltz to a form that a decade later was taken up by Carl-Maria von Weber in his *Invitation to the Dance.*

In 1800, a waltz was danced at the Paris Opera, in Étienne-Nicolas Méhul's ballet *La Dansomanie.* By 1804 "une valse, encore une valse" was the cry of young dancers in Paris. The court of Russia succumbed to its charms after the death of Catherine the Great in 1798, but the court of Berlin, though exposed to waltzing by 1794, never entirely accepted this innovation. Although the waltz was danced at Almack's Assembly Rooms by foreigners prior to 1812, London society resisted it until its appearance on the program of a ball given in July 1816 by the Prince Regent.

In the same year, Thomas Wilson, dancing master at the King's Theatre, London, published *A Description of the Correct Method of Waltzing,* giving instructions for three French waltzes and one German waltz, complete with illustrations and music, and a refutation of the evil influence ascribed to waltzing.

- In Wilson's Slow French Waltz, the man steps with the left foot from fourth position behind to the second position with a turn of the body clockwise; then he executes a slow pirouette on the right foot to fifth position behind the left; he continues turning on both feet (always on the toes) until the right foot comes around in front of the left. He then executes the three steps of the *pas de bourrée* (already known to dancers in the *menuet*), beginning with the right foot (R,L,R) on the counts 4, 5, 6. The woman performs first the *pas de*

bourrée (R,L,R) on counts 1, 2, 3, and then the steps first executed by her partner. In the first measure they dance half a circle, and in the second measure the other half, moving around the ballroom in a counterclockwise direction.

- In Wilson's second waltz, called the Sauteuse Waltz, the man springs into second position with the left foot, turning clockwise; then springs again into second position with the right foot, continuing the turn, and places his left foot in fifth position behind, still turning, (counts 1, 2, 3). He then executes the same *bourrée* as above, commencing with a spring. The woman dances the counterpart, beginning with the *bourrée*.

- In the Jetté or Quick Sauteuse Waltz, the music accelerates as the man leaps to second position with the left foot, turning clockwise. He rests the right foot behind the left ankle and hops on the left foot, still turning. He then leaps to second position with the right foot. The woman executes the reverse at the same time.

- In the German Waltz, the man steps with the left foot into second position and performs a coupé with each foot in sequence. He then steps forward through fourth position with the right foot forward, then fifth, then fourth again. The woman mirrors these steps. The woman begins by stepping forward with the right foot forward. Wilson provides engravings showing a variety of positions for holding partners in each of the waltzes.

Despite the apparent dissimilarity between waltz and minuet, it is interesting to note that Thomas Wilson used the word *bourée* (or *bourrée*) to describe the *enchaînement* of three steps used in the second measure of the waltz. This same basic *bourrée* sequence is used in the second measure of the minuet step as described by eighteenth-century dancing masters. Wilson points out that the waltz *bourrée* should be danced on the toes and does not include the "sinks" *(pliés)* required in the *bourrée* of the minuet.

The Slow French Waltz became known to dancing masters as the *"trois-temps* waltz." Wilson states that the three waltzes should be danced as a suite, with couples moving in regulated semicircles around the ballroom. To dancers restricted to the confining dimensions and exacting technique of earlier dances, the waltz represented a new-found spatial freedom. The new spirit of liberty also inspired radical shifts of fashion.

Joseph Lanner (1801–1843) and Johann Strauss the elder (1804–1849) were both members of a Viennese dance band. In 1821, Lanner established a small band of his own, to be joined later by Strauss. As their popularity grew, the band was enlarged and finally divided into two separate orchestras, with Strauss leading one and Lanner the other. Eventually rivalry separated the two partners, and their individual fame paralleled the exploding popularity of the waltz. Beginning with Weber and his *Invitation to the Dance* (1819), a series of major composers—

including Frédéric Chopin, Franz Schubert, and even Richard Wagner—wrote waltzes.

During the early nineteenth century, the original 3/8 signature time was changed to 3/4, and the typical Alberti bass gave way to a strong emphasis on the first beat, shortening the second and third beats. The melody was now expressed in the Romantic style, varied in rhythm and temperament to counteract the steady repetition of the triple beat.

The Viennese waltz was exported to all the capitals of Europe and the Americas. Johann Strauss the younger (1825–1899) conducted his first public concert at the age of nineteen, despite his father's disapproval, and took over the orchestra following his father's death five years later. His two brothers Eduard and Josef became composers of waltz music as well received as that of their father and elder brother. [*See* Strauss Family.]

The principle of couples turning together *à la valse* was soon applied to other dance steps in 2/4, 4/4, and 6/8,

WALTZ. In the early nineteenth century, the waltz was frequently performed with a variety of steps and arm positions. Pictured here are nine of these, recommended by English dancing master Thomas Wilson in his 1816 manual *A Description of the Correct Method of Waltzing*. (Private collection.)

rhythms. The ancient *chassé* step, for instance, when danced by couples turning became the *galop*, popular in ballrooms of the 1820s. The *chassé-sauté en tournant* became the basis of the polka. The *pas de basque* step danced by couples turning became the *redowa*. The mid-century schottische probably owes its inspiration to the Scottish strathspey step so similar to the *enchaînement* of *temps-levé, chassé, jeté,* and *assemblé,* which formed the basic step of the French quadrille.

The exciting, erratic rhythms and exotic harmonies of the dashing mazurka (brought to France by Polish emigrés serving in Napoleon's campaigns against Russia) rivaled the waltz briefly but proved too difficult for ballroom dancers to master. The "Cellarius Waltz," introduced in the 1850s, was an attempt to combine waltz and mazurka in a dance simple enough for all. The five-step waltz applied the turning principle to music in 5/4 time, an interesting if short-lived innovation. The polka-redowa and polka-mazurka were more successful, satisfying the mid-century craze for turning by combining simplified polka and mazurka steps to waltz tempo.

By the early 1840s, the old *trois-temps* waltz was giving way to the *deux-temps* waltz. This simplification of steps allowed dancers to turn to and fro, in and out, in all direc-

tions, relieving the endless, dizzying, somewhat monotonous rotations by half-circles which were often awkward in crowded ballrooms. The *deux-temps* waltz should not be confused with the two-step, a later dance. Waltzers often elongate the second beat of the measure to extend the length of the turn and shorten the third beat by quickening the close, a characteristic of the mazurka as well. The *deux-temps* waltz discarded the *bourrée* of Thomas Wilson's era in favor of a step and pivoting *chassé*. Both partners executed this maneuver in unison and in one measure.

By the 1870s, dancing masters were introducing variations of the waltz step, among which the Boston merits attention because of its direct relevance to the hesitation waltz, popular at the turn of the century. The Boston was a kind of limping *chassé;* the hesitation waltz called for a distinct pause on counts two and three, lending a certain languor to the endless turning motion.

Although superseded during the twentieth century by many newer dances, the waltz has continued to be taught in ballroom dancing schools and is still performed, especially by older couples, at formal occasions. It also survives in certain rural regions and among ethnic minorities who adopted it during its heyday. Several stylistic variants form part of the repertory of competitive ballroom dancers, including Viennese Waltz and American Waltz.

[*See also* Social Dance, *article on* Nineteenth-Century Social Dance.]

BIBLIOGRAPHY
Carner, Mosco. *The Waltz.* New York, 1948.
Cellarius, Henri. *The Drawing-Room Dances.* London, 1847.
Dodworth, Allen. *Dancing and Its Relations to Education and Social Life.* New York, 1885.
Nettl, Paul. *The Story of Dance Music.* New York, 1947.
Richardson, Philip J. S. *The Social Dances of the Nineteenth Century in England.* London, 1960.
Wechsberg, Joseph. *The Waltz Emperors: The Life and Times and Music of the Strauss Family.* London, 1973.
Wilson, Thomas. *A Description of the Correct Method of Waltzing.* London, 1816.

DESMOND F. STROBEL

WARING, JAMES (born 1 November 1922 in Alameda, California, died 2 December 1975 in New York), American dancer, choreographer, teacher, and designer. Waring's early dance training was in San Francisco, first with Raoul Pausé, who taught both ballet and plastique dance, and later with Welland Lathrop, the Christensen brothers, and Gertrude Shurr (for Graham technique). His first choreography was the 1946 *Luther Burbank in Santa Rosa*, to music by Gioacchino Rossini, at the Halprin-Lathrop Studio Theater in San Francisco.

In the late 1940s Waring moved to New York, where he studied at the School of American Ballet and, later, with Anatole Vilzak and Antony Tudor. His first full-scale ballet, *The Wanderers,* with music by Marga Richter, was presented in New York by the Choreographers' Workshop at the Ninety-second Street YM–YWHA, on 23 March 1952; the cast included Aileen Passloff and Marian Sarach. Like many of Waring's later ballets, this one was about performers: Passloff danced the role of a young woman who runs away from a traveling circus.

The following winter Waring and several other young choreographers, including Alec Rubin and David Vaughan, formed Dance Associates, a cooperative that presented works by themselves and others (among them Shirley Broughton and, later, Paul Taylor). For the first concert, at the Ninety-second Street Y in January 1953, Waring made *The Prisoners,* a ballet concerning "three young people introduced abruptly into an asylum," with music by Rudy Crosswell. Waring continued to present work in Dance Associates concerts, and when it ceased to operate in 1957, he gave concerts with his own company until 1969.

Many of his early dances had similarly fantastic or macabre subject matter, such as *Pastorale* (1953) to music by Hy Gubernick, and *Freaks* (1954) to music by MacRae Cook, but some were more purely romantic, such as the duet *Lamento,* (1953) suggested by a poem of Théophile Gautier to music of Croswell, or abstract, such as *Intrada* (1957) to music by Gubernick, and *Phrases* (1957) to music by Erik Satie. *Burlesca* (1953) to music by Claude Debussy was again about a company of players, but without narrative content.

Dances before the Wall (1958), Waring's first evening-long contemporary dance work, decisively established him as a leading figure in the New York avant-garde. He had always sought out young composers and painters. In 1956 he worked for the first time with the composer John Herbert McDowell, on *Adagietto: Flakes of Chance,* a solo for Toby Armour; in 1959 he first worked with the composer Richard Maxfield, on *Lunamble,* a solo for himself. Waring was to collaborate frequently with both composers. He also continued to work with existing music, especially that of Wolfgang Amadeus Mozart. In 1955, the painter Jasper Johns designed costumes for Waring's *Little Kootch Piece,* to music by Olivier Messiaen, several years before Johns first designed for Merce Cunningham. *Peripateia* (1960) with music by Maxfield had decor by George Brecht. *At the Hallelujah Gardens* (1963), to music by Maxfield, was a seventy-five-minute piece with "scenery, objects, and events" by Al Hansen and costumes and other props by Brecht, Red Grooms, Robert Indiana, Larry Poons, Robert Watts, and Robert Whitman. In the early 1960s, works such as these influenced the painters involved, and others, to create their own happenings and performance pieces.

Poet's Vaudeville (1963) to music by McDowell was another large-scale piece, with text by the poet Diane

DiPrima. Waring's company for these and other pieces at this period included David Gordon, Valda Setterfield, Yvonne Rainer, Deborah Hay, Arlene Rothlein, and Lucinda Childs. His classes in technique (an idiosyncratic yet rigorous approach to classic ballet) and in composition had a tremendous influence on those who were to be the founders of the Judson Dance Theater and subsequently the leaders of the postmodern movement in dance. (Waring gave concerts of his own at the Judson Church in New York City but was never formally part of the Judson group; in both 1978 and 1990 retrospectives of his work were presented at the Judson Church.)

In the last years of his life Waring worked with various companies, among them the Manhattan Festival Ballet, for which he made *Phantom of the Opera* (1966) to music by McDowell, *Northern Lights* (1967) to music by Arnold Schoenberg, and *Arena* (1967) to music of Igor Stravinsky. In 1969, *Purple Moment* was made to a combination of popular songs and selections from J. S. Bach and *Spookride* to music by Chopin and Ezra Sims, both for the New England Dance Theater; in 1970 they were revived, respectively, by the Netherlands Dance Theater and by the Pennsylvania Ballet. In 1971, for the Netherlands Dance Theater, Waring also made *Variations on a Landscape,* to music by Schoenberg. For New England Dinosaur, he choreographed *Novelty Sweets* (1971) to music by Scott Joplin, *A New Kind of Love* (1974) to popular music, and in 1975 a new version of *Arena*. Also in 1975 he made *Sinfonia Semplice,* to Mozart, for the Eglevsky Ballet Company.

Waring had the gift of being able to show dancers of relatively little technical accomplishment to the best advantage; for several years he taught at the arts summer school at Indian Hill (Stockbridge, Massachusetts), where he produced exquisite, witty dances for the teenage students. He was also able to perceive and utilize a professional dancer's unique qualities of physique and personality, especially in solos. As early as 1954, his *Three Pieces for Solo Clarinet* (to music of Stravinsky), for Paul Taylor, defined that dancer's individual style. Later Waring made equally personal solos for many other dancers, among them Vincent Warren, Aileen Passloff, Toby Armour, Richard Colton, Gretchen MacLane, Deborah Lee, Ze'eva Cohen, Rachel Browne, Raymond Johnson, and Elizabeth Walton.

In addition to being a dancer, choreographer, and teacher, Waring was also an accomplished collagist, and much of his choreography had the character of that medium, bringing together disparate elements. This and his use of popular music and movement led to the characterization of his work as "neo-Dada" and even as "camp," but whether in the Duncanism of *Mazurkas for Pavlova* (1967) to music by Chopin or in the pastiche of popular styles in such works as *Musical Moments* (1965) to music

WARING. In a straw hat and bow tie, Waring appeared with Deborah Lee in his *Musical Moments* (1965), a play on popular dance styles of the past. (Photograph from the Dance Collection, New York Public Library for the Performing Arts.)

by various composers or *At the Café Fleurette* (1968) to music by Victor Herbert, Waring's re-creations of past styles were free of condescension. He never had the lack of faith in the material that would justify the use of such epithets. Although it was only in his later works that he sometimes choreographed in a balletic idiom, classic ballet was always the technical base for his style; to this he added other elements, drawn from modern dance, musical comedy, vaudeville, social dance, natural movement—whatever suited his immediate purpose.

A designer and maker of costumes for his own and others' pieces, Waring was also a director and the author of plays, poems, criticism, and essays; on occasion, he was even a composer of music. Although he was a consummate craftsman and a thorough professional, his work never received the wider recognition it deserved. Yet it can safely be said that the life of anyone who knew him—as a choreographer, teacher, or friend—was deeply affected, and even changed, by the experience.

BIBLIOGRAPHY
McDonagh, Don. *The Rise and Fall and Rise of Modern Dance.* New York, 1971.

McDonagh, Don, ed. *The Complete Guide to Modern Dance.* New York, 1976.

Vaughan, David. "Remembering James Waring." *Ballet Review* 5.4 (1975–1976): 102–107.

Waring, James. "Five Essays on Dancing." *Ballet Review* 2.1 (1967): 65–77.

Waring, James. "My Work." *Ballet Review* 5.4 (1975–1976): 108–113.

DAVID VAUGHAN

WARREN, VINCENT (Vincent de Paul Warren; born 31 August 1938 in Jacksonville, Florida), Canadian-American dancer and teacher. Having begun dance training at age twelve with a local teacher in his hometown, Warren subsequently studied with a variety of internationally known teachers, including Peter Appel, Tatiana Grantzeva, Ludmilla Chiriaeff, Merce Cunningham, and Anatole Oboukhoff. Early in his career, he danced with

WARREN. John Butler's *Carmina Catulli,* staged for Les Grands Ballets Canadiens in 1968, provided Warren with one of his most effective roles. His heroic physique and expressive performing style made him well suited for Butler's dramatic choreography. (Photograph © 1968 by Jack Mitchell; used by permission.)

the Metropolitan Opera Ballet (1957–1959), the Santa Fe Opera, and the performing groups of contemporary choreographers James Waring and Aileen Passloff. In 1961, Warren joined Les Grands Ballets Canadiens in Montreal, where, except for a leave of absence in 1969–1971, he remained until his retirement from the stage in 1979.

Warren, who was noted for his fine looks, noble bearing, and dramatic gifts, performed roles in most of the wide-ranging repertory of Les Grands Ballets Canadiens, including male leads in such classical works as *Giselle, Swan Lake,* and *The Nutcracker* as well as roles in works by George Balanchine, John Butler, and other contemporary choreographers. Notably, Warren created many roles for the artistic directors and resident choreographers of the company: Ludmilla Chiriaeff, Fernand Nault, and Brian Macdonald, whose *Adieu Robert Schumann* (1978) was made for Warren's farewell performances. Warren appeared in televised performances of this and numerous other works and in the award-winning film *Pas de Deux* by Canadian animator Norman MacLaren.

During his leave of absence from Les Grands Ballets Canadiens, Warren danced with the Théâtre Français de la Danse in Paris (1969–1970) and with the Cologne Opera Ballet (1970–1971). As a guest artist, he also appeared with the Pennsylvania Ballet, the National Ballet of Guatemala, and the avant-garde Canadian company Groupe de la Place Royale.

A much-loved and respected figure in Canadian dance, Warren was awarded the Queen's Jubilee Medal in 1977. After he ceased performing, he served as chairman of the Dance in Canada Association in 1981–1982. He has since taught ballet and dance history at various institutions in Montreal, principally for the École Supérieure de Danse du Québec, where today he serves as curator of the dance library.

BIBLIOGRAPHY

Stoop, Norma McLain. "Spotlight on Vincent Warren." *Dance Magazine* (August 1973): 64–69.

Tembeck, Iro Valaskakis. *Dancing in Montreal: Seeds of a Choreographic History.* Studies in Dance History, vol. 5.2. Madison, Wis., 1994.

Warren, Vincent. "Archives of the Dance: La Bibliothèque de la Danse et l'École Supérieure de Danse du Québec, Montréal." *Dance Research* 13 (Winter 1995): 89–94.

Windreich, Leland. "Collector and Archivist Vincent Warren." *Dance International* 22.4 (1994–1995): 26.

Wyman, Max. *Dance Canada: An Illustrated History.* Vancouver, 1989.

MICHAEL CRABB

WARSAW BALLET. In 1818 Ludwik Osiński, director of the National Theater in Warsaw, founded a ballet company under the directorship of the French choreographer Louis Thierry. The company moved into Warsaw's new

Teatr Wielki (Great Theater) in 1833. Since then it has been the cradle and center of ballet in Poland. Officially named the Balet Teatru Wielkiego w Warzawie, it is known in English as the Warsaw Ballet or as the Wielki Theater Ballet.

During the Romantic period the company enjoyed special glory under the directorships of Maurice Pion (1826–1843), Filippo Taglioni (1843–1853), and Roman Turczynowicz (1853–1866). Although these choreographers closely followed the French style, they never neglected male dancing in favor of the cult of the ballerina. They also promoted character dancing and emphasized expression and action in their ballets. Most of their works were produced on a lavish scale, with a large, well-trained corps de ballet, sumptuous costumes and scenery, and ingenious stage machinery. The repertory included restagings of such famous Romantic ballets as *La Sylphide*, *Giselle*, *Esmeralda*, *Faust*, and *Le Corsaire*, as well as original works. [*See the entries on Pion and Turczynowicz.*]

A series of Italian ballet masters led the company beginning in 1869: Virgilio Calori (1869–1874), Pasquale Borri (1875–1878), José Mendes (1878–1888), Raffaele Grassi (1892–1902), and Enrico Cecchetti (1902–1905). The general decadence of western European ballet, compounded by the company's own long-standing conflict between the French and Italian traditions and its deepening financial difficulties, caused a gradual decline in its artistic standards despite the success of such works as *Jotta, Coppélia, Brahma*, and *Swan Lake*.

In the early twentieth century, the rising popularity of operetta, the mass exodus of dancers to the touring companies of Serge Diaghilev and Anna Pavlova, and the onset of World War I in 1914 dealt heavy blows to the company. Although it survived this severe crisis (from 1905 to 1918), the only high points of the period were its performances of Michel Fokine's *Eunice, Chopiniana*, and *Schéhérazade*.

From the early days of the company, the Russian rulers of Poland had stringently repressed ballets that expressed a sense of national identity. The few existing works of this nature—among them *Kraków Wedding, Pan Twardowski*, and *The Fire Feast*—were extremely popular, as were stage versions of Polish national dances executed within foreign ballets and in operas such as Stanisław Moniuszko's *Halka*. This situation changed after Poland regained its independence in 1918, and the company began to recover its brilliance under the leadership of Piotr Zajlich (1917–1934). Nationally inspired ballets, including a completely new version of *Pan Twardowski* and *The Highlanders*, now had priority in the repertory, which also included the classics and restaging of Diaghilev's ballets.

During World War II, the Wielki Theater was destroyed, and most of the company was dispersed. After 1945 Zaj-lich reassembled a small company, which worked in temporary quarters, gradually rebuilding its staff and repertory. Among the ballets produced at this time were *Romeo and Juliet* and *Le Sacre du Printemps*.

In 1965 the company returned to a restored Wielki Theater, having once more achieved a high artistic level. Its present repertory includes the classics (among them Frederick Ashton's production of *La Fille Mal Gardée*), ballets based on Polish themes (*Pan Twardowski, Kraków Wedding, Stanisław and Anna Oświęcim*, and *The Highlanders),* and contemporary works, including ballets by Serge Lifar, Maurice Béjart, Brigit Cullberg, John Neumeier, and Hans van Manen.

In 1985 the company was honored by the organization of the two-hundredth jubilee of the Polish ballet. Since then political and economic difficulties have limited its activities, and the Warsaw Ballet is fighting to survive.

[*See also* Poland, *article on* Theatrical Dance.]

BIBLIOGRAPHY

Chynowski, Paweł. "The Anniversary of Polish Ballet." *Ballet International* 8 (May 1985): 18–21.

Chynowski, Paweł, and Janina Pudełek. *Almanach baletu warszawskiego, 1785–1985 / Le ballet de Varsovie, 1785–1985*. Warsaw, 1987.

Drabecka, Maria. *Choreografia baletów warszawskich za Sasów*. Kraków, 1988.

Jasinski, Roman. "Some Recollections of *Swan Lake* in Warsaw." *Dance Chronicle* 14.1 (1991): 102–107.

Karsavina, Tamara. *Theatre Street*. Rev. and enl. ed. London, 1948.

Kinel, Lola. "Ludomir Rozycki and His *Pan Twardowski:* The First Polish Ballet Produced at the Warsaw Opera." *Musical Standard* 17 (1921): 209–210.

Mamontowicz-Łójek, Bożena. *Terpsychora i lekkie muzy*. Kraków, 1972.

Neuer, Adam, ed. *Polish Opera and Ballet of the Twentieth Century: Operas, Ballets, Pantomimes, Miscellaneous Works*. Translated by Jerzy Zawadzki. Kraków, 1986.

Pudełek, Janina. *Warszawski balet romantyczny, 1802–1866*. Warsaw, 1968.

Pudełek, Janina. *Warszawski balet w latach 1867–1915*. Warsaw, 1981.

Pudełek, Janina. *Z historii baletu*. Warsaw, 1981.

Pudełek, Janina. *Two Hundred Years of Polish Ballet, 1785–1985*. Warsaw, 1985.

Pudełek, Janina, and Jacek Luminski. "Poland: Anniversary Celebrations of Polish Ballet." *Ballett International* 9 (May 1986): 38–41.

Pudełek, Janina. "The Warsaw Ballet under the Directorships of Maurice Pion and Filippo Taglioni, 1832–1853." *Dance Chronicle* 11.2 (1988): 219–273.

Pudełek, Janina. "*Swan Lake* in Warsaw, 1900." *Dance Chronicle* 13 (Winter 1990–1991): 359–367.

Pudełek, Janina. "Crisis of Polish Dance." *Ballett International* 14 (July–August 1991): 56.

Pudełek, Janina. "Fokine in Warsaw, 1908–1914." *Dance Chronicle* 15.1 (1992): 59–71.

Pudełek, Janina, with Joanna Sibilska. "The Polish Dancers Visit St. Petersbourg, 1851: A Detective Story." *Dance Chronicle* 19.2 (1996): 171–189.

Rambert, Marie. *Quicksilver: The Autobiography of Marie Rambert*. London, 1972.

JANINA PUDEŁEK

WASHINGTON BALLET. An outstanding school has always been at the heart of the Washington Ballet. The current school was founded in 1944 by Mary Day and Lisa (Elizabeth) Gardiner, both District of Columbia natives. Day still directs both school and company.

Gardiner, a former member of the Anna Pavlova Company and a concert artist in her own right, opened her first school in 1922 and incorporated a small company called the Washington Ballet in 1938. Day had studied with Gardiner and was a member of the company. World War II put a halt to its performing until 1946. The title of Washington Ballet was resumed in 1956. A year later Gardiner became artistic adviser; she died in 1958.

In the meantime, Frederic Franklin had joined Day as co–artistic director, and for a brief time the company bore the aesthetic imprint of the Ballet Russe de Monte Carlo, with which Franklin had long been associated. By 1961, Franklin had left to form his own company, the National Ballet, also in Washington, D.C. Day meanwhile put the Washington Ballet on hold and turned her attention to developing a resident school of ballet and academic studies. It quickly earned an outstanding reputation, but a lack of funds forced its closure in 1977. The demise in 1974 of the National Ballet led Day to reestablish her Washington Ballet. Currently a twenty-four-member ensemble, the

WASHINGTON BALLET. Choo San Goh's *Momentum,* set to Sergei Prokofiev's Piano Concerto no. 1 in D-flat, entered the company's repertory in 1983. Costumes were designed by Carol Vollet Garner. (Photograph 1990 by Richard N. Greenhouse; used by permission of the Washington Ballet.)

Washington Ballet is known for its fine classical style. In addition to grooming dancers, it is consistent in its encouragement of emerging choreographers.

In 1976, while the company was deeply occupied in rebuilding its identity, Day engaged a young Sinhalese choreographer named Choo San Goh. The eleven years until his untimely death in 1987 were vital to the growth of the Washington Ballet. His presence was also beginning to be felt throughout the entire ballet world. Goh's choreographic style was both passionate and challenging. Although his ballets were in essence abstract, a strongly subjective current coursed through them. In addition, he enjoyed working with large groups of dancers and magnetizing them into vibrant responsiveness. Among his most substantial works are *Birds of Paradise, In the Glow of the Night,* and *Double Contrasts.*

Works from Goh's entire repertory are constantly being revived by the Washington Ballet. It also maintains a more modest selection of Balanchine ballets, such as *Allegro Brillante, Concerto Barocco, The Four Temperaments, Serenade,* and *Square Dance.* It is to guest choreographers, however, that the company more consistently turns. Its choices tend to be relatively conservative and have included Christian Holder, Judith Jamison, Alonso King, Monica Levy, Graham Lustig, Rick McCullough, and Martine van Hamel. The choreographic aspirations of company dancers like Lynn Cote and John Goding are also fostered.

In 1991, Mary Day began to groom her former student Kevin McKenzie to be the next artistic director of the

Washington Ballet, but American Ballet Theatre selected him for this position in 1992. Since then Day and general director Elvi Moore have worked in tandem to assure a serene future for the company.

[*See also the entry on Day.*]

BIBLIOGRAPHY
Elliot, Laura. "Dancing with Miss Day." *Washingtonian* (March 1988).
Fiorillo, Kathy. "The Woman Who Brought Ballet to Washington." *Washington Times* (3 October 1984).
Hering, Doris. "Washington Ballet's Mary Day." *Dance Magazine* (March 1992): 58–59.
Marshall, Leslie. "Mother Courage." *Washington Post* (20 November 1983).
Obituary: Choo San Goh. *New York Times* (30 November 1987).
Obituary: Lisa Gardiner. *Washington Star* (5 November 1958).

DORIS HERING

WATER STUDY. Choreography: Doris Humphrey. First performance: 28 October 1928, Civic Repertory Theater, New York City. Dancers: sixteen members of Doris Humphrey's Concert Group.

A product of Doris Humphrey's early explorations into the nonballetic possibilities of movement, *Water Study* appeared on the first program that the Humphrey-Weidman company performed independently. Although Humphrey shared Ruth St. Denis's and Isadora Duncan's interest in the flow of natural phenomena as a source for movement, her earliest experiments on nature themes were strikingly different from either the Art Nouveau–like aestheticism of St. Denis or the wholesome, bucolic youths suggested by Duncan.

In *Water Study* the movement of the individual dancer, the collective phrasing of the group, and the progression of the dance over space and time are all crafted to create water imagery on simultaneous levels of perception. The dancer's body unfolds and folds, in primal pulsations that grow from risings and sinkings to stretches, jumps, and collapsing falls. Each new movement travels through the members of the group on rhythmic upsurges that are produced and sustained by the dancers' breath—there is no musical or other accompaniment. The overall dance is a progression from slow, heavy stirrings on the floor to running leaps and falls, circling eddies, and subsidence to the floor again.

Although all the movement is "natural," *Water Study* takes great skill to perform. The dancers must have an acute sensitivity to one another and an ability to produce the dynamic cycle within themselves while also remaining responsive to the larger demands of the group.

BIBLIOGRAPHY
Davis, Martha, and Claire Schmais. "An Analysis of the Style and Composition of 'Water Study.'" *CORD Dance Research Journal* 1 (1968): 105–113.
Humphrey, Doris. *Doris Humphrey, an Artist First: An Autobiography.* Edited by Selma Jeanne Cohen. Middletown, Conn., 1977.
Kagan, Elizabeth. "Towards the Analysis of a Score: A Comparative Study of 'Three Epitaphs' by Paul Taylor and 'Water Study' by Doris Humphrey." *CORD Dance Research Annual* 9 (1978): 75–92.
Marion, Sheila. "Studying *Water Study.*" *Dance Research Journal* 24 (Spring 1992): 1–11.
Siegel, Marcia B. *The Shapes of Change: Images of American Dance.* New York, 1979.
Siegel, Marcia B. *Days on Earth: The Dance of Doris Humphrey.* New Haven, 1987.

MARCIA B. SIEGEL

WAYANG. [*This entry is limited to discussion of Balinese shadow-puppet theater and related forms of Balinese dance drama. For similar traditions in other parts of Indonesia, see* Indonesia, *article on* Javanese Dance Traditions. *For related discussion, see* Asian Dance Traditions, *article on* The Influence of Puppetry.]

In any discussion of Balinese dance and dance theater, attention must be given to the shadow-puppet theater, *wayang*, which is a major influence on most Balinese performance genres. *Wayang* is looked upon by performers as a source and guide with respect to thematic content, dramatic plot construction, vocal and movement characterization, poetic and classical language, and visual aspects such as costume and facial expression.

Balinese *wayang* is performed by a solo puppeteer, or *dalang*, who animates in movement and voice a large cast of characters, accompanied by a quartet of ten-keyed bronze metallophones *(gendér)*. The puppets *(ringgit)* are elaborately cut flat figures of buffalo- or cow-skin parchment, painted in bright colors and perforated in delicate patterns through which the light from a coconut-oil lamp

WAYANG. Children watch a daytime *wayang kulit* performance sometime in the 1920s or 1930s. The daytime *wayang*, given without lamp or screen, is said to be held for an invisible audience of the gods. (Photograph by Walter Spies / Beryl de Zoete; reprinted from Hitchcock and Norris, 1995, fig. 75.)

passes. They are silhouetted against an illuminated screen and articulated at the shoulders and elbows, punctuating their dialogue with stylized gesticulation. Some puppets have movable jaws, lips, or legs, often used for comic effect. They are manipulated by three rods fashioned from water-buffalo horn, wood, or bamboo.

Wayang performances generally last about three hours, beginning around eleven o'clock at night, though in the past performances could last until dawn. The stage is a raised bamboo platform erected for the event in the outer courtyard of a temple or palace, or on the roadside by the home of a family sponsoring the event. When the *dalang* arrives, he sits down crosslegged behind the coconut-oil lamp, which is hung just beside the white screen, and begins his preparations by reciting *mantra* prayers. Meanwhile, the musicians play introductory pieces called *gending pategak*.

WAYANG. Master puppeteer I Wayan Wija in a *wayang kulit* performance in New York City in 1992. This behind-the-scenes photograph shows how the puppeteer positions himself behind the traditional flaming lamp to keep his own shadow from falling on the screen. (Photograph © by Jack Vartoogian; used by permission.)

When the *dalang* is ready to begin the *wayang*, he signals the musicians by hitting the wooden *kropak* box in which the puppets are stored. The *kropak*, or *gedog*, lies within reach of his right foot and is hit with a wooden mallet held between the *dalang*'s two larger toes to signal sudden dramatic impulses and conduct the *gamelan* music. The opening music *(pemungkah)* is played as the Kayon puppet is waved, fluttered, twirled, and inched along the screen. The word *kayon* is derived from *kayu*, ("wood") and refers to the Tree of Life. Gunungan, another name for the same puppet, derives from *gunung* ("mountain") and refers to the mountain of the gods, Meru or Mahameru. As well as preceding the *wayang* story in a stylized dance, the Kayon serves throughout to suggest various forces of nature, unrest, or transition from a cosmic perspective.

After the Kayon is removed, the *dalang* takes his puppets one by one from the *kropak* box and assembles them side by side at either end of the screen, according to each character's allegiance in the ensuing story. Once all the Pandawa clan or Prince Rāma's followers (depending on whether the episode being enacted is from the *Mahābhārata* or *Rāmāyaṇa*) are assembled on the right, and the Kurawa clan or the demon-king Rawana and his followers) are on the left, they are all removed and the story begins.

The plays *(lampahan)* are most often taken from the Indian *Mahābhārata* epic, known in Bali as *Astadasa parwa* (The Eighteen Books). In fact, Old Javanese poems, based on episodes in the *Mahābhārata*, are the direct literary source. The most popular is *Bharata yuddha* (The Great War), dealing with the rival houses of Pandawa and Kurawa. Other *Mahābhārata*-derived stores are *Bimaswanga* and *Arjuna wiwaha*.

The other major source of *wayang* literature is the Indian *Rāmāyaṇa* epic, which requires a different set of puppets and an expanded gamelan ensemble, *wayang batel*, to portray the battles between Rawana and Rāma's allies, particularly Anoman and his army of monkeys. There are also indigenous *wayang* stories, such as *Cupak* and *Calonarang*, dealing with witchcraft. These stories utilize the *parwa* puppets, merely adding a few main characters.

A purely ritual context may require *wayang lemah*, generally performed in the afternoon using the same puppets but no screen. This brief and less dramatic genre is performed in connection with such ceremonies as toothfiling, cremation, consecration of a building, temple anniversaries, or the blessing of a child on one of its first three birthdays.

The skills of a *dalang* are extensive, and long training and experience are necessary before one is considered adept. A mystical understanding of *wayang* is crucial, and the teachings of the *Dharma pawayangan* text are generally studied in depth for this purpose. Before embarking on a performance career, a *dalang* (like other performers) goes through a *mawinten* ceremony, during which a Pedanda priest inscribes magic syllables on his tongue with the stem of a *cempaka* flower dipped in honey. The *taksu*, or psychic energy, of a *dalang* is looked for and valued by the Balinese audience.

Facility with Kawi (the old Javanese literary language) must include the ability to construct plots and subplots, *(carangan)* utilizing excerpts of poetry *(cecantungan)* to illuminate a mood or action. A *dalang* must be able to translate spontaneously back and forth between classical Kawi, High Balinese, and vernacular Balinese, since characters address each other in these varieties according to rank. The *dalang* should also be able to quote freely from Middle Javanese (Malat) poetry.

Fluency in the musical repertory enables the *dalang* to fit his singing *(tandak)* to the pentatonic tuning and melodic flow of the four *gendér;* his *tandak* phrasing has its own melodic contours which overlap the instrumental melody without joining it, pitch by pitch. A crucial aspect of the *dalang's* art is that of movement and vocal characterization *(masolah)*. In the physical and spiritual relationship initiated when the *dalang* picks up a puppet, he must "enter the soul" of the puppet and bring it to life, while the puppet in turn speaks through the *dalang* as if he were its spiritual medium. A *dalang* must have a grasp of the techniques of vocal production that will enable him to embody the particular characters at hand. Each puppet's distinct movement and gestures are coordinated with stylized voice, rhythm, and dramatic qualities.

The most important criterion of a *dalang's* skill at characterization is his relationship with the characters Tualen, Wredah, Sangut, and Delem. These four Panakawan, comic servants to the principal rival clans, are the most popular characters in the *wayang*. With their flexible jaws, these puppets have the role of translating other's Kawi language into vernacular Balinese for the audience and interpreting the story's philosophical and practical content. Although they can provide the crudest humor and silliest slapstick, the Panakawan are considered to be of divine origin, most often associated with Balinese ancestors; the other characters are all of Indian origin.

There are divergent opinions concerning the origins of *wayang*. A Central Javanese stone inscription issued by King Balitung and dated 907 CE mentions *mawayang*, the performing of *wayang*, although this does not necessarily refer to shadow-puppet theater. A Javanese charter issued by Mahārājā Sri Lokapala in 840 CE refers to *aringgit* performers. In the eleventh-century Old Javanese poem *Arjuna wiwaha*, *ringgit* is the term for leather shadow-puppets, as it is today. The origin of Indonesian *wayang* is often traced to India, where shadow theater is believed by

WAYANG. Rāma and Sītā are portrayed as extremely refined characters in *wayang wong* dramas. Both wear elaborate gilt headdresses, with winglike side pieces and bird decorations at back. (Photograph by Walter Spies / Beryl de Zoete; reprinted from Hitchcock and Norris, 1995, fig. 190.)

some to have existed at least as early as the first century BCE; others argue for independent invention, theorizing that ancient indigenous initiation or ancestral rites gave rise to Indonesian *wayang*. In any case, with the advent of Indian influence in the area, Hindu gods and legends were gradually superimposed on older Malay-Polynesian myths. Even if, as some scholars suggest, *wayang* arrived in Bali via East Java as late as the fifteenth century, it is now a distinctly Balinese genre, both ritually and dramatically.

Wayang shadow-puppet theater has influenced dance-drama characterization in general, and most profoundly in *wayang wong*, which owes its themes entirely to the *Rāmāyaṇa*. *Wayang*, literally meaning "shadow," here refers to the dramatic presentation of stories, while *wong* means "human," referring to the actors.

Wayang wong is performed in a small number of villages, the best-known groups being in Mas, Batuan, Tejakula, and Tunjuk. It is most commonly presented in connection with specific *odalan* temple festivals and during the Galungan and Kuningan holiday season, when the ancestors descend for a time to inhabit shrines. Particularly sacred are the numerous *wanara*, including the monkey army led by Anoman. *Wanara* are considered to be animals of divine origin; some are combinations of different creatures and are often linked with the sacred *barong*.

The monkey king Subali and his brother Sugriwa are strong character types, whereas Anoman (Hanumān) is of a more refined type. Other animals are lion, birds, deer, elephant, dog, pig, and snake. Jatayu, the bird hero, and the deer, which is actually the man Marica in disguise, are also important in the drama.

The principal male characters with noble, refined qualities include Rāma and his brother Laksmana, as well as Wibisana, brother of the demon-king Rawana. Refined female characters are Rāma's wife Sītā, her attendant Condong, Dewi Tara, wife of Sugriwa, and Çurpanakha, sister of Rawana. The strong *(keras)* male types are the *raksasa* king Rawana, his accomplice Marica, and Kumbakarna. Although masks for all *wayang wong* characters exist, in performance, masks are generally restricted to the animals, and the four Panakawan and are considered religious heirlooms. The music for *wayang wong* is performed by the *wayang batel* ensemble, the same collection of *gendér* and assorted percussion used for *wayang Rāmāyana.*

Parwa is a dance theater genre very similar to *wayang wong* but based on the *Mahābhārata* epic. In both genres, the actor-dancers use sung Kawi poetry for entrances, exits, and occasional proverbial quotations and stylized speech in dialogue. The poetry and text are of particular prominence, distinguishing these from other dance theater forms. In most versions of *wayang wong* and *parwa,* the dancers' movements are not as closely synchronized with the gamelan music as in other forms.

[*See also* Indonesia, *articles on Balinese dance traditions.*]

BIBLIOGRAPHY

Becker, A. L. "Text-Building, Epistemology, and Aesthetics in Javanese Shadow Theater." In *The Imagination of Reality: Essays in Southeast Asian Coherence Systems,* edited by Aram A. Yengoyan and A. L. Becker. Norwood, N.J., 1979.

Hitchcock, Michael, and Lucy Norris. *Bali, the Imaginary Museum: The Photographs of Walter Spies and Beryl de Zoete.* New York, 1995.

Hobart, Angela. *Dancing Shadows of Bali.* London, 1987.

Hooykaas, Christiaan. *Kama and Kala: Materials for the Study of Shadow Theatre in Bali.* Amsterdam, 1973.

Keeler, Ward. *Javanese Shadow Plays, Javanese Selves.* Princeton, 1987.

Keeler, Ward. "Release from Kala's grip: ritual uses of shadow plays in Java and Bali." *Indonesia* 54 (October 1992): 1–25.

McPhee, Colin. *Music in Bali.* New Haven, 1966.

Lysloff, René T. A. "A Wrinkle in Time: The Shadow Puppet Theater of Banyumas (West Central Java)." *Asian Theater Journal* 1 (Spring 1993): 49–80.

McPhee, Colin. "The Balinese Wayang Kulit and Its Music." In *Traditional Balinese Culture,* edited by Jane Belo. New York, 1970.

Pucci, Idanna. *Bhima Swarga: The Balinese Journey of the Soul.* Boston, 1992.

Robson, S. O., ed. and trans. *Wañbañ Wideya: A Javanese Pañji Romance.* The Hague, 1971.

Robson, S. O. "The Kawi Classics in Bali." *Bijdragen tot de Taal-, Land-en Volkenkunde* 128 (1972).

Sugriwa, I Gusti Bagus. *Ilmu Pedalangan/Pewayangan.* Denpasar, 1963.

Sumandhi, I Nyoman. "Gending Iringan Wayang Kulit Bali." In *Pakem wayang parwa Bali.* Denpasar, 1978.

Yayasan Pewayangan Daerah Bali. *Pakem wayang parwa Bali.* Denpasar, 1978.

Zoetmulder, P. J. *Kalangwan: A Survey of Old Javanese Literature.* The Hague, 1974.

Zurbuchen, Mary S. *The Language of Balinese Shadow Theater.* Princeton, 1987.

Zurbuchen, Mary S. "Internal Conversion in Balinese Poetry." In *Writing on the Tongue,* edited by A. L. Becker. Ann Arbor, Mich., 1989.

EDWARD HERBST

WAYBURN, NED (Edward Claudius Weyburn; born 30 March 1874 in Pittsburgh, Pennsylvania, died 2 September 1942 in New York City), American dance director of

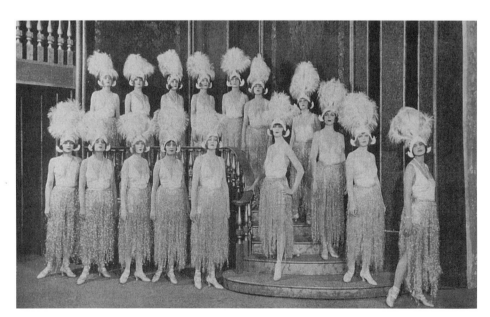

WAYBURN. Processionals were a Wayburn trademark. In various editions of the *Ziegfeld Follies* and *Midnight Frolics,* he displayed remarkable ingenuity in creating scenes that culminated in a parade of beautiful girls in beautiful costumes. These young lovelies appeared in "Bring on the Girls" in the *Ziegfeld Follies of 1922.* (Photograph reprinted from Wayburn, 1925, p. 186.)

musical shows and vaudeville acts. One of the most prolific dance directors of the twentieth century, Wayburn
staged more than three hundred musical shows and two
hundred vaudeville acts. His New York studios trained numerous performers by implementing a system he devised
for teaching his specialties: musical comedy dance, tap
and step dancing, acrobatic work, "modern Americanized
ballet," eccentric toe routines, and exhibition ballroom
displays.

As a young man in Chicago, Wayburn worked as a
draftsman for the 1893 World's Columbian Exhibition
and as an accompanist and assistant instructor at the
Hart Conway School of Acting. It was at this time that he
came into contact with the theories of François Delsarte
and the Per Henrik Ling gymnastic exercises, both of
which he incorporated into his dance training methods.

In 1896 Wayburn became a vaudeville pianist and soon
was known for his syncopation of classical music. Three
years later he choreographed his first chorus numbers for
By the Sad Sea Waves (opened 28 February 1899 at the
Herald Square). The cast included Kitty Hays, who, as
Gertrude Hoffman, worked with him on several productions. Between 1901 and 1913 Wayburn created vaudeville acts for Oscar and William Hammerstein as well as
for the theatrical syndicate of Klaw and Erlanger. He
staged spectacles in New York, Chicago, and London and
directed shows for Lew Fields and the Shubert Brothers.
Wayburn also founded the Headline Vaudeville Production Company.

Wayburn's celebrated association with Florenz Ziegfeld
and Joseph Urban began when Wayburn staged the
Ziegfeld Follies of 1916. He contributed to six editions of
the *Follies* (1916–1919, 1922, 1923), five seasons of the
Midnight Frolics (1915–1919), and three of Ziegfeld's book
musicals. The alluring step sequence known as the
"Ziegfeld walk" was a Wayburn invention.

Adept at codifying many types of information, Wayburn
established a hierarchical system for training chorus
members that made his prodigious output possible. He divided the chorus girls into five categories based on height
and at his studios had each group trained in a specific and
different technique. These classes, along with his book—
with tips on everything from diet and makeup to sample
contracts—supported his claim that he regarded "the
training of chorus girls strictly as a science." Performers
who completed some portion of their training with Wayburn included Adele and Fred Astaire, Earl Carroll, Marion Davies, the Dolly Sisters, Mary Eaton, Gilda Gray,
Gertrude Lawrence, Evelyn Law, Marilyn Miller, and Ann
Pennington.

After 1918 Wayburn experimented with the prolog, a live
performance designed to introduce a film. His efforts in
this field and the fact that most of his own choreography
involved geometrical patterns best seen from overhead
contributed to his influence on early movie musicals.

WAYBURN. Fanny Brice was one of the stars of the *Ziegfeld Follies
of 1916*, singing and clowning in two of her vaudeville numbers,
"The Hat" and "The Dying Swan," in which she satirized Anna
Pavlova's famous solo. Brice also appeared in "The Blushing Bal-
let," a scene staged by Wayburn that was a send-up of Vaslav Ni-
jinsky's most famous roles. Brice sang Gene Buck's comic song
"Nijinsky" and wore this sylphide-like costume. Nijinsky had
made his American debut with Diaghilev's Ballets Russes at the
Metropolitan Opera House only a few months before the 1916
Follies opened. (Photograph by White Studios, New York; from the Billy
Rose Theater Collection, New York Public Library for the Performing
Arts.)

[*For related discussion, see* United States of America, *article on* Musical Theater; *and* Vaudeville.]

BIBLIOGRAPHY
Cohen[-Stratyner], Barbara Naomi. "The Dance Direction of Ned
Wayburn: Selected Topics in Musical Staging, 1901–1923." Ph.D.
diss., New York University, 1980.
Wayburn, Ned. *The Art of Stage Dancing.* New York, 1925.
CAMILLE HARDY

WEAVER, JOHN (born July 1673 in Shrewsbury, England, died 24 September 1760 in Shrewsbury), English dancing master, dancer, and theoretician. Weaver was responsible for rethinking the theoretical and theatrical nature of dance in the early eighteenth century. His writings influenced the social acceptance of dance, the professional training of dancing masters, and the way in which dance would be written about in England for nearly two hundred years. His many publications are a valuable repository of information about dance in his era.

As a teacher of dance to young gentlemen and ladies throughout his life, Weaver was conversant with all aspects of his subject. During his many years as a theatrical dancer and dancing master, he introduced serious dramatic dance entertainments into the English theater, basing his experimental productions on the practice of ancient pantomimes and contemporary Italian harlequin dancers from French fairs. Those entertainments are thought to have influenced the development of the *ballet d'action* and to have introduced comic pantomime to England. Weaver wanted theatrical dance to share the lofty and edifying aims of tragic drama.

As a dancing teacher, Weaver was concerned with professional standards and the social status of dance and spent much of his career seeking to regulate, improve, and explain the practices of his colleagues. He always sought to justify the social and historical importance of dance.

Weaver was educated at Shrewsbury School, where he gained a command of ancient and modern languages and became interested in the liberal arts, science, and philosophy. Part of his childhood was also spent in Oxford, where his father was a university dancing master. In about 1696, after an apprenticeship, Weaver began his career as a dancing master in Shrewsbury. He retained his practice in the town for most of his life and in a variety of schools; even at the height of his theatrical career in London he returned to Shrewsbury for half of each year. His provincial location explains much about his need to publish and about his practical involvement with notation.

Weaver went to London in about 1700 as a theatrical dancing master; shortly thereafter he met Mister Isaac, the queen's dancing master, who became his patron. In 1706, Weaver notated and published a collection of six ball dances by Mister Isaac and in that same year, Mister Isaac also encouraged Weaver to translate Raoul-Auger Feuillet's notation manual *Chorégraphie* (Paris, 1700) under the title *Orchesography*.

An Essay towards an History of Dancing (1712) and *Anatomical and Mechanical Lectures upon Dancing* (1721), Weaver's two important theoretical publications, were both dedicated to Thomas Caverley, who led the metropolitan profession with Isaac. The former work was promoted by Richard Steele in *The Spectator*, an influential journal that also published other contributions by Weaver.

In 1717, Steele gave Weaver the opportunity to produce a serious entertainment in dancing at Drury Lane. *The Loves of Mars and Venus* was succeeded by *Orpheus and Eurydice* (1718) and *The Judgement of Paris* (1733). Weaver also produced numerous humorous entertainments, notably *The Shipwreck, or Perseus and Andromeda* (1717), *Harlequin Turned Judge* (1717), and *Perseus and Andromeda* (1728), for which Monsieur Roger provided the serious scenes.

Weaver's Work in the Theater. Beginning with the 1699/1700 season, Weaver appeared as a dancer in several London theaters, mostly in short comic interludes, character pieces, and special features such as the original Yorkshire version of the "Roger a Coverly." *The Tavern Bilkers* (1702–1703) was Weaver's first attempt at comic scene dancing and probably used characters from the *commedia dell'arte*.

More important and well documented were Weaver's experiments in serious narrative dance, all of which were performed at Drury Lane. *The Loves of Mars and Venus* (1717) was loosely based on Peter Motteux's play set to music of the same name. The part of Venus was danced by Hester Santlow, a dramatic dancer of true quality who had a principal role in Weaver's three major productions. Weaver himself danced the semicomic role of Vulcan, the cuckold. A Monsieur Dupré, a French dancer, was Mars, but it is not possible to confirm whether this was Louis Dupré.

The Loves of Mars and Venus served Steele's purpose by attracting audiences from Lincoln's Inn Fields, with which Drury Lane was in direct competition. However, Weaver was disappointed by his dancers' inability to respond fully to the unfamiliar dramatic demands of his work. The novelty of the piece lay in its lack of spoken or sung explanation: the story was conveyed by explicit manual gestures and physical expression. In addition, the plot and narrative were dramatically advanced by means of group dances, duets, and solos that established the atmosphere of each scene, as did the introductory symphonies composed for each scene by Henry Symonds.

In the scenes involving the two best dance actors, Weaver and Santlow, a complex interaction of personalities was attempted: motive was explained, the action was advanced, and the course of the plot affected. Venus performed a stylized dance, to which Vulcan reacted. His gestures became less formal and more spontaneous and instinctive as his exasperation at her insouciant disdain increased. The music for the action of each scene was supplied by Charles Fairbank, who was a dancing master as well as a composer.

Orpheus and Eurydice (1718) enjoyed comparatively little success, although Weaver prepared it meticulously.

Classical sources were established for every part of the action; the intention was to re-create an ancient fable so fully that no subtlety was lost. Weaver danced the role of Orpheus himself, incorporating some of the gestures from *The Loves of Mars and Venus*. Santlow's part, Eurydice, was relatively small, and the greater part of the entertainment depended on Weaver himself.

Weaver appeared as a comic and character dancer in the 1720s, but rather than attempt his own major works, he supported John Thurmond's rise to fame as an exponent of pantomime and collaborated as a dancer and coauthor with Monsieur Roger, also at Drury Lane. Under the influence of Thurmond, John Rich, and Lewis Theobald, the serious aims of dramatic dance were supplanted by grotesque comedy and spectacular scenic display. This genre of entertainment became known as pantomime and established itself as a permanent feature of English theatrical performance.

The Judgement of Paris (1733), adapted from William Congreve's masque of 1701, with a new score by Seedo, consisted of a succession of tableaulike scenes supported by gesture, dance, and song. Weaver demonstrated that he could adapt his theatrical principles and aims to changed circumstances. The cast was led by Philip Desnoyer as Paris and Santlow as Helen of Troy. In a variety of dramatic settings, the entertainment enjoyed sustained success.

It was Weaver's misfortune to work in a period of bitter theatrical rivalry. In addition, his theatrical career was intermittent, and his reformative ideas were hampered by the conservatism of his dancers and the vulgar expectations of London audiences. The main influence of his theatrical work was indirect: the vitality and verve of English comic pantomime as it developed under Rich, Thurmond, Theobald, and others created a dynamic dramatic impetus for theatrical dance to which even Jean-Georges Noverre and his European contemporaries, for all their high-minded disclaimers, may have been indebted.

Weaver's Publications. Weaver's theatrical works were designed to follow classical themes and methods and to promote the narrative element in dance, enabling it to convey emotions, character, and plot without spoken or sung explanation. The books published as accompaniments to Weaver's three major serious entertainments are valuable historical sources, as are those written by the exponents of comic pantomime who followed him.

The book of *The Loves of Mars and Venus* (1717) includes historical material from *An Essay towards an History of Dancing* (1712), illustrating and justifying the action and graphically describing the demonstrative gestures Weaver advocated to convey twenty-four of the "passions" and "affections" specified in the piece. The book of *Orpheus and Eurydice* (1718) includes an exhaustive historical discussion of the myth, with extensive quotations from classical sources. The printed version of *The*

Judgement of Paris (1733) is little more than an abridgment of Congreve's masque, from which Weaver's entertainment is adapted.

Weaver's nontheatrical publications are concerned with dance notation and the historical, musical, and anatomical understanding of his art. In all that he wrote, his concern was with regulating practice and with the social and artistic justification of dance.

Feuillet's *Chorégraphie* (see above) represented the most widely used system of dance notation in the eighteenth century: all dance steps in common use could be indicated by carefully contrived marks on a line, or tract, that suggested the floor pattern of the dance. The ground plan was explicitly related to the musical accompaniment, the tune of which was shown above the diagram. For its time it was an effective system, and Weaver's excellent translation (*Orchesography*, 1706) was in use for the greater part of the century. *A Small Treatise of Time and Cadence in Dancing* (1706) supersedes the brief musical section translated in *Orchesography:* Feuillet had improved his own system and published it in the preface to his *Recüeil de dances* (Paris, 1704), from which Weaver translated it. [*See* Feuillet Notation.]

A Collection of Ball-dances Perform'd at Court also appeared in 1706; Weaver's finely produced work of notation is an invaluable record of Isaac's compositions for the later Stuart court. (His notated version of Isaac's royal dance for 1707, "The Union," was published separately.)

Weaver was the champion of the provincial master; indeed, he was one himself. Notation enabled exemplary compositions to be widely studied and performed, and the possibility of teaching the most fashionable social dances gave the provincial dancing master an added claim on his pupils' patronage. The tendency to uniformity encouraged high standards of composition and performance; the very disciplines of notating and of deciphering notation made dancers and dancing masters more aware of style and precision of execution. The establishment of a body of specialized knowledge in which dancing masters required a practical working competence was part of Weaver's plan to retrain the profession. The same is true of Weaver's work in anatomy.

Weaver's lectures on anatomical and mechanical aspects of dance were read to leading members of the profession in an academy in Chancery Lane in about 1721. Weaver expected his colleagues to understand the human body in a fairly comprehensive way if they wished to train it properly and set unforced and unaffected movement on it. He therefore gave a purely anatomical description of the body and outlined the mechanical principles governing movement. From this he derived a set of reflections on the art of dance, "Rules and Institutions for Dancing," which appear at the end of the printed version of his lectures.

As early as 1706 Weaver was planning a history of dancing that would correct English social assumptions about the art that led most cultured people to dismiss it as nugatory and unworthy of serious thought. Extracts from the unfinished text of Weaver's work were freely incorporated in several issues of *The Spectator*, and Steele assiduously promoted Weaver's essay before and after its publication.

When it was finally published in 1712, *An Essay towards an History of Dancing* consisted of a conflation of sources of varying accuracy and authority that nevertheless gave the most complete account of dancing that had yet appeared in English. The essay contained a full account of Greek and Roman dance and pantomimes and sought to demonstrate, through a survey of its religious use and symbolism, that dance was one of the oldest and most fundamental human activities. Weaver also gave a full defense of dance as a social accomplishment for both gentlemen and ladies. Some of his arguments were current in courtesy literature, but they had not been fully marshaled before. Weaver found an unexpected ally in the philosopher John Locke, whose ideas on the educational benefits of dance he quoted at length, and in Francis Fuller, a physician whose fashionable promotion of exercise for purposes of health buttressed Weaver's thesis. Many other English and classical writers were cited to establish a wide and serious context for the acceptance of dance. Weaver also addressed himself to the religious and moralistic opponents of dance whose proscriptive activities were coextensive with the history of his art.

Weaver was able to draw on an impressive, if rather carefully qualified, philosophical countertradition, notably represented by Sir Thomas Elyot, that supported dance. The misgivings of ancient writers were presented as pertaining to the conditions of a different epoch. The concluding account of modern dancing is suffused with the wish to relate ancient patterns of narrative dance to contemporary practice: dance should convey meaning and address itself to matters of human moment and dignity; it should be able to encompass important themes from classical mythology and to rise to the level of the most serious art. (He regarded French figure dancing, as practiced in London by Claude Ballon and others, as contrary to his reformative purposes, calling it "meaningless motion.")

An Essay towards an History of Dancing is a remarkable document that uses material from a wide range of sources, many of them recondite and in Latin. It established a new framework within which dance could be assessed and was regarded as the standard English text on the history and defense of dancing until the late nineteenth century. (Most English works published up to that time contain either references to or extracts or borrowings from *An Essay*.)

Weaver's *History of the Mimes and Pantomimes* (1728) consists of an edited reprint of the last two chapters of *An Essay*, which deal with ancient mime and pantomime and modern dancing. It was designed to take advantage of the popularity of pantomimes, then at its height, and to make money for the author. At the same time, it recalls in a salutary way the dignified origins of mimic performance (with which many of the farcical contemporary pantomimes had little in common). The concluding "List of the modern entertainments that have been exhibited on the English stage; either in imitation of the Ancient pantomimes or after the manner of the modern Italians" is marred by several deliberate falsifications of date, designed to emphasize Weaver's priority and to represent the exponents of pantomime at Lincoln's Inn Fields as slavish imitators of the work of their rivals at Drury Lane. *The History of the Mimes and Pantomimes* has the hallmarks of a work published simply for gain; Weaver, twice married, had a large family and extravagant tastes.

Weaver was both a representative and a visionary figure; many of his ideas were not realized in his lifetime but were echoed by later writers with widely different technical and theatrical backgrounds. At the least, Weaver's publications contain a unique record of the practice of his contemporaries; at their best, his writings give a rare sense of the full potential of dance and of its capacity to serve people's physical, artistic, and spiritual natures in a socially valuable way. His apologetic methods were widely imitated for almost two hundred years. His theatrical reforms had less impact, although his part in introducing pantomime to the English stage was a permanent legacy to the theater. His anatomical lectures pointed the way to more systematic and professional teaching methods and to the further development of virtuosic performing skills.

BIBLIOGRAPHY
Chatwin, Amina, and Philip Richardson. "The Father of English Ballet: John Weaver." *Ballet Annual* 15 (1961): 60–65.
Cohen, Selma Jeanne. "Theory and Practice of Theatrical Dancing: II. John Weaver." In *Famed for Dance*, by Ifan Kyrle Fletcher et al. New York, 1960.
Dorris, George. "Music for the Ballets of John Weaver." *Dance Chronicle* 3.1 (1979): 46–60.
Foster, Susan Leigh. *Reading Dancing: Bodies and Subjects in Contemporary American Dance*. Berkeley, 1986.
Goff, Moira, and Jennifer Thorp. "Dance Notations Published in England, c.1700–1740." *Dance Research* 9 (Autumn 1991): 32–50.
Marsh, Carol. "French Court Dance in England, 1706–1740: A Study of the Sources." Ph.D. diss., City University of New York, 1985.
Ralph, Richard. *The Life and Works of John Weaver*. London, 1985.
Weaver, John. *An Essay towards an History of Dancing*. London, 1712.
Weaver, John. "The Loves of Mars and Venus" (1717). In *Dance as a Theatre Art*, edited by Selma Jeanne Cohen. New York, 1974.
Weaver, John. *The History of the Mimes and Pantomimes*. London, 1728.

RICHARD RALPH

WEDDING BOUQUET, A. Choreography: Frederick Ashton. Music: Lord Berners [Gerald Tyrwhitt]. Libretto: Lord Berners, with text by Gertrude Stein. Scenery and costumes: Lord Berners. First performance: 27 April 1937, Sadler's Wells Theatre, London, Vic-Wells Ballet. Principals: Ninette de Valois (Webster), June Brae (Josephine), Margot Fonteyn (Julia), Robert Helpmann (The Bridegroom), Mary Honer (The Bride).

The score of *A Wedding Bouquet* is a choral setting of Stein's text "They Must.Be Wedded.To Their Wife" as considerably edited and abridged by Berners, who changed words and sequences, adding or deleting repetitions to suit his musical purposes. He concocted a scenario with Ashton and Constant Lambert, not in the form of a logical narrative but rather as a series of incidents that take place at a provincial wedding in France around the turn of the twentieth century. *A Wedding Bouquet* is not a character ballet in the manner of Léonide Massine or Ninette de Valois but rather a classic ballet. The Bride and Bridegroom have a pas de deux that does not celebrate the wedding as much as prefigure the marriage—everything goes wrong; the Bride is turned upside down or faces the wrong way. There is also a pas de trois for two of the male guests and Julia's dog Pépé (named for a Mexican terrier owned by Miss Stein and her companion, Alice B. Toklas), who dons a tutu.

Among those present are the slightly demented Julia, who seems to have been seduced by the Bridegroom at some earlier date, and Josephine, who drinks too much champagne and has to be removed. The maid, Webster, whose character was evidently based on that of her original interpreter, runs the household with iron discipline.

That Ashton sometimes let the words point up a character or a situation became clear during World War II, when it was impossible to perform the ballet with a singing chorus (the ballet was no longer sharing the theater with the opera and general musical forces were reduced). Instead, Lambert recited the words while sitting at a table on one side of the stage and sipping champagne: the words were even more audible in his clear and caustic delivery. When the ballet was revived at the Royal Opera House in 1949, the chorus was briefly restored; then again, at Ashton's request, in 1983, for the centennial of Berners's birth. The ballet was in the repertory of the Royal Ballet touring section in the 1974/75 season and was revived by the Joffrey Ballet in 1978. Both productions used spoken, not sung narration. (The score has been recorded, with chorus, by the RTE Chamber Choir and Sonfonietta, conducted by Kenneth Alwyn, on a Marco Polo CD.)

BIBLIOGRAPHY
Barnes, Clive. "Ballet Perspectives No. 10: *A Wedding Bouquet.*" *Dance and Dancers* (April 1959): 20–21.
Stein, Gertrude. "They Must.Be Wedded.To Their Wife" (1931). In Stein's *Operas and Plays*. Barrytown, N.Y., 1987.

DAVID VAUGHAN

WEEME, MASCHA TER (born 17 October 1902 in Amsterdam, died 31 July 1995 in Amsterdam), Dutch dancer and ballet director. Ter Weeme received her first dance training in the schools of Mary Wigman and Émile Jaques-Dalcroze. She went regularly to Paris to study classical dance. After performing mostly in solo programs, she joined, as a soloist, the newly formed company of Yvonne Georgi, whose assistant she became. She stood out as a strong performer in character parts, which she gave a stylish, elegant flavor.

After a conflict with Georgi, ter Weeme left in 1944, started her own school, and appeared with another Georgi soloist, Tony Raedt, in dance recitals. In 1947 she and others founded the Ballet der Lage Landen; ter Weeme directed that company until it was amalgamated in 1959 with the Ballet of the Netherlands Opera to form the Amsterdam Ballet. Thus it formed a direct link between the artistic ideas of Yvonne Georgi and the new developments in Dutch dance after World War II.

Ter Weeme had no ambition to be a choreographer, a unique exception among ballet directors in the Netherlands. Her importance lies in the fact that she ascribed great value to, and had a remarkable feeling for, the emotional and theatrical side of dance. Her refined taste and eye for detail found expression in the conscientious care she gave to interpretation, decor, and costumes. This made her company quite different from others.

In 1961 ter Weeme was appointed co-director, with Sonia Gaskell, of the newly formed National Ballet, and the differences in their artistic ideas became so evident that the collaboration lasted only one season. Ter Weeme withdrew and devoted her time to teaching.

BIBLIOGRAPHY
Schaik, Eva van. *Op gespannen voet: Geschiedenis van de Nederlandse theaterdans vanaf 1900.* Haarlem, 1981.
Sinclair, Janet. *Ballet der Lage Landen.* Haarlem, 1956.
Sinclair, Janet. "A Dutch Pioneer." *The Dancing Times* (December 1982): 200–201.

INE RIETSTAP

WEIDMAN, CHARLES (Charles Edward Weidman; born 22 July 1901 in Lincoln, Nebraska, died 16 July 1975 in New York City), American dancer and choreographer. Weidman was reared and educated in Lincoln, Nebraska. He was considered a bright student and received several awards for his academic achievements. His interest in the history of architecture benefited him in the preparation, in 1919, of his first solo concert—nine ethnic dances choreographed in the style of Ruth St. Denis—whom Weidman had seen in concert in Lincoln in 1916; Weidman had been able to explain to his schoolmates the historical and architectural influences on St. Denis, those from which he drew for his own choreography.

On the basis of Weidman's solo performance, a local dance instructor invited him to study classical dance at her studio in exchange for his services as a teacher of ballroom dance. In 1920, Weidman had saved enough money for transportation to Los Angeles and tuition for summer study at Denishawn; he embarked upon a course that would change his life. Ted Shawn auditioned the tall, gawky boy with craggy eyebrows and a bony facial structure, and Weidman became a scholarship student. Before the summer session was over, Shawn sent Weidman to Tacoma, Washington, to replace a dancer who had broken his foot in the dance drama *Xochitl*.

From 1921 until 1928, Weidman's Denishawn years, his career took him to England, France, Asia, and many cities in the United States. He also served as a teacher at the Denishawn school in New York City. In 1928, Weidman and Doris Humphrey formed the Humphrey-Weidman Studio and Company. They had hoped to incorporate their ideas into Denishawn, but founders Ruth St. Denis and Ted Shawn were not receptive to their proposal.

Among Weidman's extensive contributions to American dance, his masculine approach to movement and his unique and individualistic abilities in pantomimic dance, enabled many men to enjoy dancing without following a lyrical and romantic path that some found distasteful. Some male audience members are also better able to identify with Weidman's style of dance than with much of ballet.

As a dancer, Weidman was hailed by the critic John Martin as "the most promising masculine dancer in America." He was in demand as a dance partner and it was on one such occasion that his concept of "kinetic pantomime" was brought to fruition. In a dance with Agnes

de Mille, Weidman, disturbed by the use of tangible objects, replaced them by translating ideas into movement, which gave animation to the feeling behind an idea.

Weidman choreographed and performed all types of dances—dramatic, humorous, lyrical—and was comfortable with each. *On My Mother's Side* (1940), a solo he based on members of his mother's family, embraced movement that left no doubt in the viewer's mind that Grandmother Hoffman had nimble fingers and was an artist at stitchery. In this witty commentary, Weidman introduces Great-Grandfather Walcott, the young pioneer who is quite proud; Great-Grandfather and Grandfather Hoffman; and Grandmother Hoffman, each of whom he portrays in turn. His Aunt Jessie appears next, dancing daintily to the strains of "Dear Little Buttercup," indicative of the fact that she appeared as Buttercup in one of her theatrical adventures. The final character of the dance is Weidman himself, who showed, through dance and pantomime, the young "Sonny" of Lincoln, Nebraska, who studied at Denishawn and learned Oriental dance and ballet but was not quite satisfied that this was his style of dance. He contemplates the predicament and decides that he wishes to move more freely; then, in a reminiscent fashion, he performs a few excerpts from the Humphrey-Weidman repertory while the members of the speaking chorus sum up the dance: "Then the modern creed it got him / And some think they / Might have shot him / As a leader / Of the bare / Foot and Soul."

Flickers (1942), an affectionate burlesque of silent motion pictures, was choreographed in a jerky style to approximate the movements of early moving pictures. The four scenes included in this dance were "Hearts Aflame," a takeoff on the mortgage plot of Mary Pickford movies; "Hearts Courageous," a cowboys-and-Indians western; "Flowers of the Desert," a spoof of Rudolph Valentino's sheik sagas; and "Wages of Sin," a satire on the Theda Bara–type of seductress.

Fables for Our Time (1947), a suite of four dances based on James Thurber's stories about impressionable birds, animals, and people, was the result of Weidman's being awarded a Guggenheim fellowship. The four fables Weidman included in the suite were "The Owl Who Was God," "The Shrike and Chipmunks," "The Unicorn in the Garden," and "The Courtship of Arthur and Al." *Fables* was considered one of Weidman's best efforts and received rave reviews from the critics.

Two of Weidman's later works, *Saints, Sinners, and Scriabin* and *Liebeslieder Waltzes*, both created in 1961, indicated that the master choreographer was still at work. The former work was a solo piece in which Weidman presented portrait studies of memorable characters from the past whom historians had classified as either saints or sinners. *Liebeslieder Waltzes*, dedicated to Humphrey's memory, did not contain a single traditional waltz step;

WEIDMAN. In this scene from *On My Mother's Side* (1940), a satirical suite about family members, Weidman portrayed his grandfather as a man who never relaxed—not even in death. (Photograph © 1980 by Barbara Morgan; used by permission of the Barbara Morgan Archives, Hastings-on-Hudson, New York.)

WEIDMAN. Weidman choreographed his first version of *Candide* in 1933 for a week-long Broadway run, produced by Michael Myerberg. He later restaged it for the Federal Dance Project's first season in 1936 and again in 1937 as a part of a double bill with Helen Tamiris's *How Long, Brethren?*. Pictured here is the South America scene from the 1937 production. (Photograph from the Dance Collection, New York Public Library for the Performing Arts.)

while reviewing Humphrey's beautiful fall-and-recovery technique, Weidman recalled how he had rebelled because he thought the falls were too feminine, so he decided to choreograph a suite of dances characterized by them.

When Humphrey retired as a dancer in 1945, Weidman formed the Charles Weidman Theatre Dance Company. He continued to teach and tour. For several years both his school and large company were successful, but by 1951 Weidman's alcoholism and poor management caused the company to disband. Weidman then undertook the teaching tours he continued until his death. In 1955 he joined Alcoholics Anonymous and successfully achieved sobriety, which he maintained for the remainder of his life.

In 1960 Weidman and a young avant-garde artist, Mikhail Santaro, joined forces and opened the Expression of Two Arts Theatre in New York City; Weidman's living quarters were in the rear of the second-floor loft. It was a small studio, but adequate for classes and small concerts. *Liebeslieder Waltzes* was the first major choreographic effort he made in his new quarters. Other works—*The Christmas Oratorio, The Marriage of Jacob, The Easter Oratorio, King David,* and *Visualizations from a Farm in New Jersey*—were also included in the repertory.

In 1969 a group of friends established the Charles Weidman Foundation and the Charles Weidman School of Modern Dance. In 1970 the Dance Division of the American Association of Health, Physical Education and Recreation presented Weidman with the Dance Heritage Award for his years of service to education.

[*See also entries on the principal figures mentioned herein.*]

BIBLIOGRAPHY

Becker, Svea, and Joenine Roberts. "A Reaffirmation of the Humphrey-Weidman Quality." *Dance Notation Journal* 1 (January 1983): 3–17.
"Chipmunk at Jacob's Pillow." *Time* (28 July 1947).
Code, Grant. "Humphrey-Weidman and Group." *Dance Observer* (January 1941): 8.
Hering, Doris. Review. *Dance Magazine* (April 1960): 26.
King, Eleanor. *Transformations: The Humphrey-Weidman Era.* Brooklyn, 1978.
Kriegsman, Sali Ann. *Modern Dance in America: The Bennington Years.* Boston, 1981.
Richards, Sylvia. "A Biography of Charles Weidman." Ph.D. diss., Texas Women's University, 1971.
Sherman, Jane. "Charles Weidman at Denishawn." *Ballet Review* 13 (Fall 1985): 73–82.
Smith, A. William. "*Flicker:* A Fifty-Year Old 'Flicker' of the Weidman Tradition." In *Dance Reconstructed,* edited by Barbara Palfy. New Brunswick, N.J., 1993.
Stodelle, Ernestine. "The First Duo-Drama." *Dance Observer* (December 1959): 154–155.

ARCHIVE.   Humphrey-Weidman Collection, Dance Collection, New York Public Library for the Performing Arts.

SYLVIA PELT RICHARDS

WEIDT, JEAN (Hans Weidt; born 7 October 1904 in Hamburg, died 29 August 1988 in Berlin), German dancer and choreographer. Born into the working class, choreographer Jean Weidt dedicated his career to furthering the proletarian cause through dance.

Weidt first performed in a folk dance group sponsored by a youth club. (He later wrote in *Der Rote Tänzer* [1968] that he learned "the laws of choreography" from Anna Helms and Julius Blasche, leading members of the folk dance revival movement in Germany.) As a youth he also studied with the modern dancer Sigurd Leeder (before Leeder joined Rudolf Laban and Kurt Jooss) and with the ballet mistress at the Hamburg Opera, Olga Brandt-Knaack. Throughout his choreographic career, Weidt drew upon and fused classical, folk, and modern dance, for he believed that the content of a dance determined its form, not the reverse.

In 1925, Weidt gave his first solo concert in Hamburg, including the first of "ten to twelve" versions of *The Worker*. The same year he formed a group, which included many unemployed workers, that performed in conventional theater spaces as well as at Communist Party rallies. Weidt's later groups in Berlin and Paris also performed in both types of venues. (Although he converted to the Communist cause during a workers' uprising in 1923, Weidt did not become an official party member until 1931.)

In 1929, Weidt moved to Berlin, where his group became known as The Red Dancers. The political content of his work intensified as the politics of the time became increasingly factionalized. In one solo, *Member of Parliament*, Weidt wore a mask resembling Paul Löbe, the Social Democrat leader of the Reichstag. A group work, *Potsdam*, employed masks to represent politicians on the right: Hitler, Franz von Papen, and Alfred Hugenberg. Weidt became involved with circles of other leftist artists, and in 1931 he was invited to choreograph Friedrich Wolf's play *Tai Yang Awakes*, under the direction of Erwin Piscator.

After Hitler came to power in January 1933, Weidt was arrested and jailed for several weeks. Upon his release, he received permission to travel to Sweden, but instead he journeyed to the Workers' Theater Olympiade in Moscow. From there, he made his way to Paris and formed a group to work with the French Communist Party. (At this time Weidt changed his given name from Hans to Jean.) Because of his political activities his visa was not extended, so he returned to Moscow, and then moved to Prague, where he formed another dance group. In 1937, he returned to Paris and revived his earlier French group as Les Ballets 38; among the works premiered by his company were Satie's *Parade* and Prokofiev's *Prodigal Son*.

World War II interrupted his choreographic career, for Weidt was first interned by the French and later fought in the British forces. After the war, his Paris company appeared at the 1947 International Choreographic Competition in Copenhagen and won first prize for *The Cell*, described by an American observer as "a work portraying the aspirations, nightmares and death of a common man" (Hastings, 1947).

In 1948, Weidt returned from exile to East Berlin. From 1948 to 1950 he directed the Dramatic Ballet at the Volksbühne in East Berlin. He then took positions at the opera houses in Schwerin and in Karl-Marx-Stadt. In 1958, he choreographed a work for three hundred amateur dancers in Rostock, which set the course for the remainder of his choreographic career dedicated to lay dance. From 1958 to 1966 he directed a lay dance ensemble associated with Berlin's Komische Oper, and from 1978 to 1980 he directed a workshop for young choreographers there. Along with Gret Palucca, another survivor from the 1920s Weimer era, Weidt served as an inspiration to choreographers who came of age in the Democratic Republic before the reunification of Germany in 1990.

BIBLIOGRAPHY
Hastings, Baird. "Concours à Copenhagen." *Dance Magazine* (September, 1947).
"Jean Weidt." *Tanzdrama* 5 (1988): 14–15.
Reinisch, Marion. *Auf der grossen Strasse: Jean Weidts Erinnerungen.* Berlin, 1984.
Weidt, Jean. *Der Rote Tänzer, ein Lebensbericht.* Berlin, 1968.
SUSAN A. MANNING

WELCH, GARTH (born 14 April 1936 in Brisbane), Australian dancer, choreographer, director, and teacher. Although Garth Welch made his professional debut as a performer in musical comedy and has returned to that genre on occasions in recent years, he was also Australia's first true *danseur noble*. His classical line and strong technique were enhanced by a well-proportioned body and an elegant manner of moving that marked him as a potential principal artist from the earliest days of his career as a dancer with the Borovansky Ballet.

Trained by Phyllis Danaher in Brisbane, Welch joined the Borovansky Ballet in 1952 and, apart from a period in 1958/59 when he danced in Britain with Western Theatre Ballet, he performed with Borovansky until the company folded in 1961. He was promoted to principal in 1959. While negotiations were proceeding for the establishment of the Australian Ballet, Welch danced in Europe with Le Grand Ballet du Marquis de Cuevas, returning to Australia in 1962 to join the newly formed national company as its principal male dancer.

Early in his career Welch established a luminous partnership with Marilyn Jones, to whom he was also married for a number of years. Their dancing partnership, in which they exhibited a strong emotional rapport, continued during the 1960s and 1970s until Welch retired from full-time dancing in 1973. They gave especially memorable performances in John Cranko's *The Lady and the Fool*, in which Jones played La Capricciosa and Welch played Moondog. Welch also excelled in dramatic roles such as Albrecht in *Giselle* and The Outsider in Robert Helpmann's Australian ballet *The Display*. His dramatic abilities were never more apparent, however, than in Graeme Murphy's *After Venice*, created on Sydney Dance Company in 1984. Welch, at forty-eight, played the role of the aging Aschenbach with an overwhelming strength and presence that received critical acclaim both around Australia and in the United States and Europe.

Welch has also had an important career as a choreographer, director, and teacher. He began to choreograph in earnest after spending time in 1966 and 1967 studying in the United States on a Harkness Fellowship. In New York he was influenced by Martha Graham; his first work made after his return to Australia, *Othello* (1968), was, as he said in an interview in 1990, "almost a homage to the technique I learnt from her." Othello was mounted by the Australian Ballet in 1970. Since then Welch has made many works for the Australian Ballet, Sydney Dance Company, West Australian Ballet, Ballet Victoria, Queensland Ballet, and Ballet Philippines.

His first taste of artistic directorship came in 1974 when he was associate artistic director of Ballet Victoria, a company founded as Ballet Guild by Laurel Martyn in 1946. He was also artistic director of the West Australian Ballet from 1980 through 1982. As a teacher he has worked at the Victorian College of the Arts and in a school that he and Marilyn Jones founded in Sydney in 1883. In the 1990s he has freelanced as a teacher and has taken particular interest in the careers of young dancers on the verge of a professional career.

BIBLIOGRAPHY

Laughlin, Patricia. "Dance Greats: Garth Welch." *Dance Australia* no. 84 (June–July 1996): p 28.
Pask, Edward H. *Ballet in Australia: The Second Act, 1940–1980.* Melbourne, 1982.

INTERVIEW.   Garth Welch by Michelle Potter (January 1990), National Library of Australia, Canberra (TRC 2545).

MICHELLE POTTER

WELLER, DAWN (born 16 December 1947 in Durban, Natal), South African ballet dancer and company director. First enrolled in dance classes at age two and a half, Weller received her early ballet training from Iris Manning and Arlene Spear in Durban. In 1964 she was one of the first dancers to join a company formed under the aegis of the Natal Performing Arts Council (NAPAC), one of the four provincial arts councils in South Africa. With NAPAC Ballet, Weller toured for a few months and then, in 1965, joined the larger, more competitive ballet company of the Performing Arts Council of the Transvaal (PACT). With PACT Ballet, Weller made rapid progress; she was soon dancing soloist roles and in 1968 was named a principal dancer.

During her long career with PACT Ballet, Weller's growth as an artist was steady and determined. Although her body was not ideally formed for ballet dancing, her drive to succeed, her innate musicality, and rigorous coaching by such outstanding teachers as Faith de Vil-

WELLER. As Lise in a 1982 performance of Frederick Ashton's *La Fille Mal Gardée*. Weller performed the role of Lise for many years, during which she had ample opportunity to display her marked flair for comic acting as well as her talent for expressive dancing. (Photograph © 1982 by Nan Melville; used by permission.)

liers, Denise Schultze, and Lorna Haupt helped Weller to develop into a strong and much admired performer. It was not her technical mastery, however, that made her dancing truly memorable, but her individual style and her ability to project a character. Accordingly, she shone in such roles as Titania in Frederick Ashton's *The Dream* and as the heroines of such classic ballets as *Giselle, Romeo and Juliet, Coppélia,* and *Cinderella.* In 1980 André Prokovsky gave her one of the most acclaimed roles of her career as a dancer-actress in his ballet *Anna Karenina,* for which she received both the Lilian Solomon Award and the Friends of the Ballet Award. In other works in the repertory, Weller's distinctive sense of humor was displayed in such lighthearted roles as Lise in *La Fille Mal Gardée,* Rosalinda in Ronald Hynd's ballet of the same name, and Milady in Prokovsky's production of *The Three Musketeers.*

Early in her career, Weller found it difficult to approach ballets without characters or narrative, although she later became comfortable with portraying mood and emotion in abstract ballets. Apart from Frank Staff, who worked with Weller in her first three years with PACT Ballet, the only choreographer to work creatively with her was Ashley Killar, who was ballet master with the company from 1979 to 1985. After a difficult beginning, due partly to Weller's reluctance to dance in abstract works, the success of their first ballet, *Migrations* (1980), paved the way for others, many of them non-narrative works. *The Duenna, Overture, Forgotten Summer, Sarabande, Schubert Adage,* and *Camille* were all created between 1980 and 1983.

In 1983, Weller was appointed artistic director of PACT Ballet, and in 1986 the board of directors conferred on her the title of *prima ballerina.* Not long thereafter, she was involved in a serious automobile accident, which led to her decision to retire from the stage in 1987 and to focus her energies on direction of the company. To mark her retirement, the South African government honored her with the Order for Meritorious Service, a national award for distinguished service in the public interest.

Under Weller's direction, PACT Ballet grew from strength to strength. She not only continued the policy of inviting guest artists from abroad to dance with the company, but she augmented the practice of inviting guest choreographers to mount their works for the company. As well as many revivals produced under her direction, she was responsible for enriching the repertory with the works of numerous choreographers of international renown, ranging from August Bournonville to George Balanchine, John Cranko, Choo San Goh, and David Bintley.

In 1994, Weller became director of the new PACT Ballet School, while retaining the position of artistic director of the company. Also in that year she was appointed a trustee of the national Arts and Culture Trust, and the following year, 1995, she was the center of attention at a gala performance at the State Theater in Pretoria in honor of her thirtieth year of service with PACT Ballet.

Weller's skill in coaching and producing dancers and the dramatic flair she brought to her own performances were demonstrated in 1996 in her most important production, a full-length version of *La Bayadère*, originally choreographed by Marius Petipa in Saint Petersburg in 1877. At the time of its premiere in Pretoria, Weller's production was only the third staging of the complete ballet by a company outside the republics of the former Soviet Union.

[*See also* PACT Ballet.]

BIBLIOGRAPHY

Allyn, Jane, and Nan Melville. *Dawn Weller: Portrait of a Ballerina.* Johannesburg, 1984. Includes a chronological listing of roles performed.
Borland, Eve. "CAPAB and PACT Ballet, South Africa." *Dance Gazette* (March 1985).
Cooper, Montgomery, and Jane Allyn. *Dance for Life: Ballet in South Africa.* Cape Town, 1980. Photographs by Montgomery Cooper; text by Jane Allyn.
Hurwitz, Jonathan. "Thirty Years with PACT Ballet." Program notes, PACT Ballet, 1995 season. Pretoria, 1995.

NAN MELVILLE

WELLS, DOREEN (Doreen Patricia Wells; born 25 June 1937 in Walthamstow, London), English ballerina. Trained at the Bush Davies Schools, Doreen Wells won the Adeline Genée gold medal of the Royal Academy of Dancing in 1954, and the following year she joined the Sadler's Wells Theatre Ballet. In 1956 she moved to the Royal Ballet at Covent Garden and quickly became a soloist. Exceptionally musical, petite, and beautifully proportioned, she had a sure and elegant technique and a range that extended from soubrette roles (in which she showed a delicious sense of comedy) to the most demanding of the nineteenth-century classical roles.

After her promotion to principal dancer in 1960, she led the Royal Ballet Touring Company for ten years, with David Wall as her regular partner. They were ideally matched. From 1970 to 1974 she danced with both sections of the Royal Ballet. She took the title roles in Rudolf Nureyev's 1963 staging of *Raymonda* (replacing Margot Fonteyn) and in Peter Wright's 1968 production of *Giselle.* She was a radiant Aurora, a sparkling Swanilda, a gentle Giselle, and a distinguished Odette-Odile. She also danced a wide selection of the Frederick Ashton repertory, appearing in the first casts of new productions of *Sylvia* (1963), *The Dream* (1963, Titania), and *Monotones* (1968, *Trois Gnossiennes*). She was particularly associated with the heroine of *The Two Pigeons,* a role that suited the sunny sweetness of her stage personality.

Ashton created two ballets with Wells in leading roles: *Sinfonietta* (1967), in which she danced the mysterious central Elegy, lifted and partnered through multiple configurations by four men, and *The Creatures of Prometheus* (1970). She also created roles in ballets by Kenneth MacMillan (*La Création du Monde,* 1964), Wright (*Summer Night,* 1964), Joe Layton (Mary Pickford in *The Grand Tour,* 1971), and Geoffrey Cauley. She was in the Royal Ballet Touring Company's first productions of MacMillan's *Concerto* (1967, second movement) and *La Boutique Fantasque* (1968, Can-Can Dancer), and she frequently danced the role of the Girl in MacMillan's *The Invitation.*

In 1972 she married the marquess of Londonderry, and in 1974 she retired from the Royal Ballet to become the mother of two sons. Since then she has danced at galas, as a guest with several companies (including Sadler's Wells Royal Ballet from 1980 to 1982, when she made her first appearance as the Betrayed Girl in *The Rake's Progress*), in pantomime, and in the 1984 London production of *On Your Toes,* in which she successfully followed Natalia Makarova as the Russian Ballerina.

BIBLIOGRAPHY

Buckley, Peter. "A Royal Pair: Doreen Wells and David Wall." *Dance Magazine* (March 1971): 58–61.
Clarke, Mary. "Doreen Wells." *The Dancing Times* (March 1961): 347.

Herf, Estelle. "Doreen Wells of the Royal Ballet." *Ballet Today* (May–June 1969): 18–21.
Woodcock, Sarah C. *The Sadler's Wells Royal Ballet.* London, 1991.

MARY CLARKE

WEST AFRICA. The region known as West Africa includes along the Atlantic coast the countries of Mauritania, Senegal, Gambia, Guinea-Bissau, Guinea, Sierra Leone, Liberia, Côte d'Ivoire (Ivory Coast), Ghana, Togo, Benin, Nigeria, and Cameroon; the island republic of Cape Verde off the western coast of Senegal; in the northwestern interior of the continent, Mali, Burkina Faso (formerly Upper Volta), Niger, and Chad. With more claims to diversity than threads of unity, the region encompasses environments ranging from desert and savanna to dense tropical rain forest. Sustenance is mostly derived from fishing, herding, and crop cultivation. There are effervescent urban centers and scattered quiet villages, thriving markets and desolate outposts. Christianity and Islam vie to dominate religious life. Political structures historically varied from small-scale, simply organized communities to widespread kingdoms and empires, and today include both autocracies and democracies. The peoples speak languages belonging to the Niger-Congo, Afro-Asiatic, and Nilo-Saharan families.

In West Africa, the French and British dominated in the colonial period (nineteenth to mid-twentieth century); Portugal controlled Guinea-Bissau and Cape Verde; and Germany held Togo and Cameroon. Liberia, created for and settled by freed American slaves, has been independent since 1847.

Despite this variety, West Africa has some common characteristics. The region's history is a chronicle of great indigenous kingdoms between the Sahara and the Gulf of Guinea, the longest sub-Saharan African history of contact with Europeans, the densest population (with more than 30 percent of the continent's population), and the greatest number of urban centers. Europeans arrived on the Guinea coast in the mid-fifteenth century. Trade soon flourished in gold, grain, pepper, ivory, and palm oil, and in slaves. After World War II, colonial control ended and new nations emerged, most of them retaining the European-imposed boundaries of the colonies, ignoring the territories of indigenous ethnic groups, which today overlap national borders.

Stereotypes of African dance were created in Europe and the Americas that even some westernized Africans came to accept. The dances that evoked the strongest European reaction, those therefore brought to Western theaters, were hip-swinging, pelvic-thrusting, breast-bouncing, or spear-throwing types. Through such dances, unmarried youths showed their energy, coordination, and creativity, which are believed to predict their ability to cope with life's exigencies. Nonetheless, lyrical, reserved, and stylized dances also exist here.

Although dance is common throughout West Africa, not everyone in any one society dances or moves in the same way. There are gender and class differences. Among the Wolof, highborn girls do not usually dance publicly, and when they do, their dancing is restrained. By contrast, the

WEST AFRICA. These Maxi women of Benin are Nensuxhe priestesses, devoted to the cult of the water spirits. They have left the town of Savalou and are on their way to a neighboring village, where they will join initiates into the cult in a dance to invoke the power of the spirits. (Photograph © 1992 by Judith Gleason; used by permission.)

dances of lower-class women feature sexually suggestive movements and postures. In the town of Bida in Nigeria, class prejudice precludes a man of high status from joining a dance with people of lower station.

Because African tradition is not static, but rather a changing phenomenon related to time, place, and situation, dances reported by early observers may have undergone many traditional, neotraditional, and theatrical transformations. A dance that first existed in the village may have a second form onstage in the city, a third on television, and yet a fourth on tour abroad. In contrast with dance in industrial societies, African dance tends to be enmeshed in nondance aspects of life; the sacred often blends into the secular and the aesthetic into the utilitarian. Dances with the same purpose may take different

WEST AFRICA. A masked dancer of the Guro people of central Côte d'Ivoire. His raffia skirt, wristbands, and anklebands are a brilliant red; the covering of his legs, arms, and head is banded in bright red and blue; his shawl bears black and red stripes on a white ground. He wears a spray of black feathers at the back of his head and a sculpted crown of a leopard attacking an antelope. (Photograph © 1993 by Jenny Lynn McNutt; used by permission.)

forms, and those with the same form may have different purposes.

In Western ethnographic literature, African dancing is often mentioned in conjunction with religious ritual, healing, music, storytelling, masking, dress, festivals, play, recreation, and war; the accounts of dance in these contexts vary in detail and sophistication. With growing understanding of both Africa and dance, however, reports have become less likely to stigmatize West African dance as pornography, conflict, or savagery; writers now tend to recognize the perspective of the indigenous dancer and audience. Some scholars seek to formulate a distinctly pan-African expression common to approximately a thousand societies, but such generalizations lack empirical support from ethnographic and film records.

Colonial administrators in West Africa were concerned about the propensity of music and dance to disturb the colonists' sleep, to distract Africans from going to work on time or even working for Europeans, or to ignite anti-imperialist sentiments (as in warrior dances)—so they imposed bans on dancing. The study of dance by Europeans, which might legitimize it as an art form, was not encouraged. In addition, Christian missionaries—who were aware of the deeply rooted integration of dancing with indigenous religion—tried to eliminate dancing, thereby to more easily spread Christianity.

Purposes of Dancing. Dance in West Africa conveys feelings, attitudes, concepts, and stories that emanate from everyday life, morality, myth, and legend. Dance also encapsulates essential aesthetic and social values and communicates systems of belief. Marcel Griaule (1965) recorded a Dogon elder's notions of dance as part of a coherent system of thought, a cosmological representation and vehicle for moving the world to order after the disorder of death. Team dance and masked choreography depict the Dogon conception of the world's progress. By extending movement beyond the human body, masks create the illusion or believed reality of the supernatural, inspiring reverence in performers and spectators alike. The Dogon "Storied House," one of some eight masks, rises more than ten feet (3 meters) above the dancer's head.

The dance of the Ubakala of Nigeria reflects the key tenets of their value system, mediates conflict, promotes social relations, and introduces change. The Mende, Bambara, Manika, and Nupe are among the groups that merge dance and economic activity. Dance may be intimately connected with work, interrupting or becoming part of daily tasks as an incentive to complete routine activities or initiate endeavors. Talented Nupe dancers may become professionals through the sponsorship of patrons.

Dance in West Africa plays an important educational role, too, providing a means whereby beliefs, mores, and cultural heritage are passed from adults to children. Initiation dances, performed when a boy or girl reaches puberty, usually celebrate the value of fertility, pass on lore about the initiate's new sexual powers, and describe the social responsibilities arising from the new status. For example, among the Wan, a hot and sweaty man dances with a cool and aloof female initiate on his shoulders. Opportunities for nearly mature Kuka adolescents to become acquainted and possibly marry occur in the *tadjo* dance.

In West Africa, the kind of dance that one performs expresses social rank. Prestige is usually associated with a restrained dance style. For example, the Bamana (Bambara) *segu-ka-bara* dance reflects the traditional aristocratic social structure based on gender, descent from nobility, and domestic slave status. Each Bamana social group has its own dance patterns. Low-status groups perform grotesque and obscene dances to entertain their masters; the upper-class Dahomean, however, does not dance to fast, compelling rhythms. Dances to send the deceased Igbo (Ibo) to the world of the ancestors are performed only for those believed to have earned such recognition. Dignity and age—beginning with the king, chiefs, priests and priestesses, and descending the social scale from the elderly to the young—determine the *igbin* dance sequence of the Yoruba.

In many cultures, dance promotes healing and preventive medicine. Expressing their grievances through dance is a way the Ubakala deal with stress that may lead to illness. Exercise, integral to dance, has been shown to help prevent such illnesses as heart disease, obesity, non-insulin-dependent diabetes, hypertension, and osteoporosis. In West Africa, the Tiv of Nigeria see dancing as a life force that counters disease and death, which are caused by sorcerers. The Dogon describe the rapid dance movement *gona* as "a relief, like vomiting." Possession dance is often related to physical or mental health as well as to supernatural sanction for resolving social conflict. Conversely, dance can spark conflict, as in the Ubakala second burial dances, which enact the deeds of the deceased and remind onlookers of unsettled scores.

Dance in West Africa is also linked to politics. Sponsorship of a costly dance production displays wealth and prestige and creates and validates leaders. Applying rules with sacred sanction while remaining above community factions, masquerade dancers are a medium of social control. Authorities sometimes use dance to redress grievances and control subordinates, who in turn use dance to constrain their leaders' exercise of power. For such groups as the Ubakala, Bamara, and Dahomeans, dance is a safe and sanctioned means of ridiculing the errant, conveying grievances, and proposing solutions.

As a coping mechanism for such life crises as marriage, birth, and death, dance helps individuals to contend with the foibles of humanity. For example, the *ikaki* ("tortoise") masquerade of the Kalabari presents human psychology

WEST AFRICA. Men of the Temne people in Sierra Leone instructing a group of boys in the coming-out dance that will be performed during the boys' initiation into adulthood. The boys wear woven caps and robes to protect them during the perilous, liminal state of transformation from child to adult; when the caps and robes are removed, the boys will emerge as men. (Photograph © 1975 by Frederick Lamp; used by permission.)

in animal guise; the playing of *ikaki* is a taming of human behavior.

Changes in Dance Forms. European contact has led to syncretistic dance forms—those that blend traditional and outside concepts. In Ubakala villages, where public physical contact between the sexes was considered improper, a group of young girls performed their parody of the Western man and woman embracing style of dance. In "Come Waltz with Me," instead of the Western male-female couple or Ubakala traditional circular dance pattern, the girls formed couples and parodied the Western-style waltz, clasping one another's heads, necks, shoulders, waists, hips, backs, and buttocks. Urban Nigerians and Ghanaians have merged European ballroom dance position (the embracing couple) with traditional African dance movements from many villages to create the "high-life" dance. Accompanied by indigenous and English-

WEST AFRICA. *(top)* Rose Marie Guirand, leading choreographer of the Côte d'Ivoire, posing in an outdoor setting. Guirand is the founder of the dance company called Les Guirivoires and its associated school, the École de Danse et d'Echange Culturelle, in Abidjan. *(bottom)* N'Deye-Gueye, a well-known dancer and teacher in Senegal, performing a spirited "highlife" dance. Highlife dancing is popular on social occasions throughout sub-Saharan Africa. (Top photograph © 1993 by Jenny Lynn McNutt; bottom photograph © 1996 by Jack Vartoogian; both used by permission.)

language songs, highlife dances are seen at parties and in nightclubs.

After Europeans introduced West Africans to university-level education, Western dance styles and theatrical dance forms soon appeared alongside traditional festival, ritual, and social events. Professional touring companies were developed, such as the Ghanaian concert parties (similar to *commedia dell'arte* or vaudeville) and Nigerian folk opera troupes, which present dramas featuring music, dance, and mime. Renowned practitioners of folk opera include the dramatist Duro Lapido, the actor-playwright Kola Ogunmola, and Hubert Ogunde, who is often regarded as the founder of Nigerian theater.

Theatrical Dance. Theatrical dance in West Africa may be either an aside, as in the Ghana Drama Studio's presentation of *Mother's Tears*, or an integral part of the production, as in Wole Soyinka's plays, which are more westernized than Nigerian folk opera. Soyinka's *The Lion and the Jewel* uses several arts, including dance; his *A Dance of the Forests* presents its climax through dance; and his *Death and the King's Horseman* also draws on Yoruba dance. A common pattern in West African theatrical dance companies, such as the Guinea National Ballet, is the punctuation of a simple story line with a series of traditional dances that are shortened or otherwise modified.

Dances performed in a Western-type school, government-sponsored competition, festival, or national-independence celebration are other transformations of traditional dance presented in new contexts. Apart from its manifest function as entertainment, westernized theater has also developed the covert function of encouraging nationalism.

[*See also* Aesthetics, *article on* African Aesthetics; Costume in African Traditions; Mask and Makeup, *article on* African Traditions; Music for Dance, *article on* African Music; *and* Sub-Saharan Africa. *For related discussion, see* Bamana Dance; Cameroon; Dogan Dance; Ghana; Hausa Dance; Tiv Dance; Ubakala Dance; *and* Yoruba Dance.]

BIBLIOGRAPHY

Binet, J. *Sociétés de danse chez les Fang du Gabon.* Travaux et Documents de l'O.R.S.T.O.M., no. 17. Paris, 1972.

Drewal, Henry John. "Efe/Gelede: The Educative Role of the Arts in Traditional Yoruba Culture." Ph.D. diss., Columbia University, 1973.

Fortes, Meyer. "Social and Psychological Aspects of Education in Taleland." *Africa* 11 (1938).

Gamble, David P. *The Wolof of Senegambia*. London, 1967.

Gebauer, Paul. "Dances of Cameroon." *African Arts* 4 (1971).

Griaule, Marcel. *Conversations with Ogotemmeli: An Introduction to Dogon Religious Ideas*. London, 1965.

Hanna, Judith Lynne. "African Dance as Education." *Impulse* (1965): 48–56.

Hanna, Judith Lynne. "Africa's New Traditional Dance." *Ethnomusicology* 9 (January 1965): 13–21.

Hanna, Judith Lynne. "The Highlife: A West African Urban Dance." In *Dance Research Monograph One*. New York, 1973.

Hanna, Judith Lynne. "The Anthropology of Dance Ritual: Nigeria's Ubakala Nkwa di Iche Iche." Ph.D. diss., Columbia University, 1976.

Hanna, Judith Lynne. "African Dance: Some Implications for Dance Therapy." *American Journal of Dance Therapy* 2 (1978): 3–15.

Hanna, Judith Lynne. *To Dance Is Human: A Theory of Nonverbal Communication* (1979). Chicago, 1987.

Hanna, Judith Lynne. "From Folk/Sacred to Popular Culture: Syncretism in Nigeria's Ubakala Dance-Plays." *Critical Arts* 3 (1983).

Hanna, Judith Lynne. "Movement in African Performance." In *Theatrical Movement: A Bibliographical Anthology*, edited by Bob Fleshman. Metuchen, N.J., 1986.

Hanna, Judith Lynne. *Dance and Stress: Resistance, Reduction, and Euphoria*. New York, 1988.

Harper, Peggy. *The Irigwe Dancers of Miango Village on the Jos Plateau*. Ibadan, 1968.

Harper, Peggy. *Tiv Women: The Icough Dance*. Ibadan, 1968.

Hinckley, Priscilla Baird. "The Dodo Masquerade of Burkina Faso." *African Arts* 19 (February 1986): 74–77, 91.

Horton, Robin. *The Gods as Guests*. Marina Lagos, 1960.

Horton, Robin. "The Kalabari Ekine Society." *Africa* 33 (1963).

Horton, Robin. "Igbo: An Ordeal for Aristocrats." *Nigeria Magazine* 94 (1967).

Imperato, Pascal James. "The Dance of the Tyi Wara." *African Arts* 4 (Autumn 1970).

Keil, Charles. *Tiv Song*. Chicago, 1979.

Little, Kenneth. *The Mende of Sierra Leone*. Rev. ed. London, 1967.

Meillassoux, Claude. *Urbanization of an African Community: Voluntary Associations in Bamako*. Seattle, 1968.

Nadel, S. F. *A Black Byzantium: The Kingdom of Nupe in Nigeria*. London, 1942.

Nicholls, Robert W. "Igede Funeral Masquerades." *African Arts* 17 (May 1984): 70–76, 92.

Nketia, J. H. Kwabena. "Possession Dances in African Societies." *Journal of the International Folk Music Council* 9 (1957).

Ottenberg, Simon. "Afikpo Masquerades." *African Arts* 6 (1973).

Ottenberg, Simon. "Illusion, Communication, and Psychology in West African Masquerades." *Ethos* 10 (Summer 1982).

Ravenhill, Phillip L. "The Interpretation of Symbolism in Wan Female Initiation." *Africa* 48 (1978).

Tiérou, Alphonse. *Dooplé: The Eternal Law of African Dance*. London, 1992.

Warner, Mary Jane. *Laban Notation Scores: An International Bibliography*. New York, 1984.

Wescott, Joan. "The Sculpture and Myths of Eshu-Elegba, the Yoruba Trickster: Definition and Interpretation in Yoruba Iconography." *Africa* 32 (1962).

JUDITH LYNNE HANNA

WESTERN THEATRE BALLET. *See* Scottish Ballet.

WHITE-HAIRED GIRL, THE. Choreography and libretto: Hu Rongrong, Fu Aidi, Cheng Daihui, and Lin Yangyang. Music: Yan Dinxian. Scenery: Du Shixiang and Zhu Shichang. First performance: May 1965, Shanghai School of Dancing. Principals: Cai Kuoying (Xier), Ling Guiming (Dachun), Ga Xiamei (White-Haired Girl).

Taken from a 1945 Chinese folk opera, this ballet in eight acts tells the tragic tale of Yang Bailao, an elderly and poor peasant, and his daughter Xier, in the village of Yanggezhuang in northern China during the war against Japan (1937–1945). Cruelly exploited by his despotic landlord Huang Shiren, Yang lives in abject servitude and shame. With anger smoldering in his heart, he rises against the landlord's ruthless oppression and exploitation, only to be beaten to death. Xier is seized by Huang as payment for Yang's debt and is put to work as a slave in his household. Suffering terribly, she escapes to a barren mountain, where, in the wintery conditions, her hair turns white. Only after the Eighth Red Army liberates the village does she return home to begin a new and happier life.

The White-Haired Girl was an important new attempt by Chinese choreographers in the field of national ballet and followed a fruitful experiment with the ballet *Red Detachment of Women* (1964). That work featured the integration of many colorful and locally flavorful folk dances with European classical dance techniques and used a socially forceful theme—the old society turned men into ghosts, but the new society turned ghosts into men.

The White-Haired Girl was first presented in 1964 in Shanghai by the Shanghai School of Dancing. It was filmed there in color in 1969 by the Shanghai Film Studio and released for general distribution on the Thirteenth Anniversary of Mao's Talks on Literature and Art at Yenan, 15 February 1972. With this ballet, the Shanghai Ballet Troupe toured the Democratic Republic of Korea (North Korea) in 1972 and Canada in 1977.

[*See also* China, *article on* Contemporary Theatrical Dance.]

BIBLIOGRAPHY

Brown, Estelle T. "Toward a Structuralist Approach to Ballet: *Swan Lake* and *The White-Haired Girl*." *Western Humanities Review* 32 (Summer 1978): 227–240.

Chang Keng. "My Recollection of the Production and First Performances of *The White-Haired Girl*." *Chinese Literature*, no. 9 (1977): 99–105.

Chiang Ling-chih et al. "Comments on the Ballet *The White-Haired Girl*." *Chinese Literature*, no. 8 (1966): 133–140.

Ho Ching-chih. "How *The White-Haired Girl* Was Written and Produced." *Chinese Literature*, no. 2 (1953): 110–114.

Li Hsi-fan. "An Artistic Gem Born in the Class Struggle." *China Reconstructs* 16 (September 1967): 39–43.

Snow, Lois Wheeler. *China on Stage.* New York, 1972.

Strauss, Gloria B. "Dance and Ideology in China, Past and Present: A Study of Ballet in the People's Republic." *CORD Research Annual* 8 (1977): 19–53.

Wan Kung. "How Our Revolutionary Operas and Ballets Were Produced." *Chinese Literature*, no. 5–6 (1977): 66–72.

Wan Kung. "What Chiang Ching Did to Culture." *China Reconstructs* 26 (May 1977): 2–6.

Yu Lu-yuan. "The Revolutionary Ballet *The White-Haired Girl.*" *Chinese Literature*, no. 8 (1965): 117–132.

ZHU LIREN

WHITMAN SISTERS. A family of multitalented entertainers who owned and produced their own traveling show that played major U.S. cities from 1900 to 1943, the Whitman Sisters were one of the most popular acts in black vaudeville and one of the longest-running and highest-paid acts on the Theater Owners Booking Association (TOBA) circuit. **Mabel Whitman** (died 1942), the eldest, was a singer who also handled bookings and managed the company. **Essie Whitman** (born 1881, died 7 May 1963) was a singer and comedian who designed and made costumes. **Alberta Whitman** (died 1963) was a singer, dancer, and comedian who composed music and acted as financial secretary. "Baby" **Alice Whitman** (died 1969), a singer and versatile dancer, was the show's dancing star.

From a very young age the sisters performed at church socials at the African Methodist Episcopal Church in Lawrence, Kansas, where their father was bishop of the AME Church. Essie sang jubilee songs; Mabel and Alberta played the piano. After moving to Atlanta, Georgia, where the Reverend Whitman served as dean at Morris Brown College, baby sister Alice won amateur cakewalking contests. Inspired by the enthusiastic local reception to their musical talent, Mabel and Essie formed an act and toured abroad with their mother as chaperon. Alberta joined them on their return, and in 1904 they organized themselves as the Whitman Sisters' New Orleans Troubadours. Mabel, as organizer of the group, became the first black woman to manage and continuously book her own company in leading southern houses. In 1910, Mabel organized her own show, Mabel Whitman and the Dixie Boys, which toured Germany and Australia. On her return, Alice joined the company and the Whitman Sisters were reorganized as a road show featuring all four sisters. Mabel would soon retire from the stage to manage the company.

The sisters' fast-paced show, based on a variety format of songs, dances, and comedy skits, included a cast of twenty to thirty performers, a chorus of twelve to fourteen girls, and a five- or six-piece jazz band. Alberta, or "Bert," could stop the show by patting and stamping out a Charleston rhythm for the chorus or by dancing a flashy, high-kicking strut. She cut her hair short and dressed as a man to become one of the best male impersonators in vaudeville. Essie, who excelled as a comedian in a drunk act, became famous for belting out "Some of These Days" in a resonant contralto voice that could be heard at the last row of the theater. Alice, billed as the "Queen of Taps," sang and danced tap versions of such popular black social dances as Ballin' the Jack, Walkin' the Dog, Sand, and the Shim-Sham-Shimmy. Admired for her clean, clear taps, she was considered the best female tap dancer of the 1920s. Alice married tap dancer Aaron Palmer, and their son became the last member of the family to join the show. Billed as Albert ("Pops") Whitman (1919–1950), he became a notable acrobatic tap dancer who performed cartwheels, spins, flips, and splits to swinging rhythms.

The Whitmans are considered the greatest incubators of dancing talent in black vaudeville because they gave dozens of tap dancers their first professional break into show business. Bill Robinson, Maxie McCree, Jack Wiggins, Eddie Rector, Leonard Reed, the Berry Brothers, and the legendary dancer Groundhog all served an apprenticeship with the Whitman Sisters, whose show was built on the strength of its dancing talent.

[*See also* Tap Dance.]

BIBLIOGRAPHY
Millstein, Gilbert. "Harlem Stompers." *New York World Telegram Week-End Magazine* (23 January 1937): 3.

Stearns, Marshall, and Jean Stearns. *Jazz Dance: The Story of American Vernacular Dance.* Rev. ed. New York, 1994.

CONSTANCE VALIS HILL

WIESENTHAL, GRETE (born 9 December 1885 in Vienna, died 22 June 1970 in Vienna), Austrian dancer and choreographer. Grete Wiesenthal, the daughter of the painter Franz Wiesenthal, entered the ballet school of the Vienna Hofoperntheater in 1895. After studying with Karoline Ellend, Eduard Voitus van Hamme, and Camilla Pagliero, she was accepted into the corps de ballet of the Vienna Court Opera in 1901. Matilda Kshessinska's guest performance at the Opera in 1903 spurred Wiesenthal to undertake additional studies in classical ballet with Carl Raimund. With improved technique, she was promoted to *coryphée* in 1905.

Her slender body set Wiesenthal apart from the other dancers of the Court Opera Ballet; in addition, her alert mind, interest in art history, and above all her extraordinary musicality soon led her to recognize the limits of that context. She was particularly disturbed by the lack of connection between music and choreography. "It was only a hop, skip, and jump in time to the beat, without feeling and without any idea of the music," she later wrote in her book *Der Aufstieg* (The Ascent; 1919). During this period the prime movers of American modern dance were making guest appearances in Vienna (Loie Fuller in 1898; Isadora Duncan in 1902, 1903, and 1904; Maud Allan in

1903 and 1906; and Ruth St. Denis in 1907 and 1908), but they did not provide Wiesenthal the impetus to carve out her own career.

The dancer and her sister Elsa (1887–1967), also a *coryphée* at the Court Opera Ballet, were members of the artist's alliance known as the Viennese Secession, the imagery of which may have anticipated Grete Wiesenthal's dance style. Both sisters were eager to make their own way, and an occasion soon presented itself. Gustav Mahler, in 1907, his last year as director of the Court Opera, chose Grete Wiesenthal to dance the coveted role of Fenella in Daniel Auber's opera *Die Stumme von Portici*. Subsequently the director, ballet master Josef Hassreiter, and Wiesenthal clashed, and she departed. In the spring of the same year she gave her first private program. Already in 1904 she had choreographed a dance to Chopin's Waltzes in D-flat Major; it may be more than a coincidence that Isadora Duncan had performed her Chopin program in Vienna the same year. To this program Wiesenthal added two Beethoven pieces and the Johann Strauss waltzes "By the Beautiful Blue Danube" and "Roses from the South" (the latter choreographed as a solo for Elsa Wiesenthal). This program became the core of one given at the Wiener Werkstätte cabaret, Die Fledermaus, on 14 January 1908 by Grete and her sisters Elsa and Berta, with piano accompaniment by Gertrud, another sister. The Viennese, usually not open to new developments, immediately applauded the new style of dance, which departed radically from that of the Court Opera; it was perhaps not viewed as revolutionary solely because it was in three-quarter time.

With her interpretations Wiesenthal effected a congenial transformation of the Viennese waltz into theatrical dance. The waltz was now more than the monotonous "one–two–three" done on pointe by fixedly smiling dancers laced into corsets. For Wiesenthal, waltzes were a kind of ecstasy; with unbound hair and swinging dress, she danced with a flow of movement that seemed eternal. A multiplicity of the waltz's aspects were made visible in the choreography. Waltzing was bliss, but it was also dark suspicion and even menace—an aspect of the waltz that George Balanchine was later to embody in his choreography. The waltz had now ceased to be a couple dance in which the female partner was lifted into the air on a specific beat. It became an individual giving of the self, in which stresses could be indicated even with the fists. Small or large groups moved across a gigantic stage. Waltzing became expression and development of the individual personality.

The Wiesenthal sisters soon ended their successful program at Die Fledermaus and, on the recommendation of Hugo von Hofmannsthal, turned to Max Reinhardt in Berlin. He immediately incorporated the sisters into a production and gave them an opportunity to present their program to Berliners. In addition to their dance evenings, Grete Wiesenthal, who separated from her sisters in 1910, participated in pantomimes, a genre that Reinhardt subsequently cultivated, with great popular success.

Immediately after her Berlin debut, Wiesenthal began doing guest performances. In 1908 she danced in Russia and then in the Austrian provinces. In September 1909 she made her debut in the London Hippodrome and then in the Théâtre de la Vaudeville in Paris. In 1910 she designed the movements for Reinhardt's *Sumurûn* in Berlin, in which she danced the title role. In 1912 she danced for the first time in New York. In the same year she created the role of the Kitchen Boy in Reinhardt's Stuttgart production of *Der Bürger Edelmann*. She also signed a contract with Serge Diaghilev for 1913, which she was unable to fulfill for reasons of health. She played in the 1913 film *Das fremde Mädchen*, based on a pantomime by Hugo von Hofmannsthal, which had premiered in Berlin in 1911.

WIESENTHAL. Grete Wiesenthal in her joyful "Frühlingsstimmen-walzer" (Voices of Spring Waltz). This soft-focus photograph was meticulously retouched to bring out the details of Wiesenthal's features and her unusual feathered costume. (Photograph by Rudolf Jobst; reprinted from Fritz Klingenbeck, *Unsterblicher Walzer: Die Geschichte des deutschen Nationaltanzes*, Vienna, 1940, plate 51.)

Even during World War I Wiesenthal maintained her guest appearances. She danced for the most part alone, in small genre scenes with one partner, or in small pantomime ensembles. By 1919, when she founded her first school in her native city, she had become a Viennese institution. In the dancers Willy Godlewski and Anton Birkmeyer she found partners who adapted to her style of dance; she toured all of Europe with Birkmeyer. During the 1920s she did her first work for the Salzburg Festival and also worked with Reinhardt in Berlin. Her integrated ballet interludes in Reinhardt's 1929 production of *Die Fledermaus* became famous. Wiesenthal's choreography was danced in every subsequent staging of this opera; it was revised in 1942 by George Balanchine as *Rosalinda* for performances by the New Opera Company in New York.

In 1930 Wiesenthal returned to the Vienna State Opera with her choreography for the premiere of the ballet *Der Taugenichts in Wien,* based on Joseph von Eichendorff's novel and with music by Franz Salmhofer. After a guest appearance with Willy Fränzl in the United States in 1933, in 1934 Wiesenthal agreed to lead a master class at the Academy of Music and Performing Art in Vienna. In 1938 a dance department was established at the academy. In 1945 Wiesenthal became the director of the department, a post she held until 1951. Her assistant, Maria Josefa Schaffgotsch, taught the Wiesenthal technique in the department until 1972. Even during World War II the academy had a chamber dance group that danced Wiesenthal's works almost exclusively. Its most important members included Hertha Gindl, Lia Werner, and Grete Sellier. Lisl Temple was another important interpreter of the Wiesenthal style during this period. The Grete Wiesenthal Dance Group, established in 1945, existed until 1956 and appeared as guest artists in Europe and overseas; its most important members were Vilma Kostka and Erika Kniza. Since 1977 these two have repeatedly staged Wiesenthal dances for the Vienna State Opera Ballet. Elements of Grete Wiesenthal's dance style also survive in the waltz choreographies of Dia Luca and Gerhard Senft for the Vienna Folk Opera.

BIBLIOGRAPHY

Fiedler, Leonhard M., and Martin Lang, eds. *Grete Wiesenthal: Die Schönheit der Sprache des Körpers im Tanz.* Salzburg, 1985.
Huber-Wiesenthal, Rudolf. *Die Schwestern Wiesenthal.* Vienna, 1934.
Prenner, Ingeborg. "Grete Wiesenthal: Begründerin eines neuen Tanzstils." Ph.D. diss., 1950.
Wiesenthal, Grete. *Der Aufstieg.* Berlin, 1919.
Wiesenthal, Grete. *Der ersten Schritte.* Vienna, 1947.
Witzmann, Reingard. *Die neue Körpersprache: Grete Wiesenthal und ihr Tanz.* Vienna, 1985. Exhibition catalog, Historisches Museum der Stadt Wien.

GUNHILD OBERZAUCHER-SCHÜLLER
Translated from German

WIESENTHAL TECHNIQUE. In developing her revolutionary dance technique, Grete Wiesenthal (1885–1970) was not influenced, as so many of her contemporaries were, by gymnastics, Greek culture, or folk dance, but rather by her feeling for the ecstatic, her musicality, and her childhood ballet training. Designed for female dancers (men function only as partners), the Wiesenthal technique can only be mastered from a foundation of classical training.

Wiesenthal's primary goal was to overcome the static quality of classical ballet and to dissolve all traces of posing in an endless flow of movement. She specialized in translating into dance the flowing, wavelike quality of 3/4 time as embodied in Strauss waltzes.

Wiesenthal technique comprises four areas of instruction: ballet exercises, waltz movements, turns, and leaps. In class the dancers wear sandals or soft ballet shoes.

Exercises in both balance and waltzing begin with warmup at the *barre.* Balance exercises involve slow lifts from *demi-plié* to *demi-pointe,* with torso, head, and arms inclined forward; the face followed the movement. In Wiesenthal waltz movements, the torso extends horizontally, parallel to the floor. A typical Wiesenthal turn begins from a deep bend, with head and arms hanging down; in a dynamic rising movement, the head and arms unfold upward and the dancer swings out, reaching an explosive high point. The gaze must not be fixed. Wiesenthal used this turn to unforgettable effect in "Acceleration Waltz." Another kind of turn is performed with slightly bent knees, feet parallel and on *demi-pointe,* pelvis pushed forward, and upper torso bent backward; the turn is performed slowly and with a slide. In a turn to the right, the right foot must bear most of the weight while the left slides along lightly, in an action similar to skiing.

Wiesenthal also worked out a foot technique for small, quick, sliding leaps. It requires training in classical leaps, with modifications in style and stance. Photographs show Wiesenthal in her characteristic high leaps with knees drawn in, a position she also adopted for turns. She taught these refinements only to her leading dancers.

Effortlessness, flying and swinging movement, rapture, and the capacity to be deeply moved by music were the characteristics of Grete Wiesenthal. With her technique she succeeded in integrating these into a system that could be transmitted to later generations.

BIBLIOGRAPHY

Fiedler, Leonhard M., and Martin Lang, eds. *Grete Wiesenthal: Die Schönheit der Sprache des Körpers im Tanz.* Salzburg, 1985.
Wiesenthal, Grete. *Der ersten Schritte.* Vienna, 1947.

MARIA JOSEFA SCHAFFGOTSCH
Translated from German

WIGMAN, MARY (Marie Wiegmann; born 13 November 1886 in Hanover, died 18 September 1973 in West Berlin), German modern dance pioneer. Wigman was the eldest daughter of Amalie and Heinrich Wiegmann, a prosperous merchant in Hanover. The Wiegmanns had one son, also named Heinrich, and a second daughter, Elisabeth. When Mary was nine, her father died; her mother subsequently married her husband's twin brother and business partner.

Mary attended a private girls' school and studied piano at the Hanover Conservatory. When the school director suggested that Mary enroll in the first girls' gymnasium opening in Hanover, her mother and stepfather, appalled at the thought of their daughter becoming a bluestocking, decided to send her to an English boarding school instead.

After her sojourn abroad, Mary returned to Hanover, but the glimpse of a larger world now made her feel estranged from her peers. She took up singing, but when her teacher encouraged her to seriously pursue a musical career, her parents opposed the idea. Restless, she traveled to Switzerland and Holland, became engaged, and broke the engagement, resisting her family's wishes that she marry and settle into a bourgeois life. She was "seeking," as she later wrote; seeing performances by Dalcroze students in Amsterdam and by the Wiesenthal sisters in Hanover inspired her to become a dancer.

Wigman went to the Dalcroze School in Hellerau in 1910, the year the school opened. She was almost twenty-four years old and had had little previous dance training. This was not as unusual as it may appear, for during Wigman's childhood dance was not considered an art; it was not until the early 1900s that dance experienced a revival in Germany. Enthusiastic audiences applauded guest artists Isadora Duncan, Ruth St. Denis, and Anna Pavlova as well as the Wiesenthal sisters, Clothilde von Derp, and Gertrud Louis Leistikov. Critics debated whether dance reform should proceed along the lines of "natural" or "artificial" dancing. They argued their contrary visions of dance in a spate of books on dance history and aesthetics. This theoretical orientation remained characteristic of German dance during the years of the Weimar Republic (1919–1933).

Wigman remained at the Dalcroze School for two years and earned her teacher's certificate there. She later credited Émile Jaques-Dalcroze with little influence on her work, reserving praise for her subsequent teacher Rudolf Laban. Yet Dalcroze's teaching was Wigman's first exposure to the idea that dance does not necessarily involve predetermined steps and traditional forms; it can arise from the correspondence of gesture and an internalized sense of motion based on the rhythms of music.

Wigman learned of Laban through Suzanne Perrottet, an assistant teacher at the Dalcroze School, and through Emil Nolde, an expressionist painter. Visiting Hellerau,

Nolde saw Wigman improvising and remarked that he knew a man who "dances as you do—without music." In the summer of 1913, Wigman went to Ascona, a retreat in the Swiss Alps, where Laban and his students lived communally and experimented with new ways of dancing. During this summer, the Dalcroze School asked Wigman to open a branch of the school in Berlin, but with Laban's encouragement Wigman turned down the offer, deciding to try the more uncertain career of stage dancer.

In the fall, Wigman followed Laban back to Munich to work with him there; when he fell ill, she took over his teaching for him. In the spring of 1914, for the first time, Wigman publicly presented her own compositions on a program at the Laban School. That summer of 1914, Laban and Wigman returned to Ascona for another workshop; when World War I broke out in August, the Hungarian-born Laban was stranded, and Wigman stayed with him. With few students to teach, Laban turned to work on his notation system, using Wigman as the instrument on which to test his ideas. Wigman had become not only Laban's colleague but also a collaborator.

Laban was Wigman's pedagogical model throughout her long teaching career. She adopted Laban's way of freeing students to discover their own movement through improvisation. Like Laban, Wigman based her training on gymnastics, believing that the student needed strength and flexibility to discover an individual style of movement. Like Laban, Wigman stressed the conceptual awareness demanded by dancing, an understanding of the dynamics of tension and relaxation and of the rhythms of movement through space.

Wigman was also influenced philosophically by Laban. The concept of dance as a language, as an organic unity of physical and spiritual forces, as an autonomous system with laws of its own—ideas first articulated by Laban—formed the basis of Wigman's aesthetics. Laban taught Wigman to appreciate the spatial dimension of movement as a realm independent of musical motion with a harmonic of its own. In emphasizing the spatial dimension of movement, Laban necessarily deemphasized the temporal dimension most closely akin to music, the area of Dalcroze's researches. This corresponded to Wigman's own proclivities; she later remarked that her intuitive creative work often led to discoveries paralleling Laban's theory.

Although Laban gave Wigman ways of thinking about and working with movement, he did not pass on specific structures for performance. Perhaps Wigman's first models for performance structure were the dances she and Laban saw at the Dada Gallery in Zurich in spring 1917. There, some of the dancers associated with Laban—Sophie Taeuber, Claire Walther, and Suzanne Perrottet—collaborated with Hugo Ball, Tristan Tzara, and other Dadaists in evenings of songs, dramatic sketches, and dances. The dancers were often masked and moved to the sound of a gong or a drum or in silence; the idea of the dance was primary, and all other elements—costume, scenery, music—were subordinated to it. This form seems to be the germ for the dances Wigman later evolved.

Wigman spent 1918 in solitary retreat in the Swiss mountains. She had stayed with Laban until she felt she had enough technical training to transform her body into an instrument of her creative process; like Isadora Duncan, Wigman felt compelled to create a new dance language on her own body. Having no dancers' bodies to mirror her creative process, Wigman took sole responsibility for the fusion of subjective and objective responses in the making of a dance. A special intensity marked her solos, which sprang from an inner tension. When dancing, Wigman appeared transfixed by an inner dialogue of unconscious inventing and conscious ordering.

At the end of her year of retreat, Wigman was ready to perform her dances for the public. It was at this point that she adopted the Anglicized version of her surname. Assisted by the Swiss dancer Berthe Trümpy, Wigman prepared a solo program to perform in Switzerland during the winter and spring of 1919 and then toured Germany with the program the following winter. Her first program included the solo cycles: *Dances of Night; Four Hungarian Dances* (based on Brahms); *Dance Songs,* comprising the solos "Marche Orientale," "Yaravi," and "Scherzo"; and *Ecstatic Dances,* comprising "Prayer," "Sacrifice," "Idolatry," and "Temple Dance."

The subjects of these early solos show Wigman striving toward an approach of her own. Cycles like *Four Hungarian Dances,* based on Romantic-era music, as were many Duncanesque dances, and *Dance Songs,* suggesting the pastiche of Oriental dance seen in exotic dances of the time, soon dropped out of her repertory. Increasingly, Wigman turned in the direction of *Ecstatic Dances,* where, rather than imitating religious dances of other cultures, as Ruth St. Denis often did, Wigman objectified spiritual experience without explicit reference to exotic traditions. Infused with Laban's ideas on the mystical connection between the dancer and the cosmos, Wigman continued to create dances in which "the personal life experience of the choreographer yields to the dance visualization of the incomprehensible and eternal" (Wigman, 1975, p. 93).

Within a short time Wigman found an approach of her own. She danced to silence or to a percussive accompaniment scored by Will Goetze, who joined her in 1921 as piano accompanist and composer. Wigman and Goetze collaborated in creating scores; during rehearsal Goetze would improvise accompaniment on various drums and a Javanese gong as Wigman danced, then later would set and notate the piece for performance.

Building on *Ecstatic Dances,* Wigman soon created ma-

WIGMAN. An undated studio portrait of Wigman in "Song of Destiny" from her cycle *Dance Songs* (1919). (Photograph by Charlotte Rudolph; from the Dance Collection, New York Public Library for the Performing Arts.)

ture works exemplifying her spiritual vision, such as the solos *Witch Dance* (1926) and *Monotony Whirl* (1926). In *Witch Dance,* the masked Wigman began by sitting on the floor. Convulsive jerks synchronized with percussive sounds from offstage animated her torso; it was impossible to tell whether the masked figure's movement created the sound or the sound impelled the movement. At one point the figure relaxed forward as the accompaniment of drum, gongs, and cymbals died away, and the energy of the dance seemed exhausted; but the figure came to life, swung itself to standing, then moved in circles, looming large in the space. Finally the figure sank back to the floor, but this time with its masked face staring out at the audience. In this dance Wigman did not impersonate a witch; she exemplified a spiritual state of demonism.

Similarly in *Monotony Whirl,* Wigman did more than

impersonate a whirling dervish, although this was certainly one level of association, since the dance comprised nothing but seven minutes of spinning onstage. Watching the repeated motion, the spectator could sense stillness at its center and could interpret the dance as the exemplification of the state of acting yet not acting, of being acted upon by a greater force. Like *Witch Dance, Monotony Whirl* built to several peaks of energetic motion, spinning faster and faster before subsiding; the dance ended as Wigman reached high into space and then collapsed.

Witch Dance and *Monotony Whirl* display a mode of dance that realized the theoretical ideal of the German dance movement in the early 1920s. In 1923, Laban had defined this ideal before an audience of philosophers as *Eigenkunst,* dance as "its own art"; the exemplary genre for *Eigenkunst* became dance in silence. Laban described the two-stage historical process leading to the new art: first, the rejection of ballet and dance as narrative; then, the rejection of Duncanesque dancing and music as compositional structure. Laban interpreted Wigman's dance as the exemplar of a third stage, dance discovering its own terms of expression.

Wigman ensured the independence of dance by emphasizing the spatial dimension of movement. Space became an active element in Wigman's solos; her body moved between the extremes of struggling against and giving into space. Wigman gave dramatic expression to her solo encounters with space by projecting the inner dialogue of composition in spatial terms.

Wigman achieved this mode of expressive yet absolute dance by focusing each solo around one basic movement motif and associated image, its theme. Wigman wrote that during the process of choreographing, the theme often took on a life of its own and imposed its own laws. In other words, Wigman built each dance from a motif specific to that dance rather than selecting motifs from a set vocabulary. She never codified a vocabulary, although she had a distinctive approach.

Characteristic of Wigman's approach was the cycle format, the arrangement of solos, each concentrated around a single theme, into a greater thematic whole. This format, apparent from the time of Wigman's first German tour, allowed for flexibility in building her repertory, for solos from a cycle could be presented alone or in the context of part or the whole of a cycle. To create *Witch Dance,* Wigman reworked a dance presented in 1914 at the Laban School as one solo in the *Visions* cycle (1925–1928); she then could perform *Witch Dance* either alone or in tandem with other dances from the cycle. Two years after creating *Monotony Whirl* as part of a two-dance cycle, Wigman incorporated it in the group work *Celebration* (1927–1928); once *Celebration* passed out of her repertory, Wigman still performed *Monotony Whirl* as a solo.

The cycle format reinforced other formal characteristics of Wigman's solo work. Solos arranged in a cycle displayed a series of beginnings and endings; these repeated starts and stops supported the extremes of energy marking Wigman's style. Drives toward a climax followed by a collapse often occurred; also common was the alternation of active states with periods of stillness that imperceptibly renewed the dancer's action. The arrangement of several themes into a greater whole emphasized two further structural principles in Wigman's dances: the juxtaposition of contrasting moods and movement qualities, and the recurrence of the opening image as the ending.

Wigman did not realize the possibilities of the cycle format all at once. Not until the late 1920s did she create cycles so tightly unified by interconnections from solo to solo that she could not perform the solos separately without significant loss of meaning. *Shifting Landscape* (1929) moved from an opening "Invocation" to a worshipful "Seraphic Song," then shifted to the darker mood of "Face of Night" before returning to the lighter tone of the opening, though now made more lively, in "Pastoral," "Festive Rhythm," and "Dance of Summer." "Storm Song," in which Wigman both experienced and embodied the storm, ends the idyll with a recall of the darker mood of "Face of Night."

Sacrifice (1931) reversed the pattern of light and dark presented in *Shifting Landscape.* The opening "Song of the Sword" set the note of struggle that dominated the work, then gave way to its antithesis in "Dance for the Sun"; one critic described the movement as going from the masculine to the feminine. The controlling motif of the cycle came to the fore in "Death Call," in which Wigman embodied both the force of death calling the living and the force of life resisting the call. In the following "Dance for the Earth," Wigman became a creature of nature, no longer a participant in ultimate human struggles; the critic likened this section to a Greek satyr play. "Lament" anticipated the end with a diagonal motion that became the dominant image of the final "Dance into Death." In her final solo, Wigman rushed down the diagonal against a presence that forced her to the floor, then rose and fell again, resigned to the presence.

Beyond noting the greater unity of the cycle format in *Shifting Landscape* and *Sacrifice,* critics detected a shift in the style of Wigman's solos from the early to the late 1920s. According to critic Rudolf Maack, Wigman's early dances explored pure form as a way of controlling an overflow of expressiveness, and her later dances explored the tension and reconciliation of pure form and expressiveness. Maack interpreted Wigman's early dances as the last wave of expressionism in German art and her later dances as moving toward classicism, paralleling the movement toward classicism in the other German arts.

It is clear that Maack considered Wigman's solos serious works of art. Her group works, however, received more ambivalent critical response. While some critics praised her group dances as the culmination of her art, other critics were disappointed that Wigman's group works did not achieve the heights of her solo works.

Once Wigman opened her school in Dresden in 1920 with Berthe Trümpy as codirector, a group of highly talented students gathered there, many of whom became leading dancers of their generation: Yvonne Georgi, Harald Kreutzberg, Gret Palucca, Vera Skoronel, Max Terpis. Within a few years these dancers had all left to take up positions elsewhere, mostly in opera houses. Other students left in order to open their own schools. Dance enjoyed a widespread popularity during the 1920s, which would have been unimaginable before World War I. In 1926, Trümpy decided to open her own school in Berlin, so Wigman's sister Elisabeth became codirector of the Dresden school. By 1925, Wigman's second performing group grew to about twenty dancers, including Hanya Holm, who became Wigman's assistant. This group disbanded three years later, and thereafter Wigman created new groups from among her students as needed.

Without a stable ensemble of dancers Wigman could

WIGMAN. Wearing a mask, Wigman appeared in a solo in her group work *Dance of Death* (1926). (Photograph from the Archiv der Akademie der Künste, Berlin; courtesy of Susan A. Manning.)

not build a repertory to encompass works from a period of years, so her performance repertory comprised mostly current works. Usually, Wigman toured in the fall with new solos she had created the previous summer and then rehearsed a new group work to perform on tour in the spring. The group traveled as lightly as possible: black curtains to surround whichever stage they used; costumes with simple geometric lines, often made of rich satins and brocades; and an assortment of percussion instruments. Wigman's aesthetic of dance as an independent art had a practical as well as a philosophic basis. Like the Dadaists in 1917, Wigman turned necessity into art.

Wigman's first full-scale group work, *The Seven Dances of Life* (1921), was set to a score by Heinz Pringsheim that had been commissioned by Hans Niedecken-Gebhard, a director interested in revitalizing opera by emphasizing its dance elements. Here, Wigman set a cycle of solos for herself within the framework of an overall narrative of a dancer performing for a king (represented by an effigy on stage) who promised to free her if she can dance the meaning of life. The dancer appears to have failed: a demon speaks out of the darkness and four girls bring a black veil of death; but in the final "Dance of Life" Wigman returned in a golden garment and beckoned the girls to dance with her.

Wigman's next full-scale group work, *Scenes from a Dance Drama* (1923–1924), abandoned the explicit narrative frame in favor of a series of variations entitled with abstractions such as "Circle," "Chaos," and Vision." The changing relationship of the leader to the group became the central theme in this and in many later group dances. *A Dance Fairy Tale* (1925) burlesqued this theme, when Wigman, costumed as a black magician, transformed three girls into flowers and worked other wonders in a world of fantasy. The comic-grotesque costumes that distorted the dancers' shapes recalled Oskar Schlemmer's *Triadic Ballet*, which had premiered three years earlier.

Dance of Death (1926) returned to Wigman's preoccupation with the forces of life and death. Here, life did not emerge as the clearcut victor in the struggle. Wigman, the only dancer not masked, stood between a beastlike figure of death and the group of creatures the figure commanded.

Celebration (1927–1928), Wigman's last work for her dance group of the 1920s, moved away from dramatic images and toward a structure comparable to symphonic music, a movement anticipated by *Hymns in Space* (1926). In *Celebration*, the dance images themselves made the analogy between the structures of pure dance and music, as dancers entered in procession playing musical instruments. The work was created for the Second Dancers' Congress in Essen, for an audience of peers rather than for a wider public. At the congress Wigman announced

WIGMAN. Pictured here with members of her group, Wigman appears at center in "The Prophetess," the fifth section of her *Women's Dances* (1934). (Photograph from the Dance Collection, New York Public Library for the Performing Arts.)

that her dance group was disbanding because of financial difficulties.

Wigman next turned to another form of dance created among peers, the movement choir, a dance activity for a large group of nonprofessionals, first developed by Laban. In 1929, Wigman created three studies in choric movement for her students at the Dresden School. For the 1930 Third Dancers' Congress in Munich, she integrated choric movement into a theatrical spectacle to create *Totenmal*, based on a poem and musical composition by Albert Talhoff. The theme of the dance of death recurred, but it was given more explicit reference than it had in *Dance of Death*; here, the dead were the fallen soldiers of World War I, and the chorus that called them was the women they had left behind.

Totenmal disappointed the audience of dancers at the congress, an ironic response since many of the dancers at the 1928 congress had called for dance to realign itself with the theater. At that previous congress, Wigman had described her vision of a new form of theater based on dance, and *Totenmal* was her attempt to realize that vision.

Wigman's redefinition of her aesthetic ideal around 1930 recalled her earlier collaborations with theater artists. In the early 1920s, Wigman had choreographed *A Midsummer Night's Dream* for expressionist director Berthold Viertel's production at the Berlin Schauspielhaus. During the same period, she choreographed the dance interludes for the premier of Hans Pfitzner's opera *The Rose from the Garden of Love* in Hanover. After World War II, Wigman continued her work in choric and theatrical choreography.

Wigman's aesthetic shifted significantly under the impact of National Socialism (Nazism), which became Germany's ruling political party in 1933 under the leadership of Adolf Hitler. Like many other dancers, Wigman initially embraced the new aesthetic of art arising from the so-called spirit of the Aryan race, as evidenced in her essays collected in *German Dance Art* (1935). Her one involvement with Nazi spectacle came with *Olympic Youth*, a pageant staged in connection with the opening of the Berlin Olympic Games in 1936. Ten thousand young people executed choreography contributed by Wigman, Palucca, Kreutzberg, and other dancers. Like the Nazi-sponsored dance festivals of 1934, 1935, and 1936, *Olympic Youth* was a showpiece contrived for impressionable spectators. Rather than promoting experimental work, the National Socialist spectacles glorified the Germanic past.

Wigman's group dances created in the early 1930s and her solos prior to her farewell performance in 1942 reflect the new Germanic mood of retrospection. They seem to be pastiches of earlier works rather than new works. The group cycle *Women's Dances* (1934) picks up the earlier *Witch Dance* as well as the motif of mourning women from *Totenmal*. *Autumnal Dances* (1937), a solo cycle, picks up the images of nature from *Shifting Landscape*. Hanns Hasting, who had replaced Will Goetze as Wigman's accompanist and composer in 1929, wrote the music for these works.

Wigman did little touring outside of central Europe, with the exception of three extended and well-received tours of the United States in the 1930/31, 1931/32, and 1932/33 seasons. Wigman's repertory for the first of these, which was limited to the East Coast, included solos from the *Shifting Landscape* cycle, *Witch Dance, Monotony Whirl,* and several newly composed solos. The second U.S. tour, which took in all parts of the country, included the cycle *Sacrifice,* which Wigman created in response to seeing Niagara Falls, just as *Shifting Landscape* had been created in response to an earlier trip to France. On the third U.S. tour, Wigman brought along a group of twelve dancers in a cycle created for the occasion, *The Way.*

Sponsored by Sol Hurok, Wigman's tours created a sensation among U.S. dancers and critics; for the most part, American spectators interpreted Wigman in terms of the evolution of American modern dance; they saw her as the transitional artist between the solo genius of Isadora Duncan and the early Martha Graham and Doris Humphrey. They regarded Wigman as representing the theoretical ideal of dance as an absolute art; they had had no way of seeing the changes in Wigman's work over the years or of understanding how much she had in common with her German contemporaries. With Hurok's support, Wigman's assistant Hanya Holm stayed in New York City to open a

branch of the Wigman School and reinterpret Wigman's approach for American dancers.

After 1936, Wigman received no further commissions for group works from the National Socialist party, although she continued to tour her solo programs with official support. In 1942, she gave her farewell concert and sold her school. She then moved to Leipzig, where she continued to teach through the last years and aftermath of World War II. In 1949, she moved to West Berlin and reopened her school there.

In the 1950s, Wigman staged operas at the National Theater in Mannheim as well as dance performances of *The Rite of Spring* and *Orpheus and Eurydice* in Berlin. No longer creating solos for herself, Wigman continued her work in choric theater. That Wigman now worked in the opera house says much about the changed conditions of dance in postwar Germany, since the modern dance movement was over, at least for a time. In the immediate

WIGMAN. "Men's Dance" *(below)* and "Mysterious Circle" *(opposite),* two dances from Wigman's *Rite of Spring* (1957), set to the Stravinsky score. (Photographs by Siegfried Enkelmann; from the Dance Collection, New York Public Library for the Performing Arts.)

postwar years, German dance moved in the direction of modern ballet. Only in the 1970s did a new form of modern dance emerge that went under the rubric of *Tanztheater*. The movement was inspired in part by the teaching of "survivors" from the pioneering interwar period, including Wigman herself.

Wigman shared many concerns with her generation of dancers, who built the German modern dance movement of the 1920s. They were concerned with ideas as the controlling impulse of dance; with an expressive yet absolute mode midway between narrative and abstraction; with space as an active presence in dance; with the mask and costume as transformers for the human self; and with the theme of the dance of death.

Wigman had worked more intently and had pushed her work further than did other dancers of her generation. While during the Weimar years other dancers tended either to remain touring soloists or to become ballet directors, Wigman attempted the range of choreographic forms—from solo to group to choric to stage choreography. While other dancers turned to ballet as a necessary support for theatrical dance, Wigman resisted, sustaining

a vision of modern dance as a fusion of the dancer's subjective and objective responses to the times. She did not resist the allure of National Socialist aesthetics. She presented, in dance terms, the spirit of her time and place, wavering as that spirit became transformed. Although difficult for us to accept, this fact testifies to her ability to sense and utilize the currents of her time.

[*See also* Artists and Dance, *article on* Artists and Dance, 1760–1929; Ausdruckstanz; Germany, *article on* Theatrical Dance, 1600–1945; Movement Choir; *and the entry on Laban.*]

BIBLIOGRAPHY
Bach, Rudolf, ed. *Das Mary Wigman-Werk.* Dresden, 1933.
Delius, Rudolf von. *Mary Wigman.* Dresden, 1925.
Howe, Dianne S. "The Notion of Mysticism in the Philosophy and Choreography of Mary Wigman, 1914–1931." *Dance Research Journal* 19 (Summer 1987): 19–24.
Howe, Dianne S. "Parallel Visions: Mary Wigman and the German Expressionists." In *Dance: Current Selected Research*, vol. 1, edited by Lynnette Y. Overby and James H. Humphrey. New York, 1989.
Kaut, Marion. "Lebensmoster Mary Wigman: Die Suche nach der verloren n welt." *Tanzdrama* 25 (1994): 14–19, 25 (1995): 16–19.

Linder, Kurt. *Die Verwandlungen der Mary Wigman*. Freiburg im Breisgau, 1929.

Maletić, Vera. "Wigman and Laban: The Interplay of Theory and Practice." *Ballet Review* 14 (Fall 1986): 86–95.

Manning, Susan A. *Ecstasy and the Demon: Feminism and Nationalism in the Dances of Mary Wigman*. Berkeley, 1993.

Müller, Hedwig. "At the Start of a New Era: Tenth Anniversary of the Death of Mary Wigman." *Ballett International* 6 (December 1983): 6–13.

Müller, Hedwig. *Mary Wigman: Leben und Werk der grossen Tänzerin*. Weinheim, 1986.

Müller, Hedwig. "Wigman and National Socialism." *Ballet Review* 15 (Spring 1987): 65–73.

Odom, Selma Landen. "Wigman at Hellerau." *Ballet Review* 14 (Summer 1986): 41–53.

Toepfer, Karl. "Speech and Sexual Difference in Mary Wigman's Dance Aesthetic." In *Gender in Performance*, edited by Laurence Senelick. Hanover, N.H., 1992.

Wigman, Mary. *Deutsche Tanzkunst*. Dresden, 1935.

Wigman, Mary. *The Language of Dance*. Translated by Walter Sorell. Middletown, Conn., 1966.

Wigman, Mary. *The Mary Wigman Book*. Translated and edited by Walter Sorell. Middletown, Conn., 1975.

FILM: Allegra Fuller Snyder, *When the Fire Dances between the Two Poles: Mary Wigman, 1886–1973,* includes most of the extant clips of Wigman dancing.

SUSAN A. MANNING

WILDE. A performance photograph of Wilde and members of the female ensemble of the New York City Ballet in George Balanchine's *Serenade,* c.1959. Strong and swift, with remarkable elevation, Wilde could blaze across the stage and soar through the air with thrilling effect, seeming to ride the crest of the surging strains of Tchaikovsky's "Serenade for Strings." (Photograph from the Dance Collection, New York Public Library for the Performing Arts. Choreography by George Balanchine © The George Balanchine Trust.)

WILDE, PATRICIA (Patricia Lorrain-Ann White; born 16 July 1928 in Ottawa), American ballet dancer, teacher, and company director. Patricia White began studying ballet at the age of three with Gwendolyn Osborne in Ottawa. When she was about eleven, she and her older sister Nora went to New York to continue their studies with Dorothie Littlefield. At age twelve Patricia enrolled at the School of American Ballet, where her teachers included George Balanchine and Muriel Stuart. She made her professional debut at age fifteen with the American Concert Ballet and the next year, 1944, danced in the corps de ballet of the Marquis de Cuevas's Ballet International.

In the summer of 1945 White was one a group of dancers, headed by Marie-Jeanne and William Dollar, that Balanchine took to Mexico City for a series of performances at the Palacio de Bellas Artes with the Ópera Nacional. There he mounted productions of Michel Fokine's *Les Sylphides,* his own *Concerto Barocco* and *Apollo,* and *Constantia,* a work he made jointly with Dollar, as well as staging dances in several operas. White danced a solo in the Walpurgisnacht scene in *Faust.* Upon returning from Mexico, White joined her sister Nora in the corps of Sergei Denham's Ballet Russe de Monte Carlo (changing her surname from White to Wilde to avoid confusion with her sister) and remained with this company until 1949. She then went to Europe, where she studied briefly with Olga Preobrajenska in Paris, performed as a guest artist with the Ballets de Paris de Roland Petit, and toured the Netherlands and England with the Metropolitan Ballet, a short-lived English company.

In 1950 Wilde joined the New York City Ballet. She spent the bulk of her career as a dancer with this company and with it danced many leading roles. Among those she created in Balanchine ballets were the third waltz in *La Valse* (1951), the soloist in *Scotch Symphony* (1952), the Scherzo in *Western Symphony* (1954), one of the five ballerinas in *Divertimento No. 15* (1956), and the principal female roles in *Square Dance* (1957), *Native Dancers* (1959), and *Raymonda Variations* (1961). She also originated and had great success in the pas de trois in Balanchine's staging of *Swan Lake,* which in 1959 was replaced by a solo for Prince Siegfried to the same music. She also choreographed a number of ballets, including some for the New York Philharmonic Promenade Concerts. Wilde was a mainstay of the New York City Ballet during its City Center period. She was an impeccable technician, unsurpassed in allegro, with a power and facility in aerial steps that are rare in a ballerina.

Wilde resigned from the New York City Ballet in 1965; retiring from dancing, she began a second career as an outstanding teacher by becoming director of the dance department of Harkness House for Ballet Arts, a position she held until 1967. In 1969, at Balanchine's invitation, she set up the school for the Ballet du Grand Théâtre de Genève. She was associated with the American Ballet Theatre School from 1967 until it closed in 1982—serving as director from 1979 to 1982—and between 1970 and 1976 she was a ballet mistress at American Ballet Theatre.

In September 1982 Wilde became artistic director of Pittsburgh Ballet Theatre. Her first priority as artistic director was to improve the company's technical ability so that the dancers could handle the Balanchine ballets she introduced into the repertory. She later focused on acquiring new works for inclusion in the company's mixed-bill programming.

In 1953 Wilde married George Bardyguine, at the time the New York City Ballet's production stage manager; they have two children. She became a U.S. citizen in 1957. She has served as an adviser to the New York State Council on the Arts and has been the recipient of a number of honors and cultural awards.

BIBLIOGRAPHY
Anderson, Jack. *The One and Only: The Ballet Russe de Monte Carlo.* New York, 1981.
Dacko, Karen. "Dancing on the Wilde Side: Full Steam Ahead for Pittsburgh Ballet Theatre." *Dance Magazine* (August 1986): 52–54.
Denby, Edwin. *Dance Writings.* Edited by Robert Cornfield and William Mackey. New York, 1986.
Gruen, John. *The Private World of Ballet.* New York, 1975.
Kirstein, Lincoln. *The New York City Ballet.* With photographs by Martha Swope and George Platt Lynes. New York, 1973.
Tobias, Tobi. "Patricia Wilde: A Full Life." *Dance Magazine* (September 1971): 68–74.

WILLIAM JAMES LAWSON

WILHELM, C. (William John Charles Pitcher; born 21 March 1858 in Northfleet, Kent, died 25 March 1925 in London), British costume and stage designer. C. Wilhelm was the principal designer of English ballet during the late nineteenth century, when Victorian propriety had pushed it from the opera houses into the music halls. Beginning with costume design and advancing to whole productions, his spectacular showpieces for London's Empire Theatre helped preserve a local tradition of classical dance, embedded in popular entertainment, between the eras of the Romantic ballet and the Ballets Russes.

A self-trained draftsman, Wilhelm began his career designing costumes for pantomimes at the Theatre Royal, Drury Lane. His thirty-year association with the Empire began with its opening in 1884 and advanced in 1887 with *Dilara,* in which each *coryphée* wore a white cockatoo on her wrist. His collaborations with choreographer Katti Lanner and composer Leopold Wenzel were the basis of the Empire's success, although it was in stage design that the self-declared "home of ballet" was widely agreed to surpass the larger Alhambra.

"Color is the life-blood of my art," Wilhelm said. In *Rose d'Amour* (1888) the corps de ballet were costumed as variously colored flowers, coming together into one enormous bouquet. As important as color was the spinning of whole systems of finely elaborated fantasy. He devised *Les Papillons* (1901) for the Empire's ballerina Adeline Genée with fastidious attention to actual butterfly markings, with each costume representing a different variety: Genée was the Queen Butterfly *(Vanessa imperialis),* attended by a retinue of elves and glow-worms. The dancers were always resplendent, whether costumed as fish, birds, or even fruit. Wilhelm's watercolor sketches for these costumes are as exquisite in color and detail as they are exuberant in imagination.

Wilhelm designed many of the popular contemporary ballets, such as *The Paris Exhibition* (1889), which featured the brand-new Eiffel Tower, and *The Press* (1898), in which dancers wore the symbols of contemporary London newspapers. He preferred historical romance, however, and as he became the dominant figure at the Empire, inventing scenarios as well as designs, more traditional subjects were favored. His production of *Cinderella* (1906), set in the midst of a Watteau *fête galante,* had exceptional success. The appearance of the Ballets Russes de Serge Diaghilev in London damaged the glamorous appeal of the Empire, and during World War I the ballet company was disbanded. Wilhelm retired to his watercolors in 1919; he died two years before the Empire was converted into a movie theater.

BIBLIOGRAPHY
Beaumont, Cyril W. *Five Centuries of Ballet Design.* London, 1939.
Forsyth, Gerald. "Wilhelm: A Noted Victorian Theatrical Designer." *Theatre Notebook* 11 (January-March 1957): 55–58.
Guest, Ivor. *Adeline Genée.* London, 1958.
Guest, Ivor. *The Empire Ballet.* London, 1962.
Guest, Ivor. *Ballet in Leicester Square.* London, 1992.

CLAUDIA ROTH PIERPONT

WILLIAMS, E. VIRGINIA (Virginia Ellen Williams; born 12 March 1914 in Stoneham, Massachusetts, died 8 May 1984 in Malden, Massachusetts), American ballet teacher, choreographer, and company director. Virginia Williams, who preferred to be known as E. Virginia, was the quintessential New England Yankee. Like her maternal grandfather, who owned five whaling vessels out of Salem, she was courageous and obdurate. She was also passionate about dance. This passion manifested itself early on, and although her parents frowned on a performing career, she was given the best training then available in Boston. Among her early teachers were Miriam Winslow, Dana Sieveling, and Jerrie Cragin. She also studied in New York City with Tatiana Chamié, Anatole Oboukhoff, and George Balanchine.

In 1937 Williams married Carl Nelson, with whom she had a daughter, Carla. For the next two decades she immersed herself in teaching. (Two of her early schools were in Malden and Stoneham, Massachusetts.) After divorcing Nelson, Williams married pianist Herbert Hobbs in 1955. Hobbs became musical adviser to the New England Civic Ballet, which Williams formed in 1958. When seen at the first Northeast Regional Ballet Festival in 1959, the company attracted immediate attention.

George Balanchine began to visit Williams's studio to recruit dancers for the New York City Ballet, and in 1962 he invited her to work with him privately once a month. A deep bond of mutual respect developed between them, and in 1963, with Balanchine's help, her company received a grant from the Ford Foundation that helped finance the shift from the nonprofessional New England Civic Ballet to the professional Boston Ballet. To her new status as director of the Boston Ballet Williams brought her special gifts as teacher, choreographer, and imaginative builder of repertory. She also had an infallible memory for the choreography of others.

Williams had daring dreams for the company. She invited contemporary choreographers such as Pearl Lang, John Butler, Talley Beatty, and Merce Cunningham to enrich the repertory. She also initiated the Vestris Prize Competition, which brought attention to little-known choreographers. And she encouraged well-known choreographers, such as Agnes de Mille and Choo San Goh, to take unaccustomed stylistic paths.

In 1980 Williams invited Violette Verdy to become associate artistic director of the Boston Ballet. In 1983 Williams retired, but her close connection with company and school ended only with her death the following year. Among her honors were a *Dance Magazine* Award (1976), the Distinguished Bostonian Award (1980), and several honorary doctorates.

[*See also* Boston Ballet.]

BIBLIOGRAPHY

Basco, Sharon. "E. Virginia Williams Dons New Hat." *Dance Magazine* (July 1983): 6–7.
Cash, Debra. "The Boston Ballet." *Ballet News* 5 (May 1984): 34.
Fanger, Iris M. "E. Virginia Williams." *Dance Magazine* (July 1984): 87–88.
Hering, Doris. "New England Civic Ballet: Sweet Compulsion." *Dance Magazine* (April 1960): 52–55.
Tobias, Tobi. "E. Virginia Williams and the Boston Ballet." *Dance Magazine* (June 1976): 47–58.
Williams, E. Virginia. "What Makes a Great Teacher of Classical Ballet?" *Dance Magazine* (August 1963): 20–21.

DORIS HERING

WILLIAMS, PETR (Petr Vladimirovich Williams; born 17 [30] June 1902 in Moscow, died 1 December 1947 in Moscow), Russian scenery and costume designer. Williams

PETR WILLIAMS. One of the settings that Williams designed for Leonid Lavrovsky's production of *Romeo and Juliet* at the Kirov Theater, Leningrad, in 1940. The dancers pictured are Konstantin Sergeyev and Galina Ulanova in the title roles. (Photograph from the archives of the Maryinsky Theater, Saint Petersburg.)

studied painting with Wassily Kandinsky and Konstantin Korovin, among many others. From 1941 to 1947 he was chief decor designer at the Bolshoi Theater in Moscow. Williams's signature was decor as a huge easel painting framed by a giant three-dimensional portal. His finest achievements were his decors for *Romeo and Juliet* (Kirov Ballet, 1940) and *Cinderella* (Bolshoi Ballet, 1945).

The painted backdrops for *Romeo and Juliet* were framed with a richly ornamented portal that re-created the images of the Italian high Renaissance. Sometimes Williams incorporated compositions of the great painters into his designs, for example, a copy of Sandro Botticelli's *Primavera* appeared in the backdrop for Juliet's bedroom. The costumes were so authentic that they seemed to clothe personages from Italian paintings come to life.

For the ballroom scene in *Cinderella*, drawing on Baroque magnificence and the porcelainlike delicacy of the Rococo, Williams decorated his ornamental portal frame with mirrors, candles, and sculptured figures—a triumph of sumptuous stage design. The first act, however, had been completely realistic, in accordance with the conventions for drama ballet *(drambalet)*, a genre of which Williams may be considered a typical representative in decor design. Williams was named Merited Art Worker of the Russian Federation and won the State Prize of the USSR in 1942, 1945, and 1946.

BIBLIOGRAPHY

Sidorov, Aleksandr. *Petr Viliams* (in Russian). Moscow, 1980.
Syrkina, F. Y. *Petr Vladimirovich Viliams* (in Russian). Moscow, 1953.

VIKTOR I. BEREZKIN
Translated from Russian

WILLIAMS, STANLEY (born 5 March 1925 in Chappel, England, died 21 October 1997 in New York), Anglo-Danish dancer and teacher. Son of an English father and a Danish mother, Williams immigrated with his parents to Copenhagen in 1932, when he was seven. Two years later he entered the school of the Royal Danish Ballet. There, in classes taught by Karl Merrild, Harald Lander, and others, he was thoroughly trained in the Danish school of dancing established in the nineteenth century by August Bournonville. Williams was accepted into the company in 1943, at age eighteen, and was appointed a *solodanser* (soloist, or principal dancer) in 1949, a rank he held until 1963. Among his leading roles in the Bournonville repertory were Vilhelm in *Far from Denmark*, James in *La Sylphide*, and the Ballet Master in *Konservatoriet*. He was also noted for his Mercutio in Frederick Ashton's *Romeo and Juliet*, for his Jailer in Léonide Massine's *Symphonie Fantastique* (fourth movement), and for the character role of Doctor Coppélius.

Early in his career, Williams began to go abroad for appearances as a guest artist. In 1947 and 1948, he made guest appearances in Iceland, Belgium, and Sweden, and in 1953–1954 he was the leading dancer and ballet master with George Kirsta's Ballet Comique in England. In 1955 he danced at Jacob's Pillow, in Becket, Massachusetts, with the first group of soloists of the Royal Danish Ballet to appear in the United States.

Although Williams was a skillful dancer, his greatest gift was for pedagogy. He began teaching under Lander's direction in 1950, at the age of twenty-four, but it was Vera Volkova, who came to the Royal Danish Ballet as artistic adviser in 1951, who was principally responsible for shaping him as an instructor. Volkova, a Russian dancer and teacher who had settled in England in the 1930s, was the leading authority in the West on the Vaganova system of instruction. Under her tutelage, and after an injury limited his roles onstage, Williams began to devote his energies to teaching, which he found that he greatly enjoyed. Subsequently, his teaching was influenced considerably by the work of George Balanchine, whom he met in 1956 during the New York City Ballet's visit to Denmark. Having observed Williams's classes, Balanchine invited him to come to America to teach. Williams served as guest teacher for the New York City Ballet for the 1960/61 and 1961/62 seasons, and in 1964 he became permanently affiliated with that company.

For many years Williams worked almost exclusively with the company's academy, the School of American Ballet. Long recognized as an outstanding teacher, he held for many years the prestigious appointment to the Senior Faculty Chair, an honor bestowed upon him in the 1980s. In addition to teaching daily classes, Williams frequently staged excerpts from Bournonville ballets for the school's annual Workshop Performances, and in 1977 he mounted a group of these pieces for the New York City Ballet under the title *Bournonville Divertissements*.

Williams also regularly taught company class for the New York City Ballet and served as a guest instructor with the Royal Danish Ballet and American Ballet Theatre. In class, his teaching manner was quiet and absolutely concentrated, his demeanor modest yet masterful. Over the years his reputation as a teacher achieved almost legendary status, as his skill and talent were praised by numerous famous dancers who were his students. Edward Villella, for one, credits Williams with extending his performing career by more than a decade (Villella, 1992); Peter Martins, for another, considers Williams preeminent among the world's great ballet teachers (Martins, 1982). All his students extol the fundamental simplicity of his teaching, his ability to transmit his knowledge of what has been called "the essence of technique." Yet, through his emphasis on technical purity, advanced students recognize that Williams took them beyond technique and confronted them squarely with the art of ballet dancing. Commenting on his company class for the New York City

Ballet, one dancer said that "it's like listening to Bach. It's pure, it's classical, it gets straight to the heart of things" (quoted in Schof, 1996).

BIBLIOGRAPHY

Martins, Peter, with Robert Cornfield. *Far from Denmark.* Boston, 1982.

Schof, Thomas W. "Master of the Barre." New York City Ballet *Stagebill* (January 1996): 12–13, 46.

Tobias, Tobi. "Stanley Williams: The Quality of the Moment." *Dance Magazine* (March 1981): 74–83.

Villella, Edward, with Larry Kaplan. *Prodigal Son: Dancing for Balanchine in a World of Pain and Magic.* New York, 1992.

CLAUDE CONYERS

WILLIAMS-YARBOROUGH, LAVINIA (born 1919 in Philadelphia, Pennsylvania, died 19 July 1989 in Haiti), American dancer, teacher, and choreographer. Trained in classical ballet, Williams-Yarborough performed in musical comedy and modern dance before turning to African-derived, New World dance forms as a means of reaffirming her cultural heritage. Following Katherine Dunham and Jean-Léon Destiné, she combined the religious and folkloric dances of the Caribbean—particularly those of Haiti—with European forms of theatrical dance and created a syncretic, contemporary, theatrical black dance style. She also helped to establish national dance academies in Haiti, Jamaica, Guyana, and the Bahamas.

Raised in Portsmouth, Virginia, and Brooklyn, New York, Williams-Yarborough began studying ballet when she was three years old. Tap, modern, acrobatics, singing, and acting classes soon followed. She graduated from Washington Irving High School in New York City and won a scholarship to the Art Students' League. Her dance teachers included Kay Perper (Denishawn School), Anna Sokolow, Martha Graham, Agnes de Mille, Katherine Dunham, Valerie Bettis, Lisan Kay, Helen Tamiris, African dancers Prince Almamy and Asadata Dafora, and Kyra Nijinsky (Antwerp). Her performing credits include Eugene Von Grona's American Negro Ballet (1937–1939), Ballet Theater's premiere season (in *Obeah*, choreographed by de Mille, 1940), and the Katherine Dunham Company (1940–1946, in New York City, on national tour, and in Hollywood). She appeared in the films *Stormy Weather* and *Carnival of Rhythm* (both 1943) and in several Broadway productions: *Blackbirds of 1939*, *Cabin in the Sky* (1940), *A Tropical Revue* (1943), *Blue Holiday* (1945), a 1945 United Service Organizations (USO) revival of *Shuffle Along*, *Showboat* (1946), *Finian's Rainbow* (1947), and *My Darlin' Aida* (1952).

With Haiti as her base, from 1953 to 1980 Williams-Yarborough also taught and choreographed in Jamaica (1958–1982), Guyana (1972–1976), the Bahamas (1976–1980), Antigua, Trinidad, Barbados, Montserrat, and Saint Kitts as well as in Sweden (1967) and Germany (1980–1981). She returned to the United States in 1980 and taught at the Alvin Ailey American Dance Center, Steps Studio 56, and at her own Brooklyn-based school, which opened in July 1983. In the mid-1980s she resettled in Haiti and taught at her school there until her death from food poisoning.

BIBLIOGRAPHY

Aschenbrenner, Joyce. "Katherine Dunham: Reflections on the Social and Political Contexts of Afro-American Dance." *CORD Dance Research Annual* 12 (1980).

Emery, Lynne Fauley. *Black Dance from 1619 to Today.* 2d rev. ed. Princeton, 1988.

MacDonald, Annette. "Madame Lavinia Williams: Conversations in Nassau." *Journal of Ethnic Studies* 13 (Summer 1985): 106–117.

Williams-Yarborough, Lavinia. "Haiti, Where I Teach Dance." *Dance Magazine* (October 1958): 42–44, 76–79.

ARCHIVES. Dance Collection, New York Public Library for the Performing Arts. Schomburg Center for Research in Black Culture, New York Public Library.

BRENDA DIXON GOTTSCHILD

WILSON, ROBERT (born 4 October 1941 in Waco, Texas), American theatrical designer and producer. Wilson attended the University of Texas for three years and received a bachelor of fine arts degree in 1965 from Pratt Institute in Brooklyn, New York. In 1962 he studied with George McNeil in Paris, and in 1966 with Paolo Soleri at the Arcosanti Community in Arizona. Wilson formed the Byrd Hoffman School of Byrds in 1969, a close-knit group of people from diverse backgrounds who experimented together in dance, theater, and movement.

Robert Wilson has been recognized internationally as a theatrical innovator, performer, director, writer, visual artist, and video artist. His works, which reflect his training as a painter and architect, are generally referred to as operas, although they lack the dramatic narrative and the correlation between the music and drama characteristic of traditional opera. Some of his works on an operatic scale produce the sense of total theater first described in Richard Wagner's formulation of the *Gesamkunstwerk*. Wilson's operas are structured as visual collages in which text, movement, and music are treated independently. The spectacular visual tableaux are developed through often imperceptibly slow movement by the performers, resulting in an unusual theatrical experience.

Because each tableau was complete in itself, Wilson's early productions could be rearranged, augmented, or condensed. *The King of Spain* (1969), for example, became the second act of *The Life and Times of Sigmund Freud* (1970), which was in turn incorporated into the first three acts of *Deafman Glance* (1970). *The Life and Times of Joseph Stalin*, first produced at the Brooklyn Academy of Music in 1973, was twelve hours long and included material from all five of Wilson's previous productions. His

ROBERT WILSON. A scene from Wilson's *Dr. Faustus Lights the Lights* (1992). Although few of his works include dances, Wilson exhibits a choreographic sensibility in the extreme precision with which he designs his performers' stage movement, tableaux, and abstract gestures. (Photograph © 1992 by Jack Vartoogian; used by permission.)

longest production, *Overture to KA MOUNTAIN AND GUARDenia Terrace* (1972), presented at the Shiraz Festival, Iran, lasted seven days and nights.

Einstein on the Beach (1976), one of Wilson's most celebrated works, was a collaboration with the composer Philip Glass, with choreography by Andy de Groat. The opera toured extensively in Europe before its American premiere on 21 November 1976 at the Metropolitan Opera House, New York. Revivals of *Einstein on the Beach*, with choreography by Lucinda Childs, were produced by the Brooklyn Academy of Music in 1984 and 1992.

Wilson's international opera, *the CIVIL warS: a tree is best measured when it is down*, which was to have its premiere at the 1984 Los Angeles Olympics, was canceled because of inadequate funding. Though yet to be seen in its entirety, segments of *the CIVIL warS* have been performed worldwide in Cologne, Rome, Amsterdam, Minneapolis, and New York. In 1986 Wilson was the sole nominee for the Pulitzer Prize for drama for *the CIVIL warS*, although the Pulitzer Board declined to give the award that year.

Wilson's most popular work to date was his 1990 production *The Black Rider*, with music by Tom Waits and texts by William Burroughs, for the Thalia Theater in Hamburg. Since its premiere the show has toured extensively worldwide. Wilson and Waits collaborated a second time on the Thalia's production of *Alice*, first performed in December 1992.

Among the awards and honors received by Wilson are the Bessie award (in 1984 for *the Knee Plays*); the Obie award for direction (in 1986 for *Hamletmachine*); and the Skowhegan Medal for Drawing (in 1987). He has also received fellowships from the Rockefeller Foundation (1975, 1981) and the Guggenheim Foundation (1971, 1980). In 1993 he won a Golden Lion award for sculpture at the Venice Biennale.

Major exhibitions of Wilson's work have been presented by the Museum of Fine Arts in Boston (*Robert Wilson's Vision*, 1991); the Centre Georges Pompidou in Paris (*Mr. Bojangles' Memory*, 1991); the Instituto de Valencia de Arte Moderno (1992); and the Boymans Museum, Rotterdam (1993). In 1993 Wilson was commissioned to design an installation for the Venice Biennale.

BIBLIOGRAPHY

Flakes, Susan. "Robert Wilson's *Einstein on the Beach.*" *Drama Review* 20 (December 1976): 69–82.
Kaplan, Peggy Jarrell. *Portraits of Choreographers.* New York, 1988.
Robert Wilson: From a Theater of Images. Exhibition catalog with essays by John Rockwell and Calvin Tomkins. Cincinnati, 1980.
Shyer, Laurence. *Robert Wilson and His Collaborators.* New York, 1989.

SILAS JACKSON and SETH GOLDSTEIN

WILSON, SALLIE (born 18 April 1932 in Fort Worth, Texas), American dancer and ballet director. The preeminent female interpreter of Antony Tudor's ballets during the 1960s and 1970s, Sallie Wilson became a leading dramatic ballerina during her thirty-year performing career. She began studying ballet at the age of twelve and later moved to New York, where she studied with Margaret Craske, Tudor, and Edward Caton. Accepted into Ballet Theatre in 1949, she joined the Metropolitan Opera Ballet, then under Tudor's direction, a year later. Her five years there inaugurated her intense and pivotal professional association with Tudor. Rejoining Ballet Theatre in 1955, she became a soloist the next year; her repertory included Myrtha in *Giselle* and Kristine in Birgit Cullberg's *Miss Julie.*

When the company suspended operations in 1958, Wilson joined the New York City Ballet, performing the Queen in Jerome Robbins's *The Cage,* Profane Love in Frederick Ashton's *Illuminations,* the Coquette in George Balanchine's *La Sonnambula,* and the Scherzo of his *Western Symphony.* Most notably, Martha Graham created the role of Queen Elizabeth in *Episodes* (1959) for her.

Returning to American Ballet Theatre in 1960, Wilson was promoted to principal in 1961. She had earlier danced Rosalind in *Romeo and Juliet* and "She Wore Perfume" in *Dim Lustre;* her Tudor repertory soon grew to include the lead roles in *Pillar of Fire, Jardin aux Lilas, Dark Elegies,* and *Undertow.* Hagar in *Pillar of Fire,* which she first danced in 1966, soon became Wilson's signature role; she was also acclaimed for her Lizzie Borden in de Mille's *Fall River Legend.* She danced lead roles in Fokine's *Les Sylphides,* de Mille's *Three Virgins and a Devil,* Tudor's *The Judgment of Paris,* José Limón's *The Moor's Pavane,* and Glen Tetley's *Sargasso.* She created roles in Robbins's *Les Noces* (1965), Alvin Ailey's *The River* (1970), and de Mille's *A Rose for Miss Emily.* She last performed with American Ballet Theatre in 1980.

Wilson often stages Tudor's ballets; she has assisted with American Ballet Theatre's revivals and has mounted productions for the Paris Opera Ballet and other companies worldwide. Her choreography includes *Liederspiel* (1978) and *Fête* (1979) for Arlington Dance Theatre, a three-act *Il Principe delle Pogode* (1979) featuring Carla Fracci, and *Idyll* (1986) for the Riverside Festival in New York. During the early 1980s she occasionally made guest appearances with smaller companies in New York and elsewhere.

BIBLIOGRAPHY
Gruen, John. *The Private World of Ballet.* New York, 1975.
Gruen, John. "Sallie Wilson Makes a Drama of Dance." *New York Times* (2 September 1979).
Wechsler, Bert. "Survivor: Sallie Wilson." *Ballet News* 3 (April 1982): 20–22.

SUSAN REITER

WINTERBRANCH. Choreography: Merce Cunningham. Music: La Monte Young; "Two Sounds" (April 1960). Costumes, object, and lighting: Robert Rauschenberg.

First performance: 21 March 1964, Wadsworth Atheneum, Hartford, Connecticut, Merce Cunningham Dance Company. Dancers: Merce Cunningham, Carolyn Brown, Viola Farber, Barbara Lloyd, William Davis, Steve Paxton.

Winterbranch is the last of four Cunningham works named after the seasons and the most controversial. The dance occurs in darkness; the dancers' movements are often barely visible, caught as if by accident by abruptly changing lights similar to automobile headlights suddenly illuminating objects or animals on a road at night. Robert Rauschenberg's lighting, which often used hand-held lighting instruments, was different in every performance and made an important contribution to the ambience of the work. The costumes were ordinary navy blue sweat pants and shirts, white socks, and deck shoes. Rauschenberg had the dancers put black horizontal smudges under their eyes, like those worn by football players. The effect was likened to commandos or prisoners of war.

The dance begins in silence. The stillness is broken by one and then another tape-recorded sound played at an extremely high volume over loudspeakers. One of the sounds was produced by scraping ashtrays against a mirror; the other was made by rubbing pieces of wood against a Chinese gong. The resulting sounds were so egregious that they occasionally drove people out of the theater. The movement vocabulary consists primarily of different kinds of falling, with bodies often dragged offstage. Even the leaps end in falls. A Rauschenberg "monster" (the dancers' affectionate name for a sculpture made from objects found backstage), lit from within and created anew for each performance, was pulled across the back of the stage in darkness, adding yet another menacing and mysterious element to the dance. The twenty-minute length of the dance is permanent, but its internal divisions of time and space are flexible.

Much performed on the 1964 world tour, *Winterbranch* was found haunting, strange, dramatic, disturbing, sinister, frightening; it was even likened to the Holocaust. In Essen, Germany, it received eighteen curtain calls, boos and catcalls mingling with bravos. *The Indian Express,* New Delhi (30 October 1964), called it "The most powerful and interesting work of the evening. . . . there is no way to judge it except to be exposed to it and feel its primeval impact." *Winterbranch* has no specific story, presents no particular mood. Its impact, perhaps more than with many other Cunningham works, depends upon what the individual viewer brings to the experience.

BIBLIOGRAPHY
Cunningham, Merce, in conversation with Jacqueline Lesschaeve. *The Dancer and the Dance.* New York, 1985.
Cunningham, Merce. *Changes: Notes on Choreography.* Edited by Francis Starr. New York, 1968.

CAROLYN BROWN

WIRTSCHAFT. A German court masquerade and entertainment of the seventeenth to mid-eighteenth century, the *Wirtschaft* (also *Wirthschaft, Wirtschafft;* pl., *Wirtschaften*) is lighthearted in nature and therefore was widely favored as an antithesis to the more formal court ballet. The main difference between the two forms is that in a *Wirtschaft* all present participated actively, supported by the artistic staff of the court dancing masters and their families, poets, and musicians, whereas in a ballet only a select few were performers while the rest of the court provided the audience.

The name *Wirtschaft* means "inn" or "hostelry" and set the theme for the activities. The sequence of events—some metaphorically related to the occasion (such as a princely visit or a birthday), others outright humorous, even raucous—unfolded in the setting of an inn, a *Wirtschaft*, a stopping place for a diversity of lower-class personages such as milkmaids, chimney sweeps, fools, drunkards, traveling entertainers with their monkeys, and schoolchildren, all performed by the members of the court and their guests. Characters called the *Wirt* and the *Wirtin* (innkeeper and his wife) were the official hosts of the event, played by emperor and empress (as in Austrian *Wirthschafften*), duke and duchess, landgrave and landgravine (as in Darmstadt). Both assumed additional roles during the course of the evening, as did the more prominent of the participating nobles.

The locale for a *Wirtschaft* was usually the main hall of the palace, transformed by strategically placed backdrops and props into a semblance of a rugged dining room: that the crystal chandeliers and brocade wall-coverings contradicted the feeling did not bother anyone. For such an occasion the palace itself was called *Gasthaus zum Weißen Adler* (Dresden, 9 February 1728), *Gasthaus zum Schwarzen Adler* (Vienna, before and during the reign of Maria Theresa), and the like.

On arrival the guests, lavishly attired in previously determined national, regional, and "lower-class" costumes, were greeted at the door by the *Wirt* and *Wirtin* and led to their places on chairs placed along the walls or at tables in cases where the *Wirtschaft* provided the framework for a banquet. One of the charms of this entertainment was the temporary suspension of the rigidly maintained hierarchical seating order that governed other spectacles of the period. A space was left open for the actual performance, which consisted of spoken and sung verses, reminiscent of the French *récits*, alternating with danced *entrées*, some fully laid out and carefully prepared by the court dancing master, others allowing for audience participation (*contredanses, quadrilles, cotillons*). In spite of the tendency toward increased realism in costumes, decorations, and dramatic action, *Wirtschaften* made concessions to the taste prevalent in high society: after the relaxed hilarity of the grotesque *entrées*, the final number tended to be a formal ballet, sung by a chorus accompanied by the full orchestra and danced by shepherds and shepherdesses.

The music, in every case specially composed, was written by the court composer, who also conducted the *Hofkapelle* from the harpsichord or the first violin's stand; were the size of the resident orchestra insufficient for a particularly splendid occasion (such as the *Wirthschaft* given in Darmstadt, November 1658, in honor of the visiting Cardinal Friedrich von Hessen, brother of the ruling landgrave), additional musicians were hired as reinforcements from a neighboring court or metropolis.

With the invention of the *Wirtschaft* and the stylistically related *Bauern-Hochzeit* ("peasant wedding"; see Böhme, 1886, p. 144; Gregor, 1944, p. 226), the aristocracy initiated a movement toward democratization, a conscious, albeit still playful, acknowledgment of the fact that the world of account extended beyond the palace gates. Subsequent manifestations of the same spirit were the *réceptions dans la campagne* initiated in the salon of the marquise de Mauconseil (Bie, 1919, p. 108), the *fêtes champêtres* throughout the eighteenth century, Baroque literature, and Jean-Jacques Rousseau's maxim, "Retour à la nature."

BIBLIOGRAPHY

Bie, Oskar. *Der Tanz.* 2d ed. Berlin, 1919.

Böhme, Franz M. *Geschichte des Tanzes in Deutschland.* 2 vols. Leipzig, 1886.

Gregor, Joseph. *Kulturgeschichte des Balletts.* Vienna, 1944.

Kaiser, Hermann. *Barocktheater in Darmstadt.* Darmstadt, 1951.

Kindermann, Heinz. *Theatergeschichte Europas,* vol. 3, *Das Theater der Barockzeit.* Salzburg, 1959.

Pasqué, Ernst. "Geschichte der Musik und des Theaters am Hofe zu Darmstadt." *Die Muse* (1853–1854).

Tintelnot, Hans. *Barocktheater und barocke Kunst.* Berlin, 1939.

INGRID BRAINARD

WITH MY RED FIRES. *See* New Dance Trilogy.

WOIZIKOWSKI, LEON (Leon Wójcikowski; born 20 February 1899 in Warsaw, died 23 February 1974 in Warsaw), Polish dancer, ballet master, and teacher. Trained as a dancer at the Wielki Theater School in Warsaw, Woizikowski joined the ballet company of the Wielki Theater in 1914, leaving it the following year to go to France and join the Ballets Russes de Serge Diaghilev. With the Diaghilev company, Woizikowski's remarkable gifts as a character dancer soon revealed themselves, and in the next five years he created a number of important roles in ballets of Léonide Massine. In addition to principal parts in *Las Meninas* (1916) and *Contes Russes* (1917), he created the roles of Niccolò in *Les Femmes de Bonne Humeur* (1917), the Manager in Evening Dress in *Parade* (1917), the Tarantella Dancer in *La Boutique Fantasque* (1919), the Corregidor in *Le Tricorne* (1919), and Fourbo in *Pulcinella* (1920). He frequently danced as partner to Lydia Sokolova, his offstage companion during the 1920s. A performer of enormous fire and virility who rivaled Massine in such parts as the Miller in *Le Tricorne*, he was equally memorable as the Polovtsian Chief in *Prince Igor* and in the title role of *Petrouchka*, bringing to Michel Fokine's choreography an admirable feeling for style, period, and dramatic effect.

In 1922, Woizikowski left the Ballets Russes, appearing at the London Coliseum (1922) and with Massine and Lydia Lopokova in *You'd Be Surprised* at Covent Garden (1923). Rejoining Diaghilev in 1923, he established himself as the company's leading character dancer, creating major roles in Bronislava Nijinska's *Les Noces* (1923), *Les Biches* (1924), and *Le Train Bleu* (1924) and in several George Balanchine works, including *The Prodigal Son* (1929). After Diaghilev's death, he appeared with Anna Pavlova's troupe (1929–1931), with Ballet Rambert (for which he staged Vaslav Nijinsky's *L'Après-midi d'un Faune* in 1931), with the Opéra Russe (1931), and with Colonel Wassily de Basil's Ballets Russes de Monte Carlo (1932–1934), creating roles in Massine's *Les Présages* (1933), and Balanchine's *Cotillon* (1932) and *La Concurrence* (1932). In late 1934, he left de Basil, and after a brief association with the Ballets Russes de Paris, he formed the Ballets de Léon Woizikovsky, which toured Europe and Australia under de Basil's auspices from 1936 to 1938.

Woizikowski returned to his native country in the late 1930s, heading a company of Polish dancers that performed at the 1939 World's Fair in New York. After World War II, he served as ballet master at the Warsaw State Opera, where he staged revivals of *Schéhérazade*, *Petrouchka*, and *L'Après-midi d'un Faune*. Between 1958 and his death, he worked mainly in the West, reviving, thanks to an extraordinary memory, various Diaghilev-era works for London's Festival Ballet, the Cologne Opera Ballet, and the Rome Opera Ballet, and serving on the faculty of Bonn's Rheinische Friedrich-Wilhelms-Universität.

BIBLIOGRAPHY

Garafola, Lynn. *Diaghilev's Ballets Russes*. New York and Oxford, 1989.

García-Márquez, Vicente. *The Ballets Russes: Colonel de Basil's Ballets Russes de Monte Carlo, 1932–1952*. New York, 1990.

Gockel, Eberhard. "Leon Woizikovski." *Ballet Today* (July–August 1969): 17.

Grigoriev, Serge. *The Diaghilev Ballet, 1909–1929*. Translated and edited by Vera Bowen. London, 1953.

Hall, Fernau. "Men in Ballet: Leon Woizikowski." *Ballet Today* (October 1958): 4.

Sokolova, Lydia. *Dancing for Diaghilev*. Edited by Richard Buckle. London, 1960.

Sorley Walker, Kathrine. *De Basil's Ballets Russes*. New York, 1983.

LYNN GARAFOLA

WORSAAE, JENS-JACOB (born 19 April 1946 in Jutland, died 8 August 1994 in Copenhagen), Danish stage and costume designer. Worsaae's designs for dance, which spanned the Russian classics, the works of August Bournonville, and new ballets, were characterized by elegance, lightness and sumptuous imagination. Working in Scandinavia, the United States, and elsewhere, Worsaae delighted in the process of collaboration and in using the full range of theater's resources, often combining fantasy renderings of period styles with contemporary stagecraft, such as lightweight costume materials and projections. He made imaginative use of stage space, breaking it up with subsidiary flats yet keeping a clear space for dancing. His costumes moved beautifully with the dancers and flattered individual physiques. His eye for color and detail led to dyeing techniques that produced gradations of tones, as in his costumes for Toni Lander and Bruce Marks's reconstruction of August Bournonville's *Abdallah*. He handled large-scale productions with zest and could adapt them to touring conditions.

As a youth Worsaae wanted to become a film director and haunted Copenhagen's film museum. While at the University of Copenhagen, however, he became involved with an experimental theater. He later studied at the Academy of Stage Design in Prague and gained further practical experience there. He would continue to design for drama, but he liked the freedom of dance as a less realistic art form.

His first dance design, in 1974, was for Flemming Flindt's *Felix Luna* in Göteborg, Sweden, followed by the first two of several ballets with Bruce Marks. His work in dance gained impetus in 1979 with commissions for Bournonville productions by the Soloists of the Royal Danish Ballet. Among his other designs for Bournonville works were several stagings by Kirsten Ralov, including the scenery for *A Folk Tale* by the Bolshoi Ballet.

Another of Worsaae's repeated collaborators was Anna Lærkesen, a former ballerina of the Royal Danish Ballet, who worked with him in original ballets for both that company and the San Francisco Ballet. Other major Royal Danish Ballet productions included Yuri Grigorovich's *Don Quixote* and Flindt's *Caroline Mathilde*. Worsaae also worked in various theaters with Ib Andersen, Peter Schaufuss, Elsa-Marianne von Rosen, Egon Madsen, and others. An important series of collaborations was with Helgi Tomasson at the San Francisco Ballet on *Intimate Voices, Quartette, Con Brio, Swan Lake, The Sleeping Beauty*, and *Romeo and Juliet*. Their *Swan Lake* had a Watteau-like pastoral quality and conveyed an atmosphere of heartless flirtation in the palace scenes, underscored by the refined tactile sensuousness of the costume materials.

One of Worsaae's last productions before his untimely death was a somewhat revised version of Tomasson's *The*

Sleeping Beauty for the Royal Danish Ballet. Set in Russia, it moves from the Oriental seventeenth century to Peter the Great's French-influenced eighteenth century, tempering sumptuousness with fairy-tale lightness and grandeur with Danish intimacy, and reflecting the round of the seasons, all with Worsaae's typically gracious imagination.

BIBLIOGRAPHY
Hunt, Marilyn. "Jens-Jacob Worsaae Sets a Sparkling Stage: Designing the Light Fantastic." *Dance Magazine* (April 1987): 48–52.
Matthew, Alanna. "The Magical Spaces of Jens-Jacob Worsaae." *Vandance International* 20 (Summer 1992): 12–13.

MARILYN HUNT

WRIGHT, PETER (born 25 November 1926 in London), British dancer, choreographer, director, producer, and teacher. A choreographer and producer with a gift for revitalizing the classics, Wright received his early training from Kurt Jooss and Sigurd Leeder while performing with the Ballets Jooss in England (1945–1946 and 1951–1952). He also studied with Vera Volkova and danced with several small ballet companies, including the Sadler's Wells Theatre Ballet (1949–1951 and 1952–1955), and in musicals and revues, before turning to choreography.

He made his first ballet, *A Blue Rose* (1957), for the Sadler's Wells Theatre Ballet. He made four more—of which *Mirror Walkers* and *Quintet* are the best known—for the Stuttgart Ballet, where he served under John Cranko as associate choreographer, ballet master, and teacher from 1961 to 1966. His first classical recension, the Stuttgart production of *Giselle* (1966), opened an important new chapter in his career. Highly praised for its period atmosphere and dramatic logic, it was acquired by both sections of England's Royal Ballet and by companies throughout the world.

Wright quickly followed that success with a new *Sleeping Beauty*, mounted in Cologne in 1967 and revised for the Royal Ballet, with additions by Frederick Ashton, in 1968. In 1984 Wright's first production of *The Nutcracker* was staged for the Royal Ballet.

During the late 1960s he traveled in Europe and America, teaching, choreographing, and producing the classics and his own works. He also worked extensively as a guest producer for BBC (British Broadcasting Corporation) television, where he had previously trained under Margaret Dale.

Wright returned to the Royal Ballet in 1970, as associate director in charge of the Touring Company and then as administrator of both the resident and the touring companies. In 1976 he became director of the Sadler's Wells Royal Ballet (as the Touring Company was named in that year), and he remained at the helm of that company, renamed the Birmingham Royal Ballet, from its arrival in Birmingham in 1990 until his retirement in 1995. As a ballet director he devised educational programs for young audiences and mounted new productions of *Coppélia*, *Swan Lake*, *The Sleeping Beauty*, *Giselle*, and *The Nutcracker*. He was awarded a CBE (Commander of the Order of the British Empire) in 1985 and was knighted in 1993.

BIBLIOGRAPHY
Crisp, Clement. "Peter Wright." *About the House* 3.7 (1970): 16–17.
Meisner, Nadine. "No Strings." *Dance and Dancers* (November 1990): 10–13.
Newman, Barbara. *Swan Lake: Sadler's Wells Royal Ballet.* London, 1983.
Newman, Barbara. "Speaking of Dance: Peter Wright CBE." *The Dancing Times* (March 1986): 506–507.
Thorpe, Edward. "Peter Wright, Pre-eminent Producer of the Classics." *Dance Gazette* (March 1985): 16–19.
Woodcock, Sarah C. *The Sadler's Wells Royal Ballet.* London, 1991.
Wright, Peter. "*Quintet* and *Summer's Night.*" *About the House* 1 (December 1964): 15–16.

BARBARA NEWMAN

WU XIAOBANG (born 18 December 1906 in Taicang County, Jiangsu Province, China, died 8 July 1995 in Beijing), dancer, choreographer, teacher, theoretician, and promoter of dance. Originally given the name Zupei and later Qiming, Wu took Xiaobang as his final and stage name because it sounds like "Chopin," the Polish pianist and composer, whom Wu admired both for his works and for his patriotism. Influenced by the "May Fourth" New Culture Movement in his teens and by Marxism and the goals of Sun Yat-sen (founder of the first republic of China) in his college years, Wu became an enthusiastic patriot.

Between 1929 and 1936, he went to Japan three times and studied ballet and Mary Wigman's expressionistic modern dance at the Takada Masao Dance Institute and at the Eguchi Takaya and Misako Miya Modern Dance Institute. He performed a dozen self-choreographed dances back in Shanghai, including *In a Funeral Procession*, *Puppet*, *Peace Fantasy*, *Clown*, and *Misery of Love*, laying the cornerstone for his "new dance" movement, although interest was at the time limited to elite circles.

In 1937 when the war against Japan (1937–1945) began, Wu became an activist dancer, taking part in the Shanghai National Salvation Performing Team. His solos included *March of the Volunteers* (the music of which became the national anthem of the People's Republic of China), *March of the Broadsword*, *Killing the Traitor*, *Exile Trilogy*, and *Song of the Guerrillas*. The first was danced five times at the front lines at the soldiers' request. During China's War of Liberation (civil war, 1945–1949), Wu pursued the creative and scientific methodology of German modern dance and choreographed realistic dances, using inspiration from the Tang dynasty and exposing the dark side of prerevolutionary China in such dances as *Ugly Boast of a Traitor, Messenger, Earthly Inclination, Hungry Fire, Mongolian Dance, Mongolian People's Trilogy, March Dance,* and the full-length dance dramas *Poppy Flower, Lord Tiger,* and *Pagoda and Memorial Gateway.*

After the People's Republic of China was founded in 1949, Wu devoted more time to experimental choreography, especially from 1957 to 1960, with his small experimental company, the Heavenly Horse Studio. The dances were set mainly to Chinese classical music, as music was integral with dance in Chinese tradition. He also conducted scholarly research, founding the Chinese Dance Art Research Society in 1954, and encouraged a group of young scholars to become the foundation of the Dance Research Institute. Established in 1974, it began systematic, in-depth study into ancient Chinese dance history. Sheng Jie, Wu's wife, took another group of young teachers to collect Chinese folk dances in the countryside, which laid a solid basis for the folk dance curriculum of the Beijing Dance Academy, of which Wu was appointed director of the Preparatory Committee. Wu also filmed Taoist and Confucian dances in their temples, preserving the only live images of these valuable dance rituals. He continued to teach his German-based but more realistic and political "new dance" to the first group of dance leaders in the People's Republic. Representative dances of this period included *Wintersweet Trilogy, Wild Goose in Migration, Wintersweet Drills, Happy Fisherman,* and *Ambush in All Directions.* Before and during the Cultural Revolution (1966–1976), he was persecuted for his individualism, independent tendency, emphasis on ancient themes, and works that seemed to have little to do with the excessive revolutionary fervor of the Chinese people during that period.

In 1978, two years after the Cultural Revolution ended, the Chinese Communist Party and central government began to adopt a more open policy; Wu was then appointed chairman of the China National Dance Artists Association and founding director of the Dance Research Institute, which rejuvenated him and allowed him to resume promulgating the "new dance." Unfortunately, he was over seventy by then and unable to perform. In 1982, he became the first adviser to master of arts in dance programs in China.

Wu published six books on dance theory as well as his autobiography, *My Career of Dance Art.* He also worked as editor in chief of three monumental projects in contemporary Chinese dance history: *Collection of Chinese National Folk Dances* (in more than thirty volumes), *The Chinese Encyclopaedia: Music and Dance Volume,* and *Contemporary China: Dance Volume.* In 1985 and 1990, the China National Dance Artists Association held two symposia on his lifelong contributions to all aspects of contemporary Chinese dance. He is the founder of modern Chinese theatrical dance, in both practice and theory.

[*See also* China, *article on* Contemporary Theatrical Dance.]

BIBLIOGRAPHY

Ou Jian-ping. "Dance Scholarship in China: Yesterday, Today, and Tomorrow." In *Documentation of Beyond Performance: Dance Scholarship Today,* edited by Susan Au and Frank-Manuel Peter. Berlin, 1989.

Ou Jian-ping. *The Modern Dance: Theory and Practice,* vol. 1.5, *Oh, My Great Motherland* (in Chinese). Beijing, 1994.

Ou Jian-ping. "From 'Beasts' to 'Flowers': Modern Dance in China." In *East Meets West in Dance: Voices in the Cross-Cultural Dialogue,* edited by John Solomon and Ruth Solomon. Chur, Switzerland, 1995.

Wang Ke-fen et al., eds. *A Dictionary of Chinese Dance* (in Chinese). Beijing, 1994.

Wu Xiaobang. *Introduction to the New Dance Art* (in Chinese). Shanghai, 1950. Rev. ed. Beijing, 1982.

Wu Xiaobang. *My Career of Dance Art* (in Chinese). Hong Kong, 1980. Rev. ed. Beijing, 1981.

Wu Xiaobang. *New Theory on Dance* (in Chinese). Shanghai, 1985.

Wu Xiaobang. *Anthology of Dance Theory* (in Chinese). Chengdu, 1986.

Wu Xiaobang. *Wu Xiaobang on Dance Theory* (in Chinese). Beijing, 1988.

Wu Xiaobang. *New Anthology of Dance Theory* (in Chinese). Beijing, 1989.

Ou JIAN-PING

X–Y

XIMÉNEZ-VARGAS BALLET ESPAÑOL. In 1955 a remarkable dance partnership was formed by Roberto Ximénez, a dancer of introspective dignity, and Manolo Vargas, who danced with a wild, highly personal style. Their Ximénez-Vargas Ballet Español, which lasted for a decade, was noted for its disciplined sense of theater and its attention to individual dancers. Over the years, they developed a repertory of great quality and dramatic power and some fine dramatic dancers, notably Maria Alba.

Both dancers are Mexican. Ximénez, the son of a businessman who loved the theater, attended the Escuela Nacional de Danza, studying Mexican, Spanish, Russian, and Asian dance, as well as Latin American folklore. He nearly completed a degree in chemical engineering before he returned to his interest in Spanish dance and formed his own company.

Unlike Ximénez, Vargas was discouraged by his rancher father from pursuing a dance career, but his mother, a former dancer, tutored him in secret. Later he took night classes at the Escuela Nacional. He took a job in a New York night club, where La Argentinita saw him and took him into her company in 1942.

After Argentinita's death, Vargas danced with Pilar López's Ballet Español, which Ximénez joined in 1948, replacing José Greco. The two Mexicans created a concert group in 1950 and left Lopez to form their own company in 1955, touring Europe, Asia, and the Americas. Their first United States appearance was in March 1958, and they gained immediate acclaim. Ted Shawn was particularly impressed, and they performed at Jacob's Pillow in the summers of 1958–1960, 1963, and 1964.

Both men acknowledge the profound influence Pilar López had on them, especially her uncompromising authenticity and her disciplined approach to every detail of a theatrical performance. Like Argentinita and Pilar López, their expressiveness was typical rather than individual; however, the style of their dances was very much their own and represented a new direction in the Spanish idiom. Whether tragic or humorous, their dances tended to be starkly, tersely dramatic. The two men spent hours with company members, learning their individual characteristics and exploring the motivation for each movement. The result, as critics observed, was that their dancers always seemed to know why they were onstage, and even very spare movements and gestures were highly expressive.

The most powerful of the Ximénez-Vargas dances were evocations of pure feeling. Of *Sin Quererlo Ni Buscarlo, Petenera, Petenera*—in which a courtesan meets her death in a jealous triangle—Doris Hering (*Dance Magazine*, April 1958) said, "The emotional line wove, like a surge of sea, through the innocent dance divertissements." The understated flaring and ebbing of emotional currents also characterized the humorous *De Querer Amores*, in which a rivalry between two women briefly sparks the interest of

XIMÉNEZ-VARGAS BALLET ESPAÑOL. Manolo Vargas and Roberto Ximénez in an athletic flamenco number. (Photograph from the archives at Jacob's Pillow, Becket, Massachusetts.)

men in a cafe. *La Monja Gitana*—in which two men come to life in a nun's memory, wrapping and unwrapping her in a long fabric like a cloud—is repeatedly cited for its taut symbolism.

Ximénez and Vargas were also known for their presentation of Latin American folk dances. The Spanish government granted them special permission to collect and record the regional dances of Spain.

The combination of Ximénez, Vargas, and Maria Alba, their leading female dancer from 1959 to 1963, was particularly felicitous; however, when Ximénez and Vargas began talking about retiring in late 1963, Alba and Ramon De Reyes left to form their own company. Ximénez and Vargas continued to perform in a quartet with Sara de Luis and Maria Dolores through 1964. Vargas now teaches yoga in Mexico City and continues to choreograph, including a solo version of *La Monja Gitana* for Pilar Rioja. Ximénez lives in Madrid, where he teaches dance in a private school.

BIBLIOGRAPHY

Marks, Marcia. "Ximénez-Vargas and the Dance of Spain." *Dance Magazine* (June 1962): 38–42.

Martin, John. "Dance: Spanish." *New York Times* (15 April 1962).

Pedroso y Sturdza, Dolores de. "Manolo Vargas." *Ballet* 11 (April 1951): 40–43.

Pohren, D. E. *Lives and Legends of Flamenco.* Madrid, 1964.

Reviews. *Dance Magazine* (August 1957, April 1958, January 1959, May 1962, January 1963, October 1964).

ARCHIVE. Dance Collection, New York Public Library for the Performing Arts.

JUDY FARRAR BURNS

XIMÉNEZ-VARGAS BALLET ESPAÑOL. *(above)* Manolo Vargas in a dance evoking the ancient indigenous cultures of Mexico. His elaborate ceremonial costume recalls figures from Aztec art. *(below)* Members of the Ximénez-Vargas company in a flamenco work. The couples awaiting their turn to dance provide the *palmas*, the syncopated handclapping accompaniment vital to many flamenco dances. (Photograph above by Anne-marie Heinrich; used by permission. Photograph below by John Lindquist; used by permission of the Harvard Theatre Collection, The Houghton Library.)

YAKKO AND KAWAKAMI, husband-and-wife *shinpa* company, the first Japanese theater group to tour abroad. Kawakami Otojiro (born 1 January 1864, died 11 November 1911) and his wife, Yakko (Kawakami Sadayakko; born 18 July 1871, died 7 December 1946), were colorful intercultural pioneers who opened bridges between Japanese and Western theatrical traditions at the turn of the twentieth century. While a knack for self-promotion and compromise may have resulted in an obscured place in modern theater history, their energies and achievements were significant.

Born into a poor samurai family, Kawakami came to Tokyo just as the shogunate was dissolving. Arrested numerous times for his political soapboxing, he began performing satiric songs, including his famous "Oppekeppe," as a way to continue his political attacks from a safe platform. Dabbling in *rakugo* storytelling and politics, he finally found his forte in *shinpa*, the nascent "new sect" theater movement that opposed *kabuki's* feudal themes and conservative stylization. Kawakami's barnstorming *shinpa* troupes achieved fame and intermittent fortune with productions based on contemporary political events. *Kawakami Otojiro's Battlefield Diary*, a production about Japan's success in the First Sino-Japanese War (1894–1895), featured realistic costumes and battle scenes, catapulting the young man to the largest theaters in Tokyo. *Shinpa* was highly naturalistic compared to *kabuki*: little makeup was used, the actors spoke fluidly, and stage assistants *(kurogo)* were not needed. So realistic were the costumes and acting style that there were reports that actors playing policemen and other villains were attacked by confused audience members.

Kawakami married Yakko, a spirited, high-class Tokyo geisha. In 1896, they raised funds to build the Kawakami-za, a European-style theater without the *hanamichi* (flower path) characteristic of *kabuki* theaters. Hoping to improve their flagging fortunes, husband and wife—along with a troupe of sixteen actors—embarked on a "study mission" to America and Europe in 1899. In San Francisco, Yakko joined the female impersonators onstage, to become the first Japanese woman to act since the shogunate had banned women from *kabuki* three hundred years earlier.

Attempting to distance themselves from the numerous Japanese vaudeville companies and to show their reformist interests, the troupe performed a mixture of ruthlessly edited *kabuki* standards such as *Dōjōji* and *Zingoro* (which they dubbed "A Japanese Pygmalion") and adaptations of Western drama *(Shylock, Sappho, Lady of the Camellias)*. During their eight-month tour of the United States, Kawakami refined their repertoire to give the public what it wanted—the blood-and-guts of the sword fighting, the static power of the pantomime scenes, the ele-

gance of Yakko's dancing, and numerous changes of gorgeous costumes.

Despite such exertions, the U.S. tour was poorly attended, although critics raved about Yakko's evocative dancing and heart-rending death scenes. Yakko appeared to use her geisha dance training to good effect, although the *kabuki*-like histrionics of Kawakami were often deemed unintentionally comic. Their most successful adaptation was *The Geisha and the Knight*, a combination of two *kabuki* plays, which displayed Yakko's dancing and acting talents as well as the troupe's acrobatic swordplay. The costumes, stage settings, and delicacy of emotional expression were well received, as critics marveled at these "woodblock prints come to life." Ironically, Yakko and Kawakami's "radical" *shinpa* troupe had become the promoter of *kabuki* tales of Japanese feudalism.

At the Paris Exposition of 1900, the American dancer, inventor, and producer Loie Fuller featured them at her theater, which was designed by Henride Toulouse-Lautrec. The hara-kiri death throes were so popular that Kawakami was asked to add them to every play. Fuller brought the company back a year later for a European tour, but, finding them expensive, she hired a Japanese dance-hall girl of fewer artistic pretensions, Hanako, and turned her into a star.

Meanwhile, Kawakami returned from his Western tours with pronouncements on the strengths of the European drama and a set of reforms: electric lighting, evening performances, tickets sold directly to customers (instead of through teahouse middlemen), and the separation of dance from drama. Trading on its firsthand experience with Western theater, the troupe produced Japanese versions of *The Merchant of Venice (Shylock)*, *Hamlet*—with Hamlet riding a bicycle down the *hanamichi* dressed in a contemporary school uniform—and *Othello*, with the Moor transformed into a Formosan general (the island of Formosa, now Taiwan, was then occupied by Japan, after its success in the First Sino-Japanese War).

Abroad, Yakko had been warmly received by Fanny Kemble, Eleanora Duse, Henry Irving, and Ellen Terry. Encouraged by the high esteem with which women in the acting profession were held in the West, Yakko and Kawakami in 1906 established the first Japanese school for actresses (it was taken over by the Imperial Theater in 1911).

Kawakami died of complications from appendicitis suffered in the United States. Yakko remained active in various theater reforms, giving her farewell tour as an actress in *Aïda* in 1917. She answered critics who complained of her "advanced" age (then only forty-six) by citing Sarah Bernhardt as an example.

Meanwhile, *shinpa's* revolutionary naturalism quickly became stale. *Shinpa* had caused *kabuki* to define itself as the classical theater, but the "new sect" was in turn displaced by *shingeki* as the contemporary, modern theater. *Shinpa* does continue today—but only as frozen melodramas set in the Meiji period (1868–1911).

BIBLIOGRAPHY

Berg, Shelley C. "Sada Yacco: The American Tour, 1899–1900." *Dance Chronicle* 16.2 (1993): 147–196.

Fuller, Loïe. *Fifteen Years of a Dancer's Life* (1913). New York, 1978.

Kei Shionoya. *Cyrano et les samurai: Le Théâtre Japonais en France et l'effet de retour.* Paris, 1986.

Kikou Yamata. "Sada Yacco et le Théâtre Japonais." *La revue de France* 19 (January–February 1939): 65–109.

Otojiro Kawakami and Sada Yacco. *Jiden: Otojiro Sada Yakko.* Edited by Sotetsu Fujii. Tokyo, 1984.

Pronko, Leonard C. *Theater East and West: Towards a Total Theater.* Berkeley, 1967.

Salz, Jonah. "Intercultural Pioneers: Otojiro Kawakami and Sada Yakko." *Journal of Intercultural Studies*, no. 20 (Winter 1993): 25–74.

Sevarese, Nicolas. "La peritpazazi emblematica di Sada Yacco." *Cippario Anno* 35 (1980): 5–31.

Yoko Chiba. "Sada Yakko and Kawakami: Performers of *Japonisme.*" *Modern Drama* 35 (March 1992): 35–53.

JONAH SALZ

YAKOBSON, LEONID (Leonid Veniaminovich Iakobson; born 2 [15] January 1904 in Saint Petersburg, died 17 October 1975 in Moscow), Russian dancer and choreographer. Upon graduation from the Leningrad Ballet School, where he studied under Vladimir Ponomarev, Yakobson danced at the Leningrad State Academic Theater for Opera and Ballet from 1926 to 1933, later becoming its choreographer (from 1942 to 1950 and 1956 to 1975); from 1933 to 1942 he was the choreographer for the Bolshoi Theater in Moscow. Yakobson performed several classical and character dances and roles: Puss in Boots in *The Sleeping Beauty;* the Acrobat in *The Red Poppy;* the Guest Dressed as a Bat in Fedor Lopukhov's new version of *The Nutcracker.* While still a student he began to mount concert pieces for his fellow pupils at the ballet school. When he graduated he was already a member of the Leningrad troupe and continued (without pay) as choreographer for the school. Roles Yakobson created for the junior pupils exhibited a gift for comedy and satire, while those choreographed for the senior grades attested to his enthusiasm for athletic and acrobatic movement. The second act and the dances in the first act of the ballet *The Golden Age,* staged at the Leningrad Opera and Ballet Theater in 1930 with Vasily Vainonen as artistic director, was the first important choreographic production by Yakobson. [*See* Golden Age, The.] His athletic dances for the Workers' Sport Club stadium conveyed the energy and dynamism of sporting events, expressing their competitive spirit and tension. In his one-act *Till Eulenspiegel* (1933), set to Richard Strauss's score, which he choreographed for the graduation recital at the ballet school, Yakobson

YAKOBSON. A scene from the Moscow production of *Shurale,* mounted at the Bolshoi Theater in 1955, with members of the original Bolshoi cast: Vladimir Levashev as Shurale, the wood goblin; Yuri Kondratov as Ali-Batyr, the hunter; and Maya Plisetskaya as Syuimbike, the enchanted bird-maiden. (Photograph from the A. A. Bakrushin Central State Theatrical Museum, Moscow.)

blended all of his comic dance novelties into an integral choreographic program.

The creative ideals of Yakobson's art were rooted in the trends in Soviet art in the 1920s that repudiated everything that had been created before, including classical dancing; things of the past were seen as products of courtly culture that had to be replaced by a new dance idiom capable of expressing the reality of the new era. Yakobson's preference for situations of sharp conflict along strong social, class, and political lines; his repudiation of classical dance and of the right of modern choreographers to use it; and his search for a dance idiom of his own in which dance movements were to be blended with pantomime were all reflections of those trends. Yakobson was a champion of the idea, popular in Soviet ballet in the 1930s, of injecting drama into ballet theater. He sought to invest each action with dramatic meaning and to make the portrayal of each character psychologically convincing. However, the predominant form of ballet in those years was alien to him; its forms followed the canons of classical ballet, alternating dances and pantomime scenes, and it also transplanted onto the ballet stage some of the conventional mechanics of dramatic theater. Pantomime acquired a larger role in ballet productions.

So unconventional were Yakobson's experiments that they effectively frightened off the audience. He composed little at that time, and his dance engagements were infrequent, but by the end of the 1930s he decided to compromise and make peace with classical dance, which had in the meantime regained its lead as an expressive mode in the art of dancing. He arranged and composed several recital divertissements, and in 1941 he choreographed *Shurale*, a three-act ballet with music by Farid Yarullin to be staged in Kazan. But World War II broke out, and *Shurale* was performed only at rehearsals. In 1950 it was finally presented by the Kirov Theater in Leningrad with the title *Ali-Batyr* and in 1955 by the Bolshoi Theater in Moscow. [*See* Shurale.]

Yakobson's *Solveig (The Ice Maiden)*, to Grieg's music, was produced in 1952 at the Maly Theater of Opera and Ballet in Leningrad. In it, Yakobson adhered to the themes and structure of Romantic ballet; *Shurale* had been conceived as a classical ballet. Yakobson gave a new meaning to each of these forms. The Ice Maiden, a fantastic being ruling over her kingdom, and Shurale, a wood goblin of Tatar lore, are both creatures inimical to humans. The kingdoms of ice and of the virgin forest, with evil reigning supreme in both, contrasted with the bright and merry worlds of the Norwegian and Tatar countryside. The classical dances in *Solveig* were reserved for scenes of fantastic imagery that gave beauty and an alluring appeal to the production. In *Shurale* the characters in

the scene in which the forest comes to life were grotesque, while the classical dance was used to represent birds-turned-maidens and their floating dances; classical movements were also used in the love scenes of the ballet. Although traditional in structure, both ballets asserted a new aesthetic in that their content and characters were interpreted purely by dancing.

In Aram Khachaturian's *Spartacus*, staged at the Kirov Theater in 1956 and at the Bolshoi Theater in 1962, Yakobson introduced no classical dances. Instead he developed the principles of free plastique dance and ancient dance stylization originally introduced by Isadora Duncan and Michel Fokine but disregarded in Soviet ballet for more than thirty years. Yakobson mounted a spectacular gala parade in which he juxtaposed the victorious, bellicose, and harsh Rome of patricians, the military, the troop leader Crassus, his retinue, and his sweetheart Aegina with the slaves, who were sold in the marketplace or forced to kill each other in the circus. The theme of challenging a tyrant's power was consonant with the quest for new means of expression that characterized Soviet art of the period. [*See* Spartacus.]

The new ideas and approaches introduced by Yakobson in *Spartacus* were taken a step farther in *The Bedbug* (1962), set to a score by Otkazov and Firtich, based on Vladimir Mayakovsky's eponymous comedy and some of his other poems, and in *The Twelve* (1964), to music by Boris Tishchenko, based on Aleksandr Blok's eponymous poem and staged in Leningrad by the Kirov Theater. The two ballets represented contrasting trends in Soviet postrevolutionary life: the corrupting influence of philistinism and of vulgar conventionality were the subject of

YAKOBSON. The Battle of the Gladiators from the Leningrad production of *Spartacus*, created for the Kirov Ballet in 1956. The two gladiators pictured are Yuri Maltsev (left) and Yuri Grigorovich (right), in the role of Rietiari. Yakobson's *Spartacus* was mounted in Moscow at the Bolshoi Theater in 1962 but was replaced in 1968 by a new production staged by Grigorovich. (Photograph from the Dance Collection, New York Public Library for the Performing Arts.)

The Bedbug; The Twelve celebrated the emergence of a new outlook on life and of a sense of responsibility for progress. Mayakovsky in the 1920s considered philistinism and vulgar conventionality to be vestiges of the past. Yakobson in his ballet showed how tenacious such remnants of the past were and how easily they degenerated into readiness to prey on and prosper at the expense of others.

In *The Bedbug* Mayakovsky, the central figure of the ballet, is seen by the audience inventing his characters on the stage, only to lose control over them almost immediately. The story of Prisypkin's marriage is the focal point of the ballet, which unfolds amid parasites and moneygrubbers of all sizes and shapes. Marriage is the logical culmination of Prisypkin's entire life, throughout which he excelled only as a conformist. Yet another landmark on Prisypkin's inglorious path is the suicide of Zoya Berezkina, the girl he had seduced. The climax of Prisypkin's aspirations, the episode on the vast nuptial bed that takes up the greater part of the stage evokes in the audience a feeling of disgust from watching a heap of swarming, blood-soaked bedbugs. The primacy of personal over public interests is the theme of the Red Wedding Party scene, in which the philistines march in triumph across the stage holding aloft great chunks of ham and wine bottles. The march proceeds against the background of the Russian Revolution and the civil war that followed: struck down by an enemy bullet a Red Army man drops dead; a Communist is knifed to death; a husband and wife find themselves on opposite sides of the political fence. In the revised version of *The Bedbug* (1974), set to Dmitri Shostakovich's music, Yakobson deleted the revolutionary scenes and stressed situations in which the negative and the alien were exposed and denounced.

In *The Twelve* the dynamic force of the Revolution was embodied in the figures of twelve Red Guard fighters, headed by Petrukha. In the opening scenes they are treated as a formidable and unbridled force, symbolizing the dispossessed, that is ready to destroy the old world, which is stumbling helplessly in a raging snowstorm in need of someone to guide it. In a honky-tonk scene the bar patrons register universal bewilderment in the face of the oncoming revolution and drown their fears in alcohol. Petrukha's murder of Katka, his bride-turned-prostitute, exemplifies the destruction wreaked by the Red Guards. The pangs of remorse expressed in Petrukha's solo that follows the murder scene lead to his regeneration and make him see his responsibility for all that has happened. By the finale the twelve Red Guards have turned into a well-organized force of like-minded men, and the experiences they lived through and paid for in blood make them a conscious revolutionary force with a moral right to change the world.

A follower of Fokine, Yakobson always found himself swimming against the current. He was against clichés and stereotypes in art. A choreographer whose aesthetic was expressed through choreography itself, he sought new idioms and forms and introduced into ballet the imagery and methods of related arts. Denunciation of evil and social vice became the central theme of all his creations, in which the new moral ideal of the hero was taking shape. *Love Stories* (1963), to Maurice Ravel's music, and *The Land of Miracles* (1967), to Isaac Shvarts, were among the last ballets that he choreographed for the Kirov Theater.

In mounting his productions Yakobson always included choreographic miniatures, either to introduce a theme or expand an episode, or to present an image not directly related to the theme. At the Kirov Theater in 1958 Yakobson presented his *Choreographic Miniatures,* which included his best numbers from the past and new arrangements, each of which was a short but complete ballet. The tragedy, comedy, satire, dialogue, and fairy-tale pieces were set to the music of both classical and contemporary composers and bore titles such as *Meditation, Rodin Triptych, Alborada, Skaters, Gossip,* and *Stronger Than Death.*

In 1969 Yakobson formed the troupe Choreographic Miniatures, which made its first public appearance in 1971. Although Yakobson revived some of his old pieces, the repertory was dominated by his new one-act ballets: *Exercise XX,* to Bach; *Contrasts, Traveling Circus,* and *Ebony Concerto,* to Stravinsky; *Jewish Wedding,* to Shostakovich; *Symphony of Eternity,* to Tishchenko; *The City,* to Webern; *A Brilliant Divertissement,* to Glinka; *Surprise,* to Haydn; and *Six Pas de Deux,* to Rossini, Chopin, Britten, Honegger, Lehar, and Donizetti. The best Yakobson miniatures: *Pas de Deux* to music by Mozart, *Pas de Quatre* to Bellini; *Paolo and Francesca* and *Minotaur and Nymph* to Alban Berg; *Troika,* to Stravinsky; *Baba-Yaga* to Mussorgsky; and *Snow Maiden* to Prokofiev.

Relinquishing some of the ideas of his younger days Yakobson, in the last stage of his career, made use of classical dance along with other forms of expression. He developed, transformed, and burlesqued classical dances and mounted compositions the subject matter of which could only be guessed. In the 1970s Yakobson again found himself in the forefront of Soviet ballet, anticipating its subsequent interest in the abstract presentation of humankind's spiritual and moral aspects.

BIBLIOGRAPHY

Demidov, Alexander P. *The Russian Ballet: Past and Present.* Translated by Guy Daniels. Garden City, N.Y., 1977.

Dobrovolskaya, Galina N. *Baletmeister Leonid Iakobson.* Leningrad, 1968.

Koegler, Horst. "Guests from Leningrad: Leonid Jakobson and His 'Choreographic Miniatures.'" *Ballett International* 12 (December 1989): 56–58.

Roslavleva, Natalia. *Era of the Russian Ballet* (1966). New York, 1979.

Ross, Janice. "A Survivor's Story." *Dance Magazine* (April 1988): 76–79.

Swift, Mary Grace. *The Art of the Dance in the U.S.S.R.* Notre Dame, 1968.

GALINA N. DOBROVOLSKAYA
Translated from Russian

YAKṢAGĀNA. The term *yakṣagāna* refers to several styles of dance drama in South India; this article focuses on those prevalent in the North and South districts of Kanara, Karnataka. Male performers enact stories from sacred Hindu texts, mainly the *Mahābhārata* and the *Rāmāyaṇa;* modern performances may also include local legends and new themes, as well as variations on traditional ones.

The styles of the different regions all employ vocal and instrumental music, dance, costume, makeup, and extemporaneous dialogue to tell the story; however, regional styles differ markedly in some respects. The northern style of South Kanara is known for an intricately wrapped headdress, fast steps requiring quick shifts in balance, and distinctive choreography to introduce characters; there are competitive performances in which two or more troupes portray the same stories simultaneously before the same audience. The southern style of South Kanara is famous for detailed philosophical argument, the bravado of demonic characters in varied makeup, whirling dances, and performances depicting the origin of the temple of each troupe.

The North Kanara troupes, although loyal to particular temples, are mostly family-directed. They employ flamboyant body stances, exaggerated facial expressions, and dramatic delivery of dialogue. Each troupe expresses its individuality in choreography, characters, costumes, and makeup.

Basic to traditional *yakṣagāna* is the coordination of body movement with the rhythms of the vocal and instrumental music, the latter provided by two drums—*maddale* and *caṇḍe*—and a pair of small cymbals. The story is explained through extemporaneous dialogue after each segment of music and dance, and the characters are identified through conventional costumes and makeup.

There is no recorded or oral tradition of the origin and development of *yakṣagāna.* It is generally believed that the performance was intended as an offering to a god by a patron in return for a fulfilled request. Performances took place after the rice harvest in a field where the setting was simply an area of ground demarcated by bamboo poles covered with palm frond mats, with lighting provided by torches. The play was free to the public. Although a few troupes employ similar staging to this day, most perform on raised stages in tents with spotlights and audio systems; admission is charged. About twenty-five troupes regularly perform in both Kanara districts from the end of November through May.

In the past, students attended small schools, now nonexistent, to learn the sacred texts they used in improvising dialogue. They learned music and dance from mas-

YAKṢAGĀNA. A procession of dancers from South Kanara, India, wearing characteristically elaborate headdresses. (Photograph from the archives of The Asia Society, New York.)

YAKṢAGĀNA. A *yakṣagāna* troupe includes at least two actor-dancers specializing in demon roles: a *rākṣasa vēśa* (seen here in a daylight portrait) and his demoness counterpart, the *rākṣasi vēśa*. Both men must be tall and sturdy, with broad faces, to bear the characters' heavy crowns and intricate rice-paste-and-pigment makeup. Their entrances are heightened with flaming torches, showers of crackling sparks, even small fireworks. (Photograph from the archives of The Asia Society, New York.)

ter performers in their homes and on the road from one performance to another, and by observing and participating in performances. Today there are temple, government, and privately supported schools and tutors.

Yakṣagāna has undergone many changes. Contact with the West, the impact of modern technology, and a desire to discard the old and bring in the new have influenced and altered it considerably. The adopted foreign elements and techniques obscure the remaining traditions and authentic styles of the troupes. Nevertheless, it remains a popular form of dance drama in South India.

BIBLIOGRAPHY

Ashton[-Sikora], Martha Bush, and Bruce Christie. *Yakshagana: A Dance Drama of India.* New Delhi, 1977.
Karanth, Kota Shivarama. *Yakshagana Bayalata.* Mysore, 1976.
Massey, Reginald, and Jamila Massey. *The Dances of India: A General Survey and Dancer's Guide.* London, 1989.
Massey, Reginald. "Yakshagana Indian Dance Drama." *The Dancing Times* (August 1990): 1084.

MARTHA BUSH ASHTON-SIKORA

YAMADA SETSUKO (born 25 December 1950 in Nagano City, Japan), *butō* performer and choreographer. While a student in the drama department of Meiji University in 1971, Yamada entered the Tenshi-kan *butō* training center, where she studied with Kasai Akira until 1979. She presented her first performance, *Lilac Garden,* a solo, in 1977. This was followed by dances such as *Balance of Ship* (1980), *Lion Heart* (1982), and *Crystal Vagina* (1983).

Yamada danced in Europe for the first time in 1983, when she was invited to perform at La Chartreuse in Villeneuve-lès-Avignon, France and at two festivals in Barcelona. At La Chartreuse, she received acclaim from dancer Carolyn Carlson. She toured in Europe again in 1984, earning raves as "a dancer who possesses extraordinary delicacy."

Yamada performed solo works in Seoul, Korea, in 1986 and 1987. She also choreographed for the Chang mu Dance Company, a troupe of traditional Korean dancers, and performed with them in 1988 and 1989. She collaborated with Jean-Michel Jarre in London in 1988 and with composer Carl Stone in Tokyo in 1989. From 1989 to 1991, she presented seven works in the series *Tentai no*

YAMADA SETSUKO. Wearing men's shoes, the Japanese choreographer appears here in her solo *Father* (1991). (Photograph © 1994 by Jack Vartoogian, used by permission.)

Aki. She choreographed *Father* in 1991, presenting it in Saint Petersburg, Russia, in Bucharest, Romania, as a delegate from the Japan Foundation in 1992, and in New York City in 1994.

Although her dance originated in *butō*, Yamada has created her own style with her own spatial awareness. Yamada's dances, most of which are solos, transform her inner consciousness and memory into movement. For example, her highly acclaimed *Father* was based on her recollection of her father, who had been a dancer in the Ishii Baku Modern Dance Company. The piece calmly evoked her strong tie with her father, her love for him, and complications of their relationship that could not be expressed verbally. The performance ended with lamentation.

Audiences have consistently been amazed at the beauty of Yamada's subtle movement and tensed forms and by the magnitude of the momentary metamorphoses that appear in her dances. Yamada's art is a pure dance of detailed movement and form.

BIBLIOGRAPHY
Hering, Doris. Review. *Dance Magazine* (January 1995): 112–113.
Jennings, Bernadine. "The Spirit Moves, through Sand." *Attitude* 10.4 (1994–1995): 63.

HASEGAWA ROKU
Translated from Japanese

YANG MEIQI (born 20 September 1945 in Shanghai), Chinese teacher, educator, and promoter of dance. In 1956 Yang was admitted to the National Dance Drama Section of the Beijing Dance Academy. After her graduation in 1963 she was assigned to teach Chinese folk dance at the Guangdong Dance School, where she excelled in training folk dancers. She also collected and compiled the local folk dances from fifteen areas in Guangdong Province and systematized them for teaching. In 1979, she was invited back to the Beijing Dance Academy as co-author of college-level teaching materials on Chinese folk dance. In 1983, she was invited by the Hong Kong Dance Federation to teach Chinese folk dance. A year later she was promoted to principal of the Guangdong Dance School, a position that she held until the end of 1995.

As a member of delegations of Chinese dance teachers and choreographers, Yang visited North Korea and the former Soviet Union. Early in the 1980s, when China's central government began to adopt a more open policy, she was greatly stimulated by the information that began to be available on Western modern dance; its educational and creative potential was made known by Chinese who had lived in or visited the West.

In 1986, recommended by Chiang Ching, Yang's former classmate at the Beijing Dance Academy and a New York–based Chinese-American modern dancer and choreographer, Yang had the opportunity to observe American modern dance in New York City and at the American Dance Festival, through a grant from the Asian Cultural Council. On this tour she realized that Western modern dance was indeed what she, her students, and her colleagues at home badly needed, and she determined to do everything possible to bring this creative dance form into China in a systematic way. Strongly supported by Charles Reinhart, director of the American Dance Festival, and Ralph Samuelson, director of the Asian Cultural Council, and encouraged by the Guangdong People's Provincial Government, Yang planned a four-year cooperative project—the "Guangdong Dance School: Modern Dance Experimental Class"—between the American Dance Festival and her school, begun in September 1987.

In July 1990, the Guangdong Dance School Modern Dance Practice Company was formed for the purpose of getting more stage and touring experience. The company impressed audiences at the Fifth Hong Kong International Festival of Dance Academies in July 1990, the Indian International Dance Festival at the end of the same year, and the American Dance Festival in July 1991, performing the students' own compositions. In November 1990, Qin Liming and Qiao Yang, two student members, won a gold medal for pas de deux at the Quatrième Concours International de Danse de Paris with two dances—*Taiji Impression,* choreographed by themselves, and *Ancestral,* choreographed by Willy Tsao, founder, director, and choreographer of the Hong Kong City Contemporary Dance Company.

In May 1992, the first professional modern dance company in mainland China, the Guangdong Modern Dance Company, was officially founded in Guangzhou (Canton), the capital city of Guangdong Province, with Yang as its managing director and Tsao as artistic director. A celebration gala was staged on 6 June at the local Friendship Theater. Under the leadership of Yang and Tsao, the company has successfully toured Singapore, France, Germany, Austria, Korea, and other locales, receiving acclaim from both audiences and critics. As a result of Tsao's involvement, Yang frequently took the company to Hong Kong, where they danced both independently and with the City Contemporary Dance Company.

Yang has published many articles on folk and modern dance. Her recent "Chinese Characteristics Are the Creative Root of the Guangdong Modern Dance Company" is regarded as her public manifesto on Chinese modern dance. She has also served as vice-chairman of the Guangdong Provincial Dance Artists Association, a member of the Guangzhou Municipal Arts Educational Committee, deputy director of the China National Dance Teaching Society, and a member of the China National Dance Artists Association, the Hong Kong Academic Examination and Inspection Bureau, and the Guangdong Provincial People's Political Consultative Conference.

[*See also* China, *article on* Contemporary Theatrical Dance.]

BIBLIOGRAPHY

Ou Jian-ping. *The Modern Dance: Theory and Practice*, vol. 1.5, *Oh, My Great Motherland* (in Chinese). Beijing, 1994.

Ou Jian-ping. "From 'Beasts' to 'Flowers': Modern Dance in China." In *East Meets West in Dance: Voices in the Cross-Cultural Dialogue*, edited by John Solomon and Ruth Solomon. Chur, Switzerland, 1995.

Wang Ke-fen et al., eds. *A Dictionary of Chinese Dance* (in Chinese). Beijing, 1994.

World Ballet and Dance 1–4 (1989–1993). Each volume contains an annual overview of the national dance situation in mainland China by Ou Jian-ping.

Yang Meiqi. "Chinese Characteristics Are the Creative Root of the Guangdong Modern Dance Company" (in Chinese). *Guangdong Magazine*, no. 2 (1994).

Yang Meiqi. "Bringing Modern Dance to China." In *East Meets West in Dance: Voices in the Cross-Cultural Dialogue*, edited by John Solomon and Ruth Solomon. Chur, Switzerland, 1995.

OU JIAN-PING

YAP. *See* Micronesia.

YAQUI DANCE. The Yaqui homeland is in the state of Sonora, Mexico. They had their first significant contact with Jesuit missionaries in 1617. By the mid-1600s, the Yaqui had incorporated Roman Catholicism into their religious system and had developed a Passion play (a play enacting the Passion of Jesus) that is among the oldest still being performed.

There are several Yaqui villages in Arizona established in the nineteenth century, when hundreds of Yaquis crossed the border as political refugees. In order to maintain their tribal identity and their syncretic form of Catholicism, they fled from the repressive Mexican government of Porfirio Diaz.

Men take part in Yaqui Catholic ceremonies to fulfill a vow given by or for an individual. This involves participation in one of several ceremonial groups that require public performances. Women do not fulfill their vows by dancing; instead, they participate in work or singing groups. Among the Arizona Yaqui there are four ceremonial dance groups for men: the Matachini, Fariseo, Caballero, and Fiesta dancers.

The Matachini society, dedicated to the Virgin Mary, dances several times a year. Musicians accompany the dancing with song, guitars, violins, and the Yaqui harp, while the dancers shake rattles. Matachini dance choreography is reminiscent of European folk dances, exemplified by the maypole dance performed on Holy Saturday. The Matachini are considered to be forces for good in the conflict between good and evil of the Passion play.

The Fariseo (Pharisees) personify the forces of evil in the Passion play. Actually dedicated to Jesus, the members pretend that Judas is their patron saint. Some of the members, called *chapayeka*, represent the common soldiers of ancient Rome, then the occupying force in the Near East. These masked figures are both comic and sinister. Not allowed to speak, they communicate by pantomime, hitting wooden swords and daggers together and shaking belt rattles of animal hooves. This "language" is highly stylized and is limited to the *chapayeka*.

In the numerous processions of the Passion play, both the Fariseo and Caballero society members march in file to the sounds of drum, flute, and striking wooden swords and to the noises made by the *chapayeka*. At the conclusion of the Passion play on Holy Saturday, the marching is characterized by a variety of step and tempo changes. The Caballeros change allegiance from evil to good during the final stages of the Passion play and do not participate in the dramatic procession on Holy Saturday, so their dance performances are limited.

The Fiesta dancers include the Pascola group and the Deer dancer *(maso)*. The Pascola have small masks that they wear on the sides of their heads while acting as ritual clowns and ceremonial hosts, and on their faces when they pretend to hunt the Deer dancer. During the unmasked dancing, the musicians play violins and harps. The dance includes rapid shuffling of the feet while the hands dangle near the knees. Ankle rattles and bells that hang from the waists of the Pascola dancers provide self-accompaniment. When they perform with the Deer dancer they play sistrums, and a single musician plays a flute and tambour simultaneously.

Shaking hand rattles made of gourds, leg rattles of cocoons, and hip rattles of deer hooves, the Deer dancer reacts to the music of the singers and musicians, who play rasps and a gourd water-drum. On a restricted ground space, with a deer head attached to the crown of his head, the Deer dancer combines dance movements with pantomime to suggest the motions of a deer. Like all Yaqui dancers, he dances in a ceremonial context. He and the Pascola dancers are considered to be magical forces for good.

[*See also* Matachins, *article on* Matachines Dances in the Southwestern United States; *and* Native American Dance.]

BIBLIOGRAPHY

Painter, Muriel T., and E. B. Sayles. *Faith, Flowers, and Fiestas: The Yaqui Indian Year*. Tucson, Ariz., 1962.

Painter, Muriel T. *A Yaqui Easter*. Tucson, Ariz., 1971.

Painter, Muriel T. *With Good Heart: Yaqui Beliefs and Ceremonies in Pascua Village*. Tucson, Ariz., 1986.

CARLOS LOZANO

YEMEN. Located at the southwestern corner of the Arabian Peninsula, Yemen borders on Saudi Arabia to the north and northeast, the Red Sea to the west, the Indian Ocean to the south, and Oman to the east. An estimated 13 million people live in about 205,000 square miles (528,000 square kilometers), stretching from an arid coastal zone to high mountains and a central plain. Before Islam there were a succession of wealthy South Arabian kingdoms, including the fabled home of the biblical queen of Sheba and the site of the Marib dam mentioned in the Qur'ān. In the medieval period Yemen was renowned for its agriculture and pivotal role in Red Sea–Indian Ocean trade, especially from the port of Aden. Yemen was isolated from the turmoil of the Crusades that influenced the history of much of the Middle East and the Mongol invasion that resulted in the destruction of the ʿAbbasid caliphate. The more populous North Yemen was dominated by a Zaydī religious imamate until the revolution in 1962 created the Yemen Arab Republic. The Zaydī imams, who claimed descent from the Prophet Muḥammad, were originally invited to Yemen by the tribes, who remain the dominant power brokers through the present. The South was colonized by the British in the early nineteenth century, owing to its strategic location on the sea route to India, until a Marxist revolution in 1967 created the Peoples' Democratic Republic of Yemen. Until recently, Yemen was a subsistence-based economy with few indigenous industries. During the 1970s and 1980s up to a third of the male labor force worked outside the country and sent back remittances. Oil was discovered in Yemen in 1984, although production is not as great as in the other states on the Arabian Peninsula. In 1990 North and South united into one country, the Republic of Yemen.

Traditional Dance. A strong, diverse dance tradition reflects the country's ecological and social diversity. Dancing and music are popular throughout Yemen, and the ability to dance is often equated with being Yemeni. Each community has its own dances, which may differ from each other in tempo, movements, and gestures; number and gender of performers; musical accompaniment; and in the appropriate occasions for their performance. Some dances are lively, with a fast tempo and many skips and jumps, whereas others are dignified and subdued, like the Bird Dance of Suḥār in the northern region. In this dance men, wearing robes with wide sleeves that fall like birds' wings, glide slowly and rhythmically, arms outstretched, in imitation of birds in flight. The dances may be performed by men or women. In some communities men and women dance together on a regular basis; in others they do so only in intimate contexts. Yemeni dancing is performed largely by nonprofessionals, although professional dancers are found in the southern highlands and on the Red Sea coastal plain, which is called the Tihama. As a rule, professional musicians accompany dancing on festive occasions.

Yemeni dances utilize weight shifts that are common to other Middle Eastern dance traditions, although the ways in which these are combined result in a typical Yemeni "look." The dances are characterized by intricate steps, outlined shapes on the ground, frequent turns, and moving forward and backward in a deep knee bend. Other steps include walking, the grapevine and its variations, hops, skips, and jumps. The torso is usually held erect, although some dances involve shimmying the hips or the shoulders, or swinging the head and hair with a movement initiated in the upper torso. The men usually carry daggers, sticks, or rifles when dancing. A number of dances accompany sung poetry, and most songs are set to dance music.

Traditional categories include men's dances performed to the accompaniment of drums or chanted poetry; couple dances; and dances in threes performed by men, women, or both. Solos may include the juggling of knives or other demonstrations of acrobatic skill. The religious dancing of the Sufi orders can be seen on the coastal plains and in parts of the southern highlands. *Zār* (the healing ceremony) is performed on the coastal plains. [*See* Zār.]

Dances in the eastern portions of the country include variations of the *bālah*, in which two lines of dancers are separated by a poet. The dancers repeat the verses recited by the poet and then move to the beat of drums (sometimes to other musical instruments as well), while the poet composes another verse. Several poets may compete in a contest of poetic repartee. This genre of dancing may be performed by men, women, or mixed groups, depending on the community and the context of the performance; it is known as *ẓaff* in Yafiʿ. In the northern Tihama region similar line dances, known as *farsānī*, are performed by men only.

The *zubayrī* is a couple dance performed in the evenings in the southern highlands. Another dance from this area is the *ḥawṭī*, performed by male professional dancers to the beat of drums. It involves high jumps and the twirling and juggling of daggers. In the northern highlands, only men perform line dances. Couple dances and dancing in threes are performed by men or women. In Razih, in the northermost part of the country, the *ghārah* is performed by men to sung poetry, while the *darimah* involves shooting rifles in the air. Women perform a dance in threes called *mathlūth*, in which they weave slow figure eights.

In the Ḥaḍramawt region in southern Yemen, where social stratification was traditionally more rigid than in the north, dances were classified according to the performers' social strata. Traditionally, the *zarbādī* was performed during the ibex hunting season, and the *sharḥ al-rayyid*, in which dancers run across a circle, was performed by members of the elite. This dance included high jumps and deep knee bends. The women's version of this dance is similar to the men's, with smaller changes in level. Merchants and craftsmen performed the *shabwānī*, a line dance accompanied by responsorial poetry. Laborers performed a dance called *luʿbah*, characterized by swinging the body above the waist. Another version of this dance was performed by a man and woman in the midst of a circle of men. The *sharḥ dhāhirī* resembles the *bālah* described above.

Dances performed by men in the Tihama coastal region typically include juggling acts and high jumps. A line dance that has been compared to the Levantine *dabkah* is performed in the northern Tihama.

There are dances associated with various occupations—the tobacco dance, performed by tobacco farmers, and the dances performed by fishermen. Other activities, technically not dancing, are classified as dancing in Yemen. One of these is *raqṣat al-ḥammām*, the bath dance, performed to song and a rhythmic sh-sh-sh sound voiced by the performers. This dance is not aesthetic but a way for performers to work up a sweat before taking a traditional steam bath. Another example is the footwork involved in sowing seeds; the farmer's rhythmic step is considered dancelike.

Imam Yaḥyā, the Islamic ruler of North Yemen from 1914 to 1948, banned the playing of the oud (lute) and *mizmār* (double-reed pipe) and the dancing that accompanied them. The ban was made ostensibly on religious grounds, but apparently also in reaction to the criticism

YEMEN. *(top and bottom)* Men performing a traditional *baraʿ* in a cleared area used as a parking lot in the village of Al-Ahjur. They are wearing everyday dress—a robe or shirt and skirt under a Western-style jacket—and carrying knives in their right hands. (Photographs 1978 and 1979 by Daniel Martin Varisco; courtesy of Najwa Adra.)

and revolutionary ideas aired in songs and at musical sessions. This ban had the effect of forcing urban music and dancing underground. Ironically, Yemeni dancing continued to flourish even while the ban was in effect. Windowless basement rooms were furnished to permit music and dancing that would not be heard by the imam's guards; people also stuffed their windows with cushions so that the music could not be heard outside. A smaller oud, which could be hidden under clothing, was developed. Some musicians immigrated to Ḥaḍramawt, where they established schools of Yemeni classical music, each of which is associated with a particular dance. Rural dancing continued virtually undisturbed.

The ban on dancing did not include *baraʿ*, a men's dance performed in the highlands to the beat of drums alone. Commonly, the dancers place themselves one behind the next in an open circle, wielding daggers in their right hands. They move forward, backward, and sideways. In parts of the dance they turn so that they are standing side by side and then all move together in one direction. The steps are variations of the grapevine, combined with step-together-step hops, punctuated by turns and deep knee bends. The dancers' eyes are focused on the leader, who dances near the middle of the line, directing movements and initiating changes in tempo. The performance is judged successful to the extent that the dancers achieve an extremely difficult coordination among themselves and with the drummers.

In some areas, the entire male population of a village or group of villages performs together; in others, *baraʿ* involves only two or three men at a time. Each tribe's *baraʿ* traditionally differed from that of others and served as one of the tribe's identifying markers. This dance is performed during religious and national holidays, at specific points during wedding festivities, on the road by traveling companions, at home to welcome important visitors, and during cooperative work projects (e.g., building a school or mosque, cleaning out cisterns used in agriculture). Traditionally, during work projects one half of the group would perform *baraʿ*, while the other half worked (those who worked chanted short work songs); performers and workers alternated for the duration of the project. In Yemen, *baraʿ* traditionally represented the concept of tribalism, with its emphasis on coordination and group cohesion (Adra, 1982, 1984). It does not share the connotation of frivolity that marks other genres of dancing; in fact, its performance in public is highly respectable. Even heads of state and other notables can be seen performing *baraʿ* at official functions.

In opposition to *baraʿ* are varieties of *luʿbah* couple dances accompanied by song and oud in towns or the *mizmār* in rural areas. Appropriate songs include love songs as well as praises to the Prophet Muḥammad. In many cases, song lyrics speak directly to events in the lives of the dancers. These dances are performed indoors in the evenings at weddings and other celebrations but may be performed at any small gathering of friends or relatives. Traditionally, they were also performed after the harvest. Typically, *luʿbah* is performed by two men at men's parties, two women at women's parties, or by a man and woman together in the intimacy of the home. Whereas performing *baraʿ* is considered honorable and dignified, performing *luʿbah* is considered frivolous—although not necessarily dishonorable when it is performed in appropriate contexts. Symbolically, these dances represent cultural emphases on personal autonomy and on sentiments of love and affection that stand in opposition to the ethic of responsibility and group cohesion signified by *baraʿ*.

Rapid social and economic changes in Yemen have affected dancing behavior. The traditional couple dance of the northern highlands until the 1970s was the *lāʿibīyah*. This dance is composed of a series of slow knee bends combined with small weight shifts from one foot to the other. In 1980, only older people were performing this dance. More popular dances, known simply as *luʿbah* or *raqṣ* ("dance"), focus on complicated footwork performed to intricate cross rhythms. By the late 1980s, a couple dance originally from Lahj in southern Yemen had become popular in the northern cities, where it was known as *Lahjī*. This dance is a fast-paced, light, gliding dance. It is easier to learn than the traditional northern *luʿbah*.

Changes have not been limited to *luʿbah* performance. There has also been a shift in performance contexts and in the significance of *baraʿ* in many parts of Yemen. Where tribal government has declined in importance relative to that of the national government, the primary locus of identification has shifted from the tribe to the nation: Yemenis now see themselves as Yemeni nationals first and then as members of a particular tribe. Consequently, *baraʿ* performance has shifted to towns and cities and is perceived as a national dance, representing the cohesiveness of the state.

Yemeni dancing has undergone further changes since the 1970s, with exposure to and influences from abroad. There is a decline in the amount of dancing performed at informal get-togethers at home, as television viewing fills leisure hours. The amount of dancing at formal celebrations has also declined. This is the result of both the significant rise in fees charged by professional musicians and of increased religious conservatism. Increased mobility and access to television have, however, expanded nearly everyone's knowledge of and repertory of dances, as Yemeni men and women learn to perform dances of other regions and other countries.

[*See also* Middle East.]

BIBLIOGRAPHY

Adra, Najwa. "Qabyala: The Tribal Concept in the Central Highlands of the Yemen Arab Republic." Ph.D. diss., Temple University, 1982.

Adra, Najwa. "Achievement and Play: Opposition in Yemeni Tribal Dancing." In *Proceedings of the Consulting Seminar on the Collecting and Documenting of the Traditional Music and Dance for the Arabian Gulf and Peninsula, 15–19 December 1984.* Doha, Qatar, 1984.

Adra, Najwa. "Tribal Dancing and Yemeni Nationalism: Steps to Unity." *Revue du Monde Musulman et de la Méditerranée* 67 (1993).

Botta, Paul-Émile. *Relation d'un voyage dans l'Yémen.* Paris, 1880.

Harris, Walter B. *A Journey through the Yemen and Some General Remarks upon That Country.* London, 1893.

Hunter, Frederick M. *An Account of the British Settlement of Aden in Arabia.* London, 1877.

Ingrams, Harold. "A Dance of the Ibex Hunters in the Hadramaut: Is It a Pagan Survival?" *Man* 37 (1937).

Lāmī, Majīd al-. "Al-Yaman wa-al-turāth al-shaʿbī." *Al-turāth al-shaʿbī* 5 (1974).

Myers, Oliver C. "Little Aden Folklore." *Bulletin de l'Institut Français d'Archéologie Orientale* 44 (1947).

Qāsimī, Khālid al-, and Nizār Ghānim. "Al-mūsīqā al-humāsīyah fī al-khalīj wa-al-Yaman." *Al-ma'thūrāt al-shaʿbīyah* 2 (1987).

Qāsimī, Khālid al-. *Awāṣir al-ghinā'iyah bayna al-Yaman wa-al-Khalīj.* Beirut, 1988.

Rihani, Amin. *Around the Coasts of Arabia.* London, 1930.

Scott, Hugh. *In the High Yemen.* London, 1942.

Serjeant, R. B., ed. *Prose and Poetry from Ḥaḍramawt.* London, 1951.

Serjeant, R. B. "The Ma'n 'Gypsies' of the West Aden Protectorate." *Anthropos* 56 (1961).

Serjeant, R. B. *South Arabian Hunt.* London, 1976.

Skene, R. "Arab and Swahili Dances and Ceremonies." *Journal of the Royal Anthropological Institute* 47 (1917).

Stark, Freya. *A Winter in Arabia.* London, 1941.

Stone, Francine, ed. *Studies on the Tihāmah: The Report of the Tihāmah Expedition 1982 and Related Papers.* Harlow, 1985.

NAJWA ADRA

YERMOLAYEV, ALEKSEI (Aleksei Nikolaevich Ermolaev; born 10 [23] February 1910 in Saint Petersburg, died 12 December 1975 in Moscow), dancer, choreographer, and teacher. Yermolayev studied from 1921 to 1926 at the Leningrad Choreographic Institute under the tutelage of Vladimir Ponomarev. Yermolayev's talent was manifested early. His intelligence, single-mindedness, and determination allowed him to complete in only five years the eight-year program at the school. His graduation performance was in the role of Vayu, god of the wind, in Marius Petipa's *The Talisman*, upon which he was taken into the parent company and immediately became a solo dancer.

While still a student, absorbing and perfecting the heritage of generations of dancers, he began to seek out the new. What fired his imagination was the challenge of expanding the language of male dancing by devising new movements and searching for heroic characters consonant with the new times. In 1930, when he joined the Bolshoi Theater troupe in Moscow, he was already a star. He danced the leading roles in the classical repertory but especially stood out for the range of major roles he created in his contemporaries' ballets, such as Vasily Vainonen's *The Flames of Paris* and *Mirandolina*, Rostislav Zakharov's *The Bronze Horseman* and *The Fountain of Bakhchisarai*, and Leonid Lavrovsky's *The Red Flower* and *The Tale of the Stone Flower*. The ballerina Marina Semenova, Yermolayev's contemporary, said of him that his uninhibited temperament, stamina, and technical brilliance roused audiences. His art heralded the advent of a new style that asserted the strong and heroic in classical dance. His dancing gave the impression of risk, of bold and innovative interpretations, which was true even of the traditional roles. Yermolayev's supremacy at characterization was unchallenged. The veteran Moscow Maly Drama Theater actress Elena Gogoleva said that he lived his roles; with his perfect command of technique he also offered a meticulously acted rendering of a role.

Although filled with advanced ideas, Yermolayev's choreographic output was small. At the Belarussian Opera and Ballet Theater he choreographed two ballets: *The Nightingale* (1939), to Mikhail Kroshner's score, and *Fiery Hearts* (1954), to Vasily Zolotarev's music. According to contemporary accounts, in staging these ballets he displayed daring and imaginative innovation. *Peace Will Prevail Over War* (1952) was a concert piece to the music of various composers. Directed, choreographed, and danced in by Yermolayev, it proved that modern themes could be adapted to the ballet stage. He also choreographed several *divertissements*.

Upon his retirement from dancing after a career at the Bolshoi that spanned the years 1930–1958, he channeled his energies into coaching the company from 1960 until his death, and teaching from 1968 to 1972 at the Moscow School of Choreography. There, he devised an unusual system of training dancers; his lessons and dance sessions resembled a creative laboratory in which new movements and means of expression were tested on a daily basis. Legends about Yermolayev's classes gained wide currency and are still in circulation. He schooled a galaxy of gifted dancers, among them Vladimir Vasiliev, Mikhail Lavrovsky, Vladimir Tikhonov, and Yuri Vladimirov. These dancers promoted the strong male dancing conceived by their teacher. They inherited from him a gallant attitude toward their art, a lack of complacency about their accomplishments, and the methods of rehearsing roles that he had perfected. Yermolayev is credited with instilling in them a savor for self-discovery and a stimulating creative drive, the qualities that were his hallmarks.

In 1970 Yermolayev was honored with the title People's Artist of the USSR after having won several state prizes.

BIBLIOGRAPHY

Bazhenova, T. P., ed. *Aleksei Ermolaev* (in Russian). Moscow, 1982.

Beaumont, Cyril W. "The Nightingale." In Beaumont's *Supplement to Complete Book of Ballets*. London, 1942.

Churova, Marina, ed. *Aleksei Ermolaev* (in Russian). Moscow, 1974.

Lawson, Joan. "A Short History of the Soviet Ballet, 1917–1943." *Dance Index* 2 (June–July 1943): 77–96.

Mamontov, George. "Two Dancers: Alexei Yermolayev and Vakhtang Chabukiani." In *The Soviet Ballet*, by Yuri Slonimsky et al. New York, 1947.

Smakov, Gennady. *The Great Russian Dancers*. New York, 1984.

Volkov, Nikolai D. "Distinguished Artists of the Moscow Ballet." *The Dancing Times* (October 1944): 13–14.

BORIS B. AKIMOV
Translated from Russian

YE SHAOLAN (born 1943 in Beijing), Chinese opera actor specializing in *xiaoshen* roles. Among the acknowledged stars of Chinese classical musical drama—in particular those who specialize in the *xiaoshen* role (young heroes, scholars, government officials, or generals)—Ye Shaolan is a premier artist, named by the People's Republic of China as a national treasure. Born in 1943 in Beijing, he is in the fourth generation of an established line of Beijing Opera performers, the tradition passing from father to son. His father, Ye Shenglan, was the leading man in a famous troupe that was invited to Paris, receiving adulatory critical response and the praise of Charlie Chaplin. He began to train his son in the art of young male roles when the boy was seven years old. Ye Shaolan remembers standing on one leg, the other on a high fence (undoubtedly as his father had before him), shivering in his underwear in the snow, sweating in padded winter garments in the heat of summer, training to concentrate on reciting lines and singing arias while disregarding physical discomfort. Until his father's death during China's Cultural Revolution of 1966 to 1976 (when classical opera was forbidden), the father continued to train his son secretly; with a return to normalcy, the son emerged in his father's place.

Ye Shaolan was formally educated at the Chinese Academy of Operas in Beijing, graduating in 1962; he completed further studies in the Directing Department of the Central Institute of Drama (1972). Throughout those years he was also tutored by Ru Fulan, Jiang Miaoxiang, Xiao Lianfang, Yu Zhengfei, and Yan Qinlin, all renowned artists in Beijing Opera. He had not only the best academic training available but also personal guidance from great performers. As a result, he excels in all aspects of his art, acting, singing (imitating and developing the voice skills of the great Beijing Opera actor Qiu Shengrong, especially in integrating voice and emotion), martial arts, and dance technique and interpretation. His comprehensive grasp of the form has made him a remarkable director as well; he has reworked old classics with fine dramatic effect.

Ye Shaolan's repertory includes his signature role as Lu Bu in *Lu Bu and Diao Chan,* an operatic adaptation of one of the early stories in *San Guo* (Three Kingdoms), which combine ambition and political strategy with a weakness for women, leading to subsequent downfall—a piece that provides a fine range for the *xiaoshen* performer. He has also starred with outstanding success in *An Assembly of Heroes,* another historical drama from the San Guo period; in *Liang Shanbo and Zhu Yingtai,* a Romeo and Juliet–style story; and in *The Legend of the White Snake,* an old folk tale. For these and other roles, he won the first Plum Blossom Award from the Chinese government.

In 1985, Ye was Fulbright Scholar and Artist in Residence at Bennington College in Vermont, teaching classes in movement and dance. He also gave public lectures and demonstrations: an excellent series on the art of Beijing Opera at Bennington, with shorter versions presented at nearby colleges. He adapted famous scenes from operas for his best students; toward the end of his stay, he incorporated their performances into his lectures, which he took farther afield to major universities, and to the Asia Society in New York City. He was received with popular and critical acclaim. Audiences that often had no previous experience of Beijing Opera were won over by Ye's mastery of his field, the brilliance and sincerity of his performance, and the accomplishments of the students, a real tribute to Ye as a teacher. He has made professional visits to Taiwan, Hong Kong, Singapore, Japan, Australia, and England, deepening the knowledge of cognoscenti, enlightening newcomers, and winning new fans for the art.

Ye is affiliated with the Zhan You Beijing Opera Company of Beijing. He is a member of the board of directors of the All-China Association of Dramatists and a member of the executive committee of the Conference on Political Consultation of China.

[*See also* China, *article on* Dance in Opera.]

BIBLIOGRAPHY

Arlington, L. C. *The Chinese Drama: From the Earliest Times Until Today.* Shanghai, 1930, New York, 1966.

Mackerras, Colin. *The Rise of the Peking Opera (1770–1870): Social Aspects of the Theatre in Manchuria.* Oxford, 1972.

Mackerras, Colin. *The Chinese Theatre in Modern Times: From 1849 to the Present Day.* Amherst, Mass., 1975.

Mackerras, Colin. ed. *Chinese Theater from its Origins to the Present Day.* Honolulu, 1983.

Scott, A(dolphe) C(larence). *The Classical Theatre of China.* Westport, Conn., 1957.

Yung, Bell. *Cantonese Opera: Performance as Creative Process.* Cambridge, 1989.

Zung, Cecilia S. L. *Secrets of the Chinese Drama: A Complete Explanatory Guide to Actions and Symbols, as Seen in the Performance of Chinese Dramas.* New York, 1937, 1964).

PHEBE SHIH CHAO

YOGA. The Sanskrit word *yoga* means "union with the higher reality." It is one of the six schools of Indian philosophy, and, unlike the other schools, it stresses practical methods of self-development. It advocates several paths toward the ultimate goal of communion with the Cosmic Being, the most common of which are *karmayoga*, the path of action, *bhaktiyoga*, the path of devotion, *jñānayoga*, the path of knowledge, and *haṭhayoga*. Hatha yoga is considered the lowest rung on this ladder of self-realization, but it is of particular interest to dancers and to those interested in the health and physiological condition of the human body and in the control of breath. It is not accepted as a formal school of philosophy, however, because its concentration is on *āsanas* (postures of the body), and *prāṇāyāma* (breath control).

Hatha yoga was codified systematically in the extensive work *Haṭhayogapradīpikā* by Svātmārāma between 1350 and 1550. The author of this text states that *ha* represents the sun, and *ṭha* the moon. They are also symbolic expressions of *iḍā* and *piṅgala*, the two main channels of subtle energy in the body, and of left and right, female and male, passive and active—the yin and yang of Chinese philosophy. Hatha yoga is the practice of uniting *prāṇa* and *apāna*, sun and moon.

This yoga, along with the others, finally leads to the highest yoga of all, the *rājayoga*, or "royal" yoga, which is also called *aṣṭāṅgayoga* (the Eight-Fold Path) and includes the teachings of all the paths of yoga. Hatha yoga should not be treated only as a method of bodily development, even though it expounds physical postures, but rather as the first key for the opening of the door of self-realization.

Hatha yoga prescribes from 84 to 108 *āsanas*. According to *Haṭhayogapradīpikā*, "*āsanas* make one firm, free from maladies and light of limb." This means that the body is made calm for the purpose of meditation, which is deepened if the body is in good health and free from aches and pains. In addition, the body and mind are both lightened by the removal of excess weight, and by the elimination of lethargy and depression.

BIBLIOGRAPHY

Bharata-Muni. *The Nātyaśāstra Ascribed to Bharata-Muni.* Translated by M. M. Ghosh. 2 vols. Calcutta, 1951–1961.
Eliade, Mirca. *Yoga: Immortality and Freedom.* 2d ed. Princeton, N.J., 1969.
Himalayan International Institute of Yoga Science and Philosophy. *Hatha Yoga.* Honesdale, Pa., 1977.
Vatsyayan, Kapila. *Indian Classical Dance.* 2d ed. New Delhi, 1992.

RITHA DEVI

YORUBA DANCE. One of the largest ethnic groups of southwestern Nigeria, the Yoruba make up approximately 20 percent of that nation's estimated ninety million inhabitants. According to archaeological evidence, they have been traditionally traders and farmers and to some extent an urbanized people since at least the first millennium—their lifestyle was first described to Europeans by Portuguese traders in the fifteenth century.

According to a Yoruba adage, "not standing still is dancing." In its broadest sense, Yoruba dance expresses the vitality of existence and the individual's well-being (*iwapele*, literally, "gentle or prudent character"). Thus, one of the most valued traits of a Yoruba dancer is composure, which is registered in a rhythmically controlled body, a calm, expressionless face, and a motionless head. Robert Farris Thompson (1966) called this characteristic "the aesthetic of the cool." For the Yoruba, a collected, controlled appearance reflects a composed, prudent state of mind. In dance, technical proficiency combined with improvisational flair communicates this ideal inner state.

Because of its emphasis on technical mastery and improvisation, the formal and stylistic properties of Yoruba dances override concern with narrative content; indeed, rhythm and style provide the primary content. Therefore, two dancers performing simultaneously adhere to the rhythmic structure of the music in the style appropriate to a specific context, but what they actually do within that framework is always spontaneous. Performers dance at the same time—but not necessarily together—with little concern for strict spatial, dynamic, or even rhythmic uniformity. What is most crucial is the communication between each dancer and the musicians.

Yoruba dancing is inseparable from drumming. In fact, the most frequently mentioned criterion is that dancers understand the musical structure and phrasing of the drums and match their stepping to the drum rhythms. Although the music is percussive, the dancing that accompanies it varies from highly percussive to extremely fluid, depending on the gender and status of the dancer. Men's

YOGA. A yogin, or follower of yoga disciplines, adopts an immobile posture to isolate his mind from bodily functions. (Photograph by Associated Press of India.)

dancing is usually "hard," forceful, and energetic, while women's is "cool," fluid, and delicate. (These values remain in the Yoruba-derived Candomblé dances in the state of Bahia, northeastern Brazil.)

Yoruba dance is composed of discrete rhythmic units, which can be elaborated, repeated, deleted, or condensed. The outer features of Yoruba dance include spatial and temporal segmentation, discontinuity, repetition, spontaneity, and simultaneity. The more specialized dances are also rhythmically irregular. Dancers may perform relatively simple rhythms as long as they work up to their capacity; drummers respond to the level of the dancers' proficiency, either by progressively increasing the complexity and sophistication of the music or by simplifying it.

The basis of the rhythmic units is verbal, usually in the form of drummed aphorisms or proverbs. A strong correlation is often observed between the sound qualities of the drummed verbal texts and the effort (or dynamic) qualities of the dancer, particularly in the context of a possession-trance performance, in which the dancer "becomes" the deity, to express the essence of that deity's power. Thus, the verbal basis of the music is not merely mnemonic or semantic; rather, the verbal content, the music, and the dance together represent attitudes toward time, space, weight, and flow—that is, the effort qualities appropriate to a particular context. The Yoruba use effort qualities as an expression of the metaphysical concept of the vital life force *(ase)*.

Yoruba children frequently inherit the authority to perform specialized dances, but divination also plays a crucial role in identifying and authorizing performers. Generally, the learning process involves emulating the masters. During initiations into priesthoods, however, dance training is more formal. In other contexts, students learn stepping styles and rhythms by observing and imitating their elders. With regular, sustained exposure to performances, children assimilate particular dance techniques, structures, and drum phrases; by learning to mark simple stepping patterns, they begin to perform by the age of three. Encouraged to dance, they are then rewarded with small coins and cheers from the spectators. Older, more accomplished children are usually followed closely by an adult from their lineage who makes sure that they follow the rhythms of the drums and accent the proper beats. With preadolescents, the coach watches from the side but does not hesitate to rush forward to make a correction. The performance itself therefore functions as a training session for novices.

In the interplay among Yoruba dance participants, spectators become performers and performers become spectators. Dancers or family members can tell drummers what to play, or drummers can initiate music. Spectators are free to join in the dancing. Thus individuals shape performances spontaneously, making each one fluid and unique.

YORUBA DANCE. During a ceremony in Sakete, Benin, this young man was possessed by Ṣango, a powerful deity of the Yoruba people. With upraised arms, he dances in the guise of the god. (Photograph © 1981 by Pierre Verger; used by permission)

Through Yoruba dance, spiritual forces materialize for the community's benefit. Such materializations take the form of possession trances and masquerading; possession trance is primarily within women's domain, while masking is the prerogative of men. In possession trance, the god is said to mount *(gun)* the devotee *(elegun,* literally, "one who is mounted"), and, for a time, that devotee becomes the god. Whatever a priest does from the moment of entering the trance state is thought to represent a god's own actions. Such spirit mediumship is the most significant role of a priest.

Some traits and ideals of Yoruba dance have had a significant impact on certain dance forms in the Americas. This is especially evident in Brazil, Cuba, and the United States—where aspects of Yoruba belief and the tradition of danced worship survive and flourish.

[*See also* West Africa.]

BIBLIOGRAPHY

Abiodun, Rowland. "Identity and the Artistic Process in Yoruba Aesthetic Concepts of Iwa." *Journal of Culture and Ideas* 1 (December 1983).

Abiodun, Rowland, et al., eds. *The Yoruba Artist: New Theoretical Perspectives on African Arts.* Washington, D.C., 1994.

Ajayi, Omofolabo Soyinka. "Aesthetics of Yoruba Recreational Dances as Exemplified in the Oge Dance." *Dance Research Journal* 21 (Fall 1989): 1–8.

Drewal, Henry John, and Margaret Thompson-Drewal. *Gelede: Art and Female Power among the Yoruba.* Bloomington, 1983.

Harper, Peggy. "Dance in Nigeria." *Ethnomusicology* 13.2 (1969): 280–295.

Laoye I, Adetoyese. "Yoruba Drums." *Odu* 7 (1959).

Thompson, Robert Farris. "An Aesthetic of the Cool: West African Dance." *African Forum* 2.2 (1966).

Thompson, Robert Farris. *Black Gods and Kings: Yoruba Art at UCLA.* Los Angeles, 1971.

Thompson, Robert Farris. *African Art in Motion: Icon and Act.* 2d ed. Los Angeles, 1979.

Thompson-Drewal, Margaret, and Glorianne Jackson, comps. *Sources on African and African-Related Dance.* New York, 1974.

Thompson-Drewal, Margaret. "Symbols of Possession: A Study of Movement and Regalia in an Anago-Yoruba Ceremony." *Dance Research Journal* 7 (Spring-Summer 1975): 15–24.

Thompson-Drewal, Margaret, and Henry John Drewal. "More Powerful Than Each Other: An Egbado Classification of Egungun." *African Arts* 11 (Spring 1978).

Thompson-Drewal, Margaret, and Henry John Drewal. "Composing Time and Space in Yoruba Art." In *The Relationship of the Verbal and Visual Arts among the Yoruba*, edited by Rowland Abiodun. 1987.

Thompson-Drewal, Margaret. "Dancing for Ogun in Yorubaland and in Brazil." In *Africa's Ogun: Old World and New*, edited by Sandra T. Barnes. Bloomington, 1989.

Thompson-Drewal, Margaret. *Yoruba Ritual: Performers, Play, Agency.* Bloomington, 1991.

Verger, Pierre. "Role joue par l'État d'Hebetude au cours de l'initiation des novices aux cultes des Orisha et Vodun." *Bulletin de l'Institut Français d'Afrique Noire*, Series B 16 (1954).

Verger, Pierre. *Orixás: Deuses iorubás na Africa e no Novo Mundo.* Salvador, Brazil, 1981.

MARGARET THOMPSON-DREWAL

YOUSKEVITCH. In costume for one of the princely roles in which he excelled, Youskevitch posed for this studio portrait c.1940. (Photograph from the archives at Jacob's Pillow, Becket, Massachusetts.)

YOUSKEVITCH, IGOR (Igor' Ivanovich Iuskevich; born 13 March 1912 in Pieyatin, Ukraine, died 13 June 1994 in New York), Russian-American ballet dancer, choreographer, and teacher. Youskevitch was probably the single dancer most responsible for establishing ballet as an acceptable profession for a man in the Americas. He inspired many young people to enter the profession through his masculine, unmannered, naturally elegant, and ardently romantic approach, in contrast to the highly stylized and theatrical manner of many earlier European dancers. He was instrumental in setting the style of American male classical dancers and in gaining recognition for the classics, which in the Ballets Russes tradition tended to be overshadowed by modern *demi-caractère* ballets. Edwin Denby once summed him up as follows:

His style is calm, rich and elastic. It is completely correct. . . . The trunk takes the main direction of the dance and the limbs vary the force and the drive by calculated countermovements. The changing shape of the dancing body is vigorously defined. The weight of the body and the abundant strength of it are equally clear; and the two aspects blend gracefully in the architectural play of classic sequences. The distribution of energy is intelligent and complex. In his leaps, for instance, the noble arm positions, the tilt to the head sideways or forward, make you watch with interest a whole man who leaps. . . .

The completeness of his dance education is unique among our classic male dancers. His rhythm is free, his characterization economical, his lift gracious. His stage presence has none of that hard insistence on attention that breaks the illusion and the flow of a classic ballet.   (Denby, 1949)

Backstage, Youskevitch's even temper, good manners, and detachment from petty rivalries were cited as an inspiration by his colleagues. The press made much of his athletic background (even claiming he had been in the circus) and his status as a family man. He was married to Anna Scarpova; she and their daughter Maria were both dancers.

He left his native Russia at the age of eight as a refugee from the revolution and settled in Belgrade, pursuing academic studies as far as the Royal University and becoming a champion amateur gymnast. Chosen by an adagio-style dancer, Xenia Grunt, as a concert partner, he began ballet training at age twenty, principally with Olga Preobrajenska. He overcame his late start in ballet through his gymnastics background, natural aptitude, analytical mind, and the experience gained under the guidance of Leon Woizikowski with the Ballets Russes de Paris (1934–1935), the Ballets de Léon Woizikovsky (1935–1936)—where Youskevitch became first classical dancer—and in a second company of Colonel Wassily de Basil (1936–1937) on a ten-month tour of Australia. He made an early reputation in Michel Fokine's *Le Spectre de la Rose* and danced it under the choreographer's direction as a guest with René Blum's Ballets de Monte-Carlo.

As a principal dancer of Serge Denham's Ballet Russe de Monte Carlo (1938–1944), Youskevitch created roles in such works as Léonide Massine's *Gaîté Parisienne, Seventh Symphony,* and *Rouge et Noir;* Bronislava Nijinska's *The Snow Maiden;* Aleksandra Fedorova's *Magic Swan* (*Swan Lake,* act 3); and Igor Schwezoff's *Red Poppy* (Ribbon Dance). He left the company to serve in the U.S. Navy, and upon his discharge after World War II he joined Massine's Ballet Russe Highlights (1946) and then (American) Ballet Theatre (1946–1955). He made later guest appearances with the latter, including a tour of Russia in 1960.

George Balanchine choreographed *Theme and Variations* for Youskevitch, capturing his nobility, *élan,* and technical control; the role, still a challenge to the best dancers, is considered one of his greatest, along with Albrecht in *Giselle.* He added to his repertory such varied ballets as *La Fille Mal Gardée,* the *Don Quixote* pas de deux, Nijinska's *Schumann Concerto,* Balanchine's *Apollo,* and Valerie Bettis's *A Streetcar Named Desire,* and formed an illustrious fourteen-year partnership with Alicia Alonso, both in the United States and Cuba. He appeared with Alonso's company from its inception in 1948, dancing the standard repertory, full-length classics, and Cuban works, and touring Latin America. He rejoined Ballet Russe de Monte Carlo from 1955 through 1957, becoming the company's artistic adviser. Gene Kelly's feature film *Invitation to the Dance* was released at this time, showcasing Youskevitch's dancing, of which the film remains the best record.

Youskevitch made a concert tour of South America with Nathalie Krassovska as his partner in 1961. He choreographed, restaged the classics, and established his own New York school (1960–1980), and was head of the dance program of the University of Texas at Austin (1971–1982), which honored him with a four-day tribute on his retirement. In 1983 he became the artistic director of the New York International Ballet Competition, a position in which he was active until his death. Youskevitch received a *Dance Magazine* Award in 1958 and the Capezio Award in 1992.

BIBLIOGRAPHY
Barker, Barbara. "Celebrating Youskevitch." *Ballet Review* 11 (Fall 1983): 27–29.
Cohen, Selma Jeanne. "Prince Igor: The Story of Youskevitch." *Dance Magazine* (May 1953): 14–17.
Denby, Edwin. *Looking at the Dance* (1949). New York, 1968.
Hunt, Marilyn. "Danseur Noble." *Ballet News* 3 (March 1982): 16–18.
Hunt, Marilyn. "Igor Youskevitch Dancing." *Ballet Review* 11 (Fall 1983): 32–63.
Newman, Barbara. *Striking a Balance: Dancers Talk about Dancing.* Rev. ed. New York, 1992.
Youskevitch, Igor. "Igor Youskevitch" in "The Male Image." *Dance Perspectives,* no. 40 (Winter 1969).
Youskevitch, Igor. "Former Soviet Stars as Seen by a Colleague." *New York Times* (21 February 1982).
Youskevitch, Igor. "Busing Les Ballets." *Ballet Review* 11 (Fall 1983): 30–31.

FILMS. *Seventh Symphony* (1938). *Ballets Russes de Monte Carlo* (c.1941). *Giselle,* NBC (1950). *Invitation to the Dance* (1956). Ann Barzel, *Youskevitch Gala* (n.d.), Dance Collection, New York Public Library for the Performing Arts.

MARILYN HUNT

YUAN XUEFEN (born 26 March 1922 in Zhejiang, China), Shaoxing Opera actress. One of the best known and founding actresses of *Yueju,* or Shaoxing Opera, an all-female theatrical genre and one of the most popular in China, Yuan was born into a rural teacher's family. She began her training at eleven, following a failed attempt at eight, with a male master in a local opera genre different from the then-embryonic Shaoxing Opera. Yuan played her first leading role in Hangzhou in 1936, shortly before her debut in Shanghai the same year. While her early performances were often with male partners in slightly different styles, she participated in China's first recording of the all-female Shaoxing Opera. She settled in Shanghai in 1938, concentrating on developing and refining the new female genre for urban audiences. In 1945, she founded her own Xuesheng company. In 1950, she became head of China's first state-sponsored Shaoxing Opera company—the East China Experimental Shaoxing Opera Company—and later headed the Shanghai Shaoxing Opera Theater (where she is now honorary head). She led her company on tour to East Germany and the Soviet Union (1955), Hong Kong (1960), North Korea (1961), France (1986), and to the United States (1989).

Compared to most older traditional Chinese theatrical genres, Shaoxing Opera is less conventionalized and more influenced by modern drama, especially in its use of scenery. But Yuan preferred suggestive sets, somewhere between modern drama's realism and Beijing Opera's bare stage. She also learned from *kunqu*'s (Kun opera) salient characteristic of simultaneous singing and dancing. Because in ancient China decent (noble) women were required to wear floor-length dress and walk in small steps (on bound lily feet), Yuan's characters seldom had large movements like jumping or running; instead they concentrated on the nuanced gestures of upper body, hands, and facial parts, and they played with small props such as a fan or letter. Because many of her performances were in love scenes with a male character played by a female actress, the exchange of expression between the performers was particularly delicate.

In 1953, Yuan helped conceive, choreographed, and starred in, *Liang Shanbo and Zhu Yingtai;* the subsequent film version won the Prague Film Festival prize for best musical film. In this tragedy of love, Yuan played Zhu Yingtai, who had to disguise herself as a man to leave home for school, where she fell in love with a schoolmate unaware of her feelings. Its best-known scene "Farewell," which has often been performed in excerpt, featured Yuan playing a woman faking a man trying every possible way to convey her love to a man played by a woman before leaving him. Slowly, they walked a meandering path, passing eighteen locales, such as a pond where couples of mandarin ducks swan, a well in which Zhu saw a wedding picture, and a temple with a fertility goddess. All these were indicated by Yuan's exquisite fingers, a fan, and her facial expressions mixing eagerness and bashfulness.

In Yuan's co-adaptation of the classic play *Xi Xiang Ji* (The West Chamber), she created the character of a vivacious matchmaking maid. Yuan also successfully created modern characters, the best known being Mrs. Xianglin in both stage and film versions, based on China's best writer Lu Xun's short story about a poor widow who lost everything to the oppressive society. In addition to the many young actresses trained in Yuan's theater, she also trained the first few male Shaoxing Opera actors.

BIBLIOGRAPHY
Yuan Xuefen. "Biography." Unpublished manuscript entry to *Shanghai Yueju Zhi* (records of Shanghai Shaoxing opera).
Zeng Bairong et al., eds. *Jingju Jumu Cidian.* Beijing, 1989.
Zhongguo Da Baikequanshu: Xiju, Quyi. Beijing, 1983.

WILLIAM H. SUN

YUGOSLAVIA. [*To survey the dance traditions of the former Socialist Federal Republic of Yugoslavia, this entry comprises five articles:*

> Traditional Dance
> Ballet
> Modern Dance
> Theatrical Dance since 1991
> Dance Research and Publication

The first article explores traditional dance in Macedonia and six zones that made up Yugoslavia; the second and third articles focus on the development of ballet and modern dance to 1991; the fourth article examines theatrical dance since 1991; the concluding article provides a brief history of scholarship and writing.]

Traditional Dance

The Socialist Federal Republic of Yugoslavia was created in 1918. Throughout its relatively brief national history, it was an uneasy union of diverse cultural groups critically in need of common denominators. The country comprised six republics (Croatia, Bosnia-Herzegovina, Slovenia, Serbia, Montenegro, and Macedonia) and two autonomous regions (Kosovo and Vojvodina), with three official languages (Serbo-Croatian, Macedonian, and Slovenian), two official alphabets (Latin and Cyrillic), three principal religious groups (Eastern Orthodox Christians, Roman Catholics, and Muslims), and a large number of ethnic minorities.

The scarcity of historical records prior to the ninth century makes it virtually impossible to determine what dance was like in the Balkans before the arrival of the Slavs in the sixth and seventh centuries; neither do we know what kind of dances the Slavs brought with them, or what the dance situation was in the fourteenth and fifteenth centuries, when most of the area fell to the Turks. Comparative (especially linguistic) studies, combined with empirical data collected over the past hundred years, indicate that communal group dancing was common to the Slavs in their original homeland north of the Carpathian Mountains. The chain dance (a closed or broken circle of dancers usually linked by joined hands) was the predominant form in Europe through the Middle Ages; among the Slavs it bore the name *kolo* ("wheel"). There may also have been an ancient type of couple dance without physical contact. It is highly likely, however, that the old Slavic repertory contained religious as well as purely social dancing, and that accompaniment was both vocal and instrumental. That the Slavs may not have distinguished clearly between the activities of dance and play is evidenced in the word *igra*, which has survived to the present with both meanings. In certain areas of Yugoslavia its meaning is limited to play or game, while in other areas, notably Serbia, it denotes both game and dance.

Traditional dance is defined here as folk dances, that is, social and ritual dances passed down from generation to generation primarily through imitation of culturally approved models. The period of collection of dances existing in actual practice or in the memories of the oldest informants began in the early 1930s. In remote areas, less touched by industrialization, the media, and urbanization, many of these dances survive in their latest evolved forms; in other areas they are rare in spontaneous contexts, but they are taught in schools and cultivated as living museum pieces on stage at folklore festivals. These gatherings were sponsored by the communist government for the purpose of preserving the dances under strictly-enforced rules of authenticity. The dances today thus represent an arbitrarily selected stage in the process of slow evolution.

In understanding traditional dance in Yugoslavia, it is important to bear in mind that one is seldom dealing with discrete data; rarely can one define a given dance with a single name and a single melody. Underlying structural patterns of movement have diffused over the area and beyond the national boundaries, assuming various names, tunes, styles, and modes of execution. Dances with different names found in different regions may be identical in structure and meter. The assignment of names is often an arbitrary recourse of the outsider or scholar.

The Yugoslavian dance ethnographer and choreographer Ivan Ivancan has defined six dance zones, the Dinaric, Morava, Vardar, Adriatic, Alpine, and Pannonian. (Macedonia also merits consideration as a separate zone.) The line that marks the division between the first three zones and the others coincides generally with the boundary that separated the Ottoman Empire from Europe from the fourteenth century to the late nineteenth century. In the Turkish-dominated region, the traditional patriarchal society of the Slavs remained stronger and the occurrence of ritual dances more frequent; under the Ottomans the medieval circle and chain dances continued to evolve. The other regions reflect the influence of Mediterranean and central European cultures, favoring the social and couple dances of the nineteenth and twentieth centuries. The Pannonian zone shows the influence of central Europe, often fascinatingly combined with the older *kolo* elements.

A phenomenon of the Dinaric, Morava, and Vardar regions is a rather small group of basic structural patterns upon which a larger number of discrete dances are built. For example, the *devojack* pattern has generated dozens of dances throughout the area, including some of the oldest. The *kokonjeste* pattern underlies the most famous family of dances in Serbia, variously known as *usest, sestica,* and *kukunjes.*

An important social element in these areas is the role of the male. A kind of Balkan cool and what social psychologists now call male bonding are operative, dating back to ancient times in a traditional patriarchal society. The male who pays the musicians has paid for the lead position in the dance. His performance in that role counts in acquiring and maintaining his position in the community and among his peers. The concept of the open circle, with a position for a male leader and an end man in a women's dance, is a development of this social attitude.

Dinaric Zone. The western mountain Dinaric area includes the Croatian hinterlands of Dalmatia, most of Bosnia-Herzegovina, and Montenegro. The area is rugged, life is hard, and stock breeding is the principal occupation. The dances of this area seem to be the most archaic in Yugoslavia. Chain dances made up of simple walking patterns, especially the ubiquitous Faeroe step, are performed along a curved path. They are found in other parts of the Balkans as well, and this and the features they share with the dances of other Slavs point to their great age.

In parts of Bosnia-Herzegovina, stringed instruments accompany the dances. Some of the dances are accompanied by singing for a portion and then continued in silence. Representative of this kind of dancing is *ličko kolo,* from the Dinaric highlands. As people gather after church, someone begins singing an old local song. A group of friends casually gathers in a long chain, all singing as they do the Faeroe step, moving clockwise in an ambling, casual manner. When the last verse is finished they continue dancing in silence, at first slowly, but gradually faster and with more energy. At the command of the leader they perform variations on the Faeroe step pattern in unison. The only sound is that of footfalls and perhaps the clinking of metal ornaments.

Various mimetic song-and-dance games are found everywhere in Yugoslavia, but nowhere as frequently as in the Dinaric zone. In some dance games a sole performer in the middle of a circle mimics the movements of birds or animals to the accompaniment of the circle's singing. Among the most popular of the dance games is "Paun Pase" (How the Peacock Grazes). Elaborate variants of these are practiced by the Muslim population of Bosnia-Herzegovina, among whom traditional segregation of the sexes is particularly strong.

Morava Zone. The fertile Morava zone consists of most of present-day Serbia and parts of eastern Bosnia-Herzegovina and was the route of many population shifts in the past. The open *kolo* predominates, with a leader and end man. The dances in the center of this region tend to be symmetrical; those of the eastern borderlands tend to be asymmetrical. Bagpipes, flutes, violin, and accordion provide the accompaniment. The repertory has diminished dramatically over the last two or three generations to a small number of basic patterns. *Čačak,* a

YUGOSLAVIA: Traditional Dance. Members of Tanec, the Macedonian professional folk dance ensemble, in a Croatian folk dance. (Photograph from the Dance Collection, New York Public Library for the Performing Arts.)

YUGOSLAVIA: Traditional Dance. In this exuberant folk dance, performed by the Tanec ensemble, the four couples in each group link arms in a circle and whirl around so fast that the women are able to lift both feet off the ground and fly through the air. (Photograph from the Dance Collection, New York Public Library for the Performing Arts.)

ten-measure dance, is widespread in the southeast. Turkish-dominated cities developed a culture with a strong Eastern influence. The Sumadijan style is widespread.

Vardar Zone. The Vardar zone contains all of present-day Macedonia and much of southern Serbia. Dances of this region are the open *kolo, tesko* dances in the southwest, and lighter dances in the east. There is a strict division between men's and women's dances. The most prevalent steps are *lesnoto* and Faeroe; basic patterns are Faeroe step, *berance,* and *malesevka. Zurla* (a shawm) and *tapan* (a large double-headed drum), *kavali* (a wooden, rim-blown flute), and bagpipes are used. A typical dance of the *tesko* type is performed exclusively by men. It begins slowly but then speeds up; the musicians follow the cues of the lead dancer, who sets the tempo and dynamics while the drummer matches his beats to the steps and pauses he sees performed. The music defies conventional notation.

Alpine Zone. The Alpine zone includes the republic of Slovenia and some contiguous areas of Croatia; historically it was part of the Hapsburg Empire. The dance repertory consists primarily of couple dances derived from eighteenth- and nineteenth-century central Europe, such as the polka, waltz, and mazurka, and local dances such as the *sotis, stajeris, sustarska,* and *potrkana polka.* There are also some traditional chain and circle dances, such as the *metliško kolo, žakle,* and *šivajo.* Accompaniment is provided by violin, accordion, clarinet, cymbalom, *sopile* (a double-reed wind instrument), and *mih* (bagpipe). The predominating rhythms are 2/4 and 3/4.

Pannonian Zone. The fertile plainland of northern Croatia, including Zagreb, and the autonomous region of Vojvodina make up the Pannonian zone. The most important dance type here is the *drmeš* (sometimes spelled *drmež*); the name is derived from the Serbo-Croatian verb *drmati,* meaning "to shake," "to tremble," "to vibrate," or "to bounce rapidly up and down." Its most common form is in two parts: in the first section the dancers execute some type of vertical bouncing step in place, and in the second section they spin counterclockwise. The *drmeš* is performed in couples, trios, and small circles. The closed, leaderless *kolo* is also found here.

Adriatic Zone. The Adriatic zone consists of the islands and coastal towns and villages of Croatia. The "older" dances generically known as *tanac* and *lindo* are within the repertory of the population born before the mid-twentieth century in rural, agriculturally based communities. North of Split, *tanac* dances are accompanied by *mih* or *sopile,* while in the south, *lindo* dances are accompanied by a *lijerica* (a bowed three-string instrument), although the oldest members of the population recall that the dancing was formerly accompanied also by the bagpipe. Dancing events are commonly organized during the winter season from Christmas to the beginning of Lent, also on village saints' days and at weddings. Dancing is considered a social event, which allows for acceptable contact between men and women.

Adult dancers (unmarried or married) dance in a file of side-by-side couples that traces a circular or serpentine path. During the dances there are usually reversals of direction, such as from clockwise to counterclockwise. *Tanac* and *lindo* dances have a flexible sequence of patterns in an improvised order, lead by a male (while dancing with his partner). He directs the ensemble with verbal cues or by initiating changes in pattern. Many *tanac* dances also include formations in which the men and women face each other in two lines; they all dance in place, then the members of each couple exchange places. Throughout this area, men also have an opportunity within the dance structure to demonstrate their expertise with solo dancing, performing quick footwork, lifting their arms above their heads, and spinning. The men also direct their partners into spinning turns, as well as performing pivot turns with their partners as a couple.

Under Austrian rule during the nineteenth century, the fashionable waltz *(valcer)* and polka became standard repertory at Adriatic dance events. These dances continue to be performed and in some villages have replaced the older *tanac* and *linđo*. In the second half of the twentieth century, particularly with the expansion of tourism and the construction of complexes of hotels, cafés, and nightclubs, amplified music has replaced the local instruments to cater to an international tourist clientele with contemporary pan-European music dancing. Only scattered pockets of rural communities continue to dance the older dances accompanied by traditional music. Tourism, however, is also responsible for the preservation of some dance types through seasonally organized performance groups that present programs of "traditional" dance and music for foreign visitors. Among these social dances adapted for stage performance are sword dances extant on the island of Korčula, called the *moreska* and *kumpanija*, whose roots go back at least to the fifteenth and sixteenth centuries. [*See* Moresca.]

Macedonia. Lying between Albania to the west, Bulgaria to the east, Greece to the south, and the rump Yugoslavia (Serbia and Montenegro) to the north, Macedonia has experienced successive waves of occupiers attracted by the area's ancient trade routes leading west toward the Adriatic seaports and north toward the interior of Europe as well as its rich agricultural lands and mineral deposits. The current population is composed two-thirds of Slavic, Macedonian-speaking people and one-quarter of ethnic Albanians, with Turkish, Romany (Gypsy), and Serbian minorities. The two major religions, Eastern Orthodox Christianity and Islam, are as influential in determining the types of dances performed and their social occasions as the population's various ethno-linguistic identities.

During the 1930s, more than two hundred dances were identified and described by the Janković sisters in the western, southwestern, and northern areas of Macedonia (then called South Serbia). Many of the dances tended to be segregated by sex, with the dancers linked by handholds or shoulderholds in open circles, whose path progressed counterclockwise. Tempos varied from extremely slow rubato dances to quick-paced irregular rhythmic patterns. Instrumentation for outdoor dances was usually *gajda* (bagpipe), or *zurla* (shawm) with *tapan* (drum). Urban centers with a middle-class supported mellower-sounding *calgija* orchestras (comprising violin, lutes, *kanon*, clarinet, and tambourine), which played indoors, accompanying singers for slow, walking-style dances *(lesnoto)*.

Until the 1950s the eastern, central, and western regions of Macedonia each had distinctly different dances. However, with the postwar migrations of population from mountain villages to plains areas and to urban centers, these distinctions became muted. By the 1980s a pan-Macedonian repertory had emerged at wedding celebrations, with dances (known as *oro*) often danced to newly composed songs. Weddings are lavish affairs that always feature hired musicians, and there is an expectation that everyone in attendance will dance, whether the wedding is held at the home, or in a public restaurant. Dancing is also popularly done during any public occasion when musicians are hired, such as warm evenings in the park, at a restaurant, or in an outdoor cafe, often accompanied by the singing of old and newly composed Macedonian songs.

At these occasions, a basic repertory of dance music and dances is performed by both the urban and rural populations throughout Macedonia. Men and women dance together in open circles, the dancers joined with hands held at shoulder level or with the arms down at their sides; short-phrased, repetitive step patterns progress the path of the circle in a counterclockwise direction. The pan-Macedonian dance repertory includes a variety of rhythmic patterns, for dances generically known as *lesnoto* (such as the *lesno, za ramo, teškoto,* and *pravoto,* all in 7/8 and/or 2/4 meters), *devetorka* (9/8), *beranče* (or *krsteno,* in 13/8), *eleno mome* (7/8), *pajduško* (5/8), *sitno*

YUGOSLAVIA: Traditional Dance. Dancers from the Tanec group performing a *rusalija,* a type of sword dance. (Photograph from the Dance Collection, New York Public Library for the Performing Arts.)

YUGOSLAVIA: Traditional Dance. A dancer perches atop a large drum *(tapan)* at a climactic moment in this Macedonian men's dance, the *teškoto,* performed by members of Tanec. The other musician plays a *zurla,* a loud shawm. The *tapan-zurla* repertory accompanies outdoor dancing at feasts, weddings, and circumcisions. (Photograph from the Dance Collection, New York Public Library for the Performing Arts.)

(2/4) and *čačak* (2/4). Music accompaniment tends to be by a folk orchestra composed of accordion, electric guitars, clarinet, saxophone, and trap set or *darabuka* (hourglass shaped drum) that plays newly composed music in the rhythms appropriate to each dance meter. The rhythm of the music, not the melody, determines which steps are executed.

Since 1945 Macedonian folk dances have also been performed on stage by the republic's sole professional ensemble, Tanec, as well as by a multitude of urban and village dance groups sponsored by the Cultural Artistic Societies (referred to by their collective Macedonian acronym, KUD). By 1995, approximately one hundred dance groups in Macedonian towns and villages were performing a similar choreographed repertory of Macedonian dances that represented the central, western, and eastern regions of the country. Although the population of Macedonia is multicultural, most of this stage repertory represents only the Slavic-speaking population. The principal influence on the standardization of these dances is the diffusion of the repertory of Tanec, which consists of a standardized set of regional dances established during the early 1950s from traditional sources, subjected to extensive choreographic elaboration during the 1970s and 1980s, and transmitted throughout the country. Tanec and many of the town-based KUD groups tour internationally with their programs, while other KUD and village-based groups perform in annually sponsored national and regional festival programs that offer nominally authentic dances, music, and costume to public view.

Urban Dances. In the late nineteenth century, as nationalist yearnings burgeoned among ethnic groups in the Balkans, it became clear that the only forms on which to found future national culture were the folk arts: colorful costumes, crafts, oral prose, epic poetry in the Homeric tradition, a rich stock of lyrical songs, and an immense stock of folk music and dance. One of the first things the new royal court in Belgrade undertook was the creation, based on native motifs, of dances "in the national spirit."

In their music and structure these dances reflect two main characteristics of the period: a romantic enthusiasm for the culture of the peasantry, and a desire to match the dances of the salons of Paris and Vienna. The Croatian ballroom *kolo,* for example, combined the multifigured structure of the French quadrille with movements emulating features of village dancing. From the court in Belgrade came a series of dances composed in honor of various members of the royal house. The opening dance at royal balls was "Kraljevo Oro" (The King's Solo), customarily led by the monarch himself. It consisted of the familiar Faeroe step, performed in a slow, elegant style. "Natalijino Kolo" (Queen Natalia's *Kolo*) gained immense popularity outside the court, its melody surviving as a dance tune as late as World War II, when, ironically, it was performed to the singing of patriotic revolutionary lyrics by Tito's partisans.

The Yugoslav people dance as much today as they did in the past—at family gatherings, social get-togethers, and holidays. But the types of dancing done today reflect the intense urbanization and internationalization of the country. The majority of the dancing population, the youth, now find it natural to dance their own versions of rock and roll, disco, and *sving*. In remote areas, however, many traditional dances still live.

BIBLIOGRAPHY

Dopuda, Jelena. *Narodni plesovi-igre u Bosni i Hercegovini.* Zagreb, 1990.

Dunin, Elsie Ivancich. *Dance Occasions and Festive Dress in Yugoslavia.* Los Angeles, 1984.

Dunin, Elsie. "Lindo in the Context of Village Life in the Dubrovnik Area of Yugoslavia." *Dance Research Annual* 16 (1987): 1–4.

Dunin, Elsie Ivancich and Stanimir Visinski. *Dances in Macedonia: Performance Genre—Tanec Ensemble.* Skopje, 1995.

Dunin, Elsie Ivancich, and Nancy Lee Chalfa Ruyter. *Yugoslav Dance: An Introduction and List of Sources Available in United States Libraries.* Palo Alto, Calif., 1981.

Dunin, Elsie Ivancich. "Yugoslav Dance Research Project." *Dance Research Journal* 22 (Spring 1990): 52–54.

Ivančan, Ivan. "Folk Dance among the Croats." *Narodna umjetnost,* special issue no. 2 (1988): 69–107.

Ivančan, Ivan. "Geografska podjela narodnih plesova u Jugoslaviji." *Narodna umjetnost,* no. 3 (1964–1965).

Ivančan, Ivan. "Folk Dances in Various Regions of Yugoslavia." In *The Folk Arts of Yugoslavia,* edited by Walter W. Kolar. Pittsburgh, 1976.

Janković, Ljubica S., and Danica S. Janković. *Narodne igre.* 8 vols. Belgrade, 1934–1964.

Janković, Ljubica S., and Danica S. Janković. *Dances of Yugoslavia.* New York and London, 1952.

Lawrence, Lee A. "News: Zagreb." *Dance Magazine* (November 1985).

Leibman, Robert. *Traditional Songs and Dances from the Soko Banja Area.* San Francisco, 1973.

Mladenović, Olivera. *Kolo u južnih slavena.* Belgrade, 1973.

Pajtondžiev, Gančo. *Makedonski narodni ora.* Skopje, 1973.

Ramovš, Mirko. *Plesat me pelji: Plesno izročilo na Slovenskem.* Ljubljana, 1980.

Ruyter, Nancy Lee Chalfa. "Some Musings on Folk Dance." *Dance Chronicle* 18.2 (1995): 269–279.

ELSIE IVANCICH DUNIN
(Adriatic Zone)

ELSIE IVANCICH DUNIN and STANIMIR VISINSKI
(Macedonia)

RICHARD CRUM
(all others)

Ballet

Although a permanent ballet company was not established in Zagreb until 1894, the city witnessed many performances by gymnasts, illusionists, and pantomime troupes before that time. Occasionally, foreign dancers made isolated appearances, and in 1876 the first full dance company, that of Pietro Coronelli, toured Yugoslavia. The group's ballerina, Ivana Freisinger, was engaged by the Zagreb Opera for the 1876/77 season. Remaining there into the 1880s, she provided several ballets for the standard opera repertory but attracted little interest.

In 1892 a Viennese ballet master, L. Gundlich, arrived in Zagreb and staged Josef Bayer's *The Fairy Doll* for the Croatian National Theater. Gundlich's staging repeated the success of Josef Hassreiter's original production at the Vienna Court Opera Ballet four years earlier—even though, because of the lack of a permanent ballet ensemble, he cast actors and actresses in all the roles. That situation changed two years later, when Stjepan Miletić took over the management of the National Theater and established not only a permanent dance ensemble, but also a ballet school.

Miletić engaged foreign dancers to fill the front ranks of the company, whose star became Erna Grondona, born in Budapest and trained at the Teatro alla Scala. During the next four years the company premiered *Coppélia* and *Giselle,* as well as ballets by Grondona, including *To the Plitvice Lakes* (1898), set to music by Sreácko Albini and based on a libretto by Miletić.

After Miletić left the National Theater at the turn of the century, the ballet company and school languished. Not until the 1920s, and Yugoslavia's emergence as an independent nation following the collapse of the Austro-Hungarian empire in World War I, did ballet become firmly established as a theatrical form in Zagreb, Ljubljana, and Belgrade. Immigrant dancers, mostly Russian, spearheaded the revival. While introducing works from the Russian repertory to the Yugoslav audience, they laid the groundwork for the development of a national repertory, a process that reached fulfillment after World War II.

In 1921 the Russian Margarita Froman arrived in Zagreb with her brothers Maksimilijan, Pavel, and Valentin. Maksimilijan took leading roles in her works, Pavel designed many of her productions, and Valentin followed her as a choreographer. For the National Theater Margarita staged many works from the Russian repertory, including *Schéhérazade* (1922), which Pavel designed and in which she and Maksimilijan appeared together, and *Petrouchka* (1923), also designed by Pavel after Alexandre Benois and including Valentin in the family-dominated cast.

Margarita Froman also staged works on Yugoslav themes to music by Yugoslav composers, notably *The Gin-*

gerbread Heart (1924); Krešimir Baranović wrote the libretto and composed the music, and Maksimilijan Vanka designed the scenery and costumes. Set at a Croatian village fair, the ballet shows a young man presenting a girl with a gingerbread heart and thereby winning her love. Whirling folk dances (kolos) echo their exuberance. The Gingerbread Heart became a staple in the Yugoslav repertory. [See the entry on Froman.]

At the opera house in Ljubljana a Czech, Václav Pohan, initiated a ballet revival and staged works from the international repertory, including Coppélia (1919) and Swan Lake (1921). Pohan was succeeded by choreographers who, following the lead of the Fromans in Zagreb, turned their attention toward contemporary themes. Aleksandar Trobisch staged The Flowers of Little Ida shortly after its Zagreb premiere in 1925, while Maria Tuljakova staged The Matchmaker (1925), The Gingerbread Heart (1925), and Capriccio Espagnol (1926) after Froman productions. Václav Vlček, also a Czech, took Bronislava Nijinska as precedent in his 1928 staging of Gabriel Piernés Impressions de Music-Hall, a "ballet à l'Américaine," just one year after its original production in Paris.

Jelena Poljakova, trained in Saint Petersburg, initiated the ballet revival in Belgrade with her stagings of The Nutcracker, Schéhérazade, and Les Sylphides in 1923. Although she turned her attention from choreography to pedagogy after this first season, she continued to influence the ballet revival for another two decades. Aleksandar Fortunato succeeded Poljakova as choreographer at the Belgrade Theater and staged additional works from the Russian repertory, including Coppélia (1924), the Polovtsian Dances from Prince Igor (1925), Giselle (1926), and Swan Lake (1926). In the late 1920s, Margarita Froman was invited to Belgrade and introduced ballets choreographed to music by contemporary composers, such as Manuel de Falla's El Sombrero de Tres Picos (1928), designed by Vladimir Zhedrinski.

Pia and Pino Mlakar were students of Rudolf Laban in Berlin. In 1933 they toured a program called New Ways and were invited the following year to stage Richard Strauss's Die Josephslegende and Till Eulenspiegel at the Belgrade Theater. At this time the Mlakars were ballet directors in Zurich, but they continued to stage works in Yugoslavia, notably The Devil in the Village, which was first performed in Zagreb in 1937 and in Belgrade in 1938. Set to music by Fran Lhotka, the full-length ballet integrated folk motifs, including a kolo in the concluding wedding festival. [See the entry on Mlakar.]

Meanwhile, Froman continued her choreographic efforts in all three centers of Yugoslavian ballet, and Nina Kirsanova in Belgrade joined the distinguished line of ballerina-choreographers who were also teachers. At the same time, the first generation of native dancers made its mark: Nataša Bošković, a student of Poljakova and of Olga Preobrajenska in Paris, who performed leading roles at the Belgrade Theater from 1918 to 1944; Mia Čorak-Slavenska, a student of Margarita Froman, who took leading roles in Zagreb from 1930 to 1937 (she later emigrated and became known as Mia Slavenska); and Ana Roje, a student of Froman and Poljakova who later assisted Nikolai Legat and, with her husband Oskar Harmoš, directed the Zagreb Ballet from 1945 to 1953. Roje was the last of the line of great female ballerina-choreographers who taught. Male dancers who attained distinction included Michel Panaiev and Igor Youskevitch.

After World War II, theatrical dance received generous government subsides following the Soviet model and expanded enormously. Ballet became established at theaters in Maribor, Novi Sad, Osijek, Rijeka, Sarajevo, Skopje, and Split. Audience surveys showed that in some areas interest in ballet equaled or surpassed interest in opera. The three traditional centers of Belgrade, Zagreb, and Ljubljana opened ballet schools offering extensive and rigorous training, and talented students received scholarships to finish their training in Russia. In 1959 Ljubljana became host to a biannual ballet competition.

Postwar choreography turned toward full-length contemporary ballets. Again Margarita Froman took a leading role with The Legend of Ochrid (1949). The action was set in the period of national struggle against Turkish oppression but alluded to the contemporary situation in Belgrade, which had nearly been destroyed in World War II. The work integrated folk motifs and classical ballet. The Janković sisters, early collectors of Slavic folk dances, had questioned the theatricalization of folk dances for the professional stage, but this theatricalization became an accepted practice in postwar choreography.

The Mlakars, whose The Devil in the Village had anticipated the new genre, made further contributions with The Bow (1946), The Little Ballerina (1947, and Danina, or Jocko the Brazilian Ape (1950). Other leading postwar choreographers were Franjo Horvat, who studied with Maletić and M. Zibine in Zagreb and later became director of the ballet in Sarajevo, and Dimitrije Parlić, who studied theater and dance at the Academy of Music in Belgrade and later choreographed for many theaters in Yugoslavia and abroad. [See the entry on Parlić.] Both Horvat and Parlić restaged what became the classics of the Yugoslav repertory, The Gingerbread Heart and The Legend of Ochrid, and choreographed original narrative works. Other choreographers explored the music of contemporary Yugoslav composers. Vera Kostić created Vibrations (1959) to music by Krešimir Fribec, while Nevenka Bidjin and Sonja Kastl created Symphony of a Dead Soldier (1959) to music by Branimir Sakač, The Man and His Mirror (1963) to music by Milko Kelemen, and Symphony in D (1965) to music by Luka Sorkočević.

Theatrical dance suffered a slump in the early 1980s. In the preceding decade Yugoslavia had become an exporter of dancers, but suddenly the country had to import dancers. Although technical standards remained high, artistic standards seemed to decline, except for the works of Milko Šparemblek. Especially notable were *Pjesme Ljubavi i Smrti* (Songs of Love and Death; 1981), set to music by Gustav Mahler; *The Soldier's Tale* (1983), to the score by Igor Stravinsky; and *Catulli Carmina* (1984), to the score by Carl Orff. [*See the entry on Šparemblek.*]

BIBLIOGRAPHY

Batušić, Nikola. *Hrvatsko kazaliste u Zagrebu, 1840–1992.* 2d ed. Zagreb, 1992.

Curcija-Prodanović, Nada. *Ballerina.* London, 1961.

Dragutinović, Branko. *Jedan vek Narodnog pozoriste u Beogradu, 1868–1968.* Belgrade, 1968.

Grbić-Softić, Slobodanka. *Osvajanje igre: Balet u Bosni i Hercegovini.* Sarajevo, 1986.

Gresserov-Golovin, Peter. *Moja ljuba Slovenija.* Ljubljana, 1985.

Hofmann, Wilfried. "Ballett in Belgrad." *Das Tanzarchiv* 25 (May 1977): 201–206.

Jovanović, Milica. *Balet Narodnog pozorišta u Beogradu izmedju dva rata.* Belgrade, 1976.

Lešić, Josip. *Narodno pozoriste Sarejevo, 1921–1971.* Sarajevo, 1972.

Luijdjens, Adriaan H. "Il balletto del Teatro Nazionale di Belgrado." *Balletto* 1 (November 1955): 55–63.

Magazinović, Maga. *Istorija igre.* Belgrade, 1951.

Maynard, Olga. "The Dance in Yugoslavia." *Dance Magazine* (May 1977): 67–82.

Mosusova, Nadezhda. "The Heritage of the Ballet Russe in Yugoslavia between the Two World Wars." In *Proceedings of the Eleventh Annual Conference, Society of Dance History Scholars, North Carolina School of the Arts, 12–14 February 1988,* compiled by Christena L. Schlundt. Riverside, Calif., 1988.

Rakić, Branka, and Radivoje Nikolajević. *Yugoslav Ballet.* Translated by Petar Mijušković. Belgrade, 1958.

Rakić, Branka. *Jugoslovenska baletna scena, 1950–1980.* Sarajevo, 1982.

Rakić, Branka. "Ballet." In *Zagreb Croatian National Theatre, 1860–1985.* Zagreb, 1985.

Ruyter, Nancy Lee Chalfa. "Pietro Coronelli, Dance Master of Zagreb." *Dance Research* 7 (Spring 1989): 78–81.

Sarabon, Mitja, ed. *Petdeset let slovenskega baleta.* Ljubljana, 1970. Contains Henrik Neubauer's "A Short History of the Slovene Ballet on Its Fiftieth Anniversary" (in English).

Turkalj, Nenad. "Opera and Ballet in Yugoslavia." *World Theatre* 15.5 (1966): 389–396.

Volk, Petar. *Beogradske scene.* Belgrade, 1978.

MILICA JOVANOVIĆ, PIA MLAKAR, and PINO MLAKAR

Modern Dance

In the 1930s, modern dance became an important influence on the Yugoslav dance scene. Although as early as 1921 Claudia Isačenko had introduced a Russianized form of Isadora Duncan's dancing to Belgrade, and by the mid-1920s Maga Maazinović had taught rhythmic dancing and plastique there, it was not until the 1930s that students of Rudolf Laban emerged as dancers of stature.

Ana Maletić was a student of Maazinović when she met Laban in 1924. After graduating from his school in Berlin, she returned to Zagreb, where she established a private school to teach his principles. Maletić also choreographed for her own company, staging works often based on national motifs and folklore, in close collaboration with Yugoslav composers. After World War II Maletić became attached to the Zagreb Music School. As a result of her efforts, a state school, the Zagreb School for Rhythmics and Dance, was established in 1955, the only one of its kind in the country. Some of the graduates of the school became eminent experts in their field. Among the most distinguished are Tihana Škrinjaric, Milana Broš, Lela Gluhak-Buneta, and Vera Maletić. Škrinjarić was one of the country's best-known modern dance choreographers. She also directed the school's dancers in the 1979 Mediterranean Games in Split and the 1984 Olympics in Sarajevo.

Ana Maletić's work was often inspired by national themes, as in her *Three Steles,* to music by Ivo Malec, a choreographic vision of the reliefs on medieval tombstones in Bosnia, or her choreographic satire, *Connections,* to a commissioned score by Boris Papandopulo, created in 1963 and performed in Zagreb and throughout Yugoslavia and then at Bayreuth. Her dramatic treatment of folkloric motifs is indeed her most notable achievement.

In 1962 Vera Maletić, Ana Maletić's daughter, opened the Studio of Contemporary Dance in Zagreb. The company's dancers experimented with sounds, the spoken word, and props as aural and visual components of dance. They created *Studies in Sound and Movement, After Love* (based on a poem by Vesna Parun), and *Skopje 63* (based on recollections of the disastrous earthquake in that city).

The 1960s were a decade of great experimentation and exciting innovations in the field of modern dance in Yugoslavia. Collaboration with television became an important part of the Studio's activities, and it found the demands of the medium to be very different from those of the theater. According to Vera Maletić, the International Music Council seminars and conferences in Zagreb, Vienna, and Salzburg, where numerous television ballets were screened and discussed, were tremendously stimulating and encouraging. Among the works that received critical and popular acclaim were *Connections* (Ana Maletić and Papandopulo) and *Formations* (Vera Maletić and Ruben Radica), the first co-production between TV-Zagreb and TV-Vienna, directed by Herman Lanske and presented at the Congress in Vienna in 1964; *Three Steles* (Ana Maletić and Ivo Malec) for TV-Zagreb, directed by Vladimir Seljan; and *Dessins Commentés* (Vera Maletić and Milko Kelemen), directed by Mladen Raukar; and *Équilibres* (Vera Maletić and Kelemen) for Stockholm television, directed by Arne Arnebom and screened at the Salzburg Congress in 1965.

From the beginning, the members of the Studio were aware of the need for a wider public appreciation of contemporary dance. To achieve this they started a successful collaboration with organizations concerned with arts appreciation for young people and with the wider public, such as the Musical Youth Organization, the Zagreb Theater of the Young, the Croatian State Ensemble of Folk Dance and Song, and People's University. Through these organizations they gave performances and lecture-demonstrations in schools, factories, and other places. They produced numerous programs sent on tour in Yugoslavia and abroad, consisting of works by the Studio members.

By the 1980s the Zagreb School was providing performers for Vera Maletić's company and two other professional modern dance troupes. The Studio for Contemporary Dance was then headed by Zaga Zivković and was no longer experimental, but more concerned with entertainment. Trained in both ballet and the Martha Graham technique, the dancers performed a wide-ranging repertory in concerts as well as in stage musicals and on television. The Ensemble for Free Dance (KASP), which also originated in 1962, was directed by Milana Bros. There, the emphasis was on minimalist concepts and improvisation. The Zagreb Dance Ensemble was founded in 1970 and headed by Mirna Zagar. The group performed modern works based on folk material. Zagar explained the use of folkloric themes: "These ideas are a part of our lives; they are the soul of our society and our land."

BIBLIOGRAPHY

Hofmann, Wilfried, "Ein Pionier des freien Tanzes: Smiljana Mandukic." *Das Tanzarchiv* 25 (April 1977).

Lawrence, Lee A. "News: Zagreb," *Dance Magazine* (November 1985).

Maletić, Vera. "Modern Dance Strives in Yugoslavia." *Dance News* (June 1966).

Mosusova, Nadezbda. "American Dance Abroad: A View from Yugoslavia." In *Proceedings of the Fifteenth Annual Conference, Society of Dance History Scholars, University of California, Riverside, 14–15 February 1992,* compiled by Christena L. Schlundt. Riverside, Calif., 1992.

JASNA PERUČIĆ NADAREVIĆ

Theatrical Dance Since 1991

The breakup of the former Yugoslavia began in June 1991 when Slovenia, soon followed by Croatia and later by Bosnia and Macedonia, became independent countries. Only Serbia and Montenegro continued to exist under the name Yugoslavia. Dance in Yugoslavia thus meant dance in Serbia, since Montenegro never developed professional theatrical dance.

Serbia. In Belgrade, the capital, and in Novi Sad, the second-largest city, the dance community struggled through difficult times but succeeded in maintaining a continuity in its work while the audience showed a renewed interest in theater, as is often the case in troubled times.

The cultural isolation that followed the imposition of United Nations economic sanctions created harsh conditions for dance in Serbia. While before the war a large and tightly knit dance community enjoyed frequent exchanges with a national and international dance scene, following the outbreak of hostilities Yugoslav dance activity was confined to the country's two largest cities. In Belgrade the National Theater managed to maintain the classica repertory, though few new ballet productions were mounted. The survival of modern dance, known as "alternative dance," was assisted by the enthusiasm of individuals and the form's association with long-established traditions of avant-garde theater.

Ballet. The National Theater in Belgrade presented stagings of *Coppélia, Giselle, Don Quixote, La Bayadere* and *Swan Lake.* Contemporary repertory consisted of pieces by Aleksandar Izrailovski, Krunislav Simić, and Lidija Pilipenko. Leading dancers were Ashen Ataljanc

YUGOSLAVIA: Theatrical Dance since 1991. Andjela Djaković as Odette and Denis Kasatkin as Siegfried in a performance of *Swan Lake* at the National Theater in Belgrade in 1995. (Photograph courtesy of Xenia Rakic.)

Duška Dragicĕvić, and Konstantin Koskjukov. The company's artistic directorship changed hands several times.

Elsewhere in Belgrade, Sava Centar presented an "Homage to Dimitrije Parlić," conceived and created by Višnja Djordjević, in 1993. This event was produced in an effort to conserve the work of Yugoslavia's most prolific and successful ballet choreographer. Several Broadway musicals were also staged.

In Novi Sad, the ballet company at the Serbian National Theater presented *Giselle, The Little Humpbacked Horse, La Fille Mal Gardée, Les Sylphides, The Nutcracker, Swan Lake*, and several contemporary pieces. Leading dancers included Rastislav Varga, Mihai Babuşka, Ana Kusnirova, and Oksana Storozuk.

Modern dance. Modern dance, commonly referred to as "alternative dance," developed mainly during the 1980s in Yugoslavia. By 1991 a number of modern companies and independent choreographers were established in Belgrade. Television, cultural centers, and presenters increasingly commissioned work by young modern choreographers. New dance venues included the Bitef Teatar and the Small Stage at the National Theater. There were performance spaces in concert halls (Sava Centar, Kolarac), cultural centers (the Students Cultural Center, Kud Abrašević), and traditional theaters (Atelje 212, Beogradsko Dramsko Pozorište, Yuglovensko Dramsko).

Smiljana Mandukić (1980–1992), teacher, choreographer, and founder of the Contemporary Belgrade Ballet, left a modern legacy that was developed by her students. Prominent among them is Nela Antonović, who established her own dance company, Mimart, in 1984. Other choreographers associated with Mandukić are Katarina Stojkov-Slijepčević, teacher at the Lupo Davičo National Ballet School; Vesna Milanović, who is with the Belgrade Dance Theater; and Vera Obradović, associated with the Ballet XXI Movement.

Under the auspices of the Belgrade International Theater Festival (BITEF) and its home theater, the Bitef Teatar, a number of evening-length works were created. These include *The Portrait of Dorian Grey* (1991) and *Macbeth against Macbeth* (1992), both choreographed by Dejan Pajović to music by Nenad Jeličić; *Medea* (1991), by Sonja Vukičević, former dancer at the National Theater, to music by Zoran Erić; and *Isadora* (1991), by Jelena Santić, another former National Theater dancer, to a score by Ivana Stefanović. Nada Kokotović, who left the country to work in Germany, is well known for her choreodramas, which were performed throughout the former Yugoslavia.

The Belgrade National Theater joined presenters of modern dance by offering its Small Stage to choreographers with the company's ranks of dancers. Aleksandar Isyellovski began presenting work there

YUGOSLAVIA: Theatrical Dançe since 1991. Jelena Santić in the "Death of Isadora" scene from her evening-length dance-theater work *Isadora* (1991), set to a score by Ivana Stefanović. (Photograph courtesy of Xenia Rakic.)

annually after 1990; Violeta Dubak was another dancer who choreographed for the space. In 1994, Sava Centar presented Andjelija Todorović's work *Island, Dance of Atoms*, performed by the Ister Theater.

Novi Sad has no modern dance tradition to speak of. However, after 1980 there was a surge of interest in contemporary dance forms. Jazz became popular, and several private studios that opened enrolled a large public. Choreographers organized showcases for their work and the community responded by including contemporary dance in many cultural programs and public celebrations. The gap between contemporary dance, regarded as popular entertainment, and ballet, perceived as high art, began to narrow. Most of the new studios and performing groups were directed by graduates of the national school and former members of the Serbian National Theater. At the national school itself, the curriculum was expanded to include jazz and modern dance. Excerpts from Mats Ek's *Giselle*, staged by Nada Draženta, were performed to critical acclaim at the school's recital in 1994.

A local choreographer of outstanding achievement, Tatjana Grujić, won first and second prizes for choreographer at the Yugoslav Ballet Competition held in Novi Sad in 1990. Grujić cofounded Studio Rebis with Gordana Dean Gačić in 1989. A former gymnast, she included elements of formal ballet, jazz, and modern dance in her work. Other successful studios and schools include Partizan 2, founded in 1987 by Jelena Andrejev; Lala-Znanje, founded in 1990 by Dragan Rančev; City Dance Studio, founded in 1991 by Vesna Šećerov and Vera Markuš; and the Educational Group for Modern Dance, founded in

1991 at the College of Physical Education by Professor Ljiljana Mišić.

The first International Festival of Alternative and New Theater (INFANT) was held in July 1995 as part of the Novi Sad Summer Festival. Among the companies taking part were Mimart and Ister Theater from Belgrade.

Bosnia. From the time it was founded in 1946, the Sarajevo Opera possessed a ballet group, initially directed by Eduard Venier, a dancer from Zagreb. Ubavka Milanković, a dancer from Sarajevo, directed the ballet school. At first the ballet served exclusively the needs of opera productions, but this changed in 1949 when Jitka Ivelja was named principal dancer and Franjo Horvat, a Croat, became resident choreographer. Ivelja and Horvat presented the first ballet productions. *Žetva* (Harvest), premiered in May 1950, marked the professional coming of age of the Sarajevo Ballet. A full-length work, it was choreographed by Nina Kirsanova, a guest artist from Belgrade, to the music of Boris Papandopulo, a Bosnian composer.

Over the next four decades, the Sarajevo Ballet developed into a strong regional company. The school provided the company with young dancers, but principal roles were often given to guest artists from abroad and from republics of what was then Yugoslavia. In April 1992 war erupted in Sarajevo. The ballet was then directed by Nedžad Potogija, who oversaw a new production of *Swan Lake*, staged by visiting Russian Vladimir Riabov, in December 1991. The leading roles were danced by Tatiana Kladnikina and Vladimir Grigorjiev, both guests from Russia. War interrupted all the regular functions of the national theater in Sarajevo. Nevertheless, in May 1993 Potogija presented those dancers who remained in the city in excerpts from *Carmina Burana*. Since the building housing the National Opera was damaged, this performance took place in a small theater. Dancers continued to leave the city; by 1994, only six remained. Potogija presented these six in *Boléro*, choreographed by Dragutin Boldin, at the repaired Opera in May 1994. Following the peace accord of November 1995, the National Theater resumed work. Artistic director of the ballet was Bahria Bihorac. Independently, in November 1992 choreographer and director Slavko Pervan, the ballet's former artistic director (1975–1978 and 1980–1983), caused a sensation with a production of the musical *Hair* in Sarajevo.

Macedonia. National opera and ballet companies were founded in Skopje, the republic's capital, in 1948. A year later Georgije Makedonski, who had been trained in Zagreb and Belgrade, was appointed artistic director of the ballet. He soon established a national ballet academy affiliated with the company. In 1953, the company presented its first national full-length work, *The Macedonian Tale*, choreographed by Dimitrije Parlić to music by Gligor Smokvarski. The company became one of the major troupes in Yugoslavia. Its repertory consisted of traditional nineteenth-century classics and contemporary works. Macedonian choreographers were fostered, but guests from other Yugoslav republics and abroad were also invited. Parlić maintained a connection to the company throughout his career.

YUGOSLAVIA: Theatrical Dance since 1991. Dragutin Boldin choreographed his *Boléro*, to the music of Maurice Ravel, for the last six dancers remaining in Sarajevo in May 1994, after two years of brutal Serb bombardment. The dancers were (left to right) Haris Šabanović, Adnan Džindo, and Mensud Vatić, with (kneeling) Irma Ugrinčić, Brižita Karabašić, and Tefeda Abazović. (Photograph courtesy of Xenia Rakic.)

YUGOSLAVIA: Theatrical Dance since 1991. Vojko Vidmar, Marko Omerzel, Mojmir Lasan, and Tomaž Rode of the Ballet of Ljubljana in Milko Šparemblek's *Enigma Gallus*, in a 1989 performance. The set was designed by Nenad Fabijanić, with costumes by Mojca Makuc. (Photograph courtesy of Vojko Vidmar.)

Following Macedonia's independence in September 1992, the company continued to present ballets. Many guests from Russia were invited to stage works, and several ballets by Dragutin Boldin, Iskra Sukarova, and Ekrem Husein were produced. Leading dancers of the era included Goran Božinov, Zoica Purovska, Zoran Velevski, Tanja Vujisik.

Slovenia. Following Slovenia's withdrawal from Yugoslavia in 1991, the country continued to support two ballet companies. The Ballet of Ljubljana, in the capital, had about fifty dancers, or twice the number of the troupe in Maribor. Although government funding was reduced, the company in Ljubljana continued to produce two new works a year and that in Maribor one. The Ljubljana company, which has staged more than two hundred works in a history extending back to the early years of the twentieth century, is primarily a classical troupe. Native choreographers who have worked with the company include Pino Mlakar, Milko Šparemblek, Vlasto Dedović, and Ivo Kosi. Some of their works are set to music by Slovenian composers. Works by international choreographers include Birgit Cullberg's *Romeo and Juliet;* Irina Lukashova's stagings of *Giselle* and *The Nutcracker;* Croat Dinko Bogdanović's *Don Quixote;* Toer van Schayk's *Pyrrhic Dances II, Chimera,* and *Orpheus;* and Argentine Julio López's *A Midsummer Night's Dream.*

Ballet is often aired on television; consequently, most productions exist on videotape. Many ballets are co-produced with foreign television stations; Cullberg's *Romeo and Juliet,* for example, was taped in a co-production with Swedish television, and Valery Panov's *Dreyfus: J'accuse* was a coproduction with the Bonn Ballet and English,

Swedish, and German partners. There are also some videodance festivals such as Dance Screen, Video Dance, and Prix Italia.

The country's leading ballet dancer is Vojko Vidmar, whose thirtieth year of dancing was celebrated in a telecast in which the dancer received the country's highest artist award, the Great Prešeren prize, named after France Prešeren, Slovenia's most famous poet. (Other twentieth-century ballet dancers who were similarly honored include Pia Mlakar, Pino Mlakar, Tatjana Remškar, and Mojmir Lasan.)

Maribor's renovated theater includes a modern stage and large auditorium. Major productions include *The Nutcracker,* staged by Vaslav Orlikovsky; *Don Quixote,* staged by Valery Panov; *Giselle* and *Romeo and Juliet;* and contemporary works by Vasily Solomon and Maja Milenović-Workman.

BIBLIOGRAPHY

Cerić, Zoran. "Šest 'Alternativaca'." *Borba, Kultura* (26 June 1995).
Jovanović, Milica. *Balet Narodnog Pozorišta u Beogradu.* Belgrade, 1994. See Chapter 1, "Prvih Sedamdeset Godina."
Katić-Serban, Minja. "Kako Postaješ Ratnik, ili o Sonji." *Orchestra,* no. 2 (Summer 1995): 34–35.
Maksimović, Bogdan. "Intervju Nada Kokotović." *Orchestra,* no. 3 (Winter 1996): 26–27.
Mandukić, Smiljana. *Govor Tela, Iskustvo Modernog Baleta.* Belgrade, 1990.
Marinković-Rakić, Branka, and Nikolajević Radivoje. *Yugoslav Ballet.* Belgrade, 1958.
Narodno Pozorište Sarajevo. *Sarajevski Balet 1950–1990.* Sarajevo, 1990.
Radmanović, Duška. "Pod Našim Krovom." *Pozorište,* no. 6 (February 1992): 17.
Savić, Svenka. "Studiske i Igračke Grupe u Novom Sadu." *Pozorište,* nos. 8–10 (April–June 1993): 30–31.
Savić, Svenka. "Balet Bez Pozorišta." *Pozorište,* nos. 1–2 (October–November 1994): 33.
Savić, Svenka. "Lepo I Umetnicki Ozbiljno." *Pozorište,* nos. 1–5 (September–December 1995, January 1996): 41.
"Slavko Pervan," *Svijet* (11 April 1996).
Srpsko Narodno Pozorište. "45 Godina Baleta Srpskog Narodnog Pozorišta (repertoar 1950–95)." *Pozorište,* addition to nos. 6–7 (March–April 1995): 47–78.
Zajcev, Milica. "U Devetoj Decenij Stvaralaštva." *Pozorište,* nos. 1–2, (September–October 1991): 35.
Zajcev, Milica. "Prednost Izražajnom Pokretu Tela." *Pozorište,* nos. 1–2, (September–October 1991): 36–38.
Zajcev, Milica. "Povratak Tradiciji." *Pozorište,* nos. 7–8 (March–April 1992): 61.
Zajcev, Milica. "Biliar Iza Zatvorenih Vrata." *Pozorište,* nos. 8–10 (April–June 1993): 33.
Zajcev, Milica. "Igra Uprkos Ratu." *Hello Belgrade,* no. 9 (December 1993–January 1994): 19.
Zajcev, Milica. "U Iščekivanju Novog Jutra. . . ." *Hello Belgrade,* no. 12 (April–May 1994): 21.
Zajcev, Milica. *Igra Što Život Znači: Zapisi O Beogradskim Baletskim Umetnicima.* Belgrade, 1994.
Zajcev, Milica. "Mladi Dolaze." *Pozorište,* nos. 1–5 (September–December 1995, January 1996): 41.

XENIA RAKIC, ANI UDOVICKI, and VOJKO VIDMAR

Dance Research and Publication

Research in the field of dance in the Balkans has not been very extensive. Since universities have not offered dance curricula, teachers and choreographers, not to mention dance scholars, have not been able to study dance in an academic context. Young musicologists, later responsible for dance in theater museums, learned nothing of dance in their university years. The research that has been done is mostly by dancers, choreographers, and museum workers. Most has been in the history of development of regional dance, the work of certain dance companies, and personalities on the Yugoslav dance scene.

Research in Yugoslavia before 1991. Nearly all dance publications of the communist era were published on anniversaries or other festive occasions. No dance periodicals existed, probably because Yugoslavia was a multiethnic state with three mutually unintelligible languages. Furthermore, Yugoslavia did not have a ministry of culture on the federal level. The only scientific dance institutions in the country were the institutes for folk art and folk dance in Ljubljana, Skopje, Zagreb, Sarajevo, and other cities, which pursued research and were closely connected with folk dance groups in their respective regions. These institutes issued numerous publications describing in words and Labanotation the rich variety of national dances in Yugoslavia.

There were some attempts to assemble dancers, choreographers, dance teachers, and dance critics to discuss problems facing Yugoslavian ballet. Festival Ljubljana used the occasion of the Yugoslav Ballet Biennial to organize symposiums. Every two years, dance scholarship works were presented and discussed. Festival Ljubljana also started a short-lived quarterly newsletter on dance.

In 1958 the commission for cultural relations with foreign countries published the English-language book *Yugoslav Ballet*. The authors, Branka Marinković-Rakić and Radivoje Nikolajević, wrote about the origins of ballet in Yugoslavia and described the development of ballet companies. Some books and articles written later presented more facts on regional dance. Also worth mentioning is Slobodanka Grbić-Softić's *Osvajanje igre* (Conquering the Dance), published in 1958. This history of dance in Bosnia and Herzegovina spans the period from the appearance of the first dancers in that republic until the founding of the first professional company in 1950. To commemorate the twentieth anniversary of that company, Slobodan Spirić wrote an article in 1970, "Twenty Years of the Sarajevo Ballet." Two books published in 1968 describe theater life in Belgrade. The first is *One Hundred Years of the National Theater*, for which Veroslava Petrović and Ksenija Orenković contributed articles on the Belgrade Ballet from 1918 to 1941 and from 1944 to 1968. The other book, written by Belgrade The-

ater dramatist Branko Dragutinović, is *Jedan vek Narodnog pozorista u Beogradu, 1868–1968* (A Century of National Theater of Belgrade), with a section devoted to opera and ballet. In 1976 Milica Jovanović wrote an article in *Teatron 5* entitled "Ballet of the National Theater [Belgrade] between Two Wars," using documents of that time to chronicle the Belgrade Ballet between 1922 and 1941, when German bombs destroyed the theater. The Zagreb Theater's hundredth anniversary was commemorated in *Croatian National Theater 1860–1950*, with a short article by Josip Kavur, "Ballet of the Croatian National Theater from Its Foundation till Today." Nikola Batušić wrote *Hrvatsko kazaliste u Zagrebu, 1840–1992* (History of the Croatian Theater), which briefly mentions opera and ballet.

In Slovenia, most research work in dance history was done by Henrik Neubauer. His notable articles include "Ballet Problems in Yugoslavia," and "Slavko Osterc [a composer] and the Slovene Ballet," "A Chronicle on the Development of Ballet Art in Ljubljana," and "A List of Ballet and Dance Performances in Ljubljana from the Middle of the Eighteenth Century Onward" (all 1963); "Chronological Survey of the Development of Slovene Ballet" (1970), which included lists of performances by the ballet companies in Ljubljana and Maribor; "A Short History of the Slovene Ballet on Its 50th Anniversary" (in English, 1970); and "A Chronicle of the Ballet School in Ljubljana" (1970).

Also worth mentioning are memoirs of the Russian-born Peter Gresserov-Golovin, the late ballet master and choreographer in Ljubljana and Maribor. His book *Moja ljuba Slovenija* (My Beloved Slovenia), issued in 1985 in a translation from Russian by Henrik Neubauer, evokes his life and work. It includes descriptions of dancers, choreographers, singers, directors, conductors, composers, and designers during the period from 1924 to 1951. Pino Mlakar, another former ballet master of the Ljubljana Ballet, wrote "Ballet on the Slovene Stage" (1967) for the Slovene Theater Museum.

Various articles have also been published about personalities from different Yugoslav ballet companies—Margarita Froman, Pia and Pino Mlakar, Slavko Pervan, Katarina Kocka, Stane Polik, Lidija Sotlar, Tatjana Remškar, Lidija Wisiak, Jelena Poljakova, Nada Murašova, Erika Marjaš, Radomir Vučić, Ivanka Lukatelli, and others. There are also reference works dealing with dance personalities, such as *Slovene Biographical Lexicon, Slovene Theatrical Lexicon, Music Encyclopedia, Lexicon of Yugoslav Music, Encyclopedia of Croatian National Theater, National Theater of Sarajevo 1921–1971*, and *Slovene Encyclopaedia*.

Research dedicated to folk dance is also conducted in different regions of Yugoslavia, and many books and articles describing various folk dances have been issued. Notable among the folk dance books are the eight volumes produced by Ljubica S. Janković and Danica S. Janković from 1934 to 1964, *Narodne igre*.

Research in Slovenia since 1991. Since declaring its independence in 1991 Slovenia has reorganized the system of cultural institutions it had inherited from Yugoslavia. Under the direction of the new ministry of culture, progress is being made slowly to bring Slovenia in line with other European countries in the area of dance research. The Institute for Folk Art and Folk Dance is now attached to the Slovenian Academy of Art and Science, and the Slovenian Theater Museum is gradually collecting all the materials and documents concerning theater and dance.

Most dance research is still done by Henrik Neubauer. In 1992 he published "Balet ob 100-letnici" (Ballet at the Hundredth Anniversary), included in *One Hundred Years of the Opera House in Ljubljana*, published by the Slovenian National Theater in Ljubljana. In the same year the Slovenian Theater Museum published his *Glasbeno gledališka dela slovenskih skladateljev* (Music Theater Works of Slovenian Composers), a comprehensive survey of all ballets, operas, and operettas by Slovenian composers. The book includes a chronological list of 129 works performed between 1798 and 1992 with dates and venues of their premieres, and of ninety-three never-performed works. The book's second chapter includes an alphabetical listing by composer with the names of their works, dates of composition, names of librettists, and a brief synopsis for each work. Of the 222 compositions described, sixty are ballet scores. Neubauer's book *The Development of Ballet Art in Slovenia* was published in 1997 by the Association of Ballet Artists of Slovenia. He also contributed a short article entitled "Dance Theater in Slovenia" to the *World Encyclopedia of Contemporary Theater*.

In 1993 the Ballet School in Ljubljana issued a brochure for its forty-fifth anniversary, which included "Ljubljanasha baletna šola od 1970 do 1993" (Ballet School in Ljubljana from 1970 to 1993) by Alenka Tomc, a ballet teacher. In 1993 Breda Pretnar, a ballet and dance critic, wrote "Experimental Works and Renewals (Slovenian Dance Scene)," published in English by the Slovenian Center of the International Theater Institute (ITI) in a survey on the 1992/93 theater season under the title "Slovenian Theater 1993"; Neubauer's "A Good Sign for the Future" (also in English), was included in the ITI's survey for the following season.

Henrik Neubauer

Z

ZAÏRE. *For discussion of dance in Zaïre, renamed Congo in 1997, see* Central and East Africa. *See also* Mbuti Dance *and* Sub-Saharan Africa, *article on* Popular Dance in Sub-Saharan Africa. *For dance traditions in the African diaspora, see* Brazil, *article on* Popular and Ritual Dance.

ZAJLICH, PIOTR (born 26 June 1884 in Warsaw, died 18 April 1948 in Warsaw), Polish dancer, choreographer, and ballet director. A graduate of the ballet school affiliated with Warsaw's Wielki Theater, Piotr Zajlich performed with the Warsaw Ballet from 1900 to 1910. The following year he joined Serge Diaghilev's Ballets Russes for a season, and from 1912 to 1914 he worked with Anna Pavlova's company as both principal dancer and choreographer, often under the Russian pseudonym Shouvalov. Among the works he created for Pavlova were *Invitation to the Dance, Oriental Fantasy,* and a version of Petipa's *Halte de Cavalerie.*

Zajlich spent the years from 1914 to 1917 in a German prisoner-of-war camp. Upon his release he returned to Warsaw, where he took over the direction of the Wielki Theater school and company until 1934. He reformed the curriculum by adding rhythmic gymnastics and academic classes. His pupils included Ballets Russes stars Roman Jasinski, Yurek Lazowski, and Yurek Shabelevsky. He reestablished the artistic level of the Warsaw company, producing a large repertory. Among his works were revivals of classics such as *Swan Lake, Giselle,* and *Coppélia,* as well as a selection of Diaghilev ballets, including *Les Sylphides, Schéhérazade, Petrouchka,* and *The Firebird.* In addition, he created original ballets based on Polish national tradition, and these he cultivated with special care. As a choreographer he remained traditional, even in his revisions of the Diaghilev repertory. His 1921 version of *Pan Twardowski* was especially popular, although he also set works to music of contemporary Polish composers, such as Karol Szymanowski's *Songs of Hafiz* and Ludomir Rogowski's *The Fable.* For the Polish Ballet, Zajlich restaged *Kraków Wedding* in 1938/39. After World War II, he led a small company that performed with the opera in a Warsaw theater that had escaped major damage.

[*See also* Warsaw Ballet.]

BIBLIOGRAPHY

Dąbrowski, Stanisław, and Zbigniew Raszewski, eds. *Słownik biograficzny teatru polskiego.* 2 vols. Warsaw, 1973–1994.
Kinel, Lola. "Ludomir Rozycki and His *Pan Twardowski.*" *Musical Standard* 17 (1921): 209–210.
Kinel, Lola. "The Great Polish Ballet-Pantomime, *Pan Twardowski.*" *Poland America* 4 (November 1923): 287–291, 309–310.
Mamontowicz-Łojek, Bożena. *Terpsychora i lekkie muzy.* Kraków, 1972.
Pudełek, Janina. *Z historii baletu.* Warsaw, 1981.
Pudełek, Janina. *Two Hundred Years of Polish Ballet, 1785–1985.* Warsaw, 1985.
Rebling, Eberhard. "Pan Twardowski." In *Ballet von A bis Z.* Berlin, 1966.

JANINA PUDEŁEK

ZAKHAROV, ROSTISLAV (Rostislav Vladimirovich Zakharov; born 7 September 1907 in Astrakhan, Russia, died 14 January 1984 in Moscow), dancer, choreographer, teacher, art director, and artistic director. Zakharov graduated in 1926 from the Leningrad Choreographic Institute, where he trained under Vladimir Ponomarev. His first professional positions were as a dancer with the ballet companies of Kharkov and then Kiev, where he became a soloist and essayed his first choreography for amateur groups and students, and married ballerina Maria Smirnova. Aware of the prevailing trend toward dramatizing ballet, he returned to Leningrad in 1928 to study stage directing with Vladimir Soloviev at the Leningrad Institute of Theatrical Art, and graduated in 1932. He had continued to choreograph and also began to collaborate on stage productions with the director Sergei Radlov. At the time Radlov was artistic director of the State Academic Theater for Opera and Ballet; he brought Zakharov into the company as a dancer and choreographer.

Zakharov created his first and most outstanding ballet, *The Fountain of Bakhchisarai,* for the company in 1934. Set to a score by Boris Asafiev and a libretto by Nikolai Volkov based on Aleksandr Pushkin's eponymous poem, it tells an exotic and lustful tale of love and revenge. Zakharov wrote in 1977:

> After I had the good luck to mingle with the people and witness their everyday life, traveling from town to town and visiting workers' settlements, seeing how they lived and learning of their aspirations, I realized that our art failed to portray that

seething life, those profound human emotions, but was confined to its narrow shell. I realized that ballet just as any dramatic or operatic production should have depth and should be comprehensible without recourse to program notes. The action had to be so organized that the plot could develop logically and consistently, that the protagonists could be lifelike characters in the process of interaction and conflict. I reasoned that since the ballet is theater, and theater is a public stage from which the people are told about themselves, about the beauty and cruelty of life, and about the variety of man's inner world that induces him to action, ballet has no right to stand aloof from real life.

Zakharov embodied these principles in *The Fountain of Bakhchisarai*. Before he began to choreograph he conducted research into pertinent historical material and literary sources. To prepare the work for the stage he introduced to the ballet world the principles of character development formulated by Konstantin Stanislavsky. Concepts such as "superobjective," "through-composed action," "the kernel of a role," and the actor's "period of study" were brought into play and the moral and philosophical foundations of the work explained, so that the dancers would not only dance but also act. So successful was the ballet at its premiere that it remained a company staple and was also restaged at the Bolshoi Theater in Moscow. [*See* Fountain of Bakhchisarai, The.]

In 1938 Zakharov joined the Bolshoi Theater, where he remained for twenty years, as choreographer for the ballet and the opera companies as well as a stage director for operas. There he produced other ballets based on Pushkin's works: *The Prisoner of the Caucasus* (1938) and *Mistress into Maid* (1946), both to music by Asafiev, and *The Bronze Horseman* (1949) to music of Reinhold Glière. All of them developed, each in its distinctive way, the genre of Soviet *dram-balet*, or dramatic ballet. The principles of dramatic ballet included a close link with literature, a clear-cut concept of dramaturgy and stage direction, and a reliance on the acting dancer. This implied a renunciation of the structural forms of traditional ballets: divertissements and a broad use of pantomime. In Soviet dramatic ballets the language of classical dance mingled with character dance, which was dictated by commitment to the people, realism, and social significance. Ballet sought to be lifelike and appeal to mass audiences.

In the chamber comedy ballet *Mistress into Maid* Zakharov was attracted by the lyrical theme of love, the atmosphere and style of Pushkin's epoch. The large-scale historico-philosophic ballet *The Bronze Horseman* conveyed the idea of Pushkin's poem: the indomitable Russian national spirit, symbolized by the image of Peter the Great and his capital Saint Petersburg. The ballet also incorporated elements of a fairy play. The production was replete with grandiose stage effects: scenes of a flood in Saint Petersburg, the launching of a ship, and the assem-

bly of the statue of Peter the Great. There was also a clear dramatic line in the lyrical relations between the protagonists Yegeny and Parasha.

Realism was the hallmark of Zakharov's *Taras Bulba* (1941), to music by Vladimir Soloviev-Sedoi, and *Lost Illusions* (1936), to music by Asafiev, based on works of Nikolai Gogol and Honoré de Balzac, respectively; in *Taras Bulba* Zakharov worked on a synthesis of classical dance with Ukrainian folklore. He was further the first interpreter of Sergei Prokofiev's score *Cinderella* (1945); his production was in the repertory for almost thirty years and was filmed as *The Crystal Slipper*. He produced a new version of Glière's *The Red Poppy* in 1949 as well as a revival in 1939 of the classical favorite *Don Quixote*, which is still in the Bolshoi Ballet repertory. In it, while preserving what had been created by Marius Petipa and later Aleksandr Gorsky, Zakharov reinforced the plot and added a number of new dances: a jig, a dance with guitars, and a fandango.

As a choreographer Zakharov's principles set the guidelines for the development of multinational Soviet ballet. He choreographed for the new postrevolutionary audiences but at the same time recognized the historical traditions of ballet, which proved an effective choice. Early on he collaborated with fellow choreographers such as Vasily Vainonen, Leonid Lavrovsky, Vakhtang Chabukiani, and Konstantin Sergeyev, but in practice and in theory he was the most active and consistent champion of dramatic ballet. Thus, from the 1930s to the 1950s Zakharov's art played an important role in converting ballet from what was perceived as a narrow elitist art to a popular art, close to the people ideologically and aesthetically, and his ballets were the core of his companies' repertory. He also influenced a generation of outstanding dancers. Galina Ulanova, Olga Lepeshinskaya, Marina Semenova, Olga Jordan, Natalia Dudinskaya, Tatiana Vecheslova, Raisa Struchkova, Maya Plisetskaya, Konstantin Sergeyev, Aleksei Yermolayev, Mikhail Gabovich, and many others revealed their talents in Zakharov's productions. But by the onset of the 1960s his adherence to dramatic ballet as the only correct manifestation of socialist realism came to be increasingly criticized. Only his importance as head of prominent training schools protected his position: from 1945 to 1947 he was director of the Moscow School of Choreography, and from 1946 until his death head of the choreography department, which he had founded, at the Lunacharsky Institute for Theatrical Art.

Zakharov's staging of dances in operas such as *Ruslan and Ludmila*, *Ivan Susanin*, *Aïda*, and *Carmen* was distinguished. He was also acknowledged as a fine director of operas. His 1937 production of Mikhail Glinka's *Ruslan and Ludmila* at the Bolshoi Theater was famous. The stagings of Gioacchino Rossini's *William Tell* in Kuibyshev in 1942 and at the Bolshoi in 1944 won Zakharov the State

Prize of the USSR. His production of Georges Bizet's *Carmen* at the Bolshoi in 1943 was in the repertory for many years. Zakharov also demonstrated his talent as a director in productions of large open-air performances. At world festivals of youth and students in Prague (1947), Budapest (1949), Berlin (1951), Bucharest (1953), and Moscow (1957), he was the chief director of the Soviet delegation, organizing performances that combined elements of athletic parades, massive spectacles, dance festivals, and artistic political manifestations. As a principal director of the Sixth Moscow Festival he staged the ballet *Our Flourishing Youth* at the new Lenin Stadium, in which 2,500 performers from all Soviet republics participated.

Zakharov was a prolific and often contentious writer, using the medium as a means to answer his critics. Among his books are *Iskusstvo baletmeistera* (The Art of Choreography; 1954), *Besedy o tantse* (Conversations on Dance; 1963); *Rabota baletmeistera s ispolniteliami* (The Choreographer's Work with Dancers; 1967), *Zapiski baletmeistera* (A Choreographer's Notes; 1976), *Slovo o tantse* (A Word on Dance; 1977), and *Sochinenie tantsa* (Composition of Dance; 1983.) He won the State Prize of the USSR in 1943, 1944, 1945, and 1946, and was named People's Artist of the USSR in 1969.

BIBLIOGRAPHY

Anisimov, Aleksandr I., ed. *Balet Gosudarstvennogo Ordena Lenina Akademicheskogo Bol'shogo Teatr SSSR.* Moscow, 1955.
Barnes, Clive. "Kirov Ballet Backdrop." *Dance Magazine* (September 1961): 40–47.
Brinson, Peter, ed. *Ulanova, Moiseyev, and Zakharov on Soviet Ballet.* Translated by E. Fox and D. Fry. London, 1954.
Dementieva, N. "Tvorcheskaya neutomimost." *Sovetskii balet*, no. 6 (1983).
Ivashnev, Vitalii, and Kira Ilyina. *Rostislav Zakharov: Zhizn v tantse.* Moscow, 1982.
Krasovskaya, Vera. "New Thoughts in the USSR." *Dance Magazine* (February 1966): 33–35.
Roslavleva, Natalia. "Stanislavski and the Ballet." *Dance Perspectives*, no. 23 (1965).
Roslavleva, Natalia. *Era of the Russian Ballet* (1966). New York, 1979.
Slonimsky, Yuri. *Sovetskii balet.* Moscow, 1950.
Zakharov, Rostislav. "Dramaturgy of the Ballet." *Dance Magazine* (June 1953): 24, 46–47.
Zakharov, Rostislav. *Slovo o tantse.* Moscow, 1977.
Zakharov, Rostislav. *Sochinenie tantsa.* 2d ed. Moscow, 1989.

GALINA V. BELYAYEVA-CHELOMBITKO
Translated from Russian

ZAMBELLI, CARLOTTA (Carolina Celia Luigia Zambelli; born 4 November 1875 in Milan, died 28 January 1968 in Milan), Italian dancer. While a student at the ballet school of Teatro alla Scala in Milan, Zambelli studied under Cesare Coppini. In 1894 Pedro Gailhard hired her for the Paris Opera. Already possessed of an excellent technique, she was an immediate success in a variation with a mirror in *Faust*. After her interpretation of the

Fairy of the Snows in *La Maladetta* (choreography by Joseph Hansen), in which she replaced Rosita Mauri, she was named *étoile* ("star"). She danced in numerous opera *divertissements*, including that of *La Favorite*, in which she executed fifteen *fouettés*, something never before achieved in France; in *Le Cid*, her spirit and provocative suppleness aroused wonder. She performed *L'Étoile* (choreography by Hansen) and *La Korrigane* (choreography by Louis Mérante). Invited to the Maryinsky Theater in Saint Petersburg in 1901, she danced *Coppélia*, *Paquita*, and *Giselle*, which she rehearsed with Enrico Cecchetti.

Zambelli stamped her personality on many ballets, including *La Ronde des Saisons* (choreography by Hansen), *La Fête chez Thérèse* (choreography by Madame Stichel), *Namouna* (choreography revised by Léo Staats), and *Suite de Danses* (choreography by Ivan Clustine). She was a graceful embodiment of the charming Gourouli of Mérante's *Les Deux Pigeons;* in his *Sylvia*, she ensured the

ZAMBELLI. From 1898 until 1930, Zambelli reigned supreme as *première danseuse étoile* at the Paris Opera. She posed for this charming publicity photograph around the turn of the century. (Photograph from the Dance Collection, New York Public Library for the Performing Arts.)

triumph of the haughty nymph. She was the Shade previously incarnated by Marie-Madeleine Guimard in *Castor et Pollux,* and Terpsichore (like her predecessor Marie Sallé) in *Les Fêtes d'Hébé,* performed in Monte Carlo, where she revived the French style of the eighteenth century.

Her performance in *Cydalise et la Chèvre-pied* (choreography by Staats) in 1923 remains memorable. *Impressions de Music-Hall* (choreography by Bronislava Nijinska) in 1927 was her last stage appearance. From 1920 to 1955 she taught the class of *grands sujets* and directed the training of the future dancers of the Paris Opera.

The last Italian star at the Paris Opera, Zambelli expressed herself in an incisive, pure language of movement. She was praised for her elegant precision, the vivacity of her *entrechats,* the infallibility of her acute pointe work, the audacity of her leaps, and the musical precision of her variations, which featured brilliant pirouettes and *déboulés.* As a student at the Maryinsky in 1901, Nijinska was fascinated by Zambelli's theatrical skills. Zambelli's Italian fervor was tempered by French moderation; in the words of André Levinson,

> Demonstration followed demonstration: the sparkling play of Coppélia, the radiant *entrée* of Sylvia and the liveliness of the famous pizzicato, the spiritual coquetry of Cydalise. The mischievousness of Mimi Pinson is replaced by tenderness in *La Fête chez Thérèse,* gaiety and audacity make way for a time for the romantic melancholy of Roussalka.   (Levinson, 1924)

Levinson defined her art as "that clear awareness that causes the body to move like a precision instrument with a perspicacity and a spirit of finesse that never fail." Zambelli once wrote that "dancers know, or should know, that they cannot be mediocre," a belief that governed her entire career. She was the first female dancer to be recognized by France's Légion d'Honneur, an award the press warmly welcomed. Named Chevalier of the Légion in 1926, she was made an Officier in 1956.

BIBLIOGRAPHY

Garafola, Lynn. "Dancing for the Silent Screen." *The Dancing Times* (October 1981): 26–27.

Guest, Ivor. "Carlotta Zambelli" (parts 1–2). *Dance Magazine* (February–March 1974).

Levinson, André. *La danse au théâtre.* Paris, 1924.

Vaillat, Léandre. *Ballets de l'Opéra de Paris (ballets dans les opéras—nouveaux ballets).* Paris, 1947.

ARCHIVE.   Walter Toscanini Collection of Research Materials in Dance, New York Public Library for the Performing Arts.

JEANNINE DORVANE
Translated from French

ZAMBIA. *For discussion of dance traditions in Zambia, see* Central and East Africa.

ZĀR is a healing ceremony for men and women believed to be possessed by malevolent spirits. Similar to other trance-dance traditions worldwide, *zār* is performed in many parts of the Middle East, in North Africa, and in East Africa. Dancing, often developing into trance, is an essential part of the ritual. Most of the dancing in *zār* ritual is adapted from local dance traditions and often includes parodies of stereotypical individuals.

The term *zār* refers to both the spirits and the cults dedicated to exorcising them. Individuals are said to be possessed if they are lethargic and depressed, if they lose their appetite, if they have fits of convulsion or rage, if their stomach or legs swell mysteriously, or if they display symptoms not known to be responsive to medical treatment. Women who are barren may be said to be possessed. In some regions both men and women participate in *zār*, whereas in others only women do so; however, in all regions where *zār* is practiced, most of those afflicted are women with marital problems.

Treatment for possession (*ḍarb al-zār*) includes, at a minimum, a *zār* healer-exorcist; an animal sacrifice (the patient is required to smear its blood on parts of her or his body or to drink some of the blood); dancing that leads to trance by those possessed; drums and other musical instruments; incense and other aromatics to attract spirits (jinn) and to draw the patient out of the trance; and gifts given to the possessing spirit in order to placate it. These gifts remain with the patient. The bowl lyre (*ṭanbūra*) is an integral part of *zār* ceremonies on the Arabian Peninsula and in parts of East Africa. Commonly, the healer and/or dancers wear a large belt made of goats' hooves or shells attached to leather. The hooves or shells rattle rhythmically when the pelvis is rotated in the dancing. In the Gulf region, a special house provides a focal point for the activities of the *zār* cult. In Egypt and elsewhere, special amulets made of silver and other silver jewelry are associated with the cult.

Details of *zār* ritual vary from place to place; yet the following generalizations apply to most *zār* cults. A person suspected of being possessed by spirits is taken to a healer. The healer will then ask the patient's family to arrange for a healing ceremony. This involves a large gathering with dancing and music. It may also involve sacrificing a chicken or lamb plus the giving of gifts to the healer and the patient. Guests include others who have been possessed by spirits, as well as the family and friends of the patient. The possessed are thought not to be responsible for their actions, thus unconventional behavior, such as smoking cigarettes, drinking alcoholic beverages, and/or cross-sex dressing is typical of *zār* ceremonies. Moreover, dancing during *zār* ceremonies may be less restrained than it is on other occasions.

The healer or drummers will play several rhythms. Guests who have been possessed will get up to dance to the particular beat that identifies their spirit. Eventually, the patient will begin to dance and continue dancing until she (or he) falls into a trance. The possessing spirit is identified both by the patient's symptoms and by the drum beat to which it responds. When the patient enters a trance, the spirit is questioned by the healer; it responds by presenting demands through the patient. Its demands are usually for gifts of jewelry or clothing or for family members to change their behavior toward the patient. These demands must be met by the patient's family. Failure to placate the spirit will ensure its return to plague the patient and, by extension, the family.

A special relationship is formed between the healer and a patient who has recovered. Initiates are expected to attend all *zār* ceremonies given by their healer, at which they often enjoy special status. *Zār* ritual often includes Muslim and Christian prayers, religious figures, and religious traditions; *zār* spirits are thought to respect the fasting months of Ramadan and Lent. Nevertheless, the *zār* cult is officially condemned by Muslim and Christian religious leaders.

The origin of *zār* is the subject of much scholarly debate; many believe it to have originated in Somalia or Ethiopia, where it was observed by Western travelers in the latter part of the eighteenth century. They argue that it then spread to the Niger basin, to Sudan, Egypt (where it was first reported in the late nineteenth century), the Arabian Peninsula, the Gulf region, southern Iran, Iraq, Turkey, Libya, Tunisia, Algeria, and Morocco. The presence of the bowl lyre in Mesopotamia, in ancient Sumerian inscriptions (c.3000 BCE), may indicate a possible earlier date for its spread in the region. Whatever the history of *zār*, elements of the cult appear to have been incorporated into the indigenous tradition of healing by sorcery.

[*See also* Egypt, *article on* Traditional Dance; *and* Middle East, *overview article.*]

BIBLIOGRAPHY

Ansaldi, Cesare. *Il Yemen nella storia e nella leggenda.* Rome, 1933.

Boddy, Janice. *Wombs and Alien Spirits: Women, Men, and the Zār Cult in Northern Sudan.* Madison, Wis., 1989.

Cloudsley, Anne. *Women of Omdurman: Life, Love, and the Cult of Virginity.* Rev. ed. London, 1983.

Fakhouri, Hani. "The Zar Cult in an Egyptian Village." *Anthropological Quarterly* 41 (1968).

Hadidi, Haguer el-. "The Zar Cult: An Aesthetic Expression." Master's thesis, American University of Cairo, 1996.

Hall, Marjorie, and Bakhita Amin Ismail. *Sisters under the Sun.* London, 1981.

Kahle, Paul E. "Zâr: Beschwörungen in Egypten." *Der Islam* 3 (1912).

Khoury, René. "Contribution à une bibliographie du 'zār.'" *Annales Islamogiques* 16 (1980).

Leiris, Michel. "Le culte des zârs à Gondar." *Aethiopica* 2 (1934).

Messing, Simon D. "Group Therapy and Social Status in the Zar Cult of Ethiopia." *American Anthropologist* 60 (1958).

Miṣrī, Fāṭimah al-. *Al-zār: Dirāsah nafsīyah taḥlīlīyah anthrūpūlūjīyah.* Cairo, 1975.

Nelson, Cynthia. "Self, Spirit Possession, and World-View: An Illustration from Egypt." *International Journal of Social Psychology* 17 (1971).

Qāsimī, Khālid al-, and Nizār Ghānim. "Al-mūsīqā al-humāsīyah fī al-khalīj wa-al-Yaman." *Al-ma'thūrāt al-sha'bīyah* 2 (1987).

Racy, Ali Jihad. *Tanbura Music of the Gulf.* Doha, Qatar, 1988. Companion book to audiotape.

Saleh, Magda. "A Documentation of the Ethnic Dance Traditions of the Arab Republic of Egypt." Ph.D. diss., New York University, 1979.

Saunders, Lucy Wood. "Variants in Zar Experience in an Egyptian Village." In *Case Studies in Spirit Possession,* edited by Vincent Crapanzano and Vivian Garrison. New York, 1977.

Ṭayyāsh, Fahd 'Abdallah al-. "Ḥawl irtibāṭ aghānī al-zār bi-raqṣat al-sāmirī." *Al-ma'thūrāt al-sha'bīyah* 2 (1987).

Zenkovsky, S. "*Zār* and *Tambura* as Practiced by the Women of Omdurman." *Sudan Notes and Records* 31 (1950).

VIDEOTAPE.   Magda Saleh, "Egypt Dances" (1979).

NAJWA ADRA

ZEAMI (born 1363 or 1364, died 1443 probably in Kyoto), Japanese performer, choreographer, playwright, and preeminent theoretician of *nō* theater. Together with his father Kan'ami, Zeami is credited with transforming the medieval performing art called *sarugaku* into *nō*.

Zeami, whose name has often been erroneously transliterated as "Seami" in Western publications, used several names in his lifetime. In his youth he was called Fujiwakamaru, and later Motokiyo; in his old age he signed his name as Zea, and also as Shio. Born in a family of *sarugaku* actors—who at the time were outcasts in Japanese society—he learned dancing and singing from the earliest years of his childhood. When he was eleven, he gave a performance at the Imanokumano Shrine in Kyoto that proved decisive for his career: the seventeen-year-old shogun, Yoshimitsu, was highly attracted by the beautiful and talented boy and invited him to live in the palace, starting a patronage of *nō* that became traditional at the shogun's court and among the samurai elite.

Zeami's contribution in the field of choreography was crucial in directing *nō* dance toward an ideal of highly polished, graceful elegance and simplicity with deep interior energy. As a dancer he achieved the highest recognition by the most powerful and sophisticated rulers of the time as well as by a wider public at more accessible shrine festivals. As a playwright, Zeami is credited with the authorship or adaptation of a large number of the finest *nō* dramas, including *Izutsu, Takasago, Kiyotsune,* and *Yuya.*

Beyond these achievements, Zeami is the most important author of performance theory in Japanese history. His treatises on the "Secret Tradition" of *nō*, such as *Kadensho* and *Kakyō*, reveal the pedagogical process used to train the highly talented performer who is destined to reach—and perpetuate—the sublime peak of the *nō* art. Zeami's elaboration of the central concepts of *nō* dra-

ZEAMI. A drawing, attributed to either Zeami or his brother-in-law Konparu Zenchiku, of a devil character from one of Zeami's treatises on the technique of *nō*. (Photograph from the archives of Nicola Savarese.)

Smethurst, Mae J. *The Artistry of Aeschylus and Zeami: A Comparative Study of Greek Tragedy and Nō*. Princeton, 1989.
Thornhill, Arthur H. *Six Circles, One Dewdrop: The Religio-Aesthetic World of Komparu Zenchiku*. Princeton, 1993.
Tyler, Royall, tr.. *Japanese Nō Dramas*. London, 1992.
Yasuda, Kenneth. *Masterworks of the Nō Theater*. Bloomington and Indianapolis, 1989.

BENITO ORTOLANI

maturgy *(monomane, hana, yūgen* and *kokoro),* his ranking of the styles of performance, and his insight into the essence of artistic performance are fundamental to an understanding of *nō*.

Zeami's life, after many fruitful years of favor at court, was marred by bitter disillusionment, caused by shifts of political power after Yoshimitsu's death (1408) and later by the early death of his beloved son, the heir to his art, Motomasa (died 1434). Banishment to the island of Sado (1434–1441) added new sadness to his old age. He eventually found new meaning and consolation in the art of his son-in-law Konparu Zenchiku, who became the heir to the Secret Tradition, and a great playwright and important theoretician of performance aesthetics in his own right.

[*See also* Konparu Zenchiku *and* Nō.]

BIBLIOGRAPHY

Hare, Thomas B. *Zeami's Style: The Noh Plays of Zeami Motokiyo.* Stanford, Calif., 1986.
Keene, Donald. *Nō: The Classical Theatre of Japan.* New York, 1966.
Komparu, Kunio. *The Noh Theatre: Principles and Perspectives.* New York and Tokyo, 1983.
Ortolani, Benito. *The Japanese Theatre: From Shamanistic Ritual to Contemporary Pluralism.* Rev. ed. Princeton, 1995.
Rimer, Thomas, and Yamazaki, Masakazu, trs. *On the Art of the Nō Drama: The Major Treatises of Zeami.* Princeton, 1984.
Sieffert, René, tr. *Zeami: La Tradition secrète du Nō, suivie de une journée de Nō.* Paris, 1960.

ZHOU XINFANG (born 14 January 1895 in Jiangsu, China, died 1975 in Shanghai), Chinese opera actor. A Beijing opera actor specializing in *laosheng*, old male characters, Zhou began training at six in Hangzhou and performing onstage at seven; this resulted in his stage name Qiling Tong (seven-year-old child) and later Qilin Tong (Qilin is an auspicious animal in Chinese mythology, akin to the dragon). He created the Qi school, one of the two most distinctive styles of Beijing Opera; the other is the Mei school of his frequent stage partner, Mei Lanfang.

Given the stylized nature of Beijing Opera, Zhou is best known in China for his realistic approach to characterization. He joined a modern drama group in his thirties, befriending many modern playwrights and actors. During the war against the Japanese invasion and the civil wars, he conceived and co-authored, as well as choreographed, many Beijing Opera pieces based on the ancient stories but alluding to contemporary issues, such as national defense and the peasant rebellion.

In Zhou's plays he mainly developed his robust and vigorous acting style of the righteous male hero. Zhou's voice was a bit harsh for an opera singer, but he turned this idiosyncratic feature to his advantage by integrating singing and movement as inseparable organic parts. For example, in one of his most memorable pieces, *Xu Ce Pao Cheng* (Xu Ce Runs on the City Wall), about a senior court official rushing to see the emperor for an emergency, he circles the stage alone, in various dance steps (in shoes with two-inch-thick hard soles) for about thirty minutes, while singing throughout to express his indignation, hesitation, and final determination. In indoor scenes requiring no large-scale movements, he concentrates on the dance of hands, face, and even beard and headset. In *Qingfeng Ting* (The Breeze Pavilion), when the old man he plays discovers that his wife has been murdered, his hands start trembling, pointing to her body, to the murderer, to the sky, and to his chest. Then all of a sudden he grabs some of his long beard and bites it in his mouth before crashing his head onto a pillar of the house. His other famous roles include Song Jiang, a peasant rebel leader from the classic novel *The Water Margin*, and Song Shijie, an exceptionally caring and wise official in *Si Jinshi* (Four New Officials).

Zhou was studious and learned extensively from numerous Chinese opera forms other than Beijing Opera in order to enrich his Qi school style and repertory, resulting in many of his best pieces being adaptations of other genres. In turn, his Qi school influenced generations of traditional Chinese performers of all types. He headed theater companies to tour in North Korea and the Soviet Union in 1953 and 1956, respectively. He was associate director of the Chinese Academy of Traditional Theater, head of the East China Academy of Traditional Theater, and later head of the Shanghai Beijing Opera Theater and vice-chairman of the Chinese Theater Artists Association until Mao Zedong's Cultural Revolution of 1966 to 1976, which destroyed all these and many other traditional institutions. During the Cultural Revolution, Zhou's early creation of historical character Hai Rui, a righteous official who risked his life to criticize the emperor on behalf of the people, became his "crime" against Mao. Ironically, Zhou, widely acclaimed as the reincarnation of heroes who brought justice to wronged people, was then unjustly persecuted, to die in grief.

BIBLIOGRAPHY

Liu Housheng. "Mei Zhou Xihuan Difanxi." *Xinmin Wanbao* (20 December 1994).
Zeng Bairong et al., eds. *Jingju Jumu Cidian.* Beijing, 1989.
Zhongguo Da Baikequanshu: Xiju, Quyi. Beijing, 1983.

WILLIAM H. SUN

ZIEGFELD, FLORENZ (Florenz Ziegfeld, Jr.; born 21 March 1867 in Chicago, died 22 July 1932 in Santa Monica, California), American theatrical producer. The number of his theatrical enterprises and the span of "Flo" Ziegfeld's professional career has yet to be equaled by an American. Son of the founder of the Chicago Musical College, he took the revue format from a series of topical novelty acts and developed it into a star-studded event. His productions set an unmatched standard for visual extravagance from pre–World War I seasons through the 1920s, the decade considered to have been the genre's zenith.

Ziegfeld's earliest success was as manager of the 1893 appearances of the Great Sandow, a charismatic muscle man. His first theatrical production was the 1896 revival of Charles Hoyt's *A Parlor Match* as a showcase for Anna Held (Ziegfeld's first wife), with Julian Mitchell as stage director. Teamed again with Ziegfeld and Held in 1906 for *A Parisian Model,* Mitchell evolved a formula for embellishing political and theatrical satire with musical numbers and beautiful girls. That idea later emerged as Ziegfeld's *Follies of 1907.* Influenced by Harry B. Smith

ZIEGFELD. The big hit of the *Ziegfeld Follies of 1927* was Irving Berlin's "Shaking the Blues Away." The stage setting, designed by Joseph Urban, featured a backdrop depicting a Southern plantation and a cut drop hung with skeins of Spanish moss. Singer Ruth Etting was backed up by the Jazzbow Girls (dressed entirely in red), the Albertina Rasch Dancers, the Banjo Ingenues, and Dan Healy. By the end of the number, staged by Sammy Lee, there were nearly eighty people on the stage. They were met by thunderous applause from the audience. (Photograph from the Billy Rose Theater Collection, New York Public Library for the Performing Arts.)

and later by Gene Buck, Ziegfeld adopted Mitchell's basic structure, elaborating and escalating its dimensions for his revues, which opened annually (except in 1925, 1929, and 1930) until 1931, the last edition under his personal supervision.

Known as the "Great Glorifier," Ziegfeld adorned his *Follies* with exquisite women whom he dressed in elegant gowns by Pascaud, Lady Duff-Gordon, or Erté and placed in sumptuous settings by Joseph Urban. Besides Mitchell, others who staged parts or all of the *Follies* included Leon Errol, Ned Wayburn, Ben Ali Haggin, and Michel Fokine. Singers, comics, and dancers—from art soloists to chorus girls—also were featured in Ziegfeld's book musicals. Among his headliners were Mademoiselle Daisy, Gertrude Hoffman, Bessie Clayton, Adeline Genée, Ann Pennington, Marilyn Miller, Adele and Fred Astaire, Irene Castle, Ruby Keeler, the Tiller Girls, and the Albertina Rasch Dancers.

With rare exceptions, the *Follies* were presented at the Jardin de Paris on top of the New York Theatre or at the New Amsterdam, where in 1915 Ziegfeld introduced his *Midnight Frolics* (forerunner of the modern floor show), an effort to capitalize on the era's taste for stylish naughtiness. As revues dwindled and a weakening national economy made it infeasible to stage flamboyant Broadway entertainments, many of his stars and his second wife, Billie Burke (whom he married 11 April 1914), entered films. Ziegfeld's only film was the disappointing *Glorifying the American Girl* (1929). It was live theater that kindled Ziegfeld's imagination and allowed his extraordinary abilities to mix politics, nudity, and art into a glamorous theatrical experience that subsequent revivals (1934, 1936, 1943, and 1957) have been unable to recapture.

[*For related discussion, see* United States of America, *article on* Musical Theater; *and* Vaudeville.]

BIBLIOGRAPHY
Baral, Robert. *Revue*. New York, 1962.
Carter, Randolph. *The World of Flo Ziegfeld*. New York, 1974.
Higham, Charles. *Ziegfeld*. Chicago, 1972.
Ziegfeld, Richard, and Paulette Ziegfeld. *The Ziegfeld Touch: The Life and Times of Florenz Ziegfeld, Jr.* New York, 1993.

CAMILLE HARDY

ZOLLAR, JAWOLE WILLA JO (born 1951 in Kansas City, Missouri), American dancer and choreographer. Emerging in the 1980s as one of the most innovative choreographers of modern dance, Zollar belongs to the cadre of black dancemakers whose work has avant-garde sensibilities and integrates cross-disciplinary theatrical forms. Her dances celebrate and examine the spiritual and folk traditions of the African diaspora. Her choreography is informed by grass-roots lifestyles and the musical and dance traditions of black America as well as by modern and African dance. She has cited modern dancers Dianne McIntyre, Blondell Cummings, and Kei Takei and African dancer-scholar Nontsizi Cayou as key influences.

Zollar's initial dance preparation began as a child under the direction of Joseph Stevenson, a former student of Katherine Dunham. Zollar's early training in Afro-Cuban and vernacular dance forms, supported by ample performing experiences in dance revues for social clubs and community events, began to shape her aesthetic. After graduating from high school in Kansas City, she decided to pursue a career in dance. She received a B.A. in dance from the University of Missouri at Kansas City and an M.F.A. from Florida State University.

In 1980 Zollar moved to New York City. There, she studied with Dianne McIntyre's Sounds in Motion Dance Company. She was introduced to the jazz improvisational aesthetic in modern dance and met dancers, vocalists, composers, and percussionists who were interested in performance collaboration. In 1984, a turning point in her career, she established the Urban Bush Women, a five-member ensemble whose New York premiere in July of that year received immediate critical acclaim. Revealing herself to be a cultural warrior with a strong sociopolitical consciousness, Zollar began to formulate evening-length works in which dance, a cappella vocalizations, live music, the spoken word, and visual art are assembled into multilayered dance-theater productions that explore struggle, growth, transformation, and survival of the human spirit. The work of Urban Bush Women has been described as hard-edged and straightforward. Some performances have been viewed as controversial because the company takes on such issues as abortion, racism, sexism, and homelessness. Zollar's work is characterized by a deep sense of commitment and responsibility to examine the lives of the disenfranchised, and through her choreography she seeks to "create poetry without words" based on the lives of people of color.

Zollar's creative process involves collaboration with composers, percussionists, vocalists, writers, scenic designers, and actors. She also relies on her dancers, whom she encourages to express their life experiences and choreographic voices, to help galvanize her vision. The dynamic of the dancing ranges from delicate and lyrical to bold and tough, and the content and form of the productions are based on an African-American female perspective. Recurrent themes in Zollar's work are discovery, redemption, loss, self-love, family, and survival.

Noteworthy evening-length works include *Anarchy, Wild Women, and Dina* (1986), based on the South Carolina Sea Islands folk culture; *Heat* (1988), a journey of women's lives through hope and despair, which included the acclaimed section Shelter, commissioned by the Alvin

ZOLLAR. *The Urban Bush Women* in *Praise House* (1990). Theresa Cousar is seen holding Viola Sheely in a protective embrace as (left to right) Grisha Coleman, Amy Pivar, Christine King, and Marlies Yearby surround them with warning gestures. (Photograph © by Cylla von Tiedemann; used by permission.)

Ailey American Dance Theater; *Praise House* (1990), a historical odyssey of the life of African-American painter Minnie Evans that was adapted for film and commissioned for the Public Broadcasting Service (PBS) series *Alive from Off Center;* and *Bones and Ash* (1995), based on the *Gilda Stories,* a novel by Jewelle Gomez.

Urban Bush Women has toured widely in the United States and abroad and has presented major seasons in New York at The Kitchen, the Joyce Theater, and the Brooklyn Academy of Music, and the ensemble has appeared at major festivals, such as Jacob's Pillow, Spoleto U.S.A., and the National Black Arts Festival. In 1992 Zollar and the company received the New York Dance and Performance Award (called the Bessie award) and the 1994 Capezio Award.

BIBLIOGRAPHY

Lewis-Ferguson, Julinda. "Reviews/Eye on Performance: New York City." *Dance Magazine* (October 1994): 78–79.

Osumare, Halifu. "The New Moderns: The Paradox of Eclecticism and Singularity." In *African American Genius in Modern Dance,* edited by Gerald Myers. Durham, N.C., 1993.

Shange, Ntozake. "Urban Bush Women: Dances for the Voiceless." *New York Times* (8 September 1991).

Smalls, Linda. "Blacks Enrich Modern Dance." *American Visions* (June 1989): 24–29.

Zollar, Jawole Willa Jo. "A Self-Study." In *Black Choreographers Moving: A National Dialogue,* edited by Julinda Lewis-Ferguson. Berkeley, 1991.

MELANYE WHITE-DIXON

ZORINA, VERA (Eva Brigitta Hartwig; born 2 January 1917 in Berlin), dancer and actress. The only child of a German father and a Norwegian mother, Brigitta Hartwig began her formal ballet training in Berlin at age six, studying first with Evgenia Eduardova, then with Victor Gsovsky. At age fourteen, she made her debut as the First Fairy in Max Reinhardt's production of *A Midsummer Night's Dream* (1930) and, the following year, performed in his production of *Tales of Hoffmann* (1931). Only two years later, having moved to London and continued her dance studies with Nikolai Legat and Marie Rambert, she had achieved stardom and was appearing on a West End stage with Anton Dolin in *Ballerina* (1933), a play with ballet interludes.

In 1934 she was invited by Colonel de Basil to join the Ballets Russes de Monte Carlo and thereafter was known as Vera Zorina (the easiest to pronounce of several Russianized stage names from which she had to choose). As a soloist with the Ballets Russes, she performed the Can-Can in *La Boutique Fantasque,* the Street Dancer in *Le Beau Danube,* and Action in *Les Présages,* all under the direction of Léonide Massine, with whom, offstage, she shared a brief but torrid love affair. In 1936 she left the Ballets Russes to play the temperamental Russian ballerina Vera Barnova in the London production of the Rodgers and Hart musical *On Your Toes* (1937). This production was received with great critical fanfare, and Zorina was soon being courted by film and stage producers from both sides of the Atlantic.

It was just at this time that Samuel Goldwyn, with the intention of showcasing ballet in his musical pictures, enlisted then rising star George Balanchine to choreograph a ballet sequence for his film *The Goldwyn Follies* (1938). Enticed by the prospect of working with Balanchine, Zorina signed a seven-year contract with Metro-Goldwyn-Mayer (MGM). With the combination of Zorina's grace and stylistic skill and Balanchine's ingenious choreography, Goldwyn's effort to integrate ballet into musicals proved instrumental in the popularization of ballet. In the process, Zorina—a stunning blond with a fabulous figure and a husky Germanic accent reminiscent of Greta Garbo

ZORINA. *Louisiana Purchase*, a musical comedy with music and lyrics by Irving Berlin, opened on Broadway in May 1940. Its stars were Vera Zorina, William Gaxton, and Victor Moore. Ballet choreography was by George Balanchine; "modern dances" were created by Carl Randall. In the Paramount Pictures film released in 1941, Zorina shared top billing with Bob Hope and Victor Moore. The film included Balanchine's ballet "Tonight at the Mardi Gras," in which Zorina is pictured here, but did not credit the choreographer. Zorina's appearances in film musicals of the early 1940s did much to popularize dance and to bring ballet, in particular, to audiences who might have otherwise never been able to see it. (Photograph from the Dance Collection, New York Public Library for the Performing Arts.)

and Marlene Dietrich—was thrust into Hollywood's glittering spotlight. She is perhaps most famous for her artful performance of the "Water Nymph Ballet" in *The Goldwyn Follies*, where she emerges from a pool of lilies, clad in a shift of clinging gold lamé. During the course of their work together Zorina and Balanchine became romantically involved, and they married on Christmas Eve 1938, shortly after the film was released.

From 1938 to 1944, Zorina performed in many film musicals, including *On Your Toes* (1939), *I Was an Adventuress* (1940), *Star Spangled Rhythm* (1942), and *Follow the Boys* (1944); she also appeared in several Broadway musicals, including *I Married an Angel* (1938) and *Louisiana Purchase* (1940). The majority of these productions were choreographed by Balanchine, who meanwhile had begun to secure his position in the dance world. After the term of her MGM contract expired, Zorina attempted to refocus and reinvigorate her dance career. She performed as guest ballerina in several Ballet Theatre productions, including Fokine's *Helen of Troy* and *Petrouchka* (both 1943), and on the Broadway stage she had the speaking and dancing role of Ariel in a production of *The Tempest* (1945). She came to believe, however, that her glamorous image as a Hollywood star had obscured the public's perception of her as a serious dancer.

In 1946, after long separations due to both of their work schedules, Zorina and Balanchine were divorced, and she next married Goddard Lieberson, who went on to become president of Columbia Records. She subsequently enjoyed a career as a narrator–performer of such dramatic oratorios as Honegger's *Jeanne de'Arc au Bucher*, Stravinsky's *Perséphone*, and Debussy's *Le Martyre de Saint-Sébastien*. During the 1960s and 1970s, she worked as a director of opera productions for the Santa Fe Opera, the New York City Opera, and the Norwegian Opera.

BIBLIOGRAPHY

Berg, A. Scott. *Goldwyn: A Biography*. New York, 1989.
García-Márquez, Vicente. *Massine: A Biography*. New York, 1995.
Gruen, John. "Vera Zorina." In *The Private World of Ballet*. New York, 1975.
Taper, Bernard. *Balanchine: A Biography*. Rev. ed. New York, 1984.
Zorina, Vera. "The Inward and the Outward Eye." *Dance Magazine* (December 1959).
Zorina, Vera. *Zorina*. New York, 1986.

LIZA EWELL

ZORN NOTATION. Friedrich Albert Zorn (1815–c.1900), the inventor of the system of dance notation that bears his name, was a studious and highly regarded German dance master who settled in Odessa, Ukraine. Fascinated by the subject of dance notation, he entered into an extensive correspondence with Arthur Saint-Léon. He adopted Saint-Léon's system, which he subsequently am-

plified, perfected, and published in 1887 in *Grammatik der Tanzkunst,* in Leipzig. This book is concerned fundamentally with the correct performance of dance positions and steps and reveals the terminology and execution of mid-nineteenth-century ballet. Careful verbal descriptions accompany the notated sequences.

Zorn's drawings are much more pictorial than Saint-Léon's. Instead of a staff, he used only a base line: markings on the line indicate supporting legs and those above the line indicate legs in the air. In most instances, only legwork is shown; when arm and body position are needed, the full figure is drawn. Arrows to show the direction faced, or traveling, and indications for turning, details of foot positions, and so on, are placed under the base line. Specific movement signs, such as for lifting or putting down, are added to the figure drawings. Abbreviated forms are given for commonly used steps. Timing is indicated by figure drawings placed under the appropriate note of the music's melody line.

In addition to the contradance, quadrille, minuet, and the "Gavotte de Vestris," Zorn recorded *La Cachucha,* made famous by Fanny Elssler. Reconstructions of this work reveal weaknesses in the notation: certain steps, transitions, and rhythms are not clear, perhaps because of lack of notating experience or of adequate proofreading before printing.

Zorn's book, translated into Russian and English, received wide acclaim. Recommendations by more than one dance congress that Zorn's terminology and notation should be universally adopted were never implemented, however. In his advertisements, Zorn refers to publications of notated dances, but none has yet come to light.

[*See also* Notation.]

BIBLIOGRAPHY

Amer, Rita F. "Zorn's La Gavotte de G. Vestris." *Dance Notation Journal* 5 (Spring 1987): 25–28.

Guest, Ann Hutchinson. *Fanny Elssler's Cachucha.* New York, 1981.

Guest, Ann Hutchinson. *Choreo-Graphics: A Comparison of Dance Notation Systems from the Fifteenth Century to the Present.* New York, 1989.

Vacano, E. M. "Eine Grammatik der Tanzkunst (1888)." *Das Tanzarchiv* 23 (September 1975): 289–293.

Zorn, Friedrich Albert. *Grammatik der Tanzkunst.* Leipzig, 1887. Translated by Benjamin P. Coates as *Grammar of the Art of Dancing* (Boston, 1905).

ANN HUTCHINSON GUEST

ZOTOV, RAFAIL (Rafail Mikhailovich Zotov; born 1796, died 1871), Russian ballet critic and writer. The major chronicler of ballet events during the Romantic era in Russia, Zotov was a critic for *Severnaia pchela.* His writings also appeared in *Repertuar Russkogo teatr* and in *Panteon russkikh i vsiekh evropeiskikh teatrov.* His comprehensive, detailed accounts of theater and ballet events in Saint Petersburg were complemented by a broad view of the development of ballet in Russia and a perspicacious evaluation of European influences.

Zotov's articles in *Severnaia pchela* encompassed both the development of the Russian school and the Russian tours of European dancers and choreographers. Zotov's evaluation of the Russian school focused on performances of such dancers as Elena Andreanova (1819–1857), Avdotia Istomina (1799–1848), Anastasia Novitskaya (1790–1822), and Tatiana Smirnova (1821–1871). Regarding the Russian school, Zotov noted in 1847 that although Russia had talented dancers and an excellent corps de ballet, the public's interest could be revived only by developments in choreography, specifically by the arrival of "a Didelot, a new Prometheus, a brilliant new choreographer." Despite the impoverished state of choreography, however, Zotov wrote extensively about developments in ballet technique, noting that its advances constituted a synthesis of the old and new, as was the case in contemporary music. Zotov also wrote about the performances in Russia of Marie Taglioni, Fanny Elssler, Carlotta Grisi, and Lucile Grahn, and he chronicled Jules Perrot's career in Russia.

In addition to his "Theater Chronicle" in *Severnaia pchela,* Zotov wrote two longer works. The first of these, "I moi vospominaniia o teatre" (My Theater Recollections), appeared in *Repertuar Russkogo teatr* in 1840. This work constituted a twenty-five-year account of performances in

Saint Petersburg with particular references to Didelot's work both in Russia and in Europe, to a comparative study of Istomina and Novitskaya, and to a discussion of Taglioni. Zotov's other longer article, "O nyneshem so-stoianii Sankt-Peterburgskikh teatrov" (The Contemporary State of Saint Petersburg Theaters), was published the following year in *Panteon russkikh i vsekh evropeiskikh teatrov*. This work addressed such topics in theory and perception as form versus content, audience evaluation, and the role of the critic.

[*For similar discussion, see the entries on Koni, Levinson, Svetlov, and Volynsky.*]

BIBLIOGRAPHY

Guest, Ivor. *Jules Perrot: Master of the Romantic Ballet*. London, 1984.
Swift, Mary Grace. *A Loftier Flight: The Life and Accomplishments of Charles Louis Didelot*. Middletown, Conn., 1974. Includes a complete list of Didelot's productions.
Wiley, Roland John, trans. and ed. *A Century of Russian Ballet: Documents and Accounts, 1810–1910*. Oxford, 1990.
Zotov, Rafail. "I moi vospominaniia o teatre." In *Repertuar Russkogo teatr*. Saint Petersburg, 1840.
Zotov, Rafail. "O nyneshem sostoianii Sankt-Peterburgskikh teatrov." In *Panteon russkikh i vsiekh evropeiskikh teatrov*, edited by Fedor Koni. Saint Petersburg, 1841.

SUSAN COOK SUMMER

ZOTTO, MIGUEL ANGEL. *See* Plebs and Zotto. *See also* Tango.

ZUCCHI, VIRGINIA (Virginia Eurosia Teresa Zucchi; born 10 February 1849 in Parma, died 9 October 1930 in Nice, France), Italian dancer. Renowned for the intensity of her acting and her feminine allure, Virginia Zucchi made her greatest impact in Russia, where she almost singlehandedly revived the public's flagging interest in ballet. Although few ballets were created for her, her dramatic gifts enabled her to make certain roles her own, notably the title role of Jules Perrot's *Esmeralda* and Padmana in Hippolyte Monplaisir's *Brahma*.

Zucchi studied with various teachers in Milan, though she was never admitted to the prestigious ballet school of the Teatro alla Scala. Following her debut in Varese in 1864, she began to make a name for herself in Italy. She essayed her two most famous roles early in her career—Esmeralda in Turin in 1869 and Padmana in Padua in 1873.

Zucchi first danced at La Scala in 1874 in Monplaisir's revival of *Estella*, a light ballet about a girl abducted by a rake. Despite a disappointing reception, she was invited to return the following year. From 1876 to 1878 she danced in Berlin in Paul Taglioni's *Flick und Flocks Abenteuer*, *Santanella*, and other ballets. The role of Lise in *La Fille Mal Gardée*, which Taglioni staged for her, became one of

ZUCCHI. A studio portrait, probably taken in the early 1880s in Italy. This likeness hardly does justice to the reputation of "the divine Virginia," noted for her sensual allure as much as for the artistry of her dancing. (Photograph by Schemboche; from the Dance Collection, New York Public Library for the Performing Arts.)

her favorites, as did Swanilda in *Coppélia*, for she had equal facility in comic and serious roles. In 1877 she danced Lise and Swanilda in Warsaw. She danced the role of Civilization in a revival of Luigi Manzotti's *Excelsior* at La Scala in 1883 and the title role in Manzotti's *Sieba* at the Eden-Théâtre in Paris later that year.

In 1885 Zucchi was engaged by Mikhail Lentovsky to appear at a minor theater, Kin Grust, in Saint Petersburg. Her overwhelming success led to an engagement with the Imperial Theaters that lasted for three seasons. During that time she danced in Marius Petipa's *La Fille du Pharaon* and *The King's Command;* he also choreographed a new pas de six for her standard, *Esmeralda*. Another triumph was *Fenella* (from Daniel Auber's opera *La Muette de Portici*), a favorite vehicle of actress-dancers.

The rabid excitement engendered by Zucchi's appearances in Russia was comparable to that evoked by Marie Taglioni and Fanny Elssler in an earlier day. Although Zucchi's detractors claimed that her realistic style of acting was inappropriate to the ballet, most viewers responded to her magnetism. Among her admirers were Ivan Vsevolozhsky, the powerful director of the Imperial Theaters, the future ballerina Matilda Kshessinska, and Alexandre Benois, later a key figure in the Ballets Russes. Zucchi was primarily a *terre à terre* dancer, possessed of phenomenally strong pointes; she tended to eschew steps of elevation and *batterie*. She knew how to exploit her great beauty and introduced to Russia the shorter skirts fashionable in Italy.

After her contract with the Imperial Theaters ended, Zucchi danced in smaller theaters in Saint Petersburg and Moscow. Konstantin Stanislavsky, who partnered her in an amateur production of *Esmeralda*, said that her muscular relaxation while acting taught him to eliminate his own physical and spiritual strain.

Toward the end of her career Zucchi staged and danced in the Venusberg scene of Richard Wagner's *Tannhäuser*, first in Bayreuth and then at the Paris Opera, where she appeared for the first time in 1895. She gave her final performances as a dancer in Milan in 1898. After her retirement she served on the juries of the annual examinations at La Scala's ballet school. Her niece, also called Virginia Zucchi, enjoyed a brief career at La Scala and the Teatro Colón in Buenos Aires.

BIBLIOGRAPHY

Benois, Alexandre. *Reminiscences of the Russian Ballet.* Translated by Mary Britnieva. London, 1941.
Guest, Ivor. *The Divine Virginia: A Biography of Virginia Zucchi.* New York, 1977.
Krasovskaya, Vera. "A Look at Virginia Zucchi." *Dance Chronicle* 1.1 (1977): 63–69.
Lo Iacono, Concetta. "La carne, la vita e il diavolo: I libretti dei balli di Virginia Zucchi." *La Danza Italiana* 4 (Spring 1986): 59–83.
Lo Iacono, Concetta. "Virginia Zucchi ed il teatro di danza de secondo ottocento." In *Incontri con la Danza 1993*, edited by Elena Grillo (1994): 47–57.
Wiley, Roland John, trans. and ed. *A Century of Russian Ballet: Documents and Accounts, 1810–1910.* Oxford, 1990.

ALBERTO TESTA
Translated from Italian

ZÜLLIG, HANS (born 1 February 1914 in Rorschach, Switzerland, died 8 November 1992 in Essen, Germany), Swiss ballet dancer, choreographer, and teacher. In the early 1930s, Züllig's decision to become a dancer defied common sense, as it violated social expectations for men in tradition-bound Switzerland. Consciously or not, his decision required great inner strength on the part of a youth in his teens. Züllig went to Essen, in Germany, to study with Sigurd Leeder and Kurt Jooss, whose connection with the principles of the Laban school and classical academic dance was of great importance to the young dancer.

So rapid was his progress that by 1935 Züllig had been appointed a soloist in Les Ballets Jooss, and over the next twelve years, until 1947, he danced with the troupe in its extended tours in the United States and South America. One of his most important roles was that of the Young Soldier in Jooss's *The Green Table*. Züllig also tried his hand at choreography, creating *Le Bosquet* in 1945. In 1948–1949 he danced as a soloist with the Sadler's Wells Theatre Ballet in London, and from 1949 to 1952 he was a soloist with the Folkwang Tanztheater in Essen.

In 1954, having ceased performing but still residing in Essen, Züllig began teaching at the Folkwang Schule, which was directed by Jooss. In 1956 he was engaged as teacher, dancer, and choreographer at the Universidad de Santiago de Chile, where Ernst Uthoff had been promoting the technique and work of Jooss for more than a decade. After several years in South America, Züllig returned to Europe in 1961 and resumed teaching at the Folkwang Schule, where in 1969 he was offered the post of director.

Züllig's path as a dancer was perhaps unusual for a Swiss, but his activity as a teacher of dance was in accord with a fundamental Swiss tradition, that of human development as defined by the great Swiss educator Heinrich Pestalozzi. Contrary to the Swiss impulse toward conformity, Pestalozzi sought to shape students by discovering and developing their inner strengths and abilities rather than by pressing them into an externally imposed mold. As a teacher of dance, Züllig always sought to awaken and release the inner impulses of his students, although he demanded—persistently, rigorously, and critically—that such impulses be shaped and directed with precision and not merely be allowed to burst forth haphazardly. Thus, his system of training was not aimed primarily at developing a specific style but rather at mastering body movement that, corresponding to anatomy, was functionally correct and harmoniously free. The results of his theories of teaching can be seen in the work of his students, such as Pina Bausch and Susanne Linke, who became professional dancers and choreographers.

BIBLIOGRAPHY

Barker, J. Stuart. "Ballets Jooss, 1953." *Dance and Dancers* (April 1953): 8–9.
Bartelt, Martin. "Hans Züllig." *Tanz International* 4 (February 1993): 12–15.
Pastori, Jean-Pierre. *Dance and Ballet in Switzerland.* Translated by Jacqueline Gartmann. 2d ed., rev. and enl. Zurich, 1989.
Schmülling, Friedhelm. "Stil in der Sackgasse? Mit einer Uraufführung in der Folkwang-Hochschule." *Das Tanzarchiv* 17 (June 1969): 20–21.

RICHARD MERZ
Translated from German

ZULU DANCE. *See* South Africa, *article on* Indigenous Dance.

ZURICH BALLET. The Zurich Ballet is part of the artistic ensemble of the Zurich Opera House, the cultural center of Switzerland's largest city. For the past several decades, the company has often shown promise of establishing itself as a company of international stature, but it has consistently failed to fulfill that promise. Given the sound financial resources of the opera house, this failure has been all the more frustrating, as the management of the Opera has often seemed to hinder rather than to encourage development of the ballet company, through hasty and inappropriate decisions not governed by the needs of the Zurich dance scene. In 1996, however, with the appointment of Heinz Spoerli as artistic director of the company, the outlook for the future became much brighter.

The history of the Zurich Ballet seems to reflect the sin-obsessed, anti-dance spirit of the city, as if it were haunted by the gloomy ghost of the sixteenth-century Swiss reformer Huldrych Zwingli. From 1834 to 1890, the year the old municipal theater burned down, only sixty-nine ballet performances were staged, and most of these where guest performances by outside troupes. During the first fifty years of the new municipal theater, which was dedicated in 1891, there were only a few performances of a small number of ballets, among them the biblically based *Die Josephslegende*, the most frequently performed work of all. Given a strait-laced public, it is hardly surprising that the popularity of dance was slow to develop in Zurich.

Because of the presence of the school of Rudolf Laban, Zurich became a center of the European modern dance movement in the years just before and during World War I, but the municipal theater continued to present mainly operas and operettas. Ballet was hardly ever seen. From 1934 to 1938, Pino and Pia Mlakar, both of whom were students of Laban, served as ballet directors at the Zurich Opera, and they did some significant work, including *The Devil in the Village* (1935) and *The Ballad of Medieval Love* (1937), both set to the music of the Yugoslav composer Fran Lhotka. Thereafter, during the years of World War II, ballet activity virtually ceased.

A series of ballet masters after World War II included Hans Macke, Jaroslav Berger, and Robert Mayer, but none of them made the Zurich Ballet a major part of the cultural life of the city. Zurich enjoyed its first full flowering of ballet under Nicholas Beriozoff, who was appointed artistic director in 1964. With a well-trained troupe led by the English ballerina Gaye Fulton, Beriozoff gradually built up an impressive repertory including classical and Romantic ballets as well as modern full-length works of his own choreography. After Beriozoff's departure in 1971, a lack of direction led the Opera management to engage Rudolf Nureyev to mount an expensive production of *Raymonda* (1972), in which the company's internal crisis of purposelessness was only too apparent. The next few years saw a return to instability, as another series of ballet masters—Michel Descombey (1971–1973), Geoffrey Cauley (1973–1975), and Hans Meister and Jürg Burth (1975–1978)—assumed the directorship of the company.

In 1978, the Zurich Ballet entered a new, fruitful phase when the American dancer and ballet mistress Patricia Neary assumed direction of the company. She quickly began to build a repertory of neoclassical ballets by George Balanchine, many of which had never before been danced in Europe, in addition to well-known, evening-length story ballets. Of the former, Balanchine's *Stravinsky Violin Concerto* was a notable success; of the latter, the most popular was Heinz Spoerli's production of *Giselle*, staged in 1980 with Birgit Keil and Jonas Kåge in the leading roles. Together with her sister Coleen, who served as the company's ballet mistress, Patricia Neary helped the troupe achieve a new technical standard, which was evident in its performances of Nureyev's *Manfred* and *Don Quixote* while on tour in the United States in 1985. But apparently the Zurich Opera administration wanted something different. While Neary was still in the United States, she received word that her contract would not be extended.

Uwe Scholz, a young and inexperienced choreographer from Stuttgart, assumed the post of ballet director in the fall of 1985. This meant yet one more change for a troupe that for almost a decade before Neary's arrival had experienced many changes of leadership. Thus, another line of artistic development of the Zurich Ballet was interrupted, and the company once again faced an uncertain future.

ZURICH BALLET. Using music by Giselher Klebe and a libretto by Tatjana Gsovsky, Jaroslav Berger staged *Menagerie* for the company in the early 1950s. Scenery and costumes were designed by Max Rothlisberger. (Photograph by Marka; reprinted from Horst Koegler, *Ballett International*, Berlin, 1960.)

Under Scholz, the repertory consisted largely of his own works, which displayed his skill for external brilliance, for glossy, virtuoso dancing, and for overwhelming scenic effects. Although these qualities were achieved at the cost of true artistic design and inner substance, Scholz's works found favor with the Zurich public. He remained in the post until the end of the 1990/91 season.

In 1991, Bernd Roger Bienert was appointed director of the company, and with him the Zurich Ballet once again found itself being led by a young artist with little experience in choreographing for a large troupe of dancers and no experience at all in directing a ballet company. For five years, the situation of the Zurich Ballet was difficult, both onstage and offstage. Binert's chief achievement was to bring Millicent Hodson and Kenneth Archer to Zurich to stage their brilliant reconstructions of Vaslav Nijinsky's *Le Sacre du Printemps* and Jean Börlin's *Skating Rink*. Binert left his post at the end of the 1995/96 season.

The current director of the Zurich Ballet is Heinz Spoerli, who is without question Switzerland's leading choreographer and ballet master. Soon after assuming his post in the fall of 1996 he staged his *Goldberg Variations* and then his fourth version of *A Midsummer Night's Dream*, which were both critical and popular successes. These works, one hopes, signal the beginning of a new era of high artistic achievement for the Zurich Ballet.

[*See also* Switzerland *and the entries on the principal figures mentioned herein.*]

BIBLIOGRAPHY

Bickel, Wilhelm. *100 Jahre Zürcher Stadttheater.* Zurich, 1934.
Pastori, Jean-Pierre. "The Emancipation of Dance in the Municipal Theatres." *Ballett International* 10 (June 1987): 12–18.
Pastori, Jean-Pierre. *Dance and Ballet in Switzerland.* Translated by Jacqueline Gartmann. 2d ed., rev. and enl. Zurich, 1989.
Rüegg, Reinhold. *Die Ersten fünfzig Jahre Zürcher Stadttheater, 1834–1884.* Zurich, 1925.
Scheier, Helmut. "Architecture and Choreography." *Ballett International / Tanz Aktuell* (May 1995): 32–37.
Sorell, Walter. "Watershedding the Arts." *Dance Magazine* (December 1986): 48–53.
Vollmer, Horst. "Direktorenkarussell." *Tanz und Gymnastik* 51.3 (1995): 42–46.
Whyte, Sally. "Towards a Company Style." *Dance and Dancers* (October 1987): 29–30.

RICHARD MERZ
Translated from German

ALPHABETICAL LIST OF ENTRIES

Abraxas
HORST KOEGLER

Académie de Musique et de
Poésie
MARGARET M. MCGOWAN

Académie Royale de Danse
RÉGINE ASTIER

Accompaniment for Dance
KATHERINE TECK

Adage
RICHARD GLASSTONE

Adam, Adolphe
RICHARD BONYNGE

Adama, Richard
HORST KOEGLER

Adams, Diana
ANITA FINKEL

Aerobic Dance
JUDITH B. ALTER

Aesthetics
African Dance Aesthetics
FREDERICK LAMP
Asian Dance Aesthetics
A. C. SCOTT
Islamic Dance Aesthetics
LOIS LAMYA' AL-FARUQI
Western Dance Aesthetics
CURTIS L. CARTER

Afghanistan
ANTHONY V. SHAY

Afternoon of a Faun
SUSAN AU

Aglié, Filippo D'
CLAUDIA CELI

Agon
REBA ANN ADLER

Ainu Dance Traditions
AYAKO UCHIYAMA

Åkesson, Birgit
LENA HAMMERGREN

Albania
RICHARD CRUM

Albert, Monsieur
SUSAN AU

Albertieri, Luigi
CLAUDIA CELI

Aldous, Lucette
GEOFFREY WILLIAM HUTTON

Aleksidze, Georgi
ELIZABETH SOURITZ

Alexander, Dorothy
DORIS HERING

Algeria
AISHA ALI, MARDI ROLLOW,
LEONA WOOD

Allan, Maud
LACY H. MCDEARMON

Allard, Marie
JEANNINE DORVANE

Allegro
RICHARD GLASSTONE

Allemande
REBECCA HARRIS-WARRICK

Alma
SUSAN AU

Almaszade, Gamer
VALDIMIR N. PLETNEV

Alonso, Alicia
MARILYN HUNT

Alston, Richard
ALASTAIR MACAULAY

Alta
JULIA SUTTON

Alvin Ailey American Dance
Theater
Origins to 1979
JOSEPH H. MAZO
History since 1979
HOWARD S. KAPLAN

Amagatsu Ushio
HASEGAWA ROKU

Amaya, Carmen
K. MEIRA GOLDBERG

American Ballet
ANITA FINKEL

American Ballet Theatre
DORIS HERING

American Bandstand
JOHN A. JACKSON

American Dance Festival
CHRISTOPHER CAINES

American Document
DEBORAH JOWITT

Amodio, Amedeo
VITTORIA OTTOLENGHI

Ananiashvili, Nina
IRINA KLYAGIN

Anastenárides
LAWRENCE SULLIVAN

Andreyanova, Elena
VALERY A. KULAKOV

Angiolini, Gaspero
GERHARD CROLL

Anglaise
REBECCA HARRIS-WARRICK

Anisimova, Nina
IGOR V. STUPNIKOV

Annual Collections
INGRID BRAINARD

Ansermet, Ernest
NOËL GOODWIN

Antonio and Rosario
PHILIPPA HEALE

Anwar, Rafi
SHAYMA SAIYID

Apache Dance
MARIE-FRANÇOISE CHRISTOUT

Apollo
REBA ANN ADLER

Appalachian Spring
DEBORAH JOWITT

Appia, Adolphe
IRIS M. FANGER

Après-midi d'un Faune, L'
JOAN ACOCELLA

Arabesque
ROBERT GRESKOVIC

Arabian Peninsula
ANTHONY V. SHAY

Araiz, Oscar
MARCELO ISSE MOYANO

Arbeau, Thoinot
JULIA SUTTON

Arena, Antonius de
INGRID BRAINARD

Argentina
Folk and Traditional Dance
ERCILIA MORENO CHÁ
Ballet
JUAN UBALDO LAVANGA
Modern Dance
MARCELO ISSE MOYANO

Argentina, La
PHILIPPA HEALE

Argentinita, La
JUDY FARRAR BURNS

Ari, Carina
ERIK NÄSLUND

Armed Dances
R. F. WILLETTS

Armenia
Traditional Dance
GENJA KHACHATRIAN,
EMMA PETROSSIAN
Theatrical Dance
EKATERINA L. SARIAN

Arnould-Mussot, Jean-
François
MAUREEN NEEDHAM

Arpino, Gerald
TULLIA LIMARZI

Artists and Dance
Artists and Dance,
1760–1929
MARIANNE W. MARTIN
Artists and Dance,
1930–1945
MELISSA HARRIS
Artists and Dance since
1945
ELISABETH SUSSMAN
Collaboration
MELISSA HARRIS

Asafiev, Boris
VICTOR V. VANSLOV

Åsberg, Margaretha
LENA HAMMERGREN

Ashton, Frederick
DAVID VAUGHAN

Asian Dance Traditions
An Overview
MANTLE HOOD, HAZEL CHUNG
The Influence of Puppetry
JO HUMPHREY
Religious, Philosophical,
and Environmental
Influence
A. W. SADLER

Asian Martial Arts
PHILLIP B. ZARRILLI

Assemblies
DESMOND F. STROBEL

Astaire, Fred
JOHN MUELLER

Atanassoff, Cyril
ANDRÉ-PHILIPPE HERSIN

Aterballetto
VITTORIA OTTOLENGHI

Atlanta Ballet
DORIS HERING

Attitude
ROBERT GRESKOVIC

Attitude and Shawl Dance
KIRSTEN GRAM HOLMSTÖM

Augusta, Madame
MARY GRACE SWIFT

Augustyn, Frank
MICHAEL CRABB

Aumer, Jean-Louis
MONIQUE BABSKY

Ausdruckstanz
NORBERT SERVOS

Austrialia
Ballet
JOHN CARGHER
Modern Dance
VALDA L. CRAIG
Dance Research and
Publication
VALDA L. CRAIG

Australian Aboriginal Dance
An Overview
STEPHEN A. WILD
Aborigines of Arnhem Land
MARGARET CLUNIES ROSS
Tiwi Dance
ANDRÉE GRAU
Aborigines of Cape York
Peninsula
JOHN VON STURMER

Warlpiri Dance
MEGAN LLINOS DAIL-JONES
Antakirinya Dance
CATHERINE J. ELLIS

Australian Ballet
MICHELLE POTTER

Austria
Theatrical Dance
ALFRED OBERZAUCHER
Dance Research and
Publication
GERLINDE HAID

Avant-garde Dance
SALLY BANES

Aveline, Albert
MONIQUE BABSKY

Azerbaijan
K. GASANOV,
VLADIMIR N. PLETNEV

Azuma Tokuho
MATTHEW JOHNSON

Babilée, Jean
IRÈNE LIDOVA

Baby Laurence
JANE GOLDBERG

Baker, Josephine
MARIE-FRANÇOISE CHRISTOUT

Bakst, Léon
JOHN E. BOWLT

Balanchine, George
ARLENE CROCE

Balasaraswati
LUISE ELCANESS SCRIPPS

Balet Comique de la Royne, Le
MARGARET M. McGOWAN

Ball
GRETCHEN SCHNEDER

Ballet Caravan
ANITA FINKEL

Ballet Competitions
OTIS STUART

Ballet de Collège
JEANNINE DORVANE

Ballet de Court
Ballet de Cour, 1560–1670
MARGARET M. McGOWAN
Ballet de Cour, 1643–1685
MARIE-FRANÇOISE CHRISTOUT

Ballet der Lage Landen
INE RIETSTAP

Ballet du XXᵉ Siècle
MARIE-FRANÇOISE CHRISTOUT

Ballet Imperial
REBA ANN ADLER

Ballet Nacional Español
PHILIPPA HEALE

Ballet Russe de Monte Carlo
JACK ANDERSON

Ballets Africains, Les
LOUISE BEDICHEK

Ballets de Paris de Roland
Petit
IRÈNE LIDOVA

Ballets des Champs-Élysées
IRÈNE LIDOVA

Ballets 1933
NANCY REYNOLDS

Ballet Sopianae
GEDEON P. DIENES

Ballets Russes de Monte Carlo
KATHRINE SORLEY WALKER

Ballets Russes de Serge
Diaghilev
DALE HARRIS

Ballets Suédois
SALLY BANES

Ballet Technique
Major Schools
CLAUDE CONYERS
Feet Positions
SANDRA NOLL HAMMOND
Arm Positions
SANDRA NOLL HAMMOND
Body Positions
ROBERT GRESKOVIC
Directions
RICHARD GLASSTONE
Turning Movements
ROBERT GRESKOVIC
Linking Movements
RICHARD GLASSTONE
Jumping Movements
RICHARD GLASSTONE

Ballet Technique, History of
French Court Dance
WENDY HILTON
Ballet in the Late
Eighteenth and Early
Nineteenth Centuries
SANDRA NOLL HAMMOND
Ballet since the Mid-
Nineteenth Century
RICHARD GLASSTONE

Ballet-Théâtre Contemporain
MONIQUE BABSKY

Ballo and Balletto
JULIA SUTTON

Ballon, Claude
RÉGINE ASTIER

Ballroom Dance Competition
YVONNE MARCEAU

Bamana Dance
PASCAL JAMES IMPERATO

Bandō Mitsugorō
SAMUEL L. LEITER

Bandō Tamasaburō
SAMUEL L. LEITER

Bangladesh
CLIFFORD REIS JONES

Banquet
INGRID BRAINARD

Barberina, La
KARL HEINZ TAUBERT

Baris
EDWARD HERBST

Baronova, Irina
KATHRINE SORLEY WALKER

Barre, Jean-Auguste
SUSAN AU

Barriera, Torneo, and
Battaglia
INGRID BRAINARD

Bartók, Béla
GEDEON P. DIENES,
GÉZA KÖRTVÉLYES

Baryshnikov, Mikhail
ROBERT GRESKOVIC

Basel Ballet
RICHARD MERZ

Basque Dance
CANDI DE ALAIZA

Bassedanse
INGRID BRAINARD

Bates, Peg Leg
RUSTY E. FRANK

Battement
KENNETHA R. McARTHUR

Batterie
RICHARD GLASSTONE

Bauhaus, Dance and the
DEBRA McCALL

Bausch, Pina
ANITA FINKEL

Bavarian State Ballet
HORST KOEGLER

Baxter, Richard
RICHARD RALPH

Bayadère, La
VICTOR V. VANSLOV

Bayanihan Philippine Dance
Company
REYNALDO GAMBOA ALEJANDRO

Baylis, Nadine
SUSAN AU

Beaton, Cecil
SUSAN AU

Beatty, Talley
MELANYE WHITE-DIXON

Beauchamps, Pierre
RÉGINE ASTIER

Beaujoyeulx, Balthazar de
MARGARET M. MCGOWAN

Beaumont, Cyril W.
KATHERINE M. ADELMAN

Beck, Hans
ALLAN FRIDERICIA

Beck-Friis, Regina
ANNA GRETA STÅHLE

Bedells, Phyllis
BETH ELIOT GENNÉ

Bedouin Dance
AMMON SHILOAH

Beethoven, Ludwig van
HORST KOEGLER

Behle, Anna
ANNA GRETA STÅHLE

Béjart, Maurice
MARIE-FRANÇOISE CHRISTOUT

Belarus
YULIA M. CHURKO

Belgium
Theatrical Dance
LUC VERVAEKE
Dance Education
LUC VERVAEKE

Belize
CAROL JENKINS

Bellona
JANE MINK ROSSEN

Belsky, Igor
ARKADY A. SOKOLOV-KAMINSKY

Benesh Movement Notation
TANIA INMAN

Bennett, Michael
CAMILLE HARDY

Bennington School of the
Dance
SALI ANN KIREGSMAN

Benois, Alexandre
JOHN E. BOWLT

Benserade, Isaac de
MARIE-FRANÇOISE CHRISTOUT

Berain, Jean
JÉRÔME DE LA GROCE

Bérard, Christian
PETER WILLIAMS

Beretta, Caterina
CLAUDIA CELI

Bergamasque
EMMA LEWIS THOMAS

Berger, Augustin
VLADIMÍR VAŠUT

Beriosova, Svetlana
MARY CLARKE

Beriozoff, Nicholas
HORST KOEGLER

Berk, Fred
JUDITH BRIN INGBER

Berkeley, Busby
NANCY BECKER SCHWARTZ

Berlin Opera Ballet
HORST KOEGLER

Berman, Eugene
JOHN E. BOWLT

Berners, Lord
NOËL GOODWIN

Bernstein, Leonard
GEORGE DORRIA,
KENNETH LAFAVE

Berry Brothers
RUSTY E. FRANK

Bessmertnova, Natalia
ALEXANDER P. DEMIDOV

Bettis, Valerie
THOMAS CONNORS

Bey, Hannelore
HARTMUT REGITZ

Bharata Nāṭyam
RITHA DEVI

Bhutan
LIN LERNER

Biagi, Vittorio
MONIQUE BABSKY

Bias, Fanny
MONIQUE BABSKY

Bibiena Family
GERALD L. CARR

Bible, Dance in the
MAYER I. GRUBER

Biches, Les
GUNHILD OBERZAUCHER-
SCHÜLLER

Big Apple
CYNTHIA R. MILLMAN

Bigottini, Émilie
MONIQUE BABSKY

Billy the Kid
REBA ANN ADLER

Bintley, David
CORMAC RIGBY

Bjørnsson, Fredbjørn
ERIK ASCHENGREEN

Blache Family
MONIQUE BABSKY

Blacher, Boris
HORST KOEGLER

Black Crook, The
CAMILLE HARDY

Black Hat Dance
LIN LERNER

Blair, David
BARBARA NEWMAN

Blangy, Hermine
MARY GRACE SWIFT

Blank, Gustav
HORST KOEGLER

Blasis, Carlo
ALBERTO TESTA

Blaska, Félix
MONIQUE BABSKY

Bliss, Arthur
NOËL GOODWIN

Blok, Lubov
TIM SCHOLL

Blondy, Michel
RÉGINE ASTIER

Bluebell, Miss
GEORGE PERRY

Blum, René
KATHRINE SORLEY WALKER

Bodenwieser, Gertrud
GABRIELE SCHACHERL

Bodenwieser Technique
DENISE PUTTOCK

Bodin, Louise
GUNHILD OBERZAUCHER-
SCHÜLLER

Body Therapies
An Overview
MARGARET PIERPONT
Alexander Technique
LUCY VENABLE
Bartenieff Fundamentals
PEGGY HACKNEY
Feldenkrais Method
NORMA LEISTIKO
Ideokinesis
IRENE DOWD

Skinner Releasing
Technique
ROBERT W. DAVIDSON

Bogdanov Family
VALELRY A. KULAKOV

Bolender, Todd
WILLIAM JAMES LAWSON

Bolero
JAVIER SUÁREZ-PAJARES

Bolger, Ray
DAWN LILLE HORWITZ

Bolm, Adolph
LYNN GARAFOLA

Bolshoi Ballet
ELIZABETH SOURITZ

Bonfanti, Marie
BARBARA BARKER

Bon Odori
JUDY VAN ZILE

Boquet, Louis
JÉRÔME DE LA GORCE

Borchsenius, Valborg
ERIK ASCHENGREEN

Boris, Ruthanna
LELAND WINDREICH

Borovansky, Edouard
GEOFFREY WILLIAM HUTTON

Borri, Pasquale
CLAUDIA CELI

Bosl, Heinz
HORST KOEGLER

Boston Ballet
DORIS HERING

Bourdelle, Émile-Antoine
SUSAN AU

Bournonville, Antoine
ALAN FRIDERICIA

Bournonville, August
PATRICIA MCANDREW

Bournonville Composers
KNUD ARNE JÜRGENSEN

Bourrée
MEREDITH ELLIS LITTLE

Bovt, Violetta
GALINA V. INOZEMTSEVA

Bowman, Patricia
ANN BARZEL

Boyarchikov, Nikolai
NATALIA Y. CHERNOVA

Brabants, Jeanne
LUC VERVAEKE

Bradley, Buddy
BRENDA DIXON GOTTSCHILD

Branle
JULIA SUTTON

Bravo, Guillermina
ALBERTO DALLAL

Brazil
Ritual and Popular Dance
MORTON MARKS
Ballet
KATIA CANTON,
MARILÍA DE ANDRADE
Modern Dance
KATIA CANTON
Dance Research and
Publication
KATIA CANTON,
MARÍLIA DE ANDRADE

Break Dancing
SALLY BANES

Brenaa, Hans
EBBE MØRK

Briantzev, Dmitri
ELIZABETH SOURITZ

Brianza, Carlotta
DEBRA HICKENLOOPER SOWELL

Brinson, Peter
SELMA JEANNE COHEN

Brno Ballet
VLADIMÍR VAŠUT

Brown, Carolyn
DAVID VAUGHAN

Brown, Trisha
SALLY BANES

Bruce, Christopher
STEPHANIE A. JORDAN,
BONNIE ROWELL

Bruhn, Erik
ERIK ASCHENGREEN

Bubbles, John W.
JANE GOLDBERG

Bugaku
WILLIAM P. MALM

Bulgaria
Folk and Traditional Dance
ANNA ILIEVA
Theatrical Dance
VIOLETTA KONSULOVA

Bunraku
SAMUEL L. LEITER

Burgmüller, Friedrich
OLE NØRLYNG

Burmeister, Vladimir
NIKOLAI I. ELYASH

Butler, John
KITTY CUNNINGHAM

Butō
HASEGAWA ROKU

Butsova, Hilda
KATY MATHESON

Byrd, Donald
ROBERT GRESKOVIC

Cage, John
ROY M. CLOSE

Cajun Dance Traditions
JERRY C. DUKE

Cakewalk
BRENDA DIXON GOTTSCHILD

Callot, Jacques
JEFFREY BLANCHARD

Camargo, Marie
RÉGINE ASTIER

Cambodia
AMY CATLIN

Cameroon
HANSEL NDUMBE EYOH

Campra, André
JÉRÔME DE LA GORCE

Canada
Folk and Traditional Dance
in French Canada
ELLEN SHIFRIN
Theatrical Dance
MAX WYMAN
Contemporary Theatrical
Dance
IRO VALASKAKIS TEMBEK
Dance Education
MARYJANE WARNER
Dance Research and
Publication
EVAN ALDERSON

Canary
JULIA SUTTON

Can-Can
MARIE-FRANÇOISE CHRISTOUT

Canfield
CAROLYN BROWN

Cannabich, Christian
OLE NØRLYNG

Canziani, Guiseppe
CALUDIA CELI

CAPAB Ballet
MARINA GRUT

Capoeira
IRIA D'AQUINO

Caractères de la Danse, Les
JEANNINE DORVANE

Carey Family
SUSAN AU

Caribbean Region
JAN MICHAEL HANVIK

Caricature and Comic Art
SUSAN AU

Carmagnole, La
JEANNINE DORVANE

Carnaval, Le
SUZANNE CARBONNEAU

Caroso, Fabritio
JULIA SUTTON

Cascarda
JULIA SUTTON

Castanets
MATTEO

Castle, Irene and Vernon
IRIS M. FANGER

Catarina
SUSAN AU

Caverley, Thomas
RICHARD RALPH

Cébron, Jean
HORST KOEGLER

Cecchetti, Enrico
CLAUDIA CELI

Céleste, Madame
NANCY REYNOLDS

Central and East Africa
ANDRÉE GRAU

Cerrito, Fanny
SUSAN AU

Chabukiani, Vakhtang
ÉTERI A. DUMBADZE

Chaconne and Passacaille
REBECCA HARRIS-WARRICK

Chain and Round Dances
LISBET TORP

Chaki-Sircar, Manjusri
SUNIL KOTHARI

Chalon, Alfred
SUSAN AU

Chandralekha
SUNIL KOTHARI

Chandrashekhar, C. V.
SUNIL KOTHARI

Chappell, William
PETER WILLIAMS

Character Dancing
SUSAN AU

Charisse, Cyd
LARRY BILLMAN

Charleroi/Danses
LUC VERVAEKE

Charlip, Remy
CHRISTOPHER CAINES

Charrat, Janine
IRÈNE LIDOVA

Chase, Lucia
THOMAS CONNORS

Chauviré, Yvette
IRÈNE LIDOVA

Checkmate
DAVID VAUGHAN

Cheironomia
LIBBY SMIGEL

Chen Weiya
OU JIAN-PING

Chhau
FARLEY RICHMOND

Childs, Lucinda
SALLY BANES

Chile
Folk and Traditional Dance
RAQUEL BARROS ALDUNATE
Theatrical Dance
LUZ MARMENTINI
Dance Research and
Publication
HANS EHRMANN

China
An Overview
A. C. SCOTT
Folk and Minority Dance
XU SUYIN
Dance in Opera
SOPHIA DELZA
Classical Dance
LU WENJIAN
Contemporary Theatrical
Dance
OU JIAN-PING
Dance Research and
Publication
OU JIAN-PING, ZHU LIREN

Chiriaeff, Ludmilla
CLAUDE CONYERS

Chladek, Rosalia
ALFRED OBERZAUCHER

Chladek Technique
EVA SELZER

Ch'oi Seung-hee
ALAN C. HEYMAN

Choral Dancing
WILLIAM MULLEN

Cho T'aek-won
ALAN C. HEYMAN

Christensen Brothers
DEBRA HICKENLOOPER SOWELL

Christianity and Dance
Early Christian Views
J. G. DAVIES
Medieval Views
LYNN MATLUCK BROOKS
Modern Views
ANN WAGNER

Christout, Marie-Françoise
SELMA JEANNE COHEN

Chuma, Yoshiko
BONNIE SUE STEIN

Ciceri, Pierre
SUSAN AU

Cieplinski, Jan
JANINA PUDEŁEK

Cinderella
MOLLY McQUADE

Circus
LAURENCE SENELICK

Clerico, Francesco
CLAUDIA CELI

Cleveland-San Jose Ballet
DORIS HERING

Clogging
Historical Overview
JERRY C. DUKE
Clogging in Appalachian
Dance Traditions
ROBERT G. DALSEMER

Clustine, Ivan
SUZANNE CARBONNEAU

Clytemnestra
DEBORAH JOWITT

Cocteau, Jean
ERIK ASCHENGREEN

Coe, Kelvin
MICHELLE POTTER

Cole, Jack
GLENN LONEY

Coles, Honi
JANE GOLDBERG

Collier, Lesley
DAVID VAUGHAN

Collins, Janet
YAËL LEWIN

Commedia dell'Arte
KENNETH RICHARDS

Concerto Barocco
REBA ANN ADLER

Concheros
CÉSAR DELGADO MARTÍNEZ

Congo Dances
RONALD R. SMITH

Copland, Aaron
GEORGE DORRIS,
KENNETH LaFAVE

Coppélia
CLAUDE CONYERS

Coralli, Jean
SUSAN AU

Cornazano, Antonio
INGRID BRAINARD

Corsaire, Le
ALEXANDER P. DEMIDOV

Cortesi, Antonio
CLAUDIA CELI

Costume in African Traditions
HENRY JOHN DREWAL

Costume in Asian Traditions
THERESA M. REILLY

Costume in Western
Traditions
An Overview
MALCOLM McCORMICK
Modern Dance
MALCOLM McCORMICK
Film and Popular Dance
MALCOLM McCORMICK

Cotillon
DESMOND F. STROBEL

Cotillon
DIANE J. ROSENTHAL

Country Dance
PATRI J. PUGLIESE

Country-Western Dance
JERRY C. DUKE

Courante
WENDY HILTON

Cragun, Richard
HORST KOEGLER

Craig, Gordon
ARNOLD ROOD

Cramér, Ivo
LULLI SVEDIN

Cranko, John
HORST KOEGLER

Craske, Margaret
G. B. STRAUSS

Crete
Dance in Ancient Crete
R. F. WILLETTS
Dance in Modern Crete
MARY COROS

Crofton, Kathleen
BARBARA NEWMAN

Cuba
Folk, Ritual, and Social
Dance
MORTON MARKS
Ballet before 1959
CÉLIDA PARERA VILLALÓN
Ballet since 1959
JORGE RIVERÓN
Modern Dance
SUKI JOHN

Cucchi, Claudina
CLAUDIA CELI

Cullberg, Birgit
ERIK NÄSLUND

Cunningham, Merce
DAVID VAUGHAN

Curry, John
SARAH MONTAGUE

Curz, Daniel
PAWEŁ CHYNOWSKI

Czardas
LÁSZLÓ KÜRTI

Czech Republic and Slovak
Republic
Folk and Traditional Dance
HANNAH LAUDOVÁ
Theatrical Dance
VLADIMÍR VAŠUT
Dance Research and
Publication
JANA HOŠKOVÁ

Dafora, Asadata
KENNETH K. MARTIN

Dale, Margaret
BARBARA NEWMAN

d'Amboise, Jacques
WILLIAM JAMES LAWSON

Dance and Movement Therapy
FRAN LEVY

Dance as Sport
KATHERINE FRIEDMAN

Dance Marathons
CAROL MARTIN

Dance Medicine
ALLAN J. RYAN, MD

Dance of Death
INGRID BRAINARD

Dances at a Gathering
SUSAN AU

Dance Theatre of Harlem
HILARY B. OSTLERE

Dancing Master
INGRID BRAINARD

Danielian, Leon
MARILYN HUNT

Danilova, Alexandra
JOAN ACOCELLA

Danovschi, Oleg
TEA PREDA

Danse du Ventre
ANTHONY V. SHAY

Dantzig, Rudi van
LUUK UTRECHT

Dark Elegies
DAVID VAUGHAN

Dark Meadow
DEBORAH JOWITT

Darrell, Peter
PETER WILLIAMS

Darsonval, Lycette
MONIQUE BABSKY

Dauberval, Jean
JOHN V. CHAPMAN

Davies, Siobhan
STEPHANIE A. JORDAN,
BONNIE ROWELL

Day, Mary
ANN BARZEL

Day on Earth
MARCIA B. SIEGEL

Dayton Ballet
DORIS HERING

Dayton Contemporary Dance
Company
DORIS HERING

Dean, Laura
AMANDA SMITH

Deaths and Entrances
DEBORAH JOWITT

Debussy, Claude
NOËL GOODWIN

Degas, Edgar
JANET ANDERSON

D'Egville, James Harvey
JOHN V. CHAPMAN

De Hesse, Jean-Baptiste
MARIE-FRANÇOISE CHRISTOUT

de Lavallade, Carmen
KITTY CUNNINGHAM

Delibes, Léo
NOËL GOODWIN

Dell'Ara, Ugo
VITTORIA OTTOLENGHI

Delsarte System of Expression
NANCY LEE CHALFA RUYTER

de Mille, Agnes
LELAND WINDREICH

Denby, Edwin
ARLENE CROCE

Denishawn
CHRISTENA L. SCHLUNDT

Denmark
Traditional and Social
Dance
HENNING URUP
Dance in the Faeroe Islands
WILLIAM C. REYNOLDS
Theatrical Dance
ERIK ASCHENGREEN
Dance Research and
Publication
ERIK ASCHENGREEN

Descombey, Michel
MONIQUE BABSKY

Deshayes, André
SUSAN AU

Designing for Dance
ROUBEN TER-ARUTUNIAN

Desnoyer, Philip
RICHARD RALPH

Devadāsī
RITHA DEVI

de Valois, Ninette
BETH ELIOT GENNÉ

de Vos, Audrey
DAVID VAUGHAN

Dhananjayan, V. P. and Shanta
SUNIL KOTHARI

Diable à Quatre, Le
SUSAN AU

Diable Boiteux, Le
SUSAN AU

Diaghilev, Serge
LYNN GARAFOLA

Didelot, Charles-Louis
MARY GRACE SWIFT

Dienes, Valéria
GEDEON P. DIENES

Digo Dance
VALERIE A. BRIGINSHAW

Diobono, Pompeo
ELENA GRILLO

Dithyramb
WILLIAM MULLEN

Divertimento No. 15
REBA ANN ADLER

Dmitriev, Vladimir
VIKTOR I. BEREZKIN

Dobujinsky, Mstislav
JOHN E. BOWLT

Dogon Dance
PASCAL JAMES IMPERATO

Dolgushin, Nikita
KATY MATHESON

Dolin, Anton
PETER WILLIAMS

Dollar, William
REBA ANN ADLER

Domenico da Piacenza
INGRID BRAINARD

Dominican Republic
MARTHA ELLEN DAVIS

Don Juan
INGRID BRAINARD

Don Quixote
Early Productions
CLAUDE CONYERS
Petipa Production
VICTOR V. VANSLOV
Gorsky Production
VICTOR V. VANSLOV
Balanchine Production
REBA ANN ADLER
Other Productions
CLAUDE CONYERS

Doubrovska, Felia
VICTORIA HUCKENPAHLER

Douvillier, Suzanne
MAUREEN NEEDHAM

Dowell, Anthony
BARBARA NEWMAN

Draper, Paul
JANE GOLDBERG

Dream, The
ALASTAIR MACAULAY

Drigo, Riccardo
JOSEPH GALE

Drzewiecki, Conrad
PAWEŁ CHYNOWSKI

Duato, Nacho
LAURA KUMIN

Dudinskaya, Natalia
VALENTINA V. PROKHOROVA

Dudley, Jane
SARAH ALBERTI CHAPMAN

Dumoulin Brothers
RÉGINE ASTIER

Duncan, Isadora
SUSAN A. MANNING

Dunham, Katherine
VÈVÈ A. CLARK

Dunn, Douglas
SALLY BANES

Dunn, Robert Ellis
CURTIS L. CARTER

Dupond, Patrick
ANITA FINKEL

Duport Family
JEANNINE DORVANE

Dupré, Louis
JEANNINE DORVANE

Dupuy, Dominique and
Françoise
JACQUELINE ROBINSON

Durang, John
BARBARA FERRERI MALINSKY

Durgalal
SUNIL KOTHARI

Dutch National Ballet
LUUK UTRECHT

Dying Swan, The
SUZANNE CARBONNEAU

Dyk, Peter van
JEANNINE DORVANE

Eck, Imre
GEDEON P. DIENES

Écossaise
DESMOND F. STROBEL

Ecuador
CARLOS ALBERTO
COBA ANDRADE

Edel, Alfredo
NANCY REYNOLDS

Edwards, Leslie
BARBARA NEWMAN

Egk, Werner
HORST KOEGLER

Eglevsky, André
BAIRD HASTINGS

Egorova, Lubov
LYNN GARAFOLA

Egri, Susanna
VITTORIA OTTOLENGHI

Egypt
Dance in Ancient Egypt
MAGDA SALEH
Traditional Dance
MAGDA SALEH
Contemporary Dance
Companies
MAGDA SALEH

Eifman, Boris
ELIZABETH SOURITZ

Eiko and Koma
HASEGAWA ROKU

Ek, Mats
ANNA GRETA STÅHLE

Elizabethan Progresses
ROBIN WOODARD WEENING

Elizariev, Valentin
YULIA M. CHURKO

Elssler Sisters
SUSAN AU

Elvin, Violetta
BARBARA NEWMAN

Emmeleia
LIBBY SMIGEL

English National Ballet
JANE PRITCHARD

Enigma Variations
ALISTAIR MACAULAY

Enters, Angna
GINNINE COCUZZA

Entrée
INGRID BRAINARD

Entrée Grave
WENDY HILTON

Erdman, Jean
KITTY CUNNINGHAM

Esambayev, Makhmud
YURI P. TYURIN

Escudero, Vicente
MARINA GRUT

Escuela Bolera
JAVIER SUÁREZ-PAJARES

Esmeralda, La
ELENA G. FEDORENKO

Espinosa Family
MARY CLARKE

Esplanade
ANGELA KANE

Essex, John
RICHARD RALPH, MOIRA GOFF

Estonia
LEA TORMIS, DAVID SASSIAN

Ethiopia
CYNTHIA TSE KIMBERLIN

Ethnic Dance
ANYA PETERSON ROYCE

Études
ALLAN FRIDERICIA

European Traditional Dance
WILLIAM C. REYNOLDS

Evdokimova, Eva
HORST KOEGLER

Fabre, Jan
CURTIS L. CARTER

Fadeyechev, Nikolai
BORIS A. LVOV-ANOKHIN

Faeroe Step
RICHARD CRUM

Fagan, Garth
DAVID VAUGHAN

Falla, Manuel de
NOËL GOODWIN

Fancy Free
SUSAN AU

Fan Dancing
CAMILLE HARDY

Farber, Viola
CHRISTOPHER CAINES

Farrell, Suzanne
DAVID DANIEL

Farron, Julia
BARBARA NEWMAN

Fayer, Yuri
NOËL GOODWIN

Federal Dance Project
ANNA LEE SKALSKI

Fedorova, Sofia
ELENA G. FEDORENKO

Fedorovich, Sophie
SUSAN AU

Feld, Eliot
MARILYN HUNT

Fenster, Boris
NATALIA P. SHEREMETYEVSKAYA

Fernandez, Royes
PATRICIA BARNES

Ferraris, Amalia
CLAUDIA CELI

Ferri, Olga
JUAN UBALDO LAVANGA

Feuillet Notation
RÉGINE ASTIER

Field, John
BARBARA NEWMAN

Figure Dances
INGRID BRAINARD

Fiji
DOROTHY SARA-LOUISE LEE

Fille Mal Gardée, La
JOHN V. CHAPMAN

Film and Video
Documenting Dance
VIRGINIA LORING BROOKS
Ethnographic Studies
ALLEGRA FULLER SNYDER
Choreography for Camera
NANCY BECKER SCHWARTZ

Film Musicals
Hollywood Film Musicals
JEROME DELAMATER
Bollywood Film Musicals
ALISON ARNOLD

Finland
Traditional Dance
PETRI HOPPU
Theatrical Dance
IRMA VIENOLA-LINDFORS
Dance Research and
Publication
TIINA SUHONEN

Firebird, The
Fokine Production
GALINA N. DOBROVOLSKAYA
Later Productions
SUSAN AU

Fitzjames Sisters
SUSAN AU

Flamenco Dance
NINOTCHKA BENNAHUM

Flames of Paris, The
IGOR V. STUPNIKOV

Flindt, Flemming
ERIK ASCHENGREEN

Fokine, Michel
SUZANNE CARBONNEAU

Folia
MEREDITH ELLIS LITTLE

Folk Dance History
LEEELLEN FRIEDLAND

Folk Dance Sounds
MARY ANN HERMAN

Folk Tale, A
PATRICIA MCANDREW

Folkwang Tanzstudio
NORBERT SERVOS

Fonteyn, Margot
DALE HARRIS

Footwear
SUSAN AU

Foregger, Nikolai
MEL GORDON

Forlana
REBECCA HARRIS-WARRICK

Fronaroli, Cia
CLAUDIA CELI

Forsythe, William
HORST KOEGLER

Forti, Simone
SALLY BANES

Fosse, Bob
JEROME DELAMATER

Fountain of Bakhchisarai, The
NIKOLAI I. ELYASH

Four Step Brothers
RUSTY E. FRANK

Four Temperaments, The
REBA ANN ADLER

Fracci, Carla
VITTORIA OTTOLENGHI

Franca, Celia
MICHAEL CRABB

France
Recreational Dance
YVES GUILCHER
Theatrical Dance,
1581–1789
MARIE-FRANÇOISE CHRISTOUT
Theatrical Dance,
1789–1914
MONIQUE BABSKY
Ballet since 1914
MONIQUE BABSKY
Modern Dance before 1970
JACQUELINE ROBINSON
Modern Dance since 1970
LISE BRUNEL
Classical Dance Education
MARIE-FRANÇOISE CHRISTOUT
Modern Dance Education
JACQUELINE ROBINSON
Dance Research and
Publication
MARIE-FRANÇOISE CHRISTOUT
Contemporary Criticism
LISE BRUNEL

Francisqui, Jean-Baptiste
MAUREEN NEEDHAM

Franklin, Frederic
ANDREW MARK WENTINK

Fränzl Family
RUTH SANDER

Froman, Margarita
MILICA JOVANOVIĆ

Fujima Fujiko
MATHEW JOHNSON

Fujima Kanjurō
HASEGAWA ROKU

Fuller, Loie
SALLY R. SOMMER

Fuoco, Sofia
CLAUDIA CELI

Gabovich, Mikhail
GALINA V. INOZEMTSEVA

Gabzdyl, Emerich
VLADIMÍR VAŠUT

Gadd, Ulf
ERIK NÄSLUND

Gades, Antonio
PIERRE LARTIGUE

Gagaku
ROBERT GARFIAS

Gaîté Parisienne
LISA A. FUSILLO

Galeotti, Vincenzo
ALLAN FRIDERICIA

Gallet, Sébastien
JEANNINE DORVANE

Galliard
JULIA SUTTON

Gallini, Giovanni
RICHARD RALPH

Gamelan
Balinese Traditions
EDWARD HERBST
Javanese Traditions
SUMARSAM

Gardel Family
JEANNINE DORVANE

Gardie, Anna
MAUREEN NEEDHAM

Garifuna Dance
CAROL JENKINS

Gaskell, Sonia
LUUK UTRECHT

Gaudrau, Michel
RÉGINE ASTIER

Gautier, Théophile
EDWIN BINNEY, 3RD

Gavotte
CAROL G. MARSH

Gayané
EKATERINA L. SARIAN

Geisha Dance
SACHIYO ITO

Gelabert, Cesc
NÈLIDA MONÉS I MESTRE

Geltser, Ekaterina
NATALIA Y. CHERNOVA

Genée, Adeline
IVOR GUEST

Genres of Western Theatrical Dance
SELMA JEANNE COHEN

Georgi, Yvonne
HEDWIG MÜLLER

Georgia
LAUREL VICTORIA GRAY

Georgiadis, Nicholas
CLAUDIA ROTH PIERPONT

Gerdt Family
RAISA S. STRUCHKOVA

Germany
Traditional and Social Dance
KURT PETERMAN
Theatrical Dance, 1600–1945
HORST KOEGLER
Theatrical Dance since 1945
HORST KOEGLER
Dance Education
KURT PETERS
Dance Research and Publication
CLAUDIA JESCHKE

Gert, Valeska
HEDWIG MÜLLER

Ghana
An Overview
ALBERT MAWERE OPOKU
Dance Research and Publication
SOPHIA D. LOKKO

Ghost Dance
OMER C. STEWART

Gigaku
BENITO ORTOLANI

Gigue
SUSAN F. BINDIG

Gilmour, Sally
PETER WILLIAMS

Gilpin, John
PETER WILLIAMS

Gioja, Gaetano
CLAUDIA CELI

Giriama Dance
VALERIE A. BRIGINSHAW

Giselle
SUSAN AU

Gissey, Henry
JÉRÔME DE LA GORCE

Gitana, La
SUSAN AU

Glazunov, Aleksandr
JOSEPH GALE

Glière, Reinhold
GALINA A. GULYAEVA

Gluck, Christoph Willibald
GERHARD CROLL

Glushkovsky, Adam
NIKOLAI I. ELYASH

Gogół, Jerzy
JANINA PUDEŁEK

Golden Age, The
VICTOR V. VANSLOV

Goleizovsky, Kasyan
NATALIA Y. CHERNOVA

Golovin, Aleksandr
JOHN E. BOWLT

Golovkina, Sofia
GALINA V. INOZEMTSEVA

Goncharova, Natalia
JOHN E. BOWLT

Gopal, Ram
SUNIL KOTHARI

Gordeyev, Viacheslav
ELIZABETH SOURITZ

Gordon, David
SALLY BANES

Gore, Walter
PETER WILLIAMS

Gorham, Kathleen
GEOFFREY WILLIAM HUTTON

Gorsky, Aleksandr
ELIZABETH SOURITZ

Goslar, Lotte
DORIS HERING

Gosselin Family
JOHN V. CHAPMAN

Graham, Martha
DEBORAH JOWITT

Grahn, Lucile
HENRIK LUNDGREN

Grand Ballet du Marquis de Cuevas
IRÈNE LIDOVA

Grands Ballets Canadiens, Les
MICHAEL CRABB

Grand Union
SALLY BANES

Grant, Alexander
BARBARA NEWMAN

Grantzow, Adèle
IVOR GUEST

Great Britain
English Traditional Dance
THERESA JILL BUCKLAND
Scottish Folk and Traditional Dance
GEORGE S. EMMERSON
Welsh Folk and Traditional Dance
JOHN FORREST
Manx Folk and Traditional Dance
JOHN FORREST
Theatrical Dance, 1460–1660
ALAN BRISSENDEN
Theatrical Dance, 1660–1772
JUDITH MILHOUS
Theatrical Dance, 1772–1850
JOHN V. CHAPMAN
Theatrical Dance since 1850
BETH ELIOT GENNÉ
Modern Dance
ANGELA KANE
Dance Education
PETER BRINSON
Dance Research and Publication
PETER BRINSON
Contemporary Criticism
DAVID VAUGHAN

Greco, José
JUDY FARRAR BURNS

Greece
Dance in Ancient Greece
LIBBY SMIGEL
Dance in the Roman and Byzantine Periods
ALKIS RAFTIS
Dance in Modern Greece
ALKIS RAFTIS
Ritual and Carnival Dance Traditions
TED PETRIDES
Dance Research and Publication
ALKIS RAFTIS

Green, Chuck
JANE GOLDBERG

Green Table, The
BENGT HÄGER

Gregory, Cynthia
PATRICIA BARNES

Grey, Beryl
KATHRINE SORLEY WALKER

Grigoriev, Serge
LYNN GARAFOLA

Grigorovich, Yuri
VICTOR V. VANSLOV

Gripenberg, Maggie
SAGA MIRJAM VUOIR
AMBEGAOKAR

Grisi, Carlotta
IVOR GUEST

Gruca, Witold
PAWEŁ CHYNOWSKI

Gsovsky, Tatjana
HORST KOEGLER

Gsovsky, Victor
JEANNINE DORVANE

Guatemala
CELSO A. LARA FIGUEROA

Guerra, Nicola
DEBRA HICKENLOOPER SOWELL

Guest, Ivor
SUSAN AU

Guglielmo Ebreo da Pesaro
INGRID BRAINARD

Guild Dances
INGRID BRAINARD

Guimard, Marie-Madeleine
JEANNINE DORVANE

Gusev, Petr
NIKITA DOLGUSHIN

Guyot, Marie-Catherine
RÉGINE ASTIER

Győr Ballet
GEDEON P. DIENES

Gypsy Dance
ELSIE IVANCICH DUNIN

Haiti
HENRY FRANK

Halprin, Anna
SALLY BANES

Hamburg Ballet
HORST KOEGLER

Hanako
JONAH SALZ

Hanamichi
SAMUEL L. LEITER

Hanayagi Suzushi
HASEGAWA ROKU

Hanka, Erika
ALFRED OBERZAUCHER

Han Young-sook
ALAN C. HEYMAN

Harangozó, Gyula
ZSUZSA KŐVÁGÓ,

Harkness Ballet
JUDY FARRAR BURNS

Hart, Evelyn
  MICHAEL CRABB

Hart, John
  BARBARA NEWMAN

Hartong, Corrie
  LUUK UTRECHT

Hassreiter, Josef
  GEORGE JACKSON

Hausa Dance
  VEIT ERLMANN

Hawkins, Erick
  DAVID SEARS

Haydée, Marcia
  HORST KOEGLER

Hayden, Melissa
  WILLIAM JAMES LAWSON

H'Doubler, Margaret
  NANCY LEE CHALFA RUYTER

Heinel, Anna
  JENNINE DORVANE

Helpmann, Robert
  KATHRINE SORLEY WALKER

Henie, Sonja
  ROBYNN J. STILWELL

Henry, Louis
  ELISA VACCARINO

Henze, Hans Werner
  KLAUS GEITEL

Hérold, Ferdinand
  OLE NØRLYNG

Hey
  INGRID BRAINARD

Hightower, Rosella
  IRÈNE LIDOVA

Hijikata Tatsumi
  HASEGAWA ROKU

Hill, Martha
  NANCY LEE CHALFA RUYTER

Hilverding, Franz
  SIBYLLE DAHMS

Hines, Gregory
  RUSTY E. FRANK

Hinman, Mary Wood
  SELMA LANDEN ODOM

Hoffmann, Reinhild
  HORST KOEGLER

Holm, Hanya
  NANCY MASON HAUSER

Hong Sin-cha
  ALAN C. HEYMAN

Hønningen, Mette
  ERIK ASCHENGREEN

Hopi Dance
  JOANN W. KEALIINOHOMOKU

Hornpipe
  JANIS L. PFORSICH

Horoscope
  DAVID VAUGHAN

Horschelt Family
  PIA MLAKAR

Horse Ballet
  RUTH SANDER

Horst, Louis
  JANET MANSFIELD SOARES

Horton, Lester
  LARRY WARREN

Hōshō School
  STEPHEN COMEE

House, Christopher
  MICHAEL CRABB

Houston Ballet
  DORIS HERING

Hoving, Lucas
  SUSAN REITER

Howard, Andrée
  TULLIA LIMARZI

Hoyer, Dore
  HEDWIG MÜLLER

Hugo, Jean
  PETER WILLIAMS

Hula
  AMY KU'ULEIALOHA STILLMAN

Humphrey, Doris
  MARCIA B. SIEGEL

Hungarian State Folk
    Ensemble
  LÁSZLÓ KÜRTI

Hungary
  Traditional and Popular
    Dance
    LÁSZLÓ KÜRTI
  Theatrical Dance before
    World War II
    GEDEON P. DIENES,
    GÉZA KÖRTVÉLYES
  Theatrical Dance since
    World War II
    GEDEON P. DIENES,
    ZSUZSA KŐVÁGÓ
  Modern Dance
    GEDEON P. DIENES
  Dance Education
    GÉZA KÖRTVÉLYES
  Folk Dance Research and
    Publication
    LÁSZLÓ KÜRTI

Theatrical Dance Research
    and Publication
  GEDEON P. DIENES,
  GÉZA KÖRTVÉLYES

Hurok, Sol
  THOMAS CONNORS

Husain, Ghulam
  SHAYMA SAIYID

Hus Family
  JEANNINE DORVANE

Hutchinson, Ann
  BERNICE M. ROSEN

Hynd, Ronald
  PETER WILLIAMS,
  JANE PRITCHARD

Hyporchēma
  LIBBY SMIGEL

Hyrst, Eric
  CLAUDE CONYERS

Icare
  MARIE-FRANÇOISE CHRISTOUT

Ice Dancing
  ROBYNN J. STILWELL

Iceland
  Traditional Dance
    SIGRIDUR VALGEIRSDÓTTIR
  Theatrical Dance
    ÖRN GUDMUNDSSON

Ichikawa Danjūrō
  SAMUEL L. LEITER

Ichikawa Ennosuke
  SAMUEL L. LEITER

Idzikowski, Stanislas
  LYNN GARAFOLA

Illuminations
  ALASTAIR MACAULAY

Impekoven, Niddy
  HEDWIG MÜLLER

Improvisation
  KATY MATHESON

Inbal Dance Theatre
  GIORA MANOR

Indes Galantes, Les
  JÉRÔME DE LA GORCE

India
  History of Indian Dance
    CLIFFORD REIS JONES
  Philosophy of Indian Dance
    KAPILA VATSYAYAN
  Epic Sources of Indian
    Dance
    CLIFFORD REIS JONES
  The Rādhā-Kṛṣṇa Theme in
    Indian Dance
    KAPILA VATSYAYAN

New Directions in Indian
    Dance
  SUNIL KOTHARI
Dance Research and
    Publication
  JUDY VAN ZILE,
  BETTY TRUE JONES

Indonesia
  An Overview
    EDWARD HERBST
  Balinese Dance Traditions
    EDWARD HERBST
  Balinese Ceremonial Dance
    EDWARD HERBST
  Balinese Dance Theater
    EDWARD HERBST
  Balinese Mask Dance
    Theater
    EDWARD HERBST
  Javanese Dance Traditions
    SAL MURGIYANTO
  Sumatran Dance Traditions
    SAL MURGIYANTO
  Sundanese Dance Traditions
    SAL MURGIYANTO
  Dance Traditions of the
    Outlying Islands
    SAL MURGIYANTO
  Dance Research and
    Publication
    SAL MURGIYANTO,
    GARRETT KAM

Indrani
  LUISE ELCANESS SCRIPPS

Inglesby, Mona
  PETER WILLIAMS

Intermedio
  ANGENE FEVES

International Ballet
  PETER WILLIAMS

Invitation, The
  BARBARA NEWMAN

Iran
  ANTHONY V. SHAY

Ireland
  Traditional Dance
    CATHERINE FOLEY
  Theatrical Dance
    DEIRDRE MCMAHON

Irving, Robert
  GEORGE DORRIS

Isaac, Mister
  RICHARD RALPH,
  JENNIFER THORP

Ishii Kaoru
  HASEGAWA ROKU

Islam and Dance
  AMMON SHILOAH

Israel
An Overview
JUDITH BRIN INGBER
Ethnic Dance
NAOMI BAHAT-RATZON,
AVNER BAHAT

Istomina, Avdotia
NIKOLAI I. ELYASH

Italy
Dance Traditions before
1800
CLAUDIA CELI
Theatrical Dance,
1801–1940
ALBERTO TESTA
Theatrical Dance since 1940
VITTORIA OTTOLENGHI
Classical Dance Education
ELISA VACCARINO
Dance Research and
Publication
CLAUDIA CELI

Ito, Michio
HELEN CALDWELL

Ivanov, Lev
VERA M. KRASOVSKAYA

Izmailova, Galiya
LUBOV AVDEEVA

Jacob's Pillow
KITTY CUNNINGHAM

Jamaica
REX NETTLEFORD

Jamison, Judith
HOWARD S. KAPLAN

Japan
An Overview
BENITO ORTOLANI
Ritual Dance
BENITO ORTOLANI
Folk Dance
FRANK HOFF
Ballet
USUI KENJI
Modern Dance
MIYABI ICHIKAWA
Dance Research and
Publication
MICHIKO UENO-HERR,
CARL WOLZ

Japanese Traditional Schools
SAMUEL L. LEITER

Jaques-Dalcroze, Émile
SELMA LANDEN ODOM

Jardin aux Lilas
DAVID VAUGHAN

Jazz Dance
BILLIE MAHONEY

Jeanmaire, Zizi
IRÈNE LIDOVA

Jeune Homme et la Mort, Le
IRÈNE LIDOVA

Jewish Dance Traditions
ZVI FRIEDHABER

Jhaveri Sisters
SUNIL KOTHARI

Jidaimono
SAMUEL L. LEITER

Jig
JAMES E. MORRISON

Job
DAVID VAUGHAN

Joffrey, Robert
TULLIA LIMARZI

Joffrey Ballet
TULLIA LIMARZI, ANITA FINKEL

Johansson, Christian
VALERY A. KULAKOV

Johansson, Ronny
LULLI SVEDIN

Johns, Jasper
MELISSA HARRIS

Jolie Fille de Gand, La
SUSAN AU

Jones, Bill T.
ROBERT TRACY

Jones, Inigo
GERALD L. CARR

Jones, Marilyn
MICHELLE POTTER

Jonkonnu Festival
JUDITH BETTELHEIM

Jooss, Kurt
BENGT HÄGER

Josephslegende, Die
ANDREA AMORT

Joseph the Beautiful
ELIZABETH SOURTIZ

Juba, Master
SALLY R. SOMMER

Judson Dance Theater
SALLY BANES

Kabuki Theater
SAMUEL L. LEITER

Kadman, Gurit
JUDITH BRIN INGBER

Kagura
BENITO ORTOLANI

Kain, Karen
MICHAEL CRABB

Kakul, I Nyoman
EDWARD HERBST

Kallinikos
LIBBY SMIGEL

Kamizawa Kazuo
HASEGAWA ROKU

Kan'ami
STEPHEN COMEE

Kandyan Dance
SICILLE P. C. KOTELAWALA

Kandy Perahera
SICILLE P. C. KOTELAWALA

Kanze School
STEPHEN COMEE, JONAH SALZ

Karinska, Barbara
MALCOLM MCCORMICK

Karsavina, Tamara
MARY CLARKE

Karstens, Gerda
ERIK ASCHENGREEN

Kasai Akira
HASEGAWA ROKU

Kataoka Takao
SAMUEL L. LEITER

Kathak
RITHA DEVI

Kathakaḷi
CLIFFORD REIS JONES

Kaye, Nora
ANN BARZEL

Kazakhstan
LYDIA P. SARYNOVA

Kebiar
EDWARD HERBST

Kehlet, Niels
ERIK ASCHENGREEN

Keil, Birgit
HORST KOEGLER

Kelly, Gene
JEROME DELAMATER

Kent, Allegra
WILLIAM JAMES LAWSON

Kermani, Sheema
SHAYMA SAIYID

Kermesse in Bruges
PATRICIA MCANDREW

Khachaturian, Aram
JOSEPH GALE

Khanum, Tamara
LUBOV AVDEEVA

Khōn
MATTANI MOJDARA RUTNIN

Kidd, Michael
JEROME DELAMATER

Kim Ch'un-heung
ALAN C. HEYMAN

Kim Paik-bong
ALAN C. HEYMAN

Kinesiology
An Overview
JOHN M. WILSON
Therapeutic Practices
JUDY GANTZ

King, Kenneth
SALLY BANES

Kiralfy Family
BARBARA BARKER

Kirkland, Gelsey
PATRICIA BARNES

Kirsova, Hélène
MICHELLE POTTER

Kirstein, Lincoln
NANCY REYNOLDS

Kita School
STEPHEN COMEE

Knight, Lakshmi
DONALD KNIGHT

Knust, Albrecht
RODERYK LANGE

Kochno, Boris
NANCY REYNOLDS

Kohomba Kankariya
SICILLE P. C. KOTELAWALA

Kolosova, Evgenia
NIKOLAI I. ELYASH

Kolpakova, Irina
MARINA A. ILICHEVA

Komar, Chris
DAVID VAUGHAN

Komleva, Gabriella
ARKADY A. SOKOLOV-KAMINSKY

Kondratieva, Marina
GALINA V. INOZEMTSEVA

Koner, Pauline
DAVID SEARS

Kongō School
STEPHEN COMEE

Koni, Fedor
SUSAN COOK SUMMER

Konparu School
STEPHEN COMEE

Konparu Zenchiku
STEPHEN COMEE

Konservatoriet
PATRICIA MCANDREW

Kordax
  LIBBY SMIGEL

Korea
  An Overview
    ALAN C. HEYMAN
  Masked Dance Drama
    LEE DU-HYON
  Modern Dance
    ALAN C. HEYMAN
  Dance Research and
    Publication
    ALAN C. HEYMAN, LEE DU-HYON

Koren, Sergei
  GALINA V. BELYAYEVA-
    CHELOMBITKO

Korovin, Konstantin
  JOHN E. BOWLT

Koslov, Theodore
  SUZANNE CARBONNEAU

Krakowiak
  GRÁZYNA DĄBROWSKA

Krasovskaya, Vera
  ELIZABETH SOURITZ

Kraus, Gertrud
  GIORA MANOR

Kresnik, Johann
  HORST KOEGLER

Kreutzberg, Harald
  HEDWIG MÜLLER

Kreutzer, Rodolphe
  OLE NØRLYNG

Kriger, Viktorina
  LUDMILA I. BOREL

Krishnamurthi, Yamini
  SUNIL KOTHARI

Kriza, John
  SUSAN REITER

Kröller, Heinrich
  PIA MLAKAR

Kronstam, Henning
  ERIK ASCHENGREEN

Kṛṣṇāṭṭam
  MARTHA BUSH ASHTON-SIKORA

Kshessinsky Family
  CLAUDE CONYERS

Kuchipudi
  RITHA DEVI

Kudelka, James
  PAULA CITRON

Kun, Zsuzsa
  GÉZA KÖRTVÉLYES

!Kung San Dance
  RICHARD KATZ, MEGAN BIESELE

Kunqu
  YE SHAOLAN

Kůra, Miroslav
  VLADIMÍR VAŠUT

Kurath, Gertrude Prokosch
  JOANN W. KEALIINOHOMOKU

Kurbet, Vladimir
  ELFRIDA A. KOROLEVA

Kurdish Dance
  ANTHONY V. SHAY

Kūtiyāṭṭam
  FARLEY RICHMOND

Kylián, Jiří
  LUUK UTRECHT

Kyōgen
  An Overview
    JONAH SALZ
  Kyōgen Schools
    DON KENNY

Kyrgyzstan
  ROBERT K. URASGUILDIYEV

Laban, Rudolf
  VALERIE PRESTON-DUNLOP

Labanotation
  ANN HUTCHINSON GUEST

Laban Principles of Movement
  Analysis
  VERA MALETIC

L'Abbé, Anthony
  RICHARD RALPH

Labyrinth Dances
  PENELOPE REED DOOB

Lacotte, Pierre
  MONIQUE BABSKY

La Fontaine, Mademoiselle de
  RÉGINE ASTIER

Laing, Hugh
  PATRICIA BARNES

Lake, Molly
  BARBARA NEWMAN

Lakhia, Kumudini
  SUNIL KOTHARI

Lakhǫn
  MATTANI MOJDARA RUTNIN

Lambert, Constant
  NOËL GOODWIN

Lamhut, Phyllis
  AMANDA SMITH

Lami, Eugéne Louis
  SUSAN AU

Lanchbery, John
  NOËL GOODWIN

Lander, Harald
  ALLAN FRIDERICIA

Lander, Margot
  ERIK ASCHENGREEN

Lander, Toni
  HENRIK LUNDGREN

Lang, Pearl
  SARAH ALBERTI CHAPMAN

Lanner, Katti
  BETTY JUNE MYERS

Lany Family
  JEANNINE DORVANE

Laos
  AMY CATLIN

Larionov, Mikhail
  JOHN E. BOWLT

Larsen, Niels Bjørn
  EBBE MØRK

Lassen, Elna
  HENRIK LUNDGREN

Latvia
  ERIK U. TIVUM

Lauchery, Étienne
  KURT PETERMANN

Laurencia
  ELFRIDA A. KOROLEVA

Lauterer, Arch
  MALCOLM MCCORMICK

Laval, Antoine Bandieri de
  RÉGINE ASTIER

Lavrovsky, Leonid
  MUSA S. KLEIMENOVA

Lavrovsky, Mikhail
  VALERIA I. URALSKAYA

Lazzini, Joseph
  JEANNINE DORVANE

Lebanon
  ANTHONY V. SHAY

Leclair, André
  LUC VERVAEKE

Le Clercq, Tanaquil
  WILLIAM JAMES LAWSON

Lecomte, Eugénie
  MARY GRACE SWIFT

Lecomte, Hippolyte
  SUSAN AU

Lee, Mary Ann
  BARBARA FERRERI MALINSKY

Leeder, Sigurd
  GRETE MÜLLER

Lee Mae-bang
  ALAN C. HEYMAN

Lee Sun-ock
  ALAN C. HEYMAN

Legat Family
  VICTOR V. VANSLOV

Legend of Love
  VICTOR V. VANSLOV

Legnani, Pierina
  ALBERTO TESTA

Légong
  EDWARD HERBST

Leningrad Symphony
  ARKADY A. SOKOLOV-KAMINSKY

Lepeshinskaya, Olga
  MUSA S. KLEIMENOVA

Le Picq, Charles
  JEANNINE DORVANE

Lepri, Giovanni
  CLAUDIA CELI

Lerman, Liz
  CATHRYN HARDING

Lestang, Anne-Louis
  RÉGINE ASTIER

Lester, Keith
  PETER WILLIAMS

Letter to the World
  DEBORAH JOWITT

Leventhal, Valery
  VIKTOR I. BEREZKIN

Levinson, André
  SUSAN COOK SUMMER

Levi-Tanai, Sara
  JUDITH BRIN INGBER

Lewitzky, Bella
  LARRY WARREN

Libraries and Museums
  MARY R. STROW

Libretti for Dance
  Sixteenth- and Seventeenth-
    Century Libretti
    MARK FRANKO
  Eighteenth-Century Libretti
    JUDITH CHAZIN-BENNAHUM
  Nineteenth- and Twentieth-
    Century Libretti
    SUSAN AU

Lichine, David
  LELAND WINDREICH

Liebeslieder Walzer
  REBA ANN ADLER

Liepa, Andris
  IRINA KLYAGIN

Liepa, Maris
  VICTOR V. VANSLOV

Lifar, Serge
MARIE-FRANÇOISE CHRISTOUT

Lighting for Dance
Historical Overview
CAMILLE HARDY
Theory and Practice
JENNIFER TIPTON

Limón, José
DANIEL LEWIS, LESLEY FARLOW

Linden, Anya
BARBARA NEWMAN

Lindy Hop
CYNTHIA R. MILLMAN

Linke, Susanne
HORST KOEGLER

Lithuania
Traditional Dance
DALIA URBANAVICIENÉ
Theatrical Dance
ALIODIJA RUZGAITĖ

Littlefield, Catherine
BARBARA FERRERI MALINSKY

Little Humpbacked Horse,
The
ELENA G. FEDORENKO

Liturgical Dance
CARLYNN REED

Litz, Katherine
ELIZABETH B. KENDALL

Livry, Emma
MONIQUE BABSKY

Lloyd, Maude
PETER WILLIAMS

London Contemporary Dance
Theatre
STEPHANIE A. JORDON,
BONNIE ROWELL

Longways
INGRID BRAINARD

López, Pilar
JUDY FARRAR BURNS

Lopokova, Lydia
LYNN GARAFOLA

Lopukhov, Fedor
GALINA N. DOBROVOLSKAYA

Loquasto, Santo
CLAUDIA ROTH PIERPONT

Loring, Eugene
REBA ANN ADLER

Losch, Tilly
GEORGE JACKSON

Louis, Murray
KITTY CUNNINGHAM

Louis XIV
MARIE-FRANÇOISE CHRISTOUT

Loure
WENDY HILTON

Lowski, Woytek
PAWEŁ CHYNOWSKI

Luisillo
PHILIPPA HEALE

Lukom, Elena
OLGA ROZANOVA

Lully, Jean-Baptiste
JÉRÔME DE LA GORCE

Lyonnois, Marie-Françoise
MARIE-FRANÇOISE CHRISTOUT

Macdonald, Brian
MICHAEL CRABB

Machov, Saša
VLADIMÍR VAŠUT

MacMillan, Kenneth
EDWARD THORPE

Madsen, Egon
HORST KOEGLER

Magallanes, Nicholas
ANNE MURPHY

Mahapatra, Kelucharan
SUNIL KOTHARI

Maharaj, Birju
RITHA DEVI

Makarova, Natalia
CLEMENT CRISP

Malaysia
WILLIAM P. MALM

Manen, Hans van
EVA VAN SCHAIK

Manipur
CLIFFORD REIS JONES

Manning, Frankie
CYNTHIA R. MILLMAN

Manōhrā
MATTANI MOJDARA RUTNIN

Manon
BARBARA NEWMAN

Mansingh, Sonal
SUNIL KOTHARI

Manzotti, Luigi
ALBERTO TESTA

Maori Dance
JENNIFER SHENNAN

Maracci, Carmelita
NANCY REYNOLDS

Marcel, François
RÉGINE ASTIER

Marenco, Romualdo
GEORGE DORRIS,
ALBERTO TESTA

Mario, I Ketut
EDWARD HERBST

Markó, Iván
GEDEON P. DIENES

Markova, Alicia
CLEMENT CRISP

Marks, Bruce
KATY MATHESON

Maro Akaji
HASEGAWA ROKU

Marsicano, Merle
P. W. MANCHESTER

Martin, John
SELMA JEANNE COHEN

Martins, Peter
ROBERT GRESKOVIC

Martyn, Laurel
MICHELLE POTTER

Maryinsky Ballet
Historical Overview
MARINA A. ILICHEVA
Maryinsky Style
VERA M. KRASOVSKAYA

Mask and Makeup
African Traditions
MARGARET THOMPSON-DREWAL
Asian Traditions
RON JENKINS
European Traditions
MALCOLM MCCORMICK

Maslow, Sophie
ANN VACHON

Mason, Monica
BARBARA NEWMAN

Masque and Antimasque
ANDREW J. SABOL

Masquerades
TERRY CASTLE

Massine, Léonide
LISA A. FUSILLO

Matachins
Historical Overview
JULIA SUTTON
Danza de Matlachines
CÉSAR DELGADO MARTÍNEZ
Matachines Dances in the
Southwestern United
States
JOHN FORREST

Matisse, Henri
NANCY REYNOLDS

Matsui Akira
JONAH SALZ

Matsumoto Kōshirō
SAMUEL L. LEITER

Matthews, Jessie
DAVID VAUGHAN

Maximova, Ekaterina
MARINA E. KONSTANTINOVA

May, Pamela
BARBARA NEWMAN

Mayong
WILLIAM P. MALM

Maywood, Augusta
SUSAN AU

Mazilier, Joseph
SUSAN AU

Mazurka
SUSAN AU

Mbuti Dance
COLIN M. TURNBULL

McBride, Patricia
ANNE MURPHY

McKayle, Donald
MELANYE WHITE-DIXON

Médée et Jason
RICHARD RALPH, SUSAN AU

Medieval Dance
INGRID BRAINARD

Mei Lanfang
SOPHIA DELZA

Melanesia
ADRIENNE L. KAEPPLER

Mérante, Louis
MONIQUE BABSKY

Meri, La
JUDY FARRAR BURNS

Mesopotamia
MARIE MATOUŠOVÁ-RAJMOVÁ

Messel, Oliver
SUSAN AU

Messerer, Asaf
ELLA BOCHARNIKOVA

Methodologies in the Study of
Dance
Sociology
PAUL FILMER
Cultural Context
JUDITH LYNNE HANNA
Linguistics
ADRIENNE L. KAEPPLER
Anthropology
SUZANNE YOUNGERMAN
Ethnology
COLIN QUIGLEY

New Areas of Inquiry
SUSAN LEIGH FOSTER

Metropolitan Ballet
PETER WILLIAMS

Metropolitan Opera Ballet
TULLIA LIMARZI

Mexico
Traditional Dance
AMPARO SEVILLA
Theatrical Dance
ALBERTO DALLAL
Dance Companies
ALBERTO DALLAL,
CÉSAR DELGADO MARTÍNEZ
Dance Research and
Publication
PATRICIA AULESTIA

Micronesia
ADRIENNE L. KAEPPLER

Middle East
An Overview
NAJWA ADRA
Dance Research and
Publication
NAJWA ADRA

Milhaud, Darius
JAMES RINGO

Miller, Ann
RUSTY E. FRANK

Miller, Marilyn
CAMILLE HARDY

Milloss, Aurelio
ALBERTO TESTA

Milon, Louis
MONIQUE BABSKY

Mime
THOMAS G. LEABHART

Mimus
T. DAVINA MCCLAIN

Minkus, Léon
JOSEPH GALE

Minuet
WENDY HILTON

Miranda, Carmen
FRANK W. D. RIES

Miskovitch, Milorad
IRÈNE LIDOVA

Miszczyk, Stanisław
PAWEŁ CHYNOWSKI

Mitchell, Arthur
HILARY B. OSTLERE

Mlakar, Pia and Pino
MILICA JOVANOVIĆ

Modern Dance Technique
DEBORAH JOWITT

Mōhiniāṭṭam
RITHA DEVI

Moiseyev, Igor
MARGARITA I. ISAREVA

Moldova
ELFRIDA A. KOROLEVA

Molière
MARIE-FRANÇOISE CHRISTOUT

Molnár, István
GÉZA KÖRTVÉLYES

Mommerie
INGRID BRAINARD

Moncion, Francisco
WILLIAM JAMES LAWSON

Monk, Meredith
ALLEN ROBERTSON

Monotones
ALASTAIR MACAULAY

Monplaisir, Hippolyte and
Adèle
SUSAN AU

Month in the Country, A
ALASTAIR MACAULAY

Moore, Lillian
CHRYSTELLE TRUMP BOND

Moor's Pavane, The
DANIEL LEWIS, LESLEY FARLOW

Mordkin, Mikhail
SUZANNE CARBONNEAU

Moresca
INGRID BRAINARD

Moreton, Ursula
BARBARA NEWMAN

Morlacchi, Giuseppina
BARBARA BARKER

Morocco
AISHA ALI, MARDI ROLLOW,
LEONA WOOD

Morrice, Norman
BARBARA NEWMAN

Morris, Mark
JOAN ACOCELLA

Morris Dance
JOHN FORREST

Mouret, Jean-Joseph
JÉRÔME DE LA GORCE

Movement Choir
CAROLE CREWDSON

Mudrā
SUNIL KOTHARI

Murdmaa, Mai-Ester
SELMA JEANNE CHOEN

Murphy, Graeme
VALDA L. CRAIG

Murray, Arthur
CYNTHIA R. MILLMAN

Musette
MARGARET DANIELS

Musical Offering
ANGELA KANE

Music for Dance
African Music
BARBARA L. HAMPTON
Arab Music
BARBARA RACY, ALI JIHAD RACY
Asian Music
WILLIAM P. MALM
Oceanic Music
ADRIENNE L. KAEPPLER
Western Music before 1520
INGRID BRAINARD
Western Music, 1520–1650
JULIA SUTTON
Western Music, 1650–1800
HERBERT SCHNEIDER
Western Music, 1800–1900
NOËL GOODWIN
Western Music since 1900
ROY M. CLOSE

Music Hall
British Traditions
LAURENCE SENELICK
French Traditions
MARIE-FRANÇOISE CHRISTOUT

Myanmar
ROBERT GARFIAS

Nádasi, Ferenc
GÉZA KÖRTVÉLYES

Nadezhdina, Nadezhda
ALEKSANDRA E. CHIZHOVA

Naguata
WILLIAM P. MALM

Nagrin, Daniel
CHRISTENA L. SCHLUNDT

Naharin, Ohad
GIORA MANOR

Nakamura Ganjirō
SAMUEL L. LEITER

Nakamura Kankurō
SAMUEL L. LEITER

Nakamura Kanzaburō
SAMUEL L. LEITER

Nakamura Kichiemon
SAMUEL L. LEITER

Nakamura Tomijūrō
SAMUEL L. LEITER

Nakamura Utaemon
SAMUEL L. LEITER

National Ballet of Canada
MICHAEL CRABB

National Ballet of Senegal
DORIS GREEN

Native American Dance
An Overview
GERTRUDE PROKOSCH KURATH
Northeastern Woodlands
GERTRUDE PROKOSCH KURATH,
CHARLOTTE HETH
Southeastern Woodlands
CHARLOTTE HETH
The Great Plains
WILLIAM K. POWERS
The Southwest
ADRIENNE CLANCY
California and the
Intermountain Region
RICHARD KEELING
The Northwest Coast
HENRY J. CALKINS
The Far North
THOMAS F. JOHNSTON
Dance Research and
Publication
CYNTHIA J. NOVACK

Nātyaśāstra
SUNIL KOTHARI

Nault, Fernand
CLAUDE CONYERS

Nautch
CLIFFORD REIS JONES

Navajo Dance
STEVEN A. DARDEN

Negri, Cesare
JULIA SUTTON

Němeček, Jiří
VLADIMÍR VAŠUT

Nerina, Nadia
CLEMENT CRISP

Netherlands
Folk and Traditional Dance
FEMKE VAN DOORN-LAST
Social Dance
INE RIETSTAP
Theatrical Dance before
1900
NANCY DE WILDE
Theatrical Dance,
1900–1945
EVA VAN SCHAIK
Theatrical Dance since 1945
LUUK UTRECHT

Dance Education
INE RIETSTAP

Dance Research and
Publication
CORRIE HARTONG,
EVA VAN SCHAIK

Netherlands Ballet
LUUK UTRECHT

Netherlands Dance Theater
EVA VAN SCHAIK

Neumeier, John
HORST KOEGLER

New Dance Group
DAVID SEARS

New Dance Trilogy
MARCIA B. SIEGEL

New York City Ballet
Origins to 1983
ROBERT GARIS
History since 1983
ANITA FINKEL

New Zealand
Theatrical Dance
JENNIFER SHENNAN
Dance Research and
Publication
JENNIFER SHENNAN

Nicholas Brothers
CONSTANCE VALIS HILL

Nichols, Kyra
ANITA FINKEL

Nielsen, Augusta
EBBE MØRK

Nieves and Copes
MARÍA SUSANA AZZI

Night Journey
DEBORAH JOWITT

Nijinska, Bronislava
GUNHILD OBERZAUCHER-
SCHÜLLER

Nijinsky, Vaslav
JOAN ACOCELLA

Nikolais, Alwin
KITTY CUNNINGHAM

Nō
BENITO ORTOLANI

Nobilissima Visione
LISA A. FUSILLO

Noblet, Lise
MONIQUE BABSKY

Noces, Les
GUNHILD OBERZAUCHER-
SCHÜLLER

Noguchi, Isamu
MALCOLM MCCORMICK

Nomura Mansaku II
DON KENNY

Nomura Manzō VI
DON KENNY

North Africa
AISHA ALI, MARDI ROLLOW,
LEONA WOOD

Northcote, Anna
KATHRINE SORLEY WALKER

Northern Ballet Theatre
PETER WILLIAMS, ANGELA KANE

Norway
Folk, Traditional, and Social
Dance
JAN-PETTER BLOM
Theatrical Dance before
1919
HANS-CHRISTIAN ARENT
Theatrical Dance,
1920–1958
EVA KRØVEL
Theatrical Dance since 1958
HANS-CHRISTIAN ARENT
Classical Dance Education
EMTE STAG
Dance Research and
Publication
VALDEMAR HANSTEEN

Notation
ANN HUTCHINSON GUEST

Noverre, Jean-Georges
KATHLEEN KUZMICK HANSELL

Nozze degli Dei, Le
MERCEDES VIALE FERRERO

Nuba Dance
JAMES C. FARIS

Nureyev, Rudolf
DAVID DANIEL

Nutcracker, The
Productions in Russia
ALEXANDER P. DEMIDOV
Productions outside Russia
LAURA A. JACOBS

Oboukhoff, Anatole
DAVID VAUGHAN

Ocean
NANCY DALVA

Oceanic Dance Traditions
ADIRENNE L. KAEPPLER

O'Connor, Donald
RUSTY E. FRANK

Odissi
SUNIL KOTHARI

Ogoun, Luboš
VLADIMÍR VAŠUT

Ohio Ballet
DORIS HERING

Okinawa
SACHIYO ITO

Okuni
SAMUEL L. LEITER

Ondine
SUSAN AU

Onnagata
SAMUEL L. LEITER

Onoe Baikō
SAMUEL L. LEITER

Onoe Kikugorō
SAMUEL L. LEITER

Onoe Shōroku
SAMUEL L. LEITER

Ōno Kazuo
HASEGAWA ROKU

Opera, Ballet in
DALE HARRIS

Opéra-Ballet and Tragédie
Lyrique
JAMES R. ANTHONY

Orchestra
J. MICHAEL WALTON

Orff, Carl
HORST KOEGLER

Organizations
SELMA JEANNE COHEN

Orientalism
TRUDY SCOTT

Orlando, Mariane
LULLI SVEDIN

Oswald, Genevieve
MARILYN HUNT

Otozuru
STEPHEN COMEE

Ouled Naïl, Dances of the
AISHA ALI, MARDI ROLLOW,
LEONA WOOD

Pacific Northwest Ballet
DORIS HERING

PACT Ballet
JONATHAN HURWITZ

Paeper, Veronica
NAN MELVILLE

Page, Ruth
ANDREW MARK WENTINK

Paige, Brydon
CLAUDE CONYERS

Pakistan
SHAYMA SAIYID

Palucca, Gret
HEDWIG MÜLLER

Panama
LILA R. CHEVILLE

Panigrahi, Sanjukta
SUNIL KOTHARI

Pantomime
LAURENCE SENELICK

Pantomimus
T. DAVINA MCCLAIN

Papliński, Eugeniusz
PAWEŁ CHYNOWSKI

Papua New Guinea
An Overview
DON NILES
Binandere Dance
JOHN DADEMO WAIKO
Gizra Dance
BILLAI LABA
Kaluli Dance
STEVEN FELD,
EDWARD L. SCHIEFFELIN
Maring Dance
ALLISON JABLONKO
Melpa Dance
ANDREW J. STRATHERN,
DON NILES

Paquita
SUSAN AU

Parade
MARIANNE W. MARTIN

Paris Opera Ballet
MARIE-FRANÇOISE CHRISTOUT

Park, Merle
BARBARA NEWMAN

Parlić, Dimitrije
MILICA JOVANOVIĆ

Parnell, Feliks
JANINA PUDEŁEK

Partnering
ROBERT GRESKOVIC

Pas de Deux
SANDRA NOLL HAMMOND

Pas de Quatre
JOHN V. CHAPMAN

Passepied
CAROL G. MARSH

Passo e Mezzo
JULIA SUTTON

Pastorale
REBECCA HARRIS-WARRICK

Patineurs, Les
DAVID VAUGHAN

Pavan
JULIA SUTTON

Pavaniglia
JULIA SUTTON

Pavillon d'Armide, Le
SUZANNE CARBONNEAU

Pavlova, Anna
ROBERTA LAZZARINI

Paxton, Steve
SALLY BANES

Pecour, Guillaume-Louis
RÉGINE ASTIER

Pei Yanling
WILLIAM H. SUN

Pencak
SAL MURGIYANTO

Pennsylvania Ballet
SARAH MONTAGUE

Peretti, Serge
JEANNINE DORVANE

Péri, La
SUSAN AU

Pericet Family
PHILIPPA HEALE

Perrot, Jules
IVOR GUEST

Peru
E. MILDRED MERINO DE ZELA

Petipa, Jean-Antoine
MONIQUE BABSKY

Petipa, Lucien
MONIQUE BABSKY

Petipa, Marius
VERA M. KRASOVSKAYA

Petit, Roland
IRÈNE LIDOVA

Petrouchka
MOLLY McQUADE

Petrov, Anastas
VIOLETTA KONSULOVA

Philippines
REYNALDO GAMBOA ALEJANDRO

Photography
MINDY ALOFF

Physics of Dance
KENNETH LAWS

Picasso, Pablo
ELLEN BREITMAN

Pillar of Fire
DAVID VAUGHAN

Philoblus Dance Theatre
MARA J. PEETS

Pion, Maurice
JANINA PUDEŁEK

Pistoni, Mario
VITTORIA OTTOLENGHI

Pitrot, Antoine-Bonaventure
JEANNINE DORVANE

Pittsburgh Ballet Theatre
DORIS HERING

Placide, Alexandre
MAUREEN NEEDHAM

Playford, John
GENEVIEVE SHIMER

Plebs and Zotto
MARÍA SUSANNA AZZI

Plié
SANDRA NOLL HAMMOND

Plisetskaya, Maya
AZARY MESSERER

Pointe Work
ROBERT GRESKOVIC

Pokot Dance
MARTHA E. ROBBINS

Poland
Traditional and Social
Dance
GRÁZYNA DĄBROWSKA
Theatrical Dance
JANINA PUDEŁEK
Dance Research and
Publication
PAWEŁ CHYNOWSKI

Polka
DESMOND F. STROBEL

Polonaise
SUSAN AU

Polynesia
ADRIENNE L. KAEPPLER

Poole, David
MARINA GRUT

Port de Bras
SANDRA NOLL HAMMOND

Portugal
Traditional Dance
ANA PAULA BATALHA,
FERNANDA PRIM
Theatrical Dance
JOSÉ SASPORTES

Potapova, Elena
YURI A. STANISHEVSKY

Poulenc, Francis
BAIRD HASTINGS

Poulsen, Ulla
HENRIK LUNDGREN

Powell, Eleanor
RUSTY E.FRANK

Powwow
WILLIAM K. POWERS

Practice Clothes
SUSAN AU

Praetorius, Michael
INGRID BRAINARD

Prague National Theater
Ballet
VLADIMÍR VAŠUT

Pratesi, Giovanni
CLAUDIA CELI

Precision Dancing
ROBERT D. MOULTON

Preobrajenska, Olga
VALERY A. KULAKOV

Prévost, Françoise
RÉGINE ASTIER

Price Family
HENRIK LUNDGREN

Priest, Josiah
RICHARD RALPH,
JENNIFER THORP

Primitive Dance
JOANN W. KEALIINOHOMOKU

Primitive Mysteries
DEBORAH JOWITT

Primus, Pearl
JAMES BRIGGS MURRAY

Prints and Drawings
SUSAN AU

Proco Ciortea, Vera
TEA PREDA

Prodigal Son, The
SELMA JEANNE COHEN

Prokofiev, Sergei
MICHAEL OLIVER

Psota, Ivo Váňa
VLADIMÍR VAŠUT

Psyché et l'Amour
RICHARD RALPH, SUSAN AU

Pueblo Dance
JILL D. SWEET

Puerto Rico
SUSAN HOMAR

Pugni, Cesare
IVOR GUEST

Puppenfee, Die
GEORGE JACKSON

Pucell, Henry
CURTIS A. PRICE

Pushkin, Aleksandr
GENNADY G. ALBERT

Pyrrhic
BARBARA PALFY

Quadrille
DESMOND F. STROBEL

Rábai, Miklós
GÉZA KÖRTVÉLYES

Radha
SUZANNE SHELTON

Radice, Attilia
ALBERTO TESTA

Radio City Music Hall
ROBERT D. MOULTON

Radius, Alexandra
INE RIETSTAP

Rāga
WILLIAM P. MALM

Ragini Devi
LUISE ELCANESS SCRIPPS

Rainer, Yvonne
SALLY BANES

Rake's Progress, The
DAVID VAUGHAN

Ralov, Børge
ALLAN FRIDERICIA

Ralov, Kirsten
ERIK ASCHENGREEN

Rambert, Marie
MARY CLARKE

Rambert Dance Company
ALASTAIR MACAULAY

Rameau, Jean-Philippe
JÉRÔME DE LA GORCE

Rameau, Pierre
RÉGINE ASTIER

Rao, Shanta
CLIFFORD REIS JONES

Rapanui
ADRIENNE L. KAEPPLER

Rasch, Albertina
FRANK W. D. RIES

Rās Līlā
CLIFFORD REIS JONES

Rassine, Alexis
MARINA GRUT

Rauschenberg, Robert
MELISSA HARRIS

Ravel, Maurice
NOËL GOODWIN

Ravel Family
GRETCHEN SCHNEIDER

Rayet, Jacqueline
JEANNINE DORVANE

Raymonda
KARINA L. MELIK-PASHAYEVA

Reconstruction
Use of Historical Notations
ANGENE FEVES
Use of Modern Scores
RAY COOK
Beyond Notation
LINDA J. TOMKO

Red Detachment of
Women,The
ZHU LIREN

Reddy, Raja and Radha
SUNIL KOTHARI

Red Poppy, The
ELIZABETH SOURITZ

Red Shoes, The
BARBARA NEWMAN

Reel
JAMES E. MORRISON

Reinholm, Gert
HORST KOEGLER

Relâche
SALLY BANES

Renaissance Dance Technique
INGRID BRAINARD

Renaissance Fêtes and
Triumphs
HELEN PURKIS

Rendezvous, Les
DAVID VAUGHAN

Revelations
JOSEPH H. MAZO

Revels
ROBIN WOODARD WEENING

Révérence
Origins of Modes and
Manners
INGRID BRAINARD
Early Eighteenth-Century
Modes
WENDY HILTON
Nineteenth-Century Modes
ELIZABETH ALDRICH

Riabouchinska, Tatiana
KATHRINE SORLEY WALKER

Rich, John
LAURENCE SENELICK

Richardson, Philip
BETH ELIOT GENNÉ

Rigaudon
MEREDITH ELLIS LITTLE

Riisager, Knudåge
OLE NØRLYNG

Rinaldi, Antonio
ELENA GRILLO

Rioja, Pilar
ALBERTO DALLAL

Ritha Devi
PATRICIA A. ROWE

Ritual and Dance
CYNTHIA J. NOVACK

Rivera, Chita
LARRY BILLMAN

Robbins, Jerome
DORIS HERING

Robinson, Bill
SALLY R. SOMMER

Rodeo
LELAND WINDREICH

Rodin, Auguste
NANCY VAN NORMAN BAER

Rodolphe, Jean-Joseph
OLE NØRLYNG

Roerich, Nikolai
JOHN E. BOWLT

Rogers, Ginger
CHRISTOPHER CAINES

Roman Empire
T. DAVINA MCCLAIN

Romania
Folk Dance
VERA PROCA CIORTEA
Theatrical Dance
TEA PREDA, VIVIA SĂNDULESCU
Folk Dance Research and
Publication
CONSTANTIN COSTEA

Romanoff, Dimitri
PATRICIA BARNES

Romanov, Boris
LYNN GARAFOLA

Romeo and Juliet
RITA FELCIANO

Rome Opera Ballet
VITTORIA OTTOLENGHI

Róna, Viktor
GEDEON P. DIENES

Rond de Jambe
NANCY GOLDNER

Ronzani, Domenico
BARBARA BARKER

Rosati, Carolina
ELENA GRILLO

Rose, Jürgen
CLAUDIA ROTH PIERPONT

Rosen, Elsa-Marianne von
LULLI SVEDIN

Rosenthal, Jean
CLAUDIA ROTH PIERPONT

Ross, Bertram
KITTY CUNNINGHAM

Ross, Herbert
JEROME DELAMATER

Rota, Guiseppe
CLAUDIA CELI

Round Dancing
VERONICA ANN MCCLURE

Rowe, Marilyn
GEOFFREY WILLIAM HUTTON

Royal Ballet
PETER BRINSON

Royal Ballet of Flanders
LUC VERVAEKE

Royal Danish Ballet
ERIK ASCHENGREEN

Royal Winnipeg Ballet
MAX WYMAN

Rubinstein, Ida
CHARLES S. MAYER

Rudner, Sara
ALLEN ROBERTSON

Ruskaja, Jia
VITTORIA OTTOLENGHI

Russia
Traditional Dance
VALERIA I. URALSKAYA
Siberian Dance Traditions
MARIA I. ZHORNITSKAYA
Theatrical Dance before
1917
VALERIA I. URALSKAYA,
GALINA V. INOZEMTSEVA,
ELENA G. FEDORENKO
Theatrical Dance since 1917
VICTOR V. VANSLOV
Secondary and Provincial
Dance Companies
ELIZABETH SOURITZ
Twentieth-Century Plastique
ELIZABETH SOURITZ
Dance Education
NIKOLAI I. ELYASH
Folk Dance Research and
Publication
VALERIA I. URALSKAYA

Theatrical Dance Research
and Publication
ELIZABETH SOURITZ

Sabirova, Malika
ELLA BOCHARNIKOVA

Sacre du Printemps, Le
JOAN ACOCELLA

Saddler, Donald
MARILYN HUNT

Saint-André, Adrien Merger de
RÉGINE ASTIER,
GEORGE DORRIS

St. Denis, Ruth
SUZANNE SHELTON

Saint-Léon, Arthur
MONIQUE BABSKY

Saint-Léon Notation
ANN HUTCHINSON GUEST

Sakharoff, Alexander
HEDWIG MÜLLER

Sallé, Marie
RÉGINE ASTIER

Saltarello
JULIA SUTTON

Samba
KATIA CANTON

Samburu Dance
PAUL SPENCER

Samoa
JACOB WAINWRIGHT LOVE

Samson, Leela
SUNIL KOTHARI

Sand, Inge
HENRIK LUNDGREN

San Francisco Ballet
LELAND WINDREICH

Sangalli, Rita
BARBARA BARKER

Sankovskaya, Ekaterina
NATALIA Y. CHERNOVA

Sano, Kemoko
LOUISE BEDICHEK

Sanquirico, Alessandro
NANCY REYNOLDS

Santlow, Hester
MOIRA GOFF

Sarabande
INGRID BRAINARD

Sarabhai, Mallika
SUNIL KOTHARI

Sarabhai, Mrinalini
CLIFFORD REIS JONES

Sardana
PHILIPPA HEALE

Sardono
EDWARD HERBST

Sarukkai, Malavika
SUNIL KOTHARI

Satie, Erik
ROGER SHATTUCK

Sauguet, Henri
BAIRD HASTINGS

Savignano, Luciana
VITTORIA OTTOLENGHI

Scala Ballet
LUIGI ROSSI

Scapino Rotterdam
INE RIETSTAP

Scènes de Ballet
ALASTAIR MACAULAY

Scenic Design
ARNOLD ARONSON

Schall, Claus
OLE NØRLYNG

Schanne, Margrethe
HENRIK LUNDGREN

Schaufuss Family
ERIK ASCHENGREEN

Schayk, Toer van
LUUK UTRECHT

Schéhérazade
SUZANNE CARBONNEAU

Schēma
LIBBY SMIGEL

Schilling, Tom
HARTMUT REGITZ

Schneitzhoeffer, Jean
OLE NØRLYNG

Schollar, Ludmilla
LYNN GARAFOLA

Schönberg, Bessie
DEBORAH JOWITT

Schooling, Elisabeth
BARBARA NEWMAN

Schoop, Trudi
RICHARD MERZ

Schuman, William
GEORGE DORRIS

Schwarz Family
MONIQUE BABSKY

Scott, Margaret
GEOFFREY WILLIAM HUTTON

Scottish Ballet
GEOFFREY WEST

Seguidillas
PHILIPPA HEALE

Semenova, Marina
VALERIA I. URALSKAYA

Sen, Saswati
SUNIL KOTHARI

Seraphic Dialogue
DEBORAH JOWITT

Seregi, Lázló
GÉZA KÖRTVÉYLES

Serenade
REBA ANN ADLER

Sergeyev, Konstantin
VALENTINA V. PROKHOROVA

Serrano, Lupe
PATRICIA BARNES

Setterfield, Valda
AMANDA SMITH

Seymour, Lynn
CLEMENT CRISP

Shaker Dance
SUZANNE YOUNGERMAN

Shakers, The
MARCIA B. SIEGEL

Shamanism
THERESA KI-JA KIM

Shangana-Tsonga Dance
THOMAS F. JOHNSTON

Shankar, Uday
JOAN L. ERDMAN

Sharma, Uma
SUNIL KOTHARI

Sharp, Cecil
URSULA VAUGHAN WILLIAMS

Shawn, Ted
CHRISTENA L. SCHLUNDT

Shchedrin, Rodion
ELENA N. KURILENKO

Shearer, Moira
BARBARA NEWMAN

Shearer, Sybil
ANN BARZEL

Shigeyama Family
JONAH SALZ

Shimai
CARL WOLZ

Shishimai
SAMUEL L. LEITER

Shostakovich, Dmitri
MICHAEL OLIVER

Shurale
GALINA A. GULAYAEVA

Sibley, Antoinette
BARBARA NEWMAN

Siddiqui, Nahid
SHAYMA SAIYID

Sikinnis
LIBBY SMIGEL

Sikkim
ELIZABETH GOLDBLATT

Simone, Kirsten
CLAUDE CONYERS

Sims, Sandman
SALLY R. SOMMER

Singh, Bipin
SUNIL KOTHARI

Siretta, Dan
DAVID VAUGHAN

Sitara Devi
SUNIL KOTHARI

Skeaping, Mary
PETER BRINSON

Skibine, George
IRÈNE LIDOVA

Skirt Dance
MARTIE FELLOM

Slavenska, Mia
GEORGE JACKSON

Sleeping Beauty, The
Petipa Production
VERA M. KRASOVSKAYA
Later Productions
SUSAN AU

Slonimsky, Yuri
OLEG A. PETROV

Slovak National Theater Ballet
VLADIMÍR VAŠUT

Smith, George Washington
SUSAN AU

Smith, Oliver
CLAUDIA ROTH PIERPONT

Šmok, Pavel
VLADIMÍR VAŠUT

Snoek, Hans
INE RIETSTAP

Social Dance
Court and Social Dance
before 1800
INGRID BRAINARD
Nineteenth-Century Social
Dance
GRETCHEN SCHNEIDER
Twentieth-Century Social
Dance to 1960
DON MCDONAGH

Twentieth-Century Social
Dance since 1960
SALLY R. SOMMER

Sokolova, Lydia
JOAN ACOCELLA

Sokolow, Anna
DARCY HALL

Soloviev, Yuri
ARKADY A. SOKOLOV-KAMINSKY

Somes, Michael
BARBARA NEWMAN

Somnambule, La
SUSAN AU

Sonnambula, La
SUSAN AU

Soudeikine, Serge
JOHN E. BOWLT

Souritz, Elizabeth
SELMA JEANNE COHEN

South Africa
Indigenous Dance
ANDRÉE GRAU
Ballet
MARINA GRUT
Contemporary Theatrical
Dance
ADRIENNE SICHEL

Southern Africa
JOHN BLACKING

Spagnoletta
JULIA SUTTON

Spain
Dance Traditions before
1700
LYNN MATLUCK BROOKS
Social and Theatrical
Dance, 1700–1862
PHILIPPA HEALE
Theatrical Dance since 1862
LAURA KUMIN
Dance Research and
Publication
NÈLIDA MONÉS I MESTRE,
MARTA CARRASCO BENÍTEZ

Šparemblek, Milko
PIA MLAKAR

Spartacus
VICTOR V. VANSLOV

Spessivtseva, Olga
JEANNINE DORVANE

Spindrift
ANGELA KANE

Spoerli, Heinz
RICHARD MERZ

Spohr, Arnold
MICHAEL CRABB

Square Dancing
LEEELLEN FRIEDLAND

Staats, Léo
MONIQUE BABSKY

Staff, Frank
MARINA GRUT

Starzer, Joseph
OLE NØRLYNG

Stepanov Notation
ANN HUTCHINSON GUEST

Step Dancing
Step Dancing in Great
Britain
and Ireland
JULIAN OLIVIER PILLING
Step Dancing in Cape
Breton
FRANCES MACEACHEN

Stone Flower, The
VICTOR V. VANSLOV

Strate, Grant
MICHAEL CRABB

Strauss Family
ANDREW LAMB

Stravinsky, Igor
DAVID HAMILTON

Struchkova, Raisa
GALINA V. BELYAYEVA-
CHELOMBITKO

Stuttgart Ballet
HORST KOEGLER

Subligny, Marie-Thérèse
RÉGINE ASTIER

Sub-Saharan Africa
An Overview
PEGGY HARPER
Popular Dance
DAVID COPLAN
Dance Research and
Publication
MARGARET THOMPSON-DREWAL

Suite for Five
CAROLYN BROWN

Summerspace
CAROLYN BROWN

Susana
RICHARD MERZ

Svetlov, Valerian
SUSAN COOK SUMMER

Swaine, Alexander von
HEDWIG MÜLLER

Swan Lake
Productions in Russia
ALEXANDER P. DEMIDOV
Productions outside Russia
IRIS M. FANGER

Sweden
Traditional Dance
MATS NILSSON
Theatrical Dance before
1771
MAGNUS BLOMKVIST
Theatrical Dance,
1771–1900
KIRSTEN GRAM HOLMSTRÖM
Theatrical Dance since 1900
ANNA GRETA STÅHLE
Court Theaters
MAGNUS BLOMKVIST
Dance Education
LULLI SVEDIN
Dance Research and
Publication
ANNA GRETA STÅHLE

Swiss Milkmaid, The
GUNHILD OBERZAUCHER-
SCHÜLLER

Switzerland
RICHARD MERZ

Sword Dance
JOHN FORREST

Sydney Dance Company
MICHELLE POTTER

Sylphide, La
SUSAN AU

Sylphides, Les
Russian Origins
GALINA N. DOBROVOLSKAYA
Diaghilev Production
SONDRA LOMAX

Sylvia
MONIQUE BABSKY

Symphonic Variations
ALASTAIR MACAULAY

Symphony in C
REBA ANN ADLER

Szeged Contemporary Ballet
ZSUZSA KŐVÁGÓ,
GEDEON P. DIENES

Taglioni Family
ALBERTO TESTA

Tahiti
JANE FREEMAN MOULIN

Taiwan
LIU FENG-SHUEH

Tajikistan
YURI P. TYURIN

Takarazuka
USUI KENJI

Tallchief, Maria
NANCY REYNOLDS

Tamasha
CLIFFORD REIS JONES

Tambourin
REBECCA HARRIS-WARRICK

Tamiris, Helen
CHRISTENA L. SCHLUNDT

Tanaka Min
HASEGAWA ROKU

Tango
MARÍA SUSANNA AZZI

Tankard, Meryl
MICHELLE POTTER

Tap Dance
SALLY R. SOMMER

Tarantella
SUSAN AU

Tarasov, Nikolai
RAISA S. STRUCHKOVA

Taverner, Sonia
CLAUDE CONYERS

Taylor, Paul
ANGELA KANE

Tchaikovsky, Petr Ilich
NOËL GOODWIN

Tchelitchev, Pavel
SUSAN AU

Tcherina, Ludmila
MONIQUE BABSKY

Tchernicheva, Lubov
LYNN GARAFOLA

Teatrodanza Contemporanea
di Roma
VITTORIA OTTOLENGHI

Technical Manuals
Publications, 1445–1725
INGRID BRAINARD
Publications, 1765–1859
SANDRA NOLL HAMMOND
Publications since 1887
KENNETHA R. MCARTHUR

Television
Dance on Television in
Canada
PAULA CITRON
Dance on Television in
Europe
BOB LOCKYER
Dance on Television in the
United States
BRIAN ROSE

Temple, Shirley
RUSTY E. FRANK

Tennant, Veronica
MICHAEL CRABB

Terabust, Elisabetta
VITTORIA OTTOLENGHI

Ter-Arutunian, Rouben
CLAUDIA ROTH PIERPONT

Terpsichore
LIBBY SMIGEL

Teshigawara Saburō
HASEGAWA ROKU

Tetley, Glen
ALLEN ROBERTSON

Teyyam
WAYNE ASHLEY

Thailand
MATTANI MOJDARA RUTNIN

Tharp, Twyla
LAURA SHAPIRO

Theaters for Dance
DIANNE L. WOODRUFF

Three Epitaphs
ANGELA KANE

Tibet
LIN LERNER

Tigua Dance
CARLOS LOZANO

Tikhomirov, Vasily
ELIZABETH SOURITZ

Timofeyeva, Nina
YURI P. TYURIN

Tinikling
REYNALDO GAMBOA ALEJANDRO

Tiv Dance
PEGGY HARPER

Tomasson, Helgi
KATY MATHESON

Tomaszewski, Henryk
PAWEŁ CHYNOWSKI

Tomlinson, Kellom
RICHARD RALPH,
JENNIFER THORP

Tonga
ADRIENNE L. KAEPPLER

Tordion
JULIA SUTTON

Torvill and Dean
ROBYNN J. STILWELL

Toulouse-Lautrec, Henri de
ELLEN BREITMAN

Toumanova, Tamara
KATHRINE SORLEY WALKER

Tovil
M. M. AMES

Trance Dance
ERIKA BOURGUIGNON

Travesty
MALCOLM MCCORMICK

Trefilova, Vera
LYNN GARAFOLA

Trend
NANCY MASON HAUSER

Tricorne, Le
LISA A. FUSILLO

Tripudium
DONNA LA RUE

Tudor, Antony
DAVID VAUGHAN

Tulsa Ballet Theatre
DORIS HERING

Tune, Tommy
CAMILLE HARDY

Tunisia
AISHA ALI, MARDI ROLLOW,
LEONA WOOD

Turczynowicz, Roman
JANINA PUDEŁEK

Turkey
METIN AND

Turkmenistan
N. P. RADKINA

Turner, Harold
BARBARA NEWMAN

Turnout
Physical Mechanics
JOHN M. WILSON
History and Aesthetics
SANDRA NOLL HAMMOND

Tutu
SUSAN AU

Two Pigeons, The
ALASTAIR MACAULAY

Ubakala Dance
JUDITH LYNNE HANNA

Ukraine
Traditional Dance
ANDRIY NAHACHEWSKY
Theatrical Dance
YURI A. STANISHEVSKY

Ulanova, Galina
BORIS A. LVOV-ANOKHIN

Ulrich, Jochen
HORST KOEGLER

Umewaka Makio
STEPHEN COMEE

United States of America
An Overview
GRETCHEN SCHNEIDER
African-American Dance
Traditions
BRENDA DIXON GOTTSCHILD
African-American Social
Dance
KATRINA HAZZARD-DONALD
Regional Dance Companies
DORIS HERING
Musical Theater
CAMILLE HARDY
Ballet Education
ANN BARZEL
Social, Folk, and Modern
Dance Education
NANCY LEE CHALFA RUYTER
Dance Research and
Publication
SELMA JEANNE COHEN
Contemporary Criticism
JENNIFER DUNNING

Uruguay
CLAUDIO SANGUINETTI GAMBARO

Ustinova,Tatiana
VALERIA I. URALSKAYA

Uthoff, Ernst
HANS EHRMANN

Uzbekistan
LAUREL VICTORIA GRAY

Vaganova, Agrippina
VALERY A. KULAKOV

Vainonen, Vasily
VALERY A. KULAKOV

Valberkh, Ivan
NIKOLAI I. ELYASH

Valli
SUNIL KOTHARI

van Praagh, Peggy
PETER BRINSON

Vasiliev, Vladimir
GALINA V. BELYAYEVA-
CHELOMBITKO

Vaudeville
LAURENCE SENELICK

Vedantam Satyam
SUNIL KOTHARI

Vempati Chinna Satyam
SUNIL KOTHARI

Venda Dance
JOHN BLACKING

Venezuela
BELÉN LOBO

Verchinina, Nina
KATIA CANTON

Verdon, Gwen
LARRY BILLMAN

Verdy, Violette
VICTORIA HUCKENPAHLER

Ves Dance
SICILLE P. C. KOTELAWALA

Vestris Family
JEANNINE DORVANE

Viennese Kinderballett
GUNHILD OBERZAUCHER-
SCHÜLLER

Vietnam
TRÂN VAN KHÊ

Viganò, Salvatore
CLAUDIA CELI

Villella, Edward
ROBERT GRESKOVIC

Vilzak, Anatole
LYNN GARAFOLA

Vinogradov, Oleg
ARSEN B. DEGEN

Violette, Eva Maria
SIBYLLE DAHMS

Virsaladze, Simon
VICTOR V. VANSLOV

Virsky, Pavel
YURI A. STANISHEVSKY

Vladimiroff, Pierre
SUZANNE CARBONNEAU

Vodun
HENRY FRANK

Volinine, Alexandre
LYNN GARAFOLA

Volkova,Vera
EBBE MØRK

Volta
JULIA SUTTON

Volynsky, Akim
SUSAN COOK SUMMER

Vyroubova, Nina
JEANNINE DORVANE

Waldeen
ALBERTO DALLAL

Walkaround Time
CAROLYN BROWN

Walkowitz, Abraham
NANCY VAN NORMAN BAER

Wall, David
BARBARA NEWMAN

Wallmann, Margarete
ANDREA AMORT

Walter, Erich
HORST KOEGLER

Waltz
DESMOND F. STROBEL

Waring, James
DAVID VAUGHAN

Warren, Vincent
MICHAEL CRABB

Warsaw Ballet
JANINA PUDEŁEK

Washington Ballet
DORIS HERING

Water Study
MARCIA B.SIEGEL

Wayang
EDWARD HERBST

Wayburn, Ned
CAMILLE HARDY

Weaver, John
RICHARD RALPH

Wedding Bouquet, A
DAVID VAUGHAN

Weeme, Mascha ter
INE RIETSTAP

Weidman, Charles
SYLVIA RICHARDS

Weidt, Jean
SUSAN A. MANNING

Welch, Garth
MICHELLE POTTER

Weller, Dawn
NAN MELVILLE

Wells, Doreen
MARY CLARKE

West Africa
JUDITH LYNNE HANNA

White-Haried Girl, The
ZHU LIREN

Whitman Sisters
CONSTANCE VALIS HILL

Wiesenthal, Grete
GUNHILD OBERZAUCHER-
SCHÜLLER

Wiesenthal Technique
MARIA JOSEFA SCHAFFGOTSCH

Wigman, Mary
SUSAN A. MANNING

Wilde, Patricia
WILLIAM JAMES LAWSON

Wilhelm, C.
CLAUDIA ROTH PIERPONT

Williams, E.Virginia
DORIS HERING

Williams, Petr
VIKTOR I. BEREZKIN

Williams, Stanley
CLAUDE CONYERS

Williams-Yarborough, Lavinia
BRENDA DIXON GOTTSCHILD

Wilson, Robert
SILAS JACKSON, SETH
GOLDSTEIN

Wilson, Sallie
SUSAN REITER

Winterbranch
CAROLYN BROWN

Wirtschaft
INGRID BRAINARD

Woizikowski, Leon
LYNN GARAFOLA

Worsaae, Jens-Jacob
MARILYN HUNT

Wright, Peter
BARBARA NEWMAN

Wu Xiaobang
OU JIAN-PING

Ximénez-Vargas Ballet
Español
JUDY FARRAR BURNS

Yakko and Kawakami
JONAH SALZ

Yakobson, Leonid
GALINA N. DOBROVOLSKAYA

Yakşagāna
MARTHA BUSH ASHTON-SIKORA

Yamada Setsuko
HASEGAWA ROKU

Yang Meiqi
OU JING-PING

Yaqui Dance
CARLOS LOZANO

Yemen
NAJWA ADRA

Yermolayev, Aleksei
BORIS B. AKIMOV

Ye Shaolan
PHEBE SHIH CHAO

Yoga
RITHA DEVI

Yoruba Dance
MARGARET THOMPSON-DREWAL

Youskevitch, Igor
MARILYN HUNT

Yuan Xuefen
WILLIAM H. SUN

Yugoslavia
Traditional Dance
RICHARD CRUM,
ELSIE IVANCICH DUNIN,
STANIMIR VISINSKI
Ballet
MILICA JOVANOVIĆ,
PIA MLAKAR,
PINO MLAKAR
Modern Dance
JASNA PERUČIĆ NADAREVIĆ
Theatrical Dance since 1991
XENIA RAKIĆ, ANI UDOVIĆKI,
VOJKO VIDMAR
Dance Research and
Publication
HENRIK NEUBAUER

Zajlich, Piotr
JANINA PUDEŁEK

Zakharov, Rostislav
GALINA V. BELYAYEVA-
CHELOMBITKO

Zambelli, Carlotta
JEANNINE DORVANE

Zār
NAJWA ADRA

Zeami
BENITO ORTOLANI

Zhou Xinfang
WILLIAM H. SUN

Ziegfeld, Florenz
CAMILLE HARDY

Zollar, Jawole Willa Jo
MELANYE WHITE-DIXON

Zorina,Vera
LIZA EWELL

Zorn Notation
ANN HUTCHINSON GUEST

Zotov, Rafail
SUSAN COOK SUMMER

Zucchi, Virginia
ALBERTO TESTA

Züllig, Hans
RICHARD MERZ

Zurich Ballet
RICHARD MERZ

SYNOPTIC OUTLINE OF CONTENTS

[*The outline presented on the following pages is intended to provide a general view of the conceptual scheme of this encyclopedia. Entries are arranged into nine major conceptual categories. To show the various components of the encyclopedia's coverage, each of these major categories is subdivided into a variety of sections. Because the headings for each category are not necessarily mutually exclusive, some entries in the encyclopedia are listed more than once. In general, biographical entries have been excluded because they are so numerous, except where a particular group is worthy of special mention.*]

I Lands and Peoples
Lands
Peoples

II Ritual and Religion

III Folk, Traditional, and Popular Dance, Festivals and Masquerades
Folk and Traditional Dance
Social and Popular Dance
Festivals and Masquerades

IV History of Western Dance to 1800
Ancient Mediterranean World
Europe: Middle Ages and Renaissance
Europe: From the Baroque through the Enlightenment

V Theatrical Dance
Ballet and Contemporary Theatrical Dance
Dance Drama, Mask Dance Theater, and Puppetry

VI Elements of Theatrical Dance
Costume Design
Documenting Dance
Theater, Stage, Scenery, and Lighting Design
Texts for Dance
Impresarios, Patrons, and Producers

VII Popular Entertainment

VIII Dance and other Disciplines
Aesthetics, Philosophy, and Theory
Visual Arts
Training and Education
Science and Health
Music

IX Dance Research and Publication
History of Scholarship
Dance Criticism

I LANDS AND PEOPLES

[Part I of the outline is divided into two sections by broad geographical locations: Lands and Peoples. The first section presents a geographical listing of country articles; the second section focuses on the encyclopedia's coverage of specific cultural groups.]

LANDS

Europe

Albania
Austria
  Theatrical Dance
Belarus
Belgium
  Theatrical Dance
Bulgaria
  Folk and Traditional Dance
  Theatrical Dance
Crete
  Dance in Ancient Crete
  Dance in Modern Crete
Czech Republic and Slovak Republic
  Folk and Traditional Dance
  Theatrical Dance
Denmark
  Traditional and Social Dance
  Dance in the Faeroe Islands
  Theatrical Dance
Estonia
Finland
  Traditional Dance
  Theatrical Dance
  Dance Research and Publication
France
  Recreational Dance
  Theatrical Dance, 1581–1789
  Theatrical Dance, 1789–1914
  Ballet since 1914
  Modern Dance before 1970
  Modern Dance since 1970
Germany
  Traditional and Social Dance
  Theatrical Dance, 1600–1945
  Theatrical Dance since 1945
Great Britain
  English Traditional Dance
  Scottish Folk and Traditional Dance
  Welsh Folk and Traditional Dance
  Manx Folk and Traditional Dance
  Theatrical Dance, 1560–1660
  Theatrical Dance, 1660–1772
  Theatrical Dance, 1772–1850
  Theatrical Dance since 1850
  Modern Dance

Greece
  Dance in Ancient Greece
  Dance in the Roman and Byzantine
    Period
  Dance in Modern Greece
  Ritual and Carnival Dance Traditions
Hungary
  Traditional and Popular Dance
  Theatrical Dance before World War II
  Theatrical Dance since World War II
  Modern Dance
Iceland
  Traditional Dance
  Theatrical Dance
Ireland
  Traditional Dance
  Theatrical Dance
Italy
  Dance Traditions before 1800
  Theatrical Dance, 1801–1940
  Theatrical Dance since 1940
Latvia
Lithuania
  Traditional Dance
  Theatrical Dance
Moldova
Netherlands
  Folk and Traditional Dance
  Social Dance
  Theatrical Dance before 1900
  Theatrical Dance, 1900–1945
  Theatrical Dance since 1945
Norway
  Folk, Traditional, and Social Dance
  Theatrical Dance before 1919
  Theatrical Dance, 1920–1958
  Theatrical Dance since 1958
Portugal
  Traditional Dance
  Theatrical Dance
Roman Empire
Romania
  Folk Dance
  Theatrical Dance
Russia
  Traditional Dance
  Theatrical Dance before 1917
  Theatrical Dance since 1917
  Secondary and Provincial Dance
    Companies
  Twentieth-Century Plastique

Spain
  Theatrical Dance before 1700
  Theatrical Dance, 1700–1862
Sweden
  Traditional Dance
  Theatrical Dance before 1771
  Theatrical Dance, 1771–1900
  Theatrical Dance since 1900
  Court Theaters
Switzerland
Ukraine
  Traditional Dance
  Theatrical Dance
Yugoslavia
  Traditional Dance
  Ballet
  Modern Dance
  Theatrical Dance since 1991

North Africa and Middle East

PRINCIPAL ARTICLES
Arabian Peninsula
Middle East
  An Overview
North Africa

SUPPORTING ARTICLES
Algeria
Egypt
  Dance in Ancient Egypt
  Traditional Dance
  Contemporary Dance Companies
Iran
Israel
  An Overview
  Ethnic Dance
Lebanon
Mesopotamia
Morocco
Turkey
Yemen

Sub-Saharan Africa

PRINCIPAL ARTICLES
Sub-Saharan Africa
  An Overview
  Popular Dance
West Africa
Central and East Africa
Southern Africa

SUPPORTING ARTICLES
Cameroon
Ethiopia
Ghana
  An Overview

South Africa
    Indigenous Dance
    Ballet
    Contemporary Theatrical Dance

The Caucasus, Central Asia, and Northern Eurasia

Armenia
Azerbaijan
Georgia
Kazakhstan
Kyrgyzstan
Russia
    Siberian Dance Traditions
Tajikistan
Turkmenistan
Uzbekistan

East Asia

PRINCIPAL ARTICLES
Asian Dance Traditions
    An Overview
    The Influence of Puppetry
    Religious, Philosophical, and
        Environmental Influence

SUPPORTING ARTICLES
China
    An Overview
    Folk and Minority Dance
    Dance in Opera
    Classical Dance
    Contemporary Theatrical Dance
Japan
    An Overview
    Ritual Dance
    Folk Dance
    Ballet
    Modern Dance
Korea
    An Overview
    Masked Dance Drama
    Modern Dance
Okinawa
Taiwan

South Asia

PRINCIPAL ARTICLES
Asian Dance Traditions
    An Overview
    The Influence of Puppetry
    Religious, Philosophical, and
        Environmental Influence

SUPPORTING ARTICLES
Afghanistan
Bangladesh

Bhutan
India
    History of Indian Dance
    Philosophy of Indian Dance
    Epic Sources of Indian Dance
    The Rādhā-Kṛṣṇa Theme in Indian
        Dance
    New Directions in Indian Dance
Manipur
Sikkim
Pakistan
Tibet

Southeast Asia

PRINCIPAL ARTICLES
Asian Dance Traditions
    An Overview
    The Influence of Puppetry
    Religious, Philosophical, and
        Environmental Influence

SUPPORTING ARTICLES
Cambodia
Indonesia
    An Overview
    Balinese Ceremonial Dance
    Balinese Dance Theater
    Balinese Mask Dance Theater
    Javanese Dance Traditions
    Sundanese Dance Traditions
    Dance Traditions of the Outlying
        Islands
Laos
Malaysia
Myanmar
Thailand

Oceania

PRINCIPAL ARTICLE
Oceanic Dance Traditions

SUPPORTING ARTICLES
Australia
    Ballet
    Modern Dance
Bellona
Fiji
Melanesia
Micronesia
New Zealand
    An Overview
Papua New Guinea
    An Overview
    Binandere Dance
    Gizra Dance
    Kalui Dance
    Maring Dance
    Melpa Dance

Philippines
Polynesia
Rapanui
Samoa
Tahiti
Tonga

The Americas

Argentina
    Folk and Traditional Dance
    Ballet
    Modern Dance
Belize
Brazil
    Ritual and Popular Dance
    Ballet
    Modern Dance
Canada
    Folk and Traditional Dance in French
        Canada
    Theatrical Dance
    Contemporary Theatrical Dance
Caribbean Region
Chile
    Folk and Traditional Dance
    Theatrical Dance
Cuba
    Folk, Ritual, and Social Dance
    Ballet before 1959
    Ballet since 1959
    Modern Dance
Dominican Republic
Ecuador
Guatemala
Haiti
Jamaica
Mexico
    Traditional Dance
    Theatrical Dance
    Dance Companies
Panama
Peru
Puerto Rico
United States of America
    An Overview
    African-American Dance Traditions
    African-American Social Dance
    Regional Companies
    Musical Theater
Uruguay
Venezuela

PEOPLES

Europe

Anastenáridēs
Basque Dance

Gypsy Dance
Jewish Dance Traditions

North Africa and Middle East

Bedouin Dance
Islam and Dance
Jewish Dance Traditions
Kurdish Dance
Ouled Naïl, Dances of the

Sub-Saharan Africa

Bamana Dance
Digo Dance
Dogon Dance
Hausa Dance
!Kung San Dance
Mbuti Dance
Nuba Dance
Pokot Dance
Samburu Dance
Shangana-Tsonga Dance
Tiv Dance
Ubakala Dance
Venda Dance
Yoruba Dance

East Asia

Ainu Dance Traditions

Oceania

Australian Aboriginal Dance
  An Overview
  Aborigines of Arnhem Land
  Tiwi Dance
  Aborigines of Cape York Peninsula
  Warlpiri Dance
  Antakarinya Dance
Maori Dance

The Americas

Native American Dance
  An Overview
  Northeastern Woodlands
  Southeastern Woodlands
  The Great Plains
  California and the Intermountain
    Region
  The Northwest Coast
  The Far North
Garifuna Dance
Hopi Dance
Navaho Dance
Pueblo Dance
Shaker Dance
Tigua Dance
Yaqui Dance

Melanesia
Micronesia
New Zealand
  An Overview
Oceanic Dance Traditions
Papua New Guinea
  An Overview
  Binandere Dance
  Gizra Dance
  Kalui Dance
  Maring Dance
  Melpa Dance
Polynesia
Rapanui
Samoa
Sikkim
South Africa
  Indigenous Dance
Southern Africa
Sub-Saharan Africa
  An Overview
Tahiti
Tibet
Tonga
Turkey
Vietnam
West Africa

PEOPLES
Ainu Dance Traditions
Anastenárides
Australian Aboriginal Dance
  An Overview
  Aborigines of Arnhem Land
  Tiwi Dance
  Aborigines of Cape York Peninsula
  Warlpiri Dance
  Antakarinya Dance
Bamana Dance
Basque Dance
Bedouin Dance
Digo Dance
Dogon Dance
Garifuna Dance
Gypsy Dance Traditions
Hausa Dance
Hopi Dance
Islam and Dance
Jewish Dance Traditions
!Kung San Dance
Kurdish Dance
Maori Dance
Mbuti Dance
Native American Dance
  An Overview
  Northeastern Woodlands

II RITUAL AND RELIGION

[*Part II of the outline focuses on the role of religion and ritual in dance. The* Lands *and* Peoples *listed here are particularly rich in ritual dance traditions. It is important to note that some forms originated as rituals and over time became secularized; other forms began as celebrations and festivals that in turn became expressions of popular culture. Therefore, for additional discussion, see the* Folk and Traditional Dance *articles as well as the entries under* Festivals *and* Masquerades *listed in part III of this outline; and the* Dance Drama, Mask Dance Theater, *and* Puppetry *entries listed in part V. For related information, see* Aesthetics; Costume in African Traditions; Costume in Asian Traditions; European Traditional Dance; Mask and Makeup, *articles on* African Traditions *and* Asian Traditions.]

PRINCIPAL ARTICLE
Ritual and Dance

  LANDS
Bellona
Bhutan
Brazil
  Ritual and Popular Dance
Cameroon
Central and East Africa
Cuba
  Folk, Ritual, and Social Dance

Ethiopia
Fiji
Ghana
  An Overview
Greece
  Dance in Ancient Greece
  Ritual and Carnival Dance Traditions
Indonesia
  Balinese Ceremonial Dance
  Balinese Mask Dance
Japan
  Ritual Dance

Southeastern Woodlands
The Great Plains
California and the Intermountain
  Region
The Northwest Coast
The Far North
Navaho Dance
Nuba Dance
Ouled Naïl, Dances of the
Pokot Dance
Pueblo Dance
Samburu Dance
Shaker Dance
Shangana-Tsonga Dance
Tiv Dance
Tigua Dance
Ubakala Dance
Venda Dance
Yaqui Dance
Yoruba Dance

SUPPORTING ARTICLES
Asian Dance Traditions
  Religious, Philosophical, and
    Environmental Influence
Bible, Dance and the
Black Hat Dance
Bon Odori
Christianity and Dance
  Early Christian Views
  Medieval Views
  Modern Views
Concheros

Congo Dances
Devadāsī
Guild Dances
Gigaku
Kagura
Kandyan Dance
Kandy Perahera
Kohomba Kandariya
Kathakaḷi
Khōn
Kṛṣṇāṭṭam
Kuchipudi
Kūtiyāṭṭam
Liturgical Dance
Manōhrā
Matachins
  Historical Overview
  Danza de Matlachines
  Matachines Dances in the
    Southwestern United States
Morris Dance
Moresca
Oḍissi
Shaminism
Shishimai
Tovil
Trance Dance
Tripudium
Ves Dance
Vodun
Zār

III FOLK, TRADITIONAL, AND POPULAR DANCE, FESTIVALS AND MASQUERADES

[*To describe the myriad ways people gather to dance and celebrate, part III of this outline is divided into three sections. The first section presents the encyclopedia's coverage of the rich diversity of world folk and traditional dance; the second section focuses on popular dance; the third section outlines a variety of celebrations that involve dance.*]

FOLK AND TRADITIONAL DANCE

PRINCIPAL ARTICLES
European Traditional Dance
Folk Dance History
Ethnic Dance

LANDS
Albania
Algeria
Argentina
  Folk and Traditional Dance

Armenia
  Traditional Dance
Azerbaijan
Belarus
Bhutan
Cambodia
Canada
  Folk and Traditional Dance in French
    Canada
Chile
  Folk and Traditional Dance
China
  Folk and Minority Dance

Crete
  Dance in Modern Crete
Cuba
  Folk, Ritual, and Social Dance
Czech Republic and Slovak Republic
  Folk and Traditional Dance
Denmark
  Traditional and Social Dance
  Dance in the Faeroe Islands
Dominican Republic
Egypt
  Traditional Dance
  Contemporary Dance Companies
Estonia
Finland
  Traditional Dance
France
  Recreational Dance
Georgia
Germany
  Traditional and Social Dance
Great Britain
  English Traditional Dance
  Scottish Folk and Traditional Dance
  Welsh Folk and Traditional Dance
  Manx Folk and Tradiitonal Dance
Greece
  Dance in Modern Greece
Haiti
Hungary
  Traditional and Popular Dance
Iceland
  Traditional Dance
Iran
Ireland
  Traditional Dance
Israel
  Ethnic Dance
Jamaica
Japan
  Folk Dance
Kazakhstan
Korea
  An Overview
Kyrgyzstan
Latvia
Lithuania
  Traditional Dance
Malaysia
Middle East
  An Overview
Moldova
Myanmar
Netherlands
  Folk and Traditional Dance
North Africa

Norway
  Folk, Traditional, and Social Dance
Okinawa
Pakistan
Panama
Peru
Philippines
Poland
  Traditional and Social Dance
Portugal
  Traditional Dance
Puerto Rico
Romania
  Folk Dance
Russia
  Traditional Dance
  Siberian Dance Traditions
Sikkim
Sweden
  Traditional Dance
Thailand
Tibet
Tunisia
Turkey
Ukraine
  Traditional Dance
Uruguay
Uzbekistan
Vietnam
Yemen
Yugoslavia
  Traditional Dance

  SUPPORTING ARTICLES
Ainu Dance Traditions
Basque Dance
Bolero
Branle
Capoeira
Chain and Round Dances
Clogging
  Historical Overview
  Clogging in Appalachian Dance
    Traditions
Czardas
Flamenco Dance
Folk Dance Sounds
Galliard
Hornpipe
Jewish Dance Traditions
Jig
Krakowiak
Matachins
  Historical Overview
  Danza de Matlachines
  Matachines Dances in the
    Southwestern United States

Moresca
Morris Dance
Reel
Saltarello
Sardana
Seguidillas
Shishimai
Square Dance
Step Dancing
  Step Dancing in Great Britain
    and Ireland
  Step Dancing in Cape Breton
Sword Dance
Tarantella

  BIOGRAPHIES
Hinman, Mary Wood
Kadman, Gurit
Kurbet, Vladimir
Moiseyev, Igor
Mólnar, István
Rábai, Miklós
Sano, Kemoko
Sharp, Cecil
Ustinova, Tatiana
Virsky, Pavel

SOCIAL AND POPULAR DANCE

  LANDS
Brazil
  Ritual and Popular Dance
Caribbean Region
Cuba
  Folk, Ritual, and Social Dance
Dominican Republic
France
  Recreational Dance
Germany
  Traditional and Social Dance
Ghana
  Overview Article
Hungary
  Traditional and Popular Dance
Indonesia
  Balinese Dance Traditions
Netherlands
  Social Dance
Norway
  Folk, Traditional, and Social Dance
Poland
  Traditional Dance
Sub-Saharan Africa
  Popular Dance
United States of America
  African-American Social Dance

  SUPPORTING ARTICLES
Annual Collections
Assemblies
Ball
Ballroom Dance Competition
Big Apple
Break Dancing
Cakewalk
Cajun Dance Traditions
Castle, Irene and Vernon
Cotillon
Country Dance
Country-Western Dance
Dance Marathons
Écossaise
Figure Dances
Hey
Lindy Hop
Longways
Manning, Frankie
Mazurka
Murray, Arthur
Polka
Polonaise
Quadrille
Reel
Révérence
  Nineteenth-Century Modes
Round Dancing
Samba
Social Dance
  Nineteenth-Century Social Dance
  Twentieth-Century Dance to 1960
  Twentieth-Century Social Dance since
    1960
Square Dancing
Tango
Waltz

**FESTIVALS AND
MASQUERADES**

Barriera, Torneo, and Battaglia
Bon Odori
Elizabethan Progreses
Horse Ballet
Jonkonnu Festival
Kandy Perahera
Masquerades
Mommerie
Powwow
Rās Līlā
Renaissance Fêtes and Triumphs
Teyyam
Wirtschaft

IV HISTORY OF WESTERN DANCE TO 1800

[*Part IV of the synoptic outline is divided into three sections to describe the history of dance in the ancient Mediterranean world and the development of Western court, social, and theatrical forms. For historical information on dance in non-western regions, see individual country entries.*]

ANCIENT MEDITERRANEAN WORLD

PRINCIPAL ARTICLES

Crete
    Dance in Ancient Crete
Egypt
    Dance in Ancient Egypt
Greece
    Dance in Ancient Greece
    Dance in the Roman and Byzantine
      Periods
Mesopotamia
Roman Empire

SUPPORTING ARTICLES

Aesthetics
    Western Aesthetics
Armed Dances
Cheironomia
Choral Dancing
Christianity and Dance
    Early Christian Views
Costume in Western Traditions
    An Overview
Dithyramb
Emmeleia
Hyporchēma
Israel
    Overview Article
    Ethnic Dance
Jewish Dance Traditions
Kallinikos
Kordax
Labyrinth Dances
Mimus
Music for Dance
    Western Music before 1520
North Africa
Pantomimus
Pyrrhic
Schēma
Sikinnis
Terpsichore
Theaters for Dance

EUROPE: MIDDLE AGES AND RENAISSANCE

PRINCIPAL ARTICLES

Medieval Dance
Renaissance Fêtes and Triumphs
Renaissance Dance Technique

LANDS

France
    Theatrical Dance, 1581–1789
Germany
    Theatrical Dance, 1600–1945
Great Britain
    Theatrical Dance, 1460–1660
Hungary
    Theatrical Dance before World War II
Italy
    Theatrical Dance before 1800
Spain
    Theatrical Dance before 1700
[*Virtually every European country entry contains discussion on dance in the Middle Ages and Renaissance.*]

SUPPORTING ARTICLES

Aesthetics
    Western Dance Aesthetics
Allemande
Alta
Arbeau, Thoinot
Arena, Antonius de
Ball
Ballet Comique de la Royne, Le
Ballet de Cour
    Ballet de Cour, 1560–1670
Ballo and Balletto
Banquet
Barriera, Torneo, and Battaglia
Bassedanse
Beaujoyeulx, Balthazar de
Bergamasque
Branle
Canary
Caroso, Fabritio
Cascarda
Christianity and Dance
    Medieval Views

Commedia dell'Arte
Cornazano, Antonio
Costume in Western Traditions
    An Overview
Country Dance
Dance of Death
Dancing Master
Diobono, Pompeo
Domenico da Piacenza
Elizabethan Progresses
Figure Dances
Galliard
Gavotte
Guglielmo Ebreo da Pesaro
Guild Dances
Intermedio
Jones, Inigo
Libretti for Dance
    Sixteenth- and Seventeenth-Century
      Libretti
Lighting for Dance
    Historical Overview
Longways
Masque and Antimasque
Matachins
    Historical Overview
Mommerie
Moresca
Music for Dance
    Western Music, 1520–1650
Negri, Cesare
Notation
Nozze degli Dei, le
Passo e Mezzo
Pastoral
Pavan
Pavaniglia
Prints and Drawings
Reconstruction
    Use of Historical Notations
Revels
Révérence
    Origins of Modes and Manners
Saltarello
Sarabande
Scenic Design
Spagnoletta
Social Dance
    Court and Social Dance before 1800
Technical Manuals
    Publications, 1445–1725
Theaters for Dance
Tordion
Volta

EUROPE: FROM THE BAROQUE THROUGH THE ENLIGHTENMENT

LANDS
France
  Theatrical Dance, 1581–1789
  Theatrical Dance, 1789–1914
Germany
  Theatrical Dance, 1600–1945
Great Britain
  Theatrical Dance, 1660–1772
  Theatrical Dance, 1772–1850
Hungary
  Theatrical Dance before World War II
Italy
  Theatrical Dance before 1800
Netherlands
  Theatrical Dance before 1900
Norway
  Theatrical Dance before 1919
Russia
  Theatrical Dance before 1917
Spain
  Theatrical Dane before 1700
  Theatrical Dance, 1700–1900
Sweden
  Theatrical Dance before 1771
  Theatrical Dance, 1771–1900
  Court Theaters
[*Virtually every European country entry contains discussion on dance from the Baroque through the Enlightenment.*]

SUPPORTING ARTICLES
Académie de Musique et de Poésie
Académie Royale de Danse
Aesthetics
  Western Dance Aesthetics
Allemande
Anglaise
Artists and Dance
  Artists and Dance, 1760–1929
Assemblies
Ball
Ballet de Collège
Ballet de Cour
Ballet Technique, History of
  French Court Dance
  Ballet in the Late Eighteenth- and
    Early-Nineteenth-Centuries
Banquet
Bourrée
Canary
Carmagnole, La
Chaconne and Passacaille

Christianity and Dance
  Modern Views
Commedia dell'Arte
Costume in Western Traditions
  An Overview
Cotillon
Courante
Dancing Master
Entrée
Entrée Grave
Feuillet Notation
Forlana
Gavotte
Gigue
Hornpipe
Horse Ballet
Libretti for Dance
  Eighteenth-Century Libretti
Lighting for Dance
  Historical Overview
Loure
Mask and Makeup
  European Traditions
Masquerades
Minuet
Musette
Music for Dance
  Western Music, 1650–1800
Notation
Opera, Ballet in
Opéra-Ballet and Tragédie Lyrique
Pantomime
Passepied
Pastorale
Reconstruction
  Use of Historical Notations
Révérence
  Early Eighteenth-Century Modes
Rigaudon
Sarabande
Scenic Design
Social Dance
  Court and Social Dance before 1800
Tambourin
Technical Manuals
  Publications, 1445–1725
Theaters for Dance
Turnout
  History and Aesthetics
Wirtschaft

THEATRICAL WORKS
Caractères de la Danse, Les
Don Juan
Fille Mal Gardée, La

Indes Galantes, Les
Médée et Jason
Psyché et L'Amour

PROMINENT FIGURES
Aglié, Filippo D'
Allard, Marie
Angiolini, Gaspero
Arnould-Mussot, Jean-François
Ballon, Claude
Barberina, La
Baxter, Richard
Beauchamps, Pierre
Berain, Jean
Bibiena Family
Blache Family
Blondy, Michel
Bodin, Louise
Boquet, Louis
Bournonville, Antoine
Camargo, Marie
Campra, André
Cannabich, Christian
Canziani, Giuseppe
Caverley, Thomas
Clerico, Francesco
Curz, Daniel
Dauberval, Jean
D'Egville, James Harvey
De Hesse, Jean-Baptiste
Desnoyer, Philip
Didelot, Charles-Louis
Douvillier, Suzanne
Dumoulin Brothers
Duport Family
Dupré, Louis
Durang, John
Essex, John
Francisqui, Jean-Baptiste
Galeotti, Vincenzo
Gallet, Sébastien
Gallini, Giovanni
Gardel Family
Gardie, Anna
Gioja, Gaetano
Gissey, Henry
Gluck, Christoph Willibald
Guimard, Marie-Madeleine
Guyot, Marie-Catherine
Heinel, Anna
Hilverding, Franz
Hus Family
Isaac, Mister
Kreutzer, Rodolphe

L'Abbé, Anthony
La Fontaine, Mademoiselle de
Lany Family
Lauchery, Étienne
Laval, Antoine Bandieri de
Le Picq, Charles
Lestang, Anne-Louis
Louis XIV
Lully, Jean-Baptiste
Lyonnois, Marie-Françoise
Marcel, François
Milon, Louis
Molière
Mouret, Jean-Joseph
Noverre, Jean-Georges
Pecour, Guillaume-Louis
Pirot, Antoine-Bonaventure
Placide, Alexandre
Playford, John
Prévost, Françoise

Price Family
Priest, Josiah
Purcell, Henry
Rameau, Jean-Philippe
Rameau, Pierre
Rich, John
Rinaldi, Antonio
Rodolphe, Jean-Joseph
Saint-André, Adrien Merger de
Sallé, Marie
Santlow, Hester
Subligny, Marie-Thérèse
Starzer, Joseph
Taglioni Family
Tomlinson, Kellom
Valberkh, Ivan
Vestris Family
Viganò, Salvatore
Vioilette, Eva Maria
Weaver, John

Delsarte System of Expression
Folkwang Tanzstudio
Genres of Western Theatrical Dance
Grand Union
Jacob's Pillow
Judson Dance Theater
Mazurka
Movement Choir
New Dance Group
Partnering
Pas de Deux
Plié
Pointe Work
Rond de Jambe
Technical Manuals
    Publications, 1765–1859
    Publications since 1887
Travesty
Turnout
    Physical Mechanics
    History and Aesthetics
Wiesenthal Technique

V   THEATRICAL DANCE

[Part V of this outline presents the encyclopedia's coverage of the diversity of theatrical dance found throughout the world. It is arranged in two broad sections. The first section outlines ballet and contemporary theatrical dance; the second section focuses on non-western dance drama, mask dance theater, and puppetry. For further discussion of theatrical dance on a country-by-country basis, see the Lands *section in part I of this synoptic outline. For related information on dance dramas and mask dance theater, see also* Ritual and Religion *in part II of the outline and the entries under* Festivals and Masquerades *in part III. See also the encyclopedia's index for extensive coverage of dance companies, theatrical dance works, and entries on performers and choreographers.]*

BALLET AND CONTEMPORARY THEATRICAL DANCE

PRINCIPAL ARTICLES
Ballet Technique
    Major Schools
    Feet Positions
    Body Positions
    Directions
    Turning Movements
    Linking Movements
    Jumping Movements
Ballet Technique, History of
    French Court Dance
    Ballet in the Late Eighteenth- and
        Early-Nineteenth Centuries
    Ballet from the Mid-Nineteenth
        Century
Modern Dance Technique

SUPPORTING ARTICLES
Adage
Allegro
American Dance Festival
Arabesque
Attitude
Avant-garde Dance
Ausdruckstanz
Ballet Competitions
Battement
Batterie
Bauhaus, Dance and the
Bennington School of Dance
Bodenwieser Technique
Butō
Character Dancing
Chladek Technique
Costume in Western Traditions
    Modern Dance

DANCE DRAMA, MASK DANCE THEATER, AND PUPPETRY

PRINCIPAL ARTICLES
Asian Dance Traditions
    An Overview
    The Influence of Puppetry
China
    Dance in Opera
Indonesia
    Balinese Dance Theater
    Balinese Mask Dance Theater
Japan
    An Overview
India
    An Overview
Korea
    Masked Dance Theater
Mask and Makeup
    Asian Traditions

SUPPORTING ARTICLES
Baris
Bharata Nāṭyam
Black Hat Dance, The
Bugaku
Bunraku
Chhau
Geisha Dance
Gigaku
Hōshō School

Japanese Traditional Schools
Kabuki Theater
Kanze School
Kathak
Kathakaḷi
Kita School
Khōn
Kongō School
Konparu School
Kuchipudi
Kyōgen
Kuchipudi
Kūtiyāṭṭam
Kṛṣṇāṭṭam
Lakhōn
Légong

Manōhrā
Mayong
Monhiniāṭṭam
Mudrā
Music For Dance
    Asian Traditions
Nō
Oḍissi
Onnagata
Pencak
Shimai
Shishimai
Tinikling
Ves Dance
Wayang
Yakṣagāna

Williams, Petr
Worsaae, Jens-Jacob

VI ELEMENTS OF THEATRICAL DANCE

[Part VI of this outline focuses on the encyclopedia's entries describing some of the basic components that go into the presentation of dance in a theatrical context. It is arranged in five sections:
    Costume Design
    Theater, Stage, Scenery, and Lighting Design
    Texts for Dance
    Documenting Dance
    Impresarios, Patrons, and Producers
See also the encyclopedia's index for extensive coverage of individual choreographers and performers.]

COSTUME DESIGN

PRINCIPAL ARTICLES
Costume in Asian Traditions
Costume in Western Traditions
    An Overview
    Modern Dance
    Film and Popular Dance

SUPPORTING ARTICLES
Artists and Dance
    Artists and Dance, 1760–1929
    Artists and Dance, 1930–1945
    Artists and Dance since 1945
    Collaboration
Bauhaus, Dance and the
Designing for Dance
Footwear
Mask and Makeup
    Asian Traditions
    Western Traditions
Practice Clothes
Tutu

DESIGNERS
Bakst, Léon
Baylis, Nadine

Benois, Alexandre
Berain, Jean
Boquet, Louis
Charlip, Remy
Cocteau, Jean
Dmitriev, Vladimir
Edel, Alfredo
Fedorovitch, Sophie
Georgiadis, Nicholas
Gissey, Henry
Golovin, Aleksandr
Goncharova, Natalia
Jones, Inigo
Karinska, Barbara
Lami, Eugène Louis
Larionov, Mikhail
Lecomte, Hippolyte
Loquasto, Santo
Messel, Oliver
Picasso, Pablo
Rose, Jürgen
Soudeikine, Serge
Virsaladze, Simon
Wilhelm, C.

THEATER, STAGE, SCENERY, AND LIGHTING DESIGN

SUPPORTING ARTICLES
Artists and Dance
    Artists and Dance, 1760–1929
    Artists and Dance, 1930–1945
    Artists and Dance since 1945
    Collaboration
Designing for Dance
Hanamichi
Lighting for Dance
    Historical Overview
    Theory and Practice
Orchestra
Scenic Design
Theaters for Dance

DESIGNERS
Appia, Adolphe
Bakst, Léon
Baylis, Nadine
Beaton, Cecil
Benois, Alexandre
Berain, Jean
Bérard, Christian
Berman, Eugene
Bibiena Family
Boquet, Louis
Chappell, William
Charlip, Remy
Ciceri, Pierre
Cocteau, Jean
Craig, Gordon
Dmitriev, Vladimir
Dobujinsky, Mstislav
Edel, Alredo
Fedorovitch, Sophie
Georgiadis, Nicholas
Golovin, Aleksandr
Goncharova, Natalia
Hugo, Jean
Johns, Jasper
Jones, Inigo
Korovin, Konstantin
Larionov, Mikhail
Lauterer, Arch
Leventhal, Valery
Loquasto, Santo
Messel, Oliver
Noguchi, Isamu
Picasso, Pablo
Rauschenberg, Robert

Roerich, Nikolai
Rose, Jürgen
Rosenthal, Jean
Sanquirico, Alessandro
Schayk, Toer van
Smith, Oliver
Soudeikine, Serge
Tchelitchev, Pavel
Ter-Arutunian, Rouben
Virsaladze, Simon
Wilhelm, C.
Williams, Petr
Wilson, Robert
Worsaae, Jens-Jacob

TEXTS FOR DANCE

LIBRETTI
Jidaimono
Libretti for Dance
    Sixteenth- and Seventeenth-Century
        Libretti
    Eighteenth-Century Libretti
    Nineteenth- and Twentieth-Century
        Libretti
Nātyaśāstra

BIOGRAPHIES
Arnould-Mussot, Jean-François
Cocteau, Jean
Gautier, Théophile
Leventhal, Valery

DOCUMENTING DANCE

Benesh Movement Notation
Feuillet Notation
Film and Video
    Documenting Dance
    Ethnographic Studies
    Choreography for Camera
Guest, Ann Hutchinson
Kunst, Albrecht
Laban, Rudolf
Labanotation
Laban Principles of Movement
    Analysis
Loring, Eugene
Notation
Photography
Reconstruction
    Use of Historical Notations
    Use of Modern Scores
    Beyond Notation
Saint-Léon Notation
Stepanov Notation

Television
    Dance on Television in Canada
    Dance on Television in Europe
    Dance on Television in the United
        States
Zorn Notation

**IMPRESARIOS, PATRONS,
AND PRODUCERS**

Berk, Fred
Blum, René
Chappell, William
Craig, Gordon
Diaghilev, Serge

Dmitriev, Vladimir
Gallini, Giovanni
Hilverding, Franz
Hurok, Sol
Kiralfy Family
Kronstam, Henning
Louis XIV
Rubinstein, Ida
Saddler, Donald
Shankar, Uday
Slonimsky, Yuri
Smith, Oliver
Wilson, Robert
Wright, Peter

VII   POPULAR ENTERTAINMENT

[*Part VII of this outline presents the encyclopedia's coverage of dance and Western media and popular entertainment. For discussion of specific forms of non-Western popular culture, see* Film Musicals, *article on* Bollywood; Tamasha; Takarazuka; *the entries found in part V of this outline,* Dance Drama, Mask Dance Theater, *and* Puppetry; *and the articles on other non-Western forms of dance. The line between art and popular entertainment is often hard to draw and many of the articles in the encyclopedia have broad appeal to the general public.*]

GENERAL ARTICLES
American Bandstand
Ballroom Dance Competition
Circus
Commedia dell'Arte
Costume in Western Traditions
    Film and Popular Dance
Dance Marathons
Dance as Sport
Film Musicals
    Hollywood Film Musicals
Ice Dancing
Mime
Music Hall
    British Traditions
    French Traditions
Pantomime
Radio City Music Hall
Red Shoes, The
Television
    Dance on Television in Canada
    Dance on Television in Europe
    Dance on Television in the United
        States
United States of America
    Musical Theater
Vaudeville

SUPPORTING ARTICLES
Aerobic Dance
Apache Dance
Attitude and Shawl Dance
Big Apple
Black Crook
Break Dancing
Cakewalk
Can-Can
Capoeira
Danse du Ventre
Fan Dancing
Flamenco Dance
Jazz Dance
Lindy Hop
Orientalism
Precision Dancing
Red Shoes
Samba
Skirt Dance
Tango
Tap Dance

BIOGRAPHIES
Amaya, Carmen
Antonio and Rosario
Argentina, La
Argentinita, La

Astaire, Fred
Baby Laurence
Baker, Josephine
Bates, Peg Leg
Beaton, Cecil
Bennett, Michael
Berkeley, Busby
Berry Brothers
Bluebell, Miss
Bolger, Ray
Bonfanti, Marie
Bubbles, John W.
Charisse, Cyd
Cole, Jack
Coles, Honi
Curry, John
Dale, Margaret
Draper, Paul
Dunham, Katherine
Escudero, Vicente
Fosse, Bob
Four Step Brothers
Fuller, Loie
Gades, Antonio
Gosslar, Lotte
Green, Chuck
Henie, Sonja
Juba, Master
Kelly, Gene
Kiralfy Family
Litz, Katherine
Lopez, Pilar

Losch, Tilly
Luisillo
Manning, Frankie
Murrray, Arthur
McKayle, Donald
Miller, Ann
Miller, Marilyn
Miranda, Carmen
Nagrin, Daniel
Nicholas Brothers
Nieves and Copes
Plebs and Zotto
Powell, Eleanor
Rausch, Albertina
Rivera, Chita
Robbins, Jerome
Rogers, Ginger
Robinson, Bill
Ross, Herbert
Saddler, Donald
St. Denis, Ruth
Sangalli, Rita
Schoop, Trudi
Shawn, Ted
Sims, Sandman
Siretta, Dan
Smith, George Washington
Temple, Shirley
Torvill and Dean
Tune, Tommy
Whitman Sisters
Yakko and Kawakami

India
 Philosophy of Indian Dance
Methodologies in the Study of Dance
 Sociology
 Cultural Context
 Linguistics
 Anthropology
 Ethnology
 New Areas of Inquiry

THEORISTS
Appia, Adolphe
Arena, Antonius de
Beaumont, Cyril W.
Cornazano, Antonio
Craig, Gordon
Dienes, Valéria
Domenico da Piacenza
Guglielmo Ebreo da Pesaro
Kirstein, Lincoln
Martin, John
Weaver, John
Zeami

VISUAL ARTS

GENERAL ARTICLES
Artists and Dance
 Artists and Dance, 1760–1929
 Artists and Dance, 1930–1945
 Artists and Dance since 1945
 Collaboration
Bauhaus, Dance and the
Caricature and Comic Art
Dance of Death
Photography
Prints and Drawings

ARTISTS AND DESIGNERS
Bakst, Léon
Barre, Jean-Auguste
Beaton, Cecil
Benois, Alexandre
Bérard, Christian
Berman, Eugene
Bibiena Family
Boquet, Louis
Chalon, Alfred
Degas, Edgar
Edel, Alfredo
Fabre, Jan
Gissey, Henry
Hugo, Jean
Johns, Jasper
Jones, Inigo
Lecomte, Hippolyte

VIII   DANCE AND OTHER DISCIPLINES

[*Part VIII of this outline presents the encyclopedia's coverage of the influence of dance on ancillary disciplines as well as how scholars and practioners have, in turn, been inspired by various forms of human movement. It is arranged in five sections:*

 Aesthetics, Philosophy, and Theory in Dance
 Visual arts
 Training and Education
 Science and Health
 Music

[*For related discussion on dance theory, see* Technical Manuals, *and for related discussion on visual arts, see* Designing for Dance.]

AESTHETICS, PHILOSOPHY, AND THEORY IN DANCE

PRINCIPAL ARTICLES
Aesthetics
 African Dance Aesthetics
 Asian Dance Aesthetics
 Islamic Dance Aesthetics
 Western Dance Aesthetic
Asian Dance Traditions
 Religious, Philosophical, and
  Environmental Influence

Matisse, Henri
Noguchi, Isamu
Picasso, Pablo
Rauschenberg, Robert
Rodin, Auguste
Roerich, Nikolai
Sanquirico, Alessandro
Toulouse-Lautrec, Henri de
Walkowitz, Abraham

TRAINING AND EDUCATION

LANDS
Belgium
  Dance Education
Canada
  Dance Education
Czech Republic and Slovak Republic
France
  Classical Dance Education
  Modern Dance Education
Germany
  Dance Education
Great Britain
  Dance Education
Greece
  Dance in Modern Greece
Hungary
  Dance Education
Indonesia
  Balinese Dance Traditions
  Sundanese Dance Traditions
Netherlands
  Dance Education
New Zealand
  Overview Article
Norway
  Classical Dance Education
Russia
  Dance Education
Sweden
  Dance Education
Thailand
United States of America
  Social, Folk, and Modern Dance
    Education

SUPPORTING ARTICLES
Académie de Musique et de Poésie
Académie Royal de Danse
American Dance Festival
Asian Martial Arts
Ballet de Collège
Bennington School of Dance
Dancing Master
Delsarte System of Expression

Jacob's Pillow
Pencak

BIOGRAPHIES
Albertieri, Luigi
Alexander, Dorothy
Anderson-Ivantzova, Elizabeth
Angiolini, Gaspero
Anisimova, Nina
Anwar, Rafi
Aveline, Albert
Azuma Tokuho
Ballon, Claude
Beauchamps, Pierre
Beck-Friis, Regina
Bedells, Phyllis
Behl, Anna
Belsky, Igor
Beretta, Caterina
Beriozoff, Nicholas
Berk, Fred
Blank, Gustav
Blasis, Carlo
Blondy, Michel
Bodenweiser, Gertrud
Bolm, Adolph
Borchsenius, Valborg
Bournonville, Antoine
Bournonville, August
Bowman, Patricia
Brabants, Jeanne
Bravo, Guillermina
Brenaa, Hans
Canziani, Giuseppe
Caroso, Fabritio
Caverley, Thomas
Cébron, Jean
Cecchetti, Enrico
Chabukiani, Vakhtang
Chiriaeff, Ludmilla
Chladek, Rosalia
Ch'oi Seung-hee
Cho T'aek-won
Christensen Brothers
Cieplinski, Jan
Coe, Kelvin
Collins, Janet
Craske, Margaret
Crofton, Kathleen
d'Amboise, Jacques
Dauberval, Jean
Day, Mary
Dean, Laura
Desnoyer, Philip

D'Egville, James Harvey
Descombey, Michel
de Valois, Ninette
de Vos, Audrey
Dienes, Valéria
Diobono, Pompeo
Dolgushin, Nikita
Domenico da Piacenza
Doubrovska, Felia
Drzewiecki, Conrad
Dudinskaya, Natalia
Dudley, Jane
Dunn, Robert Ellis
Durgalal
Edwards, Leslie
Eglevsky, André
Egorova, Lubov
Egri, Susanna
Erdman, Jean
Escudero, Vicente
Essex, John
Farber, Viola
Farron, Julia
Field, John
Foregger, Nikolai
Fornaroli, Cia
Franca, Celia
Froman, Margarita
Gabovich, Mikhail
Gabzdyl, Emerich
Galeotti, Vincenzo
Gallet, Sébastien
Gaudrau, Michel
Gioja, Gaetano
Glushkovsky, Adam
Gore, Walter
Gorsky, Aleksandr
Gsovsky, Tatiana
Gsovsky, Victor
Guerra, Nicola
Guglielmo Ebreo da Pesaro
Gusev, Petr
Halprin, Anna
Han Young-sook
Harangozó, Gyula
Hassreiter, Josef
Hayden, Melissa
H'Doubler, Margaret
Hightower, Rosella
Hill, Martha
Hilverding, Franz
Hinman, Mary Wood
Holm Hanya
Hong Sin-cha

Hōshō School
Hoving, Lucas
Humphrey, Doris
Husain, Ghulam
Hus Family
Idzikowski, Stanislas
Indrani
Jaques-Dalcroze, Émile
Joffrey, Robert
Johansson, Christian
Johansson, Ronny
Kadman, Gurit
Kakul, I Nyoman
Kehlet, Niels
Khanum, Tamara
Kim Ch'un-heung
Kim Paik-bong
Kirsova, Hélène
Kita School
Knight, Lakshmi
Knust, Albrecht
Kolosova, Evgenia
Komar, Chris
Komleva, Gabriella
Kongō School
Konparu School
Koslov, Theodore
Kraus, Gertrud
Kreutzberg, Harald
Kröller, Heinrich
Kronstam, Henning
Laban, Rudolf
L'Abbé, Anthony
Lacotte, Pierre
Lamhut, Phyllis
Lander, Harald
Lang, Pearl
Lanner, Katti
Laval, Antoine Bandieri de
Lavrovsky, Leonid
Leclair, André
Leeder, Sigurd
Lee Mae-bang
Lepeshinskaya, Olga
Lepri, Giovanni
Lestang, Anne-Louis
Lester, Keith
Lewitzky, Bella
Liepa, Maris
Lifar, Serge
Linke, Susanne
Lopukhov, Fedor
Loring, Eugene
Louis, Murray

Lowskik Woytek
Lukom, Elena
Mahapatra, Kelucharan
Maracci, Carmelita
Marcel, François
Mario, I Ketut
Martins, Peter
Martyn, Laurel
Mason, Monica
Matsui Akira
May, Pamela
McKayle, Donald
Mérante, Louis
Meri, La
Messerer, Asaf
Milloss, Aurelio
Milon, Louis
Moore, Lillian
Moreton, Ursula
Murray, Arthur
Nádasi, Ferenc
Nadezhdina, Nadezhda
Nagrin, Daniel
Nault, Fernand
Negri, Cesare
Northcote, Anna
Oboukhoff, Anatole
Orlando, Mariane
Paige, Brydon
Palucca, Gret
Park, Merle
Peretti, Serge
Pericet Family
Perrot, Jules
Petipa, Jean-Antoine
Petrov, Anastas
Poole, David
Potapova, Elena
Preobrajenska, Olga
Prévost, Françoise
Priest, Josiah
Proca Ciortea, Vera
Pushkin, Aleksandr
Ravlov, Kirsten
Rambert, Marie
Rameau, Pierre
Rassine, Alex
Rayet, Jacqueline
Reinholm, Gert
Romanoff, Dimitri
Romanov, Boris
Róna, Viktor
Ruskaja, Jia
St. Denis, Ruth

Samson, Leela
Sand, Inge
Sano, Kemoko
Schilling, Tom
Schollar, Ludmilla
Schönberg, Bessie
Schoop, Trudi
Schwarz Family
Scott, Margaret
Semenova, Marina
Shawn, Ted
Sharma, Uma
Singh, Bipin
Skeaping, Mary
Slonimsky, Yuri
Smith, George Washington
Sokolova, Lydia
Sokolow, Anna
Somes, Michael
Staats, Léo
Strate, Grant
Struchkova, Raisa
Susana
Taglioni Family
Tallchief, Maria
Tamiris, Helen
Tarasov, Nikolai
Techernicheva, Lubov
Tikhomirov, Vasily
Tomlinson, Kellom
Turner, Harold
Uthoff, Ernst
Vaganova, Agrippina
Valberkh, Ivan
van Praagh, Peggy
Vempati Chinna Satyam
Verdy, Violette
Villella, Edward
Vilzak, Anatole
Vladimiroff, Pierre
Volinine, Alexandre
Volkova, Vera
Vyroubova, Nina
Waldeen
Wall, David
Waring, James
Weaver, John
Wilde, Patricia
Williams, E. Virginia
Williams, Stanley
Williams-Yarborough, Lavinia
Woizikowski, Leon
Yang Meiqi
Yermolayev, Aleksei
Züllig, Hans

SCIENCE AND HEALTH

Aerobic Dance
Body Therapies
  An Overview
  Alexander Technique
  Bartenieff Fundamentals
  Feldenkrais Method
  Ideokinesis
  Skinner Releasing Technique
Dance and Movement Therapy
Dance Medicine
Kinesiology
  An Overview
  Therapeutic Practices
Physics of Dance
Shamanism
Turnout
  Physical Mechanics
Yoga

MUSIC

PRINCIPAL ARTICLES
Music for Dance
  African Music
  Arab Music
  Asian Music
  Oceanic Music
  Western Music before 1520
  Western Music, 1520–1650
  Western Music, 1650–1800
  Western Music, 1800–1900
  Western Music since 1900

SUPPORTING ARTICLES
Académie de Musique et de Poésie
Accompaniment for Dance
Bergamasque
Bournonville Composers
Carmagnole, La
Castanets
China
  Dance in Opera
Film Musicals
  Hollywood Film Musicals
  Bollywood Film Musicals
Gagaku
Gamelan
  Balinese Traditions
  Javanese Traditions
Kunqu
Musette
Naguta
Opera, Ballet in
Opéra-Ballet and Tragédie Lyrique
Rāga
Samba

Takarazuka
Tamasha
United States of America
  Musical Theater

MUSICIANS
Adam, Adolphe
Ansermet, Ernest
Asafiev, Boris
Beauchamps, Pierre
Beethoven, Ludwig van
Berners, Lord
Bernstein, Leonard
Blache Family
Blacher, Boris
Bliss, Arthur
Burgmüller, Friedrich
Cage, John
Campra, André
Cannabich, Christian
Clerico, Francesco
Copland, Aaron
Debussy, Claude
Delibes, Léo
Drigo, Riccardo
Dunn, Robert Ellis
Egk, Werner
Falla, Manuel de
Gardel Family
Glazunov, Aleksandr
Glière, Reinhold
Gluck, Christoph Willibald

Henze, Hans Werner
Hérold, Ferdinand
Horst, Louis
Irving, Robert
Jaques-Dalcroze, Émile
Khachaturian, Aram
Kreutzer, Rodolphe
Lambert, Constant
Lanchbery, John
Lully, Jean-Baptiste
Marenco, Romualdo
Milhaud, Darius
Monk, Meredith
Mouret, Jean-Joseph
Orff, Carl
Playford, John
Pugni, Cesare
Purcell, Henry
Riisager, Knudåge
Rodolphe, Jean-Joseph
Satie, Erik
Sauguet, Henri
Schall, Claus
Schuman, William
Sharp, Cecil
Shchedrin, Rodion
Shostakovich, Dmitri
Starzer, Joseph
Strauss Family
Stravinksy, Igor
Tchaikovsky, Petr Ilich

IX DANCE RESEARCH AND PUBLICATION

[*Part IX of this outline is divided into two sections. The first section presents the encyclopedia's coverage of the history of research, writing, and publication; the second section focuses on the role of criticism in understanding dance.*]

HISTORY OF SCHOLARSHIP

LANDS
Armenia
Australia
  Dance Research and Publication
Austria
  Dance Research and Publication
Brazil
  Dance Research and Publication
Canada
  Dance Research and Publication
Chile
  Dance Research and Publication
China
  Dance Research and Publication

Czech Republic and Slovak Republic
  Dance Research and Publication
Denmark
  Dance Research and Publication
Finland
  Dance Research and Publication
France
  Dance Research and Publicatin
Germany
  Dance Research and Publication
Ghana
  Dance Research and Publication
Great Britain
  Dance Research and Publication
Greece
  Dance Research and Publication

Hungary
    Folk Dance Research and Publication
    Theatrical Dance Research and
        Publication
India
    Dance Research and Publication
Indonesia
    Dance Research and Publication
Italy
    Dance Research and Publication
Japan
    Dance Research and Publication
Korea
    Dance Resesarch and Publication
Mexico
    Dance Research and Publication
Middle East
    Dance Research and Publication
Netherlands
    Dance Research and Publication
New Zealand
    Dance Research and Publication
Norway
    Dance Research and Publication
Norway
    Dance Research and Publication
Philippines
Poland
    Dance Research and Publication
Portugal
    Traditional Dance
Romania
    Folk Dance Research and
        Publication
Russia
    Folk Dance Research and Publication
    Theatrical Dance Research
        and Publication

Spain
    Dance Research and Publication
Sub-Saharan Africa
    Dance Research and Publication
Sweden
    Dance Research and Publication
Ukraine
    Traditional Dance
United States of America
    Dance Research and Publication
Yugoslavia
    Dance Research and Publication

GENERAL ARTICLES
Aesthetics
    African Dance Aesthetics
    Asian Dance Aesthetics
    Islamic Dance Aesthetics
    Western Dance Aesthetics
European Traditional Dance
Folk Dance History
Libraries and Museums
Native American Dance
    Dance Research and Publication
Organizations
Technical Manuals
    Publications, 1445–1725
    Publications, 1765–1859
    Publications since 1887

SCHOLARS
Arena, Antonius de
Beaumont, Cyril W.
Berk, Fred
Blok, Lubov
Brinson, Peter
Guest, Ivor
Koni, Fedor

Kurath, Gertrude Prokosch
Krasovskaya, Vera
Moore, Lillian
Oswald, Genevieve
Souritz, Elizabeth

DANCE CRITICISM

SPECIAL ARTICLES
France
    Contemporary Criticism
Great Britain
    Contemporary Criticism
United States of America
    Contemporary Criticism

CRITICS
Beaumont, Cyril W.
Crofton, Kathleen
Denby, Edwin
Gabovich, Mikhail
Gautier, Théophile
Koni, Fedor
Krasovskaya, Vera
Kriger, Viktorina
Levinson, André
Martin, John
Richardson, Philip
Slonimsky, Yuri
Svetlov, Valerian
Volynsky, Akim
Zotov, Rafail

INDEX

Note: Volume numbers are printed in boldface type, followed by a colon and relevant page numbers. Page numbers printed in boldface indicate a major discussion; those in italics refer to illustrations.

Aabel, Per, **4:**675
aak (Korean court tradition), **1:**166
Aamodt, Christiani, **4:**675
Aaron Diamond Foundation, **4:**623
Ababda bedouin, **2:**488–489, 492
Abai Academic Opera and Ballet
    Theater of Kazakhstan, **3:**665
abakweta dance, **5:**645
Abarca, Lydia, **2:**334, *334*
Abasheev, Petr, **5:***473*
Abatino, Pepito, **1:**252
Abazović, Tefeda, **6:***436*
'Abbasid dynasty, **4:**488
Abbas, Nadia, **2:**498
Abbe, James, **5:**183
    as photographer, **5:**45
Abbey School of Ballet, Dublin,
    3:519
Abbey Theatre, Dublin, **2:**397,
    3:519, 520
Abbots Bromley Horn Dance, **3:**242
Abbott, George, **1:**438, **5:**360, 361,
    6:281
Abbrégé de la nouvelle méthode
    (Rameau), **4:**431, **5:**308,
    6:123–124
ABC (Madrid newspaper), **5:**676
ABC-TV, **1:**77–79, **6:**139
Abdallah, **1:**510, 512
    reconstruction, **2:**388, **4:**271,
    5:433
    Worsaae designs, **6:**404
Abdelzar Suite (Purcell), **4:**458
Abdul, Paula, **2:**324, 610
Abe, Shuya, **2:**606
Abeilles, Les, **5:**95, 690
Abe Kōbō, **4:**84
Abel, Karl Friedrich, **3:**111
Abel, Katharina, **1:**239, **5:**278
Abelard and Heloise, **5:**57
Abell, Kjeld, **4:**118, **5:**238, 294, 429
Abenteuerliche Herz, Die, **3:**152
Abhijñānaśakuntala (Kālidāsa),
    1:392
Abhinavagupta, **3:**463
abhinaya, **1:**169, 274, **2:**104, **3:**448,
    4:63, **5:**582
    types, **3:**457–458, **4:**575
Abhinayacandrikā, **5:**22
Abhinayadarpaṇam (Indian text),
    3:469
Abildgård, Nicolai, **3:**105
Abirov, Daurent, **3:**665
Ablets, Isaac, **1:**485, **5:**453, **6:**312
Aboitiz, Maribel, **5:**172
Abondante, Giulio, **4:**505
Aboriginal dance. *See* Australian
    Aboriginal Dance
Aboriginal/Islander Dance Theatre
    (AIDT), **1:**212, 216

Aboriginal/Islander School. *See*
    National Aboriginal and
    Torres Strait Islander Skills
    Development Association
*Ab Ovo usque ad Mala (From Soup
    to Nuts),* **4:**482
Abrahams, Peter, **5:**572
Abrahao, Roberto, **6:**288
Abrami, Gaetana, **3:**176
Abramov, Gennady, **5:**479
Abramova, Anastasia, **1:**489,
    3:12, 207
Abramtseveo neonationalist
    colony, **4:**56
Abraxas, **1:**1, 374, **6:**353
    Bavarian State Ballet world
        premiere, **1:**1, 390, **3:**149
    Berlin Opera Ballet, **1:**436
    Bey performance, **1:**442
    as Charrat's major work, **2:**111
    Dyk choreography, **2:**471
    Egk score, **2:**478
    Schilling choreography, **5:**557
Abreu, Margarida de, **5:**234
Abricossova, Kira, **5:**265
Abruzov, Aleksei, **3:**308
Abschied, **4:**1
Absence, L', **3:**344
Absoliamova, Sania, **3:**665
Absolute Dance, **4:**91
abstract art, **1:**132, 386, **4:**644,
    6:243
abstract dance, **4:**649–650, **6:**60, 61
abstract expressionism, **1:**138–139,
    2:287, **3:**349
ABT. *See* American Ballet Theatre
Abuang kalah, **3:**475
Abujamra, Clarisse, **1:**535
Abyss, The, **3:**342
Acaac, Melinda, **5:***173*
Academia de Ballet y Bailes
    Españoles, Puerto Rico,
    5:275
Academico Inquieto di Milano,
    4:579
Academic Opera and Ballet Theater
    of Latvia, **4:**127
Académie de Musique et de Poésie,
    1:1–3, 398, **2:**338, 451
Académie des Grands Ballets
    Canadiens, **2:**152,
    3:227–228, 231
Académie Royale de Danse, **1:**3–5,
    283, 286, 288, 342, **2:**338,
    3:545, **5:**38, 39
    ballet technique, **1:**330
    Ballon chancellorship, **1:**4,
        355, 465
    Beauchamps chancellorship, **1:**4,
        355, 397
    costumes, **2:**238

Didelot *Flore et Zéphire*
    production, **2:**415
founding, **3:**81, **4:**229, **5:**86
Laval, Antoine Bandieri de,
    4:130, 131
Lestang, Anne-Louis, **4:**152
Lifar revival, **4:**186
Lully patent, **3:**66
Marcel, François, **4:**262, 263
Pecour, Guillaume-Louis, **5:**129
Saint-André, Adrien Merger de,
    5:490
Académie Royale de Musique,
    Ghent, **1:**409
Académie Royale de Musique,
    Paris. *See* Académie Royale
    de Danse; Paris Opera Ballet
Academy of Choreographic Art,
    London, **1:**462, **2:**396, **4:**463,
    5:411, 421
Academy of Dancing, London,
    1:329, **2:**83
Academy of Korean Studies, **4:**55
Academy of Mexican Dance, **1:**524,
    4:392
Academy of Music and Performing
    Art, Vienna, **6:**388
Academy of the Arts, Berlin, **3:**151
Academy of Theater and Film,
    Bucharest, **5:**389
Academy of the Pear Garden
    (Chinese tradition), **2:**130
Acadiana region, Louisiana,
    2:23–24
Acante et Céphise (Rameau), **5:**307
ACARTE (Gulbenkian Foundation),
    5:235–236
Acbar Gran Mogul, **6:**70
Accademia Filarmonica Romana,
    3:550
Accademia Nazionale di Danza,
    Rome, **3:**549–550, 552,
    554–555
"Acceleration Waltz," **6:**388
ACCESS (Canadian cable channel),
    6:132
*Acclaim to the Graces (Gratiernes
    Hyldning),* **1:**505
accompaniment for dance, **1:**5–7
    See also folk dance sounds; music
        for dance; *specific countries
        and dances*
Acconci, Vito, **1:**140
accordion, **2:**431, **3:**64, 134, 435,
    6:37, 222
Accumulation, **1:**543
Accumulation with Talking, **1:**544
*Accumulation with Talking plus
    Water Motor,* **1:**544
ACDC (Australian dance company),
    1:217

Aceh (people), **3:**499, *500*
Acharnians (Aristophanes), **3:**646
Acharyulu, C. R., **5:**521
ache lhamo, **6:**168–169
Achhan Maharaj, **5:**602
Achille, Fanny, **6:**237
Achille, **1:**202
Achille à Scyros, **2:**464, **3:**118, 358
Achille et Déidamie, **2:**34, 364, 389,
    5:40, 70
Achille et Polyxène, **4:**109, 152
Achille in Sciro (Metastasio), **3:**189
Acholi (people), **2:**86, 90
Achron, Joseph, **4:**58
Achuar (people), **2:**475
Achuff, Stephani, **5:**24
Achumawi (people), **4:**566
Acis and Galatea
    Fokine choreography, **3:**15
    Ivanov choreography, **3:**566
    Kshessinska (Matilda)
        performance, **4:***68*
    Legat (Sergei) performance,
        4:144
    Lopukhov performance, **4:**224
Acis et Galatée
    Didelot choreography, **2:**414,
        3:539
    Dupré performance, **2:**465
    La Fontaine performance, **2:**414,
        3:539
    loure, **4:**232
    Lully pastorale, **4:**235
Acocella, Joan, *as contributor,*
    1:98–100, **2:**341–343,
    4:470–472, 639–648,
    5:487–488, 636–637
Acogny, Germaine, **5:**659
Acosta, Hazel, **2:**57
Acqua Alta, **1:**406
Acquarone, Sara, **3:**553
Acrobat, The, **1:**136
acrobatics
    ballets de cour, **1:**285, 286
    break dancing, **1:**538
    Broadway musicals, **6:**286
    can-can, **2:**53
    capoeira, **2:**58
    Chinese dance, **2:**129, *135,* 144
    as choreographic device,
        4:225, 258
    circus, **2:**174, 175, 176
    Cocteau usage, **2:**182, 183
    commedia dell'arte, **2:**188
    Cuban dance, **2:**275
    Egyptian dance, **2:**485, 490,
        493–494
    Japanese dance, **3:**583, 584
    Lindy Hop, **5:**630
    Mesopotamian dance, **4:**357
    music hall, **4:***521,* 522, 523

493

acrobatics, *continued*
Romanian dance company, **5:**388
tap dancing, **6:**100
Turkish dancers, **6:**210
Uzbek dance, **6:**305
Acrobats of God, **3:**219
Acterland, **1:**412
Action Conference on Dance
Education, **3:**278
Act of Judgment, **3:**384
Act of Love, **1:**524
Actor's Equity (Great Britain),
3:280
Actors' Equity (United States),
6:270, 272
Actress, The, **3:**644, **4:**73, *73,* 547,
6:133
Acts of Light, **3:**220
ADA. *See* American Dance
Association
Adabache, Olga, **4:**185
adage, **1:***7–9,* 347, 383, **5:**101
Adagietto (Lazzini work), **4:**134
Adagietto: Flakes of Chance (Waring
work), **6:**362
adagio. See adage
Adagio (Marcello), **1:**39
Adagio d'Albinoni, **2:**114
adagio dancing (vaudeville act),
6:319, 320
Adagio Hammerklavier, **1:**402
Adalbert, prince of Prussia, **2:**504
Adam, Adolphe, **1:***9–11,* **2:**14, 136,
200, **3:**180, 315, **4:**108, **5:**135,
140, 151, 319, 558, **6:**267
Delibes as student, **2:**367
Diable à Quatre, **2:**405, **4:**341
Jolie Fille de Gand, La, **1:**10,
2:511, **3:**620
Orfa score, **4:**342
See also Corsaire, Le; Giselle
Adam, Louis, **3:**360
Adam, Tassilo, **3:**507
Adama, Richard, **1:***11,* 241, 456,
2:434, **6:**59
Adam and Eve, **3:**265, **4:**113, **6:**196
Adamawa (people), **2:**32, 33
Adameit, Luva, **5:**171, 174
'Adame Miroir, **1:**305, **2:**111, 112,
4:418
Adami, Giuseppe, **3:**51, **5:**246
Adamova, Adela, **1:**110
Adamovich, Elena, **3:**207, **4:**148
Adams, Carolyn, **2:**526, **6:***111*
Adams, David, **4:**380, **5:**434, 435,
6:131
National Ballet of Canada, **2:**38,
4:450, *540,* 541, *541*
Nutcracker performance, **5:***14*
Adams, Diana, **1:***11–12,* 68, 159,
262, **5:**265, **6:**200, 201
Agon performance, **1:**11–12, *30,*
4:436, 617
Apollo performance, **2:***244,* **4:***611*
Broadway musicals, **6:**278
Concerto Barocco performance,
4:*608*
Divertimento No. 15
performance, **2:**420
Farrell career, **2:**576
Laing marriage, **4:**110
Liebeslieder Walzer performance,
4:179, *179*
New York City Ballet,
4:616–617, 620
Adams, Doug, **4:**213
Adams, Gilbert, *as photographer,*
3:173
Adams, John (composer), **1:**411,
2:119, **4:**275, 472, 622

Adams, Lawrence and Miriam,
2:49, **4:**166
Adams, Monni, *as photographer,*
4:291, **6:**14
Adams, Phyllis, **4:**239
Adamson, Val, *as photographer,*
5:659, 660
Adam Zero, **1:**462, 463, **3:**356,
4:517, **5:**312
Adangbe (people), **3:**166
Adashevsky, Valentin, **5:**472
Adassinsky, Anton, **5:**479
Addison, Errol, **2:**261, **3:**512
Addison, Joseph, **2:**570, **3:**281
Addor, Ady, **1:**68
Ade, Sonny, **4:**487
Ade festival, **6:**19
Adélaïde, **3:**72, **5:**315
Adelaide, Australia, **1:**214
Adelaide de Borgogna, **3:**359
Adelaide di Francia, **5:**277
Adelaide Festival Center, Australia,
4:160
Adelaide Festival of the Arts,
Australia, **1:**210, 212, 214,
232–233
Adelante, **2:**580, **6:**88
Adelcrantz, Carl Fredrik, **6:**45,
46, 48
Adèle de Ponthieu, **2:**413, **3:**117,
546, **4:**695, 696
Adelman, Katherine M., *as
contributor,* **1:**398
Adelphi College, Garden City, New
York, **5:**497
Adelphi Theatre, London, **2:**85
Ad Hominem, **3:**317
Adice, Giovanni Léopold, **1:**8, 344,
345, 346, **5:**201, **6:**127
Adieu, **1:**453
Adieu Robert Schumann, **6:**364
Adjal Arduna (musical drama), **4:**87
adjinish, **4:**127
Adjustments, **4:**115
Adler, Alfred, **2:**316, 317
Adler, Clarence, **2:**196
Adler, Larry, **2:**445
Adler, Reba Ann, *as contributor,*
1:30–31, 95–96, 293–294,
452–453, **2:**193–194, 420,
425–427, 438–439, **3:**57–59,
4:179–180, 227–228,
5:570–571, **6:**65–66
Adler, Richard, **6:**281
Ad Libitum, **1:**50
ADMA (Association of Dance and
Mime Artists), **3:**275
Admète et Alceste (Noverre work),
3:257, 353, **6:**9, 331
Admetus and Alcestis (Canizani
work), **2:**55
Admiral Broadway Revue
(television program), **2:**619
Adolph Bolm Ballet, **1:**483, **3:**619
adongo, **5:**209–10
Ador, Ady, **1:**533
adoraciones, **1:**108
Adorations, **4:**121
adowa dance, **6:**24
Adra, Najwa, **4:**417
as contributor, **4:**402–413,
414–417, **6:**417–420, 444–445
as photographer, **1:**102
Adred, Shelomoh be Avraham,
3:603
Adret, Françoise
Ballet of the Amsterdam Opera,
4:591, 592
Ballet-Théâtre Contemporain,
1:349, 350, **3:**74

Cinderella production, **5:**53–54,
54, *651,* 653
students, **4:**251
Adrianova, Anna, **1:**312, 313
Adrienne Clarkson Presents
(television series), **6:**132
Ad suos compagnones studiantes
(formerly *Leges dansadi*)
(Arena), **1:**103, 107, **2:**336,
5:114, 336, 343–344, **6:**122
ADT. *See* Australian Dance Theatre
Advanced Steps in Ballet (French
and Demery), **6:**128
*Adventures of a Ballet Historian: An
Unfinished Memoir* (Guest),
3:321
Adventures of Harlequin, The,
2:192, **3:**23, 24
*Adventures of Peleus and Thetis,
The,* **4:**429
Adyrkhaev, Murat, **3:**665
Adyrkhaeva, Svetlana, **5:**567
Adzido, **3:**276
Aegeus, king of Crete, **2:**269
Aelia et Mysis, ou L'Atellane, **4:**342
Aemilianus, Scipio, **5:**374
Aenea (known as La Mouche d'Or),
1:428
Aenéas, **4:**184
Aeneid (Virgil), **4:**106, **5:**376
Aeon, **2:**293, **5:**314
aerial ballet. *See* circus
aerobic dance, **1:***12–13,* **2:**322, 324,
6:294
Aerobics (Cooper), **2:**322
Aeschylus, **2:**153, 159, 397, 453,
3:289, 300, 652, **4:**91, 476,
5:556
aesthetic calisthenics (dance),
6:294, 295
aesthetics, **1:***13–26*
African dance, **1:***13–15,*
6:19–22, 382
Arab dance, **4:**489–490
arts and dance, **1:**125–126
Asian dance, **1:***16–18,* 169, 183
Chinese Daoism, **1:**16, 17,
2:129
Chinese opera, **2:**144
Chinese philosophers, **2:**148
Indian theory, **3:***462–464,* 470,
493, **4:**575–576
Japanese *bugaku,* **2:**6
Japanese *mujo-kan,* **4:**42
Japanese *nō* influences, **3:**581,
4:42, 654–655
Javanese versus Indian, **3:**493
Korean, **4:**45–46, 47, 49
Islamic dance, **1:**18–19
Western dance, **1:***19–26*
American Progressive era,
6:241–242
ancient Greece, **2:**506
Bournonville, August,
5:426–427
British ballet, **3:**265–266, 285
Christian traditions, 165–166,
2:162
Craig, Gordon, **2:**263
Cunningham's spatial patterns,
2:287
Delsarte system of expression,
2:370–372
Duncan, Isadora, **2:**452–454,
456, 457, **6:**367
film and video, **2:**598–600
French writings, **3:**84
Germany, **3:**161–162
Humphrey, Doris, **3:**399, 404,
6:367

Judson Dance Theater,
2:290–291, **3:**634–635
Laban, Rudolf, **4:**63, 92, **6:**391
Russia, **5:**485
technical manuals, **6:**124–125
weightlessness effect, **1:**341
Wigman, Mary, **1:**25, 131, 132,
134, **3:**130, **6:**389–390, 392
See also artists and dance; avant-
garde dance; ballet technique;
ballet technique, history of;
*specific dancers and
choreographers*
Aetas (people). *See* Negritos
Afanasiev, Aleksandr, **3:**17
Affair in Trinidad (film), **1:**441
Affairs of Dobie Gillis, The (film),
3:54
Affinités Elective, Les, **1:**461
Afghanistan, **1:**18–19, **26–27,**
3:513–514
Afguden på Ceylon (Schall), **5:**552
afoxês, **1:**529
Africa. *See* African dance
influences; East and Central
Africa; North Africa; Sub-
Saharan Africa; Southern
Africa; West Africa; *specific
countries and peoples*
Africaine, L' (Meyerbeer), **5:**35, 501
African Academy of Arts and
Research, **5:**255
African-American dance traditions,
6:*253–263*
archival materials, **4:**167, 169
break dancing, **1:**538–539, **3:**447,
5:633, **6:**250–251, *263*
cakewalk, **2:**25–26, **6:**243, *255*
in character dances, **2:**108
clogging variants, **2:**179
Harlem clubs, **6:**244, *245,* 256
Harlem Renaissance, **6:**244
hip-hop, **1:**538, **2:**324, **5:**633
improvisation, **2:**324, **3:**447–448,
6:262
jazz dance, **3:**598–599
jig, **3:**607
plantation dances, **6:**254, 261
rhythm dancing, **3:**598
sacred rituals, **2:**168
sand dancing, **3:**608, **6:**98, 601
social dances, **2:**179, **5:**633,
6:256–257, *261–263*
American Bandstand, **1:**78
ballroom "fads," **2:**25
Big Apple, **1:**450
as Charleston origin, **5:**629
Lindy Hop, **4:**201–203, 254–255
as sport, **2:**324
as sub-Saharan African music
and dance influence, **6:**24
theatrical dance, **6:***258–261*
Alvin Ailey American Dance
Theatre, **1:**54–60, **4:**520,
6:259
American Dance Festival Black
Traditions project, **1:**82, 396
avant-garde, **1:**246
Beatty productions, **1:**395, 396
Broadway revues and musicals,
2:186, **6:**272, 277, 278, 280,
284, 288
Byrd choreography, **2:**19–20
college-based groups, **6:**258
Dafora's African heritage
productions, **2:**313
Dance Theatre of Harlem,
2:334–336
Dayton Contemporary Dance
Company, **2:**358

de Lavallade choreography, **2:**366–367, **4:**520
Dunham choreography, **2:**458–459, **4:**520, **6:***246*
Federal Dance Project, **2:**581, **6:**276
McKayle choreography, **4:**345–346, 520
Primus choreography, **4:**520, **5:**254–257
ragtime, jazz, and blues, **4:**519–520
tap dance, **2:**185–186, **6:**95–104
vaudeville, **6:**316–317, *316*
Zollar choreography, **6:**448–449
See also names of other specific choreographers, dancers, and groups
twisting hips movement, **5:**632, **6:***316*
white cultural exchanges, **6:**256–257
African-American Genius in Modern Dance (publication), **1:**81
African Art in Motion (Thompson), **2:**602, **6:**25
African-Brazilian dance, **1:**525–530, 537, **2:**58–59
African-Caribbean Institute, **3:**577
African Ceremonial, **5:**255
African dance traditions
  aesthetics, **1:**13–15
  African-American adaptations, **6:**253, 254, 259, 261
  African-American staged reconstructions, **6:**258
  Åkesson research and publications, **6:**258
  Ballets Africains, Les, **1:**303–304
  as Ballets Suédois inspiration, **1:**327
  Caribbean region, 63–66
  as character dance influence, **2:**108
  Chile, **2:**121
  Congo dances, **2:**195
  costume and masks, **2:**209–213
  Cuba, **2:**274–275, 280
  Dafora dance dramas, **2:**313
  Dominican Republic, **2:**430, 431
  European stereotypes, **6:**381
  filmed ethnography, **2:**601–602
  formal elements, **6:**19–22
  Garifuna dance, **3:**120–21
  Guatemala, **3:**319–320
  Haiti, **3:**333–335, **5:**355–356
  Jamaica, **3:**573–574, 575
  jazz dance, **3:**131
  jazz dance influence, **3:**599
  Jonkonnu festival, **3:**624
  Mexico, **4:**386
  music, **4:**483–487
  Peru, **5:**146
  tap dance, **3:**131
  trance rituals, **6:**185
  Uruguay, **6:**301
  See also Central and East Africa; North Africa; Southern Africa; Sub-Saharan Africa; West Africa; specific countries and peoples
African Performing Arts Center, Konama Kende, Liberia, **5:**256
African Scenario, **3:**575
African Twist (dance), **6:**263
Afro-Amerikanische Lyrik, **2:**153, 154
Afro-Caribbean Suite, **1:**60
Afro-Peruvian Folkore movement, **5:**146

After All (skating program), **6:**154
After Dark (revue), **1:**520
After Degas-Ballet Class (Sunami), **5:***183*
After Eden, **2:***16*, 17, **3:**342
After Love, **6:**433
Afternoon, **4:**230
Afternoon of a Faun (Robbins ballet), **1:**27–29, 99, 233, **2:**361, **5:**358, 363
  appraisal of, **4:**614
  contemporary perspective, **5:**362
  in Dance Theater of Harlem repertory, **2:**334
  Kehlet *demi-caractère* role, **3:**668
  Le Clercq performance, **4:**137, 416, **6:**131
  Moncion performance, **4:**619
  New York City Ballet, **4:**608
  practice clothes as costume, **2:**245
  Rosenthal design and lighting, **5:**407
  in Royal Ballet repertory, **5:**417
  in Royal Danish Ballet repertory, **5:**431
  Sibley performance, **5:**597
  videotape, **6:**131
  See also Après-midi d'un Faune, L'; Silent Cries
"After the Ball" (song), **6:**281
After Venice, **4:**479, **6:**56, 378–379
Agadati, Baruch, **3:**528–529, *529*
Agafonov, Petr, *as photographer*, **5:**470
Agamemnon (Aeschylus), **3:**652
Agamemnons Tod, **4:**91, *93*
Agamemnon Vengé, **4:**696
Agamennone, **5:**277
Agathon, **2:**159
Agee, James, **4:**26
Age of Anxiety, The (Robbins ballet), **1:**438, 478, **4:**608, **5:***360*, 361
Age of Anxiety, The (Auden poem), **1:**438, **5:**361
Age of Bronze, The (Rodin), **5:**370
Age of Gold, The. See Golden Age, The
Ages, Les, **2:**34, **5:**40
AGIS (Associazione Generale Italiana dello Spettacolo), **3:**554
Agitato, **3:**389
Aglaë, ou L'Élève d'Amour, **5:**113, **6:***73*
Aglié, Filippo d', **1:**29–30, 286
Aglié, Ludovico d', **3:**544
Agnes de Mille Heritage Dance Theatre, Winston-Salem, **2:**374, **4:**213
Agnès et Fitz-Henry, **3:**358
Agni Purāṇa (Indian text), **1:**185, **3:**465
Agnus, **1:**462
Agoglia, Esmeralda, **1:**110
Agon, **1:**30–31, **4:***613*, **5:***54*
  Adams (Diana) performance, **1:**11–12
  Aterballetto, **1:**196
  Balanchine pas de deux choreography, **5:**104
  Balanchine-Stravinsky collaboration, **1:**30, 256, 261, 262, 272, **3:**337, **4:**28, 518, 613, **6:**6
  Bolender performance, **1:**478
  costume, **2:**245
  dance aesthetics, **1:**24, 261, 262
  in Dance Theatre of Harlem repertory, **2:**334, *334*

first European performance, **3:**150
  Georgi production, **3:**133
  Hamburg Ballet Stravinsky birthday presentation, **3:**337
  Hayden performance, **3:**352, **4:**617
  Linden performance, **4:**200
  Lukanov production, **2:**11
  MacMillan production, **4:**241, **5:**417
  Mitchell performance, **4:**436
  Swope photographic record, **5:**186
Agor, Jaacov, *as photographer*, **3:**531, *533*
Agrippa, Heinrich Cornelius, **1:**22
Agrippa, Pinzuti, **3:**620
Agrippina Iakovlevna Vaganova (Krasovskaya), **4:**58
Agrippina Vaganova Leningrad Choreographic Institute, **1:**371
Agron-Levy, Hassia, **3:**531
Aguado, Alexandre, marquis de Las Marismas del Guadalquivir, **3:**5
Aguascalientes, Mexico, **4:**328
Aguilar, Rafael, **5:**674
Aguilar, Roberto, *as photographer*, **4:**396
Agulhas, Gladys, **5:**659
Ag'ya, L', **1:**60, **2:**458, **6:***246*
Aha (deity), **2:**484
Ahanta (people), **6:**19
āhāryābhinaya, **3:**457, 458
ahidous, **4:**466, *466*
Ahjolinna, Aku, **2:**633
Ahmad, Ibrāhīm Farḥān, **4:**417
Ahne, Joachim, **3:**155
ahouache (ahwash), **4:**407–408, *407*, 411, 466
Ah Q Goes West, **1:**214–215
ahwash (ahouache), **4:**407–408, *407*, 411, 466
AIAD (Associazione Italiana Attività di Danza), **3:**554
Aichinger, Manfred, **1:**240
Aichurek (opera), **4:**87
Aïda (Verdi), **2:**187, 367, 459, **4:**353, **6:**442
AIDT. *See Aboriginal/Islander Dance Theatre*
Aiello, Salvatore, **5:**436, **6:**266
Aikens, Vanoye, **2:**458, **3:**598, **6:**259
aikido, **1:**186
Ailey, Alvin, **1:***58*, **2:**4, 284, **3:**306, **4:**156, **5:**97, 432, 586, **6:**277, 324
  African-American music, **4:**520
  archival material, **4:**167
  background and early career, **1:**55
  as Byrd influence, **2:**19, 20
  costume, **2:**245
  de Lavallade dance partnership, **1:**55, *55*, **2:**367, *367*
  favorite themes, **1:**58–59
  Harkness Ballet choreography, **3:**342
  Hønningen role, **3:**373
  Horton Dance Theater, **3:***386*, 387–388, **4:**441
  Jacob's Pillow performance, **3:**571
  Jamison collaboration, **3:**577–578
  Joffrey Ballet choreography, **3:**342, 610, 611
  Mass choreography, **1:**439
  Night Creature, **2:**514
  Revelations, **5:**342

students, **2:**566
  See also Alvin Ailey American Dance Theater
AileyCamps, **1:**60
Ailey Celebrates Ellington, **3:**578
"Aimable Vainqueur," **4:**232
Aiman-Sholpan, **3:**665
Aimez-vous Bach?, **5:**435, **6:**106
Aini, S., **6:**83
Ainsi de Suite, **2:**576
Ain't Misbehavin' (musical), **6:**284
Aint' Supposed to Die a Natural Death (musical), **6:**284
Ainu dance traditions, **1:**31–32
Air for the G String, **3:**405
Air Mail Dances (Charlip series), **2:**110–111, **5:**260
Airs, **4:**482, **5:**87, 303, 680, **6:**110, 111, *111*, 112
Airs and Graces, **3:**391, 403
Airs de différents auteurs, Cinquiesme livre, **2:**98
Airs sérieux et à boire (Charpentier), **1:**364
airstep, **5:***630*
Aistros, **4:**208
Aitmatov, Chingiz, **4:**87
Ajanta Frescoes, **5:**45, 125
Ajax (Sophocles), **3:**300
Akalaitis, JoAnne, **5:**574
Akan (people), **3:**164–165, 166–167, **4:**290, **6:**12, 13, 19, 24
Akarova, Madame, **1:**410
Akbarov, Ikram, **3:**569
Ak-Bilyak (Akbilyak), **3:**568, **4:**226
Ak-Eshekli, **6:**213
Åkesson, Birgit, **1:**32–33, 145, **6:**42
Akhak kwebom (Korean text), **1:**166, **4:**52, 53
Akhmarova, N., **5:***470*
Akhtyamov, G., **5:**595
Akhundova, Rafiga, **1:**248
Akhundov Opera and Ballet Theater, Baku, **1:**48, 248
Akilova, Viktoria, **6:**307
Akimov, Boris B., **4:**360, **5:**462
  as contributor, **6:**420–421
Akira Matsui, **4:***655*
Akira Shigeyama, **4:***85*
Akkad period, **4:**356
Aksak Kulan, **3:**665
Aksakov, Sergei, **5:**516
Aksenova, Aleksandra, **5:***476*
Akses, Necil Kazim, **6:**212
Akstein, David, **6:**187
Akulenok, Petr, **1:**408
Akylbekova, Larisa, **3:**665
Alabama (people), **4:**558
Aladdin, **1:**338, **2:**60, **3:**90, **4:**667, **5:**246
Aladin, ou La Lampe merveilleuse, **1:**452, **2:**171
Ala et Lolli, **5:**267, 269
À la Française, **2:**479
Ala-Könni, Erkki, **2:**631, 634
Alam Ara (film), **2:**622
À la Mémoire d'un Ange, **2:**471–472
À la Mémoire d'un Héros, **6:**119
Alarcón, Pedro de, **2:**567
À la Recherche de . . ., **1:**405
Alaskan native dance, **4:**570–571, *572*, 573–574, *573*
À la Vue d'un Seul Oeil, **3:**79
Ala y Lolly, **4:**635
Alba, Maria, **6:**407, 408
Albaicin, Flora, **1:**94
Albania, **1:**33–35, **2:**101, *554*
Albanian State Folk Song and Dance Ensemble, **1:**34
Albee, E. F., **6:**317
Albela (film), **2:**623

Albéniz, Isaac, **1:**115, **2:**567, **5:**673
Albers, Anni, **1:**138
Albers, Josef, **1:**138, **2:**286
Albert, A., **2:**206
Albert, Alfred, **2:**198
Albert, Auguste, **1:**37
Albert, Gennady G., as contributor, **5:**282
Albert, Harry, **3:**79
Albert, Kitty, **4:**522
Albert, Monsieur, **1:**4, **35–37,** 202, 346, 455, 505, **2:**389, **5:**91
Adam ballets, **1:**9, 10
Bordeaux training, **2:**353
Cendrillon, **1:**36, 452, **2:**173
Corsaire, Le, **5:**498
Flore et Zéphire, **2:**415
Jolie Fille de Gand, La, **3:**4–5, 620
Milon productions, **4:**422, 423
notation system, **5:**502
Séducteur au Village, Le, **5:**558
students, **1:**199, **5:**498, 502
Vienna ballet choreography, **1:**237
Alberta Ballet, **2:**41, **5:**62
Albert-Bellon, Elisa, **1:**37, 238
Alberti, Andrea, **5:**231
Alberti, Luis, **2:**431–432
Alberti, Rafael, **3:**9
Albertieri, Luigi, **1:37–38, 2:**84, **4:**209, 381, **6:**128, 269
Albertina Rasch Dancers, **5:**310, **6:**273, 274, *275,* 319, 320, *447,* 448
"Albertus" (Gautier), **3:**179
Albery, Donald, **2:**510–511
Albion and Albanius, **5:**281
Albion's Triumph (masque), **4:**308
Albitz, Hans Adolf, **5:**262
Albitz, Ruth, **5:**262
Albrecht, Angèle, **1:**291, 292
Album des théâtres (libretti series), **4:**177
Album de l'Opéra, **2:**201
Alceste (Gluck), **2:**433
Canziani *intermezzi*, **2:**55
Le Picq entree, **4:**149
Noverre choreography, **4:**696
Skeaping's Drottningholm production, **6:**47
Alceste (Lully), **4:**234, 235, 509, **6:**330, 331
Alcestis, **3:**217
Alcibiade, **6:**70
Alcide, **1:**36, **2:**389
Alcidiane, **1:**287, **2:**518, **4:**234
Alcina, **4:**509
Alcina Suite, **3:**404
Alcine, **2:**34, **4:**187
Alcoceba, Felipe, as photographer, **1:**453, **3:**154, 156
Alcocer, Fracisco, **4:**326
Alcoriza, Jamin, **5:**172
Alcoseba, Raul, **5:**172
Aldar Kose, **6:**213
Aldeburgh Festival, **5:**563
Alder, Alan, **1:**38, 233
Alderson, Evan, as contributor, **2:**48–50
Aldous, Lucette, **1:**38, 210, 211, **2:**510, **5:**301
Don Quixote, **1:**231, 233, **2:**440
Aldredge, Theoni, **1:**75
Aldrich, Elizabeth, **5:**323
as contributor, **5:**347–349
Aldrich, Stanley, as photographer, **5:**632
alegrías, **3:**8
"Alegrías" (Amaya solo), **1:**61
Aleichem, Sholem, **3:**605, **4:**306

Alejandro, Reynaldo Gamboa, **5:**173, *173,* 174
as contributor, **1:**393–394, **5:**167–175, **6:**172
Aleko, **1:**49, 66, 136, **2:**245, 425, **4:**110, 269, *270,* 324, *324,* **5:**604, **6:**198
Aleksandrov, Aleksandr, **3:**665
Aleksandrov, Anatoly, **6:**344
Aleksandrov, Boris, **5:**572
Alekseev, A. Y., **3:**56
Alekseeva, Ludmila, **4:***277,* **5:**458, 465, 476–477, 478
Aleksidze, Georgi, **1:38–39, 2:**499, **3:**135, **4:**224, **5:**460, 469, 478
Aleksiutovich, K., **1:**408
alemana. See allemande
Alembert, Jean le Rond d', **1:**4, **4:**173
Alenikoff, Frances, **4:**22
Aleotti, Giovanni Battista, **5:**535
Alerte . . . Puit 21 (Warning...Shaft 21), **2:**111
Aleskovsky, Naomi, **3:**529, 530, **4:**59
Alessandri, Felice, **2:**55
Alessandri, Felippo degli, **2:**73, **4:**582, **5:**666
Alessandro, **2:**433, **3:**188, 189
Alessandro nelle Indie, **6:**339
Aleut (people), **4:**570, 571–572
Alevi sect, **6:**209, *209*
Alex, Joe, **1:**252
Alexander I, emperor of Russia, **4:**149
Alexander II, emperor of Russia, **2:**95
Alexander, Dorothy, **1:**39, 196–197, **6:**264, 265, 266
Alexander, Frederick Matthias, **1:**469, **471,** 472, 473
See also Alexander Technique
Alexander, Gerda, **6:**302
Alexander, Rod, **2:**184
Alexander, Rolf, **3:**628, 629
Alexander, Ruth, **1:**421
Alexander, Valentina, **2:**566
"Alexander's Ragtime Band" (song), **2:**79
Alexander Technique, **1:**469, 471, **472–473, 4:**17, 18, 20
Alexander the Great (English spectacle), **3:**256
Alexandra Danilova and Her Ensemble, **2:**342
Alexandre chez Apelles, **1:**201
Alexandre le Grand, **2:**113, **4:**184, **5:**95
Alexandre Nevsky, **1:**446
Alexandria, Egypt, **2:**498
Alexandrian dance (Egypt), **2:**490
Alexandrian genres, **2:**157–158
Alexandria Sporting Club, **2:**498
Alexandrova, Vera, **2:**283, **5:**406
Alexandru, Tiberiu, **2:**496
Alexeett, A. (Boris Romanov pseud.), **2:**105
Alfano, Franco, **3:**51, **5:**246
Alfieri, Eric, **3:**78
Alfieri, Vittorio, **5:**528
Alfonso, duke of Calabria, **2:**204, 205, **3:**322
Alfonso of Aragon, **2:**427
Alford, Violet, **3:**35, **5:**352
Alfred le Grand, **1:**35, 36, 202, 452, **4:**423, **5:**92
Alfvén, Hugo, **2:**263, **5:**266
Algaroff, Youly, **1:**306, **2:**114, **3:**73, 225, **5:**96
Algarotti, Francesco, **5:**89
Alger, William R., **6:**240

Algeranoff, Harcourt, **3:**25, 512, **4:**676
Algeria, **1:39–42, 2:**345, *346,* **4:**662, **5:**49–50
Algo, Julian, **3:**511
Algonkians (people), **4:**551, 554, 557, 558
Algues, Les, **2:**111, 471, 472, **3:**74
Alhambra Ballroom, Harlem, **4:**254, **6:**256
Alhambra Palace, Philadelphia, **4:**23
Alhambra Theatre (also Palace), London, **2:**249
ballet programming, **3:**261
Ballets Russes de Serge Diaghilev performances, **2:**409, **5:**611–612
Debussy commission, **2:**361
Hansen *Swan Lake* version, **6:**32
music hall events, **4:**520, *521,* 522
Alhambra Theatre, Cape Town, **5:**650
Alhamra Arts Council, Lahore, **3:**425
Alhanko, Anneli, **6:**44
Ali, Aisha
as contributor, **1:**39–42, **4:**464–469, 662–666, **5:**49–50, **6:**205–207
as photographer, **6:**206, 207
Ali, Esmat, **2:**497, 498
Ali, Mumtaz, **2:**624
Ali, Naushad, **2:**625
Alia, **3:**665
Aliaj, Agron, **1:**34
Ali-Bab (Cherubini), **2:**202
Ali Baba (musical), **6:**290
Ali Baba (Tamis work), **6:**137
Ali-Batyr. See Shurale
Alice, **1:**394, **4:**545, **5:**60, **6:**147
Alice (Wilson), **6:**401
Alice in the Garden, **5:**60
Alice in Wonderland, **1:**400, **2:**510, 514, **3:**175, **4:**668, **5:**62, **6:**137
Alice in Wonderland (Carroll), **1:**394
Aline, Reine de Golconde, **1:**202, 452, **4:**657, **6:**49
Alippi, Elías, **6:***92*
Ali Suissi ensemble, **6:**206
Alive from Off Center (television series), **2:**609, 610, **6:**139
Alkhanko, Anneli, **6:**44
Alkire, Helen, **1:**421
All about Ballet (Souritz), **5:**643
Allan, David, **4:**546, **6:**143
Allan, Ivan, **3:***611*
Allan, Maud, **1:42–43,** 212, 239, **2:**50, 360, **3:**96, **4:**520, **5:**46, 497, **6:**268, 317
Allard, Catherine, **3:***448*
Allard, Marie, **1:43–44, 3:**326, **5:**89, 105, **6:**331
Comédie Française, **3:**66
Dauberval relationship, **1:**43, **2:**352, *353*
Don Quixote performance, **2:**434–435
Lyonnois rivalry, **4:**236
Allardt, Viktor, **2:**631
All-China Association of Dance Professionals, **2:**148
All-China Association of Dance, **2:**134
All-China Dance Association, **2:**134
All-City Dance Company, Detroit, **2:**566
Allegri, Oreste, **5:**320
Allegri Diversi, **1:**453
allegro, **1:44–45,** 264, 383, **2:**268

Allegro (musical), **2:**373, **4:**120
Allegro Barbaro, **3:**386, **4:**59
Allegro Brillante, **1:**272, **2:**334, **3:**231, **4:**246, 611, 631, **6:**366
Allegro, il Penseroso, ed il Moderato, L', **4:**471
Allemagne, De l' (Heine), **2:**203, **3:**178
allemande, **1:45–47,** 342, **4:**506, 510, 511, **6:**124
Arbeau choreography, **1:**104
cotillon incorporation, **2:**253
Negri description, **4:**580
Allemann, Sabina, **1:**201
Allen, Debbie, **4:**255, **5:**517
Allen, Louis, **5:**255
Allen, Rena, **2:**329–330
Allen, Richard, **1:**216
Allen, Sarita, **1:***58,* 60
Allen, Woody, **5:**573, 592
Allerhand, Ruth, **2:**580
Allesch, Emma, **5:**278
Alessandro nelle Indie, **5:**231
Alleyne, John, **2:**42, **4:***545,* 546, 547, **6:**132
Alliances, **4:**72
Allieva D'Amore, L', **5:**498
Allis, Francis, **4:**120
allokines, **4:**367
Allouba, Samia, **2:**498
All-Star Imperial Russian Ballet, **4:**223, 459, **6:**348
All's Well That Ends Well (Shakespeare), **2:**1
Alltag und Fest, **4:**91
All that Jazz (film), **3:**55
All the Superlatives (documentary), **6:**135
Allumez les Étoiles, **5:**164
Alma, **1:**37, **47–48, 2:**93, *93,* 94, 390, **5:**136
See also Fille de Marbre, La
Alma Mater, **1:**63, **4:**612
alman. See allemande
Almanach Dansant (Guillaume), **1:**47
Almanach des spectacles, **2:**29
Almaran, Carlos, **6:***180*
Almaszade, Gamer, **1:**48, 248
Almaviva et Rosine, **1:**455, **2:**464, **3:**539
Almée, L', **4:**453, 454, 455
Almenda, Antonio de, **5:**668
al-na-'īsh, **4:**408
Aloff, Mindy, as contributor, **5:**175–188
Alone, for a Second, **2:**449, **4:**227, 674
Alonso, Alberto, **1:**493, **2:**270, 276, 277, **3:**25, **5:**205, 265, 587
Ballet de Nacional Cuba, **2:**278
Carmen, **1:**50, 73, **2:**278, 564–565
SODRE Ballet guest choreography, **6:**302
Alonso, Alicia, **1:48–50,** 86, **5:**17, 97, 275, 612, **6:**199, *200*
Ballet Russe de Monte Carlo, **1:**301, 302
Bruhn dance partnership, **2:**3
Cuban ballet, **2:**276, 277, *278,* 279, *279,* 280, **3:**306
on Eglevsky's technical feats, **2:**479
Fall River Legend, **1:**49, 68, **2:**373, *374*
Giselle, **1:**65, 68, 71, 195, **2:**276, 278, **3:***178,* 229, **4:**110
Jacob's Pillow performance, **3:**571

Jardin aux Lilas performance, **3:**597
Plisetsky dance partnership, **2:**278, *278*
Theme and Variations, **1:***67,* 68
Youskevitch dance partnership, **1:***49, 49,* 50, *65, 67,* 68, 71, 301, **3:***178,* **6:**425
Alonso, Fernando, **2:**276, 277, 278
Alonso, Laura, **2:**278, *279*
Alonzo e Cora, **2:**71
Alonzo the Brave and the Fair Imogine, **2:***412,* 414
Alophe, Marie-Alexandre, **5:**176, 261
Alotria, **2:***123,* **6:**304
Alouard, Pierre, **3:**546
Alphabet des mouvements du corps humain (Stepanov), **4:**686, **5:**693
Alpine Ballade, **1:**408
Alptraum einer Ballerina, Der, **1:**442
Also Egmont, Bitte, **4:**203
Alston, Richard, **1:**50–53
  Benesh notation use, **1:**418
  Davies (Siobhan) association, **2:**354, 355, **3:**273
  formalist choreography, **3:**274
  London Contemporary Dance Theatre, **3:**275, **4:**218, 220
  Midsummer, **5:***420*
  modern dance technique, **3:**272
  Rambert Ballet, **3:**274, **5:**302, 303, 304–305, *304*
  Sacre du Printemps, Le, **5:**488
  Second Stride, **3:**273–274
alta, **1:**53–54, **2:**74, **5:**506
altabaxo step, **1:**53
altadanza, **1:**53–54
Alter, Judith B., *as contributor,* **1:**12–13
Alterman, Barry, **4:**471
Alternativa, **4:**396, 397
Alton, Robert, **2:**108, 426, 616, **6:**275, 277, 278
Altunian, Tatul, **1:**120, 121
Alt-Wien, **1:**483
Altyn Kyz (musical drama), **4:**87
Alum, Manuel, **5:**301
Alumim, **3:**531
Alur (people), **4:***290*
alus, **1:**174, 175, *175*
Alvarenga, Oneyda, **1:**530–531
Alvarez, Anita, **3:**214
Álvarez, Tania, **3:**397
Álvarez Bravo, Lola, *as photographer,* **4:**392
Álvarez Cozzi, Fernando, **6:**302
Alveberg, Kjersti, **4:**679
Alvin Ailey American Dance Theater, **1:**54–60
  Australian tour, **1:**212
  Beatty's *Stack Up,* **1:**395
  Byrd choreography, **2:**20
  Canticle of the Elements, **2:**187
  de Lavallade guest performances, **2:**367
  Dunham works, **2:**459
  Fagan choreography, **2:**567
  Faison choreography, **6:***260*
  Jamison association, **3:**578
  Japanese tour, **3:**591
  Manning choreography, **4:**255
  racial integration of, **6:**269
  Revelations, **5:**342
  Seymour guest peformances, **5:**575
  Wedding, **5:**256
  See also Ailey, Alvin
Alwyn, Eve, **1:**211
Alwyn, Keith, **6:**375

Alzire (Alzira) (Voltaire), **1:**88, **3:**364, **4:**174
Amacher, Maryanne, **2:**289
Amadeus (musical and film), **6:**154, 286
Amadeus Monument, **5:**677
Amadis (Lully), **4:**235, **5:**39, 40, **6:**330, 331
Amadis de Gaule, **1:**456, **2:**465, **4:**109
Amadis de Grèce, **1:**355
Amad Muhammad (Javanese text), **1:**176
Amagatsu Sho, **1:**61
Amagatsu Ushio, **1:**60–61, **2:**18, **4:**271
Amahl and the Night Visitors (Menotti), **2:**16, **6:**145
Amalgam, **3:**437
Amans Surpris, Les, **6:***332*
Amants de Teruel, Les. See Lovers of Teruel, The
Amants Introduits dans le Sérail, Les, **5:**196
Amants Magnifiques, Les (Molière), **1:**288, **4:**229, 234, 447, **5:**489
Amant Statue, L', **2:**414
Amants Trompés, Les, **2:**365
Amar, Jules, **4:**15
Amarilla, **5:**125
Amaterasu, **2:**110
Amaterasu (deity), **1:**183
Amati, Olga, **5:**529
Amaturo, Aniello, **3:**320
Amaya, Carmen, **1:**61–62, 94, **3:**9, 11, **5:**674
Amaya, José ("El Chino"), **1:**61
Amaya, Juana, **3:**10
Amaya, Teresa, **4:**232–233
Amazing Adventures of Don Quixote, The, **4:**668
Amazonen, Die, **3:**358
Amazones, Les, **6:**71, 72–73
Amazonia, **2:**475
Amazonian Forest, **1:**533
Ambegaokar, Saga Miryam Vuori, *as contributor,* **3:**311–313
Amberg, George, **2:**601
Ambigu de la Folie, L', **4:**122, 694
amb kenan, **5:**84
Ambroggio, Giovanni, **3:**346, **4:**381, **5:**279
Ambrose, Saint, **2:**165
Ambrose, Kay, **1:***331, 334, 335,* **3:**200, **4:**539, *541,* **6:**128
Ambrosiny, François, **1:**410
Ambrosio, Giovanni. *See* Guglielmo Ebreo da Pesaro
Amélie, **3:**68
Ame-no-Uzume (goddess), **1:**183, **3:**579, 583, 591, **4:**40
America (extravaganza), **4:**177, 381
Americana (revue), **4:**399
American Archeology No. 1: Roosevelt Island, **4:**451
American Association of Masters of Dancing, United States and Canada, **2:**338
American Ballet, **1:**63–64, 68, 297
  Balanchine *Apollo* production, **1:**96
  Balanchine revivals, **1:**307
  Balanchine *Serenade* production, **1:***259,* 261
  Christensen brothers, **2:**160
  dancers in Ballet Caravan, **1:**279, 280
  Dollar, William, **2:**426
  founding, **4:**27–28, **6:**246
  Latin American tour, **1:**280–281, **2:***123,* 161

Loring, Eugene, **4:**227
  Moore performance, **4:**457
  practice clothes as costumes, **2:**242
  Stravinsky commission, **6:**5
American Ballet Caravan. *See* Ballet Caravan
American Ballet Center (Joffrey Ballet), **3:**609, 610, **4:**457, **5:**681, **6:***291,* 292
American Ballet Company (Feld), **1:**69, **2:**583
American Ballet Company (Fokine), **3:**22–23
American Ballet Competition, **1:**282
American Ballet Theatre (formerly Ballet Theatre), **1:**64–77, 99, 117, 149, 518, **2:**196, **4:**29, **5:**186, **6:**278, 291
  Adams, Diana, **1:**11, 12
  Alonso, Alicia, **1:**49, 50
  Balanchine *Errante* revival, **1:**307
  Ballet Caravan demise, **1:**280
  Ballet Imperial, **1:**293
  Ballet of the Red Shoes, **6:**288
  Ballet Russe de Monte Carlo competition, **1:**297
  Baryshnikov, Mikhail, **1:**73–74, 75–76, 372–373, **2:**112, **4:**24, 620
  Bayadère, La, **1:**75, *75,* 393, **4:***25*
  Billy the Kid, **1:**452, **2:**197
  Bolm performance and choreography, **1:**484
  Bruhn, Erik, **2:**3, 4
  Carnaval, Le, **2:**73
  Chagall designs, **1:**136
  Chase, Lucia, **1:**75, **2:**112
  Cinderella, **4:**226–227
  Coppélia, **2:**200
  Cranko *Romeo and Juliet,* **5:**396
  Cuban performance, **2:**279
  dancers' strike, **1:**75
  Dark Elegies, **2:**349
  de Lavallade guest performance, **2:**367
  de Mille productions, **2:**373–374, **5:**369, **6:**278
  Dolin, Anton, **1:**65, 66, 71, 437, **2:**112, 425, 426, **4:**269
  Dollar choreography, **2:**426–427
  Don Quixote, **1:**74, 76, 372, **2:***439,* 441
  Dowell guest performances, **2:**444
  Duets revival, **2:**294
  Dunning, Gary, **1:**77
  Eglevsky performances, **2:**479
  Études, **2:**536, **4:***120*
  Feld, Eliot, **2:**583
  Fernandez, Royes, **2:**586
  Firebird restaging, **1:**136, 483, **3:**2
  Fokine productions, **3:**26–27
  Fracci guest appearances, **3:**60, 61
  Franklin as artistic adviser, **3:**88
  Giselle, **1:**65, 71, 74, 373, 437, 459, **3:**60, *178, 182,* **4:**268
  Gregory, Cynthia, **3:**306
  guest solo artists in Chile, **2:**124
  Hayden, Melissa, **3:**351
  headquarters, **1:**420
  Hightower, Rosella, **3:**361
  Howard productions, **3:**392
  Italian tour, **3:**550
  Jardin aux Lilas, **1:**66, 68, **3:**597, *597*
  Jeune Homme et la Mort, Le, **3:**601
  Karinska costumes, **3:**654

Kaye, Nora, **3:**663, 664
Kidd, Michael, **4:**10
Kirkland, Gelsey, **4:**24, *25*
Kolpakova as ballet mistress, **4:**36
Kriza, John, **4:**63
Kudelka choreography, **4:**73
Laing, Hugh, **4:**109–110
Lanchbery as musical director, **4:**117
Lander (Harald) choreography, **4:**119
Lichine choreography and guest performances, **4:**178
Liepa (Andris) contract, **4:**181
Littlefield-trained dancers, **4:**209
London performances, **5:**415
Loring, Eugene, **4:**227–228
MacMillan association, **3:**267, **4:**241, 242, 243, 244
Makarova, Natalia, **4:**248–249
Markova, Alicia, **4:**268–269
Marks, Bruce, **4:**271
Massine choreography, **4:**324
McKenzie, Kevin, **1:**64–65, 74, 76, 77, **2:**441, **3:**367
Messel *Sleeping Beauty* design, **4:**357, 358, *358*
Metropolitan Opera Ballet collaboration, **4:**382
Miss Julie, **2:**283
Moor's Pavane, The, **1:**72
Mordkin Ballet origins, **1:**65, **4:**460
Nault, Fernand, **4:**576
Nijinska choreographies, **4:**638
Nureyev, Rudolf, **5:**7
Nutcracker, The, **5:**15–16
Oboukhoff, Anatole, **5:**17
On Your Toes revival, **6:**286
Patineurs, Les, **1:**69
Pleasant's credo, **1:**65
Princess Aurora, **5:**612
Raymonda, **5:**322
Robbins, Jerome, **5:**359–360, 364, 366, 367
Rodeo, **6:**247
Romanoff, Dimitri, **5:**391
Romeo and Juliet, **5:**396–398, *397*
Ross (Herbert) choreography, **5:**408
Saddler, Donald, **5:**488
school. *See* American Ballet Theatre School
Serrano, Lupe, **5:**573
Smith (Oliver) design, **5:**616
Swan Lake, **1:**66, 71, 76, 373, **6:**34
Sylphide, La, **1:**70, 71, **3:**60
Sylphides as signature piece, **3:**26, **6:**62
Tallchief, Maria, **6:**86
Taylor, Paul, **6:**112
television performances, **6:**137
Tharp, Twyla, **6:**153
Theme and Variations, **1:**67, 68, *371*
tours, **1:**65, 68–69, 70
Tudor, Antony, **5:**397–398, **6:**198–200, *198,* 202
twenty-fifth anniversary performance, **3:**577
Undertow, **1:**66, 68, **5:**562
Wilde as ballet mistress, **6:**397
Wilson, Sallie, **6:**402
world premiers, **1:**67, 68, 72
Youskevitch performances, **6:**425
Zorina performances, **6:**450
American Ballet Theatre: A Close-Up in Time (television documentary), **5:**369
American Ballet Theatre II, **1:**75

American Ballet Theatre School, **1:**75
  Danielian directorship, **2:**341
  Joffrey as faculty member, **3:**609
  Lowski as faculty member, **4:**232
  Wilde directorship, **6:**397
American Bandstand (television program), **1:**77–79, **5:**630, 632, 633, **6:**30
American Broadcasting Company. *See* ABC-TV
American Centenary Exposition (1876), **5:**45, **6:**238
American Classical Ballet. *See* Niagara Frontier Ballet
American Company, **6:**232
American Concert Ballet, **1:**478–479, **2:**426, **6:**396
American Council of Learned Societies, **6:**298
American Dance Association, **2:**579, 580, **6:**89
American Dance Asylum, **3:**621
American Dance Company, **4:**436, **6:**27
American Dance Festival, **1:**79–82, 422, 543, **6:**108, 152, 295
  archival materials, **4:**168
  Balasaraswati sponsorship, **1:**274
  Black Tradition project, **1:**81, 396, **3:**358
  Caribbean dance, **2:**66
  Chinese modern dance, **2:**146
  Critics Conference, **6:**300
  dance film and video competition, **2:**610
  Dean (Laura) association, **2:**360
  Dunn (Robert Ellis) association, **2:**461
  Graham as faculty member, **3:**219
  Horst choreography, **3:**385
  Hoyer performance, **3:**393
  Humphrey and Limón company residency, **3:**403, 404
  International Choreographers Workshop, **1:**80, **6:**251
  Koner as faculty member, **4:**39
  Lang (Pearl) association, **4:**120–121
  Limón choreography and teaching, **4:**198, *199*
  London Contemporary Dance Theatre, **4:**217
  Merce Cunningham Company residency, **2:**290
  Moor's Pavane first performance, **4:**458
  Nikolais's *Kaleidoscope* reception, **4:**649–650
  Summerspace first performance, **6:**27
American Dance Machine, **2:**245
American Dancer, The. See Dance Magazine
American Dance Therapy Association, **2:**315
American Dancing Master (Howe), **6:**239
American Delsartism. *See* Delsarte system of expression
American Document, **1:**82, 421, **3:**212, 216, 349, **4:**130, **6:**245
American Folk-Dance Society, **3:**34
American Genesis, **6:**109, 111, 112
American Heroine, An, or Treachery Punished, **2:**442, **6:**311
American Holiday, **3:**401
American Independence, or The 4th of July 1776, **6:**233

American Indian dance. *See* Native American dance
American Indian Dance Theater, **4:**575
American in Paris, An (film), **2:**616, 617, *618,* **4:**3, *3,* 4
American in Paris, An (Gershwin)
  Bolender choreography, **1:**479
  Rasch choreography, **5:**311, **6:**274, *275*
American Jubilee (extravaganza), **4:**210
American Laboratory Theater, **1:**86
American Landscapes, **6:**229
American Library Association, **4:**158
American Lyceum Movement, **2:**338
American Lyric, **3:**212
American Music Festival (1988), **1:**141, **4:**621, 622, **5:**366
American National Association of Dancing Masters, **6:**239, 290
American National Theater and Academy (ANTA), **1:**65, **4:**30
American Negro Ballet, **6:**258
American Opera Company, **2:**200, **3:**559
American Pageant Association, **6:**242, 244
American Pattern, **2:**580, **5:**59
American Physical Education Association, **6:**295
American Place, An (gallery), **1:**135
American Provincials, **3:**212, *213,* 384
American Quartet, **5:**617
American Repertory Ballet, **6:**264, 266
American School of Dance, Hollywood, **4:**228, 691
American Shakesparare Festival Theater Academy, **4:**30
American Smooth (ballroom dance position), **1:**356
American Society for Eastern Arts, Berkeley, **1:**274
American Society for the Prevention of Cruelty to Children (Geary Society), **6:**316
American Society of Composers, Authors and Publishers (ASCAP), **6:**280–281
American Society of Professors of Dancing, **2:**338, **6:**239, 290, 293
Americans We, **1:**77
American Theater Laboratory, **5:**363–364
American University, Cairo, **2:**498
American Zionist Youth Foundation, **1:**431–432, **3:**605
Ames, M. M., *as contributor,* **6:**183–184
Ame-Tsuchi, **1:**188
Amhara (people), **2:**530, 532, 533
Amherst Agricultural College, Massachusetts, **6:**248
Amiel, Josette, **5:**96, 97
Amiens, France, **1:**349, **3:**74
Amigos de la Danza, **1:**102, 112–113
Amilbangsa, Ligaya Fernando, **5:**174
Amin, Leila, **2:**498
Aminta (Tasso), **2:**368, **6:**62
Aminta et Clori (Le Picq), **4:**149
Amir, Elham al-, **2:**498
Amirkhanian, Charles, **1:**51, 52
Amirov, Fibret, **1:**248

Amis d'Argentina, Les, **1:**115
Amleth, **5:**433
Amma, Mylapore Gauri, **1:**273, **4:**257, **5:**292, **6:**321
Ammann, Dieter, **6:**53
Ammerbach, Elias Nikolaus, **4:**505
Amodio, Amedeo, **1:**82–83, 196, **3:**552, **5:**530, **6:**143
Among Company, **1:**542
Amor, **2:**82, 477, **3:***548,* **4:**258, 259, 263, **5:**246, 399, 529
Amoras, **3:**508, 511
Amor Brujo, El, **1:**115, 117, **2:**521, 567, **3:**9, 286, **5:**674, **6:**212
Amor Brujo, El (film), **3:**101
Amor Constante, Mas alla de la Muerte, **1:**412
Amore ed Arte, **4:**264
Amore e Psiche, **1:**88, **6:**70
Amorous Adventure, **3:**391
Amors og Balletmesterens Luner. See Whims of Cupid and the Ballet Master, The
Amors Triumph, **6:**75
Amors Zögling, **2:**93
Amort, Andrea, **1:**243
  as contributor, **3:**631, **6:**357–358
Amour, ou La Rose Animée, L', **2:**504
Amour à Cythere, L', **3:**358, **5:**90
Amour Constant, L', **6:**38
Amour du Moyen Age, Un, **4:**437
Amour en Espagne, L', **1:**114
Amour et Psyché, L', **2:**413, 464, **3:**112, 365
Amour et Sa Mère, L' (Daumier), **2:**71
Amour et Son Amour, L', **1:**251, **3:**73
Amour et Son Destin, L', **6:**353
Amour et Son Destub, L', **4:**185
Amour Malade, L', **1:**287, 424
Amour Médecin, L', **4:**234, 447
Amours d'Acis et Galathée, Les, **3:**365
Amours d'Antoine et de Cléopâtre, Les, **1:**202, **5:**90
Amours de Diane, Les, **2:**587
Amours de Faublas, Les, **2:**60
Amours de Franz, Les, **5:**164
Amours Déguisés, Les, **1:**288, 424, **4:**234
Amours de Jupiter, Les, **1:**305, **3:**394
Amours de Mars et de Vénus, Les (Campras), **2:**34
  See also Loves of Mars and Venus
Amours d'Enée et de Didon, Les, **3:**426
Amours des Dieux, Les, **5:**504
Amours des Vénus et Adonis, Les, ou La Vengeance de Mars, **2:**464
Amours du Bucheron et de Nicodeme, Les, **5:**198
Amour Sorcier, L', **4:**184
Amour Vaincu, L', **4:**455
Amour Vengé, ou La Métamorphose, **2:**414
Amozonen, Die, **3:**358
Amparo, Nila, **3:**286, **4:**222
Amphion, Élève des Muses, **2:**413, **5:**439
Amphitryon (Dryden), **5:**281
Amsterdam, Netherlands, **4:**591, 592
Amsterdam Ballet. *See* Dutch National Ballet
Amsterdam Municipal Theater Institute, **4:**590
Amsterdam Schouwburg, **4:**588–589
Amsterdamse Ballet Combinatie. *See* Ballet der Lage Landen

Amsterdam Theater School, **4:**594, 599
amumur, **5:**209
Amun (deity), **2:**482, 485
Amur dance traditions, **5:**449
Amynthe et Amour, **1:**36
Amzallag, David, *as photographer,* **1:**506, 511, **2:**386, **5:**431, 432
Anacreon (ancient Greek poet), **2:**414
Anacréon (Rameau), **5:**306
Anadolu Gecesi, **6:**213
Analysis of Beauty (Hogarth), **2:**527
Analysis of Country Dancing (Wilson), **2:**257
Anand, Mulk Raj, **3:**470
Ananiashvili, Nina, **1:**77, 83–84, **5:**465
  Liepa (Andris) dance partnership, **4:***180,* 181
  Moscow ballet school training, **1:**493
  Swan Lake performance, **6:**35
  Symphony in C performance, **6:**66
Ana Non, **2:**466
anapalē, **3:**291
Anaphase, **4:**532
Anar, **4:**87
Anarchy, Wild Women, and Dina, **6:**448
Anastasi, William, **1:**142, **2:**295–296
Anastasia, **1:**430, **2:**186, **4:**242, 243, *243,* **5:**417, 574, 575, **6:**117
Anastenáridēs, **1:**84–85, **2:**8, 100, 487, **3:**298, 301
Anastos, Peter, **1:**75, 76, 197, 373, **2:**333, **3:**234, **6:***191,* 266
Anatole, Madame. *See* Gosselin, Constance
Anatolia. *See* Turkey
Anatomical and Mechanical Lectures upon Dancing (Weaver), **2:**81, 527, **4:**105, **5:**518, **6:**373, 374
Anatomical Lesson, **4:**602
Anatomical Notation, The (Fee), **4:**692
Anatomy and Ballet (Sparger), **4:**17, **6:**128
Anatomy for the Dancer (Gelabert), **4:**17
Anatomy Lesson (Rembrandt), **1:**141
Anatomy Lesson, The, **6:**146
Anaya, Dulce, **2:**277
Anaya, María Elena, **4:**396
Ancestors and Descendants, **4:**266
ancestor worship, **1:**160, 227, **3:**504
  bon dances, **1:**496–497
  topéng dance, **3:**501–502
  wayang dance origination, **3:**496, 498
Ancestral, **6:**415
Anchors Aweigh (film), **4:**2, 3
Anchutina, Leda, **1:**64, **2:**479, **5:**570, 571
Ancient Airs and Dances, **4:**623
ancient civilizations. *See specific countries, empires, and regions*
Ancient Russia, **1:**297
Ancient Story, An, **4:**446
Ancient Voices of Children, **2:**1, **5:**302
Ancient Voices of Children and Black Angels, **2:**1
And, Metin, **4:**414, 416
  as contributor, **6:**208–213

Andaaz (film), **2:**622–623
And After . . ., **3:**534
Andalouse Sentimentale, **1:**115
Andalusian Center for Theater
　Documentation, **4:**162–163
Andalusian costume, **3:***70*
Andalusian dance, **4:**664–665,
　5:*672*
Andalusian Wedding, The, **1:**90
Andaluza, **1:**115
Andaxinház, **3:**421
Andermatt, Clara, **5:**236
Andersen, Frank, **1:***513,* **5:**430, 433
Andersen, Hans Christian, **1:**399,
　2:401, **3:**224, **5:**425
Andersen, Ib, **1:**96, **3:**234, **4:**180,
　615, 620, 621, 623, **6:**404
Andersen, Inger, **1:***510*
Andersen, John, **5:**428
Andersen, Reid, **2:**268, 512
Anderson, Carol, **2:**45
Anderson, Cynthia, **2:**606
Anderson, Jack
　as contributor, **1:**295–303
　Copland interview, **2:**198
　Dance Chronicle, **6:**297
　on Nijinska comeback, **4:**633
Anderson, Janet, *as contributor,*
　2:361–363
Anderson, Laurie, **1:**545, **2:**608,
　3:621
Anderson, Lea, **2:**611, **3:***275,* 276
Anderson, Maceo, **3:**57
Anderson, Maxwell, **6:**278, 281
Anderson, Nels, **4:**212
Anderson, Reid, **2:**41–42, 267,
　3:*152,* 157, **4:**73, 546–547,
　6:11
Anderson, T. J., **2:**459
Anderson, William G., **6:**240, 294
Anderson-Ivantzova, Elizabeth,
　1:85–86, **2:**11, **5:**602
Anderson-Ivantzova School of
　Dance, New York City, **1:**86
Anderson-Milton School, New York
　City, **3:**211, 212
Andersson, Benny, **1:**420
Andersson, Gerd, **6:**42, *42*
Anderton, Elizabeth, **5:**421, **6:**217
Andhara, India, **2:**394
"And I Walk in the Meadow," **5:**445,
　6:303
Andonović, Violeta, **6:**435
Andorgeus (mythic), **2:**271
And Promenade Home (de Mille),
　2:374, **6:**281
Andrade, Marília de, **1:**537
　as contributor, **1:**532–534,
　536–537
Andrade, Mário de, **1:**537
Andrade, Oswald de, **1:**533
Andrašovan, Tibor, **5:**614
André, Simon, **2:**470
Andrea de Firenze, **2:**166, **4:**349
Andreani, Domenico, **5:**424
Andréani, Jean-Paul, **5:**96
Andreanova, Elena, **4:**41, **6:**451
Andreasen, Lois, **6:**297
Andrée, Rosemary, **4:**522
Andreev, Aleksei, **1:**408
Andreini, Isabella, **2:**190
Andrejev, Jelena, **6:**435
Andreonov, Samuil, **4:**282, **5:**456,
　6:344
Andreopoulos, Argyrios, **3:**303
Andres, Jerome, **2:**447
Andrewes, John, **3:***265*
Andrews, Jerome, **2:**466, **3:**76, 83
Andrews, Julie, **2:**619, **6:**282, 283
Andrew W. Mellon Foundation,
　6:266

Andreyanova, Elena, **1:**86–87,
　5:133, 139, 147, 148, 150, 516
Fountain of Bakhchisarai
　performance, **1:**86, **3:**56,
　5:454
Giselle performance, **1:**86, **3:**181,
　4:280–281
Ivanov as protégé, **3:**560
Johansson dance partnership,
　3:618
Maryinsky provincial tours, **5:**454
Andreyev, Ivan, **1:**392, **5:**606
Andreyev, Leonid, **4:**648
Andrianov, Samuil, **1:**255
Andrien, Ruth, **2:**526
Andromeda, **3:**544
Andromeda e Perseo, **3:**176
Andronache, Doina, **5:**387
Andronicus, Livius, **4:**423, **5:**375
Andronikov, Irakly, **4:**55
"and they were not ashamed," **2:**357
Andulasian *cante,* **3:**9
Anduze, Juan, **5:**275
angaliastós, **2:**100
Angara, The, **1:**440, 441, 492, **5:**459,
　472, **6:**314
Grigorovich choreography,
　3:308–309, **5:**462
Zaslavsky and Moiseyev
　choreography, **5:**473, *473*
Ang Duong, king of Cambodia,
　2:30
Angelico, Fra, **2:**166
Angelini, Marcello, **6:**204
Angelus, Iván, **3:**421
Anger, Moŕic, **5:**245
Anger, Perrine, **2:**589
Angers, France, **1:**349, 350, 351,
　3:74, 78
Anghel, Sergiu, **5:**388–389, 389
Angika, **2:**104
āṅgikābhinaya, **3:**457
Angiolini, Fortuna, **2:**415
Angiolini, Gaspero, **1:**87–89, 123,
　2:55, **5:**270, **6:**69
　on Académie Royale de
　　Danse, **1:**4
　ballo, **3:**556
　Bodin dance partnership, **1:**468
　Curz as student, **2:**299
　Don Juan, **2:**433–434, **4:**509, **6:**48
　Galeotti as student, **3:**104, 105,
　　5:424
　Gluck collaboration, **1:**87, 88,
　　236, **3:**187, 188, 189, 190,
　　4:696
　Hilverding association, **3:**364,
　　365, **4:**174
　libretti, **4:**174
　Noverre correspondence and
　　feud, **2:**433, **3:**544, 545, 546,
　　4:696, 699
　Saint Petersburg ballet, **4:**276,
　　5:451
　Scala Ballet, **5:**528
　Starzer association, **5:**693
　students, **5:**215, **6:**311
　technical writings, **6:**124, 125
　Vienna ballet, **1:**236, 237
Angiolini, Giuseppa, **2:**209
Angiolini, Niccolò, **1:**88
Angiolini, Pasquale, **1:**88
Angiolini, Pietro, **1:**88, **5:**231
Angiolini, Romulo, **1:**88
Angkor Vat, **5:**495
Angkor Wat (Cambodia),
　2:29–30, 31
anglaise (or *angloise*), **1:**89–90,
　2:256, **4:**221
　figures, **2:**592
　as stepping dance, **5:**695

Anglebert, Jean-Henri d', **1:**517,
　3:29
Anglicanism, **2:**167
Anglo-Russian Ballet, **4:**380
Angola, **2:**86, 87–88, 89, 91
　African-Brazilian dance, **1:**525,
　　527, 529, 530
　Cuban dance, **2:**274–275
Ångström, Anna, **6:**50
Angst und Geometrie, **2:**309
Angus Dei (Bach), **1:**39
Anicetus, Actius, **5:**73
Aniel, Pierre-Jean, **1:**237, **5:**498
Anikulapo-Kuti, Fela, **4:**487
Animal Locomotion (Muybridge),
　4:*14,* 15, **5:***178*
animal mime dances
　central and eastern Africa, **2:**91
　China, **2:**140–141
　Ecuador, **2:**476
　Greece, **3:**287–288, 302
　Kazakhstan, **3:**664
　!Kung San, **5:**664
　Lepcha, **5:**599
　Native American, **1:**600, **3:***375,*
　　4:553, 563, 564, 567
　Shangana-Tsonga, **5:**579
　Siberia, **5:**446, 448
　Turkey, **6:**210, 211
　West Africa, **6:**383
　Yugoslavia, **6:**427
　See also specific animal dances
Animated Gobelin, The, **3:**15, 137,
　　4:639, **5:**121
Animated Shorts, **3:**388
Animaux Modèles, Les, **3:**132,
　　4:184, **5:**96, 237
animism, **3:**471, 472, **4:**253
　Japanese Shintō, **3:**641, 642
　Pueblo, **4:**562
Anisfeld, Boris, **3:**18, 20, **6:**41
Anisimova, Nina, **1:**90–91,
　2:11, 437
　Coppélia choreography, **2:**200
　Flames of Paris performance,
　　3:12, **4:**284
　Gayané choreography, **3:**125,
　　4:284, **5:**459, *460*
　Song of the Crane choreography,
　　5:473
Aniuta, **1:**493, **4:**336, **5:**460, **6:**314
Ankara State Ballet, **6:**212–213
Ankara State University of Music,
　4:110
ankiya nat, **4:**424
ankoku butō, **2:**17
Anna and Ostriches, **4:**81
Annaba, Algeria, **1:**41–42
Annabel Lee, **3:**226, **5:**605
Anna in Graz, **6:**132
Anna Karenina
　Kondratieva performance, **4:**38
　Leventhal scenic design, **4:**154
　Liepa (Maris) performance, **4:**182
　Nieto performance, **2:**124
　Parlić staging, **5:**101
　Pártay staging, **3:**418
　Plisetskaya choreography, **1:**493,
　　2:565, **5:**205, 206, 462, 587
　Prokovsky choreography, **1:**234,
　　4:285, **5:**410, **6:**379
　Rowe performance, **5:**410, *410*
　Shchedrin score, **5:**587–588
　Weller performance, **6:**379
Anna Karenina (film), **5:**203
Anna Pavlova (Krasovskaya), **4:**58
Anna Pavlova Company. *See*
　Pavlova, Anna
Anna Wyman Dance Theatre, **2:**40,
　45, **6:**132

Anne, queen of Great Britain,
　2:501, **3:**522, **5:**343
Anneau Magique, L', **1:**36
Anne Frank, **2:**514
Anne of the Thousand Days (film),
　5:604
Annetta e Lubino (Anetta e Lubin)
　or *Annete et Lubin),* **1:**88,
　3:326, **4:**697
Annie (musical), **5:**602, **6:**285
Annie Get Your Gun (musical),
　1:498, **4:**126, **6:**89–90, 279
Annonce Faite à Marie, L' (Claudel),
　3:596
*Annotated Bibliography of Korean
　Music, An* (Song), **4:**54
*Annotated Bibliography of Music
　and Dance in Oceana* and
　Supplement (McLean), **4:**628
annual collections, **1:**91–92
　battaglia, **1:**369
　branle, **1:**523
　contredanses, **1:**90
　cotillon, **1:**90
　country dance, **2:**255–256
　dance music, **4:**505, 510–511
　figure dances, **2:**592
　technical manuals, **6:**123
Annuario italiano della danza
　(Bucchi ed.), **3:**553
Annunciation Day, **2:**168
Annunzio, Gabriele d'. *See*
　d'Annunzio, Gabriele d'
Ano Cero, **2:**389
Anokhin, Boris, **4:**132
Anota, Philippe, **1:**375, **5:***681*
Another Goyescas, **4:**262
Another Story as in Falling, **1:**545
Another Time, Another Place, **1:**212
Another Touch of Klee, **3:**387
Anouih, Jean, **1:**305
Ansaldi, Marilena, **1:**537
Ansermet, Ernest, **1:**92–93, **4:**657,
　5:237
Ansky, S., **1:**439
ANTA (American National Theater
　and Academy), **1:**65, **4:**30
Antakirinya (people), **1:**229–230
Antar, **5:**690
Antares, **4:**397
Antes del Alba, **2:**277
Antheil, George, **3:**519
Anthony, Christine, **2:**469
Anthony, Gordon, **5:**185
　as photographer, **2:**397, 399,
　　3:305, **5:**650
Anthony, James R., *as contributor,*
　5:38–41
Anthony, Mary, **4:**212
Anthropology (Tylor), **3:**30
anthropology and dance. *See under*
　methodologies in the study of
　dance
Anthropometrics of the Blue Period
　(Klein exhibit), **1:**139
anthroposophy, **2:**18
Antic Meet, **2:**290
Antigone, **1:**429, **4:**266, 466
Antigone (Sophocles), **5:**192
Antigone/Rites of Passion (film),
　2:606, *607*
antimasque. *See* masque and
　antimasque
Antiodemes, **4:**427
Antipodes, The (Brome), **3:**252
Anti-Polkista ed i Polkamani, L',
　5:499–500
Antique Epigraphs, **4:**622,
　5:*366,* 367
Antique Feast, **3:**421

Antique Frieze, **3:**22
Antique Theater, Saint Petersburg, **1:**424, **2:**421
antiquity. *See specific countries, empires, and regions*
Antoinette Caribbean American Dance Company, L', **3:**575
Antología de Zarzuela, **1:**294
Anton, Miro, **6:**323
Antonia, **3:**203, **5:**301
Antonio and Rosario, **1:93–94**, 294, **3:**9–10, 11, **5:**674, **6:***120*
Antonio's Revenge (Marston), **3:**252
Antonolini, Ferdinand, **4:**278
Antonova, Vera. *See* Fokina, Vera
Antonović, Nela, **6:**435
Antony and Cleopatra (Barber opera), **1:**57
Antony and Cleopatra (Chernyshev ballet), **5:**472
Antwerp, Belgium, **1:**409, 410, 411
Antypova, Iroida, **6:**223
Anwar, Rafi, **1:94**, **5:**62
anyein dance theater, **4:**526–527
Anything Goes (film), **5:**163
Anything Goes (musical), **4:**419, **6:**277
Anzu, Furukawa, **2:**18
Apache (people), **4:***553*
apache dance, **1:**95, **4:**522, **5:***684*, **6:***270*, 316, 319
apala dance, **6:**16–17, 18
'aparima, **6:**79
apartheid, **2:**56, **5:**643, 655, 656, 657, 658, **6:**22
Apartment, The (film), **1:**419
Apelles et Campaspe, **4:**149, 696, **5:**371
Apelshoffer, Claudius, **1:**236
Aperova, Olympia, **6:**358
Aphin Music Library, Boston, **4:**168
Aphrodisiamania, **6:**111
Aphrodite (musical), **3:**21
Apokalyptische Reiter, **3:**152
Apolaustus, Memphis, **5:**73
Apollinaire, Guillaume, **1:**244, 323, **3:**393, **5:**237
Apollo (deity), **2:**156, **3:**287, 293, **4:**301, 499
Apollo (formerly *Apollon Musagète*), **1:95–96**, **4:***611*
Alonso (Alicia) performance, **1:**49
American Ballet premier, **1:**64, 96, *257*, 261
arabesque signature configuration, **1:**101
in Argentine ballet reportory, **1:**110
Balanchine on personal significance of, **4:**28
Balanchine revival, **4:**609, 622
in Balanchine's aesthetic progression, **1:**258, 259, 260, 261, 262, 267, 268, 269, 281, 325, **2:**410, **4:**613, **5:**208
Balanchine-Stravinsky collaboration, **1:**30, 256, **2:**407, **3:**337, **4:**516, 613, **6:**5
Bauchant costumes, **1:**95, 325, **2:***244*
Bolm performance, **1:**483, *483*
Christensen (Lew) performance, **2:**160
Craig on, **2:**263
d'Amboise performance, **2:**314
Danilova-Nikitina role alternation, **2:**342
Denby on, **2:**376
Diaghilev cuts, **1:**317
as Diaghilev production, **2:**406, 410

Doubrovska performance, **2:**441
in English National Ballet repertory, **2:**514
Farrell performance, **1:**96, **2:**576
Fernandez performance, **2:**586
Hamburg Ballet Stravinsky birthday presentation, **3:**337
Kaye performance, **3:**663
Kronstam performance, **4:**65
Le Clercq performance, **4:**137
Lifar performance, **4:**182, 620
Lukanov choreography, **2:**11
Martins performance, **4:**273
Maryinsky staging, **4:**285
in Royal Ballet repertory, **1:**155, **5:**417
in Royal Danish Ballet repertory, **5:**431
Tchelitchev design, **5:**547, **6:**119
Apollo and Daphne, **2:**414, **5:**504, 518
Apollo Distraught, **1:**52
Apollon (journal), **1:**254
Apollon et les Muses, **1:**355, **4:**149, 475
Apollon et Sa Méditation (Bourdelle), **1:**502
Apollonian Games, **4:**427
Apollon Législateur, ou Le Parnasse Réformé, **1:**284, 465
Apollon Musagète (Balanchine ballet). *See Apollo*
Apollon Musagète (Stravinsky), **5:**58
Apollo Placato, **2:**55
Apollo 65, **5:**653, 692
Apollo Theater, Harlem, **2:**186, 187, **4:**202, 629, **5:**601, **6:**317
Apologie de la danse (de Lauze), **1:**342, 523, **2:**255, 259, **3:**84, 124, **5:**345, 6, 122–123
Wildeblood translation, **3:**282
Apology (Plato), **5:**41
Apology for Dancing (Heppenstall), **3:**285
Aponte, Christopher, **3:**344
Apostate, The, **3:**391
Apothéose d'Hercule, L', **1:**236, **3:**189
Appalachian clogging, **2:**179, **180–181**, **3:**238, 608, **5:**696
Appalachian Spring, **1:96–97**, **3:***215*
archival materials, **4:**168
Copland score, **1:**96–97, **2:**196, 197–198, **3:**218, **4:**518
Cunningham performances, **2:**285, 286
Graham choreography, **1:**96, **3:**216
Hawkins performance, **3:**349
Noguchi scenic design, **1:**96, 97, 137, **3:***215*, **4:**659, **5:**547
Shaker dance, **5:**577
Speaking in Tongues comparison, **6:**109
Apparitions
Ashton production, **1:**148, 150, 152, **3:**354, 355, **5:***412*, 414
Beaton scenic design, **1:**395
English National Ballet revival, **1:**158, **2:**514
Fonteyn performance, **3:***40*, 355, **5:***412*
Helpmann performance, **3:**354, 355, **5:***412*
Karinska costumes, **3:**654
score, **4:**114
Appassionata, **2:**15, 97
Appel, Karel, **6:**90
Appel, Peter, **1:**374, **2:**470, **4:**600, **6:**364
Appel de la Montagne, L', **5:**132

Appeles e Campaspe, **4:**149
Appia, Adolphe, **1:97–98**, **3:**93, 558, 596, **4:**130, 189, **5:**540, 541, 547, **6:**161, 162
Appleton, Fanny, **5:**93
Applied Anatomy and Kinesiology (Bowen and McKenzie), **4:**16
Après-midi d'un Faune, L' (Amodio ballet), **1:**82
Après-midi d'un Faune, L' (Chouinard group choreography), **2:**46
Après-midi d'un Faune, L' (Maen ice dance), **2:**298, *298*
Après-midi d'un Faune, L' (Mallarmé poem), **1:**27, 28, 98, **4:**641
Après-midi d'un Faune, L' (Nijinsky ballet), **1:98–100**, 254, *319*, 320, 321, **2:**360, **3:**18, **4:***635*, **5:**182, *182*, 187, 192, 193, 299, 327
aesthetics, **2:**408, **4:**647, 648
Bakst decor, **1:**98, 99, 254, **2:**407, **6:**28
Chappell performance, **2:**105
choreographic description, **4:**641
Debussy music, **2:**360, 361, **4:**516, 641, 642
as Diaghilev production, **1:**98, **2:**360, 406, **3:**19
as English National Ballet production, **2:**512
Homage to Diaghilev program, **3:**75
Japanese stagings, **3:**589
Joffrey Ballet and Nureyev television program, **3:**616
Laing performance, **4:**109
Lichine performance, **4:**178
Nijinska performance, **4:**634, *635*
reconstruction and Labanotation, **4:**686, **5:**327
Robbins's *Afternoon of a Faun* vs., **1:**28, **5:**362
Rodin response, **1:**99, **5:**370
Schooling and Chappell reconstruction, **5:**560
Svetlov articles, **6:**28
Woizikowski staging, **6:**404
See also Afternoon of a Faun; Silent Cries
apsara dance, **2:**31
"Apu Inca" (dance), **5:**143, 144
Apuleius, **5:**377
aquacade, **5:**377
Aquathème, **1:**349
Aquile e Aquiloni, **6:**121
Aquino, Francisca Reyes, **1:**393, **5:**173, 174
Arab dance and music, **4:**467–468, **487–491**
bedouin dance, **1:**401–402, **2:**488–489, *488*, 492, **4:**415
Palestinians, **3:**605, **4:**358
See also Islam and dance; Middle East; North Africa; *specific countries*
Arabesk, **2:**11–12
Arabesque (journal), **4:**414
arabesque, **1:100–101**, 345, 348, **6:**62
arabesque à deux bras, **1:**100
arabesque à la lyre, **1:**100, 345
Arab Gulf States Folklore Centre, **4:**417
Arabian horse dancing, **2:**490–491
Arabian Peninsula, **1:101–102**
bedouin dance, **1:**401
combat dances, **4:**406, 407, 488
Islamic dance aesthetics, **1:**18–19

pearl fishing dance, **4:**489
Persian Gulf region, **3:**513–514
scholarly research, **4:**415, 417
Sulayb dance, **4:**408
See also Yemen
Arabic Suite, **5:**583
Arc, The, **4:**437
Aradi, Maria, **2:**470
Aragon, Louis, **1:**462
aragoto (*kabuki* style), **3:**437, 438, 439, 638, 639
Arai Shisui, **4:**333
Araiz, Oscar, **1:102–103**, **2:**39, 361, **5:**97, 200, 269, 685
Argentinian ballet, **1:**112, 113, 114
Geneva Ballet, **1:**103, **6:**52
Romeo and Juliet versions, **1:**103, **5:**398–399
Royal Winnipeg Ballet, **5:**436
Arakanese (people), **4:**524
Aranda (people), **1:**229
Araneda, Luis Eduarado, **2:**126
Aranguiz, Maria Elena, **2:**123
Aranya Amirita, **2:**102
Aranyváry, Emilia, **3:**414
Arapoff, Cyril, *as photographer*, **3:**265, **6:**196
Arapov, Pimen, **3:**539
Arashi Kichisaburō (Arashi Rikan I), **4:**537
Arashiyama, **4:**41
Ara the Beautiful, **1:**122
Araujo, Loipa, **2:**200, 279, 280
Arawak (people), **2:**62, **3:**120, 573
Arbatov, Ilya, **1:**121, **3:**125, **6:**306
Arbatova, Mia, **3:**534
Arbat Theater, Moscow, **1:**485
Arbeau, Thoinot, **1:**22, **103–107**, 146, **5:**111, 118, 244, 336, 341
on allemande, **1:**45–46
bassedanse choreographies, **1:**379
"Bouffons, Les," **1:**104–105, 369, **2:**591, **4:**460
on branle, **1:**104, 522–523, *522*, **2:**383, 471, 474, 565, 591
Caroso comparison, **2:**74
on *courante*, **2:**259
dance manual authorship, **2:**73, 74, 168, 336, 542, **5:**109, 114, 115, 338, **6:**122
on feet position, **1:**331
on figure dances, **2:**591
on function of social dances, **5:**619
on *galliard* movement, **3:***108*, 109
on gavotte, **1:**104, **3:**123
matachins choreography, **4:**326–427, *326*, *327*
on *moresca*, **4:**462
musical examples, **4:**506–507
Negri comparison, **4:**579
notation method, **4:**683–684
on pavane, **5:**620
on *révérence*, **5:**345
on Scottish branles, **2:**474
tabulature, **1:***104*
on tordion, **6:**178
on turnout, **6:**215
on *volta*, **6:**349–350, 351
Arbriscula, **4:**427
Arcade, **2:**294, 296, 469
Arcadia (Sannazaro), **5:**113
Arcana, **1:**462
Arcaño, Antonio, **2:**275
Archaic Fragments, **2:**357
Archer, Kenneth, **2:**254, 463, **3:**617, **5:**327, *327*, **6:**455
Archer, Robyn, **1:**216
Archers, The (radio serial), **4:**335
Archetypes, **1:**141

Archilochus, **2:**419, **3:**645
Archimedes, **4:**13
Archipova, Valentine, **3:**534
Architectura civilis (Furtenbach), **4:**188
architecture, **1:**132, **3:**621, 622
 kabuki theater, **3:**637–638
 See also theaters for dance
Architettura civile, L (Bibiena), **1:**447
Archive for Folk Dance (Sweden), **6:**36
Archive of Puerto Rican Composers, **5:**275
archives. *See* libraries and museums
Archives internationales de la danse, Les (journal), **5:**220
Archives Internationales de la Danse, Les (Paris), **3:**40, 72, 76, 305, 312, 507, 627, **4:**161
Arcimbolo, **4:**81
Arcona, **1:**508, 511, 515
Arcot, Suman, **5:**330
Arctic dance
 Native American traditions, **4:**551, 553, 570–574
 Siberian traditions, **2:**140, **5:**445–449
Arctic Winter Games, **4:**571
'*ardah* dance, **4:**406, 488
àrdeleana dances, **5:**380, *381*
Ardell, Anita, **1:**212
Arden, Donn, **1:**466
Arden Court, **4:**482, **6:**110, 111
Ardent Song, **3:**218
Ardolino, Emile, **1:**80, **6:**138
areito (areyto), **2:**62, 430, **4:**384, **5:**274
Arena, **4:**602, **6:**146, 363
Arena, Antonius de, **1:**103, **107–108**, **2:**336, **5:**114, 336
 branle description, **1:**522
 dance manual authorship, **6:**122
 révérence descriptions, **5:**343–344
 tordion description, **6:**178
Arends, Andrei, **3:**204
Arènes, Antoine d'. *See* Arena, Antonius de
Arens, Richard, **6:**172
Arensky, Anton, **2:**397, **3:**15, 16, 17, 186, 568, **5:**691
Arent, Hans-Christian, **4:**683
 as contributor, **4:**673–675, 676–681
Aréthuse ou La Vengeance de l'Amour, **2:**34
Areyto (dance company), **5:**275
Argentina, **1:108–114**
 ballet, **1:110–111**, 314, 315, **2:**587–588
 folk and traditional dance, **1:108–110**, **3:**35, 36
 modern dance, **1:111–114**
 tango, **1:**108, **4:**632, **5:**627, **6:**91–92, 94
 See also Teatro Colón, Buenos Aires
Argentina, La, **1:114–116**, **2:**78, 409, 521, **3:**9, 11, 72, **5:**33, 673–674
Argentine Classical Ballet Foundation, **2:**588
Argentinita, La, **1:116–117**, 296, **2:**567, **3:**9, 101, 102, **4:**395, **5:**316, 674
 Greco association, **3:**286, *286*
 Massine collaboration, **2:**108, **4:***323*, 324
 sister López (Pilar), **4:**222–223

Vargas (Manolo) association, **6:**407
Arguel, Mireille, **3:**83
Argus (Russian journal), **3:**14
Argyle, Pearl, **1:**148, 307, **2:**173
 Rambert Dance Company, **5:**296, 298, 299, *299*, 300
Ari, Carina, **1:117–118**, **5:**95, **6:**41
Aria, **1:**388, *389*
Ariadne, **4:**602
Ariadne (mythic), **2:**270, 271, **4:**106
Ariadne et Bacchus, **3:**258, **4:**276
Ariadone no Kai, **2:**18
Arianna (Gluck opera), **3:**189
Arianna in Creta, **4:**509
Arien, **1:**388, *389*
ario, **5:**78–80
Ariodante (Handel), **4:**509, **5:**35
Arion, **2:**419
Ariosto, Ludovico, **1:**285, **5:**534
Aripova, Dina, **5:**462, 472
Aris, Michael, **1:**458
Aristakessian, Vahram, **1:**120, 121
Aristophanes, **2:**234, 419, 506, **3:**288, 290, 294, 646
 kordax dances, **4:**44
 schēma, **5:**556–556
Aristotle, **1:**20, 22, **2:**419, 428, **3:**291
 on choral odes, **3:**428
 kinesiology, **4:**13
Arizona State University Dance Line, **2:***323*
Arizona Yaqui, **6:**416
arja, **1:**174, **3:482–483**, 485, 644, 645, **4:**298
Arja, Keni, **3:**502
arja telu, **3:**644
Arjuna wiwaha ringgit (Javanese poem), **6:**369
Arkas, Nikolai, **6:**224–225
Arlecchinata, **1:**483
Arledge, Sarah, **2:**604
Arlen, Harold, **1:**194, **6:**256
Arlequin, **5:**198
Arlequin, Magicien par Amour, **6:**48
Arlequin Péruvien, **5:**198
Arlequin-Pluton, **2:**365
Arlésienne, L', **2:**513, **5:**97, 164, 431
Arlichino Fortunato nell'Amore, **2:**54
arm (body part). *See* ballet technique, arm positions; *port de bras*
armadillo-shell mandolin, **2:**194
Armand, Patrick, **2:***511*, 513, **5:**394
Armand, Tylda, **1:**410
armed dances, **1:118–119**
 Albania, **1:**34
 Alexandrian, **2:**490
 Algeria, **1:**40, 41, 42
 Arbeau descriptions, **1:**104–105
 Argentina, **1:**109
 Australian Aborigines, **1:**221, 226
 Bali, **2:**232, **3:**477–478, *479*
 barriera, torneo, and *battaglia*, **1:**368–369
 bedouin, **2:**488–489, *488*
 Berber, **4:**465, 467
 as calypso antecedent, **2:**65
 central Africa, **2:**87
 China, **1:**164, **2:**129, 132
 Croatia, **6:**429, *429*
 Egypt, **2:**490, 491, 493, *493*, **4:***405*, 488
 Ethiopia, **2:**533, *534*
 European traditional, **2:***552*, 553, 554–555
 Fiji, **2:**593
 Georgia, **3:**134
 Germany, **3:**139

Ghana, 164–165
Greece, ancient, **3:***290*, 291
Japan, **1:***167*, **3:***580*
Java, **3:**495
Lebanon, **4:**136
Malaysia, **4:**249
Manipur, **4:**253
Manx, **3:**251
Maori, **4:**260–262, *260*
Melanesia, **4:***352*
Middle East, **4:**404–406, *405*
Middle Eastern women's, **4:**406
Nubian, **2:**492
Philippines, **2:**230
Russia, **5:***444*
Rwanda, **6:***20*
Sikkim, **5:**599
Turkey, **6:**211, *212*
 women's weapons dances, **4:**407
Yemen, **4:**410, 417, **6:***418*, 419
 See also Asian martial arts; Sword Dance; sword dances
Arme Fischer, Der, **6:**75
Armenia, **1:119–122**
 dance research, **1:**120–121
 theatrical dance, **1:121–122**, **3:**125
 traditional dance, **1:119–121**, **3:**513, **4:**68–69, **5:**482
Armenia, L', **3:**511
Armenian Ballet Company, **1:***122*
Armenian State Dance Ensemble, **1:**121
Armenian State Ensemble for Folk Singing and Dancing, **1:**121
Armfelt, Hélène, **3:**512
Armida, **2:**95, **4:**264, **5:**140, 425
Armida Abbandonata da Rinaldo, **2:**208
Armida e Rinaldo, **5:**231
Armidale Summer Schools (Australia), **1:**213, 217
Armide (Elssler ballet), **2:**503, **5:**134
Armide (Gluck opera), **2:**412, **3:**117
Armide (Lully opera), **4:**235
Armide et Renaud, **4:**109
Armilla, ossia La Cetra Incantata, **3:**97
Arminio, **4:**694
Armistead, Horace, **6:**201
Armitage, Karole, **1:**76, 142, **2:**19, 289, 607, 609, **4:**37, **5:**8, 98
Arm of the Blue Sky, The, **6:**145
Armory Show, New York City (1913), **6:**243, 357
Armour, Thomas, **6:**264
Armour, Toby, **3:**634, **6:**362, 363
arms (body part). *See* ballet technique, arm positions; *port de bras*
Armstrong, Kay, **4:**539, **5:**61
Armstrong, Nancy, **2:**570
Army Artistic Ensemble, Prague, **2:**309
Arnason, Jon, **3:**434
Arnaud, Baculard d', **1:**35
Arnaudova, M., **2:**11–12
Arnault, Andrew, *as photographer*, **3:**661
Arne, Thomas, **3:**378
Arnebom, Arne, **6:**433
Arnell, Richard, **2:**265
Arnheim, Daniel, **4:**17
Arnheim, D. D., **2:**330
Arnheim, Rudolf, **1:**24
Arnhem, Netherlands, **4:**596, 597
Arnhem Land, Australia, **1:**219, 220, 223–224, *223*
Arnold, Alison, *as contributor*, **2:**621–629
Arnold, Becky, **2:**605, **3:**235

Arnold, Malcolm, **2:**266
Arnold, Ronne, **1:**212
Arnon, Yehudit, **3:**532
Arnot, Paul d', **3:**76
Arnould-Mussot, Jean-François, **1:**122–124, **2:**442, 443, **5:**198
Arnout, Jean-Baptiste, **6:***158*
Arnsheimer, Johann, **5:***158*
Arnshtam, L., **4:**132
Arntz, Jan, **2:**470
Aromaa, Jukka, **2:**633, **3:***53*
Aronson, Arnold, *as contributor*, **5:**532–552
Aronson, Boris, **1:**74
Around the Coasts of Arabia (Rihani), **4:**416
Around the Hall in Texas, **5:**587
Around the World in Eighty Days (musical spectacle), **1:**496, **4:**23
Arova, Sonia, **1:**65, 306, 316, **3:**362, **4:**380, 677, **5:**5, 166
 Australian Ballet *Swan Lake* performance, **1:**210, 230
 Bruhn dance partnership, **2:**3, 4
 Japanese productions, **3:**589
Arpino, Gerald, **1:124–125**, **2:**269, **3:**360
 Bal, Le, **3:***611*
 controversial choreography, **3:**612–613
 Joffrey Ballet, **3:**610, 611, 612–615, 617
Arpino Ballet Chicago, Inc., **3:**617
Arraignment of Paris (Peele), **3:**253
arrasta-pé, **1:**529
Arrieta, Luis, **1:***533, 534*, 536
Arrivo di Venere nell'Isola di Cipro, L', **2:**55
Arrow against Profane and Promiscuous Dancing Drawn out of the Quiver of the Scriptures, An (Mather), **2:**167, 339
Arrow of Time, **2:**359
Arseniev, Mikhail, **5:**473
Arshansky, Michael, **5:**264
art. *See* artists and dance; caricature and comic art; photography; prints and drawings; scenic design; *specific artists, movements, and works*
Artaud, Antonin, **1:**135, 246, **2:**288
Art Deco, **1:**147
Art du Balet de Cour en France 1581–1643, L', **3:**283
Arteaga, Stefano, **3:**364
Arte de danzar à la francesa (Minguet e Yrol), **5:**690, **6:**124
Arte del danzare, L' (Cornazano), **1:**351
Artemis (belly dancer), **2:***344*
Artemis Troublée, **1:**255, **3:**320, **5:**438
Arte saltandi and choreas dulcendi, De (Domenico da Piacenza), **2:**427
Art et instruction de bien dancer, L' (anonymous, printed by Toulouze), **1:**378, **2:**336, **4:***683*, **5:**260, 336, **6:**122
"art-for-art's sake" movement, **1:**23, **3:**122, 180, **5:**108
Art History Institute, Bucharest, **4:**162
Arthur, John, **5:**70
Arthur Murray Dance Studios. *See* Murray, Arthur
Arthur Murray Party, The (television program), **4:**480

Artifact, **3:**52
Artifact 2, **6:**143
Art in Indonesia (Holt), **3:**506
Artistes, Les, **4:**339
Artistic Ensemble of the Polish
    Army, **3:**192
artists and dance, **1:125–144**
    ancient Greek portrayals of
        dancers, **2:***157*
    Armory Show's significance
        (1913), **6:**243
    art historians' African mask
        studies, **6:**25
    Ausdruckstanz, **1:**203–204,
        6:389–390
    avant-garde, **1:**243–244, 245, 246,
        544, 545, **6:**250
    Ballets Suédois productions,
        1:326, 327–328
    Ballet-Théâtre Contemporain,
        1:349
    Barre portrait statuettes, **1:**368
    Bauhaus, **1:**132, 138, 244,
        385–387
    Bodenwieser technique, **1:**468
    Bourdelle sculptures, **1:**502
    Brazilian Modernist movement,
        1:534, 535
    Canadian modern dance, **2:**39,
        40, 43
    caricature and comic art, **2:**67–72
    Catlin's Native American studies,
        4:*552, 553, 559*, 561
    Chalon's Romantic-era portraits
        and prints, **2:**103–104
    China, **2:***128, 129*
    collaboration, **1:141–144,**
        296–297, 298, 316–318, 327,
        544, 545, **2:**22, 241, 242,
        245, **3:**72
        Canfield, **2:**53–54
    Childs choreographies, **2:**119
    Chuma, Yoshiko, **2:**170–171
    Cocteau, Jean, **2:**182
    Cunningham, Merce, **2:**286,
        292, 607–608
    Diaghilev's Ballets Russes,
        1:133–135, 254–255, 316–317,
        318, 322–323, 422, **2:**406–410,
        3:71, 262–263, 265,
        4:124–125, 316, 317–318,
        515–516, 647, **5:**540–543
    Dunn, Douglas, **2:**460–461
    Dunn, Robert Ellis, **2:**461–462
    Fuller, Loie, **3:**92–96
    Johns, Jasper, **3:**619–620
    Lander, Harald, **4:**118
    as Massine focus, **4:**315,
        320, 324
    Noguchi and Graham, **4:**659
    See also designing for dance
    Cunningham influences, **2:**286,
        292, **6:**356
    Dances of Death iconography,
        2:331–332
    Degas's Paris Opera illustrations,
        2:361, 362–363
    early modernism, **4:**647–648
    Elssler and Taglioni depictions,
        2:503
    film use, **2:**603–612
    Foregger's influence, **3:**48
    Gauguin influence on Nijinsky,
        4:642, 644
    Karinska costume executions,
        3:653–6
    Kirstein associations, **4:**26, 27,
        28, 29–30
    Lehmann portrait of Nielsen,
        4:632

masquerade dance
    representations, **4:**315
medieval Christian portrayals of
    dancers, **2:**166
New York School, **2:**374–376
Palucca-inspired artworks
    exhibit, **5:**66
Parisian scene, **3:**71
photographic influences,
    5:178, 180
Rodin works, **5:**370–371
Russian ballet influences, **6:**456
Thorvaldsen influence on
    Bournonville, **1:**508
Walkowitz studies of Duncan,
    1:*131*, **6:**356
See also caricature and comic art;
    photography; prints and
    drawings; scenic design;
    *specific artists; specific artists
    and art works*
Artists and Models of 1924 (revue),
    6:272
Artists of the Dance (Moore), **4:**457
Art Nouveau, **1:**129
    Bakst scenic designs, **2:**241,
        5:541
    Fuller performance symbolism,
        3:92
    Korovin designs, **4:**56
    Rose designs, **5:**405
    Vienna Secessionists, **1:**239
Art of Dance, The (Hartong),
    4:600
Art of Dancing (Ferrero), **2:**571,
    6:239
Art of Dancing, The (Tomlinson),
    1:342, **4:**105, 431, 684, **5:**324,
    346, *520*, **6:**123, 175–176
Art of Indonesia (Holt), **3:**472
Art of Making Dances, The
    (Humphrey), **2:**287, **3:**404
art-of-movement schools
    (Hungary), **3:**420, 421
Art of Movement Studio,
    Manchester (later Surrey),
    3:271, 277, **4:**94, 103
"Art of Noises" (Russolo), **1:**134
Art of Terpsichore, The (Albertieri),
    1:37, **6:**128
Art of the Dance, **2:**110
Art of the Dance, The (Duncan),
    2:456
Art of the Theatre, The (Craig),
    4:189
Art of Touch, The, **2:**355–356
Arts, Les, **1:**288
Arts and Entertainment (cable
    network), **6:**140
Arts Council of England, **4:**223,
    6:136
Arts Council of Ireland, **3:**520
Arts Educational Trust, Great
    Britain, **3:**307
Arts et Mouvement center, Paris,
    4:688
Arts Florissants, Les, **5:***324*
Arts Theatre Ballet, **3:**62, **4:**110,
    153, **6:**214
Artus Company, The, **3:**421
Artus-Sage, **3:**360
Aruoba, Oya, **6:**213
Arval Brethren Hymn, **6:**193
Arval Brothers (Collegium Fratrum
    Arvalium), **3:**541
Arvanites (people), **3:**296
Arvelo, Ritva, **2:**635
Asafiev, Boris, **1:144–145**, 308,
    2:11, 72, **3:**206, **4:**226, **5:**9,
    616, **6:**310

ballet scores, **4:**517, **6:**441, 442
children's operas, **4:**641
Fountain of Bakhchisarai score,
    3:56, 192, 195, **5:**471, **6:**441
Institute of the History of the
    Arts, **5:**483
Little Humpbacked Horse pas de
    deux, **4:**212
on *Nutcracker* production, **3:**563
Prisoner of the Caucasus score,
    4:131
See also Flames of Paris, The
asafu dance, **4:**485
Asakawa, Takako, **1:**56, **3:**220, 591
Asami Maki Ballet, **3:**589
Asante (Ashanti) (people), **2:**211,
    3:164, 165, 170, **6:**24
Åsberg, Margaretha, **1:145, 6:**45
Asbestos-kan, **3:**363
As Bodas, **1:***534*
ASCAP (American Society of
    Composers, Authors and
    Publishers), **6:**280–281
Ascensio, Manola, **3:**344
Ascham, Roger, **3:**281
Aschar, Dalal, **1:**533, 537
Aschenbrödel (Cinderella), **1:**239,
    2:173, **6:**3, 335
Aschengreen, Erik, **1:**513, **2:**387,
    3:180
    as contributor, **1:**454, 497–498,
        2:2–5, 182–183, 384–386,
        386–388, **3:**12–13, 373, 657,
        667–668, **4:**64–65, 119, **5:**295,
        423–433, 553–555
As Commanded, **2:**473
Ascona colony, Lake Maggiore,
    6:51–52, 389
"Ascot Gavotte, The" (*My Fair
    Lady*), **2:**618
Asel, **2:**564, 565, **6:**171, 341
Asenjo y Barbieri, Francisco, **5:**676
As Fall Women, So Fall Women,
    5:*659*
Ásgeirsson, Jón, **3:**437
Ash, **4:**622
Ashanti region. *See* Asante
Ashbery, John, **2:**376
Ashbridge, Bryan, **1:**499, **4:**624
Ashbridge, Dorothea, **4:**627
Ashcroft, W. J., **4:**520
ashek dance, **4:**250–251
Ashentrupp, Roberto, *as
    photographer*, **4:**387
Asheville Rhododendron Festival,
    North Carolina, **2:**180
Ashigaga Yoshimitsu, **3:**650,
    6:445, 446
Ashihara Eiryo, **3:**588, 592
Ashikawa Yoko, **3:**363
Ashik-Kerib, **1:**144
Ashkenazic Judaism, **3:**526–527,
    528, 602, 605
Ashkhabad Opera and Ballet
    Theater, Turkmenistan, **6:**213
Ashley, Merrill, **1:**294, **4:**611, 618,
    621, 622, **6:**65, 129
Ashley, Robert, **1:**544
Ashley, Wayne, *as contributor*,
    6:147
Ashman, Verona, **3:**575
Ashmole, David, **5:**55
Ashmore, Catherine, *as
    photographer*, **1:**51, **2:**511,
    512, **3:**270, **5:**304, 421
Ashnak, Armenia, **1:**120
Ashour, Ahmed, **2:**497
Ashrafi, Mokhtar (Mukhtar), **2:**497,
    3:568
Ashriel, Yoav, **3:**531

Ashton, Frederick, **1:**24, 38,
    145–159, 242, **2:**269, 510,
    3:59, 285, **5:**513, 526, 564,
    639, **6:**312
    allegro style, **1:**44–45
    archival materials, **4:**164
    Beaton scenic design, **1:**395
    Beriosova roles, **1:**429–430
    Berners scores, **1:**437–438
    on *Biches, Les*, **1:**449
    as Bintley influence, **1:**453, **3:**268
    as British school exemplar, **1:**349
    Cecchetti as influence, **1:**329,
        2:84
    Chappell collaboration, **2:**105
    choreographic style, **3:**265–266,
        267, **5:**419
    choreography compared with de
        Valois's, **2:**399
    choreography compared with
        Howard's (Andrée), **3:**391
    choreography compared with
        Tudor's, **6:**195
    Cinderella en travesti role, **1:***150*,
        151, 233, **2:**174, **6:**190
    costumes, **2:**244
    Creatures of Prometheus revival,
        1:402
    as de Valois protégé, **2:**398, 401,
        3:264
    Devil's Holiday, **1:**149, 297, 437
    Don Juan, **2:**434
    Dowell roles, **2:**443–444
    English National Ballet
        productions, **1:**158,
        2:510, 514
    Enigma Variations, **2:**515–516,
        5:417
    Euclidian geometry use, **5:**531
    Façade, **5:**412, 653
    Farron roles, **2:**578
    Fedorovitch costume designs,
        2:582, 583
    film choreographies, **5:**589
    Fonteyn roles, **3:***40*, 41–42, 44,
        45, 46, 265, **5:**416
    Franklin roles, **3:**87
    Grant roles, **3:**236–237
    Helpmann roles, **3:**355, 357
    Homage to the Queen, **1:**153,
        2:590, **3:**345
    Horoscope, **1:**148, 149,
        3:379–380, **5:**414
    jazz ballet, **1:**147, 520
    Joffrey Ballet revivals, **3:**614,
        615, 616
    Karinska costumes, **3:**654
    on Karsavina's style, **3:**656
    Lambert musical collaboration,
        4:114, 115, 517
    Lanchbery musical collaboration,
        4:117
    Lloyd (Maude) roles, **4:**215
    Makarova roles, **4:**248, 249
    Markova roles, **4:**267, 268
    Masques, Les, **5:**560
    as Massine student, **4:**319
    May (Pamela) roles, **4:**336
    Messel designs, **4:**358
    musical theater productions,
        1:147, 520
    National Ballet of Canada
        productions, **4:**541, 544
    National Ballet of Canada
        repertory, **4:**541
    Nerina roles, **1:**158, **4:**485, 584
    New York City Ballet guest
        choreography, **1:**152, 153,
        4:29, 608
    Nijinska association, **4:**635,
        638, 648

Nutcracker, The, **1:**153, **5:**15
PACT Ballet repertory, **5:**653
partnering technique, **5:**104
on Pavlova, **5:**126–127
Pavlova as influence, **3:**263
Péri, La, **5:**133, 298–299
Petipa choreography as model, **5:**531
Pomona, **4:**113
Quest, The, **5:**588
Rambert association, **2:**105, **3:**263, **5:**296, 297, 298, *298,* 299, 300, 303
Rassine association, **5:**312
Royal Ballet, **1:**146–155, 155–159, 459, **2:**403, **3:**264, 267, **5:**300, 412, 413, 414–415, 417, **6:**201
Royal Swedish Ballet guest production, **6:**43, *43,* 44
Royal Winnipeg Ballet guest productions, **5:**437, *437*
Rubinstein ballet company, **4:**635
Sleeping Beauty, The, **1:**146, **5:**612, 613, **6:**137
Somes roles, **5:**639
as Soviet choreographic influence, **5:**460
Swan Lake, **5:**597
Swan Lake additions, **5:**597, **6:**33, *33*
symphonic ballet, **4:**322
television productions, **6:**137
Valse, La, **5:**316
Valses Nobles et Sentimentales, **5:**316
Wells (Doreen) roles, **6:**380
World War II service, **5:**415
See also Apparitions; Birthday Offering; Daphnis and Chloe; Dream, The; Fille Mal Gardée, La; Illuminations; Marguerite and Armand; Monotones; Month in the Country, A; Ondine; Patineurs, Les; Rendezvous, Les; Romeo and Juliet; Scènes de Ballet; Sylvia; Symphonic Variations; Two Pigeons; Wedding Bouquet, A
Ashton, Gwynne, **5:**653
Ashton, Horace D., *as photographer,* **1:**40
Ashton-Sikora, Martha Bush, *as contributor,* **4:**65–66, **6:**413–414
Ash Wednesday, **5:**211
Asian Arts Ensemble, **2:**32
Asian Cultural Council, **2:**146
Asian Dance Archive, **4:**167, **5:**48
Asian dance traditions, **1:160–184**
    aesthetics, **1:16–18**
    background and overview, **1:160–177**
    costume, **2:213–232**
    influence of puppetry, **1:178–180**
        bunraku, **2:**12–14
        See also puppetry *as separate listing*
    mask and makeup, **4:294–300**
    mime, **4:**423
    music, **4:491–495**
    notation, **4:**693
    religious, philosophical, and environmental influence, **1:180–184**
    Western dance versus, **1:**160–164
    See also specific countries
Asian Folk Dance and Music Festival, Dacca, **1:**394
Asian martial arts, **1:184–189**
    Chinese dance, **2:**129, 132, 144

Indian *chhau* dances, **2:**117–119, **3:**468
Indian *kathakaḷi* dance, **2:**223, **3:**453
Javanese *pencak,* **1:**174, 187, **3:**500–501, 503
Thai *khōn* dance, **4:**8, 10
asian Music (periodical), **4:**54
Asian New Dance Coalition, **4:**141
Asian Traditional and Contemporary Dance and Music Festival, **4:**141
Asian Traditions, **1:**274
Así Es La Vida (film), **6:***92*
As I Lay Dying, **1:**441
asimetrik. See Faeroe step
Asioli, Bonifazio, **5:**276
Asi Somos, **2:**281
As It is Forever, **4:**627
Asker, Don, **1:**213, 215, 218, **4:**602
Askew, Kelly M., *as photographer,* **2:**91, **4:**287
Askill, Michael, **4:**479
Asking the Woodsman, **2:***131*
Ask Mr. Snail, **4:**22
Askold's Tomb (Verstovsky), **1:**86
Åsmann, Egil, **4:**677
Asmat (people), **3:**471–472, 504, **4:***496,* **5:**524
Asmus, Harry, **5:***612*
Asnes, Andrew, **5:**679, 680
Aspinall, S., **2:**37, 47
Asplmayr, Franz, **3:**187, 189, **4:**696
Asquith, Herbert, **3:**558
Asquith, Ruby, **1:**279, **2:**160, 161
Assam, India, **2:**394
Assedio di Calais, L', **5:**277
assemblé, **1:**341, **3:**124
assemblies, **1:189–190,** 279
Assembly Ball, **3:**392
Assembly of Heroes, An, **6:**421
Assen, F., **2:**69
Association for the Promotion of Folk Dance, Denmark. *See* Foreningen til Folkedansens Fremme
Association of Dance and Eurhythmics, Athens, **3:**304
Association of Dance and Mime Artists (ADMA), **3:**275
Association of Dance Professionals, Brazil, **5:**43
Association of Hungarian Dance Artists, **3:**424, **4:**529
Association of Operatic Dancing of Great Britain. *See* Royal Academy of Dancing
Association of Theaters in Emilia-Romagna. *See* Aterballetto
Associazione Italiana Attività di Danza, **3:**554
Associazione Italiana par la Musica e la Danza Antiche, **3:**556
Associazione Nazionale Insegnanti Danza (ANID), **3:**552
Associazione Nazionale Liberi Insegnanti Danza (ANLID), **3:**552, 553
Associazione Teatri Emilia-Romagna. *See* Aterballetto
Assyrian Dance, **5:***122*
Astafieva, Serafina, **2:**404, 423, **3:**40, **4:**110, 152
    Nádasi dance partnership, **4:**529
    students, **4:**267, 268, **5:**296
Astaire, Adele, **1:**191–192, **2:**250, **4:**168, 229, 420, **6:**318
    Bradley choreography, **1:**520, **6:**256
    Broadway musicals, **6:**274, 275

Wayburn training, **6:**371
Ziegfeld Follies, **6:**448
Astaire, Fred, **1:**37, **190–195,** 520, **2:**80, 584, **4:**229, 419, 420, **5:**239, 630, **6:**281
    archival material, **4:**168
    Charisse (Cyd) film dance partnership, **1:**194, *194,* **2:**108, 109, *109,* 616
    dance costume, **2:**250, *250,* 251
    Hollywood musicals, **2:**613, 614, *615,* 616, 617, 618
    Kelly (Gene) film dance style comparison, **4:**2
    as MacMillan influence, **4:**239
    musical theater, **6:**273–274, 275, *275,* 276
    as photographic subject, **5:**183
    Rogers dance partnership, **1:**191, 193, 194, **5:**372, 373, *373*
    tap dance, **6:**100, 101, *101*
    vaudeville, **6:**318
    Wayburn training, **6:**371
    Ziegfeld Follies, **6:**448
Astarte, **2:**606, **3:**615, **4:**519, **5:**551
As the Audience Enters, **5:**440
As Thousands Cheer (musical), **4:**420
Astier, Régine, **5:**327, 490
    as contributor, **1:**3–5, 355–356, 396–397, 464–465, **2:**27–29, 451, 588–590, **3:**122, 329, **4:**108–109, 130–131, 152, 262–263, **5:**128–129, 248–250, 307–309, 489–490, 503–505, **6:**11
As Time Goes By, **3:**616, **6:**153
Astley, Philip, **2:**175
Astol, Félix, **2:**64
Astolfi, Luigi, **1:**237, *238,* **2:**208, **5:**499
Astolphe et Joconde, **1:**202, **3:**360, **4:**138
Aston, Hugh, **3:**376
Astral, **1:**349
Astral Convertible, **1:**545, **5:**314, *314*
Astral Years, **3:**421
Astro degli Afghan, L', **5:**245
Astuzie Femminili, Le, **5:**636
Astyanax (Kreutzer opera), **4:**61
A suos compagnones studiantes (Arena), **6:**178
Aswan High Dam, **2:**491
Asylbashev, Melisbek, **4:**87
Asylmuratova, Altynai, **4:**257, *284,* 285, 456, **5:**465
As You Like It (Shakespeare), **3:**252
At, Betrand d', **1:**308
Atah Kim, **3:**468
Atala (Chateaubriand), **3:**358
Atalanta (Ashley), **1:**544
Atalanta of the East, **4:**109, **6:**196
Ataljanc, Ashen, **6:**434
Atanasiu, Mihaela, **5:**387
Atanasoff, Cyril, **1:**195–196, 405, **2:**114, 199, **3:**82, **5:**97, **6:**64
Atelier de la Danse, L', Paris, **3:**76, 83
Ateliers de Danse Moderne de Montréal, Les, **2:**48
Atellan farce, **5:**376
A.T.E.R. *See* Aterballetto
Aterballetto, **1:**83, **96,** 446, **3:**52, 552, 553, **6:**143
Athabaskan (people), **4:**570, 573–574
Atharvaveda, **3:**453, 454
Athenaeus, **1:**20, **2:**159, 506, **3:**293, **5:**557
    on *hyporchēma,* **3:**428
    on *kordax* as vulgar, **4:**44

Atheneos, Cleo, **3:**404
Athéniens, Les, **1:**409
Athens (city-state), **2:**419, **3:**287, 288–291
Athens (modern Greece), **3:**299, 300, 301
Athletes and Dancers (Australia), **1:**214
athletic shoes, **3:**46
At Home Abroad (musical), **5:**239
Atis och Camilla, **6:**47
Atkins, Charles ("Cholly"), **2:**186, 187, **5:**632, **6:**288
Atkins, Robert, **4:**153
Atkinson, Madge, **3:**271, 277
Atkinson, Margaret F., **6:**128
At Land, **2:**603
Atlanta Ballet, **1:196–197, 2:**357
    Alexander, Dorothy, **1:**39, 196, **6:**264, 265, 266
    Blair *Swan Lake* production, **1:**71, 459, **6:**34
    Cleveland-San Jose Ballet collaboration, **1:**197, **2:**178
    Lavrovsky (Mikhail) choreography, **4:**134
    as oldest American ballet company, **6:**264
    regional ballet festival, **6:**266
Atlanta Civic Ballet Junior Group, **6:***265*
Atlanta Journal, **6:**299
Atlántida, **2:**568
Atlas (Monk opera), **4:**451
Atlas, Charles, **1:**142, **2:**294, 460, 607, 609
Atlas, Consuelo, **1:**57
Atlas Eclipticalis (Cage), **2:**23, 292
Atmanetya, **3:**497
At Midnight, **1:**72, 73, **2:**583, 584, **3:**306, **5:**47, **6:**43
Aṭrash, Farīd al-, **4:**489
Atsugewi (people), **4:**566
Atsugi Bonjin, **3:**591
Attaingnant, Pierre, **1:**369, 523, **3:**106, **4:**502, 505, **6:**178
attan, **1:**27
attaprakāras, **4:**80
Attard, Vicki, **1:**211, *232,* 235
Attaway, Larry, **4:**157
At the Café Fleurette, **6:**363
At the Hallelujah Gardens, **6:**362
At the Hawk's Well (Yeats), **3:**519, 558–559, 651, 652
    Matsui staging, **4:**332, *333*
At the Market, **5:**387
At the Periphery of Life, **3:**329
At the Still Point. See Still Point, The
At the Vintage, **3:**409
Attila, **1:**88
attitude (ballet position), **1:197–198**
attitude and shawl dance (genre), **1:198–199, 2:**176, **5:**240
Atys, **4:**109, 152, 235, **5:***324*
Au, Susan, *as contributor,* **1:**27–29, 35–37, 47–48, 368, 394, 394–395, 502, **2:**60–61, 67–72, 80, 93–95, 103–104, 106–108, 171–172, 201–204, 333–334, 389–390, 405, 405–406, 502–506, 568–569, 582–583, **3:**2–4, 4–5, 46–48, 177–184, 185, 321–322, 620, **4:**116, 138, 176–178, 338–339, 339–343, 343–344, 346–347, 357–358, 452–456, **5:**29, 85, 132–133, 223, 240–243, 257–263, 270–271, 610–613, 615–616, 640–641, 641–642, **6:**57–59, 104–105, 117–119, 216–217

Aubade, **3:**74, 601, **4:**185, **5:**237, 238
Au Bal, **5:***124*
Aubat, Robert d', **1:**409
Auber, Daniel, **1:**35, 86, 146, 202, 300, **2:**14, 80, 84, 107, 202, 209, 390, **3:**156, **4:**138, 215, 342, **5:**341, 520, **6:**387
 on Bogdanova performing style, **1:**477
 Gitana score, **3:**185
 Marco Spada score, **4:**514
 See also Muette de Portici, La
Auber, Jane, **4:**524
Aubignac, Abbé de, **3:**84
Au Bord du Precipice, **1:**58–59
Aubry, Pierre, **3:**365
Aucassin and Nicolette, **4:**268
Auckland, New Zealand, **4:**624, 626, 627, 628
Auden, W. H., **1:**438, **4:**26, **5:**361
 on Balanchine, **1:**269
 Rake's Progress libretto, **6:**6
Audeoud, Susana. *See* Susana
audiences, Asian versus Western, **1:**160–161
Audinot, Nicholas, **1:**122, **3:**66
Audran, Édmond, **3:**73, **6:**119
Auezov, Mukhtar, **3:**665
Augier, Anne-Catherine, **6:**333
Augusta, Madame, **1:**199–200, **2:**276, **4:**338, **6:**237
Augustine, Saint, **1:**20–21, **2:**163, 569
August Pace, **2:**296, **4:**37, **5:**18
Augustus Caesar, **5:**237
Augustyn, Frank, **1:**200–201
 Fille Mal Gardée pas de deux, **2:**595
 Kain dance partnership, **1:**200–201, **2:***240*, **3:**643
 National Ballet of Canada, **4:**542, 543
 Ottawa Ballet directorship, **1:**201, **2:**41
Auld Lang Syne (Burns), **3:**243
Aulestia, Patricia, *as contributor*, **4:**398–400
aulos, **3:**293, 294, 295, **4:**499
Aumer, Jean-Louis, **1:**35, 86, **201–203**, 446, 504, 507, **3:**380, **4:**657, **5:**90, 92, **6:**71
 Belle au Bois Dormant, La, **1:**202, **5:**610
 Bordeaux dance associates, **3:**68
 character dances, **2:**107
 Dauberval association, **1:**201, 202, **2:**353, 354
 Fille Mal Gardée Paris Opera production, **2:**595
 Fitzames (Nathalie) association, **3:**5
 Hérold score, **3:**360
 Lami costume designs, **4:**116
 Lecomte (Hippolyte) costume designs, **4:**138
 Manon Lescaut, **1:**202, **4:**513
 Noblet roles, **4:**657
 Paris Opera Ballet, **1:**201, 346, 452, **2:**202
 Somnambule, La, **1:**202, 505, **2:**390, **5:**640–641, 642
 Théâtre de la Porte-Saint-Martin *divertissements*, **1:**202, **3:**68
 Viennese ballet, **1:**237, **2:**389, 502
Aung, Shwei Maung Htin, **4:**526
Aura (Lithuanian modern dance company), **4:**209
Aureole, **2:**469, 514, 526, **3:**232, **4:**482, **5:**432, 678, **6:**108, *109*, 110

Auric, Georges, **1:**306, 316, 327, 390, **2:**388, 408, **3:**72, 393, **4:**33, 185, 320, 516, 517, 634, 657, **5:***95*, 96, 237, 439, **6:**183
Auriol (clown), **5:**70
Aurkhi, **4:**577
Aurora's Wedding, **1:**147, 311, 316, 324, 410, 539, **5:**553–554, *611*, 612
 Egorova performance and staging, **2:**480
 Goncharova and Benois designs, **3:**198
 Les Six, **4:**516
 Lichine performance, **4:**178
Aurore, L', **5:**136
Ausdance Guide to Australian Dance Companies, The, **1:**219
Ausdance—The Australian Dance Council, **1:**217, 218, 219
Aus der Note der Zeit, **3:**152
Ausdruckstanz, **1:**130, **203–204**, 374
 archives, **4:**161
 Bausch works, **1:**388, 389
 as Canadian modern dance influence, **2:**44
 China, **6:**405–406
 Duncan as influence, **2:**457
 East Germany, **3:**153, 155
 free dance movement, **1:**239–240, 241, 242, 243, 244, **3:**145–145, 151, 156, 161, 162, 239–240
 Georgi, Yvonne, **3:**131–133
 Graham as influence, **3:**160
 Hoyer, Dore, **3:**393
 Impekoven, Niddy, **3:**443
 as Israeli dance influence, **3:**531
 as Japanese modern dance influence, **3:**590, 591
 Kreutzberg, Harald, **4:**60, *60*
 Kröller, Heinrich, **4:**63–64
 Laban, Rudolf, **4:**90
 mask use, **4:**302
 Nazi era, **1:**204, **3:**147, 160, 161
 Netherlands, **4:**590
 Palucca, Gret, **5:**65–66, *66*
 post-World War II, **3:**148
 Russian plastique, **5:**476, 477, 479
 as Sakharoff influence, **5:**503
 scholarly sources, **3:**162
 Souritz paper on Soviet exponents, **5:**643
 Switzerland, **6:**51–52
 Weimar Republic, **3:**145–147, **6:**389–391
 See also Wigman, Mary
Ausonius, **6:**144
Austen, Jane, **1:**190
Austin, A. Everett ("Chick"), **4:**27
Austin, Anna, **2:**185, **5:**497
Austin, Ruth, **2:**379
Austin Civic Ballet, **6:**266
Australasian Dance (journal), **1:**218
Australia, **1:**205–219
 Aboriginal dance. *See* Australian Aboriginal dance
 ballet, **1:**205–211, 311, 313, 498–499
 Kirsova Ballet, **1:**208, 209, **4:**25–26
 See also Australian Ballet; Sydney Dance Company; *specific dancers*
 dance education, **1:**212, 216, 217, 218, **2:**184, **3:**89, 174, **4:**25, **6:**379
 Scott, Margaret, **5:**563–564
 dance on television, **6:**136

dance research and publication, **1:218–219**
 libraries and museums, **4:**159–160
 modern dance, **1:211–218**, 467, 468
 shamanism, **6:**185
Australia Council for the Arts, **1:**218
Australian Aboriginal dance, **1:219–230**, **5:**252
 Aboriginal Islander Dance Theatre, **1:**216
 Antakirinya, **1:229–230**
 archives, **4:**160
 Arnhem Land, **1:**219, 220, **223–224**
 background and overview, **1:219–223**
 Bangarra Dance Theatre, **1:**212, 216, **6:**56
 Cape York Peninsula, **1:**219, **225–227**
 dance training school, **1:**212
 film footage, **2:**601
 as modern dance influence, **1:**212
 Tiwi, **1:**219–220, **224–225**
 Warlpiri, **1:227–229**
Australian Archives of the Dance, **4:**160
Australian Association for Dance Education, **1:**217, 218
 Resource Center, Flemington, **4:**160
Australian Ballet, **1:230–235**
 Aldous, Lucette, **1:**38
 Baronova *Les Sylphides*, **1:**367
 Bruhn *La Sylphide*, **2:**4
 Coe, Kelvin, **2:**183–184
 Cranko *Romeo and Juliet*, **5:**396
 Dream revival, **2:**445
 foreign tours, **1:**231–232, 235
 founding, **1:**209–211, 230, 498–499
 Gemini, **3:**360
 Gorham, Kathleen, **3:**203–204
 Helpmann, Robert, **1:**207, 210, 230, 233, **3:**356–357
 Hunchback of Notre Dame, The, **2:**524
 Jones, Marilyn, **3:**623
 Lanchbery as musical director, **4:**117
 Merry Widow, The, **3:**357, 428
 Murphy, Graeme, **4:**479–480
 Nureyev restaging of *Don Quixote*, **2:**440
 Rowe, Marilyn, **5:**410
 strike, **1:**234, **2:**184
 Suite en Blanc, **1:**209
 Tankard, Meryl, **6:**95
 Tetley, Glen, **1:**214, 233, 234, 394
 Tudor, Antony, **6:**202
 van Praagh artistic directorship, **1:**209–210, 213, 499, **6:**313
 Welch, Garth, **6:**378, 379
Australian Ballet Company, **5:**563
Australian Ballet Foundation, **1:**218, 230
Australian Ballet School, **1:**38, 213, 231, 232, 234, **2:**184
 Scott (Margaret) directorship, **5:**563
Australian Bicentennial Authority, **4:**479
Australian Chapter of the World Dance Alliance—Asia Pacific Center, **1:**218
Australian Choreographic Ensemble, **1:**216, **6:**56

Australian Contemporary Dance Theatre, **1:**212
Australian Dance Council. *See* Ausdance—The Australian Dance Council
Australian Dance Theatre, **1:**214, 215, **4:**479
Australian Elizabethan Theatre Trust, **1:**230
Australian Institute of Aboriginal Studies, Canberra, **2:**601, **4:**160
Australian Institute of Classical Dance, **3:**623
Australian National University, **1:**218
Australian Opera, **2:**184, **4:**479
Australian Theatre Ballet, **3:**203
Austria, **1:235–243**
 dance research and publication, **1:242–243**, **4:**160
 folk dance sounds, **3:**38
 free dance movement, **1:**230–240, 241, 242, 243
 Chladek, Rosalia, **2:**153–154, **3:**596
 expressionism, **1:**130–131
 Wiesenthal, Grete, **6:**386–387
 popular dance music, **4:**510, **5:**625, 692–693, **6:**359–360
 See also Viennese waltz
 theatrical dance, **1:**202, **235–242**, **3:**187–190
 horse ballet, **3:**381–383
 Italian dance ties, **3:**545
 lighting, **4:**189
 Noverre influence, **4:**696, **5:**692–693
 scenic design, **5:**536
 tournaments, **3:**368
 Viennese Kinderballet, **6:**334–336
 Viganò influence, **3:**175
 Wiesenthal, Grete, **6:**387–388
 See also Hofopernballett; Vienna State Opera Ballet
 traditional Easter dancing, **2:**168
Austrian Farmer's Wedding, **6:**357
Austrian Folk Song Archives, Vienna, **1:**242
Austrian Folk Song Foundation, **1:**242
Austro-Hungarian Empire. *See* Austria; Hungary
Autobiography (Rauschenberg), **5:**314
Autobiography (Stravinsky), **6:**5
Autofocus, **6:**121
automatism, **1:**135
Automatistes, Les, **2:**39, 40, 43
automaton dance, **3:**525
Autonome Hogeschool Antwerpen, **1:**414
autos, **1:**530, **5:**230
Autre monde, Un (Grandville), **2:**70, 72
Autumn, **4:**127, 594
Autumnal Dances, **6:**393
Autumn Fields, **3:**350–351
Autumn Leaves, **5:**125, *125*
Autumn Moon Festival, **2:**223
Autumn Rhythm (Pollock), **1:**138
Autumn Song, **4:**269
Auvergne, France, **3:**35, 69
Auxerre dance, **4:**106
Au-Young, Sum Nung, **5:**497
Auzely, Yvan, **6:**44
Available Light, **2:**119, **5:**550
Avalos, Ricardo, **2:**458

avant-garde dance, **1:**243–246
  artists, **3:**197, **4:**56, 124, 515,
    6:250
  Balanchine *La Chatte*, **1:**258–259
  Ballets Suédois, **1:**326, 327–328,
    2:410
  Bauhaus, **1:**385–387
  Bausch, Pina, **1:**388–389
  Béjart, Maurice, **1:**405
  Belgium, **1:**410–411
  Brown, Trisha, **1:**543–545
  Cage-Cunningham collaboration,
    2:21–23, 287–288, 290
  Chile, **2:**122–123, 125
  choreographers, **2:**290
  composers, **4:**515–516, 519
  costume design, **2:**242,
    4:124–125, *124*
  Cunningham influence on,
    2:290–291
  Diaghilev, Serge, **1:**243, 320,
    322–323, **2:**408, 409, 410,
    4:515–516
  film dances, **2:**603–612
  Fuller influence, **3:**93, 95
  Halprin, Anna, **3:**336
  Hanayagi Suzushi, **3:**339–340
  Holm, Hanya, **3:**369–370
  India, **2:**104
  Japan, **3:**591, **4:**661
  Judson Dance Theater,
    2:290–291, **3:**633–635
  Korea, **3:**372–373
  Rainer, Yvonne, **1:**246, **2:**605,
    3:336, **6:**248
  Rainer manifesto, **2:**333
  Robbins adaptations, **2:**333
  Soviet, **1:**244, 246, **3:**48, **5:**477
  Sweden, **1:**145, **6:**42, 45
  United States, **6:**250
  Waring, James, **6:**362–363
  Zollar, Jawole Willa Jo,
    6:448–449
  See also performance art
Avatāras, **3:**465
Avdeeva, Lubov A., *as contributor*,
    3:568–569, **4:**7–8, **6:**304–307
Avdevsky, Anatoly, **6:**226
Avedon, Richard, **5:**184
Aveline, Albert, **1:**246–247, **4:**354,
    5:*92*, 95, 132, 563, 690, **6:**217
  Chauviré as student, **2:**113
  Darsonval roles, **2:**351
  Indes Galantes revival, **3:**450
  Paris Opera Ballet school,
    3:81–82
  Sylvia restaging, **6:**64
Avellaneda, Pepito (José Domingo
    Monteleone), **6:**93
Ave Maria, **2:**456
Aventures de Serail, Les, **4:**509
Aventures d'Ivan Vaffran, Les,
    3:78–79, *78*
Averof, George, **3:**303
Averty, Karin, **3:***183*
Aveugle de Palmire, L' (Rodolphe
    opera), **5:**371
Avian, Robert, **1:**420
Avila, María de, **1:**294, **2:**448, 522,
    5:673, 674
Aviles, Arthur, **3:***621*
Avilés, Nelson, **2:**126
aviso (preface), **4:**174
Avon Comedy Four, **6:**317
Avrahami, Gideon, **3:**273
Avramenko, Vasile (Vasily), **6:**223
Avril, Jane, **1:**129, **4:**523, **5:**261,
    6:181
Avui (publication), **5:**676
Awaiting, **3:**317

Awakening of Flora, The, **3:**14
Awareness Through Movement. *See*
    Feldenkrais Method
Awashima Chikage, **6:**84
Awa society, **2:**422
Awatere, Arapeta, **4:**261
Awni, Walid, **2:**498
axe dances, **1:**118
axé music, **5:**507–508
Axinte, Dorina, **5:**390
Axtmann, Ann, **4:**397
Ayala, Santiago, **1:**109
ay-aralla-buya, **4:**408, 415
Ayatsuri Sanbasō, **3:**593
Ayesha (vaudeville performer),
    6:317
Ayestaran, Lauro, **6:**301
Aykal, Duygu, **6:**212
Aymara (people), **2:**121
Ayrenhoff, Cornelius von, **6:**337
Ayres, Lemuel, **5:**551
Ayrton, Michael, **6:***280*
Ayukhanov, Bulat, **5:**460
Ayupova, Zhanna, **4:**285
'ayyālah dance, **4:**417
Ayyam al-Assiba, Al-, **2:**497
Azarel (pantomime), **4:**121
Azelia, or the Syrian Slave, **4:**453,
    454, 455
Azerbaijan, **1:**48, **247–248**, **3:**513
Azerbaijani Opera House. *See*
    Akhundov Opera and Ballet
    Theater, Baku
Azincourt, Mademoiselle d', **1:**465
Azmi, Enayat, **2:**496
Aznavour, Charles, **4:**107
Azteca. See concheros
Aztecs, **4:**327, 329, 330, 386
Azuma Kabuki, **1:**249, **4:**536
Azuma Odori, Tokyo, **3:**126
Azuma school of dance, **1:**248, 249
Azuma Tokuho, **1:248–249**
Azuma Yusaku, **3:**588
Azuolinas, **6:**301
Azuri Begum, **1:**94
AZYF. *See* American Zionist Youth
    Foundation
Azzaiolo, Filipno, **1:**428
Azzi, Maaaia Susana, *as
    contributor*, **4:**632, **5:**200–201,
    6:91–94
Azzopardi, Anthony, **4:**73, **6:**133
Azzopardi, Lydia, **3:**126–127

Baălănescu, Maria, **5:**384
Baalbeck Festival, **1:**231, 291,
    4:412
Baal-Shem, **3:**212
Baba (musical), **1:**496
Baba, Heen, **3:***649*
Baba, Meher, **2:**268, 269
Babad Dalem (Balinese text), **3:**486,
    4:146
Babaeva, Chimnaz, **1:**248
Baba-Yaga, **6:**412
"Babbity Bowster," **3:**246
Babe, Thomas, **6:**153
Babel, **3:**330
Babel-Babel, **3:**79
Babes in Arms (musical), **6:**277
Babes in Toyland (musical), **6:**268
Babes on Broadway (film), **1:**434
Babes on Broadway (musical),
    4:629
Babil and Bijoux, **2:**525
Babilée, Isabelle, **1:**251
Babilée, Jean, **1:251**, **2:**114, 277,
    3:74, **6:**143, 348
Ballet du Rhin, **3:**74

Ballets des Champs-Élyées,
    1:305, 306, **3:**73
Ballet-Théâtre Contemporain,
    1:349
Béjart ballets, **1:**292, 405
  as character dancer, **2:**106
  Don Quixote performance, **2:**440
  independent dance concerts, **3:**73
  Jeune Homme et la Mort
    performance, **1:**251, 306,
    3:601, **4:**33
  Maratona performance, **3:**359
Babilée '95 (television film), **1:**251
Babinka Group, Montevideo, **6:**302
Babitz, Sol, **4:**688
Babitz, Thelma, **4:**688
Babli, Rohini, **1:**94
Babsky, Monique, *as contributor*,
    1:201–203, 246–247, 349–351,
    445–446, *446*, 451–452,
    455–456, 461–462, **2:**350–351,
    388–389, **3:**67–72, 72–75,
    4:107–108, 214–215, 352–354,
    422–423, 656–657, **5:**147–148,
    148–149, 498–502, 562–563,
    690–691, **6:**62–64, 119–120
Babuška, Mihai, **5:**387, 390, **6:**435
"baby ballerinas," **1:**308, 310, 367,
    2:478, **5:**349, **6:**182
  See also Baronova, Irina;
    Riabouchinska, Tatiana;
    Toumanova, Tamara
Baby in der Bar, **3:**132
Baby Laurence, **1:252**
Baby Take a Bow (film), **6:**141
Bacall, Teresa, **1:**374
Bacca Pipes (sword dance), **1:**118
Baccelli, Giovanna, **3:**257, **4:***697*,
    5:260
Bacchae (Euripides), **3:**292,
    646, 652
Bacchanale, **1:**136, *137*, 296–297,
    3:22, 212, **5:**122, 123
  Karinska costumes, **3:**654
  Mordkin staging, **4:**459
"Bacchanale" (*Cléopâtre*), **3:**16
"Bacchanale" (*Samson and
    Delilah*), **4:**382
"Bacchanale" (*Tannhauser*), **4:**91
Bacchante, La, **5:**137
bacchantes (maenads), **3:**292
Bacchantes, Les, **1:**246, **2:**181
Bacchus and Ariadne (Canziani
    ballet), **2:**55
Bacchus et Ariadne (Didelot ballet),
    2:413, 414
Bacchus et Ariane, **1:**195, **2:**388
  Gallet choreography, **3:**106
  Lifar choreography, **4:**183
Bacchylides, **3:**428, 645
Bacco e Gambrinus, **5:**246
Bacewicz, Gracyna, **1:**233
Bach, Carl Philipp Emanuel, **1:**365
Bach, Ferdinand Sigismond, **3:**92
Bach, Johann Christian, **3:**111
Bach, Johann Sebastian, **1:**39,
    149, 406, 540, **3:**338, 601,
    5:163, 520
  Balanchine choreography, **1:**261,
    281, **2:**198
  bourrée composition, **1:**517
  Eck choreography, **2:**474
  Fodor choreography, **3:**418
  forlana composition, **3:**50
  Goldberg Variations, **1:**428, **4:**71,
    5:365
  Humphrey choreography, **3:**400,
    402, *403*, 404
  loure compositions, **4:**232
  Musical Offering, **1:**545,
    4:482–483

Taylor (Paul) choreography,
    2:526, **4:**482–483
Bacharach, Burt, **1:**419, **6:**284
bachata, **2:**432
Bach Cycle, **1:**484
Bachelor Belles, The (musical),
    6:270
bachelors' dances, **3:**411
Bachmann, Ingeborg, **3:**359
Bach Partita, **6:**153
Bach Suite, **2:**161
Backanaterna (Bergman), **5:**47
Backer, Friedrich, **3:**237
Background to European Ballet
    (Brinson), **1:**542
Backman, Eugène Louis,
    6:193, 194
Back Spin (break dance move),
    6:*263*
Back Water: Twosome, **5:***128*
Backyard and Beyond, **1:**215
Bacon, Faith, **2:**573, 574
Bacon, Francis, **3:**276
Bacon, Lloyd, **1:**432
Bacon, Patience Wiggin, **3:**396
Badakhstan, Afghanistan, **1:**27
Badayuni, Shakeel, **2:**625
Badekow, Holger, *as photographer*,
    3:153, 337, **4:**603
badḥan, **3:**527, 603
Badings, Henk, **2:**347, **3:**132, 133,
    4:518
Badnin, I. A., **2:**330
Badrak, Aleksei, **5:**471
Baduel-Mathon, Céline, **6:**25
Baer, Nancy Van Norman, *as
    contributor*, **5:**370–371,
    6:356–357
Baer-Frissell, Christine, **2:**153
Baervoets, Raymond, **5:**422
Báez, Aquíles, **6:***325*
Baga (people), **1:**14, **4:***286*, **6:***13*
Bagage, **6:**175
Baganova, Tatiana, **5:**475, 479
Bagmundi Purulia *chhau*,
    2:117–118
Bagnolet, France, **3:**78
Bagobo (people), **5:**168
Bagouet, Dominique, **1:**545, **3:**79,
    5:98
bagpipes
  Anastenárídēs dance, **1:**84
  Arabian Peninsula, **1:**102
  Bulgaria, **2:**9
  Cape Breton step dancing, **5:**698
  Czech and Slovak, **2:**302, 305
  France, **3:**64
  German folk dance, **3:**140
  Greece, **3:**298
  loure derivation, **4:**231
  Middle Ages, **4:**501
  musette, **4:**481
  Poland, **5:**212
  Romania, **5:**379
  Scotland, **3:**243, 249
Bagusan, Pangeran, **3:**501
Bagus Madé Geria, Ida, **5:**524
Bahamian Ministry of Tourism,
    2:65–66
Baharda Duet, **6:**213
Bahat, Avner
  as contributor, **3:**535–539
  as photographer, **3:**538
Bahat-Ratzon, Naomi, **3:**535
  as contributor, **3:**535–539
Bahía, Brazil, **1:***528*, 530, *531*,
    2:58, 59
Bahía Ballet, **1:***533*, *534*
Bahiri, Mohammed, **1:**374
Bahr, Jill Eathorne, **6:**266

Bahr, Margaretha von, **2**:632
baião, **1**:529
Baidaralim, Zhanat, **3**:665
Baïf, Jean-Antoine de, **1**:1, 2, **2**:338, **4**:172
Baikštytė, Živilė, **4**:208
bailarico, **5**:229
baile (Spanish term), **5**:667, 669
"Baile da Meia Volta," **5**:228
baile de los seizes, **2**:168
baile de palos, **2**:61, 430
baile de priprí, **2**:430, 431
Bailemos, **3**:62
Bailey, Derek, **6**:135
Bailey, Oscar, *as photographer*, **5**:548
Bailey, Pearl, **6**:277, 283
Bailey, Rona, **4**:626
Bailin, Gladys, **4**:230, 649
bailinho, **5**:229
Baillie, James, **5**:89
Baillou, Louis de, **2**:55
Bailly, Henri de, **2**:98
Báilyn, Gladys, **4**:651
Bain, Keith, **1**:211
Bainaya-darpaṇa (Indian dance treatise), **1**:168
Bainbridge, John, **3**:511
Baird, John Logie, **4**:270, **6**:134
Baiseitova, Raushin, **3**:665
Baiser de la Fée, Le, **5**:414, **6**:341
    Balanchine choreography, **1**:64, 260, 261, 262, 268, 297
    Balanchine revival, **4**:609
    Beriosova performance, **1**:429, **4**:240
    Danilova performance, **2**:342, 343
    Fonteyn performance, **3**:41
    Fracci performance, **3**:60
    Franklin performance, **3**:88
    Hynd choreography, **3**:427
    Kudelka choreography, **4**:74
    MacMillan choreography, **4**:240, 241, **5**:417
    McBride performance, **4**:345
    Nijinska choreography, **1**:148, **3**:72, **4**:635, **5**:439
    Rubinstein performance, **5**:439
    Schollar performance, **5**:559
    Seymour performance, **5**:574
    Stravinsky orchestration, **6**:5
    Vasiliov and Kasatkina production, **5**:467
Baiser pour Rien, Un, **1**:247
Bai Shuxiang, **5**:330
Baiz, Josette, **3**:79–80
baja dance type, **1**:54
Bajaja, **5**:245
Bajetti, Giovanni, **2**:209, **3**:181, **5**:137, 138, 277
Baka (Aka) (people), **2**:87
Bakalov, F., **2**:12
Bakawali, **5**:493
Baker, Dale, **1**:210, 211
Baker, George Pierce, **4**:168
Baker, Joan, **3**:634, **6**:282
Baker, Josephine, **1**:252–253, **4**:524, **6**:272, 301
Baker, Michael Conway, **4**:72
Baker, Michael J., **4**:72, 73
Baker, Peggy, **4**:73
Baker, Thomas, **1**:456
Baker's Dozen, **6**:152, 154
Bakhor (Uzbek dance ensemble), **6**:306
Bakhrushin, Yuri, **5**:483
Bakhrushin State Theatrical Museum, Moscow, **1**:463, **4**:165
Bakhti, **1**:407

Bakka, Egil, **4**:682
    as contributor, **2**:383–384
    as photographer, **4**:670, 671, 672
    notation system, **4**:693
Bakker, Gijs, **2**:245
Bakst, Léon, **1**:133, **253–255**, 424, **2**:250, 360, **3**:654, 656, **5**:125, 161, 541, 543, 690, **6**:41
    Après-midi d'un Faune, L' decor, **1**:98, 99, 254, **2**:407, **6**:28
    Carnaval decor, **2**:72, 73
    Daphnis et Chloë design, **5**:315
    Diaghilev commissions, **1**:318, 320, 322, 324, **2**:406, 407, 408, 409, **3**:16, 18, 198
    Dying Swan costume, **2**:471
    Firebird design, **2**:82, 242, **3**:1, 1, 196
    Fokine design collaborations, **2**:241, **3**:15, 20, **4**:642
    Jeux scenic design, **4**:642
    Josephslegende costumes, **3**:631
    Kocho collection, **4**:34
    Levinson biography, **4**:155
    makeup exoticism, **4**:305
    neoclassical designs, **2**:407
    Orientales costume, **4**:643
    Orientalist design, **2**:241, 242, 345, 407, **3**:17, 18, **5**:45
    prints and drawings, **5**:262
    Puppenfee design, **4**:144
    Rubinstein association, **5**:438
    Schéhérazade design, **5**:542, 556
    Sleeping Beauty designs, **5**:610, 611, 612
    Sleeping Princess designs, **3**:264
    Svetlov critiques, **6**:28
    Sylphides costume, **6**:60
    World of Art group, **5**:456
Baku, Azerbaijan, **1**:48, 248
Bakuba (people), **2**:211
Bakwele (people), **4**:365
Bakyla, **1**:461
bal. See ball
Bal, Le, **1**:260, 325, **2**:254, 342, 424, **3**:611, **4**:33, **6**:182
Bala (Kuchipudi dancer), **6**:321
Balabanova, F. I., **2**:11
Balabina, Feya, **2**:437
Balaci, Emanuela, **5**:391
Baladins, Les, **2**:388
Bālagopāla Tharaṅgam, **4**:70
bālah dance, **6**:417
Balakirev, Mily, **3**:18, 20, 135, 185
Balamat-zade, Gafur, **6**:83, 84
balance, **5**:188
Balance à Trois, **1**:251, **2**:114
Balanchine, George, **1**:7, **255–273**, 391, 395, 436, **2**:178, 421, **3**:27, 135, 344, **5**:223, 294, 485, 525, 526, 553, **6**:345
    abstract ballets, **4**:612–614
    aesthetic vision, **1**:24, 25, 245, 256–257, 258–260, 261, 262, 266–268, 325, **2**:242, 251, 457, **4**:28, 609, 610–611, **6**:243
    American Ballet, **1**:63–64, 281
    artist collaborators, **1**:141
    artistic significance, **1**:251, 272
    as Ashton influence, **1**:147
    Australian Ballet repertory, **1**:233, 234
    ballerina ideal, **4**:615, 618, **5**:419, **6**:85
    ballerinas, **1**:11, 12, 265, 269, 367, **2**:253–254, 342, 576, 577–578, **4**:136–137, 344–345, 616–619, 631, **6**:396–397, 450
    "Ballet is woman" quote, **1**:158, **4**:620

ballet motifs, **2**:254
Ballet Russe de Monte Carlo, **1**:297, 298–300, 307, **2**:342
Ballets 1933, **1**:306–307, **2**:242, **3**:72–73, **4**:33, 229, **6**:182
Ballet Society, **1**:141, **2**:161, **4**:28–29, 606, **6**:85, 247
    as Ballets Russes de Monte Carlo ballet master, **1**:308, 309, 313–314, **4**:267
    ballet technique characteristics, **1**:329, 348, **3**:130
    allegro style, **1**:45, 264
    attitude de côté, **1**:198
    double *rond de jambe en l'air*, **5**:402
    partnering, **5**:104
    pas de deux, **5**:107
    pliés, **5**:202
    pointe work, **5**:208, 209
    port de bras, **5**:227
Bérard designs, **1**:306, 426
Berners scores, **1**:437
Boston Ballet productions, **1**:501, 502
Broadway musicals, **1**:270–271, 298, 482, **2**:458, **3**:598, **4**:335, 450, 629, **5**:359, **6**:276, 277, 278, 450
as Byrd influence, **2**:19
Cecchetti method, **2**:84
Chilean premieres, **2**:123
choreographic approaches, **4**:518, 610–613
choreographic restorations, **4**:623–622
Christensen brothers association, **2**:160
Coppélia, **2**:201, **4**:610, 611, 613
costumes and designs, **2**:242, 243, 244, 245, 251
Craig appreciation of, **2**:263
critiques of, **1**:271, 299, **4**:607, **6**:352
dance legacy, **1**:255, 256–258, 262, 272
Dance Theatre of Harlem repertory productions, **2**:334
death, **4**:621, **6**:65, 264
Denby critical advocacy, **2**:376
de Valois influence, **2**:396, 401
Diaghilev's Ballets Russes productions, **1**:256, 256, 258, 317, 325, **2**:406, 410, **4**:33, 320, 321, 331, 620, **6**:32
Dollar performances, **2**:425–426
Don Quixote performances, **1**:268, **2**:438, 577
Don Quixote production, **2**:438–439
Duncan as indirect influence, **2**:457
Dutch National Ballet repertory productions, **2**:469
eclecticism and versatility, **1**:256–258, 263
Eglevsky roles, **2**:479
Electronics, **4**:519
elephant ballet, **1**:257, **2**:176
Enfant et les Sortilèges, L', **5**:316
English National Ballet productions, **2**:514
Farrell roles, **2**:576, 577–578, **3**:448, **4**:618
Flood, The, **6**:137
Fonteyn performances, **3**:43–44
as Forsythe influence, **3**:53
Franklin roles, **3**:87–88
as Geneva Ballet artistic adviser, **6**:52

Grands Ballets Canadiens productions, **3**:231, 231
Hamburg Ballet productions, **3**:150, 337, 338
as Hawkins influence, **3**:348–349
Hayden roles, **3**:352
Hollywood musicals choreography, **2**:616, 616, **5**:398, **6**:277, 450
"ideal woman" quote, **2**:438
Ivesiana, **1**:263, 268, 272, **4**:5, 274, 483
Josephslegende choreography, **3**:631
Karinska collaboration, **2**:244, **3**:653
Kaye roles, **3**:663–665
Kent roles, **4**:5
Kirkland roles, **4**:24
Kirstein association, **1**:63, 64, 141, 256, 257, 307, 399, **4**:608
Kirstein's significance in backing, **4**:26, 27
Labanotation of works, **3**:427, **4**:96
Le Clercq roles, **4**:136–137, 616
Lifar roles, **4**:182–183, 620
Littlefield association, **4**:209
London musicals, **6**:276–277
Magallanes roles, **4**:246
male classical dancing repertory, **4**:620–621
Martins association, **4**:273, 274–275, 620–621
Maryinsky Ballet, **4**:283, 284, 285
McBride roles, **4**:618
Metropolitan Opera Ballet, **4**:382
Mexican tour, **6**:396
Milhaud score, **4**:418
Mitchell roles, **4**:436
Modern Jazz: Variants, **4**:519
Molière as source, **4**:447
Moncion roles, **4**:449, 450
National Ballet of Canada repertory, **4**:541
New York City Ballet repertory, **4**:521–622, 610–613
Night Shadow. See Sonnambula, La
Noguchi scenic design, **5**:547
Nureyev, Rudolf, **5**:6
Paris Opera Ballet productions, **5**:96, 97
on Petipa (Marius), **5**:153
as photographic subject, **5**:186
Princess Aurora revision, **5**:612
program notes, **4**:177
Raymonda, **1**:298, **2**:314, **4**:610, **5**:322
regional ballet influence, **5**:131, **6**:264–265
religious beliefs, **1**:270
Robbins association, **5**:359, 361, 364, 365, 367
Romeo and Juliet versions, **5**:398
Rosalinda adaptation, **6**:388
Rosenthal lighting collaboration, **5**:407
Royal Ballet guest production, **5**:415, 417
Royal Danish Ballet repertory, **5**:238, 428, 429, 431, 599, 600
Royal Swedish Ballet repertory, **6**:42
Sand (Inge) roles, **5**:511
San Francisco Ballet association, **5**:512, 513
showmanship, **1**:257–258, 270–272
as Soviet choreographic influence, **1**:39, **5**:460

Stravinsky collaboration, **1:**30,
    95–96, 141, 256, 257, 259,
    260, 261–262, 298, 299, **2:**176,
    4:518, 606, 613, **6:**5, 6
    listing of ballets, **4:**613
Swan Lake choreographies,
    1:271, 272, **4:**610, **6:**32,
    34, 396
Sylvia: Pas de Deux, **6:**64
symphonic ballet, **4:**322
Tallchief roles, **4:**616, **6:**84–86
Tarantella, **6:**105
Tchaikovsky scores, **6:**117
Tchelitchev collaboration,
    6:118–119
as teacher, **1:**257, 263–266, 349,
    4:227, 615–616
    See also School of American
    Ballet
television productions, **6:**137,
    138, 139
Ter-Arutunian designs, **6:**144
theme reoccurences, **1:**268–269
Tomasson roles, **6:**174
Toumanova roles, **6:**182
Valse, La, **1:**272, **4:**611, **5:**316
Verdy roles, **4:**617
Villella roles, **6:**339–340, *340*
Wilde (Patricia) roles, **6:**396
Williams (E. Virginia)
    association, **6:**398
Williams (Stanley) association,
    6:399
Woizikowski roles, **6:**404
Young Ballet, **5:**458
Zorina marriage, **6:**450
Zurich Ballet repertory, **6:**454
See also Agon; Apollo; Ballet
    Imperial; Concerto Barocco;
    Cotillon; Divertimento No. 15;
    Four Temperments, The;
    Harlequinade; Jewels;
    Liebeslieder Walzer;
    Mozartiana; Nutcracker, The;
    Orpheus; Prodigal Son, The;
    Serenade; Symphony in C;
    Theme and Variations
Balanchine Celebration (1993),
    4:275, 622, 631
Balanchine's Stories of the Great
    Ballets (Mason), **4:**177
Balanchine Trust, **2:**578, **6:**264–265
Balanchivadze, Andrei, **2:**96, **3:**135
Balanchivadze, Georgii
    Melitonovich. *See*
    Balanchine, George
Balanchivadze, Meliton, **1:**255
Balanotti, R. I., **6:**225
Balasanian, Sergei, **3:**195, **6:**83
Balasaraswati, **1:**169, **273–275,**
    3:448, **6:**321
Balasaraswati-Joy Ann Dewey
    Chair for Distinguished
    Teaching, **1:**80
Balasaraswati School of Music and
    Dance, Berkeley, **1:**274
Balashova, Alexandra, **1:**488,
    2:597, **3:**207
Balásy, D., **3:**422
Balatum, **1:**412
Balazs, Beatrix, **4:**679
Balázs, Béla, **1:**370, **3:**414
Balbi, Giovanni Battista, **1:**287
Balbo, Lucia, **5:**278
Balbo, Marietta, **5:**278
Balca, **2:**125
Bal Champêtre, Le, **3:**259
Balcom, Lois, **3:**349
Balcony, The (Genêt), **1:**251
balcony design, **6:**161
Baldassarre, Luis, **1:***113*

Baldensperger, Philip, **4:**406,
    407, 416
Bal des Blanchisseuses, La, **1:**306
Baldina, Alexandra, **4:**56,
    5:119, **6:**61
Baldina, Maria, **6:**270
Baldocchino, Carlo, **5:**135
Baldrich, Hernan, **2:**125
Baldrucca (Schmelzer opera), **6:**359
Baldwin, Mark, **3:**274, 276, **4:**627
Bale, Dan, *as photographer,* **1:**313
Balé Folclórico de Bahía, **1:***531*
Bales, William, **1:**79, 421, **2:**450,
    4:306
    See also Dudley-Maslow-Bales
    Dance Trio
Balet (encyclopedia), **5:**485, 486
Balet (magazine), **5:**484, 486, 642
Balet Comique de la Royne, Le, **1:**2,
    275–277, 285, 286, 398,
    2:338, **3:**65, *66,* 130, **5:**341,
    6:156
    libretto, **4:**172
    lighting, **4:**187
    music, **4:**406
    scenic designs, **5:**533, *533,* 534
Balet Comique 1582, Le (McGowan
    introduction), **3:**283
"Balet ob 100–letnici" (Neubauer),
    6:439
Balet Prague. *See* Studio Ballet
    Prague
Balettakademien (University of
    Stockholm), **6:**48–49
Balet Teatru Wielkiego w
    Warzawie. *See* Warsaw Ballet
Balett klassisk og fri (Häger), **6:**49
Balett på Stockholmsoperas
    (Skeaping and Ståhle), **5:**604
Balfe, Michael, **2:**202
Bali. *See* Indonesia
Bali: Rangda and Barong (Belo),
    3:506
Bali: Temple Festival (Belo), **3:**506
Baliev, Nikita, **1:**85, **3:**193, **5:**642
Balinese Fantasy, **2:**378
Baliszewski, Sylwin, **5:**218
Balkan, Mehmet, **5:**422
Balkan dances, **3:**109, **6:**426–430
    See also specific countries
ball, **1:**190, **277–279, 2:***382*
    masked, **4:**313, 314, *314,* 448
    music, **4:**510–511
    Romania, **5:**383
Ball, Hugo, **6:**389
Ball, Lucille, **1:**520
Ball, Margarita, **1:**113
Ball, Mary Washington, **3:**571
Ball, The (engraving), **5:***620*
Balla, Giacomo, **1:**130, 133, 134,
    244, **2:**409, **5:**85, 399, 544
Ballabile, **3:**236, **4:**114, **5:**415
Ballad, **6:**1
Ballad about Latinca, **5:**287
Ballade, **3:**629, 664, **4:**243, 611,
    618, **5:**363
ballades, **4:**500
Ballade vom Glück, **3:**153
Ballad of a Sailor, **5:**23
Ballad of Baby Doe, The, **3:**372
Ballad of Horror, **2:**473
Ballad of Medieval Love, The, **4:**437,
    6:454
ballads, **3:**30–31, 33
Balladyna, **5:**75
ball and crane dances, **1:**167
Ballard, Hank, **5:**631, 632
Ballard, Michael, **4:**230
Ballard, Robert, **1:**275
ballare (meaning of term), **4:**348
ballare lombardo, **3:**542

Ballare lombardo, Il (Pontremoli
    and La Rocca), **3:**557
Ballarino, Il (Caroso), **1:**369, 380,
    2:50, 73–77, 189, 336, **5:***110,*
    115, *117,* 260, 338
    comprehensiveness of, **2:**74
    Negri's *Le gratie d'amore*
    comparison, **4:**581
    See also Caroso, Fabritio
ballata, **3:**541
ballerina
    Balanchine "Ballet is woman"
    quote, **1:**158, **4:**620
    costume conventions, **2:**240–241,
    6:216–217
    English usage of term, **2:**176
    physical ideals, **4:**615, 618, **5:**419,
    425, **6:**85
Ballerina (film), **3:**132, 373,
    5:600, **6:**328
Ballerina (play), **6:**449
Ballerina, The, **3:**568
Balleriñe Amante, La (Cimarosa),
    5:*231*
ballet. *See* ballet competitions;
    ballet technique; ballet
    technique, history of; genres
    of Western theatrical dance;
    specific ballets, ballet
    companies, countries,
    and works
Ballet (British publication),
    3:282, 285
Ballet (Brodovitch), **5:**184
Ballet (Peruvian-Chilean
    publication), **2:**127
Ballet (Russian encyclopedia),
    5:485, 486
Ballet: A Complete Guide to
    Appreciation (Haskell),
    3:285
Ballet: Beyond the Basics
    (Hammond), **6:**127
Ballet à Cheval des Quatre
    Éléments, **3:**381
Ballet Adagio (film), **2:**605
ballet à entrées, **2:**517, **6:**38
Ballet à la Carte, **2:**357
Ballet à la Russe, **3:**354
Ballet Alicia Alonso. *See* Ballet
    Nacional de Cuba
Ballet and Us, The (Cullberg), **2:**284
Ballet Annual (journal), **3:**321
Ballet Antologia, **1:**294
Ballet Arizona, **4:**134
Ballet Atlantique/Regine Chopinot,
    3:274
Ballet at Teatern, Göteborg, **6:**44
Ballet Austin, Texas, **6:**266
Ballet Australia Choreographic
    Competitions, **1:**217
Ballet Aztlan. *See* Ballet Folclórico
    Nacional
Ballet Ballads (musical), **3:**371,
    4:214
Ballet Belges, **1:**411
ballet blanc ("white ballet"), **2:**202,
    207, *236,* 240, **6:**189
    Coralli *pas de sylphides*
    foreshadowing, **3:**69, 180
    end of vogue, **2:**249
    evocation by *Les Sylphides,* **2:**407,
    3:180
    Ivanov's *Swan Lake* second act,
    4:282
    makeup, **4:**304
    Sylphide, La, **6:**57, 58, 74
Balletbogen (Aschengreen), **2:**387
Ballet British Columbia, **2:**41–42,
    4:546, 547

Ballet Caravan, **1:**49, 65, 96,
    279–281, 478, 498, **2:**161,
    6:291
    Balanchine productions, **1:**261,
    293, **4:**227
    Christensen (Lew) as ballet
    master, **2:**160, **4:**28
    Concerto Barocco premiere,
    2:193, *193*
    Copland's *Billy the Kid,* **2:**197
    Dollar, William, **2:**426, **4:**28
    Hawkins as founding member,
    3:349
    as Kirstein creation, **4:**28
    Loring, Eugene, **4:**28, 227, *227*
    Magallanes, Nicholas, **4:**246
    repertory, **6:**247
    Rosenthal lighting, **5:**407
    Serenade production, **5:**571
    South American tour, **2:**161, 193,
    4:28, 63
Ballet Clásico de México, **4:**394
Ballet Class (also *Class Concert*),
    4:358–359
Ballet Class for Beginners
    (videotape), **6:**129
Ballet Club, **1:**99, 146, 148, **2:**105,
    477, **3:**174, 202, 508, **4:**215,
    5:297, 298–300
    Markova roles, **4:**267, 268
    Tudor association, **6:**196, *196*
    See also Rambert Dance
    Company
Balletcoma, **6:**264
Ballet Comique, **6:**399
Ballet Company of the City of São
    Paulo, **1:**532
ballet competitions, **1:**109,
    281–282
Ballet Concierto de Puerto Rico,
    5:275
Ballet contemporain, Le (Svetlov),
    5:482, **6:**28
Ballet Contemporánea de la
    Universidad Veracruzana,
    4:397
ballet d'action, **1:**86, 123, 125, **5:**39,
    89–90, 249, 307, 518, 519, 682
    Angiolini and Noverre
    differences, **3:**545, 546
    Angiolini identification with,
    1:87, 88
    Ballon work as forerunner, **1:**355
    choreographic problem, **2:**594
    Curz, Daniel, **2:**299
    Danish performances, **5:**423–424
    Dauberval development of,
    2:354, 366
    D'Egville's performance skill,
    2:363
    different views of, **3:**546
    Don Juan importance as, **2:**433
    English performances, **3:**256,
    257–258, 259, 260
    as Galeotti influence, **3:**105
    Gallet choreography, **3:**106
    Hilverding identification with,
    2:594, **3:**365, **6:**48
    Lauchery choreography, **4:**129
    Le Picq support, **4:**150
    libretti, **4:**174–175
    Massine re-creations, **4:**320
    musical approaches, **4:**509–510,
    512
    Noverre's identification with,
    1:87, 88, **2:**239, **3:**106,
    4:699–700, **6:**9
    Saint Petersburg ballet, **4:**276,
    5:451
    Sallé, Marie, **5:**505

ballet d'action, continued
  Santlow, Hester, **5:**518
  Skeaping and Beck-Friis revivals,
    6:48
  Spoerli successes, **5:**682
  Stuttgart productions, **6:**9
  Valberkh, Ivan, **6:**311
  Viganò, Salvatore, **3:**547
  Weaver creation, **5:**603
Ballet/Danse (publication), **3:**84
Ballet de Antologia Española, **1:**94
Ballet de Bellas Artes, **1:**524, **6:**355
Ballet de Cámara de Montevideo,
  6:302
ballet de collège, **1:282–285,** 286,
  396, 464, **2:**168, 465, **3:**65, 81,
  4:130, 447
ballet de cour, **1:**2, **285–289,**
  342–344, **3:**65–67, **5:**341
  American scholarship and
    reconstructions, **6:**251
  Beaujoyeulx choreography,
    1:275–277, 285, 398
  Benserade librettos, **1:**424–425
  Callot etchings, **2:**27
  Christout scholarship, **2:**169–170,
    3:84
  costume, **2:**236–239, *236*
  dancing masters, **2:**337–338,
    3:80–81, 158, 543
  Drottningholm Court Theater
    revivals, **5:**603
  entrée and *entrée grave*, **2:**517–519
  gigues, **3:**172
  Jesuit ballet de collège,
    1:282–285, 286, 396, 464,
    2:168
  La Fontaine, Mademoiselle de,
    4:108–109
  libretti, **4:**172
  lighting, **4:**187–188
  loure, **4:**231–232
  masks and makeup, **4:**301–302,
    304, 449
  music, **4:**505, 506–507
  pastorales, **5:**113
  sarabande, **5:**520
  scenic design, **5:**533–534
  See also Louis XIV; Lully, Jean-
    Baptiste; Molière
Ballet de cour de Louis XIV, Le
  (Christout), **3:**84
Ballet de cour en France, Le
  (Prunière), **3:**84
Ballet de Cuba. *See* Ballet Nacional
  de Cuba
Ballet de Euskadi, **5:**674
Ballet de Flore, **1:**288, **6:**11
Ballet de Hanaut. *See*
  Charleroi/Danses
Ballet de la Chienne, Le, **2:**518
Ballet de la Ciudad de México,
  4:391–392, *391*
Ballet de la Délivrance de Renaud,
  Le, **1:**285, 286
Ballet de la Félicité, **6:**38
Ballet de la Nuit, Le, **1:**286, 424,
  4:229, 234
  Skeaping reconstruction, **5:**603
Ballet de la Paille, Le. See Fille Mal
  Gardée, La
Ballet de la Païx, Le, **1:**465, **2:**284,
  4:588
Ballet de la Prosperité des Armes de
  la France, Le, **1:**286
Ballet de la Reine (Gramont), **5:**270
"Ballet de la Reine de Cessile"
  (dance manuscript), **5:**336
Ballet de la Tour Eiffel, **3:**74
Ballet de la Vérité, Le, **1:**284
Ballet de l'Espérance, Le, **1:**284

Ballet de l'Harmonie Universelle,
  3:66
Ballet del INCIBA (Instituto
  National de Cultura y Bellas
  Artes), **6:**323
Ballet de l'Opéra de Paris, Le
  (Guest), **3:**321
Ballet de l'Opéra Russe, **5:**14
Ballet de l'Opéra Russe à Paris,
  4:636
Ballet del Teatro Lírico Nacional,
  Madrid, **5:**206, 674
Ballet de Lumière, **3:**93
Ballet de Marseille-Roland Petit.
  See Ballet National de
  Marseille
Ballet de Mars, Le, **1:**284
Ballet de Nice, **3:**75
Ballet der Lage Landen,
  1:289–290, **3:**203, **4:**591, 592
  Weeme, Mascha ter, **6:**375
  See also Dutch National Ballet
Ballet de Santiago de Chile,
  2:124–125, *125*, 441
  Haydée directorship, **2:**125, 127,
    3:351
Ballet des Arts, **2:**465
Ballet des Cinq Sens, **3:**66
Ballet des Comètes, Le, **1:**284
Ballet des Effets de la Nature, **3:**66
Ballet des Éléments, Le, **1:**425
Ballet des Étoiles de Paris, **3:**74,
  4:435
Ballet des Fêtes de Bacchus, Le,
  1:285
Ballet des Fragments de Mr. de Lully,
  1:46, **3:**49
Ballet des Jeux, Le, **1:**284
Ballet des Meuniers, Le, **3:**560,
  5:149
Ballet des Montagnards, **3:**544
Ballet des Muses, Les, **1:**284
"Ballet des Nations" (Le Bourgeois
  Gentilhomme*)*, **4:**231
Ballet des Noces de Pélée et Thétis,
  Le, **3:**184
Ballet des Plaisirs de la Vie des
  Enfans sans Soucy, **6:**38
Ballet des Polonais, Le, **1:**275, 398,
  409, **5:**533
Ballet des Princes Indiens, Le, **1:**409
Ballet des Saisons, Le, **1:**284, **5:**87
Ballet des Sens, Le, **1:**464, **2:**465
Ballet des Trois Arts. *See* Three Arts
  Ballet
Ballet de Victor Ullate, **5:**674
Ballet de Wallonie. *See*
  Charleroi/Danses
Ballet de Zargoza, **5:**674
Ballet d'Isoline, **6:**174
Ballet Divertissement, **1:**38
Ballet do IV Centenario de São
  Paulo, **4:**421
Ballet du Grand Théâtre de
  Genève. *See* Geneva Ballet
Ballet du Monde, Le, **1:**409
Ballet du Nord, Roubaix, **1:**462,
  3:74
Ballet du Rhin, Strasbourg, **2:**471,
  3:74, **4:**108, **5:**60
Ballet du Soleil, **2:**633
Ballet du XXᵉ Siècle, **1:**210,
  290–293, 404–406, 411, *412*,
  2:109, **5:**475, 479, 526, 677
Babilée, Jean, **1:**251
Ballet Béjart Lausanne as
  successor, **6:**54
Béjart *Romeo and Juliet*, **5:**398
Biagi, Vittorio, **1:**446
Blaska, Félix, **1:**461
  Cocteau collaboration, **2:**183

Farrell and Mejia dance
  partnership, **2:**577
Firebird, The, **3:**4
Gsovsky (Victor) teaching, **3:**318
Haydée guest performances,
  3:350
Leclair choreography, **4:**136
Markó, Iván, **4:**266
Naharin performances, **4:**531
Nureyev, Rudolf, **5:**7
Rayet, Jacqueline, **5:**320
Romeo and Juliet, **4:**335
  spectacular scenic design, **5:**551
Spectre de la Rose, Le, **3:**578
Ballet Education (Legat), **6:**128
Ballet Encyclopedia, **3:**424, **5:**643
Ballet en France, Le (Kochno), **4:**34
Ballet Español. *See* Ballet Nacional
  Español
Ballet Flor de Ceibo, **6:**301
Ballet Folklórico de la Ciudad de
  México, **4:**396
Ballet Folklórico de la Universidad
  Michoacana, **4:**396
Ballet Folklórico del Dominican
  Republic, **2:**432
Ballet Folklórico del Uruguay,
  6:301
Ballet Folklórico de México,
  4:395–396, *395*
Ballet Folklórico Nacional
  (Argentina), **1:**109, **4:**396
Ballet for All, **1:**541, **2:**354, 405,
  3:321, **5:**421, 603, 604
Ballet for Beginners (Draper and
  Atkinson), **6:**128
Ballet Franco Russe, **4:**25
Ballet Fundación Teresa Carreño
  (Ballet Nacional de Caracas),
  6:324, *324*, 325
Ballet Guatemala, **5:**62
Ballet Guild of Cleveland, **2:**178
Ballet Guild of Great Britain, **4:**110
Ballet Gulbenkian. *See* Gulbenkian
  Ballet
Ballet Guyed (Revitt), **2:**69
ballet héroïque, **5:**35, 113
Ballet High, A, **5:**436
Ballet Imperial, **1:**281, **293–294,**
  298, *299, 302*, **2:**376, 578,
  5:589, **6:**217
  Balanchine production, **1:**256,
    261, 262, 270, 293, **4:**28,
    5:415
  Balanchine revival, **4:**609
  Fonteyn performance, **3:**43
  Grey (Beryl) performance, **3:**307
  Moncion performance, **4:**449
  Nerina performance, **4:**584
Ballet in Action (Severn), **5:**184
Ballet in a Nutshell (Australia),
  1:214
Ballet Independiente de Mexico,
  4:396
Ballet in Moscow Today (Bellew),
  4:26
Ballet Internacional de Caracas,
  6:324
Ballet International, **1:**315, 430
Ballet International du Marquis de
  Cuevas. *See* International
  Ballet of New York
Ballet Intime, **1:**482, **5:**58
ballet-jazz, **2:**46
Ballet Laughs (Gard), **2:**69
Ballet Lausanne. *See* Béjart Ballet
  Lausanne
Balletlehre (Misslitz), **4:**691
Ballet Lirico Nacional. *See*
  Compañía Nacional de Danza

Ballet-Lover's Pocket-Book:
  Technique without Tears
  (Ambrose), **6:**128
Balletmakers Limited, **3:**271
Ballet Manila, **5:**172, 173
ballet master. *See* dancing master;
  specific personal names
Ballet Mécanique, Le, **1:**66, 134,
  483–484, **2:**603, **5:**546
Ballet Mêlé de Chants Héroiques,
  6:38
BalletMet, **6:**266
Ballet Nacional Chileno,
  2:123–124, *123, 124*, **3:**305,
  629, 630, **6:**304, *304*
Ballet Nacional Clásico, **1:**294, 295,
  5:674
Ballet Nacional de Caracas, **6:**324,
  324, 325
Ballet Nacional de Cuba, **1:**49, 50,
  2:276, 277–280, 586, **3:**429,
  4:398, **5:**62, 133
Ballet Nacional de México, **1:**524,
  525, **4:**392–394, 396, 397–398
Ballet Nacional Español, **1:**117,
  294–295, **3:**286, **4:**222, **5:**133,
  674, 676
Ballet Natal. *See* NAPAC Ballet
Ballet National de Marseille, **2:**200,
  3:75, 601, 643, **4:***523,* **5:**15,
  164, 613, **6:**143
Ballet National de Nancy et de
  Lorraine (formerly Ballet-
  Théâtre Français de Nancy),
  1:351, **2:**463, 576, **3:**74–75,
  4:108
Ballet National Djoliba, **1:**304,
  5:516–517
Ballet National Jeunesses
  Musicales de France, **2:**388,
  3:74, **4:**107
ballet nègre, **2:**458, 459
Ballet Nelsi Dambre, **5:**572
Ballet Nena Coronil, **6:**323
Ballet News (publication), **6:**297
Ballet Noir d'Art Dramatique, Le,
  5:516
Ballet Nuevo Mundo, **6:**324
balleto. See ballo and *balletto*
Ballet of a Grand Love, **4:**134
"Ballet of Flowers" (Rosalie), **3:**22
Ballet of Ljubljana, **6:**437, *437*
Ballet of the Amsterdam Opera,
  1:290, **4:**251, 591, 592
  See also Dutch National Ballet
Ballet of the Fourth Centennial,
  1:533
Ballet of the Great Theater in
  Warsaw. *See* Warsaw Ballet
Ballet of the Lowlands. *See* Ballet
  der Lage Landen
Ballet of the New World, **6:**324
"Ballet of the Nuns" (*Robert le*
  Diable), **2:**369, **4:**108, 514,
  6:58
Ballet of the Red Shoes, **6:**288
Ballet of the San Martín Theater.
  See San Martín Ballet
Ballet of the Stanislavsky and
  Nemirovich-Danchenko
  Musical Theater. *See*
  Stanislavsky and Nemirovich-
  Danchenko Musical Theater
Ballet of the Twentieth Century. *See*
  Ballet du XXᵉ Siècle
Ballet of the Württemberg State
  Theater. *See* Stuttgart Ballet
Ballet of Two Worlds, **3:**664, **5:**408
Balletograms, **5:**617
Ballet Oklahoma, **6:**265
Balletomania (Haskell), **3:**285

"Ballet on the Slovene Stage" (Mlakar), **6**:438
Ballet Pacifica, **6**:264
Ballet Panorama (Haskell), **3**:285
ballet-pantomime. *See* pantomime-ballet
Ballet Philippines, **5**:172, 174, **6**:379
Ballet-Plus, **5**:465, 475
Ballet Polnais, **4**:435
Ballet Populaire, **2**:125
Ballet pour Demain, **3**:75, 78
Ballet pour Tam-Tam et Percussion, **1**:462
Ballet Prague. *See* Studio Ballet Prague
Ballet Premier, **5**:684
Ballet Puertoriqqueño, **5**:275
Ballet Rambert. *See* Rambert Dance Company
Ballet Recital, **2**:347, **3**:121, **4**:251, 591, 600
See also Netherlands Ballet
Ballet Repertory Company. *See* American Ballet Theatre II
Ballet Review (journal), **5**:590, **6**:297
Ballet Royal de Wallonie. *See* Charleroi/Danses
Ballet Russe de Monte Carlo, **1**:295–303
Alonso (Alicia) guest appearances, **1**:49
Americanization of, **1**:296, 297, 302, **3**:25, **6**:264, 291
American tours, **1**:302, **6**:264
archival materials, **4**:168
Ashton productions, **1**:149, 297, 437
assessment of, **1**:301–302
Balanchine productions and influence, **1**:297, 298–300, 307
Ballet Imperial production, **1**:293, 298
Baronova guest appearances, **1**:367
Bérard designs, **1**:426
Bettis choreography, **1**:300, 441
Blum and Massine founding, **1**:295–296, 313, 466
Boris, Ruthanna, **1**:498
Canadian-trained dancers, **2**:38, 47
Carnaval, Le, **2**:73
Concerto Barocco, **2**:193
Coppélia, **2**:199
Danielian, Leon, **2**:341
Danilova, Alexandra, **2**:342, **3**:27, **4**:610
Danilova-Franklin dance partnership, **2**:342, **3**:*104*
decline and disbandment, **1**:301
Denham directorship, **1**:297, 300, 301, 313
Dolin-Markova guest performances, **2**:425
Fokine ballets, **3**:14, 21, 22, 23, 24, 25, *26*, 27, **6**:62
Franklin as *premier danseur*, **3**:87–88
Gaîté Parisienne, **3**:103–104, **4**:*320*
as Houston Ballet influence, **3**:389
leading dancers, **1**:296, 300, 301, 302, **2**:341
Markova, Alicia, **2**:425, **4**:268–269
Massine productions, **3**:103–104, **4**:323–324, 325

Mattise design, **4**:331
Nikjinska choreography, **1**:297, **4**:638
Nobilissima Visione, **4**:656
Nutcracker, The, **5**:14–15
Page, Ruth, **5**:58, *59*
as photographic subject, **5**:184
Raymonda, **5**:322
Rodeo premiere, **1**:297, **2**:197, 373, **5**:369
Serenade, **5**:571
Serrano, Lupe, **5**:572–573
Slavenska, Mia, **5**:606
Song of Norway, **1**:297–298, **6**:277
Sonnambula premiere performance, **5**:641
style, **2**:242
Swan Lake one-act production, **6**:32
Tallchief, Maria, **6**:84, 85, 86
Toumanova, Tamara, **6**:182
Youskevitch, Igor, **1**:296, 301, **6**:425
Ballet Russe Highlights, **1**:367, **4**:324, **6**:425
Ballets, Les. *See* Ballets 1933
Ballets: USA, **2**:197, **3**:242, **5**:363
Ballets Africains, Les, **1**:303–304, **4**:549, **5**:516, 517, **6**:22, 384
ballets ambulatoires, **5**:230
Ballets Américains, Les, **5**:59
Ballets anciens et modernes selon les régles du théâtre, Des (Ménéstrier), **1**:22, **3**:84
Ballets Bafia, Les, **2**:33
Ballets Bantou, Les, **2**:33
Ballets Camerounais, Les, **2**:33
"Ballets Chefs-d'oeuvre" (series), **5**:483
Ballets Chiriaeff, Les. *See* Grands Ballets Canadiens, Les
Ballets Contemporánea de la Universidad Veracruzana, **4**:394
Ballets de France, **2**:111, **3**:74, **6**:130
Ballets de la Jeunesse, **1**:284, 539, **2**:480, **3**:73, **4**:109
Ballets de la Tour Eiffel, **4**:107
Ballets de Léon Woizikovski, Les, **1**:311, **6**:404, 425
Ballets de l'Étoile, Les. *See* Ballet-Théâtre de Paris, Le
Ballets de Madrid, **1**:94
Ballets de Monte Carlo, **1**:295, 311, 313, 466, **2**:47, 449, **5**:650
Balanchine-Kochno collaboration, **4**:33
Lacotte and Thesmar joint directorships, **4**:108
Youskevitch performance, **6**:425
See also Ballet Russe de Monte Carlo
Ballets de Paris de Roland Petit, **1**:304–305, 306, **2**:111, 426, **3**:318, **5**:163, *164*
Ashton production, **1**:152
Cyrano de Bergerac, **3**:*600*
Fonteyn performances, **3**:41
founding and productions, **3**:74
Gilpin, John, **3**:175
Jeanmaire, Zizi, **3**:601
Joffrey debut performance, **3**:609
Manen, Hans van, **4**:251
Miskovitch, Milorad, **4**:435
Ballets de San Juan, **5**:275
Ballets des Champs-Élysées, **1**:305–306, **2**:440
Babilée, Jean, **1**:251, 305
Bérard designs, **1**:305, 426

Charrat, Janine, **1**:305, **2**:111, **3**:73
experimental works and performers, **3**:73–74
Grand Pas Classique, **2**:114
Gsovsky (Victor) *La Sylphide* revival, **3**:73, 318, **6**:58–59
Hugo (Jean) designs, **3**:394
Jeune Homme et la Mort, Le, **3**:601
Kochno as artistic director, **4**:33–34
Lichine choreography, **4**:178
London performances, **5**:415
Petit, Roland, **1**:304, 305–306, **3**:73, **5**:163
Ballets des Étoiles de Paris, **3**:74
Ballets des Fées de la Forêt de Saint-Germain, **2**:98
Ballets d'Esprilova, **2**:351
Ballets d'Ida Rubinstein. *See* Rubinstein, Ida
Ballets du Théâtre des Arts, **2**:150
Ballets Espagnols d'Argentina, **1**:115
ballet shoes. *See* footwear
Ballets Janine Charrat. *See* Ballets de France
Ballets Jazz de Montréal, Les, **4**:73
Ballets Jooss, **1**:111, **2**:66, **3**:40, 62, 271, **4**:93, **6**:195
Chilean tour, **2**:123
Dutch dancers, **4**:590
formation and disbandment, **3**:628–629
Hanka, Erika, **3**:340
Hoving, Lucas, **3**:390, 628, **4**:590
Leeder, Sigurd, **4**:140
Uthoff, Ernst, **6**:304
Wright, Peter, **6**:405
Züllig, Hans, **6**:453
ballet slippers. *See* footwear
Ballets Lycette Darsonval, **2**:351
Ballets Modernes de Paris, **2**:466, **3**:76
Ballets 1933, **1**:306–307, 309, 310, **2**:242, **6**:182
Balanchine repertory, **4**:229
Karinska costumes, **3**:653
Kochno involvement, **4**:33
Losch, Tilly, **4**:229
Milhaud score, **4**:418
Paris season, **3**:72–73
Ballets 1956. *See* Ballet des Étoiles de Paris
Ballet Society, **1**:300, 479, **6**:85
Cage-Cunningham commission, **2**:22, 286
Christensen, Lew, **2**:161
Dollar as ballet master, **2**:426
Four Temperaments, The, **3**:57–58, **4**:136
Kirstein and Balanchine conception, **1**:141, **4**:28–29, 606, **6**:247
Le Clercq performances, **4**:136–137
Moncion, Francisco, **4**:449, 450
Rosenthal technical supervision, **5**:407
Stravinsky commission, **6**:6
Symphony in C, **4**:65
Tallchief (Maria) as *prima ballerina*, **6**:84
See also New York City Ballet
Ballets of Valentin Elizariev, The, **2**:501
Ballet Sopianae, **1**:307–308, **2**:473–474, **3**:422
Ballets Romantiques, Les. *See* Ballet-Théâtre de Paris, Le

Ballets Russes de Colonel W. de Basil. *See* Ballets Russes de Monte Carlo
Ballets Russes de Monte Carlo, **1**:308–316, **5**:572–573
American tours, **4**:637, **6**:291
archival materials, **4**:169, 170
Aurora's Wedding, **5**:*611*, 612
Australian tours, **1**:207, 209, 235, 311, 313, 316, 498, 499, **2**:425
"baby ballerinas," **1**:308, 310, 367, **2**:478, **5**:349, **6**:182
Balanchine choreographies, **1**:256, 298, 308, 309, 313–314, 316, **2**:441, **3**:72
Ballet Russe de Monte Carlo rivalry, **1**:296
Bérard designs, **1**:311, *311*, 426
Beriozoff performances, **1**:430
Blum and Massine breaks with, **1**:295–296, 311, 312
Brazilian tour, **1**:532
Canadian tours, **2**:37
Canadian-trained dancers, **2**:38, 47
Carnaval, Le, **2**:73
Chappell designs, **2**:105
Charisse performances, **2**:108
Chiriaeff performances, **2**:150
Cieplinski association, **2**:172
Coppélia, **2**:200
Coq d'Or, **3**:20
Cotillon premiere, **2**:253
Cuban dancers, **2**:276–277
Danilova, Alexandra, **2**:201, 342
Dolin guest performances, **2**:425, **4**:269
Doubrovska performance, **2**:442
Eglevsky, André, **2**:478–479
Fernandez, Royes, **2**:586
final years, **1**:314–316
Firebird, The, **3**:1–2
first Paris season, **3**:72
Fokine and Lichine era, **1**:312–314, 316, **3**:14, 16–19, 24–25, **4**:178, **6**:62
German tour, **3**:148
Grigoriev as *régisseur*, **3**:308
Haskell involvement, **3**:285
Hightower, Rosella, **3**:361
Hugo (Jean) designs, **3**:394
inaugural season, **1**:308–309
Inglesby performances, **3**:508
Karinska costumes, **3**:653–654
Kirsova, Hélène, **4**:25
Kochno as artistic adviser, **4**:33
leading dancers, **1**:309, 310, 313, 314, 315
Lichine, David. *See* subhead Fokine and Lichine era *above*
makeup conventions, **4**:305
Markova and Dolin dance partnership, **4**:269
Massine era, **1**:207, 309–312, 316, **4**:*319*, 322–323
New Zealand tour, **4**:624
Nijinska choreography, **1**:311, 316, **4**:636–637
Noces revival, **1**:311, **4**:659
Nutcracker, The, **5**:14
Oboukhoff, Anatole, **5**:17
as Original Ballet Russe, **1**:313–316
practice clothes requirements, **5**:242
Psota, Ivo Váňa, **5**:269, 270
Riabouchinska, Tatiana, **5**:349, 350
as Sadler's Wells competitor, **5**:414
Schéhérazade, **3**:25

Ballets Russes de Monte Carlo,
  continued
 second company, **1:**311, **4:**667
 Skibine, George, **5:**604
 South American tours, **1:**110,
  314–315, 532, **2:**127
 strike, **1:**314
 style, **2:**242
 Swan Lake one-act production,
  6:32
 Tchernicheva, Lubov, **6:**120
 Teatro Colón joint ballet
  companies, **1:**110, 314, 315
 Toumanova, Tamara, **6:**182
 Woizikowski performances,
  6:404
 Zorina, Vera, **6:**449
Ballets Russes de Paris, **4:**667,
 6:425
Ballets Russes de Serge Diaghilev,
 1:316–326, 2:83
 American tour (1916), **1:**322,
  2:408–409, **4:**645, **6:**237, 243,
  271, 299
 Apollo, **1:**95–96, *95,* **2:**406
 Après-midi d'un Faune, L',
  1:98–99, *99, 319,* **2:**360, 406
 Argentine tour, **1:**110
 artistic nucleus, **1:**125, 132–134,
  135, 316–317, 323, 423–424,
  2:287, 406, 406–407, 409
  See also subhead scenic design;
  names of specific artists
 as Ashton influence, **1:**147
 Australian tours, **1:**207
 Bakst designs, **1:**253, 254–255,
  2:241, 407, **5:**541
 Balanchine choreography, **1:**256,
  256, 258, 317, 325, 348,
  2:401, 406, 410, **4:**320, 321
 Ballet Russe de Monte Carlo
  links, **1:**297
 Ballets Russes de Monte Carlo
  revivals of productions,
  1:309, 311
 Ballets Russes Orchestra, **1:**93
 ballet technique, **1:**348
 Benois designs, **1:***422,* 423–424,
  2:241
 Biches, Les, **1:**316, 449,
  2:406, 410
 Bolm, Adolph, **1:**319, 482, 483,
  2:408, 411, **3:**16, 18, 19,
  20, **6:**32
 books on, **3:**285, 308
 Brazilian tours, **1:**532
 Canadian performance, **2:**37
 Capriccio Espagnole, **1:**117
 caricatures of, **2:**70, *70*
 Carnaval, Le, **2:**73, **3:**16
 Cecchetti as principal teacher,
  1:319, 329, 348, **2:**82,
  3:547–548
 Cecchetti mime performances,
  2:82
 Cocteau libretti and
  choreographic collaboration,
  2:183
 composers, **4:**515–516
  *See also names of specific
  composers*
 contemporary critical reviews,
  3:284, 285
 Coq d'Or, Le, **5:**542, *542*
 corps de ballet, **1:**319, **2:**411
 costume innovations, **2:**241, 250
 Craske performances, **2:**268
 Danilova, Alexandra, **2:**342
 Debussy scores, **2:**360, 361
 demise of, **1:**326, **2:**411, **5:**411

de Valois, Ninette, **2:**396, 399,
 3:262
Dobujinsky designs, **2:**421
Dolin, Anton, **2:**423–424
Doubrovska, Felia, **2:**441
English National Ballet revivals
 of productions, **2:**508, 510,
 511, 512, **3:**269, **6:**404
Europeanization, **1:**323, **2:**408
Fedorova guest performances,
 2:582
film projections, **2:**603
Fokine as choreographer, **1:***317,*
 318, *318,* 319–322, **2:**406,
 3:14, 15, 16–19, 20–21,
 198, *198*
Fokine departure and brief
 return, **2:**408, **3:**19–20, **4:**641
Giselle, **3:**182
Golovin designs, **3:**196
Goncharova designs, **3:**197–198
Grands Ballets Canadiens
 repertory, **3:**233
Grigoriev as *régisseur,* **3:**308
Hungarian performances,
 3:414, 415
Idzikowski, Stanislas, **3:**441–442
Joffrey revivals, **3:**614, 616–617
Josephslegende, Die, **3:**631, **4:**316
Karsavina, Tamara, **3:**656
Kiev stagings, **6:**224
Kirstein's fascination with, **4:**26
Kochno association, **4:**32–33
Kshessinska (Matilda) guest
 performances, **4:**68
Lambert *Romeo and Juliet* score,
 4:113
Larionov designs, **4:**124–125
Levinson reviews, **4:**154–155
as London ballet influence,
 3:262–263, 279, 281
London debut (1911), **1:**319
London performances, **2:**409,
 3:262, *264,* **4:**317, 320
Lopokova, Lydia, **4:**223
makeup, **4:**305
male dancers as stars, **1:**318,
 2:408
Markova, Alicia, **4:**267
masks, **4:**302, *302*
Massine as choreographer and
 principal dancer, **1:**322, 323,
 323, 324–325, **2:**399, 410,
 4:316–318
Massine return and second
 break, **4:**320–321
Massine-type dances, **5:**636
Matisse deisgns, **4:**331
Monaco base, **2:**410
Nijinska choreography, **1:**324,
 325, 348, **2:**406, 410, 423–424,
 441, **4:**113, 633, 634, 657–659,
 5:398
Nijinska performances,
 4:634–635
Nijinsky choreography and
 performances, **1:**317, 318,
 319, 320, 321, 322, **2:**406,
 408, 409, **3:**20, **4:**639,
 641–645
Nijinsky dismissal, **4:**645
Noces premiere performance,
 4:657–659
Nutcracker segments, **5:**13
Orientalism, **2:**407, **3:**17, 18, **5:**45
Parade, **5:**85, 86
Parisian performances, **3:**71–72
Paris Opera Ballet appearances,
 5:95
Pavillon d'Armide, Le, **5:**118–119,
 6:160

Pavlova, Anna, **5:**122, 123
Petrouchka, **3:**18, *19,* 655, **4:***645,*
 5:165, 166
Picasso designs, **5:**191–192, *192,*
 262, 543–544, *543,* **6:**192
pointe work refinement, **5:**208
Polish dancers, **5:**217
Polovtsian Dances setting, **5:**372
Portugal tour, **5:**233
practice clothes requirements,
 5:241
prints and drawings, **5:**262
Prodigal Son, The, **3:**609, **5:**264
Rambert association, **3:**262,
 5:296
Ravel compositions, **5:**315
Roerich designs, **5:**372
Romanov, Boris, **4:**644,
 5:391–392
Romeo and Juliet, **1:**135, **5:**398
 as Royal Swedish Ballet
 influence, **6:**41
Sacre du Printemps, Le, **5:**327,
 487–488
scenic design, **5:**540, 541–543
 *See also names of specific
 designers*
Schéhérazade production,
 5:541, 556
Schollar, Ludmilla, **5:**558, 559
Sleeping Princess, The, **1:**255, 318,
 319, 323–324, 540, **2:**409, 480,
 3:*264,* **5:**611–612
Sololova, Lydia, **5:**636–637
South American tour, **2:**409,
 4:645
as Soviet artistic influence,
 4:320–322
Soviet emigré talent, **2:**410
Spanish influences, **5:**674
Spessivtseva, Olga, **5:**678
Swan Lake production, **6:**32
Sylphides, Les. See Sylphides, Les,
 Diaghilev production
Tchelitchev deisgns, **5:**545, *545,*
 6:118
Tchernicheva, Lubov, **6:**120
Teatro Costanzi, Rome, **5:**399
television performances, **6:**134
Tricorne, Le, **2:**567–568, **5:**674,
 6:192
Vilzak, Anatole, **6:**341
Woizikowski, Leon, **6:**403–404
 See also Diaghilev, Serge; Saison
 Russe
Ballets Suédois, Les, **1:**118, 134,
 243, **3:**326–328, 400, **2:**182,
 242, 286, 361, 410, **5:**237,
 335, *335,* 525
archives, **4:**163
artist and writer collaborators,
 1:327, **2:**399, **3:**72
Création du Monde, La, **4:**418
Fokine involvement, **3:**21, **6:**41
Hugo (Jean) designs, **3:**393
Maison de Fous, **3:**100
Mariés de la Tour Eiffel, Les, **4:**516
Milhaud scores, **1:**327, **2:**399,
 3:72, 393, **4:**418, 516
Relâche, **1:**327–328, **2:**603,
 3:614, *616*
scenic design innovations,
 5:544, *544*
Swedish dancers, **6:**41
Ballets Suédois, Les (Häger), **6:**49
Ballet Stagium, **1:**535–536, *535*
Ballets 38, Les, **6:**378
Ballets Trockadero de Monte Carlo,
 Les, **6:**190–191, *191*
Ballet-Studio de l'Opéra, **2:**388
Ballet Studio '45, **3:**121

Ballet Symphony, **2:**529–530, **4:**478
Ballets Yvonne Georgi. *See* Georgi,
 Yvonne
Ballett (journal), **3:**162
Ballett (Niehaus), **3:**161
Ballett der Bühnen der Stadt Köln,
 4:421
Ballett der Deutschen Oper am
 Rhein Düsseldorf-Duisburg.
 See Düsseldorf-Duisberg
 Ballet
Ballett der Deutschen Oper Berlin.
 See Berlin Opera Ballet
Ballett der Hamburgischen
 Staatsoper. *See* Hamburg
 Ballet
Ballett der Städtischen Bühnen
 Frankfurt am Main. *See*
 Frankfurt Ballet
Ballett der Wiener Staatsoper. *See*
 Vienna State Opera Ballet
Ballett der Wiener Volksoper. *See*
 Vienna Folk Opera Ballet
Ballett der Württembergischen
 Staatstheater Stuttgart. *See*
 Stuttgart Ballet
Ballett des Staatstheaters am
 Gärtnerplatz, Munich, **3:**157
Ballet Teatro del Espacio, **2:**389,
 4:394, 396
Ballet Teatro Municipal de San
 Juan, **5:**275
Ballet Tech, **1:**420, **2:**583, 585
ballet technique, **1:328–342**
 adage, **1:**7–9
 allegro, **1:**44–45
 arabesque, **1:**100–101
 arm positions, **1:**332, **332–333,**
  343, 345, 346
 Bournonville style, **1:**329
 corresponding to feet positions,
  1:*331*
 Dupré choreographic
  emphasis, **2:**465
  See also subhead port de bras
  below
 attitude, **1:**197–198
 battement, **1:**383–384
 batterie, **1:**384–385
 body positions, **1:**197–198,
  333–335, *334*
 capriola, **1:**384
 chaîné turns, **1:**337
 directions, **1:***335,* **335–336**
 feet positions, **1:330–332,** *331,*
  333, 396–397
 Beauchamp's definitions, **5:**87
 in pirouettes, **1:**336–337
 turnout, **6:**214–215
 fish dives, **5:**103
 fouetté turns, **5:**189, *190,* 338
 injury prevention, **2:**329–330,
  4:19
 jumping movements, **1:339–342,**
  340, 341, 343, 344, 345
 Craske approach, **1:**341, 347,
  2:268–269
 Danish school, **1:**347
 French versus Italian schools,
  1:347
 grand jeté, **5:**188–189, *189*
 as Kolpakova characteristic,
  4:36
 in Petipa (Marius)
  choreographies, **5:**152
 as Soviet school emphasis,
  1:349
 knee bend. *See plié*
 leg elevation. *See* elevation
 leg rotation. *See* turnout
 lifts, **5:**103–105, 153

linking movements, **1:338–339,** 345, 346
major schools, **1:328–330,** 333
  Bournonville, **1:**347–348, 399
  Cecchetti, **1:**347, 398, **2:**83–84
  French versus Italian, **1:**347
  Vaganova, **1:**328–329, 330, 399
partnering, **5:**101–105, 189
  See also pas de deux
physics basis, **5:**188–190
piqué turns, **5:**207, 209
pirouettes, **5:**103, 338
port de bras, **1:**332, 345, 349, **5:**226–227, **6:**62
small-scale versus large-scale poses and movements, **1:**329
soutenu turns, **1:**337
streamlined aesthetic, **1:**347, 348
technical manuals, **6:**126–127, 128–129
tours en l'air, **1:**338
turning movements, **1:***336,* **336–338**
  in attitude, **1:**198
  finger turns, **5:**103
  See also barre exercises; body therapies; notation
Ballet Technique (Karsavina), **2:**382, **6:**128
ballet technique, history of, **1:342–349**
  Balanchine approach, **1:**264–266
  Blasis method, **1:**461
  British style, **3:**258–259, 265, 267, **5:**412, 414
  caricatures and lampoons of, **2:**2.70–71
  Chinese opera, **2:**143–144
  choreographic influences, **1:**349
  costume evolution affecting, **1:**44, 347, 348, **2:**236, 238, 239, 240, 241
  Craske methods, **2:**268–269
  Eglevsky's feats, **2:**479
  England, **3:**258–259
  evolution of leg-extension emphasis, **1:**348
  evolution of streamlined look, **1:**347, 348
  Fokine approach, **3:**14, 28, **6:**62
  Fonteyn approach, **3:**43, 44
  French Conservatoire de Danse, **3:**81–82
  French court dance, **1:**285–288, **342–344,** **3:**63, 65–67, 81, 130
    American reconstructions, **6:**251
    anglaise, **1:**89–90
    Balet Comique de la Royne as first ballet, **1:**275
    ballet de cour, **1:**285–288, **2:**168
    bassedanse, **1:**378–379
    Beauchamps, Pierre, **1:**396–397
    Beaujoyeulx, Balthazar de, **1:**397–398
    bourrée, **1:**516–517
    branle, **1:**522–523
    Callot etchings, **2:**26–27
    chaconne and *passacaille*, **2:**98–99
    contredanse, **2:**255
    costume, **2:**236–239
    cotillon, **2:**251–253
    courant, **2:**259–261
    dancing masters, **2:**337–338
    de Hesse compositions, **2:**365–366
    Dupré system, **2:**465
    entrée grave, **2:**518–519
    Feuillet notation, **2:**588–589
    figure dances, **2:**591–592

folia, **3:**28, 29
forlana, **3:**49–50
gavotte, **3:**64, 123–124, 123–125
gigue, **3:**172–173, 607
  hornpipe variant, **3:**377
Italian influences, **3:**543
lighting, **4:***186,* 187
loure, **4:**231–232
menuet, **4:**431–433, 431–435, 510, 511, 512
musette, **4:**481–482
music, **4:**508–512
notation, **4:**684–685
révérence, **5:**345
rigaudon, **3:**351–352
sarabande, **5:**520
  See also France, theatrical dance, 1581–1789
Italy, **3:**542–543
  Johansson methods, **3:**618
  Lifar approach, **4:**183–184
  musical accompaniment, **1:**6
  Nijinska experiments, **4:**634
  Soviet style, **1:**329, **4:**283, 285–286
  United States, **6:**233–234
  See also aesthetics; modern dance technique
Ballet Technique for the Male Dancer (Tarasov), **6:**106, 129
Ballett-Gestalt und Wesen (Niehaus), **3:**161
Ballet Theater in Russia (Krasovskaya), **4:**58
Ballet Theatre. *See* American Ballet Theatre
Ballet-Théâtre Contemporain, **1:349–351,** 542, **2:**388, 576, **3:**77
  Babilée performance, **1:**251
  Blaska choreography, **1:**461
  founding, **3:**74
Ballet-Théâtre de Bordeaux, **3:**75
Ballet-Théâtre de l'Arche, **3:**78
Ballet-Théâtre de Paris, Le, **1:**290, 403–404, **2:**587, **3:**74
  See also Ballet du XXe Siècle
Ballet-Théâtre Français de Nancy, **1:**351, **2:**463, 576, **3:**74–75
Ballet Theatre Workshop, **1:**69
balletti. See ballo and *balletto*
Balletti, Benedetta, **2:**365, 366
Ballett Info (journal), **3:**162
Ballettinstituttet, Oslo, **4:**681
Ballett International (journal), **3:**162
Balletti Romani di Milloss, **2:**369
Ballett Journal (publication), **3:**162
balletto. See ballo and *balletto*
Ballet Today (journal), **3:**285
Ballet Transvaal, **5:**53, 652
Ballett-Variationen, **4:**517
Ballet 2000 (Spanish magazine), **5:**676
Ballettzentrum Hamburg-John Neumeier, **3:**338
"Ballet under Three Crowns" (Skeaping), **5:**603
Ballet van de Vijf Zinnen, **4:**588
Ballet van Vlaanderen. *See* Royal Ballet of Flanders
Ballet Variations, **3:**359
Ballet Victoria (Canada), **1:**208, 212, **4:**275, **5:**563, **6:**379
Ballet Waldeen, **1:**524
"ballet war" (London; 1938), **1:**296, 297, 313
Ballet West, Salt Lake City, **1:**501, **2:**388, **3:**345, **4:**435
  archival materials, **4:**170

Christensen (Willam) founding, **2:**162, **6:**264
Ford Foundation grant, **6:**265
Marks and Lander (Toni) co-directorship, **4:**120, 271
Nutcracker, The, **5:**15
Ballet Workshop, **5:**301
Ballet y baile español (Puig), **5:**676
Ballet y Bailes de España de José Greco, **3:**286
Ballet Ys, **2:**41
Ballet Yvonne Georgi. *See* Georgi, Yvonne
balli. See ballo and *balletto*
Balli di Sfessania (Callot), **2:**27, *189,* 190, **4:**312
Ball i la dansa popular a Catalunya, El (Capmany), **5:**676
Ball in Old Vienna, A, **3:**614, 628
Ballin' the Jack, **2:**25, **6:**255, 257
Balli teatrali a Venezia (score collection), **3:**556
ballo and *balletto,* **1:351–355**
  ballet origins, **3:**130
  ballo grande, **5:**529
  bassedanse versus, **1:**351, **4:**501
  Caroso dance manuals, **1:**352, **2:**74, 75, 77
  Cornazano dance manual, **2:**205, **3:**542
  dance-type components, **4:**504
  entrée, **2:**517
  as figure dances, **2:**590–591
  galliard movements, **3:**107, 108, 109
  Gluck-Angiolini collaboration, **3:**187–188, 189
  intermedio, **3:**509, 510–511, **4:**505
  Italian-style, **3:**544–545, 556, **4:**505
  music, **4:**505–506, 507
  Negri dance manual, **1:**352, **4:**579, 580–582
  pastorales, **5:**113
  suites, **5:**505, 506
Ballo Concertante, **1:**307
Ballo d'Achille, **3:**189
"Ballo del Fiore," **2:**74, **4:**507
Ballo della gagliarda (Compasso), **3:**107, **6:**122
Ballo della Regina, Il, **1:**269, **4:**611, 618
Ballo delle Ingrate, Il, **3:**544, **4:**505
Ballo d'Ercole, Il, **3:**542
Ball of the Century (marquis de Cuevas; 1953), **3:**226
Ballo in Maschera, Un (Verdi), **2:**446
ballon, **1:**44, 340, *340,* 344, 347
  Cerrito fame, **2:**93
  Nijinsky fame, **4:**646
Ballon, Antoine, **1:**355
Ballon, Claude, **1:***3,* 91, **355–356,** **4:**105, 106, **5:**41, 87, 105, 109, 129, 249, 260, 503
  Académie Royale de Danse, **1:**4, 355, 465
  as *ballet de collège* dance master, **1:**283
  ballet de cour, **1:**288, **3:**329
  Blondy association, **1:**464
  bourrée compositions, **1:**516, 517
  dance classes, **3:**81
  English performances, **3:**255
  mime, **4:**173
  nephew Laval (Antoine Bandieri de), **4:**130–131
  Subligny dance partnership, **6:**11
  Weaver on, **1:**355, **6:**374
Ballon, François, **1:**355
Ballon, Le, **3:**426

ballonné, **2:**502
Balloon, **1:**350, 542
Balloon II, **1:**542
ballos dance, **3:**296
ball-play dance, **4:***59*
Ballroom (musical), **1:**420, **6:**285
ballroom dance. *See* ball; ballroom dance competition; social dance; *specific dances*
Ball-Room Bijou, The (Durang dance guide), **2:**467, **3:**378
ballroom dance competition, **1:356–359,** **5:**631
Ball Throwing Dance, **2:**221–222
Ballum Circus, **2:**466
ballu tundu, **2:**101
Ballyhoo (revue), **1:**520
Bal Mabille, **3:**69
Bal Masqué, Le, **3:**609, 610
Bal Negré (musical), **2:**459
Balog, Klara, **6:**223
Balogh, Robert, **2:**310
Balon, Claude. *See* Ballon, Claude
Bal Paré, Le (Saint-Aubin), **1:**46, 47
Bal Poundré, **3:**15
Bals de Paris, Les, **1:**411
Baltarangio Malūnas, **4:**208
Baltatsheva, Naema, **5:**47
Baltic countries. *See* Estonia; Latvia; Lithuania
Baltimore Ballet, **5:**62
Baltimore Jazz, **6:***257*
Baluchi (people), **1:**27
Baluchistan, **3:**513–514
Balustrade, **1:**261, 314, **2:***243,* 376, **6:**119, 182
Balzac, Honoré de, **1:**144, **6:**442
Bamana dance, **1:359–361,** **4:**484, 486, **6:**12, 382, 383
Bambara dance. *See* Bamana dance
bambelô, **1:**527
Bamboche (revue), **2:**459
Bamboo Princess, The, **6:**203
bamboula dance, **2:**64
bambulá, **2:**430
BaMbuti (people), **4:**484
bambūtīyah dance, **2:**489–490, *490*
Bamileke (people), **2:**33, **4:***292*
BAMM, **2:**358
Bampton Morris Dancers, **4:**474
Bamrungtrakul, Nuchawadee, **4:**112, **6:**151
Bán, Teodora, **3:**418
Banamali, **5:**23
Banana Boy, **3:**574
Banat, **5:**379, 380, 382
Banchelli, Leopoldo, **5:**231
Banchetto musicale, **1:**364
Banda (people), **2:**87, 89, 211–212
banda dance, **3:**333–334, 335
Banda Dance (*House of Flowers*), **6:**277
bandari, **1:**102
Bandem, I Made, **2:***571*
Bandl dance, **3:**141
Bandō Minosuke IV, **1:**362
Bandō Mitsugorō, **1:361–362,** **3:**593
Bandō Mitsugorō II. *See* Ōgino Isaburō II
Bandō Mitsugorō III, **1:**361, **4:**537
Bandō Mitsugorō IV (later Morita Kan'ya XI), **1:**361, **4:**537
Bandō Mitsugorō V (Bandō Shuka I), **1:**361
Bandō Mitsugorō VI, **1:**361
Bandō Mitsugorō VII, **1:**361
Bandō Mitsugorō VIII, **1:**361
Bandoneón, **1:**388–389
Bandō Ryū, **1:**361, **3:**593

Bandō Shuka I, **1:**361
Bandō Shuka III, **1:**362
Bandō Tamasaburō, **1:362**
Bandō Tamasaburō I. *See* Bandō Mitsugorō V
Bandō Tamasaburō II, **1:**362
Bandō Tamasaburō III, **1:**362
Bandō Tamasaburō IV, **1:**362
Bandō Tamasaburō V, **1:**362, **2:***218*, **3:**439, 640, 658, **5:***29*, 30
Bandō Yasosuke V, **1:**361
Band Wagon, The (film), **1:**194–195, **2:**109, *109*, 616, **4:**10, 11, 229
Band Wagon, The (musical), **5:**310, **6:**275, *275*
Bandyoyan Purulia *chhau,* **2:**117
BaNdzabi (people), **4:**289
Banegas, Joaquín, **2:**278
Banerji, Comolata, **5:***123*
Banes, Sally, **3:**131, 304
    as contributor, **1:**243–246, 326–328, 538–539, 543–545, **2:**119–120, 460–461, **3:**54, 200–202, 336, 633–635, **4:**21–22, **5:**127–128, 292–293, 334–335
Banff Centre for Continuing Education, Alberta, **4:**238
Banff Centre for the Arts, Alberta, **4:**72, **5:**72, **6:**133
Banff Film and Video Festival, Alberta, **6:**133
Banfield, Rafaello de, **2:**426, **5:**676
"Banga" (Pot Dance), **5:***169*
Bangarra Dance Theatre, **1:**212, 215, **6:**56
Bang, Herman, **5:**553
Bangladesh, **1:**18–19, **362–363**
Bangoura, Hamidou, **1:**304
Banister, John, **5:**280
banja (song form), **2:**64
banjo, **2:**180
Banjo, **2:**289
Banjo Ingenues, **6:***447*
Bank, Liubov, **1:**489, **3:**193, **6:**106
Bankhead, Tallulah, **4:**22
Banks, Marilyn, **1:**60
Banner, Christopher, **1:**51, **3:**272
Bannerman, Kenneth, **2:**440
Banovitch, Milenko, **5:**53
banquet, **1:363–365**
    Taiwanese *yanyue,* **6:**79, 82–83
Banshee, The, **3:**398, **6:**95
Bantongha, **2:**33
Bantu (people), **2:**87–88, **5:**579, 643
Banys, Henrikas, **4:**208
banza, **2:**63
Bao Lian Deng, **5:**130
Bapov, Ramazam, **3:**665
Baptism, The, **1:**524
Baptists, **2:**167
bara', **4:**405, 410, 417, **6:***418,* 419
Bara, Charlotte, **6:**52
Barabau, **2:**399, 401, 410, **4:**182
Barabra (people), **6:**13
Baran, Ludvík, *as photographer,* **2:**304
Baran, Timir, **5:**580
Baranggay Folk Dance Group, **5:**172, 173
Baranović, Krešimir, **5:**101, **6:**432
Baratov, Leonid, **3:**186
Bar at the Folies-Bergère, The (Manet painting), **2:**400
Baratti, Filippo, **5:**404
Bar aux Folies-Bergère (de Valois ballet), **2:**105, **3:**266, 508, **4:**267, **5:**293, 299, 560
Barba, Eugenio, **2:**126, **4:**424–425, **5:**68, 130

Barba, Heen, **3:***649*
Barbà, Raoul, *as photographer,* **1:**309, **3:**26, **4:**321
Barbaja, Domenico, **2:**464, **5:**135
Barbara and Allen, **2:**364
Barbay, Ferenc, **3:**4, **6:**66
Barbeau, Marius, **2:**36
Barbe-Bleue, **3:**79, **4:**143, 144, 145, **5:**154, 157, 247
Barbee, Victor, **1:**77
Barber, Samuel, **1:**47, 57, **2:**17, **3:**218, 384, **4:**275, 518, 520, 622, **6:**342
Barberina, La, **1:**365, **2:**70, 394, **3:**545, **5:**89, 248, 353
Barber of Seville, The (Rossini), **1:**36
Barber Violin Concerto, **4:**275, 622
Barbetta, Giulio Cesare, **4:**505
Barbier, Jules, **2:**368, **6:**62
Barbier de Séville, Le, ou Figaro. See Figaro
Barbiere, Joseph, **2:**85
Barbieri, Margaret, **2:**405, **5:**55, 294, 421, 654
Barbieri, Niccolò, **2:**188
Barbon, Tito, **6:**301
Barbuta, Giocanda, **3:**233
Barceló, Antonio, **1:**109
Barcsai's Lover, **5:**287
Bardham, Shanti, **3:**468
Bardin, Micheline, **5:**96, **6:**65
Bardon, Henry, **2:**445
Bárdos, Lajos, **2:**417, **3:**421
Bardyguine, George, **6:**397
bareback riders. *See* horse ballet
Barefoot, **1:**307
barefoot dancing, **3:**214, **5:**456, 476
Baretta, Leopoldina, **4:***464*
Bari, Tania, **1:**291, 404, 406
baris, **1:**175, **366–367,** **2:**232, **3:**477–478, 479, 491, 644, 645, **4:**264
baris gedé, **3:**478, 485
Barisic, Luisa, **1:***215*
baris tumbak, **3:**478, *479*
Barker, Barbara (Barker-Warner), *as contributor,* **1:**495–496, **4:**22–24, 463–464, **5:**403–404, 514–515
Barkley, Beverly, **2:***36*
Barkleys of Broadway, The (film), **1:**194, **5:**373
Barkóczy, Sándor, **3:**417
Barlach, Ernst, **3:**152
Bârlea, Monica, **5:**387
Barley, William, **4:**505
Barlow, Ken, **5:**395
Barlow Brothers, **6:**316
Barnabé, Jocelyn, **6:**132
Barnard, Scott, **3:**617
Barnard College, New York City, **3:**385
    Greek Dance competition, **6:***241*
Barn Dance, **4:**210
Barnes, Albert C., **4:**331, 332
Barnes, Clive, **5:**131, 207
    American dance criticism, **6:**299
    on Baryshnikov, **1:**371
    on Bausch, **1:**389
    on Bennett (Michael), **1:**419
    British dance criticism, **3:**285
    on Fedorovitch designs, **2:**582
    on Fracci as "Duse of Dance," **3:**61
    on Harkness Ballet focus, **3:**42–343
    on Jamison's *Cry* performance, **3:**578
    on Lewitzky, **4:**156

on Murphy (Graeme) choreography, **6:**57
on Shawn's modern dance influence, **5:**587
Stuttgart Ballet advocacy, **2:**267
on *Walkaround Time* decor, **6:**356
Barnes, Edward, **3:**202
Barnes, Patricia, *as contributor,* **2:**586, **3:**306–307, **4:**24–25, 109–110, **5:**391, 572–573
Barnes, Theo, **6:**282
Barnes Foundation, Merion, Pennsylvania, **4:**330, 331
Barnet, Boris, **3:**48
Barnett, Dene, **6:**124
Barnett, Robert, **1:**197, **2:**178, **5:**194, *194,* **6:**265
Barnett, Sheila, **3:**574, 577
Barnett, Virginia, **1:**197
Barnfield, Richard, **3:**377
Barnum (musical), **6:**286
"Barnum" (skating program), **6:**180
Barnum, P. T., **5:**45, 318
Barnum and Bailey's Circus, **4:**24, **6:**237
Barococo Party, **5:**389
Barofsky, Jonathan, **1:**141
Baron (Stirling Henry Nahum), **5:**184
    as photographer, **1:**152, **2:**374, **3:**225, 236, **5:**91
Baron, Auguste, **3:**84
barong, **2:**232, *232,* **3:**473, **488–489,** *489, 490,* 644, **4:**249, 297, **5:**356, **6:**369
barong kékét, **3:**489–490, 491
barong landung figures, **3:**489, *489*
barong tagalog, **2:**230, 231
Baronova, Irina, **1:**207, **367–368,** **5:**248, 265, 612, **6:**182, 198
Ballets Russes de Monte Carlo, **1:**308, 310, 311, 312, 313, *313,* **3:**24, 25, **5:**349
    Cent Baisers performance, **4:**636
    Coppélia performance, **2:**200
    Fokine ballets, **3:**24, 25, 26, 27
Baron's Court, West London, **5:**422
Baroque dance
    American reconstructions, **6:**251
    ballet de cour. See subhead French court dance *below*
    Bibiena family designs, **1:**447
    costume, **2:**236
    dance reconstruction, **5:**322–325, 327, 328
    Drottningholm Court Theater revivals, **6:**46–47
    French court dance, **1:**285–289, 342–344
    horse ballet, **3:**381–383
    notation, **4:**684–685
    opéra-ballet and *tragédie lyrique,* **5:**34, 38–41
    révérence, **5:**345
    Spanish castanet style, **2:**78
    technical manuals, **6:**122–124
    theater design, **6:**156–57
    types
        allemande, **1:**45–47
        anglaise, **1:**89–90
        bergamasque, **1:**428
        bourée, **1:**516–517
        canary, **2:**51
        chaconne and *passacaille,* **2:**97–99
        courante, **1:**342, **2:**259–261
        entrée, **2:**517–518
        entrée grave, **2:**518–519
        figure dances, **2:**591, **5:**621
        folia, **3:**28–29

        forlana, **3:**49–50
        gavotte, **3:**123–125
        gigue, **3:**172–173, 607
        hornpipe, **3:**375–376
        loure, **4:**231–232
        menuet, **4:**431–433
        musette, **4:**481–482
        passepied, **5:**109
        rigaudon, **5:**351–352
        sarabande, **5:**520
        tambourin, **6:**97
    See also masquerades; subhead theatrical dance *under specific countries*
Baroque Dance Ensemble, **6:**251
Baroux, Harry, **4:**522
Barr, Alfred, **4:**27
Barr, Margaret, **1:**212, 214, **4:**626
Barra, Ray, **1:**391, 436, **2:**266, **3:**156, **5:**395, 674, **6:**10
Barrault, Jean-Louis, **3:**651, **4:**423, 425, **5:**176
Barre, Jean-Auguste, **1:**368, **2:**503, **4:**215, **5:***259*
Barredo, Maniya, **1:**197, **5:**172
barre exercises, **5:**201–202, 208–209, *337,* 338, **6:**127
    as Soviet school emphasis, **1:**349
Barrett, Maude M., **2:**284–285
Barrette, F., 373
Barretts of Wimpole Street, The (play), **3:**354
Barrez, Jean-Baptiste, **2:**405, **3:**82, 222
Barrie, J. M., **4:**463
barriera, torneo, and *battaglia,* **1:368–370,** **2:**74, 591, **3:**509, **4:**580, 581
Barrison, Gertrude, **1:**239
Barrison sisters, **1:**130, 131
Barros Aldunate, Raquel, *as contributor,* **2:**121–122
Barrow, Helen, **2:***290,* 291
Barry, Gerald, **2:**355
Barschau foundation, **1:**365
Barskov, Oleg, **4:**127
Barstow, Richard and Edith, **2:**176
Bart, Patrice, **2:**513, **3:**156, **5:**98
Barta, G., **5:**569
Bartal, Ferencné, *as photographer,* **1:**408, **3:**408, 410, 411
Bartenieff, Irmgard, **1:**469, *471,* 472–473, **2:**330, 321
    Choreometric study, **2:**602, **4:**99, 370
    Labanotation, **4:**32, 96
    Laban theory, **4:**16, 95, 97, 98, 103, 104
    movement choir, **4:**477
    students, **2:**461, **6:**25
Bartenieff Fundamentals, **1:**469, 471, **472–473,** **3:**320, **4:**18, 20, 98, 104
Bartered Bride, The (Smetana), **1:**484, **4:**239, **5:**617
Bartha, Karoly, **5:**279
Bartho, Catherina, **1:**207
Bartholin, Birger, **2:**385, **3:**657, **4:**245, **5:***554*
Bartholomin, Madame, **4:**453, 454
Bartholomin, Victor, **4:**453, 454
Bartik, Ottokar, **4:**382
Bartko, Emil, **5:**615
Bartlemas Dances, **3:**202, **5:**300
Bartók, Béla, **1:**93, 349, **370–371,** 390, 404, 479, **2:**308, 389, 473, **4:**64, **5:**527
    folk music influence, **3:**405, 423
    Harangozó productions, **3:**341, 342, 414, 415–416

music for plotless ballets, **3:**416, 417

Wooden Prince, The, **5:**569

See also Miraculous Mandarin, The; Wooden Prince, The

Bartolott, Angelo Michele, **5:**520

Bartolozzi, Lucia Elizabeth. *See* Vestris, Madame

Barton, Eddie, **3:**634

Bartosik, Kimberly, **2:***292,* **5:**17

Bartusevičiūtė, Loreta, **4:**208

Barukh, Me'ir ben, **3:**603

Baryshnikov, Mikhail, **1:371–373,** **3:**222, **5:**164, 206, 282, 574, 597

American Ballet Theatre, **1:**64, 73–76, *74,* 372–373, **2:**112, **4:**620

American Document, **1:**82

Apollo, **1:**96

Australian tour, **4:**275

Coppélia performance, **2:**201

defection from Soviet Union, **1:**372, **5:**485

Don Quixote staging, **1:**372, **2:***439,* 440–441, 444, **4:**24

films, **3:**367, **4:**117, **5:**597

Giselle performance, **1:**371–372, **3:***182*

improvisation, **3:**448

international dance competition, **1:**282

Jeune Homme et la Mort television performance, **3:**601

Kirkland dance partnership, **1:**74, *74,* 372, **2:***439,* **4:**24

Maryinsky Ballet, **4:**285

Medea performance, **3:**60

New York City Ballet, **1:**74, 379, **4:**620

Nutcracker, The, **1:**372, **4:**24, **5:**13, 15–16

Other Dances performance, **5:***364,* 366

Paris Opera Ballet, **5:**97

partnering technique, **5:***104*

partners, **1:**545, **2:**186, **5:**100, **6:**142

Pas de Duke performance, **3:**578

Petrouchka, **5:**166

Prodigal Son, The, **5:**265

Royal Ballet guest performance, **1:**158, **5:**417

Swan Lake staging, **6:**34

Sylphides restaging, **3:**26

as television documentary subject, **6:**132

Tharp, Twyla, **6:***152,* 153, 154

Three Gershwin Preludes, **5:**602

Tudor association, **6:**201, *202,* 203

White Oak Dance Project, **1:**373, **2:**294, **3:**173, 201–202, 448, **4:**471

Wild Boy performance, **4:**244

Baryshnikov & Co., **1:**373

Baryshnikov at Work (Baryshnikov), **1:**372

Baryshnikov by Tharp (television program), **6:**154

Barzel, Ann, **2:**277

as contributor, **1:**517–518, **2:**356, **3:**663–664, **5:**589–590, **6:**290–293

dance collection, **4:**168–169

Barzin, Leon, **3:**521, **4:**28, 613

Basaldella, Afro and Mirko, **4:**421

Basaraswati, **3:**571

Basarte, José, **5:**60

Basch, Peter, *as photographer,* **4:**39

Basel Ballet, **1:373–376, 2:**441, **3:**51, **6:**52

Šmok, Pavel, **5:**617

Spoerli, Heinz, **5:**681–682

Zar und Zimmerman, **5:***35*

Basel Conservatory, **2:**153

Bashir, Saad Munir, **6:**66

Bashkir Opera and Ballet Theater, **5:**472

Bashō, **4:**42

Basic Principles of Classical Ballet (Vaganova), **1:**198, 328, **6:**128, 310

Basie, Count, **1:**252, **4:**202

Basil, Colonel Wassily de. *See* de Basil, Colonel Wassily

Basilio (choreographer), **5:**172, 173

Basil of Caesarea, **2:**163, 165

Basket, **5:**575

Basket Dance, **4:**565

Baskin, Leonard, **1:**72

Basmajian, John Varoujan, **4:**15

Basner, Veniamin, **3:**193

Bason, F., **2:**366

Basque dance, **1:376–378, 2:**99, **3:**33, 69, **4:**461

Bass (dance), **5:**634–635

Bass, Paula, **2:**580

bassa, **2:**74

"Bassa et Alta" (Caroso), **1:**53

Bassani, Giorgio, **4:**244

Bassarids, The (Henze), **5:**37

bassedanse, **1:378–382,** 409, **5:**336, 505, 506, 619, 620, **6:**122

alta association, **1:**53, 54

Arena dance manual, **1:**107

ballo and *balletto* versus, **1:**351, **4:**501

Caroso dance manual, **2:**74

Cornazano dance manual, **2:**206

Domenico da Piacenza dance manual, **2:**427, 428

as figure dance, **2:**590–591

first mentioned, **4:**348

France, **1:**378–379, **3:**65

Italy, **3:**542

musical accompaniment, **4:**501

Renaissance notation, **4:**683, *684*

révérence, **5:**343–344

Bassi, Giovanna, **6:**39

Bassilla, Julia, **4:**427

Basso, Alberto, **3:**555

Bassoon and the Flute, The, **4:**238

Bastian, Michael, **3:**39

Bastien und Bastienne (Mozart), **6:**46

Bastos, Lourdes, **1:**535

Basur (performance genre), **3:**485

Bat, The, **1:**281

Ba-ta-Clan, Paris, **4:**523

"Bataille, La," **1:**369

Batak (people), **3:**499, 500, **5:**168

Batalha, Ana Paula, *as contributor,* **5:**227–230

batcha (dancing boy), **6:**305

Batchelor, Norma, **1:**375

Bat-Dor Dance Company, **2:**359, **3:**532, 533, *534,* **4:**531

Bates, Daisy, **1:**212

Bates, Peg Leg, **1:382–383, 6:**317

Bates, Ronald, **1:**293, **5:**571

Bateson, Gregory, **2:**601, **3:**505, 506, **5:**357, **6:**184, 186

Bath Assembly Rooms, England, **1:***189,* 190, 279

Baths of Caracalla, Rome, **4:**154, **5:**401

Bathtubbing, **4:**203

Bathurst Island, **1:**219, 224–225

Bathyllus, **5:**72, 73, 74

batleika, **1:**408

Batsheva Dance Company of Israel, **3:**532, 533

Embattled Garden, The, **3:***531*

Graham works, **3:**220

Kraus as artistic adviser, **4:**59

Macdonald as artistic director, **4:**238

Morris choreography, **4:**469

Naharin, Ohad, **4:**531, 532

Battaggi, Teresa, **5:**400

battaglia. See barriera, torneo, and *battaglia*

"Battaglia, La" (Caroso), **5:**341

"Battaglia, La" (Negri), **1:**369, **4:**507, 580

battement, **1:**343, 344, 345, **383–384, 2:**519

Batten, Francis, **4:**627

Batter, Parts I, II, and III, **4:**21

batterie, **1:**341, 345, **384–385,** **2:**518, **5:**338

battement exercises, **1:**383, 384

as Bournonville emphasis, **1:**347

Batteux, Charles, **1:**22–23

Bat Theater, Moscow, **3:**193

Battistino, M., **1:**369, **5:**114–115

Battle, Hinton, **2:**334, **6:**286

Battle of the Kegs, the, **2:**467

Battleship Potemkin, The, **4:**285

Batuan, Bali, **3:**475–476, 477, 644, 645

batuque, **1:**527–528, **2:**58, **6:**345

Bauchant, André, **1:**95, 325, **2:**242

Baudelaire, **1:**405

Baudelaire, Charles, **3:**122, **6:**181

Bauer, André, **1:**375

Bauer, Margaret, **2:***240,* 241

Bauhaus, dance and the, **1:**132, 138, 244, **385–388, 2:**462, **3:***146,* **4:**302

scenic design, **5:**545, 546, 547, 548

Bauhaus Dances, **1:**386, **3:**151

Baule (people), **4:**289, 290

Baul tradition, **1:**363

Baum, Morton, **4:**29, 606

Baum, Vicki, **3:**347

Bauman, Art, **3:**447

Baumann, Aja, **4:**128

Baumann, Helmut, **3:**151, **6:**228

Baumenn, Dieter, **3:**156

Baumgarten, Alexander, **1:**22

Baus, Teresa, **1:**480

Bausch, Pina, **1:**25, 143, 246, **388–390,** 414, **2:**45, 126, **3:**151, 162, 591, **5:**200, 659

as Argentine dance influence, **1:**114

Folkwang Tanztheater, **3:**40, 368, 630, **4:**203

as French modern dance influence, **3:**78

German Dance Prize, **3:**158

Sacre du Printemps, Le, **5:**488

Tankard, Meryl, **6:**95

Tanztheater Wuppertal, **2:**81, 104, **3:**151, 157, 551

as Züllig student, **6:**453

Bautista, Juan, **1:**115, **2:**431

Bauzá, Mario, **2:**276

Baužys, Mindaugas, **4:**208

Bavarian polka, **3:**142

Bavarian State Ballet, **1:390–391,** **2:**4, 197, **3:**157, **4:**96

Abraxas, **1:**1, 390, **2:**478, **3:**149

Bosl, Heinz, **1:**500

Childs choreographies, **2:**120

Cranko choreographies, **2:**268, **5:**396

director turnover, **3:**150

Forsythe choreographies, **3:**52

Grahn as ballet mistress, **3:**224

Green Table, The, **3:**305, 630

Gsovsky, Tatjana, **3:**317

Gsovsky, Victor, **3:**149, 318

Hart (Evelyn) performance, **3:**345

Hynd choreography, **3:**150, 427, 428

Josephslegende, Die, **3:**631

Knust notation of repertory, **4:**32

Kröller, Heinrich, **4:**64

Ondine, **3:**360

Sacre du Printemps, Le, **3:**149

Seymour directorship, **5:**575

Bavdilovich, Olga, **5:**474, *478,* 479

baxa dance type, **1:**54

Baxter, Ivy, **2:**566, **3:**574

Baxter, Richard, **1:391–392**

Bayadère, La, **1:**73, **392–393**

arabesques, **1:**101

Augusta (Madame) performance, **1:**199

Aumer production, **1:**202

Chabukiani choreography, **2:**96, **5:**463

character dances, **2:**108

Dowell performance, **2:**444

Gorsky versions, **1:**393, 488, **3:**206, 207

Grigorovich revival, **3:**310

Gusev revival, **3:**328, **5:**470

Karsavina performance, **3:**655

Kingdom of the Shades scene, **1:**392, 393, **5:***418,* 456

Lee (Mary Ann) performance, **4:**139

Makarova restaging, **1:**75, *75,* 393, **2:**514, **4:**117, 249, **6:**44

Maywood performance, **4:**338

Minkus score, **1:**392, 393, **4:**429, 430

Mordkin performance, **4:**459, *459*

Morlacchi and Omohundro staging, **4:**464

Nureyev performances and staging, **1:**155, 156, 393, **5:**6, *98,* 416, 417, *418*

Orientalism, **5:**45

partnering technique, **5:***104*

Pavlova performance, **5:**120, *153*

Petipa (Marius) production, **5:**120, *153,* 154, 156, 158

scenic design, **5:***540*

Semenova performance, **5:**566, *566*

Spessivtseva performance, **5:**678

as symphonic ballet, **5:**456

Taglioni (Marie) performance, **3:***258*

Vazem performance, **4:**282

Weller production, **1:**393, **5:**653, **6:**380

Bayadère, La (film), **4:**37

bayādīyah dance, **4:**406

Bayanihan Philippine Dance Company, **1:393–394, 2:**570, **5:**173

Bayard, Sylviane, **1:**375

Bayas, Anthony, **3:**335

Bayer, Josef, **3:**346, **4:**143, 144, 258, **5:**278

Bayer, Raymond, **3:**84

Bayerisches Staatsballett. *See* Bavarian State Ballet

ba yi, **2:**148

Bayle, François, **1:**349, 446

Bayley, Angela, **1:**289, 290

Baylis, Lilian, **1:**146, 148, **2:**396, **3:**264, **5:**411, 414, 416

Baylis, Nadine, **1:**394, **2:**2, 245, **5:**302, 551, **6:***146*
Baynes, Stephen, **1:**211, 235
Bayreuth Festspielhaus, **1:**97, 98, **3:**145, **4:**91, **6:**161, 453
Bays, Frank, **3:***612*
Bayside Boys, **5:**635
Bazarbayev, Cholponbek, **4:**87
Bazilis, Silvia, **1:**111
Bazzard d'Algier, Le, **2:**415
BBC. *See* British Broadcasting Corporation
BBC Television, Film, and Videotape Library, **3:**283
Beach, **4:**322
Beach Birds, **2:***294,* 296
Beach Birds for Camera, **2:**296, 608
Beach Boys, **3:**615, **4:**519
Beach Piece II, **5:**549
Beal, Tandy, **4:**651
Beale, Alan, **2:**268, **3:***150*
Beals, Margaret, **3:**447
Beaman, Patricia, **6:***250*
bear cult, **4:**550
Bear Dance, **2:**140, **3:**302, **4:**672, **5:**446
Bear Dance = Sailboat + Vase of Flowers (Severini), **1:**130
Beard, John, **5:**350
Beardsley, Aubrey, **1:**148
Beardsley, Monroe, **1:**24
Bear Festival (Ainu), **1:**32
Béarn, Countess René de, **1:**97
Beata, Francesca, **5:**476
Beatles, **2:**350
Beaton, Cecil, **1:**316, **394–395,** **2:***249,* **5:***182, 185,* 186, **6:**200
Ashton productions design, **1:***69,* 148, 150, 152, 153, **3:***40,* 442, 443, *443,* 654
as photographer, **3:**442, **4:**269
Camille designs, **4:**269
Nutcracker designs, **5:**15
Patineurs design, **1:***69,* **5:**114
Pavillon design, **1:***312*
Swan Lake design, **6:**34
Beatrice d'Este, **2:**427
Beatrix. See Jolie Fille de Gand, La
beats (beating movements). *See* *battement; batterie*
Beattie, Herbert, **4:**179
Beattie, Rolando, **4:**397
Beatty, Patricia, **2:**40, 44, 47
Beatty, Talley, **1:**81, **395–396,** **2:**358, 458, 603–604, **3:**530, **6:**137, 259
Alvin Ailey repertory choreography, **2:**55, **3:**577
Boston Ballet choreography, **1:**501, **6:**398
Israeli dance choreography, **3:**530
Beaty, Richard, **3:***231,* **6:**106, *107*
Beauchamps, Pierre (Beauchamp), **1:**396–397, **2:**338, **5:**128, 129
Académie Royale de Danse chancellorship, **1:**4, 355
on arm positions, **1:**332–333
as *ballet de collège* dance master, **1:**283, 284
ballet de cour, **1:**286, 287, 288, **4:**188
Blondy relationship, **1:**464, 465
bourrée choreography, **1:**516
comédie-ballet, **1:**288
courante notation, **2:**259
on five basic feet positions, **1:**331, 396–397
Louis XIV patronage of, **4:**229
Molière collaboration, **1:**396, **4:**447, **6:**267

notation system, **1:**91, 286, 397, 465, **2:**339, 588, **3:**81, 522, **4:**684, **6:**123
opera choreographies, **4:**235
Paris Opera Ballet, **5:**38–39, 86, 87
suit against Feuillet, **2:**588
See also Feuillet notation
Beau Danube, Le, **1:**209, 211, *297,* 305, 309, 311, 429, **5:**553
Bruhn performance, **2:**3
Danilova performance, **2:**310, 343
in English National Ballet repertory, **2:**512
Gilpin performance, **3:**175
Lichine performance, **4:**178
Lopokova performance, **4:**223
Massine first production for Soirées de Paris, **3:**72, **4:**319, 320
Massine production for Royal Danish Ballet, **5:**430
Massine restagings, **4:**322, 325, 380
Sand performance, **5:**511
Strauss (Johann the younger) score, **6:**3
Zorina role, **6:**449
Beaugency, René de, **5:**118
Beaugrand, Léontine, **2:**199, **4:**353, **5:**94
Beauharnais, Eugène de, **1:**452
Beau Ideals, **6:**318
Beaujean, Rachel, **4:***594*
Beaujoyeulx, Balthazar de, **1:**2, 364, **397–398,** **2:**337, 418, **3:**543
Balet Comique de la Royne, Le, **1:**275, 276, 285, 286, **3:**130, **4:**172
Beaulieu, Antoine de, **6:**39
Beaumarchais, Pierre-Augustin Caron de, **2:**353, 464, 499, **6:**267
Beaumesnil, Mademoiselle, **2:**352
Beaumont, Cyril W., **1:**8, 44, **398,** **5:**17, 293, 308, **6:**128
archival materials, **4:**163
on Ashton's *Sylvia,* **6:**64
ballet stories collection, **4:**177
on Bogdanova as Giselle, **1:**477
on Bolm's dance style, **1:**484
British dance history and critical studies, **3:**282, 284–285, **5:**351
Cecchetti method manual, **2:**83–84
Charing Cross Road bookstore, **3:**263, 284–285
on Fedorovitch designs, **2:**583
on *Giselle,* **3:**177
on Idzikowski as Battista, **3:**441
on Lopokova style, **4:**223
on Milon's *Nina,* **4:**422
on Nijinsky's virtuosity, **4:**646, 647
Beaumont, Édouard de, **2:**70, 71, **5:**241
Beaumont, Étienne de, **1:**309, 325, **3:**72, 103, 394, 441, **4:**223, **5:***192*
Massine association, **4:**319–320
See also Soirées de Paris, Les
Beaumont, Francis, **4:**312
Beaumont, Tessa, **1:**305, 403, **4:**435, **5:**676
Beaupré, Danseur à l'Opéra (print), **2:***236*
Beaupré, Louis-Marie, **1:**4
Beaurepaire, André, **5:***529,* 531

Beauteous Captive, The, **1:**200
Beautés de l'Opéra, Les (libretti series), **2:**104, **3:**122, 179, **4:**177, **5:**258
Beautiful Day, **2:**110, **4:**472
Beautiful People, The (Saroyan), **4:**228
Beautiful Radda, The, **1:**144
Beauty (masque), **4:**310
Beauty and the Beast, **2:**162, 265, 350, 397, **5:**225, 316, 654
Beauty Fish, The, **2:**145
Beauty of Seville, The, **3:**563
Beaux Dimanches, Les (television series), **6:**131, 132
bebarisan, **3:**477
Beccari, Filippo, **5:**452, 480
Beccaria, Carlo, **1:**235
Bechet, Sidney, **4:**107
Beck, Hans, **1:**399, 497, *504,* **2:**3, **5:**251, 295, 511
Bournonville tradition, **1:**347, 511–512, 539, **5:**427, 430
as Carey (Gustave) student, **2:**60
Cinderella performance, **2:**173
Coppélia performances, **3:**129
Coppélia staging, **2:**200
Polka Militaire debut performance, **1:**511
Royal Danish Ballet leadership, **5:**427–528
Beck, H. S., *as photographer,* **4:**351
Beck, Julian, **1:**245
Beck, R. H., *as photographer,* **5:**83, *224,* **6:**78
Beck, Richard, **1:**315
Becker, Jill, **3:**621
Becker, Mavis, **2:**57, **5:**654
Becker, Patrick, **3:***337*
Becker Schwartz, Nancy, *as contributor,* **1:**432–436, **2:**603–612
Beckett, Samuel, **3:**79, 652, **4:**332, **5:**592
kyōgen interpretations, **4:**84, *85*
Beckett, Samuel Joshua, *as photographer,* **3:**91
Beck-Friis, Regina, **1:**400, **6:**42, 47, 48, 50
Beckmann, Bettina, **3:***337*
Beckmann, Grete, **3:***147*
Becque, Don Oscar, **2:**579, 580
Bed (Rasuchenberg), **1:**140
bedaya, **1:***174,* **2:**231, **3:**493–494, *494,* 501
abstract music and dance, **4:**494
srimpi similarity, **3:**494–495
Sundanese tradition, **3:**501
Bedaya Bedah Mediun, **3:**494
Bedaya Ketawang, **3:**494
Bedaya Sayembara Sinta, **3:**494
Bedbug, The, **4:**248, 284, **5:**460, 469, **6:**411–412
Beddoes, Evor, **6:***120*
Bedells, Jean, **1:**158
Bedells, Phyllis, **1:**329, **400–401,** **2:**395, 396, 424, **3:**262, 441
Bedichek, Louise, *as contributor,* **1:**303–304, **5:**516–517
bedouin dance, **1:**401–402, **2:**488–489, *488,* 492, **4:**415
Bedtime, **4:**472
Bedu masqueraders, **6:**12
Beecham, Larl, **2:**458
Beecham, Sir Thomas, **2:**396, 401, **6:**196
Beecher, Catharine, **6:**235, 294
Beecher, Lyman, **6:**235
Beer, Henry, **3:***372*
Beerbohm, Max, **2:**262, **3:**129, 284

Beerczik, Sári, **3:**420
beer-drink dance, **5:**579
Be'er, Rami, **1:**242
Beers, Sonja van, **2:**470, **4:**600
Beer-Walbrunn, Anton, **5:**42
Beethoven, Ludwig van, **1:**402–403, 405, **2:**178, **5:**528, **6:**337, 338
ballroom dance compositions, **4:**511
contradance compositions, **2:**256
écossaises compositions, **2:**474–475
Massine symphonic ballet choreography, **4:**323
See also Creatures of Prometheus, The; Seventh Symphony
Beethoven Pas de Deux, A (Four Bagatelles), **6:***174*
Beethoven Romance, **4:**622
Beethoven's Seventh Symphony (Duncan work), **2:**456
Before Five Passed, **6:***175*
Before Nightfall, **6:**44
Befragung des Robert Scott, Die, **3:**52
Beggar's Bar (New York cabaret), **3:**163
Beggar's Opera, The (Gay), **3:**378, **5:**350, **6:**267
Begichev, Vladimir, **6:**29, 30, 115
behete dance, **4:**410
Behind the China Dogs, **3:**53, **4:**623
Behle, Anna, **1:**403, **2:**632, **3:**311, **6:**49
Behn, Aphra, **5:**518
Behr, Samuel Rudolph, **2:**51
Behra, Harekrishna, **5:**23
Behrman, David, **2:**289
Behrnes, Sonay, **4:***626*
Beibosynov, Bulat, **3:**665
Beijer, Agne, **6:**46, 48
Beijing Ballet, **2:**136–137
Beijing Dance Academy, **2:**116, 136, *141,* 145, 148–149
folk dance curriculum, **6:**406, 415
modern dance program, **2:**146
Beijing Opera, **1:**161, 164, 166, 187, **2:***131, 133, 142, 143*
costume, **2:***220*
fan and sleeve interplay, **2:**570
historical writings, **2:**148
history, **2:**132
Mei Lanfang, **1:**164, **2:**132–133, **4:**350, **6:**446
Ye Shaolan, **6:**421
Zhou Xinfang, **6:**446–447
Beiswanger, George, **1:**25, **6:**162, 299
Beit al-Din festival, **4:**136
Beja (people), **2:**488–489
Béjart, Maurice, **1:**403–407, **2:**284, **5:**234, 527, 528, 565, 676, **6:**117
as Argentine dance influence, **1:**102, 114
as Australian Ballet Company influence, **1:**210, 211, 234
Ballet du XXᵉ Siècle, **1:**210, 290–293, 404–406, 411, 446, **2:**577
Ballets de l'Étoile, **3:**74
Bartók scores, **1:**370
Berlin Opera Ballet choreography, **3:**156
Boléro productions, **1:**292, 404, 406, 410, **2:**498, 514, **4:**635, **5:**316
can-can choreography, **2:**53
choreography for Tamasaburō V, **1:**362

Christout on, **2:**170
as Cuban ballet influence, **2:**278–279
Firebird versions, **1:**403, *404*, 405, **3:***3*, 4
as French modern dance influence, **3:**77
Gaîté Parisienne, **2:**125
German Dance Prize, **3:**158
Haydée roles, **3:**351
International Ballet, **3:**512
Martyre de Saint Sébastien, Le, **2:**361
Molière as source, **4:**447
Mudra school, **1:**405, 406, 407, 412, 414
Netherlands Ballet choreography, **4:**600
Ninth Symphony, **1:**403, 405
Paris Opera Ballet, **5:**97
Plisetskaya association, **5:**206, *206*, 207
Rayet association, **5:**320
Romeo and Juliet, **1:**292, 405, **5:398**
Royal Swedish Ballet guest productions, **6:**44
Sacre du Printemps, Le, **1:**195, *290*, 404, 406, **5:**488, **6:**44
Seven Deadly Sins, The, **2:**111
spectacular scenic design, **5:**551
Spectre de la Rose, Le, **3:**578
Stuttgart Ballet guest choreography, **6:**10, *11*
Wien, Wien, nur du Allein, **1:**292, 406, **2:**104
Béjart Ballet Lausanne, **1:**407, **3:**350, **6:**54
Bek, Konstantin, **6:**306
Bekefi, Alfred, **2:**72, 107, **4:**282, **5:**455, **6:**30
Bekefi, Maria, **4:**5
Bekehrte Spiesser, Der, **3:**153
Bekker, Ron, **1:**217
beksan, **3:**496
beksan golek, **3:**497
beksan golek menak, **3:**497
Bela, **2:**585
Belans, Linda, **1:**81
Belarbi, Kader, **5:**98
Belarus, **1:407–408**, **4:**224, 226, 444, **5:**482
Belarussian Theater of Opera and Ballet, **2:**501–502, **6:**420
Belasco, David, **4:**190, **5:**491, **6:**242
Belau, **4:**400
Belcher, Ernest, **2:**38, **6:**85, 326
Belda, Patrick, **1:**291, 446
Belé, **2:**334
Belfiore, Liliana, **1:**111
Bel Geddes, Edith Lutyens, **3:***614*
Bel Geddes, Norman, **3:**399, **6:**161
Belgian Congo. *See* Congo Republic
Belgiojoso, Baldassare. *See* Beaujoyeulx, Balthazar de
Belgium, **1:408–414**
dance education, **1:**405, 406, 407, 410, **414**
libraries and museums, **4:**160
sabot dance, **2:**180
theatrical dance, **1:408–414**, **4:**136
See also Ballet du XXᵉ Siècle; Béjart, Maurice; Charleroi/Danses; Royal Ballet of Flanders
Belgrade Ballet, **6:**438
Belgrade International Theater Festival, **6:**435

Belgrade National Theater, **6:**432, 434–435, 438
Belgrade Opera, **4:**435
belian dadas, **3:**505
Belikova, Nina, **1:**441
Bélin, Alexandre, **3:***3*, *232*, 233
Belinskaya, Stanislava, **5:**9, *9*
Belinsky, Aleksandr, **1:**539
Belinsky, Vissarion, **3:**56, **5:**516
Belisa, ossia La Nuova Claudina, **2:**202, 203
Belize, **1:414–415**, **2:**61, 62, **3:**120–121
Belknap Collection for the Performing Arts, Gainesville, **4:**168
Bell, Ken, **2:**49
   as photographer, **2:**37, **3:**61, **4:**540, 541, 542, **5:**14, **6:**1, 142
Bell, Robert, **1:**315, **2:***470*
Bell, The, **3:**87
Bell, Willis, as photographer, **3:**165, 166, 169
Bella Coola (people), **4:**568, 569, *570*
"Bella della Ventola" (Italian dance), **2:**571
Bella Figura, La, **4:**81
Bella Lewitzky Company, **6:**264
Bellas Artes Ballet Company. *See* Ballet de Bellas Artes
"Belle au Bois Dormant, La" (Perrault), **5:**606
Belle au Bois Dormant, La, **2:**172, **3:**5, **5:**92, **6:**216
   Aumer staging, **1:**202, **5:**610
   Hérald score, **3:**360–361
   Lecomte (Hippolyte) costumes, **4:**138
   Noblet performance, **4:**657
   See also Sleeping Beauty, The
Belle de Liban, La, ou Le Génie de la Montague, **5:**151, 278
Belle Dorothée, La, **1:**123, 124, **2:**442, **5:**198
Belle Hélène, La (Cranko ballet), **2:**114, 266
Belle Hélène, La (Offenbach), **2:**15, 226–227, **3:**27, 70, 561, **4:**358, **5:**96
Belle Laitière, La, **2:**364
Belle of New York, The (film), **1:**194
Bellérophon, **2:**518, 519, **4:**235
Belle Rose, La, **2:**151
Belles Damnées, Les, **1:**305
Belle Vie, La, **1:**375, **5:***682*
Bellew, Hélène. *See* Kirsova, Hélène
Bellezza, Maurizio, **2:**513
Bell High, **1:**52, **5:**303
Bellini, Vincenzo, **3:**59, 360, **4:**513, **5:**277, 517, 641
Bellman, Carl Marie, **1:**509
Bellman, or the Dance at Grönalud (Bellmann, eller Polskdansen paa Grönalund), **1:**509, **6:**40
Bellona, **1:415–416**
bells
   African dancers, **4:**484, *485*, **6:***20*
   Iroquois dancers, **4:**557
   moresca and Morris dancers, **4:**461, 462, 473, *474*
   Pueblo dancers, **4:**563
   Spanish dance, **5:**669
Bells, The, **1:**300, **4:**418, 659, **5:**59
Bells Are Ringing (film), **5:**363
Bell Telephone Hour, The (television series), **6:**137
belly dance. *See danse du ventre*

Belly Roll (dance), **6:***316*
Belmondo, Muriel, **1:**349, **2:**480
Belo, Jane, **3:**506
Belo Horizonte, Brazil, **1:**535, 536
Beloscrovich, Vera, **5:**478
Belova, Valentina, **1:**411
Beloved, The, **2:**334, 425, **3:**312, 387, *387*, **4:**156
Belsky, Boris, **5:**265
Belsky, Igor, **1:416–417**, 492, **2:**470, 501, **4:**37, **5:**12, 639
   Ali-Batyr, **5:**595
   choreographic outlook, **5:**485
   Coast of Hope, The, **4:**284, **5:**460
   Ekaterinburg Opera Theater, **5:**470
   Leningrad Symphony, **4:**147–148, *283*, **5:**460
   Maly Theater Ballet, **5:**468
   Maryinsky Ballet, **4:**284
   as Soviet choreographic influence, **5:**460
Belsky, Vladimir, **3:**20
beluria ceremonies, **3:**120
Bely, Andrei, **1:**519, **4:**464, **5:**469
Belyaeva-Chelombitko, Galina V., as contributor, **4:**55, **6:**7–8, 313–315, 441–443
Bemba (people), **4:**485
Bemis, Minnie (Renwood), **3:**92
Benavente, Jacinto, **1:**116
Benavente, Toribio de, **4:**399
Benavides, Susana, **4:**397
Benchley, Robert, **6:**101
Bencini, Carlo, **5:**231
Benda, Georg, **5:**552
Benda, W. T., **4:**302
Ben-David, Ehud, **3:**532
Bender, Lauretta, **2:**320
Bender, Wim, **5:**531
Bendik og Årolilja, **4:**676
Bendongué, Fred, **3:**79
Bends, The, **3:***275*
Benedict, Laurel, **2:***470*
Benedict, Ruth, **6:**297
Benesh, Joan, **1:**417, **4:**691
Benesh, Rudolf. *See* Benesh movement notation
Benesh Institute of Choreology, **1:**417, 418, **4:**164, 691
Benesh movement notation, **1:417–418**, **4:**691
   of Bournonville style, **2:**387
   technical manuals, **6:**129
Bengalis (people), **1:**362
Ben-Gal, Nir, **3:**533, **4:**220
Benguet (people), **5:**168
Beni (dance societies), **2:**212
Beni Isguem, Algeria, **1:**41
Benin Republic
   African-Brazilian dance, **1:**525
   costume, **2:**211
   masks, **4:**288, 290
   possession dance, **6:***423*
   women's dance, **6:***15*, *381*
Beniowsky, **2:**390, **3:**260
Benishek, Lance, **1:**450, 451
   as photographer, **1:**450
Benítez, María, **3:**11
Benjamin, Fred, **6:**259
Benjamin, Roberto, **2:**195
Bennahum, Ninotchka, as contributor, **3:**6–11
Bennathan, Serge, **2:**42, 45
Bennett, Alexander, **5:**53, 653
Bennett, Armada, **1:**375
Bennett, David, **6:**273
Bennett, Hildegarde, **1:**197
Bennett, Isadora, **1:**65
Bennett, Mark, **2:**171

Bennett, Michael, **1:418–420**, **6:**204, 284, 285, 286, 287
Bennett, Richard Rodney, **1:**156, **4:**244
Bennett, Tracy, **1:**293
Bennett, Vivienne, **3:**519
Bennington College, Vermont. *See* Bennington School of the Dance
Bennington School of the Dance, **1:**6, **420–422**, **2:**71, **6:**89, 248
   American Dance Festival as successor, **1:**79
   archival collection, **4:**167
   Ballet Caravan founding, **1:**279
   Cunningham, Merce, **2:**285
   Dudley, Jane, **2:**450
   faculty mainstays, **3:**369, 399
   Graham, Martha, **3:**214–215, 219, 399, **6:**295
   Hill, Martha, **3:**364
   Holm, Hanya, **3:**369, 399
   Horst, Louis, **3:**385
   Humphrey, Doris, **3:**399–400, 401, **6:**295
   Lauterer, Arch, **4:**130
   Letter to the World, **4:**153
   Limón, José, **4:**197
   Martin (John) as faculty member, **1:**421, **4:**273, **6:**296
   modern dance technique, **4:438**, **6:**295
   New Dance Trilogy, **4:**605, 606
   Nikolais, Alwin, **4:**649
   practice clothes, **5:**243
   Schönberg as faculty member, **5:**559
   Trend, **3:**369–370, *370*
   Weidman, Charles, **3:**399–400, **4:**438
   Ye Shaolan, **6:**421
Benois, Alexandre, **1:422–424**, **5:**161, 540, 541, 556, 612
   aesthics, **5:**485
   Bakst collaboration, **1:**254
   Bourgeois Gentilhomme costumes, **4:**33
   on *Coppélia* score, **2:**369
   Diaghilev association, **1:**133, 316, 318, *318*, 320, **2:**406–407, **3:**198, 653
   Diaghilev break, **2:**408
   on Diaghilev's artistic vision, **1:**317
   Fokine collaborations, **2:**241, 244, 407, **3:**15, 16, *17*, 20
   on Hassreiter ballets, **3:**347
   Josephslegende costumes, **3:**631
   on Korovin designs, **4:**56
   Lifar as protégé, **4:**182
   makeup exoticism, **4:**305
   on Nijinsky's appearance, **4:**646
   Nutcracker design, **2:**510, **5:**14, 15
   Pavillon d'Armide design, **1:**423, 424, **2:**407, **5:**118, 119, 121
   Petrouchka designs, **1:***422*, 423–424, *423*, **2:**244, **3:**614, **5:**165, 166, 541–542, **6:**3
   prints and drawings by, **5:**262
   Romeo and Juliet design, **5:**395
   Rubinstein designs, **4:**635, **5:**439
   Sylphides design, **1:**423, **2:**244, 407, **6:**61
   World of Art group, **5:**456
   as Zucchi admirer, **2:**596, **6:**453
Benois, Nadia, **1:**150, **2:**245, 348, **3:**202, **5:**299, 612
   Lady into Fox design, **3:**392, *392*
Benoist, François, **5:**150, 500
Benpibernes Bøn, **4:***681*

Bensel, Elsie van der ten, **4:**585
Benserade, Isaac de, **1:**284, 286, **424–425, 4:**172, **5:**270
Bent, Marion, **6:**319
Bentenkozō, **3:***639*
Benthall, Michael, **3:**356
Bentley, Alys, **3:**352, **5:**359
Bentley, Muriel, **2:**568, **5:***359, 550*
bent-toe dance, **3:***133,* 134
Bentzon, Niels Viggo, **5:**294
Benvenuto Cellini, **4:**455
Benz, Rachel Berman, **5:**679
Benzin, **5:**352–353
Beolco, Angelo, **2:**189
Berañano, Cosme, **5:**676
Bérard, Christian, **1:**260, 305, 306, 316, **426–427,** 437, **2:**244, 245, **5:**163, 526, 527, 547, **6:**118
  Ballets 1933, **3:**73
  Ballets des Champs-Élysées, **3:**73
  Cotillon design, **2:**253
  Kochno relationship, **4:**33
  Seventh Symphony design, **4:***321*
  Symphonie Fantastique design, **1:**311, *311,* 426, **4:**323
Berber, Anita, **3:**162
Berber dance
  Algeria, **1:**39, 41, 42
  ethnography, **4:**415
  Morocco, **4:**407–408, *407,* 464–469, 490
  musical idiom, **4:**466–467, 663, 665–666
Berberian, Cathy, **6:**121
Berceuse, La, **3:**51
Berchoux, Joseph de, **2:**464
Berczik, Sári, **2:**480
Berech krasotu russkogo tantsa (Ustinova), **6:**303
Bereda, Eleonora Nicolaevna. *See* Nijinsky, Eleonora Bereda
Beredina, Nelli, **4:**208
Berenguer, Fátima, **1:***533*
Beresford, Ann, **2:**611
Bereska, Dussia, **3:**76, **4:**90–91, 92, 96, 103
Beretta, Caterina, **1:**427, **427,** 500, **2:**282, **3:**50, 426, **4:**145, 150, **5:**120, 248, 528, **6:**191
Berezhnoi, Sergei, **3:**162
Berezka Dance Company, **5:**445, 473, *474*
berezka step, **5:**445, 473
Berezkin, Viktor I.
  as contributor, **4:**420–421, **4:**153–154, **6:**398–399
  as photographer, **4:**154
Berezova, G. A., **6:**225
Berg, Alban, **2:**17, 471, 472, **3:**52, **4:**518, 622, **5:**367, 527, 555, 637, **6:**6
Berg, Attie van den, **4:**590
Berg, Erik, *as photographer*, **4:**676, 679
Berg, Marina de, **1:**305
Berg AB, **3:**52
bergamasque, **1:428**
Bergé, Marcel, **1:**305
Berge, Yvonne, **3:**83
Bergeest, Karl, **3:**305, 626, 628
Bergeijk, Gilius van, **5:**555
Bergen, Norway, **4:**674, 679, 680, 683
Berger, Arthur, **2:**196, 197

Berger, Augustin, **1:428–429, 2:**306, **4:**64, **5:**245, 269, **6:**30, 32
Berger, Fritz. *See* Berk, Fred
Berger, Gaston, **1:**403
Berger, Gyula, **3:**421
Berger, Hanna, **1:**240
Berger, Jaroslav, **6:**454, *454*
Berger, Ludwig, **3:**132, **6:**328
Berger, Maurice Jean. *See* Béjart, Maurice
Berger, Morroe, **4:**415
Berger, Theodor, **3:**340
bergerette, **2:**164
Bergese, Micha, **3:**274, **4:**217, 218
Bergesen, Merete, **4:**679
Berghaus, Ruth, **1:**241
Bergling, Biger, **6:***42*
Bergman, Ingmar, **2:**500, **5:**47
Bergmann, Julia, **4:**64
Berg-Peters, Inge, **3:**155
Bergsma, Deanne, **2:**515, **5:***613,* **6:**35
Bergson, Henri, **2:**417
Bergstein, Lea, **3:**530, 531
Bergström, Beata, **3:**531
  as photographer, **1:**32
berimbau, **2:**59
Berio, Luciano, **1:**82, 349, 462, **2:**388, **5:***233*
Beriocaba, **1:**38
Beriosova, Svetlana, **1:429–430,** 430, **5:**5, *104,* **6:**201
  Apollo performance, **1:**96
  Ashton ballets, **1:**158, **2:**515
  Baiser de la Fée performance, **4:***240*
  Bruhn dance partnership, **2:**3
  Checkmate performance, **2:**115
  Cinderella performance, **1:***151,* **2:***173*
  Coppélia performance, **2:**201
  Enigma Variations performance, **2:**515, *515*
  Fanciulla delle Rose performance, **5:**691
  Giselle performance, **4:**624
  Metropolitan Ballet, **4:**380
  Noces performance, **1:**430, **4:***658,* 659
  Persephone performance, **1:**155, 430
  Royal Ballet, **5:**416
  Sadler's Wells Theatre Ballet, **1:**153, 420
  "Beriozka," **5:**474
Beriozoff, Nicholas, **1:**296, 429, **430–431, 5:**527
  Don Quixote, **2:**441, **4:**545
  English National Ballet, **2:***424,* 508, 510, 511, 524, **3:**175
  Grand Ballet du Marquis de Cuevas, **3:**226
  Metropolitan Ballet, **4:**380
  Nutcracker, The, **5:***13,* 15
  Ondine choreography, **3:**360
  Romeo and Juliet, **5:**55, *652,* 653
  Stuttgart Ballet, **1:**430, **2:**266, **3:**149, **6:**9
  Swan Lake, **5:**54
  Zurich Ballet, **6:**53, 454
Beristáin, Evelia, **4:**392
Berk, Fred, **1:431–432, 3:**605, **4:**58, 164
Berkefi, Maria, **4:**4
Berkeley, Busby, **1:432–436,** 520, **2:***613,* 614, 617, **3:**559, **4:**419, 434, **5:**247, **6:**101, 274, 285, 320
Berkeley, Lennox, **5:**691

Berkenman, Paul, **5:**423
Berkoff, Steven, **1:**373
Berkshire Athenaeum, Pittsfield, **4:**168
Berkshire Ballet, **2:**359, **6:**264
Berlin, **4:**479
Berlin, Alexandre, **3:***232*
Berlin, Germany, **3:**145, 146, 147, 151, 155
  cabaret, **3:**163
  four dance companies, **3:**156
Berlin, Irving, **1:**193, 194, 323, **2:**79, 154, 618, **5:**361, **6:**271, 279, *447*
Berlin Academy of Music, **1:**456
Berlin Ballet. *See* Berlin Opera Ballet
Berlin Dance Factory. *See* Tanzfabrik Berlin
Berlin Dance Theater (Tanztheater der Komischen Oper Berlin), **1:**442, **3:**154, 155, 156, **5:**557
Berliner, Paul, **6:**25
Berlin Olympics (1936), **3:**147, **4:**61, 93, 477, 538–539, **5:**66, 218, **6:**393
Berlin Opera Ballet, **1:**110, 201, **436, 2:**441, 478, **3:**146, 150, 151, 153, 155–156, 627, 631, **5:**334
  Barberina performances, **1:**365
  Blank, Gustav, **1:**460
  Chauviré performances, **2:**114
  Childs choreographies, **2:**120
  Chiriaeff as soloist, **2:**150
  Evdokimova, Eva, **2:**561–562
  Forsythe guest choreography, **3:**52
  Gsovsky (Tatjana) school, **3:**317, 318
  Idiot, The, **3:***317,* 359
  Josephslegende, Die, **3:**631, **4:**64
  Kreutzberg, Harald, **4:**60, 61
  Kröller, Heinrich, **4:**64
  Laban as ballet master, **4:**91, 92
  MacMillan directorship, **4:**242
  MacMillan guest choreography, **3:**149
  Musical Offering in repertory, **4:**482
  Ondine, **3:**360
  Scènes de Ballet production, **5:**531
  Schaufuss, Peter, **2:**514, **3:**156, **5:**554
  Seymour performance, **5:**574
Berlin Volksbühne, **3:**151, 156
Berlioz, Hector, **2:**503, **3:**123, **5:**36
  Damnation de Faust, La, **1:**405
  Harold in Italy, **1:**301, **4:**325
  operatic ballets, **4:**514
  Romeo and Juliet, **1:**83, 405, **2:**278, **5:**392, 398
  Symphonie Fantastique, **1:**148, 311, **3:**69, 601, **4:**322–323
Berlips, Fred, **2:**470
Berman, Eugene, **1:**149, **436–437, 2:**242, **3:**653, **5:***546,* 547, **6:**118, 199
  Ballet Imperial design, **1:**293
  Concerto Barocco design, **1:**298, 437, **2:**193
  Danses Concertantes design, **1:***261,* 298, *298*
  Romeo and Juliet design, **1:**67, 437, **2:**244, **5:**397
Berman, Leonid, **1:**437
Berman, Reina, **4:**306
Bernabini, Francesca, **3:**554

Bernadelli, Fortunato, **5:**215
Bernand, B. M., *as photographer*, **4:**185
Bernanos, Georges, **5:**237
Bernard, Guy, **2:**111
Bernard, Roger, **5:**551
Bernardi, Karl, **1:**236, **3:**187, 365
Bernardin de Saint-Pierre, Jacques-Henri, **1:**201, **3:**118
Bernay, Berthe, **5:**202, **6:**128
Bern Ballet, **6:**53
Bernd, John, **3:**447
Berners, Lord, **1:**148, 150, **437–438, 6:**375
Berner Totentanz (Manuel), **4:**462
Bernhardt, Sarah, **5:**310
Berni, Francesco, **3:**106
Bernier, Françoys, **6:**130
Bernier, Nicolas, **2:**34
Bernstein, Leonard, **1:**57, 83, **438–439,** 463, **2:**287, **4:**532
  Age of Anxiety symphony, **5:**361
  Candide, **1:**439, **6:**285
  Robbins's ballet scores, **4:**518–519, **6:**279
  as Seregei influence, **5:**569
  Suite of Dances, **5:**366
  See also Fancy Free; On the Town; West Side Story
Bernstein-Serenade, **3:**337
Beron, Liljana (Lili), **2:**11, **5:**166
Berrios, Zulma, **5:***274*
Berry, Ananais ("Nyas"), **1:**439, 440
Berry, Eugene, **5:**659
Berry, Gabriel, **2:**171
Berry, Irmgard E., **4:**164
Berry, James, **1:**439, 440
Berry, Warren, **1:**439–440
Berry Brothers, **1:439–440, 6:**100, 256, 317, 386
Bert, *as photographer*, **3:**634, **4:**640, 642, 643, 644
Bert, Auguste, **5:**182
Bertali, Antonion, **3:**381
Berté, Heinrich, **3:**346
Berthe of Utrecht, **2:**165
Berthold-Baczynski, Ilse, **3:**142
Bertie, Lady Elizabeth, **3:**111
Berton, Henri-Montan, **4:**61, **5:**264
Berton, Pierre-Montan, **2:**352, **3:**190
Bertonov, Devora, **3:**531
Bertrand, A., **3:**261
berutuk, **3:**479–480, *480*
"Berzka," **5:**445
Bes (deity), **2:**484
Besard, Jean-Baptiste, **1:**523, **4:**505
Beskow, Elsa, **6:**44
Besobrasova, Marika, **1:**82, **3:**553
Besprovsany, José, **1:**412, **2:**109
Besserer, Rob, **1:**372, **6:***251*
Bessmertnova, Natalia, **1:**282, **440–441,** 493, 493, **2:**438, **3:**193, 197, **5:**321, 460
  Golden Age performance, **3:**309
  Goleizovsky ballets, **3:**195, *195*
  Grigorovich marriage, **1:**440, **3:**310
  Legend of Love, **4:**144
  Nutcracker performance, **5:**12
  Romeo and Juliet role, **1:**440, **5:**399
  Swan Lake role, **1:**440, **6:**31
Bessone, Emma, **3:**261
Bessy, Claude, **2:**199, **3:**82, **5:***91, 93,* 96, 97, **6:***216*
Best Foot Forward (musical), **4:**2
Best Little Whorehouse in Texas, The (musical), **6:**204, 285–286

Best Things in Life Are Free, The (film), **2:**314
BET (Black Entertainment Television), **2:**234
Bethke, Veit, **4:**584
Bethsabée de Rothschild Foundation, **3:**403
Bethune, Mary McLeod, **5:**255
Beti (people), **2:**32, 33
Betsuyaku Minoru, **4:**84
Bettelheim, Judith, **6:**25
    as contributor, **3:**623–624
Betterton, Mary, **3:**254
Betterton, Thomas, **4:**105, **5:**281
Better Treatment for Horses, **3:**48
Bettis, Valerie, **1:**300, **441**, **6:**90, 280
    as Holm student, **3:**369
    Hoving as student, **3:**390
    Saddler dance partnership, **5:**488–489
    Streetcar Named Desire, A, **1:**441, **2:**334, **3:**88, 664, **5:**606
Betty, ou La Jeunesse de Henri V, **3:**96, **4:**341
Betuta, **4:**78
Between Two Fires, **4:**627
Betz, Irma, **4:**96
Beuce, Paschal, **2:**337
Beuys, Joseph, **1:**139
Beveridge, Mr., **3:**377
Bewegungschöre. See movement choir
Bewick, Thomas, **5:**261
Bewicke, Hilda, **5:**637
Bey, Frank, **1:**442
Bey, Hannelore, **1:441–442**
Beyer, Marijan, **5:**54
Beyond Bach, **1:**235
Beyond Dreams, **6:**67
Beyond Good and Evil (film), **1:**82
Beyond Twelve, **2:**184, **4:**479, **5:**316
Beziehungen, **3:**351
Bezobrazov, Nikolai, **3:**561, **5:**160
Bhagavad Gītā (Indian text), **3:**466
Bhāgavata Purāṇa (Indian text), **1:**170, **3:**456, 465, 466, 467, **5:**311
Bhakti, **1:**292, 405, **3:**659
Bhāmākalāpam, **4:**70
bhāma kalapana, **1:**169, **6:**320
bhāma nṛtyam, **5:**309
bhangra dance, **2:**624, **5:**65
Bharata
    statement of aesthetic theory, **3:**463
    See also Nāṭyaśāstra
Bharata Kalanjali, Madras, **2:**404, 405
Bharatam Dance Company (Australia), **1:**216
bharata nāṭyam, **1:**94, 160, 169, *171,* 182, **442–443**, **2:**102, 104, 394, 623, **3:**457, **5:**521, 522, 580
    Balasaraswati, **1:**273, 274, **3:**448
    Chandrashekhar family, **1:**105, **2:**104
    Cole (Jack) jazz adaptations, **2:**185
    costume, **3:***460*
    Dhananjayan family, **2:**404, 405
    Gopal, **3:**199, *199*
    improvisation, **3:**448
    Kermani, Sheema, **4:**5, 6
    Knight, Lakshmi, **4:**31
    Krishnamurthi, Yamini, **4:**62, 63
    Lakhia, Kumudini, **4:**110
    Mansingh, Sonal, **4:**257
    Meri choreography, **4:**355

mime, **4:**423
modern revival, **3:**460–461, 468, 469
mōhiniāṭṭam gestures, **4:**443
notation system, **4:**693
Pakistan, **5:**62, 63
Panigrahi, Sanjukta, **5:**68
Rādhā-Kṛṣṇa theme, **3:**466–467
Samson, Leela, **5:**510, 511
Sarukkai, **5:**524–525
structured design, **3:**463
Valli, **6:**312
Bhāratārṇavaḥ (Indian text), **3:**469
Bharucha, Rustom, **2:**104
Bhavantarana (film), **4:**247
Bhavaprakāśana (Indian text), **3:**469
bhāvas, **3:**458, 462
Bhaviṣya Purāṇa, **3:**465
Bhookh, **3:**468
Bhosle, Asha, **2:**625
Bhotias (people), **5:**598
Bhūmibol Adulyadēj, king of Thailand, **4:**256
Bhutan, **1:443–445**
    Black Hat Dance, **1:**458–459
    costume, **2:**225–226
    mask, **4:***494*
Bhutto, Zulfiqar Ali, **5:**63
Biagi, Vittorio, **1:**196, 291, **445–446**
Bianca di Nevers, **4:**258
Bianchi e Negri, **4:**339, **5:**409
Biancolelli, Pietro Francesco, **2:**190
Biancolli, Louis, **3:**599
Bianconi, Lorenzo, **3:**556
Bianquet, José Ovidio (El Cachafaz), **6:**93
Bias, Fanny, **1:**202, **446**, **2:**415, **5:**91, 207
Bibalo, Antonio, **4:**677
Bibena, Antonio, **3:**161
Bibiena, Carlo, **1:**447, **4:**277
Bibiena, Ferdinando, **1:**447, **5:**537
Bibiena, Francesco, **1:**447
Bibiena, Giovanni Carlo Sicinio, **1:**447
Bibiena, Giovanni Maria, **1:**447
Bibiena, Giuseppe, **1:**447, **5:***536,* 537
Bibiena family, **1:446–448**
Bible, dance in the, **1:**20, **448–449**, **4:**365
    Christian views, **2:**165, 166, 167
    fan descriptions, **2:**569
    Greek term usage, **3:**293
    Hebrew traditions, **1:**448, **3:**526, 602, 603–604
Bible, The (film), **2:**458
Biblical Ballet, **3:**529
Biblical Pictures, **2:**263
Bibliographie de la danse théatrale au Canada (Guilmette), **2:**49
Bibliography of Dancing, A (Magriel), **6:**296
Bibliothèque Nationale, Paris, **2:**169, 204
Bicentennial, U.S., **1:**74, 232
Biche au Bois, La, **1:**457
Biches, Les, **1:449–450**
    Ballet-Théâtre Français de Nancy revival, **3:**75
    Beriosova performance, **1:**430
    de Valois performance, **2:**396
    Diaghilev's Ballets Russes, **1:**316, 324, 325, **2:**406, 410
    Dolin performance, **2:**423

Lifar and Nemchinova performances, **4:***183*
Makarova performance, **4:**248
Moncion choreography, **4:**450
neoclassicism, **4:**633, 634
Nijinska (Bronislava) choreography, **1:**324, 325, **2:**410, 574, **4:**25, 633, *637,* **5:**417
Nijinska (Irina) Dance Company of Harlem revival, **2:**334
Nijinska performance, **4:**635, **5:**237
Poulenc score, **2:**408, **4:**515, **5:**237, 238
Royal Ballet revival, **1:**155, 430, **4:**633
Sokolova role, **5:**637
vocal accompaniment, **2:**410
Woizikowski performance, **6:**404
Bickham, George, **2:**527, **5:**308, **6:**124, 176
Bicknell, Margaret, **3:**255
bid'ah, **1:**401
biddu, **3:**504
Bidjin, Neveka, **6:**432
Bidou, André, **3:**94
Bidsted, Erik, **2:**385
Bie, Oscar, **3:**161
Biedermeier style, **2:**407
Biegovitch, Iovanka, **1:**251
Bien-Aimée, La, **4:**268, 635, **5:**439, **6:**341
Bienert, Bernd Roger, **1:**241, **3:**631, **6:**53, 455
Biennial International Dance Festival, **1:**412
Bienvenus, Les, **1:**287, 424
Biernacka, Halina, **1:**532
Bierwert, T. L., as photographer, **5:**19
Biesele, Megan, as contributor, **4:**74–76
Bifurcation, **4:**107, 108
Big Apple, **1:450–451**, **6:**257, 262
"Big Apple Swing, The" (song), **1:**450
big band era, **4:**202, **5:**630–631, **6:**256, 257
big-band mambo, **2:**276
Big Bertha, **6:**109, 110
big-circle Appalachian clogging, **2:**179
Big City, **3:**614, 626, *627,* 628, **6:**304
Big Deal (musical), **3:**55, **6:**287
Big Heads (dance), **2:**121
Bighenti, Giacomo, **3:**556
Bigonzetti, Maurio, **2:**514
Bigottini, Émilie, **1:**35, 36, 202, 446, **451–452**, **4:**422, 423, 656, 657, **5:**91
Big Show, The (revue), **5:**125
Big Show of 1936, The (revue), **2:**573
Big Song (Chinese form), **2:**131
Big Top, a Circus Ballet, **5:**435
Big White Baby Dog, **3:**52
Bihari's Song, **3:**416
Bihorac, Bahria, **6:**436
Bije, Willy de, **4:**600, 601, *601*
Bijou Opera House Company, New York City, **3:**90–91
Bikos, Athanassios, **3:**303
Bilbão, Antonio el de, **2:**521
Bildungsanstalt Jaques-Dalcroze. *See* Jaques-Dalcroze Institute, Hellerau-Dresden
Bilinsky, Boris, **1:**255
Biljett till balett (Sjörgren), **6:**49
Billard, Claude, **1:**276

Billboards, **3:**617, **4:**519
Bill Haley and the Comets, **6:**249
Billion Dollar Baby (musical), **5:**360
Billioni, Mademoiselle, **5:**197
Billman, Larry, as contributor, **2:**108–109, **5:**357–358, **6:**326–327
Bill T. Jones/Arnie Zane Dance Company, **3:**620, 621
Billy Rose's Aquacades (film), **5:**247
Billy Rose's Diamond Horseshoe (film), **2:**615
Billy Rose's Diamond Horseshoe Revue (musical), **4:**2
Billy Sunday, **1:**300, 302, **3:**87, **5:**59, *59*
Billy the Kid, **1:**49, 70, 233, **452–453**, **6:**138, 204
    Christensen (Lew) performance, **2:**160
    Copland score, **1:**280, 453, **2:**196, 197, **4:**28, 518, **6:**247
    Feld performance, **2:**583
    Hawkins performance, **3:**349
    Kidd performance, **4:**10
    Kirstein libretto, **1:**452, **4:**28, 612
    Kriza performance, **4:**63
    Loring choreography, **1:**280, 452, *452,* 478, **2:**160, 196, 197, **4:**10, 63, 227, **6:**247
    Loring notation, **4:**691
Biltsin, Yuri, **4:**213
Bimba, Mestre, **2:**58
Binandere (people), **5:**78–80
Binche festival (1549), **1:**409
Binder, A., as photographer, 132
Bindig, Susan F., as contributor, **3:**172–173
Binet, Jacques, **6:**25
Binetti, Anna, **3:**365, **4:**149
Binetti, Giorgio, **5:**31
Bing, Rudolph, **1:**68, **2:**187
Bini (people), **6:**19
Binney, Edwin, 3rd, **3:**180
    as contributor, **3:**122–123
Bintley, David, **1:**437, **453–454**, **3:**233, **5:**43, 514
    Benesh notation use, **1:**418
    Birmingham Royal Ballet choreography, **3:**268
    Job choreography, **1:**454, **3:**609
    Royal Ballet choreography, **3:**268, **4:**470, **5:**418, 419, 421
Bioenergetics, **1:**469
Biography (Charlip), **2:**110
biomechanics. *See* kinesiology
Biørn, Per, **5:**314
Biracree, Thelma, **3:**211
Birch, Patricia, **5:**568, **6:**284, 285
bird (as totem), **2:**139–140
Bird, Bonnie, **2:**21, 285, **3:**214, **4:**95, 441
Bird, Dorothy, **3:**214
Bird Catcher, The, **2:**442
bird dances, **1:**14, **2:**65, **6:**417
Bird Fønix, **3:**657
bird lifts. *See* ballet technique, lifts
Birds (Aristophanes), **3:**288, 646, **4:**44
Birds, The, **3:**307, 355
Birds behind Bars, **6:**95
Birds of America, **3:**336, **5:**548
Birds of Paradise, **6:**366
Birdwhistell, Ray, **2:**602
birgas game, **2:**490
Birger Jarl, **6:**39
Biricchino di Parigi, Il, **5:**404
Birju Maharaj, **5:**568, *582,* 597
Birkmeyer, Anton, **6:**388
Birkmeyer, Michael, **1:**241, **2:**440

Birkmeyer, Toni, **1:**240
Birmingham Royal Ballet,
  3:268–269, 307
  antecedent, **4:**242–243, **5:**420
  Bintley directorship, **1:**454, **3:**268
  Kudelka choreography, **4:**74
  Peter and the Wolf restaging,
    5:692
  Wright directorship, **6:**405
Birnie, Carel, **4:**592, 600, 602
Birom (people), **6:**16
Birthday, **1:**300
Birthday Offering, **1:**154, 459
  classical tutu, **2:**244
  Fonteyn performance, **3:**44
  music arrangement, **3:**521
  Nerina solo, **4:**584
Birthday of Oberon, The, **2:**400
Birthday of the Infanta, The,
  1:482–483, **5:**58
Birthe, Froken, **3:**39
Birthnight Ball (England), **3:**522
Birth of Tragedy, The (Nietzsche),
  3:399
Birtwhistle, Harrison, **1:**53
Birtwhistle, Tara, **4:**238
Bischoff, Egon, **3:**156
Bishaō Gon-no-kami, **4:**41, 42
Bishop, Will, **3:**261
Biskop, Gunnel, **2:**631
Bismarck Archipelago. *See* Papua
  New Guinea
bis pokmbui, **3:**504
Bissell, Patrick, **1:**74, 75, **2:**441
Biswas, Anil, **2:**625, 627
Biton, Gadi, **3:**531
Bittencourt, Hulda, **1:**536
Bitter Weird, The, **2:**374, **5:**435
Bittnerówna, Barbara, **3:**316, **5:**218
Bitwin and Bitwin-2, **3:**340
Bivocality, **2:**499
Bix Pieces, The, **5:**440
Bizet, Georges, **1:**141, 545, **3:**20,
  4:33, **6:**65
  See also Carmen
Bjerkenes, Michael, **5:**436
Bjørn, Dinna, **2:**388, **3:**345, **4:**679,
  680, **5:**431, 433
Björnsdóttir, Ingibjörg, **3:**434
Bjørnsgaard, Ingunn, **4:**679
Björnson, Johanna, **6:**44
Bjørnsson, Bjønstjerne, **1:**510
Bjørnsson, Fredbjørn, **1:**454, *508,*
  512, **4:**624, **5:**295,
  430, *511*
Bjrazdylis, Vytautas, **4:**208
Blache, Alexis, **1:**86, **455–456,**
  4:280
Blache, Enrico, **1:**455
Blache, Frédéric, **1:**455, **3:**69
Blache, Giacomo, **1:**455
Blache, Jean-Baptiste, **1:**455, 505,
  3:68, 540, **4:**657, **5:**147
Blache, Mimi, **1:**455
Blache family, **1:**455–456
Blacher, Boris, **1:**241, 390, **456,**
  3:318, 340
Blacher, Deanna, **2:**57
Black, Bebey, **2:**33
Black, Maggie, **2:**404, **3:**51, **6:**292
Black, Neville, **3:**574
Black and Blue (musical), **4:**255,
  630, **6:**103, 288
Black & White, **4:**622
Black Angels, **1:**241, **4:**544
Blackbird, The, **1:**524
*Blackbirds. See Lew Leslie's
  Blackbirds*
Black Bottom (dance), **2:**25, **4:**254,
  519, **5:**629, **6:**244, 255, 256,
  262, 273, 318

Black Broadway (musical), **2:**5
Black, Brown, and Beige (television
  program), **1:**396
Black Cake, **4:**252
Black Caribs. *See* Garifuna dance
Black Crepe and Diamonds, **6:**317
Black Crook, The, **1:456–458, 2:**37,
  249, **4:**464, **5:**404, 514, 616,
  6:190, 242, 299, 315
  Bonfanti performance, **1:**456,
    457, 495, 496, **6:**267, 290
  chorus, **6:**267
  creating demand for dancers,
    6:290
  de Mille revival, **1:**457, **2:**372,
    6:267
  fan number, **2:**572
  Kiralfy brothers' exclusive rights,
    1:457, 496, **4:**23
Black Entertainment Television,
  2:234
blackface
  English border Morris dancers,
    3:242, **4:**313
  English music hall, **4:**520–521
  moresca dancers, **4:**303, 462
  mummers, **4:**313
Blackfeet style (Plains Indian
  dance), **4:**561
Black Gold, **5:**236, **6:**344
Black Hat Dance, **1:**444, **458–459,**
  2:221, 226, **6:**166, 167
Blacking, John, **3:**283, **4:**370, **6:**25
  as contributor, **5:**661–666,
    6:321–322
Black Lake, **3:**350
Black Market (Rauschenberg),
  5:313–314
Black Milk, **4:**532
Black Mountain College, North
  Carolina, **1:**138, 140, 387
  Brown, Carolyn, **1:**542
  Cage and Cunningham, **2:**286,
    287, 288–289, 292, **6:**108
  Farber, Viola, **2:**574
  Taylor, Paul, **6:**108
Black Patti's Troubadours (musical),
  6:255
Black Pirate, The, **2:**176
Black Raven of the Tombs, The,
  5:615
Black Rider, The (Wilson), **6:**401
Black Ritual (Obeah), **1:**66, **2:**373
*Black Shawl, or Infidelity Avenged,
  The,* **3:**192
Black Swan, The, **1:**209, **2:**590
Black Swan, The (film), **3:**307
Black Swan pas de deux (*Swan
  Lake*), **1:**49, 50, **4:**544, 584
  Balanchine choreography, **4:**611
  fouetté turns, **4:**338, **4:**145, **5:**68
  Hightower and Eglevsky
    performances, **3:**225
  Hightower performance, **3:**361
  Inglesby and Spurgeon, **3:**512
  Kshessinska (Matilda)
    performance, **4:**68
  Mercier and Hyrst performances,
    3:429
  Petipa choreography, **6:**31
  Serrano performance, **5:**573
  Somes and Fonteyn
    performances, **5:**640
Black Tights (film), **2:**109
*Black Tradition in American Dance,
  The* (Long), **1:**304
Black Tradition in American
  Modern Dance project,
  1:81, 396
Blagg-Huey Library, Denton, Texas,
  4:169

Blaikie, Julia, **5:**303
Blair, David, **1:459, 5:**52, 294, 531,
  6:190
  Atlanta Ballet productions, **1:**197,
    459, **6:**34
  Biches, Les, **1:**449
  Cinderella, **2:**243
  Fille Mal Gardée, La, **1:**155, **2:**597,
    4:585
  Romeo and Juliet, **5:**396
  Royal Ballet, **5:**416, *416*
  Sadler's Wells Theatre Ballet,
    5:420
  Swan Lake, **1:**71, 77, 459, **6:**34
Blair, Shareen, **2:**288
Blake, Eubie, **4:**629, **6:**276
Blake, Jack, *as photographer,* **1:**155
Blake, Michael, **2:**19
Blake, William, **2:**399, **3:**609, **5:**293
Blake, Yvonne, **5:**650
Blakstad, Kari, **4:**677, 678
Blanc, Jaime, **1:**525
Blanca, or A Marriage of Revenge,
  6:311
Blanca di Navarre, **5:**245
Blanchard, E. L., **5:**71
Blanchard, Jeffrey, *as contributor,*
  2:26–27
Blanche, Jaques-Émile, **3:**656
Blanche-Neige, **2:**176, **5:**91, 96,
  6:353
Blanco, Raymond, **1:**216
Bland, Alexander (pseud. of Nigel
  Gosling and Maude Lloyd),
  3:282, 285, **4:**215
  on Royal Ballet style and
    repertory, **5:**415, 417
Bland, James, **6:**255
Blangy, Hermine, **1:459–460**
Blank, Adele, **5:**657, 659
Blank, Carla, **3:**340
Blank, Gustav, **1:**456, **460,** 500,
  5:531
Blankenberg, *as photographer,*
  4:573
Blankert, Beppie, **4:**597
Blankov, Boris, **5:**470
Blankshine, Robert, **3:**613, *614*
Blanton, Jeremy, **1:**75, **5:**106
Blasche, Julius, **3:**142, **6:**377
Blasis, Carlo, **1:**8, 44, 86, 90, 199,
  348, **460–461,** 540, **2:**269,
  339, **5:**90, 91, 233, 404, 515,
  528, **6:**127
  on arabesque, **1:**100
  on arm positions, **1:**333
  on attitude, **1:**197–198
  on bolero, **1:**480
  Bolshoi Ballet, **1:**461, 486, **5:**455
  Bonfanti as student, **1:**495
  Bordeaux dance scene, **3:**68
  Borris as student, **1:**499
  as Cecchetti influence, **1:**328, 329
  on character dances, **2:**107
  Cucchi as student, **2:**282
  dance illustrations, **5:**260
  dance manuals, **1:**126, 344–345
  Dauberval quoted by, **2:**354
  de Valois ballet based on, **2:**400
  on feet positions, **1:**331
  Ferraris as student, **2:**587
  Fuoco as student, **3:**96
  Gardel (Pierre) influence on,
    3:119
  improvisation as interpretive
    choreographic tool, **3:**444
  Lepri as student, **4:**150
  Moscow ballet school, **5:**480
  on multiple beats, **1:**345
  on pirouettes, **1:**336, 345
  practice clothes designs, **5:**241

quadrille steps, **5:**286
  rond de jambe à terre, **5:**402
  teaching method, **1:**461, **6:**290
  technical writings, **5:**201, **6:**126
  on theatrical versus social dance
    styles, **5:**623, 624
  turnout position, **6:**215
  on weightlessness, **1:**344
Blaska, Félix, **1:**349, **461–462**
Blåskjeggs Mareritt, **4:**676
*Blast at Ballet: A Corrective for the
  American Audience* (Kirstein),
  4:28
Blatch, Cecilia, **4:**380
Blaue Reiter group, **4:**89
Blavat, Jerry, **1:**78
Blažek, Jiří, **5:**245
Blecher, Miriam, **4:**604
Blender, Todd, **1:**456
Blessing Way, **4:**578
Bless You All (musical), **1:**441,
  5:489, **6:**90
Blick, as photographer, **5:**13
Blind Beggar Woman, **5:**256
Blind Girl, **4:**149
Blindisleikur, **3:**437
Blindsight, **5:**301
Blinova, Valentina, **1:**309, *309,* 311,
  2:253, **4:**25
Bliss, Arthur, **1:462–463, 2:**115,
  397, 401, **3:**356, **4:**241, 517
Bliss, Herbert, **2:**420, **4:**619, **5:**264
Bliss, Mr. and Mrs. Robert
  Woods, **6:**5
Blitzstein, Marc, **5:**361
Blizzard, **5:**471
Bloch, Augustyn, **6:**175
Bloch, Ernest, **1:**92–93, **3:**399, **5:**57,
  6:196, *196*
Bloch, Gabrielle, **3:**95
Block, Der, **3:**159
Block Play, **1:**387
Blöde Ritter, Der, **6:**335
Blok, Aleksandr, **1:**463, **6:**411
Blok, Lubov, **1:463–464, 5:**483
Blok, Yakobson, **4:**284
Blom, Jan-Petter, *as contributor,*
  4:669–673
Blom, Marlene, **5:**659
Blomfield, John, *as photographer,*
  5:302
Blomkvist, Magnus, **1:**400, **6:**50
  as contributor, **6:**38–39, 45–48
*Blomsterfesten i Genzano. See
  Flower Festival at Genzano*
Blondy, Michel, **1:464–465, 2:**465,
  4:106, **5:**41, 87, 88, 308, 504
  as *ballet de collège* dance master,
    1:283, 284, **3:**81
  Beauchamps association,
    1:396, 397
  Camargo as student, **2:**28, 29
  Hilverding as student, **3:**364
  rond de jambe en l'air, **5:**402
Blood-Red Flower, The, **4:**143, 640
Blood Wedding (García Lorca),
  5:225, 674, **6:**28
Bloom, Phillip, *as photographer,*
  3:580
Bloomer, Ruth, **1:**79, 421
Bloomer Girl (musical), **2:**373, 374,
  6:278–279
Bloomer Polka, **5:**615
Bloomsbury Group, **4:**223
Blossom, **2:**605
Blossom, Beverly, **4:**651
Blott, Katherine, **5:**639
Blow, John, **5:**251
Blue Angel, The, **5:**164
Blue Ballet, **2:**474

Bluebeard, **2:**112, 425, **3:**26, 519, **4:**269, **5:**424, **6:**198
Bluebell, Miss, **1:465–466**
Bluebells (dance troupes), **1:**464, 466, **4:**524
Bluebird pas de deux (*Sleeping Beauty*), **1:**251, **3:**441, 442, **4:**320, 336
Blue Blouse movement, **3:**48
Blue Bonnets, **3:**247
Blue Corn Dance, **4:**565
Blue Danube, The. See Beau Danube, Le
Blue-Eyed Jack, **4:**546
Blue Grotto scene (*Napoli*), **4:***188,* 513
Blue Hall, Utrecht, **4:**597
Blue Rose, A, **6:**405
Blue Roses, **3:**391
"Blues," **3:***598*
Blue Schubert Fragments (formerly *Lay-out*), **1:**51
Blues for the Jungle, **2:**358
Blue Skin, **6:**43
Blue Snake, **2:**45, **4:**545
Blues Suite, **1:**55, *58*
Blue Studio: Five Segments (video), **2:**294
Blum, Anthony, **2:**333, **4:**619, *619*
Blum, Arthur, **5:**196
Blum, Léon, **1:**466
Blum, Odette, **6:**24
Blum, René, **1:**149, 256, 430, **466, 5:**17, 650, **6:**182
 Ballets de Monte Carlo, Les, **1:**295, 311, 313, 466
 Ballets Russes de Monte Carlo co-founding, **1:**308, 312, **4:**33
 Ballets Russes de Monte Carlo resignation, **1:**295, 311
Blume, Friedrich, **1:**456
Blunden, Jeraldyne, **2:**357, 358, **6:**264
Blunden-Diggs, Debbie, **2:**358
Blutrach, Mariana, **1:***113*
Boal, Peter, **1:**28–29, 96, **4:**623, **5:**265, **6:**66
Boalth, Annie, **4:**94
Boan, Marianela, **2:**281
Boarding House Blues, **1:**440
Boardman, Andrea, **2:***42,* **3:***234,* **4:***252*
Boas, Franz, **2:**601, **4:**370, **6:**186
Boas, Franziska, **2:**316, 320, **4:**168, 370, 649
Boatmen's Festival, The, **3:**563
Boatwright, Christopher, **6:***10,* 260
Bocaccio, Giovanni, **4:**501
Bocanne, La, **2:**260
Bocca, Julio, **1:**77, 111, **2:**124, 441
Boccherini, Luigi, **1:**310, **6:**337
Bocci, Giuseppe, **4:**258
"Bochan, Mister." *See* Cordier, Jacques
Bocharnikova, Ella V., *as contributor,* **4:**358–360, **5:**487
Bocharov, Aleksandr, **2:**107
Bocharov, Mikhail, **1:**392, **5:**480, 606, **6:**30
Bochsa, Nicholas, **4:**513
Bock, Jerry, **3:**605
Bockstaele, Martial, **2:**472
Bocobo, Jorge, **1:**393
Boda de Luis Alonso, La, **4:**222
Bodas de Sangre, **3:**101
Bodas de Sangre (film), **3:**101
Bode, Rudolf, **1:**203, **3:**147, **4:**92
Bodenwieser, Gertrud, **1:466–467**
 archives, **4:**160
 Ausdruckstanz, **1:**203–204

 Australian residency and influence, **1:**211, 467
 as Bulgarian dance influence, **2:**11
 free dance movement, **1:**239, 241
 MacTavish biography of, **4:**626–627, 629
 students, **3:**340, **4:**58, **6:**312
 See also Bodenwieser technique
Bodenwieser Dance Center, **1:**211, 215
Bodenwieser Dancers, **1:**211–212
Bodenwieser technique, **1:467–468**
Bodeuţ, Petre, **5:**385
bodhisattva, St. Denis portrayal, **2:**377
Bodick, Gay, *as photographer,* **5:**68
Bodin, Louise, **1:**236, **468, 3:**188, 189
Bodin, Pierre, **1:**468
Bodin de Boismortier, Joseph, **2:**434, **4:**122
Bodmer, Sylvia, **4:**93, 94, 103, 477
bodnártánc, **3:**412
Body, Jack, **4:**627
Body and Mature Behavior (Feldenkrais), **1:**470
Body and Soul Dance Company, **4:**213
Body Awareness in Action (Jones), **1:**473
body decoration. *See* mask and makeup
Body Language, **3:**421
body language, **4:**367–368
Body-Mind Centering. *See* Mind/Body Centering
body positions. *See* ballet technique, body positions
body suit. *See* practice clothes
body therapies, **1:468–477**
 Alexander Technique, **1:**469, 471, **472–473, 4:**17, 18, 20
 background and overview, **1:468–472**
 Bartenieff Fundamentals, **1:**469, 471, **473–474, 2:**320, **4:**17, 18, 20, 98, 104
 Delsarte system, **2:**371–372
 de Voss classes, **2:**404
 Feldenkrais Method, **1:**469, 470, **474–475, 4:**17, 18, 20
 ideokinesis, **1:**469, 470, **475–476, 4:**17, 18, 20
 kinesiological basis, **4:**17, 18–21
 Laban principles, **4:**99, 104
 movement specialists, **4:**20
 Skinner Releasing Technique, **1:476–477**
 See also dance and movement therapy; dance medicine; body tights, **1:**348
Body Weather Laboratory, **6:**90
Bodyworks, **2:**605
Boelzner, Gordon, **5:**365
Boerman, Jan, **2:**347
Boeuf sur le Toit, Le, **1:**86, 327, **2:**182, **4:**418, 516
Bogdanova, Nadezhda, **5:**140, 500, **6:**71
Bogár, Richárd, **3:**419
Bogatyrev, Aleksandr, **1:**493, **4:**360, **5:**321, 462
Bogdanov, Aleksei, **1:**486–487
Bogdanov, Konstantin, **1:**477, 485
Bogdanova, Nadezhda, **1:477–478,** 486, **4:**281, **5:**455
Bogdanov family, **1:477–478,** 486
Bogdanovich, Elena, **5:**479
Boggs, Edna Garrido, **2:**432
Boggs, Gil, **1:**77, 197

Bogianckino, Massimo, **3:**551–552, **5:**401
Bogoeva, Kalina, **2:**11
Bogusławski, Władysław, **5:**220
Bogusławski, Wojciech, **5:**220
Bohemia. *See* Czech Republic and Slovak Republic
Bohemian Girl, The, **5:**515
Bohemian Polka, **1:**459
Böhm, Karl, **4:**64
Böhme, Franz, **3:**33
Böhme, Fritz, **3:**161
Bohner, Gerhard, **2:**309, **3:**151, 162, 368
Böhn, Max von, **3:**161
Boiardo, Matteo, **3:**106
boi-bumbá, **1:**530
boi-calemba, **1:**530
boi-de-mamão, **1:**530
Boieldieu, Adrien, **1:**9, 205, **2:**414
Boieru, Martin, **1:**292
Boigne, Charles de, **6:**74
Boiko, Ivan, **6:**213
Boisgirard, Louis, **2:**353
Boitard, Louis Philippe, **3:***255*
Boîte à Joujoux, La, **1:**327, **2:**361, **3:**415
Boix, Joan, **3:***4*
Boke Named the Gouvernour (Elyot), **6:**178
Bokor, Roland, **6:**66
Bolcom, William, **3:**52
Boldin, Dragutin, **6:**436, *436,* 437
Bolender, Todd, **1:**262, 298–299, 302, **478–479, 2:**245, 361, 426, **4:**576, 619, **5:**681, **6:**137
 Age of Anxiety, **5:**360, 361
 Cologne Ballet, **3:**149
 Four Temperaments, **3:**57, *58*
 New York City Ballet choreography, **4:**608, 609
 regional ballet, **6:**265
 Souvenirs, **3:**343, *343*
bolero, **1:479–481, 2:**107, 431, *554,* **5:**133, 545, 670, 671
 See also escuela bolera
"Bolero" (skating program), **6:**180
Boléro, **1:**519, **5:**527, 565
 Argentinita performance, **1:**117
 Béjart productions, **1:**292, 404, 406, 410, **2:**498, 514, **4:**635
 Biagi performance, **1:**446
 Boldin choreography, **6:**436, *436*
 Burmeister choreography for last six dancers left in Sarajevo (1994), **2:**15
 Ciepolinski staging, **3:**416
 Fodor choreography, **3:**418
 Fokine production, **3:**24
 Hoyer "Spinning Dance," **3:**393
 Langer choreography, **4:**118
 Lifar production, **4:**184
 Nijinska choreography, **3:**72, **4:**635, *638,* **5:**439
 Page, Ruth, **5:**59
 Ravel score, **1:**117, **3:**24, 72, **4:**516, 635, **5:**315, 316
 Rubinstein performance, **5:**439
 Torvill and Dean ice dance, **3:***433*
 Vilzak, Anatole, **5:**671
Bolero de la Caleta, **5:***671*
Boleslavsky, Richard, **1:**86
Bolger, Ray, **1:481–482, 5:**184, **6:**99, 101, 277, *277*
Boliche, Antón, **5:**671
Bolksbühne, Vienna, **2:**111
Bollywood film musicals, **1:**171, **2:621–629, 3:**461
 Sitara Devi, **5:**603
Bolm, Adolph, **1:**66, 110, 136, **482–484, 3:**385, 619

Adolph Bolm Ballet, **1:**483, **3:**619
 as American dance influence, **2:**91, **6:**290
 Apollo choreography, **1:**95, **6:**5
 Ballets Russes de Serge Diaghilev, **1:**319, 482, 483, **2:**408, 411, **3:**16, 18, 19, 20, **6:**32
 Carnaval performance, **2:**73, **3:**26
 Cecchetti method, **2:**84
 as character dancer, **2:**106
 Firebird restaging, **1:**136, 483, **3:**2, **4:**269
 Metropolitian Opera Ballet stagings, **4:**382
 Pavlova association, **5:**122
 Petrouchka, **5:**166
 San Francisco Ballet, **5:**391, 511, 512
 students, **1:**400, **2:**108, 186, 357, **5:**58
 Swan Lake tour, **6:**32
Bologna, Giovanni da, **1:**197–198, 345
Bologna, Italy, **3:**552
Bologna, Joe, Jr, **5:**70
Bolotov, Mykola, **6:**222–223
Bolotov, N. A., **6:**225
Bolotov, Nikolai, **6:**344
Bolshakova, Natalia, **4:**285, **5:**462
Bolshevik Revolution (1917). *See* Russian Revolution
Bolshoi Academic Theater of Opera and Ballet, Moscow. *See* Bolshoi Ballet
Bolshoi Ballet, **1:**422, **484–495, 5:**516
 Alonso (Alberto) *Carmen,* **2:**278
 American tours, **6:**249
 Ananiashvili, Nina, **1:**83
 Anderson-Ivantzova, Elizabeth, **1:**85
 Bayadère, La, **1:**393
 Bessmertnova, Natalia, **1:**440–441
 Blasis, Carlo, **1:**461, 486, **5:**455
 Bogdanov family, **1:**477
 British tour and influence on Royal Ballet, **5:**394, 416
 Bronze Horseman, The, **3:**187, **5:***461*
 Cerrito Russian debut, **2:**95
 Chinese tour, **2:**136
 Cinderella, **2:**173, **6:**399
 Clustine, Ivan, **2:**181
 Comedians, The, **3:**187
 Coppélia, **2:**200
 Corsaire, Le, **2:**207
 Cuban dance exchanges, **2:**278, *278*
 decline toward end of nineteenth century, **5:**455
 Don Quixote, **2:**435, 437–438, *437,* **4:**429, **5:**452, **6:**442
 Elssler (Fanny) guest performances, **2:**505, **5:**516
 Elvin, Violetta, **2:**506
 Esmeralda, La, **2:**524, **3:**186
 Espinosa, Léon, **2:**525
 Fadeyechev, Nikolai, **2:**564–565
 Fayer as chief conductor, **2:**579
 Fedorova, Sofia, **2:**582
 Fille du Pharaon, La, **5:***453*
 Flames of Paris, **3:**12
 foreign tours, **6:**228
 Fountain of Bakhchisarai, The, **3:**57, **6:**442
 Gabovich, Mikhail, **3:**99
 Gayané, **3:**125
 Geltser, Ekaterina, **3:**127–128
 Giselle, **3:***179,* **6:**7

Bolshoi Ballet, *continued*
Glushkovsky as chief
choreographer, **1:**485,
3:191–192, **5:**454
Golden Age, The, **3:**193
Goleizovsky, Kasyan, **1:**489,
3:193, 194, *194,* 195, **5:**458
Golovin designs, **3:**196
Golovkina, Sofia, **3:**196–197
Gordeyev, Viacheslav, **3:**200
Gorsky, Aleksandr, **1:**393,
487–488, 489, **3:**204–207,
5:456
Gorsky reforms, **3:**204
Grey guest performance, **3:**307
Grigorovich productions,
1:492–494, **3:**308–310, **5:**399,
464, **6:**315
Gusev performances, **3:**327
historical scholarship on, **5:**483
Japanese tours, **3:**589
Joseph the Beautiful, **3:**194, *194,*
631–632, 633
Kain-Augustyn guest
performance, **3:**643
Kondratieva, Marina, **4:**38
Koren, Sergei, **4:**55
Korovin as resident designer,
4:56
Koslov, Theodore, **4:**56
Laurencia, **4:**129, *129*
Lavrovsky, Leonid, **1:**491–492,
4:131, 132
Lavrovsky, Mikhail, **4:**133
Legat, Gustav, **4:**142
Legend of Love, **4:**144
Lepeshinskaya, Olga, **4:**148–149
Leventhal scenic design, **4:**154
Liepa, Andris, **4:**180–181
Liepa, Maris, **4:**181–182
Little Humpbacked Horse, The,
4:211–212
Lopukhov, Fedor, **4:**224
Madezjdoma, Nadezhda,
4:529–530
Maximova, Ekaterina, **4:**335–336
Messerer, Asaf, **4:**358–359
Minkus compositions, **4:**429, 513
Moiseyev, Igor, **4:**443–444
Mordkin, Mikhail, **4:**459, 460
Nadezhdina, Nadezhda,
4:529–530
Nutcracker, The, **5:**10, *11,* 12
pas de deux, **5:**107
Perrot, Jules, **5:**139–141
Petipa, Marius, **5:**157
public theater origins, **5:**452
Raymonda, **5:**463
Red Poppy, The, **5:**331, 458, *458*
revival of, **5:**456
Romeo and Juliet, **5:**392–393,
393, 394, *394,* 395
Sankovskaya performances,
5:516
Semenova, Marina, **5:**566–567
Shurale, **6:**410, 411
Sleeping Beauty, **5:**610
Spartacus, **5:**677
Stone Flower, The, **3:**310, **4:**335,
5:699
Struchkova, Raisa, **6:**7, 8
style, **1:**493–494
Swan Lake first performance,
6:29–30
Swan Lake productions, **1:**486,
489, *490,* **2:**278, **6:**30–31,
30, 31
Sylphide interpretation, **5:**454
sympathy strike for Grigorovich,
3:310
Tarasov, Nikolai, **6:**105–106

Tikhomirov conservativism,
3:633, **6:**171
Ulanova, Galina, **6:**226–228
Vainonen, Vasily, **6:**310
Vasiliev, Vladimir, **5:**464,
6:313–314, 315
Williams (Petr) scenic design,
6:399
World War II, **1:**491, **5:**203, 459
Yakobson, Leonid, **1:**492,
6:410–411
Yermolayev, Aleksei, **6:**420
Zakharov, Rostislav, **1:**486,
490–491, **6:**442
Bolshoi Ballet, The (film), **6:**228
Bolshoi Ballet School, Moscow,
5:480, 527
Bolshoi Experimental Theater,
4:443
Bolshoi Theater, Moscow
theater design, **6:**160
World War II, **5:**203
See also Bolshoi Ballet
Bolshoi Theater Museum, Moscow,
4:62, 165
Bolshoi Theater, Saint Petersburg,
2:207, 414, 415
Ivanov, Lev, **3:**560–561
Johansson debut, **3:**618, **4:**281
opening, **4:**276–277
Perrot and Grisi engagement,
3:316
Perrot, Petipa, and Johansson as
premiers danseurs, **3:**560,
4:281
See also Maryinsky Ballet
Bolt, The, **1:**90, **3:**327, **4:**225
Soviet ideological critics, **5:**594
Bolte, Lisa, **1:**235
Bolton, Guy, **6:**271
Bolwell, Jan, **4:**626–627, 629
Bomarzo, **2:**185
bomba, **2:**64, **5:**274
Bombana, Davide, **1:**391
Bombay film musicals. *See* film
musicals, Bollywood
Bombicz, Barbara, **3:**330
Bon (religion), **6:**166
Bon, Arlet, **3:**84
Bonafini, Caterina, **2:**55
Bonagiunta, Elide, **1:**82
Bonaparte, Lucien, **6:**69
Bonarelli, Prospero, **2:**27
Bonaria, Marius, **5:**73
Bonati, Gina, **4:**22
Bond, Carrie Jacobs, **2:**378
Bond, Chrystelle Trump, *as
contributor,* **4:**457–458
Bond, Edward, **3:**52
bon dancing. *See bon odori*
Bondarenko, Luidmila, **6:**223
Bondarivna, **6:**344
bondialan, **1:**359
Bondoboyo, **3:**495
Bonds, **2:**473
Bondy, Luc, **2:**120
Bonefish Dance, **1:**226
bone fracture, **4:**20
Boneham, Peter, **2:**40, 43, 44
Boner, Alice, **5:**580
Bones and Ash, **6:**449
Bones in Pages, **6:**145
Bonet, María del Mar, **2:**448, **5:**234
Bonfanti, Marie (Maria),
1:495–496, **2:**572, **4:**381,
5:177, **6:**242
Black Crook performance, **1:**456,
457, 495, 496, **6:**267, 290
New York City school, **6:**290
Sangalli rivalry, **5:**514, 515
Bonfiglio, Giuseppe, **4:**382

Bonheur de Vivre (Matisse), **4:**330
Boni, Aïda, **5:**95, 690
Boniface, Charles-Étienne, **5:**649
Bonin, Louis, **2:**338, **3:**158, **6:**123,
124, 125
Bonino, Luigi, **2:**480, **3:**601
Boniuszko, Alicja, **5:**218
Bonnard, Pierre, **5:**545
Bonnart, Henry, **1:**3, **5:**260
Bonn Ballet, **2:**472
Bonne Aventure, La (*Il Trovatore*),
2:282
Bonne-Bouche, **2:**265, **3:**236
Bonnefous, Jean-Pierre, **1:**405,
4:611, **5:**97, 320, 532, **6:**292
American Music Festival (1988),
4:622
ice-dance choreography, **2:**298
McBride marriage, **4:**345
New York City Ballet, **4:**620
Paris Opera Ballet classes, **3:**82
Bonnet, Jacques, **2:**338
Bonney, William H. (Billy the Kid),
1:452
Bono (people), **4:**291
bon odori, **1:**496–497, **3:**586, *586,*
587–588
Bon Prince, Le, **2:**364
Bonsdorff, Edith, **5:**335
Bonté du Seigneur, La, **2:**413
Bonté, Patrick, **1:**412
Bontoc (people), **5:**168
Bonu Amuen masking tradition,
4:289
Bonus, Franatišik, **5:**221
Bonynge, Richard, *as contributor,*
1:9–11
Boogaloo, **6:**263
boogers, **4:**554
boogie-woogie. *See* Lindy Hop
Book 8, for the year 1785 ...
(Werner), **1:**92
Booker, Jay, **4:**252
Book Is Dead, The, **2:**110
Book of Changes (*Yijing*), **2:**128
Book of Days (film), **2:**609, **4:**451
Book of Hours, **2:**166
*Book of Ingenious Mechanical
Devices* (Ibn al-Jazarī), **3:**525
Book of Job, **3:**609
Book of Rites (*Li ji* or *Li chi*), **2:**128
Book of Songs (*Shijing* or *Shi
ching*), **2:**128
Book of the Courtier, The
(Castiglione), **1:**21–22
Booloo (film), **3:**559
Boomerang, **2:**499
boomerang dances, **2:**484
bòorii dances, **3:**348
Boorman, Joyce, **4:**168
Boorstein, William, **5:**186–187
Boosey and Hawkes, **6:**6
boot dancing, **2:**86, 212–213, **3:***133,*
134, **5:**648, *648,* **6:**22
Booth, Barton, **5:**518
Booth, Edwin, **6:**237
Booth, Hester, **3:**255
Booth, Laurie, **3:**274, 275, 276,
5:128, 305, *305*
Boothe, Power, **1:**142, **3:**201
booth stages, **5:**532–533
Booty dancing, **5:**635
Bop Dance Company, **5:**658
Bopha Devi, **2:**32
Boquet, Louis, **1:**497, **2:**238, **3:**184,
4:695, 698, **5:**270
Guimard costumes, **3:**327
Médée et Jason costumes, **4:**346
Boral, Rai Chand, **2:**622
Borani, Arthur, **6:**319

Borbélys, S., **3:**422
Borchsenius, Valborg, **1:**497–498,
5:295
Bournonville tradition, **1:**347,
512, **5:**427, 430
Folk Tale, A, **3:**39
Kermesse in Bruges, **4:**6
Konservatoriet, **4:**43
mime instruction, **5:**430
students, **1:**539, **4:**126, **5:**553
Bordéades, Les (Rameau), **6:**251
Bordeaux, France, **2:**363
Ballet-Théatre, **3:**75
choreographic activity, **3:**68
Dauberval productions,
2:352–353, **4:**174–175
Didelot performances, **6:**413
Fille Mal Gardée first
performance, **2:**594, 595, **3:**68
Hus (Eugène) stagings, **3:**426
Opera House, **3:**66, 67
Borden, Lizzie, **2:**373, 375
Borde, Percival, **5:**256
border Morris dance, **3:**241–242
Bordin, Maria, **3:**261
Borduas, Paul-Émile, **2:**39
Bordy, Ella, **3:**415
Boréades, Les (Rameau), **5:**306, 307
Borel, Ludmila I., *as contributor,*
4:62
Borelli, Giovanni Alfonso, **4:**14
Borg, Anne, **4:**677–678, 679, 680
Borg, Conny, **5:**397, **6:**42, 44
Borgatti, Jean, **6:**25
Borge, Runar, **4:**679
Borges, Jorge Luis, **6:**93
Borgonio, Tommaso, **1:**29
borica, **3:**409, 414, 422
bori cults, **6:**14
borinqueña, **2:**64
Boris, Ruthanna, **1:**498
Ballet Caravan, **1:**279, *280*
Ballet Russe de Monte Carlo,
1:298, 299, 300, *300,* 301, 302
Cakewalk, **2:**26
Metropolitan Opera Ballet
School training, **4:**381
New York City Ballet
choreography, **4:**608
Royal Winnipeg Ballet, **2:**38,
5:435
Boris Godunov (Mussorgsky
opera), **1:**317, **2:**407, **3:**195
Borisenko, Eugenia. *See* Ruskaja,
Jia
Borisoglebsky, Mikhail, **5:**483
Boris Volkoff Ballet Company, **2:**47
Borkh, Aleksandr, **5:**150
Boŕkovec, Pavel, **5:**245
Borkowski, Witold, **2:**11, 440,
5:218
Börlin, Jean, **1:**327, **2:**183, **5:**334,
335, 525, **6:**455
Ballets Suédois, **1:**326–328, 400,
2:361, 399, **3:**21, 393, 614
Milhaud collaborations, **4:**418
studies with Fokine, **6:**41
bormāyah dance, **2:**489
Borneo. *See* Malaysia
Borodin, Aleksandr, **1:**482, 483,
3:135, **4:**429, **6:**281
See also Polovtsian Dances
Borovansky, Edouard, **1:**207,
208–209, 212, 213, 230, 303,
498–499, **2:**150, **3:**203, 623,
5:563
Borovansky, Xenia, **2:**150
Borovansky Australian Ballet
Company, **1:**207, 209, 210,
212, 213, 230, 235, 498–499,
4:26

Fernandez (Royes) as *premier danseur*, **2**:586
Gorham, Kathleen, **3**:203
Jones, Marilyn, **3**:623
Martyn, Laurel, **4**:275
New Zealand performances, **4**:624
Welch, Garth, **6**:378
See also Australian Ballet
Borovik, A., **5**:*470*
Borowska, Irina, **1**:110, 302, **2**:510
Borree, Yvonne, **4**:624
Borri, Pasquale, **1**:238, 427, **499–500**, **2**:82, 587, **4**:353, 413, **5**:409
Warsaw Ballet, **1**:500, **6**:365
Borromeo, Julie, **5**:171, 172, 173
Borsa, Matteo, **3**:546
"Borsht Belt" circuit, **1**:431
Bortoluzzi, Paolo, **1**:291, 292, *404*, 405, 406, **3**:60, **5**:528, **6**:143
boru (tor-tor), **3**:500
Boruta, **5**:101
Borwicz, Bob, *as photographer*, **6**:304
Borzik, Rolf, **1**:388
Bos, Camille, **5**:95, 690
Bosch, Aurora, **2**:278, 279, 280
Bosch, Hieronymus, **1**:141
Boschetti, Amina, **1**:500, **4**:150, **5**:94, 409, 528
Bose, Madhu, **2**:623
Bose, Sadhana, **2**:623, **3**:468
Bōshibari, **1**:361
Boškovič, Nataša, **6**:432
Bosl, Heinz, **1**:391, **500–501**
Bosler, Virginia, **2**:286
Bosman, Petrus, **2**:58, **5**:651, 652
Bosnia-Herzegovina, **6**:427–428, 436, 438
bosquejo, **1**:116
Bosquet, Le, **3**:629, **6**:453
Boss, Josephine, **3**:*229*
bossa nova, **4**:520, **5**:630, **6**:251
Bosset, Vera de. See Stravinsky, Vera
Bossi, Cesare, **2**:414
Boston Ballet, **1**:201, **501–502**, **6**:264, 328
    Cunningham revised productions, **2**:294, 295, **6**:27, 398
    de Mille production, **2**:374, **6**:398
    Ford Foundation grant, **6**:265, 398
    joint Soviet *Swan Lake* production, **4**:271, **6**:35
    Lowski as principal dancer, 4232
    Marks directorship, **1**:501–502, **4**:271
    Moncion choreography, **4**:450
    Nureyev's *Don Quixote*, **2**:440
    school, **6**:292
    Sergeyev *Swan Lake* production, **5**:572
    Williams, E. Virginia, **6**:398
Boston Ballet II, **1**:502
Boston Conservatory of Music, **4**:168
Boston Evening Transcript (newspaper), **6**:299
Boston Fancy, **5**:587
Boston Grand Opera Company, **5**:125
Boston Herald (newspaper), **6**:299
Boston Lyric Opera, **3**:621
Boston, Massachusetts, **6**:233
Boston Opera, **2**:461
Boston Turnverein, **6**:240, 294
Boston Waltz, **4**:514, **6**:362

Botafogo, Ana, **1**:533, 536, 537
Botha, Andrew, **5**:*660*
Botha, Susan, **5**:659
Botka, Lola, **2**:123, **3**:205, 626, 628, 629, **5**:24, **6**:304
botoló, **3**:410
Botswana, **4**:74–75, **5**:663, 664, *664*
Botta e Risposta (film), **2**:458
Bottequin, J. M., *as photographer*, **1**:413
Botticelli, Sandro, **2**:166
Bottle Dance, **5**:287
Botto, Cecilia, **1**:533
Bottom of the Bucket, BUT...Dance Theater. *See* Garth Fagan Dance
Bouchard, Madeleine, **2**:*39*
Bouchard, Thomas, **5**:185
    as photographer, **2**:246, **3**:401
    film of *The Shakers*, **3**:405
Bouchene, Dimitri, **5**:265
Bouchet, Guillaume, **6**:350, 351
Boudoin, king of Belgium, **5**:422
Bouffes-Parisien (theater), **3**:70
Bouffons (musical troupe), **5**:306
"Bouffons, Les" (Arbeau), **1**:104–105, 369, **2**:591, **4**:460
Bougai, Marguerite, **3**:76
Bougainville, Louis-Antoine de, **2**:204
Bouïra, Algeria, **1**:41
Bou Ismail, Algeria, **1**:42
Boulanger, Nadia, **2**:196, **6**:7
Boulevard Solitude, **3**:359, **5**:37, **6**:*358*
boulevard theaters (Paris), **3**:68, **6**:267
    See also Théâtre *headings*
Boulez, Pierre, **1**:349, 405, 406, **5**:387
Bouman, Hanny, **1**:289
boumba dance, **3**:334
bouncing movements, **4**:352
Bouquet, **4**:325
Bouquet de la Reine, Le, **1**:409
Bourdais, J. D., **6**:161
Bourdelle, Émile-Antoine, **1**:502, **3**:71, **5**:261, *262*
bourée. See bourrée
"Bourée d'Achille, La" (Pecour), **1**:517
Bourgat, Alice, **5**:237
Bourgeois, Denise, **3**:*73*
Bourgeois, Jacques, **5**:563
Bourgeois, Jenne-Marie. *See* Mistinguett
Bourgeois Gentilhomme, Le, **1**:288, 298, 309, **3**:72, 522, **4**:149, **5**:489, **6**:182
    Balanchine-Kochno production, **4**:33
    Balanchine revival, **4**:622
    Balanchine-Robbins production, **4**:447, **5**:361
    Gissey costume designs, **3**:184
    Karinska costumes, **3**:653
    La Fontaine performance, **4**:109
    Lichine performance, **4**:178
    loure, **4**:231
    Lully-Molière collaboration, **4**:234, 447, **6**:267
Bourget, Barbara, **2**:41
Bourgogne, La, **2**:260
Bourguignon, Erika, **6**:185, 187
    as contributor, **6**:184–188
Bourman, Frank, **1**:502
Bourmeister, Vladimir. *See* Burmeister, Vladimir
Bourne, Jane, **5**:*55*, 56
Bourne, Matthew, **3**:276, **6**:*34*
Bourne, Val, **3**:275

Bournique, Alvar, **6**:242, 293
Bournique family, **2**:339
Bournonville, Antoine, **1**:502–503, 504, 509, **2**:412, **3**:105, **5**:425, 433, **6**:334
    Cramér-Skeaping re-creations, **1**:503, **6**:47
    Swedish theatrical dance, **6**:39, 49
Bournonville, August, **1**:503–514, **2**:596, **3**:117, **5**:149, 158–159, 294, 553, 554
    aesthetic, **5**:426–427
    on Albert, Monsieur, **1**:36, 37
    on arabesque, **1**:100
    archives, **4**:160
    on attitude, **1**:198
    autobiography, **1**:503, 505, 506, 511, **2**:387, **5**:250, 251, **6**:70
    ballerina ideal, **5**:425
    as Beck influence, **1**:399
    Bjørnsson performances and teaching of method, **1**:454
    bolero choreography, **2**:521, 522
    Borchsenius and Lander association, **1**:497–498
    as Bruhn influence, **2**:2
    Carey family association, **2**:60
    character dances, **2**:107
    choreographic approach contrasted with Galeotti's, **3**:105–106
    classifications of movements, **1**:44
    Danish composers. *See* Bournonville composers
    on Didelot's choreographic talent, **2**:412
    Don Quixote, **2**:435, **3**:222
    on *exercises d'adagio*, **1**:8
    finest works, **1**:511, **3**:39, **5**:426
    Flindt roles, **3**:12–13
    Flower Festival in Genzano restaging, **4**:380
    Grahn association and break, **3**:222–223, 224
    on Henry (Louis) works, **3**:359
    heritage, **1**:511–512, **5**:427
    See also Bournonville tradition
    Johansson association, **3**:618
    Karstens character dancing, **3**:657
    libretti, **4**:176
    Nielsen as student, **4**:631
    Paris Opera Ballet, **5**:91
    pas de deux technique, **5**:105–106
    performances of leading male roles, **5**:425, 426
    on Perrot, **5**:134
    on Petipa's (Marius) style, **5**:153
    polka choreographical use, **2**:381
    Price family and, **5**:250–251
    reconstructions of works, **2**:387–388, **4**:271, 275, **5**:43, 406, 430, *432*
    scholarly works on, **1**:513, **2**:387, **6**:297
    scores, **4**:513
    Somnambule staging, **5**:641
    style, **1**:513, 539, **5**:426
    Swedish productions and influence, **6**:40
    Taglioni family associationd, **6**:70, 71, 75, 76
    tarantella in *Napoli*, **6**:104–105
    teaching method. *See* *Bournonville-skolen*
    technical writings, **6**:127
    as Vestris (Auguste) student, **1**:329, 345–346, 347, 504, **6**:334

Vienna ballet, **1**:238
Waldemar as final dancing vehicle, **1**:509
    See also Folk Tale, A; Kermesse in Bruges; Konservatoriet; Napoli; Royal Danish Ballet; Sylphide, La; Ventana, La
Bournonville, Augusta, **1**:506, 509
Bournonville, Charlotte, **1**:506
Bournonville, Julie, **1**:236, **6**:39
Bournonville, Théodore, **6**:334
Bournonville and Ballet Technique (Bruhn and Moore), **2**:387, **4**:457, **6**:129
Bournonville Ballet Technique: Fifty Enchantments (Flindt and Jürgensen), **6**:129
Bournonville composers, **1**:514–516, **4**:513, **5**:425, **5**:552 **6**:59
Bournonville Divertissement, **2**:511, **4**:631, **6**:399
Bournonville Festival (1979), **5**:430, 433
Bournonville Festival (1992), **1**:539, **5**:433
Bournonville School, The (Ralov), **1**:513, **6**:129
Bournonville-skolen, **1**:329–330, 333, 345–346, 349, 399, 512, 513, 539, **2**:387
    arm positions, **1**:332
    ballon, **1**:340
    Beck curriculum organization, **5**:427
    French school influence on, **1**:347–348
    methods explained, **6**:129
    pirouettes, **1**:336, *336*
    technique instruction, **5**:202
    Vestris exercises, **1**:345–346
Bournonville's London Spring (Moore), **4**:457
Bournonville Summer Academy, Midland, Michigan, **2**:387
Bournonville tradition, **1**:328–330, 346, 347–348, 497–498, 511–513, 539, **2**:385, 387, **5**:427, 433
    American dance education, **6**:292
    Ashton *Romeo and Juliet*, **5**:394–395
    Beck's continuation of, **5**:427–428
    choreograpic reconstructions, **2**:387–388, **5**:430, *432*, 433, 555
    English National Ballet productions, **2**:509, 511
    Flindt's productions, **3**:13
    influence on Maryinsky Ballet, **4**:281
    Kehlet performance style, **3**:668
    Kronstam performances of repertory, **4**:65
    Lander (Harald) restagings, **4**:118
    Lander (Margot) dancing style, **4**:119
    Lander *Études*, **2**:535, **4**:118, 119, 120
    Larsen performances, **4**:125
    Lassen dancing style, **4**:126
    Moore's writings, **4**:457
    Royal New Zealand Ballet productions, **4**:624, 625
    Russian productions, **4**:281, 285, **5**:406
    Schanne, Margrethe, **5**:553
    Schaufuss (Peter) reconstructions, **5**:555
    scholarship, **2**:387

Bournonville tradition, *continued*
    Vangsaae, Mona, **5**:553
    Williams (Stanley) roles, **6**:399
    Worsaae scenic and costume
        designs, **6**:404–405
bourrée, **1**:516–517, **3**:69, **4**:235,
    510, 511
Bourrée Fantasque, **1**:198, **2**:513,
    3:654, **4**:137, *137,* 616,
    5:361, 431
Bousloff, Kira, **1**:212
Boutique Fantasque, La, **1**:66, 311,
    322, 323, *323,* 327, **5**:279,
    6:105
    Ballet-Théâtre Français de Nancy
        revival, **3**:74
    can-can, **2**:53, **4**:316
    Cecchetti mime performance,
        2:83
    Danilova performance,
        2:342, 343
    dell'Ara performance, **2**:369
    Idzikowski performance, **3**:441
    Kaye performance, **3**:663
    London premiere, **2**:409
    Lopokova performance, **4**:223
    Massine choreography, **4**:316,
        317, **5**:415, 589
    mazurka, **4**:343
    Reed performance, **4**:617
    Shearer (Moira) performance,
        4:489, **5**:588
    Sokolova performance, **5**:636
    Wells (Doreen) performance,
        6:380
    Woizikowski performance, **6**:404
    Zorina role, **4**:449
Bouvier, Joëlle, **3**:78, 79
Bouvier, Jules, **2**:93, **5**:261
bouzouki, **3**:298, 299
Bovang, Johnny, **5**:55, 56, *56*
Bovard-Taylor, Alice, **2**:319
Boven, Arlette van, **4**:602
Bovet, Maria, **2**:470
Bovet, Osip, **1**:485
Bovt, Violetta, **1**:517, **2**:15, 524,
    3:138, **5**:459
bow. *See révérence*
Bow, The, **6**:432
Bow Dance, **6**:36
Bowditch, Henry, **4**:15
Bowen, Dorothea, **3**:210, **5**:584
Bowen, Wilbur, **4**:16
Bowit, John E., *as contributor,*
    5:642
Bowles, Paul, **1**:280, 281, **2**:196,
    197, **4**:518, **6**:247
bowl lyre, **6**:444, 445
Bowlt, John E., **5**:546
    as contributor, **1**:253–255,
        422–424, 436–437, **2**:421,
        3:196, 197–199, **4**:55–56,
        124–125, **5**:372, 642
Bowman, Patricia, **1**:517–518,
    5:289
    Fokine ballets, **3**:22, 23, 26
    Mordkin Ballet, **1**:65, **4**:460
Bowne, William, **3**:386, 387, **4**:156
Box, **6**:259
Boxes, **4**:479
box-tier theater design, **6**:160–161
Boyarchikov, Nikolai, **1**:518–519,
    2:423, **4**:224, **5**:12, 460, 461,
    464, 471
    Ekaterinburg Opera Theater,
        5:470
    Maly Theater Ballet, **5**:468–469
Boyarsky, Konstantin, **4**:224, **5**:460,
    468, **6**:313
Boyce, Johanna, **2**:609

Boyce, William, **2**:401, **4**:482
Boyd, Charles, **3**:*173*
Boyd, Kimberli, **4**:*151*
Boydell, John, **2**:68
Boye, Valentina, **5**:*476*
Boyes, Peter, **4**:625
Boyfriend, The (film), **6**:204
Boy Friend, The (musical), **5**:602
Boyle, Johnny, **5**:239
Boys from Syracuse, The (musical),
    6:277
Boysse, Ernest, **1**:283
Božinov, Goran, **6**:437
Bozsik, Yvette, **3**:421, **6**:67
Bozzacchi, Giuseppina, **2**:198–199,
    3:*71*, **5**:501
    Coppélia role creation, **3**:237
Bozzolini, Cristina, **3**:553
Bozzoni, Max, **2**:351, 462, **5**:*91*,
    6:65
Braaseur, Guy, **1**:*291*
Brabants, Annie, **1**:519
Brabants, Jeanne, **1**:519, **5**:422
Brabants, Jos, **1**:519
Braceros, **1**:524, **4**:392
Bracesco, Virgilio, **2**:337, **3**:80,
    4:582
Bracho, Martha, **4**:397
Braconnier, Le, **1**:124
Brada, Ede, **3**:412, 414
Bradford, Perry, **6**:255
Bradford Civic Theatre,
    Manchester, **4**:94
Bradley, Buddy, **1**:147, 465, **520**,
    4:334–335, **6**:256–257, *257*
Bradley, Dorothy, **1**:520
Bradley, Helen, **4**:668
Bradley, Jimmy, **6**:316
Bradley, Lisa, **2**:606, **3**:610, *612*
Bradley, Wilbert, **2**:458
Bradshaw, Dove, **1**:142, **2**:296
Brady, Eileen, **3**:51, 614
Brae, June, **2**:115, **5**:114, 299, **6**:375
Bragaglia, Anton Giulio, **5**:441
Brage, Föreningen, **2**:631
Brahmā, **3**:453, 454
Brahma, **4**:455, **6**:452
brāhmānada, **3**:462
Brāhmaṇas, **3**:462, 463
Brahmanism, **1**:16
brahmans, **1**:169, **3**:459, **4**:69–71
Brahms, Johannes, **2**:584, **4**:179
    Massine symphonic ballet, **1**:310,
        4:322, 517
    See also Liebeslieder Walzer
Brahms/Handel, **4**:622, **6**:153
Brahms Handel Variations, **1**:453
Brahms Quintet, **3**:306
Brahms-Schoenberg Quartet, **2**:314,
    576, **3**:352, **4**:345, 618, **6**:340
Brahms Sonata, **4**:667
Brahms Variations, **3**:225, **4**:638
Brahms Waltzes, **2**:455
Brăiloiu, Constantin, **5**:390
Brainard, Ingrid, **1**:278, **3**:46,
    6:215, 298
    as contributor, **1**:91–92, 107–108,
        363–365, 368–370, 378–382,
        2:204–206, 331–333, 336–341,
        427–429, 433–434, 517–518,
        590–592, **3**:322–325, 325–326,
        361, **4**:221–222, 347–350,
        448–449, 460–463, 498–504,
        5:244, 336–340, 343–345,
        519–521, 619–623, **6**:121–126,
        403
Brain Waves, **4**:115
Branca, Glenn, **2**:359
Branco, Gaica, *as photographer,*
    1:232

Brancusi, Constantin, **4**:659, **5**:525
Brandão, Maria Carmen, **1**:533
Brandard, John, **2**:70, **5**:261
Brandeis University, Waltham,
    Massachusetts, **2**:287–288
Brandenburg, Hans, **3**:161, **4**:89,
    90, **5**:503
Brandenburg Concerto No. 4, **3**:404
Brandenburgs, **4**:482, **6**:110
Brandes, Christine, **6**:*250*
Brand New Dance, **2**:171
brando. See branle
Brando, Marlon, **2**:458
"Brando detto Alta Regina,"
    4:505, 581
Brandstrub, Caroline, **3**:381
Brandstrup, Kim, **2**:514, **5**:433
Brandt, Fernando, **1**:536
Brandt-Knaack, Olga, **6**:378
Brandy, Le, **2**:35
Branitska, Nathalie, **1**:311
branle, **1**:91, **520–524**, **3**:543,
    4:509, 510, **5**:222, 341,
    619–620
    Arbeau description, **1**:104,
        522–523, *522,* **2**:74, 474, 591
    cotillion as variant, **2**:251–252
    Faeroese dance similarity,
        2:383, 565
    French form, **3**:64
    gavotte, **3**:123–124
    Icelandic form, **3**:434
    intermedio, **3**:509, 511
    minuet, **4**:431
    musical accompaniment, **4**:502
    Negri description, **4**:580
    révérence, **5**:345
    Scottish form, **2**:474
    technical manuals on, **6**:122
"Branle de Poitou," **4**:431
Brant, Henry, **2**:196
Brantôme, Pierre de Bourdeilles
    de, **6**:350
Braque, Georges, **1**:316, **2**:242,
    3:*72*, **4**:33, 34, 320, **5**:544
bras à la lyre, **1**:332
bras en couronne, **1**:332
Brasileira, **2**:123
brass band movement, **6**:238
Bräuer, Lucia, **3**:89
Bräuer, Vera, **3**:154
brâulet dance, **5**:380
Braun, Editta, **1**:240
Braun, Robert, **5**:23
Braune, Christian, **4**:15
Braunfels, Walter, **4**:64
Braunschweig, Philipp, **1**:282,
    2:478, **3**:158
Braunsweg, Julian, **1**:315, **2**:425,
    507–508, 510, **3**:269
Brautfahrt, Die, **3**:625
Bravmann, René, **4**:290, 291, **6**:25
Bravo! (cable network), **6**:133, 140
Bravo, Guillermina, **1**:524–525,
    4:392–393, **6**:*355*
Bravo, Julio, **5**:676
Bravo, Petra, **5**:275, 276
Bravo, Waldeen and Guillermina,
    6:323
Bravo, Figaro!, **1**:540, **5**:467
Bray, Thomas, **2**:256, **5**:251, **6**:123
Brazil, **1**:525–537
    Association of Dance
        Professionals, **5**:43
    ballet, **1**:532–534
    Candomblé, **1**:529, 530, **6**:423
    capoeira, **2**:58–59
    Congadas, **1**:156, 157, **2**:195
    dance education, **1**:532, 533,
        534–535, 537

    dance research and publication,
        1:536–537
    as Lagos dance influence, **4**:292
    lambada, **5**:635
    modern dance, **1**:534–536,
        6:325–326
    ritual and popular dance,
        1:525–532, **6**:185, 187
        *See also specific forms and
            dances*
    samba, **5**:507–508
Brazil, Tom, **5**:186
    as photographer, **5**:276
Brazos River, **2**:575, **5**:314
"Breadalbane Ball Reel." *See* "Reel
    of Tulloch"
Bread and Puppet Theater, **1**:143
Breakaway (dance), **4**:201, 254
break dancing, **1**:538–539, **3**:447,
    5:633, **6**:250–251, *263*
Breakers, **2**:295
breaza dances, **5**:381
Brecht, Bertolt, **1**:291, 306, 375,
    2:499, **3**:163, 208, 652, **4**:118,
    241, **5**:429
Brecht, George, **6**:362
Bregvadze, Boris, **4**:284, **5**:480, 595
Breidenbach, George, **2**:602
Breinin, Raymond, **1**:66, **2**:245
Breitman, Ellen, *as contributor,*
    5:191–193, **6**:181–182
Bremen State Opera Ballet, **1**:11,
    3:151, **6**:59
Bremen Tanztheater, **3**:157, 368,
    4:59, 204
Bremer, Lucille, **1**:193, 194, **4**:209,
    5:290
Brenaa, Hans, **1**:539, **2**:200, 387,
    535, **4**:273
    Bournonville repertory, **1**:512,
        5:430
    Folk Tale, A, **3**:39
    Kermesse in Bruges, **4**:6
    Royal Danish Ballet, **5**:429
    students, **3**:667
    Sylphide, La, **6**:59
Brenda Bufalino and the American
    Tap Dance Orchestra, **6**:102
Brentano, Robyn, **2**:609, **4**:21
Bretel, Johanna, **6**:50
Breton, Jean Vostet (Arbeau
    pseud.), **1**:103–104
Brett, Steven, **5**:*305*
Bretus, Mária, **1**:308
Breuer, Marcel, **1**:385, **6**:164
Breuer, Peter, **1**:242, **5**:55
*Breve tratado de los passos del
    danzar a la española* (Minguet
    e Irol), **5**:676
Brexner, Edeltraud, **1**:241
Brézilia, ou La Tribu des Femmes,
    4:340
Brianchon, Maurice, **5**:237
Briantzev, Dmitri, **1**:539–540,
    5:401, 460, 464, 471
    Stanislavsky and Nemirovich-
        Danchenko Musical Theater,
        1:540, **5**:464, 467
Brianza, Carlotta, **1**:540–541,
    2:201, **3**:261, **5**:159, 456,
    528–529, 611
    creation of Aurora role, **1**:540,
        4:282
    Sleeping Beauty performance,
        5:506, *607,* 610
    Sylvia performance, **6**:64
Brice, Fanny, **6**:317, 319, *371*
Bridal Veil, The, **1**:86, **4**:674
Bridegroom Called Death, A, **2**:374

bridge figure, **4:**349
Bridges Go Round (film), **2:**604
Brief Fling, **1:**77
Briem, Olafur, **3:**436
Brierly, Justin, **4:**170
Brieux, Yves, **1:**461, **3:**82
Brigadoon (film), **2:**109
Brigadoon (musical), **2:**373, 374, **6:**279, 340
Brigand de Terracina, Le, **2:**390, **3:**260
Briggs, Barbara, **2:**261
Briggs, Bunny, **3:**367
Briggs, Hedley, **2:**401
Brigham Young University, Salt Lake City, **2:**169
Brighenti, Giacomo, **3:**556
Bright, Richard, **3:**409
Bright Stream, The, **1:**491, **2:**579, **3:**327, **4:**226, **5:**468
Soviet official condemnation of, **5:**594–595
Briginshaw, Valerie A., *as contributor*, **2:**417–418, **3:**177
Brijs, Frieda, **5:**422
Brik, Osip, **3:**48
Brillant, Maurice, **5:**95
Brilliant and the Dark, The, **1:**52, **3:**273
Brilliant Divertissement, A, **6:**412
Brind, Bryony, **1:**282, **5:**419
Bring in 'da Noise, Bring in 'da Funk (musical), **3:**447, **6:**103, 288
Brinnin, John Malcolm, **1:**441
Brinson, Peter, **1:**213, **541**, **2:**405, **4:**177, 678, **5:**603
as contributor, **3:**276–281, 281–284, **5:**411–422, 603–604, **6:**312–313
Brioschi, Anton, **3:**346, **5:**278
Brisbane, Australia, **1:**211, 216, 216–217
brisé, **1:**345, 384
Brissenden, Alan, *as contributor*, **3:**251–253
Bristle, **2:**19, 20
Bristol School of Ballet, **2:**349–350
Britain. *See* Great Britain
Britannia Coco-Nut Dancers, **3:**242
Britannia Triumphans (Davenant), **4:**309
Britannicus (Racine), **3:**364, **4:**174
British Ballet Organisation, **2:**525, 590, **3:**279
British Broadcasting Corporation (BBC)
dance series and productions, **2:**115, 314, 608, 611, **4:**104, 117, 132, 215, 585, **5:**114, **6:**132, 134, 135, 136
Film and Video Library, **6:**134
first televised dance, **6:**134
Giselle broadcast, **4:**585
Lambert "Third Program" broadcasts, **4:**114
Markova seventieth-birthday documentary, **4:**270
Schaufuss (Peter) production on male dancer, **5:**555
Skeaping's *Sleeping Beauty*, **5:**603
Tudor's pioneering productions, **6:**196
van Praagh productions, **6:**313
Wright (Peter) productions, **6:**405
British Columbia, Canada, **2:**38, 41, 48
British Drama League, **4:**94
British Film Institute, **4:**163

British Royal Acadmy of Dancing. *See* Royal Academy of Dancing
British Royal Ballet. *See* Royal Ballet
British school. *See* Ballet technique, major schools; Ashton, Frederick; de Valois, Ninette; Royal Ballet
British Theatre Museum, London, **3:**282
Brito, Amparo, **2:**279
Brittany, France, **2:**99, 101
traditional dance, **3:**63, 64
Britten, Benjamin, **1:**93, **2:**266, 373, **3:**203, 388, **4:**71, **6:**197, 341
Alston collaboration, **1:**52, 53
Death in Venice, **1:**157, **5:**37
Humphrey choreography, **3:**403
Illuminations score, **1:**152, **3:**442, **4:**608
opera ballet, **5:**37
Prince of the Pagodas score, **1:**374, 390, **2:**266, **4:**244, 245, 517
Staff ballets, **5:**563, 654, 692
Britton, Amanda, **5:**304, 305
Britton, Donald, **6:**218
brîul dances, **5:**379–380
Brno Ballet, **1:**541–542, **4:**77, **5:**393
Němeček, Jiří, **4:**583, 584
Ogoun, Luboš, **5:**23–24
Psota, Ivo Váňa, **5:**269, 270
Broad, Kim, **4:**625
Broadbent, Aïda, **6:**326
Broadbent, Evelyn, **4:**212
Broadsword Exercise, **3:**246
Broadway Melody of ... (film series), **1:**193, *613*, **2:**613, 615, **5:**239
Broadway Show, **1:**375
Broadway theater. *See* musical theater in the United States
Brocard, Caroline, **1:**505, **2:**390
Brocard, Monsieur, **2:**595
Broch, Frances, **6:**276
Brockway, Merrill, **1:**80, **2:**294, 375, **6:**138
Brodersen, Georg, **1:**507, **4:**6
Brodilovo, Turkey, **1:**84
Brodovitch, Alexey, **5:**184–185
Broeckx, Wim, **2:**347, **4:**252
Broken Heart, The (Ford), **3:**253
Brolga (journal), **1:**218
Brom, Rudolf, **2:**308
Broman, Diane, **1:**412
Brome, Richard, **3:**252
Bromilow-Downing, Pat, *as photographer*, **2:**56, 57, **5:**57, 654
Bronkhorts, Truus, **4:**596
Bronner, Mikhail, **1:**540
Bronx State Hospital, New York, **2:**320–321
Bronze Horseman, The, **1:**491, **2:**450, **3:**187, **4:**149, 284, **5:**459, *461*
Semenova performance, **5:**567
Sergeyev performance, **5:**572
Yermoleyev performance, **6:**420
Zakharov production, **6:**442
Brooding over This and That, **2:**473–474
Brook, The (musical revue), **6:**267
Brooker, Gary, **2:**359
Brookes, L. de Garmo, **2:**339
Brooklyn Academy of Music, **5:**187
American Ballet Company, **2:**583
New Wave Festival, **2:**566–567, **4:**471

Brooklyn Normal School of Gymnastics, **6:**240, 294
Brooks, Charles, **1:470–471**
Brooks, Louise, **5:**585
Brooks, Lynn Matluck, *as contributor*, **2:**164–166, **5:**667–670
Brooks, Peter, **5:**521
Brooks, Sheldon, **6:**255
Brooks, Virginia Loring, *as contributor*, **2:**597–600
Broomhead, Phillip, **5:**420
broomstick dancing, **5:**695–696
Broš, Milana, **6:**433, 434
Brossard, Sébastien de, **5:**506, 506–507
Brossé, Dirk, **5:**423
Brotherhood of the Rosary, **1:**526
Brothers Karamazov, The, **5:**464
Brott, Alexander, **5:**61
Broughton, Shirley, **2:**290, **6:**362
Brouillards, **2:**267, 361, **4:**1, 245
Brousson, André, **5:**94
Brouwer, Leo, **2:**279
Brown, Bruce, **3:**188
Brown, Buster, **6:**102
Brown, Carol, **1:**468, **4:**626–627
Brown, Carolyn, **1:**350, **542–543**, **2:**269
Canfield performance, **2:**53
as contributor, **2:**53–54, **6:**26, 27, 356, 402
as Cunningham dancer, **2:**286, *287*, 288, 289, 291, 293
dance film, **2:**609, **5:**440
Farber style contrast, **2:**574
Pelican performance, **1:**140
students, **5:**439
Suite for Five performance, **6:**26
Summerspace performance, **6:**27
Walkaround Time performance, **6:**356
Winterbranch performance, **6:**402
Brown, Chuck, **5:**634
Brown, David, **3:**220, **6:**114, 115
Brown, Delores, **6:**260
Brown, Doryta, **3:**76
Brown, Earle, **1:**542, **2:**289, **4:**519
Brown, Eddie, **6:**102
Brown, Esther, **3:**386
Brown, James, **5:**633
Brown, Jessie, **1:**192
Brown, Lewis, **4:**614
Brown, Lorna, **5:**433
Brown, Ralph, **6:**102
Brown, Ron, **6:**259
Brown, Trisha, **1:**143, 412, **543–545**, **3:**274, **5:**187, 243, 305
avant-garde dance, **1:**246, **3:**336, **6:**250
dance company, **1:**213, 414, 543–545
dance space and environment, **5:**548–549, *549*, 550, 551, **6:**163
film choreography, **2:**605, *605*, 608, 609
Grand Union, **3:**235, *235*
improvisation, **3:**445–446, *446*
Jones (Bill T.) collaboration, **3:**621
Judson Dance Theater, **2:**462, **3:**634
Locus, **1:**543, **6:**249
modern dance technique, **4:**442
Rauschenberg association, **1:**544, 545, **5:**313, 314, *314*, 550, 551
Brown, Vida, **5:**428
Browne, Delores, **3:**577

Browne, Harriet, **6:**102
Browne, Leslie, **4:**117, **5:**396
Browne, Louise, **4:**676
Browne, Rachel, **2:**36, 43, 48, **6:**363
Brownell, George, **6:**231
Brownskin Models, **6:**256
Bruce, Betty, **3:**22
Bruce, Christopher, **1:**375, 394, **2:1–2**, 284
Benesh notation use, **1:**419
choreography course, **3:**280
English National Ballet choreography, **2:**514, **3:**273
Geneva Ballet choreography, **6:**53
Ghost Dances, **2:**1, **5:**303, **6:**180
London Contemporary Dance Theatre choreography, **4:**220
Rambert Ballet, **2:**1, **3:**274, 275, **5:**302, 303, *303*, 304, 305, *6:134*
Bruce, Marian, **2:**1
Brücke group, **1:**131
Bruckin Party, **3:**573
Bruderfaerden i Hardanger. See Wedding Festival at Hardanger, A
Brugnoli, Amalia, **1:**36, 237, **3:**258, 359, **5:**105, 207, **6:**70, 71, 73
Bruhn, Erik, **1:**399, **2:2–5**, 443, **5:**573, **6:**174, 349
American Ballet Theatre, **1:**69, 70, 71, 73, *73*, **2:**3, 4, 280, **3:**362
archival collection, **4:**166
Australian Ballet, **1:**210, 230, 231
Bournonville ballets, **1:**329, **2:**3
on Bournonville's influence on Cecchetti, **1:**329
on Bournonville style and method, **2:**387, **4:**457, **5:**105–106, **6:**129
Bournonville training, **1:**349, **2:**2
Carmen performance, **5:**600
Chauviré dance partnership, **2:**3, 114
as Coe influence, **2:**184
Coppélia performance, **2:**200
Coppélia staging, **3:**643
Daphnis and Chloë performance, **2:**266
Don Quixote performance, **2:**436
Études performance, **2:**536
Flower Festival in Genzano, **6:**143
Folk Tale, A, **1:**508
Fracci dance partnership, **2:**3, **3:**60, *181*, **5:**107
Giselle, **3:**181, **4:**270
Harkness Ballet, **3:**342
international career, **2:**3–4
Jacob's Pillow performance, **3:**571
Metropolitan Ballet, **4:**380
National Ballet of Canada, **2:**3, 4, 42, **3:**643, **4:**542, 543, 545–546
Nerina collaboration, **4:**585
New York City Ballet, **4:**620
Norwegian National Ballet guest performance, **4:**677
Paris galas (1962), **3:**362
pas de deux technique, **5:**105–106, 107
Rome Opera mixed program performace, **5:**401
Royal Danish Ballet, **4:**273, **5:**428, 430
Royal Swedish Ballet, **2:**3, 4, **6:**42–43
Swan Lake performance, **1:**210, 230

Bruhn, Erik, *continued*
  Swan Lake production, **2:**2, 3, 4, 471, **4:**542, 543, **6:**34, 35
  Sylphide, La, **4:**542, **6:**59, *59,* 142
  Symphony in C performance, **6:**66
  Tallchief (Maria) dance partnership, **6:**86
Bruil, Michel de, **2:**337–338
brukdown, **1:**415
Brum, José, **6:**301
Brumbilla, Paolo, **3:**176
Brun, Ida, **1:**199
Brun, Victor, **5:**617
Brunati, Antonio, **6:**38
Brunel, Lise, **1:**462
  as contributor, **3:**77–80, 85–86
Brunner, Gerhard, **1:**241, 242
Bruno Ruiz, Luis, **4:**399
Bruns, Victor, **3:**153
Brunson, Perry, **4:**470
Brush Dance, **4:**567
Brusilovsky, Evgeny, **3:**665, **6:**307
Brussel, Robert, **3:**656–657
Brussels Opera, **1:**404, 405
Bruyn, Jan de, **4:**588
Bry, Theodore de, **2:***542, 550*
Bryans, Rudy, **1:**375, **2:**200
Bryant, Willie, **6:**256
Bryars, Gavin, **2:**119
Brzen Mask, The, **2:**364–365
Brzhozovskaya, Ludmilla, **1:**408
Bubble Dance, **2:**573
Bubbles, John W., **2:**5, **6:***99,* 100, 102, 317
  as Astaire influence, **1:**192
  Green (Chuck) association, **3:**304
Bubblin' Brown Sugar (musical), **2:**186, **6:**102, 284
Bubeníček, Otto and Jiří, **2:**310
Bublikov, Timofei, **3:**365, **4:**276, **5:**452
Bubois, Ninon, **6:**39
bubonic plague, **2:**331
Bucchi, Anita, **3:**553
Bucchi, Valentino, **2:**370
Buchanan, Jack, **1:**520, **4:**522, **6:**272
Bucharest Opera, **2:**343, **5:**384–385, 386, 387
Buchholtz, Hermann, **3:**302
Büchner, Georg, **2:**500, **4:**244
Buchwald, Jette, **3:***39*
Buck, Gene, **6:**448
Buck and Bubbles, **2:**5, **3:**304, **6:***99,* 317
buck-and-wing, **3:**608, **6:**96, 254, 268, 316
buck dance, **2:**179, 180, **6:**96, *97,* 254, 262
Buckland, David, **2:**355, **4:**218
  as photographer, **4:**219
Buckland, Theresa Jill, *as contributor,* **3:**238–243
Buckle, Richard, **2:**67, 73, **3:**285, 656, **4:**33, **5:**637
  on *Chant du Rossignol* 1920 production, **4:**331
  Diaghilev ballet costume exhibit, **4:**34, 125
  Diaghilev studies, **3:**282
  on Messel's *Sleeping Beauty* design, **4:**358
  on Nijinsky's *L'Après-midi d'un Faune,* **4:**648
  on Ulanova's Giselle, **6:**228
Buckmaster, Henrietta, **5:**497
Bucșan, Andrei, **5:**391
Buczyńska, Ziuta, **5:**218
Budapest Ballet, The (Körtvélyesn), **3:**424

Budapest Dance Archives, **4:**161
Budapest Dance Ensemble, **4:**448
Budapest International Ballet Competition, **3:**418
Budapest Opera Ballet, **2:**473, **3:**414–420
  foreign performance, **3:**419
  Guerra, Nicola, **3:**320
  Harangozó, Gyula, **3:**341–342, 415–416
  Kun, Zsuzsa, **4:**74
  Markó, Iván, **4:**266
  Milloss choreography, **3:**416, **4:**420–421
  Miraculous Mandarin premiere, **1:**370, **3:**415–416
  Nádasi, Ference, **4:**529
  Ondine, **3:**360
  Róna, Viktor, **5:**401–402
  Seregi, Lásló, **5:**569
  Sylvia staging, **6:**64
  training, **3:**422
Budapest Sports Palace, **4:**266
Budarin, Vadim, **4:**285, **5:**469, 472
Budaya Dance Company, **5:**524
Buddhism
  aesthetics, **1:**17, 182, **2:**287, **3:**581
  Balinese dance, **3:**471, 473, **4:**297
  Bhutanese dance, **1:**443–445, 458–459, **2:**225–226
  Burmese dance, **4:**525, 527
  Chinese martial arts, **1:**185, 186
  Dai folk dance, **2:**140
  Japanese dance, **1:**167, 168, 183, 496, **2:**6, **3:**171, 172, 579, 580–581, 588, **4:**653
  Japanese nō drama, **4:**295, 653, 655
  Korean dance, **2:**223, *223,* **4:**45, 46, 47, 48, 50–51, 299
  Sikh dance, **5:**598, 599
  Sri Lankan dance, **2:**228, *229,* **3:**649
  Thai dance, **4:**111, 255–256
  Tibetan dance, **2:**141, 221
  See also Yoga; Zen Buddhism
"Buddhist Monk Dance," **2:**223, *223,* **3:**340–341, **4:**140, 141
Buddhist Nun Craves Worldly Love, A (Chinese classical opera), **2:**143, 144
Buddy Bradley Girls, **1:**520
Buenos Aires, Argentina, **1:**102, 110–112
Bufalino, Brenda, **2:***186,* 187, **3:**367, **6:**102
Buffalo Bill (William Cody), **4:**464
buffalo cult, **4:**551
Buffalo Dance, **4:**553, 559, 560, *561,* 564, **5:**240
buffoons (Turkey), **6:**210, *210*
bugaku **1:***167,* 168, 198, **2:**5–6, **3:**579–580, *579, 580,* **6:**340
  abstract music, **4:**494
  archival manuscripts, **4:**167
  costume, **2:**213–215, *214,* **3:**579, *579, 580*
  as folk dance, **3:**586
  as form of *gagaku* tradition, **3:**102, 579
  full program, **2:**6
  gigaku traces, **3:**171–172, 579
  notation, **3:**591, 592
  togaku and *komagaku* components, **3:**102–103
Bugaku (Balanchine ballet), **2:**334, **4:**5, *616,* 617
bugei, **1:**186
Bugge, Gerd, **4:**683
Buggiano, Bettina, **2:**433
Buhlig, Richard, **2:**21

Buirge, Susan, **3:**77, 82, **4:**651
Bujeaud, Jérôme, **3:**33
Bujones, Fernando, **1:**38, 73, 74, 77, 282, 536, **2:**278, 441, **3:**306, **6:**35, 143, 324
Bukaitis, Elegius, **4:**208
Bukhara dance, **3:**537, **6:**305
Bukidnon (people), **5:**168
Bukin, Andrei, **3:**432
Bukový, Viliam, **2:**308, 473, **4:**584
bul, **5:**3
Bulan, Anna, **4:**453, 454
Bulba, **4:**444
Bulbul, Afroze, **1:**94
Bulder, Bogdan, **5:***217*
Bulgakov, Aleksei, **2:**73, 436, **3:**1, 15, **5:**119, 331
  Chopiniana performance, **6:**60
  Firebird performance, **3:**17, *18*
  Schéhérazade performance, **5:**556
Bulgakov, Sergei, **6:**30
Bulgakov and the Others, **3:**329, **4:**267
Bulgaria, **1:**85, **2:**7–12
  folk and traditional dance, **2:**7–10, 99, 100, 101, **4:**374
  theatrical dance, **2:**10–12
Bulgarian Concert Bureau, **1:**281
Bulgarian National Folk Ensemble, **2:**7, 8, 9
Bulgarian Opera Society. *See* Sofia National Opera
Bull, Jamie, **4:**627
Bull, John, **1:**428
Bull, Ole, **4:**674
Bull, Richard, **3:**447
Bull, The, **6:**175
Bullberg, Birgit, **2:**632
Buller, Edward, **2:**49
Bullet in the Ballet, A (play), **1:**367
Bullfight (film dance), **2:**604
"Bullfrog Hop, The" (song), **6:**255
bull symbol (Crete), **2:**270, 271
Bulnes, Esmée, **1:**110, 445, **2:**587, **3:**59, **5:**529
Bulton, Amanda, **1:***51*
Bulutlar Nereye Gidiyor, **6:**212
bumba-meu-boi masquerade, **1:**530, **4:**291
Bumpkin (reel), **3:**246
Bum's Rush, **1:**76
bunde, **5:**67
Bundgård, Karsten, *as photographer,* **4:**678
Bundu masking society, **4:**290
Bundy, William, **5:**396
Bungala song series, **1:**223
bunggul, **1:**223, 224
Bunin, Ivan, **2:**150
Bunny Hug (dance), **5:**627, 628, **6:**243
bu no mai dances, **2:**6
bunraku, **1:**160, 161, 179, *179,* 180, **2:**12–14, **3:**586, **4:**537
  influence on *kabuki* acting, **3:**607, 637
  mime, **4:**423
Bunster, Patricio, **1:**124, **2:**123, 125
Buonaventura, Wendy, **4:**415
Buontalenti, Bernardo, **3:**544, **4:**187, **5:**534–535
Burat de Gurgy, Edmond, **2:**405
Burchenal, Elizabeth, **3:**34, **4:**374, **5:**685–686, **6:**240, 294
Burckhardt, Jacob (filmmaker), **2:**170–171
Burckhardt, Rudy, **2:**460
Burdsall, Lorna, **2:**280, 281
Buresund, Inger, **4:**679
Burge, Lucy, **4:***470,* **5:**303
Bürger Edelmann, Der, **6:**387

Burgess, Hovey, **4:**115
Burgess, Marie (Madame Carandini), **1:**205
Burghers of Calais, The (Rodin), **1:**128, **4:**514
Burgmüller, Friedrich, **2:**14, 203, **3:**5, 177, 178, **4:**341, 513, **5:**132, 133, 157, **6:***70*
Burgon, Geoffrey, **4:**219
Burgoyne, Ollie, **6:**317
Burgtheater, Vienna, **1:**236, 237, 468, **3:**364–365
  Gluck ballets and operas, **3:**187, 188, 189
Burgundian Manuscript, **4:**683
Burgundy, France
  bassedanse, **1:**378–379, 380, 409, **4:***684*
  Renaissance banquets, **1:**364
Burhauser, Jarmil, **4:**583
Burian, Emil František, **4:**238
Buriat Ballet, **5:**473
Buried Venus, **4:**627
Burke, Billie, **1:**448
Burke, Charles H., **5:**271
Burke, Dan ("Irish Dan"), **6:**316–317
Burke, Dermot, **2:**357
Burke, Kenneth, **1:**64
Burke, Tom, **4:**464
Burkhanov, Muzafar, **6:**84
Burkhanov, Sonmas, **6:**307
Burkhardt, Ludwig, **3:**142
Burkina Faso, **4:**291
Burle d'Isabella, Le, **2:**190
Burlesca, **6:**362
burlesque
  ballet de cour, **1:**285, 286, 287, 288
  nineteenth-century variety entertainment, **6:**254
Burma. *See* Myanmar
Burma Camp (Ghana), **3:**168
Burman, S. D., **2:**625
Burman, Vladimir, **1:**540, **2:**14–16, **4:**226, **5:**97, **6:**117
  English National Ballet choreography, **2:**510
  Esmeralda, La, **2:**524, **3:**187
  Lola, **5:**459
  Stanislavsky and Nemirovich-Danchenko Musical Theater, **5:**466–467
  Swan Lake, **1:**517, **2:**388, 471, 529, **5:**463, 466, **6:**31, 34
  Tatiana, **4:**284
Burmese (people), **4:**524
Burmese National Theater, **2:**227
Burmese State Theater Troupe, **2:**227, **4:**527–528
Burn, Malcolm, **5:***54,* 55
Burnaby, Andrew, **3:**607
Burnacini, Giovanni, **5:**536–537
Burnacini, Lodovico (Ludovico), **1:**426, **5:**536
Burne, Gary, **2:**56, 57, **5:**53, 54, 55, *651,* 652
Burnett, Adrian, **1:***232*
Burnett, Catherine, **5:**56
Burney, Charles, **3:**522, **6:**343
Burnham, L. R., *as photographer,* **6:**237
Burning Bush, **1:**466
Burns, Edward, **2:**440
Burns, Judy Farrar, *as contributor,* **1:**116–117, **3:**286–287, 342–344, **4:**222–223, 354–355, **6:**407–408
Burns, Louise, **2:***289*
Burns, Robert, **2:**475, **3:**243

Bürn Theatre, Austria, **4:**189
Burr, Marilyn, **2:**404, 510, **5:***13*
Burra, Edward, **2:**401, **3:**356
Burroughs, William, **6:**401
Burrow, The, **3:**136, **4:**241, **5:**574
Burrows, Abe, **6:**281
Burrows, Jonathan, **5:**421
Burt, Francis, **1:**456
Burth, Jürg, **3:**151, **6:**228, 454
Burtner, Elizabeth, **6:**297
Burton, Anne, **1:**197, **4:***616*
Burton, Richard, **6:**283
Burundi, **2:**86, 87, *90*
Busaba-Unakan, **4:**112, **6:**151
Busby, Gerald, **6:**111
Bushmen. *See* !Kung San dance
Busida, Antonio, **4:**588
Busken, Hans van den, *as
   photographer,* **4:**591, 601
Busoni, Ferruccio, **1:**43
Busse, Edna, **1:**209, 499
Bussell, Darcey, **4:**245, **5:**419,
   420, *421*
Bussola, Maria Luigia, **5:**232
Bustillo, Gilma, **1:**375
Bustos, Isabel, **2:**281
But, **2:**388
Buta-hime, **4:**534
Butcher, Rosemary, **3:**272
Butler, Ethel, **1:**81, 421, **2:**360,
   3:216
Butler, John, **1:**214, 233, 349, 350,
   2:16–17, 41, **5:**43, 97, 131,
   234, 436, 528, 681, **6:**364
   Alvin Ailey choreography, **1:**55,
      3:577
   Amahl and the Night Visitors,
      6:145
   Boston Ballet choreography,
      1:501, **6:**398
   Broadway musicals, **6:**278
   Catulli Carmina, **3:**230
   Deaths and Entrances
      performance, **2:**360
   de Lavallade association,
      2:366, 367
   Harkness Ballet, **3:**342, 343
   Medea, **3:**60
   Netherlands Dance Theater guest
      choreography, **4:**602
   students, **6:**151
butō, **1:**168, 246, **2:17–18,** **3:**591,
   6:90
   acrobatics, **3:**583
   Amagatsu Ushio, **1:**60, 61
   American Dance Festival, **1:**80
   Eiko and Koma, **2:**499–500
   Hijikata Tatsumi, **3:**362–363
   improvisation, **3:**447
   Kasai Akira, **3:**657–658
   Maro Akaji, **4:**271–272
   masks and makeup, **2:**219
   Tanaka Min, **6:**90
   Yamada Setsuko, **6:**414–415
Butoh-ha Sebi, **2:**18
Butsova, Hilda, **1:18–19,** **4:**460,
   5:124
"Butterfly Ballet" (*Sally*), **6:**273
Butterfly Dance, **2:**223, **3:***91,* **4:**48,
   54, 565
Butterfly Love, **3:**414
"Butterfly Prelude" (*The Concert*),
   5:*360*
Button, Dick, **2:**298
buyō, **3:**639, **4:**492, 493
Buyōgaku (journal), **3:**591
buyō geki, **3:**639
Buzand, Pʻawstos, **1:**119
Buzzard Lope (dance), **2:**179, **6:**262
Byakkosha, **2:**18

Bye, Reed, **1:**142, **2:**460
Bye Bye Birdie (musical), **5:**358,
   6:283
Byelorussia. *See* Belarus
Byers, Bettina, **4:**166
bygdedanser, **4:**669–671, 672
By Jupiter (musical), **1:**419, 482
Byrd, Donald, **1:**60, 197, **2:19–20,**
   358, **5:**659, **6:**259
Byrd, William, **6:***350*
Byrd Hoffmann School of Byrds,
   6:400
Byrn, James, **5:**70
Byrne, David, **3:**339, **6:**153
Byrne, James, **2:**467, 609
Byrne, Mr. and Mrs. Oscar, **6:**233
Byron, Lord (George Gordon),
   1:36, **2:**206, 207
Bystrenina, Inna, **5:**477
By the Beautiful Sea (musical), **6:**90
By the Sad Sea Waves, **6:**371
By Word of Foot (tap festival),
   6:103
Byzantine Empire, **3:**294–296, 303,
   4:427, 428
. . . *Byzantium,* **6:**111, 113

Caamaño, Eduardo, **1:**111
Cabahug, Gloria V., **5:**174
caballo dance, **2:**64
Cabaret (film), **2:**619, *620,* **3:**55
Cabaret (musical), **6:**284
cabaret dance, **1:**131, 244
   belly dance, **2:**344, *344,* 345
   can-can, **2:**52
   France, **4:**523
   Gert, Valeska, **3:**163
   Greece, **3:**300
cabaret design, **5:**642
Cabaret Voltaire, **1:**244, **4:**90
Cabezón, Antonio de, **5:**118
cabildos (brotherhood), **2:**274
Cabin in the Sky (musical), **2:**458,
   6:277, 278
cable television. *See* television,
   dance on; *specific networks*
caboclo, **1:**530
cabriole (*capriola*), **1:**384, **2:**518
Caccia d'Enrico Quatro, La, **1:**88,
   3:105
Caccialanza, Gisella, **2:**160, **3:**57,
   5:512, 529, 571
   American Ballet, **1:**64
   Ballet Caravan, **1:**279, *280,* 293
   Four Temperaments performance,
      4:450
   Seasons performance, **2:**286
cachucha, **2:**405, 521, 522
Cachucha, La
   Barre statuette of Elssler
      performance, **1:**368
   Cañete (Juana) performance,
      1:110
   Céleste performance, **2:**85
   as character dancing popularizer,
      2:107, 203
   Duvernay performance,
      2:390, 405
   Elssler popularization, **5:**672
   as Elssler triumph, **2:**107, 203,
      390, 405, 502, 503, *503,* 522,
      3:69, 122, 185, **5:***89,* 93
   Grahn performance, **3:**224
   Labanotation of, **3:**427
   Lacotte reconstruction, **4:**108
   Lee performances, **4:**139
   twentieth-century
      reconstructions, **2:**405,
      3:321, 427

Zorn notation, **6:**451
Căciuleanu, Gheorge ("Gigi"),
   3:362, 533, **5:**388, **6:**302
Caddo (people), **4:**558
cadenas, **2:**64
Cadet Hop at West Point, A
   (Homer), **5:***260*
Cadi Ha, **3:**250
Cadmus, Fidelma, **4:**28
Cadmus, Paul, **4:**27
Cadmus et Hermione, **1:**355, **4:**109,
   234, 235, **5:**86, 128, **6:**11
Cadzow, Joan, **4:**600
Caen Biblothèque, **2:**110
Caesar, Julius, **4:**426
Caetani family, **2:**73
Caetano, Ana, **5:***235*
Café Aubette, Strasbourg, **1:**132
café cantante, **3:**708
Cafe Dances, **3:**389, **4:**547
Café de Chinitas, El, **1:**117, **3:***286,*
   4:222, *222*
Café sin Nombre (No-Name Café),
   3:7
Café Society, **4:**210
Caffin, Caroline, **6:**318
Cafi, *as photographer,* **1:**536
Cage, John, **2:21–23,** **3:**368, **4:**220,
   5:276, 526, **6:**108, 250
   avant-garde, **1:**246, **2:**287–288,
      4:519
   Brown (Carolyn and Earle)
      association, **1:**542
   chance in composition, **2:**22, 287,
      4:519, **6:**26, 108
   Cunningham collaboration,
      1:138, 140, 142, **2:**21, 22–23,
      285–296, **3:**446, **4:**519
   as Cunningham influence, **5:**548
   Dunn (Robert Ellis)
      collaboration, **2:**461, 462,
      3:633
   Erdman choreography, **2:**520
   Farber association, **2:**574
   4'33", **6:**108
   as Judson Dance Theater
      influence, **3:**634
   Ocean, **5:**18
   percussion pieces, **4:**519
   Satie as influence, **4:**516, **5:**526
   Suite for Five score, **6:**26
   Theater Piece #1 score, **5:**313
Cage, The, **1:**519, **4:**246
   appraisal of, **4:***614*
   Kaye performance, **4:**616
   as mirror of *Giselle* second act,
      5:362
   Robbins choreography, **3:**663,
      663, 664, **4:**608, **5:**358,
      361–362
   Rosenthal lighting, **5:**407
Cage aux Folles, La (musical), **6:**286
Cage/Cunningham (film), **2:**297
Cagli, Corrado, **4:**421
Cagliostro in Warsaw, **5:**75
Cagney, James, **4:**227, **6:**320
Cahan, Cora, **2:**583
Cahiers (Nijinsky), **4:**646
Cahusac, Louis de, **1:**29, 125, 126,
   3:84, **4:**174, 698, **5:**39, 40, 89,
   307, **6:**125, 126
Caignez, L. C., **1:**503
Cai Kuoying, **6:**385
Cain and Abel, **1:**315, 467, **2:**500,
   4:178, **6:**44
Caines, Christopher, **3:***372*
   as contributor, **1:**79–82,
   2:110–111, 574–576,
   5:372–373
Cairo Institute of Ballet, **4:**158

Cairón (journal), **5:**676
Cairón, Antonio, **1:**480, 481,
   5:670, 676
Cairo Opera Ballet, **2:**496, 497,
   497–498
Cairo Opera Dance Theater, **2:**498
Caiserman, Nina, **2:**47
Caitanya, Sri, **1:**183
Cajiani, Giuseppe, **5:**231
Cajun dance traditions, **2:23–25,**
   6:*250*
Cakchiquel (people), **3:**319
cak chorus, **3:**483–484
cakewalk, **2:25–26,** **4:**522, **6:**243,
   254, *255,* 258, 262, 268,
   316–317
Cakewalk, **1:**498, **2:**26
Calaucán, **2:**124, *124*
Calcium Light Night, **4:**274, 609,
   615, 619, *620*
Caldeon, Walter, **5:**408
Calder, Alexander, **1:**136–137, 252,
   3:214, **4:**27
Calderini, Renata, **2:**513
Calderón, Carmencita, **6:**93
Calderón, Pedro, **1:**54
Caldwell, Helen, *as contributor,*
   3:558–560
Caldwell, James H., **6:**237
Caldwell, Sarah, **2:**462
caleçon de précaution, **5:**240
Caledonian, **3:**517
Caledonian Country Dances
   (Walsh), **2:**256, 257
"Caledonians, The" (quadrille),
   2:475
Calegari, Maria, **4:**618, 619, 623
calembe, **3:**573
calenda dance, **2:**430, **3:**334
Caley, Thomas, **2:**296, **5:**17
Calico, **4:**594
Calico Mingling, **2:**119
Calife de Bagdad, Le, **2:**414
Calife Voleur, Le, **6:**334
California Children's Ballet
   Company, **3:**306
California Folk Dance Federation,
   4:374
California Indian dances. *See under*
   Native American dance
Californian Poppy, **5:**125
California Theater, San Francisco,
   4:189
Caligula, **4:**208
Caligula, emperor of Rome, **4:**428,
   5:73
Călin, **5:**386, 388
Calinda, La, **5:**275
Calisto, **3:**522, **5:**251, 489
Calizza, Lia, **3:**552, 553
Calkins, Henry J., *as contributor,*
   4:568–570
Callaghan, Domini, **3:**512
Callandar, Heather, **1:**217
call and response, **6:**262
Callas, **3:**368
Callas, Maria, **3:**59
callers, square dance, **5:**689
Calles de Cadiz, Las, **1:**117
Callihoé, **1:**464
Call Me Mister (musical), **4:**434
Callot, Jacques, **2:26–27,** *189,* 190,
   3:381, *543,* **4:**312, 460, **5:**1,
   258, 260, *535,* **6:**156
Calloway, Cab, **1:**440, **6:**244, 256
"Cally Waltz, The," **6:**234
Calmette, Gaston, **1:**99
Calmo, Andrea, **2:**189
Calon Arang (Indonesian text),
   3:505

Calonarang drama, **1:**174, 176, *176*, 178, **2:***232*, **3:**479, 484, **490–492**, 644–645, **4:**264, 297
Calori, Virgilio, **1:**238, **5:**217, **6:**365
Calumet Dance, **4:**554–555
căluş dances, 5, *383*, **5:**379, 382
Calvary, **3:**519
Calver, Sarah, **1:**216
Calvert, Thomas, **2:**49
Calvin, John, **2:**167
calypso, **2:**63
Calzabigi, Raniero de, **1:**87, 88, **2:**55, **3:**190, **4:**174, 696
Calzada, Alba, **2:***16*
Calzevaro, Francesco, **5:**692
Camara, Lamine, **1:**304
Cámara, Petra, **1:**480, **5:**672
Camargo, La, **2:**587, **3:***129*, 237, **4:**68, 144, **5:**157
  Legnani farewell performance, **4:**146
  Minkus score, **4:**430
  Monplaisir choreography, **4:**453
Camargo, Marie, **1:**465, **2:27–29**, 465, **3:**66, **4:**122–123, **5:**41, 88, 240, 249, 260, 504, 505, **6:**189
  debut in *Caractères de la Danse, Les*, **2:**59
  footwear, **3:**46
  Genée dance portrayal of, **3:***129, 129*
  Noverre dance partnership, **4:**694
  Sallé associate, **5:**505
  shortened skirt, **2:**238
Camargo Society, **1:**146, 148, 400
  Ashton choreography, **4:**113–114
  Chappell performances, **2:**105
  de Valois association, **2:**397, 399
  Dolin association, **2:**424
  founding, **2:**397, 424, **3:**265, 285, **5:**351
  Gore performances, **3:**202
  High Yellow jazz ballet, **1:**147, 520, **2:**65
  Job, **3:**608–609, **5:**412
  Lambert association, **5:**412
  Lloyd performances, **4:**215
  Lopokova performances, **4:**223–224
  Markova performances, **4:**268
  Rout, **1:**463
  Sadler's Wells repertory, **5:**412, 414
  Tudor performances, **6:**196
Camasse, Madameoiselle, **3:**66
Cambert, Robert, **4:**509, **5:**86, 113
cambinda de Paraíba, **1:**526
cambindas, **1:**527
Cambodia, **2:29–32**
  costume, **2:**227–228
  Royal Cambodian Ballet, **1:***161*
  shadow theater, **1:**178–179
  trance rituals, **6:**185
Cambon, Charles, **2:**198, 206, 405, **3:**620, **5:**85, 132
Cambridge (Massachusetts) Court Dancers, **5:**327
Cambridge, England, **3:**271
Cambridgeshire Molly dances, **4:**474
Caméléopard, **1:**251
Camelot (musical), **5:**616, **6:**283
Camel Walk (dance), **5:**627, 628
Camera Three (television series), **2:**186, 294, **6:**138
Cameron, Judy, *as photographer*, **3:**60
Cameron, Madeline, **6:**274
Cameron, Rachel, **1:***206*, 499

Cameroon, **1:**14, 15, **2:32–33**, 87, 274, **4:***292*
Camille, **1:**315, *315*, **2:**425, **4:**269, **5:**58, 59, **6:**380
Camille, Mademoiselle, **2:**365
Camille, Reine de Volsques (Campras), **2:**34
Cammack, Richard, **5:**513
Camp, Freddie, **1:**358
Campanelas de las Seguidillas Boleras (Téllez), **1:**479
Campanería, Miguel, **2:**278
campanero, **2:**275
Campanilla, La, **5:**133
Campanini, Barbara. *See* Barberina, La
Campbell, Joseph, **2:**520, **3:**217, **6:**297
Campbell, Joyce, **3:**575, 577
Campbell, Monica, **3:**575
Campbell, Norman, **6:**130, 131–132
Campbell, Sylvester, **2:**470, **6:**260
Camp Blue Star, North Carolina, **1:**431
"Campdre Pedro Juan" (merengue), **2:**432
Campenhout, Lut van, **1:**411
Campianu, Eva, **5:**327
Campilli, Pietro, **1:**237, **2:**93, **3:**413, 414, **4:**121, **5:**135
Campi-Mécour, Giovanna, **3:**365
Campion, Thomas, **4:**307, 309, 312, 506
camp meetings, **2:**168
Campobello, Nelly and Gloria, **1:**524, **4:**166, 391
Campos, Lourdes, **4:**392
Campos, Ronaldo, **5:**146
Campra, André, **1:**46, 425, **2:33–34**, 465, **4:**122, 475, **5:**505, **6:**46
  ballet de collège compositions, **1:**283
  bourée compositions, **1:**516
  chaconne and *passacaille* compositions, **2:**99
  forlana, **3:**49, *49*
  loure compositions, **4:**231
  opéra-ballet and *tragédie lyrique*, **5:**34, 39–40, *40*, 88
  rigaudon, **5:**352
  Télémaque, **5:***109*
Camprubí, Juan, **2:**522
Camprubí, Mariano, **1:**480, **2:**251, **5:**672
Camp Tamiment, Pennsylvania, **5:**359
Camryn, Walter, **2:**107, **4:**63, 602, **6:**292
Canada, **2:35–50**
  Cape Breton step dancing, **3:**244–245, **5:**696–698
  dance education, **2:**44–45, **46–48**
    Académie des Grands Ballets Canadiens, **2:**152, **3:**227–228, 231
    character dancing method, **2:**107
    École Supérieure de Danse du Québec, **2:**47, 152, **3:**227, **4:**577
    emigré teachers, **2:**38, 44
    National Ballet School, **2:**47, **4:**541–542, 543
    Royal Winnipeg Ballet School, **5:**436–437
  dance on television, **6:130–134**, 142, *142*
  dance research and publication, **2:**48–50, **3:**36
    libraries and museums, **4:**165–166

  French Canadian folk and traditional dance, **2:35–36**, 49, 179, **3:**36, 38
    jig step, **3:**608
    Native American dance, **4:**49, 550–551, 555, 570, 571, 573, 574, **5:**552
    theatrical dance, **2:36–43**
    theatrical dance, contemporary, **2:**40–41, **43–46**, 47
    See also Grands Ballets Canadiens, Les; National Ballet of Canada; Royal Winnipeg Ballet
Canada Council, **2:**39, 40
Canadance, **6:**132
Canadiana, **2:**151
Canadian Association for Health, Physical Education and Recreation, **2:**47, 50
Canadian Ballet Festival movement (1948–1953), **2:**39, 43, 44, **4:**538, 539, **5:**61, 435
Canadian Broadcasting Corporation (CBC), **6:**130, 132, 142, *142*, 143
Canadian Dance Teachers' Association, **2:**47, **4:**539
Canadian National Ballet. *See* National Ballet of Canada
Canadian Opera Company, **4:**479
Canaille, Die, **3:**163
Canales, Antonio, **3:**10, 11, **5:**674
Canapé, **4:**596
"Canarie pour Deux Hommes" (Pecour), **2:**51
canary (*canario*), **2:50–52**, 74, **3:**108, 510, 511, **4:**507, **5:**324, 338, 666
Canary Islands, **2:**50, 51
Canberra, Australia, **1:**214, 215, 218
can-can, **2:52–53**, 249, *249*, **3:**69
  Boutique Fantasque, **4:***316*
  Morlacchi creation, **6:**237
  popularity in Mexico, **4:**399
  as Rodin inspiration, **5:**370
Can-Can (musical), **5:**358, **6:**281, 327
Canción, **2:**279
Candal, Raúl, **1:**111
Cande, Daniel, *as photographer*, **5:**96
Candide (Bernstein), **1:**439, **6:**285
  Sokolow choreography, **5:**638
  Weidman choreography, **3:**401, **6:**337
CanDoCo, **2:**611, *611*
Candomballet, **6:**302
candombé, **6:**91, 301
Candomblé, **1:**529, 530, **6:**185, 345, 423
C&W Two-Step, **5:**634
cane dance. *See* stick dance
Cañete, Juana and José, **1:**110
Canfield, **2:53–54**, 292, 293, **3:**610
Canfield, Richard A., **2:**53, 54
Caniparoli, Val, **1:**394, **5:**513, **6:**266
Canna, D. J., **4:**691
Canna, Pasquale, **5:**537
Cannabich, Christian, **2:**54
Canner, Norma, **2:**319
Cannocchiale Aristotelico, **3:**544
Cannon, Thomas, **4:**210
Canobbio, Carlo, **2:**55
Canope, **5:**307
Canosa, Hilda, **2:**277
Canova, Antonio, **1:**126
Cansino, Angel, **4:**38, 272
Cansino, Eduardo, **1:**192, **6:**326
Cansino, Elisa, **1:**192

Cansino family, **5:**133
Cansos e bassas dansas (Raimond de Cornet), **1:**378
Cantadagio, **4:**134
Cantate Profane, **1:**349
Cantates, **1:***291*
Canterbury Tales, The (musical), **6:**204
Cantero, David Campos, **1:***413*
cantes chicos, **3:**6–7
cantes jondos, **3:**6, 7
cantica, **4:**500
Canticle, **4:**595
Canticle for Innocent Comedians, **3:**218
Canticle of the Elements, **2:**187
Cantigas, **4:**39
Cantilever, **3:**350
"Cantique de Noël" (Adam), **1:**10
Cantique des Cantiques, Le, **1:**118
Canto Hondo a España, **6:**302
Canto Indio, **3:**343
Canton, Katia, **1:**537
  as contributor, **1:**532–534, 534–536, 536–537, **5:**507–508, **6:**325–326
  as photographer, **1:**535
Cantor, Eddie, **1:**432, 433, **6:**274
Cantos, **4:**594
Canziani, Giuseppe, **2:**55, **3:**546, **4:**149, 276, **5:**480, **6:**311
Caorsi, Ettor, **5:**400
CAPAB Ballet (now Cape Town City Ballet), **2:55–58**, 265, 441, **5:**57–58, 226, 649–650, 651, 652, 654, *654*, 657, 658
  Contemporary Dance Company, **5:**657, 658
  Staff productions, **5:**692
Cap de Bonne Espérance, **2:**109
Cape, Jonathan, **6:**35
Cape Breton, Canada, **2:**179, **3:**38
Cape Breton step dancing, **3:**244–245, **5:**696–698
Čapek, Karel, **4:**648–649
Capell, Richard, **3:**284, **5:**166
Capers, **3:**372
Cape Town City Ballet. *See* CAPAB Ballet
Cape York Peninsula, Australia, **1:**219, 225–227
Capezio (ballet shoe manufacturer), **5:**209
CAPHER. *See* Canadian Association of Health, Physical Education and Recreation
Capital of the World (television program), **4:**228, **5:**573
Caplan, Elliot, **1:**142, **2:**294, 296, 297, 607–608, **6:**136
Caplet, André, **2:**361
Capmany, Aurelio, **5:**676
capoeira, **1:**527, **2:58–59**, **5:**507, 633
Capon, Gaston, **6:**331
Capote, Truman, **6:**282
Cap over Mill, **3:**202
Capriccio Espagnol, **1:**67, 117, 296, 302
  Argentinita and Massine collaboration, **2:**108, **4:**324
  film version as *Spanish Fiesta*, **4:**324
  Froman production, **6:**432
  International Ballet revival, **3:**511
  Massine and Slavenska performances, **4:***323*
Capriccio Espagnol (film), **6:**183
Capriccio Italien, **4:**615

Capricciosa, La, **2:**282
Capriccioso, **2:**425, 507
Caprices de Cupidon, Les, **2:**388
Caprices de Galathée, Les, **2:**443,
    4:149, 695, 697
Caprice Viennois, **4:**380
Caprichos (Ross ballet), **1:**69, **4:**63,
    5:408
Caprichos, Los (Petit ballet), **1:**305
capriola (cabriole), **1:**384, **5:**338
Capriol Suite, **1:**146, 147, 158,
    2:105, **5:**298, 303, 560
Caproli, Carlo, **1:**287
Capsali, Floria, **2:**343, **5:**263,
    385, *385*
Captain January (film), **6:***141,* 142
Capucilli, Terese, **3:**220
Car, Laurent, **2:***28*
Cara, La, **1:**49
Carabin, François Rupert, **3:**92
carabiné, **2:**430
Caracole, **1:**269, 426, **2:**420, 461
    See also Divertimento No. 15
caracoles, **5:**133
Caractères de la Danse, Les, **2:***28,*
    59–60, **5:**88, 105, 249, 504
Carafa, Michele, **2:**202, **3:**118, **6:**51
Carandini, Jerome, **1:**205–206
Carandini, Madame (Marie
    Burgess), **1:**205
Caras, Steven, **2:***577*
Caravan at Rest, The, **2:**414
Carbee, Brian, **4:**627
Carbezón, Antonio, **4:**505
Carbone, Giuseppe, **3:**553
Carbonneau, Suzanne, *as
    contributor,* **2:**72–73, 181–182,
    471, **3:**14–28, **4:**56, 459–460,
    5:118–119, 556, **6:**344–345
Cardel family, **2:**337
Cardell, Thomas, **2:**337
Cardella, J. F., **6:**290
Cardenas, Rosario, **2:**281
Cardiff, Cath, **4:**627
Cardiff, Jack, **5:**332
Cardiff, Wales, **3:**272
Cardona, Patricia, **4:**399
Cardoso, Iracity, **5:**235
Card Party, The, **1:**64, **4:**227
Carducci, Alessandro, **3:**381, 544
Cardus, Ana, **4:**397
Carell, Victor, **1:**218
Carey, Addison, **1:**520, **6:**257
Carey, Auguste, **1:**238
Carey, Édouard (the elder), **2:**60
Carey, Édouard (the younger), **2:**60
Carey, Fanny, **2:**60, 385
Carey, Gustave, **2:**60, **385,** **3:**346,
    413, **4:**339, **5:**232, 426, **6:**70
Carey, Isidore, **2:**60, **4:**121
Carey, Léontine, **2:**60, 385
Carey family, **2:**60–61, 385
Cargeggio . . . dal 1755 al 1797
    (Verri), **3:**546
Cargher, John, *as contributor,*
    1:205–211
Cargo X, **2:**296, **4:**37
Carib (people), **2:**62, 64–65,
    3:120–21
Caribbean Carnival (musical),
    5:255, **6:**280
Caribbean region, **2:61–67**
    as Dunham choreographic
        influence, **2:**64, 458, 459,
        3:599
    Garifuna dance, **3:**120–21, 320
    as West African dance influence,
        6:24
    Williams-Yarborough studies and
        teaching, **6:**400

See also Belize; Cuba; Dominican
    Republic; Haiti; Jamaica;
    Puerto Rico
Caribbean Rhapsody (musical),
    2:459
Carib Song (musical), **2:**459, **6:**280
caricature and comic art,
    2:67–72, 85
Caricature, La (journal), **2:**69
Carifesta programs, **1:**414
Carignan, prince de, **1:**365
carimbó, **1:**525, 530
Carina Ari Dance Library,
    Stockholm, **4:**163
Carinhas, Nuno, **5:***235*
Cariñosa, **1:**115
Caris, Nathalie, **4:***252*
cariso, **2:**65
Çark, **6:**212
Carlin, Jocelyn, *as photographer,*
    4:627
Carlo Emmanuele II, duke of
    Savoy, **1:**29
Carlos, Walter, **1:**461
Car Lot, **1:**542
Carlota, **4:**199–200
Carlotta Grisi (Lifar), **3:**123
Carlotta Grisi: In Retrospect, **4:**262
Carlson, Carolyn, **2:**470, 633, **3:**77,
    4:651, **5:**98, **6:**414
Carlson, Weit, **6:**44
Carl Theodor, elector of
    Mannheim, **2:**54
Carmagnole, La, **2:**72, **3:**67, **6:**344
Carmen
    Alonso (Alberto) production,
        1:50, 73, **2:**278, 564–565
    Berger production, **1:**428
    Brown (Trisha) choreography,
        1:545
    Bruhn performance, **2:**3
    Clavé designs, **2:**244, **5:**551
    Cranko production, **2:**267
    Danovshi staging, **5:**387
    Darrell production, **2:**350
    Flindt performance, **3:**12
    Gilpin performance, **3:**175
    gypsy theme, **3:**185
    Haydée performance, **3:**350
    Jeanmaire performance, **3:**601
    Makarova performance, **4:**248
    Page, Ruth, **5:**59
    Petit production, **1:**38, 305, 457,
        2:3, 244, 283, 513, **3:**12, 74,
        175, 601, **4:**248, **5:**163, *163,*
        431, 589, 599, *600,* 653
    Riveros production, **2:**124, 125
    Smoriginas production, **4:***208*
    Ulrich choreography, **6:**229
Carmen (Bizet opera), **1:**483, **5:**36,
    38, 587
    Appia staging, **1:**97
    Bolm choreography, **1:**484
    Brown (Trisha) choreography,
        1:545
    Collins dance performance, **2:**187
    Drigo as conductor, **2:**446
    Gades staging of dances, **3:**101
    Zakharov choreography and
        production, **6:**442, 443
Carmen (Gades film and stage
    work), **3:**101
Carmen (Mérimée novel), **3:**185
Carmen, María del, **6:**94
*Carmen Arcadiae Mechanica
    Perpetuum,* **5:**304
Carmencita, **1:***127,* **2:**572,
    6:268, 317
Carmen et Son Torero, **5:**150
Carmen Jones (film), **2:**367, **5:**408
Carmen Jones (musical), **4:**228

Carmen Suite, **1:**493, **2:***278,*
    501–502, 565, **5:**205, 587
Carmi, Maria, **3:**631
Carmiel Dance Festival, **3:**531,
    4:156
Carmina Burana
    Bintley production, **1:**454
    Butler choreography, **4:**602
    Butler production, **2:**16–17, 367
    Elizariev choreography, **5:**461
    Hanka choreography, **3:**340
    Kamel production, **2:**498
    Markó version, **3:**329, **4:**266
    Nault production, **3:**230, *230,*
        4:576
    Orff music, **1:**390, 454, **2:**474,
        502, **4:**517
    Page production, **5:**59
    Uthoff production, **2:**124, **6:**304
*Carmina Burana: Cantiones
    Profanae* (Orff), **5:**43
Carmina Catulli, **6:**364
Carmina Krleziana, **5:**677
Carmines, Al, **2:**110, **6:**282
Carmontelle (Louis Carrogis),
    5:105
Carnations, **1:**388, **2:**119
Carnaval, Le, **1:**66, 148, **2:**15,
    72–73, 273, **5:**298, **6:**214
    Bakst designs, **1:**254, **2:**407, **4:**56
    Ballets Russes de Monte Carlo
        revival, **1:**310
    Bolm performances, **1:**482, 484,
        2:73, **3:**26
    commedia dell'arte characters,
        2:*192*
    de Valois performance, **2:**396
    Dollar performance, **2:**426
    Drottningholm Court Theater
        revival, **2:**446
    Fokine as Harlequin, **3:***23*
    Fokine productions, **1:**318, 319,
        320, 321, 322, 484, **2:**72, 73,
        112, *192,* 397, 426, **3:**14, 16,
        17, 19, 23, 24, 26, 137, 511,
        4:109, 640, **5:**413, **6:**41
    Gore performance, **3:**202
    Idzikowski performance,
        3:441, 442
    Inglesby performance, **3:**508
    Karsavina performance, **3:**656
    Kirsova and Youskevitch dance
        partnership, **4:**25
    Korovin designs, **4:**56
    Króller choreography, **4:**64
    Laing peformance, **4:**109
    Markova re-creation, **4:**270
    Nijinska performance, **2:**72, 73,
        192, **4:**634, 641
    Nijinsky performance, **2:**408,
        4:640, 641
    Schollar performance, **5:**558
    Walbom's Biedermeier-style
        Danish staging, **5:**428
Carnaval des Animaux (Saint-
    Saëns), **2:**471
Carnaval de Venise, Le, **1:**451, **2:**34,
    71, **3:**49, **5:**134
    Grahn debut, **3:**222
    Milon production, **4:**423
    score, **4:**61
Carnaval et la Folie, Le, **1:**355, **5:**87
Carné, Marcel, **4:**423
"Carnegie Hall," **5:***561*
Carnegie Library Music and Arts
    Department, Pittsburgh,
    4:167
Carneval/Mascarade, Le, **1:**400
Carnevals-Abenteuer in Paris, **1:**238,
    500, **3:**346

Carnigal, Gener, **5:**173
Carniolus, Gallus, **5:**677
Carnival
    Brazil, **1:***526,* 527, 529, 530
    Congo dances, **2:**195
    Cuba, **2:**275
    Czech and Slovak, **2:**301,
        302, *305*
    Ecuador, **2:**476
    French balls, **3:**69
    French court ballet, **1:**287, 288
    Greece, **3:**298, *300,* 302, *302*
    guild dances, **3:**325
    masquerade, **4:**313, 314, 448, 449
    Mexico, **4:***387,* 388
    moresca, **4:**461
    South Africa, **6:**23
    Spain, **2:**168
    Uruguay, **6:**301
    Zurich, Switzerland, **6:**54
Carnival de Venise, Le, **5:**319
Carnival in Flanders (musical), **6:**90
Carnival of Animals, **5:**300
Carnival of Rhythm (film), **2:**458
Carnival of Rome, The, **4:**455
Carnival Scene (Tiepolo), **4:**315
carole dance, **4:**348, 501, **5:**619
Carolina Shag (dance), **4:**203
Caroline, princess of Great Britain,
    2:394
Caroline, princess of Monaco,
    2:449
Caroline Augusta, empress of
    Austria, **6:**335
Caroline Mathilde, **3:**13, **5:***431,* 433,
    6:404
Carlotta, Ikeda, **2:**18
Caron, Alfred, **5:**278
Caron, Leslie, **1:**194, **2:***618,* **5:**163
    American in Paris, An (film), **4:**3
    Ballets des Champs-Élysées,
        1:306, **3:**73–74, **4:**33
Carosello Napoletano, **2:**369
Caroso, Fabritio, **1:**22, 53, 54,
    2:73–77, 5:260, 505, 506, 621
    on *ballo* and *balletti,* **1:**352, **2:**74,
        75, 77
    Battaglia, **5:**341
    on canary, **2:**50
    on *cascarda,* **2:**74, 77, **4:**507
    on Contrapasso Nuovo step
        pattern, **2:**75
    dance collections, **1:**369, 380
    dance manuals, **1:**104, 105,
        2:73–77, 189, 336–337,
        3:542–543, **4:**684, **6:**122
        *See also Ballarino, Il; Nobiltà di
            dame*
    on dance social benefits, **4:**310
    on figure dances, **2:**591
    on figures, **2:**591
    on fundamental composition,
        3:543
    on galliard, **3:**107–109
    on *intermedio,* **3:**509, 510
    musical examples, **4:**506–507
    Negri similarities, **4:**479, 580–582
    on *passo e mezzo,* **5:**110, *110,* 111,
        112, *323*
    on *pavaniglia,* **5:**117, *117*
    Renaissance dance technique,
        5:336, 338–339
    on *révérence,* **5:**344, 345
    on rose pattern, **5:**684
    on social benefits of dance, **4:**310
    spagnoletta choreography, **5:**666
    on *tordion,* **6:**178
    on turnout position, **6:**215
Caroubel, Pierre-François, **5:**244
Carousal, **2:**296, **4:**37

Carousel (film), **2:**314, 618
Carousel (musical), **4:**59, 120, 213
 de Mille ballet, **3:**273, **6:**279
carousel de Louis XIV, **2:**238
Carozzi, Felicita, **2:**200
Carpathian Basin, **3:**407, 412, 422,
 5:379–380
Carpathians, The, **1:**510, **4:**78
Carpeaux, Jean-Baptiste, **1:**126
Carpenter, Bill, **4:**94
Carpenter, Charles, *as photographer*
 (attributed), **4:**470
Carpenter, John Alden, **1:**390,
 482–483
Carpenter, Romulus, **4:**209
Carpet-Snake Dance, **1:***222*
Carpitella, Diego, **3:**556
Carr, Gerald L., *as contributor*,
 1:446–448, **3:**621–622
Carrà, Carlo, **1:**130
Carracci, Agostino, **3:***510*
Carrafa, John, **6:**152
Carrasco, René, **2:**432
Carrasco Benítez, Marta, *as
 contributor*, **5:**675–576
Carré. *See* Carey family
Carreño, José Manuel, **1:**77,
 2:441, 514
Carreño, Lázaro, **2:**279, 280
Carreras, Guido, **4:**354
Carrey. *See* Carey family
Carrez. *See* Carey family
Carriage Discreteness, **6:***248*
Carrié, Marie-Claire, **1:**349,
 403, 446
Carrière, Eugène, **3:**92
Carris, Cynthia, *as photographer*,
 2:276
Carroboree, **1:**208
Carrogis, Louis (Carmontelle),
 5:105
Carroll, Diahann, **6:**277
Carroll, Earl, **2:**574, **6:**272, 371
 See also Earl Carroll's Vanities
Carroll, Elisabeth, **3:**342, 610,
 6:292
Carroll, Jacqui, **1:**214
Carroll, Lewis, **1:**394
Carrosse du Saint Sacrement, Le
 (Berners), **1:**437
Carrousel, Le, **4:**455
carroussels. See horse ballet
Carse, Ruth, **2:**41
Cars, Laurent, **5:**260
Carson, Barbara and David, **6:**266
Carson, Martha Faure, **4:**170
Carswell, Ed, *as photographer*,
 5:264
Carte Blanche Dance Company. *See*
 New Carte Blanche Dance
 Company
Carter, Alan, **1:**390, **3:**149, 360, 379,
 437, **5:**294
Carter, Andrew, **1:**216
Carter, Benny, **6:**256
Carter, Curtis L., *as contributor*,
 1:19–26, **2:**461–462, 563–564
Carter, Dorothy, **3:**344
Carter, Elliott, **1:**279, **4:**518, **6:**247
Carter, George, **3:**575
Carter, Jack, **1:**110, 289, **2:**510, 511,
 587, **3:**175, 620, **4:**3, 625,
 5:301, 564
Carter, Jimmy, **2:**112
Carter, Kim, **2:**358
Carter, Mrs. Leslie, **5:**491
Carter, Victoria, **3:**344
Carter, William (Bill), **3:**220, 306,
 4:179, *179*
cartes de visite, **5:**176–177

Carthage, **4:**662
Cartier, Jacques, **2:**372, **5:**58
Cartier, Jean-Albert, **1:**349, 351,
 3:74, 75
Cartier-Bresson, Henri, **5:**184, 186
cartoons, **2:**67–68, 69
Caruso, Enrico, **5:**123
Carzou, Jean (scenic designer),
 5:*92*, 551
Casa, Giovanni della, **3:**542
Casado, Germinal, **1:**291, *292*, 404,
 405, 406, **5:**398
Casagli, Serafina, **2:**81
Casanova (Giovanni Giacomo),
 1:87, **2:**465, **3:**49
Casanova. See Komödie
Casassi, Maria, **2:**55
Casati, Eugenio, **3:**261
Casati, Giovanni, **1:**237, 427, **2:**60,
 6:70
Casati, Tommasao, **1:**499
Casbah (film), **2:**458
Cascade, **1:**19, **5:**25
cascarda, **2:**74, **77**, **4:**507,
 5:506, 666
Casella, Alfredo, **1:**327, **2:**400, **3:**51,
 4:421, 635, **5:**246, 400
Casenave, Roland, **2:**469
Casentini, Maria, **1:**237
Casero-García, Estrella, **5:**676
Cases, **5:**408
Casey at the Bat, **5:**197, **6:**137, 204
Casini Ropa, Eugenia, **3:**554, 556
Casino de Paris, **1:**253, **2:**53, **3:**601,
 4:523, **5:**164
casinos, **2:**185
Casorati, Felice, **4:**421
Casorti, Giuseppe, **2:**384, **5:**250
Casorti, Pasquale, **2:**384
Caspar, Johan, **1:**517
Cassandra, **4:**39
Cassandre, **1:**287, 424, **4:**229
Cassandre, Alexandre, **2:**244, **4:**185
Cassaria, La (Ariosto), **5:**534
Cassell, Ricardo and Roberta,
 5:171
Casse-Noisette. See Nutcracker, The
Cassidy, Claudia, **6:**299
Casta Diva, **1:**406
castanets, **2:**78
 ancient Greece, **3:**293
 Argentina (La) skill, **1:**115, **2:**78
 Berber, **4:**467
 as bolero accompaniment, **1:**481
 as canary accompaniment, **2:**50
 as flamenco accompaniment,
  3:9, 11
 as *folia* accompaniment, **3:**28, 29
 Roman Empire, **4:**500
 as *sarabande* accompaniment,
  5:519, 520
 as *seguidillas* accompaniment,
  5:565
 Spain, **5:**671, 672
Castañuelas, Las (Asenjo y
 Barbieri), **5:**676
Castelli, Bertrand, **2:**111
Castelli, Victor, **1:**293
Castello di Kenilworth, **5:**277
Castiglione, Baldassare, **1:**21–22,
 523, **4:**310, 462, **5:**337
Castiglioni, Miccolò, **2:**347
Castilliana, La, **1:**200
Castillo, Mariana, **1:**480
Castillo, Mitto, **5:**172
Castle, Irene and Vernon, **1:**192,
 2:78–80, 250, **4:**480, **5:**628,
 628
 African-American musicians,
  6:256

Astaire and Rogers film
 portrayals of, **1:***191*, 193,
 2:80, **5:**373, *373*
Broadway musicals, **2:**79, **6:**270,
 271, *271*
promotion of new social dances,
 2:78, **6:**243, 270
vaudeville, **6:**318
Ziegfeld musicals, **6:**448
Castle, Josef, **2:**581
Castle, Nick, **2:**615, **4:**629
Castle, Terry, *as contributor*,
 4:313–315
Castles in Spain (extravaganza),
 4:150
Castle Walk, **2:**78
Castor et Pollux, **2:**413, **3:**106, 117,
 5:95, 306, 307
 Guerra revival, **3:**320
 Jooss production, **3:**630
 Lany (Jean-Barthélemy)
  performance, **4:**122
 Zambelli performance, **6:**444
Castren, Christian, **3:**372
Castro, Ana María de, **4:**390
Castro, Federico, **1:**525
Castro, Fidel, **2:**273, 277, 280
Castro, Valentina, **4:**397
Catà, Alfonso, **5:**681, **6:**52
Catalogue of Dance Films, A, **2:**601
Catalonia, **3:**35, 64, **5:**519
cataluña. See sardana
Catalyst, **1:**235
Catana, Doris, **1:**430
Cat and the Fiddle, The (musical),
 1:520, **6:**281
Catargi, Alexis, **5:**384
Catarina, **1:**486, **2:**80, 282, **5:**516
 Elssler (Fanny) performance,
  2:504–505
 Fuoco performance, **3:**97
 Grahn performance, **2:**80, 504,
  3:223, 224, **5:***139*
 Maywood performance, **4:**339
 Monplaisirs' American staging,
  4:455
 Perrot production, **2:**80, 82, 505,
  5:137, *139*, 141
 Pugni score, **5:**277
 Pugni score innovation, **4:**513
 Ronzani revival, **4:**339, **5:**403
 Turczynowicz version, **6:**207
Catawba (people), **4:**558
Catel, Charles-Simon, **5:**557
Catelli, Leo, **1:**140
Cateloube, Joseph, **5:**526
"Catena d'Amore, La," **4:**581
cateretê, **1:**531
Caterina Howard, **5:**403
Cathédrale Engloutie, La, **2:**361,
 4:602
Catherine II (the Great), empress
 of Russia, **2:**55, **3:**365,
 4:149, 276
Catherine de Médicis, queen of
 France. *See* Médicis,
 Catherine de
Catherine Wheel, The, **1:**72, **4:**226,
 5:440, **6:**153–154
Catholic Church. *See* Christianity
 and dance; Roman
 Catholicism
Catholic University, São Paulo,
 1:537
Catilinarian Conspiracy, **5:**377
catimbanos, **2:**121
catira, **1:**531
Catlin, Amy, *as contributor*,
 2:29–32, **4:**123–124
Catlin, George, **4:***552, 553, 559*, 561

Caton, Caroline and Philippe,
 1:110
Caton, Edward, **1:**11, 12, 65, **3:**224,
 4:449
 character dancing teaching
  method, **2:**107
 Grands Ballets Canadiens, Les,
  3:229
 Wilson (Sallie) as student, **6:**402
Cato the Younger, **5:**374
Cats (musical), **2:**251, **6:**285, 286
 Seregi's Budapest production,
  5:569
Cat's Journey, **2:**264
Catte, Efisio, **1:**427, 499
Catterina di Coluga, **2:**208
Catterson, Pat, **2:**460
Catulli Carmina, **1:**375, 390, **2:**17,
 3:230, 317, **5:**677, 43, 60
Cau, Jean, **1:**305
Caught, **5:**187
Cauley, Geoffrey, **2:**361, **4:**668,
 6:454
Causley, Marguerite, **4:**691
Cautiva, **2:**449
Cauwenberg, Ben van, **5:**422–423,
 6:53
Cauwenberg, Tom van, **5:**422–423
Cavalcante, Cybele, **1:**537
Cavalcanti, Giovanni, **1:**21–22
Cavalieri, Emilio de', **1:**353, **2:**50,
 74, **3:**108, 109, 630
 intermedio choreography, **3:**510,
  511, 543, **4:**505, 581
Cavallazzi, Malvina, **1:**37, 400,
 3:261, 284, **4:**381, **6:**270, 291
Cavalli, Francesco, **1:**287, 288,
 4:234, 510
Cavani, Liliana, **1:**82
cavaquinho, **5:**508
Cavé, Edmond, **2:**202
Cave of Sleep, The, **3:**58
Cave of the Heart, **3:**217, 221, 349
Caverley, Thomas, **2:**80–81, **337**,
 527, **3:**521, 522, **4:**106, **6:**175,
 176, 372
Caverna Magica, **1:**59
Cavos, Alberto, **1:**422, 486, **4:**281,
 6:160
Cavos, Catterino, **4:**278, 513
Cawte, E. C., **3:**240
Cawthorn, Joseph, **6:**270
caxambú, **1:**527
Cayaban, Ines V., **5:**173
Cayou, Nontsizi, **6:**448
Cayuga (people), **4:**551
Cazalet, Peter, **2:**57, **5:**57
CBC. *See* Canadian Broadcasting
 Corporation
CBS. *See* Columbia Braodcasting
 System
C Channel (cable network), **6:**133
CCP Dance Company. *See* Ballet
 Philippines
CD-Roms, **2:**612
Cébron, Jean, **2:**81, **3:**268, 630,
 4:203
Cébron, Mauricette, **2:**81
Cecchetti, Cesare, **2:**81, **4:**150,
 5:404
Cecchetti, Enrico, **1:**500, **2:**81–85,
 5:37, 159, 528, 529, 611
 Albertieri as protégé, **1:**37
 as Alston influence, **1:**52
 American performances as child,
  5:404
 Amor performance, **3:**548
 as Ashton influence, **1:**147, 329
 Ballets Russes de Serge
  Diaghilev, **1:***318*, 319, 329,
  348, **2:**82

Bournonville influence on, **1:**329
Carnaval performance, **2:**73
Cinderella choreographic
  collaboration, **2:**82,
  3:564–565
Coppélia production, **2:**82,
  200, 368
Dolin film portrayal of, **2:**425
Don Quixote performance, **2:**436
Empire Theatre, London, **3:**261
Excelsior performance, **2:**82,
  4:258
Fornaroli association, **3:**50, 51
Inediti teorico-tecnici, **3:**555
Lepri as teacher, **2:**81, 82, **4:**150
Lifar as student, **4:**182
Maryinsky Ballet, **2:**82, **4:**282,
  5:456
Massine as student, **4:**316
Nijinska as student, **4:**633
Nijinsky association, **4:**639, **5:**241
as Pavel (Elisaveta) influence,
  3:137
Pavlova association, **5:**121, 124
Petrouchka, **5:**165, 246
prominence in European dance,
  3:547–548
roles *en travesti*, **6:**190
Scala school, **3:**553
Schéhérazade performance, **5:**556
scholarship on, **3:**557
Sleeping Beauty performance,
  5:606
students, **1:**329, 400, **2:**19, 396,
  3:264, 441, 655, **4:**68, 110,
  267, 420, 463, **5:**58, 248, 288,
  296, 385, 529, 588, 636, 678,
  6:119, 143, 191
Swan Lake role, **6:**32
technical manual on
  methodology. *See* Cecchetti
  method
Warsaw Ballet, **5:**217, **6:**365
Cecchetti, Giuseppina, **6:**30
Cecchetti, Grazioso, **2:**84, **3:**557
Cecchetti, Pia, **2:**81, **5:**404
Cecchetti Council of America,
  1:329, **2:**84
Cecchetti method
  on *adage*, **1:**8–9
  on allegro, **1:**44
  on arabesque, **1:**100, 101
  on arm positions, **1:**332, 345
  on attitude, **1:**198
  batterie technique, **1:**384
  Beaumont codification, **1:**398
  Blasis method as basis, **1:**461
  on body positions, **1:**334, 348
  Craske codification, **2:**268–269
  described, **2:**83, **5:**202, 208,
    226–27
  on directions, **1:**335
  Fornaroli school, **3:**51
  French school versus, **1:**347
  influence on Australian ballet
    schools, **1:**207
  influence on Quebec Ballet
    training, **2:**47
  influence on Royal Ballet school,
    1:453, **3:**547, **4:**452, **5:**419
  influence on Russian school,
    1:347, **3:**548
  influence on South African ballet
    training, **5:**649
  as Italian school exemplar, **1:**328,
    329, 333, **3:**547–548
  Lake, Molly, **4:**110
  on leaps, **1:**347
  manual, **2:**83–84, **6:**128
  on pointe work, **1:**8–9, 347
  on *port de bras*, **5:**227–228

on turning movements, **1:**336,
  337, 347
Cecchetti Method School of
  Classical Dancing, New York
  City, **3:**51
Cecchetti Society, **1:**329, 398, **2:**84,
  3:279, **4:**110, 598, **5:**603
Cecchi, Giovanni Battista, **1:**237
Cecchini, Pier Maria, **2:**190
Cech, Adolph, **6:**32
Cech, Gisela, **1:**241
Cedar Tree, The, **3:**417, **5:**569
céilí dances, **3:**517–518
Cekwana, Boyzie Ntselileko, **5:***657,
  659*, 660
Celebration, **1:**479, **2:***65*, 314, **3:**212,
  384, **5:***184*
  Wigman choreography,
    6:391, 392
Celebrations and Ode, **1:**403, **2:**178
Celedon, Mauricio, **2:**126
celeste, **6:**117
Celeste, **2:**460
Celeste, Céline, **1:**205, **2:**71
Céleste, Madame, **2:**36, **85–86,**
  4:454, **5:**71, **6:**58, 237
Celeste-al Cabinet, The (lithograph),
  2:71, 85
Celeste and Celesthina, **2:**350
Celestin, Louis, **3:**335
Celi, Claudia, **3:**554, 555, 557
  as contributor, **1:**29–30, 37–38,
    427, 499–500, **2:**55, 81–85,
    177, 208–209, 282, 586–587,
    3:50–51, 96–97, 175–177,
    540–547, 553–558, **4:**150–151,
    5:245–246, 408–409,
    6:337–339
Çelik, Zeynep, **4:**415
Cell, **4:**217
Cell, The, **6:**378
Cellarius, Henri, **2:**339, **5:**221,
  286–287, 623, 624
"Cellarius Waltz," **6:**361
Celli, Vincenzo, **2:**586, **3:**50–51,
  5:246, 279, 529, 606
Cellule, La, 76
Celtic Ballet of Scotland, **3:**571
Celtis, Conrad, **1:**235
Celts (people), **3:**515–519
Cendrars, Blaise, **1:**327, **2:**399,
  3:72, **4:**418
Cendrillon. See Cinderella
Cenerentola, La (Rossini opera),
  1:36
çengi dancing girls, **6:**210
CENIDI-Danza, Mexico City, **4:**166
Cent Baisers, Les, **1:**311, 367, **3:**394,
  4:178, 636–637
Center for Investigation,
  Information and
  Documentation of Dance,
  Mexico, **5:**44
Center of Contemporary Art,
  Montevideo, **6:**302
Centraal Dansberaad, The Hague,
  4:599, 599–600
Central African Republic, **2:**86, 87,
  89, **4:**484
Central and East Africa, **2:86–93**
  African-Brazilian dance
    influence, **1:**523
  Digo dance, **2:**417–418
  Giriama dance, **3:**177
  Mbuti dance, **4:**344
  zār ceremony, **6:**444, 445
  See also Sub-Saharan Africa;
    specific countries
Central Ballet of China, **2:**145, 146,
  146, 147, 351, 440, *440*,
  4:158, **5:**330

Central Drama Academy, Beijing,
  2:135
Central Europe Dance Theater,
  3:421
Central Minority Nationalities
  Institute, China, **2:**149
Central Song and Dance Ensemble,
  China, **2:**136
Centre Chorégraphique de la
  Communauté Française,
  1:412
Centre de Danse Classique, Cannes,
  3:362
Centre de Documentation et de
  Recherche sur la Civilisation
  Khmere, Paris, **2:**32
Centre d'Entraînement aux
  Méthodes d'Éducation Active,
  3:65
Centre d'Études sur la Langue, les
  Arts, et les Traditions
  Populaires of Université
  Laval, **2:**49
Centre for Dance Information and
  Documentation, Mexico,
  4:400
Centre for Indian Classical Dance,
  Delhi, **4:**257
Centre International de la Danse,
  Paris, **3:**84
Centre National de Danse
  Contemporaine, Angers,
  1:349, 351, **2:**466, 575, **3:**78,
  83, **4:**650
Centre National de la Recherche
  Scientifique, Paris, **2:**601
Centre Wallon de Films
  Ethnographiques, Brussels,
  2:601
Centro di Documentazione e di
  Ricera della Danza, Turin,
  4:162
Centro Documentatzione Danza di
  Genzano, **4:**161
Centro per la Danza
  Documentazione e Ricerca,
  Turin, **3:**556
Cents Baisers, Les, **4:**33
Century of Progress International
  Exposition, Chicago (1933),
  2:573
Cephalus and Procris, **2:**105, 397,
  4:268
Ce que la Mort Me Dit, **1:**406
Ce que l'Amour Me Dit, **1:**292, 406,
  5:527
Cerale, Luigia, **1:**238–239, 429
Cerat Centhini (Javanese text),
  3:505
Cercle, Le, **4:**600
ceremonial dance. *See* ritual and
  dance
Ceremonials, **3:**212, **6:**245
Cérémonie, **2:**41, **4:**577
Ceremony of Us, **3:**336
Cereus, **6:**202
Cerezo, Sebastián, **5:**671
Černá, Michaela, **2:**310
Cernovitch, Nicholas, **2:**288
Cerny, Josette, **1:**410
Ceroli, Guido, **1:**83
Cero sobre Cero, **2:**449
Cerri, Cäcilie (Cecilia), **1:**239, **5:**246
Cerrito, Fanny, **1:**10, 477, **2:93–95,**
  5:93, 147, 528
  Alma, **1:**47–48, **2:**93, *93*, 94, 390,
    5:136
  Armida, **5:**140
  Chalon print of, **2:**103–104
  Gautier libretti, **3:**123

Gemma, **4:**353
Giselle performance, **2:**09, **3:**181
Guest biography, **3:**321
Hamburg Ballet guest
  performances, **3:**36
Hungarian performances,
  3:413, 414
King's Theatre performances,
  3:259, 260, 315
Lalla Rookh, **5:**137
Ondine, **5:**29, 136
Orfa, **4:**342
Paris Opera Ballet, **3:**69, **4:**342,
  5:89
partners, **1:**400, **2:**60, **5:**148
Pas de Quatre, **1:**103–104, **2:**94,
  103, **3:**224, 260, 315,
  5:108, 137
photographs of, **5:**177, *177*
polka performance, **5:**221
portrayal in *Pas des Déesses*,
  3:*609*, 611
Quatre Saisons, Les, **3:**260, **5:**138,
  6:76
Saint-Léon dance partnership
  and marriage, **2:**93, 94, 95,
  3:413, **5:**106, 498, 499,
  499, 500
Spanish dance performances,
  2:522
Taglioni (Marie) rivalry, **6:**74
Taglioni (Salvatore) association,
  6:70
Cervantes, Miguel de, **2:**76, 98, 401,
  434, 435, 438, 440, **4:**422,
  5:667
Cervantes Kawanago, Ignacio, **2:**62
Cesare, Gaetano, **5:**692
Cesare in Egitto, **3:**176, **5:**409, 528
Cesareso, Marie, **1:**405
Cesembasi, **2:**401
Çeşmebaşt, **6:**212
Cevera manuscript (dance
  notation), **2:**542, **4:**683
Ceylon. *See* Sri Lanka
Cezar, Adina, **5:**387, 388–389
Cezar, Cormeliu, **5:**389
Chá, Ercilia Moreno, *as
  contributor*, **1:**108–110
Chabelska, Galina, **1:**110
Chabelska, Maria, **5:**85
Chabrier, Emmanuel, **2:**253, 254,
  400, 568, **4:**33
Chabukiani, Vakhtang, **1:**34,
  2:95–97, 437, **3:**135, 665, **5:**5,
  204, **6:**310, 314, 343
  Bayadère, La, **5:**463
  Dudinskaya collaboration, **2:**449,
    450
  Esmeralda pas de deux, **2:**524
  Flames of Paris, **3:**12
  Laurencia, **4:**129, 133, 284, **5:**458
  Othello, **4:**36
  strong technique, **5:**458
  Tokyo Ballet school, **3:**589
  Zakharov collaboration, **6:**442
chacarera, **1:**108
Chace, Marian, **2:**316–317, 321
cha-cha, **4:**520, **5:**630, **6:**251
  ballroom competition standards,
    1:358
  contredanse origins, **2:**276
Ch'a Chu-hwan, **4:**53
chacona, **2:**98
Chaconne, **1:**263, **4:**197–198, *198*,
  274, 618, **5:**196
  Farrell performance, **2:**577
  Martins performance, **4:**274, 621
  Nichols performance, **4:**631
"Chaconne, A" (Isaac), **3:**522

chaconne and *passacaille*, **2:97–99,** **4:**510
  Feuillet notation, **2:***589*
  Gluck compositions, **2:**99, **3:**188, 190
  Lully compositions, **4:**235
  Rodolphe composition, **5:**371
Chaconne de Phaëton, **1:**397
Chacoon for Harlequin (Le Roussau), **5:**350
Chacun Fait le Métier d'Autruy, **1:**287
Chad, **6:**17
Chadman, Christopher, **6:**287, 288
Chaffee, George, **3:**23, **4:**28, 168
Chagall, Marc, **1:**136, 484, 486, **2:**242, 245, **3:**653, **4:**324, **5:***93,* 547, 605
  Firebird sets and costumes, **3:**3, **4:**269
chahut, **2:**52
Chahut, Le (Seurat), **5:**178
Chaib, Elie, **2:**526
Chailly, Luciano, **2:**369
chain and round dances, **2:99–102**
  Czech and Slovak, **2:**301, 302, 304, *305*
  European traditional, **2:**549–551
  Faeroe Islands, **2:**383, 565
  Faeroe step, **2:**565, **6:**427
  figures, **2:**592
  France, **3:**63–64, 65
  Hey, **3:**361
  Poland, **5:**212
  Turkey, **6:**211
  Yugoslavia, **6:**426, 427
  See also round dancing
chaîné turns, **1:**336, **337**
Chairman Dances, The, **4:**275
Chaises, Les, **1:**406
Chakiris, George, **5:**398
Chaki-Sircar, Manjusri, **2:102–103,** **3:**468
chakkar, **1:**171
Chalet, Le (Adam opera), **1:**9, 10
Chaliapin, Fedor, **1:**317, 487, **2:**150, **4:**56
Chalif, Louis, **6:**128, 269, 294
Chalif Text Book of Dancing, The (Chalif), **6:**128
Challet, Jacqueline, **4:**96
Chalon, Alfred, **2:**71, **103–104,** 239, **3:***609,* **5:**260, 261, **6:**74
Cham (pseud. of Amédée de Noé), **2:**71
cham (sacred Tibetan dance), **1:**458–459, **2:**221, **5:**599, **6:**167–168
chamamé, **1:**109
chamarrita, **1:**109, **5:**229
Chamber Ballet, Moscow, **1:**411, **5:**458
Chamber Ballet of the Hungarian State Opera, **3:**418
Chamber Dances, **4:**217
Chamberlain, Sonia, **2:**498
Chamber Music No. 1, **3:**418, **5:**569
Chambers, Barbara, **1:**232
Chambon, Philip, **2:**1, **5:**305
Chambre, La, **1:**241, 305
Chameleon Dance Company, **5:**174
Chameroy, Marie-Adrienne, **3:**105, **6:**333
Chamié, Tatiana, **1:**39, *296,* 300, **6:**398
Chamorro (people), **4:**401
Chamo System of Dance Notation (U Chang Sop), **4:**693
Champagne Charlie (film), **1:**438
Champêtres Plaisirs, Les, **5:**88
Champion, **4:**306

Champion, Arthur M., **3:**177
Champion, Gower, **2:**108, 619, **5:**358, **6:**277, 282–283, 287
Champion, Marge, **2:**619, **6:**205, 287
Championship Wrestling after Roland Barthes, **4:**471
chamrieng, **2:**31–32
Chan, Kai Tai, **1:**214–215
chance procedures (choreographic and compositional), **2:**22, 287, 288, **3:**446, **4:**519, **5:**548, **6:**26, 108
Chandalika, **2:**102, **3:**468, **6:**321
Chandidas (film), **2:**622
Chandrabhanu, Dr., **1:**216
Chandralekha, **2:104,** **3:**468
Chandralekha (film), **2:***621*
Chandrashekhar, C. V., **2:104–105**
Chandrashekhar, Chitra, **2:**105
Chandrashekhar, Jaya, **2:**105
Chandrashekhar, Manjari, **2:**105
Chanel, Coco, **1:**307, 323, 419
Chaney, Lon, **6:**102
Chaney, Stewart, **1:**96
Chang, Mabel Dai Chee, **1:**114
Changa, Evgeny, **1:**122, **4:**127, 132, **5:**470
Change of Address, **2:**296, **4:**37
Changing Pattern Steady Pulse, **2:**358
Changing Planes, **5:**521
Changing Steps (video), **2:**294, 608, **4:**37
Changing-woman, **2:**520
Chang mu Dance Company, **6:**414
Ch'ang Mu Hoe, **4:**52
Chang Sa-hun, **4:**54
Channell, Luke, **5:**251
Channels/Inserts (film dance), **2:**294, 607, **4:**37
Channel Z, **3:**446
Channing, Carol, **6:**281, 283
Chanova, Ruth, **4:**382
Chanson de l'Éternelle Tristesse, La, **6:**353
Chansons de Bilitis, Les, **2:**361, **3:**186, **4:**646
Chansons Madacasses (Duato work), **2:**448
Chansons Madécasses (Robbins work), **5:**366
Chant du Compagnon Errant, Le, **1:**292, 405–607
Chant du Rossignol, Le, **1:**93, 135, 322
  Markova debut, **4:**267, 331
  Massine choreography, **4:**317, **6:**3
  Matisse designs, **4:**331, **5:**544, **6:**3
  Sokolova performance, **5:**636
  Stravinsky score, **4:**516, **6:**3
Chant Funèbre, **5:**547
Čhantharaprahpā, Somphop, **4:**112
Chants de l'Amour et de la Mort, **5:**677
Chants de Maladoror, Les, **1:**461
Chao, Phebe Shih, *as contributor,* **6:**421
Chao Huey-ren, **6:***81*
Chao-Kang, **2:**60, 203, **3:**358
Chapell, William, **2:**400
Chaperon, Philippe, **6:**62
Chaplin, Charlie, **4:**522, **5:**317
Chapman, George, **4:**312
Chapman, John V., **2:**50, **3:**180
  as contributor, **2:**351–354, 363–365, 594–597, **3:**208–209, 257–261, **5:**108–109
Chapman, Sarah Alberti, *as contributor,* **2:**450–451, **4:**120–121

Chapman, Wes, **1:**77
Chappell, William, **2:105,** **3:**202, 263, 508, 511, 520, **5:**414, 560
  Patineurs, Les, **2:**105, **5:**113, 114
  Rambert, Marie, **5:**296, 298, 299
  reconstructions, **5:**560
  Rendezvous, Les, **5:**341
Chapple, Margaret, **1:**211
character dancing, **2:106–108**
  as balletic version of folk dance, **6:**295
  Belsky, Igor, **1:**416–417
  Bintley, David, **1:**453
  Bjørnsson, Fredbjørn, **1:**454
  Bolm, Adolph, **1:**482–484
  Cachucha, La, **2:**107, 203, 502
  Camryn's American Character Dance course, **6:**292
  Copland scores, **2:**108, 196, 197
  Coppélia, **2:**106, 108, 198, 200, 368
  costumes, **2:**239, 241, 244, 251, *251,* **393**
  Denishawn programs, **2:**378, *379*
  Edwards, Leslie, **2:**477–478
  Elssler performances, **2:**107, 502, 504, **3:**69
  escuela bolera, **2:**521–522
  Gogół, Jerzy, **3:**192
  Goleizovsky choreography, **3:**195
  gypsy portrayals, **3:**330
  Jota Aragonesa, **3:**21
  Karstens, Gerda, **3:**657
  Koren, Sergei, **4:**55
  Kshessinsky family, **4:**66, 67
  Larsen, Neils Bjørn, **4:**125–126, *125*
  Little Humpbacked Horse, The, **4:**211, **5:**501
  makeup, **4:***304*
  Maryinsky dancers, **4:**282
  mazurka, **4:**343
  Minkus scores, **4:**513–514
  Noblet, Lise, **4:**657
  Russian nineteenth-century ballet, **5:**453
  Shiriaev, Aleksandr, **2:**107, **4:**282
  Sokolova, Lydi, **5:**636
  as Soviet dramatic ballet element, **4:**284, **6:**442
  Staff productions, **5:**654
  Taglioni (Marie) *Gitana* performance, **3:**185
  Thamar, **3:**18–19
  Ukrainian ballet, **6:**225
  Woizikowski, Leon, **2:**106, **6:**404
Characteristic Dances (Tchaikovsky), **6:**114
charanga orchestra, **2:**275
Charbonneau, Pierre, **2:**603
Charbonnier, Pierre, **6:**118
Charchevnikova, Manya, **5:**124
Charda, **3:**195
Chardin, Jean-Baptiste-Siméon, **1:**126
Charisse, Cyd, **1:**194, *194,* **2:108–109,** 251, *251,* 616
Charisse, Nennette, **4:**120
Charisse, Nico, **2:**108, **5:**488
Charivari, Le (journal), **2:**69
Charleroi/Danses, **1:**411, 412, **2:109–110,** 120, 171, 471
Charles I, king of England, **1:**286, **3:**622, **4:**307, **5:**343
Charles II, king of England, **2:**570, **3:**253, 254, 522, **4:**315
Charles VI, emperor of Austria, **3:**383

Charles IX, king of France, **1:**1, **2:**338, 418
Charles X, king of France, **5:**371
Charles X Gustav, king of Sweden, **6:**38
Charles XI, king of Sweden, **6:**38
Charles XVI Gustav, king of Sweden, **6:**44
Charles, Jacques, **4:**524
Charles, Lynne, **2:**512
Charles d'Angolème, **3:**166
Charles the Bold, duke of Burgundy, **1:**364, **3:**322
Charleston, **1:**358, 450, *450,* **2:**25
  African-American origins, **2:**262, **6:**244, 255
  Broadway musicals, **6:**256, 273
  caricatures, **2:**70
  Egyptian *bambūtīyah* dance, **2:**489–490, *490,* **4:**411
  jazz basis, **4:**519
  as Lindy Hop antecedent, **4:**201, 254
  slide, **5:***629*
  social significance, **5:**629
  vaudeville, **6:**318
Charleston French Theatre, South Carolina, **3:**86, **5:**198, 199, **6:**232
Charles University Dance Company, Prague, **2:**308
Charles VI (Halévy), **4:**341
Charles Weidman Theatre Dance Company, **6:**377
Charlip, Remy, **2:**69, 72, **110–111,** **3:**391, **4:**218, **5:**260, 262
  Cunningham association, **2:**289, 290, **5:**548
  Suite for Five performance, **6:**26
  Summerspace performance, **6:**27
Charlot Revue of 1926, **2:**424, **6:**272–273
Charlotte (mixed *branle*), **1:**522
Charlotte, **1:**462
Charlotte Brontë, **3:**428
Charmers of the Age, The (Hogarth), **2:**70, 394
Charmoli, Tony, **6:**137
Charnley, Michael, **1:**411, **2:**509, 510, **3:**175, **5:**301
Charpentier, Gabriel, **6:**130
Charpentier, Gustave, **3:**50
Charpentier, Marc-Antoine, **1:**283, 364, 516
Charpentier, Olga, **4:**148
Charrat, Janine, **1:**110, 456, **2:111–112,** **3:**73, 74, **5:**98, 162, 526, 606, 676, **6:**348
  Abraxas production, **1:**1, *1,* 436, **2:**111, 478
  Adame Miroir, **1:**305, **2:**111, 112, **4:**418
  Ballets de France, **3:**74, **6:**130
  Ballets de Paris, **1:**305
  Ballets des Champs-Élysées, **1:**305, **2:**111, **3:**73
  Béjart association, **1:**290, 291, 403, 411
  Budapest Opera Ballet, **3:**416
  Duel, The, **2:**246
  Dyk association, **2:**471
  as Egorova student, **2:**480
  Enfant et les Sortilèges, L', **5:**316
  Geneva Ballet, **6:**52
  Grand Ballet du Marquis de Cuevas, **3:**225
  independent dance concerts, **3:**73
  Lifar association, **4:**184, 185
  Róna dance partnership, **5:**402
Charrière, Monsieur, **1:**205
Chartreuse de Parme, La, **1:**247

Chäs, **5:**682–683, **6:***52*
Chase, Alida, **1:**233, **4:**602
Chase, Alison, **5:**194
Chase, Barrie, **1:**195
Chase, Doris, **2:**606
Chase, Lucia, **2:112–113, 3:**571, **5:**193
   American Ballet Theatre, **1:**64, 65, 67, 75, **2:**374, **3:**26, **4:**241, **6:**34, 200
   Bluebeard performance, **3:**26
   Fall River Legend performance, **2:***374*
   Mordkin Ballet, **4:**460
   Pillar of Fire performance, **6:***199*
   Romeo and Juliet performance, **5:**397
   Swan Lake role, **6:**34
   Three Virgins and a Devil performance, **2:***373*
Chase, William Merritt, **1:***127*
"Chase around the Table," **5:**213
chassé, **1:**339, 345
Chasse-Croise, **2:**109
Chasseur Royal, Le, **5:**518
chastushka dance, **6:**303
Chatal, Yuri, **3:**437
Chat Botté, Le, **1:**122
Chateaubriand, René de, **3:**358
Chateauneuf, Maria, **2:**394
Châtel, Krisztina de, **4:**594, 597
Chatfield, Philip, **1:**429, **4:**624, 625
Chatillon Festival, **1:**461
"Chattanooga Choo Choo" (song), **4:***630*
Chatte, La, **5:**208, 526
   Balanchine stylistic identification, **1:**258–259, **4:**33
   black oilcloth costumes, **1:**325
   Gabo and Pevsner design, **5:**544–545
   Hynd production, **2:**512
   Lazzini re-creation, **4:**134
   Lifar performance, **4:**182
   Markova performance, **4:**267
   Sauguet score, **4:**517
   Spessivtseva performance, **5:**678
Chatte Blanche, La, **1:**9
Chatte Métamorphosée en Femme, La, **1:**459, **2:**105, 203, 503, **4:**340
Chatterjee, Meera Devi, **1:**94
Chatterly, Monsieur, **5:**69
Chaudes-Aigues, J., **3:**178–179
Chaudhary, Tara, **3:**199
Chaudhury, Salil, **2:**625
Chaufour, Serge, **1:**350
Chaumière Hongroise, La, **1:**86, **2:**415, **3:**560, **4:**277–278
Chausson, Ernest, **2:**280, **3:**597, **6:**196
Chautauqua movement, **6:**240
Chauteaubriand, **3:**7
Chauve-Souris (variety theater), **1:**85
Chauve-Souris, La, **3:**601, **5:**164
Chauviré, Yvette, **1:**300, **2:**111, **113–115,** 341, **4:**68, 354, **5:**606
   Atanasoff dance partnership, **1:**195, **2:**114
   Ballets des Champs-Élysées, **1:**306
   Béjart association, **1:**403
   Bruhn dance partnership, **2:**3, 114
   English National Ballet guest performances, **2:**508, 510
   Giselle role, **2:**351, 561, **3:***182*

Grand Ballet du Marquis de Cuevas, **3:**225
   Lifar association, **2:**113–114, **4:**184, 185
   Mirages role, **3:***73*, **4:**185
   PACT Ballet guest performance, **5:**652
   Paris Opera Ballet, **5:***92*, 95, 96, 97, **6:**352
   partners, **5:**53, 132, 313
   Pas de Quatre performance, **3:**59
   students, **2:**114
   Swan Lake performance, **3:**318
Chavalillos Sevillanos, Los. *See* Antonio and Rosario
Chavanne, G. M. de, **6:**124
Chávez, Carlos, **1:**524, **2:**349, **4:**518
chaya-chaya, **2:**121
Chayan, Rubén, **1:**111
Chazarreta, Andrés, **1:**110
Chazin-Bennahum, Judith, *as contributor,* **4:**172–176
Cheats, The, or *The Tavern Bilkers* (pantomime), **5:**350
Chebreau, Urban, **6:**38
Check, **1:**140
Checker, Chubby, **5:**632, **6:**249
Checkmate, **2:115,** 401
   Bliss score, **1:**462, **2:**115, **4:**517
   de Valois production, **2:**105, 115, *400,* **4:**515, **5:**414
   Grey (Beryl) performance, **2:**115, **3:**307
   Helpmann performance, **3:**357, **5:**414
   Lambert score arrangement, **4:**114
   Makarova performance, **4:**248
   Mason performance, **4:**307
   May performance, **4:**336, *336*
   televised production, **6:**134
   Turner performance, **6:**214
Checkpoint, **4:**243
Check to the King, **5:**24
Cheek to Cheek, **4:**627, *627*
cheerleading, **2:**322–324
Cheetham, Keith, **6:**135
cheganças, **1:**527
cheironomia, **2:115–116,** **3:**289, 291
Chekhov, Anton, **3:**565, **5:**419, 456, 588
Chekrygin, Aleksandr, **3:**187, 196, 665, **4:**148, **5:**282, 480, 610
Chellis, Pauline, **3:**404
Chelyabinsk State Institute of Art and Culture, **4:**165
Chemin, Le, **5:**681
Chemin de la Lumière, La, **1:**390, **2:**471, **3:**318, **4:**185, **5:**96
Chemins de la Creation, Les, **1:**461
Chenchikova, Olga, **4:**285
Chen Chuen-mey, **6:***81*
Chenevière, Jacques, **1:**98
Cheng Daihui, **6:**385
Cheng Guey-mei, **6:***81*
Cheng Ten-shiang, **6:***81*
Cheng Yanqiu, **1:**164
Chenier, Clifton, **2:**24
Chen Weiya, **2:116**
Chercheuse d'Esprit, La, **1:**43, **3:**117
Cherepin, Aleksandr, **5:**485
Chéret, Jules, **3:**92, **5:**261, **6:**62
Chéri, **2:**350, **5:**565
cherkessia, **3:**528
Cherneshova, Lidia, **6:**223
Chernetskaia, Inna, **5:**458, 477
Cherniavsky, Felix, **2:**50
Chernobrovkina, Tatiana, **5:**467
Chernoff, John, **1:**14, 15
Chernova, Alla, **5:**479

Chernova, Natalia Y., **5:**483, 484
   as contributor, **1:**518–519, **3:**127–128, 193–196, **5:**515–516
Chernyshev, Igor, **4:***282,* **5:**12, 460, 462, 472
Cherokee (people), **4:**551, 553, 554, 556, 558, 559
Cherrier, René, **5:**518, **6:**175
Cherubini, Luigi, **2:**202, **5:**558
Chervinsky, Nikolai, **5:**572
Cheselka, Anna, **2:**507
Cheshire Morris dance, **4:**474
Chesnakov, Vasily, **3:**192, **4:**283, **5:**594, **6:**227
Chesnakov, Vladimir, **6:**310
Chesnaye, sieur de la, **1:**275
Chess (Rice), **1:**420
Chess-Game, **5:**471
Chesterfield, Lord, **3:**281, **4:**263, 431
Chestnut Street Theatre, Philadelphia, **2:**467, **6:**159, 232–233
Chesworth, John, **2:**440, **4:***470,* **5:**301, 302, 303
Cheval d'Argile, **3:**79
Chevalier, Maurice, **1:**253, **4:**523, **5:**237
Chevalier Errant, Le, **2:**440, **4:**185
Chevalier et la Demoiselle, Le, **2:**113, **4:**184
Chevigny, Geneviève, **2:**413, **5:**90
Cheville, Lila R., *as contributor,* **5:**66–68
Cheyenne (people), **3:**170, 171
Chez Joséphine (New York City cabaret), **1:**253
Chez Joséphine (Paris cabaret), **1:**252
chhau, **2:117–119, 3:**453, *467,* 468, **4:**6, 299
Chiang Ching, **1:**33, **6:**415
Chiang Lee, **3:**355
chiaranzana, **2:**74, **3:**542
Chiarle, Angelo, **3:**556
Chiaroscuro, **4:**623, **5:**606
Chiaveri, Luigi, **5:**231
chica dance, **2:**62
Chicago (musical), **3:**54, 261, **5:**358, **6:**288, 327
Chicago Allied Arts, **1:**483, **5:**58
Chicago Brass, **1:**52, **5:**303
Chicago City Ballet, **2:**173, **4:**168, **5:**60, **6:**86, 265
Chicago Civic Opera Ballet, **1:**482–483, 518, **4:**63, 210
Chicago Daily Tribune (newspaper), **6:**299
Chicago Dance Archive, **4:**168
Chicago Dance Collection, **4:**169
Chicago Federal Dance Project, **2:**580, **4:**63, 120, **6:**245
Chicago Grand Opera Company, **6:**291
Chicago Lyric Opera Ballet, **1:**37, **2:**577, **5:**59, *398,* **6:**86
Chicago Opera Ballet, **5:**59, 60, **6:**86
Chichimeca (dance). *See concheros*
Chichimeca (people), **2:**194
Chichinadze, Aleksei, **1:**517, **3:**187, **4:**132, **5:**461, 467, 470
Chickasaw (people), **4:**558, 559
Chicken (dance), **4:**561, **5:**632, **6:**263
Chief, The, **1:**139
Chieftains, The, **3:**520
Chiesa, Antonio, **4:**688
Chiesa, Noberto, **3:***272,* **4:**217–218
Chigo no Shoshi, **3:**657

Chikamatsu Monzaemon, **2:**13, 14, **3:**637, 639, **4:**533
Chikamatsu-za, **4:**533
Chikazane Koma, **3:**171
Childe Harold, **4:**1
Childerhose, Diane, **4:**325, *540*
Childhood of Erik Menved, The, **1:**514
Child of the Air, The, **1:**460
Child of the Wreck (melodrama), **2:**85
Children of Men, **5:**684
Children's Album, **5:**9
Children's Ballet. *See* Viennese Kinderballett
children's dances
   Finland, **2:**629
   Japan, **2:**6
   Nigeria, **6:**14
   traveling step, **2:**101
   United States, **6:**239
Children's Folk Ballet of Seoul, **2:**572
children's literature, **2:**111
Children's Theater, Moscow, **3:**193
Childs, Lucinda, **1:**391, **2:119–120,** 462, **3:**274, **5:**24, 187, 305, 550
   Einstein on the Beach choreography, **1:***143,* 144, **6:**401
   film and video use, **2:**605, 608
   as French modern dance influence, **3:**78
   Judson Dance Theater, **3:**635, **6:**282
   Light Explosion choreography, **1:**436
   Waring's Dance Associates, **6:**363
Chile, **2:121–127**
   dance research and publication, **2:**127, **3:**35, **4:**171
   folk and traditional dance, **2:121–122,** 127, **3:**35, **5:**310
   theatrical dance, **2:122–126,** **4:**140, **6:**453
Chilean National Ballet. *See* Ballet Nacional Chileno
Chilkat dance blankets, **4:**572, *573*
Chilkovsky, Nadia, **2:**580, **4:**96, 604, **5:**661
Chime Bell Music and Dance, **2:**145
Chimène (opera), **2:**413
Chimera, **4:**230
Chin (people), **4:**524
China, **1:**164–166, **2:127–150**
   aesthetics, **1:16–17, 2:**148
   audiences, **1:**161, **2:**146
   background and overview, **1:**164–166, **2:127–138**
   cartoon personification as ballet dancer, **2:**70
   castanet counterpart, **2:**78
   classical dance, **2:144–145, 4:**350
   contemporary theatrical dance, **2:**136–138, **145–147**
   Australian ballet tour, **1:**232
   ballet education, **2:**133, 136, 137, 145, 149, **3:**328
   Boston Ballet tour, **1:**501
   Chen Weiya, **2:**116
   costume, **2:**220–221
   English National Ballet tour, **2:**513
   first avant-garde presentation, **3:**373
   Grey as first Western ballerina guest artist, **3:**307
   modern dance, **2:**145–146, 147, 149

China, *continued*
    Red Detachment of Women, The,
      5:330
    Sylvia staging, **6:**64
    White-Haired Girl, The, **6:**385
    Wu Xiabang, **6:**405–406
    costume, **2:**219–221
    court dance, **1:**129–130,
      2:131, 148
    dance in opera, **1:**164–165, 166,
      179–180, 187, **2:***131,* 132, *133,*
      141–144, 148, 219–220
    kunqu, **4:**76
    makeup and color symbolism,
      4:296
    Mei Lanfang, **1:**164, **2:**132–133,
      4:350, **6:**446
    mime, **4:**423
    Shaoxing Opera, **6:**425–426
    Ye Shaolan, **6:**421
    Zhou Xinfang, **6:**446–447
    dance notation, **2:**129, 148, **4:**693
    dance research and publication,
      2:147–150, **4:**158–159, **6:**406
    fan usage, **2:**570
    folk and minority dance, **1:**165,
      2:134–136, **138–141,** 148,
      149–150
    costume, **2:**220
    martial arts, **1:**185–186, *185,*
      187, 188
    puppetry, **1:**179–180, *179*
    sword dances, **1:**118, 164
    women's feet-binding custom,
      2:131
    See also Taiwan; Tibet
Chinafarerne (Schall), **5:**552
China National Arts Academy,
    2:148, 149
China National Dance Artists
    Association, **2:**148, 149, **6:**406
Chinese Academy of Traditional
    Theater, **6:**447
Chinese Dance Art Research
    Society, **6:**406
Chinese Encyclopedia Publishing
    House, **2:**149
Chinese Festival, The, **5:**537
Chinese Folk Artists Troupe, **2:**136
Chinese opera. *See* Beijing Opera;
    China, dance in opera
Chinese Performing Arts Company,
    2:*134,* 146
Chinese Poem, **3:**384
Chinese Theater Institute, **4:**159
Chinnammumma, Srimati, **3:**508
chinos (brotherhood), **1:**109, **2:**121
Chiriac, Mircea, **2:**343
Chiriaeff, Alexis, **2:**150, **3:**229
Chiriaeff, Ludmilla, **2:150–153,**
    5:61, **6:**106
    film dance, **2:**605, **3:***228*
    Grands Ballets Canadiens, Les,
      2:*38,* 39, 42, 47, 150–152,
      3:227–229, 230, 231, **6:**364
    Hyrst association, **3:**429
    Nault as co-artistic director,
      4:576
    Quebec dance school, **4:**577
    television series, **6:**130, *130,*
      131, *131*
Chirico, Giorgio de', **1:**133, *312,*
    316, 325, 327, 437, **2:**242,
    4:421, **5:**544, 545
chiropractor, **4:**20
Chirpaz, Jean-Luc, **1:**374
chisungu initiation ceremony, **2:**89
chitimacha (people), **4:**558
Chitlin Circuit, **6:**257

Chitra, **5:**472
Chitrangada, **3:**468
chivalry, **1:**368
chivo, **2:**431
Chizhova, Aleksandra E., *as*
    contributor, **4:**529–530
Chladek, Rosalia, **1:**204,
    2:153–154, 6:29, 52
    Basel Ballet, **1:**374
    free dance movement, **1:**239,
      240, 241
    Hellerau school, **3:**596
    students, **1:**211
Chladek technique, **2:**153, **154–155**
Chmiel, Manja, **2:**500
Cho Chi-hun, **3:**341
Choco (people), **5:**67
Chocolate Dandies, The (musical),
    1:252
Chocolate Soldier, The (musical),
    4:450
Choctaw (people), **4:**558, 559, *559*
Cho Dae-hyung, *as photographer,*
    3:372, **4:**52
Chodyna, Jaček, *as photographer,*
    5:212
chodzony, **5:**213
Choeur Dansé, **5:**587
Choice of a Bride, The, **3:**193
Ch'oi Seung-hee, **2:155–156,**
    4:12, 51
Choisy, abbé de, **1:**284
Chokwe (people), **2:**86, 89
Cholmondeleys, **3:**275, 276
Cholpon, **4:**87
Chomsky, Noam, **4:**367
Chong, Ping, **1:**143, **4:**451
chongjae, **1:**167, **4:**49
chong'joong'dong, **4:**49
Chong Pom-t'ae, **4:**54
Chopi (people), **5:**661, *662,*
    6:*21,* 664
Chopin, Frédéric, **1:**316, **2:**426,
    4:117, **5:**125, *125*
    Ashton's choreography, **4:**456
    Duncan dances, **2:**453
    Fokine ballet. *See Sylphides, Les*
    mazurka compositions, **4:**343
    polka compositions, **5:**221, 223
    Robbins's choreography, **2:**333,
      4:*364,* 614, **5:**358, *360, 362,*
      365, 366
    waltz compositions, **6:**360
    Wiesenthal's choreography, **6:**387
Chopin Concerto, **1:**297, **4:**633, 638,
    6:85
Chopiniana. See as subhead under
    Sylphides, Les
Chopinot, Régine, **3:**77, 79
Chopin Piano Concerto, **2:**273
Chopin Prelude, **4:**634
choral dancing, **2:**153, **156–159**
    Argentina, **1:**108
    costume, **2:**234
    dithyramb, **2:**419, **3:**291
    Etruscan, **2:**374
    Grecian, **3:**288–289, 290, **4:**499
    Greek reconstruction, **3:**300
    hyporchēma, **2:**158, **3:**428
    kallinkos, **3:**645–646
    schēma, **5:**557
    sikinnis, **5:**598
    See also movement choir
chorea major, **4:**348
choreare (meaning of term), **4:**348
Choreartium, **1:**310, *310,* **2:**342,
    3:72, **4:**322, 517, **6:**182
Chorearum molliorum collectanea
    (Phalèse), **3:**49
chorēgos, **3:**288, 289

Chorégraphie. See Feuillet, Raoul-
    Auger; Feuillet notation
Chorégraphie (Laban). *See*
    Choreographie
Chorégraphie: Studi e ricerche sulla
    danza (journal), **3:**555
"choreodrama," **5:**528
choreographers
    American Dance Festival
      residence program, **1:**80
    analyses of styles, **4:**99, 101
    ballet history, **3:**130–131
    computer use, **2:**296, 608
    copyright law, **3:**92, 370
    film use, **2:**603–612
    improvisation, **3:**446–447
    theatrical, **6:**277–279
    theatrical director combination,
      6:281–282, 284
    See also dancing master;
      notation; *specific companies,*
      choreographers, and works
Choreographer's Notes, A
    (Zakharov), **5:**480
Choreographer's Workshop, **1:**69,
    3:609
Choreographic Art of the 1920's
    (Souritz), **5:**643
Choreographic Centre, The, **1:**215
Choreographic Concert Ensemble
    "Young Ballet." *See* Moscow
    State Theater of Classical
    Ballet
Choreographic Institute Laban,
    4:103
Choreographic Miniatures, **4:**286,
    5:460, **6:**412
Choreographic Miniatures, Saint
    Petersburg, **5:**467, 469, **6:**412
Choreographic Offering, A, **4:**199
Choreographic Suite, **1:**38
Choreographic Theater, Berlin,
    3:156
Choreographie (Laban), **3:**161, **4:**92,
    99, 686
Choreographisches Institut, Berlin,
    4:92
Choreographische Vorstellung der
    englischen und französischen
    Figuren in Contretänzen
    (Lange), **2:**256
Choreography for the Camera (film
    dance), **2:**603–604, 605
Choreography Workshops (ABT II),
    1:75
Choreola (journal), **3:**555–556
choreology. *See* Laban Movement
    Analysis
Choreometrics Project, **2:**602, **4:**90,
    99, 104, 370–371, 374
Choreostruction, **4:**602
Choretones (television dance), **4:**39
Choreutics (Laban), **4:**94, 98,
    100, 103
Choreutics (Laban concept), **4:**99,
    101, 103, 140, **6:**162
chorines. *See* chorus girls
Chorley, Henry F., **3:**284
chōros, **1:**60, 448, 536, **2:**459, **4:**450
Choros (periodical), **3:**304
chorovod, **2:**301, 302
Chorus Equity, **5:**247
Chorus for Furies, **3:**384
Chorus for Maenads, **3:**384
Chorus for Supplicants, **3:**384
chorus girls, **2:**249–250, 613, **6:**267,
    267, 269, *272*
    tap dancing, **6:**99, 101
    Wayburn training system, **6:**371
    See also precision dancing

Chorus Line, A (musical),
    1:419–420, **4:**191, **6:**285, *285*
chorus lines. *See* chorus girls
Chorus of Masks, **1:**386–387
Chorus of Youth-Companions,
    3:384
chosun dance, **1:**167
Cho T'aek-won, **2:**159–160, **4:**51
Chota Roustaveli, **2:**114, **4:**185
Chouchous, Claudio, **2:**586
Chou dynasty. *See* Zhou dynasty
Chouinard, Marie, **2:**40, 46, **4:**628,
    6:132
Choura, Randy, *as photographer,*
    5:197
Chout, Le, **1:**93, **2:**409, **4:**124, 634,
    5:267, 269, 541, 542
Chouteau, Yvonne, **1:**302, **3:**362
Chowdhry, Nighat, **3:**425, **5:**63–64
Cho Won-kyung, **4:**54
choyong dance, **1:**167, **4:**12
Chrimes, Pamela, **5:**56, 650,
    651, 652
Chrissie Parrott Dance Company,
    1:216
Christa, Gabri, **2:**65
Christchurch, New Zealand, **4:**626
Christe, Nils, **4:**593, *595,* **5:**530,
    530, **6:**44
Christensen, Christian, **1:**507, 539,
    2:160, **3:**39, **5:**429
Christensen, Gyda, **4:**673, 674,
    682, 683
Christensen, Harold, **1:**279, *280,*
    2:160, 161–162, **5:**512,
    6:247, 264
Christensen, Lars Christian, **2:**160
Christensen, Lew, **1:**63, 452, *452,*
    2:160, 161–162, **5:**51, **6:**247
    Apollo, **1:**64, 96, *257*
    archival materials, **4:**170
    Ballet Caravan, **1:**279, 280, *280,*
      281, **4:**28, **6:**247
    Don Juan, **2:**434
    Filling Station, **1:**478, **2:**160, 314,
      4:227, **6:**247
    Four Temperaments performance,
      2:161, **3:**57
    Lady of Shalott, The, **1:**463
    New York City Ballet
      choreography, **4:**608
    Nutcracker version, **2:**162, **5:**15
    Pocahontas, **1:**279, 498, **3:**349,
      6:247
    San Francisco Ballet, **2:**161–162,
      5:512–513, *512,* **6:**264
    Swan Lake role, **2:**160, **6:**34
Christensen, Moses, **2:**160
Christensen, Willam, **2:160–161,**
    162, **4:**435, **6:**247
    archival materials, **4:**170
    Ballet West, **5:**162, **6:**264
    Coppélia production, **2:**200
    Nutcracker production, **2:**160,
      5:15, 16
    Romeo and Juliet choreography,
      5:398
    Salt Lake City Ballet, **6:**264
    San Francisco Ballet, **5:**511–512,
      512, 513
    Swan Lake choreography, **2:**160,
      6:34
    University of Utah faculty, **6:**292
Christensen brothers, **2:160–162,**
    6:247, 264
Christiakova, Valeria, **5:**484, 485
Christian IV, king of Denmark,
    2:384, **4:**673
Christian V, king of Denmark,
    2:384

Christian VII, king of Denmark, **5:**423–424

Christian VIII, king of Denmark, **1:**509

Christian, John, **3:**572

Christianity and dance, **2:162–169**
  Dances of Death, **2:**331–332
  early Christian views, **2:162–164,** 165, 540, 631, **3:**294–295, 541, **4:**428, 499
    opposition to *pantomimus,* **5:**74
    prohibitions against women onstage, **6:**188
  medieval views, **2:164–166,** 168, 540
    aesthetics, **1:**20–21
    labyrinth dances, **4:**106–107
  modern views, **2:166–169,** **4:**212–213
    marginalization of dance, **2:**541, **3:**227, 228
    nineteenth-century American evangelism, **6:**234–235
    syncretism, **1:**525–526, **2:**121–122, **4:**386, 387
  tripudium, **6:**194
  See also Bible, dance in the; liturgical dance; Protestantism; ritual and dance; Roman Catholicism; *other specific denominations and festivals*

Christian Science, **5:**491–492

Christian Science Monitor (newspaper), **2:**273, **6:**299

Christie, Keith, **6:**132

Christie, Niels, **2:**514

Christie, William, **5:**324

Christina, queen of Sweden, **6:**38

Christine of Lorraine, **2:**570, **3:**510, *510*

Christmas
  English Sword Dance, **6:**55
  Jonkonnu festival, **2:**62, 65, **3:**120–121, 121, 623
  liturgical dance, **2:**164
  mommerie (mummery), **4:**448, 449
  Nutcracker tradition, **2:**160, **4:**606, 678, **5:***11,* 12, 13, 15, **6:**44, *139*
  popular dancing, **2:**165, 168
  revels, **4:**343

Christmas Carol, A, **2:**57, **4:**668, **5:**57

Christmas Eve, **1:**144, **2:**15, **4:**226

Christmas Eve Dream, A, **1:**429, **5:**245

Christout, Marie-Françoise, **2:169–170,** **3:**84
  as contributor, **1:**95, 252–253, 287–289, 290–293, 403–407, 424–425, **2:**52–53, 365–366, **3:**65–67, 80–83, 84–85, 431, **4:**182–186, 229–430, 236, 447–448, 523–524, **5:**86–100

Christy's Minstrels, **6:**91

Chronica, **3:**629, *630*

Chronicle, **3:**212, **4:**659

chronophotography, **4:***14,* 15

Chroscript (Nikolai notation system), **4:**649

Chrysis, **3:**186, **5:**477

Chrysostom, John, **2:**163, 165

Chryst, Gary, **2:***124,* **3:**614, 615, *615*

Chuck and Chuckles, **3:**304

Chueco, El, **4:**392

Chujoy, Anatole, **1:**280, 281, **2:**39, **4:**355, **6:**266, 296

Chukchi (people), **5:**446, 448

chula, **5:**229

Chulalongkorn (Rama V), king of Siam, **4:**111, 112

Chulalongkorn University, Thailand, **6:**150

Chu Luhae, **2:***133*

Chuma, Yoshiko, **2:170–171**

chumba, **3:**121

ch'unaeng-mu, **4:**12

Chung, Hazel, *as contributor,* **1:**160–177

Chunsa Chum, **2:**572

Chun Ying Chuan, **6:***81*

Chuperchuk, Iaroslav, **6:**223

Church, Esmé, **4:**94

Church, George, **3:**23, **6:**278

Churchill, Caryl, **5:**440, 574, **6:**205

Churcko, U., **3:**44

Churko, Yulia M., *as contributor,* **1:**407–408, **2:**501–502

churra, **2:**533

Chūshingura, **3:**439, 607, 637, 658, **4:**334, 532, 533, 535, 536

Chutkan, Noelle, **3:**575

Chu Tsai-yü, **6:**81

Chynowski, Paweł, **5:**221
  as contributor, **2:**299, 447–448, **3:**316–317, **4:**232, 435, **5:**75, 220–221, **6:**175

Ciaccona, **1:**88

Cibber, Colley, **5:**69

Cicariticis, **5:**432

Ciceri, Pierre, **1:**36, **2:171–172,** 405, **3:**69, 177, 620, **5:**91, 92
  Giselle design, **5:**538
  Somnambule design, **5:**640
  Sylphide design, **2:**172, **5:**538, *539,* **6:**57

Cicero, **4:**426, 499, **5:**374–375, **6:**193

Cid, Le (Massenet), **1:**88, **4:**354, **5:**35, **6:**433

CID-Danza-INBA (Mexico), **4:**400

CID-UNESO, **6:**135

Ciechomski, Stanisław, **5:**220

Cie Irène K, **1:**412

cielito, **1:**108

Cieplinski, Jan, **2:**172, **3:**415, 416, **5:**218

Cimarosa, Domenico, **2:**409, **3:**175, **5:**231, 684

Cimarosiana, **1:**312, **4:**267

cimbalom, **6:**4

Cimber, Alphonse, **5:**256

Cincinnati Ballet, **3:**88, **5:**60

Cincinnati (Ohio) Court Dancers, **5:**327

Cincinnati Summer Opera Company, **4:**457

Cinderella (Cendrillon), **2:172–174**
  Adret production, **5:**53–54, *54, 651,* 653
  Albert staging, **1:**36, 452, **2:**173, **4:**657, *591*
  Aldous performance, **1:**38
  Ashton production, **1:**151, *151,* 153, **2:**173, *173,* 243, 574, **3:**307, *356,* **4:**248, **5:***54,* 55, 299, 415, *415,* 574, 589, **6:**44, 137
    stepsisters as travesty roles, **1:***150,* 233, **2:**174, 184, **3:**355, *356,* **6:**190
  Baryshnikov-Anastos staging, **1:**76, 373
  Beriozoff production, **1:**430
  Bias performance, **1:**446

Bigottini performance, **1:**452

Bintley performance, **1:**453

Blair performance, **1:**459

Cecchetti-Petipa-Ivanov production. *See subhead* Petipa-Cecchetti-Ivanov production division *below*

Chiriaeff productions, **2:**151

Clustine revival, **2:**181

Collier performance, **2:**186

Corder production, **2:**514

costumes, **2:**243, *243*

Darrell production, **2:**350

demi-caractère performance, **5:**299, 300

de Warren production, **4:**668

Dyk choreography, **2:**471

Evdokimova performance, **2:**561

Fokine production, **1:**313, **3:**25

Fonteyn performance, **3:**44

Fracci performance, **3:**59, **5:**529

Franca production, **3:**62, **4:**542, **6:**142, *142*

Gable production, **4:**668

Gogół production, **3:**192

Grant performance, **3:**237

Grey (Beryl) performance, **3:**307

Hart (Evelyn) performance, **3:**345

Helpmann *demi-caractère* role, **3:**355, *356*

Howard *demi-caractère* performance, **3:**392

Hullin-Sor staging, **1:**485

Ivanov production. *See subhead* Petipa-Cecchetti-Ivanov production division *below*

Jones (Alun) staging for Tulsa Ballet Theatre, **6:**204

Kolpakova performance, **4:**36

Kondratieva performance, **4:**38

Lavrovsky (Leonid) ice dance, **4:**132

Lavrovsky (Mikhail) performance, **4:**133

Legnani performance, **3:**565, **4:**145

Lepeshinskaya performance, **4:**149

Leventhal scenic design, **4:**153

Loloviev performance, **5:**639

Loquasto costumes, **4:**226–227

Maclès designs, **2:**243

Makarova performance, **4:**248

Meyer production, **4:**667

Mezincescu choreography, **5:**386

Noblet performance, **4:**657

Nureyev choreography, **2:**463

Page production, **5:**58

Panov production, **2:**561

Petipa-Cecchetti-Ivanov production division, **1:**338, **2:**82, **3:**564–565, 565, **5:**154

Placide production, **5:**199

popularity with Soviet provincial companies, **5:**463

Prokofiev conception, **2:**173–174

Prokofiev score, **1:**151, 153, **2:**173–174, **4:**517, **5:**268, 269, **6:**442

Riabouchinska performance, **5:**350

Rodriguez staging, **5:***54,* 529

Semenova performance, **5:**567

Sergeyev and Dudinskaya performance, **2:**449

Sergeyev choreography, **4:**284, **5:**572, **6:**639

Seymour debut performance, **5:**574

Shearer (Moira) performance, **5:**589

Spies staging, **3:**153

Staff *demi-caractère* role, **5:**651, 692

Stevenson production, **2:**124, 173, 174, 514, **3:**389, **4:**547

Stowell production, **6:**252

Strauss (Johann the younger) score, **1:**239, **2:**173, **6:**3

television productions, **6:**137, 142, *142*

Ulanova performance, **6:**226

Vasiliev version, **5:**474

Vinogradov production, **4:**153, 285, **6:**341, 342

Wilhelm staging, **6:**397

Williams (Petr) scenic design, **6:**399

Zakharov staging, **1:**491, **3:**99, **4:**335, **5:**459, 567, **6:**442

Cinderella (Asafiev children's opera), **4:**641

Cinderella (Rodgers and Hammerstein), **2:**619, **5:**72

Cinderella Story, A (Neumeier ballet), **4:**604

Cinder-Ellen Up to Date (burlesque), **4:**520

Ciné-Bijou, **1:**305, **5:**163

cinema. *See* film musicals

Cinéma, **2:**351, **5:**525

Ciné Qua Non, **6:**133

Cinesias, **2:**419

Cinq Soltanes, Les, **4:**696

Cinquantaine, La, **3:**117

Cinsielli's Circus, **2:**176

Cintolesi, Otavio, **2:**124, 127

Ciocca, Giovanna, **5:**615

CIOFF (International Council of Folk Festivals), **2:**546

Ciorgio Cini Foundation, Venice, **4:**162

Cippolino, **4:**38, 154, 182

Ciprés, Pablo, **1:**480

Ciranda de Paraty, **1:**529

Circassian dance, **3:**537

Circe, **3:***218,* 219, **5:**282, 407

Circé, ou Le Balet Comique de la Royne. See Balet Comique de la Royne, Le

Circle Dance, **2:**358

Circles, **1:**542

Circle the Earth, **3:**336

Circo, El, **1:**49

Circo Orrin, **4:***391*

Circul, Mila, **3:**76

Circulo de Iniciaçao Coreográfica, **5:**234

circumcision ritual
  Algeria, **1:**42
  Australian Aborigines, **1:**227, 228–229
  central Africa, **2:**88, 89
  central African women, **2:**211–212
  Egypt, **2:**492
  Shangana-Tsonga, **5:**579

Circumnavigation: Lisbonne-Vigo (film dance), **2:**611

circus, **2:174–177**
  Australian physical theater groups, **1:**217
  Balanchine-Stravinsky elephant ballet, **1:**257, **2:**176
  as visual artists' theme, **1:**131, 135, 136, 137

Circus, **1:**387, **5:**546

Circus Horseman, The, **1:**136

Circus Oz (Australia), **1:**217
Circus Polka (Stravinsky), **2:**176, **6:**6
Circus Scene, **3:**208
Cirebon, Central Java, **3:**501–502
Cirklen, **5:**430
Cirque, Le, **2:**57, **5:**226
Cirque de Deux, **1:**300, 301, 498
Cirque d'Hiver, **2:**176
Cirque Napoléon, **2:**176
Cirque Olympique, **2:**175, 176
Cirque Royal, Brussels, **1:**405
Cisne Negro, **1:**535, 536, *536*
Cisneros, Evelyn, **5:**398, *513*
Citron, Paula, *as contributor*, **4:**71–74, **6:**130–134
City, The, **6:**412
City Center Joffrey Ballet. *See* Joffrey Ballet
City Center of Music and Drama, New York City
 Alvin Ailey Dance Theater, **1:**56
 Ballet Russe de Monte Carlo, **1:**297, 298, 300
 Dance Theatre of Harlem, **2:**334
 Encores! concert productions, **6:**288
 Joffrey Ballet, **3:**611, 613, 617
 Kirstein, Lincoln, **4:**30
 Merce Cunningham Dance Theater, **2:**294
 New York City Ballet, **1:**262–263, 271, **4:**29, 606
CITYDANCE, **1:**502
City Dionysia (Athens), **3:**288–290
City of Angels (musical), **6:**287
City Portrait, **4:**28, 227
City Projects Council, **2:**580
City Symphony, A, **4:**59
City Theater, Stockholm, **2:**284
City Theatre, Charleston, **6:**159, 233
City Waits, A, **4:**59
Ciuleandra, The, **5:**385
Civil War, American (1861–1865), **6:**238
CIVIL warS: a tree is best measured when it is down, the (Wilson), **6:**401
Cladiwowa, Irina, **3:***149*
Claid, Emilyn, **2:**576, **3:**272
Clair, René, **1:**134, 328, **2:**603, **3:**72, 614, **5:**334, 335, 525, 545
Clair de Lune, **1:**75, 292
"Clair de Lune" (Debussy), **2:**361, 573
Cláirière, **2:**388
Clancy, Adrienne, *as contributor*, **4:**562–565
clappers, **3:**514, **4:**500
Clara, José, **3:**71
Clara, or Return to Virtue, **6:**311
Claremont College, California, **4:**688
Claretie, Jules, **2:**361
Clarey, Martine, **3:**82
Clarinet Concerto (Copland), **2:**197
Clari, ou La Promesse de Mariage, **1:**35, *35*, 446, **3:**180, **5:**91
 Bigottini performance, **1:***451*
 Kreutzer score, **4:**61
 Milon production, **4:**423
 Noblet performance, **4:**657
Clark, Barbara, **1:**475
Clark, Dick, **1:**77–79, **5:**632
Clark, Michael, **1:**52, 142, **2:**514, 607, **3:**274, **5:**304
Clark, Murray, **4:***217*
Clark, Peggy, **4:**191
Clark, Sibyl, **2:**592

Clark, Vèvè A., *as contributor*, **2:**458–460
Clarke, Hope, **1:***58*, **6:**259, 288
Clarke, Jeremiah, **5:**252
Clarke, Kenneth, **1:***450*
Clarke, Martha, **5:**194, 305
 ADF/Tokyo, **1:**80
 American Dance Festival, **1:**80
 Blaska association, **1:**462
 visual artworks as inspirations, **1:**141
Clarke, Mary, **1:**462, **3:**285, **4:**177
 as contributor, **1:**429–430, **2:**525–526, **3:**655–658, **5:**295–297, **6:**380–381
 on Fonteyn's *Cinderella* characterization, **2:**174
 Sadler's Wells Ballet, **3:**282, **5:**484
Clarke, Mrs. Michael, **1:**205
Clarke, Paul, **2:**512, **5:**421
Clarke, Phillippa, **1:**216
Clarke, Shirley, **2:**604, 606
Clarkson, Priscilla M., **2:**330
Clary, ou Le Retour à la Vertu Récompensé (d'Arnaud), **1:**35
class acts (tap dancing), **6:**100
Class Concert. See Ballet Class
classe de perfectionnement (class of perfection), **3:**81–82, **4:**143, 214, **5:**282
Classes in Classical Ballet (Messerer), **4:**360, **6:**129
Classical and Contemporary Ballet Ensemble, Constanza, **5:**387
Classical and Folk Dances of India (Anand ed.), **3:**470
Classical Ballet (Lawson), **2:**382
Classical Ballet Center (Greece), **3:**300
Classical Ballet of Moscow. *See* Moscow State Theater of Classical Ballet
Classical Ballet: The Flow of Movement (Karsavina), **2:**382, **5:**596–597, **6:**128
Classical Ballet, The: Basic Technique and Terminology (Stuart and Kirstein), **6:**128–129
Classical Dance (Tarasov), **5:**480
Classical Dance: Past and Present (Blok), **1:**463, 464
Classical Dance Ensemble of Kazakhstan, **3:**665
Classical Greek drama. *See* Greek drama; choral dancing
Classical Symphony, **1:**479, **2:**11, **3:**417, **4:**132
Classic Ballet, The (Stuart), **5:**208
Claudel, Paul, **1:**327, **3:**72, 596, **4:**417, **5:**439
Clauss, Heinz, **2:**268, **6:**10
Clavé, Antoni, **1:**306, **2:**244, **3:**74, **5:**60, 551
Clavier, Josette, **4:**107, **5:***91*
Clavijo, Antonio, **2:**476
Clay, Edward W., **5:**258
Clayden, Pauline, **3:***236, 355*
Clayton, Bessie, **6:**269, 318, 448
Clear Lake, Dark Woods, **2:**469
Clegg, Peter, **4:**667, **5:***165*
Cleisthenes, **2:**116
Clément, Jean-Marie, **6:**330, 331
Clementi, Muzio, **3:**15
Clementine, **3:**192
Cleopatra, **1:**37, **3:**186, **5:**409
Cleopatra's Nightmare (music hall act), **4:**522

Cléopâtre, **1:**317, 319, **2:**299, **3:**16, **5:**45, 122
 Bakst decor and costumes, **1:**254, 255, **2:**241, 407, **3:**15, 16, 18
 Fedorova performance, **2:**582
 Fokine performance, **3:***22*
 Fokine production in Sweden, **6:**41
 Karsavina performance, **3:**656
 Koslov pirated version of Fokine production, **4:**56
 Rubinstein performance, **5:**438
 as *Une Nuit d'Égypte* in Maryinsky repertory, **3:**15, 568
Clérambault, César, **1:**283
Clerc, Elsie, **4:**334
Clerc, Florence, **2:**114, **5:**97
Clerici, Fabrizio, **4:**421
Clerico, Francesco, **1:**237, **2:**177, **3:**546
Clerico, Gaetano, **2:**177
Clerico, Joseph and Louis, **1:**466
Clerico, Rosa, **2:**177
Cleveland, C. H., **2:**339
Cleveland Foundation, **2:**178
Cleveland–San Jose Ballet, **1:**73, 197, **2:**177–178, **3:**306
Clever Mokanu, The, **4:**444
Clifford, Henry, **4:**178
Clifford, Jack (vaudeville performer), **6:**318
Clifford, John (ballet dancer), **2:**333, **4:**24, 609, 611, *619*, **6:**66
Clinic of Stumble (film dance), **2:**604
Clinics in Sports Medicine (publication), **4:**17
Clinton, Bill, **1:**60, 545
Cliquet-Pleyel, Henri, **5:**526
Cloche de Hamana, La, **1:**304, **5:**517
Clochette, La, **3:**360
Clock Symphony, **1:**426, **3:**236
Clockwise, **4:**271
clogging, **2:**178–181, **6:**251
 Appalachian traditional, **2:**179, **180–181**, **3:**238, 608, **5:**696
 England, **3:**240, **4:**520, 522, **5:**694–695
 historical overview, **2:178–180**
 hornpipe variant, **2:**179, **3:**379
 jig variant, **2:**179, **3:**608
 South African gumboot dancing, **2:**86, **5:**648, *648*, **6:**22
 tap dance variant, **3:**633, **6:**96, 254
 vaudeville acts, **6:**316, 319
 Wales, **5:**695–696
Clorinda, **5:**120
Clorindy, or The Origin of the Cakewalk (musical), **2:**25, **6:**255
Close, Roy M., *as contributor*, **2:**21–23, **4:**515–520
clothing. *See* costume *headings*; practice clothes; tutu
Clouchard, Le, **2:**388
Cloud 9 (musical), **6:**205, 286
Cloud Cover, **4:**596
Cloud Dance, **4:**565
Cloud Gate Dance Theater, **6:**82, 83
Cloud Installation #72513 (Nakaya), **1:**544, *544*
Clouds (Aristophanes), **4:**44
Cloudsley, Anne, **4:**415
Clouser, James, **2:**4, 357, **3:**389
Cloven Kingdom, **2:**526, **3:**232, **4:**219, **6:**110, 111, 165

clowns, Native American ceremonial, **4:**554
Clowns, The, **3:**612, *614*, 615
Clowns and Other Fools, **3:***208*
club dance, **5:**635–636, *635*
Club des Amis du Septième Art, Le, **1:**466
Cluj Romanian Opera House, **5:**384–385
Clunies Ross, Margaret, *as contributor*, **1:**223–224
Clurman, Harold, **2:**196
Clustine, Ivan, **1:**246, 487, 540, **2:181–182**, **5:**14, *45*, 95, 455, **6:**443
 Adélaïde, **5:**315
 Assyrian Dance, **5:***122*
 Gavotte, **5:***120*, 125
 Pavlova association, **5:**124, 125, *126*
 Puppenfee, Die, **5:**279
 Sleeping Beauty abridged version, **5:**610
 students, **5:**636, **6:**119
Clytemnestra, **2:**182, **3:**217, *217*, **4:**659, **5:**407
Cmiral, Ilja, **2:**264
CNDC. *See* Centre National de Danse Contemporaine
Coach with the Six Insides, The, **2:***519*, 520
coals, dancing on live, **1:**84, **2:**487, **3:**298
Coast, John, **3:**645, **4:**264, 265
Coast of Happiness, The, **1:**517, **2:**15–16, **6:**310
Coast of Hope, The, **1:**416, **4:**36, 37, 284
 choreographic significance, **5:**460
Coast Zone (film dance), **2:**294, 607, *608*
Coates, Albert, **3:**521
Coba Andrade, Carlos Alberto, *as contributor*, **2:**475–477
Coblet, Anton, **3:**364
Cobos, Antonia, **1:**300, 301, 302
Cobras, **3:***153*, **5:**46, 492
Coca, Imogene, **4:**434
Cocambo, **1:**455, **5:**317
Cocceji, Charles-Louis de, **1:**365
Cochois, Marianne, **1:**365
Cochran, Charles B., **1:**115, 271, 395, 426, 520, **2:**105, 572, **4:**229, 334, 357–358, **5:**294, **6:**277, 278
Cochran, Mary, **4:**482, **5:**679
Cochran's Revues, **4:**33, 183, 320, 358, **6:**277
Cocia, Aurelio, **1:**192
Cock, Jean de, **2:**109, **4:**136
Cockrill, Andrew, *as photographer*, **5:**305, **6:**34
coco, **1:**525
Coco (musical), **1:**419
coco de roda, **1:**527
cocoyé, **2:**275
Cocteau, Jean, **1:**301, 535, **2:**67, **182–183**, 244, **3:**427, 656, **5:**237, 525, 527, **6:**4
 Ballets des Champs-Élysées, **3:**73, **4:**33
 Ballets Suédois, **1:**327, **3:**72
 Boeuf sur le Toit, Le, **1:**86, 327, **2:**182, **4:**418
 caricatures of dancers, **2:**70, 71
 Diaghilev collaborations, **1:**323, 325, **2:**183, 409, **3:**18, **4:**317, 515
 Hugo (Jean) designs, **3:**393, 394
 Imre ballet memorializing, **6:**66

Jeune Homme et la Mort libretto, **2**:183, **3**:601, **5**:163
on Lifar's *Joan de Zarissa*, **4**:184
Parade, **2**:409, **4**:516, **5**:85
on *Parade* costumes, **5**:543
Phèdre design, **4**:185, **5**:95, **6**:183
Picasso association, **5**:191
prints and drawings by, **5**:262
on *Sacre du Printemps* premiere riot, **4**:644
as subject of Murphy ballet *Poppy*, **4**:479, **6**:56
Cocteau—Opium, **3**:61
Cocuzza, Ginnine, *as contributor*, **2**:516–517
Codanza, **2**:281
Code of Terpsichore, The (Blasis), **1**:8, 328, 460, **2**:107, 339, 400, **6**:126
Codex (film), **2**:610
Codreanu, Lizica, **1**:244
Cody, William (Buffalo Bill), **4**:464
Coe, Kelvin, **1**:210, 211, *232*, 233, **2**:183–184, **5**:410
Coe, Robert, **3**:201
Coeur à Barbe, Le, **1**:244
Coeur de la Marquise, Le, **1**:254
Cofini, Marcello, **3**:556
cofradías (brotherhoods), **2**:195, **4**:388
Coggan, Forrest, **4**:212
Çoğul, **6**:212
Cohan, George M., **6**:269, *269*, 272, *315*, **7**:273
Cohan, Robert, **1**:394, **3**:*272*, 274, 275, 280, **5**:562, *564*, **6**:134
Batsheva Dance Company, **3**:532
London Contemporary Dance Theatre, **4**:216, 217–218, *217*, 219, 220, 221
Martha Graham Dance Company, **3**:218, **5**:407
students, **6**:121
Cohan Revue of 1916, The, **6**:272
Cohen, Bonnie Bainbridge, **3**:54, **4**:17, 20
Cohen, Fritz (Frederick), **3**:40, 305, 625, 626, 627, 628, 629, **5**:265
Cohen, Gabriella, **2**:480
Cohen, Harvey, **1**:57
Cohen, Leonard, **6**:133
Cohen, Nathan, **2**:49
Cohen, Selma Jeanne, **1**:24, **4**:104, **6**:127, 300
as contributor, **1**:541, **2**:169–170, **3**:130–131, **4**:272–273, 478–479, **5**:43–44, 264–266, 642–643, **6**:296–298
Dance Perspectives, **6**:297
Cohen, Sol, **5**:497
Cohen, Viki, **3**:531
Cohen, Yardena, **3**:529, 530
Cohen, Ze'eva, **1**:501, **2**:576, **3**:532, **6**:363
Coisas do Brasil, **1**:536
Coker, Norman, **5**:256
colam, **1**:171
Colasse, Pascal, **1**:425, **2**:465, **4**:235
Colberg, Ana Sánchez, **5**:275
Colbert, Claudette, **5**:175
Colby, Gertrude, **6**:242, 295
Cold War era. *See* Soviet era
Cole, Bob, **6**:21
Cole, Herbert M., **2**:212
Cole, Jack, **2**:184–185, 251, **5**:497, **6**:327
as Ailey influence, **1**:55
Hollywood musicals, **2**:615, 616, *617*, **4**:3, 4

jazz dance, **3**:598, 599, 600, **6**:281
Kismet, **6**:281
Man of La Mancha, **6**:283
Cole, Michael, **2**:294, **5**:17
Coleman, Cy, **1**:419, **6**:283
Coleman, Grisha, **6**:*449*
Coleman, Michael, **5**:531
Coleman, Ross, **1**:214
Coleone, Bartolommeo, **2**:204
Coles, Honi, **1**:252, **2**:185–186, **3**:304, 447, **5**:632, **6**:100, 102
Coles, Jeremy, **5**:55, *55*, 56, *154*
Coles, Marion, **2**:186, **6**:102
Coles and Atkins, **2**:185, 186, **5**:632
Colet, John, **3**:281
Colet Gardens, London, **4**:143
Colette, **1**:252, **3**:512, **4**:523, **5**:238
Colimbinade, **3**:630
Colin, Paul, **5**:262
Colinette, Marie Rose, **2**:414, 415
Colinette à la Coeur, **6**:360
Colker, Deborah, **1**:*536*
Coll, Adriana, **6**:301
Collaborative Event, A, **3**:*634*
collage, **1**:142
Collage, **2**:288
Collage Dansekompani, **4**:679
Collan, Anni, **2**:631
Collatet, Guillaume, **3**:66
Colleano, Con, **2**:175
Collection of Ayres, Compos'd for the Theatre, and upon Other Occasions (Purcell anthology), **5**:282
Collection of Ball-dances Perform'd at Court, A (Weaver and Isaac), **3**:522, **6**:373
Collection of Chinese National Folk Dances (Wu), **6**:406
collections. *See* annual collections
Collective Symphony, **2**:347–348, **4**:*596*, **5**:555
Collector's History of Fans, A (Armstrong), **2**:570
Colleen (film), **6**:*100*
Collège de Clermont. *See* Collège de Louis-le-Grand
Collège de Coqueret, **1**:2
Collège de Louis-le-Grand, **1**:282–283, 284, 286, 396, 464, **2**:34, 465, **5**:128
"College Hornpipe," **3**:376, *377*, 378
Collegiate (dance), **4**:201, 254
Collegio Romano, **3**:544
Collegium Fratrum Arvalium (Arval Brothers), **3**:541
Collenette, Beatrice, **6**:151
Collet, Antoine-François-Auguste, comte de Saint-James, **1**:199
Collet, Henri, **5**:525
Colletet, Guillaume, **1**:285
Collett, John, **2**:70
Collier, Cliff, **2**:49
Collier, John, Jr., **2**:601
Collier, Lesley, **1**:158, *159*, **2**:186, **4**:257, **5**:419
Collin, Darja, **4**:590, 591
Collingwood, Robin George, **1**:24
Collins, Arthur, **5**:72
Collins, Darja, **6**:29
Collins, Dorothy, **1**:419
Collins, Eugene, **1**:302
Collins, Harold, **1**:211
Collins, Janet, **2**:186–188, 269, 458, **4**:382
Collins, Jeremy, **1**:77
Collins, Leon, **6**:102
Collins, Lottie, **4**:520, **5**:72

Collum, Jan, **6**:264
Colman, George, **1**:122
Colman, John, **3**:629
Colmbiad, **3**:384
Colochea, Marcela, **2**:125
Colognato, Lucia, **5**:401
Cologne Dance Forum, **3**:151, 157, **6**:228–229
Cologne, Germany, **3**:161
Cologne State Opera Ballet, **1**:479, **3**:149, 151, **5**:681, **6**:228, 404
Colohan, Nancy, **4**:73
Colomba, Innocenzo, **4**:346, **5**:270
Colombe, La, **5**:237
Colombo, Regina, **3**:51
Colomé, Delfi, **5**:676
Colon, Nancy, **1**:*372*
Colon Theater. *See* Teatro Colón, Buenos Aires
color
  Chinese costume and makeup, **2**:219, 220, **4**:296
  Imperial Russian Ballet School practice dress rankings, **5**:241
  Indian *kathakali* costume, **2**:224
  Japanese costume, **2**:214
  lighting, **4**:193
  set design, **4**:193, **5**:541, 543
Colorado Ballet, **4**:478, 577, **6**:266, 292
Colorado College, **3**:371, **6**:295
Colorful Sculpture of Dunhuang, **2**:145
Color Harmony, **3**:398–399
Colour Moves, **5**:303
Colour Symphony, A (Bliss), **1**:463
Colt, Alvin, **2**:245, **5**:360
Colton, Richard, **6**:152, *152*, 363
Columbia Broadcasting System (CBS), **6**:137, 138, 139
Columbia Pictures, **2**:185, 616, **3**:598
Columbia University
  Choreometrics project, **2**:602
  International Council for Traditional Music, **4**:370
  Oral History Research Office, **4**:167
  Teachers College, **3**:385, **4**:16, **6**:242, 295
Columbine. *See* pantomime
Columbine Invisible, **5**:198
Columbus, **3**:389
Columbus, Christopher, **2**:62, 429, **3**:418
Column, The (dance group), **5**:263
Comanche (people), **3**:171, **4**:554
Combat, Le (The Duel), 3532, **1**:110, **2**:426, **4**:435
Combat à la Barrière, Le (Callot), **2**:26, 27
combat dances. *See* armed dances; Asian martial arts
Combat de Tancredi, **4**:107
Combat of Forms, **6**:66
Combat Review/Witches' Response, **6**:259
Combattimento di Tancredi e Clorinda, Il, **3**:544
Combes, Paul, **5**:526
Comden, Betty, **1**:438, **2**:616, **5**:360
Come and Get the Beauty of It Hot, **1**:395
"Come Ashore, Jolly Tar" (tune), **3**:249
Come Dance with Me (de Valois), **2**:395, 403

Comedia Balletica (formerly *Musical Chairs*), **1**:298–299, 478–479
Comedians, The, **1**:498, **3**:187
comédie-ballet, **1**:342, **6**:267
  Lully compositions, **4**:234
  Molière, **1**:288, **3**:66, **4**:234, 447, **6**:267
Comédie Française, **1**:43, 406, **2**:369
  Ciceri scenic design, **2**:171
  dancer roster (seventeenth- and eighteenth-century), **3**:66
  Deshayes (Jacques-François) as ballet master, **2**:389
  Guimard, Marie-Madeleine, **3**:66, 326
Comédie Italienne, **2**:365, 366, **3**:66, 67
comedy (Greek drama), **2**:158, **4**:44, 301
comedy (Roman Atellan farce), **5**:376
comedy tap dancing, **6**:99–100
Comee, Stephen
  as contributor, **3**:388, 646–647, 650, 653, **4**:30–31, 39–40, 41–42, 42, **5**:48–49, **6**:229–230
  as first non-Japanese professionally trained *nō* actor, **6**:229
Comelin, Jean-Paul, **3**:74, **5**:51
Come Out, **4**:596
Comerio, Luca, **4**:258
Come Summer (musical), **1**:482, **2**:373
Come Sunday, **2**:367
Comforts of Bath, The (Rowlandson), **1**:*189*
Comfort Zone, The, **4**:73, **5**:*513*
comic art. *See* caricature and comic art
Comic Opera, Berlin. *See* Berlin Dance Theater
Comic Tunes (Walsh), **3**:256
Coming Back from the Depths, **2**:343
Coming Together, **2**:449
Comin' Uptown (musical), **3**:366
comique, defined, **2**:106, 107
Commandant d'Oleq, Le, **4**:149
commedia dell'arte, **1**:188–193
  Baxter, Richard, **1**:391
  Beaumont study, **3**:282
  bergamasque as Baroque form, **1**:428
  Callot prints, **2**:27, *189*, 190
  chaconne, **2**:98, 99
  de Hesse productions, **2**:365–366
  Denmark, **2**:384, 385, **5**:423
  England, **3**:254, *256*
  as *Fille Mal Gardée* ancestor, **2**:594
  as Fokine *Carnaval* basis, **3**:23
  improvisation, **3**:444
  Italian style, **3**:544–545
  as masque influence, **4**:312
  masquerade, **4**:*314*, 315
  as Massine influence, **4**:317, 319, 418
  Mazurier, Charles-François, **5**:318
  mime, **4**:423, 425
  as Nureyev *Don Quixote* basis, **2**:440
  Soviet, **3**:48
Commedia dell'Arte. See Farces
Commentaries on Nature, **1**:524
"Commodore Perry's March," **6**:234
Commonplace Quintet, **4**:596

Commonwealth Arts Festival, London, **1:**230, 231
Commotion Dance Company, **4:**627
Commune Warrior, **3:**590
communism. *See* socialst realism; Soviet era
community dance, **3:**32, 280, **4:**94, 151–152
movement choirs, **4:**476–477
Como, Anna, **5:**423
Como, Antonio, **5:**423
Como, Perry, **2:**619
Como, William, **4:**168
Comoedia, **1:**462
Comoro Islands, **6:**187
Compaan, Evert, **4:**590
Compagnia del Balletto Italiano da Camera, **3:**51
Compagnie Azanie, **3:**79
Compagnie de l'Ésquisse, **3:**79
Compagnie Jerome Andrews, Le, **3:**76
Compagnons de la Danse, Les, **3:**76, 230
Compan, Charles, **1:**123, 383, **2:**336, **5:**39, 105, 285, 507, **6:**126
on *entrée,* **2:**517
on *rigaudon,* **5:**352
Russian translation, **5:**486
technical manual, **6:**126
Companhia de Dança de Lisboa, **5:**235
Companhia Nacional de Bailado. *See* National Ballet of Portugal
Compañía Nacional de Danza, Madrid, **2:**448, 449, **5:**674, *674,* 676
Compania Teatrale de Torino, **1:**446
Company (musical), **1:**419, **6:**285
Company at the Manor, **1:**402, **3:**629
Company B, **6:**110, 111, 112, 113, *113, 140*
Company Dance Theatre, **3:**575–576
Company of the General Disasters, **3:**421
Company Sarbo, **3:**421
comparsas groups, **2:**275
Compasso, Lutio, **2:**74, 75, 337, **3:**107, **5:**339, **6:**112
Compendio de las principales reglas del baile (Cairón), **5:**676
Competing with the Sylph: Dancers and the Pursuit of the Ideal Body Form (Vincent), **2:**330
competitions. *See* ballet competitions; ballroom dance competition; cheerleading; dance marathons; ice dancing
Complaint about the Destruction of the Town of Ur, **4:**77
Complete Book of Ballets (Beaumont), **1:**398, **3:**284, **4:**177
Completely Birdland, **3:**274, **5:**305, *305*
Complete System of English Country Dancing, The (Wilson), **2:**257
Complete Writings of Nomura Manzō, The, **4:**661
Composition for Group, **6:**88
Compositions in Dance Form, **2:**516
Compot et manuel kalendrier (Breton; Arbeau pseud.), **1:**104
Compton, Gardner, **2:**606
Compton, R. M., **5:**649

computer applications
choreography, **2:**296, 608
dance websites, **2:**612, **6:**300
Labanotation software, **4:**158
lighting effects, **4:**190–191
movement research, **4:**17
research resources, **4:**158, 167
Comstock, Ray, **6:**271
Comtesse d'Escarbagnas, La, **4:**447
Comus, **3:**355, **4:**114, 358
Con Amore, **2:**161–162, **6:**204
"Conception of the Sphere in Movement, The" (Laban), **4:**100
Concerning Oracles, **6:**201
Concert, The, **1:**233, 478, **2:**333, **3:**391
Kent performance, **4:**617
Le Clercq performance, **4:**137
"Mistake Waltz," **4:**358
Moncion performance, **4:**450
Robbins choreography, **4:**608, **5:**358, *360,* 365
in Royal Ballet repertory, **5:**417
Concertante Musik, **1:**456
Concert Dance Company of Boston, **2:**359
Concert Dancers' League, **6:**89
Concert Dances, **5:**25
Concert de Danse, **1:**305
Concert Ensemble "Classical Ballet" of the USSR. *See* Moscow State Theater of Classical Ballet
Concert for Piano and Orchestra (Cage), **2:**23
Concerti, **4:**179
concertina, **4:**485
Concertino, **4:**107, **5:**24
Concerto, **1:**69, **2:**277, 426, 473
Charrat performance, **2:**111, 112
Kaye performance, **3:**664
Kriza performance, **4:**63
MacMillan production, **4:**242, **6:**380
Ross (Herbert) choreography, **5:**408
Tchelitchev design, **5:**547
See also Constantia
Concerto aux Étoiles, **2:**114, 334
Concerto Barocco, **1:**281, **2:**193–194, 376, **3:**226, **4:**71, *608,* 618, **5:**97
Balanchine revival, **4:**609
in Balanchine's aesthetic progression, **1:**256, 261, 262, 263, 267, 270, 272, **4:**613
Ballet Caravan, **4:**28
Ballet Russe de Monte Carlo, **1:**298
Berman design, **1:**298, 437, **5:**547
in Grands Ballets Canadiens repertory, **3:**231
practice clothes as costume, **2:**193, 245
in Royal Danish Ballet repertory, **5:**431
in Washington Ballet repertory, **6:**366
Concerto Burlesco, **3:**174
Concerto de Grieg, **3:**74
Concerto dell'Albatro, **5:**196, 527
Concert of Dance (1962), **3:**633–634
Concerto for Charlie, **5:**57
Concerto for Flute and Harp, **2:**267
Concerto for Piano, Accordian and Orchestra, **6:**67
Concerto for Two Solo Pianos, **4:**274, 615, 619

Concerto Grosso (Limón dance), **4:**198
Concerto Grosso (Schnitke), **1:**38
Concerto Grosso en Ballet, **4:**179
Concerto in F (Gershwin), **1:**59, 479
Concerto in F Dur (Vivaldi), **1:**38
Concerto in G (Robbins ballet), **5:**366
Concerto in White, **2:**423
Concerto Six Twenty-Two, **3:**233
Concerto the Rainbow, **2:**473
Concert Royal, **6:**250
concerts, public, **5:**625
Concert Varieties, **6:**279
Concha, Gaby, **2:**125
Concha y Petro Cortes, La, **3:**11
concheros, **2:**194–195, **4:**386
Concierto de Mozart, **1:**110, **6:**119
Concierto Madrigal, **2:**448
Concise & Easy Method of Learning the Figuring Part of Country Dances, A, **2:**255–256
Concordia University, Quebec, **2:**48
Concours, Le, **1:**211
Concurrence, La, **1:**309, **2:**479, **3:**72, 653, **6:**182
Condé, Jean, **6:***189*
Condé, Sekou-Ouien, **5:**516
Conder, Charles, **2:**574
Condes Ballet, Las, **2:**125
Condeza, Luz, **2:**126
condición, **1:**108
condong, **1:**174, **3:***181,* 182, 191, **4:**146
Condos, Steve, **3:**367, **6:**102
Cone, Grace, **2:**507, 578
Coney, Miranda, **1:**211, 235
Conference on Preservation and Dissemination of American Dance (1980), **5:**48
Confesse, Mister, **2:**337, **3:**252, **4:**307, 310
Confessional, **3:**174, 202–203, **5:**300
Confidencen (formerly Ulrisdal Court Theater), **6:**48
Configurations, **1:**75
Confrairie de Maîtres de Danses & Joueurs d'Instrumens, **2:**338
confraternities, Chile, **2:**12
Confrères de la Passion, **3:**65
Confucianism
aesthetics, **1:**16–17, 183
Chinese music and dance, **2:**128–129, 132, 148
Korean dance, **4:**45, 48, 494
ritual music, **1:**164, 167, **2:**132, **3:**102
Taiwanese dance, **4:**494
tōgaku and *komagaku* dances, **2:**6
yayue ritual dance, **1:**164, **3:**102, **6:**79, 80–82
conga, **2:**275, **4:**520
Congadas. See Congo dances
Congaroo Dancers, **4:**255
Congdon, Mary Redwing, **4:**555
Congo (formerly Zaïre), **2:**86, 87, *88,* 89, 90, 91, **6:**24
African-Brazilian dance influences, **1:**525, 527
costume, **2:**211
masks, **2:**91
sounds accompanying dance, **4:**484
"Congo Beat" style, **6:**24
Congo dances, **1:**526, 527, **2:**195–196, 275, **3:**335, **4:**486

circle dance, **6:***18*
makeup, **4:***290*
congos, **5:**67
Congo Square, New Orleans, **6:**261
"Congo Tango Palace" *(Come and Get the Beauty of It Hot),* **1:**395
congregational dance, **4:**213
Congregationalism, **2:**167
Congress on Research in Dance (CORD), **4:**370, 575, **5:**44, **6:**297
Congreve, William, **6:**373
Coniglio, Mark, **2:**612
Coninx, Stijn, **5:**423
Conjugación, **2:**278
Conklin, John, **6:**35
Conmee, Ivy, **5:**52, 649, 650
Conn, Robert, **4:***72*
Connecticut College, New London. *See* American Dance Festival
Connections, **6:**433
Connors, Thomas, *as contributor,* **1:**441, **2:**112–113, **3:**424–425
Conolly, Karen, **2:**125
Conquest, **2:**285, **3:**387
Conquest, George, **5:**71
Conquest of Granada, The (Dryden), **3:**252
Conquista, La (dance drama), **3:**319
Conquista di Malacca, La, ossia I Portoghesi nell'Indie, **6:**70
Conrad, Karen, **1:**65, **3:**597, **4:**209
Conradi, August, **5:**499
Conran, Jasper, **1:**454
Consagración de la Primavera, **1:**102, 103
Conscience, **4:**584
Consecration, **1:**484
Conservatoire de Danse de l'Opéra, Paris, **3:**81
Conservatoire de Danse Marius Petipa, Paris, **3:**82
Conservatoire de La Rochelle, France, **3:**83
Conservatoire de Musique d'Alexandrie, Egypt, **2:**498
Conservatoire de Musique de Genève, **3:**594
Conservatoire National de Musique, Paris, **3:**82, **5:**371, 563
Conservatoriet. See Konservatoriet
Conservatorio Nacional de Música y Arte Escénico, Buenos Aires, **1:**109
Conservatory of Dancing, Brussels, **1:**410
Consoer, Dianne, **3:***609,* 610, *611*
Consort, The, **2:**584, **6:**43
Consort Lessons, **3:**233
Constable, William, **1:**499
Constance and Almazor, **2:**364
Constance et Alcidonis, **3:**258
Constant, Marius, **1:**305, 462, **5:**163
Constantia, **1:**110, **2:**426, **3:**224, **6:**396
Constantin Brăiloiu. *See* Ethnography and Folklore Institute, Bucharest
Constantine, Roman emperor, **2:**163, **3:**541
Constantine, Hélène, **1:**305, 315
Constantine, Manos, *as photographer,* **2:**341, 551, **5:**46
Constantine, Saint, **1:**84
Constantinescu, Paul, **2:**343, **5:**385
Constantinople, or The Revels of the East (musical spectacle), **4:**24
Constanza's Lament, **3:**61

Constellation Dance, **2:**138
Constrastes, Les, **2:**153
Construction 231, **3:**590
constructivism, **1:**133, 244, **2:**242, **5:**544–545, *545,* 547
  Balanchine choreography, **1:**258–259, 260, 262
  Erdman scenic design, **3:**194, *194,* 632, *632*
  Fujime choreography, **3:**590
  Stravinsky's *Le Sacre du Printemps,* **6:**4
Consuelo, Beatriz, **1:**533
Consul, The (Menotti), **2:**16
Contact, **4:**651
contact improvisation, **3:**446–447, *447,* **5:**127–128
Contact Quarterly (publication), **3:**447
Conté, Pierre, **4:***687,* 688
Conte di Montecristo, Il, **2:**282, **5:**409
Contempodanza, **4:**397
Contemporary Ballet of the San Martín Theater. *See* San Martín Ballet
Contemporary Ballet Theater of France. *See* Ballet-Théâtre Contemporain
Contemporary Belgrade Ballet, **6:**435
Contemporary Dance Association of Japan, **3:**591
Contemporary Dance Company of Australia, **1:**212
Contemporary Dancers of Winnipeg, **2:**42, 43, 48
Contemporary Dance Trust, **3:**275
Contemporary Suite, **3:**420, **6:**301–302
Contesa dell'Aria e dell'Acqua, La, **3:**381
Contes de Ma Mère l'Oye, **5:**690
Contes Russes, **1:**322, **4:**124, 304, 635
Contessa di Egmont, La, **2:**282, **5:**409
contextual pattern of dance, **4:**363
Conti, Marietta, **3:**176
Conti, Natale, **1:**275
"Continental, The," **5:***630*
Continental Ballet, **4:**110
Continuo, **6:**202
Continuous Process Altered Daily (Morris), **1:**140
Continuous Project—Altered Daily (Rainer choreography), **1:**140, **3:**235, 446, **5:**293
Contrabandiera, La (Pugni), **5:**277
Contrabandier Espagnole, Le, **4:**454
contradance. *See* contredanse
Contradanza, **4:**397, **6:**302, 323
contrapasso, **2:**74
"Contrapasso Nuovo, Il," **2:***75,* **5:**621
Contrasten, **2:**470
contrasto, **3:**541
Contrasts, **3:**329, **6:**412
Contre, **1:**462
Contrebandier, Le, **1:**115
Contredances, **6:**146
contredanse (contradance), **2:**255–257, **4:**511
  as Argentine dance influence, **1:**109
  Argentine form, **1:**108
  bourrée, **1:**516, 517
  Cajun version, **2:**24–25
  in Campra *opéra-ballet,* **2:**34

Canadian variation, **2:**35
Caribbean versions, **2:**62, 64
Chilean adaptation, **2:**121
Cuban forms, **2:**275–276
Czech variation, **2:**301
Danish form, **2:**382
Dominican Republic form, **2:**430, 431
figure patterns, **2:**591, 592, **5:**621
flamenco stylistic similarities, **3:**6
four-couple. *See* quadrille
France, **3:**63, 65
French longways adaptation, **4:**221
French versus English, **1:**89, *89,* 90, 91, **2:**254, 255–257
Germany, **3:**141
Italy, **3:**545
modern, **2:**257
Norwegian form, **4:**671
notation, **4:**684–685
Polish adaptation, **6:**211–212
Russian versions, **5:**445
square form, **2:**256–257
on tightrope, **2:***175*
United States, **3:**35
See also country dance
Contredanse (organization), **1:**414
contredanse allemande. See allemande
contredanse française. See cotillon
Contreras, Gloria, **4:**394, 397
Contreras, Irma, **6:**323
Contreras, Margot, **6:**323
contretemps, **1:**339, **3:**172
Contrition, **3:**212
Contugy, Marie-Geneviève, **1:**397
Conus, Natalia, **3:**437, **6:**42
Convento Veneziano, Il, **5:**246
Conversations, **5:**440
Convolutions, **6:**203
Conway, Edmund H., **2:**592, **6:**237
Conyers, Claude, **5:**53
  as contributor, **1:**328–330, 373–376, **2:**150–153, 198–201, 434–435, 439–441, **3:**428–430, **4:**66–69, 576–578, **5:**61–62, 599–601, **6:**106–107, 399–400
Conyngham, Barry, **4:**479
Cook, Bart, **1:**141, **2:**162, **4:**180, 620, 621, 623
Cook, Charles (Cookie), **3:**447, **6:**102
Cook, Ray, *as contributor,* **5:**325–326
Cooking French, **1:**351
Cook Islands. *See* Polynesia
Cool for Cats (television series), **2:**349
Coolidge, Elizabeth Sprague, **1:**95, **3:**218, **6:**5
Coolidge Collection, Washington, D.C., **4:**168
Coon, Carleton, **4:**467
"coon show," **4:**520, **6:**255
Cooper, Adam, **6:**34
Cooper, Bill, *as photographer,* **2:**2, 514, **3:**273, **5:**420, 564
Cooper, David, *as photographer,* **2:**42, **3:**234, 344, **4:**82, 252, **5:**399, 435, 437
Cooper, Douglas, **5:**193
Cooper, George, **6:**317
Cooper, James Fenimore, **1:**9, **3:**5
Cooper, Kenneth, **1:**13, **2:**322
Cooper, Ralph, **6:**255
Coopersmith, Jacob, **2:**62
Coordination Method of Dance Notation, The (Wu and Gao), **4:**693

Coorlawala, Uttara Asha, **3:**469
Copasetics, The, **2:**186, **5:**369
Cope, Jonathan, **5:***420*
Copeau, Jacques, **1:**98, **3:**75, **4:**190, 423–424, 426, **5:**547
Copen, Ilona, **1:**282
Copenhagen, Denmark, **2:**384
Copenhagen Opera, **5:**552
Copère, Madame, **2:**390, 523
Copes, Juan Carlo. *See* Nieves and Copes
Coplan, David, *as contributor,* **6:**23–24
Copland, Aaron, **2:**154, **196–198,** 584
  Appalachian Spring score, **1:**96–97, **2:**196, **3:**218, **4:**518
  Billy the Kid score, **1:**280, 453, **2:**196, **4:**28, **6:**247
  Day on Earth score, **2:**356, **3:**402
  Graham commissions, **3:**213, 384, **4:**518
  Page association, **5:**59, 60
  Rodeo score, **1:**297, **2:**196, 373, **5:**369
Coplande, Robert, **1:**45, 378, **2:**336, **5:**343, **6:**122
Coppée, François, **3:**71
Coppélia, **2:**198–201
  Albertieri production, **1:**37
  Alonso (Alicia) staging, **1:**49
  Anisimova choreography, **1:**91
  Balanchine choreography, **2:**201, **4:**611, 613
  Balanchine remounting, **4:**610, **6:**174
  Ballets Russes de Monte Carlo revival, **1:**313
  Baryshnikov performance, **1:**372
  Beck production, **1:**399, **5:**427
  Bennett's PACT Ballet production, **5:**653
  Beriosova performance, **1:**429
  Bjørnsson performance, **1:**454
  Blair performance, **1:**459
  bolero from act 2, **2:**522
  Borchsenius performance, **1:**497
  Borg production, **4:**678
  Bozzacchi performance, **3:***71*
  Bruhn performances, **2:**3, 4
  Bruhn staging, **2:**4, **4:**73
  Budarim staging, **5:**472
  Campilli production, **3:**414
  Carter (Jack) productions, **1:**110, 289, **2:**511
  Cecchetti production, **2:**82, 200, 368, **4:**145
  Chappell designs, **2:**105
  character role and dancing, **2:**106, 108, 198, 200, 368
  Christensen (Willam) choreography, **2:**160, **5:**512
  Clegg adaptation, **4:**667
  Clustine reconstruction, **2:**181
  Danilova performance, **2:***199,* 201, 342, *342,* 343
  Delibes score, **1:**390, **2:**198, 200, 201, 368, 369, **3:**70–71, **4:**226, 514, **5:**501
  Descombey mounting, **2:**388
  de Valois performance, **2:**399
  de Valois production, **1:**146, **2:**401–402, **3:**265
  Dobujinsky designs, **2:**421
  Ferri performance, **2:**588
  first production, **1:**390
  Franca performance, **3:**62
  Franca staging, **4:***541*
  Franklin performance, **2:**342
  Gadd-Goude production, **3:**100

Genée performance, **3:**128–129, 261, *262*
Georgi production, **3:**123
Golovkina-Martirosian-Radunsky revival, **3:**197
Grantzow illness, **3:**237
Grey (Beryl) performance, **3:**307
Harangozó production and performance, **3:**341, 342, 415
Hynd production, **2:**512, *512,* **3:**428
Inglesby *demi-caractère* role, **3:**512
Ivanov *demi-caractère* role, **3:**560
Kain performance, **2:**200, **3:**643
Kalina choreography, **5:**614
Kudelka character performance, **4:**73
Lacotte reconstruction, **4:**108
Lander (Harald) production, **2:**510
Lander (Margot) performance, **4:**119
Larsen character role, **4:**125
Lassen performance, **4:**126
Last staging, **4:***676*
Legnani performance, **4:**145
Lopokhova performance, **2:**200, **4:**224
Lopukhov version, **2:**369, **3:**327, **4:**226, **5:**468
Makarova performance, **4:**248
Martinez staging, **1:**72, 77, **3:**233
Martins performance, **4:**274, *274*
McBride performance, **4:**618
Norwegian National Ballet stagings, **4:***676,* 678, **5:***676*
Parés production, **1:**436, **3:**70–71
Parnell performance, **5:**101
as Pavlova and Mordkin Metropolitan Opera debut vehicle, **4:**382, 459
Petipa-Cecchetti version, **4:**145
Petipa version, **2:**200, 368, 369, **5:**158
Petit production, **3:**75, **5:**164
Petrov, Anastas, **5:**166
Rambert production, **5:**301
Saint-Léon production, **5:**94, 501, 502
Saint-Léon's mazurka choreography, **4:**343
Sand performance, **5:**511, *511*
Schauffus (Frank) performance, **5:**554
Schwarz (Solange) performance, **5:**563
Sergeyev (Nicholas) revival, **3:**511
Sofia National Opera staging, **2:**11
Spoerli production, **1:**375, *375,* **5:**682
Staff performance, **5:**692
Taglioni (Paul) production, **3:**145
Tarasov's staging as *The Doll,* **4:***674*
Tomasson *demi-caractère* role, **6:**174
travesty role, **2:**199, 368
Uthoff expressionist version, **2:**124
Vinogradov production, **4:**285
Williams (Stanley) role, **6:**399
Zucchi performance, **6:**452
Coppi, Carlo, **3:**261, **4:**258, **5:**72
Copping, Kit, **2:**36
Coppini, Achille, **3:**50

Coppini, Cesare, **4:**258, **6:**443
Coppola, Giovanni Carlo, **5:**1
Coprario, John, **4:**309, 311
Coptic Christians, **4:**402–403
copyright law, **3:**92, 370
Coq de Village, Le, **3:**426
Coq d'Or, Le, **1:**367, 424, **6:**118
  Bolm stagings, **1:**110, 482, 484,
    4:382, **5:**511
  Cecchetti mime performance,
    2:83
  Fokine stagings, **1:**312, 322, **3:**20,
    24–25, 28
  Goncharova design, **2:**408, **3:**197,
    5:542, *542*
  Karsavina performance, **3:**656
  Riabouchinska performance,
    5:350
Coquina, **1:**142
Coquinera, La, **1:**117
Coquis, André, **2:**367
Cora and Alonso, **2:**416
Čorak-Slavenska, Mia. *See*
    Slavenska, Mia
Coralia. See Undine
Coralli, Eugène, **2:**204, **4:**341, **5:**93
Coralli, Giovanni. *See* Coralli, Jean
Coralli, Jean, **1:**10, 86, 237, *237,*
    2:201–204, 503, **3:**5, 156, 176,
    223, **5:**221, 319, 498, 615
  ballet themes, **3:**180
  Diable Boiteux, Le, **2:**201, 203,
    390, 405, 502, 503, **3:***70*
  Faust sylphides ballet, **2:**202,
    3:69, 180, **6:**58
  Giselle as career pinnacle, **2:**201,
    203, **3:**177, 178, 314, 547
  Grisi roles, **3:**314, 315
  Kehlet roles, **3:**668
  Lami watercolor, **4:**116
  Lee as student, **4:**139
  libretti, **4:**176
  Maywood as student, **4:**338
  Mazilier roles, **4:**339, 340, 341
  Paris Opera Ballet, **5:**92, 93, 136
  Pugni scores, **4:**513
  Tarentule, La, **2:**201, 203, 504,
    5:148, **6:**104
  Théâtre de la Porte-Saint-Martin,
    2:202, **3:**68–69
  "white ballet," **3:**69, 180
  See also Giselle; Péri, La
Coralli, Teresa, **1:**237, **2:**201, 202,
    3:176, 547
Corbin, Patrick, **5:**679, 680
Corby (comic dancer), **4:**453, 454
CORD (Congress on Research in
    Dance), **4:**370, 575, **6:**297
Cordeiro, Analivia, **1:**537
Corder, Michael, **1:**394, **2:**514,
    4:470, **5:**421
Cordier, Alain, *as photographer,*
    4:398
Cordier, Denys, **3:**81
Cordier, Jacques ("Mr. Bochan"),
    2:260, 337, **3:**81, 252,
    4:307, 310
Cordier, Jean, **2:**337
Córdoba, Edmée de, **4:**392
Corella, Angel, **2:**441
Corelli, Arcangelo, **3:**29
coreodramma, **5:**517, **6:**338
Corey, Winthrop, **4:**71
Corida, La, **1:**114
Corigliano, John, **1:**82
Corinna, **2:**158
Corinne and Delphine (de Staël),
    1:199
Corisande (opera), **2:**413
Cork Ballet Company, **3:**519–520

Cormani, Lucia, **1:**329, 400, **3:**261
Cornazano, Antonio, **1:**53, 351,
    352, 380, **2:204–206,** 336,
    427, 517, **3:**542, **4:**501, 683,
    5:337, 506, 620, **6:**121
Corn Dance, **4:**551, 565
Corneille, Pierre, **1:**355, 425, **4:**234,
    475, **5:**503
Corneille, Thomas, **4:**447
Cornell, Heather, **6:**102
Cornell, Joseph, **1:**137, **5:**177
Cornell, Katharine, **3:**216
Cornell University, **3:**505
Corner, Philip, **3:**635
Cornero, Vincent, **2:**269
Corn Grinding Dance, **4:**565
Cornichon (cabaret), **5:**560
Corniol, Antoine, **4:**588
Cornish, Nellie, **6:**243
Cornish College of the Arts, Seattle,
    2:285, **6:**243
Cornlius-Knudsen, Britta, **5:**394
Corn Maiden Dance, **4:**565
Coronela, La, **4:**392, **6:**355
Coronelli, Pietro, **6:**431
Coronil, Nena, **6:**322, 323
Coros, Mary, *as contributor,*
    2:271–272
Corot, Camille, **1:**127
Corot, Jean Baptiste, **2:**571
Corpus Christi procession, **2:**164,
    168, **4:**461
Correa, Marcos, **2:**125
Correia, Don, **6:**287
Correlations, **4:**21
Correo español, El (publication),
    5:676
corridinho, **5:**228, 229
Corriveau, La, **5:**61
corroborees, **1:**221, *221,* 227
Corsair, The (Byron), **1:**36,
    2:206, 207
Corsaire, Le, **1:**36, **2:**96, 136,
    206–208, 513, **5:**93, **6:**116
  Adam score, **1:**10, **2:**206, 207,
    368, **4:**342
  Blankov reconstruction, **5:**470
  Clustine choreography, **2:**181
  Cucchi performance, **2:**282
  Delibes musical additions,
    2:207, 368
  Fonteyn and Nureyev
    performances, **3:**45, *45*
  Gorsky versions, **2:**207, **3:**206
  Grantzow performance, **3:**237
  Grigorovich revival, **3:**310
  Gusev revival, **3:**328
  Ivanov performance, **3:***561*
  lighting effects, **4:**189
  Mazilier choreography, **2:**206,
    207, 282, 368, **4:**189, 339,
    342, **5:**403, 405
  Mazilier revival, **4:**343
  Moiseyev choreography, **5:**471
  Mordkin performance, **4:**459
  Nureyev performances, **5:**6
  Orientalism, **5:**45
  Perrot staging, **4:**280, **5:**140, 141
  Petipa (Marius) interpretation,
    4:279, **5:**150, 151, 156,
    157, 158
  Ronzani performance, **5:**403, 404
  Ronzani restaging, **5:**616
  Rosati performance, **5:**405
  Sergeyev revival, **5:**572
  Tikhomirov performance, **6:**171
Corsican Brothers, The (film), **1:**484
Corso, Rinaldo, **6:**349
Cort Adeler in Venice, **1:**515
Cortège Hongrois, **3:**352, **4:**610, 631

Cortegiano, Il (Castiglione), **1:**523,
    4:310, **5:**337
Cortés, Fernando, **4:**330, 386,
    388, 399
Cortesi, Antonio, **2:**93, **208–209,**
    505, **3:**181, **4:**453, **5:**528
Cortés, Joaquín, **5:**674
Cortez, Hernando, **5:**679
Corti, Gino, **2:**74
Cortijo, El, **3:**286
Corvino, Alfredo, **1:**51, **2:**574
Corybantes (Crete). *See* Curetes
Corybantic, **3:**403
coryphées, **1:**457
Cosaques, Les, **5:**424
Cosi, Liliana, **2:**201, **3:**553,
    5:527, 529
cosmetics, **4:**303–305
Cosmopolites, Les, **3:**316
Cosmo-Sileo Associates, *as*
    photographers, **5:**289
Cossa, Gabor, **3:**628
Cossack dance
  Old Babylonian, **4:**356, *357*
  Ukraine, **6:***222*
"Cossack's Dance," **5:**444
Cossacks on the Rhine, **3:**191
Costa, Alice, *as photographer,* **5:**232
Costa, David, **1:**456
Costa, Giacoma, **1:**345, **6:**126
Costa, Madame, **1:**456
Costa, Mario Pasquale, **3:**51, **5:**246
Costa, Michael, **1:**47, **5:**138
Costa e Selva, José, **5:***231*
Costantini, Angelo, **2:**190
Costanzi, Domenico, **5:**399
Costas, *as photographer,* **4:**622
Costé, A., **1:**276
Costea, Constantin, **5:**391
  as contributor, **5:**390–391
Costea, Irina, **5:**390
costume in African traditions,
    2:209–213
  Cameroon, **2:**32, 33
  central and eastern Africa,
    2:90, *90*
    Digo dance, **2:**418
    Giriama dance, **3:**177
    Tiv dance, **6:**173
  Egypt, ancient, **2:**482, 484, 485
  Egyptian *ghawāzī,*
    2:494–495, 495
  Ethiopia, **2:***532,* 533, *534*
  North Africa, **4:**666
    Algeria, **1:**40, 41–42
    Berber dances, **4:***465,* 466
    Ouled Naïl dancers, **2:***346,* **5:**50
    Tunisia, **6:**206, 207
  South Africa, **5:***643,* 644, 645,
    646, 647
  southern Africa, **5:**661, 662, *663*
  sub-Saharan Africa, **6:**12, 15,
    15, *382*
costume in Asian traditions,
    2:213–233
  Bali, **1:***366,* 377, **3:**474–475,
    477–478, 480, *480,* 485,
    486–487, *486,* 488, 489–490,
    489, **4:**146
  Bellona, **1:***415,* 416
  Bhutan, **1:**445, *445,* 458,
    2:225–226
  Black Hat Dance, **1:**458
  Cambodia, **2:**30, *30,* 31, *31*
  China, **2:**130, *130,* 132, 140, *140,*
    141, 144, 219–221
  India, **1:**443, **2:**223–225, **3:**457,
    458, 460, 460, **4:**70–71, *70,*
    5:23, *582,* 598, 599
  Indonesia, **2:**231–232, **3:**644, *644.*
    See also subheads Bali; Java

Japan, **5:***591,* 592, *592,* 593, *593*
  bon dances, **2:**214–215
  bugaku, **2:**214–215, **3:**579,
    579, *580*
  butō dancers, **2:**18, 219
  kabuki, **2:**217–219, **3:**638–639,
    639, 640, **4:**493, **5:**29, 30
  kyōgen, **4:**83, *83*
  modern dance, **3:**590
  nō, **2:**2.2157–217
  shishimai, **5:**593
  tōgaku and *komagaku* dances,
    2:6
Java, **3:**493, *493*
Korea, **1:**166, 167, **2:**221–223,
    4:47, 48, 49, *49,* 51
Malaysia, **2:**229–230
Myanmar, **2:**226–227, **4:***526,*
    527, 528
Nepal, **2:**226
Oceania, **4:**352, **5:***19*
Pakistan, **2:**226
Papua New Guinea, **5:***76,* 80, 81,
    82, *82,* 83, *83*
Philippines, **2:**230
Sikkim, **5:**598, 599
Sri Lanka, **2:**228–229, **3:**647,
    648, 649
  tovil ritual, **6:***183*
  ves dance, **6:***329, 329*
Tahiti, **6:**78
Taiwan, **5:**80, 81–82
Thailand, **2:**227, **4:**110, 111, 112,
    255, **6:***149*
Tibet, **1:**458, **2:**221, **5:**599, **6:**167,
    168, 169, 169
Turkey, **6:**210, *210*
costume in Central Asian
    traditions, **6:***306*
costume in Middle Eastern
    traditions
  Arabian Peninsula, **1:**101
  danse du ventre (belly dance),
    2:344, *344,* 345, *345*
  Israeli ethnic dance, **3:**536
costume in Native American
    traditions, **5:***585*
  Arctic areas, **4:**571, 572, *572*
  Athabaskan, **4:**574
  Brazil, **1:**530–531
  California and intermountain
    region, **4:***566,* 567, *567*
  Hopi, **3:**374
  matachines, **4:**329
  Northwest Coast, **4:**569, *570*
  Pueblo dance, **4:**563, *564,* 565,
    5:273
costume in Western traditions,
    2:233–251, 392–393, **5:***647*
  background and overview,
    2:234–345, **5:**542, 543, 546
  film and popular dance,
    2:248–251
    apache style, **5:***684*
    ballroom dance competition,
      1:356
    club dancing (1990s), **5:***635*
    jazz age, **5:**629
  folk and social dance
    Algeria, **1:**41–42
    American square dance,
      5:687, 689
    Basque, **1:**376
    break dancing, **1:**538
    Byzantine Empire, **3:**295
    country-western dance, **2:**258
    Crete, **2:**272
    danza de Matlachines, **4:**28
    Garifuna, **3:**121
    Georgia, **3:***133,* 134, *134*
    Greece, **2:**100, **3:**300

Ireland, **3:***517*, 518, *518*, **5:***696*
Lithuania, **4:***205*
masquerade, **4:**313–314
Mexico, **2:**194, **4:**328, *328*, *387*, 388, *388*, *390*, 391
moresca, **2:**235, **4:**461, *461*, 462
Morris dance, **3:**33, 250, **4:**461, 473, 474, *474*
Northumbria rapper dance, **6:**55
Peru, **5:***143*, *144*, *145*
Russia, **5:**443, *443*
Scottish Highland competitions, **3:**249
Spanish traditional, **5:***584*, 615, *670*, *671*
upper Rio Grande *matachines*, **4:**329
modern dance, **2:245–248**
  Cunningham productions, **2:***287*, *288*, 290, 292, 296
  Delsarte movement, **2:**371, 452
  Duncan drapery, **2:***453*, 454
  Fuller's use of fabric, **2:**50, 246–247, *246*, **3:**91–93, *91*, *93*, 95, 96
  Graham productions, **2:**245, 248, **3:***209*, 211, *211*, 214, 218, 220, *220*
  Jaques-Dalcroze student productions, **3:**596
  practice clothes, **5:***683*
  St. Dennis draperies, **5:***492*, *494*
  St. Dennis's Orientalism, **5:***493*, *495*, *497*
theatrical dance
  Andalusian dancer, **3:***70*
  archival materials, **4:**167
  artist collaborators, **1:**135, 136, 140, 141, 142, 323, 497, **2:**242, 244, 245, *288*, *289*
  Bakst designs, **1:**254–255, *254*, 318, **2:***82*, **3:**196
  Balanchine ballets, **1:***259*, *261*, *263*, 298, *298*, **2:**193, 242, **3:**3
  ballerina conventions, **2:**240–241, **392–393**, **5:**241, 242, **6:**161, **216–217**
  ballet costume classification, **2:**244–245, **392–393**, **6:**216–217
  ballet de collège, **1:**283
  ballet de cour, **1:**285, 288
  ballet technique evolution and changes in, **1:**44, 347, 348
  Baylis designs, **1:**394
  Benois designs, **1:***422*, 423–424
  Berain designs, **1:**424–425, **2:**238
  Bérard designs, **1:**426
  Berman designs, **1:**437
  body tights, **1:**348, **2:393**, *442*
  Boquet designs, **1:**497, **2:**238
  cabaret belly dance, **2:***344*, 345
  caricature, **2:**67, 413
  Chalon's artworks as inspiration, **2:**104
  for character dancer, **2:**106, **393**
  Diaghilev's Ballets Russes, **1:**318, 321, 323, 325, **2:**241–242, **3:**196, **4:***302*, **5:***372*, 541, 543
  Didelot innovations, **2:***412*, 413, 414, *415*
  Edel designs, **2:**477
  Enigma Variations naturalistic Victorian dress, **2:**516
  Fedorovitch designs, **2:**582–583
  flamenco, **1:***62*, *62*, **3:**8, *9*, *10*

Fokine aesthetics, **3:**14, 15
footwear, **3:**46–48
Gissey designs, **3:**184
Guimard's style-setting, **3:**326, 327
Karinska designs, **3:**653–654
Lami designs, **4:**116, *116*
Larionov designs, **4:**124–125, *124*
Lecomte (Hippolyte) designs, **4:**138
masque, **3:**622, *622*, **4:***311*
Matisse designs, **4:**331, 332
Nikolais *decentralization* theory, **5:**548
pantomime, **5:**70
pantomimus, **5:**72, 73
practice clothes as, **1:**348, **2:**193, 242, *244*, 245, 247, 251, 292, **393**, **3:**58, *58*, **4:**226, **5:**240–243
Renaissance court dances, **2:**75
Roman dance, **5:**376
skirt dance, **5:**605
Soudeikine designs, **5:**642
Tchelitchev design, **5:**547
travesty, **6:**188–191
Virsaladze designs, **6:**343
Worsaae designs, **6:**404–405
See also mask and makeup; nudity; tutu
Cotarelo y Mori, Emilio, **5:**669, 676
Cote, Lynn, **6:**366
Côte d'Ivoire, **4:**288, 289, 291, *291*, 292, **6:**12, *14*, 382, 384
Cotgrave, Randle, **1:**520, **4:**313
cotillon, **2:251–253**, **5:**624, 685
  anglaise, **1:**89–90
  annual collections, **1:**91, 92, 523
  figures, **2:**591
  Le Grand Rond, **2:**252, **252**
  as quadrille ancestor, **2:**256, 257, 554, **5:**285–286
  square form, **2:**256
  United States, **6:**237
Cotillon, **1:**260, 268, **2:253–254**, **3:**617, 653, **5:**326, 327, **6:**182, 183, 203
  in Balanchine aesthetic progression, **4:**613
  Balanchine-Kochno collaboration, **4:**33
  Ballets Russes de Monte Carlo premiere, **1:**308, 309, *309*, **2:**253, **3:**72
  Bérard design, **1:**426, **5:**547
  Joffrey Ballet reconstruction, **3:**617
  Karinska costumes, **3:**653
  Lichine performance, **4:**178
  Woizikowski performance, **6:**404
"Cotillon, Le," **3:**124
"Cotillon des Fêtes de Thalie, Le," **2:**256
Coton, A. V., **3:**282, 285, **4:**637, **6:**65
Cotswold Morris dance, **4:**473, 474
Cotton Club, Harlem, **1:**439, 440, **3:**57, **4:**629, **6:**244, 256, 257
Cotton Club, The (film), **3:**366
Cotton Club Revues, **5:**368
Cotton-Eyed Joe, **2:**259, **5:**634, **6:**251
Coudy, Douglas, **1:**279, 280, **4:**209
Coudyzer, Ruphin, *as photographer*, **5:**658
Coughran, Brian, **1:**216–217
Coulin, Antoine Louis, **2:**523
Coulisses Scandaleuses, Les (Jullian), **2:**71

Coulon, Antoine, **2:**390
Coulon, Eugène, **5:**221, 623
Coulon, Jean-François, **1:**446, **3:**81, 208, 209, **5:**91
  students, **3:**358, **6:**69, 71, 75
  teaching methods, **6:**127
Council for Dance Education and Training, London, **3:**280, 307
Count Castelli, or The Criminal Brother, The, **6:**311
Counterswarm, **6:**111
Count Nulin (film), **4:**55, 149
country and western music, **6:**251
country dance, **2:254–258**
  American "collections," **6:**247
  anglaise, **1:**89–90
  annual collections, **1:**92
  Danish *engelskans*, **2:**381
  England, **3:**3, 34, 256, 377, **4:**581
  figures and patterns, **2:**591, 592, **3:**361, **5:**621
  Finland, **2:**630
  France, **4:**510
  Iceland, **3:**435
  jig versus, **3:**608
  longways, **4:**221
  modern, **2:**257
  New England, **3:**35
  Playford, John, **5:**200
  reels, **5:**333, 334
  Scotland, **3:**247–249, 377
  See also contredanse; quadrille
Country Dance and Song Society, Massachusetts, **2:**257
Country Dance Book, The (Sharp), **2:**257, **3:**238, 239, **6:**247
Country of Wonder, **4:**248
Country Song and Dance Society of America, **6:**247
country-western dance, **2:258–259**, **5:**634
coupé, **1:**339, 345
Couperin Suite, **1:**390
couple dancing. *See* social dance
courante, **1:**342, **2:259–261**, **4:**510, 511, **5:**341
  Arbeau choreography, **1:**104
  Argentine adaptation, **1:**108
  menuet derivative, **4:**431
  Negri description, **4:**580
  révérence, **5:**345
Courlander, Harold, **3:**333, **6:**345
"Courrant Sarabande," **5:**520
Course, **3:**212
Court, Louisa, **1:**505
Court, Paula, **5:**186
court ballet. *See ballet de cour*
court dance. *See* ballet technique, history of; Baroque dance; Renaissance court dance; *under* social dance; *under* specific countries
Court Dance Company of New York, **5:***323*, 327
Courtenay-Ehrenkreutz-Jędrzejewiczowa, Cezaria Baudouin de, **5:**211, 220
courtesy. *See révérence*
Courtier, The, **4:**310
Courtney, Anne, **3:**520
Courtney, Inez, **6:***319*
Court of Jah, **3:**575
Court of Love, The, **5:**575
courtship dances
  Bulgaria, **2:**7
  Cuba, **2:**275
  Ethiopia, **2:**533
  European medieval costume, **2:**235
  galliard variations, **3:**108

Garifuna as, **3:**120
Germany, **3:**141
Indonesia, **3:**475, 480, 500
Kenya, **2:**89, 212
minuet as, **4:**432
Morocco, **4:**408–409
Norway, **4:**670, 672
Papua New Guinea, **5:**83, 84
Renaissance, **2:**74, 75
Russia, **5:**444–445
spagnoletta as, **5:**666
sub-Saharan Africa, **6:**13, *17*
Turkey, **6:**212
See also wedding dances
Courville, Joachim Thibault de, **1:**1, 2, 275, **2:**338
Cousar, Theresa, **6:***449*
Cova, Fiorella, **5:**196
Covan, Willie, **4:**419
Covarrubias, Miguel, **4:**264, 399
Covarrubias Horozco, Sebastián de, **1:**54, **3:**29
Covent Garden, London (Royal Opera House)
  Adam opera productions, **1:**9
  Albertieri, Luigi, **1:**37
  Albert, Monsieur, **1:**37
  Ballets Russes de Monte Carlo appearance, **1:**311, 313, 315, **3:**508
  Bintley as resident choreographer, **1:**454
  Dance Theatre of Harlem, **2:**334
  D'Egville production, **2:**364–365
  Desnoyer, Philip, **2:**394
  de Valois performances, **2:**396
  Library and Museum, London, **4:**163
  lighting, **4:**189
  post-World War II reopening performance, **4:**114
  Rich (John) pantomime stagings, **5:**350
  Royal Ballet (Sadler's Wells) as resident dance company, **1:**150, **2:**402, **3:**267, **5:**415, 416–417, *417*, 420
  Royal Ballet School expansion, **5:**422
  theatrical dance (1600–1772), **3:**255–256
Covent Garden Russian Ballet. *See* Ballets Russes de Monte Carlo
Covento Veneziano, Il, **3:**51
Cover Girl (film), **2:**616, **4:**2
Covey, Edna, **6:**318
Covey, Adjetey, **3:**170
Coward, Noël, **1:**520, **2:**510, **4:**320, 334, **6:**272
cowboy dance. *See* country-western dance
Cowboy Dances (Shaw), **6:**247
Cowboys, The, **1:**540
Cowboys, Dreams and Ladders, **3:**448
Cowboy Two-Step, **2:**24, 258–259
Cowell, Henry, **2:**21, 520, **3:**384, **4:**519
Cowen, Donna, **3:**614
Cowrie, Christa, *as photographer*, **4:**394
Coyle, Grant, **5:**56
Crabb, Michael, **2:**49
  as contributor, **1:**200–201, **3:**61–62, 227–234, 344–345, 388–389, 643–644, **4:**237–238, 538–548, **5:**684–685, **6:**1–2, 142–143, 364
Crăciun, Cristina, **5:**390

Cracovienne, La
  Elssler popularization of, **2:**107, 504, *505,* **4:**57, 340
  kwakowiak element, **4:**57
  Lacotte reconstruction, **4:**108
  Lee performances, **4:**139
Cracoviens et Cosaques, Les, **2:**299, **5:**215
Cracow Wedding. See Kraków Wedding
Craft, Ben, **1:***51,* **5:***304*
Craft, Robert, **5:**488, **6:**6
Cragom, Jerrie, **6:**398
Cragun, Richard, **1:**436, *453,* **2:**125, **261–262,** **5:**586
  Berlin Opera Ballet, **3:**156
  Cranko Medal, **2:**268
  Haydée dance partnership, 2, 267, **2:**262, **3:**351, *351,* **6:**9
  Initialen R.B.M.E., **2:**267, **5:***102,* 107
  Onegin performance, **2:**512
  Orpheus performance, **3:***152*
  Stuttgart Ballet, **2:**266, 267, *267,* **3:***152,* **6:**9, 10, *10*
  Tetley's *Rite of Spring* performance, **6:***146*
Craig, Gordon, **1:**97, **2:262–263,** 454, **3:**93, 519
  archival materials, **4:**170
  lighting and scenic design, **4:**189, **5:**540
Craig, Valda L., *as contributor,* **1:**211–218, 218–219, **4:**479–480
Crait (ballet shoe manufacturer), **3:**47
Cramér, Ivo, **2:263–265, 283,** **5:**234, 265–266
  Drottningholm Court Theater choreography, **1:**503, **6:**42, 47–48, 50
  Förlarade Sonen production, **2:**263, **264,** **5:**265–266
  Norwegian National Ballet commissions, **4:**676, 677
  Royal Swedish Ballet, **6:**36, 42, 43, 47–48
Cramér Ballet, **6:**45
Crampton, C. Ward, **6:**240
Crandall, Milton, **2:**324–325
crane (totemic), **2:**139–140
Crane, Hart, **2:**197, **4:**26
Crane, Ivy and Douglas, **6:**318
Crane, The, **2:**159
Crane Dance, **3:**341
Cranko, John, **1:**72, 375, 420, **2:**41–42, 262, **265–268,** 478, **5:**96, 225, 301, 528, 531, 651
  Australian productions, **1:**210, 230, 233, 499
  Batsheva Dance Company, **3:**532
  Beauty and the Beast, **5:**316
  Belle Hélène, La, **2:**114, 266
  Benesh notation use, **1:**418
  Beriosova roles, **1:**429
  Birmingham Royal Ballet choreography, **3:**268
  Blair roles, **1:**459
  Bosl roles, **1:**500
  Brouillards, **2:**267, 361
  Daphnis and Chloe, **2:**266, **5:**316
  de Valois association, **2:**403
  Fonteyn role, **3:**45
  Hamburg Ballet productions, **3:**338
  Haydée roles, **3:**350–351, **6:**9, 10
  Joffrey Ballet revivals, **3:**616
  Keil roles, **4:**1, 2
  as Kylián influence, **4:**81

Lady and the Fool, The, **2:**57, 266, **3:**623, **4:**65, **5:**431, **6:**378
  MacMillan association, **4:**240, 242, 243
  Madsen roles, **4:**245
  National Ballet of Canada productions, **4:**547
  Nutcracker staging, **5:**15
  Onegin, **1:**201, 391, **2:**267, 512, **3:**345, **4:**546, **5:**405, 433, **6:**9, 117
  Pineapple Poll, **1:**209, 459, **2:**57, 265, *266,* **3:**203, *268*
  Romeo and Juliet, **2:**39, 125, 266, 267, *267,* **3:***150,* **4:**547, **5:**394, **395–396,** 405, **6:**9, 142
  Rose design collaborations, **5:**405
  Royal Ballet productions, **3:**236, **5:**417, 420
  Royal Danish Ballet guest productions, **5:**431, 433
  Royal Swedish Ballet guest productions, **6:**43
  Scott association, **5:**563, 564
  South African ballet productions, **5:**650, 651, 654
  Stuttgart Ballet, **2:**266–267, **3:**149, 150, **4:**1, **6:**9–10
  Swan Lake, **6:**34–35
  Taming of the Shrew, The, **2:**124, 267, 514, **4:**547, **6:**9, *9,* 43
  Tritsch-Tratsch, **5:***650*
  as van Praagh protégé, **6:**313
  video documentary on, **2:**314
Cranks, **2:**266
Crapo Collection, Ontario, **4:**166
Crapshooter, The, **2:**378
Crash, **1:**103
Crash into Zero, **2:**171
Craske, Dorothy, **3:***262*
Craske, Margaret, **1:**147, **2:268–269, 5:**298, **6:**128
  Cecchetti Society founding, **2:**84
  on jumps, **1:**341, 347, **2:**268–269
  Metropolitan Opera Ballet School, **4:**381, 382
  New York dance school, **6:**292
  students, **1:**542, **2:**134, 269, 574, **3:**508, **4:**109, 271, 667, **5:**602, 603, 649, **6:**29, 107, 145, 312, 402
Craske-Ryan School, London, **2:**268
Crawford, Cheryl, **6:**278
Crawford, Michael, **6:**180
Crazy for You (musical), **6:**289
Création, La, **1:**306, **4:**178
Creation, The (de Lavallade ballet), **2:**367
Creation, The (Haydn oratorio), **1:**402
Création du Monde, La, **5:**545
  Bölin choreography, **1:**327, **2:**373, **4:**418
  de Valois choreography, **2:**397, 399–400, **3:**265
  Imre choreography, **3:***419*
  jazz elements, **4:**519
  Léger design, **5:***544,* 545
  MacMillan version, **2:**242, **6:**380
  Milhaud score, **2:**373, **4:**418, 516
Creation of Eve, The, **2:**42
Creation of the World, The, **2:**12, 502
  Baryshnikov performance, **1:**371
  Bolender choreography, **1:**479
  Kasatkina and Vasiliov staging, **1:**371, **3:**418, **4:**36, 285, 336, **5:**461, 467, 470
  Kolpakova performance, **4:**36

Maximova performance, **4:**336
  Soloviev performance, **5:**639
Creations (Sarabhai), **5:**522
"Creative Dance" (Boas), **2:**320
Creative Nation (Australian program), **1:**217
Créatures de Prométhée, Les, **5:**95
Creatures of Prometheus, The (*Die Geschöpfe des Prometheus*), **3:**132, **5:**528
  Ashton revival, **1:**402
  Beethoven score, **1:**157, 237, 402, **2:**172, 401, **3:**414, 547, **4:**421, **5:**512–513, **6:**388
  Guerra staging attempt, **3:**414
  Lanchbery score revision, **4:**117
  Lifar choreography and performance, **4:**183
  Milloss revival, **1:**402, **3:**416, **4:**420, *421*
  Miskovitch staging, **4:**435
  Viganò production, **1:**237, 402, **2:**401, **3:**175, 547, **6:**338
  Wells performance, **6:**380
Crébillon, **3:**364, **4:**174
Crededio, Conchita, **6:**323
Credo in Us, **2:**285
Cree (people), **4:**559
Creek (people), **4:**558, 560
Creeley, Robert, **2:**460
Cregan, Kevin, **2:***347*
Créole, La (Offenbach), **1:**253
Creoles
  Belize, **1:**414, 415
  Brazil, **1:**530
  cakewalk, **6:**243
  Caribbean region, **2:**64
  Dominican Repbulci, **2:**431
  Louisiana, **2:**23, 24
Creole Show, The (musical), **2:**25, **6:**255
Crespé, Marie-Madeleine. *See* Théodore, Mademoiselle
Cressida, **2:**111
Creston, Louise, **3:**214
Crete, **2:**101, **269–272**
  ancient dance, **2:269–271,** 419, **3:**287, 428, **4:**106
  modern dance, **2:**100, **271–272,** **3:**296, 299
Creutz, Gustav Philip, **6:**47
Creutzfeldt-Jakob disease, **1:**257
Crevier, Gérald, **2:**47, **4:**238
Crewdson, Carole, *as contributor,* **4:**475–477
Crianca y virtuosa dotrina, La (Gracia Dei), **1:**53
Crichton, Michael, **3:**619–620
Crickmay, Anthony, *as photographer,* **1:**150, 159, **2:**355, **3:***272,* **4:**216, 217, **5:**303, 596
Crime and Punishment, **4:**478
Crimean War, **1:**486
Crimogaea (Jonsson), **3:**434
Crimson Sails, **1:**487, 491, **4:**149, **5:**459
criolla dance, **2:**431
Crises, **2:**290
Crises, Paired, **2:**574
Crisp, Clement, **3:**285, **4:**177
  as contributor, **4:**247–249, 267–271, 584–585, **5:**574–575
Cristobal Colon, **3:**127
Cristoforo, **3:**418
Cristoforo Colombo, **4:**455
Critical Observations on the Art of Dancing (Gallini), **2:**252, 256, **3:**111
Critical Path, **4:**21

criticism, dance
  aesthetics, **1:**24–25
  contemporary in United States, **6:**298–300
  Dance Critics Association, **6:**300
  International Dance Critics Conference, **1:**81
  See also methodologies in the study of dance; *subhead dance research and publication under specific countries; specific critics*
Croatia, **1:**370
  circle dance, **2:***548*
  modern dance, **6:**433–434
  traditional dance, **6:***427,* 428, *428,* 430–431
Croatian National Theater, **6:**431
Croatian National Theater 1860–1950, **6:**438
Croce, Arlene, **1:**389, **4:**622, 631, **5:**602, **6:**152
  Ballet Review, **6:**297
  as contributor, **1:**255–273, **2:**375–376
  New Yorker dance essays, **6:**299
Croce, Benedetto, **2:**188
Crockett, Barbara and Deane, **6:**264, 266
Croff, Giovanni Battista, **5:**138
Crofton, Kathleen, **2:272–273**
Crofts, James, duke of Monmouth, **5:**489
croisé, **1:**333–334
Croll, Gerhard, *as contributor,* **1:**87–89, **3:**187–191
Crombé, Françoise, **2:**306
Cronin, Timothy, **2:***584*
Cronley, Connie, **6:**204
Cropley, Eileen, **2:**526
Croqueuse de Diamants, La, **3:**601
Croquis, **6:**67
Croquis de Mercure, **3:**174
Crosby, Bing, 615–616
Crosby, Bob, **1:**194
Crosfield, Domini, **3:**303
Cross, Gertrude, **4:**688
Cross Channels (television program), **2:**611
Crosset, Ann, **2:**386
Cross-Garter'd, **3:**174, **4:**215, **5:**300, **6:**195
Crossing, The, **2:**1, **3:**575
Crossmann-Hecht, Eva, **3:**52
Crossroads, **2:**423
Crow Hop, **5:**240
Crowley, Paul, *as photographer,* **1:**232
Crowne, John, **3:**522, **5:**251, 489
Crow style (Plains Indian dance), **4:**561
Crucible, **3:**445
Crucified Virgin Mary, **3:**657
Crucifixion, **6:**88
Crucinom, **3:**429
Cruel Garden, **2:**1, **5:**302, **6:**134
Cruel World, **4:**73
Cruikshank, George, **2:**69, 70
Crum, Richard, *as contributor,* **1:**33–35, **2:**565–566, **6:**426–431
Crumb, George, **2:**1, 4, **5:**302
Cruse, Mildred, **6:***262*
Crux, Peter Anton, **1:**237
Cruz, Eric V., **5:**172, 173
CRWDSPCR, **2:**290, 296, *296,* 608, **4:**37
Cry, **1:**56–57, **3:**577–578, **577**
Cry and Silence, **4:**478, 479

Crystal Palace, The, **1:**507, 510
Crystal Slipper, The (film), **6:**442
Csáki Biró Lánya, **3:**413
csárdás. See czardas
Csarnóy, Katalin, **3:**418
Csinády, Dóra, **3:**415
Csokonai Theater of Debrecen, **3:**419
Csongor and Tünde, **3:**417
Csupajáték, **4:**420–421
Cuadro Flamenco, **1:**323, **2:**378, 379, **5:**192, *584*
cuando, **1:**108
Cuando, El, **2:**122
Cuatro Soles, Los, **3:**391, **4:**198
Cuba, **2:**273–282
 ballet, pre-1959, **2:**66, **276–277,** 504
 ballet, post-1959, **2:277–280**
  Uruguayan ballet exchanges, **6:**302
  See also Ballet Nacional de Cuba
 folk, ritual, and social dance, **2:**62, *63,* 64, **273–276,** 280, 281, 430
  Macarena, **5:**635
  rumba, **5:**629
  Santería, **6:**185, 345
 modern dance, **2:280–282**
Cuban motion, **1:**357, 358
Cuban National Ballet, **5:**406
Cubanola Glide, **6:**316
cubism, **1:**133, 323, **2:**242, **4:***302,* 516
 scenic design, **5:**543, *543*
cubo-futurists, **1:**244, **2:**408
Cucchi, Claudina, **1:**238, 500, **2:282, 5:**141, 455, 528
Cuckson, Mary, **4:**160
cuculi, **2:**121
cucumbis, **1:**526
cueca, **1:**109
Cueca, La (Garrido), **2:**127
Cuerdos. *See* concheros
Cueto, Elena del, **2:**277
Cuevas, George, marquis de, **1:**315, **3:**224, 227
 See also Grand Ballet du Marquis de Cuevas
Cugat, Xavier, **1:**194
Cugley, Ian, **1:**212
Cui, César, **4:**429
Cukor, George, **4:**3
Cullberg, Birgit, **1:**370, **2:**263, **283–284, 5:**234, 386, 599
 Medea, **2:**283, **4:**608, 676, **5:**431
 Moon Reindeer, **2:**283, **3:**373, **4:**120, **5:**431, 553
 Norwegian National Ballet productions, **4:**676, 677
 Riisager scores, **5:**353
 Royal Danish Ballet guest choreography, **2:**283, **5:**431
 Royal Swedish Ballet productions, **2:**283, **6:***41,* 42, 43–44
 son Ek (Mats), **2:**500–501
 television productions, **6:**135
 See also Miss Julie
Cullberg Ballet, **2:**1, 284, **6:**45
 Ek, Mats, **2:**500–501, **6:***44*
 Gadd as guest choreographer, **3:**100
 Green Table revival, **3:**630
 Summerspace revival, **2:**294, **6:**27
Cullen, Philippa, **1:**217
Culmann, Karl, **4:**15
Culpo, Madeline, **6:**264
Cultural Center, Kumasi, **3:**170

Cultural Center of the Philippines Dance Workshop Company. *See* Ballet Philippines
cultural evolution theory, **3:**30, 35
Cultural Revolution (China; 1966–1976), **1:**164, **2:**132, 149
 background, **2:**137
 classical opera ban, **6:**421
 persecution of Wu, **6:**406
 persecution of Zhou, **6:**447
 revised opera, **2:**137, 142
cultural studies. *See* methodologies in the study of dance
cultural theory, **4:**376–379
Culture musicali: Quaderni di etnomusicologia (journal), **3:**556
Cultuur Kamer, Netherlands, **4:**590
Culver, Andrew, **2:**296, **5:**17, 18
cumbia, **1:**109, **2:**24, **5:**67
Cummings, Alma, **2:**324, 327
Cummings, Blondell, **1:***245,* **3:**448, **5:**659, **6:**259, 448
Cuna (people), **5:**67
Cunliffe, Alan, *as photographer,* **4:**470
Cunningham, Kitty, *as contributor,* **2:**16–17, 366–367, 519–520, **3:**571–572, **4:**230–231, 648–652, **5:**407–408
Cunningham, Merce, **2:284–297,** **3:**387, **4:**608, 186, 234, *243,* 276, 526, 573, **6:**278
 as Alston influence, **1:**50, 51
 American Dance Festival, **1:**79
 Appalachian Spring performance, **1:**97, **2:**285, 286
 as Argentine dance influence, **1:**114
 as Australian dance influence, **1:**212–213
 avant-garde dance, **1:**246, **2:**287–288, 290, **6:**249, 250
 Bennington School, **1:**421
 Boston Ballet choreography, **1:**501, 502, **6:**398
 Brown (Carolyn) dance partnership, **1:**542
 Cage collaboration, **1:**138, 140, 142, **2:**21, 22–23, 285–296, **3:**446, **4:**519
 Canfield, **2:**53–54, 292
 chance procedures in choreography, **2:**287, 288, **3:**446, **4:**519, **5:**548, **6:**26
 as Chilean modern dance influence, **2:**125
 choreographic abstraction, **3:**131
 choreography course, **3:**280
 computer-assisted choreography, **2:**296
 as Cuban modern dance influence, **2:**280
 dance aesthetics, **1:**25, 128, **2:**287, 288, 293, **6:**249
 Deaths and Entrances performance, **2:**360, **3:***214*
 Denby profile of, **2:**375
 Duets, **1:**75, **5:**105
 Duncan as indirect influence, **2:**457
 Dunn (Robert Ellis) association, **2:**461, 462
 elevation technique, **2:**285
 Erdman association, **2:**520
 Farber association, **2:**574
 films and videos, **2:**294, 607–608
 as French modern dance influence, **3:**77, 78
 as Graham Dance Company member, **3:**216, 218, **4:440**

improvisational rarity, **3:**447
 as Judson Dance Theater influence, **3:**634
 Lauterer scenic design, **4:**130
 Letter to the World performace, **4:**153
 modern dance technique, **2:**285, 289, **3:**274, **4:440,** **441**
 music and movement simultaneity, **2:**288
 Ocean, **2:**296, **5:**17–18
 Paris Opera Ballet, **5:**97, 98
 partnering technique, **5:**105
 performance design, **5:**547, 548, *548*
 performance spaces, **2:**287, **6:***162,* 163–164
 practice clothes as costumes, **2:**248
 Rambert Dance Company, **3:**274, **5:**303, 305
 Rauschenberg association, **1:**140, 142, **2:**22, 245, 290, 292, 293, **5:**313, 314
 Russian students, **5:**465
 Satie scores, **2:**286, 287, 289, **4:**516
 Seasons, **2:**286, **6:**402
 Signals, **1:**372, **2:**294
 students, **1:**212, **2:**119, 358, 466, **3:**201, 339, **4:**37, 115, **5:**127, 292, 439, 602, **6:**151, 364
 Suite for Five, **6:**26, **2:**287
 television productions, **6:**139
 Variations V, **2:**292, 605, **4:**519
 Winterbranch, **1:***542,* **2:**294, **5:**314, **6:**402, **402**
 See also Merce Cunningham Dance Company; *Summerspace; Walkaround Time*
Cunningham, Ron, **1:**501
Cunningham Dance Foundation, **2:**292, 294, 296, **6:**136
Cunningham Dance Technique (videotape), **2:**294
cunquen, **2:**121
Cupak (performance genre), **3:485**
Cupid and Psyche (Ashton and Berners ballet), **1:**148, 150, 438
Cupid and Psyche (Didelot ballet). *See Psyché et l'Amour*
Cupid and Psyche (Staff ballet), **5:**691
Cupido Trionfatore, o Sia Apollo e Dafne, **2:**55
Cupid Out of His Humor, **1:**403, **6:**38, *46,* 47
Cupid's Prank, **3:**563
Cupid's Revenge, **1:**423
cupid headdress, **4:**329
cup/saucer/two dancers/radio, **4:**21
Cura, Therese, **6:**164
Curaçao, **2:**61, 63
curaçao (dance), **2:**64
curcunabaz, **6:**210
Curetes (Crete), **2:**270
Curie, Marie and Pierre, **3:**94
curing ceremonies. *See* medicinal rites
Curious School of Theatrical Dancing, **2:**45
curiquinga dance, **2:**476
Curlew River (Britten), **3:**388
Curran, Alvin, **2:**170–171
Curran, Sean, **6:***260*
Curriculum Aeternum, **2:**154
Currier, Nathaniel, **1:***200,* **2:***94,* **5:**261
Currier, Ruth, **3:**403, 404, **4:**198

Curry, John, **1:**28, **2:297–299,** 359, 584, **3:**428, *433,* **4:**274, **5:**187, **6:**154
Curtis, Edward, **2:**601, **5:**180
Curtis, Margaret, **3:**663, **4:**381, 457, **5:**637
curtsy. *See révérence*
cururu, **1:**531
Curz, Daniel, **2:**299, **5:**215
cushion dance, **3:**246
Cushman, Flora, **3:**534
cutti, **3:***457*
Cutting the Sugar Cane, **5:**586
Cutting Up, **1:**373
Cuvilliés Theater, Munich, **1:**390, 391
Cuyjet, Marion, **3:**577
Cvejičová, Máša, **1:**541
Cvetanov, C., **2:**11, **5:**166
Cybele, **3:**292
Cycle of Unrest, **6:**88
Cycles (dance group), **3:**272–273
Cycles, **2:**460
Cycle, The (de Valois), **2:**403
Cyclops, **3:**290, **5:**557
Cydalise et le Chèvre-pied, **1:**247, **5:**690, **6:**444
Cygne, Le (ballet solo). *See Dying Swan, The*
Cyklop, **3:**625
Cymbal Dance (Korea), **4:**48
cymbals, **3:**298, 475, 514, **4:**664
Cyprus, **2:***550,* **3:**296, *297*
Cyrano de Bergerac, **3:***600,* **4:**65, **5:**163, 431, 600
Cyrca, **3:**321
Cythère Assiégée, La, **1:**87, **3:**188, 190
Cytheris, Volumnia, **4:**427
czardas (csárdás), **2:299–301,** *553,* **3:**408, 409, 412
 in *Coppélia,* **2:**200, 368
 "Czardas" (Ivanov choreographic poem), **3:**567, 568
Czarnowski, Lucile K., **6:**247
Czarny, Charles, **4:**602, **5:**51, 530–531
Czechoslovak State Ensemble of Song and Dance, **2:**309
Czech Republic and Slovak Republic, **2:301–311**
 dance education, **2:**310
 dance research and publication, **2:**311, **4:**160
 libraries and museums, **4:**160
 folk and traditional dance, **2:301–305**
  chain and round dances, **2:**100, 101, 102, 301, 302, *305*
  research, **2:**311
 touring companies, **2:**309–310
 vocal sounds, **2:**38
 theatrical dance, **2:306–311**
  See also Brno Ballet; Prague National Theater Ballet; Slovak National Theater Ballet; *names of specific choreographers and dancers*
Czerniawski, Karol, **4:**57
Czerny, Karl, **2:**535, 536, **5:**353
Czernyana, **3:**174, **5:**54, 300, 691
Czernyana II, **5:**300, 691
Czernyana III, **5:**692
Czobel, Lisa, **3:**146, 305, 626, 628, **6:**29

Daan, Léa, **1:**411, 519
da'assa (dance step), **3:**449
Dabh, Halim el-, **2:**182, **3:**218

Dabh, Michael al-, **2:**498
dabkah, **3:**538, *538,* 605, **4:**79, 410, 411
 common forms, **4:**406–407
 Lebanon, **4:**135–136, *135*
 structure, **4:**490
Dabney, Ford, **2:**78, 79, **6:**256
Dąbowski, Zygmunt, **5:**218
Dąbrowska, Grażyna, **5:**211, 220
 as contributor, **4:**57, **5:**210–215
dabus dance, **4:**249
Da Capo al Fine, **4:**218
Dacia, Fulda, **5:**384
Dacian, Eleana, **5:**386
daCosta, Yvonne, **3:**574
Dada Gallery, Zurich, **6:**52, 389
Dadaism, **1:**133, 134–135, 244, 246, 327–328, **2:**182, 287, 564, 603, **3:**163, **4:**90, 516, **5:**545, **6:**356, 389–390
Daddy Long Legs (film), **5:**163
Dadishkiliani, Otar, **1:**408, **4:**154, **5:**471
Daedalus (mythic), **2:**270, 271, **4:**106
Daffy, Brett, **1:***215*
Dafne (Rinuccini and Peri), **5:**113
Dafora, Asadata, **2:**313, **5:**255, **6:**258
Daganova, Ella, **2:**356, **5:**359
dagger dance, **1:**176, **4:***291,* 465, 468, **6:**417, *418,* 419
Dagger Society, The, **2:**116
Daghestan, **3:**513
d'Aglie, Filippo. *See* Aglié, Filippo d'
Dagomba (people), **2:**210
Dagon, Gadi, *as photographer,* **3:**535
Daguerre, Louis-Jacques-Mandé, **2:**171
Daguin, Sophie, **6:**40
Dah-Dah-Sko-Dah-Dah, **6:**145
daḥīyah dance, **1:**401
Dahl, Christian Florus Balduin, **1:**516
Dahl, Hugo, **2:**631
Dahl, Viking, **3:**100
Dahlen, Caro, **5:**425
Dahlia Bleu, Le, **5:**151, 278
Dahms, Sibylle, *as contributor,* **3:**364–366, **6:**342–343
Dahomean (people). *See* Fon
Dahomey. *See* Benin Republic
Dai (people), **2:**140
Dai Ailian, **2:**134, 135–136
Daihannya, **3:***651,* **4:***654*
Daija, Tish, **1:**34
Dai Rakudakan, **1:**61, **2:**17–18, 18, **4:***271–272,* 272
Daisy, Mademoiselle, **6:**448
Dakin, Christoper, **3:**220
Daks, Nicholas, **1:**518
Dalada Maligawa Perahera. *See* Kandy Perahera
dalang, **1:**173, 179, **3:**476, 496, **6:**367
 necessary skills, **6:**368–369
Dalayrac, Nicolas, **3:**175, **6:**337
Dalcroze, Émile. *See* Jaques-Dalcroze, Émile
Dalcroze Institute. *See* Jaques-Dalcroze Institute
Dalcroze method. *See* eurhythmics; Jaques-Dalcroze, Émile

Dale, Grover, **5:**366
Dale, Jim, **6:**286
Dale, Margaret, **2:314, 6:**134, 135, 405
Dale, Virginia, **1:**193
d'Alembert, Jean le Rond, **5:**306, **6:**123, 125
Daleng, Rolf, **4:**677
D'Aler, Francesca, **1:**411
d'Alessandri, Blanche, **6:**119
Dali, Salvador, **1:**136, *137,* 291, 296–297, 437, **3:**224, 343, 654, **5:**547, 551, **6:**199
Dalia Folk Dance Festival, **3:***528,* 530, 531, 532, 641, **4:**155
DALICA (Canza Libre de Cámara), **6:**302
Dallal, Alberto, **4:**399
 as contributor, **1:**524–525, **4:**389–395, 395–398, **5:**353–354, **6:**355–356
Dallapiccola, Luigi, **4:**421
Dall'Argine, Constantino, **4:**455
Dallas Ballet, **3:**13, **4:**435, **6:**264, 265, 266
Dallas Public Library, **4:**169–170
Dallas Push, **4:**203
Dallas Starlight Theater, **1:**518
Dalle, Stephane, **5:***683*
dalloukah, **4:***663*
Dally, Lynn, **6:**102
Dalman, Elizabeth, **1:**214
Dalsemer, Robert G., *as contributor,* **2:**180–181
Dalva, Nancy, *as contributor,* **5:**17–19
Daly, Augustin, **1:**496, **2:**452, **5:**46, **6:**242
Daly Brothers, **6:**316
Dalza, Joan Ambrosio, **4:**502, **5:**114, 115
dama dances, **2:**422, **4:***288*
Damarwulan, **3:**497–498, 502
Damase, Jean-Michel, **2:**596, **3:**226, **5:***604*
Damba Festival,, Ghana, **3:**164
d'Amboise, Charlotte, **2:**315
d'Amboise, Christopher, **2:**315, **5:**132, **6:**286
d'Amboise, Jacques, **1:**12, **2:314–315, 3:**521, **4:**273, **5:**316, **6:**131, 138
 Apollo performance, **1:**96
 Ballet Imperial, **1:**293
 Farrell dance partnership, **2:**576, **4:**611
 Karinska costumes, **3:**654
 Medea performance, **4:***614*
 New York City Ballet, **4:**609, 611, 619, 620, 623
 Nichols (Kyra) as protégée, **4:**631
Dambre, Nelsi, **5:**572–573
Dame à la Licorne, La, **1:**301, **2:**183
Dame aux Camélias, La (Dumas *fils* novel), **1:**155, **4:**339
Dame aux Camélias, La (Gsovsky ballet), **5:**97
Dame aux Camélias, La (Rubinstein ballet), **1:**424
Dame Blanche, La (Boieldieu), **1:**9
Dame de Pique, La, **5:**164
Dames (film), **1:**432, 433, 434, *434*
Dames at Sea (musical), **6:**284
Damgaard, Holger, *as photographer,* **4:**43
Damian, Vella C., **5:**172
Damiró, Casandra, **2:**432
Damitse Ngacham, **1:**445
Damm, Palle, **4:**677
Damme, André van, **1:**519

Dämmern. See Twilight
Dämmernden Rhythmen, **4:**91
Damnation de Faust, La (Berlioz), **1:**405
Damn Yankees (film), **3:**54
Damn Yankees (musical), **3:**54, **6:**281, 288, 327, *327*
Damoiselle Élue, La, **2:**361
Damon, Ben, *as photographer,* **6:**265
Dämon, Der, **3:**625
Damond, Geneviève Lespagnol, **4:**256
Dämon Maschine, **1:**467
Dan (people), **1:**15
 masked stilt dancing, **4:***287,* 288, 289
Dana, Jerilyn, **3:**233
Danaher, Phyllis, **6:**378
Dana Porter Library, London, Ontario, **4:**166
Danbury Mix, **4:**623, **6:**111, 112
"Dança do Castelo," **5:**228
"Dança do Rei David," **5:**228
"Dança dos Pauliteiros," **5:**228, 229
Dançar (magazine), **1:**537
Dance (film and live dance), **2:**608
Dance (Matisse painting). *See Danse I and II, La*
Dance: An Historical Survey of Dancing in Europe, The (Sharpe and Oppé), **5:**583
Dance: A Short History of Classical Theatrical Dancing (Kirstein), **4:**27, **6:**246
Dance, Nathaniel, **6:***332*
Dance, The (Lucian), **1:**20
dance accompanists. *See* accompaniment for dance
dance aesthetics. *See* aesthetics
Dance against Time, A (Solway), **3:**617
Dance Alliance, Johannesburg, **5:**659
Dance and Dancers (journal), **3:**283, 285
Dance and Human History (film), **2:**602
dance and movement therapy, **1:**469, **2:315–322,**
 Ausdruckstanz exercises, **1:**203
 Bodenwieser technique, **1:**467–468
 Chladek technique, **2:**153, 154–155
 improvisation, **3:**444–445
 kinesiological basis, **4:**18–21
 Laban principles, **4:**97, 99, 104
 Schoop, Trudi, **5:**560–561
 See also body therapies
Dance and the Child International, **5:**44
dance animation movement, **3:**278
Dance Anzu Machine, **4:**271–272
Dance Archives, Academy of Arts, Leipzig, **4:**161
Dance around the Golden Calf (Nolde picture), **1:**131
Dance as an Art Form (film), **4:**230
Dance as a Theatre Art (Cohen), **6:**127
Dance Associates, **3:**362, **6:**107
Dance Association, **4:**156
dance as sport, **2:322–324**
 aerobic dance, **1:**12–13, **2:**322, **6:**294
 capoeira, **2:**58, 59
 gymnastics dance, **6:**294
 See also gymnastics movement; physical education, physical conditioning

Dance at the Gym, **2:**20
Dance Australia (magazine), **1:**218
Dance Autobiography, A (Makarova), **4:**248
dance-band highlife. *See* highlife
Dance Base, Sydney, **1:**217
Dance Book of Margaret of Austria (Burgundian Manuscript), **4:**683
DanceBrazil, **2:**59
Dance Butter, **2:**18
Dance Canada: An Illustrated History (Wyman), **2:**49
Dance Center, The, New York City, **5:**359
Dance Centre, Vancouver, **6:**133
Dance Chromatic (film dance), **2:**604
Dance Chronicle (publication), **3:**285, **6:**297
dance circles, England, **4:**477
dance clubs, **3:**167, **5:**635–636, **6:**13–14
dance collections. *See* annual collections
Dance Company of New South Wales. *See* Sydney Dance Company
dance competitions. *See* ballet competitions; ballroom dance competition; dance marathons; ice dancing
Dance Concert Company, **5:**172
Dance Consort, **4:**39
Dance Council of Wales, **3:**307
dance criticism. *See* criticism, dance; *specific countries and critics*
Dance Critics Association, **6:**300
Dance Design, **4:**679
Dance Dialects of India (Ragini Devi), **5:**292
Dance Documentation Center, Genzano, **4:**161
Dance Drama Company, **1:**479
Dance Dream, **1:**85
dance education. *See under specific countries; specific dance schools*
Dance Encyclopedia, The (Martin), **6:**300
dance epidemics (dancing manias), **2:**168, **3:**292, **4:**348, **6:**185, 187
Dance Exchange, **1:**215, **4:**151, 152
Dance Factory, Johannesburg, **5:**648, 659
Dance Fairy Tale, A, **6:**392
Dance Film and Video Guide (catalog), **4:**167
Dance Films Association, **2:**610, **4:**167
Dance Findings (videodance collection), **2:**462
Dance for Life, **4:**267
Dance for One Figure, Four Obects and Film Sequences, **2:**606
"Dance for the Amazon Warriors," **4:**23
Dance for the Camera, **6:**136
Dance Forum, Hungary, **3:**419
Dance Forum of the Cologne State Opera. *See* Cologne Dance Forum
dance games
 Faeroe Islands, **2:**383, 384
 Finland, **2:**629–630
 Iceland, **3:**434–435
 Lithuania, **4:**206
 Russia, **5:**442–443, 481
 Siberia, **5:**447–448

Yugoslavia, **6:**427
See also children's dances
Dance Group, Montevideo, **6:**302
Dance Hall, **5:**634
Dance Heritage Coalition, **4:**158, **5:**44
Dance Horizons, **3:**282, **6:**298
Dance House (television series), **2:**611, **6:**136
Dance House, Melbourne, **1:**217
Dance House, The, **1:**454
Dance in America (television series), **2:**294, 359, 459, **5:**513, **6:**138–139, 140, *140,* 300
Clytemnestra, **2:**182
Joffrey Ballet, **3:**616
Lamentation, **3:**213
Pennsylvania Ballet, **5:**132
Pilobolus Dance Theatre, **5:**195
Promised Land, The, **3:**621
Villella, Edward, **6:**340
Dance in Ancient Greece, The (Lawler), **3:**302–303, **6:**297
"Dance in Bali" (McPhee), **6:**297
Dance in Canada (journal), **2:**49
Dance in Canada Association, **2:**43, 49
Dance Indaba, Cape Town, **5:**656
Dance Index (magazine), **4:**28, **5:**177, **6:**297
Dance Index for Research, **2:**462
Dance-Information-Danse (Hungarian annual), **3:**424
Dance in India: An Annotated Guide to Source Materials (Van Zile), **3:**470
Dance Injuries: Their Prevention and Care (Arnheim), **2:**330, **4:**17
Dance Ink (journal), **6:**297
Dance in Psychotherapy (Rosen), **2:**320
Dance in Tahiti (Moulin), **4:**628–629
Dance in the Sun (film), **2:**604
"Dance into Death," **6:**391
"Dance Is a Man's Sport, Too," **6:**154
Dance Journal (publication), **1:**398
Dance Kaleidoscope, **6:**266
dance kinesiology. *See* kinesiology
Dance Librarians Discussion Group, **4:**158
Dance Library of Israel, Tel Aviv, **4:**164
Dance Magazine
on *For Bird With Love,* **1:**59
founding and focus, **6:**296, 300
William Como Collection, **4:**168
Dancemakers, **2:**42, 45
Dancemakers, The (television series), **6:**133
dance mania. *See* dance epidemics
dance manuals. *See* technical manuals; *specific authors*
dance marathons, **2:**324–328
dance master. *See* dancing master
dance medicine, **2:**328–331
causes of injury, **4:**19–20
injury types, **4:**20
kinesiology, **4:**13–21
practitioners, **4:**20–21
See also body therapies; dance and movement therapy; medicinal rites
Dance Medicine: A Comprehensive Guide (Ryan and Stephens eds.), **2:**330
Dance Medicine—Health Newsletter, **4:**17

Dance Moketi, **5:**656
Dance Museum (Dansmuseet), Stockholm, **4:**163, **6:**49, 50
Dance News (New Zealand publication), **4:**629
Dance News (U.S. publication), **3:**285, **6:**296
Dance North, **1:**215
dance notation. *See* notation
Dance Notation Bureau, New York, **1:**471, **3:**427, **4:**95, 96, 98, 104, **5:**44
library, **4:**167
qualification levels, **4:**687
Dance Notation Record, The (magazine), **4:**96
Dance Now (British quarterly), **3:**285
Dance Observer (periodical), **1:**6, **3:**385, **6:**297
Dance of Court and Theatre (Hilton), **3:**283
Dance of Death, **2:**165, **331–333,** **3:**180, **4:**348, **6:**667
carole, **4:**501
Green Table, The, **3:**305
Rowlandson masquerade representation, **4:**315
Dance of Death (Holbein the Younger), **5:**258, 259
Dance of Death (Wigman *Totentanz*), **3:**392, **4:**161, **6:**392
"dance of death and resurrection" (Jewish traditional), **3:**603, 605
Dance of Exorcism, **3:**341
Dance of Garuda, **3:**199
Dance of Machines, **3:**48, **5:**477
Dance of Our Pioneers (Ryan), **6:**247
"Dance of Phra Phirāp," **6:**151
Dance of Salomé, The, **3:**62
Dance of Silence (Hong), **3:**373
Dance of Society, The (DeGarmo), **5:**624, *625*
Dance of the Ages (film), **5:**583
Dance of the Ages (Shawn dance), **5:**586
Dance of the Black and Gold Sari, **5:**496
Dance of the City, **6:**87
Dance of the Cloud Gate, **2:**138
Dance of the Conquest. *See concheros*
Dance of the Court Lady, **4:**12
Dance of the Eight Manifestations, **1:**444
Dance of the Five Senses, **5:**46
Dance of the Forests, A (Soyinka), **6:**384
"Dance of the Furies" (*Don Juan*), **2:**34
"Dance of the Future, The" (Duncan), **2:**453
Dance of the Great Birds, **2:**231
Dance of the Great Tenochtitlan. *See concheros*
"Dance of the Hours" (*La Gioconda*), **2:**84, 187
Dance of the Hundred Animals, **2:**140
"Dance of the Jesters" (*Don Juan*), **2:**34
"Dance of the Little Swans" (*Swan Lake*), **3:**566, *566,* 567
Dance of the Moors, **3:**120
"Dance of the Moors and Christians." *See* "Moros y Cristianos"
Dance of Theodora, The, **2:**378

Dance of the People, **6:**81, 82
"Dance of the Seven Mannequins" (*Roberta*), **6:**276
"Dance of the Seven Veils" (*Salomé*), **2:**120, **3:**20, **4:**114, **5:**438, **6:**270
Dance of the Siren, **6:**317
Dance of Work and Play, **1:**421
"Dance of Yamoto" (*Kazuraki*), **3:**653
Dance on Disc (CD-ROM catalog), **4:**167
Dance-on-Line (web site), **2:**612
Dance Online, **6:**300
Dance Overture, **2:**357, **3:**391
Dance Pacific, **4:**627
Dance Pageant of Egypt, Greece, and India, **5:**494
Dance Panels, **2:**197
Dance Perspectives (journal), **6:**297
Dance Perspectives Foundation, **6:**298
Dance Players, **2:**161, **4:**10
dance poems, **3:**558
"Dance Portraits" (Nagrin solos), **4:**530
Dance Primer for Korean Children, A (Ch'oi), **2:**155
"Dancer and Musician" (Spencer), **3:**30
Dancer and Spheres (Calder), **1:**137
Dancer as Athlete, The (Shell), **2:**330
Dancer at the Bal Tabarin (Severini), **5:**180
Dance Repertory Theater, **3:**25, 399, **6:**88
dance research. *See specific authors and works; under specific countries*
Dance Research (journal), **3:**283, 285, 321, **6:**297
"Dance Research in Italy" (Sparti and Veroli), **3:**553
Dance Research Institute, China, **2:**148, 149, **6:**406
Dance Resources in Canadian Libraries (Giulmette and Collier), **2:**49
Dancers (film), **3:**664, **5:**408
Dancer's Adventure, The, **3:**129
Dancers and Musicians of Peliatan, The, **3:**645
Dancer's Book of Health, The (Vincent), **2:**330
Dancers' Collective, **4:**597
Dancers Company, The, **1:**234, **3:**623
Dancer's Complete Guide to Healthcare and a Long Career, The (eds. Ryan and Stephens), **2:**330
Dancers Congress (1928), **3:**626
Dancers' Emergency Association, **6:**89
Dancers En Route, **4:**649
Dancers' Guild, India, **2:**102
Dancer's Heritage, The (Guest), **3:**321
Dancers of Mercury: The Story of Ballet Rambert (Clarke), **3:**282
Dancers of the Australian Ballet. *See* Dancers Company, The
Dancers on a Plane (Johns), **3:**620
Dancer Tying Her Shoe (Degas), **5:**262
Dances, **2:**119
Dances at a Gathering, **2:**333–334, 444, **4:**248, **5:**104, 187, **6:**328, 340
appraisal of, **4:**614
Leland performance, **4:**618

Martins performance, **4:**273
McBride performance, **4:**345
Robbins choreography, **2:**333, **4:**5, 609, 614, *619,* **5:**358, *362,* 364, 365
in Royal Ballet repertory, **5:**417
Sibley performance, **5:**597
Verdy performance, **4:**617–618
Dances before the Wall, **6:**362
Dances Born from Need, **6:**67
Dance Screen, **6:**135
Dances for Isadora, **4:**199
Dances for Men, Women, and Moving Door, **1:**141
Dances for Women, **3:**447
Dances from Napoli, **2:**511
Dance Shongololo, Durban, **5:**656
Dances of Albion-Dark Night: Glad Day, **6:**146
Dances of Early California Days (Czarnowski), **6:**247
Dances of England and France (Dolmetsch), **3:**282
Dances of Galánta, **3:**318, **4:**380
"Dances of Haiti, The" (Dunham), **2:**458
Dances of Korea (Cho and Wolz), **4:**54
Dances of Love and Death, **4:**217
Dances of Many Nations (Esambayev program), **2:**520
Dances of Night, **6:**390
Dances of Spells, **1:**524
Dances of the Hungarians (Rearick), **3:**423
Dances of the Kawakiutl (film), **2:**601
Dances of the Three Jumps, **3:**410
Dances of the Three-Thousand-League Land (Heyman), **4:**54
Dances of Work and Play, **4:**130
Dance Sonata, **1:**421, **4:**130
Dance Songs, **6:**390
Dance-Sound-Word, **4:**89
Dances . . . Patrelle, **5:**399
Dance Spectrum (Taplin), **2:**50
dance spiritual, **6:**258
Dance-State Series, **6:**90
Dance Suite (Bartók), **3:**417
Dances Were Choreographed by László Seregi, The (film), **5:**569
Dances with Words and Music, **5:**59
dance symphonism. *See* symphonic ballet
Dance Symphony (Copland), **2:**196
Dance Symphony (Lopukhov). *See Magnificence of the Universe, The*
Dance Technique and Injury Prevention (Howse and Hancock), **2:**330
Dance Theater (Horton-Lewitzky-Bowne-Reynolds), **4:**156
Dance Theater of Detroit, **2:**566
Dance Theater Workshop, New York, **5:**559, **6:**251
Dance Theatre ERI (Turku), **2:**633
Dance Theatre Journal (British quarterly), **3:**283, 285
Dance Theatre of Harlem, **2:**334–336, **5:**60, **6:**139, 260
archives and library, **4:**167
Beloved, The, **3:**387
Biches, Les, **1:**450
Billy the Kid, **1:**453
character dances, **2:**108
de Lavallade choreography, **2:**367
Fagan choreography, **2:**567
Fall River Legend, **2:**374
Franklin staging of *Giselle,* **3:**88

Dance Theatre of Harlem,
    continued
    Giselle setting, **3:**183
    Le Clercq teaching post, **4:**137
    Mitchell founding, **4:**436
    Schönberg, Bessie, **5:**559
    Serenade, **5:***570*
    South African dance ties,
        5:657, 660
    Taras's *Firebird* production, **3:**4
    Troy Game, **4:**218
Dance Theatre Philippines, **5:**172
dance therapy. *See* dance and
    movement therapy
Dance! Therapy for Dancers (Dunn),
    2:330
Dance, Thought, and Times
    (Messerer), **4:**360
Dance Through Time, **5:**327
Dance Today in Canada, **2:**49
Dance to the Piper (de Mille), **2:**372,
    373, 374, **4:**262, **5:**299
Dance Touring Program, **6:**300
Dance Umbrella, London, **2:**450,
    3:275, 276
Dance Umbrella, South Africa,
    5:656
Dance Umbrella, Toronto, **6:**133
Dance Umdudo, Grahmstown,
    5:656
Dance Unit, **5:**637
Dance United Kingdom, **3:**280
Dance View (journal), **6:**297
Dance with a Torch, **3:**16
Dance without Tourism, **1:**524
Danceworks, **1:**215–216, *217*
Dancin' (musical), **3:**54, **6:**284, 327
Dancing (Frazer), **2:**570
Dancing (Grove), **3:**31
Dancing: A Man's Game (television
    program), **4:**3
"dancing actor" principle, **5:**466
*Dancing and Its Relation to
    Education and Social Life . . .*
    (Dodworth), **5:**627
*Dancing and Writing (On
    Hermaphrodites)*, **4:**22
dancing boys, **1:**26, 27, **6:**210, 305
dancing choir, **4:**212–213
dancing circle (orchestra), **5:**532
Dancing Class, The (Degas), **2:***362*
Dancing Doll, The, **4:**121, **5:**279
Dancing for Balanchine (Ashley),
    6:129
Dancing for Diaghilev (Sokolova),
    3:262, **5:**241, 636, 637
Dancing Girl (film), **2:**155
Dancing Ink, **4:**531
"Dancing in the Dark" *(The Band
    Wagon)*, **6:***275*
Dancing in the Mist, **5:**63, 597–598
*Dancing in the Streets of London
    and Paris, Continued in
    Stockholm and Sometimes
    Madrid*, **3:**447, **6:**152
Dancing Lesson, The (Cruikshank),
    2:*69, 70*
dancing manias. *See* dance
    epidemics
dancing master, **2:**336–341
    as assembly host, **1:**190
    masque productions, **4:**310
    musical accompaniment, **1:**5,
        4:507
    Negri documentation of
        contemporaries, **4:**580
    pochette stringed instrument,
        4:*509*
    professionalization, **5:**626
    on *révérence*, **5:**343–349

step description, **4:**684
*See also ballet de cour; specific
    countries and personal names;
    technical manuals*
Dancing Master, The (Essex), **5:**518,
    6:123, 176
Dancing Master, The (Playford;
    formerly *English Dancing
    Master*), **1:**91–92, **3:**254,
    5:200, 285, 520, 621
    colonial North American copies,
        6:231–232
    as Sharp influence, **3:**239
    See also Playford, John
*Dancing-Master; or, The Art of
    Dancing Explained* (Essex),
    2:527, **3:**262
Dancing Masters of America, **6:**290
Dancing on My Grave (Kirkland
    and Lawrence), **4:**25
"Dancing on the Ceiling" *(Ever
    Green)*, **4:**335
*Dancing on the Front Porch of
    Heaven*, **6:**44
Dancing Part Time, **5:***440*
Dancing School, The, **6:**40
Dancing Space, **2:**512
"Dancing Through Barriers" (trade
    mark) program, **2:**335
*Dancing through Danger: A Guide
    to the Prevention of Injury for
    the Amateur and Professional
    Dancer* (Featherstone and
    Allen), **2:**329–330
Dancing Times, The (publication),
    3:283
    Clarke editorship, **3:**285
    de Valois articles, **2:**398
    founding, **5:**351
    Guest as editorial adviser, **3:**321
    Richardson editorship, **3:**263,
        282, 284, **5:**351
Dancing Wor(l)ds, **4:**21–22
Dandré, Victor, **1:**313, 498, **5:**121,
    123, 124, 126, 678
Dandridge, Dorothy, **6:**255
Daneau, Lambert, **2:**167
Dangerous Games, **1:**349
Dangerous Liaisons, **1:**52, **5:**303
Dangeville, Madamoiselle, **3:**66
Danhoff, Christiaan, **5:**55
Dani (people), **3:**471–472, **5:**524
Daniel, David, *as contributor*,
    2:576–578, **4:**4–9
Daniel, Faye, **5:**55
Daniel, Monsieur, **6:**38
Daniel, Samuel, **4:**308, 310
Daniele, Graciela, **6:**286, 287, 288
Danieli, Fred, **1:**293, *452*, **3:**57,
    4:*227*, 608, **6:**265
Danielian, Leon, **1:**65, 306, 498,
    2:314, **3:**41
    academic teaching post, **6:**292
    Ballet Russe de Monte Carlo,
        1:298, 299, *300*, 301, 302
    Ballets Russes de Monte Carlo,
        1:314
Daniels, Bebe, **2:***614*
Daniels, Danny, **6:**286
Daniels, Margaret, *as contributor*,
    4:481–482
Daniels, Pauline, **2:**576, **4:**596
Danilova, Alexandra, **2:**277,
    341–343, **5:**208, 237, 241
    Apollo performance, **1:**95, **2:**342
    Ashton ballets, **1:**158, 437
    Aurora's Wedding performance,
        5:*611*
    Balanchine liasion, **1:**257, **2:**342

Ballet Russe de Monte Carlo,
    1:296, *296, 297*, 298, 299,
    300, 301, *301*, 302, **2:**342,
    342, **3:**22, *27*, **4:**610
Ballets Russes de Monte Carlo,
    1:310, 311, 312, **2:**342
Ballets Russes de Serge
    Diaghilev, **1:**256, **2:**342,
    410, 411
Beaton photograph of, **1:**395
Beau Danube performance,
    1:310, **2:**343
Christensen (William)
    association, **2:**160
Coppélia role, **2:**199, 201, 342,
    342, 343
Dallas Ballet, **6:**264
Dance Theatre of Harlem
    stagings, **2:**334
Danses Concertantes, **1:***261*
Denby profile of, **2:**375
Eglevsky dance partnership,
    2:479
English National Ballet guest
    performances, **2:**508
Franklin dance partnership,
    1:296, *297*, 302, **2:**342, *342*,
    3:88, *104*, **5:**107
Gaîté Parisienne, **3:**104, *104*
Harkness classes, **3:**342
Jacob's Pillow performances,
    3:571
as Legat (Nikolai) student, **4:**143
leg warmer invention, **5:**243
Metropolitan Ballet guest
    performance, **4:**380
Metropolitan Opera Ballet guest
    choreography, **4:**382
Mozartiana, **1:***258*, 307, **2:**342
musical theater, **6:**277
Nutcracker performances, **5:**15,
    512
Raymonda performances, **5:**322
Sonnambula performances, **5:**641
students, **2:**586
Swan Lake performance, **6:**32
Sylphides restaging, **6:**62
Danilova, Maria, **2:**464, **4:**36, 279,
    5:207, 453
Danilova, Natalia, **3:**125, **5:**472
Danilowa (Adam), **1:**9
*Danina, oder Jocko der
    Brazilianische Affe* (Taglioni
    ballet). *See Jocko, the
    Brazilian Ape*
Danish Association for the
    Promotion of Folk-Dancing.
    See Foreningen til
    Folkedansens Fremme
Danish Ballet Club, **5:**43
Danish Ballet Company. *See* Royal
    Danish Ballet
Danish Ballet School. *See* Royal
    Danish Ballet School
Danish Children's Ballet, **4:**246
Danish Dance History Archives,
    Copenhagen, **4:**160
Danish Folk Dancers, **2:**381
Danish Folklore Archives,
    Copenhagen, **4:**160
Danish Royal Ballet. *See* Royal
    Danish Ballet
Danish school. *See* ballet
    technique, major schools;
    Bournonville, August;
    Bournonville-skolen; Royal
    Danish Ballet
Dankevich, Konstantin, **6:**225
d'Annunzio, Gabriele d', **2:**360,
    3:20, **5:**438, 439

Danny Grossman Dance
    Company, **2:**40
Danovschi, Oleg, **2:**343–344, **5:**384,
    386, 387
    National Competition for Young
        Dancers, **5:**390
Dans (magazine), **6:**60
Dansa a Catalunya, La (Capmany),
    5:676
Dans à Dal (line dance), **2:***555*
Dansbeskrivningar (Heikel), **2:**631
Danscentrum, **6:**45
Danscompany, The, **4:**306
Dansconcept, **1:**414
Danscore (Saunders notation
    system), **4:**690
Danse (Carpeaux), **1:**126
Danse (Graham solo), **3:**213
Danse, La (Bourdelle), **1:**502
Danse, La (Genée performance),
    3:129
Danse, La (Picasso), **5:**192–193
Danse, ou Les dieux de l'Opéra, La
    (Berchoux), **2:**464
Danse I and II, La (Matisse), **1:**35,
    130, 135, **4:**330, 331, *331*
Danse Américaine, **2:**378, **5:**587
Danse ancienne et moderne, La
    (Cahusac), **3:**84, **4:**698
Danse Assyrienne. See Dance with a
    Torch
Danse au Canada (journal), **2:**49
Danse au théâtre, La (Bernay),
    6:128
Danse Baroque Toronto, **5:**327
Danse Blanche, La (Fuller dance),
    3:92
Danse Cité, Montreal, **4:**73
Danse classique, La (Meunier),
    4:688
Danse Creation, **3:**84
Danse de Pierrot en Panniers, **5:**319
danse des cheveux, **4:**408, 415
danse du barbier, **2:**35
Danse du Feu, La. See Fire Dance
danse du ventre (belly dance),
    2:344–346, **4:**406, 409, 410,
    411, 662–663
    Algeria, **1:**40, 41
    Chicago World's Columbian
        Exposition (1893), **2:**572
    Egypt, **2:**344–345, 345–346, *345*,
        494–495, *494–495*, **4:***403*,
        662–663
    flamenco link, **3:**6
    Iranian comic, **3:***514*
    kheliji similarity, **1:**102
    Lebanon, **4:**135
    Martinique and Guadeloupe,
        2:64
    Orientalism, **5:**45
    Ouled Naïl dancers, **4:**409, **5:**50
    scholarship, **4:**415–416
    Turkey, **6:**211
Danse en Voyage, La, **5:**390
Danse et Culture, **3:**76
Danse et les ballets, La (Castil-
    Blaze), **3:**84
Danse grecque antique, La
    (Prudhommeau), **3:**302
Danse grecque antique, La
    (Séchan), **3:**302
*Danse grecque antique d'après les
    monuments figurés*
    (Emmanuel), **3:**302
Danse Iberienne, **1:**115
danse infernale (The Firebird), **3:**3
danse languide, **3:**211
danse macabre. See Dance of Death
Danse Macabre, **5:**650

Danse Macabre (film), **1:**483, **5:**58
danse noble. See ballets de cour
Danse Noble, **1:**484
"danse normande," **2:**85
Danseorganisationernes Fællersråd, **2:**381
danse orientale. See danse du ventre
Danser (publication), **3:**85
Danseries, Les, **2:**35
Danse Sacrée et Danse Profane, **2:**397, 399
Dansescenen, **2:**386
Danses Concertantes, 298, **1:**349, 461, **2:**342, 376, **5:**225, **6:**6
  Balanchine productions, **1:**256, *261,* 298, *298,* **4:**602
  Balanchine revival, **4:**621
  Franklin performance, **3:**88
  Georgiadis design, **3:**136
  MacMillan choreography, **4:**240, **5:**431
Danses de Cour, **4:**623
Danses Lumineuses, **6:**161
Danses pour l'année (Dezais), **2:**256
Danses Slaves et Tziganes, **1:**311
Danses sur la Musique de Chopin, **3:**16
danse taquetée, **2:**502
Danse traditionelle au Québec, La (Séguin), **2:**49
Danse traditionelle dans l'est du Canada, La: Quadrilles et cotillons (Voyer), **2:**49
Danseur, Le, **1:**407
Danseur du Roi, Le, **3:**5, **5:**500
danseur noble
  defined, **2:**106, 107
  distinctive costume, **2:**241, *243,* 244
  Eglevsky as foremost (1930s), **2:**479
danseur sérieux, distinctive costume, **2:**239
danseuse, distinctive costume, **2:**239
danseuse en travesti. See travesty
Danseuses Viennoises, Les, **2:**37, 405, **6:**334, 335–336, *335*
danse vivante technique, **3:**83
Dansgille, **1:**327
Dansgroep Léa Daan, **1:**411
Danske Folkedansere. *See* Danish Folk Dancers
Danskroniek (magazine), **4:**599
Dansmuseet, Stockholm. *See* Dance Museum
Dansnöjen genom tiderna (Beck-Friis, Blomkvist, Nordenfelt), **1:**400
Dansomanie, La, **1:**237, **2:**264, 389, **3:**68, 118, 119, **4:**588, **5:**90, 149, **6:**71, 333
  Cramér-Skeaping revival, **6:**47, *47*
  waltz choreography, **6:**360
Dans tidningen (magazine), **6:**50
Danstoneel, **1:**411
Dansu waku (journal), **3:**591
Dante, Nicholas, **1:**419
Dante Alighieri, **1:**149, **2:**166, **3:**20
Dantes, Theo, **5:**654
Dante Sonata, **1:**149, 150, **2:**583, **4:**114, 336, **5:**639
Danton, Henry, **1:**150, **4:**380, **6:**64, 323
D'Antuono, Eleanor, **1:**73, 302, **4:**232
Dantzari Dantza, **1:**376
Dantzig, Rudi van, **1:**241, **2:**39, 58, **346–348,** 350, 361, **3:**343, **4:**600, **5:**301, 555, 565
  Collective Symphony, **4:**596

Dutch National Ballet, **2:**469, 470, **4:**593
  Hart (Evelyn) roles, **3:**344
  Netherlands Ballet, **4:**600
  Netherlands Dance Theater, **4:**601
  Royal Danish Ballet guest choreography, **5:**431
  Royal Winnipeg Ballet guest productions, **5:**436
  Swan Lake, **2:**470, **4:**593
D.A.N.Z. (Dance Aotearoa New Zealand), **4:**629
danza, **2:**62, **5:**274, 667, 669
Danza Abierta, **1:**113, **2:**281
Danza Antiqua, **1:**519
Danza come modo di essere (Ruskaja), **5:**441
Danza Contemporánea de Cuba, **2:**280, 281
Danza del Abago, **2:**476
danza de la muerte. See Dance of Death
Danza de la Muerte (Limón work), **4:**649
"Danza de las Cintas," **4:***385*
Danza del Ojos Verdes, La, **1:**115
Danza de los Abagos de Cumbas, **2:**476
"Danza del Santissimo Nacimiento de Nuetro Señor" (Suárez de Robles), **5:**667
Danza de Matlachines, **4:**327, 328
Danza Estudio, **2:**397
"Danza General," **5:**667
Danzahoy, **6:**324, 325, *325*
Danza italiana, La (journal), **3:**447, 555
Danza Libre, **2:**281
Danza Libre Universitaria, **4:**397
Danza Lorca, **5:**654
Danza, Luz, Sonidos, **6:**302
Danzantes de Pujili, **2:**476
Danza por Correro, **2:**110
Danza Propettiva, **1:**446
danzas de cascabeles, **5:**669
Danzas Eslavas, **1:**315
Danza '75 (Venice), **3:**550–551
Danza Sì (journal), **3:**554
Danzas populares argentinas, Las (Vega), **1:**110
Danza y Rito, 2448
danzón, **2:**275, 276, 430–431, **3:**320
Danzón Cubano, **2:**196
Daoism
  aesthetics, **1:**16, 17, **2:**129
  as Dunn (Robert Ellis) influence, **2:**461
  as Hawkins influence, **3:**349
Daphne, **3:**51
Daphnis and Céphise, **1:**36
Daphnis and Chloe
  Ashton production, **1:**152, *153,* **2:**44, **5:**416
    Fonteyn performance, **3:**42, 44
  Cranko production, **2:**266, **5:**316
  Field performance, **2:**590
  Grant performance, **3:***236,* 237
  Kovačev choreography, **2:**11
  Littlefield production, **4:**210
  Murphy choreography, **6:**56
  Tetley production, **4:**1, **5:**316, **6:**146
  See also Daphnis et Chloë
Daphnis et Alcimadure, **3:**117
Daphnis et Chloë
  Bakst design, **1:**254, **2:**407
  choreographers, **5:**316
  Fokine production for Diaghilev, **1:**247, 316, 322, 482, **3:**18, 19, **4:**641, **5:**113, 315

  Fokine unproduced scenario, **3:**14, 15, 19, **5:**541, **6:**541
  Neumeier production, **5:**316
  Ólafsdóttir production, **3:**437
  as pastoral ballet, **5:**113
  Ravel score, **1:**152, 316, **2:**408, **3:**19, **4:**515, 516, **5:**315
  Skibine choreography, **3:**342, **5:***93,* 605
Daphnis et Eglé (Rameau), **5:**307
DaPron, Louis, **5:**21
daqq al-ḥabb, **4:**489
d'Aquino, Iria, *as contributor,* **2:**58–59
Dar, Noa, **3:**534
Darago, Vicente, **1:**109–110
Darangan Cultural Troupe, **5:**172
Darbes, Johannes, **3:**105
Darbois, Dominique, *as photographer,* **6:**15
Darby, Eileen, *as photographer,* **6:**277, 280
Darby, Eyrick, **3:**574
Darciel, Elsa (also Dewette), **1:**410–411
D'Arcy, Mary, **6:**287
Dardanus (Rameau), **1:**365, **3:**116, 119, **5:**40, 306, 307, **6:**331
Darden, Steve, *as contributor,* **4:**578–579
D'Argo, Enrichetta, **1:**207
Darius, Adan (Harvey Krekfets), **1:**289
darjah dance, **4:**412, 417
Dark Diamond, The (Adolphe opera), **1:**9
Dark Elegies, **1:**66, **2:348–349**
  Chase performance, **2:**112
  de Mille performance, **2:***348,* 372
  Gilmour performance, **3:**174
  Laing performance, **4:**109, 110
  Lloyd pas de deux, **4:**215
  Mahler's *Kindertotenlieder,* **2:**348, 349, **5:**299, **6:**197
  modern dance costuming, **2:**245
  in National Ballet of Canada repertory, **2:**37, **4:**541
  in Rambert Company repertory, **5:**299, 300, 301, 303, 305
  Tudor choreography, **6:**197, 198, 202, 203
  Tudor performance, **6:***198*
  van Praagh role, **6:**312
  Wilson (Sallie) performance, **6:**402
Dark Eyes (film), **1:**367
Dark Forest, The, **4:**627
Darkling, The, **4:**238, **5:**435
Dark Meadow, **2:349,** **3:**217, 349, **4:**659
Dark Night of the Soul (de la Cruz), **1:**405
Dark Rhythms, **5:**256
Darktown Follies, **6:**256
Dark Waves, **4:**625, *626*
Darmstadt State Theater, **3:**151
Darpena Academy of the Performing Arts, **4:**159, **5:**522
Darrell, Peter, **1:**370, **2:349–350,** **4:**667, **5:**43, 301, 565
  Chéri, **5:**565
  Home, **5:**564
  Jeux, **2:**361
  Prisoners, The, **5:**564
  Scottish Ballet, **5:**564
  Sun into Darkness, **5:**564
  Tales of Hoffmann, **1:**73, **2:**350, **4:**117

Western Theatre Ballet, **3:**270, **4:**585
Darsonval, Lycette, **1:**348, **2:350–351,** **4:**354
  Béjart association, **1:**403
  Don Quixote performance, **2:**440
  Lifar association, **4:**184
  Palais de Cristal performance, **2:**351, **6:**65
  Paris Opera Ballet, **5:**95, 96
  Sylvia version, **5:**96, **6:**64
Dartington Hall, Devon, **1:**51, **2:**283, **3:**277, 628–629, **4:**93
  Jooss-Leeder Dance School, **4:**96, 103, 140
  as Laban refuge, **4:**93–94, 477
Darwin, Australia, **1:**217
Darwin, Charles, **1:**127, 128, **3:**30
Das, Deba Prasad, **3:**508, **4:**247, **5:**23
Das, Pankajcharan, **4:**62, 247
Das, Prahlad, **2:**102
Daśarūpa (Indian text), **3:**469
Das Blümenmädchen im Elsass, **5:**499
dāsiāṭṭam. See bharata nāṭyam
Dasté, Jean, **4:**425
D'Auban, John, **5:**72, 605, **6:**268
Daubeny, Peter, **5:**296
Dauberval, Jean, **1:**154, 284, 455, **2:**269, **351–354,** 366, **3:**66, 67, 117, 546, **4:**122, **5:**147
  Académie Royale de Danse membership, **3:**81
  Allard relationship, **1:**43, **2:**352, *353*
  Ashton tribute to, **2:**597
  Aumer association, **1:**201, 202, **2:**353, 354
  Comédie Française, **3:**66
  D'Egville association, **2:**353, 363, 364, 389
  Didelot association, **2:**413
  English dance choreography, **3:**256, 257–258, 259
  Gardel (Maximilien) association, **3:**117
  Hus (Eugène) as assistant, **3:**426
  Noverre on, **4:**150, **5:**105
  Noverre rivalry, **4:**696
  Paris Opera Ballet, **2:**352, **5:**89
  pas de deux, **5:**105
  as Petipa (Marius) influence, **5:**149
  Psyché et l'Amour version, **5:**270
  realistic libretti, **4:**174–175
  students, **1:**460, **2:**354, 363
  Stuttgart Ballet, **6:**9
  Swedish opera-ballet dancer training, **6:**39
  Viganò (Salvatore) association, **6:**337
  See also Fille Mal Gardée, La
Daughter of Castile, A, **3:**187
Daughter of Eve, A, **2:**397
Daughter of the Snow, **4:**430
Daughter of Virtue, **4:**214
Daughters of the Lonesome Isle, **2:**520
Daujotytė, Kira, **4:**208
Daumer, Friedrich, **4:**179
Daumier, Honoré, **2:**71
Da un'altra faccia del tempo, **2:**564
Dausset, Carmen ("Carmencita"), **1:***127*
Dauty, François-Édouard, **2:**198
Davenant, Charles, **5:**282
Davenant, William, **3:**622, **4:**309, **5:**251
Davenport, Mary, **3:**519

David, **3:**420, **4:**153
David (Hebrew scriptures), **1:**20
  dance references, **1:**448, **2:**165,
  3:526
David, Félicien, **4:**341, 342, **5:**137
David, Hal, **1:**419
David, Jacques-Louis, **1:**126, **5:**89
David and Bathsheba (film), **6:**327
David and Goliath, **5:**439
David of Sasun, **1:**122
Davidson, Robert, *as contributor,*
  1:476–477
Davidsson, Olafur, **3:**434, 436
David's Victory over Goliath, **2:**176
David Triomphant, **2:**113, **4:**184,
  5:95
Davies, Dudley, **5:**53, 653–654
Davies, Grayham, **5:**659
Davies, Iva, **4:**479
Davies, J. G., *as contributor,*
  2:162–164
Davies, John, **2:**254, 256, **5:**619
Davies, Marion, **6:**371
Davies, Martha Hill. *See* Hill,
  Martha
Davies, Moll, **5:**251
Davies, Peter Maxwell, **1:**52, **3:**13,
  4:219
Davies, Siobhan, **1:**50, **2:354–355,**
  514, **4:**217, **5:**302, 305
  choreographic style, **3:**274, **4:**218
  London Contemporary Dance
  Theatre, **2:**354, 355, **3:**273,
  4:218, *219*
  Second Stride, **3:**273–274
Davioud, Gabriel, **6:**161
Davis, Carl, **4:**668
Davis, Charlie (Chuck), **6:**257, 258
Davis, Coleen, **2:**470, *470*
Davis, Donald, **1:**450
Davis, Gussie L., **6:**255
Davis, Joan, **3:**520
Davis, John Freeman, **2:**47
Davis, Lynda, **3:**520
Davis, Martha, **2:**320, **4:**104
Davis, Martha Ellen
  as contributor, **2:**429–433
  as photographer, **2:**61, 430, 431
Davis, Mike, *as photographer,* 509,
  2:508
Davis, Peter Maxwell, **5:**433
Davis, Sammy, Jr., **3:**367
Davis, Toots, **6:**256
Davis, William, **2:**288, **6:**402
davluri dance, **3:**134
Davydov, Yuri, **6:**115
Dawn, **2:**97, **4:**447
Dawn, The (group), **5:**448, 449
Dawn Dazzled Door, **3:**350
Dawn in New York, **3:**404
Dawson, Nancy, **3:**378
Day (Hodler), **1:**129
Day, Ernestine, **2:**379
Day, Jennifer, **4:**679
Day, Mary, **2:**356, **6:**264, 366–367
Dayak (people), **3:**471–472, 504,
  5:524
Day at the Carnival in Venice, A,
  6:73
Daydé, Bernard, **1:**404, **3:**362, **5:**60,
  551, **6:**64
Daydé, Liane, **1:**247, 251, **5:**91, 96
Day in a Southern Port, A,
  4:113–114
*Day in Hollywood, A Night in the
  Ukraine* (musical), **6:**204, 286
Day Is Breaking, **5:**287
Day of Madness, A, **2:**499, **5:**469
Day of the Kings (January 6),
  1:526–527
Day on a Ship, A, **4:**444

Day on Earth, **2:356–357,**
  3:402–403, **4:**198
  Labanotation example, **4:**97
Day Sin, **1:**540
Days of Glory (film), **6:**183
Daystar (Rosalie Jones), **4:**555
Dayton Ballet, **2:357–358,** **6:**264
Dayton Contemporary Dance
  Company, **2:**358, **6:**264
Dazie, Mademoiselle, **6:**268, 269
de. *For names with this prefix not
  found below, see main element*
Dead Ballerinas, **4:**627
Dead Dreams of Monochrome Men,
  2:611, **3:**274
Dea del Valhalla, La, **1:**500, **2:**82
Deadly Sins, **4:**115
*Dead Sea, The-Vienna Waltz and
  Ghosts,* **5:**34
Deafman Glance (Wilson opera),
  6:440
Deakin, Irving, **5:**512
Deakin University—Rusden
  Campus, Australia, **1:**212
de Alaiza, Candi, *as contributor,*
  1:376–378
Dean, Beth, **1:**212
Dean, Christopher. *See* Torvill and
  Dean
Dean, Dora, **2:**25
Dean, Laura, **2:**299, **358–360,** 608,
  5:24
  ADF/Tokyo, **1:**80
  American Music Festival (1988),
  4:623
  avant-garde dance, **1:**246
  Joffrey Ballet choreography,
  2:359, **3:**615, 616, 617
  Orientalism, **5:**46
Dean Dance and Musician
  Foundation. *See* Laura Dean
  Dancers and Musicians
Deane, Derek, **2:**513, 514, **3:**269,
  5:401
De Angelo, Ann Marie, **3:***612*
*Dean Martin Presents the
  Golddiggers* (television show),
  6:204
Dean Martin Show, The (television
  program), **1:**419
De architectura, **4:**187
Dearly, Max, **1:**95, **4:***523*
De arte gymnastica (Mercurialis),
  4:460
De arte saltandi (Domenico), **1:**351
Death. *See* Dance of Death
Death, **3:**469
Death and King's Horseman
  (Soyinka), **6:**384
Death and the Maiden, **1:**66, **2:**374,
  3:391–392, 418, **4:**667, **5:**300
Death in Venice (Britten opera),
  1:157, **5:**37
Death in Venice (Flindt ballet),
  3:13, **6:**95
Death in Venice (Mann novel),
  1:157, **6:**56
Death of Adonis, The, **5:**584, *584*
Death of Klinghoffer, The (Adams
  opera), **1:**411, **4:**472
Deaths and Entrances, **2:**285, **360,**
  3:*214,* 216, 349, **4:**130
  program notes, **4:**177
Death Wedding, **3:**418
Deaver, Sherri, **4:**415
Debalke, Tsegaye, **2:**530
de Basil, Colonel Wassily, **1:**110,
  149, 367, 466, **5:**17, **6:**182
  co-founding of Ballets Russes de
  Monte Carlo, **1:**308, **4:**33
  conflict with Blum, **1:**295

conflict with Massine, **1:**295,
  312–313
  death, **1:**316
  Massine choreographic copyright
  suits, **1:**312
  rival Ballet Russe company,
  1:296, 311, 313
  See also Ballets Russes de Monte
  Carlos
Debatte, Anne Marie, **3:**84
debka, **3:**529.
  See also dabkah
Debka Dayagim, **3:**529
Deboo, Astad, **3:**469
Debret, François, **6:**158–159, *158*
Debucourt, Philibert, **2:**68
Deburau, Charles, **5:**176
Deburau, Jean Gaspard, **4:**424,
  425, 426
Debureau, Gaspard, **3:**75
Debussy, Claude, **1:**82, 479,
  2:360–361, 573, **5:**367, 520,
  526, **6:**111
  Diaghilev collaboration, **1:**316,
  2:360, 406, 408, **4:**515–516
  Falla friendship, **2:**567, 568
  Jeux score, **1:**320, 321, 325, 326,
  2:361, 408, 427, **4:**641,
  642, 643
  Martyre de Saint-Sébastien score,
  2:360, **3:**20, **5:**438
  Monotones II orchestration,
  4:452
  musical idiom, **4:**516
  Satie association, **5:**525
  Stravinsky friendship, **6:**3, 5
  Suite Bergamasque score, **1:**428
  *See also Prélude à l'Après-midi
  d'un Faune*
Débutante, La, **1:**477, **5:**140
Decade, **1:**421, **3:**401, **4:**130
Decameron (Boccaccio), **4:**501
DeCarlo, Yvonne, **1:**419
de Caro, Maria, **5:**207
Decay of Lying, The, **4:**625
Deceived Village Doctor, The, **5:**452
Decembrist Revolution, **5:**453, 454
Decent of Hebe, The, **5:**560
Dechuli, P. L., **5:**449
De civilitate morum puerilium
  (Erasmus), **3:**281
Déclamation théâtrale, La, **2:**465
Decombe, François. *See* Albert,
  Monsieur
decor, ballet. *See* scenic design
DeCouflé, Philippe, **2:**607, 610–611
Decroux, Étienne, **3:**75, **4:**423,
  424–425
Dedalo, **6:**338
de doi schimbat dances, **5:**380–381
Dedović, Vlasto, **6:**437
Deege, Gisela, **1:**436, **3:**318
Deep End, The, **6:**95
Deep in My Heart (film), **2:**109,
  6:183
Deep Song, **3:**212, 213
"Deer Dance," **1:**415, **4:**396, 551,
  5:272, **6:**416
Deer Dance (Bhutan), **1:**444, **2:**225
Deer-Hunting Dance, **2:**228
Deering, Jane, **4:**209
Defago, Jean-Jacques, **3:***153*
De Fanti, Luciana, **3:**553
Defoe, Daniel, **4:**315
de Garmo, William B., **2:**339, **5:**624
Degas, Edgar, **1:**6, *126,* 127–128,
  437, **2:361–363,** 480, **5:**191,
  241, **6:**181
  effects of photography on,
  5:180, *180*
  Perrot as subject, **5:**141

prints and drawings, **5:**259,
  262, *262*
Degen, Arsen B., **5:**486
  as contributor, **6:**341–342
De generatione animalium
  (Aristotle), **4:**13
de Glehn, Wilfred, **3:**656
de Groat, Andy, **6:**401
D'Egville, James Harvey, **2:**175,
  353, **363–365,** 389, 414, 435,
  5:70
  ballets d'action, **3:**259
  dance school, **3:**279
  Fille Mal Gardée productions,
  2:595
D'Egville, Peter, **2:**363
De Haven, Mr. and Mrs. Carter,
  6:318
de Hesse, Jean-Baptiste, **1:**288,
  2:365–366, 594, **3:**66
Dehn, Mura, **2:**579
De humani corporis fabrica
  (Vesalius), **4:**14
De incessu animalium (Aristotle),
  4:13
Deipnosophists, The (Athenaeus),
  1:20, **4:**44
Deitering, Carolyn, **4:**213
Déjà Vu, **4:**230, *230*
Déjazet, Virginie, **1:**9
Déjeuner sur l'Herbe, Le, **5:**163
de Jong, Bettie, **2:**526, 605
de Keersmaeker, Anne Teresa, **1:**25,
  403, 412, 414, **2:**611
Dekkhr, Kekso, **5:***683*
de Kooning, Elaine, **1:**138, **2:**286
de Kooning, Willem, **1:**138, 139,
  2:286, 375–376
De Koven, Reginald, **6:**269
Delacroix, Eugène, **3:**180, **5:**141
De la danza (Gasch), **5:**676
de la Fay, Julie Alix, **1:**503
de La Gorce, Jérôme, *as
  contributor,* **1:**425–426, 497,
  2:33–34, **3:**184, 450–451,
  4:234–236, 475, **5:**305–307
Delakova, Katya, **1:**431, **3:**605
Delalande, Michel-Richard, **1:**364,
  2:34
Delamater, Jerome, *as contributor,*
  2:612–621, **3:**54–55, **4:**2–4,
  10–11, **5:**408
Del amor y de la Muerte, **3:**226
Deland, Louis Joseph, **6:**40
Delannoy, Marcel, **5:**237
De La Pena, George, **6:**286
de Lappe, Gemze, **2:**374, **4:**214,
  6:278
de Lara, Reyes, **1:**217
Delarova, Eugénie, **1:**296, **3:**104,
  4:321, 322
Delasalle, Sandy, **1:**375
De la saltation théâtrale (Aulmaye),
  3:84
de la Torre Bueno, J. R., **6:**298
Delaunay, Sonia and Robert, **5:**544
de Lavallade, Carmen, **2:366–367**
  African-American music, **4:**520
  as Ailey dance partner, **1:**55, *55,*
  2:367, *367*
  Horton dance company, **3:**387,
  387, **4:**156, 441
  Jacob's Pillow performance,
  3:571
  Metropolitan Opera Ballet, **4:**382
  Rainbow 'Round My Shoulder
  performance, **4:***346*
Delavalle, Hugo, **5:**395
Deldevez, Édouard, **2:**14, 204,
  4:341, 428, 429, 514, **5:**85
Deldevez, Marie-Ernest, **5:**150

Delerue, George, **5:**422
De l'état actuel de la danse (Saint-Léon), **5:**500
Delf, Harry (The Kid Romeo), **6:**316
Delfau, André, **5:**60
Delfini, Laura, **3:**558
del Frate, Bice, **3:**51
Delgado Martínez, César, *as contributor,* **2:**194–195, **4:**328–329, 395–398
Delibes, Léo, **1:**9, 518, **2:**207, **367–369, 5:**160
  Balanchine ballets, **4:**611
  Corsaire music, **4:**343
  Fiammetta score collaboration, **4:**429
  Fille Mal Gardée score, **2:**594, 596
  "Jardin Animé" score *(Le Corsaire),* **2:**207, 368
  Minkus collaborations, **4:**429, 514
  St. Denis choreography, **5:**288
  Saint-Léon collaboration, **5:**501, 502
  Soir de Fête score, **5:**690
  success as ballet and opera composer, **4:**514
  See also Coppélia; Sylvia
Delibes Divertissements, **4:**615
Délices, **3:**77, 79
Deliciae theatrales (Lambranzi), **2:**190
Deli Commedia (videodance), **2:**294, 607
Délire d'un Peintre, ou Le Portrain Animé, La, **1:**477, **2:**95, **4:**142, 453, **5:**139, 277
Delisle, Mademoiselle, **2:**465
Delius, Frederick, **1:**67, 148, **4:**113, **5:**392, 397, **6:**199
della Bella, Stefano, **2:**238, **3:**184, **5:**1, 2, *2,* 260
Della Casa, Giovanni, **5:**324
Della nobiltà di dame (Caroso). *See Nobiltà di dame*
dell'Ara, Ugo, **2:**201, **369–370, 3:**60, 553, **5:**529
della Robbia, Luca, **2:**166
Della Seta, Fabrizio, **3:**556
Della tragedia antica e moderna (Martello), **3:**546
Deller, Florian, **4:**695, **5:**371
Dell'Era, Antonietta, **5:**9, 94, 106
Dellert, Kjerstin, **6:**48
Dello Joio, Norman, **3:**218, 384, **4:**10, 518, **5:**568
Delman, Judith, **4:**605
Delmar, Frank, **5:**585
Delmar, John, **5:**585
Delnira Agustini, **6:**302
DeLoatch, Gary, **1:**59, 60
de Los Angeles, Victoria, **2:**280
Delos, Greece, **2:**270
Delouche, Dominique, **2:**114
De Louis, Sara, **3:***8*
de Loutherbourg, Philip James. *See* Loutherbourg, Phillipe Jacques de
Delphic Festival, Greece, **3:**300
Delphin, Marguerite, **1:**237
Delsarte, François, **1:**128, **6:**240
  as Bodenwieser influence, **1:**466, 467, 468
  as free dance movement influence, **1:**239, **2:**452, **3:**160
  as Jaques-Dalcroze influence, **3:**594, 595
  life and career, **2:**370–371
  students, **1:**470, **2:**316

Delsarte system of expression, **1:**128, **2:370–372, 3:**211
  Duncan, Isadora, **2:**452–453
  movement classification, **4:**439
  as St. Denis influence, **5:**490, 491, 494
  as Shawn influence, **5:**584, 586, *586*
  in United States, **2:**371–372, **6:**240, 295
  as Wayburn influence, **6:**371
Delsartism. *See* Delsart system of expression
"Delsartismus," **1:**239
Delta, **2:**359, **6:**213
del Tredici, David, **4:**545
Déluge (television production), **6:**133
Delvaux, Louise, **1:**411
Delvaux, Paul, **1:**305
Delza, Sophia, *as contributor,* **2:**141–144, **4:**350
Demagogue, The (El Demagogo), **1:**524, **4:**392–393
Demama, Kol, **3:**532
De Manthe, Bernard, **1:**4
DeMarco, Tony, **1:**518, **4:**434
De Marco, Tony and Renée, **6:**318
de Maria, Warren, **1:**232
de Martino, Ernesto, **6:**104
de Masson, Paul, **1:**235
Demby, Constance, **4:**21
Demcsák, Ottó, **3:**330
De Meaux, Jean, **6:**256
Demeney, G., **1:**130
Dementev, Aleksandr, **5:**460
Dementev, Anatoly, **5:**460, 472
Demery, Felix, **6:**128
Demeter, **1:**456, **3:**133
Demeter (mythic), **3:**288
Demetrios of Skepsis, **2:**270
de Meyer, Adolf, **5:**182, *182,* 183, 187
de Mey, Michèle Anne, **1:**412
demi-caractère
  Christensen (Willam) use of, **2:**161
  Danielian (Leon) roles, **2:**341
  defined, **2:**106, 107
  de Valois performances, **2:**399
  distinctive costume, **2:**239, 241
  Douvillier (Madame Placide) roles, **2:**443
  Farron roles, **2:**578
  Franca roles, **3:**62
  Gore roles, **3:**202
  Grant roles, **3:**236–237, **4:**544
  Helpmann roles, **3:**355
  Italian popularity, **3:**545
  Kehlet roles, **3:**667–668
  Kshessinska (Matilda) roles, **4:**68
  Loring roles, **4:**227
  Massine ballets, **4:***316,* 317, 319
  Sand (Inge) roles, **5:**511
  Scarpetta, La, **5:**501
  Schaufuss (Peter) roles, **5:**554
  Villella roles, **4:**620
Demidov, Alexander P., **5:**483
  as contributor, **1:**440–441, **2:**206–208, **5:**9–12, **6:**29–31
de Mille, Agnes, **1:**421, 497, **2:**269, **372–375, 3:**385, 571, **5:**300, 386
  American Ballet Theater, **1:**65, 66, 67–68, 73, **2:**367, 373–374
  archival materials, **4:**167
  Black Crook revival, **1:**457, **2:**372, **6:**267
  Bolm association, **1:**483
  Boston Ballet choreography, **2:**374, **6:**398

Broadway musicals, **1:**482, **2:**251, 373, **5:**369, **6:**278–279, 281, 283, 288
  character dances, **2:**108
  choreography for Jooss, **3:**629
  Copland score, **2:**196, 197, 198
  Dance Repertory Theater, **3:**399, **6:**88
  Dark Elegies performance, **2:**372, **3:***348*
  on director-choreographers, **6:**281
  on Franklin, **3:**88
  Hollywood musicals, **2:**618
  Jamison discovery, **3:**577
  Juilliard dance division, **5:**561
  Koslov training, **4:**56
  Litz association, **4:**213
  on Maracci, **4:**262
  Oklahoma! choreography as theatrical dance milestone, **6:**248, 278, *278*
  as photographic subject, **5:***183*
  on *Primitive Mysteries,* **5:***253*
  Rambert Dance Company, **2:**372, **5:**299
  Royal Winnipeg Ballet productions, **2:**374, 375, **5:**435
  Shearer (Sybil) association, **5:**589
  students, **1:**11, **6:**312
  Tally-Ho, **2:**112, 373, **4:**110
  television performances and productions, **6:**137, 138, 197
  Three Virgins and a Devil, **2:***373,* **6:**278
  Tudor association, **6:**195, 197
  Weidman association, **6:**376
  Wilson (Sallie) roles, **6:**402
  See also Fall River Legend; Rodeo
De Mille, Cecil B., **2:**372, **4:**56, **6:**243
de Mille, William Churchill, **2:**372
demi-plié. See plié
demi-pointes. See pointe work
Demmenie, Lizzy, **5:**531
Demmy, Lawrence, **4:**432
Demoazela Mãriutza, **5:**385
Demoiselles de la Nuit, Les, **1:**305, **3:**74, **5:**163, 164
Demon, The, **2:**97, **3:**391, **6:**66
Demon Machine, The, **1:**211
de Moor, Teda, **5:**657
de Moroda, Friderica, **6:**128
de Mosa, Noëlle, **3:**628, 629, *630*
Demosthenes, **3:**293, **4:**44
De mota animalium (Borelli), **4:**14
Dempster, Carol, **5:**494
Dempster, Elizabeth, **1:**218
Dempster, Stuart, **2:**296
De musica (Plutarch), **1:**2
Demuth, Norman, **3:**508, 511
Denard, Michaël, **2:**199, **3:**156, **5:**97
  Apollo, **1:**96
  Firebird, The, **1:**405, **3:**3
  Grand Cirque performance, **4:**185
  Romeo and Juliet performance, **5:**396
Denby, Edwin, **2:**145, **375–376, 5:**184, 265, **6:**85, 199, 202, 352
  on Argentinita, **1:**117
  on Ashton, **1:**155
  on Baby Laurence, **1:**252
  on Balanchine, **1:**261, 299
  on Chagall set designs, **1:**136
  on dance aesthetics, **1:**25
  on Danilova's *Coppélia* performance, **2:**201
  as dean of American dance criticism, **6:**300

on Dollar, **2:**426
  on filmed dance, 599
  on Fonteyn, **3:**42
  on Hawkins, **3:**349
  intrinsic school of dance criticism, **6:**300
  on *Jardin aux Lilas,* **3:**597
  on Nijinska's *Les Noces* choreography, **2:**375, **4:**658–659
  on *On Stage!,* **4:**10
  on Robbins's *Dances at a Gathering,* **5:**365
  on St. Denis, **5:**497
  on *Sleeping Beauty,* **5:**612
  on Youskevitch's dance style, **6:**424
Déné (people), **4:**573
dengaku, **3:**584, **584,** 585, **4:**83
Deng Kei-fu, **6:***82*
Deng Yu-lin, *as photographer,* **6:**82
Denham, Sergei, **1:**367, 426, **6:**182
  Ballet Russe de Monte Carlo directorship, **1:**295, 297, 300, 301, 313, **4:**323
Denis, Maurice, **1:**437
Denishawn, **2:376–380,** 457, **5:**46, 171, **6:**243, *244,* 295
  archival materials, **4:**168
  Asian tours, **2:**146, 377, **5:**496, 584, 585
  costumes, **2:**247–248
  founding, **5:**583–584
  Graham association, **3:**210–211
  Horst as musical director, **3:**384
  as Horton influence, **3:**386
  Humphrey association, **3:**397
  Humphrey-Lawrence-Weidman break, **3:**397, **5:**496, **6:**376
  Job, **2:**184, **3:**609
  St. Denis, Ruth, **5:**494–496
  Shawn departure, **5:**496–497
  Sherman reconstruction of program, **5:**587
  souvenir programs, **2:**378
  students, **5:**494, 584
  technique classes, **5:**496
  Weidman association, **6:**376
  See also Shawn, Ted
Denishawn House, New York City, **5:**496
Denishawn Repertory Dancers, **2:**379
Denisova, Alexandra, **1:**313, **2:**277
Denju no Mon, **3:**657
Denman, Judith, **2:***584*
Denmark, **2:380–388**
  dance in the Faeroe Islands, **2:**99, 100, 101, **383–384,** 386
  dance on television, **6:**134, 135
  dance research and publication, **2:386–388**
  on Bournonville heritage, **1:**512–513
  on Faeroese dance, **2:**384
  folk dance, **3:**33–34
  libraries and museums, **4:**160
  dancing masters, **5:**600
  theatrical dance, **2:384–386**
    allegro style, **1:**44
    Bournonville ballet reconstructions, **2:**387–388
    character dancing classes, **2:**107
    costume, **2:***240,* 243
    court ballet, **2:**384
    Danish Ballet Club, **5:**43
    first ballet school, **5:**424
    music for ballet, **4:**513

Denmark, *continued*
    See also Bournonville, August;
        Bournonville tradition; Royal
        Danish Ballet; *specific
        choreographers and dancers*
    traditional and social dance,
        2:380–383, 386–387, **3:**33–34
Dennis, Harry, **4:**522
Dennis, Ruth Hull, **5:**490
de Nobili, Lila, **1:**154, **2:**244, **5:**551
DeNoe, Mister, **4:**310
Denoier, Monsieur. *See* Desnoyer,
    Philip
Denoyer, Philip. *See* Desnoyer,
    Philip
D'Ensemble, **4:**668
Densy, Monette, **2:**109
Dent, Edward J., **5:**280
Dent, Nancy Lima, **2:**47
de Nunes, Silva, **5:**61
Denvers, Robert, **1:**290, *405,* **5:**423
Denys, Maxine, **5:**55
Deobhakta, Kanan, **4:**628
deodhanis, **2:**394
Deo Gratias, **1:**197
De oratore (Cicero), **4:**426
De Oteyza Company, **5:**172
de Palma, Bryan, **5:**573
Depanis, Giuseppe, **4:**258
*Départ d'Énée, ou La Didon
    Abandonnée,* **1:**87
De partibus animalium (Aristotle),
    4:13
Depero, Fortunato, **4:**125, **5:**544
De poesi fennica (Porthan), **2:**629
De Pol, John, **4:**463
Deposits, The, **1:**243
De practica seu arte tripudii
    (Guglielmo Ebreo), **1:**351,
    3:322, 323, 542, 557,
    6:193, 194
De Profundis, **6:**153
De Querer Amores, **6:**407–408
Derain, André, **1:**306, 316, 322,
    2:242, 406, **3:**653, 654, **5:**526
    Ballets 1933, **3:**73
    Épreuve d'Amour, L', **3:**24
    scenic design, **4:**317, 319,
        5:544, 547
derba, **4:**468, *469*
Derbas, Frank, *as photographer,*
    5:476
Derby, **3:**418
Dérèglement des Passions, Le,
    1:287, 396
Deren, Maya, **1:**395, **2:**601,
    603–604, 605, 606
Derevianko, Vladimir, **3:**156
De Reyes, Ramon, **6:**408
deRham, William, **5:**627
de Ribere, Lisa, **5:**190, 197, 514,
    6:266
de Rivas, Elena, **1:**259, **5:**571
Derman, Vergie, **2:**445
Dernier Bal, Le (Adam), **1:**10
Deroc, Jean, **4:**59
Derossi, Giuseppe, **2:**202
Derp, Clotilde von, **1:**204, **3:**146,
    5:503
Derra de Moroda, Friderica, **2:**84,
    4:160
Derra de Moroda Archives,
    Salzburg, **4:**160
Derval, Paul, **1:**465, 466, **4:**524
Derviche, **1:**326
dervishes. *See* Sufi dance; whirling
    dervishes
Derzhavin, Konstantin, **3:**125
Desai, Darshini, **4:**111
Desai, Shubha, **4:**111
Desai, Vasant, **2:**625

Des Arts Décoratifs, **1:**466
Descartes, René, **6:**38
Descent into the Dream, **3:**404
Descent of Hebe, The, **4:**109, 215,
    5:560, **6:**196, *196,* 197, 203
"Descent of Rhythm and Harmony,
    The" (de'Cavalieri *ballo*),
    3:108
Descent to Hell, **2:**473
Descombey, Michel, **1:**349, 350,
    2:388–389, **4:**396, **5:**97
    Atanassoff association, **1:**195
    Ballet Teatro del Espacio, **2:**389,
        4:396
    Coppélia choreography, **2:**199
    Enfant et les Sortilèges, L', **5:**316
    Zurich Ballet, **3:**88–389, **6:**454
*Description of the Correct Method of
    Waltzing, A* (Wilson),
    6:360, *361*
Descueve, El, **1:**114
Desenamoradas, Las, **2:**358
Desenamorados, Las, **6:**259
*Déserteur, ou La Clémence Royale,
    Le,* **1:**202, **2:**352, 353, 413,
    3:258, 358, **4:**149, 175, **5:**90,
    6:311
Desert of Love, The, **1:**308
Déserts, **1:**82, 349, **2:**388
Desert Song, The (Romberg), **6:**273
Deshayes, Alain, **1:**349
Deshayes, André, **1:**4, 9, 36, 47,
    2:93, 364, **389–390,** **3:**180,
    258, **4:**106, 423, **5:**70,
    134, 136
    early symphonic ballet, **4:**517
    King's Theatre, London, **3:**258,
        259, 260, 313
Deshayes, Jacques-François, **1:**455,
    2:389, 412, **3:**81, 358, **5:**91
Deshayes, Jean-Baptiste. *See* de
    Hesse, Jean-Baptiste
Deshevov, Vladimir, **2:**585, **4:**225
De Shou Gongwa Pu (Court Dance
    Notation . . .), **2:**148
designing for dance, **2:**390–393
    artist collaborators, **1:**132–135,
        135–138, 139, 140, **2:**171
    See also costume in Western
        tradition; footwear; lighting
        for dance; scenic design;
        specific designers
Designs with Strings, **1:**429, **2:**3,
    3:74, **4:**117, 380
Désir, **4:**72–73
Desiree, Laura, **5:**197
Desjardins, Pauline, **6:**290
Deskey, Donald, **5:**289
Deslys, Gaby, **4:**523
Desmarets, Henri, **2:**51, **5:**352
Desmatins, Claude, **1:**464
Desmatins, Mademoiselle, **5:**260
Desnoyer, Philip, **2:**70, **394,** **5:**518,
    6:232, 373
Desnoyers, Danielle, **2:**43
De Sola, Carla, **4:**213
Desormière, Roger, **5:**525, 526
Désossé, Valentin de, **1:**95, **2:**53
Desperate Heart, The, **1:**441
Desplaces, Henri, **1:**36, 47
Despléchin, Édouard, **2:**198, 206,
    405, **5:**85, 132
Despréaux, Jean-Étienne, **1:**464,
    3:326
Desrat, G., **1:**278, **2:**53, **6:**128
Desrosiers, Robert, **2:**45, **4:**545
Dessins Commentés, **6:**433
Dessins pour les Six, **3:**226
d'Este, Isabella, **6:**178
Destiné, Jean-Léon, **2:**458,
    6:259, 400

Destinn, Emmy, **5:**123
Destouches, André Cardinal, **1:**516,
    2:465, **4:**122, 509, **5:**88,
    113, 352
d'Estrée, Jean. *See* Estrée, Jean d'
De Strouper, Paul, **4:**238
Detbegynte med dansen (Ibsen),
    4:682
Detik . . . Detik . . . Tempo . . .,
    5:524
Detrich, Tamas, **6:**11
Detroit Contemporary Dance
    Company, **2:**566
Detroit Public Library, **4:**169
Deuce Coupe, **3:**615–616, **4:**519,
    5:437, 440, *440,* **6:**153
Deuce Coupe II, **3:**615
Deuil en 24 Heures, **5:**163, 164
Deutsche (allemandes), **1:**45, 46–47
Deutsche Oper am Rhein. *See*
    Düsseldorf-Duisberg Ballet
Deutsche Oper Berlin. *See* Berlin
    Opera Ballet
Deutscher Komponistenverband,
    2:478
Deutscher Tänzerbund, **4:**93
Deutsches Opernhaus,
    Charlottenburg, **1:**436
Deutsche Staatsoper (East Berlin),
    3:152, 156
    See also Berlin Opera Ballet
Deutsche Tanzbühne, **4:**91
"Deutsche Tänze," **3:**132, **6:**360
Deutsche Werkbunde Exhibition,
    Cologne, **4:**90
Deux Créoles, Les, **1:**201, **2:**107,
    3:68
Deuxième Concerto, **1:**461
Deuxième Légende, **3:**79
Deux Petits Savoyards, Les, **3:**358
Deux Pigeons, Les, **1:**6, **2:**113, 351,
    4:354, **5:**94, **6:**443
    See also Two Pigeons, The
Deux Roses, Les, **4:**454
devadāsī, **1:**162, 169, **2:**104,
    394–395, **3:**459
    bharata nāṭyam, **1:**442–443, **2:**394
    Oḍissi, **5:**22, 23
de Valois, Ninette, **2:**56, 265,
    395–404, 590, **5:**5, 14, 114,
    298, 560, 588
    Abbey Theatre, Dublin, **2:**397,
        3:519
    Ashton's style comparison, **2:**399
    autobiography, **2:**403
    Ballets Russes de Serge
        Diaghilev, **3:**262
    Benesh notation use, **1:**417
    Bliss scores, **1:**462, 463, **4:**517
    British ballet development,
        3:264–265
    on British dance style, **5:**412, 414
    as British school influence, **1:**349,
        3:263, **5:**414–415
    Camargo Society, **3:**265
    Cecchetti Society founding, **2:**84
    Chappell association, **2:**105
    choreographies, **2:**399–401, 445
    Creatures of Prometheus revival,
        1:402
    demi-caractère roles, **2:**399
    Don Quixote one-act version,
        2:440
    Espinosa family association,
        2:525
    eurhythmics, **3:**597
    Fedorovitch designs, **2:**582, 583
    Fonteyn roles, **3:**41, 42, 265
    Haunted Ballroom production,
        5:413, 414, 650
    Helpmann association, **3:**354

Irish dance, **2:**397, **3:**520, 529
    Jooss as influence, **3:**628
    on Lambert as musical director,
        4:114
    as Legat (Nikolai) student, **4:**143
    MacMillan mentorship,
        4:239, 240
    Markova roles, **4:**267, 268
    Massine association, **4:**319
    Moreton as assistant, **4:**463
    Prospect before Us, The, **2:**72,
        401, *402*
    Rambert collaboration, **3:**266
    Rambert dancers, **5:**300
    Rassine roles, **5:**312
    reaction to Tudor's early
        choreography, **6:**196
    Rendezvous performance, **5:**342
    as Royal Ballet director, **6:**313
    Royal Ballet founding, **1:**146,
        148, 149, 155, **2:**105, 314,
        397–404, **3:**264, **5:**411–416
    Royal Ballet retirement, **5:**417
    Royal Ballet School, **3:**277, **5:**421
    Sadler's Wells Theatre Ballet,
        1:151, **2:**402
    Sergeyev (Nicholas)
        reconstruction of Maryinsky
        classics, **2:**401–402,
        3:264–265, **5:**14, 413, 414,
        6:33
    Sleeping Beauty productions,
        2:186, **3:**268, **4:**243, **5:**612
    Toronto ballet company
        founding, **4:**539
    Turkish ballet, **6:**212
    Wedding Bouquet performance,
        6:375
    Yeats collaboration, **3:**519
    See also Checkmate; Job; Rake's
        Progress, The
*Development of Ballet Art in
    Slovenia, The* (Neubauer),
    6:439
développés, **1:**7, 8
Devéria, Achille, **1:**368, **2:**201,
    5:259, 261
Devil Dance, **2:**221
Devil in the Village, The, **4:**437,
    6:432, 454
Devil is an Ass, The (Jonson), **5:**520
de Villers, Stephen, **2:**58
de Villiers, Faith, **5:**52, 53–54, 651,
    652, 653, **6:**379
de Villiers, James, *as photographer,*
    5:652, 653
*Devil on Two Sticks, The. See Diable
    Boiteau, Le*
Devil's Auction, The (musical),
    1:496, **4:**463, **5:**404, **6:**290
Devil's Holiday (Le Diable S'amuse)
    Ashton choreography, **1:**149,
        297, 437
    Berman design, **1:**437, **5:**547
    Franklin performance, **3:**87
Devil's Violin, The, **1:**460
*Devil to Pay, The. See Diable à
    Quatre, Le*
Devin du Village, Le (Rousseau
    opera), **2:**413, **3:**106
devishnik dance, **5:**442
Devi Yim, **2:**30
Devoirs de Vacances, **1:**306
devojack pattern, **6:**427
de Vos, Audrey, **2:**404, **3:**307, **5:**573
Devoto, Daniel, **5:**519
Devreese, Frederik, **5:**422
de Warren, Robert, **1:**463,
    4:667, 668
Dew Drop, or La Sylphide, The,
    4:338

Dewette, Elsa. *See* Darciel, Elsa
Dewey, John, **1:**471, **4:**94, **6:**241
de Wilde, Nancy, **4:**600
  as contributor, **4:**588–589
Dewinne, Henri, **3:**261
Dexter, Van, **2:***519*
Dey, Manna, **2:**625
Dezais, Étienne-Joseph, **2:**589,
  5:621
Dezais, Jacques, **1:**90, 91, **6:**114
  bourrée compositions, **1:**517
  on country dance, **2:**255, 256, 591
de Zela, E. Mildred Merino, *as
  contributor,* **5:**142–147
de Zoete, Beryl
  as photographer, **3:**474, 478, 480,
    481, 482, 484, 486, 487, 488,
    489, 491, **6:**367
  Hellerau association, **3:**596
  writings on Mario (I Ketut),
    4:264
Dhabkar, **3:**468
Dhadhap Alus, **3:**495
Dhanam, Veena, **1:**273
Dhananjayan, Satayjit, **2:**405
Dhananjayan, V. P. and Shanta,
  2:404–405
Dhanurveda, **1:**185, **3:**453–454
dharma, **3:**459
dharma pawayangan, **6:**368–369
dhikr, **2:**486–487, 492, **4:**416, 490,
  6:305
Dhir, Rakhi Badal, **2:**468
Dhiraj (film), **5:**603
Diable Amoureux, Le, **3:**5,
  4:338–339, 340–341, 657
Diable à Quatre, Le, **2:405,** **3:**188,
  315, **5:**148, *260,* 516
  Adam (Adolphe) score, **1:**10
  Andreyanova performance, **1:**86
  Beretta performance, **1:**427
  Grisi performance, **3:**315
  Mazilier choreography and
    performance, 593, **2:**405,
    4:339, 340, 341, 343
  mazurka, **4:**343
  Monplaisirs' American
    performances, **4:**453, 454
  Petipa (Lucien) and Grisi dance
    partnership, **5:**418
  Petipa (Marius) restoration,
    5:158
  Ravel family performances, **5:**319
  Turczynowicz version, **6:**207
Diable Boiteux, Le, **1:**200, 459,
  2:107, **405–406,** **3:**69, 122,
  5:93, 498
  Andalusian costume, **3:***70*
  Coralli creation, **2:**201, 203, 390,
    405, 502, 503, **3:***70*
  Duvernay performance, **2:**390
  Elssler performance, **2:**203, 390,
    405, 502, 503, **3:**69, **4:**340
  Maywood performance, **4:**338
  Mazilier leading roles, **4:**340
  See also Cachucha, La
Diable dans le Beffroi, Le, **3:**321
*Diable S'Amuse, Le. See Devil's
  Holiday*
diablitos (spirits), **2:**274
Diablos de los Espejos, Los, **2:**195
"Diablos Limpios, Los," **5:**67
"Diablos Sucios, Los," **5:**67
Diack, Michael, **3:**249
Diaghilev, Serge, **1:**192, 271, 437,
  540, **2:406–412, 5:**37, 525,
  526, 544
  aesthetic vision, **1:**318, 320, 325,
    2:406
  Ansermet premieres, **1:**93

Après-midi d'un Faune, L', **1:**98,
  2:360, 406, **3:**19
  archival materials, **4:**168
  artist collaborators, **1:**316–318,
    2:241, 242, 406–407, 408, 410,
    4:331, 332, **5:**541–544, 642
  artistic change of direction,
    1:320, **2:**408, 409, 410
  artistic significance, **1:**317–318
  avant-garde, **1:**243, 320, 322–323,
    2:408, 409, 410
  Bakst collaboration, **1:**254, 255,
    2:409
  as Ballets Suédois influence,
    1:326
  Ballet-Théâtre de Français de
    Nancy homage production,
    3:75
  Benois collaboration, **1:**422,
    423–424
  book collection, **2:**410
  as British ballet influence,
    3:262, 281
  Buckle studies of, **3:**282
  caricatures of, **2:**70, *70*
  Cocteau collaboration, **2:**183
  composer collaborators,
    4:515–516
  constructivism, **1:**259
  death, **1:**326, **2:**411, **5:**547
  Debussy commissions, **2:**361,
    408, **4:**515
  as de Valois influence, **2:**395,
    396, 401
  Dolin's one-man show on, **2:**425
  on Duncan as Fokine influence,
    3:15
  Fokine break with, **1:**319, 320,
    2:408, **3:**17–18, 19–20
  Fokine relationship, **2:**406,
    3:16–18
  Fokine reunion, **1:**321–322, **3:**20
  Golovin designs, **3:**196
  Goncharova association,
    3:197, 198
  Grigoriev collaboration, **3:**308,
    6:32
  Haskell biography of, **3:**285
  Karsavina relationship, **3:**656
  Kirstein compared with, **4:**26
  Kirstein fascination with,
    4:26, 27
  Kochno relationship, **1:**306–307,
    2:411, **4:**32–33
  Korovin designs, **4:**56
  Lambert musical collaboration,
    4:113
  Larionov commissions,
    4:124–125
  legacy, **2:**406, 411
  Levinson's critiques, **4:**154–155
  Lifar relationship, **2:**410, 411
  Lopokova association, **4:**223, 224
  Markevitch relationship,
    2:410, 411
  Maryinsky dispute and
    resignation, **6:**64
  masks, **4:**302
  Massine break, **4:**318–319
  Massine relationship, **1:**317, 318,
    322, 323, **2:**408, 409, 411,
    4:33, 315, 316–318
  Massine return and second
    break, **4:**320–321
  Milhaud scores, **4:**418, 515
  musical interests, **2:**406, 407–408,
    409, 410, **4:**515–516
  Nijinska disputes, **4:**635
  Nijinsky relationship, **1:**317, 318,
    319–320, 321, 322, **2:**406, 408,
    411, **4:**316, 641–645

  observation of Jaques-Dalcroze
    school, **3:**596
  one-act productions, **1:**318, **2:**411
  Pavlova, Anna, **5:**122
  Poulenc collaboration, **5:**237
  Prokiev collaborations,
    5:267, 268
  Rambert association, **5:**296, 298
  Ravel commissions, **2:**408, **4:**515,
    5:315
  rejection of *Job* production,
    3:609
  Roerich collaboration, **5:**372
  Rubinstein association, **5:**438
  Russian scholarly views on, **5:**483
  Sokolova memoir, **5:**637
  Stravinsky commissions, **1:**316,
    2:406–407, **3:**17, **6:**3–5, 7
  Svetlov association, **6:**28
  Théâtre du Châtelet redesign,
    6:160
  view of Viennese ballet, **3:**347
  Vladimiroff association, **6:**345
  See also Ballets Russes de Serge
    Diaghilev; Saison Russe
Diaghilev Ballet, The (Grigoriev),
  3:308
Diaghilev et les Ballets Russes
  (Kochno), **4:**34
"Diaghilev Exhibition, The"
  (Edinburgh; 1954), **4:**34, 125
Diaghilev Observed (Macdonald),
  3:284
"Diaghilev Period, The" (Kirstein),
  4:26
Diaghilev's Ballets Russes. *See*
  Ballets Russes de Serge
  Diaghilev
Diaghilews Ryska Balett, **3:**100
diagonal point perspective, **5:***538*
Dialectology, **3:**423
Dialogo, **2:**389
Dialogues, **1:**69, **3:**391, 664, **5:**408
Dialogues des Carmélites,
  5:237, 238
Dialogues on Stage Affairs (Di
  Somi), **4:**187
Diamants de la Couronne (Auber),
  2:80
Diamond, David, **3:**384
Diamond, Dennis, **2:**608, **3:**201
Diamond, Emma, **2:***292,* **5:**17
"Diamond Project" (New York City
  Ballet), **4:**623
Diamonds (*Jewels* section), **2:**576,
  4:612, 618, 631, **5:**223
Diana and Actaeon, **5:**6
Diana e Endimione, **2:**177
Diane de Poitiers, **3:**24, **5:**439
Diane et Endymion, **2:**413
Diane la Chasseresse, **1:**200
Diario 16 (publication), **5:**676
Diary (Pepys), **3:**255
Diary of One Who Disappeared,
  2:309
Dias, Linneu, **1:**537
Diaspora, **3:**526, 535, 602, 605
Diavolina, **4:**353, **5:**94, 501
Diavolo a Quattro, Il, **1:**88
Díaz, Lydia, **6:**302
Díaz del Castillo, Bernal, **4:**328,
  386, 399
Dibakoane, Carly, **5:**656, 660
Dibbuk (play), **3:**312
di Bona, Linda, **1:**375
Dicello, Robert, **3:**3
Dichterliebe, **1:**406
Dickens, Charles, **3:**633
Dickey, Mary (La Petite Adelaide),
  6:318

Dickinson, Emily, **4:**153
Dickson, H. R. P., **4:**415
Dick Whittington (pantomime),
  4:520, **5:**72
*Dictionary Catalog of the New York
  Public Library Dance
  Collection,* **4:**167
Dictionary of Canadian Dance
  (Officer ed.), **2:**49
Dictionary of Kinetography Laban
  (Knust), **4:**32
*Dictionary of Theatre Anthropology,
  A* (Barba), **5:**130
Dictionnaire de danse (Compan),
  2:336, **5:**285, 486, **6:**126
Dictionnaire de la danse (Desrat),
  1:278, **6:**128
Dictionnaire de la langue française
  (Littré), **1:**384
Dictionnaire de musique
  (Rousseau), **3:**50, **5:**520
Didelot, Charles (father), **2:**412,
  5:614, **6:**39
Didelot, Charles-Louis, **2:412–417,**
  3:68, 112, 560, **5:**91, 105, 270,
  319, **6:**158, 160
  ballet d'action, **1:**86, **2:**363
  Blok writings on, **1:**463, 464
  Bournonville (Antoine)
    correspondence, **1:**503
  caricature of, **2:**71
  Cendrillon, **2:**163
  choreographic innovations,
    4:278
  choreography anticipating
    Romantic ballet, **4:**278, 280
  costumes, **2:***412*
  Dauberval association, **2:**353,
    354, 412
  Don Quixote production, **2:**435
  Fille Mal Gardée performance,
    2:595, 596
  Flore et Zéphire, **1:**35, 86, 110,
    2:71, 464, **4:**277, 279, **5:**91
  Glushkovsky association,
    3:191, 192
  as Istomina mentor, **3:**539
  King's Theatre, London, **2:**413,
    414, **3:**258, 259, 326
  Kolosova association, **4:**35–36
  Koni reviews, **4:**41
  libretti subjects, **4:**175
  Paris Opera Ballet, **5:**91
  pas de deux choreographies,
    5:105
  Prisoner of the Caucasus, The,
    1:485, **3:**540
  Russian themes, **5:**453–454
  Saint Petersburg ballet,
    4:277–278, 279, 280, 285–286,
    422, 483, 513, **5:**453–454, 480,
    6:452
  score collaborations, **4:**513
  students, **1:**477, **2:**416, **3:**191,
    539, **5:**480
  Swedish opera-ballet, **2:**412–413,
    6:39
  Swift biography of, **6:**297
  as Vestris (Auguste) student,
    6:334
Didelot, Rose, **3:**258
Diderot, Denis, **3:**545–546
  dance aesthetics, **1:**22, 23, 123,
    125–26
  Encyclopédie, **1:**4, 47, **4:**173–174,
    379, **6:**123, 125
  on Feuillet notation, **2:**588
  on middle-class drama, **4:**175
  as Noverre influence, **4:**698
Dido, **1:**88

Dido and Aeneas (Purcell), **2:**337, **3:**368, 630, **4:**114, 470, **5:**280
Morris (Mark) danced version, **4:**471
"Sailor's Dance," **3:**376
Dido and Aeneas (television production), **6:**133
Didon, **2:**51, **4:**109
Didone Abbandonata (opera), **1:**87, **4:**347, **5:**424
Dieckelmann, Heinrich, **3:**142
Dienes, Gedeon P., **3:**419, 424
as contributor, **1:**307–308, 370–371, **2:**417, 473–474, **3:**329–330, 341–342, 413–415, 415–420, 420–421, 423–424, **4:**266–267, **5:**401–402
Dienes, Valéria, **2:**417, **3:**420–421
Dies, Martin, **2:**581
Diéterle, Jules, **2:**405, **5:**85, 132
Dietrich, Urs, **3:**151, 157, **4:**204
Dieu Bleu, Le, **1:**254, **2:**183, 407, 408, **3:**18
Dieu et la Bayadère, Le, **1:**86, 199–200, **2:**84, **3:**5, **4:**657, **6:**72, 74
Dieux Mendiants, Les, **4:**178
Dieux Rivaux, Les, **4:**61
Díez, Rafael, **4:**391
Different Drummer, **4:**244
Different Trains, **3:**275
Digby Morality of Wisdom, **3:**377
Diggity, **6:**111
Dignan, Pat, **2:**171
Digo dance, **2:417–418**
Dijk, Peter van. *See* Dyk, Peter van
Dijon Opera House, **3:**66
Dilara, **6:**397
Dilbar, **6:**84
Dill, Gerlinde, **5:**279
Dillen, Bianca van, **4:**596, 597
Diller, Elizabeth, **1:**412
Dilley, Barbara, **3:**234, *235,* 446, **5:***548*
Dillingham, Charles, **1:**482, **2:**79, 80, **3:**424, **4:**420, **5:**125, **6:**273
Dillon, Fannie Charles, **2:**21
Dilu (people), **2:**86
Dimacale, Rene, **5:**172
Dimanches Classiques (television series), **6:**132
Dimas, Elias, **3:**303
Dime a Dance, **2:**289
Dimitrov, Aleksandŭr, **2:**10
Dim Lustre, **2:**376, **4:**63, 110, 608, **6:**199, *201*
Dimoglou, Nelly, **3:**296
Dimond, Charlie, **6:**316
Dimova, Maria, **2:**11
Dine, Jim, **1:**139
Dingxian, China, **2:**135
Dinizulu, Nana, **6:**258
Dinka (people), **2:**86–87
dinki-mini, **3:**573
Dinzel, Los (Gloria and Rodolfo), **6:**94
Diobono, Pompeo, **2:**337, **418,** **3:**80, 543, **4:**579
Diodorus Siculus, **6:**144
Diógenes ante et Tonel, **2:**278
Dionysia, **4:**56
Dionysian cults, **6:**185
Dionysiaques, **3:**399
Dionysios, **3:**85
Dionysius the Areopagite, **1:**21
Dionysus (deity), **2:**158, 419, **3:**287, 288, 289, 292, 293, **4:**301, 499
Dionysus, **3:**195
dioramas, **4:**189
Dior, Christian, **1:**306, **2:**244
Dipping Wings, **5:***304*

DiPrima, Diane, **6:**362–363
"Dipsy Doodle" (song), **1:**450
Director, The (magazine), **6:**239, 293
Dirk Dance, **3:**251
Dirtl, Willy, **1:***240,* 241, *241*
Dirty Dancing (film), **2:**620
Dis, or Eros and Death, **3:**156
Disappearances, **2:**461
Discépolo, Enrique Santos, **6:**93
Disciples of Christ, **2:**167
disco dance, **1:**78, **5:**630, 633, *634*
discotheques, **6:**251
Discourses II, **1:**82
Discs, **1:**543
Discursos sobre el arte del danzado (*Discursos sobre el arte del dançado;* Esquivel Navarro), **2:**337, **5:**116, 345, 668, 670, **6:**123
Disdéri, André Adolph-Eugene, **5:**176, 177, *177*
Diseases and Injuries of Ballet Dancers (Thomasen), **2:**330
Diseases of the Workers (Ramazzini), **2:**328
Disertore Svizzero, Il (Pugni), **5:**277
Disgenoten, **4:**600
dish-shaped pit design, **6:**161
Disinclinations, **4:**115
dislocation, bone, **4:**20
Dislocations, **4:**115
Disney, Walt, **1:**402, **3:**373, **5:**16, 600
Display, The, **1:**208, 210, 230, 231
Gorham performance, **3:**204
Helpmann production, **3:**356
Welch performance, **3:**378
Dispute, The, **6:**175
Disquieting Muses, **4:**272
Distant Dances (Osato), **5:**241–242
Distant Planet, The, **4:**37, **5:**572
Distratto, Ill, **2:**162
District of Columbia. *See* National Ballet; Washington Ballet
District Storyville, **2:**358, **4:**345, **6:**259
Ditchburn, Ann, **3:**643, **4:**544, **6:**133
Di Tella Institute (Argentina), **1:**103, 112, 113
dithyramb, **2:**158, **419–420,** **3:**288–289, 291, 292
Dithyrambic, **2:**196, **3:**213
Divergence, **1:**235
Divers Entretiens de la Fontaine de Vaucluse, Les, **1:**287
Diversion of Angels, **3:**218, 221
Diversions, **1:**463, **4:**241
Diversité des Fols, La, **1:**288
Divertimento, **1:**281, 446, **3:**416, **4:**450, 608
Divertimento Campestre, Un, **1:**88
Divertimento del Sur, **5:**274
Divertimento from "Le Baiser de la Fée", **4:**608, 613, 618, 620, **6:**174
Divertimento No. 15 (originally *Caracole*), **1:**426, **2:**420
Balanchine production, **1:**266, 269, **2:**420, **4:**613, **5:**104
Balanchine revival, **4:**609
Hayden performance, **3:**352
Kent performance, **4:**5
Le Clercq performance, **2:**420, **4:**137
Nichols performance, **4:**631
Wilde role, **6:**396
Divertissement (1986), **2:***247*
Divertissement (Gaevsky), **5:**483, 484

Divertissement à la Cour, **2:**114
Divertissement d'Auber, **2:**162
Divertissement de Petipa, **4:**184
divination, **6:**423
Divine, **3:**351
Divine, The: An Homage to Garbo, **1:**406
Divine Altar Dance, **2:**129
Divine Comedy (Dante), **2:**166, **3:**20
Divine Dunham, The (television documentary), **2:**459
Divine Horsemen, The, **1:**233, **6:**202
Divine Horsemen: The Living Gods of Haiti (Deren), **2:**601, **6:**202
Divine Idiot, The, **5:**586–587
Divining, **1:**59, **3:**578
Division of Angels, **3:**221
Divorce Me, Darling, **1:**520
diwan, **3:**536
Dix contredanse engloises et deux françoises (Gautier), **2:**256
Dix Entretiens... Dixey, Phyllis, **2:**574
Dixie to Broadway (musical), **6:**256
Dixit, Madhuri, **2:**625
Dixit Dominus, **3:**630
Dixon, Bill, **3:**448
Dixon, Harland, **4:**522
Dixon, Lee, **2:**2615
Dixon, Norman, **2:**200, **5:**234, 235
Dixon, Ray, **3:**233
Dixon Place, New York City, **2:**171
Djambidj song series, **1:**223, 224
djangi, **1:**247
Djawa (periodical), **3:**505
djinn (spirits), **4:**291
Djordjević, Višnja, **6:**435
Dlugoszewski, Lucia, **3:**349
D-Man in the Waters, **3:**621
Dmitriev, Vladimir, **1:**64, 256, **2:420–421,** **3:**12, 72, **5:**10, **6:**343
do (martial arts), **1:**186
Doanna de Aur, **5:**384
Dobiecki, Paweł, **3:**316
Doble Corchea, **6:**324, *324*
Doboujinsky, Mstislav, **4:**178
Dobrievich, Louba and Pierre, **1:**290
Dobrovolskaya, Galina N., **5:**483, 484, 485
as contributor, **3:**1–2, **4:**224–226, **6:**59–61, 410–413
Dobrowolski, Adam, **5:**220
Dobrudja, **5:**379
Dobujinsky, Mstislav, **1:**254, 293, **2:**241, **3:**26, 656, **4:***207,* **5:**301, 541
Doce Pares de Francia, Los (dance drama), **3:**319
Docherty, Peter, **1:**73, **2:**512, **3:**427, **5:**55
Dockeley, Peter, **4:**602
Doctor Aibolit. See Doctor Oh-It-Hurts
Doctor Faustus. *See* Faust legend
Doctor Oh-It-Hurts, **2:**11, 585, **3:**665, **5:***466,* 471
Documenta choreologica (Petermann ed.), **3:**161
Dodd, Patricia, **2:**299
Dodds, Baby, **2:**286, **3:**446
Dodds, Eric, **6:**186
Dodecanese, **2:**101
Dodge, Roger Pryor, **2:**579
Dodi Li, **3:**531
Dodworth, Allen, **2:**339, **5:**623, 627, **6:**234, 238, 293
Dodworth, T. George, **5:**627, **6:**242
Dodworth Academy, New York City, **5:**627

doe (song form), **2:**64
Doesburg, Theodore van, **1:**132
Dogon dance, **2:421–422,** **4:**288, *288,* 291–292, 485, **6:**382, 383
Dogra, Urmila, **2:**468
Dogrib (people), **4:**552
Dogue d'Angleterre, **5:**198
Dohnányi, Ernő, **1:**541, **2:**426, **4:**674, **5:**569
Do Homem ao Poeta, **1:**536
Dohrn, Wolf and Harald, **3:**595
Do I Hear a Waltz? (musical), **5:**408
Doima. *See* Zhok
Doing, Ruth, **2:**450
Dokoudovsky, Vladimir, **1:**65, 315, 316, **4:**656
Doktor Faust, **5:**245
Doktor Faust, Der: Ein Tanzpoem (Heine), **1:**1
Dolgany (people), **5:**447
Dolgushin, Nikita, **2:422–423,** **5:**282, 460
as contributor, **3:**327–329
Giselle, **2:**152, **4:**247
Dolin, Anton, **1:**49, 117, 148, 207, 300, 400, 411, **2:**19, 396, **423–425,** 586, **3:**101, 571, **4:***184,* **5:**17, 107, 108, 386, 678, 681, **6:**312, 449
American Ballet Theatre, **1:**65, 66, 71, 437, **2:**112, 425
autobiography, **2:**425
as Ballets Russes de Monte Carlo guest artist, **1:**310, *312,* 313, 315, *315,* **2:**425
Chopiniana performance, **2:***507*
Coppélia performance, **2:**200
Diaghilev's Ballets Russes, **1:**318, 325, **2:**411, 423–424, **3:**262
Dublin City Ballet, **3:**520
English National Ballet, **2:507–510,** **3:**175, 269
Fils Prodigue, Le (The Prodigal Son), **5:**264, 265
Fokine ballets, **3:**26, 27
Fracci as protégée, **3:**59
Genée dance partnership, **3:**129
Giselle, **1:**315, **2:**152, 424, *508,* 509–510, **3:**59, 182, *182,* 437, **5:**512, 650
Grands Ballets Canadiens, Les, **3:**229
Icelandic stagings, **3:**437
Job performance, **2:**399, 424, **3:**354, 608, 609, **5:**412
as Legat (Nikolai) student, **4:**143
Markova association, **4:**267, 268, 269
Markova dance partnership, **2:**425, **3:**182, 265, *267,* **4:**268, 269–270
Nutcracker performances, **5:**15, *15*
on pas de deux, **3:**354
Pas de Quatre reconstruction, **2:**104, 112, 425, **3:**59, 229, 437, **4:**269, **5:**431, 553, **6:**353
Petrouchka, **2:**425, **5:**166
Princess Aurora, **5:**612, *612*
Rome Opera Ballet directorship, **2:**425, **5:**401
Royal Ballet, **5:**411, 413, **6:**33
Scènes de Ballet production, **5:**531
South African tour, **5:**561
students, **2:**134, 341, **3:**87, **4:**63, 152, **5:**650
Swan Lake, **6:**33
television performances, **6:**137

Zéphire et Flore performance, **4:**320
See also Markova-Dolin Ballet
Dolinskaya, Evgenia, **2:**596
Dolinský, Jozef, **5:**615
Dolivet, **1:**286, 287
Doll, Isabelle, **5:**660
Doll, The, **4:**674
Dollar, William, **1:**64, 110, **2:425–427, 3:**352, **4:**209, 435, **5:**29, **6:**396
American Concert Ballet, **1:**478
Ballet Caravan, **1:**280, 281, 293, **4:**28
Concerto Barocco, **2:**193
Duel, The, **5:**573
Four Temperaments performance, **2:**426, **3:**57, 59
Grand Ballet du Marquis de Cuevas, **3:**73, 224, 225, 226
New York City Ballet choreography, **4:**608
Romeo and Juliet film, **5:**398
Doll's House, A (Ibsen), **5:**425
Dolly Sisters, **6:**270, 319–320, 371
Dolmetsch, Arnold, **2:**453
Dolmetsch, Mabel, **3:**282
Dolores, María, **3:***8*, **6:**408
Dolphine, Marguerita, **3:**413
Domashev, N. P., **2:**436
Domashov, Nikolai, **1:**487, **5:**455, **6:**105
Do masking society, **4:**291
Dombrowsky, Jacques, **1:**349
Dome, The, **5:**586
Domeika, Egidijus, **4:**208
Domenico, Giuseppe, **2:**190
Domenico da Ferrara. *See* Domenico da Piacenza
Domenico da Piacenza, **1:**22, 351, 352, **2:**204, 205, 336, **427–429,** 517, **3:**542, **5:**336, 337, 506, 621, **6:**121, 122
ballo music, **4:**501
dance manuels, **6:**683
figure dances, **2:**591
Guglielmo Ebreo da Pesaro association, **3:**322, 323
on *révérence,* **5:**344
Domínguez, Jorge, **4:**397
Dominic, Zoë, *as photographer,* **3:**43, **4:**240, **5:**416, 418
Dominican order, **2:**165
Dominican Republic, **2:**62, **429–433**
baile de palos, **2:**61
merengue, **2:**61, *193,* 430, 431, 432
Dominic, Zoë, **5:**184
as photographer, **5:**100, 104, **6:**217
Dominique, Madame, **2:**198, **3:**81, 82, 237, **4:**214
Dommisse, Hermien, **5:**52, 53
Domnişoara Nastasia, **5:**386
Dom Sébastien (Donizetti), **4:**514
Donahue, Jack, **4:**420, **5:**239
Doña Inés de Castro, **3:**226, 361, **5:**604
Donald Byrd/The Group, **2:**19–20
Donat, Robert, **3:**356
Donato, Signor, **1:**205
Donaverus, Christoph, **5:**244
Don Carlos (Didelot ballet), **3:**539
Don Carlos (Verdi opera), **2:**120, **4:**514, **5:**35, 38, 148
Don Chischiotte, **2:**435
Don des Etoiles, Le. *See* Gala des Etoiles, Le
Don Domingo, **2:**425, **4:**269, 324
Don Domingo de Don Blas, **1:**66–67
Donen, Stanley, **2:**616, **4:**3, **6:**287

Doner, Kitty, **4:**38–39, **6:**137
Donetsk Ballet, **6:***225*
Don Euthichio della Castagna, **5:**277
Dong Fang Art Ensemble, **2:**136
Don Giovanni (Mozart), **1:**406, **2:**95, 202, **3:**118, 223, **4:**509, 511, 639, **6:**360
Dong Xijiu, **2:**149
Donizetti, Gaetano, **1:**461, **2:**202, 475, **3:**5, 175, 176, 314, 360, **4:**108, 513, 514, 657, **5:**517
Donizetti Variations, **4:**610, **5:**431, 600, **6:***51, 328*
Don Juan, **1:**151, 446, 517, **2:433–434,** 470, **5:**528
Andreyanova performance, **1:**86
Babilée performance, **1:**251
Ballet Russe de Monte Carlo repertory, **1:**295
Beck-Friis revival, **1:**400, **6:**48
Eck productions, **2:**473, 474
Fokine production, **2:**434, **3:**24
Fonteyn performance, **3:**44
Gades production, **3:**101
Hanka production, **3:**340
Kröller production, **1:**240
Laban production, **4:**91, 92, 94
Neumeier production, **4:**604
Rosen production, **5:**432
Simone performance, **5:**600
Wallmann production, **6:**357
Don Juan, ou Le Festin de Pierre, **1:**87, **3:**187, 188, 190
Angiolini *aviso* (preface), **4:**174
Angiolini-Bodin dance partnership, **1:**468
Angiolini production, **1:**236, **2:433–434, 4:**509, **6:**48
Douvillier performance, **2:**443
Gluck score, **2:**433–434, **4:**509
Noverre's *Jugement de Pâris* preceding, **4:**695
Don Juan Fantasia, **3:**391
Don Juan Reigen, **2:**434
Don Juan's Shadow upon Us, **4:**266
Donker, Greetje, **1:**289, 290, **5:**531
Donkey's Tale (avant-garde group), **3:**197, **4:**124
Don Morte, **3:**146, **4:**60
Donn, Jorge, **1:***404,* 405, 406, **5:**97
Balanchine performance, **1:***268*
Ballet du XXᵉ Siècle, **1:**291, 292, *292*
Donne di Buon Umore, Le (The Good-Humored Ladies), **3:***550,* **6:**214
Donnet, Vera, **5:**296
Donneybrook! (musical), **2:**185
Dono del Re dell'Alpi a Madama Reale, Il, **1:**29
Don Pedro I, emperor of Brazil, **1:**532
Don Pedro di Portugallo (Drigo), **2:**446
Don Quichotte et Sancho Pança, **1:**456
Don Quichotte, **2:434–441, 5:***470, 471,* 473, 554
Balanchine production, **1:**268, *268,* **2:438–439, 4:**610, 613
Farrell role, **1:***268,* **2:**438, 439, 576, *577,* **4:**618
Moncion performance, **4:**450
Nabokov score, **4:**613
Bart staging, **3:**156
Baryshnikov, **1:**74, 76, 372, **2:***439,* 440–441, 444, **4:**24
Bavarian State Ballet, **1:**391
Beriozoff, **2:**441, **4:**545

Blank's first German production, **1:**460
Bournonville, **1:**515, **2:**435, **3:**223
Bräuer production, **3:**154
Cairo ballet, **2:***497*
Central Ballet of China, **2:**147, 440, *440*
Chabukiani choreographic changes, **2:**96
Cole musical, *Man of La Mancha,* **6:**283
de Valois, **2:**401, 440, **5:**312
early productions, **2:434–435**
Didelot choreography, **2:**414
Milon libretto, **2:**435, **4:**422
Eifman production, **5:**469
Gable-Moricone version, **4:**668
Gorsky production, **1:**90, 372, **2:436–438,** 439, 440, 441, 582, **3:**206, 207, **4:**133, 148, 336, **5:**161, *452*
Fedorova performance, **5:***452*
as Gerdt (Pavel) last performance, **3:**136
Lavrovsky (Mikhail) performance, **2:**438, **4:**133
Lepeshinskaya performance, **4:**148, *148*
Lopukhov revival, **4:**224
Maximova performance, **4:**336
Messerer performance, **4:***148,* 358, *359*
Mordkin roles, **4:**459
Plisetskaya performance, **5:**204, *205*
Helpmann performance, **3:**357
Hightower, **3:**362
Krätke, **3:**153–154
Makarova performance, **4:**248
Markova-Dolin pas de deux, **4:**269
Nureyev, **1:**38, 210, *231,* 232–233, 241, **2:**440, **3:**60, 357, **4:**117, 678, **5:**7, **6:**454
Oboukhoff, **5:**17
Paeper, **2:**57, 441
Panov, **6:**437
Pavlova performances, **1:**207, **2:**439
Petipa production, **2:**435, **435–436,** 437, 438, 440, 441, **4:**429, **5:***152,* 157
Bolshoi Ballet, **1:**486, *486,* **2:**435
character dances, **2:**108
Kitri's fan solo, **2:***570,* 574
Minkus score, **4:**429, 430
Vergina performance, **2:**436, **4:**282
Starzer scores, **5:**693
Spoerli, **1:**375, **2:**441
Vasiliev, **1:**77
Vienna State Opera Ballet, **1:**241, **2:**440
Zakharov revival, **6:**442
Don Quixote (film), **1:**210, *231,* 233
Don Quixote at Camacho's Wedding, **2:**435
Don Quixote de la Mancha (Cervantes), **2:**434, 435, 438
Don Redlich Dance Company, **3:**372
Don't Bother Me, I Can't Cope (musical), **1:**395
Dontsuki, **3:**593
Don Zeffiro, **5:**501
Doob, Penelope Reed, *as contributor,* **4:**106–107
Doo Dah Day, **2:**585
Dooley, Rae, **6:**316

Doorn-Last, Femke van, **4:**598
as contributor, **4:**585–586
Doors (rock group), **2:**563
Dooyes, Max, **1:**289
Doppelgänger, Der, **5:**557
Doppler, Franz, **1:**500
d'Or, Henriette, **2:**525, **5:***151*
Doraldina (vaudeville performer), **6:**317
Dora Stratou Society Library and Archives, Athens, **3:**303, **4:**161
Dorat, Claude Joseph, **2:**465, **6:**49
Dorat, Jean, **1:**2
Dorati, Antal, **1:**310, **3:**26, **4:**10, **5:**397, 562
Dorazio, Ralph, **3:**349
Dorcy, Jean, **3:**76
Doré, Gustave, **2:**71, **3:**7
Doreen Bird College of Performing Arts, Kent, England, **3:**280
Dorella, Oriella, **5:**530
Dorival, Anne, **5:**35
Dorje Phurba (deity), **1:**458–459
Dorner, Willi, **1:**240
Dornröschen—Die Schlfende Schönheit, **6:**53
Dorofeeva, Inna, **2:**208
Dorothée, **2:**595
Dorothy Alexander Concert Group. *See* Atlanta Ballet
Dorp de Weyer, Henk van, **4:**589–590
Dorris, George
as contributor, **1:**438–439, **2:**196–198, **3:**520–521, **4:**263–264, **5:**489–490, 561–562
Dance Chronicle, **6:**297
Dorsay, Peggy, **5:**279
D'Orschwiller, Hippolyte, **5:**132
Dorsey, Jimmy, **6:**275
Dorsey, Tommy, **1:**450, **5:**631
Dortoir, Le (film), **2:**610
Dorvane, Jeannine, *as contributor,* **1:**43–44, 282–285, 259–60, 72, 464–465, 465–466, **3:**106, 116–119, 318–319, 326–327, 353, 426, **4:**122–123, 134–135, 149–150, **5:**132, 196, 320, 678–679, **6:**330–334, 352–353, 443–444
Dorze (people), **2:***534*
Dosza, Istvan, **2:**127
Dotson, Dancing, **1:**520
Douai, Jacques, **3:**65
Douanes, **2:**397, 399, 400
Double Contrasts, **6:**366
Double Jump (photograph), **5:***179*
double one-legged song and dance, **6:**316
Double Quatuor, **3:***233*
double rond de jambe en l'air sauté, **5:**402
Doubles, **2:**290, 294, 295, **3:**274
Double Violin Concerto in D Minor (Bach), **1:**281, **2:**193
double work. *See* partnering; pas de deux
Doublework, **1:**51–52, **4:***218*
Doubrovska, Felia, **1:**95, 110, *256, 324,* **2:**410, **441–442, 5:**241, **6:**345
Ballets Russes de Monte Carlo, **1:**309
Biches performance, **5:**237
Metropolitan Opera Ballet, **4:**382
Noces performance, **4:**636, 657
Nutcracker performance, **5:**14
Prodigal Son performance, **5:**264
Dougill, David, **3:**285
Dougla, **2:**334, 335

Douglas, Anita, **2:**519
Douglas, Ann, **2:**379
Douglas, Helen, **1:**75
Douglas, Mona, **3:**250
Douglas, Scott, **1:**69, *71*, 72, 75, **2:**161
Douglas Dunn and Dancers, **2:**460
Douglass, Stephen, **6:**327
Dougletoss, **2:**296
Doula (people), **2:**32
Doutreville, Emma, **5:**318
Douvillier, Louis, **3:**87
Douvillier, Suzanne (Mademoiselle Théodore), **1:**124, **2:**352–353, 413, **442–443**, **3:**81, 258, **5:**198, **6:**333
   Fille Mal Gardée performance, **2:**594
   Francisqui association, **3:**86, 87
Dove, Ulysses, **2:**463, 514, **3:**577, **5:**98, **6:**44
Doves, The, **1:**493
Doves of Peace, **2:**135
Døving, Anderz, **4:**680
Dow, Simon, **6:**35
Dowd, Irene, **4:**17
Dowell, Anthony, **2:443–444**, **5:**55, 100, *104*, **6:**135, 143, 146, 201
   as American Ballet Theatre guest artist, **1:**74, 75
   Dream performance, **2:**443, 445, 446, **5:**596, 597
   Enigma Variations performance, **2:**515
   Makarova roles, **4:**248
   Manon performance, **4:**256, 257, *257*
   Monotones performance, **4:**452
   Month in the Country performance, **4:**456, *456*
   Romeo and Juliet performance, **5:**396
   Royal Ballet, **1:**156, 157, 159, **2:**443–444, 445, **3:**262, 268, **4:**24, *242*, 470, **5:**396, 417, 418–420, *421*
   Sibley dance partnership, **1:**156, 157, 158, **2:**444, 445, **4:***244*
   Sleeping Beauty staging, **5:**420
   Swan Lake performance, **3:**567, **6:***33*
   Swan Lake staging, **5:**420, **6:**35
Dowland, John, **2:**76, **3:**109, **4:**505, **5:**115, 683
Down Argentine Way (film), **2:**615, **4:**434, 629, **6:***92*
Downes, Bob, **4:**219
Downes, John, **5:**251
Downes, Olin, **4:**272
Downhill, Jed, *as photographer*, **2:**290, 291, 293, 296, 297, **3:**220
Downrocking (break dance move), **6:**263
Downs, Brandon, **4:***238*
Downs, William, **4:***201*
Down to Earth, **2:**184, 616
downtown dance movement, **2:**170–171
Doyle, Desmond, **2:**515, **3:**512, *513*, **5:**396
D'Oyly Carte, Richard, **4:**189
Doyon-Ferland, Madeleine, **2:**36
Do You Love Me Still? . . . Or Do You Love Me Moving? (Charlip), **2:**110
Dózsa, Imre, **2:**124, **3:**418, 422, **6:***43*
Drabecka, Maria, **5:**211, 220
Drábek, Ivan, *as photographer*, **2:**310, **5:**618

Dracula, **2:**574, **4:**214, 668
Draghi, Giovanni Battista, **5:**280
Dragićević, Duška, **6:**435
Dragi Miha, **5:**677
dragon (totemic), **2:**139
Dragon and Jana, The, **2:**11, **5:**166
Dragon Dance, **2:**139, 140
Dragonfly, The, **5:***121*, 125
drag shows, **6:**190
Dragutinović, Branko, **6:**438
Drake, Alfred, **6:**278
Drake, Samuel, **6:**237
Drama Action Centre, Sydney, **4:**627
Drama of Motion, **3:**399
dramatic ballet, **1:**517, **4:**283, 284, **5:**458, 460, 484, 485, **6:**410–411
   pantomime as element, **5:**458, **6:**411, 442
   Slonimsky concept, **6:**614
   Zakharov statement on principles of, **6:**441–442
Dramatic Ballet, Volksbühne, East Berlin, **6:**378
Dramaturgy of 20th Century Ballet (Slonimsky), **3:**328
drambalet. *See* dramatic ballet
Drambalet (Moscow company), **5:**458, 466, 477
Dramma per Musica, **2:**114, **4:**185, *185*, **5:**96, **6:**353, *353*
Dramnyen Chotse, **1:**444
Drapal, Julia, **1:**240
Drapeau, Jacques, **3:***233*, **4:***71*
Drapeau, Jean, **3:**227
Draper, Muriel, **2:**444, **4:**26
Draper, Nancy, **6:**128
Draper, Paul, **2:444–445**, **6:***100*
Draper, Ruth, **2:**444
Drapier, Le (Halévy), **3:**5
draping. *See* attitude and shawl dance
Drastic Classicism, **1:**142, **4:**37
Draupadi, **4:**257
drawings. *See* prints and drawings
Drawn Blinds, **3:**429
Drayton, Thaddeus, **1:**520
Dražeta, Nada, **6:**435
Dream, The (Ashton ballet), **1:**156, **2:**443, **445–446**, **5:**417, 437, *596*, 597, **6:**175
   Aldous performance, **1:**38
   Australian popularity, **1:**233
   Coe performance, **2:**183
   Dowell performance, **2:**443, 445, 446, **5:**596, 597
   Lanchbery musical arrangement, **4:**117
   Lopukhov staging, **4:**224
   National Ballet of Canada staging, **4:**544
   Royal Winnipeg Ballet mounting, **4:**537, **5:***437*
   Weller performance, **6:**379
   Wells performance, **6:**380
Dream, The (Graham work), **4:**531
Dream about Kafka, **6:**67
dream ballets, **3:**620, **6:**278
Dreamboat (film), **6:**327
Dream Collector, **2:**359
Dream Dance, **4:**552, 558
Dream Dances, **4:**81, 602
Dreamers, **1:**517
Dreamgirls (musical), **1:**420, **6:**286, 287
Dream in a Sculptor's Studio, A, **2:**528
Dreaming Boys (Kokoschka illustrations), **1:**131

Dreaming of the Bones, The (Yeats), **3:**519
Dream Is Over, The, **2:**1
Dream Night, **4:**266
Dream of Galilei, **3:**51
Dream of Roses and Butterflies, A, **3:**129
Dreams, **1:**64, **3:**348, 532, **5:**638
Dreams—Dream of Fear and Dream of Desire, **1:**466
Dreams of Glory, **3:**342, 610
Dreams of Harmony, **4:**72
Dreams with Silences, **4:**218
Dream Team, **3:**421
Dreamtime (Australian Aborigines), **1:**227–228, 229–230, **5:**252
Dreamtime, **4:**81
Drechin, Semen, **1:**408
dreher, **1:**46
Drei Schwangeren, **3:**155
Dreisteirer dance, **3:**141
Dresden, Germany, **3:**146, 152, 153, 154
   Wigman school, **4:**95, 440, **6:**392, 393
   See also Jaques-Dalcroze Institute, Hellerau-Dresden
Dresden Brücke group, **1:**131
Dresden State Opera Ballet, **3:**154, 156, **4:**64
dress. *See* costume *headings*; practice clothes
Dress, The, **6:**175
Dressed to Kill, **4:***216*
Drew, David, **2:**445
Drew, Leonardo, **2:**296
Drewal, Henry John, **1:**14, **6:**25
   as contributor, **2:**209–213
Drewal, Margaret. *See* Thompson-Drewal, Margaret
Dr. Faustus Lights the Lights (Wilson opera), **6:***401*
Drie Diere, **2:**57, **5:**57
Drift, **1:**543, **4:**126
Drigo, Riccardo, **1:**301, 539, **2:**207, **446–447**, 596, **3:**562, **4:**226, 615, **5:**123, 160, 161, 246, **6:**30
drills, musical, **6:**240
Drilon, Mercy, **5:**172
Drinking Horn, The, **3:**519
Drink to Me Only with Thine Eyes, **1:**76
Driscoll, John, **2:**461
Driscoll, Stephan, *as photographer*, **3:**201
Driver, Senta, **2:**608
Drive Series, **6:**90
drmeš, **6:**428
dro, **6:**168, 169–170
Droit du Seigneur, Le, **5:**149
Drommebilleder, **5:**427
"Drops of Brandy" (tune), **3:**245
Dror, Liat, **3:**533, 534
Drosselbart, **3:**626, 628, **6:**304
Drottnerová, Marta, **3:**100, **5:**245
Drottningholm Court Theater, Stockholm, **1:**503, **6:45–48**
   Amors og Balletmesterns Luner staging, **3:**105
   archive, **4:**163, **6:**50
   Beck-Friis choreography, **1:**400
   Cramér productions, **2:**264
   Gustav III, king of Sweden, **6:**39
   lamps, **4:**188
   Skeaping reconstructions, **5:**603–604, **6:**38, 42, *46*
Drottning Kristina, **3:**100
Drouet, Jean-Pierre, **1:**462, **2:**575
Droulers, Pierre, **1:**412

Drozdova, Margarita, **5:**462, 467
Druet, *as photographer*, **5:**438
Drug Addict, **3:**469
Drugasheva, Maria, **3:***205*
Drum Dance (Korea), **2:**222, **4:**48
Drum Is a Woman, A (television program), **1:**396
Drumming, **2:**358, *359*
Drumscore, **3:**575
Drums of the War, **2:**102
Drums Sound in Hackensack, **3:**629, **6:**278
"Drunken Skipper," **5:**695
Drury Lane theatre, London, **5:**518
   Adam ballets, **1:**9, 10
   Albert, Monsieur, **1:**37
   Ballet Russe de Monte Carlo, **1:**296, 297, 313
   dance programs, **3:**256
   D'Egville production, **2:**364
   Desnoyer, Philip, **2:**394
   Essex, John, **2:**527
   lighting reforms, **4:**188–189
   Noverre stagings, **4:**695
   pantomime stagings, **1:**37, **5:**350, **6:**374
   Promenade Concerts, **5:**625
   Weaver productions, **6:**372–373, 374
Druze dance, **3:**538, *538*
Dryad, The, **2:**162
Dryden, John, **3:**252, **5:**281, 490
Drzewiecki, Conrad, **2:447–448**, 470, **5:**219, *219*
D35–D36 (Prague theater), **4:**238–239
Dtt Dygn, **3:**619
Duato, Nacho, **1:**234, **2:448–449**, **3:**234, **4:**602, **5:***234*, 674, **6:**10, 131
du Barry, Madame, **1:**122, **2:**352
DuBarry Was a Lady (film), **4:**2
DuBarry Was a Lady (musical), **6:**277
Düben, Andreas, **6:**38
Dubeneckienė, Olga, **4:**208
Dubey, Gopan, **3:***467*
Dubinon, Manuela, **2:**251, **5:**672
Dublin City Ballet, **3:**520
Dublin City Ballet School, **3:**520
Dublin Contemporary Dance Theater, **3:**520
Dublon, Ilse, **3:**531
Dubois, Leopold, **5:**605
Du Bois, W. E. B., **2:**168
Dubos, Abbé (Jean-Baptiste Du Bos), **1:**22, **4:**235, **5:**39
DuBoulay, Christine, **6:**292
Dubourg, Matthew, **3:**522
Dubreuil, Alain, **2:**513, **5:**421
Dubreuil, Pierre, **5:**260
Dubrovnin, Ivan, **2:**343
Dubrovsky, **5:**471
Duchamp, Marcel, **1:**134, 137, *141*, 244, 246, **2:**287, 292, 564, **3:**620, **5:**180, 335, 525, 543, **6:**356
Duchemin, Elisabeth, **2:**389
Duchenne, Guillaume Benjamin Amand, **4:**15
Duchesnay, Paul and Isabelle, **3:**432, **6:**180
Duckland, David, *as photographer*, **4:***218*
Ducos, Coralie, **2:**176
Ducoté, A., 270
Ducrow, Andrew, **2:**175, 176
Ducy-Barre, Louise, **5:**615, 616
Duddy, Kimberly, **1:**241

Dudinskaya, Natalia, **1:**502, **2:**174, **449–450, 4:**247, **5:**321
Ali-Batyr peformance, **5:**595
Don Quixote performance, **2:**437
Flames of Paris performance, **3:**12
Gayané performance, **3:**125
joint Soviet-American *Swan Lake* production, **6:**35
Laurencia performance, **4:**129, 284
Maryinsky school, **5:**480
Nureyev as partner, **5:**4–5
Path of Thunder performance, **5:**462
Sergeyev dance partnership and marriage, **5:**572, *572*
strong technique, **5:**458
students, **5:**47
Zakharov as influence, **6:**442
Dudko, Mikhail, **3:**56, *56*, **4:**283
Dudley, Alice, **2:**185
Dudley, Jane, **1:**79, 421, **2:**360, **450–451, 4:**153, **5:***184*
Batsheva Dance Company, **3:**532
London Contemporary Dance School, **4:**220
Martha Graham Dance Company, **2:**450, **3:**214, 216, **4:**441
New Dance Group, **4:**605
Dudley-Maslow-Bales Dance Trio, **1:**79, 421, **2:**450, **4:**306, 605
Duel, The (*Le Combat*), **1:**110, **2:**426, *426*, **3:**352, **5:**573
Duell, Daniel, **2:**357, **4:**274, 620, *620*
Chicago City Ballet, **6:**265
Nichols marriage and dance partnership, **4:**631
Duell, Joseph, **2:**357, **4:**180, 609, 631
Duende, **3:**437
duende (trance), **3:**6
Duenna, The, **6:**380
Duero, Edwin, **5:**172
Due Sindaci, Li, ossia La Vendemmia, **6:**69
Duet, **2:**470, **6:**108
Duet for One, **2:**605
Duets, **1:**75, **2:**294, **4:**37, **5:**105
Duett, **5:**677
Duetto in Nero, **6:**121
Dufay, Guillaume, **1:**364
Duff, Arthur, **3:**519
Dufort, Catherine, **4:**130
Dufort, Elisabeth, **4:**130
Dufort, Giambattista, **3:**545, **5:**324, **6:**123
Dufort, Marie, **1:**355
Du Four Brothers, **4:**522
Dufrenne, Mikel, **1:**24
Du Fu, **2:**132
Dufy, Raoul, **1:**316, **4:**418, **5:**544, 547
Dugied, Jean-Luc, *as photographer,* **3:**77, 78
dugu ceremony, **3:**121
Du Gul, **3:**195
Dukas, Paul, **2:**567, **3:**21, 72, **5:**125, 133
Duke, Jerry C., *as contributor,* **2:**23–25, 178–180, 258–259
Duke, Nicholas, **2:**255–256
Duke, Vernon, **5:**398
Dukelsky, Vladimir, **1:**316, **2:**410, **4:**320
Duke of Iron, **5:**255
Dukes, Ashley, **5:**296, 297, 298, 299
Dukes, Lulu, **2:**173
Duke's Motto, The (musical), **5:**404

Duke University, Durham, North Carolina, **1:**80
dukia dance, **4:**400–401
dukkala dance, **4:**408
Dulac, Edmund, **3:**558–559
Dulaine, Pierre, **5:***630,* **6:***288*
Dullin, Charles, **4:**425
Dulongpré, Louis, **2:**47
Dumanoir, Guillaume, **1:**4, **3:**81, **4:**511
Dumas, Alexandre (*fils*), **1:**155
Dumas, Russell, **1:**213, 215
Dumbadze, Éteri A., *as contributor,* **2:**95–97
Dumba festival, **6:**19
Dumbarton Oaks concerto (Stravinsky), **6:**5
Dumb Girl of Portici, The (film), **5:**125
Dumesny, Louis Gaulard, **4:**235
Dumilâtre, Adèle, **1:**10, 36, 37, **5:**148
Coralli ballets, **2:**203, 204
Giselle performance, **3:**177, 179
Gypsy, La, **2:***201*
Dumitrescu, Corina, **5:**390
Dumos, Madame F., **2:**176
Dumoulin, David, **2:***451,* 465, **3:**450, **5:**87
Dumoulin, François, **1:**516, **2:**451, **4:**106, **5:**87
Dumoulin, Henri, **2:**451, **5:**87
Dumoulin, Pierre, **2:**451, **5:**87
Dumoulin brothers, **2:**451, **3:**81, **5:**41, 87
Dumpe, Inessa, **4:**128
Dun, Barclay, **2:**257
Duncan, Elizabeth, **1:**239, **2:**452, 456, **3:**83, 160, **5:**476, 477
Duncan, Irma, **1:**39, **2:**146, *454,* 456, **3:**83, **5:**477
Duncan, Isadora, **1:**239, **2:451–458, 5:**37, 541
archival materials, **4:**167, 170
Argentine tour, **1:**111
artist collaborations, **1:**128, 130, 131, 502, **3:**71
as Ashton influence, **1:**149, 153, 158–159
as avant-garde dance influence, **1:**244, 410
barefoot dancing, **3:**46
as Behle influence, **1:**403
as Bodenwieser influence, **1:**466
Brazilian tour, **1:**534, **6:**295
as British dance education influence, **3:**277
costumes, **2:**245–246, 247, *453,* 454, 572
Craig relationship, **2:**262, 263, 454
dance aesthetics, **1:**25, **2:**263, 452–454, 456, 457, **6:**243
dance legacy, **2:**456–457, **6:**299
Delsarte system, **2:**371, 372, 452–453
as Dienes influence, **2:**417
as exemplifier of new American spirit, **6:**243
Finnish tour, **2:**632, **3:**311
as Fokine influence, **2:**457, **3:**14–15, 18, 20
as French modern dance influence, **3:**75, 83
Fuller association, **3:**93, 96
German performances and school, **3:**145, 160
as Hawkins influence, **4:**441
Hungarian tour, **3:**420
improvisational elements, **3:**445

as Italian dance influence, **3:**552
as Ito influence, **3:**558
as Jaques-Dalcroze influence, **3:**595
as Korean dance influence, **4:**51
Levinson reviews, **4:**155
Moscow school, **5:**458, 465, 476, 477, 484
music and dance concept, **4:**515, 518
Netherlands performances, **4:**589
Orientalism, **5:**46
Paris performances, **3:**71, 72
performance space preferences, **6:**161
as photographic subject, **5:**181, 182–183, *182*
political vision, **2:**456
practice clothes worn, **5:**241
as print and drawing subject, **1:***131,* **5:**261, *262,* **6:**356
as Rodin inspiration, **5:**370
Russian plastique, **5:**476, 477, 484
as St. Denis influence, **5:**494, 495
as Spessivtseva influence, **5:**679
students, **1:**211, **2:**456, **5:**560
Svetlov description, **6:**28
Swedish tour, **6:**41, 49
Ubekistan performances, **6:**306
Walkowitz drawings and watercolors, **1:***131,* **6:**356
Duncan, Kenn, **5:**183
as photographer, **6:**205
Duncan, Lisa, **3:**75, 77
Duncan, Margherita, **2:**456
Duncan, Maria-Theresa, **4:**21–22, **5:**181
Duncan, Nancy, **3:**274, **4:**220
Duncan, Raymond, **2:**417, **3:**420, **5:**181, *182,* 296, 385
Duncan Center Conservatory, Prague, **2:**310
Duncan Dancers, **2:**456
Dune, **2:**575
Dune Dance (film), **1:**542, **2:**609, **5:**440
Dunedin Dance Theatre, **4:**626–627
Dunham, Christine, **1:**77
Dunham, Katherine, **1:**421, **2:458–460,** 603, **6:***246,* 255
African-American music, **4:**520, **6:**258–259, 400
as Ailey influence, **1:**55, 59–60
archival materials, **4:**169
Australian tour, **1:**212
Balanchine collaboration, **6:**277
cakewalk use, **2:**26
Caribbean dance, **2:**64, 458, 459
dance ethnology, **4:**373
Federal Dance Project, **2:**580, **6:**246
jazz dance, **3:**598, 599
Metropolitan Opera Ballet guest choreography, **4:**382
musical theater, **6:**276, 278, 280
students, **1:**395, **5:**489, **6:**259
television performances and productions, **6:**132, 137, 139
Vodun ritual sources, **3:**335, **5:**356
Dunham School of Dance and Theater, New York City, **2:**458, **6:**258–259
Dunham Company, **2:**458, 459
Dunhoft, Dietmar, **4:**161
Duni, Egidio Romualdo, **2:**594
Dunin, Elsie Ivancich, **2:**602–603, **4:**374, 375
as contributor, **3:**330–331, **6:**426–431

Dunkles Danser, Den, **3:**100
Dunlop, Barbara, **5:**54
Dunn, Beryl, **2:**330
Dunn, Douglas, **1:**142, **2:460–461,** 607, **5:**98
Gordon collaboration, **3:**201
Grand Union, **3:**235, *235*
Dunn, James, **6:**141
Dunn, Judith, **1:**25, **2:**290, 462, 605, **3:**448, 635
Dunn, Robert Ellis, **1:**25, **2:**290, **461–462**
improvisation, **3:**445
Judson Dance Theater, **3:**633
postmodernism, **4:**519
students, **2:**119, **3:**54, 201, **5:**127, 292
Dunning, Gary, **1:**77
Dunning, Jennifer, **2:**20
as contributor, **6:**298–300
Duo (film dance), **2:**611
Duo Concertant, **4:**274, 608, 613, 618
Duo Éclatant, **6:**317
Duplessis, Maurice, **2:**39
Duplessis, Paul, **3:**230
Duponchel, Henri, **2:**171–172, **3:**5, 69, **5:**93, 499
Dupond, Patrick, **1:**59, 282, **2:462–463, 3:**75, *82,* 601, **4:**108, **5:**97, *97,* 98, 682
Dupont, *as photographer,* **1:**406
Dupont, Alexis, **5:**92
Dupont, Gabriel, **5:**690
Dupont, Jacques, **6:**217, 218
du Pont, Paul, **5:**58
Dupont, Pierre Landrin, **1:**5
Duport, Louis-Antoine, **1:**237, 409, 455, **2:**389, **464, 3:**68, 86, 191, 426, **5:**90, 91, 215
children's ballet, **6:**335
Vestris (Auguste) rivalry, **2:**464, **6:**333, *333*
Duport, Marie-Adélaïde, **2:**464
Duport, Paul, **5:**316
Duport family, **2:464–465**
Du Pradel, Abraham, **1:**4
Dupré, Eléonore, **3:**106
Dupré, Giovanni, **2:**433
Dupré, Jean-Denis, **2:**465
Dupré, Louis, **1:**283, 284, 365, 465, **2:465–466, 3:**67, **5:**41, 88, 215, 518
Académie Royale de Danse membership, **3:**81
Indes Galantes, Les, **3:**450
students, **2:**29, 465, **4:**694, **6:**331, 332
Dupré, Monsieur, **5:**105
Dupree, Roland, **5:**21
Duprés, Maedée, **1:**52, **3:**275
Dupuy, Dominique and François, **2:466, 3:**76, 84
Duquesnay, Lanchlin, **2:**596
Duran, Adelina, **2:**277
Durán, Diego, **4:**384, 385, 398–399, **5:**519
Durand, Eugene, **1:**460
Durand, José, **5:**146
Durang, Charles, **2:**339, 467, **3:**378, 379, **5:**199, 318, 623, 625, **6:**233, 237, 239, 290
Durang, John, **2:**36, **466–468,** **6:**233
"Durang's Hornpipe," **2:**467, **3:**378, 379, **6:***233*
Durante, Jimmy, **6:**182
Durante, Viviana, **2:**441, **4:**257, **5:**420
Durazzo, Giacomo, **1:**468, **3:**190, 365

Durban, South Africa, **5:**651, 654, 658–659
Durbin, Deanna, **2:**615
Dürer, Albrecht, **5:**259
Durey, Louis, **5:**237
D'Urfey, Thomas, **5:**251
Durgalal, **2:468**
Durkheim, Émile, **5:**357
Durko, Zsolt, **1:**233
Duroc, Gérald-Christophe-Michel, **1:**452
Durocher, Dominique, *as photographer*, **4:**71
Duryea, Oscan, **5:**628
Duschenes, Maria, **1:**535
Duse, Eleanora, **2:**263
Duse, Riccardo, **1:**375, **3:**345, **6:**53
Du Shixiang, **6:**385
Dushkin, Samuel, **6:**5
Dusmetov, Takhir, **6:**307
Dussasana Vadhan, **3:***662*
Düsseldorf-Duisberg Ballet, **2:***208*, **3:***4*, 132, 149, 157, *157*, 340, 360
  Josephslegende, Die, **3:**631
  Spoerli directorship, **5:**683
  Walter as ballet director-chief choreographer, **6:**358
Düsseldorf Neuer Tanz, **3:**157
Dust, **2:**526, **6:**111
Dust Bowl Ballads, **4:**306
"Dusty Miller, The" (song), **3:**376
Dutacq, Jean, **2:**414
Dutan, Joan, **4:**588
Dutch Association of Dance Teachers, **4:**587
Dutch Ballet, The, **5:**452
Dutch Festival of Improvisation, Dance, and Music, **4:**595
Dutch National Ballet, **1:**290, **2:468–470**, **4:**594, *596*, *597*
  archives, **4:**600
  Baiser de la Fée, Le, **3:**427
  Dantzig, Rudi van, **2:**347–348, **4:**593
  formation, **4:**592, 600
  Four Temperaments, The, **3:**58
  Gaskell, Sonia, **3:**121–122
  Green Table revival, **2:**469, **3:**630
  Manen, Hans van, **4:**251, 593
  Netherlands Dance Theater versus, **4:**592–593
  Noces revival, **4:***594*, 659
  Nureyev, Rudolf, **5:**7
  repertory, **2:**469, 470, 536, **4:**659
  Schayk, Toer Van, **5:**555–556
  Swan Lake, **2:**470, **4:***593*
  Weeme, Mascha ter, **2:**468, 469, **4:**592, **6:**375
Dutch Reflex Dance Company, **2:**171
Dutch Scapino Ballet. *See* Scapino Rotterdam
Du Tertre, Estienne, **4:**505
Duthe, Miss, **3:**86
Dutiful Ducks, **1:**52
Du Tillet, Madame, **6:**39
Dutot, Noël, **2:**589
Du Tralage, Jean Nicolas, **4:**108
Dutta, Raghu, **5:**23
Duttj, Geeta, **2:**625
Duval, Jean-Baptiste, **3:**49
Duvernay, Pauline, **1:**36, **2:**202, 203, 390, 405, **4:**340, **5:**93
Duvernoy, Anne M., **1:**461
DV8 Physical Theatre, **3:**274, 276
Dvořák, Antonín, **2:**309, **3:**51, **5:**269
Dvořák Variations, **2:**512, **3:**427
Dwarf Grenadier, The, **3:**414
dwarfs (ancient Egyptian performers), **2:**484

Dwyer, Thomas, **4:***151*
Dyad, **4:**115
Dybbuk (Dybbuk Variations), **4:**345, **5:**366, 408, **6:**174
  Berstein score, **1:**439, **4:**519
  Robbins choreography, **4:**614
Dybdal, Annemarie, **5:**430
Dyer, Sammy, **6:**257
Dying Swan, The (Le Cygne or *La Mort du Cygne)*, **1:**300, 306, 446, **2:***113*, 395, **471**
  American Ballet Company repertory, **3:**22
  Bowman performances, **1:**518
  Charrat performances, **2:**111, 112
  Fokine choreography, **2:**471, **3:**15, 16, 565, 568, **4:**282, **5:**227
  Henie ice skating version, **3:**357
  Ivanov *Swan Lake* "white scene" as influence, **4:**282
  Markova performance, **4:**269
  Nerina performance, **4:**584
  Pavlova's Australian performance, **1:**207
  as Pavlova's signature role, **2:**471, **3:**15, 16, **5:***119*, 121, 123, 125
  Ulanova performance, **4:**226
  Vyroubova performance, **6:**353
Dyk, Peter van, **2:471–472**, **3:**150, 318, **5:**96, 97, 320, 531, **6:**353
  Geneva Ballet, **2:**471–472, **6:**52
  Hamburg Ballet, **2:**471, **3:**337
  Henze collaboration, **3:**359
Dylan, Bob, **2:**1
Dynalix, Paulette, **2:**199
Dynamic Breathing and Harmonic Gymnastics (Stebbins), **1:**470
Dyrehavsbakken, Copenhagen, **2:**384
dyshe. See valle dyshe
Dyson, Clare, **1:**219
Dzharishvili, David, **3:**135
Dzieciństwo Jezusa, **5:**219
Dzieje Teatru Narodowego (Bogusławski), **5:**220
Džindo, Adnan, **6:***436*

E=MC², **4:**134
Eadeyechev, Nikolai, **1:***492*
Eadie Was a Lady, **2:**184
Eager, Janet, **3:**274
Eagle, Arnold, *as photographer*, **3:**215
Eagle Dance, **4:**554, 555, 563, *564*, 568, **5:**240
Eagling, Wayne, **2:**468, 470, **4:***245*, 470, **5:***100*
Eakins, Thomas, **5:**178, *179*
Eames, Marian, **6:**297
Eanal, **3:**154
Earl Carroll's Vanities (revue), **2:**572, **6:**112
Earle, David, **2:**40, 44, 47, 350, **4:**545, **5:**57, **6:**133
"Earl of Erroll, The," **3:**246, **5:**695
Early, Teresa, **3:**271
Early Departures, **3:**389
Early Floating, **3:**349, 350
Early Memoirs (Nijinska), **4:**646
Early Music movement, **5:**326, 327
Early Reign of Oleg, The, **2:**55, **4:**276
Earth Dreaming, **1:**214
Earth Mother (African deity), **6:**18
Easdale, Brian, **5:**331
East, Alison, **4:**628

East Africa. *See* Central and East Africa; *specific countries*
East Anglia, England, **3:**242
East Asia. *See* China; Japan; Korea
East Berlin Komische Oper, **1:**1, **2:**471, **3:**317
Easter
  English traditional dance, **3:**242
  linear *moresca*, **4:**461
  liturgical dance, **2:**164
  pagan fertility rites, **2:**165
  tradititional dancing, **2:**168
  Ukrainian dance, **6:**221
Easter Freeway Processional, **2:**566
Easter Island. *See* Rapanui
Eastern Europe. *See* European traditional dance; *specific countries*
Eastern Orthodox Church, **2:**537, 540, **3:**294–295, **6:**429
Eastern Regional Sacred Dance Association, **4:**212
Easter Parade (film), **1:**194–195, **4:**419
East Germany (former). *See* Germany
Eastin, Evelin, **4:**391
East Java. *See* Indonesia
Eastman School of Music, Rochester, **3:**211, 212
East Midlands Mobile Arts (EMMA), **3:**273
East River, **2:**134
Easy to Love (film), **1:**435
E.A.T. (Experiments in Art and Technology), **5:**314
Eaters of Darkness, **3:**203, 520
Eatin' Rain in Space, **3:**448
Eaton, Mary, **6:**371
Ebara Tomoko, **3:**591
Ebbelaar, Hans, **2:**470, **4:**602, **5:**290
Ebb och Flod, **3:**100
ébéng, **1:**174
Eberhard, Christian, **6:**294
Ebers, John, **1:**446, **2:**389, 401
Ebner, Doris, **1:**240
Eboina della Siberia, L', **2:**81
Ebony Concerto (Stravinsky), **6:**6, 412
Ebreo da Pesaro, Guglielmo. *See* Guglielmo Ebreo da Pesaro
Ebru, **6:**213
Ebsen, Buddy, **2:**615, **6:**101, 141, *141*, 142, 320
ecarté, **1:**334
Ecce Homo, **4:**134
eccentric tap dancing, **6:**99
Eccentrique, **1:**73, **2:**583
Eccles, Andrew, *as photographer*, **5:**573, 635
Ecco, **4:**479
Echelle, L', **5:**676
Echigo Jishi, **1:**361
Echo, **2:**461
Echoes of American Ballet (Moore anthology), **4:**457
Echoes of a Night Sky, **2:**1
Echo et Narcisse (Gluck), **3:**190
Echoing of Trumpets, **2:**512, **6:**42, 42, 201
Echo Point, **6:**95
Echos de Pologne, **2:**368
Echo und Narzissus, **1:**98
Eck, Imre, **1:**307, 308, 370, **2:**473–474, **3:**360
  Budapest Opera Ballet stagings, **3:**417
  choreographies to Bartók music, **3:**416
  Miraculous Mandarin performance, **3:***416*

Eckensteher, **3:**155
Eckl, Shirley, **2:**568
Eckner, Babette, **3:**380
Eckstein, Clare, **2:**375
Eclogues (Virgil), **5:**112, 113
École-Atelier Rudra Béjart Lausanne, **1:**407, **6:**54
École d'Arcueil, **5:**526
École de Loie Fuller, **3:**94–95
École de Minerve, L', **1:**284
École de Mouvement, Kiev, **4:**634
École des Amants, L', **4:**236
École de Vieux-Colombier, L', Paris, **4:**423–424, 425, 426
École Royale de Chant, **5:**371
École Supérieure de Danse du Québec, **2:**47, 152, **3:**227, **4:**577
École Supérieure d'Études Chorégraphiques, **3:**84
Ecos, **2:**449
écossaise, **2:**301, **474–475**, **5:**445
écosse, écossaise vs., **2:**474
Écriture de la dance théâtrale (Conté), **4:**687, 688
Ecstasy of Purpose, An (MacTavish), **4:**626–627, 629
Ecstasy of Rita Joe, The, **5:**436
Ecstatic Dances, **6:**390
ecstatic dancing, **6:**185–186
  ancient Greece, **3:**292
  Egyptian *dhikr*, **2:**486–487
  Hasidim, **3:**528
  as liturgical dance, **4:**213
  Shaker, **5:**575–577
  Sufi, **3:**524–525, **4:**79, 403
  Turkey, **6:**209
  See also whirling dervishes
Ecstatic Orange, **4:**275, 622
Ecuador, **2:475–477**
Ecumeur des Mers, L', **1:**86, **3:**180, **6:**73
Écuyère, L', **2:**114
Eddy, Glen, **4:**602
Edel, Alfredo, **2:**477, **4:**258
Edelson, Mary Beth, **1:**140
Eden, **4:**677
Eden, Dottie, **1:***450*
Eden-Concert, Paris, **4:**523
Edge, **1:**51
Edgerton, Harold E., **5:**178
Edinburgh, Scotland, **3:**248, 249
Edinburgh International Ballet, **6:**313
Edinburgh International Festival, **2:**267, **5:**415
Edinoff, Ellen, **4:**593, 594, 597
Edison, Thomas Alva, **2:**601, **4:**189
Edna M, **3:**575
Edo period (Japan), **3:**637, 638, 650, **4:**30, 41, 86
EDRIN 1992, **3:**424
Ed Sullivan Show, The (television program), **1:**382, 419, **2:**619, **5:**632, **6:**137
Eduardova, Evgenia, **1:**460, **2:**150, **3:**147
  fan collection, **2:**571
  students, **4:**529, **5:**166, **6:**29, 357, 449
education, dance. *See as subhead under specific countries; names of specific ballet companies, schools, and teachers*
Educational Ballets Limited. *See* Ballets Russes de Monte Carlo
Education and Community Program (English National Ballet), **2:**513

Education Institute of Music and Dance, Paris. *See* Institut de Pédagogique Musical et Choréegraphique, Paris
Education of the Girlchild, **4:**451
Edur, Thomas, **2:**514, *514*
Edvardsen, Sølvi, **4:**679
Edward II, **1:***452*, 453
Edwards, Bettina, **4:**624
Edwards, Gus, **5:**238
Edwards, Leslie, **2:**477–478, **3:**427, **4:**470
Edwards, Winifred, students, **5:**596, **6:**106
Edwige, o Il Sogno, **3:**620
Edwin Strawbridge Ballet, **1:**39
Edye, Stephanie, **1:**211
Een, Robert, **2:**171
E. F. Albee syndicate, **6:**99
Efe (people), **2:**87, **6:**12
effacé, **1:**198, 333–334
Effects of Love for the Motherland, The, **4:**35
Effort (Laban-Lawrence), **4:**94, 101–102
Effort-Shape analysis (Laban), **4:**97, 98, 104
affinities, **4:**103–104
eight basic actions, **4:***101*, 102
Effort Theory (Laban), **4:**94, 101
Efimov, Nikolai, **1:**256, **2:**342, **4:***317*
Efimov, Vasily, **3:**194
Efrati, Moshe, **1:**350, **3:***531*, 532
Efremova, Svetlana, **4:**285
Eger, Lise, **4:**679, *680*
egg dance, **2:***550*, **6:**316
Egiazarian, G., **1:**122
Egk, Werner, **1:**1, 436, **2:**111, 471, **478**, **3:**149, 340, **4:**184, 517, **6:**202
Eglè, Queen of Grass Snakes, **4:**208
Eglevsky, André, **1:**49, **2:478–479**, **3:**343–344, **4:**68, **5:**17, 279, 606, **6:**348
Apollo performance, **1:**96, **2:***244*, **4:***611*
as Ballets Russes de Monte Carlo guest artist, **1:**310, 315
Brahms Variations performance, **3:***225*
Cuban ballet school, **2:**277
Cuban performance, **2:**279
Denby profile of, **2:**375
Fokine ballets, **3:**24
Grand Ballet du Marquis de Cuevas, **3:**225
on Legat's teaching methods, **4:**479, **6:**128
New York City Ballet, **4:**479, 620, **6:**64
Nutcracker roles, **5:**14
Pas de Trois performance, **4:**269
Swan Lake role, **6:**34
Tallchief (Maria) dance partnership, **4:**616, **6:**85, *85*
technical feats, **2:**479, *479*
television performances, **6:**137
World's Fair (1940), **1:**498
See also Eglevsky Ballet Company
Eglevsky, Marina, **2:**479, **5:**436
Eglevsky Ballet Company, **2:**587, **4:**24, **6:**340, 363
Egorova, Lubov, **2:479–480**, **6:**344
Ballets de la Jeunesse, **3:**73
Diaghilev's *Sleeping Beauty* performance, **2:**409, **5:**611
Maryinsky Ballet, **4:**282
Paris dance studio, **3:**82
as Rayet influence, **5:**320

students, **1:**403, 498, 518, 532, 539, **2:**111, 150, 341, 350, 447, 478, 480, **3:**87, 121, 350, 391, 508, 626, **4:**107, 110, 178, 182, 209, 336, 457, 529, **5:**553, 603, 606, **6:**352
Egri, Susanna, **2:480–481**, **3:**553
Eguchi, **3:**647
Eguchi Takaya, **3:**339, 590, **5:**33
Egúngún (people), **6:**12
Egypt, **2:479–499**
ancient dance, **2:481–486**, 493
accompaniments, **4:**498
castanet origin, **2:**78
costume, **2:**234, 485
danse de ventre, **4:**662–663
fan usage, **2:**569
mime, **4:**423
contemporary dance companies, **2:495–499**
dance research and publication, **4:**416
libraries and museums, **4:**158
music and song types, **4:**489
traditional dance, **1:**401, **2:486–495**, **4:***403, 404*, 485–486, 488, 491
combat dance, **4:***405, 406*, 407
danse du ventre (belly dance), **2:**344–345, *345–346*, *345*, 494–495, *494–495*, **4:***408*, 409, 410, 411, 662–663, 664
Reda troupe, **4:**412, 417, 490
zār, **2:**487–488, **4:**466, 488, **6:**445
trance rituals, **6:**185
Egypta, **5:**493, 494, 583
Egypt Dances (film), **4:**414
Egyptian Nights. *See Nuit d'Égypte, Une*
Egypt through Centuries (spectacle), **5:**491, 493
Ehrenburg, Ilya, **3:**590
Ehrenswärd, Count (Sweden), **6:**39
Ehrfur, Manon, **4:**58
Ehrmann, Hans, *as contributor*, **2:**127, **6:**304
Eifman, Boris, **2:**499, **3:**125, **5:**460, 461, 462
choreographic style, **5:**464–465
Saint Petersburg Theater of Contemporary Ballet, **5:**469
Eigenkunst (Laban concept), **6:**391
8, *Letters from Eight*, **4:**171
Eight-Animal Dance, **2:**141
Eight Beatitudes, **2:**417, **3:**421
Eight by Benny Goodman, **5:**25
Eight Clear Places, **4:**350
Eight Column Line, **4:**649
Eight Easy Pieces, **4:**615
18 basses dances (Attaingnant), **6:**178
18 Happenings in 6 Parts (Kaprow), **1:**139
Eight Hands Round, **3:***245*
Eighth Eclogue, **3:**418
Eight Jelly Rolls, **5:**440, **6:**153
Eight Lancashire Lads, **4:**522
Eight Solos, **5:**440
Eiko. *See* Eiko and Koma
Eiko and Koma, **2:499–500**, **5:**46
Eilber, Janet, **2:**606, **3:**220
Eine Kleine Nachtmusik, **5:**58
Einem, Gottfried von, **1:**456, **3:**132, 152, 317, 340, **4:**517
Eine vision des Irdischen Glücks, **3:**152
Eine Weltgeschichte des Tanzes (Sachs), **3:**161, 583
Einhorn, der Drache und der Tigermann, Das, **3:**133

Einstein on the Beach (Glass and Wilson), **1:***143*, 144, **2:**119, **6:**401
Eis, Alice, **6:**317, 319
Eisenstein, Sergei, **2:**133, 191, **3:**48
Eisler, Lee, **6:**134
Ejagham (people), **2:**274
Ek, Anders, **2:**500
Ek, Mats, **2:**284, **500–501**
Giselle, **1:**391, **2:**500, **3:**183
Kibbutz Contemporary Dance Company choreography, **3:**532
Royal Swedish Ballet, **6:**44, *44*
Sleeping Beauty, **3:**338
Ek, Niklas, **1:**292, **2:**501
Ekaterinburg Opera Theater, **5:**470
Ekaterinburg State Choir, **5:**474
Ekiti Yoruba (people), **6:**12
Ekman, Marie-Louise, **2:**501
Ekon av Trumpeter. *See Echoing of Trumpeters*
Ekstasis, **3:**212
Ekston, Anna, **2:**528
El. *For names and titles with this prefix, see key word*
Elagabalus, **5:**74
Elamites, **4:**357
Elbéniz, Isaac, **5:**673
Elbers, Johan, *as photographer*, **1:**103, 143, 526, 543, 544, **2:**19, 46, 120, 247, 289, 359, 461, 463, **3:**13, 446, 586, **4:**22, 531, 548, **5:**33, 106, 128, 131, 440, 447, 464, 508, **6:**140, 163
Elbow Room, **1:**142
Elda, ossia Il Patto degli Spiriti, **3:**224
Eldorado, Paris, **4:**523
Elective Affinities (Goethe), **1:**199, 442
See also Affinités Electives, Les
Electra (Sophocles drama), **3:**216, 385
Electra (Taglioni ballet), **3:**315, **6:**75
electrical stage lighting. *See* lighting for dance
electric boogie, **1:**538, **5:**633
Electric Dance Ensemble, **1:**217
electric guitar, **6:**249
Electro-Bach, **1:**461, 462
electromyography, **4:**15
Electronic Ballets, **3:**132
Electronic Love (Kozma), **5:**569
electronic music, **1:**403, **2:**20
Cunningham experiments, **2:**288, 289, 296
Georgi choreography, **4:**518
Gsovska choreography, **4:**519
London Contemporary Dance Theatre, **4:**219
Nikolai use, **4:**519, 650
Electronics, **4:**519, **6:**340
Elegaic Song, **5:**24
Elegia, **4:**602
Elegiac Blues, **4:**113
Elegy upon My Friend Mr. John Playford (Purcell), **5:**200
Elejar, Eddie, **5:**171, 172, 173
Elekes, Edit Weber, **3:**412
Elektra (Strauss), **3:**205, **4:**585, **5:**512
Élémens de la danse (Pauli), **1:**90
Element (film dance), **2:**606
elementarism, **1:**132
Elementary Treatise (Blasis), **2:**254, **5:**90
Elementos de la ciencia contradanzaria (Iza Zamácola), **5:**676

Éléments, Les, **1:**288, 464, **2:**95, 465, **3:**24, 180, 260, 315, 329, **4:**475, **5:**138
Elements of the Art of Dancing (Strathy), **6:**126
Eleonora Duse—Isadora Duncan: Adieu et au Revoir, **3:**61
Eleo Pomare Company, **1:**212, 214
Elerz e Zulmida, **5:**277, *538*
Eleta, Angel, **1:**315
elevation (*élévation*), **1:**339, 340, 341, 343, 347, 348
Cerrito facility, **2:**93
Cunningham technical skill, **2:**285, *285*
Maywood's abilities, **4:**338
Messerer virtuosity, **4:***359*
Nijinsky abilities, **3:**18, **4:**646
See also leaps
élevé. *See* elevation
Eleven, **2:**296
Elf, The, **5:**385
Elfelt, Peter, **1:**399
as photographer, **1:**507, 509, **4:**6, **5:**250
Elfes, Les, **2:**587, **3:**22–23, 24, **4:**269, 342
Elgar, Edward, **2:**400, **3:**428
Amoras score, **3:**508, 511
Sanguine Fan score, **2:**574
See also Enigma Variations
Elgeyo (people), **2:**86
Elias, Brian, **4:**245
Eliasen, Johnny, **3:**13, **5:**432, 433
Eliash-Chain, Meira, **3:**534
"Elie Nadelman: Sculptor of the Dance" (Kirstein), **4:**28
Eliot, Maine, **6:**248
Eliot, T. S., **3:**356, **5:**488, **6:**286
Eliot Feld Ballet. *See* Feld Ballets/NY
Elisir d'Amore, L' (Donizetti), **3:**360
Elite Syncopations, **4:**243, 519
Eliza, **4:**332
Elizabeth, empress of Russia, **3:**365, **4:**276
Elizabeth I, queen of England, **2:**76, 255, 337, 501, **4:**307, **5:**340
Elizabeth II, queen of Great Britain, **1:**153, **2:**179, 403, 509, **5:**433
Elizabethan progresses, **2:501**, **5:**343
Elizabethan theater, **3:**607
Elizariev, Valentin, **1:**408, **2:501–502**, **4:**36, **5:**460, 461
Elkayam, Oshra, **4:**499, 532, 533
Elkin, Adolphus P., **1:**223
as photographer, **1:**223
Elkins, Doug, **2:**609
Ellend, Karoline, **6:**386
Ellingerová, Růžena, **5:**270
Ellington, Duke, **4:**107, 113, 117, 202, 254–255, **6:**256
Alvin Ailey Company scores, **1:**56, 57, 59, 196, **3:**578
Beatty collaboration, **1:**396
Berry Brothers, **1:**439
Four Step Brothers, **3:**57
Nutcracker jazz version, **1:**454
Queenie Pie musical, **2:**567
Sophisticated Lady, **2:**578
Ellington, Mercedes, **6:**286
Ellingtonia, **1:**396
Elliniko choroi (Sakellariou), **3:**303
Elliott, Donald, **2:**71, 72
Elliott, G. H., **4:**520
Elliott & Fry, London, *as photographer*, **3:**129
Elliott-Clarke, Shelagh, 2, 590

Ellis, Angela, **5**:301
Ellis, Catherine J., **1**:230
    as contributor, **1**:229–230
Ellis, David, **5**:301
Ellis, Ed, *as photographer*, **2**:42
Ellis, Lucille, **2**:458, **6**:259
Ellis, Richard, **3**:379, **6**:292
Ellis Island (film), **2**:609, **4**:451
Ellmerich, Luis, **1**:537
Ellwood family, **3**:240
Ellys, John, **5**:519
Elman, Mischa, **6**:32
Elmhirst, Dorothy and Leonard,
    4:93, 94
Elmolo (people), **2**:86
Éloge à la Folie, **1**:305, 461, **5**:163
Eloy, Jean-Claude, **1**:461
Elseeta (The American Dancing
    Girl), **6**:316
Elson, Sandra, **6**:179
Elssler, Anna, **2**:502
Elssler, Fanny, **1**:44, 86, 199,
    2:502–506, **3**:618, **4**:139,
    5:150, 516, 528, 640, **6**:71
    American tour, **2**:504, **6**:160, 237,
        269, 298–299
    Barre statuette of, **1**:365
    Bavarian Ballet guest
        appearance, **1**:390
    Belgian performances, **1**:410,
        5:147
    La Cachucha dance, **2**:107, 203,
        405, 502, 503, *503*, 522, **3**:69,
        122, 185, **5**:89, 93, 672, **6**:451
    Carey (Gustave) dance
        partnership, **2**:60
    caricatures of, **2**:69
    Catarina performance, **2**:80, 505
    Cerrito pas de deux, **2**:94
    as character dancing popularizer,
        2:107, 504, 522, **3**:69
    Cortesi *Giselle* production, **2**:209
    Cracovienne popularization,
        2:107, 504, *505*, **4**:57, 340
    Cuban performance, **2**:276, 504
    Diable Boiteux performance,
        2:203, 390, 405, 503
        See also subhead La Cachucha
        dance above
    Esmeralda performance, **2**:95,
        502, 503, 504, 505, 524,
        4:453, **5**:403
    Faust performance, **2**:60, 505,
        4:339
    Fille Mal Gardée performances,
        1:486, **2**:502, 503, 596, **3**:360
    Fitzjames (Nathalie) association,
        3:5
    Fra Diavolo performance, **2**:390
    Gautier's championship of,
        3:122–123
    Gipsy performance, **2**:504, **3**:185,
        4:340
    Giselle performances, **1**:410, 486,
        2:502, 504, 505, **3**:180, 181,
        4:453
    Guest biography of, **3**:321
    Hamburg Ballet guest
        performances, **3**:336
    Hungarian performances,
        3:413, 414
    King's Theatre (London)
        performances, **3**:259, 260
    Koni reviews, **4**:41
    Lami watercolor of, **4**:116
    Mazilier dance partnership,
        4:340
    Mazilier roles, **5**:340
    Monplaisir dance partnership,
        4:453
    Nina performances, **2**:503, **3**:180

Noblet rivalry, **4**:657
Paris Opera Ballet, **3**:69, **5**:89, 93
Paris Opera debut in *La Tempête*,
    2:202–203
partners, **6**:335
Perrot association, **5**:134, 136,
    137, 138, 139
Plisetskaya comparison, **5**:204
popularity compared with
    Madame Céleste's, **2**:85
practice clothes worn, **5**:241
Romantic era identification,
    2:440, 502, 503, **5**:70, *89*
Ronzani ballets, **5**:403
Russian tours, **1**:486, **2**:505,
    4:280, **5**:454, **6**:451
La Scala appearances, **5**:528
Smith (George Washington)
    association, **5**:615
Swiss Milkmaid performance,
    2:505, **6**:50, 51
Taglioni (Marie) contrasted with,
    2:502, **3**:123, 185, **6**:74
Taglioni (Marie) rivalry, **2**:405,
    503, 504, **3**:69, 185, **5**:93,
    6:51, 73, 74
tarantella performance, **6**:104
technical strengths, **2**:502, **3**:222
Viennese ballet, **1**:237, 238, *239*,
    2:464, 502, 505, **3**:358, 380
Elssler, Thérèse, **2**:502–504, 505,
    3:358, **4**:340, **5**:134, 150
"Elssler Quadrilles, Selected from
    Her Favorite Dance," **6**:234
Elssler sisters, **2**:502–506
Elverhøj, **1**:539
Elvin, Violetta, **1**:459, **2**:115, **506**,
    5:294, 313, 416, 639
Elvira Madigan, **1**:400
Elvire, **1**:247, **2**:351, **5**:132
Elyash, Nikolai I., **5**:483
    as contributor, **2**:14–16,
        3:191–192, 539–540, **4**:35–36,
        5:479–481, **6**:311–312
Elyot, Sir Thomas, **2**:167, **3**:281,
    6:178, 374
Emard, Sylvain, **2**:43
Emaux et camées (Gautier), **3**:122
Embarque, **2**:355
Embarquement pour Cythère, L',
    2:413
Embassy Ballet. *See* Continental
    Ballet
Embattled Garden, **3**:218, 221, *531*,
    5:407
Embleton, Lloyd, **5**:*564*
embolima, **2**:159
*Embrace Tiger and Return to
    Mountain*, **4**:602, **5**:305,
    6:43, 146
Emeralds (*Jewels* section), **4**:345,
    450, 612, 617, *618*
Emerson, Billy, **6**:319
Emerson, Ralph Waldo, **2**:504
Emerson, Lake, and Palmer, **5**:406
Emilia-Romagna, Italy. *See*
    Aterballetto
EMMA (East Midlands Mobile
    Arts), **3**:273
Emmanuel, Maurice, **3**:302
emmeleia, **2**:506–507, **3**:289, **4**:499,
    5:598
Emmer, Milly, **4**:600
Emmerson, George S.
    as contributor, **3**:243–250
    as photographer, **3**:244, 245,
        247, 248
Emmert, Richard, **4**:333
Emmons, Beverly, **2**:292, **4**:191
Emond, G., **1**:283

"Emperor Destroys the
    Formations, The" (dance),
    6:82–83
Emperor Jones, The (play), **3**:391,
    4:198, **5**:256
Emperor Norton, **2**:162
Emperor Quin, The, **2**:116
"Emperor's New Clothes, The"
    (Andersen), **2**:401
"Emperor Waltz" (Strauss), **6**:3
Empire de la Mode, L', **1**:465
Empire de la Sagesse, L', **1**:465
Empire Theatre, London, **1**:37
    Bedells as first British *prima
        ballerina*, **1**:400
    Cecchetti performances, **2**:82
    closure, **2**:395
    Genée performances, **3**:128,
        4:522
    Lanner as ballet mistress, **4**:121
    music hall, **4**:522
    Sylvia abridged version, **6**:64
    Wilhelm scenic and costume
        designs, **3**:261, **4**:121, 522,
        6:397
Emprises de l'Amour, Les (Bernard),
    6:331
Empty, **2**:449
Empty Place, **1**:241
Empty Speech, **3**:52
Empty Winds (Cage), **2**:23
Empyrean Dances, **3**:617
Enas, **3**:351
En Blanc, **3**:205
En Blanc et Noir, **1**:462
Encarnado, **3**:389
Encatadora de Madrid, La, **5**:499
Enčeva, P., **5**:166
enchaînement. *See* ballet technique,
    linking movements
Enchanted Forest, The, **2**:299, 446,
    480, **3**:562
Enchantements d'Alcine, Les, **5**:439
En Choro (periodical), **3**:304
encomium, **2**:158
Encontros ACARTE, **5**:235
Encore! Encore! (Canadian
    project), **2**:49
Encores! (American musical
    theater series), **6**:288
"Encounter" (skating program),
    6:180
Encounter pas de deux, **4**:71
Encuentro Coreográfico (Chile),
    2:126
Encyclopedia of Kinetorgraphy
    (Knust), **4**:32
*Encyclopedia of Theatre Dance in
    Canada* (Adams and Adams
    eds.), **4**:166
Encyclopedia of the Ballet
    (Espinosa), **2**:525
Encyclopédie (Diderot and
    d'Alembert), **1**:4, 47, **2**:589,
    3:545–546, **4**:173–174, 379,
    6:123, 125
Encyclopédie méthodique, **6**:126
*Encyclopédie pitoresque de la
    musique*, **1**:481
End, The, **4**:73
Endangered Species, **1**:462, **2**:45
Endechas de canario (Pisador), **2**:51
Endicott, Josephine Ann, **1**:389
Endymion, **3**:508, 511, 563,
    6:331, 332
Enea, Mademoiselle, **5**:71
Enea in Italia, **3**:365
Enekes, Istvan, **3**:421
Enemy in the Figure, **1**:216

Enemy Way, **4**:578
Enescu, George, **2**:343, **5**:386
Enfance du Christ, L' (Berlioz),
    5:*219*
Enfant et les Sortilèges, L', **1**:446,
    4:81, **5**:315, 316
Enfant Prodigue, L', **3**:118
    Auber score, **5**:342
    Gardel (Pierre) version, **5**:264,
        6:333
    Gluck-Sandor version, **5**:266
Enfants du Paradis, Les (film),
    4:423, **5**:176
Enfin . . . Une Revue (musical),
    2:79
Eng, Frank, **3**:387
Engdahl, Horace, **6**:50
Engel, Johann Jakob, **3**:556
Engel, Lehman, **5**:59, **6**:276
Engelmann, Godefroi, **1**:*202*
engelskdans, **2**:*381*, **4**:671
England. *See* Great Britain
English Country Dance Society,
    2:592, **4**:221
English Dance of Death, The
    (Rowlandson), **4**:315, **5**:259
English Dance Theatre, **3**:273
English Dancing Master (Playford).
    See Dancing Master, The
English Folk Dance and Song
    Society, London, **2**:257, **3**:34,
    238, 239, **5**:582, 695, **6**:247
    Vaughan Williams Memorial
        Library, **4**:163
English Folk Dance Society of
    America, **3**:367, **6**:247
*English Folk Song: Some
    Conclusions* (Sharp), **5**:582
English jig, **5**:507
English National Ballet (formerly
    London Festival Ballet),
    1:420, **2**:507–515, **5**:554, 603
    Aldous, Lucette, **1**:38
    Ashton productions, **1**:158,
        2:510, 514
    Beatrix (*La Jolie Fille de Gand*),
        3:620
    Bruce choreography, **2**:1, **3**:273
    Coppélia performance, **2**:200
    Darrell choreography, **2**:349, 350
    Davies (Siobhan) choreography,
        2:355
    Diaghilev production revivals,
        2:508, 510, 511, 512, **3**:269,
        6:404
    directors, **3**:269
    Evdokimova performances,
        2:561, 562
    Ferri performance, **1**:110
    Flindt, Flemming, **3**:12
    Fokine and Massine works,
        2:424, 508, 510, 512
    foreign tours, **2**:509, 513
    Fracci guest *Giselle* performance,
        3:59
    Gilpin, John, **3**:*174*, 175
    Grigoriev as *régisseur*, **3**:308
    Hynd choreography, **2**:511, 512,
        514, **3**:427
    Kun guest performance, **4**:74
    Lander (Harald) choreography,
        4:119
    Larsen guest performances,
        4:125, 126
    Lichine choreography, **4**:178–179
    Markova-Dolin ensemble as
        antecedent, **4**:270
    Nureyev productions, **2**:511, 513,
        5:7, 398
    Nutcracker, The, **3**:*270*, **5**:*13*, 15

origins, **2:**425, 507, **3:**269, **4:**270
repertory, **2:**509–510, 512–514, 524, 536
Romeo and Juliet, **5:**398
Royal Danish Ballet ties, **2:***511,* **3:**269
Sanguine Fan, The, **2:**574
Schaufuss, Peter, **5:**554, 555
Seymour performance, **5:**575
Skeaping *Giselle* production, **5:**603
Symphony in Three Movements, **3:**273
Terabust, Elisabetta, **6:**143
Woizikowski revivals of Diaghilev works, **6:**404
English National Opera, **3:**269
English school. *See* Ballet technique, major schools; Ashton, Frederick; de Valois, Ninette; Royal Ballet
English Society for Dance Research, **1:**541
English traditional dance. *See under* Great Britain
Englund, Richard, **1:**75
Englund, Sorella, **3:**39, **5:**431
engravings. *See* prints and drawings
Enigma Gallus, **5:**677, **6:**437
Enigma Variations, **2:515–516,** **5:**187, 300
   Ashton production, **1:**156–157, *158,* **5:**417
   Beriosova performance, **1:**430
   Dowell performance, **2:**444
   Elgar score, **1:**156, **2:**515–516, **5:**691
   Mason performance, **4:**307
   Staff version, **5:**691
Enkelmann, Siegfried, *as photographer,* **1:**1, **3:**317, **6:**394
Enken i Spejlet, **1:**539, **5:**294, 429
Enlaces, **2:**279
Enlèvement d'Adonis, L', **2:**389
Enlèvement de Prosperpine, L', **5:**504
Enlightenment, **1:**125, **5:**35
en manège, **1:**347
Enman'i-za, **4:**41
Ennosuke Jūhachiban, **3:**441
En'o Jūshu, **3:**441
Enrietty, J., *as photographer,* **4:**636, 638
Enrôlement, L', **2:**299
En Saga, **4:**275
ENSA (Entertainments National Service Association), **3:**271, **4:**110
Ensayo Sinfónico, **1:**49
Ensemble for Free Dance (KASP), Zagreb, **6:**434
Ensemble of Song and Dance of the Polish Army, **3:**192
enskanye dance, **4:**557
Enstone, Edward, **2:**167
Enter, **2:**295, 296, **4:**37
Enters, Angna, **2:516–517,** **3:**559
Entr'ácte (Clair film), **1:**134, **2:**603, **3:**614, 620, **5:**545
Entr'acte (Johns painting), **3:**619, 620
Entrance to the Labyrinth, **6:**175
Entrata, **4:**602, **5:**43
en travesti. See travesty
entrechats. See batterie
Entre Deux Rondes, **4:**184, **5:**95
entrée, **2:517–518**
   ballet de cour, **1:**288
   bourrée, **1:**516

Lully compositions, **4:**234
Molière compositions, **4:**447
in St. Léon notebooks, **1:**346
entrée grave, **2:**517–518, **518–519**
"Entrée pour un Berger et une Bergère," **4:**481
entremet, etymology of, **1:**363
Entre-Six, **2:**41
Entries from an Early Diary (Kirstein), **4:**26
Entropy, **2:**474
Entsy (people), **5:**447
environmental dance concept, **5:**548–550
Enzinger, George, **2:**80
Éoline, ou La Dryade, **2:**70, 587, **3:***222,* 224, **5:**137, 277
   Gautier description of, **5:**140–41
Eonta, **1:**349
Epa masqueraders, **6:**12
épaulé, **1:334**
épaulement, **1:**335, 347, **6:**42
Epic, **6:**113
Epidauros, Greece, **3:**300, **6:**155
Epigraphes Antiques, **2:**361
Epiphany, **1:**526–527, **2:**7, 164
epirus, **2:**101, **3:**296
Episodes, **2:**245, 314, **3:**217, **4:**608, **6:**107, 112, 328
   Adams performance, **4:**617
   Balanchine choreography, **1:**263, 271, **4:**613
   Balanchine revival, **4:**609, 621
   Hayden performance, **3:**352
   Kent performance, **4:**5, 617
   Moncion performance, **4:**450
   Taylor performance, **4:**620
   Wilson (Sallie) role, **6:**402
Episodes of an Artist's Life. See Symphonie Fantastique
Episodio di San Michele, Un (Pugni), **5:**277
Epitaaf, **2:**347
Epitaph, **3:**329
Epithalame, **3:**76
Époque, Martine, **2:**40, 45, **6:**132
Épreuve, ou La Jambe de Bois, L', **2:**415
Épreuve d'Amour, L', **1:**295, **3:**24, **5:**17
Épreuve Villageoise, L', **1:**451, **4:**422–423
Equator, **2:**359
equestrian ballet. *See* horse ballet
Équilibres, **6:**433
Equinox, **6:**110
"Equipment" Dances, **5:**549
Equivalences (later *Bakyla*), **1:**461
Era of the Russian Ballet (Roslavleva), **5:**483
Erasmus, Desiderius, **3:**276, 281, **5:**345
Erbse, Heimo, **3:**132
Erbstein, Boris, **5:**458
Ercole Amante (Cavalli), **4:**234, 510
Erdélyi, Sándor, **3:**418
Erdman, Boris, **1:**489, **2:**174
   Joseph the Beautiful design, **3:**194, *194,* 631, 632–633, *632*
Erdman, Jean, **1:**421, **2:**22, 110, 285, 290, **519–520, 3:**216, 385
   Letter to the World performance, **4:**153
   students, **5:**523
Erdman, Joan L., *as contributor,* **5:**580–581
Erevan, Armenia, **1:**120, 121
Erevan Choreographic School, **1:**121

Erevan State Pedagogical Institute, **1:**121
Erich Weinert Ensemble, **3:**154
Erick Hawkins Dance Company, **1:**373, **4:**594
Erigone, **2:**365
Erik XIV, king of Sweden, **2:**264
Erik Menveds Barndom, **1:**509
Eriksen, Anne Grete, **4:**679
Erikson, Betsy, **5:**513
Erkin, Ulvi Cemal, **6:**213
Erkomaishvili, Anzor, **3:**135
Erlanger, Frédéric d', **1:**316, **3:**25, 394, **4:**33, 636
Erler, Stefan, **1:**390, 391
Erlmann, Veit, *as contributor,* **3:**347–348
Erlo, Louis, **1:**446
Ermecheo, Keyla, **6:**324
Ernie Smith Collection, **4:**167
Ernst, Max, **1:**135, 316–317, **2:**242, **4:**113, **5:**544
Eros, **3:**20, **4:**68, **5:***455,* **6:**28, 344
Eros-Thantos, **1:**406
Erotikon (film), **1:**118
Erotokritos (Cretan epic), **2:**269
Errand into the Maze, **1:**467, **3:***216,* 217, **4:**107
Errante, L', **1:**64, 260, 279, 281, 306, 307, **4:**229, **5:**547, **6:**118
Errecacho, Carmelo, **5:**676
Errol, Leon, **6:**271, 319, 448
Erschaffung der Welt, Die, **3:**153
Ersky, F. A. d', **3:**302
Erwartung, **3:**368
Erweiterung der Kunst nach der Chorographie zu tanzen (Feldtenstein), **6:**124
Esala Perahera, **3:**649
Esalen Institute, California, **1:**470
Esambayev, Makhmud, **2:**520
Esaulova, Ksenia, **5:**471
Escauríaza, Oscar, **6:**304
Escobar, Daniel, **1:**111
escolas de samba. See samba schools
escondido, **1:**109
Escott Opera Company, **5:**404
Escudero, Rosario, **5:**674
Escudero, Vicente, **1:**115, **2:520–521, 3:**9, 11, 102, **5:**674
escuela bolera, **1:**294–295, 479, 480, **2:521–522, 5:**133, 671, 672–673
   flamenco, **3:**6, 9, 11
   publications, **5:**676
   ronde de jambe en l'air, **5:**402
   Susana performances, **6:**27–28
Escuela de Camagüey, **2:**278
Escuela de Danza Ballet Nacional, Havana, **2:**277
Escuela de Danza Moderna, Havana, **2:**278
Escuela Nacional de Arte, Havana, **2:**277, 280, 281
Escuela National de Danzas Folklóricas, Argentina, **1:**109
Escuela Provincial de Ballet, Havana, **2:**277–278
Escuelas Polivalentes de Arte, Argentina, **1:**109
Escursioni, **1:**82
Eshel, Ruth, **3:**533, 535
Eshkol, Noa, **3:**534, **4:**692

Eshkhol-Wachman movement notation, **3:**534, **4:***690,* 692
Eshmukhambetov, Bourdzhan, **3:**665
Eskimo (Inuit)
   Arctic Circle, **4:**551, 553, 570–571
   Canadian, **4:**551, 553, 571
   dance characteristics, **5:**252
   Siberian, **5:**446, 447
ES, le 8ème Jour, **1:**350, **2:**388
Esmeralda, La, **1:**110, 477, 486, 489, 517, **2:**509, **523–525,** **5:**137, *138,* 141, 156, 160, 319, 499
   Beriozoff production, **2:**510, 524, **3:**175
   Bräuer choreography, **3:**154
   Brianza performance, **1:**540
   Burmeister choreography, **2:**15, 524, **3:**187
   Carey (Gustave) performance, **2:**60
   Cerrito performance, **2:**95
   Clustine performance, **2:**181
   Cucchi performance, **2:**282
   Drigo compositions, **2:**446
   Elssler (Fanny) performance, **2:**95, 502, 503, 504, 505, 524, **4:**453, **5:**403
   Geltser performance, **2:**524, **3:**128
   Grisi performance, **2:**95, 405, 505, 523, **3:**315
   gypsy theme, **3:**185
   Ivanov performance, **3:**560
   Kshessinska (Matilda) performance, **4:**68, *69,* 341
   Libonati version, **5:**232
   Maywood performance, **4:**339
   Monplaisir troupe staging in United States, **4:**452, 453–454
   Perrot production, **1:**540, **2:**60, 95, 505, 523, 524, **3:**185, 260, 315, **4:**280, **5:**403
   Pugni, Cesare, **5:**277
   Ronzani restaging, **5:**403, 516
   Russian and Soviet interpretations, **2:**524, **3:**186–187
   score, **3:**186–187
   Semenova role, **5:**566–567
   Smith performance, **5:**616
   Tikhomorov revision, **6:**171
   Turczynowicz version, **6:**207
   Vaganova revival, **6:**309
   Zucchi performance, **6:**452, 453
   See also Notre-Dame de Paris
Espacio y Movimiento, **2:**278
Espagnolade, L', **1:**117, **4:**222
España, **3:**198, **5:**94, 690
Espenak, Liljan, **2:**316, **3:**318
Esperance Working Girls Club, East London, **3:**238
Espinosa, Brigette, **2:**525
Espinosa, Édouard, **1:**384, 400, **2:**396, 525, **3:**264, **6:**128
   Empire Theatre, London, **3:**261
   English ballet advocacy, **3:**263, **5:**351
   Royal Academy of Dancing, **1:**329, **2:**395
   students, **5:**639
Espinosa, Geoffrey, **2:**525
Espinosa, Judith, **2:**525, **3:**61, 345, 508
Espinosa, Lea, **2:**525
Espinosa, Léon, **2:**435, 525, **4:**455, **6:**269, 290
Espinosa, Marius, **2:**525
Espinosa, Nicholas, **2:**525
Espinosa, Ray, **2:**525

Espinosa, Yvette, **2:**525
Espinosa family, **2:525–526, 5:**318
Espla, Oscar, **1:**115
Esplanade, **2:526–527, 4:**219, 482, **5:**680, **6:**109, 110, *110*, 111
Esposizione, **5:**548
Esquivel, Jorge, **1:**49, **2:***278*, 280
Esquivel Navarro, Juan de, **1:**53, 54, 523, **2:**51, 337, **3:**109, **4:**507, **5:**116, 668, 669, 670, 675, 688, **6:**123
  on *matachins*, **4:**326
  on *révérence*, **5:**345
Essai sur l'orchestique grecque (Emmanuel), **3:**302
Essakow, Hubert, **5:**57
Essay for the Further Improvement of Dancing (Pemberton), **2:**81, **3:**522, **4:**433
Essay towards an History of Dancing, An (Weaver), **2:**81, 527, **3:**111, **6:**372, 373, 374
Essen, Germany. *See* Folkwang Tanzstudio
Essen, Viola, **1:**65, **3:***225*, 597, **4:**460
essence (tap step), **6:**98
Essence, **4:**115
Essen Folkwang Schule. *See* Folkwang Tanzstudio
Essen Folkwang Tanzbühne. *See* Folkwang Tanzbühne, Essen
Essen Opera, **3:**627
Essex, John, **2:**255, 338, **527**, **3:**522, **4:**105, 684, **5:**308, 324, 518, **6:**123, 124, 176, 232
Estamos Todos Solos, **1:**112
estampie, **4:**348
Estampío, El, **5:**672
Estampio, Juan, **6:**27
Estay, Patricia, **4:**397
Este, Ercole d', **2:**204
Esté, Rein, **1:**241–242
Este family, **2:**427
Esterházy family, **3:**413
Esteve, Enrique, **3:**101
Esteves, Nora, **1:**533
Estévez, Carlos Alberto (Petróleo), **6:**93
Estey, Audrée, **6:**264
Esther, queen of Persia, **3:**603
Esto Armonico, **3:**74
Estonia, **2:527–530, 4:**160
Estonia Theater Ballet, Tallinn, **2:**529, 530, **4:**278
Estrée, Jean d', **1:**523, **4:**505, **5:**244
Estri, **3:**418
Estro Armonico, L', **2:**267
Estruscan culture, **3:**540
Estudio Religioso, Un, **4:**635
Étapes, **4:**238
Etchévery, Jean-Jacques, **1:**411, **2:**360, **3:**73, **5:**98
Eterbak Udiw, The, **1:**72
Eternal Circle, **4:**161
Eternal Idol, The, **3:**306
Eternal Prodigal, The, **2:**580
Eternal Song, The, **5:**462
Eternal Traveler, **3:**330
Eternity Bounce, **4:**519
Etherege, Sir George, **5:**490, 518
Etheridge, Dorothy, **1:***298*, **5:**369
Ethiopia, **2:**86, 90, **530–534, 4:**485–486
  zār, **6:**185, 445
Ethiopian Orthodox Christian Church, **2:**533
Ethiopian Serenaders, **3:**633
ethnic dance, **2:534–535**
  as balletic character dancing, **2:**106–108

Chinese, **2:**138–141
costume, **2:**244
cross-cultural comparisons, **2:**547
Greek, **3:**296
interethnic or cross-cultural diffusion, **2:**544
Meri presentations, **4:**355
methodologies in study, **4:**374
ownership of cultural material issue, **2:**546
terminology definition, **2:**539
  See also folk dance history; *names of specific peoples; under specific countries*
Ethnic Dance Arts, Barnstable, Massachusetts, **4:**355
Ethnikon Theatron (National Theater), Athens, **3:**300
ethnochoreography, **4:**372, 374, 375, **5:**391
ethnochoreology, Poland, **5:**211, 220
Ethnographia (Hungarian journal), **3:**422
Ethnographic Ensemble, Armenia, **1:**120
Ethnographic Film (Heider), **2:**600
ethnography and dance, **4:**372–375
  anthropology versus, **4:**373
  cultural context, **4:**362–366, 374–375
  European folk dance research, **3:**422–423, **4:**374
  European traditional dance, **2:**537, 537–540, 541, 545–547, **3:**35
  films and videos, **2:**600–603
  Kurath studies, **4:**78, 370, 372–373
  Native American dance, **4:**574–575
  Ustinova studies, **6:**303–304
"Ethnography and Exhibitionism at the Expositions Universelles" (Çelik and Kinney), **4:**415–416
Ethnography and Folklore Institute, Bucharest (formerly Folklore Institute), **5:**390–391
Ethnography of the Hungarians (Gönyey and Lajtha), **3:**422
Ethnologic Dance Center, **4:**354, 355
ethnomusicology, **4:**575, **6:**25
etilogwu dance, **6:**16
etiquette
  bows and curtsies, **5:**343–349
  dance accomplishments linked with, **3:**281, **6:**236–237, 293, 374
  dance manuels on, **1:**105, 107, **2:**73, 74, 75
  fan holding, **2:**570–571
  Italian court dance, **3:**542–543
  nineteenth-century social dance, **5:**624
  as reflection of social power, **1:**278, **6:**237
Étoile, L', **3:**522
Étoile de Messine, L', **1:**500, **2:**587, **4:**353
Étoile de Séville, L', **2:**202
Étoile du Nord, L' (Meyerbeer), **5:**114, 645
Etra, Bill, **2:**606
Étrange Farandole, L'. See Rouge et Noir
Etruscans, **5:**373–374, *374*
Etting, Ruth, **1:**433, **6:***447*
Ettore Fieramosca, **6:**70

etu, **3:**573
Étude
  Nijinska production, **1:**297, **4:**635, 636
  Struchkova and Lapauri performances, **6:**8
  Verchinina choreography, **1:**313
Études, **1:**70, *70*, 539, **2:**124, **535–536, 4:**271, **5:**96, **6:**217
  battements, **1:**383
  Bruhn performances, **2:**3
  Gilpin performance, **3:***174*, 175
  Gorsky production, **2:**457
  Hønningen performance, **3:**373
  Lander (Harald) production, **2:**509, 510, 513, 535–536, 586, **4:**118, 119, 120, *120*, **5:**429, *429*
  Riisager score, **5:**353
  soutenu turns, **1:**337
Études (Scriabin), Duncan choreography, **2:**456
Etudes Australes (Cage), **2:**23
Études chorégraphiques (Bournonville), **1:**8, 44, **6:**127
Études in Blue, **2:**473
Études No. 2, **2:**473
Eubie! (musical), **3:**366, **6:**284
Eucharis, **2:**204
Eudes, Roger, **1:**305, **5:**163
Eugene Onegin (Cranko ballet). *See Onegin*
Eugene Onegin (Pushkin), **4:**279
Eugene Onegin (Tchaikovsky opera), **5:**37, 626
Eugenia, Victoria, **5:**674
Eukinetics (Laban-Jooss concept), **4:**101–102, 103, 140
Eula, Joe, **2:**333, **4:***619*
Eunice, **3:**15, **4:**68, 640, **5:**121, 456
Eunice and Petronius, **3:**205, **4:**459
eurhythmics, **1:**97, 128–129, **2:**18, **3:**301, *595, 596*
  Ausdruckstanz, **1:**203
  Chladek technique, **2:**153
  as dance therapy influence, **2:**316
  French dance genre, **3:**76
  Hinman school, **3:**367
  Jaques-Dalcroze development, **3:**593–594, 596
  Kasai Akira studies, **3:**657, 658
  as Nijinsky *Sacre du Printemps* choreographic influence, **4:**644
  Rambert study, **5:**296
  Rouché introduction to Paris Opera, **5:**95
  as Russian plastique influence, **5:**476
  as St. Denis influence, **5:**495
  See also Jaques-Dalcroze Institute, Geneva; Jaques-Dalcroze Institute, Hellerau-Dresden
Eurhythmics, Art and Education (Jaques-Dalcroze), **3:**596
Euripides, **2:**153, 159, 419, **3:**289, 290, 292, 294, 645–646, 652, **5:**557
EuroDance Foundation, **1:**370, **3:**418, 419
Europa (Kaiser), **3:**305
Europa (mythic), **2:**270
Europe, James Reese, **2:**79, **6:**256
European Association of Dance Historians, **5:**44
European dance traditions. *See* genres of Western theatrical dance; *specific countries, dances, and personal names*

European Folk Dance (Lawson), **2:**382
European traditional dance, **2:536–561**
  armed dances, **1:**118
  branle, **1:**91, 520–524
  Caribbean adaptations, **2:**62
  chain and round dances, **2:**99–102, 549–551
  classification, **2:**549–555
  clogging, **2:**278–281
  dances of earth, **2:**331–332
  evolution and diffusion, **2:**543–544, 549
  Faeroe Islands, **2:**383–384
  Faeroe step, **2:**565
  figure dances, **2:**590–592
  folk dances versus, **3:**296
  function classification, **2:**555–558
  galliard, **2:**560, **3:**109–10
  history and historical records, **2:**540–543
  hornpipe, **3:**375–379
  jig, **3:**607–608
  linguistic analogies, **4:**367
  methodologies of study, 475, **4:**370, 371, 373–474, 375
  moresca, **4:**460–463
  Morris dance, **4:**473–475
  musical accompaniment. *See* music for dance
  preservation and scholarship, **2:**544–549, **3:**142, **6:**240
  reel, **5:**333–334
  religious dances, **2:**168
  saltarello, **5:**505–507
  structural classification, **2:**547–555
  See also Christianity and dance; folk dance history; folk dance sounds; social dance; *specific countries*
Europe Galante, L' (Campra), **5:**34, 40, *40*, 87, 105
Europe Galante, L', **1:**409, 425, **2:**33, 34, **4:**231, **5:**505, **6:**46
Eurythmy (Hodler), **1:**129
Euthyme et Eucharis, **2:**413, **4:**696, 698
Euzkadi!, **1:***377*
Evangeline (musical), **2:**572
evangelism, **2:**167, **6:**234–235
Evans, Arthur, **5:**41
Evans, Bill, **6:**266
Evans, Blanche, **2:**316, **317–318**
Evans, Charie, **2:**42, **4:***82*
Evans, Edwin, **3:**263, 265, 282
Evans, Minnie, **6:**449
Evans, Walker, **4:**26
Evans-Pritchard, E. E., **4:**369
Evdokimov, Gleb, **4:**133
Evdokimova, Eva, **1:**282, **2:**513, **561–562, 3:**75, **5:**55, 431
Evelyn, John, **3:**522
Evelyn, Mary, **3:**274, 522, **5:**304, *304*
Eagenement du jeudi, Le (publication), **3:**85
Evening in the Spinnery, **3:**406, **5:**287
Evenings at Békés, **5:**287
Evening's Songs, **2:**309
Evening's Waltzes, An, **4:**24, 614
"Evening with Bertram Ross, An," **5:**408
Evening with the Royal Ballet, An (film), **3:**45
Evenki (people), **2:**139, 140, **5:**446, 447

Event (Cunningham program), **2:**288, 292, 294, 297, *297*, **3:**446, **6:***162*
Éventail de Jeanne, L', **5:**237, **6:**182
"Event for Television" (television segment), **2:**294
Event of the Year (film), **2:**315
Eveny (people), **5:**446, 447
Eve of Saint Agnes, The, **3:**62, **4:**117
Ever-Fresh Flowers, **3:**206
Ever Green (musical), **1:**520, **4:**334, 335
Evergreen Dance, **6:**170
Everlast, **1:**76
Every Little Movement: A Homage to Delsarte, **2:**110
Everyman, **3:**508–509, 511
Everyone Says I Love You (film), **5:**573
Every Soul Is a Circus, **2:**285, **3:**216, 349
Evil Queen, The (television ballet), **2:**284
Evina, Wanda, **3:**441, 442
Evita (musical), **5:**423, **6:**285
Evocazioni, **2:**369
Evolución del Movimiento, **4:**178
Evolution of Consciousness through the Ages Cruise, **3:**336
Evolution of Dance, The, **3:**193
Evrar, Jeanne, **1:**502–503
Ewe (people), **3:**167
Ewell, Liza, *as contributor,* **6:**449–450
Ewha Women's University, Seoul, **4:**51, 55
Examiner (journal), **3:**284
Excavations Continued, **5:**128
Excelsior, **1:**37, 110, 239, **2:**249, **5:**180, 245, 246, 529, 540
Brianza performances, **1:**540
Cecchetti performance, **2:**82, **4:**258
dell'Ara reconstruction, **2:**369, **3:**60
Fracci performance, **3:**60
Manzotti-Edel-Marenco collaboration, **2:**477, **3:**548, **4:**258, 263, 264
revivals and versions, **4:**258
Teatro Costanzi, Rome, **4:**399
Zucchi performance, **3:**71, **6:**452
Excelsior (musical), **2:**572
Excerise XX, **6:**412
"Excerpts from an African Journey," **5:**256
Exchange, **2:**294, **4:**37
Excursion à Paris (film), **1:**252
exercises d'aplomb, **1:**8
Exercises de plastique animée (Jaques-Dalcroze), **3:**596
Exhibition of Historical Portraits (1905), **2:**407
Exiles, The, **4:**198, **5:***638,* **6:**43
Exiner, Johanna, **1:**212
Ex Machina, **1:**412
Exodus, **6:**66–67
exorcisms, **2:**165
Shangana-Tsonga dance, **4:**580
Sri Lanka *tovil* rite, **2:**228, *229*
Expectation, **6:**67
Experiment (formerly Theater of Modern Dance, Perm), **5:**475, 479
Experimental Ballet Troupe, Beijing, **2:**136
Experimental Studios of Dance, Romania, **5:**387
Experimental Workshop of Dance and Theater, **2:**125

Experiments in Art and Technology. *See* E.A.T.
Expo 67 (Montreal), **1:**49, 232, **2:**152, **3:**228, 229, 230, **4:**576
Express, L' (publication), **3:**85
expressionism
Argentine modern dance, **1:**112
avant-garde dance, **1:**244, 246
ballet technique development, **1:**348
Belgian dance, **1:**410–411
Chilean dance, **2:**122–123, 124
dance aesthetics, **1:**24, **2:**370–372
French modern dance, **3:**75, 77
German artists, **1:**130–131, 385, **3:**131–133, 163, **6:**391
Japanese modern dance, **3:**590
modern dance technique, **3:**131
United States, **6:**240, 243, 295
See also Ausdruckstanz; Delsarte system of expression; Duncan, Isadora
Expression of Emotions in Man and Animals, The (Darwin), **1:**127
Expression of Two Arts Theatre, **6:**377
Expressions Dance Company, **1:**216
expressive dance. *See* Ausdruckstanz; free dance movement
"Expulsion" (Holbein the Younger), **5:**258
Ex-Romance (videodance), **2:**607
Exsultate Jubilate, **3:**232
Extempory Dance Company, London, **2:**576
extensions, **1:**345, 348
See also arabesque
Extenzion, **4:**668
Exter, Alexandra, **4:**634, **5:**546, **6:**118
Exulta filia sion (Monteverdi), **4:**504
Eyak (people), **4:**570
Eyck, Jan van, **5:**230
Eyden, Deirdre, **5:**419
Eyen, Tom, **1:**420
Eyoh, Hansel Ndumbe, *as contributor,* **2:**32–33
Eyoun Bahīyah, **2:**497
Ezio (Gluck), **3:**189
Ezralow, Daniel, **2:**463, **3:**532, **5:***187*
Ezz, Magda, **2:**497
Ezzat, Ahmed, **2:**498

fa'ahiula, **4:**496
Fabbri, Paolo, **3:**556
Fabella, Antonio, **5:**173
Fabergé, Irène, **3:**104
Fabian, Joseph, **3:**156
Fabian family, **5:**376
Fabião, José, *as photographer,* **5:**235
Fabijanić, Nenad, **6:***437*
Fable, The, **6:**441
Fables for Our Time, **6:**376
Fabre, Jan, **1:**25, 412, **2:**470, **563–564**
Fabrications, **2:***291,* 296, **4:**37
Fabula Atellan. See Atellan farce
Facade (Sokolow work), **5:**637
Façade
Ashton choreography, **1:**146, *146,* 147, 148, 149, **5:**411
Australian Ballet repertory, **1:**209
Camargo Society, **3:**265, **5:**411
Chappell performance, **2:**105
Fonteyn and Helpmann performances, **3:**46, 357

Gore performance, **3:**202
Helpmann performance, **3:**357
Joffrey Ballet, **3:**614
Lopokova performance, **4:**224
Markova performance, **4:**268
PACT Ballet repertory, **5:**653
tango in Walton score, **4:**520
Walton dedication to Lambert, **4:**113
Facciuto, Eugene Louis. *See* Luigi
Face à Face, **1:**412
Face, Face, Face, **3:**523
Face of Violence, **2:**366
face paint. *See* mask and makeup
Face Tunes, **3:**54
Face Value, **4:**627
Fâcheaux, Les (Molière), **1:**288, 325, **2:**423, **4:**33, 234
Massine version, **4:***317,* 320
Molière and Beauchamps production, **1:**396, **4:**447
Nijinska choreography, **4:**447, 634
facial expression, **3:**514
facial makeup. *See* mask and makeup
Facsimile, **3:***663,* **4:**63, 110, **5:**360
Berstein score, **1:**438, **4:**519
Fact and Fancy, **6:**165–166
Faculdade de Mortricidade Humana, **5:**228
Fadetta, **4:**131
Fadeyechev, Aleksei, **1:**83, 493, **4:**360, **5:**465
Fadeyechev, Nikolai, **1:**491, **2:564–565,** **4:**360, 585, **5:***203,* 459, **6:***30*
Faedrelandets Muser. See National Muses
Faerie Queene, The (Spenser), **1:**150
Faeroe Islands, **2:**99, 100, 101, 383–384, 386, 565, **3:**30
Faeroe step, **2:565–566**
Albania, **1:**33, 34
Norway, **4:**671–672
Yugoslavia, **6:**427, 428, 431
Fagan, Garth, **2:**65, **566–567,** **3:**574, **4:**628, **6:**259, 266
Fagerholt, Arne, **4:**680
Fahbulleh, Miatta, **4:**487
Fail, Noël de, **5:**109
failli, **1:**339
Fair at Sorochinsk, **2:**112, **4:**178
Fairbairn, Flora, **5:**588
Fairbank, Charles, **6:**372
Fair in Sofia, A, **2:**12
Fair Maid of Perth, The, or the River Lovers, **1:**205
Fair Quaker of Deal, The, **5:**518
Fairy Doll, The. See Puppenfee, Die
Fairy of the Rondane Mountains, The, **4:**285
Fairy of the Tarn (Jókai), **3:**414
Fairy Queen, The (Ashton ballet), **3:**44
Fairy Queen, The (Purcell), **2:**400, **3:**391, 630, **4:**114, 215, **5:**251, 281
fais do-do, **2:**24
Faisi, A., **5:**595
Faison, George, **1:**57, 439
Fait Accompli, **4:***190,* **5:**440, **6:***153*
Faithful Shepherd, The, **1:**411
Faivre, A., **1:***278*
Faiz, Faiz Ahmad, **5:**63
Faizi, Wadoud, **2:**497, 498
Fajardo, Libertad, **1:**394, **5:**174
Falco, Louis, **1:**351, 501, **3:**577, **4:**199, 602, **5:**98, 301, 528, **6:**56

Faliero, Nina, **3:**594
Falik, Yri, **1:**38
Falk, Benjamin, **5:**180
Falk, Jeanna, **2:**283
Falk, Loti, **5:**196
Falla, Manuel de, **1:**115, 118, **2:**408, 409, **567–568,** **3:**101, **5:**673, **6:**192, 212
Diaghilev collaboration, **4:**515
flamenco reconstruction, **2:**567, **3:**9, 11
Massine ballet, **4:**317
See also Amor Brujo, El; *Tricorne, Le*
Falling Angels, **4:**81
"Falling Leaves," **1:**482, **5:**58
Fallis, Barbara, **2:**277, 583, **5:**439
Fall Like Rain, **4:**220
Fall of Babylon, The (spectacle), **4:**23
Fall of Icarus, The, **1:**412
Fallo, Un, **2:**282, **5:**409
Fall River Legend, **2:**374
Alonso (Alicia) performance, **1:**49, 68, **2:**373, *374*
American Ballet Theatre, **1:**67, 68
Chase (Lucia) performance, **2:**112
de Mille production, **1:**49, 67, 68, **2:**112, 334, 373–374, **3:**61, **4:**63, **5:**435, *550,* 551, **6:**402
Fracci performance, **3:**61
Johnson (Virginia) performance, **2:**334
Kaye performance, **3:**663
Kriza performance, **4:**63
Smith (Oliver) scenic design, **5:***550,* 551, 616
television productions, **2:**375
Wilson (Sallie) performance, **6:**402
False Bridegroom, The, **2:**585
False Face (Wooden Face) society, **4:**553, 554, 557, *557*
Falstrom, Oyvind, **2:**606
Famille Cardinal, La (Halévy), **2:**362–363
Famille Mante, La (Degas), **2:**363
Family Business, The, **3:**202
fan (use in dance). *See* fan dancing
Fan, The (Callot), **2:**27
Fanciulla delle Rose, **1:**429, **4:**380, **5:**691
Fancy Dress (Ghanian masking), **4:**292–293
fancy dress balls. *See* masquerades
Fancy Free, **1:**68, **2:**376, **568–569**
Bernstein score, **1:**438, 439, **2:**568, **4:**519
contemporary costume, **2:**245
Feld performance, **2:**583
jazz dance, **2:**108
Kidd performance, **4:**10, **5:***539*
Kriza performance, **2:**568, *568,* **4:**63, **5:***359*
original cast, **5:***359*
Robbins choreography, **2:**245, 376, 568–569, *568,* **4:**614, **5:**358, *359,* 360
Smith (Oliver) scenic design, **5:**551, 616
tap dance, **3:**131
See also On the Town
Fan Dance, **2:**573, *573,* **4:**12
fan dancing, **2:569–574**
Bali, **4:**264
Fiji, **2:**593
Japanese *kabuki,* **2:**219, **3:**650, **4:**493
Japanese *kyōgen,* **4:**84
Korea, **4:***45*

fandango (*fandango*), **1:**479, **4:**671, **5:**229, **6:**104
  Brazilian adaptations, **1:**525, 528, 529
  Caribbean variants, **2:**64
  Egyptian *ghawāzi* similarity, **4:**664
  evolution of, **2:**62
  Mexican adaptation, **4:**384
  Spain, **5:**671
Fandango, **1:**60, **4:**353, 541, **6:**202
Fandango de Candil, El, **1:**115
fandango do Paraná, **1:**529
fandanguillo, **2:**64
Fandino, Luis, **4:**394, 396
Fanfare, **1:**478, **4:**5, 608, **5:**362
Fanfare for the Common Man, **4:**151
Fanfare für Tanzer, **3:**428
Fan Festival (*dengaku* type), **3:**585
Fang (people), **1:**15
Fanga, **5:**256
Fanger, Iris M., *as contributor,* **1:**97–98, **2:**78–80, **6:**31–35
Fångne Cupido, Den, **1:**403, **6:**38, 46, 47
Fa Nguan, prince of Laos, **4:**123
Fanny (musical), **6:**90
Fanø Island, **2:**382
Fantasca, **6:**76
Fantasia (Balanchine ballet), **2:**123
Fantasia (film), **1:**402, **5:**16
Fantasia Brasileira, **4:**421
Fantasie, **2:**4, **3:**630
Fantasien, **4:**1
Fantasies, **6:**359
Fantastic Art, Dada and Surrealism (exhibition), **1:**135
Fantastic Gardens, **2:**605
Fantasticks, The (musical), **6:**282
Fantastic Scenes from the Legend of Pan Twardowski, **6:**175
Fantastic Toyshop, The. See Boutique Fantasque, La
Fantasy (television film), **5:**203
Fantasy and Fugue in C Minor, **3:**391
Fantasy of the Western Pilgrimage, **2:**116
Fantôme de l'Opéra, Le, **5:**164, 554
"Fantômes, Les" (Hugo), **3:**178
Fārābī, Abū Naṣr al-, **3:**525, **4:**488
Farah, **1:**292
farandole, **2:**100, **3:**64, 70, **5:**619
Faraona, La, **1:**61
Farber, Viola, **1:**350–351, **2:**269, 287, 289, 292, **574–576,** **3:**78, 83, **5:**314
  Suite for Five performance, **6:**26
  Summerspace performance, **6:**27
  Winterbranch performance, **6:**402
Farces, **2:**151
Far Eastern University Folk Dance Group, **5:**173
Far Eastern University Modern Experimental Dance Group, **5:**172
Farelli, Jacqueline, **2:**150
Farewell, The, **4:**39
Far from Denmark, **1:**497, 510, 510, 511, **5:**426
  Brenaa production, **1:**539
  character dances, **2:**107
  Lander (Margot) performance, **4:**119
  Lumbye finale score, **4:**513
  Price (Juliette) performance, **5:**425
  Schanne performance, **5:**553
  Williams (Stanley) performance, **6:**399

Far from the Madding Crowd (Bintley ballet), **1:**454
Far from the Madding Crowd (Hardy novel), **1:**454
Fargion, Matteo, **2:**356
Farha, Clint, **2:**470
Faria, Arthur, **6:**284
Farida Feisol, **5:**523
Faris, James C., *as contributor,* **5:**3–4
Farjeon, Herbert and Eleanor, **2:**173
Farkas, Ferenc, **3:**415
Farley, Alice, **2:**65–66
Farley, Richard, **6:**217
Farlow, Lesley, *as contributor,* **4:**197–200, 458
Farmaniants, Evgenia, **5:**461
Farmaniants, Georgi, **3:**12, **5:**459
Farmer, Peter, **2:**445, **4:**216, 217–218
farmers' dance (Korea), **1:**166, 167, **4:**46–47
Farmers' Dances, **1:**411
Farnell, Brenda, **4:**368
Faro, Antonio José, **1:**537
Faroese step. *See* Faeroe step
Farrally, Betty, **2:**38, 47, **5:**434, 435, 684, 685
Farrel, Billy, **4:**522
Farrell, Suzanne, **1:**12, 257, **2:**314, **576–578,** **5:**97, **6:**86
  Apollo, **1:**96, **2:**576
  Balanchine marriage and breakup, **2:**576–577
  Balanchine productions, **1:**96, 268, 271, **2:**576, 577–578, **3:**448, **4:**611, 612, 618
  Ballet Imperial performance, **1:**293
  Béjart productions, **1:**292, 292, 405, 405, 406, **2:**577
  Cinderella performance, **2:**173
  Diamonds performance, **4:**612
  Don Quixote performance, **1:**268, **2:**438, 439, 576, 577, **4:**618
  interpretation spontaneity, **3:**448
  Liebeslieder Walzer performance, **4:**180, 615
  Martins dance partnership, **2:**577–578, **4:**273, 274, **5:**102, 364
  New York City Ballet, **4:**611, 612, 618, 623
  Nichols's interpretation of Balanchine roles, **4:**631
  Nutcracker tutu, **3:**654
  Robbins choreography, **4:**615, 622, **5:**364, 367
  Romeo and Juliet performance, **5:**398
  Symphony in C significance, **6:**66
  Vienna Waltzes performance, **4:**612
Farren, Fred, **3:**261, **6:**64
Farron, Julia, **2:**115, **578,** **5:**294, 396
farruca dance, **1:**61
Fars, **5:**513–514
Faruqi, Lois Lamya' al-, **4:**404, 416
  as contributor, **1:**18–19
Fascilla, Roberto, **3:**552, 553
Fascist regime (Italy), **3:**549–550, 552, **5:**400, 441
Fassi, Carlo, **2:**298
Fassler, Gregoria, **2:**125
Fast Blues, **3:**446
Fastes, **1:**306, **4:**517
Fast Footwork, **5:**636
Fata Căpitanului, **5:**384

Fata Nix, La, **5:**233
Fatauros, Jorge, *as photographer,* **2:**469, **4:**593, 594, 597
Father, **6:**414, 414, 415
Father Hubbards Tales (Middleton), **2:**254
Fathers and Sons, **1:**60
Fatimah, Djemille, **6:**317
Fattah, Heba Abdel, **2:**497
Fatum, Ole, **5:**395
Faulkner, William, **1:**441
Faun, The, **2:**397, **5:**555
Faune, La, **1:**446, **5:**301, 303
Fauré, Gabriel, **3:**392, **4:**243, **5:**236
Faust, **1:**9, 208, 477
  Blasis staging, **1:**461
  Borri performance, **1:**499
  Bournonville staging, **1:**507, 515, **5:**425, **6:**40
  Coralli *pas de sylphides,* **2:**202, **3:**69, 180, **6:**58
  Deshayes (André) staging, **2:**390, **3:**260
  as Elssler's (Fanny) farewell performance, **2:**60, 505
  Ferraris performance, **2:**587
  Ivanov performance, **3:**560
  Kirsova staging, **4:**26
  Lanner staging, **4:**121
  Maywood performance, **4:**339
  Perrot interpretation, **5:**134, 138, 140, 141, 403, 404
  Ronzani revival, **5:**403, 404
  Taglioni (Salvatore) version, **6:**70
  Tudor version, **6:**196
Faust (Gounod opera), **1:**300, **5:**36, 37
  Walpurgis Night, **2:**510, 511, **4:**381, **5:**569, **6:**8
Faust, Lotta, **2:**79
Faust legend
  Abraxas, **1:**1, **2:**478
  Béjart works, **1:**405, 406
  Black Crook, The, **1:**458
  Doktor Faust, **5:**245
  Dr. Faustus Lights the Lights, **6:**401
  Harlequin Doctor Faustus, **5:**350, 518
  Laban movement choirs, **4:**476
  Mephistophela, **5:**59, 60
  Polish *Pan Twardowski,* **5:**217, 217
  See also Faust
Faust's Departure, **6:**175
Fausts Erlösung, **4:**91
Faust Symphony, **2:**473
Faustus, or The Demon of Dragonfels, **1:**456
Fauvism, **4:**330
Favart, Charles-Simon, **2:**366, **4:**122, **5:**90, **6:**38
Favier, Jean, **1:**397, **4:**263, 696, **6:**123
Favola d'Orfeo (Poliziano), **5:**113
Favor (Roman mime), **4:**426
Favorite, La (Donizetti), **1:**461, **3:**314, **4:**108, 514, 657, **6:**443
Favrilin, Valery, **5:**471
Fay, Maria, **2:**561
Faye, Alice, **1:**433, **2:**615, **6:**142
Fayer, Yuri, **1:**491, **2:**579, **4:**444
Faye-Theresa, **4:**628
Fayolle, Peter, **3:**86
Fazer, Edvard, **2:**632
FDP. *See* Federal Dance Project
Fearful Symmetries, **4:**275
Feast for the Dead (Athabaskan), **4:**573–574
Feast of Ashes, **3:**342, 610, 611
Feast of Fools, **2:**165, 523, **4:**448

Feast of Saint John, **2:**476
Feast of the Assumption, **4:**328
Feast of the Dead (Borneo), **4:**298
Feast of the Pheasant, **1:**364, **4:**449
Feather Dance, **4:**559
Feather of the Dawn, **2:**378, **5:**585
Featherstone, Donald F., **2:**329–330
Featherstonehaughs, **3:**275, 276
Feats Unlimited Company, **1:**217
Febvre, Michèle, **2:**49
fecioreasca deasă, **5:**382
Fedelma, **2:**397
Feder, Abe, **4:**191
Federal Dance Project, **2:579–582,** **4:**30, 209, **6:**245–246
  African dance, **2:**313
  Humphrey-Weidman Company, **3:**401
  Lang, Pearl, **4:**120
  musical theater, **6:**276
  Tamiris, Helen, **6:**89, 89
Federal Street Theatre, Boston, **6:**233
Federal Study Group on Austrian Folk Dance, **1:**242
Federal Theatre African Dance Troupe, **2:**313
Federal Theatre Project (FTP), **2:**579, 580, **5:**59, 407, **6:**276
Federal University of Bahía, **1:**534–535, 537
Federal University of Rio de Janeiro, **1:**535
Federal Writers' Project, **3:**35
Federated Union of Black Arts (FUBA) Dance Company, **5:**659
Fédération des Loisirs-Danse du Québec, **2:**35
Fédération Française de Danse, **3:**84
Fedicheva, Kaleria, **2:**570, **4:**282, 285
Fedorenko, Elena G., *as contributor,* **2:**523–525, 582, **4:**211–212, **5:**449–457
Fedor Lopukhov (Dobrovolskaya), **5:**484
Fedorov, Ivan, **2:**410
Fedorov, Michael, **5:**264
Fedorova, Aleksandra, **1:**48, 124, **3:**609, **4:**457, 667, **6:**425
  Latvian ballet, **4:**127
  Nutcracker staging, **5:**14
Fedorova, Natalia, **5:**478
Fedorova, Sofia, **1:**488, **2:**436, **582,** **3:**202, 205, 207, **5:**452, **6:**32
Fedorovitch, Sophie, **1:**145, 148, 149, 153, **2:**244, 401, **582–583,** **5:**296, 298, 298, 299
  Endymion designs, **3:**511
  Horoscope design, **3:**379, 380
  Howard collaboration, **2:**582, 583, **3:**392
  Symphonic Variations design, **6:**64, 65
Fedorovsky, Fedor, **6:**343
Fedra, **1:**88, **4:**208
Fedra and the Twilight Nights (film), **6:**171
Fedro, Maria, **3:**628
Fee, Mary, **4:**692
Feest, Claudia, **3:**156
feet. *See* ballet technique, feet positions; footware; point work; turnout
feet-binding, **2:**131
Fehl, Fred, **5:**186
  dance and theater photograph collection, **4:**169

as photographer, **1:**8, 264, 265, 267, 268, 269, 270, 295, **2:**568, **3:**182, 208, **4:**120, 425, 609, 615, 616, 617, 618, 619, **5:**361, 612, **6:**201, 328, 340
Feidman, Giora, **4:**532
feier, **4:**671
Feiffer, Jules, **2:**69, 70, **5:**243
Feigay, Paul, **5:**360
Feigl, Eva Maria. *See* Violette, Eva Maria
Feinblatt, Eric, *as photographer,* **2:**439
Feintuch, Robert, **5:**440
Feist, Herta, **4:**91
Felciano, Rita, *as contributor,* **5:**392–399
Feld, Eliot, **1:**69, 72–73, 370, 420, **2:583–585,** **3:**299, 306, 448, 605, **4:**542, **5:**398, 436, **6:**281
  American Music Festival (1988), **4:**623
  Royal Swedish Ballet guest productions, **6:**43
  See also Feld Ballets/NY
Feld, Steven, **4:**498
  as contributor, **5:**80–82
  as photographer, **5:**81, 82
Feld Ballets/NY, **2:**583–584, *584, 585,* **6:**139
  Baryshnikov guest appearances, **1:**373
Feldenkrais, Moshe, **1:**469, **470,** **4:**692
Feldenkrais Method, **1:**469, 470, **474–475,** **4:**17, 18, 20
Feldman, Morton, **2:**289, **4:**214, 519, **6:**27
Feldtenstein, C. J., **6:**124
Felicita Lusitana, La, **5:**231
Feliksdal, Benjamin, **2:**470
Felipe el Loco, **3:**403
Felis, Stefano, **5:**500
Felix, Joji, **5:**172
Felix, Seymour, **2:**615, **6:**101, 274
Felix Luna, **6:**135, 404
Fellerman, Stan, *as photographer,* **1:**198
Fellini, Federico, **3:**60, **5:**196
Fellom, Martie, *as contributor,* **5:**605
Felsenstein, Walter, **3:**155, **5:**557
Female Forty Thieves, of the Daughters of the Golden West, The, **4:**455
female impersonation
  kabuki theater. *See onnagata*
  Kuchipudi dance, **6:**320–321
  travesty, **6:**188–191
  Turkish boys, **6:**210
Female Saylor, **1:**89
Feminism in a Traditional Society (Chaki-Sircar), **2:**103
feminist theory
  dance analysis, **4:**378–379
  performance art, **1:**140
Femme et Son Ombre, La, **2:**111
Femmes d'Alger, Les, **1:**316
Femmes de Bonne Humeur, Les, **1:**254, 311, 322, **2:**409, **5:**399
  Cecchetti mime performance, **2:**82
  Idzikowski performance, **3:**441
  Lopokova performance, **4:**223
  Massine choreography, **4:**317
  Pulcinella versus, **6:**5
  Woizikowski performance, **6:**493
Fenella, **6:**452
Fénelon, Eugène Baptiste, **5:**317
Feng Ying, **2:***147, 440*

Fenice, La. *See* Teatro La Fenice, Venice
Fenice Rinovata, La, **1:**29
Fenollosa, Ernest, **3:**558, **6:**229
Fenolt, Jeff, **6:**284
Fenonjois, Roger, **3:**600, **5:**96, **6:**301
Fenster, Boris, **1:**144, **2:**529, **585–586,** **4:**226, 284, **5:**459, 468
Fenster, Nancy, **2:**605
Fenton, William, **4:**78
Feodorova, Eugenia, **1:**533
Feodorova, Sofia, **5:**556
Ferand, Ernst, **2:**153
Feranne, Claire, **2:**472
Feraris, Amalia, **1:**499
Ferchiou, Sophie, **4:**416–417
Ferdinand II, emperor of Austria, **1:**235
Ferdinand II, grand duke of Tuscany, **3:**544
Ferdinand II, king of Spain, **3:**6
Ferdinand III, emperor of Austria, **1:**235
Ferdinand VII, king of Spain, **3:**69
Fere, Vladimir, **4:**87
Fereh, V., **5:**595
Ferendzhi, **3:**48, 135, **5:**472
Ferghana dance, **6:**305
Ferguson, Austin, *as photographer,* **3:**576
Ferguson, Constance, **2:**108
Fergusson, Francis, **1:**420
Ferin, Louis, **5:**318
Fern, or Midsummer Night, The, **1:**486, **4:**514
Fernández, Félix, **2:**409, **4:**317
Fernandez, James, **1:**15, **6:**25
Fernandez, José, **1:**66, 281, **6:**198
Fernández, Las, **1:**480
Fernandez, Royes, **1:**69, 70, **2:**277, 279, **586,** **5:**573, **6:**34, 292
Fernández de Rojas, Juan, **5:**676
Ferrabosco, Alfonso, **4:**309, 311, 506
Ferracin, Michela, **3:**554
Ferrari, Benedetto, **3:**544
Ferrari, Giacomo, **2:**209
Ferrari, Victor, **1:**110
Ferrari, Virginia, **1:**110
Ferrario, Giulio, **3:**176
Ferraris, Amalia, **1:**500, **2:586–587,** **3:**70, 123, **4:**150, 455, **5:**93–94, 140, 148, 405, 528
  Elfes debut performance, **2:**586, **4:**342
  Marco Spada performance, **4:**342
Ferraro, Adelaide, **1:**200
Ferrer, José, **2:**458
Ferrer Adevoso, Carmen, **5:**172
Ferrero, Edward, **2:**339, 571, **6:**239
Ferrero, Mercedes Viale. *See* Viale Ferrero, Mercedes
Ferri, Alessandra, **1:**77, 282, **4:**244, **5:**419, 530
Ferri, Olga, **1:**110–111, *111,* **2:**510, **587–588,** **3:***317*
Ferriol y Boxeraus, Bartolomé, **2:**51, **5:**670, 676
Ferro, António, **5:**233
Ferroud, Pierre-Octave, **5:**237
Ferry, J., **4:**415
Ferté, Denis Papillon de la, **5:**89
fertility rites
  Argentine choral dances, **1:**108
  armed dances, **1:**118
  central and eastern Africa, **2:**91
  Chinese *yangke,* **1:**165
  as Christian Easter dances basis, **2:**165

Finland, **2:**629
  Greece, ancient, **3:**287–288
  Pueblo dance, **4:**565
Festa d'Alceste, La, **3:**189
Festa del Himeneo, La, **2:**394
Festa della Rosa, **1:**499
festas juninas, **1:**529, 530
Feste dei Polli (Feast of Fools), **3:**541
Feste Royal, **6:**38
Festes de L'Amour et de Bacchus, Les, **5:**489
Festin, Le, **3:**16, **4:***643*
Festin de l'Araignée, Le, **1:**247, **3:**62, 392, **5:**95
Festin de la Sagesse, La, **5:**439
Festin de Pierre, Le. See Don Juan
Festin i Albano, **1:**508
Festival (television series), **6:**131
Festival Ballet. *See* English National Ballet
Festival Ballet Company, Ottawa, **4:**238
Festival Ballet House, London. *See* Markova House
Festival de Beweeging, Antwerp, **1:**412
Festival de Lausanne. *See* Lausanne International Ballet Competition
Festival des Baux-de-Provence, **2:**466
Festival in Albano, **6:**40
Festival International de Danse, Paris, **3:**75, 77
Festival International de Nouvelle Danse, Montreal, **2:**46, **6:**132
Festival in the Maryina Grove, **1:**485
Festival Ljubljana, **6:**438
Festival of Britain (1951), **2:**508
Festival of Contemporary Dance, Jassy, **5:**390
Festival of Folk Dances of the USSR, Moscow, **4:**444
Festival of India, **2:**104, 468, **5:**525
Festival of Mandarins, **1:**370, **3:**419
Festival of Nervi, **1:**82–83
Festival of the Banners, **2:**476
Festival of the Sun (Raymi), **2:**475, 476
Festival of Two Worlds. *See* Spoleto Festival
Festival Theatre, Cambridge, England, **2:**396–397
Festliche Tanzsuite, **2:**153
Fest-Polonaise, **4:**118, 119, **5:**429, 600
Festspielhaus. *See* Bayreuth Festspielhaus
Festus, Sextus Pompeius, **4:**427, **6:**193
Fest von Coqueville, Das, **3:**154
Festzug des Handwerkes und der Gewerbe, Vienna, **4:**91–92
Fête au Village, Le (pantomime-ballet), **5:**319
Fête Bohème, **3:**511
Fête Carignan (*Hangman's Reel*), **3:**231, **4:**238
Fête chez Thérèse, La, **1:**246, **5:**95, **6:**443
Fête de Juin, La (1914 Geneva pageant), **1:**98
Fête d'Hébé, La (Baum opera), **1:**482
Fête du Faisan, La (allegorical banquet), **1:**364, **4:**449
Fête Étrange, La, **1:**429, **2:**583, **3:**392, **4:**215, **5:**300, 691
Fête Galante, **3:**318

Fête Hongroise, La, **1:**202, **2:**107, 151
fêtes. *See* Renaissance fêtes and triumphs
Fêtes, **1:**424, **2:**361, **6:**402
Fêtes, ou Le Triomphe de Thalie, Les, **4:**475
Fêtes Chinoises, Les, **3:**59, 66, 255, 256, **4:**188, 694, 695, 697
Fêtes de Bacchus, Les, **1:**287, **4:**229
Fêtes de Flore, Les, **3:**106
Fêtes de l'Amour et de Bacchus, Les, **4:**231, 234, **5:**86, 113
Fêtes de l'Hymen et de l'Amour, Les (Rameau), **5:**39, 307
Fêtes de Polymnie, Les, **4:**236, **5:**285, 307
Fêtes de Tempe, Les, **2:**413, **4:**698
Fêtes d'Hébé, Les, **1:**365, **2:**29, **4:**122, 236, **5:**88, 306, 307, 690, **6:**444
Fêtes du Tempe, Les, **3:**258
Fêtes Grècques et Romaines, Les, **1:**365, 464, **3:**326, **4:**236
Fêtes Polonaise, **2:**399
Fêtes Provençales, Les, **2:**413, **4:**698
Fêtes Vénitiennes, Les, **1:**464, **2:**34, 465, **3:**49, **4:**262–263, 475, **5:**40, 105, **6:**11
Fetters, **3:**420
Feuchères, Léon, **2:**405
feudalism, **2:**538
Feu d'Artifice, **5:**85
Feuervogel, Der. See Firebird, The
Feuillet, Raoul-Auger
  annual collections, **1:**91
  Chorégraphie, **1:**342, 343, 397, 465, **2:**338, 588, **3:**81, 545, **5:**39, 109, 129, 201, 308, 323, 329, 621, **6:**123, 126, 215
  Weaver's English translation, **2:**81, 588, 589, **3:**522, **4:**684, **6:**232, 372, 373
  See also Feuillet notation *below*
  on country dances, **1:**90, 91, **2:**255, 591, **4:**510
  on *entrée grave,* **2:**518
  on feet positions, **1:**331, 333
  folie d'Espagne, **3:**29
  on "Le Cotillon," **1:**523, **2:**251–252
  Recüeil de contredances, **6:**124
  on turnout positon, **6:**215
Feuillet notation, **1:**91, 342, 343, 397, 465, **2:**339, 588–589, **588–590,** **4:**684, *685,* **5:**39, 109, 129, 201, 329, 503, 505, 506, *520,* **6:**123
  anglaise steps, **1:**90
  Ballon use of, **1:**355
  Beauchamps petition, **1:**397, 465, **2:**588
  Blondy rejection, **1:**465
  bourrée, **1:**517, **4:***685*
  canary examples, **2:**51
  chaconne and *passacaille* choreographies, **2:**99
  country dance figure reconstruction, **2:**591
  courante, **2:**259, 260
  entrées, **2:**517–518
  Essex use of, **2:**527
  folia, **3:***28,* 29
  forlana, **3:**50
  "French-style" hornpipes, **3:**377
  galliard, **3:**109
  gavotte, **3:**124, *124*
  gigue, **3:**172, *173*
  as historical dance record, **2:**542

Feuillet notation, *continued*
  Isaac (Mister) dance collection,
    3:522
  as Labanotation basis, **4:**92, 99
  loure, **4:**231
  for Pecour dances, **3:**122
  rigaudon, **5:**352
  sarabande, **5:***520*
  Spanish dance, **5:**670
  tambourin, **6:**87
  track drawings as basis, **4:**684
  translations, **2:**589, **4:**684
Feun, Anton, *as photographer*,
  5:657
Feux d'Artifices, Les, **5:**399
Feux Follets, Les, **2:**36
Feves, Angene, *as contributor*,
  3:509–511, **5:**322–325
Fewster, Barbara, **6:**129
Fiadeiro, João, **5:**236
Fiammetta, ou L'Amour du Diable,
  2:282, 367, **3:**237, **4:**429,
  5:501
Fiancée du Diable, La, **1:**305, **5:**163
Fichman, Niv, **6:**133
Ficino, Marsilio, **1:**21
Fick, Adolf E., **4:**15
Ficzere, Attila, **2:**39
Fidanzata Valacca, La, **5:**501
fiddle. *See* violin
Fiddler on the Roof (musical),
  3:605, **5:**363, 364, **6:**281,
  284, 288
Fidlovčka, **2:**303
Field, John, **1:**152, 429, **2:**590,
  3:318, **4:**380, **5:**529
  Birmingham Royal Ballet, **3:**268
  English National Ballet, **2:**511,
    513, **3:**269
  Grey (Beryl) dance partnership,
    2:590, **3:**307
  Norwegian National Ballet, **4:**678
  Royal Ballet, **5:**416, 417, **6:**357
Field, Lila, **2:**395
Field, Ronald, **1:**418, **6:**284
Field and Figures (Cunningham
  work), **2:**296
Field, Chair and Mountain, **1:**76
Field Dances, **2:**119, *291*, **3:**446
Field Figures (Tetley work), **5:**417,
  6:146
Fielding, Henry, **5:**70
Fielding Sixes, **2:**294, **5:**303
Field of Grass, **6:**112, 113, 165
Fields, Dorothy, **1:**419, **6:**256, 283
Fields, Lew, **2:**78, 79, **6:**371
Fieldworks Performance Group,
  1:216
Fiera di Barcellona, La, **6:**337
Fieroiu, Florin, **5:**390
Fiery Hearts, **6:**420
Fiesta, **1:**291, **6:**137
Fiesta (film), **2:**108
Fiesta de Pendones, **2:**476
Fiesta de San Juan, **2:**476
Fiesta Filipino Dance Troupe, **5:**173
fife, **1:**105
Fife, Lord, **2:**71
Fifield, Elaine, **1:**210, 232, 429,
  2:*266*, **5:**420, *650*
Fifteen Heterosexual Duets, **4:**72, 73
Fifteen Years of Dancer's Life
  (Fuller), **3:**94
Fifth Hong Kong International
  Dance Conference (1990),
  5:44
Fifth Position (film), **2:**315
Fifth Symphony (Tchaikovsky),
  1:310, **4:**322, 517
Fifty Russian Folksongs
  (Tchaikovsky), **6:**114
figaro, **4:**671

Figaro (Duport ballet), **1:**455,
  2:389, 464
Figaro, Le (Paris newspaper), **1:**99,
  3:85
Figarová, Mirka, **5:**270, 393
Fighting the Waves (Yeats), **3:**519
Figlio dello Shak, Il, **6:**70
Figliuol Prodigo, Il, **5:**266
Figuera, Gabriela, **2:**125
Figueroa, Celso A. Lara, *as*
  contributor, **3:**319–320
Figueroa, Graciela, **6:**302
Figura Dance, **6:**170
Figural Cabinet, **1:**385, 386
figure dances, **2:590–592,**
  5:620–621
  anglaise, **1:**89–90
  country dance, **2:**255–257
  French, **3:**64, 65
  Hay, **3:**361
  longways, **4:**221
  medieval, **4:**349
  Norway, **4:**671
  quadrille, **5:**285–287
  Russian, **5:**444
  Scottish, **3:**247–248
  See also Morris dance; reel;
    square dancing; Sword Dance
Figure in the Carpet, The, **1:**263,
  266, **2:**314, **4:**344, 617, **6:**340
figure skating. *See* ice dancing
Fiji, **2:593–594**, **4:**351, **5:**224
Filandre (Parisian poet), **1:**365
*Filatka and Fedora on the Swings at
  Novinsk*, **3:**191
Filiou, Robert, **1:**139
Filipinescas, **2:**230, **5:**171
Filipinescas Dance Company,
  5:173, 174
Filipiniana Dance Company of
  Hawaii, **5:**173
Filipiniana Folk Music and Dance
  Committee, **1:**393–394
Fille de Marbre, La, **1:**48, 460, **2:**95,
  5:277, 499
  See also Alma
Fille des Neiges, La, **5:**151
Fille du Danube, La, **1:**9, **2:**209,
  3:123, **5:**232, 516, **6:**73, 74
  Lacotte reconstruction, **4:**108
  Lee's American performances,
    4:139
  mad scene, **3:**180, **4:**176
  Mazilier and Taglioni
    performances, **4:**340
Fille du Pharaon, La, **2:**446, 582,
  3:206, **4:**68, 144, **5:***453*
  Mordkin performance, **4:**459
  Pavlova performance, **5:**120
  Petipa (Marius) choreography,
    5:151, 155–156
  Petipa (Marius) performance,
    5:*150*
  Pugni score additions, **5:**278
  tutu decoration, **6:**217
  Zucchi performance, **6:**452
*Fille Fugitive, ou La Laitière
  Polonaise*, **1:**455
Fille Mal Gardée, La, **2:594–597**
  Ashton production, **1:**154–155,
    2:594, 597, **3:**321, 418, **4:**117,
    5:417, 431
  Aldous performance, **1:**38
  Augustyn performance, **1:**200,
    2:595
  Australian Ballet repertory,
    1:*231*, 233
  Bavarian State Ballet repertory,
    1:391
  Bintley performance, **1:**453
  Blair performance, **1:**459
  Coe performance, **2:**183

  Collier performance, **2:**186
  Grant farewell performance,
    3:237
  Holden performance, **6:**190
  Joffrey Ballet revival, **3:**616
  Jones (Marilyn) performance,
    3:623
  Kain performance, **2:***295*, **3:**643
  Karsavina role, **3:**656
  Larsen performance, **4:**126
  National Ballet of Canada
    repertory, **4:**543
  Nerina performance, **1:**55,
    2:597, **4:***584*, 585
  Nureyev performance, **5:**6
  PACT Ballet repertory, **5:**54
  Park performance, **5:***417*, **6:***190*
  Royal Danish Ballet repertory,
    5:431
  Royal Swedish Ballet repertory,
    6:43, *43*
  Schaufuss (Peter) roles, **5:**554
  televised performances, **1:**200,
    6:134
  Usher performance, **5:***417*
  Warsaw Ballet repertory, **6:**365
  Weller performance, **6:**379, *379*
  Aumer staging, **1:**202, **5:**92
  Bey performance, **1:**442
  Caton staging, **3:**229
  character roles and dances,
    2:106, 107
  Cramér production, **2:**264
  as Dauberval creation,
    2:353–354, 594, 595, **3:**258
  Elssler (Fanny) performance,
    1:486, **2:**502, 503, 596
  first performance, **2:**594, **3:**68
    first Argentine performance,
      1:110
    first Canadian performance,
      2:36
    first English performance,
      3:258
    first Mexican performance,
      4:399
    first Portuguese performance,
      5:232
    first Russian performance,
      2:596
    first U.S. performance, **2:**597
  Guest scholarship, **3:**321
  Hérold score, **3:**360, **4:**117, **5:**513
  Hus (Eugène) staging, **2:**595,
    3:426
  Lazzini reconstructions, **4:**134
  libretto, **4:**174–175
  Mazilier performance, **4:**340
  Mordkin production, **2:**597,
    4:459, 460
  Nault productions, **1:**73, **2:**597,
    4:576
    Chiriaeff final stage
      performance, **2:**152
  Nijinska production, **1:**66, **2:**597,
    4:638
  Papliński production, **5:**75
  Parés production, **1:**436
  Rochefort production, **4:**588
  Romanoff (Dimitri) production,
    5:391
    Markarova performance, **1:***92*,
      4:248
  Russian productions and
    reproductions, **1:**34, **2:**11, 36,
    596–597, **3:**197, 206, **5:**39
    Clustine performance, **2:**181
    Fenster performance, **2:**585
    Gorsky production, **2:**596,
      3:206, **4:**358
    Istomina performance, **3:**539,
      4:279

    Kshessinska performance,
      4:68, 640
    Legat (Nikolai) and Pavlova
      performance, **4:***142*
    Legat (Sergei) role, **4:**144
    Messerer production, **4:**358
    Nijinsky performance, **4:**640
    Petipa staging, **5:**158
    Sergeyev staging in Latvia, **4:**127
    Vinogradov production, **4:**285
    Zucchi performance, **6:**452
  scores, **2:**594, 595, 596, 597,
    3:321, 360
  Spoerli production, **1:**375, **2:**596,
    596, **5:**682
    Dupond performance, **2:**463
  Taglioni (Paul) revised version,
    2:594, 596, **3:**145
  Taglioni (Salvatore) restaging,
    6:70
  travesty role in, **6:**190, *190*
  Viganò production, **1:**390, **4:**285
Fille Sauvage, La, **2:**364
Filleule des Fées, La, **1:**10, 86, **2:**60,
  505, **3:**315–316, **5:**93,
  138–139, *140*, 148, **6:**70
Filling Station, **1:**280, 281, **5:**512,
  6:247
  Christensen (Lew) choreography
    and performance, **1:**478,
    2:160, 162
  d'Amboise performance, **2:**314
  Hawkins performance, **3:**349
  Kirstein libretto, **4:**28
  Loring performance, **4:**227
  Thomson score, **4:**518
Film about A Woman Who . . .
  (film), **5:**293
film and video, **2:597–612**
  avant-garde dance, **1:**244, **3:**95,
    96, **4:**452
  choreography for camera,
    2:603–612
    Cunningham-Atlas
      collaboration, **2:**294, 607
    Gordon videodances,
      3:201, 202
    Hollywood musicals, **2:**613,
      616, 617
    Tharp, Twyla, **6:**139, 154
  documenting dance, **1:**134,
    2:597–600
    Amsterdam Theater School,
      4:599
    archival collections, **4:**163, 167,
      168–169, 170
    Béjart stagings, **1:**403, 407
    Bournonville and Beck styles,
      1:399
    Choreometric project, **4:**374
    Cunningham productions,
      2:294, 296
    Dale productions, **2:**314
    d'Amboise productions,
      2:314–315
    de Keersmaeker works, **1:**412
    de Mille productions,
      2:374–375
    Egyptian cabaret dance
      sequences, **2:**345–346
    Graham works, **3:**213
    Humphrey works, **3:**404–405
    movement studies, **1:**130,
      134, 140
    Nikolais/Louis technique, **4:**230
    Nutcracker versions, **5:**16
    Relâche, **1:**134–135, 244
    Robbins Film and Videotape
      Archive, **5:**363
    technique study, **6:**129
  ethnographic studies, **2:600–603**
    African dance styles, **6:**25

Balinese dance, **3:**507
Chinese dance, **2:**148
Egyptian dance, **4:**414
Eskimo (Inuit) dance, **4:**571
European traditional dance, **2:**543
Pakistani dance, **5:**64, 65
mixed media, **1:**140, 142
music videos, **1:**78, **2:**610, 620, **5:**631
See also film musicals; photography; television
Film Archive, **5:**48
Filmer, Paul, *as contributor*, **4:**360–362
filmi dance, **5:**64, 65
film musicals, **2:612–629**
See also Bollywood film musicals, Hollywood film musicals
Films for Ethnographic Teaching (Heider), **2:**602
Filosofov, Dmitri, **2:**406, 407, 411
Fils de l'Air, ou L'Enfant Changé en Jeune Homme, **2:**183
Fils Prodigue, Le. See Prodigal Son, The
Fin, **2:**45
Financial Times (British newspaper), **3:**285
Finart, Enrique and Ana Trabattoni, **1:**110
Finch, Dianne, **5:**55, *154*
Finding of the Moon, The, **1:**212
Findings, **4:**238
Findlay, Elsa, **3:**596
Fin du Jour, La, **4:**243, **5:**315
Fine, Toby, **5:**652
Fine, Vivian, **1:**421, **2:**196
finger-cymbal dance, **2:***494–495*, 495
Fini, Léonor, **1:**152, 305, **2:**244, **3:**74, **4:**421, **5:**60, 65
Finian's Rainbow (musical), **4:**10, 120, **6:**279–280
Fink, Hector, **4:**396
Finkel, Anita, *as contributor*, **1:**11–12, 63–64, 279–281, 388–390, **2:**462–463, **3:**610–618, **4:**621–624, 630–631, **5:**411–422
Finkel, Heinz, **3:**76, 83
Finland, **2:629–635**
dance research and publication, **2:**386, 631, **634–635**, **4:**160
theatrical dance, **2:631–634**, 635, **3:**311–313
traditional dance, **1:**118, **2:629–631**, 634–635
Union of Finnish Dance Artists, **5:**43
See also Finnish National Ballet
Finlayson, Victoria, **2:***291, 293*
Finn, David A., **5:**679
Finnegans Wake (Joyce), **2:**295, 520
Finnell, Carrie, **2:**572–573
Finney, Charles G., **6:**235
Finnish National Ballet, **2:**632–633, *633*, 635
Beriozoff as ballet master, **1:**430
Don Quixote, **2:**441
Finnish Theater Academy, **2:**632
Finnissy, Michael, **4:**219
Finta Giardiniera, La (Mozart), **2:**372
Finta Pazza, La, **4:**229, **6:**157
Finto Feudatorio, Il, **1:**460, **5:**528
Fiocre, Eugénie, **2:**198, 199, **5:**94, 501
Fior di Maria, **2:**209
Fiorello! (musical), **6:**282, 288
Fiorentino, Pier-Angelo, **4:**215, **5:**499

Fiorilli, Tiberio, **2:**190, **3:**254
Fire, **2:**359, **3:**616
Fire and Ice (television program), **6:**180
Firebird, The, **3:1–4**
Ashton production, **5:**416
Ananiashvili performance, **1:**83
Beriosova performance, **1:**429
Blair performance, **1:**459
Fonteyn performance, **3:**2, 42, 44, **5:**416
Somes performance, **5:**639
Balanchine productions, **1:**271, **2:**245, **3:**2–3
innovative approach, **4:**608–609
Kirkland performance, **4:**24
Moncion performance, **4:**450
revival and restoration, **4:**621
Robbins collaboration, **5:**631
Stravinsky collaboration, **4:**613
Tallchief (Maria) performance, **3:**2, *2, 3*, **4:**609, 616, **6:**85
Verdy performance, **4:**617
Barbay choreography, **3:**4, **6:**66
Béjart productions, **1:**292, 403, *404*, 405
Belin performance, **3:***3*
Denard performance, **3:***3*
Markó performance, **4:**266, *266*
Bolm stagings, **1:**136, 484
Markova performance, **4:**269
character role, **2:**106
Dyk choreography, **2:**471
Fokine production, **1:**316, 320, **3:1–2**, 4, 14, 16, 17, *18*, **5:**208
Balanchine performance, **4:**26
Bolm performance, **1:**482
Cecchetti mime performance, **2:***82*, 83
Danilova role, **2:**342
Diaghilev collaboration, **1:**311, **2:***242*, 406, 407
Golovin designs, **2:***82*, **3:***1, 1*, 196
Karsavina role, **3:**656
Lassen performance in Denmark, **4:**126
Spessivtseva performance, **5:**678
Stravinsky score, **4:**515–516, **6:**3
Fokine production revivals
Ananiashvili performance, **1:**83
Goncharova designs, **3:**197, *198*, **5:**543
Grigoriev-Tchernicheva revival, **3:**308
Liepa (Andris) revival, **4:**181
Haydée choreography, **2:**125
Holm (Eske) choreography, **5:**432
Lifar choreography, **4:**185, **6:**353
Lopukov production, **2:**342, **4:**224
Macdonald staging, **3:**343
makeup conventions, **4:***305*
Nebrada production, **3:**4
Neumeier production, **1:**241
Poole production, **5:***652*
Spoerli production, **1:**374, **3:***4*
Stier choreography, **6:**41
Stravinsky score, **1:**93, **2:**407, **3:**1, 2, 4, **4:**515–516, 609, **6:**3
Taras production, **2:**334, **3:**4
Tetley production, **3:**4
Fire Ceremony, **4:**568
Fire Dance (Fuller dance), **2:**37, 92–93, **3:***93*
Fire Dancer, The, **2:**11, 12
fire-dancing rituals, **1:**84, **2:**8, 100, 487
Greece, **3:**298
Hungary, **3:**411
trance dance, **6:**187, 188

Fire Feast, The, **6:**365
Fireflies, **5:**525
Fire in the Snow, **4:**214
Firestone Library, Princeton, New Jersey, **4:**167
Fireworks, **1:**244, **2:**409, **5:**544
Fireworks Suite, **1:**197
Firqa al-Qawmīyah Lil Funun al-Shaʿbīyah, **2:**496
Firqat al-Alaʿat al-Shaʿbīyah, **2:**496
Firqat al-Fellahin. *See* Firqat al-Alaʿat al-Shaʿbīyah
Firqat al-Raqṣ al-Hadith, **2:**498
First Ball, The, **1:**456
First Construction (in Metal) (Cage), **2:**21
First Encounter of Danza Callejera Contemporánea, **4:**397
First Intermezzo (Callot), **2:**27
First International Congress of Sports Medicine (1928; Amsterdam), **2:**328
First International Symposium on Orthopaedic and Medical Aspects of Dance (1979), **2:**328
First Love, **5:**470
First New York Theatre Rally, **1:**542
First Physical Theatre Company, **5:**657
First Principles (Spencer), **1:**127
First Shoot, The, **1:**395
First Steps in Ballet (French and Demery), **6:**128
First Symphony (Shostakovich), **4:**324, 517
First Time Painting (Rauschenberg), **5:**314
First World Festival of Negro Arts (1966; Dakar), **1:**55
Fischer, Anne, *as photographer*, **2:**265
Fischer, Eberhard, *as photographer*, **2:**210
Fischer, Ferdinand, **1:**517
Fischer, Lindsay, **2:**470
fish dives. *See* ballet technique
Fisher, Clyde, *as photographer*, **4:**564
Fisher, Constance, **4:**212
Fisher, Otto, **4:**15
Fisher, Robert, **2:**470
Fisherman, The (Paradisi ballet), **5:**452
Fisherman, The, or The Girl from the Archipelago (Cramér ballet), **2:**264
Fisherman and His Soul, The, **6:**1
Fiskarena, **1:**503, **6:**47
Fisk, Jim, **5:**514
Fisk University, **6:**258
Fissi, Dario, **3:**97
Fistoulari, Anatole, **1:**315
Fitt, Sally, **4:**17
Fitzgerald, F. Scott, **1:**252
Fitzjames, Alexandrine, **3:**5
Fitzjames, Louise, **3:**4–5
caricature of, **2:**69
Fitzjames, Nathalie, **1:**9, **2:**203, **3:***5, 5*, 179, **4:**340, **5:**558
Fitzjames sisters, **3:**4–5
Fitz-Simmons, Foster, **1:**112, **5:**585
Fitzwilliam Virginal Book (Byrd), **1:**523, **6:***350*
Five American Sketches, **5:**586, 587
Five Boons of Life, The (later *The Five Gifts*), **2:**426
Five Brahms Waltzes in the Manner of Isadora Duncan, **1:**158–159, **4:**244, **5:**303, 437
Five Car Pile-Up, **2:**171
Five Civilized Tribes, **4:**559

5 dance constructions + some other things, **3:**54
Five Études for Cymbale, **1:**307
Five Faces of Eurydice, **5:***52*, 53, 54, 692
Five-Legged Stool, **5:**548
Five Stone Wind, **2:**292, 296, **4:**37
Five Tangos, **3:**344, **5:**436
Fjeld, **3:**389
Fjeldsted, Caroline, **1:**509, **5:**425
Fjelstuen, eller Tyveaar. See Mountain Hut, The
Fjernt fra Danmark, eller Et Costumebal Ombord. See Far from Denmark
Flaccus, Aulus Clodius, **5:**73–74
Flach, Hans, **3:**302
Flade, Tina, **1:**441
Flagg, Laura, **6:**265
Flaherty, Robert, **2:**601
Flahooley (musical), **6:**90
Flakelar, Barrie, *as photographer*, **5:**15
Flamand, Frédérick, **1:**411, 412
Flamenco, **1:**294
Flamenco (film), **5:**674
flamenco dance, **3:6–11**
accompanying vocal sounds, **3:**38
Amaya, Carmen, **1:**61–62
Antonio and Rosario, **1:**92–93
Argentinita, La, **1:**116, 117
Escudero, Vicente, **2:**520–521
escuela bolero, **2:**522, **3:**6, 9, 11
Gades, Antonio, **3:**101–102
Greco, José, **3:**286
improvisation, **3:**448
Massine choreography, **4:**317
Rioja, Pilar, **5:**353–354
Spain, **5:**671, 672, *673*, 674, 674–675
Ximénez-Vargas Ballet Español, **6:***408*
Flamenco Dances, **2:**378
Flamenco Puro (musical), **6:**288
Flamencos en Route, **6:**28
Flament, Édouard, **4:**657
Flames of Paris, The, **1:**90, 490, 491, *491*, **2:**72, **3:12**, **6:**310
Asafiev score, **1:**144, **4:**517
Chabukiani performance, **2:**96
Dmitriev libretto, **2:**421, **3:**12
Dudinskaya performance, **2:**449
Fayer conducting, **2:**579
film, **2:**97
Gabovich performance, **3:**99
Golovkina performance, **3:**197
Lavrovsky (Mikhail) performance, **4:**133
Lepeshinskaya performance, **4:**148
Semenova performance, **5:**557
Sergeyev performance, **5:**571
as Soviet-era ballet, **4:**283, 284, **5:**458
Vainonen production, **3:**417, **4:**283, **5:**458, *459*
Yermolayev performance, **6:**420
flamingo (as totem), **2:**476
Flammand, Frédéric, **2:**109
Flanagan, Hallie V., **2:**579, 580, 581
Flanders. *See* Belgium
Flapper and the Quarterback, The, **5:**58
Flare-Up, **4:**627
Flashdance (film), **1:**538, **2:**620
flash tap dancing, **6:**100
Flat, **5:**127
flatfooting, **2:**179, 180
Flathead (people), **4:**554
Flatow, Herb, *as photographer*, **6:**138
flat wing and groove, **5:***534*, 535

Flaubert, Gustave, **2:**345
Flauto Danzante, Il, **1:**83
Flaxman, John, **1:**149
Fledermaus, Die (Strauss the younger), **4:**126, **6:**268
  Page choreography, **5:**59
  Wiesenthal choreography, **6:**388
Fleet, **3:**388
Fleischmann, Aloys, **3:**520
Fleischmann, Julius, **1:**295
Fleisheimer, Kurt, **4:***156*
Fleming, Gladys Andres, **4:**168
Flemings (people), **1:**408, 409, 412
Flemish Royal Opera House. *See* Royal Flemish Opera
fleshings (tights), **5:**240–241
Flesh Is Heir (Kirstein), **4:**26
Fletcher, Nicky, **1:***217*
Fletcher, Tom, **5:**368, **6:**254
Fleuret, Maurice, **2:**466
Fleurs, Les, **3:**450, **4:**119
Fleurs Animées, Les, **1:**460
Fleurs de Peau, **2:**45
Fleurs du mal, Les (Baudelaire), **3:**122
Fleury, Elise, **5:**233
Fleury, Louise, **1:**37
Flexmore, J. H., **1:**206
Flexmore, Richard, **5:**70
Flextime (film and live dance), **2:**608
Flickers, **6:**376
Flick und Flocks Abenteuer, **3:***144*, 145, **5:**514–515, **6:**75–76, 452
Flier, Frieda, **3:**214, 216, **5:***184*
Flier, Jaap, **1:**214, **4:**600, 601, *601*, 602, **5:**302, **6:**56
Flier, Yakov, **5:**587
Fligg, Anny, **1:**211
Flindt, Flemming, **1:**50, 111, 454, **2:**245, 284, 350, 387, **3:12–13**, 657, **5:**98, **6:**135
  Bournonville heritage, **1:**512
  Caroline Mathilde, **3:**13, **5:***431*, 433
  Coppélia performance, **2:**201
  Danish composers, **5:**425
  English National Ballet, **2:**509, 510, **3:**12
  Hønningen roles, **3:**373
  Kermesse in Bruges, **4:**6
  Lesson, The, **3:**668, **5:***430*, 564
  Norwegian National Ballet choreography, **4:**678
  Nutcracker performance, **5:***13*
  Riisager scores, **5:**353
  Romeo and Juliet performance, **5:**394
  Royal Danish Ballet, **5:**430–431, 600
  showmanship, **3:**13
  Triumph of Death, The, **5:**511
  Volkova influence, **5:**430
  Worsaae designs, **6:**404
Flindt, Vivi, **3:**13, **5:**432, **6:**129
Floating Lady, The, **2:**602
Flood (Linke solo), **4:**203
Flood, The, **3:**328, **6:**6, 137
Floodlight (musical), **1:**520
Floodtide (film), **3:**521
Floor Plastique, **5:**587
Floradora (musical), **6:**269
Floral Design (Johns artwork), **3:**619–620
Floralia (Roman festival), **4:**427, **5:**376
Flora Macdonald's Fancy, **3:**247, *248*, 249
Flore (1669), **4:**234
Flore et Armide, **5:**231
Flore et Zéphire, **2:***415*, **5:**113, 319, **6:**216

Didelot production, **1:**35, 86, 110, **2:**71, 464, **4:**277, 279, **5:**91
  Duport performance, **2:**464
  first performance, **2:**414
  Gosselin (Geneviève) performance, **3:**208
  Istomina performance, **4:**279
  Mazilier choreography, **4:**342
  Paris production, **2:**415, *415*
  restaging. *See Zéphire et Flore*
  Taglioni (Marie) costume, **2:**239
  Thackeray caricature, **2:**71
Florence, Italy, **3:**544, 553
Florentine Spring, The, **5:**503
Florentinische Frühling, Der, **5:**503
Flores Canelo, Raúl, **4:**394, 396
Flores Guerrero, Raúl, **4:**399
Floresta do Amazonas, A, **1:**535
Flore Subsimplici, **3:**51
Florian (film), **1:**367
Florida, **5:**151
Florieux, François, **5:**422
Florio, John, **2:**50, **4:**326, **5:**111, 115, **6:**178
Flotow, Friedrich von, **2:**14, **4:**341, 514
Flower Arrangement, The, **2:**378
Flowerburger, **3:**336
Flower Crown Dance, **2:**222
Flower Dance, **4:**567
Flower Drum Song (musical), **4:**3, **6:**282
Flower Festival (*kagura* type), **3:**585
Flower Festival in Genzano, **2:**511, **5:**427
  Bournonville production, **1:**510, 511, 514
  Bruhn pas de deux staging, **2:**4
  Paulli score, **1:**515
  Ralov and Bjørnsson pas de deux, **5:**295
  Rosen re-creation, **4:**380
  Terabust performance, **6:**143
Flower Lantern Dance, **2:**139
Flowers, **1:**58, **5:**575
Flowers, Verla, **4:**470
Flowers of Granada, The, **3:**193
Flowers of Little Ida, The, **6:**432
Flowing Landscapes, **1:**374
Flow of Movement, The (Karsavina). *See Classical Ballet: The Flow of Movement*
Flucht vor Göttern, **3:**155
flute, **1:**6, 164
  Bamana dance, **4:**484
  Basque, **1:**376, 377, *377*
  Berber, **4:**467
  as *folia* accompaniment, **3:**28
  France, **3:**64
  gamelan, **3:**112, 114, 475
  Garifuna dance, **3:**120
  Greece, ancient, **3:**290
  Japan, **3:**585, 587, **4:**492, 652
  Middle Ages, **4:***501*
Flute of Krishna, **3:**211
Flute of Pan, **3:**220
Flute That Calmed Ten Thousand Waves, **4:**12
Fluxus, **1:**139, 141–142, **3:**54, 634
Fly (dance), **1:**78
Flying Down to Rio (film), **1:**192, 193, **5:**373, **6:**92
Flying into the Middle, **4:***151*
Flying Trapeze, The (revue), **1:**520
Flynn, Carlos, *as photographer*, **1:**114
Flynn, Patrick, **2:**441
Focus I to V, **4:**594
Fodeba, Keita, **4:**549
Fodor, Antal, **1:**307, **3:**418, **4:**285
Fodor, Iris, *as photographer*, **6:**291

foeroyskur dansur, **2:**101
Fogel, Vladimir, **3:**48
Fogliazzi, Maria Teresa, **1:**87, 236
Föhn, **3:**368
Foire Espagnole, **3:**198
Fojo de Flores, Felipe, **5:**676
Fokina, Vera, **1:**518, **3:**1, 14, *20*, 21–22, 23, *24*, **5:**95, 428
  Chopiniana performance, **6:**60
  Josephslegende performance, **3:**631
  Schéhérazade performance, **5:**556
  Swedish Royal Ballet, **6:**41
Fokine (Haskell ed.), **4:**27
Fokine, Isabelle, **4:**181, **5:**556
Fokine, Leon, **1:**255, 498
Fokine, Michel, **3:14–28**, **5:**17, *158*, 247, 559, 614, 650, 678, 693, **6:**191, 217
  abstract ballet, **6:**60, 61
  aesthetic vision, **1:**25, 239, 318, 320–321, 322, **3:**14, 28, 130, **4:**63, 64, **5:**456
  American Ballet Company, **3:**22–23
  American Ballet Theatre, **1:**65, 66, *71*, **2:**112, **3:**26–27
  as American dance influence, **6:**290, 291
  American musicals and revues, **3:**21–22
  Argentine tour, **1:**110, **3:**24
  artistic significance, **3:**28
  attitude devant, **1:**198
  Ballets Russes de Monte Carlo, **1:**295, 312–314, 316, **3:**14, 24–25, **4:**667
  Ballets Russes de Serge Diaghilev, **1:***317*, 318, *318*, 319, 320–321, **2:**406, 441, **3:**14, 16–19, **5:**391
  Ballets Russes de Serge Diaghilev resignation, **1:**98, 319–320, **3:**19–20, **4:**641
  Ballets Russes de Serge Diaghilev return, **1:**321–322, **3:**20–21
  ballet technique, **6:**195
    pas de deux, **5:**107
    pointe work, **5:**208
    port de bras, **5:**227, **6:**62
  Benois association, **1:**423
  Blok critique of, **1:**464
  Bolm interpretations, **1:**482, 483, 484
  as Börlin influence, **1:**326
  Bowman roles, **1:**518
  Cecchetti mime roles, **2:**82
  character dances, **2:**108, **3:**18–19, 21
  charity events, **3:**15–16, 19, 22
  as Chiriaeff influence, **2:**150
  Chopiniana as signature, **1:**327, 492, **3:**14, 15, *20*, **4:**283, **6:**62
    See also Sylphides, Les, Russian origins
  choreographic intent, **1:**320–321, 322, 348, **3:**130, **6:**62
  Cléopâtre, **5:**45, 122
  commedia dell'arte characters, **2:**191, *192*
  concert repertory, **3:**21
  concerts, recitals, and lecture-performances, **3:**21–22
  Coq d'Or staging, **3:**20
  costume authenticity, **2:**241, **3:**14
  critical assessments, **3:**27–28, **5:**483, **6:**352
  Diaghilev quarrel, **1:**319, 320, **2:**408, **3:**17–18, 19–20

Dollar performances, **2:**426
Don Juan version, **2:**434, **3:**24
Duncan as stylistic influence, **2:**457, **3:**14–15, 18, 20, **5:**542
Eglevsky audition for, **2:**478
  on Eglevsky's technique, **2:**479
English National Ballet revivals, **2:**510, 512
Eunice, **5:**121
Fedorova roles, **2:**582
Firebird choreography. *See Firebird, The*
Firebird performance, **3:**1, *1*, 17, *18*
  first choreography, **3:**15
Five Principals of ballet reform, **3:**14
Francesca da Rimini, **6:**117
Gerdt (Pavel and Elisaveta) association, **3:**14, 15, 137
Goleizovsky as student, **3:**193
Golovin designs, **3:**196
Goncharova designs, **3:**198
Gorsky artistic similarity, **1:**487
Graham aesthetic disagreement, **3:**28
influences seen in Lopukhov's work, **4:**225
International Ballet repertory, **3:**511
Ivanov choreographic vision as similar, **3:**568
Josephslegende, Die, **3:**631
Karsavina roles, **3:**656
Kaye association, **3:**663
Kirstein as student, **4:**27
Koslov unauthorized ballet versions, **4:**56
Kshessinska (Matilda) roles, **4:**68
Laing roles, **4:**109, 110
as Lander (Harald) influence, **4:**118
Lassen roles, **4:**126
Latvian ballet, **4:**127
as Legat (Nikolai) student, **4:**143
Legat caricature drawings of, **2:**69
Legat rivalry, **3:**16
libretti, **4:**176
Liepa (Andris) reconstructions, **4:**181
Markova association, **4:**268, 269, 270
Maryinsky Ballet, **1:**319, **3:**14–16, 19–20, **4:***280*, 282, 283, 639, **5:***455*, 456
Maryinsky resignation, **1:**319, **3:**18
Maryinsky teaching methods revision, **5:**480
Massine choreographic vision versus, **1:**322
memoir, **5:**483
as Nijinska influence, **4:**633, 634
Nijinsky roles and interpretation, **4:**639, 640, *642*, 646–647
Nutcracker choreography, **5:**13
one-act ballet, **3:**205
Orientalism, **5:**45
Paris Opera Ballet appearances, **5:**95
Petipa ballets versus, **6:**62
Préludes, Les, **5:**124
Puppenfee, Die, **5:**279
Riabouchinska roles, **5:**350
Romanov roles and choreographic influence, **5:**391, 392
Royal Danish Ballet guest productions, **5:**428, **6:**62
Royal Swedish Ballet restagings, **3:**20, **6:**41, 62

Rubinstein roles, **5:**438
Russian scholarly views on, **5:**483
Saison Russe (1909) ballet choreography, **2:**407
Schollar roles, **5:**558
Seven Daughters of the Mountain King, The, **5:**124
Shaw on, **3:**284
Spectre de la Rose, **3:**14, 18, *24,* 73, *668,* **5:**413
Stepanov system as inadequate for recording choreography, **5:**693
students, **1:**39, 117, **2:**160, 341, 426, **3:**14, 22, **4:**38, 126, 223, 233, 674, **5:**391, 558, 674, **6:**41, 120, 341
Svetlov's critical support, **6:**28
Swan Lake performance, **6:**32
Swedish dance and theatrical influence, **6:**41
training and early career, **3:**14–16
Volynsky's criticism of, **6:**352
Ziegfeld Follies staging, **6:**448
See also Carnaval, Le; Daphnis et Chloë; Dying Swan, The; Firebird, The; Pavillon d'Armide, Le; Petrouchka; Polovtsian Dances; Schéhérazade; Sylphides, Les
Fokine, Vera. *See* Fokina, Vera
Fokine, Vitale, **3:**22, 23
"Fokine and His Time" (Slonimsky), **3:**21
Foley, Catherine E., **3:**519
  as contributor, **3:**515–519
  as photographer, **5:**695, 696
folia, **3:**28–29, 51
Folie d'un Peintre, La, **4:**454
Folies-Bergère, Paris, **4:**523
  Baker, Josephine, **1:**252, 253
  Bluebell, Miss, **1:**465
  Fuller, Loie, **3:**71, 92, **4:**524
"Folies d'Espagne," **3:***28,*29, **5:**520
Folies d'Espagne, Les, **2:**107
Foligno dance collection, **1:**380
Folio (television series), **6:**131, 132
Folk Army, Hungary, **4:**448
Folkdance (Byrd ballet), **1:**60, **2:**20
Folk Dance (Coudy ballet), **1:**280
folk dance clubs (Sweden), **6:**36, 37
folk dance history, **3:**29–38
  Argentina, **1:**108–110
  Armenia, **1:**119–121
  Austria, **1:**242–243
  Azerbaijan, **1:**247–248
  Bangladesh, **1:**363
  Bartók studies, **1:**370
  Basque, **1:**376–278
  Belarus, **1:**407–408
  Belgium, **1:**409
  bourrée form, **1:**517
  Cambodia, **2:**29, *32,* 227, 228
  chain and round dances, **2:**99–102
  China, **2:**138–141, 149–150, 220–221, **6:**406, 415
  clogging, **2:**178–181
  Crete, **2:**271–272
  Cuba, **2:**273–276
  Czech Republic and Slovak Republic, **2:**301–305
  Dances of Death, **2:**331–332
  Denmark, **2:**382, 386–387
  Dominican Republic, **2:**430–431, 432
  Egyptian Reda troupe, **4:**412, 417, 490
  England, **3:**238–243, 256, **5:**695
  Estonia, **2:**527–528, 530

Europe, **2:**540–543, **3:**29–34, 109–10, **4:**374
European historical records, **2:**541–543
European marginalization, **2:**540–541
European peasant dance, **5:**624
Faeroe Islands, **2:**383–384, **3:**30
Faeroe step, **2:**565
Finland, **2:**629–630, 631, 634
first use of *folk dance* as term, **3:**31
folklorism and folkloristics, **2:**537–540, 542, 543, 559, **3:**29–36
France, **1:**520, 522, **3:**63–65
gavotte, **3:**125
Germany, **3:**29, 139–140, 142, 160, **6:**377–378
Greece, **3:**296–298, 303, 304
Haiti, **3:**333–336
Hinman studies, **3:**367–368
Hungary, **2:**299–300, **3:**405–407, 407–413, 422–423, **4:**448, **5:**287
Iceland, **3:**435–436
India, **2:**225
Iran, **3:**513–514
Ireland, **3:**518–519
Israel, **3:**530–531, 532, 537–539, 605, 641, **4:**155–156
Japan, **1:**496–497, **2:**219, **3:**585–588
Kazakhstan, **3:**664
Korea, **1:**167, **4:**46–48, 50
Kyrgyzstan, **4:**86, 87
Latvia, 128, **4:**126–127
Lebanese "new" folkloric dance, **4:**489–490, *490,* 491
Lithuania, **4:**204–207
Malaysia, **4:**250
Mexico, **4:**395–396
Moiseyev Dance Company, **4:**445
Moldova, **4:**78, 446
Morocco, **4:**469
Myanmar, **4:**525
Native American, **4:**555, 570, 571
Netherlands, **4:**585–586, 598
North Africa, **4:***664,* 666
Norway, **4:**669, 672, 682
notation systems, **4:**691–693
Okinawa, **5:**26
Pakistan, **2:**226, **5:**63, 64–65
Peru, **5:**142–146
Philippines, **1:**394, **5:**167–169, 170, *171,* 173, 174
Poland, **4:**57, 343, **5:**210–214, *218,* 220
primitive dance versus, **3:**30, 31, 32, **5:**252–253
Romania, **5:**379–383, 390–391
Russia, **4:**530, **5:**442–445, 449–450, 452, 473–474, 481–482, **6:**303–304
Scotland, **3:**243–250
Sharp collections, **5:**582–583
square dancing, **5:**585–690
Sri Lanka, **4:**34–35
Sweden, **6:**36–37, 40, 49
Taiwan, **5:**80
technical manuals, **6:**128
Thailand, **2:**227, **6:**147, 148
Tibet, **6:**169–170
traditional dance versus, **3:**296
Tunisia, **6:**207
Turkey, **6:**208–209, 211
Turkmenistan, **6:**213
Ukraine, **6:**222–223, 224–226
United States, **6:**240, 242, 245–246, 247–248, 294–295, 297
Uruguay, **6:**301

Uzbekistan, **6:**305, 306, 307
Vietnam, **6:**336, 337
Wales, **3:**250
Yugoslavia, **6:**426–431, 438–439
See also ethnic dance; European traditional dance
Folk Dances of All Nations, **6:**245–246
folk dance sounds, **3:**38–39
  Africa, **4:**484
  Albania, **1:**34
  Amirkhanian text-and-sound, **1:**52
  Arabian Peninsula, **1:**101, 102
  Australian Aboriginal, **1:**225, 226, 228, 229
  Cape Breton step dancing, **5:**698
  Guatamalan whistles, **3:**319
  Middle East, **4:**403–404
  See also clogging
Folk Dancing in Elementary and Secondary Schools (Sharp), **5:**582
Folk Dancing Is for Everyone (Schwalbe-Brame), **4:**693
Folkedanslitteratur i Norden (newsletter), **2:**386
Folkemusikhusringen, Denmark, **2:**382
Folk Ensemble of the Trade Unions, Hungary, **4:**448
Folkerts, Jessica, **2:**470
Folkesangen på Færoerne (Thuren), **2:**384, 565
folkevisedans, **4:**671, 672
Folk Festival Council of New York, **3:**368
Folklore Group of the National University of Engineering, Peru, **5:**146
Folklore Institute, Bucharest. *See* Ethnography and Folklore Institute
folklorism and folkloristics, **2:**537–540, 541, 542, 543, 545, 547, 559, **3:**29–36
Folkloristes du Québec, Les, **2:**36
Folk Opera Ballet, Vienna, **1:**241, **6:**388
Folksagen, Et. See Folk Tale, A
Folksay, **4:**306, *605*
Folk Singing in Schools (Sharp), **5:**582
Folktale (1984), **1:**479
Folk Tale, A (1854), **1:**497, **3:**39–40, 185, **5:**251, 295, 426, 433, 555, 600
  Bjørnsson performance, **1:**454
  Bournonville production, **1:***508,* 509, 510, 511
  Evdokimova performances, **2:**561
  Gade music, **1:**515
  Price (Juliette) performance, **5:**425
  reconstruction, **2:**387, **4:**119
  Worsaae designs, **6:**404
Folk Theater, Berlin. *See* Berlin Volksbühne
FOLKUNI (Folklore Group of the National University of Engineering; Peru), **5:**146
Folkuniversitet, Stockholm, **6:**48–49
Folkwang Schule, Essen, **3:**157, 626, 629–670
  Knust, Albrecht, **4:**32
  as Laban central school, **4:**92, 103
  Leeder, Sigurd, **4:**140
  Linke studies, **4:**203
  Züllig directorship, **6:**453

Folkwang Tanzbühne, Essen, **3:***625,* 627, 628
  See also Ballets Jooss
Folkwang Tanzstudio, **1:**386, 411, 460, **2:**81, **3:**40, 149, 151, 368, 630, **4:**203, **6:**453
  Hoffmann, Reinhild, **3:**368
  Jooss, Kurt, **3:**626, 630
  Linke, Susanne, **4:**203
Follets des Alpes, Les (later *The Goblin of the Alps*), **4:**454
Folletta, or The Enchanted Bell, **4:**454–455
Follia di Orlando, La, **1:**82, 349–350, **2:**369, **5:**529
Follies (musical), **1:**419, **6:**285
Follies of 1907 (musical revue), **2:**572, **6:**269, 447
  See also Ziegfeld Follies
Follow the Boys (film), **6:**450
Follow the Girls (musical), **4:**210
Follow the Sun (musical), **1:**395, 520
Fomin, Evstigney, **5:**452
Fomin, William, **3:**329
Fon (people), **1:**529, **2:**274, **6:**383
Fonaroff, Nina, **1:**97, 421, **2:**285, 290, 360, **3:**214, 216, 385, **4:**220
Fondazione Giorgio Cini, Venice, **3:**556
Fondo Nacional para el Desarrollo de la Danza Popular Méxicana (FONDAN), **4:**399–400
Fonseca, Barbara, **3:**574
Fonseca, Peter, **1:**75, **2:**356
Font, Francisco, **5:**672
Fonta, Laure, **5:**94
Fontaine, Mademoiselle de la, **4:**235
Fontaine de Jouvence, La, **3:**66, **4:**695
Fontano, Joseph, **6:**121
Fontenla, Norma, **1:**110
Fonteyn, Felix, **2:**58
  as photographer, **1:**154
Fonteyn, Margot, **3:**40–46, 220, **5:**163, 299, 565, 612, **6:**198
  Apparitions performance, **3:**40, 355, **5:***412*
  Ashton collaboration, **1:**148, 158, **3:***40,* 41–42, 44, 45, 46, 265, **5:**416
  Australian Ballet tours, **1:**210, 231, 499, **2:**183
  Ballet de Santiago guest appearance, **2:**124
  Ballet Imperial performance, **1:**293
  Ballets de Paris guest performance, **1:**305, **3:**74
  ballet training in Shanghai, **2:**133, 145
  Bayadère performance, **5:***418*
  Beaton photograph, **1:**395
  on Bosl's dance qualities, **1:**500–501
  Cinderella performance, **2:**174, *243*
  Coppélia performance, **2:**201
  Demoiselles de la Nuit performance, **1:**305, **3:**74
  as de Valois protégée, **2:**398, **3:**41, 42
  Don Quixote performance, **2:**440
  English National Ballet guest performances, **2:**508, 511
  Fernandez dance partnership, **2:**586
  Firebird performance, **3:**2, 42, 44, **5:**416

Fonteyn, Margot, *continued*
  first solo role, **3:**41
  as Fracci influence, **3:**59
  Helpmann dance partnership,
    3:*42*, 43, 46, 355, *355*, 357
  Horoscope performance, **3:**379,
    4:114
  international stardom, **5:**416
  Jacob's Pillow performance,
    3:572
  Japanese performances, **3:**589
  Karsavina role coaching, **3:**656
  Kshessinska (Matilda) as teacher,
    4:68
  as Legat (Nikolai) student, **4:**143
  Marguerite and Armand
    performance, **3:***42*, *44*, 45
  Nureyev dance partnership,
    1:155, **3:***43*, *44*, 45–46, *45*,
    5:*5*, 6, 7, 97, 107, 164, 416
  Nutcracker performance, **5:**14
  Ondine performance, **3:**41, *42*,
    43, 44
  partners, **5:**312
  Patineurs, Les, **5:**114
  Petrouchka, **5:***165*
  as photographic subject, **1:**395,
    5:*185*
  Poème de l'Extase performance,
    5:405, **6:***10*
  Pomona performance, **4:**113
  proportions and style, **5:**419
  Rake's Progress performance,
    5:294
  Rambert Ballet guest
    performances, **3:**266
  Rendezvous performance, **5:**342
  Romeo and Juliet performance,
    4:242, **5:**396
  Róna dance partnership, **5:**402
  Royal Ballet, **1:***147*, *149*, 150,
    151, 152–153, 154, 155, *155*,
    156, 459, **2:**402, **3:**40–46, 265,
    5:*414*, 416
  Scènes de Ballet performance,
    5:531–532
  Shearer (Moira) as Cinderella
    replacement, **5:**589
  60th Birthday Tribute, **3:**46, 357
  Sleeping Beauty performances,
    3:*41*, 42, 43, 59, *266*, 362,
    5:*55*, *413*, 414, 612, **6:***134*
  Somes dance partnership,
    5:*639*, *640*
  Swan Lake roles, **3:**41, *42*, 43, 44,
    5:*640*, **6:***33*, 35
  Sylvia performance, **6:***63*, 64
  Symphonic Variations
    performance, **3:***42*, 44, **5:**588,
    6:*64*, 65
  television performances, **1:**400,
    6:137
  as Volkova student, **6:**349
  Wedding Bouquet performance,
    6:375
Fonteyn: Impressions of a Ballerina
  (Chappell), **2:**105
Font, Francisco, **2:**251
Fonti, La, **4:**342, 353, **5:***405*
Fonti della danza, Le (journal),
  3:554
Fonti musicali in Italia, Le (journal),
  3:554
Fool (*moresca* and Morris dance),
  4:461, 462, 473, 474
Football Player, The, **1:**490, **4:**359,
  359, 444, *444*
Footlight Parade (film), **1:**432, 433,
  434
footlights, **4:**188
Footloose (film), **2:**620, **5:**408

Footnote Dance Company, **4:**627
Foot Notes: The Classics of Ballet
  (television series), **1:**201,
  6:133
Foot Rules, **2:**460
Footstep of Air, A, **2:**584
footwear, **3:46–48**
  ballet shoe development,
    5:152, 207
  Chinese opera, **2:**220
  Gorsky barefoot choreography,
    5:456
  Graham company bare feet,
    3:214
  gumboots, **2:***86*, 212–213, **5:**648,
    648, **6:**22
  heeled, **2:**236, 238, 249, **3:**46, 47
  Japanese *kabuki,* **3:**640
  Korean costume, **2:**223
  leather boots, **3:***133*, 134
  pointe shoe evolution, **1:**347, 513
  poulaine shoe, **5:**336
  soft-shoe dancing, **3:**517, *517*,
    4:520–521
  step dancing, **5:**694–698
  tap dancing, **6:**98–99
  See also clogging
forains, **5:**69
Forains, Les, **1:**305, 426, **4:**517,
  5:163, 527, **6:**352
Foray Forêt, **1:**545
Forbes, Earle, *as photographer,*
  5:589
For Bird with Love, **1:**59
Force Field, **2:**359, **3:**616
force platform, **4:**15–16
Forces of Rhythm, **2:**108, 334
Ford, Henry, **3:**35, **5:**686, 688,
  6:242
Ford, John, **3:**253
Ford Center for the Performing
  Arts, New York City, **6:**289
Ford Foundation
  Joffrey Ballet grant, **3:**611
  New York City Ballet grant, **4:**607
  Omnibus television program
    sponsorship, **6:**138
  Pennsylvania Ballet grant, **5:**131
  regional grants, **6:**264–265, 398
  San Francisco Ballet grant, **2:**162
  School of American Ballet grant,
    1:271, **4:**607, **6:**265
Ford Motor Company, **1:**280, **6:**137
Foregger, Nikolai, **1:**134, 244, 489,
  3:48–49, **5:**458, 477
Foreman, Donlin, **3:**220
Foreman, Richard, **1:**143, 245,
  5:574
Föreningen Brage, **2:**631
Foreningen til Folkendansens
  Fremme, Denmark, **2:**381,
  3:33
Forest, Kurt, **3:**153
Foresta d'Hermanstadt, La, **6:**70
Forestier, Jane, **2:**84
Forest of Three, **4:**649
Forest Song, The, **5:**236, **6:**226
*Fôret Enchantée, La. See Enchanted
  Forest, The*
Fôret Noire, La, **1:**124, **2:**442, 467,
  5:198, **6:**233
Forgotten Land, **4:**1
Forgotten Summer, **6:**380
Forgotten Time, **3:**578
Forion Ensemble, **4:**396–397
Forkins, Morty, **5:**368
Forladte Dido, Den, **3:**105, **5:**424
forlana, **2:**107, **3:49–50**
*Förlorade Sonen, Den. See Prodigal
  Son, The*
Forma, **2:**277

formal dance. *See* ball
formalist dance aesthetics, **1:**24,
  3:274
Forman, Milos, **6:**154
Formations, **6:**433
For M. C.: The Movie, **1:**545
Form Dance, **1:**386
For Me and My Gal (film), **1:**432,
  4:2
Forme et Ligne, **2:**513
Formosa. *See* Taiwan
Formosa Aboriginal Dance Troupe
  of Taiwan, **6:***80*
Fornaroli, Cia, **2:**84, **3:50–51,**
  4:667, **5:**246, 288, 529
Fornicon, **6:**57
Forray, Gábor, **3:**417, *417*
Forrest, George, **1:**298
Forrest, John, *as contributor,* **3:**250,
  250–251, **4:**329–330, 473–475,
  6:54–55
Forrester, Gladys, **6:**130, 132
forró, **1:**529
For Spirits and Kings, **4:**115
Forster, Caroline, **3:**179
Förster, Lutz, **1:**389, **3:**157
Forsyne, Ida, **2:**25
Forsythe, William, **1:**25, 196, 216,
  234, 242, 375, 389, **2:**42, 563,
  3:51–53, **5:**8, 98, 514, 674,
  6:53, 143
  American Music Festival (1988),
    4:623
  CD-ROM Interactive Dance, **2:**612
  Frankfurt Ballet, **3:**52–53, 151
  improvisation, **3:**448
  Joffrey Ballet choreography,
    3:616
  as Kylián influence, **4:**81
  National Ballet of Canada
    choreography, **4:**547
  New York City Ballet guest
    choreography, **4:**623
  Orpheus, **3:**52, *152*, 360
  Stuttgart Ballet, **2:**268, **3:**51–52,
    150, **6:**10
Forsythia, **3:***621*
Fort, Syvilla, **1:**395, **2:**21, 458,
  3:599, **4:**519, **6:**259
*For the Further Improvement of
  Dancing* (Essex), **2:**255, 527
"For the further Improvement of
  Dancing... (Pemberton),
  2:591
for these who die as cattle, **2:**1
Forti, Simone, **3:**54, 336, *444*,
  445, 634
Fortier, Paul-André, **2:**40, 45
Fortún, Julia Elena, **5:**142
Fortuna, Uranio, **3:**314, **5:**135
Fortunato, Aleksandar, **6:**432
Fortune Ballet, **4:**308
Fortune Teller, The (Herbert), **6:**268
Fortune Vient en Dormant, La,
  3:358
Fortuny, Mariano, **3:**123, **4:**189
Fort Worth–Dallas Ballet, **6:**264,
  265, 266
  See also Dallas Ballet
40 Grades de la Sombra, **6:**324
Forty-Nine Dance, **4:**561
42nd Street (film), **1:**432, 434,
  2:614, *614*, **6:**287
42nd Street (musical), **6:**102, 287
Fosca, Igor, **1:**306
Foss, Lukas, **3:**42
Foss, Wilson Perkins, **6:**25
Fossano, Il. *See* Rinaldi, Antonio
Fosse, Bob, **2:**618–619, **3:54–55,**
  5:363, **6:**284, 287
  archival material, **4:**168

  Chicago, **3:**54, **6:**288
  Dancin', **3:**54, **6:**284
  Pajama Game, **3:**599, *599*, **6:**281
  Sweet Charity, **6:**283, *283*
  Verdon association, **6:**327, *327*
Fossen, Maïté, **3:**84
Foster, Allan K., **5:**246
Foster, Pamela, **2:**404
Foster, Stephen, **4:**472
Foster, Susan Leigh, **5:**329
  as contributor, **4:**376–379
Foto-album, **4:**596
Foucault, Michel, **5:**329
Foucher, Paul, **5:**85
Fou d'Elsa, L', **1:**462
fouetté turns, **1:**8, 336, **338,**
  341, 345
  mechanics of, **5:**189, *190*
  Renaissance dance technique,
    5:338
  virtuoso feats, **1:**338, 347, **3:**261,
    565, **4:**68, 145, 282, **6:**443
Foula Reel, **3:**245
Foulkes, Cathy, **2:***298*, 299
Foundation Contemporary Dance,
  4:593–594, 594, 596
Foundation Dance Production,
  4:594, 596–597
Foundation for the Open Eye,
  2:520
Fountain of Bakhchisarai, The,
  1:34, 86, 91, 308, 491, **2:**176,
  3:56–57, 5:557, 616
  Andreyanova performance, **1:**86,
    3:56, **5:**454
  Arseniev choreography, **5:**473
  Asafiev score, **1:**144, **3:**56, 192,
    195, **4:**517, **5:**471, **6:**441
  Belsky performance, **1:**416
  Bulgarian stagings, **2:**11, 12
  Burmeister performance, **2:**15
  Chabukiani performance, **2:**96
  Dudinskaya performance, **2:**449
  Fayer conducting, **2:**579
  Gabovich performance, **3:**99
  Gogół choreography, **3:**192
  Goleizovsky production, **3:**195
  Gusev performance, **3:**327, *328*
  Kondratieva performance, **4:**38
  Lavrovsky (Leonid) staging,
    2:497
  Lavrovsky (Mikhail)
    performance, **4:**133
  Maximova performance, **4:**335
  Parnell production, **5:**101
  Plisetskaya's versus Ulanova's
    performance styles, **5:**204
  Polish premiere, **5:**218
  popularity with Soviet provincial
    companies, **5:**463
  Protsenko choreography, **4:**446
  as Soviet-era ballet, **4:**283, **5:**458
  Ulanova performance, **5:**204,
    6:226, 227
  Yermolayev performance, **6:**420
  Zakharov production, **4:**283,
    5:458, **6:**441–442
Fouquet, Louis, **4:**447
4 Solos for 4 Women, **2:**406
Four Bagatelles (*A Beethoven Pas de
  Deux*), **6:***174*
Fourberies de Scapin, Les, **4:**185,
  447, **5:**96, **6:**353
Four Brubeck Pieces, **4:**230
Four Chorale Preludes, **3:**402
Four Cohans, **6:***315*
Four Corners, **6:**263
*Four Dances Based on American
  Folk Music,* **5:**587
Four Elements, **2:**119
4 Epitaphs, **5:**313

"Four Hundred" (dancers), **5:**629
Four Hungarian Dances, **6:**390
Four Images of the Seasons, **4:**134
Four Insecurities, **6:**245
Four Insincerities, **3:**213
Four Kemptons, **4:**522
Four Last Songs, **2:**514, **3:**344, *390,* **5:**436, **6:**201
Four Little Salon Pieces, **5:**637
Four Lovers, or The Harvest Home (pantomime-ballet), **5:**319
Four Marys, The, **2:**367, 374, **3:**577
4'33" (Cage), **6:**108
Four Piano Blues (Copland), **2:**197
Four Plays for Dancers (Yeats), **3:**519
Four Saints in Three Acts (Stein and Thomson opera), **1:**147, **4:**436, **6:**278
Four Seasons, The, **1:**427, **2:**511, **3:**13, 21
  Calciuleanu production, **6:**302
  Loquasto costumes, **4:**226
  MacMillan production, **4:**243
  Moiseyev (Igor) suite, **4:**444
  Nichols and Duell dance partnership, **4:**631
  Perrot ballet. *See Quatre Saisons, Les*
  Robbins choreography, **4:**345, 615, 619, **5:**358, *364*
Four Step Brothers, **3:**57
Fourteen-Year-Old Dancer (Degas), **2:**363
Four Temperaments, The, **1:**478, **3:**57–59, **5:**97
  Balanchine production, **1:**256, 270, 272, **3:**57–59, **4:**28, 613
  Balanchine revival, **4:**609, 618
  Christensen (Lew) performance, **2:**161
  in Dance Theatre of Harlem repertory, **2:**334
  Dollar performance, **2:**426, **3:**57, 59
  Dyk performance, **2:**471
  Gorey caricature of, **2:**71
  in Grands Ballets Canadiens repertory, **3:**231
  Hart (Evelyn) performance, **3:**345
  Hindemith score, **1:**141, **3:**57
  Le Clercq performance, **4:**136, 616
  Moncion and Caccialanza performances, **4:**450
  Ralov choreography, **5:**294
  in Royal Danish Ballet repertory, **5:**431
  in Washington Ballet repertory, **6:**366
Fourth Book of the New Flute Master, The (1703), **1:**92
Fourth Symphony (Brahms), **1:**310, **4:**322, 517
Fourth Symphony of Gustav Mahler, The, **4:**604
Four Tokens, **6:**136
Four Valiant Brothers. See Quatre Fils Aymons, Les
Four Virtues, **1:**276
Four Walls, **2:**286, **4:**130
Fox, Della, **2:**250
Fox, George L., **4:**22, 23, **5:**514
Fox, Harry, **2:**258, **5:**628
Fox Dance, **4:**553
Fox Movietone Follies (film), **2:**613
fox trot, **5:**627, **6:**243, 251
  African-American origins, **6:**256
  ballroom competition standards, **1:**358

Castle style, **2:**78, **6:**270
Faeroe step pattern, **2:**565
Finland, **2:**630
  inception, **5:**628
  ragtime influence, **4:**519
  Texas Two-Step variant, **2:**258
Foxtrot A (Mondrian), **1:**132
Foye, Christian, **1:**305
Foyer de la Danse (Ashton ballet), **1:**437, **4:**267, **5:**299
Foyer de la Danse (Egri television ballet), **2:**480
Foyer de la Danse (Paris Opera salon), **5:**93, 95
  Lami watercolor, **4:**116
  Lifar's closure of, **4:**184
Fracci, Carla, **1:**49, 71, 72, **2:**183, **3:**59–61
  acting strength, **3:**60, 61
  Amodio collaborations, **1:**82
  Bruhn dance partnership, **2:**3, **3:**60, *181,* **5:**107
  Butler collaboration, **2:**17
  Cinderella performance, **5:**529, *529*
  Coppélia performance, **2:**200, 201
  English National ballet guest performances, **2:**510
  Giselle performance, **3:**59, *60, 181*
  as Italy's leading *prima ballerina,* **3:***549, 550,* 551, 552
  Miskovitch dance partnership, **4:**435
  Pistoni roles, **5:**195, 196
  Romeo and Juliet performance, **5:**395
  Rome Opera mixed program performance, **5:**401
  Scala Ballet, 529, **5:**527
  Scala training, **3:**553
  Sylphide role, **3:***549*
Fractions I and II (videodance), **2:**294, 607
fracture, **4:**20
Fra Diavolo (Auber), **2:**390, **4:**514
Fragments (Tragedy and Comedy), **3:**384
Fragments of a Biography, **6:**314
Fragments Psychologiques (Berners), **1:**438
Fragonard, Jean-Honoré, **3:**68
Fragrance of Spring, **2:**159
Frail Quarry, The, **2:**367
Frame, Peter, **6:**112
Frames, Poppy, **5:**52, 650
Frames of Mind, **4:**547
Framework, **1:**142–143, **3:**201
Fra Mina, **3:**23
Frampton, Eleanor, **3:**404
Franca, Celia, **2:**49, **3:**61–62, *62,* 511, **4:**117, *540,* 541, *541*
  archival collection, **4:**166
  artistic vision, **4:**539
  Metropolitan Ballet, **4:**380
  National Ballet of Canada, **2:**39, 42, 47, **3:**61, *62,* **4:**539–543, *540,* **5:***14,* **6:**1
  Peter and the Wolf role, **5:**691
  Rambert Dance Company, **5:**299, 300, 301
  Rose design collaboration, **5:**405
Françaix, Jean, **1:**305, 310, 316, **2:**401, **4:**517
Francalanci, Andrea, **3:**556, 557
France, **3:**62–68
  Académie de Musique et de Poésie, **1:**1–3
  Académie Royale de Danse, **1:**3–5, 286, 288, **3:**81
  apache dance, **1:**95, **5:***684*

ballet de collège, **1:**282–284, 286, **2:**168
ballet de cour, **1:**285–288, **2:**517–518, 518–519
Ballet-Théâtre Contemporain, **1:**349–351
  as Canadian dance influence, **2:**35–36
can-can, **2:**52–53, **3:**69
circus, **2:**174–175, 176
classical dance education, **3:**80–83
  Cecchetti method, **2:**84
  Chauviré, Yvette, **2:**114–115
  dancing masters, **2:**337–339, **3:**80–81
  Egorova school, **2:**480
  French versus Italian school, **1:**347
  influence on Danish school, **1:**347
  menuet importance, **4:**512
  Schwarz family, **5:**562–563
  See also ballet technique, history of; *subhead* major schools *under* ballet technique
contemporary criticism, **3:**85–86
court and theatrical dance, 1581–1789, **1:**5, 6, **3:**65–67
  accompaniment, **1:**5, 6, **4:**506–507
  Beauchamps notation, **1:**397
  ballet in opera, **5:**34–35
  Baroque theater design, **6:**156–157
  canary, **2:**250
  chaconne and *passacaille,* **2:**97, 98–99
  costume, **2:**238–239
  commedia dell'arte, **2:**188, 191
  dance manuals, **1:**103–105, 107
  Feuillet notation, **1:**397
  first *Don Quixote,* **2:**434–435
  galliarde, **3:**107–109
  gavotte, **3:**123–125
  gigue, **3:**172–173
  horse ballet, **3:**381
  Italian dance exchanges, **3:**381
  libretti, **4:**172–175
  lighting, **4:**187–188
  Louis XIV interests, **4:**229
  masks, **4:**301–302, *301*
  opéra-ballet and *tragédie lyrique,* **5:**34, 38–41
  pastorales, **5:**13
  political role, **1:**286, 288
  revels, **4:**343
  révérence, **5:**343–344
  See also subhead ballet de cour above; names of specific dance types; and subhead French court dance *under* Ballet technique, history of
dance research and publication, **3:**84–85
  bassedanse manuscript, **1:**378
  Block's works, **1:**463
  Christout's works, **2:**169–170
  folk dance, **3:**35, 64–65
  libraries and museums, **4:**160–161
Grand Ballet du Marquis de Cuevas, **3:**225–227
liturgical dance, **3:**162, 164
medieval dance, **5:**112, 533–534
mime, **4:**423–426
modern dance, **2:**466, **3:**75–80
modern dance education, **2:**575, 576, **3:**83–84
  Delsarte theories, **2:**370

music hall, **4:**523–524
Petit companies, **1:**304–306, **3:**74–75, **4:**33–34
recreational dance, **3:**63–65
  annual collections, **1:**91–92
  ballet influence, **3:**69
  balls, **1:**278–279
  Basque, **3:**376–378
  chain and round dances, **2:**99, 100, **3:**63–64, 65, 67
  contredanse, **2:**255–258, **5:**621
  cotillon, **5:**621, 685
  dance manuals, **1:**103–105, 107
  Dans B Dal, **2:**555
  folk dance studies, **3:**33, 35
  mazurka, **3:**70
  polka, **3:**69
  schottische, **3:**70
  waltz, **3:**68, 69
  See also names of specific French court dances
Renaissance fêtes and triumphs, **5:**340
scenic design, **5:**536, 538–539, *539,* 547
theaters for dance, **6:**156, 157–159
theatrical dance, nineteenth and twentieth centuries, **2:**239–241, **3:**67–75
  ballet in opera, **5:**35–37
  music, **4:**513
  lighting, **4:**189
  See also subheads court and theatrical dance *and* modern dance *above;* Paris Opera Ballet; *specific choreographers and performers*
France, Hélène, **1:**208, 499
France, Tatiana, **1:***536*
France/Dance, **3:**52
Francés, Esteban, **2:**438, **4:**28, 613
Francesca da Rimini, **1:**144, 517, **3:**20–21, **4:**178, **5:**195, 470, **6:**117, 121
  Mérante *divertissement,* **4:**353
  Messel design, **4:**358
Francesca da Rimini (d'Annunzio), **5:**438
Franchetti, Raymond, **3:**82, **5:**97
Franchi, Paolo, **2:**435
Franchi, Valborg, **5:**47, 406, **6:**46
Francini, Tomaso, **6:**156–157
Francis I, king of France, **4:**187
Francis II, emperor of Austria, **2:**467
Francis, William, **2:**467
Francis, Xavier, **4:**394, 396
Francis, William, **6:**232–233
Franciscan order, **2:**165, **3:**541
Francis of Assisi, Saint, **4:**322, 656, **5:**587
Françisque, Anthoine, **4:**505
Francisqui, Jean-Baptiste, **2:**442–443, 467, **3:**86–87, 119, **5:**198, **6:**232, 233
Francis Robinson Collection of Theatre, Music, and Dance, **4:**169
Francis W. Parker School, Chicago, **3:**367, 397
Franck, César, **1:**150, 301, **3:**24, **6:**64–65
Franck, Daniel, **3:**82
Franck, Paul, **4:**523
Franck, Yvonne, **5:**237
Franco, Francesco, **3:**9, 10
Franco, Francisco, **1:**101, **2:**522
Franco, Giacomo, **5:**260
Franco, Marília, **1:**532

Franco-American Bilateral Young Choreographers/Dancers Exchange Project, **1:**81
Franconetti, Silverio, **3:**7
Franconi, Antoine, **2:**175, 176
Franconi, Laurent, **2:**176
Franconi, Minette, **2:**175, 176
Franco-Prussian War (1870), **3:**71
Frandsen, Edite, **4:**245, **5:**431
Frank, Bill, **4:**230
Frank, Edgar, **3:**625, 628, **4:**91, 92
Frank, Henry, *as contributor,* **3:**333–336, **6:**345–348
Frank, Rusty E., *as contributor,* **1:**382–383, 439–440, **3:**57, 366–367, **4:**418–419, **5:**21–22, 238–239, **6:**141–142
Frankel, Dora, **5:**661
Frankel, Emily, **1:**479
Frankenstein (Shelley), **2:**200
Frankenstein, the Modern Prometheus, **2:**470
Frankenthaler, Alfred, **6:**299
Frankfurt Ballet, **1:**414, 479, **2:**563–564, **3:**149, 157, **4:**64
  Firebird, The, **3:**3
  Forsythe as artistic director, **3:**52–53, 151
  Madsen directorship, **4:**246
  Neumeier as ballet director, **4:**603
  Neumeier *Nutcracker,* **5:**15
  New Zealand tour, **4:**624
  Romeo and Juliet, **5:**396
Frankfurt Städtische Bühnen, **3:**203
Frankfurt Theater am Turm, **3:**151
Frankie and Johnny, **1:**210, 298, 302, **2:**334, 580, **3:**88, **5:**59, 691, **6:**204
Franklin, Aretha, **3:**52
Franklin, Frederic, **1:**258, 261, **3:**87–88
  Ballet Imperial revival, **1:**293
  Ballet Russe de Monte Carlo, **1:**296, 296, 297, 298, 299, 301, 302, **3:**87–88
  Cinderella travesty role, **2:**174
  Coppélia performance, **2:**201, 342
  Dance Theatre of Harlem stagings, **2:**334, 335, **3:**88
  Danilova dance partnership, **1:**296, 297, 302, **2:**104, 342, 342, **3:**88, **5:**107
  Gaîté Parisienne performance, **3:**104, 104, **4:**320
  Giselle staging, **2:**335, 335, **3:**88
  Jacob's Pillow performance, **3:**571
  Metropolitan Ballet guest performance, **4:**380
  musical theater, **6:**277
  National Ballet, **3:**88, **6:**366
  Nobilissima Visione performance, **4:**656
  Page ballets, **5:**59, 60
  Pittsburgh Ballet Theatre co-artistic directorship, 5196
  Rodeo performance, **3:**87, **5:**369
  Streetcar Named Desire performance, **5:**606
  Washington Ballet, **6:**366
Franklin, James L., Jr., **5:**73
Franklin, Lidija, **6:**325
Franko, Mark, **5:**329
  as contributor, **4:**172
Franko Opera and Ballet Theater, **6:**226
Franková, Kateřina, **2:**309
Franks, Arthur, **4:**179
Frantz, Patrick, **5:**196

Franz, Joseph, **3:**571, *572*
Fränzl, Fritzi, **3:**88
Fränzl, Hedy, **3:**88
Fränzl, Philipp, **3:**88
Fränzl, Rudi, **3:**88–89
Fränzl, Willy, **1:**240, **3:**89, 631, **5:**279, **6:**388
Fränzl family, **3:**88–89
Französische Suite, **2:**478
Franz Stefan, emperor of Austria, **3:**188, 189
Frappart, Louis, **1:**239, **3:**347, **4:**381, **5:**278
Frasa, Alina, **2:**631
Fraser, John, **4:**166, 543
Fraser, Moyra, **1:**207
Fraser, Pat, **2:**45
Fraser, Peggy, **4:**73
Fra Siberien til Moskau. See From Siberia to Moscow
Frasquillo (Francisco Léon), **1:**93, 115, **5:**672
Fratellini Détectives, Les, **2:**176
Fratellini en Afrique, Les, **2:**176
Fratres, **4:**604
Frauen-Carossel, **3:**382–383
Frauhauf, Aline, **2:**70–71
Fraunces Tavern, New York City, **3:**120
Frazer, James, **4:**369
Frazer, Lady Lilly Grove, **2:**570, **3:**31, 33
Frazier, George, **6:**101
Frazier, Sir James, **3:**31
Freaking, **5:**635
Freaks, **6:**362
Frédéric, Carolina and Charlotta, **4:**588, 588
Frédérick (Antoine Lemaître), **5:**134, 138
Frederick, prince of Great Britain, **2:**394
Frederick, prince of Hessen, **4:**632
Frederick II, king of Denmark, **2:**384
Frederick II (the Great), king of Prussia, **1:**365, **4:**122, 694
Frederick III, king of Denmark, **2:**384
Frederick III, king of Germany, **2:**338
Frederick IV, king of Denmark, **2:**384
Frederick VI, king of Denmark, **1:**504, 508
Fredericks, William S., **1:**200
Frederick William III, king of Prussia, **2:**414
Frederick William IV, king of Prussia, **1:**10
Fred Fehl Collection of Theatre and Dance Photographs, **4:**169
Fredmann, Martin, **6:**266
Fredowa, Vera, **6:**355
Fredstrup, Axel and Petrine, **1:**507
Fredstrup, Carl, **1:**507, **5:**425
Free Ballet School, New York City, **2:**182
Freebury, Jean, **2:**296, **5:**17
Free Chamber Dance. *See* DALICA
free dance movement, **3:**156–157, 160, 161, 162, 163
  Austria, **1:**239–240, 241, 242, 243, **2:**153–154, **6:**386–387, 389
  Finland, **3:**312
  France, **3:**75
  Italy, **5:**441
  modern dance as, **3:**131

Russian plastique, **5:**476–479, 484
  See also Ausdruckstanz
Freed, Arthur, **2:**108, 109, 616, 618
Freedman, Deborah, **5:**440
Freedman, Harry, **3:**231, **4:**238, **6:**131
Freedom Sanctuary, **4:**127, 128
Freefall, **5:**302
Free Flight Dance Company, **5:**657
Free French, **1:**253
Freelance Dance, **3:**446, **5:**127
Freeman, Gillian, **4:**244
Freemasonry, **1:**203
Freeny, Philip, **4:**668
Free Radicals, **6:**56
FreeStyle dances, **5:**635, 636
Free Theater, **3:**652
Freier Tanz. See free dance movement
Freischütz, Der (Weber), **1:**457, **4:**341, **5:**36
Freisinger, Ivana, **6:**431
Frejtag, Maria, **5:**216
Fremde Mädchen, Das (film), **6:**387
French, Bert, **6:**317, 319
French, Jared, **1:**452
French, Leslie, **3:**508, 511, **5:**411
French, Norman, **4:**523
French, Ruth, **1:**207, **3:**41, **6:**33, 128
French-Canadian ballet. *See* Grands Ballets Canadiens, Les
French-Canadian composers, **2:**151
French-Canadian folk dance, **2:**35–36, 49, **3:**36
  vocal sounds, **3:**38
French-Canadian modern dance, **2:**39, 40, 43–44, 45, 49
French Cancan (film), **2:**53
French Guiana, **2:**65
French Opera Academy, **1:**532
French Revolution (1789), **1:**503, **2:**595
  dance, **2:**72, **3:**67
  dress reforms, **2:**239
  effects on Daubervals, **2:**352, 413
  English dance effects, **3:**258
  Flames of Paris, The, **3:**12, **5:**439
  Gardel (Pierre) Paris Opera post during, **3:**119
  libretto realism, **4:**174
  Noverre retirement, **4:**698
  romanticized nationalism in wake of, **3:**29
French school. *See* Ballet technique, major schools; Paris Opera Ballet
French Spy, The (melodrama), **2:**85, **4:**464
French Dancing Master, The (Walsh), **1:**92
French Mitty and Tillo, **6:**318
Frenetic Rhythms, **3:**214
Frère Humains, Les, **2:**388
Frescobaldi, Girolamo, **2:**98, **3:**29, **6:**195
Frescoes, **3:**220
Fresnel, Augustin Jen, **4:**190
Fresnel lens, **4:**190
Freud, Sigmund, **1:**466, 469, **2:**316, **6:**195, 241
Freund, Herbert, **1:**241
frevo, **1:**527
Frey, Frank, **3:**151
Frey, Leonard, **2:**519
Fribec, Krešimir, **6:**432
Fri Dans (Kjølaas), **4:**682
Fridericia, Allan, **2:**385, 387
  Bournonville curriculum, **1:**539

Bournonville reconstruction, **5:**433
  as contributor, **1:**399, 502–503, **2:**535–536, **3:**104–106, **4:**118–119, **5:**294
  on mime roles, **1:**511
  Skandinaviska Balletten, **5:**406
  wife, Elsa-Marianne von Rosen, **5:**406
Fridolin, **3:**155
Fridolin en Route (Schoop dance group), **5:**560
Fried, Joshua, **2:**461
Fried, Malvina, **2:**581, *581*
Fried, Michael, **1:**140
Friedberk, Ekaterina, **2:**306, **5:**140
Friedhaber, Zvi, *as contributor,* **3:**602–606
Friedland, Aleksand, **5:**470
Friedland, LeeEllen, *as contributor,* **3:**29–38, **5:**685–690
Friedman, Gene, **2:**605
Friedman, Judith, **4:**616
Friedman, Katherine, *as contributor,* **2:**322–324
Friedman, Lise, **6:**297
Friedman, Sharon, **5:**659
Friedrich Horschelt Kinderballett, **6:**334
Frieman, Alexandre, **3:**563
Friends and Enemies of Modern Music, **4:**649
Friendship Dance, **4:**560, 563
Friends of Swedish Folk Dance. *See* Svenska Folkdansens Vänner
Friese, Jovita Sison, **5:**173
Frigerio, Ezio, **5:**398
Frigga, **2:**413
Friml, Rudolf, **6:**271, 273, 274
Frisbie, Charlotte, **4:**575
Frisco, Joe, **6:**320
Fritz, **1:**388
Fröbel, Friedrich, **3:**159
Froberger, Johann Jakob, **4:**507
Froelich, Biancha, **6:**270
Froger, François, **4:**286
Frogs and the Ballet (Elliott), **2:**70
Frohlich, Anine, **5:**425
Frohman, Charles, **2:**79
Froilan, Nonoy, **5:**172
Fröliche, Johannes Frederik, **1:**514
Fröliche Kreis, Der, **1:**242
Frolicking Gods, **3:**22, **6:**341
Frolova, Zinaida, **5:**160
From an Island Summer (videodance), **2:**607, 609
Froman, Maksimilijan, **2:**11, **3:**89, **5:**614, **6:**431
Froman, Margarita, **2:**11, **3:**89, **4:**459, **5:**14, 605, **6:**431–432, 438
Froman, Pavel, **3:**89, **6:**431
Froman, Valentin, **1:**309, 311, **2:**253, **3:**89, **5:**14, **6:**431
From Before, **2:**567, **6:**259
From Fable to Fable, **5:**245
Fromm, Erich, **3:**217
From Morning to Midnight, **2:**154
From Sea to Shining Sea, **6:**109, 112
From Siberia to Moscow, **1:**511, 513, **5:**425
From the Book of Ruth, **4:**306
From the Most Distant Time, **3:**51
From the Sources of Yemen, **4:**155
From the White Edge of Phrygia, **2:**120
Fronde, John, **1:**456
Frontier, **1:**137, 463, **3:**212, 384, **5:**175
  American theme, **6:**245

Graham performance, 4:*660*
Horst score, 4:518
Noguchi scenic design, 3:214, 4:659, *660*, 5:547
Frossard, Louis, 2:412, 6:38, 39
Frou-Frou (musical), 6:242
Fruen fra Havet, 5:353
Frug (dance), 5:630, 6:251
"Frühlingsstimmenwalzer," 6:387
Frühman, Leopold, 1:237
Fruits of Labour, The, 6:66
Frythe, Richard, 2:337
FTP. *See* Federal Theatre Project
Fu Aidi, 6:385
Fuazien, C. R., *as photographer,* 5:225
FUBA (Federated Union of Black Arts Dance Company), 5:659
Fuchs, Alexandre, 6:70, 71
Fuchs, Augusta. *See* Augusta, Madame
Fuchs, Ernst, 3:631
Fuchs, Livia, 3:424
Fuchs, Marianne, 6:53
Fuente, Luis, 3:*612*, 613
Fuente Ovejuna (Lope de Vega), 2:96, 3:187, 4:129
Fuentes, comte de, 1:452
Fuera de Balance, 2:281
Fuerst, Eugene, 1:315
Fué Una Vez, 5:270
Fugitive, The, 5:300
Fugl Fønix, 4:118
Fugue, The, 1:76, 5:440, 6:153
Fugue for Four Cameras, 4:215, 6:135, 196
Führer Kult, 4:118
Fuingiri, 4:536
Fuji, 6:229
Fuji Junko, 5:32
Fujikage Shizue. *See* Fujime Shizue
Fujima Fujiko, 3:89–90, 582, 640
Fujima Kanbei, 3:90, 593
Fujima Kanbei III, 3:593
Fujima Kan'emon II, 3:89, 593, 4:333
Fujima Kan'emon III, 3:593
Fujima Kan'emon IV. *See* Onoe Shōroku II
Fujima Kan'emon V, 3:593
Fujima Kan'emon VI, 3:89
Fujima Kanjūrō, **3:90**
Fujima Kanjūrō I, 4:537
Fujima Kanjūrō VI, 3:90
Fujima Kanjūrō VII, 3:90
Fujima Koko. *See* Fujima Kanjūrō VII
Fujima Masaya II, 1:248
Fujima Ryū, 3:593
Fujima school. *See* Fujima *headings above*
Fujime Shizue, 3:582, 590
Fujimusume, 3:90, 639
Fujito no Ura, 1:249
Fukkatsu, 4:30
Fukugawa Hideo, 3:589
Fukuhara Tetsuro, 2:18, 72
Fula, Samba Diallo, 4:549
Fulgens and Lucres (Medwall), 3:251
Fulkerson, Mary, 1:51, 3:272
Fullemann, John, 2:295
Fuller, Buckminster, 2:286, 4:27
Fuller, Francis, 6:374
Fuller, Larry, 6:285
Fuller, Loie, **3:90–96**
American musical theater, 6:268
Amsterdam performances, 4:589
artistic connections, 1:128, 129, 130, 131, 134, 239, 243, 3:92–93

British music hall performances, 4:522
Butterfly Dance, 2:*223*, 3:*91*
Canadian performance, 2:37
diaresis in name, 3:92
as Duncan influence, 2:454, 3:93, 96
floating fabrics, 2:246–247, *246,* 250, 3:91, *91,* 92–93, 95
as French dance influence, 3:71
French music hall performances, 4:524
Hanako sponsorship, 3:338, 6:409
as Jaques-Dalcroze influence, 3:595
legacy of, 3:95–96
lighting design, 3:92–93, 94, 96, 4:*189,* 5:547, 548
MacMillan ballet parody of, 4:244
Mexican tour, 4:390, 399
musical choices, 2:361, 3:95
on "natural dancing," 3:94–95
as Nikolais influence, 5:548
Orientalism, 5:45, 46
patented costume and lighting designs, 3:92
photographs of, 5:181
props and transparencies, 2:572, 573, 3:93
as Rodin inspiration, 5:370
as St. Dennis influence, 5:491, 492
Serpentine Dance, 2:250, 572, 3:71, 91, 92, 4:*522,* 6:268
skirt dance, 2:250, 3:91, 5:605, 6:268
theater and scenic design, 6:161, 317
Toulouse-Lautrec lithographs of, 1:129, 3:*71,* 92, 5:*261,* 6:*181*
as Yakko and Kawakami sponsor, 6:409
Fuller v. Bemis (1892), 3:92
Full Moon in March, A (Yeats), 3:519
Fülöp, Viktor, 3:415, *417,* 4:266, 5:472
Fülöp, Zoltán, 3:415, 417
Fulton, Gaye, 1:375, 2:174, 3:96, 6:454
Funa Benkei, 1:187
Funck, Pauline, 4:43
Funck, Poul, 1:504
Funck, Wilhelm Erik, 3:39, 4:43
Functional Integration. *See* Feldenkrais Method
Fundamentals of Character Dance (Shiriaev, Bocharov, Lopukhov, and Ivanovsy), 5:480
Fundamentals of Character Dance (Slonimsky and Lopukhov), 5:614
Fundamentals of Classical Dance (Vaganova), 5:480
Fundamentals of Physical Education (Glassow), 4:16
Funérailles, 3:418
Funeral March for a Rich Aunt (Berners), 1:437
funerary dances
Africa, 2:212, 3:166–167, 4:484, 6:13
Native American, 4:568
Funky Butt (dance), 5:634
"Funky Butt, The" (song), 5:634
Funny Face (film), 1:194–195, 2:617, 4:228
Funny Face (musical), 6:286

Funny Girl (musical), 5:363, 6:274, 283–284
Funny Papers, 6:112
Funtastique, 5:57
Fuoco, Sofia, 2:70, 282, **3:96–97,** 4:341, 5:85, 148, 232
Fura dels Baus, La, 5:*675*
Furber, Norman, 2:58, 5:652
Furijan, Stefan, 5:677
Furioso, 1:214, 6:95
Furioso, Pierre, 5:316
furlana. See forlana
"furniture music," 5:525
Furno, Loredana, 2:480
Furse, Roger, 2:401, *402,* 3:356
Furst, Lilian R., 3:180
Furt, Jorge, 1:110, 3:35
Furtenbach, Josef, 4:188, 5:534
Furth, George, 1:419
Furtseva, Ekaterina, 5:205
furyū no, 3:585, 586–587, 637, 4:652
Fusai-kai, 1:248
Fusco, Mara, 3:553
Fuseli, Henry, 5:640
Fushi kaden (Zeami), 3:652
Fusillo, Lisa A., *as contributor,* 3:103–104, 4:315–325, 656, 6:192–193
Fusion, 2:605
Füssel, Andreas, 1:507, 4:6, 5:425
futurism, 1:130, 133, 134, 243–244, 246, 3:96
scenic design, 3:197, 198, 5:543, 544
Futurist Painting: Technical Manifesto, 1:130
Futurist Reconstruction of the Universe, The (Balla), 1:130
"Futurist Scenography" (Prampolini), 5:544
Futurities, 2:460
Fux, María, 1:112
Fu Xi, 2:138, 139
Fu Yi, 2:148
Fuzelier, Louis, 3:450
Fuzz, 4:594
Fy, Varian, 4:26

Ga (people), 6:13, 19
Gabichvadze, Ravaz, 1:38
Gabin, Jean, 1:253
Gable, Christopher, 1:155, 3:512, 4:*241,* 242, *668,* 5:6, 396, *396,* 421
as Northern Ballet Theatre artistic director, 4:668
Seymour dance partnership, 5:*217,* 574, *574*
Two Pigeons performance, 6:217, *217,* 218
Gabler, Clar, 4:64
Gabo, Naum, 1:133, 258, 317, 2:242, 5:526, 544
Gabon, 1:15, 2:86, 87, 91, 4:289
gabor, 1:175, 3:477
Gabovich, Mikhail, 1:489, 2:173, 3:99, 4:360, 5:483, 610, 6:106
Romeo and Juliet performance, 5:*303,* 574
students, 3:99, 6:313
Zakharov as influence, 6:442
Gabriel, Israel, 5:171
Gabriel, Onni, 3:312
Gabriella di Vergy, 2:208, 3:175, 176
Gabriella la Fioraia, 1:427
Gabrielli, Luigi, 5:232
Gabrielli, Nicolò, 1:500, 2:95
Gaby, *as photographer,* 3:429
Gabzdyl, Emerich, **3:99–100,** 5:269

Gac, Yann le, 1:292, 406, *406*
Gačić, Gordana Dean, 6:435
Gáczy, Éva, 3:419
Gad, Rose, 1:*506,* 5:*431,* 433
Gadd, Ulf, 2:4, 284, 529, **3:100–101**
Götebog Ballet at Teatern, 6:44
Royal Swedish Ballet, 6:41, 43, 44
Gade, Joseph, 4:274
Gade, Julia and José Claudio, 6:302
Gade, Ludvig, 1:399, 507, 511, 5:427
Gade, Niels Wilhelm, 1:514–515, 3:39, 4:513
Gades, Antonio, 1:50, 294, 3:10, 11, **101–102,** 4:222, 5:674
Gadeskov, Iril (Richard Vogelesang), 4:590, 598
Gadfly, The, 1:416
Gadget, 1:536
Gaelic League, 3:517
Gaevaya, Valentina, 1:408
Gaevsky, Vadim, 1:464, 5:483, 484, 485
Gafner, Frédéric, 2:*296,* 5:17
gagá, 2:431
gagaku, 1:168, 180, 2:5, 216, **3:102–103,** 579–580, 591
Gagarin, Sergei Sergeevich, 2:416
Gagliano, Marco da, 1:353
gagliarda. See galliarde
"Gagliarda di Spagna" (Caroso), 3:108–109
gaguntangan, 3:667
Gai, Loris, 1:82, 3:60
Gaica, Branco, *as photographer,* 1:*209,* 213, 234, 4:*479,* 6:56
Gaïda, Fanny, 5:98
Gaiety Theatre, London, 3:91
Gailhard, Pedro, 5:94, 6:443
Gaillard, Félix, 3:426
Gain, Richard, 1:375, 3:610
Gains, "Bubba," 1:252
Gainsborough (singer), 3:601
Gainsborough, Thomas, 5:260
Gaîté Parisienne, 1:68, **3:103–104**
Béjart production, 1:292, 2:125
can-can, 2:53
Danilova performance, 2:*341,* 342, 343, 3:104
in English National Ballet repertory, 2:512
film version, 4:324
Franklin performance, 3:87, 104
International Ballet revival, 3:511
Massine production, 1:295, 301, 302, 3:72, 226, 511, 4:*320,* 323, 6:204
Youskevitch role, 6:425
GAKhN. *See* Moscow State Academy of Art Science
Gakkaroku (Japanese text), 3:591
Gál, Andor, 3:*416*
Gala, 1:291, 446
Gala, Giuseppe Michele, 3:555–556
Ga-Labadi (people), 3:165
Gala des Etoiles, Le, 1:201
Galambos, Tibor, 3:419
Galand du Désert, Florent, 1:3
Galand du Désert, François, 1:3, 4, 397
Galanta, Ekaterina de, 1:110
Galante Gartner, Den, 1:503
Galanterie du Temps, La, 1:287
Galanteries, 1:453
Gala Performance, 1:49, 3:663, 4:109, 215, 540, 5:431
television broadcast, 6:134
Tudor production, 6:198, 200, *200,* 202
van Praagh role, 6:312

Gala Performances of Ballet. *See* English National Ballet
Galarza, Guillermina, **4:**396
Galasso, Michael, **2:**119
Galatea (televised ballet), **1:**539, **4:**336, **5:**460
Galateo (Della Casa), **5:**324
Gala Variations, **5:**353
Galavresi, Savina, **3:**426
Gale, Amy, **4:**595, 597
Gale, Joseph, *as contributor*, **2:**446–447, **3:**185–186, **4:**6–7, 428–431
Galen, **4:**13–14
Galeotti, Vincenzo, **1:**507, **2:**387, 388, **3:**104–106, **4:**696, **5:**270, 392, 552, **6:**126
  ballet d'action, **4:**175, **5:**424
  Bournonville (Antoine) performances, **1:**503
  Bournonville (August) stage debut, **1:**503
  as Danish dance influence, **3:**546
  Don Juan version, **2:**434
  Romeo and Juliet, **3:**105, **5:**392, 424
  Royal Danish Ballet, **5:**424–525
  Whims of Cupid and the Ballet Master, The, **2:**107, 594, **3:**657, **5:**424, 426, **6:**47
Galetskaya, Valentina, **1:**491, **3:**12
Galileo (film), **3:**208
Galileo Galilei, **4:**14
Gall, Iwo, **6:**175
Galla (people). *See* Oromo
Gallagher, Helen, **6:**283
Gallant Assembly, **6:**197
Gallé, Émile, **3:**71
Gallegos, Beverly, *as photographer*, **5:**364
Gallegos, Christina, **4:**397
Gallenberg, Wenzel Robert, **3:**176
Gallery, **4:**303, 479
Gallery of Romantic Ballet, A (Guest catalog), **3:**321
Gallet, Sébastien, **2:**202, **3:**106
  Didelot roles, **2:**412, 414
  English ballet choreography, **3:**257, 258
  Noverre on, **4:**150
  Viennese ballet choreography, **1:**237
Galletti, Annetta, **5:**404
Galli, Giovanni Maria, **5:**537
Galli, Rosina, **1:**37, 428, **3:**663, **4:**382, 457
galliarde (gagliarda), **2:**560, **3:**106–111, 542, **5:**506, 620
  Argentinian adaptation, **1:**105, 108
  basic pattern, **3:**108
  for *intermedio*, **3:**510, 511
  musical compositions, **4:**504, 506
  Negri instructions, **3:**107–108, 109, **4:**580, 580, 581, **5:**323
  Renaissance dance technique, **5:**338, 339
  révérence, **5:**345
  tordion similarity, **6:**178
  See also passo e mezzo; pavaniglia
Galliard, Johann Ernst, **5:**350
Gallini, Giovanni, **3:**111–112, 378, 546, **6:**125
  on *allemande*, **1:**47
  on *cotillon*, **2:**252, 256
  on forlana, **3:**49
Gallizia, Bianca, **3:**50, 552, **5:**400
Gallo, Fortune, **1:**314
Gallo, Suzanne, **2:**296
Gallodier, Louis, **1:**400, **6:**38, 39, 40
gallop, **5:**624

Gallopade, **2:**293
Gallotta, Jean-Claude, **3:**78–79, *78*
Galopp (Rauth), **1:***130*
Galster, Amalia, **6:**75
Galstian, Vilen, **1:**122, **3:**125, **5:**460, **6:**302
Galvan, Roberto, **6:**67
Galvani, Luigi, **4:**14
Galzerani, Giovanni, **2:**93, 208, **5:**277
Gambarelli, Maria, **1:**37, **4:**382
gambuh dance drama, **1:**175–176, **3:**480–482, *481, 482*
  arja as offshoot, **3:**483
  Cupak similarity, **3:**485
  Kakul, I Nyoman, **3:**644–645
  légong links, **4:**146, 147
Gambuzzi, Innocenzo, **5:**424, **6:**69
Game, The, **5:**436
Game Animals Dance, **4:**553
Gameche, Abelardo, **6:**325
gamelan, **3:**112–116, 501
  Balinese traditions, **1:**175, 177, **2:**112–114, **3:**479, **4:**492, *493*
    arja dance, **3:**483
    baris dance, **1:**366, **3:**477–478
    gambuh dance, **3:**482
    kebiar dance, **3:**666–667, *666,* **4:**264–265
    légong dance, **4:**146–147
    rejang dance, **3:**477
    wayang puppets, **6:**368, 370
  instruments, **3:**114, *115,* 472, 475
  Javanese traditions, **1:**172, 174, **3:**114–116, 494, 496, 499, 503
Gamelan (Joffrey work), **3:**610
gamelan gaguntangan, **3:**483
gamelan gambuh, **3:**482
gamelan gong gede, **3:**478
gamelan gong kebiar, **1:**177, **3:**666, 667
gamelan pelégongan, **3:**479
gamelan selundéng, **3:**475, 477
games. *See* children's dances; dance games; singing games
Games, **4:**345, 451, **6:**259
Games of the Peoples of the USSR (Vsevolodsky-Gerngross), **5:**481
Gamil, Soleiman, **2:**496
Gamle Minder, eller En Laterna Magica, **1:**509
Gamliel, Eliyahu, **3:**531
gammeldans, **4:**670–671, *670, 671,* 672, **6:**36
Gamson, Annabelle, **2:**455
Gaṇapati, **3:**464
Gandara, Babil, **3:**520
Gāndharvaveda, **3:**453
Gandini, Pietro, **2:**190
gandrung, **3:**475, 505
gandrung banyuwangi, **3:**504
Ganesan, Kandappa, **1:**273
Ganesh (deity), **1:**178
gangar, **4:**669, 670, *670*
gang dances (Romania), **5:**381
Gänge, **3:**52
Gänge I, **3:**52
Gangl, Ott, *as photographer*, **5:**24
Gang's All Here, The (film), **1:**433, 434, **4:**229, 434
Ganithalankara, **3:**647–648
Ganjirō Jūnikyoku, **4:**532
Ganjou Brothers and Juanita, **4:**532
Ganti, Ni Nyoman, **3:***481*
Gantner, Carrillo, *as photographer*, **1:**179
Gantz, Judy, *as contributor*, **4:**18–21
Gao Chun Lin, **4:**693
gaoqiang, **1:**164

Gappō, **4:**538
gar, **6:**167, 168
Garafola, Lynn, *as contributor*, **1:**482–484, **2:**406–412, 479–480, **3:**307–308, 441–442, **4:**223–224, **5:**391–392, 558–559, **6:**120–121, 191, 341, 348, 403–404
Garbish, Melodie, *as photographer*, **3:**233
Garborg, Arne, **4:**677
García, Carmita, **2:**521
García, Felix, **5:***671*
García, Frank, **4:**648
García, Manuela, **2:**522
García, Marta, **2:**279, *279,* 280
García, Miguel, **4:***544*
García Lorca, Federico, **1:**93, 116, 117, **2:**1, 568, **3:**101, 611, **4:**242, **5:**302, **6:**529
  Blood Wedding, **5:**674
  on flamenco, **3:**6, 9, 11
  Madrid Ballet, **4:**222
  Markó choreographic homage, **4:**266
  Susana choreography, **6:**28
García Matos, Manuel, **3:**6
García Otzet, Montse, **5:**676
García Victorica, Victoria, **2:**127
Garçonne, La, **4:**268
Gard, Alex, **2:**69
Gardano, Antonio, **4:**502, 505
Gardel, Agathe, **3:**117
Gardel, Carlos, **6:**94
Gardel, Marie, **3:**118, 119, **5:**90
Gardel, Maximilien, **1:**43, 123, 504, **2:**352, 389, 413, 443, **3:**67, 116–117, **4:**122, **5:**35
  Cramér-Skeaping revival of *La Dansomanie*, **6:**47, *47*
  disuse of mask, **4:**302
  Guimard roles, **3:**326
  libretti, **4:**175
  Noverre rivalry, **4:**696
  Paris Opera Ballet, **5:***86,* 89–90
  Paris Opera intrigues, **4:**149
  Stuttgart Ballet, **6:**9
Gardel, Pierre, **1:**237, 507, **2:**269, 389, 464, **3:**112, 117–119, **5:**35, 319, **6:**69
  Aumer rivalry, **1:**201, 202, **3:**68
  Bournonville (Antoine) friendship, **1:**503
  Bournonville (August) training, **1:**504, 505
  Conservatoire de Danse directorship, **3:**81
  Enfant Prodigue, L', **5:**264, **6:**333
  Gallet as assistant ballet master, **3:**106
  Henry rivalry, **3:**358
  Milon association, **3:**118, 119, **4:**422, 423
  opera *divertissements*, **4:**657
  Paris Opera Ballet, **1:**35, 346, 446, 451, 452, 455, 460, **2:**389, 413, **3:**68, 117–119, **5:**90–91, 92
  as Petipa (Marius) influence, **5:**147, 149
  pirouettes, **1:**336
  Psyché et l'Amour, **5:**270
  Swedish dance influence, **6:**40
  Vestale pas de deux choreography, **5:**105
  Vestris (Auguste) roles, **6:**333
Gardel family, **3:**116–119
Gardemeister, Mila, **3:**100
Garden, Pierre, **1:**201
Garden, The, **4:**272

Garden of Earthly Delights, **1:**141, 462, **5:**305
Garden of Love, The, **6:**175
Garden of the Finzi-Contini, The (Bassani), **4:**244
Garden of Weeds, **3:**368
Garden Party, The, **4:**273
Gardens of the Night, **2:**350
Garden State Ballet, **6:**265
Gardie, Anna (Madame Gardie), **2:**467, **3:**86, 119–120, **6:**233, 298
Gardiner, John, **1:***372*
Gardiner, Lisa, **1:**70, 518, **2:**356, **6:**264, 366
Gardiner, Sally, **1:**218
Gardini, Carlo, **4:**339
Gardner, Robert, **2:**601, 602
Gardon, Anne, **3:**76
Gárdonyi, G., **3:**422
Gare, **2:**361
Garfias, Robert, *as contributor*, **3:**102–103, **4:**524–528
Gargi, Balawant, **4:**63
gargouillade, **4:**236, **5:**402
Garide, Louis Stephen, **3:**120
Garifuna dance, **1:**415, **2:**62, **3:**120–121, 320
Garis, Robert, *as contributor*, **4:**606–621
Garland, Judy, **1:**194, 432, **2:**5, 616, **4:**191
Garland of Flowers, The, **4:**127
garments. *See* costume *headings*
Garner, Carol Vollet, **6:***366*
Garnett, David, **3:**174, 392
Garnier, Charles, **6:**159
Garnier, Jacques, **1:**349, **5:**98
Garrand, Mimi, **4:**230
Garren, Elizabeth, **6:***249*
Garrett, Betty, **4:**434
Garrick, David, **1:**126, **3:**254, 256, 378, **5:**70, **6:**343
  lighting reforms, **4:**188, 189
  Noverre association, **4:**695–696, 697, 698
Garrick Gaieties, The, **6:**272
Garrido, Arturo, **4:**397
Garrido, Pablo, **2:**127
Garry, Liliane, **3:**82
Garten, David, *as photographer*, **2:**63, 273, 274, 281
Gartenfest, **1:**72
Garth, Charles, **5:***323*
Garth Fagan Dance, **2:**566, **4:**624, **6:**266
Garzia, Urbano, **2:**202
Gasanov, K., *as contributor*, **1:**247–248
Gascard, Michel, **1:**292, 407
Gasch, Sebastiàn, **5:**676
Gascony, France, **3:**63
Gaselda, ou Les Tziganes, **1:**477
Gaskell, Sonia, **2:**346–347, **3:**121–122, **4:**598
  Ballet Recital, **4:**591, 592
  Dutch National Ballet, **2:**468, 469, 470, **4:**592, 593, **6:**375
  Netherlands Ballet, **4:**600
  students, **4:**251, **5:**555
gas lighting, **2:**171, 172, **3:**92, **4:**189
  makeup use, **4:**304
  Paris Opera Ballet, **3:**69, **5:**91
  as Romantic ballet component, **5:**538–539, **6:**57, 58
Gassmann, Florian, **3:**187, 189, 365
Gassmann, Remi, **4:**519
Gastoldi, Giovanni, **3:**109
Gaston, Lydia Madarang, **5:**172
gatbec-deya, **4:**127
Gates of Hell, The (Rodin), **1:**128

"Gathering Peascods," **5:**621
gato, **1:**108
Gatti-Casazza, Giulio, **4:**381, 382
Gatutkaca Gandrung, **3:**495
Gaucho, **3:**657, **4:**118, 445, **5:**429
gaucho dances, **3:**35
Gaudefroy-Demombynes, Maurice, **4:**416
Gaudibert, Eric, **5:**681
Gaudrau, Michel, **2:**338, **3:122,** **5:**129, 402, **6:**123
Gauguin, Paul, **4:**642, 644
Gaukelei, **3:**627, **4:**91, 92
Gauklerin, Die (La Giocoliera), **1:**499–500
Gaul, Franz, **1:**540, **3:**346, **5:**278
Gaultier, Ennemond, **4:**505
Gaultier, J. P., **3:**79
Gaumond, Diane, **3:**429
Gauthier, Anastasie, **1:***410*
Gautier, P. N., **2:**256
Gautier, Théophile, **1:**23, 122, 123, 392, **2:**95, 587, **3:**7, **122–123,** **5:**640
on acrobatics-ballet comination, **2:**176
on *Aeila et Mysis,* **4:**342
"art for art's sake," **3:**180, **5:**108
on Beretta's dance technique, **1:**427
on Bogdanova performing style, **1:**477
on bolero performances, **2:**521
on *Cachucha,* **2:**503
on Cerrito's arms, **2:**93
Coralli collaboration, **2:**203, **4:**176
critical reviews, **3:**84
Elssler (Fanny) and Taglioni (Marie) comparison, **2:**502, **6:**74
on Elssler sisters, **2:**503–504
on Elssler's *Nina,* **3:**180
Éoline description, **5:**140–41
on Fuoco's Paris Opera debut, **3:**96–97
Giselle libretto, **3:**69, 123, 177, 178, 179, 182–183, 314, **5:**135, 148
on Grahn, **3:**222
Grisi (Carlotta) friendship, **3:**123, 314, 316
Grisi (Ernesta) marriage, **3:**313
Guest translations and editing of, **3:**321
libretti, **4:**176
Livry elegy, **4:**215
on Maywood's elevation, **4:**338
on Mérante's mime skill, **4:**353
Pavillon d'Armide story, **5:**118
Péri libretto, **2:**14, **3:**123, **4:**176, **5:**93, 132
on pointe shoes, **3:**47
on Saint-Léon, **5:**499, 500
Spectre de la Rose, Le, **3:**18
Taglioni (Marie) and Elssler (Fanny) comparison, **2:**502, **6:**74
Gauvin, Noël, **6:**130
Gavarni, Paul (pseud.), **2:**71
gavotte, **3:**123–125, **4:**510, 511
Arbeau choreography, **1:**104, **3:**123
Caribbean adaptation, **2:**62
France, **3:**64, **4:**510
Rodolphe composition, **5:**371
Gavotte, **5:***120,* 125
"Gavotte de Vestris," **3:**125, **4:***686,* **5:**319
"Gavotte du Roi, Le," **3:**124
Gavrilin, Valery, **2:**499

Gavrilov, Aleksandr, **2:**12, **3:**14
Gavrilov, Asser, **5:**166
Gawalewicz, Marian, **5:**220
Gawlik, Roland, **1:**442
Gawlikowski, Philippe, **2:**339
Ga Xiamei, **6:**385
Gay, John, **3:**378, **5:**350, **6:**267
Gayané, **1:**90–91, **2:**450, **3:125–126,** **4:**7, 284, **5:**459, *460,* **6:**310
Khachaturian score, **3:**153, 312, **4:**517
Kondratieva performance, **4:**38
"Saber Dance," **1:**90, **3:**125, **4:**7, 517
Gay Divorce (musical), **1:**192, 193, **6:**276
Gay Divorcee (film), **1:**193
Gayevsky, Vadim, **5:**203, 204
Gay Parisian, The (film), **3:**104
gazelda, **3:**316, **5:**139, 141, 278
Gazier, Marat, **5:**471
Gazulina, A., **5:**595
Gazzelloni, Severino, **1:**83
Gba gba masking tradition, **4:**289–290
Gbain masking society, **4:**291
Gbaya (people), **2:**89, 211–212
gburka, **6:**173
Gé, George, **2:**441, 632, **6:**46
Geary Society, **6:**316
Geblendeten, Die, **3:**624, **4:**91
Gedé Mandra, Anak Agung, **4:**265
Gedeonov, Stepan, **4:**429–430
Gedé Raka, Anak Agung, **3:**644
Gedit, I Dewa Ketut, **3:**644
Gedong Kirtya Library, Singaraja, **4:**158
Geems, Joyce van, **5:**52
Geertz, Clifford, **4:**369, **5:**354–355, 357
Gefangene im Kaukasus, Der, **3:**154
Gehry, Frank, **1:**144, **2:**119, **5:**550
Geidenreikh, Ekaterina, **5:**471
Geiger, Andreas, **1:***239*
Geiler, Johann, **2:**165
Geisha and the Knight, The, **6:**409
geisha dance, **3:**126, 338
Geissler, Fritz, **3:**153
Geitel, Klaus, *as contributor,* **3:**359–360
Geiten, Lydia, **5:**455
geki nō, **4:**652
Gelabart-Azzopardi Company, **3:**126–127
Gelabert, Cesc, **3:126–127,** 156, **5:**675
Gelabert, Raoul, **4:**17
Gelasius I, pope, **5:**376
Geldard, Kathleen, **1:**232
Gelede (people), **4:**288
Gelencsér, Ágnes, **3:**424
Gellerman, Jill, **4:**104
Gelobt Sei, **2:**472
Gelovani, G., **4:**447
Geltman, Fanya, **2:**580
Geltser, Anatoly, **5:**610
Geltser, Ekaterina, **1:**85, **3:127–128,** **5:**331, **6:**106, 171, 348
Bolshoi Ballet, **1:**487, 488, 489, **3:**207, **5:**458
Corsaire, Le, **2:**207, 208
Esmeralda performance, **2:**524, **5:**128
Gorsky ballets, **3:**204–205
as Johansson student, **3:**618
Moiseyev (Igor) dance partnership, **4:**444
Mordkin All-Star Imperial Russian Ballet, **4:**459, **6:**32

Salammbô performance, **3:**204–205
Swan Lake performance, **6:**32
Geltser, Vasily, **1:**486, **2:**435, **3:**127, **5:**455
photograph of, **5:**178
Swan Lake libretto, **6:**29, 30, 115
gelungan (headdress), **3:**474–475, 477, 489
Gémier, Firmin, **1:**98
Gemini, **1:**233, **3:**360, **5:**410
Géminis, **6:**324
Gemma, **2:**95, **3:**123, **4:**353, **5:**93
Gencsy, Eva von. See von Gencsy, Eva
Gendai Okinawa buyō, **5:**28
gendér. See metallaphones
gender and dance
Africa, **4:**290, **6:**381–382
American women's physical education curriculum, **6:**235, 294
Balkan male leadership, **6:**427
cheerleading and aerobic dance, **2:**324
Chinese all-female Shaoxing Opera, **6:**425–426
chorus lines, **6:**267, 269
close social dancing, **5:**628
cultural context, **4:**364–365
dance marathons, **2:**327
Delsarte system, **2:**371, 372
entrée grave technique, **2:**518–519
female body image, **2:**330
flamenco styles and costumes, **1:**61, 62, *62*
galliard pyrotechnics, **3:**107, 108
Hindu proscriptions, **3:**459
Japan, **6:**409
Jewish traditions, **3:**527, 536–537
Middle East, **4:**403, 404–409, 415–417, 488–489
movements and movement qualities, **4:**378–379
Native American role division, **4:**552–553, *554,* 555, 557, 559, 560, 561, 563, 564, 566, 571
North Africa, **4:**468, 664
proscriptions against women onstage, **6:**188
See also travesty
Roman critics of sensuality, **4:**428, **5:**378
Roman mime actresses, **4:**427
Ubakala symbolic patterns, **6:**219
See also armed dances; circumcision ritual; courtship dances; *danse du ventre;* wedding dances
gender studies, **4:**378–379
gendér wayang ensemble. See metallaphones
Gendlin, Eugene, **2:**319
Genée, Adeline, **2:**385, **3:128–130,** **4:**382, 674, **5:**238
Albertieri dance partnership, **1:**37
American musical theater, **6:**268, 269, 270
as Astaire influence, **1:**192
Australian tour, **1:**207
as Bedells mentor, **1:**400
contemporary critical review of, **3:**284
Coppélia performance, **2:**200, **3:**128–129, 261, *262*
as de Valois influence, **2:**395
Empire Theatre (London) performances, **3:**128, 279, **4:**522
Guest biography, **3:**321

on Hassreiter, **3:**347
impact on British dance, **3:**261–262, 279
New Zealand tour, **4:**625
Papillons costume, **6:**397
photography of, **5:**177
Royal Academy of Dancing, **1:**329, 330, **3:**129
Volinine dance partnership, **6:**348
Ziegfeld Follies, **6:**448
Genée, Alexander, **1:**400, **3:**128, **4:**674
General San Martín Municipal Theater, Buenos Aires. See San Martín Ballet
General Wu Says Farewell to His Wife, **5:**496
Genesis, **1:**49, **2:**187
Genet, Jean, **1:**69, 251, 305, **2:**111, **3:**363, **4:**418
Geneva Ballet, **1:**103, **2:**1, 111, 471–472, **5:**681, **6:***51,* 52–53, 397
Geneva Dalcroze Institute. See Jaques-Dalcroze Institute, Geneva
Geneviève de Brabant, **1:**124, **5:**525
génggong, **3:**475
Genghis Khan, **2:**139
Génie, Le, **2:**465
Genio Anarak, Il, **5:**409
Genji Monogatari, **3:**439
Genkle, Bodil, **4:**394
Gennaro, Peter, **2:**458, **3:**599–600, *599,* **5:**290, 358, **6:**137, *137,* 281, 282, 285
Genne (Buddhist priest), **4:**86
Genné, Beth Eliot, *as contributor,* **1:**400–401, **2:**395–404, **3:**261–271, **5:**351
Genoa, Italy, **3:**552
genres of Western theatrical dance, **3:130–131**
aesthetics, **1:**22, 23–24
ancient Greek choral odes, **2:**157–158
Asian dance versus, **1:**160–164
ballet character dancing, **2:**106–108
collaborative visual artists, **1:**135–136
costume, **2:**233–251
Craig antiballet articles, **2:**263
first ballet in Canada, **2:**36
first ballets, **1:**275–277, 284, **2:**427
first use of term *ballet* in modern sense, **2:**205
television productions, **6:**134–136
theater design, **6:**155–161
See also avant-garde; ballet technique; ballet technique, history of; jazz dance; modern dance technique; tap dance; *specific countries and dances*
Genroku Chūshingura, **3:**658
Gens de Mon Pays, Les, **2:**36
Genthe, Arnold
archival materials, **4:**168
as photographer, **2:**455, **5:**183
photographs of Duncan and Pavlova, **5:**182–183
Genther, Shirley, **2:**319
Gentilhommes, Les, **4:**275
Gentlemen Prefer Blondes (film), **2:**615
Gentlemen Prefer Blondes (musical), **2:**186, **6:**281
Gentner, Norma, **4:**209

Gentry, Eve, **1:**421, **3:**369, **6:**191
Genzmer, Harald, **1:**350
Geoffrey, Charles, **4:***554*
Geoffroy, Julien-Louis, **1:**201, 202, **3:**68
Geography of Noon, **3:**350
Geologists, The, **1:**492, **5:**463
George I, king of Great Britain, **4:**105
George II, duke of Saxe-Meiningen, **5:**540
George II, king of Great Britain, **4:**105, 313
George, Carolyn, **2:**161, 315
George, Henry, **2:**372
George, Ken, *as photographer*, **4:**260
George Dandin, **3:**184, **4:**234
George Frideric, **2:**1
George M! (musical), **6:**283
George Sand, **6:**324
Georges Dandin, **1:**288, **4:**447
George White's Scandals (film), **5:**239
George White's Scandals (revue), **1:**482, 518, **2:**572, 613, **4:**419, **5:**239, **6:**272
Georgi, Yvonne, **1:**11, 204, 289, 456, **2:**357, **3:131–133,** 146, *147,* 149, 345, 625, **4:**60–61, 518
    Dutch dance dominance, **4:**590
    Nazi collaboration charges, **4:**590, 591
    ter Weeme association, **6:**375
    Wigman training and tours, **5:**65, **6:**392
Georgia (republic), **3:133–136,** 513
    folk dance choreography, **5:**482
    Hellerau school association, **3:**596
Georgiadis, Nicholas, **1:**76, **3:136,** 512, **4:**240, *241,* 242, **5:**551
    Manon design, **4:**256
    Nutcracker design, **5:**15
    Romeo and Juliet design, **5:**396, 405
Georgian State Dance Company, **3:***133, 134,* 135
Georgieva, S., 211
Geranium, **2:**119
geranos, **2:**270
Gérard, Christine, **3:**84
Gérard, Jean-Ignace-Isidore, **2:**70
Gerbek, Robert, **5:**393, 595, 677
Gerber, Nikolai, **5:**466
Gerber, Rudolf, **3:**189
Gerber, Yuri, **4:**514
Gerbl, Erna, **1:**500
Gerdt, Elisaveta, **1:**490, **2:**11, **3:**136, **136–138,** 480
    as Fokine student, **3:**14
    Maryinsky Ballet, **4:**283
    students, **1:**517, **2:**341, 506, **3:**138, **4:**74, 335, **5:**203, **6:**7
Gerdt, Pavel, **1:**392, *392,* 540, **2:**11, 181, **3:136–137,** 561, **5:**118
    Don Quixote pas de deux, **2:**436
    Fokine roles, **3:**15
    Imaginary Dryads, **5:**120
    as Johansson student, **3:**618
    Maryinsky Ballet, **5:**456, 480
    as Maryinsky *premier danseur*, **4:**282
    Nutcracker performance, **5:**9, 106
    as Petipa (Jean-Antoine) student, **5:**148
    Raymonda, **5:**320
    Seasons performance, **5:***161*
    Sleeping Beauty performance, **5:**606

    students, **1:**255, 482, **3:**14, 137, 655, **4:**142, 144, 639, **5:**119, **6:**170, 309
    Swan Lake performance, **6:**30
    Sylvia collaboration with Ivanov, **3:**568
Gerdt family, **3:136–138**
Gerges, Mona, **2:**498
Gerges, Safwat, **2:**498
Gergiev, Valery, **6:**342
Gerhard, Roberto, **2:**401
Gerle, Conrad, **4:**505
Germain, Louis, **5:**490
German Academy of the Arts, East Germany, **5:**66
German cotillon, **2:**253
German Dance Archive, Cologne, **4:**161
German Dance Art (Wigman), **6:**393
"German expressionist dance." *See Ausdruckstanz*
German Master Workshops for Dance, Berlin, **3:**147
German Opera Ballet. *See* Berlin Opera Ballet
German Opera on the Rhine. *See* Düsseldorf-Duisberg Ballet
German Society for Dance Research, **3:**162
Germany, **3:138–163**
    Abraxas, **1:**1, **2:**478
    aesthetics, **1:**23
    Ausdruckstanz, **1:**130–131, 203–204, **3:**131–133, 146–147, 160, **5:**65–66
    Bauhaus, **1:**132, 138, 385–388
    dance education, **3:158–160**
        dancing masters, **2:**336, 337–338, 339, **3:**158–159
        East Germany (former), **3:**152–153, 160, **5:**66
    Folkwang Tanzstudio, **3:**40
    Gsovsky school, **3:**317, 318
    John Cranko Ballet School, **2:**267–268
    Laban schools, **4:**92
    Schlemmer, Oskar, **5:**546
    See also Jaques-Dalcroze Institute; Hellerau-Dresden
    dance research and publication, **3:160–163**
        folk dances, **3:**33, 35, 36, 142
        libraries and museums, **4:**161
        liturgical dance, **2:**164
        theaters for dance, **6:***157,* 158, 161
    theatrical dance, **3:143–158**
        circus, **2:**174
        dance on television, **6:**134
        Duncan influence, **2:**457, **3:**146
        East Germany (former), **3:**152–155, 156–157, 161–162, 317, **6:**378
        music, **4:**507, 517
        notation, **4:**685–686
        tournaments, **1:**368
        West Germany (former), **3:**148–152, 157–158, 161, 162, 318
        Wigman movement, **6:**389–395
    Wirtschaft, **6:**403
    See also Bavarian State Ballet; Berlin Opera Ballet; Hamburg Ballet; Stuttgart Ballet; *specific choreographers and performers*
    traditional and social dance, **2:***552,* **3:138–143**
        allemande origins, **1:**45, 46–47
        country dance, **2:**256

        East Germany (former), **3:**142, 160
        guild dances, **3:**325
        Herder *das volk* concept, **3:**29
        ländler and waltz, **5:**627
        movement choirs, **4:**475–476
        Sword Dance, **6:**55
        vocal sounds, **3:**38
        waltz, **6:**359
    See also Nazi era
Germinación, **1:***112*
Germinations, **5:**521
Gernreich, Rudi, **4:156–157**
gerreh, **3:**573
gerrehbenta, **3:**575
Gerschel, *as photographer*, **1:**320, **4:**646
Gershmaya, M., *as photographer*, **5:**5
Gershwin, George, **1:**59, 192, 540, **2:**5, 154, 513, 584, 618, **3:**135, **4:**133, 611, **5:**59, 602, **6:**205, *205*
    American in Paris score, **1:**479, **5:**311, **6:**274, *275*
    musical theater, **6:**271, 273, 274–275, 277, 281, 286, 289
    Rasch choreography, **5:**310–311
    Ravel (Maurice) on, **5:**315
    Rhapsody in Blue score, **2:**424, **4:**622–623, **5:**311
Gershwin, Ira, **1:**192, **2:**616, **5:**602, **6:**274, 275
Gershwin Concerto, **4:**615, 619
Gert, Valeska, **1:**204, **3:**146, 162, **163–164,** **6:**52
Gertrud Kraus Dance Group. *See* Kraus, Gertrud
Gertz, Jenny, **4:**92
Gerusalemme Liberata, **3:**544, **5:**1, 2
Gervaise, Charles-Hubert, **2:**34
Gervaise, Claude, **1:**523, **4:**505
Gervasi, Elio, **1:**240
Gerzer, Anny, **4:**64
Gerzson-Kovács, Péter, **3:**421
Gesamtkunstwerk concept, **1:**254, 318, 325, **2:**406, 453, **5:**540, 541
Geschöpfe des Prometheus, Die. See Creatures of Prometheus, The
Gest, Morris, **3:**21, **4:**460
Gestos Transitorios, **2:***281*
Gesture Dance, **1:**386
Gesture Language of Hindu Dance, The (Meri), **4:**355
Gestures in Red, **2:**460
Get Together (revue), **3:**21–22
Get Up Early, **6:**229
Geur, George de, **3:**92
Geurtze, Cher, **2:**386
Geva, Tamara, **1:**256, **2:**342
    archival materials, **4:**168
    Balanchine marriage, **1:**257
    musical theater, **6:**277
Gevanim Hadashim Bemahol, **3:**533
Geverfde Vogels, **2:**347
Gevergeyeva, Tamara. *See* Geva, Tamara
geza music, **3:**640
Gezira Sporting Club, Cairo, **2:**498
Ghana, **3:164–170,** **6:**12, 13, 19
    background and overview, **3:164–169**
    as Caribbean dance influence, **2:**62
    costume, **2:**210, 211
    dance education, **6:**19–20
    dance research and publication, **3:**169–170, **6:**24
    dance theater, **6:**21, 384

    Haouka cult, **6:**186
    highlife (popular dance), **4:**293, **6:**23–24, 383–384
    libraries and museums, **4:**158
    masking, **4:**290, 291, 292–293
Ghanaba, Kofi, **4:**487
Ghana Dance Ensemble. *See* National Dance Company of Ghana
Ghana Drama Studio, **6:**384
Ghanshyams (Indian dance team), **5:**62–63
ghārah dance, **6:**417
gharānā kathak, **2:**468, **4:**110
ghawāzī dancers, **2:**345, *345,* 493, 494–495, *494–495,* **4:**403, *403,* 488, 664
Gheho, Philip, **3:**167
Ghent, Belgium, **1:**409, 410, 414
Ghéon, Henri, **1:**255
Gheorghiu, Marie-Christine, **3:**79
Ghosh, Manomohan, **3:**470
Ghost Dance, **3:170–171,** **4:**562, 567–568, 574, **6:**185
Ghost Dances, **2:**1, **5:**303, **6:**180
Ghost Town, **1:**297, 302
Ghyssens, Vinciane, **1:***413*
Giacomelli, *as photographer*, **5:**400
Giannini, A. Christina, **5:**24
Giannone, Mary, **1:**75
Giants, dance of the, **2:**121
Giara, La, **4:**635, **5:**400
Gibasa, **3:**363
Gibbs, Linda, **4:**217
Gibson, Burt ("Gip"), **6:**102
Gibson, Darren, **2:**584
Gibson, Glenn, **4:***540*
Gibson, Ian, **1:**302, **2:**38, **3:**27
Gibson, Jon, **2:**289, **3:***444*
Gicheva, Lydia, **5:**478
Gidali, Marika, **1:**533, 535, *535,* 536
gidayū bushi style, **3:**639
Gide, André, **1:**155, **3:**628, **5:**438, **6:**5
Gide, Casimir, **1:**9, **2:**405
Gidén, Tomas, **6:**50
Giebel, Dolf, **3:**142
Gielgud, John, **3:**656
Gielgud, Maina, **1:**210–211, 234–235, *292*
    Checkmate, **2:**115
    English National Ballet, **2:**513
    as Royal Danish Ballet artistic director, **5:**433
Giese, Al, **5:**187
Gift of the Magi, **3:**663, **4:**63
giga, **3:**172
gigaku, **1:**167–168, **3:171–172,** 579
Gigantes, Los, **3:**319
Gigantesques (La Danse de la Sorcière), **3:**95
Gigault, Nicolas, **4:**234
Gigorovich, Yuri, **2:**441
gigue, **3:172–173,** **4:**511
    French vs. Italian, **3:**172–173, 607
    loure vs., **4:**231
    as Quebecois dance form, **2:**35
    theatrical use, **4:**509
    See also jig
Gigue (Massine ballet), **4:**319, 320
Gikuyu (Kikuyu) (people), **2:**86, **4:**365
Gil, Jean-Charles, **6:**143
Gilbert, Eliza. *See* Montez, Lola
Gilbert, Melvin Ballou, **5:**223, **6:**240, 293, 294, 295
Gilbert, W. S., **2:**250, **6:**267, 268
Gilbert Islands. *See* Kiribati
Gil Blas (magazine), **1:**466
Gilda Stories (Gomez), **6:**449

Gilded Bat, The (Anastos ballet),
  3:234
Gilded Bat, The (Gorey book),
  2:71, *71*
Giles, Thomas, **2**:337, **3**:252,
  4:307, 310
Gilfond, Edythe, **1**:82, 96,
  2:349, 360
  Graham costumes, **3**:218, **4**:153
Gilgamesh, **6**:175
"Gille Calluim" (Scottish dance),
  1:118, **3**:246, *247*
Gillert, Aleksander, **5**:75
Gillert, Arnold, **6**:29
Gillert, Victor, **4**:633
Gilles des Binches, Les, **1**:409
Gillespie, Dizzy, **4**:630
Gillian, Marie (La Belle Marie),
  6:317
Gillies, Don, **6**:130
Gillis, Christopher, **4**:482, **5**:681,
  6:*111, 112*
Gillis, Margie, **2**:17, 40, 46, **6**:132
Gillot, Claude, **1**:425, 497, **2**:191,
  3:184
Gillray, James, **2**:68, 71, 414
Gilmore, Rosamund, **3**:151
Gilmour, Sally, **2**:173, 510,
  3:*173–174*, 203, **5**:560
  Lady into Fox performance,
    3:174, 392, *392*
  Peter and the Wolf role, **5**:691
  Rambert Dance Company, **5**:299,
    300, 301
Gilpin, John, **2**:200, **3**:*174–175*,
  5:196, 301
  Dublin City Ballet, **3**:520
  English National Ballet, **2**:507,
    509, 510, **3**:59, 175
Gilpin Players, **4**:648
Gils, Flip, *as photographer*, **2**:563
Gilson, Étienne, **1**:24
Ginat Egoz, El, **4**:155
Gindler, Elsa, **1**:469, 470
Gindl, Hertha, **6**:388
Ginetti-Guerri, Madame, **5**:215
Gingerbread Heart, The, **3**:89, **5**:101,
  6:431–432
Gini, Angelina, **3**:50, **5**:288
Ginling College for Girls,
  Shanghai, **2**:133
Ginner, Ruby, **3**:271, 277
Ginsburg, Michael, *as
  photographer*, **6**:263
Ginslov, Jeannette, **5**:659
Gin, Woman, Distress, **1**:214
Giocca, Giovanna, **5**:615
Giocoliera, La (Die Gauklerin),
  1:499–500
Gioconda, La (Ponchielli),
  2:84, 187
Gioja, Gaetano, **2**:202, 208,
  3:*175–177*, 547, **5**:231, *231*,
  277, 528, **6**:70
  Cesare in Egitto, **3**:276, **5**:409
  as Henry (Louis) influence,
    3:68, 358
  I Minatori Valacchi, **3**:176, **6**:50
  Viennese ballet choreography,
    1:237
Giordano, Gloria, **3**:554
Giorgini, Jean-Claude, **1**:350
Giorgio manuscript (c.1470), **1**:351
Giorza, Paola, **1**:499, 500, **5**:409
Giouba, **6**:254
Giovanna d'Arco, **6**:339
Giovanna Maillote, **5**:499
Giovanni in London, **6**:189
Gipsy, La (Mazilier ballet), **2**:*505*,
  4:339, 340
  Cracovienne, La, **4**:57, 108, 340

Elssler role, **2**:504, **4**:340
Gitana comparison, **3**:185
Giraffe Dance, **5**:355
Girard, Françpois, **2**:610
Girard Brothers, **6**:316
Giraudet, Eugène, **6**:128
Giraudoux, Jean, **5**:527
Giriama dance, **3**:177
Girl Crazy (musical), **5**:372, **6**:289
Girl Danced into Life (film), **5**:569
Girl from the Woods, **2**:264
Girl in the Pink Tights, The
  (musical), **1**:458, **3**:601
Girl of the Golden West, A
  (Belasco), **6**:242
Girls, Les (film), **4**:3
Girl's Circle Dance, **2**:223
gisalo, **5**:81–82, *82*
gisaro, **5**:355
Giselle, **1**:110, 111, 146, 451, **2**:503,
  3:122, 145, **177–184**,
  5:499, 500
  adage examples, **1**:8
  Adama staging, **1**:11
  Adam score, **1**:9, 10, **2**:203, 390,
    500, **3**:5, 177, 178, 314, **4**:513,
    5:558
  Alonso (Alicia and Fernando)
    staging, **2**:276, 278, *279*
  Alonso (Alicia) title role
    identification, **1**:48, 49, 50,
    65, 68, 71, **2**:278
  Alonso on Eglevsky's technical
    control, **2**:479
  American Ballet Theatre, **1**:*65*,
    66, 71, 74, 373, 451, **3**:*178*,
    182, **4**:24
  Andreyanova as first Russian
    dancing title role, **1**:86, **3**:181,
    4:280–281
  arabesques, **1**:101
  Atanassoff performance, **1**:195
  Augusta (Madame) performance,
    1:200
  Augustyn and Kain
    performances, **1**:200, **3**:643
  Azuma staging, **3**:589
  Baryshnikov interpretation,
    1:371–372, **3**:*182*
  Basel Ballet staging, **1**:374–375
  BBC telecast, **4**:585
  Benois designs, **1**:424
  Berman designs, **1**:437
  Bessmertnova performance,
    1:440, *440*
  bird lift technique, **5**:103
  Blair performance and staging,
    1:71, 459
  Blangy performances, **1**:459
  Bogdanova performance, **1**:477
  Bolshoi corps de ballet
    formation, **1**:*494*
  in Boston Ballet repertory, **1**:501
  Bruhn performances and staging,
    2:3, 4
  Burgmüller's peasant pas de deux
    score, **2**:14, **3**:5, **4**:513
  Byrd's *Life Situations*, **2**:20
  Cage as mirror of, **5**:362
  Carey (Gustave) production,
    2:60, **5**:426
  caricatures and parodies, **2**:71,
    3:183
  Cerrito in La Scala's first
    production, **2**:93, **3**:181
  Chappell designs, **2**:105
  Chauviré's identification with,
    2:113, 114, 351
  as Chiriaeff's final stage
    appearance, **2**:152
  Ciceri design, **2**:172, **5**:538

Clustine performance, **2**:181
Collier performance, **2**:186
Coralli and Perrot collaboration,
  2:201, 202, 203, **3**:314, 547
Cortesi production, **2**:93, 209,
  4:253
Danilova performance, **2**:342
Darsonval performance, **2**:351
Davies production, **5**:654
Deane production, **2**:514
Deshayes (André) and Perrot
  London production, **2**:390
de Valois production, **2**:401–402,
  3:265
Dolgushin staging, **2**:423
Dolin performances, **2**:424, *508*,
  3:*182*, **4**:268, *268*, 269
Dolin production, **1**:315, **2**:152,
  509–510, **3**:59, 229, 437,
  5:401
Doubrovska performance, **2**:442
Egorova performance, **2**:480
Ek production, **1**:391, **2**:500,
  3:183
Elssler (Fanny) performances,
  1:410, 486, **2**:502, 504, 505,
  3:180, 181
Elssler and Monplaisir
  (Hippolyte) performance,
  4:453
Evdokimova performance,
  2:561–562
Ferri performances, **2**:587, 588
first American staging, **3**:181,
  5:615
first London production, **2**:390,
  3:180
first Royal Danish Ballet
  production, **2**:60
first South African performances,
  5:650, 652
Fitzjames (Nathalie)
  performance, **3**:5, *5*, 179
Fonteyn and Nureyev
  performances, **3**:45, **5**:416
Fracci performance, **3**:59, *60*
Franca performance, **3**:*61*, 62
Franklin staging, **2**:335, *335*, **3**:88
Gabovich and Ulanova
  performances, **3**:99
Gautier libretto, **3**:69, 123
Gielgud production, **1**:234
Gilmour performance, **3**:174
Gilpin and Dolin production,
  3:520
Gorsky productions, **1**:488, 490,
  3:206, 207, *207*, **4**:459
Grantzow performance,
  3:237, 238
Grey performance and staging,
  3:307
Grigorovich revival, **3**:310
Grisi performances, **2**:203, 390,
  3:69, *70*, 123, 177, 178, 179,
  314, *314*, 316
Gusev revival, **3**:328
Hart (Evelyn) performance,
  3:344, 345, **5**:436
Hassreiter performance, **3**:346
Haydée production, **3**:351, **4**:1
Kain performance, **1**:200, **3**:*643*
Karsavina performance, **3**:182,
  183, 656, **4**:*641*
Kerr staging, **4**:624
Kirkland performance, **4**:24
Kondratieva performance, **4**:38
Kun performance, **4**:74
Lacotte reconstruction, **4**:108
Laine production, **4**:678
Laing performance, **4**:110

Lander (Harald) choreography,
  3:226
Lander (Margot) performance,
  4:119
Lander (Toni) performance,
  4:120
Lanner performance, **4**:121
Lavrovsky (Leonid)
  choreography, **1**:491, **4**:74,
  132, **5**:463
Lavrovsky (Leonid) restaging,
  2:11
Lavrovsky (Mikhail)
  performance, **4**:133
Lee's American performance,
  4:139
libretto, **3**:69, 177, 178, 182–183
Lifar restaging, **4**:184
Makarova and Baryshnikov
  performance, **1**:74, 372
Makarova performances, **1**:74,
  372, **3**:*182*, 183–184,
  4:247, 248
Markova performances, **2**:*508*,
  509, **3**:182, *182*, 183, **4**:268,
  268, 269, 270, **5**:512, 650
as Maryinsky repertory favorite,
  4:218
Maywood performances, **4**:339
Mérante performance, **4**:353
Minkus score additions, **4**:429
modern scenic design, **5**:550–551
Mordkin performances,
  4:459, 460
Nerina performances, **4**:585
Neumeier staging, **3**:338
Nijinska performance, **4**:634
Nijinsky costume dispute, **4**:641
Nijinsky performance, **4**:640, *641*
Nureyev performance, **5**:*5*, 6
Paris Opera Ballet, **2**:203, **3**:69,
  177–179, 181, *182, 183*,
  5:93, 95
Pavlova performance, **1**:207,
  3:183, **5**:141
Perrot productions, **2**:201, 203,
  390, **3**:5, 177, 180, 181, 260,
  314, **5**:135–136, 141
Petipa (Lucien) performance of
  Albrecht, **3**:*70*, 177, 179,
  5:148
Petipa (Marius) productions,
  3:181, 182, 183, **4**:286, 353,
  429, **5**:141, 157
as quintessential Romantic
  ballet, **2**:201, 203, **3**:69, 177,
  179, 180
Ralov's portrayal of Albrecht,
  5:294
Romanov staging, **5**:392
Russian productions, **3**:*179*, 181,
  182, 183, **4**:280, 281
Saint-Léon staging, **5**:499, 500
Schanne performance, **5**:553
Selby's burlesque version, **2**:85
Semenova performance, **5**:566
Sergeyev production, **1**:247
Sergeyev revival, **3**:511, **5**:413
Seymour performance, **5**:574
Shearer (Moira) performance,
  5:*588*, 589
Skeaping act 2 staging, **6**:47
Skeaping re-creation, **5**:603
Somes performance, **5**:639
Spessivtseva performance, **5**:678,
  679, *679*
Spoerli production, **5**:*681*, 682,
  6:454
Spohr production, **5**:685
Struchkova performance, **6**:7
Teatro Colón staging, **1**:111

Giselle, continued
  television productions, **6:**137
  Terabust performance, **6:**143
  Titus staging, **4:**280
  Toumanova performance, **6:**182
  Tudor production, **1:**436
  Turczynowicz staging, **6:**207
  Ulanova performance, **6:**226,
    228, *228*
  van Praagh production, **1:**210,
    231, 232
  Verdy performance, **6:**328
  Vienna State Opera Ballet,
    1:*240*, 241
  Volinine guest production for
    Royal Danish Ballet,
    5:185, 294
  Vyroubova performance, **6:**353
  Wells performance, **6:**380
  "white scene," **2:**202
  Wright staging, **2:**470, **3:**344,
    4:*543*, **5:**436, **6:**380, 405
  Youskevitch performance, **6:**425
Giselle, oder Die Wilis. See Giselle
*Giselle, or The Phantom Night
  Dancers. See Giselle*
Giselle and I (Markova), **4:**269
Giselle's Revenge, **3:**183
Giselle und die Wilis. See Giselle
Gismonti, Egberto, **2:**359
Gissey, Germain, **3:**184
Gissey, Henry, **1:***285*, 287, 288, 425,
    426, **2:**238, **3:**184, **5:**70, 536
Gistelinck, Elias, **5:**422
Gisvova, Nina, **2:**124
Gīta Govinda (Indian text), **3:**466,
    467, 468, **5:**22, 23, 311
Gitana, La, **1:**86, **2:**93, 504, **3:**185,
    618, **4:**340, **5:**528, **6:**73, *73*, 74
Gitanos, Los, **4:**390
Gitanos de la Alpujarra, **4:**233
Git on Board, Lil Chillen, **6:**88
Giudizio di Paride, Il, **2:**55, **5:**1
Giuliano, Juan, **1:**349, **2:**109, **3:**82
Giulio Cesare, **4:**455
Giuocatore, Il, **2:**81, **5:**409
Giuochi Istmici, I, **6:**338
Giurchesco, Anca, **2:**386–387,
    5:391
Giuri, Adelina, **1:**487, **5:**455
Giuri, Maria, **1:**347, **2:**200
Giuseppe Ebreo, **3:**322, 323
Giussani, Paolina, **3:**59
Giusto syllabique, Le (Brăiloiu),
    5:390
Give a Girl a Break (film), **3:**54
givha, **6:**322
Gizra (people), **5:**80
Glacial Decoy, **1:**143, 544, **2:**608,
    5:313
Gladkov, Aleksandr, **1:**539
Gladkovsky, Arseny, **2:**585, **6:**309
Gladly, Sadly, Badly, Madly, **3:**273,
    5:575
Gladstein, Robert, **5:**513
Gładysz, D., *as photographer*, **4:**57
Glagolin, Boris, **4:**227
Glagolitic Mass, **4:**81
Glasco, Kimberley, **4:***545*
Glasemann, Max, **2:**200, **5:**427
Glasgow, Scotland, **3:**270, 275
Glashuset, Stockholm, **6:**45
*Glas im Kopf wird vom Glas: The
  Dance Sections, Das*,
    2:563, *563*
Glass, Philip, **2:**359, 608, **3:**201,
    202, **4:**597, **5:**367, 573, 683
  Einstein on the Beach, **1:***143*, 144,
    2:119, **6:**401
  In the Upper Room score, **6:**153
Glass Blew In, The, **3:**275

Glass Dance, **1:**387
Glasser, Sylvia, **5:***656*, 659
Glass Houses, **3:**388
Glassie, Henry, **4:**313
Glassman, William, **5:**364
Glassow, Ruth, **4:**16
Glass Pieces, **4:**615, **5:**367
Glass Slipper, The, **2:**173, **5:**163
Glasstone, Richard, **2:**404, **5:**530,
    652, **6:**212
  CAPAB Ballet productions,
    2:56, 57
  on Cecchetti-Massine-Ashton
    link, **1:**329
  as contributor, **1:**7–9, 44–45,
    335–336, 338–339, 339–342,
    347–349, 384–385
Glaucus (mythic), **2:**271
Glazer, Diane, *as photographer*,
    1:*445*, **4:**294
Glazunov, Aleksandr, **1:**298, 486,
    2:73, **3:**16, 17, 21, **185–186**,
    428, **4:**634, **5:**120, 123
  Birthday Offering musical
    arrangement, **3:**521
  Gorsky ballet scores, **3:**205
  Petipa (Marius) ballet
    commissions, **3:**186, **4:**515
  Raymonda score, **4:**610, **5:***159*,
    160, 320, 321
  Sylphides orchestration, **6:**60, 61
Gleason, Johnny and Bertha, **6:**316
Gleason, Judith, *as photographer*,
    6:16, 381
Glebov, Evgeny, **2:**502, **5:**471
Glebova, Tamara, **5:**476
gledir, **3:**434, 435
Gleede, Edmund, **1:**390, **3:**150
Gleisner, Martin, **4:**93, 103, 477
Glen, The, **4:**153
Glen, William, **6:**292
Glevob, Evgeny, **1:**408
Glevob, Igor (Boris Asafiev pseud.),
    1:144
Gli Amori di Adone e Venere, **1:**461
Gli Dispetti Amorosi, **5:**231
Glière, Reinhold, **2:**579,
    3:186–187, **5:**266, **6:**171
  Bronze Horseman score, **6:**442
  musical idiom, **4:**517
  Red Poppy score, **1:**297, **3:**186,
    187, **4:**225, 283, 517, **5:**331,
    6:442
Glikman, Isaak, **3:**193
Glinka, Mikhail, **1:**86, 144, **2:**568,
    5:277, 471, **6:**5
  Fokine ballets, **3:**15, 16, 21, 196
  nationalistic music, **5:**455
  operatic ballets, **4:**514
  waltz and polonaise
    compositions, **5:**626
  See also Ruslan and Ludmila
Glinka Pas de Trois, **4:**622
Glinka State Central Museum of
  Music Culture, Moscow,
    4:165
Glinkiana, **4:**345
Gli Orazi e Curiazi, **3:**175–176
glissade, **1:**339
glissé, **1:**343
Glisson, Francis, **4:**14
Gli Strelizzi, **5:**232, **6:**338
Gli Uccelli, **3:**51, **5:**400
Global Groove (video art), **4:**141
Gloger, Zygmunt, **5:**210
Gloire, La, **1:**68, 402–403, **3:**664,
    4:608, **6:**200–201
Gloom, Passion, Marseillaise, **5:**477
Gloria, **4:**72, 243, *245*, 471, 627,
    6:302
Gloria and Eduardo, **6:**94

Gloria and Rodolfo, **6:**94
Glorifying the American Girl (film),
    6:448
Gloucestershire, England, **3:**607,
    4:473
Glover, Amelia, **6:**317
Glover, Savion, **3:**447, **6:**103, *103*,
    288, *289*
Głowacki, Stanisław, **5:**221
Glowing Planets, **4:**266
Gluck, Christoph Willibald, **1:**468,
    2:412, **3:187–191**
  Angiolini collaboration, **1:**87, 88,
    236, **3:**187–190, **4:**696
  chaconne and *passacaille*
    compositions, **2:**99,
    3:188, 190
  dance in opera, **3:**189–190,
    5:35, 39
  dance theory, **1:**126
  Don Juan, ou Le Festin de Pierre,
    1:87, **2:**433–434, 443, 473,
    474, **3:**187, 188, 190, **4:**509,
    695, **6:**48
  Drottningholm preserved scenery
    and costumes, **5:**603
  gavotte composition, **3:**124
  libretti, **4:**174
  Noverre collaboration,
    3:189–190, **4:**696, **5:**371
  operatic reform, **5:**35
  pantomime ballet, **1:**236,
    3:187–188
  Schall comparison, **5:**552
  Schneitzhoffer borrowings, **5:**558
  Skeaping's Drottningholm Court
    Theater productions, **6:**47
  as Swedish Gustavian opera
    influence, **6:**39
  See also Alceste; Orfeo ed Euridice
Gluck, Rena, **3:**531, 532, 535
Glück-Sandor, Senia, **2:**579, 580,
    5:266, 359
Glück, Tod und Traum, **3:**132
Gluhak-Buneta, Lela, **6:**433
Glushak, Nanette, **5:**565
Glushkovsky, Adam, **1:**477,
    3:191–192
  Bolshoi Ballet, **1:**485, **3:**191–192,
    5:454
  as Didelot's student, **2:**416, **3:**191,
    192, **5:**454
  folk *divertissements*, **5:**453
  memoirs, **5:**483
  Moscow Imperial Theatrical
    School, **5:**480
  Ruslan and Ludmila, **3:**191, 540,
    5:454
  Russian literary sources, **5:**454
  as Valberkh student, **6:**312
  glyph shorthand, **4:**78
Gnatt, Poul, **1:**231, 316, **4:**380, 626,
    5:56, 172, 430
  Napoli restaging, **4:**678
  Royal New Zealand Ballet,
    4:624, 625
Gnawa brotherhood,
    4:468–469, *469*
Gnesin, Mikhail, **4:**7
Gnossienne, **2:**378, **5:***583*, 586
Gnosticism, **1:**1, **2:**163
Goat Dance, **3:***302*
Goat Horn, The, **2:**11
Goatlegged, The, **3:**193
Gobbis, Sebastiano, **3:**545
Gockel, Eberhard, **3:**162
Goda, Gábor, **3:**421
Goddard, Colette, **5:**34
Goddard, Paulette, **1:**193
Goddard, P. E., *as photographer*,
    5:272

Goddard College, Vermont, **1:***245*
Godden, Mark, **2:**41, 42, **3:**234,
    5:437
Godenski, or The Skaters of Wilna,
    5:318, 319
Godfrey, Louis, **2:**510, **5:**54, 55, 653
Goding, John, **6:**366
Godkin, Paul, **6:**137
Godlewski, Carl, **1:**239, 466, **2:**173
Godlewski, Willy, **6:**388
Godogan, **3:**475–476
Go Down, Moses, **6:**88
Godoy, Alejandro, **6:**301
Godoy, Marised, **2:**281
Godreau, Miguel, **1:**56
God's Favorite (Simon), **1:**419
Gods Go a-Begging, The, **2:**342, 401,
    3:307, **4:**33
Godspell (musical), **6:**284
Godunov, Alexander, **1:**59, **3:**578
Godwin, Dwight, *as photographer*,
    3:104
Godwin, Edward W., **2:**262
Goebbels, Josef, **3:**147
Goethe, Johann Wolfgang von,
    1:126, 199, 406, 442, 458,
    461, 507, 515, **3:**180,
    4:179, 476
Goetze, Will, **6:**390, 393
Goff, Moira, *as contributor*,
    1:391–392, **2:**80–81, 527,
    5:518–519
Gofflot, L. V., **1:**283, 284
Go-Go, **5:**634
Gogoleva, Elena, **6:**420
Gogół, Jerzy, **3:**192, **5:**219
Gogol, Nikolai, **1:**144, 519, **6:**442
Goh, Choo San, **1:**55, 75, 373,
    6:266
  Boston Ballet choreography,
    6:398
  Washington Ballet, **2:**356, **6:**366
Gohiiki Kanjinchō, **4:**296
Goi Teru, **2:**18
Gojo Tamami, **3:**590
Gojo Tamami, **3:**590
Gokhtn, Armenia, **1:**119
Go-Komatsu, emperor of Japan,
    6:229
Goldberg, Jane, **6:**103
  as contributor, **1:**252, **2:**5,
    185–186, 444–445, **3:**304
Goldberg, K. Meira, *as contributor*,
    1:61–62
Goldberg, Maurice, *as
  photographer*, **3:**147
Goldberg Variations
  Kirkland performance, **4:**24, 618
  Robbins production, **4:**273, 345,
    614, **5:**358, 364–365
  Spoerli production, **5:**683, *683*,
    6:455
  Tomasson performance, **6:**174
Goldberg Variations (Bach), **1:**428,
    4:71, **5:**365
Goldblatt, Elizabeth, *as contributor*,
    5:598–599
Gold Coast. *See Ghana*
Gold Diggers of . . . (film series),
    1:432, 433, *433*, 434, 435,
    2:614
Gold Eagle Guy, **6:**88
Golden, Donny and Barbara, **3:***518*
Golden, Miriam, **3:**26, **4:**209
Golden Age, The, **1:**492, **3:192–193**
  Bessmertnova performance,
    1:440–441
  Chabukiani performance, **2:**96
  de Mille choreography, **2:**374
  Grigorovich revival, **3:**193,
    309, *309*
  Shostakovitch score, **5:**594

as Soviet-era ballet, **4:**283, **5:**462
Ulanova performance, **6:**227
Vainonen choreography,
    3:192–193, **4:**283, **6:**227,
    310, 410
Yakobson choreography,
    3:192–193, **4:**283, **5:**594,
    6:410
Golden Apple, The, **3:**372
Golden Ass, The (Apuleius), **5:**377
Golden Bough, The (Frazer), **3:**31
golden calf, **2:**166
"Golden Chain, The," **6:**303
Golden Cockerel, The, **2:**512
Golden Fleece, The, **3:**371, **4:**130
Golden Hoop, The, **6:**225
Golden Horse, The, **5:**403, 404
Golden Ring, The, **6:**344
Golden Round, The, **1:**441
Goldfish, The, **2:**112, **3:**132, **4:**281,
    429, 460
Goldfish of Divine Play, The, **4:**272
Golding, Annette, **4:**627
Goldman, James, **1:**419
Goldman, Sherwin M., **1:**71
Goldman, Vera, **3:**530
Goldmark, Károly, **3:**418, **5:**569
Goldmark, Rubin, **2:**196
Goldner, Nancy, **6:**299–300
    as contributor, **5:**402–403
Gold of the Incas, The, **4:**127
Goldoni, Carlo, **2:**409
Goldoni, Lelia, **3:**387
Goldovsky, Boris, **2:**462
Goldsmith, Lillian, **6:**317
Gold Standard, **5:**58
Goldstein, Seth, *as contributor,*
    6:400–401
Goldwyn, Samuel, **1:**271,
    6:243, 450
Goldwyn Follies of 1938, The (film),
    1:64, **2:**426, 616, *617,* **5:**398,
    6:450
Goldwyn Hollywood Regional
    Library, **4:**170
Goléa, Anne, **1:***291*
Goleizovsky, Kasyan, **1:**28, 244,
    2:410, **3:**193–196, **4:**634,
    5:206
    athletic and acrobatic
        choreography, **4:**259
    choreographic renovations, **5:**460
    Don Quixote revival, **2:**437
    folk dance choreographic
        descriptions, **5:**481
    Gabovich roles, **3:**99
    Golden Age, The, **1:**441
    *Images of Russian Folk
        Choreography,* **5:**445
    Joseph the Beautiful, **1:**255, 489,
        3:631, 632–633, **4:**443, **5:**458
    Leili and Medzhnun, **1:**492, **3:**195,
        195, 569, **4:**133, **5:**460, 487,
        6:8, 84, 313
    Maximova roles, **4:**336
    Moscow Chamber Ballet, **1:**489,
        3:193
    Polovtsian Dances, **1:**485, **3:**195
    Souritz analysis of work, **5:**653
    Stanislavsky and Nemirovich-
        Danchenko Musical Theater,
        5:466
    students, **6:**344
    Tajikistan ballet, **6:**83, 84
    Tikhomirov opposition to
        innovations, **6:**171
    Vasiliev role, **6:**313
golèk, **1:**174
Golem, The, **3:**133
Goleminov, Marin, **2:**11
Golestan, **1:**292, 406

Golgotha, **2:**264
Golikova, Tatiana, **3:**193
Goli masking tradition, **4:**289, 290
Golinelli, Giovanni, **1:**238, **3:**346
Gollner, Nana, **1:**68, 124, 314, 315,
    3:512, **4:**56, **5:**612, 650,
    6:33, 199
Golonka, Wanda, **3:**157
Golovin, Aleksandr, **2:**241, 436,
    3:196, **5:**161
    Firebird designs, **2:***82,* **3:**1, *1,* 196
    World of Art group, **5:**456
Golovine, Serge, **2:**633, **3:**82,
    6:52, 353
Golovkina, Sofia, **1:**440, 491, **2:**438,
    3:196–197
    Flames of Paris performance,
        3:12
    Moscow ballet school, **5:**480
Golts, Nikolai Osipovich, **1:**392,
    2:436, **3:**185, **4:**279–280
"Golubets," **5:**444–445
Golubin, Dmitri, **5:**466
Golubov, Vladimir, **5:**485
gomba, **1:**359
Gombár, Judit, **1:**308, **3:**330, **4:**266
Gomberg, Sydelle, **1:**502
Gomez, Carmen de (La Josalito),
    1:115
Gomez, Jewell, **6:**449
Gomez, Tommy, **2:**458, *459,* **6:**259
Gomon, Aleksei, **6:**226
gona dance movement, **6:**383
Goncharov, George, **2:**133, 145,
    3:40
Goncharov, Leonid, **4:**224
Goncharova, Natalia, **1:**85, 133,
    322, **2:**241, 406, 409, **3:**20,
    197–199, **4:**34, 56, 316
    Agadati costume designs, **3:**529
    Coq d'Or design, **2:**408, **3:**197,
        5:542, 547
    Diaghilev Ballets Russes designs,
        5:542–543
    Firebird design, **3:**197, *198,* **5:**543
    Fokine ballets, **3:**20, 24, 25
    Larionov relationship, **3:**197,
        198, **4:**124, 125
    Noces design, **4:**657
Goncourt, Edmond de, **3:**326
Goncourt brothers, **2:**363
gonda dance, **3:**177
Gondowerdoyo play, **3:**497
Gondwanaland, **1:**214
gong, Korean, **4:**47, 48, 494
Gong Belaluan ensemble, **4:**265
gong-chime ensembles, **1:**172, **2:**31,
    3:112–116, *115,* 472, 475,
    4:264
gong kebiar, **1:**177, **3:**112
Gong Pangkung of Tabanan,
    4:264, 265
Gonta, Leonide, **1:**500
Gontard, Helen, **2:**176
Gönyey, Sándor, **3:**422
Gonzaga, Peter (Pietro), **2:**435,
    4:278
Gonzales, Guillermo, **3:***232*
Gonzalez, Nila Claraval, **5:**172
Gonzalez, Onesimo, **4:**397
Gonzalve de Cardoue, **6:**334
Good, Alan, **2:***290, 293*
Good Companions, The (film),
    4:335
Good Evening Beautiful Mask,
    2:264
Good Government, The (Lorenzetti
    fresco), **4:**348–349
Good-Humored Ladies, The, **3:**550,
    6:214

Goodman, Benny, **4:**202,
    5:630–631, **6:**256, 275
Goodman, Erika, **3:***612,* 614
Goodman, Lord, **2:**510
Goodman, Nelson, **1:**24
Goodrich, Joan, **4:**94
Goodspeed Opera House,
    Connecticut, **5:**602
Good Treatment for Horses, **3:**48
Goodwin, Noël
    as contributor, **1:**92–93, 437–438,
        462–463, **2:**360–361, 367–369,
        567–568, 579, **4:**113–115,
        116–118, 512–515, **5:**315–316,
        6:114–117
    as photographer, **3:**23
goombay, **3:**573
Gopak, **4:**444, **5:***574*
Gopal, Ram, **3:**199–200, *455,*
    4:110, 111, 270, 354
Gopalakrishna, **5:**23
Gopal Krishna (film), **2:**622
gopīs, **3:**465, 467, 468
Goquingco, Leonor Orosa, **5:**168,
    171–172, 173, 174, **6:**172
góralski, **5:**212, 213
Gorbachev, Mikhail, **5:**463
Gorbanev, Gennady, **4:**128
Gorborg, Hulda, **4:**672, 682
Gorda, **2:**96, 97
Gordian Knot Untied, The (Purcell),
    4:458
Gordo, Don Miguel. *See* Gaudrau,
    Michel
Gordon, Ain, **3:**202, **5:***574*
Gordon, David, **1:**142–143, **2:**460,
    3:200–202, 274, **5:**187, 305,
    573, *573,* 574
    American Ballet Theatre,
        1:76, 373
    avant-garde dance, **1:**246, **6:**250
    Dunn (Douglas) collaboration,
        2:460, **3:**201
    film and video, **2:**608, **3:**201
    Grand Union, **3:**201, 235, *235*
    improvisation, **3:***446*
    Judson Dance Theater, **2:**462,
        3:634, 635
    Waring's Dance Associates,
        6:363
Gordon, Gary, **5:**657, 660
Gordon, Gavin, **5:**293
Gordon, Mel, *as contributor,*
    3:48–49, 201
Gordon, Michael, **5:**683
Gordon, Mikhail, **4:**147
Gordova, A. A., **4:**529
Gorecki, Henryk Mikolaj, **5:**683
Gore, Walter, **2:**173, 350,
    3:202–203, 520, **4:**667, **5:**226,
    530, 565
    Ballet der Lage Landen, **1:**289
    Dark Elegies performance, **2:**348,
        3:*348*
    Frankfurt Ballet, **3:**149
    Gilmour roles, **3:**174
    Gulbenkian Ballet artistic
        directorship, **5:**234, 235
    Lady into Fox performance, **3:***392*
    Nutcracker, The, **5:**653
    Rake's Progress performance,
        2:401, **5:**293, 294
    Rambert Ballet, **1:**146, **3:**61, 62,
        174, **5:**296, 298, 299, 300, 301
    Royal Ballet, **5:**414
    Scapino Rotterdam
        choreography, **5:**530
    Vic-Wells Ballet, **5:**300
Górecki, Henryk, **2:**1, 120, 563

Goren, Ayalah, **3:**641
Gorey, Edward, **2:**71, *71*
Gorham, Kathleen, **1:***208,* 209, 211,
    230, 231, 232, 499, **3:**203–204
Goring, Marius, **5:**331
Gorky, Arshile, **2:**376
Gorky, Maxim, **1:**144, **5:**456
Gorky Central Park of Culture and
    Recreation, Moscow,
    5:460, 478
Gorlina, Inna, **6:**307
Gorny, Sergei (Aleksandr Otsup
    pseud.), **2:**150
Gorodetsky, Sergei, **5:**267
Gorp, Bert van, **1:**412
Gorriz, Ana Marie de, **5:**436
Gorschkov, Aleksandr, **3:**432
Gorshenkova, Maria, **1:**392, **3:**99,
    4:282, **5:**456
Gorsky, Aleksandr, **1:**74, 90, 255,
    3:17, 186, **4:**204–207
    archival materials, **4:**165
    artistic ideal, **1:**487, **3:**204, 207,
        4:459, **5:**456
    Bayadère, La, **1:**393, 488, **3:**206,
        207
    Bolshoi Ballet, **1:**487–488, 489,
        3:204–207, **5:**456
    Clorinda, **5:**120
    Coppélia, **2:**200
    Corsaire, Le, **2:**207, **3:**206
    critical appraisals of, **5:**483
    Dance Dream, **1:**85
    Don Quixote. See Don Quixote,
        Gorsky production
    Duncan as stylistic influence,
        2:457
    Études, **2:**457
    Fedorova roles, **2:**582
    Fille du Pharaon revival, **5:**453
    Fille Mal Gardée, La, **2:**596, **3:**206,
        4:358
    Geltser association, **3:**127–128,
        204–205
    Goleizovsky as student, **3:**193
    Little Humpbacked Horse, The,
        2:582, **3:**206, **4:**211–212
    as Moiseyev (Igor) influence,
        4:443
    Mordkin association, **1:**488,
        3:204, 207, **4:**459
    Moscow school, **4:**459, **5:**480
    Nutcracker, The, **1:**489,
        3:205–206, **5:**10, 11
    Raymonda, **3:**206, **5:**321
    Sleeping Beauty revival, **5:**610
    Souritz analysis of work, **5:**693
    Stanislavsky acting method,
        5:480
    Stepanov notation, **5:**693
    students, **3:**99, 655, **4:**358, **6:**348
    Swan Lake, **3:**206–207, *206,*
        4:358, 459, **6:**31
    Tikhomirov opposition to
        innovations, **6:**171
Gorzanis, Giacomo, **1:**428, **4:**505
Goslar, Lotte, **2:**81, **3:**146,
    207–208, 571
Gosling, Nigel. *See* Bland,
    Alexander
Gosschalk, Käthy, **4:**596, **5:**531
Gossec, François-Joseph, **3:**190
Gosse de Paris, **4:**107
Gosselin, Constance, **3:**209, 259
Gosselin, Geneviève, **1:**35, 455,
    2:415, **3:**208–209, **5:**91, 207,
    6:74
Gosselin, Louis François, **1:**505,
    2:71, 80, 523, **3:**81, 209
Gosselin family, **3:**208–209**

Gösta Berlings Saga (Lagerlöf),
  3:100, **6**:36, 44
Goswami, Mohan, **4**:246
gota, **5**:229
Gotēborg Opera (formerly Stora
  Teatern), **3**:100, 101, **5**:406
Göteborg, Sweden, **6**:44, 45, 48
Goth, Trudy, **1**:69
Gothenburg University, **6**:37
gōtipūas, **5**:22
Goto Hideo (Kanze Hideo), **3**:652
Götterdämmerung (Wagner), **1**:423
Gottesman, Jane, **2**:324
Gottschalk, Louis Moreau, **1**:479,
  2:289
Gottschild, Brenda Dixon, *as
  contributor*, **1**:520, **2**:25–26,
  6:253–261, 400
Goubé, Paul, **3**:73, 82
Gouda, Gamal, **2**:497, **4**:603
Goudar, Ange, **3**:546
Goudar, Sarah, **1**:123
Goude, Svenerik, **3**:100
Gouden Zwaan, De, **5**:618
Goudovitch, Alexander, **1**:*298*
Gough, Orlando, **3**:274
Goulart, Simon, **1**:397–398
Gould, Diana, **5**:296, 298
Gould, Glenn, **5**:128
Gould, Morton, **1**:63, **5**:*53*, 360
Gould, Norma, **5**:583
Gould, R. A., *as photographer*, **1**:222
Gouliaev, Alexander, **2**:470
Goulue, La (Louise Weber), **1**:95,
  2:*249*, **5**:176, 261, **6**:181
Gounod, Charles, **1**:247, 300,
  4:514, **5**:36, 94
Gounod Symphony, **1**:256, *265*,
  4:617, 621
Goupy, Louis, **3**:522
Gourd Dance, **5**:240
gourd masks, **2**:223
Gourdoux-Daux, J. H., **1**:345, **6**:126
Gourgaud, Françoise Rose, **6**:332
Gourma (people), **4**:290
Govari, Smulik, **3**:531
Governour, The (Elyot), **3**:281
Govozdev, Aleksei, **5**:483
Govrin, Gloria, **4**:618
Gowans, John-Marc, **5**:305
Gowing, Lawrence, **6**:197
Goya, **6**:229
Goya, Carola, **2**:78, **3**:11, 286, 571
Goya, Francisco, **1**:69, **5**:259
goyam kapeema, **2**:229
Goya Pastorale, **4**:229, **6**:198
Goyescas (Argentinita dance), **1**:66,
  115, **6**:198
Goyescos (Guerra ballet),
  3:320–321
Gozzi, Carlo, **2**:191–192, **4**:60
Graaf, Tom de, **5**:531
Graafland, Tanja, **5**:56, *56*, 653
Grabinska, Vera, **1**:110
Grable, Betty, **2**:251, 615,
  6:277, 327
Grabu, Louis, **5**:281
Graca, Francis, **5**:233
Graces (mythic), **3**:287, **6**:145
Grâces, Les, **1**:87, **3**:316
Gracheva, Nadezhda, **5**:465
García, Ana, **5**:*274*, 275
Gracia, Miguel, *as photographer*,
  6:323, 324
Graduation Ball, **1**:*205*, **2**:273,
  6:190
  Australian world premiere,
    1:207, 313
  Ballet Russe de Monte Carlo,
    1:300
  Bjørnsson performance, **1**:454

Brenaa performance, **1**:539
Lichine performance and
  choreography, **1**:300, 313,
  314, 315, 316, 539, **2**:334,
  510, **3**:229, **4**:178, *178*, **5**:431,
  511, **6**:3
Riabouchinska performance,
  5:380
Sand role, **5**:511
Strauss (Johann the younger)
  score, **6**:3
Gradus, Lawrence, **2**:41, **3**:230
Graeb, Emilio, **1**:540, **2**:173
Graeme, Joyce, **1**:208, **2**:404, **5**:565
Graeske Hyrde, Den, **1**:503
Graf Dracula, **6**:229
Graff, Grace and Kurt, **2**:580
Graff, Jens, **4**:678–679, 680, **6**:43
Graffin, Guillaume, **1**:77
graffiti, **1**:538
Graham, Geordie (Georgia), **2**:378,
  3:210
Graham, Margaret, **6**:301
Graham, Martha, **2**:119, 463,
  3:209–222, 619, **4**:608, **5**:7,
  254, 289, 559, 577, **6**:83, 144,
  272
  American Dance Festival, **1**:79,
    2:461
  American Document, **1**:82, 421,
    3:212, 216, 349, **4**:130, **6**:245
  analysis of choreographic style,
    4:101, 102–103
  archival materials, **4**:168
  artist collaborators, **1**:136–138,
    3:214, 217–218
  as Béjart influence, **1**:403–404
  Bennington School, **1**:79, 421,
    3:369, **4**:438, **6**:295
  as Bravo influence, **1**:524
  as British modern dance
    influence, **3**:271, 278, **4**:216,
    217, 218, 220
  as Butler influence, **2**:16
  as Chilean modern dance
    influence, **2**:280
  Clytemnestra, **2**:182, **3**:217, *217*,
    4:659, **5**:407
  commissioned scores, **3**:218,
    4:518
  Copland collaboration, **2**:196,
    197, **4**:518
  costume, **2**:245, 248, **3**:*209*, 211,
    211, 214, 218, 220, *220*
  as Cuban modern dance
    influence, **2**:280
  as Cullberg influence, **2**:283
  Cunningham association, **2**:285,
    286, **3**:216
  dance aesthetics, **1**:25, **2**:44,
    3:216, 218, 220
  dance company. *See* Martha
    Graham Dance Company
  Dance Repertory Theater, **3**:399,
    6:88
  dance technique, **3**:130–131,
    213–214, **4**:358, **439**, *440*, 442
  Dark Meadow, **2**:349, **3**:217, 349,
    4:659
  Deaths and Entrances, **2**:285, 360,
    3:*214*, 216, 349, **4**:130, 177
  Denishawn, **2**:376, 378,
    5:494, 495
  Duncan as modern dance
    influence, **2**:457
  Fokine aesthetic disagreement,
    3:28
  Fonteyn role, **3**:45
  as French modern dance
    influence, **3**:77
Frontier, **4**:*660*, **5**:175, 547

as German modern dance
  influence, **3**:151, 160
Hawkins collaboration and
  marriage, **3**:216, 218, 349
as Hill influence, **3**:364
Horst collaboration, **3**:210, 211,
  212, 214, 218, 384–385, **4**:518
Imagined Wing, **4**:418
influence on Czech dance, **2**:308
Irving (Robert) musical
  collaboration, **3**:521
as Israeli dance influence, **3**:531,
  532, **5**:531
as Japanese modern dance
  influence, **3**:583, 591
Korean modern dance students,
  4:51
Lauterer collaboration, **4**:130
liturgical dance, **5**:356
as major modern dance pioneer,
  3:369, 384, **6**:245, 299
makeup skill, **4**:305
method, **5**:657
musical accompaniment, **4**:518
Noguchi set designs, **3**:214, *215*,
  217, 218, **4**:659, **5**:175, 547,
  548, 562, **6**:162–163
Orientalism, **5**:46
partnering technique, **5**:105
performance space, **6**:162–163
as photographic subject,
  5:183–184, 185
piano accompaniment, **1**:6, **3**:214
program notes, **4**:177
Rosenthal lighting collaboration,
  5:407
Sacre du Printemps, Le,
  3:215–216, *219*, 220, **4**:*318*,
  322, **5**:488
as Schönberg influence, **5**:559
Schuman musical collaboration,
  5:561, 562
Seraphic Dialogue, **5**:568
Shawn association, **5**:584
students, **1**:55, 212, 213, 535,
  2:40, 347, 358, 566, **3**:339,
  4:272, 469, **5**:637, **6**:145, 151
stylistic impact, **6**:265
Taylor (Paul) rejection of,
  6:107–108
television performances and
  productions, **6**:138, 139
on *Three Virgins and a Devil*,
  2:373
as Welch influence, **6**:379
*See also Appalachian Spring;
  Letter to the World; Primitive
  Mysteries*
Graham, Melanie, **3**:575
Graham-Brown, Sarah, **4**:416
Grahn, Lucile, **3**:145, **222–224**,
  5:499, **6**:71, 451
  Bavarian State Ballet, **1**:390
  Catarina performance, **2**:80, 504,
    3:*223*, 224, **5**:*139*
  Don Quixote performance, **2**:435
  Giselle performance, **3**:181, **5**:425
  Hamburg Ballet, **3**:336
  Hungarian performances, **3**:414
  lithograph of, **5**:258
  Meistersinger choreography, **5**:37
  Nielsen comparison, **4**:631
  Paris Opera Ballet, **3**:69
  Pas de Quatre performance, **2**:94,
    103, 104, **3**:*224*, 260, 315,
    5:108, 137
  Pas des Déesses portrayal of,
    3:*609*, 611
  photographs of, **5**:176
  Prague performances, **2**:306

Royal Danish Ballet, **1**:507, 508,
  3:222–223, **5**:425
Spanish dance performances,
  2:522
Sylphide performance, **6**:59
Waldemar performance, **3**:223,
  5:425
Grain, **5**:434
Grainger, Percy, **3**:281
Gramaphone Company of India,
  2:627
Grame, Joyce, **2**:173
Grammaire de la danse, La
  (Darsonval), **1**:348
grammar, generative and
  transformational, **4**:367–368
Grammar of the Art of Dancing,
  (*Grammatik der Tanzkunst*,
  Zorn), **3**:159–160, **4**:685–686,
  5:222, 626, **6**:128, 290, 451
Gramont, Scipion de, **5**:270
Granados, Enrique, **1**:115, **5**:673
Gran Ballo (Cavilieri *intermedio*),
  3:510, 511
Gran Circo Teatro, **2**:126
Gran Compañia Coreográfica
  Italiana, **1**:110
Grand Adagio (Pas de Deux),
  1:*298*
Grand Ballet d'Amour, **2**:394, **5**:518
Grand Ballet de Monte Carlo. *See*
  Grand Ballet du Marquis de
  Cuevas
Grand Ballet de Psyché, Le, **1**:288
*Grand Ballet des effects de la Nature,
  Le* (Colletet), **1**:285
Grand Ballet du Marquis de
  Cuevas, **1**:110, 410, 420,
  2:426, 586, **3**:73, **224–227**,
  318, **4**:29
  archival materials, **4**:169
  Charrat performance, **2**:112
  Eglevsky performances, **2**:479
  Haydée, Marcia, **3**:350
  Hightower, Rosella, **3**:361–362
  Jones, Marilyn, **3**:623
  Lander (Harald) choreography,
    3:226, **4**:119
  Markova guest performances,
    4:270
  Moncion performance, **4**:449
  Nijinska association, **3**:224, *225*,
    226, 227, **4**:638
  Nureyev performances, **5**:5
  Skibine, George, **5**:*604*, 605
  Vyroubova, Nina, **6**:353
Grand Canyon, The, **2**:585
Grand Cirque, Le, **4**:185
Grand Duo, **4**:472
Grande, Dora del, **1**:110, 315
Grande Jatte, La, **1**:247, **2**:351
grande pirouettes à la seconde,
  1:337
Grande Salle du Louvre, **6**:156
Grande Théâtre, Brussels. *See*
  Théâtre de la Monnaie,
  Brussels
Grand Hotel (play and musical),
  2:109, 195, **3**:154, **6**:205,
  287, *288*
Gran Diablos, **2**:195
grand jeté, **1**:341, *341*,
  5:188–189, *189*
Grand Kabuki of Japan, **6**:287
Grandma Always Danced, **3**:208
Grand-Maître, Jean, **2**:42, **3**:234,
  4:547
Grand Music Hall of Israel, **3**:531
Grand Ole Opry, **2**:180
grand opera. See opera, ballet in

Grand Pas Classique, Le, **1:**300, 306, **2:**114, **4:**185, **5:**96
  Gregory performance, **3:**306, *306*
  Gsovsky (Victor) choreography, **3:**318
Grand Pas d'Auber. See Grand Pas Classique
grand pas de deux, **5:**105, 106–107
Grand Pas de Kossuth, **4:**455
Grand Pas de Quatre, **1:**49, 50
grand pas des cygnes. See Swan Lake
grand plié. See plié
Grand Prix International Vidéo Danse, **2:**610, **6:**135
Grand Rond, Le, **2:**252, 254
grand rond de jambe en l'air, **1:**8, **5:**402
Grands Ballets Canadiens, Les, **2:***38, 41, 151, 152,* **3:227–234**
  Alonso (Alicia) guest performances, **1:**49
  archival materials, **4:**165
  Chiriaeff, Ludmilla, **2:**150–152, **3:**227
  collective direction, **3:**231–232
  Firebird, The, **3:**3
  founding and growth, **2:**39, 42, 150–152, **3:**227–229
  Guest association, **3:**389
  Hyrst, Eric, **3:**429
  In Paradisum, **4:***71,* 72
  Jacob's Pillow performance, **3:**571
  Kudelka, James, **4:**72–73, 544
  Lorrain history of, **2:**49
  Macdonald, Brian, **3:**230–231, **4:**238
  Nault, Fernand, **3:**229–230, 231, **4:**576–577
  Nault's *Nutcracker* holiday tradition, **3:**229, 334, **4:**576, *577,* **5:***15*
  Paige, Brydon, **5:**61, 62
  Popa, Magdalena, **5:**387
  Rhodes, Lawrence, **3:**233–234
  schools, **2:**47, 152, **3:**213, 227–228
  Shawn *Polonaise,* **5:**586
  Spoerli, Heinz, **5:**681
  Symphony of Psalms, **4:**576–577, *576*
  television performances, **6:**131, 132
  touring company, **3:**230
  Warren, Vincent, **6:**364
Grand Street Follies, The (revues), **6:**272
Grand Tarentella, **1:**479, **5:**319
Grand Théâtre, Bordeaux, **2:**112
  Dauberval's and Didelot's performances, **2:**352–353, 413
  Fille Mal Gardée first performance, **2:**594, 595
Grand Théâtre de Genève. *See* Geneva Ballet
Grand Théâtre, Nancy, **3:**362
Grand Trio, **1:**241
Grand Union, **1:**142, **3:235–236**, **5:**127, 292, 573
  Brown, Trisha, **1:**543
  Dunn, Douglas, **2:**460
  Gordon, David, **3:**201
  improvisation, **3:**446, *446*
Grand Union Dreams, **5:**293
Grandville (pseud. Jean-Ignace-Isidore Gérard), **2:**70, 72
Grand Voile, La (La Mer), **3:**95
Grand Waltz in E-flat Major (Chopin), **6:**60, 61, 62
Granero, José, **5:**674

Granet, Marcel, **2:**128
Grange Eve, **2:**296
Granger, Pierre, **5:**692
Granier, François, **4:**695
Grant, Alexander, **2:**515, **3:236–237,** **4:**72, 456, **5:***165, 294, 596,* **6:**143
  as character dancer, **2:**106
  Dance performance, **2:**445
  Don Quixote performance, **2:**440
  Fille Mal Gardée, La, **1:**155
  National Ballet of Canada, **2:**42, **3:**237, **4:**543–545
  Petrouchka performance, **4:**624
  Royal Ballet, **5:**416
  Sylvia role, **6:**64
  Wedding Bouqet, **1:***148*
Grant, Freda, **4:**336
Grant, Gloria, **2:**41
Grantzeva, Tatiana, **1:**290, **6:**364
Grantzow, Adèle, **2:**198, **3:**145, **237–238,** **4:**343, **5:**94, 455, 501
Grantzow, Gustav, **3:**237
Granville-Barker, Harley, **3:**596, **4:**190
Graphic Ballet, Moscow, **5:**479
Grasheva, Nadia, **3:**197
Grass Dance, **4:**552, 555, **5:**240
Grasser, Erasmus, **4:**461
Grassi, Paolo, **3:**551–552
Grassi, Raffaele, **3:**50, **5:**217, **6:**365
Gratie d'amore, Le (Negri), **1:**46, 369, 380, **2:**73, 189, 337, 418, **3:**543, **4:**579, **5:**323, *337,* 338, 668, **6:**122
  musical examples, **4:**506–507
  reissued as *Nuove inventioni di balli,* **3:**107, **4:**579
  sections, **4:**579–582
  Spanish translation, **4:**582
  See also Negri, Cesare
Gratiernes Hyldning, **1:**505
Grau, Andrée, **5:**661
  as contributor, **1:**224–225, **2:**86–93, **3:**643–649
Grau, Maurice, **1:**37
Graun, Karl Heinrich, **1:**365
Gravat, Pascal, **3:**78
Graves, Michael, **2:**359
Graves, Morris, **2:**286, 293
Graves, Nancy, **1:**143, 545
Graves, Robert, **3:**217
Gravier, Jean-Paul, **2:**471
Gravity, **2:**359
Gravity and Grace, **4:**627
gravity, center of, *419,* **4:**15
Gray, Daryl, **1:**75
Gray, Diane, **3:**220, **4:***633*
Gray, Gilda, **1:**520, **3:**22, **6:**317, *317,* 371
Gray, Laurel Victoria, *as contributor,* **3:**133–136, **6:**304–307
Gray, Terence, **2:**397
Gray Angel, The, **3:**226
"Gray's Inn Masque," **4:**505
Graz, Austria, **1:**241–242
Graziana, **3:**664
Graziella, ou Les Dépits Amoureux, **5:**500, 501
Graziosa, **2:**587, **5:**148
Grbiç-Softić, Slobodanka, **6:**438
GRCOP. *See* Groupe de Recherche Chorégraphique de l'Opéra de Paris
Grease (musical), **6:**284, 288
Great American Broadcast, The (film), **2:**615, **4:**629
Great American Goof, The, **1:**65, **2:**112, **4:**227–228, **6:**198

Great Britain, **3:238–286**
  Christian churches view of dance, **2:**167
  circus, **2:**174, 176
  contemporary criticism, **3:284–286**
  dance and movement therapy, **2:**321
  dance caricatures, **2:**70
  dance education, **3:276–281,** 283–284
    Bedells, Phyllis, **1:**400
    Bodenwieser technique, **1:**468
    Bradley tap dance school, **1:**520
    Brazilian ballet influence, **1:**533
    Caverley, Thomas, **2:**80–81
    Cecchetti school and influence, **2:**83–84
    in character dancing, **2:**107
    Craske, Margaret, **2:**268
    creative-dance movement, **4:**95
    Crofton, Kathleen, **2:**272–273
    dancing masters, **2:**337, 338–339, **3:**239, 246–247, 248–249, 252, 254, 276, 281, 521–522
    de Vos, Audrey, **2:**404
    English National Ballet program, **2:**513
    Espinosa syllabus, **2:**525
    Farber, Viola, **2:**575
    Genée, Adeline, **1:**330, **3:**129, 261, 279, 1329
    Jooss school, **3:**277, 628–629
    Laban Centre, **4:**95, 103, 104
    Laban Movement System, **4:**94
    Lanner, Katti, **4:**121
    Legat (Nikolai) school, **4:**143
    Massine dancing school, **4:**319
    modern dance, **3:**273, 278, **4:**220
    Northcote, Anna, **4:**667
    Royal Academy of Dancing, **5:**43, **6:**128
    Royal Academy of Dancing roots, **2:**396, **3:**263, 279
    Royal Ballet school, **2:**403
    social dance, **5:**631
    Sokolova, Lydia, **5:**636–637
    See also ballet technique, history of; ballet technique, major schools
  dance research and publication, **3:281–284**
    anthropological studies, **4:**369–370
    Brinson, Peter, **1:**541
    dance sociology, **4:**362
    folk dance studies, **3:**33, 281–282
    Guest, Ivor, **3:**321–322
    libraries and museums, **4:**163–164
    Richardson, Philip, **5:**351
    Sharp, Cecil, **5:**582–583
    Weaver, John, **6:**373–374
    See also Dancing Times, The; English Folk Song and Dance Society
  Elizabethan progresses, **2:**501
  English traditional dance, **3:238–243**
    anglaise, **1:**89–90
    branle, **1:**523
    as Canadian folk dance influence, **2:**35
    canary, **2:**50
    clogging, **2:**178–179, 180, **3:**240, **5:**694–695
    country dance, **2:**254–257, **3:**256, **5:**620, 621

    English measure or *almaine,* **5:**620
    figure dances, **2:**591, 592
    folk song revival, **5:**582
    galliard patterns, **3:**107
    Hey, **3:**361
    Horn Dance, **2:***558*
    hornpipe, **3:**375–379, **5:**694
    jig, **3:**607
    labyrinth dances, **4:**107
    longways, **4:**220, **5:**520, 620
    Morris dance, **3:**240, 241–242, *241,* **4:**313, 461, 462, 473–475, **5:**582, 695
    mummery, **4:**449
    pavane, **5:**620
    in physical education curriculum, **3:**276
    reels, **5:**333, 334, 695
    revival movement, **3:**34
    romantic nationalism, **3:**29, 30
    saraband, **5:**520
    step dancing, **5:**694–696
    Sword Dance, **1:**118, **2:***551,* **3:**240–241, *240,* **4:**313, **6:**54–55
    sword dances,, **5:**695
    theatrical use, **3:**254, 256
  liturgical dance, **2:**164
  Manx folk and traditional dance, **3:250–251**
  masque and antimasque, **2:**236, *236,* **3:**622, **4:**307–313, 343, **5:**113, 340
  modern dance, **3:271–275**
    Laban *Ausdruckstanz,* **1:**204
    movement choir, **4:**477
    See also London Contemporary Dance Theatre; *specific choreographers and performers*
  music, **4:**506, 517, **5:**625
  musical theater. *See* musical theater in Great Britain
  music hall, **4:**520–523
  pantomime, **2:**396, **3:**254, *256,* **5:69–72,** 350, **6:**373, 374
  Renaissance fêtes and triumphs, **5:**340
  Scottish folk and traditional dance, **2:**592, **3:243–250**
    in Canada, **2:**35, **3:**244–245
    Hey, **3:**361
    Highland dance, **3:**243–247, **5:**695
    hornpipe, **3:**376, 377–378, 379, **5:**695
    as Netherlands dance influence, **4:**585–586
    reels, **5:**333, 334, 695
    step dance, **5:**695
    See also Scotland
  social dance
    annual collections, **1:**91–92
    assemblies, **1:**189–190
    ballroom dance competitions, **1:**356, **5:**631
    balls, **1:**278, 279
    public balls, **4:**314
    révérence (Honour), **5:**345–347
    waltz, **6:**360
  television and video, **2:**314, **6:**134–135, 136
  theaters for dance, **6:**159
    See also specific theaters
  theatrical dance, **3:251–271**
    allegro style, **1:**44–45
    as Australian dance influence, **1:**213, 230–231
    Bedells as first British *prima ballerina,* **1:**400, **2:**396

Great Britain, *continued*
British style, **3:**265, 267, **5:**412, 414
costume, **2:**243
Desnoyer, Philipe **2:**394
de Valois role in developing, **2:**395–404, **5:**412, 414
Isaac, Mister, **3:**521–522
Jooss influence, **3:**628
L'Abbé, Anthony, **4:**105–106
libretti, **4:**173
lighting, **4:**188, 189–190
Santlow, Hester, **5:**518–519
skirt dance, **5:**605
Sorin and Baxter, **1:**391
Weaver, John, **6:**372–374
See also English National Ballet; International Ballet; King's Theatre, London; Metropolitan Ballet; Northern Ballet Theatre; Rambert Dance Company; Royal Ballet; *specific choreographers and dancers*
Welsh folk and traditional dance, **2:**592, **3:**250
clog dance, **5:**695–696
hornpipe, **3:**376, 379
Great Campaign, The (musical), **6:**90
Great Chain of Being, **2:**591
Great Dance of Zhou, **2:**129
Great Depression (1930s)
dance marathons, **2:**324, 325–326
Federal Dance Project, **2:**579–582
Great Detective, The, **2:**314
Great Fugue (Beethoven opus 133), **1:**403
Great Galloping Gottschalk, **1:**75
Great Lady (musical), **1:**49, **3:**663, **5:**359, **6:**277
Great Ode of Emperor Yao, **2:**138
Great Peacock, The, **5:**226
Great Performances (television series), **2:**375, **5:**195
Great Plains Indians. *See* Great Plains *under* Native American dance
Great Russian Ball, The, **6:***236*
Great Soviet Encyclopedia, **5:**643
Great to Be Alive (musical), **1:**441, **6:**90
Great Waltz, The (film), **5:**310, *311,* **6:**276
Great Waltz, The (musical), **2:**160, **5:**310, **6:**276
Greco, El, **1:**326–327
Greco, José, **1:**117, **3:**9, 10, 11, 286–287, **4:**222, **5:**674, **6:**407
Greco, Lola, **5:**674
Grecof, Renato, **3:**553
Gredelue, Adrien, **5:**233
Gredelue, Émile, **3:**560, **4:**455, **5:**501
Greece, **3:**287–304
ancient, **3:**287–294
as American dance influence, **6:**241, *241*
castanet origins, **2:**78
cheironomia, **2:**115–116
choral dancing, **2:**156–159, **3:**300
classical models, **1:**2
comedy, **2:**158, **4:**44, 301
costume, **2:**234, *236*
as Craig dance theory basis, **2:**263
Cretan influences, **2:**269–272
dance aesthetics, **1:**19–20, **2:**506

as dance costume influence, **2:**239, 244, 452, *453*
dance training, **3:**291
as Delsartist inspiration, **2:**452
dithyramb, **2:**419
drama, **3:**288, 289–290, 293, 300
as Duncan influence, **2:**453, **3:**15
emmeleia concept, **2:**506
fan representations, **2:**569
as Fokine influence, **3:**15
as Graham influence, **4:**632–633
as Humphrey influence, **3:**399
hyporchēma, **2:**158, **3:**428
as Islamic cultural influence, **4:**488
kallinikos, **3:**645–646
kōmos, **5:**598
kordax, **4:**44
labyrinth dances, **4:**106
as libretti subjects, **4:**174
masked dance, **3:**290, **4:**301, **5:**375
mime, **4:**423, 426
Muses and Graces, **3:**287, **6:**144–145
musical accompaniment, **4:**499, *499*
orchestra, **5:**41–42, **6:**155
pastorales, **5:**112
pyrrhic, **5:**282–283
revivals of drama, **3:**300
schēma, **5:**556–557
scholarly research on, **3:**302–303, **6:**297
sikinnis revel, **5:**598
stage design, **5:**532–533
Terpsichore, **6:**144–145
theaters, **6:**155, *155*
travesty, **6:**188
vase paintings, **5:**259
See also neoclassical *headings*
dance research and publication, **3:**302–304, **4:**161, **6:**297
modern, **3:**296–301
folk dance education, **3:**301
folk dance vocal sounds, **3:**38
syrtós dance, **1:***100,* 101–102, **2:**271–272, **3:**296, 300
traditional men's dance, **2:**551
ritual and carnival dance traditions, **2:**100, *100,* **3:**298, 300, **301–302**
Dionysian cults, **6:**185
trance dances, **6:**185, 186, 187
Roman and Byzantine periods, **3:**294–296, 303, 541, **5:**374–375, 376
mime, **4:**426
Greek Civil War (1947–1949), **3:**296
Greek Dance Theater, Athens, **3:**304
Greeks (ethnic), **3:**296
Greek Veil Plastique, **2:**378
Green, **4:**1
Green, Adolph, **1:**438, **2:**616, **5:**360
Green, Chuck, **3:**304, 447, **5:**601, **6:**102
Green, Doris, *as contributor,* **4:**548–549
Green, George Hamilton, **1:**52
Green, John, **2:**616
Green, Lili, **4:**589–590, 598
Green, Paul, **6:**276
Green, Ray, **1:**82, 421
Green, Stanley, **6:**102
Green Altars, **1:**197
Greenaway, Peter, **4:**451
Greenberg, Clement, **1:**135

Green Bushes, or A Hundred Years Ago, The (melodrama), **2:**85
Green Corn Ceremony, **4:***552,* 557, 559
Greene, Robert, **3:**377
Greene, Sean, **4:***156*
Greenfield, **2:**116
Greenfield, Amy, **2:**460, 606, *607,* 609, **5:**187
Greenfield, Lois, **5:**186
as photographer, **2:**295, 585, **5:**187
Green Grow the Lilacs (Rigg), **2:**373
Greenhood, Henrietta, **4:**96
Greenhouse, Richard N., *as photographer,* **6:**366
Greening, **2:**513, 561, **3:**373, **4:**1, *156,* **6:**146
Greenland, **4:**571
Greenlee, Rufus, **1:**520
Green Mansions (film), **2:**458
Green Mill Dance Project, **1:**217
Green Monster, The, **5:**317–318
Green Queen, The, **1:**251
"Green Room Ballet" (*The Street Singer*), **6:**274
Green Season, The, **1:**501
Green-Stone Mountain, The (Beijing Opera), **2:**220
Green Table, The, **1:**331, 386, **2:**58, 82, 123, **3:**305–306
Archives Internationales first prize award, **3:**40, 72, 76, 305, 627
Ausdruckstanz, **3:**147
Bavarian State Ballet revival, **3:**305, 630
Dutch National Ballet revival, **2:**469, **3:**630
Joffrey Ballet staging, **3:**305, 614, 616, 617, **6:**630
Jooss revival, **3:**630
mask use, **3:***626,* **4:**302
Mirror as sequel, **3:**629
two-piano score, **4:**517
Uthoff performance, **6:**304
Züllig role, **6:**453
Greenwich Village, New York City
Halloween Parade, **2:**171
Judson Memorial Church, **1:**79, 139, **3:**633–634, *634*
Greenwich Village Follies, **5:**495
Greenwich Village Follies of 1919 (revue), **6:**272
Greenwich Village Follies of 1923 (revue), **3:**211, **6:**272
Greenwich Village Follies of 1924 (revue), **4:**460
Greenwich Village Follies of 1928 (revue), **1:**520, **2:**572
Greenwood, Charlotte, **6:**142, 319
Greenwood, Dennis, **3:**272
Greeting Dance, **6:**170
Grégoire, Carboche, **2:**69
Gregory, Cynthia, **2:**161, **3:**306–307, **5:**513
American Ballet Theatre, **1:**72, *72, 73, 73,* **2:**3, 4, **3:**306
Cuban dance performance, **3:**306
as Maracci student, **4:**262
Gregory, Gillian, **6:**287
Gregory, Jill, **3:**519
Gregory, John, **2:**479, **6:**128
Gregory, Jon, **3:**599
Gregory of Nazianzus, **4:**106
Gregory the Great, pope, **2:**165
Grein, J. T., **1:**43
Greive, Pieter, **4:**588
Grekowski, Mikołaj, **5:**215
Gremina, Nina, **2:**15, **5:**458
Grendel, Wanda, **4:**597
Grenke, David, **5:**679, 680

Grenoble, France, **1:**462, **3:**78
Grenot, Lesme, **2:**281
Greskovic, Robert, *as contributor,* **1:**100–101, 197–198, 333–335, 336–338, 371–373, **2:**19–20, **4:**273–275, **5:**101–105, 207–209, **6:**339–341
Gresserov-Golovin, Peter, **6:**438
Gretchen, **5:**233
Grete Wiesenthal Dance Group. *See* Wiesenthal technique
Gretna Green, **5:**353
Grétry, André-Ernest-Modeste, **1:**306, **4:**514, **5:**198, **6:**360
Greuze, Jean Baptiste, **1:**126
Greve, Dane Kenneth, **5:**8
Grey, Beryl, **2:**404, **3:**307, **5:**312, 639, 652
Ballet Imperial, **1:**293
Beijing Ballet classes, **2:**137
Checkmate, **2:**115, **3:**307
English National Ballet, **2:**508, 511, 512, 513, **3:**269, 427
Field dance partnership, **2:**590, **3:**307
PACT Ballet guest *Swan Lake* performance, **5:**53
Royal Ballet, **5:**413, 416
Sleeping Beauty staging for Swedish Royal Ballet, **6:**44
Grey, Geoffrey, **5:**555
Grey, Joel, **2:**620, **6:**284
Grey-Cullert, Dyane, **1:**292
Greyling, Eduard, **2:**58, **5:**652, *653*
Griaule, Marcel, **4:**291, **6:**382
Gribler, Jeff, **2:**357
Griboedov, Aleksandr, **4:**279
Gribov, Aleksandr, **4:**144, 285, **5:**459, 699
Gridelino, o Ballet du Griselin, Il, **1:**29, **3:**544, **5:**2
Gridin, Anatoly, **4:**144, 285, **5:**459, 699
Grieg, Edvard, **1:**297, 298, 374, **2:**21, 112, **3:**17, 511
Grierson, John, **2:**601
Gries, Lance, **5:**314
Griesbach, Karl-Rudi, **3:**153
Grieve, William, **1:**47, **2:**390, 523, **5:**29
Griffin, Hayden, **3:**609
Griffin, Verlon and Berlon (Griffin Twins), **6:***319*
Grigny, Jean de, **1:**3
Grigolati, Madame, **5:**71
Grigoriev, Serge, **1:**308, 311, 312, 315, **3:**307–308, **5:**118, 166, **6:**120
Ballets Russes de Monte Carlo stagings, **3:**24, *25*
Diaghilev association, **3:**308, **6:**32
English National Ballet, **2:**510
Firebird restaging, **3:**2
on Goncharova's *Les Noces* designs, **3:**198
on Kochno's role in Diaghilev company, **4:**33
view of Viennese ballet, **3:**347
Grigoriev, Vladimir, **6:**436
Grigoriev, Yuri, **5:**150, 467
Grigorieva, Tamara, **1:**315, **3:**25, **4:**659, **5:**265, **6:**301
Grigorovich, Yuri, **1:**248, 416, **2:**11, 422, **3:**308–311, **5:**97, 282, 461, 473, 639
ballet themes, **1:**493, **4:**284–285, **5:**462, 485
Bessmertnova marriage, **1:**440, **3:**310
Bolshoi Ballet, **1:**492–494, **3:**308–311

as Bolshoi Ballet director, **6:**315
choreographic revivals skill,
     3:309–310, **5:**463
Golden Age revival, **3:**193,
     309, *309*
Gordeyev roles, **3:**200, *200*
International Theatre Institute,
     3:610
Kondratieva roles, **4:**38
Lavrovsky (Mikhail) roles, **4:**133
Liepa roles, **4:**180–181
Maryinsky Ballet, **4:**284
Novosibirsk Ballet
     choreographies, **5:**472
Nutcracker, The, **3:**309, **4:**435,
     5:10, *11*, **12**, 463, **6:**314
Plisetskaya, Maya, **5:**205, 206
Raymonda, **1:**492, **3:**310,
     5:321–322, 463
Romeo and Juliet, **1:**492, **3:**309,
     5:399
Sleeping Beauty versions,
     3:309–310, **5:**463, 610
as Soviet ballet influence, **5:**460
Spartacus, **3:**308, **4:**7, 38, 182,
     335, **5:**677–678, **6:***411*
Stone Flower, The, **4:**38, *282*, 284,
     335, *335*, **5:**460, **6:**42
Stone Flower as choreographic
     debut, **5:**699
Swan Lake production, **3:**309,
     4:38, **5:**463, **6:**31
Swedish guest staging, **6:**42
symphonic dance, **4:**284–285
Vanslov study of, **5:**484, 485
Vasiliev roles, **6:**313, 314
Virsaladze design collaboration,
     6:343
     See also Legend of Love
griha (musical style), **4:**468
Grike, Mirdza, **4:**127
Grille d'Egout (Manhole Grating),
     1:95, **2:***249*
Grillo, Elena, **3:**555
     as contributor, **2:**418, **5:**353,
          404–405
Grimaldi, Enriquetta, **1:**429, **5:**245
Grimaldi, Giuseppe, **5:**70
Grimaldi, John Baptiste (Nicolini),
     5:70
Grimaldi, Joseph, **5:**70
Grimaldi family, **2:**410
Grimberg, Luisa, **1:**112
Grimm, Friedrich Melchior von,
     3:117, 326, **5:**196
Grimm, Jacob Ludwig Carl and
     Wilhelm Carl, **5:**624
Grimm, Thomas, **6:**134
Grind (dance), **5:**634
Gringo Tango, **5:**587
Grinwis, Paul, **1:**315, 410, **5:**54
Griot New York, **2:**566–567
Gripenberg, Maggie, **2:**632, *632*,
     3:311–313
Gripsholm Court Theater,
     Stockholm, **6:**39, 48
Gris, Juan, **1:**316, **2:**242
Grise-aile (Lorentz caricatures),
     2:71, **3:**183
Griseldis, ou Les Cinq Sens, **1:**10,
     3:315, **4:**340, 341
Gris-Gris Ceremonial, **6:**88
Grisi, Carlotta, **1:**10, 508, **2:**71,
     3:313–316, 359, **4:**340, **5:**93,
          150, 499, 528
     dance style and technique, **3:**315,
          316, **5:**103
     daughters, **3:**314, 316
     Diable à Quatre performance,
          2:405, **4:**341
     Electra performance, **6:**75

Elssler (Fanny) comparison,
     2:504
Esmeralda performance, **2:**95,
     405, 505, 523, **3:**315
flying leap, **3:**315, 316
Gautier love for, **3:**123
Giselle performances, **2:**203, 390,
     504, **3:**69, *70*, 123, 177, 178,
          179, 180, 181, 314, *314*, 316,
          5:135–136, 148
Jolie Fille de Gand performances,
     1:36, 37, **3:**5, 620
King's Theatre (London)
     appearances, **3:**259, *259*, 260,
          313, 314, 315, 316
Mazilier roles, **4:**341
mazur solo, **5:**216
Métamorphoses performance,
     6:75
Paquita performance, **5:**85, 93
Pas de Quatre performances,
     2:94, *103*, 104, **3:**224, 260,
          315, **5:**108, 137
Péri performances, **2:**204, 405,
     3:315, **5:**132, 133, *148*
Perrot relationship, **2:**203, 390,
     3:313–314, 315, **5:**106,
          135–136, 137, 138, *138*, 139
polka, **5:**221
Polka pas de deux, **3:**315, *315*
Quatre Saisons performance,
     3:260, **5:**138, **6:**76
Rossignol performances, **2:**390,
     3:*259*
Saint Petersburg guest
     performances, **4:**280, **5:**454,
          6:451
Taglioni (Salvatore) roles, **6:**70
Grisi, Ernesta, **3:**123, 313
Grisi, Giulia, **5:**616
Grisi, La, **1:**247, **5:**132
Grivickas, Vytautas, **4:**208
Grizzly Bear (dance), **5:**628, **6:**255
Grohg, **2:**196
Grondona, Erna, **6:**431
Groniero, David, **3:***232*
Groningen, Netherlands, **4:**597
Grönlund, Erna, **6:**50
Grooms, Red, **3:**202, **6:**362
Groot, Pauline de, **4:**218, 593,
     594–595
Gropius, Karl, **6:**29
Gropius, Walter, **1:**132, 385, **5:**546,
     6:162, *162*
Grosch, Karla, **1:***386*
Gross, Grete, **1:**239
Gross, Mimi, **1:**142, **2:**460
Gross, Sally, **3:**446, 634
Gross, Valentine, **3:**393, **4:**642, 644
Grossatesta, Gaetano, **3:**545, 554
Grosse, Ernst, **4:**369
Grosse Fuge, **1:**403
Grossi, A., **4:**453
Grossman, Danny, **2:**45, **4:**545,
     6:133
Grossmann, Mechtild, **1:**389
Grosser, Philip, **1:**75
Grosz, Alexander, **2:**454
Grosz, Wilhelm, **3:**132
groteschi, **1:**341
grotesque dance, **3:**256, 545, 546,
     5:251, 280
     technical manuals, **6:**126
     See also demi-caractère
Grotowski, Jerzy, **3:**652
ground bass, **2:**97
Groundhog (dancer), **6:**386
Ground Level Overlay, **2:**296, **5:**17
Group Activities, **6:**152
Group Concertante de Balle, **6:**302

Groupe de Ballet, Conservatoire
     National Supérieure de la
     Musique, Lyon, **2:**575
Groupe de la Place Royale, Le,
     2:40, 43–44, 45
Groupe de Recherche
     Chorégraphique de l'Opéra de
     Paris (GRCOP), **2:**293, **5:**98
Groupe de Recherche Théâtrale de
     l'Opéra de Paris (GRTOP),
     3:77, **5:**98
Groupe Émile Dubois, Grenoble,
     3:78
Groupe Gripenberg, **3:**312, *312*
Groupe Nouvelle Aire, Le, **2:**40, 45,
     6:132
Group Gymnasium, **5:**388, *388*
group improvisation, **3:**447
Group Primary Accumulation,
     1:543
Group Rhythmic Movment
     Relationship, **2:**316
Group Theater, **6:**88, 276, 278
Grove, Lilly, **2:***570*, **3:**31, 33
Groves, John L., **1:**243
Growing Up in Public, **2:**110, **3:**391
Grown Gentlemen Taught to Dance
     (Collett), **2:**70
Groza (Ostrovsky), **6:**114
GRTOP. *See* Groupe de Recherche
     Théâtrale de l'Opéra de Paris
Grube, Elisabeth, **4:**60
Gruber, Lilo, **3:**153
Gruber, Mayer I., *as contributor,*
     1:448–449
Gruca, Witold, **3:**316–317, **5:**219
Gruen, John, **4:**177
Gruenberg, Louis, **6:**200
Grujić, Tatjana, **6:**435
Grunberg, Eugène, **3:**225
"Grundprinzipien der
     Bewegungsschfit" (Laban),
     4:99
Grüne Heinrich, Der, **4:**64
Grünen Clowns, Die, **4:**90, 91
Grunt, Xenia, **6:**424
Grupo Corpo, **1:**535, *535*, 536
Grupo Espiral, **2:**281
Grupo Experimental de Bailado,
     5:234
Grupo Folklórico de Guadalajara,
     4:396
Grupo Gestus, **6:**302
Grupo Gulbenkian de Bailado. *See*
     Gulbenkian Ballet;
     Gulbenkian Foundation
Grupo Moebius, **6:**302
Grusis (people), **4:**290
Grut, Marina (Keet), *as contributor,*
     2:55–58, 520–521, **5:**225–226,
          312–313, 649–655, 691–692
     See also Keet, Marina
Gruzenberg, Sergei, **1:**437
Gsovsky, Tatjana, **1:**110, 445–446,
     456, **2:**114, 434, 441,
          3:317–318, **4:**134, 517, **5:**43,
               97, 334
     Ballet du XXᵉ Siécle, **1:**290
     Berlin Opera Ballet, **1:**436, **2:**114,
          3:149, 150, 152, 318, 359
     electronic music score, **4:**519
     Henze commissions, **3:**359
     Nazi era, **3:**147
     Ondine choreography, **3:**360
     Paris dance studio, **3:**82
     students, **2:**471, **3:**318, **5:**263
Gsovsky, Victor, **1:**300, 390, 456,
     2:114, **3:**318–319
     Ballets des Champs-Élysées,
          1:306, **3:**73, 318, **4:**34
     marriage, **3:**317, 318

Metropolitan Ballet, **4:**380
Munich State Opera, **3:**149, 318
students, **1:**251, 460, **2:**113, 447,
     587, **4:**136, 420, **6:**449
Taglioni's *La Sylphide*
     reconstruction, **3:**73, 318,
          6:58–59
Gstettner, Bert, **1:**240, 306
Guacanagari (Taino leader), **2:**62
Guadeloupe, **2:**64
guaguancó, **2:**275
Guangdong Dance Academy,
     China, **1:**81
Guangdong Modern Dance
     Company, **1:**81, **2:**146, **3:**373,
          6:415
Guangzhou Ballet, **2:**146
guaracha, **2:**521
guarapo, **2:**430
Guarini, Giovanni Battista, **5:**113
Guasch, Elizabeth, **5:**171
Guatemala, **3:**319–320
Guatemala Ballet Academy, **5:**62
Guaymi (people), **5:**67
Gubaidulina, Sofia, **2:**564, **5:**479
Gubstkaya, Vera, **6:**306
Gudarnas Högtid, **6:**38
Gudim, Ketil, **4:***676*
Gudmundsson, Örn, *as contributor,*
     3:436–437
Gudonov, Alexander, **1:***198*
Gudule's Daughter, **1:**488, **2:**582,
     3:204, *205*, **4:**459, **5:**456
guedra, **1:**42, **4:**408, 465–466,
     465, 490
Guélis, Jean, **1:**306
Guepard, Le, **5:**164
Guerard, Roland, **1:**296, *296*,
     309, 311
Guéré (people), **4:**291
Guérin, Isabelle, **2:**114, **3:***183*,
     5:7, 98
Guérinot, Théodore, **1:**477, 485
Guerra, Antonio, **1:**238, **2:**93, **5:**498
     Budapest Opera Ballet, **3:**414
     Gitana restaging, **3:**185
     Maywood dance partnership,
          4:339
     Mohicans, Les, **1:**9, **3:**5
Guerra, Juan Luis, **2:**432
Guerra, Maximiliano, **1:**111, **3:***273*
Guerra, Nicola, **3:**320–321, 414,
     4:420, 529, **5:**95, 400
Guerra, Ramiro, **2:**277, 280
Guerra d'Amore, **3:**381
"Guerre, La" (Janequin), **1:**369
Guerrero, Félix, **2:**279
Guerrero, Manuel, **1:**480
Guerrero, Margarita, **1:**112
Guest, Ann Hutchinson. *See*
     Hutchinson, Ann
Guest, Ivor, **1:**541, **3:**321–322,
     6:216
     on Albert, Monsieur, **1:**36
     as contributor, **3:**128–130,
          237–238, 313–316, **5:**134–142,
               276–278
     on Bias, **1:**446
     on *Fille Mal Gardée,* **2:**594, 597,
          3:321
     on *fouetté* virtuosity, **1:**347
     on Grahn, **3:**223
     historical research, **3:**282
     on López and Ballet Español,
          4:222
     on Noblet's persona, **4:**657
Guests, The, **4:**608, **5:**361, 362
Gueullette, Thomas-Simon, **2:**365
Guevara, Taormina, **6:**325
Gueye, Pathe, **4:**549
Guglielmi, Alessandro, **5:**231

Guglielmo Ebreo da Pesaro
(Giovanni Ambrosio), **1:**45,
351, 352, **2:**74, 336, 427,
3:322–325, 542, **5:**337, 621
ballo tunes, **4:**501
dance manuals, **4:**683, **6:**121, 122
figure dances, **2:**591, **3:**110
Jewish background, **3:**527, 603
révérence, **5:**344
treatise scholarship,
3:553–554, 557
on *tripudium,* **6:**193, 194
Guiablesse, La, **2:**458
Guide chorégraphique, Le (Conté),
4:688
Guidetti, Giovanni Battista, **3:**545
Guidi, Antonia, **3:**104, **5:**424
Guidi, Ronn, **6:**266
Guido, Beatriz, **3:**512
Guido et Ginevra (Halévy opera),
4:340
Guignol et Pandore, **4:**184–185
Güije, El, **2:**278
Guilbert, Yvette, **4:**523
Guilcher, Yves, *as contributor,*
3:63–65
guild dances, **3:325–326**
Athens, **3:**291
England, **4:**473
German, **4:**92
Germany, **3:**140–141
Hungary, **3:**411–412
sub-Saharan African, **6:**13
Guillablesse, La, **5:**59
guillatun, **2:**121
Guillaume, Simon, **1:**45, 47, **6:**124
Guillaume Tell (Rossini opera),
1:35, 409, **4:**514, 631, 657,
5:35, **6:**442–443
Guillem, Sylvie, **2:**441, 501, **4:**257,
456, **5:**7, 99, 419, **6:**66
Guillemain, Louis-Gabriel, **2:**365
Guillemin, Charles, **3:**145
Guillet, Claude, **3:**313
Guillot, Geneviève, **3:**82
Guilmette, Pierre, **2:**49
Guimard, Marie-Madeleine, **2:**353,
413, **3:**112, 117, **326–327,**
4:149
Comédie Française, **3:**66
popularity, **6:**189
Vestris (Auguste) relationship,
6:333
Vestris (Gäetan) dance
association, **5:**35, 89,
6:331, 332
Guinea, **1:**14
Ballets Africains, **1:**303–304,
5:659, **6:**20, 384
as Caribbean dance influence,
2:64
masks, **4:**286, **6:**13
Guinea, Laurenţiu, **5:**390
Guinea National Ballet. *See* Ballets
Africains, Les
Guinguette, La, **2:**366, 366
Guiot, Mademoiselle, **1:**516
Guipúzcoan dances, **1:**376, **3:**33
Guipúzkoa 'ko Dantzak (Iztueta),
1:376
Guirand, Rose Marie, **6:**384
Guirlande, La (Rameau), **5:**307
guitar, **1:**6
electric, **6:**249
flamenco, **1:**61, 62, **3:**6, 8, 9, 10
folia, **3:**28
Garifuna dance, **3:**120
Hawaiian steel, **4:**497
West African urban dance, **6:**24
guitar-band highlife, **6:**24
Guizerix, Jean, **1:**462, **2:**293, **5:**97

Gulak-Artemovsky, Semen, **6:**344
Gulandom, **4:**7
Gulbenkian, Calouste, **5:**234
Gulbenkian Ballet, **3:**203, **5:233,**
234, *234,* 235, *235,* 677
Gulbenkian Foundation, **1:**217,
541, **3:**278, 279–280, 283,
4:217, **5:**230, 234, 235
Gulf Cooperation Council Folklore
Centre, **4:**417
Gulf states and emirates. *See*
Arabian Peninsula
Guliandom, **6:**306–307
Gulick, Luther, **3:**34, **6:**240
Gull, The, **4:**435
Gulliver, **2:**202
Gulliver's Travels, **3:**329
Gulyaev, Vadim, **4:**285, **5:**462
Gulyaeva, Galina A., *as contributor,*
3:186–187, **5:**595–596
Gulyás, László, **2:**473
gumboot dancing, **2:**86, 212–213,
5:648, *648,* **6:**22
Gumbo Ya Ya, **4:**346
Gumiel, Renée, **1:**535
Gumpenhuber, Philipp, **3:**365
Gundeberga, **3:**176
Gundersen, Mona, *as photographer,*
4:680
Gundersen, Niklas, **4:**681
Gundlich, L., **6:**431
Guneya, Nittawala, **5:**309
Gungl, Joseph, **6:**2
gunjai, **3:**121
Gunn, Nicholas, **2:**526
Guns and Castanets, **2:**580, **5:**59
Gunshol, Jeffrey, **4:**151
Günther, Dorothee, **1:**204, **4:**92,
5:42
Güntherschule, Munich, **5:**42
"Guoji Shinduan Pu" (Qi Rushan),
2:148
Gurage (people), **2:**530, 532
Gurdjieff, G. I., **4:**89
Gurevitch, Anatol, **3:**529
Gurindji (people), **1:**221
Guro (people), **4:**292, **6:**382
Gurri dances, **4:**485–486
guru (people), **2:**210
gurukkal, **1:**186
Guruvayur Temple, Kerala,
4:65, 66
Gurzau, Elba Farabegoli, **6:**104
Gusev, Petr, **1:**248, 490, 491,
3:327–329, **5:**236
Bayadère reconstruction, **3:**328,
5:470
Chinese ballet students, **2:**136,
145, **3:**328
Corsaire staging, **4:**279
Don Quixote revival, **2:**437
Lopukhov influence, **4:**283
Maly Theater Ballet, **5:**468
Maryinsky Ballet, **5:**458
Novosibirsk Ballet, **2:**422
Seven Beauties, **5:**459–450
Gusmann, Rosina, **1:**500
Gustav (Auber), **4:**657
Gustav III, king of Sweden, **1:**503,
2:264, **4:**313, 698, **5:**425,
6:39, 48
assassination as curbing Swedish
ballet development, **6:**39–40
court theaters, **6:**46, 48, 50
Didelot dance stagings,
2:412, 413
Swedish Academy founding, **6:**49
Gustav IV Adolph, king of Sweden,
6:40
Gustave, **6:**72
Gustave III, **3:**426

Gustav Vasa, **1:**456
Gutelius, Phyllis, **3:**220
Gutes, Nuri, **2:**126
Guthrie, Tyrone, **2:**445, **3:**355, 356
Guthrie, Woody, **4:**306
Gutierrez, Carmen, **2:**604
Guttuso, Renato, **4:**421, **5:**400
Guy, Edna, **6:**258
Guy, Geoffrey, **6:**202
Guyer, Charles, **6:**316
Guyot, Marie-Catherine, **2:**465,
3:329, **4:**231, **5:**41, 248, 249
Guys, Constantin (pseud.), **2:**71
Guys and Dolls (film), **4:**10
Guys and Dolls (musical), **2:**251,
4:10, **6:**281
Guy-Stéphan, Marie, **4:**342, **5:**500
Güzelleme, **6:**212
Guzmán, Martín Luis, **4:**391
Guzmán Mexía, Fernando, **5:**519
Gvaramadze, Elena L., *as
contributor,* **3:**133–136
Gwyn, Nell, **3:**253, 255
Gyinna-Gyinna, **4:**291
Gyllich, Valdemar, **1:**504
Gymnasion. *See* Column, The
Gymnasium. *See* Group
Gymnasium
Gymnastic Kinesiology
(Skarstrom), **4:**16
gymnastic movements, **5:**476,
6:235, 240, 242, 294, 389
Gymnastics and Folk Dancing
(Hinman), **3:**368
Gymnastiklehre (Misslitz), **4:**691
Gymnastik und Tanz (Laban),
4:92, 99
gyōdō, **3:**171
Gyöngyösbokréta, **3:**412
Győr Ballet, **3:329–330,** 422,
4:266–267
Györgyfalvay, Katalin, **1:**370
Gypsies, The (Kholfin ballet), **2:**15
"Gypsies, The" (Pushkin poem),
1:136
Gypsy (musical), **5:**363, **6:**282, 288
Gypsy, La (Coralli ballet), **2:**201
Gypsy Ballads, The (Garcïa Lorca),
3:6
Gypsy dance, **3:330–331,**
5:667, 695
Argentinita, La, **1:**116, 117
Bartók studies, **1:**370
as English dance influence, **3:**240
Falla scores, **2:**567
flamenco, **3:**6–11, 7
North Africa, **4:**664
Gypsy theme. *See Carmen;
Esmeralda, La; Gipsy, La;
Gitana, La*
Gyrowetz, Adalbert, **1:**202, **6:**50
Gyulshen, **1:**48, 248
Gzhel folk dance ensemble, **5:**473

Ha'aheo, Pua, **3:**396
Haakon, Paul, **1:**498, 518, **3:**22, 23
Háas, Andréa, **2:**122–123
Haas, Gerd, **1:**211
Haas, Henn, **3:**152
Haas, Olga de, **2:**470
Haase, L., **3:**144
habanera, **2:**63, 275, **6:**91
Haber, David, **4:**543
Häberli, Ema, **6:**302
Haçen ben Salomo, **2:**336
Hachimonjiya Jisho, **3:**591
Hachirobei Tatsumatsu, **2:**13
Hackett, Janette, **6:**319
Hackney, Peggy, *as contributor,*
1:473–474

Haddakin, Lillian, **3:**285
Haddington Masque, The (Jonson),
4:312–313
Haderlap, Zdravko, **1:**240
Hadiwijaya, **3:**494
Hadjidakis, Manos, **3:**299
Hadley, Susan, **6:**251
hadrah dance, **4:**250
Hadyńa, Stanisław, **5:**212
Hadžiev, Paraslikev, **2:**12
Haeffner, Johann Christian
Friedrich, **6:**39
Hagemann, Frederick, **5:**659
Hagen, Pina, **3:**78
Hagenmaier, Emily, **5:**512
Häger, Bengt, **4:**163, **6:**49
as contributor, **3:**305–306,
624–631
Häggbom, Nils-Åke, **6:**43, *43,*
44, *46*
Haggin, Ben Ali, **2:**572, **6:**448
Haggin, B. H., **6:**299
Häggman, Ann-Marie, **2:**631
Hagoromo, **4:**40, 41
Hague, Netherlands, **4:**591, 592,
597, 598, 600
Hague Municipal Library, **4:**162
Hahn, David, **3:**306
as contributor, **2:**77, **4:**504–508,
6:178–179
Hahn, Reynaldo, **3:**18
Haid, Gerlinde, *as contributor,*
1:242–243
Haida (people), **4:**470
Haider-Pregler, Hilde, **3:**381
Haidouk Song, A, **2:**11, 12
Haieff, Aleksei, **2:**286, **4:**28
Haieff Divertimento, **4:**622
Haifa, Israel, **3:**529, 534
Haigen, Kevin, **2:**514, **3:**578, 631
Hai-Kai, **1:**251, 349
Hail and Farewell, **6:**201
Hail to the Conquering Hero, **5:**51
Haines, Alfred, **6:**213
Haines, Jackson, **3:**431, *432*
Hair (film), **6:**154
Hair (musical), **6:**284
Sarajevo performance, **6:**436
Sokolow original choreography,
5:638
Hair Dance, **6:**80
hair styles. *See* costume *headings*
Haiti, **2:**62–63, 64, 65, **3:333–336**
Dunham dance studies, **2:**458,
459, **3:**335
filmed ethnography, **2:**601
ritual dance, **5:**356–357
trance rituals, **6:**185, 187
Vodun, **5:**355–356, **6:**185, 188,
345–348
as Williams-Yarborough dance
base, **6:**400
haivky, **6:**221, 222
hajduch, **2:**301
hajdútánc, **3:**407, 422
haka, **4:**261, **5:**510
Håkansson, Helene Frederikke,
1:505
Hakmu, **3:**341
hakobi, **5:**592
Håkon Jarl, **1:**503
Hakutobo, **2:**18
Halanzier, Olivier, **5:**94, **6:**63
halay dance, **6:**211
Hale, Chester, **1:**478, **2:**19, **5:**247
Hale, George, **6:**275
Halévy, Fromental (Jacques),
1:202, **2:**202, **3:**5, 316, **4:**340,
341, 513, **5:**404, **6:**71
Juive, La, **4:**631, 657
Manon Lescaut score, **4:**513, **5:**92

Halévy, Léon, **3:**5
Halévy, Ludovic, **2:**362–363, **3:**26
Halevy, Moshiko, **3:**531
Haley, Jack, **6:**142
Half a Sixpence (musical), **6:**283
Halffter, Ernesto, **1:**115, **2:**568
Halfway House (film), **1:**438
Halifax, England, **4:**668
Halil and Hajiria, **1:**34
Halka (Moniuszko), **5:**75, 216,
     6:207, 365
Hall, Andria, **2:**513, **5:**422
Hall, Arthur, **6:**259
Hall, Darcy, *as contributor*,
     5:637–638
Hall, Fernu, **3:**282
Hall, Frank, **4:**367
Hall, G. Stanley, **6:**241, 295
Hall, Lucy Duncan, **3:**367
Hallam, Lewis, **2:**467
Hallberg, Ulrika, **2:**633, *634*
Halle, Adam de la, **5:**112, **6:**267
Halle, Charles, **2:**453
Halle, Germany, **3:**154–155
Hallelujah, **2:**613
Haller, Albrecht, **4:**15
Haller, Lelia, **2:**586
Haller, Robert, *as photographer*,
     2:607
Hallet-Eghayan, Michel, **3:**79
halling (laus), **4:**669, *669*
hallisaka, **3:**466
Halloween, **2:**171
Hällström, Raoul, **2:**635, **3:**312
hallucenogenic mushrooms, **4:**550
Halman, Talat, **4:**416
Halprin, Anna, **1:**421, 543, **3:**54,
     336, 5:547, 548, **6:**249
     improvisation, **3:**445
     as Judson Dance Theater
        influence, **3:**634
     liturgical dance, **3:**356
     students, **3:**339, **4:**230, **5:**292
Hälsingehambon, **6:**37
Halsman, *as photographer*, **3:**225
Halston, **2:**182, **3:**220
Halte de Cavalerie, **3:**137, 328, **4:**67,
     68, 144, 145, 459, **5:***158*, 160,
     6:442
Hamada Koji, **3:**523
Hamadisha, **3:**525
Hamadryaden, Die, **1:**10
hamamah, al-, **2:**489
Hamar (people), **2:**530, 533
Hamar, Norway, **4:**676
Hamatsa Dance, **4:***570*
hambo dance, **6:**36, 37
Hamburg Ballet, **1:**460, **2:**420, 441,
     463, **3:336–338**
     Artus-Sage, **3:**360
     Balanchine guest choreography,
        3:150, 337
     Dyk, Peter van, **2:**471, **3:**337
     Gsovsky (Victor) guest
        choreography, **3:**318
     Hanka, Erika, **3:**340
     Hoyer directorship, **3:**149–150,
        337, 393
     Josephslegende, Die, **3:**578
     Lanner, Katti, **3:**336, **4:**121
     Neumeier, John, **3:**150, 157,
        337–338, **4:**603–604, **6:**35
     Ondine, **3:**360
     Swan Lake, **6:**35
Hamburger Bewegungschöre
     Laban, **4:**91, *93*
Hamburger Tanzschreibstube, **4:**32
Hamburg State Opera. *See*
     Hamburg Ballet
Hamburguer, Claudia, **1:**537
Hamed, Nader, **2:**498

Hamengku Buwana I, sultan of
     Jogjakarta, **3:**496
Hamengku Buwana II, sultan of
     Jogjakarta, **3:**494
Hamengku Buwana VIII, sultan of
     Jogjakarta, **3:**496
Hamengku Buwana IX, sultan of
     Jogjakarta, **3:**497
Hamilton, Chico, **1:**194
Hamilton, David, *as contributor*,
     6:3–7
Hamilton, Gordon, **1:**207, 305,
     3:340
Hamilton, Lady (Emma Hart),
     1:126, 199
Hamilton, William, **1:**199, **2:**328
Hamlet, **1:**156, 390, 436, 456,
     5:*57*, 58
     Biagi choreography, **1:**446
     Chabukiani production, **2:**97
     Dolgushin performance, **2:**423
     Franca performance, **3:**62
     Georgi choreography, **3:**133
     Gsovsky productions, **3:**318
     Hart (John) performance, **3:**345
     Helpmann choreography and
        performance, **3:**355, *355*, 356,
        5:312, **6:**117
     Henry (Louis) production, **3:**358
     Lacotte choreography, **4:**107
     Lifar choreography, **6:**117
     Nijinska choreography, **4:**636
     Schaufuss (Peter) production,
        5:433, 555
     Sergeyev choreography, **2:**423,
        5:572
     Soviet-era productions, **5:**462
Hamlet (Shakespeare), **3:**177, 180,
     356, **4:**332, **5:**518
     Yakko and Kawakami
        production, **6:**409
Hamlet (Tchaikovsky concert
     piece), **6:**117
Hamlet (Thomas opera), **5:**148
Hamlet Connotations, **2:**4,
     3:338, 351
Hamlet—Irony and Mourning,
     6:175
Hamletmachine (Wilson), **6:**401
Hamlisch, Marvin, **1:**419
Hamme, Andries van, **4:**589
Hamme, Eduard Voitis van, **1:**410,
     5:278
Hammer, Signe, **1:***245*
Hammer and Sickle Works,
     Moscow, **5:**461
Hammergren, Lena, **6:**50
     as contributor, **1:**32–33, 145,
        2:429
Hammerich, Alice, **3:***147*
Hammerstein, Oscar I, **6:**270, 371
Hammerstein, Oscar II, **4:**420,
     5:72, **6:**271
     Kern collaboration, **6:**273, 274
     Rodgers collaboration, **2:**619,
        4:3, **5:**72, 362, 369, **6:**281, 288
Hammerstein, William, **6:**371
Hammond, Mark, **6:**133
Hammond, Paul, **1:**218, 499, **4:**380,
     5:563
Hammond, Sandra Noll, **6:**127
     as contributor, **1:**330–332,
        332–333, 344–347, **5:**105–108,
        201–202, 226–227, **6:**126–127,
        215–216
Hampshire, June, **2:**443
Hampton, Barbara L., *as
     contributor*, **4:**483–487
Hampton Institute Creative Dance
     Group, **2:**25–26, **6:**258

Han (people), **2:**138–139, 141, **6:**79,
     80–81, 82
hana (aesthetic concept), **1:**17,
     4:654–655
Hanago, **5:**591
Hanako, **1:**128, **3:338–339, 6:**409
hanamichi, **3:339,** 637–638
Hana no Kai, **3:**651
Hanauer, Mark, *as photographer*,
     5:314
Hanayagi Buyō Kenkyū Kai, **3:**593
Hanayagi Jūsuke II, **3:**593
Hanayagi Jūsuke III, **3:**593
Hanayagi Ryū, **3:**593
Hanayagi Suzushi, **3:339–340,** 583
Hanayagi Yoshijirō (also Nanayagi
     Jūsuke I), **3:**593
hanbok, **2:**223
Hançerli Hanum, **6:**212
Hancock, Bill, **1:**252
Hancock, Shirley, **2:**330
Hand, The, **5:**391
Handbook of Irish Dances, A
     (O'Keeffe and O'Brien), **3:**518
Handbuch der Tanzkunst (Klemm),
     4:686
Handel, George Frideric, **3:**376,
     629, **4:**482, 509, **5:**352, 504,
     680, **6:**47, 679
Handel—A Celebration, **6:**174
Handel Variations, **3:**388
hand gestures
     India, **1:**443, **3:**457, **4:***478*, 489,
        493, 777–478
     Polynesia, **4:**495–496
handkerchief dances
     Algeria, **1:**41
     Argentina, **1:**109
     Armenia, **1:**120
     Bulgaria, **2:**10
     Ecuador, **2:**476
     English Morris dance, **3:**241,
        4:461, 473, *474*
     Indonesia, **3:**504–505
     Jewish traditional, **3:**527, *528*
     Lebanon, **2:**135, 136
     Scottish Sword Dance, **3:**246
     Turkey, **6:**211
     Welsh Morris dance, **3:**250
Han dynasty, **2:**129–130, 144, 148
Handy, W. C., **6:**255
Haney, Carol, **2:**109, 184, **3:**54, 599,
     5:363, **6:**281, 283
hangjang dance, **1:**167
Hanguk chont'ong muyong (Song),
     4:54
Hanguk chont'ong muyong yon'gu
     (Chang), **4:**54
Hanguk Munhwa Poho Hyophoe,
     4:53
Hanguk muyongsa (Kim), **4:**54
Hanguk muyong yon'gu (journal),
     4:53
Hanguk Muyong Yon'guhoe, **4:**53
Hangukui myongmu (Ku), **4:**54
Hang Up, **4:**220
Hanhart, M. and N., **5:***139*
Hani, János, **3:**330, **4:**267
Hanka, Erika, **1:**240–241, 456,
     3:336, **340,** 628, 631, **5:**43
Hank Ballard and the Midnighters,
     5:631
Hanke, Susanne, **6:**10
Hanlon, Lindley, **2:**608
Hanna, Judith Lynne, **4:**370, 371,
     373, **6:**24–25, 186
     as contributor, **4:**362–366, **6:**219,
        381–385
Hannah, David, **1:**141
Hannah, Nigel, **5:***55*
Hannam, Selva, **5:***659*

Hanninen, Maija, **2:**633
Hannon, Théodore, **1:**410
Hannukah Festival, New York City,
     4:306
Hanover family (Great Britain),
     2:394
Hanover Opera Ballet, **1:**11, **3:**132,
     133, 146, 149, **4:**60
Hanover Square Rooms, London,
     3:111
Hanover Theater, Germany, **3:**132
hansam, **1:**166, **2:***223*
Hansberry, Lorraine, **6:**284
Hansel and Gretel (Humperdinck),
     2:265, 396, **4:**627
     Spohr choreography, **5:**684
Hansell, Kathleen Kuzmick, **3:**175
     as contributor, **4:**694–700
Hansen, Al, **6:**362
Hansen, Emil, **1:**399, 497, 511,
     3:105, **5:**427
Hansen, Erwin, **3:**154
Hansen, Joseph, **1:**486, **2:**200,
     3:261, **5:**94, 455, **6:**443
     students, **5:**248, 690
     Swan Lake choreography, **6:**30,
        32, 116
Hansen, Laura, **1:***113*
Hansli le Bossu, **2:**177
Han Song-Jun, **3:**340, 341, **4:**12
Hanson, Willy Blok, **6:**130
Hansteen, Valdemar, **4:**683
     as contributor, **4:**682–683
Hantam, Vincent, **5:**657
Hanţiu, Delia, **5:**387
Hanuš, Jan, **4:**583
Hanvik, Jan Michael, *as
     contributor*, **2:**61–67
Hanya Holm School of Dance, New
     York City, **3:**369, 370–371,
     4:95, 96, **6:**395
Han Young-sook, **3:340–341, 4:**141
ha odori, **5:**27
Haole, **2:**460
Haouka cult, **6:**186
Ha-Poel, **3:**530, 641
Happee, Nellie, **4:**397
happenings, **1:**139, 141–142, 245,
     3:54, 634, **4:**21, **6:**362
Happiness, **1:**121, **3:**125
*Happy Birthday Kirk—Yours,
     Lifetimes, Tina*, **5:**440
*Happy Marriage: The Masked Ball at
     Wanstead* (Hogarth), **4:**315
Happy Repentance, A, **6:**311
Haqqaq, Diane, **2:**497, 498
Haramat Masach, **3:**533
Harangozó, Gyula, **1:**308, 370,
     3:341–342, 412, 415–416,
     419, **4:**529, **5:**402, 569, **6:**66
Harangozó, Gyula, Jr., **3:**418, 419
Harapes, Vlastimil, **5:**245
Haraszti, Emil, **3:**423
Hara Vilasa, **6:**321
Harbin, China, **2:**145
Harbinger, **1:**72, **2:**583, 584
Harbour View Dance Centre, **3:**575
Harding, Cathryn, *as contributor*,
     4:151–152
Harding-Irmer, Patrick, **4:**217
Hard Nut, The, **1:**411, **4:**471, **5:**16
Hardy, Camille, *as contributor*,
     1:418–420, 456–458,
     2:569–574, **4:**186–192,
     419–420, **6:**204–205, 267–290,
     370–371, 447–448
Hardy, Thomas, **1:**454
Harem, **4:**596
Hargitai, Ákos, **3:**421
Hari, Eugene, **5:***561*
"Haricots, Les" (song), **2:**24

Harijs-Suna, **4:**128
Hariraya Dance Company, **5:**172
Harivaṃśa (Indian text), **3:**466
Harju, Otto, **2:**631
Harkarvy, Benjamin, **2:**468, 470,
 5:684
 eclectic style, **6:**292
 Harkness Ballet, **3:**343, 344
 Netherlands Dance Theater,
  4:592, 600, 601, 602, **5:**290
 Pennsylvania Ballet, **5:**131,
  131, 132
 Royal Winnipeg Ballet, **2:**38,
  5:435
Harkness, Rebekah, **2:**404,
 3:342, 610
Harkness Ballet, **1:***478*, **3:342–344**
 Ailey choreography, **1:**57, **3:**577
 Bruhn choreography, **2:**4
 de Mille choreography, **2:**374
 Joffrey Ballet association,
  3:610, 611
 Macdonald as artistic director,
  4:238
 Macdonald choreography, **3:**3
 Saddler, Donald, **5:**489
 Skibine, George, **5:**605
Harkness Foundation, **3:**342, 610,
 611, **5:**489
Harkness House for Ballet Arts,
 New York City, **3:**343, **6:**397
Harkness Youth Dancers, **3:**343,
 344, 389
Harlekins Reise (Hoffmann), **2:**191
Harlem, New York, **2:**334–335,
 4:202, 254, 336, **5:**368, **6:**256
 See also Apollo Theater; Savoy
  Ballroom
Harlem Highlanders, **1:**252
Harlem Nutcracker, The, **2:**20
Harlem Renaissance, **6:**244
Harlequin. *See commedia dell'arte*;
 pantomime
Harlequin, **2:**110, 265
Harlequin, Magician of Love, **2:**264
harlequinade (generic), **1:**391,
 2:191
Harlequinade, **1:**49, 272, 301
 Balanchine choreography, **1:**272
 Balanchine remounting, **4:**610
 Darrell revised version, **2:**349
 Graham solo, **3:**213
 Gusev revival, **3:**328
 Lichine choreography, **2:**509,
  510, **4:**179
 Lopukhov choreography, **2:**585,
  4:226, **5:**468
 McBride performance, **4:**345, 618
 Petipa choreography. *See Millions
  d'Arlequin, Les*
 Ter-Arutunian scenic design,
  6:144
 Vainonen production, **6:**310–311
 Villella performance, **4:**620,
  6:340, *340*
Harlequin à la Watteau
 (pantomime), **2:**85, **5:**71
*Harlequin and Mother Goose, or
 The Golden Egg* (pantomime),
 5:70
"Harlequin Chacoone," **1:**92
Harlequin Doctor Faustus,
 5:350, 518
Harlequin Executed (pantomime),
 5:69, 350
Harlequin for President, **1:**279,
 4:227
Harlequin in April, **1:**459
Harlequin in the Street, **3:**654, **4:**114
Harlequin's Death, **2:**264
Harlequin's Masks, A, **6:**175

*Harlequin's Millions. See Millions
 d'Arlequin, Les*
Harlequin's Museum (pantomime),
 5:70
Harlequin Sorcerer (pantomime),
 5:350
Harlequin Turned Judge, **6:**372
Harlingue-Viollet, *as photographer*,
 2:249
Harmonica Breakdown, **2:**450
Harmonice musices odhecaton
 (Petrucci), **4:**502
Harmonie universelle (Mersenne),
 1:2, 523, **2:**260, **3:**84, 125
"harmonius gymnastics"
 (Alekseeva technique), **5:**476
Harmony of the Spheres, The, **3:***510*
Harmoš, Oskar, **5:**676, **6:**432
Harnasie, **5:**75
Harney, Liam, **3:**518
Harnick, Sheldon, **3:**605
Harold in Italy (Berlioz), **1:**301,
 4:325
Haroun al-Raschid, **1:**455
Harper, Herbie, **3:**598, **6:**257
Harper, Leonard, **1:**520, **6:**257
Harper, Meg, **2:**53, **6:**356
Harper, Peggy, **2:**602, **5:**657,
 6:24, 25
 as contributor, **6:**12–22, 172–174
Harper, Ves, **5:**342
Harper and Stencil, **6:**316
Harpoon Dance, **2:**138
Harpsicord Concerto, **3:**609, 610
Harrington, Rex, **4:***73*, *545*
Harris, Augustus, **5:**72
Harris, Charles K., **6:**281
Harris, Dale, **3:**27
 as contributor, **1:**316–326,
  3:40–46, **5:**34–38
Harris, Diane, **6:**318
Harris, Henry (British dancer),
 3:254
Harris, Henry B. (St. Denis
 manager), **5:**493
Harris, Hilary, **2:**602, 604, 606
Harris, Joan, **4:**676–677, 681
Harris, Lee, **5:**194
Harris, Melissa, *as contributor*,
 1:135–138, 141–144,
  3:619–620, **5:**313–315
Harris, Roy, **5:**561
Harrison, Jane, **4:**369
Harrison, Kate, **4:**217
Harrison, Lanny, **1:***245*
Harrison, Lou, **2:**22, 110, 574
Harrison, Ray, **4:**214
Harrison, Rex, **6:**282
Harris-Warrick, Rebecca, *as
 contributor*, **1:**45–47, 89–90,
  2:97–99, **3:**49–50, **5:**112–113,
  6:87
Harrold, Robert, **6:**212
Harrowing of Hell and
 Resurrection, **4:**106
Harsymchuk (Harasymczuk),
 Roman, **6:**223
Hart, David, **4:**415
Hart, Emma (Lady Hamilton),
 1:126, 199
Hart, Evelyn, **3:344–345,**
 5:436, 685
Hart, Harvey, **6:**132
Hart, John, **1:**155, **3:**345, **5:**54, 55,
 6:64
Hart, Larry, **1:**271, **4:**334, **6:**449
Hart, Oliver, **2:**167
Hartford Ballet, **6:**266
Hartford Opera Guild, **4:**649
Hartford Parks Marionette Theatre,
 4:648

Hartley, Edgardo, **5:**55
Hartley, Marsden, **6:**320
Hartley, Russell, **4:**170
Hartman, Louis, **4:**190
Hartman, Thomas, **4:**143
Hartmann, Emil (Wilhelm Emilius
 Zinn), **1:**515
Hartmann, Jan, **2:**308
Hartmann, Johan Peter Emilius,
 1:510, 514, 515, **3:**39
Hartmann, Leopold, *as
 photographer*, **1:**504
Hartmann, Sadakichi, **5:**182
Hartong, Corrie, **3:345–346,** **4:**590,
 598, 599
 Art of Dance, The, **4:**600
 as contributor, **4:**598–600
Hartt School of Music, Hartford,
 4:649
Haruaki Kai, **3:**440
Haru-pin Ha, **2:**18
Harvard Society for Contempory
 Art, **4:**27
Harvard Summer School of
 Physical Education, **6:**240
Harvard Theater Collection, **2:**387,
 4:168
Harvard University, **4:**26
 Film Study Center, **2:**601–602
 Stravinsky lectures, **6:**5
Harvest 1935, **6:**88
Harvest According, The, **1:**68, **2:**374
Harvest Fête, The, **6:***335*
Harvest Moon Ball, **4:**202
Harvest Time, **4:**63
Harvey, Cynthia, **1:**75, 77, **2:**441,
 6:35
Harvey, Peter, **2:**438
Harvey Girls, The (film), **2:**108
Harwood, Vanessa, **4:**542, **5:***554*
Hasakawa, Itomi, **1:**291, 405
Hasburgh, Rabana, **1:***63*, 279, *280*
Hasegawa Roku, *as contributor*,
 1:60–61, **2:**17–18, 499–500,
  3:90, 339–340, 362–363, 523,
  646, 657–658, **4:**271–272,
  5:33–34, **6:**90, 145, 414–415
Hashi no Kai, **3:**653
Hashiri-mai dances, **2:**6
Hashish, **5:**245
Hasidim, **3:**528, 536, 537, 603, 604,
 4:213
Haskell, Arnold, **1:**310, **2:**401,
 3:263, 391, **4:**27
 British dance history and critical
  study, **3:**282, 285
 Camargo Society founding,
  2:397, **3:**265, 285, **5:**351
 on Losch dance style, **4:**229
 as Netherlands Ballet adviser,
  4:600
 on Nijinska choreographic style,
  4:637–638
 on program notes, **4:**177
 Royal Ballet School directorship,
  5:422
Haskin, Harold, **3:**22
Hass, Henn, **3:**154–155
Hassall, Nanette, **1:**51, 213, 215,
 216, **3:**272
Hassan, Pansy, **3:**574
Hasse, Johann Adolf, **1:**236, 365,
 4:694, 698
Hasselquist, Jenny, **5:**406, **6:**41
Hasson, Thomas, **5:***361*
Hassreiter, Carl, **3:**346, 347
Hassreiter, Josef, **2:**173, **3:**89,
 346–347
 criticisms, **3:**347
 one-act ballet programs, **3:**347
 Red Shoes, The, **1:**540

 as Viennese ballet master, **1:**239,
  240, **6:**387
 See also Puppenfee, Die
Hastalakṣanadīpikā, **4:**80
hastas. See mudrā
Hasting, Hanns, **6:**393
Hastings, Baird, **4:**28
 as contributor, **2:**478–479,
  5:236–238, 526–527
Hatala, Milan, **5:**55
Hata no Kōkatsu, **4:**41
Hata no Ujiyasu, **4:**41
Hatch-Billops Collection, **4:**167
haṭhayoga, **6:**422
Hathor (deity), **2:**482, 483–484
Hatilius, Lucius, **5:**375
Hattori Yuko, **3:**592
"Hat Trick" (skating program),
 6:180
Haubert, Alaine, **1:**77
Hauer, Josef Matthias, **2:**289
Hauer, Steffan, **2:**338
Hauffe, Adolfine, **5:**278
Haugtussa, **4:**677
Haunted Ballroom, The, **1:**540,
 2:105, 400, 590, **3:**41
 de Valois production, **5:**413,
  414, 650
 Helpmann performance, **3:**354
 Markova performance, **4:**268
Haupt, Lorna, **5:**54, 55, 653, **6:**379
Haupt, Walter, **4:**59
Hausa dance, **3:**347–348, **6:**185
Hauser, Nancy Mason, *as
 contributor*, **3:**368–372,
  6:191–192
Hauts de Hurlevent, Les, **5:**164
Haut Voltage, **1:**404
Havana, Cuba, **2:**275, **3:**87
Havas, Ferenc, **3:**417
Haver, June, **4:**420
Have Steps, Will Travel, **4:**546
Havi, Mihály, **3:**412
Havoc, **6:**260
Havoc, June, **2:**326
Hawaiian dance traditions,
 4:496–497
Hawaii Archives of Ethnic Music,
 Honolulu, **4:**170
hawk (as totem), **2:**139
Hawkins, Alma, **1:**421, **2:**316, *319*
Hawkins, Erick, **3:348–350**
 American Document
  performance, **1:**82
 Appalachian Spring performance,
  1:97, **3:***215*
 avant-garde choreography, **2:**290
 Ballet Caravan, **1:**279, 280, *280*
 Bennington School, **1:**421
 dance company, **1:**373, **4:**594
 Dark Meadow performance,
  2:349
 Deaths and Entrances
  performance, **2:**360, **3:***214*
 Graham relationship, **3:**216, 218,
  349, **4:**441
 Letter to the World performance,
  4:153
 liturgical dance, **3:**356
 mask use, **4:**302, *303*
 modern dance technique, **4:441**
 Night Journey performance,
  4:632
 Noguchi scenic design, **4:**659
 Oklahoma! performance, **6:**278
 students, **6:**151
 television documentary on, **6:**137
Hawkins, Frances, **1:**279
Hawkins, John, **3:**376
Hawkins, Mark, **5:**659
Hawkins, Matthew, **6:**66

Rambert Ballet, 1:146, 3:174, 391, 392, 5:298, 299, 299, 300
as Rambert protégé, 3:263
Howard, David, 6:129
Howard, Holly, 1:96, 257, 259, 5:570, 571
Howard, Leslie, 5:274
Howard, Robin, 3:275, 4:216, 220, 221
Howard, Ruth Eleanor, 6:296
Howard University, 6:258
Howe, Elias, 2:257, 339, 6:239
Howes, Dulcie, 2:55, 56, 57, 58, 5:52, 56, 225, 226, 649–650, 651, 657
How Long, Brethren?, 2:580, 6:89, 89
How Near Heaven, 1:77
How Now, Dow Jones? (musical), 1:419
How on Earth, 4:627, 628
Howse, Justin, 2:330
Howson, Mrs. Frank, 1:205
How Steel Was Tempered (Ostrovsky), 2:585
How to Pass, Kick, Fall and Run, 2:292
How to Succeed in Business without Really Trying (musical), 3:54, 6:284
How to Walk an Elephant, 1:59
Hoxha, Enver, 1:33
Hoy Ballet, 1:102–103
Hoyer, Czeslaw and Jan, 4:635
Hoyer, Dore, 1:102, 112, 113, 3:148, 162, 393
Ausdruckstanz, 1:204, 3:393
Hamburg Ballet, 3:149–150, 337
Linke dance re-creations, 4:204
as Linke influence, 4:203
Moses and Aaron Golden Calf dance choreography, 1:436
Schilling association, 5:557
Wigman Dresden school, 3:152, 393
Hoyer, Jean, 1:311
Hoyland, John, 5:304
Hoyos, Cristina, 3:101, 5:674
Hoyt, Charles, 6:268, 270, 447
Hpa (people), 4:566
hringbrot, 3:434
Huaibei Municipal Dance Company, 2:116
Huang, Al, 1:188
Huang Shuquin, 5:130
huapango dance, 4:386
Huayano, El, 1:117, 4:222
Hubay, Jenő, 3:341, 415
Hubbard, John, 1:52
Hubbard Street Dance Company, Chicago, 4:73, 168, 6:266
Hübbe, Nikolaj, 1:506, 2:386, 4:623–624, 5:431, 432
Hubeau, Jean, 1:305, 5:163
Huber, Francie, 5:679
Huberman, Bronisław, 3:529, 4:164
Hubin, Pascale, 2:611
Huckenpahler, Victoria, as contributor, 2:441–442, 6:327–329
Huddle, 3:54, 445
Hudson, Richard, 2:98, 3:29
Hudson Review (publication), 6:299
Hudy, Wolfgang, 3:153
Huelster, Laura, 1:475
Huespedes, 6:325
Huet, Michel, as photographer, 2:87, 4:288, 290, 6:17, 20
Huet-Villiers, François, 2:389
Huffman, Gregory, 3:612, 614, 616

Hawley, Guy, 6:316
Haxho, Zoica, 1:34
Hay. See Hey
Hay, Alex, 1:140, 2:605
Hay, Deborah, 1:215, 243, 2:605, 3:446, 634, 6:363
hayashi, 4:530, 5:592
Haycock, Hill, 1:210
Haydée, Marcia, 3:350–351
as Ballet de Santiago artistic director, 2:125, 127, 3:351
Béjart ballets, 1:292, 406
Brazilian background, 1:533, 4:1
Cragun dance partnership, 2:262, 267, 3:351, 351, 5:102, 107, 6:9
Cranko Medal, 2:268
Initialen R.B.M.E. performance, 2:267
Onegin performance, 2:512
Romeo and Juliet performance, 5:395
Stuttgart Ballet, 2:266, 267, 267, 3:150, 150, 157, 4:1, 5:395, 6:9, 10
Hayden, Melissa, 1:267, 2:269, 426, 3:351–352, 4:610, 5:51, 290, 6:137, 174
Agon performance, 1:30, 4:613
Ashton ballets, 1:152, 159, 3:442, 442
Canadian background, 2:38, 47
Divertimento No. 15 performance, 2:420
Illuminations performance, 3:442, 442
Liebeslieder Walzer performance, 4:179, 179
Medea performance, 4:614
National Ballet of Canada guest performances, 4:541
New York City Ballet roles, 4:616, 617, 617
Haydn, Franz Joseph, 1:46, 237, 402, 2:401, 595, 4:510, 6:338
ballroom dance compositions, 4:511
Markó choreography, 4:266
waltz composition, 6:359–360
Hayes, William B., 3:90, 91
Hayland, John, 1:51
"Haymaker's Jig," 3:517, 5:334
Hayman-Chaffey, Susana, 2:53
Haymarket, London, 4:314
Haymarket Theatre, Boston, 3:86
Haynes, Edward, 2:174
Haynes, Jo, 3:255
Hays, David, 2:420, 4:179
Hays, Kitty. See Hoffman, Gertrude
Haythorne, Harry, 4:625
Hayworth, Rita, 1:193, 193, 441, 2:251, 616
Hazana, 3:271, 4:469, 5:301
Hazard, Paul H., 6:290
Hazelius, Arthur, 3:33, 6:36
Hazen, Shelomoh, 3:603
Hazlitt, William, 5:539
Hazzard-Donald, Katrina (Hazzard-Gordon), 1:450
as contributor, 6:261–263
H'Doubler, Margaret, 2:319, 3:336, 352–353, 444–445, 4:438, 627, 6:242, 295
Headline Vaudeville Production Company, 6:371
Headlong, 1:51
Heads Up (musical), 1:482

Heale, Philippa, 2:405
as contributor, 1:93–94, 114–116, 294–295, 4:232–233, 5:133, 522–523, 565, 670–672
Healey, Katherine, 1:241, 2:513, 513, 5:394
Healey, Sue, 1:215
Healing and the Arts (television series), 3:621
healing rites. See medicinal rites
Healthful Art of Dancing, The (Gulick), 6:240
Healy, Dan, 6:447
Hearn, Fred, 5:585
Hearn, Lafcadio, 4:332
Heart of Maryland, The (Belasco), 6:242
Heart of the Hills (formerly Mzechabuki), 2:96, 97, 3:135, 6:343
Heart of the Matter, The, 4:72
Heart's Labyrinth, 4:81
Hearts of Palm, 4:115
Hear Ye! Hear Ye!, 2:196–197, 5:59
Heat, 6:448–449
Heath, Dave, 5:683
Heath, Ida, 4:520
Heath, William, 5:69
Heathcote, Steven, 1:211, 235
Heather Cornell's Manhattan Tap, 6:102
Heaton, Anne, 3:512, 5:420
Heavenly Horse Studio, 6:406
Hebbel Theater, Berlin, 3:156
Hebei bangzi, 5:130
Heberle, Therese, 1:238, 2:202, 3:313, 6:50, 71, 335
Hébert, Bernar, 6:133
Hebraica Dance Company, 1:431, 3:605
Hebrew scriptures. See Bible, dance in the
Hebridean Weaving Lilt, 3:245
Heckel, Erich, 1:131
Heckelman, Strelsa, 1:206, 208, 499
Heckroth, Hein, 3:305, 625, 627, 5:265, 331, 332
Hecuba, 2:112
Hedda, 4:677, 678
Heeley, Desmond, 2:512
Hegel, G. W. F., 1:23
Heger, Robert, 4:64
Heggawi, Zakariah al-, 2:496
Hegyesi, Aranka, 3:418
Heian period, 2:214, 215, 216, 217
Heiberg, Johanne Luise, 2:502
Heiberg, Peter Andreas, 5:552
Heich, William, 2:601
Heid, Grete, 3:624
Heidegger, "Count" John James, 4:314
Heider, Karl G., 2:600, 6:202
Heikel, Yngvar, 2:631
Heike Monogatari, 4:661
Heike Nyogo no Shima, 3:440
Heine, Heinrich, 1:1, 2:203, 478, 3:175, 180, 5:92, 138, 149
Heine, Thomas T., 1:131
Heinel, Anna, 3:353, 5:35, 89, 6:9, 331
pirouette à la seconde, 1:337
Heinemann, Helen, 3:344
Heinrich, Annemarie, as photographer, 1:111, 5:222, 673, 6:408
Heinz Bosl Foundation, 1:391
Heinzerling, Scott, 5:24
Heise, Peter (Arnold), 1:515
Heistad, Targeir, 4:670
Heitkamp, Dieter, 3:156

Held, Anna, 2:250, 6:268, 269, 447
Held, John, Jr., 1:63
Heldenleben, Ein, 3:215
Helen, 4:358
Helen, Saint, 1:84
Helena and Paris, 2:202, 4:176
Hélénè de Sparte (Helen of Sparta), 1:254, 5:438
Helen of Troy, 1:66, 67, 2:112, 479
Feld performance, 2:583
Fokine production, 3:27
Lichine restaging, 4:178
Robbins performance, 5:359–360
Zorina performance, 6:450
Héliogabale, ou L'Anarchiste Couronné, 1:292, 406, 5:527
Helios, 5:294, 432
Hell, Jutta, 3:156
Hellé, André, 2:361
Hellenism. See Greece, ancient; neoclassical headings
Hellerau Institute. See Jaques-Dalcroze Institute, Hellereau-Dresden
Hellerau-Laxenburg School, 1:98, 239, 2:153, 3:156, 393, 596
Helliniko Choreodrama, 3:300
Helliwell, Rosemary, 4:668
Hellman, Lillian, 1:439
Hello, Dolly! (film), 4:3, 10, 11, 6:204
Hello, Dolly! (musical), 5:373, 6:283
Hello, Everybody (revue), 3:22
Hello, Frisco, Hello (film), 2:615
Hellzapoppin' (film), 4:254
Hellzapoppin' (musical), 4:201, 6:275
Helms-Blasche, Anna, 3:142, 6:377
Helnwein, Gottfried, 4:59
Helpmann, Robert, 1:38, 231, 3:353–357, 4:335, 585, 5:564, 588, 639
American Ballet Theatre Sleeping Beauty revisions, 1:74
Apparitions performance, 5:412
Australian background, 1:207, 3:353–354
Australian Ballet choreography and joint artistic directorship, 1:210, 230, 233, 234, 2:233, 3:356–357, 428
Checkmate performance, 2:115, 3:357
Cinderella travesty role, 2:174, 3:355, 356, 5:55, 6:190
Coppélia performance, 2:200
Display, The, 1:208, 210, 230, 6:378
Don Quixote performance, 1:231, 233, 2:440
emphasis on dramatic expression, 3:265
Fonteyn dance partnership, 3:42, 43, 46, 355, 355
Gorham roles, 3:204
Hamlet, 5:312, 6:117
Hamlet choreography, 1:156, 3:62, 345, 355, 356
Job performance, 3:354, 609
Messel designs, 4:358
Nutcracker performance, 5:14
Patineurs performance, 5:114
Pomona performance, 4:113
Prospect before Us performance, 2:401
Rake's Progress performance, 2:398, 401, 3:354, 354, 5:294
Rambert Ballet guest performances, 3:266, 5:299
Rassine roles, 5:312

Red Shoes (film) performance, 4:325, 5:331, 332, 332, 6:119
Rendezvous performance, 5:342
Royal Ballet, 1:147, 148, 150, 151, 2:401, 403, 3:42, 265, 354–356, 357, 5:414, 415
Sleeping Beauty, 3:227, 5:413, 612
Swan Lake staging and performance, 3:42, 6:33, 33
technique, 3:355
theatrical acting and directing, 3:353–354, 355, 356, 357
travesty roles, 6:190
Wedding Bouquet performance, 6:375
Helsinki City Theater, 2:633
Helsinki College of Dance, 2:632
Helsinki International Ballet Competition, 1:281, 282
Helsinki Theater Museum, 4:160
Helsted, Edvard Mads Ebbe, 1:514, 4:513
Helston Furry Dance, 3:242
Helu, Futa, 4:628
He Makes Me Feel Like Dancin' (film documentary), 2:314–315
Hemminger, John, 3:306
Hempel, Wily, 3:149
Henderson, Betty, 1:450
Henderson, Fletcher, 6:256
Hendrix, Jimi, 6:259
Hendrix Project, The, 6:259
Henery, Salwa, 2:498
Hengler Sisters, 6:316
Henie, Sonja, 3:357–358, 4:210
henna ceremony and dance, 2:489, 3:527, 536, 537
Hennessy, Christine, 5:435, 436
Henney, Jeannette, 6:186
Henningsen, as photographer, 3:559
Hen-Pecks, The (musical), 2:79
Henri II, king of France, 2:570, 3:80, 5:536
Henri III, king of France, 1:2, 275, 276, 277, 398, 2:418
Henri IV, king of France (Henri de Navarre), 1:285, 364, 397
Henrietta, queen consort of England, 1:288
Henriksen, Elvi, 2:387
Henri-Lartigue, Jacques, 5:180–181
Henríque, Graciela, 6:323
Henry, Jenny, 4:217, 5:304
Henry, Louis, 1:237, 2:203, 503, 3:68, 358–359
Paris Opera Ballet, 5:90, 91
Pugni score, 5:277
Taglioni (Filippo) plagiarism accusations, 6:72
Teatro San Carlo ballet school, 6:70
Henry, Pierre, 1:403, 405, 2:288, 4:613
Henry, Sweet Henry (musical), 1:419
Henry, Teuira, 6:77
Henry VIII, king of England, 3:251, 4:307, 313
Henry VIII (Shakespeare), 3:253
Henry IV, or Virtue Rewarded, 6:311
Henry Street Playhouse, New York City, 4:230, 649, 650
Henry Yu Dance Company, 6:83
Hensel, Wilhelm, 5:260
Hentazová, Marie, 1:428
Henze, Hans Werner, 2:267, 471, 3:359
ballet music compositions, 4:517, 5:37
Forsythe ballet scores, 3:51, 522

Holtzinger, Derek, **1:**216
hołubce, **4:**343
Holy Etudes, **4:**635
Holy Women, **4:**627
Holz, Emmy, **2:**528
Holzbachová, Mira, **2:**307
Holzbauer, Ignaz, **1:**236
Holzgeschnitzte Prinz, Der, **2:**153
Homage to a Princess, **2:**510
Homage to Brancusi, **5:**386
Homage to Cervantes, **1:**525
Homage to Chopin, **1:**453
Homage to David Tudor, **3:**619, **5:**314
"Homage to Dimitrije Parlić," **6:**435
Homage to Stravinsky (Ballet-Théâtre Contemporain, 1972), **1:**350
Homage to Stravinsky (Biagi work), **1:**446
Homage to the Queen
  Ashton production, **1:**153, **2:**590, **3:**44, 345, **5:**312
  Messel designs, **4:**358
  Nerina performance, **4:**584
Homage to the Romantic Ballet (Cornell artwork), **1:**137
Homar, Susan, *as contributor,* **5:**273–276
Home, **2:**358, **4:**585, **5:**564
Home Ground, **1:**52
Home Guard, or Love of the Homeland, The, **5:**453
Homelands, **6:**56
Homemade, **2:**605
Homenaje a Schubert, **5:**267
Homer, **2:**269, 270, **3:**287, 291, 293, 372, **4:**106, **5:**41
Homer, Winslow, **2:***53,* **5:***260*
Homerische Symphonie, **3:**340
Hommage à Dore Hoyer, **4:**204
Hommage à Jérôme Bosch, **4:**134
Hommage à Loïe Fuller, **2:**110
Hommage à Meredith Monk, **3:**421
"Hommage à Ravel," **5:**316
Hommage aux Belles Viennoises, **2:**399
Homme au Sable, L', **3:**95
Homme aux Loups, L', **1:**462
Homme et Son Désir, L', **1:**327, **4:**418
Homme Instruit par les Spectacles, L', **1:**284
Homura Yasuyuki, **3:**646
Honda Toshio, **4:**332
Honda Yasuji, **3:**583, 585, 592
Honduras, **2:**64, **3:**120–21
Honegger, Arthur, **1:**93, 327, **3:**24, 213, 394, 590, **4:**64, 517, **5:**132, 237, 294, 438, 439
  Icare orchestration, **3:**431, **4:**184
  as Les Six member, **4:**516
  modern dance scores, **3:**384
Honegger Concertino, **4:**450
Honer, Mary, **2:**200, **5:**113, 414, **6:**375
Honey Dance, **4:**344
Hong Kong, **2:**134, 136
Hong Kong City Contemporary Dance Company, **6:**415
Hong Kong Dance Company, **2:**116
Hong Kong Dance Federation, **6:**415
Hong Kong International Arts Festival, **2:**171
Hong Sin-cha, **3:**372–373, **4:**52
Honi Soit qui Mal y Pense, **2:**595
Honkanen, Anatti, **2:**633
Hønningen, Mette, **3:**373, **5:**430, *430*

Hurok, Sol, **1:**62, 117, 367, **2:**155, 374, 458, **3:**424–425, **4:**29, 51, **5:**193, 205, 580, **6:**198
  American Ballet Theatre, **1:**66, 297
  Ballet Russe de Monte Carlo, **1:**296, 297
  Ballets Russes de Monte Carlo, **1:**310, 313, 315, **2:**37, **4:**269
  Canadian bookings, **2:**37
  Fokine sponsorship, **3:**21, 23
  Holm sponsorship, **3:**369
  Inbal Dance Theater, **3:**449, 532
  international cultural exchanges, **6:**249
  on Maracci, **4:**262
  Nureyev representation, **4:**543
  Royal Ballet, **5:**415
  Royal Winnipeg Ballet, **5:**435
  Sadler's Wells, **3:**267
  Wigman tour, **6:**274, 394
Hu Rongrong, **6:**385
Hürrem Sultan, **6:**212
Hurry, Leslie, **2:**243, **3:**355, *355,* **5:**551, **6:**33
Hurwitz, Jonathan, *as contributor,* **5:**51–56
Hus, Auguste (1735–1781), **3:**426
Hus, Auguste (*fl.* 1820–1850), **1:**238, 427, **2:**282, **3:**426, **5:**514
Hus, Eugène, **2:**353, 413, 464, **3:**68, **5:**147
  Fille Mal Gardée, La, **2:**594, 595, **3:**426
Hus, Pierre, **3:**426
Husain, Ghulam, **3:**425, **5:**63
Husein, Ekrem, **6:**437
Hus family, **3:**426
Hussars, **5:**518
Hussar's Ballad, The, **1:**539
Hustle (dance), **2:**259, **5:**630, 633, **6:**251, 257
"Hustle, The" (song), **5:**633
Hutchinson (Guest), Ann, **3:**426–427, **5:**502
  as contributor, **4:**95–98, 683–684, 683–694, **5:**502–503, 693–694, **6:**450–451
  Bennington School, **1:**421
  Dance Notation Bureau, **4:**95
  Guest marriage, **3:**321
  Jooss ballet notation, **4:**96
  Juilliard dance division, **5:**561
  Labanotation, **4:**95, 97
  Language of Dance Centre, **3:**427, **4:**97, 693
  musical theater, **6:**278
  reconstruction of *Après Midi d'un Faune,* **5:**237
  reconstruction of *La Cachucha,* **2:**405
  reconstruction of *La Vivandière* pas de six, **3:**614, **5:**502
Hutchinson, Michael, **6:**179
Hutchinson, Oatrucua, **4:**229
Hutin, Francisque, **2:**85
Hutton, Betty, **1:**194
Hutton, Geoffrey William, *as contributor,* **1:**38, 230–235, 498–499, **3:**203–204, 622–623, **4:**275–276, **5:**410–411, 563–564
hutzul dance, **3:**38
Huxley, Aldous, **1:**471, **6:**6
Huxley, Hugh Esmor, **4:**15
Hwang Buyng-ki, **3:**372
Hwela (people), **4:**291
Hyakuman, **5:**49
hyangak, **1:**166, **4:**49
Hyatt, Gigi, **3:**337

Hyde, Anne, **4:**602
Hyksos nomads, **2:**490–491
Hyla, Marcus Amplius, **5:**74
Hyman, Prudence, **5:**296, 298
Hymenaei (Jonson masque), **4:**310
Hymen de Zéphire, ou Le Volage Fixé, L', **2:**464
Hymenée et Cryseus, **4:**149
Hymn, **1:**60, **3:**578
Hymnen, **1:**349, **2:**388
Hymns in Space, **6:**392
Hynd, Ronald, **1:**38, 500, **3:**427–428
  Bavarian State Ballet, **1:**390, **3:**150, 427, 428
  English National Ballet, **2:**511, 512, 514, **3:**427
  Merry Widow choreography, **3:**357, 428, **4:**117, 546, **5:**410
  PACT Ballet, **5:**55, 56
  Romeo and Juliet performance, **5:**396
  Sanguine Fan choreography, **2:**574
  Valses Nobles et Sentimentales, **5:**316
Hyper-Dance, **6:**90
Hypernestra, **6:**9
Hypnotic Circus, **3:**79
Hypocrisy, **6:**87
hyporchēma, **2:**158, **3:**428
Hyppomène et Atlante, **2:**364
Hyrst, Eric, **2:***38, 150,* **3:**228, *228,* 229, **428–430,** **4:**380, **6:***130,* 131
Hyvärinen, Nina, **2:**633

Iakobson, Leonid. *See* Yakobson, Leonid
I Am a Dancer (film), **6:**146
I Am a Hotel, **6:**133
I Am Coming Tomorrow, **6:**175
Iancu, Gheorghe, **3:**61, **5:**390
Iancu Jianu, **2:**343, **5:**387
Ianegic, Raluca, **5:**389
Ian Spink Group, **3:**273
Ibbetson, Amy, **1:**459
Iberia, **1:**326
Iberian Monotone, **5:**58
Ibert, Jacques, **1:**305, 460, **2:**440, **3:**24, 394, **4:**3, 517, 635, **5:**60, 237, 439, **6:**201
ibing kursus, **3:**504
ibing rampak, **5:**130
Ibn al-Jazarī, **3:**525
Ibn Khaldūn, **1:**401, **4:**416
Ibsen, Henrik, **4:**674, 678, **5:**425
Ibsen, Lillebil, **4:**674, *674,* 675, 682
I Can Get It for You Wholesale (musical), **5:**408
Icare, **1:**313, 437, **3:431,** **4:**184, **5:***90,* 95, 193, 547, **6:**203
Icaro, **4:**396
Icarus (mythic), **2:**270
Icarus, **1:**416, 493, **3:**391, **4:**36, 37, **5:**639, **6:**314
  Kondratieva performance, **4:**38
  Leventhal scenic design, **4:**154
  Maximova performance, **4:**336
  Vasiliev choreography, **4:**336, **5:**461
ice dancing, **3:431–433**
  Afternoon of a Faun, **1:**28
  Broadway musical, **6:**270
  Curry, John, **2:**297–299
  Dean choreography, **2:**359
  Feld choreography, **2:**584
  Henie, Sonja, **3:**357–358
  Hynd choreography, **3:**428

  Lavrovsky (Leonid) choreography, **4:**132
  Littlefield choreography, **4:**210
  Martins choreography, **4:**274
  Murphy (Graeme) choreography, **4:**479
  Swan Lake, **6:**34
  Torvill and Dean, **6:**179–180
Ice Dancing (Curry show), **2:**299, **4:**274
Ice Follies, **5:**247
Icehouse (rock group), **4:**479
Iceland, **3:434–437**
  theatrical dance, **3:436–437**
  traditional dance, **2:**386, **3:434–436**
Icelandic Dance Company, **3:**437
Ice Maiden, The, **2:**423, **3:**327, **4:**225, **5:**457
Ice Moves, **2:**298
Ice Theater of New York, **2:**299, 359
"Iceworks" (skating program), **6:**180
Ichikawa Danjūrō, **3:437–440,** 593
Ichikawa Danjūrō I, **3:**437, 637
Ichikawa Danjūrō II, **3:**437
Ichikawa Danjūrō III, **3:**437
Ichikawa Danjūrō IV, **3:**437, **4:**333
Ichikawa Danjūrō V, **3:437–438,** **4:**333
Ichikawa Danjūrō VI, **3:**438
Ichikawa Danjūrō VII, **3:438**
Ichikawa Danjūrō VIII, **3:**438
Ichikawa Danjūrō IX, **3:438–439,** 440, **4:**537, **5:**31
Ichikawa Danjūrō X, **4:**439
Ichikawa Danjūrō XI, **3:***439,* **4:**333, 439, **5:**33
Ichikawa Danjūrō XII, **1:**162, 362, **3:439–440,** *582,* 638
Ichikawa Danshirō IV, **3:**441
Ichikawa Ebizō, **3:**437
Ichikawa Ennosuke, **3:440–441**
Ichikawa Ennosuke I, **3:**440
Ichikawa Ennosuke II, **3:**440, **4:***492,* **5:**593
Ichikawa Ennosuke III, **3:**440, **440–441,** **4:**296, 535
Ichikawa Kakitsu VI, **5:**30
Ichikawa Kodanji IV, **5:**31
Ichikawa Ryū, **3:**593
Ichikawa Sadanji I, **5:**31
Ichikawa Sadanji II, **5:**30
Ichikawa Sadanji III, **5:**33
Ichikawa Shinnosuke VI, **5:**32
Ichikawa Somegorō V. *See* Matsumoto Kōshirō VIII
Ichikawa Somegorō VI. *See* Matsumoto Kōshirō IX
Ichimura Uzaemon XV, **1:**248
I Ching (Chinese divination book), **2:**22, 23, 128
Ichinohe, Saeko, **6:**266
Ichinotani Futaba Gunki, **2:**13
Ichiyama Ryū, **3:**593
Ichiyanagi, Toshi, **2:**289
Ich Schenk Mein Herz, **3:**368
Icosahedron, Zuni, **2:**171
icough, **6:**173
ICTM. *See* International Council for Traditional Music
Idang, **3:**341
Ida Rubinstein Ballet. *See* Rubinstein, Ida
Ide, Letitia, **2:**356, **3:**402, 404, **4:**198, 605
Idéal, **2:**471
Idee, Die, **3:**154
Ideen zu einer Mimik (Engel), **3:**556

ideokinesis, **1:**469, 470, **475–476,** **4:**17, 18, 20
Idestam-Almquist, Bengt, **6:**49
idiophones, **3:**114
Idiot, The, **2:**561, **3:***317,* 318, **4:**517
  Eifman staging, **2:**499, **5:**462, 464, 469
  Henze score, **3:**359
Idol's Eye, The (Herbert), **6:**268
Idoménée (Campra), **2:**34
Idoménée (Crébillon), **3:**364, **4:**174
Idomeneo, Rè di Creta (Mozart), **1:**390, **2:**99, **3:**144, **5:**35
Idylle, **3:**226, **5:**605
Idyllic Song, **2:**286, 289
Idzikowski, Stanislas, **1:**146, 428, **3:441–442,** **4:**268, **5:**166, 611
  book on ballet theory, **5:**221, **6:**128
  Cecchetti method manual, **1:**8, 398, **2:**83–84
  International Ballet repertory, **3:**511
  as Massine-type dance, **5:**636
  Polish background, **5:**217
  Rendezvous performance, **5:**342
  students, **2:**2, **3:**61, **5:**312
  Tricorne, Le, **6:**192
Ieharu Tokugawa, **3:**650
ieomoto, **3:**583, 640
Ife (people), **4:**289
If Iphigenia, **4:**21
Ifugao (people), **5:**168
If You Couldn't See Me, **1:**545
Igagoe, **4:**534
Igbo dance, **3:**335, **4:**484, **6:**14, 16, 17, 20, 219
Iglesias, Roberto, **1:**94
Igorot (people), **5:**167–168, *169*
Igrouchki, **3:**22, 24, 27
Ihara Saikaku, **3:**581
Ihy (deity), **4:**498
Ijo (people), **6:**16
Ika (people), **6:**13
ikaki masquerade, **6:**383
Ikayama Prefecture, Japan, **3:**587–588
Ikeda Masuo, **3:**363
ikhien-ani-mhin masquerades, **6:**12, 15–16
Ikkyū, **4:**42
Ikonina, Maria, **2:**414, 416, **5:**453
Ikoon, **4:**596
Ilalaole, Joseph, **3:**396
Ilaminga, **2:**476
Ilbak, Ella, **2:**528
Ileana Cosînzeana, **5:**384
Île des Pirates, L', **2:**503, **3:**358–359, **4:**116, 340
Ileria, **2:**587
Ilga, **4:**127
Iliad (Homer), **3:**287, 293, 372, **4:**106, 499, **5:**41, 283
ilib kuwo, **5:**81, 82
Ilicheva, Marina A., *as contributor,* **4:**36–37, 276–285
Iliescu, Ileana, **5:**386, 387
Ilieva, Anna, *as contributor,* **2:**7–10
I Lived in Those Days, **2:**473
illumination. *See* lighting for dance
Illuminations (Ashton ballet), **1:**152, **3:442–443**
  Beaton scenic design, **1:**395, **3:**442, 443
  Joffrey Ballet staging, **3:**614
  Laing performance, **4:**110
  Le Clercq performance, **3:**442, *442,* **4:**137, **5:**185
  Lynes's photographs of, **5:***185,* 186

Magallanes performance, **4**:246
  as New York City Ballet repertory
    staple, **4**:608
Illuminations, Les (Béjart ballet),
  1:406
Illuminations, Les (Lazzini ballet),
  4:134
Illuminations, Les (Rimbaud
  poems), **3**:442
Illusion d'une Peintre, L', **1**:459
Illusions perdues, Les (Balzac),
  1:144
Illustres Fugitifs, Les, **3**:426
il-mu, **4**:48
Ilongot (people), **5**:168
Ilusion d'un Pientre, L', **5**:232
Ilyushchenko, Elena, **3**:193
Images, **2**:526, **6**:111, 165
Images of a Man, **1**:524
Images of Dance (Moore), **4**:457
Images of Love, **1**:156, **4**:242
*Images of Russian Folk
  Choreography* (Goleizovsky),
  5:445, 481
Imaginaires, Les, **3**:72, **4**:178
Imaginary Dryads, **5**:120
Imaginary Landscape No. 4 (Cage),
  2:22
Imagined Wing, **4**:418
Imago, **4**:650
Imago Danseteater, **4**:679, *680*
Imari, Bamaga, **5**:80
I Married an Angel (musical),
  6:277, 450
Imbrek with the Nose, **3**:89
Imelda e Bonifacio, **2**:209
Imene Deificato, **2**:202
*Imitation Tang Dynasty Music and
  Dance*, **2**:145
Immediate Tragedy, **1**:421, **3**:212
Immigrant, **3**:212, **6**:245
Immortality, **4**:87
Immortal Pierrot, The, **3**:22
Imoseyama, **4**:538
Impact: Hurling Dervishes
  (videodance), **2**:609, *610*
Impatience, L', **1**:288, 424
Impekoven, Niddy, **1**:204, **3**:146,
  443
Imperato, Pascal James, **4**:291–292
  as contributor, **1**:359–361,
    2:421–422
Imperatrice aux Roches, L', **5**:438
Imperial Academy of Music,
  France, **5**:90
Imperiale Regia Accademia di
  Ballo, Milan, **1**:344, **2**:338
Imperial Gesture, **3**:212
Imperial Opera, Vienna. *See*
  Hofopernballett
Imperial Russian Ballet. *See*
  Imperial Theater School,
  Saint Petersburg; Imperial
  Theaters, Russia; Maryinsky
  Ballet
Imperial Society of Dancing. *See*
  Royal Academy of Dancing,
  Great Britain
Imperial Theater of Warsaw, **2**:82
Imperial Theater School, Saint
  Petersburg, **1**:330
  Canziani as teacher, **2**:55
  character dancing classes, **2**:107
  Didelot's students, **2**:416
  Fokine as student and teachers,
    3:14, 15, 16
  Fokine's *Les Sylphides*
    performance, **4**:60
  Legat (Nikolai) class of
    perfection, **4**:143

Nijinsky as student, **4**:639
Nijkinska as student, **4**:633
Stepanov notation, **5**:693–694
Imperial Theaters, Russia, **1**:477,
  478, 485
  Canziani productions, **2**:55
  Diaghilev post, **2**:406–407
  Drigo ballet conducting,
    2:446–447
  end of monopoly by, **5**:159
  Golovin as resident artist, **3**:196
  Minkus as staff composer,
    4:429, 430
  Pavlova leadership of dancers'
    protest, **5**:120–121
  Perrot association, **5**:138,
    140, 141
  Petipa, Jean-Antoine,
    5:147–148, 150
  Petipa, Marius, **5**:150, 151, 159,
    160–162
  Pugni as staff composer, **4**:513,
    5:277
  Saint-Léon post, **5**:500
  Tchaikovsky, Petr Ilich,
    6:115, 116
  Vsevolozhsky abolishment of
    staff composer post,
    4:430, 515
  Zucchi guest performances,
    6:452–453
  See also Maryinsky Ballet
Imperial Theater, Tokyo, **3**:583,
  588, 590
Imperio, Pastora, **2**:521, 567,
  4:222, **5**:674
"Impermanent Art, The"
  (Cunningham), **2**:284–285
Impresario (Hurok), **3**:425
Impressing the Czar, **3**:52
impressionism
  Debussy music, **2**:360, **4**:516
  as Korovin design influence, **4**:56
Impressions de Music-Hall, **1**:247,
  4:635, **5**:95, **6**:432, 444
Impressions of a Buddhist Monk,
  2:159
Impressions of Modern Russia,
  5:476
Impressions of the Bull Ring, **6**:87
Impromptu, **3**:448
Improved Treatment for Horses,
  3:48
improvisation, **3**:443–449
  African-American forms, **2**:324,
    3:447–448, **6**:262
  African music, **4**:486
  Balinese dance, **3**:483, 484
  Brown, Tricia, **1**:543
  commedia dell'arte, **2**:188–189,
    3:444
  contact, **3**:446–447, *447*
  Grand Union, **3**:235–236
  group, **3**:447
  Holm technique, **3**:371
  Humphrey choreography, **3**:404
  Iranian dance, **3**:513–514
  Jooss, Kurt, **3**:625
  Laban productions, **4**:91
  Lebanese solo, **4**:135
  Mbuti dance, **4**:344
  medieval instrumental music,
    4:501, 502
  Middle Eastern dance, **4**:404
  modern dance training, **4**:442
  Negri endorsement, **4**:580
  Palucca, Gret, **5**:65
  southern African dance, **5**:662
  step dances, **3**:518
  Yemenite dance, **3**:449
Improvisation and Aria, **2**:473

*Improvisations on a Chicken Coop
  Roof*, **1**:543
Impulse (journal), **4**:17
Impulse Dance Company, **4**:627
Imre, Zoltán, **3**:419, *419*, **4**:470,
  6:66–67
IMZ. *See* International Music
  Center
IMZ Dance Screen, **2**:610, 611, 612
In a Rehearsal Room (film), **3**:306
Inbal Dance Theatre, **3**:449–450,
  532, 533, *533*, 537, **4**:155–156,
  5:201, 638
Inca (people), **2**:475, 476,
  5:142–143
Incantations, **2**:466
Incas du Pérou, Les, **3**:450
Incense, **5**:46, 206, 492, 497
Inceste, L', **2**:45
In Circles, **6**:282
Incohérence, **4**:577
Incompatibles, Les, **4**:447
Inconnue, L', **1**:403, **4**:63
Inconsequentials, **2**:374
Incontri con la danza (Grillo ed.),
  3:555
*Incoronazione di Corinna in Roma,
  L'*, **4**:258
Incubus, **3**:610
Indagine Classica, **3**:389
In Dahomey (musical), **2**:25,
  5:180, *181*
indang, **3**:500
Indarsabha, **5**:582
In Defense of Murena (Cicero),
  5:374
In Defense of the Poet Archias
  (Cicero), **5**:374–375
*Indépendance Americain, ou
  L'Apothéose de Washington, L'*,
  2:443
Independent (British newspaper),
  3:285
Independent (dance company),
  5:475
Indes Galantes, Les, **1**:247, **2**:238,
  3:50, 365, **450–451**, **4**:119,
  122, **5**:34, 88, *92*, 96, 306,
  307, **6**:87, 331
  Favart parody, **4**:122
  Lyonnois performance, **4**:236
  Mouret parody, **4**:475
Indeterminant Figure, **4**:531
Index (film dance), **2**:605
Index to Dance Periodicals (Hall),
  4:167
India, **3**:451–470
  audiences, **1**:161
  bharata nāṭyam, **1**:443–444
  Bollywood film musicals,
    2:621–629
  castanet counterpart, **2**:78
  chhau, **2**:117–119
  Chinese dance, **2**:136
  costume, **2**:223–225, **4**:70–71, *70*
  dance research and publication,
    3:469–470, **4**:159, **5**:510–511
  notation, **4**:693
  devadāsī, **2**:394–395
  epic sources of dance, **1**:160, 161,
    168, **2**:118, **3**:464–466
  kathakali, **1**:162, 170, 181–182,
    188, **2**:223–224, **3**:660–663
  yakṣagāna, **6**:413
  history of dance, **1**:168–171,
    181–182, **3**:451–461, **6**:86–87
  avant-garde, **2**:104
  body movements, **1**:162,
    4:477–478
  bon odori origination, **1**:496
  fan usage, **2**:570, *571*

folk dance costume, **2**:225
improvisation, **3**:448
Islamic influence, **1**:171, 182
mime, **4**:424
modern dance, **5**:521, 580–581
musical accompaniment, **4**:494
shadow theater, **1**:178, *178*
Sikh tradition, **5**:598–599
See also Nāṭyaśāstra
kathak, **2**:224, 468, *468*, 623,
  3:658–660
kṛṣṇāṭṭam, **1**:171, **3**:456, 464, 465,
  467, **4**:65–66
Kuchipudi, **1**:169, **3**:468, 508,
  4:69–71, **5**:330, **6**:320–321
kūṭiyāṭṭam, **3**:456, *459*, 660,
  4:79–80
martial arts, **1**:185, 186, 187–188
mask and makeup, **4**:298–299
mōhiniāṭṭam, **1**:170, **3**:457, *460*,
  468, 508, **4**:443
nautch concept, **1**:178, **4**:578
new directions in dance,
  3:468–469, **4**:355
Odissi, **5**:22–23
philosophy of dance, **1**:16, 169,
  3:461–464, 470
Rādhā-Kṛṣṇa theme in dance,
  1:94, 160, **3**:464–468
rās līlā, **5**:311, *312*
Teyyam, **6**:147
yoga, **6**:421–422
See also Manipuri dance drama;
  *specific performers and dance
  types*
Indiana, Robert, **6**:362
Indianapolis Ballet, **4**:478
Indiana University, **1**:430, **6**:292
Indian Dance Theatre, New York
  City, **5**:292
Indian Hill, Stockbridge,
  Massachusetts, **6**:363
Indian Morning, **6**:73
Indians, American. *See* Native
  American dance
Indian Summer, **5**:602
*Indigenous Performing and
  Ceremonial Arts in Canada: A
  Bibliography* (Buller ed.), **2**:49
Indio-American Folklore
  Association, **6**:301
indlamu, **5**:644
Indomitable Agnes, The (television
  documentary), **2**:375
Indonesia, **3**:470–507
  background and overview,
    1:172–177, **3**:471–473
  Chinese dance exchanges,
    2:136
  costume, **2**:231–232
  fan usage, **2**:570, *571*
  influence on Malaysan dance,
    2:229
  pencak movement system,
    5:130–131
  baris, **1**:366, **2**:232, **3**:644
  barong, **2**:232, *232*, **3**:473, **4**:297
  Balinese ceremonial dance,
    3:447–480, **5**:356, 357
  costume, **2**:231–232
  trance rituals, **6**:185, 186,
    187, 188
  Balinese dance theater,
    1:175–176, **3**:480–486,
    4:264–265
  Balinese dance traditions, **1**:160,
    163, 174–177, **2**:571, **3**:471,
    472, **473–477**, 505
  anthropological studies, **4**:369
  dance education, **3**:476
  rhythmic patterns, **4**:492

Indonesia, *continued*
Balinese mask dance theater,
3:486–492, **4:**297–298, *297*,
5:356
Calonarang, **1:**174, 176, *176*, 178
dance research and publication,
3:505–507, **4:**158, 159, **5:**167,
6:297
libraries and museums,
4:158–159
gamelan, **3:**112–116, 472
Javanese dance traditions,
1:162–163, 172–174, *175*,
2:228, **3:**471, 472, **492–499,**
504, 505, **5:**357, 523–524
abstractions, **4:**494
costume, **2:**231
court dances, **3:**493–496
dance education, **3:**504
martial arts, **1:**187
masks, **4:**298, *298*
rhythmic patterns, **4:**492
theatrical dance, **3:**496–499
trance ritual, **6:**188
Javanese puppet play, **1:**160,
172–174, 179, **4:**298
jangér, **3:**484, 485
kebiar, **3:**666–667, **4:**264
légong, **1:**160, 175, **2:**231–232,
231, **4:**146–147
outlying islands, **3:**504–505
Sumatran dance traditions,
3:471, **499–501,** 504, 505
Sundanese dance traditions,
1:174, **3:**501–504, **4:**297, 497
topéng, **4:**297–298, *297*
wayang, **1:**179, **3:**476, 485,
6:367–370
*Indorf et Rosalie, ou L'Heureuse
Ruse, L',* **2:**415
Indrani, **1:**442, **3:**507–508
Indus Europa, **5:**64
Inediti teorico-tecnici (Cecchetti),
3:555
Inès di Castro, **2:**55, 208–209, **4:**279
Inesitia, **3:***10*
Infante C'est Destroy, **6:**132
Infernal Games, **6:**66
Inferno (Dante), **1:**149
Infinity, **2:**359
Informer, The, **2:**374
In Full Swing, **5:**25
Ingber, Judith Brin, **3:**535
as contributor, **1:**431–432,
3:526–535, 641, **4:**155–156
Ingegneri, Angelo, **4:**188
Ingegno supera l'Età, L', **3:**176
Ingemann, Bernhard Severin,
1:507
Ingemarsson, Evan, **6:**45
Ingenieros, Cecilia, **1:**112
Inglesby, Mona, **3:**508–509, **5:**588
International Ballet, **1:**403, **2:**525,
3:269, 442, 511
on Sergeyev (Nicholas) *Swan
Lake* reconstruction, **6:**33–34
Swan Lake performance, **3:***512*
Inglestone, Ruth, **4:**306
In G Major (formerly *Concerto in
G*), **4:**615, 618, **5:**366
ingough, **6:**172–173
Ingres, Jean Auguste, **2:**571
In Honor of Dance (Slonimsky),
3:328
Inigo, Corazon Generoso,
5:172, 173
Initialen R.B.M.E., **2:**267, *267*,
3:350, **4:**1, 245
Initiation, The, **5:***255*, 256
initiation dances
Balinese males, **3:**479–480

central and east Africa, **2:**87, 88,
89, 91, *91*, 211–212
!Kung San, **5:**664
Melanesia, **4:**352
Native American, **4:**550, 567, 568
southern Africa, **5:**579, *645*, 646
sub-Saharan Africa, **6:**13
West Africa, **6:**382–383, *383*
See also circumcision ritual;
puberty ritual injuries. *See*
dance medicine
*Inkas, oder Die Eroberung von Peru,
die,* **2:**202
Inkoe and Yarico, a Historical Ballet
(opera), **2:**64
Ink Spots, **1:**52
Inlets and *Inklets 2,* **2:**293, **5:**18
Inman, Tania, *as contributor,*
1:417–418
In Memoriam (Tesla), **2:**53, 54
In Memory of . . ., **4:**622, **5:**367
Inner Appearances, **5:**293
Inner Mongolia, **2:**135–136, *139*
"Innocent Ivan and His Two
Brothers," **1:**324
In Nomine, **2:**512
Innsbruck, Austria, **1:**241–242
Inns of Court, London, **4:**309, 312
Manuscripts, **1:**104, **5:**115, 116,
118, 345, **6:**350
In Old Kentucky (vaudeville show),
5:368
I Not I, **3:**575
Inoue Yachiyo, **3:**339
Inozemtseva, Galina V., *as
contributor,* **1:**517, **3:**99,
196–197, **4:**38, **5:**449–457
In Paradisum, **4:**71, 72
In Performance from Wolf Trap
(television series), **6:**139
Inquest, **3:**402
Inquisition, **3:**6, **4:**386, 664
*Insalade. See Salade
Insan-Insan,* **6:**212
Insatiate Countess (Marston), **3:**253
Inscape, **4:**157
Insect Comedy, The, **3:**371
Insects and Heroes, **6:**108, *108*
Inside Dance (Louis), **4:**230
Inside U.S.A. (revue), **1:**395, 441,
6:90, 280
Insolvent River, **4:**627
Inspector-General, The, **4:**185,
5:462, **6:**342
Installations, **2:**296
Institut Chorégraphique, Paris. *See*
Université de la Danse
Institut de Teatro de Barcelona,
5:675
Institute de Recherche et de
Coordination Acoustique
Musique, Paris, **1:**406
Institute for Popular Culture,
Hungary, **3:**423
Institute for Theater Research,
Bergen, **4:**683
Institute for Theatre Research,
Copenhagen, **2:**387, 388
Institute of African Studies, Ghana,
3:167, 168, 170, **4:**158
Institute of African Studies, Kenya,
4:158
Institute of Archaeology and
Ethnography, Armenia, **1:**121
Institute of Folk Studies, Germany,
4:161
Institute of Musicology, Folk Dance
Department, Hungary, **3:**423,
4:373
Institute of Research in the Arts,
Moscow, **5:**483

Institute of Theater, Music, and
Cinema, Leningrad, **5:**483
Institute of Theater Arts, Moscow,
5:483
Institute of Theater Studies,
Vienna, **1:**243
Institute of the History of the Arts,
Saint Petersburg, **5:**483
Institutes of Rhythm, Moscow and
Leningrad, **5:**478
Institut für den Wissenschaftlichen
Film, Göttingen, **2:**601
Institutional Linkages Program,
1:80–81
Institut Jaques-Dalcroze, Geneva.
See Jaques-Dalcroze Institute,
Geneva
Instituto Nacional de Bellas Artes
of Mexico, **4:**198
Instituto Nacional Superior del
Profesorado de Folklore,
Argentina, **1:**109
instruction books. *See* technical
manuals
Intabulatura de lauto (Dalza),
4:502, **5:**114
*Integrative Action of the Nervous
System, The* (Sherrington),
4:15
Interconnexions, **3:***574*, 575
Interdenominational Church, San
Francisco, **4:**212
Intérieur, **4:**602
Interim, **4:**531–532
Intermède, **4:**107–108, **5:**684
Intermediate and Advanced
(videotape), **6:**129
Intermediate Steps in Ballet (French
and Demery), **6:**128
intermedio, **1:**353, **2:**191,
3:509–511, 542, 543
Negri choreography, **3:**511,
4:505, 581
pastorales, **5:**113
scenic designs, **5:**534–535
Intermezzi (Callot), **2:**27
*intermezzo. See intermedio
Intermezzo,* **1:**73, **2:**584, *584*
intermissions, introduction of, **3:**69
Intermittences du Coeur, Les, **3:**643,
5:164
International Archive of Dance,
Paris. *See* Archives
Internationales de la
Danse, Les
International Ballet, **1:**403, **2:**525,
3:62, 269, 442, 508–509,
511–512
Nijinska's *Brahms Variations,*
4:638
Sergeyev (Nicholas) *Swan Lake*
re-creation, **3:**511, *512*,
6:33–34
Shearer, Moira, **5:**588
Turner, Harold, **6:**214
World War II inception,
3:508, 511
International Ballet du Marquis de
Cuevas. *See* Grand Ballet du
Marquis de Cuevas
International Ballet of New York,
3:224, *225*
International Center for African
Music and Dance, Ghana,
3:168, 169
International Choreographers
Commissioning Program,
6:251
International Choreographers
Workshop, **1:**80, **6:**251

International Choreography
Competition, **1:**502, **3:**305
International Council for
Traditional Music, **2:**386–387,
3:36, **4:**367, 370, 371
Study Group on
Ethnochoreology, **2:**546,
4:375, **5:**211, 220
International Council of Ballroom
Dancing, **5:**351
International Council of Folk
Festivals, **2:**546
International Council of
Kinetography Laban, **3:**427,
4:32, 94, 96
International Council of the USA
International Ballet
Competition, **3:**610
International Cultural Society of
Korea, **4:**55
International Dance Council,
5:44, 48
International Dance Critics
Conference, **1:**81, **6:**251
International Dance Teachers
Association, Great Britain,
3:279
Internationale (anthem), Duncan
choreography, **1:**232
International Festival of Dance,
Paris, **1:**232, **3:**419, **4:**607
International Film and Videotape
Dance Festival (1981), **5:**48
International Folkloristisch
Danstheater, **4:**586, 598
International Folk Music Council.
See International Council for
Traditional Music
International Modern Dance
Festival, **1:**81, **6:**251
International Music Center (IMZ),
Vienna, **2:**610, **6:**135
International Music Festival,
Venice, **3:**51
International Revue, The, **1:**117,
2:424
International Sailors, **4:**444
International Symposium on the
Scientific Aspects of Dance,
4:17
International Theater Institute,
1:281, **3:**419, 610, **5:**44
Internet, dance web sites, **2:**612,
6:300
Interplay (Mounsey), **5:**53
Interplay (Robbins), **1:**338, **2:**376,
5:360, **6:**279
Joffrey Ballet revival, **3:**614
Kidd performance, **3:**10
Kriza performance, **4:**63
New York City Ballet revival,
4:608
practice clothes as costume,
2:245
interpretive dance. *See*
Ausdruckstanz; free dance
movement
Interrupted Song, The, **2:**499, **5:**462
In the Company of Angels, **1:***217*
In the Glow of the Night, **6:**366
In the Land of the War Canoes
(Curtis), **2:**601
In the Middle, Somewhat Elevated,
3:53
In the Midst, **2:**309
In the Name of the Holocaust, **5:**18
In the Night, **4:**273, 285, 345, 614,
618, **5:**364, 365, 597
In the Upper Room, **1:**76, 77, **6:**153,
153, 154

Intimate Letters, **2:**308, **5:**575, **6:**43
Intimate Theater, Moscow, **3:**193
intore dance, **6:**20
Into the Hopper, **1:**141
Into the Life, **3:**578
Into the Woods (musical), **6:**287
Intrada, **6:**362
intrata/intrada, **2:**517
Intravaia, Toni, **4:**212
Intrecerea, **5:**388
Intro-Dans (formerly Studio L.P.), **4:**594, 595, 598
Introdução ao Princípio das Coisas, **5:**235
Introduction et Allegro, **3:**416
Introspection, **2:**604
Inuit (people). *See* Eskimo
I Nuovi Balli Italiani del Maestro Nicola Guerra, **3:**321
Inupiaq (people), **4:**570, 571
învârtita dances, **5:**379, 380, *380,* 381
Invention, **3:**403
Inventions, **2:**296, **4:**37
Inverzinni, Pepa, **2:**199
In Vienna, **2:**161
Invisible Dance, **2:**609
Invisible Frontiers, **5:**436
Invitation, The, **3:512–513**
 Georgiadis scenic design, **3:**136, 512
 MacMillan choreography, **4:**241
 Mason performance, **4:**307
 Seymour performance, **5:**574, *574*
 Wall performance, **6:**357
 Wells performance, **6:**380
Invitation to Butō, **3:**657
Invitation to the Ballet (de Valois), **2:**397
Invitation to the Ballet (Kelly film), **4:**3
Invitation to the Dance (film), **4:**3, **6:**183, 425
Invitation to the Dance (Mazumdar), **3:**175
Invitation to the Dance (Weber), **3:**19, **6:**360
Invitation to the Dance (Zajlich ballet), **6:**441
Invocation to the Thunderbird, **5:**585
Iofiev, Moissey, **4:**38, **5:**485
Iolanta (Tchaikovsky), **6:**116
Ionesco, Eugène, **3:**12, **5:**432
Ionian islands, **3:**296
Iorgulescu, Liliana, **5:**389
Ipermestra (Hasse), **1:**236
Iphigenia in Aulis (Humphrey-Weidman choreography; 1935), **3:**399
Iphigenia in Tauris (Bausch choreography; 1975), **1:**388
Iphigénie (Gluck-Angiolini ballet pantomime), **3:**187, 188–189
Iphigénie en Aulide (Gluck opera), **5:**35, **6:**47
 Noverre choreography, **1:**87, 89, **2:**363, **3:**117, 188, 190, 257, 353, **4:**698, 700
Iphigénie en Tauride (Gluck opera), **3:**188–189, 190, **6:**47
 Blondy choreography, **1:**464
Ipi Tombi (musical), **6:**22
Ippen, Evelyn, **1:**468
Ippolita, duchess of Calabria, **2:**204, 205
Ippolito, **5:**683
Ippolitov-Ivanov, Mikhail, **3:**186
Ippon Gatana, **4:**534
Ira di Achille, L', **6:**70

irama concept, **3:**116
Iran, **3:513–515**
 hobby-horse dance, **4:**406
 Islamic dance aesthetics, **1:**18–19
 Kurdish dance, **4:**78–79
Irani, Ardeshir, **2:**622
Iranian National Ballet, **2:**427
Ireland, **3:515–520**
 dancing masters, **3:**516
 theatrical dance, **2:**397, **3:519–520**
 traditional dance, **3:515–519**
 clogging antecedents, **2:**179
 costume, **5:**696
 hornpipe, **2:**379
 jig, **2:**35, 179, **3:**607, 608, *608*
 reels, **5:**333, 334
 research and publication, **3:**518–519
 step dancing, **3:**517–518, *517, 518,* 519, **5:**694–696, 695, *698*
 wedding festivities, **3:**33
Ireland, David, **1:**141, **2:**461
íreme (spirit), **2:**274
Irene (musical), **6:**272, 273
Irene Holm, **5:**432, 553
Irian Jaya, **3:**504, **4:**496
Iribarne, Fraga, **1:**101
Iribiri, **1:**536
Irigwe (people), **6:**13
Irina Kolpakova (film), **4:**36
Iris, **5:**384
Irish Ballet Company. *See* Irish National Ballet
Irish Dancing Commission, **3:**517
Irish Fantasy, **2:**314, **4:**631
Irish jig, **2:**35, 179, **3:**249, 607, 608, *608*
Irish National Ballet, **3:**518, 520
Irish Republic. *See* Ireland
Irish Theatre Ballet, **3:**520
"Irish Washerwoman, The" (tune), **3:**249
Irish World Music Center, Limerick, **3:**519
Irkutsk Story, The (Abruzov), **3:**308
irmandades, **1:**526
Ironic Rite, **4:**271
Ironside, Robin and Christopher, **1:**153, *154,* **2:**243, **6:**63, 64
Iroquois dance, **4:**554–555, 556–557, *557,* 574
 False Faces, **4:**554
 gender roles, **4:**553
 Kurath studies, **4:**78
Irsaliev, Arstanbek, **4:**87
Iruya, Salta, **1:**109
Irving, Henry, **2:**262, 525, **4:**190
Irving, Robert, **2:**368, **3:520–521,** **4:**29, 114, 115, 179, 613, 623
Irwin, Bill, **2:**609, **4:**425
Irwin, Robert T., **3:**104
Isaac, Mister, **2:**337, 338, **3:521–523,** **4:**106, **5:**251, 506, 518, 519, 621, **6:**175
 bourrée compositions, **1:**517
 hornpipe, **3:**377
 minuet, **4:**433
 Weaver as protégé, **6:**372, 373
Isabella d'Este, **3:**322, 509
Isabella of Aragon, queen of Spain, **1:**364, **3:**6
Isabelle's Dance, **3:**52
Isaby, *as photographer,* **1:**327, **5:**335
Isačenko, Claudia, **6:**433
Isadora, **1:**292, **4:**243–244, **5:**100, 187, 206, 418, **6:**435, *435*
Isadora Duncan Dancing (Walkowitz), **1:***131*

"Isadora Duncan School in Moscow, The" (Roslavleva), **5:**484
Isaev, Stanislav, **5:**467
Isakov, Pavel, **2:**435
Isaksen, Lone, **3:**342, 610
Isamu Kawai, *as photographer,* **3:**339
Isareva, Margarita I., *as contributor,* **4:**443–446
Isatchenko, Claudia, **3:**317
Isaura. See Filleule des Fées, La
Isbert, Pär, **6:**44
iscathamiya, **5:**648
Ise *kagura* tradition, **3:**584, 642
Isfahānī, al-, **4:**416
Isham, Mark, **2:**359
Ishan (people), **6:**12, 15–16
Ishii Baku, **2:**155, 159, **3:**523, 590, **4:**51, **5:**33
Ishii Baku Dance Company, **3:**523, **6:**415
Ishii Kaoru, **3:**523
Ishii Maki, **3:**523
Ishii Mitsutaka, **2:**18
Ishikiri Kajiwara, **3:**658, **4:**535
Ishtar, **2:**378, **5:**438, **6:**66
Ishtar of the Seven Gates, **5:**495
Isidore of Seville, **6:**193
Isin-Larsa period, **4:**356
Isis (deity), **2:**482
Isis, **1:**464, **2:**465, **4:**235, **5:**39
iskesta, **2:**531–532, 533
Iskusstvo baletmeistera (Zakharov), **6:**443
Isla, Camaron de la, **3:**10
Isla de los Ceibos, La, **5:**270
Islam and dance, **523–526,** **4:**402, 403, 410
 aesthetics, **1:**18–19
 Afghanistan, **1:**26–27
 African masking, **4:**291
 Algeria, **1:**40–42
 Arabian Peninsula, **1:**101–102
 Arabic music, **4:**487–488
 Bangladesh, **1:**362
 Brazilian Moorish influences, **1:**527
 Cameroon, **2:**33
 Egypt, **2:**487–490, 491–492
 European traditional dance, **2:**537, 551, 552
 flamenco link, **3:**6
 Ghana, **3:**164, **6:**19
 Hindu artistic interaction, **3:**659, 660
 India, **1:**171, 182, **3:**452, 659, 660
 Indonesia, **1:**176, 179, **2:**231, **3:**471, 493, 499, 500, 501, 504
 Iranian prohibitions, **3:**514–515
 as Jewish ethnic dance influence, **3:**537
 Kurds, **4:**79
 Macedonia, **6:**429
 Malaysia, **4:**249–250
 Nigeria, **3:**347–348
 North Africa, **4:**664–665, 666
 Philippines, **2:**230
 research and publication, **4:**416–417
 Turkey, **6:**208, 209, *209*
 Yemen, **6:**417, 418–419
 See also Sufi dance
Islamey, **3:**20
Islamova, A., **6:**83
Island Birds, Eshkol-Wachman notation, **4:***690*
Island, Dance of Atoms, **6:**435
Island of Dance, Gorky Park, Moscow, **5:**460, 478
Isle of Man, **3:**250–251

Isle of the Amazons, The, **5:**216, **6:**73
Ismael Ivo Company, Stuttgart-Weimar, **3:**157
Ismail, Omar, **4:***250*
Ismailov, Gainula, **3:**665
Ismatova, Yulduz, **6:**307
Ismène, **3:**116
Isoko (people), **4:**289
Isouard, Nicolò, **2:**171
Israel, **3:526–539**
 background, **3:526–535**
 dance education, **3:**535
 Eshkol-Wachman notation system, **4:**690, 692
 ethnic dance, **1:**431, 432, **3:535–539,** 641, **5:**638
 folk dance movement, **3:**530–531, 537–539, 605, 641
 Kraus, Gertrud, **4:**58–59
 Levi-Tanai, Sara, **4:**155–156
 Inbal Dance Theatre, **3:**449–450, 532
 libraries and museums, **4:**164
 theatrical dance, **2:**509, **3:**528–530, **4:**58–59, 531, 532
 Yemenite, **3:**449, 527, 529, 531, 531–352, 535, 536–539, **4:**155
 See also Jewish dance traditions
Israel Ballet, **3:**534, **4:**58
Israel Ballet Theatre, **3:**530
Israel Dance Library, **3:**535
Israel Dance Quarterly (periodical), **3:**535
Israel Ethnic Dance Project, **3:**537, 641
Israel Festival, Jerusalem, **3:**534
Israel Folk Dance Institute, **1:**432, **3:**605
Israeli Dance Festival, **1:**431
Israilovski, Aleksandar, **6:**434, 435
Issé (Destouches), **5:**113
Isse Moyano, Marcelo, *as contributor,* **1:**102–103, 111–114
Istanbul State Ballet, Turkey, **6:**212
Ištar, **2:**113, **3:**72, **4:**184, **5:**245, 690
Ister Theater, Belgrade, **6:**436
Istomina, Anna, **1:**302
Istomina, Avdotia, **1:**86, **2:**596, **3:539–540,** **4:**36, 279, 280, **5:**207, 453, 567, **6:**451, 452
Istomina, Maria (Cyd Charisse pseud.), **2:**108
Istoriia tantsev (Khudekov), **5:**482
Italian Beggar, **4:**459
Italian National Academy, **3:**552, 553
Italian Opera House, London, **6:**159
 See also King's Theatre
Italian Radio-Television, **2:**480
Italian school. *See* ballet technique, major schools; Cecchetti method; Scala Ballet
Italian Suite, **2:**507
Italian-Viennese Ballet (Irene Sironi Ballet), **3:**50
Italy, **3:540–558**
 classical dance education, **3:**551, **552–553**
 Caroso dance manuals, **2:**73
 Cornazano dance manuals, **2:**204–205
 dancing masters, **2:**336–337, 338, 380, 527, 542–543, 603, **4:**579–583
 Italian versus French schools, **1:**347
 Viganó (Salvatore) and Henry (Louis) royal school, **3:**358

Italy, *continued*
    See also ballet technique,
        history of; ballet technique,
        subhead major schools;
        Cecchetti method
    dance research and publication,
        3:553–558, **5**:505–506
    libraries and museums,
        4:161–162
    music, **4**:505–506
    opera, **1**:287–288, **2**:446
    Renaissance and Baroque dance
        traditions, **3**:542–545
        ballo and *balletto*, **1**:351–355
        barriera, torneo, and *battaglia,*
            1:368–369, **4**:580
        bassedanse, **1**:379–380, **5**:620
        bergamasque, **1**:428
        branle, **1**:523
        canary, **2**:50–51
        ciacona and *passacaglio,* **2**:98
        commedia dell'arte, **2**:188–189
        figure dances, **2**:591
        forlana, **3**:49
        galliard, **3**:107–109, **4**:580, *580*
        giga, **3**:*172, 607*
        intermedio, **3**:509–511
        libretti, **4**:173, 174
        notation, **4**:683
        pastorales, **5**:113
        Renaissance fêtes and
            triumphs, **5**:340
        révérence, **5**:344–345
        saltarello, **5**:505–507
        tarantella, **6**:104–105
        turnout position, **6**:215
    Roman era. *See* Roman Empire
    stage design and machinery,
        5:534–537
    theaters for dance,
        6:155–156, *159*
    theatrical dance, **3**:552–553
        Aterballetto, **1**:196
        dance on television, **6**:134
        Fracci as first diva, **3**:60
        theatrical lighting, **4**:187–188
        See also subhead Renaissance
            and Baroque dance traditions
            above; Rome Opera Ballet;
            Scala, La; Teatrodanza
            Contemporanea di Roma;
            *specific choreographers and
            performers*
Itan Kahanai, **5**:521
Itchū, **3**:646
It Doesn't Wait (videodance),
    2:609
Itelman, Ana, **1**:112
Itelmeny (people), **5**:447
It Happens on Ice (ice show), **4**:210,
    6:34
Itineraries, **1**:349
Ito, Michio, **1**:482, **3**:211, 385,
    558–560, 5:46
    Hellerau association, **3**:596
    Horton association, **3**:386
    Noguchi masks, **4**:659
    students, **2**:516, **3**:559, **4**:38
Ito, Robert, **4**:*540*
Ito, Sachiyo, *as contributor,* **3**:126,
    5:25–28
Ito, Teiji, **2**:520
It's Always Fair Weather (film),
    2:109, **4**:3, 10–11
Itten, Johannes, **1**:132, 385
Ivancan, Ivan, **6**:427
Ivanitsky, P. I., **6**:224
Ivanov, Ivan, **5**:150
Ivanov, Konstantin, **5**:9, 150, 320,
    557, 606

Ivanov, Lev, **1**:45, 74, 255, 486,
    3:560–568, 5**:149
    archival materials, **4**:165
    ballet technique, **5**:227
    Cecchetti collaboration, **2**:82
    choreographic symphonism,
        5:456
    Cinderella second act
        choreography, **2**:82, **3**:565
    Coppélia revision, **2**:200
    Don Quixote performance, **2**:436
    Drigo compositions, **2**:446
    Fille Mal Gardée, La, **2**:596
    first *La Bayadère* performance,
        1:392
    Fokine's choreographic vision in
        continuum of, **3**:562, 568
    Gerdt (Pavel) roles, **3**:137
    Golovin designs, **3**:196
    Labanotation of works, **3**:427
    Little Humpbacked Horse
        divertissement, **3**:562, 567,
        4:211
    musical talent, **3**:562
    Nutcracker choreography,
        3:563–564, **5**:9, 10, 106, 107,
        160, **6**:117
    Petipa collaborations, **2**:108,
        3:15, 560, **4**:282, **5**:149, 456
    Polovtsian Dances choreography,
        3:561–562, **4**:282, 515
    port de bras innovation, **5**:227
    students, **4**:68, 144, **5**:247, **6**:309
    Swan Lake choreography, **2**:15,
        3:207, 560, 565–566, *567,* 568,
        4:*278,* 282, 286, **5**:456,
        6:30–31, 114
    Sylvia collaboration with Gerdt,
        3:568, **6**:64
    Tulip of Haarlem, The, **1**:540,
        2:82, **3**:562
Ivanov, Mikhail, **5**:160
Ivanov, Vladimir, **1**:408
Ivanova, Sonia, **2**:498
Ivanova-Glushkovskaya, Tatiana,
    5:454
Ivanov-Raikov, Gavrila, **1**:484,
    5:452
Ivanovsky, Aleksandr, **3**:192
Ivanovsky, Nikolai, **3**:14, **4**:247,
    5:480
Ivan Susanin (Glinka opera),
    4:514, **5**:455, 471, **6**:442
Ivan the Terrible, **1**:440, 492, **3**:308,
    5:461, **6**:314
Ivantzov, Ivan, **1**:85
"Ive Gotta Hear That Beat" *(Small
    Town Girl),* **4**:419, *419*
Ivelja, Jitka, **6**:436
Ives, Charles, **2**:196, 584, **4**:274,
    613, 615, **6**:111, 112
Ives, James Merritt, **5**:261
Ives, Simon, **4**:311
Ives, Songs, **4**:622, **5**:366
Ivesiana, **1**:263, 268, 272, **4**:5,
    274, 483
Iwai Hanshirō V, **5**:30
Iwanson, Jessica, **4**:680
Iwanson Dance Company, Munich,
    3:157
*I Want to Dance (Suite
    Nostalgique),* **6**:314
I Was an Adventuress (film),
    6:34, 450
I Watched Myself Grow Up, **2**:357
iwo, **5**:82
Ixion (revue), **6**:267, 315
"I Yi Yi Yi Yi" (song), **4**:434
Izayoi Seishin, **3**:658
Iza Zamácola, Juan Antonio de,
    5:676

Izenour, George, **4**:190
Izmailova, Galiya, **3**:568–569,
    6:306, *306,* 307
Iztuela, Juan Ignacio, **1**:376, **3**:33
Izumi school, **4**:85–86, 660–662
Izumo Kagura Dance, **2**:219,
    3:584, 642
Izutsu, **6**:445
Izzo, Filippo, **3**:620

Jablochkoff candles, **4**:189
Jablonko, Allison, **2**:602
    as contributor, **5**:82–84
Jack and the Beanstalk, **4**:3, **6**:107
*Jack at the Cape, or All Alive among
    the Hottentots,* **5**:649
Jackdaw Songs, **3**:54
Jackie Gleason Show, The
    (television program), **6**:*138*
Jack-in-the-Box, **3**:442, **4**:516,
    5:208, 525, 526
Jack of Diamonds (avant-garde
    group), **3**:197, **4**:124
Jack Pudding, **3**:359, **4**:517
Jackson, Alfred, **1**:465
Jackson, Andrew, **2**:71, 85
Jackson, Barry, **3**:356
Jackson, Calvin, **6**:130
Jackson, Clarence, **6**:109
Jackson, Clay, **2**:*585*
Jackson, Daniel, **2**:42, **3**:231–232
Jackson, George, **6**:259
    as contributor, **3**:346–347,
        4:228–229, **5**:278–279,
        605–606
Jackson, Glorianne, **6**:25
Jackson, Holbrook, **4**:520
Jackson, Jennifer, **5**:421
Jackson, John, *as contributor,*
    1:77–79
Jackson, John W. (clogging troupe
    manager), **4**:522
Jackson, Laurence. *See* Baby
    Laurence
Jackson, Michael, **2**:610, 620
Jackson, O. D., **1**:252
Jackson, Rowena, **1**:499, **4**:624,
    625, **5**:*107*
Jackson, Silas, *as contributor,*
    6:400–401
Jackson Girls, **1**:465
Jackson International Ballet
    Competition, **1**:281, 282
Jackson Library, Greensboro, **4**:168
"Jacky Tar" hornpipe, **3**:376, 378
Jacob, Maria, **2**:405, **4**:341
Jacob, Max, **5**:237, 526
Jacobi, Georges, **3**:261, **6**:32
Jacobi, Inga, **4**:675
Jacobi, Lotte, **5**:185
Jacobilli, Ludovico, **3**:107
Jacob in Horan, **3**:449, *533*
Jacobs, Laura A., *as contributor,*
    5:13–16
Jacobs, Matt, **3**:*390*
Jacobs, Winni, **5**:422
Jacobsen, Palle, **2**:385, **5**:431
Jacobson, Edmund, **2**:319
Jacobson, Irena, **5**:514
Jacobson, Leonid. *See* Yakobson,
    Leonid
Jacobson, Mark, **4**:153
Jacob's Pillow, **1**:81, **2**:367,
    3:571–572, **5**:559, 564, **6**:295
    Alvin Ailey Dance Theater, **1**:55
    archival materials, **4**:168
    Atlanta Ballet, **1**:39, 197
    Caribbean dance, **2**:66
    Cébron association, **2**:81

Chandralekha appearance, **2**:104
Dayton Contemporary Dance
    Company grant, **2**:358
Grands Ballets Canadiens, **2**:151,
    3:229
Joffrey Ballet, **3**:611
Joffrey choreography, **3**:609
Lang, Pearl, **4**:120
Markova-Dolin summer school,
    4:269
Meri, La, **4**:355
Moore, Lillian, **4**:457
National Ballet of Canada, **4**:541
Royal Danish Ballet soloists,
    6:399
Royal Winnipeg Ballet, **5**:435
San Francisco Ballet, **2**:162
Shawn, Ted, **5**:497, 583, 585
Ximénez and Vargas, **6**:407
Jacoby, Ann, **6**:251
Jacoby, Heinrich, **1**:470
Jacques, Christian, **6**:119
Jaeger, A. J., **2**:516
Jaffe, Susan, **1**:75, 77, **2**:471
Jagata, Uljis, **4**:128
Jäger, Marion, **6**:*11*
Jag ville gorna telefonera, **5**:127
Jahn, Thomas, **3**:52
*Jahrbuch des östrreichischen
    Volksliedwerkes* (journal),
    1:242
"J'ai Deux Amours" (song), **1**:253
jaipongan, **3**:503
Jaipur style (India), **2**:468
Jai Somnath, **3**:606
Jaka Bluwo, **3**:498
Jákai, Mór, **3**:414
Jaka Penjaring, **3**:498
Jakarta, **3**:502
Jakarta Arts Center, Taman Ismail
    Marzuki, **5**:523
Jakarta Institute of the Arts, **4**:159
Jal Bin Machhli, Nritya Bin Bijli
    (film), **2**:*627*
Jaleo de Jerez, El, **3**:223, **4**:657
jaleos, **5**:133
Jalousies du Sérail, Les, **4**:695, 696
Jaloux Puni, Le, **2**:363–364, **6**:*189*
Jamaica, **2**:62, 65, **3**:573–577,
    5:634, **6**:400
    See also Jonkonnu festival
Jamaica (musical), **1**:55, **2**:185
Jamaica Cultural Development
    Commission, **3**:576–577
Jamaica Dance Company, **3**:575
Jamaican National Dance
    Company, **2**:566
Jamaica School of Dance, **3**:577
James I, king of England, **1**:286,
    2:236, 501, **3**:252
    masques and revels, **4**:307, 308,
        5:343
James II, king of England, **1**:424
James, Bernard, **1**:213
James, Edward, **1**:306, 307, **3**:72,
    4:229
James, Frances, **2**:582, **5**:301
James, Freddy, **3**:57
James, Henry, **4**:26, 72
James, Leon, **4**:202
James, Martin, **4**:626
James, William, **6**:241
James the Apostle, Saint, **2**:194
James Waring Dance Company. *See*
    Waring, James, **6**:282
Jamieson, Karen, **2**:41, 46
Jamison, Judith, **1**:292, **3**:577–578,
    5:256, **6**:286
    Alvin Ailey American Dance
        Theater, **1**:56–57, *57,* 58, 59,
        60, **3**:577–578

Josephslegende performance, **3:**631
as Washington Ballet guest choreographer, **6:**366
Janáček, Leoš, **2:**308, **4:**239, **5:**245, 617, **6:**202
Janeiro, Violeta, **1:**111
Janequin, Clément, **1:**369
jangér dance drama, **3:***484*, 485
Janíček, Albert, **3:**100
Janietz, Erich, **3:**142
Janin, Jules, **1:**477, **2:**503, **5:**93, 500
Janinet, Jean-François, **3:***326
Jankó, János, **3:**412
Janković, Ljubica and Danica, **3:**35, **6:**429, 432, 439
Janmaat, Martinette, **4:**602
Jannequin, Clément, **1:**352
Jannides, Chris, **4:**627
Jan of Lublin, **5:**210
János Háry (Kodály), **3:**412
Jansenism, **3:**228
Janssen, Werner, **6:**6
Janssen-Audeoud, Susana. *See* Susana
Jansson, Carina. *See* Ari, Carina
Jan Veen-Katrine Amory Hooper Memorial Dance Collection, **4:**168
Japan, **3:**578–592
 Ainu, **1:**31–33
 audiences, **1:**161
 background and overview, **1:**167–168, **3:**578–583
 ballet, **3:**588–590
 bon odori, **1:**496–497, **3:**586–588
 castanet counterpart, **2:**78
 costume, **2:**213–219
 dance aesthetics, **1:**17, 182, **2:**6, **4:**42, 46
 dance research and publication, **3:**591–592, **4:**159
 fan usage, **2:**569, 570, *571*
 first woman actors, **6:**409
 folk dance, **3:**585–588
  costume, **2:**219
  journals, **3:**592
  vocal sounds, **3:**38
 geisha dance, **3:**126
 gigaku, **3:**171–172
 kagura, **3:**583–584, 641–642
 kusemai, **5:**49
 libraries and museums, **4:**159
 martial arts, **1:**186, 187
 mask and makeup, **4:**295–296, *296*
 modern dance, **3:**583, **590–591**
  Hanayagi Suzushi, **3:**339–340
  Ishii Kaoru, **3:**523
  Ito Michio, **3:**558–559
  Kamizawa Kazuo, **3:**646
  See also butō
 ritual dance, **1:**160, 167–168, **3:**583–585
 sword dances, **1:**118
 See also bugaku; bunraku; gagaku; Japanese traditional schools; kabuki theater; kyōgen; nō; specific performers and works
Japan Actors' Association, **4:**537
Japanese Actor 17th Century, **3:**385
Japanese Imperial Household Agency, **3:**102
Japanese Kabuki Troupe, **6:**249
Japanese Spear Dance, **5:**585, 586
Japanese traditional schools, **3:**593–594, 640, 650
 Azuma Tokuho, **1:**248–249
 Bandō Mitsugorō, **1:**361
 Bandō Tamasaburō, **1:**362

Fujima tradition, **3:**89–90
 See also kyōgen, schools; *nō*
Japan Foundation, **2:**171
Japarov, Kosha, **6:**213
Jaque, Juan Antonio, **5:**670, **6:**123, 124
Jaques-Dalcroze, Émile, **3:594–597**
 Appia design collaboration, **1:**97–98, **5:**540, **6:**161
 archival materials, **4:**163
 artist associates, **1:**127–128, 128–129
 Ausdruckstanz, **1:**203
 as avant-garde dance influence, **1:**244, **2:**122–123
 Behle studies with, **1:**403
 as Bodenwieser influence, **1:**466, 467
 as British dance education influence, **3:**276
 as Chladek influence, **2:**153
 contribution, **3:**596–597
 as free dance movement influence, **1:**239
 as French modern dance influence, **3:**75
 Netherlands performances, **4:**589
 Nijinsky studies with, **2:**408, **3:**596, **4:**644
 as St. Denis influence, **5:**495
 as Schönberg influence, **5:**559
 students, **2:**632, **3:**131, 596, **5:**46, 296
 as Swiss dance influence, **6:**51
 theater design input, **6:**161
 Wigman studies with, **2:**316, **3:**596
 See also eurhythmics; Jaques-Dalcroze Institute, Geneva; Jaques-Dalcroze Institute, Hellerau-Dresden
Jaques-Dalcroze, Gabriel-Émile, **3:**594
Jaques-Dalcroze Institute, Geneva, **1:**98, 128–129, **3:**596, **6:**51
Jaques-Dalcroze Institute, Hellerau-Dresden, **2:**153, **3:**145–146, 156, 160, 311, 317, 369, 558
 move to Vienna outskirts. *See* Hellerau-Laxenburg School
 program and philosophy, **3:**595–596
 students and faculty, **3:**596
 Wigman as student, **6:**389
Jaques-Dalcroze Theater, Hellerau, **1:**98, **3:**596, **5:**540, **6:**161
Jar, The, **2:**400, **3:**202
Jara, Victor, **2:**499
jarabe dance, **4:**384, 386, 391
Jarabe Tapatio, **4:***390, 391
jarana dance, **4:**386
jaran kepang (prajuritan), **1:**174
Jarash festival (Jordan), **4:**136
"Jardin Animé, Le" (*Le Corsaire*), **2:**207, *207*
Jardin aux Lilas, **3:597–598**, **6:**197, *197*, 198, *198*, 200, 201, 202, 203, 312
 Alonso (Alicia) performance, **1:**49
 American Ballet Theatre premiere production, **1:**66, *68*
 Aterballetto staging, **1:**196
 Edwards performance, **2:**477
 Fernandez performance, **2:**586
 Gilmour performance, **3:**174
 Hart (Evelyn) performance, **3:**345
 Kaye performance, **3:**663, **4:**616
 Kirkland performance, **4:**24
 Laing performance, **4:**109, 110

Lander (Toni) performance, **4:**120
Lloyd (Maude) performance, **3:**597, **4:**215, **6:***197*
Markova performance, **4:**269
Marks performance, **4:**271
Maryinsky staging, **4:**285
 in National Ballet of Canada repertory, **4:**540, *540*
New York City Ballet revival, **4:**608
 in Rambert Ballet repertory, **5:**300, 301
Royal Ballet revival, **1:**155
 in Royal Danish Ballet repertory, **5:**431
 in Royal Winnipeg Ballet repertory, **5:**437
Wilson (Sallie) performance, **6:**402
JardinCour, **4:**204
Jardin Encantado, El, **4:**390
Jardi Tancat, **2:**448, **4:**602, **5:***234
Jarman, Derek, **1:**156
Jarre, Jean-Michel, **6:**414
Jarre, La (La Giara), **1:**327
Jarret, Keith, **1:**56
Jarrett, Henry, **5:**514
Jarrett, Henry C., **1:**457
Jarvis, Lilian, **4:***540
Jarzynówna-Sobczak, Janina, **5:**219
Jasinski, Roman, **1:**307, 309, 313, 315, **4:**659, **5:**218, **6:**203, 204, 264
 Ballets 1933, **3:**72–73
 Rubinstein ballet company, **4:**635
 Tulsa Ballet Theatre, **6:**264
 as Zajlich student, **6:**441
Jaska, Marialuise, **1:**241
Jason, Josephine, **1:**232, *232*
jātaka tales, **2:**226, **4:**111, 255
jauk, **3:489–490**
Java. *See* Indonesia, Javanese dance traditions
Java, **1:**52, **3:**273, **5:**303, *304*
Java Forever, **3:**601
javali, **1:**442
Javelli family, **5:**317
Javotte, **3:**71, 137, **5:**94, 247, 690
Jay, Letitia, **3:**304, **4:**691
Jayadeva, **3:**466, **5:**22, 311
Jayammal, **1:**273
Jayasmedi, **3:**496
Jayme, Ernest August, **6:**124
Jayteens Dance Workshop, **3:**575
Jazzart Dance Theatre Company, **5:**657, *657*, *658*
Jazzbow Girls, **6:**447
Jazz Café, **4:**133
Jazz Calendar, **1:**156, **5:**417
Jazz Concert, **4:**450
jazz dance, **3:598–600**
 African-American origins, **6:**244, 256
 American musical theater, **6:**272
 Ashton-Bradley ballet, **1:**520
 Baby Laurence tap dance, **1:**252
 ballet scores, **2:**46, **4:**516, 519
 Ballets Suédois ballets, **1:**327
 Béjart use of, **1:**404
 Belgium, **1:**411
 Bintley use of, **1:**454
 body movements and rhythms, **3:**131
 Bubbles tap routines, **2:**5
 Castle arrangements, **2:**78
 Charleston, **5:**629
 Cole use of, **2:**185, **3:**598, 599, 600, **6:**281

Fosse choreography, **6:**281
 France, **3:**76
 improvisation, **3:**447–448
 McKayle choreography, **6:**286–287
 Nicholas brothers, **4:**629–630
 Robbins balletic use, **2:**108, **3:**599, **5:**360
 sub-Saharan Africa, **6:**24
 Verdon, Gwen, **6:**327
 See also Lindy Hop
Jazz Dance (Stearns and Stearns), **1:**520
jazzercise. *See* aerobic dance
Jazz Hoofer (film), **1:**252
Jazz Hot, Le, **1:**498
Jazz Impressions, **1:**446
Jazz Play, **2:**480
Jazz Six Syncopated Movements, **4:**622, *623*
Jazz Tap Ensemble, **2:**186, **3:**448
Jazz Tillana, **5:**521
J. C. Williamson Theatres, Ltd., **1:**206, 207, 208, 209, 230, 498, 499, **3:**353–354
Jeakins, Dorothy, **3:**654
Jean, **4:**625
Jean de Paris (Boieldieu), **1:**205
Jean Erdman Dance Company, **2:**520
Jean-Jean, **1:**455
Jeanmaire, Zizi (Renée), **1:**315, **3:600–601**, **4:**524, **6:**348
 Ashton ballets, **1:**152, 159
 Ballet National de Marseille, **4:***523
 Ballets de Paris de Roland Petit, **1:**305, **3:**74
 Ballets des Champs-Élysées, **3:**73
 Carmen performance, **3:**74, **5:***163
 Grand Ballet du Marquis de Cuevas, **3:**225
 Jeune Homme et la Mort television performance, **3:**601
 Lifar association, **4:**184, 185
 Petit relationship, **5:**163, *163*, 164
 Sleeping Beauty performance, **5:**613
Jeanne au Bûcher (Lifar oratorio), **4:**185
Jeanne au Bûcher (Rubinstein commission), **5:**439
Jeanne d'Arc, **1:**517, **2:**15–16, 151, **5:**294
Jeannette and Jeanot, **5:**319
Jean Vilar House, Avignon, **4:**161
Jefferies, Stephen, **5:**55, 294, *652*
Jelgerhuis, Johannes, **4:**588, 589
Jelín, Lía, **1:**112
Jelinek, Victor, **3:**229
Jelly's Last Jam (musical), **3:**366, **6:**103, 288, *289*
Jelyotte, Pierre, **3:**450
Jemnitz, Sándor, **3:**416
Jemparing Ageng, **3:**495
Jena, Suredranath, **5:**23
Jenčik, Josef, **2:**307, 308, **5:**245
Jenden, Paul, **4:**627, *627*
Jenkins, Carol, *as contributor*, **1:**414–415, **3:**120–121
Jenkins, Joe, **1:**212
Jenkins, Margaret, **6:**266
Jenkins, Ron, *as contributor*, **4:**294–300
Jenkinson, Philip, **5:**332
Jenney, Neil, **2:**292
Jenny, ou Le Mariage Secret, **1:**201, **2:**354, **3:**68
Jenny from Westphalen, **5:**406
Jensen, Anina. *See* Genée, Adeline
Jensen, Chris, **1:***374*, 375, **2:**200

Jensen, Dagny, **5:**599
Jensen, Elna Jørgen, **5:**352
Jensen, Gunilla, **6:**50
Jensen, Lillian, **5:**394, *395, 424,* 430
Jensen, Mariane, **1:**503
Jensen, Michael, *as photographer,* **1:**228
Jensen, Svend Erik, **2:**535, 536, **5:***395,* 430
Jensson, Liv, **4:**682
Jephté, **1:**464, **5:**306
Jeppesen, Lis, **2:***385,* **5:**430, **6:**349
Jeremiah Symphony (Bernstein), **1:**438, 439
Jerk (dance), **5:**633, **6:**263
Jero Gedé (Big Man) mask, **3:**489, *489*
Jero Luh (Female Person) mask, **3:**489, *489*
Jerome, king of Westphalia, **1:**202
Jerome Robbins' Broadway, **5:**366, **6:**288
Jerschik, Andrei, **1:**241, **2:**434
Jerusalem, **3:**526, *527,* 534
Jérusalem (Verdi opera), **4:**341
Jerusalem Delivered (Tasso), **2:**426
Jerusalem Ensemble, **3:**534
Jeschke, Claudia, **5:**327
   as contributor, **3:**160–163
Jeschke, Colette, **6:***51*
jesters, **3:**541
Jest of Cards, **2:**162
Je Suis Né à Venise, **1:**407
Jesuits
   Algonkian culture, **4:**557
   ballet de collège, **1:**282–284, 286, 396, 464, **2:**34, 168, **3:**544
   Brazilian syncretic dance, **1:**530, 531
   dance theatrical productions, **3:**544, **5:**230
Jesus, the Son of Man, **3:**329, **4:**267
Jesus Christ Superstar (musical), **5:**423, **6:**284
   Korean dance version, **4:**51
   Reinthaller staging, **6:**66
Jesús Moctezuma, Maria de, **4:**399
Jesus of Nazareth, **2:**163, **4:**106
"Jesus Sold by Judas" (song), **5:**210
jetés, **2:**518, **3:**172, **5:**337
Jeu de Cartes, **1:**297, 305, 442, **2:**111
   Balanchine revival, **4:**609
   Charrat version, **3:**73, 74, 416
   Chiriaeff production, **2:**151
   Cranko production, **2:**267, **5:**431, *431*
   Danilova performance, **2:**342
   Kehlet *demi-caractère* role, **3:**668
   Keil performance, **4:**1
   Kirstein commission, **4:**28
   Madsen performance, **4:**245
   Raibayev choreography, **3:**665
   Reed performance, **4:**617
   Stravinsky score, **4:**28, 518, **6:**5
Jeu de Robin et de Marion, Le (de la Halle), **5:**112, **6:**267
Jeune Dalmate, ou Le Retour au Village, La, **4:**454
Jeune Fille et la Mort, La, **3:**79
Jeune Homme et la Mort, Le, **1:**461, **3:***601,* **5:**163
   Babilée performance, **1:**251, 306, **3:**601
   Cocteau staging ideas, **2:**183, **3:**601
   costume, **2:**245
   Petit production, **3:**73, 601, **4:**33
Jeux, **1:**316, 320, 321, 322, 325, **2:**71
   Ballets Suédois performance, **1:**326

choreographers, **2:**361
   costumes, **2:**242, **4:**642, *646*
   Darrell production, **5:**564
   Debussy music, **2:**361, 408, **4:**515, 516, 641, 642
   Dollar choreography, **2:**427
   failure of, **4:**643
   Nijinska on place in ballet history, **4:**648
   Nijinsky choreography, **1:**320, 321, 325, 326, **2:**361, **4:**641–643, 644, *646,* 647, **5:**558
   Schayk choreographer, **5:**555
Jeux d'Eglé, Les, **1:**202
Jeux de Massacre (Ionesco), **3:**12
Jeux d'Enfants, **1:**247, 309, **6:**182
   Massine choreography, **4:**322
   Massine-Kochno collaboration, **4:**33
   Miró sets and costumes, **1:**135, *136,* **4:**33
   Moncion choreography, **4:**450
   Riabouchinska performance, **5:**350
Jeux de Printemps, **4:**418
"Jeux des Papillons" pas de deux (*La Source*), **4:**640
Jeux Forains, **3:**233, 389
Jeux Venetiens, **3:**133
Jewels, **1:**263, 271, **2:**314, **6:**328, 340
   assessment of, **4:**612
   Diamonds section, **2:**576, **4:**612, 618, 631, **5:**223
   Emeralds section, **4:**345, 450, 612, 617, *618,* 619
   Rubies, **1:**269, **4:**612, 613, 618, 620, **5:***653*
Jewish Dance Guild, New York, **1:**431, **3:**605
Jewish dance traditions, **3:**526–528, 539, **602–606**
   Ashkenazic versus Sephardic, **3:**526–527, 602–603
   Berk, Fred, **1:**431–432, **3:**605
   biblical, **1:**448, **3:**526, 602, 604
   Hasidim, **3:**528, 536, 537, 603, 604
   Israeli folk dance movement, **3:**530–531, 605, **4:**58–59
   "wedding house," **3:**602–603, **4:**349
   Yemenite, **3:**449, 527, 529, 531, 531–532, 536–537
   See also Israel
Jewish Theological Society, New York City, **1:**431
Jewish Wedding, **6:**412
Jewkes, Josephine, **2:***511,* **3:**273
Jew Süss (play), **2:**105
Jezek, Jaroslav, **2:**310
Jha, Prakash, **2:**468, **6:**312
Jhanak Jhanak Payal Baje (film), **2:**623, *623*
Jhaveri sisters, **3:**606, **5:**601
Jhung, Finis, **2:**162, **3:**51, 342, 610
Jiang Miaoxiang, **6:**421
Jiang Qing, **2:**137
Jiang Zuhui, **5:**471
Jibe, **2:**606
jidaimono, **3:**440, **606–607,** 637, **4:**333, 334, 532, 536, 537
jidai-sewamono, **3:**607
jig, **3:**607–608**
   Americas, **3:**607–608
   clogging variant, **2:**179, **3:**608
   derivation of term, **3:**172
   England, **3:**238, 241, 607, **4:**473
   hornpipe versus, **3:**379, 607

Ireland, **2:**35, 179, **3:**249, 517, 607, 608, *608*
   musical theater, **6:**268
   Scottish dances, **3:**243, 247, *248,* 249
   as step dance, **5:**695, *695*
   tap dance origins, **3:**131, 633, **6:**96, 97
   See also gigue
Jilek, Victor, **2:**470
Jílek, Vlastimil, **5:**245, 270
Jillana, **2:**438, **4:**179, *179,* 616, 617
Jilliling, **2:**24
Jiménez, José, **3:**10
Jimmy Durante Show, The (television program), **4:**210
Jingle Dress Dance, **5:**240
Jingpo (people), **2:**141
Jinx, **2:**161, **5:**512
Jirsíková, Nina, **2:**308, 434
jitterbug. *See* Lindy Hop
jive. *See* jazz dance
Jive, **2:**583–584
Jivin' Jacks and Jills, **5:**21
Jiyu Gekijō (*kabuki* troupe), **3:**440
Joana d'Arc, **5:**384
Joan de Zarissa, **2:**113, 351, **5:**96
   Egk score, **2:**478, **3:**340, **4:**517
   Lifar production, **4:**184
   Miskovitch performance, **4:**435
Joan of Arc (film), **3:**654
Job, **1:**146, **3:608–609,** **5:**293, 415
   Bintley production, **1:**454, **3:**609
   Camargo Society commission, **5:**412
   Chappell performance, **2:**105
   de Valois production, **2:**397, 399, **3:**265, 608, 609, **4:**517, **5:***411,* 412
   Dolin performance, **2:**399, 424, **3:**354, 608, 609, **5:**412
   Gore performance, **3:**202
   Helpmann performance, **3:**354, 609
   Lambert musical arrangement, **4:**114
   Richardson (Philip) performance, **5:**351
   Shawn production, **2:**184, **3:**609
   Vaughan Williams score, **3:**608, 609, **4:**517, **5:**412
Jobe, Tom, **1:**394, **4:**217
Jobst, Rudolf, *as photographer,* **6:**387
joc dance, **5:**380, 382–383
Jockey Club, Paris, **2:**199, **4:**514
Jockey du Diable, Le, **4:**455
Jocko, ou Le Singe du Brésil (*Jocko, or The Ape of the Brazils;* pantomime-ballet), **1:**455, **3:**69, 69, **5:**147, 318, 319
Jocko, the Brazilian Ape (Taglioni ballet; 1826), **1:**390, **3:**144, **4:**138, **5:**72, **6:**73
   Mlakar reconstruction (1950), **4:**437, **6:**432
   Stuttgart premiere, **6:**9
"Jocky Said to Jenny" (song), **3:**376
Joe, **2:**45, **6:**132
Joe Miller the Younger, **2:**70
Joe Nash Black Dance Collection, **4:**167
Joffe, Diana, **1:**75
Joffre, Dennis, **4:***71*
Joffrey, Robert, **3:609–610,** **5:**301, 327, 437
   American Ballet Center, **4:**457
   Arpino relationship, **1:**124–125, **3:**610
   illness and death, **3:**617
   Jooss collaboration, **3:**614

multimedia, **2:**606, **3:**615, **4:**519
   See also Joffrey Ballet
Joffrey Ballet, **1:**99, **3:610–618**
   Ailey choreography, **1:**57
   Araiz *Romeo and Juliet,* **1:**103, **5:**398–399
   Arpino, Gerald, **1:**124–125, **3:**610, 611, 612–615, 617
   Ashton ballets, **3:**614, 617
   Astarte, **5:**551
   Billy the Kid, **1:**453
   Cotillon reconstruction, **2:**254
   Cranko *Romeo and Juliet,* **5:**396
   dance reconstructions, **5:**326–327, *327*
   Dean choreography, **2:**359, **3:**615, 616, 617
   de Mille choreography, **2:**374, **3:**614
   Dream revival, **2:**446
   Feld production, **2:**583–584
   financial problems, **3:**611, 617
   formation, **3:**610
   Forsythe training, **3:**51
   Green Table, The, **3:**305, 614, 616, 617, 630
   Harkness association, **3:**342, 610
   Illuminations revival, **1:**152, **3:**443, 614
   Kudelka choreography, **4:**72
   Noces revival, **4:**659
   Nureyev, Rudolf, **5:**7
   Parade, **5:**526
   Pas des Déesses, **3:**609, *609*
   Poppet, The, **3:**360
   Robbins ballet revivals, **3:**614
   rock music scores, **4:**519
   Sacre du Printemps revival, **4:**644, **5:**437, 488
   school. *See* American Ballet Center
   summer workshop, **2:**404, **3:**342
   television performances, **3:**616
   Tharp choreography, **3:**615–616, 617, **6:**153
   Wedding Bouquet revival, **6:**375
Joffrey Ballet Chicago, **1:**125, **3:**617
jogéd, **1:**174, **3:***474,* 505
jogéd bumbung, **3:**475
joget gamelan, **2:**229
joget social dances, **4:**250
Jogjakarta, Java, **1:**172, 173, **3:**495, 496, 497, 498–499
jo ha kyū (aesthetics), **2:**6
Johannesburg Ballet Theatre, **5:**52, 650–651
Johannesburg City Ballet. *See* PACT Ballet
Johannesburg Dance Factory. *See* Dance Factory, Johannesburg
Johannesburg Dance Foundation, **5:**659
Johannesburg Festival Ballet, **5:**52, 650
Johannes de Groccheo, **4:**500
Johannesen, Augusta, **4:**675
Johannesen, Ina Chriostel, **4:**679
Johannesnatten, **5:**406
Johannes og Anima, **4:**677
Johannis Ambrosio. *See* Guglielmo Ebreo da Pesaro
Johansen, Birthe, **2:**387
Johansen, Jahn Magnus, **2:**470, *470*
Johansen, Svend, **4:**118
Johansson, Anna, **3:**618, **5:**95
Johansson, Christian, **1:**392, 508, 510, **3:**127, **618–619, 4:**143, **5:**150
   Fokine as student, **3:**14
   Gerdt family association, **3:**136, 137

influence on Russian school,
   1:330, **3**:560, 618, **4**:281,
   5:456, 480, **6**:40
Petipa collaboration, **3**:618
   students, **3**:618, 655, **4**:68, 142,
   144, **5**:119, 247, **6**:309
Swedish ballet, **3**:618, **6**:40
Johansson, Ronny, **3**:619
Johansson, Vera, **2**:341
John V, king of Portugal, **5**:230
John, Suki, *as contributor*,
   2:280–282
John Brown, **3**:349
John Butler Dance Theatre, **2**:16
John Canoe festival. *See* Jonkonnu
   festival
John Chrysostom. *See* Chrysostom,
   John
John Cranko Ballet School,
   Stuttgart, **2**:267–268
John Cranko Gesellschaft, **2**:268
John Curry's Theatre of Skating.
   See Ice Dancing
John Falstaff, **1**:375, **5**:683
Johnny Johnson (musical), **6**:276
Johns, Jasper, **2**:53, **3**:619–620,
   5:313, 314, **6**:107, 250
   Cunningham association, **1**:142,
      2:22, 292, 293, **3**:619, 6120,
      5:548
   Walkaround Time set, **1**:*141*
   Waring designs, **6**:362
Johnsen, John R., *as photographer*,
   2:385, **5**:424
John Somebody, **4**:219
Johnson, Ann, **4**:*201*
Johnson, Carole, **1**:212, 216
Johnson, Charles, **2**:25
Johnson, Edward, **1**:64
Johnson, Hazel, **3**:574
Johnson, Hunter, **1**:421, **2**:360,
   4:153
Johnson, Jack, **6**:102
Johnson, James Weldon, **2**:367
Johnson, Kate, **1**:*372*, **4**:482, **6**:*112*
Johnson, Kenneth, **5**:*60*, **6**:292
Johnson, Louis, **1**:59, **2**:108, 334,
   356, **6**:259
Johnson, Matthew, *as contributor*,
   1:248–249, **3**:89–90
Johnson, Nicholas, **4**:394
Johnson, Nora, **1**:419
Johnson, Philip, **4**:26, 27, 29, 382
Johnson, Raymond, **6**:363
Johnson, Robert, **4**:309, 311
Johnson, Steve, **5**:194
Johnson, Sylvester ("Happy"), **3**:57
Johnson, Virginia, **1**:*100*, **2**:334,
   335, 356, **6**:260
Johnson and Dean, **2**:25, **6**:316
Johnsson, Anna, **1**:247, **5**:690
Johnston, Jill, **3**:635, **6**:299
Johnston, Thomas F., *as
   contributor*, **4**:570–574,
   5:579–580
Johnstone, Mary, **5**:374
John Street Theatre, New York
   City, **6**:233
John the Baptist, **2**:166
John the Baptist, **5**:57
Joite, Eckhard, *as photographer*,
   3:535, 537
Jóka's Devil, **5**:287
Joleo, Ande, **1**:93
Jolie Bordelaise, La, **5**:150
Jolie Fille de Gand, La, **3**:69, **620**,
   5:148
   Adam score, **1**:10, **2**:511, **3**:620
   Carter choreography, **2**:511,
      3:175
   Cerrito performance, **5**:89

Fitzjames (Louise) performance,
   3:4–5
Grisi performance, **1**:36–37, **3**:5,
   314, 316, 620
Lee's American performances,
   4:139
Mazilier character performance,
   4:340
Jolivet, André, **4**:517
Jolles, Thea, **4**:246
Jolley, Jay, **2**:162
Joly, Anténor, **3**:314
Jomfrukilden, **5**:432
Jomon Sho, **1**:61
Jommelli, Niccolò, **2**:54, **4**:347,
   695, 698, **5**:371, **6**:9
Jonas, Joan, **5**:548, 549
Jones, Alun, **6**:204, 266
Jones, A. M., **1**:15
Jones, Betty, **1**:519
   Limón Dance Company, **4**:198
   Moor's Pavane performance,
      4:199, 458, *458*
   Night Spell performance, **3**:403
   videotape profile of, **1**:81
Jones, Betty True, *as contributor*,
   3:469–470
Jones, Bill T., **1**:59, **2**:609,
   3:620–621
   American Dance Festival, **1**:80
   Boston Ballet choreography,
      1:502
   dance themes, **6**:259–260
   improvisation, **3**:448
Jones, Cheryl, **2**:*584*
Jones, Clifford Reis
   as contributor, **1**:362–363,
      3:451–461, 464–466, 660–663,
      4:253–254, 578, **5**:309,
      311–312, 522, **6**:86–87
   as photographer, **4**:299
Jones, Frank Pierce, **1**:473
Jones, Inigo, **2**:236, *236*, 400,
   3:*251*, 252, *252*, **621–622**,
   4:188, **5**:2, 535
   masque designs, **4**:307, *308*,
      311, 312
Jones, John, **3**:577, *612*, **5**:260,
   6:260
Jones, Kenn, **5**:*651*
Jones, Marilyn, **1**:209, 210, 211,
   230, 231, 233, 234, 499,
   3:622–623, **6**:378, 379
Jones, Pamela, *as contributor*,
   2:50–52
Jones, Robert Edmond, **1**:483,
   4:190, 645
Jones, Rosalie, **4**:555
Jones, Susan, **1**:75, 76, **2**:441
Jones, Tom, **6**:282, 283
Jones, William, **2**:337
Jones Beach, **5**:361
jongo, **1**:525, 527
Jonkers, Mark, **3**:156
Jonkonnu festival, **2**:62, 65,
   3:120–121, **623–624**
Jonsdóttir, Minerva, **3**:435, 436
Jonson, Ben, **1**:286, **2**:591, **3**:*251*,
   252, 361, 622, **4**:107, 307,
   308, 309, 310, 312–313, **5**:520
Jonsson, Arngrimur, **3**:434
Jonsson, Per, **6**:44, 45, *45*
jooks, **6**:262
Jooss, Anna. *See* Markard-Jooss,
   Anna
Jooss, Kurt, **1**:99, 204, 402, 436,
   3:162, **624–631**, **5**:24,
   225, 439
   Batsheva Dance Company, **3**:532
   as British modern dance
      influence, **3**:271, 277

Canadian performances, **2**:37
Chilean audience, **2**:123
Coton study of, **3**:285
Cuban performances, **2**:66
as Cullberg influence, **6**:42
Dartington Hall school, **3**:277,
   628–629, **4**:93
expressionist dance, **2**:122
Fils Prodigue, Le, **5**:265
Folkwang Tanzstudio, **3**:40, 149,
   626–627
German dance, **3**:146
as influence on Cullbert,
   2:283, 284
Joffrey production of *Green Table*,
   3:614, 616
Laban association, **4**:15, 91, 92,
   93, 103, 477
Labanotation development, **4**:96
Labanotation of works, **3**:427,
   4:32, 96
Leeder collaboration, **4**:140
mask use, **3**:*625, 626*, **4**:302
as Netherlands dance influence,
   4:590, 598, 600
Nijinska's style comparison,
   4:634
prize for *Green Table*
   choreography, **3**:40, 72, 76,
   305, 627
Spring Tale, A, **3**:629, *629*
   students, **1**:388, 411, 460, 519,
   535, **2**:44, 109, 134, **3**:390,
   4:597, **5**:263, **6**:405
Uthoff association, **6**:304
Züllig association, **6**:453
See also Ballets Jooss; *Green
   Table, The*
Jooss-Leeder Dance School. *See*
   Dartington Hall, Devon
Jooss Ballet. *See* Ballets Jooss
Jooste, Johan, **2**:*56*
Joplin, Janis, **1**:58
Joplin, Scott, **2**:459, 512, **4**:243,
   5:266
Jora, Mikhail, **2**:343, **5**:386
Jordan, Diana, **4**:94
Jordan, Marguerite, **3**:301
Jordan, Olga, **3**:12, 56, 193, **4**:232,
   6:31, 442
Jordan, Stephanie A., **3**:285
   as contributor, **2**:1–2, 354–356,
   4:216–221
Jordan, Susan, **4**:627, 629
Jorge, Armando, **5**:*61*, 235
Jørgen-Jensen, Elna, **5**:*427*, 428
Jorgensen, Nels, **3**:610
Jorgensen, Øyvind, **4**:680
jōruri styles, **3**:639
José Antonio (Ruiz), **5**:654, 674
José Limón Dance Company. *See*
   Limón Dance Company
Joseph II, emperor of Austria, **1**:89,
   236, 237, 409, **3**:188, 365
*Joseph and the Amazing Technicolor
   Dreamcoat* (musical), **2**:1
Joséphine (revue), **1**:253
Josephslegende, Die, **1**:240, 241,
   316, **2**:124, 408, **3**:20, **631**
   Cieplinski production, **3**:415
   Fornaroli performance, **3**:51
   Gabzdyl performance, **3**:99
   Hanka production, **3**:340
   Kröller production, **4**:64
   Massine performance, **4**:316
   Mlakar staging, **6**:432
   Neumeier choreography,
      3:578, 631
   Pratesi choreography, **5**:246
   Shaw on, **3**:284
   Strauss (Richard) score, **4**:515

Toumanova performance, **6**:183
Tudor version, **6**:201
Wallmann production, **6**:357
Zurich Ballet staging, **3**:631, **6**:454
Joseph the Beautiful, **1**:255, 489,
   3:194, *194*, **631–633**, **4**:443,
   5:458
Joshua Fit de Battle ob Jericho, **6**:88
jota, **1**:377, 378, **3**:6
Jota (Brabants ballet), **1**:519
Jota Aragonesa (Fokine ballet),
   3:21, 24, 196, 205
Jota Aragonesa (Moiseyev dance),
   4:445
jota moncadeña, **2**:231
Jota Valenciana, **1**:115
Joubert, Gillian, **5**:54, *651*, 659
Joukowski, Antony, **1**:241, 315
Journal, **1**:407
*Journal of Sports Medicine and
   Kinesiology for Dance, The*,
   4:17
Journée de l'Amour, La, **2**:413
Journey, **3**:664, **4**:241
Journey on Horseback (Chinese
   opera), **2**:144
Journeys from Berlin/1971 (film),
   5:293
Journey to Avalon, **2**:512
Journey to the Fatherland (Chinese
   opera), **2**:*143*
Jour ou Deux, Un, **2**:293, 294
Joute, ou Les Amours d'Été, La,
   3:426
Jouvancy, Joseph de, **1**:283
Jouvet, Louis, **5**:527
Jovanović, Milica, **6**:438
   as contributor, **3**:89, **4**:437,
   5:100–101, **6**:431–433
Jovanovits, Mara, **6**:52
*Jovita, ou Les Boucaniers
   Mexicains*, **1**:427, **4**:342, 353,
   5:405, 500
Jowitt, Deborah, **2**:585, **3**:391,
   5:131, **6**:152, 300
   as contributor, **1**:82, 96–97, **2**:182,
   349, 360, **3**:209–222, **4**:153,
   437–443, 632–633, **5**:253–254,
   559–560, 568
Joy, **6**:260
Joy, S. M., **5**:258
Joyce, James, **2**:295, 520, **3**:520,
   5:18
Joyce/Cage Festival, Zürich, **2**:296
Joyce Trisler Dance Company. *See*
   Trisler, Joyce
Joyeuse, duc de, **1**:2, 275
Joyful Noise, A (musical), **1**:419
Joyner, Jerry, **2**:111
Juan Darién (musical), **6**:289
Juba, Master, **3**:608, **633**, **6**:98,
   237–238, *238*, 254, 258, 262
juba dance, **3**:334, 335
Jubilee (musical), **5**:310
Judaism. *See* Israel; Jewish dance
   traditions
Judas Tree, The, **4**:245
Judd, Donald, **1**:143, 544, 545
Jude, Charles, **5**:7, 97, *97*, 98
judengas, **5**:228
Judenkunig, Hans, **4**:502
Judge, Bronwyn, **4**:626–627
Judgement of Paris, The (Weaver
   ballet), **2**:394, **5**:518,
   6:372, 373
Judgment Day, **1**:141
Judgment of Paris, The (Tudor
   ballet), **1**:66, **2**:55, 112,
   372–373, **4**:109, 455, 541,
   5:301, 303, **6**:197, 198, 202
   See also Jugement de Pâris, Le

Judgment of Solomon, **1:**503
Judith (Graham dance), **2:**58,
  3:217, 218
  Noguchi set, **5:**562
  Schuman music, **5:**562
Judith (Serov opera), **3:**20
Judith: The Triumph of the Spirits,
  1:411
Judith Marcuse Repertory
  Company, **6:**132
Judith Wright—Australian Poet,
  1:212
Judson, Arthur, **2:**377
Judson, Stanley, **3:**608, 609, **4:**519,
  5:342, 414
Judson Dance Theater, **3:633–635,**
  5:127, 292, 313, **6:**282, 606
  aesthetic, **2:**290–291, **3:**633–635,
    634–635
  artist collaborators, **1:**139, 140,
    141–142
  aural eclecticism, **4:**519
  as British dance influence, **3:**272
  Brown, Trisha, **1:**543, **4:**442
  Childs, Lucinda, **2:**119
  choreographic influences,
    3:54, 634
  choreographic silence, **4:**519
  choreography using film, **2:**605
  Dunn, Robert Ellis, **2:**461, 462,
    3:634, **4:**519
  Gordon, David, **3:**201
  Grand Union members, **3:**235
  improvisation, **3:**445, 446
  legacy, **3:**635
  Litz, Katherine, **4:**214
  performance spaces, **6:**163
  scenic design, **5:**548–549
  Tharp performances, **6:**152–153
  Waring's influence, **6:**363
  What Happened, **3:**201, **6:**282
Judson Flag Show (exhibition),
  5:293
Judson Memorial Church, New
  York City, **1:**79, 139,
  3:633–634, *634,* **6:**282
  See also Judson Dance Theater
Judson Poets' Theater, New York
  City, **2:**110, **6:**282
Juego de los Congos, El, **2:**195
Juego de los Voladores, **4:***383*
Juerga, **1:**115
Jugar con Fuego (Playing with Fire),
  1:*113*
Jugement de Midas, Le, **2:**364
Jugement de Pâris, Le, **1:**505, **2:**389,
  413, 464, **3:**117–118, **4:**695,
  5:137, 277, 319, 499
  Cerrito, Taglioni, and Grahn
    performances, **2:**94–95,
    3:223, 260
  Glushkovsky performance, **3:**191
  intermedii, **3:**509
  as Joffrey's *Pas des Déesses*
    inspiration, **3:**609, *609*
  Noverre performance in
    Hungary, **3:**413
  in Swedish ballet repertory, **6:**40
Juggler, The, **1:**500
juglares, **5:**667
Juice, **4:**451, **5:**549
Juif Errant, Le, **6:***70,* 71
Juilliard Dance Theater, **3:**403–404
Juilliard School, New York City,
  3:364, 385
  Humphrey dance classes, **3:**404
  Koner as faculty member, **4:**39
  Labanotation use, **4:**96
  Limón as faculty member,
    4:198, 199
  research materials, **4:**167

Schönberg as faculty member,
  5:559
Schuman (William) presidency,
  5:561
Juive, La (Halèvy), **4:**631, 657
juju music, **6:**24
Juke Box, **1:**281
Jukun (people), **6:**14
Julian the Apostate, emperor of
  Rome, **2:**163
Julie, Fair Girl, **3:**420
Julien, A.-M., **5:**96
Julius Caesar (Handel), **2:**153
Jullian, Philippe, **2:**71
Jullien, Louis Antoine, **3:**123, **5:**625
Julnar and the Sea, **5:**584
Jumbo (film), **1:**432, 435
Jumla, Nepal, **2:**226
Jump Dance, **4:**566
Jump for Joy dance, **2:**179
Jumping Dance, **2:**358
jumping dances
  Asian, **2:**164
  Czech, **2:**301, 302
  East African, **2:**86, 90, *90,* 212,
    6:18
  Hungarian, **3:**410, 411
  Middle Eastern, **4:**404
  Romanian, **5:**379
  Sotho, **5:***646*
  southern African, **5:**661–662, *662*
jumps. *See* ballet technique,
  jumping movements
Jump Start, **1:**77
Juncker-Jensen, Sophus, *as*
  photographer, **1:**505, **5:**427
Junction, **2:**526, **4:**482, **6:**108,
  110, 112
June Taylor Dancers, **6:***138,* 320
June Taylor School, **3:**600
Jung, Carl, **2:**316, 317, 349,
  3:161, 217
  Laban theory, **4:**94, 102
Jungen, Andrea, **4:**600
Junger, Esther, **1:**421
Jungian dance movement,
  2:315, 317
Jungle, **2:**347
Jungmann, Flora, **4:**64, **5:**279
Jungwiwiathanaporn, Parichat,
  4:112, **6:**151
Junk Dances, **4:**230
Juno (musical), **6:**145
Juno and the Paycock (musical),
  2:374
Juozapaitytė, Marija, **4:**208
*Jupiter and Europa, or the Intrigues
  of Harlequin,* **5:**70, 350
Jürgensen, Knud Arne, **1:**512,
  2:388, **3:**556, 557, **6:**129
  as contributor, **1:**514–516
Juriens, Henny, **2:**42
Juronics, Tamás, **6:**66, 67
Jurou, **3:***312*
Jurriëns, Henny, **2:**470, **5:**437
Just a Play, **4:**421
Just around the Corner (film), **6:**142
Just Call Me Dance, **3:**578
Justinian I, emperor of Rome, **4:**427
Jüstrich, Andreas, **4:**595, **5:***530*
Juvarra, Filippo, **5:**537
Juvenal, **4:**427, 499, 662, **5:**377
Juventud, **3:**629

Kàan, Jindřich, **5:**245
Kaán, Zsuzsa, **3:**424
kaati-koopi dance, **2:**629
Kabbalah, **1:**1, **3:**605
Kabdelaj, o La Figlia del Profeta,
  3:97

Kabeláč, Miloslav, **1:**56
Kabuki (Béjart), **1:**406
kabuki theater, **1:**168, **3:**586,
  637–641, 5:591, 592
  architectural features, **3:**637–638
  Azuma Tokuho, **1:**248, 249
  Bandō Mitsugorō, **1:**361
  Bandō Tamasaburō, **1:**362,
    2:*218*
  bon dance choreography,
    3:586, 588
  bunraku association, **1:**180, **2:**12,
    13, 14
  costumes, **2:**217–219
  dance (*nihon buyō*), **3:**89, 90, 338,
    639–640
  first dancer, **3:**581
  Fujima school, **3:**89–90,
    582–583
  hanamichi (raised walkway),
    3:339
  Hanayagi school, **3:**583
  historical background,
    3:581–583, 637
  Ichikaawa Danjūrō,
    3:437–440, *582*
  Ichikawa Ennosuke, **3:**440–441,
    4:*296*
  jidaimono category, **3:**606–607
  Kataoka Takao, **3:**658
  kyōgen influence, **4:**84
  lion dances, **5:**593
  makeup styles, **4:**295–296, *296*
  martial arts technique,
    1:187, *187*
  Matsumoto Kōshirō, **4:**333–334
  mime, **4:**423
  as modern dance group basis,
    3:590, 591
  music, **4:**492–493, *492,* 494
  nagauta music, **4:**530
  Nakamura Ganjirō, **4:**532–533
  Nakamura Kankurō, **4:**533–534
  Nakamura Kanzaburō, **4:**534
  Nakamura Kichiemon,
    4:534–535
  Nakamura Tomijūrō, **4:**536
  Nakamura Utaemon, **4:**537–538
  "new," **4:**535, 536
  Okuni, **5:**28–29
  onnagata, **3:**581, 637, *638,*
    5:29–30
  Onoe Baikō, **5:**30–31
  Onoe Kikugorō, **5:**31–32
  Onoe Shōroku, **5:**32–33
  performance technique,
    3:638–640
  scholarship, **3:**592
  sewamono category, **3:**606
  shinpa reform movement,
    6:409–410
  style, **1:**160, 161, *162,* 168,
    182, *361*
  traditional schools, **3:**593, 640
  as *ukiyo* symbol, **3:**581
  video documentary, **2:**314
  See also nō
Kabu zuinō ki (Konparu Zenchiku),
  4:42
Kachin (people), **4:**524
kachina. See katsina dancers
Ka Cho Fu Getsu, **5:**33, 34
Kaddish Symphony (Bernstein),
  1:439
Kadensho (Zeami), **3:**591, **4:**295,
  6:445
Kadlets, Andrei, **3:**15, 566, **6:**32
Kadman, Gurit (Gert Kaufmann),
  3:530, 537, **641**
Kadyrova, Maira, **3:**665

Kaeppler, Adrienne L., **4:**366, 367,
  368, 370, 371, 372, 373,
  375, 628
  as contributor, **4:**351–352,
    366–368, 400–402, 495–498,
    5:19–21, 223–225, 310,
    6:176–178
  as photographer, **4:**401, 496, **5:**77,
    509, **6:**176, 177
  on trance dance, **6:**184, 186
Kaesen, Philip, **2:**470
Kaesen, Robert, **2:**469, 470
kaf al-'Arab dance, **2:**488, 489
kaf/kaffafah dance, **2:**489, 492
Kafka, Franz, **1:**373, **3:**523,
  4:241, 266
Kafka, Lubomír, **2:**310
Kagai, **3:**646
Kagamijishi, **3:**593, 639, **5:**593, *593*
Kagamiyama, **4:**538
Kagan, Elizabeth, **4:**99, 104
Kaganat sa Darangun, **2:**570
Kagawa Prefecture, Japan, **3:**588
Kåge, Jonas, **1:**375, **5:**396, **6:**43,
  44, 454
Kagekiyo, **3:**89–90
Kagotsurube, **4:**535
kagura, **1:**183, **3:**578–579, 583–584,
  584, 585, **641–643**
Kahl, Elsa, **3:**40, 305, 625, 626, 628
Kahn, Albert E., *as photographer,*
  1:492, **4:**281
Kahn, Otto, **1:**322, **2:**409, **4:**645
Kahn, Stanley, **4:**690
*Kahnotation: The K Symbols for
  Writing Tap Dancing* (Kahn),
  4:690
Kai, Una, **4:**625
Kaier, Avi, **1:**412
kaiko, **5:**83, *83*
kailao, **4:**496
Kailish Dance Company, **1:**216
Kain, Karen, **3:643–644, 5:***242,*
  6:133
  Augustyn dance partnership,
    1:200–201, **2:***40,* **3:**643
  Coppélia performance, **2:**200,
    3:643
  Fille Mal Gardée pas de deux,
    2:*595*
  Kudelka choreography, **4:**73, *73*
  National Ballet of Canada,
    4:542, 543
Kaiser, Georg, **3:**305
Kaiser, Roy, **5:**132
Kaitani Ballet, **3:**589
Kajiwara, Mari, **1:**57, **4:***531*
kakelik, **4:**265
Kakul, I Nyoman, **3:***476,* **644– 645**
Kakyō (Zeami), **4:**42, **6:**445
Kalabari (people), **6:**14, 383
Kalākaua, David, king of Hawaiian
  Islands, **3:**394
Kalakshetra Institute, India, **2:**104,
  105, 404, 405, **3:**468,
  5:510, 511
kalamatianós, **2:**101–102, **3:**296
kaḷarippayaṭṭu, **1:**185, *185,* 186,
  187, **3:**468
kālas, **3:**457
Kalavati Devi, **5:**601
Káldy, Gyula, **3:**422
Kaleidoscope (Boris ballet), **1:**498
Kaléidoscope (Chiriaeff ballet),
  2:*150,* 151, **3:**429
Kaleidoscope (Nikolais dance
  work), **4:**649–650
Kalendrier des bergers (Breton;
  Arbeau pseud.), **1:**103–104
Kalev, Arie, **3:**530

Kalevala (Finnish epic), **1:**453, **2:**629, 631
Kalevala (Gadd ballet), **3:**100
Kalevala (Walter ballet), **6:**359
Kalevipoeg, **2:**15, 529, *529*
Kalfaktorn, **2:**500
Kālidāsa, **1:**392
Kalimantan, Indonesia, **3:**504, 505
Kalimos, Leon, **5:**51, 513
Kalina, Václav, **5:**614
kalinda, **2:**65
Kalinga (people), **5:**168, *169, 171*
Kalinin, Leonid, **6:**223
Kalioujny, Alexandre, **4:**185, **5:**96, **6:**65
Kalipayan Dance Company, **5:**172, 173
Kalkabrino, **1:**540, **4:**68, 430
Kalkaman and Mamyr, **3:**665
Kállai, Lilli, **3:**420
Kallas, Aino, **3:**597
kallinikos, **3:**645–646
Kallman, Chester, **6:**6
Kalmar, Bert, **1:**192
Kalmykova, Evdokia, **6:**30
Kalninjs, Alfreds, **4:**127
Kalninjs, Imant, **2:**499
Kalnojns, Janis, **4:**127
Kalojan's Daughter, **2:**11
Kalpana (film), **2:**623, **5:**581
Kaluli (people), **4:**498, **5:**80–82, *82,* 355
kalushari dances, **2:**8
Kalyanpur, Suman, **2:**625
Kalyansundaram, Guru, **5:**524
Kam, Garrett, *as contributor,* **3:**505–507
kama (songs), **5:**4
Kamabara, **5:**591
Kamadeva, **6:**321
Kamadjojo, Indra, **4:**599
Kamakura era, **4:**83–85
Kamakura Sandaiki, **4:**535
Kamal, Seema, **5:**64
kamalabari satra dance, **5:**354
Kamau'u, Hoakalei, **3:**396
Kamba (people), **2:**89
Kambar and Nazym, **3:**665
Kambari (people), **2:**212, **6:**15, 18
Kamel, Abdel Monem, **2:**497, 498
Kameliendame, Die (ballet). *See Lady of the Camellias, The*
Kameliendame, Die (film), **3:**351
Kamenetsky, Aleksandr, **4:**78
Kamenny Theater. *See* Bolshoi Theater, Saint Petersburg
kami (spirit), **3:**642
Kami, **2:**57, **5:**226
Kamien, Ana, **1:**113
Kamigata *kabuki,* **3:**658, **4:**532–533, 536
Kamilov, Usta Alim, **3:**568, **4:**8, 226, **6:**306
Kami no Kyujitsu, **3:**646
Kamińska, Elwira, **5:**212
Kaminski, Heinrich, **5:**42
Kamiyui Shinza, **4:**533, 534
Kamizawa Kazuo, **3:**646
Kamizawa Modern Dance Institute, **3:**646
Kamkova, Natalia, **6:**171
Kammer, Hanna, **1:**241
Kammer, Renée, **3:**300
Kammermusik Nol 2, **4:**619
Kammerspiele des Deutschen Theater, Berlin, **1:**85
Kammertanzbühne Laban, **4:**91
Kamo, **4:**42
Kamogawa Odori, Kyoto, **3:**126
Kampen (Sylt Island), Germany, **3:**163

Kamula (people), **5:**77
Kamuro, **3:**90
Kanaçi, Panajot, **1:**34
Kanaele, Mary, **3:**396
kanaga mask, **4:**288
Kanahele, Keaka, **3:**396
Kanahele, Pualani Kanaka'ole, **3:**396
Kanaka'ole, Edith, **3:**396
Kanaka'ole, Nālani, **3:**396
Kan'ami, **1:**17, **3:**580, **646– 647,** 650, **6:**445
  Otozuru influence, **5:**48, 49
kanant, **5:**83
Kanász Tánc (sword dance), **1:**118
Kanbei school. *See* Fujima Kanbei
Kanda, Akiko, **3:**218, 591
Kandappa Pillai, **1:**273
Kandaurova, Margarita, **1:**489, **3:**207, **6:**106
Kandinsky, Wassily, **1:**132, 385, **5:**66, **6:**399
Kandyan dance, **2:**601, **3:647–649,** **6:**330
Kandy Perahera, **3:**647, **649**
  costume, **2:**228, **3:**649
Kane, Angela, *as contributor,* **2:**526–527, **3:**271–275, **4:**482–483, 667–668, **5:**679–681, **6:**107–114, 164– 166
Kane, Anita M., **5:**171
Kanegamisaki, **2:**218
Kanemaki Dōjōji, **3:**90
Kan'emon. *See* Fujima Kan'emon
Kaneto Shindo, **3:**652
Kangaroo Dance, **1:**220
Kangaroo Dip, **5:**628
kangen, **2:**5, **3:**102
kanjan halu, **3:**504
Kanjinchō, **1:**162, **3:**438, 593, 637, 658, **4:**333, 533, 536
Kankariya Temple, **3:**647
Kanneberg, Ludwig, **2:**338
Kansas City Ballet. *See* State Ballet of Missouri
Kanteletar (Finnish song collection), **2:**631
Kanuri (people), **6:**14–15
Kanze Akeo, **3:**653
Kanze Gasetsu, **3:**650, 652
Kanze Hideo, **3:**650, 651, **652–653**
Kanze Hisao, **3:**339, 650, **650–652,** **6:**230
Kanze Kasetsu, **3:**650, 652
Kanze Kiyotaka, **3:**650
Kanze Koykazu, **3:**650
Kanze Oribe Kiyohisa, **3:**650
Kanze school, **3:**646–647, **650–653,** **4:**41, 42
  Umewaka Makio, **6:**229–230
Kanze Tetsunojō VII. *See* Kanze Gasetsu
Kanze Tetsunojō VIII (Kanze Shizuo), **3:**650, 651, **653,** **6:**230
Kaondé (people), **2:**89, 90
Kaoru Matsumoto, **4:**83
Kaoshan (people), **6:**79
kapanska, **2:**10
Kapel, d'Oude, **1:**414
Kaplan, Graciella, **4:**668
Kaplan, Howard S., *as contributor,* **1:**58–60, **3:**577–578
Kaplan, Richard, **2:**324
Kaplan, Semyon, **5:**321
Kapliński, Jerzy, **5:**219
Kaplow, Maurice, **5:**131
Kapoor, Raj, **2:**624, *624*
Kapoor, Shammi, **2:**624
Kaposi, Edit, **3:**424, **4:**161
Kaposvár region, **3:**422

Kapp, Eugen, **2:**15
Kaprow, Allan, **1:**139, **6:**250
Kapustina, Nadezhda, **1:**491, **2:**97, **3:**12
Karabašić, Brižita, **6:**436
Karabolinova, Kamysh, **3:**665
Karaev, Kara, **3:**327
Karakulova, Maira, **3:**665
Karalli, Vera, **1:**488, **4:**459, **5:**119, 384
Karamojong (people), **2:**86, 87
karaṇas, **1:**168, **4:**575
karate, **1:**186
Karavan, Danni, **3:**449, *534*
Karawang, **3:**502
Karczag, Eva, **1:**544, **3:**272
Karczmarewicz, Barbara, **3:**316
Kardjono, S., **5:**523
Kârdzali, **2:**12
Kare (Toposa) (people), **2:**86
karéj, **3:**409
Karelian Ballet, **5:**473
Karelskaya, Rimma, **5:**435, 459
Karetu, Timoti, **6:**629
Karger, George, *as photographer,* **1:**48
karg/karj dance, **2:**490
Karhánek, Rudolf, **1:**542, **5:**270
kari (female demons), **4:**298
karička, **2:**100, 101, **3:**410
karikatánac, **3:**410
karikázo, **2:**100, **3:**409, *410*
Karin, Janet, **1:**232
Karina, Lilian, **5:**47
Karinska, Barbara, **1:**96, *263,* 293, **2:**243, 244, 420, **3:653–655,** **4:**613, **6:**144
  Don Quixote costumes, **2:**438
  Liebeslieder Walzer costumes, **3:**654, **4:**179, 180, *615*
  Nutcracker costumes, **4:**617
  Serenade costume design, **5:**571
  Sylvia costumes, **6:**64
  Symphony in C costumes, **6:**65
Karklin, Hortense, **1:**63
Karl, Ludwig, **1:**241
Karlberg, Rolf, *as photographer,* **4:**669
Karl et Lisbeth, **2:**415
Karl Eugen, duke of Württemberg, **4:**346, 347, 695, **6:**9
Karlholm, Göran, **6:**36
Karl-Marx-Stadt, germany, **3:**155
Karlsson, Gustav, **6:**36
Karmon, Yonatan, **3:**530, 531
Karnataka, India, **2:**225, 394, **3:**464
  See also yakṣagāna
Karnetzky, Vladimir, **1:**410
Karnilova, Maria, **3:**26, **4:**382
Kärntnertor Theater, Vienna, **1:**236, 237, **3:**379
  Cerrito performance, **2:**93
  Cucchi as *prima ballerina,* **2:**282
  Duport (Louis-Antoine) directorship, **2:**464
  Elssler sisters, **2:**502, 505
  Gluck association, **3:**187
  Hilverding association, **3:**364–365
  Hus (Auguste) association, **3:**426
  Noverre association, **4:**696
Karok (people), **4:**566
Karp, Poel, **5:**485
Karpakova, Pelagia, **6:**115
Karpakova, Polina, **1:**486, **2:**435, **5:**455
  Swan Lake first performance, **6:**29, 30
Karpakova, Tatiana, **1:**485–486
Karpeles, Maud, **3:**239, **5:**582, 688
Karr, James, **4:**482

Karras, Vicki, **5:**659
Karsavin, Platon, **1:**482, **3:**14, 204, 655, **6:**170
Karsavina, Tamara, **1:**85, 146, 154, 427, 463, **2:**11, 207, 424, 436, **3:**618, **655– 658,** **4:**56, 144, **5:**220, 636
  Ashton ballets, **1:**152, 158
  Benois association, **1:**423
  Carnaval, Le, **2:**72, 73, **3:**202, 656
  Chalon's works as inspiration, **2:**104
  Chopiniana performance, **6:**60
  Coq d'Or performance, **3:**20, 656
  Diaghilev's Ballets Russes, **1:317, 318,** 319, **2:**183, 411, **3:**18, 19, 20, 656, **4:**113, 463
  English National Ballet productions, **2:**510
  Fille Mal Gardée performance, **2:**597, **3:**656
  Firebird costume, **3:**196
  Firebird performance, **3:**1, *1, 2,* 17, 656
  Fokine ballet roles, **3:**15, 16, 18, 656
  Fokine mentorship, **3:**655, 656, **5:**456
  Fracci portrayal of, **3:**60
  Gerdt (Pavel) as teacher and influence, **3:**137, 655
  Giselle performance, **3:**182, 183, 656, **4:**641
  Haskell monograph on, **3:**285
  Jeux performance, **4:**642, 643, 646
  Josephslegende, **3:**631
  on Kshessinska's (Matilda) dance and acting skills, **4:**68
  Legat (Nikolai) association, **4:**142, 143
  on Legnani's virtuosity, **4:**145
  Lester dance partnership, **4:**152
  Lifar dance partnership, **4:**182
  London performances, **1:**263
  Maryinsky Ballet, **4:**283
  partners, **5:**17, **6:**213, 345
  Pavillon d'Armide performance, **5:**118
  Petrouchka performance, **3:**18, *19,* 655, 656, **5:**165
  on practice clothes, **5:**241, 243
  Rambert association, **5:**296, 297, 298, 299, **6:**213
  Royal Academy of Dancing syllabus, **1:**329, 400
  Schéhérazade performance, **5:**556
  as Shearer (Moira) coach, **5:**589
  Spectre de la Rose performance, **3:**18, 656, *656,* **4:**644
  students, **3:**173, 354, 357, **4:**457, **5:**238, **6:**312
  Swan Lake role, **6:**31
  Sylphides performances and staging, **1:**317, **6:**60, 61, 62
  Thamar performance, **3:**18–19
  Tricorne performance, **6:**192
  Turner dance partnership, **6:**213, 214
  video documentary on, **2:**314
  writings on dance, **2:**382, **5:**596, **6:**128
karsilamas dance, **3:**296, 299
Karsten, Sofia, **6:**40
Karstens, Gerda, **3:657, 5:**430
Karstens, Judith, **3:**3, *232*
kartala, **1:**174–175
kartal halayi, **6:**211
kartuli dance, **3:**134
Karussell. See horse ballet
Karyeva, Bernara, **6:**306

karyōbin dance, **2:**6
Karzcag, Eva, **1:**51
Kasai Akira, **2:**17, 18, **3:**591, **657–658, 6:**414
Kasami Yasuko, **3:**591
Kasane, **3:**593
Kasatkin, Denis, **6:***434*
Kasatkina, Natalia, **1:**371, 492, **3:**418, **4:**285, 335, 363, **5:**460, 472
   Creation of the World, The, **4:**336, **5:**461
   Ekaterinburg Opera Theater, **5:**470
   Moscow State Theater of Classical Ballet, **5:**461, 464, 467
   Sacre du Printemps, Le, **5:**488
Kaschmann, Truda, **1:**421, **3:**445, **4:**648–649
Kashani, Esfandiar, **5:***460*
Kashkin, Nikolai, **6:**116
Kashmir Legend, The, **3:**568
kaska, **4:**666
Kašlík, Václav, **2:**434
Kasoaka City, Japan, **3:**687–588
Kass, Jerome, **1:**420
Kassite period, **4:**356–357
Kasteeva, Zarema, **3:**665
Kastl, Sonja, **6:**432
kastrinós. *See maleviziótikos*
Kastuar, Jayant, **2:**468
Kasuga Shrine, Nara, **3:**646, **4:**41
Kasyan Goleizovsky (Vasilieva and Chernova), **5:**484
kata, **3:**638, **4:**84
Kata Kádár, **5:**287
Katakinas, Jonas, **4:**208
Katalyse, **2:**266
Kataoka Nizaemon XIII, **3:***640,* 658, **4:**536
Kataoka Takao (Kataoka Nizaemon XV), **1:**362, **3:**658
Kataoka Takatarō, **3:**658
Katcharoff, Michel, **1:**298, **5:**641
Katchourovsky, Leonid, **1:**410, 411
Katerina (Arkas opera), **6:**224–225
Katerina (Lavrovsky ballet; 1935), **4:**131
Katerina Ismailova 77, **5:**101
kathak, **1:**94, 171, **2:**102, 623, *623,* **3:**453, 467, 468, **658–660, 5:**510, 568, 580, 581
   costume, **2:**224, **3:**660
   Durgalal, **2:**468, *468*
   flamenco link, **3:**6
   Husain, Ghulam, **3:**425
   improvisation, **3:**448
   Kermani, Sheema, **4:**5, 6
   Lakhia, Kumudini, **4:**110–111
   Lucknow school, **5:**602
   Maharaj, Birju, **4:**247
   modern innovations, **3:**468
   Pakistan, **5:**62, 63, 64
   Sen, Saswati, **5:**568
   Sharma, Uma, **5:**581, 582
   Siddiqui, Nahid, **5:**597
   Sitara Devi, **5:**602–603
   structured design, **3:**463
kathakaḷi, **1:**162, 170, 178, 181–182, 188, **3:**199, *456,* 460, **660–663, 5:**292, 309
   costume, **2:**223–224, **3:***347,* 458
   epic sources, **3:**464, 458, 660–661
   kṛṣṇāṭṭam similarity, **4:**65
   makeup, **4:**298–299
   mime, **4:**423
   modern innovation, **3:**468
   mōhinīāṭaṃ as feminine equivalent, **4:**443
   mudrā meaning, **4:**478

New Zealand dance tour, **4:**628
   physical training for, **3:**453
   scholarship, **3:**470
   structured design, **3:**463
   teaching center, **3:**468
Kathak Ensemble, **3:**131
Katherine Dunham Museum, East Saint Louis, Illinois, **2:**459
Kathleen, **4:**593
Kato Miyako, **3:**591
Katrilli, Helsinki, **2:**633
katsina dancers, **3:**374–375, *374,* **4:**565, **5:**271, **6:**170
katsura (kabuki wig), **2:**218
Katsura Kan, **2:**18
katsureki geki, **3:**607
Kattfuss, Heinrich, **2:**339
katti (demon character), **4:**298, *299*
Katz, Alex, **1:**143, **6:**108, 109
Katz, Madeleine, **6:**60
Katz, Richard, **5:**661
   as contributor, **4:**74–76
Kauffer, E. McKnight, **2:**115, *400,* 401
Kauffman, Claudia Vall, **1:**431
Kaufman, George S., **6:**274, 275
Kaufmann, Gert. *See* Kadman, Gurit
Kaunitz, Prince, **1:**87
Kaushalya, **5:**330
Kavan, Albia, **1:**279
kāvya, **1:**168
Kawakami. *See* Yakko and Kawakami
Kawakamiza, **6:**409
Kawarazaki Gonjūrō I. *See* Ichikawa Danjūrō IX
Kawarazaki Gonnosuke VI, **3:**438
Kawatake Mokuami, **3:**593, 638
Kawatake Shigetoshi, **3:**592
Kaweski, Jan, **2:**122
Kay, Barry, **1:**233, **2:**440, **4:**242
Kaya, **5:**137
Kayaert, Robert, *as photographer,* **1:**290, 291
Kayapó Indians, **1:**531
Kayaw Group of the Montanosas, **5:**172
Kaye, Nora, **1:**11, 49, **2:**269, 277, 373, **3:**571, **663–664, 5:**290, **6:**137, 328
   American Ballet Theater, **1:***66,* 67, 68, 69, 75, **3:**26
   archival material, **4:**168
   Bruhn dance partnership, **2:**3
   Fokine association, **3:**22, 23, 663
   Japanese tour, **3:**589, 664
   Jardin aux Lilas performance, **3:***597*
   MacMillan ballets, **4:**241
   Metropolitan Opera Ballet School training, **4:**381
   New York City Ballet, **1:**68, **4:**616
   Pillar of Fire performance, **3:**663, **4:***109*
   Princess Aurora performance, **5:**612, *612*
   Robbins ballets, **5:**360, 361, 362
   Romeo and Juliet performance, **5:**397
   as "thinking dancer," **3:**663
   Tudor ballet roles, **5:**193, **6:**198, *198, 199, 199,* 200, *200,* 201
   Tudor mentorship, **3:**663, **4:**616
Kaye, Pooh, **1:**25, **2:**609
Kayon puppet, **6:**368
Kazakhstan, **3:**664–665
Kazan, Elia, **6:**278
Kazan Opera and Ballet Company, **5:**472–473

Kazarian, Tovmas, **1:**120
Kazhlayev, Murad, **6:**341
Kazukuri Yuko, **2:**18
Kazunobi Yanagi, *as photographer,* **2:**500
Kazuraki, **3:**653
K Danse, **5:**64
Kealiinohomoku, Joann W., **4:**370, 373, 374
   as contributor, **3:**373–375, **4:**77–78, **5:**252–253
Kean (musical), **2:**185
Kean, Rebekah Harkness. *See* Harkness, Rebekah
Keane, James, **5:**695
Keane, Elizabeth, **6:**266
Keene, Christopher, **2:**583
Keep Fit Association, **4:**94
Keep Going, **5:***233*
Keep Off the Grass (musical), **5:**359, **6:**277
Keersmaeker, Anne Teresa de. *See* de Keersmaeker, Anne Teresa
Keesmaat, Hannie, **4:**595
Keet, Marina, **2:**57, **5:**652, 654
   as contributor. See Grut, Marina
Kehlet, Niels, **2:**201, **3:**667–668, **5:**430, *431*
Keil, Birgit, **2:**266, **3:**351, **4:**1–2, **6:***136*
   Cranko Medal, **2:**268, **4:**2
   Giselle performance, **6:**454
   Initialen R.B.M.E. performance, **2:**267, **4:**1
   Stuttgart Ballet, **6:**10, *10*
Keil, Gerhard, **3:**154
Kéita, Fodéba, **1:**303, 304, **5:**516
Kei Takei, **5:**46
Keith, B. F., **6:**99, 317
Keith, Jens, **1:**456, **4:**91
Keith's vaudeville circuit, **2:**376, **6:**317
Kékesi, Mária, **3:**418
Kekisheva, Galina, **4:***277*
Kela, Reijo, **2:**634
Kelaa M'Gouna (people), **4:**466
Kelantan, Malaysia, **2:**229, **4:**337
Kelbauskas, Bronius, **4:**208
Kelder, Diane, **1:**447
Kelemen, Milko, **5:**676, **6:**433
Kelland, Eve, **2:**525
Kelland-Espinosa, Edward, **2:**525
Kellaway, Leon, **3:**203
Keller, Maurice, **3:**16, **6:**60
Kellgren, Jessica, **2:**633
Kellgren, Johan Henrik, **6:**49–50
Kelly, Anthony, **5:**691
Kelly, Bridget, **3:**512
Kelly, Desmond, **2:**174
Kelly, Ellsworth, **1:**143

Kelly, Gene, **1:**194, 432, **2:2–4,** 108, 251, **4:**419
   archival material, **4:**168
   Broadway musicals, **6:**278
   dance style, **4:**3–4
   as film director, **6:**183
   Hollywood musicals, **2:**613, 616, 617–618, *618, 619,* **4:2–3,** **6:**287
   Invitation to the Dance film, **4:**3, **6:**425
   Pas des Dieux, **2:**388, **4:**3, **5:**97
   Singin' in the Rain, **5:**21, *21*
   as tap dancer, **6:**101
   television performances, **6:**138
   video documentary on, **1:**194, **2:**314
Kelly, Grace, **2:**509, 510
Kelly, Joanne, **4:**627
Kelly, Kevin, **1:**419
Kelly, Margaret. *See* Bluebell, Miss
Kelly, Ned, *as photographer,* **1:***215*
Kemoko, Sano, **516–517**
Kemp, Lindsay, **2:**1, 45, **5:**302, **6:**134
Kemp, Travis, **4:**110
Kempe, William, **3:**60, **4:**462
kemshoole, **2:**474
kenan, **5:**84
Kendall, Elizabeth B., *as contributor,* **4:**213–214
kendo, **1:**186, 188
Kenebel, Virginie, **2:**176
Kenessey, Jenő, **3:**416
Kengmo, Paul, **2:**33
Kenilworth, **2:**390, **3:**176, 260
Ken Murray's Blackouts, **1:**382, *382*
Kennard, C., *as photographer,* **2:**571
Kennedy, Douglas, **2:**592, **3:**239
Kennedy, Jacqueline (later Onassis), **1:**70
Kennedy, James (pseud. of James Monahan), **3:**285
Kennedy, John F., **1:**55, 70, **3:**611
Kennedy, Patrice, **4:**596
Kennedy, Peter, **2:**592
Kennedy, Sherilyn, **4:**626
Kennedy Center, Washington, D.C., **1:**74, 75, **4:**168
Kennedy Center Tonight (television series), **2:**334
Kenney, Colleen, **4:***540*
Kenny, Don, *as contributor,* **4:**85–86, 660–661, 661–662
Kenosha, David, **4:**558
Ken Pierce Baroque Dance Company, **5:**327
Ken-si and Tao, **2:**414
Kent, Allegra, **4:4–5**
   Afternoon of a Faun performance, **1:**29, **6:**339
   Bugaku performance, **4:***616,* 617
   Dances at a Gathering performance, **2:**333, **4:**5, *619*
   Divertimento No. 15 performance, **2:**420, **4:**5
   as Maracci student, **4:**262
   New York City Ballet roles, **4:**617
   Sonnambula performance, **4:**5, 617
   Symphony in C performance, **6:**66
   Villella dance partnership, **6:**339, 340
Kent, Julie, **1:**77
Kent, Linda, **4:**482
Kenton, Stan, **4:**116, 240
Kentucky Running Set, **5:**329
Kenya, **2:**86, 87, 89, *90,* 91, 212
   Digo dance, **2:**417–418
   Giriama dance, **3:**177

libraries and museums, **4:**158
music for dance, **4:**484
national dance company, **6:**22
Kenyan, Neal, **6:**284
Kenzi et Tao, **4:**277–278
Keppler, Céleste. *See* Céleste,
Madame
Kerala, India, **2:**223, **3:**459, 463,
468, 470, **4:**65–66, 79–80, 443
See also kathakali
Kerala Kalmandalam, **3:**661
Keral Kala Mandalaem, Kerala,
3:468
keras, **1:**174, 175
kerauhan. See trance dance, Bali
Kerche, Cecilia, **1:**533
Kerchief, The, **3:**341, 415, **5:**472
kerchief dance. *See* handkerchief
dance
keren (*kabuki* special effects), **3:**440
Keres, Imre, **3:**125, 360
Keresley, Leo, **1:**289
keris dancers, **1:**176, **3:**491
Kermani, Sheema, **4:**5–6, **5:**63,
64, *64*
Kermesse, La (Petipa ballet), **1:**410,
5:147
Kermesse in Bruges (Bournonville
ballet), **1:**454, 510, 511, **4:**6,
5:250–251
Brenaa production, **1:**539
Karstens character dancing,
3:657
Paulli score, **1:**515
Schanne performance, **5:**553
Simone performance, **5:**600
Kern, Jerome, **1:**193, 194, 520,
2:281, 618, **4:**335, 420, **5:**602,
6:271, 272, 273, 274, 277, 289
Kerr, Harrison, **1:**421
Kerr, Joan, **4:**225
Kerr, Mary, **4:**166, **5:**435
Kerr, Russell, **4:**624, 625, 626
Kerridge, Jeremy, **4:**668
Kerry Set, **3:**517
Kersands, Billy, **6:**254
Kersley, Leo, **1:**289, **3:**511, **6:**196
Kertesz, André, **5:**186
Kesselheim, Silvia, **1:**388, 389
Kessler, Harry, **3:**20, 631, **5:**493
Kesten, Hilde, **3:**529, 530, *530*
Kestenberg, Judith, **2:**321, **4:**104
Kestenberg Movement Profile,
2:321
Keth, Jens, **3:**625
Ketly, of the Mountain Rose, **4:**455
ketuk tilu, **3:**503, **5:**130
Keuter, Cliff, **4:**602, **5:**301, 302, 316
Keveházi, Gábor, **3:**418, 419
Kevorkov, Sergei, **1:**48, 248, **5:**472
Kewley, Vanya, **5:**575
Key, Guillermo, **4:**392
Keynes, Geoffrey, **2:**399, **3:**608,
608–609
Keynes, John Maynard, **4:**223–224
Keys Arenas, Guillermo, **4:**397
Kgaga (people), **5:**643, 646
Khachatrian, Genja, *as contributor,*
1:119–121
Khachaturian, Aram, **1:**90–9,
2:502, 579, **4:**6–7, **5:**268, 569,
6:310
first Armenian national ballet,
1:121
Gayané score, **3:**125, 153, 312,
4:517
musical idiom, **4:**517
Prisoner of the Caucasus score,
3:226
Soviet choreographies, **4:**285, 517

Spartacus score, **3:**308, *417,* **4:**7,
284, 444, **5:**569, 677, 678,
6:411
Khadra, **3:**62
Khalfouni, Dominique, **1:**405,
2:114, **3:**75, **5:**97, *97*
Khalīj al-aghānī, **4:**414
Khalil, Mohammed, **2:**496
Khamma, **2:**360, 361
Khamsin, **4:**219
Khan, Ashique Hussain, **4:**110
Khan, Ustad Allauddin, **5:**580
Khandekar, Renuker, **4:**63
Khanum, Koutchouk, **2:**345
Khanum, Tamara, **3:**568, **4:**7–8,
6:306, *306*
Kharkevitch, Kyra, **1:**292
Kharkov, Ukraine, **6:**225, 226
Khasi (people), **1:**362
kheliji, **1:**102
Khevsur dance, **3:**134
Khmer Empire. *See* Cambodia
Khmer Rouge, **2:**29, 30
Khodasevich, Valentina, **3:**56
Khodasevich, Vera, **3:**192, **5:**677
Khodot, Olga, **4:**133
khoduchi dance, **5:**444
Khokar, Mohan, **3:**470
Khoklov, Boris, **5:**435
Kholfin, Nikolai, **1:**144, **2:**11, 15,
4:86–87, **6:**213
"dancing actor" principle, **5:**466
Kholfina, Serafima, **4:**38
khomba rites, **5:**579
khōn, **1:**179, **2:**227, 228, *228,*
4:8–10, **6:**148, *148, 149*
ethnographic film, **2:**602
khora, **4:**446
Khorasan, **3:**513–514
Khoreograficheskie otkrovennosti
(Lopukhov), **4:**225
Khorezm dances, **6:**305
Khoroshki company, **1:**408
khorovod dance, **5:**443, 444, 445
Khorumi (Moiseyev choreography),
4:445
khorumi dance, **3:**134
Khory Fetelor, **4:**78
Khovantchina, **1:**482, **5:**37
Khrennikov, Tikhon, **6:**341
Khudekov, Sergei, **1:**392, **4:**145,
5:153, 482
ki (life force), **1:**184
ki-ak dance, **1:**167
Kibbutz Contemporary Dance
Company, **3:**532–533,
4:59, 532
Kibbutz Dalia, **3:**530, 641
Kibbutz Ga'aton, **3:**532
kibbutzim, **3:**528, *528,* 529,
530, 535
Kibbutz Ramat Hakovesh, **4:**155
Kibbutz Ramat Yohanan, **3:**531
Kibbutz Teachers Seminary, Tel
Aviv, **3:**535
Kichiemon. *See* Nakamura
Kichiemon
Kick Dance, **4:**567
kickin' (term). *See* country-western
dance
Kidd, Michael, **1:**482, **2:**245, 616,
3:664, **4:**10–11, **6:**137, 327
American Ballet Theatre, **1:**68
Ballet Caravan, **4:**10
Band Wagon choreography, **2:**109
Broadway musicals, **2:**251,
6:279–280, 284
Fancy Free performance, **4:**10,
5:359
film choreography, **4:**3,
6:280, 281

Guys and Dolls choreography,
6:281
Interplay performance, **6:**279
as musical director-
choreographer, **6:**281, 284
Yankee Clipper, **4:**227
Kid Millions (film), **4:**629
Kidung Sunda (East Javanese
poem), **3:**477
Kiefer, Otto, **5:**377
Kieselhausen, Lucy, **1:**239
Kiesler, Fredrick, **5:**568
Kiev, Ukraine, **6:**225, 226
Kiev Opera Ballet, **4:**634, **5:**236,
6:224, 225
Kikimora Theater Company,
1:85
Kikta, Valery, **5:**471
Kiku, **1:**248
Kikugorō Gekidan troupe, **5:**30
Kikujido, **3:**89–90
Kilányi, Lajos, **3:**414
Kilar, Wojciech, **1:**349
Kilian, Gundel, *as photographer,*
1:375, **2:**208, 596, **3:**4, 174,
5:682, 683, **6:**11, 52
Kilian, Hannes, *as photographer,*
6:10
Kiliński, Zbigniew, **5:**218
Killar, Ashley, **2:**267, **3:**150, **4:**625,
5:55, 659, **6:**10, 379–380
Killing of the Children, The
(medieval play), **3:**251
Kill What I Love, **1:**350
Kilowatt Magic, **5:**434
Kilpatrick, David, **3:**303
kilt, Scottish, **3:**249
Kim, Theresa Ki-ja, *as contributor,*
5:578–579
Kimball, Renee, **6:**109
Kimberlin, Cynthia Tse, *as*
contributor, **2:**530–534
Kim Chong-yon, **4:**54
Kim Ch'un-heung, **4:**12
Kim Hae Shik, **3:**3
Kim Hyon-ok, **4:**52
Kim-Ka, **4:**455
Kim Ka, or the Adventures of an
Aeronaut (pantomime-ballet),
5:319
Kim Keum-ha, **4:**48
Kim Ku, **2:**155
Kim Mae-ja, **4:**52, 54
Kim On-kyong, 454
kimono, **3:**638, 639, 640
Kim Paik-bong, **4:**12–13
Kimura, Naomi, **2:**36
Kimura, Yuriko, **3:**216, 220, 591
Kinaesonata, **4:**156
"Kinakulangan" (dance), **5:**171
Kinal, Sylvie, **2:**605
Kinch, Myra, **2:**581, **3:**183
Kincses, József, **1:**307
Kinder, Jenny, **1:**216
Kinderballett. *See* Viennese
Kinderballett
kindergartens, **3:**159, **6:**239
Kindermann, Johann Erasmus,
4:507
Kindertotenlieder (Mahler song
cycle), **2:**348, 349, **5:**299,
6:197
Kindertotenlieder (Rückert poem),
2:348
Kindes Gymnastik und Tanz, Des
(Laban), **4:**92, 99
Kindī, Abū Yūsuf Ya'qūb al-, **4:**488
Kindo, Christopher, **5:**657
kinemes, **4:**366–367, 368
kinesemes, **4:**367–368

Kinesiography (Loring and Canna),
4:691
kinesiology, **4:**13–21
as academic discipline, **4:**16–17
background and overview,
4:13–18
ideokinesis, **1:**469, 470, 475–476,
4:17
Laban, Rudolf, **4:**89–90, 91, 94,
95, 97, 98–105
linguistic analogies, **4:**366–368
orchestics, **2:**417, **3:**420–421
physics basis, **5:**188–191
therapeutic practices, **1:**471–472,
476, **4:**18–21, 97
Kinesiology for Dance (Fitt), **4:**17
Kinesiology for Dance (newsletter),
2:329, **4:**17
kinesphere (Laban term), **4:**100
Kinetic Molpai, **5:**586, 586
Kinetikos Dance Theatre, **1:**217
Kinetographisches Institut, Essen,
4:32
Kinetography Laban. *See*
Labanotation
King, Alonso, **6:**366
King, Audrey, **5:**54, 652, 653, 659
King, Christine, **4:**449
King, Eleanor, **1:**421, **3:**404, **4:**130
King, Harold, **3:**269
King, John, **1:**142
King, Kenneth, **2:**358, 462, 608,
609, **3:**447, 634, **4:**21–22
King, Liz, **1:**240
King, Mary Perry, **2:**371
King, Mazie, **6:**318
King, Theresa, *as photographer,*
2:575
King and I, The (film), **5:**363
King and I, The (musical), **5:**362,
6:281, 282, 288–289
King Arthur, or The British Worthy
(Purcell), **5:**251, 281
King Arthur's Knights, **6:**175
King Candaule, **5:**251
Kingdom of Pagodas, The, **1:**52
Kingdom of the Shades scene (*La*
Bayadère), **1:**392, 393,
5:418, 456
King John (Shakespeare), **3:**356
King Kamehameha Traditional
Hula and Chant Competition
(Hawaii), **3:**395
King Lear, **2:**423
King of Spain, The (Wilson opera),
6:400
King of Sweden (Scottish dance),
3:246
King of the Clock Tower, The
(Yeats), **2:**397, **3:**519
King Roger, **4:**479
Kings and Queens, **3:**368
King's Command, The, **6:**452
King Sejong University, **3:**341
King's Jester, The, **5:**219
King's Lifguards on Amager, The,
5:251
"Kings of Man," **3:**251
King Solomon: The Fall of
Jerusalem (musical
spectacle), **4:**23
King's Theatre, London (also Her
Majesty's Theatre), **1:**35,
36, 505
as ballet center, **3:**257–261
Cerrito dance triumphs, **2:**93, 94
Chalon caricatures of dancers,
2:103
choreographic residencies, **3:**256
contemporary reviews of
performances, **3:**284

King's Theatre, London, *continued*
dance school, **3:**279
Dauberval productions, **2:**352,
3:257–258
D'Egville association, **2:**363–364,
365, **3:**279
Deshayes (André) association,
2:389, 390
Didelot association, **2:**413, 414,
3:258, 259, 326
Elssler sisters' performances,
2:502–503
first ballet produced, **3:**257
Fitzjames (Nathalie) as principal
dancer, **3:**5
Gallet association, **3:**106
Gallini association, **3:**111, 112
Giselle restaging, **3:**180, 314
Gitana restaging, **3:**185
Grisi debut, **3:**313
Grisi performances, **3:**314,
315, 316
Guimard performances, **3:**326
Heinel performances, **3:**353
L'Abbé as dancing master, **4:**105
Le Picq performances and
productions, **4:**149
Noblet guest performances, **4:**656
Noverre productions, **3:**112, 117,
256, 257, 258, **4:**697, 698
Pas de Quatre performance, **3:**224
Perrot and Deshayes
collaboration, **2:**389, 390
Perrot association, **2:**94,
3:*259*, 260
programs and libretti, **4:**177
Pugni, Cesare, **5:**277
Ronzani as ballet master, **5:**403
Saint-Léon productions, **3:**260,
5:498, 499
Sangalli performances, **5:**514
Taglioni (Marie) performances,
2:502–503, **3:***258*
King's Volunteers on Amager, The,
1:*399*, 511, *512*, 539, **4:***513*,
5:426, 600
Kinjiki, **2:**17, **3:**362–363
Kinkan Shonen, **1:**60, 61
Kinney, Leila, **4:**415
Kinney, Sharon, **6:***109*
Kinoshita Junji, **4:**661, **5:**591
kinpira jōruri, **2:**13
Kinsey, Carol, **2:***56*, 58
Kinsky, Joseph, **6:**335
Kinsky, Klaus, **3:**359
Kintakamardawa, **3:**497
Kintzel, Renée Odic, **3:**76
Kioi Jishi, **3:**593
Kiowa Indians, **3:**171
Kiradžieva, Nadežda (Nina), **2:**11,
12, **5:**166
Kiralfy, Arnold, **4:**24
Kiralfy, Bolossy, **4:**22–23, *23*, 24
Kiralfy, Calvin, **4:**24
Kiralfy, Emilie, **4:***23*
Kiralfy, Haniola, **4:***23*, **4:**22, 23,
23, 177
Kiralfy, Imre, **2:**477, **4:**22–23,
23, 24
Kiralfy, Katie, **4:***23*
Kiralfy, Marie, **4:***23*
Kiralfy, Veronica, **4:**24
Kiralfy family, **4:**22–24
Black Crook, The, **1:**457, *457*, 496,
4:*23*
Excelsior, **2:**540
Kiralfy Kiddies, **4:**24
Kirare Yosa, **1:**362, **3:**439
Kirasova Ballet, **1:***206*
Kirby, Monsieur, **5:***69*
Kirby's Flying Ballet, **5:**71

Kirchhoff, Christian, **3:**302
Kirchner, Ludwig, **1:**131
Kirghizia. *See* Kyrgyzstan
kiriba, **2:**418
Kiribati, **4:**400, *401*, 497
Kiri Hitoka, **4:**537
Kirillov, Vladimir, **5:**467
Kirjonen, Juha, **2:**633
Kirk, Mette-Ida, **5:**430
Kirkaldie, Michela, **1:**210
Kirkenær, Jorunn, **4:**681
Kirkland, Gelsey, **1:***270,* **4:**24–25
American Ballet Theatre, **1:**68,
73, 74, *74,* 75
Baryshnikov dance partnership,
1:74, *74,* 372, **2:***439,* **4:**24
Coppélia, **2:**201
Don Quixote performance, **2:***439,*
441, **4:**24
Dowell dance partnership, **2:**444,
4:24
Firebird performance, **3:**3
Goldberg Variations performance,
4:24, 618
Makarova as influence, **1:**73
New York City Ballet, **4:**618
Nutcracker performance, **5:**16
Tomasson dance partnership,
6:174, *174*
as Tudor muse, **6:**202, *203*
Kirkwood, James, **1:**419
Kirnbauer, Susanne, **1:**241
Kirokuda, **5:**591
Kirova, S. M., **4:**276
Kirova, Vera, **2:**11
Kirov Ballet. *See* Maryinsky Ballet
Kirov Palace of Culture, Leningrad,
5:461
Kirov State Academic Theater for
Opera and Ballet, Saint
Petersburg. *See* Maryinsky
Ballet
Kirsanova, Nina, **6:**432, 436
Kirsanova, Vera, **3:**317
Kirsova, Hélène, **1:**207–208, 309,
311, 313, 499, **3:**24, **4:**25–26
Kirsova Ballet, **1:**208, 209, **4:**25–26
Kirsta, George, **1:**316, **4:**380, **6:**399
Kirstein, Lincoln, **2:**26–30, **5:**186,
297, **6:**118–119, 129
on *Agon,* **1:**30
American Ballet, **1:**63–64,
280–281, **4:**27–28
American ballet scenarios, **4:**612
on *American Document,* **1:**82
archival materials, **4:**167
Balanchine association, **1:**63, 64,
141, 256, 257, 263, 280–281,
300, 307, **4:**26, 27, 608
Ballet Caravan, **1:**279, 280, **2:**160,
4:10, 28
ballet education, **6:**292
Ballet Society, **1:**141, **2:**161,
4:28–29, 606, **6:**247
Billy the Kid libretto, **1:**452,
4:28, 612
Boston Ballet, **1:**501
Cage-Cunningham
commissioned work,
2:22, 286
on character dancing, **2:**106
Christensen (Lew) association,
2:161
dance history studies, **4:**27,
6:246, 296, 297
on Farrell's dancing, **2:**577
as Fokine student, **3:**22
libretti, **1:**452, **4:**27, 28, 612
Loring association, **4:**227
Metropolitan Opera Ballet, **4:**382

New York City Ballet, **1:**152,
2:265, 606, **3:**442, **4:**623
on Nijinsky's modernism,
4:647–648
principal contribution to
American dance, **4:**26
Rosenthal lighting collaboration,
5:407
School of American Ballet, **1:**263,
6:246, 292
Stravinsky commissions, **6:**5, 6
Tudor commission, **6:**198
on Villella's dance portrayals,
6:339, 340
*Kirsten Piil, eller To
Midsommerfester,* **1:**509, 514
kisaeng, **1:**166
Kisch, Istvan, **6:**43, *46*
Kismet (musical), **2:**185, **6:**281, 285
Kiss, János, **3:**329, 330
Kiss, Nora, **1:**290, **3:**82, **4:**251,
5:320
Kisselgoff, Anna
on Ailey, **1:**58, 60
on Balanchine Celebration
(1993), **4:**622
on Balasaraswati, **1:**274
dance criticism, **6:**299
on Hawkins, **3:**350
on Kudelka choreography, **4:**73
on Lifar technique, **4:**183
on Maslow choreography, **4:**306
Kissing Bandit, The (film),
2:108, *251*
kissing reel, **3:**246
Kiss Me, Kate (film), **3:**54, *55*
Kiss Me, Kate (musical), **2:**186,
6:145
Holm choreography, **3:**370,
371–372, **6:**280, *280*
Kiss My Eyes Goodnight, **2:**358
Kiss of the Spider Woman
(musical), **5:**358, **6:**288
Kistler, Darci
Afternoon of a Faun, **1:**29
Apollo, **1:**96
Martins marriage, **4:**623
New York City Ballet roles, **4:**618,
622, 623
Sleeping Beauty performance,
4:622, *622*
Kitāb al-aghānī (al-Isfahānī), **4:**416
kita dance, **3:**334
Kita Minoru, **4:**30
Kita Nō Theater Company, **2:**215,
3:*581*
Kita Roppeita XIV, **3:**652, **4:**30
Kita Roppeita XV, **4:**30–31, *31*
Kita school, **1:**187, **3:***581*, 651, 652,
4:30–31, 332
Kita Shichidayū, **4:**30
Kitchell, Iva, **2:**70
Kitcher, Barry, **1:***208*
Kitchy-Koo of 1918 (revue), **6:**272
Kith and Kin, **6:**113
kithara, **3:**293, 295
Kithsiri Megawanna, king of
Kandy, **3:**649
Kitri's Wedding. See Don Quixote
Kitt, Eartha, **2:**458
Kitti, Tommi, **2:**634
Kitty Tango (Charlip), **2:**72
Kitzinc, Minna, **3:***144*
KIUBATA troupe, **2:**91
kiva, **4:**563
Kivelä, Sempo, **2:**633
Kivitt, Ted, **1:**73
kiyomoto style, **3:**639
Kiyotsune, **6:**445
Kjaerligheds og Mistankens Magt,
3:105

Kjelberg, Ellen, **4:***678*
Kjølaas, Gerd, **4:**675–676, *675*
kkaekki dance, **4:**50
Klachte de Levenden, **1:**411
Kladivova, Irina, **1:**1
Kladnikina, Tatiana, **6:**436
Klagenfurt, Austria, **1:**241–242
Klakegg, Øystein, *as photographer,*
4:681
Klamt, Jutta, **3:**531, **4:**208
Klapstuk, **1:**412, 414
Klár, Jan, **2:**309
*Klassichesky tanec: Istoriia i
sovremennost* (Blok), **1:**463
Klatzow, Peter, **2:**57, **5:**57, 58
Klaus, François, **6:**53
Klavsen, Verner, **5:**47, **6:**42, *46*
Kleban, Edward, **1:**419
Klebanov, Dmitri, **3:**197
Klebe, Giselher, **1:**456
Kleczyński, Jan, **5:**220
Klee, Paul, **1:**132, 385, **3:**387, **5:**66
Klee Wyck: A Ballet for Emily, **6:**132
Kleiber, Walter, **5:**681
Kleimenova, Musa S., *as
contributor,* **4:**131–132,
148–149
Klein, Aleksandr, **2:**15
Klein, Erika, **6:**162
Klein, Ernst, **6:**36, 49
Klein, Michael, **3:**163
Klein, Thomas, **5:***674*
Klein, Yves, **1:**139
Kleine Diebin, Die, **6:**335
Kleine Passion, **2:**154
Kleine Tänze mit Vorübungen, **4:**96
Klein Kunst (Small Art), **4:**115
Klein Zack, **3:**133
Kleist, Heinrich, **1:**134
Klekovic, Patricia, **5:***60*
Klemm, Bernard, **4:**686
klezmorim, **3:**605
Klimentová, Daria, **2:**310, **5:**57
Klimova, Marina, **3:**432
Klimt, Gustav, **3:**387
Kline, Franz, **1:***138*, 139
Kloborg, Eva, **5:***106, 432*
Klodt, N. A., **2:**436
Kloepper, Louise, **1:**421, **3:**369,
371, **4:**130, **6:**191
Klono Topéng, **3:**495, 498–499
Klos, Vladimír, **2:**308, **4:**1
Klosty, James, **2:**609, **5:**186
as photographer, **1:**141, **6:**162
Kloubek, Vladimír, **2:**309
klumpfen dance, **2:**180
Klunder, Andy, **4:**245
Klüver, Billy, **5:**314
Klyagin, Irina, *as contributor,*
1:83–84, **4:**180–181
Kmhmu (people), **4:**123
Knaifel, Aleksandr, **1:**39
Knee Deep in Thin Air, **1:**215
Knee Plays, The (Wilson), **3:**339,
6:401
kng kui, **5:**85
Kniaseff, Boris, **1:**111, 315, **2:**11,
113, **3:**82, 601, **4:**68, 435,
5:678
Noces performance, **4:**659
students, **2:**343, 471, **5:**553
Kniazeva, Olga, **5:**474
Knickerbocker Holiday (musical),
6:278
knife dance. *See* dagger dance
Kniga likovanii (Volynsky), **5:**482–
483, **6:**352
Knight, Alethea, **5:***659*
Knight, Aniruddha, **1:**274
Knight, Arthur, **2:**603

Knight, Donald, *as contributor,*
4:31–32
Knight, Douglas, 4:31
Knight, Lakshmi, 1:274, **4:31–32**
Knight, Laura, 5:262
Knight Errant, **6:**201–202
Knight in a Tiger Skin, The
(Vinogradov ballet), 4:285
Knight in Panther Skin, The
(Rustaveli), 3:134
Knighton, Bit, 2:566
Knighton, Marian, 1:421
Knight's Ballad, 5:614
Knill, Hans, 4:81, 602
Knipper, Ellen. *See* Tels, Ellen
Knipper, Lev, 5:473
Knipschildt, Else, 2:385
Kniza, Erika, 6:388
Knoben, Marly, 4:602
Knossos, Crete, 2:270
KNOW (Knowledge Network),
6:132–133
Knowles, Alison, 2:22
Knowles, Ian, 5:55
Knra, Vivek, 4:628
Knust, Albrecht, 1:390, 411, **4:32,**
91, 96, 103
movement choir, 4:476
personal archives, 4:164
Ko, Murobushi, 2:18
ko:luba, 5:81, 82
Koasati (people), 4:558
Kobayashi Ichizo, 6:84
Kobayashi Saga, 3:363
Köbbler, Jeannette and Nanette,
4:588–589
Kobborg, Johan, 1:*506,* 5:433
Kobelev, K., 4:*634*
Koberwein, Katharina, 3:380
Kobi, Maria, 5:677
Kobold, Der, 1:238, 3:314, 5:135
Kobylansky, Catherine, 5:278
köçek, 6:210
Köçekce, 6:213
Koch, Friedrich Ernst, 1:456
Kochanowski, Jan, 5:210
Kochetovsky, Aleksandr, 2:11,
4:634, 6:224
Kochno, Boris, 1:426, 3:394,
4:32–34, 5:163, 526, 527, 679
Ballet Russe de Monte Carlo,
1:295
Ballets des Champs-Élysées,
1:305–306, 3:73
Ballets 1933, 1:306–307, 3:72
as Ballets Russes de Monte Carlo
artistic adviser, 1:308, 326
Chatte libretto, 1:258, 5:526
Cotillon libretto, 2:253
as Diaghilev assistant, 2:410, 411,
4:33
Prodigal Son libretto, 5:264,
265, 266
reconstruction of Taglioni's *La
Sylphide,* 6:58–59
Zéphire et Flore re-creation idea,
4:320
kochō dance, 2:6
Kochōmai, 4:494
Kocka, Katarina, 6:438
Kodalii, Nevit, 2:401, 6:212, 213
Kodály, Zoltán, 2:473, 474, 3:318
Budapest Opera Ballet
productions, 3:415
folk music influence, 3:405
Hungarian folk dance research,
3:423
János Háry, 3:412
modern dance scores, 3:384
Kodi, Hema Kaiser, 1:94
kodīah, 2:487

kŏdŭrŭm dance, 4:50
Koe, A. de, 4:585
Koechlin, Charles, 2:360, 5:236,
526, 6:201, *202*
Koegler, Horst, 3:162, 424
as contributor, 1:1, 11, 390–391,
402–403, 430–431, 436, 456,
460, 500–501, 2:81, 261– 262,
265–268, 478, 561–562,
3:51–53, 143–148, 148– 158,
317–318, 336–338, 350–351,
368, 4:1–2, 59–60, 203–204,
245–246, 602–604, 5:42–43,
334, 6:8–11, 228–229,
358–359
Koehne, Graeme, 4:479
Koesun, Ruth Ann, 1:69, 2:*374*
Kogan, Timur, 1:539
Kohler, Marie, 2:173
Köhler-Richter, Emmy, 3:154
Kohlkopp (Berlin cabaret), 3:163
Kohomba Kankariya, 2:228, 3:647,
4:34–35, 6:329
Kohoutek, Barbora and Vendula,
2:310
Koichi, Tamano, 2:18
Koje, Aicha, 4:487
Kojiki (Japanese text), 3:578, 591
Kokaji, 3:441
K.O.K.A.R. (Konservatori Karwitan
Indonesia Bali), 3:476
Kokata (people), 1:229
kōken, 3:639
Kokhlova, Olga, 5:192
Kokitch, Casimir, 3:104, 5:369
Kokkonen, Timo, 2:633
Kokonin, Vladimir, 1:493, 6:315
kokonjeste pattern, 6:427
kokoro (Japanese concept),
4:654, 655
Kokoschka, Oskar, 1:131, 466,
6:146
Kokotović, Nada, 6:435
Koktem, 3:665
Kol, Siki, 3:532
kolam-natima masked dance, 4:300
Kolář, Petr, 2:309
Kolb, Wolfgang, 2:611
kolbaşı, 6:210
Kolben, Amir, 3:534
Kolberg, Oskar, 5:210, 6:223
Kolčakova, L., 5:166
Koldamova, Krasimira, 1:349, 2:11
Koleda Folk Ensemble, 4:470
koleso, 2:100, 101
Koleva, R., 2:10
Köllinger, Bernd, 3:162, 5:557
Kölling, Rudolf, 3:*149,* 415
Kollwitz, Käthe, 3:152
Kolnik, Paul, 5:186
as photographer, 4:623, 5:265, 366
kolo, 2:100, 101, 6:426, 428,
430–431
Kolodin, Irving, 5:163
kolomeyka, 3:38
Kolosova, Evgenia, 3:539, **4:35–36,**
36, 279, 280, 5:453, 6:312
Kolossánszky, János, 3:413
Kolpakova, Irina, 1:77, 231, 2:437,
441, **4:36–37,** 144, 285, 5:459
Giselle performance, 5:5
Nutcracker performance, 5:12
Stone Flower performance, 5:699
Kołpikówna, Miła, 5:75
Kølpin, Alexander, 5:433
Koltai, Chrissie, 1:214
Koltsova, Mirra, 5:473
Koly, Souleymane, 5:517
Koma. *See* Eiko and Koma
Koma, 3:440
komagaku, 1:168, 2:5, 6, 102–103

Komaki Masahide, 3:589
Komar, Chris, 2:*289,* 294, **4:37**
Komarova, Hélène, 1:315
Komischen Oper Berlin. *See* Berlin
Dance Theater
Komkov, Vladimir, 1:408
Komleva, Gabriella, 2:437,
4:37–38, 147, 285, 5:460
Kommen und Gehen, 4:81
kommos, 3:289
Komödie, 4:91, 92
Komori, 3:593
kōmos, 3:287, 293, 4:*499,* 5:598
Komparu Yasuaki, 4:*653*
Kompiang, Gusti, 4:265
Konaraka Dance Festival, 4:247
Kondratieva, Marina, 1:491, **4:38,**
5:459, 567, 595
Kondratov, Yuri, 1:490, 491, 5:595,
6:*410*
*Konek Gorbunok. See Little
Humpbacked Horse, The*
Koner, Pauline, 1:421, 2:269, 3:23,
391, 402, 559, **4:38–39,** 6:137
Jacob's Pillow performance,
3:571
Limón Dance Company, 4:198
Moor's Pavane performance,
4:*199,* 458, *458*
koneri, 5:26
Kongelige Danske Ballet, Den
(Krogh and Kragh-Jacobsen),
2:387
Kongen paa Jagt, 3:105
Kongens Nytorv troupe, 2:384
Kongo (people), 1:14, 526–527,
529, 530
as Cuban dance influence,
2:274–275
geographic regions, 2:86
shoulder dance emphasis, 2:90
Kongō Gon-no-kami, 4:40
Kongō Iwao I, **4:40**
Kongō Iwao II, 3:*40,* 4:40
Kongō school, 4:30, **39–40**
Kongō Ujiakai, 4:40
Kongō Ujikatasu, 4:40
Kongress Karussell, 3:383
Koni, Fedor, **4:40–41**
Konigsmark, 4:625
Königstanz, 3:625
Konings, Hennie, 4:595
Koninklijke Muntschouwburg,
Brussels, 4:136
Koninklÿk Ballet van Vlaanderen,
1:411
Koninsberg Aroeste, Matilde, 4:399
konkoma dance, 3:167
Kononovich, Vladimir, 1:144
konopice, 2:301–302
Konparu Gon-no-kami, 4:41, 42
Konparu Mitsutarō Hachijō, 4:41
Konparu Nobutaka, **4:41–42**
Konparu school, 3:650, 651,
4:41–42
Konparu Yasuburō, 4:42
Konparu Zenchiku, 3:581, 4:41, 86,
6:446
Konparu Zenpō, 4:41, *42*
Konservatoriet, 1:345, 510, 511,
2:535, 3:43, 5:250, 553, 554
Australian Ballet revival, 1:231
ballet class scene, 1:329–330
Brenaa production, 1:539
Gnatt production, 4:626
Paulli score, 1:515
Price (Juliette) performance,
5:425
Vangsaae staging, 2:511
Williams (Stanley) performance,
6:399

Konstantinova, Marina E., 5:483
as contributor, 4:335–336
Konstantin Sergeyev Ballet
Foundation, 4:165
Konsulova, Violetta, *as contributor,*
2:10–12, 5:166
Kontakhof, 1:*388*
Kontakion, 4:218
kontro, 5:211–212
kontsovka step, 5:445
Konyus, Natalia, 5:487
Konzertantes Duo, 1:241
Kopelow, *as photographer,* 2:39
Kopiński, Mikołaj, 2:447
Koppel, Thomas, 3:13
Koppers, Maria, 2:470
Koralli, Vera, 3:207
Korçë, Albania, 1:34
Korchmarev, Klimenty, 4:225,
6:213
Kord, Henry, *as photographer,* 5:61
kordax, 2:506, 3:290, 293, **4:44,**
5:598
Korea, **4:44–55**
background and overview,
1:166–167, **4:44– 50**
costume, 2:214, **221–223,** 4:47,
48, 49, *49, 51*
court dance, 1:167, 2:214, 3:102,
4:49
costume, 2:221–223
Kim Chu'un-heung, 4:12
scholarship, 4:54
dance research and publication,
4:52–55, 159
fan usage, 2:570, *572*
folk dance, 4:46–48, 50
Han Young-Sook, 3:340–341
libraries and museums, 4:159
masked dance drama, 2:222–223,
222, 4:45, 46, 47, **50–51,** 53,
299, **299–300**
scholarship, 4:54
modern dance, **4:51–52**
Ch'oi Seung-hee, 2:155–156
Cho T'aek-won, 2:159–160
Hong Sin-cha, 3:372–373
Kim Paik-bong, 4:12–13
North Korea, 2:155–156, 4:44, *48*
ritual dance, 4:45, 46, 47, 48,
49, 494
shamanism, 6:185
Korea Journal, 4:53, 54
Koreana (periodical), 4:54
Korean Culture (periodical), 4:54
Korean Culture and Arts
Foundation, 4:55
Korean Dance Arts Association,
2:159
Korean Dance Festival, 4:52
Korean Folk Arts Company,
2:159, *572*
Korean Folk Arts Institute, 3:341
Korean Foundation, 4:55
Korean Musical Arts Conservatory,
Seoul, 3:341
Koreans (ethnic), 2:139–140
Korean Traditional Performing
Arts Center (formerly
National Classical Music
Institute of Korea), 4:12,
49, 53
Korean War (1950–1953), **4:44,** 46
Korean Zen Festival, 4:142
Korecká, Anna, 1:429, 2:306
Koren, Sergei, 1:490, **4:55,** 131,
5:394
Koreshchenko, Arseny, 3:196,
5:161
Koriak (people), 5:446–447,
446, 448

Koribut-Kubitovich, Pavel, **2:**411
Körmagyar, **3:**412
Kornfield, Lawrence, **6:**282
Korniss, Péter, *as photographer,* 553
Koro, Henry, *as photographer,*
2:230, **3:**231
Koroleva, Elfrida A., *as contributor,*
4:78, 129–130, 446–447
Korolewicz-Waydowa, Janina,
5:220
Korovin, Konstantin, **1:**487, **2:**241,
4:55–56, **5:**161, 541, **6:**399
Bayadère scenic design, **1:**393
Corsaire decor and costumes,
2:207
Don Quixote design and costume,
2:436, 439
Gorsky collaboration, **3:**204
Sleeping Beauty design, **5:**610
students, **5:**642
World of Art group, **5:**456
Korrigane, La, **3:**71, **4:**353, *353,*
5:94, **6:**443
Kortárs Tánc Szinház Egyesület,
3:421
Kortlandt, Ed, **1:**389
Kortner, Fritz, **3:**163
Körtvélyes, Géza, **3:**424
as contributor, **1:**370–371,
3:413–415, 421–422, 423–424,
4:74, 448, 529, **5:**287,
569–570
Korty, Sonja, **1:**410, **5:**43
körverbunk, **3:**409
Koryŏ dynasty, **2:**222, **4:**46, 47, 52
Koryosa akchi (Korean text),
4:52, 53
Kósa, György, **3:**421
Kosh, The, **4:**628
koshare, **4:**554
Koshiji Fubuki, **6:**84
Kosi, Ivo, **6:**437
Kosiuk, B., *as photographer,* **6:**224
Koski, Seppo, **2:**632
Koskinen, Emil, **2:**631
Koskinen, Irja, **2:**632
Koskjukov, Konstantin, **6:**435
Kosloff, Alexis, **6:**273
Koslov, Leonid, **4:**620
Koslov, Theodore (Fedor Koslov),
3:655, **4:**56, 200, 420, **5:**636,
6:270
ballet school in United States,
6:291
students, **2:**372, **3:**655, **5:**391,
488, **6:**355
unauthorized Fokine ballet
versions, **3:**21
Koslov Ballet, **4:**56
Kosma, Joseph, **1:**306, **5:**163
Kostas (photographer), **5:**186
Kostenko, Vladimir, **1:**296, **6:**278
Kostić, Vera, **6:**432
Kostka, Vilma, **6:**388
Kostrovitskaya, Vera, **1:**329, **4:**37,
5:487, **6:**129
Kosugi, Takehisa, **2:**289, 296
Kőszegi, Ferenc, **3:**415
Kosztka, Tivadar Csontváry, **3:**417,
5:569
Kotarbiński, Józef, **5:**220
Kotce Theater, Prague, **2:**306
Kotelawala, Sicille P. C., **3:**648
as contributor, **3:**647–649, 649,
4:34–35, **6:**329–330
Kothari, Sunil, **3:**470
as contributor, **2:**102–103, 104,
104– 105, 404–405, 468,
3:199–200, 468–469, 606,
4:62–63, 110–111, 246–247,
257–258, 477–478, 575–576,

5:22–23, 68–69, 330–331,
510–511, 521–522, 524–525,
568, 581–582, 601–602,
602–603, **6:**312, 320–321, 321
Kothera, Lynn, **6:**135
"Kotini on Riia Raa" (singing
game), **2:**629
Kotliarevsky, Ivan, **6:**222, 224
Koukoules, Phaidon, **3:**303
Koussevitzky, Serge, **1:**438
kouta odori, **3:**587
Koutev Bulgarian National
Ensemble, **2:**99
koutsós chorós, **2:**101
Kovačev, Bogdanov, **2:**11, 12
Kovach, Nóra (Kovács), **2:**508, 510,
3:415, **4:**624
Kővágó, Zsuzsa, *as contributor,*
3:341–342, 415–420, **6:**66–67
Kovalev, Vladimir, **5:**472
Kovalev, Yuri, **3:**665
Kovařovic, Karel, **5:**245
Kovtun, Valery, **1:**519
Kovtunov, Ivan, **2:**520
kovyrialochka step, **5:**445
Kowroski, Maria, **4:**624
Koželuh, Leopold, **2:**306
Kozensha, **2:**18
Kozhukhova, Maria, **1:**440, 517,
5:480
Kozielec, Tadeusz, **5:**218
Kozlovsky, Albert and Nina, **4:**128,
5:47, 406
Kozma, Joseph, **5:**569
Kpledzo festival, **6:**19
Kraanerg, **1:**214, **4:**479, *542,* **6:**56
Kraemer, Franz, **6:**130
Kraetzmer, Andrea, **5:**425
Krafft, Per, **1:**503
Kragh-Jacobsen, Svend, **2:**387,
5:238
krakowiak, **2:**368, **3:**528, **4:**57,
5:210, 212, 213, *213,* 214, 216
cracovienne derived from, **2:**107
*Kraków Wedding (Cracow
Wedding),* **5:**75, 195, 215–216,
216, 219, **6:**365, 441
krama, **2:**228
kramadīpikās, **4:**80
Kramar, Ivan, **2:**469
Kramar, Leonie, **2:**470, **4:**600
Kramarevsky, Lev, **1:**408, **3:**665,
4:87
Krámer, György, **3:**329, 419,
6:66067
Kranig, Saima, **2:**530
Krannerg, **5:**574
Krap, Arnost, **5:**393
Krapivin, Mikhail, **5:**467
Krapivina, Galina, **5:**467
Krapnik, Eugeniusz, **2:**563, 564
Krapp's Last Tape, **5:**592
Krasnodar Experimental Theater,
3:317
Krasnoe Selo, Russia,
3:562–563, 567
Krasovskaya, Vera, **4:**58
aesthetics, **5:**485
on Baryshnikov ("before Adam"),
1:371
on Bogdanova as Giselle, **1:**477
on Brianza's dance style, **1:**540
as contributor, **3:**560–568,
4:285–286, **5:**149–162,
606–610
on Dolgushin's style, **2:**423
on Fedorova's temperament and
acting, **2:**582
on Fokine's ballets, **5:**483
history of western European
ballet, **5:**484–485

on Petipa's *Raymonda* structure,
5:456
*Sovetskii baletnyi teatr,
1917–1967,* **5:**484
Krassovska, Nathalie (Natalie
Leslie)
Ballet Russe de Monte Carlo,
1:296, 300, *301*
Ballets 1933, **1:**307
Dallas Ballet, **6:**264
English National Ballet,
2:507, 509
Étude performance, **4:**636
Grand Ballet du Marquis de
Cuevas guest appearance,
3:226
Youskevitch dance partnership,
6:425
Kratak, Nicola, **5:**421
Kratina, Valeria, **1:**239, 240, **2:**11,
153, **3:**596
Kratinus, **2:**159
Krätke, Grita, **3:**152, 153
Kratt, **2:**529, **3:**100
Kratz, Corinne A., *as photographer,*
2:90
Kraul, Earl, **4:**540
Kraus, Gertrud, **1:**239, 240, 431,
3:529–530, 531, **4:**58–59,
5:606
Kraus, Joseph Martin, **6:**39, 47
Kraus, Lisa, **1:**544
Kraus Dance Troupe, **1:**431
Krause, Johann, **3:**302
Krausenecker, Adele, **1:**240
Kraus-Natschewa, Helen, **1:**500
Krauss, Ernst, **4:**590
Krauss, Ruth, **2:**110
Krauter, Marvin, **5:**612
Krauze, Zygmunt, **2:**120
Krazy Kat, **1:**483, 484
Krebs, Stephanie, **2:**602
Kreidweis, W., **3:**154
Kreiger, Johann, **1:**517
Krein, Aleksandr, **2:**15, 96, **4:**129
Kreisler, Fritz, **5:**121
Kreitsele, **4:**78
Krekfets, Harvey, **1:**289
Kremlin Ballet, **5:**465, 474, **6:**314
Kremlin Palace of Congresses,
Moscow, **1:**494
Kremzov, Ellen, **2:**176
Krenek, Ernst, **1:**390, **2:**161,
4:64, 649
Kresnik, Johann, **3:**151, 156, **4:**59–
60, **5:**43
Kressig, Thorsten, **6:**53, *53*
Kreutzberg, Harald, **1:**111, 204,
537, **2:**357, **3:**146, *147,* 340,
385, **4:**60–61, **5:**33, 59, 289,
6:195, 355
Canadian performances, **2:**37
as Egri influence, **2:**480
Eternal Circle, **4:**161
Georgi collaboration, **3:**132
Italian recital, **3:**550
as Limón influence, **4:**197
Nazi era, **4:**93, **6:**393
students, **2:**150, **3:**348, **5:**263
Wigman training, **6:**392
Kreutzer, Rodolphe, **4:**61, **5:**513
Kreutzer Sonata, **5:**617, *617*
Krevoff, Sammy, **6:**319
Kricskovics, Antal, **1:**370
Krida Beksan Wirama, Jogjakarta,
1:172–173, **3:**496
Krieger, Henry, **1:**420
Kriegsman, Alan, **6:**299
Kriegsman, Sali Ann
as contributor, **1:**420–422

as Jacob's Pillow executive
director, **3:**572
Kriegsmann, James J., *as
photographer,* **6:**98
Kriger, Viktorina, **1:**489, **2:**11, 15,
132, 528, **4:**62, **5:**454, 458,
6:106, 344
Mordkin American tour, **4:**460
Stanislavsky and Nemirovich-
Danchenko Musical Theater,
5:466
Krilova, Olga, **2:**278
Krimov, Nikolai, **5:**541
Kringloop, **2:**470
Krips, Henry, **4:**26
Krishan, Rajendra, **2:**625
Krishna, Gopi, **2:**623, *623*
Krishna and Radha, **5:**123, 580
Krishnamurthi, Jiddu, **1:**467
Krishnamurthi, Jyotishmati, **4:**62
Krishnamurthi, Yamini, **4:**62–63,
5:23
Krishna Parijata, **6:**321
Kristina Talking Pictures (film),
5:293
krithis, **1:**442
krīyas, **4:**80
Kriza, John, **1:**68, 69, 86, **2:**279,
4:63
Billy the Kid performance, **1:**452
Cuban ballet school, **2:**277
Fancy Free 2.568, 2.*568*
performance, **4:**63, **5:**539
Interplay performance, **6:**279
Krogh, Torben, **2:**387
Krokover, Rosalyn, **4:**177
Kröller, Heinrich, **4:**63–64
Bavarian State Ballet, **1:**390
Don Juan version, **2:**434
Impekoven association, **3:**443
Josephslegende version, **3:**631,
4:64
Losch roles, **4:**228
Ruinen von Athen choreography,
1:402
students, **3:**619, **5:**65, **6:**357
Vienna State Opera Ballet, **1:**240,
3:89, **4:**228
Kronbruden (Strindberg), **6:**36
Kronstam, Henning, **1:**154,
4:64–65, 273, **5:**341, 394, 430,
430, 432–433, **6:**349
krookeltussu dance, **2:**629
Kropivnitsky, M. L., **6:**224
Kropivnitsky, Jarmila, **2:**153, 307
Kroshner, Mikhail, **1:**408, **4:**226,
6:420
Krotkov, Nikolai, **5:**160
Krøvel, Eva, **4:**682
as contributor, **4:**675–676
Kṛṣṇa (deity), **4:**65, 69, 70, 253, *424*
kṛṣṇāṭṭam, **1:**171, **3:**456, 464, 465,
467, **4:**65– 66
Krugel, David, **5:**658
Kruger, Elsa, **5:**392
Krum, Daniel, **1:**497
Krupa, Gene, **6:**275
Krupska, Diana, **5:**550
Krutikov's Circus, **2:**176
Kryvokhyzha, Anatolii (Anatole),
6:223
Krzesiński, Feliks. *See* Kshessinsky,
Feliks
Krzyszkowska, Maria, **5:**218
Kshessinska, Julia, **4:**67
Kshessinska, Matilda, **1:**308, 311,
392, **2:**82, 436, 597, **3:**618,
4:*67,* 67–69, *68, 69,* 267, **5:**13,
94, 154, 247, 279, 606,
6:191, 341
Cecchetti method use, **2:**84

Diaghilev Ballets Russes guest
performance, **6**:32
Eros performance, **5**:*455*
on father's mazurka
performance, **4**:66–67
Fille Mal Gardée performance,
4:68, 640
Fokine ballet roles, **3**:15, 16
Karsavina as protégée, **3**:655
Legat (Nikolai) association, **3**:16,
4:142
Legat (Nikolai) caricature
drawings of, **2**:69
Maryinsky Ballet, **4**:282, **5**:456
Paris dance studio, **3**:*81*, 82, **4**:68
students, **2**:478, **3**:354, 508, **4**:68,
336, **5**:349, 350, **6**:357
Swan Lake performance, **6**:32
Sylphides performance, **6**:60
Vladimiroff, Pierre, **6**:345
as Zucchi admirer, **6**:453
Kshessinsky, Feliks, **3**:560, **4**:57,
66–67, *67*, 282, **5**:571
Kshessinsky, Iosif, **4**:67, **5**:571
Kshessinsky family, **4**:57, 66–69
kuarup, **1**:531, 535–536
Kubicová, Ivana, **2**:308
Kubiesa, Maria, **5**:*218*
Kubik, Gerhard, **2**:88, 212, **6**:25
Kübler-Ross, Elisabeth, **1**:462
Kuch, Richard, **1**:375, **5**:681
Kuchipudi, **1**:169, **3**:468, 508,
4:69–71, **5**:330, 521, 522,
6:320–321
Krishnamurthi, Yamini, **4**:62, *62*
Kuchipudi Art Academy, **6**:321
Kuckelsom, Alexandre, **2**:384
kuda kepang dance, **4**:249
Kudelka, James, **1**:75, **2**:39, 42,
3:232–233, 234, 616, **4**:71–74,
5:*513*, 514, **6**:133, 143
Actress, The, **3**:644, **4**:73, *73*, 547
Grands Ballets Canadiens, Les,
4:72–7, 544
Monotones performance, **4**:*544*
National Ballet of Canada,
4:71–72, 73, 74, 544, 547
Nutcracker, The, **4**:73, *546*, 547
Pastorale, **1**:403, **4**:73, 547
kudoki, **3**:588, 639
Kudriavtseva, Valentina, **1**:489,
3:206, 207
Ku Hi-so, **4**:54
Kuhn, Hans Peter, **5**:128, *305*
Kuhn, Karolos, **3**:300
Kuhnau, Johann, **4**:507
Kuiruchuk, **4**:87
Kujawa, Teresa, **5**:219
kujawiak, **5**:213, 214, *218*
Kuka (people), **6**:383
kukavula dance, **5**:*662*
Kuki (people), **1**:362
Kuksu (deity), **4**:567
Kulakov, Valery A., *as contributor*,
1:86–87, 477–478, **3**:618–619,
5:247–248, **6**:309–310,
310–311
Kulichevskaya, Klavdia, **2**:341,
4:633, 639, **5**:456, 558
Kulturkreislehre theory, **4**:374
kumadori (facial makeup), **2**:217–
218, **3**:437, 638, **4**:*296*
Kuma Eha, **3**:531
Kumagai Jinya, **3**:440, **4**:533, 536
Kumakawa Tetsuya, **3**:589
Kumar, Dilip, **2**:622–623
Kumar, Hemant, **2**:623
Kumar, Kishore, **2**:625
Kumar, Krishna, **4**:110
Kumar, Narendra, **1**:94
Kumar Shambhava, **4**:110

Kumasi, Ghana, **3**:167, 170
Kumin, Laura, *as contributor*,
2:448–449, **5**:672–675
kumina, **3**:573, 575, **6**:345
kumi odori, **5**:27
kumpanija, **6**:429
Künstlerlist, **3**:320
Kumuznikov, Abderachman, **4**:600
Kun, Zsuzsa, **3**:415, 422, **4**:74,
5:472
Kunakova, Liubov, **4**:285
Kunavičius, Henrikas, **4**:208
kundu (drum), **4**:497
Kundum festival, **6**:19
Kungnip Kugagwon. *See* Korean
Traditional Performing Arts
Center
!Kung San dance, **4**:74–76, 484,
485, **5**:252, 355, 661, 664, *665*
Kuni Masami, **3**:590, 646
Kuningan festival, **2**:231
kunqu, **1**:161, 164, **4**:76
Kunshan Opera. *See kunqu*
Kunst, Jaap, **4**:585
Kunzen, Friedrich, **5**:552
Kuosmanen, Elo, **2**:632
Kupferberg, Sabine, **4**:82, 602
Kupka, Karel, **5**:617
Kuprin, Aleksandr, **1**:144
Kůra, Miroslav, **1**:542, **4**:77,
5:245, 270
Kurashakova, Margarita, **5**:469
Kurath, Gertrude Prokosch, **2**:49,
4:77– 78, 370
as contributor, **4**:550–556,
556–558
ethnomusicology, **4**:575, **6**:297
"Panorama of Dance Ethnology,"
4:372–373
Kurbet, Vladimir, **4**:78, 446
Kurdish dance, **3**:513, **4**:78–79,
407, 410
combat dance, **4**:406
Jewish ethnic, **3**:537, *537*
Kurgapkina, Ninel, **4**:277, 284,
5:5, *98*
Kurilenko, Elena N., **5**:485
as contributor, **5**:587–588
Kuril Island, Japan, **1**:31
Kurilko, Mikhail, **5**:331
Kurilov, Ivan, **2**:15
Kurkela, Vesa, **2**:634–635
Kurkjian, Samuel, **1**:501
kurogo, **3**:639
Kurokami, **5**:29
Kurō Shigefusa, **3**:388
Kurová, Jana, **2**:310
Kurozuka, **3**:441, **4**:*296*
kurraj dance, **2**:491
Kursi, **5**:64
Kurtág, György, **2**:473
Kurtanas (Indian music treatise),
1:171
Kürti, László, **4**:367
as contributor, **2**:299–301,
3:405–407, 407–413, 422–423
Kurtisanen, **5**:294
Kurtz, Efrem, **1**:310
Kurtz, Elizabeth, *as contributor*,
3:106–111, **4**:326–328
Kuruma Biki, **4**:535, *536*
Kurup, Kunju, **3**:199, **5**:522
Kurut's Tale, **3**:415
Kurylewicz, Andrzej, **2**:120
Kuryło, Edward, **5**:221
Kurz, Daniela, **3**:157, **4**:2
kuse, **3**:646
kusemai, **3**:646, **5**:49
Kusnirova, Ana, **6**:435
Kusumo, Sardono W. *See* Sardono
Kusumokesowo, R. T., **5**:523

Kusunoki Masashige, **3**:646
Kuswaraga, **3**:497
kūṭiyāṭṭam, **3**:456, *459*, 660,
4:79–81
Kuttubayev, Bolot, **4**:87
Kuusela, Marjo, **2**:633
Kuzmin, Mikhail, **3**:193
Kuznetsov, Anatoly, **2**:497
Kuznetsov, Andrei, **5**:475
Kuznetsov, Dmitri, **2**:435, **5**:455
Kuznetsov, Maria, **3**:20, 631
Kuznetsova, Raissa, **3**:25
Kuznetsova, Svetlana, **5**:*471*
kvaedadansleikir, **3**:434
Kvarnström, Kenneth, **2**:611, 633
Kvernadze, Aleksandr, **1**:38
Kvietys, Yone, **2**:44, 47
Kwakiutl (people), **2**:601, **4**:553,
568, 569, 569, **6**:186
Kwakiutl of British Columbia, The
(film), **2**:601
Kwaśnicowa, Zofia, **5**:211, 220
Kyaksht, Georgi, **4**:282–283
Kyakuraika (Zeami), **3**:591, **4**:42
Kyasht, Lydia, **1**:400, 482, **3**:15,
261, **4**:67, 640
as Legat (Nikolai) student, **4**:143
Lester dance partnership, **4**:162
students, **3**:87
Sylvia performance, **6**:64
Kykunkor, **2**:313, **6**:258
Kylián, Jiří, **1**:233, 234, 391, **2**:41,
267, 284, 309, 310, 632,
3:150, 234, **4**:81–82, **5**:235,
305, 437, 565, 674
choreographic sources, **3**:131
Geneva Ballet choreography, **6**:43
Joffrey Ballet choreography,
3:616
Keil roles, **4**:1
Kibbut Contemporary Dance
Company choreography,
3:532
L'Enfant et les Sortilèges, **5**:316
Netherlands Dance Theater
artistic directorship, **4**:81,
593, 602
Royal Swedish Ballet guest
choreography, **6**:43
Silent Cries, **2**:361
Stuttgart Ballet, **6**:10
Symphony of Psalms, **4**:592
kyōdo buyō, **3**:585
kyōgen, **3**:*581*, 642, **4**:84–86
background, **3**:637, **4**:83–85
costumes, **2**:217
masks, **4**:295, 661
mime, **4**:423
Nomura family, **4**:660–662
schools, **4**:85–86
Shigeyama family, **5**:590–592
Kyōkunshō (1233 compendium),
3:171
Kyoto, Japan, **3**:126
Kyr, **2**:532
Kyrgyzstan, **4**:86–87, **5**:482
Kyrie Eleison, **4**:1
kyudo, **1**:186
Kyū-i (Zeami), **4**:655
Kyukunsho (Japanese text), **3**:591
kyutei buyō, **5**:26
Kyzzhibek, **3**:665

La. *For names and titles with this
prefix, see key word*
La Argentina Sho, **5**:33–34
Laba, Billai
as contributor, **5**:80
"free rhythm" parade, **1**:239
Laban, Azra, **4**:32, 96

Laban, Rudolf, **4**:89–95, **6**:83
aesthetic vision, **4**:63, 89–90, 92,
6:391
archival materials, **4**:163, 164
Ascona colony, **6**:51–52
Ausdruckstanz development,
1:203, 204, **3**:161, 162
avant-garde dance, **1**:244,
4:91, 94
Berlin State Opera, **3**:146
as Bodenwieser influence,
1:466, 467
body therapies, **1**:469, 471, 473
as Brazilian dance influence,
1:535, 537
British dance education, **3**:276,
277, 278, 283
British modern dance, **3**:271
as Bulgarian dance influence,
2:11
choreographic silence, **6**:390
as dance therapy influence,
2:316, 320
Don Juan version, **2**:434
escape from Nazis, **3**:628,
4:93–94, 477
as Forsythe influence, **3**:53
as French modern dance
influence, **3**:75, 83
as Holm influence, **4**:440
Hutchinson association,
3:426–427, **4**:96, 97
improvisation, **3**:445
as Japanese modern dance
influence, **3**:646
Jooss association, **3**:624–625,
627, 628, **4**:91, 92, 103
as Jooss influence, **3**:40, 626, **4**:15
legacy, **4**:94, 95
male dancers, **4**:92
movement choirs, **3**:147, **4**:89,
91, 92, 93, 96, 103, 475–477
movement efficiency, **4**:15, 16, 97
as Netherlands dance influence,
4:590, 598
notation system. *See*
Labanotation
on performance environment,
6:161–162
Ritterballett choreography, **1**:402
as Rome Opera Ballet technical
influence, **5**:400
schools, **3**:146, 160, **4**:92, 103
students and colleagues, **1**:132,
134, 203, 310, 411, **2**:44,
4:103–104, 420, 437, **5**:603,
6:304, 326, 433
Wigman association, **6**:389–390
See also Laban Principles of
Movement Analysis
Labananlysis Research Workshop
(Ohio State University), **4**:104
Laban Art of Movement Guild,
4:477
Labanator, The (publication), **4**:96
Laban/Bartenieff Institute of
Movement Studies, New York
City, **1**:471, **4**:95, 104
archives, **4**:167
Laban Central School, Berlin, **4**:32
Laban Centre for Movement and
Dance, London, **1**:541, **3**:279,
280, 283, 284, 625, **4**:95, 104,
5:559
archival collections, **4**:164
dance sociology course, **4**:362
Laban Chamber Dance Theatre,
4:103
Laban Collection, London, **4**:95
Laban Guild, Manchester, **4**:94
Laban International, **4**:104

Laban-Lawrence Effort Assessment test, **4:**103
Laban Movement Analysis. *See* Laban Principles of Movement Analysis
Labanotation, **1:**120, 387, **3:**147, **4:**15, 16, 90, 92, **95–98**, 99, 104, 686–687, *689*, **5:**325
of *Après-midi d'un Faune*, **5:**327
Bereska contribution, **4:**103
of Bournonville style, **1:**513, **2:**387
of *bugaku*, **3:**592
of *Carnaval, Le*, **2:**73
comparative ethological dance research, **4:**374
diagrammatic example, **4:***97*
direction symbols, **4:***689*
of *Green Table*, **3:**305
Holm use of, **3:**370
of Humphrey dances, **3:**404
Hutchinson development, **3:**426–427
of Icelandic dance, **3:**436
of Irish step dances, **3:**519
Jooss contribution, **3:**625, **4:**103
Knust development, **4:**32, 96
of Korean dances, **4:**54
Kurath ethnographic studies, **4:**78
Leeder contribution, **3:**625
of Mlakar choreography, **4:**437
movement analysis inclusion, **4:**97–98
nationalistic rejections of, **2:**542
of Romanian folk dances, **5:**391
software LabanWriter, **4:**158
technical manuals' use of, **6:**129
textbooks, **4:**98
of Trinidadian dance, **2:**62
Wigman collaboration, **6:**389
Labanotation (Hutchinson), **3:**426–427
Laban Principles of Movement Analysis, **1:**471, **2:**320, 321, **3:**271, **4:**92, 95, **98–105**
Bartenieff Fundamentals, **1:**471, 474, **2:**320, **4:**16, 17
Bodenwieser interpretation, **1:**467–468
Canadian dance education, **2:**47, 48
choreology, **1:**417–418, **4:**95
components, **4:**97
conceptions, **4:**98–99
diagram, **4:***100*
kinesiology, **4:**15, 16, 18–19
as Leeder influence, **4:**140
Netherlands dance education, **3:**346
South Africa, **5:**657
See also Effort-Shape analysis; Labanotation
Laban School, Hamburg, **4:**32, 91, 92
Laban School, Stuttgart, **4:**91
La Barre, Michel, **3:**49
Labarre, Théodore, **5:**148
Labasse, Claude and Madame, **6:**237
Labat, Ana, **1:**102–103
Labat, Jean-Baptiste, **2:**430
Labayen, Enrico, **5:**173
L'Abbé, Anthony, **1:**92, **2:**339, **3:**377, **4:**105–106, 433, **5:**518, 519, 621, **6:**123, 175
bourrée compositions, **1:**517
English dance, **3:**255, 256
LaBelle, Ronald, **3:***232*
Laberinto, El, **4:**107
Laberius, Decimus, **4:**426

Labis, Attilio, **5:**97, 652
Labitzky, Joseph, **6:**2
Laboire, Monsieur, **3:**258
"Labor" (*Impressions of Modern Russia*), **5:**476
Laborde, Jean-Benjamin, **3:**117, **5:**221
Labor Festival, A, **4:**444
Laborintus, **2:**388, **4:**107, **5:**417, **6:**146
Labor Symphony, **5:**586
Labour and Machinery, **3:**468, **5:**580
Labour Party (Great Britain), **3:**281
Labroca, Mario, **3:**550
Labyrinth, **1:**136, 139, 297, **3:**87, 359, **4:**107, **5:**436, **6:**175
labyrinth dances, **2:**269, 270, 271, **4:**106, **5:106–107**
Labyrinthe, **3:**429
Labyrinthian Dances, **2:**289, **4:**107
Lacasse-Morenoff, Maurice, **4:**576
Lacauchie, Alexandre, **2:***206*, **5:***135*, 261
Lac de Fées, Le, **5:**498
Lac des Cygnes, Le. See Swan Lake
Lac des Fées, Le, **1:**86, 459, 460, **2:**202, **3:**156, **6:**73
Lacey, Ethel, **5:**588
Lachaise, Gaston, **4:**27, 30
Lachapelle, Louis, **4:**588
Lachian Dances, **4:**239
Lacombe, Louis, **1:**532
Lacoste, Eugène, **6:**62
Lacotte, Pierre, **1:**111, **2:**199, **3:**75, 156, **4:**107–108, **5:**301, 502
Paris Opera Ballet, **5:**96, 97
Swiss Milkmaid reconstruction, **6:**51
Sylphide "reconstitution," **2:**588, **3:**74, **4:**108, **5:***94*, **6:***58*, 59
La Cour, Lise, **5:**433
La Cour, Marian, **2:**576
Lacy, John, **2:**337, **3:**254, 255
Lacy, Steve, **2:**460, 575
Ladányi, Andrea, **3:**419
Ladies and Me, The, **3:**448
Ladies' Better Dresses, **4:**210
Ladies Garment Workers Union, **6:**276
Ladislau of Gielnów, **5:**210
Ladlisharanji, Rasadhari, **5:**581
ladrang gongan, **3:***116*
Lads' Dance from Györgyfalva, **5:**287
lads' dances, **5:**379
Lady, The, **3:**421
Lady among the Shadows, **5:**24
Lady and the Fool, The, **1:**230
Cranko choreography, **2:**57, 266, **3:**623, **4:**65, **5:**431, **6:**378
Jones (Marilyn) performance, **3:**623, **6:**378
Kronstam performance, **4:**65
Welch performance, **6:**378
Lady, Be Good (film), **1:**439
Lady, Be Good! (musical), **1:**192, **5:**602, **6:**274
Lady Comes Across, The (musical), **4:**335, **6:**277
Lady from the Sea, **1:**70, **2:**586, **3:**62, **5:**431, 573, **6:**85
Lady Henriette, ou La Servante de Greenwich, **2:**14, **4:**341, 514
Lady in the Dark (film), **3:**654
Lady in the Dark (musical), **5:**310, **6:**278
Lady in the Ice, **1:**305
"Lady in the Tutti-Frutti Hat" (*The Gang's All Here*), **1:***433*, **4:**434
Lady into Fox, **1:**66, **3:***173*, 174, 391, 392, *392*, **5:**300

Lady Macbeth of the Mtsensk District (Shostakovitch), **5:**594
Lady of Shalott, The, **1:***147*, 462, 463, **2:**162, **4:**215
Lady of the Camellias, The, **1:**68, **2:**114, **3:**351, **6:**200
Dolin and Markova production, **4:**269
Laing performance, **4:**110
Madsen performance, **4:**246
Neumeier production, **6:**10
Rose design, **5:**405
Rubinstein performance, **5:**438
Sauguet score, **4:**517
Tudor choreography, **4:**608
Lady of the House of Sleep, The, **3:**220
Lady of the Slipper, The (musical), **2:**79
Lady with a Lapdog, The, **1:**493, **5:**462, 588
Laecke, Frank van, **5:**423
Lærkesen, Anna, **2:***386*, **5:***395*, 431, 433, **6:**404
LaFave, Kenneth, **4:**117
as contributor, **1:**438–439, **4:**117
Lafayette Theatre, Harlem, **6:**256
Lafon, Madeleine, **2:**388, **5:**96, **6:**65
La Fontaine, Mademoiselle de, **4:**108–109, **5:**40–41, 87
La Fortune, Brahams ("Bravo"), **5:***635*
LaFortune, Sylvain, **2:**605, **3:***233*
La Fosse, Robert, **1:**75, 391, **4:**623, **5:**265, *265*, 396
Lag ba-'Omer, **3:**536, 605
Lagerbourg, Anne-Marie, **5:**266
Lagerlöf, Selma, **6:**36, 44
Lagertha, **1:**503, **3:**105, **5:**424, 552
Lagoutine, Claire, **5:**232
Laguerre, John, **5:**70
Laguna, Ana, **6:**44
Laguna, Philippines, **2:**231
Lagut, Irène, **1:**327, **3:**393
L'Ag'Ya, **2:**580
lā'ibīyah dance, **6:**419
Laiderette, **4:**230, **5:**301
Lai Haraoba ceremonies, **4:**253
Lailson, Philippe, **2:**443, **3:**86
Laima, **4:**127
Laine, Doris, **1:**282, **2:**633, **3:**156, **4:**678
Laing, Hugh, **1:**11, **2:**269, 348, **4:109–110**, 369, **5:**193, 248, 299, 300
Aleko, **4:***270*
de Mille dance partnership, **2:**372
Facsimile, **5:***360*
Jardin aux Lilas performance, **3:**597, *597*, **4:**109, 110
New York City Ballet, **1:**68, **4:**620
Pillar of Fire, **1:**67–68, **4:**109, 110
Princess Aurora, **5:***612*
Romeo and Juliet performance, **5:**397, *397*
Tudor roles, **6:**196, *196*, 197, *197*, 198, 199, *199*, 200, *200*, 201, 202
Undertow, **1:**66, 68
Laitière Suisse, La. See Swiss Milkmaid, The
Lajtha, László, **2:**473, **3:**422
lakalaka, **4:**495, **6:**177, *177*
Lakatos, Gabriella, **3:**415, *416*
Lakatos, Sándor, **3:**412
Lake, Maliki Aiu, **3:**396
Lake, Molly, **2:**84, **4:**110, 667, **5:**53, 411

Lake School of Dancing, London, **4:**110
Lakhia, Kumudini, **3:**199, 468, **4:110–111**
lakhǫn, **1:***161*, **2:**227, 229, **4:**9, 111–113, 255, **6:**148–149
Lakmé (Delibes opera), **2:**369, **5:**288
Lakota (people), **4:**561
Lakota Rosebud Reservation, South Dakota, **4:**555
Lakshmi. *See* Knight, Lakshmi
La La La Human Steps, **2:**45, 610, **6:**132
Lalande, Michel-Richard de, **5:**520
Lalauze, Charles, **3:**255, **5:**70
Lalla Rookh, **2:**94, **3:**260, **5:**137, 499
Lalo, Édouard, **5:**149
Lalor, Joyce, **3:**575
"Lamadas," **6:**301
Lamaist Buddhism, **2:**141, 221
Lamartine, **3:**20
Lamb, Andrew, *as contributor*, **6:**2–3
Lamb, Betty, **5:**100
Lamb, Warren, **2:**320, 321, **4:**95, 97, 98, 103, 104, 163
lambada, **4:**520, **5:**635
Lambeck, Michael, **6:**187
Lambert, Constant, **3:**355, **4:113–115**, **5:**113, **6:**196
Ashton collaboration, **1:**15, 146, 148, 149, 152, 153, 155, **4:**114, 115, 517, **6:**375
book *Music Ho!*, **3:**285
Camargo Society, **2:**265, **5:**412
de Valois collaboration, **2:**400, 401
Diaghilev commissions, **2:**408, 410
Horoscope score and libretto, **3:**379–380, **4:**114
as Irving (Robert) influence, **3:**520
Job orchestration, **5:**412
Romeo and Juliet score, **4:**635, **5:**398
Royal Ballet, **5:**412
Lambert, Gary, **5:***304*
Lambert, Hugh, **6:**284
Lambert, Madeleine, **4:**234
Lambert, Margery, **5:**61
Lambert, Michel, **4:**234
Lambin, Petr, **1:**392, **5:**320
Lambranzi, Gregorio, **1:**428, **2:**190, 191, 338, **3:**257, **5:**201, 260, 318, **6:**124
forlana composition, **3:**50
New and Curious School of Theatrical Dancing, **3:**365, 544–545
Lambrou, Lambros, **2:**41, **6:**266
Lame Little Devil, The, **6:**73
Lamellaphones, **2:**91
Lament, **1:**59, 484, **3:**405
semiotic analysis, **4:**377
Lamentation, **2:**119, **3:***211*, 212, 213
Lament for Ignacio Sánchez Mejias, **3:**402, 403, **4:**197
Lament for the Dead, **4:**477
Lamenting Forest, **5:**524
Lamento, **6:**362
Lamers, Luger, **5:***235*
Lamet, Armand, **6:**256
Lamhut, Phyllis, **3:**445, **4:115–116**, 230, 442, 649, 650, **6:**266
Lami, Eugène Louis, **2:**239, **4:**116, **5:**92, **6:**57, 216
Lamiral, Jean, **5:**480
Lämmel, Rudolf, **3:**132
Lammersen, Kiki, **1:**391

Lamont, Deni, **1:**302, **2:**438
La Morris, Claude, **3:**200
Lamotte, Andrée, **3:**84
Lamour, Dorothy, 615–616
Lamoureux, Louise, **5:**404
Lamp, Frederick, **6:**25
  as contributor, **1:**13–15
  as photographer, **4:**286, **6:**13, 383
Lampinen, Elina, **1:**7
Lampugnano, Giulio Cesare, **2:**337
Lamp unto My Feet (television series), **6:**138
lamvong, **4:**123
Lamy, Martine, **4:***72, 547*
Lanari, Alessandro, **3:**313
"Lancashire Clog Dance," **2:**180, **3:***379,* **5:***694*
"Lancashire Hornpipe," **5:***695*
Lancashire Morris dance, **4:**474
Lancaster, Mark, **1:**142, **2:***292, 293, 296*
Lancaster, Osbert, **2:***266, 597*
Lancelot, Francine, **5:***324*
Lanceray, Eugene, **1:**422
Lancers
  British, **2:**592, **3:**239
  Cajun, **2:**25
  Cape Breton Square Set, **5:**697
  Caribbean, **2:**63
  Danish, **2:**381
  Irish, **3:**517
  Russian, **5:**445
Lanchbery, John, **4:116–118, 5:**55, 526, **6:**217
  Don Quixote score arrangement, **1:**233
  Dream score arrangement, **2:**445
  Fille Mal Gardée libretto and score, **1:**155, **2:**597
  Hynd choreographies, **3:**428
  Mayerling score arrangement, **4:**243
  Metropolitan Ballet, **4:**380
  Monotones orchestration, **4:**452
  Month in the Country score arrangement, **4:**456
Lancret, Nicolas, **2:***28, 190,* **5:**260
Land, Alan, **2:**470
Land, Dave, **5:**683
Landa, Anita, **2:**510
Landa, María Julia, **5:**275
Landé, Jean-Baptiste, **4:**276, **5:**423, 451, 480, **6:**38
Lander, Harald, **1:**247, **2:**114, 388, **4:118–119**
  Bournonville repertory reproduction, **1:**497–498, 512, 539, **5:**430
  Coppélia restaging, **2:**200
  Danish composers, **5:**425
  English National Ballet productions, **2:**509, 510, **4:**119
  Études, **1:**70, *70,* 337, 383, 539, **2:**3, 124, 509, 510, 535–536, 586, **3:***174,* 175, 373, **4:**118, 119, 120, *120,* **5:**429, *429*
  Fokine influence, **5:**428
  Folk Tale, A, **3:**39
  Grand Ballet du Marquis de Cuevas choreography, **3:**226, **4:**119
  Hop-Frog, **1:**251
  Indes Galantes revival, **3:**450, **4:**119, **5:***92,* 96
  Karstens character dancing, **3:**657
  Kermesse in Bruges, **4:**6
  Konservatoriet, **4:**43
  Paris Opera Ballet choreography, **5:**96, 429

Paris Opera Ballet School directorship, **3:**82
  Ralov's interpretation of Petrouchka role, **5:**294
  Riisager musical collaboration, **5:**353, 429
  Royal Danish Ballet, **1:**512, **4:**118, 119, **6:**349, 429–430
  students, **1:**454, **2:**2, **3:**12, **4:**64, **5:**295, 406, 511, 553, **6:**399
  Sylphide, La, **3:**362, **6:**59
  Whims of Cupid staging, **3:**105, **4:**119
  wives, **4:**118–119, 120
Lander, Margot, **1:**539, **2:**201, 535, **4:***43,* 118–119, **119,** **5:**294, 429
Lander, Toni, **1:**70, 501, **2:**201, 387, 509, **4:**119, **120,** **5:**429, 432
  Bournonville heritage, **1:**512, **2:**388, **5:**433, **6:**404
  Études performance, **5:***429*
  Marks marriage, **4:**271
  Paris Opera Ballet classes, **3:**82
  Swan Lake performance, **6:**34
Landers, Dennis, **5:**585
Laneville-Johnson Union Brass Band, **6:**164
Landi, Gina, **3:**551
Landing, **2:**460
Landings, **2:**609
Ländler, **1:**46, **3:**141, **4:**510, 514, **5:**627, **6:**359, 360
Land of Milk and Honey, The, **3:**657, **5:**295
Land of Miracles, The, **6:**412
Landon, Jane, **5:**421
Landory, Véronique, **5:***61*
Landriani, Paolo, **2:**435, **5:**537
Landrover, **2:**292, 293, **4:**37
Landry, Richard, **1:**545, **5:**314
Landsbymøllerne i Provense, **1:**503
Landscape of Longing, **3:**387
Landscapes, **1:**59
Landschap (Landscape), **5:**555
Lane, Edward, **4:**416, 664
Lane, James Richard, **2:**103
Lane, Maryon, **5:**52, 294, 652, **6:**34
Lane, William Henry. *See* Juba, Master
Lanfranco, Bishop, **5:**115
Lang, Andrew, **3:**30–31
Lang, Erwin, **1:**131
Lang, Harold, **2:**568, *568,* **3:**371, **5:**513, **6:**279
Lang, Herbert, *as photographer,* **2:**88, 89, **6:**18
Lang, Maria, **6:**43
Lang, Pearl, **3:**385, **4:120–121,** **6:**132
  Appalachian Spring, **1:**97
  Bennington School, **1:**421
  Boston Ballet choreography, **1:**501, **6:**398
  Deaths and Entrances, **2:**360
  Dutch National Ballet choreography, **2:**469, 470, **3:**122
  Graham Dance Company, **3:**216, 218, **4:**441
  Jacob's Pillow performance, **3:**571
  Marks association, **4:**271
  musical theater, **6:**278
Lang, Tup, **4:**626, 629
Lang Dharma, **1:**458
Langdown, Dawn, **5:***657,* 659
Lange, Carl, **2:**256
Lange, Miriama, **4:**628
Lange, Roderyk, **4:**32, 96, **5:**211, 220
  as contributor, **4:**32

Langen Asmara, **3:**498
langendriya dance drama, **3:**497–498
langen mandra wanara, **1:**163, 173, **3:**498
Langen Pranasmara, **3:**498
Langer, Hans-Klaus, **3:**154
Langer, Susanne K., **1:**24
Langford, Helen, **4:**627
Lango (people), **2:**86
Language of Dance, The (Wigman), **4:**476
Language of Dance Centre, London, **3:**427, **4:**97, 693
Languages of Art (Goodman), **1:**24
Languedoc, France, **2:**99
Lanier, Nicholas, **4:**309
lanku dance, **6:**12
Lan Ling theme, **2:**130
Lanner, Jörg, **1:**291
Lanner, Joseph, **3:**261, 628, **4:**121, **5:**625, **6:**2, 335, 360, 361
Lanner, Katti, **1:**37, 238, **2:**82, **3:**128, 145, **4:121–122,** **5:**233
  Dancing Doll production, **5:**279
  Empire Theatre choreography, **3:**261, 347
  Hamburg Ballet choreography, **3:**336, **4:**121
  pantomime spectacles, **5:**72
  students, **5:**248
  Wilhelm collaboration, **6:**397
Lansac, Régis, **1:**214, **6:**95
Lansbury, Angela, **6:**284
Länsivuori, Kare, **2:**633
Lanske, Herman, **6:**433
Lansley, Jacky, **3:**272
Lantern Dance, **2:**139
Lantern of Lotus, **2:**145
Lantern, Rotterdam, **4:**597
Lany, Charlotte, **1:**365, **4:**122
Lany, Jean-Barthélemy and Louise-Madeleine, **1:**43, 365, **2:**352, 412, **3:**81, **4:122–123,** 236, 694, **5:**89, **6:**331, 333
Lányi, Ágoston, **5:**423
Lanz, Joseph, **2:**256, 257, 592
Laokoon Dance Group, **3:**151
Laos, **2:**31, **4:123–124,** **6:**185
Lapauri, Aleksandr, **1:***489,* **3:**56–57, **5:**460, **6:**106
  Struchkova marriage and dance partnership, **6:**8, *8*
  students, **4:**74
Lapido, Duro, **6:**21, 384
Lapine, James, **6:**287
Lapitsky, I. M., **6:**225
Lapitzki, Eugen, **4:**635
Laplante, C., **3:**7
La Plata School, Argentina, **1:**113
Laporte, Pierre, **1:**9
Lapzeson, Noemi, **4:**216
Lara, Gregory, **5:***314*
Larche, François-Raoul, **3:**92
Larcher, Pierre, **1:**504, **3:**222, **5:**426
La Redd, Cora, **6:**256
Large Glass, The (Duchamp), **1:***141,* **2:**292, **3:**620, **6:**356
laridés, **2:**101
Laríi, Marion, **3:***232*
Larionov, Mikhail, **1:**93, 133, 322, 323, **4:**34, 56, **124–125,** **5:**267, 485
  caricature of Diaghilev, **2:**70
  Chout design, **5:**541, 542
  Diaghilev commissions, **2:**406, 408, 409, **4:**124–125, **5:**262, 541, 542–543
  Goncharova relationship, **3:**197, 198, **4:**124, 125

Massine ballets, **4:**316
  rayonism, **5:**542
Lark Ascending, The, **1:**56
Larkin, Moscelyne, **1:**302, **3:**362, **6:**203, 264
Larkina, Moussia, **1:**315
La Rocca, Patrizia, **3:**557
Laroche, Michael Johann, **6:**335
Larrain, Raymundo de, **3:**226–227, *226,* 362
Larrain, Vicky, **2:**125
Larrieu, Daniel, **3:**79
Larsen, Gerd, **4:**675, **5:**396
Larsen, Mike, **3:**362
Larsen, Niels Bjørn, **1:**49, **2:**201, 385, *511,* **4:125–126,** **5:***424*
  Ashton *Romeo and Juliet,* **1:**158, **5:**394
  mime training, **5:**430
  Royal Danish Ballet, **5:**430
Larsen, Sven Aage, **5:**428
Larson, Bird, **2:**316, **3:**444, **5:**637
Larsson, Johan, **6:**36
Larthe, Paul, **3:**431, **5:**563
Lartigue, Pierre, *as contributor,* **3:**101–102
La Rue, Donna, *as contributor,* **6:**193–195
Larven, **3:**625
Las. *For names and titles with this prefix, see key word*
Lasan, Mojmir, **6:**437, *437*
La Scala Ballet. *See* Scala Ballet
Lascaux, **4:**134
Laschilin, Lev, **1:**489, 490, **2:**579, **3:**207, **4:**444, **5:**331, 567
  Gabovich roles, **3:**99
  Red Poppy choreography, **3:**128, 187
Lasica, Margaret, **1:**212
Laskey, Charles, **1:**259, 279, *280,* 518, **5:**570–571
Laskin, Aleksandr, **5:**483
Lasky, Jesse L., **6:**243
Lasmane, Milda, **4:**128
Lassen, Elna, **4:126,** **5:**428, 429
Lassiat, Caroline. *See* Dominique, Madame
lassú, **3:**411
Last, Brenda, **4:***676,* 678, **5:**421
Last Ball, The (Adam), **1:**10
Last Gone Dance, The, **1:**142
Lasthénie (Hérold), **3:**360
Lastiverc'i, Aristakes, **1:**119
Lastivka, Darii (Dare), **6:**223
Last Judgment, The, **2:**331, 332, **6:**357
Last Look, **6:**109, 111
Last Night on Earth (Jones), **3:**621
Last Seven Days, The, **3:**523
Last Supper at Uncle Tom's Cabin/The Promised Land, **3:**621, **6:**259
Last Vision, The, **1:**233
Las Vegas, Nevada, **1:**466
Lászaky, Andrea, **3:***419*
László, Péter, **1:**308, **3:**418
Latcham, Ricardo E., **2:**121
Lateral Pass, **1:**143, 545
Lathrop, Welland, **1:**421, **3:**336, **6:**278, 362
Latin American dances, **5:**630, 636
  ballroom competition, **1:**357, 358, 359
  folk dance collection, **3:**35–36
  popularity as U.S. social dances, **6:**246, 251
  See also specific dances
Latouche, John, **1:**439
Latour, Pamela, **6:**319

Latte, Kurt, **3**:302
Latvia, **4**:126–128, **5**:482
Lauchengco, Mercy, **5**:171
Lauchery, Albert, **4**:129
Lauchery, Étienne, **2**:54, **3**:144, **4**:128–129
Lauchery, Stephen, **4**:128
Laudes Evangelii, **2**:369–370, **4**:324
Laudisio, China, **5**:17
Laudová, Hannah, *as contributor*, **2**:301–305
Lauener, John, *as photographer*, **2**:44
Lauer, Eleanor, **1**:421
Laughing Eyes, **3**:296
Laughing Stone Dance Theater Company, **3**:373, **4**:52
Laughton, Charles, **3**:208
Launer, Marinette, **2**:595–596
Laura and Henry, **2**:415
Laura Dean Dancers and Musicians, **2**:358–359
Laura et Lenza, **2**:414
Laura Sauve (balletto), **2**:51
Laurencia, **1**:34, **3**:135, **4**:129–130, **5**:204, **6**:343
  Chabukiani production, **2**:96, 97, 97, **4**:129, 133, 284, **5**:458
  Dudinskaya performance, **2**:449
  Lavrovsky (Mikhail) performance, **4**:133
  Nureyev performance, **5**:4–5
  Sergeyev performance, **5**:571
  as Soviet-era ballet, **5**:458
Laurençin, Marie, **1**:449, **2**:242, **5**:237, 544
Laurent, Jean-Pierre, **1**:403, **2**:380, 386, **3**:74, **5**:424, 425
Laurents, Arthur, **1**:439, **5**:362
Laureolous (mime play), **4**:428
Lauret, Jeannette, **1**:296, **3**:24, 26, 104, **4**:656
Lauretta, **1**:88
Lauri clan, **5**:70
Laurie, Joe, Jr., **6**:316
Laurikainen, Terttu, **2**:634
Laurin, Ginette, **2**:43, 45, **6**:133
Lauro, Antonio, **2**:279
laus (halling), **4**:669, 669
Lausanne, Switzerland, **1**:407, **6**:53–54
Lausanne International Ballet Competition, **1**:281, 282, **6**:53
Lauterer, Arch, **1**:82, **2**:286, **4**:130
  Bennington School, **1**:420, 421, **4**:130
  Deaths and Entrances design, **2**:360
  Graham scenic design, **3**:216, **4**:153
  Trend stage design, **6**:162, 191, 192
Lauze, François de, **1**:105, 342, 523, **2**:259, **3**:84, 282, **4**:507, 582, **5**:201, **6**:215
  on *branle/gavotte*, **3**:124
  on *contredanse*, **2**:255
  dance manual, **6**:6, 122–123
  on *galliarde*, **3**:109
  on *port de bras*, **5**:227
  on *révérence*, **5**:345
  See also Apologie de la danse
Laval, Antoine Bandieri de, **1**:4, 283, 355, **2**:59, 465, **4**:130, **130–131**, **5**:88, 105, 249, 504
Laval, Michel Jean Bandieri de, **1**:4, **3**:106, **4**:131
Lavalle, Josefina, **4**:392, 393, 396
La Vallière, Louise de. *See* Vallière, Louise de la
Lavasseur, André, **2**:244

Lavender Leotard, The (Gorey), **2**:71
Lavery, Sean, **4**:180, 620, 623, 631, **5**:397
La Villemarqué, Théodore Hersart, **3**:33
Lavoie, Serge, **1**:375
Lavrovsky, Leonid, **1**:144, 440, **2**:11, 596, **4**:131–132, **5**:316, 571
  as Bolshoi chief choreographer, **1**:491–492, 493, **4**:131, 132
  Cairo Ballet production, **2**:497
  campaign against choreographic innovation, **5**:484
  choreographic renovations, **5**:460
  Diana and Acteon, **1**:493
  Faust choreography, **5**:37
  Fayer conducting, **2**:579
  Fenster association, **2**:585
  Gabovich roles, **3**:99
  Giselle, **1**:491, **2**:11, **4**:74, 132, **5**:463
  Maly Theater Ballet stagings, **5**:468
  Paganini, **4**:38, 132
  Prokofiev working relationship, **5**:268, 269
  Raymonda, **4**:132, **5**:321, 463
  Red Poppy, The, **2**:579, **3**:197, **4**:132, **5**:331, **6**:226
  Romeo and Juliet, **1**:488, **3**:99, **4**:74, 132, 281, 284, 335, **5**:268, 392, **393–394**, 395, 396, 458, **6**:226, 227, 398
  scholarly analyses of, **5**:484
  son Mikhail, **4**:133
  Stone Flower, The, **5**:269, 699
  as Yermolayev student, **6**:420
  Zakharov collaboration, **6**:442
Lavrovsky, Mikhail, **4**:132–134, **5**:89, 460, **6**:106
  Don Quixote performance, **2**:438, **4**:133
  Grigorovich ballets, **1**:493, **4**:133
  Nutcracker performance, **5**:12
  Tbilisi ballet directorship, **3**:135, **4**:133
Lavry, Marc, **3**:529
Law, Evelyn, **6**:319, 371
Lawes, William and Henry, **4**:309, 311, 506
Lawler, Lillian, **2**:270, **3**:292, 302–303, **6**:297
Lawrence, Byran, **1**:232
Lawrence, F. C., **4**:94, 101–102, 103
Lawrence, Gertrude, **4**:334, **6**:272–273, 278, 371
Lawrence, Greg, **4**:25
Lawrence, Monica, **3**:576
Lawrence, Pauline, **2**:246, 356, 378
  Humphrey-Weidman association, **3**:397–398, 401
  Limón marriage, **3**:402, **4**:197
  Moor's Pavane costumes, **4**:199, 458, 458
  Shakers score, **5**:577
Laws (Plato), **5**:283
Laws, Kenneth, **4**:17
  as contributor, **5**:188–191
Lawson, Joan, **2**:330, **3**:282, **6**:128
Lawson, William James, *as contributor*, **1**:478–479, **2**:314–315, **3**:351–352, **4**:4–5, 136–137, 449–450, **6**:396–397
Lawung Ageng, **3**:495
LaYacona, Maria, **3**:575
  as photographer, **3**:624
Layag, Luis, **5**:172

Lay of Thrym, The, **1**:497, 508, 510, 511, 511, 512, **5**:251, 426, 433
  Hartmann score, **1**:515
  reconstruction (1990), **5**:600
Lay-out (later *Blue Schubert Fragments*), **1**:51
Layton, Joe, **6**:283, 286, 380
laywä dance, **4**:488
Lazarov, Itchko, **1**:350
lazgi dance, **6**:305
Lazo, Agustín, **4**:391
Lazowski, Yurek, **1**:313, **2**:107, **3**:25, 26–27, 614, **5**:166, 218, **6**:441
Lazy Madge, **2**:460
Lazzarini, Roberta, *as contributor*, **5**:119–127
Lazzini, Joseph, **1**:251, 349, 411, **3**:74, **4**:134, **134–135**, **5**:98
Leabhart, Thomas G., *as contributor*, **4**:423–426
Leach, Al, **6**:317
Leacock, Rick, **2**:606
Lead Us Not into Penn Station, **2**:575
League of Nations, **3**:34
Leahy, Leonie, **1**:232
leaps. *See* ballet technique, jumping movements; jumping dances
Lear, Edward, **4**:6
Least Flycatcher, The, **5**:313
leather boots, **3**:133, 134
Leaves Are Fading, The, **1**:68, **2**:244, **4**:24, 285, **6**:202, 203
Lebah, Madé, **4**:265
Lebanon, **4**:135–136, 412, 489–490, 491
Lebedev, Leonid, **5**:469, **6**:342
Lebedeva, Praskovia, **1**:486, **3**:237, 618, **5**:455, 501
Lebedinoe Ozero. See Swan Lake
Lebègue, Nicolas-Antoine, **1**:517
Leben für den Tanz, Ein (Laban), **4**:93
Lebercher, Louis, **1**:315, **3**:24
LeBlond, Richard, **5**:513
Le Boeuf, Bernard, **4**:588
Lebrun, Charles, **1**:397
Le Cerf de La Viéville, Jean-Laurent, **5**:38, 39, 129
Leclair, André, **1**:291, **4**:136, **5**:422
Le Clerc, Marianna, **2**:433
Le Clercq, Tanaquil, **1**:28, 159, 262, 263, **2**:291, **4**:136–137, **6**:131, 201
  Apollo performance, **2**:244, **4**:611
  Balanchine marriage, **1**:257, **4**:137
  Balanchine roles, **4**:616
  Concerto Barocco performance, **4**:608
  Divertimento No. 15 performance, **2**:420, **4**:137
  Four Temperaments performance, **3**:57, **4**:136
  Illuminations performance, **3**:442, 442, **4**:137, **5**:185
  Robbins ballets, **5**:360, 361
  Seasons performance, **2**:286
Lecomte, Eugénie, **4**:137–138, 139, **5**:147, 149, 259, **6**:216, 290, 298
Lecomte, Hippolyte, **4**:116, **138**, **5**:147, 149, 259, 640, **6**:216
Lecomte, Nathalie, **3**:85
Leçon, La, **5**:98
Lecoq, Charles, **2**:244
Lecoq, Jacques, **1**:350, **4**:425
Lecouvreur, Adrienne, **5**:249

Le Coz, André, *as photographer*, **2**:152, **3**:232
Leda, **5**:206
Leda and the Swan, **1**:158, **5**:575
Leda-no-Kai, **5**:33
ledek, **3**:504
Lederer, George, **6**:268, 269
Ledezma, José, **2**:110, **6**:323
Le Doux, François Gabriel, **2**:299, **5**:215
Lee, Ann (Mother Ann), **5**:575, 577
Lee, Deborah, **3**:634, **6**:363, 363
Lee, Dorothy Sara-Louise, *as contributor*, **2**:593–594
Lee, Gypsy Rose, **2**:573, **6**:282
Lee, Keith, **6**:260
Lee, Larisa, **3**:665
Lee, Mary Ann, **3**:181, **4**:139–140, 338, **5**:615, **6**:237, 290
Lee, Mignon, **2**:160
Lee, Ming Cho, **5**:551
Lee, Rem, **3**:275
Lee, Sammy, **2**:613, **6**:101, 273, 274, 447
Lee, Spike, **4**:255
Leech, John, **2**:68
Lee Ching-chun, **6**:82
Leeder, Sigurd, **1**:145, 519, **2**:263, **4**:140
  as British modern dance influence, **3**:271, 277
  Folkwang Tanzstudio, **3**:40, 626, **5**:24
  Jooss association, **3**:625, 626, 628, 629, **4**:140
  Laban association, **4**:92, 140
  Labanotation use, **4**:96
  students, **2**:81, **4**:140, **6**:378, 405, 453
Lee Du-hyon, **4**:54
  as contributor, **4**:50–51, 52–55
Lee Hye-gu, **4**:53
Lee Jung-hee, **4**:52
Lee Kuo-hsing, **2**:143
Lee Kyung-ok, **4**:52
Lee Mae-bang, **2**:223, **4**:140–141
Leersun, Emy van, **2**:245
Leese, Elizabeth, **2**:39–40, 42, 47, 3:62, **4**:238, 576
Lee Sun-ock, **4**:55, **141–142**
Leeuw, Boris de, **2**:470, 470
Leeuwen, Hannie van, **4**:601
Lefebre, Dominique, **5**:480
Lefebre, Jorge, **2**:109, 279
Lefevre, Auguste, **3**:313
Lefèvre, Brigitte, **5**:98
LeFevre, Fernanda, **1**:480, **2**:521
Le Flaneur, G., **1**:446
Lefler, Heinrich, **2**:173
Left-handed Craftsman, The, **5**:470
Left Hand, Right Hand (Sitwell), **2**:525
Legacy, **2**:575
Legallois, Amélie, **1**:202, **2**:203, 390, 405, **4**:340, 657, **5**:91, 640
Legat, Gustav, **2**:181, **4**:142, **5**:455
Legat, Nadine Nikolaeva. *See* Nikolaeva, Nadine
Legat, Nikolai, **1**:44, 255, **2**:142–143, **3**:618, **5**:94, 279, 456
  caricature skill, **2**:69, 143
  Eglevsky and Gregory book on, **2**:479, **6**:128
  Fokine rivalry, **3**:16, 20, **6**:352
  Golovin designs, **3**:196
  Maryinsky Ballet, **4**:282, 639, **5**:456, **6**:352
  Pavlova association, **5**:122, 123
  Puppenfee, Die, **4**:143, 144

students, **1:**518, **2:**272, 341, 396, **3:**14, 87, 264, 354, 508, 655, **4:**56, 143, 145, 152, 182, 224, 267, 529, 639, 667, **5:**248, 282, 385, 588, **6:**105, 309, 449
Swan Lake tour, **6:**32
teaching methods, **6:**128
Volynsky support, **6:**352
Legat, Sergei, **2:**69, **3:**618, **4:143–144,** 282, 639, **5:**279, 456
Nutcracker performance, **5:**9, *9*
Raymonda performance, **5:**320
students, **6:**344
Legat family, **4:142–144, 5:**279
Legat Saga, The (Gregory), **6:**128
Legat School, England, **5:**75
Lege, Jean-Marie, **3:**86, **6:**233
Legende de Cerfs, La, **1:**349
Legende von der Wegwarte, **3:**154
Legend of Aziade, The, **3:**193, **4:**459, **5:**45, 123
Legend of Joan of Arc, The, **5:**572
Legend of Joseph. See Josephslegende, Die
Legend of Judith, The, **3:**217, **5:**407
Legend of Love, **1:**492, **3:**569, **4:144–145**
Bessmertnova performance, **1:**440
choreographic significance, **5:**460
Grigorovich choreography, **3:**308, **4:**144, 181–182, 284, **5:**460, 472
Kolpakova performance, **4:**36
Kondratieva peformance, **4:**38
Liepa (Maris) performance, **4:**181–182
Plisetskaya performance, **5:**205
Timofeyeva performance, **6:**171
Legend of Lovers' Leap, **3:**575
Legend of Ochrid, The, **3:**89, **4:**437, **5:**101, **6:**432
Legend of the Lake, The, **1:**91, **2:**11
Legend of the Peacock, **5:**493
Legend of the Taj Mahal, The, **4:**110
Legend of the White Snake, The, **6:**421
legényes, **3:**411
Léger, Fernand, **1:**134, 141, 327, **2:**603, **3:**72, **4:**418, **5:**544, 545
Legerton, Henry, **1:**206
Leges dansadi (Arena). *See Ad suos compagnones studiantes*
Leggenda di Giuseppe, La. See Josephslegende, Die
Leggenda di Sakuntala, La, **3:**51, **5:**246
legmania, **6:**316, 319
Legnani, Pierina, **1:**427, 540, **3:**618, **4:145–146, 5:**456, 528
Cecchetti-Petipa-Ivanov *Cinderella,* **2:**82, **3:**565, **4:**145
Petipa ballet roles, **5:**154, 159, 160
Raymonda performance, **5:**159, 320
Swan Lake role, **1:**145, **3:**566, **4:***145,* **6:**30, **5:**106
thirty-two *fouetté* turns, **1:**338, 347, **3:**261, 565, **4:**145, 282
Legnani, Ria Teresa, **3:**51
légong, **1:**160, 175, **2:**231–232, *231,* **3:***474,* 475, 479, 485, 487, **4:146– 147,** 264
Legrain, Victorine, **2:**282
Legrand, Peter, **1:**390, **3:**144
Legrée, Françoise, **4:**134
Legris, Manuel, **5:**7, 98
legs
 arabesque, **1:**100–101, 345, 348

attitude, **1:**197–198
battement, **1:**383–384
batterie, **1:**384–385
evolution of whole leg use, **1:**348
extension height, **1:**348
plié, **1:**8, 343, 344, **5:**201–202
practice clothes, **5:**243
rond de jambe, **5:**402
Soviet school, **1:**349
taboo against showing woman's, **2:**249
See also ballet technique, feet positions; ballet technique, jumping movements; elevation
Legs On the Wall (Australian company), **1:**217
leg warmers, **5:**243
lehaka, **3:**538
Lehár, Franz, **6:**268, 269
Lehmann, Edvard, **3:**39, **4:**6, 632
Lehmann, Maurice, **3:**450, **5:***92,* 96
Lehnert and Landrock, *as photographers,* **5:**49
Lehnhof, Klaus, **2:**120
Leibovici, Marcel, **1:**464–466
Leica, **5:**184
Leicester, England, **3:**275
Leicester University, **3:**284
Leichner, Ludwig, **4:**305
Leigh, Robert Devore, **1:**420
Leigh Warren and Dancers, **1:**214, 216
Leili and Medzhnun, **1:**492, **3:**195, *195,* 569, **4:**133, **5:**460, 487, **6:**8, 84, 313
Leipoldt, C. Louis, **2:**57
Leipzig, Germany, **3:**152, 153, 154, 161
Leipzig Ballet, **3:**156–157
Leipzig Theater Ballet, **3:**154
Leistiko, Norma, *as contributor,* **1:**474–475
Leistikov, Gertrud, **3:**345, **4:**590, 598
Leitch, Helen, **1:***63,* **5:**571
Leiter, Samuel L., *as contributor,* **1:**361–362, *362,* **2:**12–14, **3:**339, 437–440, 440–441, 593–594, 606–607, 637–641, 658, **4:**333–334, 532–533, 533–534, 534, 534–535, 536, 537–538, **5:**28–29, 29–30, 30–31, 31–32, 32–33, 593
Leiva, Maruja, **6:**323
Lewisohn Stadium, New York City, Denishawn performances, **5:**496
Le Jay, Gabriel-Thomas, **1:**283
Lejeune, Eugène, **2:**503, **3:**620
Lekain, Henri-Louis, **1:**497
Lekh (film), **5:**603
Lekis, Lisa, **2:**62
Leland, Sara, **2:**333, **4:**612, 618, *619,* **5:**360
Lelu, Pierre, **2:**353
Lemaître, Antoine. *See* Frédérick
Lemaître, Gerard, **4:**602
Lemaître, Jules, **5:**107–108
Lemanis, Osvald, **4:**127
Lemanski, Thomas, **2:***584*
Lemay, Jacqueds, **5:***435*
Lemay, Maurice, **3:**3
Lemberge, Alexander, **4:**127, 128
Lemieux, Jacqueline, **2:**41
Lemming, Carl Frederick, **5:**649
Lemon, Mark, **5:**71
Lemon, Ralph, **1:**502, **2:**576, **6:**56, 259, *260*
Lender, Marcelle, **6:**181
Lengyel, Menyhért, **1:**370

Leningrad. *See* Saint Petersburg
Leningrad Academic Theater of Opera and Ballet (Kirov Ballet). *See* Maryinsky Ballet
Leningrad Ballet Ensemble. *See* Saint Petersburg Theater of Contemporary Bllet
Leningrad Chamber Ballet. *See* Saint Petersburg Chamber Ballet
Leningrad Choreographic Institute, **3:**137–138, **4:**224, **5:**571, 614
Leningrad Conservatory. *See* Saint Petersburg Conservatory
Leningrad Maly Academic Theater of Opera and Ballet. *See* Maly Theater Ballet
Leningrad Music Hall, **1:**416
Leningrad State Theater of Ballet. *See* Saint Petersburg Theater of Contemporary Ballet
Leningrad Symphony, **4:147–148,** **5:**23, 470
Belsky production, **1:**416, **4:**147–148, *283,* 284, **5:**460
choreographic significance, **5:**460
Komleva performance, **4:**37
Ogoun production, **1:**542
Soloviev performance, **5:**639
Leningrad Theater of Contemporary Ballet. *See* Saint Petersburg Theater of Contemporary Ballet
Leninism. *See* socialist realism; Soviet era
Lennon, John, **2:**1
Leno, Dan, **3:**249, **4:**520, **5:**72
Lenoir, Alexandre, **5:**89
Le Noire, Rosetta, **6:**276
Lense, Adolph Frederick, **1:***505*
Lensky, Aleksandr, **3:**195, **5:**437, **6:**83, 84
lenso, **3:**504–505
Lent, **2:**10–11, 164–165
See also Carnival
Lent, Patricia, **2:***291, 292*
Lentovsky, Mikhail, **6:**452
Lentulus, **4:**427
Lenya, Lotte, **1:**306, 441
Lenzi, Sabrina, **1:***453*
Leo and Lotus (musical spectacle), **4:**121
Léocadie, **1:**461, **2:**202, **4:**340
León, Francisca González (La Quica), **1:**115
León, Francisco (Frasquillo), **1:**115
Léon, Hélène, **4:**657
Leonardo da Vinci, **4:**14
Leone de 'Sommi, **2:**337
Leoneff, Peter, **4:**598
Leonidoff, Ileana, **5:**400
Leonidoff, Leon, **5:**289
Leonilda, ossia La Fidanzata del Filbustiere, **1:**427, **2:**587
Leonora of Toledo, **4:**502
Leonova, Marina, **3:**197
Leontev, Leonid, **6:**352
Leontiev, Leonid, **1:**255, **2:**72, 73, 585, **4:**225
Leontieva, Anna, **2:**277
Leontieva, Maria, **5:**480
Leontjev, Sacha, **1:**240
Leopold I, emperor of Austria, **1:**235–236, **3:**189, 381
Leopold I, king of Belgium, **1:**410
Leopold II, emperor of Austria, **1:**237, 409
Léotard, Jules, **4:***521,* **5:**242
leotards. *See* practice clothes
Leoussi, Eleni, *as photographer,* **3:**274

Lépaulle, Gabriel, **6:**72
Lepcha (people), **5:**598–599
Lepczyk, Billie, **4:**102–103
Lepeshinskaya, Olga, **1:***486, 487,* 490, 491, **3:**195, **4:148–149**
Cinderella performance, **2:**173
Don Quixote performance, **2:**438, **4:**148, *148*
Flames of Paris performance, **3:**12
Hungarian ballet instruction, **3:**422
strong technique, **5:**458
students, **4:**74
Zakharov as influence, **6:**442
Le Picq, Charles, **1:**237, **2:**55, 107, 299, **3:**256, 365, **4:**35, **149–150,** 696, **5:**215, 270, **6:**311
Didelot association, **2:**414, 416
Don Juan version, **2:**434
Médée et Jason revival in Saint Petersburg, **3:**347
Naples ballet, **3:**546, **4:**149
Noverre influence, **3:**545, **4:**149–150, 276
Saint Petersburg ballet, **4:**276, **5:**451–452
Lepkoff, Danny, **3:***447*
Lepo-leh-leh, **1:***122*
Lepomme, Linda, **5:**423
Lepri, Giovanni, **1:**461, **2:**81, 82, 269, **4:**150, **150–151,** 399
Leptri, Amalia, **4:**150
Le Riche, Nicolas, **5:**98
Lerina, Lina, **1:**313
Lerman, Liz, **4:151–152**
Lermontov, Mikhail, **1:**144, **2:**97, **3:**135, 196
Lerner, Alan Jay, **1:**419, 439, **6:**279, 282
Lerner, Lin, *as contributor,* **1:**443–445, 458–459, **6:**166–170
Le Roussau, F., **1:**92, **5:**350, **6:**123
Leroux, Pauline, **1:**9, **2:**203, 204, 390, 405, **3:**620, **4:**340
Le Roy, Adrian, **1:**275, **4:**505
Le Roy, Bernard, **4:**588
Leroy, Hal, **6:**101
Le Roy, Mervyn, **1:**432
Le Roy, Rita, **6:**319
Lert, Ruth Clark, **4:**170
Léry, Jean de, **1:**530
Les. *For names and titles with this prefix, see key word*
Lesage, Alain-René, **2:**203, 405, **5:**504
Leschetizky, Theodor, **4:**430
Le Seuer, Suzette, **5:**659
Lesgart, Gustavo, **1:***113*
Leshkov, Denis, **5:**150
Leskov, Nikolai, **5:**470
Leskova, Tatiana, **1:**313, 315, 532–533, **2:**127, **3:**73, 350
Leslie, Fred, **3:**296, **4:**159
Leslie, Joan, **1:**193
Leslie, Lew, **1:**117, 520
Blackbirds revue, **1:**382, 439, **2:**572, **4:**629, **6:**272
Leslie, Natalie. *See* Krassovska, Nathalie
Leslie-Spinks, Lesley, **6:**50
as photographer, **2:**500, **6:**44
lesnoto dances, **6:**428, 429
Lessing, Florence, **2:***184,* 185
Lessons (Feldenkrais), **4:**692
Lesson, The, **1:**454, **3:**12, 373, 668, **4:**65, **5:***430,* 432, 564, **6:**135
Lestang, Anne-Louis, **1:**397, **3:**81, **4:**109, **152**

Lestang, Louis, **1:**288, **4:**235, **5:**87, 260

Lester, Edwin, **1:**297, 298

Lester, Eugene, **3:**218

Lester, Keith, **1:**110, **2:**425, **4:**110, **152–153,** 268, **5:**108

Lester Horton Dance Theatre. *See* Horton, Lester

LeStrange, Sir Nicholas, **4:**310–311

Lesznowski, Antoni, **5:**220

LeTang, Henry, **3:**366, 367, **6:**286, 288

L. et Eux, La Nuit (L. and Them, The Night), **3:**362

"Let's Face the Music and Dance" (skating program), **6:**179

Lettera Amorosa, **1:**292

Letters from the Front, **5:**471

Letters on Dancing (Théleur), **4:**685, **5:**207, **6:**126–127

Letters on Dancing and Ballets (Noverre), **2:**107

Letter to the World, **1:**421, **2:**285, 519, **3:**216, 349, **4:**130, 153, **153,** **5:**407, **6:***246*

Let the Righteous Be Glad, **4:**210

Lettre . . . à Monsieur Noverre, **1:**88

Lettres à Sophie (Baron), **3:**84

Lettres sur la danse et sur les ballets (Noverre), **1:**4, 126, **2:**238–239, **3:**14, 84, **4:**122, 149, 694–695, 699–700, **5:**270, **6:**124

critical reception, **4:**699

on function of theatrical dance, **4:**698

Italian translation, **3:**546

on libretti, **4:**174

on Marcel, **4:**263

Médée et Jason, **4:**346, 347

stance against mask use, **4:**301–302, 699

Stuttgart and Lyon publication, **3:**143–144, **4:**695

Swedish translation of portion, **6:**49

Letukaitė, Birutė, **4:**208–309

Leuven, Adolphe de, **2:**405, **4:**341

Le Vacher, Thomas, **1:**3

Levashev, Vladimir, **1:**491, **5:**459, 595, **6:***410*

Levasseur, André, **3:**226

Levasseur, Henri, **3:**92

Levastre, Antoine, **2:**198

Léveillé, Daniel, **2:**40, 45

Leventhal, Marcia B., **2:**319

Leventhal, Valery, **4:153–154**

Levier, Nancy, **4:**346

Levin, David Michael, **1:**24

Levinson, André, **1:**247, 464, **3:**84, **4:154–155**

aesthetics, **1:**23, 24, **5:**485

on Baker (Josephine), **1:**252

on Bakst's design, **1:**255

on Ballet 1933, **1:**307

on Egorova, **2:**480

on Lifar's innovations, **4:**184

on Lifar's personal style, **5:**95

on Nijinska's *Étude,* **4:**636

on *Schéhérazade* design, **5:**541

on Spessivtseva, **5:**679

on stiff classical tutu, **5:**217

on Toumanova's virtuosity, **5:**182

on Trefilova's technique, **5:**191

on turnout, **5:**215

writings on Russian ballet, **5:**482

on Zambelli's art, **6:**444

Levitan, Isaak, **3:**565

Levi-Tanai, Sara, **3:**449, *449,* 450, 531–532, 537, **4:155–156**

Levitoff-Dandré Russian Ballet, **4:**667

Levitov Russian Ballet, **5:**650

Levitsky, Dmitri, **2:**407

Levkoyeva, Natalia, **2:**174

Levogt, Heinrich, **5:**606, **6:**30

Levsha, **5:**572

Levy, Diana, **4:**382

Levy, Fran, **2:**321
as contributor, **2:**315–322

Levy, Monica, **6:**366

Levy, Yakov, **3:**531

Lewicki, Jan, **5:***211*

Lewin, Joseph L., **2:**385

Lewin, Yaël, *as contributor,* **2:**186–188

Lewis, André, **2:**42, **5:**437

Lewis, Daniel, **4:**199
as contributor, **4:**197–200, 458

Lewis, Dio, **6:**235, 294

Lewis, Gilbert, **5:**356

Lewis, Lloyd, **3:**446

Lewis, Matthew ("Monk"), **2:**414

Lewis, Nancy, **3:**235, *235,* 446

Lewis, Noenoelani Zuttermeister, **3:**396

Lewis, Penny, **2:**321

Lewis C., **6:**229

Lewisohn, Alice, **6:**243

Lewisohn, Irene, **3:**215, 399, **5:**559, **6:**243

Lewisohn Stadium, New York City, **1:**64, 518, **3:**23

Lewitan, Joseph, **3:**147, 161

LeWitt, Sol, **1:**144, **2:**119, 608

Lewitzky, Bella, **2:**285, **3:**386, 387, **4:156–157,** **6:**264, 266

modern dance technique, **4:**441

Lew Leslie's Blackbirds (revue), **1:**382, 439, **2:**572, **4:**629, **6:**272

Ley, Maria, **1:**239

Leyte Filipiniana Dance Troupe. *See* Kalipayan Dance Company

Leyton, Marie, **4:**522

"Lezghinka" *(Le Festin),* **4:***643*

Lezhnina, Larissa, **2:**470

Lhotka, Fran, **6:**432, 454

Liadov, Anatol, **2:**73, **6:**61, 310

Liadov, Konstantin, **3:**560

Liadova, Vera, **3:**560–561

Liaisons Amoureuses, Les, **3:**428

Liang Bolong, **4:**76

Liangjiang College, Shanghai, **2:**133

Liang Shanbo and Zhu Yingtai (opera and film), **6:**421, 426

Liaoning Ballet, **2:**146

Liapis, Vangelis, **3:**303

Liatoshinsky, Boris, **6:**225, 344

Libellus spectaculorum (Martial), **4:**428

Liberalités des Dieux, Les, **6:**38

Libération (publication), **3:**85

Liberation of Tirreno and Arnea, The, **5:**535

Liberazione di Lisbona, La, **2:**209

Liberazione di Tireno, La, **5:**1

Liberia, **1:**15, **4:**288, 290

Liberté Tempérée, **4:**577

Liberty, or the Four Quarters of the World, **4:**454

Liberty Tree, **3:**349

Libeskind, Daniel, **3:**53

Libidins, David, **1:**295

Libonati, Beatrice, **1:**389

Libonati, Nicola, **5:**232

Libraire du Pont-Neuf, Le, **1:**287

libraries and museums, **4:157–171**
BBC Film and Video, **6:**134

Native American collections, **4:**555

service organizations, **5:**44

Library of Congress, Washington, D. C., **4:**168

Library of the Academy of Arts and Music, Berlin, **4:**161

Library of the Arsenal, Paris, **4:**161

libretti for dance, **4:172–178**
sixteenth- and seventeenth-century, **4:**172

eighteenth-century, **4:172–176**

nineteenth- and twentieth-century, **4:176–178**
Cocteau, Jean, **2:**183

Gautier, Théophile, **3:**123

Grigorovich, **3:**309, 310

Kirstein, Lincoln, **4:**27, 28

Paris Opera Ballet, **3:**69

Slonimsky, Yuri, **5:**614

Libro de buen amor (Ruiz), **1:**53

Libro de danzar (Jaque), **6:**123

Libro dell'arte del danzare (Cornazano), **1:**380, **2:**204–205, 427, **5:**337, 620

Libro di gagliarda, tordiglione, passo è mezzo canario è passeggi (Lupi da Caravaggio), **6:**122

Libro primo di chitarra spagnola (Bartolott), **5:**520

Libya, **2:**485, 486, **4:**666

Licaone, **3:**359, **5:**277

Li Chengxiang, **5:**330

Li chi (Book of Rites), **2:**128

Lichine, David, **1:**67, 110, 395, 426, **3:**74, **4:178–179,** **5:**61, 681
Aurora's Wedding performance, **5:***611*

Australian tours, **1:**205, 207, 313, 499

Ballets des Champs-Élysées, **1:**306

Ballets Russes de Monte Carlo, **1:**309, *309,* 310, 311, 315, 316, **2:**108, 253, 342, **3:**25, 72, **4:**33

choreographies, **1:**311, 312, *312,* 313, 316, **2:**112, 509, **3:**27, **4:**270

English National Ballet, **2:**509, 510

Francesca da Rimini, **6:**117, 121

Harlequinade, **2:**509, 510, **4:**179

Messel designs, **4:**358

Nutcracker, The, **5:**15

Présages performance, **4:***319*

Prodigal Son, The, **5:**265

Riabouchinska marriage and dance partnership, **4:**178, **5:**349, 350

Rubinstein ballet company, **4:**178, 635

See also Graduation Ball

licht (light) dances, **3:**247–248

Lichtwende, **4:**91

Liciu, Irinel, **5:**386

ličko kolo, **6:**427

Lida, oder Das Schweizer Milchmädchen. See Swiss Milkmaid, The

Lidell, Jeanette, **1:**212

Lidji, Jacques, **1:**64

Lido, Las Vegas, **1:**466

Lido, Paris, **4:**524

Lido, Serge, *as photographer,* **3:**226, 600, **5:**145

Lidova, Irène
Ballet des Champs-Élysées, **1:**305, **4:**33

Ballet des Étoiles de Paris, **3:**74

as contributor, **1:**251, 304–305, 305–306, **2:**111–112, 113–115, **3:**224–227, 361– 362, 600–601, 601, **4:**434–435, **5:**162–165, 604–606

Soirées de la Danse, **1:**251, 305, **3:**73, **5:**162

Lidström, Kerstin, **6:**43, *43*

Lieber, Edward G., **2:**328

Liebermann, Rolf, **3:**337, **5:**96

Lieberson, Goddard, **6:**450

Liebeslieder Waltzes (Weidman choreography), **6:**376–377

Liebeslieder Walzer (Balanchine production), **1:**11, 263, 270, 272, **3:**352, 521, **4:**179–180, **179–180,** 613, 615

Irving (Robert) onstage piano performance, **3:**521

Karinska costumes, **3:**654, **4:**179, 180, *615*

Magallanes performance, **4:**246

Nichols performance, **4:**623, 631

restaging, **4:**621, 631

Verdy performance, **4:**617, **6:**328

Liebes Sender (film), **2:**458

Liebestraum, **3:**208, **5:**494

Liebowitz, Annie, **5:**187

Lieb und Leid und Welt und Traum, **4:**604

Liechtenstein, Princess Eleonore, **1:**89

Lieder eines Fahrenden Gesellen, **6:**44

Liederspiel, **6:**402

Lied von der Erde, Das (Song of the Earth, The), **2:**267, 444, **3:**192, 350, **4:**242, *242,* 246, 248, **6:**9

Liefting, Astrid, **2:**470

Liège Opera Ballet, **4:**134

Liens, Les, **2:**111

Liepa, Andris, **1:**83, 493, **4:180–181,** **5:**465, 556

Liepa, Ilsa, **4:**181

Liepa, Maris, **4:181–182,** 360, **5:***204,* 460, **6:**106
Grigorovich ballets, **1:**493, **4:**144, 181–182

son Andris, **4:**180

Spartacus performance, **5:**677

Liepaja Opera House, **4:**128

Lieszkovszky, Aranka, **4:**529

Lieutenant Kijé, **6:**8

Lieutenant Kijé Suite (Prokofiev), **3:**27

Lifar, Serge, **1:**28, 70, 110, 207, 247, 426, 437, **2:**401, **3:**74, **4:182–186,** **5:**237, 526, 563, 606, 691, **6:**345
Académy Royale de Danse resurrection, **3:**81

Apollo performance, **1:**95, *95,* **4:**182, 620

Après-midi d'un Faune, L', **1:**99
archival materials, **4:**163, 167–168

athletic and acrobatic choreography, **4:**259

Balanchine choreography, **1:**258, 259, **4:**182–183, 620

Ballet Russe de Monte Carlo, **1:**296, 300

Ballets Russes de Monte Carlo
Australian appearances, **1:**207, 313

Beaton photograph of, **1:**395

Berman design collaboration, **1:**437

Biches performance, **4:***637*

on Blache (Alexis), **1:**455–456

Boléro, **5:**316

Cairo Ballet production, **2:**497
Cantique des Cantiques, Le, **1:**118
as Charrat influence, **2:**111
Chatte, La, **1:**258–259, **4:**182
Chauviré association, **2:**113–114
Cocteau artistic disagreement, **2:**183
Creatures of Prometheus revival, **1:**402, **4:**183
Daphnis et Chloë, **2:**388, **5:**316
Darsonval association, **2:**350–351
Diaghilev relationship, **2:**410, 411
Diaghilev's Ballets Russes, **1:**318, *325,* 326, **2:**411, **3:**656, **4:**33, 113, 182–183
Don Quixote version, **2:**440
Dyk association, **2:**471
Egk collaboration, **2:**478
on feet positions, **1:**331
Firebird restaging, **3:**2
Grand Ballet du Marquis de Cuevas, **3:**73
Grisi biography by, **3:**123
Hamlet, **6:**117
Icare, **3:**431, **4:**184, **5:**90
Indes Galantes revival, **3:**450
as Legat (Nikolai) student, **4:**143
on leg elevation, **1:**348, **4:**183
Markova dance partnership, **4:**269
Molière as choreographic source, **4:**447
Nouveau Ballet de Monte Carlo, **3:**225, 601
Paris Opera Ballet, **3:**73, *73,* **4:**183–186, **5:**90, *91, 92, 93, 95–96, 96*
partners, **5:**288
Pastorale, La, **1:***256*
Peretti, Serge, **5:**132
Petit as protégé, **5:**162, 164
Phèdre, **6:**183
Prodigal Son performance, **4:**183, *183,* 620, **5:**264
Romeo and Juliet, **6:**117, 119, 353
Spessivtseva dance partnership, **5:**678, 679
students, **2:**471, **4:**107
Sur le Borysthène, **5:**268
Sylvia, **6:**64
Valses Nobles et Sentimentales, **5:**316
on Vestris (Auguste), **6:**333
Vyrouboya roles, **6:**352, 353
writings on dance, **3:**431, **4:**184, **6:**128
Lifar on Classical Ballet (Lifar), **6:**128
Life, **1:**251, 292, 405, 496, **2:**162, 347, **5:**555
Life and Culture of the Byzantines (Koukoules), **3:**303
Life and Death, The, **2:**258
Life and Times of Joseph Stalin, The (Wilson opera), **6:**400
Life and Times of Sigmund Freud, The (Wilson opera), **6:**400
Life and Works of John Weaver, The (Ralph), **3:**283, 522
Life Begins at 8:40 (musical), **1:**482
Life Continues, **3:**312
Life Crises, **5:**256
LifeForms (computer program), **2:**296, 608
Life for the Tsar, A (Glinka), **5:**626
Life of a Flower, **3:**208
Life of Fanny Elssler, The (television program), **2:**587
Life of the Bee, **3:**398
Life of the Buddha, The, **5:**581
Life of the Insects, The, **1:**467

Life Situations, **2:**20
lifts, **5:**103–105
 Petipa (Marius) innovations, **5:**153
 Renaissance dance, **5:**338
Ligbi (people), **4:**291
Li Gepia, **5:**471
Ligeti, György, **1:**349, **2:**347, **3:**51, **6:**111
Lighetti, Iosif, **5:**384
Light, **1:**292, 406, **4:**597
Light and Shadow, **3:**329, **5:**407
light dancing. *See* soft-shoe dancing
Light Explosion, **1:**436
Lightfall, **1:**543
Light Fantastic, **3:**203
lighting for dance, **2:**393–394, **4:186– 197**
 Appia, Adolphe, **1:**97–98, **4:**189
 Balla innovation, **5:**544
 color, **4:**193
 Fuller innovations, **1:**243, **2:**250, **3:**71, 92–93, *93,* 94, 96, **4:**189
 historical overview, **3:**69, 90–91, **4:186–192,** **6:**57, 58
 Lauterer, Arch, **4:**130
 Loutherbourg approach, **5:**537, 538–539
 makeup needs, **4:**304, 305
 masking, **4:**192–193
 Nikolais concepts, **4:**650, *651,* **5:**547–548
 Rauschenberg design for *Winterbranch,* **6:**402
 Romantic era, **5:**538–539, **6:**57, 58
 as scenic design component, **5:**536, *536,* 537, 538–539, 540, 544–545, 547, 548, 551
 Shankar contribution, **5:**581
 side-lighting effects, **4:**217–218
 theory and practice, **4:192–197**
 while touring, **4:**196
light shows, **1:**244
Lignes et Pointes, **5:**62
Lignière, Aimé de, **1:**414, **5:**422
Li ji (Confucian Book of Rites), **1:**17, **2:**128
Li Jinghan (Li Ching-han), **2:**135
Like Will to Like, **3:**252
Li Keyhu, **5:**330
Likhutina, Anastasia, **4:**36
Likhutina, Natalia, **4:**279
Lilac Garden. See Jardin aux Lilas
Lilangika, **3:**468
Lilavati, **2:**104, **3:**630
Lilea (Lileya), **6:**225–226
Lilius, Margit, **2:**632
Lillebil (Mjøen), **4:**682
Lillie, Beatrice, **6:**272
Lilo, **6:**281
Lily, The, **3:**237, **4:**429
Lily Dance, **2:**246
Lily Marlene in the Jungle, **2:**46
Lily Queen, The, **4:**139
Lima Dent, Nancy, **2:**44, 47
Limarzi, Tullia, *as contributor,* **1:**124–125, **3:**391–393, 609–610, 610–618, **4:**380–382
Limbs Dance Company, **4:**626, 627
Limido, Giovannina, **2:**82, **4:**258
Li Ming-hsun, *as photographer,* **6:**82
Limon, Jean-Marie, **1:**290, 292
Limón, José, **1:**55, 519, **2:**4, 461, **4:197–200,** **5:**116, 127, 187, **6:**83, 132
 all-male casts, **4:**198
 American Dance Festival, **1:**79, **4:**198

as Araiz influence, **1:**102
 archival materials, **4:**166, 167, 169
 Batsheva Dance Company, **3:**532
 Bennington School, **1:**79, 421, **4:**197, 649
 Broadway musicals, **6:**276, 277
 Cébron association, **2:**81
 Chaconne performance, **4:**198
 dance company. *See* Limón Dance Company
 Day on Earth performance, **2:**356
 as Humphrey protégé, **3:**398, 404, 405, **4:**197–198, 199
 Humphrey-Weidman Company, **3:**398, 399, 402, **4:**197–198
 Jacob's Pillow performance, **3:**571
 Juilliard dance division, **5:**561
 Lawrence marriage, **3:**402, **4:**197
 Mexican dance residency, **4:**393
 modern dance technique, **4:**440, 442
 New Dance Variations choreography, **4:**605
 Night Spell performance, **3:**403
 Royal Swedish Ballet guest productions, **6:**43
 students, **1:**535, **2:**566
 See also Moor's Pavane, The
Limón Dance Company, **4:**197–199
 Australian tour, **1:**212
 British appearances, **4:**216
 Fagan choreography, **2:**567
 formation, **3:**402–404, **4:**198
 Hoving, Lucas, **3:**390, 391, 402, 403
 Humphrey choreography, **3:**402, 403, 404, **4:**198
 Japanese tour, **3:**591
 Koner, Pauline, **4:**39
 Linke guest works, **4:**203
Limpid Stream, The. See Bright Stream, The
Lincke, Andreas Frederik, **1:**516
Lincke, Paul, **5:**120
Lincoln Center, New York City, **1:**263, 271, **4:**29, 30
 Schuman presidency, **5:**561–562
 See also Juilliard School; Metropolitan Opera House; New York Public Library for the Performing Arts Dance Collection; New York State Theater
Lincoln Memorial, Washington, D.C., **4:**151
Lincoln Portrait, **2:**357
Lincoln's Inn Fields, London, **4:**105, **5:**350, **6:**372, 374
Linda, Bertna, **1:**238
Lindbergh, Charles, **4:**201, **5:**629
Lindbohm, Valdemar, **2:**631
Linden, Anya, **4:**200–201
Linden, John, **5:**659
Lindesköld, Erik, **6:**38
Lindfors, Tiina, **2:**530, 634
Lindgren, Erik, **6:**42
Lindgren, Gunnel, **6:**42
Lindgren, Robert, **1:**302, **6:**265
lindo dance, **6:**428, 429
Lindquist, John, *as photographer,* **1:**55, 340, 501, **6:**408
Lindqvist, Maria, **6:**44
Lindström, Georg, *as photographer,* **5:**426
Lindström, Rune, **6:**406

Broadway musicals, **6:**273
Cajun, **2:**24
 Four Step Brothers tap style, **3:**57
 Manning, Frankie, **4:**254–255
 Whitey's Lindy Hoppers, **1:**451, **4:**254, **6:***262*
Linea, O King, **1:**462
line-formation dances, **5:**619–620, 635
 branle, **1:**521
 Central and East Africa, **2:**89, *91*
 clogging, **2:**179–180
 conga, **2:**275
 country-western, **2:**259, **5:**634
 Dances of Death, **2:**332
 disco, **5:**633
 European traditional, **2:**552–554, *555*
 Finland, **2:**629
 Greece, **3:**296–298, *299*
 horo, **2:**9
 Indonesia, **1:**366, **2:**232
 Iran, **3:**514
 Israel, **3:**528
 Lebanon, **4:**135–136, *135*
 Macarena, **5:**635
 matachines, **4:**328, 329
 medieval, **4:**348–349, 501
 Mexico, **4:**387
 Middle East, **3:**538, **4:**404, 406–410, **5:**405–406
 moresca, **4:**461, 462
 Papua New Guinea, **5:**76, 77
 Shangana-Tsonga, **5:**579
 Slovakia, **2:**302
 South Africa, **5:**644–645, 646–647, *647*
 southern Africa, **5:**661, 662
 Turkey, **6:***211*
Lines, **4:**597
Line Up, **1:**544
Ling, Per Henrik, **6:**371
Ling Guiming, **6:**385
linguistics and dance. *See* methodologies in the study of dance, linguistics
Lin Hwai-min, **6:**82
Linke, Susanne, **1:**412, **2:**126, **3:**40, 151, 157, **4:203–204,** **5:**200
 Folkwang Tanzstudio, **3:**368, **4:**203
 as Züllig student, **6:**453
linking movements. *See* ballet technique, linking movements
Linn, Bambi, **3:**370, **6:**278, *278*
Linné, Carl von (Linnaeus), **6:**36
Lin Shou-shiang, **6:***81*
Liński, Henryk, **5:**220
Linstrom, Rune, **5:**266
Lin Yangyang, **6:**385
Linz, Austria, **1:**241–242
Lion Amoureux, Le, **4:**33
Lion and the Jewel, The (Soyinka), **6:**384
lion dance (Japan). *See shishimai*
lion dance (Korea), **2:**222, 223, **4:**47, 300
Lion King, The (musical), **6:**289
lion masks, **3:**584, 642
Li Pao-chun, **6:***142*
Lipinski, Dolores, **5:***60*
Lipkovska, Tatiana, **4:**659
Lipman, Sandra, **5:***53,* 54
Lippincott, Gertrude, **1:**421, **3:**385, **4:**169
Lippold, Louise, **2:**286
Lippold, Richard, **1:**138, **2:**286
Lisbell, ou La Nouvelle Claudine, **2:**202

Lisereux, Julie, **5:**233
Lis et la Rose, Le (Campra), **2:**34
Lisitsian, Srbhi, **1:**120, 121, **4:**688, **5:**482
Liška, Ivan, **2:**512, **3:***153*, 157, *337*
Lisle, Rouget de, **3:**118
Lissim, Simon, **1:**255
Liszt, Franz, **2:**473, **3:**20, 24, 29, **5:**124
  Hungarian dance stagings, **3:**418
  Ivanov adaptations, **3:**567–568, **4:**211, 282
  Lanchbery adaptations, **4:**117
  sponsorship of Glazunov, **3:**185
Listziana, **3:**195
Litavkin, Sergei, **5:**160
lithography. *See* prints and drawings
Lithuania, **4:**204–209
  theatrical dance, **4:207–209**, 224
  traditional dance, **4:204–207**, **5:**482
Lithuanian Dance Information Center, **4:**209
Lithuanian Folkculture Centre, **4:**207
Lithuanian National Ballet. *See* National Ballet of Lithuania
Litny Miniature Theater, Saint Petersburg, **5:**391, 392
Little, Cleavon, **6:**284
Little, Keith, **1:**214
Little, Meredith Ellis, *as contributor*, **1:**516–517, **3:**28–29, **5:**351–352
Little, Sue, **3:**273
Little Ballerina, The, **4:**437, **5:**603, **6:**432
Little Ballet, The (Once Upon a Time), **1:**372, **6:**153
Little Colonel, The (film), **5:**368, *368,* **6:**100, 142
Little Dancer, Aged Fourteen, The (Degas bronze), **1:***128*
Little Egypt (dancer), **2:**346, 572
Littlefield, Carl, **4:**209, 210
Littlefield, Caroline, **4:**209
Littlefield, Catherine, **2:**426, 480, **3:**357, **4:209–211**, 246, **5:**279, 612, **6:**291
Littlefield, Dorothie, **4:**209, 210, **6:**292, 396
Littlefield Ballet. *See* Philadelphia Ballet
Littlefield School, Philadelphia, **4:**209, 210
Little Group (Humphrey students), **3:**404
Little Hall, Arnhem, **4:**597
Little Humpbacked Horse, The, **1:**416, 486, 492, **4:211–212**, **5:**278, **6:**311, 313
  Briantzev version, **1:**539, **5:**401
  Gorsky production, **2:**582, **3:**206, **4:**211–212
  Ivanov *divertissement,* **3:**562, 567, **4:**211, 282
  Korovin design, **4:**56
  Mordkin performance, **4:**459
  Nijinsky performance, **4:**640
  Radunsky production, **4:***211,* 212
  Radunsky rechoreography, **5:**587
  as Russian national ballet, **2:**108
  Saint-Léon production, **4:**211, 281, **5:***450,* 455, 501
  Semenova performance, **5:**666
  Shchedrin score, **5:**587
Little Improvisations, **6:**202
Little Jack Shepherd (musical), **3:**90

Little Johnny Jones (musical), **6:***269*
Little Kootch Piece, **3:**619, **6:**362
Little Me (musical), **3:**54
Little Mermaid (statue), **1:**399
Little Mermaid, The, **1:**399, **5:**427
Little Miss Broadway (film), **6:**142
Little Night Music, A (musical), **6:**289
Little Peggy's Love, **2:**414
Little Prince, **5:**471
Little Princess, The (film), **6:**142
Little Princess Hollyhock, **3:**414
Little Prince, The, **4:**154
Littler, William, **2:**49
Little Show of 1929 (revue), **1:**520
Littlest Rebel, The (film), **6:**142
Little Theatre Company of Harper Avenue, Chicago, **2:**458
Little Theatre Movement (Jamaica), **3:**574
Little Tich (George Relph), **4:**521
Littlewood, Joan, **4:**94
Littlewood, Letty, **4:**380
Littré, Emile, **1:**384
liturgical dance, **2:**162–169, **4:212–213**
  cultural context, **4:**365
  Ethiopian Orthodox Christian Church, **2:**533
  medieval, **2:**164, 166, 168, 540, **4:**106–107, **5:**533
  Roman Catholic countries, **2:**168–169
  Roman Empire, **3:**541, **5:**376–378
  Shaker, **2:**168, **5:**575–577, **6:**236
  Spain, **5:**667
  tripudium, **6:**193–195
  See also Jewish dance traditions; ritual and dance
Liturgie, **2:**408, **3:**198, **4:**316, 324
Litvinenko, Vasily, **3:**136, **6:**225
Litvinova, Evgenia, **2:**528
Litvinsky, Georgi, **5:**473
Litz, Katherine, **1:**421, **2:**110, 286, 290, 574, **4:213–214**, 605, **5:**573
Liu Enbo, **2:**149–150
Liu Feng-Shueh, **6:**81, *81,* 82, *82*
  as contributor, **6:**79–83
Liu Jen-ying, **6:***81*
Liu Mengdie, **2:**149
Liu Shaoji, **2:**137
Liu Tsu-chu, **2:***143*
Live, **1:**411, **4:**252
Live for the One Who Bore You, **4:**262
Live from Lincoln Center (television series), **6:**139
Live from Studio 8H (television series), **6:**139
Liverpool Ballet Club, 2, 590
Lives of Performers (film), **5:**293
Living Movement, **2:**385
Livingston, William, **6:**232
Living Theater, **1:**245, **2:**110, **3:**633
Livre de la contredance présenté du Roy (Lorin), **6:**123
livrets. *See* libretti for dance
Livry, Emma, **1:**368, **4:**107, **214–215**, 343, 353
  burns from gas jets, **3:**70, **4:**189, 215, **5:**94
  Nadar photographs of, **4:**176, *176*
  Papillon performance, **3:**70, **4:**215, **5:**94
  Paris Opera Ballet, **5:**94
  Sylphide performance, **6:**58
  as Taglioni (Marie) protégée, **4:**214–215, **5:**94, **6:**74–75
Livshits, Yakov, **5:**472

Livy, **5:**373–374, 375, 377–378, **6:**193
liyuan (pear garden), **2:**130
Lizardo, Fradique, **2:**432
Liza with a Z (television program), **2:**619, **3:**55
Li Zhongmei, **2:***140*
Liz Lerman Dance Exchange, **4:**151, 152
Lizon, Philippe, **1:**292
Lizzie Borden: A Dance of Death (de Mille), **2:**373, 374
Ljubljana Ballet, **6:**432, 437, 438, 439
Ljung, Viveka, **4:**479
Llacer, Tony, **5:**171
Lland, Michael, **1:**69, 75, **4:**394
Llompart, Gloria, **5:**275, 276
Llorente, Maria Elena, **2:**279, *279,* 280
Lloyd, Barbara, **1:**315, **6:**356, 402
Lloyd, Gweneth, **2:**38, 47, **5:**434, 435, 684, 685
Lloyd, Margaret, **1:**116, **4:**306, **6:**88, 299
Lloyd, Maude, **2:**348, *348,* **3:**285, **4:215**, **5:**649, 692
  Jardin aux Lilas performance, **3:**597, **4:**215, **6:***197*
  as London Ballet director, **6:**198, 312
  Rambert Ballet, **5:**296, 298, 299, 300
  students, **5:**312
  television performances, **6:**135, 196
  Tudor association, **6:**196, *196,* 197, *197*
Lloyd, Norman, **1:**421, **3:**402, 403, **5:**559
Lloyd, Ruth, **5:**559
Lloyd Webber, Andrew, **1:**76, **2:**251, **4:**244, **6:**284, 285, 286, 287–288
LMA. *See* Laban Principles of Movement Analysis
loa, **5:**355
Lobanov, Ivan, **5:**453
Lobi (people), **4:**290
Lobo, Belén, **6:**323
  as contributor, **6:**322–325
Locale (film dance), **2:**294, 607
Locardi, Elide, **1:**102, 113
Locatelli, Giovanni, **5:**451
Lock, Édouard, **2:**40, 45, 470, 610, **3:**234, **6:**132, 180
Locke, John, **3:**276, 281, **6:**374
Locke, Matthew, **3:**376, **5:**280
Lockende Phantom, Das, **4:**228
Lockyer, Bob, **6:**1, 133–134, 136
  as contributor, **6:**134–136
Lőcsei, Jenő, **3:**418
Locsin, Agnes, **5:**172, 173
Locsin, Carmen, **5:**172
Locus, **1:**543, **6:***249*
Loder, Edward James, **3:**183
Lodoïska (Kreutzer opera), **4:**61, **6:**71
Lodowka, Vallya (pseud.), **4:**589–590
Loeber, Vivien, **5:**422
López Mateos, Adolfo, **4:**396
Loesch, Ilse, **4:**92
Loeser, Ruth, **3:**340, **4:**103
Loesser, Frank, **5:**561, **6:**281
Loeszer, Gert Ruth, **4:**91, 92
Loewe, Frederick, **1:**539
Loftier Flight, A (Swift), **6:**297
Logan, Billie, **2:**319
Logan, Joshua, **6:**182
Logar province, Afghanistan, **1:**27

Lohengrin (Wagner), **1:**510
Loiko, Antoni, **1:**408
lokadharmī, **3:**456–457, **4:**575
Lokko, Sophia D., *as contributor,* **3:**169–170
Loktak Lake, **3:**468
Lola, **1:**517, **2:**15, 16, **5:**459, 466, **6:**83
Lola Coming! Europe Farewell! America I Come (caricature), **2:**69
Lola Tajik Dance Company, **6:**84
Lolita, **5:**475
Lolle, Jens, **3:**105, **5:**425
Lomax, Alan, **2:**602, **4:**99, 370, 374
Lomax, Sondra, *as contributor,* **6:**61–62
Lombardi alla Prima Crociata, I, **4:**514
Lombardin, Raymonde, **3:**76
Lombok, Indonesia, **3:**504, 505
Lommel, Daniel, **1:**292, 293
Lommi, Enrique, **1:**110, **3:***317*
Londesborough, Lord, **2:**525
London Archives of Dance, **4:**163
London Arts Council, **2:**511, 513
London Ballet, **2:**349, **3:**203, 392, **4:**215, **5:**300, **6:**197–198, 312
London blitz (1940–1941), **3:**511
London Calling (Coward revue), **4:**334
London Casino Revue, **1:**467
London City Ballet, **3:**269
London Coliseum, **2:**409, 424, 511
London Contemporary Dance School, **2:**450, 575, **3:**273, 278, 279, 283, **4:**110, 216, 220, **5:**559
London Contemporary Dance Theatre, **2:**1, **3:**221, *272,* 273, 278, **4:216–221**, **5:**575, **6:**134
  Alston, Richard, **1:**50, 51, 53
  Davies, Siobhan, **2:**354, 355, **3:**273
  evolution, style, and members, **3:**272, 273, 274–275
  Phantasmagoria, The, **1:**394
London Festival Ballet. *See* English National Ballet
London Morning, **2:**510, **3:**175
London School of Contemporary Dance. *See* London Contemporary Dance School
London's Festival Ballet. *See* English National Ballet
London Studio Centre, **3:**280
London Sunday Times (newspaper), **1:**398
London *Times* (newspaper), **3:**285
London Weekend Television, **6:**135
Lonely Shadow, **3:**590
Lonely Won't Leave Me Alone, **5:***659*
Loney, Glenn, *as contributor,* **2:**184–185
Long, Julie-Anne, **1:**215
Long, Larry, **5:**60
Long, Richard, **1:**304
Longchamp, Gaston, **5:**570
Longfellow, Henry Wadsworth, **2:**504
Longhorns (film dance), **2:**605
Long, Long Ago (Gladkov), **1:**539
Longley, Suzanne, **2:**356
long-sword dance, **3:**240, **6:**54, 55
Long Undressing, A, **4:**627
longways, **4:221–222**
  as country dance, **2:**254–256, 257, **5:**685, 686
  English traditional, **3:**238, 239, **4:**473, 474
  "minor sets," **4:**221

New England traditional, **3:**35
Scottish Lowlands, **3:**248
See also anglaise; Morris dance; quadrille; *sarabande*
Look, Ma, I'm Dancin' (musical), **5:**361, **6:**279
Look for the Silver Lining (musical), **4:**420
Loomis, Clarence, **5:**59
Loomis, Margaret, **5:**494
Looring, Lillian, **2:**528
Loosestrife, **2:**296, **4:**37
loosestrife plant, **2:**489
Lopen, **4:**597
López, Hercilia, **6:**323
López, Israel (Cachao), **2:**276
López, Julio, **5:**275
López, Lila, **4:**397
Lopez, Lourdes, **4:**619, **5:**265
López, Nacho, *as photographer*, **4:**393
López, Nancy, **1:**111
Lopez, Orestes, **2:**276
López, Pilar, **1:**117, 294, **2:**521, **3:**9, **4:**222–223, **5:**316, 674
  Gades association, **3:**101, 102
  Greco association, **3:**286, *286*
  Ximénez and Vargas association, **6:**407
Lopez, Sony, **5:**172
López Julvez, Encarnación. *See* Argentinita, La
López Lomba, Violeta, **6:**301–302
Lopokova, Evgenia, **6:**348
Lopokova, Lydia, **1:***323*, **5:**223–224, **6:**348
  American musicals, **3:**21, **4:**223
  American tour, **4:**223
  Ashton ballets, **1:**158, **4:**224, 268
  Carnaval, Le, **2:**73, *192*
  Coppélia, **2:**200, **4:**224
  de Valois friendship, **2:**397, 401
  Diaghilev's Ballets Russes, **2:**410, **4:**223, **5:**13, 611
  dramatic roles, **4:**224
  as Fokine student, **3:**14, **4:**223
  Idzikowski dance partnership, **3:**441
  Keynes marriage, **4:**223–224
  as Legat (Nikolai) student, **4:**143
  London performances, **3:**263, **4:**223–224
  Massine association, **4:**319
  as Massine-type dance, **5:**636
  Mordkin's All-Star Imperial Russian Ballet, **4:**459
  Parade performance, **5:**85
  Sleeping Beauty performance, **5:**611
Lopresti, Ronald, **1:**50
Lopukhov, Andrei, **5:**393, 480, 614
Lopukhov, Fedor, **1:**38, 90, 244, 402, **2:**200, **4:**224–226, **5:**236, 614, **6:**314, 348
  Blok on, **1:**464
  Bolshoi Ballet, **1:**491, 492, **2:**579
  Burmeister collaboration, **2:**15
  character dancing classes, **2:**107
  choreographic training program, **5:**480
  Coppélia version, **2:**369, **3:**327, **4:**226, **5:**468
  dance symphony concept, **1:**258, 416, **5:**457–458
  Danilova performances, **2:**342
  Dmitriev collaboration, **2:**421
  Dolgushin tribute to, **2:**423
  Don Quixote revival, **2:**437
  as Fokine student, **3:**14

Gerdt (Elisaveta) roles, **3:**137
  as Grigorovich choreographic influence, **3:**308
  as Gusev choreographic influence, **3:**327
  as Legat (Nikolai) student, **4:**143
  Lukom association, **4:**233
  Maly Theater Ballet, **5:**467–468, 595
  Maryinsky Ballet, **4:**224, 226, 283–284, **5:**457–458
  Nutcracker, The, **5:**10–11, 12
  Raymonda, **5:**321
  scholarly writings on, **5:**484
  Shostakovich ballets, **5:**594–595
  sister Lopokova (Lydia), **4:**223
  Sleeping Beauty design, **5:**610
  Souritz analysis of work, **5:**653
  Spring Tale, **5:**459
  students, **2:**585, **4:**224
  Swan Lake production, **4:**224, **6:**31
  on Volynsky, **6:**352
Lopukhova, Evgenia, **4:**223
Loquasto, Santo, **2:**245, 441, **4:**226–227, **5:**551, **6:**112
  Don Quixote sets, **1:**74
  Other Dances costume, **4:**248
  Relâche re-creation, **3:**616
  Spindrift design, **5:**679, 680–681
Lorber, Marcel, **1:**467
Lorber, Martha, **3:**21, 22
Lorca, Alberto, **1:**294, **4:**222
Lorca, Federico García. *See* García Lorca, Federico
Lorca, Luz, **2:**125, 127
Lorca, Nana, **3:**286, **4:**222, **5:**674
Lorcia, Suzanne, **4:**184, **5:**95, **6:**64
Lord, Jane, **2:**470
Lord of Burleigh, The, **1:**147, **3:**41
Lord's Masque, The (Campion), **4:**312
Lord's Prayer, The, **2:**264
Loreley, **1:**427
Lorentz, Alcide Joseph, **2:**71, **3:**183
Lorenze, Johnny, **6:**316
Lorenzetti, Ambrogio, **4:**348–349, 501
Lorezzo, **1:**88
Lorges, Nicolas de, **1:**3, 287, 288, **5:**87
Lorin, André, 4, 684, **1:**90, 189, **2:**255, 256, 337, **6:**123
Lőrinc, György, **3:**422, 424, **6:**66
Lőrinc, Katalin, **3:**419, 421
Loring, Eugene, **1:**49, 65, 233, **2:**109, 112, **4:**227–228, **5:**573, **6:**137, 138, 198
  archival materials, **4:**170
  Ballet Caravan, **1:**279, **4:**28, **6:**247
  Dance Players, **2:**161
  Fokine association, **3:**22, 23
  Hawkins roles, **3:**349
  Hollywood musicals, **2:**616, **4:**4
  notation system, **3:**427, **4:**691
  Silk Stockings, **6:**282
  students, **6:**151
  Yankee Clipper, **4:**227, **6:**247
  See also Billy the Kid
Lormeau, Jean-Yves, **5:**96, 98, **6:**64
Lormier, Paul, **2:**405, **3:**177, 620, **5:**92, 132
Lorrain, Claude, **5:**517
Lorrain, Jean, **3:**92
Lorrain, Roland, **2:**49
Lorraine, Eva, **3:**306
Lorrayne, Vyvyan, **1:**156, **2:**515, **4:**452
Lőrubc, Katalin, **6:**67
Los. *For names and titles with this prefix, see key word*

Los Angeles, California
  Federal Dance Project, **2:**581
  Horton modern dance, **3:**386–387
Los Angeles Ballet Theatre, **4:**179
Los Angeles Dance Center, **1:**11
Los Angeles Museum of Contemporary Art, **2:**110
Los Angeles Music Center, **3:**611, 617
Losch, Tilly, **1:**240, **4:**228–229
  Balanchine choreography, **1:**306, 307, **3:**72
  Beaton photograph of, **1:**395
  "Dancing in the Dark," **6:**275, *275*
Los Del Rio, **5:**635
Loss of Small Detail, The, **3:**52
Lost, Found, Lost, **6:**111
Lost Illusions, **2:**96, 421, 449, **5:**571, **6:**442
Lost in the Stars (musical), **3:**621, **6:**281
Lotharingen, Karel van, **1:**409
Lotsy, Anne, **1:**292
Lotte Goslar Pantomime Circus, **3:**207–208
Lotuko (Otuho), **2:**86
Lotus Dance, *2:134*, 136
Lotus I, II, III, IV, **4:**142
Lotus VI: Taming the Bull, **4:**142
Loudières, Monique, **5:**98
Louis II, prince of Monte-Carlo, **2:**253
Louis XIII, king of France, **1:**285, 286, 287, **2:**169–170, 236, **3:**81
Louis XIV, king of France, **1:**90, 409, **4:**229–230, 684
  Académie Royale de Danse founding, **1:**3, 286, 288, **2:**338, **3:**81, 545, **4:**229
  ballet de collège, **1:**283, 284
  ballet de cour, **1:**285, 286, 287, 288, 342–344, **3:**65, 66, **4:**109, **5:**520, 620
  banquets, **1:**364
  Beauchamps as ballet intendant, **1:**396–397
  Benserade as ballet librettist, **1:**424–425
  Berain as designer, **1:**425
  bourrée dance type, **1:**516
  commedia dell'arte ban, **2:**188
  Conservatoire de Danse founding, **3:**81
  costumes, **2:**236, 238
  courante, **2:**259, 260
  dancers' makeup, **4:**304
  dance skills, **1:**286, 287, 424, **3:**63, 66, **4:**229, **5:**489
  definition of dance, **1:**283
  folia dance, **3:**28, 29
  Gissey costume designs, **3:**184
  horse ballets, **3:**381
  lighting for dances, **4:**188
  loures, **4:**231, 232
  Lully as dancing master, **2:**337, **4:**234, 586
  menuet, **4:**431, *432*
  Molière commissions, **4:**447
  Paris Opera Ballet regulations, **5:**87–88
  rigaudon, **5:**351
  scenic design, **5:**536
  Subligny performance, **6:**11
Louis XV, king of France, **1:**122, 288, 425
  Ballet de la Nuit, Le, **5:**603
  Ballon as ballet master, **1:**355
  Barberina performances, **1:**365
  costume design, **2:**238
  de Hesse ballets, **2:**365

masquerades, **4:**313
Mouret's composition of coronation dances, **4:**475
Prévost as dancing master, **3:**81
Louis XVI, king of France, **2:**72, 238, 239, 353, **3:**66, **5:**89
Louis XVIII, king of France, **5:**91
Louis, Murray, **3:**445, **4:**115, 168, **230–231**, 441, **5:**316, 432
  Nikolais association, **4:**230, 649, 650–651
  Nureyev, Rudolf, **5:**7, *8*
  Pilobolus Dance Theatre, **5:**194
Louis, Victor, **6:**158
Louise (Charpentier), **3:**50
Louisiana. *See* Cajun dance traditions
Louis-le-Grand. *See* Collège de Louis-le-Grand
Louis Phillippe. *See* Napoleon III
Louisville Arts Council, **3:**218
Louisville Ballet, **5:**62, **6:**266
Louisville Civic Ballet, **4:**577
Loup, Le, **1:**305, **3:**12, 74, 133, **5:**163, 431, **6:**328
Loup et l'Agneau, Le, **6:**119
loure, **4:**231–232**, 511
Lourié, Eugène, **1:***310*
Louisana Purchase (film), **6:**450, *450*
Louther, Dudley, **3:**219
Louther, William, **4:**216
Loutherbourg, Philippe Jacques de, **4:**189, **5:**537, 538
Loutzaki, Irene, **3:**303, 304, **4:**367
Loutzaki, Rena, **3:**303
Louvain, Belgium, **1:**414
Louÿs, Pierre, **2:**360, **3:**186
Love, Ellen, **3:**402
Love, Jacob Wainwright, *as contributor*, **5:**509–510
Love, Kermit, **2:**245, 438, 568
Love, M'Pongo, **4:**487
Love and Death (Savitri), **6:**151
Love Ballad, **4:**226
Love Charm, The, **3:**568
Love! Despair! and Champagne! (later *Spleen and Champagne*), **4:**454
Lovedu (people), **5:**643, 646
Love for Three Oranges, The, **3:**24
Love in a Tub, **2:**364
Love Is Quick!, **4:**459
Løvenskjold, Herman Severin, **1:**515, **4:**513, **6:**59
Love of Three Oranges, The (Prokoviev), **2:**192
Loveraker, **3:**520
Lovers' Gallery, The, **2:**2–3, **4:**380, **5:**691
Lovers Made Men (Jonson masque), **4:**309, 310, 312
Lovers of Teruel, The (film), **6:**119–120, *120*
Love's Labour's Lost (Shakespeare), **2:**1
Loves of Mars and Venus, The (Weaver ballet-pantomime), **2:**465, **4:**173, **5:**69, **6:**372, 373
  dancer characterizations, **5:**105
  Santlow performance, **5:**518
  Skeaping re-creation, **5:**603
Love Song, The, **3:**129, **5:**58
Love Songs (Forsythe ballet), **6:**53
Love Sonnets, **3:**317
Love Stories, **6:**412
Love's Triumph through Callipollis (Jonson), **4:**312
Lovisa Ulrika, queen of Sweden, **6:**39, 46, 48

Low countries. *See* Belgium; Netherlands
Low Down Dirty Rag, **2:**19
Lowe, Frederick, **6:**279, 282
Lowe, Joseph, **4:**629
Lowe collection (New Zealand), **4:**629
Lowen, Alexander, **1:**469
Lowie, Robert H., *as photographer*, **3:**374
Lowry, Corinna, **5:**659
Lowry, L. S., **4:**668, *668*
Lowry, W. McNeil, **5:**513
Lowski, Woytek, **1:**291, **4:**232
Lozano, Amalia, **6:**301
Lozano, Carlos, *as contributor*, **6:**170, 416
Lozano, Silvia, **4:**396
Lozi (people), **2:**90
LSCD. *See* London School of Contemporary Dance
Luahine, Iolani, **3:**396, **5:**225
Luahine, Keahi, **3:**396
Luang Prabang Palace dancers, **4:**123
Luba (people), **1:**527
luʿbah dance, **4:**406, 408–409, *408*, 417, **6:**419
Lubala (people), **2:**87–88
Lubitsch, Ernst, **2:**613
Lubovitch, Lar, **1:**291, 350, **2:**284, 299, **3:**233, **5:**301, 432
　Alvin Ailey Dance Theater choreography, **1:**55, 60, **3:**578
　American Music Festival (1988), **4:**622–623
　Ballet of the Red Shoes, **6:**288
　Dutch National Ballet choreography, **2:**469
　Gulbenkian Ballet guest choreography, **5:**234
　Into the Woods choreography, **6:**287
　Rudner as guest artist, **5:**440
Lu Bu and Diao Chan (opera), **6:**421
Luca, Dia, **1:**241, 402, **6:**388
Lucas, Carolyn, **5:***314*
Lucas, David, **4:***238*
Lucas, Leighton, **4:**256
Lucas, Sam, **6:**254
Lucas et Laurette, **3:**119, **4:**422
Lucas Hoving and Dance Company, **3:**391
Luccioni, Denise, **3:**362
Luce, **5:**246
Luce, Clare Boothe, **1:**192, **3:**559, **6:**276
Lucea, Oliver, **5:***683*
Lucena, Elvira, **2:**522
Lucerne Ballet, **6:**53
Lucezarskaya, Ira, **5:**263
Lucia, Paco de, **3:**10
Lucia di Lammermoor (Donizetti), **2:**367, **3:**5, 180
Lucian, **1:**20, **2:**116, 270–271, **3:**428, **5:**72–73, 74
Luciani, Rafaello, **3:**554
Lucian of Samosata, **3:**541
Lucier, Alvin, **2:**575
Lucifer, **3:**45
Lucila, Jojo, **5:**172
Lucile, Jean, **2:**261
Lucile Marsh Concert Group, **1:**39
Lucinda Childs Dance Company, **2:**119, *120*
Lucio Silla (Mozart), **5:**693
Luciuk, Juliusz, **6:**175
"Luck Be a Lady Tonight" *(Guys and Dolls)*, **6:**281
Lucke, Virginia, **4:**212

Lucky Seven, **2:**186
Lucy, countess of Bedford, **4:**310
Lucyan (people), **2:**62
Luʿdayati (people), **2:**86
Lüders, Adam, **4:**620, 623, 631, **5:**430, **6:**349
Ludi Apollinares. *See* Apollonian Games
Ludlow, Conrad, **2:**161, **4:**179, *179*, 611, *618*, 619–620, **5:**513
Ludlow, Noah, **1:**459, **2:**85, 443, **6:**237
Ludmilla, Anna, **2:**424
Ludovico company, **1:**110
Ludt, Finn, **4:**677
Ludwig, Arnold, **6:**184
Ludwig: Fragments of a Puzzle, **4:**427
Ludwig of Bavaria, **1:**297, **5:***175*
Luengo, Paul, **1:**480
Luengo, Sandalio, **1:**480
Luening, Otto, **1:**420
Luft, Uriel, **3:**229
Lugbara (people), **2:**90
Lugossy, Emma, **3:**423
Luigi (Eugene Louis Facciuto), **3:**600, **6:**151
　See also jazz dance
Luipart, Marcel, **1:**1, 390, **2:**478, 561, **3:**149
Luis, Sara de, **6:**408
Luisa Strozzi, **3:**426
Luiseño (people), **4:**568
Luisillo, **4:**232–233, **5:**654, 674
Lukanov, P., **2:**11, 12
Lukatelli, Ivanka, **6:**438
Lukcso, David, **2:***584*
Lukin, Lev, **5:**476
Lukom, Elena, **3:**14, **4:**233–234, 283, **5:**458
Łukowicz, Aleksander, **5:**217
Lully, Jean-Baptiste, **1:**46, 424, **2:**202, **4:**234–236
　Atys, **5:***324*
　ballet de cour, **1:**286, 287, 288, 342, **2:**518, **3:**66, **4:**188, 234–235
　Beauchamps collaboration, **1:**396, 516
　Berain costume designs, **1:**425
　bourrées, **1:**516
　canaries, **2:**51
　chaconne and *passacaille* development, **2:**98–99
　commedia della'arte reciprocal influences, **2:**191
　dancing master post, **2:**337
　Drottningholm Court Theater revival, **4:**47
　entrée grave, **2:**518, 519, **4:**234
　gavottes, **3:**124
　gigues, **3:**172
　Gissey costume designs, **3:**184
　importance in dance development, **1:**342, **3:**545, **4:**508, 509
　Louis XIV patronage, **2:**337, **4:**234, **5:**86
　loures, **4:**231, 232
　menuets, **4:**431, 511
　Molière collaboration, **4:**234
　Molière rivalry, **4:**447, **6:**267
　musicianship, **4:**509
　Paris Opera, **2:**338, 465, **3:**81, **5:**86–87, 88
　position on opera ballets, **5:**34, 38–40, 306, 307
Lully, Louis de, **4:**443
Lulu (Berg opera), **2:**17
Lulu (Ulrich ballet), **6:**229

Lumbye, Hans Christian, **1:**516, **4:**513, **5:**428
Luminaire (videodance), **2:**609
Lumley, Benjamin, **1:**47, **3:**224, 260, 279, **5:**108, 136, 137, 138, 277
"Luna, La," **5:**527
Luna Arroyo, Antonio, **4:**399
Lunacharsky, Anatoly, **1:**246, 489, **6:**352
Lunacharsky Institute of Theatrical Art, Moscow, **5:**480, **6:**8, 442
Lunacharsky Museum, Saint Petersburg, **4:**165
Lunacharsky Theater Technicum, Saint Petersburg, **2:**15, **6:**106
Lunamble, **6:**362
Luna Park, **1:**437, **4:**33
Lunceford, Jimmie, **4:**202, **6:**256
Lund, Alan and Blanche, **6:**130
Lund, Gun, **6:**45
Lund, Jørgen Gad, **2:**381
Lund, Sweden, **6:**45
Lund, Troels, **3:**39
Lunda (people), **2:**86, 89, 91
Lundgren, Henrik, *as contributor*, **3:**222–224, **4:**120, 126, **5:**238, 250–251, 511, 553
Lundqvist, Eva, **6:**45
Lundsten, Ralph, **2:**264
lundú, **1:**528, 530
Lundy, William, **6:**323
Lunn, Jonathan, **4:**220
Lunsford, Bascom Lamar, **2:**180
Lunyu (Confucius), **2:**148
Luo (people), **4:**484
luo sacrificial dance, **2:**140
Lupercalia, **3:**541, **5:**376
Lupi da Caravaggio, Livio, **2:**73, 75, 337, **3:**107, **4:**580, **5:**339
　on canary, **2:**50
　on *cascarda*, **2:**77
　dance manual, **6:**122
　on *passo e mezzo*, **5:**110, 111
　on tordion, **6:**178
Lupino, George, **5:**70–71
Lupo, Thomas, **4:**311
Lupovsky, Vladimir, *as photographer*, **5:**478
Lurçat, Jean, **1:**259, **5:**570
Lure, The, **4:**214
Lurie, Liane, **5:**55
Lurline, **4:**464
Luscombe, Jean, **4:**628
Lustig, Graham, **4:**668, **6:**366
lute, **1:**6
　Caroso and Negri tablature, **2:**73, 75, **4:**507
　gamelan, **3:**112, 114
　Mesopotamia, **4:**498
　Middle Ages, **4:**501, 502
　Renaissance, **4:**505, *506*
　Roman, **4:**500
Lutgerink, Ton, **4:**595, 597
Lutheranism, **2:**167, 537, 552, **3:**436
Luther Burbank in Santa Rosa, **6:**362
Luti di Sulmona, Prospero, **2:**73, 75, 337, **3:**107, **4:**580, **5:**339, **6:**122
Lutin de la Vallée, Le, **5:**500, *501*
Lutosławski, Witold, **5:**302
Lutry, Michel de, **1:**500, **3:**512
Lutte Éternelle, La, **1:**313
Lutton, F., *as photographer*, **4:**353
lutuki, **1:**527
Lutyens, Elisabeth, **4:**115
Lützelberger, Hans, **5:**258, 259
Lu Wenjian, *as contributor*, **2:**144–145

Lux, Stephan, **3:**155
Luxe I and *II, La* (Matisse), **1:**130
Luxembourg, **2:**164, 168
Luyt, Jan van, **1:**411
Luyth, Jaak van, **1:**519
Luzon, Philippines, **2:**230
Luzzati, Emanuele, **1:**83
Lvov, Prince Pavel Dmitrievich, **4:**641
Lvov, Ukraine, **6:**226
Lvov-Anokhin, Boris A., **4:**55, **5:**204
　as contributor, **2:**564–565, **6:**226–228
Lyadov, Anatoly, **6:**3
Lyadov, Konstantin, **5:**150
Lyavonikha, **4:**444
Lyceum (Lykeion) of Greek Women, **3:**296
Lyceum movement, **6:**235
Lyceum Theatre, London, **2:**395, 525
Lycko-Priis, **6:**38
Lydia (1951), **1:**49
Lydie (1828), **1:**35, **3:**360
Lyle, Bernie, **5:**654
Lyman, Peggy, **3:**213, 220
Lynch, Claudia, **3:**88
Lynch, Ventura, **1:**109
Lynes, George Platt, **5:**183, 185–186
　as photographer, **2:**244, **4:**607, 611, **5:**185
Lynn Dally's Jazz Tap Ensemble, **6:**102
Lynne, Gillian, **4:**668, *668*, **5:**589, **6:**286, 287
Lyon, Annabelle, **1:**63, 64, 279, *280*, **2:***373*, **5:**193, 571, **6:***199*
　Fokine association, **3:**22, 23
　Holm studies, **3:**370
Lyon, France
　modern dance, **3:**79
　national dance conservatory, **3:**82
　See also Lyon Opera Ballet
Lyonnet, Henry, **1:**122
Lyonnois, Marie-François, **4:**236
Lyon Opera Ballet, **1:**446, **3:**66, 67, **5:**399
　Blache (Jean-Baptiste) productions, **1:**455
　Childs choreographies, **2:**120
　Hus family, **3:**426
　Jones (Bill T.) as resident director, **3:**621
　New Zealand tour, **4:**624
　Noverre, Jean-Georges, **4:**695
lyre *(lyra)*, **3:**293, 294, 295, **4:**499, **6:**444, 445
lyrical chanting, **5:**375
Lyrical Company of the Bucharest National Theater. *See* Bucharest Opera
Lyrical Poem, A, **3:**205
Lyric Suite, **5:**637, **6:**229
Lyric Theater, Israel, **3:**532, **5:**638
Lys de la Vie, La (film), **3:**95, 96
Lysenko, Mykola, **6:**225, 344
Lysistrata, **1:**456, 460
　Chappell design, **2:**105
　Humprhey-Weidman choreography, **3:**399
　Markova performance, **4:**267
　Tudor production, **5:**299, 300, **6:**195
Lyster, William Saurin, **1:**206
Lys, The, **2:**368
Lytton, Madeleine, **3:**77
Lytton, Ulrike, **1:**235

M (Cage), **2:**23
Maack, Rudolf, **6:**391
Maácz, László, **3:**424
Maazinovič, Maga, **6:**433
Mabel Whitman and the Dixie Boys, **6:**386
Mabille, Auguste, **2:**203, 204, **3:**5, *5*, 179, **5:**93, 114, **6:**71
Mabille, Charles, **4:**338, 339
Mabille, Madame. *See* Maywood, Augusta
Mabry, Iris, **1:**421
mabuang, **3:**477
Ma Bugi (film), **2:**602
mabumbumbu dance, **3:**177
Mac an Fhosair, **3:**246
Macarena (dance), **5:**635
Macarrona, La, **1:**61, **3:**7, **5:**672
Macaulay, Alastair, **3:**285, **5:**16
as contributor, **1:**50–53, **2:**445–446, 515–516, **3:**442–443, **4:**452, 456–457, **5:**297–305, 531–532, **6:**64–65, 217–218
MacBean, Ian, **1:**400
Macbeth (Boyarchikov ballet), **1:**518, **5:**464, 468
Macbeth (Didelot ballet), **2:**414
Macbeth (Galeotti ballet), **3:**105, **5:**424
Macbeth (Shakespeare)
Federal Theatre production, **2:**313
Priest dance choreography, **5:**251
witches' dance, **3:**253
Macbeth (Vasiliev ballet), **1:**493, **3:**418, **5:**452, **6:**314
Leventhal scenic design, **4:**154
Timofeyeva performance, **6:**171
Macbeth (Verdi opera), **1:**461, **4:**514
Macbeth against Macbeth, **6:**435
Macbetto, **5:**277
MacCracken, Joan, **5:**290
MacDonald, Betty, **3:**211
Macdonald, Brian, **1:**349, 350, **3:**230–231, **4:**237–238, **5:**62, 685, **6:**324
Adieu Robert Schumann, **6:**364
Firebird production, **3:**3
Harkness Ballet, **3:**342, 343
Joffrey Ballet, **3:**610, 611
Norwegian National Ballet, **4:**677
Royal Swedish Ballet, **4:**238, **6:**42
Royal Winnipeg Ballet, **2:**39, 42, **5:**435, 436
Taverner roles, **6:**106
television dance choreographies, **6:**130, 131, 133
MacDonald, Elaine, **5:**565
Macdonald, Nesta, **3:**284
Macdonian Tale, The, **6:**436
Mace, Thomas, **5:**520, **6:**125
MacEachen, Frances, *as contributor*, **5:**696–699
MacEachen, Ronald, **5:**697
Macedonia, **1:**84, **2:**101, **3:**296, 298, 299, **6:**428, 429–430, 436–437
Macero, Teo, **5:**638
MacFarlane, John, **4:**602
MacFlecknoe (Dryden), **5:**490
MacGillivray, David, **4:***82*
Machandel, **3:**368
Macharovský, Rudolf, **5:**614
Machaut, Guillaume de, **1:**364
Machavariani, Aleksei, **1:**540, **6:**342
Mâche, François-Bernard, **2:**120
Macheret, Elena, **5:**471
Machherndl, Robert, **2:**470
"machine dances," **1:**134
Machito, **2:**276
machitun, **2:**121

Machov, Saša, **2:**307, 308, **4:**77, **238–239, 5:**245, 270
Maciek i Baśka, **5:**195
Maciunas, George, **1:**139
Mackaye, James Steele, **2:**371
Macke, Hans, **6:**454
MacKenzie, Kenneth, **1:**314, 315
Mackenzie, Ruth, **1:**365
Mackerras, Charles, **2:**265
Mackie, Joyce, **2:**498
Mackinnon, Sheila, **2:***36*, **5:**435
Mackintosh, Keith, **2:**58, **5:***652*
Mackrell, Judith, **3:**285
"Mack Sennett Ballet" (*High Button Shoes*), **6:**279, *279*
mackshun (dance), **2:**64
MacLachlan, Ewen, **3:**247
MacLaine, Shirley, **6:**327
MacLane, Gretchen, **3:**634, **6:**363
Maclaren, Euphan, **4:**667
MacLaren, Norman, **6:**364
MacLeary, Donald, **1:***151*, **4:***240*, **5:***104*, 421, 654
Apollo, **1:**96
Beriosova dance partnership, **1:**429
Romeo and Juliet performance, **5:**396
MacLeish, Archibald, **3:**216, **4:**26
Maclès, Jean-Denis, **2:**243
Macmahon, Diamond, and Clemence, **6:**319
MacMaster, Buddy, **5:**698
MacMaster, Chris Rankin, **5:**697
MacMaster, Minnie (Beaton), **5:**698
MacMillan, Kenneth, **1:**38, 234, 370, 463, **3:**268, **4:**239–245, **5:**225–226, 301, 563, 564
American Ballet Theatre, **1:**76, **3:**664, **4:**244
Anastasia, **4:**117
Benish notation use, **1:**417
Beriosova roles, **1:**429, 430
Berlin Opera Ballet, **1:**436, **3:**149, **4:**242
Birmingham Royal Ballet choreography, **3:**268
Carousel dances choreography, **6:**288
choreographic style, **3:**267
de Valois association, **2:**403
Fin du Jour, La, **5:**315
Georgiadis collaboration, **3:**136, **4:**240, *241*, 242, 256, **5:**396
Gloria, **4:**72
Haydée ballets, **3:**350–351
Hermanas, Las, **5:**564
ice-dance choreography, **2:**298
Images of Love, **1:**156
Invitation, The, **3:**512–513, **4:**241, **5:**574, *574*
Jeux reconstruction, **4:**643
Lanchbery musical arrangements, **4:**117
Linden roles, **4:**200
Makarova roles, **4:**248
Manon, **1:**77, **4:**243, *244*, 256–257, 547, **6:**44
Mason roles, **4:**306, 307
Mayerling, **5:**418, *419*
National Ballet of Canada choreography, **4:**542
partnering technique, **5:**104–105
ragtime ballet, **4:**519
Romeo and Juliet, **1:**459, **2:**186, 444, **3:**136, **4:**24, *241*, 242, 244, 248, **5:**6, 394, *396*, **396**, **6:**43, *43*
Royal Ballet, **5:**416, 417–418, 419
Royal Ballet co-directorship, **2:**590, **3:**267, **4:**242–243

Royal Danish Ballet guest productions, **5:**431
Royal Swedish Ballet guest productions, **4:**242, 243, **6:**43, *43*, 44
Sacre du Printemps, Le, **5:**488
Sadler's Wells Royal Ballet, **5:**420
Seymour roles, **4:**241, 242, 243, **5:**574, 575
Sibley roles, **5:**597
Sleeping Beauty, The, **1:**77, 436, **6:**44
Stuttgart Ballet productions, **2:**267, **3:**149, **6:**9
Swan Lake, **1:**436
Valses Nobles et Sentimentales, **5:**316
van Praagh association, **6:**313
Verdi Variations, **6:**143
Wells roles, **6:**380
Winter Dreams, **5:***421*
See also Manon
MacMillan's "Mayerling" (documentary), **6:**135
MacOrlan, Pierre, **1:**252
Macrodance (Macrodanza), **6:**136, 323
MacTavish, Shona Dunlop, **4:**626–627, 629
Macuja, Lisa, **5:**172
Maculele, **1:***530*
Macumba, **6:**185, 345
Madalengoitia, Pablo de, **2:**127
Madama Butterfly (Belasco production), **5:**491
Madama Butterfly (Puccini opera), **3:**339, 356
Madam Chrysanthème, **1:**153
Madame Butterfly (film), **3:**559
Madame La Lune, **6:**119
Madan Vera, Olga, **6:**302
Madara Horseman, **2:**11
Madden, Diane, **5:***314*
Maddox, Michael, **1:**485, **5:**452
Madé Geria, Ida Bagus, **5:**524
Made in Malaysia: A Shamanistic Journey, **4:***250*
Madej, Krystyna, **5:***213*
Mädel, Ernst Chr., **2:**339
Madeleine, **6:**119
Mademoiselle Dazie (Daisy Peterkin), **6:**318
Mademoiselle de Maupin (Gautier), **3:**122, 179
Madé Netra, **5:**524
Madé Pasek Tempo, **5:**524
Mader, Raoul, **3:**346
Máder Rezső, **3:**346
Mad Genius, The (film), **1:**484
Madhumati (film), **2:**626
madhura bhakti cult, **4:**69
Madl, Roderich, **1:**240
Madonna, **2:**610
Madras Music Academy, **1:**273
Madras Music Academy Journal, The, **3:**469
Madres Polacas, **4:**392
Madrid Ballet, **1:**117, **4:**222
Madrona, Victor, **5:**172
Madroños, **1:**300
mad scenes, **3:**180, *181*, 183
Madsen, Egon, **2:**266, 385, **4:**245–246, **5:**55, **6:**10, 44
Cranko Medal, **2:**268
Initialen R.B.M.E., **2:**267
Romeo and Juliet, **5:**395, 396
Stuttgart Ballet, **6:**10, *10*
Worsaae designs, **6:**404
Mad Tristan, **1:**136, **4:**449
Madura, East Java, **3:**499
Madzsar, Alice, **3:**420

Maen, Norman, **1:**28, **2:***298*
maenads (bacchantes), **3:***288*, 292, 541
maengket, **3:**505
Maestra Rural, La, **4:**392
Mafai, Mario, **4:**421
Magallanes, Nicholas, **1:***152*, 293, **2:**420, **4:**246
Ballet Russe de Monte Carlo, **1:**298, 299, 302
Cage performance, **3:**663
Don Quixote performance, **2:**438
Illuminations performance, **3:**442, *442*
Liebeslieder Walzer performance, **4:**179, 179
New York City Ballet, **4:**246, 619
Orpheus performance, **4:***607*, 619
Sonnambula performance, **5:***641*, *641*
Square Dance performance, **4:***612*
Sylvia: Pas de Deux performance, **6:**64
Magazi, Simpiwe, **5:***657*
Magdalena (musical), **2:**185, **6:**327
Maggie, Dinah, **3:**76
Maggio Musicale, Florence, **1:**251
Maggior Impresa d'Ercole, o Sia Admeto e Alceste, La, **2:**55
maggots (dances), **3:**377
"Maggott, The" (Isaac dance), **3:**522
Magic, **6:**119
Magic Bird of Lolita, The, **4:**127
Magic Dreams, **2:**181
Magic Fairy Tale, The, **5:**119
Magic Flute, The
Béjart choreography, **1:**292, 480, **6:***11*
Martins choreography, **4:**615
Magic Flute, The (Mozart opera), **1:**406
Magic Goldfish, The, **3:**328
Magic Lotus Lantern, The, **2:**136
Magic Mirror, The, **3:**196, **4:**639, **5:**161
Magic of Dance, The (television series), **1:**400, **3:**321
Magic of Katherine Dunham, The (Ailey dance program), **2:**459
Magic Pills, The, **4:**430
Magic Shoes, The, **2:**181
Magic Shop, The, **5:**452
Magic Swan, The (*Swan Lake* third act), **1:**297, **6:**425
Magic Veil, The. See Miraculous Bridal Veil, The
Magier, Antoni, **5:**220
Magische Suite, **3:**153
maglalatik, **2:**231
Maglie Rapita, La (Drigo), **2:**446
Magnificat, **4:**397, 606, **5:**677
Magnificence of the Universe, The (also *Dance Symphony*), **1:**258, 402, **2:**342, 423, **3:**327
Balanchine performance, **4:**283
Lopukhov conception, **4:**224, **5:**457
Magny, Claude Marc, **1:**397, **2:**253, **5:**285, 621, **6:**126
Magri, Francesco, **6:**62
Magri, Gennaro, **1:**197, 341, 344, 345, 384, **3:**527, **5:**604, 621, **6:**46
on arm-leg opposition, **1:**333
Beck-Friis technique re-creation, **6:**48
on country dances, **2:**257, 591
dance manual, **1:**197, 344, **2:**257, **3:**545, **6:**123, 124, 125, 126
on *demi-caractère*, **3:**545

Magri, Gennaro, *continued*
on feet positions, **1:**331, 344
on minuet, **4:**433
Magriel, Paul, **4:**28, **6:**296
Magriñá, Juan, **5:**673
Magritte, René, **1:**141
Magritte, Magritte, **1:**141
Magro, Cristina del, **1:**111
Magyar balett történetéből, A (Vályi ed.), **3:**423–424
Magyar Opera House, Cluj-Napoca, **5:**385
Magyars (people), **3:**407
Magyarság táncai (Réthei), **3:**422
Magyar tánchagyományok (Molnár), **3:**422–423
Mahabharata, The (play), **5:**521
Mahābhārata (Indian epic), **1:**161, 168, 170, 172, 173, 178, **3:**451–452, **464**
Balinese dance source, **3:**160, 174, 473–474, 484, 489, 666
Balinese *wayang* puppetry source, **6:**368, 370
baris dance, **1:**366
Javanese dance, **3:**492, 495, 497, 498, 499, 502
kathakaḷi, **3:**660–661
Kṛṣṇa figure, **3:**466
Purulia *chhau*, **2:**118
yakṣagāna, **6:**413
Maha Buta, **5:**524
Mahakala (deity), **1:**444
Mahapatra, Kelucharan, **4:246–247,** 257, **5:**23, 68, 525, **6:**321
Mahapatra, Maheshwara, **5:**22
Maharaj. *See* Husain, Ghulam
Maharaj, Acchan, **3:**425, **4:**247
Maharaj, Birju, **3:**468, **4:**110, **247**
Maharajah Serfoji Sarasvathi, Madras, **4:**159
Mahārāsa, **3:**467
mahari nṛtya, **2:**394
Mahavamsa chronicle, **2:**228, **3:**647, 649
Mahdaviani, Miriam, **4:**622
Maheu, Gilles, **2:**610, **6:**132
Mahgoub, Ahmed, **2:**498–499
Mahi dance, **3:**334
Mahit, **3:**50
Mahler, Donald, **4:**382
Mahler, Elfreda, **2:**280, 281
Mahler, Fritz, **4:**39
Mahler, Gustav, **1:**131, 307, **3:**51, **6:**197, 200, 387
Béjart stagings, **1:**406
as critic of Hassreiter, **3:**347
Hofoperntheater directorship, **1:**239
Kindertotenlieder, **2:**348, 349, **5:**299, **6:**197
Neumeier ballets, **4:**604
See also Lied von der Erde, Das
Mahler, Roni, **1:**302
Mahler 4: Eternity Is Now, **3:**344, **5:**436
Mahoganny, **5:**527
maḥol, **1:**448
Mahoney, Billie, *as contributor*, **3:**598–600
Mahzar, Fahreda. *See* Little Egypt
Maiden's Dance, **4:**107
maiden-song, **2:**158
Maiden's Tower, The, **1:**48, 248
Maid in America (musical), **4:**56
Maid of Cashmere, The, **1:**199, **4:**138, 139, 338, 338
Maid of Pskov, The, **3:**196
Maids, The, **1:**69, **2:**583, **5:**408

Maid to Measure (revue), **4:**335
Maidwell, Keith, **2:**58
Maijuku company, **6:**90
Maillol, Arostode, **4:**182
Maillot, Monsieur, **5:**240–241
Mail Order Dances (Charlip), **2:**110–111, **5:**260
Maimonides, **3:**526
Maimouna, **5:**690
Maimuna, **3:**537
maindo, **2:**33
Mainerio, Giorgio, **4:**505
Maintenon, Madame de, **2:**238
Maiorano, Robert, **2:**333, **4:***619*, **5:***362*
Maison de Fous, **1:**326, **3:**100
Maison de la Culture, Amiens, **1:**349
Maison de la Culture, Grenoble, **1:**462
Maison de la Danse, **3:**78
Maison Paquin, **4:**642
Maître à danser, Le (Rameau), **1:**333, 342, 396–397, **2:**59, 259, 527, 588, **3:**81, 124, 172, 545, **4:**106, 431, **5:**260, 308, *308*, 324, 346, **6:**123, 176
Maître de Danse, Le, or the Art of Dancing Cotillons (Conway), **2:**592
Maîtres Fous, Les (film), **6:**186
Maizel, Boris, **5:**572
Maja, La, **5:**133
Maja de Seville, La, **5:**615–616
Majaphahit Empire, **1:**160
"Majesty Invests the Four Seas" (martial dance), **6:**81
Majewicz, Steven, **5:***131*
Majiltons, the, **5:**70, **6:**316
Majorana, La, **1:**117
Majoros, István, **3:**419
Majorowa, M., 211
Makarov, Askold, **4:**284, **5:**435, 461, *462*, 469, 595, 677
Makarova, Natalia, **4:247–249,** **5:**565, **6:**146
American Ballet Theatre, **1:**72, 73–74, 75, *75*, 77, 372, **4:**248–249
Ashton ballets, **1:**158, 159
Australian tour, **4:**275
Baryshnikov dance partnership, **5:***104*
Bayadère staging, **1:**75, *75*, 393, **2:**514, **4:**117, 249, **6:**44
Blue Angel performance, **5:**164
Bruhn dance partnership, **2:**3, 4
Checkmate performance, **2:**115
Coppélia performance, **2:**201
defection from Soviet Union, **1:**372, **4:**248, **5:**485
Don Quixote performance, **2:**441
Dowell dance partnership, **2:**444
Dying Swan interpretation, **2:**471
Giselle performances, **1:**74, 372, **3:***182*, 183–184, **4:**247, 248, **5:**55
international ballet competition, **1:**282
Manon performance, **4:**248, 257
Maryinsky Ballet, **4:**285
Month in the Country performance, **4:**456
Onegin performance, **2:**512
On Your Toes performance, **4:**249, **6:**286
Other Dances performance, **5:***364*, 366
Paris Opera Ballet guest performance, **5:**97
pas de deux, **5:***107*

Royal Ballet guest performance, **5:**417
Sleeping Beauty performance, **4:***277*
Swan Lake film, **3:**345
Swan Lake staging, **1:**158, **2:**514, 562
Makedonski, Gerije, **6:**436
Make Mine Music (film), **4:**179
makeup. *See* mask and makeup
Makhalina, Yulia, **4:**285, **5:**465
Makhayeva, Agrafina, **5:**453, **6:**312
Makiadi, Luambo (Doctor Franco), **4:**487
Making and Doing, **3:**447
Making Ballet (documentary film), **4:**73, **6:**133
Making Television Dance (television program), **6:**139, 154
Makio. *See* Umewaka Makio
makishi masks dances, **2:**87–88
Makletsova, Ksenia, **4:**460
Makonde (people), **2:**91, *91*, **4:***287*, 289
makossa, **2:**32
Makron, **3:***288*
Makua (people), **2:**91
Makuc, Mojca, **6:***437*
makuta, **2:**274
makwaya, **5:***579*
mak yong, **2:**229
Malade Imaginaire, Le (Molière), **4:**447, 459
Malade Jaloux, Le, **5:**198
Maladetta, La, **5:**94, **6:**443
Malaga, La, **2:**174
Malakhov, Vladimir, **1:**77, 241, **5:**464, 465, 467, **6:**132
malambo, **1:**109
Malang, East Java, **3:**499
Malashenko, Camille, **3:**429
Malati Madhava, **4:**110
Malat literature, **3:**481, 482
Malavergne, Pierre-Frédéric, **3:**560
Malawi, **2:**86, 87, **4:**291, **5:***663*
Malay (people), **3:**499
malaya, **4:**291
Malaysia, **4:249–251**
costume, **2:**229–230
masks, **4:**298
mayong dance drama, **4:**337, 491–492
trance dance, **4:**249, 494
trance rituals, **6:**185, 187
Malbekov, Eduard, **3:**665
Malcev, Viktor, **5:**270
Malchugina, Varvara, **3:**561
Malcolm X (film), **4:**255
Maldoom, Royston, **4:**209
Maldoror, **1:**305
Mal du Pays, ou La Batalière de Brientz, Le (Adam), **1:**9
Maldybayev, Abdfyias, **4:**87
Male and Female Rituals, **3:**336
Malec, Ivo, **1:**349, **6:**433
Malek, Mary Abdel, **2:**498
Malena, La, **1:**61, **3:**7
Maleras, Anna, **5:**675
Maletić, Ana, **6:**433
Maletić, Vera, **4:**96, 99, **6:**433–434
as contributor, **4:**98–105
Malevich, Kazimir, **3:**197
maleviziótikos, **2:**271–272
Malfleuroy, Clotilde, **3:**119, **5:**90
malhão, **5:**229
Mali
animal-spirit masqueraders, **6:**12
Bamana dance, **1:**359–360
Dogon dance, **2:**421–422, **4:**291–292, 485
masked stilt dancing, **4:**288

Malibran, Maria, **5:**277
mali dance, **3:**121
Malidor, Lisette, **4:**524
Maligawa Perahera, **3:**649
Malina, Judith, **1:**245
Mali National Folk Troupe, **2:**422, **4:**291–292
Malinche, **4:**329–330, 388, 388–389
Malinche, La, **3:**391, **4:**39, 198, 396
Malini, Hema, **2:**627
Malinsky, Barbara Ferreri, *as contributor*, **2:**466–468, **4:**139–140, 209–211
Malipiero, Gian Francesco, **3:**51, **4:**421
Maliszewski, Witold, **5:**101
Malkowski, François, **3:**83
Mallarmé, Stéphane
dance aesthetics, **1:**23, 26, 125, 129, 130, **5:**107
on Fuller, **1:**243, **3:**92
poem *L'Après-midi d'un Faune*, **1:**27, 28, 98, **4:**641
Mallarmé III, **1:**292
Mallet, Daniel, **4:**447
Malling, Otto, **2:**173
Malm, William P., *as contributor*, **2:**5–6, **4:**249–251, 337–338, 491–495, 530, **5:**291
Malmgren, Gert, **3:**628–629
Malmö, Sweden, **6:**48
Malmö Stadsteatern, **5:**406, **6:**44–45
Malpied, **1:**332–333, **6:**123, 126
Maltaire brothers. *See* Malter brothers
Maltakva, **3:**135
Malter, François-Louis, **1:**283, 284, 464, **4:**130
Malter brothers, **3:**67, **5:**88
Maltsev, Yuri, **6:***411*
Malvezzi, Cristofano, **4:**505
Maly Theater Ballet (Modest Mussorgsky Theater of Opera and Ballet), **2:**585, **5:467–469**
Belsky choreography, **1:**416–417
Boyarchikov as chief choreographer, **1:**518–519, **5:**464, 468–469
Dolgushin as soloist, **2:**423
Gayané, **3:**125
Gusav performance, **3:**327
Lopukhov, Fedor, **4:**224, 226, 595, **5:**467–468
Maman, Shlomo, **3:**531
Mamat, Idris, **4:***250*
Mamay, Gally de, **6:**322
mambo, **2:**274, 275–276, **4:**520, **5:**630, 636
Mambo (film), **2:**458
Mame (musical), **4:**419, **5:**373, **6:**284
Mamelles de Tirésias, Les (Poulenc), **5:**238
Ma Mère l'Oye (Ravel), **5:**315, 316
Mammon, **1:**390
Mamonovsky Miniature Theater, Moscow, **3:**193
Mamontov, Savva, **1:**487, **3:**204, **4:**55, 56, **5:**456, 471, 541
Mamontowicz-Łojek, Bożena, **5:**221
Mamoulian, Rouben, **6:**278
Mamprussi (people), **2:**210
Mampuloria, **6:**323
Mam'zelle Angot, **1:**38, **3:**44, 236, **5:**415
Man, A (Fallaci), **2:**1
managa dance, **5:**579
Managué, Soumah, **5:**516

Manaka, Nomsa Kupi, **5:**660
"Man and Art Figure"
    (Schlemmer), **5:**546
Man and His Mirror, The, **6:**432
Man and Woman, **3:**665
Manas (Kyrgyz epic), **4:**86
manchegas, **5:**133
Manchester, England, **3:**270, 271,
    277, **4:**94
    Northern Ballet Theatre,
        4:667–668
Manchester, P. W., **2:**187, **3:**285,
    6:296
    as contributor, **4:**272
Manchester Dance Circle,
    4:103, 477
Manchester Guardian (British
    newspaper), **3:**285
Manchus, **2:**131
Mandala, **2:**388
maṇḍala, **6:**167
Mandan (people), **4:**554, 561, 562
Mandara-Uta 2 and *Mandara-Uta-3,*
    3:523
*Mandarin Merveilleux, Le. See
    Miraculous Mandarin, The*
*Mandarin Merveilleux, Lear-
    Prospero, Le,* **1:**407
Mandel, Sonia, **1:**292
Mandela, Nelson, **2:**1, **5:**643, 655
Mandelberg, Evgeny, **4:**129
mandiani, **1:**359
Mandinian, Edward, *as
    photographer,* **5:**413
mandolin, **2:**194
Mandoline, **2:**56, **5:**652
Mandragora, **3:**317
Mandukić, Smiljana, **6:***435*
Manen, Hans van, **1:**55, 241, 242,
    370, 375, 391, 436, **2:**39,
    347–348, **4:251–253, 5:**131,
    234, 290, 530, 555, 674, **6:**146
    choreography for Béjart, **1:**291
    Collective Symphony, **4:**596
    Dutch National Ballet, **2:**469,
        470, **4:**593
    German Dance Prize, **3:**158
    Grosse Fuge and *Adagio
        Hammerklavier,* **1:**403
    John Falstaff role, **5:**683
    Netherlands Dance Theater,
        2:448, **4:**592, 601, 602
    Royal Winnipeg Ballet
        productions, **5:**436
    Sacre du Printemps, Le, **5:**488
    Stuttgart Ballet, **6:**10
Månerenen, **4:**677, **5:**353
*Maner of dauncyinge of bace
    daunces after the vse of
    fraunce and other places . . .*
    (Coplande), **1:**45, 378
*Manessesche
    Minnesängerhandscrhift*
    (medieval manuscript),
    4:*347, 348*
Manet, Édouard, **2:**400, **5:**259, 262,
    293, 672, **6:**181
Manez, Linda, **4:**600
Manfred, **1:**97, **5:**387, **6:**117, 454
Manfredi, Barbara, **2:**427
Manfredini, Vincenzo, **3:**365
Mangaldas, Aditi, **4:**111
Mangbetu (people), **2:***88,* **4:***486*
Mangeshkar, Lata, **2:**623, 625
Mangkubumi, prince of Jogjakarta,
    3:494, 498
Mangkunagara I, prince of
    Surakarta, **3:**494
Mangkunagara IV, prince of
    Surakarta, **3:**498

Mangkunagaran court, Java, **3:**505
Mangolte, Babette, **5:**187
    as photographer, **5:**549, **6:**163,
        249
Mangrove, **3:**446
Mangué, Soumah, **5:**516
mangulina, **2:**430
Manhattan Celebration, **4:**306
Manhattan Festival Ballet, **1:**542,
    6:363
Manhattan Opera Company, **6:**270
Manhattan School of Dance, **2:**268
Manhattanville College of The
    Sacred Heart, New York,
    2:187
maní, **2:**275
Manie de la Danse, La (Debucourt),
    2:68
*Manière de composer et faire réussir
    les ballets, La* (Saint-Hubert),
    3:84
Manifeste du chorégraphie, Le
    (Lifar), **3:**431, **4:**184
"Manifesto of the Futurist Dance"
    (Marinetti), **1:**244
Manika (people), **6:**382
manikay, **1:**223
Manila Ballet Company, **5:**172
Manings, Muriel, *as contributor,*
    2:280–282
Man in the Moon, The (musical),
    6:268
Manipur, **1:**94, 170–171, *173,* 363,
    2:223, **3:**468, **4:253–254**
    costume, **2:**224–225
    dance drama, **1:**94, 170–171, *173,*
        2:224–225, **3:**606
    dance style, **5:**580, 601
    Jhaveri sisters, **3:**606
    modern innovation, **3:**468
    Pakistan, **5:**62, 63
    Rādhā-Kṛṣṇa theme, **3:**467, 468
    rās līlā (play genre), **5:**311
    structured design, **3:**463
manis, **1:**174
Manitoba Square-dancer (journal),
    2:49
Mankunagara I, prince of
    Surakarta, **3:**497
Manley Morris Dancers, **3:***241*
Mann, Erika, **3:**208
Mann, Madge, **5:**649, 650
Mann, Thomas, **1:**157, **6:**56
*Manners and Customs of the
    Modern Egyptians* (Lane),
    4:416
Mannheim court orchestra, **2:**54
Mannheim National Theater, **4:**91
Mannila, Elina, **2:**634
Manning, Frankie, **1:**451, **2:**203,
    4:*201,* 202, **254–255, 5:***630,*
    6:*262,* 288
Manning, Iris, **6:**379
Manning, Susan A., *as contributor,*
    2:451–453, **4:**377–378,
    389–396
Manobo (people), **5:**168
Man of Action, **4:**531
Man of La Mancha (musical),
    4:334, **6:**283
Man of Mode, The (Etherege),
    5:490, 518
Manōhrā, **4:**251, **255–256,** 492,
    6:*149*
Manokhin, Fedor, **1:**486, **3:**135,
    5:455
Manokhina, Maria, **5:**516
Manolache-Lux, Betty, **5:**387
Manolescu, Cosmin, **5:**390
Manolov, A., **5:**166

Manolov, Emanuil, **2:**11, 12
Manolov, H., **5:**166
Manon, **4:256–257**
    Collier performance, **2:**186
    Dowell performance, **2:**444
    Dyk choreography, **2:**472
    Georgiadis designs, **3:**136, **4:**256
    MacMillan production, **1:**77,
        4:243, *244,* 256–267, *257,* 547,
        5:418, **6:**44
    Makarova performance,
        4:248, 257
    Wall performance, **6:**357
Manon Lescaut
    Aumer production, **1:**202, **4:**513
    Halévy score, **4:**513, **5:**92
    Lami costume designs, **4:**116
    Lecomte (Hippolyte) costume
        designs, **4:**138
    score innovations, **4:**513
Manor, Giora, **3:**535
    as contributor, **3:**449–450,
        526–535, **4:**58–59, 531–532
Manosa, Inday Gaston, **5:**172
Manou, Rallou, **3:**300
Man + Machine, **5:**5466
Mansaka (people), **5:**168
Mansaku. *See* Nomura Mansaku II
Mansfield, Portia, **3:**385, **6:**248
Mansingh, Sonal, **4:257–258, 5:**23
Mansurian, T., **1:**122
Mante, Suzanne, **2:**363
Mantegna, Andrea, **5:**259
Mantero, Vera, **5:**236
Mantis Moon, **5:**692
Mantsoe, Vincent Sekwati,
    5:*656,* 660
Mantuano, Paulo, **1:***536*
*Manual of the Theory and Practice
    of Classical Theatrical
    Dancing, A* (Cecchetti,
    Idzikowski, and Beaumont),
    1:8, 398, **2:**83–84, **6:**128
manuals. *See* technical manuals
Manuel, Nicolaus, **4:**462
Manuel, Roland, **4:**452
Manuel complet de la danse
    (Blasis), **1:**199, **6:**126
*Manuel des exercises de danse
    théâtrale* (Cecchetti), **6:**128
Manukian, Edward, **1:**120, 121
Manuscripts of the Inns of Court,
    London, **1:**104, **5:**115, 116,
    118, 345, **6:**350
Manuscrit de Cervera (notation
    book), **5:**675
*Man Walking Down the Side of a
    Building,* **1:**543
Man Who Dances, A (television
    program), **6:**340
Man Who Envied Women, The
    (film), **5:**293
Manx folk and traditional dance.
    See under Great Britain
Manyanani dancers, **2:**86
Manzotti, Luigi, **1:**37, 540, **2:**82,
    249, 369, 572, **3:**60,
    4:258–259, 5:529, **6:**190
    Edel collaboration, **2:**477
    Marenco collaboration, **3:**548,
        4:263–264
    Pratesi performances, **5:**245–246
    Rome Opera Ballet, **5:**399
    spectacles, **3:**71, **4:**258–259
    Zucchi roles, **6:**452
Manzù, Giacomo, **4:**421
Mao Fu-kuei, **2:***131*
Maor, Yehudah, **5:**529
Maori dance, **4:260–262,** 629
Mao Zedong, **2:**134, 137

mapantsula dance, **5:**648
mapia, **3:**504
Maple, Charles, **1:**74, 375
Maple Leaf Rag, **3:**220
Mapleson, James, **4:**121
Mapplethorpe, Robert, **2:**119,
    5:187
Mara, Thalia, **2:**19, **3:**23
marabi dance, **5:**648
maracatú, **1:**525, 527
Maracatu Dances, **1:**533
Maracci, Carmelita, **2:**186, 366,
    3:306, **4:**4, **262**
    eclectic style, **6:**292
    students, **4:**262, **5:**488, **6:**327
maradjiri ritual. *See rom* ritual
Marais, Marin, **3:**29, **4:**433,
    443, 481
Marajó island, Brazil, **1:**530
Maranao Sining Pananadem,
    5:172
Marani, Jerónimo, **4:**390, 399
maranji dance, **6:**15
marathons. *See* dance marathons
Maratona, **3:**359–360
Maravi (people), **4:**291
Maravilla, Luis, **4:**222
Marble Maiden, The, **1:**10, 37
Marbury, Bessie, **6:**271
Marbury, Elizabeth, **2:**79
Marcade, Caroline, **3:**79
Marcadet, Jean, **6:**39, 40, 48, 49
Marceau, Marcel, **2:**174, **3:**75,
    4:425, *425*
Marceau, Yvonne, **5:***630,* **6:***288*
    as contributor, **3:**356–359
Marcel, François, **3:**81, 111, **4:**106,
    262–263, 263, **5:**402
Marcel, Jacques (father), **4:**262
Marcel, Jacques-Antoine (son),
    4:262, 263
Marcel-Dubois, Claudie, **1:**517
Marcelino, Benito, **6:***11*
Marcello, Benedetto, **1:**39
Marchand, Colette, **1:**305, 349,
    2:246, **3:**318, **4:**184, 380,
    5:163
Marchand, Joseph, **1:**397
Marchand, Pierre, **1:**464
Marchant, Adam, **1:**235
Marchant, Claude, **5:**255, **6:**259
Marchaund's Tale, The, **4:**380
Marche, Ulrich Roboam de la,
    2:338
Marché des Innocents, Le, **4:**353,
    5:94, 151
Marche Funèbre, **2:**421
Marche Slav, **2:**456
Marchiolli, Sonja, **2:**470
Marchiori, *as photographer,* **5:**34
March of Single Women, **5:**474
March of the Volunteers, **4:**405
Marchowsky, Marcia, **1:**139
Marcinkowa, Janina, **5:**211, 220
Marco Spada, **2:**587, **3:**70, **5:**93
    Auber score, **4:**514
    Lacotte reconstruction, **4:**108
    Mazilier choreography,
        4:339, 342
    Mérante performance, **4:**353
    Rosati performance, **5:**405
Marco Viscounti, **6:**70
Marcu, Vasile, **5:**386, 387
Marcus, Joan, *as photographer,*
    6:113
Marcus, Julia, **3:**76
Marcuse, Judith, **2:**40, 46,
    3:232, 233
Marcy, George, **5:***361*
Mardi Gras, **3:**392, **4:**584

Maré, Rolf de, **1:**134, 326, 327, 328, **2:**263, 287, 410, **3:**21, 72, **4:**93, **5:**237
Archives Internationales de la Danse, **3:**72, 76, **4:**161
Indonesian dance documentation, **3:**507
scenic design innovations, **5:**545
Swedish dance museum, **4:**163
See also Ballets Suédois, Les
Maréchal des Logis, Le (The Old Soldier), **1:**123, 124
Maréchal, Magdeleine, **2:**412
Marenco, Romualdo, **4:**263–264, **5:**246, 529
Edel and Manzotti collaborations, **2:**477, **3:**548, **4:**258
Marenzio, Luca, **5:**683
Maretzek, Max, **3:**5, **5:**403, **6:**335
Marey, Étienne Jules, **1:**130, **4:**15, **5:**178, *179*
Marg (periodical), **3:**469, 470
Margaret Eaton School, **2:**47
Margaret Jenkins Dance Company, **6:**266
Margaret Morris Movement, **3:**271
Margaret of Austria, **1:**409
Margaret of Connaught, **1:**403
Margaret of York, **1:**364
Margarita Teresa, infanta of Spain, **3:**381
Margarit-Mudances, Angels, **5:**675
Margenat, Beatriz, **1:***291*
Marginalii (Romanian group), **5:**390
Marginoni, Edda, **3:**59
Margolies, Linda, **3:**218, **5:**568
Margolin, Yaron, **3:**529, 533, 534
Margolis, Joseph, **1:**24
Margrete II, queen of Denmark, **3:***39*, **5:**433
Marguerite and Armand (Ashton production)
Beaton scenic design, **1:**395
Fonteyn and Nureyev performances, **1:**155, **3:**42, *44*, 45–46, **5:**6, 7
Somes mime role, **5:**640
Marguerite de Valois, **1:**397, **3:**80
Mar-Haim, Jossi, **3:**449
Maria, Giuseppina de (Giuseppina Cecchetti), **2:**82, *83*, 84, **4:**150
Maria, Maria, **1:**536
Maria Chapdelaine, **6:**130
Maria Cristina, duchess of Savoy, **1:**29
María de la O (film), **1:**61
Maria del Mar Bonet, **3:**234
Mariage au Temps de la Régence, Un, **5:**151
Mariage dans la Vicaria de Madrid, Le (Fortuny), **3:**123
Mariage Forcé, La, **1:**288, **4:**234
Mariage Méxicain, Le, **2:**364
Mariage per Capitulation, Le (Rodolphe opera), **5:**371
Marianas Islands, **4:**401
Maria Theresa, empress of Austria, **1:**236, 409
horse ballet, **3:**382–383
masquerades, **4:**313
Maribor, Slovenia, **6:**437, 438
Marichiyo, **3:**126
Marie (Hérold), **3:**360
"Marie" (song), **1:**450
Marie, queen of Romania, **3:**93, 95, 96
Marie Antoinette (film), **5:**310

Marie Antoinette, queen of France, **1:***236*, **2:**72, 238, 352, **3:**365, **4:**61, 696
Marie-Jeanne, **1:**96, 280, 281, 293, 452, **2:***193*, **5:**571, **6:**396
Mariemma, Luisillo, **1:**294
Marie Rambert Dancers. *See* Rambert Dance Company
Mariés de la Tour Eiffel, Les, **1:**327, **2:**182, 183, **3:**393–394, **4:**418, 516, **5:**237, 238
Marie Stuart (Niedermeyer), **2:**202
Mariette, Mademoiselle, **5:**88
Marimba, **1:**291
Marin, Antonio, **1:**82
Marin, Maguy, **1:**291, 292, 389, 412, **2:**470, **3:***78*, 79, 329, **5:**8, 98, **6:**57
Marin Ballet, **6:**264
"Marinera, La," **5:**145
Marinetti, Filippo, **1:**130, 134, 244
Maring (people), **5:**82–84, *83*
Maring in Motion, **2:**602
Marini, Ernest, **4:**675
Marini, Marilú, **1:**113
Marinka (musical), **5:**310
Marinković-Rakić, Branka, **6:**438
Mario, Giovanni, **5:**616
Mario, I Ketut, **3:**666, **4:**264–266
Mario, I Nyoman, **1:**176–177
Mario and the Magician, **1:**251, 460, **3:**154
marionettes. *See* puppetry
Marion Rice Dancers, **5:**586
Mario the Magician (film), **2:**369
Mario und der Zauberer (ballet). *See Mario and the Magician*
Mariquita (ballet author), **5:**278
Maritain, Jacques, **5:**525
Mariti, Luciano, **3:**556
Marius Vitorinus, **4:**106
Marjaš, Erika, **6:**438
Márk, Tivadar, **3:**417, *417*
Marka, *as photographer*, **4:**421, 437, **5:**165, **6:**454
Markard, Anna. *See* Markard-Jooss, Anna
Markard, Herman, **3:**305, 630
Markard-Jooss, Anna, **2:**58, **3:**305, 627, 630, **5:**652
Markaz al-Funun al-Shaʿbīyah, Egypt, **2:**496
Markert, Russell, **2:**426, **5:**247, 289–290
Market Place, The, **2:**343
Market Theatre, Johannesburg, **5:***658*
Markevitch, Igor, **2:**410, 411, **5:**268
Markham, Dewey ("Pigmeat"), **6:**255
Markham, Pauline, **1:**457
Markham, Philip, **5:***52*, 54
Markman, Hillel, **3:**534
Mark Morris Dance Group. *See* Morris, Mark
Markó, Iván, **1:**292, 370, **3:**329–330, **4:**266–267
Markova (documentary), **6:**135
Markova, Alicia, **2:**586, **3:**442, 571, **4:**267–271, **5:**107, 293, 294, 526, 604, 612, 684, **6:**198
Ashton association, **1:**146, 147, 148, 158, 437, 520
Ballet Russe de Monte Carlo, **1:**296, 300, *301*, **4:**268–269
as Ballets Russes de Monte Carlo guest artist, **1:**315, *315*
Bluebeard performance, **3:**26
Bruhn dance partnership, **2:**3
Chopiniana performance, **2:**507

Cuban ballet school, **2:**277
Denby profile of, **2:**375
de Valois productions, **2:**400, **4:**267, 268
Diaghilev Ballets Russes, **2:**411, **3:**262, **4:**267, 331
Dolin dance partnership, **2:**425, **3:***182*, 265, *267*, **4:**268, *268*, 269–270
Dying Swan performance, **2:**471, **4:**269
English National Ballet, **2:**507–508, 509, 512, **3:**269
Fonteyn as Royal Ballet successor, **3:**41, 42
Giselle performances, **2:**508, 509, **3:***182*, *182*, 183, **4:**268, *268*, 269, 270, **5:**512, 650
Grand Ballet du Marquis de Cuevas guest appearance, **3:**226, **4:**270
Idzikowski dance partnership, **3:**442, **4:**268
as Legat (Nikolai) student, **4:**143, 267
Lloyd as role successor, **4:**215
Metropolitan Opera Ballet directorship, **4:**270, 382
Miskovitch dance partnership, **4:**435
Northern Ballet Theatre coaching, **4:**667
Nutcracker performances, **5:**14, 15
Pas de Quatre performance, **3:**59, **4:**268, 269, *269*
Radha Krishna performance, **3:**199
Rambert association, **5:**299
Rambert Ballet guest performances, **3:**266
Rendezvous performance, **5:**341–342
Romeo and Juliet performance, **1:**67, **5:**397, **6:**199
Royal Ballet, **3:**354, **4:**268, **5:**413, 414, **6:**33
Royal Winnipeg Ballet guest performance, **5:**435
Scènes de Ballet performance, **5:**531
South African tour, **5:**650
students, **1:**231
Swan Lake performance, **6:**33
Sylphides revival, **2:**512, **4:**269, 270, **6:**62
television performances and profiles, **6:**134, 135, 137
Markova-Dolin Ballet, **2:**425, 586, **3:**87, 265, **4:**110, 268
Gsovsky (Victor) as ballet master, **3:**318
Lester, Keith, **4:**153
Lloyd, Maude, **4:**215
Nijinska revival productions, **4:**638
tours, **4:**269, 270
See also English National Ballet
Markova House, London, **2:**513
Markowski (dancing master), **5:**221
Marks, Bruce, **1:**72, *72*, **2:**269, 387, **4:**120, *120*, **271**, **5:**432
Ballet West, **4:**271
Boston Ballet artistic directorship, **1:**501–502, **4:**271
Bournonville ballet reconstruction, **2:**388, **4:**271, **5:**433, **6:**404
joint Soviet-American *Swan Lake* production, **4:**271, **6:**34, 35
Worsaae designs, **6:**404

Marks, Morton, *as contributor*, **1:**525–532, **2:**273–276
Marks, Victoria, **2:**611
Markuš, Vera, **6:**435
Marlière, Andrée, **5:**422
Marlowe, Christopher, **1:**454
Marmentini, Luz, **2:**126
as contributor, **2:**122–126
Marney, Denis de, *as photographer*, **2:**266
Maro Akaji, **1:**61, **4:**271–272
Maroons, **3:**120, 575
Maros, Rudolf, **2:**473
Marova, Winja, **4:**598
Marozzi, Mario, **5:**401
Marques, Isabel, **1:**537
Marquet, Louise, **6:**62
Marquet, Sophie, **1:**375
Márquez, Antonio, **5:**674
Márquez, Lidya, *as photographer*, **1:**112
Marquez, Luis, *as photographer*, **4:**384, 385
"Marquis of Huntly's Highland Fling, The," **3:**245
Marrakesh (Marrakech) Festival, Morocco, **4:**407, 469
Marre, Pamela, **2:**2
Marriage, The, **1:**519, **5:**468
Marriage d'Aurore, Le, **5:**678
Marriage de Figaro, Le (Beaumarchais), **2:**353, 499, **6:**267
Marriage of Figaro, The (Mozart), **4:**511, **6:**267
marriage rituals. *See* wedding dances
Married Beau, The, or The Curious Impertinent (Crowne), **5:**282
Mars (deity), **5:**377–378
Marsalis, Wynton, **2:**567
Marschall, Barak, **3:**450
"Marseillaise" (French anthem)
Duncan choreography, **2:**454, 456
Fujime choreography, **3:**590
Gardel interlude based on, **3:**118
Marseille, France, **2:**200, **3:**74, 75
Marseille Ballet of Roland Petit. *See* Ballet National de Marseilles
Marseille Opera Ballet, **1:**461, **3:**66, 67, 362, **4:**134
Mars et l'Amour, **6:**334
Mars et Vénus, **1:**455, **3:**426, **4:**138, 657, **5:**92
Schneitzhoeffer score, **5:**558
Marsh, Carol G., *as contributor*, **3:**106–111, 123–125, **5:**109, 114–116
Marshall, Charles, **2:**80
Marshall, John, **2:**602
Marshall, Lorna, **5:**661
Marshall, Madeleine, **2:**516
Marshall, Minnie, **1:**56
Marshall, Rob, **6:**288
Marshall, Susan, **1:**502, **2:**609
Marshall Islands, **4:**401
Marsia, **1:**82
Marsicano, Merle, **1:**139, **4:**272
Marston, John, **3:**252, 253
Marsyas, **5:***400*
Marteau sans Maître, Le, **1:**406, **3:**274, **5:**387
Martelletta, Luigi, **3:***551*, **5:**401
Martello, Pier Jacopo, **3:**546
Marteny, Fred, **1:**242
Martha (Flotow), **4:**341, 514

Martha Graham Dance Company,
    1:97, **3:**212–222
    Baryshnikov guest appearances,
        1:373
    British performances, **4:**216
    Butler, John, **2:**16
    as Canadian dance influence,
        2:37, 40, 44
    Cunningham, Merce, **2:**22, 285,
        3:216
    Dark Meadow, **2:**349
    Deaths and Entrances, **2:**360
    Denishawn dance re-creations,
        2:379
    Dudley, Jane, **2:**450, **3:**214, 216
    Erdman, Jean, **2:**519–520
    Hawkins, Erick, **3:**216, 349
    Hill, Martha, **3:**214, 364
    Japanese tour, **3:**583, 591
    Lang, Pearl, **4:**120, 121
    Lauterer scenic design, **4:**130
    Letter to the World, **4:**153
    male members, **3:**216, *217,* 218,
        219–220, 390, **5:**407
    Rosenthal lighting, **3:**216, **4:**191,
        5:407
    Ross, Bertram, **5:**407–408
    scenic design, **3:**214, *215,*
        217–218
    Schönberg, Bessie, **5:**559
    Seraphic Dialogue, **5:**568
    Sokolow, Anna, **5:**637
    Taylor (Paul) performances,
        6:107
    women members, **3:**214, 218, 220
Martha Graham School of
    Contemporary Dance,
    3:218–219, 532, **4:**216, 439
Martha Graham Technique
    (copyright), **4:**442
Martial, **4:**428, 662, **5:**377
martial arts. *See* Asian martial arts
martial dances. *See* armed dances;
    Sword Dance; sword dances
Martin, A., **2:**206
Martin, Alex, **2:**178
Martin, Bob, *as photographer,*
    5:54, 55
Martin, Carol, *as contributor,*
    2:324–328
Martin, Elsa, **2:**122–123
Martin, Erin, **5:**364
Martin, Frank, **1:**93, **4:**242
Martin, György, **1:**370, **2:**530,
    3:407, 423, **4:**367, 371, 375
Martin, Jacqueline, **5:**512, **6:**34
Martin, Jean-Baptiste, **1:**497,
    2:*236,* 238, **3:**184, **5:**424
Martin, John, **1:**25, **4:**272–273
    on American Ballet, **1:**63, 64, 281
    on Argentinita, **1:**117
    on Balanchine ballets, **1:**299, 307
    as Bennington School faculty
        member, **1:**421, **4:**273, **6:**296
    on Bolger, **1:**482
    on Bruhn-Markova *Giselle*
        performances, **2:**3
    championship of modern dance,
        4:273, **6:**296, 300
    on choreographic notation, **3:**427
    on communicative power of
        dance, **6:**296
    as dean of American dance
        criticism, **6:**299, 300
    on Denishawn style, **5:**496
    on Duncan, **2:**246
    on Duncan's dance aesthetic,
        2:456
    on expressive dance, **3:**131
    on fan dancing, **2:**573
    on Graham's technique, **3:**214

    on Holm's *Trend,* **3:**370, **6:**192
    importance in American dance
        world, **4:**26
    on Inbal Dance Theatre, **3:**449
    on Kolpakova, **4:**36
    on Koner's solo debut, 38
    on Maracci, **4:**262
    on Nijinska's *Chopin Concerto,*
        4:638
    on Nijinska's *Étude,* **4:**636
    on *On Stage!,* **4:**10
    on Page's originality, **5:**60
    on Palucca's style, **5:**66
    on Primus's debut, **5:**254
    on *Radha,* **5:**288
    on Rasch, **5:**310
    on Robbins's *Facsimile,* **5:**360
    on Shawn's complexity, **5:**583
    on Shearer (Sybil), **5:**589
    sociopolitical works, **5:**521
    on *Sonnambula, La,* **5:**641
    on symbolism of pas de deux,
        5:107
    on Tallchief (Maria), **6:**85
    on Tamiris, **6:**88
    on Tudor, **6:**198
    on Ulanova's Juliet, **6:**228
    on Weidman's dance potential,
        6:376
    "white man's art" quote, **6:**258
Martin, Jules, **4:**137, 138, **6:**290
Martin, Julia, **5:**676
Martin, Keith, **2:**445
Martin, Kenneth K., *as contributor,*
    2:313
Martin, Marianne W., *as*
    contributor, **1:**125–135,
    5:85–86
Martin, Mary, **6:**278, 281
Martin, Maxine, **1:***450*
Martin, Theodore, **5:**232
Martin, Tony, **2:**108, 109
Martindale, Coral, **4:**649
Martínez, Cristina, **6:**302
Martínez, Cuca, **2:**277
Martínez, Enrique, **1:**49, 73, 76–77,
    2:200, 277, **3:**233, **4:**394
Martínez, Graciela, **1:**113
Martínez, José, **3:**57
Martínez, Menia, **1:**290, **2:**278
Martínez Cabreras, Guillermina
    (Mariemma), **2:**522
Martini, D., **2:**176, 17626144
Martini, Giovanni, **1:**428
Martini, Jean-Baptiste, **5:**424
Martini, Vincenzo. *See* Martín y
    Soler, Vicente
Martiniková, Marcela, **2:**308
Martinique, **2:**64
Martino, Celestino de, **1:**110
Martinoli, Lida, **1:**110, 315
Martins, Peter, **1:***271,* 391, 399,
    4:273–275, **6:**117, 349
    Afternoon of a Faun, **1:**28
    Apollo, **1:**96
    Ballet Imperial, **1:**293
    ballet technique, **5:***102, 106*
    Calcium Light Night, **4:**274, 609,
        615, 619, *620*
    Coppélia, **2:**201
    Farrell dance partnership,
        2:577–578, **4:**273, 274, **5:***364*
    Four Seasons, **5:***364*
    ice-dance choreography, **2:**298
    New York City Ballet, **4:**29,
        274–275, **5:**364
    administration, **4:**275, 608,
        621, 623
    choreography, **4:**615, *620,* 622,
        631, **6:***622*

    dance roles, **4:**615, 620–621,
        621
    Nutcracker, The, **3:***654*
    On Your Toes revival
        choreography, **6:**286
    Paris Opera Ballet, **3:**82, **5:**97
    restagings, **4:**275
    Sleeping Beauty, **5:**613
    Sylphide, La, **5:**132, **6:**59
    television performances, **6:**154
    Volkova influence, **5:**430
    Williams (Stanley) influence,
        4:273, **6:**399
Martín y Soler, Vicente (Vincenzo
    Martin), **3:**68, **4:**510, **6:**360
Martinetti family, **5:**317
Martirosian, Maxim, **3:**125, 197,
    5:460
Martyn, Laurel, **1:**207, 208, 209,
    212, 499, **4:**275–276, **6:**379
Martyrdom of Saint Sebastian, The
    (Hanayagi dance), **3:**339
Martyre de Saint-Sébastien, Le
    (d'Annuzio-Fokine-Debussy-
    Rubinstein production), **2:**360,
    3:20, **5:**438, 439
Martyre de Saint-Sébastien, Le
    (Spoerli ballet), **2:**361
Martyrs, Les (Donizetti), **2:**202, **3:**5,
    4:514
marujada, **1:**525, 527
Maruschkatänzer figurines
    (Grasser), **4:**461
Marusya Boguslavka, **6:**226
Maruti, **5:**523
Marweg, Carl (Karl Marwig),
    5:490–491, **6:**293
Marx, Roger, **3:**92
Marxism. *See* socialist realism;
    Soviet era
Mary (musical), **6:**273
Maryinsky Ballet (formerly Kirov
    Ballet), **1:**96, 207, 328, 422,
    423, 427, 493, **3:**327, **4:**165,
    276–286
    Aleksidze, Georgi, **1:**38
    Anisimova, Nina, **1:**90–91
    archival materials, **4:**165
    Balanchine productions,
        4:*284,* 285
    ballet scores, **4:**513
    Baryshnikov, Mikhail, **1:**371–372
    Belsky, Igor, **1:**416
    Benois designs, **1:**423
    Bournonville admiration for,
        1:510
    Bournonville ballet
        reconstructions, **4:**281, 285,
        5:406
    Briantzev, Dmitri, **1:**539
    Brianza, Carlotta, **1:**540
    Bronze Horseman, The, **3:**187
    caricature drawings of dancers,
        2:69
    Carnaval original production,
        2:72, **3:**16
    Cecchetti as principal dancer,
        2:82
    Cecchetti debut, **2:**82, **4:**282
    Cecchetti imprint, **2:**82, **4:**282,
        5:456
    Chabukiani, Vakhtang, **2:**96
    Chopiniana, **3:**16, 19, *20,* **6:**59–61
    Cinderella, **2:**173–174
    Coppélia, **2:**200
    Corsaire, Le, **2:**207, *207,*
        4:*279,* 280
    dancers' strike (1905), **4:**67, 144
    Didelot, Charles-Louis,
        4:277–278, 279, 280, 285–286,
        513, **5:**453–454

    Dolgushin performances,
        2:422, 423
    Don Quixote, **2:**436, 437, 439, 440
    Dudinskaya, Natalia, **2:**449–450
    Egorova, Lubov, **2:**480, **4:**282
    Esmeralda, La, **2:**524, **3:**186–187
    Farrell's Balanchine program,
        2:578
    Fenster, Boris, **2:**585–586
    Fille Mal Gardée, La, **1:**155
    first *Dying Swan* performance,
        2:471
    Flames of Paris revivals, **3:**12
    Fokine, Michel, **1:**319, **3:**14–16,
        18, 19–21, **4:**282, 283, **5:**456
    Fokine innovations, **5:**456
    "Fokintsy" versus "Imperialitsy,"
        3:16
    Fountain of Bakhchisaraï, The,
        3:56–57, **4:**283, **6:**441–442
    Gayané, **3:**125
    Gerdt, Elisaveta, **3:**137, **4:**283
    Gert, Pavel, **3:**136–137, **4:**282
    Giselle, **5:**5
    Giselle prominence in repertory,
        4:281
    Grey guest performance, **3:**307
    Grigorovich choreography, **3:**308
    historical overview, **4:**276–285,**
        5:450–452
    historical research and writings
        on, **5:**483
    Ivanov, Lev, **3:**560–568, **4:**282
    Japanese tours, **3:**589
    Johansson, Christian, **3:**618,
        4:281
    Karsavina, Tamara, **3:**655, **4:**283
    Kolpakova, Irina, **4:**36
    Komleva, Gabriella, **4:**37
    Kshessinsky family, **4:**66–67,
        68, 282
    Laurencia, **2:**97, **4:**129, 284
    Lavrovsky, Leonid, **4:**131, 132
    Legat, Nikolai, **3:**16, 20, **4:**282
    Legat family, **4:**142–144, 282,
        5:456
    Legend of Love, **4:**144
    Legnani, Pierina, **4:**145
    Leningrad Symphony,
        4:147–148, *283*
    Le Picq, Charles, **4:**149, 150, 347
    Little Humpbacked Horse, The,
        4:211, 212, 281
    Lopukhov, Fedor, **4:**224, 226,
        283–284, **5:**457–448
    Lukom, Elena, **4:**233, 283
    Makarova, Natalia,
        3:247–248, 249
    Maryinsky style, **4:**283, **285–286**
        Cecchetti influence, **4:**347
        late nineteenth-century
            virtuosity, **5:**456
        technique history, **1:**347
        training, **2:**396, **5:**480
        See also Vaganova method
    Médée et Jason popularity, **4:**347
    members in Diaghilev
        productions, **1:**319
    musical compositions, **4:**513–514
    New Zealand tour, **4:**624
    Nijinska, Bronislava, **4:**633–634
    Nijinsky dismissal, **4:**641
    Nijinsky performances, **4:***280,*
        283, 634, 640–641
    Nureyev, Rudolf, **5:**4–5, 8
    Nutcracker, The, **5:**10, *10,* 11–12
    Path of Thunder, **5:**462
    Pavlova, Anna, **5:**120–122
    Perrot choreography, **4:**280–281,
        5:454

Maryinsky Ballet, *continued*
  Petipa (Marius) heritage,
    4:281–283, 285, *451,*
    5:157–162, 455–456
  Petipa's *Coppélia* production,
    2:200, 201
  Polovtsian Dances, **3:**561–562,
    4:282, 283
  Polovtsian Dances revival, **3:***563*
  Prisoner of the Caucasus, The,
    5:*472*
  provincial tours, **5:**454
  Pushkin, Aleksandr, **5:**282
  Romanov, Boris, **5:**391, 392
  Romeo and Juliet, **5:**268, 393,
    6:*398,* 399
  Rosati performances, **5:**405
  Royal Ballet exchanges, **5:**416
  Saint-Léon productions, **4:**281,
    5:*450,* 455, 500–501
  Schollar, Ludmilla, **5:**558–559
  Sergeyev, Konstantin, **4:**284, **5:**5,
    571–572
  Sergeyev (Nicholas) notation and
    reproduction of repertory,
    3:264–265, 511, **5:**413, 693,
    6:32–34
  Sleeping Beauty, The, **4:**277,
    5:606–610
  Soloviev, Yuri, **5:**639
  Spartacus, **5:***462,* 677, **6:**411, *411*
  Spessivtseva, Olga, **5:**678
  Stepanov notation, **5:**693,
    693–694, 694
  Stone Flower, The, **5:**699
  Swan Lake, **4:**278, **5:***464,*
    6:30–31, 32
  Sylphide, La, **4:**280, **5:**454
  Sylphide interpretation, **5:**454,
    6:58
  Sylvia, **6:**64
  Theme and Variations, **2:**578,
    4:*284,* 285
  tours, **4:**285, **6:**249
  Vaganova, Agrippina, **4:**286,
    5:456
  Vinogradov artistic directorship,
    4:285, **6:**341, 342
  Virsaladze, Simon, **6:**343
  Volynsky criticisms, **6:**352
  Warsaw Ballet one-way
    arrangement, **5:**217
  Western choreographers, **4:**285,
    5:463–464
  as world's second oldest ballet
    company, **5:**425
  World War II evacuation to Perm,
    4:284, **5:**459, 471
  Yakobson choreography, **6:**411,
    411, 412
  Zakharov, Rostislav, **6:**441–442
  Zambelli guest performances,
    6:443
  Zotov performance criticisms,
    6:451–452
  Zucchi, Virginia, **5:**529
  See also Bolshoi Theater, Saint
    Petersburg; Imperial Theater
    School, Saint Petersburg;
    Imperial Theaters, Russia
Maryinsky Theater, Saint
  Petersburg
  building of, **4:**281
  See also Maryinsky Ballet
Maryland Ballet, **2:**273
Maryland Dance Theatre, **1:**542
Marymount Manhattan College,
  New York, **2:**187
Mary of Egypt (Nolde), **1:**131
Mary of Hungary, **1:**364, 409
Mary, Queen of Scots, **2:**350, **5:**565

Mary Wigman Central Institute,
  Dresden, **3:**369, 393
Mary Wigman in Leipzig (Rannow
  and Stabel, eds.), **3:**162
Mary Wigman Society, **3:**162,
  5:43–44
Marzio Coriolano, **6:**338
Marzouq, Fatma, **2:**498
Masaba (people), **2:**86
Masada, **4:**546
Masai (people), **2:**210, **4:**484, **5:**509
Masakado, **3:**90
Masaniello (Deshayes ballet), **2:**209,
  390, 3:260
*Masaniello, or The Dumb Girl of
  Portici* (Auber). *See Muette de
  Portici, La*
Mascagno, Stefano, **2:**160, **5:**202,
  511, **6:**290
Mascall, Jennifer, **2:**40
Mascarade, **3:**318
máscaras, **5:**668, 688
Maschera, o Le Notti di Venezia, La,
  5:409
Masekela Language, **3:**577
Mashed Potato (dance), **5:**630,
  6:263
Mask, The (periodical), **2:**263
mask and makeup, **4:286–306**
  African traditions, **1:**14, **2:**210,
    210, 211, **4:286–294**, **6:***13,* 14,
    15–16
  art historian studies, **6:**25
  Bamana dance, **1:**359, 360
  Bantu ritual dances, **2:**87–88
  Cameroon, **2:**32
  Central and East Africa, **2:**91
  Cuban dance, **2:**274
  dance aesthetics, **1:**14
  Dogon dance, **2:**422
  Jonkonnu festival, **3:**623, *624*
  "sound masks," **4:**484
  South Africa, **5:**643, *6:23*
  southern Africa, **5:**661
  West Africa, **4:**288, *289,* 292,
    6:*12–13, 382,* 383, 423
  Asian traditions, **1:**166, 167,
    4:294–300, **5:**592, 593
  Afghanistan, **1:**27
  Ainu tatoos, **1:**32, **2:**189
  Bali, **2:**231, 232, **3:**475–476,
    480, **4:486–492**, 645, **4:**146,
    146, 297–298, *297,* **5:**356,
    6:370
  Bhutan, **1:**445, *445,* **2:**226
  Cambodia, **2:**31, 228
  China, **1:**179, **2:**129, 140, 220,
    4:296–297
  Cirebonese, **3:**501–502
  India, **1:**170, 178, **2:**117, 118,
    118, 223–224, **3:***457,* 458, *662,*
    4:65, 66, *66,* 298–299, **6:***414*
  Japan, **4:**295–296
  Japanese *bugaku,* **2:**213, *214,*
    3:579, *579*
  Japanese *butō,* **2:**18, 219
  Japanese folk dance, **2:**219
  Japanese *gigaku,* **3:**171–172
  Japanese *kabuki,* **3:**437, 638,
    4:295–296, *296,* **5:**30
  Japanese *kagura,* **3:**584, *584,*
    585, 642, *642*
  Japanese *kyōgen,* **4:**83, 661
  Japanese *nō* drama, **1:***169,* 179,
    2:216–217, **3:**581, **4:**295, 652,
    653, 654, 655
  Java, **3:**499
  Korea, **2:**222–223, *222,* **4:**45,
    46, 47, 50–51, *51,* 53, 54,
    299–300, *299*
  Malaysian *mayong,* **4:**337

Myanmar, **2:**226, 227, **4:**527
  Papua New Guinea, **5:**76, *76,* 84
  Sri Lanka, **2:**228–229, **4:**300,
    300
  Sumatra, **3:**500
  Sundanese, **3:**501–502
  Thailand, **2:**227, *228,* **4:**8–10,
    6:148–149, *148, 149*
  Tibet, **2:**221, **6:**166, 167, *168,*
    169, *169*
  European traditions, **4:301–306**
  commedia dell'arte, **2:**188,
    191, 192
  Greco-Roman, **3:**294
  Greece, ancient, **3:**290, **4:**301,
    5:*375*
  jazz age cosmetics, **5:**629
  Jooss choreography, **3:***625, 626,*
    4:302
  Laban's *Grünen Clowns,* **4:***90*
  matachins, **4:**327
  mime white-face, **4:**425, *425,*
    426
  mommerie (mummery),
    4:448–449
  moresca, **4:**303, 461, 462
  pantomime and pantomimus,
    5:3, 69, 72
  Paris Opera Ballet
    discontinuance, **2:**352, 354,
    4:302, 609, **5:**89
  Roman Empire, **5:**376
  Romania, **5:**382
  theatrical makeup, **4:**303–305
  travesty roles, **6:**188
  Weidt choreography, **6:**378
  Wigman choreography, **4:**302,
    6:390, *392*
  See also masquerades
Mesopotamia head coverings,
  4:355
Mexican body painting, **4:**385
Mexican masks, **4:***387,* 388
Native American traditions,
  4:550–551, 553, 557, *557, 561*
  Arctic people, **4:**571, 572, 573,
    573, 574
  kachina mask, **4:**565, **5:**271
  male body painting, **4:**564
  Northwest Coast, **4:**569, 570,
    570
  Tigua, **6:**173
  Yaqui, **4:**554, **6:**416
Oceanic traditions, **4:**496
  Australian Aborigine body
    painting, **1:**221, 228, 229
Mask Dance, **4:**574
Maske, Hans, **5:**654, 692
masked ball, **4:**313, 314, *314*
*Masked Ball at the Cracow Redoubt,
  The,* **5:**453
masking (lighting), **4:**192–193
maskaradak, **1:**377, 378
Maske and Kothurn (journal), **1:**243
Masken des Luzifer, Die, **1:**467
maskota, **2:**230
Mask Play of Yangju, **2:**223
Masks, Props, and Mobiles, **4:**649
Maslow, Sophie, **1:**79, 421, **2:**360,
  450, **3:**214, 216, 605, **4:306,**
  345, **5:***184*
  New Dance Group, **4:**605
  See also Dudley-Maslow-Bales
    Dance Trio
Mason, Charles, **6:**126
Mason, Francis, **4:**177, **6:**297
Mason, Monica, **2:**115, **4:**241–242,
  242, **306–307,** **5:**5
masque and antimasque,
  4:307–313
  antimasque, **4:**311–312

configurations, **2:**591
  costumes, **2:**236, *236,* **4:***311*
  England, **3:**251–253, *251,* 254,
    622, **5:**113, 340
  intermedio, **3:**509–511
  Job, **3:**608–609
  labyrinthine dances, **4:**107
  mommerie (mummery), **4:**449
  music, **4:**505, 506
  revels, **4:**307, **5:**343
  scenic design, **5:**535
  *Masque in Honour of the Marriage
    of Lord Hayes* (Campion),
    4:309
  Masque of Beauty (Jonson), **4:**308
  Masque of Beauty and the Shepherd
    (lithograph), **2:**161–162
  Masque of Blackness, **3:**622
  Masque of Comus, The, **3:**511
  Masque of Oberon (Jonson), **3:***251*
  "Masque of the Deities," **5:**518
  *Masque of the Inner Temple and
    Gray's Inn, The* (Beaumont),
    4:312
  *Masque of the Middle Temple and
    Lincoln's Inn* (Jonson), **4:**312
  Masquerade, **2:**450, 586, **3:**196,
    4:36, **5:**572
  Masquerade, The (Khachaturian-
    Ognessian score), **4:**7
  masquerades, **4:313–315**
    ballet de cour borrowings, **1:**286
    Benserade collaborations, **1:**424
    mommerie (mummery),
      4:448–449
    Saint Croix plantation dance, **2:**64
    See also mask and makeup
  Masquerade Ticket (Hogarth), **4:**315
  Masques, Les, **1:**147, 148, **3:**174,
    4:267, **5:**299, 560
  Masreliez, Adrien, **6:**46
  Mass (Bernstein), **1:**57, 439
  Mass, Vladimir, **3:**48
  Massacre des Amazones, Le, **2:**111
  Massarano, Isacchino, **2:**337
  Massen, Gaetan, **2:***42*
  Massenet, Jules, **2:**200, **3:**123, 346,
    4:256, 514
  Mass for the Young, **5:**387
  Massicotte, Édouard-Zotique, **2:**36
  Massine, Léonide, **1:**38, 49, 93,
    306, 411, **3:***73,* **4:**27, 29,
    315–325, **5:**511, 636, **6:**117
  Aleko, **5:**604
  American Ballet Theatre,
    1:66–67, 68
  Argentine dance company, **1:**110,
    532, **4:**318
  Argentinita collaboration, **1:**117,
    296, **2:**108
  artist collaborators, **1:**135–136,
    136, 137, 322, 426, **2:**568,
    4:316, 317, 320, 324, 331, 332
  Ashton association, **1:**145, 146,
    147, 148, 149, 329, **4:**319,
    5:296
  athletic and acrobatic
    choreography, **4:**259
  Ballet Russe de Monte Carlo,
    1:149, 295, *295,* 296, 301,
    302, **2:**242, 342, **4:**268–269,
    323–324, 325, **6:**182
  Ballet Russe Highlights, **1:**367
  Ballets Russes de Monte Carlo,
    1:207, 309–312, 316, **3:**72,
    361, **4:**322–323, **6:**404
  Ballets Russes de Serge
    Diaghilev, **1:**322, 323, *323,*
    324–325, **2:**342, 408, 409, 410,
    441, **4:**32–322, 33,
    316–318, 657

Beau Danube, Le, **1:**209, *297*, 305, 309, 429, **2:**406, **3:**175, **4:**319, 325, **5:**554, **6:**3
Boutique Fantasque, La, **3:**74, **4:***316,* 317, 343, **5:**589
Bowman roles, **1:**518
break with de Basil, **1:**295, 312–313
can-can choreography, **2:**53
Cecchetti influence on, **1:**329, **4:**316
Cecchetti mime roles, **2:**82
Chant du Rossignol, **6:**3
Chappell association, **2:**105
as character dancer, **2:**106, 108
character dancing choreography, **2:**107, 108
children of, **4:**324, 325
choreographed film projections, **2:**603
choreographic copyright suits against de Basil, **1:**312
choreographic intent, **1:**322
choreographic style and themes, **4:**315
choreographies, **2:**408
choreography for Béjart, **1:**291
Danilova roles, **2:***341,* 342, 343
as de Valois influence, **2:**397, 399
Diaghilev break with, **4:**318–319
Diaghilev relationship, **1:**317, 318, 322, 323, **2:**406, 408, 409, 411, **4:**33, 315, 316–318, 321–322
Don Juan version, **2:**434
Eglevsky roles, **2:**478–479
English National Ballet revivals, **2:**508, 512
Fonteyn roles, **3:**44
Franklin roles, **3:**87
Gaîté Parisienne, **1:**295, 301, 302, **2:***341,* **3:**103–104, **4:***320,* 323
gear-and-piston "factory" dances, **1:**259
Goncharova collaboration, **3:**198
Gore association, **3:**202
Grand Ballet du Marquis du Cuevas choreography, **3:**224, 226
International Ballet revivals, **3:**511
Joffrey Ballet revival stagings, **3:**614, 617
Josephslegende performance, **3:**20, 631, **4:**316
Karinska costumes, **3:**654
Kochno collaboration, **4:**33
Labanotation of works, **3:**427
Laing roles, **4:**110
Larionov collaboration, **4:**124
Lichine roles, **4:**178
Lopokova roles, **4:**223
Lovers of Teruel, The (film), **6:***120*
Mam'zell Angot, **3:**236
mazurka choreography, **4:**343
Messel designs, **4:**357, 358
as Metropolitan Ballet guest artist, **4:**380
Nobilissima Visione, **1:**296, 302, **4:***322,* 323–324, 656, **6:**119
Ode, **5:**545, *545,* **6:**118, *118*
Parade, **1:**323, **2:**182, **4:***302,* 317, 516, **5:**85, 191, *192*
Pas d'Acier, Le, **5:**267
Petrouchka, **5:**166
Pulcinella, **2:**192, **4:**317, **5:***543,* **6:**5
Rake, The, **5:**294
Rambert association, **5:**296, **6:**213

Red Shoes film role and choreography, **4:**324, *325,* **5:**331, 332, *332,* **6:**119
Riabouchinska roles, **5:**350
Royal Ballet productions, **3:**236, **5:**415
Royal Danish Ballet guest productions, **2:**3, **4:**125, **5:**430
Rubinstein commissions, **4:**321, **5:**438, 439
on Rubinstein's dance limitations, **5:**438
Sacre du Printemps, Le, **5:**488
Satie scores, **5:**525, 526, 527
Shearer (Moira) roles, **5:**589
Soirées de Paris, **3:**72, **4:**319–320, 418
Sokolova roles, **5:**636
Soleil de Nuit, **5:**233
Stepanov notation, **4:**686, **5:**693–694
symphonic ballets, **1:**310, *310,* 311, **4:**322–324, 517, 518, 636
Tricorne, Le, **2:**568, **4:**317, *323,* **6:**192–193
wives, **4:**318, 319, 320, 321, 324
Woizikowski roles, **6:**503–404
Zorina romance, **6:**449
Massine, Lorca, **1:**291, **3:**74, 360, **4:**324, 325, 609
Massine, Tatiana, **4:**324, 325
Massine on Choreography (Massine), **4:**325
Masson, André, **4:***319,* 322
Masson, Colette, *as photographer,* **3:**82, 183, **4:**523, **5:**94, 95, 97, 98, 152, 206, **6:**58
Mass Study, **6:**88
Master and Margarita, The, **2:**499, **5:**469
Master Juba. *See* Juba, Master
Masters of the Georgian Ballet (film), **2:**97
Masterson, Peter, **6:**204
Mastery of Movement (Laban; Ullmann revision), **4:**99, 102
Mastery of Movement on the Stage (Laban), **4:**94, 99, 102
MASTFOR (Moscow), **3:**48
Mastroianni, Umberto, **4:**421
Mas'ūdi, Abū al-Ḥasan al-, **3:**525
Mata, Norda, **1:**211
Mata, Ruth, **5:***561*
Mata and Hari, **5:***561,* **6:**320
matachins, **4:**325–330
danza de matlachines, **2:**332, **4:**328–329, 388–389
historical overview, **4:**326–328
masques, **4:**312
Morris dance similarity, **4:**474–475
in southwestern United States, **4:**329–330, 473–474, **6:**416
Mata Hari, **1:**241
Maṭar, Būlus Anṭūn, **4:**414
Matas, Marcos, **5:**64
matatoros dance, **2:**64
Match, **1:**442, **5:**557
Matchmaker, The, **6:**432
Matelots, Les, **4:**33, 182, 320, **5:**636
matenik, **2:**304
Materialy po istorii russkogo baleta (Borisoglebsky), **5:**483
Mather, Increase, **2:**167, 339
Mathesius, Michelle, **2:**379
Matheson, Katy, *as contributor,* **2:**18–19, 422–423, **3:**443–449, **4:**271, **6:**174–175
Mathias, Yrca, **1:**485, 486
Mathilde, **1:**446
Mathinna, **1:**208

Mathura, India, **3:**467, 468
Matin de Paris, Le (journal), **3:**85
mating dances. *See* courtship dances
Matinsky, Mikhail, **5:**452
Matirosian, Maxim, **1:**122
Matisse, Henri, **1:**130, 133, 135, 296, 316, 322, **2:**242, 406, **3:**653, **4:**34, 324, 330–332, **5:**544, 547, **6:**3
"Matjažev Rejc," **3:**412
Matlage, Louise, **2:**212
Matlagova, Eva, students, **6:**203
Matos, Jasmim de, **5:***232*
Matoušová-Rajmová, Marie, *as contributor,* **4:**355–357
Matray, Ernst, **4:**675
Matribhumi (Indian weekly), **3:**470
Matsui Akira, **4:**332–333
Matsukaze, **3:**646
Matsumoto Hakuō I (Matsumoto Kōshirō VIII), **4:**334, **5:**33
Matsumoto Kintarō. *See* Ichikawa Danjūrō
Matsumoto Kōshirō, **3:**593, **4:**333–334, **5:**496
Matsumoto Kōshirō I, **3:**437, **4:**333
Matsumoto Kōshirō III. *See* Ichikawa Danjūrō V
Matsumoto Kōshirō IV, **4:**333
Matsumoto Kōshirō V, **4:**333, 535
Matsumoto Kōshirō VI, **4:**333
Matsumoto Kōshirō VII, **3:**439, **4:**333
Matsumoto Kōshirō VIII, **3:**439, **4:**333, *334,* **334,** 535
Matsumoto Kōshirō IX, **4:**334, 535, *535*
Matsumoto Ryū, **3:**593
Matsumoto Somegorō VI, **4:**334
Matsumoto Yazō. *See* Ichikawa Danjūrō IV
Matsuri (publication), **3:**591
Matsuyama Ballet, **2:**440, **3:**589, **6:**64
Matteo
as contributor, **2:**78
flamenco reconstruction, **3:**11
"Hindu" *Swan Lake* performance, **4:***354*
Matter, Herbert, *as photographer,* **5:**309
Matthes, Walther, **4:**64
Mattheson, Johann, **1:**90, 517, **6:**125
Matthews, Jessie, **1:**520, **4:**334–335
Matthews, Lawrence, *as photographer,* **2:**324
Matthews, Sara, **1:***51*
Matthew the Goose-Boy, **3:**341
Matthus, Siegfried, **5:**557
Mattie the Gooseboy, **3:**416
Matton, Roger, **2:**151
Mattox, Matt, **2:**184, **3:**600
Matumoto Yazō. *See* Ichikawa Danjūrō IV
Matus, Donn, **5:**262
Matyatin, **3:**317
Matzinger, Ruth, **1:**243, **2:**174
Mauclair, Camille, **5:**541
Maude-Dioula (people), **4:**291
Maude Russell and Her Ebony Steppers, **6:***245*
Maudrik, Lizzie, **5:**288
Mauggallena (Mokuren), **1:**496
Maule, Michael, **2:**277, **5:***612*
mā'ulu'ulu, **4:**495, **6:**177
Mauri, Rosita, **1:**347, **2:**522, **3:**81, **4:**353–354, *353,* **5:**94, 95, 673, **6:**64, 191, 217
Maurice, Charles, **1:**44, **2:**502

Mauricio, Joao, **4:**482
Maurin, Elisabeth, **4:**134, **5:**98
Mauritania, **4:**408
Mauvet, Maurice, **6:**318
Maver, Marilyn Rowe. *See* Rowe, Marilyn
Mavı Düşler, **6:**213
Mavra (Stravinsky), **2:**410, **6:**4–5
mawlawīyah, **3:**524
mawlids, **2:**487, 490, 491, 493
Max and Moritz, **3:**193
Maxfield, Richard, **2:**461, **6:**362
Maxi (people), **6:***381*
Maximilian I, Holy Roman emperor, **4:**449, 462
Maximilian II, emperor of Austria, **1:**235
Maximova, Ekaterina, **1:**405, 539, **3:**138, 195, **4:**335–336, 360, **5:**97, 164, 460, **6:**324
Don Quixote performance, **2:**438, **4:**336, **5:***102*
Faust performance, **5:**37
Grigorovich ballets, **1:**492, 493, **3:***310*
Nutcracker performance, **5:**12
Onegin performance, **2:**512
Romeo and Juliet performances, **4:**335
Spartacus performance, **5:**677
Swiss Milkmaid performance, **5:***467,* **6:**51
on Ulanova's coaching, **6:**228
Vasiliev dance partnership and marriage, **5:***102,* **6:**314, *314*
maxixe, **1:**528, **2:**78, **5:**624, 627, **6:**246, 269, 270
Maxon, Norman, *as photographer,* **4:**346
Maxwell, Carla, **4:**115
May, Betty, **3:**210, **5:**584
May, Deborah, *as photographer,* **2:**611
May, Herida, **1:**316, **3:**512
May, Pamela, **1:***149,* **2:**115, **3:**379, **4:**336–337, **5:**114, 588, 596, 639
Royal Ballet, **5:**414, *414,* 416
Symphonic Variations performance, **6:**64, 65
Maya (people), **1:**414, 415, **3:**319
Maya, Mario, **3:**9, 10, 11, **5:**674
Maya, Vera, **1:**244, **4:**8, **5:**458, 477, 478
Mayakovsky, Vladimir, **3:**48, **5:**331, **6:**411, 412
May B, **3:***78,* 79
Mayday, **2:**120
May Day, **3:**33, 242, 250
May Day, or A Holiday in Sokolniki, **3:**191
May Day on the Mall. See Fanfare for the Common Man
Mayer, Angioletta, **6:**335
Mayer, Charles S., *as contributor,* **5:**437–439
Mayer, Daniel, **2:**376, 377, 378, **5:**495, 496
Mayer, David, **5:**70
Mayer, Gilbert, **3:**82
Mayer, Louis B., **5:**239
Mayer, Robert, **5:**531, **6:**454
Mayer, Timothy, **6:**205
Mayerling, **2:**186, **5:**100, **6:**135
Georgiadis designs, **3:**136
Lanchbery score adaptations, **4:**117
MacMillan production, **4:**243, *244,* 245, **5:**418, *419*
Seymour performance, **5:**575
Wall performance, **6:**357

Mayerová, Milča, **2:**307
Mayette, Bob, *as photographer*, **4:**620
mayimayiwane dance, **5:**579
Mayim Mayim, **3:**531
Maynard, Olga, **4:**170
May Night, **1:**482
Mayo, Glen, **4:***628*
Mayo, Sonje, **5:**657, 659, 660, *660*
Mayol, Oslo, **4:**675
Mayol, Paris, **4:**523
mayong, **4:***250*, 251, **337–338**, 491–492
Mayor, A. Hyatt, **4:**26
Mayoral and Elsa María, **6:**94
mayores, **2:**431
Mayorov, Henrik, **1:**493, **4:**38, 154, **5:**460, 467
Maypole dancing, **2:**254
  colonial North America, **6:**231, 232
  Ecuador, **2:**476
  England, **3:**242
  European folk dance history, **3:**31
  Haiti, **3:**335
  Jamaican form, **3:**573
  Mexico, **4:***385*, 399
  Sweden, **6:**37
Mayr, Thomas, **1:**391
Mayseder, Joseph, **5:**498
Ma Yunhong, **5:**330
Mayurbhanj *chhau*, **2:**117, 118
Mayuzumi, Toshirō, **2:**388, **4:***616*
Maywood, Augusta, **2:**60, **4:338–339**, **5:**138, 232, 384, **6:**290
  Borri dance partnership, **1:**499
  Hungarian performance, **3:**413
  international fame, **6:**237
  Lee rivalry, **4:**139, 338
Mazarin, Jules Cardinal, **1:**286, 287, 288, **4:**229, **5:**536
Maze, Georges, **1:**504, **3:**81
Mazepa (Polish ballet), **5:**219
Mazeppa (Tchaikovsky opera), **6:**116
mazes. *See* labyrinth dances
Mazhikov, Kairat, **3:**665
Mazia, Marjorie, **1:**97, **3:**214, 216
Mazilia, **3:**261, **5:**134
Mazilier, Joseph, **1:**455, **2:**503, **3:**70, 96, **4:339–343**, **5:**139, 148, 319, 516
  Cerrito roles, **1:**10, **4:**342
  Coralli association, **2:**202, 203, 204, **5:**339–340
  Corsaire, Le, **2:**206, 207, 282, 368, **4:**189, 339, 343, **5:**120, 140, 403
  dance partnerships, **4:**340
  Diable Amoureux, Le, **4:**340–341, 657
  Diable Boiteux, Le, **2:**405, **4:**340
  Elfes, Les, **2:**587
  Elssler (Fanny) roles, **2:**504, *505*, **3:**185, **4:**57, 340
  Elssler dance partnership, **5:**340
  Fitzjames (Nathalie) roles, **3:**5
  Gipsy, La, **4:**339, **5:**340
  Grisi roles, **3:**315, 316, **4:**341
  Jolie Fille de Gand, La, **3:**5
  Lacotte reconstruction, **4:**108
  Marco Spada, **4:**339, 342, 358
  mazurka choreography, **4:**343
  Mérante roles, **4:**353
  mime skills, **5:**92
  Orfa choreography, **2:**95, **4:**342
  Paquita, **3:**315, **4:**339, 428, **5:**85, 93, 120, 150
  Petipa (Lucien) association, **5:**148

Rosati roles, **5:**405
  scores, **4:**514
  students, **1:**477, **4:**338
  Sylphide performance, **4:**116, 339, 340, **5:**134, **6:**57
  Taglioni (Marie) dance partnership, **4:**340, **6:**73
  See also Diable à Quatre, Le
Mazilli und Orisko, **6:**337
Mazilu, Răzvan, **5:**390
Mazloum, Nelly, **2:**498
Mazlová, Ruzena, **6:**359
Mazo, Joseph H., *as contributor*, **1:**54–57, **5:**342
Mazoń, Janusz, **3:**337
Mazowsze Song and Dance Ensemble, **5:**75, 212
Mazulme, **5:**615, 616
Mazumdar, Maxim, **3:**175
mazur. *See* mazurka
Mazurier, Charles-François, **1:**455, **3:**68, **4:**339, **5:**134, 149
  Coralli choreography, **2:**202
  Jocko, ou Le Singe du Brésil, **3:***69*
  as Ravel family influence, **5:**317, 318, 319
mazurka, **4:343–344**
  Argentina, **1:**108
  Brazil, **1:**530
  Cajun, **2:**24
  Coppélia, **2:**200, 368
  Elssler (Fanny) popularization of, **2:**107, 504
  Finland, **2:**630
  France, **3:**70
  Germany, **3:**142
  as Kshessinsky family specialty, **4:**66–67, *67*
  Poland, **5:**210, 212, 213, 214, 216
  United States, **6:**235
  waltz popularity versus, **6:**361
Mazurka, **2:**584, **3:**22, **4:**336
Mazurka in C Major (Chopin), **6:**60, 62
Mazurka in C-sharp Minor (Chopin), **6:**60
Mazurka in D Major (Chopin), **6:**660
Mazurka of 1890, **1:**117
Mazurkas for Pavlova, **6:**363
Mazza, Giovanni, **2:**435
Mazzantini, Luigi, **3:**412, 414
Mazzarelli, Victoria, **3:**375
Mazzo, Kay, **1:***28*, 29, 96, **2:**333, **4:**618, *619*, **5:***362*
Mazzucchelli, Ettorina, **5:**529
mbenga, **1:**527
mbuji, **2:**91
Mbunda (people), **2:**87–88
Mbuti dance, **2:**87, *88*, 210, **4:**344
Mbuyiselwa, Jackie, **5:**660
McAllister, David, **1:**211, 235
McAndrew, Patricia, **2:**387
  as contributor, **1:**503–514, **3:**39–40, **4:**6, 43
McArthur, Kennetha R., *as contributor*, **1:**383–384, **6:**127–129
McBean, Angus, **4:**168
McBirney, Mara, **2:**47
McBride, Patricia, **2:**333, **4:344–345**, **619**, **5:***362*, 532, **6:**105, 137, 174, *201*, *340*
  Afternoon of a Faun performance, **1:**29
  Balanchine ballets, **1:***269*, **4:**611, 618
  Ballet Imperial performance, **1:**293
  Coppélia performance, **2:**201
  Jacob's Pillow performance, **3:**571

Liebeslieder Walzer performance, **4:**180, *615*
  New York City Ballet, **4:**618, 623
  Rubies performance, **4:**612
  Symphony in C performance, **6:**66
McBride, Robert, **1:**280, 421, **2:**197
McCabe, John, **1:**454, **2:**350, **5:**565
McCaffrey, Ken, **1:**216–217
McCall, Debra, *as contributor*, **1:**385–388
McCandless, Stanley, **4:**191
McCann, Cathy, **4:**482
McCay, Winsor, **5:**613
McClain, T. Davina, *as contributor*, **4:**426–428, **5:**72–75, 373–378
McClure, Veronica Ann, *as contributor*, **5:**409–410
McColl, Ewan, **4:**94
McCormack, Wilbur, **5:**585
McCormick, Malcolm, *as contributor*, **2:**234–245, 245–248, 248–251, **3:**653–655, **4:**130, 301–306, 659–660, **6:**188–191
McCoy, Bessie, **2:**79, **6:**317
McCoy, Van, **5:**633
McCracken, Joan, **4:**209, **6:**278
McCraw, Charles, **4:**692, *692*
McCree, Maxine, **6:**386
McCullagh, Shona, **4:**626, 627
McCulloch, Deborah, **4:**626, 627
McCullough, Rick, **4:**602, **6:**366
McCurnie, Beryl, **5:**254
McDearmon, Lacy H., *as contributor*, **1:**42–43
McDermott, William, **1:**315
McDonagh, Don, *as contributor*, **5:**626–631
McDonald, Anthony, **2:**355, **3:**274, **5:**304
McDonald, Eddy, *as photographer*, **5:**274
McDonald, Gene, **2:**182
McDonald, Gertrude, **6:***319*
McDonald, Rufus Lee ("Flash"), **3:**57
McDowell, John Herbert, **6:**362, 363
McDowell, Norman, **1:**289, 290, **2:**174, 511
McEwen, Mary, **2:**467, 468
McFall, John, **1:**75, 197, 373, **5:**513
McFarlane, James, *as photographer*, **1:**232
McFee, Graham, **1:**24
McGehee, Helen, **2:**182, 466, **3:**218, 385, **5:**568
McGhee, Brownie, **2:**450
McGill, John, **3:**378–379
McGill, Kristina Gjems, **4:**680
McGill University, **2:**47
McGoldrick, Larissa, **2:**293
McGowan, Margaret M., **3:**283
  as contributor, **1:**1–3, 275–277, 285–287, 397–398
McGowan, Monica, **3:**574
MC Hammer, **2:**610
McHose, Caryn, **4:**17
McHugh, Jimmy, **6:**256
McIndoe, Thomas, **2:**47
McIntyre, Chuna, **4:**571
McIntyre, Colin, **2:**42, **3:**231–232, 233–234
McIntyre, Dianne, **2:**358, **3:**448, **6:**89, 259, 448
McKayle, Donald, **1:**55, **2:**110, 358, **3:**577, **4:345–346**, **6:**132
  African-American music, **4:**520
  de Lavallade dance partnership, **2:**367

Rainbow 'Round My Shoulder, **2:**358, **4:**345, *346*, 520, **6:**259
Raisin, **6:**284
  San Martín Ballet repertory works, **1:**113
  social content, **6:**259
  Sophisticated Ladies, **6:**286–287
  students, **6:**388
  videotape profile of, **1:**81
McKechnie, Donna, **1:**419, **6:***285*, 288
McKechnie, Shirley, **1:**212, 216
McKendry, Mary, **2:**513
McKenzie, Jean, **5:**434
McKenzie, Kevin, **6:**129
  American Ballet Theatre, **1:**65–65, 74, *76*, 77, **2:**441, **3:**367
  Washington Ballet, **2:**356, **6:**366–367
McKenzie, Robert Tait, **4:**16
McKerrow, Amanda, **1:**77, 282, **2:**356, 441
McKim, Ross, **3:**273
McKinzie, Edith, **3:**396
McLain, David, **2:**357
McLaren, Coralee, **3:***389*
McLaren, Norman, **2:**605
McLaughlin, Frederick, **2:**80
McLaughlin, John, **2:**499
McLauren, Barbara, **2:**355
McLean, Jane, **1:**542
McLean, Mervyn, **4:***628*
McLerie, Allyn Ann, **5:**361, 369, **6:**277
McMahon, Deirdre, *as contributor*, **3:**519–520
McMartin, John, **1:**419
McMicken, David, **1:**216
McMillan, Geyvan Yılmas, **6:**212–213
McNair, Dorothy, **5:**653
McNair, John, **5:**653
McNeil, George, **6:**400
McNutt, Jenny Lynn, *as photographer*, **2:**492, **6:**382, 384
McPhee, Colin, **3:**506, **6:**297
McPherson, Joy, **2:**38
McPherson, J. W., **4:**416
McQuade, Molly, *as contributor*, **2:**172–174, **5:**165–166
McRae, Edna, **6:**291
McShann, Jay, **1:**60
McTavish, Shona Dunlop, **1:**468
Meacham, Joseph, **5:**576
Mead, Margaret, **2:**601, **3:**505, 506, **4:**369, **5:**357
Mead, Robert, **1:**156, **2:**515, **4:**452, *658*, 659
Meade Brothers, *as photographers*, **5:**175
Meadow Dance, **3:**344
Meadowlark, **2:**583, **5:**436
Meadow of Proverbs, **1:**453
Meadows of Gold and Mines of Gems (al-Masʿūdi), **3:**525
Me and My Girl (musical), **6:**287
Mean Street on Earth, **5:**521
Measured Pace, A: Towards a Philosophical Understanding of the Arts of Dance (Sparshott), **1:**24
Measuring the Speed of a Swordthrust by Means of Photochronography (photograph), **5:***179*
Mecca (musical), **3:**21
Mechanical Ballet. *See Ballet Mécanique, Le*
"mechanical" dances, **5:**458

Mechanical Lectures upon Dancing (Weaver), **6:**372
Mechanical Man, The, **3:**420
Mechanical Organ, The, **4:**651
Mechanics of Normal and Pathological Locomotion in Man (Steindler), **4:**16
Meck, Galina von, **6:**116
Meck, Nadezhda von, **2:**360, **6:**116
Meckel, Arnold, **1:**115
Medea, **1:**38, 39, **2:**17, **5:***658,* 674, **6:**323, 328
  Cullberg choreography, **2:**283, **4:**676, **5:**431
  Cullberg restaging for New York City Ballet, **4:**608, *614*
  Fracci performance, **3:**60
  Haydée performance, **3:**351
  Neumeier choreography, **4:**604
  Roger performance, **4:**677
  Vukičević production, **6:**435
Medea (Seneca), **3:**652
Médée (Paige ballet), **5:**61, *61*
Médée et Jason, **1:**43, 236, **2:**414, **3:**117, 257, **4:346–347, 697, 5:**270, **6:**311, 331
  Boydell engraving of, **2:**68
  Guimard performance and costume, **3:**326
  Le Picq and Noverre collaboration, **4:**149, 276
  popularity in Stuttgart, **4:**695, 696
  productions throughout Europe, **4:**695
  Rodolphe score, **4:**346, **5:**371
  Saint Petersburg performance, **5:**451
  Stuttgart premiere, **6:**9
Medes (people), **1:**247
media caña, **1:**108
Medical Aspects of Dance, The (report), **2:**330
medical treatments. *See* dance medicine; medicinal rites
Medici, Cosimo de', **4:**502
Medici, Cosimo II de, **2:**26, **3:**381
Medici, Cosimo III de, **3:**381
Medici, Ferdinand de', **3:**510, *510*
Medici family, **3:**544
  See also Médicis, Catherine de
medicinal rites
  Central and East Africa, **2:**91
  Christian, **2:**165, 168
  Dogon dance, **4:**485
  !Kung San, **4:**74–75, 485, **5:**664, *665*
  Native American, **4:**552, 558, 567, 578, 579
  Ubakala, **6:**383
  zār, **2:**487–488, *4:*488, **6:**444–445
Medicine Lodge Ceremony, **4:**558
Médicis, Catherine de, **1:**2, 397, 409, **5:**536
  Balet Comique de la Royne commission, **1:**275, **3:***66*
  banquet, **1:**364
  court ballet patronage, **1:**285
  dancing master, **2:**337, **3:**80
  folding fan, **2:**570
Médicis, Marie de, **1:**364
Medieros, John, **1:**57
medieval dance, **4:347–350**
  aesthetics, **1:**20–21
  Armenia, **1:**119
  banquets, **1:**363
  barriera, torneo, and *battaglia,* **1:**369–370
  bassedanse, **1:**378–382
  Christian, **2:**164–166, 168, 540
  cosmetics prohibitions, **4:**303

costume, **2:**234–235
  Dance of Death, **2:**332
  dancing manias, **6:**185, 187
  dancing masters, **2:**336
  guild dances, **3:**325
  Iceland, **3:**436
  India, **3:**466–468
  Islamic, **3:**525
  Japan, **3:**580–581, 584
  jesters and traveling players, **3:**541
  Jewish, **3:**602–603
  labyrinth dances, **4:**106–107
  liturgical stagings, **2:**164, 166, 168, 540, **5:**533
  masks and makeup, **4:**301, 448, 449
  mime, **4:**423
  mommerie, **4:**448, 449
  moresca, **4:**460–461
  music, **4:**500–502
  performance spaces, **6:**155
  Poland, **5:**213–214
  Scandinavia, **2:**629
  sword dances, **1:**118
  technical manuals, **6:**121–122
Medina, Juan, **4:**390, 399
Medina, Maria, **1:**237, **2:**353, 413, **5:**105
  Fille Mal Gardée, La, **1:**390
  Hungarian performances, **3:**413
Medina, Narciso, **2:**281, *281*
Medinj, M. Janis, **4:**127
Meditation, **2:**314, 576, **4:**611, 618
"Meditation" (Massenet), **1:**157
Meditation on Violence (film dance), **2:**604
Meditations (Dolgushin ballet), **2:**423
Meditations of Arjuna, The, **3:**496
Mediterranean Legends, **5:**387
Medium, The, **6:**66
Medley, **3:**447, **6:**152
Medusa, **3:**23, *23,* 340
Medwall, Henry, **3:**251
Medzhnun, **6:**84
Meehan, John, **1:**74, 208, 211, 213, 214, 233, **2:**42, **5:**437
Meeker, Jess, **5:**585, 586
Meer, Deen van, *as photographer,* **2:**470, **4:**596
Meer, Marjolin van der, **5:**676
Meester, Johan de, **1:**410
Meeting Places, **4:**667
Meeting Point, **2:**1, **5:**305
Meet Me in Las Vegas (film), **2:**109
Meet Me in St. Louis (film), **2:**616
me'etu'upaki, **4:**496
Mefistofeles, **3:**127
megerengue redondo, **2:**431
Meghasandesh, **2:**105
Mehlman, Lillian, **3:**214, **6:**245
Mehmood, Talat, **2:**625
Mehnen, Holger, **1:***510*
Méhul, Étienne-Nicolas, **2:**264, 435, **3:**360, **6:**360
Meija, Paul, **2:**173
Meiji Restoration of 1868, **2:**6, **3:**582, 585, 638, 650, **4:**30, 41, **6:**410
Meiji Shrine, Tokyo, **3:**103
Mei Lanfang, **1:**164, **2:**132–133, **4:350, 5:**496, **6:**446
Meilhac, Henry, **3:**26
Mei-no-Kai, **3:**651, 652, **4:**661
Mei school (Beijing Opera). *See* Mei Lanfang
Meishar, Yaron, **3:**535
Meissner, Alexander, **1:**242
Meister, Hans, **6:**454

Meistersinger von Nürnberg, Die (Wagner), **1:**510, **2:**367
Meitei tradition. *See* Manipur
Meja, Daniel, **6:**35
Mejia, Paul, **2:**576, 577, **5:***398,* **6:**86, 265, 266
mejorana, **5:**67
meke, **2:**593
Mekeo (people), **5:**76
mek mulung, **4:**251
Melancholy, **3:**590
Mélancolie, La, **1:**515
Melanesia, 19–20, **2:**593, **4:351–352,** 495, 497–498
Melanin, Andrei, **5:**473
Melanippides, **2:**419
Melato, Mariangela, **5:**527
Melaveh Malka, **3:**528–529
Melbourne, Australia, **1:**208, 209, 211, 212, 213, 215–216, 217, 498, **3:**623
Melbourne Ballet Club, **1:**498, **4:**275
Melbourne Cup, **1:**230
Melby, Ernest O., **1:**79
Meleagro, ossia La Vendetta di Diana, **1:**499
mele hula, **4:**496
Mélicere, **4:**447
Méliès, Georges, **2:**603
Melikov, Arif, **3:**569, **4:**144, **6:**341
Melik-Pashayeva, Karina L., *as contributor,* **5:**320–322
Mellado, Paulina, **2:**126
Mellan Tvd Trädgårdar, **6:**45
Mellor, Hugh, **3:**250
Melnikov, Kirill, **1:**391
Melò, Maria, **3:**51
Melodeon Company, **5:**616
Mélodrama, **4:**625
Melodrama for Two Men and One Woman, **1:**524
Melody, **4:**359
Melpa (people), **5:**84–85
Melsher, JoAnne, **2:***286*
Melson, B., **2:**316
Melvana Çelal Eddin Rumi and the Whirling Dervishes (Halman and And), **4:**416
Melville, Nan
  as contributor, **5:**56–58, **6:**379–380
  as photographer, **5:**652, **6:**379
Melville Island, **1:**219, 224–225
Member of Parliament, **6:**378
memendet, **3:**477
Mémoires historiques (Speer), **3:**409
Memoirs (Fokine), **6:**62
Memoirs of the Life of Barton Booth (Booth), **5:**518
Memoirs on the State of France under Charles IX (Goulart), **1:**397–398
Memoria, **1:**56, 58, *59,* **5:**432
Memorial to Zapata, **1:**524
Memories from Puna (Hong), **3:**373
Memories of Youth, **2:**500
Memory, **2:**359
Memphis Students Band, **6:**256
Menagerie, **6:***454*
Menagerie of Empress Philissa, The, **6:**175
Mena Gujarati (film), **5:**521
Menaka, Madame, **3:**468
Menak Chino, **3:**497
Menak Djinggo, **1:**173
Menak stories, **1:**173–174, **3:**493, 494, 497, 501
Mencken, H. L., **2:**573
Men Dancers, **3:**571
Mende (people), **6:**382

Mendel, Deryk, **3:**76
Mendel, Olive, **4:**626
Mendeleev, Dmitri, **1:**463, 464
Mendelssohn, Felix, **2:**445, **4:**429
Mendelssohn Concerto, **2:**427
Mendes, José, **1:**487, **2:**181, 524, **3:**127, **6:**365
mendèt, **1:**175
Méndez, Alberto, **1:**50, **2:**279, 280, 281, **5:**133, 275
Méndez, Josefina, **2:**279, 280
Mendez, Julieta, **5:**511
Mendoza, Cesar, **5:**172
Menegatti, Beppe, **3:**59, 60, 61
Ménéstrier, Claude-François, **1:**22, 23–24, 29, **3:**84, 544, **5:**230, **6:**125
  ballet de collège, **1:**283
  on *ballet de cour,* **1:**287
  on horse ballet, **3:**381
Mengarelli, Julius, **5:**266, **6:***41,* 42
Mengarelli, Mario, **6:**42, *42*
Men in Her Life, The (film), **1:**484
Menomini (people), **4:**558
Menon, K. P. S., **3:**470
Menon, Padma, **1:**216, **6:**321
Menon, P. Ramunni, **5:**309
Menotti, Gian-Carlo, **1:**467, **2:**183, **3:**101, 224, **4:**28–29, **6:**145
  Butler association, **2:**16
  Graham commissions, **3:**384, **4:**518
  Spoleto Festival, **3:**550, **5:**363
Mensch und seine Sehnsucht, Der, **2:**153
"Men's Dance," **6:**394
Mensendieck, Bess, **1:**203, **3:**145, 420, **4:**92
mental health therapies. *See* dance and movement therapy
Mental Mode, **3:**52
menuet. See minuet
Menus Plaisirs, Les, **5:**327
Menut, Adolphe, **4:***214*
Menyhárt, Jacqueline, **3:**417
Menz, Meta, **2:**69
Menzelli, Elizabetta, **5:**58, **6:**290
Mephisto, **1:**484
Mephisphela, **5:**59, *60*
Mephistopheles, or The Evil Spirit, **1:**461
Mephisto Valse, **1:**147–148, *148,* **2:**510, 324, **4:**109, 267, 269, 646, **5:**299
Mer, La, **1:**442, **2:**361, **5:**557
Mérante, Louis, **1:**500, 540, **2:**38, 113, 351, 363, 587, **4:352–354, 5:**515, **6:**70
  Deux Pigeons, Les, **5:**94, **6:**21
  Paris Opera Ballet, **3:**71, **4:353–354, 5:**94, 141, **6:**443
  Petipa (Lucien) choreography for, **5:**148, 149
  students, **5:**690
  Sylvia, **2:**368, **6:**62, 64
Mercandotti, Maria, **1:**35, 36, **2:**71, 521
"Mercanzia, La," **2:**427
Mercé, Antonia. *See* Argentina, La
Merce Cunningham Dance Company, **2:**289–296
  Australian tour, **1:**212–213
  Belgian modern dance, **1:**412
  Brown, Carolyn, **1:**542, **2:**289
  Cage management, **2:**22, 23
  Charlip, Remy, **2:**110, 289
  former members in Grand Union, **3:**235
  founding, **2:**289
  funding, **1:**542, **2:**292
  Japanese tour, **3:**591

Merce Cunningham Dance
Company, *continued*
Johns as artistic adviser,
3:619–620
Komar, Chris, **4:**37
resident filmmaker, **2:**294
Setterfield, Valda, **5:**573
Suite for Five, **6:**26
Summerspace, **6:**27
Winterbranch, **6:**402
world tours, **2:**291–292, 293
See also Cunningham, Merce
Mercedes Molina Company, **5:**654
Mercer, Johnny, **1:**194
Mercé y Luque, Antonia. *See*
Argentina, La
Merchant of Venice, The
(Shakespeare(, **3:**356
Yakko and Kawakami
production, **6:**409
Mercier, Jean, **1:**98
Mercier, Louis, **4:**404, 414
Mercier, Margaret, **2:**605, **3:**228,
342, 429, *429*
Mercure (periodical), **5:**504
Mercure, **1:**325, **4:**319, 320, 516,
5:192, 299, 304, 525, 543
Mercure, Pierre, **2:**151, **5:**62, **6:**130
Mercuric Tidings, **5:**678, **6:**110, 111
Mercurio, Paul, **1:**216, **6:**56
Mercury (deity), **1:**198
Mercury Ensemble, **5:**302
Mercury in Flight (Bologna),
1:197–198, 345
Mercury Theater, New York City,
6:276
Mercury Theatre, London, **2:**105
*Mercury Vindicated from the
Alchemists* (Jonson masque),
4:310
Mercy, Dominique, **1:**350,
388–389, *389*
Meredith, Margaret, **4:**153
Meredith Monk Vocal Ensemble,
4:451
"Mère Gigogne et les Polichinelles,
La" *(The Nutcracker)*, **3:**565
merengue, **5:**630, 636
Domincan Republic, **2:**61, *193*,
430, 431, 432
Virgin Islands, **2:**64
Merényi, Zsuzsa, **3:**422
Merger de Saint-André, Adrien. *See*
Saint-André, Adrien
Merger de
Meri, La, **3:**199, **4:**168, **354–355**,
415, **5:**497, **6:**34, 327
Mérida, Ana, **1:**524, **4:**392
Mérida, Carlos, **4:**391, **6:***355*
as photographer, **4:**391
Merimée, Prosper, **3:**7, 185
Merino de Zela, E. Mildred. *See* de
Zela, E. Mildred Merino
Merino Santos, Rosalia, **5:**172
Merlin, Olivier, **5:**691
Mermaid, The, **5:**75, 300
Merman, Ethel, **6:**182, 277, 279
Merrick, David, **1:**419, **6:**281, 287
Merrie Monarch Festival (Hawaii),
3:395
Merrild, Karl, **1:***510*, **5:***427*, 428,
6:399
Merrill, Bruce, **5:**52
Merry Andrew (film), **4:**10, 11
Merry-Go-Rounders, **1:**432,
3:404, 605
Merry Mount, Massachusetts,
6:231
Merry Widow, The, **1:**38, 210, 234,
6:143

Balanchine choreography, **6:**277
Béjart production, **1:**291, 405
Helpmann staging, **1:***233*,
3:357, 428
Hynd choreography, **3:**357, 428,
4:546, **5:**410
Keil performance, **4:**2
Lanchbery score adaptation,
4:117
Markova performance, **4:**270
Rowe performance, **1:***233*, **5:**410
waltz popularization, **6:**268–269
Merry Widow, The (film), **5:**310
Merry Wives of Windsor, The, **2:**15
Merry Wives of Windsor, The
(Japanese version), **4:**661
Mersenne, Marin, **1:**2, 46, 523,
2:51, 260, **3:**84, 109, 124,
5:112, 115, 116, **6:**6, 125
Mersy, Adelaide, **2:***415*
Meruntsika, **4:**78
Merwe, Marianne van der, **5:**54
Meryl Tankard Australian Dance
Theatre, **1:**214, **6:**95
Meryl Tankard Company,
1:214, 215
Merz, Richard, *as contributor*,
1:373–376, **5:**560–561,
681–684, **6:**27–28, 51–54, 453,
454–455
mésa éxo, **2:**100
Meshes of the Afternoon (film),
2:601, 603
Mesopotamia, **4:**355–357, 423,
6:445
Mesquakie (people), **4:**551
Messac, Magali, **1:**75, **5:***131*
Message, The (also *Biblical
Pictures*), **2:**263
Messager, André, **1:**6, 155, **4:**354,
5:94, **6:**217
Mess Around (dance), **4:**254
Messe en Jazz, **2:**389
Messel, Oliver, **1:**316, **4:357–358**,
5:294, 413, 415, 551, 612
American Ballet Theatre, **1:**73,
4:357, *358*
Royal Ballet (Sadler's Wells)
designs, **1:**150, **2:**243, **3:***266*,
355, **4:**357, 358
Messenger, Dalley, **1:**218
Messenger Feast, **4:**571
Messe pour le Temps Présent, **1:**405,
6:131
Messerer, Asaf, **1:**38, 445, 489,
2:605, **4:358–360**, **5:**107, 202,
331, 480, 487, 610, **6:**106
Ballet du XXᵉ Siècle, **1:**290
ballet technique text, **1:**329,
4:360, **6:**129
Don Quixote, **4:***148*, 358, *359*
strong technique, **4:**359, *359*,
5:458
students, **3:**523, **4:**360, **6:**313, 344
Swan Lake, **1:***490*, **4:**358
Messerer, Azary, **5:**202
as contributor, **5:**202–207
Messerer, Sulamith, **2:**596, **3:**589,
5:202
Messiaen, Olivier, **2:**471, **6:**362
Messisbugo, Cristoforo di, **1:**363
Mestey, Oscar, **5:**275, 276
mestizada dance, **1:**415
Mestral, Patrice, **4:**461
Mestre, Gloria, **4:**392
Meta, **1:**386, **3:***146*
Métaboles, Les, **2:**471, **4:**134, 243
Meta Ecology, **5:**524
Metaforen, **5:**290
Metal Dance, **1:**386, 387

metallophones *(gendér)*, **3:**112, 113,
114, 475, 485, **6:**367, 369,
370
metamorphose (transvestite ball),
4:314
Métamorphose, La (Didelot ballet),
2:414
Metamorphoses (Balanchine
ballet), **4:**137
Metamorphoses (Fodor ballet),
3:418
Metamorphoses (Georgi ballet),
3:133
Metamorphoses (Ovid), **3:**15,
5:113
Métamorphoses, Les (Taglioni
ballet), **2:**413, **3:**145, **6:**75
Metamorphosis (Imre
choreography), **6:**66
Metamorphosis (Medina
choreography), **2:**281, *281*
"Metamorphosis, The" (Kafka),
1:373, **3:**523
Metaphor, **5:**553
metaphysical art, **1:**133
Metastaseis & Pithoprakta, **2:**576
Metastasio, Pietro, **1:**87, **3:**189,
5:231
Météora, **1:**477, **5:**500
Méthode de Vestris (Bournonville),
6:127
Méthode Jaques-Dalcroze (Jaques-
Dalcroze), **3:**595, 596
Methodik des klassischen Tanzes
(Merényi), **3:**422
Methodism, **2:**167, **4:**376–379
Method of Lighting, A
(McCandless), **4:**191
methodologies in the study of
dance, **4:360–379**
anthropology, **4:**360, **368–372**
African dance studies, **6:**25
American dance historians,
6:297
Dunham studies, **2:**458
ethnology versus, **4:**373
film and video tape records,
2:597–598
functionalist approach, **4:**371
Labanotation, **4:**104
on ritual dance, **5:**357
cultural context, **4:362–366**, 371,
374–375
Bartók folk dance analyses,
1:370
European folk dance history,
3:32–36
Hungarian folk dance, **3:**423
symbolic devices, **4:**364
ethnology, **2:**534–535, 538–540,
541, 545–547, **3:**35, 422–423,
4:78, 369, **372–376**
anthropology versus, **4:**373
dance reconstruction,
5:328–329
films and videos, **2:**600–603
Kurath studies, **4:**78, 370, 372,
575, **6:**297
Native American dance,
4:574–575
Romanian ethnochoreography,
5:391
See also ethnography and dance
linguistics, **4:366–368**, 371,
376–377
semiotic analysis, **4:**367–368,
371, 376, 377
new cultural theory, **4:376–379**,
6:298
sociology, **4:360–362**

See also European traditional
dance; *subhead* dance
research and publication
*under specific countries and
geographic areas*
Métral, Corine, **3:**78
Métraux, Alfred, **3:**333, **5:**356
Metrobius, **4:**426
Metro-Goldwyn-Mayer (MGM),
3:54
film musicals, **2:**613, 614, 615,
616, 618, 619
Great Waltz production, **6:**276
Kelly, Gene, **4:**2–3
Rasch, Albertina, **5:**310
Metropolitan Ballet, **1:**420, **4:**380
Beriosova performances, **1:**429
Bruhn as guest performer, **2:**2, 3
Fraca as soloist and ballet
mistress, **3:**62, **4:**380
Hyrst as principal dancer, **3:**429,
4:380
Staff as resident choreographer,
5:691
Wilde performances, **6:**396
Metropolitan Ballet of Canada,
3:429
Metropolitan Daily, **3:**370
Metropolitan Museum of Art, New
York City, **4:**30
Metropolitan Opera Ballet,
4:380–382
Aïda choreography, **2:**459
Albertieri, Luigi, **1:**37
ballet in opera, **5:**38
Berger, Augustin, **1:**428
Boris, Ruthanna, **1:**498
Collins (Janet) solo dances,
2:187, **4:**382
Coppélia as Pavlova debut
vehicle, **2:**200, **4:**382
de Lavallade performances and
choreography, **2:**367
Doubrovska, Felia, **2:**442
Lacotte performances, **4:**107
Markova directorship, **4:**270, 382
Marks, Bruce, **4:**271
Moore, Lillian, **4:**457
Page as guest soloist, **5:**58
Pavlova and Mordkin guest
performances, **4:**382, 459,
6:243, 270
Pavlova performances, **5:**122–123
practice clothes requirements,
5:242
Romanov as ballet master, **5:**391
Salome choreography, **2:**120,
6:270
Serrano roles, **5:**573
Wallmann association, **6:**357
Wilson, Sallie, **6:**402
Metropolitan Opera Ballet School,
New York City, **1:**68, **2:**273,
4:381, 382, **6:**270, 291
Metropolitan Opera Company,
6:299
Metropolitan Opera House, New
York City
Alvin Ailey Dance Company
performances, **1:**57, 59
American Ballet as resident
dance company, **1:**64, 65, 68,
74, 279, 297, **2:**160, **4:**28
Ballet Russe de Monte Carlo
performances, **1:**296, 297,
300, 301
Ballets Russes de Monte Carlo
performances, **1:**311–312, 315
Ballets Russes de Serge Diaghilev
performance, **2:**408–409,
6:271

Dance Theatre of Harlem, **2:**335
  Massine's *Le Sacre du Printemps* performance, **4:***318,* 321–322
  Mordkin *Swan Lake* production, **6:***32*
  Sadler's Wells appearances, **1:**149
  See also Metropolitan Opera Ballet
Metropol Theater, East Berlin, **3:**154
Metro Theater Circus, St. Louis, **2:**110
Métru, Nicolas, **4:**234
Metsis, Yiannis, **3:**300
Mettler, Barbara, **1:**421, **3:**445, **4:**212
Metzger, Márta, **3:**418
Meudtner, Sabine, **3:**154
Meunier, Antonine, **1:**347, 348, 384, **4:**688
Meunier, Hipoḷit, **5:**216, 217
Meuniers, Les, **1:**455
Mevlevi Dervish (Shawn dance), **5:***46,* 586
Mevlevi dervishes, **4:***410,* **6:**187, *208,* 209
Mexican Archives of Dance, **4:**166
Mexican Ball Game, **1:**525
Mexican Center for Investigation, Information and Documentation of Dance (CENIDI-Danza, Mexico City), **4:**166, **5:**44
Mexican National Opera, **1:**117
Mexican Tavern, The, **4:**224
Mexico, **4:***382–400*
  dance companies, **4:**395–398, **6:**355
    Ximénez-Vargas Ballet Español, **6:**407–408
  dance research and publication, **4:398–400**
    ethnological, **4:**78
    libraries and museums, **4:**166, **5:**44
  theatrical dance, **4:389–395**
    Limón choreography, **4:**198
    modern dance, **5:**637
    See also specific performers
  traditional dance, **4:383–389**
    concheros, **2:**194
    matachines, **4:**327, 328, **6:**416
    vocal sound, **3:**38, **4:**389
    Zapotec, **2:**535
Mey, Thierry de, **1:**412
Meyberg, Edzard, *as photographer,* **5:**56, 154, 653, 655, 659
Meyen, Henry, **2:**339
Meyer, Baron Adolf de, *as photographer,* **1:**99, 319, **4:**635
Meyer, Hannes, **1:**387, **6:***52*
Meyer, Laverne, **3:**271, **4:**667, **5:**564
Meyer, Marcelle, **4:**657
Meyerbeer, Giacomo, **1:**86, 461, 477, **2:**172, 369, **3:**4, 69, 176, **4:**514, **5:**35, 113, 114, 277
  See also Robert le Diable
Meyerhold, Vsevolod, **1:**85, 244, **2:**72, 183, 191, 420, **3:**20, 196, **5:**10, 267, 268, 438
Meyer-Riehl, Anuschka, **6:***52*
Meygra entrepriza (Arena), **1:**107
Mezentseva, Galina, **2:**471, **4:**285, **5:**462
Mezincescu, Alexa, **5:**386, *386,* 387
M.F., **5:**477
mganga, **2:**212
MGM. *See* Metro-Goldwyn-Mayer
Mhlongo, Ndaba, **6:**288
Miami Ballet, **6:**264, 265
Miami City Ballet, **1:**96, **6:**340–341

Mians, Moses, **5:**256
Miatsakanian, Mark, **1:**122
Michaeli, Katia, **3:**531
Michael Todd's Peep Show (musical), **6:**281
Michaud, J. F., **1:**123
Michaud, Marcel, **2:**466
Michaut, Pierre, **2:**480, **4:**636
Michel, Léon. *See* Saint-Léon, Léon-Michel
Michelet, Louis, **5:**141
Michelson, Bruce, **1:***51*
Michio Ito's Pinwheel Revel, **3:**559
michiyuki, **3:**639
Micolaides, Melisa, **2:**356
Micronesia, 19–20, **4:400–402,** 495, 497
Midas, **1:**322, **2:**421, **3:**20, 62
Middle Ages. *See* medieval dance
Middle East, **4:402–417**
  Arabian Peninsula, **1:**101–102
  Arab music, **4:**487–491
  background and overview, **4:402–413**
  bedouin dance, **1:**401
  biblical dance, **1:**448
  dance classifications, **4:**405–410
  dance research and publication, **4:414–417**
  dance research and publications, libraries and museums, **4:**164
  folk dance sounds, **3:**38
  Islamic dance aesthetics, **1:**18–19
  Kurdish dance, **4:**78–79
  Mesopotamia, **3:**355–357
  zār ceremony, **6:**444–445
  See also North Africa; *specific countries*
Middlesex University, **3:**284
Middleton, Lucille, **6:**262
Middleton, Thomas, **2:**254, **3:**252
Middleton, T. M., **5:**351
Midlands, England, **3:**272–273
Midnight Follies, The (revue), **6:**272, 371
Midnight Frolics (revue), **6:**448
Midnight Masquerade (public ball), **4:**314
Midnight Sun, The. See Soleil de Nuit, Le
Midsummer, **1:**52
Midsummer Day Eve, **2:**12, **4:**436, 450
Midsummer Marriage, The (Tippett), **5:**37
Midsummer Night's Dream, A (ballet), **1:**12, 308, 374, 391
  Ashton production. *See Dream, The*
  Balanchine production, **1:**263, 267, **3:**352, **4:**436, 450, 610, 613, *616*
    Magallanes performance, **4:**246
    McBride performance, **4:**345
    Verdy performance, **6:**328
    Villella performance, **6:**620, **6:**340
  Cohan production, **5:***564*
  Daly production, **2:***452,* **5:**345
  Fokine revision of Petipa's production, **3:**15
  Fuller production, **3:***94*
  Kehlet *demi-caractère* role, **3:**668
  Mingus arrangement of Mendelssohn's score, **4:**429
  Neumeier production, **2:**463, **3:**668, **5:**406, 432, 644
  Paeper production, **5:**58
  Petipa (Marius) production, **4:**429

Poole production, **2:**57, **5:**226, 652
  Rose design, **5:**406
  Scholes production, **4:**625
  Seregi staging, **3:**418
  Spoerli versions, **3:***157,* **5:**681, 683–684, **6:**455
  Wigman choreography, **6:**393
Midsummer Night's Dream, A (Britten opera), **2:**266, **5:**37
Midsummer Night's Dream, A (Shakespeare), **1:**156, 428
  as basis of Ashton's *The Dream,* **2:**445
  dances, **3:**253
  Fokine choreography, **3:**23
  Helpmann acting role, **3:**355
  Messel design, **4:**358
  nō adaptation, **4:**332
  Reinhardt productions, **4:**60, 229, 449, **5:**391, **6:**29
Midsummer's Day dances, **1:**529, 2:8
Midsummer's Eve dances, **5:**211, **6:**36, 37
Mid-West Ballet Workshop, Limerick, **3:**520
Midwives' Day (Bulgaria), **2:**7–8
Mieczyńska, Janina, **5:**217
Miel, Juan C., **5:**174
Mielziner, Jo, **2:**242, 249, **4:**191, **5:**193, 547, **6:***199*
Mien (people), **4:**123
Mierzyńska, Julia, **5:**215
Mies van der Rohe, Ludwig, **1:**385
Miettinen, Jukka, **2:**635
  as photographer, **4:**298, 525, **6:**149, 150
Migawari Zazen, **1:**361, **3:**658
Migdoll, Herbert, **5:**183, 262
  as photographer, **5:**327, **6:***152,* 285
Mighty Aphrodite (film), **5:**573
Migrations, **6:**380
Mijikenda Segeju (people), **2:**418
Mikado, The (dance version), **1:**301
mikagura, **3:**578, 584, 642
Mikhail Gabovich (Gabovich), **5:**483
Mikhailov, Aleksandr, **4:**143
Mikhailov, Mikhail, **2:**422, **3:**327
Mikhailova, Varvara, **5:**452
Mikhailovsky, Mikhail, **4:**247
Mikhailovsky, Valery, **5:**465
Mikhalchenko, Alla, **3:**197, **4:**360, **5:**462
miko, **3:**579, 642
Mila, Lidija, **5:**677
Miladova, Milada, **4:***320*
Milán, Louis de, **4:**505
Milan, Italy, **3:**546, **4:**696, **5:**579
Milanković, Ubavka, **6:**436
Milanović, Vesna, **6:**435
Milberg, Barbara, **4:**450
Milchin, L., **5:**595
Milenoff, Georges, **2:**277
Milenović-Workman, Maja, **6:**437
Miletić, Stjepan, **6:**431
Milezinar, Jo, **2:**244
Milhaud, Darius, **1:**305, 306, 479, **2:**279, 397, 408, **3:**393, 596, **4:417–418,** **5:**60, *164,* 237, 439, 525, 526, **6:**111
  Ballets 1933 collaboration, **3:**73
  ballet scores, **3:**399, **4:**515, 517
  Ballets Suédois collaborations, **1:**327, **2:**399, **3:**72, 393, **4:**418, 516
  Claudel collaboration, **4:**417, **5:**439
  Création du Monde score, **2:**373, **4:**418, 516
  Diaghilev commissions, **4:**515

  Graham commission, **4:**518
  Humphrey scores, **3:**399
  as member of Les Six, **4:**516
  musical idioms, **4:**516
  Nijinska ballets, **4:**634, 635
Milhous, Judith, *as contributor,* **3:**253–257
Mili, Gjon, **5:**178
Militsa, **1:**90, 144, **2:**450, **4:**284, **6:**310
Milk Fund Ball (1933; Chicago), **2:**573
Mill, Natalia, **3:**186
Miller, Amanda, **3:**52, 151, 157, **4:**220
Miller, Ann, **3:***55,* **4:**418–419, **6:**101
Miller, Bebe, **1:**502, **5:**659, **6:**259
Miller, Buffy, **2:**585
Miller, Buzz, **1:**305, **3:**599, *599,* **4:***214*
Miller, Elizabeth, **5:**113, 294, 414
Miller, Glenn, **5:**631, **6:**275
Miller, Henry, **4:**681
Miller, Irvin C., **6:**256
Miller, Laurie, **5:***197*
Miller, Marie. *See* Gardel, Marie
Miller, Marilyn, **3:**22, **4:419–420,** **6:**270, 273, *274,* 371, 448
Miller, Norma, **4:**202, 203
Miller, Patricia, **2:**356, **5:**420, 653–654
Miller, Samuel A., **3:**572
Milliand, Jacqes, **1:**411
Milligan, Jean, **3:**249
Million Dollar Mermaid, The (film), **6:**85
Millions d'Arlequin, Les, **1:**399, 539, **2:**447, 480, **5:**160, 247, 427
  See also Harlequinade
Millman, Bird, **2:**175
Millman, Cynthia R., *as contributor,* **1:**450–451, **4:**201–203, 254–255, 480–481
Millner, Odette, **5:***54*
Milloss, Aurelio, **1:**82, 110, 241, 411, 533, **2:**480, **3:**149, 340, **4:420–422,** **5:***34,* 266, 288
  Budapest Opera Ballet, **3:**415, 416, 418, **4:**420–421
  Creatures of Prometheus revival, **1:**402, **3:**416, **4:**420, *421*
  dell'Ara association, **2:**369
  Don Quixote version, **2:**440
  Italian Fascist-era ballet scene, **3:**550
  Laban Choreographisches Institut training, **4:**92
  Maggio Musicale, **1:**251
  Miraculous Mandarin production, **1:**370, **4:**420
  Rome Opera Ballet, **4:**400, 421
  Scala Ballet, **4:**421, **5:**529
Milloss Collection, **3:**556
Mills, Florence, **2:**25, **4:**113
Mills, Harry, **2:**19
Mills, Stephanie, **6:**284
Mills College, Oakland, California, **1:**420, **2:**285, **3:**364, 369, 387, 402, **4:**418, **6:**248
Milon, Louis, **1:**35, 201, 202, 446, **3:**68, **4:422–423**
  Bigottini association, **1:**451, **4:**422, 423
  Bournonville (August) training, **1:**504, 505
  Bournonville friendship, **1:**503
  Conservatoire de Danse, **3:**81
  Don Quixote libretto, **2:**435, **4:**423
  Gardel (Pierre) association, **3:**118, 119, **4:**422, 423, **5:**91, 92

Milon, Louis, *continued*
  Henry (Louis) rivalry, **3:**358
  Paris Opera Ballet, **1:**455, **3:**68,
    4:422–423, **5:**92
Milon de Crotone, **1:**455
Milwaukee Ballet, **4:**37, **5:**60, 132,
  6:292
Mimart, Novi Sad, **6:**435, 436
Mimashi, **3:**171
Mimasuya Hyōgo (Ichikawa
  Danjūrō I pseud.), **3:**437
mime, **4:423–426**
  antimasque, **4:**307
  Armenia, **1:**121
  Asian dance gestures, **4:**493
  attitude and shawl dance, **1:**199
  Australia, **1:**206
  ballet choreographic purpose,
    3:130
  ballet scenarios, **4:**173, 176,
    5:640, 693
  barriera, torneo, and *battaglia,*
    1:369
  Battaglia (Caroso), **5:**341
  Bournonville tradition,
    1:511–512, **2:**385
  branles, **1:**104
  break dancing, **1:**538
  Cecchetti roles, **2:**82
  character dancing, **2:**107
  Chauviré roles, **2:**114–115
  China, **2:**129–130
  Chinese dance theater, **2:**132
  dance therapy use of, **2:**318
  Danish ballet tradition, **1:**497,
    5:425, 430
  as Didelot emphasis, **2:**413
  Edwards's skill, **2:**477, 478
  Elssler (Fanny) skills, **2:**502,
    503, 504
  French traditional theater, **3:**75,
    4:423–426
  Ghanan storytelling dance, **3:**167
  Grisi's skills, **3:**316
  Helpmann's skills, **3:**354, 355
  Indian *nrtya,* **1:**169, **3:**463
  intermedio, **3:**509
  Italian acting companies, **3:**66
  Italy, **3:**545
  Japanese *gigaku,* **3:**172
  Japanese *kabuki,* **3:**639
  Mata and Hari, **5:**561
  Mérante talents, **4:**353
  mimus, **4:**426–428
  modern dance, **5:**492, 503
  Mordkin dramatic
    characterizations, **4:**459
  Native American dances, **4:**553,
    572, 573
  Papua New Guinea dances, **5:**77
  Paris Opera Ballet, **5:**90
  Petipa's (Marius) use of, **5:**152
  Price family, **5:**250
  Rameau, Jean-Philippe, **5:**307
  Ravel family, **5:**317–319
  Ronzani, Domenico, **5:**403
  Sakharoff modern dance, **5:**503
  Samoa, **5:**510
  Schoop, Ruth, **5:**560
  Scottish folk reels, **3:**245
  Shangan-Tsonga dance, **5:**579
  Shawn's *Labor Symphony,* **5:**586
  Shigeyama Sensaku IV, **5:**591
  Siberian dances, **5:**448
  social dances, **5:**632
  southern African dance, **5:**661,
    662, *662, 663*
  Soviet dramatic ballet, **5:**458,
    6:411, 442
  Spain, **5:**667
  theater design effects on, **6:**155

Tomaszewski, Henryk, **6:**175
travesty, **6:**190
Turkish dance, **6:**211
Valberkh, Ivan, **6:**311
Viennese ballet, **1:**239
Wiesenthal, Grete, **6:**387
See also animal mime dances;
  pantomime; pantomime-
  ballet
Mime (Lawson), **2:**382, **4:**176
mimoplastic art. *See* attitude and
  shawl dance
mimukku (painted characters),
  4:298
Mimunah, **3:**537
mimus, **4:426–428**
Minahasa, Indonesia, **3:**505
Minamoto family, **3:**607
Minangkabau (people), **3:**499, 500
Minardo, Stefania, **5:**401
Minarik, Jan, **1:**389
Minataree (people), **4:***552*
Minatori Valacchi, I, **3:**176, **6:**50
Mind/Body Centering, **4:**17, 20
Mind Is a Muscle, The, **5:**293
mine dances, **5:**643, 661, *663*
Minenkov, Andrei, **3:**432
Miners and Sunlight, **2:**116
Miners' Ballad, **2:**473
Minetti, María, **6:**302
Ming dynasty, **2:**131–132, 144, 219,
  4:76
Minghella, Anthony, **4:**220
Ming Huang, emperor of China,
  2:130
Minguet e Irol, Pablo, **5:**670, *670,*
  676, **6:**124
Mingus, Charlie, **2:**480, **6:**175
Miniatures, **3:**329
Minikin Fair, **6:**111
minimalism
  dance, **4:**596–597
  music, **2:**119–120, **5:**367, 526
  sculpture, **1:**140
Miniño, Josefina, **2:**432
Miniyakan, Les, **2:**33
Minkus, Léon, **1:**9, **2:**298, **4:**146,
  428–431, 5:123, 501, 607,
  690, **6:**116
  Bayadère score, **1:**392, 393,
    4:429, 430
  Delibes collaboration, **2:**367, 368,
    4:514
  Don Quixote score, **2:**57, 435,
    436, 439, 440, 441, **4:**117,
    429, 430, 668
  Fille Mal Gardée score, **2:**594, 596
  musical idioms and methods,
    4:513–514
  Petipa (Marius) association, **5:**85,
    150, 151, *152, 153, 154,* 155,
    158, 159, 160
  Swan Lake, **6:**115
Minkus Pas de Trois, **4:**622
Minnelli, Liza, **2:**619
Minnelli, Vincente, **2:**616, **4:**3
Minnesota Dance Theater, **5:**51,
  6:264
Minns, Al, **4:***201,* 202
Minoan religion, **2:**270, 419
Minor Characters, **2:**355
Minos, king of Crete, **2:**269, 270
Minotaur (mythic), **2:**269, **4:**106
Minotaur, The, **4:**107, 518, **6:**175
Minotaur and Nymph, **6:**412
Minotauros, **1:**32
Minsk ballet school, **1:**408
Minsk Opera and Ballet Theater,
  4:226
Minstrel Show, The, **2:**19–20

minstrelsy, **6:**97–98, 254–255, 316
  cakewalk, **2:**25, **6:**254
  circus antecedents, **2:**174
  jig, **3:**608
minuet *(menuet),* **3:**125, **4:431–433**
  annual collection, **1:**92
  Argentine form, **1:**108
  assembly dancing, **1:**190
  dance manuel descriptions, **6:**124
  Danish treatises, **2:**380, *380,* 381
  England, **3:***255*
  Finland, **2:**630
  French court dance, **1:**344, **2:**238,
    3:63, **4:**508, 510, 511
  Marcel's refinement of, **4:**263
  opéra-ballet and *tragédie lyrique,*
    5:38, 40
  Pecour variation, **5:**129
  popularity as social dance, **4:**511
  Scottish strathspey, **3:**244
  social importance, **4:**508, **6:**237
  Spanish illustration, **5:***670*
Minuit, **1:**304
Minutiae, **2:**290, **5:**314
Minwalla, Panna and Amy, **5:**65
Minz, Alexander, **1:**111, 390,
  2:441, 587
minzoku buyō, **5:**26
Minzoku geino (publication), **3:**591
Miracle, **4:**152, 229, 322
Miracle in the Gorbals, **5:**312, 588
  Bliss score, **1:**462, 463, **3:**356,
    4:516
  Edwards performance, **2:**477
  Franca performance, **3:**62
  Helpmann production,
    3:*355,* 356
Miracle of Bali (film series), **3:**507
Miracolo d'Amore, **1:**462
*Miraculous Bridal Veil, The (The
  Magic Veil),* **1:**91
Miraculous Mandarin, The, **1:**375,
  479, **5:**527
  Bartók score, **1:**370, **5:**529, 569
  Bozsik choreography, **3:**421
  Bruhn performance, **2:**4
  Bulgarian performances, **2:**12
  Descombey production, **2:**389
  Dupuy choreography, **2:**466
  Eck production, **2:**473, 474
  festival presenting fifteen
    versions, **3:**419
  Flindt choreography, **3:**12
  Gadd staging, **3:**100
  Harangozó production, **3:**342,
    415–416, *416,* 419
  International Dance Festival
    prize, **3:**419
  Kudelka choreography, **4:**73, 547
  Lazzini choreography, **4:**134
  Lőrinc staging, **6:**66
  Markó choreography, **4:**266
  Milloss version, **3:**418, **4:**420
  Murdmaa choreography, **4:**478
  Ogoun production, **2:**308, **5:**23
  Parlić production, **5:**401
  Pistoni production, **5:**195–196
  score complexity, **3:**416
  Seregi rechoreography, **3:**417,
    5:569
  symbolic plot, **3:**416
  Ulrich choreography, **6:**229
Mirage Blanc, **4:**115
Mirages, Les, **2:**114, *114,* **3:**73,
  4:185, 517, **5:**96
Miraglia, Vincent, *as photographer,*
  4:358
Miralles, Francisco, **2:**522
Miranda, **6:**73
Miranda, Carmen, **1:**433,
  4:433–434

Miranda, Jésus, **5:**275
Miranda, Regina, **1:**537
Mirandolina, **3:**60, **4:**149, **5:**567,
  6:8, 310, 420
Mirasi (people), **5:**65
Miriam (Old Testament), **1:**20,
  3:526
Mir iskusstva (World of Art), **1:**254,
  318, 319, 422, 437, 487,
  2:406–407, 408, 421, **3:**16,
  196, 197, **4:**56, **5:**372, 456,
  541–542, 642
Mirk, Shonach, **1:**292, 406
Miró, Joan, **1:**135, *136,* 316, 317,
  2:242, 410, **4:**33, 113,
  5:544, 547
Miroglio, Francis, **1:**349
Mirova, Vera, **1:**483, **2:**458
Mirra, o sia La Vendetta di Venere,
  3:176, **5:**528, **6:**338
Mirror, The, **3:**629
Mirror Dance, **2:**483–484
Mirror for Witches, A, **3:**392
"Mirror Image" (skating program),
  6:180
Mirrors, **3:**445
Mirror Walkers, **6:**405
Mirza, **1:**123, **2:**443
Mirza et Lindor, **4:**175
Misa Flamenca, **2:**57
Misanthrope, Le (Molière), **4:**447
Mischievous Students, **3:**341, 415,
  5:402
*Mise en scène du drame Wagnérian,
  La* (Appia), **1:**97
Misguided, **3:**312
Mishima Yukio, **3:**363, 657, **4:**332,
  5:592
Mishkin, *as photographer,* **3:**22,
  5:120
Mishnah, **3:**526
Mišić, Ljiljana, **6:**436
Misión Konrad, **1:**49
Miskocl National Theater, **3:**419
Miskovitch, Milorad, **1:**290, 305,
  404, **2:**111, 112, **4:**270,
  434–435
  Ballet des Étoiles de Paris, **3:**74
  Chauviré dance partnership,
    2:114
  International Ballet, **3:**512
Misra, Shanta Rati, **5:**330–331
Miss 1917 (revue), **1:**482, **2:**80, **5:**58
Missa Brevis in Tempore Belli,
  4:199, **6:**43
Missa Luba, **2:**358
Miss Carter Wore Pink, **4:**668
Miss Hook of Holland (musical),
  5:694
"Missing" (skating program),
  6:*179,* 180
Mission Indians, **4:**568
Mission to Moscow (film), **2:**108
Mississippi Gambler (film), **6:**327
Miss Julie, **3:**75, **4:**65
  Cullberg production, **1:**70, *73,*
    2:3, 283, 284, 561, **3:**437,
    4:677, **5:**341, 406, *406,* 599,
    6:*41,* 328
  Lander (Toni) performance,
    4:120
  MacMillan production, **4:**242
  Marks performance, **4:**271
  Rosen performance, **5:**406, *406*
  in Royal Danish Ballet repertory,
    5:431
  Simone performance, **5:**599
  television production, **6:**135
Miss Liberty (musical), **5:**361

Misslitz, Walter Paul, **4:**690–691
Miss Loie Fuller (Toulouse-Latrec),
     6:181
Miss Mǎriuţze, **5:**387
Miss Natasia, **2:**343
"Mistake Waltz" (The Concert),
     5:358
Mistinguett, **1:**95, **3:**87, **4:**523, *523*,
     675, **5:**176
Mistress into Maid, **1:**144, **5:**567,
     6:442
misura, **1:**351, 352
Miszczyk, Stanisław, **4:**435, **5:**219
Mitchell, A. Cosmo, **4:**164
Mitchell, Arthur, **1:***12, 30*, 266, 267,
     2:334, 458, **4:436–437, 616,**
     620, **6:**138, 277
Mitchell, David, **4:**180
Mitchell, Jack, **5:**183
     as photographer, **1:**542, **6:**107,
          109, 137, 364
Mitchell, James, **2:**109, 374
Mitchell, Julian, **2:**572, **6:**268, 269,
     270, 271, 272, 273, 281,
     447–448
Mitchell, Steven, **4:**255
Mitsu Men Komori, **3:**593
Mitsuyama, **3:**653
mitsvah dances, **3:**527, 536,
     602, 603
Mitsvah Tanz, **3:**527
Mittanian dance, **4:**357
Mitterhuber, Alois, **1:**241
Mittertreiner, Johan, **1:**290
Mit Theaterliv (Bournonville),
     1:503, 505, 506, 511
Mitysková, Mimi, **5:**393
Mix Detail, **2:**119
mixed-media theater. *See*
     multimedia
Miyabi Ichikawa, *as contributor*,
     3:590–591
Miyagi, **5:***26*
Miyagi Prefecture, Japan,
     3:586–587, 587
Miyagi Troupe, **5:**27
Miyake family, **4:**85
Miyako Odori, Kyoto, **3:**126
Miya Misako, **5:**33
Miyoshi Shōraku, **3:**637
Mjøen, Reidar, **4:**682
Mlada, **2:**82, **4:**68, 430, **5:**37, 158
Mladova, Milada, **1:**296, 302,
     5:369
Mlakar, Pia and Pino, **1:**390, **4:**32,
     437, 6:438
     "Ballet on the Slovene Stage,"
          6:438
     as contributors, **3:**63–64,
          380–381, **5:**676–677,
          6:431–433
     Laban as resident notator, **4:**96
     Laban Choreographisches
          Institut training, **4:**92
     Yugoslavian ballet, **6:**432, 437
     Zurich Ballet directorship, **4:**437,
          6:454
Mlakar, Veronika, **1:**305, **3:**74,
     4:435, 437, **5:**193, 676
Mlotkovsky, L. I., **6:**224
Mnatsankanian, M., **4:**132
Mnester, **5:**73
Mniszchówna, Urszula, **5:**220
M.O., **1:**542
Moana (film), **2:**601
Mobiles and Cycles, **1:**211
mock-battle dances. *See* armed
     dances; *moresca*
Moderna Dansteatern, Stockholm,
     1:145, **6:**45

modern dance. *See Ausdruckstanz;*
     avant-garde; genres of
     Western theatrical dance;
     modern dance technique;
     postmodern dance; *specific
     companies, countries, dancers,
     and works*
Modern Dance, The (Martin),
     6:296, 300
Modern Dance Association of
     Korea, **4:**51
*Modern Dance Forms in Relation to
     the Other Modern Arts*
     (Horst), **3:**385
Modern Dance Holiday Courses,
     4:94
modern dance technique,
     3:130–131, **4:437–443**
     aesthetics, **1:**25
     Alston, Richard, **3:**272
     Bennington School, **1:420–422,**
          4:438
     Bodenwieser, Gertrud, **1:**466–468
     Chladek, Rosalia, **2:**153, 154–155
     costume, **2:**245–246,
          245–248, *247*
     Cunningham, Merce, **2:**285, 289,
          3:274, **4:**440, **441**
     dance and movement therapy,
          2:316
     Denishawn classes, **5:**496
     Duncan, Isadora, **2:**455
     Dunham's movement sources,
          2:459
     footwear, **3:**46, 47
     Fuller as forerunner, **3:**93,
          94–95, 96
     Graham, Martha, **3:**213–214, 220,
          4:437, 438, **439**, 442
     Gripenberg style, **3:**313
     Hawkins, Erick, **4:441**
     Holm, Hanya, **3:**369, 370,
          4:440–441
     Horton, Lester, **1:**212, **4:441–442**
     Humphrey, Doris, **3:**398, 399,
          4:437, **439–440**, **6:**367, 377
     Hungary, **3:**420–421
     improvisational activity,
          3:445–446, **4:**442
     improvised musical
          accompaniment, **1:**6
     jazz dance, **3:**598–599, 600
     Limón, José, **4:**197, 198, 440, 442
     London Contemporary Dance
          Theatre, **4:**220, 221
     Marsicano, Merle, **4:**272
     Netherlands, **2:**469
     New Dance Group curriculum,
          4:604
     Nikolais, Alwin, **4:**440, 442
     Orientalism, **5:**45–46
     percussion accompaniment, **1:**6,
          4:518, 519
     performance spaces, **6:**162–164,
          162, 163, 192
     photographic studies, **5:**175,
          185, 187
     practice clothes worn, **5:**242–243
     St. Denis early innovations, **5:**491
     spatial patterns, **2:**287
     tap dance, **6:**102
     teaching programs, **2:**575–576,
          4:94
     Weidman, Charles, **4:**437, 438,
          439–440, **6:**376
     Züllig, Hans, **6:**453
Modern Dance, The (Martin), **4:**273
*Modern Dance Tutor: or, Society
     Dancing, The* (Davis), **2:**47
*Modern Dance: Theory and Practice,
     The* (Ou Jian-ping), **2:**149

Modern Educational Dance
     (Laban), **4:**94, 100, 102
Modern English Ballet (Hall), **3:**282
Modern Grace (Gillray), **2:**71
modernism, **1:**99, 323, **2:**408, 409,
     6:243, 244
     Brazilian dance, **1:**534
     dance aesthetics, **1:**24
     Duncan concept, **2:**457
     Nijinsky kinship, **4:**647, 648
Modern Jazz: Variants, **4:**519
Modern Jazz Quartet, **4:**519
Modern Music (journal), **2:**375,
     6:300
Modest Mussorgsky Theater of
     Opera and Ballet. *See* Maly
     Theater Ballet
Modo de Andar por la Vida, Un,
     6:324
Modori Kago, **3:**593
Mods and Rockers, **2:**350
Mohanty, Kum Kum, **5:**23
Mohave (people), **4:**566
Mohicans, Les, **1:**9, **3:**5
mōhiniāṭṭam, **1:**170, **3:**457, *460*,
     468, 508, **4:**443, **5:***309*
Mohiyuddin, Zia, **5:**597
mohlam, **4:**123
mohobelo, **5:**646, *646*
Mohr, Matthew, **5:**17
Mohr von Venedig, Der, **1:**241, **3:**133
moieties, **4:**557, 572
Moïse, **4:**418
Moiseyev, Igor, **1:**233, 539, **2:**596,
     4:443–446, 446, **5:**205, 473
     Bolshoi Ballet, **1:**490, 492,
          4:443–444
     Kharkov ballet company, **6:**225
     Lebanese folkloric dance, **4:**489
     Moscow State Theater of
          Classical Ballet, **5:**467
     State Ensemble of Folk Dance,
          4:444, **5:**481
     See also Moiseyev Dance
          Company
Moiseyev, Mikhail, **3:**665,
     5:470, 471
Moiseyeva, Irina, **3:**432
Moiseyeva, Olga
     Legend of Love performance,
          4:144
     Maryinsky Ballet, **4:**284
     Royal Winnipeg Ballet guest
          performance, **5:**435
Moiseyev Dance Company, **2:**308,
     423, 496, 559, **4:**445, *445*,
     5:473, *474*, **6:**249
Moi zapiski (Kriger), **4:**62
Moja ljuba Slovenija (Gresserov-
     Golovin), **6:**438
Mokuren (Mauggallena), **1:**496
molapo, **5:***646*
Molas, Nicholas de, **6:**198
Molasso, Giovanni, **6:**319
Molchanov, Konstantin, **3:**418
Moldavia (Romania),
     5:379–380, 381
Moldobasanov, Kalyi, **4:**87, 584,
     5:472
Moldova, **4:**78, **446–447**
Moldovan Opera and Ballet
     Theater, **4:**446–447
Molé, Marijan, **4:**416
Molière, **1:**298, 403, 424, **2:**202,
     4:447–448, **5:**38, 270
     ballet de collège as influence,
          1:283, **4:**447
     ballet du cour, **1:**288, **4:**188, 447

     Beauchamps association, **1:**396,
          4:447
     Béjart production, **1:**406
     comédie-ballet, **1:**288, **3:**66, **4:**234,
          447, **6:**267
     commedia dell'arte reciprocal
          influences, **2:**188, 191
     Don Juan drama, **2:**433
     Gissey costume designs, **3:**184
     Lully collaboration, **4:**234
     matachins use, **4:**326
Molière Imaginaire, Le (Béjart
     ballet), **1:**292, 406, 407,
     4:447
Molin, Ya'aqov ha-Levi, **3:**527, 603
Molina, Antonia, **1:**480
Molina, Joseph, **1:**480
Molina, Ricardo, **3:**6
Molina, Tirso de, **2:**433
Molino Room, The, **1:**76
Mollajoli, Gustavo, **1:**111
Møller, Carl Christian, **1:**516
Møller, Grete and Mette, **4:**677
Mollerup, Mette, **1:***508*
Mollica, Fabrio, **3:**558
Mollier, Louis de, **1:**286, 287
Molloy, Felicity, **4:**627
molly dancing, **3:**242, **4:**474
Molnár, István, **1:**370, **3:**413,
     422–423, **4:448**
Molnár, Lajos, **1:**370
Molodov, Aleksandr, **4:**208
mølya, **5:**84
Mombasa, **2:**212
Môme Fromage, La, **1:**95
Moment, **5:**316
Moment in Love, A (film dance),
     2:604
*Moment of Truth, The: Ceremony
     and Ritual for F. G. Lorca*,
     4:266
Momentos Hostiles, **6:**324
Moment Rustica, **3:**212
Moments, **5:**8
Momentum, **6:**88, *366*
Momijigari, **1:**361, **2:**215, **5:**496
Momix, **6:**57
mommerie (mummery),
     4:448–449, 462
     Ireland, **3:**33
     masques, **4:**312, 313
Mompou, Federico, **4:**117
Momus (deity), **4:**448
Monaco
     English National Ballet royal
          performance, **2:**509, 510
     Grand Ballet du Marquis de
          Cuevas, **3:**224–225
     See also Ballet Russe de Monte
          Carol; Ballets Russes de
          Monte Carlo
Monahan, James, **3:**285
Monakhov, Aleksandr, **3:**196
Monakhov, A. M., **1:**90
Monaldi, Gino, **2:**209
     on Beretta, **1:**427
Monarchy, Monarchy, **3:**330
monastic dances, Tibet, **6:**166,
     167–168
Mona-Tymga troupe, **2:**176
Moncada, Antonio, **4:***398*
Moncado, Philippines, **2:**231
Moncion, Francisco, **1:**28, *28*,
     2:438, **4:449–450**
     Emeralds pas de deux, **4:**450, 612
     Firebird performance, **3:**2
     Four Temperaments performance,
          3:57
     New York City Ballet roles,
          4:609, 619

Moncion, Francisco, *continued*
  Prodigal Son performance, **4**:450, *610*, 619, **5**:265
  Robbins ballets, **5**:361
Mönckeberg-Kollmar, Vilma, **4**:476
Moncrieff, William, **3**:183
Moncrieffe, Barry, **3**:574
Monde, Le (French newspaper), **3**:85
Monde Reiovi, Le, **6**:38
Mondo Festiggiante, Il, **3**:381
Mondonville, Cassanea de, **1**:483
Mondonville, Jean-Joseph, **2**:365, 366, **3**:117
Mondrian, Piet, **1**:132
Monés i Mestre, Nèlida, *as contributor*, **3**:126–127, **5**:675–676
Monet, Claude, **1**:129
Money, Keith, **5**:187
  as photographer, **3**:433
Mongolia, **2**:*221*
Mongols (people), **2**:131, 139, 141
Mongut, Rama IV, king of Siam, **4**:111
Monin, Janine, **1**:404
Moniteur universel, Le (Parisian newspaper), **3**:122
Moniuszko, Stanisław, **2**:368, **5**:75, 216, **6**:207, 365
Monja Gitana, La, **6**:408
Monk, Meredith, **1**:143, 245, *245*, **2**:462, **4**:450–452
  dance aesthetics, **1**:25
  eurhythmics, **3**:597
  films, **2**:609, **4**:451
  Judith Dance Theater, **3**:634
  Schönberg as influence, **5**:559
  students, **4**:53
  Vessel, **5**:549–550
Monkey (dance), **1**:78, **5**:630, **6**:257, 263
Monkey and His Shadow, **4**:595
monkey army (Bali), **6**:369–370
"Monkey Dance" (*kécak*), **1**:176, **3**:471, 483–485, *483*, **4**:494
Monkey Dances, The (Cunningham), **2**:289
Monkey Dramas, **2**:142
Monkey King, The, **2**:*133*
Monk's Dance (*sungmu*), **2**:223, *223*, **4**:140, 141
Monnaie. *See* Théâtre Royal de la Monnaie, Brussels
monomane (aesthetic concept), **4**:295, 654, 655
Monosanhchetana, **2**:30
Monotones, **1**:156, 157, **2**:444, **4**:117, 452, *452*, 544, *544*, **5**:104, 417, 526, **6**:380
Monotony Whirl, **6**:390–391, 391, 394
Monplaisir, Hippolyte and Adèle, **1**:427, **2**:587, **4**:452–456
Monroe, Marilyn, **2**:184, 615, **6**:281
Monsieur de Pourceaugnac, **1**:288, **2**:202, **4**:234, 326, 447, **5**:147
Monsieur Deschalumeaux, **5**:147
"Monsieur Marcelle of Paris" (pseud.), **1**:92
Monsieur Molinet, or A Night of Adventures, **5**:319
Monsigny, Pierre-Alexandre, **5**:90, 198
Montagnon, Patrice, **6**:10
Montague, Sarah, *as contributor*, **2**:297–299, **5**:131–132
Montague, Stephen, **2**:120
Montalban, Ricardo, **2**:108, *251*
Montalvo, Beaucaire, **1**:39
Montanara, Carlo, **4**:258

Montansier, Marguerite Brunet, **2**:413, **6**:158
Monte, Elisa, **1**:55, 59, **3**:220, 578
Monteaux, Pierre, **1**:93
Monte Carlo, Monaco. *See* Ballet Russe de Monte Carlo; Ballets Russes de Monte Carlo; Ballets Russes de Serge Diaghilev
Monte Carlo Opera Ballet, **1**:251, 295, **2**:342
Monte Carlo Russian Ballet. *See* Ballets Russes de Monte Carlo
Montéclair, Michel Pignolet de, **5**:306
Monte Cristo, **3**:138
Montefiascone codex, **3**:554
Monteleone, José Domingo. *See* Avellaneda, Pepito
Montenegro. *See* Yugoslavia
Montepulciano Festival, **3**:51
Monterey Ballet, **3**:306–307
Monterossi, Giuseppe, **4**:588
Montes, Henry, **2**:*607*
Montesardo, Girolamo, **2**:98
Montessu, François, **2**:389
Montessu, Julia de Varennes, **5**:92
Montessu, Pauline, **1**:202, 455, **2**:390, 596, **4**:138, **5**:92, 134, 640, **6**:216
Monteverdi, Claudio, **1**:52, 353, **2**:76, 455, **3**:51, 52, 109, 418, **6**:66
  dramatic ballets, **3**:544, **5**:505–506
  galliard rhythm use, **4**:504
  Orpheus as opera subject, **4**:581, **6**:359
Monte Verità, Switzerland, **1**:203, **4**:89
Montevideo Chamber Ballet. *See* Ballet de Cámara de Montevideo
Montevideo, Uruguay, **6**:301, 302
Montez, Lola, **1**:205, **2**:69, **5**:175, *175*, 615
Montezuma, ou La Conquête du Mexique, **1**:88
Montgomery, Frank, **6**:257
Montgomery, Lokalia, **3**:396
Montgomery and Stone, **6**:319
Montgomery Variations, **1**:395
Month in the Country, A (Ashton ballet), **1**:157, **2**:244, **3**:236, **4**:117, 248, **456–457**
Month in the Country, A (Turgenev play), **1**:157, **2**:421, **4**:456
Monticelli, Genoveva, **5**:232
Monticello College Foundation, **6**:266
Monticini, Antonio, **1**:499
Monticini, Giovanni, **2**:208
Montjoie, Louis, **2**:390, **5**:640
Montoya, Carlos, **1**:117
Montoya, Pepe, **6**:301
Montpensier, Mademoiselle de, **4**:234
Montplaisir Ballet, **5**:318, **6**:237
Montreal, Canada, **2**:35, 36, 39–41, 42–43, 44, 45, 46, 47, 49, 150–151, 152
  See also Grands Ballets Canadiens, Les
Montreal Theatre Ballet, **4**:237
Montresor, Beni, **2**:124, **5**:401, **6**:*201*
Mon Truc en Plumes (revue), **3**:601, **5**:163
Montsoe, Vincent Sekwati, **5**:660
Monty, Paul, **4**:416

Monument for a Dead Boy (*Monument voor een Gestorven Jongen*), **2**:347, **3**:343, **5**:431, 555
Monumentum pro Gesualdo, **4**:613, 617, 618
Monvel, Boutet de, **6**:39
Monvel, Jacques-Marie, **6**:337
Mooch (dance), **5**:634, **6**:255
Mooche, The, **1**:58, *58*
Moods, **4**:273
Moody, Dwight, **5**:491
Moog synthesizer, **4**:650
Moonbine, **6**:110, 165
Moongates III, **2**:606
Moon Il-chi, **4**:54
Moon Is Quicksilver, The, **6**:145
Moon over Miami (film), **2**:*184*, 615, 617
Moon Reindeer, **2**:283, **3**:373, **4**:120, **5**:431, 553
Moonshine, **2**:1
Moon Skate (ice ballet), **2**:584
Moonsong, **4**:120
Mooré (people), **4**:290
Moore, Bonnie, **2**:356
Moore, Charles, **1**:215, **2**:458, **6**:258
Moore, Eloise, **2**:580
Moore, Elvi, **6**:367
Moore, Gene, **4**:482
Moore, Geoff, **3**:272
Moore, Hannah, **1**:279
Moore, Henry, **5**:363
Moore, John F., **1**:79
Moore, Kathleen, **1**:77
Moore, Lillian, **1**:124, **2**:329–330, 387, **4**:28, **457–458**, **6**:69, 85, 129
  American dance historical studies, **6**:296, 298
  archival materials, **4**:167
  British dance historical articles, **5**:351
  on Camargo's shoes, **3**:46
  on Monplaisirs in North America, **4**:455
  on nineteenth-century ballet in United States, **6**:233, 237
Moore, Mary, **1**:216
Moore, Peter, **5**:187
  as photographer, **1**:243, 244, **3**:634, **6**:248
Moore, Robert, **1**:419
Moore, Thomas, **5**:141
Moorish dancing. *See moresca*; Morris dance
Moormann, Lucie, **3**:78
Moor of Venice, The, **1**:436, 456, **3**:318, 340, 418
Moors, **1**:527, **4**:664–665
"Moors and Christians." *See* "Moros y Cristianos"
Moor's Pavane, The, **1**:72, 80, **2**:4, 423, 514, 586, **3**:391, **4**:458
  award, **4**:200
  Koner performance, **4**:39, *199*, 458, *458*
  Kronstam performance, **4**:65
  Lander (Toni) performance, **4**:120
  Marks performance, **4**:271
  premiere performance, **4**:198, *199*
  Royal Danish Ballet repertory, **5**:432
  Royal Swedish Ballet repertory, **6**:43
Moragas, Ricard, **5**:673
Morales, Estrella, **1**:524
Morales, Mil, **2**:20
Morales, Paul, **5**:172

Moralia: Table Talk, **1**:20
moran (warriors), **5**:509
Moravec-Alberti, Vojtěch, **2**:306
Moravia, **2**:100, 101, **6**:*234*
Moravski, Roman, **5**:384
Morbihan (France), **3**:63
Morca, Teo, **3**:11
Morcom, James Stewart, **2**:420
Mordente, Tony, **5**:358
Mordkin, Michael (son), **4**:460
Mordkin, Mikhail, **1**:393, 518, **2**:19, 436, **3**:16, **4**:459–460, **5**:119, 122–123, **6**:171, 348
  All-Star Imperial Russian Ballet, **4**:223, 459
  American Ballet Theatre origins, **1**:65, **4**:460
  ballet school in United States, **6**:291
  Bolshoi Ballet, **4**:459, 460, **5**:456
  Chase (Lucia) association, **2**:112
  dramatic interpretation, **4**:459
  Fille Mal Gardée, La, **2**:597, **4**:459, **5**:391
  Geltser association, **3**:128
  Goleizovsky as librettist, **3**:193
  Gorsky association, **1**:488, **3**:204, 207, **4**:459
  Kiev ballet productions, **6**:225
  Metropolitan Opera House performance, **4**:382, 459, **6**:243, 270
  Pavlova touring partnership, **4**:382, 459, 522, **6**:243, 270
  Salammbô, **5**:454
  students, **2**:341, 426, **4**:136, 272, **5**:636
  Swan Lake production, **6**:32
  Valse Caprice, **3**:*263*
Mordkin Ballet Company, **1**:518, **2**:112, 341, **4**:460, **5**:391
  as Ballet Theatre basis, **1**:65, **4**:460
Moreau, Jacqueline, **1**:306
Moreau de Saint Méry, M. L., **2**:430, **3**:334
Moreau-Desproux, Pierre-Louis, **6**:157
Moreira, Leal, **5**:*231*
Morel, Horace, **3**:66
Moreland, Barry, **1**:211, 213, **2**:512–513, **4**:218, 219, **5**:266
Morell, Paco, **5**:654
Morelli, Cosimo, **1**:484, **5**:215, 452
Morelli, Francesco, **1**:484, **5**:452
morenos, **2**:121
moresca, **1**:104, 369, 527, **2**:74, **3**:542, **4**:460–463
  costume, **2**:235, **4**:461, *461*, 462
  Death and the Devil association, **2**:332
  folia linkage, **3**:29
  guild dances, **3**:325
  intermedio, **3**:509, 510, 542
  masks and face painting, **4**:303, 449
  matachins, **4**:326
  morisca, **1**:118, **4**:78, 386
  Portugal, **5**:228
  Renaissance conventions, **5**:337, 341
  Spain, **5**:667–668
  stick dance, **2**:555
  Yugoslav form, **6**:429
  See also Morris dance
Moresca quarta deta la Bergamasca, **1**:428
Moresi, Guglielmo, **5**:234
Moreton, Ursula, **4**:463, **5**:293, 411

Morgan, Barbara, **5:**175, 183, *184*, 185
  as photographer, **2:**285, 313, **3:**211, 212, 213, 214, 370, 371, 400, 403, **4:**303, 440, 660, **5:**253, 254, 638, **6:**246, 376
Morgan, Lady, **2:**80
Morgan, Lewis Henry, **4:**574
Morgan, Mary Rice, **4:**168
Morgan, Willard, **5:**185
Morgan Memorial Library, Hartford, **1:**63
Mori, Elisabetta, **3:**557
Mori, Mademoiselle, **2:**521
Morianoff, Adam, **3:**300
Moriarty, Joan Denise, **3:**518, 519, 520
Moricone, Massimo, **4:**668
Morin, Jean-Louis, **2:**605
Morin, Pierre, **6:**130, 131, 132
morisca. See moresca
Mori Shigeya, **2:**18
Morishita, Yoko, **1:**292, **3:**589, *589*
morisque. See moresca
Morita Kan'ya XI, **1:**361
Morita Kan'ya XII, **1:**361, 362
Morita Kan'ya XIII, **1:**362
Morita Kan'ya XIV, **1:**362, **3:**439
Morita Toshirō, as photographer, **3:**653, **4:**31, 40, 653, **6:**229
Moritsuna Jinya, **3:**440, **4:**535
Mørk, Ebbe, as contributor, **1:**539, **4:**125–126, 631–632, **6:**349
mørl, **5:**84
Morlacchi, Giuseppina, **4:463–464,** **5:**404, **6:**237, *237*, 242, 290
Morlaye, Guillaume, **3:**376, **4:**505
morlbo pipi, **5:**80
Morley, Christopher, **2:**372
Morley, Thomas, **4:**315, 505, **5:**111
Mormonism, **2:**169
Morning: Dance of the Nymphs, A (Corot), **1:**127
Morning in the Camp, **5:**569
Morning Prayer, **3:**529
Morocco, **4:**408–409, 411–412, **464–469,** 666
  Berber dance, **4:**407–408, *407*, 465–469, 490, 666
  Jewish ethnic dance, **3:**537
  shikhat entertainers, **4:**468, 664, 665
  Sufi dance, **3:**525, **4:**490
  transvestite performers, **4:**665
Moroni, David, **3:**344, **5:**436–437
moros (Philippine Muslims), **5:**167, 168
Morosco, Oliver, **3:**559
Morosini, Livio, **1:**499
Morosoff, Serge, **3:**296
Morosova, Olga, **1:**309, 315
Moross, Jerome, **1:**421, **5:**59, 60
"Moros y Cristianos," **3:**319, **4:***384*, 386, 460–461, 473, **5:**667–668
morphokines, **4:**366–367, 368
Morrice, Norman, **1:**213, 394, **2:**186, 201, 444, **4:469–470,** **6:**146
  Rambert Ballet, **3:**271–272, **4:**469, **5:**301, 302, *302*
  Royal Ballet directorship, **3:**267–268, **4:**469–470, **5:**418
Morris, Lenwood, **2:**458, **6:**259
Morris, Margaret, **3:**271
Morris, Mark, **1:**25, **4:470–472,** **5:**16, 329, 514, **6:**133, 251
  American Ballet Theatre, **1:**76, 373
  American Dance Festival, **1:**80

Batsheva Dance Company choreography, **3:**532
Boston Ballet choreography, **1:**502
Grands Ballets Canadiens choreography, **3:**234
Hard Nut (Nutcracker version), **4:**471, **5:**16
improvisation, **3:**447, 448
Pièces en Concert, **6:***251*
Théâtre Royal de la Monnaie, **1:**411
White Oak Dance Project, **1:**373, **3:**448
  See also Mark Morris Dance Group
Morris, Marnee, **2:**606, **4:**618
Morris, Monica, **2:**526
Morris, Robert, **1:**139, 140, **2:**605, **3:**336, 635
Canfield, **2:**53, 54, 292, **3:**620
Morris, Simone. See Forti, Simone
Morris Book, The (Sharp), **3:**238
Morris dance, **3:**240, 241–242, *241*, **4:473–475,** **5:**582
  bells, **4:**461, 473, *474*
  clogging variant, **2:**179
  costume, **3:**33, 250, **4:**461, 473, *474*, 474
  country dance similarities, **2:**255
  English revival, **3:**34, 241–242
  as English social dance, **4:**462
  etymology, **4:**473
  Fool's solo, **4:**462, 474
  galliard footwork, **3:**109
  handkerchiefs, **3:**241, **4:**461, 473, *474*
  jig, **3:**607, **5:**695
  masque link, **4:**313
  matachins link, **4:**326
  moresca versus, **1:**118
  Scotland, **3:**249
  Wales, **3:**250
Morrison, Christopher, **2:**566
Morrison, Helen, **5:**589
Morrison, James E., **2:**592
  as contributor, **3:**607–608, **5:**333–334
Morrison, Jim, **1:**58–59
Morrison, Toni, **3:**621
Morrow, Carl, **6:***56*
Morskaya, Maria, **1:**430
Morskoï Rasbonick, **1:**10
Mort de'Arlequin, La, **6:**48
Mort d'Hercule, La, **6:**331
Mort d'Orphée, La, **3:**426
Mort du Cygne, La. See Dying Swan, The
Mort du Cygne, La (film), **5:**606
Morte di Cleopatra, La, **4:**174
Morte di Masniello, La, **4:**258
Morte di Procotieff, La, **5:**403
Morte du Capitaine Cook, La, **1:**123, 124
Mortimer, John, **5:**564
Morton, Edward, **2:**71, **3:***222*, **5:***258*
Morton, James, **2:**176
Morton, Jelly Roll, **5:**637
Morton, Lawrence, **6:**4
Morton, Thomas, **6:**231
Morton, Ursula, **3:**268
Mosa, Noëlle de, **4:**590
Moschen, Michael, **2:**609
Moscow Art Ballet. See Stanislavsky and Nemirovich-Danchenko Musical Theater
Moscow Art Theater, **1:**424, 487, **2:**421, **3:**186, 204, **4:**459, **5:**456, 476, 541

Moscow Ballet School, **3:**99, 197, **5:**480, **6:**106
Moscow Center of Musical Movement, **5:**478
Moscow Chamber Ballet, **1:**28, 489, **3:**193
Moscow Choreographic Institute, **1:**83, **2:**11
Moscow Classical Ballet. See Moscow State Theater of Classical Ballet
Moscow Conservatory, **4:**429
Moscow Free Theater, **4:**459
Moscow Ice Revue, **4:**132
Moscow Imperial Theatrical School. See Moscow State Theater of Classical Ballet
Moscow Institute for the History of the Arts, **5:**480, 642
Moscow Operetta Theater, **4:**133
Moscow Orphanage, **5:**452, 480
Moscow Renaissance Ballet, **5:**474
Moscow School of Choreography, **4:**132, 358, 359, **6:**420, 442
Moscow State Academy of Art Science (GAKhN), **5:**477–478
Moscow State Theater of Classical Ballet, **1:**539, **4:**445, **5:**461, 464, **467,** 480
  Lacotte *Swiss Milkmaid* reconstruction, **6:**51
  Maximova performances, **4:**335, 336
Moscow Theater School, **1:**477, **2:**181
Mosè in Egitto (Rossini), **1:**461, **4:**657, **5:**36
Moser, Kolo, **1:**131
Moses (Rossini). See Mosé in Egitto
Mose's Dream, **5:**616
Moses und Aron (Schoenberg), **1:**436, **2:**120, **3:**393, **5:**37, **6:**359
Mosheh ben Maimon. See Maimonides
Mosheh ben Naḥman. See Nahmanides
moshing. See slam dancing
Mosolov, Aleksandr, **4:**134
Mosolova, Vera, **4:**443
Moss, Carlton, **2:**581, *581*
Moss, David, **3:**446, **5:**128, *128*
Mossanen, Moze, **6:**133
Mossolov, Alexandre, **1:**483
Mostel, Zero, **6:**284
Moszkowski, Moritz, **3:**508, 511
Moszkowski Waltz, **6:**8, *8*, 310
mot (Korean aesthetic), **4:**47
motalochka step, **5:**445
Mot Ballade, **4:**675, 676
Moteur et les bases scientifiques du travail professionel (Amar), **4:**15
Mother Ann. See Lee, Ann
"Mother Ginger and Her Children" *(The Nutcracker)*, **3:**565
Mother Goose Suite (Ravel), **1:**478
Mother of Korea, **2:**155
Mother of Three Sons, **3:**621
Mothers, Daughters, and Other Women, **5:**521
Mother's Field, **4:**87, 584, **5:**462, 472
Mother's Tears, **6:**384
motion pictures. See film and video; film musicals
motion study, **4:**94
Motive Power, **1:**524
Motley, **2:**242, **3:**354
Motley, Polly, **5:**128

Motographia (Chiesa), **4:**688
Motomasa, **4:**42, **6:**446
Motoshige (On'ami), **4:**42
Motown Records, **5:**632, 633
Motown Return to the Apollo (television program), **3:**366
Motta, Pietro della Levastori, **1:**236
Motta, Sonia, **1:**536
Motte, Claire, **1:**461, **5:**96, 97
Motte-Fouqué, Friedrich de La, **5:**141
Mottl, Felix, **2:**254
Motto, Francesco, **2:**435
Mo-tzu (Mozi), **1:**183, **2:**148
Mouche d'Or, La (Aenea), **1:**428
Moulid, Al-, **2:**497
Moulids of Egypt, The (McPherson), **4:**416
Moulin, Geneviève, **1:**313, 315, **3:**73
Moulin, Jane Freeman, **4:**628–629
  as contributor, **6:**77–79
Moulinet Elegancies of Quadrille Dancing (Cruikshank), **2:**70
Moulin Rouge, Paris, **2:**53, 249, *249*, **4:**523
Moulton, Charles, **1:**142, **2:**609, **3:**617, **5:**24
Moulton, Ethel, **3:**397
Moulton, Robert D., as contributor, **5:**246–247, 289–290
Moulton, William, **1:**7
Mounier, Mathilde, **2:**576
Mounsey, Yvonne, **4:**610, 616, 617, **5:**52, 54, 265, 651, 653
Mountain Dance and Folk Festival, North Carolina, **2:**180
Mountain Girl, The, **1:**34, **4:**37, 285
Mountain Goblin, The, **3:**380
Mountain Hut, or Twenty Years, The, **1:**510, 511, 515–516, **5:**251
Mountain Trainers, **3:**646
Mountain Way, **4:**578
Mourão, Noemia, **4:***421*
Mouret, Iris, **6:**302
Mouret, Jean-Joseph, **2:**465, **4:**122, **475,** **5:**88, 504
mourisca. See moresca
"Mourner's Bench" *(Southern Landscape)*, **1:**395
Mourner's Bench, **2:**358
Mourning Ceremonial, **6:**88
mourning rites, **4:**568
Mousetrap, The (pantomime), **5:**69
Moussoux, Nicole, **1:**412
Mouth to Tail: The Dance World of Hong Sin-cha (Hong), **3:**373
Mouvement Perpetuel, **2:**397
Mouzaki, Rozanna, **3:**303
*Movement, 1:**32
Movement and Metaphor (Kirstein), **4:**27, 29
movement choir, **3:**147, **4:**89, 91, 92, 93, 96, 103, **475–477,** Wigman choreography, **6:**393
Movement Company (Bewegingsgroep) Bart Stuyf, **4:**594, 595
movement efficiency, **4:**15, 97
movement in space. See space harmony
Movement Notation (Eshkol and Wachman), **4:**692
Movement Notation (Morris), **4:**687
Movement Notation Society, Israel, **4:**692
movement notation systems. See Labanotation; notation

movement psychotherapy. *See* dance and movement therapy
Movements (Stravinsky), **6**:6
Movements Dance Company, **3**:575
Movements for Piano and Orchestra, **1**:12, **2**:314, 576, **4**:613
movement specialists, **4**:20
movement study. *See* kinesiology
Moves, **2**:197, **3**:614, **4**:219, **5**:422
Movie Movie (film), **4**:10, 11
movies. *See* film musicals
Moving Being, **3**:272
Moving into Dance Company, **5**:*656*, 659
Moving Pictures Festival of Dance on Film and Video, Toronto, **6**:133
Moving Target, **1**:412
Moving Visions, **3**:273
Moyers, Bill, **3**:621
Moylan, Mary Ellen, **1**:498
  Ballet Imperial performance, **1**:293
  Ballet Russe de Monte Carlo, **1**:299, 301, 302
  Four Temperaments performance, **3**:57
  Metropolitan Opera Ballet, **4**:382
Moyle, Richard, **4**:628
Mozambique, **2**:86, 91, **5**:661, 662, *662, 663*
  ngodo dance, **6**:*21*
  Shangana-Tsonga dance, **5**:579–580
Mozart, Leopold, **2**:54
Mozart, Wolfgang Amadeus, **1**:46, 406, **2**:54, 151, 372, **6**:46
  as *Amadeus* (play and film) subject, **6**:286
  ballet-divertissement, **4**:509–510
  bourrée composition, **1**:517
  chaconne and *passacaille* composition, **2**:99
  contradance composition, **2**:256
  Divertimento No. 15, **2**:420
  Don Giovanni, **1**:406, **2**:95, 202, **3**:118, 223, **4**:509, 511, 639, **6**:360
  Fokine choreography, **3**:21
  gavotte composition, **3**:124–125
  on Gluck's musical genius, **3**:190
  Idomeneo, Rè di Creta, **1**:390, **2**:99, **3**:144
  Marriage of Figaro, The, **4**:511, **6**:267
  popular dance compositions, **4**:511, **6**:360
  Rodolphe association, **5**:371
  Starzer themes, **5**:693
Mozart and Themes from "As You Like It," **3**:338
Mozartiana, **4**:613, **6**:182
  Andersen (Ib) performance, **4**:621
  Balanchine versions, **1**:256, 257, 260, 261, 270, 298, **4**:609, 613, 614
  Balanchine world premiere, **1**:256, 306, **3**:73
  Bérard designs, **1**:426
  Danilova performance, **1**:*258*, 307, **2**:342
  Farrell performance, **4**:618
  Franklin performance, **3**:87
  Hawkins performance, **3**:348
  Nichols performance, **4**:631
  Yakobson choreography, **5**:469
Mozartissimo, **6**:302
Mozart Violin Concerto, **6**:203
Mozi (Collection of Works by Mo), **1**:183, **2**:148

Mrig Trishnaa (film), **2**:*627*
Mr. Johnson, **5**:256
Mr. Punch, **3**:174, 203
Mr. Scrooge, **4**:626
Mr. Worldly Wise, **5**:420
M S Method, **4**:693
MTV (Music Television Network), **1**:78, **2**:324, 610
Much Ado about Nothing (Shakespeare), **3**:253
muchongolo dance, **5**:579, 646, *646*, 661, 662–663
Mucius Scaevola, **1**:409
Muckross House—Folk Museum, Killarney, **3**:519
Mudarra, Alonso, **4**:505
mudrā, **1**:443, **3**:457, **4**:477–478, 489, 493
Mudra Afrique, Dakar, **1**:405, **6**:20
Mudra Centre, Brussels, **1**:292, 405, 406, 407, 412, 414, **6**:54
Mueller, John, **2**:605
  as contributor, **1**:190–195
Muette, La (Béjart), **1**:292, 406
Muette de Portici, La (Auber), **1**:35, 86, 202, *239*, 410, 495, **2**:85, 172, 390, **5**:35
  character dances, **2**:107
  Elssler (Fanny) mime performance, **2**:503
  Grahn debut, **3**:222
  Lecomte (Hippolyte) costumes, **4**:138
  Livry burns from gas jet, **4**:189, 215
  Masaniello ballet version, **2**:390
  Monplaisir troupe's American performances, **4**:454
  Noblet performance, **4**:657
  Teleshova performance, **4**:279
  Zucchi *Fenella* performance, **6**:452
Muffat, George, **6**:125
mugen nō, **4**:652
Mughal, Madhavi, **5**:510, **6**:312
mugopta, **4**:46
Muḥammad ʿAlī Pasha, **2**:492, 495
Mujeres, **6**:323
mujo-kan, **4**:46
mujra, **5**:64, 65
mukabele, **3**:524
Mukesh, **2**:625
Mukhamedov, Irek, **1**:493, **2**:441, **3**:193, **5**:419, *421*, 465
  Golden Age performance, **3**:*309*
  Mayerling performance, **4**:245
mukimi guma makeup, **4**:*296*
Mukunda Raja Tamburan, Manakkulam, **3**:661
Mul, Jan, **4**:600
Mula & Haramaty, *as photographer*, **3**:533, 534
Mullen, William, **6**:145
  as contributor, **2**:156–159, 419–420
Müller, Charles, **3**:*145*
Müller, Ernest, **3**:118, 119
Müller, Grete, **4**:140
  as contributor, **4**:140
Müller, Hedwig, **3**:192
  as contributor, **3**:131–133, 163–164, 393, 443, **4**:60–61, **5**:65–66, 503, **6**:29
Muller, Jennifer, **1**:113, **4**:199, 602, **5**:200
Muller, Konstantin, **5**:470
Müller, Leticia, **5**:56
Müller, Veit-Ulrich, **3**:155
Mulligan, Gerry, **1**:404
Mulligan, Janette, **2**:513
Mullins, Carol, **2**:460–461

Mullowny, Kathryn, **1**:64, *259*, 279, **5**:570–571
Mulqueen, Laura, **5**:*696*
multiculturalism, **3**:276
Multigravitational Experiment Group, **5**:549
multimedia, **1**:139–142
  Ballets Suédois, **1**:327–328
  Bernstein *Mass*, **1**:439
  Childs choreographies, **2**:119
  Chile, **2**:125
  Einstein on the Beach, **1**:143–144, **2**:119
  Great Britain, **3**:272
  Halprin, Anna, **3**:336
  Joffrey's *Astarte*, **2**:606, **3**:615, **4**:519
  Jones, Bill T., **3**:621
  Judson Dance Theater, **3**:635
  Sweden, **1**:32
  Sydney Ballet, **6**:56
Multi Media. *See* Movement Company (Bewegingsgroep) Bart Stuyf
Mulys, Gérard, **3**:73
Mumaw, Barton, **3**:571, *572*, **5**:585, 586
Mumford, Peter, **1**:52, **2**:355
Muminov, Akbar, **6**:307
Muminov, Kadir, **6**:307
Mumma, Gordon, **2**:289, 574
mummenschanz. *See* mommerie
mummery. *See* mommerie
Mumtaz, Zohra, **5**:580
"Munadzhat," **6**:305
mundasu (headdress), **2**:225, *225*
Mundo, El (Spanish publication), **5**:676
Mundy, James, **6**:256
Munekiyo, **3**:593
Mungalova, Olga, **3**:327, **4**:283, **5**:11, 458
Mungiki and Mungaba. *See* Bellona
Munhon Tonggo (Korean text), **4**:45
Munich, Germany, **3**:144, 146, 157, 224
  See also Bavarian State Ballet
Munich Academy of Music, **1**:460
Munich Ballet Festival, **3**:4
Munich Hof- und Nationaltheater, **3**:380
Munich State Opera Ballet. *See* Bavarian State Ballet
Municipal Ballet of Rio de Janeiro, **1**:532, 533, 534, 536
Municipal Dance Archive, Santiago, Chile, **2**:127, **4**:171
Municipal Institute for Ballet, Belgium, **1**:414, 519
Municipal Opera of West Berlin, **2**:471, 478, **3**:318
Muni Mekhala, **2**:30
Munkacsi, Martin, **5**:184
Munn, Denise, **4**:456
Munschin, Jules, **4**:419
Münster, Germany, **3**:146
Munster, Jan van, **4**:597
Münster Opera, **3**:625
Munteanu, Alma, **5**:390
Munza (king of Congo), **2**:90
Murad, Tharwat, **2**:498
murādah dance, **4**:407
Murakami, emperor of Japan, **4**:41
Murasaki Shikibu, **2**:5
Murašova, Nada, **6**:438
Murat, Joachim, **3**:358, **6**:69, 70

Muravieva, Marfa, **2**:95, **3**:181, **4**:281, **5**:94, 140, 141, 177, 455
  Little Humpbacked Horse performance, **4**:211
  Paris Opera Ballet performances, **4**:353
  Saint-Léon ballets, **5**:501
Muray, Nickolas, **5**:183
Murder, **1**:76, **5**:574
Murder, the Hope of Women
  Kohoschka pantomime, **1**:131
  Tetley ballet, **6**:146
Murder and Murder (film), **5**:293
Murderers, The, **2**:499, **5**:465, 469
Murder in the Cathedral (Eliot), **3**:256
Murdmaa, Mai-Ester, **2**:530, **4**:478–479, **5**:460
Murdock, William, **4**:189
Murena, Lucius, **5**:374
Mürer, Henny, **4**:677
Mureşianu, Iacob, **5**:384
Murgiyanto, Sal, **5**:523, 524
  as contributor, **3**:492–499, 499–501, 501–504, 504–505, 505–507, **5**:130–131
Murguia, Francisco, *as photographer*, **4**:397
Murobushi Ko, **4**:271–272
Muromachi era, **2**:215–216, **4**:83–85, 85
Murphy, Anne, *as contributor*, **4**:246, 344–345
Murphy, Dudley, **1**:483
Murphy, George, **5**:*239*, **6**:141, 142
Murphy, Gerald, **1**:134
Murphy, Graeme, **1**:*208*, 213, *213*, **2**:184, **4**:479–480, 625, **5**:316, **6**:180
  After Venice, **4**:479, **6**:56, 378–379
  Nutcracker production, **1**:211, 235, **4**:479
  Sydney Dance Company, **1**:214, **4**:479, **6**:56–57
Murphy, Megan, **5**:*584*
Murray, Arthur, **2**:339, **4**:480–481, **5**:628
  box-step instructional pattern, **6**:*294*
Murray, C., **1**:456
Murray, G. W., **4**:416
Murray, James Briggs, *as contributor*, **5**:254–257
Murray, Jan, **3**:275
Murray, M. A., **4**:416
Murray, Mae, **6**:318
Murray, Michele, **1**:57
Murray, Nicholas, *as photographer*, **1**:115
Murray, Owen, **2**:58, **5**:653
Murray, R. N. M., **3**:281
Murray, Ruth, **1**:421, **4**:168
Murray, Tommy, *as photographer*, **5**:53, 651
Murray Louis Company. *See* Louis, Murray
murrungurru, **1**:228
Mursius, Johannes, **3**:302
Musaeva, Gulbakhar, **6**:213
Musard, Philippe, **5**:625
muscle action, **4**:14–15, 19, 20, 99
Muscle Function (Wright), **4**:16
Muscles Alive (Basmajian), **4**:15
musculoskeletal injuries, **4**:20
Museo Teatrale of La Scala, **5**:517
Muse Protette dal Genio d'Austria, Le, **1**:87, **3**:189
Muses, Les, **1**:424, **2**:34, **5**:40
Muse of dance, **3**:287, **6**:144–145
  choral dancing, **2**:156

musette, **4:**481–482, 510, 511, **5:**113
"Musette par M. Pécour, La," **4:**481–482
Museum Event No. 1, No. 2, No.3, **2:**291–292
Museum of Modern Art, New York City, **4:**27
  Dance Archives, **4:**28, 30
Museum of the Performing Arts of Serbia, Belgrade, **4:**164
museums. *See* libraries and museums; *specific museums*
Musgrave, Thea, **2:**350, **5:**565
Mush, Armenia, **1:**120
Mushel, Georgi, **3:**568
Mushi, **3:**440
Musica en la Noche (film), **2:**458
Musical Chairs (later *Comedia Balletica*), **1:**298–299, 478–479
Musical Clown, Equilibristics, **1:**387, *387*
musical drills, **6:**240
Musica libri septem (Salinas), **3:**29
Musical May Festival, Florence, **4:**421
Musical Moments, **6:**363, *363*
Musical Offering, **4:**482–483, **6:**110, 111, 112
  Brown (Trisha) dance, **1:**542
Musical Offering (Bach), **4:**482–483
Musical Snuffbox, The, **6:**310
Musical Suite, **4:**115
Musical Theater, Braşov, **5:**385
musical theater in Great Britain
  as American musical theater influence, **6:**268, 269
  Ashton engagements, **1:**147
  Balanchine choreography, **6:**276–277
  Bradley choreography, **1:**520
  Coles, Honi, **2:**186–187
  Matthews, Jessie, **4:**334–335
  Tiller Girls, **4:**24, 520, 524, **6:**268, 273, *273*
musical theater in the United States, **6:**242, **267–290**
  African-American traditions, **6:**255–257, 272, 278, 284, 288
  Ailey and de Lavallade performances, **1:**55
  Alonso (Alicia) performances, **1:**49
  Astaire, Fred, **1:**192
  Balanchine choreography, **1:**270–271, 298, 482, **2:**458, **4:**335, **6:**276, 278
  Ballet Russe dancers in *Song of Norway*, **1:**297–298, **6:**277
  Beatty choreography, **1:**395
  Bennett, Michael, **1:**418–420
  Bernstein scores, **1:**438–439
  Black Crook significance, **1:**456–458, 495, 496
  Bolger, Ray, **1:**482
  Bruce choreography, **2:**1
  cakewalk, **2:**25, **6:**268
  Céleste tour, **2:**85
  chorus lines and precision dancing, **6:**242
  Cole, Jack, **2:**185
  costumes, **2:**245, 248–251
  de Mille, Agnes, **2:**373, **5:**369, **6:**248
  director-choreographers, **6:**281–282, 284
  Dunham performance and choreography, **2:**458, 459
  Durang, John, **2:**466–468
  fan dances, **2:**572–574
  first Pulitzer Prize winner, **6:**275

Fokine (Michel and Vera) productions, **3:**21–22
Fosse, Bob, **3:**54, 55
Fuller, Loie, **3:**90–96
Hines, Gregory, 367, **3:**366
Hollywood adaptations, **2:**618–619
Holm, Hanya, **3:**371–372
jazz dance, **3:**598–600
Jeanmaire, Zizi, **3:**601
Kaye performance, **3:**663
Kelly, Gene, **4:**2, 3
Kidd, Michael, **2:**251, **4:**10, **6:**279–280
Kirafaly family, **4:**22–24
Koslov choreography, **4:**56
Lang, Pearl, **4:**120
lighting designs, **4:**191
Lindy Hop, **4:**202
Littlefield choreography, **4:**210
Loring choreography, **4:**228
Manning, Frankie, **4:**255
Manzotti choreographic antecedents, **4:**259
McKayle, Donald, **4:**345
Miller, Ann, **4:**419
Miller, Marilyn, **4:**419–420
minstrel shows, **6:**97–98
Nagrin, Daniel, **4:**530
operettas, **6:**268, 270, 271, 273, 276
precision chorus line, **5:**247, **6:**257, 273, *273*
Rasch, Albertina, **5:**310
revivals, **6:**287–288
Rivera, Chita, **5:**358
Robbins, Jerome, **5:**358, 359–360, 360, 361, 362, 363, 364, 366
Robinson, Bill, **4:**368
Rogers, Ginger, **5:**372
Ross, Herbert, **5:**408
Saddler, Donald, **5:**488–489
Siretta, Dan, **5:**602
Tamiris, Helen, **6:**89–90
tap dance, **2:**185–186, **6:**97–98, 102
Tune, Tommy, **6:**204–205
Verdon, Gwen, **6:**327
Wayburn, Ned, **6:**242, 271, 272, 273, 370–371
Ziegfeld, Florenz, **6:**447–448
See also Hollywood film musicals
Musical Theater, Karlín, **4:**584
Musical Theater of Karelia, **5:**473
Musicamera (television series), **6:**131
Music and Choreography of Contemporary Ballet (anthology), **5:**643
Music and the Art of the Theater (Appia), **1:**97–98
Music Box Revue, The, **5:**58, **6:**272
Music for a Birthday (film), **4:**182
music for dance, **1:**5–7, **4:483–520**
  African, **2:**88, 91, **4:**75, **483–487**
  African-American, **6:**256
  ancient Greece, **2:**419, **3:**290, 293–294, **4:**499
  Arab, **1:**101, 102, **4:**467–468, **487–491**
  Asian, **1:**163, 168, 169, 366, **491–495**
  Balanchine approach, **1:**256, 260–261, 266–267
  Ballets Suédois collaborations, **1:**327
  Baroque, **1:**5–6, **4:508–512**
    ballet de collège, **1:**283
    courante, **2:**260
    entrée, **2:**517–518

entrée grave, **2:**518–519
folia, **3:**29
gigue, **3:**172–173
loure, **4:**231–232
minuet, **4:**432–433
rigaudon, **5:**351–352
See also specific dance types
  Bournonville composers, **1:**514–516
  Byzantine, **3:**295
  Childs (Lucinda) collaborations, **2:**119–120
  Christian liturgical, **2:**540, 543
  concert music, **4:**517–518
  Cunningham collaborations, **2:**21–23, 286, 287, 288, 289, 296
  Diaghilev commissions, **1:**317–318, 325, **2:**406–407, 409, 410, 411, **3:**263, **4:**515–516
  ethnomusicology, **4:**575
  first publisher, **4:**502
  Fuller's (Loie) choice of composers, **2:**361, **3:**95
  Graham commissions, **3:**218, 383–385
  Hollywood musicals, **2:**618
  hornpipe, **3:**375–379
  modern dance composers, **3:**384
  Native American, **4:**551–552, 557, 559–560, 561, 563, 566, 571, 575, **5:**273, **6:**416
  Mesopotamia, **4:**355–356, 498
  Middle Ages and early Renaissance, **4:**500–502
  Oceanic, **4:**352, **5:**77–78, 83, 84, **495–498**
  Portugal, **5:**229
  Renaissance, **1:**5–6, **4:**502–508
    for *Balet Comique de la Royne, Le*, **1:**276
    for *ballo* and *balletto*, **1:**351
    bataille genre, **1:**368–369
    Caroso dance manuals on, **2:**75–76
    galliard, **3:**108–109
    masques, **4:**309, 311
    Renaissance drum rhythms, **1:**105
  Roman Empire, **5:**72, 73, 375–376
  Soviet modernists versus proletarians, **5:**594
  taped recorded sounds, **1:**403
  waltz, **6:**2–3, 359–361
  western, **4:498–520**
  See also countries, instruments, musicians, peoples, titles of works, and specific composers
"Music for Eighteen Instruments," **1:**59
Music for Piano 1 (Cage), **2:**22, 287
Music for Piano 8–84 (Cage), **6:**25
Music for Strings, Percussion, and Celesta (Bartok), **3:**416, 417
Music for the Theatre (Copland), **2:**196
music hall, **4:520–524**
  British traditions, **4:520–523**
    clog dancing, **3:**240, **4:**520, 522
    early ballet, **3:**261
    skirt dance, **5:**605
    See also musical theater in Great Britain; vaudeville
  French traditions, **3:**71, **4:523–524**
    Baker, Josephine, **1:**252–253
    can-can, **2:**52–53
    Fuller, Loie, **3:**92
    travesty, **6:**190

Music Ho! (Lambert), **3:**285, **4:**114
"Musician's Day, A" (Satie), **5:**526
Musiciens du Nil, Les, **2:**496
Music in Bali (McPhee), **3:**506
Music in My Heart (musical), **4:**246, **5:**59
Music Masters Chorus (Harlem Branch YMCA), **5:**342
Music of Changes (Cage), **2:**22
Music of the City, **2:**581
Music Television Network. *See* MTV
Music Theater Ballet. *See* Stanislavsky and Nemirovich-Danchenko Musical Theater
music videos, **4:**631
music visualizations, **2:**377, 378, **3:**384, 397, **4:**518, **5:**495
Musik und die Inszenierung, Die (Appia), **1:**97–98, **4:**189
Musil, Karl, **1:**241, **2:**111, 510
Musings, **4:**73, 547
musique concrète, **1:**403
Musique de table (Telemann), **1:**364
Musitz, Suzanne, **1:**214, **6:**56
Muslims. *See* Islam and dance
Mussen, Tharon, **4:**191
Mussorgsky, Modest, **1:**318, 324, 486, 518, **2:**151, 407, **3:**16, **4:**226, 429, **5:**406
Mussorgsky Theater Ballet. *See* Maly Theater Ballet
Mussot, François. *See* Arnould-Mussot, Jean-François
Mustel, Auguste, **6:**116
Musume Dōjōji, **3:**639
"Muszette à Deux, La" (Pecour), **4:**481
Mut (deity), **2:**482
Mutation, **2:**470, **4:**594
Mutations, **2:**245, **4:**252, 602
Muteki-sha, **2:**18
Mute Wife, The, **1:**300
Mutiny (musical), **2:**1
Muus, Henriette, **5:**396
Muybridge, Eadweard, **1:**130, **3:**201, **4:***14*, 15, **5:**178, *178*, 180, 184, 187
Muzzarelli, Amalia, **6:**338
Muzzarelli, Antonio, **1:**237, **6:**337
mvet, **2:**33
Myal, **3:**575
Myanmar, **1:**178, 179, **4:524–528**
  Chinese dance exchanges, **2:**136, 137
  costume, **2:**226–227, **4:**526, 527, 528
  trance rituals, **6:**185
Myaskovsky, Nikolai, **5:**268
My Brother, Moughy, **3:**665
My Brother, My Sisters, **4:**243, **6:**9
My Career of Dance Art (Wu), **6:**406
Mycenaean civilization, **3:**287
My Dancing Days (Bedells), **1:**400
Mydtskov, H. J., as photographer, **5:**428
Mydtskov, Rigmor, **1:**508
  as photographer, **2:**4, **3:**39, **5:**395, 429, 430, 431, 600, **6:**59
Myers, Betty June, as contributor, **4:**121–122
Myers, Edward, **4:**367
Myers, Gerald, **1:**81
Myers, Martha, **1:**79
My Fair Lady (film), **2:**618
My Fair Lady (musical), **1:**539, **3:**372, **5:**423, 489, 616, **6:**282
My Father's Vertigo, **4:**220
My Fur Lady (revue), **4:**237
My Husband (Castle), **2:**80
My Life in Ballet (Massine), **4:**325

My Mother, **5:**34
My One and Only (musical), **2:**186, **6:**102, 204, 205, *205,* 286
My Sister Eileen (film), **3:**54
Mystères, **1:**251
Mystères de Paris, Les (Sue), **1:**500
Mystères Dionysiaques, Les, **5:**585
Mysteries and Rapture, **4:**346
Mysteries and What's So Funny, The?, **3:**202
"Mysterious Circle," **6:**394
mystery plays, **4:**448, 462
mysticism, **2:**165, **3:**523–525, 605
Myth, **5:**437
My Theater Life (Bournonville), **1:**503, 505, 506, 511, **2:**387, **3:**222, **5:**250, 251, **6:**70
Mythical Hunters, **1:**196, **3:***533,* **4:***602, 677, **6:***135,* 146
Myth of Modern Dance, The (Dunn solo), **2:**460
Mythologiae (Conti), **1:**275
Mythologies, **1:**52, **4:***471*
Mzechabuki. See Heart of the Hills
Mziri (television film), **4:**133
mzumbano dance, **2:**418

Naas el-Ghiwam ("new" music group), **4:**469
Nabarawi, Mervat, **2:**498
Nabi Chum, **2:***223*
Nabila, **6:***207*
Nabokov, Nicolas, **1:**316, **2:**410, 438, **4:**33, 518, 613
Nabucco (Verdi opera), **2:**187
Nacht, **4:**91, 94
Nacht aus Blei, Die, **1:**375, **3:**52
Nachteiland, **2:**347, **4:**600
Nachtigall, Die, **5:**557
Nächtlichen, Die, **4:**60
Nachtzug, **3:**630
Naculík, Libor, **5:**615
Nadal, Alexandra, **5:**436
Nadan, o L'Orgoglio Punito, **6:**70
Nadar (Félix Tournachon), **5:**176, *176*
Nadarević, Jasna Peručić, as contributor, **6:**433–434
Nádasi, Ferenc, **2:**480, **3:**414, 415, 416, 417, **4:**529
   school and students, **2:**473, **3:**421, **4:**74, 529, **5:**401
Nádasi, Marcella, **5:**569
Nadav, Rachel, **3:**529
Nadeau, Louise, **6:***252*
Nadelman, Elie, **4:**27, 28, 30
Nadezhdina, Nadezhda, **4:**529–530, **5:**445, 473, *474*
Nadi al-Shams Ballet, **2:**498
Nadirov, Ivan, **3:**665, **5:**480
Nafana (people), **6:**12
Na Floresta (film), **6:**131
Náfrádi, László, **1:**370
Naga (people), **4:**253
Nagano Chiaki, **5:**33
Nagar, Urmila, **5:**581
Nagarakertagama (Javanese text), **3:**505
Naga Raksha, **4:***300*
Nagaraksa mask, **2:**228–229
nagauta, **3:**639, **4:**530
Nagel, Lauri, **3:***444*
Nago dance, **3:**334, **6:**345
Nagoya Sanzaburō, **5:**28
Nagrin, Daniel, **2:**604, **3:**447, **4:**530–531, **6:**89–90
Nagy, György, **3:**419
Nagy, Iván, **1:**72, **2:**201, **3:**306, **4:**25, **5:**55, **6:**143, *203*
   American Ballet Theatre, **1:***72,* 73

Ballet de Santiago, **2:**124, 127
   English National Ballet, **2:**513, 514, **3:**269
Nagys, Biroute, **2:**47
Nahachewsky, Andriy
   as contributor, **6:**220–224
   as photographer, **6:**221
Naharin, Ohad, **3:**532, **4:**531–532, **6:**53, 56
Nahat, Dennis, **1:**73, 197, 403, **2:**177, 178, **3:**306, **6:**266
Nahmanides, **3:**603
Nahum, Stirling Henry. *See* Baron
Nahuatl culture, **4:**384–386
Nahumck, Nadia Chilkovsky, **4:**96
Naïad and the Fisherman, The, **2:**181, **5:**139, 141
Naiad Queen, The, **1:**456
Naïads, Les, **1:**199
Naidu, Chinnayya, **1:**273
Naidu, Shobha, **6:**321
Naïla, **2:**368, **4:**429
Nair, Ramunni, **5:**292
Nair, the Slave, **1:**43
NAISDA (National Aboriginal and Torres Strait Islander Skills Development Association), **1:**216
Naissance de la Lyre, La, **4:**635
Naissance de la Paix, La, **6:**38
Naissance de Vénus, La (1665), **1:**286, 288, **4:**234
Naissance de Vénus, La (1826), **2:**365
Naissance de Vénus et l'Amour, La (1821), **1:**410, **5:**147
Naissance d'Osiris, La, **5:**306
naiyandi dance, **3:**647, 650
Nakajima Natsu, **2:**18
Nakamura Baigyoku IV, **4:**538
Nakamura Ganjirō, **4:**532–533
Nakamura Ganjirō I, **4:**532
Nakamura Ganjirō II, **3:***640,* **4:**533
Nakamura Ganjirō III, **4:***532,* 533, 536
Nakamura Hirotarō, **4:**533
Nakamura Kankurō, **4:**533–534
Nakamura Kanzaburō, **4:**534
Nakamura Kanzaburō I, **4:**534
Nakamura Kanzaburō XVII, **4:**534
Nakamura Kichiemon, **4:**534–535
Nakamura Kichiemon I, **4:**334, 533, **534,** 535, 537, **5:**31
Nakamura Kichiemon II, **4:**334, **534–535,** *535*
Nakamura Kikaku I, **4:**536
Nakamura Mannosuke I. *See* Nakamura Kichiemon II
Nakamura Matagorō II, **4:***535*
Nakamura Matsue V, **4:**538
Nakamura Nakazō I, **3:**593
Nakamura Ryū, **3:**593
Nakamura Shikan IV, **4:**537
Nakamura Shikan VII, **4:**534
Nakamura Tomijūrō, **4:**536
Nakamura Tomijūrō I, **4:**536
Nakamura Tomijūrō II, **4:**536
Nakamura Tomijūrō III, **4:**536
Nakamura Tomijūrō IV, **4:**536
Nakamura Tomijūrō V, **1:**249, **4:**533, *536,* **536**
Nakamura Tomotarō, **4:**533
Nakamura Utaemon, **4:537–538**
Nakamura Utaemon I, **4:**537
Nakamura Utaemon II, **4:**537
Nakamura Utaemon III, **1:**361, **4:**537
Nakamura Utaemon IV, **1:**361, **4:**537
Nakamura Utaemon V, **1:**362, **4:**537

Nakamura Utaemon VI, **4:***537,* **537–538,** **5:**30
Nakanishi Natsuyuki, **1:**61
Nakaya, Fujiko, **1:**143, 544, *544*
Naked Leopard, **3:**350
nakhkh dance, **4:**408, 415
na Lazar, **2:**100
Namaskar, **2:**104
Namboodiri, Shankaran, **5:**580
Nambutiri, Kaplingad, **3:**661
Namiki Sōsuke, **3:**637
Nam Jeong-ho, **4:**52
Namouna, **4:**184, **5:**149, 515, **6:**443
Nana, **2:**463, **3:**643, **5:**164
Nana Odori, **5:**28
Nanas, Effie, **5:**172
nanayila dance, **5:**579
Nancy, France, **1:**351, **3:**74, 362
Nandanji, Rasadhari Devaki, **5:**581
Nandi, Amala, **5:**581
nandir, **4:**146
Nanjing, China, **2:**133–134
nanxi, **4:**76
Naoussa, Greece, **3:**298
Naozamurai, **3:**439, *638*
NAPAC Ballet, **5:**651, 653–654, 692, **6:**379
   Contemporary Dance Company, **5:**659, **6:**657
   Staff productions, **5:**692
Naples, Italy, **3:**545, 546, 551, 553
Napoleão, Marcos, **1:***533*
Napoleon I, emperor of France, **1:**452, **2:**72, **3:**176, **4:**423
   balls and spectacles, **3:**68
   costume reform, **2:**239
   Gnatt restaging, **4:**678
Napoleon III, emperor of France, **3:**69, 70, **4:**215
Napoleonic Wars, **5:**453, 480
Napoli, **1:**454, **5:**295, 425, 426, 427, 553, 554, 555, 600, **6:**104
   Blue Grotto scene, **1:**514–515, **4:***188,* 513
   Bosman staging, **2:**58
   Bournonville production, **1:***506,* 508–509, 511, 512, 514–515, **2:**387, **5:**406, *432*
   Bruhn performance in student production, **2:**2
   Bruhn staging of pas de six, **2:**4, 443
   composers, **4:**513
   costume authenticity, **2:***240*
   English National Ballet versions, **2:**510, 511
   Flindt performance, **3:**12
   Gade score for Blue Grotto scene, **1:**514–515
   Lander (Margot) performance, **4:**119
   Lassen performance, **4:**126
   lighting and set design, **4:***188*
   Paulli score, **1:**515
   Rosen stagings, **2:**285, **5:**406
   Schaufuss (Peter) staging, **2:**511, **4:**545
   Skoog staging, **5:**401
   Wall performance, **6:**357
Nápravík, Eduard, **2:**436
Nápravík, Georgi, **2:**439
Nápravil, Olrich, **5:**393
Nara, Japan, **4:**41, 42
Narayanan, Kalanidhi, **6:**312
NARB. *See* National Association for Regional Ballet
Narcisse, **1:**254, 322, **2:**407
   Fokine choreography, **3:**18, 19, **4:**634
   Nijinsky performance, **2:**408

Narcissus (film dance), **2:**605
Narcissus (Fokine ballet). *See Narcisse*
Narcissus and Echo, **1:**49
Nardi, Wanda, **3:**51
Narenta, **2:**82
Narisaranuwadhiwong, prince of Siam, **4:**9
Narkissos, **6:**340
Narodne igre (Janković and Janković), **6:**439
Narodni Dom, Saint Petersburg, **4:**634
Narragansett (people), **4:**555
Narrenspiegel, **4:**91, 92
Narukami, **3:**439, **4:**536
Nascimento, Milton, **1:**536
Nash, Beau, **1:**190
Nash, Chris, as photographer, **3:**275
Nash, Ogden, **6:**278
Nash balet (Pleshcheyev), **5:**482
Nashe, Thomas, **4:**114
Nasib, as photographer, **6:**257
NASIDA (National Aboriginal and Torres Strait Islander Skills Development Association), **1:**216
Nasidze, Sulkhan, **1:**38
Näslund, Erik, **6:**50, 60
   as contributor, **1:**117–118, **2:**283–284, **3:**100–101
Nasr, Seyyed Hossein, **1:**14, 15
Nasser, Esther, **3:***655,* **6:**659
Nasser, Gamel Abdel, **2:**345, 497
Nasturtiums and the "Dance" (Mastisse), **4:**331
Nasu no Yoichi no Katari, **4:**660
Nasvytyte, Danute, **4:**208
nāṭaka, **1:**168
Natalia Makarova (anthology), **5:**485
Natalka Poltavka (Kotliarevsky), **6:**222, 224
Natal Performing Arts Council. *See* NAPAC Ballet
Nataraja (film), **3:**200
nātasin, **6:**147, 148, 149–150
Natasin School of Music and Drama, Vientiane, **4:**123
Natchez (people), **4:**558
nat festival (Myanmar). *See nat pwe* ceremonies
Nathalie. See Swiss Milkmaid, The
Nathan, Adèle, **2:**282
National Aboriginal and Torres Strait Islander Skills Development Association (NAISDA), **1:**216
National Academy of Dance, Rome, **5:**441
National Academy of Performing Arts, Bangladesh, **1:**362
National Association for Regional Ballet, United States, **1:**39, **2:**357, **3:**610, **6:**249, 266–267
National Association of Dance Teachers, Italy, **5:**43
National Association of Fiddlers, **4:**672
National Ballet (Ireland), **3:**520
National Ballet (Washington, D.C.), **2:**174, 587, **3:**88, **6:**265, 366
National Ballet Company (Panama), **5:**68
National Ballet of Brazil, **4:**436
National Ballet of Cairo. *See* Cairo Opera Ballet
National Ballet of Canada, **2:**37, 38, *40,* 45, **4:538–548,** **5:**434
   Anderson (Reid) directorship, **4:**546–547

archives, **4**:166
artistic directors, **2**:3, 4, 39, 42
Augustyn, Frank, **1**:200–201, **2**:*40*
Baylis costume designs, **1**:394
Bruhn artistic directorship, **4**:545–456
Bruhn productions, **2**:3, 4, 42, **3**:643, **4**:542, 543, 545–546, **6**:35
Cranko *Romeo and Juliet,* **5**:396
Dark Elegies revival, **2**:349
Farrell as guest artist, **2**:577
Fille Mal Gardée, La, **2**:595, **4**:544
founding, **2**:39, 47, **3**:62, **4**:538–539
Franca directorship, **3**:62, **4**:539–453
full-scale productions of classics, **3**:228–229, **4**:538, 539–540, 542
Giselle, **3**:*61*, 62
Grant (Alexander) directorship, **2**:42, **3**:237, **4**:543–545
Guest choreography, **3**:389
Hart, Evelyn, **3**:345
Hayden guest performances, **3**:352
Jacob's Pillow performance, **3**:571, **4**:541
Jardin aux Lilas, **4**:540, *540*
Kain, Karen, **3**:643
Kudelka as artistic director, **4**:547
Kudelka productions, **4**:71–72, 73, 74, 544, 547
Macdonald, Brian, **4**:237, 238
Nureyev, Rudolf, **5**:*6*, 7
Nutcracker, The, **4**:73, *546*, **5**:*14*
Romeo and Juliet, **4**:542
Schaufuss, Peter, **5**:554
school, **2**:47, **4**:541–542
Seymour guest peformances, **5**:574
Strate as resident choreographer, **6**:1
style and image, **4**:542
Swan Lake, **6**:35
television appearances, **6**:131–132
Tennant, Veronica, **6**:142–143
Tetley productions, **1**:394, **2**:42, **4**:544, 545, *545*, 546, **6**:146–147
Tudor productions, **4**:540–541, 547
writings on, **2**:49
National Ballet of Chile. *See* Ballet Nacional Chileno
National Ballet of China, **6**:64
National Ballet of Finland. *See* Finnish National Ballet
National Ballet of Guinea. *See* Ballets Africains, Les
National Ballet of Lithuania, **1**:430, **4**:*207*, 208, **5**:17
National Ballet of Marseille. *See* Ballet National de Marseille
National Ballet of Portugal, **5**:62, 235
National Ballet of Senegal, **4**:548–549, **6**:21–22
National Ballet of Spain, **3**:101
National Ballet of the Netherlands. *See* Netherlands Ballet
National Ballet of Venezuela, **6**:323
National Ballet School of Canada, **2**:47, **4**:541–542, 543
National Broadcasting Company (NBC), **6**:137, 139
National Bunraku Theater, Osaka, **2**:14

National Center for the Conservation and Promotion of Folk Creation, Bucharest, **5**:391
National Choreography Plan (U.S.), **6**:266
National Classical Music Institute of Korea. *See* Korean Traditional Performing Arts Center
National Contemporary Dance Center, Mexico, **4**:396
National Contemporary Dance Center, Querétaro, **1**:524
national costume. *See* costume
National Council of Dance Teacher Organizations (U.S.), **5**:631
National Council on the Arts (U.S.), **1**:545
National Cultural Center, Cairo, **2**:496
National Dance College of Bali, **4**:158
National Dance Company of Ghana, **3**:167–168, *169*, 170
National Dance Company of Havana. *See* Danza Contemporánea de Cuba
National Dance Company of Korea, **4**:12
National Dance Company of Senegal. *See* National Ballet of Senegal
National Dance Ensemble of Cameroon, **2**:33
National Dance Ensemble of Iraq, **1**:48
National Dance Institute, **2**:314–315
National Dance School, Mexico City, **4**:391, 392
National Dance School, Montevideo, **6**:301
National Dance Theatre Company of Jamaica, **2**:65, **3**:574–575, *574, 575,* 576
National Educational Television (NET), **6**:138
National Endowment for the Arts (U.S.), **1**:70–71, **2**:374, 575, 609, 610, **3**:610, 611, **4**:115
Dance Program, **6**:250, 300
National Choreographic Project, **4**:271, **6**:266
National Ensemble of Popular Arts, Tunisia, **6**:207
National Film Board of Canada, **6**:133
National Folk Art Ensemble of the German Democratic Republic, **3**:152, 154
National Folk Ballet of Korea, **2**:570
National Folk Dance Ballet, Dominican Republic, **2**:432
National Folklore Festival, Marrakech, **4**:*407*, 469
National Folkloric Troupe (Egypt). *See* Firqa al-Qawmīyah Lil Funun al-shaʿbīyah
National Folk Theatre (Ireland), **3**:518
National Foundation on the Arts and Humanities Act of 1966 (U.S.), **6**:250
National Geographic Society, **5**:200
National Ghana Dance Ensemble. *See* National Dance Company of Ghana

National Institute for Dance Pedagogy. *See* Autonome Hogeschool Antwerpen
National Institute of Mental Health (U.S.), **2**:602
nationalism (national dance). *See* ethnic dance; folklore history; *specific countries*
National Kabuki Theater of Japan, **4**:661
National Library, Sydney, **4**:159
National Library of Braidense, Milan, **4**:162
National Muses, **1**:507, 514
National Museum of Dance, Saratoga Springs, New York, **4**:167
National Nō Theater, Tokyo, **3**:592
National Opera (Greece), **3**:300
National Opera House, Oslo, **4**:676
National Organisation for Dance and Mime. *See* Dance United Kingdom
National Playground Association, **3**:367
National Resources Centre for Dance (Surrey University), **4**:95, 163
National School of Dramatic Art, New Delhi, **4**:159
National Socialism. *See* Nazi era
National Square Dance Repository (U.S.), **4**:170
National State College of Ballet (Norway), **4**:677
National Theater, Belgrade, **6**:432, 434–435, 438
National Theater, Brno (formerly State Theater), **1**:542
National Theater, Budapest, **3**:413, 414, 420
National Theater, Helsinki, **3**:311–312
National Theater, Munich, **1**:390, 391
National Theater, Oslo, **4**:674, 675, 681
National Theater, Prague. *See* Prague National Theater Ballet
National Theater, Reykjavik, **3**:436–437
National Theater, Zagreb, **6**:431
National Theater Ballet, Yugoslavia, **5**:100
National Theater of Japan, Tokyo, **3**:592
National Theater of the Deaf, **2**:110
National Theatre Ballet, Melbourne, **1**:208
National Theatre Ballet Company, Australia, **5**:563
National Theatre Ballet School, Melbourne, **3**:204, 623
National Theatre of Kenya, **6**:22
National Training School for Dancing, London, **4**:121
National Troupe of the People's Republic of China, **4**:256
National Youth Dance Company, London, **2**:575
Native American Center for the Living Arts, Niagara Falls, **4**:555
Native American dance, **4**:549–575
Alaska and Arctic area, **4**:570–574
Argentina, **1**:108, 109
background and overview, **4**:550–556

ballet dancers from Oklahoma, **3**:362
Brazil, **1**:529, 530–531
California and intermountain region, **4**:565–568
Canada, **2**:49, **4**:49, 550–551, 555, **5**:552
Caribbean region, **2**:62, 64–65
Chile, **2**:121
dance research and publication, **4**:555, 570, 571, **574–575**
anthropological studies, **4**:369, 372, **6**:297
ethnographic film, **2**:601, 602, **4**:571
ethnological studies, **4**:78, **5**:574–575
diffusion and borrowing, **4**:555, 560
fan use, **2**:569–570
as Garifuna dance influence, **3**:120, 121
Ghost Dance, **3**:170–171, **4**:562, 567–568, **6**:185
Great Plains, **4**:550, 551, *552,* 553, *554,* **560–562**
Guatemala, **3**:319
as Hawkins influence, **3**:349, 350
Hopi, **1**:600, **3**:373–375
Kwakiutl people, **6**:186
Mexico, **4**:384–386
music, **4**:551–552
Navajo, **2**:601, **4**:552, 578–579
Northeastern Woodlands, **4**:550, 551, **556–558**
Northwest Coast, **4**:550, **568–570**
Panama, **5**:67
powwow, **4**:555, 561, **5**:239–240
Pueblo, **5**:271–273
as Shawn influence, **5**:585, *585*
Southeastern Woodlands, **4**:558–560
Southwest, **4**:550, 553, **562–565**
dance literature, **4**:575
matachines, **4**:329–330
See also subheads on specific tribes
Sun Dance, **6**:187
Tigua, **6**:170
trance rituals, **6**:185
tribal dance photographs, **5**:180
Yaqui, **6**:416
Native Dancers, **6**:396
Native Green, **1**:142, **2**:296, **4**:37
nat pwe ceremonies, **2**:226–227, **4**:525, *525,* 527
Natural History of the Ballet-Girl, The (Smith), **5**:241
Natural Movement, **3**:271
Nature Dances, **2**:1
nature dances, **5**:599
Natya (Krishnamurthi), **4**:63
nātya, **1**:442, **4**:70
nātyadharmī, **3**:456–457, **4**:575
Nātyaratnakośa (Indian text), **3**:658–659
Nātyaśāstra (Bharata), **1**:168, 187–188, **3**:451, 452–453, 455, 457, 458, 658, **4**:575–576
aesthetics, **1**:16, 17, **3**:462, 659
on *mudrā,* **4**:477
subject matter, **3**:469, 658
nau catarinetas, **1**:527
Naufrage de la Méduse, Le, **3**:426
Naughton, Louise, **5**:436
Naughty Little Princess, The, **4**:673
Naughty Marietta, **6**:270

Nault, Fernand, **1:**70, 73, **2:**597, 605, **3:**342, **4:576–578**, **5:**43, 681, **6:**106, 131
   Carmina Burana, **3:**230, *230*, **4:**476
   Grands Ballets Canadiens, Les, **2:**39, 42, 152, **3:**228, 229–330, 231, **4:**576–577, **6:**364
   Joffrey Ballet, **3:**610
   Nutcracker staging, **3:**229, 234, **4:**576, *577*, **5:***15*
   Tommy, **2:**39, **3:**230, **4:**576
Nauman, Bruce, **2:**292, **3:**620, **5:**548
Naumann, Johann, **1:**88, **5:**552, **6:**39
Naumov, Pavel, **1:**437
Naushad, **2:**622
Nausicaa (Sophocles), **2:**159
nautch, **1:**178, **4:**578, **5:**46
Nautch, The, **5:**492, 496
Nautéos, **2:**114, **4:**185, **5:***92*, 96
Navagraha, **2:**104
Navajo dance, **4:**552, **578–579**
Navajo Yeibechai Dance, **2:**601
navanṛtya, **2:**102
Navarra, Gilda, **5:**275
Navarre dance, **1:**377
Navarro, Aníbal, **2:**276–277
Navarro, Armando, **5:**530–531
Navarro, Esquivel. *See* Esquivel Navarro, Juan de
Navarro, Victor, **1:**536
Navas, Cassia, **1:**537
Nave, La (d'Annunzio), **5:**438
Navette, Nellie, **4:**520
Navoi, Alisher, **6:**305, 306
Navoi Theater, Tashkent, **4:**226
Navruz festival (Uzbek), **6:**305
Nayyar, O. P., **2:**625
Nazareth, **1:***535*
Nazi era (1933–1945), **3:**147–148, 161
   Ausdruckstanz, **1:**204, **3:**147, 160, 161
   ballet productions, **4:**517
   Bauhaus closing, **1:**387
   Berlin Olympics (1936), **3:**147, **4:**61, 93, 477, 538–539, **5:**66, 218, **6:**393
   dance emigrés, **1:**239–240, 431, 467, 498, **3:**277, **4:**93, 103, 477, **6:**304, 357
   French dance persecutions, **1:**466
   German dance exiles, **3:**147, 627–628, **6:**378
   Henie association, **3:**357
   Holocaust victims, **1:**431, 466
   Laban in Germany, **4:**91, 93, 477
   Laban refuge in England, **3:**628, **4:**93–94, 103, 477
   Lander (Harald) antifascist works, **4:**118, 119
   Netherlands arts suppression, **4:**590, 598
   Norwegian dance closures, **4:**676
   official dance policy, **4:**93
   Palucca school closure, **5:**66
   Paris Opera Ballet, **3:**73, **4:**184–185, **5:**96
   Polish ballet effects, **5:**218, **6:**365
   ritualized dances, **5:**357
   Royal Danish Ballet's symbolic works, **5:**429
   Warsaw Ballet effects, **6:**365
   Wigman productions, **4:**93, 477, **6:**393, 394, 395
   See also World War II
Nazirov, Kagraman, **1:**248
Nazirova, Nela, **1:**248, **5:**460
Nazzaro, Nat, **3:**304

NBC. *See* National Broadcasting Company
NBC Concert Hall (television series), **6:**137
Ndau (people), **5:***663*
Ndebele (people), **5:**643, 644, 661, **6:**13
Ndembu (people), **5:**357
N'Deye-Gueye, **6:***384*
NEA. *See* National Endowment for the Arts
Neal, Mary, **3:**238, 241
Neal, Philip, **4:**631
Neapolitanischen Fischer, Die, **3:**314, **5:**135
Nearly Beloved, **6:**56
Nears, Colin, **6:**134, 135
Neary, Coleen, **1:**293, **4:**618–619, **6:**454
Neary, Patricia, **1:**196, 293, **2:**42, **4:**612, 618, **5:**265, 653
   Geneva Ballet, **6:**52
   Zurich Ballet, **6:**53, 454
Nebesky-Wojkowitz, René de, **1:**458
Nebrada, Vicente, **2:**39, 514, **6:**323, *323*, 324, *324*
   Firebird production, **3:**4, **5:**436
   Harkness Ballet, **3:**344
   Joffrey Ballet, **3:**610
   National Ballet of Canada production, **4:**544
   Royal Winnipeg Ballet productions, **5:**436
Necessary Weather, **5:**440
Nécrologe des hommes cèlèbre, **2:**27, 28, 29
Necromancer, or Harlequin Dr. Faustus, The (pantomime), **5:**350
Nedbal, Oskar, **2:**308, **3:**346, **5:**245, 614
Nedbaliana, **2:**308
Nederlandsch Indie Oud en Nieuw (periodical), **3:**505
Nederlandsche Ballet (1954–1961). *See* Netherlands Ballet
Nederlandse Beroepsvereniging van Danskunstenaars, **4:**592
Nederlandse Opera, **2:**120
Nederlandse Vereeniging van Dansleraren, **4:**587
Ned Wayburn's Gambols (revue), **6:**272
Needham, Carole, **2:**445
Needham, Joseph, **3:**240
Needham, Maureen, *as contributor*, **1:**122–124, **2:**442–443, **3:**86–87, 119–120, **5:**197–199
Neel, Darlene, **4:**157
Neels, Sandra, **2:**53, **6:**356
Nefte, ossia Il Figliuol Prodigo, **2:**282
Neggo, Gerd, **2:**528
Neglia, José, **1:**110, *111*
Negreiros, Almada, **5:**233
Negri, Cesare, **1:**54, 235, **2:**73, **4:579–583**, **5:**324, 621, 666, 668
   on *ballo* and *balletti*, **1:**352, **4:**579, 580–582
   on *brando*, **1:**523
   on canary, **2:**50
   dance collections, **1:**46, 369, 380
   dance manuals, **1:**104, 105, **2:**73, 74, 75, 189, 337, **3:**542–543, **6:**122
   See also Gratie d'amore, Le
   on Diobono as teacher, **2:**418
   figure dances, **2:**591

   on galliard movements, **3:**107, 107–108, 109, **4:**580, *580*, 581, **5:**323
   intermedi choreography, **3:**509, 511, **4:**505, 581
   listing of contemporary dance artists, **3:**543
   on *matachins*, **4:**326
   musical examples, **4:**506–507
   on *pavane*, **5:**115
   pavaniglia, **5:**112, 117
   as Renaissance dance technique source, **5:**336, *337*, 338–339, **6:**349, 350
   on *révérence*, **5:**344–346
   sobriquet, **4:**579
   on *spagnoletta*, **5:**666
   on *tordion*, **6:**178
   on *volta*, **6:**349, 350
Negri, Pola, **5:**220
negrilla, **2:**1, 50
Negritos (people), **2:**230, **5:**168
"Negro Dance" (*Amors og Balletmesterns Luner*), **3:**105
Negro Dance Group, **2:**458
Negro-Jazz Ballet, A. See Création du Monde, La
Negro Rhapsody, **2:**458
Negro Sculpture, **2:**458
"Negro Speaks of Rivers, The" (Hughes), **5:**254, 255
Negro Spirituals, **2:**480
Negry, Gabriel, **5:**385, *385*
   students, **5:**263
Neher, Caspar Rudolph, **1:**306
Neige, La, **2:**202, **4:**339, **5:**318
Neighborhood Playhouse, New York City, **3:**212, 385, 399, **5:**637, **6:**243
Neighbors, **2:**292, 296
Neil, Sara, **4:**624
Neisvestne Diaghilevy ili konets tsitaty (Laskin), **5:**483
Nélida and Nelson, **6:**94
Nelidova, Lydia, **1:**98, *99*, *319*
Nelidova, Vera, **1:**312
Nell Gwynne, **5:**57–58
Nelson, Gene, **1:**419
Nelson, Lisa, **1:**215, **5:**128
Nelson, Peter, **2:**161
Nelson, Terez, **3:**520
Nema, **4:**218
Nembe (people), **6:**14
Nemchinova, Vera, **1:**207, 313, 430, **3:**24, **4:***207*, 208, **5:**237, 650
   Biches, Les, **1:**449, 450, **4:***183*
   Dolin association, **2:**424
   Lifar dance partnership, **4:***182*, *183*
   Mordkin Russian Ballet tours, **4:**460
   Oboukhoff marriage, **5:**17
Néméa, ou L'Amour Vengé, **4:**353, 429, **5:***94*, 501
Němeček, Jiří, **1:**542, **2:**11, **4:583–584**, **5:**245
Nemeitz, J. C., **2:**451, **5:**38
Nemesis, **2:**264
Nemirovich-Danchenko, Vladimir, **1:**487, **5:**456, 466, 514
   dramatic realism, **1:**517, **3:**56
   as Kriger influence, **4:**62
Nemirovich-Danchenko Musical Theater. *See* Stanislavsky and Nemirovich-Danchenko Musical Theater
Nena, La (Manuela Perca), **2:**522, *569*, **5:***671*, 672
nenbutsu dance, **3:**588
Nentsy (people), **5:**447
Nénuphar, Le, **2:**582, **5:**160

neoclassical ballet, **2:**410, **3:**258
   Nijinska style development, **4:**634
   Nijinska's *Les Biches* as keystone, **4:**633
neoclassical costume, **2:**235, 236, 238, 239, 244, 246
   Bakst design, **2:**407
   Balanchine ballet, **2:***244*
   Delsartean, **2:**452
   Didelot innovations, **2:**413, 414, *414*, *415*
   Duncan drapery, **2:***453*, 454
   Fokine hybrids, **3:**15
   Greek dance competition, **6:***241*
neoclassical music, **2:**409
Neo-Classic Dance Company, **6:**83
neoclassicism
   Gluck operatic reform, **5:**35
   Sakharoff, Alexander, **5:**503
   scenic design, **5:**537
neohumanism movement, **1:**426
neonationalism, **4:**56
Neoplatonism, **4:**505
neoprimitivism, **2:**409
neoromantic school of design, **5:**547
Nepal, **2:**226, **5:**598, **6:**185–186
Nephete, o Il Figliuol Prodigo, **1:**500
Nepveu, Clazina, **2:**470
Nerina, Nadia, **2:**404, **4:584–585**, **5:***5*, 416, 531, 652
   Ashton ballets, **1:**158, **4:**584
   Blair dance partnership, **1:**459
   Fille Mal Gardée, La, **1:**155, **2:**597, **4:***584*, 585
   Firebird makeup, **4:***305*
   Rassine dance partnership, **5:**313
   Soviet Union performances, **4:**585
   Swan Lake performance, **6:**34
Nermut, Jiří, **5:**270
Nero, emperor of Rome, **5:**376
Nero, or The Fall of Babylon (musical spectacle), **4:**23
Nerodenko, Volodymyr, **6:**223
Nerta, **5:**690
Neruda, Josef, **5:**221
Neruda, Pablo, **1:**536
Nervi festival, **3:**550, 553
Nesbit, Evelyn, **6:**318
Nesterov, Andrei, **4:**276, **5:**451
Nesterov, Arkady, **5:**471
Nestinal (fire dance), **2:**8
Nestinarski celebration, **1:**85
NET. *See* National Educational Television
Netherlands, **4:585–600**
   dance education, **4:597–598**
      folk dance, **4:**598
      Groot, Pauline de, **4:**594
      Hartong, Corrie, **3:**345, 346, **4:**598
   dance on television, **6:**136
   dance research and publication, **4:598–600**
      folk dance, **4:**585, 586
      libraries and museums, **4:**162, 600
   folk and traditional dance, **4:585–586**
      clogging variant, **2:**180
   social dance, **4:586–588**
   theatrical dance, pre-1900, **4:588–589**
   theatrical dance, 1900–1945, **3:**132, 133, **4:589–590**
   theatrical dance, post-1945, **1:**289–290, **3:**121–122, **4:591–597**
      modern dance, **4:**593–507, 602

Scapino Rotterdam, **5:**530–531, 618
See also Dutch National Ballet; Netherlands Ballet; Netherlands Dance Theater; *specific choreographers and performers*
Netherlands Antilles, **2:**63
Netherlands Ballet, **4:**590, 592, 600, **600–601, 5:**555, 618
See also Dutch National Ballet
Netherlands Dance Institute, **4:**600
Netherlands Dance Theater, **1:**215, **2:**347, 500, **3:**122, **4:***591, 592,* 596, **601–602, 5:**290
Duato, Nacho, **2:**448–449, **4:**602
focus versus Dutch National Ballet, **4:**592–594
formation, **4:**592, 600, 601
Forsythe guest choreography, **3:**52
as German modern dance influence, **3:**151
Jacob's Pillow performance, **3:**571
Kylián as artistic director, **4:**81, 593, 602
Manen, Hans van, **4:**251–252, 602, **5:**592
New Zealand tour, **4:**624
Tetley, Glen, **6:**146
Waring choreography, **6:**363
See also Dutch National Ballet
Netherlands Documentation Center for the Dance, **4:**162
Netherlands Institute for Dance, **4:**597
Netherlands Opera Foundation, **2:**469
Netherlands Professional Association of Dance Artists, **4:**592
netotiliztli, **4:**384–385
Netsu no Katachi, **1:**61
Nettl, Paul, **5:**221
Nettleford, Rex, **2:**65, **3:**574, 576
as contributor, **3:**573–577
as photographer, **2:**65
Nettleton, Beryl, **4:**624
Nettleton-Edwards Studio, Auckland, **4:**624
Neubauer, Henrik, **6:**438, 439
as contributor, **6:**438–439
Neue Odysee, **3:**153
Neue Silhoutten, **4:**64
Neueste Art zur Galanten und Theatralischen Tanzkust, Die (Bonin), **6:**123
Neue Tanzbühne, Die, **3:**625
Neue und curieuse theatralische Tanz-Schul (Lambranzi). *See New and Curious School of Theatrical Dancing*
Neue und Curieuse Theatralische Tanz-Schul (Ulrich choreography), **6:**229
Neumann, Therese, **2:**464
Neumeier, John, **1:**25, 241, 350, 406, 463, **2:**39, **3:**156, **4:602–604, 5:**97, 565, 685, **6:**349
Benesh notation use, **1:**418
Daphnis et Chloë, **5:**316
Don Juan version, **2:**434, **4:**604
Don Quixote choreography, **2:**441
Firebird versions, **3:**3
Hamburg Ballet, **3:**150, 157, 337–338, 360, **4:**603–604
Hamlet Connotations, **2:**4, **3:**338, 351
Josephslegende, Die, **3:**578, 631

Kehlet *demi-caractère* roles, **3:**668
Midsummer Night's Dream, A, **2:**463, **3:**668, **5:**406, 432, **6:**44
National Ballet of Canada guest choreography, **4:**542, 547
Nutcracker conception, **1:**391, 500, **5:**13, 15, 16, 436
Peer Gynt, **4:**604, **6:**44
Romeo and Juliet, **3:**668, **5:**394, **396–397,** 432
Rose design collaboration, **5:**405–406
Royal Danish Ballet guest productions, **5:**432, 433
Royal Swedish Ballet guest productions, **6:**44
Royal Winnipeg Ballet guest choreography, **5:**436
Sacre du Printemps, Le, **5:**488
Saint Matthew Passion, **3:***153,* **4:**604
Stages and Reflections, **3:**343, **4:**603
Stuttgart Ballet, **2:**267, **4:**603, **6:**10
Swan Lake, **3:**337, **6:**35
Vaslav, **2:**463
neurophysiology, **4:**15
Neuschnee in Troja, **1:**376
Neuvième Symphonie, **1:**292
Nevada, **2:**460
Nevada, Anna, **1:**305
Nevaro, Annie, **6:**319
Neve, Trotraut de, **3:**151
Never on Sunday (film), **3:**299
Neville, Edgar, **5:**676
Neville, John, **5:**602
Neville, Phoebe, **2:**462, **3:**634
Nevin, Ethelbert, **2:**452
New American Bandstand, The (television program), **1:**79
New Amsterdam Theater, New York City, **6:**289, 448
New and Curious School of Theatrical Dancing (Lambranzi), **1:**428, **3:**257, 365, 544–545, **5:**260, **6:**124
Newark, **1:**545
"new artistic dance." *See Ausdruckstanz*
New Ballet, The (Coton), **3:**282, 285
"New Ballet, The" (Fokine), **3:**14
New Ballet School, New York. *See* Ballet Tech
Newberry Library, Chicago, **4:**168
New Britain. *See* Melanesia
New Caledonia. *See* Melanesia
New Carte Blanche Dance Company, **4:**679–680, *681*
Newcastle, England, **3:**273, 275
Newcater, Graham, **2:**57, **5:**54
New Collection (L'Abbé), **4:**106
New Collection of Dances, A (Le Rousseau), **4:**105
Newcomers, **4:**238, **6:**133
new dance
Denmark, **2:**385–386
Germany, **3:**145
Japan, **3:**593
New Dance (Humphrey dance work), **1:**421, **2:***246,* **3:**399, 400, 401, *401,* 403, 404, **4:**518, 605, **606**
New Dance (publication), **3:**272, 275, 283
New Dance Ensemble, Minneapolis, **2:**576
New Dance Group, **2:**450, 520, **4:**306, 345, **604–605,** 626, **6:**245
New Dance Group of Toronto, **2:**40

New Dance League, **6:**89
New Dance Trilogy, **2:**285, **3:**399–400, 401, *401,* 403, *403,* 404, **4:605–606**
See also New Dance: Theatre Piece; With My Red Fires
New Danish Ballet, **2:**385
New Danish Dance Theater, **2:**386
New Delhi, India, **4:**159
New Delhi (film), **2:**623, 624
New Directions in Dance (Taplin), **2:**50
New Directions in Dance Research: Anthropology and the Dance— The American Indian, **4:**373
New Dramatic Opera in Serious and Grotesque Characters, Call'd Amadis, or the Loves of Harlequin and Columbine, A, **5:**350
New England
folk dance collection, **3:**34
longways country dance, **2:**257, **3:**35
New England Civic Ballet. *See* Boston Ballet
New England Dance Theater, **6:**363
New Galileo, **3:**276
New Gallery, London, **2:**453, 455
Newgeordnet künstlich Lautenbuch, Ein, **5:**110
New Girl in Town (musical), **3:**54, **6:**327
New Group (Royal Ballet), **4:**242–243
New Guinea. *See* Indonesia, outlying islands; Papua New Guinea
New Gymnastics, **6:**235, 294
New Hampshire, **3:**35
Newhborhood Playhouse, New York City, **3:**215
New Heptachor, **5:**478
New Heroine, A, or The Cossack Woman, **6:**311
New Ireland. *See* Melanesia
"new" *kabuki* (*shin kabuki*), **4:**535, 536
New Kind of Love, A, **6:**363
Newland, Peter, *as photographer,* **1:**510, 512
New London Ballet, **2:**350
Newlove, Jean, **4:**94
Newman, Barbara, *as contributor,* **1:**459, **2:**272–273, 314, 443–444, 477–478, 506, 578, 590, **3:**236–237, 345, 512–513, **4:**110, 200–201, 256–257, 306–307, 336–337, 463, 469–470, **5:**100, 331–333, 560, 588–589, 596–597, 639–640, **6:**213–214, 357, 405
Newman, Claude, **3:**414
Newman, Ernest, **3:**284
Newman, Rosalind, **2:**608, **4:**219
New Midsummer Night's Dream, A, **1:**442, **5:**557
New Movement (theater), **2:**262–263
New Narcissus, The, **2:**60
New Negro Art Dancers, **6:**258, *258*
New Odyssey, **5:**617
New Opera House, Cairo, **2:**497, 498
New Orleans, Louisiana, **3:**86–87
New Orleans Opera Ballet, **2:**586, **3:**87
New Penelope, The, **1:**509
Newport, Vivienne, **3:**151
Newport Jazz Festival, **2:**5

New School for Social Research, New York City, **2:**196, 290
Dance Committee, **3:**385
"Dances of Many Peoples" course, **3:**368
Martin (John) modern dance lectures, **4:**273
"new sect" theater (Japan). *See shinpa*
Newsidler, Hans, **4:**505, **5:**110
New Sleep, **3:**52
New Society for Ballet and Dance, Germany, **5:**43
Newson, Lloyd, **2:**611, **3:***274,* 276
New South Wales, Australia, **1:**214, 217
See also Sydney Dance Company
Newsreview (Korean periodical), **4:**54
New Sterne, The, **4:**278, **6:**311
New Television (television series), **6:**139
New Testament. *See* Bible, dance in the
New Time Shuffle, **3:**336
Newton, Christopher, **3:***615*
Newton, Isaac, **4:**14
laws of motion, **5:**188, 189
Newton, Joy, **5:**411
New Victory Theater, New York City, **6:**289
New Wave, **1:**78, **5:**390
New Wave Festival. *See* Brooklyn Academy of Music
New Werther, The, **4:**35, 278, **6:**311
New Year (Tippet), **3:**621
New Year's Carnival, **6:**23
New Year's Sacrifice, **2:***146*
New York Baroque Dance Company, **5:**327, **6:***250,* 261, 298
New York City
downtown dance movement, **2:**170–171
early dance presentations, **6:**232–233
Federal Dance Project, **2:**579, 580, **6:**245
libraries and museums, **4:**166–167
See also specific dance companies, schools, sections, and theaters
New York City Ballet, **1:**141, **4:**29, **606–624, 6:**247, 278
Adams, Diana, **1:**11–12
Afternoon of a Faun, **1:**28–29
Agon, **1:**30, *30,* **4:**28
allegro style, **1:**45
American Music Festival (1988), **1:**141, **2:**359, **5:**366
Ananiashvili and Liepa performances, **1:**83
Apollo, **1:**96, **4:***611*
Ashton guest choreography, **1:**152, 153, **4:**29
Balanchine administrative role, **4:**608
Balanchine as dominant creative force, **3:**29, **4:**608
Balanchine Celebration (1993), **4:**275, 622, 631
Balanchine company class, **4:**615–616
Balanchine founding and legacy, **1:**256, 257, 262–264, 270, 271–272, **4:**26, 29, 606–621
Balanchine repertory, **4:**621–624, 631
Balanchine-Stravinsky mode, **1:**71

New York City Ballet, *continued*
  Ballet Imperial revivals,
    1:293–294
  as Ballet Russe de Monte Carlo
    competition, **1:**301
  Baryshnikov, Mikhail, **1:**74, 372,
    4:620
  Bolender, Todd, **1:**478, 479,
    4:608, 609
  Boris productions, **1:**498
  choreographic festivals,
    4:622–623
  Coppélia, **2:**201
  costumes, **2:**242–243
  Cranko production, **2:**265
  d'Amboise, Jacques, **2:**314, 315,
    4:609
  Dances at a Gathering, **2:**333
  Danilova *Les Sylphides* restaging,
    6:62
  Danish dancers, **5:**430
  Diamond Project, **2:**42
  Divertimento No. 15, **2:**420
  Dollar choreography, **2:**425–426
  Don Quixote premiere, **2:**438–439
  Duel, The, **2:**246, *246*
  Eglevsky, André, **4:**479, 620, **6:**64
  Farrell, Suzanne, **2:**576, 577–578
  Firebird, The, **3:**2–3, *2*
  Ford Foundation grant, **1:**271,
    6:265
  foreign tours, **4:**29, 607
  former American Ballet Theatre
    dancers, **1:**68
  Forsythe guest choreography,
    3:53
  Four Temperaments, The, **3:**58–59
  Gorey caricatures of repertory,
    2:71
  Gounod Symphony, **1:**265
  Hayden, Melissa, **2:**47,
    3:351–352, **4:**617
  home theater, **6:**164
  "Hommage à Ravel," **5:**316
  Illuminations, **3:**442–443
  Irving (Robert) as principal
    conductor, **3:**521, **4:**29, 613
  Italian tour, **3:**550
  Japanese tours, **3:**589
  Jardin aux Lilas revival, **3:**597
  jazz evenings, **4:**519
  Karinska costumes, **3:**654
  Kaye, Nora, **3:**664
  Kent, Allegra, **4:**5, 617
  Kirkland, Gelsey, **4:**24
  Kirstein as general director, **4:**26,
    28, 29
  Laing, Hugh, **4:**110
  Le Clercq, Tanaquil, **4:**137
  Liebeslieder Walzer, **4:**179, 180
  Liepa (Andris) and Ananiashvili
    guest performances, **4:**181
  Magallanes, Nicholas, **4:**246, 619
  male dancers, **4:**619–620
  Martha Graham company co-
    production, **6:**107
  Martins, Peter, **4:**29, 273–275,
    609, 614, 615, **5:**364
  Martins directorship, **4:**274, 275,
    608, 621, 622
  McBride, Patricia,
    4:344–345, 618
  Medea, **2:**283
  Mitchell, Arthur, **4:**436
  Moncion, Francisco,
    4:449–450, 609
  musical quality, **4:**613
  Nichols Kyra, **4:**615, 618, 619,
    622, 623, 631
  Nutcracker, The, **1:**264, **4:**29, 606,
    617, **5:**13, 15, 16, **6:***139,* 144

On Your Toes revival, **6:**286
Orpheus, **4:**28
  as photographic subject, **5:**186
Ravel Festival (1975), **4:**607,
  5:366
Raymonda, **5:**322
repertory development, **4:**609
Robbins, Jerome, **4:**29, 608–609,
  614–615, 621, 622, **5:***360,* 361,
  364–367, **6:**288
Robbins Festival (1990), **5:**367
Rosenthal lighting designs, **4:**191,
  5:407
San Francisco Ballet exchange
  program, **2:**161
Scènes de Ballet, **5:**531–532
scenic design deemphasis, **4:**613
Schaufuss, Peter, **5:**554
school. *See* School of American
  Ballet
seasons, **4:**606–607
Serenade as signature work,
  4:*609,* **5:**571
Shadow'd Ground, **2:**197
Sleeping Beauty, **5:**613
Stravinsky commissions, **6:**6
Stravinsky Festival (1972), **1:**437,
  479, **3:**521, **4:**29, 274,
  607–608, 613, **5:**366
Stravinsky scenario decisions,
  4:613
stylistic and technical standards,
  4:615–616
Summerspace revised production,
  2:294, **6:**27
Swan Lake version, **6:**34
Sylphides restaging, **6:**62
Sylvia: Pas de Deux, **6:**64
Symphony in C, **6:**65–66
Tallchief, Maria, **6:**84–86
Taras, John, **4:**609
Tchaikovsky Festival (1981),
  4:274, 607, **5:**366
television performances,
  6:132, 138
Tomasson, Helgi, **6:**174
Tudor, Antony, **4:**29, **6:**200–201
Verdy, Violette, **6:**328
Villella, Edward, **4:**609,
  6:339–340
West Side Story Suite, **6:**288
Wilde, Patricia, **2:**38, **4:**617,
  6:396–397
Williams, Stanley, **6:**399–400
New York City Ballet, The (Kirstein),
  4:26
New York City Center of Music and
  Drama. *See* City Center of
  Music and Drama, New York
  City
New York City Opera, **1:**124, **6:**289
  Cole production of *Bomarzo,*
    2:185
  Joffrey as resident
    choreographer, **3:**610
New York City's First Ballet Season
  (Moore), **6:**233
New York City Winter, **4:**151
New York Dance Festival, **5:**489
New Yorker (magazine), **1:**297,
  3:285, 402, **6:**299
New Yorker, The (Massine ballet),
  3:87, **4:**324
New York Export: Opus Jazz, **3:**343,
  614, **4:**519
New York Herald Tribune
  (newspaper), **2:**376, **4:**457,
  6:299, 300
New York International Ballet
  Competition, **1:**281, 282,
  6:425

New York Opera Company, **2:**426
New York Philharmonic Orchestra,
  1:438, 439
New York Post (newspaper), **6:**299
New York Public Library for the
  Performing Arts, Dance
  Collection, **2:**462, **4:**28,
  166–167, **6:**300
  Oswald as founder, **5:**48
  Moore as acting curator, **4:**457
  Other Dances benefit
    performance, **5:**366
  Robbins Film and Videotape
    Archive, **5:**363
New York School, **2:**375–376
New York Society of Teachers of
  Dancing, **5:**627
New York State Theater, New York
  City, **1:**263, 264, 271, **4:**28, 29,
  6:164
  New York City Ballet residency,
    4:606, 607
New York State University system.
  See State University of New
  York
New York Swing Dance Society,
  4:255
New York Times (newspaper),
  4:272–273, **6:**296, 299, 300
New York University, **6:**292
  Dance Education Program,
    1:141, **6:**297
New York University–Connecticut
  College School of the Dance,
  1:79, **3:**364
New Zealand, **4:**624–629, **5:**510
  dance education, **4:**625–626, 628
  dance research and publication,
    4:628–629
  Maori dance, **4:**260–261
  Oceanic dance traditions,
    5:*20,* 225
  theatrical dance, **4:**624–628
  See also Royal New Zealand
    Ballet
New Zealand Association of Dance
  Teachers, **5:**43
New Zealand School of Dance,
  4:625–626
Next Ice Age Company, **2:**359
Nezha (film), **5:**130
Nga (people), **6:**16
Nganasany (people), **5:**447
Ngatatjara tribe (Australian
  Aborigine), **1:***220,* 222
Ngbaka (people), **2:**89, 211–212
Ngejuk Captung, **4:**265
Ngema, Mbongeni, **5:**648
Ngesti Pandawa, **1:**174
ngibing, **3:***474,* 475
ngodo dance, **5:***661, 662,* **6:***21*
Ngombe (people), **2:**90
Nguni (people), **5:***663*
Nguni dance, **5:**644–645, 661–662
Ngurah Raka, I Gusti, **4:**265
Ngwa, Liza, **2:**33
Ni—Woman of Destiny, **3:**575
Niagara Frontier Ballet, **2:**273,
  4:270, 638
Niblo's Garden, New York City,
  1:456, 457, 459, 495,
  4:23, 121
Nicaragua, **2:**64
Nice, France, **3:**75
Nice Opera Ballet, **2:**351, **4:**134
Nichili, Carlos, **5:**232
Nicholas I, emperor of Russia,
  1:10, **4:**57, 66
Nicholas II, emperor of Russia,
  4:68

Nicholas, Harold, **3:**367
Nicholas Brothers, **1:**440, **2:**615,
  3:367, **4:**629–630, **6:***100,*
  277, 288
Nicholas Nickleby (film), **1:**438
Nicholas Roerich Museum, New
  York City, **5:**372
Nichols, Betty, **2:**291
Nichols, Kyra, **1:**294, **2:**314, **4:**180,
  630–631
  inheritance of Farrell roles, **4:**631
  New York City Ballet roles, **4:**615,
    618, 619, 622, 623, 631
Nicholson, William, **5:**294
Nichomachean Ethics (Aristotle),
  2:428
Nicks, Walter, **2:**458
Nicol, Noleen, **5:**54
Nicolaeva, Nadine, **5:**588
Nicolet, Jean-Baptiste, **2:**174,
  5:197, 198
Nicolini. *See* Grimaldi, John
  Baptiste
Nicoll, Allardyce, **2:**188
Nicoll, Charles, **2:**177, 178
Nicoloau, Marina, **1:***413*
Nico Malan Opera House, Cape
  Town, **2:**57
Nid d'Amours, Le, **3:**426
Nieblas de Niño, **3:**79
Niedecken-Gebhard, Hans,
  6:392
Niedermeyer, Louis-Abraham,
  2:202, **3:**5
Niehaus, Max, **3:**161
Niels Bjørn Balletten, **4:**126
Nielsen, Augusta, **1:**508, 509,
  3:223, **4:**631–632, **5:**425
Nielsen, Carl, **2:**173, **5:**294, 352
Nielsen, Lavina, **3:**391
Nieman, Daniel, **4:**595
Nieminen, Arja, **2:**633
Nieminen, Pasi, **2:***284*
Nierenberg, George, **5:**601
Nieri, Pietro, **4:**588
Nierra, Douglas, **5:**172
Nieto, Angel, **1:**115
Nieto, Sara, **2:**124, 125
Nietzsche, Friedrich Wilhelm,
  1:127, 130, **2:**453
  as Humphrey aesthetic influence,
    3:399, **4:**439
Nietzsche, Gernot, **3:**142
Nieuwenhuis, G. J., **3:**506
Nieuwkerk, Karin van, **4:**415
Nieves and Copes, **4:**632, **6:**93, 94
Ni Fleurs, Ni Couronnes, **1:**405
Nifontova, Lucia, **2:**632
Nigeria, **1:**14, **6:**13, 14–16
  as African-Brazilian dance
    influence, **1:**525
  as Caribbean dance influence,
    2:62, 274
  children's dance, **6:**14
  costume, **2:**211, 212
  dance research and publication,
    6:24–25
  dance theater education, **6:**20
  diversity of ethnic groups, **6:**15
  filmed dance, **2:**602
  gender and class dance
    proscriptions, **6:**382
  Hausa dance, **3:**347–348
  highlife, **6:**24, 384
  libraries and museums, **4:**158
  masks, **4:**288–289, *289,* 292,
    6:12–13
  music for dance, **4:**484
  opera companies, **6:**21, 384
  popular dance, **6:**24
  theatrical dance, **6:**384

Tiv dance, **6:**172–174, 383
trance rituals, **6:**185
Ubakala dance, **6:**219, 383
See also Yoruba dance
Night, **2:**359, **5:**123
"Night," **4:**33
"Night and Day" (Porter song),
    1:192
Night and the Silence, The, **5:**226
Night City, **1:**492, **4:**132, **6:**171
Night Creature, **1:**56, 196, **2:**514
Night Dancers, The, **3:**183
Nightingale, The, **1:**408, **4:**226,
    6:420
Nightingale and the Rose, The,
    2:424, **4:**127
"Nightingale Dance," **2:**222, **4:**12
Nightingale's Song, The, **5:**617
Night Journey, **2:**574, **3:**217, *218*,
    349, **4:**632–633, **632–633**,
    5:407, 562
Nightmare, The (Fuseli painting),
    5:640
Night Moves, **1:**453
Night Music, **1:**52, **5:**303
Night on the Bare Mountain, **1:**324,
    3:205, **4:**185, 225
    Moiseyev (Igor) production,
    4:445
Night Porter, The (film), **1:**82
Nightshade, **2:**575, **6:**111
Night Shadow (Balanchine). *See
    Sonnambula, La*
Night Shadow, The (Bournonville).
    See Somnambule, La
Night Song, **4:**450
Night Spell, **3:**391, 403
Night with Waning Moon, **2:**1
nihon buyō, **3:**89, 90, 338, 639
Nihon minzoku geino jiten
    (Honda), **3:**592
Nihon Minzoku Geino Kai, **3:**592
Nijhuis, Bob, **1:**289
Nijinska, Bronislava, **1:**49, 51, 70,
    93, 367, **4:**633–639, **5:**606
    American Ballet Theatre
    productions, **1:**65, 66, **4:**638
    analyses of choreographic style,
    4:101
    Après-midi d'un Faune, L',
    1:98–99, **3:**19, **4:**634, *635*,
    5:362
    in Argentina, **1:**110, **4:**635
    Ashton association, **1:**146, 147,
    4:633, 638
    as Ashton influence, **3:**380, **4:**648
    athletic and acrobatic
    choreography, **4:**259
    Baiser de la Fée choreography,
    1:148, **3:**72, **4:**635, **5:**439
    Ballet Polonaise, **4:**435, **5:**218
    Ballet Russe de Monte Carlo
    productions, **1:**297, **4:**638
    Ballets Russes de Monte Carlo
    productions, **1:**311, 316,
    4:636–637
    Ballets Russes de Serge Diaghilev
    performances, **4:**634, *634*
    Ballets Russes de Serge Diaghilev
    productions, **1:**324, 325, 348,
    2:183, 410, 423–424, **3:**18,
    4:33, 634, **5:**217
    Beriosova roles, **1:**430
    Boléro, **5:**315
    brother, Nijinsky, **4:**633, 634, 639,
    641, 642, 645, 646, 648
    Carnaval performance, **2:**72, 73,
    192, **4:**634
    Chappell association, **2:**105
    criticism of Kshessinska
    (Matilda) style, **4:**68

de Valois sponsorship, **2:**396
Diaghilev association, **1:**317,
    2:399, 406, **4:**634, 635
dismissal of comparisons with
    Massine's symphonic ballets,
    4:636
Early Memoirs, **4:**646
on Egorova's *Giselle*, **2:**480
Fille Mal Gardée, La, **2:**594, 597,
    4:638
Fokine association, **3:**14, 16, 18
on Goncharova's *Les Noces*
    designs, **3:**198
Grand Ballet du Marquis de
    Cuevas, **3:**224, *225*, 226, 227,
    4:638
Hugo (Jean) designs, **3:**394
Impressions de Music-Hall, **1:**247,
    4:635, **5:**95, **6:**432, 444
on *Jeux*, **4:**648
Kochno association, **4:**33
Lambert scores, **4:**113
as Legat (Nikolai) student, **4:**143
Lifar as student, **4:**182
Markova-Dolin Ballet, **4:**268
Markova roles, **4:**269
Molière source, **4:**447
Nutcracker choreography, **5:**14
Paris Ballet choreographies, **5:**95
Polish background, **5:**217
Polish Ballet, **4:**435, **5:**218
productions in Kiev, **4:**634, **6:**224
Renard, Le, **3:**441, **4:**124, *124*
Romeo and Juliet, **4:**113, **5:**398,
    6:196
Rondo Capriccioso, **1:**484, **3:**361,
    4:638
Royal Ballet productions, **4:**633,
    658, **5:**417, **6:**438
Rubinstein ballet choreography,
    3:72, **4:**635–636, **5:**438–439
on *Sacre du Printemps*
    choreography, **4:**644
Sacre du Printemps performance,
    4:635, 643
Schéhérazade performance, **5:**556
Sleeping Beauty, **3:**227, **4:**633, 634
Sleeping Beauty reconstruction,
    5:611
students, **2:**108, **3:**264, **4:**4, 178,
    182, **6:**326
Swan Lake role, **6:**32
Sylphides performance, **6:**60
Tallchief as protégée, **6:**84, 85
Tchaikovsky piano concerto
    choreography, **6:**117
in United States, **6:**291
Valse, La, **5:**315
Woizikowski roles, **6:**404
*See also Biches, Les; Noces, Les;
    Train Bleu*
Nijinska, Irina, **2:**334, **4:**4, 634
Nijinska Ballets, **4:**636
Nijiński, Tomasz. see Nijinsky,
    Foma
Nijinsky (film), **2:**425, 512, **3:**60,
    664, **5:**408, 560
Nijinsky (Kline portrait). *See
    Portrait of Nijinsky*
Nijinsky (Krasovskaya), **4:**58
Nijinsky (Rodin sculpture),
    1:128, *128*
Nijinsky, Eleonora Bereda, **4:**633,
    639, **5:**217
Nijinsky, Foma (Tomasz Nijiński),
    2:176, **3:**56, **4:**633, 639, **5:**217
Nijinsky, Kyra, **5:**299, **6:**196
Nijinsky, Paul, **5:**171
Nijinsky, Romola de Pulszky, **4:**27,
    645–646, **5:**241

Nijinsky, Vaslav, **4:639–648**
    aesthetics, **4:**647–648
    American debut performance,
    4:645
    androgyny, **4:**647
    assessment of talents, **4:**646–647
    Ballets Russes de Serge
    Diaghilev, **1:**317, 318, 319,
    320, 321, 322, **2:**183, 408,
    409, **3:**18, 19, 20, 308, **4:**639,
    5:217
    as Béjart choreographic
    inspiration, **1:**292, *292*,
    405, 406
    Benois collaboration, **1:**423
    Bourdelle sculpture of, **1:**502
    caricatures of, **2:**70, 71, 72
    Carnaval performance, **2:**72,
    73, 408
    Chopiniana performance, **3:**16,
    6:60
    choreographic arm angularity,
    3:18, **5:**227
    choreographic influence, **4:**648
    choreographic intent, **1:**320, 321,
    4:647
    choreographies, **2:**408, **4:**645–646
    costuming innovations,
    2:241–242, **4:**642, *646*
    dance performance influence,
    4:648
    Daphnis et Chloë performance,
    3:19
    Diaghilev relationship, **1:**317,
    318, 319, 320, 321, 322,
    2:406, 408, 411, **3:**17, 631,
    4:316, 641–645
    diary, **4:**646
    Didelot Scholarship, **2:**416
    Dowell film portrayal of, **2:**444
    films on, **2:**512, **3:**60, **5:**408
    Fokine association, **3:**15, 16, 17,
    18, 19, 20, 28, **5:**456
    Fokine roles and interpretation,
    4:639, 640, *642*, 646–647
    Giselle, **3:**182
    as Ito inspiration, **3:**558
    Jeux, **1:**320, 321, 325, 326, **2:**361,
    4:641–643, 644, *646*, 647,
    5:558
    Kirstein writings on, **4:**27
    Kline portrait of, **1:***138*, 139
    last public performance, **4:**645
    leaps, **2:**71, **4:**639, 646
    as Legat (Nikolai) student,
    4:143, 639
    London performances, **3:**263,
    4:645
    makeup versatility, **4:**305
    marriage, **4:**645–646
    Maryinsky Ballet, **4:***280*, 283,
    634, 640–641
    Neumeier ballet on, **2:**463
    notation system, **4:**645, 646, 686
    Nutcracker solo, **5:**13
    observation of Jaques-Dalcroze
    school, **2:**408, **3:**596, **4:**644
    Pavillon d'Armide, Le, **5:**118,
    119, 121
    Pavlova as partner, **5:**121,
    122, 123
    Petrouchka performance, **1:***318*,
    3:18, *19*, **5:**165, 166
    as photographic subject,
    5:182, *182*
    Polish background, **5:**217
    practice outfit, **5:**241
    Rodin sculpture of, **1:**128, *128*,
    5:370
    on Roerich's designs, **5:**372
    Roi Candaule, Le, **5:***151*

Sacre du Printemps, Le, **1:**52, 259,
    320, 322, **2:**408, **3:**616–617,
    5:296, *327*, 372, 487–488,
    6:4, 455
Schéhérazade performance, **5:**556
schizophrenia diagnosis, **4:**646
sister, Nijinska, **4:**633, 634,
    639, 645
Spectre de la Rose performance,
    2:71, 408, **3:**18, *656*,
    4:*644*, 645
Swan Lake performance, **6:**32
Sylphides performance, **3:**16,
    4:640, **6:**60, 61
teachers, **5:**17
technical feats, **4:**646
Till Eulenspiegel, **1:**322,
    4:645, 647
See also Après-midi d'un Faune, L'
Nijinsky, Clown de Dieu, **1:**292, *292*,
    405, 406
Nijinsky Dancing (Kirstein), **4:**27,
    5:297
Nijinsky Galas (Hamburg Ballet),
    3:338
Nijinsky Memorie di Giovinezza,
    3:61
Nikaronova, Nina, **6:**325
Nikita Dolgushin (Krasovskaya),
    4:58
Nikitin, Eraclito, **4:**339
Nikitin, I. D., **3:**127
Nikitina, Alice, **1:**95, *95*, 437, **2:**410,
    5:392, 526
    Apollo performance, **2:**342
    Zéphire et Flore performance,
    4:320
Nikitina, Varvara, **4:**282, **5:**160, 606
Nikitin's Circus, **2:**176
Nikolaeva, Alexandra, **2:**150
Nikolaeva, Nadezhda, **5:**282
Nikolaeva, Nadine, **3:**520, **4:**143,
    6:128
Nikolaeva, Olga, **1:**486, **5:**455
Nikolais, Alwin, **1:**140, 143, 351,
    421, **2:**119, 290, **4:648–652**,
    5:97, **6:**249
    on early modern dance practice
    clothes, **5:**243
    electronic music, **4:**519, 650
    film and videodance, **2:**605,
    4:230, **6:**135
    as French modern dance
    influence, **3:**77, 78, 83
    as Holm student, **3:**369, 371,
    4:95, 441, 442, 649
    improvisation, **3:**445
    lighting, **4:**547–548, 650, *651*
    Louis association, **4:**230, 649,
    650–651
    mask use, **4:**302, *303*
    notation system, **4:**649, 688, 690
    scenic design, **5:**545, 547–548
    students, **4:**52, 115, **6:**151
    Totem costume, **2:**247
Nikolais and Murray Louis Dance
    Company, **4:**230, 651
Nikolais Dance Theatre (formerly
    Playhouse Dance Company),
    4:115, 230, 649, **5:***600*, *657*,
    658–659, 660, *660*
Nikolajević, Radivoje, **6:**438
Nikolská, Jelizaveta, **2:**307, **4:**238,
    583, **5:**245
Nikolska, Lila, **6:**323
Nikotina, **5:**245
Nikova, Rina, **3:**528, 529, 532
Nilanowa-Sanftleben, Nika, **1:**1
Niles, Don, *as contributor*, **5:**76–78,
    84–85
Niles, Doris, **3:**559

Nilsson, Hans, **6:**44
Nilsson, Mats, *as contributor,* **6:**35–37
Nimbus, **6:**200
Nimura, Yeichi, **1:**39, **3:**559, **4:**38, **5:**359
Nin, Joaquín, **1:**115
Nina Ananiashvili and International Stars Company, **1:**83
Nina, eller Den Vanvittige of Kærlighed, **5:**425
Nina, ou La Folle par Amour, **1:**35, 505, **3:**175, **5:**425
  Bigottini performance, **1:**451, **5:**91
  Bournonville (August) debut, **1:**505
  Elssler (Fanny) performance, **2:**503, **3:**180
  mad scene, **3:**180
  Milon production, **4:**422, **5:**91
Nine (musical), **6:**205
Nine Evenings: Theater and Engineering, **2:**119, 605–606, **6:***248*
Nine Sinatra Songs, **1:**77, **5:**440
Nine Songs, **6:**82
Nine Tangos and . . . Bach, **1:**540
1931 Revue, **1:**520
Ninette à la Cour, **3:**353, 426, **4:**175, **5:***86, 90*
Ninety-second Street YM-YWHA, New York City, **1:**431, **2:**187, **3:**404, 605, 609, 610
  dance resources, **4:**167
  Dunham's first New York concert, **6:**258
  Primus debut, **6:**259
  Waring works, **6:**362
Nine Variations on a Dance Theme, **2:**602, 604, 605
Ninfa dell 'Acqua, La, **1:**499
Ninfa Eco, La, **1:**461
Nini-Patte-en-l'Air (Nini Foot-in-the-Air), **1:**95
Ninth Symphony, **1:**403, 405, 446
Nirschy, Emilia, **3:**414, 423
Nishikawa Koisaburō, **5:**30
Nishikawa Ryū, **3:**593
Nishikawa Senzō I, **3:**593
Nishikawa Senzō II, **3:**593
Nishikawa Senzō IV, **3:**593
Nishikawa Senzō V, **3:**593
Nishikawa Yoshijirō, **3:**593
Niskanen, Toivo, **2:**632
Nisnevich, Anatoly, **5:**401
Nissinen, Mikko, **2:**633
Niva (literary journal), **6:**28
Nivelon, Francis, **3:***255,* **4:***346,* **5:**70, 346
Nivelon, Louis, **1:**4, **3:**117, **5:**90
Nivkh (people), **5:**448, *448*
Nixon, David, **6:**266
Nixon, Richard M., **2:**137
Nixon in China (Adams opera), **4:**472
Niyazi, Khamza Khakimzadeh, **4:**8
Nizhniy Novgorod, Russia, **5:**471
nizzarda, **4:**580, **6:**350
Nkake, Adolph, **2:**33
Nketia, J. H. Kwabena, **3:**166, 167, **6:**25
Nketsia, Nana Kobina, **3:**167, 168
nkisi (deities), **1:**529
Nkrumah, Kwame, **3:**167, 169–170
nkwa dance play, **6:**219

nō, **1:**160, 161, 168, *169,* 179, 182, 183, **3:**642, **4:652–656**, **5:**49, 590, 592
  aesthetics, **1:**17, **3:**581, **4:**442, 654–655
  bugaku elements, **3:**580
  costumes, **2:**215–217, *215*
  dance movement, **4:**653–654
  dengaku and *sarugaku* elements, **3:**584
  historical background, **3:**580, 584, 637
  Hōshō school, **3:**388
  Kabuki versus, 295
  Kan'ami, **3:**646–647
  Kanze school, **3:**646, 650, **4:**42
  Kita school, **1:**187, **3:***581,* **4:**30–31
  Kongō school, **4:**39–40
  Konparu school, **4:**41–42
  Konparu Zenchiku, **4:**42
  kuse climactic dance, **3:**646
  kyōgen interludes, **4:**83
  lion dances, **5:**593
  martial techniques, **1:**187
  masks, **1:***169,* 179, **2:**216–217, **3:**581, **4:**295, 652, *653,* 654, *655*
  Matsui Akira, **4:**332–333
  mime, **4:**423
  musical accompaniment, **4:**494, 652
  performance training, **4:**655
  primary sources, **3:**591
  repertory and play structure, **4:**652
  Robbins's choreographic tribute, **5:**365
  shamanistic and spiritual traditions, **4:**652–653
  shimai, **5:**592
  Umewaka Makio, **6:**229–230
  as Yeats influence, **3:**519, 558–559
  Zeami as preeminent theoretician, **6:**445–446
  See also kabuki theater; Zeami
Noack, Kjeld, **5:**394
Noah's Minstrels, **6:**112
Nobbe, Walter, **2:**2, 448, **4:**602
Nobilissima Visione, **1:**296, 302, **4:***322,* 323–324, **656**
  Tchelitchev design, **5:**547, **6:**119
Nobiltà di dame (Caroso), **1:**369, 380, **2:**73–77, 336, **5:**107, *110,* 112, *117, 323,* 324, 338, **6:**122
  Negri's *Le gratie d'amore* comparison, **4:**581
  scholarly value of, **2:**74
  See also Caroso, Fabritio
Noble, Duncan, **6:**278
Noblet, Lise, **1:**35, 202, 455, **2:**71, 389, **4:**422, **656–657**, **5:***87,* 91, **6:**57
Nobody Home (Kern and Bolton), **6:**271
Nobody Knows de Trouble I See, **6:**88
Noce è Nantes, La, **5:**149
Noce di Benevento, Il, **5:**232, **6:**338
Noces, Les, **1:**52, 93, 155, 519, **4:***636,* **657–659**
  Anderson-Ivantzova choreography, **1:**86
  Bahía Ballet performance, **1:***534*
  Ballets Russes de Monte Carlo revival, **1:**311, **4:**659
  Basel Ballet performance, **1:**375
  Béjart's Paris Opera staging, **5:**97

Beriosova performance, **1:**430, **4:***658,* 659
Biagi choreography, **1:**446
Chiriaeff productions, **2:**151, 152, *152,* **3:**228, 429, **6:**131
  choreographic constructivism, **1:**259
  costumes, **2:**244
  Cunningham version, **2:**288
  Denby article on, **2:**375, **4:**658–659
  as Diaghilev production, **2:**406, 410, **4:**657
  Doubrovska performance, **2:**441, *442*
  Dutch National Ballet revival, **4:**594, 659
  Feld revival, **2:**585
  four-piano accompaniment, **4:**657; **6:**4
  Goncharova designs, **3:**197–198, **4:**657
  Nijinska choreography, **1:**155, 259, 323, 324, *324,* **2:**410, **4:**633, 634, 657–659, **5:**417, **6:**4
  Robbins choreography, **1:**70, **5:**358, 364, 367, **6:**43
  Royal Ballet revival, **1:**155, 430, **3:**267, **4:**633, 659
  in Royal Swedish Ballet repertory, **6:**43
  Stravinsky score, **2:**407, **4:**516, 657, **5:**43, **6:**4
  vocal accompaniment, **2:**410
  Wilson (Sallie) performance, **6:**402
  Woizikowski performance, **6:**404
Noces d'Argile, **3:**79
Noces de Gamache, Les, **1:**201, **2:**435, **4:**422, **5:**157
Noces de Pélée de Thétis, Les, **1:**287, 424, **5:**534
Noces de Psyché et de l'Amour, **1:**424, **5:**439
Noces de Village, Les, **4:**236
Noces di Benevento, Il, **2:**480
Noces Fantastiques, Les, **2:**471, 472, **4:**185, **6:**353
Noche de San Juan, **2:**124
Noches en los Jardines de España (Falla), **2:**567
Noctambules, **3:**136, **4:**200, 240, 584, **5:**416
Nocturnal Dances, **4:**219
Nocturne (Ashton ballet), **1:**148, 150
Nocturne (Gsovsky ballet), **1:**300, **3:**318
Nocturne (Lichine ballet), **2:**342, **4:**178
Nocturne (Nijinska ballet), **5:**439
Nocturne (Robbins ballet), **5:**206
Nocturne for a Blind Pierrot, **5:**391
Nocturne in A-flat Major (Chopin), **6:**60, 61
Nocturne in F Major (Chopin), **6:**60
Nocturnes (Cunningham choreography), **2:***288,* 289, 574
Nocturnes (Vainonen choreography), **6:**310
Nocturno Flamenco, **4:**233
Nocturnos, **2:**277
Nodier, Charles, **6:**58
Noé, Amédée de. *See* Cham
No Exit, **4:**625
No Exit (Sartre), **1:**404
No Fire Escape in Hell (stage piece), **1:**142

No-gaku genryu-ko (Nose), **3:**591
nogongoti stilt dance, **4:**287
Noguchi, Isamu, **2:**182, **4:**27, **659–660**, **5:**60, 551
  Appalachian Spring design, **1:**96, 97, 137, **3:**215, **4:**659
  Dark Meadow design, **2:**349, **4:**659
  Frontier, **3:**214, **4:**659, *660,* **5:**547
  Graham set designs, **3:**214, *215,* 217, 218, **4:**659, **5:**175, 547, 548, 562, **6:**162–163
  Night Journey design, **2:**574, **4:**632, 659
  Orpheus design, **1:**141, **2:**245, **4:**607, 660, **5:**547
  Seasons design, **2:**286
  Seraphic Dialogue design, **5:**568
Noho Theater Group, Kyoto, **5:**592
Noiject, **6:**145
Noir et Blanc, **2:**511
Noiret, Michèl, **1:**412, **2:**109
noisy shoe. *See* clogging
Noja, Simona, **1:**241, **3:***4, 53,* **5:**390
No-ja-li (also *Le Palais du Silence*), **2:**361
Nolan, Sidney, **1:**210, 230, **3:**356
Nolde, Emil, **1:**132, **6:**389
Noli Dance Suite, **5:**172
Noli Me Tangere, **3:**389
Nomaden, **4:**81
No Maps on My Taps (film), **3:**304, **5:**601
Nomius the Syrian, **5:**73
No More Play, **4:**81
Nomos Alpha, **1:**292
Nomura family, **3:**651, 652, **4:**85, 660–662
Nomura Mansaku II, **3:**651, **4:660–661**
Nomura Manzō V, **4:**661
Nomura Manzō VI, **4:661–662**
Nonas, Richard, **5:**128
Non-Cordless, **5:**276
None But the Lonely Heart, **3:**23
nongak (farmers' dance), **1:***166,* 167, **4:**46–47
Nono, Luigi, **3:**318, **5:**479
No, No, Nanette, **3:**559
No, No, Nanette (musical), **1:**433, **5:**489, 602, **6:**102, 274, 285
Nonquase, **5:**55
nonverbal communication studies, **3:**104, **4:**361–362, 367–368
Noorjahan, **2:**625
Noppe, Henri, **5:**659
Nōrā. See Manōhrā
Noram, Manuel, **5:**55
Norbertine, Goho, **4:***291*
Nordal, Lise, **4:**679
Nordenfelt, Birgitta, **1:**400
Nordgren, Erik, **2:**535, **4:**118
Nordheim, Arne, **4:**677, **5:**302, **6:**146
Nordic Museum, Sweden, **6:**36
Nordic Society for Folk Dance Research, **2:**386, **4:**160, 682
Nordic Star Dance Theater, **2:**530
Nordic Tales (Suhm), **1:**503
Nordic tradition, **1:**508, 510, 515, **3:**105, **5:**426
Nordiska Museet, Stockholm, **6:**36, 49
Nordisk Forening for Folkedansforskning, **2:**386, **4:**160, 682
Nordmann, Asta, **3:**436
Nordoff, Paul, **2:**373
Nordseth, Un-Margit, **4:**679
Nordström, Anders, **3:***337,* **6:**44
Noregs Ungdomslag, **4:**672

Nō Renaissance Kai, **3:**651
Nørgård, Per, **5:**432
Norheim, Arne, **4:**677, 678
Noriaibune, **1:**361, **3:**593
Noriega, Elena, **2:**280
Norlind, Tobias, **6:**36
Nørlyng, Ole, **2:**387
    as contributor, **2:**14, 54,
        3:360–361, **4:**61, **5:**352–353,
        371–372, 552, 557–558,
        692–693
Norman, Frank, **2:**47
Norman, Gary, **1:**210, 211, *231*, 233
Norman, Ingvar, **6:**36
Norman, Jessye, **1:**59
Norman, Leona, **6:**264
Normandy, France, **3:**63
Norris, George P., **1:**200
Norske Ballett, Den, **4:**676
Norske dansetradisjonar (Bakka),
    4:682
Norske Theater, Oslo, **4:**679
North, Alex, **1:**421, **5:**637
North, Marion, **4:**94, 95, 102,
    103–104
North, Robert, **2:**234, 514, 632,
    3:273, 274, 329, **5:**575
    Death and the Maiden, **3:**418
    London Contemporary Dance
        Theatre, **4:**217, 218
    Rambert Dance Company
        directorship, **5:**302, 303, 304
    Swedish ballet, **6:**44
North Africa, **4:662–666**
    combat dances, **4:**406
    euphemisms for dancing, **4:**403
    Islamic dance aesthetics, **1:**18–19
    scholarship, **4:**415
    zār ceremony, **6:**444–445
    See also Algeria; Egypt; Libya;
        Morocco, Tunisia
Northanger Abbey (Austen), **1:**190
North Carolina. *See* Appalachian
    clogging
North Carolina Dance Theatre,
    6:265
North Carolina School of the Arts
    de Mille productions, **2:**374
    Hayden as teacher, **3:**352
    Koner as artist in residence, **4:**39
Northcote, Anna, **3:**307, **4:667**
Northcott, Kilda, **4:**627, *628*
North Dakota style (Plains Indian
    dance), **4:**561
Northeast Regional Ballet Festival
    (Pennsylvania), **1:**501
Northern Arapho, **4:**561, 562
Northern Arts, **3:**273
Northern Ballet Theatre, **3:**270,
    4:667–668, **5:**589
Northern Divertissement, **5:**473
Northern Folk Choir, **5:**474
Northern Ireland, **3:**515
Northern Lights, **6:**363
"Northern Oklahoma style (Plains
    Indian dance), **4:**561, 562
Northern Paiute Indians,
    3:170, 171
"Northern Round Dances," **6:**303
Northern Territory, Australia, **1:**216
    Aboriginal dance, **1:**223–224,
        227–229
Northern Wakashan (Bella Bella),
    4:568
North Korea. *See* Korea
North Netherlands Dance Group,
    4:597
North Queensland, Australia, **1:**215
Northumbria, England, **6:**55
Norton and Margot, **6:**256, 257

Norway, **4:668–683**
    classical dance education, **4:**677,
        681–682
    dance research and publication,
        2:383, 386, **4:682–683**
    folk, traditional, and social
        dance, **2:**382, **4:**669–673, 682
    theatrical dance, **4:673–681**
Norwegian Ballet Union, **4:**676
Norwegian National Ballet, **1:**394,
    2:440, **3:**13, 203, **4:**677–679,
    681, **5:**433
    forerunners, **4:**674, 675–476
Norwegian National Opera, **4:**679,
    680, 681
Norwegian Youth League, **4:**672
Norwood, Lily (Cyd Charisse
    pseud.), **2:**108
Nose Asaji, **3:**591
Nosferatu (film), **2:**196
Nostradamus, **4:**455
No Super, No Boiler, **2:**575
Nosyrev, Mikhail, **5:**472
Notari, Gianni, **5:**401, **6:**143
notation, **2:**339, **3:**36, 426–427,
    4:90, **683–694**
    balli, **3:**545
    Bauhaus, **1:**387
    Beauchamps-Feuillet
        controversy, **1:**397, 465, **2:**588
        See also Feuillet notation
    Beauchamps system, **1:**91, 286,
        397, 465, **2:**339, 588, **3:**81,
        522, **4:**684, **5:**239, **6:**123
    Benesh movement, **1:**417–418,
        2:387, **4:**691, **6:**129
    bolero reconstruction, **1:**481
    Bournonville ballets, **1:**498, 511,
        512, 513, **2:**388
    bourrées, **1:**516, 517
    castanet, **2:**78
    Caverley dances, **2:**81
    Chinese ancient dance, **2:**129,
        148, **4:**693
    courante, **2:**259, 260–261
    dance reconstruction, 322–329
    Eshkol-Wachman system, **3:**534,
        4:690, 692
    ethnographic, **4:**78, 575
    European folk dance, **2:**542–543
    film or videotape supplement,
        2:597
    first based on music notes, **4:**686
    folia, **3:**29
    folk dance movement, **3:**36
    folkloristic collections, **2:**542, 543
    Georgian choreography, **3:**135
    gigue, **3:**172
    historical dance reconstructions,
        4:297–298
    history, **1:**342, 345
    Indian dance, **1:**168
    Japanese dance, **3:**591
    loure, **4:**231
    Massine system, **4:**325
    Negri dance manuel, **4:**579
    Nijinsky system, **4:**645, 646, 686
    Nikolais system, **4:**649, 688, 690
    Saint-Léon system, **4:**685, **5:**500,
        502, **6:**450–451
    Spain, **5:**670, 675
    Stepanov system, **2:**401, **3:**511,
        4:686, **5:**693–694
    technical manuals,
        6:123–124, 129
    Théleur system, **1:**345, **4:**685
    Zorn system, **4:**685–686,
        6:450–451
    See also Feuillet notation;
        Labanotation

Notations (Cage), **2:**22
Notebooks of Martha Graham,
    2:182, **3:**217
Notes upon Dancing (Blasis), **1:**345,
    460, 465
Nothin' Doing Bar, **2:**161
No Time for Love (film), **5:**175
"Notions sur la danse ancienne et
    moderne" (Dorat), **6:**49
Not Necessarily Recognizable, **5:**574
Notre-Dame de Paris (Hugo novel),
    1:488, **2:**523, 524, **3:**185,
    204, 315
Notre-Dame de Paris (Petit ballet),
    1:195, **2:**524, **4:**248, 285,
    5:97, 163
Notre Faust, **1:**292, 406, *406*
Nourrit, Adolphe, **1:**505, **2:**203,
    405, **6:**57, 58, 72
Nouveau Ballet de Monte Carlo,
    2:111, 113–114, **3:**73, 225
    Hightower, Rosella, **3:**361
    Jeanmaire, Zizi, **3:**601
    Lifar directorship, **4:**185
    See also Grand Ballet du Marquis
        de Cuevas
Nouveau Ballets Suédois, Les,
    3:100
Nouveau Robinson, Le, **1:**455
Nouveau Zydeco, **6:**250
Nouvel, Serge, **3:**285
Nouvel, Walter, **2:**411, **6:**5
Nouvelles Aventures, **4:**602
Nouvel observateur, Le
    (publication), **3:**85
Nouvel Opéra-Comique de Baxter
    et de Sorin, Le, **1:**391
Novack, Cynthia J., *as contributor*,
    4:574–575, **5:**354–357
Nova Ensemble, **1:**216
Novák, Ferenc, **1:**370
Novak, Nina, **1:**301, *302*, **6:**324–325
Novák, Vítězslav, **5:**245, 269
Novaro, Luciana, **5:**529
Novelty Sweets, **6:**363
November Night's Dream, A, **6:**175
November Steps, **4:**81, 602
Noverre, Augustin, **2:**47
Noverre, Jean-Georges, **1:**4, 43,
    122, 123, 503, **2:**299, 306,
    366, 443, 567, **4:**510,
    694–700, **5:**505
    Académie Royale de Danse, **3:**81
    Angiolini correspondence and
        feud, **2:**433, **3:**544, 545, 546,
        4:696, 699
    archival materials, **4:**163
    Armida, **5:**140
    Ashton dance impersonation of,
        1:149
    assessment of, **4:**698–699
    on Aumer ballets, **1:**201
    Austrian ballet, **1:**236–237, 241
    ballet d'action, **1:**87, 88, **2:**239,
        594, **3:**106, 365, 544, 546
    ballet de collège, **1:**283
    on ballet technique, **1:**331, **5:**227,
        6:215
    Berlin ballet, **1:**365
    on Bigottini dance technique,
        1:451
    Boquet costume designs, **1:**497
    Boydell engraving of *Jason et
        Médée*, **2:**68
    on Camargo's appearance and
        technique, **2:**27
    on character dancing, **2:**107
    children's ballet, **6:**334
    as Clerico influence, **2:**177
    composer collaborators, **5:**371

on costume excess, **2:**238–239
criticisms of, **4:**696–697
dance aesthetics, **1:**23, 125, 126,
    3:14, **4:**698, 699
dance theories, **4:**698–699
Dauberval association, **2:**351,
    352, 354, **5:**105
D'Egville performances, **2:**363
diatribe against masks,
    4:301–302
Didelot collaboration, **2:**413
on Dumoulin (David) style,
    2:451, **5:**87
on Duports (Louis-Antoine and
    Marie-Adélaïde)
    performances, **2:**464
on Dupré's technique, **2:**465
fame from *Lettres sur la danse*,
    4:695, 699
    *See also Lettres sur la danse et
        sur les ballets*
on feet positions, **1:**331, **6:**215
on Feuillet notation, **2:**588
Gallet association, **3:**106
on Gardel (Marie) dance
    technique, **3:**119, **5:**90
on Gardel (Maximilien)
    choreography, **3:**117
on Gardel (Pierre) choreography,
    3:119
German ballet, **3:**143–144, **4:**695,
    6:9
Gluck collaboration, **3:**189–190,
    4:696, **5:**371
Guimard roles, **3:**326
Heinel roles, **3:**353
on Heinel's harmonious
    movements, **3:**353
Hungarian performances, **3:**413
Iphigénie en Aulide, **1:**87, 89,
    2:363
King's Theatre (London)
    performances, **3:**112, 117,
    255, 256, 257, 258, **4:**697,
    698, **6:**333
on Lanys (Jean-Barthélemy and
    Louise-Madeleine)
    performances, **4:**122–123
Le Picq association,
    4:149–150, 276
on Le Picq's style, **4:**150
on libretti, **4:**174
Lisbon ballet, **5:**231
on Lully's dance music, **5:**39
on Marcel, **4:**263
Médée et Jason, **3:**326, **4:**149,
    346–347, 695
on Milon ballets, **4:**422, 423
on movements designating
    emotion, **3:**130, **5:**227
neoclassical themes, **3:**258
Opéra-Comique productions,
    3:66
on pantomime-ballet, **4:**698, 700
Paris Opera, **4:**696–697, 699–700,
    5:89
as Petipa (Marius) influence,
    5:149
on *port de bras*, **5:**227
on Prévost (Françoise), **5:**248
Psyché et l'Amour, **5:**270
on Rinaldi (Il Fossano), **5:**353
Rodolphe scores, **5:**371
Russian ballet influence, **4:**276,
    5:451
scholarship on, **3:**557
on stage versus private
    choreographies, **5:**623
Starzer collaboration, **5:**691–693
Stuttgart Ballet, **4:**695, **6:**9, 331

Noverre, Jean-Georges, *continued*
  Swedish opera-ballet influence,
    6:39, 49
  technical manual, **5:**270, **6:**124,
    125, 126
    See also Lettres sur la danse et
      sur les ballets
  theaters utilized, **6:***157*, 158
  Vestris family association,
    6:331, 333
  Vienna engagement, **4:**696
    *See also Fêtes Chinoises, Les;
      Jugement de Pâris, Le*
Noverre Society, Stuttgart, **6:**9, 10
Novikoff, Laurent, **1:**489,
    2:160, 272
  "Bacchanale" performance, **3:**16
  Don Quixote staging, **2:**439
  Metropolitan Opera Ballet,
    4:382, 457
  Pavlova association, **5:***45*, 123,
    124, *126*
  students, **2:**404, **3:**317, 354,
    5:603
  Swan Lake one-act production,
    6:32
Novi Sad, Yugoslavia, **6:**434,
    435–436
Novi Sad Summer Festival (1995),
    6:436
Novissimo, Giovanni, **1:**495
Novitskaya, Anastasia, **2:**416,
    4:279, 453, **6:**451, 452
Novoi State Academic Theater of
    Uzbekistan, **3:**568, 569
Novosibirsk Opera and Ballet,
    2:136, 422, **5:**459, **471–472**
Nowak, Lionel, **1:**421
Now and Then, **4:**547, 604
Nowhere Slowly, **3:**272
Now Is the Hour, **4:**627
Nowotny, Richard, **5:**56
Nowy, Arthur, **3:**142
Nozze degli Dei, Le, **3:**544, **5:**1–3,
    260, **6:**156
Nozze di Bacco e Arianna, Le, **1:**499
Nozze di Ninetta e Nane, Le, **3:**97
Nozze di Zefiro e Flora, Le, **2:**202
Nozze Slave, **1:**540
N+N Corsino, **2:**611
Nritanjali (Ragini Devi), **5:**291
Nritya Kaustubha, **4:**63
Nørlyng, Ole, *as contributor,* **2:**14,
    54, **3:**360–361
nrtta, **1:**169, 170, 442, **3:**463,
    4:63, 70
nrtya, **1:**169, 170, 442, **3:**463, **4:**70
Ntoré, **2:**212
Nuages, Les, **1:**484, **2:**361, **4:**1
*Nuances of the Tang Dynasty, Series
    I and II,* **2:**116
Nuba dance, **2:**210, **5:**3–4
nūbah dance (Morocco), **4:**491
Nubian dance, **2:**485–486, 491–492
Nucleodanza, **1:**113, 114
*Nude Couple Dancing with Young
    Girl Holding a Mask* (Picasso),
    1:*139*
Nude Descending a Staircase
    (Duchamp), **1:**137
Nude Descending a Staircase No. 2
    (Duchamp), **5:**180
Nude Prince, The, **3:**317
nudity, **2:**234, 235, 241, 393
  as costume illusion, **2:**245
  Didelot's costuming, **2:***414*
  Duncan dance concept, 246
  Egypt (ancient) dance, **2:**485
  fan dancing, **2:**572, 573

film dance, **2:**606
Flindt choreography, **3:**12, 13, *13*
Laban dance students, **4:**91, 92
Mesopotamian dance, **4:**355,
    356, 357
musical revue performers'
    seminudity, **2:**250
musical theater, **6:**272
Shawn dance concept, **2:**247
Nuer (film), **2:**602
Nuer (people), **2:**86, 210,
    4:484, 486
Nuestros Valses, **6:***323*, 324
Nuevo Balletto di Roma, **1:**446
nuin, **2:**121
Nuit, La, **1:**426, **4:**183, 517, **5:**527
Nuit de Bal, Une, **2:**93
Nuit d'Égypte, Une (*Egyptian
    Nights*), **3:**15, 19, 568, **4:**283,
    640, **5:**247
Nuit de Saint-Jean, La, **1:**326
Nuit de Walpurgis, La, **1:**446
Nuit Ensorcelée, La, **5:**690
Nuit Est un Socière, La, **4:**107
Nuit et le Jour, La, **5:**158
Nuit Obscure, La, **1:**405
Nuits, **1:**350
Nuit sur le Mont Chauve, **2:**151
Nuitten, Jan, **1:**414
Nuitter, Charles, **2:**198, 367, 368,
    5:501
Nuit Transfigurée, La, **5:**164
Nuit Venitienne, La, **2:**351
Numa Pompilius, king of Rome,
    5:377
Numbers (Johns artwork), **3:**619
Numeros, **4:**108
N/um Tchai (film), **2:**602
Nunca Más, **4:**398
*Nuova inventione d'intavolatura per
    sonare li balletti sopra la
    chitarra spagniuola*
    (Montesardo), **2:**98
Nuova sposa persiana, La
    (Noverre), **4:**696
Nuove inventioni di balli (formerly
    Le gratie d'amore) (Negri),
    3:107, **4:**579
*Nuovo e curiosa scuola de' balli
    teatrali* (Lambranzi). *See New
    and Curious School of
    Theatrical Dancing*
Nupe (people), **6:**15, 382
Nur and Anitra, **4:**459
Nuremberg, Germany, **6:**55
Nureyev, Rudolf, **1:**292, **3:**220,
    5:4–9, 187, 206, 282, 555,
    565, 575, **6:**146, 324
  Alonso (Alicia) dance
    partnership, **2:**280
  American stage debut, **5:**59
  Apollo, **1:**96
  Après-midi d'un Faune, L', **1:**99
  Australian ballet tours, **1:**210
  Austrian ballet, **1:**241, 243
  Bayadère performance, **5:***418*
  Bayadère staging, **1:**155, 156, 393,
    5:416, 417, *418*
  Beaton photograph of, **1:**395
  as Boston Ballet guest artist,
    1:501
  Bruhn friendship, **2:**4
  Checkmate, **2:**115
  Cinderella staging, **2:**174
  as Coe influence, **2:**184
  Collier dance partnership, **2:**186
  in Cramér productions, **2:**264
  defection to West, **1:**372, **5:**5,
    416, 485

Don Quixote, **1:**38, 232–233,
    2:440, **3:**60
  Dupond rivalry, **2:**463
  English National Ballet
    productions, **2:**511, 513, 514
  Evdokimova association, **2:**561
  Ferri dance partnership, **2:**587
  film appearance, **2:**444
  Flindt choreography for, **3:**13
  Fonteyn dance partnership,
    1:155, **3:**43, *44*, 45–46, *45*,
    5:5, *6, 7,* 97, 107, 164, 416
  Fracci dance partnership, **3:**60
  Georgiadis design collaboration,
    3:136
  Giselle performance, **2:**114, **5:**5
  Homage to Diaghilev program
    (1982), **3:**75
  Jeune Homme et La Mort
    television performance, **3:**601
  Joffrey program, **3:**616
  Kain dance partnership, **3:**643
  Karsavina association, **3:***656, 656*
  last stage performance, **3:**418
  Manfred, **6:**117
  Manon performance, **4:**257
  as National Ballet of Canada
    influence, **4:**543
  Norwegian National Ballet guest
    performance, **4:**677
  Nutcracker production, **1:**111,
    436, **2:**587, **5:**7, 13, 15
  Paris galas, **3:**362
  Paris Opera Ballet, **2:**463, **5:**7–8,
    97, *97, 98*
  partners, **5:***94,* 100, 290, **6:**143
  Petrouchka, **5:**166
  Raymonda, **1:**73, 231, 232, **2:**114,
    3:306, **5:**7, 97, *159*, **6:**380,
    454
  Romeo and Juliet, **2:**114, 511,
    514, **3:**46, 60, **4:**242, **5:**394,
    396, 398
  Rome Opera mixed program
    performance, **5:**401
  Royal Ballet productions,
    1:155, 156
  Sleeping Beauty, **1:**200, **2:**114,
    511, 513, **3:**136, 362, **4:**543,
    5:*5, 6, 7,* **6:**132, 142, 353
  Swan Lake, **4:**34, 35
Nuristani (people), **1:**27
Nurkalev, Timur, **3:**665
Nurkhon, **6:**306
Nurmyov, Chary, **4:**87
Nursery Suite, The, **2:**400
Nurymov, Chary, **4:**87
Nusa Tenggara, Indonesia, **3:**504
Nutcracker, The, **5:**9–16, 597, 611
  character role, **2:**106
  as Christmas tradition, **2:**160,
    3:121, **4:**576, *577,* 606, 678,
    5:*11,* 12, 13, 15, 407,
    6:44, *139*
  film versions, **5:**16
  grand pas de deux, **5:**106
  Orientalism, **5:**45
  productions in Russia, **5:**9–12
    Ananiashvili performances,
      1:83
    Belsky production, **1:**417
    Bessmertnova performance,
      1:440
    Boyarchikov production, **5:**23
    character dances, **2:**108
    Dmitriev design, **2:**421
    Gerdt (Pavel) performance,
      3:137
    Gorsky production, **1:**489,
      3:205–206, **5:**10, 11

    Grigorovich conception, **3:**309,
      4:335, **5:**10, *11, 12,* 463, **6:**314
    Ivanov conception, **3:**563–564,
      564, **5:***565*
    Lopukhov version, **2:**421,
      3:327, **4:**225, **5:**10–11, 12
    Maximova performance, **4:**335
    Petipa-Ivanov collaboration,
      2:108, **3:**563–564, **5:**9, 10,
      160, **6:**117
    Vainonen production, **2:**421,
      5:10, *10,* **10–12,** 11–12, 15,
      6:310, 311, 343
  productions outside Russia,
    5:13–16
    Amodio production, **1:**83
    Ashton production, **1:**153, **5:**15
    Balanchine production, **1:**197,
      264, 270, 271, **2:**342, 574,
      577, **3:***654,* **4:**29, 246, 274,
      606, 610, *617,* **5:**13, 15, 16,
      407, 512, **6:***139,* 144, 265
    Ballet der Lage Landen, **1:**289
    Ballet Russe de Monte Carlo,
      1:297, 301
    Baryshnikov version, **1:**372,
      4:24, **5:**13
    Basel Ballet, **1:**374, 375
    Biagi performance, **1:**446
    Bintley one-act production,
      1:454
    Bjørn staging, **4:**679
    Blair performance, **1:**459
    Bruhn performances, **2:**3
    Byrd's *Harlem Nutcracker,* **2:**20
    Christensen brothers'
      choreographies, **2:**160, 162,
      5:15, 16, 512, *512,* 513
    Christmas tree effect, **5:**407
    de Valois stagings, **1:**146,
      2:401–402, **3:**264
    English National Ballet, **2:**509,
      509, 510, 511, 512, 514, **3:**270
    first full-length in West, **5:**14
    Flindt production, **3:**13
    Franca choreography, **3:**62,
      4:542
    Gore production, **3:**203
    Hightower production, **3:**362
    Hynd production, **3:**428
    Isbert Swedish version, **6:**44
    Joffrey re-creation of
      Petipa-Ivanov version, **3:**617
    Karinska costumes, **3:***654*
    Kronstam performance, **4:**65
    Kudelka production, **4:**73, *546,*
      5:547
    Lichine choreography, **2:**510,
      4:179
    Martins performance, **4:**274
    Morris's *Hard Nut* version,
      1:411, **4:**471, **5:**16
    Murphy (Graeme) production,
      1:211, 235, **4:**479
    Nault for Grand Ballets
      Canadiens, **3:**229, 234,
      4:576, *577*
    Neumeier production, **1:**391,
      500, **5:**13, 15, 16, 436
    Nureyev production, **1:**111,
      436, **2:**587, **5:**7, 13, 15
    Orlikovsky staging, **6:**437
    Ottawa Ballet, **1:**429
    Paeper choreography, **5:**58
    Page production, **5:**59
    Petit staging, **3:**75, **5:**15, 164
    Poole staging, **5:**651
    Prokovsky staging, **4:**667
    Romanov production, **2:**105

Rosenthal lighting, **5:**407
Schaufuss (Peter) production,
    1:436, **2:**514, **3:**156, *270*
Schayk version. *See Nutcracker
    and the Mouse King, The*
Sergeyev revival, **5:**413
Spoerli staging, **5:**682
Stevenson production, **2:**514
Teatro Colón, **1:**111
Ter-Arutunian scenic design,
    6:144
Vainonen's in Budapest, **3:**417
Vainonen's in Norway,
    4:677–678
Wright production, **2:**186,
    6:405
Snowflakes waltz, **1:***264*,
    3:*564, 564*
Tchaikovsky score, **3:**135, **4:**515,
    6:114, 116–117
travesty role, **6:**190
*Nutcracker and the Mouse King,
    The,* **2:**470
Nutcracker Suite (Tchaikovsky),
    5:16
Nuti, **1:**214, **6:**95
Nü Wa, **2:**139
Nuyts, Jean, **1:**290
Nyankole (Ankole) (people), **2:**86
Nye engelske danse (Danish dance
    manual), **2:**380–381
*Nye Narcis, Det. See New Narcissus,
    The*
*Nye Penelope, Den. See New
    Penelope, The*
N.Y. Export, Opus Jazz, **2:**108,
    5:363
Nyman, Michael, **2:**1, 119, **5:**305
Nymph and the Faun, The, **2:**60
Nympheas, **3:**272
Nymph Errant, **2:**372
Nymphet, **2:**474
Nymphe und der Schmetterling, Die,
    3:313–314, **5:**135
Nymph of Świteź Lake, The, **3:**192,
    5:75
Nymphs of Diana, The, **6:**334
Ny Norsk Ballett, **4:**676
Nyonga, Alice, **5:**305
Nyoro (people), **2:**90
Nyrittya Tale Tale (television
    program), **5:**63
Nyts, Jan, **5:**422
Nyungwe (people), **5:**663–664
Nzakara (people), **4:**484
Nzema (people), **6:**19

Oakes, Percy, **6:**319
Oakie, Jack, **6:**142
Oakland Ballet, **6:**266
Oaks, Agnes, **2:**514, *514*
Oak Street Beach, **5:**59
Oath of the Horatii, The (David),
    1:126, **5:**89
Oatka Trail, **2:**567
Obadia, Regis, **3:**79, 83
Oba Oba (musical), **6:**288
Obarzanek, Gideon, **6:**56
Obasute, **4:**42
Obeah. See Black Ritual
Oben und Unten, **3:**624–625
oberek, **5:**213, *218*
Oberlin Dance Collective, **6:**266
Oberon, **1:**247
Oberon (Weber opera), **4:**514
Oberon, the Fairy Prince (Jonson
    masque), **4:**312, 313
obertas, **5:**213, 214
Oberzaucher, Alfred, *as contributor,*
    1:235–242, **2:**153–154, **3:**340

Oberzaucher-Schüller, Gunhild, *as
    contributor,* **1:**242–243,
    449–450, 468, **4:**633–639,
    657–659, **6:**50–51, 334–336,
    386–388
Obey, André, **2:**450
Objects, **2:**292
Objem (film), **5:**677
Objet Poétique (Miró), **1:**135
obliquement, **1:**335
oboe, **4:**47, 50
O-bon festival, **1:**496
Oboukhoff, Anatole, **1:**110, 313,
    430, **2:**444, **3:**16, 51, **4:***207,*
    208, 449, **5:**17, 392, **6:**292,
    364, 398
O, Boy! (musical), **6:**271
Obradović, Vera, **6:**435
Obrant, Aleksandr, **4:**224
*Obrazy russkoi narodnoi
    khoreografi* (Goleizovsky),
    3:196
O'Brien, Art, **3:**518
O Brother Sun and Sister Moon,
    5:587
*Observations sur les modes et les
    usages de Paris* (print),
    2:*175*
Observer (British newspaper),
    3:282, 285
Obukhov, Mikhail, **4:**283, 639, **5:**17,
    391, **6:**60, 344
Obukhova, Evgenia, **3:**568
Obusan, Ramón, **5:**173, 174
    as photographer, **5:**169, 171
Occioni, Fernando, **1:**237
*Occupational Marks and Other
    Physical Signs* (Ronchese),
    2:328
Ocean, **2:**296, **5:**17–19
Oceanic dance traditions, **5:**19–21
    anthropological studies,
    4:369, 628
    Bellona, **1:**415–416
    hula, **3:**394–397
    Melanesia, **4:**351–352
    Micronesia, **4:**400–402
    musical accompaniment,
    4:495–498
    Okinawa, **1:**186, **2:**219, **5:**25–28
    research and publication,
    4:628–629
    See also Australia; New Zealand;
    Polynesia; Samoa
Ocellus, **5:***197*
ochitsuita, **4:**46
Ochner, Berta, **2:**580
ōchōmono, **3:**607
Ochre Dusk, **1:**215, *215*
Ochrid legend, **5:**617
O Come All Ye Faithful, **3:**575
O'Connell, Daniel, **2:**70
O'Connor, Donald, **5:**21–22,
    6:101, 287
Octandre, **1:**461
October Legend, **6:**344
October Revolution (1917). *See
    Russian Revolution*
Octoroons, The (musical), **6:**255
odalan, **2:**232
Odalisa, o La Figlia del Soldato,
    1:499
O'Day, Kevin, **3:**234, **4:**623
Ode, **1:**348, **2:**410, 441, *442,* **4:**33,
    5:242, 545, 547
    choreographed film projections,
    2:603
    Lifar performance, **4:**182
    Tchelitchev design, **2:**603,
    6:118, *118*

Ødegaard, Marit Schade, **4:***680*
O'Denishawn, Florence, **6:**272
Odenthal, Johannes, **3:**162
"Ode on Mira Dancing" (Booth),
    5:518
Odessa, Ukraine, **6:**225, 226
Ode to Glory, **1:**66
"Ode to Joy" (Schiller), **1:**402
Ode to Taylor Jones (Dunham and
    Redmond), **2:**459
Odetta, **2:**60, 367
Odetta, **2:**505, 587, **5:**403
*Odetta, o La Demenza di Carlo VI
    Re di Francia,* **5:**138
Odissi, **1:**170, **2:**394, **3:**467, 468,
    507, 508, **4:**5, 6, 62, 63, 257,
    5:22–23, 525
    Mahapatra performances,
    4:246–247
    Pakistan, **5:**62, 63
    Panigrahi, Sanjukta, **5:**22, 23,
    68–69
    Ritha Devi performance, **5:**354
    Valli, **6:**292
Odom, Selma Landen, **2:**49, **3:**321
    as contributor, **3:**367–368,
    594–597
odori, **3:**586–587, *586,* 637, 639
    See also bon odori
odu tonnolo dance, **2:**422
Odyssey (Homer), **3:**291, 327
odzemek, **2:**301
Oedipus Rex (Sophocles), **3:**652
Oedipus Rex (Stravinsky), **2:**183,
    410, **6:**5
Oehlenschläger, Adam, **1:**503, 515
Oenone et Paris, **1:**36
"O'er the Water to Charlie," **3:**247
Oeuf à la Coque, **4:**320
Oeuvre d'art vivant, L' (Appia), **1:**98
Of Blessed Memory, **1:**235
*Of Bright & Blue Birds & the Gala
    Sun,* **6:**112
Offenbach, Jacques, **1:**253, **2:**15,
    60, **4:**418, **5:**57
    Belle Hélène, La, **2:**15, 226–227,
    3:27
    can-can, **2:**249
    Fokine ballets, **3:**26, 27
    Gaîté Parisienne, **3:**103
    operettas, **6:**268
    Orpheus in the Underworld, **2:**57
    polka compositions, **5:**221
    popularity, **3:**70
    Tales of Hoffmann, **1:**405, **6:**268
Offenbach Follies, **4:**136
Offenbach in the Underworld, **1:**68,
    3:62, 614, 664, **4:**540, *541,*
    6:201
Offenbach Overtures, **6:**111
Offerlunden, **1:**327
Office, The, **4:**472
Officer, Jillian, **2:**49
Official Doctrine (film dance), **2:**605
Offrande à la Liberté, **3:**118
Offrande à L'Amour, L', **3:**564
Offrande à Terpsichore, L', **3:**258
Offrande Chorégraphique, **1:**291
Offrandes à l'Amour, Les, **2:**112,
    413, **4:**698

*Off the Ground: First Steps to a
    Philosophical Consideration of
    the Dance* (Sparshott), **1:**24,
    2:50
Of Mice and Men (film), **2:**197
Of Thee I Sing (musical), **6:**275, 281
Ogan, Banu, **5:**17
Ogenblikken, **4:**596
Oggetto Amato, **1:**82
Ogilby, John, **2:**337, **3:**254, 521
Ōgino Isaburō II, **1:**361
Ognessian, E. S., **4:**7
Ogoun, Luboš, **1:**542, **2:**308,
    5:23–24, 617
Ogunde, Herbert, **6:**21, 384
Ogunmola, Kola, **6:**21, 384
Ohanian, Mademoiselle Armen,
    6:*318*
O'Hara, Frank, **2:**376
Ohara Gokō, **4:**42
Ohara Noriko, **3:**589, **5:***564*
Ohardieno, Roger, **2:***459*
Oh Boy! (musical), **5:**602
Oh, Captain (musical), **2:**343
Ohio Ballet, **2:**120, 359, **5:**24–25
Ohio State University, **4:**95,
    104, 169
Oh Julie!, **3:**296
Oh, Kay! (musical), **5:**602
Oh, Lady! Lady!! (musical), **6:**271
Ohman, Frank, **1:**293, **4:***615*
Oh, My, Murder?, **2:**357
Ohn, Gérard, **1:**306
Ohya, Masako, **1:**282
Ohns, Elly, **1:**1
"O Holy Night" (Adam), **1:**10
O'Horgan, Tom, **6:**284
Ohya, Masako, **1:**282
oiemono, **3:**607
Oimatsu, **3:**90
Oiseau Bleu, L', **4:**320
Oiseau de Feu, L'. See Firebird, The
Oiseau Phoenix, L', **2:**151
Oiseleurs, Les, **5:**196
Ojibwe (people), **4:**553
Okantomi, **2:**281
O'Keefe, J. G., **3:**518
O'Keefe Center. *See* Hummingbird
    Centre, Toronto
O-kee-pah (Catlin), **4:**561
okeoke pati, **1:**415
*Okhrana truda i zdorov'ia artistov
    baleta* (Badnin), **2:**330
Okie, William B. Jr., **5:**570
Okiek (people), **2:**90
Okina, **6:**229
Okinawa, **5:**25–28
    folk dance, **2:**219
    martial arts, **1:**186
Oklahoma! (film), **2:**618
Oklahoma! (musical), **1:**11, **2:**251,
    373, **4:**126, 213, **5:**369, **6:**248,
    278, *278,* 281, 285, 287
Oklahoma Territory, **4:**555, 556,
    558, 560
Okpela (people), **4:**288
Okpodu (people), **6:**16
Oksana, **6:**226
Oktett, **5:**683
Okunev, Herman, **4:**87
Okuneva, V., **5:**481
Okuni, **3:**581, 637, **5:**28–29
Ōkura family, **4:**86
Ōkura school, **4:**85, *86,* **5:**90–592
Ōkura Torakazu, **4:**86
Ōkura Yaemon, **4:**86
Ōkura Yataro, **4:**86
Ólafsdóttir, Nanna, **3:**437
Olafsen, Inge, **5:***429*
Olafsson, Eggert, **3:**434
Oláh, Gusztáv, **3:**415, 416–417

Olalde, Patricia, **6:**266
Olason, Vesteinn, **3:**436
Olatunji, Michael, **6:**258
Olaus Magnus, bishop of Sweden, **6:**36
Olavarría y Ferrari, Enrique, **4:**399
Olbrei, Rahel, **2:**528–529
Old American Company, **2:**467, **5:**198
Old Babylonian period, **4:**356
Oldenburg, Claes, **1:**139
Oldenburg, Petr, **2:**207
Old Globe Theater, San Diego, **6:**288
Oldham, Arthur, **2:**265, **5:**301
Old in Age, but Still Young in Spirit, **2:**155, 159
Old Memories, **1:**509
Old Polish Encyclopedia (Gloger), **5:**210
Olds, Elizabeth, **5:**399, 437
Old Soldier, The (*Le Maréchal des Logis*), **1:**123, 124
Old Tango, The (television ballet), **1:**539, **4:**336
Old Testament. *See* Bible, dance in the
Old Vic Theatre, London
    de Valois association, **2:**396, 397, **3:**264, **5:**411
    first all-ballet evening, **1:**146
    Helpmann acting roles, **3:**356
    See also Royal Ballet
Oleaga, Milton, *as photographer*, **4:**651
Oleg Tumulilingan, **3:**666
olender, **5:**214
Oleneva, Maria, **1:**532, 533
olés, **5:**133
Olé Toro, **3:**22
Olga Roriz Companhia de Dança, **5:**235
O, Libertad!, **5:**586
Olimi festival, **4:**288
Olimpiade (Manfredini), **3:**365
Oliosa, Elionora, **1:**533
Oliphant, Betty, **2:**47, **4:**541, **6:**1
Oliva, Pepita de, **2:**306, 522, **4:**414, **5:***671*, 672
Olivares, Luis, **3:**286
Oliveira, Roberto de, **6:**10
Oliver, Enrique Senis, **3:**343
Oliver, Michael, **5:**594–595
    as contributor, **5:**266–269, 594–595
Oliver, Thelma, **6:**283
Oliveros, Pauline, **2:**53, 54, 289
Olivet, François d', **2:**337
Olivet, Louis-Hilaire d', **1:**3, **4:**235, **5:**39, 490
Ollantay, **5:**144
Oller-Metros, Ramón, **5:**675
Olo (people), **5:**76
Olrich, April, **1:**315
Olsen, Andrea, **4:**17
Olsen, Ole, **2:**4
Olson, Charles, **2:**288
Olsovská, Vera, **5:**393
Olsson-Åhrberg, Cissi, **6:**46
Oltenia, **5:**379, 380
Oluşum, **6:**212
Olympia Theatre, London, **4:**24
Olympic Games, **1:**127, 291
    Berlin (1936), **3:**147, **4:**61, 93, 477, 539–540, **5:**66, 218, **6:**393
    Heracles as originator, **3:**645
    ice dancing, **3:**431, 432, 433
    International Committee, **5:**62
    Mexico City, **3:**167

Olympics, **3:***612*, 613
Olympic Youth (Wigman pageant), **6:**393
Olympie, **1:**452
Omagiu lui Brâncuşi, **5:**386
Omaha Dance, **4:**561
Oman, Julia Trevelyan, **1:**156, **2:**244, 515, 516, **4:**456
Omatsu Kyōran, **3:**593
Ombra du Tsi-Ven, ossia La Costanza Premiata, L', **6:**70
Ombre, L', **1:**86, **3:**95, **4:**455, **6:**58, 73
Omega Liturgical Dance Company, **4:**213
Omerzel, Marko, **6:**437
O-Mika, **2:**572, **5:**493
Omkarlal, Pandit, **2:**468
Omnibus (television series), **1:**452, **2:**375, **6:**137–138, 154
Omodokaya Jūshu, **3:**441
Omohundro, John ("Texas Jack"), **4:**464
Omorosōshi, **5:**26
Omote, **1:**61
Om Shiva (film), **3:**200
On a Clear Day You Can See Forever (musical), **5:**408
On'ami. *See* Montoshige
On an Island with You (film), **2:**108
On Baile's Strand (Yeats), **2:**397
"On Ballet Dramaturgy" (Slonimsky), **5:**614
On Brighton, **3:**261
Once Group, **1:**141
Once More, Frank, **1:**73
Once on This Island (musical), **6:**288
Once Upon a Time (*The Little Ballet*), **1:**372
On Death and Dying (Kübler-Ross), **1:**462
Ondine, **1:**86, 375, **2:**356, **5:**29, 136, 277, 498
    Ashton production, **1:**154, *156*, **3:**41, 42, *43*, 360, **5:**29
    Bavarian State Ballet, **1:**390
    Beriozoff production, **1:**430
    Bey performance, **1:**442
    Cerrito performance, **2:**93, 94, **3:**260
    costumes, **2:**244
    Dollar choreography, **2:**426
    Fonteyn performance, **3:**41, 42, *43*, 44
    Gerdt (Pavel) performance, **3:**136
    Henry (Louis) production, **3:**358
    Henze score, **3:**360, **4:**517
    Neumeier choreography, **4:**604
    Perrot production, **2:**94, 95, **5:**29, 136, 277
    Romantic tradition, **2:**207, **3:**260
    Saint-Léon staging and performance, **3:**413
    Taglioni (Paul) production, **3:**145
    various productions and choreographers, **3:**360
Ondine (Tchaikovsky), **6:**29, 114
Ondine, ou La Naïade. See Ondine
ondo-tori, **3:**588
One Damn Thing after Another (musical), **1:**520, **4:**334
One Extra Company, The, **1:**214–215
Onegin, **1:**201, 391, 500
    Cranko production, **2:**267, **3:**150, 350, **4:**245, 249, 546, 2498, **5:**405, 430, **6:**9, 43, 117
    English National Ballet annual performance, **2:**512

Hart (Evelyn) performance, **3:**345
    Haydée performance, **3:**350
    Madsen performance, **4:**245
    Makarova performance, **4:**248, 249
    Rose designs, **5:**405
    Tennant performance, **6:**143
One Good Turn, **5:**440
100 Men and a Girl (film), **2:**615
110 in the Shade (musical), **6:**283
O'Neill, Dan, **3:**275
O'Neill, Kitty, **6:**316
O'Neill, Michael, *as photographer*, **2:**292, 294, **4:**451
O'Neill, Nellie, **6:**316
One Kikugarō VI, **4:**534
One More Gaudy Night, **3:**219
One Part of the Matter, **3:**201
one-step, **2:**630, **6:**243
One Story as in Falling, **1:**545
One Touch of Venus (musical), **2:**373, **4:**120, **6:**278
1–2–3, **5:**301
Oni Kembei (Demon Sword Dance), **3:**587
Only Jealousy of Emer, The (Yeats), **3:**519
On Music (Augustine), **1:**20–21
On Music and Musicians (Falla), **2:**568
On My Mother's Side, **6:**376, *376*
onnagata, **3:**658, **5:**29–30
    as *kabuki* tradition, **3:**581, 637, *638*, 640
    makeup, **4:**296
    Nakamura Ganirō II, **4:**533
    Nakamura Tomijūrō, **4:**536
    Nakamura Utaemon, **4:**537–538, *537*
Onna Goroshi Abura no Jigoku, **3:**658
onna kabuki, **3:**637
Onne, Madeleine, **6:**44
Onoe Baikō, **5:**30–31
Onoe Baikō V, **5:**30
Onoe Baikō VI, **5:**30
Onoe Baikō VII, **4:**538, **5:**30
Onoe Kikugorō, **5:**31–32
Onoe Kikugorō I, **5:**31
Onoe Kikugorō II, **5:**31
Onoe Kikugorō III, **5:**30, 31
Onoe Kikugorō IV, **5:**31
Onoe Kikugorō V, **3:**438–439, **4:**537, **5:**31
Onoe Kikugorō VI, **1:**361, **3:**90, **4:**533, 534, **5:**31, 31–32, 33
Onoe Kikugorō VII, **3:**439, *638*, **5:**30, 32
Onoe Kuroemon II, **5:**30
Onoe Ryū, **3:**593
Onoe Shōroku, **5:**32–33
Onoe Shōroku I, **5:**32–33
Onoe Shōroku II, **3:**593, **4:**333, 536, **5:**30, *32*, 33
Onoe Tatsunosuke, **3:**439
Onoe Tatsunosuke I. *See* Fujima Kan'emon V
Onoe Tatsunosuke I, **5:**32
Onoe Tatsunosuke III. *See* Fujima Kan'emon VI
Ōno Kazuo, **2:**17, 18, **3:**363, 591, 657, **5:**33–34
Onomasticon (Pollux), **2:**116
Onondaga (people), **4:**551
Ono no Komachi, **3:**647
Onorati, Giacomo, **2:**414
On Stage!, **1:**68, **2:**245, **3:**664, **4:**10, 11, 63
Onsum, Gary, **3:**372
Ontario, Canada, **2:**48

On the Art of the Theatre (Craig), **4:**189
On the Brink of Time, **4:**156
On the Chorus (Sophocles), **2:**159
On the Path of Modern Dance Art (Körtvélyes), **3:**424
On the Periphery of Life, **4:**267
On the Radio, **6:**121
On the Riviera, **2:**184
On the Seashore, **4:**208
On the Town (stage and film musical), **2:**617
    Berstein score, **1:**438
    Fancy Free as basis, **2:**568, **6:**279
    Kelly film performance, **4:**3, 4
    Miller (Ann) performance, **4:**419
    Neumeier choreography, **4:**604
    Robbins choreography, **3:**599, **5:**360, **6:**279
    Seregi staging, **3:**418, **5:**569, **6:**66
    Smith (Oliver) design, **5:**616
On with the Dance (revue), **3:**202, **4:**320, **5:**294
On Your Toes (film), **6:**450
On Your Toes (musical), **2:**262, **3:**598, **5:**489, **6:**276
    Balanchine choreography, **1:**271
    Bolger performance, **1:**482, **6:**277
    Makarova performance, **4:**249, **6:**286
    revival, **6:**286
    Stuttgart Ballet production, **4:**2
    Wells performance, **6:**380
    Zorina performance, **6:**449
Onze Tijd, **1:**410
Onzia, Koen, **2:**2, 514, **5:**422
Oomori Masahide, **2:**18
Opal Loop, **1:**143, 544, *544*, **3:**274, **5:**305
Opanasenko, Aleksandr, **1:**408
Open British Championship (ballroom dancing), **1:**356
Openhaus, Mark, **2:**609
Opening Dance, **1:**421
openings of the (eye), **3:**349
Open Score (Rauschenberg), **5:**314
open (solo) dancing, **1:**78
open space design, **5:**532
opera
    Adam, Adolphe, **1:**9, 10
    Appia scenic design, **1:**97–98
    Australia, **1:**205, 206, 207
    Austria, **1:**236, 240
    ballet score borrowings from, **4:**513, 514
    Bulgaria, **2:**10
    China, **1:**164–165, 179–180, 187, **2:**19–220, *131*, 132, 141–144, 148
    comic, **2:**250
    Diaghilev productions, **2:**407, 410
    Drigo, Riccardo, **2:**446–447
    English masques, **3:**254
    first French, **4:**509
    French operetta popularity, **3:**71
    French preference for dance, **1:**287–288
    French provincial houses, **3:**66–67
    French scenic and lighting innovations, **2:**171–172, **3:**69
    Gluck reform, **3:**188
    Helpmann direction, **3:**356, 357
    Korea, **1:**166
    Kreutzer, Rodolphe, **4:**61
    libretto reforms, **4:**174
    Lully, Jean-Baptiste, **4:**234, 235
    mad scenes, **3:**180
    pastorales influence on development of, **5:**113
    Prague, **2:**306, 307

Romanian companies, **5:**385
Sweden, 39, **6:**38, 47
Tibetan folk works, **6:**168–169, *168, 169*
Ukraine, **6:**225
Wilson (Robert) productions, **6:**400–401
Yoruba, **6:**21
Zakharov direction, **6:**442
See also specific composers and opera titles
opera, ballet in, **4:**514, **5:**34–38
Ailey choreography, **1:**57
Béjart staging, **1:**404, 405, 406
Belgian productions, **1:**410
Blasis *divertissements*, **1:**461
Campra compositions, **2:**34
canaries, **2:**51
Canziani compositions, **2:**55
chaconnes and *passacailles*, **2:**98–99
Childs choreographies and direction, **1:**120
Chladek choreographies, **2:**153, 154
composers, **4:**514
Coralli choreographies, **2:**202
divertissements, **4:**514
first in America, **6:**233
French popularity, **3:**70
French sixteenth- and seventeenth-century characteristics, **4:**235
Gardel (Pierre) choreography, **3:**118
Gioja compositions, **3:**175–176
Gluck, Christoph Willibald, **3:**188–190
Mazilier *divertissements* choreographies, **4:**341
Page, Ruth, **5:**58, 59
as Paris Opera convention, **4:**514, **5:**148–149
Petipa, Lucien, **5:**148–149
Portugal, **5:**230–231
Purcell, Henry, **5:**280–282
Seregi choreographies, **5:**569
Zakharov stagings, **6:**442
See also opéra-ballet and *tragédie lyrique*
Opera Atelier, **5:**327, **6:**132, 133
Opéra au XIXᵉ siècle (Beaumont), **2:**70, 71
Opéra au XIXᵉ Siècle, L' (print series), **5:**241
Opera and Ballet Theater of Belarus, Minsk, **1:**408
opéra-ballet and *tragédie lyrique*, **5:**34, 38–41
ballet de cour, **1:**2, 287–288
Ballet des Saisons, **5:**87
Berain designs, **1:**446
Campra compositions, **2:**34
entrée term, **2:**517
Indes Galantes, Les, **3:**450
Lully inauguration, **4:**234–235, 509
Mouret compositions, **4:**475
music, **4:**509
Paris Opera Ballet, **5:**86, 87
pastorales, **5:**113
Rameau, Jean-Philippe, **5:**38, 40, 306–307
Rodolphe composition, **5:**371
Sweden, **6:**39, 47
Operaballeten, **4:**676
Opera bellissima . . . di gagliarda (Luti di Sulmona), **6:**122
opéra-comique (genre), **5:**37, 113
See also operetta

Opéra-Comique, Paris
Adam compositions, **1:**9
Arnould-Mussot ballets, **1:**122
Biagi as *premier danseur étoile*, **1:**446
Charrat performance, **2:**111
Darsonval performance, **2:**351
Fleurs revival, **3:**450
Hérold compositions, **3:**360–361
Khamma, **2:**360
Lacotte reconstruction, **4:**108
Noverre productions, **3:**66
Paris Opera association, **5:**98
post-World War II, **3:**73
Schwarz family, **5:**562–563
Opera della Accademia Nazionale di Danza, **3:**555
Opéra de Monte-Carlo, **2:**253
Opera Descuartizada, La, **2:**389
Operama Productions, **5:**62
Opéra Russe, **1:**308, **5:**17
opera seria (genre), **5:**35
Opérateyr Chinois, L', **2:**365
operetta, **5:**217, **6:**267–628, 270, 271, 273, 276
Operetta Theater, Budapest, **3:**422
Operti, Giuseppe, **1:**456
Opfermann, Franz, **4:**589
Ophelia, **1:**394
Opoku, Albert Mawere, **3:**167, 169, 170
as contributor, **3:**164–169
Oposnasky, Yuri, **2:**176
Opportunity Makes the Thief, **1:**400
Oprichnik, The (Tchaikovsky), **6:**114
Optimistic Tragedy, **1:**540, **5:**464, 467
Opus 1, **2:**267, **4:**1, **5:**431
Opus 19/The Dreamer, **1:**372, **4:**345, **5:**366–367
Opus 34 (Balanchine work), **5:**407
Opus 35 (Spoerli work), **1:**375
Opus 43, **5:**677
Opus 51, **1:**421
Opus 58, **4:**602
Opus McShann, **1:**60
Opus Piat, **2:**448–249
Oraciones, **6:**324
Oracle, **1:**394
oral history, **3:**32
Oral History Project, **5:**48
O'Ramsey, Georgia, **6:**272
O Rangasayee, **3:**447, **4:**471, *471*
Orange Free State, South Africa, **5:**651, 654
Oratorio, **2:**116
Orbis sensualium pictus (book), **6:***156*
Orbs, **1:**403, **6:**109, 112
Orcaizaguirre, Jorge (Virulazo), **6:**93, 94
orcheomai, **1:**448
Orchesis, **3:**352, **6:**295, 296
Orchésographie (Arbeau). *See* Arbeau, Thoinot
Orchesography (Weaver trs. of Feuillet *Chorégraphie*), **2:**81, 588, 589, **3:**522, **4:**105, 684, **6:**372, 373
Orchestics Foundation, **2:**417
Orchestics Movement Theater, **3:**421
orchestics system, **2:**417, **3:**420–421
orchestra, **5:**41–42, **6:**155, 157, 161
Orchestra (Davies), **2:**254, 269, **5:**619
Orchestre de la Suisse Romande, L', **1:**93

Ordelaffi, Pino de, **2:**427
Order of the Golden Fleece, **4:**449
Ordman, Jeannette, **3:**532
Ordre du Roi, L', **3:***562*, **5:**154
O'Reilly, Mary Jane, **4:**625, 626, 627
O'Reilly, Robert Bray, **2:**353
Orenković, Ksenija, **6:**438
Oreste, **4:**509
Oresteia, **1:**38, **2:**397, **3:**289
Orestes, **3:**399, **5:**432
Orezzoli, Héctor, **6:**94, 287, 288
Orfa, **1:**10, 477, **2:**95, **4:**342
Orfeo (Alonso ballet), **2:**277
Orfeo (Cavalli), **1:**287
Orfeo (Monteverdi), **2:**455, **3:**418, **5:**34, 6:**349
Orfeo (Romanov ballet), **5:**392
Orfeo ed Euridice (Gluck opera), **1:**87, 98, 153, 253, 268, **2:**64, 153, 401, 433, 455, **3:**20, 188, 189, 353, 372, 596, **4:**270, **5:**35, 246, 558, **6:**95, 119
"Dance of the Furies," **4:**509
Drottningholm Court Theater re-creations, **6:**47
Metropolitan Opera Ballet, **4:***381*
as reform opera, **5:**35
Swedish premiere production, **6:**39
Orff, Carl, **1:**390, **2:**124, **3:**318, **5:**42–43, 677
Catulli Carmina, **1:**375, 390, **2:**17, **3:**230, 317
Egk as student, **2:**478
trilogy, **3:**230
See also Carmina Burana
Orff-Instrumentarium, **5:**42
Organisation for Irish Dance, **3:**517
Organisian, Edgar, **1:**122
organizations, dance service, **5:**43–44
organized-play movement, **3:**34
Organ Tablature (Jan of Lublin), **5:**210
Orgie, L', **2:**202, 203, **3:**180, **4:**116, 340
O'Riada, Sean, **3:**520
Oriane et le Prince d'Amour, **2:**351, **4:**184, **5:**95
Oriental America (musical), **6:**255
Oriental Dances, **3:**23
Orientales, Les, **4:**641, *643*, **5:**45
See also Carnaval, Le
Oriental Fantasy, **6:**441
Oriental Impressions, **5:**123, 125
Orientalism, **5:**44–47
Bakst designs, **2:**241, *242*, 345, 407, **3:**17, 18, **5:**541, 556
cabaret belly dance, **2:***344*, 345
Denishawn programs, **2:**378
ghāwāzi dancers, **6:***403*
Khachaturian compositions, **4:**7
Philippine dance traditions, **5:**168
St. Denis dance motifs, **5:**491, 492, *493, 495, 497*
Schéhérazade design, **5:**541, 556
scholarly writings, **4:**415–416
vaudeville acts, **6:***318*
Orient/Occident, **3:**428
Origen de las danzas folklóricas, El (Vega), **1:**108
Original Ballet Russe. *See* Ballets Russes de Monte Carlo
Original Ballet Russe en América Latina, El (García Victorica), **2:**127
"Original Black Bottom Dance, The" (song), **6:**255
Original Sin, **2:**162
Origine des Jeux, L', **1:**284

Origin of Design, The, **2:**400
"Origns and Development of the Technique of Classical Dance, The" (Blok), **1:**463, 464
orijent, **2:**101
Orion Ballet Company, **5:**389
Orione (Bach), **3:**111
orishas (spirits), **2:**273, 274, *274, 280*
Orissa, India, **2:**394, **3:**467, **5:**22, 68
Orixá (Arrieta ballet), **1:***533*
orixás (spirits), **1:**529
Orlando, Mariane, **5:**47–48, **6:**42, 43
Orlando Innamorato (Boiardo), **3:**106
Orléans, France, dancing masters, **3:**81
Orlikovsky, Vaslav, **1:**241, 242, **5:**681, **6:**437
Basel Ballet, **1:**374, **6:**52
English National Ballet productions, **2:**510
Orlin, Robyn, **5:**659–660
Orloff, Alexandre, **3:***19*, **5:**165
Orloff, Nicholas, **1:**313, *314, 318*, **5:**397
Norwegian National Ballet, **4:**676
Orlova, Sophie, **1:**95
Orlovskaya, Natalia, **4:**600
Ørnberg, Leif, **4:***43*, **5:**429
Ornelli, Otto, **4:**64
Ornstein, Robert, **2:**319
Ornstein, Shoshana and Yehudit, **3:**531
orô, **1:***528*, 529
orodri, **3:***586*
Oromo (people), **2:**530, 532–533, *534*
Orosa, Leonor, **2:**230
Oroscopo, L', **2:**93
Orosz, Adél, **3:**417, **5:**402
Orozco, Gladiola, **4:**396
Orozco, José Clemente, **4:**391, **5:**253
Orozco Romero, Carlos, **4:**391
Orphée (Béjart ballet), **1:**404
Orphée (Cocteau film), **2:**183
Orphée (Staats choreography), **1:**404
Orphée aux Enfers (Balanchine ballet), **1:**367
Orphée aux Enfers (Offenbach operetta), **3:**70
Orphée et Euridice (Gluck opera). *See Orfeo ed Euridice*
Orphelin de la Chine, L', **1:**88, 123, **3:**105, **5:**424
Orpheus, **1:**241, **5:**554, **6:**85
Balanchine-Stravinsky-Noguchi collaboration, **1:**30, 141, 268, **3:**337, **4:**28, 29, 518, 606, *607*, 613, **6:**6
Basel Ballet, **1:**375
Boyarsky staging, **5:***468*
costume design, **2:**245
Cranko production, **4:**1
Duncan works, **2:**455
as first ballet performed by Russians, **5:**450
Forsythe choreography, **3:**52, *152*, 360
Gadd choreography, **6:**44
Hamburg Ballet Stravinsky birthday presentation, **3:**337
Henze score, **3:**360, **5:**683
Jaques-Dalcroze student production, **3:**596
Le Clercq performance, **4:**137
MacMillan choreography, **4:**244

Orpheus, continued
Magallanes performance,
4:246, 619
Moncion performance,
4:450, 619
Murphy choreography, **4:**625
Negri *intermedi*, **4:**581
Noguchi design, **5:**547
Noguchi scenic design, **1:**141,
2:245, **4:**607, 660
Rubinstein mime drama, **3:**196
Spoerli choreography, **5:**683
Tetley production, **1:**394
See also Orfeo ed Euridice
Orpheus and Eurydice, **5:**70, 518,
547, **6:**331
American Ballet, **1:***63,* 64
Andrašovan, **5:**614
Angiolini production, **3:**546
Balanchine production costumes,
2:244
Bausch choreography, **1:**388
Beck-Friis choreography, **1:**400
Boyarchikov choreography, **5:**471
Christensen (Lew) performance,
2:160
de Valois choreography,
2:401, 583
Eck choreography, **2:**474
Georgi choreography, **3:**133
Tchelitchev design, **5:**547
Valberkh, Ivan, **4:**311
Weaver ballet, **6:**372–373
Orpheus and Rhodolpe, **2:**11, **5:**166
Orpheus Descending (Williams),
1:251
Orpheus Dionysos, **6:**357
Orpheus in the Underworld,
2:57–58, *57,* **5:**57
Orpheus Portrait, **5:**51
Orpheus Returning from the Shades
(Richmond), **2:**455
Orpheus Singing and Dreaming,
1:53
Orpheus und Eurydike (Basel
Ballet), **1:**375, **5:**682
Orpheus und Eurydike (Gluck
opera). *See Orfeo ed Euridice*
Orr, Terrence (Terry), **1:**72, 75, 77
Orr, Terry, **2:**161, **3:**306, **5:**513
Orta, Carlos, **6:**324, 325
Ortega, Rafael, **4:**222
Ortega y Gasset, José, **1:**116
Orthodox Church. *See* Eastern
Orthodox Church
orthopedics. *See* dance medicine
orthopedic surgeon, **4:**20
Orthwine, Rudolf, **1:**65, **4:**460
Ortigoza, Luis, **2:**125
Ortiz, Alfonso, **4:**575
Ortiz, Angeles, **5:**237
Ortiz, Diego, **4:**505
Ortiz, Vanessa, **5:**275
Ortolani, Benito, *as contributor,*
3:171–172, 578–583, 583–585,
641–643, **4:**652–656,
6:445–446
Ortutay, Zsuzsa, **3:**423
Osaka, Japan, *bunraku,* **2:**12, 13, 14
Osaka International Ballet
Competition, **1:**281, 282
Osamu Muranaka, *as photographer,*
4:83, 333, **5:**591
O Sărbătoare la Țară, **5:**384
Osato, Sono, **1:***312, 312,* 313, 438,
5:242, 360, 397, **6:**278, 279
O Say, Can You See? (revue), **6:**246
Osborne, Greg, **4:***544*
Osborne, Gwendolyn, **2:**38, 47,
6:396

Osborne, Nigel, **1:**52
Osborne, Rowland, **2:**337
"Oscar Tango" (skating program),
6:180
Osenham, Andrew, **2:**49
Osiński, Ludwik, **6:**364
Osipenko, Alla, **4:**285, **5:**459, 699
Osiris (deity), **2:**569
Oslo, Norway, **4:**673, 674, 675, 676,
677, 679, 680, 683
Oslo Opera Ballet, **4:**675, **5:**402
Oslo Philharmonic, **4:**674
Osnovy kharakternogo tantsa
(Bekefi, Lopukhov, and
Bocharov), **2:**107
Osome, **5:**593
*Osservazioni sopra la musica ed il
ballo* (Goudar), **3:**546
Ossian, **2:**364
Ossona, Paulina, **1:**112, *112*
Ossorio, Robert, **2:**268
Östberg, Jens, **6:**45
osteopathic physician, **4:**20
Osterberg, Martin Bergman, **3:**276
Østergaard, Solveig, **2:**201, **3:**668
Österreichische Musikzeitschrift
(journal), **1:**243
Östgötateatern, **6:**45
ostinato, **2:**97
Ostlere, Hilary B., *as contributor,*
2:334–336, **4:**436–437
Ostrava, Czechoslovakia, **3:**99, 100
Ostrovsky, Aleksandr, **1:**486, **2:**510,
5:470, **6:**114
Ostrovsky, Nikolai, **2:**585
Ostrowski-Naumoff, Jan, **5:**220
Osuga Isamu, **4:**271
O'Sullivan, Louis, **3:**520
Osvajanje igre (Grbić-Softić), **6:**438
Oswald, Genevieve, **4:**166–167,
5:48
Ota Hisa. *See* Hanako
O tańcu (Idzikowski), **5:**221
'ōte'a, **6:**79
Otello (Verdi opera), **4:**514, **5:**36
Otello (Viganò ballet), **5:**528,
6:338–339
See also Othello (for other
productions)
Otera, José, **1:**93
Otéro, Carolina, **2:**572, **3:**71, **4:**523,
6:268, 317
Otero, Decio, **1:**535, *535,* 536
Otero, Manuel and Antonio, **2:**522
Otero Aranda, José, **5:**676
Oteyza, Remedios de (Totoy), **5:**172
Othello, **2:**335, **5:**518
Briantzev production, **1:**540,
5:464, 467
Chabukiani production, **2:**96, 97,
4:36, **6:**343
Darrell production, **2:**350
Henry production, **3:**358
Kolpakova performance, **4:**36
Němeček production, **4:**583
Neumeier production, **3:**338
Virsaladze design, **6:**343
Welch production, **6:**379
*See also Moor's Pavane, The;
Otello*
Othello (Rossini opera), **4:**341
Othello (Shakespeare), **4:**533, **6:**409
Other, The, **2:**374
Other Dances, **1:**74, **4:***248,* 614, 631,
5:*364,* 366, 437
Otomì (people), **2:**194
Otowa Nobuko, **6:**84
Otozuru, **3:**646, **5:**48–49
Otsup, Aleksandr, **2:**150
Ottawa (people), **4:**558

Ottawa, Canada, **2:**40, 43, 47
Ottawa Ballet (formerly Theatre
Ballet of Canada), **2:**47
Augustyn directorship, **1:**201,
2:41
Beriosova *Nutcracker*
performance, **1:**429
financial collapse, **2:**41
Otte, Gerald, **4:***649*
Otte-Betz, Irma, **4:**103
Ottmann, Peter, **4:**544
Otto, king of Greece, **3:**299
Ottolenghi, Vittoria, *as contributor,*
1:82–83, 196, **2:**369–370,
480–481, **3:**59–61, 549–552,
5:195–196, 399–401, 441,
527–528, **6:**121, 143–144
Ottoman (Turkish) tradition
Algerian costumes, **1:**41–42
Armenian dance, **1:**119
buffoons and dancing boys and
girls, **6:**209–210
cultural autonomy policy,
3:295
North African dance, **4:**665
Ottonelli, Giovanni Domenico,
2:188
Ottone Ottone I & II, **1:**412
Ottrubay, Melinda, **3:**415, 423
otufo initiation rites, **6:**13
Oude Nederlands volksdansen
(Sanson-Catz and de Koe
eds.), **4:**585
Ouéru, Guillaume, **1:**3
Ou Jian-ping, **2:**146, 149–150,
3:373
as contributor, **2:**116, 145–147,
147–150, **6:**405–406, 415–416
Oukhtomsky, Vladimir, **6:**183
Oukrainsky, Serge, **5:**58, *120,* 511,
6:291
Ouled Naïl, dances of the, **1:***40,*
2:345, *346,* **4:**409, 415, *662,*
5:49–50
Oumansky Ballet, **4:**667
Our Cell, **6:**67
Our Flourishing Youth, **6:**443
"Our Jockye Sale Have Our Jenny"
(song), **3:**377
Our Lady's Juggler, **3:**391, **5:**300
Our Town (film), **2:**197
Our Waltzes, **2:**514, **5:**436
Outlaw, The, **1:**209
Outlet Dance (Australia), **1:**216
Outline for a Funeral March,
1:524–525
Outline of Polish Ballet History
(Ciepliński), **2:**172
Out of Line (Mackrell), **3:**285
Out of the Inkwell (cartoon series),
3:559
Out of This World (musical), **2:**187
Outside In, **2:**611, *611*
Outsider, The, **1:**453
Outwitted Miller, The, **5:**452
Ouyang Yuqian, **2:**148
Oved, Margalit, **2:**449, 532, 537
Oven, Louki van, **4:**600
Overcoat, The, **3:**13
Overlees, Frank, **5:**585
Overskou, Thomas, **1:**506–507
Over the Pavement, **2:**584
O Vertigo, **2:**45
Overture, **2:**380
*Overture to KA MOUNTAIN AND
GUARDenia Terrace* (Wilson
opera), **6:**401
Ovid, **3:**15, **5:**113
Ovid Metamorphoses, **1:**69, **5:**408
Owen, Michael, **1:**77

Owen, Robert, **3:**276
Owen, Walter E., *as photographer,*
1:262, 263, 301, **2:**426, **4:**268
Owerło, Paweł, **5:**220
"Owl and the Pussycat, The"
(Lear), **4:**6
Owl Dance, **4:**561, **5:**240
O World, **1:**467
Owo Yoruba (people), **6:**13, 14
Oxenham, Andrew, *as
photographer,* **4:**544, 545, 546
Oxfordshire, England, **3:**607
Oxfordshire Morris dance,
4:473, *474*
Oxford University, **3:**283
Oxford University Ballet Club,
3:202
Oxóssi (deity), **1:**529
oyama. See onnagata
oyin dance, **6:**305
Ozaï, **3:**315
ozilla, **2:**33

pacca (divine characters), **4:**298
Pacham, **1:**444–445
Pachelbel, Johann, **6:**202
Pacific Festival of Arts, **5:**20
Pacific Islands. *See* Melanesia;
Micronesia; Oceanic dance
traditions; Polynesia
Pacific Northwest Ballet, **2:**162,
4:631, **5:**51, **6:**264
Childs choreographies, **2:**120
Cunningham production revival,
2:294
Stowell choreographies, **5:**399,
6:*252,* 265, 266
Pacific Overtures (musical), **6:**285
PACOFS Ballet, **5:**57, 651, 654, 692
PACT Ballet, **5:**203, **5:**51–56, *651,*
652–653, *655,* 658, *659*
Bayadère, La, **1:**393, **5:**653, **6:**380
Coppélia, **5:**653, 692
Dream revival, **2:**445
Giselle, **5:**652
Hart (John) as artistic director,
3:345
Hynd choreography, **3:**428, **4:**117
Nureyev's *Don Quixote,* **2:**440
Paeper choreography, **5:**57
Rubies, **5:***653*
Staff, Frank, **5:**652, 691–692,
6:379
Swan Lake, **5:***651,* 652, 653
Weller, Dawn, **6:**379–380
PACT Ballet School, **6:**380
PACT Dance Company, **5:**653, *655,*
657, 658
padams, **1:**442, **3:**466–467
Padenie Parizha (Ehrenburg), **3:**590
Padmalingpa, **1:**444–445
Padmasambhava, **1:**443–444, 445,
2:221, **6:**166
Padmāvatī (Roussel), **4:**516
Padmavati Srinivasa Kalyanam,
6:321
Padovan, Maurizio, **3:**554, 556
Padron, Lilian, **2:**281
Padula, Edward, **1:**419
Paean, **1:**69, **3:**664, **5:**408, 573
electronic music, **4:**519
Paekche Kingdom, **2:**221
Paeper, Veronica, **2:**57–58, 441,
5:56–58
Apollo 65 performance,
5:653, 692
CAPAB Ballet, **5:**57, 652, 653,
654, 658, 692
Pagan Greece, **2:**516

Paganini, **1:**313, *313*, 492, 493, **3:**25, **5:**460, **6:**203
  Kondratieva performance, **4:**38
  Lavrovsky (Leonid) production, **4:**132
  Riabouchinska performance, **5:**350
  Vasiliev performance, **6:***313*
Paganini, Camilla, **2:**433
Paganini, Niccolò, **5:**498, 558
Paganini, Raffaele, **4:**394, **5:**401
Paganini Variations of 1947, **1:**456
Pagan Poem, A, **3:**215
Pagava, Ethéry, **1:**305, **3:**73, 74, **5:**162, 605
Page, Annette, **1:**390
Page, Ashley, **3:**443, **4:**470, **5:**304, 419, *420*
Page, Barbara, **1:**421
Page, Ralph, **4:**168, **6:**247
Page, Ruth, **1:**482, 483, 518, **2:**334, **3:**385, **4:**77, **5:58–61, 6:**137
  archival materials, **4:**169
  Ballet Russe de Monte Carlo, **1:**298, 300
  Ballets des Champs-Élysées, **1:**306
  design elements, **5:**548
  Dunham as student, **2:**458
  English National Ballet, **2:**510, **3:**175
  Federal Dance Project, **2:**580, **4:**210
  as Fokine student, **3:**22
  Franklin roles, **3:**87, 88
  Hear Ye! Hear Ye!, **2:**196–197
  Kriza association, **4:**63
  Noguchi scenic design, **4:**659
  Ravinia Park Ballet, **2:**357
Page, Stephen, **1:**216, **6:**56
pageants, **6:**244
Page Blanche and Page Noire, **1:**446
Page Inconstant, Le, **1:**202, 452, **2:**353, 354, **4:**657
Page 1—Love Songe—Old Records, **3:**52
Pages du Duc de Vendôme, Les, **1:**199, 202, 446, 507, **5:**92
  Bigottini performance, **1:**452
  character dances, **2:**107
  Fitzjames (Louise) debut, **3:**4
  Milon performance, **4:**423
Pages from a Life, **4:**132, 133
Paghetti family, **5:**231
Pagliero, Camilla, **5:**278
paian, **4:**499
Paige, Brydon, **2:**41, *150,* **3:**229, **5:**43, **61–62, 6:***130*
Paik, Nam June, **1:**139, **2:**605, 606, **3:**54, **4:**141, 142
Pai Ming-ta, **6:***81*
Painlevé, Jean, **4:**688
Painted Princess, The (film), **2:**609
Painter, Eleanore, **3:**559
Painter, Walter, **6:**287
painting. *See* artists and dance
Paint Your Wagon (musical), **6:**281
Paischeff, Mary, **2:**632
Paisey, Karen, **5:**419
Paisiello, Giovanni, **1:**88, **2:**55, **4:**698
Paiute. *See* Northern Paiute Indians
Paiute Round Dance, **3:**171
Paiwan (peole), **6:**80
paizō, **1:**448
Pajama Game, The (film), **3:**54
Pajama Game, The (musical), **3:**54, 599, *599,* **6:**281
"Pajarillas, Las" (dance drama), **5:**67

pajeng, **1:**366
Pajović, Dejan, **6:**435
Paka, Toots, **6:**317
Pakhomova, Ludmila, **3:**432
Pakhta (pantomime), **6:**306
Pakistan, **5:62–65**
  costume, **2:**226
  Husain, Ghulam, **3:**425
  kathak, **5:**597
  Kermani, Sheema, **4:**5–6
  Siddiqui, Nahid, **5:**597–598
Pakistan American Cultural Center, **1:**94
Pakistan International Airlines, **5:**62
Palace, The, **3:**611
Palace Academy, France, **1:**2
Palace of the Legion of Honor (San Francisco museum), **3:**95
Palace Theater, New York City, **6:**283, 320
Palace Theatre, London, **6:**161
Paladins, Les (Rameau), **5:**306, 307
Palais de Cristal, Le. See Symphony in C
Palais de Glace (Saddler ice dance), **2:**298
Palais d'Électricité (Paris Exposition), **3:**91
Palais des Glaces (Charrat dance), **2:**112
Palais du Louvre, **6:**156
Palais du Silence, Le (also *No-ja-li*), **2:**361
Palais Royal, Versailles, **6:**156, 157–158
palalaibilli dance, **2:**476
Palanquin Bearers, The, **5:***64*
Palasovszky, Ödön, **3:**420
Palau, Thérèse, **3:**65
Palazzo della Ragione, Padua, **4:**349
Palczewska, Antonina, **5:**215
Pale Boy, The, **6:**145
Paléologue, Jean de, **3:**92
Palermo, Italy, **3:**552
Palestine. *See* Israel; Middle East
Palestine, Charlemagne, **3:**54
Palestine Folk Opera, **3:**529
Palestine Orchestra, **3:**529
Palestinians, **3:**538, 605
Pálffy, Ferdinand, **6:**335
Palfy, Barbara, **6:**297
  as contributor, **5:**282–283
Palgyi Doije, **1:**458
Paliashvili, Zakhary, **1:**38
Paliashvili Theater of Opera and Ballet, Tbilisi, **2:**96, **4:**133
Palisades Amusement Park, New Jersey, **4:**23
Pal Joey (musical), **3:**54, **4:**2, **6:**278
Palladino, Emma, **3:**261
Palladium, New York City, **2:**276
Pallavicino, Leo, **4:**579
Pallay, Anna, **3:**414
Pallerini, Antonia, **2:**208, **3:**176, **4:**263, **6:**338, 339
Palm, Jan Gerard, **2:**63
Palma, Susanna di, **3:**11
Palmer, Aaron, **6:**386
Palmer, A. M., **5:**514
Palmer, Bee, **6:**317
Palmer, David, **5:***55*
Palmer, Henry, **1:**457
Palmina, ossia La Figlia del Torrente, **5:**232
Palmstedt, Eric, **6:**48
"palm wine" highlife, **6:**24
Palóc dances, **3:**422

Paloma Azul, La, **5:**637
palotás, **3:**412
Palo Volador, El, **3:**319
Paltenghi, David, **3:**307, **5:**301
Paltrinieri-Bergrova, Giulietta, **1:**429, **5:**245, **6:**32
Palucca, Gret, **1:**132, 204, **3:**132, 146, 147, 152, 153, 156, **5:65–66, 6:**378
  Hoyer as student, **3:**393
  Nazi era, **4:**93, **6:**393
  Schilling association, **5:**557
  students, **5:**263
  Wigman training, **6:**392
pambiche, **2:**431
Pamiés, Pauleta, **5:**673
Pan (Chernetskaya dance), **5:**477
Pan (deity), **3:**287
Pan, Hermes, **1:**82, **2:**615, 618, **3:**357, 551, **4:**419
  Astaire collaboration, **1:**191, *192,* 195
  Miranda (Carmen) collaboration, **4:**434, *434*
  Rogers tap dubbing, **5:**373
panaderos de la flamenco, **5:**133
Panaiev, Michel, **1:**296, 313, **3:**306, **6:**432
Panama, **2:**195, **5:66–68**
Panama Hattie (film), **1:**440
Panamerica, **2:**314, **4:**450
panasar, **1:**174–175, **3:**487
pancar, **3:**504
Panchakaya, **4:**257
Panchamahabhuta, **2:**105
Pancho Fierro troupe, **5:**146
Pandae, Mohan Lal, **1:**94
Pandji Semerang, **1:**177
Pandolfi, Vito, **2:**188
Pandor, Miriam, **2:**356, **4:**198
Pandora, **3:**358, 629
Panduvasdeva, king of Ceylon, **4:**34
Panembahan Senopati, **3:**494
Panfilov, Evgeny, **5:**475, 479
Panic (MacLeish), **3:**216
Panigrahi, Raghunath, **5:**68, 69
Panigrahi, Sanjukta, **5:**22, 23, **68–69**
Panikkar, Krishnan, **5:**309
Panis, Aleluia, **5:**173
Panizza, Giacomo, **5:**138, 277
Panji, **1:**173, 174, **3:**502
Panji-Bogis, **5:**130
Panji cycle, **1:**174, 176, **3:**495, 498, 499, 502, 505
Panji Semirang, **3:**666
Pan Kanevsky, **6:**225
Pankararu (people), **1:**530–531
Pankov, Gradimir, **6:**52–53
Pankova, Elena, **1:**391
Pankrat, Janita Janina, **4:**128
pannier, **2:**236, *236,* 238, 239
Panorama, **1:**136, 421, **3:**212, 214, **4:**130
Panorama of Contemporary Ballet, Focşani, **5:**389
"Panorama of Dance Ethnology," **4:**372–373
Panorama of Naples, A, **5:**216, **6:**73
På Norrbotten, **2:**500
Panov, Valery, **1:**436, **4:**275, **5:**55, *102,* 282
  as character dancer, **2:**106
  Don Quixote, **6:**437
  Evdokimova roles, **2:**561
  Maryinsky Ballet, **4:**285
  Orpheus performance, **5:***468*
  Romeo and Juliet, **1:**413, **5:**422
  Royal Ballet of Flanders, **5:**422
  Sacre du Printemps, Le, **5:**488

Panova, Galina, **4:**275, **5:**55, 422, **6:**53
Panoveriana, **5:**422
panpipes, **5:**663–664
p'ansori, **1:**166
Pantages and the Palace Present TWO-A-DAY, The, **1:**125
Pantanal, **1:**536
Pantheon Theatre, London, **2:**353
pantheru dance, **3:647,** 650
Pantins de Violette, Les, **1:**10
pantomime, **5:69–72,** 503, 614
  Denmark, **2:**384–385, **5:**423
  Glass Slipper, The, **2:**173
  Great Britain, **2:**396, **3:**254, *256,* **5:**350, **6:**373, 374
  Greco-Roman, **3:**294
  Greek *cheironomia* identified with, **2:**115, 116
  Harlequin role, **5:**615
  Rich, John, **5:**350–351, **6:**373
  Roman Empire. *See pantomimus* in United States, **5:**198, 199
  See also commedia dell'arte; mime; *pantomimus*
pantomime-ballet
  Angiolini, Gaspero, **1:**87, 88–89
  Arnould-Mussot, Jean-François, **1:**122–123
  de Hesse, Jean-Baptiste, **2:**365–366
  Douvillier, Suzanne, **2:**442, 443
  Duport, Louis-Antoine, **2:**464
  first tragic, **1:**236
  Gluck, Christoph Willibald, **3:**187–188, 190
  libretti, **4:**173
  Noverre, Jean-Georges, **4:**695–696, 698, 700
  Quatre Fils Aymons, Les, **1:**122–123, 124
  Sweden, **6:**40
  Viganò (Salvatore) transformation of, **3:**547
Pantomime Circus, **3:**207–208
Pantomime Theater. *See* Tivoli Gardens Pantomime Theater, Copenhagen
pantomimus, **4:**426–428, **5:72–75,** 375–376
Pantry Ballet (for Jacques Offenbach), A (Cornell), **1:**137
pantum bersambut recitations, **3:**499
Pan Twardowski, **3:**192, **4:**435, **5:**101, 217, *217,* 218, 219, **6:**365, 441
Panufnik, Andrej, **1:**453, **4:**242
Panurge auf der Laterneninsel, **1:***238*
Panyāsa-Chādok (Buddhist tales), **4:**111
Panyembrama, **3:**666
Panzier, Lorenzo, **2:**177
pā'ō'ā, **6:**79
Paolo and Francesca, **6:**412
Paoluzi, Gianfranco, **2:**480
Papa, Tony, **6:**132
Papachristou, Vassilios, **3:**303
Papammal, **1:**273
Papandopulo, Boris, **6:**433, 436
Papanti, Louis, **2:**339
Papa Stour (dance), **3:**249
Papathanassiou, Vangelis, **3:**351
Papendick, Ruth, **5:***150*
Paper Bag Players, **2:**110
Papillon (Fuller dance), **3:**92
Papillon, Le
  Lacotte reconstruction, **4:**108
  Livry performance, **3:**70, **4:**215, **5:**94

Papillon, Le, continued
  Mérante performance, **4:**353
  as Pavlova dance, **5:**123
  Petipa (Marius) choreography,
    5:153, 157
  Taglioni (Marie) choreography,
    1:390, **3:**70, **4:**108, 215, 353,
    5:94, **6:**73, 75
Papillons, Les, **1:**322, **2:**421,
  3:20, 428
  Wilhelm design, **6:**397
Papillons de Nuit, Les, **4:**646
Papinta (vaudeville performer),
  6:317
Papko, Yuri, **3:**99
Papliński, Eugenieusz, **5:**75, 219
Papliński's Polish Theater, **3:**317
Papp, Joseph, **6:**282, 284
Pappacena, Flavia, **3:**555, 557, 558
Pappe, Alan, *as photographer,* **6:**283
Papua New Guinea, **5:**76–85
  background and overview,
    5:76–78
  Binandere dance, **5:**78–80
  costumes, **4:**352
  Gizra dance, **5:**80
  Kaluli dance, **5:**80–82, 355
  Maring dance, **5:**82–84
  Melpa dance, **5:**84–85
  rhythmic dance accompaniment,
    4:498
  shamanism, **6:**185
  See also Melanesia
Pâquerette, **2:**95, **3:**123, **5:**158, 500
Paquin, **1:**321
Paquita, **3:**414, **4:**430, 639, **5:**85,
  401, **6:**225
  Danilova staging, **1:**300, **2:**334
  Dolgushin staging, **2:**423
  Fokine debut in pas de quatre,
    3:14
  grand pas, **5:**107, *154*
  Grisi performance, **3:**315, **4:**341,
    5:93
  Legat (Sergei) performance,
    4:144
  Makarova *grand pas de deux*
    staging, **1:**77, **4:**249
  Mazilier choreography,
    4:339, 341
  Petipa (Lucien) performance, **3:**5,
    5:148
  Petipa (Marius) staging, **1:**86,
    300, **4:**429, **5:**147, 150, 154
  Pribylov version, **5:**474
  score, **4:**428–429
Pará, Brazil, **1:**530, 531
Parable in Blue, **4:**210
Parac, Frano, **5:**677
Parachute (journal), **2:**49
Parade, **1:**93, 196, 244, 291, 327,
  2:289, **5:**85–86
  avant-garde elements, **2:**409
  Cocteau's choreographic input,
    2:182, 183, 409, **4:**317
  Diaghilev's Ballets Russes, **1:**316,
    322, 323, **2:**287, 406, 408, 409
  in English National Ballet
    repertory, **2:**512
  Joffrey Ballet revival, **3:**614
  Massine choreography, **4:**317
  Picasso designs, **2:**409, **3:**614,
    4:*302,* 317, **5:**191–192,
    192, 543
  Satie score, **2:**408, 409, **4:**317,
    516, **5:**525, 526
  Woizikowski performance, **6:**403
Parade (March), **3:**401
Parades and Changes, **3:**336
Paradiesgärtlein (Orff), **5:**43

Paradis d'Amour, **1:**275, 397
Paradise Gained, **3:**520
Paradise Lost. See Paradis Perdu, Le
Paradise of the Drowned-Tlalocan,
  The, **1:**524
Paradisi, Leopold, **5:**452, 480
Paradis Perdu, Le, **3:**45, 133, **5:**97,
  163–164
Paradossi kai Techni (periodical),
  3:304
Paradox, **4:**81
Parafango (video), **1:**142
Paramount on Parade (film), **2:**613
Paramount Pictures, **2:**616
Paravicini, Monique, **1:**115
Parc, Mademoiselle de, **4:**447
Parc, Père du, **1:**284
Pardave, Eva, **4:***394*
Pardon My Sarong (film), **2:**458
Paredes, Marcos, **4:**25
Parekh, Anne Marie, **5:**408
pareng, **1:**171
Parenté d'Arlequin, La, **2:**365
Parera Villalón, Célida, *as*
  contributor, 276–277
Parés, José, **1:**290, 436, **2:**278,
  5:275
Parfaict brothers, **1:**355, 464,
  4:152, 263, **5:**87, 128
Parfango (videodance), **2:**607
Paride ed Elena (Gluck), **2:**433,
  3:189, 190
  Noverre choreography, **4:**696
Parigi, Alfonso, **3:**622, **5:**535
Parigi, Alfonso (the younger),
  5:1, 260
Parigi, Giulio, **2:**27, **3:***543,* 622, **5:**1,
  258, 535
Parijata Harana, **1:**169
Parikh, Ishira, **4:**111
Paris, **1:**148, **2:**111, **4:**451
Paris, Carl, **5:**675
Paris, Lucius Domitius, **5:**73, 74
Paris, Thomasso, **5:**384
Paris Autumn Festival (1973),
  2:293
Pariserpolka (social polka), **2:**381
Paris Exhibition, The, **1:**37, **4:**121,
  6:397
Paris Exposition (1900), **5:**45,
  6:409
Paris Exposition Universelle
  (1889–1890), **3:**91, 93
Parisiana, **4:**325
Parisian Model, A (musical),
  6:269, 447
Parisien, Le (publication), **3:**85
Paris International Dance Festival,
  2:293, **5:**436
Paris-Londres (revue), **1:**253
Paris Mes Amours (revue), **1:**253
Paris Opera Ballet, **5:**86–100
  Adam compositions, **1:**9, 10
  Afternoon of a Faun, **1:**28
  Ailey choreography, **1:**57, 59
  Albert, Monsieur, **1:**35, 36
  Allard, Marie, **1:**43
  Alma, **2:**95
  Alonso (Alicia) productions, **1:**49
  Apollo, **1:**96
  Après-midi d'un Faune, L', **1:**99
  Ari performances, **1:**118
  Atanassoff, Cyril, **1:**194
  Atys, **5:***324*
  Augusta (Madame) debut, **1:**199
  Aumer, Jean-Louis, **1:**201
  Aveline, Albert, **1:**246–247
  ballet de collège, **1:**284
  Ballon, Claude, **1:**355, 464
  Barberina, La, **1:**365

Bayadère, La, **1:**393
Beauchamps choreography,
  1:396
Béjart productions, **1:**405
Berain design, **1:**425
Bias, Fanny, **1:**446
Bigottini, Émilie, **1:**451–452
Blache, Jean-Baptiste, **1:**455
Blangy, Hermine, **1:**459
Blasis, Carlo, **1:**460
Blaska choreography, **1:**462
Blondy, Michel, **1:**464, 465
Bogdanova performances, **1:**477
Boquet designs, **1:**497
Bournonville, August, **1:**347,
  504–505
Burmeister's *Swan Lake,* **2:**15
Camargo, Marie, **2:**28–29
Campra as orchestral director,
  2:33–34
Caractères de la Danse, Les, **2:**59,
  4:130
Carey (Édouard) debut, **2:**60
Cerrito, Fanny, **1:**48, **2:**93, 94, 95
Charrat performances, **2:**111, 112
Chauviré, Yvette, **2:**113, 114–115
Childs choreographies, **2:**120
Ciceri scenic innovations,
  2:171–172, **3:**69, **5:**538–539
Cinderella productions,
  2:173, 174
Clustine as ballet master and
  teacher, **2:**181
Cocteau and Lifar artistic
  disagreement, **2:**184
composers, **1:**6, **4:**516–517, **5:**513
Coppélia, **2:**198–199, **3:**70–71,
  5:501, 502
Coralli, Jean, **2:**201, 202–204
  costume, **2:**239, 243–244,
    4:116, 138
Cranko's *Romeo and Juliet,* **5:**396
Cucchi, Claudina, **2:**282
Cunningham productions,
  2:293, 294
Dark Elegies revival, **2:**349
Darsonval, Lycette, **2:**350, 351
Dauberval, Jean, **2:**352, **5:**89
Degas paintings, **2:**361, 362–363
Delibes association, **2:**367–368
Descombey, Michel, **2:**388–389
Deshayes, André, 289–390
development and Parisian dance
  monopoly, **3:**66, 67, 68
Diaghilev's *Boris Godunov*
  production, **1:**317, **2:**407
Diaghilev's Russian Historical
  Concerts, **1:**317, **2:**407
Didelot debut performance,
  2:413
Don Quixote productions, **2:**434,
  435, 440
Douvillier, Suzanne, **2:**443
Dumoulin brothers, **2:**451
Dupond, Patrick, **2:**462–463, **3:**75
Dupré, Louis, **2:**465
Dyk, Peter van, **2:**471
early twentieth-century
  productions, **3:**71–72
Elssler (Thérèse) choreography,
  2:95, 502, 503
Elssler, Fanny, **1:**44, **2:**503, 504,
  3:185
Études, **2:**535, 536
  exercises, **1:**346
Ferraris, Amalia, **2:**587
Fille Mal Gardée, La, **2:**595–596,
  5:682
Fille Mal Gardee reconstruction,
  4:134

Firebird versions, **3:**2, *3,* 4
first *Don Quixote,* **2:**434–435
first professional female dancers,
  4:235, **5:**40
Fitzjames sisters, **3:**4–5
Flindt, Flemming, **3:**12
foreign-born nineteenth-century
  ballerinas, **3:**69, 70
Forsythe guest choreography,
  3:52, 53
as French school exemplar,
  1:330, 347
Fuoco, Sofia, **3:**96–97
Gallet, Sébastien, **3:**106
Gardel, Marie, **3:**119
Gardel, Maximilien, **2:**352, **3:**68,
  116–117, **4:**302
Gardel, Pierre, **3:**117–119
gas lighting, **3:**69, **5:**91
Gautier libretti, **3:**123
Gautier reviews of productions,
  3:122
genre classification of dancers,
  2:106
Giselle, **2:**203, **3:**177–179, 181,
  182, 183
Gosselin, Geneviève, **3:**208–209
Grahn debut, **3:**223
grand défilé du corps de ballet,
  5:690
Grisi performances, **3:**314–315
Guerra, Nicola, **3:**320, 330
Guest's offical history of, **3:**321
Guimard, Marie-Madeleine,
  3:326–327
Guyot, Marie-Catherine, **3:**329
Heinel, Anna, **3:**333
Hightower as artistic director,
  3:362
Indes Galantes, Les, **3:**450
Italian school influence on, **1:**347
Jardin aux Lilas revival, **3:**597
Jeune Homme et la Mort, Le,
  3:601
Jolie Fille de Gand, La, **3:**620
Kelly's *Pas des Dieux,* **4:**3
Kröller performances, **4:**64
Lacotte reconstructions, **4:**108
Lami costume designs, **4:**116
Lander (Harald) as ballet master
  and choreographer, **3:**105,
  4:119, **5:**429
Lany, Jean-Barthélemy, **4:**122
Lany, Louise-Madeleine,
  4:122–123
Laval, Antoine Bandieri de, **4:**130
Lecomte (Hippolyte) costumes,
  4:138
Le Picq, Charles, **4:**149
Lestang, Anne-Louis, **4:**152
libretti and programmes as style-
  setters, **4:**173
Lifar directorship, **3:**73,
  4:183–186, **5:**691
Lifar dismissal, **4:**185
Lifar reforms, **4:**183–184
lighting, **4:**189
Livry, Emma, **4:**214–215
Lully founding and exclusive
  license, **2:**338, **4:**234, 235
Lyonnois, Marie-Françoise, **4:**236
MacMillan productions, **4:**243
Marcel, François, **4:**263
mask discontinuance, **2:**352, 354,
  4:302, **5:**89
masked dancers, **4:***301*
Maywood, Augusta, 4, **4:**338–339
Mazilier, Joseph, **4:**339, 340–343
Mérante, Louis, **4:**353–354
Milon, Louis, **1:**455, **3:**68,
  4:422–423

mime, **5:**90
Minkus and Delibes collaborations, **4:**429
minuets and gavottes, **3:**125
museum and library, **4:**160–161
New Zealand tour, **4:**624
Nielsen performances, **4:**631
Nijinska choreography, **4:**635
Nikolais choreography, **4:**650
Noblet, Lise, **4:**656–657
Notre-Dame de Paris, **2:**524
Noverre criticisms of, **4:**699–700
Noverre engagement, **4:**696–697
Nureyev, Rudolf, **2:**463, **5:**7–8, **6:**34, 35
opera ballet conventions, **4:**514, **5:**148–149
opera ballets, **2:**282, **4:**514, **5:**35–36, 113
Palais de Cristal, Le, **6:**65, 66
Pecour, Guillaume-Louis, **1:**516, **5:**128
Perrot, Jules, **5:**134, 135–136, 138–139, 141
Petipa, Lucien, **5:**93, 94, 135, 148
Petit, Roland, **5:**96, 97, 164
public balls, **1:**278–279
Pulcinella, **2:**460
rarity of women choreographers, **2:**95
Romantic movement, **3:**69
See also Romantic era
Romeo and Juliet, **3:**309, **5:**396
Róna as ballet master, **5:**402
Rosati, Carolina, **5:**404–505
Rouché directorship, **5:**678
Sacre du Printemps, Le, **1:**404
Saint-Léon, Arthur, **4:**341–342, **5:**499, 500, 501–502
Sallé, Marie, **5:**504
Sangalli, Rita, **5:**515
scenic design and lighting, **2:**171–172, **3:**69
Schneitzhoeffer compositions, **5:**558
school. *See* Paris Opera Ballet School
Schwarz family, **5:**562–563
Skibine, George, **5:**605
Spessivtseva, Olga, **5:**678
Staats, Leo, **5:**690–691
structure (chart), **5:**88
Subligny, Marie-Thérèse, **6:**11
Swan Lake, **6:**34, 35
Sylphide premiere performance, **3:**69, **6:**57–58
Sylphide revivals, **6:**58, 59
Sylvia, **6:**62–64
technique history, **1:**346, 347
theaters used, **6:**156, 157–159, *158*
Three Graces (Baillie) lithograph, **5:**89
Tudor tribute, **6:**202
Venetian themes, **3:**49, 50
Verdy, Violette, **6:**328
Vestris family, **5:**89, **6:**330, 331, 332–333
Vyroubova, Nina, **6:**352–353
waltz choreography, **3:**68, **6:**360
as world's oldest ballet company, **5:**425
World War II, **3:**73
Zambelli, Carlotta, **3:**71, *71*, **6:**443–444
Zucchi guest performance, **6:**453
Paris Opera Ballet School, **2:**113, 114, 351, **5:**562
Aveline directorship, **1:**247, **3:**82
Deshayes (Jacques-François) directorship, **2:**389

Gardel (Pierre) directorship, **3:**119
history, **3:**81–82, *82*
Lacotte association, **4:**107, 108
Lander (Harald) directorship, **4:**118, 119
Taglioni (Marie) as faculty member, **4:**214–215
Parisot, Mademoiselle, **2:**71, 364, *412*, **3:**258
Parissi, Norah, **4:**323
Paris-Soir, **3:**202
Paris World Exposition (1924), **6:**306
Park, Merle, **4:**456, **5:**5, 55, **100,** 654, **6:**201
Fille Mal Gardée performance, **5:***190*, 417
Isadora performance, **4:**244
Romeo and Juliet performance, **5:**396
Wedding Bouquet, **1:***148*
Park, Rosemary, **1:**79
Park Avenue (musical), **6:**90
Parker, Charlie, **1:**59
Parker, Clifton, **2:**173
Parker, Dorothy, **4:**177
Parker, H. T., **4:**60–61, **6:**299
Parker, James, **1:**218
Parker, Peter, **4:**668
Parkes, Albert, **4:**23
Parkes, R. B., **5:**519
Parkes, Ross, **3:**220, **6:***135*
Parkinson, Georgina, **1:**75, 77, **2:**266, 515, **6:**129
Monotones performance, **4:**452
Romeo and Juliet performance, **5:**396
Swan Lake performance, **3:**567, **6:***33*
Parkman, Francis, **2:**569
Park Theater, New York City, **6:**159
parlampanes, **2:**121
parle, **5:**80
Parliament of the Birds, The, **2:**427
Parlić, Dimitrije, **1:**241, **2:**114, **5:**100–101,** 401, **6:**432, 436
Parlor Match, A (musical), **6:**447
Parmain, Martine, **1:**349
Parmegiani, Bernard, **1:**349, 446
Parmenter, Michael, **4:**627
Parmer, Vidar, **4:**682
Parnas, Estelle, **4:**604
Parnaso Confuso, Il (Gluck), **3:**365
Parnassus (Mantegna), **5:**259
Parnassus Triumphans, **6:**38
Parnell, Feliks, **5:**101, *217*, 218, 219, **6:***175*
Parnell's Ballet. *See* Polish Ballet of Parnell
Parody Show, The, **3:**48
Parr, André, **1:**327, **5:**545
Parra, Marianno, **3:**11
Parrott, Chrissie, **1:**216
Parry, Jann, **3:**285
Parsifal (Wagner), **2:**360
Parsi, Hector Campos, **5:***274*
Parsloe, Charles, **1:**200
Parson, Annie B., **3:***372*
Parsons, David, **1:**76, **3:**448, **4:**482, **5:**8, 187
Parsons Dance Company, **6:**57
Pärt, Arvo, **1:**462, **4:**532
Pártay, Lilla, **3:**418, 419
Particular Reel, **2:**119
partido alto, **1:**527
Partie de Chasse d'Henri IV, La, **2:**299, **4:**149
Partisan Days, **1:**90, 144, **2:**96, **6:**310

Partisans, The, **4:**444–445
Partita, **2:***386*
Partita for Four, **3:**611
Partita in G Minor, **3:**402
partnering, **5:101–105,** 189
Part Real—Part Dream, **3:**219
P.A.R.T.S. (Performing Arts Research and Training Studios), **1:**414
Party, A, **4:**71–72
parwa, **6:**370
Pas, Jacoba van der, **4:**589, 598
Pasacaglia, **2:**473
Pasarić, Irena, **5:**677
pas battu, **1:**384, **3:**172
Pas Battu, Le (Degas), **5:**180
pas brisés volés, **1:**384–385
Pasch, Johann, **2:**338
Pascha en de Beer, De, **5:**618
Paschner, Johann Georg, **2:**190
Pascua, Arizona, **4:**329
Pas d'Acier, Le, **1:**259, 316, 324–325, **2:**342, 410, **4:**38, 182, 225, **5:**267, 544, 545
Massine-Prokofiev collaboration, **4:**320–321
pas d'action
Perrot as inventor of, **5:**136, 141
in Petipa's (Marius) works, **5:**153–154
Pas d'Action, **6:**106
Pas d'Arbre d'Or, Le (tournament), **1:**364
pas de bourrée, **1:338–339, 5:**323
pas de Brabant, **1:**53, **5:**506
pas de chaconne, **1:**356
Pas de Demons (The Black Crook), **1:**495
Pas de Derviche au Tambour, **5:**319
Pas de Deux (Dolin book), **3:**354
Pas de Deux (film dance), **2:**605
Pas de Deux (Grand Adagio), **1:**298
Pas de Deux (Mordkin), **5:**122–123
Pas de Deux (Yakobson miniature), **6:**412
pas de deux, **5:105–108**
Balanchine choreographies, **4:**611, 613–614
Dolin and Helpmann on importance of, **3:**354
evolution of classical, **1:**347
partnering, **5:**101
in Petipa's (Marius) works, **2:**436, **5:**152, 153
Pas de Deux and Divertissement, **4:**611
"Pas de Deux des Jeunes Paysans" (Burgmüller), **2:**14
Pas de Dix, **4:**610, 616, **6:**85
Pas de Duke, **1:**73, **3:**578
Pas de Pepsi, **4:**531
Pas de Quatre, **1:**49, 300, *301*, **2:**70, **5:108–109,** 150, **6:**353
Ballet Nacional de Cuba cast, **2:***279*
caricature, **2:**70
Central Ballet of China, **2:***146*
Cerrito, Grahn, Grisi, and Taglioni as cast members, **1:**103–104, **2:**94, *103*, **3:**224, 260, 315
Chalon print of, **1:***103*, **2:**103–104
Dolin reconstruction, **2:**104, 112, 425, **3:**59, 229, 437, **4:**269, **5:**431, 553, **6:**353
Fuoco, Rosati, Vente, and Taglioni as cast members, **3:**96
King's Theatre performance, **3:**260

Lester reconstruction, **4:**110, 153, 268
Perrot production, **5:**108, 137, 277
Pribylov version, **5:**475
Rosati as Grahn replacement, **5:**404
Yakobson miniature, **6:**412
pas de Scaramouche, **2:**190
pas de schall, **1:**199
Pas des Déesses, **3:**609, *609*, 610, 611, **4:**153, 5:437
Pas des Dieux (Kelly ballet), **2:**388, **4:**3, **5:**97
Pas de Trois, **4:**269
Pas de Trois Classique, **5:**197
Pas de Trois Cousines, **1:**509, **5:**250
Pas de Trois for Piano and Two Dancers, **6:**119
Pas d'Extrase, or Ministerial Fascination, **2:**70
Pas Espagnol, **3:**22
Pas et Lignes, **1:**70
Pasetti, Carlo, **3:**381
Pasetti, Leo, **4:**64
Pash, Margaret, *as contributor*, **1:**520–524
Pashkevich, Vasily, **2:**55
Pashkova, Lydia A., **5:**320
Pashtun (people), **1:**27
Pasiphaë (mythic), **2:**270
Pasiphaë, **3:**427
Pasloff, Aileen, **6:**282
Paso, **2:**466
paso doble, **1:**359
Pasqual, Alida, **1:**358
Pasricha, Avinash, *as photographer*, **2:**468
Passacaglia in C Minor, **1:**421, **3:**400, 401, 402, 403, *403*, **4:**130
program notes, **4:**177
passacaille. See chaconne and passacaille
"Passaccille pour une Femme" (Feuillet notation), **2:***589*
Passage Nord Theater, **4:**679
Passagens, **5:**235
Passage through the Gong, **5:**524
passepied, **4:**510, 511, **5:**40, **109,** 113
Caribbean adaptation, **2:**62
Passing Show, The (revues), **1:**482, **4:**56, **6:**269, 270, 272
Passion (Kůra ballet), **4:**77
Passion (medieval play), **3:**251
Passion (Sondheim musical), **6:**289
Passion According to Saint Matthew (Bach), **2:**474
Passion for Dance, A (Krishnamurthi), **4:**63
Passion play (Yaqui), **6:**416
Passion Play, **4:**627
Passion selon Saint-Jean, **1:**446
Passloff, Aileen, **4:**214, **6:**362, 363
passo de canario, **2:**51
passo e mezzo, **2:**74, 75, 76, 591, **4:**504, **5:110–112,** 115, 117–118, *323*
galliard relationship, **3:**108, 109
Pas Tartare, **5:**319
Pastelli Coreografici, **3:**320
Pastor, Tony, **6:**315, 316
pastorale, **5:112–113**
Pastorale, **1:**403, **4:**73, 450, 547, **6:**362
Pastorale, La (1926), **1:**256, 259–260, **4:**33
Pastorale Comique, La, **4:**447

Pastorale d'Issy, La (Perrin and Cambert), **5:**113
Pastorela, **1:**281
Pastorela Fedele, La, **2:**55
Pastor Fido, Il, **4:**509, **5:**113, **6:**47
Pastori, Jean-Pierre, **4:**108
Pasuka, Berto, **3:**574
Pásztor, Vera, **3:**415
Patchwork, **4:**134
Pate, Kiko, **5:**310
Paterson, Susan, **4:**627
Pather, Jay, **5:**658, 659
Path of the Choreographer (Lopukhov), **4:**225
Path of Thunder, **2:**449, **4:**149, 284, **5:**462, 487, 572, 614
Path of Thunder (Abrahams), **5:**572
Patin, Jacques, **1:**275–276, **3:**66, **5:**260, 533, *533*, **6:**156
Patín, Mariano, **1:**114
patinada, **3:**300
Patineurs, Les, **1:**148, 149, **4:**544, **5:**113–114, 414, 653, **6:**214
   American Ballet Theatre staging, **1:**69
   Chappell scenic design, **2:**105
   Joffrey Ballet staging, **3:**614
   May performance, **4:**336
   music score, **4:**114
   National Ballet of Canada staging, **4:**544
   Turner performance, **6:**214
Patisson, Mamert, **1:**275
"Patlong" (dance), **5:**171
Pâtre et l'Hamadryade, Le, **2:**414, 415
Patrelle, Francis, **5:**399
Patria (film), **2:**79–80
Patrick, Thomas, **5:**679
Patrick's Fourth Dansing Dance (Orestes' Spell), **4:**22
Patrik, Janaki, **3:**131
Patrona Hungariae, **3:**421
Patsalas, Constantin, **3:**643, **4:**544, 546, **6:**132, 133, 143
Patterns of Change, **2:**359
Patterns of Culture (Benedict), **6:**297
Patterson, Orlando, **3:**576
Patterson, Randi, **2:**386
Pattin' Juba, **6:**254
Pauels, Irina, **3:**157
Paukenschlag, **3:**234
Paul, Saint, **2:**161
Paul, Annette av, **3:**231, 233, *233*, **4:**238, 546, **6:**43, *43*
Paul, Antoine, **1:**36, 455, 505, **2:**390, **5:**91
Paul, Henri, *as photographer*, **3:**228, **6:**130, 131
Paul, Marie Rose, **2:**412, *412*, 413, 414
Paul, Mimi, **4:**611, 612, 618, **6:**66
Paul, Monsieur ("The Aerial"), **2:**353
Paul, Pauline. *See* Montessu, Pauline
Paulaharju, Samuli, **2:**629
Paulay, Forrestine, **4:**99, 104, 370
Paul et Virginie
   Gardel choreography, **1:**35, 451, 507, **3:**68, 118, **4:**61, **6:**333
   Kreutzer score, **4:**61
   Petit choreography, **5:**162
   Valberkh choreography, **4:**278
Paul et Virginie (Bernardin de Saint-Pierre), **1:**201, **3:**118
Paul et Virginie (Kreutzer opera), **4:**61
Pauli, Carl, **1:**47, 90
Paulini, Béla, **3:**412, **4:**420

Paulli, Holger Simon, **1:**515, 516, **4:**6, 43, 513
Paul Sanasardo Dance Company, **5:**439
Paul Taylor Dance Company, **2:**358, **5:**679
   Esplanade, **2:**526–527
   Japanese tour, **3:**591
   Musical Offering, **4:**482–483
   television performances, **6:**139, *140*
   Tharp, Twyla, **6:**151
"Paun Pase" ("How the Peacock Grazes"), **6:**427
Paüs, Torbjørg Åmlid, **4:**670
Pausé, Raoul, **6:**362
Pautret, Andres, **4:**399
Pauwels, Eric, **1:**412
pavan (*pavane*), **2:**74, **5:114–116,** 620, **6:**122
   Kiss Me, Kate choreography, **6:**280, *280*
   music, **4:**502, 506
   See also passo e mezzo; pavaniglia
Pavana para un Amour Muerto, **2:**389
Pavane, **4:**622, **5:**58
Pavane, Lisa, **1:**208, 211, 235
Pavane for a Dead Infanta (Jooss ballet), **3:**614, 626
Pavane pour une Infante Défunte (Bolm ballet), **1:**483
Pavane pour une Infante Défunte (Ravel), **5:**116, 316
Pavane pour une Infante Défunte (Tudor ballet), **6:**196
pavaniglia, **2:**74, **3:**109, **5:**112, 115, **117–118**
Pavelcová, Vlasta, **3:**100
Pavel's Piece, **5:**617
Pavillon, Le, **1:**311, *312*, **4:**33, 178
Pavillon d'Armide, Le, **5:118–119,** 542, 612
   Benois scenic design, **1:**423, 424, **2:**407, **5:**118, 119, 121
   Diaghilev's Ballets Russes, **1:**317–318, 319, 324, **3:**16
   Fokine production, **3:**15, 16, *17*, 137, **5:**118, 119, 121, 456, **6:**160
   Massine choreography, **2:**407
   Mordkin performance, **4:**459
   Nijinsky performance, **4:**280, 639, 640, *640*
   Pavlova performance, **4:**280, **5:**118, 121
Pavinoff, Rovi, **3:**511
Pavley, Andreas (pseud.), **4:**589–590, **5:**58, **6:**291
Pavley-Oukrainsky Company, **5:**391, **6:**264
Pavlova, Anna, **1:**110, 427, 482, **2:**85, 207, 521, 573, 574, **4:**145, 159, **5:119–127,** 171, 247, 278, 610, 650, **6:**182
   American debut, **2:**200, **4:**382, **5:**243, **6:**243, 270
   American tours, **6:**237, 291, 299
   archival materials, **4:**163, 167
   as Ashton influence, **1:**145, 149, 158
   Australian tour, **1:**207, 209, 498, **2:**439, **3:**353
   "Bacchanale" as signature work, **3:**16
   Bakst designs, **1:**254, 255
   Bayadère performance, **5:**120, *153*
   Brazilian tours, **1:**532
   as British dance influence, **3:**263, 279
   Butsova association, **2:**18, 19

Canadian tours, **2:**37
   caricature drawing of, **2:**70
   as Cecchetti pupil, **3:**547
   Chilean tour, **2:**122
   Chinese appearance, **2:**145
   Clustine choreography, **2:**181–182
   Coppélia performance, **2:**200
   Cuban tour, **2:**66, 276
   as de Valois influence, **2:**395, 396
   Diaghilev's Ballets Russes, **1:**319
   Don Quixote performance, **2:**207, 436, 439
   Dying Swan as signature role, **2:**471, **3:**15, 16, **5:**121
   Fille Mal Gardée performance, **2:**597
   as Finnish ballet influence, **2:**632
   Fokine association, **5:**456
   Fokine choreography, **3:**15, 16, 20
   Fokine dance partnership, **3:**14
   French performances, **3:**72
   Gerdt (Pavel) as teacher, **3:**137
   German appearances, **3:**145
   Giselle interpretation, **1:**207, **3:**183, **5:**141
   Helpmann association, **3:**353
   as Henie influence, **3:**357
   homage to Cecchetti, **2:**82
   Hungarian performances, **3:**414
   Hurok management, **3:**424
   interpretive improvisation, **3:**445
   as Italian dance influence, **3:**552
   Japanese tour, **3:**588
   as Johansson student, **3:**618
   as Kirstein inspiration, **4:**26
   as Kshessinsky (Iosif) student, **4:**67
   Legat (Nikolai) dance partnership, **4:**142, *142*
   Legat (Nikolai) caricature drawings of, **2:**69
   as Legat (Nikolai) student, **4:**143
   Lopukhov dance partnership, **4:**224
   Maryinsky Ballet, **3:**655, **4:**280, 283
   Mexican tour, **4:**390, 391
   Mordkin touring partnership, **4:**382, 459, 522, **6:**243, 270
   New Zealand tour, **4:**624
   Nijinsky as partner, **5:**121, 122, 123
   Nutcracker performance, **5:**14
   observation of Jaques-Dalcroze school, **3:**596
   Orientalism, **5:**45, 45, 122, 123
   Page (Ruth) association, **5:**58
   Paris Opera Ballet appearances, **5:**95
   partners, **5:**17
   Pavillon d'Armide performance, **4:**280, **5:**118, 121
   as photographic subject, **5:**178, 183, *183*, 187
   practice clothes worn, **5:**241
   Puppenfee performance, **5:**279
   as Romanoff inspiration, **5:**391
   as Shankar (Uday) influence, **5:**580
   Sleeping Beauty abridged performance, **5:**610–611
   Snowflakes performance, **5:**14
   South African tour, **5:**650
   South American tours, **5:**275, **6:**322
   students, **1:**400, **5:**124, 636
   Swan Lake tour, **6:**32
   Swedish performances, **6:**41

Sylphides performances, **6:**60, 61, *61*
   Valse Caprice performance, **3:**263
   vaudeville performances, **6:**319
   video documentary on, **2:**314
   Vladimiroff as partner, **6:**345, *345*
   Volinine as partner, **6:**348
   Zajlich association, **6:**441
Pavlova, Claudia, **5:**392
Pavlova, Eliana, **3:**588
Pavlova, Nadezhda, **1:**493, **2:**438, **3:**200, 588, **5:**462, 567
Pavlova, Nina, **1:**408
Pavlova Ballet, **5:**124–125, 126
Pavlova Gavotte (Hoffman), **1:**132
Pavlovich, Constantine, **2:**415
Pavon, Pastora, **3:**7
pavoneggiare, **5:**339
Pawelak, Lydia, *as photographer*, **4:**72, 73
Pawnee (people), **4:**554
Paxton, Steve, **1:**215, *243*, 412, 543, **2:**288, 606, **5:127–128,** 313, **6:**250
   British dance classes, **3:**272
   Grand Union, **3:**235, *235*
   improvisation, **3:**446–447, *447*, **4:**442
   Judson Dance Theater, **2:**462, **3:**634, 635
   Winterbranch performance, **6:**402
Payal (television program), **5:**63
Payne, Jimmy, **6:**102
Paysanne Supposée, La, **2:**389
Payse, **2:**151
Paz, Nira, **3:**530
Pazik, Thomas (Tom), **1:**197, **6:**266
PBS. *See* Public Broadcasting System
P. D. Q. Bach (Schickele pseud.), **4:**482
Peabody. *See* ballroom dance competition
Peabody Museum Film Study Center (Harvard University), **2:**601–602
Peace Drum dances, **2:**141
Peace of Westphalia (1648), **6:**38
peace-pipe dances, **4:**550
Peace Will Prevail over War, **6:**420
peacock (as totem), **1:**140, **2:**139
Peacock, Francis, **3:**246–247, **4:**105
Peacock, James, **5:**357
Peacock, Sue, **1:**216
Peacock, The, **2:**378
Peacock and a Girl, A, **5:**75
Peacock Dance, **2:**140
Peacock of Dursad, **2:**32
Peacock Theatre, Dublin, **3:**519
Peaks, **5:**75
Pearl, Kenny, **2:**40
Pearl Fishers, The (Bizet opera), **3:**20
Pearlman, Karen, **1:**216
Pearl of Tokay, The, **4:**22
Pearl Primus Dance Language Institute, **5:**256
Pearl Primus School of Primal Dance, **5:**256
Peasant Couple Dancing, The (Dürer), **5:**259
peasant dance. *See* folk dance history
Peasant Dance (Vsevolodsky-Gerngross), **5:**481
Peasant Feast near Kielce, **6:**207
Peasant Gospel, **2:**264
peasant pas de deux (*Giselle*), **2:**14, **3:**5, **4:**513
Peasant Revolt of 1514, **2:**473
Pease, Esther, **1:**421

Peasley, Colin, **5:**56
Peau et les Os, La, **3:**79
Peaver, Munroe P., **4:**190
Pecour, Guillaume-Louis, **2:**465, 518, **4:**106, 107, 109, **5:128–129,** 308, 506, 621, **6:**123
   allemande choreography, **1:**47, **2:**338
   as *ballet de collège* dance master, **1:**283, 284
   on ballet scenario source, **4:**173
   Blondy as Paris Opera successor, **1:**464
   bourrée compositions, **1:**516, 517
   Camargo as student, **2:**28, 29
   "Canarie pour Deux Hommes," **2:**51
   choreography for Campra *opérasballet,* **2:**34
   courante choreography, **2:**260
   dance classes, **3:**81
   figure dances, **2:**591
   folia notation, **3:**29
   French ballroom dances, **1:**91
   gargouillade, **5:**402
   Gaudrau collection of dances, **3:**122
   gigue choreography, **3:**172, 173
   Lestang collaborations, **4:**152
   Louis XV coronation dance choreography, **4:**475
   loures, **4:**231, 232
   as Lully protégé, **4:**235, **5:**39, 87
   menuet, **4:**431, 433
   musette choreography, **4:**481
   Paris Opera Ballet, **5:**39, 87
   pas de deux scores, **5:**105
   passepieds, **5:**109, *109*
   pavanes, **5:**116
   Recüeil de Danses, **1:**355, **6:**124
   tambourins, **6:**87
Pécs Summer festival, Hungary, **1:**308, **2:**474
Peculiar Closet, The, **6:**175
pedalangan, **3:**496
Pedanda, Ida, **3:**644
Pédant, Le, **2:**365
Pedenchuk, Larisa, *as photographer,* **1:**440, 494
Pederneiras, Rodrigo and Paulo, **1:**536
Pedersen, Thorolf, **4:***188*
Pedi (people), **5:**643, *646,* 663
Pedrilla e Rosetta, overo Un Peccato di Desiderio, **1:**427
Pedro de Gracia Dei, **1:**380
Peel, Sir Robert, **2:**70
Peele, George, **3:**253
Peep at the Parisot with Q in the Corner, A (Queensbury), **2:**71
"Peerdesprong," **4:**586
Peer Gynt, **3:**338
   Budarin staging, **5:**472
   Klaus staging, **6:**53
   Neumeier choreography, **4:**604, **6:**44
   Orlikovsky choreography, **1:**374, **2:**510–511
   Ulrich choreography, **6:**229
Peer Gynt (Ibsen and Grieg), **1:**298
Peets, Mara J., *as contributor,* **5:**194–195
Peggy, Edith, **6:**93
Peicam de Bressoles, Chevalier, **2:**353, 595, **4:**35
Peiko, Nikolai, **2:**16, **5:**572
Peintre et Son Modèle, Le, **1:**306
Pei Yanling, **5:129–130**
pejoge, **3:**505
Pekalis, Coco, **1:***245*

Peking. *See* Beijing *headings*
Peking Ballet School, **3:**328
pelandok, **3:**505
pelegongan, **3:**667
Pelham, Peter, **2:**339, **6:**231
Pelican, **1:**140, 542, **5:**314
Pélin, Mademoiselle, **1:**43
Pelléas et Mélisande, **1:**82, **2:**471, **3:**45
Pellegrin, Abbé, **5:**306
Pellegrina, La, **1:**353, **3:**108, 509, *510*
Pellia e Mileto, **5:**277
Pelo, Mal, **5:**675
Peloponnesian Folklore Foundation, **3:**304
Peloponnesian War, The, **4:**531
Peloponnesus, **3:**296
pelota, **4:**106
Pelt, Joost, **5:**436
Pelus, Marie-Jeanne. *See* Marie-Jeanne
Pembe Kadın (A Woman Called Rosy), **6:**212
Pemberton, Edmund, **1:**92, **2:**81, 338, 591, **3:**281, 522, **4:**105, 433, **5:**252
Pemberton-Billing, Noël, **1:**43
penaché, **1:**7
Penalver, Rosario, **6:**301
pencak, **1:**174, 187, **3:**500–501, 503, **5:130–131**
pencak-randai, **3:**500
pencak-silat, **1:**187, **3:**500
Penderecki, Krzysztof, **3:**51, **5:**302, 683
Pendlebury, J. D. S., **2:**269
Pendleton, Francis, **2:**337
Pendleton, Moses, **3:**614, *616,* **5:**98, 194, *194,* 335, 526
Pêne du Bois, Raoul, **2:**242, **3:**656
Penescu Liciu, Elena, **5:**384
Penger, Rafael, **2:**632
penglembar dances, **3:**490
Peng Song, **6:**82
Peninsula (film), **2:**155
Penitente, El, **1:**421, **2:**285, **3:**216, 221, 349, 384, **4:**120, 130
   Horst score, **4:**518
   Noguchi scenic design, **4:**659
Penman, Robert, **3:**283
Penn, Arthur, **2:**285
Pennewell, Norwood, **2:**566
Penney, Jennifer, **3:**443, **4:***245,* 257
Pennies from Heaven (film), **5:**408
Pennington, Ann, **6:**270, 371, 448
Pennsylvania Ballet, **2:**315, **5:131–132,** **6:**139, 264
   Cunningham choreography, **2:**294
   Ford Foundation grant, **1:**271, **6:**265
   Martins's *La Sylphide* reconstruction, **4:**275
   Moncion choreography, **4:**450
   Waring choreography, **6:**363
Penobscot (people), **4:**554
Pen Song, **2:**149
Penta Theater, **4:**594, 595
pentazalis, **2:**269
Pentecostal dances, **2:**164, **3:**241, **4:**213
Pentheus, king of Thebes, **3:**292
pentozalis, **2:**271–272
Penzi, Giuliana, **3:**552, 553, 555
People Like Us, **1:**215
People Long for Liberation, The, **2:**155
People's Republic of China. *See* China
People's Theater movement, **6:**161

People's Theater of the Gorky Palace of Culture, Leningrad, **5:**461
Pépin, Clermont, **2:**151
Pepin's Circus, **2:**174
Peppermill, The (revue), **3:**208
Pepys, Samuel, **2:**337, **3:**254, 255
Perca, Manuela. *See* Nena, La
Percival, John, **1:**394, **3:**285
Percussion for Six Men, **6:**324
Percussion Instrument Étude, **3:**312
percussive dances. *See* clogging; flamenco dance; step dancing; tap dance
Perdacher, Walter, **5:***682*
Perea, Manuela. *See* Nena, La
Pereira, Vincent, *as photographer,* **2:**605
Pereira Sales, Eugenion, **2:**121
Perelman, S. J., **6:**278
pereplias dance, **5:**444
Peretti, Serge, **1:**195, **2:**351, 447, **3:**318, **4:**184, **5:**95, 96, **132,** 676, 678, 690
Pereyaslavec, Valentina, **1:**65, **4:**63
Perez, Andrés, **2:**126
Perez, David, **5:**231
Pérez, Julián, **6:**323
Perez, Xavier, **5:**676
Pérez Borjas, Elías, **6:**323, 324
Pérez Castillo, Carlos, **2:**522
Pérez Gurri, Delfina, **2:**276
Pérez Padilla, Rosario Florencia. *See* Antonio and Rosario
performance art, **1:**139–140, 143–144, 199
   as avant-garde, **1:**245
   Chile modern dance, **2:**126
   Chuma, Yoshiko, **2:**170–171
   Farber, Viola, **2:**575
Performing Arts Collection of South Australia, **4:**160
Performing Arts Council of the Transvaal. *See* PACT Ballet; PACT Dance Company
Pergolesi, Giambattista, **2:**409, **4:**317, 318, 516, **5:**306, **6:**5
Pergolesi, Giovanni, **5:**683, **6:**175
Péri, Jacopo, **4:**581, **5:**113
Péri, La, **1:**50, 86, 246, **3:**72, **4:**185, **5:132–133**
   Ashton production, **5:**133, 298–299
   Bakst costume design, **1:***254,* 255
   bird lift technique, **5:**103
   Burgmüller score, **2:**14, 203, **4:**513
   caricature of, **2:**71
   character dance, **2:**107
   Coralli production, **2:**14, 107, 201, 203–204, **3:**315, **4:**176, 513, **5:**93, 132, 133
   Darrell production, **2:**350
   first American production, **5:**616
   Gautier libretto, **2:**14, **3:**123, **4:**176, **5:**93
   Grisi performance, **3:**315, 316, **5:**93, 132–133
   Markova performance, **4:**267
   Pavlova orientalization of, **5:**45
   Pavlova performance, **5:**125
   Petipa (Lucien) performance, **5:**132, 133, 148, *148*
Péri, Panchita de, **1:**290, **2:**470
Pericet, Antoine, **5:**133
Pericet, Luisa, **2:**522
Pericet, Raphael, **2:**522
Pericet Carmona, Angel, **1:**93, 294–295, **2:**522, **5:**133, 672
Pericet Jiménez, Angel, **2:**522, **5:**133, 672

Pericet family, **2:**522, **5:133**
Périchole, La (Offenbach), **2:**15
Periclean Theater, Athens, **5:**42
pericón, **1:**108, 109
Pericona, La, **2:**122
perico ripiao, **2:**431
Perihippikes (Xenophon), **2:**490
Perillo, Mary, **2:**609
Perilous Night, **4:**220
Perini, Mana I., **3:**135
periniṭa dance, **5:**382
period modernism, **2:**409
Peripateia, **6:**362
Perisynthyon, **1:**230, **3:**357
Perkins, Dorothy, **3:**361
Perkins, William, **2:**167
Perkun, G., **1:**34
Perle, La, **3:**318, **4:**145, **5:**160
Perls, Frederick, **1:**470
Perm Ballet School, **5:**471
Perm Opera and Ballet Theater, **1:**38, **5:470–471**
   Boyarchikov as chief choreographer, **1:**518–519
"Pernambuco" *(Where's Charley?),* **6:**277
Pernikoff, Serge, **3:**22
Perottet, Suzanne, **3:**596
Perrault, Adélaïde, **6:**69
Perrault, Charles, **1:**36, 425, **2:**172, **5:**9, 606
Perrault, George, **1:**305
Perrault, Michel, **2:**151, **3:**227
Perrault, Serge, **1:**305, **2:**350, **3:**318, **4:**380
Perreault, Jean-Pierre, **2:**40, 44, 45–46, **6:**132
Perrin, Émile, **2:**198, **5:**94
Perrin, Pierre, **1:**396, **5:**86, 113
Perron, Wendy, **2:**247
Perrot, Jules, **1:**35, 86, 505, **2:**202, 339, 363, **4:**339, **5:**91, **134–142,** 149, 319
   Adam ballets, **1:**9, 10
   Alma, **1:**37, 47–48, **2:**390
   ballet training, **5:**91, **6:**334
   Bogdanova roles, **1:**477
   Carey (Gustave) roles, **2:**60
   caricatures, **2:**70
   Catarina, **2:**80, 82, 505
   Cerrito association, **2:**93, 94–95
   choreographic emphasis on dancing, **3:**180
   Coralli association, **2:**201, 202, 203, 204
   Corsaire, Le, **2:**206, 207, **4:**280
   Deshayes (André) collaboration, **2:**389, 390
   divertissements, **3:**260
   Elssler (Fanny) collaboration, **2:**503, 504, 505
   Esmeralda, La, **1:**540, **2:**60, 95, 505, 523, 524, **3:**185, 315, **5:**403, 516, 528, **6:**452
   Esmeralda restaging in United States, **4:**452
   Faust, **1:**461, 499, **2:**60, 505
   Ferraris roles, **2:**587
   Flore et Zéphire performance, **2:**415
   Gerdt (Pavel) roles, **3:**136–137
   Giselle, **2:**201, 203, 390, **3:**5, 177, 180, 181, 260, 314, **5:**135–136, 141
   Grahn roles, **3:**224
   Grisi relationship, **2:**390, 405, **3:**313–314, 315, 316, **5:**106, 135–136, 137, 138, 139, 221
   Guest biography, **3:**321
   Ivanov roles, **3:**560

Perrot, Jules, *continued*
  Johansson as acting student,
    3:618
  King's Theatre (London)
    association, **2**:94, 389, 390,
    3:*259*, 260
  Kobold, Der, **1**:238
  Maywood roles, **4**:339
  Nielsen as student, **4**:631
  Ondine, **2**:94, 95, **5**:29, 136, 277
  Parisian debut, **3**:68
  Paris Opera Ballet, **5**:93
  Pas de Quatre, **5**:108, 137, 277
  polka, **5**:221
  Polka pas de deux, **3**:315, *315*
  practice clothes requirements,
    5:241
  Pugni scores, **5**:277, 278
  Ronzani choreographic
    reproductions, **5**:403
  Rossignol, Le, **3**:259
  Saint-Léon association, **5**:498,
    499, 502
  Saint Petersburg ballet, **3**:316,
    560, **4**:280–281, **5**:454, **6**:451
  students, **1**:205
  Swiss Milkmaid production, **6**:51
  Taglioni family association, **6**:70,
    73, 75
  Vienna Hofoper, **3**:313–314
Perrot, Marie-Julie, **3**:314
Perrottet, Suzanne, **1**:203, **4**:90, 91,
  103, **6**:389
Perry, Charlotte, **3**:385, **6**:248
Perry, George, *as contributor,*
  1:465–466
Perry, Ronald, **2**:334, **6**:260
Perry Como Show, The (television
  series), **6**:137, *137*
Perry-Mansfield School of Theatre,
  3:385, **6**:248, 295
Persée, **2**:98, 465, **3**:106, **4**:109, 235,
  5:105
Persephone (mythic), **3**:288
Perséphone
  Ashton choreography, **1**:155, 430
  Joffrey choreography, **3**:609
  Jooss revised (1954) version,
    3:630
  Jooss-Rubinstein (1934)
    production, **3**:628, **5**:439, **6**:5
  Lang choreography, **2**:470
  Rubinstein production, **6**:5
Perseus and Andromeda, **1**:391,
  6:372
Persia. *See* Iran
Persian Angel, **1**:518, **3**:23
Persian Gulf region. *See* Arabian
  Peninsula
Persians (Aeschylus), **3**:289
Persisches Märchen, Ein, **3**:625
personal dance prayer, **4**:213
Persons and Structures, **4**:651
perspective, angled, **5**:*536*, 537
perspective painting, **5**:534
Perspectives, **3**:212
Persson, Bodil, **6**:50
Persuasian (Austen), **1**:190
Persuis, Louis-Luc de, **4**:61,
  422, 423
Perth, Australia, **1**:211, 212,
  216, 217
Perth Glovers' Dance, **3**:249
Pertoldi, Erminia, **3**:261
Peru, **2**:62, **3**:35, **5**:142–147
Peru Negro, **5**:146
peruperu, **4**:261
Pervan, Slavko, **6**:436, 438
Pescanny, Gennady, **5**:479
Pescht, Rudolf, **2**:123, **3**:626, 628,
  628, 629, **5**:265, **6**:304

Peshkov, Nikita, **1**:485
Pesovár, Ernő and Ferenc, **3**:423,
  4:367, 371
Pessoa, Fernando, **5**:233
Pestalozzi, Johann Heinrich, **3**:159,
  6:453
Pestekhin, Serge, **1**:408
Pestelli, Giorgio, **3**:556
Pestov, Petr, **3**:100, 200
peteneras, **5**:133
Peter I (the Great), emperor of
  Russia, **5**:450, **6**:442
Peter III, emperor of Russia, **4**:276
Peter, Frank-Manuel, **3**:161
Peter, Zoltan, **2**:470
Peter (film), **1**:539
Peter and the Wolf (Prokofiev), **1**:66,
  5:54, 300
  Bolm choreography, **1**:484
  Cramér production, **2**:264
  Larsen choreography, **4**:126
  Loring performance, **4**:227
  Staff production, **3**:62, 174,
    5:691, 692
Peterich, Gerda, **5**:185
  as photographer, **5**:256
Peterka, Anni, **3**:154
Peterkin, Daisy (Mademoiselle
  Dazie), **6**:318
Petermann, Kurt, **2**:386, **3**:161–162
  as contributor, **3**:138–143,
    4:128–129
  Dance Archives, Leipzig, **4**:161
Peter Pan (musical), **4**:420, **6**:281,
  285, 288
Peter Pan and the Butterfly, **5**:58
Peters, Bernadette, **6**:284, 286, 287
Peters, Kurt, **3**:161–162
  as contributor, **3**:158–160
  dance archives, **4**:161
Peters, Larry, **6**:186
Peters, Michael, **1**:420
Petersburg, **1**:519, **5**:464, 469
Petersen, Britta, **3**:261
Petersen, Conrad, **3**:*232*
Petersen, Jan Ludwig, **5**:649
Peterson, Kirk, **6**:266
Peterson, Sidney, **2**:604
Petersson, Allan, **6**:43
pethilan, **3**:495
Pethő, László, **3**:418, 419
Petipa, Jean-Antoine, **1**:410, **3**:136,
  560, **4**:138, **5**:147–148, 149,
  150, 319
Petipa, Lucien, **1**:10, 392, 410,
  2:71, 282, **5**:147, 148–149,
  221, 515
  bird lift technique, **5**:103
  Coralli ballets, **2**:203, 204
  Diable à Quatre performance,
    2:405
  Ferraris association, **2**:587
  Gemma, **2**:95
  Giselle performance, **3**:70, 177,
    179, **5**:148
  Grisi dance partnership,
    3:314, 315
  Jolie Fille de Gand, La, **3**:5, 620
  Mazilier ballets, **4**:341, 342
  Mérante as Paris Opera
    successor, **4**:353
  Paquita, **3**:5, **5**:85, 148
  Paris Opera Ballet, **5**:93, 94, 135,
    148–149
  Péri performance, **3**:315, **5**:132,
    133, 148, *148*
  Sacountala, **3**:123, **5**:94, 148, 158
Petipa, Marie (daughter of Marius),
  2:436, **3**:14, 15, 561, 618, **5**:37
  character dancing, **4**:282, **5**:160
  Disdéri photograph of, **5**:177

husband Legat (Sergei), **4**:144
Pâquette performance, **5**:500
Seasons performance, **5**:*161*
Sleeping Beauty performance,
  5:606–610
Petipa, Marius, **1**:45, 73, 74, 147,
  255, 410, 486, **2**:181, 446,
  525, **5**:141, 147, **149–162,**
  531, 557, 572, 614
  archival materials, **4**:165
  Armida, **5**:140
  as Ashton influence, **1**:151, 154,
    3:267
  as Balanchine influence, **1**:263,
    272, 293
  as Baryshnikov influence, **1**:373
  Bolshoi Theater, Saint
    Petersburg, **3**:560
  Bournonville relationship, **1**:510
  Camargo, La, **3**:237
  Cecchetti association, **2**:82
  character dances, **2**:108
  Cinderella choreographic
    collaboration, **2**:82,
    3:564–565
  Coppélia, **2**:200, 368, 369
  Corsaire, Le, **2**:207–208
    criticisms, **3**:347
  Drigo compositions, **2**:446, 447
  Elssler (Fanny) roles, **2**:505
  Esmeralda revivals, **2**:524
  Fille du Pharaon, La, **5**:120, *150,*
    151, 155–156
  Fille Mal Gardée, La, **2**:594, 596
  Fokine as successor, **1**:319
  Fokine choreography versus, **6**:62
  Fokine's early career, **3**:14
  Gerdt (Pavel) roles, **3**:137
  Giselle, **5**:141, 157
  Giselle restaging, **3**:181, 182, 183
  Glazunov score commission,
    4:515
  Golovin designs, **3**:196
  grand pas de deux, **5**:106
  influences seen in Lopukhov's
    work, **4**:225
  Ivanov as assistant, **3**:560, 562,
    4:282
  Ivanov collaborations, **2**:108,
    3:15, 560, **4**:282
  Ivanov roles, **3**:561
  Johansson collaboration, **3**:618
  Kshessinska (Matilda) roles, **4**:68
  Labanotation of works, **3**:427
  Lecompte (Eugénie) association,
    4:138
  legacy, **5**:162, 455–456
  Legat (Nikolai) as Maryinsky
    Ballet successor, **4**:143
  Legat (Sergei) roles, **4**:144
  Legat caricature drawings of,
    2:69
  Legnani roles, **4**:145, 146
  Little Humpbacked Horse, The,
    4:211
  Marché des Innocents, Les,
    5:94, 151
  Maryinsky Ballet, **4**:281–283,
    286, **5**:157–162, *161–162, 451,*
    566–456
  Minkus scores, **4**:30, 429
  Nutcracker conception, **2**:108,
    3:563–564, **5**:9, 10, 160
  Paquita, **1**:86, 300, **4**:429, **5**:85,
    147, 150, 154, *154*
  Pavlova as protégée, **5**:119
  pointe work refinement,
    5:152, 207
  Pugni association, **5**:277
  Rambert's early championship of,
    3:263

Raymonda, **5**:154, 157, 159, *159,*
  160, 320
Raymonda as last great
  production, **5**:456
as Russian school exemplar,
  1:328–329, **5**:480
Seasons, The, **5**:120, 160, *161*
Spanish dance influences, **2**:522
Stepanov notation of repertory,
  4:686, **5**:693, **6**:32–34
Swan Lake, **2**:574, **3**:566, **4**:*278,*
  6:30–31, 32
Swiss Milkmaid production, **6**:51
Sylphide version, **6**:58
Trilby, **3**:237
  tutu, classical, **2**:244
Two Stars, The, **5**:119
  wife Surovshchikova, **4**:281,
    5:140, 141, 150, 455
  *See also Bayadère, La; Don
    Quixote; Sleeping Beauty, The*
Petipa, Vera, **5**:162
Petipa family, **3**:68
Petit, Anatole, **1**:36, **3**:209
Petit, Baptiste, **2**:464
Petit, Charles, **3**:82
Petit, Constance, **1**:505
Petit, Dominique, **2**:126
Petit, Jean-Baptiste, **1**:237
Petit, Madame. *See* Duport, Marie-
  Adélaïde
Petit, Michel, *as photographer,*
  2:278
Petit, Roland, **1**:195, 426, **2**:109,
  3:156, **5**:162–165, 527, **6**:352
  'Adame Miroir, **4**:418
  Babilée association, **1**:251
  Ballets des Champs-Élysées,
    1:305–306, **3**:73, 394, **4**:33
  Béjart association, **1**:403
  Benesh notation use, **1**:418
  Carmen, **1**:38, 305, 454, **2**:3, 244,
    283, **3**:12, 74, 601, **5**:*164,* 589,
    599, *600,* 653
  Charrat association, **2**:111
  Cocteau association, **2**:183
  Coppélia revised version,
    2:200, 201
    costume, **2**:245
  Cyrano de Bergerac, **4**:65
    designers, **3**:74
  Dupond roles, **2**:463
  Flindt roles, **3**:12
  Fonteyn roles, **3**:45
  independent dance concerts, **3**:73
  Jeanmaire relationship, **3**:601
  Jeune Homme et la Mort, Le,
    3:73, 601
  Jeux, **2**:361
  Kehlet roles, **3**:668
  as Lifar student, **4**:184
  Makarova performances, **4**:248
  Notre-Dame de Paris, **1**:195,
    2:524, **4**:285
  Nutcracker, The, **5**:15, 164
  Paris Opera Ballet, **5**:96, 97, 164
  Plisetskaya role, **5**:206
  Rayet role, **5**:320
  Royal Ballet guest productions,
    3:236, **5**:415
  Royal Danish Ballet guest
    productions, **5**:431
  Sleeping Beauty, The, **5**:613
  Taglioni's *La Sylphide*
    reconstruction, **6**:58–59
  See also Ballet du XXᵉ Siècle;
    Ballet National de Marseille;
    Ballets de Paris de Roland
    Petit
Petit Ballet, **2**:277

Petit Carnaval de Venise, Le, **5:**134
Petite Bohémienne, La, **5:**149
Petite Fadette, Le, **4:**110
Petite Mort, **4:**81, **5:**305
Petit Musée de Vélasquez, Le, **6:**133
Petits Danaïdes, Les, **5:**147
Petits mystéres de l'Opéra, Les (Second), **5:**241
Petits Riens, Les, **2:**396, **3:**206, **4:**509–510, 697, **5:**89, 603
petits tours, **1:**337
Petit Suite, La, **5:**95
Pet of the Village, The, **1:**460
Petrassi, Goffredo, **1:**350, **2:**440, **4:**421, **5:**400, 529
Petrides, Ted, **3:**303
  as *contributor,* **1:**84–85, **3:**301–302
Petrobelli, Pierluigi, **3:**556
Petroff, Nicholas, **6:**292
Petroff, Paul, **1:**124, 309, 313, 315, *367,* **3:**512, **4:**208, **6:**33
Petrograd-Leningrad Opera and Ballet Theater. *See* Maryinsky Ballet
Petronio, Stephen, **1:***544*
Petro rite, **3:**334–335
Petrossian, Emma, as *contributor,* **1:**119–121
Petrouchka, **1:**66, *207,* 374, **5:165–166,** 246, 294, **6:**313
  Bavarian State Ballet premiere, **1:**390
  Béjart production, **1:**292, 406
  Benois designs, **1:***422,* 423–424, *423,* **2:**244, **5:**541–542, **6:**3
  Bintley performance, **1:**453
  Bjørnsson performances, **1:**454
  Blair performance, **1:**459
  Bolm staging and performance, **1:**482, 483, **4:**382
  Bosman production and performance, **2:**58
  Brada production, **3:**414
  Bruhn performance, **2:**4
  Cecchetti mime performances, **2:**83, 84
  character role, **2:**106, **4:**125
  Chiriaeff production, **2:***151*
  as Diaghilev production, **2:**406, 407, **3:***655*
  Eglevsky performance, **2:**579
  English National Ballet revivals, **2:**507–508, 512
  Fokine productions, **1:***138,* 318, *318,* 320, 321, *422,* 423, 482, **2:**112, 191, 244, *424,* **3:**14, 18, *19,* 21, 26, 75, 226, **4:**126, **5:**165, 166, **6:**3–4
  Fornaroli performance, **3:**51
  Froman staging, **6:**431
  Grands Ballets Canadiens, **2:**38
  Grant performance, **3:**236
  Grigoriev-Tchernicheva revival, **3:**308
  Idzikowski performance, **3:**441
  Joffrey Ballet-Nureyev television program, **3:**616
  Joffrey Ballet restoration and staging, **3:**614
  Karsavina performance, **3:***655,* 656
  Kehlet *demi-caractère* role, **3:**668
  Kerr production, **4:**625, 626
  Kirsova performance, **4:**25
  Koslov pirated version, **4:**56
  Kovaček choreography, **2:**11
  Krätke production, **3:**153
  Laing performance, **4:**110
  Lassen performance, **4:**126
  Liepa (Andris) reconstruction, **4:**181
  Lifar performance, **4:**182
  Lopokova performance, **4:**223
  Milloss production, **3:**415
  Nijinska performance, **4:**634, *634*
  Nijinsky performance, **1:***138,* **2:**408, **4:***645*
  orchestration, **1:**93
  "Petrouchka chord," **4:**516
  port de bras, **5:**227
  Robbins performance, **5:**360
  Rome Opera Ballet revival, **5:**400
  Stravinsky rescoring, **6:**6
  Stravinsky score, **2:**407, **4:**516, **6:**3–4
  Uthoff expressionist version, **2:**124, **6:**304
  Vashegyi choreography, **3:**416
  Vinogradov choreography, **4:**285
  Woizikowski performance, **6:**404
  Zorina performances, **6:**450
Petrov, Anastas, **2:**11, 12, **5:166**
Petrov, Andrei, **2:**499, 502, **5:**460, 465, 474
Petrov, Nicholas, **5:**196, 398, 531
Petrov, Oleg A., **5:**465, 475, 482
  as *contributor,* **5:**613–614
Petrov, Pavel, **3:**196
Petrov, Vasiklko, **3:**560
Petrova, Galina, **4:**38, **5:**480
Petrova, Ninel, **4:**284
Petrovic, Emil, **2:**473, 474
Petrović, Veroslava, **6:**438
Petrovsky Theater, Moscow, **1:**484–485, **5:**452
Petrov-Vodkin, K. S., **2:**420
Petrucci, Ottaviano, **4:**502
Pettinati, Gaetano, **5:**215
Pettoletti, Philippo, **2:**385
Petukhov, Yuri, **5:**469
Peu de Chagrin, La, **2:**471
Peuls (people), **4:**548
Peurel, Paul, **4:**507
Peut-on Danser une Paysage, **6:**90
Pevsner, Antoine, **1:**133, 258, 317, **2:**242, **5:**544
Pevsner, Nicolas, **5:**526
Peyer, Fritz, as *photographer,* **6:**7
peyote cactus, **4:**550
Pezzoli, Francesca, **5:***403*
Pfeiffer, Edith, **4:**127
Pfitzner, Hans, **6:**393
Pforsich, Janis L., as *contributor,* **3:**375–379
Pfundmayr, Hedy, **1:**240, **4:**229, 457
Phaedra (mythic), **2:**271
Phaedra and Hippolytus, **4:**279
Phaëton, **2:**465, **4:**109, 235
Phalèse, Pierre, **3:**49
Phallic Mythology, **4:**272
Pham Anh Phuong, **1:***215*
Phantasmagoria, The, **1:**394, **4:**217
Phantom Dancers, The, **2:**85
Phantom of the Opera, The (musical), **2:**251, **6:**287
Phantom of the Opera, The (Waring ballet), **6:**363
Pharaoh's Daughter. See Fille du Pharaon, La
phaulos, **2:**506
Phèdre, **2:**183, 351, **4:**185, **5:**95, 96, **6:**183, 353
Phèdre et Hippolyte, **4:**35
Pheloung, Barrington, **4:**219
Phende (people), **2:**91
Phifer, Cassandra, **3:***387*
Philip III, king of Spain, **4:**579
Philadanco, **2:**358, **4:**96, **6:**264
Philadelphia, Pennsylvania
  Federal Dance Project, **2:**581
  nineteenth-century dance, **4:**139, **6:**232–233, 290
Philadelphia Academy of Music, **5:**403–404, **6:**291
Philadelphia Ballet, **4:**209–210, **5:**612, **6:**264
Philadelphia Civic Ballet. *See* Philadelphia Ballet
Philadelphia Dance Company. *See* Philadanco
Philadelphia Dancing Assemblies, **6:**232
Philadelphia La Scala, **4:**209
Philadelphia Opera Company, **4:**209
Philastre, Humanité, **2:**405, **3:**620, **5:**85, 132
Philebois, Alexander, **1:**236, **3:**364
Philebois, Antoine, **3:**365
Philebois, Franz Anton, **1:**236
Philebois, Maria, **1:**236
Philidor, André, **4:**510
Philip, king of Macedon, **3:**293
Philip II, king of Spain, **2:**76, **4:**579, **5:**230
Philip III, duke of Burgundy, **1:**364, **4:**449
Philip IV, king of Spain, **1:**409, **5:**668, 670
Philippart, Nathalie, **1:**251, 305, **2:**277
  Amour et Son Amour performance, **3:**73
  Don Quixote performance, **2:**440
  Jeune Homme et la Mort performance, **3:**601, **4:**33
Philippine Ballet Theater, **5:**172, 174
Philippine Dance Company of New York, **5:**173, *173,* **6:***172*
Philippine Folk Dance Society, **5:**44
Philippine Life, Legend, and Love in Dance, **5:**171
Philippines, **5:167–175**
  Bayanihan Philippine Dance Company, **1:**393–394, **2:**570, **5:**173
  costume, **2:**230–231
  dancing with fans tradition, **2:**570
  libraries and museums, **4:**159
  tinikling dance, **2:**231, **6:***172*
Philippine Women's University, **1:**393, 394
Phillips-Gutkin, as *photographer,* **5:**684
Phillipe, M., **1:**284, 456
Phillipini, Rosalie, **1:**206–207
Phillips, Arlene, **6:**287
Phillips, Ethel, **4:**272
Phillips, Jared, **5:**17
Phillips, Maggi, **1:**217
Phillips-Gutkin, as *photographer,* **5:**434
Philly Dog, **6:**257, 263
Philochoros, **6:**37
Philosophy Lesson, The, **4:**239, **5:**245
Philotis, **1:**246, **2:**181
Philoxenus, **2:**419
Philpot, Gly, **3:**656
Phimphilalai, **4:**112, **6:**151
Phina and Her Picks, **6:**317
Phipps, Aimée, **6:**312
Phi Project, **4:**21
Phithī Wai Khrū, **4:**9
Phoenix, or The Morning of a Journalist (Shakhovsky vaudeville), **3:**539–540
Phol, Elsa, **5:**637
phorminx, **3:**293, **4:**499
Photographer, The, **3:**201, **5:**187, 573
photography, **5:175–188**
  Beaton, Cecil, **1:**395
  film dance, **2:**603–612
  kinesiology application, **4:***14,* 15–16
  Kirstein interest, **4:**30
  Sweden, **6:**50
  See also film and video
Phra Phirāp, **4:**9
Phra Phrot Rūsī, **4:**9
Phrases, **1:**142, **2:**295–296, **6:**362
Phrynichus, **2:**159, **5:**556
Phumiphol, king of Thailand, **4:**10
physical anthropology. *See* anthropology *under* methodologies in the study of dance
physical conditioning
  aerobic dance, **1:**12–13
  as *Ausdruckstanz* basis, **1:**203
  body therapies, **1:**468–477
  capoeira dance as, **2:**58–59
  dance as sport, **2:**322–324
  Delsarte system of expressions, **2:**370–372, *370,* **6:**240
  kinesiology, **4:**17
  Laban movement system, **4:**92, 94, 97, 104
  See also dance as sport
physical education
  ancient Sparta, **3:**291
  British dance curriculum, **3:**276–278
  folk dance in curriculum, **3:**34, 35, **6:**294–295
  French modern dance option, **3:**83
  German dance curriculum, **3:**159, 160
  Greek folk dance, **3:**301, 303, 304
  kinesiology, **4:**16
  Mexican dance training, **4:**391
  square dancing, **5:**688–689
  U.S. dance curriculum, **3:**352–353, **6:**235, 239, 240–241, 248–249, 291, 294, 295
physical therapist, **4:**20
Physical Things, **4:**21
physicians. *See* dance medicine
physics of dance, **5:188–191**
  See also kinesiology
Physics of Dance, The (Laws), **4:**17
Physiologie des mouvements (Duchenne), **4:**15
PIA Arts Academy, **1:**94
Piacentini, Marcello, **5:**399
Piacenza. *See* Domenico da Piacenza
Pian, Leonidas, **3:**300
piano
  Cage "prepared," **2:**21–22, **4:**519
  dominance in Graham dance scores, **3:**214
  four in *Noces* score, **4:**657, **6:**4
  as rehearsal instrument, **1:**6, 7, **4:**438, **5:**480
Piano Circus, **5:***235*
Piano Concerto in E Minor (Chopin), **4:**633, 638
Piano Concerto no. 1 (Tchaikovsky), **6:**117

Piano Concerto no. 2 (Tchaikovsky). *See Ballet Imperial*
Piano Pieces, **4:**615, 619, **5:**366
Piano-Rag-Music, **1:**479, **4:**274
Piano Rag Music (Stravinsky), **4:**519
Piano Sonata, **4:**479, **6:**56
Piano Variations (Copland), **2:**196
Pianovsky, Mečislav, **4:**127
piantone, **3:**109
Piatnitsky, Mitrofan, **5:**474
Piatnitsky Folk Choir, **5:**474
Piatnitsky State Academic Russian Folk Choir, **6:**303
Piattoli, Vincenzo, **5:**424
Piazzolla, Astor, **1:**540, **4:**632, **6:**93, 94
Picabia, Francis, **1:**134, 328, **2:**603, **3:**72, 614, *616*, **5:**334, 335, *335*, 525, 545
Picard, Bernard, **6:**132
Picassiana, **5:**617
Picasso, Pablo, **1:**133, *139*, 141, 252, **2:**67, 242, **3:**393, 653, **5:**191–193, 259
  ballet caricature drawings, **2:**71
  Diaghilev commissions, **1:**316, 317, 322, 323, **2:**406, 409, 568, **4:**317, 515, **5:**191–192, *192*, 262, 525, 527, 543, *543*, 547, **6:**192
  Escudero friendship, **2:**521
  Kochno association, **4:**33, 34
  Mercure designs, **4:**320
  Parade designs, **2:**409, **3:**614, **4:***302*, 317, 516, **5:**85, 86, 191–192, *192*
  Pulcinella designs, **2:**192, **6:**5
  Soirées de Paris, **3:**72
  Tricorne drop curtain, **2:**568, **5:**192, **6:**192
Piccagliani, Erio, *as photographer*, **3:**549, 550, **5:**529
Piccinini, Alessandro, **4:**505
Piccinni, Niccolò, **5:**371
Piccola Scala, Milan, **3:**601
Piccoli, **1:**315, **3:**601
Piccolo et Mandolines, **2:**388
Pichaut, Alexandre, **2:**436
Pichler, Gusti, **1:**240, **3:**347
Picken, L. E. R., **6:**82
Pick-Mangiagalli, Riccardo, **3:**50, 51
Pick-Up Company, **3:**201, **5:**573
Picnic, **4:**380
Picnic at Tintagel, **1:**153, 395, **2:**314, **4:**608
Picnic Polka, **2:**289
Pictorial History of Turkish Dancing, A (And), **4:**414
picture-frame stage design, **6:**161
Picture of Goya, **1:**117
Pictures, **2:**295
Pictures and Doubles, **4:**37
Pictures at an Exhibition, **4:**226, **5:**406
Pictures from a Cry, **3:**421
Pictures from the Past, **4:**444
pidihtós. See malevizióitkos
Pie, Bertrand, **1:**292
Piece by Pina Bausch, A, **1:**388
Pièce Chorégraphique, **2:**471
Piece Period, **6:**108–109
pièces à machines, **3:**66
Pièces en Concert, **6:***251*
Pièces Pittoresques (Chabrier), **2:**254
Piedigrotta, **1:**134
Pied Piper, The, **2:**197, **4:**608, **5:**245, 358

Pied Piper of Hamelin, The, **3:**123
Piège de Lumière, **3:**226, 361
Piège de Méduse, Le (Satie), **2:**285
Pie, Pie, Blackbird (film), **4:**629
Pierce, Billy, **1:**520
Pierce, Ken, **5:**202
Pierce, Tina, **3:**175
Pierné, Gabriel, **1:**93, **4:**635, **6:**432
Pierpont, Claudia Roth, *as contributor*, **3:**136, **4:**226–227, **5:**405–406, 407, 616, **6:**144, 397
Pierpont, Margaret, *as contributor*, **1:**468–472
Pierre, Dorathi Bock, **4:**170
Pierre de Médicis (opera), **2:**587
Pierre de Provence et la Belle Maguelonne, **1:**124
Pierre et Catherine (Adam), **1:**9
Pierrot de la Lune, **2:**151
Pierrot Forlorn, **2:**378
Pierrot in the Dead City, **5:**586
Pierrot in the Park, **2:**264
Pierrot Lunaire, **2:**1, **3:**368, 609, 610, 651, 668, **4:**602, **5:**301, *303*, 432, **6:**145–146
Pierrot Macabre, **1:**410
Pierrot show, **2:**191
Pierson, Louise, **6:**71
Pierstorff, Erik, **4:**682
Pierus, Marcus Pileius, **5:**74
Pietas, **4:**156
Piétragalla, Marie-Claude, **5:**98
Pietro Micca, **4:**258
Pietrovsky, Adrien, **5:**392
Pigafetta, Antonio, **5:**167
Pigeon Dance, **4:**408, 409, 410, 415
Pignard, Jean, **1:**103
Pihl, Toni, **2:**536
pihuang, **1:**164
Piissimi, Vittoria, **2:**190
Pike, Kenneth, **4:**366
Pilates Method, **4:**20
Pilcer, Harry, **4:**524
Piletta, Georges, **1:**461, 462, **5:**97
Pilgrim's Progress (musical version), **4:**380
Pilgrim's Progress, The (Howard), **2:**3
Pilipenko, Lidija, **6:**434
Pillai, Chandashekhar, **1:**94
Pillai, Chokkalingam, **3:**508, **6:**312
Pillai, Conjeervaram Elappa, **4:**62
Pillai, Elappa, **2:**104
Pillai, Govind Rai, **1:**94
Pillai, Kundappa, **5:**580
Pillai, Maruthappa, **2:**102
Pillai, Meenakshi Sundaram, **3:**199, **5:**309, 522
Pillai, Muthukumaran, **5:**522
Pillai, Subbaraya, **6:**312
Pillai, Swamimalai Raharatnam, **5:**524
Pillai, Tanjore Kitappa, **4:**62
Pillar of Fire, **5:**193, **6:**198, *199*, 200, 202, 203
  Australian Ballet staging, **1:**233
  Chase performance, **2:**112
  historical costuming, **2:**244
  Kaye performance, **3:**663, **4:***109*, **6:**198, *199*
  Laing performance, **1:**67–68, **4:***109*, 110, **6:***199*
  Marks performance, **4:**271
  original cast, **6:***199*
  Wilson (Sallie) performance, **6:**402
Pillet, Léon, **1:**446, **2:**204
Pillette, El, **1:**49
Pilling, Julian Olivier, *as contributor*, **5:**694–696

Pillows and Comforter, **2:**110
Pilloy, Daniel, **2:**384
Pilobolus, **5:**194
Pilobolus Dance Theatre, **5:194–195**
  Blaska-Clarke duet, **1:**462
  Rudner performance, **5:**440
  television performances, **6:**139
  Untitled, **5:***24*
Pilot, **2:**355, **4:**218
Pilteri, Giovannina, **3:**261
Piltz, Marie, **3:**14, **4:**487, 643
Pilules du Diable, Les, **5:**159–160
Pimble, Toni, **1:**197
Pimenov, Aleksandr, **3:**136, 560
Pimenta, Emanuel Dimas de Melo, **2:**289
Pina Bausch Tanztheater Wuppertal. *See* Tanztheater Wuppertal
Pinchard, Léontine, **3:**316
Pindar, **2:**158–159, *159*, **4:**499, **6:**145
  dithyrambs, **2:**419
  hyporchematic odes, **3:**428
  kallinkos, **3:**645
pindin, **5:**67–68
Pineapple Poll, **1:**209, 459, **2:**57, 265, *266*, **3:**203, *268*, **5:**225
pinggan-pinggan, **2:**230
Pini, Enrico, **3:**414
Pink Floyd (rock group), **2:**499
Pink Floyd Ballet, **3:**75
Pink Lady, The (musical), **6:**270
Pinocchio, **2:**471, **4:**677
Pinos Nuevos, Los, **2:**274
pin peat ensemble, **2:**31
Pins and Needles (musical), **6:**276
Pintér, Sändor, **3:**422
Pinto, Clarice, **1:**537
Pinto, Francisco, **5:**500
Pintupi tribe, **1:***222*
Pinucci, Pietro, **1:**484, **5:**452
Piollet, Wilfride, **1:**462, **2:**293, **5:**97
Pion, Eugenia, **5:**195
Pion, Maurice, **1:**408, **5:**195, 216, 217, **6:**365
Piotrovsky, Adrien, **5:**393
pipe (musical instrument), **2:**332
Pipe-of-Peace Dance. *See* Calumet Dance
Piper, John, **1:**150, **2:**265, 266, **3:**609, **5:***411*
Piperno, Elsa, **6:**121
Pippin (film), **5:**358
Pippin (musical), **3:**54, **6:**284
Pippin Press, **4:**2
Piquet, Jean-François, **1:**3
piqué turns, **1:**336, **337–338**
Piraïkon Theatron (Piraeus Theater), **3:**300
Pirandello, Luigi, **1:**327, **2:**400
Pirate, The (film), **4:**2
Pirate's Isle, The, **1:**199, 200
Pirchan, Emil, **3:**631
Pirnitzer, Daisy, **1:**211, 212
Piron, Alexis, **5:**306
Pirosmani, **1:**38
pirouette à la seconde, **1:**337, 343
pirouette en dedans, **1:**336, 337, 338
pirouette en dehors, **1:**336, 337, 338
pirouette renversé, **1:**337
pirouettes, **1:336–337**, 342, 343, 344, 345
  in attitude, **1:**198
  can-can, **2:**53
  in *entrée grave*, **2:**519
  Renaissance dance, **5:**338
  See also ballet technique, turning movements

pirouette sur la pointe, **1:***336*, 347, 366
Pisador, Diego, **2:**51
Pisanella, La (d'Annunzio), **3:**20, **5:**438
Pisarev, Aleksei, **3:**308, **6:**129
Pisarev, Vadim, **2:***208*
Piscator, Erwin, **5:**548, **6:**378
Pischl, A. J., **6:**297
Piscopo, Tullio de, **1:**83
Pisis, Filippo de, **4:**421
Pisoni, Jospeh, **4:**390
Pisotón, **5:**275
Pistolees de las Seguidillas Boleras (Téllez), **1:**480
Piston, Walter, **2:**196
Pistoni, Mario, **3:**60, 552, 553, **5:195–196**, 395, 401, 527, 529
Pit and Bolster, **6:**175
Pitcher, William John Charles. *See* Wilhelm, C.
Pite, Crystal, **2:**41, 42
Pithey, Doug, *as photographer*, **2:**86, **6:**23
Pithoprakta, **4:**618
Pitjantjatjara (people), **1:**229
Pitoeff, Ludmilla and George, **1:**565*319*
Pitrot, Antoine-Bonaventure, **1:**236, **2:**366, 435, **3:**67, 365, **5:**196
Pitrot, Dominique, **5:**196
Pitt, Daryl, *as photographer*, **1:**166
Pittner, Rudolf, *as photographer*, **1:**240
Pitts, Bryan, **6:**265
Pittsburgh Ballet Theatre, **5:**60, **196–197**, 398, **6:**265, 292, 397
piva, **1:**351–352, **5:**506
Pivar, Amy, **6:***449*
pive, **3:**542, **4:**502
Pixérécourt, Guilbert de, **1:**202, **3:**68
Pizarre, **3:**258
Pizzaro (Pixérécourt), **1:**202, **3:**68
Pizarro, Inés, **1:**111
Pizzetti, Ildebrando, **3:**51
Pizzi, Pier Luigi, **3:***550*
Pjesme Ljubavi i Smrti, **5:**677
Plá, Mirta, **2:**279, *279*, 280
Place, **2:**292
Place de l'Opéra, Paris, **6:**159
Place in the Desert, A, **4:**469
Place Theatre, London (The Place), **1:**53, **3:**272, 274, 275, 276, **4:**216, 220
Placide, Alexandre, **1:**124, **2:**174, 442, 443, 467, **5:197–199**, **6:**233
  Francisqui partnership, **3:**86, **6:**232
Placide, Madame. *See* Douvillier, Suzanne
Plain and Fancy (musical), **4:**530, **6:**90
Plain of Prayer, **3:**219
Plains Daybreak, **3:**350
Plains Indians. *See* Great Plains *under* Native American dance
Plains Ojibwe (people), **4:**551
Plaisance, **3:**174, 203
Plaisirs, Les, **1:**287, 424
Plaisirs de l'Hiver, Les, **6:**75
Plaisirs de l'Île Enchantée, Les, **1:**288, 424, **4:**234, 447, **5:**536
Plaisirs Troublés, Les, **1:**287
Plamya Lyubvi, **5:**501
Plamya Parizha. See Flames of Paris, The
Planche, James Robinson, **2:**85, **5:**70
Planes, **1:**543

Planes/Configurations, **5:**25
Planet, **3:**54
Planetary Dance: A Prayer for Peace, **3:**336
Planetomania, **3:**508, 511
Planeton, Die, **4:**61
Planets, The, **3:**265, 351, **4:**109, 215, **5:**300, **6:**196, 197, 203, 312
Plan K (Brussels company), **1:**411
Plantation Dances, **2:**26
Plantation Revelry, **3:**575
Plasquinade, **2:**378
Plastic Complex + Dance + Merriment (Bala), **1:**130
Plastic Jungle, The, **5:**524
plastique
  as Bulgarian dance influence, **2:**11
  Russian twentieth-century, **5:**456, 476–479, 484, 485
Plateau (Brussels dance center), **1:**411–412, 414
Platée, **1:**400, 446, **4:**236, **5:**306, **6:**47
Platel, Alain, **1:**412
Platel, Elisabeth, **1:**405, **5:**7, 98
Platens, **1:**21
Plato, **1:**2, **2:**506, **3:**292, 293, **5:**41, 283, 598
  aesthetics, **1:**19–20
  moral condemnation of *kordax,* **4:**44
Platt (Platoff), Marc **1:**296, 297, **2:**184, **3:**25, **4:**335, **5:**290, **6:**278
Playboy of the Western World, The (Moriarty ballet), **3:**518, 520
Players Project, **5:**638
Playfair, Nigel, **5:**298
Playford, Henry, **1:**92, **2:**254, **5:**200
Playford, John, **1:**5, 91–92, **3:**34, 238, **4:**585, **5:**199–200, 285, 345, 520, 621, **6:**123
  on country dances, **2:**254, 255, *255,* 256, 591, **3:**238, 248, **4:**221, 410, 581
  dance collection, **2:**542, **3:**522, **4:**505, 510
  dance step descriptions, **4:**684
  first use of term "square dance," **2:**592
  on hornpipes, **3:**376, 777
  revival of publications, **5:**582
  on saraband, **5:**520
  See also Dancing Master, The
Playground, **4:**243
Playground Association of America, **3:**34, **6:**242
Playground Recreation Association of America, **6:**242
Playhouse, **4:**72
Playhouse Company, Durban, **5:**658–659
Playhouse Dance Company. *See* Nikolais Dance Theatre
Playing with Fire (Jugar con Fuego), **1:***113*
Pleasant, Richard, **4:**109
  American Ballet Theatre, **1:**64, 65, 66, **2:**112, 373
  Mordkin Ballet, **4:**460
Pleasuredome, **4:**117, 380
Pleasure Reconciled to Virtue (Jonson masque), **2:**591, **3:**361, **4:**107, 310
Pleasures of Counterpoint No. 2, **3:**385
Plebs and Zotto, **5:**200–201, **6:**93
Pleiades, Les (Blasis students), **3:**96
Pleitez, S., *as photographer,* **4:**665

plena, **5:**274
Pleshcheyev, Aleksandr, **1:**541, **3:**562, **5:**160, 482
Plessi, Fabrizio, **1:**412
Pletin, Constance, **5:**453, **6:**312
Pletnev, Vladimir N., *as contributor,* **1:**48, 247–248
pliaska (Russian dance term), **5:**442, 445
plié, **1:**8, 343, 344, **5:**201–202
  as Korean traditional dance position, **4:**48
Pliny the Younger, **5:**73
Pli Selon Pli, **1:**406
Plisetskaya, Maya, **1:**490, 491, **2:**448, **3:**195, **4:**360, **5:**97, 164, **202–207,** 459, 587, 588
  Anna Karenina choreography, **2:**565, **5:**462
  Ballet del Teatro Lírico Nacional, **5:**674
  Béjart ballets, **1:**292, 406
  Chinese tour, **2:**136
  Don Quixote performance, **2:**437, 438
  Dying Swan interpretation, **2:**471
  Fadeyechev dance partnership, **2:**564
  Fountain of Bakhchisarai performance, **3:**56–57, *328*
  Gerdt (Elisaveta) as teacher, **3:**138
  grand jeté, **1:***341*
  Grigorovich ballets, **1:**493
  Lady with a Lapdog staging, **1:**493, **5:**462, 588
  Laurencia performance, **4:**129, *129*
  Legend of Love, **4:**144
  Leventhal scenic design, **4:**154
  Little Humpbacked Horse film, **4:**212
  personal creative theme, **1:**493
  Raymonda performance, **5:***463*
  Rome Opera Ballet, **5:**401
  Seagull staging, **5:**462, 588
  Shchedrin marriage, **5:**587
  Shurale performance, **5:**595, **6:***410*
  Stone Flower performance, **5:**699
  Swan Lake role, **6:***30,* 31
  Zakharov as influence, **6:**442
Plisetsky, Azari, **1:**49, 290, 111
  Alonso (Alicia) dance partnership, **2:**278, *278*
Plotinus, **1:**21, **2:**116
Plough Dance, **2:**138
Plough Monday, **3:**242
Plovdiv, Bulgaria, **2:**11
Plovdiv Opera, **2:**12
Plucos, Karij, **4:**127
Plum Productions Inc., **1:**419
Plunkett, Adeline, **1:**500, **2:**204, **4:**341, **5:**148
Pluque, Édouard, **5:**94
Pluque, Ernest, **2:**363
Plus Loin que la Nuit e le Jour, **2:**480
Plutarch, **1:**2, 20, **2:**163, 270, **4:**106, **5:**557, **6:**144
Pluto, **3:**373
Plutus (Aristophanes), **3:**290
Plzáková, Markéta, **2:**309
PNB. *See* Pacific Northwest Ballet
PNB Offstage, **5:**51
Pocahantas, **2:**160, **3:**349
  Carter (Elliott) score, **4:**518
  Christensen (Lew) choreography, **1:**279, 498, **3:**349, **6:**247
  Kirstein libretto, **4:**28
Pocamania, **3:**575

pochette, **3:**80, **4:***509*
Pochini, Carolina, **1:**238, 499, 500, **5:**409
Podgoretskaya, Nina, **1:**489, **3:**193, **6:**106
Podhale, **5:**75
Poe, Edgar Allan, **1:**300, **4:**60
Poelvoorde, Rita, **1:**292, **5:**422
Poem, **5:**637
Poem-Ballet, **2:**97
Poème, **2:**471, 472, **3:**597
Poème de l'Exstase, **3:**45, **5:**405, **6:***10*
Poème Lyrique, **3:**88
Poems of 1917, **3:**212
Poems of Love and the Seasons, **5:***131*
Poesio, Giannadrea, **3:**557
Poète et Sa Muse, La, **2:**183
Poetic Meditations (Lamartine), **3:**20
Poetics (Aristotle), **1:**20, 22, **2:**428, **3:**290
poetry
  ancient Greece, **3:**294, **4:**499
  Middle East, **4:**405, 408
  Oceanic chanted/sung, **4:**495, 496–497
  Yemeni *bālah* genre, **6:**417
Poet's Dream, The, **3:***530,* **4:**59
Poet's Vaudeville, **6:**282, 362–363
Pogany, Willy, **3:**21
Pohan, Václav, **6:**432
Pohnpei dance, **4:**400–401
Pohren, D. E., **1:**117
Point and Line to Plane (Kandinsky), **1:**132
Pointe by Pointe (videotape), **6:**129
pointe work, **1:**343, **5:**207–209
  Balanchine style, **1:**264–265
  Bournonville style, **1:**513
  Cecchetti on, **1:**8–9, 347
  chaîné turns, **1:**337
  costume evolution, **2:**241
  Diaghilev ballet repertory absence of, **1:**348
  Flore et Zéphire among first to use, **2:**415
  fouetté turns, **1:**338
  of Gosselin (Geneviève), **3:**209
  of Grahn, **3:**222, *222,* 224
  of Grisi, **3:**316, **4:**341
  history, **1:**130, 341, 345, 347, **3:**69
  Lifar policies, **4:**184
  Mazilier choreography, **4:**341
  Paris Opera Ballet, **5:**93
  in Petipa's (Marius) works, **5:**152, 207
  piqué turns, **1:**337–338
  pirouette, **1:**336, *336,* 347
  as Romantic ballet characteristic, **2:**239, **3:**69, 130, 547, *548,* **6:**57, 58
  shoe evolution, **1:**347, 513, **3:**46–47
  Sylphide, La, **3:**47, 547, *548,* **6:**57, 58, 59
  Taglioni family, **3:***548,* **6:**58, 71–72, 74
  weightlessness aesthetic, **1:**341
Point of Departure (television series), **6:**132–133
Point of the Wind, The, **6:**145
Pointois, Noelle, **6:**64
Point Park College, Pittsburgh, **5:**196, **6:**292
Points in Space, **2:**294, 296, 608, **4:**37

Poireau, Auguste, **5:**453, **6:**311
Poirier, Claude, **3:**229
Poirier, Hélie, **6:**38
Poker Game, **5:**300
Pokot dance, **209–210**
Pokryshkina, Galina, **5:***102*
Polajenko, Nicholas, **3:**342
Poland, **5:**210–221
  dance research and publication, **4:**162, **5:**211, **220–221**
  theatrical dance, **2:**299, **3:**192, **4:**435, **5:**215–220**
  mime, **6:**175
  See also Polish Ballet, Warsaw Ballet
  traditional and social dance, **5:**210–215,** *218,* 223
  Hasidic dance, **3:**528
  krakowiak, **4:**57
  mazurka, **4:**343
Polaris, **2:**526, **6:**110, 111
Polarity, **2:**296
polca-lundú, **1:**528
Polden, Rodney, *as photographer,* **2:**42
Pole Dance, **1:**387
pole dancing. *See* Maypole dancing
polen, **2:**232
Poli, Nives, **3:**51
Poliakov, Valery, **4:**446
Poliakova, Elena, **5:**556
Polichinel Vampire, **1:**455
Polik, Stane, **6:**438
Poliński, Aleksander, **5:**220
Polish Academy of Sciences, Warsaw, **5:**211, 220
Polish Ballet (Nijinska), **4:**435, **5:**218
Polish Ballet (Parnell), **5:**101
Polish Dance Company, **3:**317, **5:**75
Polish Dance Theater, **2:**447, **5:**219, *219,* 220
Polish Devils, **5:**75
Polish Theater Museum, **4:**162
political cartoons, **2:**70, 72
Political Pas de Quatre, The, **2:**70
political revue, **4:**59
politicized dance, **4:**365, 378
Politics (Aristotle), **1:**20
Politrevue, **3:**151
Poliziano, Angelo, **5:**113
Poljakova, Jelena, **4:**420, 437, **6:**432, 438
polka, **5:**221–223
  Argentina, **1:**108
  Brazil, **1:**528, 529, 530
  Caribbean region, **2:**63
  caricatures, **2:**70
  Castle style, **2:**78, **6:**270
  country-western, **2:**259
  Croatia, **6:**428–429
  Czech and Slovak Republics, **2:**301, 304–305
  Denmark, **2:**381
  Dodworth's dislike of, **5:**627
  Finland, **2:**630
  France, **3:**69
  Germany, **3:**142
  Israeli adaptation, **3:**528
  Norway, **4:**670–671
  Poland, **5:**213
  Protestant sectarian condemnation, **2:**167
  quadrille, **5:**625
  as social dance, **5:**624, 627, 686
  social dance popularity, **4:**514
  Strauss (Johann the younger) classics, **6:**2
Polka, **3:**315, *315,* **5:**137
polkabal, **5:**169
Polka Comique, La, **1:**200
Polka Militaire, **1:**509, 511

Polka with a Little Ball, **3:**15
Poll, Heinz, **5:**24–25, **6:**266
Pollins, Harvey, **1:**421
Pollock, Benjamin, **5:***71*
Pollock, Jackson, **1:**138, **2:**287, 375–376
Pollux, **2:**116, **5:**557
polo, **1:**479
polonaise *(polonaise),* **2:**382, **4:**510, **5:***223,* 586, 626
    Finland, **2:**630
    Israeli kibbutzim adaptation, **2:**528
    Poland, **5:**210, *211,* 214, 223
Polonaise in A Major (Chopin), **6:**60, 61, 62
polonez. See polonaise
Polonia, **1:**453
Polovtsian Dances (Prince Igor)
    Bartik choreography, **4:**382
    Beriozoff staging of Fokine's choreography, **4:**380
    Bolm performance, **1:**482, 483, *483,* **3:**16
    Clustine choreography, **2:**181
    Fedorova performance, **2:**582
    Fokine production, **1:***321,* 482, 483, *483,* **2:**57, 407, 582, **3:**16, 19, 24, *26,* **4:**283, **5:**391, 650
    Fokine's conception versus Ivanov's, **3:**562, 568
    Goleizovsky choreography, **1:***485,* **3:**195
    Grigoriev and Tchernicheva revival, **3:**308
    Harangozó re-creation, **3:**341, 342, 415, **6:**66
    Ivanov original production, **3:**561–562, **4:**282, 515
    Kirov Ballet revival, **3:***563*
    Lepeshinskaya film performance, **4:**149
    Moiseyev (Igor) production, **4:**445
    Orientalism, **2:**407
    Poole reconstruction of Fokine choreography, **2:**57
    Roerich design, **4:**643, **5:**372
    Romanov performance, **5:**391
    Woizikowski performance, **6:**404
pols, **2:**382, **4:**669, 671
polska, **2:**630
"Polska-tänze in Finnland, Die" (Ala-Konni), **2:**631, 634
Poltroon, The, **4:**243
Polubentsev, Aleksandr, **5:**460, 469, 475
Polunine, Elizabeth, **1:***310*
Polyakov, Evgeny (Eugène), **3:**552, **5:**98
Polyandrion, **2:**196
Polyanka, **4:**444
Polyeidus (mythic), **2:**271
Polymorphia, **3:**418
Polynesia, **4:**495–496, **5:**223–225
    Bellona, **1:**415–416
    dance traditions, **5:**19–20
    Fiji, **2:**593
    Rapanui, **5:**310
    Samoa, **2:**593, **4:**369, 628, **5:**225, 509–510
    Tahiti, **6:**77–79
    Tonga, **6:**177–178
Polzunets, **6:**225
Pomaks (people), **3:**296
Pomare, Eleo, **1:**212, 214, **2:**358, **6:**259
Pomarès, Jean, **3:**79
Pomes Penyeach, **3:**520
Pomiès, George, **3:**75–76

Pomme d'Or, La, **5:**296
Pomo (people), **2:**602
Pomo d'Oro, Il (Cesti), **1:**236, **5:**34, 536
Pomona, **1:**146, **2:**424, **4:**113, 517, 635
Pomone, **1:**396, **4:**509, **5:**86
Pompadour, Madame de, **1:**288, **2:**365, 366
Pomponius, Lucius, **5:**375
Pona, Vladimir, **5:**474
Ponchielli, Amilcare, **2:**84
Pondick, Rona, **5:**440
Pongor, Ildikó, **3:**418
pongsan, **2:**222–223, *222,* **4:**299, *299*
Pongsan t'al'ch'um, **4:**47, 50–51, *51, 299*
Pongsan t'al'ch'um mubo (Kim), **4:**54
Poniatowski, Józef, **2:**587
Ponnelle, Jean-Pierre, **3:**359, **5:**43
Ponomarenko, Sergei, **3:**432
Ponomarev, Vladimir, **2:**596–597
    Red Poppy, The, **4:**225
    students, **2:**96, 585, **3:**327, **4:**55, 131, 283, **5:**282, 571, **6:**310, 410, 420, 441
Ponomaryov, Evgeny, **6:**30
Ponorogo, Java, **2:**231
Pons, Aurora, **5:**673, *674*
Ponsan Mask Dance-Drama Dance Notation (Kim), **4:**13
Pontois, Noëlla, **1:**195, **2:**114, 511, **5:***96,* 97, *152,* 396
Pontozó, **5:**287
Pontremoli, Alessandro, **3:**555, 557
Pony (dance), **1:**78, **5:**632, **6:**257
Pony Ballet, **6:**268
Poole, David, **2:**56–57, 58, *266,* **5:***56,* 57, **225–226,** 294, 420
    CAPAB directorship, **5:**651, 652, *652*
Poole, Dennis, **2:**127
Poole, Robert, **5:***304*
Poole Brothers, **6:**316
Poons, Karel, **1:**289, 290, **4:**598, **5:**530
Poons, Larry, **6:**362
Poor Eddie, **2:**574–575
Poor Little Rich Girl (film), **6:**142
Popa, Magdalena, **1:**349, **5:**387
Popard, Irène, **3:**76
pop art, **1:**139, **3:**615, **4:**21
Pop Beat, **4:**602
Pope Joan, **2:**11
Popescu, Aliss, **5:**387
Popescu, Stere, **5:**387
Popiel, Jan, **5:**216
Popko, Nikolai, **1:**490, 491, **3:**197, **5:**203, 459
Pop Locking, **6:**263
Popol Vuh (Maya chronicle), **3:**319
Popova, Nina, **3:**389, **6:**264
Poppet, The, **3:**360
Poppie Nongena (musical), **6:**22
popping, **1:**538
Popping and Locking, **5:**633
Poppin' the Hips, **6:**263
Poppy, **1:***213,* 214, **4:**479, **6:**56
popular dance
    folk dance versus, **3:**32
    See also social dance; *specific dances*
popular music. *See specific types*
Poquelin, Jean-Baptiste. *See* Molière

Pór, Anna, **3:**424
Porcelain Dialogues, **4:**230
Porcher, Le, **1:**327, **5:**353
Porcher, Nananne, **1:**30, **5:**397
Porcile, Mario, **3:**550
Porée, Père, **1:**284
Porgy and Bess (Gershwin), **2:**5, *5*
    Lavrovsky (Mikhail) production, **3:**135, **4:**133
Por la danza (Spanish magazine), **5:**676
Poro masking society, **4:**290
Portal, Michel, **2:**575
port de bras, **1:**332, 345, 349, **5:226–227**
    Fokine expansion, **5:**227, **6:**62
    Kshessinska (Matilda) emphasis on, **4:**68
    Nijinsky *Spectre de la Rose* performance, **3:**18
Port de Marseille, Le, **3:**188
Porte-bonheur, Le, **5:**246
Portefeuille englischer Taenze (Lanz), **2:**256
Porter, Cole, **1:**192, 193, 307, 327, **2:**187, 616, **3:**280, 371, **4:**334, **6:**271, 277, 281
Porter, Marguerite, **4:**456, **5:**419
Porter, Thomas, **3:**254
Porte-Saint-Martin, Paris, **3:**358
Porthan, H. G., **2:**629
Portillo, Alberto, **4:**222
Portinari, Candido, **5:**571
Portinari, Maribel, **1:**537
Portland, Washington, **2:**581
Porto, Luigi da, **5:**392
Portrait de Don Quichotte, Le, **1:**306, **2:**440
Portrait du Grand Monarque, Le, **1:**284, **2:**465
Portrait of a Lady with the C.B.E., **1:**212
Portrait of Billie, **2:**17, 367
Portrait of Chess Players (Duchamp), **1:**137
Portrait of Dorian Grey, The, **6:**435
Portrait of Nijinsky (Kline), **1:***138,* 139
Portraits, **3:**380
Portraits in Reflection, **2:**119
portraiture. *See* artists and dance; caricature and comic art; photography
Portugal, **5:227–236**
    as Brazilian dance influence, **1:**525, 527, 528, 532
    dancing master, **2:**337
    libraries and museums, **4:**162
    mouriscas as social dances, **4:**462
    theatrical dance, **5:230–236**
    traditional dance, **5:227–230**
Porzia, **2:**55
Posada, José Guadalupe, **4:**392
posidelki dance, **5:**444
positions des bras. See ballet technique, arm positions
positions des pieds. See ballet technique, feet positions
Positivism, **4:**258
Posniakov, Nikolai, **5:**476, 477, 478, 485
Posokhov, Yuri, **1:**493
Pospekhin, Lev, **1:**490, 491, **3:**197, **5:**203, 459
Possessed, The, **4:**121
possession trance. *See* trance dance
Post-Chaise Driver, The, **5:**452
postcolonial discourse analysis, **4:**375, 378

Postillon de Longjumeau, Le (opera), **1:**200
postmodern dance
    aesthetics, **1:**25, 246, **3:**131, **6:**252
    African-American dancers, **6:**259
    Australia, **1:**215–216, *217*
    as avant-garde, **1:**243, 246
    Brown, Trisha, **1:**543–545
    Cage and Cunningham collaboration, **4:**519
    Canada, **2:**40–41
    Chile, **2:**125
    Chuma, Yoshiko, **2:**170–171
    contemporary criticism, **6:**299
    Cunningham link, **2:**290–291
    as Feld influence, **2:**585
    film and videotape incorporation, **2:**608, 609
    France, **3:**77–78
    Great Britain, **3:**272, 273
    Hawkins's masks, **4:**302, *303*
    Japan, **3:**591
    Judson Dance Theater influence, **3:**635, **4:**519
    mime, **4:**426
    Norway, **4:**679
    Rainer, Yvonne, **5:**292–293
    scenic design, **5:**548–550
    Sweden, **1:**145
    United States, **6:**251
poststructural thought, **6:**25
poststudio movement, **1:**140
Pösztenyi, Emöke, **3:**155
Potapova, Elena Mikhailovna, **5:**236
Poté, Aurilla Colcord, **5:**490
potlatch, **4:**550, 568, 572, 573, *573*
Potogija, Nedžad, **6:**436
Potsdam, **6:**378
Potteiger, Jack, **4:**209
Potter, Lauren, **4:***218*
Potter, Michelle, **1:**218, **6:**95
    as contributor, **1:**38, 230–235, 498–499, **2:**183–184, **3:**203–204, 622–623, **4:**25–26, 275–276, **5:**410–411, 563–564, **6:**56–57, 95, 378–379
Potter, Sally, **3:**272
Potts, Nadia, **4:**542, *544*
Potts, Nellie, **2:**313
Pougny, Jean, **5:**278
poulaine (shoe), **5:**336
Poulenc, Francis, **2:**397, **4:**243, **5:236–238,** **6:**111
    Ballets Suédois commissions, **1:**327, **3:**72, 393
    Biches score, **1:**316, 325, 449–450, **2:**408
    Diaghilev commissions, **2:**406, **4:**515
    as Les Six member, **4:**516
Poulsen, Johannes, **5:**238
Poulsen, Ulla, **5:238,** 428, 429
Pound, Ezra, **5:**558
Pour Deux Orchestres à Cordes et Deux Danseurs, **4:**134
Pourfarrokh, Ali, **2:**41
Poussin, Nicolas, **5:**517
Pouvoir de l'Amour, Le, **2:**82
Pouyanne, Alberto, **6:**301
Powell, Dick, **1:**432, **2:***614*
Powell, Eleanor, **1:**193, 520, **2:**615, **5:238–239,** **6:**101
Powell, Jane, **1:**194
Powell, Michael, **5:**331, **6:**119
Powell, Ray, **1:**230, 233, **2:**184, **5:**564
Powell, Robert, **3:**219, **4:**216, **6:**146
Powers, William K., *as contributor,* **4:**560–562, **5:**239–240

power tapping, **6:**103
powwow, **4:**555, 561, **5:239–240**
Pozhitskaya, Bronislava, **4:**459
Poznań Opera Ballet, **2:**447, **3:**316, 523, **5:**75
Prabuwijaya, prince of Surakarta, **3:**498
practice clothes, **5:240–243**
  ballet schools, **6:**292
  as costume, **2:**193, 242, *244,* 245, 247, 248, 292, **393, 3:**58, *58,* **4:**226, **6:**62
  Danilova restaging of *Les Sylphides,* **6:**62
  Jaques-Dalcroze student productions, **3:**596
  as mainstream fashion, **2:**251
Practise for Dauncing (Ramsey), **5:**666
Prado, Pérez, **2:**276
Praetorius, Michael, **1:**523, **5:**109, 111, **244, 6:**125
  on canary, **2:**50–51
  on *entrée,* **2:**517
  on *gavotte,* **3:**123
  Lithuanian folk dance engravings, **4:**204
  on *menuet,* **4:**431
  saraband music, **5:**520
  terpsichore, **4:**507
Prague Chamber Ballet, **2:**309, 310, **5:**617, *617, 618*
Prague City Theaters, **5:**617
Prague Dance Conservatory, **2:**310
Prague National Theater Ballet, **2:**306, 309, 310, **5:245**
  Berger, Augustin, **1:**428, 429
  first *Swan Lake* production outside Russia, **4:**632
  Kůra, Miroslav, **4:**77
  Machov, Saša, **4:**238, 239
  Němeček, Jiří, **4:**583–584
  Ogoun, Luboš, **5:**23
Prague-Nusle, **4:**584
praiá, **1:**530
Prairie, **4:**228
Praise House, **6:**449, *449*
Praise Songs, **3:**575
prajuritan (jaran kepang), **1:**174
praleng dances, **1:**178
Pram, Christen, **3:**105
Prāmoj, Mom Rātchawong Kukrit, **4:**9–10
Prampolini, Enrico, **4:**421, **5:**544
prāṇa (life force), **1:**184
Prana, **2:**104
Prantl, Sebastian, **1:**240
Prasad, Sundar Pundit, **1:**94
Pratesi, Ferdinando, **1:**540, **4:**258, 263, **5:**245
Pratesi, Giovanni, **2:**84, **3:**51, 261, **4:**263, **5:245–246**
Pratesi family, **5:**404
Pratinas, **2:**159, **5:**556
Prato, Giovanni Andrea da, **5:**114
Pratsika, Koula, **3:**301
Pratt, John, **5:**60
pravo horo dance, **2:**100, 101
Praying Mantis Dreaming, **1:**216
Pré aux Clercs, Le (Hérold opera), **3:**360
Prebil, Zarko, **1:**111, **5:**401
Précieuses Ridicules, Les, **4:**447
Precious Lotus Lantern, The, **5:**471
Precious Stones, The, **4:**127
precision dancing, **4:**522, **5:246–247,** 289–290, **6:**242, 257
  clogging, **2:**179, 180–181
  June Taylor Dancers, **6:***138,* 320

Rockettes, **4:**24, **5:**247, 289–290, *289,* **6:**242, 268, 285
  tap, **6:**99, 101
  Tiller Girls, **6:**268, 273, *273*
Pre-Classic Dance Forms (Horst), **3:**385
Preda, Tea, *as contributor,* **2:**343–344, **4:**384–390, **5:**263–264, 384–390
Predators, **4:**667
Prefectural Troupe of Macenta, **5:**516
Preger-Simon, Marianne, **2:***286,* **6:**26
prehistoric cave drawing, **2:***541*
Preisser, Suse, **1:**500
Prejudice Conquered, **5:**451
Prejudice for Ballet, A (Coton), **3:**285
Preljocaj, Angelin, **1:**391, 418, **2:**611, **4:**220, **5:**399, **6:**57
Prélonge, Michèle, **3:**77
Prelude (Fagan choreography), **2:**567
Prélude (Leeder ballet), **1:**519
Prelude (Pederneiras ballet), **1:**536
Prélude à l'Après-midi d'un Faune (Debussy), **1:**27, 28, 98, 99, **2:**360, 361, **4:**516, 641, 642, **5:**362
Prelude in A Major (Chopin), **6:**60, 61
Preludes, **4:**667
Préludes, Les, **3:**20, **5:**124
Preludes and Songs, **2:**1
Préludes d'Eginhard, **4:**452
Prelude to Swing, **2:**581, *581*
Preludios, **2:**277
prémbon, **3:**488, **4:**298
Premice, Josephine, **5:**255
Première Classique, **3:**429
Premiere Dance Theatre, Toronto, **6:**164
Premier Navigateur, Le, **2:**413, **5:**90
Preobrajenska, Olga, **1:**110, 305, **2:**82, 207, 597, **5:**94, **247–248,** 279, 320, 676
  Cecchetti method, **2:**84
  Chopiniana performance, **5:**247, 248, **6:**60
  Don Quixote performance, **2:**436
  Finnish tour, **2:**632
  Fokine roles, **3:**15
  as Gerdt (Elisaveta) influence, **3:**137
  improvisational skill, **3:**444
  as Johansson student, **3:**618
  Legat (Nikolai) dance partnership, **4:**142
  Maryinsky Ballet, **4:**282, **5:**456
  Paris dance studio, **3:**82
  students, **1:**308, 310, 367, 498, 519, **2:**272, 341, 350, 396, 466, **3:**264, 317, 350, 354, 391, **4:**336, 420, 435, 529, 667, **5:**312, 604, 606, **6:**119, 182, 309, 326, 352, 357, 396, 424
  Swan Lake performance, **6:**32
  Sylvia performance, **6:**64
Preobrajensky, Vladimir, **1:**491, **5:**699
Pre-Romantic Ballet, The (Winter), **3:**283
Présages, Les, **1:**150, 310, 316, **3:**617, **4:***319,* **5:**350, **6:**404
  as Massine's first symphonic ballet, **4:**322
  Tchaikovsky's Fifth Symphony, **4:**517
  Zorina role, **6:**449

Presbyterianism, **2:**167
Présence, **3:**350
presja me tagana, **1:**34
Presley, Elvis, **2:**618
Presnyakov, Valentin, **1:**121
Press, The, **6:**397
Pressburger, Emeric, **5:**331
Presse, La (Parisian newspaper), **3:**122, 314
Pressel, Esther, **6:**187
Presser, Gábor, **3:**418
Pressman, Louis P., **2:**328
Prestigiatore, Il, **3:**97
Preston-Dunlop, Valerie, **4:**94, 96, 101, 103–104
  as contributor, **4:**89–95
Pretnar, Breda, **6:**439
Pretoria Ballet Club, **5:**52, 650
Pretoria Technikon Dance Department, **5:**659
Pretty Prentice, The, **3:**129
Pretty Ugly Dancecompany, Frankfurt, **3:**157
Preuss, Brigitte, **3:**155
Previl, Zoltan, **2:**470
Previn, André, **1:**419, **2:**616, **4:**3
Previous Night, The, **4:**220
Prévost, Françoise, **1:**355, **3:**329, **5:**41, 87, **248–250,** 503, 504
  Camargo studies with, **2:**28, 29
  Caractères de la Danse, Les, **2:**59, **4:**130
  dance classes, **3:**81, **5:**88, 105
  as Louis IV's dancing master, **3:**81
  mime, **4:**173
Prévost, Henri, **1:**3
Pribylov, German, **5:**465, 475
Price, Amalie, **1:**509
Price, Curtis A., *as contributor,* **5:**280–282
Price, Ellen, **1:**399, *509,* **2:**173, **4:**6, **5:***250,* 426, 427, 553
Price, James, **2:**384
Price, Janey, **4:**96
Price, Juliette, **1:**509, 510, **3:**39, **4:**6, **5:**250–251, *250,* 553
  Konservatoriet performance, **4:**43, **5:**425
Price, Julius, **1:**239, 509, **5:**278
Price, Roland, **5:**421
Price, Sophie, **1:**509
Price, Waldemar, **5:**251
Price de Plane, Ellen. *See* Price, Ellen
Price family, **1:**507, 509, **2:**384, **5:250–251**
Priede, Anna, **4:**127–128
Priest, Helen, **1:**421, **4:**96
Priest, Josiah, **2:**337, **3:**254, **4:**433, **5:**251–252, 280, 281, 489
Prikhunova, Anna, **5:**140
Prim, Fernanda, *as contributor,* **5:**227–230
Prima Ballerina, La, **1:**300, **6:**75
Primal Energy, **2:**104
Primavera (van Wyk), **2:**57
Primedia, **6:**132, 133
Prime Movers (Mazo), **6:**113
primitive dance, **5:252–253**
  folk dance versus, **3:**30, 31, 32
Primitive Mysteries, **3:**212, 215, 384, **4:**518, **5:253–254,** 559, **6:**245
Primitive Suite, **1:**211
primitivism, **4:**644, 647
Primo viaggio interno al mondo (Pigafetta), **5:**167
Primrose, George, **6:**317

Primus, Pearl, **1:**55, 79, **2:**22, 313, **4:**520, **5:254–257**
  African-American music, **4:**520, **6:**259
  dance ethnology, **4:**373
  Harkness Foundation support, **3:**342
  as McKayle influence, **4:**345
  musical theater, **6:**280
  students, **2:**566
Prina, Anna Maria, **5:**527, 529
Prince (musician formerly known as), **2:**359, **3:**617, **4:**519
Prince, Harold, **1:**419, **6:**287–288
Prince, Robert, **4:**519
Prince and Pauper, **2:**343
Prince Argyle, **3:**414
Prince du Désert, Le, **5:**604
Prince Igor (Borodin). *See Polovtsian Dances*
Prince of the Pagodas, The, **1:**374, 390, **2:**266
  Beriosova performance, **1:**429
  Blair performance, **1:**459
  Britten score, **1:**374, 390, **2:**266, **4:**244, 245, 517
  Bussell performance, **5:**419
  Georgiadis designs, **3:**136
  MacMillan production, **4:**244–245, **5:**419
Prince Oleg's Reign, **5:**451–452
Princess Audrey (singer), **4:**487
Princess Aurora, **3:**654, **5:**612, *612*
Princess Cygne, La, **4:**635, **5:**439
Princesse de Carisme, La, **5:**504
Princesse d'Élide, La, **1:**464, **4:**234, 447
Princesse de Navarre, La, **5:**306, 307
Princess's Magic Mirror, The, **6:**265
Princess's Passpied, **2:**527
Princess Tam-Tam (film), **1:**252
Princess Theater, New York City, **6:**271, 276, 281
Princess Turandot, **3:**152, 317
Princess Wencheng, **2:**145
Princess Who Never Laughed, The, **3:**421
Princess Zondilda and Her Entourage, The, **2:**286
Princeton Book Company, **6:**298
Princeton University, **4:**167
Principal Dancers of the Russian State Ballet, **2:**342
Principes et notions élémentaires sur l'art de la danse (Gourdoux-Daux), **6:**126
Principles of Dance and Movement Notation (Laban), **4:**99
Pringsheim, Heinz, **6:**392
Prinses op de Erwt, De, **5:**530
Prinster, Katti, **2:**505
Printemps, Yvonne, **4:**523
Print-Out, **4:**21
prints and drawings, **5:257–263**
  commedia dell'arte illustrations, **2:**27, *189,* 190, 191
  dance caricatures, **2:**68–69, *69,* 70, *70,* 71, *71,* 85
  Dances of Death, **2:**331–332, *332*
  technical manuals, **6:**124
  See also artists and dance; *specific artists*
Prinz, John, **2:**333, **4:**612, *619,* **5:***107, 362*
Prinzregenten Theater, Munich, **1:**391
Priora, Olimpia, **4:**341, 342
prisiadka, **5:**696, **6:**220
Prism, **4:**650
Prismatic Variations, **4:**624
Prisoner, The, **6:**362

Prisoner of the Caucasus, The,
  1:485, **2:**416, 579, 585, **5:***472*
  Asafiev score, **1:**144, **4:**517
  Didelot production, **4:**278, 279,
    280, **5:***453–454*
  Gabovich performance, **3:**99
  Glushkovsky production, **3:**192
  Istomina performance, **3:**540,
    4:*279*
  Lavrovsky (Leonid)
    choreography, **4:**131
  Pushkin poem as basis,
    5:*453–454*
  Semenova performance, **5:**567
  Skibine choreography, **3:**226,
    5:605
  Zakharov production, **6:**442
Prisoners, The, **5:**564
Prisonniers de Guerre, **4:**339
Pritchard, Jane, *as contributor,*
  2:507–515, **3:**427–428
Private Domain, **6:**112
Private Life of Sherlock Holmes, The
  (film), **6:**183
Private Opera, Moscow, **1:**487
Private Relations, **2:**575
Privilege (film), **5:**293
Prix, ou L'Offrande de Terpsichore,
  L', **2:**389
Prix de la Danse, Le, **3:**188
Prize Fight Studies, **6:**87
Prmitive Mysteries, **3:**212
Próba, **3:**418, **4:**285
Problemy russkogo baleta
  (Volynsky), **6:**352
Proca Ciortea, Vera, **5:263–264,**
    385, 388
  as contributor, **5:**379–384
  ethnochoreography, **5:**390–391
  Romanotation system, **4:**691–692
Procanotation (Romanotation),
  4:691–692
Process, The, **4:**602
processional
  as ancient Greek choral genre,
    2:158, **3:**287, **4:**499
  Balinese ceremonial dance,
    3:477–478, *478*
  in Christian tradition, **2:**164, 168
  Ghanian Fancy Dress, **4:**293
  Greek linking dances,
    3:297–298, 302
  Japanese Taki Tenmangu shrine
    festival, **3:**588
  moresca form, **4:**461
  Morris, **4:**473–474
  Spain, **5:**519–520, 667–668
  Sri Lankan Kandy Perahera,
    2:228, **3:**649–650
  Yaqui Passion play, **6:**416
Procession and Rite, **1:**395
Proche-Guisbilei, Augustine, **5:**318
Procopius, **4:**427
Procris, **2:**105
Proctor, F.F., **6:**317
Prodigal (Byrd dance), **2:**20
Prodigal Son, The, **1:**251, **2:**71,
    5:264–266
  Australian world premiere,
    1:207, 313
  Balanchine productions, **1:**258,
    260, 268, 270, **2:**410, **3:**609,
    4:33, 609, *610,* 613, 621,
    5:264–265, *264,* 267–268, 361,
    431, **6:**339–340
  Baryshnikov performance, **1:**372
  Bulgarian staging, **2:**12
  costume design, **2:**245
  Cramér Swedish production,
    2:263, *264,* **5:**265–266

Diaghilev's Ballets Russes, **1:**316,
    317, 325, *325,* **2:**406, 410,
    3:609, **4:**33
  Dolin performance, **2:**424
  Doubrovska performance, **2:**441
  Gardel version, **5:**264
  Hønningen performance, **3:**373
  Jooss production, **3:**627, 628,
    628, **5:**265
  Kehlet *demi-caractère* role, **3:**668
  Kirstein description, **4:**26
  Laing performance, **4:**110
  Lichine choreography and
    performance, **4:**178, **5:**265,
    6:203
  Lifar performance, **4:**183,
    183, 620
  Moncion performance, **4:**450,
    610, 619, **5:**265
  Mounsey performance, **4:**617
  Murdmaa choreography, **4:**478
  Prokofiev score, **2:**408, **3:**627,
    4:525
  Robbins performance, **5:**361
  Royal Danish Ballet repertory,
    5:431
  Tomaszewski version, **6:**175
  Uthoff choreography, **6:**304
  Wall performance, **6:**357
  Woizikowski performance, **6:**404
Prodigal Son (in Ragtime), The,
    2:512, **5:**266
Proença, Laura, **1:**291, *291,* 404,
    405, 533
Profeta, Laurențiu, **2:**343
Profiles, **6:**111, 165
program notes
  libretti pamphlets, **4:**176–177
  twentieth-century, **4:**177
progresses, Elizabethan. *See*
  Elizabethan progresses
Progressive, **2:**258, 259
progressive dances, **3:**325
progressive education movement,
  6:241, 295
Progressive era (1901–1930),
  6:240–242
Prohibition, **5:**629
Proia, Alexandre, **1:**282
Proie, La, **4:**107
Prokeš, Zdeněk, **1:**542
Prokhorova, Valentina V., *as*
    contributor, **2:**449–450,
    5:571–572
Prokhorova, Violetta, **3:**429
Prokofiev, Sergei, **1:**479, **2:**579, **4:**7,
    5:266–269, **6:**341
  Alexandre Nevsky, **1:**446
  Boyarchikov collaboration, **1:**518
  Chiriaeff choreographies, **2:**151
  Cinderella conception, **2:**173–174
  Diaghilev's commission, **1:**316,
    317, **2:**406, 408, 410, 411,
    4:515
  Gala Performance, **6:**198
  Ivan the Terrible, **3:**308
  Lieutenant Kijé, **3:**27, **6:**8
  Love of Three Oranges, The, **2:**192
  Lysistrata, or The Strike of Wives,
    6:195
  Massine collaboration, **4:**320–321
  Peter and the Wolf, **1:**483,
    5:691, 692
  Prodigal Son, The, **1:**251, 316,
    317, **3:**627, **5:**264, 265, 266,
    267–268
  Romeo and Juliet, **1:**103, 153,
    446, *488,* 518, 541, **2:**266,
    347, **3:**309, **4:**132, 133, 517,
    5:393, 394, 395, 396, 398,
    401, 422

on Semenova's *Cinderella,* **5:**567
  Soviet choreographies, **4:**285
  Stone Flower score and libretto,
    5:699
  Tale of the Stone Flower,
    1:491–492
  See also Cinderella
Prokofiev by Two (video), **4:**73
Prokovsky, André, **1:**234, **2:**510,
    511, 513, **3:**623, **4:**625, **5:**54,
    401, 652
  Anna Karenina, **4:**285, **5:**410,
    6:379
  New York City Ballet, **4:**620
  Nutcracker staging, **4:**667
  Sleeping Beauty production,
    5:401
Prologue, **3:**521
promenade (dance movement), **1:**7
Promenade, **1:**280, *280,* **2:**401, 426,
    5:312, 588, **6:**282
Promenade Concert, **3:**341, 342
Promenade Concerts, Drury Lane
    Theatre, London, **6:**625
promenades. *See* ballet technique,
    turning movements
Prometeo, **3:**547, **6:**338
Prométhée, **1:**98, 404
Prométhée II, **1:**291
Prometheus, **4:**87, **5:**422, 528
Prometheus (Aeschylus), **4:**91, 476
Prometheus (film), **4:**133
Prometheus Bound (Aeschylus),
    3:300
Promised Valley, The (musical), **6:**90
Promises, Promises (musical),
    1:419, **6:**284
Pro Musica Antiqua, **4:**30
Pronk, Leon, **2:***347*
Propert, W. A., **2:**441
Prophet Dance, **3:**170–171
Prophète, Le (Meyerbeer), **5:**114
Prophetess, The, or The History of
    Diocletian (Purcell), **5:**251,
    280–281
proscenium stage, **5:**535–536, *535*
Proserpine, **1:**400, **4:**235, **5:**558
Prosperine, **1:**452, **2:**465, **4:**109,
    5:558
Prospérité, La, **2:**465
Prospero, **3:**329, **4:**267
Prospero, Salvador, **4:**396
prostitution, **3:**514, 581, 637
Protecting Veil, The, **6:**57
Protecult (Proletarian Culture
    Association), **5:**476–477
Protée, **1:***312,* 313, **4:**178
Protestantism, **2:**166–168, 537
  dance prohibitions, **2:**167, 168,
    540, **4:**212
  Native American syncretism,
    4:557–558
  See also specific denominations
    and sects
Protiv techeniaa (Fokine), **5:**483
Protsenko, Aleksandr, **4:**446
Provence, France, **2:**99, 107,
    3:64, 70
Proverbes, Les, **1:**286, 287, 424
Provincial Dances, Ekaterinburg,
    5:475, 479
Provocation, The, **5:**70
Proxy, **5:**127
Prozerpi, P., **2:**176
Prudence, **3:**79–80

Prudhommeau, Germaine, **2:**157,
    3:302
Prud'hon, Jean, **3:***118*
Prüme, François Humbert, **1:**515
Pruna, Pedro, **2:**410, **4:**320
Prunières, Henry, **3:**84, **6:**337, 338
Prussian Fairy Tales, **1:**456, 460
Pruvot, Marie-Louise, **2:**109
Prybilov, German, **2:**565
Pryde, James, **2:**262
Prynne, William, **2:**167
Psalmen Symphonie, **4:**602, **5:**677
Pseudo-Dionysius, **2:**165
Psiche a Manhattan, **1:**83, **6:**143
Psota, Ivo Váňa, **1:**315, 429, 542,
    2:307, 308, **4:**77, 583, **5:**268,
    269–270
  Romeo and Juliet choreography,
    1:541, **5:**393
Psyché, **1:**287, 424, 451, 514, **2:**389,
    464, **3:**24, 117, 119, **5:**489
  Bournonville libretto notes, **4:**176
  Gardel choreography, **5:**90, **6:**333
  Gissey costume designs, **3:**184
  Gosselin (Geneviève)
    performance, **3:**208
  Lully score, **4:**234, 235
  Molière-Corneille composition,
    4:447
  popularity, **4:**175
  Shadwell production, **5:**280
  Theilade production, **5:**430
Psyché et l'Amour, **5:270–271**
  Didelot production, **2:**412,
    414–415, **4:**277
  productions throughout Europe,
    4:695
  Rodolphe score, **5:**371
psychoactive plants, **4:**550, 568
psychodramatic movement
    therapy, **2:**321
psychological ballet, **6:**195
psychotherapy. *See* dance and
    movement therapy
Ptaszek, Jan, **5:***213*
puberty ritual
  African, **4:**484
  Native American, **4:**566, 567, 568
  Romanian, **5:**381
publications. *See* technical
    manuals; *subhead dance
    research and publication
    under specific countries; titles
    of specific publications*
"public" balls, **1:**278–279, **4:**314
Public Broadcasting System (PBS),
    2:294, 359, 375,
    6:138–139, 140
  Alive from Off Center, **2:**609, 610,
    6:139
  National Educational Television,
    6:138
  See also Dance in America
Público, La, **3:**127
Pucci, Peter, **2:**41, **3:**617
Puccini, Giacomo, **5:**246
Puck, Eva and Harry, **6:**316
Pudełek, Janina, **5:**221, **6:**73
  as contributor, **2:**172, **3:**192,
    5:101, 195, 215–220,
    6:207–208, 364–365, 441
Pudelko, Edith, **1:**533
Pueblo dance, **4:**551, 553, 562–565,
    5:271–273
  borrowings and diffusion, **4:**554
  ceremonial clowns, **4:**554
  dance literature and scholarship,
    4:575
  Hopi, **3:**373–375
puellae gaditanae, **5:**667
Puertollano, Lulu, **5:**172

Puerto Rico, **2:**62, 64, 430, **5:273–276**
Puertorrico, **2:**61–62
Pugh, Kevin, **4:**544, **6:**260
Pugliese, Patri J., *as contributor*, **2:**254–258
Pugni, Cesare, **2:**80, 207, 446, 523, **5:276–278,** 315, 498, 499, 500, 607
  Corsaire score, **5:**140, 151
  Esmeralda score, **3:**186
  Fille du Pharaon score, **5:***150,* 278
  Fille Mal Gardée score, **2:**594, 596
  Little Humpbacked Horse score, **4:**56, 211, 212
  Minkus comparison, **4:**429, 430
  musical idioms and methods, **4:**513–514
  Ondine score, **3:**136, **5:**29, 277
  Pas de Quatre score, **5:**108, 277
  Perrot collaborations, **5:**136, 137, 139, 277, 278
  Petipa (Marius) collaborations, **5:**151, 155, 277, 278
  Swiss Milkmaid score, **5:**148
  Two Stars score, **5:**119
Pugni, Leontina, **5:**278
Pugni, Nikolai, **5:**278
Puig, Alfonso, **5:**676
puirt-a-beul (mouth music), **5:**698
pukkitantsu dance, **2:**629
pukkumina, **3:**573
Pukui, Mary Kawena, **3:**396
Pulcinella, **1:**52, 93, 375, **5:**192, 304, *530,* **6:**143, 340
  Balanchine-Robbins production, **5:**361
  Bavarian State Ballet premiere, **1:**390
  Béjart staging, **1:**404
  Berman design, **1:**437
  Cecchetti mime role, **2:**83
  Christe choreography, **4:***595*
  Comedia Balletica (Musical Chairs), **1:**299
  Dmitriev design, **2:**421
  Dunn production, **1:**142, **2:**460
  Gerdt (Elisaveta) performance, **3:**137
  Idzikowski performance, **3:**441
  Jooss version, **3:**630
  Karsavina performance, **3:**656
  Kshessinsky (Iosif) performance, **4:**67
  Lopukhov choreography, **4:**225, **5:**457
  Massine choreography, **1:**322, **2:**192, **4:**317–318
  Picasso set design, **5:***543*
  Šparemblek choreography, **5:**677
  Steier choreography, **6:**41
  Stravinsky orchestration, **1:**52, 390, 404, **2:**192, 409, **4:**317–318, 516, **6:**5
  Tetley production, **2:**513
  Woizikowski performance, **6:**404
Pulcinella Variations, **1:**72
Pulkkinen, Aasko, **2:**631
Pullman community, Illinois, **6:**236
pulotu ta'anga, **4:**495
Punch (journal), **2:**69, 70
Punch and Judy, **1:**421, **3:**349
Punch and Judy Get Divorced (musical), **3:**202
Punch and the Judy, **2:**285, 519, **3:**216, **4:**120, 130
Punch and the Street Party, **1:**437
Punch Bowl, The (revue), **2:**424
punk music, **2:**19
punta dance, **3:**320

punta rhythmic pattern, **2:**62, **3:**120
punto, **5:**67
Pupille Espagnole, La, **2:**299
Puppenfee, Die (The Fairy Doll), **1:**37, 110, 239, 241, 254, **2:**181, **3:**89, 145, **5:**184, **278–279**
  Gundlich staging, **6:**431
  as Hassreiter creation, **3:**346, 347, **5:**278–279
  Legats' production, **4:**143, 144
  popularity in Hungary, **3:**414
  popularity in Switzerland, **6:**51
  Pratesi staging, **5:**246
Puppenladen, Im, **5:**278
puppet (dance), **1:**538, **2:**226, **3:**347
puppetry
  Asia, **1:178–180**
    Balinese, **1:**160, 179, **3:**367–370, **4:**485, **6:367–370**
    Burmese, **4:**525–526, 527
    Chinese, **1:**179–180
    Japanese, **1:**160, 161, 179, *179,* 180, **2:**12–14, **3:**586, 637
    Javanese, **1:**172–174, **3:**496–497, *497,* **4:**298
  Europe
    Beaumont study, **3:**282
    Belarus, **1:**408
    Falla opera, **2:**568
    Italian futurists, **1:**243–244
Purāṇas, **3:**451–452, 464, **465–466,** 660
Pura Penataran Topéng temple, Blahbatu, **3:**486
Purbaningrat, Tumenggung, **3:**497
Purcell, Florence, **1:**358
Purcell, Henry, **1:**52, 517, **2:**400, **3:**254, **5:**251, **280–282,** **6:**47
  Dido and Aeneas, **2:**337, **3:**376, 630, **4:**114, 470
  elegy composed for Playford, **5:**200
  Fairy Queen, The, **2:**400, **3:**391, 630, **4:**114, 215, **5:**251, 281
  hornpipe compositions, **3:**376
  as *Moor's Pavane* score source, **4:**458
  rigaudon compositions, **5:**352
Purcell Opera Society, **2:**262, 263, **4:**215
Pure, Michel de, **3:**84, **6:**125
Puri, Rajika, **4:**368
Purim, **3:**526, 529, 603–604
Puritani, I (Bellini), **3:**180
Puritanism, **2:**167, **4:**212, **6:**231
Purkis, Helen M. C., *as contributor,* **5:**340–341
Purlie (musical), **6:**284
Purovska, Zoica, **6:**437
Purple Moment, **1:**363
purpuri dance, **2:**630
Pursianov, Akhmed, **6:**213
purtatas, **5:**380, 381
Purulia *chhau,* **2:117–118,** *118*
Purwadiningrat, Raden Tumenggung, **3:**498
Puryear, Martin, **2:**567
Püschner, Johann Georg, **5:**260
Push Comes to Shove, **1:**74, 74, 372, **2:**463, **4:**226, **6:***152,* 153
Pushkin, **4:**36, **5:**467, 470
Pushkin, Aleksandr (dancer), **5:282**
  Baryshnikov as student, **1:**371
  Maryinsky school, **5:**480
  Nureyev as student, **5:**4
  students, **1:**441, **2:**422, **4:**232, **5:**4, 282, 401, **6:**341
Pushkin, Aleksandr (poet), **2:**416, **3:**20, 186, 187, **4:**324, **5:**264, **6:**5

admiration for Elsslner, **2:**596
admiration for Kolosova, **4:**35
as *Aleko* source, **1:**136
Asafiev scores, **1:**144
Boyarchikov choreography of poems, **1:**518
as *Bronze Horseman* source, **1:**491
definition of ballet, **3:**539
Didelot ballets, **4:**278, 279
as *Fountain of Bakhchisarai* source, **3:**56, **6:**441
Glushkovsky choreography of poems, **1:**485, **3:**191–192, **5:**454
Istomina as muse, **3:**539, 540, **4:**279
Lavrovsky (Leonid) choreography of poem, **4:**131
Nizhniy Novgorod estate, **5:**471
as *Prisoner of the Caucasus* source, **5:**453–454
as Soviet ballet source, **3:**56, **4:**284, **5:**454, 464, **6:**441, 442
as Ulanova inspiration, **6:**227
writings on ballet, **5:**486
Puss in Boots, **4:**143
Puti baletmeistera (Lopukhov), **4:**225
Putman, Todd, **6:***250*
putri (puteri) dance, **4:**249, 494
Putro, Susetyo Hario, **3:***496*
putul nautch dance, **1:**178
Puttke, Martin, **3:**158
Puttock, Denise, *as contributor,* **1:**467–468
Puuur, Helmi, **2:**529
Puvigné, Mademoiselle, **2:**365, **6:***330,* 331
Puymaigre, Théodore de, **3:**33
Puzakov, Yuri, **5:**475
pwe, 4, 525–526, **4:***526,* 527
Pye, David, **1:**216
Pygmalion, **1:**201, 400, 451, 540, **3:**68, 318, 413, **4:**380, **5:**504
  Hilverding choreography, **3:**365
  Milon production, **4:**422
Pygmalion (Rameau), **5:**306, 307
Pygmalion (Shaw), **6:**282
Pygmy dance, **2:**32, 33, 87, *88,* **4:**357
  See also Baka; Efe; Mbuti dance
Pygram, John, **5:**653
Pylades, **5:**72, 73, 74
Pynchon, Thomas, **2:**474
pyöl sandae nori (masked dance drama), **4:**50, 300
pyolsin masked drama, **4:**299–300
Pyramiderna, **1:**145
Pyramides, **6:**45
Pyramus and Thisbe (Pyrame et Thisbé), **2:**55, 465, **4:**276
pyrrhic, **3:***290,* 291, **4:**499, **5:282–283**
  Arbeau theory linking *matachins* with, **4:**326
  cheironomia identified with, **2:**116
  emmeleia versus, **2:**506
  Roman Empire, **5:**376
  Syrian men, **4:**405
Pyrrhic Dances, **5:**555

Qaartsiluni, **2:**388, **4:**118, 125, **5:**96, 353, 429
"Qabyala: The Tribal Concept in the Central Highlands of the Yemen Arab Republic" (Adra), **4:**417
Qāsimī, Khḻid al-, **4:**417

qi (life force), **1:**184, 186
Qiao Yang, **6:**415
qidrah. See guedra
Qing dynasty, **2:**19, 131, 132, **4:**76
Qingfeng Ting (opera), **6:**446
Qin Liming, **6:**415
Qi Rushan (Ch'i Ju-shan), **2:**132, 148
Qi school (Beijing Opera), **6:**446, 446–647
Qi Shufang, **2:***220*
Qiu Shengrong, **6:**421
Quack, M.D. (play), **3:**91, 92, **6:**268
quadernaria, **1:**351, **4:**501, **5:**506
Quadri, Alicia, **1:**111
quadrille, **5:285–287,** 624, *625,* 685, 688
  Argentinian form, **1:**108
  Brazilian form, **1:**529
  can-can as form of, **2:**52, **3:**69
  Caribbean form, **2:**63, 431, **3:**335
  as *cotillon* form, **2:**253, 256, 257
  Danish form, **2:**381
  Dutch form, **4:**586
  écossaise form, **2:**474–475
  European traditional, **2:**554
  figures, **2:**591, 592
  Finnish form, **2:**630
  France, **3:***63,* 69
  French Canada, **2:**35
  German notation, **4:***685*
  Germany, **3:**141
  Irish form, **3:**516
  Jamaican form, **3:**573
  Lancers, **2:**592
  Lithuania, **4:**206
  Mexican form, **4:***388*
  music, **4:**514
  New England four-couple, **3:**35
  Protestant sectarian denuciation, **2:**167
  Russia, **5:**445, 474
  square dance, **5:**685–686, 688
Quadrille and Cotillion Panorama (Wilson), **5:**286
Quadrille des Nations, Le (masque), **5:**285
quadrille réaliste, **1:**95
"Quaestiones convivales" (Plutarch), **5:**557
Quaglio, Giovanni Maria, **2:**433
Quaglio, Giulio, **1:**87
Quantum, **2:**359
Quantz, Johann Joachim, **6:**87
Quarry, **4:**451
Quartet, **2:**293, **4:**244, 667
Quartet Opus 59, No. 3, **1:**524
Quasi-Waltz, **3:**398
quaternaria, **3:**542
Quatre Fils Aymons, Les
  Arnould-Mussot pantomime, **1:**122–123, 124
  Béjart and Charrat production, **1:**291
  Hus (Auguste) production, **3:**426
Quatre Images, **5:**431
Quatre Saisons, Les (Perrot ballet), **2:**95, **3:**180, 260, **5:**138, **6:**76
  See also Four Seasons, The
Quatrième Concert Royal, **2:**151
Quatuor, **5:**676
Quéariau, Marie, **3:**358
Quebec, Canada, **2:**35–36, 40–41, 47, 48, 49, 152, 179, **3:**36
Quebec City, Canada, **2:**35, 36, 37, 47, **3:**228
Queen, John, **6:**316
Queenie Pie (Ellington musical), **2:**567
Queen of Hearts, **1:**139
Queen of Spades, The, **1:**518, **2:**463

Queens (Jonson), **4:**312
Queensbury, duke of, **2:**71
Queensland Ballet, **1:**211, 215, **4:**479, **6:**379
Queensland Modern and Contemporary Dance Company, **1:**216–217
Queen's Theatre, London. *See* King's Theatre, London
Queen's University, Belfast, **3:**283
Queen Walks in the Garden, The, **6:**87
Quelques Fleurs, **1:**300, 498
Queretaro, Mexico, **2:**194
Queriau, Madame, **2:**595
Querida, Monique, **4:**136
Quest (Weidman dance), **1:**421
Quest, The (Ashton ballet), **1:**150, **2:**477, **3:**307, **5:**312, 588, **6:**326
Quica, La, **3:**286
Quiché (people), **3:**319
Quick Change Artists, **2:**110
Quicksilver, **2:**1
quickstep, **1:**358
Quiet Flows the Don, **1:**519, **5:**468–469
Quiet Place, A (Bernstein), **1:**438
Quigley, Colin, *as contributor,* **4:**372–376
Quilanti, Francesco, **3:**545
Quilter, Roger, **5:**294
Quinault, Philippe, **2:**412, **4:**234, **5:**86, 307
Quinault, Robert, **5:**98
Quincunx, **3:**234
Quintet (Wright ballet), **6:**405
Quintet, or The Adventures of Don and Dolores from New York to Hollywood and Back, **1:**66, **2:**425
Quintilian family, **5:**319, 376
Quito, Ecuador, **2:**475
Quotidien, Le (publication), **3:**85
Qu Yuan, **2:**145

Raab, Riki, **1:**240, 243, **2:**347, **5:**279
Raatikko Dance Theater of Vantaa, **2:**633
Rábai, Miklós, **3:**405, 406, **5:**287
Rabbit Dance, **4:**561, **5:**240
Rabel, Daniel, **2:**236, **3:**184
Raben, Peter, **4:**59
Rabenek, Ellen. *See* Tels, Ellen
Rabenek studio, **5:**476, 477
Rabin, Linda, **2:**40, **3:**232, 233
Rabinal Achí (dance drama), **3:**319
Rabindrik, **3:**468
Rabinovitch, Isaac, **6:**118
Rabinovszky, Máriusz, **3:**420, 423
Rabovsky, István, **2:**508, **3:**415, **4:**624
Raccolta di varij balli (formerly *Nobilità di dame*), **2:**73
Race, The, **4:**627
Race of Life, The, **2:**580, **3:**401, 404, **4:**177
Rachmaninov, Sergei, **1:**158, **3:**25, 29, **4:**132
Rachou, Ruth, **1:**535
Racine, Jean, **3:**188, 189, 364, **4:**174
Racoon Dance, **4:**553
Racy, Ali Jihad, *as contributor,* **4:**487–491
Racy, Barbara, *as contributor,* **4:**487–491
RAD. *See* Royal Academy of Dancing
Radaic, Felicitas L., **5:**172, 173

Rada rite, **3:**334, *334,* 335
Radcliffe-Brown, A. R., **4:**369
Raden, Kanjeng, **3:**497
RAdeoA.C.Tiv(ID)ty, **4:**21
Rader, Patricia Weeks, *as contributor,* **1:**53–54, 520–524, **6:**349–351
Rådet for Folkemusik og Foledans, Norway, **4:**682
Radford, Karen, **2:**291
Rādhā (deity), **3:**467, 468, **4:**253
Radha, **5:**46, **288,** 492, *492,* 494, 495
Radha Krishna (Gopal dance), **3:**199
Rādhā-Kṛṣṇa theme, **1:**94, 160, **3:**466–468, **4:**253
Radice, Attilia, **3:**51, **5:288–289,** 400, **6:**143
radio "barn-dance" programs, **5:**688
Radio City Music Hall, New York City, **5:289–290**
  Bowman as *prima ballerina,* **1:**518
  Buck and Bubbles as first black performers, **2:**5
  Kaye as ballet corps member, **3:**663
  precision dancing, **5:**247
  Rockettes, **4:**24, **5:**247, 289–290, *289,* **6:**242, 268, 285
Radio City Revels (film), **4:**419
Radio-Québec, **6:**132
Radio Republik Indonesia, **3:**483
Radiotelevision Italia (RAI), **3:**554, **6:**134
Radium Dances, **3:**94
Radius, Alexandra, **2:**470, **4:**602, **5:290**
Radkina, N. P., *as contributor,* **6:**213
Radlov, Sergei, **3:**12, **5:**268, 392, 393, **6:**441
RAD method, **5:**649
Radnai, Miklós, **3:**414
Radoev, Pešo, **2:**10
Radojevic, Danilo, **1:**74, 233, **6:**202
Răducanu, Miriam, **5:**388, *388*
Radunsky, Aleksandr, **1:**490, 491, 492, **3:**197, **5:**203, 459, 587, **6:**311
  Little Humpbacked Horse, The, **4:***211,* 212
Radziwill, Prince Léon, **3:**316
Radzynski, Jan, **6:**111
Rae, Bernadette, **4:**629
Raedt, Tony, **6:**375
Raeves, Eric, **1:**412
Rafael, **1:**509
Raff, Emma Scott, **2:**47
Raffé, W. G., **6:**104
Raffinerie du Plan K, La, **1:**411
Raffinot, François, **3:**156
Raffles, Thomas Stamford, **3:**502–503, 506
Rafi, Mohammad, **2:**625
Raft, George, **6:**320
Raftis, Alkis, **3:**302, 303
  as contributor, **3:**294–296, 296–301, 302–304
  as photographer, **2:**100
Raft Piece, **6:**163
rāga, **1:**169, **3:**463, 662, **4:**79, **5:**22, **291**
Ragamuffin, **5:**634
Ragghianti, Carmen, **1:**83
Raghavan, V., **3:**470
Ragini Devi, **3:**507, **5:291–292**
Ragir, Judith, **6:***249*
Ragozina, Galina, **4:**285

Ragragsakan, **5:***169*
Rags, **1:**350
ragtime, **4:**519, **5:**628, **6:**244
Ragtime (film), **6:**154
Ragtime (musical), **6:**289
Rag-Time, **2:**289
Ragtime Dance Company, **4:**519, 625
Raguenet, François, **1:**396
Rah, Kavisurya Baladeva, **5:**23
Raḥbānī brothers, **4:**489
Rahman, Fasih-ur, **3:**425
RAI (Radiotelevision Italia), **3:**554, **6:**134
Raibayev, zaur, **3:**665
Raices Profundas, **2:***273*
Raičev, Aleksandŭr, **2:**11
"Raiding the Dragon King's Palace" (*The Monkey King*), **2:**133
Raillerie, La, **1:**287, **4:**234
Raimond de Cornet, **4:**348
Raimondi, Ezio, **3:**557
Raimund, Carl, Jr., **1:**240
Raimund, Carl, Sr., **1:**239
Rainbow Bandit, **1:**51, 52
Rainbow Pass, **2:**142
Rainbow Ripples, **1:**52, **5:**303
Rainbow 'Round My Shoulder, **2:**358, **4:**345, *346,* 520, **6:**259
Raincheck, **4:**306
Rainer, Yvonne, **1:**140, **5:292–293,** 313, 573, 606
  American Dance Festival, **1:**79
  aural eclecticism, **4:**519
  avant-garde dance, **1:**246, **2:**333, 606, **3:**336, **6:***248,* 250
  dance aesthetics, **1:**25
  as French modern dance influence, **3:**78
  Gordon association, **3:**201
  Grand Union, **3:**235
  improvisation, **3:**445, 446
  as Japanese postmodern dance influence, **3:**591
  Judson Dance Theater, **2:**462, **3:**634, 635, **6:**282
  Room Service, **1:**244
  Three Seascapes, **4:**519
  Trio, **2:**247
  Waring's Dance Associates, **6:**363
Rainey, F., *as photographer,* **4:**572
RainForest, **2:**290, 292, **3:**620, **5:**548, *548*
Rainier, prince of Monaco, **2:**509, 510
Rainier, Priaulx, **3:**403
Rainoldi, **1:**237
Rain Queen, The, **2:**56, 57, **5:**226, 692
Rain Sacrificial Dance, **2:**140
Raisin (musical), **6:**284
Raistrick, Martin, **5:**55
Raizenberg, Lindy, **5:**652, 660
Raj, Sheela, **2:**460
Raja, K. Kunjunni, **3:**470
Rajah (vaudeville performer), **6:**317
Rajah de Benares, Il, **6:**70
Rajala, Maj-Lis, **2:**632
Rajamani, Madanlal, **1:**94
rāja nartakis, **1:**169
rajang, **3:**485
Rajka, Peter, **6:**50
Rajkumar, Priyagopal, **3:**468
Raj Nartaki (film), **2:**623
Rajnartaki (Jhaveri sisters), **3:**606
Raka, **5:**54, 692
Raka Rasmin, Ni Gusti Ayu, **4:**265, *265*
Rake, The, **5:**294
Rake's Progress, The, **5:293–294**
  Blair performance, **1:**459

CAPAB Ballet mounting, **2:**56
Chappell performance, **2:**105
de Valois production, **1:**148, **2:***396,* 400–401, **4:**625, **5:**413, 415
Gore performance, **2:**401, **3:**202
Grant performance, **3:**236
Helpmann performance, **2:***396,* 401, **3:**354, *354*
Markova performance, **4:**268
Moreton performance, **4:**463
Staff role, **5:**691
Turner roles, **5:**293, 294, **6:**214
Wall performance, **6:**357
Wells performance, **6:**380
Rake's Progress, The (Hogarth engraving), **2:***396,* 401, 527, **6:**6
Rake's Progress, The (Stravinsky opera), **6:**6
Rakhimova, Gavkhar, **6:**307
Rakic, Xenia, *as contributor,* **6:**434–437
Rákoš Rákoczy, **1:**429, **5:**245
Rakusin, Debbie, **5:**659
Rall, Tommy, **4:***11,* **3:**55, **5:**21
Ralov, Børge, **1:**399, *508,* **3:**657, **4:**118, 119, **5:**166, 238, **294,** 353, 428
  Coppélia performance, **2:**200
  Enken i Spejlet, **1:**539, **5:**429
  Konservatoriet performance, **4:***43*
  Royal Danish Ballet, **5:**294, 429
Ralov, Kirsten, **1:**454, **3:**39, **5:295,** *428,* 429, **6:**129
  Bournonville heritage, **1:**512, 513, **3:**387, **5:**430, **6:**292
  Royal New Zealand Ballet guest performances, **4:**624
  turning movement, **1:**336
  Worsaae designs, **6:**404
Ralph, Richard, **3:**283, 522
  as contributor, **1:**391–392, **2:**80–81, 394, 527, **3:**111–112, 521–523, **4:**105–106, 346–347, **5:**251–252, 270–271, **6:**175–176, 372–374
  London Contemporary Dance School, **4:**220
Rāma, **3:**465
Ramaccini, Annunciata, **1:**460, **2:**282, 587, **3:**547
Ramaiah, Kalyanasundaram, **1:**273
"Ramaiya Vastavaiya," **2:***624*
Rāmakian (Sanskrit epic), **4:**9, 10, 112
rāmanāṭṭam, **3:**465
Ramaniranjan, **5:**23
Rama-Sida, **4:**10, 112, **6:**151
Rāmāyaṇa (Indian epic), **1:**168, 170, 172, 173, 176, 182, **3:464–465,** **5:**523, 524
  Balinese dance, **1:**160, 174, **3:**473–374, 483–485, 666, **6:**321, 368, 369, 370
  baris dance, **1:**366
  Burmese dance drama, **2:**226, *227,* **4:**527
  Cambodian *reamker* dance, **2:**31
  Indian dance, **3:**451–452
  Javanese dance, **3:**492, 495, 497, 498
  kathakaḷi, **3:**660, **4:**298–299
  puppetry, **1:***178,* **2:**226
  Purulia *chhau,* **2:**118
  Thai dance, **2:**227
  yakṣagāna, **6:**413
Ramazin, Boris, **2:**496
Ramazzini, Bernardino, **2:**328

Rambert, Marie, **1:**52, **5:295–297**
  Ashton association, **1:**145, 146, 147
  Ballets Russes de Serge Diaghilev, **3:**262
  Cecchetti Society founding, **2:**84
  Chappell as student, **2:**105
  choreographic protégés, **3:**263
  de Valois collaboration, **3:**266
  Franca association, **3:**61
  Gore association, **3:**202
  Hellerau school, **3:**596
  Joffrey association, **3:**611
  Karsavina friendship, **3:**656
  memoirs, **5:**220
  as Nijinsky assistant, **2:**408, **4:**644
  Sacre du Printemps, Le, **5:**327, 488
  Staff association, **5:**691
  students, **2:**372, **3:**173, 427, 508, **4:**109, 215, **5:**296, 298, 573, **6:**195, 213, 449
  Tudor as protégé, **3:**263
  video documentary on, **2:**314, **6:**135
Rambert at Fifty (documentary), **6:**135
Rambert Dance Company (formerly Ballet Rambert), **5:**296–297, **297–305**
  Aldous, Lucette, **1:**38
  Alston, Richard, **1:**51, 52–53, **3:**273, 274
  archives, **4:**163–164
  Ashton, Frederick, **1:**145, 146, 147
  Australia-New Zealand tour, **1:**208, 213, **4:**624
  Baylis, Nadine, **1:**394
  Bournonville *La Sylphide* revival, **5:**406
  Bruce, Christopher, **2:**1, **3:**274, 275, **5:**302, 303, *303*, 304, 305, **6:**134
  Childs choreographies, **2:**120
  Cinderella, **2:**173
  Coppélia, **2:**200
  Cunningham productions, **2:**294, 295, **3:**274
  Dark Elegies, **2:**348–349, 372
  Davies, Siobhan, **2:**355, **3:**273
  de Mille, Agnes, **2:**372
  de Valois choreography, **2:**400
  development, **3:**263–264, 266
  Don Quixote, **2:**440
  Enigma Variations, **2:**515
  Franca, Celia, **3:**61–62
  funding, **2:**510
  as German modern dance influence, **3:**151
  Gilmour, Sally, **3:**174
  Gilpin, John, **3:**174
  Gore, Walter, **3:**202, 203
  Howard, Andrée, **3:**391–392
  Hynd, Ronald, **3:**427
  Jacob's Pillow performance, **3:**571
  Jardin aux Lilas, **3:**597
  Joffrey choreography, **3:**609
  Karsavina guest performances, **3:**656, **6:**62
  Lacotte choreography, **4:**107–108
  Lady into Fox, **3:**173, 174
  members in modern dance groups, **3:**273
  modern dance style, **3:**274, 275, 278
  Morrice, Norman, **3:**271–272, **4:**469
  Planets, The, **3:**265
  repertory revision, **3:**274
  role in development of British ballet, **3:**263–264, 265
  Sadler's Wells reciprocity, **3:**266
  school, **3:**273, 279, 280
  Schooling, Elisabeth, **5:**560
  Scott, Margaret, **5:**563
  Seymour choreography, **5:**575
  Staff, Frank, **5:**691
  telecasts, **6:**134
  Tetley, Glen, **5:**301, 302, 303, *303*, **6:**146
  Tudor, Antony, **5:**296, 298, 299, 300, **6:**195, 196, 197, *198*
  Woizikowski, Leon, **6:**404
  World War II activity, **3:**266, **5:**515
Ramchandra, C., **2:**623, 625
Rameau, Jean-Philippe, **1:**43, 46, **3:**36, 106, **5:**34, **305–307,** 504, 520
  ballet music, **4:**509, 511
  Boquet costume design, **1:**497
  bourrée compositions, **1:**516
  chaconne and *passacaille* compositions, **2:**99
  on *courante*, **2:**259–260, 261
  dances for La Barberina, **1:**365
  Drottningholm Court Theater production, **6:**47
  gavotte, **3:**124
  Hippolyte et Aricie, **3:**117, **4:**107, 122, **5:**38, 88, 306, 307
  on hornpipe, **3:**377
  individualization of dance types, **4:**509
  loure compositions, **4:**232
  Lyonnois roles, **4:**236
  musette compositions, **4:**481
  music for Gardel family ballets, **3:**116, 117, 119
  music for Lany family ballets, **4:**122
  nautical *forlana* composition, **3:**50
  as Noverre influence, **4:**694, 698
  opéra-ballet and *tragédie lyrique*, **5:**38, 40, 306–307
  Paris Opera Ballet, **5:**87, 88
  reconstruction of dances, **2:**51, **6:**250
  rigaudon, **5:**352
  as Rodolphe influence, **5:**371
  tambourins included in works, **6:**87
  technical writings, **6:**125
  Temple de la Gloire, Le, **1:**284, **4:**236, **6:**250
  Zaïs, **5:**113, 306, 307
  See also Castor et Pollux; Indes Galantes, Les
Rameau, Pierre, **1:**396–397, **2:**338, **5:**201, **307–309**
  on ballet technique, **1:**331, 333, 343
  on *branle/gavotte*, **3:**124
  dance manuals, **1:**342, **2:**527, 588, **3:**81, 545, **4:**106, **6:**123–124, 126
  on *galliarde*, **3:**109
  on *gigue*, **3:**172
  Maître à danser, Le (dance manual), **5:**260, 308, *308*, 324, **6:**123, 176
  on *menuet*, **4:**431, 432
  on *port de bras*, **5:**226
  on Prévost, **2:**59, **5:**248, 249
  on *révérence*, **5:**345, 346
  on *rond de jambe à terre*, **5:**402
  See also Maître à danser, Le
Rameau, **4:**593

Ramírez, Eduardo, **6:**301, 302
Ramírez, Francisco, **4:**391
Ramírez, Raquel, **2:**126
Ramishvili, Nina, **3:**135
Rām Līlā pageants, **3:**465
Ramón Obusan Folkloric Group, **5:***169, 171,* 172, 173
Ramos, Francisco, **5:**668
Ramos, Vivan, **2:**63
Ramos Smith, Maya, **4:**399
Ramov, Alexi, **6:**266
Ramsay, Susie, **2:**612
Ramsden, Pamela, **4:**97
Ramsey, John, **3:**107, **5:**666, **6:**350
Ramunni Menon, Pattiykkantoi, **3:**661
Ramuz, C. F., **1:**93, **6:**4
ramvong (Cambodia), **4:**123
ramwong (Thailand), **2:**227, **6:**148
Rančev, Dragan, **6:**435
ranchos, **1:**527
ranchos folclóricos, **5:**228, 229
Rand, Sally, **2:**569, 573–574, *573*, **3:**559, **6:**318
randai, **3:**500, **5:**130
Randall, Lew, **6:**316
Randazzo, Anthony, **5:***513*
Randazzo, Peter, **2:**40, 44, 47, **3:**219
Randoli Perahera, **3:**649
Random Breakfast, **3:**201
Ranganathan, **1:**273
Rangda, **3:**473, 490, *490,* 491–492, **5:**356
  mask, **4:**297
Ranger, T. O., **2:**212, **6:**25
Rangga Lawe (Javanese text), **1:**176
Ránki, György, **2:**473
Ranney, Donald A., **4:**17
Rannow, Angela, **3:**162
Ranta, Tarja, **2:**633
rants (Scottish reel), **3:**243
Rao, Korada Narasimha, **3:**508
Rao, Shanta, **3:**199, *460,* **5:**309
Raoul, or The Magic Star, **5:**318, 319
Raoul, Signor de Crechi, ossia La Tirannida Represa, **4:**175
Raoul Barbe-Bleue, **4:**35, **6:**311
Raoul de Créquis, **2:**416, **4:**35, 277–278
Rapanui, **5:**310
Rapee, Erno, **5:**289
Rape of Lucrece, The, **4:**72
Rape of Lucretia, The (Britten opera), **2:**373
Raphael ("El Gato"), **1:**61
rap music, **1:**538, **3:**447, **5:**633
Rapp, Richard, **2:**438, **4:***613*
Rappel, Carolyn, **1:**232, 233
rapper dance, **3:**240–241, 608, **6:**54, 55
rapping, **1:**538, **6:**250
Rapport, **2:***284*
Rappresentazione di Anima et di Corpo, **3:**510, 544, 630
Rapsodie Espagnole (Ravel), **5:**316
Raptus, 2448
raqs, **4:**408, 487, **6:**305
raqs al-kurra, **3:**525
raqs al-samāḥ, **4:**411
raqs al-sham 'eddan, **2:**494, **4:***411*
raqsat al-nahlah, **2:**494
"Rara Tonga" (*Tropical Revue*), **2:***459*
rasa (concept), **1:**16, 169, **3:**458, 462, 463, 466, **4:**575
rasābhivyakti, **3:**462
rasānubhāva, **3:**462

Rasch, Albertina, **1:**37, **2:**342, 613, **5:**246–247, **310–311, 6:**273, 274, 275, *275,* 276, 278
  See also Albertina Rasch Dancers
Rasch, Ellen, **6:**42
Rashkovsky, Mikhail, *as photographer*, **4:**208
Rashomon, **5:**575
rasika, **3:**463
Rasky, Harry, **6:**132
rās līlā, **3:**467, 468, 606, **5:311–312,** 581–582, 601
Rasmussen, Angeline, **4:**179
Rasmussen, Clara, **1:***507*
rasoutapati, **3:**462
Rasputin, the Holy Devil, **2:**4
Rassadin, Konstantin, **5:**469
Rassemblement, **2:**42
Rassine, Alexis, **4:**584, **5:312–313,** 652
Rastafarians, **3:**573, 575
Rastas, Jarmo, **2:**633, *634*
Rastignac, **3:**92
Ratcliff, Carl, **1:**197
Rathner, Wilhelmine, **5:**278
rationalism, **1:**22
rational recreation movement (England), **3:**241
Rat Passage, **3:**574
Rats (d'Opéra) (Doré), **2:**71
Rättvik Folklore Festival (Sweden), **6:**37
Raub der Proserpina, Der, **6:**9
Rauchwerger, Mikhail, **4:**87
Raukar, Mladen, **6:**433
Raul, Signore de Crechi, **6:**337
Raun Raun Theatre, Goroka, New Guinea, **4:**352
Rauschenberg, Robert, **1:**143, 542, **2:**462, 608, **5:**187, **313–315,** **6:**108, 250
  Brown (Trisha) design collaboration, **1:**544, 545, **5:**550, 551
  celebrity of, **2:**292
  Cunningham association, **1:**140, 142, **2:**22, 245, *287,* 288, *288,* 290, 291, 292, 293, **5:**548, **6:**26, 27
  Farber collaboration, **2:**575
  film and dance, **2:**606
  Johns collaboration, **3:**619
  Lucinda Childs Dance Company, **2:**120
  Taylor (Paul) association, **6:**107, 164, 165
  Winterbranch lighting, **6:**402
Rausmaa, Pirkko-Liisa, **2:**631
Raut, Mayadhar, **4:**247, **5:**23
Rauth, Leo, **1:***130*
Ravel, Antoine and Jerome, **4:**455
Ravel, Maurice, **1:**478, 483, **2:**397, **3:**416, **4:**7, **5:**237, **315–316,** 525, **6:**326
  Diaghilev collaborations, **1:**316, **2:**406, **4:**515, 516
  Falla friendship, **2:**567
  musical idiom, **4:**516
  Nijinska choreography, **4:**635–636
  pastoral ballet, **5:**113
  Pavane pour une Infante Défunte, **5:**116, 316
  Satie association, **5:**525
  Stravinsky friendship, **6:**3
  Valse, La, **2:**20, **3:**24, **4:**635–636
  Valses Nobles et Sentimentales, **1:**148, 151, **2:**426, **3:**72, 429
  See also Boléro; Daphnis et Chloë
Ravel family, **5:316–320, 6:**236, 237, 238

Ravel Festival (1975), **4:**607, **5:**366
"Ravel Polka Quadrilles," **6:**234
raven cult, **4:**550
Raven Dance, **4:**553
Ravenscroft, John, **3:**376
Raverat, Gwen, **3:**608, 609, **5:***411*
Ravinia, Menasha, **4:**164
Ravinia Opera, **5:**58
Ravinia Park Ballet, **2:**357
Ravlov, Borge, **4:**270
Ravlov, Kirsten, **5:**394
Ravodna, Madame (Ray Espinosa),
　2:525
rawa. See Hausa dance
Rawat, Harish, **2:**468
Rawe, Tom, **6:**152
Raw-Edged Woman, **2:**607
Rawlings, John, **2:**526, **6:**109
Rawlings, Margaret, **3:**354
Rawsthorne, Alan, **4:**115
Ray, Man, **1:**327, **5:**335
Ray, Mavis, **6:**278
Ray, Satyajit, **5:**568
Rayet, Jacqueline, **1:**290, 292, 462,
　2:*472*, **5:**97, **320**
Raymi festival (Inca), **2:**475, 476
Raymonda, **1:**48, **3:**22, **5:**247,
　320–322
　Balanchine production, **1:**298,
　　2:314, **4:**610, **5:**322
　Bessmertnova performance,
　　1:440
　Bujones production, **1:**77
　CAPAB stagings, **2:**11
　character dances, **2:**108
　Chauviré mime role, **2:**114
　Danilova performance, **2:**342
　double *tours en l'air*, **1:**338
　Fayer conducting, **2:**579
　Franklin performance, **3:**88
　Geltser performance, **3:**128
　Gerdt (Pavel) performance, **3:**137
　Glazunov score, **3:**186, **4:**610
　Gorsky versions, **3:**206, **5:**321
　Gregory performance, **3:**306
　Grigorovich stagings, **1:**492,
　　3:310, **5:**321–322, 463
　Gusev performance, **3:**327
　Lavrovsky (Leonid) version,
　　4:132, **5:***463*
　Legat (Sergei) performance,
　　4:*143*, 144
　Legnani performance, **4:**145
　Lopukhov revival, **4:**224
　Mordkin performance, **4:**459
　Nichols performance, **4:**631
　Nureyev staging and
　　performances, **1:**73, 231, 232,
　　373, **3:**136, **5:**7, 97, *159*
　as Petipa's last great production,
　　5:456
　Petipa staging, **5:**154, 157, 159,
　　159, 160
　Plisetskaya open-air production,
　　4:154, **5:**401
　Rodrigues production, **2:**58
　Semenova performance, **5:**566
　Sergeyev (Konstantin)
　　choreography, **5:**321, 463,
　　572, **6:**343
　Sergeyev (Nicholas) preservation,
　　4:284
　Vainonen restaging, **5:**321, **6:**311
　Wells performance, **6:**380
　Zvereff staging, **4:**207
Raymonda (film), **6:**171
Raymonda Variations, **4:**610, 617,
　631, **6:**396
Raynal, Guillaume, **1:**3
Raynal, Jean, **1:**3
Rayon de Lune, **1:**118

Rayon d'Or, **2:***249*
rayonism, **1:**133, **4:**124, **5:**542
Raysse, Martial, **1:**305
Razeq, Aleya Abdel, **2:**497, 498
Razsokhiskaya Collection, **4:**165
Razzanelli, Assunta, **5:**409
Read, John B., **4:**217, *218*
*Reading Dance: The Birth of
　Choreology* (Benesh), **4:**691
Ready, Eddie, **4:**522
Reagan, Ronald, **1:**60
Real, Elvira, **4:**222
Real, Maria Therese del, **2:**514
"Realistic Manifesto" (Gabo and
　Pevsner), **2:**255
Re alla Caccia, Il, **1:**87–88, **3:**105
Realm, **4:**545
Realms of Choice, **1:**394
Real McCoy, The, **2:**584
*Real Story of Little Red Riding
　Hood, The*, **5:**475
Real Teatro de São Carlos, **5:**231,
　231, 232–233, 234
Reamker dance drama, **2:**31
Reardon, William, **2:**80
Rearick, Elizabeth C., **3:**423
rebec, **4:**501
Rebecca of Sunnybrook Farm (film),
　6:142
Rebekah Harkness Foundation. *See*
　Harkness Foundation
Rebel, Jan, **5:**530, 531
Rebel, Jean-Féry, **1:**516, **2:**59, 465,
　5:249
Reber, Napoléon Henri, **5:**150
rebetika (dance genre),
　3:298–299, *299*
Rebling, E., **4:**599
Rebus, **2:**293
*Réception d'une Jeune Nymphe à la
　Cour de Terpsichore*, **6:**71, 73
Recherche en danse, La (journal),
　3:85
Recht des Herrn, Das, **3:**153
Rechtschaffener Tantzmeister, Der
　(Taubert), **1:**342, **2:**259, *338*,
　6:123, 124
Recife, Brazil, **1:**527, 530, **2:**58
*Recital for Cellist and Eight
　Dancers*, **4:***591*
Récit—Chapter 5, **3:**523
Recke, Elise von der, **5:**220
Reclbefore ou Oedipe
Recollections of a Beloved Place,
　5:563
Reconctres Internationales de
　Danse Contemporaine, **3:**84
reconstruction, **5:**322–330
　historical notations, **5:**322–325
　modern scores, **5:**325–326
　beyond notation, **5:**326–330
　"to dance by the book," **2:**592
　See also notation
Recontre, Le (Lichine ballet), **4:**33
*Recontre, ou Oedipe et le Sphinx,
　La*, **1:**426, **3:**74
Recontre Imprévue, La (Gluck), **1:**87
Recontres, Les (Nijinska), **4:**635
Recontres Internationales de Danse
　Contemporaine, **2:**466
record industry, **2:**620, 627
recreational dance. *See* folk dance
　history; social dance
"Recruit's Dance," **2:**304
Rector, Eddie, **1:**252, 520,
　6:256, 386
Recüeil de contredances (Feuillet),
　1:89, 90, 91, **2:**255, 256, 591,
　5:621, **6:**124
　Essex translation, **2:**527

Recüeil de danses (Pecour), **1:**355,
　6:124
*Recüeil de danses de bal pour
　l'année 1700* (Feuillet), **3:**172
*Recüeil de danses de bal pour
　l'année 1703* (Feuillet), **1:**91
*Recüeil de danses de bal pour
　l'année 1706* (Feuillet), **1:**90,
　91, **4:**510
*Recüeil de danses de bal pour
　redoua 1708* (Feuillet), **2:**255
Recüeil de danses pour l'année 1719
　(dance collection), **6:**87
Recüeil de nouvelles contredances
　(Dezais), **2:**255
Reda, Mahmoud, **2:**499, **4:**412,
　417, 490
Reda troupe, **4:**412, 417, 490
Red Cloak, The, **3:**318
Red Curtain Up (Grey), **3:**307
Red Dancers, The, **1:**204, **3:**146,
　6:245, 378
Red Detachment of Women, The,
　2:70, 116, *146*, **5:**330, **6:**385
　costumes, **2:**220–221
　Cultural Revolution production,
　　2:137
Reddy, Kamala, **6:**321
Reddy, Raja and Radha, **5:**330–331
Red Earth, **1:**234
Redel, Mariëtte, **5:***530*
Redes, **4:**198
Red Flower, The, **5:**331, **6:**420
Redford, John, **3:**252
Redhead (musical), **3:**54, **6:**327
Redi, Nancy, **5:**342
Redina, Mirra, **2:**15
Redlich, Don, **2:**606, **3:**369, 445,
　4:441
Redman, Don, **6:**256
Redmond, Eugene, **2:**459
Redon, Odilon, **1:**99
redoutes, **2:**62
redowa, **5:**498, 624, **6:**235
Red Poppy, The, **1:**408, 489–490,
　2:11, **5:**331, *458*, **6:**171
　Ballet Russe de Monte Carlo,
　　1:297
　Fayer conducting, **2:**579
　first Czech production, **1:**541
　Gabovich role in creating, **3:**99
　Geltser performance, **3:**128
　Gerber (Nikolai) revival, **5:**466
　Glière score, **1:**297, **3:**186, 187,
　　4:517
　Golovkina performance, **3:**197
　Gusev performance, **3:**327
　Kharkov premiere staging, **6:**225
　Kshessinsky (Iosif) direction,
　　4:67
　Lavrovsky (Leonid)
　　choreography, **2:**579, **3:**197,
　　4:132, **5:**331, **6:**226
　Lepeshinskaya performance,
　　4:148
　Lopukhov production, **4:**225
　Lukom performance, **4:**233
　Moiseyev (Igor) performance,
　　4:444
　Moiseyev (Mikhail)
　　choreography, **5:**470, **6:**225
　"Russian Sailors' Dance," **4:**517
　Semenova performance, **5:**567
　significance in Soviet ballet,
　　3:187, **4:**283, **5:**458
　Ulanova performance, **6:**226, 227
　Youskevitch performance, **6:**425
　Zakharov version, **6:**442
Red Roses and Red Noses (Berners),
　1:438

Red Shoes, The (film), **3:**356, **4:**324,
　325, **5:**331–333, 588–589,
　6:119
Red Shoes, The (Hassreiter ballet),
　1:540
Red Silk Dance, The, **1:***165*
Red Steps, **5:***219*
Red Whirlwind, The, **3:**137, **4:**225,
　5:457
Red Wine in Green Glasses, **2:**284,
　6:135
Reed, Carlynn, *as contributor*,
　4:212–213
Reed, Janet, **2:**160, 568, **4:**10, **5:**51,
　359, 398
　Interplay performance, **6:**279
　New York City Ballet roles,
　　4:616, 617
　San Francisco Ballet, **5:**511,
　　512, 513
　Swan Lake performance, **6:**34
Reed, Leonard, **1:**252, **6:**257, 386
Reed, Thomas, **2:**336
reed-pipe dances, **5:**646, *646*,
　663–664, *664*
reel, **5:**333–334
　clogging variant, **2:**179, 180
　England, **3:**238, 239
　Hey, **3:**361
　Iceland, **3:**435
　Ireland, **3:**517
　Norway, **4:**671
　Scotland, **3:**243–245, 247, 249
　as step dance, **5:**695, *696*, 698
　Wales, **3:**250
"Reel, The" (*The King's Volunteers
　on Amager*), **1:**399
"Reel of Tulloch, The," **3:**243–244, 249
Reese, Kitty, **3:**214
Reformation, **2:**166, 540
　See also Protestantism
Refuge of Virtue, The, **4:**451
Refugiados a Ras de Suelo, **2:***126*
Refus global, Le (Les Automatistes
　manifesto), **2:**39, 43, 49
Regal, Betty, **1:**456
Regan, Jayne, **4:**668
Regan, John and Jean, **3:**520
Regatta, **1:**146
Rège, Paul de, **3:**80
Regel, Heinrich, **3:**346
Regeling, Siegfried, *as
　photographer*, **3:**58
Regenmakers, **4:**595
reggae, **1:**415, **3:**573–574, **5:**634
Reggini, Margherita, **2:**208
Reggio Emilia, Italy. *See*
　Aterballetto
Regional Ballet Festival
　Association. *See* National
　Association for Regional
　Ballet
Regional Dance America, **1:**39,
　6:266
regional dance companies, U.S. *See
　under* United States of
　America; *specific companies*
Regitz, Hartmut, **3:**162
　as contributor, **1:**441–442, **5:**557
Reglas de danzar (anonymous),
　1:54
*Reglas utiles para los aficionados a
　danzar* (Ferriol y Boxeraus),
　5:676
Règles pour faire des ballets
　(Pecour), **4:**173
Regli, Francesco, **1:**500, **2:**208
Régnier, Henry, **6:**217
Rehearsal, The (Degas), **1:**6
Rehearsal, The (de Mille
　documentary piece), **2:**374

Rehman, Indrani, **5:**330, 331
Rehnberg, Mats, **6:**36, 49
Reich, George, **1:**305
Reich, Steve, **1:**59, 412, **2:**119, 358, 359, 585, **4:**596, **5:**367, 683
Reich, Wilhelm, **1:**469
Reid, Albert, **6:**356
Reid, Derek, **2:**42
Reid, Dianne, **1:**217
Reid, Rex, **1:**208, 230
Reigen, **2:**120
Reign of Terror (1792), **2:**72, **3:**67
Reilly, E. B., **6:**239
Reilly, Sheila, **4:**602
Reilly, Theresa M., *as contributor,* **2:**213–233
Reiman, Elise, **1:**64, 96, 483, **2:**161, **3:**57, **5:**570–571
Reimann, Aribert, **1:**456
Reinach, Baron de, **2:**368, **6:**62
Reinagle, Alexander, **6:**232
Reine-Adelaide, Odile, **6:**260
Reine de Golconde, La, **2:**415
Reine des Îles, La, **5:**101
Reine verte, La (Béjart), **1:**405
Reinhardt, Max, **1:**85, **3:**163, 596, **4:**126, **5:**493, **6:**161
  Ibsen (Lillebil) coaching, **4:**674
  lighting innovations, **4:**190
  Losch association, **4:**229
  Midsummer Night's Dream productions, **4:**60, 229, **5:**931, **6:**29, 449
  Nijinska choreographic work, **4:**636
  Swaine association, **6:**29
  Wiesenthal association, **6:**387, 388
Reinhart, Charles, **1:**79, 90, **3:**572, **6:**415
Reinhart, Stephanie, **1:**79, 80
Reinholm, Gert, **1:**436, **5:**334
  Berlin Opera Ballet, **1:**436, **3:**150, 155–156, 318
Reinhold, H. A., **2:**631
Reinking, Ann, **6:**284, 288
reinlender, **4:**671, *671*
Reinshausen, Fedor, **1:**486
Reinthaller, Eva, **6:**66
Reisen, Maria, **1:**489, **3:**207
Reisenhofer, Heinrich, **5:**657
Reisinger, Julius, **1:**486, **5:**455, **6:**115
  Swan Lake choreography, **6:**29, 30, 32
Reisinger, Václav, **5:**245
Reisner, Bohumil, **2:**309
Reiss, François, **3:**85
Reiter, Susan, *as contributor,* **3:**390–391, **4:**63, **6:**401–402
Reiter-Soffer, Domy, **2:**404, **3:**520, 532
Reitz, Dana, **1:**373, **3:**447, 448, **5:**128, 440
Reizinger, V., **2:**176
rejang, **1:**175, **3:**476, 477, *478*
rejdovák, **2:**301
rejog, **2:**231
Réjouissance, **4:**602
Relâche, **1:**134–135, 244, **2:**287, **5:**334–335, 525, 526
  Ballets Suédois, **1:**327–328, **2:**603, **3:**614
  film use, **2:**603, **3:**620
  Joffrey revival, **3:**614, *616*
  Picabia modernist set design, **3:**72, *616,* **5:**545
  Satie score, **4:**516
Relative Calm, **2:**120
Relay, The, **2:**355, **4:**218, **6:**135

release technique, **3:**272
relevé, **1:**336, **5:**208–209
religious dance. *See* liturgical dance; ritual and dance
Relph, George. *See* Little Tich
Remar, Stanislav, **5:**614
Rembrandt, **1:**141
Remember, **5:**462
Remington, Mamye, **5:**368
Reminiscence, **4:**227
Reminiscences of a Hardly Used Clothes Line, The, **6:**67
Reminiscences of Old Puya, **2:**159
Remislavsky, Kasimir, **1:**430
Remisoff, Nicolas, **1:**483, **5:**60
Remley, Rob, **2:**289
Re-Moves, **5:**439
Remšar, Tatjana, **6:**437, 438
Rémy, Marcel, **1:**43
Remy Charlip Dance Company. *See* Charlip, Remy
Ren-ai Butō-ha, **6:**90
Renaissance Ballet, **2:**565, **5:**465
Renaissance Ballroom, Harlem, **6:**256
Renaissance court dance. *See* social dance, court and social dance before 1800
Renaissance dance technique, **5:**336–340
  aesthetics, **1:**21–22
  Arbeau dance manual, **1:**103, 104–105
  Arena dance manual, **1:**107
  Balet Comique de la Royne, Le, **1:**275–277
  Caronazano manuals, **2:**204–205
  Caroso manuels, **2:**73–77
  dancing masters, **2:**336–337
  figure dances, **5:**621
  Guglielmo Ebreo da Pesaro manuals, **3:**322–325, 603
  historical notation, **5:**322–325
  intermedio, **3:**509–511
  Italy, **3:**542
  Jewish dancing masters, **3:**527
  technical manuals, **6:**121–122, 349–350
Renaissance fêtes and triumphs, **3:**542, **5:**340–341
  Florentine float, **3:**543
  horse ballet, **3:**381–382
  labyrinthine dances, **4:**107
  makeup, **4:**303–304
  masks, **4:**301, 304
  masque and antimasque, **4:**307–313, **5:**113, 340
  mommerie, **4:**449
  moresca, **4:**460
  scenic design, **5:**533–534
Renaissance theaters, **6:**155–156
Renard, Le, **1:**93, 325, 350, 460
  Dmitriev scenic design, **2:**421
  Idzikowski performance, **3:**441
  Larionov costumes, **4:**124, *124*
  Lifar choreography, **4:**182
  Lopukhov choreography, **4:**225, **5:**457
  Nijinska choreography, **4:**634
  Nijinska performance, **4:**635
  Stravinsky score, **4:**516, 634, **6:**4
Renate Schottelius and the Experimental Group of Contemporary Dance, **1:**112
Renaud, Guillaume, **1:**3
Renaud, Jean (Académie Royale dancing master), **1:**3
Renaud, Jeanne (Canadian dancer), **2:**39, 40, 42, 43, *43,* **3:**232, **6:**131

Renaud, Madeleine, **4:**425
Renaud et Armide, **3:**117, **4:**695, **5:**371, **6:**9
Renault, Michel, **1:**247, **3:**73, **4:**185, 354, **5:**96, **6:**65
Rencher, Derek, **1:**157, **2:**445, *515,* 516, **4:**255, 456, **5:**396, **6:**35, 201
Rencontre, La, **4:**178, **5:**527
Rencontre, ou Oedipe et le Sphinx, **1:**306
Rencontres, Les, **5:**95
Rendez-vous, **1:**306
Rendezvous, Les, **1:**146, 147, 148, 230, **3:**442, **5:**163, **341–342**
  Ashton production, **1:**146, 147, 148, **2:**57, **5:**114, 341, 342, 413, 414, 651
  CAPAB Ballet staging, **2:**57
  Chappell scenic design, **2:**105
  Markova performance, **4:**268
  score, **4:**114
Rendezvous, Les (film), **6:**119
René Blum's Ballets de Monte Carlo. *See* Ballet Russe de Monte Carlo; Ballets Russes de Monte Carlo
René d'Anjou, **2:**202
renga, **4:**83
Renjishi, **1:**361, **4:**533, **5:**593
Renmin Yinyue Chubanshe, **2:**149
Rennell. *See* Bellona
Renner, Suzanne, **4:**627
Renoir, Jean, **2:**53
Rent (musical), **6:**289
rentaks, **3:**500
Renvall, Johan, **1:**74, 77
renversé, **1:**8
Renzi, Marta, **2:**609
Reparateur de Radio, **1:**306
Repercussion Unit, **5:**235
Repertory Theatre, Auckland, **4:**624
Répétz, **5:**472
Repo, Riitta, **2:**635
Report, **6:**44
Reppa, David, **5:**366
Represa, Jorge, *as photographer,* **2:**248, **5:**674
Représentations en musique anciennes et modernes, Des (Ménéstrier), **3:**84
Reprieve, **2:**374
Republic (Plato), **1:**19–20
Requa, Barbara, **3:**574, 577
Requejo, **1:**480
Request Concert, **2:**104
Requiem, **1:**76, 349, 446, **3:**351, 437, **4:**243, 244, 604, **5:**478, **6:**9, 67
Requiem (Verdi), **1:**446, **2:**473–474
Requiem Canticles, **2:**576, **5:**366
Requiem de Verdi, **1:**446
Requiem senza Parola, **1:**446
Rescoldo, **4:**393
research. *See* libraries and museums; methodologies in the study of dance; *subhead* dance research and publication *under specific countries; names of specific programs and writers*
Research and Classification of Dance Motifs (Martin), **3:**407
Resemblances, **5:**313
Respighi, Ottorini, **3:**51, 355
responsa literature, **3:**526, 527, 602, 603
Response Dance, **2:**358
Ress, Sabine, **2:**150, **3:**154

Restoration (England), **3:**253–257
Resurrection, The, **4:**285
Retablo de Maese Pedro, El, **2:**568
Retablo para Romeo y Julieta, Un, **2:**278
Retazos, **2:**281
Réthei Prikkel, Márián, **3:**422
retiré positions, **1:**348
Retour de la Paix, Le, **1:**409
Retour des Lys, Le, **5:**91
Retour de Zéphire, Le, **2:**464
Retour d'Ulysse, Le, **4:**422
Retour du Printemps, Le. See Return of Spring, The
Retrato, **6:**302
Return from the Deep, **5:**386
Return of Spring, The, **4:**276
  Skeaping reconstructed versions, **5:**603, 604, **6:**47
  Taglioni (Filippo) production, **5:**604, **6:**47
Return of the Soldier, The, **5:**57
Return to Mountain, **5:**305, **6:**146
Return to the Strange Land, **4:**1, *82*
Retzsch, Moritz, **5:**141
Reuling, Karl, **6:**297
ReUnion, **3:**446
Revalles, Flora, **1:**482
Revanche, La, **1:**306
Rêve de la Marquise, Le, **3:**21, 22
Rêve de Léonor, Le, **1:**152, **3:**175
Réveil de Flore, Le, **3:**565
Revelations, **1:**55, *56,* 57, **2:**574, **3:**577, **4:**520, **5:**342
revels, **4:**307, **5:**343
Revenge, **5:**59
Revenger's Tragedy (anonymous), **3:**252
révérence, **5:**343–349**
  menuet, **4:**431, 432, 433
  See also etiquette
Reverend, Abbé, **3:**409
Revid, Sonia, **1:**211
Revilla, Lydia, **6:**301
Revista musical chilena (journal), **2:**127
Revitt, Peter, **2:**69
revivalism, **2:**167, 168
Revived Greek Dance (movement), **3:**271
Revolt, **6:**245
Révolte au Sérail, La, **1:**86, **3:**5, **4:**340, **5:**134, **6:**72–73, 74
Revolutionary Étude, **2:**377, **3:**210
Revolutionary March, **6:**88
Revue de Roland Petit, La (revue), **5:**164
Revueltas, Silvestre, **1:**461, **2:**367, **4:**392, **6:**355
Revue Nègre, Le (revue), **1:**252
Rewendt, Margot, **2:**150
Rey, Federico (Freddie Wittup), **1:**117
Rey, Louise, **5:**196
Rey, Mademoiselle, **3:**66
Reyde, Gwendolyn, **6:**276
Reyer, Ernest, **5:**148
Reyes, Alice, **5:**172, 173
Reyes, Benjamin. *See* Villanueva, Benny
Reyes, Denisa, **5:**172, 173
Reyes, Rodolfo, **4:**394
Reyno, Spikerman, **6:**301
Reynolds, Debbie, **5:**21, **6:**287
Reynolds, Greg, **2:**526
Reynolds, Nancy, *as contributor,* **1:**306–307, **2:**85–86, 477, **4:**26–30, 32–34, 262, 330–332, **5:**517–518, **6:**84–86
Reynolds, Newell, **3:**387, **4:**156

Reynolds, Nora, **4:**_156_
Reynolds, Pearl, **2:**458
Reynolds, William C., **2:**386–387, 536–561
  as contributor, **2:**383–384, 536–561
Rezvani, Medjid, **4:**414
Rgveda, **1:**168, **3:**453
Rhallys, Pierre, **2:**112
rhambela phikezano dance, **5:**579
Rhapsodie Espagnole, **1:**305, **5:**554
Rhapsody, **1:**158, _159,_ **6:**66
  Chappell scenic design, **2:**105
  Collier-Baryshnikov dance partnership, **2:**186
  Ivanov production of score, **3:**568
Rhapsody (musical), **4:**179
Rhapsody in Blue (Gershwin), **2:**424, **5:**311
Rhapsody in Blue (Lubovitch ballet), **4:**622–623
Rheinländer dance, **3:**142
Rhif Wyth, **3:**250
Rhine Ballet. *See* Ballet du Rhin Strasbourg
Rhoden, Dwight, **2:**358
Rhodes, **3:**296, 297
Rhodes, Lawrence, **1:**302, 350, **2:**_16,_ 42, **6:**292
  Grands Ballets Canadiens, Les, **3:**233–234, **4:**72
  Harkness Ballet, **3:**342, 343
  Joffrey Ballet, **3:**610
Rhodin, Teddy, **5:**47, 266, **6:**42, 44
Rhombus Media, **6:**133
Rhur-Ort, **4:**204
rhythm-and-blues (R&B) music, **4:**203, 519–520
Rhythme akasak, Le (Brăiloiu), **5:**390
Rhythmen-Zyklus (solo dance), **2:**153
rhythmical gymnastics. *See* eurhythmics
Rhythmic Choir, **5:**497
Rhythm in Joy (Samson), **5:**510–511
Rhythm, Music and Education (Jaques-Dalcroze), **3:**596
Rhythm of a Russian Dance (van Doesburg), **1:**132
Rhythm of Life, **5:**580
rhythmoplastique. *See* plastique
Rhythms of Objects (Carrà), **1:**130
Rhythms of the Bow (Balla), **1:**130
rhythm tap dancing, **6:**100
Riabouchinska, Tatiana, **1:**_205,_ 207, 308, 310, 312, 313, _314,_ 315, 367, **3:**_81,_ **4:**68, **5:**17, **539–350,** **6:**182
  English National Ballet guest performances, **2:**508, 510
  Fokine ballets, **3:**24, 25
  Lichine marriage and dance partnership, **4:**178, **5:**349, 350
Riabov, Vladimir, **6:**436
Riabtsev, Vladimir, **1:**489
Rianne, Patricia, **4:**625, 626
Riaz, Fehmida, **5:**63
Ribbon Dance, **2:**_137,_ **4:**559
ribbon dances, **1:**_165,_ **3:**141
  See also Morris dance
Ribeiro, Paulo, **5:**236
Ribera, Ramón (Fina), **6:**93
Rib of Eve, **1:**68
Ricarda, Ana, **3:**226, **6:**353
Ricaux, Gustave, **1:**246, 251, **4:**107, **5:**95, 132, 690, **6:**119
Ricci, Agnioli, **3:**544, **5:**1
Ricci, Nina, **5:**474

Riccoboni, Luigi, **2:**188, 191, **3:**365, **5:**38, 88
Rice, Edward N., **2:**572
Rice, H. S., *as photographer,* **3:**395, **4:**561
Rice, Marion, **1:**542
Rice, Peter, **5:**394
Rice, Tim, **1:**420, **6:**284
Ricercare (Tetley), **1:**72, **4:**602, **5:**301, **6:**43
Ricercare a Nove Movimenti (Amodio), **1:**82, 196
Richard Coeur-de-Lion, **2:**413
Richard Löwenherz, König von England, **6:**337
Richards, Gryfydd, **3:**250
Richards, Kenneth, *as contributor,* **2:**188–193
Richards, M. C., **2:**286, 288
Richards, Sylvia Pelt, *as contributor,* **6:**375–377
Richardson, David, **1:**77
Richardson, Philip (P. J. S.), **5:**351
  archives, **4:**164
  on Bedells, **1:**400
  Camargo Society founding, **2:**397, **3:**265, 285, **5:**351
  dance scholarship, **3:**282
  Dancing Times column, **3:**284, **5:**351
  on de Valois, **2:**395, **5:**351
  English ballet advocacy, **2:**396, **3:**263, **5:**351
  on Espinosa (Édouard), **2:**525
  Royal Academy of Dancing founding, **2:**395, **5:**351
  on Volinine, **6:**348
Richelieu, Cardinal, **1:**286, **5:**520
Riching's Opera Company, **5:**515
Richmond, Farley
  as contributor, **2:**117–119, **4:**79–81
  as photographer, **4:**424
Richmond, Kevin, **2:**_2,_ 514, **3:**_270_
Richmond, Sir William, **2:**455
Richter, Hans, **2:**516
Richter, Marga, **6:**362
Ricker, Billie, **4:**_201_
Ricker, Willamae, **4:**_201,_ 202
Ricketts, Patsy, **3:**575
Ricketts Circus of Philadelphia, **2:**36, 467
Rico, Pat, **3:**367
ridées, **2:**101
Ride of the Valkyries (Wagner), **3:**92
Riegger, Wallingford, **1:**421, **3:**384, **4:**518, 605, 606, **6:**191, 192
Riel, Franz van, *as photographer,* **5:**122, 125
Riepel, Joseph, **4:**512
Ries, Frank W. D., **3:**183
  as contributor, **4:**433–434, **5:**310–311
Rieti, Vittorio, **1:**298, **2:**254, 401, 408, 410, **5:**641
Rietstap, Ine, **1:**290, **4:**600, **5:**531
  as contributor, **1:**289–290, **4:**586–588, 597–598, **5:**290, 530–531, 618, **6:**375
Rietz, Dana, **1:**215

Rif dancing, _468,_ **4:**467
rifle dances, **1:**_40,_ **4:**406, 467, **6:**417
  North Africa, **4:**406, **6:**206
  Turkey, **6:**211, _212_
Rift, **3:**578
Riga Operetta Theater, **4:**128
rigaudon, **2:**64, **3:**65, **4:**510, 511, **5:**40, 113, 169, **351–352**
Rigby, Cormac, *as contributor,* **1:**453–454
Rigg, Lynn, **2:**373
Riggins, Lloyd, **1:**_511,_ **5:**396, _432,_ 433
Rignold, Hugo, **4:**117
Rigo, J., **2:**_201_
Rigoletto (Verdi), **2:**369
Rigonda, **4:**127
Rihani, Amin, **4:**416
Riisager, Knudåge, **2:**535–536, **4:**118, 125, **5:**294, **352–353,** 429
Rijksleergang voor Danspedagogiek. *See* Autonome Hogeschool Antwerpen
Riksföreningen för Folkmusik och Dans, **6:**37
Riksteatern, **2:**263–264, **6:**45
Rikud, **4:**220
Rikugi (Zeami), **4:**42
ril (reel), **4:**671
Riley, Bridget, **5:**303
Riley, Daisy, **3:**574
Riley, Terry, **2:**359
Rimbaud, Arthur, **1:**152, **3:**442, 443
Rimmer, William, **4:**30
Rimsky-Korsakov, Nikolai, **2:**73, 82, 404, 407, **4:**429, 430, **6:**115
  Fokine choreographies, **3:**16, 20, 22
  Glazunov as student, **3:**185
  Golovin designs, **3:**196
  Legend of Aziade, The, **5:**123
  Massine choreography, **4:**316
  Schéhérazade score, **5:**556
  Stravinsky as student, **6:**3
Rimsky-Korsakov Conservatory of Music, Saint Petersburg, **1:**91, **5:**480
Rinaldi, Antonio (Il Fossano), **1:**365, **3:**545, **4:**276, **5:**89, 353, **353,** 451
Rinaldo and Armida, **1:**153, **3:**358
Rindi, I Wayan, **4:**265
ringah, **2:**492–493
Ringen, **3:**100
Ringer, Jenifer, **4:**624
Ringer, Rolf Urs, **5:**683
ringgit. See wayang
Ringling Brothers, Barnum & Bailey, **2:**176, **6:**6
Ringo, James, *as contributor,* **4:**417–418
ring shout, **1:**450
Ring um den Ring, **1:**407
Rink, The (musical), **5:**358, **6:**286, 287
Rinker, Kenneth, **2:**608, **6:**152
Rinuccini, Ottavio, **5:**113
Rinuccini, Pierfrancesco, **3:**544
Rio de Janeiro, Brazil, **1:**527, 528–529
  ballet, **1:**532, 533
  capoeira, **2:**58
  Carnival, **1:**527, 530
  Concerto Barocco premiere performance, **2:**193
  dance education, **1:**537
  modern dance, **1:**534

Rio Grande (Ashton ballet), **1:**147, 148, **3:**41, **4:**517
Rio Grande, The (Lambert concert piece), **4:**113, 114
Rioja, Pilar, **3:**11, **5:**353–354, **6:**408
Rioja dances, **1:**376, 377
Riopelle, Françoise, **2:**39, 40, 43, **6:**131
Rio Rita (musical), **4:**420, **5:**310, **6:**273
Rios, Tomas, **4:**222–223
Rio y el Bosque, El, **2:**279, _279_
Ripening Seed, The (Colette), **3:**512
Ris, Otto, **1:**375
Ris et Danceries, **5:**_324,_ 327
r̄ishī, **4:**408
Rising Sun, The, **4:**210
Risley, Professor (Richard Carlisle), **2:**176
Riss Dance Company, **4:**683
Rita, **6:**70
Rita Gauthier, **4:**339
Rite of Spring. *See Sacre du Printemps, Le*
Rites, **4:**120
Rites de Passage, **2:**458
Ritha Devi, **1:**_171,_ **5:**23, 46, **354**
  as contributor, **1:**442–443, **2:**394–395, **3:**658–660, **4:**69–71, 247, 443, **5:**580–581, **6:**421–422
Ritiger et Wenda, **5:**215
ritirate jumps, **1:**341, 347
Ritmografia: L'arte di scrivere la danza (Chiesa), **4:**688
Ritmo Jondo, **3:**403
Ritmo Oriental, **5:**635
Ritorni, Carlo, **6:**338
Ritorno di Ulisse in Itaca, Il, **3:**176, **6:**70
Ritrovata di Due Nobili Amante Jiulietta i Roméo (Porto), **5:**392
Rittenberg, Harald, **4:**128
Ritterballett, **1:**402, **4:**91
Ritter Pázmán (Strauss), **6:**3
Ritual, **2:**57
ritual and dance, **5:354–357**
  cultural context, **4:**365
  definitions, **2:**540
  European folk dance origins, **3:**30, 31, 32
  Haitian Vodun, **6:**346–347
  morescas, **4:**461
  ritual definitions, **5:**354–355
  theatrical, **5:**356–357
  trancelike states, **6:**185–186
  See also liturgical dance; shamanism; *specific countries and peoples*
Ritual Dances of the Province of Santiago (Urrutia Blondel), **2:**127
"Ritual Fire Dance" (Falla), **2:**567
Ritual in Transfigured Time (film dance), **2:**604
"Ritual of Good Fortune," **4:**48
Rituals, **4:**243
Ritu Samhara, **2:**105
Ritus Paganus, **4:**136
Ritz, Roger, **1:**195, **6:**65
Ritz Brothers, **5:**398
Rival Artistes, The (Ducoté), **2:**70
Rivals, The, **2:**11, 15
Rivano, Magaly, **2:**125
Rivarola, María and Carlos, **6:**93, 94
River, The, **1:**59, **2:**4, 245, **3:**306, **6:**402
Rivera, Chita, **2:**458, **5:357–358,** 398, **6:**283, 286

Rivera, Eduardo, **2:**281
River Dance, **3:**518
Rivére, Théodore,, 81
Riverón, Jorge, **2:**278, 279, *279*
    as contributor, **2:**277–280
Riveros, Hilda, **2:**124, 125, 441
Riveros, James, **5:**55
Rivers, Frank, **6:**616
Riverside, **1:**60, **3:**578
Riverside Nights, **1:**145
Rives, Michel, **4:**588
Rivière, Jacques, on *Sacre du
    Printemps*, **5:**488
Rivière, Théodore, **3:**92, **4:**644
Rivoire, Mary, **3:**214, **5:**254
Riwikin, Stockholm, *as
    photographer*, **3:**628
Rizzo, Marlene, **3:**342
RKO Studios, **2:**613, 614
RM Arts, **6:**132
Roach, Max, **3:**621
road dances, **1:**121
Road of Phoebe Snow, The, **1:**395
Road of the Child, **3:**421
Roadrunners, **2:**290, 293
Roads, **5:**287
Road series (films), **2:**615–616
Roaming, **3:**421
*Roaratorio: An Irish Circus on
    Finnegans Wake*, **2:**23, 295,
    4:37, **5:**18
Robatto, Lia, **1:**537
Robbers, The, **1:**518, **5:**319,
    464, 468
Robbins, Jerome, **1:**233, 234, 372,
    391, **2:**361, 463, **3:**343, **5:**97,
    358–368, 437, 513, 597, **6:***174*
    Age of Anxiety, **5:***360*, 361
    American Ballet Theatre, **1:**68,
        70, 74, **5:**359–360, 364, 367
    Archive of the Recorded Moving
        Image, **4:**167
    Balanchine association, **5:**359,
        361, 363, 364, 367
    Batsheva Dance Company, **3:**532
    Bernstein collaboration, **1:**438,
        439, **4:**518, 518–519, **5:**360,
        362, 366
    Bolender performances, **1:**478
    as Broadway director-
        choreographer, **6:**281–282
    Broadway musicals, **5:**358,
        359–360, *360*, 361, 362, 363,
        364, 366, **6:**277, 279, 281–282,
        284, 288–289
    Cage, The, **3:**663, 664, **5:**358,
        361–362, 407
    character dance, **2:**108
    Concert, The, **2:**333, **4:**137, **5:**358
    Copland score, **2:**197
    Dance Theatre of Harlem
        repertory, **2:**334
    Dybbuk (Dybbuk Variations),
        1:439, **5:**366
    Fiddler on the Roof, **3:**605,
        5:363, 364
    Film and Videotape Archive,
        4:363
    film choreography, **5:**362–363
    Firebird revision, **3:**3
    Goldberg Variations, The, **4:**24,
        273, **5:**358, 364–365
    Guests, The, **5:**361
    Hollywood musicals, **2:**618
    Interplay, **1:**338, **2:**376, **5:**360,
        6:279
    In the Night, **4:**273, 285,
        5:364, 365
    Israeli dance survey, **3:**449, 532

jazz dance, **2:**108, **3:**599, 600,
    4:519
Jerome Robbins' Broadway, **6:**288
Joffrey Ballet revivals, **3:**614
Kirkland roles, **4:**24
Kriza roles, **4:**63
Labanotation of works, **3:**427
Loquasto costumes, **4:**226
"Mack Sennett Ballet" (*High
    Button Shoes*), **6:**279, *279*
Makarova roles, **4:**248, *248*
Martins roles, **4:**273
McBride roles, **4:**345
New York City Ballet, **4:**29, 608,
    608–609, 614–615, 618–619,
    621, 623, **5:***360*, 361, 364–367,
    6:65
    administration, **4:**621
    resignation as co-ballet master,
        4:623
Noces, Les, **1:**70, **2:**244, **5:**358,
    364, 367, **6:**43
Other Dances, **1:**74, **4:***248*,
    5:*364*, 366
partnering, **5:**104
pas de deux, **5:**107
Pas de Trois, **4:**269
Pied Piper, **2:**197, **4:**608, **5:**358
Plisetskaya roles, **5:**206
Prodigal Son performance, **5:**264,
    264, 361
Ravel piano concerto
    choreography, **5:**316
Romeo and Juliet performance,
    5:397
Rosenthal lighting, **5:**407
Royal Ballet repertory, **5:**417
Royal Danish Ballet repertory,
    5:431
Royal Swedish Ballet staging,
    6:43
"Small House of Uncle Thomas"
    (*The King and I*),
    choreography, **5:**362, **6:**281
as Soviet choreographic
    influence, **5:**460
television productions, **6:**138
Tharp collaboration, **6:**153
Tomasson roles, **6:**174, *174*
Verdy roles, **4:**617–618
Watermill, **2:**245, **3:**538, **5:**358,
    363, 365–366
West Side Story, **3:**600, **5:**358, 398,
    6:281–282
    See also *Afternoon of a Faun*;
        Dances at a Gathering; *Fancy
        Free*
Robbins, Martha E., *as contributor*,
    5:209–210
Robbins, Sonya, **5:**359
Robe à la Guimard, **3:**326
Roberday, François, **4:**234
Robert, Adrien, **2:**339
Robert, Grace, **4:**177
Robert, Louis Léopold, **2:**80, **5:**141
Roberta (film), **1:**193
Roberta (musical), **6:**276
Robert and Bertram, or Two Thieves,
    4:66
Robert Bruce (Rossini opera), **4:**341
Robert Joffrey Ballet Concert. *See*
    Joffrey Ballet
Robert le Diable (Meyerbeer opera),
    1:86, 459, 477, **3:**69, **5:**35, 93,
    6:72, *158*
    "Ballet of the Nuns," **4:**514, **6:**58
    dell'Ara re-creation, **2:**369
    Lacotte re-creation, **4:**108
    Fitzjames (Louise) role, **3:**4
    Lecomte performance, **4:**137, 139

Lee performance, **4:**139
Monplaisir troupe's American
    performances, **4:**454
Noblet's *divertissement*
    performance, **4:**647
scenic design, **2:**172
Roberts, Denise, **5:**679
Roberts, James, **5:**86
Roberts, Joan, **6:**278
*Robert Schumann's
    "Davidsbündlertänze"*, **1:**266,
    268, **2:**314, 577, **4:**274,
    614, 618
Robertson, Allen, *as contributor*,
    4:450–452, **5:**439–441,
    6:145–147
Robertson, Pandora, **5:***24*
Robies, Miguel, **1:**114
Robilant, Claire de, **2:**127,
    4:163, 171
Robin, Jean, **1:**306
Robinson, Alma, **1:***57*
Robinson, Bill ("Bojangles"), **2:**615,
    4:419, **5:368–369**, 601, **6:***98*,
    100, 141, 142, 244, 256, 272,
    276, 284, 317, 386
Robinson, Cecily, **5:**225, 312, 313,
    650, 651
Robinson, Chase, **2:**53
Robinson, Clarence, **1:**520, **6:**257
Robinson, Harold, **4:**626
Robinson, Henry R., **2:**71, **5:**258
Robinson, Jacqueline, **3:**76, 83
    as contributor, **2:**466, **3:**75–77,
        83–84
Robinson, Tedd, **2:**43
Robinson, Thomas, **1:**523, **3:**376
Robinson Crusoe, **1:**495, **3:**358,
    6:137
Robinson Crusoe dans Son Isle
    (c.1791), **1:**124
Robitaille, Louis, **3:***234*
Robledo, Antonio, **6:**28
Robles, María Teresa, **5:***275*
Robot, **6:**263
robot dancing, **1:**538
Roboz, Ágnes, **3:**419
Robst, Robert, **4:**92
Roca, Renée, **3:**433
Roche, David, **1:**218
Roche, Pierre, **3:**92
Rochefort, Jean, **4:**588
Rochefoucauld, Sosthène de La,
    5:91
Rochemont, Ben de, **1:**290, **2:**470
Rochepkina, Nadia, **2:**278
Rochois, Marie le, **4:**235
Rochon, Roger, **6:***130*
Rock, Judith, **4:**213
Rockabye (Beckett), **4:**332
rock-and-roll, **1:**359, **2:**618, **4:**203,
    519, **6:**249, 250
    musical theater, **6:**284, 288
    Naharin choreography, **4:**532
    nontouch dancing, **5:**630,
        631, 633
Rock and the Spring, The, **3:**404
Rockefeller, John D., **6:**242
Rockefeller, Nelson, **1:**64, 280
Rockefeller Foundation, **2:**374
Rockettes, **4:**24, **5:**247, 289–290,
    289, **6:**242, 268, 285
rocking. *See* break dancing
Rocking Horse, The, **6:**175
rocking waltz (*valse chaloupée*),
    1:95
Rock Steady Crew, **1:***538*
Rockwell, John, **6:**153
Rod, Antoine, **2:**47

Rodarte, Pablo, **3:**11
rodat dance, **3:**504, **4:**250
Rodchenko, Aleksandr, **3:**48
Rode, Lizzie, **2:***284*
Rode, Tomaž, **6:***437*
Rodenbach, Georges, **3:**92
Rodeo, **5:369–370**, **6:**204
    Ballet Russe de Monte Carlo
        premiere, **1:**297, **2:**197, **5:**369,
        6:278
    character dancing, **2:**108, 197
    Copland score, **2:**196, 197, **4:**518
    costume design, **2:**245
    de Mille performance, **5:**369
    de Mille production, **1:**297,
        2:108, 197, 245, 373, **3:**87,
        4:369, **5:**369, 435, **6:***247*, 278
    Franklin performance, **3:**87,
        5:369
    Joffrey Ballet revival, **3:**614
    scenic design, **5:**616
    significance in American ballet,
        1:302
Roders, Jennifer, **5:**531
Rodgers, Richard, **1:**271, 482, **5:**72,
    6:272
    See also Rodgers and Hammerstein;
        Rodgers and Hart
Rodgers, Rod, **6:**259
Rodgers and Hammerstein, **2:**619,
    4:3, **5:**72, 362, 369, **6:**281, 288
Rodgers and Hart, **1:**271, **4:**334,
    6:449
Rodice, Attilia, **5:**529
Rodin, Auguste, **3:**71, **5:**181, 259,
    261, **370–371**
    on *Après-midi d'un Faune, L'*,
        1:99
    Fuller friendship, **3:**93–94, 95
    Hanako busts, **3:**338
    sculpture of Nijinsky, **1:**128, *128*,
        5:370
    Yakobson choreography, **5:**469
Rodolfo, **1:**427, 500
Rodolphe, Jean-Joseph, **4:**346, 347,
    5:270, **371–372**
Rodrigo, Florrie, **1:**289, **4:**590, 598
Rodrigo, Joachín, **2:**434
Rodrigues, Alfred, **2:**58, **3:**59, 60,
    5:*54*, 225, *529*, 650, 652
Rodriguez, Antonio and Yolande,
    1:212
Rodriguez, Beatrice, **3:**615
Rodriguez, Elizabeth, **2:**126
Rodriguez, Jon, **2:**357, **6:**266
Rodriguez, Marcelo, **2:**126
Rodríguez, Nélida, **6:***94*
Rodríguez, Rodolfo, **2:**277, **6:**324
Rodríguez, Zhandra, **6:**323,
    323, 324
Rodríguez Cravanzola, Ana Rosa,
    6:302–303
Rodríguez de Ayestaran, Flor de
    María, **6:**301
Rodríguez Turchi, María, **4:**390
Rodzinski, Artur, **1:**438
Roehampton Institute, London,
    3:284, 285, **4:**164
Roemers, Willy, **5:**531
Roempke, Gunilla, **6:**43–44, 50
Roerich, Nikolai, **1:***321*, **2:**241,
    3:16, 196, **4:**34, **5:**372
    Sacre du Printemps design, **2:**242,
        4:643, 644, **5:**327, 372, 487,
        542, **6:**4
Roessler, Anton, **2:**306
Roessler, Tehilla, **3:**531
Roger, Edith, **4:**677
Roger, Monsieur, **6:**372, 373
Roger et Bradamante, **5:**693

Rogers, Ginger, **1:**_191_, 193, 194, 432, **2:**80, 250, _250_, 584, 614, _615_, **4:**239, **5:372–373**, 630, **6:**101
Rogers, Helen Priest, **4:**95
Rogers, Houston, _as photographer_, **2:**243, 515, **3:**513, 567, **4:**584, **5:**417, 613, **6:**33, 190
Rogers, Lela, **5:**372
Rogers, Natalie, **2:**566
Rogers, Wendy, **5:**440
Roger-Viollet, _as photographer_, **5:**92, 93, **6:**353
Rogge, Bianca, **2:**44, 47
Rogge, Florence, **5:**290
Rogneda, **1:**408, **2:**502
Rogoff, Tamar, **4:**209
Rogowski, Ludomir, **6:**441
Rogue Song (film), **5:**310
Rohauer, Raymond, **1:**432
Roi Candaule, Le, **2:**525, **5:**151, _151_, 154, 157, 278
Roi Carotte, Le (Offenbach), **2:**60
Roi des Gourmets, **6:**143
Roi d'Yvetot, Le, **5:**148
Roi et le Fermier, Le, **1:**88, **4:**174
Roi Nu, Le, **2:**113, 314, 401
Roi S'Amuse, Le (Hugo), **2:**369
Rojas, Carmen, **1:**94
Roje, Ana, **5:**676, **6:**432
Rök, **2:**501
Rokdim (magazine), **3:**535
Roklin, G. D., **2:**328
Rokurin ichiro (Konparu), **4:**42
Roland, **3:**106, **4:**109, 235, **5:**34, 38, **6:**11, 330, 331
Roland, Ashley, **5:**_187_
Roland, Catherine Violanta, **3:**394
Roland, Elina, **3:**179
Roland, Madame, **5:**232
Roland and Morgana, **2:**414
Rolandi Collection, Venice, **4:**162
Roland-Manuel, Alexis, **5:**237, 526, **6:**5
Rolf, Ida, **1:469–470**
Rolf Blaaskæg, **5:**424, 552
Rolla, **2:**82, **4:**258
Rolla, Allessandro, **5:**276, 277
Roller, Alfred, **1:**131
Roller, Andreas, **1:**392, **4:**211, 280, **5:**156
Roller, Franz Anton, **3:**159
Rollers, **5:**54
roller skates, **1:**455
Rollin, Charles, **1:**284
Rolling Stones (music group), **2:**1, **4:**220
Rollow, Mardi, _as contributor,_ **1:**39–42, **4:**464–469, 662–666, **5:**49–50, **6:**205–207
Roman, Gil, **1:**292
Roman, Johan Helmich, **6:**47
romana, **5:**384
Roman Catholicism, **2:**537
  antidance writers, **2:**167
  Argentine dance, **1:**108–109
  ballet de collège, **1:**282–284, **2:**168
  Brazilian-African syncretized dance, **1:**526–527, 529, 530, 531
  Chilean dance, **2:**121–122
  dance prohibitions, **2:**165
  early church, **2:**162–164
  European traditional dance, **2:**540
  Guatemalan dance, **3:**319
  hostility toward _commedia dell'arte,_ **2:**189
  hostility toward Grands Ballets Canadiens, 227, 228
  hostility toward pantomimes, **5:**74
  Inquisition dance prohibitions, **4:**386, 664
  Irish dance, **3:**516
  liturgical drama staging, **5:**533
  Mexican dance, **2:**194, **4:**386, 388–389, **6:**416
  Middle Ages, **2:**162–164, 168, **3:**541
  modern era, **2:**167, 168
  Native American syncretism, **4:**557, 558
  Philippines dance, **2:**230–231
  ritual fan, **2:**569
  Yaqui dance, **6:**416
  See also Christianity and dance
Romance, **2:**36
Romance of the Infanta, The, **4:**56
Romance of the Rosebud, The, **2:**447
Romance of the Yarn-Washing Girl, **4:**76
Roman Empire, **3:**540–541, **5:373–378**
  Atellan farce, **5:**376
  cheironomia misinterpretation, **2:**116
  costume, **2:**234, **5:**376
  as dance costume influence, **2:**238, 239
  early Christian views of dance, **2:**163
  Etruscan influence, **5:**373–374
  feather fans, **2:**569
  festivals, **5:**376–377
  Greco-Roman period, **3:**294–296, 541, **5:**374–375, 376
  kordax performances, **4:**44
  labyrinth dances, **4:**106
  literary dramas, **5:**375–376
  mime, **4:**423, 426–428
  music, **4:**499–500
  North African dance, **4:**662–663, 664
  orchestra, **5:**42
  pantomimus, **5:**72–74, **6:**155
  theaters, **6:**155
  See also Byzantine Empire
Romani, Petro, **3:**176
Romania, **5:378–389**
  folk dance, **2:**101, _101, 548, 553,_ **5:379–384**
  Israeli hora origins, **3:**528
  notation systems, **4:**691–692, **43:**692–693
  as theatrical dance influence, **5:**385
  vocal sounds, **3:**38
  folk dance research and publication, **5:**263–264, **390–391**
  libraries and museums, **4:**162
  theatrical dance, **2:**343–344, **5:384–390**
  "Romanian educated dance" system, **5:**263, 385
Romanian Opera of Bucharest. _See_ Bucharest Opera
Romanian Rhapsody, **2:**343, **5:**386
Romanoff, Dimitri, **1:**65, 67, **4:**56, 460, **5:**166, **391**
Romanotation (Proca-Ciortea system), **4:**691–692
Romanotation (Vasilescu system), **4:**692–693
Romanov, Boris, **1:**49, 301, **5:391–392,** 642
  in Argentina, **1:**110

Ballets Russes de Monte Carlo choreography, **1:**309, **2:**105
  Goncharova designs, **3:**199
  Metropolitan Opera Ballet, **4:**382, 457, **5:**391
  Nutcracker, The, **5:**14
  Petrouchka choreography, **3:**51
  Prokofiev, Sergei, **5:**267
  Rome Opera Ballet, **4:**457, **5:**392, 399
  Russian Romantic Ballet, **5:**17
  Volynsky's criticism of, **6:**351–352
Romanov, Roman, **5:**384
Romanova, Maria, **1:**48, 90, **6:**349
Romanovsky, Anton, **4:**420
Romanovsky, Yakov, **5:**470
Romanow, **6:**70
Romanowski, Anton, **2:**343
Roman Scandal (film), **1:**433
Romans XII (dance group), **4:**213
Romantic Adventure of an Italian Ballerina and a Marquis, A, **3:**199
Romantic Age, **2:**425, **4:**63, 269
Romantic Ballet in England, The (Guest), **3:**321
Romantic Ballet in France, The (Guest), **3:**321
Romantic era
  Adam ballet music, **1:**9, 10
  art and dance, **1:**127, 129, **2:**103–104
  Austrian ballet, **1:**238
  ballet blanc ("white scenes"), **2:**202, 207, **4:**116, 138, 304, **6:**74, 189
  Bournonville composers, **1:**514
  Cerrito, Fanny, **2:**93–95
  as character dancing high point, **2:**107
  characteristics and motifs, **2:**200, 202, 203, 207, 239, **3:**180, **6:**57
  costumes, **2:**239–241, **6:**57
  dance aesthetics, **1:**23
  dance reconstruction, **5:**328
  Didelot ballets as forerunners, **4:**278, 280
  Elssler (Fanny) as sensual aspect of, **2:**440, 502, 503, **5:**89
  English ballet, **3:**260
  folklorism, **2:**538, **3:**29–30, 32
  Fracci as modern personification of, **3:**59–60, _60_
  French popular theater, **3:**68
  Gardel (Pierre) ballets as precursors, **3:**118
  gas lighting effects, **4:**189, **5:**538–539, **6:**57, 58
  German ballet, **3:**145
  Giselle epitomizing, **2:**201, 203, **3:**69, 177, 179, 180
  Guest histories, **3:**282, 321
  Italian ballet, **3:**547, _548,_ 557–558
  Lacotte reconstructions, **4:**108
  leading ballerinas, **5:**89
  Lecomte (Hippolyte) costumes as forerunners, **4:**138
  mad scenes, **3:**180, _181_
  makeup conventions, **4:**302, 304, 305
  Mazilier roles, **4:**340
  national culture movement, **3:**29–30
  notation systems, **4:**685–686
  Paris Opera Ballet, **2:**202, **3:**69, **4:**340, **5:**92–94
  Pas de Quatre, **1:**103–104, **2:**103–104, **5:**108–109
  pointe work, **2:**239, **3:**69, 130, 547, _548,_ **6:**57

popularity of Scottish themes, **2:**474, 475
  prints and drawings, **5:**258, 261
  Russian ballet, **5:**454–455, 480
  scenic design, **5:**537–542, _539_
  Schanne's style personifying, **5:**553
  shadow dance, **5:**29
  social dances, **5:**624, 625
  Swan Lake second act as climax, **3:**565
  Swedish ballet, **6:**39–40
  Sylphide, La, **2:**202, 207, **3:**69, 547, _548,_ **4:**657, **6:**57–58
  Sylphides as Diaghilev's homage to, **3:**16
  Sylphides motif, **6:**60, 61, 62
  Taglioni (Marie) personifying, **2:**239, 369, 502, 503, **3:**547, _548,_ **4:**340
  technical manuals, **6:**126
  Three Graces (Baillie) lithograph, **5:**89
  tutu, **5:**241, **6:**161, 216–217
  Warsaw Ballet, **5:**216, 217, **6:**365
Romantic Rosette, **2:**_633_
Romanyuk, V., **5:**595
Romberg, Sigmund, **6:**271, 273, 280–281
Rome, ancient. _See_ Roman Empire
Rome, Italy, **3:**553
Roméca, **2:**202
Romeev, K., _as photographer,_ **6:**306
Romeo and Juliet, **5:392–399**
  Aldous performance, **1:**38
  Alonso (Alberto) choreography, **2:**277
  Alonso (Alicia) performance, **1:**49
  American Ballet Theatre repertory, **1:**76
  Ananiashvili performance, **1:**83, _84_
  Araiz versions, **1:**103, **5:**269, 398–399
  Ashton production, **1:**153–154, 158, **2:**_513,_ 514, **3:**269, **4:**65, 125–126, **5:**269, **394–395,** _395,_ 431, 433, 553, 554, 555, **6:**399
  Aterballetto repertory, **1:**83
  Augustyn performance, **1:**201
  Balanchine versions, **5:**398
  Bartholin production, **5:**_554_
  Basel Ballet repertory, **1:**375
  Baylis (Nadine) design, **1:**394
  Béjart production, **1:**292, 405, **4:**335, **5:**398
  Beriozoff production, **1:**430, **5:**_652,_ 653
  Berlioz music, **1:**83, 405, **2:**278, **5:**392, 398
  Berman design, **1:**67, 437, **2:**244, **5:**397, 547
  Bessmertnova performance, **1:**440, **5:**399
  Bey performance, **1:**442
  Biagi choreography, **1:**446
  Blair performance, **1:**459
  Bosl performance, **1:**500
  Bournonville staging, **1:**507
  Boyarchikov choreography, **1:**518, **5:**471
  Bruhn and Fracci balcony scene, **5:**401
  Changa choreography, **4:**127
  Chase performance, **2:**112
  Chauviré performances, **2:**114
  Christensen (Willam) choreography, **5:**398
  Cocteau staging, **2:**183, **3:**394

Collier performace, **2:**186
Cranko production, **2:**39, 125, 266, 267, *267,* **3:***150,* 350, 616, **4:**73, 542, **5:**394, 395–396, 405, 565, **6:**9, 142
Dantzig productions, **2:**347, *347,* **3:**344, **5:**436
Delius music, **1:**67, 68, **5:**392, 397
Diaghilev production, **1:**135
Dowell performance, **2:**444
Dyk version, **2:**472
Farron character role, **2:**578
first historically significant production, **5:**392
first staging of Prokofiev score, **4:**132
Galeotti production, **3:**105, **5:**392, 424
Georgiadis design, **3:**136, **5:**396, 405
Gogół production, **3:**192
Grigorovich production, **1:**492, **3:**309, **5:**399
Harangozó production, **3:**341
Haydée performance, **3:**350
Herczog production, **1:**308
Joffrey Ballet revival, **3:**616
Karsavina performance, **3:**656
Kasatkina and Vasiliov choreography, **4:**335, **5:**472
Kaye performance, **3:**663
Kehlet acting technique, **3:**668
Kirkland performance, **4:**24
Kondratieva performance, **4:**38
Kronstam performance, **4:**65
Kun performance, **4:**74
Kūra performance, **4:**77
Kylián version, **4:**593
Laing performance, **4:**110
Lambert score, **4:**113
Larsen performances, **4:**125–126
Lavrovsky (Leonid) productions, **1:***488,* 491, 493, **2:**579, **3:**99, **4:**132, 133, 284, 335, **5:**392, **393–394,** 458, 571, **6:***227,* 398, 399
Lavrovsky (Mikhail) performances, **4:**133
Leventhal design, **4:**153–154
Liepa (Andris) performance, **4:***180,* 181
Lifar production, **4:**184, **6:**117, 119, 353
Macdonald production, **4:**238
Machov choreography, **4:**239
MacMillan production, **1:**459, **2:**186, 444, **3:**136, **4:**24, *241,* 242, 244, 248, **5:**394, 396, *396,* 574, 640, **6:**43, *43*
Makarova performance, **4:**248
Markova performance, **4:**269
Maximova performance, **4:**335
Němeček production, **4:**584
Neumeier production, **3:**338, 668, **5:**394, 396–397, 432
Nijinska choreography, **4:**113, **5:**398, 637, **6:**196
Nureyev production, **2:**511, 513, 514, **3:**46, 60, **5:**6, 7, *7,* 269, 394, 396, 398
Page choreography, **5:**59
Panov production, **1:***413,* **5:**422
Parlić choreography, **5:**101
Plisetskaya performance, **5:**204, *206*
popularity with Soviet provincial companies, **5:**463
Prokofiev score, **1:**103, 153, 446, 518, 541, **2:**266, 347, **3:**309, 393, **4:**132, 133, 517, **5:**268, 392–394, 395, 398, 401, 422

Psota choreography and performance, **1:**541, **5:**269, 393
Robbins's contemporary version, **3:**599, 600, **5:***361,* 363, 393, 398
Rose design, **5:**405
Royal Swedish Ballet repertory, **5:**396, **6:**43, *43*
Schilling production, **5:**557
scores, **5:**392, 398
Seregi staging, **3:**418
Sergeyev performance, **5:**571
Seymour performance, **5:**574
Shakespeare's play as inspiration, **5:**392, 394, 395, 396, 397
Sokolova role, **5:**637
Somes's mime role, **5:**640
Sophia national opera choreographers, **2:**11
Soviet-era versions, **5:**462, 470
Soviet film, **6:**227
Soviet popularity, **4:**517
Šparemblek performance, **5:**676
Spoerli productions, **5:**682, 685
Staff production, **2:**56, 57, **5:**652, 692
Tchaikovsky score, **5:**392, 398, 399
television productions, **5:**513, **6:**142
Tomasson choreography, **6:**174
Tóth production, **1:**308
Tudor production, **1:**67, 68, **2:**244, 376, **4:**110, 269, **5:**397–398, *546,* **6:**199, 200, 203
Ulanova performance, **4:***281,* **6:**226, 227, *227,* 228, *398*
Valberkh staging, **4:**278, **6:**311
Vinogradov choreography, **4:**153, **5:**471–472, **6:**341, 342
Williams (Petr) scenic design, **6:**399
Williams (Stanley) performance, **6:**399
Wubbe production, **4:**593, **5:**531
Romeo and Juliet (film), **2:**372, **4:**133, **6:**227, 278
Romeo and Juliet (Shakespeare), **1:**439, **3:**253, **4:**132, **5:**362, 392, **6:**281
Roméo et Juliette (Gounod opera), **1:**247, **5:**36
Romeo og Giulietta. See Romeo and Juliet
Rome Opera Ballet, **1:**82, **2:**4, 369, 463, **5:**100, 206, **399–401,** **6:**404
  Bogianckino as director, **3:**552, **5:**401
  Dolin as director, **2:**425, **5:**401
  Milloss as director, **4:**421, **5:**400
  Pistoni as director, **3:**552, **5:**401
  Plisetskaya, Maya, **5:**401
  Radice, Attilia, **5:**288
  Romanov as director, **5:**400
  Terabust, Elisabetta, **6:**143–144
Rome Opera Ballet School, **3:**551, 553, **5:**400, 401
Romeo und Julia und die Finsternis, **3:**154
Romero, Carmencita, **2:**458, **6:**259
Romero, Cesar, **4:**434, **6:**319
Romero, Miguel, **5:**24
Romieu, Auguste, **3:**4
Rommett, Zena, **4:**115
Romoli, Wilfried, **4:**134
Romplis Mude, **3:***500*
rom ritual, **1:**223

Róna, Viktor, **3:**417, 419, **4:***677–678, 678,* **5:401–402**
Ronaldson, James, **4:***540*
Roncal, Virginia, **2:**123
Ronchese, Francisco, **2:**328
Ronda, Lola de, **3:**286, **4:**222
Ronda de Toros, **6:**28
rond de jambe, **5:402–403**
rond de jambe à terre, **1:**344, **5:**402
Ronde, La (Schnitzler), **1:**72, **6:**147
Ronde, La (Tetley ballet), **4:***545,* 546
rondeaux, **4:**500
Ronde des Saisons, La, **6:**443
Rondel, August, **4:**161
Rondella, La, **1:**200
Rondinelli, F., **5:**1
Rondiris, Dimitrios, **3:**300
Rondo, **2:**296, **5:**436
Rondo Capriccioso, **1:**484, **3:**361, **4:**638
Roné, Elvira, **6:**352
ronggeng, **3:**499–500, 502, 503–504, 505, **4:**250, **6:**369
rongo, **2:**492–493
ronquido, **2:**275
Ronsay, Jeanne, **2:**111
Ronström, Owe, **6:**50
Ronzani, Domenico, **1:**238, 499, **2:**60, 81, 587, **4:**339, 464, **5:403–404,** 616, **6:**237
Rood, Arnold, *as contributor,* **2:**262–263
Rood, Robert, **2:**528
Roof Piece, **1:**543, **5:**549, *549*
Rooms, **3:**532, **4:**602, **5:**637, **6:**138
Room Service, **1:**244, **5:**293
Rooney, Mickey, **4:**419, 434
Rooney, Pat, **6:**319
Roope, Clover, **3:**271, **4:**667
Roos, Nel, **4:**598
Roosevelt, Eleanor, **2:**313, **5:**255
Roosevelt, Franklin D., **2:**579, 581, **6:**245
Roosevelt, Theodore, **6:**241
Rootzén, Kajsa, **6:**49
Rope and People (Miró), **1:**135
rope dancing, **2:**174–175, *175,* **5:***448*
  Placide, Alexandre, **5:**198
  Ravel family, **5:**316
Roper, June, **2:**38, 47
Ropes, **1:**124, **3:**612
Roritz, Olga, **2:**514, **5:***232,* 235, *235*
Rosa, **1:**412
Rosa, Hebe, **6:**302
Rosa, María, **3:**9, 10
Rosa, Salvator, **2:**80
Rosa d'Amore, **2:**477, **4:**258
Rosado, Manolo, **5:**172
Rosai, Georgi, **5:**13, 118, 119
Rosalba, or The Masked Ball, **1:**477, **5:**539
Rosalia Chladek Dance Group, **2:**154
Rosalia Chladek International Company, **2:**153
Rosalie (film), **5:**310
Rosalie (musical), **3:**22, **4:**420, **6:**273, *274,* 280–281
Rosalinda, **2:**125, **3:**428, **4:**117, **5:**55, **6:**379
  Balanchine adaptation of Wiesenthal choreography, **6:**388
Rosanova, Berta, **1:**533
Rosario. See Antonio and Rosario
Rosario's Spanish Dance Company, **5:***673*
Rosas, **1:**412, **4:**624

Rosa Silber, **3:**359
Rosati, Carolina, **5:**93, 108, 148, **404–405,** 528, **6:**75
  Corsaire, Le, **1:**10, **2:**206, *206,* 282, **5:**405
  Éléments performance, **3:**315
  Ferraris rivalry, **2:**587, **5:**405
  Fonti performance, **4:**342
  French productions, **3:**70, **4:**353, **5:**404–405
  Pas de Quatre performances, **3:**96, **5:**404
  Quatre Saisons performance, **3:**260, **5:**138, **6:**76
  Russian ballet performances, **5:**455
  Saint-Léon ballets, **5:**500
Rosati, Francesco, **5:**404
Rosato, Genesia, **3:**443, **4:***244,* 456
Roschberg, Paal and Leif, **4:**675
Roscius, Quintus, **5:**374–375
Rose, Bert, **3:**574, 577
Rose, Billy, **4:**269, **5:**531, **6:**279
  Stravinsky commission, **6:**6
Rose, Brian, *as contributor,* **6:**136–141
Rose, Carl, **3:**402
Rose, Francis, **1:**148
Rose, Jürgen, **2:**266–267, 268, **5:405–406**
Rose, Mademoiselle, **2:**174
Rose Colored Dance, **3:**657
Rose d'Amour, **4:**397
Rose des Vents, La, **4:**418, **5:***164*
Rose et le Bouton, La, **3:**426
Rose for Emily, A, **2:**374, **6:**402
Rose from the Garden of Love, The (Pfitzner), **6:**393
Rose Girl, The (musical), **3:**21, **4:**223
Rose Latulippe, **4:**238, *238,* **5:**435, **6:**131
Rose Malade, La, **5:**164, 206
Rose-Marie (Friml), **6:**273
Rose Mourante, La, **5:**123
Rosen, Bernice M., *as contributor,* **3:**426–427
Rosen, Elizabeth, **2:**320
Rosen, Elsa-Marianne von, **2:**283, 284, 385, 387, **3:**105, **4:**245, **5:**266, 294, **406–407,** **6:**44, 47
  Bournonville reconstructions, **4:**285, 380, **5:**406, 433, **6:**59, 404
  Don Juan, **5:**600
  Irene Holm, **5:**553
  Miss Julie performance, **5:**406, *406,* **6:**41
  Royal Danish Ballet choreography, **5:**432
  Royal Swedish Ballet, **6:***41,* 42
Rosen, Heinz, **1:**110, 301, 374, 390, 500, **2:**197, **3:**150, **5:**43
  Cocteau collaboration, **2:**183
  Folkwang Tanztheater, **3:**626, 628
  Josephslegende production, **3:**631
Rosenbach, Ulrike, **1:**140
Rosenberg, Douglas, **1:**81
Rosenberg, Harold, **1:**135, 138
Rosenfeld, Sydney, **6:**269
"Rosenkavalier" section (*Vienna Waltzes*), **4:**612, 631
Rosenthal, Diane J., *as contributor,* **2:**253–254
Rosenthal, Jean, **1:**28, 96–97, **2:**182, 349, 360, 420, **3:**57, **4:**191, **5:**407, **407,** **6:**163
  Cage design, **5:**361
  Graham Company lighting, **3:**216, **4:**191, **5:**407

Rosenthal, Jean, *continued*
  Seraphic Dialogue lighting, **5:**568
  Serenade lighting design, **5:**571
Rose of Margitta, The, **4:**143
Rose of Turaids, The, **4:**127
rose pattern (dance progression), **4:**684
Roses, **6:**110
Roses, Les, **5:**526
Roses and Butterflies, **4:**639
Rose Variations, **2:**513
Roshanara, **1:**482
Ro-Shibari (play), **1:***170*
Rosicrucianism, **4:**89
Rosida, ou Les Mines de Syracuse, **2:**94, **5:**499
Rosière de Gand, La, **3:**620
Rosina, Mademoiselle, **5:**71
Rosina et Lorenzo, **1:**201
Roske-Cho, W. S., **4:**46
Roslavets, Nikolai, **5:**594
Roslavleva, Liubov, **1:**393, 487, **2:**436, **5:**455
  Little Humpbacked Horse performance, **5:***450*
  on Vaganova's legacy, **1:**329
Roslavleva, Natalia, **5:**483, 484
Ross, Bertram, **2:**182, 606, **3:**218, **4:**216, 633, **5:407–408,** 562, 568
Ross, Charles, **1:***244,* **3:***634,* **5:**293
Ross, Elisabeth, **2:**609
Ross, Hal J., **2:**325
Ross, Herbert, **1:**195, 370, **2:**367, 583, **3:**551, **5:**408, 573
  archival material, **4:**168
  Caprichos, **1:**69, **4:**63
  Kaye association, **3:**664
  Nijinsky film, **2:**425, 512, **3:**60, 664, **4:**643, **5:**408
Ross, Jerry, **6:**281
Rosse, Helena, **1:**440
Rosseel, Danny, **5:**423
Rossellat, Robert, **3:**306
Rossen, Jane Mink, *as contributor,* **1:**415–416
Rossen, Keith, **5:**55
Rossi, Domenico, **3:**175, 546, **5:**231
Rossi, Gertrude, **4:**149
Rossi, Giovanni V., **3:**583, 588, 590
Rossi, Luigi, *as contributor,* **5:**528–530
Rossi, Madame, **3:**258
Rossi, Tino, **4:**524
Rossi, Venceslao de, **5:**231
Rossignol, Le, **1:**158, 350, 424, **2:**390, **3:**127
  Grisi-Perrot performance, **3:***259,* 313
  Makarova performance, **4:**249
  Romanov performance, **5:**391
  Stravinsky score, **6:**3
Rossignol et la Rose, Le, **5:**162
Rossini, Gioacchino, **1:**36, 461, 503–504, **2:**14, 409, 435, **4:**341, **5:**36, 517, 528, **6:**197
  as *Boutique Fantasque* influence, **4:**317
  as Hérold influence, **3:**360
  operatic ballets, **4:**514, 657
  See also Guillaume Tell
"Rostiboli" (Domenico), **1:**352
Rostislava, **5:**236, **6:**226
Rostock, Germany, **3:**152, 154
Rostora, Lubov, **2:**253
Rostov, Dmitri, **1:**313, *313,* 315, **3:**25, **5:**265, 400
Rostova, Lubov, **1:**296, 307, 309, **4:**656
Rostrand, Maurice, **5:**438

Rot, **1:**82
Rota, Giuseppe, **1:**238, **2:**81, 282, **4:**339, **5:408–409**
Rota, Nino, **4:**421
Rotardier, Kelvin, **1:**56, *57*
rotation, **1:**8
Rote Mantel, Der, **4:**1
Rothenstein, William, **2:**262
Rothlein, Arlene, **3:**634, 635, **6:**363
Rothlisberger, Max, **6:***454*
Roti (film), **2:**622, **5:**603
rotta, **4:**348
Rotterdam Ballet Ensemble, **4:**591–592
Rotterdam Dance Academy, **3:**391
Rotterdam Dance Center, **4:**593, 596
Rotterdam Dance School, **3:**345
Rotterdamse Dansgroep, **4:**594, 596, 598
rotuma, **5:**80
Rouault, Georges, **1:**316, 325, **2:**242, 245, **4:**33, **5:**264, 265
Roubaix, France, **1:**462, **3:**74
Rouch, Jean, **2:**600, 601, **6:**186
Rouché, Jacques, **3:**72, 81, 320, **4:**183, 185, **5:**95, 96, 563, 678, 690
Roudenko, Lubov, **5:**369
Rouen Opera House, **3:**66
Rouge et Noir, **1:**135, 296, 300, 301, **6:**317
  Franklin performance, **3:**87
  Markova performance, **4:**269
  Massine choreography, **4:**324
  Matisse design, **4:**324, 332
  Shostakovich First Symphony, **4:**517
  Youskevitch role, **6:**425
Rouget, Gilbert, **6:**185
Rough for Theatre I, **4:**332
roughhouse dancing, **6:**316
Rouillier, Quentin, **3:**79, 82
Roulin, Yane-Claude, **4:**209
Roundabout, **3:**342, 610
Round Dance, **4:**561, **5:**240
Round Dances (Gilbert), **5:**223
round dancing, **5:409–410,** 481
  Argentina, **1:**109
  Protestant sectarian objections, **2:**167
  Romania, **5:**379
  Russia, **5:**443, *443,* 449, 473
  See also chain and round dances
Roundelay, **1:**498
Round the Town, **4:**121
Rousanne, Madame, **1:**403, **2:**113, 150, 350, **3:**82, **4:**107, **6:**327
Rouselles, Céleste des. *See* Céleste, Madame
Rousseau, Henri, **1:**141
Rousseau, Jean-Jacques, **1:**517, **2:**51, 352, **4:**173–174, **5:**306, 520, **6:**38
  on forlana, **3:**50
  opera *Le Devin du Village,* **2:**413, **3:**106
Roussel, Albert, **2:**388, **3:**72, **4:**516, 635, **5:**237, 525
Roussel, Louis, **6:**232
Roussel Suite, **3:**401, 404
Rousset, Calestina, **1:**110
Rousset, Carolina, **1:**110
Rousset, Giovanni, **2:***415*
Rousset, Jean, **1:**110
Rousset troupe, **5:**318
Roustand, Joelle, **5:**551
Rout, **1:**462, **2:**397–398

Roux, Aline, **1:**349
Roval, Adolfo, **2:**278
Rover, The (Behn), **5:**518
Rovinsky, Dmitri, **5:***442*
Rowe, Cynthia, **2:**57
Rowe, Mannie, **1:**197, **3:***3,* 232
Rowe, Marilyn, **1:**210, 211, *231,* 233, *233,* 234, **2:**183, **5:**410, 410–411
Rowe, Patricia A., *as contributor,* **5:**354
Rowe, Punky and Betty, **3:**574
Rowell, Bonnie, *as contributor,* **2:**1–2, 354–356, **4:**216–221
Rowell, Kenneth, **1:**232, **4:***240*
Rowlandson, Thomas, **1:***189,* **2:**68, 72, **4:**315, **5:**259, 293
Rowse, Anne, **4:**626
Roxana (Defoe), **4:**315
Roxander, David, **4:**544
Roxane, la Belle de Montenegro, **5:**151
Roxo, Josef, **1:**480
Roxo de Flores, Felipe, **5:**670
Roxy Theater, New York City, **4:**321
Roy, Pierre-Charles, **5:**40
Roy, Sheila, **2:***519*
Royal, Tairoa, **4:**626, 627
Royal Academy of Dancing, Australia, **3:**174
Royal Academy of Dancing, Great Britain, **1:**329, 400, 533, **2:**48, 84, 497, **3:**279, **4:**164, **5:**43, 631, **6:**128
  Bedells vice-presidency, **3:**262
  character dancing method, **2:**107
  Cranko choreography, **2:**265
  dance medicine, **2:**330
  Farron administrative post, **2:**578
  Field directorship, **2:**590
  Fonteyn presidency, **3:**45
  founding, **2:**338, 395, 525, **3:**263, **5:**351
  Genée presidency, **1:**329, 330, **3:**129, 261
  Grey presidency, **3:**307
  Guest association, **3:**321
  Karsavina syllabus, **3:**656
  Lester association, **4:**153
  library and archives, **4:**164
  Netherlands branch, **4:**598
  Richardson (Philip) association, **2:**395, **5:**351
  Sibley presidency, **5:**597
  Wall directorship, **6:**357
  See also Royal Ballet School
Royal Academy of Music, **5:**128
Royal Albert Hall, London, **2:**514
Royal Alexandra Theatre, Toronto, **4:**542
Royal Ballerinas (Australia), **1:**206, 207
Royal Ballet (formerly Sadler's Wells Ballet), **5:411–422**
  Aldous, Lucette, **1:**38
  Alston choreography, **1:**52
  American tours, **1:**152, 158, **2:**402, **3:**41, 42, *42,* 267, **4:**115, **5:**415–416, **6:**249
  Apollo, **1:**96
  archival materials, **4:**163
  Ashton, Frederick, **1:**146–155, 155–159, 329, **2:**173, 397, 403, **3:**267, **4:**65, **5:**412, 417
  Baiser de la Fée, Le, **4:***240,* 241
  ballerinas, **5:**419, 420
  Ballet Imperial production, **1:**293
  Benesh notation use, **1:**417, **4:**691
  Beriosova, Svetlana, **1:**429–430

Bintley, David, **1:**453, 454, **3:**268, **5:**418
Blair, David, **1:**459
Bliss scores, **1:**462, 463
books on, **3:**282, 285
Cecchetti training, **1:**453, **4:**452, **5:**419
Chappell, William, **2:**105
Checkmate, **2:**115
Cinderella, **2:**173
Collier, Lesley, **1:**158, *159,* **2:**186, **5:**419
composers, **4:**517
Coppélia productions, **2:**200
costumes, **2:**243, **3:***40*
Covent Garden residency, **1:**150, **2:**402
Cranko guest choreography, **2:**265, 266, **5:**417, 433, *650*
Dale, Margaret, **2:**314
Dark Elegies revival, **2:**349
de Valois (Ninette) development of, **2:**397–404, **3:**263, 265–266, **5:**411–416, **6:**313
Dolin, Anton, **2:**424–425, **3:**265, **4:**269–270, **5:**411, 412
Don Quixote productions, **2:**440, 441
Dowell, Anthony, **2:**443–444, **3:**268, **5:**418–420
Dream, The, **2:**445–446
educational section, **5:**603
Edwards, Leslie, **2:**477–448
Elvin, Violetta, **2:**506
as English school exemplar, **1:**329, 349, **3:**263, **5:**412
Enigma Variations, **2:**515–516
European tours, **5:**415
Farron character dancing, **2:**578
Fedorovitch designs, **2:**582–583
Field, John, **2:**590
Fille Mal Gardée, La, **1:**155, **2:**597, **3:**321, **5:**417
Firebird restaging, **3:**2, 198
Fonteyn, Margot, **3:**40–46, 265, **5:**416, 419
formation as Vic-Wells Ballet, **1:**146, 148, **3:**263, 264–265, **5:**411–414
founding date, **5:**411
Franca *demi-caractère* roles, **3:**62
Georgiadis designs, **3:**136, **4:**256
Giselle, **3:**182
Grant, Alexander, **3:**236–237, **4:**544
Grey, Beryl, **3:**307
Hart, John, **1:**155, **3:**345
Helpmann, Robert, **3:**265, 354–356, 357, **5:**414, 415
Horoscope, **3:**379–380
Howard, Andrée, **3:**391, 392
Hynd, Ronald, **3:**427
Illuminations revival, **3:**443
Invitation, The, **3:**512–513
Irving (Robert) as principal conductor, **3:**521
Jardin aux Lilas revival, **3:**597
Job, **3:**609
Kirkland guest performances, **4:**24, 25
Lambert as conductor and music director, **4:**114–115, 517, **5:**411–412
Lanchbery as conductor, **4:**117
MacMillan, Kenneth, **3:**267, **4:**239–246, **5:**396, 417–418, 419
Makarova guest performances, **4:**248
male dancers, **5:**414, 416, 419

Manon, **4:**256–257
Markova, Alicia, **3:**265, **4:**268, 269–270, **5:**413, 414, **6:**62
Mason, Monica, **4:**306–307
Massine productions, **4:***316*, 324, **5:**415
May, Pamela, **4:**336–337
Messel *Sleeping Beauty* design, **4:**357
Monotones, **1:**156, 157, **2:**444, 452, **5:**417
Month in the Country, A, **4:**456–457
Morrice directorship, **3:**267–268, **4:**469–470, **5:**418
name changes, **1:**149, **3:**167, **5:**416
as National Ballet of Canada influence, **2:**39, **4:**542
Nerina, Nadia, **4:**584–585
New Zealand tour, **4:**624
Nijinska revivals, **4:**633, 638, *658*, 659
Nureyev, Rudolf, **5:**5–6, 7, 416
Nutcracker, The, **5:**14, 15, **6:**405
Ondine, **3:**360
Patineurs, Les, **5:**114
practice clothes, **5:**242
Prospect before Us, **1:**149, **2:**72, 401, *402*
Rabert Ballet reciprocity, **3:**266
Rake's Progress, The, **2:**396, 400–401, **3:***354*, **5:**691
Raymonda, **5:**322
Rendezvous, Le, **5:**342
Romeo and Juliet, **5:**396, *396*
as Rome Opera Ballet influence, **5:**401
royal charter (1956), **1:**154, **2:**403, **3:**44, 267, **5:**416–417
Russian connections, **5:**416, 417, 419
Russian tour, **4:**585
Scènes de Ballet, **5:**531–532
Sergeyev (Nicholas) Maryinsky reproductions, **5:**413, 414, **6:**33, 35
Seymour, Lynn, **5:**574–575
Shakespeare 400th anniversary program, **1:**156, **2:**445
Shearer, Moira, **5:**588, 589
Sibley, Antoinette, **5:**596–597
Skeaping, Mary, **5:**603
Sleeping Beauty productions, **5:**612–613, *613*
1946, **1:**324, **2:**243, 401–402, **3:***41*, 42, *266*, **5:**415
1977, **2:**403, **3:**268
Sleeping Princess (1939) production, **1:**324
Somes, Michael, **5:**639–640
star dancers, **2:**402
Stravinsky program, **4:**244
style, **5:**414–415, 418–419
Swan Lake, **1:**71, 429–438, **3:***42*, **6:**33, *33*, 35
Sylphides, Les, **3:**41, **6:**62
Sylvia, **2:**369, **3:***567*, **6:***63*, 64
Symphonic Variations, **6:**64–65
televised repertory, **6:**134, *134*, 137
Tetley choreography, **6:**146
Tharp choreography, **5:**420
as Toronto ballet inspiration, **4:**539
Troy Game, **4:**218
Tudor, Antony, **6:**196, 201–202
Turner, Harold, **6:**214
van Praagh, Peggy, **6:**312–313
Wall, David, **6:**357

Wedding Bouquet, **1:**437, **6:**375
Wells, Doreen, **6:**380
World War II losses, **1:**149, **2:**115, 402, **3:**266–267, **4:**114
Wright, Peter, **6:**405
See also Birmingham Royal Ballet; Sadler's Wells Royal Ballet
Royal Ballet, The (Bland), **3:**282
Royal Ballet, The (film), **1:**429
Royal Ballet Choreographic Group, **4:**470
Royal Ballet New Group, **1:**459
Royal Ballet of Flanders, **1:**411, *413*, **5:**422–423
Brabants directorship, **1:**519
Leclair choreography, **4:**136
Nureyev's *Don Quixote*, **2:**440
Royal Ballet School (Great Britain), **1:**329, 453, **2:**403, **3:***277*, 279, 280, 285, **4:**325, 463, **5:**100, 416, 419, 421–422
Royal Cambodian Ballet, **1:***161*, 414
Royal Circus, Brussels, **1:**405
Royal Comic Opera Company (Australia), **1:**206
Royal Danish Ballet, **2:**384, 385, 386, **5:**423–433
Ailey choreography, **1:**57
Alonso (Alicia) guest performances, **1:**49–50
Alston choreography, **1:**52
Anisimova choreography, **1:**91
annual ballet festival, **5:**430
Apollo, **1:**96
Ashton's *Romeo and Juliet*, **1:**153–154, 158, **5:**394–395, *395*, 431, 555
Aurora's Wedding, **2:**480
Balanchine guest productions, **5:**428, *429*, 431
ballon, **1:***340*
Beck as ballet master, **1:**399, **5:**427–428
Bjørnsson, Fredbjørn, **1:**454
Borchsenius, Valborg, **1:**497–498, **5:**430
Bournonville, Antoine, **1:**503, 504, **5:**425
Bournonville, August, **1:**504, 505–511, **5:**425–427
Bournonville Festivals, **1:**539, **5:**430, 433
Bournonville tradition, **1:**329–330, 346, 347–348, 497–498, 511–513, 539, **2:**385, 387, **5:**427–428, 430, *432*, 433
Brenaa, Hans, **1:**539, **5:**429
Bruhn, Erik, **2:**2, 3, 4, **5:**430
Carey, Gustave, **2:**60, **5:**426
Cinderella, **2:**173
Coppélia, **2:**200
costume authenticity, **2:***240*, 243
Cullberg choreography, **2:**283, **5:**431
dance accompaniment, **1:**6
dance medicine, **2:**330
Danish repertory, **1:**399, 506, 509
Dean choreography, **2:**359
Don Quixote productions, **2:**435, 441
English National Ballet ties, **3:**269
Études, **2:**535–536
Evdokimova, Eva, **2:**561
Feld production, **2:**583
Firebird, The, **3:**4
first *Giselle* production, **2:**60
Flindt, Flemming, **3:**12–13, **5:**431–432, 600

Flindt's stylistic innovations, **5:**431–432
Fokine guest productions, **5:**428, **6:**62
Folk Tale, A, **3:***39*, **5:**426
Galeotti, Vincenzo, **3:**104, 105–106, 546, **5:**424–425, 426
Grahn, Lucile, **3:**222–223
guest productions, **5:**431–432, 433
historical background, **5:**423–425
Hønningen, Mette, **3:**373
Jacob's Pillow performance, **3:**571, 572
Karstens, Gerda, **3:**657
Kehlet, Niels, **3:**667–668
Kermesse in Bruges, **4:**6
Konservatoriet, **4:**43, *43*
Kronstam, Henning, **4:**64–65, **5:**432–433
Lander, Harald, **1:**512, **4:**118, 119, **5:**429–430
Lander, Margot, **4:**119, **5:**429
Lander, Toni, **4:**120, **5:**429
Larsen, Niels Bjørn, **4:**125, 126, **5:**430
male dancers' footwear, **3:**47
male dancing tradition, **1:**399, 454, **5:**426
Marks, Bruce, **4:**271
Martins's debut performance, **4:**273
Martins's *Swan Lake*, **4:**275
Massine guest productions, **2:**3, **4:**125, **5:**430
mime tradition, **5:**425, 430
modern dance productions, **5:**432
music compositions, **4:**513
Napoli, **2:***240*, **5:**426
Nazi occupation, **4:**118, 119, **5:**429
Nielsen, Augusta, **4:**631–632
Pantomime Theater ties, **2:**385
post-1915, **5:**428–430
post-Bournonville, **5:**427–428
Ralov, Børge, **5:**294, 429
Ralov, Kirsten, **5:**295
Riisager scores, **5:**352–353
Romeo and Juliet, **1:**153–154, 158, **5:**392, 394–395, 424, 432, 433
Russian classics, **5:**430
Sand, Inge, **5:**511
Schanne, Margrethe, **5:**553
Schaufuss (Peter) as artistic director, **5:**433
Schaufuss family, **5:**553–555
scholarly studies of, **2:**387
Simone, Kirsten, **5:**599–600
Skeaping directorship, **5:**603
Sylphide, La, **1:***504*, 507, **2:***385*, **3:**222, **4:**125, *125*, 126, **5:**426, 433, **6:***59*
television productions, **2:**386, 387, **6:**134, 146
Ten Soloists, **3:**572, 573
Tetley production, **6:**146
Tomasson's *Sleeping Beauty*, **6:**404–405
tours abroad, **5:**431
Vangsaae, Mona, **5:**553
Williams, Stanley, **6:**399
as world's third oldest ballet company, **5:**425
Worsaae design, **6:**404–405
Royal Danish Ballet School, **1:**399, *506*, 512, 513, 539, **2:**2, 386, 387, **5:**406, 425, 427, **6:**349
Volkova as faculty member, **5:**430, **6:**349

Williams (Stanley) training, **6:**399
Royal Drama School, Stockholm, **1:**403
Royal Dramatic Theater, Sweden, **2:**500
Royal Festival Hall, London, **2:**509, 511
Royal Flemish Opera, **1:**411, 414, **5:**422
Brabants dance school and company, **1:**519
Leclair choreography, **4:**136
See also Royal Ballet of Flanders
Royal Khōn Troupe, Siam, **4:**9
Royal New Zealand Ballet, **4:**479, 624–625, 626, 629
Royal Offering, **1:**463
Royal Opera Ballet, Vienna. *See* Hofopernballett
Royal Opera House, Ghent, **1:**410, 411
Royal Opera House, London. *See* Covent Garden
Royal Opera, Stockholm, **1:**118, **6:**48
See also Royal Swedish Ballet
Royal Schouwburg, The Hague, **4:**589
Royal Scottish Academy of Music and Dance, Glasgow, **4:**164
Royal Scottish Country Dance Society, Edinburgh, **2:**257
Royal Swedish Ballet
Åkesson, Birgit, **1:**32, 145, **6:**42
Anisfeld decor, **6:**41
archival materials, **4:**163
Beck-Friis choreography, **1:**400
Béjart choreography, **1:**403
Bournonville, Antoine, **1:**503, 510, **5:**425, **6:**39, 49
Bruhn as artistic director, **2:**3, 4, **6:**42–43
Carnaval, Le, **2:**73
Cramér, Ivo, **2:**263, 264, **6:**36, 42, 43
Cullberg choreography, **2:**283, **6:**41, 42, 43–44
Dark Elegies revival, **2:**349
Dream revival, **2:**446
Drottningholm Court Theater revivals, **6:**38, 42, 46–48
Ek choreography, **2:**500, **6:**44
Firebird, The, **3:**3
Fokine restagings, **3:**20, **6:**41, 62
Gadd, Ulf, **3:**100, **6:**44
Grey *Sleeping Beauty* staging, **3:**307, **6:**44
history, **6:**39–41, 41–45
Johansson, Christian, **3:**618, **6:**40
Macdonald as artistic director, **4:**238, 642
MacMillan productions, **4:**242, 243, **6:**44
Romeo and Juliet, **5:**396, **6:**43, *43*
Madsen as artistic director, **4:**246
Nureyev productions, **5:**7, 15
Orlando, Mariane, **5:**47
Rosen, Elsa-Marianne von, **5:**406
Schauffuss as ballet master, **5:**553
scholarship on, **6:**49
Selinder as first native-born ballet master, **6:**40
Skeaping directorship, **5:**603, **6:**41, 42
Tudor productions, **5:**397, 603, **6:**42, *42*
Royal Swedish Ballet School, **6:**44, 48

Royal Theater, Copenhagen, **1:**511, 515
  Archives and Library, **4:**160
Royal Theater, Stockholm. *See* Swedish Royal Ballet
Royal Troupe of Morocco, **2:**459
Royal Winnipeg Ballet, **2:**36, 39, 42, **4:**538, **5:**62, **433–437**, **6:**132
  Araiz productions, **1:**103, *103*, **5:**436
  archives, **4:**166
  artistic directors, **2:**42, **5:**435
  Boris choreography, **1:**498
  de Mille productions, **2:**374, 375, **5:**435
  Feld production, **2:**583, **5:**436
  Firebird production, **3:**4
  founding and early repertory, **2:**38–39, 47, **5:**434–435
  Hart, Evelyn, **3:**344, 345, **5:**685
  Hyrst, Eric, **3:**429
  Macdonald, Brian, **2:**39, 42, **4:**238, **5:**435, 436
  Neumeier productions, **5:**436
  Neumeier's *Nutcracker*, **5:**15
  school, **2:**47, 404, **5:**436–437
  Spoerli as soloist, **5:**681
  Spohr directorship, **5:**684–685
  tours, **5:**435, 436
  Wyman history of, **2:**49
  youth-oriented image, **5:**436
Royce, Anya Peterson, **4:**370, 373
  as contributor, **2:**534–535
Royeca, Rosario, **5:**172
Royer, Joseph, **1:**365
Rozanova, Olga I., *as contributor*, **4:**233–234
Rozhdestvensky, Gennady, **5:**677
Rozier, Jean, **1:**202, **5:**105
Rozier, Théodore, **6:**50
Rózsavökgtu, Márk, **3:**412
Różycki, Ludomir, **5:***217*
Ruanne, Patricia, **2:**512, **5:**55, 398
Ruanova, María, **1:**102, 110, 315
Rubaiyat of Omar Khayyam, **2:**452, **5:**46
Rubato, **3:**156
Rubble Dance, Long Island City, **2:**460
Rubé, Jules, **6:**62
Rubens, Peter Paul, **5:**259
Rubenstein, Carol, **6:**164
Rübezahl, **1:**499
Rubicon, Göteborg, **6:**45
Rubies (*Jewels* section), **1:***269*, **4:***612*, 613, 618, 619, 620, **5:***653*
Rubin, Alec, **3:**362
Rubin, Harold, **5:**300
Rubin, Marcel, **4:**59
Rubin Academy of Music and Dance, Jerusalem, **3:**534–535, **4:**59
Rubinstein, Anton, **2:**596, **3:**15, 622, **5:**123, **6:**114
Rubinstein, Ida, **1:**146, 148, 424, **2:**360, **3:**196, 431, **4:**25, **5:**95, 315, **437–439**, 559, **6:**326, 341
  Bakst designs, **1:**254, 255
  Boléro production, **4:***638*
  Chappell association, **2:**105
  Fokine productions, **3:**16, 20, 24, **5:**438
  Istar, **5:**690
  Jooss choreography, **3:**628, **5:**439
  Leeder association, **4:**140
  Lester association, **4:**152–153
  Lichine association, **4:**178, 635
  Massine choreography, **4:**321, **5:**438, 439

Nijinska as chief choreographer, **3:**72, **4:**635–636, **5:**438–439
  Schéhérazade performance, **5:**556
  Scholar as principal dancer, **5:**559
  Stravinsky commissions, **6:**5
Rubinstein, Martin, **1:**209, 499
Rubinstein, Nikolai, **6:**114
Rubtsova, Lydia, **5:**9
Rückert, Friedrich, **2:**348
Rückkehr ins Fremde Land, **4:**81
Rudenick, Catherine A., **1:**451
Rudenko, Aleksandr, **2:**564
Rudiments of Genteel Behaviour (Nivelon), **3:***255*, **5:**346, *346*
Rudkin, David, **5:**564
Rudner, Sara, **2:**460, **4:**442, **5:439–441**, **6:**152
Rudneva, A., **5:**481
Rudneva, Stefanida, **5:**478
Rudolf II, emperor of Austria, **1:**235
Rudolph, Charlotte, **5:**66
  as photographer, **3:**159, **6:**390
Rudolph, Hermann, **3:**155
Rudolph, Johann Joseph, **4:**695
Rudzka, Yanka, **1:**534, 537
Ruffin, Elena, **3:**556, 557
Ru Fulan, **6:**421
Rugg, Harold, **2:**319
Ruggieri brothers, **1:**284
Ruggieri di Sansverino, Alfonso, **3:**544
Rug Maker's Daughter, The (film), **1:**43
ruhunu dances, **2:**228
Ruinen von Athen, Die, **1:**402
Ruins and Visions, **3:**391, 403, 405, **4:**39, 198
Ruiz. *See* José Antonio
Ruiz, Antonio (19th-century flamenco dancer), **1:**294, **2:**522
Ruiz, Brunilda, **3:**342, *609*, 610, *611*
Ruiz, Dorita, **4:**222
Ruiz, Juan, **1:**53
Ruiz Soler, Antonio. *See* Antonio and Rosario
Rukmini Devi, **2:**104, 105, 404, 405, **3:**468, **4:**62, **5:**68, 510
Rukmini Devi (Samson), **5:**511
Rulegame 5, **1:**543
"Rules and Institutions for Dancing" (Weaver), **6:**373
rull, **4:**669
Rulowa, Shura, **6:**319
rumada dance, **6:**16
rumba, **2:**275, *275*, **4:**520, **5:**629, **6:**246
  ballroom competition standards, **1:**358
"Rumba" (skating program), **6:***180*
Rūmī, Jalāl al-Dīn, **3:**524, **5:**63, **6:**209
Rumjantseva, Marianna, **2:**632
Rummage Sale and the Floor of the Forest, **5:**549
Rumnev, Aleksandr, **5:**476
Rumours, **6:**56
random, **4:**669
Rune (Cunningham dance), **2:**290, 574, **4:**37
Runes (Taylor dance), **2:**526, **6:**111
Runich, Nina, **2:**265
Runkov, A., **3:**56–57
Run, Little Chillun, **6:**276
running set, **3:**238, **5:**687
Runnin' Wild (revue), **5:**629, **6:**256

ruoia, **4:**497
Rupprecht, Martin, **5:***682*
rusali dances, **2:**8
rusalija dance, **6:***429*
Ruse, Bulgaria, **2:**11
Ruse of Medusa, The (Satie), **2:**285
Ruse People's Opera, **2:**12
Ruses d'Amour, Les, **2:**363, **3:**186, **4:**145, **5:**160
rush-bearing procession, **3:**241, **4:**474
Rushes, **2:**355
rusīyah technique, **2:**490
Ruskaja, Jia, **3:**549–550, 552, 554, 555, **4:**688, **5:**441
Ruslan and Ludmila (Glinka opera), **1:**86, 485, **3:**21, **5:**36, 37
  dances, **4:**514
  Fokine choreography, **4:**283
  Glushkovsky choreography, **3:**191, 540, **4:**279, **5:**454
  Zakharov production, **6:**442
Ruspoli, Prince Allesandro, **1:**305
Russakoff, Senia, **1:**481
Russalka, **2:**181
Russell, Francia, **2:**578, **5:**51, **6:**265
Russell, Henrietta and Edmund, **2:**371
Russell, Joan, **4:**103–104, 477
Russell, Lillian, **2:**250
Russell, Maude, **6:**244, *245*
Russell, Paul, **2:**334, **6:**260
Russell, Rhoda Winter, **2:**319
Russell Market Girls, **6:**101
Russia, **5:**216–217, **441–486**
  ballet in opera, **5:**37
  Blok dance histories, **1:**463–464
  cartoon personification as dancer, **2:**70, 72
  dance aesthetics, **5:**485
  dance education, **5:**463, **479–481**
    Canziani as teacher, **2:**55
    Cecchetti method, **2:**84
    character dancing, **2:**107
    Chinese ballet instruction, **2:**133, 136, 145, 149
    Clustine as teacher, **2:**181
    early French and Italian school influences on, **1:**347
    first ballet school (1738), **4:**276, **5:**451, 480
    first Moscow school, **5:**452, 480
    Gerdt family, **3:**137–138
    Goleizovsky studio, **3:**193
    Golovkina as Moscow Ballet School head, **3:**197
    Gusev as teacher, **3:**328
    Johansson system, **3:**618
    Kolosova as first woman teacher, **4:**35–36
    Messerer's classes, **4:**359–360
    Perm Ballet School, **5:**471
    plastique, **5:**476
    Saint Petersburg Conservatory, **4:**224
    Semenova as teacher, **5:**567
    Vaganova and Russian school, **1:**328–329, 347, 348–349, **6:**309–310
    See also ballet technique, history of; Vaganova method
  folk dance research and publication, **5:481–482**
    Goleizovsky, Kasyan, **3:**195–196, **5:**445
    Nadezhdina, Nadezhda, **4:**530
    Ustinova, Tatiana, **6:**303–304
  libraries and museums, **4:**164–165

modern dance. *See subhead* twentieth-century plastique *below*
  scenic design, **5:**540–547, *545*
  secondary and provincial dance companies, **5:**459, 463, **465–475**
  Siberian dance traditions, **2:**140, **5:445–449**
  shamanism, **5:**578–579
  theatrical dance, pre-1917, **5:449–457**
    Bolshoi Ballet, **1:**484–488, **3:**204–205
    Brianza performances, **1:**540
    Canziani productions, **2:**55
    character dancing, **2:**108
    circus, **2:**176
    commedia dell'arte influences, **2:**191–192
    costume, **2:**241–242, **4:**124–125
    Diaghilev Parisian exhibition, **1:**317–318, **2:**407
    Diaghilev's Ballets Russes links, **1:**319, **2:**407–409
    Didelot productions, **2:**414–415, 416
    Don Quixote versions, **2:**435–438
    Fille Mal Gardée popularity, **2:**596
    Giselle productions, **3:**181, 183, **4:**281
    Gorsky reforms, **3:**204
    Ivanov as "soul of," **3:**560
    Kshessinska (Matilda) as last imperial-age great ballerina, **4:**68
    Maryinsky Ballet, **4:**276–283
    music for ballet, **4:**513–515
    partnering technique development, **5:***102*, 103–104
    Petipa (Marius) influence, **5:**152–153, 158–159
    photography of, **5:**180
    practice clothes, **5:**241, 243
    Rinaldi (Il Fossano) choreography, **5:**353
  theatrical dance, post-1917, **5:457–465**
    avant-garde, **1:**244, 246, **3:**48
    Bolshoi Ballet, **1:**488–494, **3:**205–207
    Canadian tours, **2:**38
    Chilean company, **2:**124–125
    circus, **2:**176
    classical ballet revivals, **4:**224
    Corsaire popularity, **2:**206, 207
    costume, **2:**242, 244
    Don Quixote popularity, **2:**437–438
    Duncan involvement, **2:**456
    Fille Mal Gardée popularity, **2:**596–597
    Giselle productions, **3:**182
    ice dancing, **3:**432, 434
    Maryinsky Ballet, **4:**283–285
    Moiseyev (Igor) folk dance ensemble, **4:**444–445
    music, **4:**517, **5:**594
    See also Soviet era
  theaters for dance, **6:**160, *160*
  theatrical dance research and publication, **5:482–486**
    Koni, Fedor, **4:**40–41
    Krasovskaya, Vera, **4:**58
    Slonimsky, Yuri, **5:**613–614
    Souritz, Elizabeth, **5:**642–643
    Stepanov Notation, **5:**693–694
    Zotov, Rafail, **6:**451–452

traditional dance, **3:**39,
  5:442–445, 449–450, 452
classical dance synthesis, **4:**530
folk dance ensembles,
  4:444–445, **5:**473–474
Georgian dance, **3:**135
twentieth-century plastique,
  5:456, 465, **476–479,** 484, 485
Russian Ballet. *See* Ballets Russes
  de Monte Carlo
Russian Ballet, Moscow company,
  3:200, 442, **5:**465
Russian Ballets (Stokes), **3:**285
Russian Chamber Ballet, Moscow,
  5:465, 475, 479
Russian Dances (Nadezhdina),
  4:530
*Russian Folk Round Dances and
  Dances* (Okuneva), **5:**481
Russian Honeymoon, A, **5:**180
Russian Imperial Geographic
  Society, **5:**481
Russian Journals (de Mille), **2:**374
Russian Opera and Ballet Troupe,
  4:276
Russian Opera House. *See* Kiev
  Opera
Russian Revolution (1905), **2:**407
Russian Revolution (1917), **2:**11,
  409, 456, **3:**193–194, **5:**442
effects on Bolshoi, **3:**205–206,
  5:458
effects on Maryinsky, **4:**283,
  5:457–458
exiles in United States, **6:**291
Stravinsky exile in Paris, **4:**4
See also Soviet era
Russian Romantic Theater, Berlin,
  5:392
*Russian Round Dances and Round
  Dance Songs* (Bachinskaya),
  5:481
"Russian Sailors' Dance" *(The Red
  Poppy),* **4:**517
Russian school. *See* ballet
  technique, major schools;
  Petipa, Marius; Vaganova
  method
Russians in Germany, **4:**35,
  6:311–312
Russian Soldier, The, **3:**26–27
Russian State Library of Art,
  Moscow, **4:**165
Russian Toys. See Igrouchki
Russian Version, The (Cheliabinsk
  company), **5:**474
*Russia's Triumph, or the Russians
  in Paris,* **4:**278
Russillo, Joseph, **5:**528
*Russkaia baletnaia kritika kontsa
  XVIII-pervoy poloviny XIX
  veka* (Petrov), **5:**482
Russkie tantsy (Ustinova), **6:**303
Russkii baletnyi teatr
  (Krasovskaya), **5:**483
Russkii balet v karikatura (Legat
  and Legat), **2:**69
Russkii narodnyi tanets (Ustinova),
  6:303
Russolo, Luigi, **1:**134
Rustaveli, Shota, **3:**134
Ruth, **3:**132
Ruthenian folk dance, **1:**370
Rutherford, Richard, **5:**436
Ruth Page Foundation for Dance,
  5:59–60
Ruth Page's International Ballet,
  5:59, 60
Ruth Page's Invitation to the
  Dance, **5:**59

Ruth St. Denis Concert Dancers,
  2:377, 378, **5:**495
Ruth St. Denis School of the Dance
  and Its Related Arts. *See*
  Denishawn
Rutledge, Richard, *as photographer,*
  2:287, 288
Rutnin, Mattani Mojdara, **4:**10,
  112, **6:**151
  as contributor, **4:**8–10, 111–113,
  255–256, **6:**147–151
Rutt, August, **2:**328
Rutt, Steve, **2:**606
Rütter, Fredrik, **4:**680
Ruud, Tomm, **2:**196, **5:**513
Ruyter, Nancy Lee Chalfa, *as
  contributor,* **2:**370–372,
  3:352–353, 363–364,
  6:293–296
Ruzgaitė, Aliodija, *as contributor,*
  4:207–209
Ruzimatov, Farukh, **4:**285, **5:**465
Rwanda, **2:**86, 90, 212, **6:**20
Ryabinkina, Elena, **2:**136, **3:**195
Ryan, Allan J., **2:**330
  as contributor, **2:**328–331
Ryan, Grace Laura, **5:**686, **6:**247
Ryan, Patricia, **3:**520
Ryan, Peggy, **5:**21
Ryberg, Flemming, **2:**385, 387, 388,
  5:430, 433
Rydberg, Enar Merkel, **6:**50
  as photographer, **2:**284, **5:**47, 406,
  6:41, 42, 43, 46, 47
Ryder, Mark, **1:**479, **3:**216, **4:**632
Ryerson Polytechnic University,
  Ontario, **2:**48
Rykhliakova, Varvara, **2:**341
Ryman, Cheryl, **3:**577
Ryman, Rhonda, **2:**49–50, **4:**17
Ryndin, Vadim, **6:**343
Ryom, Heidi, **1:***506,* **5:***432,* 433
Ryskind, Morris, **6:**275
Ryskulov, Anvarbek, **4:**87
Ryukyu buyō, **5:**26, 28
Ryzhenko, Natalia, **1:**517, **2:**565,
  4:133, **5:**460, 587

Saal, Hubert, **5:**489
Saarinen, Tero, **2:**634
Sabaliauskaiė, Genovaitė, **4:**208
Šabanovič, Haris, **6:***436*
sabaragamuwa dance, **2:**228
Sabas, Hazel, **5:**172
Sabbatini, Nicola, **4:**188, **5:**534
Sabella Morali, José, **4:**390, 399
"Saber Dance" *(Gayané),* **1:**90,
  3:125, **4:**7, 517
Sabícas, **1:**62
Sabin, Evelyn, **3:**211
Sabin, Robert, **3:**349, 384
Sabine in Roma, Le, **6:**339
Sabine Women, **4:**648
Sabino, Paolo, *as photographer,*
  5:235
sabio, **5:**82
Sabirova, Malika, **4:**360, **5:487,**
  6:84, 228
Sable, **1:**251
Sablon, Marcel, **6:**119
Sabol, Andrew J., *as contributor,*
  4:307–313
sabot dance, **2:**180
Sabungan Ayam, **2:**359
Saburov, Andrei, **5:**140
Sacchetti, Lorenzo, **5:**538
Sachs, Curt, **5:**560
Sacountala, **5:**94, 148, 158
Sacred Grove on Mount Tamalpais,
  3:612–613

*Sacre du Printemps, Le (Rite of
  Spring),* **5:487–488**
Alston version, **1:**52, **5:**303
Araiz version, **1:**102, 103, **5:**436
Atanassoff performance, **1:**195
audience riot at premiere, **4:**644,
  6:4
Bausch choreography, **1:**388
Béjart choreography, **1:**195, 290,
  290, 292, 404, 406, **5:**97, **6:**44
Beriozoff performance, **1:**431
Biagi choreography, **1:**446
Chen Weiya version, **2:**116
choreographic constructivism,
  1:259, 262, **6:**4
Chouinard group choreography,
  2:46
controversial score, **4:**516, **6:**4
dancers' dislike of, **4:**644
Eck staging, **3:**417
Flindt television production, **3:**13
Gadd chamber version, **3:**100
Georgi production, **3:**132
Graham performance, **3:**215–216,
  220, **4:***318,* 322
Graham production, **3:***219,*
  220–221
Hodson reconstruction, **4:**644,
  645, **5:**327, *327,* 488, **6:**455
Horton choreography, **3:**386
hostile reaction to, **1:**321, **6:**4
Hoyer performance, **3:**393
Joffrey ballet re-creation,
  3:616–617, **5:**326
Kasatkina and Vasiliov
  choreography, **1:**492,
  5:460, 467
Kölling production, **3:***149*
MacMillan choreography,
  4:241–242, **5:**417
Mason performance, **4:**306–307
Massine choreography, **1:**323,
  3:215, **4:***318, 318,* 321–322
Nijinska choreography, **4:**635, 643
Nijinsky choreography, **1:**52, 259,
  320, *320,* 321, 322, **2:**242,
  408, **3:**616, **4:**641–642,
  643–644, 647, 648, **5:**4, 97
Ogoun choreography, **5:**23
Rambert work with Nijinsky, **6:**97
Roerich costumes and scenic
  design, **2:**242, **4:**643, **5:**372,
  487, 542, **6:**4
Sokolova role, **5:**636
Stravinsky score, **2:**407, **4:**516,
  6:4
Tanaka choreography, **6:**90
Tetley choreography, **1:**73, **2:**245,
  5:432, **6:**146, *146*
Tóth production, **5:**614
Walter choreography, **6:**359
Vienna State Opera Ballet, **1:**241
Wigman production, **1:**436,
  3:393, **6:***394*
Zurich Ballet staging, **6:**455
*Sacre du Printemps, Le (The
  Rehearsal)* (Taylor work),
  6:109, 110, 111, 165
Sacrifice, **6:**391, 394
*Sacrifice Indien, La, ou La Veuve de
  Malabar,* **3:**358
"Sad Art, A" (Fokine), **3:**28
Sada Yakko. *See* Yakko and
  Kawakami
Saddler, Donald, **1:**86, 439, **2:**298,
  3:27, **4:**262, **5:488–489**
Harkness Ballet, **3:**342
Joffrey Ballet, **3:**610
On Your Toes choreography,
  6:286

Sadko (Rimsky-Korsakov), **5:**37
Sadko—Au Royaume Sousmarin,
  1:482, **3:**18, **4:**56
Sadla (Settler) Beni (people), **2:**212
Sadler, A. W., *as contributor,*
  1:180–184
Sadler's Wells Ballet. *See* Royal
  Ballet
Sadler's Wells Ballet, The (Clarke),
  3:282, **5:**484
Sadler's Wells Opera Ballet. *See*
  Sadler's Wells Royal Ballet
Sadler's Wells Royal Ballet
  (formerly Sadler's Wells
  Theatre Ballet), **1:**151, 153,
  3:267, **5:**415, 417, 420–421
Beriosova performances, **1:**429
Cranko, John, **2:**265, **5:**420
Dale choreography, **2:**314
Darrell, Peter, **2:**349
as de Valois smaller company,
  2:402
Macmillan, Kenneth, **4:**239, 240,
  5:420
Moreton role in launching, **4:**463
New Zealand tour, **4:**624
original function, **5:**420
Pineapple Poll, **2:**266
Seymour, Lynn, **5:**574, 575
Somes's *Summer Interlude,* **5:**639
tours, **5:**420
Wall, David, **5:**421, **6:**357, 380
Wedding Bouquet, The, **6:**375
Wells, Doreen, **6:**380
Wright, Peter, **6:**405
Züllig performances, **6:**453
See also Birmingham Royal
  Ballet
Sadler's Wells Theatre Ballet. *See*
  Sadler's Wells Royal Ballet
Sadler's Wells Theatre, Islington,
  5:411, 420
Sadoff, Simon, **4:**458
Sadovska, Hélène, **1:**305
Sad Young Man in a Train
  (Duchamp), **1:**137
Saeko Ichinohe, **3:***590*
Sa Erp, Helenita, **1:**535
Sæther, Marte, **4:**677
Saeverud, Harald, **4:**676
Saez, Vicente, **3:**156
saff (sahge), **3:**538
Saffo, o sia Il Salto di Leucade,
  3:176
Sagatov, Mansur, **3:**665
Sager, Peggy, **1:***206,* 208, 209, 499,
  4:380, **5:**563
Sage's Threshing Floor (Estonian
  dance), **2:**528
Sagirova, Damira, **6:**307
Sagi school, **4:**85
Sagrificio di Dirces, Il, **1:**88
Sahagún, Bernardino de, **4:**398
sa'hjī dance, **4:**407
Sahm-Ch'un-Li Dancers and
  Musicians of Korea, **3:**341,
  4:12
sahṛdaya, **3:**463
saias, **5:**229
Saidazimov, Ata Hoja, **4:**8
Saigal, Kundan Lal, **2:**625
Saiga Toshiko, **6:**145
"Sailor's Dance" *(Dido and Aeneas),*
  3:376
Sailor's Fancy, **3:**629
"Sailor's Hornpipe," **3:**249, 375,
  376, 378, **6:***233*
Sailor's Return, The, **3:**174, 392,
  5:301
saing ensemble, **4:**527
Sainsbury, John, **4:**200

Saint-Aignan, duc de, **1:**4, 288, 424
Saint-Amans, Louis-Joseph, **3:**118
Saint-André, Adrien Merger de, **3:**255, 522, **4:489–490, 5:**251
Saint Auben, Gabriel de, **2:**366
Saint-Aubin, Augustin, **1:**46, 47
Saint Cecilia Society of Charleston, South Carolina, **6:**232
St. Clair, Sallie, **4:**454
Saint Croix (island), **2:**63, 64
St. Denis, Ruth, **1:**204, 239, **2:**377, **3:**93, 559, **5:490–498,** 583–585, **6:**299
American musical theater performance, **6:**269
archival materials, **4:**167, 168, 169, 170, **5:**498
British music hall appearances, **4:**522
Canadian vaudeville circuits, **2:**37
costume, **2:**245, 247, 572, 574
dance aesthetics, **1:**25, **2:**377–378, **6:**243
Delsarte system, **2:**371, 372
eurhythmics, **3:**596
exoticism, **2:**572
German performances, **3:**145
as Graham influence, **3:**210, 211
as Humphrey influence, **3:**397
interpretive improvisation, **3:**445
on Johansson, **3:**619
Kiralfy brothers' influence, **3:**24
Korean dance, **2:**155, 159
liturgical dance, **2:**169, **4:**212, **5:**356
makeup skill, **4:**305
Meri association, **4:**354
music visualizations, **2:**377, 378, **3:**384, 397, **4:**518, **5:**495
nautch choreographic use, **4:**578
Orientalism, **5:**46, *46*
as photographic subject, **5:**183
Radha, **5:**46, 288
Shawn marriage, **2:**376, **5:**494, 495, 496, 497
students, **4:**272
vaudeville performances, **6:**317
Weidman association, **6:**375, 376
See also Denishawn
Sainte-Claire, Joséphine, **2:**60
Saint Francis. See Nobilissima Visione
Saint Gall Ballet, **6:**53
Saint George and the Dragon, **2:**500, *500*
Saint-Georges, marquis de. *See* Vernoy de Saint-Georges, Jules-Henri
Saint George's Day, **2:**8
Sainthill, Loudon, **4:**26
Saint-Hubert, Monsieur de, **2:**517, **3:**84
St. James's Ballet, **2:**265
Saint Job guild, **1:**409
Saint John Island, **2:**63
Saint John's dance, **4:**348
Saint John the Divine, Church of the, New York City, **4:**213
Saint Joseph's Oratory, Montreal, **3:**228, **4:**576, 577–578
Saint Joseph's School for the Deaf, New York, **2:**187
Saint-Julien, Alfred de, **3:**316
Saint-Juste, Serge, **3:**335
Saint-Laurent, Yves, **1:**305
Saint-Léon, Arthur, **1:**6, 37, 48, 331, 455, 477, 478, **2:**523, **5:498–502**
arm positions, **1:**332, **5:**227

ballet technique definitions, **5:**201, 227
Bolshoi Ballet, **1:**486
Bolshoi Theater, **5:**151
Cerrito dance partnership and marriage, **2:**93, 94, 95, **5:**106, 498–500
character dances, **2:**108
Coppélia, **2:**181, 198, 199, 200, 368, **3:**70–71, **4:**343
on *coupé* exercises, **1:**345
Delibes collaboration, **5:**501, 502
on *enchaînements,* **1:**346
Fiammetta staging, **4:**429
on *Flick und Flocks Abenteuer,* **6:**75–76
Gerdt (Pavel) roles, **3:**137
Grantzow roles, **3:**237–238
Hungarian performances, **3:**413
Ivanov roles, **3:**561
King's Theatre, London, **3:**260, **5:**498, 499
Lacotte choreographic reconstructions, **4:**108
Lalla Rookh performance, **5:**137
Little Humpbacked Horse, The, **4:**211, 281, **5:**450, 498
mazurka choreography, **4:**343
Minkus-Delibes collaborations, **4:**429
Netherlands performances, **4:**589
notation system. *See* Saint-Léon notation
Pâquerette choreography, **3:**123
Paris Opera Ballet, **4:**341–342, 353, **5:**93, 94, 499, 500, 501–502
pas de deux, **5:**106
polka, **5:**221
portrayal in *Pas des Déesses,* **3:**609, 611
in Portugal, **5:**232–233
Pugni, Cesare, **5:**277–278
Rendezvous, Les, **5:**342
Saint Petersburg ballet, **4:**281, 514, **5:**141, 455, 500–501
Source, Le, **2:**368
Taglioni, Louise, **6:**70
technical writings, **5:**227, **6:**127, 128
as violinist, **5:**498, 499, *499*
Vivandière, La, **2:**94, **3:**427, 614
Saint-Léon, Léon-Michel, **1:**345, 346, **5:**105, 106, 498, **6:**127
Saint-Léon notation, **1:**37, **4:**685, **5:**227, 500, **503–503, 6:**127, 128, 450–451
Saint-Lot, Emile, **3:**335
Saint Louis Municipal Opera, **1:**518
Saint Louis Shag, **4:**203
St. Louis Woman (musical), **4:**630
Saint-Mard, Rémond de, **5:**40, 88
Saint Mary's Eve (melodrama), **2:**85
Saint Matthew Passion, **3:**153, 338, **4:**604
Saint Nicholas's Day, **2:**7
Saint Petersburg, Russia
dance training, **5:**480
environmental influence on Petipa, **4:**286
metamorphose (transvestite ball), **4:**314
See also Maryinsky Ballet
Saint Petersburg Academy, **5:**480
Saint Petersburg Arcade (Matinsky opera), **5:**452
Saint Petersburg Ballet. *See* Maryinsky Ballet
Saint Petersburg Cappella, **1:**38, 39

Saint Petersburg Chamber Ballet, **1:**38, 518, 540, **5:**475
Saint Petersburg Conservatory Rimsky-Korsakov, **1:**416, **2:**423
Saint Petersburg school traditions. *See* Vaganova, Agrippina; Vaganova method
Saint Petersburg State Museum of Theater and Music, **4:**165
Saint Petersburg State Theater of Ballet, **5:**461, 464
Saint Petersburg Theater of Contemporary Ballet, **2:**499, **5:469**
Saint Petersburg Theater School, **3:**137, **5:**480
Saint-Phalle, Niki de, **1:**305, **3:**619, **5:**314
Saint Pierre, Dianne de, **3:**429
Saint-Point, Valentine de, **1:**134
Saint-Romain, Angelica, **6:**71
Saint-Saëns, Camille, **2:**471, **3:**16, 24, **5:**121, 520, **6:**117
Saints and Lovers, **1:**350
Saint Sebastian's Day, **1:**520
Saints, Sinners, and Scriabin, **6:**376
Saint Thomas (island), **2:**63, 64
Saint-Victor, Paul de, **4:**214
Saint Vincent (island), **2:**62, 65, **3:**120, **6:**186, 187
Saint Vitus's dance, **4:**348
sairei buyō, **5:**26
Saishiki buyō, **5:**26
Sai Shoki (Ch'oi Seung-hee), **2:**155
Saison en Enfer, Une, **4:**134
Saison Russe (Paris), **1:**98, 317–318, **2:**407, **3:**128, **4:**233, **6:**348
Cléopâtre, **3:**568
composers, **4:**515–516
Firebird, **6:**3
Fokine association, **3:**15, 17, *17,* 21, **4:**283
Lopokova's Bluebird pas de deux, **4:**223
Mordkin performance, **4:**459
one-act ballet, **3:**205
Svetlov written accounts, **6:**28
Sylphides premiere performance, **6:**61–62, *61*
Saisons, Les, **1:**288, 424, 425, **4:**68
Legat (Nikolai) revival, **4:**143
Saisons de la danse, Les (journal), **3:**85
Śaiva cult, **3:**465–466
Saiyid, Shayma, **5:**64
as contributor, **1:**94, **3:**425, **4:**5–6, **5:**62–65, 597–598
Saiz, Jean-Louis, **3:**299
Sajuriana, La, **2:**122
Sakara, **4:**537
Sakari Viika, *as photographer,* **1:**176
Sakata Tōjūrō, **3:**637
Sakato Kongō, **4:**40
Sakato-za, **4:**39
Sakellariou, Charalambos, **3:**303
Sakhalin Island, **1:**31
Sakharoff, Alexander, **1:**111, **3:**76–77, 146, **5:503, 6:**52, 301, 302
Sakharoff, Clotilde, **1:**111, **3:**76–77, **6:**52, 301, 302
Sakhianova, Larisa, **5:473**
Saklin, Peter, **2:**438
Sakon Motoakira, **3:**650
Sakura-hime, **1:**362
Sakura Hime Azuma Bunshō, **3:**658
Sakurama Banba, **3:**388, 650, **4:**41, **6:**229

Sakurama Michio, **4:**41
Sala, Eugenia, **3:**51
Sala, Oscar, **4:**519
Sala B, **6:**121
Salade, **2:**267, **3:**341, 415, **4:**184, 319, 418, **5:**95
Salama, Gamal, **2:**497
Salaman, Susan, **5:**298, 299, 300
Salammbô, **1:**488, **2:**582, **3:**128, 204–205, **4:**444, **5:454**
Mordkin performance, **4:**459
Salamoni, Giuseppe (the elder), **1:**236, **2:**596, **3:**365
Salamoni, Giuseppe (the younger), **3:**365, 449, **4:**696
Saland, Stephanie, **4:**180, 619, 623
Salanga, **4:**639
Salas, Roger, **5:**676
Salavisa, Jorge, **5:**234–235
Salazar, Adolfo, **4:**399
Saldoni, Rafaela, **1:**480
Saleh, Magda, **2:**496, 497, *497,* 498, 499, **4:**414, 416
as contributor, **2:**481–486, 486–495, 495–499
Salem, Lori Anne, **4:**416
Salgado, Olando, **2:**280
Saliba, Paul, **1:**213, 232
Salii brotherhood, **3:**541
Salimbaev, Vladimir, **1:**519, **5:**471
Salin, Klaus, **2:**632
Salinas, Francisco de, **3:**29
Salish (people), **4:**568
Sallay, Zoltán, **3:**415, *416*
Salle, David, **1:**142
Sallé, Francis, **6:**175
Sallé, Marie, **2:**29, 465, **5:**35, **503–505, 6:**175, 189
Caractères de la Danse, Les, **2:**59, **4:**130, **5:**105
costume, **2:**238
debut, **3:**66
Handel ballet music, **4:**509
Indes Galantes, Les, **3:**450
as Noverre influence, **4:**694, 698
Paris Opera Ballet, **5:**41, 88
pas de deux, **5:**105
Phaëton, **5:**505
as Prévost protégée, **5:**248, 249
retirement in wake of La Barberina's success, **1:**365
Salle Pleyel, **3:**82
Salles des Machines (Tuileries), **4:**188, **6:**157
Salle du Petit Bourbon, Versaille, **6:**156, 157
Salle Favart. *See* Opéra-Comique, Paris
Sally (musical), **4:**209, 420, **6:**273
Salmacida Spolia, **3:**622, **5:**2
Salmhofer, Franz, **4:**59
Salmirs, Deborah, **3:78**
Salmon, Jacques, **1:**275
salmon cult, **4:**550
"Salmon Leap, The," **3:**251
Salome (biblical figure), **1:**20, 448, **2:**166
Salomé (Allan dance), **1:42,** 43
Salome (film), **1:**441
Salomé (Flindt dance drama), **3:**13
Salomé (Fuller dance), **2:**94, **3:**92
Salomé (Lazzini dance), **1:**349
Salomé (Strauss opera), **1:**406, **5:**246
"Dance of the Seven Veils," **2:**120, **3:**20, **4:**114, **5:**438, **6:**270
Salomé (Wilde play), **3:**20, 163, **5:**493
Horton dance versions, **3:**386, 387

Lambert incidental music, **4:**114
Rubinstein production, **5:**438
See also Tragédie de Salomé, La
Salomini, Giuseppe ("di Vienna"), **3:**545
Salomonoff, Senia, **2:**581
Salomons, Elsie, **2:**47
Salon d'Automne, Gran Palais, Paris, **1:**317, **2:**407, **3:**197
Salonen, Toivo, **2:**631
Salón México, El, **2:**196, **3:**402
Salón Variedades de Sevilla, **1:**61
sal-p'uri, **3:**341, **4:**47–48
salsa, 276, **2:**274, **5:**636, **6:**251
saltare derivations, **4:**348
Saltarelli Ensemble, **1:**400
saltarello, **1:**351, **4:**348, **5:**505–507
  allemande, **1:**45
  alta association, **1:**53
  bassedanse pairing, **1:**380, **4:**501
  Caroso dance manuals, **2:**74
  cascarda similarity, **2:**77
  Cornazano dance manual, **2:**05, **3:**542
  forlanas, **3:**49–50
  galliarde versus, **3:**109
  music, **4:**502
Saltarello, ou O Maniaco po la Dança, **5:**500, 501
Saltarello dito il Bergamasco, **1:**428
saltarello tedesco, **1:**45
saltatas, **4:**476
Saltatina, **1:**411
Salter, Humphrey, **3:**376
Salt Lake City ballet. *See* Ballet West
saltos al lado, **1:**53
Saltsame Haus, Das, **3:**132
Saltykov-Shchedrin, Mikhail, **5:**516
Salucci, **2:***415*
Salud, La, **1:**61, 62
Salutation to the Depths, **3:**404
Salut au Monde, **6:**89
Salut d'Amour à Margot Fonteyn, **3:**46
Salute of the Sun, The, **5:**46
Salute to "Dancers for Life", A (television program), **6:**132
Salvadori, Andrea, **3:**381
Salvioni, Guglielmina, **1:**238, **3:**346, 426, **5:**94, 455, 501
Salz, Jonah, *as contributor*, **3:**338–339, 650–652, 652–653, **4:**83–85, 332–333, **5:**590–592, **6:**409–410
Salzburg, Austria, **1:**241–242
Salzburg Festival, **3:**630, **4:**60, **6:**357
Salzedo, Carlos, **5:**302
Salzmann, Alexander von, **1:**98, **3:**558
Samai fu (Japanese text), **3:**591
saman, **3:***500*
Samar, Devilal (Udaipur), **5:**580
Samara Opera and Ballet Theater, **5:**472
Samaritanti, PierLuigi, **1:**75, **4:**249
Samarkand, Uzbekistan, **6:**306
Samaropoulo, Persephone, **2:**498
Samaryaa (Nigeria), **3:**348
Sāmaveda, **3:**453
samba, **4:**520, **5:**507–508, 630, **6:**246
  ballroom competition standards, **1:**359
  Brazil, **1:**527–529, 530
samba de caboclo, **1:**530
samba de gafieira, **1:**527–528

samba de roda, **1:**527
sambai, **3:**121
samba schools, **1:**526, 527
Samblaceno, Vinencio, **5:**172
Samburu dance, **2:**89, 210, 211, 212, **4:**484, **5:**509
Sámdor, Ivánka, **3:**418
Samedi C (television series), **6:**132
Samengo, Paolo, **1:**36, 237, **3:***258*
Same Old Story, **3:**52–53
Samev, A., **2:**11
Sami, Magda, **2:**498
Samkov, Vladimir, **5:**483
Samoa, **2:**593, **4:**369, 628, **5:**225, **509–510**
Samody (peoples), **5:**447
Sampih, I., **4:**265, *265*
Sampo, **5:**473
Samson, **3:**358, **5:**306
Samson, Leela, **5:**510–511
Samsonarson, Jon, **3:**436
Samson et Dalila (Saint-Saëns), **2:**187, 367, **3:**24
  Metropolitan Opera centennial performance, **4:**382
Samsova, Galina, **2:**510, 511, **4:**541, **5:**53, 55, 421, 565
  Swan Lake performance, **5:***651*, 653
Samuels, Heather, **4:**22
Samuelson, Ralph, **6:**415
samurai, **1:**160, 168, **2:**216, 217, **3:**580–581, 606–607, **4:**653, **6:**445
Samurai, **4:**266
Samusara, **3:**523
San (people), **2:**210, 602
Sanasardo, Paul, **1:**350, 388, **2:**358, 604, **5:**234, 439, **6:**121
Sanbasō, **3:**593, **4:**660
Sanborn, John, **2:**609
San Carlo Opera Ballet, Naples, **4:**134
sañchāri bhāvas, **3:**462
Sanchez, Juan, **5:**54
Sanchez, Pedro, *as photographer*, **5:**323
Sanchez de Badajoz, Diego, **2:**1
Sanctum, **4:***649*
Sand, Inge, **1:**316, *508*, **5:**295, *428*, 429, **511**
  Bjørnsson dance partnership, **1:**454
Sand, Monique, **2:**470
sandae-dogam tradition, **4:**50
sandals, **3:**46
sand dance, **3:**608, **5:**601, **6:**98
Sande masking society, **4:**290
Sanderlings, **4:**595
Sander, Ruth, *as contributor*, **3:**88–89, 381–383
Sanders, Dirk, **1:**251, 349, 403, **3:**359, **4:**601, 602
Sanderson, Julia, **6:**270
Sandhya, **2:**623, *623*
San Diego Ballet, **3:**345
sand jig dancing, **6:**316
"Sandmann, Der" (Hoffmann), **2:**198
Sandmen, The, **3:**193
Sandrini, Emma, **2:**199
Sand Skin, **4:**220
Săndulescu, Vivia, **5:**390
Sandys, George, **2:**269
Sandys, William, **3:**33
Sanesi, Ireneo, **2:**188
Sanford, Eric, *as photographer*, **1:**395
Sanford, Ralph, **1:**481

San Francisco Arts Education Project, **2:**110
San Francisco Ballet, **1:**73, 96, **2:**161, 273, **5:**511–514, **6:**264, 265
  archival materials, **4:**170
  Balanchine works in repertory, **5:**513
  Bliss score, **1:**462, 463
  Bolm, Adolph, **1:**484, **5:**511
  Christensen brothers, **2:**160, 161–162, **5:**511–512, 513, **6:**264
  Collins choreography, **2:**187
  Coppélia, **2:**200, **5:**512
  Ford Foundation grant, **1:**271, **6:**265
  Forsythe guest choreography, **3:**52
  full-length *Swan Lake*, **6:**34
  Giselle, **5:**512
  Gregory, Cynthia, **3:**306
  Job, **3:**609
  Kudelka productions, **4:**72, 73
  Martins's *La Sylphide* reconstruction, **4:**275
  New York City Ballet exchange program, **2:**161
  Nutcracker, The, **5:**15, *512*
  Oukrainsky, Serge, **5:**511–512
  Reed, Janet, **5:**511
  Romanoff performances, **5:**391
  Romeo and Juliet, **5:**398, 514
  Sleeping Beauty, The, **5:**613
  Swan Lake, **5:**512, 514
  Tomasson, Helgi, **5:**513–514, **6:**174
  Worsaae designs, **6:**404
San Francisco Ballet School, **1:**483, **2:**161, **5:**559, **6:**292
San Francisco Chronicle (newspaper), **6:**299
San Francisco Civic Ballet, **1:**484
San Francisco Performing Arts Library and Museum, **4:**170
Sangai, **3:**468
sangaku, **3:**584, **4:**83
Sangalli, Rita, **1:**347, **3:**71, 261, **4:**353, **5:**94, 149, **514–515**, **6:**62, 64, 242
  Black Crook performances, **1:**456, **5:**514, **6:**267
Sang an der Sonne, **4:**90–91
Sangeet Natak (journal), **3:**469
Sangeet Natak Akademi, **5:**43
Sanggar Tari Nyoman Kakul, **3:**645
sang hyang dedari, **2:**231–232, **3:**473, 479, **4:**146
sangig, **2:**230
Sangīta-ratnākara (Indian dance treatise), **1:**168
Sangree, Walter H., **6:**25
Sanguet, Henri, **2:**410, **5:**163
Sanguine Fan, The, **2:**512, 513, 574, **3:**428
Sanguinetti, Inés, **1:***113*
Sanguinetti, Julio María, **6:**302
Sanguinetti Gambaro, Claudio, *as contributor*, **6:**301–303
San Guo (opera), **6:**421
Sanguozhi (Chinese text), **4:**45
Sanja Matsuri, **1:**361, **3:**90
sanjo, **1:**166
San Jose Ballet. *See* Cleveland–San Jose Ballet
San Juan, Olga, **6:**93
Sanjukta Panigrahi, **5:**68–69
Sanjust, Filippo, **5:**396
Sankai Juku, **1:***60*, 61, 246, **2:**18, *18*, **4:**628

sankīrtan, **4:**254
Sankovskaya, Ekaterina, **1:**485, 486, **4:**454, **5:**454, **515–516**
Sankt Gallen, Switzerland, **6:**52
Sankurō (Sanjūro), **5:**28
Sanlaville, Marie, **2:**199, **4:**354, **6:**62
San Martin, José de, **2:**122
San Martín Ballet, **1:**102, 103, 112, 113, 114
San Miguel, Lolita, **5:**275
Sannazaro, Jacopo, **5:**113
sanni dances, **2:**229, **4:**300
sanni yakuma dances, **4:**300
Sanoja, Sonia, **6:**323
Sano, Kemoko, **1:**304, **5:**516–517
San Pedro Manrique, Soria, **1:**85
Sanquirico, Alessandro, **2:**208, **3:**547, **5:**517–518, 537, *538*, **6:**338–339
  costume design library, **4:**162
Sanskrit literature. *See* India, epic source of dance
Sansom, Bruce, **5:***420*
Sanson-Catz, Anne, **4:**585, 599
Sans Titre, **1:**350
Santa Cruz, Nicomedes, **5:**146
Santa Cruz, Victoria, **5:**146
Santalicante, Rafaella, **5:**409
Santamaria, Elvira, **6:**93
Santamaria, Mary Anne, **5:**172
Santana, Carlota, **3:**11
Santanella. See Métamorphoses, Les
Santaro, Mikhail, **6:**377
Santa Rosa, Isabel, **5:**234, 235
Santee, David, **2:**299
Santería, **2:***63*, 280, **6:**185, 345
Santhal (people), **1:**362
"Santiago" (dance), **5:**144
Santiago, Chile, **2:**124–125
Santiago, Sonia, **3:***153*
Santić, Jelena, **6:**435, *435*
Santillán Ortiz, Canuto, **4:**328
Santlow, Hester, **2:**394, **5:**105, **518–519**, **6:**372, 373
Santo, Iván, **5:**275
Santo Domingo. *See* Dominican Republic; Haiti
Santolini, Emma, **5:**404
Santons, Les, **1:**247, 534
Santoro, Claudio, **6:**326
Santos Rivera, Antonio, **4:**328
São Paulo, Brazil, **1:**532, 533, 534, 535, 537
sapateia, **5:**229
sapateo dances, **1:**529
Saplain, Dimitri, **2:**136
Saporta, Karine, **2:**611, **3:**79
Sapozhnikov, Sergei, **3:**193
Sapphire, Olga, **3:**589
Sappho et Phaon, **2:**414
Sappington, Margo, **3:**617, **6:**324
Saqui, Madame, **2:**174, **4:**523
Sara (people), **6:**17
sarabande, **4:**507, 510, 511, 664, **5:**519–521, 620, 669, **6:**380
Sarabande, **3:**398, **4:**81
Sarabhai, Mallika, **4:***70*, **5:**521–522
Sarabhai, Mrinalini, **3:**199, 468, **5:**521, **522**
Saracco, Giorgio, **5:**610, **6:**64
Sarach, Marian, **3:**362
"Saracumbe" (dance drama), **5:**67
Sarafina! (musical), **5:**648, **6:**288
Sarah, duchess of Marlborough, **4:**431
Sarah Lawrence College, **2:**111, 575, **3:**385, **5:**559, 561, **6:**164
Saraiva, Eduardo, *as photographer*, **5:**233, 234

Sarajevo Ballet, **6:**436, 438
Sarakatsani (people), **3:**296
Sarambo, **2:**430
sarao, **5:**668
Sarasate, Pablo, **4:**59
Saratoga, **1:***296,* 297, **3:**87, **5:**616
Saratoga Performing Arts Center, New York, **4:**607
Saratov Ballet Company, **5:**472
Saray Eğlenceleri, **6:**213
Sarbagishev, Uran, **4:**87, **5:**460, 462
Sarcinelli, Ferdinando, **5:**1
sardana, **2:**101, **3:**35, 65, 69–70, **5:522–523**
Sardinia (Italy), **2:**99, 101
Sardoni, Alessandra, **3:**557
Sardono, **5:523–524**
Sarfoji II, king of Thanjavur, **1:**442
Sargasso, **1:**72, **4:***601*
Sargent, Dudley A., **6:**294
Sargent, John Singer, **3:**7, 656, **5:**262
Sargent, Malcolm, **3:**520
Sari, Wirahma, **3:**504
Sarian, Ekaterina L., *as contributor,* **1:**121–122
Sarje, Aino, **2:**635
Sarkisian, Viktor, **1:**408
Sarkissian, Rousanne. *See* Rousanne, Madame
Sarkoff, Sacha, **1:**410
Sarma, Pasumarti Venugopal Krishna, **5:**330
Sarma, Prahlad, **5:**330, **6:**320
sarongs, **2:**229
Sarony, Otto, **5:**177
as photographer, **5:**515
Sárosi, Bálint, **2:**530
Saroyan, William, **1:**65, **4:**227–228
Sarracenia, **2:**388
Sarracenia, But, **1:**195
Sarry, Christine, **1:**72, **2:**583, **4:**262, **5:**369
Sarstädt, Marianne, **4:**602, **5:**531
Sarti, Giuseppe, **2:**55
Sartorio, Giulio Aristide, **5:**438
Sartre, Jean-Paul, **1:**404
sarugaku, **3:**584, **5:**49, **6:**445
Sarugaku Dangi, **4:**40
Sarugaku-no-za, **3:**653
saruguma makeup style, **4:***296*
Sarukkai, Malavika, **5:524–525**
Saruwaka Kanzaburō, **4:**534
Saruwaka Ryū, **3:**593
Sarwiti, Sandrut Bin, **3:***502*
Saryan, Katarineh, *as contributor,* **1:**121–122, **3:**125–126
Sarynova, Lydia P., *as contributor,* **3:**664–665
Sasaki family, **4:**85
Sasanka, **5:**660
Sasha Waltz & Guests, **3:**156
Saskatchewan, Canada, **2:**48, **4:**166
Sasportes, José, **3:**555, 557
as contributor, **5:**230–236
Sasraprawira, **3:**497
Sassian, David, *as contributor,* **2:**527–530
Sasson, Jack M., **1:**448
Sastri, Vedantam Lakshminarayana, **1:**273, **6:**321
śāstrīya, **3:**455
Sasun, Armenia, **1:**120, 122
Satanilla, ou L'Amour et l'Enfer, **1:**86, **5:**147–148, 150
Satan's Ball, **3:**421
Satan with All His Devices, or The Lessons of the Sorcerer, **1:**477

Satie, Erik, **1:**134, 156, 196, 246, 438, **3:**393, **5:**85, 191, 237, **525–526,** 527, *674*
Ballet Suédois scores, **1:**328
Cunningham collaborations, **2:**286, 287, 289, **4:**516
Diaghilev commission, **1:**316, 323, **2:**408, 409, **4:**515, 516
Foundation Contemporary Dance program, **4:**594
Mercure score, **4:**320, 516
modern dance scores, **3:**384, **4:**516
Monotones score, **4:**452
musical idiom, **4:**516
Relâche score, **2:**603, **3:**614, **4:**516, 334, 335
as Sauguet influence, **4:**517
Trois Gnossiennes score, **1:**156, **4:**117
Vexations score, **2:**574
See also Parade
satire. *See* caricature and comic art
Satisfyin' Lover, **5:**127
satokagura, **3:**578, 584, 642
satriya nrttya, **5:**354
Sats, Ilya, **3:**193
Satsumanokami, **4:**83
sāttvikābhinaya, **3:**457–458
Saturday Night Fever (film), **2:**620, **5:**186, *186,* 633
Saturday Review (British journal), **3:**284
Saturday Review/World (American publication), **6:**299
Saturn (deity), **5:**378
Saturnalia, **3:**541, **5:**376
Satyam, Tadepalli Pariya, **6:**321
Satyavati, **3:**199
satyrs, **2:**158, 234, **3:**287, *288,* 290, **5:***375,* 598
Sauce Tartare (revue), **1:**520, **4:**335
Saudades do Brazil, **3:**132
Saudi Arabia. *See* Arabian Peninsula
Sauguet, Henri, **1:**305, 306, **2:**111, **4:**33, **5:526–527**
Ballets 1933, **3:**73
ballet scores, **4:**517
Chatte, La, **1:**258
Diaghilev commissions, **2:**408
Lazzini productions, **4:**134
Mirages, Les, **2:**114
Saul, Peter, **2:**574, **4:**115
Saul, Pinise, **4:**487
Saulnier, Victoire, **5:**90
Saunders, George, **4:**189
Saunders, Job, **4:**394
Saunders, Richard Drake, **4:**690
Saunier, Vicent, **4:**695
Saura, Carlos, **3:**10, 101, **5:**674
Saurin-Sorani, *as photographer,* **6:**358
Sause, Judson, **6:**239
Sausin, Jacques, **1:**290, **2:**109, **4:**136
Saussure, Ferdinand de, **4:**376–377
Sauterelle, La, **2:**249
Sauti (people), **3:**500
sauts. See ballet technique, jumping movements
Sauvage, Henri, **6:**161
Sauvage, Marcel, **3:**93
Sauvage, Thomas, **5:**135
Sauvages, Les, **3:**450, **4:**423
"Sauvages, Les" (Rameau), **5:**306, 307
Sauvages, ou Le Pouvoir de la Danse, Les, **3:**117
Sauvages de la Floride, Les, **3:**68, 358

Sauvé, Bernard, **4:***82*
Sauveterre, François, **5:**231
Sauveur, Marie-Louise, **4:**694
Sauveur, Nicolas, **4:**9
Sava Centar, Belgrade, **6:**435
Savage, Archie, **2:**458
Savage, Nelly, **3:**23
Savage, Richard Temple, **2:**368
Savage Rose (music group), **3:**13, **5:**432
Savannah, **5:**660
Savarese, Nicola, **3:**556
Savaria, Georges, **5:**61
Savignano, Luciana, **1:**292, **3:**553, 601, **5:**196, **527–528,** 529–530
Savina, Vera, **2:**409, **4:**318, 319, 320
Savino, Jo, **2:**109, **5:**55
Savinskaya, Tatiana, **3:**186
Savitri, **4:**112, **6:**151
Savitskaya, Liubov, **5:**157
Savoy, duchy of, **3:**544
Savoy Ballroom, Harlem, **4:**202, 254, **5:**629–630, **6:**256, *262*
Savoy Theatre, London, **4:**189
Savrovsky, Leonid, **5:**699
Sawicka, Olga, **5:**218
șawt dance, **4:**412
Saxelin, Alexander, **2:**632
saxophone, **1:**10, **2:**368, 431
sayare, **2:**121
"Sayaw sa Bangko" (Bench Dance), **5:***173*
Say Bye-Bye, **3:**52
Sayette, Howard, **1:**519
Sayın, Hidayet, **6:**212
Sayings of Mao Tse Tung, The (Krauss), **2:**110
Saylor, Bess, **6:**266
Sayo Iura, Caroline, **2:**470, *470*
sayuun dance, **4:**571
Sazonova, Evgenia, **3:**539
sbarra. See barriera, torneo, and *battaglia*
Sbarra, Francesco, **3:**381
Scaccheri, Iris, **1:**112, 113
Scafidi, Nadia, **3:**558
Scala, Flaminio, **2:**190
Scala Ballet, **1:**82, 420, **2:**111, **3:**552, **5:**515, 517, **528–530,** **6:***159*
Angiolini, Gaspero, **1:**88, **3:**546, **5:**528
Aumer production, **1:**202
Beretta performances, **1:**427
Blasis, Carlo, **1:**344, 460, **3:**547, **5:**528
Borri, Pasquale, **1:**499–500
Brianza, Carlotta, **1:**540, **5:**528–529
Canziani, Giuseppe, **2:**55
Carey, Gustave, **2:**60
Cecchetti as ballet school director, **2:**84, **5:**529
Cecchetti as principal dancer, **2:**82
Cerrito debut and performances, **2:**93, 94, **3:**181, **5:**528
Cinderella, **5:***529*
contemporary directors, **3:**551–552
Coralli family, **2:**202
Cortesi versions of *Giselle* and *La Sylphide,* **2:**209
Cranko's *Romeo and Juliet,* **2:**266, **5:**395–396
dancing master, **2:**338
dell'Ara, Ugo, **2:**369
Don Quixote productions, **2:**435, 440
Edel designs, **2:**477

Elssler (Fanny) performances, **2:**504, 505, **5:**528
Ferraris debut and final performances, **2:**587
Field as ballet director, **2:**590
Fokine choreography, **3:**24
Fornaroli, Cia, **3:**50–51
Fracci, Carla, **3:**59–60, *550,* 551, 552, **5:**527, 529, *529*
Fuoco, Sophia, **3:**96, 97
Gioja, Gaetano, **3:**175, 176
Giselle staging, **2:**93, **3:**181
Grisi, Carlotta, **3:**313, 314
Gsovsky (Tatjana) production, **3:**317
Henry, Louis, **3:**358
Hightower as artistic and ballet director, **3:**362
Hus, Auguste, **3:**426
Jeune Homme et la Mort, Le, **3:**601
Legnani, Pierina, **4:**145
Lepri, Giovanni, **4:**150
library, **4:**162
Manzotti, Luigi, **4:**258–259, **5:**529
Marenco, Romualdo, **4:**263–264
Maywood, Augusta, **4:**339
Milloss directorship, **4:**421, **5:**529
Monplaisir, Hippolyte, **4:**453, 455
Nureyev performances, **5:**7
Nutcracker, The, **5:**14, 15
opera premieres, **5:**517
Perrot productions, **1:**461, **5:**528
Pugni, Cesare, **5:**277
Romanov as ballet master, **5:**392
Romantic era, **5:**517, 528
Róna as ballet master, **5:**402
Ronzani, Domenico, **5:**403–404
Rota choreography, **5:**409
Sanquirico scenic design, **5:**517, 517–518, 537, *538*
Savignano, Luciana, **5:**527, 529–530
school, **3:**551, 553
Sleeping Beauty, The, **5:**606–610
Sylvia, **6:**64
Terabust, Elisabetta, **3:**552, **5:**401, **6:**144
Viganò, Salvatore, **5:**517, 528, **6:**338
virtuosity emphasis, **1:**347
Wallmann choreography, **6:**357
Zucchi, Virginia, **5:**529, **6:**452
Scandal (musical), **1:**420
Scandals of. . . . See George White's Scandals
Scandella, Misha, **2:**369
Scandinavia
folk dance society, **2:**386
labyrinth dances, **4:**107
See also Denmark; Finland; Norway; Sweden
Scandinavian Ballet, **2:**385, **4:**245
Scangiarusca, **1:**214
Scapino Rotterdam, **4:**252, 591, 593, 595, *595,* 598, **5:530–531,** 618
Scaramouche, **1:**287, **2:**388, **3:**609, **4:**447
Scaramuzo, Desiderius, **1:**235
Scarecrows, **2:**561
Scarlatti, Alessandro, **6:**119
Scarlatti, Domenico, **1:**291, **2:**355–356, 409, **3:**29, 447, **5:**230, **6:**5
Scarlatti, Giuseppe, **3:**187, **4:**509
Scarlatti Portfolio, **2:**162
Scarlet Letter, The, **5:**7
Scarpova, Anna, **6:**424
scena per angolo, **1:**447

Scenario, **4**:*651*
scenarios for dance. *See* libretti for dance
Scène de Ballet (Degas), **5**:180
Scene in the Czarda, **3**:341, 415, **6**:66
Scène Javanaise, **3**:384
scenery. *See* scenic design
Scenes and Dances, **3**:208
Scènes Dansées, **1**:118
Scènes de Ballet, **2**:425, **5**:**531–532**, 589
  Ashton production, **1**:151, 152, **5**:415
  choreographic style, **3**:265–266
  Fonteyn performance, **3**:42, 44
  Keil performance, **1**:4
  Markova-Dolin performance, **4**:269
  Somes performance, **5**:639
Scènes de Ballet (Stravinsky), **6**:6
Scenes from a Dance Drama, **6**:392
Scenes from Childhood, **3**:433
scenic design, **2**:390–392, **5**:**532–552**
  archival materials, **4**:167, 169
  artist collaborators, **1**:132–140, **2**:22
  ballet de collège, **1**:283
  ballet de cour, **1**:288
  Ballets Suédois influence, **5**:545
  Bauhaus and space interaction, **5**:546
  Budapest Opera Ballet, **3**:416–417
  caricature, **2**:67
  choreographer's role, **2**:390, 392
  constructivism, **3**:194, *194*, 631, *632*
  costume design linkage, **5**:543
  cubism, **5**:543, *543*
  Cunningham productions, **2**:*287*, 290, 291, 292
  curtain use, **5**:539, 543
  as Diaghilev's emphasis, **1**:318, 320, 322–323, 324, 325, **5**:540–543
  Fuller innovations, **3**:92–93, 94, 96
  Graham Dance Company productions, **3**:214, 216
  introduction of intermissions, **3**:69
  Léger's influence, **5**:545
  lighting, **5**:537, 538–539, 540, 544, 545, 547, 548, 551
  modern dance, **5**:547–548
  Noguchi's influence, **4**:659–660, **5**:547, 548
  nontraditional spaces, **5**:548–550
  perspective, **5**:*536*, 537, 538, *538*, 540
  Petipa choreographies, **5**:155–56
  proscenium arch, **5**:535–536
  Russian art influence, **5**:541–543
  Russian theatrical, **4**:277, 278, 280
  scenery changes, **5**:534–536, *535*, 539
  Soviet realism, **5**:*458*
  stage machinery, **5**:*534*, 535, 537, 539, **6**:38, 39, 46, 48
Schabel, John, **2**:609
Schacherl, Gabriele, *as contributor*, **1**:466–467
Schade, Maja, **2**:319
Schadow, Johann Gottfried, **1**:126, **5**:260
Schaeffer, Pierre, **1**:403, **2**:288, **4**:600

Schaffgotsch, Maria Josefa, **6**:388
  as contributor, **6**:388
Schaik, Eva van, **4**:599, 600
  as contributor, **4**:251–253, 589–590, 598–600, 601–602
Schall, Claus, **2**:380, **3**:105, **5**:392, 424, **552**
Schall, Margrethe, **5**:425
Schandorff, Silja, **1**:*511*, **2**:*386*, **3**:*39*, **5**:433
Schanne, Margrethe, **1**:*508*, **2**:3, **5**:*428*, 429, **553**
  Pas de Quatre performance, **3**:59
  Sylphide performance, **6**:59
Scharaff, Harald, **1**:507
Schartz, Michael, **2**:609
Schaufuss, Frank, **2**:385, **4**:380, **5**:394, *429*, 430, **553**
Schaufuss, Peter, **1**:158, 196, **2**:387, 561, **4**:244, **5**:97, 394, 553, *554*, **554–555**, 575, **6**:143, 349
  Berlin Opera Ballet, **1**:436, **3**:156
  English National Ballet, **2**:*510*, 511, *511*, 513, *513*, 514, **3**:269, 270
  Napoli staging for National Ballet of Canada, **4**:545
  New York City Ballet, **4**:611, 620
  as Royal Danish Ballet artistic director, **5**:433
  Swan Lake film, **3**:345
  Sylphide, La, **2**:511, *511*, 561, **4**:2, 125, **5**:401, 433, **6**:59
  Volkova influence, **5**:430
  Worsaae designs, **6**:404
Schaufuss family, **5**:**553–555**
Schawinsky, Alexander, **1**:387, **5**:546
Schayk, Toer van, **2**:347, 348, 469, 470, **4**:593, *593*, *596*, **5**:**555–556**
Schedel, Hartmann, **2**:*332*
Scheepers, Martin, **1**:290
Scheerer, Bobby, **5**:21
Schéhérazade, **1**:248, 410, **2**:15, 176, 441, **5**:**556**
  Anisimova choreography, **1**:91
  Bakst designs, **1**:254, 255, **2**:241, 407, **4**:*642*, **5**:541, 556
  Ballet Russe de Monte Carlo, **1**:301
  Ballets Russes de Monte Carlo revival, **1**:311, **2**:334
  Bolm production, **1**:484
  Bowman performance, **1**:518
  Cecchetti mime role, **2**:83
  Dance Theatre of Harlem revival, **2**:334
  English National Ballet revival, **2**:512
  Fokine production, **1**:318, 319, 320, **2**:582, **3**:14, 16, 17, 18, 24, *25*, 545, 208, 556
  Liepa (Andris) reconstruction, **4**:181
  in Sweden, **6**:41
  Froman staging, **6**:*4331*
  Harangozó production, **3**:341, 416
  Karsavina performance, **3**:656
  Kelly (Gene) adaptation, **4**:3
  Kölling expressionist production, **3**:415
  Koslov pirated version, **4**:56
  Kröller choreography, **4**:64
  Nijinsky performance, **2**:408, **4**:*642*
  Rimsky-Korsakov score, **2**:407
  Rubinstein performance, **5**:438, *438*
  Schollar performance, **5**:556, 558

Scheiffelin, Edward, **5**:355
Schein, Johann Hermann, **1**:364, **4**:507
Schell, Boris, **3**:562
Schellenberg, Ilke, **3**:*147*
Schema, **4**:650
schēma, **3**:289, **5**:**556–557**
Schemboche, *as photographer*, **6**:452
Schergen, Janek, **5**:56
Scherillo, Michele, **2**:188
Schering, Arnold, **1**:456
Scherzer, Birgit, **3**:156, 158
Scherzo, **4**:198
Scherzo à la Russe (Stravinsky), **6**:6
Scherzo Fantastique, **4**:24
Scherzo Waltz, **2**:378
Scheuermann, Lilly, **1**:241
Schiassi, Gaetano, **5**:231
Schickele, Peter, **4**:482
Schiefflen, Edward L., *as contributor*, **5**:80–82
Schiel, Margared and Rolf, **3**:303
Schiff, Jeffrey, **1**:141, **2**:461
Schiff-Faludi, Susan, *as photographer*, **4**:650
Schifrin, Lalo, **2**:389
Schild, Ludolf, **3**:76, 83
Schilder, Paul, **2**:320
Schiller, Beatriz, **6**:260
  as photographer, **1**:389, **2**:170, 247, **3**:447, **4**:151, 190, 471, **6**:153
Schiller, Johann Christoph von, **1**:402, **5**:464
Schilling, Tom, **1**:1, 441–442, **3**:154, 155, 156, 158, 360, **5**:**557**, **6**:53
Schillinger, Joseph, **4**:688
Schillinger System of Musical Composition, The, **4**:688
Schindowski, Bernd, **3**:157
Schiørring, Nils, **2**:387
Schipp, William, *as photographer*, **6**:108
Schippers, Thomas, **1**:101
schlacht. *See barriera, torneo*, and *battaglia*
Schlafende Prinzessin, Die, **4**:517
Schlagobers, **1**:240, **4**:228
Schläpfer, Martin, **1**:375, **6**:*52*, 53
Schlee, Albert, **3**:161
Schlee, Alfred, **4**:92
schleifer, **1**:46
Schlemiel the First (musical), **3**:202
Schlemmer, Oskar, **1**:132, 133–134, 204, 244, **5**:66, 184, 546, 548, **6**:162
  on Bauhaus theater, **1**:386, 387
  masks, **4**:302
  Triadic Ballet, **1**:*133*, 134, 385–386, *385*, **4**:161, **6**:9, 392
Schlesinger, Maurice Adolphe, **1**:9
Schlicher, Susanne, **3**:162
Schlömer, Joachim, **1**:376, **6**:52
Schloss Atelier, *as photographer*, **2**:451
Schlottman, Jeanette, **1**:79
Schlundt, Christena L., **6**:297
  as contributor, **2**:376–380, **4**:530–531, **5**:583–587, **6**:87–90
Schmais, Claire, **2**:320–321
Schmelzer, Heinrich, **3**:381
Schmelzer, Johann Heinrich, **4**:510
Schmelzer, Joseph, **6**:359
Schmid, Bernhard, **4**:505
Schmidt, Beverly, **2**:605, **3**:445, **4**:649
Schmidt, Harvey, **6**:282, 283
Schmidt, Hermann, **3**:185

Schmidt, Jochen, **3**:162
Schmidt, Jules, **1**:206
Schmidt, Kurt, **5**:546
Schmitt, Florent, **3**:94, **5**:237, 642
Schmolz, Halina, **1**:207
Schneemann, Carolee, **3**:634
Schneider, Gretchen, *as contributor*, **1**:277–279, **5**:316–320, 623–626, **6**:230–253
Schneider, Herbert, *as contributor*, **4**:508–512
Schneider, Karin, **3**:340
Schneider, Yurgen, **1**:75
Schneitzhoeffer, Jean, **2**:203, 435, **4**:108, 513, 514, **5**:319, **557–558**
  Sylphide score, **1**:9, 455, **5**:513, 558, **6**:57
Schnell, Betty (Hennings), **5**:425
Schnetz, Peter, *as photographer*, **1**:374, **5**:681, **6**:53
Schnitke, Alfred, **1**:38
Schnitzler, Arthur, **1**:72, 85, 86
Schoeller, J. C., **1**:239
Schoenberg, Arnold, **2**:21, 57, 471, **4**:244, 517, 613, **5**:37, 193, 407, 527, 679, 680, **6**:145
  Laban aesthetic similarities, **4**:89
  modern dance scores, **3**:384
  Moses und Aron, **1**:436, **2**:120, **3**:393
  Stravinsky twelve-tonal experimentation, **4**:6
  See also Pierrot Lunaire; Verklärte Nacht
Schoenfeld, Rina, **3**:532, 533
Schofield, Derek, *as photographer*, **3**:240, 241
Schola Cantorum, **3**:388
Scholar's Companion and Ball-Room Guide (Hillgrove), **6**:239
scholarship, dance. *See* libraries and museums; methodologies in the study of dance; *subhead* dance research and publication *under specific country names*
Scholes, Peter, **4**:625
Scholl, Tim, *as contributor*, **1**:463–464
Schollar, Ludmilla, **1**:48, 110, 429, **2**:72, **4**:457, **5**:**558–559**, **6**:341
  Jeux performance, **4**:642, *646*
  Nijinska choreography, **4**:*634*, 635, 659
  Schéhérazade performance, **5**:556
  students, **3**:351, 663
  Swan Lake role, **6**:32
Scholz, Friedrich, **3**:191, 192
Scholz, Uwe, **1**:391, **2**:361
  Leipzig Ballet, **3**:156–157
  Seventh Symphony, **1**:403
  Stuttgart Ballet, **2**:268, **3**:150, **6**:10
  Zurich Ballet, **6**:53, 454–455
Schomburg Center for Research in Black Culture, New York City, **4**:167
Schönberg, Bessie, **1**:421, **3**:214, 596, **5**:**559–560**
Schonfield, Derek, *as photographer*, **4**:474
Schönwald, Andreas, **2**:339
School for Dance, Leipzig, **3**:153
School for Husbands, **2**:185, **6**:276
Schooling, Elisabeth, **5**:299, **560**, 691

School of American Ballet, New
York City
Balanchine, George, **1:**257, 263,
266, 268, 271, **6:**246, 292
Collins as faculty member, **2:**187
Concerto Barocco inception,
2:193
Danilova teaching, **2:**343
Doubrovska and Vladimiroff as
faculty members, **2:**442
Eglevsky teaching, **2:**479
faculty, **6:**292
Ford Foundation grant, **1:**271,
4:607
founding, **1:**63, 64, 257, 263, 266,
271, **6:**246
Kirstein directorship, **4:**26, 27, 29
Littlefield as faculty member,
4:209
Schollar as faculty member,
5:559
Serenade premiere performance,
1:268, **4:**27, **5:**570–571
significance of, **6:**292
training style, **4:**615–616
Vladimiroff as faculty member,
6:344, 345
Williams (Stanley) men's classes,
1:330, **6:**399–400
School of Classical Dance
(Kostrovitskaya and Pisarev),
1:329, **6:**129
School of Contemporary Dancers,
Winnipeg, **2:**47–48
School of Fine Arts, Mexico City,
6:29
School of Hard Knocks, **2:**171
School of Natya, New York City,
4:354, **5:**497
School of Performing Arts, Ghana,
3:168
School of the Pennsylvania Ballet,
5:131
Schoon, Théo, **4:**626
Schoop, Raimond, **5:**54
Schoop, Trudi, **2:**40, 44, 316,
318–319, **4:**125, **5:560–561,**
561, **6:**52
Schorer, Suki, **2:**161, **4:**612,
616, 618
schotis, **2:**430
Schotte, Marie-Anne, **1:**414
Schottelius, Renate, **1:**102, 112
schottische, **5:**624, 627
Caribbean adaptation, **2:**63
Czech, **2:**301
écossaise vs., **2:**474
Finnish, **2:**630
French, **3:**70
German, **3:**141–142
Jamaican, **3:**573
Scottish Highlands, **3:**244
Schreyer, Lothar, **1:**132, 385
Schrifttanz (Laban newsletter),
3:161, **4:**92, 96, 686
Schröder, Wilhelmine, Betty, and
Auguste, **6:**335
Schubert, **4:**230
Schubert, Barbara S., **5:**25
Schubert, Franz, **2:**374, 475, **6:**360
Schubert Adage, **6:**380
Schubert Dances, **3:**388
Schubertiade, **1:**72, **4:**275
Schubertiana, **2:**356, **4:**459
Schüler, Henriett Hendel, **1:**199
Schüller, Gunhild, **1:**243
Schuller, Gunther, **4:**519
Schuller, Otto, **3:**305
Schultz, Carolyn, *as photographer,*
5:634

Schultz, Friedrich, **5:**220
Schultz, Marianne, **4:**627, *628*
Schultze, Denise, **5:**52, 54, 55, 653,
6:379
Schulwerk (Orff), **5:**42
Schulz, Johann, **5:**552
Schuman, William, **1:**66, **3:**218,
4:518, 632, **5:561–562,** **6:**199
Schumann, Robert, **5:**162, **6:**202
Schumann Concerto, **1:**49
Schuplattler dance, **2:**552, **3:**141
Schurman, Nona, **1:**421, **4:**440
Schutte, Terry, **5:**187
Schütz, Heinrich, **5:**244
Schwabe, Randolphe, **3:**656
Schwaen, Kurt, **3:**153
Schwalbe-Brame, Marilyn, **4:**693
Schwarcz Knab, **2:**332
Schwartz, Alexander, **4:**397
Schwartz, Michael, **2:**610
Schwartz, Nancy. *See* Becker
Schwartz, Nancy
Schwartz, Sheldon, **1:**374, 375
Schwarz, Hermene and Joseph,
2:357, 358, **6:**264
Schwarz, Jeanne, **5:**562, 690
Schwarz, Jhanyne (Jane), **5:**562
Schwarz, Josephine, **6:**266
Schwarz, Juanina (Christiane),
5:562
Schwarz, Nelly, **5:**562
Schwarz, Solange, **1:**1, **2:**199, 480,
3:73, 82, **5:**95, **562–563**
Béjart association, **1:**403
Lifar association, **4:**184, **6:**64
Schwarze Vögel, **1:**442, **5:**557
Schwarz family, **5:**357, **562–563**
Schween, Lione, **6:**51
Schweizerische Dachverband, **6:**54
Schweizer Milchmädchen, Das. See
Swiss Milkmaid, The
Schwerin, Germany, **3:**152
Schwertsik, Kurt, **4:**59
Schwetzinger Festival, **3:**630
Schwezoff, Igor, **1:**297, 313, **4:**590,
598, **5:**331, 573, **6:**151
Schwingende Tempel, Der, **4:**91
Scialoja, Toti, **4:**421, **5:***400*
Sciascia, Gaylene, **4:**627, 628
Science of Dance Training (Clarkson
and Skrinar eds.), **2:**330, **4:**17
Scintilla, o Il Demone Seduttore,
1:499
Scirocco Dance Group, **4:**679
Scoglio, Joseph, **5:**302
Scolaro, Il, **4:**507
Scope (television series), **6:**130, 131
*Scoporta del America du Cristofor
Columbo, La* (Angiolini),
4:174
Scoreography (McCraw notation
system), **4:**692, *692*
"Scores of Dunhuang, The"
(dance), **6:**82
Scotch Four (set dance), **5:**697
Scotch reel, **3:**243, 244–245, 249,
5:333
Scotch snap, **3:**243, 249
Scotch Symphony, **1:**272, **2:**578,
4:285, 610, 614, 617,
6:85, 396
Scotland, **3:**243–250
as Athabaskan dance influence,
4:574
Canadian dance forms, **2:**35,
3:244–245
country dances, **2:**256, 257,
3:247–250, 361
dancing masters, **3:**246–247,
248–249

écossaise derivation, **2:**474–475
folk dance sounds, **3:**38
Highland dance, **3:**243–247,
377–378
Highland dance competitions,
3:249
Highland music vogue, **2:**474
hornpipe, **3:**376, 377–378
Lancers, **2:**592
libraries and museums, **4:**164
as Netherlands dance influence,
4:585–586
as popular Romantic-era theme,
2:413, 474–475
stepping dances, **5:**695
See also Scottish Ballet
Scott, A. C., **1:**188
as contributor, **1:**16–18,
2:127–138
Scott, Blake, **5:**58
Scott, Jack, **3:**23
Scott, Lincoln, **3:**235
Scott, Margaret, **1:**208, 210, 213,
230, 231, **2:**184, **5:563–564**
Scott, Trudy, *as contributor,*
5:44–47
Scott, Virginia, **5:**69
Scott, Sir Walter, **2:**390, 475, **5:**624
Scott Brothers, *as photographers,*
2:424
Scottish Ballet (formerly Western
Theatre Ballet), **1:**290, **2:**110,
3:270, 271, **5:564–565**
Cranko's *Romeo and Juliet,* **5:**396
Darrell, Peter, **2:**350, **4:**117,
5:564–565
Glushak as guest director, **5:**565
MacMillan choreography,
4:241, 242
modern dance synthesis, **3:**271
Nerina guest performance, **4:**585
Welch performances, **6:**378
Scottish Country Dance Society,
2:592, **3:**249
Scottish Fantasy, **2:**4
Scottish History of James IV
(Greene), **3:**377
Scottish measure, **3:**376
Scottish Official Board of Highland
Dancing, **3:**245–246, 249
Scottish reel, **2:**35
Scottish Theatre Ballet. *See*
Scottish Ballet
Scott Library, Toronto, **4:**166
Scouine, La, **4:**577
Scouts of the Prairie (drama), **4:**464
Scramble, **2:**292, **3:**446, 620, **4:**37
Scranton Ballet, **6:**266
Scrapbook, **2:**580
Scrapped Ship, **3:**646
Screenplay, **4:**602
Screws Loose, **3:**447
Scriabin, Aleksandr, **2:**456, **3:**384,
6:66
Scriabiniana, **1:**492, **3:**195
Scriabin Preludes and Studies,
4:218
Scribe, Eugène, **1:**9, 202, **3:**69,
5:35, 92, **6:**267
Muette de Portici libretto, **4:**657
Somnambule libretto, **3:**360,
5:640, 641
Scripps, Luise Elcaness, **4:**693
as contributor, **1:**273–275,
3:507–508, **5:**291–292
Scripting the Dreams, **4:**626
Scudorama, **6:**108, 109, 165
Scully, Vincent, **4:**575
sculpture. *see* artists and dance
Scuola di Ballo, **1:**310, **4:**322

*Scuola Olandese, ossia L'Amante in
Statua, La,* **6:**69
Scylla, **1:**464, **2:**465, **4:**231, 232
Scythian Suite, **1:**38, **4:**36
Seda, Madame, **2:**314, 341
Sea Alliance, **1:**501
Sea Change, **2:**265, **5:**651
Seafall (film dance), **2:**606
Sea Gallows, **3:**429
Seagull, The, **1:**82, 493, **5:**205–206,
387, 588
Leventhal scenic design,
4:154, *154*
Plisetskaya staging, **5:**462
Sea Legend, **3:**511
Seale, Humphrey, **1:**402
Sea Maid, The, **2:**145
Seami. *See* Zeami
Séance, **5:**654, 692, **6:***82*
"Sean Triubhas" (Scots dance),
3:243, 246, 249
Sea of Tears, **3:**329
Searle, Humphrey, **4:**115, 240
Sears, David, *as contributor,*
3:348–350, **4:**38–39, 604–605
Sea Sand, **4:**595
Sea Shadow, **1:**124, **3:**611, 612
Season for Six, **5:**637–638
Season of the Stags, **5:**387
Seasons (Haydn Getanzt), **4:**266
Seasons, The, **1:**372, **2:**22, 293,
5:120, 123, 160, *161*
Cunningham staging, **2:**286,
6:402
Glazunov score, **3:**186, **4:**515
Golovin designs, **3:**196
Hynd arrangement, **3:**428
Keil performance, **4:**1
Seasons, The (Johns artwork),
3:620
Seattle, Washington, **6:**307
Seattle Public Library Dance
Collection, **4:**170–171
Sebastian, **1:**110, **2:**16, **3:**224, 343,
4:449, *450,* **5:**573, 604
Sebastian, Mister, **4:**310
Sebastian, Stuart, **2:**357, **6:**266
sebu', **2:**493
Šećerov, Vesna, **6:**435
Séchan, Charles, **2:**405, **5:**85, 132
Séchan, Louis, **3:**302
Seckler, Beatrice, **3:**402, 404,
4:198, 605
Second, Albéric, **5:**241
Second Dancers' Congress, Essen,
6:392
Second Detail, The, **4:**547
Second Great Awakening
(1790s–1830s), **6:**234
Second Hand, **1:**542, **2:**292
Second Hardy Tune Book, **3:**379
Second Hungarian Rhapsody
(Liszt), **4:**282
Second Lieutenant Romashov,
2:499
Second Mesa, **1:**141, **2:**461
Secondo libro di toccate
(Frescobaldi), **2:**98
Second Piano Concerto
(Tchaikovsky), **1:**261, 281
Second Stride, **1:**52, **2:**354–355,
3:273–274, 275
Secret des Muses (Vallet), **2:**98
Secret Detour, **4:**22
Secret du Sphinx, Le (Rostrand),
5:438
Secret of the Waterfall (videodance),
1:142, **2:**460, 607
Secret Pastures, **3:**621
Secrets (Charlip), **2:**110

Section d'or, La (journal), **1:**466
Secular Games, **3:**219
Seda, Magdalena. *See* Malena, La
Sedaine, Michel-Jean, **3:**117
Sedova, Julia (Julie), **3:**655
    Chopiniana performance, **6:**60
    Maryinsky Ballet, **4:**282, **5:**456
    Mordkin's All-Star Imperial
        Russian Ballet, **4:**459
    Nijinsky "Jeux des Papillons" pas
        de deux, **4:**640
    students, **2:**341, **5:**604, **6:**119
Séducteur au Village, Le, **1:**36, **5:**558
Sedunova, Tatjana, **4:**208
See-Saw (Forti choreography),
    3:54, 445
Seesaw (musical), **1:**419, **4:**594,
    6:204
See Ya Next Century, **1:**216
Sega, Roberto, **4:***222*
Segal, Roni, **3:**529
Segarelli, Domenico, **2:**206, 282,
    4:342
Segarra, Ramón, **5:**275
Segawa Kikunojō II, **5:**30
Segeeva, Aksinia, **4:**276
Segeju (people), **2:**418
Segerström, Per-Arthur, **6:**44, *46*
Segni, Lidia, **1:**111
Segonzac, André Dunoyer de, **5:**261
Segovia, Claudio, **6:**94, 287, 288
Segovia, Enrique, **5:**654
Segovia, Rosita, **1:**94, **5:**673
Seguidilla de Cuatro, **2:**122
seguidillas, **5:**133, **565,** 669, 671
    Mexican adaptation, **4:**384
seguidillas bolera, **1:**479, 480–481,
    2:421
seguidillas manchega, **1:**479, 480
Séguin, Robert-Lionel, **2:**36, 49
seguito breve, **2:**74
Segura, Felipe, **4:**397
Segura, Maestra, **5:**133
Sehgal, Mohan, **2:**624
Sehgal, Sarla, **1:**181–182
Seiber, Matyas, **3:**512
Seidl, Anna, **2:**470, **4:***597*
Seifutdinova, Bibian, **3:**665
Seigneuret, Michèle, **1:**291,
    403, 404
Seigneur Généreux, Le, **2:**389
Sei Koshyaku (Ankoku Buyō), **3:**363
Sein, Kenneth, **4:**520
Sein, U Po Sein, **4:**526, *526*
seis dance, **2:**64, **5:**274
seis-ocho dance, **3:**320
Sejong University, Korea, **4:**55
sekar alit, **3:**483
sekarans, **3:**493
Sekh, Yaroslav, **1:**491, **5:**459, **6:**106
Sekidera Komachi, **1:***179*
Seki no To, **3:**90, 593
Seko, K., *as photographer,* **5:**218
Sekolah Tinggi Seni Indonesia,
    3:481
Selby, Charles, **2:**85
Selico, ossia Il Buon Figlio, **3:**358
Seligmann, Kurt, **1:**141, **3:**57,
    58, 371
Selim, Maya, **2:**497, 498
Selim, Yousri, **2:**498
Selimov, Nikolaus, **1:**240
Selina, **3:**392
Selinder, Anders, **3:**618, **6:**37, 40
Selivanova, E., **5:***469*
Seljan, Vladimir, **6:**433
Sellars, Peter, **4:**472
Sellier, Carl Joseph, **1:**236
Sellier, Franz Joseph, **1:**236
Sellier, Grete, **6:**388

Sellier, Joseph, **6:**342
Sellinc, Anna, **3:***144*
Selling, Caj, **1:**230, **5:**47, **6:**42
Seltsames Septett, **3:***625*
Selva, **6:**324
Selva sin Amor, La, **1:**409
Selver, Charlotte, **1:**469, **470–471**
Selzer, Eva, *as contributor,*
    2:154–155
Selznick, David O., **4:**2
semasiology, **4:**367–368
Semb, Klara, **4:**672, 682
sembah, **1:**163
Šemberová, Zora, **1:**541, **4:**81,
    5:269, 393
Semenoff, Simon, **1:**296, 437,
    2:200, 201, **4:**63, 656
Semenov, Nikolai, **4:**657
Semenov, Viktor, **1:**517, **2:**96, 341,
    506, **3:**196, **4:**148
Semenova, Luda, **3:**48
Semenova, Marina, **1:**83, 490,
    2:597, **3:**12, **5:**95, 282,
    566–568, **6:**106
    Cinderella role, **5:**567
    Esmeralda role, **5:**566–567
    Flames of Paris performance,
        5:567
    Giselle performance, **5:**566
    as Kondratieva coach, **4:**38
    Sleeping Beauty performance,
        5:566
    students, **4:**74, **5:**236
    Swan Lake role, **6:**31
    virtuosic dramatic dancing,
        5:458
    on Yermolayev's dance style,
        6:420
    Zakharov as influence, **6:**442
    Zweig on, **5:**566
Semenova, Tatiana, **3:**389, **6:**264
Semenyaka, Ludmila, **1:**493, **4:**360,
    5:12, 462, **6:**228
Sémeté (Marais), **4:**481
Seminole (people), **4:**554, 558,
    559, 560
semiotic dance analysis, **4:**367–368,
    371, 377, **6:**25
Semira, **4:**276
Semiramide del Nord, La, **1:**427
Sémiramis, **1:**87, 88–89, **2:**433, 465,
    3:24, 187, 188, 189, 190,
    4:153, **5:**148, 424, 439, 528
Semizorova, Nina, **1:**493, **5:**567,
    6:228
Semmler, Max, **3:**99
Semyonova, Marina. *See*
    Semenova, Marina
Sen, Bhaswati, **5:**568
Sen, Saswati, **5:**568
Sendak, Maurice, **5:**51
séndratari, **3:**471, 666, 667
Sendratari Rāmāyaṇa, **3:**484, 666
Seneca, **3:**652, **4:**499, **5:**73, **6:**193
Seneca-Cayuga (people), **4:**556,
    557, 558
Senefelder, Alois, **5:**261
Senegal, **4:**663–664, **6:**20, *384*
    as Caribbean dance influence,
        2:62
    national dance company,
        4:548–549, **6:**21–22
Senelick, Laurence, **5:**318
    as contributor, **2:**174–177,
        4:520–523, **5:**69–72, 350–351,
        6:315–320
Senez, Sylvain, **3:**233, *233*
Senfl, Ludwig, **5:**683
Senft, Gerhard, **1:**241, **6:**388
sengenya dance, **2:**418

Senghor, Leopold Sedar, **4:**548
Senghor, Maurice Sonar, **4:**548–549
Senra, Carmen, **5:**675
Sensemaya, **1:**461, **2:**367
Sensory Awareness, **1:**469,
    470–471
Sentimental Bloke, The, **1:**208
Sentimental Journey, A (Sterne),
    6:311
Sentot Sudiharto, **5:**523, 524
Sen-Tsuru combination, **4:**533, 536
Seostri, **6:**70
Seoul National University, **4:**55
Separate Journeys, **4:**603
Sephardic Judaism, **3:**526–527, 603
Sephardic Song, **3:**605
Seprődi, János, **3:**422
Septet, **2:**286, 289, 294, **3:**274
Septimino, **2:**208
*Sept Péchés Capitaux, Les. See
    Seven Deadly Sins, The*
Septuor, **4:**185
Sequenza, **2:**388
Sequoio, Ron, **2:**269, 361
Seraikella *chhau,* **2:**117
Seraitce la Mort?, **1:**405
serampang dua belas, **3:**500
Seraphic Dialogue, **3:**217, **5:**407,
    547, **568**
Seraphic Song, **2:**584
Seraphita, **3:**657
Séraphite, **1:**292
Șerbănescu, Felicia, **5:**387
Serbia, **1:**370, **2:**101
    folk dance sounds, **3:**38
    theatrical dance since 1991,
        6:434–435
    traditional dances, **6:**426–428
Serbian National Theater, **6:**435
Serebriakova, Zinaida, **1:**422
Seregi, László, **1:**211, 242, 370,
    5:469, **569–570,** **6:**66
    Budapest Opera Ballet,
        3:417–418
    Cedar Tree, The, **5:**569
    Miraculous Mandarin
        rechoreography, **5:**569
    Serenade, **5:**569
    Spartacus, **3:**417, *417,* **5:**402, 569
    Sylvia, **3:**417, **4:**678, **6:**64
Serenade (Balanchine), **1:**63, 155,
    197, 258, 259, *259,* 260,
    260–261, 266, 281, **2:**244,
    3:418, **4:***609,* **5:**431, 569,
    570–571, **6:**217
    Balanchine revival, **4:**609
    in Balanchine's aesthetic
        progression, **1:**262, 267–268,
        272, **4:**27, 613
    Bruhn production, **2:**4
    in Dance Theatre of Harlem
        repertory, **2:**334
    Farrell performance, **2:**576
    feet position, **1:**331
    Franklin performance, **3:**87
    in Grands Ballets Canadiens
        repertory, **3:**231
    Hart (Evelyn) performance,
        3:345
    Hawkins performance, **3:**348
    Lavrovsky reconstruction, **3:**135
    as New York City Ballet signature
        work, **4:***609*
    piqué turns, **1:**338
    School of American Ballet
        premiere performance, **1:**268,
        4:27, **5:**570–571
    Simone performance, **5:**600
    in Washington Ballet repertory,
        6:366
    Wilde performance, **4:***609,* **6:***396*

Serenade (Neumeier), **4:**604
Serenade (Seregi), **5:**569
Serenade Andalouse, **1:**115
"Serenade for Strings"
    (Tchaikovsky), **1:**260
Serenade für Streicher, **3:**153
Serenade in A, **1:**479
Serenata Morisca, **3:**210, 211, **5:**587
Serers (people), **4:**548
Serf Ballerina, The, **4:**67, 225
serf dancers and theaters, **1:**408,
    5:452
Sergava, Katherine, **6:**278, *278*
Sergeant Early's Dream, **2:**1, **5:**303
Sergava, Aksinia, **5:**451
Sergei Diaghilev i russkoe iskusstvo
    (Silverstein and Samkov),
    5:483
Sergeyev, Konstantin, **1:**248, 371,
    502, **2:**422, **4:**67, **5:**5, 268,
    386, **571–572**
    Ali-Batyr, **5:**572, 595
    archival materials, **4:**165
    Boston Ballet joint production, 4,
        271, **6:**35
    Bronze Horseman, The, **3:**187
    Cinderella, **2:**174, **4:**284,
        5:572, 639
    Don Quixote performance, **2:**437
    dramatic dancing, **5:**458
    Dudinskaya collaboration, **2:**449,
        450, **6:**35
    Dudinskaya marriage and dance
        partnership, **5:**572, *572*
    Flames of Paris performance,
        3:12
    Fountain of Bakhchiserai
        performance, **3:**56
    Gayané performance, **3:**125
    Giselle performances, **4:**248, 585
    Hamlet, **2:**423
    Maryinsky directorship, **4:**284
    Maryinsky school, **5:**480
    Path of Thunder, **5:**462
    Raymonda staging, **5:**321, 463,
        572, **6:**343
    Romeo and Juliet performance,
        4:*281,* 284, **5:**393, **6:***398*
    Sleeping Beauty version, **5:**610
    Swan Lake performance and
        stagings, **4:**271, 284, **6:**31, 35
    Ulanova dance partnership,
        5:571
    Zakharov collaboration, **6:**442
Sergeyev, Nicholas (Nikolai), **1:**247,
    324, 329
    Coppélia production, **2:***199,* 200
    de Valois contract to reproduce
        Russian classics, **2:**401–402,
        3:264–265, **5:**413, 414, **6:**33
    Diaghilev productions, **2:**409
    Giselle revival, **3:**181–182, **4:**268,
        5:95
    International Ballet, **3:**269,
        511, *512*
    Latvian staging of *La Fille Mal
        Gardée,* **4:**127
    Markova roles, **4:**268
    Nutcracker reconstruction, **5:**13,
        14
    Sleeping Beauty reconstructions,
        3:511, **4:**284, **5:***413,* 611,
        6:*613*
    Stepanov notation of Maryinsky
        repertory, **5:**693, **6:**32–34, 35
    students, **3:**429, 508
    Swan Lake reconstruction, **3:**511,
        512, **4:**413, **5:**414, **6:**33–34, 35
Sergeyev, Sergei, **3:**125
Serglio, Sebastiano, **3:**622

Seril, Bruna P., **5**:173
Serjeant, R. J., **1**:401
Serkabaev, Almaz, **3**:665
Serling, Craig, **5**:436
Serlio, Sebastiano, **4**:187, **5**:534
Serov, Aleksandr, **3**:20, **4**:430, **5**:140
Serov, Valentin, **1**:254, 487, **3**:656, **5**:541, **6**:61
Serova, Lisa, **1**:312, **3**:265, **6**:196
Serpentine Dance (Fuller), **2**:250, 572, **3**:71, 91, 92, **4**:522, **6**:268
Serpentine Dance (Severini), **1**:130
Serpent of the Nile: Women and Dance in the Arab World, **4**:415
Serra, Richard, **6**:90
Serral, Dolores, **1**:480, **2**:251, **5**:672
Serrano, Eduardo, **4**:222
Serrano, Lupe, **1**:69, 71, *71*, 392, **2**:3, 279, 426, *436*, **4**:397, **5**:572–573, **6**:34
Serre, Jean-Claude, **3**:85
serrés, **1**:383
Serry, Jean, **3**:76, 83
Serse (Cavalli), **4**:234
Sert, José Maria, **3**:631
Sert, Misia, **2**:411
Servandoni, Giovanni-Niccolò, **3**:450, **4**:695
Servandoni, Jean-Nicolas, **5**:537, 538
Servante Justifiée, La, **1**:35, **4**:61
Servant of Two Masters, The, **4**:583, 625
Serva Padrona, La, **5**:306
servikos dance, **3**:299
Servos, Norbert, *as contributor*, **1**:203–204, **3**:40
Sese, Eddie, **5**:173
Sessions, Roger, **2**:196
Set and Reset, **1**:143, 545, **2**:608, **5**:313, 314, 551
set design. *See* scenic design
Seter, Mordecai, **3**:218
Sette Canzoni, **2**:356
Setterfield, Valda, **1**:51, **2**:53, 404, **3**:201, *201*, 202, 235, **5**:573–574, **6**:356, 363
Setting Sun, **3**:199
Setti Peccati Capitali, I, **4**:264
seudati, **3**:499
Seul, **2**:309
Seurat, Georges, **5**:178
Sevastianov (Severn), German (Gerry), **1**:313, 367, **3**:25, **5**:193
Seven Ballet Stories (Slonimsky), **3**:328
Seven Beauties, **3**:327, **5**:459, 471
Seven Brides for Seven Brothers (film), **2**:314, **4**:10, 11, *11*, **6**:280, 281
Seven Dances of Life, The, **6**:392
Seven Daughters of the Mountain King, The (The Three Palms), **3**:20, **5**:124
Seven Deadly Sins, The (Les Sept Péchés Capitaux), **1**:260, 271, 291, 388, 446, **6**:144
Balanchine world premiere, **1**:306, 307, **3**:73
Charrat performance, **2**:111
costume design, **2**:245
Gsovsky (Tatjana) production, **3**:318
Jenden-Solino choreography, **4**:627
Lander (Harald) choreography, **4**:118, **5**:429
Lander (Margot) performance, **4**:119

Linden performance, **4**:200
Losch performance, **4**:229
MacMillan choreography, **4**:241, 243
Nault production, **4**:577
Tanztheater Wuppertal revival, **3**:*151*
Vogelsang production, **3**:152
Seven Heroes, **3**:628
Seven Lively Arts, The (revue), **2**:425, **4**:269, **5**:531, **6**:6
Seven New Dances, **2**:526, **3**:619, **5**:680, **6**:107, 108, 113, 165
Seven Seals, **3**:657
Seven Silences of Salome, **2**:514
Seven Sisters, The (spectacle), **1**:456, **5**:616
1776 (musical), **6**:283
1789 . . . et nous, **1**:407
Seventh-Day Adventists, **1**:415
Seventh Symphony, **5**:547
  Azuma staging, **3**:589
  Bérard designs, **1**:426, **5**:547
  Franklin performance, **3**:87
  Markova performance, **4**:269
  Massine choreography, **1**:295, 300, 301, **4**:*321*, 323
  Scholz (Uwe) choreography, **1**:403
  Shostakovich music, **5**:595
  Skibine performance, **5**:604
  Youskevitch performance, **6**:425
Seventh Symphony (Petersson), **6**:43
Seventh Thursday after Easter, or Popular Festivities at Maryina Roshcha, The, **5**:453
Severini, Gino, **1**:130, **4**:421, **5**:180
Severn, Margaret, **4**:302
Severn, Merlyn, **5**:184
  as photographer, **4**:485, **5**:579, 645, 646, 647, 662, 663, 664, **6**:21, 22
Severnaia pchela (Saint Petersburg newspaper), **6**:451
Severskaya, Anna. *See* Northcote, Anna
Sévigné, Madame de, **5**:87, 298, *298*
Sevilla, Amparo, **4**:399
  as contributor, **4**:383–389
Sevilla, Cojo de, **6**:27
sevillanas, **5**:565
Sevillanas (film), **5**:674
Sevillano, Trinidad, **2**:513
sewamono, **3**:606, 637, **4**:352, 533, 536
Seward, C., **1**:456
Seyffert, Dietmar, **3**:155
Seyfried, Robert, **3**:*78*
Seymour, Kate, **4**:520, **6**:317
Seymour, Lynn, **1**:58, 390, **3**:150, 273, **5**:6, 193, 303, 574–575, **6**:217, *217*, 218
  Ashton ballets, **1**:155, 157, 158–159, **3**:267, **4**:456
  Invitation performance, **3**:512, 513, *513*
  MacMillan ballets, **4**:241, *241*, 242, 243, *243*, 244, 257, **5**:306, 396, *419*
  Month in the Country performance, **4**:456, *456*
  Sadler's Wells Theatre Ballet, **5**:421
Seymour, Maurice, **5**:183
  as photographer, **1**:296, 302, 315, **2**:113, 436, **3**:362, **4**:178, 322, 324, **5**:369, **6**:182
Sezefreda, Estela, **1**:532
Sferes, Andrea, **2**:612

Sforza, Alessandro, **3**:322
Sforza, Bianca Maria, **3**:322
Sforza, Francesco, **2**:204, 427, **3**:322
Sforza, Giangaleazzo, **1**:364
Sforza, Ippolita, **2**:427, **3**:322
Sforza, Tristano, **2**:427
Sforza family, **3**:322, 603
Shab Drung, **1**:444
Shabelevsky, Yurek, **1**:66, 309, 313, **3**:512, **4**:635, **5**:218, **6**:301, 441
Shabelska, Gala, **6**:301
shabwānī, **1**:401, **6**:418
Shadanova, O., *as photographer*, **5**:473
Shadow, The, **2**:11, 266
shadowboxing (cheironomia), **2**:115–116
"Shadow Dance" (pas de l'ombre), **2**:94, *94*
shadow dances, **3**:94, 95, **5**:29
Shadow'd Ground, **2**:197
Shadow of the Wind, **6**:200
Shadow on the Prairie, **5**:435
Shadowplay, **1**:68, **3**:444, **4**:24, **5**:417, **6**:201, 202, *202*
Shadow Reach, **3**:520
Shadows of Forgotten Ancestors, The, **6**:226
shadow theater, **1**:178–179, *178*, 180, **3**:476
  Balinese *wayang*, **1**:172, 173, 174, 179, **3**:476, 485, *487*, 501, 502, 504, **6**:367–370
  Javanese puppetry, **3**:496–497, 502, **4**:298
  Thai puppetry, **4**:8
Shadwell, Charles, **5**:518
Shadwell, Thomas, **5**:280, 489
Shafei, Abdel Rahman el-, **2**:496
Shāferin, Die, **4**:674
Shaffy Theater, Amsterdam, **4**:597
Shaft, **6**:44
Shag (dance), **1**:450
Shagonaby, Susan, **4**:558
Shaham, Rina, **3**:530, 531
Shahani, Kumar, **4**:247
Shahn, Ben, **5**:262
Shahzada, Laila, **1**:94
Shaievsky, Valery, **5**:265
Shake (dance), **6**:249
shake-a-leg, **5**:252
Shaker dance, **2**:168, **5**:575–577, **6**:185, 236
Shakers, The, **3**:399, *400*, 403, 404, **5**:577–578
  choreographic analysis, **4**:103
  film of, **3**:405
Shakespeare, ossia Un Sogno di una Notte d'Estate, **1**:427, **2**:60, **6**:70
Shakespeare, William, **5**:640
  bergamasque mention, **1**:428
  canary mentions, **2**:50
  dance performances within plays, **3**:252–253
  details for dance reconstructions, **1**:104, **2**:76
  Galeotti ballets, **3**:105
  galliard reference, **3**:106–7
  Hungarian productions, **3**:418
  mad scenes, **3**:180
  Neumeier ballet choreographies, **3**:338
  Old Vic productions, **2**:396
  Royal Ballet 400th anniversary program, **1**:156, **2**:445, **3**:392, **4**:242

Soviet-era productions, **4**:132, **5**:462
  on *volta*, **6**:351
  See also specific works
Shakhovsky, Aleksandr, **3**:539–540
Shakhuda, **6**:306
"Shakin' the Blues Away" (song), **4**:419, **6**:*447*
shakkyō mono, **5**:593
Shakti, **2**:105, **5**:521
Shalabi, Nagwa, **2**:498
Shall We Dance? (film), **2**:615
Shall We Dance? (Neumeier ballet), **4**:604
shamanism, **1**:183, **5**:578–579
  Central Asia, **6**:305
  China, **2**:140–141
  cross-cultural dance similarities, **4**:494
  Ecuador, **2**:475
  film documentation, **2**:602
  India, **3**:455
  Japan, **3**:578–579, 583–584, 641–642, **4**:652–653
  Korea, **4**:48, *48*, 494
  !Kung San, **4**:74, 75, *75*
  Malaysia, **4**:249
  Native Americans, **3**:171, **4**:550, 566, 567
    Arctic peoples, **4**:571–572, 573
  Siberia, **5**:447, 448–449
  Taiwan, **6**:80
  Tibet, **6**:166
  Turkey, **6**:208, 209
  Vietnam, **6**:336
  See also trance dance
Shambhu Maharaj, **5**:581, 602
shamisen, **2**:12, 13, **3**:126, 639, **4**:*492*
  nagauta music, **4**:530
Shams Sporting Club, Cairo, **2**:498
Sham's Twin, **3**:340
Shan (people), **4**:524
Shanahan, Julie, **1**:389
Shangaan (people), **5**:661
Shangana-Tsonga dance, **5**:579–580, 643, 661, 662–663
Shanghai, China, **2**:133–134, 145
Shanghai Ballet, **2**:146, **6**:385
Shanghai Beijing Opera Theater, **6**:*447*
Shanghai Dongnan Physical Training School, **2**:133
Shanghai School of Dance, **2**:135, 137, **6**:385
Shanghai Shaoxing Opera Theater, **6**:425
Shanghai Wenyi Chubanshe, **2**:149
Shango, **2**:458
Shango cult, **2**:62, **6**:185, 345, *423*
Shangshu (Book of Records), **2**:148
Shanguine, Ivan, **2**:435, **6**:29
Shankar, Ananda, **5**:581
Shankar, Kanaklata, **5**:580
Shankar, Mamata, **5**:581
Shankar, Ravi, **5**:235, 580
Shankar, Sachin, **3**:468, **5**:580
Shankar, Uday, **1**:273, **2**:623, 625, **3**:468, **5**:45, *123*, **580–581**
Shankarscope (mixed media), **5**:581
Shantaram, V., **2**:623
Shaoxing Opera, **6**:425–426
Shape of Love, The (Kirkland and Lawrence), **4**:25
Shapero, Harold, **4**:450
Shapero, Lillian, **3**:214
shaping (Laban concept), **4**:99
Shapiro, Laura, *as contributor*, **6**:151–155
Shapiro, Sophiline, **2**:32
Shaporin, Yuri, **5**:587

Shaposhnikova, Aleksandra, **3:**137
Sharaff, Irene, **1:**28, **2:**245, 249, **5:**362
shararán dance, **2:**476
Shards, **2:**20, 296
Sharett, Rena, **3:**449
sharḥ al-rayyid dance, **6:**418
Sharir, David, **3:**449
Sharma, Bharat, **3:**469
Sharma, Narendra, **3:**468, 469
Sharma, Uma, **5:581–582**, 601
Sharma, Venugopalakrishna, **4:**62
Sharman, Frank, *as photographer*, **3:**512
Sharon, Mirali, **3:**531, 532
Sharp, Cathy, **1:**374, *374*, 375
Sharp, Cecil, **1:**118, **2:**257, 542, 546, 591, **3:**34, 281, **5:**329, **582–583**
  American square dances, **5:**687–688
  dance reconstructions, **3:**239, 241, 242
  English Folk Dance Society of America, **6:**247
  English traditional social dances, **3:**238, 239, 242
  Hinman association, **3:**367
  on minor sets, **4:**221
  on Morris dance, **4:**473
  summer dance camps, **6:**248
Sharp, Madeline, **3:**307
sharqī, **4:**490, 491
Shashikala, **6:**321
Shataranj ke khilari (film), **5:**568
Shatilov, Konstantin, **2:**497, **4:**284
Shatin, Anatoly, **1:**144
Shattuck, Roger, *as contributor*, **5:**525–526
Shavrov, Boris, **1:**464, **3:**125, 193, **4:**129
  Lukom dance partnership, **4:**233
  Maryinsky Ballet, **4:**283, **5:**458
  students, **3:**308, **5:**487, 638
Shavu'ot, **3:**641
Shaw, Artie, **1:**194, **5:**631
Shaw, Brian, **1:**150, **2:**515, **4:**452, **5:***107*, 416, **6:**64
Shaw, George Bernard, **3:**284, 596, **6:**282
Shaw, John, **5:**518, **6:**175
Shaw, Lloyd, **5:**689, **6:**247
Shaw, Martin Fallas, **2:**262
shawl dances. *See* attitude and shawl dance
Shawn, Allen, **2:**119
Shawn, Ted, **1:**55, 212, **2:**184, *377, 379*, **3:**396, **5:583–587, 6:**357, 407
  American musical theater performance, **6:**269
  archival materials, **4:**167, 168, 169
  Canadian vaudeville circuits, **2:**37
  costumes, **2:**247–248
  Delsarte system of expression, **2:**371
  as Graham teacher, **3:**210
  Jacob's Pillow, **2:**81, **3:**571–572, **5:**497, 586
  Job choreography, **2:**184, **3:**609
  Labanotation of works, **3:**427
  liturgical dance revival, **4:**212, **5:**356
  Orientalism, **5:**46, *46*
  St. Denis collaboration, **5:**583–584
  St. Denis marriage, **2:**376, **5:**494, 495, 496, 497

Weidman association, **6:**376
  See also Denishawn
Shawnee (people), **4:**556, 557
Shay, Anthony V., **4:**415
  as contributor, **1:**26–27, 101–102, **2:**344–346, **3:**513–515, **4:**78–79, 135–136
Shaytan's Captive, **3:**22
Shchedrin, Rodion, **1:**492, 539, **2:**278, **4:**212, **5:**205, 587–588
Shchepkin, Mikhail, **5:**515–516
Shcherbachev, Konstantin, **31:**5
Shcherbachev, Nikolai, **4:**224
Shcherbinin, Boris, **5:**471
Shchors, **6:**344
Shchukin, Sergei I., **4:**330
She (film), **3:**559
Shea, Mary Jane, **1:**478, **2:**193, *193*, 426
Sheaf of Dreams, A (film), **5:**589–590
Shearer, Joy, **5:**654
Shearer, Moira, **5:**331, 332, *332*, **588–589**, 639, **6:**119
  Cinderella performance, **2:**174, **5:***415*
  English National Ballet, **2:**510
  on *Giselle* interpretation, **3:**183
  Giselle performance, **5:***588*, 589
  International Ballet, **3:**511
  Red Shoes (film), **4:**324, *325*, **5:***588*, 589
  Sadler's Wells, **1:**150, 151, 158, **5:***414*, 416
  Scènes de Ballet performance, **5:**531
  Simple Man performance, **4:**668
  Symphonic Variations performance, **6:**64, 65
Shearer, Sybil, **1:**79, 421, **2:**290, **3:**404, **4:**213, 602, 605, **5:589–590**
Shebalin, Vissarion, **6:**116
shedding (beat), **3:**246
Sheehy, Carolyn, **4:**168
Sheely, Viola, **6:***449*
Sheep Spring, **4:**460
sheet music, **5:**625–626
Shekera, Anatoly, **5:**460, **6:**226
Sheleen, Laura, **3:**83–84
Shelem, Matityahu, **3:**531
Shelest, Alla, **3:**56–57, 138, **4:**247, **5:**5, 459, 595, 677
Shell, Caroline G., **2:**330
Shelley, Mary, **2:**200
Shellman, Eddie J., **2:***335*
Shelly, Mary Josephine, **1:**79, 420, 421
Shelomoh ben Avraham Adret, **3:**526
Shelter, **1:**60
Shelton, Beth, **1:**216
Shelton, Suzanne, *as contributor*, **5:**288, 490–498
Sheng Jie, **2:**148, **6:**406
Shennan, Jennifer, **4:**628, 629
  as contributor, **4:**260–262, 624–628, 628–629
Shen Nong, **2:**138
shensa, **5:**645
Shenyan, Fedor, **2:**435
Shepard, Ernest Howard, **2:**71
Shepherds Content (Barnfield), **3:**377
"Shepherd's Dance," **5:**695
Shepherd's Paradise, The, **2:***236*, **3:***252*
Shepp, Archie, **1:**349
sher, **3:**528

Sheremetyevskaya, Natalia E., **5:**484
  as contributor, **2:**585–586
Sherlott, Henry, **2:**339
Sherman, Jane, **2:**379, **5:**496, 586, 587
Sherman, Louis, **4:**179
Sherman, Maxine, **6:***260*
Sherrington, Charles, **4:**15
Sherry Brothers, **4:**522
Sherwood, Benson, **1:**456
Shestakowa, Nina, **4:**391
Shestdesiat let v balete (Lopukhov), **4:**225
Sheta, Hassan, **2:**498
Sheta, Reda, **2:**497
Sheth, Daksha, **3:**468, **4:**111
Shevanti, **3:**199
Shevchenko, Taras, **6:**224–225
Shevchenko Opera and Ballet Theater, Kiev, **6:**226
She Was Black, **2:**501
Shibaraku, **3:**437, 438, **4:***296*
Shibusawa Tatsuhiko, **3:**363
Shick, Vicky, **5:***440*
Shidohāgaku, **5:**591
Shield Dance, **5:**240
shield dances, **5:**662, **6:**211
Shifrin, Ellen, **2:**36
  as contributor, **2:**35–36
Shifting Landscape, **6:**391, 393, 394
Shigayama Mansaku, **3:**593
Shigayama Ryū, **3:**593
Shigeko Sasada, **1:**94
Shigeyama Akira, **5:**592
Shigeyama family, **4:**86, **5:590–592**
Shigeyama Sengorō. *See* Shigeyama Sensaku IV
Shigeyama Sennojō II, **5:***591*, **591–592**
Shigeyama Sensaku II, **5:**590
Shigeyama Sensaku III, **5:**590
Shigeyama Sensaku IV, **4:***83*, **5:590–591**, *591*
Shigosen no Matsuri (Kinoshita), **4:**661
Shigyo Masatoshi, **3:**590
Shih Kun-cheng, **6:***82*
Shih Show-tseng, **6:***81*
Shijima, **1:**61
Shijing (*Shih ching*; Book of Songs), **2:**128
shikhat (female entertainers), **4:**468, 664, 665
Shiki no Tameno 27 Ban, **2:**17, **3:**363
Shilluk (people), **2:**86, **4:**484, 485
Shiloah, Amnon, **4:**416
  as contributor, **1:**401–402, **3:**523–526
Shilpakala Academy, Bangladesh, **1:**362
shimai, **5:592–593**
Shimer, Genevieve, *as contributor*, **5:**199–200
Shimmy (dance), **4:**519, **6:**244, 255, 317, *317*
Shimotakahara, David, **5:**24
Shinbashi Enbujō, **3:**658
shin buyō movement, **3:**593
Shing-a-ling, **6:**263
Shingandi, **4:**56
shingeki theater, **6:**410
Shining Dark, The, **4:**39
Shining People of Leonard Cohen, The, **2:**39, **3:**231, **4:**238, **5:**436
shin kabuki ("new" *kabuki*), **4:**535, 536
Shin Kabuki Jūhachiban (Ichikawa Danjūrō IX), **3:**439
shinmyong, **4:**47

shinpa, **6:**409–410
Shintō, **1:**167, 183, **2:**6, 13, 214, 570, **3:**578–579, 581
  gagaku music and dance, **3:**102, 103
  kagura dance, **3:**583–584, *584*, 641
  nō drama, **4:**295
Shinzei kogaku zu (scroll), **2:**5
Shio Kazako, **3:**658
Shiokumi, **3:**593
Shipwreck, or Perseus and Andromeda, The, **5:**69, **6:**372
shirabyōshi, **4:**83, **5:**48–49
shira dance, **3:***535*
Shirah, **2:**469, **4:**120
Shiraishi *bon* dance, **3:**587–588
Shirali, Vishnudass, **5:**580
Shiralieva, Tamilla, **1:**248
Shiriaev, Aleksandr, **1:**90, **2:**72, 596, **5:**153, **6:**60
  character dancing, **2:**107, **4:**282
  Fundamentals of Character Dance, **5:**480
  Polovtsian Dances performance, **3:**562
  students, **2:**96, **3:**14, 327, **5:**636, **6:**170
Shiripina, Elena, **4:**247, **5:**480, 487
Shirley, James, **4:**309, 310
shishimai, **3:**584, 642, *642*, **5:**593
shishi odori, **3:**586
Shishkov, Matvei, **1:**392, **5:**540, 606
Shitadashi Sanbasō, **3:**593
Shiva. *See* Śiva
Shives, Will, **5:***197*
Shizuka Gozen, **5:**48–49
Shizuka Monogatari, **1:**248–249
Shizuka-na Ie, **3:**363
Shleuh (people), **4:**466, 467
shoes. *See* footwear
Sholokhov, Mikhail, **1:**519
Shona (people), **5:**580, 661, **6:**12, 664
Shook, Karel, **2:**469, **4:**600
  Harlem dance school, **2:**334, **4:**436
  as Netherlands Ballet ballet master, **4:**600
  students, **1:**55
Shore, Dinah, **2:**619
Shore of Hope, The, **5:**471
Short Essay on the French Danse de Société, A (Mason), **6:**126
Short Lecture and Demonstration on the Evolution of Ragtime as Presented by Jelly Roll Morton, **5:**637
Short Stories, **5:**440
Shorty-George, **6:**262
shosagoto, **3:**637, 639
Shoshone (people), **3:**171
Shostakovich, Dmitri, **1:**296, 416, 542, **2:**266, 471, 579, **4:**7, **5:**268, **594–595**, **6:**310
  Bright Stream, **4:**226
  as Glazunov student, **3:**186
  Massine choreography, **4:**324, 517
  musical idiom, **4:**517
  Soviet choreographies, **4:**285
  See also *Golden Age*; *Leningrad Symphony*
Shota and Azem Galicia, **1:**34
shoulder dance
  Berber, **4:**467
  Ethiopia, **2:**531–532, *531*
  Giriama, **3:**177
  Korean movements, **4:**49
  Kurdish movements, **4:**407

shoulders (ballet technique). *See épaulé; épaulement*
Shouvalov (pseud.). *See* Zajlich, Piotr
Show Boat (musical), **1:**395, **6:**90, 271, 274, 279, 281, 289
Show Boat (play), **5:**255
Show Girl, The (musical), **5:**310, **6:**274, *275*
Show of Shows (film), **2:**613
Show Piece, **1:**280, **3:**349
Shrew, The, **1:**215
Shuar (people), **2:**475
Shubert, J. J., **6:**270
Shubert, Lee, **3:**286, **4:**420, **6:**270
Shubert, Sam, **6:**270
Shubert organization, **6:**270, 271, 272, 371
Shubert Theater, New York City, archives, **4:**167
Shuffle Along (musical), **1:**252, **6:**256, *272*
Shuga, **3:**665
Shūgyoku Tokka (Zeami), **4:**42
Shuhplattler, **3:**141
shuimo qiang, **4:**76
Shukhevych, Volodymyr, **6:**223
Shukurbekova, Aidai, **4:**87
Shumka dancers, **6:**133
Shunkan, **3:**639, **4:**533
"Shuo Wu" (Wen Yiduo), **2:**148
Shurale (later *Ali-Batyr*), **1:**492, **2:**450, **5:**460, **595–596**
Belsky performance, **1:**416
Kondratieva performance, **4:**38
Tagirov and Zhukov choreography, **5:**472
Yakobson choreography, **4:**284, **5:**472, 572, **6:***410,* 411
S. Hurok Presents (Hurok), **3:**425
Shurr, Gertrude, **1:**124, **3:**214, **6:**362
Shutta, Ethel, **1:**419
Shyama, **3:**468
Siamese Suite, **2:**378
Siamsa Tire (Irish National Folk Theatre), **3:**518
Siang-Sin, **5:**95, 690
Sibelius, Jean, **1:**38, 453, **2:**265, **3:**100
Siberia. *See* Russia, Siberian dance traditions
"Siberian Polka," **6:**303
Sibley, Antoinette, **2:**515, **5:**5, *104,* **596–597**
Ashton ballets, **1:**158, **2:**445, **3:**267
Dowell dance partnership, **1:**156, 157, 158, **2:**444, 445, **5:***421,* 597
Dream as signature role, **5:**597
Manon performance, *257,* **4:**243, *244,* 256
Monotones performance, **4:**452
Month in the Country performance, **4:**456
Romeo and Juliet performance, **5:**396
Scènes de Ballet performance, **5:**531
Siboney (people), **2:**62
Sichel, Adrienne, *as contributor,* **5:**655–661
Sicilien, Le, ou L'Amour Peintre, **1:**36, 505, **3:**138, **4:**234, 447, **5:**558, **6:**72
Sicily, **5:**377
Sickle Dance, **3:**297
Siddhas of the Upper Air, **5:**586
Siddhendra Yogi, **4:**69, 70

Siddiqui, Nahid, **3:**425, **5:**63, **597–598**
Sidney, Sir Robert, **2:**255
Sidorenko, Yuri, **4:**446
Sidorov, Aleksei, **5:**485
Sidorov, Ivan, **1:**489
Sieba, **1:**540, **2:**82, **4:**258, 263, **5:**399, **6:**452
Sieben Todsünden, Die. See Seven Deadly Sins, The
Sieben Todsünden der Kleinbürger, Die (Krätke ballet), **3:**153
Siedlecki, Franciszek, **5:**221
Sieg des Neptun, Der, **6:**9
Sieg des Opfers, Der, **4:**90
Siège de Cythère, Le, **2:**414, **3:**259
Siegel, Marcia B., **2:**171, 584, 606, **3:**343
as contributor, **2:**356–357, **3:**397–405, **4:**605–606, **5:**577–578, **6:**367
dance criticism seminars, **6:**300
Siegel, Mary, **5:**531
Siege of Corinth (Rossini), **4:**657
Siege of Ennis, The, **3:**517
Siegert, Arila, **3:**155, 156
Siegmeister, Elie, **5:**637
Siegrist, Topsy, **2:**79
Siembra, **6:**355
Sierra, Maria, **3:**9
Sierra, Martinez, **6:**192
Sierra Leone, **1:**14, **3:**25, **4:**290, **6:**25, *383*
Siete Canciones Populares (Falla), **2:**567
Siete Pares de Francia, Los, **3:**319
Siete Puñales, Los, **6:**28
Sietsma, Maggie, **1:**216
Sieveling, Dana, **6:**398
Sieveling, Earle, **1:**293, **4:***620*
Siflis, József, *as photographer,* **3:**419
Sifnios, Duška, **1:**291, **4:***437*
Sigalova, Alla, **5:**475, 479
sighanós, **2:**271–272
Signals, **1:**372, **2:**294
Signature, **2:**355
signature choreography, **3:**325
Signatures, **4:**73
Signorina Gioventù, **5:**245, 269
Sign Writer, The (publication), **4:**693, *693*
Sigrid, **4:**275, **5:**552
Sigurdsson, Jon, **3:**436
siheq, **1:**448
Siimola, Aino, **3:**40, 625, 626, 627, 628, 630
Si J'etais Roi, **1:**10
Si Jinshi (opera), **6:**446
Sikelianos, Angelos, **3:**00
Sikelianos, Eva Palmer, **3:**300
sikinnis, **2:**158, 506, **3:**290, **5:**598
Sikkim, **598–599**
sikyi dance, **6:**13
Silappadikāram (Tamil epic), **3:**469
Silas Green from New Orleans (show), **6:**256
silat, **5:**130
Silayan Philippine Dance Company, **5:***170*
Silberstein, Ilya, **5:**483
Silence (Cage anthology), **2:**23, **6:**26
Silence Is the End of Our Song, **2:**1
Silent Cries, **3:**361
Silent Partners, **2:**355
Silent Screams, Difficult Dreams, **2:**564
Sîlfide, La, **2:**122, **3:**358
Silfverberg, Seija, **2:**632
Silk Road, **2:**129

Silk Road Flower Rain, **2:**145
Silk Stockings (film), **2:**109, **4:**228
Silk Stockings (musical), **6:**282
Silla, La, **1:**461
Sills, Bettijane, **4:***620*
Silo: The Path of Life, **1:**304
Silva, José, **4:**392
Silva, Marco Antonio, **4:**397
Silva, Ricardo, **4:**392, **6:***355*
Silvana (Weber), **4:**514
Silver Birch, **1:**315
Silver Shoes, The, **2:**12
Silvester, Victor, **4:**522
Silvestre, Israël, **1:**287
Šimek, Petr, **2:**310
Simhat Torah, **3:**526
Simić, Krunislav, **6:**434
Simkie (Simone Barbier), **5:**580
Simmonds, David, *as photographer,* **1:**217
Simmons, Stanley, **1:**72
Simon, Anton, **2:**436, **3:**204
Simon, François, **2:**179
Simon, John, **6:**153
Simon, Neil, **1:**419, **5:**408, **6:**283
Simón, Pedro, **1:**50
Simone, Kirsten, **1:***508,* **2:**3, **4:**65, **5:**430, **599–601,** **6:**292, 349
Simone Forti and Troupe, **3:**54
Simonet, Adélaïde, **4:***697,* **5:**86
Simonet, François, **1:**237
Simonet sisters, **2:**353
Simon Fraser University, British Columbia, **2:**48, 49
Simoni, Renato, **4:**258
Simonov, Ruben, **5:**203
Simonov, Yuri, **3:**193
Simons, John, **2:**58
Simons, Ton, **4:**596
Simonson, Lee, **1:**98
"Simosilla" (singing game), **2:**629
Simov, Viktor, **5:**541
"Simple Gifts" (song), **2:**197, **5:**577
Simple-Hearted Villager, The, **5:**452
Simple Man, A, **4:**668, *668,* **5:**589
Simple Symphony, **3:**174, 203, **4:**107, 108, **5:**300
Simplizissimus (magazine), **1:**131
Simpson, Bruce, **5:**55
Simpson, Fay, **3:**574
Simpson, Thomas, **1:**364
Sims, Sandman, **3:**367, **5:**601, **6:**102
simultaneous staging, **5:**533, *533*
Sinatle, **2:**96
Sinatra, Frank, **4:**419
Sinatra Suite, **6:**153
Sinbad the Sailor, **1:**206, **3:**354
Sinceretti, Francis, **2:**470
Sinclair, Upton, **3:**596
sinding, **3:**501
Sinding, Christian, **3:**17
Sind jhooman, **2:**226
Sinfonia, **2:**162, 471
Sinfonia dei Salmi, **5:**677
Sinfonia Eroica, **1:**412
Sinfonia Semplice, **6:**363
Sinfonia Sevillana, **4:**233
Sinfonietta, 82, **1:**156, **2:**401, **4:**81, 82, **6:**212, 380
Sing, Karen, **4:***649*
Singer, Alice, **4:**367
Singer, Isaac Bashevis, **3:**202
Singer, Paris, **2:**525
Singh, Amobi, **5:**580
Singh, Bipin, **3:**606, **5:**601–602
Singh, R. K. Singhjit, **3:**468
Singh, S., *as photographer,* **6:**168
Singh Bhuller, Darshan, **1:**394, **4:**217, *218,* 220

singing. *See* accompaniment for dance; song dances
singing games
Faeroe Islands, **2:**383, 384
Finland, **2:**629–630
Iceland, **3:**434–435
Singin' in the Rain (film), **2:**109, 616, 617–618, *619,* **4:**3, 4, *4,* **5:**21–22, *21,* **6:**287
Singin' in the Rain (musical), **6:**154, 287
singkil, **2:**230, 231, **5:***170*
Singleton, Trinette, **2:**606, **3:***612,* 613, 615
singsing (Melanesia), **4:**352
Sinha, Nabakumar, **4:**253
Sinha, Priya Gopal, **1:**94
Sinhala dance. *See* Sri Lanka
Sinisalo, Ilmer, **5:**473
Sinke, Johann Wenzel, **1:***238*
Sin Quererlo Ni Buscarlo, Petenera, Petenera, **6:**407
Siobhan Davies Dance Company, **2:**354, 355–356, **3:**273
Sioux (people), **3:**171
si pecut langkah empat, **5:**130
sîrba, **2:**101
Sircar, Ranjabati, **2:**102
Sire Huon, **3:**264
Sirène des Tropiques, La (film), **1:**252
Sirènes, Les, **1:**150, 438, **2:**361, **3:**236, **5:**312
Siretta, Dan, **5:**602
Siris, Paul, **1:**92, **2:**338, **4:**684, **6:**123, 175
širo kolo, **2:**100
Sironi, Irene, **1:**239
"Sir Roger de Coverly" (dance), **5:**334
Sismani, Iro, **3:**300
Sismani Ballet, **3:**300
Sissle, Noble, **1:**252
Sistonen, Anu, **2:**633
Sisyphus, **2:**46
Sītā, **1:***178,* **3:**465
Sītā Harāna, **5:**68
Sitara Devi, **3:***659,* **5:602–603**
Sita's Daughters (performance piece), **5:**521
Site and Pastoral: Et Al, **2:**605
sitting dance, **2:**593, *593*
Sitwell, Edith, **4:**113
Sitwell, Osbert, **2:**525
Sitwell, Sacheverell, **4:**113
Šiva (deity), **1:***178,* **2:**227, 394
Indian dance portrayals, **3:**454, *454, 455*
Shawn portrayal, **2:**377
Thai dance mask, **4:**9
Sivaram, Ananda, **3:***456,* **4:**628
Šiva Tripurāntaka, **3:***455*
Siwela Sonke Dance Company, **5:**659
Six, Les, **1:**325, 327, **2:**182, 410, **3:**95, **4:**418, 516, **5:**236–237, 352, 525
Six Dances, **4:**81
Six Dances Composed by Mr. Kellom Tomlinson (print collection), **6:**175
Six Merry Scotchmen (later Harlem Highlanders), **1:**252
Six Pas de Deux, **6:**412
Six Sketches of Mademoiselle Taglioni (Chalon), **2:**103
Sixteen Dances for Soloist and Company of Three, **2:**287
1600 Pennsylvania Avenue (musical), **1:**439

16 Millimeter Earrings, **4:**451
Sixth Symphony of Gustav Mahler, The, **4:**604
Six Volts (music group), **4:**627
Sizova, Alla, **4:**285, **5:**4
Sjöberg, Henry, **6:**36, 49
Sjörgen, Margareta, **6:**49–50
Skálová, Olga, **1:**542, **5:**270
Skalski, Anna Lee, *as contributor,* **2:**579–582
Skandinaviska Baletten, 5406
Skandinavisk balett (Sjörgren), **6:**50
Skansen, Stockholm, **3:**33, **6:**36
Skares, George, **2:**379
Skarstrom, William, **4:**16
Skate (dance), **5:**632
Skating Rink, **1:**327, **5:**545, **6:**455
Skauge, Therese, **4:**680
Skazka pro Shuta. See Chout
Skeaping, Mary, **1:**73, 403, 541, **5:**299, 327, 406, **603–604**
  Beck-Friis association, **1:**400, **6:**42
  Cramér collaboration, **1:**503, **2:**264, **6:**47–48
  Royal Swedish Ballet directorship, **6:**41, 42
  Swan Lake staging, **2:**277, **5:**406
  Swedish court ballet revivals, **1:**503, **6:**38, 42, 46–47, *46,* 50
Skelton, Red, **2:**326
Skelton, Thomas, **2:**333, **4:**191, **5:**24, 365
Sketches from the People, **3:**212
Skibine, Boris, **5:**604
Skibine, George, **1:**111, 313, 315, 349, **2:**480, **3:**26, 74, **4:**269, **5:**96, 248, **604–605**, **6:**348
  Ballets de la Jeunesse, **3:**73
  Dallas Ballet, **6:**264
  Daphnis et Chloë choreography, **3:**342, **5:**93, 605
  Grand Ballet du Marquis de Cuevas, **3:**225, *225,* 226
  as Harkness Ballet artistic director, **3:**342, 343
Skid, **1:**142
Skidmore College, **3:**352, **6:**292
"Skin Kompasse" (sword dance), **1:**118
Skinner, Joan, **1:**476, **4:**17
Skinner, Marsha, **2:**296, **5:**17
Skinner Releasing Technique, **1:476–477, 4:**17
skinnkompass dance, **2:**630
Skinny, **3:**52, *52*
Skirmantas, Petras, **4:**208
skirt dance, **2:**249–250, 250, **3:**91, **5:605, 6:**268, 317
Skofitz, Franz, **3:**346
Skofitz, Karoline, **5:**278
Skøien, Kjetil, **4:**679
skok, **2:**301
Sköld, Berit, **5:**397, **6:**42
skomorokhs, **5:**450, **6:**220
Škomrlj, Ika, **5:**677
Skoog, Matz, **2:**2, 514, **4:**625, **5:**401
Skopje 63, **6:**433
Skopje, Macedonia, **6:**436
Skorik, Irène, **1:**305, 306, **2:**510, 511, **3:**73, 74, 318
Skoronel, Vera, **3:**146, 531, **6:**392
Skouratoff, Vladimir, **1:**305, 306, 315, **2:**114, **3:**73, 601, **4:**185, 270
Skrinar, Margaret, **2:**330
Škrinjaric, Tihana, **6:**433
Skrušny, Václav, **5:**393
Sky Eye, **2:**460–461
Skyscrapers, **1:**390

Slack, Freddie, **1:**194
slam dance, **5:**633–634
Slant Board, **3:**54
Slaraffenland, **4:**118, **5:**353
Śląsk, **5:**212, *213, 218*
Slater, William J., **5:**74
Slaughter of the Innocents, **5:**637
Slaughter on MacDougal Street, **1:**142
"Slaughter on Tenth Avenue" *(On Your Toes),* **1:**271, 482, **2:**576, **3:**598, **6:**276, 287
Slavenska, Mia, **2:**277, **5:**292, **605–606**
  Ballet Russe de Monte Carlo, **1:**296, 300, *301*
  Capriccio Espagnol performance, **4:**323
  Dallas Ballet, **6:**264
  English National Ballet guest performances, **2:**508
  Franklin dance partnership, **3:**88
  as Kraus student, **4:**58
  Mort du Cygne, La (film), **2:**113
  students, **2:**186, 358, **5:**439
  Yugoslavian ballet, **6:**432
Slavenska-Franklin Ballet, **3:**88, **5:**606
slavery
  cakewalk, **2:**25
  Caribbean social dance restrictions, **2:**62
  Congo dances, **2:**195
  Cuban dance, **2:**274–275
  Dominican dance, **2:**429, 430
  Jamaica, **3:**573
  jig, **3:**607
  Jonkonnu festival, **3:**121, 623–624
  plantation dances, **6:**254, 261, *261*
  sacred dancing, **2:**168
  urban dances, **6:**261
Slavery, **3:**312
Slavin, Eugene, **1:**302
Slavinsky, Tadeo (also Thadée Slavinsky; Tadeusz Slaviński), **1:**93, 323, **2:**409, **4:**637, **5:**217, 267
Slavonia, **2:**100
Slavonic Dances, **5:**269
Slavs (people), **1:**407, **6:**426–427
Slayton, Jeff, **2:**53, 575, **6:**356
Sleep, Wayne, **2:**515, **4:**456
Sleeping Beauty, The, **5:606–613**
  character role, **2:**106
  double *tours en l'air,* **1:**338
  fish dive movement, **5:**103
  later (post-Petipa) productions, **5:610–613**
  Alonso (Alicia), **1:**49
  Ananiashvili performance, **1:**83
  Anderson-Ivantzova performance, **1:**85
  Arova staging in Japan, **3:**589
  Ashton, **1:**146, **5:**612–613, **6:**137
  Bakst designs, **1:**254, 255
  Balabanova staging, **2:**11
  Balanchine, **6:**612
  Ballets des Champs-Élysées, **1:**305
  Benois designs, **1:**424
  Beriosova performance, **1:**429, *430*
  Blair performance, **1:**459
  Bruhn performance, **2:**2, 3
  CAPAB Ballet production, **5:**653
  Chabukiani choreographic changes, **2:**96

  Chauviré performance, **2:**114
  Collier performance, **2:**186
  Cragun performance, **2:**262
  Darsonval performance, **2:**351
  de Valois performance, **2:**396
  de Valois stagings, **1:**324, **2:**186, 243, 401–402, 403, **3:**264, **4:**243, **5:**415
  Diaghilev, **2:**396, 409, **5:**611–612
  Edwards's character role, **2:**447–448
  Eks staging, **3:**338
  Farron performance, **2:**578
  Fonteyn performance, **3:**41, *41, 42, 43, 46, 59*
  Froman staging, **2:**11
  Gadd version, **3:**100
  Goleizovsky, **3:**195
  Grey performance and staging, **3:**307, **6:**44
  Gusev revival, **3:**328
  Haydée choreography, **2:**262, **3:**351, **6:**10
  Helpmann and Fonteyn performances, **3:**355, **5:**414
  Helpmann and Nijinska choreography, **3:**226–227, *226*
  Hightower performance, **3:**362
  Hightower staging, **3:**362
  Hynd staging, **2:**514
  Kressig's *Dornröschen—Die Schlafende Schönheit,* **6:**53
  Kronstam performance, **4:**65
  Larrain staging, **3:**362
  Lifar excerpts, **4:**183
  Littlefield, **4:**210, **5:**612
  MacMillan, **1:**76, 436, **4:**242, 243, **6:**44
  Markova and Dolin performances, **4:**269–270
  Martins staging, **4:**275, 622, *622,* **5:**613
  May performance, **4:**336
  Messel designs, **2:**243, **4:**357, 358, *358*
  Mordkin performance, **4:**459
  Nerina performance, **4:**584
  Neumeier staging, **3:**337, **5:**405–406
  Nureyev, **1:**200, **2:**114, 511, 513, **3:**136, 362, **4:**543, **5:**5, *6,* 7, **6:**132, 142, 353
  Pavlova, **1:**255
  Petit, **3:**601, **5:**164
  Prokovsky, **5:**401
  Rassine, **5:**313
  Róna staging, **3:**419
  Rose design, **5:**405, 406
  Rosen staging, **5:**406
  as Royal Ballet signature production, **1:**150, 152, **3:**266, **5:**413, 415
  Schaufuss, **3:**156
  Semenova performance, **5:**566, *567*
  Sergeyev (Konstantin) version, **5:**572, *572,* 610, **6:**343
  Sibley performance, **5:**596
  Skeaping, **1:**73–74, **5:**603
  Soloviev performance, **5:**639
  Spessivtseva performance, **5:**611, 679
  Stevenson for English National Ballet, **2:**511
  Teatro Colón, **1:**110, 315, 424
  television, **5:**603, **6:**132, *134,* 137, 142
  Tomasson, **5:**613, **6:**174, 404–405

  Ukrainian, **6:**224
  Vainonen, **6:**311
  Wright staging, **2:**470, **4:**597, **5:**613, **6:**405
  See also Sleeping Princess, The
  pas brisés volés, **1:**384–385
  Petipa production, **4:**277, **5:**9, 154, *155,* 156, 157, 158, 159, 160, **606–610**, **6:**116
  as Ashton influence, **1:**151, 154
  attitude derrière, **1:**198
  as Baryshnikov influence, **1:**373
  Brianza creation of Aurora role, **1:**540, **4:**282
  Cecchetti dual roles in first complete performance, **2:**82
  Clustine abridged version, **2:**182
  as de Valois influence, **2:**401
  Diaghilev *divertissement Aurora's Wedding,* **1:**324
  Diaghilev's staging as *The Sleeping Princess* (1921), **1:**255, 318, 319, 323–324, 540, **2:**409, 410, 423, **3:**264
  Gerdt (Elisaveta) performance, **3:**137, *138*
  Gerdt (Pavel) performance, **3:**137
  Gorsky revival, **5:**610
  Grigorovich revivals, **3:**309–310, **5:**463, 610
  Kshessinska (Matilda) performance, **4:**68
  Lopukhov revival, **4:**224
  Maximova performance, **4:**335
  Nijinska alterations, **4:**633, 634
  Nijinska performance, **4:**635
  Nijinsky performance, **4:**640
  Sergeyev (Nicholas) reconstructions, **3:**511, **4:**284, **5:**413, 611, *613*
  symphonic structure, **5:**456
  Tchaikovsky mazurka composition, **5:**343
  pre-Petipa productions. *See Belle au Bois Dormant, La*
  Tchaikovsky score, **5:**9, 606, 607–610, **6:**114, 116
  travesty role, **6:**190
Sleeping Beauty, The (Carafa opera), **3:**118
Sleeping Beauty, The (Perrault), **5:**9
Sleeping Princess, The, **5:**13, **6:**341
  British Vic-Wells production, **1:**324, **5:**414
  Diaghilev production, **1:**255, 318, 319, 323–324, 540, **2:**409, 410, 423, 480, **3:**264, 285, **5:**611–612
  as financial disaster, **4:**319
  impression on Haskell, **3:**285
  Lopokova performances, **4:**223
  Schollar performance, **5:**559
  significance of, **1:**324
  Spessivtseva performance, **5:**678
sleeve-dancing styles
  China, **2:**129, 130, *130,* 132
  Korea, **2:**223, **4:**49, *49*
  Nigeria, **2:**211
Slezak, Anna, **5:**221
Šlezingerová, Jiřina, **5:**270
Śliwiński, Bonifacy, **5:**75
Slobin, Mark, **1:**26
Slobodian, Nikolai, **3:**56–57
Slodtz brothers, **5:**306
ślokams, **1:**442
Slonimsky, Yuri, **1:**408, **2:**585, **3:**21, **4:**28, **5:**321, 454, **613–614,** **6:**311

Slonimsky, Yuri, *continued*
  on Balanchine, **1:**258, **5:**485
  on Fokine, **3:**21
  as Grigorovich choreographic
    influence, **3:**308
  scholarly writings, **3:**328, **4:**58,
    5:483, 485
  students, **5:**642
Sloot, Pieter van der, **1:**289, 290
Slorer, Henriette, **4:***680*
Slovák, Boris, **5:**614
Slovak Folk Art Collective,
  2:309–310
Slovakia. *See* Czech Republic and
  Slovak Republic
Slovak National Theater Ballet,
  5:614–615
Slovenia, **6:**428, 437, 438, 439
Slovenian Acadmy of Art and
  Science, **6:**439
Slow Minuet (Caverley dance
  notation), **2:**81
slow waltz. *See* waltz
Sluiter, Ineke, **4:**593
Slutsker, Peter, **6:**287
Slyde, Jimmy, **6:**102, *102*
Smadbeck, Paul, **4:**532
Smakov, Gennady, **1:**371
Smalakys, Edvardas, **4:**208, *208*
Small Gallows, **2:**309
"Small House of Uncle Thomas"
  (*The King and I*), **5:**362, **6:**281
Small Town Girl (film), **4:**419
*Small Treatise of Time and Cadence
  in Dancing, A* (Weaver), **6:**373
Smeraldi, Cesare, **4:**420
Smetana, Bedřich, **2:**309, **4:**239,
  5:221, 617
Smifnoff, Xenia, **1:**498
Smigel, Libby, *as contributor*,
  2:115–116, 506–507,
  3:287–294, 428, 645–646,
  4:44, **5:**556–557, 598,
  6:144–145
Smile (film), **4:**11
Smiles (musical), **4:**420
Smiling Immortal, **4:***470*
Smiling Workman (Dine), **1:**139
Smirnov, Edvald, **5:**465, 475, 479
Smirnov, Igor, **5:**473
Smirnova, Elena, **1:**110, **3:**14, 15,
  560, **5:**392
Smirnova, Maria, **6:**441
Smirnova, Svetlana, **5:**467
Smirnova, Tatiana, **6:**451
Smirnov-Golovanov, Viktor, **1:**517,
  2:565, **4:**133, **5:**460, 587
Smit, Leo, **1:**300
Smit, Margie, **4:**596
Smith, Adam, **1:**22
Smith, Albert, **5:**241
Smith, Alexis, **1:**419
Smith, Amanda, *as contributor*,
  2:358–360, **4:**115–116,
  5:573–574
Smith, Andrea Ciel, **2:**45
Smith, Anna Deveare, **1:**60, **3:**578
Smith, A. William, **3:**553–554
Smith, Bessie, **6:**256
Smith, Campbell, **1:**218
Smith, Cecil, **6:**299
Smith, Chris, **6:**255
Smith, Ernie, **4:**202
Smith, Frank, **5:**687
Smith, George Washington, **4:**139,
  5:133, 178, 404, **615–616**,
  6:237, 269
Smith, Harry B., **6:**447
Smith, Jack, **5:**304
Smith, Joe, **6:**317

Smith, Joseph, **5:**616
Smith, Kaj, **1:***510*, **5:**335, 428–429
Smith, Kathleen, **2:**470
Smith, Lois, **4:***540*, 541, *541*, **5:***14*,
  6:131
Smith, Lowell, **3:**387
Smith, Merrilee, **1:**197
Smith, Oliver, **2:**249, **5:**547, **616**,
  6:200
  American Ballet Theatre, **1:**64,
    67, 70, 72, 75, 76, **2:**242
  Fall River Legend design, **5:***550*,
    551, 616
  Fancy Free design, **2:**568
  Messel commission, **4:**357
  Noces design, **5:**364
  On the Town design, **5:**360
  Rodeo design, **2:**373, **5:**369, **6:***247*
  West Side Story design, **5:**362
Smith, Queenie, **6:**274
Smith, Raymond, **4:**544, **6:**143
Smith, Richard, **1:**52, **5:**303
Smith, Ronald R., *as contributor*,
  2:195–196
Smith, Rowena, **1:**441
Smith, Solomon, **6:**237
Smith College, **4:**168
Smithells, Philip, **4:**627
Smithsonian Institution,
  Washington, D.C., **2:**601
Smits, Thierry, **1:**412
Šmok, Pavel, **1:**308, 374, **2:**308,
  309, 310, **5:**23, 469, **616–618**
Smolenska, La, **4:**139, *139*
Smoliak, A. V., **5:**448
Smoltsov, Ivan, **5:**331
Smoltsov, Viktor, **1:**489, **6:**170
Smoriginas, Jurijus, **4:**208
Smuin, Michael, **1:**73, **2:**162, **3:**306,
  5:51, 107
  Harkness Ballet choreography,
    3:342
  Romeo and Juliet choreography,
    5:398
  San Francisco Ballet, **5:**513
Sophisticated Ladies, **6:**286
Snaith, Yolande, **3:**275, 276
Snake (dance), **5:**628
Snake Dance, **1:**600, **2:**475, **3:**375,
  4:551, 554, 555, **5:**240
Snake Hips, **6:**262, 263, *316*
Snapshots from the City
  (Oldenburg), **1:**139
sneakers, **3:**46, 47
Snell, Gertrud, **4:**92
Snell, Onni Gabriel, **3:**312
Snicker, Raija, **2:**634
Snidwongsēnī, Khunying Phaeo,
  4:256
Snijders, Ronald, **2:**470, **4:**600
Snoek, Hans, **4:**590, 591, 592, 593,
  5:530, **618**
Snow, Graham, **5:***305*
Snow, Valaida, **1:**439
Snowden, Shorty, **4:**201, 202
Snow Fantasy (ice show), **4:**132
Snowflake and the Seven Dwarfs,
  1:493
Snowflakes, **5:**14
Snow Maiden, The, **1:**297, **2:**15,
  510, **4:**638, **5:**37, 62,
  6:412, 425
Snow Queen, The, **1:**122, 453, **2:**59,
  4:641, **5:**226
Snow White, **4:**185, **6:**111
Snyder, Allegra Fuller, **4:**374–375
  as contributor, **2:**600–603
Snyder, Don, **1:**349
Snyder, Gene, **5:**290
Snyder, Ted, **1:**323

Soane, George, **3:**183
S.O.A.P. Dance Theater, Frankfurt,
  3:157
Soap-Powders and Detergents, **4:***471*
Soares, Janet Mansfield, *as
  contributor*, **3:**383–386
Soaring, **2:**377, **3:**210, 232, 403,
  5:495
Sobakina, Arina, **5:**452
Sobeka (Kochno *nom de plume*),
  4:32
Sobel, Bernard, **6:**320
Sobeshchanskaya, Anna, **1:**486,
  2:207, 435, **5:***152*, 455,
  6:30, 115
Sobinova, Natasha, **1:**313
Sobol, M. A., **6:**225
Sobotka, Ruth, **3:***663*, **5:**362
"Sobria, La," **2:**427
Soby, James Thrall, **4:**26
Sochiku-Otani Library, Tokyo,
  4:159
social dance, **5:619–636**
  as caricature and comic art
    subject, **2:**70
  Christian churches' views, **2:**165,
    167–168
  court and social dance before
    1800, **5:619–623**
  ancient Greece, **3:**291–292
  anglaise, **1:**89–90
  annual collections, **1:**91–92
  assemblies, **1:**189–190
  ball, **1:**278–279
  ballo and *balletto*, **1:**352–355
  barriera, torneo, and *battaglia*,
    1:369
  bassedanse, **1:**378–382
  bolero, **1:**480
  bourrée, **1:**516–517
  branle, **1:**520–523
  canary, **2:**50–51
  carscarda, **2:**77
  colonial North American,
    6:231–232
  cotillon, **2:**251–253
  country dance, **2:**254–257
  dance manuals, **1:**103–105,
    2:73–77
  etiquette, **1:**105, 107, **2:**73, 74
  fandango variants, **1:**528
  figure dances, **2:**592–592, **3:**68
  forlana, **3:**49–50
  French, **1:**285–289, 342–344,
    3:63
  galliarde, **3:**108
  gavotte, **3:**15, 124
  gigue, **3:**172–173
  improvisation, **3:**444
  makeup, **4:**303–304
  Malaysia, **4:**250–251
  masks, **4:**301, 304
  masquerades, **4:**313–315
  medieval, **2:**165
  minuet, **4:**431–433
  moros y cristianos, **4:**473
  mouriscas, **4:**462
  musical accompaniment,
    4:500–502, 504–508, 509,
    510–512
  notation, **4:**683–684
  pirouettes, **1:**342
  Renaissance fètes and
    triumphs, **5:**341
  revels, **4:**307, **5:**343
  révérence, **5:**345–347
  technical manuals,
    6:122–124, 126
  dancing masters, **2:**336–339,
    3:521–522
  definitions, **2:**539–540, **3:**32

European traditional, **2:**551–552,
  553–554, *553*, *554*, **4:**670–672
  England, **3:**238–243, 254, 256
  folk dance versus, **3:**332
  France, **3:**63–65
  Gypsy, **3:**330–331
  Hungary, **3:**409
  Iceland, **3:**435
  Lithuania, **4:**205–208
  Netherlands, **4:**586–587
  Norway, **4:**670–672
  Poland, **4:**343
  Russia, **5:**445
  Scotland, **3:**243–250
  Sweden, **6:**36–37
  figure dances, **2:**590–592
  historical notation, **5:**323
  nineteenth-century, **5:623–626**
    African-American traditions,
      6:254, 255, 261–262
    assemblies, **1:**190
    balls, **1:**279, **3:**68, 69
    Caribbean region, **2:**63–64, 275,
      430–431
    cotillon, **2:**253
    Denmark, **2:**380–381, *381*
    figure dances, **2:**592
    Finland, **2:**630
    France, **3:**68, 69–70
    Greece, **3:**299
    mazurka, **4:**343
    Mexico, **4:**399
    notation, 684–685
    polka, **1:**529, **4:**514
    quadrille, **2:**592, **5:**285–287
    square dancing, **5:**685
    United States, **6:**235–236,
      254, 293
    waltz, **6:**359–362
  twentieth-century, **5:626–636**
    African-American traditions,
      2:25, **6:**244, 256–257, 262–263
    American Bandstand, **1:**77–79
    ballroom dance competition,
      1:356–359
    ballroom dance teaching,
      4:480–481, **6:**294, *294*
    balls, **1:**279
    Big Apple, **1:**450–451
    break dancing, **1:**538
    Castles' popularization, **2:**78,
      5:628, *628*, **6:**243, 270
    Charleston, **5:**629, *629*
    in China, **2:**133–134
    country-western, **2:**258–259
    Cuban-based, **2:**274, 275–276
    Denmark, **2:***382*
    Dominican Republic,
      2:431–432
    Finland, **2:**630–631, 634–635
    French Canada, **2:**35
    Indonesia, **3:**475
    jazz dances, **4:**519
    Lindy Hop, **4:**201–203,
      5:629–630, *630*
    Murray instruction method,
      4:480–481
    musical theater popularizing,
      6:269–270
    Romania, **5:**383
    samba, **1:**528–529, **4:**520
    South Africa, **5:**656–657
    square dancing, **5:**686–589
    sub-Saharan Africa, **6:**23–24
    tango, **4:**520, **5:**629
    technical manuals, **6:**128
    United States, **6:**242–243, 246,
      249, 250, 256–257,
      269–270, 273
    waltz popularity, **4:**514
social Darwinism, **3:**30

socialist realism
  Albanian dance, **1**:34–35
  avant-garde dance, **1**:246
  Burmeister productions, **2**:16
  Chinese opera and dance, **1**:164, 165, **2**:135, 137, 145, 220–221
  Ch'oi Seung-hee dance dramas, **2**:155–156
  Dmitriev scenic design, **2**:421
  East German dance, **3**:153, 155
  Golden Age, The, **4**:283
  Lavrovsky (Leonid) ballets, **4**:131
  Red Poppy, The, **3**:187, **4**:283
  Romeo and Juliet conception, **5**:392, 394
  Soviet scenic design, **5**:*458*
  Spartacus, **4**:7
  Yakobson choreography, **6**:410–411
  Zakharov championship, **5**:485, **6**:442
  See also dramatic ballet; Soviet era
Socialist Revolution of 1917. *See* Russian Revolution; Soviet era
Sociedad Pro-Arte Musical, Havana, **1**:48, **2**:276–277
Société des Bains de Mer de Monte Carlo, **2**:410, **3**:225
Société Radio-Canada, **3**:227, **6**:130–131, 132
Society for Dance Research, **3**:283, 285
Society for Movement Culture, **2**:417
Society Islands, **5**:20
Society of Dance Arts, **1**:214
Society of Dance History Scholars, **6**:297, 298
Society of Korean Dance Studies, **4**:53
Society of Spiritual Arts, **5**:497
Society of Teachers of the Alexander Technique, **1**:473
sociology of dance. *See under* methodologies in the study of dance
Socrate, **2**:286, **5**:525
Socrates, **3**:292, 293
Sode, Pietro, **6**:232
Söderbaum, Ulla, **3**:614, 628, 629
Sodi, Pietro, **1**:236, 365, **3**:365
SODRE Ballet, **6**:301–302
Soelberg, Louise, **3**:596–597
Soe Loep Ons, **5**:657
Sofia, Bulgaria, **2**:11
Sofia Folk Opera House, **1**:91
Sofia National Opera, **2**:10, 11, **4**:182, **5**:166
Soft Bruising, **4**:479
soft-shoe dancing, **4**:520–521, **6**:98, 316
Software Dragon, **1**:216
Soga no Taimen, **4**:296
Sōgi, **4**:42
Sogno d'Ines, Un, **3**:620
Sogno, Un, **3**:620
sohbah, **2**:490
Sohl, Marty, *as photographer,* **5**:512
Sohl-Donnell, Linda, **6**:102
Sohlke, Gus, **6**:268, 281
Soir de Fête, **2**:368, **5**:690, 691
Soirée Debussy, La, **5**:164
Soirée Musicale, **4**:109, 215, **6**:197–198, 312
Soirées de Paris, Les, **1**:243, 251, 305, 309, 325, **3**:73, 394, 441, **4**:223, **5**:162, 543
  Massine productions, **3**:72, **4**:319–320, 418

Soirées de Vienne, **4**:117
Soisson, Charles, **4**:588
Sōke Fujima Ryū. *See* Fujima Kanjūrō
Sökmen, Sait, **6**:212
Sokol, Jan, **5**:393
Sokolov, Oleg, **4**:285
Sokolov, Sergei, **1**:486, **2**:435, **4**:514
Sokolova, Evgenia, **3**:562, 655, **5**:150, 456
Sokolova, Lydia, **1**:311, 437, 449, **2**:411, **5**:241, **636–637**, **6**:120
  British origins, **3**:262
  as character dancer, **2**:106
  Diaghilev-era memoir, **5**:637
  Massine association, **4**:319
  as Massine-type dance, **5**:636
  Mordkin's All-Star Imperial Russian Ballet, **4**:459
  Sacre du Printemps role, **5**:636
  students, **3**:87, 318, **6**:312
  Train Bleu performance, **4**:*637*
  witch makeup, **4**:*304*
  Woizikowski dance partnership, **6**:404
Sokolov-Kaminsky, Arkady A., *as contributor,* **1**:416–417, **4**:37–38, 147–148, **5**:638–639
Sokolow, Anna, **1**:141, 214, **4**:345, **5**:301, **637–638**
  as ADF videotape subject, **1**:81
  as Ailey influence, **1**:55
  archival collection, **4**:166
  Bennington School, **1**:421
  Boston Ballet choreography, **1**:501
  film dance, **2**:604
  Inbal Dance Theatre, 532, **3**:449
  Israeli dance, **3**:532, 534
  London Contemporary Dance Theatre choreography, **4**:218
  Martha Graham Dance Company, **3**:214
  as Mexican modern dance influence, **4**:392
  Netherlands Dance Theater guest choreography, **4**:602
  students, **1**:145, 388, **2**:450
  teaching in Israel, **5**:638
  televised dance, **6**:137, 138
Sol, Laura del, **3**:101
Sol, Maria del, **1**:294
Solan, Jeanne, **4**:602
Solane, Janine, **3**:76, 83
Solange Rose, **2**:415
Solano, Rafael, **2**:432
Solar, Willie, **6**:319
Solari, Malucha, **2**:123
Solaris/Lakota group, **4**:555
Soldatenmis, **4**:602
Soldier and Peasant (Soldat og Borde), **1**:505, 507
Soldier and the Gypsy, The, **1**:280
Soldier's Mass, **4**:81
Soldier's Tale, The, **1**:292, **4**:81, 181, **5**:294, 677
  Cranko production and performance, **2**:265, *265,* **5**:650
  Feld production, **2**:583, 584
  Helpmann choreography, **3**:356
  Holm performance, **3**:369
  Šmok choreography, **5**:617
  Stravinsky score, **1**:93, 251, 453, **2**:265, **3**:356, **6**:4, 5
Soledad, **6**:28
Soleil de Nuit, Le (later *Midnight Sun*), **1**:311, 322, **2**:108, 408, **4**:124, 316, 657, **5**:233
Soleil des Eaux, Le, **1**:349
Soler, Antonio, **6**:202

Soleri, Paolo, **6**:400
Solh, Indji Al-, **2**:498
Soliannikov, Nikolai, **5**:118
Solid Gold (television program), **5**:633
Solimano (Angiolini), **1**:88, **5**:528
Solimano, Il (Bonarelli), **2**:27
Solino, Louis, **4**:626, 627, *627*
Solitaire, **4**:200, 240, **5**:341
Solitaire premier (de Tyard), **1**:2
Solitaire second (de Tyard), **1**:2
Solitary Song, **4**:39, *39*
Soliva, Carlo, **5**:276
Sollertinsky, Ivan, **5**:614
Solomon, Vasily, **6**:437
Solomoni, Giuseppe, **1**:484
Solomon Islands. *See* Bellona; Melanesia
Solomonoff-Menzelli Ballet, **1**:39
Solomons, Gus, Jr., **2**:19, 606, **6**:259, 356
So Long Eden, **6**:112
Solo Ride, **4**:218
Solo Suite in Space and Time. See Suite for Five
Solov, Zachary, **2**:187, **4**:382
Soloviev, Yuri, **1**:147, 285, **5**:460, **638–639**, **6**:441
Solo with Sofia, **3**:368
Soloviev-Sedoi, Vladimir, **6**:442
Solway, Diane, **3**:617
Solymosi, Tamás, **1**:241
Solymosi, Zoltán, **2**:470, **5**:419
Şomâcescu, Simona, **5**:390
Somalian trance rituals, **6**:185
Somani, La Ciba, **3**:574
Somantri, Radan Cece, **3**:504
Sombart, Alexander, **4**:249
Somba Sebit, **3**:496
Sombert, Claire, **1**:251, **3**:82, **4**:3, 435, **5**:53, 163
Sombras, **2**:277
Sombreros, **1**:301
Somdet Phra Phuttha Lōēt Lā, king of Siam, **4**:112
Somebody's Coming to See Me Tonight, **4**:472
Somers, Harry, **5**:62, **6**:1
Somes, Michael, **5**:**639–640**, **6**:*134,* 137
  Australian guest appearances, **1**:499
  Ballet Imperial, **1**:293
  Cinderella performance, **2**:174
  Fonteyn dance partnership, **3**:*41, 43, 43, 266,* **5**:639, 640
  Horoscope performance, **3**:379
  Japanese performances, **3**:589
  Karsavina role coaching, **3**:656
  Romeo and Juliet performance, **5**:396
  Royal Ballet, **1**:*149,* 150, 155, *155, 156,* 459, **2**:443, **5**:396, *414,* 416
  Scènes de Ballet, **5**:531–532, 639
  Sibley dance partnership and marriage, **5**:596
  Sylvia performance, **6**:*63,* 64
  Symphonic Variations performance, **6**:64
Something to Do, **3**:272
Something to Shout About (film), **2**:108
Something to Tell, **2**:355, **4**:218
Some Thoughts Concerning Education (Locke), **3**:281

Sommer, Sally R., *as contributor,* **3**:90–96, 633, **5**:368–369, 601, 631–636, **6**:95–104
Somnambule, La, **5**:92, **640–641**, 642, **6**:216
  Augusta (Madame) performance, **1**:199
  Aumer choreography, **1**:202, 505, **2**:390, **5**:640–641, 642
  Bournonville (August) production, **1**:505, **5**:641
  Deshayes (André) restaging, **2**:390
  Fitzjames (Nathalie) performance, **3**:5
  Hérold score, **3**:360
  Lecomte (Hippolyte) costumes, **4**:138
  Scribe libretto, **3**:69
Somnambulism, **4**:117, 240
son, **2**:275, **3**:319
Sonata, **4**:71–72, **5**:677
Sonata for Two Pianos and Percussion (Bartok), **1**:404
Sonata of Death and Movement, The, **3**:193
Sonata Pathetique, **2**:377
Sonatas, **1**:412
Sonatas and Interludes (Cage), **2**:22
Sonata Tragica, **2**:378, **3**:397
Sonate, **1**:292
Sonate à Trois, **1**:404
Sonate di Scarlatti, **4**:615
Sonatina, **1**:115
Sonatine, **4**:611, 617, **6**:328
Sondheim, Stephen, **1**:419, 439, **5**:362, **6**:282, 285, 287, 289
son duro dance, **2**:64
Sonen, Pat, **4**:212
sones dances, **4**:384, 386, 387
Sonezaku Shinjū, **4**:533
Song, **2**:1, 359, **3**:220
Song and Dance (musical), **6**:286
Songbook, **5**:245
song dances, **2**:100, 629, **3**:436
  Berber, **4**:466–467, 663
  Native American, **4**:557, 560, 561, 563, 566
  Norway, **4**:671–672
songdans, **4**:672
Song dynasty, **2**:130–131, 144, 148
Songe, Un, **5**:300, 691
Songe d'Ossian, Le, **1**:202
Songes, Les, **1**:306, **4**:418, **6**:182
Song Kyong-rin, **4**:54
Song of a Wayfarer, **2**:513–514
Song of Ceylon, The (film), **2**:601
Song of Deborah, **4**:*121*
"Song of Destiny," **6**:*390*
Song of Goat Tragedy, **3**:646
Song of Happiness, A, **4**:7
Song of Hybrias the Creta (Pendlebury), **2**:269
Song of Liberation, **2**:155
Song of Mohenjodaro, The, **4**:5, **5**:63
Song of Norway (musical), **1**:297–298, **2**:584, **3**:88, **4**:246, **6**:277
Song of Songs (Bible), **1**:448
Song of Songs (Eck choreography), **2**:474
Song of Songs (Levi-Tanai choreography), **3**:449, 450
Song of Stalin (Khachaturian), **4**:7
Song of the Crane, **1**:91, **5**:459, 473
Song of the Earth, The. See Lied von der Erde, Das
Song of the Guerrillas, **6**:405
Song of the Nightingale, The, **2**:245
Song of the West, **3**:403

Song of the World, **2:**155
Song of the Yimeng Mountain, The, **2:**116
Song of Triumphant Love, The, **5:**472
Song of War, **3:**401
Songs and Dances, **4:**218
Songs for a Dark Voice, **5:**62
Songs of Auvergne, **4:**275
Songs of Hafiz, **6:**441
Songs of the Ghetto, **3:**529, **4:**58
Songs of the Plantation, **2:**581
Songs of the Russian Revolution, **2:**454
Songs with Mara, **6:**95
Songs without Words, **5:**436
Songulashvili, Aleksidze, **3:**135
Sonic Arts Union, **1:**141
son-montuno, **2:**274, 276
Sonnabend, Yolanda, **6:**35
Sonnambula, La (Bellini opera), **3:**59, 360, **5:**641
Sonnambula, La (Balanchine ballet; originally *Night Shadow*), **1:**74, 198, 268, 298, **2:**254, **3:**74, 226, **4:**613, **5:**431, 553, **641–642,** **6:**353
  Balanchine revival, **4:**609, 621
  Danilova performance, **2:**342, 343
  Fonteyn performance, **2:**511
  Franklin performance, **3:**87
  Jillana performance, **4:**617
  Kent performance, **4:**5, 617
  Kronstam performance, **4:**65
  Magallanes performance, **4:**246
  Schanne performance, **5:**553
  Skibine performance, **5:**604
Sonnenfels, J. V., **3:**189
Son of Gone Fishin', **1:**143, 544
Sonora, Mexico, **6:**416
Sons of Ishmael (Murray), **4:**416
Sønstervold, Gunnar, **4:**676
Soohih, Anatole and May, **3:**574
Sophie Amalie, queen of Denmark, **2:**384
Sophie Maslow and Company. *See* Maslow, Sophie
Sophie of Brabant, **2:**442
Sophisticated Ladies (musical), **1:**58, **3:**366, 578, **6:**102, 103, 286
Sophocles, **2:**153, 159, **3:**216, 289, 300, 652
Sor, Fernando, **1:**36, 479, 480, 481, **2:**521
Sorbonne, Paris, **3:**83, 85, **4:**186
Sorcerer, The, or The Loves of Pluto and Prosperine, **5:**350
Sorcerer's Apprentice, The, **3:**21, 23, 24, **6:**175
  Lander (Harald) staging and symbolism, **4:**118, **5:**429
  nō adaptation, **4:**332
Sorceress, The, **6:**133
Sorceress of Dirah, The, **5:**524
Sorel, Cécile, **4:**524
Sorel, Felicia, **2:**579, 580, **5:**359
Sorel, Ruth Abramowitz, **2:**39, 44
Sorensen, Jacki, **1:**12–13, **2:**322
Sörensen, Margareta, **6:**50
Sorex, Norbanus, **4:**426
Sorgente, La, **4:**429
Sorin and Baxter, **1:**391
Sorley Walker, Kathrine, **4:**178
  as contributor, **1:**308–316, 367–368, 466, **3:**307, 353–357, **4:**667, **5:**349–350, **6:**182–183
Sorokina, Nina, **1:**493, **3:**197, **5:**460, 567
šorový, **2:**302

Sorrentino, Giuseppe, **5:**232
Sorrow of India, The, **2:**155
Sortilèges, Les, **2:**36
Sortis, Bettina de, **4:**380
Sospiri, **1:**501
Šoth, Ondrej, **2:**310, **5:**614
Sotho dance, **5:**643, 646, 663, **6:**646
Sotlar, Lidija, **6:**438
Soto, Hilda, **2:**127
Soto, Jock, **4:**623
Soto, Merián, **2:**65
Soto, Pepita, **5:**133, 615–616
Sotoba Komachi, **3:**646–647
šotyš, **2:**301, 304
Souard, Francine, **2:**388
Soudeikine, Serge, **1:**85, 86, **2:**241, **3:**25, **4:**32, **5:**642
Soule dance, **1:**377
Soulier, Achille, **4:**588
Soul Kiss, The (musical), **3:**129
Soul of Africa, **5:**660
Soul Train (television program), **1:**78, **5:**633
Soumoud, Al-, **2:**497
Sounddance, **2:**289, 293, **4:**37, **5:**18
Sound Delay, **5:**549
Sounding, **2:**355
Soundings (Rauschenberg), **5:**314
Sound of Music, The (film), **2:**618
Sound of Music, The (musical), **6:**282
Sound of One Hand Clapping, The, **2:**563
Sounds in Motion Dance Company, **6:**448
Sound Ventures, **6:**132, 133
Source, La, **2:**198, 201, **3:**441, **5:**94, 501, 515, 566, **6:**328
  Balanchine pas de deux, **4:**611
  Degas painting, **2:**361
  Grantzow role, **3:**237, 238
  Mérante performance, **4:**353
  as Nijinsky debut vehicle, **4:**639–640
  score, **2:**367–368, 368–369, **4:**429, 514
  Verdy performance, **4:**617
Sourde Supposée, La, **2:**55
Souritz, Elizabeth, **5:**483, 484, **642–643**
  as contributor, **1:**38–39, 484–495, 539–540, **2:**499, **3:**200, 204–207, 631–633, **4:**58, **5:**331, 465–475, 476–479, 482–486, **6:**170–171
sousa (song and dance), **2:**64
Sousa, John Philip, **1:**256, **6:**271
  as two-step influence, **5:**627–628
soústa, **1:**519, **2:**271–272
Sous valley, Morocco, **4:**467
soutenu turns, **1:**336, 337
South Africa, **5:**643–661
  ballet, **5:**649–655**
    See also CAPAB Ballet; PACT Ballet
  contemporary theatrical dance, **5:**655–661**
  indigenous dance, **5:**643–649,** **6:**22
    costume, **2:**212–213
    gumboot, **2:**86, 212–213, **5:**648, 648, **6:**22
    Shangana-Tsonga, **5:**579–580
    Venda, **6:**321–322
South African Ballet Company, **5:**52, 651
South African Broadcasting Company, **5:**53
South African National Ballet, **5:**650, 691, 692

South America. *See* Latin American dances; *specific countries*
"South American Way" (song), **4:**434
South before the War, The (vaudeville show), **5:**368
South Dakota style (Plains Indian dance), **4:**561, 562
Southeast Asia
  dance traditions, **1:**161, 162–163, **171–177**
  Islamic dance aesthetics, **1:**18–19
  See also specific countries
Southeastern Regional Ballet Association, **1:**197
Southern, David, *as photographer,* **1:**449
southern Africa, **5:**661–666**
  African-American music influence, **6:**24
  !Kung San dance, **4:**74–75, **5:**664, 665
  Shangana-Tsonga dance, **5:**579–580, 662–663
Southern Ballet Theatre, Christchurch, **4:**626
Southern Drama (Chinese form), **2:**130
Southern Illinois University, **2:**459
Southern Landscape, **1:**395, 395
South Korea. *See* Korea
Southland, **2:**458–459
South Pacific (musical), **6:**281
South Seas Evangelical Church, **1:**415
Soutzo, Olga, **2:**199
Souvenirs, **1:**478, 479, **2:**245, **3:**343, 343, **4:**520
"Souvenirs de Ratisbon" (Burgmüller), **2:**14
Souza, Ignace de, **4:**487
Sovedu (people), **5:**643
Sovetskii balet (Slonimsky), **5:**483
Sovetskii baletnyi teatr, 1917–1967 (Krasovskaya ed.), **5:**484
Soviet Ballet (journal), **5:**642
Soviet Choreographers in the 1920s (Souritz), **5:**484, 643
Soviet Encyclopedia of Ballet, **2:**524, **4:**58
Soviet era (1917–1991), **5:**457–465
  Albanian dance, **1:**33, 34
  Alonso (Alicia) as first Western guest ballerina, **1:**49
  Alvin Ailey American Dance Theater tour, **1:**57
  American Ballet Company tour, **1:**70
  Armenian dance, **1:**121
  Australian Ballet tours, **1:**233
  avant-garde dance, **1:**244, 246, **3:**48
  Azerbaijan dance, **1:**247, 248
  ballet competitions, **1:**282
  Baryshnikov stardom, **1:**371–372
  Belarussian dance, **1:**408
  Belsky choreographic influences, **1:**416–417, **5:**460
  Bolshoi Ballet, **1:**488–494
  Bulgarian ballet, **2:**11–12
  Burmeister, Vladimir, **2:**15–16
  Chinese dance, **2:**133, 135, 145
  choreographic innovations, **4:**283–285
  circuses, **2:**176
  classical ballet revivals, **4:**224, **5:**462–463, 464
  companies in constituent republics, **4:**224, 226, **5:**459, 463
  constructivist design, **5:**544–545

Corsaire popularity, **2:**206, 207
  costume, **2:**244
  Cuban ballet and modern dance, **1:**49, **2:**278–279, 280–282
  Czechoslovakia, **2:**308–310
  dance aesthetics, **5:**485
  dance criticism, **5:**613–614
  dance defectors, **1:**372, **2:**342, **4:**248, **5:**5, 416, 485
  dance emigrés to Israel, **3:**534
  dance technique, **1:**329, 348–349, 384, **4:**283
    batterie, **1:**384
    as major emphasis, **1:**44, 349
    Messerer classes, **4:**359–360
  Dance Theatre of Harlem tour, **2:**335
  Diaghilev dance relations, **2:**410
  Don Quixote popularity, **2:**438
  dramatic ballet, **1:**517, **4:**283, 284, **5:**458, 460, 484, 485, 614, **6:**410–411, 442
  Duncan dances, **2:**456
  Egyptian folk dance and ballet, **2:**496–497
  Esmeralda productions, **2:**524
  Fadetta as choreographic landmark, **4:**131
  first English ballerina as guest artist at Kirov and Bolshoi theaters, **3:**307
  first U.S. dance tour, **2:**96
  first Western ballet company to tour Eastern Europe, **5:**436
  Flames of Paris as revolutionary classic, **3:**12, **5:**458, 459, **6:**310
  Fokine recognition, **3:**21
  folk dance choreography, **4:**530
  folk dance research, **3:**423, **4:**448, **5:**481
  Foregger choreography, **3:**48
  foreign ballet critiques, **5:**484–485
  Gayané, **3:**125
  Geltser, Ekaterina, **3:**128
  Georgian ballet, **3:**135
  German dance, **3:**152–155
  German folk dance, **3:**142
  Giselle interpretation, **3:**182
  Glière scores, **3:**186–187
  Goleizovsky choreography, **3:**194–195
  Golovkina performances, **3:**197
  Gorbachev cultural reform effects, **5:**463
  Grigorovich choreographic style, **3:**308–309, **5:**460
  Hungarian ballet, **3:**416, 417–418
  Hungarian folk dance research, **3:**423, **4:**448
  Hungarian modern dance, **3:**421
  ice dancing, **3:**432, 433
  ideological critiques of Shostakovich ballets, **5:**594
  as influence on Diaghilev's Ballets Russes, **4:**320–321
  Japanese dance schools, **3:**589
  Joffrey Soviet Union tour, **3:**611
  joint American-Soviet *Swan Lake,* **6:**35
  Khachaturian, Aram, **4:**6–7
  Kirov Ballet (later Maryinsky), **4:**276
  Kyrgyzstan dance, **4:**86–87
  Latvian dance, **4:**127–128
  Laurencia, **4:**129, **5:**458
  Lavrovsky, Leonid, **1:**144, 440, **2:**11, 596, **4:**131–132, **5:**484
  Leningrad Symphony, **4:**147–148
  Lepeshinskaya style, **4:**148–149

literary classics as dance
    subjects, **5:**461–462, 468–469
Little Humpbacked Horse
    versions, **4:**212
Lopukhov influence,
    4:224–226, 283
Lukom dance influence, **4:**233
modern dance, **5:**477–478, *477*
modernist versus proletarian
    music split, **5:**594
Moiseyev, Igor, **4:**444–445
Moldovan dance, **4:**446–447
Moscow teachers, **5:**480
music, **4:**517, **5:**594
New York City Ballet tour, **4:**607
Nureyev's unorthodoxy, **5:**5
Prokofiev, Sergei, **5:**268
provincial ballet companies,
    5:470–473
Pushkin poetry-based ballets,
    3:56
Red Poppy significance, **3:**187,
    4:283, **5:**331, 458, *458*
revolutionary themes, **5:**458
Romanian dance, **5:**385–386
Romeo and Juliet as
    representative ballet,
    5:392, 394
Shakespearean ballets, **4:**132,
    5:462
Shostakovich, Dimitri, **5:**594–595
Shurale choreographic influence,
    5:596
Spartacus, **5:**463, 471, 677–678
Stravinsky return visit, **4:**6
Swedish productions, **6:**42
symphonic ballet, **2:**11, **4:**225,
    283, 284–285, 517
theatrical dance research and
    publication, **5:**483–485
Ukrainian dance, **6:**222
Ulanova performances,
    6:226, 227
Ustinova folk-based dance
    choreography, **6:**303–304
Uzbek dance, **6:**306
Western dance influences, **5:**460
Yakobson choreography,
    6:410–411
Yermolayev, Aleksei, **6:**420
Zakharov, Rostislav, **5:**484,
    6:441–443
Sovietskii balet (magazine), **6:**8
Soviet Union. *See* Russia; Soviet
    era; *specific former republics*
Sovremenny balet (Svetlov), **5:**482,
    6:28
Sowell, Debra Hickenlooper, *as*
    contributor, **1:**540–541,
    2:160–162, **3:**320–321
Soweto, **2:**500
Soweto Dance Theatre, **5:**660
Soweto Street Beat Company,
    5:660
Soyinka, Wole, **6:**384
Space, **2:**359, **4:**623
Space at City Center for Music and
    Dance, New York City, **6:**164
Space City, **2:**609, **4:**21
Space Dance, **1:**386
Space Harmony (Laban concept),
    3:53, **4:**96, 99–100, 102,
    103, 140
Space Rhythm (Laban concept),
    4:99
Spaces Between, **4:**156
Spadavecchia, Antonio, **2:**15, **6:**310
Spade Dance, **6:**316
spagnoletta, **2:**74, **5:**666
Spaight, Dennis, **1:**75

Spain, **5:667–676**
    Basque dance, **1:**376–378
    bolero, **1:**479–481
    castanet styles, **2:**78
    Catholic Church views of dance,
        1:167, **2:**164, 429, 430
    dance notation, **4:**683
    dance on television, **6:**136
    dance research and publication,
        5:675–676
    libraries and museums,
        4:162–163
    dancing masters, **2:**337, **5:**668,
        669, 670, 671
    escuela bolera, **2:**521–522, *554*,
        5:671–673
    flamenco dance, **1:**61–62, 116,
        117, **2:**520–521, **3:**6–11,
        101–102, **5:**672, *673*, 674
    folia, **3:**29
    folk dance sounds, **3:**38, 39
    as influence on Argentine dance,
        1:109
    as influence on Caribbean dance,
        2:62
    as influence on Dominican
        Republic dance, **2:**430, 431
    as influence on Garifuna dance,
        3:120
    as influence on Guatemalan
        dance, **3:**319
    as influence on Mexican dance,
        4:399
    as influence on North African
        dance, **4:**664–665
    as influence on South African
        dance, **5:**654
    as influence on Uruguayan
        dance, **6:**301
    liturgical dances, **2:**168
    matachins, **4:**327
    moresca stick dance, **2:***555*
    "Moros y Cristianos," **4:**473
    processional dances, **2:**164, 168
    révérence, **5:**345
    Sephardic Jewish dance, **3:**603
    theatrical dance, **5:667–675**
        alta, **1:**53–54
        fan usage, **2:***569*, 571
        Italian influences, **3:**543
        modern dance, **5:**674–675
        pastorales, **5:**113
        South African influences, **5:**654
        Susana, **6:**27–28
    See also Ballet Nacional
        Español
Špalíček, **2:**307, **4:**77
SPAM. *See* Sociedad Pro Arte
    Musical, Havana
Spanda, **5:**510
Spanier auf der Insel Christina, Die,
    6:338
Spanish Association for Dance
    Medicine, **2:**329
Spanish Dance (Kraus
    choreography), **4:**59
Spanish Dance (Nagrin solo), **4:**531
Spanish Dance Company, **1:**101,
    5:673
Spanish Dance Society, South
    Africa, **5:**654
Spanish Dancing (Meri), **4:**355
Spanish Encounter, **5:**54, 692
Spanish Fiesta (film), **4:**324, **6:**183
Spanish Grenadiers, **2:**15
Spanish Riding School, Vienna,
    3:383
Spanish Sketches, **3:**205
Spanish Student, The (Longfellow),
    2:504
Spanish Suite, The, **1:**90, **2:**378

Šparemblek, Milko, **1:**349, **3:**74,
    344, **4:**435, **5:**98, 234, 235,
    676–677, 6:437, *437*
Sparger, Celia, **4:**17, **6:**128
Sparling, Peter, **1:**75, **3:**220
Sparshott, Francis, **1:**24, **2:**49, 50
Sparta, **2:**158, **3:**287, 291
Spartacus, **2:**502, **4:**87, **5:**57–58,
    205, *462*, 470, **677–678,**
    6:171, 314, *314*
    Australian Ballet, **1:**211
    Bessmertnova performance,
        1:440
    Bolshoi production, **1:**492
    Changa choreography, **4:**127
    Fayer conducting, **2:**579
    Gordeyev performance, **3:***200*
    Grigorovich libretto and
        choreography, **3:**308, **4:**7,
        5:472, 677–678
    Khachaturian score, **3:**308, **4:**7,
        284, 444, **5:**569, 677, 678,
        6:411
    Kondratieva performance, **4:**38
    Lavrovsky (Mikhail)
        performance, **4:**133, *133*
    Liepa (Maris) performance,
        4:*181*, 182
    Maximova performance, **4:**335
    Moiseyev (Igor) staging, **4:**444
    Paeper choreography, **5:***654*
    popularity with Soviet provincial
        companies, **5:**463, 471
    Róna performance, **5:**402
    Seregi production, **3:**417, *417*,
        5:402, 569
    Yakobson choreography, **4:**7, 284,
        5:460, 677, **6:**411, *411*
Spartak. See Spartacus
Sparta Purulia Chhau Dance
    Museum, **4:**159
Sparti, Barbara, **3:**553, 554, 557,
    5:327
    as contributor, **1:**351–355,
        5:505–507
Spatt, Leslie E., **5:**184
    as photographer, **2:**347, 513, **4:**1,
        244, 257, **5:**104, 419, **6:**146
Spaulding, Bridget, **3:**574
Spaziani, Jeanne, **5:***305*
Speaking about Dance (Hartong),
    4:600
Speaking in Tongues, **6:**109, 110,
    111, 112
"Speaking of Dance—
    Conversations with the
    Masters" (videotapes), **1:**81
Speak to Me, Dance with Me, **2:**374
Spear, Arlene, **6:**379
spear dances, **1:**118, 167, **2:**232,
    593, **3:***103*, 479
Spears, Warren, **2:**386
Specimen Days, **4:**451
Spectacle Berio, **2:**388
Spectacles du Parnasse, Les, **1:**284
Spectator, The (journal), **2:**570,
    6:372, 374
Spectre de la Rose, Le, **1:**251, 292,
    5:298, **6:**213
    Bakst designs, **1:**254, **2:**407
    Ballets Russes de Monte Carlo
        revival, **1:**311
    Béjart choreography, **3:**578
    Beriozoff staging of Fokine's
        choreography, **4:**380
    Bowman performance, **1:**518
    English National Ballet revival,
        2:510, 512
    Fokine productions, **1:**318, 320,
        2:424, **3:**14, 18, 24, *24*, 26, 75,
        226, *668*, **5:**413

Koslov pirated version, **4:**56
    in Sweden, **6:**41
Idzikowski performance,
    3:441, 442
Japanese stagings, **3:**589
Joffrey Ballet and Nureyev
    television production, **3:**616
Karsavina performance,
    3:656, *656*
Kehlet performance, **3:***668*
libretto, **3:**73
Liepa (Andris) reconstruction,
    4:181
Liepa (Maris) revival, **4:**182
Lifar restaging, **4:**184
Lopokova performance,
    4:223, *223*
Nijinsky leap, **2:**71, **4:***644*
Nijinsky performance, **2:**408,
    3:18, *656*, **4:***645*
Shearer (Moirer) performance,
    5:589
Spessivtseva performance, **5:**678
Youskevitch performance, **6:**425
Spectrum (television series), **6:**131
Speed, Francis, **2:**602, **6:**25
Speer, Daniel, **3:**409
Spell, **1:**59, **3:**578
Spellbound by Rhythm
    (Gripenberg), **3:**313
Spellbound Child, **4:**136
Spell for Opening the Mouth of N,
    2:461
Spelman College, **6:**258
Spencer, Audrey, **1:**453
Spencer, Baldwin, **2:**601
Spencer, Herbert, **1:**127, **3:**30,
    6:241
Spencer, Paul, *as contributor*, **5:**509
Spencer, Penelope, **1:**437
Spencer, Prince, **3:**57
Spencer-Edwards, Barbara, **3:**175
Spender, Stephen, **3:**403
Spendiarov, Aleksandr, **3:**20, **5:**124
Spenser, Edmund, **1:**150
Speransky, P., **5:**595
Speranzeva, Ludmilla, **2:**458
Sperling, Jody, *as contributor*,
    2:603–612
Spessivtseva, Olga, **1:**110, 207, 247,
    3:24, **5:**17, 95, 132, 526,
    678–679, 6:128, 344
    Camargo Society, **2:**424, **4:**268
    Diaghilev's Ballets Russes, **2:**409,
        410, 411, **4:**267
    as Dolin influence, **2:**423
    Don Quixote performance, **2:**437
    as Fokine student, **3:**14
    Giselle interpretation, **3:**183
    Giselle performance, **2:**424,
        5:678, 679, *679*
    Lester dance partnership, **4:**152
    Lifar dance partnership, **4:**182,
        183, 184
    Maryinsky Ballet, **4:**283
    Nijinska choreography, **4:**635
    Sleeping Beauty performance,
        2:409, **5:**611, 679
    Swan Lake performance, **6:**31, 32
Spherical Expansion (Centrifugal)
    (Severini), **1:**130
Sphinx, **1:**196, **2:**355, *355*, 513, 561,
    3:273, **4:**178, 218, 242,
    6:143, 146
"Spider and the Fly, The," **3:**354
Spider dance, **3:**334
Spider's Web, **2:**473
Spiegel, De, **2:**470
Spier, Leslie, **3:**170–171
Spies, Daisy, **3:**153
Spies, Leo, **2:**441, **3:**154

Spies, Walter, *as photographer*, **3:**474, 478, 480, 481, 482, 484, 486, 487, 488, 490, 491, **6:**367
Spiess, Adolph, **6:**235
Spillane, Douglas, *as photographer*, **4:**237
Spinacuta, Laurent, **3:**86, **5:**199
Spindrift, **5:679–681, 6:**110, 111, 112
Spink, Ian, **1:**213, 214, **2:**354, **3:**273–274, **5:**304
spinning. *See* ballet technique, turning movements
Spinning Dance, **2:**358
spinning dances, **2:**303, *303*
Spinzi, Henrietta, **4:**529
Spira, Phyllis, **2:**56, 58, **5:**53, 54, 652, *653*
Spiral, **6:***163*
Spiral Hall, Tokyo, **1:**61
Spirić, Slobodan, **6:**438
Spiriditis, **4:**127
Spirit Dance, **2:**141, **4:**573
Spirit of the Factory, The, **1:**484
Spirit of the Rose, The, **2:**378
Spirit of the Sea, The, **2:**378
Spirit of the Times (journal), **6:**298
spirituals, **6:**258
Spivey, Billy, **1:**450, *450*
Spivey, Creighton, **1:***450*
Spizzo, Christine, **1:**75
Spleen and Champagne, **4:**454
Spoerli, Heinz, **1:**242, **2:**200, 561, **5:***35*, 43, **681–684, 6:***51, *136*
Basel Ballet, **1:**374–375, **2:**441, **6:***52, 52*
Düsseldorf-Duisberg Ballet, **3:**157
Fille Mal Gardée, La, **2:**596, *596*
Firebird, The, **3:***4*
Giselle, **6:**454
Josephslegende, Die, **3:**631
Keil roles, **4:**1
Sackgasse, **6:***10*
Zurich Ballet, **6:**454, 455
Spohr, Arnold, **2:**39, 42, **5:**434, 435, 436, 437, **684–685**
Spohr, Louis, **2:**14, **5:**555
Špokaitė, Eglė, **4:**208, *208*
Spontini, Gaspare, **2:**435, **4:**61, **5:**558
Spookkar, **1:**411
Spookride, **6:**363
Spork, Martin, **3:**153
Špork Theater, Prague, **2:**306
Sport, **2:**477, **4:**258, 259, 264, **5:**529
sports. *See* dance as sport
sports medicine. *See* dance medicine
Sports of England, The, **3:**261, **4:**121
Sposa Rapita, La, **6:**69
spotlights, **4:**189
spotting (timing), **1:**336
spoudaios, **2:**506
Sprache des Tanzes, Die (Wigman), **3:**161
sprain, **4:**20
Spread It Abroad (revue), **3:**61, 202
Spreckles, Alma, **3:**95
Spring, **2:**529, **5:**511
springar, **2:**382, **4:**669–670
Spring Awakening, **4:**73, 547
Spring Azure, **3:**350
springdans, **4:**669, 671
Springer, Dominik, **3:**365
Springer, Julia, **2:**306
Spring Fairy Tale, **2:**449, **5:**572
Springfield (Missouri) Civic Ballet, **3:**429
Spring Loaded, **3:**276

Spring 1975, **2:**473
Springplank, **4:**602
Spring Tale, **3:**629, *629*, **4:**226, 284, **5:**459, **6:**343
Spring Waters, **5:**107
Spura, Alfred, **4:**128
"spur dance," **3:**411
Spurgeon, Jack, **1:**316, **3:***512*
Square Dance, **1:**262, 271, **2:**334, 358, 514, **4:**246, *612*
Balanchine revisions, **4:**611, 618, 619
Cook (Bart) solo, **4:**621
Nichols performance, **4:**623
in Washington Ballet repertory, **6:**366
Wilde performance, **4:**617, **6:**396
Square Dances, **3:**401
Square Dance, Walking Dance, **2:**358
square dancing, **1:**47, 521, **5:**625, **685–690**
American "calling" of figures custom, **2:**257
American revival as recreational dance, **3:**35, **6:**247
clogging teams, **2:**180
cotillion elements, **2:**252, 253, 256
as country dance form, **2:**256–257
European roots, **2:**554
figures, **2:**592
French-Canadian, **2:**35
jig dance steps, **3:**608
northeastern, **5:**685–686
Protestant sectarian condemnation, **2:**167
quadrille, **5:**285
reels, **5:**333
Rodeo use of, **2:**108, **5:**369
round variant, **5:**409–410
southeastern, **5:**686–688
western, **5:**688–689
Square Deal, **3:**52
Squaregame, **2:**294
Squaregame Video, **2:**284, 607
Square Order Shuffle, **5:**576
squat dance, **4:**356, *357*
Squaw Man, The (film), **6:**243
Srabhai, Mrinalini, **3:**468
srandul, **1:**174
Srbljenović, Maja, **5:**677
SRC. *See* Société Radio-Canada
Sri, **2:**104
Sri 420 (film), **2:**624
Sri Lanka, **1:**178
costume, **2:**228–229
Kandyan dance, **3:**647–649
Kandy Perahera, **3:**649–650
Kohomba Kankariya, **2:**228, **3:**647, **4:**34–35
masks, **4:**300, *300*
tovil ritual, **6:**183–184
trance rituals, **6:**185
ves dance, **6:**329–330
Sri Mangkunagara VII, sultan of Surakarta, **3:**496
srimpi, **1:**174, **3:**494–495
Srimpi Anglirmendung, **3:**494
Sri Ram Bharatiya Kala Kendra, **2:**468, **5:**510
Sri Suwela, **3:**496
Sritensky, Genrikh, **4:**333
Sri Wedari (Surakarta park), **3:**497
Sri Weeraparakrama Narendrasinghe, king of Kandy, **3:**647–648
SRT. *See* Skinner Releasing Technique

Staats, Léo, **1:**246, 247, **3:**71, 82, **5:**132, 315, **690–691**
Paris Opera Ballet, **4:**64, **5:**94, 95, *96*
Soir de Fête, **2:**368
students, **1:**403, **4:**25, 209, **5:**385
Sylvia production, **2:**351, **6:**64
Staatsopernballett (State Opera Ballet, Vienna), **1:**238–241, *240*, **5:**683
Adama, Richard, **1:**11, 241
Alonso (Alicia) productions, **1:**49
Charrat performances, **2:**111
Checkmate revival, **2:**115
Chladek stagings, **2:**153, 154
Don Quixote productions, **2:**435, 440
Firebird, The, **3:**3
Forsythe guest choreography, **3:**52
Fränzl family, **3:**88–89
Gioja productions, **3:**175–176
Hanka, Erika, **3:**340
Hassreiter, Josef, **3:**346–347
Henry (Louis) productions, **3:**358
Hungarian performances, **3:**413–414
Josephslegende, Die, **3:**631, **4:**64
Kröller, Heinrich, **4:**64
Losch, Tilly, **4:**228–229
Milloss as ballet master, **4:**421
Noverre, Jean-Georges, **4:**696
Nureyev-Georgiadis *Swan Lake* production, **3:**136, **6:**35
Parlić directorship, **5:**100
Viganò productions, **3:**175
Wallmann choreography, **6:**357
Wiesenthal sisters, **6:**388
Staatsoper Unter den Linden. *See* Berlin State Opera
Stabat, **5:**617
Stabat Mater (Pergolesi), **6:**66
Stabel, Ralf, **3:**162
Staburadze, **4:**127
Stach i Zośka, **5:**195
Stackhouse, Sarah, **4:**199
Stack-Up, The, **1:**395, **2:**358
sta dío, **2:**101
Stadler, Brigette, **1:**241
Staël, Madame de, **1:**199
Staff, Frank, **1:**429, **2:**56, **4:**306, 667, **5:**226, **691–692**
Cinderella performance, **5:***651, 692*
Czernyana, **3:**174
Enigma Variations, **2:**515
Lovers' Gallery, The, **2:**2–3
Metropolitan Ballet, **4:**380
Peter and the Wolf, **3:**62, 174, **5:**691, 692
Rain Queen, The, **2:**57
Rambert Dance Company, **1:**146, **5:**299, 300
Schooling revivals, **5:**560
South African ballet, **5:**52, 53, 54, 650, 651, 653, 654, 691–692, **6:**379
students, **5:**56
staff dances. *See* stick dance
Stag, Emte, *as contributor*, **4:**681–682
stage design. *See* scenic design
Stage for Dancers, **1:**432
stage machinery, **5:***534*, 535, **6:**38, 39, 46, 48
Stages, **4:**217
Stages and Reflections, **3:**343, **4:***603*
stage space. *See* theaters for dance
Stagg, Mr. and Mrs. Charles, **6:**231
Staggins, Nicholas, **5:**251

Stagium. *See* Ballet Stagium
Ståhle, Anna Greta, **6:**49
as contributor, **1:**400, 403, **2:**500–501, **5:**41–45, 49–50
Staines, Mavis, **4:**541–542
stair dance, **5:**368, **6:**100, 317
Stålhammar, Charlotte, **2:***284*
Stalinism. *See* socialist realism; Soviet era
Stalinsky, Oleg, **4:**634
Stalinsky, Vsevolod, **4:**634
stambeli, **6:**206
Stamina (foundation), **4:**597
Stamitz, Anton, **4:**61
Stamitz, Johann, **2:**54
Stamping Dance, **2:**358
stamping dances, **5:**646, 661
Stamping Ground, **4:**81
Standard Dictionary of Folklore, Mythology, and Legend, **4:**373
Stand Up and Cheer (film), **6:**141
Stanevicius, J. A., **6:**301
Stanishevsky, Yuri A., **5:**482, **6:**224–226
as contributor, **5:**236, **6:**344
Stanislavska, Maria, **2:**181, **4:**112
Stanislavsky, Konstantin, **1:**85, 487, **2:**132, 263, **5:**456, 516, 529, 541, **6:**195
Dobujinsky scenic design, **2:**421
dramatic realism, **1:**517, **3:**56
as Gorsky influence, **5:**480
as Kanze brothers' influence, **3:**652
as Kriger influence, **4:**62
as Martin (John) influence, **4:**272–273
method analysis as Kaye influence, **3:**663
as Soviet ballet influence, **4:**283, **5:**466, 480, **6:**442
on Zucchi's technique, **6:**453
See also Moscow Art Theater
Stanislavsky and Nemirovich-Danchenko Musical Theater, **5:**456, 464, **466–467,** 475
Bovt, Violetta, **1:**517
Briantzev, Dmitri, **1:**540, **5:**464, 467
Burmeister, Vladimir, **2:**15–16, **5:**466–467, **6:**31, 34
Esmeralda, La, **2:**524
Kriger, Victorina, **4:**62
Lopukhov, Fedor, **4:**224, 226
repertory, **5:**464
Swan Lake production, **6:**31, 34
Stanisław II Augustus, king of Poland, **5:**215, 220
Stanisław and Anna Oświęcim, **6:**365
Stanley, Charles, **3:**634
stantipes, **4:**500
Stanton, Anna, **5:**58
Stapelton, Leonora, **2:***19*
Star! (film), **4:**10
Starace, Maria-Anna (Nina Faliero), **3:**594
Stara Zagora, Bulgaria, **2:**11
Starbuck, James, **5:**513, **6:**137
Starbuck, Jo Jo, **2:**299, **4:**274
Star Cross'd, **4:**238
Starer, Robert, **3:**218
Starlight Express (musical), **2:**251, **6:**287
Stars, **2:**181
Stars and Stripes, **1:**256, 262, 271, **2:**314, **3:**352, **4:**612, 617, *621*, 631
Star's End, **4:**275

Stars in Your Eyes (musical), **1:**49, **3:**663, **6:**182
Stars of the Ballet with Markova and Dolin, **2:**425
Stars of the Bolshoi, **1:**372
Stars of the Russian Ballet (film), **2:**97
"Star Spangled Banner, The" (*Ziegfeld Follies* staging), **6:**271
Star Spangled Rhythm (film), **2:***250*, 458, **6:**277, 450
Startzman, Jane, **5:***24*, 25
Starye gody (journal), **1:**422
Starzer, Joseph, **1:**236, **2:**435, **3:**187, 189, **5:**371, **692–693**
  Hilverding ballet scores, **3:**365
  Noverre association, **4:**696
STAT. *See* Society of Teachers of the Alexander Technique
State Academic Piatnitsky Folk Choir, **5:**474
State Academic Theater of Opera and Ballet (later Kirov). *See* Maryinsky Ballet
State Ballet Institute, Hungary, **3:**417, 421–422, **4:**529
State Ballet of Missouri (formerly Kansas City Ballet), **1:**479, **3:**429, **6:**265, 266
State Ballet of Oregon, **3:**429–430
State Ballet School, East Berlin, **3:**153
State Central Archives of Literature and Arts, Moscow, **4:**165
State Choir of the Urals, Ekaterinburg, **5:**474
State Concert Ensemble "Moscow Classical Ballet" of the USSR. *See* Moscow State Theater of Classical Ballet
State Ensemble of Folk Dance, Russia, **5:**481
State Ensemble of Folk Singing and Dancing, Armenia, **1:**120
State Fine Arts Schools, Mandalay and Rangoon, **4:**527–528
State Folk Dance Company, Turkey, **6:**209
State Folk Dance Ensemble of the Ukrainian S.S.R.. *See* Ukrainian State Folk Dance Company
State Folk Dance Ensemble of the USSR, **4:**444
State Folk Song and Dance Ensemble, Albania, **1:**34, 35
State Institute of Theater, Music and Cinematography, Saint Petersburg, **4:**165
State Musical Theater, Kazakhstan, **3:**665
State Opera and Ballet Theater, Albania, **1:**34, 35
State Opera and Ballet Theater, Armenia, **1:**122
State Opera Ballet, Vienna. *See* Staatsopernballett
State Opera of Istanbul, **1:**479
State Opera of Jassy, **5:**385
State Opera of Timişoara, **5:**385
State School of Advanced Ballet, Norway, **4:**681–682, 683
State School of Dance Art, Athens, **3:**301
States of Grace, **4:**73
State Theater, Brno. *See* National Theater, Brno
State Theater of Ballet of the USSR. *See* Moscow State Theater of Classical Ballet

State Theater of Opera and Ballet. *See* Tbilisi Theater of Opera and Ballet
State University of Campinas, São Paulo, **1:**537
State University of New York, Brockport, **1:**7, **4:**370
State University of New York, Purchase, **1:**543, **6:**292
State Zagora Opera, **2:**12
staticule, **3:**434
Stati o balete (Krasovskaya), **5:**485
Stations of Life, The, **1:**308
Stations of the Cross, **4:**266
Statkiewicz, Maksymilian, **5:**85, 218
sta tría (three steps), **2:**101
Statua di Venere, La, **2:**202
Statue Amoureuse, La, **3:**123
Statue de Chypre, La, **5:**158
Stavonin, Gennady, **5:**472
Stead, J. H., **4:**520
Steadfast Tin Soldier, The (Andersen), **3:**224
Steadfast Tin Soldier, The (Balanchine ballet), **4:**611, 618, **5:**554
Steamboat Springs, Colorado, **6:**248
"Steam Heat" (*Pajama Game*), **3:**599, *599*, **6:**281
Stearns, Jean, **1:**252, 520, **4:**201
Stearns, Linda, **2:**42, **3:**231–232, 233–234
Stearns, Marshall, **1:**252, 520, **4:**201, **6:**101
Stearns, Michael, **4:**21
Stebbins, Genevieve, **1:**470, **2:**371, **5:**491, 493
stechen. See barriera, torneo, and *battaglia*
Stedelaube, Anna, **4:**128
Steele, Jeannie, **2:***296*, **5:**17
Steele, Richard, **1:**391, **2:**81, **3:**281, **6:**372, 374
Steele, Robert, **1:***501*
Steele, Tommy, **6:**283
Steel Pier (musical), **6:**289
Stefani, Jan, **5:**215
Stefanović, Ivana, **6:**435
Steggel, Amanda, **2:**612
Steichen, Edward, **5:**181, 183
Steier, Lisa, **6:**41, 46
Stein, Bonnie Sue, *as contributor*, **2:**170–171
Stein, Gertrude, **1:**147, 437–438, **4:**114, **5:**85, **6:**118, 278, 282, 375
Stein, I. F., **6:**224
Stein, Peter, **2:**120
Steinberg, Maximillian, **3:**20
Steindler, Arthur, **4:**16
Steinem, Gloria, **5:**290
Steiner, Anne, **4:**59
Steiner, Rudolf, **1:**203, **2:**18, **3:**658
Steiner, Ulrich, **3:**162
Steinhoff, Tom, **6:**266
Steinlen, Théophile-Alexandre, **5:**262
Steinweg, Gertrud, **3:**154, **5:**269
Stekelman, Ana Maria, **1:**114
Steletsky, Dmitri, **3:**196
Stella, **2:**95, **5:**278
Stella, Frank, **2:**22, 292, **3:**620, **5:**548
Stella, ou Les Contrebandiers, **5:**500
Stella Maris Dance Ensemble, **3:**576
Stelldichein, Das, **3:**314, **5:**135
Stendahl, **2:**464, **5:**528

Stenhouse, William, **3:**376
Stenka Razin, **1:**489, **3:**21, 205
Sténochorégraphie, La (Saint-Léon), **1:**37, **4:**685, **5:**227, 500, 502, **6:**127, 128
Stens, Olga, **3:**76
Štěpáková, Helena, **5:**23
Stepanenko, Galina, **3:**197, **5:**465
Stepanov, A., *as photographer*, **5:**474
Stepanov, Les, **5:**473
Stepanov, Vladimir Ivanovich, **5:**693
Stepanova, Tatiana, **1:**313, 315, 324
Stepanov notation, **2:**401, **3:**511, **4:**686, **5:**693–694, **6:**32–34, 35
Stepan Razin, **5:**461, 472
Step by Step (de Valois), **2:**403
step dancing, **5:694–699**
  African-American, **6:***261*
  Cape Breton, **2:**179, **5:696–699**
  clogging, **2:**179, 180
  Great Britain and Ireland, **3:**239–240, 517–518, *517, 518, 519*, **5:694–696**
  hornpipe, **3:**375–379
  Morris dance, **4:**473
  Scotland, **3:**247, 377
  Normandy, **3:**63
  Quebec, **2:**179
  reels, **5:**334
  tap dancing versus, **6:**96
Stephen, Saint, **3:**407, 412
Stephen, Edith, **5:**292
Stephen Acrobat, **3:**349
Stephens, Robert E., **2:**330
Stephensen, Magnus, **3:**434
Stephenson, Allan, **5:**58
Stephenson, Geraldine, **4:**94, 103, 104, 477
Step into My Dream, **3:**448
Stepney, Francis, **2:**339
Steppin' Out (musical), **6:**205, 287
Steptext, **3:**52
Step Wise Motion, **1:**142
Sterile Cloud, The, **1:**524
Sterling, Awilda, **5:**275, 276
Stern, Bert, *as photographer*, **4:**616
Sternberg, Amy, **2:**47
Sterne, Laurence, **6:**311
Sterneveld, Daan, **5:**422
Sternfield, Moshe, **3:**449
Stesichorus, **2:**158
Stevens, Dorothy, **1:**453
Stevens, Erin, **4:**255
Stevens, Housely, Jr., **1:**82
Stevenson, Ben, **1:**394, **2:**124, 174, **4:**547, **5:**51, **6:**292
  English National Ballet, **2:**511, 514
  Harkness Ballet, **3:**344
  Houston Ballet, **3:**389, 390, *390*, **6:**264
Stevenson, Dorothy, **1:**209, 499, **3:**511
Stevenson, Hugh, **2:**173, **3:**597, **5:**299, **6:**33, 196, *197*
Stevenson, Jenny, **4:**628
Stevenson, Joseph, **6:**448
Stevenson, Robert, **5:**519
Stevenson, Terry, *as photographer*, **2:**608
Stewart, Ian, **5:***304*
Stewart, Martin, *as photographer*, **4:**625, 626
Stewart, Maybelle, **3:**92
Stewart, Nora, **3:**353
Stewart, Omer C., *as contributor*, **3:**170–171
Stewart, Robert, **4:**667

Stewart, Ysobel, **3:**249
Steyn, Val, **5:**657
Stičeva, T., **2:**12
Stichel, Madame, **1:**246, **5:**95
stick dance
  Algeria, **1:**41, 42
  Basque, **1:**376–377, **4:**461
  Egypt, **2:**484, 493, **4:***405*
  England, **3:**241, *241*, 242, **4:***473*, 474
  Ethiopia, **2:**533, *534*
  Europe, **2:**552, 554
  Haiti, **3:**335
  Hungary, **2:***556*, **3:**410
  Micronesia, **4:**401
  Middle East, **4:**406
  moresca, **4:**461
  North Africa, **4:***653, 665*, 666
  Spain, **2:***555*
  Swazi, **5:**662
  Yemen, **6:**417
  Zulu, **5:***644*
Stick Dance (Athabaskan). *See* Feast for the Dead
Sticks on the Move (film), **2:**609
Stiefel, Ethan, **4:**623, **6:**66
Stieglitz, Alfred, **1:**135
Stier, De, **2:**470
Stier, Theodore, **5:**124
Stierle, Edward, **3:**617
Stiernhielm, George, **6:**38
Stikhira, **5:**474
Still, William Grant, **5:**59
Still Crossing, **4:**151
Stiller, Mauritz, **1:**118
Still/Here, **3:**621, **6:**259
"Still Life" at the Penguin Café, **1:**454
Still Life with Moonbeams, **2:**57, **5:**57
Still Life with the "Dance" (Matisse), **4:**331
Stillman, Amy Ku'uleialoha, *as contributor*, **3:**394–397
Still Moves (Australian dance company), **1:**217
Still Point, The, **1:**479
stilt-dance, **4:**287, 288–289, **6:**210
Stilwell, Robynn J., *as contributor*, **3:**357–358, 431–433, **6:**179–181
Stimmung, **1:**406
Stines, L'Antoinette, **3:**575
Stober, Mandy, **2:**57
Stock, Cheryl, **1:**215
Stock, Gailene, **1:**210, 232
Stockhausen, Karlheinz, **1:**349, 350, **2:**388, **4:**517, 594, **5:**302
Stockholm Royal Theater. *See* Royal Swedish Ballet; Sweden, court theaters
Stockholmsposten (Swedish journal), **6:**49
Stock im Eisen, Der, **1:**500
Stöckli, Peter, *as photographer*, **5:**35
Stodelle, Ernestine, **3:**384, 404, **4:**440, **6:**258
Stodelle, Martin, **6:**258
Stoelen, De, **4:**600
Stoinov, A., **2:**11
Stojkavo-Slijepčević, Katarina, **6:**435
Stokes, Adrian, **1:**23, **3:**285
Stokkermans, Jaap, **4:**600
Stokowski, Leopold, **3:**215
Stoll, Oswald, **2:**409, **5:**611, **6:**277
Stollwitzer, Wolfgang, **3:***153*
Stölzl, Gunta, **1:**385

Stom, Mascha, **1:**289
Stomp (musical), **6:**288
Stomp Dance, **4:**559, 560, 561,
  5:240
Stompin' at the Savoy (television
  film), **4:**255
Stone, Barton W., **2:**168
Stone, Bentley, **1:**298, **2:**334, 580,
  4:63, 602, **5:**59, 299, **6:**292
Stone, Carl, **6:**414
Stone, Cynthia, **6:**27
Stone, Paddy, **5:**434
Stone, Ruth M., **6:**25
Stone, Sandra, **4:**482, **5:**679–680
Stone-Camryn Ballet, **4:**168
Stone Dance, **4:**107
Stone Flower, The, **1:**492, *492*,
  2:579, **3:**60, **4:**132, **5:**205,
  268–269, 639, **699**, **6:**226,
  313, 343
  choreographic significance, **5:**460
  Grigorovich choreography, **3:**308,
    310, **4:**282, 284, **5:**460, 472
  Grigorovich staging in Sweden,
    6:42
  Kolpakova performance, **4:**36
  Kondratieva performance, **4:**38
  Lavrovsky staging, **1:**491–492
  Maximova performance,
    4:335, *335*
  Muller choreography, **5:**470
  Yermolayev performance, **6:**420
Stone Guest, The, **1:**144
Stone Idol, The, **5:**471
Stone Ruler, The, **6:**226
Stone the Crow, **4:**627
Stone Work Fragments, **4:**595
Stoolgame, **2:**309, **4:**602, **5:**437
Stopani, Donato, **6:**46
"Stop in the Name of Love" (song),
  5:632
Stoppato, Lorenzo, **2:**188
Stoppiello, **2:**612
Stop Press (revue), **3:**354
stop times, **6:**98
Stop Violence against Women!,
  5:517
Stora genius, Den, **6:**38
Stora Teatern, Gotëborg. *See*
  Gotëborg Opera
Storer, Robert, **4:**212
Storm, The, **2:**513
Stormen, **4:**677, 678, *678*
Stormy Weather (film), **2:**458, **4:**629
Storozuk, Oksana, **6:**435
Story, **2:**291, **3:**446, **5:**314, 548
Story of Lin Chung, The, **2:**142
Story of Mankind, The, **3:**402
Story of Narcissus, The, **2:**452
Story of Ruth, The, **3:**449, 450
Story of the Russian School, The
  (Legat), **4:**143
Story of Three Loves, The (film),
  5:589
Story of Vernon and Irene Castle,
  The (film), **1:***191*, 193, **2:**80,
  5:373, *373*
Stotchewsky, Joachim, **4:**164
Stovepipe Hat (musical), **6:**90
Stowe, Harriet Beecher, **4:**339,
  5:409
Stowell, Kent, **2:**162, **5:**51, 399,
  6:*252*, 265, 266
Stowitts, Hubert, **5:***122*, 125
Strada, La (film), **3:**60
Strada, La (Pistoni ballet), **3:**60,
  5:195, 196
Stradella (Niedermeyer), **2:**202, **3:**5
strain (pulled muscle), **4:**20
Strakhova, Nathalie, **2:**253–254
Strakosh Opera Company, **1:**496

Stramboe, Adolf, **1:**507, **5:**425
Stramboe, Edvard, **1:**507, **3:**39,
  5:425
Stramboe, Laura, **1:**507
Strange, Frederick, **4:**520
Strange American Funeral, **5:**637
Strange Fish (dance drama), **2:**611
Strange Fruit, **5:**255
Strange Guest, **4:**59
Strange Hero, **4:**531
Stranger I Came, A, **2:**514
Strangers, **4:**602
Strangler, the, **3:**349, **5:**24
Stranić, Lane, **5:**677
Strasbourg, France, **2:**471, **3:**74
Strate, Grant, **2:**39, 48, **4:**540, *540*,
  6:1–2, 297
Stratford Festival, Ontario, **4:**238,
  5:435
Strathern, Andrew J., *as*
  contributor, **5:**84–85
strathspey, **2:**474, **3:***245*, **5:**697, 698
  Scotland, **3:**243, 244, 245, 249
Strathspey reel, **3:**243, 244, 245
Strathspey Twasome, **3:**249
Strathy, Alexander, **6:**126
Stratou, Dora, **3:**296, 303, **4:**161
Stratton, Eugene, **4:**520
Straus, Anna, **5:**216
Straus, Karolina, **5:**216
Straus, Oscar, **3:**346
Strauss, Eduard, **5:**625, **6:**2, 361
Strauss, Gloria B., *as contributor*,
  2:268–269
Strauss, Johann (the elder), **3:**361,
  5:221, *311*, 625, **6:**2, 276,
  335, 360
Strauss, Johann (the younger),
  1:239, **2:**265, **4:**612, **5:**221,
  286, *311*, 625, **6:**2–3, 114, 276
  Cinderella composition, **2:**173
  Fledermaus, Die, **4:**126, **5:**59,
    6:268, 388
  polka, **5:**221
  waltzes, **6:**361, 387, 388
  as *Le Beau Danube* basis, **4:**319
Strauss, Josef, **5:**625, **6:**2, 361
Strauss, Richard, **1:**240, 390, 402,
  406, **2:**347, **3:**509, 511, **4:**612,
  5:246, 512, **6:**199, 201
  Bourgeois Gentilhomme, **4:**33
  Diaghilev commission, **1:**316,
    2:408, **4:**515
  Don Juan, **2:**434
  Don Quixote, **2:**441
  Josephslegende, **3:**20, 51, 631,
    4:64, 515
  Kröller collaboration, **4:**64
  Salomé, **2:**120
  Till Eulenspiegel, **1:**322, **4:**645
  Vienna State Opera Ballet, **4:**228
Strauss family, **3:**360, 361, **4:**514,
  6:2–3, 290
  social dance music, **5:**625, 626
  See also Strauss, Johann
Straussiana, **2:**15
Stravinsky, Igor, **5:**186, 527,
  6:3–7, 326
  Agon, **1:**11, 30, 261, **4:**64, 518, **6:**6
  Alston Dance Company, **1:**53
  Ansermet association, **1:**93
  Apollo, **1:**49, 95–96, 259, 260,
    261, 267, 317, 483, *483*,
    4:516, **5:**58, **6:**5
  Baiser de la Fée, Le, **1:**148, 260,
    261, **4:**635, **6:**5
  Balanchine collaboration, **1:**30,
    71, 95–96, 256, 257, 259, 260,
    261–262, 267, 298, 299, **2:**176,
    4:28, 518, 613, **6:**5, 6
  Berners friendship, **1:**437

Collective Symphony, **5:**555
  Diaghilev commissions, **1:**316,
    320, **2:**406–407, 409, 411,
    3:17, **4:**124, 515–516, **5:**399,
    6:3–5, 7
  eightieth birthday celebration,
    3:150, 337
  Falla friendship, **2:**567
  fame from *Firebird*, **3:**17,
    4:515–516, **6:**3
  Firebird (1945) revision, **4:**609
  Firebird orchestration, **4:**516
  Flood, The, **6:**137
  on Fokine as "exhausted artist,"
    3:19
  on Fokine's *Petrouchka* staging,
    1:321
  as Henze influence, **3:**359
  as influence on Lambert's *Romeo*
    and Juliet score, **4:**113
  Jeu de Cartes, **3:**73, 416, **4:**28,
    518, **6:**5
  Kirstein commission, **4:**28
  legacy, **4:**6–7
  Massine collaborations,
    4:317–318
  Movements for Piano and
    Orchestra, **1:**12
  on musical expression, **1:**269
  Nijinska choreography,
    4:634, 635
  Noces, Les, **1:**70, 86, 446, **2:**151,
    152, 288, **4:**657–659, **5:**364,
    6:4
  octatonic scale, **6:**4
  Oedipus Rex, **2:**183, 410
  Orff comparison, **5:**43
  Orpheus, **5:**318, 606
  Pas d'Acier, Le, **1:**259, 316
  Perséphone, **1:**155, 430, **3:**628,
    5:439, **6:**5
  Petrouchka, **5:**165
  Pulcinella, **1:**52, 390, 404, **2:**192,
    409, **4:**317–318, 516, **6:**5
  Renard, Le, **4:**516, 634, **6:**4
  on Roerich designs, **5:**372
  Rossignol, Le, **1:**158, 424, **6:**3
  Royal Ballet program, **4:**244
  Rubinstein commissions, **6:**5
  Russian folk music, **6:**3, 4, 5
  Sacre du Printemps origination,
    4:643
  Sacre du Printemps score,
    5:487, 488
  Sacre du Printemps score
    sensation, **4:**644
  Scènes de Ballet, **1:**151, **2:**425,
    5:269
  Scènes de Ballet score, **5:**531
  Soldier's Tale, The, **1:**93, 251, 453,
    2:265, **3:**356, **5:**294, **6:**4
  Sylphides orchestration, **1:**316,
    6:61
  Symphony of Psalms, **3:**228,
    4:576–577
  years in France, **6:**4–5
  years in United States, **6:**5–6
  See also Firebird, The; Petrouchka;
    Rake's Progress, The; Sacre du
    Printemps, Le
Stravinsky, Vera, **6:**5, 6
Stravinsky Centennial Celebration
  (1982), **4:**274
Stravinsky Concerto for Two Solo
  Pianos, **4:**619
Stravinsky Festival (1937), **1:**64,
  4:28
Stravinsky Festival (1972), **1:**437,
  479, **3:**521, **4:**29, 274,
  607–608, 613, **5:**531

"Stravinsky in the Theater" *(Dance*
  Index), **4:**28
Stravinsky Pas de Deux, **2:**162
Stravinsky Violin Concerto, **1:**261,
  268, **4:**608, 618, 621, **6:**454
"straw-boys" (Irish mummers),
  3:33
Strawbridge, Edwin, **5:**58
Straw Hat Revue, The (musical),
  5:359
Straw Hearts, **2:**583
Strayhorn, Billy, **6:**256
Strazatkowski, Zbigniew, **5:**218
Strazhenetskaya, Tatiana, **5:**699
Stream, **5:**305
Streamline (revue), **1:**395, **4:**229
Streams, **1:**56
Streb, Elizabeth, **2:**609–610
Strebinger, Thérèse Ferdinand,
  1:205–206
Stree, **3:**468, **5:**582
Street, David, *as photographer*,
  4:577
Streetcar Named Desire, A, **1:**441,
  2:334, **3:**88, 351
  Kaye performance, **3:**663, 664
  Neumeier production, **6:**10
  Slavenska performance, **5:**606
Street Dance, **2:**119
Streets, Sally, **4:**630
Street Singer, The (musical), **6:**274
Streets of Paris, The (musical),
  4:434
"Strega, La" (melodic theme),
  5:558
Strelecki, Jean de, *as photographer*,
  2:192
Strender, **4:**677
Strepponi, Giuseppina, **3:**60
Stresiand, Barbra, **6:**285
Stretton, Ross, **1:**77, 211, 235
Strichmänchen (stick figure)
  system, **3:**160
Strider, **1:**50–51, **2:**354, **3:**272, 273
Striding Out (Jordan), **3:**285
strikes
  Actors' Equity, **6:**272
  American Ballet Theatre, **1:**75
  ASCAP, **6:**280–281
  Australian Ballet, **1:**234, **2:**184
  Ballets Russes de Monte Carlo,
    1:314
  Bolshoi Ballet, **3:**310
  Maryinsky Ballet, **4:**67, 144
Strike Up the Band (musical),
  6:274–275, 281
Strindberg, August, **2:**283, **6:**36
String, A, **2:**605
String Quartet (Bloch), **3:**399
String Quartet (Debussy), **2:**361
String Quartet Concerto
  (Schoenberg), **5:**679, 680
Stripsmania, **6:**121
striptease
  American twentieth-century,
    6:254
  American vaudeville, **2:**573
  Egyptian dancing girls, **2:**495
  French music hall, **4:**523
"Strip the Willow," **3:**245, **5:**334
Strobach, Hans, **1:**370
Strobel, Desmond F., *as*
  contributor, **1:**189–190,
  2:251–253, 474–475,
  5:221–223, 285–287,
  6:359–362
Strobel, Fredric, **6:**106
Strode, Irene, **4:**127, 128
Stroganova, Nina, **1:**65, 315, 316
Strogova, Pauline, **1:**312

Strohlendorf, Elsa von, **1:**240, **3:**347
Strok, Asway, **2:**377
Stroman, Susan, **6:**289
Strømberg, Johan Peter, **4:**673
Strømgren, Jo, **4:**679
Strong, Roy, **3:**180
Strong Language, **1:**52, **5:**305
Stroud, Tom, **2:**43
Strow, Mary R., *as contributor,* **4:**157–171
Struchkova, Raisa, **1:**83, *489,* 491, *492,* **2:**514, **3:**138, **5:**236, 459, **6:7–8**
  as contributor, **3:**136–138, **6:**105–106
  Flames of Paris performance, **3:**12
  Fountain of Bakchisarai performance, **3:**56–57
  Zakharov as influence, **6:**442
Structural Integration (Rolfing), **1:469–470**
Structure/Light Field, **2:**359
Structures, **5:**521
Struggle, **3:**418
Strüss, Karl, *as photographer,* **4:**647
Strüweer, Astrid, **6:**43
S.T.S.I. (Sekola Tinggi Seni Indonesia), **3:**476
Stuart, Meg, **1:**412
Stuart, Muriel, **1:**421, **4:**120, 227, 449, 457, **5:**124, 208, **6:**129, 291, 292, 396
Stuart, Otis, *as contributor,* **1:**281–282
Stuart dynasty (England), **3:**522, 622, **4:**307–312, 343
Stubenrauch, Philipp, **6:**50
Stucco Moon, **2:**461
Stuck, Leslie, **3:**53
Studenten-Schmaufs, **1:**364
Student Prince, The (Romberg), **6:**273
Studies in Ballet (Chappell), **2:**105
Studies in Dance History (periodical), **6:**297
Studies in Nigerian Dance (film), **2:**602
Studies in Sound and Movement, **6:**433
Studio Ballet Prague, **2:**308, **5:**23, 617
Studio Dance Group, **5:**171
Studio DCM, **5:**390
Studio '45, **4:**591
Studio for Contemporary Dance, Zagreb, **6:**434
Studio Group (Leeder students), **4:**140
Studio L.P. (later Intro-Dans), **4:**595
Studio of Contemporary Dance, Zagreb, **6:**433–434
Studio of Dance Arts, New York City, **4:**460
Studio Rebis, Novi Sad, **6:**435
Studio Wacker, Paris, **3:**82, **5:**248
Study Group for Ethnochoreology, **2:**386–387
Study in Choreography for Camera, A (film), **1:**395
study of dance. *See* methodologies in the study of dance
Stueng, Jens, **4:***680*
Stuhlmüller, Anton, **6:**9, 71, 335
Stukolkin, Timofei, **2:**436, **3:**560, **4:**282, **5:**9
Stukolkin, Vasily, **5:**9
Stumme von Portici, Die (Auber opera), **6:**387

Stundesløse Per Aabel, Den (Aabel), **4:**682
Stupnikov, Igor V., **5:**486
  as contributor, **1:**90–91, **3:**12
Sturman, Marjorie, **2:**265, **5:**52, 53, 649, 650, 652
Sturman, Rivka, **3:**531
Stürmer, Heinrich, **5:**260
Sturm und Drang aesthetics, **1:**23
Stuttgart, Germany, **3:**143–144, **4:**695
Stuttgart Ballet, **1:**420, **3:**127, **6:8–11**
  Anderson (Reid) directorship, **4:**547, **6:**11
  Ballet de Santiago exchanges, **2:**125
  Beriozoff as ballet director, **1:**430, **2:**266, **3:**149, **6:**9
  Bosl performances, **1:**500
  Cobra, **3:***154*
  Cragun, Richard, **2:**262, 266, **3:**351, **6:**9
  Cranko, John, **2:**265–267, **3:**149, 150, **6:**9–10
  Cranko *Romeo and Juliet,* **5:**395, 405
  directors, **3:**157
  Forsythe as resident choreographer, **2:**268, **3:**51–52, **6:**10
  Haydée, Marcia, **3:**350–351, **4:**1, **6:**9, 10
  Jürgen designs, **5:**405
  Keil, Birgit, **4:**1–2
  Kylián debut, **4:**81
  Lied von der Erde, Das, **4:**242
  MacMillan choreography, **4:**242, 243, **6:**9
  Madsen, Egon, **4:**245–246
  Noverre, Jean-Georges, **4:**695, **6:**9
  Nutcracker, The, **5:**15
  Orpheus, **3:***152,* 360
  Scholz, Uwe, **6:**10
  Swan Lake, **6:**35
  Taglioni productions, **6:**9
  Tetley, Glen, **6:**10, 146, *146*
  Wright, Peter, **6:**405
Stuyf, Bart, **4:**595
Stuyf, Koert, **2:**469, 470, **4:**593, 594, 595, 597
style troubadour, le, **2:**239, 241, 244
Styne, Jule, **6:**279, 282
Suanda, Endo, **4:**297
Suárez, Finita, **2:**277
Suarez, Petronilla S., **5:**174
Suárez, Rosario, **2:**280
Suárez de Robles, Pedro, **5:**667
Suárez-Pajares, Javier, *as contributor,* **1:**479–481, **2:**521–522
sua sua, **2:**230
Subligny, Marie-Thérèse, **1:**355, 516, **3:**255, **4:**109, 231, **5:**11, 87, 105, 260
Submission, The, **3:**256
Subotnick, Morton, **5:**302
Subra, Julia, **2:**199, **4:**354
Subrahmanyana, **4:**693
sub-Saharan Africa, **6:12–26**
  background and overview, **6:12–22**
  costume, **2:**211
  dance aesthetics, **1:13–15,** **6:**19–22, 382
  dance research and publication, **6:24–26**
  masks, **4:**286–293, **6:**12–13, *13, 14,* 15–16
  Mbuti dance, **4:**344
  Moroccan black dances, **4:**468

music, **4:**483–487
popular dance, **6:23–24**
Ubakala dance, **6:**219
See also Central and East Africa; Southern Africa; West Africa; *specific countries*
Subways Are for Sleeping (musical), **6:**284
Sucena, Eduardo, **1:**537
Such Sweet Thunder, **4:**107
Suciptahening Mintaraga, **3:**496
Sucking Doctor (film), **2:**602
Sudakov, Gennady, **5:**469
Sudan, **2:**86, 92
  costume, **2:**210
  libraries and museums, **4:**158
  Nuba dance, **5:**3–4
  Pigeon Dance, **4:**408, 409, 415
  ringah dance in Egypt, **2:**492–493
  trance rituals, **6:**185
  zār rites, **2:**487–488, **4:**488, **6:**445
sudmalinyas, **4:**127
Sue, Eugène, **1:**500
Sue's Leg, **2:**245, **4:**226
Suetonius, **4:**106, 428, **5:**73, 376
Suez henna dance, **2:**489
Sufi dance, **2:**486–487, **3:523–525,** *524,* 659, **4:**79, 213, 402, 403, 410, 411, 488, 489, **5:**598
  scholarship on, **4:**416
  Turkey, **4:***410,* **5:**46, **6:**187, *208,* 209
  Uzbekistan, **6:**305
  Yemen, **6:**417
Suganuma, Pele Pukui, **3:**396
Sugar Babies (musical), **2:**574, **4:**419, **6:**102
Sugawara, **1:**362, **4:**537
Sugawara Michizane, **3:**588
Suhm, Peter, **1:**503
Suhonen, Tiina, **2:**635
  as contributor, **2:**634–635
Suhrawardy, G. H., **5:**62
Suite Argentine, **1:**115
Suite Bergamasque (Debussy), **1:**428
Suite by Chance, **1:**542
Suite Canadienne, **2:**151, **3:**429
Suite de Danses, **5:**95, **6:**182
  Clustine choreography, **1:**246, **2:**181, **6:**443
  de Valois choreography, **2:**399
  Dyk choreography, **2:**471
  Zambelli performance, **6:**443
Suite de Trio de Différents Auteurs (Philidor), **4:**510
Suite en Blanc, **1:**209, **2:**113, 351, **4:**184, **5:**96, **6:**353
Suite for Five, **2:**287, **6:**26
Suite Lyrique, **2:**471, 472
Suite Nostalgique (I Want to Dance), **6:**314
Suite No. 3, **6:**340
Suite of Dances (Robbins), **5:**366
Suite of Sonatas, **1:**94
Suite Otis, **6:***260*
Suite Romantique, **1:**306
Suite Saint-Säens, **3:**612
Suite Yoruba, **2:**280
sujiguma makeup, **4:**296
Sukarova, Iskra, **6:**437
Sukeroku, **3:**658, **4:**296, 538
Sukhishvili, Iliko, **3:**135
Sukkot, **3:**602
Sukra, Pan, **4:**265
Sukraka, Gedé, **3:***666*
Sulaberidze, Fridon, **3:**135
Sulamyth, **1:**144
Sulawesi, Indonesia, **3:**504, 505
Sulayb dance, **4:**406, 408

Suleiman II, **3:**546
Suleimanov, Kemel, **4:**87
Sulich, Vassili, **4:**435, **5:**676
Sulima, Vadim, **2:**124
Súlkari, **2:**281
Sulkunen, Pekka, **2:**634
Sulla, **4:**426, **5:**376
Sullivan, Arthur, **2:**250, 265, **6:**267, 268
Sullivan, Ed, **1:**382
Sullivan, Françoise, **2:**39, 40, 42, **6:**131
Sullivan, Harry Stack, **2:**316
Sullivan, Lawrence, *as contributor,* **1:**85–86
Sultanpuri, Majruh, **2:**625
sulubba dance, **4:**415
Sulzer, Johann Georg, **5:**352
Sulzman, Mona, **6:***249*
Sumanasantaka (Javanese text), **3:**505
Sumarsam, *as contributor,* **3:**114–116
Sumatra. *See* Indonesia, Sumatran dance traditions
sumbali, **2:**230
Sumbeka, or the Subjugation of the Kazan Kingdom, **3:**540
Sumer. *See* Mesopotamia
Sumidagawa, **3:**388
Summer. See Death and the Maiden
Summer, Susan Cook, *as contributor,* **6:**40–41, 154–155, **6:**28, 351–352, 451–452
Summer Evening, **2:**473
Summer Interlude, **5:**639
Summer Night, **5:**25
Summers, Elaine, **2:**605, 609, **3:**446, 634, 635, **6:**282
Summers, Justine, **1:***232*
Summer's Last Will and Testament (Lambert), **4:**114
Summer's Night Dream, A, **5:**24
Summer Solstice, **2:**512
Summerspace, **2:**245, 290, 292, 294, **4:**37, 608, **5:**314, 548, **6:**27
  performances by other companies, **2:**294, **6:**27
"Summertime" (skating program), **6:**180
Summer Widowers, The (musical), **2:**79
Sumurûn, **6:**387
Sun, William H., *as contributor,* **5:**129–130, **6:**425–426, 446–447
Sunal, Evinç, **6:**213
Sunami, Soichi, **5:**183–184, *183*
  as photographer, **3:**398, **4:**60
Sun and Earth, **3:**347
Sunan Kalijaga, **3:**498, 501
Sunda (people), **3:**501–504
Sun Dance, **3:**170, **4:**550, 552, 561, 562, **6:**187
Sundances, **2:**42
Sundanese (people), **1:**174, **3:**501–504, **4:**297, 494
Sundarprasad, **2:**468, **5:**581
Sunday Afternoon, **2:**575
Sunday *hora,* **5:**383
Sunday Times (London newspaper), **3:**282, 285
Sundberg, Lovisa, **1:**503
Sunde, Erling, **6:**357
Sune, H., **5:**482
Sunflowers, **6:**202
Sung Hae-oh, **4:**45
sungmu, **2:**223, *223,* **3:**340–341, **4:**140, 141
Sun into Darkness, **2:**350, **5:**564
Sun Jingchen, **2:**149

Sun Music, **1:**230, **3:**357
Sunni Islam, **4:**69
Sunny (musical), **4:**420, **6:**273
Sunset, **6:**111, *112*
Sunset Boulevard (musical), **6:**287
Sunshine Girl, The (musical), **2:**79, **6:**270
Sunshine Sammy, **3:**57
Sun Valley Serenade (film), **2:**615, **3:**357, **4:***630*
SUNY. *See* State University of New York
Suomalainen kisapirtti (Collan ed.), **2:**631
Suomalaisen Kansantanssin Ystaavaat, **2:**631
Suomen Nuorisoseurojen Liitto, **2:**631
Suotoshi, **5:**591
supper clubs, **2:**185
Suppliants, The (Aeschylus), **2:**453, **3:**300
supported adagio, **5:**101
Supree, Burt, **2:**605
Supremes (music group), **5:**632
Sur, Gorsha, **3:**433
Suradas, **5:**582
Surakarta, Java, **1:**172, 173, **3:**494, 495, 496–497, 498, 499, 505
Surasena, **6:***329*
Surǎţia (brotherhood), **5:**381
sure-footing, **2:**179
Suren, Ann, **3:**512
Suriaatmaja, Raden Maman, **3:**504
Surinach, Carlos, **3:**218, **4:**518
Surinam, **2:**64, 65
Sur le Borysthène, **5:**268
sur les pointes. See pointe work
Sur les Pointes (Kandinsky), **1:**132
Sur O/Sur, **5:***675*
Surovshchikova, Maria, **4:**281, **5:**140, 141, 150, 455
Surprise, **6:**412
Surprises de l'Amour, Les (Rameau), **5:**307
Surratt, Valeska, **6:**317
surrealism, **1:**133, 135, 136, **2:**242
Automatistes, Les, **2:**39
avant-garde performances, **1:**243, 244
Cocteau aesthetics, **2:**182
music and dance influences, **4:**516
sur-réaliste (Apollinaire term), **1:**244
Survivors, **1:**59
Susana, **6:27–28**
Susanna and the Barber, **5:**59
Susa-no-o (deity), **1:**183
Susato, tylman, **1:**409, **4:**505
Susie Q., **6:**262
Suspect Terrain, **5:**128
Suspicious Husband, The (Garrick), **3:**254
Suspinul, **5:***390*
Sussman, Elisabeth, *as contributor,* **1:**138–141
Süssmayr, Franz Xaver, **6:**338
Susugigawa, **5:**590
Susuhunan Paku Buwana X, sultan of Surakarta, **3:**497
sutartinès, **4:**205–206
Sutherland, Geoffrey, **5:**659
Sutherland, Graham, **1:**150
Sutherland, Paul, **3:**610
Suttie, Richard, **4:***679*
Sutton, Julia, **5:**327
as contributor, **1:**53–54, 103–107, 351–355, 520–524, **2:**50–52, 73–77, 77, **3:**106–111, **4:**326–328, 504–508, 579–583,

5:110–112, 114–116, 117–118, 505–507, 666, **6:**178–179, 349–351
Sutton, Valerie, **4:**693
Sutton Movement Shorthand (notation system), **4:**693, *693*
Suūzadètinè, **4:**208
Suve, Enn, **2:**529, 530
Suzanne Dellal Center, Tel Aviv, **3:**533–534
suzu-furi players, **3:**587
Suzuki, D. T., **2:**285
Suzuki Tadashi, **3:**652
Svabo, J. C., **2:**384
Svadebka, **4:**81
Svalberg, Göran, **6:**44
Svanetish Legend, The, **1:**38
Svavarsdóttir, Hlíf, **3:**437
Svedbert, Brit, **6:**50
Svedin, Lulli, *as contributor,* **2:**263–265, **3:**619, **5:**47–48, 406–407, **6:**48–49
Svenska baletten, Den (Rootzén), **6:**49
Svenska Balettskolan, **5:**47
Svenska dagbladet (Swedish newspaper), **4:**49, 50
Svenska Folkdansens Vänner, **3:**33, 34
Svenska Folkdansring, Finland, **2:**631
Svenska Ungdomsringen för Bygdekultur, **6:**37
Svenska Visarkivet, **6:**49
Svensk balett (Idestam-Almquist), **6:**49
Svensk Folkdansensamble, **6:**36
Sventickaitè, Tamara, **4:**208
Sverdlik, Daniel Ira, **1:***245*
Sverdlovsk Opera and Ballet Theater, **5:**470
Svetlana (1939), **1:**490, **3:**197, **4:**148, **6:**226
Svetlana, The Slavic Princess (1886), **1:**486–487
Svetlov, Valerian, **5:**120, 482, 642, **6:**28, 191, 309
Svetlova, Marina, **1:**313, **4:**382, **6:**191, 264
Sviridov, Georgi, **5:**471
Svoboda, Josef, *as photographer,* **2:**307, 309
Svoboda, Viacheslav, **1:**85
Swados, Elizabeth, **2:**119
Swain, Eva, **4:**381
Swaine, Alexander von, **3:**146, **6:**29
Swamp, **3:**274
swan (as totem), **2:**139
Swan, Joseph William, **4:**189
*Swan, The. See Dying Swan, The
Swan and Skylark, The,* **1:**197
Swan Dance, **4:**555
Swan Lake, **6:29–35**
arabesques, **1:**101
Blok's writings on, **1:**463
character dances, **2:**106
character role, **2:**106
grand pas de deux, **5:**106
Odette's characteristic pose, **3:**565–566
pas de deux, **5:**107
petits battements battus, **1:**383
productions in Russia, **6:29–31**
Ananiashvili performances, **1:**83
Anderson-Ivantzova performance, **1:**85
Bessmertnova performance, **1:**440, **6:**31
Bolshoi Ballet versions, **1:**486, 489, *490,* **2:***278*

Bovt performance, **1:**517
Burmeister, **1:**517, **2:**388, 471, 529, **5:**463, 466, **6:**31, 34
Chabukiani choreographic changes, **2:**96
character dances, **2:**108
Dmitriev designs, **2:**421
Dudinskaya performance, **2:**449
Ek choreography, **2:**500
Fokine additional choreography, **3:**18
fouettés virtuosity, **1:**338, 347, **4:**145
Gerdt (Pavel) performance, **3:**137
Golovin designs, **3:**196
Gorsky versions, **3:**206–207, *206,* **4:**358, 459, **6:**31
Grigorovich conception, **3:**309, **4:**38, **5:**463, **6:**31
Gusev revival, **3:**328
Ivanov choreography. *See* subhead Petipa-Ivanov collaboration *below*
Kondratieva performance, **4:**38
Kshessinska performance, **4:**68
Legnani performance, **4:**145, *145*
Lopukhov productions, **4:**224, **6:**31
Messerer performance, **4:**358
Mordkin performance, **4:**459
original production, **6:**29–30
Petipa-Ivanov collaboration, **2:**15, 108, **3:**207, 560, 565–566, *566,* **4:**145, *278,* 282, 286, **5:**157, 159, 160, 456, **6:**30–31, 32, 34
Plisetskaya performance, **5:***203,* 204
revival popularity, **5:**463
Semenova performance, **5:**566
Sergeyev (Konstantin) performance and choreography, **5:**571, 572, **6:**343
Vaganova, **6:**31, 309
productions outside Russia, **4:**31–35
Alonso (Alicia) and Youskevitch pas de deux, **1:***49*
Alonso (Alicia) performance, **1:**49, 50
American Ballet Theatre, **1:**66, 71, 76, 373
Anisimova production, **1:**91
Australian Ballet first season, **1:**230
Australian four-act productions, **1:**208, 209–210, 211
Balanchine productions, **1:**271, 272, **4:**610, **6:**32, 34, 396
Ballet der Laage Landen, **1:**289
Ballet Russe de Monte Carlo, **1:**297, 301
Barnett and Nahat collaboration, **1:**197
Baryshnikov staging, **1:**373, **6:**34
Basel Ballet, **1:**374, 375
Bavarian State Ballet, **1:**391
Béjart performance, **1:**403
Berger second-act choreography, **1:**429
Beriosova and MacLeary partnership, **1:**429
Beriosova performance, **1:**429
Berlin Opera Ballet, **1:**436
Blair performance, **1:**459

Blair production, **1:**71, 77, 459, **5:**573, **6:**34
Boston Ballet, **1:**501, 502
Bruhn conception, **2:**2, 3, 4, 471, **4:**542, 543, *544,* **6:**34, 35
Burmeister version, **2:**15, 388
Carter (Jack) staging for Teatro Colón, **1:**110
Chinese students, **2:**136, 137
Christensen (Lew) performance, **2:**160, **6:**34
Christensen (Willam) choreography, **2:**160, **5:**512, **6:**34
Cleveland-Atlantic Ballet collaborative production, **2:**178
Collier performance, **2:**186
Conus staging in Sweden, **6:**42
Cranko version, **6:**34–35
Dantzig staging, **2:**470, **4:***593*
de Valois staging, **2:**401, **3:**264
Diaghilev's Ballets Russes repertory, **6:**32
Dowell staging, **5:**420, **6:**35
English National Ballet versions, **2:**510, 511, 512, 514
Evdokimova performance, **2:**562
Farron character role, **2:**578
Field production, **2:**511, 590, **4:**678, *678*
first, **6:**32
first full-length American version, **6:**34
Flindt staging, **3:**13
Fonteyn performance, **3:**41, *42,* 43, 44
Franklin staging, **2:**334
Graff, **4:**678–679
Gregory performance, **3:**306–307
Grey (Beryl) performance, **2:**511, **3:**307
Gsovsky (Victor) restaging, **3:**318
Hart (Evelyn) performance, **3:**344, *344,* 345
Helpmann-Markova performances, **3:**354
Hightower staging for La Scala, **3:**362
Hønningen performance, **3:**373
Keil performances, **4:***1,* 2
Kerr, **4:**626
Komaki staging in Japan, **3:**589
Kronstam performance, **4:**65
Labis staging, **2:**58
Lander (Harald) choreography, **3:**226
Lifar performance, **4:**182
MacMillan, **1:**436, **4:**242, **5:**574
Makarova staging, **1:**158, **2:**514
Markova act 2 performance, **4:**267, 268
Marks performance, **4:**271
Martins's full-length, **4:**275
May performance, **4:**336–337
Meri's "Hindu" version, **4:***354,* 355
Miszczyk, **4:**435
Nahat choreography, **2:**178
Nerina performance, **4:**584
Neumeier staging, **3:**337, **6:**35
Nieto performance, **2:**124
Nureyev-Georgiadis staging, **3:**136
Nureyev performance and production, **5:**6, 7, **6:**34, 35
one-act reductions, **6:**32
PACT Ballet, **5:***651*

Parlić, **5:**101
Psota, **5:**269
Rosen performance, **5:**406
Royal Ballet, **1:**146, 156, **2:**243, **3:**354
Royal Danish Ballet, **1:**539
Royal Winnipeg Ballet, **5:***434*
Schaufuss, **3:**156
Sergeyev (Nicholas) reconstruction of Maryinsky version, **3:**511, *512*, **4:**271, **5:**413, 414, **6:**33–34, 35
Serrano performance, **5:**572
Sibley performance, **5:**596, 597
Skeaping staging, **2:**277, **5:**406
Somes performance, **5:**639, *640*
Spessivtseva performance, **5:**678
Spohr production, **5:**685
Tallchief (Maria) performance, **4:**616
Tomasson, **6:**174
Toumanova, **6:**183
tours of Russian productions, **6:**32
Vámos for Budapest Opera Ballet, **3:**419
Vienna State Opera Ballet, **1:**241
Wilde pas de trois, **6:**396
revisionist productions, **6:**34–35
semiotic analysis, **4:**377, 378
Tchaikovsky score, **2:**368, **4:**514–515, **6:**29–31, 32, 34, 114, 115–116
Tchaikovsky score revision, **6:**30, 32
television productions, **6:**131–132
third act *(The Magic Swan),* **1:**297, **6:**425
See also Black Swan pas de deux
Swan Lake (film), **3:**345
Swann, Lynn, **6:**154
Swan of Tuonela, The (Bintley ballet), **1:**453
Swan of Tuonela, The (Sibelius tone poem), **1:**38, 453
Swans, The, **6:**32
Swansong, **2:**1, *2,* 514
Swapnakosha, **3:**469
Swātani, Bunnāk, **4:**256
Swazi (people), **5:**643, 644, 661, 662, 664
Sweden, **6:**35–50
court theaters, **1:**400, **6:**39, **45–48,** 50
See also Drottningholm Court Theater, Stockholm
dance education, **6:**44, **48–49**
Behle, Anna, **1:**403
Johansson, Ronny, **3:**619
seventeenth- and eighteenth-century theatrical, **5:**603
dance research and publication, **2:**386, **6:**49–50
folk culture, **3:**33, **6:**36, 49
libraries and museums, **4:**163, **6:**50
Skeaping, Mary, **5:**603–604
modern and postmodern dance, **1:**32, 145, 403, **2:**294
theatrical dance, **1:**503, **3:**21, **6:**38–45
traditional dance, **6:**35–37, 40, 49
See also Ballets Suédois; Royal Swedish Ballet
Swedish Academy, **6:**49
Swedish Ballet and Dance (Engdal), **6:**50
Swedish Ballet School. *See* Royal Swedish Ballet School

Swedish Choreographical Institute, **1:**32
"Swedish Dance" (reel), **5:**334
Swedish Dance Teachers Association, **3:**619
Swedish Dance Theater, **2:**263, 283
Swedish Folk Dance Ensemble., **6:**36
Swedish Folk Music and Folk Dance Association, **6:**37
Swedish National Library, Stockholm, **4:**163
Swedish National Theater Center, **2:**284
Swedish Royal Ballet. *See* Royal Swedish Ballet
Swedish Royal Opera. *See* Royal Opera, Stockholm
Swedish Youth Clubs for Country Culture, **6:**37
Swedisk Riksteatern, **2:**263–264, **6:**45
Swedlund, Helga, **3:**336, 337
Sweeney Todd (musical), **2:**266, **6:**285
Sweet, Jill D., **4:**575
as contributor, **5:**271–273
Sweet Adeline (musical), **5:**602
Sweet Charity (film), **2:**618, **3:**54–55, **5:**358
Sweet Charity (musical), **3:**54, 55, **5:**358, **6:**283, *283,* 287, 327
Sweet Dancer, **3:**203
Sweete, Barbara Willis, **6:**133
Sweethearts (film), **5:**310
Sweet Rosie O'Grady (film), **2:**615
Sweet Sorrow, **4:**625
Sweigard, Lulu, **1:**469, **470,** 475, **2:**328, **4:**17
Swift, Jonathan, **2:**202
Swift, Kay, **1:**63
Swift, Mary Grace, **6:**297
as contributor, **1:**199–200, 459–460, **2:**412–417, **4:**137–138
Swim (dance), **5:**632, **6:**263
Swimmer, Eddie, **5:***240*
swing band era, **6:**246
swing dance. *See* Lindy Hop
Swinging Wife, The, **2:**130
Swing It (musical), **6:**276
"Swing Low, Sweet Chariot" *(Prelude to Swing),* **2:***581*
Swing Low, Sweet Chariot, **6:**88
Swing Mikado, The (musical), **6:**276
Swing Time (film), **2:**614
Swinson, Cyril, **4:**200
Swinston, Robert, **2:***290, 293,* **5:**17
Swiss Milkmaid, The (Nathalie, ou La Laitière Suisse), **1:**200, 237, **2:**502, 505, **3:**180, **4:**30, 108, 336, **5:***135,* 148, 426, *467,* **6:**50–51, 71, 72, 75
Swiss Theater Collection (Berne), **4:**163
Switzerland, **6:**51–54, 53
archival material, **4:**163
castanet counterpart, **2:**78
Christian churches' views of dance, **2:**167
eurhythmics, **1:**98, 128–129, **3:**596
folk dance revival, **3:**35
folk dance sounds, **3:**38, 39
See also Basel Ballet; Geneva Ballet; Zurich Ballet
Swoboda, Maria, **3:**577
Swope, Martha, **5:**186
as photographer, **1:**12, 28, 266, **2:**577, 584, **4:**436, 614, **5:**102,

186, 190, 360, 361, 362, 363, **6:**288
sword dances, **2:**46, 222, **6:54–55**
Albania, **1:**34, **2:***554*
Algeria, **1:**41, 42
Arabian Peninsula, **1:**101, **4:**406
Arbeau choreography, **1:**104–105, 369
Basque, **1:**376
bedouin, **2:**488–489, *488*
Brazil, **1:***530*
China, **1:**118, 164, **2:**129, 132
circus performers, **2:**174
Croatia, **6:**429, *429*
Czech and Slovak, **2:**302, *305*
Egyptian Jewish brides, **3:**603
England, **1:**118, **2:***551,* **3:**34, 240–241, *240,* 608, **4:**473–475
Ethiopia, **2:**533, *534*
Europe traditional, **2:**554–255
furriers of Breslau, **3:**325
Greece, **3:***300*
India, **2:**117
Isle of Man, **3:**251
Japan, **1:**188, **3:**587
Korea, **1:**167, **2:**222
Lebanon, **4:**136
matachins, **4:**326–328
Middle Eastern women, **4:**406, 410
moresca, **4:**460–463
Morris dancers, **4:**313
Norway, **4:**672
Persian, **3:***515*
Scotland, **3:**243, 246, *247,* 249
as stepping dance, **5:**695
Sweden, **6:**36
symbolic, **1:**118
Tunisia, **6:**206
Turkey, **6:**211, *212*
See also stick dances
Sword Dances of Northern England, The (Sharp), **3:**238
Sword of the Spirit, **4:**141
Sydney, Australia, **1:**207–208, 209–210, 212, 214, 215, 217, **2:**439, **4:**25, 26, 159–160, 627
Sydney Dance Company, **2:**184, **4:**624, **6:56–57,** 379
Murphy (Graeme) as artistic director, **1:**214, **4:**479, **6:**56–57
Sydney on the Wupper (film), **6:**95
Sydoff, Angèle, **4:**590
Sygietyński, Antoni, **5:**220
Sygietyński, Tadeusz, **5:**212
Sylfiden. See Sylphide, La
Syllabus of Stage Lighting, A (McCandless), **4:**191
Sylphide, La, **1:**110, 373, 390, **5:**94, 134, 319, 642, **6:57–59**
American Ballet Theatre, **1:**70, 71, **4:**24
Augusta (Madame) performance, **1:**199
Ballets de Champs-Élysées, **1:**306
Blangy performance, **1:**459
Bogdanov and Bogdanova performances, **1:**477
Bolshoi Ballet, **1:**485
Borchsenius performance, **1:**497
Bournonville production, **1:***504,* 507, 511, 515, 539, **2:***4,* **3:**222, 657, **5:**425, 426, *426,* 565, **6:**59
Bournonville production reconstructions, **2:**385, *385,* 387, *510,* **4:**275, **5:**406, 433, **6:**59
Bournonville score, **4:**513, **6:**59
Bowman performances, **1:**518

Bruhn performances and production, **2:**3, 4, *4,* **3:**60, **4:**542, **6:**59, *59,* 142
Céleste performance, **2:**85
Cerrito in La Scala's first production, **2:**93
Cerrito performance, **5:**528
Chalon print series of, **2:**103
character dances within, **2:**106
character role, **2:**106, **4:**125, *125,* 126, **5:**425
Ciceri design, **2:**172, **5:**538, *539,* **6:**57
Cortesi production, **2:**93, 209
costume designs, **4:**116, *116,* **5:**241, **6:**57
as costume influence, **2:**239–240, 244
Crombé staging in Prague, **2:**306
Elssler performance, **1:**410, **2:**502, 504, **3:**123
Evdokimova performance, **2:**561–562
Ferraris debut performance, **2:**587
Flindt performance, **3:**12
Fracci performances, **3:**59, 60, *549*
as *Giselle* inspiration, **3:**180
Grahn performances, **3:**222, 224, **5:**425
Gsovsky (Victor) revival, **3:**73, 318, **4:**34
Hart (Evelyn) performance, **3:**345
Henry's *Silfide* versus, **3:**358
Hullin-Sor choreographer, **5:**516
Keil performance, **4:**2
King's Theatre (London) premiere, **3:**260
Kirkland performance, **4:**24
Komleva revival, **4:**38
Lacotte reconstruction, **2:**588, **3:**74, **4:**108, **6:***58,* 59
Lander (Harald) choreography, **3:**226, 362, **6:**59
Lander (Toni) performance, **4:**120
Larsen's witch performance, **4:**125, *125,* 126
Livry performance, **3:**70, **4:**214
Løvenskjold score, **1:**515
Markova performance, **4:**270
Martins staging, **5:**132
Mazilier performance, **4:**339, 340, **6:**57
Monplaisir troupe's American staging, **4:**455
Moscow versus Saint Petersburg interpretations, **5:**454
Nielsen performance, **4:**631
Noblet performance, **4:**657, **6:**57
Nourrit scenario, **1:**505, **2:**203, **6:**57, 58
Paris Opera premiere, **3:**69, **6:**57–58
pointe work, **3:**47, 547, *548,* **6:**57, 58, 59
Romantic tradition, **2:**202, 207, 239, **3:**69, **4:**657, **6:**67–58
Rosen staging for Maryinsky Ballet, **4:**285, **6:**59
Saint-Léon performance, **5:**499
Sankovskaya performance, **5:**454, 516
Sankovskya-Taglioni comparison, **1:**485
Schanne performance, **5:**553
Schaufuss (Peter) staging, **2:**511, *511,* 561, **4:**2, **5:**401, 433, 555, **6:**59

Sylphide, La, continued
Schneitzhoeffer score, **1:**9, 455, **4:**513, **5:**513, 558, **6:**57
Somes performance, **5:**639
Sonnambula kinship, **5:**642
symbolism of, **5:**642, **6:**58
Taglioni (Filippo) choreography, **4:**340, **5:**454, 499, 640–641, **6:**57, 58, 72, 73
Taglioni (Marie) print series, **2:**103
Taglioni (Marie) role identification, **1:**485, **2:**202, 502, **3:**47, 69, 547, *548*, **5:***89*, 93, 528, **6:**57, *57*, 58, 72, *72*, 73, 74, 216
Taglioni (Marie) statuette, **1:**368
Titus staging for Maryinsky, **4:**280, **5:**454, **6:**58
Vyroubova performance, **6:**352
Weber's *Silvana* anticipating, **4:**514
"white scene," **2:**202, 207, 240, **3:**180, **6:**57
Williams (Stanley) performance, **6:**399
Sylphide, La: Souvenir d'Adieu de Marie Taglioni (Chalon), **2:**103
Sylphides, Les, **6:59–62**
as abstract ballet, **6:**62
as American Ballet Theatre signature piece, **3:**26
Ballet der Lage Landen, **1:**289
Ballets Russes de Monte Carlo, **1:***309*
Baronova staging, **1:**367
Baryshnikov restaging, **3:**26
Börlin reconstruction, **1:**327
Bruhn performances, **2:**2, 3
Chopiniana, **1:***492,* **2:**112, 244, 407, 457, 507, **3:**137, **4:**37, 283, 335, **5:**121, **6:59–61,** 62
Bessmertnova debut performance, **1:**440
Fokine choreography, **3:**14, 15, 16, 19, *20,* 21, 24
Fokine lighting and makeup effects, **4:**305
Nijinska performance, **4:**634, **6:**60
Nijinsky performance, **3:**16, **4:**640, **6:**60
Pavlova performance, **5:**121, 123, *126,* **6:**60, 61, *61*
Preobrajenska performance, **5:**247, *248,* **6:**60
Vaganova revival, **6:**309
Dances at a Gathering comparison, **2:**333
de Valois production, **4:**268
Diaghilev production, **1:**65, *71,* 198, *206,* 316, 317–318, *317,* 319, 320, 321, *492,* **2:**406, 457, **3:**16, 511, **4:**68, **6:61–62**
Benois designs, **1:**423, **2:**244, 407, **6:**61
as company's signature piece, **6:**61
Grigoriev-Tchernicheva revival, **3:**308
Idzikowski performance, **3:**441
Karsavina performance, **3:**656
Nijinsky performance, **4:**640, **6:**61
Pavlova performance, **5:**122
Stravinsky orchestration, **1:**316, **6:**61
Eglevsky performance, **2:**479
English National Ballet, **2:**507, *507*
first Japanese staging, **3:**589

first South African performance, **5:**650
Fokine choreographic innovations, **6:**62
as Fokine masterpiece, **3:**14, **4:**27, **6:**59
Fokine Royal Swedish Ballet production, **6:**41, 62
Fokine use of Romantic tutu, **6:**217
Kirosova Ballet, **1:***206*
Koslov pirated version, **4:**56
Lander (Harald) choreography, **3:**226
Lopokova performance, **4:**223
Markova revival, **2:**512, **4:**269, 270, **6:**62
Nijinsky choreography, **4:**645
Nureyev performance, **5:**6
Picasso caricature drawing of, **2:**71
Pribylov version, **5:**475
Rambert Dance Company, **5:**298, 299, **6:**62
Romanticism of, **6:**60, 61, 62
Royal Ballet production, **3:**41, **6:**62
Russian origins. *See subhead Chopiniana above*
Spessivtseva performance, **5:**678
television productions, **6:**134
Sylvain, James, **2:**504, **4:**139, **5:**615
Sylvaine, Maria, **2:**470
Sylvestersson, Elsa, **2:**632
Sylvia, **1:**247, 540, **5:**94, *96,* 515, **6:62–64**
Ashton production, **1:**153, *154,* **2:**243, 368–369, 401, **3:**345, **4:***416,* 584, **5:**416, *416,* **6:***63,* 64
Balanchine choreographies, **3:**44, **4:**611, 662, **6:**64
Bintley production, **1:**454
Campilli production, **3:**414
Darsonval restaging, **2:**351
Delibes score, **1:**153, 390, **2:**201, 368–369, **4:**353, 514, **5:**58, 569, **6:**62, 63–64
Diaghilev projected production, **1:**254, **2:**407
first production, **1:**390
Gerdt and Ivanov collaboration, **3:**137, 568
German productions, **3:**145
Hart (John) performance, **3:**345
Kröller choreagraphy, **4:**64
Larsen choreography, **4:**126
Lifar production, **4:**184
Martyn choreography, **4:**275
Mérante choreography, **4:**353, **6:**62, 64
Milloss staging, **3:**416
Nerina performance, **4:**584, 585
Seregi production, **3:**417, **4:**678, **5:**569, **6:**64
Staats production, **5:**690
Wells performance, **6:**380
Zambelli performance, **6:**443–444
Sylvia: Pas de Deux, **3:**44, **4:**611, 662, **6:**64, 85, *85*
Sylvia in Hollywood, **5:**58
Sylvie, **1:**43, **2:**352, **5:**105, 113
Sylwan, Kari, **6:**42
"Symbolism and the Dance" (Campbell), **6:**297
symbolists, **1:**128, 148, 243, **3:**96
Symbols for the Notation of Georgian Choreography (Chabukiani), **3:**135
symmetry, **5:**536, *536*

Symonds, Henry, **6:**372
symphonic ballet
Bulgarian choreography, **2:**11
Choreatium, **1:**310, **4:**322
Duncan as influence, **4:**518
Ivanov development, **5:**456
Lopukhov concept, **1:**258, 416, **5:**457–458, 468
Massine choreographies, **1:**310, *310,* 311, **4:**322–324, 517
Neumeier choreographie of Mahler, **4:**604
Nijinska's choreography as anticipating Massine's, **4:**636
Petipa examples, **5:**456
Présages, Les, **1:**150, 310, **4:***319*
Soviet choreography, **4:**225, 283, 284–285, **5:**457–458, 484
Symphonie Fantastique as example, **1:**311, *311,* **4:**323, **5:**430
Symphonic Dances, **4:**622
Symphonic Impressions, **4:**179, 270
Symphonic Variations (Ashton ballet), **1:***149,* 150, 151, 152, 156, **2:**244, **5:***414,* 415, 588, 639, **6:64–65**
choreographic style, **3:**265–266, **6:**65
Fedorovitch designs, **2:**582, 583, **6:**64, 65
Fonteyn performance, **3:**42, 44, **5:**639, **6:**64, 65
May performance, **4:**336, **6:**64
Somes performance, **5:**639
three leading ballerinas, **5:**588
Symphonic Variations (Franck orchestral work), **1:**150, 301
Symphonic Variations (Tudor ballet), **4:**547
Symphonie Allégorique, **4:**134
Symphonie Concertante, **1:**12, 256, 269, 478, **2:**420, **4:**136, 518, **5:**97
Symphonie en Trois Mouvements, **2:**109
Symphonie Fantastique (Berlioz), **1:**148
Symphonie Fantastique (Caciuleanu choreography), **6:**302
Symphonie Fantastique (Massine ballet), **1:**148, 311, *311,* **4:**322–323, **5:**430
Bérard designs, **1:**311, 426, **4:**323, **5:**547
Bruhn performance, **2:**3
Larsen performance, **4:**125
Toumanova performance, **6:**182, 183
Vangsaae performance, **5:**553
Verchinina performance, **6:***326*
Williams (Stanley) role, **6:**399
Symphonie Fantastique (Petit ballet), **3:**601
Symphonie pour un Homme Seul, **1:**403, **2:**287, **3:**74
Symphonies of Wind Instruments (Stravinsky), **6:**5
Symphony, **4:**242, **5:**417
Symphony for Fun, **2:**510, **3:**175
Symphony for Strings, **3:**391, **5:***428*
Symphony in C, **1:**141, **6:65–66**
Balanchine choreography, **1:**256, 266, **4:**25, 613, 619, **6:**65–66
battements, **1:**383, **3:**69
classical tutu, **2:**244
Darsonval performance, **2:**351, **6:**65
in English National Ballet repertory, **2:**514

Hart (Evelyn) performance, **3:**345
Komleva performance, **4:**37
Le Clercq performance, **4:**137, 616
Maryinsky staging, **4:**285
Moncion performance, **4:**450
Nichols performance, **4:**631
as *Palais de Cristal,* **2:**351, **5:**96, **6:**65, 66, 183
in Royal Danish Ballet repertory, **5:***428,* 431
Toumanova performance, **6:**183
Symphony in D, **1:**233, **4:***601,* **6:**432
Symphony in Three Movements, **1:**291, **3:***293,* **4:**608, 613, **5:**290, **6:**6, 340
Symphony in Waves, **2:**470
Symphony Movements, **1:**241
Symphony of a Dead Soldier, **6:**432
Symphony of Eternity, **6:**412
Symphony of Psalms, **3:**228, **4:**81, 576–577, *576, 592,* **6:**5
Synácová, Marta, **2:**308
Synaphai, 2448
Synergy (group), **4:**479
Synergy with Symphony, **4:**479
Synergy with Synergy, **6:**56
Synge, J. M., **3:**518, 520
"synthetic dance" (Chernetskaya style), **5:**477
Syrena, **5:**101
syrtaki ("Zorba dance"), **3:**299
syrtós dance, **1:***100,* 101–102, **2:**271–272, **3:**296, 300
Syrus, Publilius, **4:**426
Sysyfos, **1:**32
Syzygy, **5:**680, **6:**110, 111, 112
Szabadi, Edit, **3:**418
Szabados, Károly, **3:**414
Szabó, Iván, students, **5:**569
Szabo, Michel, *as photographer,* **5:**324
Szakály, György, **3:**418, 419
Szalay, Karola, **3:**415, 423
Szargut, Zygmunt, *as photographer,* **5:**214
Szeged Contemporary Ballet, **6:66–67**
Szeged National Theater, Budapest, **3:***419,* 422
Szeged Studio Ballet, **6:**67
Szendrey Ákos, **3:**423
Szentimrei, Jenő, **3:**412–413
Szentpál, Mária, **3:**424, **4:**96
Szentpál, Olga, **3:**412, 420, 423
Szervánszky, Endre, **6:**66
Szilard, Paul, **3:**664
Szilka, Adolf, **3:**414
Szmolc, Halina, **5:**218
Szögi, Csaba, **3:**421
Szokolay, Sánder, **2:**473
Szöllősi, Lajos Szabó, **3:**412
Szöllősy, András, **2:**473
Szozda, Andrzej, **5:***219*
Szumrák, Vera, **3:**417
Szyfer, Georges, **3:**431, **4:**184, **5:***90*
Szyfman, Arnold, **5:**218
Szymanowski, Karol, **2:**172, **5:**218, **6:**441
Szymanowski, Wacław, **5:**220
Szymańska, Irena, **5:**218
Szymanski, Stanisław, **5:**218

Tabacco, Il, **1:**29
Tabachnik, Ken, **5:**314
Tabatière, La, **4:**634
Taber (photographer), **5:**180
Taberna del Toro, La, **1:**94

Table, A, or Dreams of a Fetus, **5:**34
Tableau Allégorique des Moeurs, Le, **1:**465, **5:**308
Tableau d'une Exposition, **2:**151
tableaux vivants, **3:**541
Taboos and Fetishes, **3:**329, **4:**266
Tabourot, Jehan. *See* Arbeau, Thoinot
Tabulae, **2:**448, 449
Tabula Rasa, **4:**532
tabulation, **1:**104
Tachibana Ryū, **3:**593
Tachibana, Sahomi, **6:**203
tachimawari, **1:**187
tachiyaku, **3:**438, **4:**537
Tacitus, **3:**139, **5:**74
Taco, **4:**549
Tadatsugu Sasaki, **3:**589
Tadmor, Ido, **3:**534, *535*
Taegener, Edith, **3:***147*
Taeger-Berger, Gisela, **5:**659
Taeuber, Sophie, **1:**134, **6:**389
Tafelmanieren, **4:**596
Taffel-Consort (Simpson), **1:**364
tafiatrenazh (movement grids), **3:**48
Tagbanwa (people), **5:**168
Tagirov, Gay, **5:**471, 595
Taglicht, Gisa, **4:**626
Taglioni, Amalia, **6:**58, 237, 298
Taglioni, Carlo, **6:**69
Taglioni, Filippo, **1:**86, 202, 390, 477, **2:**202, 369, **3:**358, 547, **4:**657, **5:**134, 319, 499, 516, 640, **6:**69, **71–73,** 207
  "Ballet of the Nuns" choreography, **6:**58
  Borri dance partnership, **1:**500
  choreographies, **3:**260
  as daughter Marie's mentor, **6:**71, 72–73, 74
  Gitana, La, **2:**93, 504, **3:**185, 618, **4:**340
  Henry (Louis) plagiarism accusations, **6:**72
  Jocko, the Brazilian Ape, **1:**390, **3:**144
  Lacotte reconstructions, **4:**108
  Paris Opera Ballet, **5:**91, 92, 93, **6:**72–73
  pas de deux technique, **5:**105
  Pion association, **5:**195, 216
  Saint Petersburg stagings, **4:**280, **5:**454, 483
  scores for ballets, **4:**513
  Skeaping reconstructions, **6:**47
  students, **1:**199, **3:**4
  Stuttgart Ballet productions, **6:**9
  Swedish ballet, **6:**40
  Swiss Milkmaid, The, **5:***135,* 426, **6:**50–51, 72
  Viennese ballet debut, **1:**237
  Warsaw Ballet, **5:**216, **6:**73, 365
  See also Fille du Danube, La; Sylphide, La
Taglioni, Giuseppa, **6:**69
Taglioni, Louise, **6:**69, 71
Taglioni, Louise (the younger), **6:***70,* **70–71**
Taglioni, Marie, **1:**35, 202, 390, **2:**85, 596, **3:**358, 618, **5:**70, 122, 499, 516, 640, **6:**73–75
  Adam ballets, **1:**9, 10
  ballet blanc costume, **2:**236, 239–240, **3:***548,* **4:**138, **6:**216
  Barre statuette of, **1:**368
  Bournonville (August) on, **1:**505
  Carey (Gustave) dance partnership, **2:**60
  Cerrito rivalry, **2:**94
  Conservatoire de Danse de l'Opéra organization, **3:**81

Cortesi's *La Fille du Danube,* **2:**209
  debut performance, **6:**71
  Dieu et la Bayadère performance, **1:**86, **4:**657
  Elssler rivalry, **2:**405, 503, 504, **3:**69, 185, **5:**93, **6:**51, 73, 74
  Elssler's style versus, **2:**502, **3:**123, 185, **6:**74
  father (Filippo) as mentor, **6:**71, 72–73, 74
  Fitzjames sisters as colleagues, **3:**4, 5
  Flore et Zéphire performance, **2:**415
  Fracci in tradition of, **3:**60
  Gitana performance, **3:**185, **6:**73
  Gosselin (Geneviève) comparison, **3:**209
  Hamburg Ballet guest performances, **3:**336
  Hungarian performances, **3:**414
  Jocko, the Brazilian Ape performance, **3:**144
  Jugement de Pâris, Le, **6:**70
  King's Theatre (London) performances, **2:**502–503, **3:***258,* 259, 260
  Koni reviews, **4:**41
  Levinson biography of, **4:**155
  Livry as protégée, **4:**214–215, **6:**74–75
  Markova portrayal, **4:**268, *269*
  Mazilier dance partnership, **4:**340
  mazur solo, **5:**216
  operatic ballet performances, **4:**514
  Papillon choreography, **1:**390, **3:**70, **4:**108, 215, 353, **6:**73, 75
  Paris Opera Ballet, **3:**69, **5:**89, 92, 93, 94, **6:**69, 72, 74–75
  partners, **5:**134–135, 195, **6:**333
  Pas de Quatre performances, **2:**94, 103–104, **3:**96, 224, 260, 315, **5:**108, 137
  pointe work, **2:**369, **3:**47, 69, 222, 547, *548,* **5:**207, **6:**72, 74
  portrayal in *Pas des Déesses,* **3:**609, 611
  prints and drawings of, **2:**103–104, *103,* 239, **5:***259,* 260
  Robert le Diable performance, **2:**369, **6:**58
  as Romantic ballet prototype, **2:**239, 369, **3:**547, *548,* **4:**340
  Saint Petersburg guest performances, **4:**280, **5:**454, **6:**451, 452
  Sankovskaya comparison, **1:**485
  Scala Ballet performances, **5:**528
  Spanish dance performances, **2:**522
  Stuttgart Ballet guest performances, **6:**9
  Swiss Milkmaid performance, **6:**51
  Sylphide role, **1:**368, 485, 507, **2:**103, 202, 502, **3:**69, 547, *548,* **4:**116, 340, 657, **5:***89,* 93, 528, **6:**57, *57,* 58, 72, *72,* 73, 74
  technical strengths, **2:**502, **3:**69
  triumph in Sweden, **6:**40
  tutu costume, **4:**138, **6:**216
  Ulanova (Galina) comparison, **5:**204
  Vienna ballet debut, **1:**237, **2:**464
Taglioni, Marie (the younger), **1:**238, **3:**260, **5:**138, **6:***76,* **76**

Taglioni, Paul, **1:**238, 427, **2:**435, 587, **3:**145, 237, **5:**138, 195, 514, **6:**71, **75–76**
  American tours, **6:**237, 298
  Fille Mal Gardée, La, **2:**594, 596, **3:**145
  Grisi roles, **3:**315, 316
  Hungarian performance, **3:**414
  King's Theatre performances, **3:**260
  Royal Danish Ballet production, **5:**426
  Royal Swedish Ballet production, **6:**40
  Swiss Milkmaid production, **6:**51
  Sylphide performance in United States, **6:**58
  Zucchi roles, **6:**452
Taglioni, Salvatore, **2:**60, 435, **3:**620, **5:**277, 517, **6:**69–70, **69–70**
Taglioni chez Musette, La, **1:**247
Taglioni family, **6:**69–77
Taglioni's Jewel Casket (Cornell), **1:**137
Tagore, **4:**546, **6:**147
Tagore, Rabindranath, **2:**102, 117, **3:**468, **4:**253–254, **5:**292, 354
Tahina Can, **6:**326
Tahiti, **5:**225, **6:77–79**
tahṭīb, **2:**492, 493, **4:**405, *405,* 488
Tai Ai-Lien. *See* Dai Ailian
taibubu, **5:**80
Taigensho (Japanese text), **3:**591
Taiheiki Chūshin Kōshaku, **3:**441
Taiji Impression, **6:**415
taijiquan (Buddhist discipline), **1:**17, *185,* 186, 188, **3:**272
Taillandet, Suzanne. *See* Douvillier, Suzanne
Tailleferre, Germaine, **1:**327, **3:**393, **4:**516, **5:**237
Tailors Wedding, A (Rowlandson), **2:**70
Tain, The, **3:**520
Taíno (people), **2:**62, 429, 430
Taipan Snake–Blue-tongued Lizard Dance, **1:**226
Taira family, **3:**607
Tamiris and Her Group, **6:**88, 89, *89*
Tairov, Aleksandr, **1:**85, **2:**183, 191, **3:**48, 197, **4:**190, **5:**267
Tairova, Rosa, **4:**87
Tait, Marion, **5:**193
Taiwan, **4:**159, 494, **6:79–83**
Tai Yang Awakes, **6:**378
Tajakant (people), **1:**42
Tajik (people), **1:**27
Tajikistan, **1:**27, **6:83–84**
Takada Masao, **3:**590
Takada Masao Dance Institute, **6:**405
Takada Seiko, **3:**590
Takahashi Yasunari, **4:**661
Takahashi Yuji, **3:**523
Takahime, **3:**651, 652
takai dance, **6:**13
Takai Tomiko, **2:**18
takak, **1:**531
Takarazuka, **6:**84
Takasago, **4:***653,* **6:**445
Takashi, Otake. *See* Eiko and Koma
Takashi Sasaki, **3:***642*
Take a Master Class with David Howard (videotape), **6:**129
Takechi Kabuki troupe, **4:**533, 536
Takechi Tetsuji, **4:**533, 536, **5:**590, 591

Takeda Izumo, **3:**637
Takehara Han, **3:**339
Takei, Kei, **2:**606, **3:**449, 620, **6:**448
Take Me Out to the Ball Game (film), **4:**2, 4
Takemoto Gidayū, **2:**13
Take-Off from a Forced Landing, **2:**358
"Taking a Chance on Love" (tap routine), **2:**186
takirari, **1:**109
taksu, **4:**297–298
Taktakishvili, Otar, **1:**38
tāla, 568, **1:**169, **3:**457, 463, 662, **4:**492
Talard, Philippe, **3:**158
t'al'ch'um, **4:**46, 47, *47,* 50–51, *51*
T'al'ch'um taesajip (Korean text), **4:**53
Tale about Jack, **5:**245
taledek, **1:**174, **3:**504, 505
Tale of Fortune Found, The, **1:**429
Tale of Found Happiness, The, **5:**245
Tale of Genji (Murasaki), **2:**5
Tale of the Russian Land, A (Ustinova ballet), **6:**303
Tale of the Russian Land, The (Livshits ballet), **5:**472
Tale of the Stone Flower, The. See Stone Flower, The
Tale of the Supernatural Sea-Dappled Horse, The, **4:**272
Tales from the Vienna Woods (Strauss), **4:**612
Tales of Beatrix Potter, **1:**157, **3:**236–237, **4:**117
Tales of Hoffmann (Darrell ballet), **1:**73, **2:**350, **4:**117
Tales of Hoffmann (Offenbach opera), **1:**405, **6:**268
Tales of Hoffmann (Petit ballet), **5:**164
Tales of Hoffmann, The (film), **5:**589, **6:**119
Talhoff, Albert, **3:**369, **6:**393
Talisman, The, **3:**14, **4:**67, 143, 145, 640, **5:**160
Talking Heads, **3:**78
Tall Arches III, **2:**606
Tallchief, Maria, **1:**70, **2:**472, **5:**96, 264, **6:84–86**
  Apollo performance, **1:**96, **2:**244, **4:***611*
  Balanchine marriage, **1:**257
  Balanchine roles, **4:**616
  Ballet Imperial, **1:**293
  Ballet Russe de Monte Carlo, **1:**298, 299, 301, 302, **3:**87
  Bruhn dance partnership, **2:**3
  Chicago Lyric Opera Ballet, **2:**577
  Eglevsky dance partnership, **2:**479, **4:**616
  Étude performance, **4:**636
  Firebird performance, **3:**2, 3, **4:**609, 616
  Gounod Symphony, **1:**265
  Guests performance, **5:**361
  Harkness Ballet, **3:**342
  Native American roots, **3:**362
  New York City Ballet, **4:**610, 616
  Orpheus performance, **4:**607
  Sonnambula performance, **5:**641
  Swan Lake role, **6:**34
  Sylvia: Pas de Deux performance, **6:**64
Tallchief, Marjorie, **1:**315, **2:**277, 480
  Grand Ballet du Marquis de Cuevas, **3:**73, 225, *225*

Tallchief, Marjorie, *continued*
  Native American roots, **3:**362
  Skibine marriage and dance
    partnership, **5:***604,* 605
Taller Coreográfico de la
  Universidad Autónoma de
  Puebla, **4:**397, *398*
Taller Coreográfico de la
  Universidad Nacional
  Autónoma de México,
  4:394, 397
Taller de Danza Antigua, Chile,
  2:125–126
Taller de Danza Contemporánea,
  Caracas, **2:**110, **6:**323
Taller de Histriones, Puerto Rico,
  5:275
Taller de Otra Cosa, Puerto Rico,
  5:276
Taller Mouret, **6:**302
Talley, Dale, **6:**324
Talley, Jean, **1:**217
Tallulah Deconstruction, The, **4:**22
Tally-Ho, **2:**112, 373, **4:**110
Talmud, **3:**526, 602
Talmud, Blanche, **5:**637
Talos (mythic), **2:**271
Tamagusuku Chokun, **5:**27, 28
Tamamoto Yasue, **4:**661
Tamanrasset, Algeria, **1:**42
Tamaprawira, Panji, **3:**497
Tamara, **3:**205
Tamar-Jerusalem, **3:**534
Tamasha, **6:**86–87
Tamasik, László, **3:**3
Tamberg, Einó, **2:**530, **4:**478
Tamblyn, Russ, **6:**281
tambor-de-crioula, **1:**527
tamborito, **5:**67
tambourin, **4:**511, **6:**87
tambourine, **3:**242, 504, **4:**501, *506,*
  5:212
tambu, **3:**573
Tambuli Cultural Dance Troupe of
  Ligaya Fernando Amilbangsa,
  5:172
Tamburini, Antonio, **2:**93
"Tamburini row," **2:**93
Tambutti, Susana, **1:**113, 114
Tameng Towok, **3:**495
Tamerlane, **1:**119
tamhawst, **4:**466
Tamil Nadu, India, **1:**442–443,
  2:394, **3:**464, 468
Taming of the Shrew, The, **1:**215,
  2:124, 514, **5:**55, 387
  Cragun performance, **2:**262, **6:**9
  Cranko production, **2:**267, **3:**150,
    616, **4:**2, 547, **6:**9, *9,* 43
  Haydée performance, **3:**350, **6:**9
  Joffrey Ballet revival, **3:**616
  Keil performace, **4:**2
  Seregi choreography, **3:**418,
    5:569
  Wall performance, **6:**357
Tamiris, Helen, **1:**79, 395, 421, 441,
  2:461, **4:**15, 531, **6:**87–90, 137
  Dance Repertory Theater,
    3:215, 399
  Federal Dance Project, **2:**579,
    580, **6:**246
  as Fokine student, **3:**22
  Horst musical collaboration,
    3:385
  importance in modern dance
    world, **6:**245
  musical theater, **6:**279
Tammany (opera), **1:**495, **2:**467,
  6:233
Tampa, Florida, **2:**581
Tam Ti Delam, **3:**231, **4:**238

tanac dance, **6:**428, 429
Tanagra, **3:***209,* 211, *289*
Tanaka Min, **3:**447, 591, **6:**90
ṭanbūrah dance, **4:**488–489
Tanc, Cengiz, **6:**212
Táncművészet (Hungarian
  periodical), **3:**423, 424
Tancred and Clorinda, **3:**52
Tancrède, **2:**34, 465, **3:**329, **5:**40
Tancredi, **3:**359, **4:**517, **5:**7
tandak. See ronggeng
Tandy Beal and Dancers, **2:**110
Tanec ensemble, **4:**630, *630,*
  6:*427, 428*
Taneční listy (periodical), **2:**311
Tanec Praha, **2:**310
tanets (meaning of word), **5:**442
Tanets, pantomima, balet
  (Dobrovolskaya), **5:**485
Tanets na estrade
  (Sheremetyevskaya), **5:**484
Taneyev, Sergei, **3:**16, 186, **5:**266
tangak (Tang music), **1:**166
Tanga Port Authority Cultural
  Troupe, **2:***91*
Tang dynasty, **1:**166, **2:**129, 130,
  130, 131
Tangiayeva-Birzniece, Elena,
  4:127, 128
tango, **6:**91–94
  Argentina, **1:**108, **4:**632, **5:**627,
    6:91–92, 94
  ballet scores, **4:**520
  ballroom competition standards,
    1:358
  caricatures, **2:**70
  Castle style, **2:**78
  Christian sectarian
    condemnation, **2:**168
  Façade, **1:**146, 147
  Finland, **2:**630
  Nieves and Copes, **4:**632
  origination, **3:**629
  Plebs and Zotto, 5.200–201
  social dance popularity, **4:**520,
    5:627, **6:**243, 270
  Valentino popularization, **5:**628
Tango (film), **5:**200
Tango Andalou, **1:**115
Tango Argentino (musical), **4:**632,
  5:200, **6:***93,* 94, *94,* 287
Tango Buenos Aires, **3:**100
Tango-Tango, **4:**274
Tango × 2, **5:**200, **6:**94
Tanguay, Eva, **6:**317
Tanguera, La, **1:**61
Tani, Gino, **5:**246
Tani Ballet, **3:**589
Taniec (Idzikowski), **5:**221
Tanigawa Toshiyuki, **4:**271
Tanimura Tatsuro, **4:**272
tanish, **4:**568
Tanjore style, **1:**273
  See also Thanjavur Quartet
Tankard, Meryl, **1:**213, 214, 389,
  6:95
Tank Dive, **6:**151
Tanner, Richard, **1:**75, **3:**448, **4:**24,
  609, 623
Tanner, Virginia, **1:**421, **4:**168
Tannhäuser (Wagner). *See*
  Venusberg scene
Tanning, Dorothea, **1:**298, **5:**641
Tano festival, **4:**50–51
Tano Hideko, **3:**591
"Tanovar," **6:**305
Tansman, Alexandre, **3:**628
Tantaquidgeon, Harold and Gladys,
  4:555
Tantric Buddhism, **1:**443–445
  Black Hat Dance, **1:**458–459

Tantric Geography, **2:**293
Tantz-Schul, **1:**241
Tanz, Der (periodical), **3:**142, 161,
  162, **4:**92
Tanz Aktuell (journal), **3:**162
Tanzania, **2:**86, 87, 89, 91, **4:**484
  masked stilt-dance, **4:**287, 289
Tanzarchiv, Das (periodical),
  3:161–162
Tanzbibliographie (Petermann ed.),
  2:386, **3:**161
Tanzblätter (periodical), **1:**243
Tanzbühne Laban. *See* Laban
  School
Tanzdrama (journal), **3:**162
Tänze für alle (Gleisner), **4:**103, 477
Tänze für Käthe Kollwitz, **3:**393
Tänzer-Kollectiv, **6:**357
Tanzfabrik Berlin, **3:**156
Tanzfest, Der (Zatzinger), **5:**259
Tanzfigurenschrift (Misslitz), **4:**691
Tanzforschung (Klein ed.), **3:**163
Tanz-Forum der Oper der Stat
  Köln. *See* Cologne Dance
  Forum
Tanzhaus (Tanz-Hauß), **3:**602–603,
  4:349
Tanzmärchen, **1:**540
Tanzspiel, **4:**622
Tanzsuite, **3:**132
Tanztheater (dance genre), **3:**156,
  157, 162, **6:**52, 53
TanzTheater (Schlicher), **3:**162
Tanztheater Basel. *See* Basel Ballet
Tanztheater Bochum, **3:**157
Tanztheater der Komischen Oper
  Berlin. *See* Berlin Dance
  Theater
Tanztheater in Deutschland
  (Schmidt), **3:**162
Tanztheater Schauspiel Haus
  Leipzig, **3:**157
Tanztheater Wuppertal, **1:**214, 246,
  388–389, 414, **3:**40, 149, 151,
  151, 157, **6:**95
  Cébron as ballet master, **2:**81
  Indian tour, **2:**104
  Italian performances, **3:**551
  Ondine, **3:**360
  Walter as ballet master-
    choreographer, **6:**358
Tanztherapie: Theorie und Praxis
  (Willke ed.), **3:**163
Tanz-Ton-Wort, **4:**89
Taoism. *See* Daoism
Tap (film), **3:**367, **5:**601, **6:**103
Tapalova, Nursula, **3:**665
Tapa Sudana, **5:**524
tap dance, **5:**632, **6:**95–104
  Baby Laurence, **1:**252
  Bates, Peg Leg, **1:**382, *382*
  Bradley, Buddy, **1:**520
  Bubbles, John W., **2:**5
  clogging relationship, **2:**180
  Coles, Honi, **2:**185–186
  Darktown Follies, **6:**256
  Draper, Paul, **2:**444–445
  Four Step Brothers, **3:**57
  Green, Chuck, **3:**304
  Hines, Gregory, **3:**366–367
  Hollywood musicals, **2:**613, 615
  improvisation, **3:**447
  jazz element, **3:**598
  Juba, Master, **3:**633, **6:**254
  Kahn notation, **4:**690
  Miller, Ann, **4:**418–419
  musical theater, **6:**274
  Nicholas brothers, **4:**629–630
  Powell, Eleanor, **5:**238–239, **6:**101
  rhythms and sources, **3:**131
  Robinson, Bill, **5:**368–369

Rodeo cadenza, **5:**369
  shoes, **3:**47
  Sims, Sandman, **5:**601
  step dancing as influence, **5:**696
  Temple, Shirley, **6:**141–142
  Whitman Sisters, **6:**386
  See also precision dancing
Tap Dance in America (television
  program), **3:**366
Tap Dance Kid, The (musical),
  6:102, 286
Tap Dance Kid, The (television
  film), **2:**186
taped music. *See* electronic music
Taper, Bernard, **1:**325
"Tap Happenings" (Hotel Dixie),
  3:304, **6:**102
Taplin, Diana, **2:**50
taqueté, **1:**44
taraf, **5:**379
Tarahumara (people), **4:**389
Tarakanova, Nina, **1:**310,
  3:103–104, 511
taralala, **2:**593
Taranda, Gediminas (Gedeminas),
  3:193, *309,* **5:**321
tarantella, **2:**107, **6:**104–105
  Céleste performances, **2:**85
  Elssler popularization, **2:**107, 504
Tarantella, **4:**345, 611, 620
Tarantism, **6:**104, 185, 187
Taranto, **2:**279
Taras, John, **1:**76, 110, 315, 395,
  2:245, 425, **3:**74, **4:**5, 24, **5:**97,
  316, 512, 526, **6:**200
  Ballets des Champs-Élysées,
    1:306
  Ballets Russes de Monte Carlo,
    4:269
  Berlin Opera Ballet, **1:**436
  Copland score, **2:**197
  Designs with Strings, **1:**429, **2:**3,
    3:74, **4:**117, 380
  Firebird staging, **2:**334, **3:**4
  as Fokine student, **3:**22
  Grand Ballet du Marquis de
    Cuevas, **3:**226
  Jeux, **2:**361
  Karinska costumes, **3:**654
  Lanchbery musical arrangemnt,
    4:117
  New York City Ballet, **4:**609
  Scènes de Ballet production,
    5:531–532
Taras Bulba, **2:**585–586, *586,* **3:**99,
  187, **4:**148, 226, 284, **5:**23,
  567, 571, **6:**225, 344, 442
Tarascan, dance of the, **2:**121
Tarascans, The, **4:**395
Tarasov, Ivan, **6:**105
Tarasov, Nikolai, **1:**489, **4:**133, 181,
  6:105–106, 129
  ballet technique text, **1:**329
  Bolshoi Ballet, **4:**89
  Norwegian ballet company, **4:**674
Tarasova, Olga, **5:**460, **6:**8
Tarcan, Bülent, **6:**212
Tarchi, Angelo, **2:**435
Tarcia, Celia, **1:**112
tardah game, **2:**490
Tardif, Danielle, **2:**610
Tarantella, **4:**345, **6:**105, 340
Tarantella in A-flat Major
  (Chopin), **6:**60
Tarentule, La, **1:**200, **5:**148, **6:**104
  Coralli production, **2:**201,
    203, 504
  Elssler (Fanny) performance,
    2:502, 504, **4:**340
  Lecomte company performance,
    4:138

Maywood performance, **4:**338
Mazilier performance, **4:**340
Target (avant-garde group), **3:**197, **4:**124
tari kursus, **3:**504
tari piriang, **3:**500–501
tari ragam, **4:**251
Tarlac, Philippines, **2:**231
Tarnowski, Aleksander, **5:**216
Tarnowski, Antoni, **5:**216
Tarrant, Deirdre, **4:**627
Tartans, The, **5:**300, 691
Tartini il Violinista, **4:**589, **5:**499, 500
Taruna, **1:**177
Taruskin, Richard, **6:**4
Tasfi, Gabor, **5:**677
Tashkent Choreographic Institute, **6:**306
Tashkent Institute of Culture, **6:**306
Tashköprüzäde, **3:**525
Tasso, Torquato, **1:**285, **2:**73, 95, 368, 426, **3:**544, **5:**1, **6:**62
Taste, **5:**316
Tata, **4:**118
Tatai, Mária, **3:**421
Tataradze, Avtandil, **3:**133
Tate, Marion, **5:**421
tateshi, **1:**187
tati (comic characters), **4:**298
Tatiana, **2:**15, **4:**284
Tatjana Gsovsky Ballet School, Berlin, **3:**317
Tatler (British journal), **3:**284
tatoos. *See* mask and makeup
Tatsonas, Eustathios, **3:**303
Tatsunokuchi, **4:**30
Tatum, Art, **1:**252
Tatyana and the Others, **6:**67
taualuga, **5:**510
Täuber, Sophie, **4:**90, **6:**52
Taubert, Gottfried, **1:**342, **2:**259, 338, *338*, **3:**158, **4:**431, **5:**227, 520, **6:**123, 124
Taubert, Karl Heinz, **3:**161
   as contributor, **1:**365
   dance archives, **4:**161
Taubert, Manfred, **2:**478
taue odori, **3:**586–587
Taugenichts in Wien, Der, **6:**388
tau'olunga movement, **4:**495
Tavata (people), **2:**418
tavernas, **3:**299
Tavern Bilkers, The (pantomime), **5:**69, **6:**372
Taverner, Sonia, **3:***231*, **6:106–107**
Taviani, Ferdinando, **2:**188
tavşan rakşı, **6:**211
Tawhīd concept, **1:**18
taxi dancing, **2:**133–134
Taylor, Basil, **5:**53
Taylor, Billy, **3:**448
Taylor, Cecil, **3:**448
Taylor, Jonathan, **1:**214, **4:**275, 625, **5:**302
Taylor, June, **3:**600
Taylor, Margaret Fisk, **4:**212
Taylor, Maxwell D., **5:**561
Taylor, Paul, **1:**234, **2:**269, **3:**122, **4:**218, 219, **5:**7, 303, 574, **6:107–114**, 249
   American Dance Festival, **1:**79
   American Music Festival, **4:**623
   Aureoloe, **2:**514
   avant-garde, **2:**290
   Boston Ballet choreography, **1:**501
   choreographic style analysis, **4:**99
   Clytemnestra, **2:**182, **3:***217*
   collaborative visual artists, **1:**140, 143, **2:**290, **3:**619

Cunningham Dance Company, **2:**289
Esplanade choreography, **2:**526–527
Graham Dance Company, **2:**182, **3:***217*, 218, 219
modern dance technique, **4:**442
Musical Offering, **4:**482–483
Netherlands Ballet choreography, **4:**600
New York City Ballet, **4:**620
Orbs, **1:**403
partnering technique, **5:**105
Rauschenberg collaboration, **1:**140, **3:**619, **5:**313
Royal Danish Ballet guest productin, **5:**432
Sacre du Printemps, Le, **5:**488
Spindrift, **5:**679–681
Ter-Arutunian association, **6:**144
Three Epitaphs, **6:**107, 108, 110, 164–166
Waring association, **6:**362, 363
See also Paul Taylor Dance Company
Taylor, Philip, **3:**157
Taylor, Robert, **6:***263*
Taylor, Victoria, **6:***56*
Taylor, William, **2:**353, 364
Taylor-Corbett, Lynne, **1:**75, 197, **2:**358, **4:**625, **5:**24, **6:**266, 289
Taylor 2, **6:**113
Taymor, Julie, **6:**289
tayub, **3:**503–504
tbila dance, **4:**466
Tbilisi Theater of Opera and Ballet, **1:**38, **3:**135, **4:**133
T'boli (people), **5:**168
Tchaikovsky, **2:**499, **4:**469, **5:**465
Tchaikovsky (film), **5:**203
Tchaikovsky, Modest, **6:**30
Tchaikovsky, Petr Ilich, **1:**9, 486, **5:**315, 626, **6:**5, **114–117**
   Balanchine choreographies, **1:**260–261, 281, 293, 298, *299*, 306, **4:**609, 611, 613
   Berlin Opera Ballet commemorative productions, **1:**436, **3:**156
   Children's Album, **5:**9
   dancer style preferences, **1:**540
   as Debussy inspiration, **2:**360
   Delibes's ballets as inspiration, **2:**200, 368, **4:**514, **6:**63–64
   Dolgushin ballets, **2:**423
   Duncan choreography, **2:**456
   Fokine choreography, **3:**20–21, 22, 23
   Georgian musical inspiration, **3:**135
   as Glazunov influence, **3:**186
   Grigorovich revivals, **3:**309–310
   Ivanov's versus Petipa's attitudes toward ballet scores by, **3:**563–564
   Little Humpbacked Horse, The, **5:**588
   Massine symphonic ballets, **1:**310, **4:**322, 517
   mazurka composition, **5:**343
   Romeo and Juliet, **5:**392, 398, 399
   Serenade score, **5:**571–572
   on *Sylvia* score, **6:**63–64
   Vsevolozhsky's ballet commissions, **4:**515
   waltz and polonaise compositions, **5:**626
   See also Nutcracker, The; Sleeping Beauty, The; Swan Lake

Tchaikovsky Festival (1980–1981), **4:**274, 607, **5:**366
Tchaikovsky Memorial Ballet School, Tokyo, **3:**589
Tchaikovsky Pas de Deux, **3:**231, **4:**611, **6:**340
Tchaikovsky Piano Concerto No. 2, **1:**256, 293, **4:**613, 618, 619, 631
   See also Ballet Imperial
Tchaikovsky Suite No. 2, **2:**314, **4:**631
Tchaikovsky Suite No. 3, **1:***270*
Tchaikovsky Symphony No. 1, **4:**615
Tchaikovsky Piano Concerto No. 2. *See Ballet Imperial*
Tchaikovsky's First Symphony ("Winter Dreams"), **6:**114
Tchaikovsky's Suite No. 3 ("Theme and Variations"), **5:**223
Tchelitchev, Pavel, **1:***63*, 64, 133, 306, 316, 437, **2:**242, 406, **3:**58, **5:**242, **6:117–119**
   Balustrade designs, **1:**314, **2:***243*
   body tights design, **1:**348, **2:**442
   Diaghilev commission, **2:**410, **4:**3
   on *Errante's* reception, **1:**307
   Kirstein association, **4:**27, 30
   Nobilissima Visione design, **4:**656
   Ode decor, **2:**603, **6:**118, *118*
   Orpheus and Eurydice costumes, **2:**244
   scenic design, **5:**545, *545*, 546, 547
Tcherepnin, Alexander, **1:**467, **3:**401, **5:**45, 118, 121, 163
Tcherepnin, Nikolai, **2:**73, **3:**16, 18, 24, **6:**61
Tcherina, Ludmila, **1:**291, 305, **3:**18, **4:**184, **5:**332, 676, **6:119–120**
Tcherkas, Constantin, **5:**98, 562, 563
Tcherkassky, Marianna, **1:**74, *74*, 77, **2:**356, **5:**16, **6:***152*
Tchernicheva, Lubov, **1:**95, 207, **4:**267, **6:120–121**
   Ballets Russes de Monte Carlo, **1:**311, 313, 315
   Biches, Les, **1:**449
   English National Ballet, **2:**510
   Firebird restaging, **3:**2, 308
   as Fokine student, **3:**14
   Grigoriev marriage, **3:**308
   Noces performance, **4:***636*
   Petrouchka staging, **5:***165*, 166
   Royal Ballet stagings, **3:**308
   Schéhérazade performance, **5:**556
Tchernichov, Igor, **1:**371
Tchernichova, Elena, **1:**75
Tchernikoff, Paul, **1:**518
Tchikaboumskaya, Olga, **6:***191*
Tchinarova, Tamara, **1:**311, 499, **4:**26, **5:**265
Tchulaki, Michail, **4:**583
Teachers College (Columbia University), **3:**385, **4:**16, **6:**242, 295
Teaching of Classical Ballet (Lawson), **2:**330, **6:**128
Teaching Young Dancers (Lawson), **2:**330, **6:**128
tea dance, **5:**628, **6:**251
Tease, **3:**578
Teatri Shtetëror i Operës dhe Baleti, Albania, **1:**34, 35
Teatro alla Scala, Milan. *See* Scala Ballet
Teatro Colón, Buenos Aires, **1:**110, 111, 112, 424, **2:**111, **3:**317, **5:**58, **6:**119

Araiz directorship, **1:**103
Ballets Russes de Monte Carlo joint residency, **1:**314, 315
Bolm productions, **1:**483
Doubrovska performance, **2:**441
Ferri, Olga, **2:**587, 588
Fokine productions, **3:**24
Hoyer, Dore, **3:**393
Josephslegende, Die, **3:**631
Lacotte reconstruction, **4:**108
Nijinska choreography, **4:**635
Noces revival, **4:**659
Nutcracker, The, **2:**587, **5:**15
Wallmann choreography, **6:**357
Teatro Comunale, Florence, **3:**552, **4:**246
Teatro Costanzi, Rome. *See* Rome Opera Ballet
Teatro Danza Company, Montevideo, **6:**302
Teatrodanza Contemporanea di Roma, **6:**121
Teatro de la Danza del Caribe, Santiago, Chile, **2:**281
Teatro del Casinó Municipale, San Remo, **3:**51
Teatro dell'Opera, Rome. *See* Rome Opera Ballet
Teatro del Silencio, **2:**126
Teatro de São Carlos, Lisbon, **5:**500
Teatro di Apollo, Rome, **5:**404, 409
Teatro Farnese, Parma, **4:**188
Teatro García Lorca, Havana, **2:**279
Teatro Grande, Trieste, **5:**403
Teatro La Fenice, Venice, **1:**291, 427, 460, 640, **3:**551, **4:**108
   Rota choreography, **5:**408, 409
Teatro La Pergola, Florence, **3:**176
Teatro Lirico, Rio de Janeiro, **1:**532
Teatro Massimo, Palermo, **1:**446, **2:**369, **3:**552
Teatro Mercandante, Naples, **3:**61
Teatro Municipale, Reggio Emilia, **1:**196
Teatro Pagliano, Florence, **1:**427
Teatro Reale dell'Opera di Roma, **5:**392, 399–400
Teatro Regio, Naples, **2:**93
Teatro Regio, Turin, **1:**427, **2:**208
Teatro Regio Ducal, Milan, **4:**696
Teatro San Carlo, Naples, **3:**61, 176, 426, 552, **5:**196
   ballet school, **3:**551, 553, **6:**70
Teatro San Cassiano, Venice, **6:**156
Teatro San Materno, Switzerland, **6:**52
Teatro San Samuele, Venice, **2:**55
Teatro São Carlos, Lisbon, **1:**85, **2:**208
Teatro Teresa Carreño, Venezuela, **6:**324–325
Teatro Verdi, Trieste, **3:**552
Teatro y Danzas Negras del Peru, **5:**146
Technical Dictionary of Dancing (Espinosa), **6:**128
technical manuals, **6:121–129**, 239–240, 349–350
   Baroque, **1:**342, 344–345
   Cecchetti method, **1:**329, **2:**83, 84
   colonial North American, **6:**231–233
   for *commedia dell'arte* players, **2:**189
   on court etiquette, **3:**542–543
   on dance social benefits, **4:**310
   musical examples, **4:**506–507
   prints illustrating, **5:**260
   for historical reconstructions, **5:**323

technical manuals, *continued*
Renaissance, **1:**22, 103–104, 105, 107, **2:**73–77, **5:**336–337, 338
on *révérences,* **5:**343–349
See also annual collections; ballet technique, history of; dancing master; notation; *specific authors and countries*
technique. *See* ballet technique; ballet technique, history of; modern dance technique; Renaissance dance technique; *specific techniques*
Technique for the Ballet Artiste (Spessivtseva), **6:**128
Teck, Katherine, *as contributor,* **1:**5–7
Teck, Le, **1:**404
Tedeev, Vadim, **5:**467
tedesco. See allemande
Tedjoekoesoemo, Prince, **5:**522
Ted Shawn and His Men Dancers, **5:**585–586
Ted Shawn Theatre, Jacob's Pillow, **3:**571, 572, *572*
Teduh, I Wayan, **4:**297
Teeters, Jim, **4:**649
Tehias Hemesim, **3:**603
Tehillim, **2:**359
Teika, **4:**42
Teitelbaum, Carol, **2:***292*
Te Kanawa, Kiri, **6:**133
teke dance, **6:**211
Tekin, Altan, **6:**213
Tekna (people), **1:**42
Tel Aviv, Israel, **3:**528, 529, 532, 533, 534, 535, **4:**58
Telemachus in the Island of Calypso. See Télémaque dans l'Île de Calypso
Telemaco, **1:**87, **3:**189
Telemann, Georg Philipp, **1:**364, **4:**511
Télémaque dans l'Île de Calypso, **2:**353, 364, 413, 414, 465, **3:**117, 118–119, *118,* 426, **5:***198*
Télèphe, **2:**34
Telephone, The, **3:**427
Teleshova, Ekaterina, **4:**279, 280, **5:**453
television, **6:**130–141
dance in Canada, **6:**130–134
Augustyn productions, **1:**201
Ballets Chiriaeff, Les, **2:**150–151, **3:**227, *228*
dance in Europe, **6:**134–136
Béjart stagings, **1:**404
Briantzev productions, **1:**539
British programming. *See* British Broadcasting Corporation
Danish productions, **2:**386, 387, **3:**12, 13, **5:***430,* 432
Flindt's ballets, **3:**12, 13
Fonteyn series, **1:**400
Fracci documentary, **3:**60–61
Italian productions, **2:**480, **3:**551, 554
Russian productions, **4:**133, 336, **5:**460
Swedish productions, **1:**32–33, 400, **2:**284, 294, 501
Yugoslav productions, **6:**433, 437
dance in United States, **6:**136–141
Alive from Off Center program, **2:**609, 610
American Ballet Theatre documentary, **5:**369

American Bandstand, **1:**77–79, **5:**630, 632, 633, **6:**30
American Dance Festival workshop, **1:**80
Astaire specials, **1:**195
Beatty-Ellington specials, **1:**396
Bennett productions, **1:**419
Billy the Kid filmed presentation, **1:**452
Coles features, **2:**186
Cunningham productions, **2:**294
Dance in America series, **2:**294, 359, 459, **3:**616, 621, **6:**300
dance popularizations, **5:**632, 633
first live modern dance performance, **3:**370
Giselle version, **3:**60, *60*
Joffrey Ballet programs, **3:**616
musicals and musical revues, **2:**619–620
San Francisco Ballet productions, **5:**513
See also film and video
Teliakovsky, Vladimir, **3:**14, **5:**160–161
Telle, Carle, **1:**238, **3:**346, 347
Telle, Constantin Michel, **3:**144
Telle, Johanna Dulan, **5:**278
Téllez, Marcos, **1:***479, 480*
Tell Me a Tale, **4:***625, 625*
Tels, Ellen (also Knipper and Rabenek), **1:**239, **3:**83, **5:**476, 560
Te Maia, **4:**625
tembang, **3:**483, 485
Tembeck, Iro Valaskakis, **2:**49
as contributor, **2:**43–46
Temne (people), **1:**14, **6:**25, *383*
Tempe Restored (masque), **3:**622
Tempest, The, **1:**394, **2:**463, **5:**280
Howard choreography, **3:**392
Nureyev production, **5:**7
Rambert Dance Company, **5:**302, **6:**146
Tetley staging as *Stormen,* **4:**677, *678,* **6:**44
Tempest, The (Shakespeare), **2:**203, **3:**252, 253, **6:**450
Tempest, The (television production), **5:**513
Tempesta, Le, **3:**316, **5:**404–405
Tempest of Rhythms, A, **5:**517
Tempête, La, **1:**44, **2:**202–203, 503, **4:**340
Templ, Lisl, **6:**388
Temple, Shirley, **2:**615, **5:**368, *368,* **6:**100, 141–142
Temple de la Fortune, Le, **2:**465, **4:**236
Temple de la Gloire, Le (Rameau), **1:**284, **4:**236, **5:**307, **6:***250*
Temple de la Paix, Le, **1:**288, 425, **4:**109, 235
Temple in Jerusalem, **3:**526, 536, 602
Temple of Universal Happiness, The, **2:**55
Templeton, Fay, **6:**276
Tempo di Valse, **4:**5
Temps, Le, **1:**287, 424
temps d'adage, **1:**8
temps de chaceone, **1:**8
temps de courante simples et composés, **1:**8, 345
temps de courante sur les pointes, **1:**8–9
temps levé, **1:**339, 341
tendonitis, **2:**328, **4:**20
Tenisheva, Maria, **2:**408, **5:**372

Tennant, Cecil, **1:**367
Tennant, Veronica, **4:**71, 542, **5:***106,* **6:**132, **142–143**
Ten New Fashionable Irish Dances (Bray), **2:**256
Tenniel, Sir John, **1:**394
Tennis, **1:**518, **3:**23
Tennis Court Theater, Stockholm, **6:**39
Tenorio, Iván, **2:**279, **5:**615
Tent, **4:**650, **5:**548
Tentai no Aki, **6:**414
Tentation, La, **2:**202, **4:**116
Tentation de Saint Antoine, La (Béjart), **1:**407
Tentations de la Bergère, La, 2, 424, **4:**634
Ten Virgins, **2:**417
Teolinda, **3:**194
teppu (painted characters), **4:**298
Terabust, Elisabetta, **1:**83, 196, **2:**513, **4:**244, **5:**15, 289, 527, **6:143–144**
Nutcracker performance, **5:**15
Rome Opera Ballet, **5:**401
Rome Opera Ballet School, **3:**553, **5:**401
Scala, La, **3:**552, 553, **5:**401
Ter-Arutunian, Rouben, **1:**72, 293, **2:**245, **5:**532, 551, **6:144**
as contributor, **2:**390–393
Balanchine *Nutcracker* scenery design, **4:***617*
Swan Lake design, **6:**34
Terayama Shuji, **4:**84
Terechkovitch, Constantin, **1:***310*
Terekhova, Tatiana, **2:***207,* **4:**285, **6:**35
Terence, **5:**375
Terentieva, Elena, **5:**476, 478
Teresi, Stefano, **3:***551*
Termanini, Filippo, **4:**339
Terminal, **4:**210
Terminal City Dance, **2:**40
Terminal Velocity, **1:**216
Ternicheva, Lubov, **4:**657
terno dress, **2:**231
Terpis, Max, **4:**60, **5:**166, 263, **6:**392
Terpsichore, **6:144–145**
Terpsichore, **2:**50–51, 381, **3:**123, **4:**91, 431, 507, 509, **5:**109, 244, 520
Terpsichore (Sangalli preface), **5:**515
Terpsichore, or Ball Room Guide (Durang), **2:**339, **3:**379, **6:**239
terpsychoretrance therapy, **6:**187
Terra Australis, **1:**209
Terrade, Federico Nadi, **6:**40, 48
Terra del rimorso, La (de Martino), **6:**104
Terrades, Jean-Antoine, **3:**546
Terra Firma, **4:**73
Terrain, **3:**446
terre à terre steps, **1:**339–340
Terre Battue, **3:**79
Terrible Tom, **4:**625
Terror, **2:**474
Terry, Ellen, **2:**262, 263, **4:**189
Terry, Emilio, **1:**306
Terry, Sonny, **2:**450
Terry, Walter, **2:**376, **4:**177, **5:**163, **6:**85, 198
on Alonso (Alicia), **1:**50
on Chase (Lucia), **2:**112
on Collins (Janet), **2:**186
Danielian quote, **2:**341
as dean of American dance criticism, **6:**299, 300
on de Lavallade (Carmen), **2:**366
on Franklin (Frederick), **3:**88

on Holm as teacher, **3:**370
Jacob's Pillow, **3:**572
on Karinska costumes, **3:**654
on Loring's *Prairie,* **4:**228
on Maracci, **4:**262
on Meri, **3:**355, **4:**354
Moore as associate dance critic, **4:**457
St. Denis association, **5:**497
Terschellinger volksleven (Kunst), **4:**585
Tersicoreide (Guerra), **3:**320
Ter-Stepanova, Ksenia, **3:**665
Tertulia, La, **3:**226
Tertullian, emperor of Rome, **4:**428
terukkūttu, **3:**464
Tervamäki, Minna, **2:**633
ter Weeme, Mascha. *See* Weeme, Mascha ter
Tesauro, Emanuele, **3:**544
Teseo in Creta, **4:**88, **4:**107
Teshigahara Hidroshi, **3:**653
Teshigawara Saburō, **3:**591, **6:**145
teškoto dance, **6:**428, 429, *430*
Tesla, Nikola, **2:**53, 54
tesoura, **1:**527
Tessari, Roberto, **2:**188
Tessenow, Heinrich, **1:**98
Tessitore, Gabriella, **3:***551*
Testa, Alberto, **3:**555, 556
archival material, **4:**162
as contributor, **1:**460–461, **3:**547–549, **4:**145–146, 258–259, 263–264, 420–422, **5:**288–289, **6:**69–77, 452–453
Test Match, **5:**653
Tesunojō family, **3:**650
Tetart, John, **2:**337
Tetley, Glen, **1:**55, 141, 196, **2:**269, 561, **3:**351, **4:**252, **5:**97, 513, 528, **6:**145–147, 250
American Ballet Theatre, **1:**72, 73
Australian Ballet productions, **1:**214, 233, 234, 394
Baylis design association, **1:**394
Benesh notation use, **1:**418
as Bruce influence, **2:**1
choreography course, **3:**280
costume, **2:**245
Daphnis and Chloe, **4:**1, **5:**316, **6:**146
de Lavallade performance, **2:**366, 367
English National Ballet productions, **2:**513
Firebird version, **3:**4, **6:**134, 146
Gemini, **3:**360, **5:**410
Holm association, **3:**370
Hønningen roles, **3:**373
Joffrey Ballet, **3:**609, 610
Keil roles, **4:**1
as Kylián influence, **4:**81
Mythical Hunters, **3:***533,* **6:***135,* 146
National Ballet of Canada, **1:**394, **2:**42, **4:**544, 545, *545,* 546
Netherlands Dance Theater, **4:***601,* 602
Norwegian National Ballet choreography, **4:**677
Pierrot Lunaire, **5:**301, *303,* **6:**145–146
Pulcinella, **6:**143
Rambert Dance Company, **5:**301, 302, 303, *303,* **6:**146
regional choreographic conferences, **6:**266
Royal Ballet repertory, **5:**417
Royal Danish Ballet guest productions, **5:**432

Royal Swedish Ballet guest productions, **6:**43, 44
Sacre du Printemps, Le, **5:**488
San Francisco Ballet guest choreography, **5:**513
Sphinx, **6:**143
students, **5:**388
Stuttgart Ballet, **6:**10
Ter-Arutunian, Rouben, **6:**144
Voluntaries spontaneity, **3:**448
Ziggurat, **1:**394
Tew (people), **4:**575
Tewsley, Robert, **4:***547*
Texas Cowboy, **2:***176*
Texas Fourth, **1:**73, **2:**108, 374
Texas Jack (John Omohundro), **4:***464*
Texas Swing, **2:**258
Texas Ten-Step, **5:**634
Texas Tommy, **2:**259, **4:**201, **6:**319
Texas Two-Step, **2:**24, 258–259, **6:**251
Texas Woman's University, Denton, **4:**169
textual analysis, **4:**377–378
textual pattern of dance, **4:**363
Teyyam, **6:**147
teyyam kettu, **4:**299
Tezaab (film), **2:**625
TFO (cable network), **6:**132, 133
Thabal Chongbi, **1:***173*
Thackery, William Makepeace, **2:**67, 71
Thailand, **1:**178, 179, **6:147–151**
costume, **2:**227, *228,* **4:**255
influence on Cambodian dance, **2:**30, 31, 228
influence on Malaysian dance., **2:**229
lakhŏn dance, **4:**111–112, **6:**148–149
libraries and museums, **4:**159
Manōhrā dance drama, **4:**251, 255–256, 492
trance rituals, **6:**185
Thaïs (Massenet), **1:**157
Thalberg, Irving, **2:**372
Thalia, Rita, **1:**290
Thamar, **1:**482
Bakst costume design, **1:**254, **2:**241, 407, **3:**18
Ballets Russes de Monte Carlo revival, **1:**311
Doubrovska performance, **2:**441
Fokine choreography, **3:**18
Georgian dance, **3:**135
Thamar, queen of Georgia, **3:**134
Thammasat University, Thailand, **6:**150
Thammasat University Khōn Troupe, **4:**10
Thanatopsis (film dance), **2:**605
thang-ta, **3:**468
Thanjavur Quartet (Tanjore), **1:**273, 442
Tharp, Twyla, **1:**391, **2:**19, 463, 609, **3:**448, **4:**622, **5:**437, **6:**139, **151–155**
Amadeus dances, **6:**286
American Ballet Theatre, **1:**73, 74, *74,* 76, 77
American Dance Festival, **1:**79
archival materials, **4:**169
avant-garde dance, **1:**245, 246
Baryshnikov roles, **1:**372
Boston Ballet choreography, **1:**502
Brief Fling, **1:**77
choreographic style analysis, **4:**99
costume, **2:**245, **4:**226
Cutting Up, **1:**373

dance company, **1:**213
Deux Coupe, **4:**519
group improvisation, **3:**447
ice-dance choreography, **2:**298
Joffrey Ballet choreography, **3:**615–616, 617
lighting for dance, **4:***190*
Loquasto collaboration, **4:**226
modern dance technique, **4:**442
New Zealand performance, **4:**628
Nine Sinatra Songs, **1:**77
Royal Ballet choreography, **5:**420
Rudner association, **5:**439–449, 441
Singin' in the Rain direction and choreography, **6:**287
See also Push Comes to Shove
That Certain Feeling, **2:**513
That Is the Show, **5:**301
That Night in Rio (film), **4:**434
That's Dancing (film), **6:**205
That's Entertainment (film), **1:**195
That Was Fast (Australian dance company), **1:**216
Théa, ou La Fée aux Fleurs, **6:**75, 76
Theater (Russian journal), **5:**642
Theater an der Wien, **1:**237, 241, **3:**380
Theater and Its Double, The (Artaud), **1:**135, **2:**288
Theater auf der Wieden, **1:**237
Theater for New Dance, Music, and Design, A, **6:**107
Theater 14, **6:**161
Theater Guild, **6:**276
Theater in der Josefstadt, Vienna, **1:**237
Theater in der Leopoldstadt, Vienna, **1:**237
Theater Instituut Nederland, **4:**162
Theater Musick (Walsh), **1:**92
Theater Nollendorf, **2:**150
Theater of Chamber Dance, Vladivostok, **5:**478, 479
Theater of Contemporary Ballet, Saint Petersburg, **5:**467
Theater of Dance, Moscow, **5:**478
Theater of Dionysus, Athens, **5:**41, 42
Theater of Modern Dance, Perm, **5:**475
Theater of Northern Greece, Thessalonike, **3:**300
Theater of Plastique Arts, Moscow, **5:**479
Theater of the Four Masks, Moscow, **3:**48
Theater of the Open Eye, New York City, **2:**520
Theater of the Sanctuary of Apollo, Delphi, **6:***155*
Theater Owners' Booking Association (TOBA), **6:**99, 256
Theater Piece, **1:**421, 422, **2:**580, **3:**399, 400, 404, **4:**605, *606*
Theater Piece Number 1, **5:**313
Theater Piece Number 2, **3:**391
theaters for dance, **6:155–164**
ballet de collège, **1:**283, 284
ballet de cour, **1:**286
ballet directions, **1:**335
bunraku playhouses, **2:**12, 14
kabuki layout, **3:**637–638
nō drama, **4:**652
orchestra, **5:**41–42, **6:**155, 157, 161
Swedish court theaters, **6:**45–48
See also specific theater names
Theater Unga Klara, **2:**501
Theatre, **1:**73

Theatre Action, **4:**627
Theatre Advancing, The (Craig), **4:**189
Theatre Arts Monthly, **6:**299
Theatre Ballet of Canada. *See* Ottawa Ballet
Thèâtre Beaulieu, Lausanne, **6:**53–54
Thèâtre Choréographique, Paris, **4:**635
Theatre Comique, Boston, **4:**463, 464
Thèâtre de la Danse Nijinska, **4:**636, 659
Thèâtre de la Gaîté, Paris, **2:**464, **3:**68
Thèâtre de l'Amibigu-Comique, Paris, **2:**412, **3:**66, 68
Thèâtre de la Monnaie, Brussels. *See* Théâtre Royal de La Monnaie, Brussels
Thèâtre de la Porte-Saint-Martin, Paris, **1:**201, 202, 455, **2:**525
choreographic and dance performance talent, **3:**68
Ciceri scenic design, **2:**171
Coralli as ballet master, **2:**202, **3:**68–69, **4:**339, 340
Fille Mal Gardée production, **2:**595, **3:**426
Gautier libretto, **3:**123
Hus (Eugène) as ballet master, **3:**426
Mazilier performances, **4:**339, 340
Thèâtre de la Ville, Paris, **1:**462, **3:**77
Thèâtre de l'Empire, Paris, **3:**226
Thèâtre de Loïe Fuller, Le (Paris Exposition), **3:**93
Thèâtre de l'Opéra-Comique. *See* Opéra-Comique, Paris
Thèâtre de Monte-Carlo. *See* Ballets Russes de Monte Carlo
Thèâtre des Arts, Paris, **6:**158–159, *158*
Thèâtre des Champs-Élysées, Paris
Baker appearance, **1:**252
Balanchine premieres, **1:**306, **3:**72–73
Ballets Suédois first performance, **1:**326
Bourdelle frieze and façade sculptures, **1:**502
See also Ballets des Champs-Élysées
Thèâtre du Châtelet, Paris. *See* Théâtre Musical du Châtelet
Thèâtre du Nicolet, Paris, **4:**523
Thèâtre du Silence, **2:**294, **3:**77, **6:**27
Thèâtre et la danse en Iran, Le (Rezvani), **4:**414
Theatre for a Voyage, **5:**562
Théâtre Italien, Le, **2:**190
Thèâtre Kursaal, Geneva, **2:**150
Thèâtre Municipal, Lausanne, **2:**150
Theatre Museum, London, **4:**163
Thèâtre Musical du Châtelet, Paris, **3:**53, 72, **6:**160, 191
Theatre of Angna Enters, The, **2:**516
Theatre of Chamber Dance, Vladivostok, **5:**474
Theatre of the Tuileries. *See* Salle des Machines
Theatre Omnibus, **3:**520
Theatre Piece, **1:**542, **4:**518, 605
Theatre Research Studies II, **2:**387

Theatre Royal, Hobart, Tasmania, **1:**205
Theatre Royal, Liverpool, **2:**85
Theatre Royal, London. *See* Drury Lane Theatre, London
Théâtre Royal de la Monnaie, Brussels, **1:**290, 292, 404, 406, 407, 410, 411, 412, **2:**111, **5:**147, 148, 149
Childs's debut as opera director, **2:**120
Hansen's *Coppélia,* **2:**200
Messerer teaching and choreography, **4:**359
Morris directorship, **4:**471
Theatre Street (Karsavina), **2:**382, **3:**655
theatrical dance. *See under specific countries; specific dances*
Theft, **4:***238*
Theilade, Nini, **1:**296, 539, **3:**657, **4:**656, **5:**391, 430, 553
Théleur, E. A., **1:**331, 333, 345, 346, **4:**685, *686,* **5:**201, 202, 207, 226, **6:**126–127
Theme and Variations, **1:**38, 256, **4:**271
Alonso (Alicia) and Youskevitch partnership, **1:**49, 67
American Ballet Theatre, **1:**68, *371*
Balanchine choreography, **1:**256
Balanchine revival, **1:**256
double *rond de jambe en l'air,* **5:**402
double *tours en l'air,* **1:**338
Fernandez performance, **2:**586
in Grands Ballets Canadiens repertory, **3:**231, *231*
Kirkland performance, **4:**24
Maryinsky staging, **2:**578, **4:**284, 285
Nichols performance, **4:**623, 631
Youskevitch performance, **6:**425
Theobald, Lewis, **5:**350, **6:**373
Theocritus, **5:**112
Theodora, empress of Rome, **4:**427
Theodorakis, Miskis (Miskis, Michel), **2:**266, **3:**299, **6:***120*
Theodore, Lee, **1:**419
Théodore, Mademoiselle. *See* Douvillier, Suzanne
Theogony (Hesiod), **6:**144
Theolinda, **4:**443
Théolinde l'Orpheline, **5:**500–501
Théonis et Zélinde, **3:**353
Théorie de la gymnastique de la danse théâtrale (Adice), **1:**8, **6:**127
Theory and Practice of Allegro in Classical Ballet, The (Craske), **2:**268, **6:**128
therapy. *See* body therapies; dance and movement therapy; *specific types*
There Goes the Bride (film), **4:**335
There Is a Cliff Over There, **4:**52
There Is a Time, **1:**519, **3:**232, 391, **4:**39, 198, **6:**43
Theresa, the Orphan of Geneva, **5:**404
Thérèse, Mademoiselle (Schmidt), **1:**205, 206
There's No Business Like Show Business (film), **2:**615
Therrien, Cheryl, **5:**17
thés dansants. See tea dance
These Charming Sounds, **1:**493, **6:**314
Thésée, **3:**329, **4:**107, 235, **5:**34, 39, 105

Thésée en Crète, **4**:174
Thésée et Ariane, **1**:88, **2**:465
Theseus (mythic), **4**:106
Thesmar, Ghislaine, **2**:199, **4**:107, 108, **5**:94, 97, **6**:58
Thespis, **2**:159, **5**:556
Thétis et Pélée, **1**:202, **2**:465, **4**:109, 152, **5**:160, **6**:46
They Seek after the Sun, **2**:155
They Too Are Exiles, **3**:370
They Who Are Not Named, **4**:272
Thibault de Courville, Joachim. *See* Courville, Joachim Thibault de
Thibon, Nanon, **5**:95
Thieben, Carletto, **1**:534
Thief Who Loved a Ghost, The, **1**:69
Thieme, Otto, **5**:278
Thierry, Joseph, **2**:206
Thierry, Louis, **5**:195, 215, **6**:364
Thieves (musical), **1**:419
Thimey, Erika, **2**:69, 574, **4**:212
Thin Ice (film), **3**:357
Thinking Body, The (Todd), **1**:470, **4**:17, 441
3rd Rotation, **1**:141
Third Dancers' Congress, Munich, **6**:393
Third Symphony (van Dyk ballet), **2**:471
Third Symphony of Gustav Mahler, The (Neumeier ballet), **4**:603, 604
Third Time Painting (Rauschenberg), **1**:140
Thiriet, Maurice, **2**:351
Thirteen (Charlip and Joyner), **2**:111
30–30, **4**:391
Thirty Year's Musical Recollections (Chorley), **3**:284
This Year of Grace (Coward), **4**:334
Thom, Brigitte, **5**:54
Thomajohn, Dale, **2**:109
Thomas, Allan, **4**:629
Thomas, Eddy, **3**:574, 575
Thomas, Emma Lewis, *as contributor*, **1**:428
Thomas, Richard, **2**:583, **5**:439, **6**:151
Thomas, Robert, **1**:291
Thomasson, Helgi, **2**:385
Thomas Aquinas, Saint, **1**:21
Thomasen, Elvind, **2**:330
Thomee, Eeke, **4**:598
Thompson, Anne, **1**:218
Thompson, Betty Lynd, **1**:421
Thompson, Clive, **1**:56, **3**:219, 574
Thompson, Ella, **1**:56
Thompson, Frank, **1**:74, **2**:245
Thompson, Liz, **3**:571
Thompson, Lydia, **2**:572, **6**:267
Thompson, Norman, **2**:161
Thompson, Robert Farris, **1**:15, **2**:602, **4**:289, **6**:25, 422
Thompson, Sada, **1**:419
Thompson, Ulysses ("Slow Kid"), **6**:317
Thompson, William, **5**:61
Thompson annual collection, **1**:92
Thompson-Drewal, Margaret, **1**:14, **6**:24, 25
as contributor, **4**:286–294, **6**:24–26, 422–424
Thomsen, Paul Arnt, **2**:245
Thomson, Virgil, **1**:280, **2**:196, 197, 374, **5**:526, 527
on Ballets 1933, **1**:307
Cage relationship, **2**:22
Filling Station score, **2**:160, **4**:518, **6**:247

Four Saints in Three Acts, **1**:147, **4**:436, **6**:278
Kirstein association, **4**:27
Thor, Janine van, **4**:600
Thoreaux, Thérèse, **1**:350
Thoresen, Otto, **5**:406
Thornton, Asa, **2**:581
Thornwaite, J., **5**:86
Thorp, Jennifer, *as contributor*, **3**:521–523, **5**:251–252, **6**:175–176, 251–252
Thorpe, Edward, *as contributor*, **4**:239–245
Thorpe, Jonathan, **4**:667
Thorsteinsson, Bjarni, **3**:436
Thorthwaite, J., **6**:332
Thorvaldsen, **4**:118
Thorvaldsen, Bertel, **1**:508
Those Loved by the Sun, **3**:329, **4**:266
Thoss, Stefan, **1**:391, **3**:156, **6**:10
Thought in the Night, A, **6**:145
Thoughts out of Season, **4**:214
Thousand and One Nights, A. See Schéhérazade
Thousands Cheer (film), **2**:108
Thousand Times Neigh!, A (World's Fair show), **1**:280, **4**:246
Thrace, **2**:7, 9, **3**:296, **5**:382
Threads, **5**:408
Three Arts Ballet, **3**:62
Three Belts, or The Russian Cinderella, **3**:192, **5**:454
Three Cards, The (film), **6**:171
Three-Cornered Hat, The. See Tricorne, Le
Three Dances (film dance), **2**:605
Three Epitaphs, **6**:107, 108, 110, **164–166**
Three Fat Men, **1**:490, **4**:148, 444
Three Gershwin Preludes, **5**:602
Three Girdles, or The Russian Cinderella, **3**:192, **5**:454
Three Gopi Maidens, **3**:211
Three Graces (Canova), **1**:126
Three Graces, The (Baillie), **5**:89
Three Italian Comedians (Callot), **2**:27
Three Ivans dance (*Sleeping Beauty*), **5**:611, 612
Three Jumps, **5**:287
Three Latin American Sketches (Copland), **2**:197
Three Little Words (film), **1**:194–195, **6**:101
Three Musketeers, The, **1**:234, 518, **3**:13, 623, **5**:600, **6**:379
Three Musketeers, The (Friml musical), **6**:274
Three Palms, The. See Seven Daughters of the Mountain King
Three Parables, **2**:480
Threepenny Opera, The (Brecht and Weill), **1**:441, **2**:499
Three Pieces for Solo Clarinet, **6**:363
Three Poems of the East, **3**:384
Three Preludes, **3**:389
Three Seascapes, **4**:519
Three Songs for One, **2**:367
Three Steles, **6**:433
Three Step (*Shipwreck*), **2**:576
3 × 3, **5**:363
Three Virgins and a Devil, **1**:112, **2**:373, 373, **3**:10, **4**:227, **5**:359, **6**:278
Three Wise Fools (film), **2**:108
Three Wishes for Jamie (musical), **4**:228
Threshold, **1**:233
Through Interior Worlds, **5**:51

Through Me Many Voices, **4**:22
Through the Bamboo Curtain (Grey), **3**:307
Through the Crystal Ball (television series), **6**:137
Thrymskvilden. See Lay of Thrym, The
Thunderbird, **3**:21–22
Thundermove, **5**:683
Thurber, James, **3**:401, **6**:376
Thuren, Hjalmar, **2**:384, 565
Thurmond, John, **5**:518, **6**:373
Thurston, Doris, **6**:164
"Tiajuana" Pete, **5**:601
Tian, Talia, **5**:477
Tianjin Ballet, **2**:146
Tibbett, Lawrence, **5**:256
Tibbs, Gerald, **4**:602
Tiberius, **5**:74
Tibet, **1**:443, **5**:599, **6**:166–170**
Black Hat Dance, **1**:458–459
costume, **1**:458, **2**:221
totem dances, **2**:139
Tibetan Religious Dances (Nebesky-Wojkowitz), **1**:458
Tibetans (people), **2**:139, 141, **5**:598–599
Tibol, Raquel, **4**:399
ticumbis, **1**:526
Tidboald, David, **2**:57, **5**:57
Tiempo Azul, **2**:110
Tiepolo, Giambattista, **2**:191
Tiepolo, Giovanni Domenico, **4**:315
Tietböhl, Volker, **3**:155
Tiffany, Jackson, **2**:606
Tiffany, Louis, **4**:189, **5**:493
Tiger Balm, **1**:51
Tiger Lily, **5**:81
tightrope performers. *See* ropedancing
tights (practice clothes), **5**:240–241, 242, 243
Tigré (people), **2**:530, 531, 532, 533
Tigua dance, **4**:329, 330, 551, 554, 563, 565, **6**:170
Tihai, **5**:597
Tiina, **2**:529
tiiroo dance, **2**:629
Tiitinen, Sakari, **2**:634
Ti-Jean, **2**:151
Tikar (people), **2**:32, 33
Tikhomirov, Vasily, **2**:436, 579, **5**:331, **6**:170–171**
Bayadère, La, **1**:393
Bolshoi Ballet, **1**:487, 488–489, **3**:207, 633, **5**:456, 458
Corsaire, Le, **2**:208
Esmeralda, La, **2**:524, **3**:186
Gabovich association, **3**:99
Geltser dance partnership, **3**:128, 204
Latvian ballet, **4**:127
Moscow ballet school, **5**:480
Red Poppy, The, **3**:128, 187, **5**:567
Sleeping Beauty revival, **5**:610
students, **1**:489, **4**:62, **6**:348
Tikhonov, Vladimir, **2**:136, **5**:205, **6**:420
Tikkanen, Matti, **2**:633
tikkuristi dance, **2**:630
Tikopia, **1**:416
Tileston, Nathaniel, **5**:187
tillānā, **1**:442
Tiller, John, **4**:520, **5**:246, 290, **6**:268, 273
Tiller Girls, **4**:24, 520, 524, **5**:289–290, **6**:268, 273, 273, 448
Tiller in the Fields, The, **1**:75, **4**:24, **6**:202
Tillers of the Soil, **5**:494, 497, 587

Till Eulenspiegel
Babilée choreography, **1**:251, 306
Balanchine production. *See Tyl Ulenspiegel*
Elizariev choreography, **1**:408, **2**:502, **4**:36, **5**:461
Köhler-Richter staging, **3**:154
Leventhal design, **4**:154
Mlakar staging, **6**:432
Nijinsky choreography, **1**:322, **2**:463, **4**:645, 647
Panov choreography, **5**:422
Schläpfer performance, **1**:375
Sokolova performance, **5**:637
Yakobson choreography, **6**:410
Till the Clouds Roll By (film), **2**:108
Timaeus (Plato), **1**:2
Tímár, Sándor, **1**:308, **3**:406
Timbuktu (musical), **6**:285
Time and Ebb, **5**:51
Time Cycle, **3**:42, **5**:597
Time In, **3**:578
Time of Parting, A, **2**:58
Time of Snow, **5**:407
Time of Your Life, The (film), **2**:245
Time of Your Life, The (musical), **4**:2
Time Out, **2**:460, **3**:578
Time out of Mind, **3**:342, 610, 611
time rhythm (Laban concept), **4**:99
time step, **6**:98
Time Table, **1**:281, **2**:196, **4**:63, 608, **6**:198, 200
Timme, Elisaveta, **3**:15
Timofeyeva, Avdotia, **5**:451
Timofeyeva, Nina, **4**:129, **5**:459, 567, **6**:171, 227
Grigorovich ballets, **1**:492, 493, **3**:310
Leningrad training, **1**:493
Spartacus, **5**:677
Timon of Athens (Shakespeare), **3**:253
"Timonya," **6**:303
Timotheus, **2**:419
Timoyko, Noanim, **6**:94
Timur and His Team, **5**:471
Tinge, **4**:594
Tinggian (people), **5**:168
Tinguely, Jean, **1**:305, **3**:619, **5**:314
tinikling, **2**:231, **6**:172
Tin Pan Alley (film), **2**:615
Tin Soldier, The, **1**:201
Tiomkin, Dimitri, **5**:310
Tiongson, Nicanor, **5**:174
Tippet, Clark, **1**:73
Tippett, Michael, **1**:52, **3**:621, **5**:37
Tippoo-Saeb, **6**:70
Tip Toes (musical), **5**:602
Tipton, Jennifer, **2**:441, 526, **4**:190, **5**:128, 394, **6**:112, 153
as contributor, **4**:192–197
lighting design, **4**:191
Musical Offering lighting, **4**:482
on performance spaces, **6**:163
Rudner collaboration, **5**:440
tirana, **1**:479
tirasila (curtain), **1**:170
Tired Death, **4**:59
Tiresias, **1**:152–153, **3**:44, **4**:115, 517
Tirsi e Clori, **4**:505, 506, 518–582
Tirtza Hodes, **3**:530
Tiruray (people), **5**:168
Tishchenko, Boris, **5**:468, **6**:342, 411
Tis Maria, **3**:298
'Tis Goodly Sport, **4**:625
'Tis Pity She's a Whore, **3**:52
Titan (Laban choral work), **4**:91, 476

Titani, I, **5:**517, 528, **6:**339
Titanic (musical), **6:**289
Titenia (vaudeville performer), **6:**318
Titl, Anton Emil, **6:**335
Tito, 1:88
Titus, Antoine, 1:86, 237, 477, **2:**502, **3:**144–145, **4:**280
Giselle staging, **3:**181, **4:**280, **5:**454
Swiss Milkmaid stagings, **6:**50–51
Sylphide staging, **5:**454, **6:**58
Titus Feuerfuchs, **3:**340
Tiv dance, **6:**172–174, 383
Tivoli Gardens Pantomime Theater, Copenhagen, 1:539
ballet performances, **2:**385
Carey family, **2:**60, 385
commedia dell'arte, **2:**384, 385, **5:**423
founding, **2:**385
Larsen choreography, **4:**126
Madsen, Egon, **4:**245
Tivum, Erik U., *as contributor,* **4:**126–128
Tiwi (people), 1:219–220, **224–225**
Tiyyāṭiyāṭṭam, **3:**453
Tjoddansafelag Reykjavikur, **3:**435
Tkachenko, Tamara, **5:**480
Tkanova, Nina, **3:**82
Tleubaev, M., **3:**665
Tlingit (people), **4:**570, 572–573
Toaduff, Jackie, **5:**695
To a Young Dancer (de Mille), **2:**374
TOBA (Theater Owners' Booking Association), **6:**99, 256
Tobias, Roy, 1:*30,* **2:**420, **5:***360*
Tobias, Tobi, 1:513, **2:**387, **5:**108, 131–132
Tobi-za, **3:**388
Tobo Batak dance, **3:***501*
"TOBY-Time," **6:**256
"Toccata" (*Come and Get the Beauty of It Hot*), 1:395
Toccata and Fugue, **2:**4
točivé, **2:***303*
"to dance by the book" (construction method), **2:**592
Todaro, Antonio, **6:**93
Todd, Mabel Elsworth, 1:469, *470,* 475, 476, **3:**349, **4:**16–17, 441
Todd, Michael, **6:**276, 281
Todorović, andjela, **6:***434,* 435
toe dance (Georgian), **3:***133,* 134
toe shoes. *See* pointe work, shoes
tōgaku, 1:168, **2:***5,* 6, **3:**103–103
Tōgan Boto, **3:**653
Togo, **4:**290
Toguri, David, **4:**667
Tōhō Gekidan (*kabuki* troupe), **3:**439, **4:**334
Tohoku Kabuk Keikaku, **3:**363
Tohvelmann, Helmi, **2:**529, *529*
Toilette de Vénus, La, **4:**697
Toin Kai troupe, **3:**590
Toison d'Or, La, **3:**66
Toissant, Auguste, 1:532
To José Clemente Orozco, 1:*55,* **3:**387
tokiwazu style, **3:**90, 639
Toklas, Alice B., **6:**375
Tokombayeva, Aisulu, **4:**87
Tokugawa family, **4:**85
Tokugawa Ieyasu, **3:**581
Tokugawa shogunate, **2:**215, 217, **3:**581, 637, 638, 650, **4:**30
Tokyo Ballet, 1:406, **2:**388, **3:**428, 589
Tokyo Ballet School, **3:**589
Tokyo City Ballet, **3:**589
Tokyo Conservatory, 1:362

Tokyo Dance Theater, **3:**523
Toláda Dance Company, **3:**156
Toledo, Mariana, 1:*536*
Toller, Ernst, **2:**397
Tolman, Beth, **6:**247
Tolstoy, Leo, 1:24, **2:**464, **3:**135
Tolv med Posten, **5:**294, 353
Tolzer, Johanna, **4:**64
Tomalonis, Alexandra, **6:**297
Tomaquog Museum, Ashaway, Rhode Island, **4:**555
Tomari Matir Kanya, **2:**102, **3:**468
Tomasson, Helgi, **2:**201, **3:**342, 437, 610, **6:**174–175
choreographies, **6:**266
New York City Ballet, **4:**609, 620, 621, 623
San Francisco Ballet, **5:***512,* 513–514, **6:**265
Sleeping Beauty production, **5:**613
Worsaae design collaborations, **6:**404–405
Tomaszewski, Henryk, **2:**470, **5:**218, **6:**175
Tomayo, Aleida, **2:***63*
tombé, 1:343
Tombeau (Béjart; 1973), 1:292
Tombeau de Couperin, Le (Balanchine), 1:326
Tombeau de Couperin, Le (Ravel), **5:**316
Tombeaux (Bintley; 1993), 1:453, 454
Tombi, Chao, **3:**468
Tomc, Alenka, **6:**439
Tomijūrō. *See* Nakamura Tomijūrō
Tomita Makiko, **3:**579
Tomkins, Calvin, **2:**287, **5:**314
Tomko, Linda J., *as contributor,* **5:**326–330
Tomlinson, Ernest, **4:**667
Tomlinson, Kellom, **2:**51, 80, 81, 337, 338, **6:**123, **175–176**
dance manual authorship, 1:342, **3:**256, 281, **4:**105, 431, 629, 684, **5:**324, 346, *520,* **6:**123, 175–176
on galliard, **3:**109
L'Abbé dances, **4:**105
on minuet, **4:**431, 432, 433
notation, **4:**684
on *révérence* (Honours), **5:**346
on sarabande, **5:***520*
Tomlinson, Mel, **2:**334, *334,* **6:**260
Tommasini, Vincenzo, 1:149, **6:**5
Tommy (rock opera), **2:**39, **3:**230, *232,* **4:**576, **6:**288
Tomo Yakko, **3:**593
Tompkins, Beatrice, **3:**57, *609,* 610, *611*
Toms, Carl, **2:**511, **6:***33*
Tom Sawyer, **2:**585
Tomsky, Aleksandr, **6:**306
Tom Thumb (pantomime), **5:**71–72
Tona, La, **3:**10
tonal portraits, **5:**526
Tonantzintla, **4:**393
Tondokusumo, Raden Mas Hario, **3:**498, 498–499
Tone, Yasunao, **2:**289
Tonga, **2:**593, **4:**495–496, 628, 629, **5:**225, **6:**176–178
Tonight and Every Night (film), **2:**616
"Tonight at the Mardi Gras" (*Louisiana Purchase*), **6:**450
Tonight the Ballet (Stokes), **3:**285
Tonight We Sing (film), **6:**183
Tonin, Boris, **2:**109

Tonkin, Fiona, 1:211, 235
tonnelet, **2:***236,* 238
Toodle-oo (dance), **6:**318
Too Many Girls (musical), **3:**654
Toorn, Pieter van den, **6:**4
Tootikian, Karoun, 1:*122*
Topaz, Muriel, **4:**96, *97*
topéng, 1:174, **2:**232, **3:***486,* **486–488,** *487,* 501–502, *502*
Kakul, I Nyoman, **3:**645
mask, **3:***476, 486, 487,* **4:**297–298, *297*
topéng barangan, **3:**498, 501, 502
topéng dalang. See wayang topéng
topéng pajegan, **3:**488
Topham, John, **6:**175
Top Hat (film), **2:**614
Toporkov, Afanasy, **5:**451
Toppe, Andris, 1:*210,* **3:**3
Top Speed (film), **5:**372
Torah, **3:**526
tordiglione. See tordion
"Tordiglione, Il," **4:**580, 582
tordion, **2:**74, **3:**108, 109, **5:**506, 620, **6:**178–179
Tordis, Ellinor, 1:239
Toreador, The (*Toreadoren*), 1:*10,* 408, 497, *505,* 511, 514, **2:**521, **3:**13, 373, **4:**126, **5:**425
Nielsen performance, **4:**631, 632
Royal Swedish Ballet mounting, **4:**60
Torelli, Antonia, **5:**404
Torelli, Giacomo, 1:287, 426, **4:**188, **5:***534,* 535, 536, **6:**157
torém, 1:530
Torenbosch, Chris, **2:**470
torero, el, **5:**133
Tori, Rita, **4:**676
Toribeyama Shinjū, **3:**439, **4:**533
"Torito, El" (dance drama), **5:**67
Toritos, Los, **3:**319
Torke, Michael, **4:**275, 622
Tormis, Lea, *as contributor,* **2:**527–530
Torn Curtain (film), **6:**183
torneo. See barriera, torneo, and battaglia
"Torneo Amoroso," 1:369
Torniai, Renato, **3:**541
Toronto, Canada, **2:**38–45, 47, 48, **4:**166, 553–539
See also National Ballet of Canada
Toronto Dance Theatre, **2:**40, 44, 47
House, Christopher, **3:**388–389
Kudelka choreography, **4:**72, 73
Toronto Independent Dance Enterprise, **2:**40
Toropchenova, Maria, **5:***476*
Torp, Lisbet, **2:**386–387
as contributor, **2:**99–102
Torres Strait Islanders. *See* Australian Aboriginal dance
Torse, **2:**293, 294, **4:**37
tor-tor, **3:**500
Torvill, Jayne. *See* Torvill and Dean
Torvill and Dean, **3:**432, 433, *433,* **6:**179–181
Murphy (Graeme) choreography, **4:**479
Tosar, Héctor, **6:**301
Toscanini, Arturo, **2:**84, **3:**50, 529, 553, **5:**529, 561
Toscanini, Walter, **3:**51
Toschi, Andrea, **3:**557
Toschi, Mónica, 1:*113*
Toschi, Paolo, **2:**188

Tossed as It Is Untroubled, **5:**18
Toss Quintet, **3:**388
Tosti, Kenneth, **4:**482
Total Eclipse, **5:***655*
Total Theater, **6:**162, *162*
Totem, **2:**247, 605, **3:**329, **4:**266, 650
Totem (film), **2:**605
Totem Ancestor, **2:**285
totemism, **2:**139
Australian Aboriginal dance, 1:221, *222,* 226, 227–229
Native American dance, **4:**550
"Totem Tom-Tom" (*Rose-Marie*), **7:**273
Totenklage, **3:***147*
Totenmal, Das, **3:**369, **6:**393
Totentanz. See Dance of Death
Totentanz (Wigman dance). *See* Dance of Death
Tóth, Karol, **5:**614
Tóth, László, *as photographer,* **3:**416
Tóth, Sándor, 1:307, 308, **2:**473
To the Dance, **2:**580, **3:**401
To the Plitvice Lakes, **6:**431
Totto, Alejandro, 1:111
Touch and Go (musical), **6:**90
Touchbase, **2:**294–295, 296, **3:**274, **5:**305
Touissant, Caroline and Jean, 1:110
Toulouse-Lautrec, Henri de, **5:**191, 260–262, **6:**181–182
apache dancer depictions, 1:95
lithographs of Fuller (Loie), 1:129, **3:**71, 92, **5:**261, **6:**181
poster, 1:*129*
Toulouze, Michel, 1:378, **4:**501, **5:**336, 343, **6:**122
Toumanova, Tamara, 1:*8,* 207, **5:**17, 96, 248, **6:**65, **182–183,** 353
Ballet Russe de Monte Carlo, 1:*295,* 296
Ballets 1933, 1:307, 309, **3:**72
Ballets Russes de Monte Carlo, 1:*308, 309,* 310, 311, 312, 314, 367, **4:**33, **5:**349
Cotillon, **2:**253–254
Denby profile of, **2:**375
English National Ballet guest performances, **2:**508
film *Invitation to the Dance* performance, **4:**3
Giselle performance, **4:**110
Grand Ballet du Marquis de Cuevas guest appearance, **3:**226
Kochno collaboration, **4:**33
Phèdre, **2:**351, **4:**185
San Francisco Ballet guest appearances, **5:**512
Toumine, Lorne, **3:***232*
Toumine, Nesta, **2:**38, 47
Toumine, Sviatoslav, 1:*296*
Tour: Dedicated to Dinosaurs, **5:**549
Tour in Ireland, A (Young), **3:**516
Tournachon, Adrien, **5:**176
Tournachon, Félix. *See* Nadar
tournaments. *See barriera, torneo, and battaglia*
Tourniaire, Louise and Adelheid, **2:**176
Touron, Patrice, 1:292, **3:**578
tour piqué or *tour posé. See* piqué turns
tours. See ballet technique, turning movements
tours chaînes déboulés, 1:337
tours déboulés, 1:347
tours en l'air, 1:336, **338,** 341, **5:**402

Tout Satie, **3:**75
Toverfluit, De, **5:**618
tovil, **2:**228, *229,* **4:***300,* **6:183–184**
Toward the Light, **6:**88
Tower, The, **3:**445, 619, **5:**313
Towlandson, Thomas, **2:**401
Town, Harold, **6:***1*
Towson State University, **2:**423
Toye, Geoffrey, **2:**400, **3:**354
Toye, Wendy, **3:**87, 174, **4:**268
toyi-toyi dance, **5:**648
Toyne, Gabriel, **3:**354
Toyotomi Hideyoshi, **3:**388, 650, **4:**30, 41
Tozzi, Antonio, **2:**55
Tozzi, Lorenzo, **3:**555, 557
Traces, **3:**3350
Tracey, Andrew, **5:**661
Tracey, Hugh, **2:**602, **5:**661
Tracey, Margaret, **4:**623
Trackers, **2:**296, **4:**37
Tracks (Australian dance project), **1:**216
Tracy, Martin, **4:**17
Tracy, Michael, **5:**194, *194*
Tracy, Robert, *as contributor,* **3:**620–621
Traczewski, Włodzimierz, **5:***217*
Tradimento Punito, Il, **2:**55
Traditional Balinese Culture (Belo), **3:**506
traditional dance. *See* European traditional dance; folk dance history; methodologies in the study of dance, ethnology; *under specific countries*
Traetta, Tommaso, **1:**87
Traffic in Souls, **2:**396
Trafieri, Giuseppe, **1:**237, **3:**175
Tragédie à Verone, Une, **5:**605
Tragédie de Salomé, La, **2:**351, **3:**94, 320, **5:**95, 391
    Soudeikine design, **5:**642
    Spessivtseva performance, **5:**678
tragédie en ballet. See ballet d'action
tragédie en musique. See opera-ballet and *tragédie lyrique*
tragedy (Greek drama), **2:**158, **3:**399, **4:**301
tragedy (Roman drama), **5:**375
Tragedy of Fashion, A, **1:**145, 437, **2:**582, **3:**263, **5:**296, 298, *298*
Tragedy of Romeo and Juliet, The (Tudor ballet), **5:***546*
Trager, Philip, **5:**187
Tragic Exodus, **3:**370, **4:**130
Tragic Patterns—Three Choric Dances for an Antique Greek Tragedy, **3:**212, 384
Trăilescu, Cornel, **2:**343
Trailine, Hélène, **1:**306, 404, **3:**74, 75
Trail of Tears, **4:**558
Train Bleu, Le, **1:**323, 325, **2:**71, 183, **4:**61, **5:**192
    Dolin performance, **2:**423
    Georgi and Kreutzberg collaboration, **3:**132
    Milhaud score, **4:**418, 515
    Nijinska choreograpy, **4:**634, *637*
    Nijinska performance, **4:**635
    Sokolova role, **5:**637
    Woizikowski performance, **6:**404
Trainor, Jimmy, **5:**602
Trainor, Susan, **4:**627
Trait d'Union, Un (film), **2:**611
Traité (Josson), **3:**125
Traité (Malpied), **6:**123
Traité de la danse (Giraudet), **6:**128
Traité de la danse académique (Lifar), **1:**348

Traité des études (Rollin), **1:**284
Traité élémentaire, théorique et pratique de l'art de la danse (Blasis), **1:**100, 197–198, 328, 336, 344, 460, **2:**107, **6:**126
Traité sur l'art de la danse (Malpied), **1:**332–333
Traitor, The, **3:**391, **4:**198
Trancard, Nancy, **1:**237
Trance and Dance in Bali (film), **2:**601, **3:**506
trance dance, **3:**421, **5:**580, **6:**25, **184–188**
    Bali, **1:**174, 176, 178, **3:**473–474, 477, 479, 484, 492, **5:**356
    Brazil, **1:***528,* 529
    Central and East Africa, **2:**91–92
    flamenco *duende,* **3:**6
    Haitian Vodun, **5:**355–356
    Japan, **3:**583–584, 642
    Malaysia, **4:**249
    Myanmar, **4:**525
    Native American, **4:**550, 565
    South Africa, **5:**643
    Sri Lanka, **4:**300
    sub-Saharan Africa, **4:**290, **6:**12
    Sufi, **3:**524, 525
    West Africa, **6:**383, 423
    zār ceremony, **6:**444–445
    See also shamanism
Tranceformations, **5:***656*
Trangama-Fanga (radio play), **2:**313
Transcendence, **1:**64, **4:**27
transcendentalism, **2:**452, 453, **6:**235
Transfigured Night. See Verklärte Nacht
Transformation Dance, **2:**572, **6:**316
Transformations of Medusa, The, **2:**520
Transit, **1:**50, **3:**273
Transitory, **1:**462
Transkei Traditional Music Association, **5:**648
Translation of Nine of the Most Fashionable Quadrilles, A (Dun), **2:**257
Transposed Heads, **5:**521
transvestite performers, **4:**665
Transylvania, **1:**370, **2:**100, 101, **3:**410–411, 412, 412–413, 414, 422, **5:**379–380, 381, 382, 383
Trân Van Khê, *as contributor,* **6:**336–337
TrANZFORM, Stuttgart, **3:**157
Trápaga, Luis, **2:**276, 277
trapdance, **4:**546
Trapèze, Le, **5:**267
tráta, **2:**100
Trattato del ballo nobile (Dufort), **5:**324, **6:**123
Trattato teorico-prattico di ballo (Magri), **1:**197, 344, **2:**257, **3:**545, **4:**433, **6:**123, 124, 126
    Skeaping translation, **5:**604, **6:**48
Trauma, **1:**350
Traüme, **4:**1, **6:***136*
Travail et Culture, **3:**76, 83
Traveler of the Desert, **4:**267
Traveling Circus, **6:**412
Traveling Dancer-Actress, of the Three Sister-Brides, A (vaudeville act), **3:**549
traveling dance steps, **2:**100–101, 102
Travelogue, **2:**293, **4:**37, **5:**314
Travelogue Series, The, **4:**451

Travels in America (Dickens), **3:**633
Travels in Lower Hungary (Bright), **3:**409
Travers, Cathie, **1:**216
Travers, Cathie, **1:**216
travesty, **6:188–191**
    Ballets Russes de Serge Diaghilev ending tradition, **2:**408
    Coppélia role, **2:**199, 368
    Elssler (Thérèse) roles, **2:**502, 503
    masks, **4:**301
    Renaissance standard dance costume, **2:**235
    Turkish traditional dances, **6:**210–211
    women's nineteenth-century costume, **2:**241
    See also onnagata
Traviata, La (Verdi), **1:**406, **4:**339, **5:**512
Travolta, John, **2:**620, **5:**186, *186*
Trayectodanza, Caracas, **4:**171
Treacher, Arthur, **6:**142
Tread, **2:**292, **3:**620, **5:**548
Treading, **1:**59
Treatise on the Art of Dancing, A (Gallini), **3:**111, 378, 546
Treatise on Theatres (Saunders), **4:**189
Tree Grows in Brooklyn, A (musical), **5:**408
Treemonisha (Joplin), **2:**459
Trefilova, Vera, **1:**427, **2:**82, 597, **5:**279, **6:**191
    Diaghilev's *Sleeping Beauty,* **2:**409
    Haskell monograph on, **3:**285
    Maryinsky Ballet, **3:**655, **4:**282, 639, **5:**486
    Paris dance studio, **3:**82
    Sleeping Beauty performance, **5:**611
    students, **2:**341, **3:**391, **4:**110, 182, **5:**603, **6:**352
    Svetlov marriage, **6:**28
Tregubov, N. I., **5:***472*
Treize Dances, **1:**306
Treman, Robert E., **2:**80
Treize Dances, **1:**306
Treman, Robert E., **2:**80
Trend, **1:**421, 441, **3:**369–370, *370,* **4:**130, **6:**162, **191–192**
Trend: Return to Native, **5:**172
Trénis, La (figure), **2:**592
Trentin, Giovanna, **2:**177, **3:**556, 557
Trepak, **4:**460
Trepykhalin, Yuri, **5:***466*
Tres, **6:**323
tresca, **4:**348
Tres Pascualas, Las, **2:**124
Trespass, **2:**355
Tre Sultane, Le, **3:**359
Trevaskis, Cherie, **1:**391
Trevor, Ted (English Ted), **6:**318
Trevor, Walter, **4:**624
Trévoux, Carole, **3:**85
Triad, **4:**243
Triadic Ballet: Figurines in Space, **1:**134, 385–386, *385,* 387
    archival materials, **4:**161
    Bohner staging, **3:**151
    costumes, **6:**392
    masks, **4:**302
    Schlemmer design, **5:**546
    Stuttgart premiere, **6:**9
Trial, J.-C., **2:**352
Triana, **1:**115, **3:**198
Triana, Antonio de, **1:**117
Triangle Dance, **6:**88
"Tribal [Savage] Rites" (skating program), **6:**180
Tribute (Franklin work), **1:**301, **3:**88
Tribute, The (Morrice work), **4:**469

"Tribute to Fred and Ginger" (skating program), **6:**180
"Tribute to John Lennon" (skating program), **6:**180
Trickster Coyote, **3:**349, **4:***303*
Tricorne, Le, **1:**67, 93, 117, *295,* 310, 322, 323, 326, **2:**15, 506, **5:**192, 674, **6:192–193**
    Argentinita and Massine performances, **4:***323*
    in English National Ballet repertory, **2:**512
    Falla score, **2:**408, 409, 567, **4:**515
    Fonteyn performance, **3:**44
    Gades choreography and performance, **3:**101
    Harangozó productions, **3:**415
    Idzikowski performance, **3:**441
    Joffrey revival, **3:**614
    Karsavina performance, **3:**656, **5:**636
    Massine choreography, **3:**319, **4:**317
    Massine production for Royal Ballet, **5:**415
    Massine revival, **4:**325
    Picasso design, **2:**409, 568
    Sokolova performance, **5:**636
    Spanish dances choreography, **2:**107, 108, 409
    Toumanova performance, **6:**183
    Turner performance, **6:**214
    vocal accompaniment, **2:**410
    Woizikowski performance, **6:**404
Triegaardt, Elizabeth, **2:**58, **5:***652*
Trieste, **3:**552
Trilby, **3:**237, **6:**58
Trillium, **1:**543, 545, **3:**445–446
Trilogie M.R., **4:**604
Trilogy, **2:***500*
Trimmer, Jon, **4:**625, *625, 626*
Trincheiras, Carlos, **5:**234, 235
Trinidad, **2:**62, 63, 65, **6:**185
Trinity, **1:***124,* **3:**612, 615
Trio A, **5:***292,* 293
Triofono di Afrodite (Orff), **5:**43
Trio for Saki, **4:**156
Trio in G Minor, **2:**309, *310*
Triomphe d'Alcide, Le, **4:**235
Triomphe de l'Amour, Le, **1:**288, *343,* 425, **2:**518, 519, **4:**108, 109, 235, **5:**40, 87, **6:**11
Triomphe de Minerve, **6:**157
Triomphe de Trajan, Le, **3:**119
Trionfo d'Amore, Il, **1:**236, **3:**365
trionfo della morte. See Dance of Death
Trionfo di Afrodite, **1:**390, **3:**230, 318, **5:**677
Trionfi di Petrarcha, I, **1:**292, 406
Trio Pericet, **5:**133
Trios (Ghanan dance company), **6:**20
Trip to Chinatown, A (musical), **6:**268, 270
Trip to Coontown, A (musical), **6:**255
tripudium, **3:**541, **4:**106, **6:193–195**
Trisha Brown Dance Company. *See* Brown, Trisha
Trisler, Joyce, **1:**55, 58, *59,* 459, **2:**367, **5:**586
    Dansecompany, **4:**306
    Horton Dance Theater, **3:**386, 387, **4:**441
Trissino, Giangiorgio, **1:**352
Tristan, **1:**69, 456, **2:**267, **3:**664
    Henze score, **3:**360, **4:**517

Tristan and Iseult (Darrell ballet), **2:**350
Tristan Fou, **3:**224, 226
Tristan und Isolde (Wagner), **1:**98
?Tristan und Isolde?, **4:**204
Tritsch-Tratsch, **2:**265, **5:***650*
Triumph des Frühlings, Der, **3:**365
Triumph of Death, The, **2:**245, **3:**12–13, *13*, 657, **5:**432, 511
Triumph of Love, The, **4:**127
Triumph of Neptune, The, **1:**437, **2:**342, **4:**33, **5:**637
Triumph of Peace, The (masque), **4:**309, 310
Triumph of Russia, or Russians in Paris, The, **5:**453
Triumph of St. Joan, The, **3:**218
Triumph of the Muses, The, **1:**485
Triumph of the Russians, or The Military Camp at Krasnoye, **3:**191
triumphs. *See* Renaissance fêtes and triumphs
Triumphs of the Prince d'Amour, The (Davenant), **4:**309
Trivelin, **1:**287
Trninić, Dušan, **4:***437*
Trobisch, Aleksandar, **6:**432
Trofimova, Natasha, **3:**318
Troika, **6:**412
Trois Gnossiennes (Satie), **4:**117, 452, **5:**525, 526
    Graham choreography, **3:***209*, 211
    Manen choreography, **2:***470*
    See also Monotones
Trois Grâces, Les (Lejeune lithograph), **2:**503, **3:**620
Trois Gymnopédies (Satie), **1:**156, **4:**452, **5:**525, 526
Trois Siècles de Danse a l'Opéra, **2:**351
Trois Valses Romantiques, **2:**254
Trojan Incident, **2:**580, **6:**88
Trojan Women, The (Euripides), **3:**652
Troldmandens Laerling. See Sorcerer's Apprentice, The
Trombone, Il (Negri sobriquet), **4:**579
Trommler, Birgitta, **3:**151
trompong (gong-chime), **4:**264
Trophy I (for Merce Cunningham) (Rauschenberg), **5:**314
Tropical Pas de Deux, **1:**49
Tropical Revue (musical), **2:**459, *459*
Tropicana, **1:**395
Tropics and Le Jazz Hot (musical), **2:**459
tropotianka, **3:**409
Tropp, Sven, **6:**41, 46
Trott (Deer-Hunting Dance), **2:**228
Trotta, Giovanna, **2:**427
trotto, **4:**348
Trottoir, **4:**594
Trouble in Tahiti (Bernstein), **1:**438
Trouhanova, Natalia, **1:**246, **3:**72, **5:**315
Troupe de Mademoiselle Églantine, La, **1:***129*
Troupe des Danseurs du Roi, **5:**198
Trovatore, Il (Verdi), **1:**306, **2:**282, **4:**514, **5:**36
Troyan, Yuri, **1:**408
Troy Game, **2:**334, **3:**273, **4:**218, **5:**376
Truckin', **6:**262
Trudel, Jean, **2:**36
Truglia, Lucia, **2:**513, **3:***551*, **5:**401

Truitte, James, **1:***56*, 57, 212, 215, **2:**358, **3:***387*, **4:**441
Trujillo, Teresa, **6:**302
Trujillo Molina, Rafael, **2:**62, 431–432
TRUK Ballet. *See* PACT Ballet
Trumble, Tim, *as photographer*, **2:**323
Trümpy, Berthe, **1:**203, **3:**146, **5:**65, **6:***392*
Trunoff, Vassilie (also Vasily), **1:**208, 209, 499, **2:**512
Truth (Hodler), **1:**129
Truth about the Russian Dancers, The (Barrie), **4:**463
Truyol, Antonio, **1:**110
Truzzi, William, **2:**176
Truzzi's Circus, **2:**176
Trying Times, **1:**142, **3:**201
Tsao, Willy, **6:**415
Tsar Boris, **1:**518, **2:**423, **5:**461, 464, 468, 471
Tsar-Maiden, The. See Little Humpbacked Horse, The
Tschernischova, Elena, **1:**241
Tserenyaske, **4:**78
Tsigane, **2:**577
Tsimshian (people), **4:**470
Tsinguirides, Georgette, **2:**268
Tsintsadze, Sulkhan, **1:**38
tsiphteteli dance, **3:**299
tso, **2:**33
Tsoi, Svetlana, **5:**467
Tsonga (people). *See* Shangana-Tsonga dance
Tsou (people), **6:**80, *80*
Tsoukalas, Nicholas, **4:**120
Tsubouchi Shōyō, **3:**582, **4:**537
Tsuchigumo, **4:***31*, *296*
Tsuda Nobutoshi, **3:**590
Tsukimizato, **5:**591
Tsumbomi Kai study group, **4:**538
Tsunemasa, **3:**90, **4:***40*
Tsuneo Ishifuku, **3:**592
Tsuri-Gitsune, **4:**84, 660, 661
Tsuruya Nanboku IV, **5:**31
Tsvetaeva, Valeria, **5:**477
Tswa (people), **5:***663*
Tswana (people), **5:**643, 663
Tsygany, **5:**471
Tuareg (people), **1:**42, **4:**465, *468*, 665, 666
Tu Auras Nom Tristan, **2:**111
Tub, The, **4:**320
Tu be-Av, **3:**602
Tubin, Eduard, **2:**529
Tuccaro, Arcangelo, **4:**348
Tucker, Barbara, **5:***635*
Tucker, Earl ("Snake Hips"), **6:**263, *316*, 317
Tucker, Gregory, **1:**421
Tucker, Joan, **1:**316
Tucker, Richard, *as photographer*, **1:**257, 299
Tuckett, Wiliam, **2:**361
Tucson Swing, **5:**634
Tudor, Antony, **3:**285, 571, **5:**107, 564, 565, **6:195–203**
    American Ballet, **1:**281, **2:**269
    American Ballet Theatre, **1:**11, 65–68, 75, **3:**26
    Ashton comparison, **6:**195
    Australian Ballet, **1:**230, 233, 234
    Bluebeard performance, **3:**26
    Cecchetti as influence, **2:**84
    costumes, **2:**244, 245
    de Mille association, **2:**372–373
    film choreography, **2:**604
    Giselle, **1:**436
    Gloire, La, **1:**68, 402–403

Howard (Andrée) comparison, **3:**391
Icare, **1:**437
Josephslegende, Die, **3:**631, **6:**201
Juilliard dance division, **5:**561
Kaye association, **3:**663, 664, **4:**616
Kirkland roles, **4:**24
Labanotation of works, **3:**427
Laing collaboration, **4:**109–110
Leaves Are Fading, The, **4:**24
Lloyd roles, **4:**215
Markova roles, **4:**269
Metropolitan Opera Ballet School, **4:**381, 382
National Ballet of Canada guest choreography, **2:**37, 39, **4:**540–541, 547
New York Ballet guest choreography, **4:**29, 608
Offenbach in the Underworld, **3:**62, 614
psychological ballets, **6:**195
Rambert association, **1:**146, **3:**263, **5:**296, 298, 299, 300, **6:**195, 196, 197, *198*
Romeo and Juliet, **1:**67, 68, 437, **2:**376, **4:**110, 269, **5:**397–398, **397–398**, *546*
Royal Ballet guest choreography, **1:**155
Royal Danish Ballet guest productions, **5:**431
Royal Swedish Ballet productions, **5:**603, **6:**41, 42, *42*
Saddler roles, **5:**488
Schuman collaboration, **5:**561, 562
Shadowplay, **2:**444, **4:**24, **5:**417
students, **1:**48, 388, 542, **3:**61, 173, 577, **4:**271, **5:**602, **6:**107, 145, 362
Teatro Colón, **1:**110
television works, **6:**135, 196, 197
Tiller in the Fields, The, **1:**75, **4:**24
Time Table, **2:**196
Undertow, **1:**66, 68, **2:**376
van Praagh association, **6:**196, 197, *197*, 198, 312
Wilson (Sallie) association, **6:**401–402
    See also Dark Elegies; *Descent of Hebe, The*; *Jardin aux Lilas*; *Judgment of Paris, The*; *Pillar of Fire*
Tuerlings, Hans, **4:**596
Tuffin, Michael, **2:**57
Tufts University, **1:**473
Tugal, **3:**72
Tugearu, Ion, **5:**387, 389
Tugelov, Nurdin, **4:**87
Tukai, Gabdulla, **5:**595
Tukbulatova, Svetlana, **4:**87
Tukmanova, Arina, **6:**312
Tulaelis, Natacha (Cyd Charisse pseud.), **2:**108
Tulip of Haarlem, The
    as Cecchetti's Maryinsky debut performance, **2:**82
    Ivanov role in production, **1:**540, **2:**82, **3:**562
Tuljakova, Maria, **6:**432
Tullochgorm, **3:**247
Tullus Hostilius, king of Rome, **5:**377
Tulsa Ballet Theatre, **5:**60, **6:203–204**, 264, 292

Tulubieva, Sofia, **5:**470
tumba, **2:**61, 431
Tumbuka Dance Company, **5:**659
Tumsa Nahin Dekha (film), **2:**624
Tumulilingan, **1:**177, **4:**265
Tumulilingan Mengisep Sari, **4:**265, *265*
Tune, Tommy, **6:204–205**, 285–286, 287
tū ngārahu, **4:**261
Tunica (people), **4:**558
Tunisia, **4:***664*, **6:205–207**
Tunisian National Folklore Troupe, **4:***664*
Tunnellen, **4:**680
Tupin, Wassil, **1:**110
Tupine, Oleg, **1:**313, 315
Turandot (Gozzi ballet), **4:**60
Turandot (Puccini opera), **5:**246
Turangalia, **2:**471, 472
Turangalîla, **5:**97, 164, 320
Turbyfill, Mark, **2:**458
Turc Généreux, Le, **3:**365, 450
Turchi, Peregrino, **4:**390, 399
Turchi, Vincenzo, **2:**433
Turczynowicz, Konstancja, **5:**216, **6:**207
Turczynowicz, Roman, **5:**216, 217, **6:207–208**, 365
turdanser, **4:**671, 672
Tures, Les, **3:**188
Turfanda, Oytun, **6:**212
Turgenev, Ivan, **1:**157, **4:**457
Turgunbaeva, Mukarram, **4:**226, **6:**306, *306*
Turin, Italy, **2:**480, **3:**546, 552, 553, 556
Turjak, Zdenko, **5:**676
Turkana (people), **2:**86, 91
Turkestan. *See* Uzbekistan
Turkey, **6:208–213**
    as Algerian dance influence, **1:**41–42
    Byzantine music, **3:**295
    castanet counterpart, **2:**78
    dance education, **4:**110
    danse du ventre, **4:**409
    folk dance sounds, **3:**38
    Islamic dance aesthetics, **1:**18–19
    Kurdish dance, **4:**78–79
    musical traditions, **4:**489
    trance rituals, **6:**187
    whirling dervishes, **4:***410*, **5:**597–598, **6:**187, *208*, 209
    See also Ottoman (Turkish) tradition
Turkey Trot, **2:**25, **5:**627, 628, **6:**243, 255, 262, 270, 316
Turkish State Ballet, **2:**401, 403
Turkmenistan, **3:**513–514, **4:**224, **6:213**
Turkoman (people), **1:**27
Turnabout Theater, Hollywood, **3:**208
Turnbull, Colin M., *as contributor*, **4:**344
Turnbull, Julia, **5:**615, **6:**237
"turned-out body" principle, **1:**24
Turner, Harold, **2:**261, **6:213–214**
    Arts Theatre Ballet, **4:**153
    Baiser de la Fée performance, **1:**148
    Checkmate performance, **2:**115
    International Ballet, **3:**511
    Patineurs performance, **5:**113–114
    Rake's Progress role, **5:**293, 294, **6:**214
    Rambert association, **5:**296, 298
    Revelations performance, **5:**342
    Royal Ballet, **2:**443, **5:**300, 414

Turner, Joan, **2:**125
Turner, Victor, **5:**357, **6:**25
Turney, Matt, **1:**56, **2:**182, **3:**218, **5:**568
Turning Point, The (film), **1:**38, **3:**664, **4:**117, **5:**408, 597
Turning Shuffle, **5:**576
turnout, **1:**24, **3:***64*, **5:**402, **6:214–216**
attitude, **1:**198
history and aesthetics, **1:**344, **6:215–216**
physical mechanics, **6:214–215**
turns. *See* ballet technique, turning movements
Turocy, Catherine, **6:**251, 298
Turos, Judith, **1:**391
Turpio, Lucius Ambivius, **5:**375
Turquoisette, or A Study in Blue, **1:**206–207
Turska, Irena, **5:**221
Turtle (break dance move), **6:***263*
Turtle's Walk, **2:**530
Turu (people), **2:**91
Turuh, Ida Bagus Kakiang, **3:**644
turundus, **1:**526
Tuskegee Institute, **6:**258
Tutankhamun, king of Egypt, **2:**569
Tutelo (people), **4:**551
Tuteur Trompé, Le, **2:**107, **4:**149
Tutor, The (Roman play), **4:**426
Tutore Sorpresa, Il, **1:**88
Tutsi (Watusi; people), **2:**86, 90, *90,* 212, **4:**365, **6:***20*
Tutti Coreografi, **5:**409
Tutto Liscio, **4:**596
tutu, **2:***243,* **6:216–217**
classical vs. romantic, **2:**244
earliest prototype, **2:**239, 241, 244
Karinska design, **3:***654*
Lami missing sketch, **4:**116
Lecomte (Hippolyte) progenitor, **4:**138
musical comedy adaptation, **2:**250
as practice outfit, **5:**241, 242
Romantic, **5:**241, **6:**161, 216–217
Sylphide, La, **6:**57, *57, 58*
Sylphides, Les, **6:**60
types described, **2:**392–393
Tuvia, Ovadia, **3:**449, **4:**155
Tuzer, Tanju, **3:**344
Tüzün, Ferit, **2:**401, **6:**212
TVA (Canadian televison network), **6:**132
Tverskoi, Michel, **6:**119
TV5 (cable network), **6:**133
TVOntario (cable network), **6:**132, 133
TV Reel (film and live dance), **2:**608
twosomes (Scottish couples dancing), **3:**244
Tweedie, Penny, *as photographer,* **1:**221
Tweedie, Valrene, **1:**217, **2:**277
Twelfth Night (ballet), **2:**499, **3:**511, **5:**469
Twelfth Night (Shakespeare), **3:**106–107, 174, **5:**411
Twell, Olga, **2:**58
Twelve, The, **4:**284, **5:**460, **6:**411, 412
Twelve Months, The, **2:**585
Twelve Temptations, The, **1:**496
Twelve Ton Rose, **1:**545
Twelve with the Mail Coach, **3:**657
Twentieth Century Bacchante, **6:**87
Twentieth Century–Fox, **2:**615, **6:**327

Twenty Eight Contra Dances Largely from the New England States (Burchenal), **6:**240
23, 24, 25, et 26 Septembre, Le, **1:**410, **5:**147
Twiggy, **6:**204, 205, *205,* 286
Twigs (Furth), **1:**419
Twilight, **4:***252,* **5:**436
Twist (dance), **1:**78, 450, **5:**627, 630, 631–632, *631,* **6:**249
African-American origins, **6:**257, 262, 263
Finland, **2:**630
"Twist" (song), **5:**631, 632
Two, **4:**36
Two Ballets' Trust (London), **2:**511
Two Brothers, The, **3:**271, **4:**469, **5:**301, *302*
Two Coppélias, The, **3:**321, **4:**678
2 Dance Plus, **1:**216
Two Days in Venice, **4:**429
Two Drums for Babylon, **3:**575
Two Ecstatic Themes, **3:**399
Two Feet, **6:**95
Two for Yesteryears, **4:**594
Two on the Aisle (musical), **1:**498
Two Philosophers and the Merry Girl, **5:**199
Two Pigeons, The, **2:**186, **6:217–218,** 357
Ashton conception, **1:**155
Australian Ballet repertory, **1:**233
National Ballet of Canada repertory, **4:**544
Seymour-Gable dance partnership, **1:**155, **5:**574
Wells performance, **6:**380
See also Deux Pigeons, Les
2 + 3 Part Inventions, **4:**622
Two Roses, The, **6:**83–84
Two Sosias, The (Dryden), **5:**281
Two Stars, The, **5:**119
two-step, **5:**627, 686
Cajun, **2:**24
Finland, **2:**630
Texas, **2:**258–259
Two Step (Cunningham work), **2:**289
Two-Step (Plains Indian dance), **4:**561
Tyard, Pontus de, **1:**2
Tyc, Petr, **2:**309
Tyi wara dancers, **1:**360
Tylor, Edward Burnett, **3:**30, **4:**369
Tyl Ulenspiegel (Balanchine ballet)
Laing performance, **4:**110
Robbins performance, **5:**361
See also Till Eulenspiegel
tympanum, **3:**294, 295
TYRANA (Khmer dance troupe), **2:**32
Tyrant, The, **1:**431
Tyrolerne, **1:**507
Tyrwhitt-Wilson, Gerald. *See* Berners, Lord
Tyschsen, Anna, **1:***504*
Tyurin, Yuri P., **5:**205
as contributor, **2:**520, **6:**83–84, 171
Tyven, Gertrude, **1:**302
Tyzenhauz, Antoni, **5:**215
Tzaddik, **2:**584, **3:**605
Tzara, Tristan, **6:**389
Tzigane, **1:**269, **2:**577, **4:**274
Tzutsiang, **3:**328

Ubaid period, **4:**356
Ubakala dance, **6:**25, **219,** 382, 383
Ubaldo Lavanga, Juan, *as*

contributor, **1:**110–111, **2:**587–588
ubi-ogazu dance, **6:**16
Ucelli, 2448
U Chang Sop, **4:**693
Uchida, Christine, **6:**152, *154*
Uchiyama, Ayako, *as contributor,* **1:**31–32
UCT/CAPAB Ballet. *See* CAPAB Ballet
Udaeta, José, **6:**27
udarata dance, **2:**228
Uday Shankar Company of Hindu Dancers and Musicians, **5:**580
uddekki dance, **2:**228, **3:647,** 650
Udegeitsy (people), **5:**449
Udovicki, Ani, *as contributor,* **6:**434–437
Uemura Bunrakuken, **2:**12, 14
Ueno-Herr, Michiko, *as contributor,* **3:**591–592
ufari dance, **6:**305
UFBA. *See* Federal University of Bahia
Uganda, **2:**86, 87, 90
Ugetsu—Hell Rising to Heaven, **4:**272
Ugly Boast of a Traitor, **6:**406
Ugray, Klotild, **3:**415
Ugric (people), **3:**407
Ugrinčić, Irma, **6:***436*
ugrós, **3:**410–411
Uhlendorff, Gustav, **4:***6,* **5:***426,* 428
Uhrik, Dóra, **1:**308
Uighurs (people), **2:**141
ukanshin odori, **5:**26–27
Ukhov, Vsevolod, **4:**284
ukiyo, **3:**581
Ukraine, **6:219–226**
folk dance, **6:**222–223, 224, 225, 226
folk dance research, **5:**482
libraries and museums, **4:**165
theatrical dance, **6:224–226**
traditional dance, **3:**38, **6:220–224,** 344
Ukraine Folk Ensemble, Prešov, **2:**310
Ukrainian Maiden, The, or The Magic Castle (opera), **6:**224
Ukrainian Musical Drama, Kiev, **6:**225
Ukrainian State Folk Dance Company, **6:**222–223, 225
Ukrainian Suite, The, **4:**445, **5:***474*
'ukulele, **4:**497
Ukyō Ujiyasu, **4:**40
ula, **5:**510
Ulanova, Galina, **3:**665, **4:**360, **5:**268, **6:226–228**
Bolshoi Ballet, **1:**491, *491,* 492
Chinese tour, **2:**136
Chopiniana performance, **1:**440, 492
Denby profile of, **2:**375
dramatic dancing, **5:**458
Dying Swan interpretation, **2:**471
Esmeralda pas de deux, **2:**524
Fadeyechev dance partnership, **2:**564
Flames of Paris performance, **1:***491*
Fountain of Bakhchisarai performance, **3:**56, *56,* **6:**226, 227
on *Fountain of Bakhchisarai* role, **6:**227
Gabovich dance partnership, **3:**99
Giselle performance, **3:***179,* 183

Golden Age performance, **3:**193
Goleizovsky ballet roles, **3:**194, 195
Nutcracker performance, **5:**12
Romeo and Juliet film, **4:**132
Romeo and Juliet performance, **1:***488,* 491, **4:***281,* 284, **5:**393, 394, *394,* **6:**226, 227, *227,* 228, *398*
Sergeyev dance partnership, **5:**571
Stone Flower performance, **4:**335, **5:**699
students, **5:**487, **6:**228, 313
style contrasted with Plisetskaya's, **5:**204
Swan Lake performance, **6:**31
Tokyo Ballet School, **3:**589
Zakharov as influence, **6:**442
Ulbrich, Werner, **3:**360
Ul'chi (people), **5:**448
Ullate, Victor, **1:**291, 292, **2:**448, **5:**674
Ullman, Chinita, **1:**534
Ullmann, Lisa, **3:**271
archival material, **4:**164
Laban association, **4:**93, 94, 95, 96, 99, 102, 103–104, 477
on movement choir, **4:**476
Ullring, Gunvor, **4:**675
Ulrich, Jochen, **1:**241, 242, **3:**151, 437, **6:228–229**
Ulriksdal Court Theater, Stockholm, **6:**39, 48
Ultima Vez, **1:**412
Ultimo Giorno di Missolungi, L', **2:**209
Ultimo Trem, **1:**536
Ulvaeus, Bjorn, **1:**420
Ulysse 84, **3:**79
Ulysse dans l'Île de Circé, **5:**196
Ulysses, **1:**241
Umai fu (Japanese text), **3:**591
Umanoff, Nancy, **4:**471
Umbanda, **1:**529, 530, **6:**185, 187
umbigada dance, **1:**528, **2:**275, **5:**507, 508
umdudo men's dance, **5:**645
Umeda (people), **4:**352
Umewaka Makio, **6:229–230**
Umewaka Manzaburō II, **6:**229
Umewaka Minoru, **3:**388, **4:**41
Umewaka Minoru I, **3:**650, **6:**229
Ummidia Quadratilla, **5:**73
Umnov, Eugene, *as photographer,* **5:**37
Umpateedle, **3:**609
umteyo dance, **4:**485
Una Cosa Rara (Martín y Soler), **3:**68, **4:**510, **6:**360
Unamerican Activities, **1:**51
Unanswered Question, The, **4:**623
Unanue, Alfonso, **2:**125
Uncle Celestine (play), **3:**91–92
Uncle Tom's Cabin (Stowe), **4:**339, **5:**409
Unconquered, The, **2:**97
Unconsummated Act, The (Danse Macbre), **1:**244
Under Jorden, **5:**431
Underdahl, Eivor, **3:**303
Understanding Kuchipudi (Sarabhai and Acharyulu), **5:**521
Understudy, **5:**617
Under the Clear Blue Sky, **2:**155
Under the Italian Sky, **5:**236
Undertow, **2:**376
Adams (Diana) role, **1:**11
Alonso (Alicia) performance, **1:**49

American Ballet Theatre,
1:66, 68
Laing performance, **4:**110
modern dance costuming, **2:**245
Schuman score, **5:**561, 562
Tudor choreography, **6:**199,
200, 202
Wilson (Sallie) performance,
6:402
*und Farben, die mitten in die Brust
leuchten,* **5:**683
Undine (ballet). *See Ondine*
Undine (Coralia), **6:**75
UNESCO Information Service,
Paris, **4:**435
Unetsu, **1:**61
Unfinished Dance, The (film), **2:**108,
4:179
Unfinished Life, An (St. Denis),
5:497
Unfinished Symphony, **2:**471, 472,
5:320
ungaresca dance genre, **3:**407
Unger, Serge, **4:**635
UNICAMP. *See* State University of
Campinas, São Paulo
*Unicorn, the Gorgon, and the
Manticore, The,* **1:***103,* **2:**16
Union de l'Amour et des Arts, L',
3:117, **4:**149
Union Jack, **1:**271, **2:**314
Balanchine's conception,
4:611–612
Martins performance, **4:**274, 621
Union of Finnish Dance Artists,
5:43
Union of Soviet Socialist Republics
(former). *See* Russia; *Soviet
era; specific former republics*
Union Pacific, **1:**310, **2:**478, **4:**178,
322, 518
United Kingdom. *See* Great Britain
United Scenic Artists (USA),
4:191–192
United States, **3:**202, **5:**573
United States of America,
6:230–300
African-American dance
traditions, **6:**253–263
See also as separate listing
Appalachian clogging, **2:**179,
180–181, **3:**608, **5:**696
Arnould-Mussot ballet
pantomime performances,
1:124
as Australian modern dance
influence, **1:**212–213
avant-garde dance, **1:**245, 246
background and overview,
6:230–253
Ballet Caravan's dance
significance, **1:**279, **6:**247
ballet education, **6:**246–247,
290–293
Balanchine role, **1:**257,
263–266, 329, 349, **6:**264–265
See also School of American
Ballet
Cecchetti method, **2:**84, **3:**51
character dancing teaching
methods, **2:**107
Christensen brothers, **2:**161
Craske teaching, **2:**69
Crofton schools, **2:**273
Eglevsky school, **2:**479
Fokines' students, **3:**22
Harlem Dance Theatre,
2:334–335
Koslov school, **4:**56
major schools, **1:**329

Metropolitan Opera Ballet
School, **1:**68, **4:**381, 382,
6:270
Mordkin studios, **4:**460
Philadelphia nineteenth-
century school, **4:**137, 138,
6:290
technique, **1:**329
Ballet Russe de Monte Carlo
strong influence, **6:**264
Ballets Russes de Serge Diaghilev
tour impact (1916), **1:**322,
2:408–409, **4:**645, **6:**237,
243, 271
Basque dances, **1:**377–378
break dancing, **1:**538
Cajun dance traditions, **2:**23–25,
6:*250*
as Canadian dance influence,
2:37, 38
Caribbean migration, **2:**61, 65
character dances, **2:**108
Christian views of dance, **2:**167,
168, **6:**234–235
circus, **2:**176
contemporary criticism,
6:298–300
American Congress on
Research and Dance, **5:**44
country-western, **2:**258–259
dance as sport, **2:**322–324,
6:298–300
Dance Heritage Coalition, **5:**44
dance marathons, **2:**324–327
dance medicine specialization,
2:328
Dance Notation Bureau, **5:**44
dance on television, **6:**136–141
American Bandstand, **1:**77–79
dance research and publication,
5:624, **6:**251–252, **296–298**
anthropological studies,
4:369, 370
court-dance reconstructions,
6:251
ethnological studies, **4:**373
folk dance studies, **6:**240,
247–248
Kirstein, Lincoln, **4:**26–30,
6:246, 296
landmarks, **6:**300
libraries and museums,
4:166–171
Moore, Lillian, **4:**457,
6:233, 296
Sachs, Curt, **6:**246
dance therapy, **2:**316–321,
5:560–561
dancing masters, **2:**338, 339
Delsartism, **2:**371–372
early choreographers, **3:**86–87
Elssler (Fanny) tour, **2:**504,
6:237, 269, 298–299
Federal Dance Project, **2:**579–582
first American-born *premier
danseur,* **5:**615–616
first native-born ballerina,
4:139–140, **6:**237
first native-born theatrical
dancer, **2:**466, **6:**233
first *Nutcracker* stagings, **5:**15
first serious ballet presentation,
6:233
first Soviet dancers to tour, **2:**96
first truly American classical
ballet company, **1:**63–64
first woman ballet professional to
tour, **2:**442
folk dance education, **3:**367–368,
4:374

Ford Foundation scholarships,
6:264–265
historical theatrical touring
circuits, **4:**452–455, 463–464,
6:233, 235–236, 237
Hollywood musicals. *See* film
musicals, Hollywood
human movement analysis,
4:16–17
international cultural exchanges,
6:249
jazz dance, **3:**598–600
jig, **3:**607–608
Labanotation, **4:**96, 98
Laban theory, **4:**95, 103, 104
major companies. *See* American
Ballet Theatre; New York City
Ballet
modern dance
Federal Dance Project, **2:**579,
580, **6:**245–246
five pioneers, **3:**369, **6:**245.
See also Graham, Martha;
Holm, Hanya; Horst, Louis;
Humphrey, Doris;
Weidman, Charles
idiosyncratic approaches,
6:249, 250
Progressive Era inception,
6:242
regional companies, **6:**265–266
White Oak Dance Project, **1:**373
See also Bennington School of
Dance; Jacob's Pillow; *specific
choreographers and
companies*
movement choir, **4:**477
musical theater, **6:**237–238, 242,
267–290
See also as separate listing
Native American dance,
3:170–171, **4:**549–575
oldest classical ballet company,
1:196–197
Orientalism, **5:**45–46
regional companies, **6:**249,
264–267, 300
Atlanta Ballet, **1:**39, 196–197
Boston Ballet, **1:**501–502
Canadian Dance Festival
influence, **2:**39
Cleveland–San Jose Ballet,
2:177–178
Crofton association, **2:**273
Dayton Ballet, **2:**357
Dayton Contemporary Dance
Company, **2:**358, **6:**264
Houston Ballet, **3:**389–390
Joffrey teaching posts, **3:**610
Philadelphia Ballet, **4:**209–210
San Francisco Ballet,
2:161–162
*See also separate listings for
specific companies*
Ronzani dance troupe, **5:**403–404
round dancing, **5:**409–410
Shaker dance, **5:**575–577
social dance. *See* social dance;
specific dances
social, folk, and modern dance
education, **3:**34, 35,
4:437–443, **6:**235, 239, 240,
293–296
Bennington School of the
Dance, **1:**420–422
dance reconstruction, **5:**329
Duncan, Isadora, **2:**457
Dunham School of Dance and
Theater, **2:**458
Farber, Viola, **2:**575, 576

H'Doubler, Margaret,
3:352–353
Hill, Martha, **3:**363–364
Holm, Hanya, **3:**370–371
Horst, Louis, **3:**385
Martha Graham Company
School, **3:**218–219
reels, **5:**333
Soviet dance defectors, **1:**372
square dancing, **5:**621, 685–690
tap dance, **6:**95–104
theaters for dance, **6:**159–160
UNited We Dance (festival), **5:**514,
6:174, 325
Universal Art, Inc. (formerly World
Art, Inc.), **1:**295, 313, 466
See also Ballet Russe de Monte
Carlo
Universal Studios, **2:**615
Universidad de Santiago de Chile,
6:453
Universidad de Sonora,
Hermosillo, **4:**397
Université de la Danse, Paris,
2:466, **4:**186
Université de Montréal, **2:**45
Université du Québec à Montréal,
2:48
Université Laval, **2:**36
University of Arizona, Tucson,
4:170, **6:**292
University of Auckland, **4:**624, 628
University of Calgary, Alberta,
2:48, 49
University of California, Berkeley,
2:602, **5:**494
University of California, Irvine,
4:170, 228, 346
University of California, Los
Angeles, **2:**319, **4:**17
archives, **5:**498
dance archives, **4:**170
dance ethnology studies, **2:**602,
4:373
University of California, Riverside,
6:297
University of Cape Town Ballet. *See*
CAPAB Ballet
University of Chicago, dance
history graduate studies,
6:297
University of Chile, **2:**123, 125, 127,
4:140, 171, **6:**453
University of Copenhagen, **2:**387,
388, **4:**160
University of Denver, Colorado,
4:170
University of Ghana, **3:**168, 170,
4:158
University of Illinois, Champaign,
Urbana, **4:**169
University of Indiana,
Bloomington, **4:**63
University of Kent, **3:**278, 283, 284,
4:220
University of Limerick, **3:**519
University of London, **4:**103–104
University of Maryland, **3:**556
University of Minnesota Libraries,
Saint Paul, **4:**169
University of Paris, **1:**2, 284
University of Stockholm,
6:48–49, 50
University of Surrey, **3:**278, 283,
285, **4:**95, 163
University of Texas, Austin, **2:**341,
4:169, **6:**292, 425
University of Utah, **2:**162, **5:**512,
6:292
University of Washington, Seattle,
1:498, **4:**660, 661

University of Wisconsin, **2:**319, **3:**352, **6:**242, 295
Un Jour ou Deux, **2:**293, 294
Unknowing Steps, **4:**627
Un Sucre ou Deux?, **3:**79
Unsung, The, **4:**199
Untitled, **1:**140, **5:**24
Untitled Solo, **2:**289
untitled theater piece (Cunningham). *See* Event
Untitled Trio, **2:**119
upaj ang, **5:**582
Uotinen, Jorma, **2:**633, **6:**67
upaj ang, **5:**582
Upaniṣads, **3:**462
Upavedas, **3:**453–454
Up in Central Park (musical), **6:**89, 90, 279
Upper Atmospheric Disturbances, **4:**22
Upper Xingu, Brazil, **1:**531
Up the River, **3:**261
Urakova, A. P., **6:**60
"Ural Shestera," **6:**303
Uralskaya, Valeria I., **5:**484
as contributor, **4:**132–134, **5:**442–445, 449–457, 481–482, 566–568, **6:**303–304
Urasguildiyev (Urazgildeez), Rogert K., **5:**482
as contributor, **4:**86–87
Urbach, S., **6:**83
Urbain, James, **1:**349
Urban, Joseph, **2:**249, **6:**271, 273, 274, 371, *447*, 448
Urbanavičienė, Dalia, *as contributor*, **4:**204–207
Urban Bush Women, **3:**448, **6:**448–449, *449*
Urbani, Giuseppe, **1:**402, 456, **3:**360, 553
Urbel, Ida, **2:**529
Urdaneta, Adriana and Luz, **6:**323–324, *325*
Urdapilleta, Laura, **4:**397
Urhobo (people), **6:**15
Uribe, Bárbara, **2:**126
Uriella, **2:**282, **4:**121, **5:**403
Uris, Victoria, **1:**75
Urlicht, **3:**51
Urlo, L', **2:**369
Urreta, Pilar, **4:**397
Urrutia Blondel, Jorge, **2:**127
Urseanu, Tilde, **5:**384, 386, 387
Ursuliak, Alexander, **2:**268
Urtula, Lucrecia Reyes, **1:**394, **5:**173, 174
Uruguay, **4:**171, **6:**301–303
Urup, Henning, **2:**386–387
as contributor, **2:**380–383
Urusov, Prince Petr, **1:**485
USA: Dance (television series), **6:**138
Usana Bali, **3:**486
Usha, **3:**606
Ushakov, Aleksandr, **5:**157
Usha Parinayam, **6:**320
Usher, Graham, **4:***417*
Usova, Maia, **3:**432
Ussher, Jane, *as photographer*, **4:**628
USSR. *See* Russia; Soviet era; *specific former republics*
Ustinova, Tatiana, **5:**445, 474, **6:**303–304
Usui Kenji, *as contributor*, **3:**588–590, **6:**84
Utah Ballet Archives, **4:**170
Ute Indians, **3:**171

Uthoff, Ernst, **5:**24, 266, **6:304**
Ballets Jooss, **3:**628, 629
Chilean ballet, **2:**123–124, **3:**305, 629, **6:**453
Folkwang Tanztheater, **3:**626
Green Table, The, **3:**305, 614
Uthoff, Michael, **2:**606, **3:**614
'Uthmān ibn Fūdī, **3:**348
Utrecht, Luuk, **4:**599, 600
as contributor, **2:**346–348, 468–470, **3:**121–122, 345–346, **4:**81–82, 591–597, 600–601, **5:**555–556
Utrillo, Maurice, **1:**316, **5:**544
Utsubo Zaru, **4:**84, 660, 661
Uttini, Francesco Antonio, **6:**38, 39, 46, 49
Uytiepo, Pancho and Elsie, **5:**172
Uzbek (people), **1:**27
Uzbek Dance and Culture Society, **6:**307
Uzbek Ethnographic Company, **6:**306
Uzbekistan, **3:**568, **4:**8, 224, **6:304–307**
folk dance choreography, **5:**482
libraries and museums, **4:**165
Uzbek Opera and Ballet Theater, **6:**306
Uzmanbaş, Ilhan, **6:**212
Uzume, **4:**40

Vacarescu, Elena, **5:**384
Vaccarino, Elisa, *as contributor*, **3:**358–359, 552–553
Vachon, Amy, *as contributor*, **4:**306
Vachon, Nicole, **5:***61*
vācikābhinaya, **3:**457
vacunao, **2:**275
Vadasy, Tibor, **2:**530
Vaes, Alain, **6:**34
Vagabond King, The (Friml), **6:**273
Vaganova, Agrippina, **1:**90, 533, **5:**203, 208, 248, 279, **6:309–310**, 352
Basic Principles of Classical Ballet (Vaganova), **1:**198, 328, **6:**128, 310
Blok's writings on, **1:**463, 464
Cecchetti method, **2:**84
Chopiniana, **1:**440
Esmeralda staging, **2:**524, **3:**186–187
as Gerdt (Pavel) student, **3:**137
on Italian pointe work, **1:**347
as Legat (Nikolai) student, **4:**143
Maryinsky Ballet, **4:**282, 286, **5:**456, 480
Raymonda, **5:**321
school curriculum. *See* Vaganova method
students, **2:**341, 449, 506, **4:**36, 58, 529, **5:**282, 566, 567, 678, **6:**349
Swan Lake production, **6:**31
Ulanova as student, **6:**226
as Vazem student, **4:**282
Vaganova Ballet Academy, **1:**416
Vaganova method, **1:**328–329, 330, 399, **5:**480
arabesque, **1:**100–101
arm positions, **1:**332, 345
attitude, **1:**198
body positions, **1:**334
Cecchetti influence, **1:**347
Chilean ballet school, **2:**124
directions, **1:**335
Dudinskaya application, **2:**450

French and Italian schools as influence, **1:**348
Hungarian adaptation, **3:**417, 421, **4:**529
jumps, **1:**341, 347
pointe work, **1:**347
port de bras, **5:**226, 227
as Russian school exemplar, **1:**328–329, 333
as Soviet school basis, **1:**348–349
turning movements, **1:**337, 338
Volkova as western exponent of, **6:**349
Vágnerová, Věra, **5:**270
Vailenko, K., **5:**482
Vaillancourt, Angela, **5:**680
Vaillat, Léandre, **4:**353, **5:**690, **6:**69, 71
Vainio, Riitta, **2:**633
Vainonen, Vasily, **1:**74, 90, 144, **2:**96, 421, 449, 579, **4:**422, **6:310–311**
Asafiev score, **4:**517
Bolshoi Ballet, **1:**490, 491, *491*
Budapest Opera Ballet, **3:**417
Flames of Paris, The, **3:**12, 197, 417, **4:**133, 148, 283, **5:**458, *459*
Gabovich roles, **3:**99
Gayané production, **3:**125
Golden Age, The, **3:**192–193, **4:**283, **6:**227, 410
Militsa, **4:**284
Mirandolina, **5:**567
Nutcracker, The, **3:**417, **4:**677, **5:**10, *10*, **11–12**, 15, **6:**310, 311, 343
Raymonda, **5:**321, **6:**311
students, **5:**614
Zakharov collaboration, **6:**442
Vain Precautions. *See Fille Mal Gardée, La*
Vainqueurs, Les, **1:**412
Vaiṣṇava Hinduism, **3:**465–466, **4:**253–254
Vajiravudh, Rama VI, king of Siam, **4:**9, 112
vakamalolo dance, **2:**593
vakara ni iri, **2:**593
Vakhtangov, Evgeny, **2:**191, **4:**190, **5:**10
Vakula the Smith (Tchaikovsky), **6:114–115**
Val, Jean-Baptiste, **6:**233
Val, Madame, **3:**86
Valberkh, Ivan, **1:**485, **2:**55, **3:**191, **6:311–312**
ballet themes, **4:**278, **5:**453
as first Russian ballet master, **4:**276, 278, **5:**453
memoirs, **5:**483
Saint Petersburg Theatrical School, **5:**480
students, **4:**35
Valchanov, Yassen, **4:**134
Valcroze, Raymond, **5:**594
Valda and Misha, **5:**574
Valdeke, Heinrich von, **1:**364
Valeikaitė, Jolanta, **4:**208
Valence, Lola de, **5:**262
Valencia, Tórtola, **5:**675
Valente, Alfredo, *as photographer*, **1:**62, **2:**424, **3:**286
Valentin, Susanne, **6:**45
Valentine, Dennis, *as photographer*, **3:**574, 575
Valentine's Eve, **1:**148, 151, **4:**109, 215
Valentin le Désossé, **6:**181
Valentino (film), **2:**444

Valentino, Rudolph, **5:**628
Valeriani, Giuseppe, **4:**277
Valéry, Paul, **1:**23, 24, **2:**360, **3:**84, 431, **4:**186, **5:**180
Valev, Bulat, **3:**665
Valgeirsdóttir, Sigridur, **3:**434–435, 436
as contributor, **3:**434–436
Väljapts, Udo, **2:**530
Valk, Netty van der, **4:**592
Valkay, Francisc, **5:**389, 553
Vâlkova-Beševič, **2:**11
Valkuil, **4:**602
Valkyrie, The
Borchsenius performance, **1:**497
Bournonville production, **1:**508, 510, 511, 512, **5:**426
Hartmann score, **1:**515
Price (Juliette) performance, **5:**425
Valladolid, Anna, **1:**391
Vallarino, Elsa, **6:**301, 302
Vallathol Narayana Menon, Mahākavi, **3:**468, 661
valle dyshe, **1:**33–34
Vallerand, Jean, **2:**151
Vallet, Adam, **2:**337
Vallet, Nicolas, **2:**98
Valley of Shadows, **4:**244
Valli, **6:**312
Vallière, Louise de la, **1:**288, 424
Válmīki, **3:**464
Valois, Marguerite de. *See* Marguerite de Valois
Valois, Ninette de. *See* de Valois, Ninette
Valse, La, **2:**20, 244, 254, 277, **3:**24, **5:**58, 563, **6:**341
Ashton production, **5:**316
Balanchine production, **1:**272, **4:**611, **5:**316
La Clercq performance, **4:**137, 616
Magallanes performance, **4:**246
Moncion performance, **4:**450, 619
Nijinska choreography, **3:**72, **5:**439
Rosenthal lighting, 5407
Wilde role, **6:**396
"Valse à Cinque Temps" (*Catarina*), **4:**513
Valse Caprice, **2:**151, 378, **3:***263*, **5:**123
valse chaloupée, **1:**95, **4:***523*
Valse Directoire, **2:**378
Valse-Fantaisie, **4:**611, 622
Valse Finale, **3:**174, 202, **5:**300
Valses de Beethoven, Les, **1:**306, **4:**229
Valses de Ravel, Les, **3:**75
Valses Nobles et Sentimentales, **1:**148, 151, **2:**426, **3:**72, *229*, 429, **5:**316
Valse Triste (Gripenberg solo), **3:**312
Valse Triste (Verchinina ballet), **6:**326
Valse Vienoise, **4:**110
Valtonen, Martti, **2:**632
Valtýsson, Helgi, **3:**434, 435, 436
Valupin, Evgeny, **3:**99
Vályi, Rózsi, **3:**423–424
Valz, Karl, **6:**29
Vámos, Youri, **1:**375–376, 391, **3:**157, 419, **5:**43, **6:**52, 66
Vampire Dance, **6:**319
Vampiro, Il, **5:**409
Van, Bobby, **3:**55
Vanaver Caravan, **5:**586, 587

Van Buren, Martin, **2:**504
van Cauwenburgh, Tom, **2:**58
Vance, Norma, **6:***200*
Vancouver, Canada, **2:**37, 38, 40, 41–42, 45, 46, 47, 48, 423
Native American dance, **4:**569
Vancouver Ballet Society, **4:**166
Vancouver Public Library, **4:**166
Vanda, Queen of Poland, **5:**215
Vandeghinste, Mia, **1:**414
Vandekeybus, Wim, **1:**412
van den Berg, Chris, **5:***651*
VanDerBeek, Stan, **2:**605
Vanderbilt University, **4:**169
Vandergucht, Gerard, **6:**176
van Druten, John, **6:**199
Van Dyke, Dick, **6:**283
Vane, Daphne, **1:***63,* 64, 96, *257*
Vanel, Hélène, **1:**244
Vanemuine Theater, Tartu, **2:**529, 530
van Geems, Joyce, **5:**651
van Gelder, Bernice, **6:**191
Van Grove, Issac, **5:**60
Vangsaae, Mona, **1:**154, *508,* **2:**3, 511, **4:**65, **5:**394, *428,* 429, 431, *553,* **554**, **6:**66
Vanguardia (publication), **5:**676
van Hamel, Martine, **1:**73, 74, *74,* 282, **4:**542, **6:**146, 366
van Heerden, Augustus, **5:**657
Vanier, Luc, **5:**24
Vanina Vanini, **5:**460
Vanities. See Earl Carroll's Vanities
Vanka, Maksimilijan, **6:***4332*
van Lennep, William Bird, **4:**168
van Lund, John, as photographer, **4:**45
vannams, **3:**647–648
Vanner, Wilhelm, **2:**435
Vano, I., **5:**595
van Praagh, Peggy, **2:**265, **4:**369, **5:**299, 300, 563, **6:**95, **312–313**
Australian Ballet, **1:**209–210, 213, 217, 218, 230, 231, 232, 234, 499, **3:**203–204, 623
Birmingham Royal Ballet, **3:**268
Dark Elegies performance, **2:**348, *348*
de Valois association, **2:**403
Helpmann association, **3:**356
Jardin aux Lilas performance, **3:**597
London Ballet, **4:**215
Sadler's Wells Theatre Ballet, **5:**429
Tudor association, **6:**196, 197, *197,* 198, 312
Van Riper, Peter, **3:**54
Vanrunxt, Marc, **1:**412
Van Scott, Glory, **2:**458
Vanslov, Victor V., **5:**321
as contributor, **1:**144–145, 392–393, **2:**435–436, 436–438, **3:**192–193, 308–311, **4:**142–144, 144–145, 181–182, **5:**457–465, 677–678, 699, **6:**343
on Grigorovich and *drambalet,* **5:**484, 485
van Tieghem, David, **2:***247*
van Tonder, Tossie, **5:**659
Vantukh, Miroslav, **6:**225
Vantukh, Mykola, **6:**223
Van Tuyl, Marian, **1:**421, **2:**604, **4:**130
Vanuatu. *See* Melanesia
van Ultzen, Karen, **1:**218

Van Vechten, Carl, **5:**186, **6:**299
as photographer, **2:**5, **3:**58, 330, **4:**270, 450, **6:**198, 259, 317
van Wyk, Arnold, **2:**57
Van Zile, Judy, **4:**375
as contributor, **1:**496–497, **3:**469–470
Dance In India, **3:**470
van Zon, Boujke, **4:**626
van Zon, Carla, **4:**626
Vaque-Moulin, Elise, **6:**71, 73
Vardi, Yair, **3:**533
Varela, Florence, **6:**302
Vären, 5429, **4:**118, 119
Varèse, Edgard, **1:**82, 349, 461, 462, **2:**388, **4:**519, **6:**111, 192
Varga, Rastislav, **6:**435
Varga, S. F., **3:**423
Vargas, Josefa, **5:**672
Vargas, Juana. *See* Macarrona, La
Vargas, Manolo, **1:**117, **3:***10,* **4:**222, **5:**674, **6:**407–408, *408*
See also Ximénez-Vargas Ballet Español
Variations, **2:**351, **4:**185, **5:**96, **6:**6
Variations, Les, **4:**636
Variations and Fugue on a Theme by Handel, **1:**301
Variations Classiques, **1:**301
Variations Diabelli, **2:**472
Variations Don Giovanni, **1:**292
Variations for Four, **2:**425, 510, **3:**175, **5:**401
Variations for Men, **5:**226
Variations for Orchestra, **2:**576
Variations IV (Cage), **2:**292
Variations on a Landscape, **6:**363
Variations on an Encounter, **2:**473
Variations on a Nursery Song, **3:**418, **5:**569
Variations on a Theme by Purcell, **1:**153, **4:**584
Variations on a Theme of Frank Bridge (Britten), **3:**203
Variations on Euclid, **6:**119
Variations on the Theme of Othello. *See Moor's Pavane, The*
Variations pour une Porte et un Soupir, **1:**292, **6:**144
Variations sur un Thème de Haydn, **3:**429, **6:***130*
Variations V, **2:**292, 605, **4:**519
Variations within Space, **2:**57
variety dancing, **5:**491
Variety Show (musical), **1:**142, **6:**277
Varii Capricci, **1:**158, **2:**444, **5:***421*
Varisco, Daniel Martin, as photographer, **4:**408, **6:**418
Varkas, Leon, **1:**65
Varkony, as photographer, **2:**38, 151, **3:**229
Varkovitsky, Vladimir, **1:**144, **4:**55, 224, 447
Varlamov, Aleksei, **3:**200, 589
Värmlänningarna (Selinder), **6:**37, 40
Varna, Bulgaria, **2:**11
Varna International Ballet Competition, **1:**281
varṇam, **1:**442
Varney, Linn, **1:***245*
Våroffer, **6:***44*
Varona, Jose, **5:***512*
Varone, Doug, **2:**358
Varro, Taddea de, **2:**204
Varsity Drag, **5:**629
varsovienne (*varsoviana*), **2:**258, 259, **5:**624

Vartoogian, Jack, **6:**260
as photographer, **1:**58, 59, 60, 74, 75, 76, 84, 100, 162, 165, 167, 169, 170, 173, 179, 185, 294, 371, 405, 513, **2:**6, 13, 18, 30, 32, 125, 131, 133, 134, *135,* 137, 141, 143, 147, 207, 215, 223, 231, 284, 334, 335, 440, 566, 572, 595, **3:**79, 133, 200, 219, 306, 387, 457, 467, 497, 500, 502, 581, 582, 587, 589, 615, 616, 621, 642, 651, 662, 666, **4:**66, 70, 180, 230, 250, 296, 303, 410, 445, 513, 523, 654, **5:**8, 25, 29, 240, 243, 275, 421, 440, 444, 513, 523, 530, 554, 570, 675, **6:**94, 103, 110, 111, 112, 152, 154, 191, 225, 250, 251, 368, 414
Vartoogian, Linda, as photographer, **1:**366, 530, 531, **2:**17, 30, 218, 220, 278, 279, 394, **3:**3, 52, 396, 483, 494, 496, 498, 502, **4:**274, 601, 621, **5:**242, **6:**80, 93, 202
Varugalamo, **2:**405
Vasant Rāsa, **3:**467
Vasarely, Victor, **4:***542*
Vashegyi, Ernő, **3:**415, 416, *416*
Vasikov, Yuri, **5:**469
Vasilenko, Sergei, **2:**15, **3:**194, 631, 632–633, **4:**226, **5:**472, 567, **6:**310
Vasilescu, Theodor, **4:**692–693
Vasileva, A. I., **5:**472
Vasilieva, A. I., **5:**472
Vasiliev, Vladimir, **1:**493, **3:**61, **4:**360, **5:**97, *102,* 164, *204,* 460, **6:**313–315
Béjart ballets, **1:**292, 406
Bolshoi Ballet, **1:**493, **3:**200
Budapest Opera Ballet, **3:**418
Cinderella version, **5:**474
Don Quixote, **1:**77, **2:**438, 441
as Gabovich student, **3:**99
Goleizovsky ballets, **3:**195, *195*
Grigorovich ballets, **1:**493
Icarus, **4:**336, **5:**461
international ballet competition, **1:**282
Leventhal scenic design, **4:**154
Little Humpbacked Horse performance, **4:***211,* 212
Macbeth, **1:**493, **3:**418, **4:**154, **5:**452, 462
Nutcracker performance, **5:**12
Shurale performance, **5:**595
Spartacus, **5:**677
Stone Flower performance, **4:***335*
as Ulanova student, **6:**228
wife Maximova, **4:**336
as Yermolayev student, **6:**420
Vasilieva, Vera, **5:**484
Vasilieva-Rozhdestvenskaya, Margarita, **5:**480
Vasiliov, Vladimir
Bolshoi Ballet choreographies, **1:**492, **5:**460
Creation of the World, The, **1:**371, **3:**418, **4:**36, 285, 336, **5:**461
Ekaterinburg Opera Theater choreography, **5:**470
Moscow State Theater of Classical Ballet, **1:**371, **5:**461, 464, 467
Novosibirsk Ballet choreography, **5:**472
Sacre du Printemps, Le, **5:**488
Vaslav, **2:**463
Vasnetsov, Viktor, **1:**487, **5:**541
Vasquez, Manolo, **2:**281

Vasquez, Michel, **5:**94
Vasquez, Porfirio, **5:**146
Vast, **1:**214, **4:**479
Västanå Teater, Sweden, **6:**36
Vašut, Vladimir, **2:**308, **5:**23, 617
as contributor, **1:**428–429, 541–542, **2:**306–311, **3:**99–100, **4:**77, 238–239, 583–584, **5:**23–24, 245, 269–270, 614–615, 616–618
as photographer, **5:**617
Vasylenko, Kim, **6:**223
Vasyuchenko, Yuri, **4:**360
Vater, Jürgen, **3:**52
Vatič, Mensud, **6:***436*
Vatsyayan, Kapila, **3:**470
as contributor, **3:**461–464, 466–468
Vaudemont, Mademoiselle de, **1:**275
vaudeville, **6:315–320**
African-American circuit, **1:**520, **6:**255, 256, 257
Bates, Peg Leg, **1:**382
Black Crook significance, **1:**457, 458
Bournonville ballets, **1:***512,* 516
Bubbles, John W., **2:**5, **3:**304
Canadian circuits, **2:**37
careers in dance, **6:**291
Christensen brothers, **2:**160, *161*
Denishawn tours, **2:**376–377, 378
fan dances, **2:**572, 573
Federal Dance Project, **2:**579–580
flamenco dance, **3:**8–9
Fokines' tour, **3:**22
Irish jig, **3:**608
Robinson, Bill, **4:**368
Russian ballet performances, **4:**56
tap dancing, **6:**99
travesty, **6:**190
Wayburn stagings, **6:**371
Whitman Sisters, **6:**386
See also music hall; tap dance
Vaudeville of the Elements, **4:**650, *650*
Vaudoyer, Jean-Louis, **3:**73
Vaughan, David, **2:**73, 110, **3:**27, 362, **6:**282
as contributor, **1:**145–159, 542–543, **2:**115, 186, 284–297, 348–349, 404, 566–567, **3:**284–286, 379–380, 597–598, 608–609, **4:**37, 334–335, **5:**17, 113–114, 193, 293–294, 341–342, 602, **6:**195–203, 362–364, 375
Vaughan, Kate, **5:**605, **6:**268, 317
Vaughan Williams, Ralph, **1:**52, 56, **2:**397, 399
archival materials, **4:**163
Job score, **3:**608, 609, **4:**517, **5:**412
Vaughan Williams, Ursula, as contributor, **5:**582–583
Vaussard, Christiane, **3:**73, 82, **4:**354, **5:**96, 690
Vāyu Purāṇa, **3:**465
Vazem, Ekaterina, **1:**392, **3:**137, 561, **5:**150
Bayadère performance, **4:**282
Maryinsky Ballet, **5:**456
students, **4:**282, **5:**119, **6:**309
Vázquez, Raquel, **4:**397
Vázquez, Viveca, **5:**275, 276, *276*
V Comme, **1:**291
Vecchia Milano, **3:**51, **5:**246
Vecheslova, Tatiana, **4:**247
on Alonso (Alicia), **1:**49
American tour, **2:**96

Vecheslova, Tatiana, *continued*
  Esmeralda performance, **2:**524
  Fountain of Bakhchisarai
    performance, **3:**56, *56*
  Tatiana performance, **4:**284
  Zakharov as influence, **6:**442
Vedantam Satyam, **6:320–321**
Vedas, **3:**453, 462
Veddha (people), **4:**34
veduta per angolo, **1:**447
Veen, Jan (Hans Wiener), **1:**211,
  2:461, **3:**385, **4:**438
Veen, Marie-Jeanne van der, **1:**289
Vega, Alejandro, **4:**222
Vega, Carlos, **1:**108, 110
Vega, Leticia de la, **1:**110, 315
Vega, Lope de, **4:**129
Vega, Mario de la, **1:**294
Végvári, Zsuzsa, **1:**308
Veiga, Laura, **1:**114
Veigl, Eva Maria. *See* Violette, Eva
  Maria
veil dances, **1:**41, **2:**488, 489
Veil of Pierrette, The, **1:**85, 541
Veit, Louis, **3:***144*, **6:**76
Veitía, Carlos, **5:**275
Vejsada, Igor, **2:**310
Vekilova, Leila, **1:**248
Vela, Pablo, **1:***245*
Velevski, Zoran, **6:**437
Velikanov, Vasily, **3:**665
velikdensko horo, **2:**100
Velikovsky, M. I., **6:**225
Velloso, Fernando, **1:**536
Velox, **1:***536*
Veloz and Yolanda, **6:**257
Veltchek, Vaslav, **1:**532, 533, **3:**350,
  6:301
Velvet Lady, The (musical), **6:**272
Vempati Chinna Satyam, **6:**321
Vempati Ravi Shankar, **6:**321
Venable, Lucy, **4:**96
  as contributor, **1:**472–473
Venda dance, **4:**365, **5:**643, 661,
  663, **6:321–322**
Vendange, La, **5:**150
Vendetta, La (Pugni), **5:**277
Vendetta Ingegnosa, o La Statua di
  Condillac, La, **1:**88
Vendrig, Yvonne, **2:**470
Venema, Mea, **4:**602
Venere, Bacco e Amore, **2:**587
Veneziana, **3:**392
Venezuela, **4:**171, **6:322–325**
Venezuelan School of
  Contemporary Dance,
  6:323
Vengeance of Diana, The, **1:**459
Venice, Italy, **3:**552, 556
  Danza '75 festival, **3:**550–551
  forlana, **3:**49–50
  Italian and French schools of
    ballet, **3:**546
Venier, Eduard, **6:**436
vénitienne, **3:**49–50
Vénitienne, La, **3:**49
Ventaglio, Il, **3:**197
Ventana, La, **2:**535, **5:**250, 295, 600,
  6:75, 324
  Bournonville production, **1:**509,
    511, 516, **2:**574
  Brenaa production, **1:**539
  Bruhn pas de trois staging, **2:**4
  fan use, **2:**574
  Lander (Margot) performance,
    4:119
  Nichols pas de trois
    performance, **4:**631
Vent de Folie, Un (revue), **1:**252
Vente, Carolina, **3:**96

Ventura, Domenico, **1:**236
Ventura, Johnny, **2:**432
Ventura, Pep, **3:**64
Ventura, Santo, **1:**235, 236
Venu, G., **4:**693
Venua, Frédéric-Marc, **2:**389, 415
Venusberg scene (*Tannhäuser*),
  1:390, 446, **3:**19, 22, 206,
  6:563
  as ballet, **5:**36, *36*, 37, 38, 569
  Béjart choreography, **1:**405
  Bournonville Danish production,
    1:510
  Duncan performance, **3:**145
  Fokine staging, **3:**19, 22
  Grahn staging, **3:**224
  Laban choreography, **4:**91
  Paris Opera controversy, **4:**514,
    5:148–149
  Staats *grand défilé du corps de*
    ballet, **5:**690
  Zucchi choreography, **6:**453
Vénus et Adonis, **1:**201, **2:**366
Venza, Jac, **6:**138
Veola, Helen, **1:**498, **3:**286, **5:**359
Vêpres Siciliennes, Les (Verdi),
  2:282, **4:**514
Vera, Domingo, **6:**301, 302
Vera, Ilona, **3:**415
Vera-Ellen, **1:**194, **2:**251, **4:**419,
  5:290, **6:**101
Verano Porteño (Piazzola), **4:**632
Vera Storia, La, **3:**127
Vera Violetta (musical), **4:**459
Verbist, Felyne, **1:**410
Verbova, Zinaida, **5:**476
Verbrugge, Bob, **5:**531
verbunkos, **2:**304, **3:**408–409, 411
Verchinina, Nina, **1:**534, **2:**127,
  277, **5:**511, **6:325–326**
  Ballets Russes de Monte Carlo,
    1:309, 310, *311*, 315
  Présages solo, **4:**322
Verdaguer, Jacinto, **2:**568
Verdak, George, **3:**617, **6:**292
verde-gaio, **5:**229
Verde Gaio Company, **2:**263,
  5:233–234
Verdi, Giuseppe, **1:**406, 461, **2:**120,
  282, 367, 369, 446, 459,
  473–474, **4:**339, 341, **5:**36
  ballets for Paris Opera
    productions, **4:**514
  television biography, **3:**60
Verdi Ballets, The (Jürgensen),
  3:556
Verdi Variations, **4:**244, 631, **6:**143
Verdon, Gwen, **2:**184, **5:**358, **6:**281,
  283, **326–327**
  archival material, **4:**168
Verdy, Violette, **1:**69, 501, **2:**333,
  3:59, 318, **5:**97, 163, **6:**174,
  327–329
  Ballets de Paris de Roland Petit,
    3:74
  Ballets des Champs-Élysées,
    1:305, 306
  Black Swan pas de deux, **4:**611
  Boston Ballet, **6:**398
  Bruhn dance partnership, **2:**3
  Coppélia, **2:**200
  Dances at a Gathering
    performance, **2:**333, **4:***619*
  Emeralds performance, **4:**612,
    617, *618*
  English National Ballet guest
    performances, **2:**508
  Firebird performance, **4:**617
  Liebeslieder Walzer performance,
    4:179, *179*

Medea performance, **4:***614*
  New York City Ballet roles,
    4:611, 617
  Paris Opera Ballet classes, **3:**82
  Sonnambula performance, **5:***641*
  Sylvia revival, **6:**64
Veredon, Gray, **2:**267, **3:**150, 151,
  4:519, 625, **6:**10, 228
Vereen, Ben, **6:**284
verevochka step, **5:**445
Vergani, Bice, **4:**258
Vergelul ritual, **5:**381
Verger, Pierre
  Andes dance photography, **3:**35
  as photographer, **1:**528, **3:**334,
    335, **4:***289*, **5:**143, 144, 146,
    6:346, 347, 423
Vergil. *See* Virgil
Vergina, Aleksandra, **2:**436, **5:**456
Verhoeven, Pauline, **4:**381, **6:**270
Verikundova, N. V., **5:**236
Veriovka, Grigory, **6:**226
Veriovka Ukrainian National Dance
  Company, **6:**226
Verita Nemica dell'Apparenza
  Sollevata dal Tempo, La, **1:**29
Verkhovinets, V. N. (Verkovynets),
  6:223, 225
Verklärte Nacht (Schoenberg),
  1:375, **2:**561, **4:**81, 244, 517
  Kylián choreography, **4:**602
  Šmok choreography, **5:**617
  Spoerli choreography, **5:**683
  Staff choreography, **5:**692
Verklungene Feste, **1:**390
Verlorene Sohn, Der, **3:**153, **5:**265
  See also Prodigal Son, The
Vermigli, Pietro, **2:**167
vernacular dance, **3:**32
Vernal Floods, **4:**359
Verneuil, Catherine, **1:**290
Vernon, Bettina, **1:**468
Vernon, Jack, **4:**479, 480
Vernon, Janet, **1:**214, **6:**56, 57
Vernon, Konstanze, **1:**390–391,
  3:150, 157, 318
Vernoy de Saint-Georges, Jules-
  Henri, **1:**36, **2:**203, 206,
  5:135, 151
  Diable Amoureux libretto,
    4:340–341
  Gipsy libretto, **4:**340
  Giselle libretto, **3:**69, 177, 178
  Jolie Fille de Gand libretto, **3:**620
  Lady Henriette libretto, **4:**341
  Mazilier collaborations, **4:**342
  Papillon libretto, **4:**215
Veroli, Patrizia, **3:**553, 556
Véron, Eugène, **1:**24
Véron, Louis, **2:**202, 464, **3:**4,
  4:116, **5:**92, 134, **6:**71, 74,
  159
Veronese, Antonia, **2:**190
Verreist, **3:**368
Verret, François, **3:**79, 362
Verri, Pietro and Alessandro, **3:**546,
  4:696
Ver Sacrum (arts journal), **1:**131
Verses to the Beautiful Lady (Blok),
  1:463
Vershinina, Irina, **5:**485
Verso, Edward, **3:**614
Verstegen, Aart, **4:**380, 592, 600,
  601, **5:**530, 531
Verstovsky, Aleksei, **1:**86
Vertée, **3:**79
Vertès, Marcel, **2:**242, **3:**26
Vertpré, **1:**286, 287, 288
Vertue, George, **6:**176
Vert-Vert, **3:**316, **5:**341

Vervaeke, Luc, **1:**414
  as contributor, **1:**408–414, 414,
    519, **2:**109–110, **4:**136,
    5:422–423
Very Eye of Night, The (film dance),
  2:604
Very Good Eddie (musical), **5:**602,
  6:271
Verzet, **1:**289
Vesak, Norbert, **2:**39, 41, **4:**382,
  5:436, 685, **6:**266
Vesalii Icones, **4:**219
Vesalius, Andreas, **4:**14
ves dance, **2:**228, **3:***647*, *649*,
  4:34–35, **6:329–330**
Vespasian, emperor of Rome, **4:**426
Vespers, **5:**57
Vessel, **1:**245, **4:**451, **5:**549–550
Vessel, Anne Marie, **5:**433
Vestale, La, **1:**451, **5:**105, 160,
  6:338, 339
Vestrian Dish, A, or Caper Sauce
  for a Goose Pye (Assen and
  Jones), **2:**69
Vestris (ballet), **1:**371
Vestris, Adolphe, **3:**353
Vestris, Angiolo, **3:**66, **4:**695, **6:**330,
  331, 332
Vestris, Armand, **1:**237, **2:**415, 521,
  5:105, **6:**334
  dance *tours de force*, **3:**259
Vestris, Auguste, **1:**4, 371, 409,
  3:106, 5:260, 264, 316, **6:**330,
  331, *332*, **332–334**, *333*
  Bournonville (August) as student,
    1:329, 345–346, 347, 504,
    6:334
  Bournonville's exercise treatise,
    1:345–346
  Conservatoire de Danse, **3:**81, 82
  Didelot association, **2:**413, 416
  Don Quixote, **2:**435
  Duport (Louis-Antoine) rivalry,
    2:464
  Fitjames (Louise) as last
    pupil, **3:**4
  Gardel family association,
    3:118, 119
  King's Theatre choreography,
    3:256, 258
  Konservatoriet exemplifying
    choreographic school, **4:**43
  mother, Marie Allard, **1:**43, **2:**352
  Paris Opera Ballet, **5:**89, 90, 91
  Psyché et l'Amour, **5:**270
  puns on name, **2:**69
  students, **5:**134, 149, **6:**71, 334
  teaching methods, **6:**127
Vestris, Bernard, **1:**238, **2:**435,
  5:232
Vestris, Charles, **6:**237
Vestris, Gaëtan, **1:**236, **3:**81, 189,
  326, 546, **5:**35, 89, **6:330–331**
  Allard relationship, **1:**43, **2:**352
  Didelot as student, **2:**413
  as Dupré's student, **2:**465
  Gardel (Maximilien) comparison,
    3:117
  gavotte performance, **3:**125
  Heinel relationship, **3:**353
  King's Theatre (London)
    choreography, **3:**256, 258
  Lany (Jean-Barthélemy) rivalry,
    4:122
  Médée et Jason performance,
    4:346, 347, 697
  Paris Opera intrigues, **4:**149
  pirouettes, **1:**336
  students, **5:**215, **6:**334
  Stuttgart Ballet, **4:**695, **6:**9

Vestris, Jean-Baptiste, **6:**330
Vestris, Madame (Lucia Elizabeth Bartolozzi), **5:**70, **6:**189, 334
Vestris, Marie Ronzi, **6:**237
Vestris, Thérèse, **6:**330, 331
Vestris family, **6:**237, **330–334**
Vestris Prize Competition, **1:**501, **6:**398
Veszprém Dance Workshop, **3:**419
Veszter, Sándor, **3:**412, 414
Veteranen, eller Det Gaestfrie Tag, **1:**507
Vétéran, ou Le Bûcheron Déserteur, Le, **1:**124
Vial, Sara, **2:**125
Via la Vita, **3:**418
Viale, Rosina, **4:**258
Viale Ferrero, Mercedes, **5:**517
as contributor, **5:**1–3
Vianna, Klaus, **1:**535, 537
Vicente, Gil, **5:**230
Vice Puni, ou Le Nouveau Festin de Pierre, Le, **1:**124
Victim, **3:**418
Victimes Cloîtrées, Les, **1:**409
Victim of Jealousy, The, **3:**56
Victoria, Tomás Luis, **2:**434
Victoria University, New Zealand, **4:**629
Victoria and Albert Museum, London, **4:**163
Victorine, ou La Nuit Porte Conseil, **3:**620
Victory Boogie Woogie (Mondrian), **1:**132
Victory Dances (Berk), **1:**431
Victory Drum Dance, **2:**222
Vic-Wells Ballet. *See* Royal Ballet
Vida, Edna, **5:**172
Vida Breve, La, **1:**115
Vida Genera Danza, La, **4:***394*
Vidal, Lorena, **4:**668
video. *See* film and video
Video (television ballet), **5:**294
Video Dictionary of Classical Ballet, The (videotape set), **6:**129
Video Opera (Paik), **3:**54
Videotape for a Man and a Woman, **2:**406
videotaping
ethnographic, **2:**602–603
experimental film and dance, **2:**606–607
Vidmar, Vojko, **5:**677, **6:**437, *437*
as contributor, **6:**434–437
Vidor, King, **2:**613
Vidyapati (film), **2:**622
Vie de Polichinelle, La, **4:**184, **5:**95
Vieira, Jelon, **1:***530*
Vielhauer, Heidrun, **3:**151
vielle, **4:**50
Vienna, **1:**297, **4:**269
Vienna, Austria, **1:**131, 236–241
See also Austria, theatrical dance; Viennese waltz
Vienna, Lorenzo, **5:**232
Vienna: Lusthaus, **1:**462
"Vienna Blood" (Strauss), **6:**3
Vienna Conservatory, **2:**153
Vienna Court Ballet. *See* Hofopernballett
Vienna 1814, **4:**324
Vienna Festzug des Handwerke und der Gewerbe (1929), **4:**476
Vienna Folk Opera Ballet, **1:**241, **6:**388
Vienna Institute for Music and Dramatic Arts, **2:**153–154
Vienna Opera Ball, **3:**89

Vienna Secessionists, **1:**239
Vienna State Academy of Music and Dramatic Art, **1:**467
Vienna State Opera Ballet (Wiener Staatsopernballett), **1:**238–241, *240,* **5:**683
Adama, Richard, **1:**11, 241
Alonso (Alicia) productions, **1:**49
Charrat performances, **2:**111
Checkmate revival, **2:**115
Chladek stagings, **2:**153, 154
Don Quixote productions, **2:**435, 440
Firebird, The, **3:**3
Forsythe guest choreography, **3:**52
Gioja productions, **3:**175–176
Hanka, Erika, **3:**340
Hassreiter, Josef, **3:**346–347
Henry (Louis) productions, **3:**358
Hungarian performances, **3:**413–414
Josephslegende, Die, **3:**631, **4:**64
Kröller, Heinrich, **4:**64
Losch, Tilly, **4:**228–229
Milloss as ballet master, **4:**421
Noverre, Jean-Georges, **4:**696
Nureyev-Georgiadis *Swan Lake* production, **3:**136, **6:**35
Parlić directorship, **5:**100
Viganò productions, **3:**175
Wallmann choreography, **6:**357
Wiesenthal choreography, **6:**388
Viennese Kinderballett, **1:**238, **6:334–336**
Horschelt, Friedrich, **2:**202, 237, **3:**380
Viennese School of Applied Art, **1:**131
Viennese Secession, **6:**387
Viennese waltz, **1:**46, 239, **3:**89, 141, 361, **6:**359, 360
ballroom competition standards, **1:**358
operettas as popularizers, **4:**269–270, **6:**268
popularity, **4:**514
Strauss family, **4:**514, **6:**2–3, 361
Wiesenthal technique, **6:**387, *387,* 388
Vienola-Lindfors, Irma, **2:**635
as contributor, **2:**631–634
Vie Parisienne, La (Offenbach), **3:**70, **6:**268
Vierges Folles, Les, **1:**326–327
Vier Letzte Lieder, **2:**347, *469*
Viertel, Berthold, **6:**393
Vier Temperamente, Die, **2:**154
Vies, Abraham van der, **5:**530
Vietnam, **6:336–337**
libraries and museums, **4:**159
Stock (Cheryl) dance activities, **1:**215
trance rituals, **6:**185
Viewers, **4:**81, 602
Viganò, Adelaide, **3:**50
Viganò, Maria Medina, **5:**260, **6:**337, 338
Viganò, Onorato, **2:**208, 433, 434, **3:**546, 556
Viganò, Salvatore, **1:**126, 460, **2:**202, 208, 363, **3:**546, **5:**105, 260, 517, **6:337–339**

ballet d'action, **3:**547, **4:**175
Creatures of Prometheus, The, **1:**237, 402, **2:**401, **3:**175, **4:**513
Dauberval association, **2:**353
Didelot association, **2:**413
Egri ballet reconstruction, **2:**480
Fille Mal Gardée, La, **1:**390, **2:**596
Gioja's influence compared with, **3:**175, 176
as Henry (Louis) influence, **3:**68, 358
Hungarian performances, **3:**413
Otello, **5:**528, **6:**338–339
Prometheus, **5:**528
as Rota influence, **5:**409
Sanquirico collaboration, **5:**537
synthesis of Angiolini and Noverre styles, **3:**547
Viganò family, **1:**126, **3:**67, 546
Vigarani, Carlo, **1:**288, 425, 426, **5:**86, 536
Vigarani, Gasparo, **5:**536, **6:**157
Vigarani, Lodovico, **5:**536
Vigée-Lebrun, Élisabeth, **6:**331, 334
Vignale Monferrato festival, **3:**553
Vigne, La, **3:**15, 562
Vigrani, Gaspare, **4:**188
Vi har ikke tid, **4:**677
Vijeya, **3:**647
Vijf Schetsen, **5:**290
Vikivakar og vikivakakvaedi, **3:**436
vikivaki, **3:**434, 435, 436
Viktorka, **4:**239, **5:**245
Vilar, Jean, **1:**405
Vilariño, Numen, **6:**302
Vilcinja, Velta, **4:**128
Vile Parody of Address, The, **3:**52
Vilia, **2:**510, **3:**175
Vilimaa, Ülo, **2:**528, 530, **5:**460
Villa, Guiseppe, **5:**232
Villadolid, Anna, **5:**172
Villaflor, Lourdes, **1:**394
Village Apothecary, The, **5:**404
Village Bride, The (Greuze), **1:**126
Village I Knew, The (Maslow), **3:**605, **4:**306
Village of Whispers, **4:**649
Village Voice (newspaper), **2:**69, 70, **3:**635, **6:**299, 300
Villain, The (Porter), **3:**254
Villa-Lobos, Heitor, **1:**533, **6:**326
villancico, **2:**1
Villano Rincivilito, Il, ossia Il Barone Molletta di Rocca Antica, **6:**69
Villanueva, Benny (Benjamin Reyes), **5:**171
Villarica, Fe Sala, **5:**172
Villaruz, Basilio Esteban, **5:**174
Villegas, Quevedo, **5:**667
Villella, Edward, **1:***30,* 372, **2:**333, **5:**202, 265, **6:***201,* **339–341**
Afternoon of a Faun performance, **1:**28
Apollo performance, **1:**96
Bugaku performance, **4:***616*
Dances at a Gathering performance, **2:**333, **4:***619*
Jacob's Pillow, **3:**571
McBride dance partnership, **4:**345, 611, 612, **6:**340, *340*
Miami Ballet, **6:**265
Midsummer Night's Dream, A, **1:**267
New York City Ballet roles, **4:**609, 611, 619
partners, **6:**143, 340
Rubies perfrmance, **1:**269, **4:**612
Symphony in C performance, **6:**66

Tarantella performance, **6:**105, 340
television performances, **6:**137, 340
triple *tours en l'air,* **1:**338
on turnout position, **6:**215
Verdy as partner, **6:**328, 340
Watermill performance, **5:***363,* 365
on Williams (Stanley) teaching skill, **6:**399
Villeneuve-lès-Avignon, **3:**77
Villeroy, marquis de, **1:**288, 424
Villoch, Aida, **2:**278
Villon, **3:***232*
Villumsen, Arne, **2:**385, **5:**430
Vilmorin, Louise de, **5:**237
Vilnius Ballet School, **4:**208
Viltsak, Valentina, **3:**568
Vilzak, Anatole, **1:**48, 110, 301, **2:**410, 444, **3:**24, **4:**182, 457, **5:**237, 611, 650, **6:**341
Biches, Les, **1:**449
Latvian ballet, **4:**127
Nijinska works, **4:**635, 659
Schollar marriage, **5:**559
students, **1:**478, **3:**351, 663, **4:**227, **6:**362
Vilzak-Schollar School, New York, **1:**429
Vilzak Variations after Petipa, **6:**341
Vincent, L. M., **2:**330
Vincent, René, **2:**470
Vincenti, Vittorio de, **3:**284
Vincitori dei Giuochi Olimpici, I, **1:**88
Vine, Carl, **4:**479
Vines, Ricardo, **5:**236
Vingt-cinq Ans des Grands Ballets, Les (documentary), **6:**132
Vingt-quatre Préludes, **2:**471
Vinogradov, Oleg, **1:**371, **2:**11, 200, 422, 423, 564, **4:**36, **5:**460, **6:341–342**
Inspector-General, The, **5:**462
Leventhal collaboration, **4:**153–154
Maly Theater Ballet directorship, **5:**468
Maryinsky Ballet artistic directorship, **4:**285, **5:**463-464
Mountain Girl, The, **4:**285
Novosibirsk Opera and Ballet Theater, **5:**471-472
Viola, Norma, **1:**109
Viola Alone, **4:**623
Violence, **2:**45
Violet (Fuller dance), **3:**92
Violette, Eva Maria, **6:342-343**
Violette, Ferdinand, **6:**343
violin, **1:**121, **2:**180, 382, **3:**64
Cape Breton step dancing, **5:**697, 698
as dance lesson accompaniment, **1:**6, **3:**80
Garifuna dance, **3:**120
as Irish jig accompaniment, **3:***608*
Kreutzer, Rodolphe, **4:**61
Norwegian dance accompaniment, **4:**670
Poland, **5:**212
Saint-Léon's skills, **5:**498, 499, *499*
Scottish dance, **3:**243
Swedish dance accompaniment, **6:**37
Ukraine, **6:**222
Violin Concerto, **1:**24, **4:**274, 613
Violin Concerto in E Major, **3:**418

Violin Phase, **1:**412
Violon, **1:**305
Violoncelo não Acompanhado em Suite de Luxo, **5:***232*
Violon du Diable, Le, **1:**6, **2:**95, **5:***499,* 500, 516
Violostries, **1:**349, *350*
Viora, **3:**414
Viotti, Emmanuele, **1:**499, **2:**587
Viotti, Giovanni Battista, **4:**61
vira, **5:**228, 229
viraha concept, **1:**169
Virgil, **4:**106, **5:**112, 113, 376
Virginia Dance Society, **4:**39
Virginia Essence, **6:**254
"Virginia Reel" (dance), **5:**333, 334
Virginia Sampler, **1:**300, 302, 441
Virgin Islands, **2:**63, 64
Virgin of Andacollo festival, **1:**109
Virgin of Guadalupe festival, **2:**194
Virgin of the Immaculate Conception feast day, **1:**529
Vironmäki, Susanna, **2:**633
Virsaladze, Simon, **3:**193, 310, **4:**129, 144, **5:**12, 321, **6:343**
    Sleeping Beauty design, **5:**610
    Spartacus design, **5:**677
    Stone Flower design, **5:**699
Virsky, Pavel, **6:**222-223, 225, 226, **344**
Virsky Academic Dance Company of Ukraine, **6:***224*
Virulazo and Elvira, **6:**94
visa, **6:**322
Visability . . . by Chance, **2:**470
Visage, **2:**388
Visages de Femmes, **2:**466
Vis-A-Vis Dance Canberra, **1:**215
Visayan, Philippines, **2:**230
Visconti, Luchino, **2:**369, **3:**59
Viscusi, Achille, **3:**99, **5:**245, 614, **6:**32
Visentini, Catherine-Antoinette, **2:**365
Visentini, Tommaso Antonio, **2:**190
Vishnevsky, Vsevolod, **1:**540
Vishnu. *See* Viṣṇu
Vishvabharati University, **4:**253
Vishwa Bharati-Shantiniketan, **3:**468
Visibility by Chance, **4:**594
Visinski, Stanimir, *as contributor,* **6:**426-431
Vision (cable network), **6:**133
vision dances, **4:**551, 568-569
Vision of Chopin, **2:**510, **4:**179
Vision of Delight, The (masque), **4:**310
Vision of Marguerite, **2:**510, **3:**175
Vision of Salomé, The, **1:**42, 43, **4:**522, **5:**46
Vision of the Aissoua, The, **2:**378
Vision of the Apocalypse, **3:**212
Vision of the Twelve Goddesses, The (masque), **4:**308, 310
vision quest, **4:**568
Visions, **3:**511, **6:**391
Visions of a Poet, The, **6:**309
Visit, The, **3:**391
Visitation, The, **3:**391, **4:**39, 198
Visite à Bedlam, La, **2:**202, **4:**339, 341
Viski, Károly, **3:**422
Vislocky, Dorothy, **3:**445
Viṣṇu (deity), **2:**394, **3:**465, 466, 467, **4:**253, 298
Viṣṇudharmottara Purāṇa, **2:**454-455
Viṣṇu Purāṇa (Indian text), **3:**465, 466

visual arts. *See* artists and dance; prints and drawings
Viswanathan, **1:**273
Vita di Maria Vergine (Cornazano), **2:**204
Vita Futurista, La (film), **1:**134
Vitak, Albertina, **3:**23, 349
Vitali, Giovanni Battista, **4:**511
Vitalis, **4:**427
vitalism, **1:**127, 130
Vitányi, Iván, **3:**424
Vitková, Michaela, **2:***309*
Vitolinjs, Janis, **4:**127
Vitols, Jarol, **4:**127
Vitruvius, **4:**186
Vittadini, Franco, **3:**51, **5:**246
Vittoria, La (Paisiello), **4:**698
Vittorio Amedeo I, duke of Savoy, **1:**29
Vittuci, Matteo Marcellus. *See* Matteo
Vityn, Tamara, **4:**127
Viva Afrika Borwa, **5:***660*
Vivaldi, Antonio, **2:**388, 426, **3:**13, 51
Vivaldi Concerto Grosso, **2:**162
Vivandiera, La (1842), **1:**499
Vivandière, La, **1:**460, 477, **5:**158, **6:**127
    Cerrito choreography, **2:**93, 94, 95
    Ivanov as Petipa replacement, **3:**560
    Joffrey revival of pas de six, **3:**614, 617
    Labanotation of pas de six, **3:**427
    Lacotte and Guest reconstruction, **4:**108, **5:**502
    Saint-Léon choreography, **5:**498, 500
Viva Tu Madre, **4:**262
Viva Vivaldi, **3:**612, 613
Vives, Amedeo, **2:**567
Vives, Juan Luis, **2:**167
Vives, María, **1:**480
Vizcayan dances, **1:**376
Vlachs (people), **3:**296
Vláčilová, Hana, **2:**310
Vlad, Roman, **4:**421, **5:**387
Vladimiroff, Pierre, **2:**160, **4:**63, 184, 227, **5:**126, 611, **6:344–345**
    Australian tour, **1:**207
    Doubrovska marriage, **2:**441, 442
    Eros performance, **5:**455
    as Fokine student, **3:**14, **5:**456
    Maryinsky Ballet, **4:**283
    Mordkin Russian Ballet tours, **4:**460
    School of American Ballet, **6:**292
    students, **4:**178, 449, 457
Vladimirov, Yuri, **1:**493, **5:**12, 460, **6:**420
Vladimirov-Klimov, S., **5:**473
Vlady, Lawrence, **2:**438
Vlaslova, Ludmila, **1:***493*
Vlasnova, Eleonora, **2:**15
Vlasov, Stanislav, **1:***493*
Vlasov, Vladimir, **4:**87, **5:**595, **6:**341
Vlassi, Christiane, **1:**405, **3:**82
Vlassof, Anton, **4:**369
Vlaş, Traian, **5:**387
Vlček, Václav, **6:**432
"Vleegert," **4:**586
"Vlöggelen," **4:**585
Vltava, **1:**499, **4:**275
Vluegels, Donald, **3:**520
vocal choreography, **5:**632
vocal sounds. *See* folk dance sounds; song dance

Voce Umana, La, **5:**527
Vodehnal, Andrea, **1:**302
vodena râčenica, **2:**101
Vodery, Will, **6:**256
Vodun, **1:**538, **2:***431,* **3:**333-336, **6:345-348**
    as Dunham dance source, **3:**335
    filmed record, **2:**601
    ritual dances, **5:**355-356, 357
    trance dance, **6:**185, 188
vodunsi (spirit), **2:**274
Voegtlin, W. T., **6:**267
Voema, Lorenzo, **1:**427
Vögel, Die, **4:**64
Vogelesang, Richard. *See* Gadeskov, Iril
Vogelsang, Marianne, **3:**152, 153
Voguing (dance), **5:**187, 636
Voice of Firestone, The (television series), **6:**137
Voices and Light Footsteps, **1:**52
Voices of Spring, **1:**65, **2:**23, **4:**460
"Voices of Spring" (Strauss waltz), **6:**3
V.O.I.D. (Velocity of Interfering Data), **4:**595
Voigt, Michael, **5:**244
Voiture, Vincent, **1:**425
Voix Humaine, La (Cocteau), **4:**427
Vojáčková, Hana, **1:**541
Vokes, Fred, **5:**71-72
Vokes family, **5:**71-72
Volange family, **5:**215
Volans, Kevin, **2:**355
volé, **1:**384-385
Volga Boatmen, The, **2:**454
Volgendo il Ciel, **4:**505
Volière, La, **2:**38, 503-504, **4:**340
Volinine, Alexandre, **1:**489, **3:**129, **4:**223, **5:**14, *120,* 124, 294, 604, 611, **6:**348
    Australian tour, **1:**207
    Bolshoi Ballet, **5:**456
    Cuban tour, **2:**276
    Mordkin's All-Star Imperial Russian Ballet, **4:**459
    Paris dance studio, **3:**82
    Royal Danish Ballet guest production, **5:**439
    students, **1:**251, **2:**19, 426, 478, **5:**312, 349, **6:**348
volk concept, **3:**29
Volkersen, Niels Henrik, **2:**385
Volkoff, Boris
    archival papers, **4:**166
    students, **3:**351
    Toronto ballet scene, **2:**38, 39, 47, **4:**538
Volkoff Canadian Ballet, **2:**38
Volkonsky, Sergei, **4:**68, **5:**160
Volkov, Nikolai, **2:**421, **3:**12, 14
    Fountain of Bakhchisarai libretto, **3:**56, **6:**441
    Spartacus libretto, **5:**677
    students, **3:**204, **4:**142
Volkova, Anna, **1:**313, 315
Volkova, Natalia, **5:**469
Volkova, Vera, **5:**53, 529, **6:349**
    Harkness classes, **3:**3342
    Hønningen mentorship, **3:**373
    influence on English and Danish schools, **1:**330, 348, **5:**430
    PACT Ballet guest productions, **5:**652
    Royal Danish Ballet school, **5:**430
    students, **1:**48-49, 231, 330, **2:**2, 262, 561, **3:**12, 59, 429, 667, **4:**64, 603, **5:**312, 430, 554, 599, **6:**312, 349, 405
    teaching in China, **2:**145

Vaganova method, **1:**330, 399, **6:**399
    as Williams (Stanley) teacher, **6:**399
Volksbühne. *See* Berlin Volksbühne
Volksopernballett (Folk Opera, Vienna), **1:**241, **6:**388
Vollmar, Jocelyn, **2:**161, **5:**513
volta, **1:**104, **3:**109, **5:**338, **6:349-351,** 359
Voltaic peoples, **4:**290
Voltaire, **2:**589, **3:**364, **4:**174, **5:**249, 306, 424, 505
    on Camargo, **5:**505
Voluntaries, **1:**72, **2:**335, 470, **3:**351, 373, 448, **6:**146
    Keil performance, **4:**1
    Makarova performance, **4:**248
Volusian, **1:**276
Volven, **4:**679
Volynsky, Akim, **1:**23, 24, 464, **3:**564, **6:**309, **351-352**
    aesthetics, **5:**485
    Kniga likovany, **5:**482-483
    students, **5:**282, **6:**349
Volzhsky Folk Choir, **5:**474
Vom Tauwind und der Neuen Freude (Laban movement choir), **4:**93
von. *For names with this prefix not found below, see main element*
von Aroldingen, Karin, **3:**318, **4:**618, 623
Vondersaar, Jeannette, **2:**470
Vondruška, Petr, **2:**308
von Gencsy, Eva, **2:**46, *150,* **3:**228, **5:***434, 684*
Von Grona, Eugene, **6:**258, *259*
von Loggenburg, Dudley, **2:**513
von Sturmer, John, *as contributor,* **1:**225-227
von Tiedemann, Cylla, *as photographer,* **2:**59, **3:**389, **4:**547, **6:**449
Voodoo. *See* Vodun
Voodoo Ceremonial, **3:**386
Voor een verloren Soldaat (van Dantzig), **2:**348
Voos, Hanna, **2:**109
Voos, Isa, **1:**411
Voremberg, Reuven, **2:**469, 470
Voronezh Ballet Company, **5:**472
Voronezh Russian Choir, **5:**474
voronezhsky step, **5:**445
Voronina-Ivanova, Aleksandra, **5:**454
Vorster, John, **5:**53
Vos, Irène d', **2:**470, **4:**600
Voskovec, Jiří, **2:**307, **4:**239
Voskresenskaya, Svetlana, **5:**475, 479
Voskresenskaya, Vera, **3:**186
Vosseler, Heidi, **1:***63,* **2:**445, **5:**570-571
Vostell, Wolf, **1:**139
Vostřák, Zbyněk, **5:**245
Vouras, Mary, **5:**303
Vox Maris, **2:**343
Voyage, **5:**562
Voyage au Coeur d'un Enfant, **1:**404
Voyagers in Southern Seas, **1:**496
Voyage to Spain (Gautier), **2:**251
Voyer, Simonne, **2:**36, 49
Voyeurisme, **2:**45
Voyevoda (Tchaikovsky), **6:**114
Voytek, **2:**440
Vranický, Pavel, **2:**306
Vretos, Anne-Marie, **5:**390
Vrije Universiteit, Brussels, **1:**414
Vrindavan, India, **3:**467, 468

Vronsky, Vakhtang, **1:**248, **6:**226
Vroom, Jean-Paul, **4:**253
Vroubel, Mikhail, **5:**541
vrták, **2:**304
Vrubel, Mikhail, **1:**487
Vsevolodsky-Gerngross, Vsevolod, **5:**473, 481
Vsevolozhsky, Ivan, **2:**82, 446, **3:**563, **4:**430, 515, **5:**160, **6:**453
 Nutcracker libretto, **5:**9, 10
 Sleeping Beauty libretto, **5:**606, **6:**116
Vu-An, Eric, **1:**406, **3:**61, 75, 601, **5:**99
Vučić, Radomir, **6:**438
Vudyarthi, Reba, **5:**568
Vuillard, Édouard, **1:**437
Vuillet-Baum, Marcelle, **4:**529
Vuillier, Gaston, **3:**67, **5:**222
Vujicsics, Tihamér, **2:**473
Vujisik, Tanja, **6:**437
Vukičević, Sonja, **6:**435
Vukový, Viliam, **4:**584
Vumba (people), **2:**418
Vyāsa, **3:**464
Vyjayantimala, **2:**624, *626*
Vyncke, Karin, **1:**412
Vyroubova, Nina, **1:**305, 306, **2:**472, **5:**91, 96, 162, 248, 401, **6:**191, **352–353**
 Phèdre performance, **4:**185
 Sylphide revival performance, **3:**73, 318, **4:**34

Wachman, Abraham, **3:**534, **4:**690, 692
Waddle (dance), **6:**263
Wadia, J. B. H., **2:**623
Wadlington, Jeff, **4:**482, **6:**112
Wadsworth Athenaeum, Hartford, **1:**63, **4:**167–168, 186
Waehner, Karin, **3:**76, 83, **5:**388
Waelterlin, Oskar, **1:**98
Waffentantz, **4:**61
Waggoner, Dan, **1:**215
Waghle, Rohini, **1:**94
Wagner, Ann, *as contributor*, **2:**166–169
Wagner, Cosima, **1:**97, **5:**37
Wagner, Gertrud, **5:**36
Wagner, Heinrich, **1:**392
Wagner, Richard, **1:**97, 98, 390, 407, **2:**360, **3:**19, 92, **5:**36, 148, **6:**161
 dance aesthetics, **1:**127, 129, **2:**453
 Danish productions of operas, **1:**510
 Gesamtkunstwerk concept, **5:**540, 541
 Grahn collaboration, **3:**224
 influence on Diaghilev, **2:**406
 Laban dance choreography, **4:**91
 Paris Opera ballet requirement, **4:**514
 Tannhäuser. See Venusberg scene
 waltz compositions, **6:**360
Wagner, Robin, **1:**420
Wagner, Shauna, **1:**375
Wagner, Thelma, **2:**47
Wagner, Wieland, **5:**36
Wagoner, Dan, **3:**274, **5:**303, **6:**109
 choreographic style analysis, **4:**99
 London Contemporary Dance Theatre, **4:**218, 220
wagoto, **3:**637
Wague, Georges, **4:**523
Wahhāb, 'Abd al-, **4:**489

Wahlverwandtschaften, **1:**442, **5:**557
waiata kori (waiata-a-ringa), **4:**261
Waiko, John Dademo, *as contributor*, **5:**78–80
Wainrot, Mauricio, **1:**114, **2:**514
Waissel, Matthäus, **4:**505
Waiting, **2:**1
Waiting for Godot (Beckett), **3:**652
Waiting for the Dawn, **2:**417, **3:**421
Waits, Tom, **6:**401
Wajda, Andrzej, **1:**361
wakashu kabuki, **3:**637
Wakayagi Ryū, **3:**593
Wake Up and Dream (musical), **4:**334
Wakhevitch, Georges, **3:**601, **4:**33
Walbom, Emilie, **2:**173, **4:**674, **5:**427–428
Walbrook, Anton, **5:**331, 332
Walczak, Jan, **5:**217
Waldeen, **4:**392, *392*, 394, **6:**355–356
 archival collection, **4:**166
 Bravo discovery by, **1:**524
Waldemar, **1:**497, 507, 508, 509, 511, 512, 514, **3:**222, 223, **5:**425
Waldman, Anne, **1:**142, **2:**460, **3:**52
Waldman, Max, **5:**183
 as photographer, **1:**271, **2:**16, 444, **3:**216, 351, 577, **4:**25, 248, 633, 649, **5:**102, 398, **6:**203
Waldman, Toos, **5:**531
Waldstein, count von, **1:**402
Waldteufel, Émile, **6:**2
Waléry (photographer), **5:**182
Wales, **3:**250
 clog dancing, **5:**695–696
 folk dance study, **3:**33
 Lancers, **2:**592
 Morris dance, **4:**474
walk-around, **6:**254
Walkaround Time, **1:**141, 542, **2:**292, **3:**620, **6:**356, **356**
 film of, **2:**294
Walker, Ada Overton, **5:**180, *181*
Walker, Carol, **6:**292
Walker, David, **2:**445–446, 514
Walker, David Hatch, **3:**220
Walker, George, **1:**439, **4:**25, **5:**180, *181*, **6:**99–100, 255, 256
Walker, James, **3:**304
Walker, John III, **4:**27
Walker, Kathrine. *See* Sorley Walker, Kathrine
Walker, Kim, **6:**56
Walker, Margareth, **4:**590
Walker, Nancy, **5:**361, **6:**279
Walker, Norma, **6:**262
Walker, Norman, **5:**43, 234, 586, **6:**266
 Boston Ballet choreography, **1:**501
 Jacob's Pillow, **3:**572
 Trionfo di Afrodite, **3:**230
Walker, William, **3:**57, **4:**668
Walking Dance for Any Number, **2:**605
Walking on the Wall, **1:**543
"Walkin' the Dog" (song), **6:**255
Walkowitz, Abraham, **1:**131, **5:**261, **6:**356–357**
Walks and Digressions, **3:**201
Walk This Way, **1:**76
Wall, David, **2:**401, **3:**267, **5:**100, 294, **6:**202, **357**
 Manon roles, **4:**255, 256, **6:**357
 Mayerling performance, **4:**243, 244, **5:**419, **6:**357
 Month in the Country performance, **4:**456–460

Sadler's Wells Theatre Ballet, **5:**421, **6:**357, 381
Wells dance partnership, **6:**357, 380
Wall, The, **4:**267
Wallaby Dance, **1:**226
Wallachia, **2:**301, **5:**379, 381
Wallen, Errolyn, **2:**1
Wallenstein, Alfred, **5:**562
Wallin, Börje, **6:**36
Wallis, Lynn, **1:**456, **2:**42, **4:**546
Wallmann, Margarete, **1:**110, 112, 240, 518, **2:**568, **3:**89, 146, 631, **5:**248, **6:**357, **357–358**
Walloons (people), **1:**408
Wall Street Journal, The (Hanayagi-Blank dance), **3:**340
Walong, Bernadette, **1:**215
Walpiri (people), **1:**227–229, 228
Walpurgisnacht, **5:**58, *204*
Walpurgisnacht Ballet, **2:**577, **4:**611, 618, 631
Walpurgis Night, **2:**510, **4:**381, **5:**569, 6:8
Walsh, Christine, **1:**235
Walsh, John, **1:**92, **2:**256, **3:**522
Walsh, Thommie, **6:**204, 205, 285, 286
Walter, Bruno, **1:**438, **4:**64
Walter, Erich, **2:**361, **3:**149, **6:**358–359**
 Creatures of Prometheus revival, **1:**402
 Don Juan version, **2:**434
 Ondine choreography, **3:**360
Walter Gore Ballet, **3:**203
Walters, Charles, **2:**616
Walther, Claire, **6:**389
Walton, Elizabeth, **6:**363
Walton, Florence, **6:**318
Walton, J. Michael, *as contributor*, **5:**41–42
Walton, Jude, **1:**218
Walton, Liz, **6:**109
Walton, William, **1:**149, 150, 158, **4:**113, 520
Walt Whitman Suite, **6:**88
waltz, **6:**359–362
 Argentina, **1:**108, 109
 ballroom competition standards, **1:**358
 Cajun, **2:**24
 Caribbean region, **2:**63, 64
 caricatures, **2:**70
 Castle style, **2:**78
 Coppélia score, **2:**368
 Croatia, **6:**428–429
 Czech, **2:**301
 Denmark, **2:**381
 Deutsche precursors, **1:**46–47, **3:**141
 development, **5:**627
 Finland, **2:**630
 France, **3:**68, 69
 Germany, **3:***142*
 Iceland, **3:**435
 music compositions, **4:**514
 Norway, **4:**670–671
 Protestant sectarian condemnation, 167
 as social dance, **5:**626, 627, 686
 social dance popularity, **4:**514
 stage choreographies, **3:**68, **6:**268–269
 Strauss family, **6:**2, 3
 United States, **6:**235, 251
 Viennese opera, **6:**268
 volta comparison, **6:**351
 Wiesenthal choreography, **6:**387, 388
 See also Viennese waltz

Waltz, Sasha, **3:**151, 156
Waltz Academy, **3:**664, **4:**63, 616
waltz clog, **6:**98
Waltz Dreams, **6:**229
Waltzes from Vienna, **2:**342
Waltz in C-sharp Minor (Chopin), **6:**60, 62
Waltz in G-flat Major (Chopin), **6:**60, 62
"Waltz of Limeric, The," **3:**517
"Waltz of the Snowflakes" (*The Nutcracker*), **1:**264, **3:**564, *564*, **5:**10, 12, *13*, 15
Waltz Project, The, **4:**622
Walz, Karl, **2:**208, **5:**610
Wan (people), **4:**290, **6:**383
wanara, **6:**369
wanaragua, **2:**62, **3:**120, 121
wanarunga, **3:**320
Wanderer, The (Ashton ballet), **1:**150, **2:***424*
Wanderers, The (artist group), **1:**486
Wanderers, The (Waring ballet), **6:**362
Wandji, Myrian, **3:**79
Wandtke, Harald, **3:**155
wangarr, **1:**223, 224
Wanger, Walter, **5:**372
Wang Guohua, **5:**330
Wangh, Anne Wilson, **3:**535, **4:**164
Wang Kefen, **1:**149, 149–150
wang topéng, **3:**487
Wang Xixian, **5:**330, 471
Wanner, Wilhelm, **1:**486
Wan Qiwu, **5:**330
Wanting to Tell Stories, **2:**355
Wantke, Harald, **3:**155
Wapping Landlady, The, **3:**378
WAR, **5:**293
Waramba: L'Opéra Mandingue, **5:**517
War and Peace (Tolstoy), **2:**464
Warburg, Edward M. M., **1:**63, 64, **4:**27, 28, 382, **6:**246
Warby, Ros, **1:**217
Ward, Kevin, **2:**358
War Dance, **4:**555, 561, **5:**240
War Dance of the Apaches against the Navajos (Catlin), **4:**553
war dances. *See* armed dances
Warden and the Ward, The, **1:**500
ware, **5:**85
War Hero, The, **5:**431
Warhol, Andy, **2:**290, 292, **3:**620
 Rainforest set design, **5:**548, *548*
Waring, Fred, **2:**619
Waring, James, **2:**119, 269, 290, **3:**200–201, 619, 634, **4:**519, 602, **5:**292, 573, **6:**107, 282, **362–364**
Warlock, Peter, **1:**146
Warlock, Thomas, **4:**311
Warman, Arturo, **4:**386
Warner, MaryJane, *as contributor*, **2:**46–48
Warner Brothers Studios, **2:**613, 614
War of Beauty, The (Callot), **2:**27
War of Love, The (Callot), **2:**27
War of the Women, The, **3:**316, **5:**139, 278
Warren, Harry, **1:**194
Warren, Larry, *as contributor*, **3:**386–388, **4:**156–157
Warren, Leigh, **1:**213, 214, **4:**602
Warren, Robert, **2:**337
Warren, Thomas, **2:**337
Warren, Vincent, **2:**41, 605, **3:**228, 233, **4:**165, **6:**107, 363, **364**

Warren, William, **2:**337
warrick, **3:**573
warrine, **3:**121
warrior dances. *See* armed dances
Warsaw Ballet, **1:**297, 500, **2:**172,
   3:316, 317, **5:**75, 195,
   6:364–365
Ballets of Valentin Elizariev, The,
   2:501
   Berger as artistic director, **1:**428
   Blasis choreography, **1:**460–461
   Bogdanova guest appearance,
      1:477
   Borri directorship, **1:**500, **6:**365
   Chopin Concerto, **4:**638
   Gogół, Jerzy, **3:**192
   school, **6:**441
   Turczynowicz, Roman, **5:**216,
      217, **6:**207–208
   Woizikowski as ballet master,
      6:404
   Zajlich, Piotr, **6:**441
Warsaw Ghetto, **4:**156
Warsaw Opera Ballet. *See* Warsaw
   Ballet
Warsaw Rhapsody, The, **5:**75
Wartski, Sheila, **5:**657
Warwick, Dionne, **3:**52
Washburn, Watson, **1:**295
Washington, Ernest L., **2:**328–329,
   6:267
Washington, Ford Lee ("Buck"),
   2:5, **6:**99, 317
Washington, Shelley, **6:**152, *154*
Washington, Vernon, **6:**284
Washington Ballet, **1:**65, **2:**356,
   3:88, **4:**450, **6:**264, **366–367**
   Savannah premiere, **5:**660
   Serrano as teacher, **5:**573
Washington Ballet Guild, **1:**70
Washington Irving High School,
   New York City, **3:**215
Washington Post, **6:**299
Washington School of Ballet, **1:**70,
   2:356, **5:**559
Washington Square (James novel),
   4:72
Washington Square (Kudelka
   ballet), **2:**463, **4:**71, 72,
   544, 547
"Washington Square" (television
   series), **1:**482
waṣlah dance, **4:**491
Wasps (Aristophanes), **2:**506, **4:**44,
   5:556
Wasteland, **4:**596
Watch Hill, Rhode Island, **3:**342,
   610, 611
Watch Your Step (musical), **2:**79,
   6:271, *271*
water ballets, **5:**377
Waterbodies (film), **2:**609
Waterbury, John, **4:**417
*Waterless Method of Swimming
   Instruction*, **4:**217, *217*
Water Lilies, **5:**34
Waterman, Jill, **5:**659
Water Margin, The (opera), **6:**446
Watermill, **2:**245, **3:**538, **4:**614,
   5:363, 365–366, **6:**340
Water Motor, **1:**544
Water Music (Handel), **3:**376
"Water Nymph Ballet" (*The
   Goldwyn Follies*), **6:**450
water puppets, **1:**179
Waters, Edmund, **2:**364
Waters, Elizabeth, **3:**369, **4:**649,
   6:191
Waters, Ethel, **6:**244, 255, 256, 278
Waters, Simon, **1:**52, **5:***304*
Waters, Sylvia, **2:**20

Water Study, **3:**399, 403, **5:**680,
   6:367
Wa'Thionogo, Ngugi, **6:**22
Watkins, Mary F., **6:**299
Watson, Graeme, **1:**214, 215
Watteau, Jean-Antoine, **2:**191,
   4:481, **5:**259
Watts, Alan, **1:**470
Watts, Heather, **3:**448, **4:**274, 618,
   619, *620*, 623
Watts, Jonathan, **1:***30*, **3:**51, **4:**179,
   179, *613*, 619
Watts, Robert, **6:**362
Watts, Usher, **6:**317
Watusi (people). *See* Tutsi
Watusi (dance), **5:**633, **6:**263
Way, Jennifer, **4:**442, **6:**152
Way, The, **6:**394
Wayan Diya, **5:**523, 524
wayang, **1:**172, 173, 174, 179,
   3:485, *487*, 501, 502, 504,
   6:367–370
wayang golek puppets, **3:**497, *497*,
   4:298, 494
wayang kulit, **3:**368, **6:***367*
wayang lemah, **6:**368
wayang purwa wong, **1:**173
wayang topéng, **3:***487*, **498–499**,
   501–502, **4:**298
wayang wong, **1:**174, *175*, 179,
   3:*493*, 496, **496–497**, 498,
   502, 644–645, 670, **4:**298, *298*,
   6:369
wayang wong golek menak,
   3:497, 498
Wayan Pugra, **5:**524
Wayburn, Ned, **6:**98, 242, 271, 272,
   273, 318, **370–371**, 448
Wayne, Dennis, **1:***124*, **5:**528
wayno, **5:**145, *146*
Wè (people), **6:***14*
weapons dances. *See* armed
   dances; Sword Dance
Weathersby, Eliza, **2:**572
Weaver, Jenifer, **5:**17
Weaver, John, **1:**23, 92, **2:**338, 363,
   3:111, **4:**106, **5:**69, 105, 251,
   518, 519, **6:372–374**
   ballet d'action, **5:**518, 519, 603
   on Ballon, **1:**355, **6:**374
   on Caverley, **2:**80–81
   Essex association, **2:**527
   Feuillet translation, **2:**81, 588,
      589, **3:**522, **4:**684, **6:**372, 373
   Isaac (Mister) dance collection,
      3:522, **6:**373
   on L'Abbé, **4:**105
   libretto, **4:**173, **6:**373
   Loves of Mars and Venus, **2:**465,
      4:173, **6:**372, 373
   on *port de bras*, **5:**227
   publications, **2:**527, **3:**256, 281,
      4:105, **6:**123, 124, 125, 232,
      282, 373, 373–374
   Ralph scholarship on, **3:**283
   on Santlow, Hester, **5:**518
   on Sorin and Baxter, **1:**391
weaver's dance, **3:**435
Weavil, Bruce, **3:***232*
Weaving Dance, **6:**36
Webb, Clifton, **1:**520, **4:**420,
   6:256, 318
Webb, Elida, **6:**257
Webb, Helen, **5:**312, 649, 650, 691
Weber, Carl Maria von, **1:**457,
   2:173, **3:**18, **4:**514, **5:**36, *299*,
   6:360
Weber, Lois, **5:**125
Weber, Louise. *See* Goulue, La
Weber, Ruth, **1:**374, 375
Weber and Fields, **6:**268, 270, 271

Webern, Anton, **1:**349, 405, 545,
   4:517, 594, 613, **6:**6
Webern Op. 5, **2:**513, **5:**97, 320
Webre, Septime, **6:**266
Webster, Benjamin, **2:**85
Webster, David, **3:**521, **4:**242, 607
Webster, John, **3:**356
Webster, T. B. L., **2:**156–157
We Can't All Be Swans, **4:**203
Wecker, Hans Jacob, **4:**505
Wedding, **3:**368, **5:**256
Wedding at Ecser, **3:**406, *408*, **5:**287
Wedding Bouquet, A, **6:**375
   Ashton production, **1:**148, *148*,
      151, 437, **3:***615*, **5:**414, **6:**375
   Berners score, **1:**437, 438
   de Valois *demi-caractère* role,
      2:399
   Farron performance, **2:**578
   Helpmann performance,
      3:355, 357
   Joffrey Ballet staging, **3:**614, *615*
   Lambert musical arrangement,
      4:114
   May performance, **4:**336
   Shearer (Moira) performance,
      5:589
   Somes performance, **5:**639
wedding dances
   African music, **4:**484
   Armenia, **1:**121
   Berber, **4:**467, *468*
   black Moroccan, **4:**468
   Cape Breton stepping, **5:**697
   Egypt, **2:**489
   Finland, **2:**630
   Greece, **3:**297–298, 301, 302
   Gypsy, **3:**331
   Hungary, **2:***549*, 553, **3:**410–411
   Ireland, **3:**33
   Jewish traditional, **3:**526–527,
      536, *536*, 537, 602–603, 605,
      4:349
   Macedonia, **6:**429
   Middle East, **3:**538, **4:**403, 409
   Moldova, **4:**446
   Nubian traditional, **2:**491–492
   Philippines, **2:**230
   Poland, **5:**211, *214*
   Romania, **5:**381–382
   Russia, **5:**442
   Siberia, **5:**447
   Turkey, **5:**211
   Ukraine, **3:**38, **6:**221, *221*, 222
   Yemen, **4:***408*, 410
   Zulu, **5:**644
Wedding Festival at Hardanger, A,
   1:497, *507*, 510, 511, **3:**13,
   6:40
Wedding in the Carpathians, **2:**343,
   5:385
Wedding Party, The (film), **5:**573
Weddings, **4:**239
Wedekind, Frank, **4:**73
Wedekind, Lotte, **4:**93
Weege, Fritz, **3:**302
Weekend, **2:**1
Weekend in Havana (film), **4:**434
Weeme, Mascha ter, **6:**375
   Ballet der Lage Landen, **1:**289,
      290, **3:**203, **4:**591, 592, **6:**375
   Dutch National Ballet, **2:**468,
      469, **4:**592, **6:**375
Weening, Robin Woodard, *as
   contributor*, **2:**501, **5:**343
Weeping Willow (Willow Tree), **1:**91
Weese, Miranda, **4:**624
Weetering, Conrad van de, **2:**470,
   4:600
Weetsering, Conrad van de, **4:**600
Weg im Nebel, **3:**630

Wegmann, Mats, **2:***284*, **6:**44
Wehe, Oliver, **1:**391
Weidman, Charles, **2:**110, **3:**354,
   4:130, 214, **5:**254, **6:375–377**
   American Dance Festival, **1:**79
   archival materials, **4:**169
   Bennington School, **1:**421, **3:**369
   Cole association, **2:**185, **3:**598
   Dance Repertory Theatre, **6:**88
   dance technique, **4:**437, 438,
      439–440, **6:**376, 377
   Denishawn, **2:**376, 378, 379, *379*,
      3:210, **5:**495, 496, 584, 587
   Federal Dance Project, **2:**580,
      6:246
   Graham association, **3:**210, 215
   Horst score, **3:**385
   Humphrey collaboration,
      3:397–399, *401*, 402, 404,
      6:376
   as major modern dance pioneer,
      3:369, 384, **6:**245
   New Dance Trilogy, **2:**285,
      4:605, 606
   Orientalism, **5:**46
   Shakers performance, **5:**577–578
   Shawn influence, **5:**584
   students, **1:**55, **2:**357, **4:**457,
      5:589
   See also Humprhey-Weidman
      Company
Weidt, Jean, **2:**466, **3:**76, 83, 152,
   155, **6:377–378**
   Red Dancers, **1:**204, **3:**146,
      6:245, 378
Weigel, Christoph, **3:***143*
weightlessness aesthetic
   ballet technique, **1:**341, 344
   Korean dance, **4:**45, 46
weight rhythm (Laban concept),
   4:99
Weigl, Joseph, **1:**402, **6:**337, 338
Weigl, Petr, **4:**77
Weilandt, Julius, **2:**338
Wei Liangfu, **4:**76
Weill, Kurt, **1:**291, 306, 446, **3:**153,
   4:241, **5:**429, 527, **6:**197,
   278, 281
Weilson, Robert, **2:**119
Weimar ballet, **3:**154
Weimar Theater of Dance, **3:**152
Wein, George, **2:**5
Weiner, Jody, **2:**609
Weiner, Leó, **2:**473
Weininger, Andreas, **1:**387, *387*
Weinstein, Arnold, **3:**202
Weinstein, Larry, **6:**133
Weinstock, Maria, **4:**595
Weir, Mary, **1:**206
Weisberger, Barbara, **5:**131, 132,
   6:264, 266
Weiss, Adolph, **2:**21
Weiss, Josefine Maudry, **1:**238,
   5:605, **6:**334, 335–336
Weiss, Robert, **1:**141, **4:**620, 622,
   5:132
Weiss, Ulli, *as photographer*, **1:**388,
   3:151
Weitzmann, Jean, **2:**174
Welander, Karl, **1:**232
Welch, Damian, **3:**623
Welch, Garth, **1:**208, 209, 211, 213,
   214, 230, 231, 233, 499,
   3:623, **4:**275, **6:**56, 378,
   378–379, 379
Welch, Stanton, **1:**211, *232, 234*,
   235, **3:**623
Welk, Lois, **3:**620, 621
Well, Franziska, **5:**278
Wellenkamp, Vasco, **5:***233*,
   234, 235

weller, **1:**46, **6:**359
Weller, Dawn, **1:**393, **6:379–380**
  PACT Ballet, **5:***52,* 53, 54, *54,*
    55–56, *652,* 653, 654, 658
Welles, Orson, **2:**313
Wellesz, Egon, **3:**132, 625
Wellington, duke of, **2:**70, **5:**232
Wellington, New Zealand,
  4:624, 626
Wellington Performing Arts Center,
  4:628
Wellingtons (boots). *See* gumboot
  dancing
Well, Jan van, **4:**588
Wells, Bruce, **1:**234, 501, **2:**524,
  3:623, **5:**196–197, **6:**266
Wells, Dickie, **1:**252
Wells, Doreen, **2:**404, **5:***159,* 421,
  6:357, **380–381**
Wells, Harriet and Henri, **5:**318
Wells, Henry, **3:**181
Wells, Kenn, **2:**512
Wells, Mary Ann, **1:**124, 421, **3:**609
Wellschen tenntz, Die, **2:**336
Welsh, Joseph, **2:**373
Welsh folk and traditional dance.
  See under Great Britain
Weltbühne, Die (periodical),
  3:153, 305
Weltchronik (Schedel), **2:***332*
Welt des Tänzers, Dies (Laban),
  3:161, **4:**90, 99
Wemyss, Francis Courtney,
  4:138, 139
Wendel, Heinrich, **6:**359
Wenders, Wim, **3:**78
Wendy Hilton Dance Company,
  5:327
Wengerd, Tim, **3:**220, **4:***633*
Wentink, Andrew Mark, *as*
  contributor, **3:**87–88, **5:**58–61
wenwu, **1:**164
Wen Yiduo, **2:**148
Wenzel, Leopold, **4:**121
Werberg, Otto, **1:**112
Werich, Jan, **2:**307, **4:**239
werl, **5:**84
Werner, Francis, **1:**92
Werner, Lia, **6:**388
Wertmüller, Lina, **1:**545
Wer will Frau Wahrheit herbergen?,
  1:467
Wesele Krakowskie. See Kraków
  Wedding
Wesleyan University, **1:**274
Wesleyan University Press, **6:**298
West, Elizabeth, **2:**349–350, **5:**564
West, Geoffrey, *as contributor,*
  5:564–565
West, Mae, **1:**520
West, Victoria, **4:**668
West Africa, **6:**13, 14, **381–385**
  as African-Brazilian dance
    influence, **1:**525–530, **6:**24
  Ballets Africans, Les, **1:**303–304
  Bamana dance, **1:**359–360, **4:**484,
    486, **6:**12, 382, 383
  as Caribbean dance influence,
    2:62, 64, 65, 274
  costume, **2:**210–211
  Dafora dance dramas, **2:**313
  dance research and publication,
    6:24–25, 382
  Dogon dance, **2:**421–422, **4:**288,
    288, 291–292, **6:**382, 383
  Hausa dance, **3:**347–348
  highlife (dance style), **4:**293,
    6:23–24
  masks, **4:**287–293, **6:**423
  professional theaters, **6:**20–21
  Tiv dance, **6:**383

Ubakala dance, **6:**25, 219,
  382, 383
See also specific countries; sub-
  Saharan Africa
West African Frontier Force, **6:**24
West Australian Academy of
  Performing Arts, **1:**38
West Australian Ballet, **1:**211, 212,
  3:307, **4:**379, **6:**379
Westberg, Maria, **1:**511, **5:**425
West Berlin Academy of Arts, **1:**456
West Berlin German Opera,
  2:561, 562
West Berlin Hochschule für Musik,
  2:478
West Berlin Municipal (City)
  Opera, **1:**460, **3:**149
Westbeth (videodance), **2:**294, 607
Westbury, Ian, *as photographer,*
  2:41, **3:**3
West Coast Swing, **4:**203
Western Association of Normal
  School Masters of Dancing,
  2:338, **6:**239
Western Folk Suite, **4:**198
Western Michigan University, **4:**169
Western Oklahoma style (Plains
  Indian dance), **4:**561
Western Sahara, **4:**663–664
Western square dance, **5:**688–689
Western Symphony, **1:**271, **2:**314,
  3:654, **4:**137, 246, 612, 621
Western Theatre Ballet. *See*
  Scottish Ballet
West Germany. *See* Germany
Westhuizen, Annette van der, **5:**54
West Indies. *See* Caribbean region;
  specific countries
West Java. *See* Indonesia
Westnes, Sissel, **4:***676*
West Side Story (film), **2:**618, **5:***361,*
  362–363, 398, **6:**281–282
West Side Story (musical), **1:**212,
  463, **2:**583, **3:**419, **5:**616,
  6:281–282
  Bernstein score, **1:**438, 439,
    3:338, 599, **5:**358, 362, 398,
    6:281
  McKayle performance, **4:**345
  Neumeier production, **3:**338,
    4:604
  Rivera performance, **5:**358
  Robbins choreography, **3:**599,
    600, **5:***361,* 363, 398
  Romeo and Juliet basis, **5:**398
West Side Story Suite (Bernstein),
  4:622, **6:**288
Westwood, Jean, **3:**432
Westyergaard, Arlene, **5:**659
WGBH (PBS television station),
  6:139
Whacking, **5:**636
whale cult, **4:**550
whale dances, **4:**571–572
whale festival, **4:***572,* **5:**446
What Happened, **3:**201, **6:**282
What Is under Your Head?, **1:**307
What's So Bad about Feeling Good?
  (film), **1:**419
What to Do till the Messiah Comes,
  5:436
Wheatley, William, **1:**457
Wheeldon, Christopher, **5:**419
Wheeler, Pearl, **5:**495
Whelan, Wendy, **4:**623
When the Dancing Had to Stop
  (television documentary),
  5:575
When the Grapes Grow Ripe, **5:**385
When We Were Very Young, **4:**226,
  6:153

Where's Charley? (film), **4:**10
Where's Charley? (musical), **1:**482,
  6:277, *277*
"Where's Raymond?" (television
  program), **1:**482
Where the Rainbow Ends, **2:**510,
  4:270, **5:**684
Where the Wings Grow (de Mille),
  2:372, 374
Wherlock, Richard, **6:**53
Whims of Cupid and the Ballet
  Master, The, **2:**107, 388, 594,
  3:546, 657, **5:**424
  Drottningholm Court Theater re-
    creation, **6:**47
  Galeotti choreography, **3:**105,
    5:424, 426, **6:**126
  Lander (Harald) staging, **3:**105,
    4:119
Whirling Dance (Native American),
  4:568
whirling dervishes, **3:**524, **4:**402,
  410, 411
  scholarly studies, **4:**416
  Turkey, **4:***410,* **6:**187, *208,* 209
Whirlwind, The, **3:**195
Whisper Moon, **3:**52
Whistle in the Wind (musical),
  6:287–288
Whistler, Rex, **1:**149, **2:***398,* 401,
  3:509, 511, **5:**293–294
Whitcomb, Bess, **2:**581
White, Charlie, **6:**257
White, Elissa, **2:**320–321
White, Eric, **1:**259
White, Frederick, **5:***415*
White, George. *See George White's*
  Scandals
White, Herbert ("Whitey"), **1:**451,
  4:202, 254
White, Howard, **2:**397
White, Josh, **5:**255
White, Miles, **2:**249
White, Myrna, **1:***56*
White, Nora, **2:**38, **6:**396
White, Onna, **2:**161, **5:**513,
  6:283, 284
White, Patricia. *See* Wilde, Patricia
White, Patrick, **1:**210
White, Peter, **3:**512
"white ballets." *See ballet blanc*
White Bird Featherless, **2:**355
Whitebirds of 1927 (revue), **2:**396
White Boys Mummers, **3:**251
White Cat, The, **5:**69
White City, London, **4:**24
White Dance, **2:**500
White Deer Dance, **4:**566, *567*
White Devil, The (Webster), **3:**356
White-Dixon, Melanye, *as*
  contributor, **1:**395–396,
  4:345–346, **6:**448–449
White Fawn, The, **1:**457, 495
Whitefield, George, **3:**167
White-Haired Girl, The, **2:**70, 116,
  6:385–386
  costumes, **2:**220–221
  Cultural Revolution production,
    2:137
  history, **2:**135
  operatic version, **2:**142
Whitehouse, Mary, **2:**316, **3:**318
White Jade, **2:**377, **5:**496
White Lily, The, **4:**143
Whitelocke, Sir Bulstrode, **4:**309
Whiteman, Paul, **6:**256
White Man Sleeps, **2:**355
Whitener, William, **2:**42, **5:**437,
  6:152
White Nights (film), **2:**514, **6:**103,
  154, **2:**514, **3:**367, **4:**133

White Oak Dance Project, **1:**373,
  2:294, **3:**201–202, 448, **4:**471
White Paintings (Rauschenberg),
  5:313
White Peacock, **4:**355
White Rose, The, **1:**509
White Russia. *See* Belarus
White Studios, **5:**183
White Witch of Rose Hall, The,
  3:576
Whitey's Lindy Hoppers, **1:**451,
  4:*201,* 202, 254, **6:***262*
Whitman, Albert ("Pops"), **6:**386
Whitman, Alberta, **6:**386
Whitman, Alice, **6:**386
Whitman, B. F., **5:**514
Whitman, Essie, **6:**386
Whitman, Mabel, **6:**386
Whitman, Martha, **2:**450
Whitman, Paul, **6:**6
Whitman, Robert, **2:**606, **3:**54,
  6:362
Whitman, Simone. *See* Forti,
  Simone
Whitman, Walt, **2:**85, 453
Whitman Sisters, **6:**256, **386**
Whitney, Salem Tutt, **6:**256
Whitsuntide, **2:**164, 168, **3:**241,
  4:474
Whittaker, Herbert, **2:**49
Whittaker, James, **5:**576
Who, The (music group), **3:**130,
  4:571
Who Cares?, **1:**272, **2:**314, 514,
  4:345, 611, *620*
  McBride performance, **4:**345, 618
  Villella performance, **4:**620
Whoopee (film), **1:**432
Whoopee (musical), **6:**274
Whoops-de-Doo, Les, **5:**435
Why Is the Willow Tree Weeping?,
  6:225
Whylie, Marjorie, **3:**575
Whyltington, R., **3:**281
Whyte, Raewyn, **4:**629
Whyte, Rowland, **2:**255
Wichita Public Library, Kansas,
  4:169
Wichitwathakān, Luang, **4:**112
Wickoff, Henry, **2:**504
Widow in the Mirror, The, **5:**238
Wiegmann, Marie. *See* Wigman,
  Mary
Wieland, Clara, **4:**520
Wieland, George, **5:**70
Wielki Theater Ballet. *See* Warsaw
  Ballet
Wiener, Elizabeth, **1:**211, 212
Wiener, Hans. *See* Veen, Jan
Wiener, Nina, **1:**75
Wiener Hofopernballett. *See*
  Hofopernballett
Wiener Staatsopernballett. *See*
  Vienna State Opera Ballet
Wiener Walzer, **1:**239
Wiener Werkstätte, **1:**131
Wien Film, **5:**279
Wieniawski, Henri, **4:**429
Wien, Wien, nur du Allein, **1:**292,
  406, **2:**104, **3:**351
Wiesbaden State Opera, **2:**471,
  3:359
Wiesenthal, Berta, **6:**387
Wiesenthal, Elsa, **1:**239, **2:**11, **6:**387
Wiesenthal, Gertrud, **6:**387
Wiesenthal, Grete, **4:**228,
  6:386–388
  as Bulgarian dance influence,
    2:11
  criticism of Hassreiter, **3:**347

Wiesenthal, Grete, *continued*
   free dance movement, **1:**239, 240, 242, **6:**389
   as Jaques-Dalcroze influence, **3:**595
Wiener Werkstätte, **1:**131
Wiesenthal technique, **6:388**
Wiesner, Daniel, **1:**542
Wiesner, Theodora, **1:**79, 421
wig
   Egypt, ancient, **2:**482
   kabuki, **2:**218, **3:**639
   kathakai, **2:**224
   Louis XIV vogue, **2:**238
Wigeliew, Eugen, **1:**374
Wiggers, Ton, **4:**596
Wiggins, Jack, **1:**520, **6:**386
Wigman, Elisabeth, **6:**392
Wigman, Mary, **1:**112, **3:**162, **5:**43, **6:**83, 195, **389–396**
   as American modern dance influence, **4:**438
      See also New Dance Group
   American tour, **6:**274, 393–394
   archival collections, **4:**161, 166
   Ascona colony, **6:**51–52, 389
   Ausdruckstanz, **1:**203, **3:**146, 147, 161, **6:**389–393
   avant-garde dance, **1:**244, **2:**122
   Bauhaus, **1:**132
   as British modern dance influence, **3:**271
   as Bulgarian dance influence, **2:**11
   as Canadian modern dance influence, **2:**30, 37, 44
   choral dancing, **4:**476, **6:**393, 394
   choreographic silence, **6:**390
   costume, **2:**245, 248
   dance aesthetics, **1:**25, 131, 132, 134, **3:**130, **6:**389–390, 392, 393, 395
   dance caricatures by, **2:**69
   as dance therapy influence, **2:**316, **3:**317
   design elements, **5:**548
   East German dance studios, **3:**152
   as French modern dance influence, **3:**75, 76, 83
   Gert (Valeska) contrasted with, **3:**163
   group dances, **6:**392–393
   Hellerau school, **3:**596
   as Holm influence, **3:**369, **4:**95, 440–441
   Hoyer association, **3:**393
   improvisation, **3:**445
   Kreutzberg association, **4:**60
   Laban as influence, **4:**15, 90, 103, 476
   as Linke influence, **4:**203
   Mary Wigman Society, **3:**162, **5:**43–44
   masks, **4:**302, **6:**390, *392*
   modern dance technique, **4:**440–441
   Nazi era, **4:**93, 477, **6:**393, 394, 395
   as Netherlands dance influence, **4:**590, 598
   New York City school, **6:**395
   as Nikolais influence, **4:**648
   Palaccua's style versus, **5:**65
   Palucca association, **5:**65
   percussive accompaniment, **4:**518, **6:**390
   Sacre du Printemps production, **1:**436, **5:**488, **6:**393
   solo dances, **6:**389, 390–391, 393

students, **1:**211, 403, 441, 534, **2:**44, 357, **3:**132, *159,* 657, **4:**228, **5:**166, 263, 557, **6:**375, 392
Totentanz, **4:**161
Wallmann association, **6:**357
Women's Dances, **3:**147
Wignell, Thomas, **6:**232
Wihtol, Robert, *as photographer,* **2:**232
Wiinblad, Bjørn, **1:**539, **3:**13
Wija, I Wayan, **6:**368
Wikström, Jan-Erik, **6:**44
Wilbur, Richard, **1:**439
Wilckens, Friedrich, **4:**60
Wild, Stephen A., *as contributor,* **1:**219–223
Wild Boy, **4:**244
Wild Dove, The, **5:**617, *618*
Wilde, Oscar, **1:**43, **3:**20, 163, **4:**114, **5:**438, 493
Wilde, Patricia, **1:**299, 302, **2:**38, 47, 420, **5:**196, 197, **6:396–397**
   Balanchine marriage, **6:**397
   New York City Ballet roles, **4:**616, 617
   Pittsburgh Ballet Theatre, **6:**265
   Serenade performance, **4:**609, **6:**396
   Square Dance performance, **4:**612
Wildeblood, Joan, **3:**282
Wilder, Billy, **1:**419
Wilder, Valerie, **2:**42, **4:**546
Wilderijckx, Marie-Louise, **1:**411, **5:**422
Wilderness, **6:**56
Wild Flower, The, **5:**473
Wildlife, **1:**52, **5:**303
Wildor, Sarah, **5:**420
Wild Rose (musical), **3:**449, **4:**335
Wild Translations, **2:**355
Wild West, The, **6:**137
Wild West shows, **4:**464
Wiles, Harold, **1:**450
Wiley, Roland John, **6:**35, 115
Wilhelm, C., **2:**249, **3:**128, 129, *129,* **6:**397
   Empire Theatre ballet designs, **3:**261, **4:**121, 522, **6:**397
Wilhelm Tell, **3:**358
Wilk, Gérard, **1:**292
Wilkerson, Raven, **6:**260
Wilkes-Barre Ballet Guild, **6:**266
Wilkinson, Raven, **1:**302
Willems, Tom, **3:**52, 53
Willets, R. F., *as contributor,* **1:**118–119, **2:**269–271
Willful Wife, The. See Diable à Quatre, Le
Willi I, **2:**574–575
William III of Orange (king of England), **3:**522, **4:**588
Williams, Al, **3:**57
Williams, Bert, **1:**439, **2:**25, **5:**180, *181,* **6:**99–100, 255
Williams, Billy, **6:**262
Williams, Celeste. *See* Celeste, Mademoiselle
Williams, Charles H., **6:**258
Williams, Derek, **4:**668
Williams, Drid, **4:**367, 370, 371, 372, 373
Williams, Dudley, **1:**56, 60, **3:**219
Williams, Esther, **1:**435
Williams, E. Virginia, **1:**501, 502, **6:**264, **397–398**
Williams, Jack, **5:**601
Williams, Jerome, **6:**262
Williams, Lavinia, **2:**65, 458, **3:**574

Williams, Lottie, **5:**180
Williams, Margaret, **2:**611
Williams, Peter, **4:**222
   as contributor, **1:**426–427, **2:**105, 349–350, 423–425, **3:**173–174, 174–175, 202–203, 393–394, 427–428, 508–509, 511–512, **4:**152–153, 380, 667–668
   Dance and Dancers editorship, **3:**285
Williams, Petr, **2:**173, **5:**393, **6:**343, **398–399**
Williams, Rudolph ("Sarsaparilla"), **3:**574
Williams, Sheri, **2:**358
Williams, Stanley, **1:**330, *508,* **3:**667, **5:**428, 430, 554, **6:**349, **399–400**
   Bournonville Divertissement, **2:**511, **4:**631, **6:**399
   as Martins influence, **4:**273, **6:**399
Williams, Tennessee, **1:**251, **3:**163
Williamsburg, Virginia, **6:**232
Williams Mix (Cage), **2:**22
Williamson, Esther, **1:**421
Williamson, James Cassius, **1:**206, 207, 208
   See also J. C. Williamson Theatres Ltd.
Williamson, Malcolm, **1:**156, 210, 230, **2:**350, **3:**356
Williams-Yarborough, Lavinia, **2:**566, **6:**255, 259, **400**
William Tell (Rossini opera). *See Guillaume Tell*
William Tell Divertissement, **1:**539, **4:**657
William the Hebrew. *See* Guglielmo Ebreo da Pesaro
Willibrord, Saint, **2:**164, 168
Willis, Gordon, **6:**287
Willke, Elke, **3:**163
Willner, A. M., **3:**346
Will-o'-the-Wisp, **1:**498
Willow Tree (Weeping Willow), **1:**91
Will Rogers Follies, The (musical), **6:**205
Wills, Alexander, **2:**256
Wilson, Billy, **1:**59, 60, **2:**470, **3:**578, **6:**260, 284
Wilson, Dorothy, **2:**47
Wilson, Edmund, **1:**262
Wilson, G. B. L., **4:**164
Wilson, John (Joffrey dancer), **3:**610, *611*
Wilson, John (Wovoka), **3:**171
Wilson, John M., **4:**17
   as contributor, **4:**13–18, **6:**214–215
Wilson, Linley, **1:**212
Wilson, Lucretia, **6:**191
Wilson, Margo, **5:**52
Wilson, Mitzi, **4:**179
Wilson, Robert, **1:**143–144, 245, 389, **2:**463, **3:**339, **5:**38, 574, **6:400–401**
Wilson, Sallie, **1:**72, 77, **2:**269, 375, **4:**381, **5:**193, **6:401–402**
Wilson, Sandy, **1:**520
Wilson, Thomas, **2:**257, 339, **3:**361, **4:**221, **5:**286, 623, **6:**360
Wilson, Tony, **3:**576
Wilson, Ural, **2:**458
Wilson, Zane, **3:**344, **6:**323
Wilson, Keppel, and Betty, **4:**522
Winckelmann, Johann Joachim, **5:**517
Wind, Edgar, **1:**126
Winding, August Henrik, **1:**515

Wind in the Mountains, **2:**374
Wind Is Rising, The, **6:**66
Windmill Theatre, London, **4:**153
Windows, **2:**296
Windreich, Leland, *as contributor,* **1:**498, **2:**372–375, **4:**178–179, **5:**369–370, 511–514
Windsong, **4:**120
Windward Islands, **2:**62
Wind Witches, **6:**45
Winfield, Hemsley, **6:**258, *258*
Winfield, Raymond, **1:**252
Winged, The, **4:**199
Wing Suite, **2:**356
Winkel, Kit, **3:**346, **4:**598
Winkler, Dean, **2:**609
Winkler, Gerhard, **1:**243
Winkler, John, **3:**289
Winkler-Betzendahl, Madeline, *as photographer,* **3:**152
Winnebago (people), **4:**558
Winnipeg, Canada, **2:**39, 42, 43, 47–48, **5:**433
Winnipeg Ballet Club. *See* Royal Winnipeg Ballet
Winnipeg Contemporary Dancers, **6:**132
Winnsboro Cotton Mill Blues, **2:**355
Winogrand, Garry, **5:**186
Winqvist, Nisse, **6:**46
Winslow, Miriam, **1:**112, 113, **6:**398
Winslow Ballet, **1:**112
Winsome Widow, A (musical), **6:**270
Winter, Ethel, **2:**182, 450, **3:**216, 218, **4:**216
Winter, Marian Hannah, **2:**202, **3:**283, **4:**28, **5:**70
Winter, Peter von, **5:**276
Winterbranch, **1:**542, **2:**294, **5:**314, **6:**402, **402**
Winter Carnival, **2:**161
"Winter Dreams" (Tchaikovsky's First Symphony), **6:**114
Winter Dreams, **4:**245, **5:**419, *421*
Winter Fantasy (ice show), **4:**132
Winter Garden Theater, New York City, **6:**270, 285
Winter in Lisbon, The, **1:**60
Winter Night, **3:**174, 203
Winter Pool (Rasuchenberg), **1:**140
Winters Court, **2:**583
Winter's Eve, **3:**663, 664, **4:**63, 241
Winter's Tale, The (Shakespeare), **3:**253
Winther, Charles, **5:**318
Winti dances, **2:**64
Wirakusumah, Raden Sambas, **3:**504
Wirama, Krida Besa, **3:**498
wireng, **3:**495
Wireng Tameng Gleleng, **3:**495
Wirthmüller, Kitty, **1:**500
Wirtschaft, **6:**403
Wir Warren—Liebeslied aus einer Schlechten Zeit, **1:**374, 375
Wisconsin (film), **1:**140
Wisdom (medieval play), **3:**251
Wisdom of Terpsichore, The (television series), **4:**37
Wise Virgins, The, **1:**149, 150, **5:**639
Wisiak, Lidija, **6:**438
Wit and Science (Redford), **3:**252
Witch, The, **2:**265
Witch Boy, The, **2:**510, 511, **3:**175, **4:**625
Witch Dance, **6:**390, 391, 393, 394
   as *Ausdruckstanz* example, **1:**203
witches sabbath, **2:**166
Witch of Endor, The, **5:**562
Wither and *Wither 2,* **3:**523

Within the Grove, **3:**664
Within the Quota, **1:**327
With My Red Fires, **1:**421, 422,
  2:580, **3:**399, 400, 401, 403,
  403, **4:**518, 605, *606*
Without Dowry, **5:**470
*With Timbrel and Dance Praise His
  Name*, **2:**358
Withy, John, **4:**311
Witkowsky, Gisella, **4:***544*
Witness, **1:**59, **3:**373
Witt, Eduard, **4:**589
Witt, Gunilla, **6:**45
Witte Salamander, De, **4:**600
Wittgenstein, Victor, **2:**196
Wittup, Freddie (Federico Rey),
  1:117
Witty, Fedorovitch, **1:**147
Witwatersrand gold mine dances,
  5:643, *663*, **6:**661
Witwicki, Władysław, **5:**221
Wizard of Oz, The (1903–1904
  musical), **6:**268
Wizard of Oz, The (film), **1:**482
Wiz, The (musical), **6:**102, 284
Władysław IV Vasa, king of
  Poland, **5:**215
WNET (PBS television station),
  6:132, 139, 154
Wodehouse, P. G., **6:**271
Wodsiwob, **3:**171
Woelfl, V. A., **3:**157
Woetzel, Damian, **2:**201, **4:***622*,
  623, 631, **5:**43
Wöfl, V. A., **4:**59
Wohltaetige Fee, Die, **2:**93
Woisen, Bernhard, **3:**154
Woizikowska, Hélène, **4:**635
Woizikowska, Sonia, **1:**311
Woizikowski, Leon, **1:**207, 309,
  312, 449, **2:**253, **3:**316, **4:***183*,
  5:85, 166, 237, 264,
  6:403–404
  Australian tour, **1:**311, **4:**25
  Biches performance, **4:***637*, **6:**404
  Carnaval performance, **3:**202
  as character dancer, **2:**106, **6:**404
  as Massine-type dancer, **5:**636
  Noces performance, **4:***636*, 657,
    6:404
  Polish background, **5:**217
  Polish Ballet, **5:**218
  Rambert, Marie, **5:**298, 299
  students, **4:**59, 232
  Train Bleu performance, **4:***637*,
    6:404
  Tricorne, Le, **6:**192
  Youskevitch association, **6:**425
Wolbers, Mary Jane, **4:**212
Wolf, Frederick, **6:**378
Wolfangle, Karla, **4:**482, 483
Wolfe, George, **6:**103
Wolfe, Julia, **5:**683
Wolff, Christian, **2:**120, 289, **4:**519
Wolff, Jules, **4:**15
Wolfgang Amadeus, **4:**625
Wolfie, **5:**575
Wolfram, Richard, **4:**372
Wolf's Bride, **2:***634*
Wolfsohn, Leopold, **2:**196
Wolken, Jonathan, **5:**194, *194*
Wolkonsky, Prince Serge,
  2:406–407, **3:**596
Wolliaston, Elsa, **2:**460
Wolof (people), **4:**548, **6:**381
Wolz, Carl, **3:**592, **4:**54, **5:**44
  as contributor, **3:**591–592,
    5:592–593
Woman, The, **4:**478
Woman, Demon, Human (film),
  5:130

Woman of the Clear Vision, **4:**151
Woman's Love—Woman's Fate, **6:**66
Women, **3:**520
*Women and Children in a Bengal
  Village* (Chaki-Sircar), **2:**103
Women Beware Women
  (Middleton), **3:**252
Women's Choreography Initiative,
  1:60
Women's Dances, **3:***147*, **6:**393, *393*
women's dances. *See* gender and
  dance
women's feet-binding, **2:**131
women's studies. *See* feminist
  theory
Women's War II, **1:**215
Women's War of 1929 (Ubakala),
  6:219
Wonder Bar (film), **1:**432, 435–436,
  435
Wonder Children (troupe), **2:**395
Wonderful Town (musical),
  1:438–439, **5:**489
Wong, Mel, **2:**53
Wood, Betty, **1:**451
Wood, Christopher, **4:**113
Wood, David, **2:**182, **3:**218
Wood, Dawn M., **2:**358
Wood, Donna, **1:**57, 58, *59*, **2:**357,
  6:*260*
Wood, Leona, **4:**415
  as contributor, **1:**39–42,
    4:464–469, 662–666, **5:**49–50,
    6:205–207
Wood, Marilyn, **6:**27
Wood, Melusine, **2:**255, **3:**282
Wood, Raegan, **4:**358
Wood, Roger, as photographer,
  1:156, 314, **2:**479, 508, **3:**392,
  4:608, 610, **5:**412, 415
Woodberry, David, **2:**609
woodcuts. *See* prints and drawings
Wooden Face Society. *See* False
  Face (Wooden Face) Society
wood engravings. *See* prints and
  drawings
wooden masks, **2:**217, 228–229,
  4:288
Wooden Prince, The, **1:**390, **2:**11,
  473, **3:**341, 342
  Bartók score, **1:**370, **5:**569
  Budapest Opera Ballet, **3:**414,
    415, 416, 417
  International Dance Festival
    prize, **3:**419
  Róna performance, **5:**402
  score complexity, **3:**416
  Seregi rechoreography, **3:**417,
    5:569
  symbolic plot, **3:**416
wooden shoes. *See* clogging
Woodford, Charles Francis, **3:**398
Woodford, Charles Humphrey,
  3:398
Woodpecker Dance, **4:***566*
Woodruff, Dianne L., **2:**49
  as contributor, **6:**155–164
Woodstock Music and Art Fair,
  New York (1969), **5:**633
Woodward, Henry, **5:**70
Woolford, Louisa, **2:**175–176
Wooliaston, Elsa, **3:**84
Woollcott, Alexander, **6:**272
Woolliams, Anne, **2:**184
  Australian Ballet directorship,
    1:210, 211, 233–234
  Austrian State Opera Ballet
    directorship, **1:**241
  Cranko Medal, **2:**268
  as Stuttgart Ballet ballet mistress,
    2:266, **3:**149, **6:**9

Woolmer, Robin, **5:**531
Wooster Group, **1:**245
Wordell, Bertha, **2:**581
Wordraid, **3:**447
Words and Music (film), **2:**108
Words and Music (musical), **1:**520
Words on Mime (Decroux), **4:**425
Work and Play, **3:**370, *371*
Work Center Dance. *See*
  Rotterdamse Dansgroep
Worker, The, **6:**378
Workers Dance League, **4:**604,
  5:637, **6:**245
Workers Dance Movement, **1:**246
Workers Educational Association,
  Plymouth, England, **4:**477
Workgroup, **3:**447
Workman, Jenny, **5:**369
Works Progress Administration
  (WPA), **2:**579, 581, **4:**30, 63,
  6:245, 276
World Art, Inc. *See* Universal Art,
  Inc.
World Book of Modern Ballet
  (Martin), **4:**273
World Completely Reformed (civil
  dance), **6:**81
World Dance Alliance, **5:**44, 48
World Dance History Makers (Ou
  Jian-ping), **3:**373
World Festival of Negro Arts
  (Dakar, Senegal), **2:**459
World History of the Dance (Sachs),
  3:161, **4:**369, **5:**560, **6:**246
"World in Masquerade, The"
  (print), **4:***314*
World Journal Tribune (newspaper),
  6:299
World of Art group. *See* Mir
  iskusstva
World of Pleasure, A (musical), **4:**56
World's Columbia Exposition
  (1893), Chicago, **2:**572
World's End (Sinclair), **3:**596
World's Fair (1939–1940), New
  York, **1:**280, **2:**574, **4:**210, 246
World's Fair (1940), San Francisco,
  1:498
World Stars in Opera (gala), **3:**418
World Trade, **3:**447
World War I
  American musical theater's
    patriotic themes, **6:**271
  Ballets Russes de Serge
    Diaghilev, **1:**322, **2:**409
  Castle (Vernon) RAF service and
    death, **2:**79, 80
  as Duncan dance influence, **2:**456
  Fuller relief work, **3:**95
  Gorsky ballets, **3:**205
  Rubinstein care of wounded,
    5:438
  Scholar Red Cross service,
    5:558–559
  Shawn military service, **5:**495
World War II
  Ashton career, **1:**148, 149–150,
    5:415
  Australian ballet emigrés,
    1:498, 499
  Baker (Joseph) activities, **1:**253
  Ballet Russe de Monte Carlo
    move to United States,
    1:296, 302
  Bolshoi Ballet effects, **1:**491, **5:**459
  Brazilian ballet emigrés,
    1:532–533
  British ballet effects, **3:**266–267,
    5:415
  British ballet morale-building
    tours, **5:**415

Chinese patriotic dance,
    2:135, 146
  Chiriaeff's hardships, **2:**150
  Danish ballet effect, **4:**118, 119,
    5:429
  Deutsches Opernhaus bombing,
    1:436
  Gore military service, **3:**203
  International Ballet founding,
    3:508–509, 511
  Italian dance effects,
    3:549–550, 552
  Japanese policy toward Korean
    performers, **2:**155, 159
  Japanese theatrical activity halt,
    3:589
  Jooss internment in England,
    3:629
  Kirstein military service, **4:**28
  Korean occupation by Japanese,
    4:44
  Laban movement efficiency
    application, **4:**15, 94, 97
  Latin American ballet emigrés,
    2:127
  Leningrad Symphony,
    4:147–148, *283*
  Lepeshinskaya front-line troop
    entertainment, **4:**149
  Maryinsky Ballet effects, **4:**284,
    5:459
  Netherlands dance effects, **4:**586,
    590, 598
  Nikolais military service, **4:**649
  Partisans, The, **4:**444–445
  Red Poppy, The, **1:**297
  Rome Opera Ballet effects, **5:**400
  Sadler's Wells losses, **1:**149,
    2:115, 402, **3:**266–267, **4:**114,
    5:415
  square dancing as recreation,
    5:689
  Youskevitch's U.S. naval service,
    6:425
  See also Holocaust; Nazi era
*World We Live In (or The Life of the
  Insects)*, **4:**648–649
World Wide Web, **4:**158
Worm Chambers Group, **3:**574
Worsaae, Jens-Jacob, **5:**514,
  6:404–405
Worthington, Rozeane, **4:**626
Wounded Knee Creek massacre
  (1890), **3:**171, **4:**562
Wovoka (John Wilson), **3:**171
Wozniuk, Esteban, **1:***114*
Wozzeck (Berg opera), **5:**527
Wozzeck (Büchner play), **4:**244
WPA. *See* Works Progress
  Administration
Wright, Barbara, **6:**187
Wright, Basil, **2:**601
Wright, Belinda, **2:**200, *508*, 510,
  5:301
Wright, Daniel, **3:**376
Wright, Douglas, **4:**482, 625, 627,
  6:56
Wright, Judith, **1:**212
Wright, Peter, **1:**391, 454, **5:**226,
  6:405
  Benesh notation use, **1:**418
  Birmingham Royal Ballet, **3:**268,
    4:243
  Dutch National Ballet, **2:**470
  Giselle, **2:**470, **3:**344, **4:**542–543,
    5:436, **6:**380, 405
  Nutcracker, The, **2:**186, **6:**405
  Sadler's Wells Royal Ballet, **5:**421,
    6:405
  Scottish Ballet, **5:**564

Wright, Peter, *continued*
  Sleeping Beauty, 2:266, 4:597,
    5:613, 6:405
  Stuttgart Ballet, 3:149, 6:9, 405
  Wells roles, 6:380
Wright, Rebecca, 2:357, 3:615
Wright, Robert, 1:297
Wright, Rose Marie, 6:152
Wright, Wilhelmine, 4:16
Wrighten, Charlotte, 5:199
Writings on Dance (Coton), 3:285
Writings on Dance (journal), 1:218
Writing through Finnegans Wake
  (Cage), 2:23
Wrocław Mime Theater, 6:175
Wroe, Edna, 4:272
Wrught, Douglas, 4:628
wu, 2:140
Wubbe, Ed, 4:593, 5:531
Wudao (periodical), 2:149
Wudao luncong (periodical), 2:149
Wudao xinlun (Wu Xiaobang),
  2:149
Wudao xuexi ziliao (periodical),
  2:149
Wudao Yanjiusuo. *See* Dance
  Research Institute
Wudao yishu (journal), 2:149
Wuehrer, Ully, 2:440
Wu Fu (Fu Yi), 2:148
Wu Ji Mei, 4:693
Wulff, Käthe, 4:90, 91
Wünder auf der Alameda, 6:304
Wuppertal Dance Theater. *See*
  Tanztheater Wuppertal
Wurg, Walter, 3:305
Württemberg State Library, 4:161
Württemberg State Theaters. *See*
  Stuttgart Ballet
wu shu, 2:129, 132
wuwu, 1:164
Wu Xiaobang, 2:145, 146, 148, 149,
  6:405–406
Wu Zuqiang, 5:330
www//alenikoffking.com, 4:22
Wyatt, Olivia, 2:36
Wycichowska, Ewa, 5:219, 220
Wyckoff, Bonnie, 5:436
Wyman, Anna, 2:40, 44–45, 6:132
Wyman, Max, 2:49
  as contributor, 2:36–43,
    5:433–437
Wynne, Shirley, 6:251
Wysocka, Tacjanna, 5:217, 221
Wyss, Pierre, 3:157

X6 (dance collective), 3:272,
  273, 275
xando, 1:529
Xangô (deity), 1:529, 6:185
Xenakis, Iannis, 1:214, 349, 350,
  2:120, 3:428, 4:613, 5:302
Xenophon, 2:115–116, 490, 3:290,
  292, 5:556
Xerxes, 3:289
Xerxes (Cavalli), 1:287
xhensa dance, 5:645, 664
Xhosa (people), 4:485, 5:643,
  644–645, 645, 661, 664
Xiao Lianfang, 6:421
xichayachaya dancing, 5:579
xifase competitive dance, 5:579
xigubu dance, 5:579
Xijing Fu (Zhang Heng), 2:148
xiju, 2:148
xilala, 5:579
Xi Liong, 4:626
Ximénez, Roberto, 4:222, 5:674,
  6:407–408, *408*

Ximénez-Vargas Ballet Español,
  3:9, *10*, 5:674, **6:407–408**
Xin wudao yishu gailun (Wu
  Xiaobang), 2:149
Xi Xiang Ji (Chinese play), 6:426
X.N.Tricities, 2:514
Xochitl, 2:378, 3:210, 5:584, 585,
  6:376
Xorenac'i, Movsēs, 1:119
Xu Ce Pao Cheng (opera), 6:446
Xue Qinghua, 5:330
Xu Erchong, 2:149–150
Xu Gang, 2:147, *440*
Xun Kuang, 2:148
Xu Suyin, *as contributor*, 2:138–141
xylophones, 2:31, 91, 3:114,
  472, 475

"Yablochko" ("Russian Sailors'
  Dance"), 6:310
Yachyo Inoue III, 3:126
Yadonashi Danshichi, 4:533
Yaffa Publishing Group, 1:218
Yagnik, Alka, 2:625
yajña, 3:462, 468
Yajurveda, 3:453, 453–454
Yakko, Sada. *See* Yakko and
  Kawakami
Yakko and Kawakami, 1:128,
  2:454, 3:93, 96, 338, 5:45,
  491, **6:409–410**
Yakobson, Leonid, 1:144, 2:520,
  4:446, 5:205, 206, 461, 639,
  6:213, 227, 310, **410–413**
  Ali-Batyr (originally *Shurale*),
    5:595
  Bedbug, The, 6:411–412
  Bolshoi Ballet, 1:492, 6:410–411
  choreographic innovations,
    5:460, 6:410–411, 412
  Choreographic Miniatures, 5:467,
    469, 6:412
  choreography for Baryshnikov,
    1:371
  choreography for Lepeshinskaya,
    4:149
  dramatic ballets, 4:284,
    6:410–411
  Golden Age, The, 3:192–193,
    4:283, 5:594, 6:410
  Makarova roles, 4:248
  Maly Theater Ballet, 5:468
  Maryinsky dramatic ballet
    revivals, 4:284
  scholarly writings on, 5:484
  Shurale, 4:284, 5:460, 472, 595,
    6:410, 411
  Spartacus, 4:7, 284, 5:460, 462,
    677, 6:411
yakṣagāna, 3:453, 460, **6:413–414**
  costume, 2:225, *225*, 3:458, 6:414
  epic sources, 3:464, 6:413
Yakulov, Georgi, 2:410, 5:267
Yakulov, Yuri, 5:544
Yakusha rongo (Hachimonjiya),
  3:591
Yakut Dance Theatre, 5:448
Yakuts (people), 5:447
Yakutsk Ballet, 5:473
Yale Repertory Theatre Company,
  2:367
Yale University, 2:367
yally, 1:247
Yamabashi Kagura group, 3:584
yamabushi, *642*, 3:586
Yamada Kosaku, 3:590
Yamada Setsuko, 2:18, **6:414–415**
Yamaguchi Katsuhiro, 3:340
Yamamoto family, 4:86

Yamato *sarugaku*, 3:646
Yamato Takeru, 3:441
Yamauba, 3:90
Yamawaki family, 4:85
Yamawaki Motoyasu, 4:85
yambú, 2:275
Yami (people), 6:80
Yampilov, Buadorzhi, 5:473
Yampolski, Berta, 3:534
Yan Dinxian, 6:385
Yánez, Ana María, *as photographer*,
  6:325
yangge, 2:134–135, 139, 140
Yangju masked dance drama,
  4:50–51
yangke theater, 1:165
Yang Meiqi, **6:415–416**
Yang Shi, 1:179
Yang Xiaolou, 1:164
Yanka Kapula Theater, 1:408
Yankee Bluebritches, 3:349
Yankee Clipper, 1:280, 3:349, 4:28,
  227, 227, 518, 6:247
Yanko le Bandit, 6:123
Yano, Hideyuki, 3:79, 84
Yanomano Series (film), 2:602
Yanovsky, Boris, 5:472
Yan Qinlin, 6:421
Yantra, 1:292, 2:104
yanvalou dance, 3:334, *334*, 335
Yanvallou, 1:538
yanyue, 6:79, 82–83
Yao (people), 2:86, 89, 91
Yap (people), 4:401
Yaqui dance, 4:396, **6:416**
  masks, 4:554, 6:416
  matachines, 5:329–330
  musical instruments, 4:552
Yara, 1:315, 5:270
Yarborough, Sara, 1:57, 59
Yard, The, Martha's Vineyard, 5:559
Yaroslavna, 2:423, 5:461, 468,
  6:342
Yarovoff, Nicholas, *as
  photographer*, 6:345
Yarullin, Farid, 5:472, 595, 6:411
Yasha Kai, 4:536
Yashin, Kamil, 6:306
Ya Sin, 1:462
Yaskaz, 1:61
Yasko, Jeanne, 2:530
Yastrebova, Nonna, 4:277, 284
Yasuna, 3:593
Yasushi Maruishi, 4:85
Yates, Frances, 1:2
Yavorsky, Evgeny, 5:485
Yavorsky, Nikolai, 1:48, 2:276, 277
yayue, 1:164, 3:102, 6:79, 80–82
Yazīdī (people), 4:79, 410
Yazvinsky, Georgi, 5:470, 471
Yazvinsky, Jan, 1:295, 296, 2:34
Yck, Lou van, 4:590
Yeager, Cheryl, 1:75
Yearbook for Traditional Music,
  4:375
Yearby, Marlies, 6:*449*
Year from Monday, A (Cage), 2:23
Yearsley, Ross, 6:*252*
Yeatman, Ken, 5:659
Yeats, William Butler, 2:397, 3:462
  nō drama, 3:519, 558–559, 651,
    652, 4:332, *333*, 5:592
  poetic dance imagery, 3:519
Yedda, 3:71, 4:353, 5:515
Ye Fang, 6:81
Yeh Funjun, 2:*131*
Yella, Gabriele, 5:140
Yellowbelly, 1:543
Yellow Book, The (quarterly), 1:148

Yellow Whale, 4:595
Yelyagin, Anatoly, 3:422
Yemen, **6:417–420**
  bedouin dance, 1:401
  dance characteristics, 1:101, *102*,
    4:403, 405, 406, 408, 409, 410
  Jewish traditional dances, 3:449,
    527, 529, 531, 531–352, 535,
    536–537, 4:155
  scholarly publications, 4:414, 417
  wedding dance, 4:408, 410
Yemenite Wedding, 3:449, 532,
  4:155
Yen, Alma Mock, 3:575
Yerma, 1:441, 3:520, 6:229
Yermolayev, Aleksei, 1:408, 2:436,
  4:133, 5:5, 6:106, 314,
  420–421
  Bolshoi Ballet, 1:*486*, 490, 491,
    6:420
  Don Quixote performance, 2:438
  dramatic virtuosic dancing,
    5:458, 6:420
  Flames of Paris performance,
    3:12
  Nightingale, The, 4:226
  Romeo and Juliet Bolshoi
    performance, 5:*393*, 394
  Romeo and Juliet film, 4:132
  Stone Flower performance, 5:699
  students, 6:313, 420
  Zakharov as influence, 6:442
Yermolov, Ivan, 5:455
Yershov, Petr, 4:211
Ye Shaolan, **6:421**
  as contributor, 4:76
Ye Shenglan, 6:421
Yes, Virginia, Another Piano Ballet,
  2:333, 6:*191*, 204
yeve dance, 1:538
Yi (people), 2:139
Yi Dance, 6:81
Yi dynasty, 4:46, 47, 48, 49, 53
Yi Dynasty Royal Music
  Conservatory, 4:12, 49
Yijing (*I Ching, Book of Changes*),
  2:22, 23, 128
yin and *yang*, 2:132
Yin Mei, 2:*137*
Yirrkala and Sabai Islands, 1:216
YM-YWHA. *See* 92nd Street Y, New
  York City
yoga, 1:175, 3:462, 468, 469,
  6:421–422
Yogi, The, 5:492
Yoh'ai, Shim'on bar, 3:605
Yohannes, Yoel, 2:530
yoi, 1:224
Yolanda (film), 1:367
Yolanda and the Thief (film),
  1:193, 194
Yordanova, Galina, 3:344
York, Donald, 6:110, 111, 112
York, Lila, 2:526, 5:51, 6:110
York Dance Review (journal), 2:49
Yorkin, Pavel, 3:568, 5:470, 471,
  6:226
Yorkshire, England, 3:240, 6:55
York University, Toronto, 2:45, 48,
  49, 4:166
  graduate program in dance
    history, 6:1–2, 297
Yoruba dance, 1:14, 529, 2:211,
  212, 274, 280, 313, 3:57, 334,
  6:13, 16–18, 185, **422–424**
  masks, 4:288, *289*, 292,
    6:12–13, 423
  opera companies, 6:21
  trance dances, 4:290, 6:25, 423
Yoshi and Company, 1:188

Yoshida Minosuke III, **1:**_179_
Yoshida Miyako, **3:**589
Yoshihiro Hosomi, *as photographer,* **4:**85
Yoshimoto Daisuke, **2:**18
Yoshitsune Senbon Zakura, **3:**441
Yoshizawa Ayame, **3:**637, **5:**30
yosim, **3:**504
Yotsuya Kaidan, **5:**31
You Can See Us, **1:**545
You Can't Always Get What You Want, **2:**470
Youchkevitch, Nina, **1:**311
You'd Be Surprised, **6:**404
Youmans, Vincent, **6:**274
Young, Andy, *as photographer,* **1:**528
Young, Arthur, **3:**516
Young, Betty, **4:**649
Young, Calvin Norris, **2:**358
Young, Dorren, **2:**122
Young, Douglas, **3:**427, 428
Young, Friedrich, **3:**224
Young, Irene Vera, **1:**211, **4:**160
Young, John, **2:**254, **5:**200
Young, La Monte, **2:**461, **3:**54, **6:**402
Young, Laura, **1:**_501,_ 502
Young, Stark, **3:**349
Young, William, **4:**311
Young Ballet, **1:**256, **2:**421, **5:**458
Young Ballet of Baku, **1:**248
Young Choreographers and Composers in Residence Program and the Emerging Generation Program, **1:**80
Young Classical Ballet, Leningrad, **4:**108
Young Composers Group, **2:**196
Youngerman, Suzanne, **4:**103, 104, 373
    as contributor, **4:**368–372, **5:**575–577
Young Girl and Death, The, **5:**472
Young Ladies Conduct. . . . (Essex), **2:**527, **5:**324
Young Loves, The, **1:**501
Young Man Must Marry, The, **3:**12, 373, **5:**432, **6:**135
Young Man of Manhattan (film), **5:**372
Young Omelet, **2:**110
Young People (film), **6:**142
Young People's Art Theater Seigen, **3:**652
Young Stars' Kabuki, **3:**658
Young Tramps, **2:**580, _580_
Your Arm's Too Short to Box with God (musical), **1:**395
You're a Good Man, Charlie Brown (musical), **6:**284
You're My Everything, **1:**440
Your Eyes, **2:**634
Your Hit Parade (television series), **2:**620, **6:**137
Your Legs, Musiah, **4:**156
Your Move (Hutchinson), **4:**97
Your Own Thing (musical), **1:**419
Your Show of Shows (television series), **6:**137
Yourth, Linda, **4:**_616_
You Shuyan, **1:**164
Youskevitch, Igor, **1:**282, 311, **3:**104, **5:**248, **6:**137, _424–425_
    academic teaching post, **6:**292
    Alonso (Alicia) dance partnership, **1:**49, _49,_ 50, 65, 67, 68, 71, 301, **3:**_178,_ **6:**425
    Ballet Russe de Monte Carlo, **1:**296, 301, **6:**425

Coppélia performance, **2:**201
Cuban ballet, **2:**277
Denby profile of, **2:**375, **6:**424
Giselle performance, **3:**_178,_ **6:**425
Invitation to the Dance (film) performance, **4:**3, **6:**425
Kirsova dance partnership, **4:**25
Markova dance partnership, **4:**269
Zagreb Ballet, **6:**432
Youskevitch, Maria, **6:**424
Youssef, Wagih, **2:**498
Youth, **2:**585, **4:**583, 584, **5:**236, 459, 617
youth dance movement (Britain), **3:**279, 280
you thei, **4:**525, 527
You Were Never Lovelier, **2:**616
Yovanovitch, Irina, **6:**323
Yoz Döngü, **6:**212
Yri Grigorovich i problemy khoreografi (Vanslov), **5:**484
Yrmolov, Ivan, **1:**486, **6:**170
Yuan dynasty, **2:**131, **4:**76
Yuan Xuefen, **6:**_425–426_
Yuchi (people), **4:**558
Yueji (Gongsun Nizi), **2:**148
Yueju (Shaoxing Opera), **6:**425–426
Yue Lun (Xun Kuang), **2:**148
Yuelü quanshu (Zhu), **1:**17
Yugen (ballet), **1:**38, 230, **3:**204, 357
yūgen (Japanese aesthetic term), **1:**17, **4:**654, 655
    masks expressing, **2:**217, **4:**295
Yugmadwandwa, **5:**68
Yugoslavia, **6:**_426–439_
    ballet, **3:**89, **4:**437, **6:**431–433
    dance research and publication, **6:**438–439
    libraries and museums, **4:**164
    modern dance, **6:**433–434
    theatrical dance since 1991, **6:**434–437
    traditional dance, **2:**101, 102, **6:**426–431
    vocal sounds, **3:**38–39
    See also Bosnia-Herzegovina; Croatia; Macedonia; Serbia; Slovenia
Yugoslav National Opera, Zagreb, **5:**605, 606
yuka, **2:**274
Yuki (creator figure), **4:**567
Yukunina, Lubov, **2:**15
Yuk Wan-sun, **4:**51
Yu Leidi, **5:**330
Yulianti Parani, **5:**523
Yung, Danny, **2:**171
Yunkuntjatjara (people), **1:**229
Yupik (people), **4:**570, 571, 574
Yuragi, **1:**61
Yurésha, Anjelkō, **2:**_508_
Yurieva, Maria, **2:**11
Yuri Grigorovich i problemy khoreografi (Grigorovich), **5:**484
Yuriko (Anemiya Yuriko), **1:**97, **2:**182, **3:**216, 218, 385, **4:**388, 659
Yuriko Kimura. *See* Kimura, Yuriko
Yurka, Blanche, **3:**216
Yurok (people), **4:**566
Yusupov, Ibrahim, **6:**307
Yusupov, Prince Nikolai, **4:**429
Yuthawong, Ornchuma, **4:**112
Yutkevich, Sergei, **3:**48
Yuya (Mishima), **4:**332, _655,_ **6:**445
Yūzaki-za troupe, **3:**646, 650
Yu Zhengfei, **6:**421

Yūzuru, **4:**661
Yvaral, **4:**_542_
Yves P., **3:**78
Yvette Chauviré: Une Étoile pour l'Exemple, **2:**114–115
Yvonne Georgi Ballet, **4:**590
Yẓuru, **5:**591

Zacharias, Gerhard, **3:**161
Zack, Leon, **5:**_124_
Zadara, Remy, **4:**688
zaff, **6:**417
Zagar, Mirna, **6:**434
Zagorsky, V., **4:**447
Zagreb Ballet, **2:**114, **6:**431, 432, 438
Zagreb Ballet School, **5:**676
Zagreb Dance Ensemble, **6:**434
Zagreb Music School, **6:**433
Zagreb School for Rhythmics and Dance, **6:**433
Zaïde, Reine de Granade, **1:**365, **2:**120
Zaïre. *See* Congo
Zaïs (Rameau), **1:**43, **3:**116–117, **5:**113, 306, 307
zajqc, **6:**213
Zajetz, Konstantin, **2:**440
Zajko, Jozef, **5:**614, 615
Zajlich, Piotr, **5:**75, 124, 125, 218, **6:**365, **441**
zaju, **4:**76
zaka dance, **3:**334, 335
Zakharov, Rostislav, **1:**34, 144, 416, **2:**11, 15, 96, 449, **4:**127, **5:**268, 331, **6:**441–443
    Bolshoi Ballet, **1:**_486,_ 490–491, **6:**442
    Bronze Horseman, The, **3:**187, **4:**284, **5:**459, _461,_ 567, **6:**442
    Cinderella, **2:**173, **4:**38, 133, 149, **5:**459, 567, **6:**226, 442
    Don Quixote revival, **2:**437, **6:**442
    Gabovich role, **3:**99
    Lunacharsky Institute of Theatrical Art, **5:**480
    Mistress into Maid, **5:**567
    Prisoner of the Caucasus, The, **5:**567
    Semenova roles, **5:**567
    Soviet "realistic" ballets, **5:**484, 485, **6:**441–442
    students, **4:**133, 478, **6:**171, 313
    Taras Bulba, **5:**567
    See also Flames of Paris, The; Fountain of Bakhchisarai, The
Zakharov, Vladimir, **5:**473
zakhkhah (*dabkah* phase), **4:**490
Zaklinsky, Konstantin, **4:**_284,_ 285, **5:**465, **6:**35
Zakynthos, Greece, **3:**298
Zaleski, Antoni, **5:**_216_
Zalewski, Jan, **5:**58
Zali, Lila, **6:**264
Zalinsky, Konstantin, **4:**249
zălul[c]ta, **2:**101
zamba, **1:**108
zambé, **1:**527
Zambelli, Carlotta, **1:**246, 247, 347, **2:**199, **4:**354, **6:**217, **443–444**
    classe de perfectionnement, **3:**81, 82
    fouettés, **6:**443
    Impressions de Music-hall as last Paris Opera performance, **4:**635, **6:**444
    Impressions de Music-hall role origination, **5:**95
    Mordkin's All-Star Imperial Russian Ballet, **4:**459

Paris Opera Ballet, **3:**71, _71,_ **4:**64, **5:**94, 95
    Staats dance partnership, **5:**690
    students, **2:**113, 350, **4:**107, **6:**327
    Sylvia performance, **6:**64
Zambia, **2:**86, 87–88, 89, 90, 91, **4:**485
Zambo, Italo, **1:**304
Zambon, Rita, **3:**557
"Zambra Dance," **3:**254
"Zambra Mora," **4:**664
Zampakos, Stanley, **1:**498
Zampa, ou La Fiancée de Mabre (Hérold), **3:**360
Zanaida (Bach), **3:**111
Zande (people), **2:**86, 92
Zane, Arnie, **1:**59, **3:**620, 621
Zanella, Renato, **1:**241, **6:**10
Zanetti, Gasparo, **4:**507
Zanfratti, Francesca, **4:**463
Zanfretta, Enrico, **1:**48
Zanfretta, Francesco, **3:**261, **5:**603
Zanfretti Ballet Company, **2:**579
Zangretta, Marietta, **2:**174
Zanini, Gerson, *as photographer,* **1:**535
Zannoni, Guido, **1:**196
Zansa, **5:**304
Zantzinger, Gei, **2:**602
Zanuzzi, Santina, **1:**236, **3:**365
Zanza, **1:**_51,_ 52
Zapadno-evropeisky baletny teatr (Krasovskaya), **4:**58
zapateado, **1:**94, **2:**50, **3:**286
Zapateado de Cádiz, La, **2:**522
zapateo, **2:**64, 275, 504
Zapatera y el Emborazo, La, **4:**222
zapin, **3:**504, **4:**250
Zapis dvizhenija (Lissitzian), **4:**688
Zaplin, Viktor, **2:**278
Zaporogerne, **4:**118
Zaporozhe Cossack beyond the Danube, The, **6:**225, 344
zaporozhtsi, **6:**222
Zapotec dance, **2:**535, **4:**389
Zappolini, Walter, **3:**553, **5:**400, _400,_ 401
zaqqalīn, **2:**489
zār, **4:**402, 404, **6:**185, **444–445**
    Egypt, **2:**487–488, **4:**466, 488, **6:**445
Zara (people), **4:**291
Zara, **6:**75
zarabanda. See sarabande
Zaraspe, Héctor, **1:**111, **2:**587
Zarathustra. See Zoroastre
zarbādī dance, 6, 417–418
Zarema, Juliet, **4:**128
Zarrilli, Phillip B.
    as contributor, **1:**184–189
    as photographer, **1:**185, 186
Zar und Zimmerman (Lortzing), **5:**35, 37
zarzuela, **1:**480
Zaslavsky, Mikhail, **2:**520, **5:**459, 473
zat pwe, **4:**525, 527
Zatzinger, Martin, **5:**259, _344_
Zauberfell, Das, **3:**152
Zauberflöte, Die. See Magic Flute, The
Zauberring, Der, **1:**36
Zauberschwestern im Beneventer Walde, Die, **6:**338
zauli mask, **4:**292
Zavadiková, Marie, **5:**393
zavivat berezky, **5:**443, _443_
Zeami, **2:**217, **3:**580, 581, 591, 650, 652, 653, **4:**40, **6:**445–446

Zeami, *continued*
aesthetic principles, **1:**17,
4:654–655
father, Kan'ami, **3:**646–647, **6:**445
Konparu Zenchiku as artistic
successor, **3:**581, **4:**41, 86,
6:446
kyōgen, **4:**83
mask aesthetics, **4:**295
on *nō* performer's training, **4:**655
treatises, **4:**42, 655,
6:445–446, *446*
Zeami Nijusan Bushi (Zeami), **1:**17
Zeche I, **3:**368
Zeche Z, **3:**368
Zechmeister, Freusa, **1:**536
Zechmeister, Gustav, **1:**243
Zéire et Azor, **2:**390
Zelaschi, Rosana, **1:***114*
Zelenko, A., **5:**481
Zelensky, Igor, **4:**623
Zelia, ossia Il Velo Magico, **1:**499
Zélis, ou La Forêt aux Aventures,
2:415
Zélis et Alcindor, **2:**415
Zemach, Benjamin, **3:**559, **6:**355
Zemer Atik, **3:**531
Zémire et Azor, **4:**423, **5:**92, 558
Zemp, Hugo, **1:**15
Zen Buddhism
aesthetics, **1:**17, 182, **3:**581
as Cage-Cunningham influence,
2:286–287, 288
as Dunn (Robert Ellis) influence,
2:461
as Konparu Zenchiku influence,
4:42
Lee Sun-ock dance, **4:**141–142
martial arts, **1:**186
nō drama, **4:**653
Zenchiku. *See* Konparu Zenchiku
Zenchiku Keigorō, **4:**86
Zen Dance: Meditation in Movement
(Lee), **4:**141
Zen Dance/Zen Painting, **4:**141
Zenobia (Tozzza), **2:**55
Zenzinov, Vladimir, *as
photographer,* **5:**469
Zéphire (Duport ballet), **2:**464
Zéphire et Flore (Didelot restaging),
2:415, *415,* 464, **3:**539, **4:**109
Zéphire et Flore (Massine ballet),
2:410, 424, 441, **4:**33, 320
Lifar performance, **4:**182
Messel mask designs, **4:**357
Zéphyr e l'Amour, **2:**60
Zéphyr Inconstant Puni et Fixé,
2:415
Zerara, Catherine, **1:**375, **5:***681*
Žetva, **6:**436
Zeus (deity), **1:**118, **3:**287
"Zevensprong," **4:**585
zeybek dance, **6:**211
zeybekikos dance, **3:**298–299
Zhadnov, Leonid, *as photographer,*
5:204, 205
Zhalbyr, **3:**665
Zhang Heng, **2:**148
Zhang O's Flight to the Moon,
2:132–133
Zhang Shiwen (Chang Shi-wen),
2:135
Zhan You Beijing Opera Company,
6:421
Zhdanov, Leonid, *as photographer,*
3:195
Zhdanov, Yuri, **1:**491, 539, **4:**131,
5:459, 461, 467, **6:**7, 106, *227*
Zhedrinski, Vladimir, **6:**432

Zhenkulova, Shara, **3:**665
Zhirkov, Mark, **5:**473
Zhivago, **2:**58
Zhok (dance troupe), **4:**78, 446
zhok dance, **4:**446
Zhok Ferarilor, **4:**78
Zhongguo Wudao Shi (Chinese
text), **2:**148, 149
Zhong Runliang, **5:**330
Zhornitskaya, Maria I., *as
contributor,* **5:**445–449
Zhou dynasty, **2:**128, 130, 141,
147–148
Zhou Xinfang, **6:**446–447
Zhukov, Alexei, **2:**496–497
Zhukov, Leonid, **1:**85, **3:**665
Bolshoi Ballet, **5:**458
Latvian ballet, **4:**127
Shurale, **5:**472, 595–596
Zhukov, Yuri, **5:**512
Zhukova, Vera, **2:**341
Zhukovsky, Vasily, **3:**192, **5:**454
Zhulin, Aleksandr, **3:**432
Zhu Liren, **2:**149–150
as contributor, **2:**147–150, **5:**330,
6:385–386
Zhu Shichang, **6:**385
Zhu Zaiyu, **1:**17
Zialcita, Malot, **5:**172
Zia ul-Haq, Muḥammad, **5:**63
Zibine, M., **6:**432
Zide-Booth, Rochelle, **4:**626
Ziegenstall (Kampen cabaret),
3:163
Ziegfeld, Florenz, **1:**482, **2:**80, 175,
250, 572, 574, **4:**209, 420,
6:242, 273, 289, **447–448**
competitors, **6:**272
Mitchell (Julian) association,
2:572, **6:**268, 269, 270,
447–448
Mitchell break, **6:**271
production galas, **6:**273
Urban collaboration, **6:**274
Wayburn association, **6:**271, 272,
273, 371
Ziegfeld Follies (film), **1:**93, 193,
194, **2:**108, 613
Ziegfeld Follies (musical revues),
2:5, 250, 572, 613, **3:**22,
4:209, 420, 629, **5:**628, **6:**242,
256, 270
Berlin's "Shaking the Blues
Away" (1927), **6:**447
first (1907), **2:**572, **6:**269, 447
Kern compositions, **6:**272
last supervised by Ziegfeld
(1931), **6:**275, 448
significance of 1914 *Follies,* **6:**271
Tiller Girls, **6:**273, 448
Wayburn staging, **6:***370, 371*
Ziegfeld's Midnight Frolic, **2:**572
Ziegfeld Theater, New York City,
6:273
"Ziegfeld walk," **6:**371
Ziegler, Fred, **5:**52
Ziehrer, Carl Michael, **6:**2
Ziemsky, Andrzej, **1:**292
Zigeunernes Lejr, **5:**424
Ziggurat, **1:**394, **5:**302, **6:**146
Ziino, Agostino, **3:**558
Zijlstra, Joke, **4:**602
Zijwind, **4:**596
Ziković, Zaga, **6:**434
"Zikr." *See dhikr*
zil-badu, **5:**80
Zilcher, Hermann, **5:**42
zil-kerlam, **5:**80
zil-paza, **5:**80

Zimbabwe, **5:**661, **6:**12
Zimin, Sergei, **5:**471
Zimine, Victor, **6:**118
Zimińska, Mira, **5:**212
Zimmerl, Christi, **1:**241, *241*
Zimmerman, Joanne, **2:**470
Zimmermann, Bernd Alois, **2:**563
Zimmermann, Susana,
1:102–103, 113
Zimmermann, Walter, **2:**309
Zimmer Nr. 13, **3:**626
Zinck, Otto, **2:**435
Zingara, La, **5:**403, **6:**203
Zingarelli, Niccolò, **2:**435
Zingaro, **3:**314, **5:**135, *136*
Zinkeisen, Doris, **3:**508, 509, 511
Zipper, Trudy Dubsky, **5:**171
Zipprodt, Patricia, **2:**244, 245,
6:*203*
žita, **2:**100
zither, **4:***489*
Ziv-Eyal, Ruth, **3:**533
Zizi, Je T'aime (revue), **5:**164
Znamenacek, Wolfgang, **1:**1
Znamensky Theater, Moscow,
1:485
Zöbisch, Otto, **1:**370, **3:**414
Zoder, Raimund, **1:**242
Zola, Émile, **2:**361
Zolan, Miro, **3:**520
Zollar, Jawole Willa Jo, **1:**60, **3:**448,
578, **6:**448–449
Zolotarev, Vasily, **6:**420
Zolotaya Rybka, **5:**501
Zolotoe runo (journal), **3:**197
Zolotova, Natalia, **1:**83
Zomosa, Maximiliano, **2:**606,
3:614, 615
Zone of Silence, **3:**421
zonzo ternero, **2:**121
zoppa, **2:**45
Zoraide o La Schiava Circassa,
1:427
Zorango, **1:**93
Zoraya, **4:**430, **5:**158
"Zorba dance," **3:**299
Zorba the Greek (film), **3:**299
Zorina, Elizabeta, **5:**451
Zorina, Vera, **2:***616,* **6:**449–450
Balanchine marriage, **1:**257,
6:450
Ballets Russes de Monte Carlo,
1:311, **6:**449
costumes, **2:***250*
films, **2:**426, **5:**398, **6:**34, 450, *450*
musical theater, **6:**277, 449, 450
Norwegian background, **6:**449
Wanderer, The, **2:***424*
Zoritch, George, **1:**518, **6:**292
Ballet Russe de Monte Carlo,
1:296
Ballets Russes de Monte Carlo,
1:*311*
zorkhana, **1:**247
Zorn, Friedrich Albert, **2:**405,
3:159–160, **4:**161, 685, **5:**201,
222, 626, **6:**128, 290
Zorn notation, **4:**685–686,
6:450–451
Zoroastre, **4:**236, **5:**306, 307
Zorongo Gitano, El, **4:**222
Zotov, Rafail, **6:**451–452
Zotto, Miguel Angel. *See* Plebs and
Zotto
Zouzou (film), **1:**253, *253*
Zoželuh, Petr, **2:**308
Zsedényi, Károly, **3:**415, **6:**66
zubayrī dance, **6:**417

Zubkovskaya, Inna, **4:***277,* 284,
5:*401,* 480, 595, 677
Zubkovsky, Nikolai, **1:**539
Zuccari, Federico, **6:**350
Zucchi, Virginia, **1:**500, 540, **2:**572,
4:*150, 282,* 430, 455, **5:**37, 94,
159, 456, 529, **6:**452–453
Excelsior performance, **3:**71,
6:452
Fille Mal Gardée performance,
2:596, **6:**452
Guest biography, **3:**321
Saint Petersburg triumph,
6:452–453
Zucchi, Virginia (niece), **6:**453
Zuckerman, Michael, **6:**231
Zuimaaluti, **6:**326
Zuiver, Johanna, **4:**600
Zuleika, **3:**97
Zulfugarov, Khumar, **1:**248
Zulima und Azem, **3:**175
Züllig, Hans, **3:**40, 628, 629, 630,
4:597, **6:***304,* **453**
*Zulma, eller Krystalpaladset. See
Crystal Palace, The*
Zulu dance, **5:**643, 644, *644,* **6:**13
Boot Dance, **2:**86, 212–213,
5:*648,* 661, **6:**22
filmed ethnology, **2:**602
shamanism, **5:**580
sounds accompanying, **4:**484
stamping, **5:**661
Zummo, Peter, **1:**545
Zunga (dance drama), **2:**313
zungure (dance drama), **2:**313
Zuñi dance, **4:**565
Zuo Qiming, **2:**147
Zuozhuan (Chronicle of Zuo),
2:147
Zurich, Switzerland, **1:**134, **6:**454
Zurich Ballet, **6:**454–455
Beriozoff, Nicholas, **6:**53, 454
Descombey, Michel, **2:**388–389,
6:454
Don Quixote, **2:**440
Josephslegende, Die, **3:**631, **6:**454
Mlakar, Pia and Pino, **5:**547,
6:454
Neary, Patricia, **6:**53, 454
Nureyev-Georgiadis productions,
3:136, **6:**454
Ondine, **3:**360
Scholz, Uwe, **6:**53, 454–455
Spoerli, Heinz, **5:**683, **6:**454, 455
Sylvia staging, **6:**64
Zurich Opera House, **6:**454
Zuska, Petr, **2:**309, 310
Zuttermeister, (Emily) Kau[soq]i,
3:396
Zvereff, Nicholas, **1:**411, 449,
2:466, 587, **4:**107, *207,* **5:**85
Grands Ballets Canadiens, Les,
3:227
Lithuanian ballet choreography,
4:*207,* 208
Paris dance studio, **3:**82
Zvezdnie khorovody (Ustinova),
6:303
Zvyagina, Susanna, **3:**12
Zweig, Stefan, **5:**566
Zwiefachen dance, **3:**141
Zwischenräume, **4:**604
Zybine, Hipólito, **4:**391
Zydeco, **2:**24, **6:***250*
Zydower, Astrid, **5:**297
Zyklus, **2:**388
Zyriab, **3:**6